Electrical service &
repair. Domestic
c1991-
V.1
33305012687137
CU   09/30/99

ELECTRICAL SERVICE & REPAIR

1999 Domestic Vehicles

Santa Clara County
LIBRARY

Renewals:
(800) 471-0991
www.santaclaracountylib.org

CHRYSLER CORP.

JEEP

HOW TO FIND
THE INFORMATION

3 Quick Steps

1 On facing page, you'll find the Contents of this manual arranged according to manufacturer. Locate the manufacturer of the vehicle you're working on...notice it has a Black square next to it.

CHRYSLER CORP.

2 THUMB INDEX RECTANGLE

Looking along the right-hand edge of the manual, you'll notice additional Black squares. Match the Black square of the appropriate manufacturer with the Black squares in line with it on the manual's edge. Turn directly to the first page (Contents Page) of that manufacturer's "section".

3 Scan the Subjects listed in the Contents page: then turn to the page indicated for the Specific Information you desire.

Information Company

ELECTRICAL SERVICE & REPAIR

1999 Domestic Vehicles

GENERAL INFORMATION

CHRYSLER CORP.

JEEP

Information Company

ACKNOWLEDGMENT

Mitchell Repair Information Company thanks the domestic and import automobile and light truck manufacturers, distributors, and dealers for their generous cooperation and assistance which make this manual possible.

MARKETING

Senior Vice President
David Peterson

Directors
David R. Koontz
Daniel Ramirez

Product Managers
Catherine Smith
Victor Addison
Nick DiVerde
Robert Gardner
Brian Warfield

TECHNICAL LIBRARIAN
Debbie Hickman

EDITORIAL

Director, Annual Data Editorial
Mike Mancini

Director, Special Product Editorial
Ronald E. Garrett

Senior Editors
Chuck Vedra (ASE-Quadruple Master)
Ramiro Gutierrez
John M. Fisher (ASE)
Tom L. Hall (ASE-Quadruple Master)
James A. Hawes (ASE-Quadruple Master)
Eddie Santangelo (ASE)

Technical Editors
Thomas L. Landis
Scott A. Olsen (ASE)
Bob Reel
David W. Himes (ASE)
Alex A. Solis (ASE)
James R. Warren (ASE)
Bobby R. Gifford (ASE)
Linca M. Murphy (ASE)
Donald Lawler (ASE)
Wayne D. Charbonneau (ASE-World Class)
Sal Caloca (ASE)
Bud Gardner (ASE)
Robert L. Eller (ASE-Quadruple Master)
John Schartz (ASE)
Richard C. Hamilton (ASE-Quadruple Master)
Leonid A. Shneyder (ASE)
Brian Yockey (ASE)
John Howard (ASE)
Todd Mercer (ASE)
James Barrow (ASE)
Demian Hurst (ASE)
Jeff Wyatt (ASE)
Patrick Bolton (ASE)
David Steckling (ASE)
Tim Flannery (ASE)
Robert Therieau
Susan Schalk (ASE)
Andrew Smith (ASE)

WIRING DIAGRAMS
Manager
Matthew M. Krimple

PRINT COMPOSITION
Brian Henderson
Julia Gillis (ASE)

TECHNICAL SUPPORT
Bob Pilz

PRODUCT SUPPORT
Product Specialists
James A. Wafford (ASE)
Jeff Hicks
David Block (ASE)
Carol Menickelly
Matt Mathews (ASE)
Bill Belliston (ASE)

GRAPHICS
Manager
Judith A. La Pierre
Supervisor
Ann Klimetz
Graphic Specialists
Sally Muhlbaier
Lynn Plummer
Percella Kuhns
Carmen Rusnak
Deb Eaton
Edder Naguit
Jordan Butcher
Cheryl Griffin
Jean Petaja
Robert Taylor

Published By

MITCHELL REPAIR INFORMATION COMPANY
9889 Willow Creek Road
P.O. Box 26260
San Diego, California 92196-0260

ISBN 0-8470-2215-3

© 1999 Mitchell Repair Information Company, LLC
All Rights Reserved

Printed in U.S.A.

COPYRIGHT: No part of this publication may be reproduced, stored in a retrieval system, or transmitted in any form or by any means, electronic, mechanical, photocopying, recording, or otherwise, without the prior written permission of the copyright holder.

Customer Service Numbers
For Subscription, Billing or Technical Information call:
1-888-724-6742 Toll Free or 858-549-7809
Or Write: P.O. Box 26260, San Diego, CA 92196-0260

DISCLAIMER OF WARRANTIES: Although the information contained within this volume has been obtained from sources generally believed to be reliable, no warranty (expressed or implied) can be made as to its accuracy or completeness, nor is any responsibility assumed by Mitchell Repair Information Company or anyone connected with it for loss or damages suffered through reliance on any information contained in this volume.
SPECIFICALLY, NO WARRANTY OF MERCHANTABILITY, FITNESS FOR A PARTICULAR PURPOSE OR ANY OTHER WARRANTY IS MADE OR TO BE IMPLIED WITH RESPECT TO THIS VOLUME AND ITS CONTENTS.
In no event will Mitchell Repair Information Company be liable for any damages, direct or indirect, consequential or compensatory, including, without limitation, lost profits, for any representations, breaches or defaults arising out of the use of this volume. Customer agrees to indemnify Mitchell Repair Information Company and hold it harmless against all claims and damages, including without limitation, reasonable attorney's fees arising out of the use of this volume, unless such claims or damages result from the infringement of any copyright or other proprietary right of any third party.
"This publication contains material that is reproduced and distributed under a license from Ford Motor Company. No further reproduction or distribution of the Ford Motor Company material is allowed without the express written permission from Ford Motor Company."

1999 GENERAL INFORMATION
Contents

GENERAL INFORMATION

ALL MODELS

Computer Relearn Procedures

INTRODUCTION

Vehicles equipped with engine or transmission/transaxle computers may require a computer relearn procedure after the vehicle battery is disconnected. Vehicle computers memorize and store vehicle operation patterns for optimum driveability and performance. When the vehicle battery is disconnected, this memory is lost, resulting in a driveability problem. Depending on the vehicle and how it is equipped, the following driveability problems may exist:

- Rough or unstable idle.
- Hesitation or stumble.
- Rich or lean running.
- Poor fuel mileage.
- Harsh or poor transmission/transaxle shift quality.

Default data is used until NEW data from each key start is stored. As the computer restores its memory from each new key start, driveability is restored.

Driveability problems may occur during the computer relearn stage. To accelerate computer relearn process after battery removal and installation, specified computer relearn procedures should be performed. See appropriate procedures under specified manufacturer.

CHRYSLER CORP.

ALL MODELS

NOTE: *Read all procedures listed to determine why each procedure is to be performed before proceeding.*

Vehicle Driveability Computer Relearn Procedure – Manufacturer does not provide a specified computer relearn procedure for obtaining proper driveability. If vehicle battery was disconnected or Powertrain Control Module (PCM) was replaced, driving the vehicle will enable the PCM to perform a computer relearn procedure for obtaining proper driveability. Inform customer that driveability may differ from what they are accustomed to until the PCM completes the computer relearn procedure.

NOTE: *If Powertrain Control Module (PCM) was replaced, the correct vehicle mileage and Vehicle Identification Number (VIN) must be programmed into the PCM to prevent Diagnostic Trouble Codes (DTCs) from being set in the Anti-Lock Brake System (ABS) module and Supplemental Restraint System (SRS) module. To program PCM and clear DTCs from ABS and SRS modules, proceed to appropriate procedure listed. If replacing Powertrain Control Module (PCM) on models equipped with a Smart Key Immobilizer Module (SKIM), the secret key data must also be updated to enable engine starting. To update secret key data, proceed to appropriate procedure listed.*

Programming PCM & Clearing DTCs From ABS & SRS Modules – Connect scan tool to Data Link Connector (DLC) below driver's side of instrument panel. Using scan tool, enter correct VIN and mileage into PCM. Using scan tool manufacturer's instructions, clear DTCs from ABS and SRS modules.

Updating Secret Key Data – Connect scan tool to Data Link Connector (DLC) below driver's side of instrument panel. Go to ENGINE, then MISC menu on scan tool. Place the SKIM in SECURED ACCESS MODE by using the appropriate Personal Identification Number (PIN) for this vehicle. PIN may be obtained from the owner, vehicle's invoice, or

from the manufacturer. Select UPDATE THE SECRET KEY DATA. The data will be transferred from Smart Key Immobilizer Module (SKIM) to the PCM.

NOTE: *If 3 attempts are made to enter the SECURED ACCESS MODE using the incorrect Personal Identification Number (PIN), the SECURED ACCESS MODE will be locked out for one hour. To exit this locked-out mode, leave ignition switch in the ON position for one hour with all accessories turned off. It may be necessary to monitor battery state and connect a battery charger.*

FWD CARS & FWD VANS

Transaxle Shift Quality Quick Learn Procedure (All FWD Cars Except Avenger & Sebring Coupe, & All FWD Vans) – 1) Transaxle shift quality quick learn procedure must be performed to provide proper transaxle operation if any of the following have been done:

- Vehicle battery was disconnected.
- Transaxle assembly was replaced.
- Transmission Control Module (TCM) was replaced.
- Solenoid assembly was replaced.
- Valve body was reconditioned or replaced.

2) Transaxle shift quality quick learn procedure must be performed using Chrysler's Diagnostic Readout Box III (DRB-III) scan tool. Following conditions must be met when performing transaxle shift quality quick learn procedure:

- Brakes must be applied.
- Engine speed must be greater than 500 RPM.
- Throttle position sensor angle must be less than 3 degrees.
- Shift lever must remain in designated position until prompted to shift to overdrive.
- Shift lever must remain in overdrive after the shift to overdrive until scan tool indicates procedure is complete.
- Calculated oil temperature must be within 60-200°F (16-93°C).

3) Connect scan tool to Data Link Connector (DLC) below driver's side of instrument panel. For DLC location, see appropriate SELF-DIAGNOSTICS article in ENGINE PERFORMANCE.
4) Go to TRANSMISSION display on scan tool. Go to MISCELLANEOUS display on scan tool. Select QUICK LEARN PROCEDURE display on scan tool. Follow instructions displayed on scan tool to perform transaxle shift quality quick learn procedure. Remove scan tool.

Transaxle Shift Quality Quick Learn Procedure (Avenger & Sebring Coupe) – 1) Transaxle shift quality quick learn procedure must be performed to provide proper transaxle operation after replacing or overhauling transaxle. After transaxle work is completed, clear any Diagnostic Trouble Codes (DTCs) as necessary. Connect Chrysler's Diagnostic Readout Box III (DRB-III) scan tool to Data Link Connector (DLC) below driver's side of instrument panel. For DLC location, see appropriate SELF-DIAGNOSTICS article in ENGINE PERFORMANCE.
2) Select SPECIAL FUNCTION on scan tool. Set scan tool to QUICK LEARN mode. Follow scan tool manufacturer's instructions to perform transaxle shift quality quick learn procedure. Remove scan tool.

Pinion Factor Procedure (All FWD Cars Except Avenger & Sebring Coupe, & All FWD Vans) – 1) Electronic pinion factor procedure must be performed to provide proper speedometer operation if Transmission Control Module (TCM) is replaced. If pinion factor procedure is not performed, improper speedometer readings may exist or speedometer may not operate. Pinion factor procedure must be performed using Chrysler's Diagnostic Readout Box (DRB-III) scan tool.
2) Connect scan tool to Data Link Connector (DLC) below driver's side of instrument panel. For DLC location, see appropriate SELF-DIAGNOSTICS article in ENGINE PERFORMANCE.
3) Select TRANSMISSION system, MISCELLANEOUS functions, then PINION FACTOR. Scan tool will now display tire size. If tire size is incorrect, press ENTER key and select correct size. Press PAGE BACK key to exit procedure.

Pinion Factor Procedure (Avenger & Sebring Coupe) – 1) Transaxle uses rotation speed of output shaft to calculate vehicle speed and cumulative distance travelled. Therefore, it is necessary to input or update tire size into TCM memory after TCM has been replaced or tire size has been changed.

2) Select SPECIAL FUNCTION on Chrysler's Diagnostic Readout Box (DRB-III) scan tool. Set scan tool to PINION FACTOR mode. Input tire size into TCM memory.

NOTE: New TCMs do not have tire size input into memory. TCM may also be referred to as EATX module.

FORD MOTOR CO.

NOTE: When battery is disconnected and reconnected, some abnormal drive symptoms may occur while vehicle relearns its adaptive strategy. Vehicle may need to be driven for approximately 10 miles or more to relearn strategy.

NOTE: New Generation Star (NGS) tester will not store information for more then 24 hours.

ALL MODELS (PROGRAMMING PCM)

NOTE: Before performing PCM programming procedure, check for any applicable Technical Service Bulletins (TSBs) that may apply to vehicle application.

Description – Flash Electronically Erasable Programmable Read Only Memory (EEPROM) is contained in an Integrated Circuit (IC) inside of Powertrain Control Module (PCM). The EEPROM contains the vehicle strategy and any calibration information specific to vehicle. The IC is reprogrammable, and at times it may become necessary to reprogram or reflash the entire contents. This is usually due to an after-production strategy change or the Vehicle Identification (VID) area has been previously reprogrammed and has reached its limit. The VID block can be tailored to accommodate various hardware changes made since vehicle production. This procedure can only be performed using Ford's Service Bay Technical System (SBTS) or equivalent.

A replacement PCM will have a label stating PROGRAMMING REQUIRED. This indicates that it is necessary to retrieve VID data from the original PCM before removing PCM from vehicle. This procedure can be performed using New Generation Star (007-00500) tester or equivalent. See FLASH VEHICLE IDENTIFICATION (VID) BLOCK PROCEDURE. If original PCM is nonfunctional, it will be necessary to manually reprogram VID block. This procedure can only be performed using Ford's Service Bay Technical System (SBTS) or equivalent.

NOTE: If using a generic scan tool, follow scan tool manufacturer's instructions to perform FLASH VEHICLE IDENTIFICATION (VID) BLOCK PROCEDURE.

Flash Vehicle Identification (VID) Block Procedure – 1) To perform this procedure, NGS tester, Ford Service Function (FSF) card and NGS

Flash Cable (007-00531) must be used. Plug flash cable into NGS tester. Plug other end of flash cable into Data Link Connector (DLC), located under instrument panel next to steering column. From the NGS tester main menu, select SERVICE BAY FUNCTIONS, PCM-POWERTRAIN CONTROL MODULE and then PROGRAMMABLE MODULE INSTALLATION.

2) NGS tester display should show 2 selections. The first selection is for old PCM information to be retrieved and stored. The second selection is for storing new PCM with information that has been retrieved from the old PCM. Follow scan tool display instructions or refer to instruction sheet included with FSF card. If Vehicle Identification (VID) block has been reprogrammed previously, NGS tester will display a message indicating the need to reflash entire Integrated Circuit (IC). This procedure can only be performed using Ford's Service Bay Technical System (SBTS) or equivalent.

CONTINENTAL

Customer Driven Preferences – There are customer preferences that can be configured on this vehicle. Some items the customer may or may not want to have enabled. To carry out customer configuration process, connect New Generation Star (NGS) tester to Data Link Connector (DLC), located under instrument panel next to steering column. Insert Ford Service Function (FSF) card into NGS tester. Using NGS tester, set customer preferences as necessary. See CUSTOMER PREFERENCE INDEX (CONTINENTAL) table.

Driver's Door Module (DDM) Programming – Prior to removal of DDM, upload module configuration information to the New Generation Star (NGS) tester using manufacturer's instructions. Once module has been replaced, download module configuration information from NGS tester into new module.

NOTE: Permanent entry code programmed in driver's door module is taped to driver's door module or on wallet card provided with owner's manual.

Keypad Programming – 1) Enter 5-digit permanent entry code at keypad. Within 5 seconds of pressing last digit, press 1/2 button on keypad to activate programming mode. Hold 1/2 button for more than 2 seconds to erase all stored customer codes. Door locks will lock and unlock to confirm all codes are erased. Existing codes do not need to be erased to program new codes.

2) Enter new 5-digit keypad code. To associate new code with personality position No. 1 or 2, within 7.5 seconds of entering last digit of new code, press 1/2 button for position No. 1 or 3/4 button for position No. 2. Doors will lock and unlock to confirm new code is programmed. If another code is to be programmed, begin entering code within 7.5 seconds of pressing last button.

CUSTOMER PREFERENCE INDEX (CONTINENTAL)

Module	Configurable Item	State
Driver's Door Module	Remote Transmitter Programming	ID Code (TIC) Value
Lighting Control Module	Headlights On With Wipers	Enabled, Disabled
Lighting Control Module	Daytime Running Lights	Enabled, Disabled
Lighting Control Module	Bulb Out Strategy	Enabled, Disabled
Remote Emergency Satellite Cellular Unit Module	Vehicle Identification Number (VIN) Download	Enter VIN
Restraint Control Module	Side Air Bags	With Or Without
Instrument Cluster	Enter Security Access	Enter Security Access
Instrument Cluster	Ignition Key Code Program	Program Ignition Keys
Instrument Cluster	Ignition Key Code Erase	Erase All Stored Ignition Keys
Instrument Cluster	Spare Key	Enabled, Disabled
Instrument Cluster	Parameter Reset	Reset Security

Computer Relearn Procedures (Cont.)

3) After all new codes are programmed, a new remote transmitter can be programmed within 7.5 seconds of pressing last digit in keypad code. To exit program mode, press keyless entry keypad buttons 7/8 and 9/0 at the same time or wait 7.5 seconds for DDM to exit automatically.

NOTE: *This procedure is used when a customer needs keys programmed into system and does not have 2 programmed ignition keys available, or when programmed ignition keys have been lost and/or ignition switch assembly has been replaced. This procedure will erase all programmed ignition keys from memory and prevent vehicle from starting until 2 keys have been programmed. Ignition keys must have correct mechanical key cut for vehicle and must be an encoded key. If additional key(s) are to be programmed, perform KEY PROGRAMMING – USING 2 PROGRAMMED KEYS. If remaining keys are with customer and not with vehicle, instruct customer to see owner's manual to program spare key(s).*

Key Programming – Erase All Keys & Program 2 Keys – 1) Insert Ford Service Function (FSF) card into NGS tester. Turn ignition switch from LOCK to RUN position. With NGS tester connected to vehicle, enter VIC then select SECURITY ACCESS PROCEDURE. This procedure will take 10 minutes to perform. After the security access procedure has been completed, a new menu will be displayed with command options. Select IGNITION KEY CODE ERASE.

2) Turn ignition switch to LOCK position and disconnect NGS tester. Insert first encoded ignition key into ignition lock cylinder. Turn ignition switch to RUN position for 30 seconds. Turn ignition switch to LOCK position and remove first encoded key.

3) Insert second encoded ignition key into ignition lock cylinder. Turn ignition switch to RUN position for 30 seconds. Turn ignition switch to LOCK position and remove second encoded key. Both encoded ignition keys should now start vehicle.

NOTE: *Security access must be granted to erase ignition keys, enable/disable spare key programming switch, or perform parameter resets for instrument cluster or PCM. This procedure has a 10-minute time delay prior to granting security access during which the New Generation Star (NGS) tester must remain connected to vehicle. After security access has been granted, security access command menu is displayed which offers various command options. Multiple security access commands can be executed (if necessary) prior to exiting security access command menu. Execution of all necessary security access commands prior to exiting command menu avoids the performance of an additional security access procedure and the associated 10-minute time delay. Security access for the instrument cluster and security access for the PCM must be obtained separately as needed (each will require a 10-minute time delay).*

Key Programming – Security Access Procedure – Insert Ford Service Function (FSF) card into NGS tester. Turn ignition switch from LOCK to RUN position. With NGS tester connected to vehicle, enter VIC then select SECURITY ACCESS PROCEDURE. This procedure will take 10 minutes to perform. After the security access procedure has been completed, a new menu will be displayed with command options. Select as many functions as required before exiting this menu. Once this menu is exited, security access procedure must be performed again to perform additional commands.

NOTE: *The spare key programming switch is a programmable switch which provides the capability to enable/disable the normal customer spare key programming procedure detailed in the owner's manual. This programmable switch is provided as a convenience for rental company fleets or other fleet purchasers who may not want the spare key programming procedure available to the vehicle driver. The spare key programming switch state can be viewed using VIC PID SPARE_KY.*

Key Programming – Spare Key Programming Switch – Insert a programmed ignition key into the ignition lock cylinder. Insert Ford Service Function (FSF) card into NGS tester. Turn ignition switch from LOCK to RUN position. With NGS tester connected to vehicle, enter VIC then select SECURITY ACCESS PROCEDURE. This procedure will take 10 minutes to perform. After the security access procedure has been completed, a new menu will be displayed with command options. The default setting on all new vehicles is ENABLE. Select SPARE KEY PROGRAMMING SWITCH. Set SPARE KEY PROGRAMMING SWITCH to ENABLE to allow keys to be programmed or DISABLE to make key programming not accessible.

NOTE: *This procedure will only work if 2 or more programmed ignition keys are available and there is a need to program additional keys. If 2 keys are not available, perform KEY PROGRAMMING – ERASE ALL KEYS & PROGRAM 2 KEYS. PID SPARE_KY must be enabled for this procedure to operate. To enable this PID, perform KEY PROGRAMMING – SPARE KEY PROGRAMMING SWITCH and enable spare key programming switch. If programming procedure is successful, new key(s) will start vehicle and THEFT indicator will illuminate for 3 seconds. If programming procedure is not successful, new key(s) will not start vehicle and THEFT indicator will flash for one minute (after flashing for one minute, THEFT indicator will flash fault code). If necessary, repeat programming procedure. If programming of key(s) is still unsuccessful, perform self-diagnostics. See SELF-DIAGNOSTIC SYSTEM in PASSIVE ANTI-THEFT SYSTEMS – CONTINENTAL article in ACCESSORIES & EQUIPMENT. Maximum of 8 keys can be programmed into system. If procedure is not performed as outlined, programming procedure will end. Ignition keys must have correct mechanical key cut for vehicle and must be an encoded key.*

Key Programming – Using 2 Programmed Keys – 1) Insert the first programmed ignition key into ignition lock cylinder. Turn ignition switch from LOCK to RUN position (ignition switch must stay in RUN position for one second). Turn ignition switch to LOCK position and remove ignition key from ignition lock cylinder.

2) Within 5 seconds of turning ignition switch to LOCK position, insert second programmed ignition key into ignition lock cylinder. Turn ignition switch from LOCK to RUN position (ignition switch must stay in RUN position for one second). Turn ignition switch to LOCK position and remove second ignition key from ignition lock cylinder.

3) Within 10 seconds of turning ignition switch to LOCK position, insert a NEW unprogrammed ignition key into ignition lock cylinder. Turn ignition switch from LOCK to RUN position (ignition switch must stay in RUN position for one second). Turn ignition switch to LOCK position and remove ignition key from ignition lock cylinder. The NEW ignition key should now be programmed. To program additional key(s), repeat key programming procedure from step **1)**.

NOTE: *NGS tester will only store module configuration information for 24 hours.*

Lighting Control Module (LCM) Programming – Prior to removal of LCM, upload module configuration information to the New Generation Star (NGS) tester using manufacturer's instructions. Once module has been replaced, download module configuration information from NGS tester into new module.

PCM Programming – For Powertrain Control Module (PCM) programming procedures, see ALL MODELS (PROGRAMMING PCM).

NOTE: *Permanent entry code programmed in driver's door module is taped to driver's door module or on wallet card provided with owner's manual.*

NOTE: *Driver's Door Module (DDM) will erase all previously programmed remote transmitters when a new remote transmitter is programmed. If adding an additional remote transmitter, all existing remote transmitters must be reprogrammed at the same time.*

Transmitter Programming – 1) Enter 5-digit permanent entry code at keypad. Within 5 seconds of pressing last digit, press 1/2 button on keypad. Hold 1/2 button for more than 2 seconds to erase all stored

GENERAL INFORMATION
Computer Relearn Procedures (Cont.)

customer codes. Door locks will lock and unlock to confirm all codes are erased. Existing codes do not need to be erased to program new codes.

2) Press and hold any button on remote transmitter within 5 seconds of pressing 1/2 button. Doors will lock and unlock to confirm programming. Driver door module will automatically associate remote transmitters to a personality setting. The first remote transmitter to be programmed will be position No. 1, and the second remote transmitter will be position No. 2. Remaining remote transmitters, if programmed, will not be associated to a personality setting.

3) If additional remote transmitters are to be programmed, press any button on next remote transmitter to be programmed within 7.5 seconds of pressing button on last transmitter. If programming is successful, doors will signal by locking and unlocking.

4) After all remote transmitters are programmed, a new keyless entry keypad code can be programmed within 7.5 seconds of pressing button on last remote transmitter. To exit program mode, press keyless entry keypad buttons 7/8 and 9/0 at the same time or wait 7.5 seconds for DDM to exit automatically.

NOTE: Virtual Instrument Cluster (VIC) may also be referred to as instrument cluster. Passive anti-theft system MUST be reconfigured after replacement of the VIC. See PASSIVE ANTI-THEFT SYSTEMS – CONTINENTAL article in ACCESSORIES & EQUIPMENT. Also all keys to be used MUST be reprogrammed. See KEY PROGRAMMING – ERASE ALL KEYS & PROGRAM 2 KEYS.

Virtual Instrument Cluster (VIC) Programming – 1) Turn ignition switch to LOCK position. Using NGS tester, retrieve and record continuous DTCs. Clear continuous DTCs and perform instrument cluster self-test. If DTC B2139 is retrieved, go to next step. If DTC B2139 is not retrieved, system is okay at this time.

2) Perform security access for instrument cluster. See KEY PROGRAMMING – SECURITY ACCESS PROCEDURE. Using NGS tester, select PARAMETER RESET command for instrument cluster. Using NGS tester, select PARAMETER RESET command for PCM. Turn ignition switch to RUN position for 30 seconds. Turn ignition switch to LOCK position. Using NGS tester, perform instrument cluster self-test. If DTC B2139 is not retrieved, system is okay at this time. If DTC B2139 is retrieved, verify PCM calibration is correct for vehicle. If calibration is okay, replace instrument cluster. If DTC B2139 still exists, replace PCM.

CONTOUR & MYSTIQUE

NOTE: This procedure is used when a customer needs keys programmed into system and does not have 2 programmed ignition keys available, or when programmed ignition keys have been lost and/or ignition switch assembly has been replaced. This procedure will erase all programmed ignition keys from memory and prevent vehicle from starting until 2 keys have been programmed. Ignition keys must have correct mechanical key cut for vehicle and must be an encoded key. If additional key(s) are to be programmed, perform KEY PROGRAMMING – USING 2 PROGRAMMED KEYS. If remaining keys are with customer and not with vehicle, instruct customer to see owner's manual to program spare key(s).

Key Programming – Erase All Keys & Program 2 Keys – 1) Insert Ford Service Function (FSF) card into NGS tester. Turn ignition switch from LOCK to RUN position. With NGS tester connected to vehicle, enter PCM then select SECURITY ACCESS PROCEDURE. This procedure will take 10 minutes to perform. After the security access procedure has been completed, a new menu will be displayed with command options. Select IGNITION KEY CODE ERASE.

2) Turn ignition switch to LOCK position and disconnect NGS tester. Insert first encoded ignition key into ignition lock cylinder. Turn ignition switch to RUN position for 3 seconds. Turn ignition switch to LOCK position and remove first encoded key.

3) Within 5 seconds, insert second encoded ignition key into ignition lock cylinder. Turn ignition switch to RUN position for 3 seconds. Turn ignition

switch to LOCK position and remove second encoded key. Both encoded ignition keys should now start vehicle.

NOTE: Security access must be granted to erase ignition keys, enable/disable spare key programming switch, or perform parameter resets for PCM. This procedure has a 10-minute time delay prior to granting security access during which the New Generation Star (NGS) tester must remain connected to vehicle. After security access has been granted, security access command menu is displayed which offers various command options. Multiple security access commands can be executed (if necessary) prior to exiting security access command menu. Execution of all necessary security access commands prior to exiting command menu avoids the performance of an additional security access procedure and the associated 10-minute time delay.

Key Programming – Security Access Procedure – Insert Ford Service Function (FSF) card into NGS tester. Turn ignition switch from LOCK to RUN position. With NGS tester connected to vehicle, enter PCM then select SECURITY ACCESS PROCEDURE. This procedure will take 10 minutes to perform. After the security access procedure has been completed, a new menu will be displayed with command options. Select as many functions as required before exiting this menu. Once this menu is exited, security access procedure must be performed again to perform additional commands.

NOTE: The spare key programming switch is a programmable switch which provides the capability to enable/disable the normal customer spare key programming procedure detailed in the owner's manual. This programmable switch is provided as a convenience for rental company fleets or other fleet purchasers who may not want the spare key programming procedure available to the vehicle driver. The spare key programming switch state can be viewed using PCM PID SPARE_KY.

Key Programming – Spare Key Programming Switch – Insert a programmed ignition key into the ignition lock cylinder. Insert Ford Service Function (FSF) card into NGS tester. Turn ignition switch from LOCK to RUN position. With NGS tester connected to vehicle, enter PCM then select SECURITY ACCESS PROCEDURE. This procedure will take 10 minutes to perform. After the security access procedure has been completed, a new menu will be displayed with command options. The default setting on all new vehicles is ENABLE. Select SPARE KEY PROGRAMMING SWITCH. Set SPARE KEY PROGRAMMING SWITCH to ENABLE to allow keys to be programmed or DISABLE to make key programming not accessible.

NOTE: This procedure will only work if 2 or more programmed ignition keys are available and there is a need to program additional keys. If 2 keys are not available, perform KEY PROGRAMMING – ERASE ALL KEYS & PROGRAM 2 KEYS. PID SPARE_KY must be enabled for this procedure to operate. To enable this PID, perform KEY PROGRAMMING – SPARE KEY PROGRAMMING SWITCH and enable spare key programming switch. If programming procedure is successful, new key(s) will start vehicle and THEFT indicator will illuminate for 3 seconds. If programming procedure is not successful, new key(s) will not start vehicle and THEFT indicator will flash for one minute (after flashing for one minute, THEFT indicator will flash fault code). If necessary, repeat programming procedure. If programming of key(s) is still unsuccessful, perform self-diagnostics. See SELF-DIAGNOSTIC SYSTEM in PASSIVE ANTI-THEFT SYSTEMS – CONTOUR & MYSTIQUE article in ACCESSORIES & EQUIPMENT. Maximum of 8 keys can be programmed into system. If procedure is not performed as outlined, programming procedure will end. Ignition keys must have correct mechanical key cut for vehicle and must be an encoded key.

Key Programming – Using 2 Programmed Keys – 1) Insert the first programmed ignition key into ignition lock cylinder. Turn ignition switch from LOCK to RUN position (ignition switch must stay in RUN position

Computer Relearn Procedures (Cont.)

for one second). Turn ignition switch to LOCK position and remove ignition key from ignition lock cylinder.

2) Within 5 seconds of turning ignition switch to LOCK position, insert second programmed ignition key into ignition lock cylinder. Turn ignition switch from LOCK to RUN position (ignition switch must stay in RUN position for one second). Turn ignition switch to LOCK position and remove second ignition key from ignition lock cylinder.

3) Within 5 seconds of turning ignition switch to LOCK position, insert a NEW unprogrammed ignition key into ignition lock cylinder. Turn ignition switch from LOCK to RUN position (ignition switch must stay in RUN position for one second). Turn ignition switch to LOCK position and remove ignition key from ignition lock cylinder. The NEW ignition key should now be programmed. To program additional key(s), repeat key programming procedure from step **1)**.

NOTE: This procedure is used when customer needs extra keys programmed and 2 programmed keys are not available, but system has 2 ignition keys programmed. A maximum of 8 keys can be programmed. If 8 keys are already programmed, this procedure will not allow any more keys to be programmed. The number of programmed keys can be determined by accessing PCM PID NUMKEYS with NGS tester.

Key Programming – Without Using 2 Programmed Keys – Insert unprogrammed key in ignition and turn ignition switch to START position. Connect New Generation Star (NGS) tester to Data Link Connector (DLC), located under instrument panel next to steering column. Insert Ford Service Function (FSF) card in NGS tester. Perform security access procedure. See KEY PROGRAMMING – SECURITY ACCESS PROCEDURE. Select IGNITION KEY CODE PROGRAM. Turn ignition switch to LOCK position. Disconnect NGS tester. Key should now be programmed and be able to start vehicle.

PCM Programming – For Powertrain Control Module (PCM) programming procedures, see ALL MODELS (PROGRAMMING PCM).

NOTE: To enter programming mode, ensure battery is fully charged and anti-theft system (if equipped) is not armed or triggered. Up to 4 transmitters may be programmed.

Transmitter Programming – 1) Turn ignition switch to RUN position. Locate programming connector located next to electronic door lock module above glove box. Momentarily connect both terminals on programming connector. Horn will sound to verify program mode has been entered successfully. Press any button on remote transmitter.

2) Horn will sound again to verify remote transmitter has been programmed successfully. To program additional remote transmitters, press any button on next remote transmitter. Horn will sound again to indicate new transmitters have been programmed. Turn ignition switch to LOCK position. Horn will sound again to confirm program mode has exited.

COUGAR

NOTE: This procedure is used when a customer needs keys programmed into system and does not have 2 programmed ignition keys available, or when programmed ignition keys have been lost and/or ignition switch assembly has been replaced. This procedure will erase all programmed ignition keys from memory and prevent vehicle from starting until 2 keys have been programmed. Ignition keys must have correct mechanical key cut for vehicle and must be an encoded key. If additional key(s) are to be programmed, perform KEY PROGRAMMING – USING 2 PROGRAMMED KEYS. If remaining keys are with customer and not with vehicle, instruct customer to see owner's manual to program spare key(s).

Key Programming – Erase All Keys & Program 2 Keys – 1) Insert Ford Service Function (FSF) card into NGS tester. Turn ignition switch from LOCK to RUN position. With NGS tester connected to vehicle, enter PCM then select SECURITY ACCESS PROCEDURE. This procedure will take 10 minutes to perform. After the security access procedure has been completed, a new menu will be displayed with command options. Select IGNITION KEY CODE ERASE.

2) Turn ignition switch to LOCK position and disconnect NGS tester. Insert first encoded ignition key into ignition lock cylinder. Turn ignition switch to RUN position for 3 seconds. Turn ignition switch to LOCK position and remove first encoded key.

3) Within 5 seconds, insert second encoded ignition key into ignition lock cylinder. Turn ignition switch to RUN position for 3 seconds. Turn ignition switch to LOCK position and remove second encoded key. Both encoded ignition keys should now start vehicle.

NOTE: Security access must be granted to erase ignition keys, enable/disable spare key programming switch, or perform parameter resets for PCM. This procedure has a 10-minute time delay prior to granting security access during which the New Generation Star (NGS) tester must remain connected to vehicle. After security access has been granted, security access command menu is displayed which offers various command options. Multiple security access commands can be executed (if necessary) prior to exiting security access command menu. Execution of all necessary security access commands prior to exiting command menu avoids the performance of an additional security access procedure and the associated 10-minute time delay.

Key Programming – Security Access Procedure – Insert Ford Service Function (FSF) card into NGS tester. Turn ignition switch from LOCK to RUN position. With NGS tester connected to vehicle, enter PCM then select SECURITY ACCESS PROCEDURE. This procedure will take 10 minutes to perform. After the security access procedure has been completed, a new menu will be displayed with command options. Select as many functions as required before exiting this menu. Once this menu is exited, security access procedure must be performed again to perform additional commands.

NOTE: The spare key programming switch is a programmable switch which provides the capability to enable/disable the normal customer spare key programming procedure detailed in the owner's manual. This programmable switch is provided as a convenience for rental company fleets or other fleet purchasers who may not want the spare key programming procedure available to the vehicle driver. The spare key programming switch state can be viewed using PCM PID SPARE_KY.

Key Programming – Spare Key Programming Switch – Insert a programmed ignition key into the ignition lock cylinder. Insert Ford Service Function (FSF) card into NGS tester. Turn ignition switch from LOCK to RUN position. With NGS tester connected to vehicle, enter PCM then select SECURITY ACCESS PROCEDURE. This procedure will take 10 minutes to perform. After the security access procedure has been completed, a new menu will be displayed with command options. The default setting on all new vehicles is ENABLE. Select SPARE KEY PROGRAMMING SWITCH. Set SPARE KEY PROGRAMMING

GENERAL INFORMATION
Computer Relearn Procedures (Cont.)

SWITCH to ENABLE to allow keys to be programmed or DISABLE to make key programming not accessible.

NOTE: This procedure will only work if 2 or more programmed ignition keys are available and there is a need to program additional keys. If 2 keys are not available, perform KEY PROGRAMMING – ERASE ALL KEYS & PROGRAM 2 KEYS. PID SPARE_KY must be enabled for this procedure to operate. To enable this PID, perform KEY PROGRAMMING – SPARE KEY PROGRAMMING SWITCH and enable spare key programming switch. If programming procedure is successful, new key(s) will start vehicle and THEFT indicator will illuminate for 3 seconds. If programming procedure is not successful, new key(s) will not start vehicle and THEFT indicator will flash for one minute (after flashing for one minute, THEFT indicator will flash fault code). If necessary, repeat programming procedure. If programming of key(s) is still unsuccessful, perform self-diagnostics. See SELF-DIAGNOSTIC SYSTEM in PASSIVE ANTI-THEFT SYSTEMS – COUGAR article in ACCESSORIES & EQUIPMENT. Maximum of 8 keys can be programmed into system. If procedure is not performed as outlined, programming procedure will end. Ignition keys must have correct mechanical key cut for vehicle and must be an encoded key.

Key Programming – Using 2 Programmed Keys – 1) Insert the first programmed ignition key into ignition lock cylinder. Turn ignition switch from LOCK to RUN position (ignition switch must stay in RUN position for one second). Turn ignition switch to LOCK position and remove ignition key from ignition lock cylinder.
2) Within 5 seconds of turning ignition switch to LOCK position, insert second programmed ignition key into ignition lock cylinder. Turn ignition switch from LOCK to RUN position (ignition switch must stay in RUN position for one second). Turn ignition switch to LOCK position and remove second ignition key from ignition lock cylinder.
3) Within 5 seconds of turning ignition switch to LOCK position, insert a NEW unprogrammed ignition key into ignition lock cylinder. Turn ignition switch from LOCK to RUN position (ignition switch must stay in RUN position for one second). Turn ignition switch to LOCK position and remove ignition key from ignition lock cylinder. The NEW ignition key should now be programmed. To program additional key(s), repeat key programming procedure from step **1)**.

NOTE: This procedure is used when customer needs extra keys programmed and 2 programmed keys are not available, but system has 2 ignition keys programmed. A maximum of 8 keys can be programmed. If 8 keys are already programmed, this procedure will not allow any more keys to be programmed. The number of programmed keys can be determined by accessing PCM PID NUMKEYS with NGS tester.

Key Programming – Without Using 2 Programmed Keys – Insert unprogrammed key in ignition and turn ignition switch to RUN position. Connect New Generation Star (NGS) tester to Data Link Connector (DLC), located under instrument panel next to steering column. Insert Ford Service Function (FSF) card in NGS tester. Perform security access procedure. See KEY PROGRAMMING – SECURITY ACCESS PROCEDURE. Select IGNITION KEY CODE PROGRAM. Turn ignition switch to LOCK position. Disconnect NGS tester. Key should now be programmed and be able to start vehicle.
PCM Programming – For Powertrain Control Module (PCM) programming procedures, see ALL MODELS (PROGRAMMING PCM).

NOTE: Once programming mode has been enter and transmitter button is pressed for the first time, all previously stored transmitter codes will be erased. All transmitters to be used with this system must be programmed at the same time (maximum of 4 transmitters).

Remote Transmitter – 1) Open driver's window. Turn ignition switch to RUN or ACC position. Access programming connector. Programming connector is behind left trunk trim panel, attached to relay panel. Using jumper wire, momentarily short the 2 terminals of programming connector together. Both doors should lock then unlock to confirm program mode has been entered.
2) Press any button on keyless entry remote transmitter. Both doors should lock then unlock to confirm that transmitter has been programmed.
3) Repeat step **2)** to program all other transmitter (maximum of 4 transmitters) to be used with this system before exiting programming. To exit programming, turn ignition switch to LOCK position. To confirm programming mode has been exited, both doors should lock then unlock.

CROWN VICTORIA & GRAND MARQUIS

Customer Driven Preferences – There are customer preferences that can be configured on this vehicle. Some items the customer may or may not want to have enabled. To carry out customer configuration process, connect New Generation Star (NGS) tester to Data Link Connector (DLC), located under instrument panel next to steering column. Insert Ford Service Function (FSF) card into NGS tester. Using NGS tester, set customer preferences as necessary. See CUSTOMER PREFERENCE INDEX (CROWN VICTORIA & GRAND MARQUIS) table.

NOTE: NGS tester will only store module configuration information for 24 hours.

Driver's Door Module (DDM) Programming – Prior to removal of DDM, upload module configuration information to the New Generation Star (NGS) tester using manufacturer's instructions. Once module has been replaced, download module configuration information from NGS tester into new module.

NOTE: This procedure is used when a customer needs keys programmed into system and does not have 2 programmed ignition keys available, or when programmed ignition keys have been lost and/or ignition switch assembly has been replaced. This procedure will erase all programmed ignition keys from memory and prevent vehicle from starting until 2 keys have been programmed. Ignition keys must have correct mechanical key cut for vehicle and must be an encoded key. If additional key(s) are to be programmed, perform KEY PROGRAMMING – USING 2 PROGRAMMED KEYS. If remaining keys are with customer and not with vehicle, instruct customer to see owner's manual to program spare key(s).

Key Programming – Erase All Keys & Program 2 Keys – 1) Insert Ford Service Function (FSF) card into NGS tester. Turn ignition switch from LOCK to RUN position. With NGS tester connected to vehicle, enter PATS then select SECURITY ACCESS PROCEDURE. This procedure will take 10 minutes to perform. After the security access procedure has been completed, a new menu will be displayed with command options. Select IGNITION KEY CODE ERASE.

CUSTOMER PREFERENCE INDEX (CROWN VICTORIA & GRAND MARQUIS)

Module	Configurable Item	State
Driver's Door Module	Remote Transmitter Programming	ID Code (TIC) Value
Driver's Door Module	Horn Chirp	Enabled, Disabled
Driver's Door Module	Autolocks	Enabled, Disabled
Passive Anti-Theft System Module	Enter Security Access	Enter Security Access
Passive Anti-Theft System Module	Ignition Key Code Program	Program Ignition Keys
Passive Anti-Theft System Module	Ignition Key Code Erase	Erase All Stored Ignition Keys
Passive Anti-Theft System Module	Spare Key	Enabled, Disabled
Passive Anti-Theft System Module	Parameter Reset	Reset Security ID

2) Turn ignition switch to LOCK position and disconnect NGS tester. Insert first encoded ignition key into ignition lock cylinder. Turn ignition switch to RUN position for 3 seconds. Turn ignition switch to LOCK position and remove first encoded key.

3) Within 5 seconds, insert second encoded ignition key into ignition lock cylinder. Turn ignition switch to RUN position for 3 seconds. Turn ignition switch to LOCK position and remove second encoded key. Both encoded ignition keys should now start vehicle.

NOTE: Security access must be granted to erase ignition keys, enable/disable spare key programming switch, or perform parameter resets for PATS and PCM. This procedure has a 10-minute time delay prior to granting security access during which the New Generation Star (NGS) tester must remain connected to vehicle. After security access has been granted, security access command menu is displayed which offers various command options. Multiple security access commands can be executed (if necessary) prior to exiting security access command menu. Execution of all necessary security access commands prior to exiting command menu avoids the performance of an additional security access procedure and the associated 10-minute time delay.

Key Programming – Security Access Procedure – Insert Ford Service Function (FSF) card into NGS tester. Turn ignition switch from LOCK to RUN position. With NGS tester connected to vehicle, enter PATS then select SECURITY ACCESS PROCEDURE. This procedure will take 10 minutes to perform. After the security access procedure has been completed, a new menu will be displayed with command options. Select as many functions as required before exiting this menu. Once this menu is exited, security access procedure must be performed again to perform additional commands.

NOTE: The spare key programming switch is a programmable switch which provides the capability to enable/disable the normal customer spare key programming procedure detailed in the owner's manual. This programmable switch is provided as a convenience for rental company fleets or other fleet purchasers who may not want the spare key programming procedure available to the vehicle driver. The spare key programming switch state can be viewed using PATS PID SPARE_KY.

Key Programming – Spare Key Programming Switch – Insert a programmed ignition key into the ignition lock cylinder. Insert Ford Service Function (FSF) card into NGS tester. Turn ignition switch from LOCK to RUN position. With NGS tester connected to vehicle, enter PATS then select SECURITY ACCESS PROCEDURE. This procedure will take 10 minutes to perform. After the security access procedure has been completed, a new menu will be displayed with command options. The default setting on all new vehicles is ENABLE. Select SPARE KEY PROGRAMMING SWITCH. Set SPARE KEY PROGRAMMING SWITCH to ENABLE to allow keys to be programmed or DISABLE to make key programming not accessible.

NOTE: This procedure will only work if 2 or more programmed ignition keys are available and there is a need to program additional keys. If 2 keys are not available, perform KEY PROGRAMMING – ERASE ALL KEYS & PROGRAM 2 KEYS. PID SPARE_KY must be enabled for this procedure to operate. To enable this PID, perform KEY PROGRAMMING – SPARE KEY PROGRAMMING SWITCH and enable spare key programming switch. If programming procedure is successful, new key(s) will start vehicle and THEFT indicator will illuminate for 3 seconds. If programming procedure is not successful, new key(s) will not start vehicle and THEFT indicator will flash for one minute (after flashing for one minute, THEFT indicator will flash fault code). If necessary, repeat programming procedure. If programming of key(s) is still unsuccessful, perform self-diagnostics. See SELF-DIAGNOSTIC SYSTEM in PASSIVE ANTI-THEFT SYSTEMS – CROWN VICTORIA & GRAND MARQUIS article in ACCESSORIES & EQUIPMENT. Maximum of 8 keys can be programmed into system. If procedure is not performed as outlined, programming procedure will end. Ignition keys must have correct mechanical key cut for vehicle and must be an encoded key.

Key Programming – Using 2 Programmed Keys – 1) Insert the first programmed ignition key into ignition lock cylinder. Turn ignition switch from LOCK to RUN position (ignition switch must stay in RUN position for one second). Turn ignition switch to LOCK position and remove ignition key from ignition lock cylinder.

2) Within 5 seconds of turning ignition switch to LOCK position, insert second programmed ignition key into ignition lock cylinder. Turn ignition switch from LOCK to RUN position (ignition switch must stay in RUN position for one second). Turn ignition switch to LOCK position and remove second ignition key from ignition lock cylinder.

3) Within 5 seconds of turning ignition switch to LOCK position, insert a NEW unprogrammed ignition key into ignition lock cylinder. Turn ignition switch from LOCK to RUN position (ignition switch must stay in RUN position for one second). Turn ignition switch to LOCK position and remove ignition key from ignition lock cylinder. The NEW ignition key should now be programmed. To program additional key(s), repeat key programming procedure from step **1)**.

NOTE: This procedure is used when customer needs extra keys programmed and 2 programmed keys are not available, but system has 2 ignition keys programmed. A maximum of 8 keys can be programmed. If 8 keys are already programmed, this procedure will not allow any more keys to be programmed. The number of programmed keys can be determined by accessing PATS PID NUMKEYS with NGS tester.

Key Programming – Without Using 2 Programmed Keys – Insert unprogrammed key in ignition and turn ignition switch to RUN position. Connect New Generation Star (NGS) tester to Data Link Connector (DLC), located under instrument panel next to steering column. Insert Ford Service Function (FSF) card in NGS tester. Perform security access procedure. See KEY PROGRAMMING – SECURITY ACCESS PROCEDURE. Select IGNITION KEY CODE PROGRAM. Turn ignition switch to LOCK position. Disconnect NGS tester. Key should now be programmed and be able to start vehicle.

NOTE: NGS tester will only store module configuration information for 24 hours.

Lighting Control Module (LCM) Programming – Prior to removal of LCM, upload module configuration information to the New Generation Star (NGS) tester using manufacturer's instructions. Once module has been replaced, download module configuration information from NGS tester into new module.

NOTE: NGS tester will only store module configuration information for 24 hours.

Passive Anti-Theft System (PATS) Module – Prior to removal of PATS module, upload module configuration information to the New Generation Star (NGS) tester using manufacturer's instructions. Once module has been replaced, download module configuration information from NGS tester into new module. After module has been installed and module configuration information has been downloaded, all ignition keys to be used with vehicle MUST be reprogrammed. See KEY PROGRAMMING – ERASE ALL KEYS & PROGRAM 2 KEYS.

PCM Programming – For Powertrain Control Module (PCM) programming procedures, see ALL MODELS (PROGRAMMING PCM).

NOTE: This procedure will erase all transmitters that are programed. Ensure all transmitters to be used with vehicle are available before beginning this procedure.

Transmitter Programming – Open driver's window. Turn ignition switch from LOCK to RUN position 4 times within 3 seconds ending in RUN position. Door locks will lock then unlock to verify programming mode has been entered. Press any button on transmitter to be programmed. Within 7.5 seconds, press any button on next transmitter to be programmed and so on until all transmitters are programmed. To exit programming mode, turn ignition switch to START position or wait for more than 7.5 seconds.

ECONOLINE

PCM Programming – For Powertrain Control Module (PCM) programming procedures, see ALL MODELS (PROGRAMMING PCM).

ESCORT & TRACER

PCM Programming – For Powertrain Control Module (PCM) programming procedures, see ALL MODELS (PROGRAMMING PCM).

Transmitter Reprogramming – To reprogram all transmitters, cycle ignition switch from LOCK to RUN position 8 times within 10 seconds, ending in RUN position or LOCK to START position 4 times in 10 seconds, ending in RUN position. After doors lock and unlock, press any button on all remote transmitters (up to limit of 4). With each button

press on remote transmitter, door locks should cycle (lock/unlock) to confirm programming. Once completed, turn ignition switch to LOCK position. Door locks should cycle (lock/unlock) one last time to confirm completion of programming. All transmitters must be reprogrammed at the same time.

EXPEDITION & NAVIGATOR

Customer Driven Preferences – There are customer preferences that can be configured on this vehicle. Some items the customer may or may not want to have enabled. To carry out customer configuration process, connect New Generation Star (NGS) tester to Data Link Connector (DLC), located under instrument panel next to steering column. Insert Ford Service Function (FSF) card into NGS tester. Using NGS tester, set customer preferences as necessary. See CUSTOMER PREFERENCE INDEX (EXPEDITION & NAVIGATOR) table.

NOTE: NGS tester will only store module configuration information for 24 hours.

Generic Electronic Module (GEM) Programming – Prior to removal of GEM, upload module configuration information to the New Generation Star (NGS) tester using manufacturer's instructions. Once module has been replaced, download module configuration information from NGS tester into new module.

NOTE: This procedure is used when a customer needs keys programmed into system and does not have 2 programmed ignition keys available, or when programmed ignition keys have been lost and/or ignition switch assembly has been replaced. This procedure will erase all programmed ignition keys from memory and prevent vehicle from starting until 2 keys have been programmed. Ignition keys must have correct mechanical key cut for vehicle and must be an encoded key. If additional key(s) are to be programmed, perform KEY PROGRAMMING – USING 2 PROGRAMMED KEYS. If remaining keys are with customer and not with vehicle, instruct customer to see owner's manual to program spare key(s).

Key Programming – Erase All Keys & Program 2 Keys – 1) Insert Ford Service Function (FSF) card into NGS tester. Turn ignition switch from LOCK to RUN position. With NGS tester connected to vehicle, enter instrument cluster then select SECURITY ACCESS PROCEDURE. This procedure will take 10 minutes to perform. After the security access procedure has been completed, a new menu will be displayed with command options. Select IGNITION KEY CODE ERASE.

2) Turn ignition switch to LOCK position and disconnect NGS tester. Insert first encoded ignition key into ignition lock cylinder. Turn ignition switch to RUN position for 3 seconds. Turn ignition switch to LOCK position and remove first encoded key.

CUSTOMER PREFERENCE INDEX (EXPEDITION & NAVIGATOR)

Module	Configurable Item	State
Remote Anti-Theft Personality Module	Autolocks	Enable, Disabled
Instrument Cluster	Enter Security Access	Enter Security Access
Instrument Cluster	Ignition Key Code Program	Program Ignition Keys
Instrument Cluster	Ignition Key Code Erase	Erase All Stored Ignition Keys
Instrument Cluster	Spare Key	Enabled, Disabled
Instrument Cluster	Parameter Reset	Reset Security ID

Computer Relearn Procedures (Cont.)

3) Within 5 seconds, insert second encoded ignition key into ignition lock cylinder. Turn ignition switch to RUN position for 3 seconds. Turn ignition switch to LOCK position and remove second encoded key. Both encoded ignition keys should now start vehicle.

NOTE: Security access must be granted to erase ignition keys, enable/disable spare key programming switch, or perform parameter resets for instrument cluster and PCM. This procedure has a 10-minute time delay prior to granting security access during which the New Generation Star (NGS) tester must remain connected to vehicle. After security access has been granted, security access command menu is displayed which offers various command options. Multiple security access commands can be executed (if necessary) prior to exiting security access command menu. Execution of all necessary security access commands prior to exiting command menu avoids the performance of an additional security access procedure and the associated 10-minute time delay.

Key Programming – Security Access Procedure – Insert Ford Service Function (FSF) card into NGS tester. Turn ignition switch from LOCK to RUN position. With NGS tester connected to vehicle, enter instrument cluster then select SECURITY ACCESS PROCEDURE. This procedure will take 10 minutes to perform. After the security access procedure has been completed, a new menu will be displayed with command options. Select as many functions as required before exiting this menu. Once this menu is exited, security access procedure must be performed again to perform additional commands.

NOTE: The spare key programming switch is a programmable switch which provides the capability to enable/disable the normal customer spare key programming procedure detailed in the owner's manual. This programmable switch is provided as a convenience for rental company fleets or other fleet purchasers who may not want the spare key programming procedure available to the vehicle driver. The spare key programming switch state can be viewed using instrument cluster PID SPARE_KY.

Key Programming – Spare Key Programming Switch – Insert a programmed ignition key into the ignition lock cylinder. Insert Ford Service Function (FSF) card into NGS tester. Turn ignition switch from LOCK to RUN position. With NGS tester connected to vehicle, enter instrument cluster then select SECURITY ACCESS PROCEDURE. This procedure will take 10 minutes to perform. After the security access procedure has been completed, a new menu will be displayed with command options. The default setting on all new vehicles is ENABLE. Select SPARE KEY PROGRAMMING SWITCH. Set SPARE KEY PROGRAMMING SWITCH to ENABLE to allow keys to be programmed or DISABLE to make key programming not accessible.

NOTE: This procedure will only work if 2 or more programmed ignition keys are available and there is a need to program additional keys. If 2 keys are not available, perform KEY PROGRAMMING – ERASE ALL KEYS & PROGRAM 2 KEYS. PID SPARE_KY must be enabled for this procedure to operate. To enable this PID, perform KEY PROGRAMMING – SPARE KEY PROGRAMMING SWITCH and enable spare key programming switch. If programming procedure is successful, new key(s) will start vehicle and THEFT indicator will illuminate for 3 seconds. If programming procedure is not successful, new key(s) will not start vehicle and THEFT indicator will flash for one minute (after flashing for one minute, THEFT indicator will flash fault code). If necessary, repeat programming procedure. If programming of key(s) is still unsuccessful, perform self-diagnostics. See SELF-DIAGNOSTIC SYSTEM in PASSIVE ANTI-THEFT SYSTEMS – EXPEDITION & NAVIGATOR article in ACCESSORIES & EQUIPMENT. Maximum of 8 keys can be programmed into system. If procedure is not performed as outlined, programming procedure will end. Ignition keys must have correct mechanical key cut for vehicle and must be an encoded key.

Key Programming – Using 2 Programmed Keys – 1) Insert the first programmed ignition key into ignition lock cylinder. Turn ignition switch from LOCK to RUN position (ignition switch must stay in RUN position for one second). Turn ignition switch to LOCK position and remove ignition key from ignition lock cylinder.

2) Within 5 seconds of turning ignition switch to LOCK position, insert second programmed ignition key into ignition lock cylinder. Turn ignition switch from LOCK to RUN position (ignition switch must stay in RUN position for one second). Turn ignition switch to LOCK position and remove second ignition key from ignition lock cylinder.

3) Within 5 seconds of turning ignition switch to LOCK position, insert a NEW unprogrammed ignition key into ignition lock cylinder. Turn ignition switch from LOCK to RUN position (ignition switch must stay in RUN position for one second). Turn ignition switch to LOCK position and remove ignition key from ignition lock cylinder. The NEW ignition key should now be programmed. To program additional key(s), repeat key programming procedure from step **1)**.

NOTE: This procedure is used when customer needs extra keys programmed and 2 programmed keys are not available, but system has 2 ignition keys programmed. A maximum of 8 keys can be programmed. If 8 keys are already programmed, this procedure will not allow any more keys to be programmed. The number of programmed keys can be determined by accessing instrument cluster PID NUMKEYS with NGS tester.

Key Programming – Without Using 2 Programmed Keys – Insert unprogrammed key in ignition and turn ignition switch to RUN position. Connect New Generation Star (NGS) tester to Data Link Connector (DLC), located under instrument panel next to steering column. Insert Ford Service Function (FSF) card in NGS tester. Perform security access procedure. See KEY PROGRAMMING – SECURITY ACCESS PROCEDURE. Select IGNITION KEY CODE PROGRAM. Turn ignition switch to LOCK position. Disconnect NGS tester. Key should now be programmed and be able to start vehicle.

CUSTOMER PREFERENCE INDEX (EXPLORER & MOUNTAINEER)

Module	Configurable Item	State
Anti-Lock Brake Control Module	Tire Size (Revolutions/Mile)	List Of Tires
Anti-Lock Brake Control Module	Tone Ring Size (Number Of Teeth)	8.8"
Anti-Lock Brake Control Module	Option Information	4WABS
Anti-Lock Brake Control Module	Vehicle Program	Explorer/Mountaineer
Central Timer Module	Tire Size (Revolutions/Mile)	List Of Tires
Central Timer Module	Tone Ring Size (Number Of Teeth)	8.8"
Central Timer Module	Option Information	4WABS
Central Timer Module	Vehicle Program	Explorer/Mountaineer
Passive Anti-Theft System Module	Enter Security Access	Enter Security Access
Passive Anti-Theft System Module	Ignition Key Code Program	Program Ignition Keys
Passive Anti-Theft System Module	Ignition Key Code Erase	Erase All Stored Ignition Keys
Passive Anti-Theft System Module	Spare Key	Enabled, Disabled
Passive Anti-Theft System Module	Parameter Reset	Reset Security ID

PCM Programming – For Powertrain Control Module (PCM) programming procedures, see ALL MODELS (PROGRAMMING PCM).

Transmitter Programming – Open driver's window. Cycle ignition key from LOCK to RUN 8 times within 10 seconds ending in RUN position. Doors will lock, then unlock to verify program mode has been entered. Press any button on transmitter. Doors will lock, then unlock to confirm transmitter has been programmed. Turn ignition switch to LOCK position or wait 5 minutes to exit program mode. Doors will lock, then unlock to confirm program mode has been exited.

EXPLORER & MOUNTAINEER

Customer Driven Preferences – There are customer preferences that can be configured on this vehicle. Some items the customer may or may not want to have enabled. To carry out customer configuration process, connect New Generation Star (NGS) tester to Data Link Connector (DLC), located under instrument panel next to steering column. Insert Ford Service Function (FSF) card into NGS tester. Using NGS tester, set customer preferences as necessary. See CUSTOMER PREFERENCE INDEX (EXPLORER & MOUNTAINEER) table.

NOTE: NGS tester will only store module configuration information for 24 hours.

NOTE: Vehicle will have a CTM or a GEM depending on what features vehicle is equipped with.

Central Timer Module (CTM)/Generic Electronic Module (GEM) Programming – Prior to removal of CTM/GEM, upload module configuration information to the New Generation Star (NGS) tester using manufacturer's instructions. Once module has been replaced, download module configuration information from NGS tester into new module.

NOTE: This procedure is used when a customer needs keys programmed into system and does not have 2 programmed ignition keys available, or when programmed ignition keys have been lost and/or ignition switch assembly has been replaced. This procedure will erase all programmed ignition keys from memory and prevent vehicle from starting until 2 keys have been programmed. Ignition keys must have correct mechanical key cut for vehicle and must be an encoded key. If additional key(s) are to be programmed, perform KEY PROGRAMMING – USING 2 PROGRAMMED KEYS. If remaining keys are with customer and not with vehicle, instruct customer to see owner's manual to program spare key(s).

Key Programming – Erase All Keys & Program 2 Keys – 1) Insert Ford Service Function (FSF) card into NGS tester. Turn ignition switch from LOCK to RUN position. With NGS tester connected to vehicle, enter PATS then select SECURITY ACCESS PROCEDURE. This procedure will take 10 minutes to perform. After the security access procedure has been completed, a new menu will be displayed with command options. Select IGNITION KEY CODE ERASE.

2) Turn ignition switch to LOCK position and disconnect NGS tester. Insert first encoded ignition key into ignition lock cylinder. Turn ignition switch to RUN position for 3 seconds. Turn ignition switch to LOCK position and remove first encoded key.

3) Within 5 seconds, insert second encoded ignition key into ignition lock cylinder. Turn ignition switch to RUN position for 3 seconds. Turn ignition switch to LOCK position and remove second encoded key. Both encoded ignition keys should now start vehicle.

NOTE: Security access must be granted to erase ignition keys, enable/disable spare key programming switch, or perform parameter resets for PATS module and PCM. This procedure has a 10-minute time delay prior to granting security access during which the New Generation Star (NGS) tester must remain connected to vehicle. After security access has been granted, security access command menu is displayed which offers various command options. Multiple security access commands can be executed (if necessary) prior to exiting security access command menu. Execution of all necessary security access commands prior to exiting command menu avoids the performance of an additional security access procedure and the associated 10-minute time delay.

Key Programming – Security Access Procedure – Insert Ford Service Function (FSF) card into NGS tester. Turn ignition switch from LOCK to RUN position. With NGS tester connected to vehicle, enter PATS then select SECURITY ACCESS PROCEDURE. This procedure will take 10 minutes to perform. After the security access procedure has been completed, a new menu will be displayed with command options. Select as many functions as required before exiting this menu. Once this menu is exited, security access procedure must be performed again to perform additional commands.

NOTE: The spare key programming switch is a programmable switch which provides the capability to enable/disable the normal customer spare key programming procedure detailed in the owner's manual. This programmable switch is provided as a convenience for rental company fleets or other fleet purchasers who may not want the spare key programming procedure available to the vehicle driver. The spare key programming switch state can be viewed using PATS PID SPARE_KY.

Key Programming – Spare Key Programming Switch – Insert a programmed ignition key into the ignition lock cylinder. Insert Ford Service Function (FSF) card into NGS tester. Turn ignition switch from LOCK to RUN position. With NGS tester connected to vehicle, enter PATS then select SECURITY ACCESS PROCEDURE. This procedure will take 10 minutes to perform. After the security access procedure has been completed, a new menu will be displayed with command options. The default setting on all new vehicles is ENABLE. Select SPARE KEY PROGRAMMING SWITCH. Set SPARE KEY PROGRAMMING

Computer Relearn Procedures (Cont.)

SWITCH to ENABLE to allow keys to be programmed or DISABLE to make key programming not accessible.

***

NOTE: This procedure will only work if 2 or more programmed ignition keys are available and there is a need to program additional keys. If 2 keys are not available, perform KEY PROGRAMMING – ERASE ALL KEYS & PROGRAM 2 KEYS. PID SPARE_KY must be enabled for this procedure to operate. To enable this PID, perform KEY PROGRAMMING – SPARE KEY PROGRAMMING SWITCH and enable spare key programming switch. If programming procedure is successful, new key(s) will start vehicle and THEFT indicator will illuminate for 3 seconds. If programming procedure is not successful, new key(s) will not start vehicle and THEFT indicator will flash for one minute (after flashing for one minute, THEFT indicator will flash fault code). If necessary, repeat programming procedure. If programming of key(s) is still unsuccessful, perform self-diagnostics. See SELF-DIAGNOSTIC SYSTEM in PASSIVE ANTI-THEFT SYSTEMS – EXPLORER & MOUNTAINEER article in ACCESSORIES & EQUIPMENT. Maximum of 8 keys can be programmed into system. If procedure is not performed as outlined, programming procedure will end. Ignition keys must have correct mechanical key cut for vehicle and must be an encoded key.

***

Key Programming – Using 2 Programmed Keys – 1) Insert the first programmed ignition key into ignition lock cylinder. Turn ignition switch from LOCK to RUN position (ignition switch must stay in RUN position for one second). Turn ignition switch to LOCK position and remove ignition key from ignition lock cylinder.

2) Within 5 seconds of turning ignition switch to LOCK position, insert second programmed ignition key into ignition lock cylinder. Turn ignition switch from LOCK to RUN position (ignition switch must stay in RUN position for one second). Turn ignition switch to LOCK position and remove second ignition key from ignition lock cylinder.

3) Within 5 seconds of turning ignition switch to LOCK position, insert a NEW unprogrammed ignition key into ignition lock cylinder. Turn ignition switch from LOCK to RUN position (ignition switch must stay in RUN position for one second). Turn ignition switch to LOCK position and remove ignition key from ignition lock cylinder. The NEW ignition key should now be programmed. To program additional key(s), repeat key programming procedure from step **1)**.

***

NOTE: This procedure is used when customer needs extra keys programmed and 2 programmed keys are not available, but system has 2 ignition keys programmed. A maximum of 8 keys can be programmed. If 8 keys are already programmed, this procedure will not allow any more keys to be programmed. The number of programmed keys can be determined by accessing PATS PID NUMKEYS with NGS tester.

***

Key Programming – Without Using 2 Programmed Keys – Insert unprogrammed key in ignition and turn ignition switch to RUN position.

Connect New Generation Star (NGS) tester to Data Link Connector (DLC), located under instrument panel next to steering column. Insert Ford Service Function (FSF) card in NGS tester. Perform security access procedure. See KEY PROGRAMMING – SECURITY ACCESS PROCEDURE. Select IGNITION KEY CODE PROGRAM. Turn ignition switch to LOCK position. Disconnect NGS tester. Key should now be programmed and be able to start vehicle.

PCM Programming – For Powertrain Control Module (PCM) programming procedures, see ALL MODELS (PROGRAMMING PCM).

Transmitter Programming – Open driver's window. Cycle ignition key from LOCK to RUN 5 times within 10 seconds ending in RUN position. Doors will lock, then unlock to verify program mode has been entered. Press any button on transmitter. Doors will lock, then unlock to confirm transmitter has been programmed. Turn ignition switch to LOCK position or wait 20 seconds to exit program mode. Doors will lock, then unlock to confirm program mode has been exited.

MUSTANG

Customer Driven Preferences – There are customer preferences that can be configured on this vehicle. Some items the customer may or may not want to have enabled. To carry out customer configuration process, connect New Generation Star (NGS) tester to Data Link Connector (DLC), located under instrument panel next to steering column. Insert Ford Service Function (FSF) card into NGS tester. Using NGS tester, set customer preferences as necessary. See CUSTOMER PREFERENCE INDEX (MUSTANG) table.

***

NOTE: This procedure is used when a customer needs keys programmed into system and does not have 2 programmed ignition keys available, or when programmed ignition keys have been lost and/or ignition switch assembly has been replaced. This procedure will erase all programmed ignition keys from memory and prevent vehicle from starting until 2 keys have been programmed. Ignition keys must have correct mechanical key cut for vehicle and must be an encoded key. If additional key(s) are to be programmed, perform KEY PROGRAMMING – USING 2 PROGRAMMED KEYS. If remaining keys are with customer and not with vehicle, instruct customer to see owner's manual to program spare key(s).

***

Key Programming – Erase All Keys & Program 2 Keys – 1) Insert Ford Service Function (FSF) card into NGS tester. Turn ignition switch from LOCK to RUN position. With NGS tester connected to vehicle, enter instrument cluster then select SECURITY ACCESS PROCEDURE. This procedure will take 10 minutes to perform. After the security access procedure has been completed, a new menu will be displayed with command options. Select IGNITION KEY CODE ERASE.

2) Turn ignition switch to LOCK position and disconnect NGS tester. Insert first encoded ignition key into ignition lock cylinder. Turn ignition switch to RUN position for 3 seconds. Turn ignition switch to LOCK position and remove first encoded key.

CUSTOMER PREFERENCE INDEX (MUSTANG)

Module	Configurable Item	State
Instrument Cluster	Enter Security Access	Enter Security Access
Instrument Cluster	Ignition Key Code Program	Program Ignition Keys
Instrument Cluster	Ignition Key Code Erase	Erase All Stored Ignition Keys
Instrument Cluster	Spare Key	Enabled, Disabled
Instrument Cluster	Parameter Reset	Reset Security ID

GENERAL INFORMATION
Computer Relearn Procedures (Cont.)

3) Within 5 seconds, insert second encoded ignition key into ignition lock cylinder. Turn ignition switch to RUN position for 3 seconds. Turn ignition switch to LOCK position and remove second encoded key. Both encoded ignition keys should now start vehicle.

NOTE: Security access must be granted to erase ignition keys, enable/disable spare key programming switch, or perform parameter resets for instrument cluster and PCM. This procedure has a 10-minute time delay prior to granting security access during which the New Generation Star (NGS) tester must remain connected to vehicle. After security access has been granted, security access command menu is displayed which offers various command options. Multiple security access commands can be executed (if necessary) prior to exiting security access command menu. Execution of all necessary security access commands prior to exiting command menu avoids the performance of an additional security access procedure and the associated 10-minute time delay.

Key Programming – Security Access Procedure – Insert Ford Service Function (FSF) card into NGS tester. Turn ignition switch from LOCK to RUN position. With NGS tester connected to vehicle, enter instrument cluster then select SECURITY ACCESS PROCEDURE. This procedure will take 10 minutes to perform. After the security access procedure has been completed, a new menu will be displayed with command options. Select as many functions as required before exiting this menu. Once this menu is exited, security access procedure must be performed again to perform additional commands.

NOTE: The spare key programming switch is a programmable switch which provides the capability to enable/disable the normal customer spare key programming procedure detailed in the owner's manual. This programmable switch is provided as a convenience for rental company fleets or other fleet purchasers who may not want the spare key programming procedure available to the vehicle driver. The spare key programming switch state can be viewed using instrument cluster PID SPARE_KY.

Key Programming – Spare Key Programming Switch – Insert a programmed ignition key into the ignition lock cylinder. Insert Ford Service Function (FSF) card into NGS tester. Turn ignition switch from LOCK to RUN position. With NGS tester connected to vehicle, enter instrument cluster then select SECURITY ACCESS PROCEDURE. This procedure will take 10 minutes to perform. After the security access procedure has been completed, a new menu will be displayed with command options. The default setting on all new vehicles is ENABLE. Select SPARE KEY PROGRAMMING SWITCH. Set SPARE KEY PROGRAMMING SWITCH to ENABLE to allow keys to be programmed or DISABLE to make key programming not accessible.

NOTE: This procedure will only work if 2 or more programmed ignition keys are available and there is a need to program additional keys. If 2 keys are not available, perform KEY PROGRAMMING – ERASE ALL KEYS & PROGRAM 2 KEYS. PID SPARE_KY must be enabled for this procedure to operate. To enable this PID, perform KEY PROGRAMMING – SPARE KEY PROGRAMMING SWITCH and enable spare key programming switch. If programming procedure is successful, new key(s) will start vehicle and THEFT indicator will illuminate for 3 seconds. If programming procedure is not successful, new key(s) will not start vehicle and THEFT indicator will flash for one minute (after flashing for one minute, THEFT indicator will flash fault code). If necessary, repeat programming procedure. If programming of key(s) is still unsuccessful, perform self-diagnostics. See SELF-DIAGNOSTIC SYSTEM in PASSIVE ANTI-THEFT SYSTEMS – MUSTANG article in ACCESSORIES & EQUIPMENT. Maximum of 8 keys can be programmed into system. If procedure is not performed as outlined, programming procedure will end. Ignition keys must have correct mechanical key cut for vehicle and must be an encoded key.

Key Programming – Using 2 Programmed Keys – 1) Insert the first programmed ignition key into ignition lock cylinder. Turn ignition switch from LOCK to RUN position (ignition switch must stay in RUN position for one second). Turn ignition switch to LOCK position and remove ignition key from ignition lock cylinder.

2) Within 5 seconds of turning ignition switch to LOCK position, insert second programmed ignition key into ignition lock cylinder. Turn ignition switch from LOCK to RUN position (ignition switch must stay in RUN position for one second). Turn ignition switch to LOCK position and remove second ignition key from ignition lock cylinder.

3) Within 5 seconds of turning ignition switch to LOCK position, insert a NEW unprogrammed ignition key into ignition lock cylinder. Turn ignition switch from LOCK to RUN position (ignition switch must stay in RUN position for one second). Turn ignition switch to LOCK position and remove ignition key from ignition lock cylinder. The NEW ignition key should now be programmed. To program additional key(s), repeat key programming procedure from step **1)**.

NOTE: This procedure is used when customer needs extra keys programmed and 2 programmed keys are not available, but system has 2 ignition keys programmed. A maximum of 8 keys can be programmed. If 8 keys are already programmed, this procedure will not allow any more keys to be programmed. The number of programmed keys can be determined by accessing instrument cluster PID NUMKEYS with NGS tester.

Key Programming – Without Using 2 Programmed Keys – Insert unprogrammed key in ignition and turn ignition switch to RUN position. Connect New Generation Star (NGS) tester to Data Link Connector (DLC), located under instrument panel next to steering column. Insert Ford Service Function (FSF) card in NGS tester. Perform security access procedure. See KEY PROGRAMMING – SECURITY ACCESS PROCEDURE. Select IGNITION KEY CODE PROGRAM. Turn ignition switch to LOCK position. Disconnect NGS tester. Key should now be programmed and be able to start vehicle.

Matching Security Identification Between Instrument Cluster & PCM – 1) Using NGS tester, perform instrument cluster self-test. If DTC B2139 is retrieved, go to next step. If DTC B2139 is not retrieved, system is okay at this time.

2) Perform security access for instrument cluster. See KEY PROGRAMMING – SECURITY ACCESS PROCEDURE. Using NGS tester, select PARAMETER RESET command for instrument cluster. Using NGS tester, select PARAMETER RESET command for PCM. Turn ignition switch to RUN position for 3 seconds. Turn ignition switch to LOCK position. Using NGS tester, perform instrument cluster self-test. If DTC B2139 is not retrieved, system is okay at this time. If DTC B2139 is retrieved, verify PCM calibration is correct for vehicle. If calibration is okay, replace instrument cluster and repeat this test. If DTC B2139 still exists, replace PCM.

PCM Programming – For Powertrain Control Module (PCM) programming procedures, see ALL MODELS (PROGRAMMING PCM).

NOTE: Performing this test will erase all previously programmed transmitters from memory of GEM. All remote transmitters to be used with vehicle MUST be programmed at the same time.

Transmitter Programming – Open driver's window. Cycle ignition key from LOCK to RUN 8 times within 10 seconds ending in RUN position. Doors will lock, then unlock to verify program mode has been entered. Within 7.5 seconds, press any button on transmitter. Doors will lock, then unlock to confirm transmitter has been programmed. Turn ignition switch to LOCK position or wait 5 minutes to exit program mode. Doors will lock, then unlock to confirm program mode has been exited.

Computer Relearn Procedures (Cont.)

PICKUP

NOTE: This procedure is used when a customer needs keys programmed into system and does not have 2 programmed ignition keys available, or when programmed ignition keys have been lost and/or ignition switch assembly has been replaced. This procedure will erase all programmed ignition keys from memory and prevent vehicle from starting until 2 keys have been programmed. Ignition keys must have correct mechanical key cut for vehicle and must be an encoded key. If additional key(s) are to be programmed, perform KEY PROGRAMMING – USING 2 PROGRAMMED KEYS. If remaining keys are with customer and not with vehicle, instruct customer to see owner's manual to program spare key(s).

Key Programming – Erase All Keys & Program 2 Keys – 1) Insert Ford Service Function (FSF) card into NGS tester. Turn ignition switch from LOCK to RUN position. With NGS tester connected to vehicle, enter instrument cluster then select SECURITY ACCESS PROCEDURE. This procedure will take 10 minutes to perform. After the security access procedure has been completed, a new menu will be displayed with command options. Select IGNITION KEY CODE ERASE.

2) Turn ignition switch to LOCK position and disconnect NGS tester. Insert first encoded ignition key into ignition lock cylinder. Turn ignition switch to RUN position for 3 seconds. Turn ignition switch to LOCK position and remove first encoded key.

3) Within 5 seconds, insert second encoded ignition key into ignition lock cylinder. Turn ignition switch to RUN position for 3 seconds. Turn ignition switch to LOCK position and remove second encoded key. Both encoded ignition keys should now start vehicle.

NOTE: Security access must be granted to erase ignition keys, enable/disable spare key programming switch, or perform parameter resets for instrument cluster and PCM. This procedure has a 10-minute time delay prior to granting security access during which the New Generation Star (NGS) tester must remain connected to vehicle. After security access has been granted, security access command menu is displayed which offers various command options. Multiple security access commands can be executed (if necessary) prior to exiting security access command menu. Execution of all necessary security access commands prior to exiting command menu avoids the performance of an additional security access procedure and the associated 10-minute time delay.

Key Programming – Security Access Procedure – Insert Ford Service Function (FSF) card into NGS tester. Turn ignition switch from LOCK to RUN position. With NGS tester connected to vehicle, enter instrument cluster then select SECURITY ACCESS PROCEDURE. This procedure will take 10 minutes to perform. After the security access procedure has been completed, a new menu will be displayed with command options. Select as many functions as required before exiting this menu. Once this menu is exited, security access procedure must be performed again to perform additional commands.

NOTE: The spare key programming switch is a programmable switch which provides the capability to enable/disable the normal customer spare key programming procedure detailed in the owner's manual. This programmable switch is provided as a convenience for rental company fleets or other fleet purchasers who may not want the spare key programming procedure available to the vehicle driver. The spare key programming switch state can be viewed using instrument cluster PID SPARE_KY.

Key Programming – Spare Key Programming Switch – Insert a programmed ignition key into the ignition lock cylinder. Insert Ford Service Function (FSF) card into NGS tester. Turn ignition switch from LOCK to RUN position. With NGS tester connected to vehicle, enter instrument cluster then select SECURITY ACCESS PROCEDURE. This procedure will take 10 minutes to perform. After the security access procedure has been completed, a new menu will be displayed with command options. The default setting on all new vehicles is ENABLE. Select SPARE KEY PROGRAMMING SWITCH. Set SPARE KEY PROGRAMMING SWITCH to ENABLE to allow keys to be programmed or DISABLE to make key programming not accessible.

NOTE: This procedure will only work if 2 or more programmed ignition keys are available and there is a need to program additional keys. If 2 keys are not available, perform KEY PROGRAMMING – ERASE ALL KEYS & PROGRAM 2 KEYS. PID SPARE_KY must be enabled for this procedure to operate. To enable this PID, perform KEY PROGRAMMING – SPARE KEY PROGRAMMING SWITCH and enable spare key programming switch. If programming procedure is successful, new key(s) will start vehicle and THEFT indicator will illuminate for 3 seconds. If programming procedure is not successful, new key(s) will not start vehicle and THEFT indicator will flash for one minute (after flashing for one minute, THEFT indicator will flash fault code). If necessary, repeat programming procedure. If programming of key(s) is still unsuccessful, perform self-diagnostics. See SELF-DIAGNOSTIC SYSTEM in PASSIVE ANTI-THEFT SYSTEMS – PICKUP article in ACCESSORIES & EQUIPMENT. Maximum of 8 keys can be programmed into system. If procedure is not performed as outlined, programming procedure will end. Ignition keys must have correct mechanical key cut for vehicle and must be an encoded key.

Key Programming – Using 2 Programmed Keys – 1) Insert the first programmed ignition key into ignition lock cylinder. Turn ignition switch from LOCK to RUN position (ignition switch must stay in RUN position for one second). Turn ignition switch to LOCK position and remove ignition key from ignition lock cylinder.

2) Within 5 seconds of turning ignition switch to LOCK position, insert second programmed ignition key into ignition lock cylinder. Turn ignition switch from LOCK to RUN position (ignition switch must stay in RUN position for one second). Turn ignition switch to LOCK position and remove second ignition key from ignition lock cylinder.

3) Within 5 seconds of turning ignition switch to LOCK position, insert a NEW unprogrammed ignition key into ignition lock cylinder. Turn ignition switch from LOCK to RUN position (ignition switch must stay in RUN position for one second). Turn ignition switch to LOCK position and remove ignition key from ignition lock cylinder. The NEW ignition key should now be programmed. To program additional key(s), repeat key programming procedure from step **1)**.

NOTE: This procedure is used when customer needs extra keys programmed and 2 programmed keys are not available, but system has 2 ignition keys programmed. A maximum of 8 keys can be programmed. If 8 keys are already programmed, this procedure will not allow any more keys to be programmed. The number of programmed keys can be determined by accessing instrument cluster PID NUMKEYS with NGS tester.

Key Programming – Without Using 2 Programmed Keys – Insert unprogrammed key in ignition and turn ignition switch to RUN position. Connect New Generation Star (NGS) tester to Data Link Connector (DLC), located under instrument panel next to steering column. Insert Ford Service Function (FSF) card in NGS tester. Perform security access procedure. See KEY PROGRAMMING – SECURITY ACCESS PROCEDURE. Select IGNITION KEY CODE PROGRAM. Turn ignition switch to LOCK position. Disconnect NGS tester. Key should now be programmed and be able to start vehicle.

PCM Programming – For Powertrain Control Module (PCM) programming procedures, see ALL MODELS (PROGRAMMING PCM).

GENERAL INFORMATION
Computer Relearn Procedures (Cont.)

CUSTOMER PREFERENCE INDEX (RANGER)

Module	Configurable Item	State
Anti-Lock Brake Control Module	Tire Size (Revolutions/Mile)	List Of Tires
Anti-Lock Brake Control Module	Tone Ring Size (Number Of Teeth)	[1]
Anti-Lock Brake Control Module	Option Information	4WABS
Anti-Lock Brake Control Module	Vehicle Program	Ranger
Generic Electronic Module/Central Timer Module	Tire Size (Revolutions/Mile)	List Of Tires
Generic Electronic Module/Central Timer Module	Tone Ring Size (Number Of Teeth)	[1]
Generic Electronic Module/Central Timer Module	Option Information	4WABS
Generic Electronic Module/Central Timer Module	Vehicle Program	Ranger
Passive Anti-Theft System Module	Enter Security Access	Enter Security Access
Passive Anti-Theft System Module	Ignition Key Code Program	Program Ignition Keys
Passive Anti-Theft System Module	Ignition Key Code Erase	Erase All Stored Ignition Keys
Passive Anti-Theft System Module	Spare Key	Enabled, Disabled
Passive Anti-Theft System Module	Parameter Reset	Reset Security ID

[1] – On 2.7L and 3.0L, tone ring size is 7.5″. On 4.0L, tone ring size is 8.8″.

RANGER

Customer Driven Preferences – There are customer preferences that can be configured on this vehicle. Some items the customer may or may not want to have enabled. To carry out customer configuration process, connect New Generation Star (NGS) tester to Data Link Connector (DLC), located under instrument panel next to steering column. Insert Ford Service Function (FSF) card into NGS tester. Using NGS tester, set customer preferences as necessary. See CUSTOMER PREFERENCE INDEX (RANGER) table.

NOTE: This procedure is used when a customer needs keys programmed into system and does not have 2 programmed ignition keys available, or when programmed ignition keys have been lost and/or ignition switch assembly has been replaced. This procedure will erase all programmed ignition keys from memory and prevent vehicle from starting until 2 keys have been programmed. Ignition keys must have correct mechanical key cut for vehicle and must be an encoded key. If additional key(s) are to be programmed, perform KEY PROGRAMMING – USING 2 PROGRAMMED KEYS. If remaining keys are with customer and not with vehicle, instruct customer to see owner's manual to program spare key(s).

Key Programming – Erase All Keys & Program 2 Keys – 1) Insert Ford Service Function (FSF) card into NGS tester. Turn ignition switch from LOCK to RUN position. With NGS tester connected to vehicle, enter PATS then select SECURITY ACCESS PROCEDURE. This procedure will take 10 minutes to perform. After the security access procedure has been completed, a new menu will be displayed with command options. Select IGNITION KEY CODE ERASE.

2) Turn ignition switch to LOCK position and disconnect NGS tester. Insert first encoded ignition key into ignition lock cylinder. Turn ignition switch to RUN position for 3 seconds. Turn ignition switch to LOCK position and remove first encoded key.

3) Within 5 seconds, insert second encoded ignition key into ignition lock cylinder. Turn ignition switch to RUN position for 3 seconds. Turn ignition switch to LOCK position and remove second encoded key. Both encoded ignition keys should now start vehicle.

NOTE: Security access must be granted to erase ignition keys, enable/disable spare key programming switch, or perform parameter resets for PATS module and PCM. This procedure has a 10-minute time delay prior to granting security access during which the New Generation Star (NGS) tester must remain connected to vehicle. After security access has been granted, security access command menu is displayed which offers various command options. Multiple security access commands can be executed (if necessary) prior to exiting security access command menu. Execution of all necessary security access commands prior to exiting command menu avoids the performance of an additional security access procedure and the associated 10-minute time delay.

Key Programming – Security Access Procedure – Insert Ford Service Function (FSF) card into NGS tester. Turn ignition switch from LOCK to RUN position. With NGS tester connected to vehicle, enter PATS then select SECURITY ACCESS PROCEDURE. This procedure will take 10 minutes to perform. After the security access procedure has been completed, a new menu will be displayed with command options. Select as many functions as required before exiting this menu. Once this menu is exited, security access procedure must be performed again to perform additional commands.

NOTE: The spare key programming switch is a programmable switch which provides the capability to enable/disable the normal customer spare key programming procedure detailed in the owner's manual. This programmable switch is provided as a convenience for rental company fleets or other fleet purchasers who may not want the spare key programming procedure available to the vehicle driver. The spare key programming switch state can be viewed using PATS PID SPARE_KY.

Key Programming – Spare Key Programming Switch – Insert a programmed ignition key into the ignition lock cylinder. Insert Ford Service Function (FSF) card into NGS tester. Turn ignition switch from LOCK to RUN position. With NGS tester connected to vehicle, enter PATS then select SECURITY ACCESS PROCEDURE. This procedure will take 10 minutes to perform. After the security access procedure has been completed, a new menu will be displayed with command options. The default setting on all new vehicles is ENABLE. Select SPARE KEY PROGRAMMING SWITCH. Set SPARE KEY PROGRAMMING

Computer Relearn Procedures (Cont.)

SWITCH to ENABLE to allow keys to be programmed or DISABLE to make key programming not accessible.

NOTE: This procedure will only work if 2 or more programmed ignition keys are available and there is a need to program additional keys. If 2 keys are not available, perform KEY PROGRAMMING – ERASE ALL KEYS & PROGRAM 2 KEYS. PID SPARE_KY must be enabled for this procedure to operate. To enable this PID, perform KEY PROGRAMMING – SPARE KEY PROGRAMMING SWITCH and enable spare key programming switch. If programming procedure is successful, new key(s) will start vehicle and THEFT indicator will illuminate for 3 seconds. If programming procedure is not successful, new key(s) will not start vehicle and THEFT indicator will flash for one minute (after flashing for one minute, THEFT indicator will flash fault code). If necessary, repeat programming procedure. If programming of key(s) is still unsuccessful, perform self-diagnostics. See SELF-DIAGNOSTIC SYSTEM in PASSIVE ANTI-THEFT SYSTEMS – RANGER article in ACCESSORIES & EQUIPMENT. Maximum of 8 keys can be programmed into system. If procedure is not performed as outlined, programming procedure will end. Ignition keys must have correct mechanical key cut for vehicle and must be an encoded key.

Key Programming – Using 2 Programmed Keys – 1) Insert the first programmed ignition key into ignition lock cylinder. Turn ignition switch from LOCK to RUN position (ignition switch must stay in RUN position for one second). Turn ignition switch to LOCK position and remove ignition key from ignition lock cylinder.

2) Within 5 seconds of turning ignition switch to LOCK position, insert second programmed ignition key into ignition lock cylinder. Turn ignition switch from LOCK to RUN position (ignition switch must stay in RUN position for one second). Turn ignition switch to LOCK position and remove second ignition key from ignition lock cylinder.

3) Within 5 seconds of turning ignition switch to LOCK position, insert a NEW unprogrammed ignition key into ignition lock cylinder. Turn ignition switch from LOCK to RUN position (ignition switch must stay in RUN position for one second). Turn ignition switch to LOCK position and remove ignition key from ignition lock cylinder. The NEW ignition key should now be programmed. To program additional key(s), repeat key programming procedure from step 1).

NOTE: This procedure is used when customer needs extra keys programmed and 2 programmed keys are not available, but system has 2 ignition keys programmed. A maximum of 8 keys can be programmed. If 8 keys are already programmed, this procedure will not allow any more keys to be programmed. The number of programmed keys can be determined by accessing PATS PID NUMKEYS with NGS tester.

Key Programming – Without Using 2 Programmed Keys – Insert unprogrammed key in ignition and turn ignition switch to RUN position. Connect New Generation Star (NGS) tester to Data Link Connector (DLC), located under instrument panel next to steering column. Insert Ford Service Function (FSF) card in NGS tester. Perform security access procedure. See KEY PROGRAMMING – SECURITY ACCESS PROCEDURE. Select IGNITION KEY CODE PROGRAM. Turn ignition switch to LOCK position. Disconnect NGS tester. Key should now be programmed and be able to start vehicle.

PCM Programming – For Powertrain Control Module (PCM) programming procedures, see ALL MODELS (PROGRAMMING PCM).

NOTE: Performing this test will erase all previously programmed transmitters from memory of GEM. All remote transmitters to be used with vehicle MUST be programmed at the same time.

Transmitter Programming – Open driver's window. Cycle ignition key from LOCK to RUN 8 times within 10 seconds ending in RUN position. Doors will lock, then unlock to verify program mode has been entered. Within 20 seconds, press any button on transmitter. Doors will lock, then unlock to confirm transmitter has been programmed. Turn ignition switch to LOCK position or wait 20 seconds to exit program mode. Doors will lock, then unlock to confirm program mode has been exited.

SABLE & TAURUS

Enabling & Disabling Features On Remote Anti-Theft Personality Module – Enable/disable mode allows technician to set alarm configuration to match the laws for alarm operation in the country where vehicle is to be driven. Enable/disable mode will also enable/disable autolock. Alarm configurations are set by assembly plant for regulations in expected destination and should not be modified for use in other countries. Remote keyless entry transmitter PANIC will share exterior lights and horn characteristics. PANIC alarm will also turn on interior lights in all cases for 25 seconds.

NOTE: Step 2) must be completed within 30 seconds of turning ignition switch to RUN position in step 1). While in enable/disable mode, RAP module will not have any other functionality except enabling/disabling features. Enabling a new alarm configuration will automatically disable previous alarm configuration.

1) Ensure anti-theft system is not armed or triggered. Turn ignition switch to LOCK position. Close all doors. Turn ignition switch from LOCK to RUN position.

2) Press power door UNLOCK button 3 times. Turn ignition switch from RUN to LOCK position. Press power door UNLOCK button 3 times. Turn ignition switch back to RUN position. If enable/disable mode has been entered successfully, horn will chirp.

3) Press power door UNLOCK button number of times associated with function you would like to enable or disable as shown in table. See ENABLE/DISABLE FUNCTIONS table. Press power door LOCK button once after last UNLOCK button press in order to enter enable/disable code. System will confirm altered function by chirping horn same number of times as number of unlock presses registered. If function has been enabled, a long horn sound will follow sequence of horn chirps. If function has been disabled, no horn sound will follow sequence of horn chirps.

4) After horn chirp sequence has occurred in enable/disable mode, another function may be enabled or disabled. To exit enable/disable mode, turn ignition switch to LOCK position or allow 5 minutes to pass after entering enable mode. After exiting, system will confirm exit with horn chirp if a function has been changed.

ENABLE/DISABLE FUNCTIONS

Function	Press Unlock Button
Autolock/Relock	1 Time
North America/Gulf Coast/Korea Alarm [1]	5 Times
Europe/Australia Alarm [1]	6 Times

[1] – Locations not listed use North America standards.

NOTE: This procedure is used when a customer needs keys programmed into system and does not have 2 programmed ignition keys available, or when programmed ignition keys have been lost and/or ignition switch assembly has been replaced. This procedure will erase all programmed ignition keys from memory and prevent vehicle from starting until 2 keys have been programmed. Ignition keys must have correct mechanical key cut for vehicle and must be an encoded key. If additional key(s) are to be programmed, perform KEY PROGRAMMING – USING 2 PROGRAMMED KEYS. If remaining keys are with customer and not with vehicle, instruct customer to see owner's manual to program spare key(s).

Key Programming – Erase All Keys & Program 2 Keys – 1) Insert Ford Service Function (FSF) card into NGS tester. Turn ignition switch from LOCK to RUN position. With NGS tester connected to vehicle, enter PATS then select SECURITY ACCESS PROCEDURE. This procedure will take 10 minutes to perform. After the security access procedure has been completed, a new menu will be displayed with command options. Select IGNITION KEY CODE ERASE.

2) Turn ignition switch to LOCK position and disconnect NGS tester. Insert first encoded ignition key into ignition lock cylinder. Turn ignition switch to RUN position for 3 seconds. Turn ignition switch to LOCK position and remove first encoded key.

GENERAL INFORMATION
Computer Relearn Procedures (Cont.)

3) Within 5 seconds, insert second encoded ignition key into ignition lock cylinder. Turn ignition switch to RUN position for 3 seconds. Turn ignition switch to LOCK position and remove second encoded key. Both encoded ignition keys should now start vehicle.

NOTE: Security access must be granted to erase ignition keys, enable/disable spare key programming switch, or perform parameter resets for PATS module and PCM. This procedure has a 10-minute time delay prior to granting security access during which the New Generation Star (NGS) tester must remain connected to vehicle. After security access has been granted, security access command menu is displayed which offers various command options. Multiple security access commands can be executed (if necessary) prior to exiting security access command menu. Execution of all necessary security access commands prior to exiting command menu avoids the performance of an additional security access procedure and the associated 10-minute time delay.

Key Programming – Security Access Procedure – Insert Ford Service Function (FSF) card into NGS tester. Turn ignition switch from LOCK to RUN position. With NGS tester connected to vehicle, enter PATS then select SECURITY ACCESS PROCEDURE. This procedure will take 10 minutes to perform. After the security access procedure has been completed, a new menu will be displayed with command options. Select as many functions as required before exiting this menu. Once this menu is exited, security access procedure must be performed again to perform additional commands.

NOTE: The spare key programming switch is a programmable switch which provides the capability to enable/disable the normal customer spare key programming procedure detailed in the owner's manual. This programmable switch is provided as a convenience for rental company fleets or other fleet purchasers who may not want the spare key programming procedure available to the vehicle driver. The spare key programming switch state can be viewed using PATS PID SPARE_KY.

Key Programming – Spare Key Programming Switch – Insert a programmed ignition key into the ignition lock cylinder. Insert Ford Service Function (FSF) card into NGS tester. Turn ignition switch from LOCK to RUN position. With NGS tester connected to vehicle, enter PATS then select SECURITY ACCESS PROCEDURE. This procedure will take 10 minutes to perform. After the security access procedure has been completed, a new menu will be displayed with command options. The default setting on all new vehicles is ENABLE. Select SPARE KEY PROGRAMMING SWITCH. Set SPARE KEY PROGRAMMING

SWITCH to ENABLE to allow keys to be programmed or DISABLE to make key programming not accessible.

NOTE: This procedure will only work if 2 or more programmed ignition keys are available and there is a need to program additional keys. If 2 keys are not available, perform KEY PROGRAMMING – ERASE ALL KEYS & PROGRAM 2 KEYS. PID SPARE_KY must be enabled for this procedure to operate. To enable this PID, perform KEY PROGRAMMING – SPARE KEY PROGRAMMING SWITCH and enable spare key programming switch. If programming procedure is successful, new key(s) will start vehicle and THEFT indicator will illuminate for 3 seconds. If programming procedure is not successful, new key(s) will not start vehicle and THEFT indicator will flash for one minute (after flashing for one minute, THEFT indicator will flash fault code). If necessary, repeat programming procedure. If programming of key(s) is still unsuccessful, perform self-diagnostics. See SELF-DIAGNOSTIC SYSTEM in PASSIVE ANTI-THEFT SYSTEMS – SABLE & TAURUS article in ACCESSORIES & EQUIPMENT. Maximum of 8 keys can be programmed into system. If procedure is not performed as outlined, programming procedure will end. Ignition keys must have correct mechanical key cut for vehicle and must be an encoded key.

Key Programming – Using 2 Programmed Keys – 1) Insert the first programmed ignition key into ignition lock cylinder. Turn ignition switch from LOCK to RUN position (ignition switch must stay in RUN position for one second). Turn ignition switch to LOCK position and remove ignition key from ignition lock cylinder.

2) Within 5 seconds of turning ignition switch to LOCK position, insert second programmed ignition key into ignition lock cylinder. Turn ignition switch from LOCK to RUN position (ignition switch must stay in RUN position for one second). Turn ignition switch to LOCK position and remove second ignition key from ignition lock cylinder.

3) Within 5 seconds of turning ignition switch to LOCK position, insert a NEW unprogrammed ignition key into ignition lock cylinder. Turn ignition switch from LOCK to RUN position (ignition switch must stay in RUN position for one second). Turn ignition switch to LOCK position and remove ignition key from ignition lock cylinder. The NEW ignition key should now be programmed. To program additional key(s), repeat key programming procedure from step **1)**.

NOTE: This procedure is used when customer needs extra keys programmed and 2 programmed keys are not available, but system has 2 ignition keys programmed. A maximum of 8 keys can be programmed. If 8 keys are already programmed, this procedure will not allow any more keys to be programmed. The number of programmed keys can be determined by accessing PATS PID NUMKEYS with NGS tester.

Key Programming – Without Using 2 Programmed Keys – Insert unprogrammed key in ignition and turn ignition switch to RUN position. Connect New Generation Star (NGS) tester to Data Link Connector (DLC), located under instrument panel next to steering column. Insert Ford Service Function (FSF) card in NGS tester. Perform security access procedure. See KEY PROGRAMMING – SECURITY ACCESS PROCEDURE. Select IGNITION KEY CODE PROGRAM. Turn ignition switch to LOCK position. Disconnect NGS tester. Key should now be programmed and be able to start vehicle.

Computer Relearn Procedures (Cont.)

PCM Programming – For Powertrain Control Module (PCM) programming procedures, see ALL MODELS (PROGRAMMING PCM).

NOTE: When programing remote transmitters, all transmitters MUST BE programmed at the same time. Failure to program all transmitter at the same time will render all other transmitters inoperative.

Remote Transmitter – 1) Ensure anti-theft system is not armed. Turn ignition switch from LOCK to RUN position 8 times within 10 seconds ending in RUN position. The system will indicate entry into program mode by locking and unlocking all doors.

2) Press any button on remote transmitter within 20 seconds. Doors will lock and unlock to confirm transmitter has been programmed. Repeat procedure to program additional transmitters.

3) Turn ignition switch to LOCK position to exit program mode. If a new set of transmitters have been programed, RAP module will lock and unlock all doors one last time to confirm programing was successful. If system does not program successfully, repeat procedure. If system will not program, repair remote keyless entry system as necessary. See appropriate wiring diagram in REMOTE KEYLESS ENTRY SYSTEMS article in ACCESSORIES & EQUIPMENT.

TOWN CAR

Customer Driven Preferences – There are customer preferences that can be configured on this vehicle. Some items the customer may or may not want to have enabled. To carry out customer configuration process, connect New Generation Star (NGS) tester to Data Link Connector (DLC), located under instrument panel next to steering column. Insert Ford Service Function (FSF) card into NGS tester. Using NGS tester, set customer preferences as necessary. See CUSTOMER PREFERENCE INDEX (TOWN CAR) table.

NOTE: NGS tester will only store module configuration information for 24 hours.

Driver's Door Module (DDM) Programming – Prior to removal of DDM, upload module configuration information to the New Generation Star (NGS) tester using manufacturer's instructions. Once module has been replaced, download module configuration information from NGS tester into new module.

NOTE: After HEC has been replace, Passive Anti-Theft System (PATS) module MUST be reconfigured.

Hybrid Electronic Instrument Cluster (HEC) Programming – 1) Turn ignition switch to LOCK position. Connect NGS tester to Data Link Connector (DLC), located under instrument panel next to steering

column. Using NGS tester, retrieve and record continuous DTCs. Clear continuous DTCs and perform instrument cluster self-test. If DTC B2139 is retrieved, go to next step. If DTC B2139 is not retrieved, system is okay at this time.

2) Perform security access for instrument cluster. See KEY PROGRAMMING – SECURITY ACCESS PROCEDURE. Using NGS tester, select PARAMETER RESET command for instrument cluster. Perform security access for Powertrain Control Module (PCM). See KEY PROGRAMMING – SECURITY ACCESS PROCEDURE. Using NGS tester, select PARAMETER RESET command for PCM. Turn ignition switch to RUN position for 30 seconds. Using NGS tester, clear continuous DTCs. Turn ignition switch to LOCK position. Using NGS tester, perform instrument cluster self-test. If DTC B2139 is not retrieved, system is okay at this time. If DTC B2139 is retrieved, verify PCM calibration is correct for vehicle. If calibration is okay, go to next step.

3) Repeat step 2). If DTC B2139 is still exists, replace instrument cluster. If DTC B2139 does not exist, system is okay at this time. If any other DTCs are retrieved, perform appropriate test. See INSTRUMENT CLUSTER DTC INDEX table under DIAGNOSTIC TROUBLE CODE (DTC) DEFINITIONS in MODULE COMMUNICATIONS NETWORK – TOWN CAR article in ACCESSORIES & EQUIPMENT.

NOTE: This procedure is used when a customer needs keys programmed into system and does not have 2 programmed ignition keys available, or when programmed ignition keys have been lost and/or ignition switch assembly has been replaced. This procedure will erase all programmed ignition keys from memory and prevent vehicle from starting until 2 keys have been programmed. Ignition keys must have correct mechanical key cut for vehicle and must be an encoded key. If additional key(s) are to be programmed, perform KEY PROGRAMMING – USING 2 PROGRAMMED KEYS. If remaining keys are with customer and not with vehicle, instruct customer to see owner's manual to program spare key(s).

Key Programming – Erase All Keys & Program 2 Keys – 1) Insert Ford Service Function (FSF) card into NGS tester. Turn ignition switch from LOCK to RUN position. With NGS tester connected to vehicle, enter instrument cluster then select SECURITY ACCESS PROCEDURE. This procedure will take 10 minutes to perform. After the security access procedure has been completed, a new menu will be displayed with command options. Select IGNITION KEY CODE ERASE.

2) Turn ignition switch to LOCK position and disconnect NGS tester. Insert first encoded ignition key into ignition lock cylinder. Turn ignition switch to RUN position for 3 seconds. Turn ignition switch to LOCK position and remove first encoded key.

CUSTOMER PREFERENCE INDEX (TOWN CAR)

Module	Configurable Item	State
Driver's Door Module	Remote Transmitter Programming	ID Code (TIC) Value
Lighting Control Module	Daytime Running Lights	Enabled, Disabled
Restraint Control Module	Side Air Bags	With, Without
Instrument Cluster	Enter Security Access	Enter Security Access
Instrument Cluster	Ignition Key Code Program	Program Ignition Keys
Instrument Cluster	Ignition Key Code Erase	Erase All Stored Ignition Keys
Instrument Cluster	Spare Key	Enabled, Disabled
Instrument Cluster	Parameter Reset	Reset Security ID

GENERAL INFORMATION
Computer Relearn Procedures (Cont.)

3) Within 5 seconds, insert second encoded ignition key into ignition lock cylinder. Turn ignition switch to RUN position for 3 seconds. Turn ignition switch to LOCK position and remove second encoded key. Both encoded ignition keys should now start vehicle.

NOTE: Security access must be granted to erase ignition keys, enable/disable spare key programming switch, or perform parameter resets for instrument cluster and PCM. This procedure has a 10-minute time delay prior to granting security access during which the New Generation Star (NGS) tester must remain connected to vehicle. After security access has been granted, security access command menu is displayed which offers various command options. Multiple security access commands can be executed (if necessary) prior to exiting security access command menu. Execution of all necessary security access commands prior to exiting command menu avoids the performance of an additional security access procedure and the associated 10-minute time delay.

Key Programming – Security Access Procedure – Insert Ford Service Function (FSF) card into NGS tester. Turn ignition switch from LOCK to RUN position. With NGS tester connected to vehicle, enter instrument cluster then select SECURITY ACCESS PROCEDURE. This procedure will take 10 minutes to perform. After the security access procedure has been completed, a new menu will be displayed with command options. Select as many functions as required before exiting this menu. Once this menu is exited, security access procedure must be performed again to perform additional commands.

NOTE: The spare key programming switch is a programmable switch which provides the capability to enable/disable the normal customer spare key programming procedure detailed in the owner's manual. This programmable switch is provided as a convenience for rental company fleets or other fleet purchasers who may not want the spare key programming procedure available to the vehicle driver. The spare key programming switch state can be viewed using instrument cluster PID SPARE_KY.

Key Programming – Spare Key Programming Switch – Insert a programmed ignition key into the ignition lock cylinder. Insert Ford Service Function (FSF) card into NGS tester. Turn ignition switch from LOCK to RUN position. With NGS tester connected to vehicle, enter instrument cluster then select SECURITY ACCESS PROCEDURE. This procedure will take 10 minutes to perform. After the security access procedure has been completed, a new menu will be displayed with command options. The default setting on all new vehicles is ENABLE. Select SPARE KEY PROGRAMMING SWITCH. Set SPARE KEY PROGRAMMING SWITCH to ENABLE to allow keys to be programmed or DISABLE to make key programming not accessible.

NOTE: This procedure will only work if 2 or more programmed ignition keys are available and there is a need to program additional keys. If 2 keys are not available, perform KEY PROGRAMMING – ERASE ALL KEYS & PROGRAM 2 KEYS. PID SPARE_KY must be enabled for this procedure to operate. To enable this PID, perform KEY PROGRAMMING – SPARE KEY PROGRAMMING SWITCH and enable spare key programming switch. If programming procedure is successful, new key(s) will start vehicle and THEFT indicator will illuminate for 3 seconds. If programming procedure is not successful, new key(s) will not start vehicle and THEFT indicator will flash for one minute (after flashing for one minute, THEFT indicator will flash fault code). If necessary, repeat programming procedure. If programming of key(s) is still unsuccessful, perform self-diagnostics. See SELF-DIAGNOSTIC SYSTEM in PASSIVE ANTI-THEFT SYSTEMS – TOWN CAR article in ACCESSORIES & EQUIPMENT. Maximum of 8 keys can be programmed into system. If procedure is not performed as outlined, programming procedure will end. Ignition keys must have correct mechanical key cut for vehicle and must be an encoded key.

Key Programming – Using 2 Programmed Keys – 1) Insert the first programmed ignition key into ignition lock cylinder. Turn ignition switch from LOCK to RUN position (ignition switch must stay in RUN position for one second). Turn ignition switch to LOCK position and remove ignition key from ignition lock cylinder.

2) Within 5 seconds of turning ignition switch to LOCK position, insert second programmed ignition key into ignition lock cylinder. Turn ignition switch from LOCK to RUN position (ignition switch must stay in RUN position for one second). Turn ignition switch to LOCK position and remove second ignition key from ignition lock cylinder.

3) Within 5 seconds of turning ignition switch to LOCK position, insert a NEW unprogrammed ignition key into ignition lock cylinder. Turn ignition switch from LOCK to RUN position (ignition switch must stay in RUN position for one second). Turn ignition switch to LOCK position and remove ignition key from ignition lock cylinder. The NEW ignition key should now be programmed. To program additional key(s), repeat key programming procedure from step **1)**.

NOTE: This procedure is used when customer needs extra keys programmed and 2 programmed keys are not available, but system has 2 ignition keys programmed. A maximum of 8 keys can be programmed. If 8 keys are already programmed, this procedure will not allow any more keys to be programmed. The number of programmed keys can be determined by accessing instrument cluster PID NUMKEYS with NGS tester.

Key Programming – Without Using 2 Programmed Keys – Insert unprogrammed key in ignition and turn ignition switch to RUN position. Connect New Generation Star (NGS) tester to Data Link Connector (DLC), located under instrument panel next to steering column. Insert Ford Service Function (FSF) card in NGS tester. Perform security access procedure. See KEY PROGRAMMING – SECURITY ACCESS PROCEDURE. Select IGNITION KEY CODE PROGRAM. Turn ignition switch to LOCK position. Disconnect NGS tester. Key should now be programmed and be able to start vehicle.

NOTE: NGS tester will only store module configuration information for 24 hours.

Lighting Control Module (LCM) Programming – Prior to removal of LCM, upload module configuration information to the New Generation Star (NGS) tester using manufacturer's instructions. Once module has been replaced, download module configuration information from NGS tester into new module.

PCM Programming – For Powertrain Control Module (PCM) programming procedures, see ALL MODELS (PROGRAMMING PCM).

NOTE: After first remote transmitter is programmed, all other remote transmitters will be erased. All remote transmitters must be programmed at the same time. Up to 4 transmitters may be programmed at one time.

Transmitter Programming – 1) Cycle ignition switch from LOCK to RUN positions 4 times within 3 seconds. Locks will lock and unlock to confirm programming mode has been entered. Press any button on remote transmitter.

2) If additional remote transmitters are to be programmed, press any button on remaining remote transmitters within 7.5 seconds. To exit programming mode, turn ignition switch to START position or wait 7.5 seconds.

3) To set a remote transmitter to also operate a memory set position, press SET button on memory switch then press any button on remote transmitter then press appropriate memory button (1 or 2). To unassociate a transmitter, repeat this step.

Computer Relearn Procedures (Cont.)

VILLAGER

PCM Programming – For Powertrain Control Module (PCM) programming procedures, see ALL MODELS (PROGRAMMING PCM).

NOTE: Performing this procedure will erase all previously programmed transmitters. All remote transmitters must be programmed at the same time. Up to 4 transmitters may be programmed at one time.

Transmitter Programming – 1) While inside of vehicle, closed and lock all doors. Insert and remove key in ignition switch 6 times within 10 seconds. Parking lights will flash 2 times to confirm programming mode has been entered. Turn ignition switch to ACC position.

2) Press any button on remote transmitter to be programmed. Parking lights will flash 2 times to confirm remote transmitter has been programmed. To program additional remote transmitters, unlock then lock driver's door at driver's door lock switch. Press any button on additional remote transmitter(s) to be programmed. Parking lights will flash 2 times to confirm remote transmitter has been programmed. Open driver's door to exit programming mode.

WINDSTAR

Customer Driven Preferences – There are customer preferences that can be configured on this vehicle. Some items the customer may or may not want to have enabled. To carry out customer configuration process, connect New Generation Star (NGS) tester to Data Link Connector (DLC), located under instrument panel next to steering column. Insert Ford Service Function (FSF) card into NGS tester. Using NGS tester, set customer preferences as necessary. See CUSTOMER PREFERENCE INDEX (WINDSTAR) table.

NOTE: NGS tester will only store module configuration information for 24 hours.

Front Electronic Module (FEM) Programming – Prior to removal of FEM, upload module configuration information to the New Generation Star (NGS) tester using manufacturer's instructions. Once module has been replaced, download module configuration information from NGS tester into new module.

NOTE: This procedure is used when a customer needs keys programmed into system and does not have 2 programmed ignition keys available, or when programmed ignition keys have been lost and/or ignition switch assembly has been replaced. This procedure will erase all programmed ignition keys from memory and prevent vehicle from starting until 2 keys have been programmed. Ignition keys must have correct mechanical key cut for vehicle and must be an encoded key. If additional key(s) are to be programmed, perform KEY PROGRAMMING – USING 2 PROGRAMMED KEYS. If remaining keys are with customer and not with vehicle, instruct customer to see owner's manual to program spare key(s).

Key Programming – Erase All Keys & Program 2 Keys – 1) Insert Ford Service Function (FSF) card into NGS tester. Turn ignition switch from LOCK to RUN position. With NGS tester connected to vehicle, enter instrument cluster then select SECURITY ACCESS PROCE-

DURE. This procedure will take 10 minutes to perform. After the security access procedure has been completed, a new menu will be displayed with command options. Select IGNITION KEY CODE ERASE.

2) Turn ignition switch to LOCK position and disconnect NGS tester. Insert first encoded ignition key into ignition lock cylinder. Turn ignition switch to RUN position for 3 seconds. Turn ignition switch to LOCK position and remove first encoded key.

3) Within 5 seconds, insert second encoded ignition key into ignition lock cylinder. Turn ignition switch to RUN position for 3 seconds. Turn ignition switch to LOCK position and remove second encoded key. Both encoded ignition keys should now start vehicle.

NOTE: Security access must be granted to erase ignition keys, enable/disable spare key programming switch, or perform parameter resets for instrument cluster and PCM. This procedure has a 10-minute time delay prior to granting security access during which the New Generation Star (NGS) tester must remain connected to vehicle. After security access has been granted, security access command menu is displayed which offers various command options. Multiple security access commands can be executed (if necessary) prior to exiting security access command menu. Execution of all necessary security access commands prior to exiting command menu avoids the performance of an additional security access procedure and the associated 10-minute time delay.

Key Programming – Security Access Procedure – Insert Ford Service Function (FSF) card into NGS tester. Turn ignition switch from LOCK to RUN position. With NGS tester connected to vehicle, enter instrument cluster then select SECURITY ACCESS PROCEDURE. This procedure will take 10 minutes to perform. After the security access procedure has been completed, a new menu will be displayed with command options. Select as many functions as required before exiting this menu. Once this menu is exited, security access procedure must be performed again to perform additional commands.

NOTE: The spare key programming switch is a programmable switch which provides the capability to enable/disable the normal customer spare key programming procedure detailed in the owner's manual. This programmable switch is provided as a convenience for rental company fleets or other fleet purchasers who may not want the spare key programming procedure available to the vehicle driver. The spare key programming switch state can be viewed using instrument cluster PID SPARE_KY.

Key Programming – Spare Key Programming Switch – Insert a programmed ignition key into the ignition lock cylinder. Insert Ford Service Function (FSF) card into NGS tester. Turn ignition switch from LOCK to RUN position. With NGS tester connected to vehicle, enter instrument cluster then select SECURITY ACCESS PROCEDURE. This procedure will take 10 minutes to perform. After the security access procedure has been completed, a new menu will be displayed with command options. The default setting on all new vehicles is ENABLE. Select SPARE KEY PROGRAMMING SWITCH. Set SPARE KEY PROGRAMMING SWITCH to ENABLE to allow keys to be programmed or DISABLE to make key programming not accessible.

CUSTOMER PREFERENCE INDEX (WINDSTAR)

Module	Configurable Item	State
Front Electronic Module	Smart Locks	On, Off
Front Electronic Module	Automatic Locks	On, Off
Front Electronic Module	Illuminated Exit (As Of 3/99)	On, Off
Driver's Door Module	Horn Chirp	On, Off

GENERAL INFORMATION
Computer Relearn Procedures (Cont.)

NOTE: This procedure will only work if 2 or more programmed ignition keys are available and there is a need to program additional keys. If 2 keys are not available, perform KEY PROGRAMMING – ERASE ALL KEYS & PROGRAM 2 KEYS. PID SPARE_KY must be enabled for this procedure to operate. To enable this PID, perform KEY PROGRAMMING – SPARE KEY PROGRAMMING SWITCH and enable spare key programming switch. If programming procedure is successful, new key(s) will start vehicle and THEFT indicator will illuminate for 3 seconds. If programming procedure is not successful, new key(s) will not start vehicle and THEFT indicator will flash for one minute (after flashing for one minute, THEFT indicator will flash fault code). If necessary, repeat programming procedure. If programming of key(s) is still unsuccessful, perform self-diagnostics. See SELF-DIAGNOSTIC SYSTEM in PASSIVE ANTI-THEFT SYSTEMS – WINDSTAR article in ACCESSORIES & EQUIPMENT. Maximum of 8 keys can be programmed into system. If procedure is not performed as outlined, programming procedure will end. Ignition keys must have correct mechanical key cut for vehicle and must be an encoded key.

Key Programming – Using 2 Programmed Keys – 1) Insert the first programmed ignition key into ignition lock cylinder. Turn ignition switch from LOCK to RUN position (ignition switch must stay in RUN position for one second). Turn ignition switch to LOCK position and remove ignition key from ignition lock cylinder.

2) Within 5 seconds of turning ignition switch to LOCK position, insert second programmed ignition key into ignition lock cylinder. Turn ignition switch from LOCK to RUN position (ignition switch must stay in RUN position for one second). Turn ignition switch to LOCK position and remove second ignition key from ignition lock cylinder.

3) Within 5 seconds of turning ignition switch to LOCK position, insert a NEW unprogrammed ignition key into ignition lock cylinder. Turn ignition switch from LOCK to RUN position (ignition switch must stay in RUN position for one second). Turn ignition switch to LOCK position and remove ignition key from ignition lock cylinder. The NEW ignition key should now be programmed. To program additional key(s), repeat key programming procedure from step **1)**.

NOTE: This procedure is used when customer needs extra keys programmed and 2 programmed keys are not available, but system has 2 ignition keys programmed. A maximum of 8 keys can be programmed. If 8 keys are already programmed, this procedure will not allow any more keys to be programmed. The number of programmed keys can be determined by accessing instrument cluster PID NUMKEYS with NGS tester.

Key Programming – Without Using 2 Programmed Keys – Insert unprogrammed key in ignition and turn ignition switch to RUN position. Connect New Generation Star (NGS) tester to Data Link Connector (DLC), located under instrument panel next to steering column. Insert Ford Service Function (FSF) card in NGS tester. Perform security access procedure. See KEY PROGRAMMING – SECURITY ACCESS PROCEDURE. Select IGNITION KEY CODE PROGRAM. Turn ignition switch to LOCK position. Disconnect NGS tester. Key should now be programmed and be able to start vehicle.

PCM Programming – For Powertrain Control Module (PCM) programming procedures, see ALL MODELS (PROGRAMMING PCM).

NOTE: NGS tester will only store module configuration information for 24 hours.

Rear Electronic Module (REM) Programming – Prior to removal of REM, upload module configuration information to the New Generation Star (NGS) tester using manufacturer's instructions. Once module has been replaced, download module configuration information from NGS tester into new module.

Transmitter Programming – Open driver's window. Cycle ignition key from LOCK to RUN 8 times within 10 seconds ending in RUN position. Doors will lock, then unlock to verify program mode has been entered. Within 20 seconds, press any button on transmitter. Doors will lock, then unlock to confirm transmitter has been programmed. Turn ignition switch to LOCK position or wait 20 seconds to exit program mode. Doors will lock, then unlock to confirm program mode has been exited.

GENERAL MOTORS (CARS)

NOTE: Before performing Electronically Erasable Programmable Read Only Memory (EEPROM) programming procedure, check for any applicable Technical Service Bulletins (TSBs) that may apply to vehicle application. Body Control Module (BCM) must be programmed with proper Regular Production Option (RPO) configurations. Follow instructions on Techline Terminal and scan tool to program BCM.

ALERO, CUTLASS, GRAND AM & MALIBU

NOTE: Read all procedures listed to determine why and when each procedure is to be performed before proceeding.

Electronically Erasable Programmable Read Only Memory (EEPROM) Programming (2.4L) – 1) If Powertrain Control Module (PCM) was replaced, the EEPROM in the PCM must be programmed. If EEPROM is not programmed, a Diagnostic Trouble Code (DTC) will be set in the PCM or PCM may be damaged. Perform EEPROM programming using the Techline equipment manufacturer's instructions and latest software applicable for the vehicle model.

2) Once EEPROM is reprogrammed, the Crankshaft Position (CKP) sensor variation learn procedure must be performed using proper procedure.

Electronically Erasable Programmable Read Only Memory (EEPROM) Programming (3.1L & 3.4L) – 1) If Powertrain Control Module (PCM) was replaced, the EEPROM in the PCM must be programmed. If EEPROM is not programmed, a Diagnostic Trouble Code (DTC) will be set in the PCM.

2) Ensure battery is fully charged. If battery is being charged, ensure battery charger is disconnected before performing EEPROM programming procedure.

3) Ensure cable is properly connected on Data Link Connector (DLC). Turn ignition on. Perform EEPROM programming using the Techline equipment manufacturer's instructions and latest software applicable for the vehicle model.

4) Once EEPROM is reprogrammed, perform powertrain On-Board Diagnostic (OBD) system check. See POWERTRAIN ON-BOARD DIAGNOSTIC (OBD) SYSTEM CHECK in appropriate SELF-DIAGNOSTICS article in ENGINE PERFORMANCE. Ensure engine is idling for one minute before checking for DTCs when performing powertrain OBD system check.

NOTE: If EEPROM programming fails, ensure all electrical connections on PCM are okay. Check Techline for latest software. If EEPROM programming still fails, replace PCM.

Crankshaft Position (CKP) Sensor Variation Learn Procedure (2.4L) – 1) Procedure must be performed if any of the following have been done or exist:
- EEPROM was reprogrammed.
- If Diagnostic Trouble Code (DTC) P1336 exists.
- If crankshaft, crankshaft position sensor, engine or Powertrain Control Module (PCM) have been replaced.
- Any repairs have been performed that disturbs the crankshaft or vibration damper to the crankshaft position sensor relationship.

2) CKP sensor variation compensating values are stored in Powertrain Control Module (PCM) after a learn procedure has been performed. If actual CKP sensor values are not within specification, Diagnostic Trouble Code (DTC) P0300 will be stored in the PCM.

3) Ensure battery is fully charged. Ensure cable is properly connected on Data Link Connector (DLC). Apply parking brake. Block front wheels. Ensure hood is closed.

4) Place transaxle in Park or Neutral. Ensure all accessories are off. Start engine and warm engine until engine coolant temperature is at least 185°F (85°C).

Computer Relearn Procedures (Cont.)

5) Apply service brakes. With engine idling, use scan tool to select and enable CKP sensor variation learn procedure.

6) Accelerate engine until CKP sensor variation learn procedure fuel cut off is obtained and engine starts to decelerate or cut out. Quickly release throttle to idle position once CKP sensor variation learn procedure is obtained and engine decelerates or cuts out. Once CKP sensor variation values are learned, the PCM will return engine control to the operator and engine will respond to throttle position.

CAUTION: Ensure throttle is quickly released to idle position once CKP sensor variation learn procedure fuel cut off is obtained and engine starts to decelerate or cut out.

7) Using scan tool, verify that CKP sensor variation learn procedure was completed. If CKP sensor variation learn procedure was not completed, go to next step. If CKP sensor variation learn procedure was completed, shut engine off and remove scan tool.

8) If CKP sensor variation learn procedure was not completed, repeat entire procedure up to 10 times. If PCM will not learn the CKP sensor variation compensating values, a DTC P1336 should be stored in the PCM. Perform test procedures for DTC P1336 and repair as necessary. See appropriate SELF-DIAGNOSTICS article in ENGINE PERFORMANCE.

Crankshaft Position (CKP) Sensor Variation Learn Procedure (Alero 3.4L & Grand Am 3.4L) – 1) Procedure must be performed if any of the following have been done or exist:

- EEPROM was reprogrammed.
- If Diagnostic Trouble Code (DTC) P1336 exists.
- If crankshaft, crankshaft position sensor, engine, Powertrain Control Module (PCM) or vibration damper have been replaced.

2) CKP sensor variation compensating values are stored in Powertrain Control Module (PCM) after a learn procedure has been performed. If actual CKP sensor values are not within specification, Diagnostic Trouble Code (DTC) P0300 will be stored in the PCM.

3) Using scan tool, check for stored DTCs. If no DTCs exist, or if DTC P1336 exists, go to next step. If any DTCs exist except for P1336, perform test procedures for specified DTC and repair as necessary. See appropriate SELF-DIAGNOSTICS article in ENGINE PERFORMANCE. Ensure all DTCs are cleared from PCM. Go to next step.

4) Ensure ignition is off. Apply parking brake. Block front wheels. Ensure hood is closed. Start engine and warm engine until engine coolant temperature is at least 158°F (70°C). Turn ignition off.

NOTE: Ensure engine coolant temperature is at least 158°F (70°C) before performing CKP sensor variation learn procedure.

5) Apply service brakes. Using scan tool, select and enable CKP sensor variation learn procedure. Follow instructions displayed on scan tool.

6) If CKP sensor variation learn procedure was not terminated, go to next step. If CKP sensor variation learn procedure was terminated, this may be caused by PCM detecting a problem in cam signal causing DTC P0341, 3X crank signal causing DTC P1374 3X or 24X crank signal causing DTC P0336 24X. Using scan tool, check for stored DTCs. Perform test procedures for specified DTCs and repair as necessary. See appropriate SELF-DIAGNOSTICS article in ENGINE PERFORMANCE.

7) Check scan tool for status of DTC P1336. If scan tool indicates DTC P1336 ran and passed, CKP sensor variation learn procedure is complete. If scan tool indicates DTC P1336 failed or was not run, check for any other DTCs. See appropriate SELF-DIAGNOSTICS article in ENGINE PERFORMANCE. If any other DTCs exist, perform test procedures for specified DTC and repair as necessary. If no other DTCs exist, repeat CKP sensor variation learn procedure.

Password Learn Procedure For Anti-Theft System (Cutlass & Malibu) – 1) Password learn procedure must be performed if Body Function Controller (BFC) is replaced. A password is communicated between BFC and Powertrain Control Module (PCM) to provide engine operation. If BFC is replaced, the PCM must learn the password from the BFC. If password learn procedure is not performed, Diagnostic Trouble Codes (DTCs) P1631 and P1632 may be set in the PCM when attempting to start the engine.

2) Attempt to start engine and then leave ignition on. DO NOT turn ignition off. The THEFT SYSTEM indicator light will flash for about 10 minutes and then turn off. THEFT SYSTEM indicator light is located on instrument panel, just to the left of tachometer.

NOTE: If PCM is replaced, the Electronically Erasable Programmable Read Only Memory (EEPROM) should be programmed. When EEPROM is programmed, the PCM will learn the password when ignition is initially turned on. Password learn procedure is not required when replacing the PCM and EEPROM is programmed.

3) Once THEFT SYSTEM indicator light stops flashing, turn ignition off. Attempt to start the engine. If engine starts, the password learn procedure is complete.

4) On Malibu 2.4L, if password is not learned, a Diagnostic Trouble Code (DTC) P1626, P1632 and U1064 may be set in PCM. Perform test procedures for specified DTC and repair as necessary. See appropriate SELF-DIAGNOSTICS article in ENGINE PERFORMANCE.

5) On Cutlass 3.1L and Malibu 3.1L, if password is not learned, a Diagnostic Trouble Code (DTC) P1610, P1626 and P1632 may be set in PCM. Perform test procedures for specified DTC and repair as necessary. See appropriate SELF-DIAGNOSTICS article in ENGINE PERFORMANCE.

Password Learn Procedure For Anti-Theft System (Alero 3.4L & Grand Am 3.4L) – 1) Password learn procedure must be performed if Body Function Control (BFC) or PCM is replaced. A password is communicated between BFC and PCM to provide engine operation. PCM must learn the password from the BFC.

2) Attempt to start vehicle. Engine will stall. Leave ignition on until theft system light turns off (about 10 minutes). Turn ignition off. Start vehicle. Password is now in memory.

3) If engine does not start, ensure procedure was properly followed. If procedure was properly followed, check for any DTCs. If any DTCs exist, perform test procedures for specified DTC and repair as necessary. See appropriate SELF-DIAGNOSTICS article in ENGINE PERFORMANCE.

Vehicle Driveability Computer Relearn Procedure (A/T Models) – 1) If vehicle battery was disconnected or Powertrain Control Module (PCM) was replaced, turn ignition off. Reconnect PCM battery feed. Turn A/C off. Set parking brake and block drive wheels. Start engine.

2) Idle engine until it reaches operating temperature. Shift transmission into Drive. Allow engine to idle for 5 minutes. Shift transmission selector into Park. Allow engine to idle another 5 minutes. Turn engine off for 30 seconds. Vehicle should now be returned to learned idle.

Vehicle Driveability Computer Relearn Procedure (M/T Models) – 1) If vehicle battery was disconnected or Powertrain Control Module (PCM) was replaced, turn ignition off. Reconnect PCM battery feed. Turn A/C off. Set parking brake and block drive wheels. Shift transmission into Neutral.

2) Start engine. Idle engine until it reaches operating temperature. Allow engine to idle for 5 minutes. Turn engine off for 30 seconds. Vehicle should now be returned to learned idle.

AURORA & RIVIERA

NOTE: Read all procedures listed to determine why and when each procedure is to be performed before proceeding.

Electronically Erasable Programmable Read Only Memory (EEPROM) Programming (3.8L) – 1) If Powertrain Control Module (PCM) was replaced, the EEPROM in the PCM must be programmed. If EEPROM is not programmed, a Diagnostic Trouble Code (DTC) will be set in the PCM.

2) Ensure battery is fully charged. Ensure cable is properly connected on Data Link Connector (DLC). Turn ignition on. Perform EEPROM programming using the Techline equipment manufacturer's instructions and latest software applicable for the vehicle model.

GENERAL INFORMATION
Computer Relearn Procedures (Cont.)

3) Once EEPROM is reprogrammed, the Crankshaft Position (CKP) sensor variation learn procedure must be performed using proper procedure.

NOTE: If EEPROM programming fails, ensure all electrical connections on PCM are okay. Check Techline for latest software. If EEPROM programming still fails, replace PCM.

Electronically Erasable Programmable Read Only Memory (EEPROM) Programming (4.0L) – 1) If Powertrain Control Module (PCM) was replaced, the EEPROM in the PCM must be programmed. If EEPROM is not programmed, a Diagnostic Trouble Code (DTC) will be set in the PCM or PCM may be damaged. Perform EEPROM programming using the Techline equipment manufacturer's instructions and latest software applicable for the vehicle model.

2) Once EEPROM is programmed, use scan tool to clear DTC P0603 from PCM. Engine oil life interval and transaxle fluid life interval must now be reprogrammed using proper procedure. Turn ignition off. Wait 30 seconds to ensure all memory learn procedures occur.

Crankshaft Position (CKP) Sensor Variation Learn Procedure (3.8L) – 1) Procedure must be performed if any of the following have been done or exist:
* EEPROM was reprogrammed.
* If Diagnostic Trouble Code (DTC) P1336 exists.
* If crankshaft, crankshaft position sensor, engine, Powertrain Control Module (PCM) or vibration damper have been replaced.

2) CKP sensor variation compensating values are stored in Powertrain Control Module (PCM) after a learn procedure has been performed. If actual CKP sensor values are not within specification, Diagnostic Trouble Code (DTC) P0300 will be stored in the PCM.

3) Using scan tool, check for stored DTCs. See appropriate SELF-DIAGNOSTICS article in ENGINE PERFORMANCE. If no DTCs exist, or if DTC P1336 exists, go to next step. If any DTCs exist except for P1336, perform test procedures for specified DTC and repair as necessary. See appropriate SELF-DIAGNOSTICS article in ENGINE PERFORMANCE. Ensure all DTCs are cleared from PCM. Go to next step.

4) Ensure ignition is off. Apply parking brake. Block front wheels. Ensure hood is closed. Start engine and warm engine until engine coolant temperature is at least 158°F (70°C). Turn ignition off.

NOTE: Ensure engine coolant temperature is at least 158°F (70°C) before performing CKP sensor variation learn procedure.

5) Using scan tool, select and enable CKP sensor variation learn procedure. Start engine. Apply service brakes. Ensure transaxle is in Park.

6) Accelerate engine until CKP sensor variation learn procedure fuel cut off is obtained at 5150 RPM. Quickly release throttle to idle position once CKP sensor variation learn procedure fuel cut off is obtained and engine starts to decelerate. Once CKP sensor variation values are learned, the PCM will return engine control to the operator and engine will respond to throttle position.

CAUTION: Ensure throttle is quickly released to idle position once CKP sensor variation learn procedure fuel cut off is obtained.

7) If CKP sensor variation learn procedure was not terminated, go to next step. If CKP sensor variation learn procedure was terminated, this may be caused by PCM detecting a problem in cam signal causing DTC P0341, 3X crank signal causing DTC P1374, 3X or 18X crank signal causing DTC P0336 18X. Using scan tool, check for stored DTCs. Perform test procedures for specified DTCs and repair as necessary. See appropriate SELF-DIAGNOSTICS article in ENGINE PERFORMANCE.

8) Check scan tool for status of DTC P1336. If scan tool indicates DTC P1336 ran and passed, CKP sensor variation learn procedure is complete. If scan tool indicates DTC P1336 failed or was not run, check for any other DTCs. See appropriate SELF-DIAGNOSTICS article in ENGINE PERFORMANCE. If any other DTCs exist, perform test procedures for specified DTC and repair as necessary. If no other DTCs exist, repeat CKP sensor variation learn procedure.

Engine Oil Life Interval Programming (4.0L) – 1) Engine oil life interval programming must be performed if any of the following have been done:
* Battery voltage was disconnected from PCM before ignition switch was placed in LOCK position for a minimum of 30 seconds.
* EEPROM was reprogrammed.
* PCM was replaced.

2) Engine oil life interval is calculated by the Powertrain Control Module (PCM). The PCM uses many engine parameters to determine the percentage of engine oil life remaining before engine oil should be changed.

3) Engine oil life interval may be read by the operator by depressing ENG button on Driver Information Center (DIC). The DIC is located above the climate controls at center of instrument panel. Engine oil life interval will be displayed as a percentage when DIC indicates OIL LIFE.

4) If battery voltage was disconnected from PCM before ignition switch was placed in LOCK position for a minimum of 30 seconds, or PCM was replaced, engine oil life interval must be reprogrammed or reset. Engine oil life interval may be programmed or reset by using a scan tool or the DIC.

5) If using scan tool to reprogram or reset engine oil life interval, use scan tool manufacturer's instructions and reprogram or reset engine oil life interval back to the closest original interval index that was recorded on original PCM. Scan tool may reset engine oil life interval index in 10 percent intervals.

NOTE: Scan tool may reset engine oil life interval index in 10 percent intervals. The DIC can only reprogram or reset engine oil life interval to 100 percent.

6) If using DIC to reprogram or reset engine oil life interval, ensure ignition is on. Depress ENG button on DIC until displays OIL LIFE percentage. Depress and hold RESET button on DIC for 5 seconds. The word RESET will be displayed and then OIL LIFE 100 percent will be displayed. Release all buttons. The DIC can only reprogram or reset engine oil life interval to 100 percent.

Transaxle Fluid Life Interval Programming (4.0L) – 1) Transaxle fluid life interval programming must be performed if any of the following have been done:
* Battery voltage was disconnected from PCM before ignition switch was placed in LOCK position for a minimum of 30 seconds.
* EEPROM was reprogrammed.
* PCM was replaced.

2) Transaxle fluid life interval is calculated by the Powertrain Control Module (PCM). The PCM uses many engine parameters to determine the percentage of transaxle fluid life interval remaining before fluid should be changed.

3) When PCM determines transaxle fluid should be changed, a signal is sent to the instrument cluster and warning light is displayed. If battery voltage was disconnected from PCM before ignition switch was placed in LOCK position for a minimum of 30 seconds, or PCM was replaced, transaxle fluid life interval must be reprogrammed or reset.

4) To reprogram or reset transaxle fluid life interval to original interval set in the PCM, connect scan tool to Data Link Connector (DLC). Using scan tool manufacturer's instructions and reprogram or reset transaxle fluid life interval back to the closest original interval index that was recorded on original PCM.

Vehicle Driveability Computer Relearn Procedure (All Models) – Manufacturer does not provide a specified computer relearn procedure for obtaining proper driveability. If vehicle battery was disconnected or Powertrain Control Module (PCM) was replaced, driving the vehicle will enable the PCM to perform a computer relearn procedure for obtaining proper driveability. Inform customer that driveability may differ from what they are accustomed to until the PCM completes the computer relearn procedure.

Computer Relearn Procedures (Cont.)

BONNEVILLE, EIGHTY EIGHT & LE SABRE

NOTE: Read all procedures listed to determine why and when each procedure is to be performed before proceeding.

Electronically Erasable Programmable Read Only Memory (EEPROM) Programming – 1) If Powertrain Control Module (PCM) was replaced, the EEPROM in the PCM must be programmed. If EEPROM is not programmed, a Diagnostic Trouble Code (DTC) will be set in the PCM.

2) Ensure battery is fully charged. If battery is being charged, ensure battery charger is disconnected before performing EEPROM programming procedure.

3) Ensure cable is properly connected on Data Link Connector (DLC). Turn ignition on. Perform EEPROM programming using the Techline equipment manufacturer's instructions and latest software applicable for the vehicle model.

4) Once EEPROM is reprogrammed, perform powertrain On-Board Diagnostic (OBD) system check. See POWERTRAIN ON-BOARD DIAGNOSTIC (OBD) SYSTEM CHECK in appropriate SELF-DIAGNOSTICS article in ENGINE PERFORMANCE. Ensure engine is idling for one minute before checking for DTCs when performing powertrain OBD system check. Also after EEPROM is reprogrammed, the Crankshaft Position (CKP) sensor variation learn procedure must be performed using proper procedure.

NOTE: If EEPROM programming fails, ensure all electrical connections on PCM are okay. Check Techline for latest software. If EEPROM programming still fails, replace PCM.

Crankshaft Position (CKP) Sensor Variation Learn Procedure – 1) Procedure must be performed if any of the following have been done or exist:
- EEPROM was reprogrammed.
- If Diagnostic Trouble Code (DTC) P1336 exists.
- If crankshaft, crankshaft position sensor, engine, Powertrain Control Module (PCM) or vibration damper have been replaced.

2) CKP sensor variation compensating values are stored in Powertrain Control Module (PCM) after a learn procedure has been performed. If actual CKP sensor values are not within specification, Diagnostic Trouble Code (DTC) P0300 will be stored in the PCM.

3) Using scan tool, check for stored DTCs. If no DTCs exist, or if DTC P1336 exists, go to next step. If any DTCs exist except for P1336, perform test procedures for specified DTC and repair as necessary. See appropriate SELF-DIAGNOSTICS article in ENGINE PERFORMANCE. Ensure all DTCs are cleared from PCM. Go to next step.

4) Ensure ignition is off. Apply parking brake. Block front wheels. Ensure hood is closed. Start engine and warm engine until engine coolant temperature is at least 158°F (70°C). Turn ignition off.

NOTE: Ensure engine coolant temperature is at least 158°F (70°C) before performing CKP sensor variation learn procedure.

5) Using scan tool, select and enable CKP sensor variation learn procedure. Start engine. Apply service brakes. Ensure transaxle is in Park.

6) Accelerate engine until CKP sensor variation learn procedure fuel cut off is obtained at 5150 RPM. Quickly release throttle to idle position once CKP sensor variation learn procedure fuel cut off is obtained and engine starts to decelerate. Once CKP sensor variation values are learned, the PCM will return engine control to the operator and engine will respond to throttle position.

CAUTION: Ensure throttle is quickly released to idle position once CKP sensor variation learn procedure fuel cut off is obtained.

7) If CKP sensor variation learn procedure was not terminated, go to next step. If CKP sensor variation learn procedure was terminated, this may be caused by PCM detecting a problem in cam signal causing DTC P0341, 3X crank signal causing DTC P1374 3X or 18X crank signal causing DTC P0336 18X. Using scan tool, check for stored DTCs.

Perform test procedures for specified DTCs and repair as necessary. See appropriate SELF-DIAGNOSTICS article in ENGINE PERFORMANCE.

8) Check scan tool for status of DTC P1336. If scan tool indicates DTC P1336 ran and passed, CKP sensor variation learn procedure is complete. If scan tool indicates DTC P1336 failed or was not run, check for any other DTCs. See appropriate SELF-DIAGNOSTICS article in ENGINE PERFORMANCE. If any other DTCs exist, perform test procedures for specified DTC and repair as necessary. If no other DTCs exist, repeat CKP sensor variation learn procedure.

Vehicle Driveability Computer Relearn Procedure – Manufacturer does not provide a specified computer relearn procedure for obtaining proper driveability. If vehicle battery was disconnected or Powertrain Control Module (PCM) was replaced, driving the vehicle will enable the PCM to perform a computer relearn procedure for obtaining proper driveability. Inform customer that driveability may differ from what they are accustomed to until the PCM completes the computer relearn procedure.

CAMARO & FIREBIRD

NOTE: Read all procedures listed to determine why and when each procedure is to be performed before proceeding.

Electronically Erasable Programmable Read Only Memory (EEPROM) Programming – 1) If Powertrain Control Module (PCM) was replaced, the EEPROM in the PCM must be programmed. If EEPROM is not programmed, a Diagnostic Trouble Code (DTC) will be set in the PCM.

2) Ensure battery is fully charged. Ensure cable is properly connected on Data Link Connector (DLC). Turn ignition on. Perform EEPROM programming using the Techline equipment manufacturer's instructions and latest software applicable for the vehicle model.

3) On 3.8L, once EEPROM is reprogrammed, perform powertrain On-Board Diagnostic (OBD) system check. See POWERTRAIN ON-BOARD DIAGNOSTIC (OBD) SYSTEM CHECK in appropriate SELF-DIAGNOSTICS article in ENGINE PERFORMANCE. Ensure engine is idling for one minute before checking for DTCs when performing powertrain OBD system check.

NOTE: If EEPROM programming fails, ensure all electrical connections on PCM are okay. Check Techline for latest software. If EEPROM programming still fails, replace PCM.

4) On 5.7L, once EEPROM is reprogrammed, perform powertrain On-Board Diagnostic (OBD) system check. See POWERTRAIN ON-BOARD DIAGNOSTIC (OBD) SYSTEM CHECK in appropriate SELF-DIAGNOSTICS article in ENGINE PERFORMANCE. Ensure engine is idling for one minute before checking for DTCs when performing powertrain OBD system check. Also, after EEPROM is reprogrammed, the idle learn procedure and then Crankshaft Position (CKP) sensor variation learn procedure must be performed using proper procedures.

Idle Learn Procedure (5.7L) – 1) Idle learn procedure must be performed to provide proper positioning of Idle Air Control (IAC) valve to obtain proper engine idle. If idle learn procedure is not performed, engine idle may become unstable. Procedure must be performed if any of the following have been done:
- Vehicle battery was disconnected.
- PCM was disconnected or PCM looses battery voltage. On A/T models, go to next step. On M/T models, go to step **4)**.

2) On A/T models, ensure ignition is off. Restore battery voltage to PCM. Ensure A/C is turned off. Apply parking brake. Block rear wheels. Start engine. Place transmission in Drive. Allow engine to idle for 5 minutes. Place transmission in Park.

3) Allow engine to idle for 5 minutes. Shut engine off for 30 seconds. Clear Diagnostic Trouble Codes (DTCs) from PCM. Perform powertrain On-Board Diagnostic (OBD) system check. See POWERTRAIN ON-BOARD DIAGNOSTIC (OBD) SYSTEM CHECK in appropriate SELF-DIAGNOSTICS article in ENGINE PERFORMANCE. Ensure engine is idling for one minute before checking for DTCs when performing powertrain OBD system check.

GENERAL INFORMATION
Computer Relearn Procedures (Cont.)

4) On M/T models, ensure ignition is off. Restore battery voltage to PCM. Ensure A/C is turned off. Apply parking brake. Block rear wheels. Place transmission in Neutral. Start engine. Allow engine to idle for 5 minutes.

5) Shut engine off for 30 seconds. Clear Diagnostic Trouble Codes (DTCs) from PCM. Perform powertrain On-Board Diagnostic (OBD) system check. See POWERTRAIN ON-BOARD DIAGNOSTIC (OBD) SYSTEM CHECK in appropriate SELF-DIAGNOSTICS article in ENGINE PERFORMANCE. Ensure engine is idling for one minute before checking for DTCs when performing powertrain OBD system check.

Crankshaft Position (CKP) Sensor Variation Learn Procedure (3.8L) – **1)** Procedure must be performed if any of the following have been done or exist:

- EEPROM was reprogrammed.
- If Diagnostic Trouble Code (DTC) P1336 exists.
- If crankshaft, crankshaft position sensor, engine, Powertrain Control Module (PCM) or vibration damper have been replaced.

2) CKP sensor variation compensating values are stored in Powertrain Control Module (PCM) after a learn procedure has been performed. If actual CKP sensor values are not within specification, Diagnostic Trouble Code (DTC) P0300 will be stored in the PCM.

3) Using scan tool, check for stored DTCs. If no DTCs exist, or if DTC P1336 exists, go to next step. If any DTCs exist except for P1336, perform test procedures for specified DTC and repair as necessary. See appropriate SELF-DIAGNOSTICS article in ENGINE PERFORMANCE. Ensure all DTCs are cleared from PCM. Go to next step.

4) Ensure ignition is off. Apply parking brake. Block rear wheels. Ensure hood is closed. Start engine and warm engine until engine coolant temperature is at least 158°F (70°C). Turn ignition off.

NOTE: *Ensure engine coolant temperature is at least 158°F (70°C) before performing CKP sensor variation learn procedure.*

---

5) Using scan tool, select and enable CKP sensor variation learn procedure. Start engine. DO NOT start engine until instructed to do so by scan tool. Apply service brakes. Ensure transmission is in Park.

6) Accelerate engine until CKP sensor variation learn procedure fuel cut off is obtained at 5150 RPM. Quickly release throttle to idle position once CKP sensor variation learn procedure fuel cut off is obtained and engine starts to decelerate. Once CKP sensor variation values are learned, the PCM will return engine control to the operator and engine will respond to throttle position.

CAUTION: *Ensure throttle is quickly released to idle position once CKP sensor variation learn procedure fuel cut off is obtained.*

---

7) If CKP sensor variation learn procedure was not terminated, go to next step. If CKP sensor variation learn procedure was terminated, this may be caused by PCM detecting a problem in cam signal causing DTC P0341, 3X crank signal causing DTC P1374 3X or 18X crank signal causing DTC P0336 18X. Using scan tool, check for stored DTCs. Perform test procedures for specified DTCs and repair as necessary. See appropriate SELF-DIAGNOSTICS article in ENGINE PERFORMANCE.

8) Check scan tool for status of DTC P1336. If scan tool indicates DTC P1336 ran and passed, CKP sensor variation learn procedure is complete. If scan tool indicates DTC P1336 failed or was not run, check for any other DTCs. See appropriate SELF-DIAGNOSTICS article in ENGINE PERFORMANCE. If any other DTCs exist, perform test procedures for specified DTC and repair as necessary. If no other DTCs exist, repeat CKP sensor variation learn procedure.

Crankshaft Position (CKP) Sensor Variation Learn Procedure (5.7L) – **1)** Procedure must be performed if any of the following have been done:

- EEPROM was reprogrammed.
- If crankshaft position sensor was removed or replaced.
- Powertrain Control Module (PCM) has been replaced.

2) Install scan tool on Data Link Connector (DLC). Apply parking brake. Block rear wheels. Ensure hood is closed. Ensure transmission is in Park (A/T models) or Neutral (M/T models). Start engine and allow engine to idle until engine coolant temperature is at least 150°F (65°C). Ensure all accessories are off.

3) Apply brakes. Ensure brakes remain applied during remaining duration of this procedure. Using scan tool, select and enable CKP sensor variation learn procedure.

4) Gradually accelerate engine to 4000 RPM. Quickly release throttle to idle position once CKP sensor variation learn procedure is obtained and engine starts to decelerate. Once CKP sensor variation values are learned, the PCM will return engine control to the operator and engine will respond to throttle position.

5) If CKP sensor variation learn procedure was not terminated, turn ignition off for at least 15 seconds. CKP sensor variation learn procedure is complete. If CKP sensor variation learn procedure was terminated, turn ignition off. Refer to Diagnostic Trouble Code (DTC) P1336 for additional diagnostic information. See appropriate SELF-DIAGNOSTICS article in ENGINE PERFORMANCE.

Vehicle Driveability Computer Relearn Procedure (All Models) – Manufacturer does not provide a specified computer relearn procedure for obtaining proper driveability. If vehicle battery was disconnected or Powertrain Control Module (PCM) was replaced, driving the vehicle will enable the PCM to perform a computer relearn procedure for obtaining proper driveability. Inform customer that driveability may differ from what they are accustomed to until the PCM completes the computer relearn procedure.

CATERA

NOTE: *Read all procedures listed to determine why and when each procedure is to be performed before proceeding.*

Electronically Erasable Programmable Read Only Memory (EEPROM) Programming – **1)** The replacement Powertrain Control Module (PCM) comes with the EEPROM already programmed. However, the PCM must be programmed, with proper immobilizer signal for anti-theft system before the vehicle will start. See appropriate ANTI-THEFT SYSTEMS article in ACCESSORIES & EQUIPMENT for programming immobilizer signal.

2) Once PCM is programmed, perform powertrain On-Board Diagnostic (OBD) system check. See POWERTRAIN ON-BOARD DIAGNOSTIC (OBD) SYSTEM CHECK in appropriate SELF-DIAGNOSTICS article in ENGINE PERFORMANCE.

Sun Roof Actuator Programming – **1)** Procedure must be performed when vehicle battery is disconnected. Turn ignition on.

2) Rotate knob on sun roof control switch to CLOSED position. Sun roof control switch is located on the overhead console near the windshield. After sun roof is fully closed, press and hold knob on sun roof control switch inward for 3 seconds.

3) Rotate knob on sun roof control switch to the VENT position. After sun roof moves to the vent position, press and hold knob on sun roof control switch inward for 3 seconds.

4) Rotate knob on sun roof control switch to the OPEN position. After sun roof full opens, press and hold knob on sun roof control switch inward for 3 seconds.

5) Rotate knob on sun roof control switch to CLOSED position. After sun roof is fully closed, press and hold knob on sun roof control switch inward for 3 seconds.

6) Sun roof actuator is now programmed. If after programming the sun roof actuator, the sun roof opens after being closed, it may be necessary to reprogram actuator up to 3 more times.

Vehicle Driveability Computer Relearn Procedure – Manufacturer does not provide a specified computer relearn procedure for obtaining proper driveability. If vehicle battery was disconnected or Powertrain Control Module (PCM) was replaced, driving the vehicle will enable the PCM to perform a computer relearn procedure for obtaining proper driveability. Inform customer that driveability may differ from what they are accustomed to until the PCM completes the computer relearn procedure.

CAVALIER & SUNFIRE

NOTE: Read all procedures listed to determine why and when each procedure is to be performed before proceeding.

Electronically Erasable Programmable Read Only Memory (EEPROM) Programming – 1) If Powertrain Control Module (PCM) was replaced, the EEPROM in the PCM must be programmed. If EEPROM is not programmed, a Diagnostic Trouble Code (DTC) will be set in the PCM or PCM may be damaged. Perform EEPROM programming using the Techline equipment manufacturer's instructions and latest software applicable for the vehicle model.

2) Once EEPROM is reprogrammed, the Crankshaft Position (CKP) sensor variation learn procedure must be performed using proper procedure.

Crankshaft Position (CKP) Sensor Variation Learn Procedure – 1) Procedure must be performed if any of the following have been done or exist:

- EEPROM was reprogrammed.
- If Diagnostic Trouble Code (DTC) P1336 exists.
- If crankshaft, crankshaft position sensor, engine or Powertrain Control Module (PCM) have been replaced.
- Any repairs have been performed that disturbs the crankshaft or vibration damper to the crankshaft position sensor relationship.

2) CKP sensor variation compensating values are stored in Powertrain Control Module (PCM) after a learn procedure has been performed. If actual CKP sensor values are not within specification, Diagnostic Trouble Code (DTC) P0300 will be stored in the PCM.

3) Ensure battery is fully charged. Ensure cable is properly connected on Data Link Connector (DLC). Apply parking brake. Block front wheels. Ensure hood is closed.

4) Place transaxle in Park (A/T models) or Neutral (M/T models). Ensure all accessories are off. Start engine and warm engine until engine coolant temperature is at least 185°F (85°C).

5) Apply service brakes. With engine idling, use scan tool to select and enable CKP sensor variation learn procedure.

6) Accelerate engine until CKP sensor variation learn procedure fuel cut off is obtained and engine starts to decelerate or cut out. Quickly release throttle to idle position once CKP sensor variation learn procedure is obtained and engine decelerates or cuts out. Once CKP sensor variation values are learned, the PCM will return engine control to the operator and engine will respond to throttle position.

CAUTION: Ensure throttle is quickly released to idle position once CKP sensor variation learn procedure fuel cut off is obtained and engine starts to decelerate or cut out.

7) Using scan tool, verify that CKP sensor variation learn procedure was completed. If CKP sensor variation learn procedure was not completed, go to next step. If CKP sensor variation learn procedure was completed, shut engine off and remove scan tool.

8) If CKP sensor variation learn procedure was not completed, repeat entire procedure up to 10 times. If PCM will not learn the CKP sensor variation compensating values, a DTC P1336 should be stored in the PCM. Perform test procedures for DTC P1336 and repair as necessary. See appropriate SELF-DIAGNOSTICS article in ENGINE PERFORMANCE.

Password Learn Procedure For Anti-Theft System – 1) Password learn procedure must be performed if Instrument Panel Cluster (IPC) is replaced. A password is communicated between IPC and Powertrain Control Module (PCM) to provide engine operation. If IPC is replaced, the PCM must learn the password from the IPC.

2) Attempt to start engine and then leave ignition on. DO NOT turn ignition off. The THEFT SYSTEM indicator light will flash for 10 minutes.

NOTE: If PCM is replaced, the Electronically Erasable Programmable Read Only Memory (EEPROM) should be programmed. When EEPROM is programmed, the PCM will learn the password when ignition is initially turned on. Password learn procedure is not required when replacing the PCM and EEPROM is programmed.

3) On Cavalier, THEFT SYSTEM indicator light is located on IPC, just above the vehicle mileage indicator. On Sunfire, THEFT SYSTEM indicator light is located on IPC, just above the temperature gauge.

4) On all models, once THEFT SYSTEM indicator light stops flashing, attempt to start the engine. If engine starts, the password learn procedure is complete. If engine does not start, ensure procedure was properly followed. If procedure was properly followed, check for any DTCs. If any DTCs exist, perform test procedures for specified DTC and repair as necessary. See appropriate SELF-DIAGNOSTICS article in ENGINE PERFORMANCE.

Vehicle Driveability Computer Relearn Procedure – Manufacturer does not provide a specified computer relearn procedure for obtaining proper driveability. If vehicle battery was disconnected or Powertrain Control Module (PCM) was replaced, driving the vehicle will enable the PCM to perform a computer relearn procedure for obtaining proper driveability. Inform customer that driveability may differ from what they are accustomed to until the PCM completes the computer relearn procedure.

CENTURY, GRAND PRIX, INTRIGUE, LUMINA, MONTE CARLO & REGAL

NOTE: Read all procedures listed to determine why and when each procedure is to be performed before proceeding.

Electronically Erasable Programmable Read Only Memory (EEPROM) Programming (All Models) – 1) If Powertrain Control Module (PCM) was replaced, the EEPROM in the PCM must be programmed. If EEPROM is not programmed, a Diagnostic Trouble Code (DTC) will be set in the PCM.

2) Ensure battery is fully charged. If battery is being charged, ensure battery charger is disconnected before performing EEPROM programming procedure.

3) Ensure cable is properly connected on Data Link Connector (DLC). Turn ignition on. Perform EEPROM programming using the Techline equipment manufacturer's instructions and latest software applicable for the vehicle model.

4) Once EEPROM is reprogrammed, perform powertrain On-Board Diagnostic (OBD) system check. See POWERTRAIN ON-BOARD DIAGNOSTIC (OBD) SYSTEM CHECK in appropriate SELF-DIAGNOSTICS article in ENGINE PERFORMANCE. Ensure engine is idling for one minute before checking for DTCs when performing powertrain OBD system check. On 3.5L and 3.8L, after EEPROM is reprogrammed, the Crankshaft Position (CKP) sensor variation learn procedure must be performed using proper procedure.

NOTE: If EEPROM programming fails, ensure all electrical connections on PCM are okay. Check Techline for latest software. If EEPROM programming still fails, replace PCM.

Crankshaft Position (CKP) Sensor Variation Learn Procedure (3.1L) – 1) Procedure must be performed if any of the following have been done or exist:

- EEPROM was reprogrammed.
- If Diagnostic Trouble Code (DTC) P1336 exists.
- If crankshaft, crankshaft position sensor, engine, Powertrain Control Module (PCM) or vibration damper have been replaced.

2) CKP sensor variation compensating values are stored in Powertrain Control Module (PCM) after a learn procedure has been performed. If actual CKP sensor values are not within specification, Diagnostic Trouble Code (DTC) P0300 will be stored in the PCM.

3) Using scan tool, check for stored DTCs. See appropriate SELF-DIAGNOSTICS article in ENGINE PERFORMANCE. If no DTCs exist, or if DTC P1336 exists, go to next step. If any DTCs exist except for P1336, perform test procedures for specified DTC and repair as necessary. See appropriate SELF-DIAGNOSTICS article in ENGINE PERFORMANCE. Ensure all DTCs are cleared from PCM. Go to next step.

4) Ensure ignition is off. Apply parking brake. Block front wheels. Ensure hood is closed. Start engine and warm engine until engine coolant temperature is at least 158°F (70°C). Turn ignition off.

NOTE: Ensure engine coolant temperature is at least 158°F (70°C) before performing CKP sensor variation learn procedure.

5) Using scan tool, select and enable CKP sensor variation learn procedure. Start engine. Apply service brakes. Ensure transaxle is in Park.

6) Accelerate engine until CKP sensor variation learn procedure fuel cut off is obtained at 5150 RPM. Quickly release throttle to idle position once CKP sensor variation learn procedure fuel cut off is obtained and engine starts to decelerate. Once CKP sensor variation values are learned, the PCM will return engine control to the operator and engine will respond to throttle position.

CAUTION: Ensure throttle is quickly released to idle position once CKP sensor variation learn procedure fuel cut off is obtained.

7) If CKP sensor variation learn procedure was not terminated, go to next step. If CKP sensor variation learn procedure was terminated, this may be caused by PCM detecting a problem in cam signal causing DTC P0341, 3X crank signal causing DTC P1374 3X or 24X crank signal causing DTC P0336 24X. Using scan tool, check for stored DTCs. Perform test procedures for specified DTCs and repair as necessary. See appropriate SELF-DIAGNOSTICS article in ENGINE PERFORMANCE.

8) Check scan tool for status of DTC P1336. If scan tool indicates DTC P1336 ran and passed, CKP sensor variation learn procedure is complete. If scan tool indicates DTC P1336 failed or was not run, check for any other DTCs. See appropriate SELF-DIAGNOSTICS article in ENGINE PERFORMANCE. If any other DTCs exist, perform test procedures for specified DTC and repair as necessary. If no other DTCs exist, repeat CKP sensor variation learn procedure.

Crankshaft Position (CKP) Sensor Variation Learn Procedure (3.5L & 3.8L) – 1) Procedure must be performed if any of the following have been done or exist:

- EEPROM was reprogrammed.
- If Diagnostic Trouble Code (DTC) P1336 exists.
- If crankshaft, crankshaft position sensor, engine, Powertrain Control Module (PCM) or vibration damper have been replaced.

2) CKP sensor variation compensating values are stored in Powertrain Control Module (PCM) after a learn procedure has been performed. If actual CKP sensor values are not within specification, Diagnostic Trouble Code (DTC) P0300 will be stored in the PCM.

3) Using scan tool, check for stored DTCs. See appropriate SELF-DIAGNOSTICS article in ENGINE PERFORMANCE. If no DTCs exist, or if DTC P1336 exists, go to next step. If any DTCs exist except for P1336, perform test procedures for specified DTC and repair as necessary. See appropriate SELF-DIAGNOSTICS article in ENGINE PERFORMANCE. Ensure all DTCs are cleared from PCM. Go to next step.

4) Ensure ignition is off. Apply parking brake. Block front wheels. Ensure hood is closed. Start engine and warm engine until engine coolant temperature is at least 158°F (70°C). Turn ignition off.

NOTE: Ensure engine coolant temperature is at least 158°F (70°C) before performing CKP sensor variation learn procedure.

5) Using scan tool, select and enable CKP sensor variation learn procedure. Start engine. Apply service brakes. Ensure transaxle is in Park.

6) Accelerate engine until CKP sensor variation learn procedure fuel cut off is obtained at 4300 RPM (3.5L) or 5150 RPM (3.8L). Quickly release

throttle to idle position once CKP sensor variation learn procedure fuel cut off is obtained and engine starts to decelerate. Once CKP sensor variation values are learned, the PCM will return engine control to the operator and engine will respond to throttle position.

CAUTION: Ensure throttle is quickly released to idle position once CKP sensor variation learn procedure fuel cut off is obtained.

7) If CKP sensor variation learn procedure was not terminated, go to next step. If CKP sensor variation learn procedure was terminated, this may be caused by PCM detecting a problem in cam signal causing DTC P0341, 3X crank signal causing DTC P1374 3X or 18X crank signal causing DTC P0336 18X. Using scan tool, check for stored DTCs. Perform test procedures for specified DTCs and repair as necessary. See appropriate SELF-DIAGNOSTICS article in ENGINE PERFORMANCE.

8) Check scan tool for status of DTC P1336. If scan tool indicates DTC P1336 ran and passed, CKP sensor variation learn procedure is complete. If scan tool indicates DTC P1336 failed or was not run, check for any other DTCs. See appropriate SELF-DIAGNOSTICS article in ENGINE PERFORMANCE. If any other DTCs exist, perform test procedures for specified DTC and repair as necessary. If no other DTCs exist, repeat CKP sensor variation learn procedure.

Vehicle Driveability Computer Relearn Procedure (All Models) – Manufacturer does not provide a specified computer relearn procedure for obtaining proper driveability. If vehicle battery was disconnected or Powertrain Control Module (PCM) was replaced, driving the vehicle will enable the PCM to perform a computer relearn procedure for obtaining proper driveability. Inform customer that driveability may differ from what they are accustomed to until the PCM completes the computer relearn procedure.

CORVETTE

NOTE: Read all procedures listed to determine why and when each procedure is to be performed before proceeding.

Electronically Erasable Programmable Read Only Memory (EEPROM) Programming – 1) If Powertrain Control Module (PCM) was replaced, the EEPROM in the PCM must be programmed. If EEPROM is not programmed, a Diagnostic Trouble Code (DTC) will be set in the PCM.

2) Ensure battery is fully charged. Ensure cable is properly connected on Data Link Connector (DLC). Turn ignition on. Perform EEPROM programming using the Techline equipment manufacturer's instructions and latest software applicable for the vehicle model.

3) Once EEPROM is reprogrammed, perform powertrain On-Board Diagnostic (OBD) system check. See POWERTRAIN ON-BOARD DIAGNOSTIC (OBD) SYSTEM CHECK in appropriate SELF-DIAGNOSTICS article in ENGINE PERFORMANCE. Ensure engine is idling for one minute before checking for DTCs when performing powertrain OBD system check. Also after EEPROM is reprogrammed, the password learn procedure for the anti-theft system must be performed.

NOTE: If EEPROM programming fails, ensure all electrical connections on PCM are okay. Check Techline for latest software. If EEPROM programming still fails, replace PCM.

Password Learn Procedure For Anti-Theft System – 1) Password learn procedure must be performed if Powertrain Control Module (PCM) is replaced. A password is communicated between Body Control Module (BCM) and PCM to provide engine operation. If PCM is replaced, the PCM must learn the password from the BCM. If password learn procedure is not performed a Diagnostic Trouble Code (DTC) may be set in the PCM when attempting to start engine.

2) Using Tech 2 scan tool, select NEW BCM setup and program BCM with correct RPO code configuration. Turn ignition switch to ON position with engine off for 11 minutes. Turn ignition switch to OFF position for 30 seconds.

NOTE: Ensure battery is fully charged before proceeding. Performing this procedure will cause a DTC P1630 to be set in the PCM. It will be necessary to use scan tool to check for DTC P1630 when performing this procedure.

3) Turn ignition switch to ON position with engine off for 11 minutes. Turn ignition switch to OFF position for 30 seconds.

4) Turn ignition switch to ON position with engine off for 11 minutes or until DTC P1630 is set. Turn ignition switch to OFF position for 30 seconds.

5) Turn ignition switch to ON position with engine off for 30 seconds. Attempt to start engine.

6) If engine starts, go to next step. If engine does not start, check for any other DTCs. If any DTCs exist, perform test procedures for specified DTC and repair as necessary. See appropriate SELF-DIAGNOSTICS article in ENGINE PERFORMANCE.

7) Clear DTCs from PCM. Turn ignition switch to OFF position for 30 seconds. Attempt to start engine.

8) If engine does not start, ensure procedure was properly followed. If procedure was properly followed, check for any DTCs. If any DTCs exist, perform test procedures for specified DTC and repair as necessary. See appropriate SELF-DIAGNOSTICS article in ENGINE PERFORMANCE.

Vehicle Driveability Computer Relearn Procedure (All Models) – Manufacturer does not provide a specified computer relearn procedure for obtaining proper driveability. If vehicle battery was disconnected or Powertrain Control Module (PCM) was replaced, driving the vehicle will enable the PCM to perform a computer relearn procedure for obtaining proper driveability. Inform customer that driveability may differ from what they are accustomed to until the PCM completes the computer relearn procedure.

DEVILLE, ELDORADO & SEVILLE

NOTE: Read all procedures listed to determine why and when each procedure is to be performed before proceeding.

Electronically Erasable Programmable Read Only Memory (EEPROM) Programming – **1)** If Powertrain Control Module (PCM) was replaced, the EEPROM in the PCM must be programmed. If EEPROM is not programmed, a Diagnostic Trouble Code (DTC) will be set in the PCM or PCM may be damaged. Perform EEPROM programming using the Techline equipment manufacturer's instructions and latest software applicable for the vehicle model.

2) To verify proper EEPROM programming, start engine. If engine starts, go to next step. If engine fails to start, ensure all electrical connections on PCM are okay and all fuses are okay. Check Techline for latest software. Once engine is repaired so it will start, go to next step.

3) Once EEPROM is programmed, use scan tool to clear DTC P0603 from PCM. Engine oil life interval and transaxle fluid life interval must now be reprogrammed using proper procedure.

Engine Oil Life Interval Programming – **1)** Engine oil life interval programming must be performed if any of the following have been done:

- Battery voltage was disconnected from PCM before ignition switch was placed in LOCK position for a minimum of 30 seconds.
- EEPROM was reprogrammed.
- PCM was replaced.

2) Engine oil life interval is calculated by the Powertrain Control Module (PCM). The PCM uses many engine parameters to determine the percentage of engine oil life remaining before engine oil should be changed.

3) Engine oil life interval may be read by the operator by depressing INFO button on Driver Information Center (DIC). The DIC is located above the stereo. Engine oil life interval will be displayed as a percentage when DIC indicates OIL LIFE LEFT.

4) If battery voltage was disconnected from PCM before ignition switch was placed in LOCK position for a minimum of 30 seconds, or PCM was replaced, engine oil life interval must be reprogrammed or reset. Engine oil life interval may be programmed or reset by using a scan tool or the DIC.

5) If using scan tool to reprogram or reset engine oil life interval, use scan tool manufacturer's instructions and reprogram or reset engine oil life interval back to the closest original interval index that was recorded on original PCM. Scan tool may reset engine oil life interval index in 10 percent intervals.

NOTE: Scan tool may reset engine oil life interval index in 10 percent intervals. The DIC can only reprogram or reset engine oil life interval to 100 percent.

6) If using DIC to reprogram or reset engine oil life interval, depress INFO button on DIC. Depress and hold INFO RESET button on DIC until 100 percent OIL LIFE LEFT is displayed on instrument panel. Release all buttons. The DIC can only reprogram or reset engine oil life interval to 100 percent.

Transaxle Fluid Life Interval Programming – **1)** Transaxle fluid life interval programming must be performed if any of the following have been done:

- Battery voltage was disconnected from PCM before ignition switch was placed in LOCK position for a minimum of 30 seconds.
- EEPROM was reprogrammed.
- PCM was replaced.

2) Transaxle fluid life interval is calculated by the Powertrain Control Module (PCM). The PCM uses many engine parameters to determine the percentage of transaxle fluid life interval remaining before fluid should be changed.

3) When PCM determines transaxle fluid should be changed, a signal is sent to the instrument cluster and warning light is displayed. If battery voltage was disconnected from PCM before ignition switch was placed in LOCK position for a minimum of 30 seconds, or PCM was replaced, transaxle fluid life interval must be reprogrammed or reset.

4) To reprogram or reset transaxle fluid life interval to original interval set in the PCM, connect scan tool to Data Link Connector (DLC). Using scan tool manufacturer's instructions and reprogram or reset transaxle fluid life interval back to the closest original interval index that was recorded on original PCM.

Vehicle Driveability Computer Relearn Procedure (All Models) – Manufacturer does not provide a specified computer relearn procedure for obtaining proper driveability. If vehicle battery was disconnected or Powertrain Control Module (PCM) was replaced, driving the vehicle will enable the PCM to perform a computer relearn procedure for obtaining proper driveability. Inform customer that driveability may differ from what they are accustomed to until the PCM completes the computer relearn procedure.

METRO

NOTE: Powertrain Control Module (PCM) does not have a reprogrammable EEPROM. No special procedures are required for programming the PCM.

Vehicle Driveability Computer Relearn Procedure – Manufacturer does not provide a specified computer relearn procedure for obtaining proper driveability. If vehicle battery was disconnected or Powertrain Control Module (PCM) was replaced, driving the vehicle will enable the PCM to perform a computer relearn procedure for obtaining proper driveability. Inform customer that driveability may differ from what they are accustomed to until the PCM completes the computer relearn procedure.

GENERAL INFORMATION
Computer Relearn Procedures (Cont.)

PARK AVENUE

NOTE: Read all procedures listed to determine why and when each procedure is to be performed before proceeding.

Electronically Erasable Programmable Read Only Memory (EEPROM) Programming – 1) If Powertrain Control Module (PCM) was replaced, the EEPROM in the PCM must be programmed. If EEPROM is not programmed, a Diagnostic Trouble Code (DTC) will be set in the PCM.

2) Ensure battery is fully charged. If battery is being charged, ensure battery charger is disconnected before performing EEPROM programming procedure.

3) Ensure cable is properly connected on Data Link Connector (DLC). Turn ignition on. Perform EEPROM programming using the Techline equipment manufacturer's instructions and latest software applicable for the vehicle model.

NOTE: If EEPROM programming fails, ensure all electrical connections on PCM are okay. Check Techline for latest software. If EEPROM programming still fails, replace PCM.

4) Once EEPROM is reprogrammed, perform powertrain On-Board Diagnostic (OBD) system check. See POWERTRAIN ON-BOARD DIAGNOSTIC (OBD) SYSTEM CHECK in appropriate SELF-DIAGNOSTICS article in ENGINE PERFORMANCE. Ensure engine is idling for one minute before checking for DTCs when performing powertrain OBD system check. Also after EEPROM is reprogrammed, the Crankshaft Position (CKP) sensor variation learn procedure must be performed using proper procedure.

Crankshaft Position (CKP) Sensor Variation Learn Procedure – 1) Procedure must be performed if any of the following have been done or exist:

- EEPROM was reprogrammed.
- If Diagnostic Trouble Code (DTC) P1336 exists.
- If crankshaft, crankshaft position sensor, engine, Powertrain Control Module (PCM) or vibration damper have been replaced.

2) CKP sensor variation compensating values are stored in Powertrain Control Module (PCM) after a learn procedure has been performed. If actual CKP sensor values are not within specification, Diagnostic Trouble Code (DTC) P0300 will be stored in the PCM.

3) Using scan tool, check for stored DTCs. See appropriate SELF-DIAGNOSTICS article in ENGINE PERFORMANCE. If no DTCs exist, or if DTC P1336 exists, go to next step. If any DTCs exist except for P1336, perform test procedures for specified DTC and repair as necessary. See appropriate SELF-DIAGNOSTICS article in ENGINE PERFORMANCE. Ensure all DTCs are cleared from PCM. Go to next step.

NOTE: Ensure engine coolant temperature is at least 158°F (70°C) before performing CKP sensor variation learn procedure.

4) Ensure ignition is off. Apply parking brake. Block front wheels. Ensure hood is closed. Start engine and warm engine until engine coolant temperature is at least 158°F (70°C). Turn ignition off.

5) Using scan tool, select and enable CKP sensor variation learn procedure. Start engine. Apply service brakes. Ensure transaxle is in Park.

6) Accelerate engine until CKP sensor variation learn procedure fuel cut off is obtained at 5150 RPM. Quickly release throttle to idle position once CKP sensor variation learn procedure fuel cut off is obtained and engine starts to decelerate. Once CKP sensor variation values are learned, the PCM will return engine control to the operator and engine will respond to throttle position.

CAUTION: Ensure throttle is quickly released to idle position once CKP sensor variation learn procedure fuel cut off is obtained.

7) If CKP sensor variation learn procedure was not terminated, go to next step. If CKP sensor variation learn procedure was terminated, this may be caused by PCM detecting a problem in cam signal causing DTC P0341, 3X crank signal causing DTC P1374 3X or 18X crank signal

causing DTC P0336 18X. Using scan tool, check for stored DTCs. Perform test procedures for specified DTCs and repair as necessary. See appropriate SELF-DIAGNOSTICS article in ENGINE PERFORMANCE.

8) Check scan tool for status of DTC P1336. If scan tool indicates DTC P1336 ran and passed, CKP sensor variation learn procedure is complete. If scan tool indicates DTC P1336 failed or was not run, check for any other DTCs. See appropriate SELF-DIAGNOSTICS article in ENGINE PERFORMANCE. If any other DTCs exist, perform test procedures for specified DTC and repair as necessary. If no other DTCs exist, repeat CKP sensor variation learn procedure.

Password Learn Procedure For Anti-Theft System – 1) Password learn procedure must be performed if Powertrain Control Module (PCM), Pass-Key® III module, ignition lock cylinder, steering column assembly or ignition key are replaced. A password is communicated between Pass-Key® III module and PCM to provide engine operation. If PCM is replaced, the PCM must learn the password from the Pass-Key® III module.

2) Insert a valid mechanical coded unlearned ignition key in the ignition switch. Place ignition switch in the RUN position. The SECURITY indicator light will come on for 10 minutes for the length of the auto learn timer. SECURITY indicator light is located on instrument panel, just below the fuel gauge.

3) When auto learn timer expires and SECURITY indicator light goes off, place ignition switch in OFF position. Remove ignition key from ignition. Wait 10 seconds.

4) Repeat steps **2)** and **3)** two more times, for a total of 30 minutes. Insert the newly learned ignition key in ignition switch.

5) Place ignition switch in RUN position. The SECURITY indicator light should remain off to indicate the ignition key was learned. If security indicator does not remain off, repeat procedure.

Vehicle Driveability Computer Relearn Procedure – Manufacturer does not provide a specified computer relearn procedure for obtaining proper driveability. If vehicle battery was disconnected or Powertrain Control Module (PCM) was replaced, driving the vehicle will enable the PCM to perform a computer relearn procedure for obtaining proper driveability. Inform customer that driveability may differ from what they are accustomed to until the PCM completes the computer relearn procedure.

PRIZM

NOTE: Powertrain Control Module (PCM) does not have an reprogrammable EEPROM. No special procedures are required for programming the PCM.

Vehicle Driveability Computer Relearn Procedure – Manufacturer does not provide a specified computer relearn procedure for obtaining proper driveability. If vehicle battery was disconnected or Powertrain Control Module (PCM) was replaced, driving the vehicle will enable the PCM to perform a computer relearn procedure for obtaining proper driveability. Inform customer that driveability may differ from what they are accustomed to until the PCM completes the computer relearn procedure.

SATURN

NOTE: Read all procedures listed to determine why and when each procedure is to be performed before proceeding.

Electronically Erasable Programmable Read Only Memory (EEPROM) Programming – 1) EEPROM must also be programmed if replacing Powertrain Control Module (PCM) or changing Transaxle Control (TC) calibrations. If EEPROM is not programmed, a Diagnostic Trouble Code (DTC) will be set in the PCM.

Computer Relearn Procedures (Cont.)

2) Ensure battery is fully charged. Ensure cable is properly connected on Data Link Connector (DLC). Perform EEPROM programming using the SSS equipment manufacturer's instructions and latest software applicable for the vehicle model.

CAUTION: PCM may be damaged if programming procedure is interrupted during the downloading procedure. Ensure cable for scan tool is securely connected to Service Stall System (SSS) equipment and power supply for SSS is securely connected to power supply before proceeding.

NOTE: Ensure original PCM has the correct Vehicle Identification Number (VIN), vehicle tire size and vehicle options prior to programming the EEPROM. If original PCM is not available or incapable of communicating, the VIN, vehicle tire size and vehicle options must be manually entered into the replacement PCM.

NOTE: On A/T models, when replacing PCM for an engine related problem, the transaxle adaptives should be transferred from original PCM to replacement PCM. Transaxle adaptives should be reset if replacing PCM for transaxle related failure, transaxle, transaxle line pressure actuator, transaxle valve body or transaxle is overhauled. Transaxle adaptives may be reset using Service Stall System (SSS) equipment or a scan tool.

3) Once EEPROM is reprogrammed, check for any Diagnostic Trouble Codes (DTCs). See appropriate SELF-DIAGNOSTICS article in ENGINE PERFORMANCE. Also, after EEPROM is reprogrammed, crankshaft learn procedure and vehicle driveability computer relearn procedure must be performed.

NOTE: Once EEPROM is reprogrammed, the SERVICE indicator light on instrument panel will flash. This is a normal function, as the PCM must learn the crankshaft notches for engine misfire diagnosis. SERVICE indicator light is located on instrument panel, just to the left of the speedometer.

Crankshaft Learn Procedure – 1) The PCM uses crankshaft velocity calculations to determine engine misfire and to operate engine misfire self-diagnostics. PCM must know precisely the variation between notches on the crankshaft. PCM contains crankshaft learn procedure which learns the variation between notches on crankshaft. The crankshaft learn procedure must be reset if PCM, crankshaft, or crankshaft position sensor are replaced.

2) If crankshaft learn procedure is being performed as a result of replacing the crankshaft, reset crankshaft learn procedure using Service Stall System (SSS) equipment and manufacturer's instructions. If replacing PCM with a replacement PCM, procedure will be prompted automatically. Allow engine to idle until SERVICE light flashes. Hold engine speed between 3000-4000 RPM until light goes off after about 10-20 seconds.

NOTE: If any Diagnostic Trouble Codes (DTCs) exist that relate to an engine misfire, crankshaft learn procedure will not be initiated. Any DTCs for engine misfire must be corrected before performing crankshaft learn procedure.

Vehicle Driveability Computer Relearn Procedure – 1) If vehicle battery was disconnected or Powertrain Control Module (PCM) was replaced, driving the vehicle will enable the PCM to perform a computer relearn procedure for obtaining proper driveability and engine idle. Until PCM has completed computer relearn procedure, driveability or idle may differ from standard vehicle operation. On A/T models, transaxle shift qualities must be relearned.

2) On all models, start engine and warm engine to normal operating temperature. Perform 10 sets of upshifts (1-2, 2-3 and 3-4) at about 30 percent throttle.

3) On DOHC engine, while coasting at 35 MPH, slowly accelerate to 1/2 throttle to achieve a 4-3 downshift. Place gearshift in "D3" while coasting at 20 MPH, slowly accelerate at 3/4 throttle to achieve a 3-2 downshift.

4) Repeat step **3)** 5 times. Vehicle driveability computer relearn procedure is now complete.

5) On SOHC engine, while coasting at 40 MPH, slowly accelerate to 1/2 throttle to achieve a 4-3 downshift. Place gearshift in "D3" while coasting at 30 MPH, slowly accelerate at 1/2 throttle to achieve a 3-2 downshift.

6) Repeat step **5)** 5 times. Vehicle driveability computer relearn procedure is now complete.

GENERAL MOTORS (TRUCKS & VANS)

NOTE: Before performing Electronically Erasable Programmable Read Only Memory (EEPROM) Programming procedure, check for any applicable Technical Service Bulletins (TSBs) that may apply to vehicle application. Body Control Module (BCM) must be programmed with proper Regular Production Option (RPO) configurations. Follow instructions on Techline Terminal and scan tool to program BCM.

ASTRO & SAFARI

NOTE: Read all procedures listed to determine why and when each procedure is to be performed before proceeding.

Electronically Erasable Programmable Read Only Memory (EEPROM) Programming – 1) If Vehicle Control Module (VCM) was replaced, the EEPROM in the VCM must be programmed. If EEPROM is not programmed, a Diagnostic Trouble Code (DTC) will be set in the VCM.

2) Ensure battery is fully charged. Ensure cable is properly connected on Data Link Connector (DLC). Turn ignition on. Perform EEPROM programming using the Techline equipment manufacturer's instructions and latest software applicable for the vehicle model.

3) Once EEPROM is reprogrammed, Crankshaft Position (CKP) sensor variation learn procedure and password learn procedure for anti-theft system must be performed using proper procedure.

NOTE: If EEPROM programming fails, ensure all electrical connections on VCM are okay. Check Techline for latest software. If EEPROM programming still fails, replace VCM.

4) Once Crankshaft Position (CKP) sensor variation learn procedure and password learn procedure for anti-theft system are performed, perform powertrain On-Board Diagnostic (OBD) system check. See POWERTRAIN ON-BOARD DIAGNOSTIC (OBD) SYSTEM CHECK in appropriate SELF-DIAGNOSTICS article in ENGINE PERFORMANCE.

Crankshaft Position (CKP) Sensor Variation Learn Procedure – 1) Procedure must be performed if any of the following have been done:

- EEPROM was reprogrammed.
- If crankshaft position sensor was removed or replaced.
- Vehicle Control Module (VCM) was replaced.

2) Install scan tool on Data Link Connector (DLC). Apply parking brake. Block rear wheels. Ensure hood is closed.

3) Place transmission in Park (A/T models) or Neutral (M/T models). Start engine and warm engine until engine coolant temperature is at least 150°F (65°C). Ensure all accessories are off.

4) Apply service brakes. With engine idling, use scan tool to select and enable CKP sensor variation learn procedure.

5) Gradually accelerate engine to 4000 RPM. Quickly release throttle to idle position once CKP sensor variation learn procedure is obtained and engine starts to decelerate. Once CKP sensor variation values are learned, the VCM will return engine control to the operator and engine will respond to throttle position.

CAUTION: Ensure throttle is quickly released to idle position once CKP sensor variation learn procedure fuel cut off is obtained and engine starts to decelerate.

6) If CKP sensor variation learn procedure was completed, turn ignition off for at least 15 seconds and remove scan tool. If CKP sensor variation learn procedure was not completed, a DTC P1336 should be stored in the VCM. Perform test procedures for DTC P1336 and repair as necessary. See appropriate SELF-DIAGNOSTICS article in ENGINE PERFORMANCE.

Password Learn Procedure For Anti-Theft System – 1) Password learn procedure must be performed if Vehicle Control Module (VCM), passlock module or passlock sensor is replaced. A password is communicated between VCM and passlock module to provide engine operation. If VCM is replaced, the VCM must learn the password from the passlock module.

2) Momentarily rotate ignition switch to CRANK position, but do not start engine. Release switch to RUN position, but do not turn off. Wait 10 minutes and observe SECURITY indicator.

NOTE: Ensure battery is fully charged before proceeding. Ensure steps are followed in correct order or procedure may need to be repeated.

3) If passlock sensor was replaced, SECURITY indicator will flash for 10 minutes. If passlock module was replaced, SECURITY indicator will flash for a few seconds, then remain on for 10 minutes. If VCM was replaced with a new programmed VCM and connected to vehicle for the first time, vehicle will start and this procedure is not necessary. If replacement VCM was connected to any vehicle at any other time, SECURITY indicator will flash for a few seconds, then remain on for 10 minutes.

4) Of ignition remains on, SECURITY indicator will transition from flashing on briefly to off after 10 minutes. Turn ignition off and wait 10 seconds.

5) Repeat programming procedure 2 more times. New security code is ready to be communicated. New password is learned on next ignition switch lock cylinder from OFF to CRANK to ON.

Vehicle Driveability Computer Relearn Procedure – Manufacturer does not provide a specified computer relearn procedure for obtaining proper driveability. If vehicle battery was disconnected or Vehicle Control Module (VCM) was replaced, driving the vehicle will enable the VCM to perform a computer relearn procedure for obtaining proper driveability. Inform customer that driveability may differ from what they are accustomed to until the VCM completes the computer relearn procedure.

BLAZER, BRAVADA, ENVOY, JIMMY, PICKUP & SONOMA

NOTE: Read all procedures listed to determine why and when each procedure is to be performed before proceeding.

Electronically Erasable Programmable Read Only Memory (EEPROM) Programming (2.2L) – 1) If Powertrain Control Module (PCM) was replaced, the EPROM in the PCM must be programmed. If EEPROM is not programmed, a Diagnostic Trouble Code (DTC) will be set in the PCM. Perform EEPROM programming using the Techline equipment manufacturer's instructions and latest software applicable for the vehicle model.

2) Once EEPROM is reprogrammed, the Crankshaft Position (CKP) sensor variation learn procedure must be performed using proper procedure.

Electronically Erasable Programmable Read Only Memory (EEPROM) Programming (4.3L) – 1) If Vehicle Control Module (VCM) was replaced, the EEPROM in the VCM must be programmed. If EEPROM is not programmed, a Diagnostic Trouble Code (DTC) will be set in the VCM.

2) Ensure battery is fully charged. Ensure cable is properly connected on Data Link Connector (DLC). Turn ignition on. Perform EEPROM programming using the Techline equipment manufacturer's instructions and latest software applicable for the vehicle model.

3) Once EEPROM has been reprogrammed, Crankshaft Position (CKP) sensor variation learn procedure and password learn procedure must be performed using proper procedure. Once Crankshaft Position (CKP) sensor variation learn procedure and password learn procedure are performed, perform powertrain On-Board Diagnostic (OBD) system

check. See POWERTRAIN ON-BOARD DIAGNOSTIC (OBD) SYSTEM CHECK in appropriate SELF-DIAGNOSTICS article in ENGINE PERFORMANCE.

NOTE: If EEPROM programming fails, ensure all electrical connections on VCM are okay. Check Techline for latest software. If EEPROM programming still fails, replace VCM.

Crankshaft Position (CKP) Sensor Variation Learn Procedure (2.2L & 4.3L) – 1) Procedure must be performed if any of the following have been done:
- EEPROM was reprogrammed.
- If crankshaft position sensor was removed or replaced.
- Vehicle Control Module (VCM) was replaced.

2) Install scan tool on Data Link Connector (DLC). Apply parking brake. Block rear wheels. Ensure hood is closed.

3) Place transmission in Park (A/T models) or Neutral (M/T models). Start engine and warm engine until engine coolant temperature is at least 150°F (65°C). Ensure all accessories are off.

4) Apply service brakes. With engine idling, use scan tool to select and enable CKP sensor variation learn procedure.

5) Gradually accelerate engine to 4000 RPM. Quickly release throttle to idle position once CKP sensor variation learn procedure is obtained and engine starts to decelerate. Once CKP sensor variation values are learned, the VCM will return engine control to the operator and engine will respond to throttle position.

CAUTION: Ensure throttle is quickly released to idle position once CKP sensor variation learn procedure fuel cut off is obtained and engine starts to decelerate.

6) If CKP sensor variation learn procedure was completed, turn ignition off for at least 15 seconds and remove scan tool. If CKP sensor variation learn procedure was not completed, a DTC P1336 should be stored in the VCM. Perform test procedures for DTC P1336 and repair as necessary. See appropriate SELF-DIAGNOSTICS article in ENGINE PERFORMANCE.

Password Learn Procedure For Anti-Theft System (2.2L) – 1) Password learn procedure must be performed if Truck Body Controller (TBC) or passlock sensor is replaced. A password is communicated between TBC and Powertrain Control Module (PCM) to provide engine operation. If TBC has been replaced, the PCM must learn the password from the TBC. If password learn procedure is not performed, a Diagnostic Trouble Code (DTC) may be set in the PCM when attempting to start the engine.

2) Attempt to start engine and then leave ignition on. DO NOT turn ignition off. The SECURITY indicator light will flash for 4 seconds and then remain on steady for about 10 minutes and then turn off. SECURITY indicator light is located on center of instrument panel, just above the turn signal indicators. Once SECURITY indicator light turns off, turn ignition off.

NOTE: If PCM has been replaced, the Electronically Erasable Programmable Read Only Memory (EEPROM) should be programmed. When EEPROM has been programmed, the PCM will learn the password when ignition is initially turned on. Password learn procedure is not required when replacing the PCM and EEPROM is programmed.

3) Repeat step **2)** two more times. When SECURITY indicator light turns off on the third ignition cycle, attempt to start the engine. If engine starts, the password learn procedure is complete. If password is not learned, a Diagnostic Trouble Code (DTC) may be set in PCM. Perform test procedures for specified DTC and repair as necessary. See appropriate SELF-DIAGNOSTICS article in ENGINE PERFORMANCE.

Password Learn Procedure For Anti-Theft System (4.3L) – 1) Password learn procedure must be performed if Vehicle Control Module (VCM), Truck Body Controller (TBC) or passlock sensor is replaced. A password is communicated between TBC and VCM to provide engine operation. If VCM has been replaced, the VCM must learn the password from the TBC.

Computer Relearn Procedures (Cont.)

2) Attempt to start engine. Engine will start and then stall. After engine stalls, leave ignition on for 10 minutes. After engine stalls the SECURITY indicator light will come on for 10 minutes and then go off. The SECURITY indicator light is located on center of instrument panel, just above the turn signal indicators.

NOTE: Ensure battery is fully charged before proceeding. Ensure steps are followed in correct order or procedure may need to be repeated.

3) After SECURITY indicator light goes off, turn ignition off for 30 seconds. Attempt to start engine and then leave ignition on. After engine has stalled, leave ignition on for 10 minutes. SECURITY indicator light will come on for 10 minutes and then go off. After SECURITY indicator light goes off, turn ignition off for 30 seconds.

4) Attempt to start engine and then leave ignition on. After engine has stalled, leave ignition on for 10 minutes. SECURITY indicator light will come on for 10 minutes and then go off.

5) Turn ignition off for 30 seconds. Turn ignition on and wait 30 seconds. Attempt to start engine. If engine starts, password learn procedure is complete. If engine does not start, ensure procedure was properly followed. If procedure was properly followed, check for any DTCs. If any DTCs exist, perform test procedures for specified DTC and repair as necessary. See appropriate SELF-DIAGNOSTICS article in ENGINE PERFORMANCE.

Vehicle Driveability Computer Relearn Procedure (2.2L) – Manufacturer does not provide a specified computer relearn procedure for obtaining proper driveability. If vehicle battery was disconnected or Powertrain Control Module (PCM) was replaced, driving the vehicle will enable the PCM to perform a computer relearn procedure for obtaining proper driveability. Inform customer that driveability may differ from what they are accustomed to until the PCM completes the computer relearn procedure.

Vehicle Driveability Computer Relearn Procedure (4.3L) – Manufacturer does not provide a specified computer relearn procedure for obtaining proper driveability. If vehicle battery was disconnected or Vehicle Control Module (VCM) was replaced, driving the vehicle will enable the VCM to perform a computer relearn procedure for obtaining proper driveability. Inform customer that driveability may differ from what they are accustomed to until the VCM completes the computer relearn procedure.

CUTAWAY, EXPRESS, RV CUTAWAY & SAVANA

NOTE: Read all procedures listed to determine why and when each procedure is to be performed before proceeding.

NOTE: References to California models apply to California emission vehicles, which may be verified by underhood Emission Control label. California emissions may be available in other states.

Electronically Erasable Programmable Read Only Memory (EEPROM) Programming (4.3L, 4.8L, 5.0L, 5.3L, 5.7L & 6.0L) – 1) If Vehicle Control Module (VCM) was replaced, the EEPROM in the VCM must be programmed. If EEPROM is not programmed, a Diagnostic Trouble Code (DTC) will be set in the VCM.

2) Ensure battery is fully charged. Ensure cable is properly connected on Data Link Connector (DLC). Turn ignition on. Perform EEPROM programming using the Techline equipment manufacturer's instructions and latest software applicable for the vehicle model.

3) Once EEPROM is reprogrammed, Crankshaft Position (CKP) sensor variation learn procedure and password learn procedure for anti-theft system must be performed using proper procedure.

NOTE: If EEPROM programming fails, ensure all electrical connections on VCM are okay. Check Techline for latest software. If EEPROM programming still fails, replace VCM.

4) Once Crankshaft Position (CKP) sensor variation learn procedure and password learn procedure for anti-theft system are performed, perform powertrain On-Board Diagnostic (OBD) system check. See

POWERTRAIN ON-BOARD DIAGNOSTIC (OBD) SYSTEM CHECK in appropriate SELF-DIAGNOSTICS article in ENGINE PERFORMANCE.

Electronically Erasable Programmable Read Only Memory (EEPROM) Programming (7.4L) – 1) If Vehicle Control Module (VCM) was replaced, the EEPROM in the VCM must be programmed. If EEPROM is not programmed, a Diagnostic Trouble Code (DTC) will be set in the VCM.

2) Ensure battery is fully charged. Ensure cable is properly connected on Data Link Connector (DLC). Turn ignition on. Perform EEPROM programming using the Techline equipment manufacturer's instructions and latest software applicable for the vehicle model.

NOTE: Crankshaft Position (CKP) sensor variation learn procedure should ONLY be performed on Except Calif. models. DO NOT perform CKP sensor variation learn procedure on Calif. models. Verify vehicle application by using underhood Emission Control label.

NOTE: If EEPROM programming fails, ensure all electrical connections on VCM are okay. Check Techline for latest software. If EEPROM programming still fails, replace VCM.

3) Once EEPROM is reprogrammed, use scan tool to reset Idle Air Control (IAC) valve. On Calif. models, go to next step. On Except Calif. models, go to step **5)**.

4) Once EEPROM is reprogrammed, password learn procedure for anti-theft system must be performed using proper procedure. Once password learn procedure for anti-theft system has been performed, perform powertrain On-Board Diagnostic (OBD) system check. See POWERTRAIN ON-BOARD DIAGNOSTIC (OBD) SYSTEM CHECK in appropriate SELF-DIAGNOSTICS article in ENGINE PERFORMANCE.

5) Once EEPROM is reprogrammed, Crankshaft Position (CKP) sensor variation learn procedure and password learn procedure for anti-theft system must be performed using proper procedure. Once Crankshaft Position (CKP) sensor variation learn procedure and password learn procedure for anti-theft system are performed, perform powertrain On-Board Diagnostic (OBD) system check. See POWERTRAIN ON-BOARD DIAGNOSTIC (OBD) SYSTEM CHECK in appropriate SELF-DIAGNOSTICS article in ENGINE PERFORMANCE.

Powertrain Control Module (PCM) Programming (6.5L Diesel) – 1) If PCM was replaced, the PCM must be programmed. If PCM is not programmed, a Diagnostic Trouble Code (DTC) will be set in the PCM.

2) Ensure battery is fully charged. Ensure cable at Data Link Connector (DLC) and power supply for scan tool are properly connected. Turn ignition on. Perform EEPROM programming using the Techline equipment manufacturer's instructions and latest software applicable for the vehicle model.

3) Perform password learn procedure for anti-theft system using proper procedure. Once PCM is programmed, if only the PCM was replaced, go to next step. If the crankshaft position sensor, engine or PCM with fuel injection pump were replaced, perform TDC offset learn procedure.

NOTE: If PCM programming fails, ensure all electrical connections on PCM are okay. Check Techline for latest software. If EEPROM programming still fails, replace PCM.

4) Start engine and warm engine until engine coolant temperature is at least 170°F (77°C). This will allow TDC offset to be programmed into the PCM if necessary. The PCM has the ability to determine the amount of offset required to bring the engine to TDC. PCM uses the TDC to determine proper fuel injection pump timing. If TDC offset is not programmed, a Diagnostic Trouble Code (DTC) P1214 will be set in the PCM.

TDC Offset Learn Procedure (6.5L Diesel) – 1) Procedure must be performed if any of the following have been done or exists:

- If sent here from Diagnostic Trouble Code (DTC) P1214.
- Engine has been replaced.
- Crankshaft position sensor or engine front cover has been replaced.

GENERAL INFORMATION
Computer Relearn Procedures (Cont.)

- Powertrain Control Module (PCM) and fuel injection pump have been replaced.

NOTE: DO NOT perform procedure unless sent here from DTC P1214 or one of the components listed above have been replaced.

2) The PCM has the ability to determine amount of offset required to bring the engine to TDC when TDC offset is not present or has been cleared. This procedure must be performed to allow PCM to be updated with the correct TDC offset for vehicle application.

3) Install scan tool on Data Link Connector (DLC). Start engine and warm engine until engine coolant temperature is at least 170°F (77°C). Using scan tool, clear DTCs from PCM. Turn ignition on with engine off. Fully depress and hold throttle at full throttle for at least 45 seconds.

4) Turn ignition off for 30 seconds. Start engine. Verify scan tool indicates TDC offset has been cleared to zero. If TDC offset has been cleared to zero, go to next step. If TDC offset has not been cleared to zero, repeat step 3) until TDC offset has been cleared to zero.

5) With engine running, use scan tool to verify engine coolant temperature is greater than 170°F (77°C). It may be necessary to drive vehicle to obtain correct engine coolant temperature if engine coolant temperature is less than specified.

6) As soon at engine coolant temperature is greater than 170°F (77°C) and engine speed is less than 1500 RPM, the PCM automatically learns a NEW TDC offset. The NEW TDC offset will overwrite the previous TDC offset. Using scan tool, note NEW TDC offset. TDC offset should be -.25 to -.75.

7) Shut engine off. If TDC offset is not within specification, go to next step. If TDC offset is within specification, TDC offset learn procedure is complete.

8) Using Flange Nut Wrench (J41089), loosen fuel injection pump retaining nuts. Fuel injection pump must be rotated to change TDC offset. Rotating fuel injection pump .039" (1.00 mm) will change TDC offset about 2 degrees. Rotating fuel injection pump toward driver's side of vehicle will produce a positive (+) number and rotating fuel injection pump toward passenger's side of vehicle will produce a negative (–) number.

9) Using Fuel Injection Pump Wrench (J 29872-A), slightly rotate fuel injection pump. Tighten fuel injection pump retaining nuts.

10) Repeat step 3) through 9) until TDC offset is within specification. If proper TDC offset cannot be obtained, check the following:

- Ensure engine coolant temperature is greater than 170°F (77°C).
- Electric connectors at PCM are properly installed.
- Electric connectors at injection timing stepper motor on side of fuel injection pump is correctly installed.
- Ensure latest Techline software was used.
- Check for proper base installation of fuel injection pump. The electric engine shutoff solenoid on top of fuel injection pump should be approximately straight up and down.
- Fuel injection pump may be defective, although manufacturer states this is highly unlikely.

Crankshaft Position (CKP) Sensor Variation Learn Procedure (4.3L, 5.0L, 5.7L & 7.4L Except Calif.) – 1) Procedure must be performed if any of the following have been done:

- EEPROM was reprogrammed.
- If crankshaft position sensor was removed or replaced.
- Vehicle Control Module (VCM) was replaced.

2) Install scan tool on Data Link Connector (DLC). Apply parking brake. Block rear wheels. Ensure hood is closed.

3) Place transmission in Park (A/T models) or Neutral (M/T models). Start engine and warm engine until engine coolant temperature is at least 150°F (65°C). Ensure all accessories are off.

4) Apply service brakes. With engine idling, use scan tool to select and enable CKP sensor variation learn procedure.

5) Gradually accelerate engine to 4000 RPM. Quickly release throttle to idle position once CKP sensor variation learn procedure is obtained and

engine starts to decelerate. Once CKP sensor variation values are learned, the VCM will return engine control to the operator and engine will respond to throttle position.

CAUTION: Ensure throttle is quickly released to idle position once CKP sensor variation learn procedure fuel cut off is obtained and engine starts to decelerate.

6) If CKP sensor variation learn procedure was completed, turn ignition off for at least 15 seconds and remove scan tool. If CKP sensor variation learn procedure was not completed, a DTC P1336 should be stored in the VCM. Perform test procedures for DTC P1336 and repair as necessary. See appropriate SELF-DIAGNOSTICS article in ENGINE PERFORMANCE.

Password Learn Procedure For Anti-Theft System (4.3L, 5.0L & 5.7L) – 1) Password learn procedure must be performed if Vehicle Control Module (VCM), passlock module or passlock sensor is replaced. A password is communicated between VCM and passlock module to provide engine operation. If VCM is replaced, the VCM must learn the password from the passlock module.

2) Attempt to start engine. Engine will start and then stall. After engine stalls, leave ignition on for 10 minutes. After engine stalls the SECURITY indicator light will come on for 10 minutes and then go off. The SECURITY indicator light is located on right corner of instrument panel, just to the right of battery charge indicator.

NOTE: Ensure battery is fully charged before proceeding. Ensure steps are followed in correct order or procedure may need to be repeated.

3) After SECURITY indicator light goes off, turn ignition off for 30 seconds. Attempt to start engine and then leave ignition on. After engine has stalled, leave ignition on for 10 minutes. SECURITY indicator light will come on for 10 minutes and then go off. After SECURITY indicator light goes off, turn ignition off for 30 seconds.

4) Attempt to start engine and then leave ignition on. After engine has stalled, leave ignition on for 10 minutes. SECURITY indicator light will come on for 10 minutes and then go off.

5) Turn ignition off for 30 seconds. Turn ignition on and wait 30 seconds. Attempt to start engine. If engine starts, password learn procedure is complete. If engine does not start, ensure procedure was properly followed. If procedure was properly followed, check for any DTCs. If any DTCs exist, perform test procedures for specified DTC and repair as necessary. See appropriate SELF-DIAGNOSTICS article in ENGINE PERFORMANCE.

Password Learn Procedure For Anti-Theft System (6.5L Diesel) – 1) Password learn procedure must be performed if Powertrain Control Module (PCM), passlock module or passlock sensor is replaced. A password is communicated between PCM and passlock module to provide engine operation. If PCM is replaced, the PCM must learn the password from the passlock module.

2) Attempt to start engine. Engine will start and then stall. After engine stalls, leave ignition on for 10 minutes. After engine stalls the SECURITY indicator light will come on for 10 minutes and then go off. SECURITY indicator light is located on right corner of instrument panel, just to the right of battery charge indicator.

NOTE: Ensure battery is fully charged before proceeding. Performing this procedure will cause a Diagnostic Trouble Code (DTC) P1630 to be set in the VCM. It will be necessary to use scan tool to check for DTC P1630 when performing this procedure. Ensure steps are followed in correct order, or procedure may need to be repeated.

3) After SECURITY indicator light goes off, turn ignition off for 30 seconds. Attempt to start engine and then leave ignition on. After engine has stalled, leave ignition on for 10 minutes. SECURITY indicator light will come on for 10 minutes and then go off. After SECURITY indicator light goes off, turn ignition off for 30 seconds.

4) Attempt to start engine and then leave ignition on. After engine has stalled, leave ignition on for 10 minutes. SECURITY indicator light will come on for 10 minutes and then go off or until DTC 1630 is set in PCM.

Computer Relearn Procedures (Cont.)

5) Turn ignition off for 30 seconds. Turn ignition on and wait 30 seconds. Attempt to start engine. If engine starts, password learn procedure is complete. Ensure DTC 1630 is cleared from PCM by turning ignition off for 30 seconds and then turning ignition on again. If DTC 1630 is not cleared from PCM, perform test procedures for DTC 1630 and repair as necessary. See appropriate SELF-DIAGNOSTICS article in ENGINE PERFORMANCE.

NOTE: DTC 1630 will be set in PCM as result of this procedure. DTC P1630 may be cleared from PCM by turning ignition off for 30 seconds and then turning ignition on again.

6) If engine does not start, ensure procedure was properly followed. If procedure was properly followed, check for any DTCs. If any DTCs exist, perform test procedures for specified DTC and repair as necessary. See appropriate SELF-DIAGNOSTICS article in ENGINE PERFORMANCE.

Password Learn Procedure For Anti-Theft System (7.4L) – 1) Password learn procedure must be performed if Vehicle Control Module (VCM), passlock module or passlock sensor is replaced. A password is communicated between VCM and passlock module to provide engine operation. If VCM is replaced, the VCM must learn the password from the passlock module.

2) Attempt to start engine. Engine will start and then stall. After engine stalls, leave ignition on for 10 minutes. After engine stalls the SECURITY indicator light will come on for 10 minutes and then go off. SECURITY indicator light is located on right corner of instrument panel, just to the right of battery charge indicator.

NOTE: Ensure battery is fully charged before proceeding. Performing this procedure will cause a Diagnostic Trouble Code (DTC) P1630 to be set in the VCM. It will be necessary to use scan tool to check for DTC P1630 when performing this procedure. Ensure steps are followed in correct order or procedure may need to be repeated.

3) After SECURITY indicator light goes off, turn ignition off for 30 seconds. Attempt to start engine and then leave ignition on. After engine has stalled, leave ignition on for 10 minutes. SECURITY indicator light will come on for 10 minutes and then go off. After SECURITY indicator light goes off, turn ignition off for 30 seconds.

4) Attempt to start engine and then leave ignition on. After engine has stalled, leave ignition on for 10 minutes. SECURITY indicator light will come on for 10 minutes and then go off or until DTC 1630 is set in VCM.

5) Turn ignition off for 30 seconds. Turn ignition on and wait 30 seconds. Attempt to start engine. If engine starts, password learn procedure is complete. Ensure DTC 1630 is cleared from VCM by turning ignition off for 30 seconds and then turning ignition on again. If DTC 1630 is not cleared from VCM, perform test procedures for DTC 1630 and repair as necessary. See appropriate SELF-DIAGNOSTICS article in ENGINE PERFORMANCE.

NOTE: DTC 1630 will be set in VCM as result of this procedure. DTC P1630 may be cleared from VCM by turning ignition off for 30 seconds and then turning ignition on again.

6) If engine does not start, ensure procedure was properly followed. If procedure was properly followed, check for any DTCs. If any DTCs exist, perform test procedures for specified DTC and repair as necessary. See appropriate SELF-DIAGNOSTICS article in ENGINE PERFORMANCE.

Vehicle Driveability Computer Relearn Procedure (4.3L, 5.0L, 5.7L & 7.4L) – Manufacturer does not provide a specified computer relearn procedure for obtaining proper driveability. If vehicle battery was disconnected or Vehicle Control Module (VCM) was replaced, driving the vehicle will enable the VCM to perform a computer relearn procedure for obtaining proper driveability. Inform customer that driveability may differ from what they are accustomed to until the VCM completes the computer relearn procedure.

Vehicle Driveability Computer Relearn Procedure (6.5L Diesel) – Manufacturer does not provide a specified computer relearn procedure for obtaining proper driveability. If vehicle battery was disconnected or

Powertrain Control Module (PCM) was replaced, driving the vehicle will enable the PCM to perform a computer relearn procedure for obtaining proper driveability. Inform customer that driveability may differ from what they are accustomed to until the PCM completes the computer relearn procedure.

ESCALADE, PICKUP, SIERRA, SILVERADO, SUBURBAN, TAHOE & YUKON

NOTE: Read all procedures listed to determine why and when each procedure is to be performed before proceeding.

NOTE: References to California models apply to California emission vehicles, which may be verified by underhood Emission Control label. California emissions may be available in other states.

Electronically Erasable Programmable Read Only Memory (EEPROM) Programming (4.3L, 5.0L & 5.7L) – 1) If Vehicle Control Module (VCM) was replaced, the EEPROM in the VCM must be programmed. If EEPROM is not programmed, a Diagnostic Trouble Code (DTC) will be set in the VCM.

2) Ensure battery is fully charged. Ensure cable is properly connected on Data Link Connector (DLC). Turn ignition on. Perform EEPROM programming using the Techline equipment manufacturer's instructions and latest software applicable for the vehicle model.

3) Once EEPROM is reprogrammed, Crankshaft Position (CKP) sensor variation learn procedure and password learn procedure for anti-theft system must be performed using proper procedure.

NOTE: If EEPROM programming fails, ensure all electrical connections on VCM are okay. Check Techline for latest software. If EEPROM programming still fails, replace VCM.

4) Once Crankshaft Position (CKP) sensor variation learn procedure and password learn procedure for anti-theft system are performed, perform powertrain On-Board Diagnostic (OBD) system check. See POWERTRAIN ON-BOARD DIAGNOSTIC (OBD) SYSTEM CHECK in appropriate SELF-DIAGNOSTICS article in ENGINE PERFORMANCE.

Electronically Erasable Programmable Read Only Memory (EEPROM) Programming (7.4L) – 1) If Vehicle Control Module (VCM) was replaced, the EEPROM in the VCM must be programmed. If EEPROM is not programmed, a Diagnostic Trouble Code (DTC) will be set in the VCM.

2) Ensure battery is fully charged. Ensure cable is properly connected on Data Link Connector (DLC). Turn ignition on. Perform EEPROM programming using the Techline equipment manufacturer's instructions and latest software applicable for the vehicle model.

3) Crankshaft Position (CKP) sensor variation learn procedure should ONLY be performed on Except Calif. models. DO NOT perform CKP sensor variation learn procedure on Calif. models. Verify vehicle application by using underhood Emission Control label. If EEPROM programming fails, ensure all electrical connections on VCM are okay. Check Techline for latest software. If EEPROM programming still fails, replace VCM. Once EEPROM is reprogrammed, use scan tool to reset Idle Air Control (IAC) valve. On Calif. models, go to next step. On Except Calif. models, go to step **5)**.

4) Once EEPROM is reprogrammed, password learn procedure for anti-theft system must be performed using proper procedure. Once password learn procedure for anti-theft system has been performed, perform powertrain On-Board Diagnostic (OBD) system check. See POWERTRAIN ON-BOARD DIAGNOSTIC (OBD) SYSTEM CHECK in appropriate SELF-DIAGNOSTICS article in ENGINE PERFORMANCE.

5) Once EEPROM is reprogrammed, Crankshaft Position (CKP) sensor variation learn procedure and password learn procedure for anti-theft system must be performed using proper procedure. Once Crankshaft Position (CKP) sensor variation learn procedure and password learn procedure for anti-theft system are performed, perform powertrain On-Board Diagnostic (OBD) system check. See POWERTRAIN ON-BOARD DIAGNOSTIC (OBD) SYSTEM CHECK in appropriate SELF-DIAGNOSTICS article in ENGINE PERFORMANCE.

Powertrain Control Module (PCM) Programming (4.8L, 5.3L & 6.0L) – 1) Ensure battery is fully charged. Turn ignition on. Program PCM using the Techline equipment manufacturer's instructions and latest software applicable for the vehicle model.

2) Once PCM is reprogrammed, Crankshaft Position (CKP) sensor variation learn procedure, password learn procedure for anti-theft system, and PCM idle learn procedure must be performed.

NOTE: If programming fails, ensure all electrical connections on PCM are okay. Check Techline for latest software. If programming still fails, replace PCM.

Powertrain Control Module (PCM) Programming (6.5L Diesel) – 1) If PCM was replaced, the PCM must be programmed. If PCM is not programmed, a Diagnostic Trouble Code (DTC) will be set in the PCM.
2) Ensure battery is fully charged. Ensure cable at Data Link Connector (DLC) and power supply for scan tool are properly connected. Turn ignition on. Perform EEPROM programming using the Techline equipment manufacturer's instructions and latest software applicable for the vehicle model.
3) Perform password learn procedure for anti-theft system using proper procedure. Once PCM is programmed, if only the PCM was replaced, go to next step. If the crankshaft position sensor, engine or PCM with fuel injection pump were replaced, perform TDC offset learn procedure.

NOTE: If PCM programming fails, ensure all electrical connections on PCM are okay. Check Techline for latest software. If EEPROM programming still fails, replace PCM.

4) Start engine and warm engine until engine coolant temperature is at least 170°F (77°C). This will allow TDC offset to be programmed into the PCM if necessary. The PCM has the ability to determine the amount of offset required to bring the engine to TDC. PCM uses the TDC offset to determine proper fuel injection pump timing. If TDC offset is not programmed, a Diagnostic Trouble Code (DTC) P1214 will be set in the PCM.

TDC Offset Learn Procedure (6.5L Diesel) – 1) Procedure must be performed if any of the following have been done or exists:
- If sent here from Diagnostic Trouble Code (DTC) P1214.
- Engine has been replaced.
- Crankshaft position sensor or engine front cover has been replaced.
- Powertrain Control Module (PCM) and fuel injection pump have been replaced.

NOTE: DO NOT perform procedure unless sent here from DTC P1214 or one of the components listed above has been replaced.

2) The PCM has the ability to determine amount of offset required to bring the engine to TDC when TDC offset is not present or has been cleared. This procedure must be performed to allow PCM to be updated with the correct TDC offset for vehicle application.
3) Install scan tool on Data Link Connector (DLC). Start engine and warm engine until engine coolant temperature is at least 170°F (77°C). Using scan tool, clear DTCs from PCM. Turn ignition on with engine off. Fully depress and hold throttle at full throttle for at least 45 seconds.
4) Turn ignition off for 30 seconds. Start engine. Verify scan tool indicates TDC offset has been cleared to zero. If TDC offset has been cleared to zero, go to next step. If TDC offset has not been cleared to zero, repeat step **3)** until TDC offset has been cleared to zero.
5) With engine running, use scan tool to verify engine coolant temperature is greater than 170°F (77°C). It may be necessary to drive vehicle to obtain correct engine coolant temperature if engine coolant temperature is less than specified.
6) As soon at engine coolant temperature is greater than 170°F (77°C) and engine speed is less than 1500 RPM, the PCM automatically learns a NEW TDC offset. The NEW TDC offset will overwrite the previous TDC offset. Using scan tool, note NEW TDC offset. TDC offset should be -.25 to -.75.
7) Shut engine off. If TDC offset is not within specification, go to next step. If TDC offset is within specification, TDC offset learn procedure is complete.

8) Using Flange Nut Wrench (J41089), loosen fuel injection pump retaining nuts. Fuel injection pump must be rotated to change TDC offset. Rotating fuel injection pump .039" (1.00 mm) will change TDC offset about 2 degrees. Rotating fuel injection pump toward driver's side of vehicle will produce a positive (+) number and rotating fuel injection pump toward passenger's side of vehicle will produce a negative (–) number.
9) Using Fuel Injection Pump Wrench (J 29872), slightly rotate fuel injection pump. Tighten fuel injection pump retaining nuts.
10) Repeat steps **3)** through **9)** until TDC offset is within specification. If proper TDC offset cannot be obtained, check the following:
- Ensure engine coolant temperature is greater than 170°F (77°C).
- Electric connectors at PCM are properly installed.
- Electric connectors at injection timing stepper motor on side of fuel injection pump is correctly installed.
- Ensure latest Techline software was used.
- Check for proper base installation of fuel injection pump. The electric engine shutoff solenoid on top of fuel injection pump should be approximately straight up and down.
- Fuel injection pump may be defective, although manufacturer states this is highly unlikely.

Crankshaft Position (CKP) Sensor Variation Learn Procedure (4.3L, 4.8L, 5.0L, 5.3L, 5.7L, 6.0L & 7.4L) – 1) Procedure must be performed if any of the following have been done:
- EEPROM was reprogrammed.
- If crankshaft position sensor was removed or replaced.
- Vehicle Control Module (VCM) was replaced.

2) Install scan tool on Data Link Connector (DLC). Apply parking brake. Block rear wheels. Ensure hood is closed.
3) Place transmission in Park (A/T models) or Neutral (M/T models). Start engine and warm engine until engine coolant temperature is at least 150°F (65°C). Ensure all accessories are off.
4) Apply service brakes. With engine idling, use scan tool to select and enable CKP sensor variation learn procedure.
5) Gradually accelerate engine to 4000 RPM. Quickly release throttle to idle position once CKP sensor variation learn procedure is obtained and engine starts to decelerate. Once CKP sensor variation values are learned, the VCM will return engine control to the operator and engine will respond to throttle position.

CAUTION: Ensure throttle is quickly released to idle position once CKP sensor variation learn procedure fuel cut off is obtained and engine starts to decelerate.

6) If CKP sensor variation learn procedure was completed, turn ignition off for at least 15 seconds and remove scan tool. If CKP sensor variation learn procedure was not completed, a DTC P1336 should be stored in the VCM. Perform test procedures for DTC P1336 and repair as necessary. See appropriate SELF-DIAGNOSTICS article in ENGINE PERFORMANCE.

Password Learn Procedure For Anti-Theft System (4.3L, 4.8L, 5.3L & 6.0L) – 1) Password relearn procedure must be performed if passlock sensor, Body Control Module (BCM), PCM or Vehicle Control Module (VCM) are replaced. Ensure battery is fully charged.
2) Using scan tool, erase Diagnostic Trouble Codes (DTCs). Turn ignition switch from OFF to CRANK position, allowing vehicle to try and start. Vehicle will start and then stall. Leave ignition on while observing SECURITY indicator on instrument panel. When security indicator turns off (after about 10 minutes), turn ignition off. Wait 10 seconds. Repeat this step 3 more times. New password will be learned on next start attempt.

Password Learn Procedure For Anti-Theft System (5.0L, 5.7L & 7.4L) – 1) Password learn procedure must be performed if Vehicle Control Module (VCM), passlock module or passlock sensor is replaced. A password is communicated between VCM and passlock module to provide engine operation. If VCM is replaced, the VCM must learn the password from the passlock module.
2) Attempt to start engine. Engine will start and then stall. After engine stalls, leave ignition on for 10 minutes. After engine stalls, the SECURITY indicator light will come on for 10 minutes and then go off. The

Computer Relearn Procedures (Cont.)

SECURITY indicator light is located on upper right corner of instrument panel, just above battery charge indicator.

NOTE: *Ensure battery is fully charged before proceeding. Performing this procedure will cause a Diagnostic Trouble Code (DTC) P1630 to be set in the VCM. It will be necessary to use scan tool to check for DTC P1630 when performing this procedure. Ensure steps are followed in correct order, or procedure may need to be repeated.*

3) After SECURITY indicator light goes off, turn ignition off for 30 seconds. Attempt to start engine and then leave ignition on. After engine has stalled, leave ignition on for 10 minutes. SECURITY indicator light will come on for 10 minutes and then go off. After SECURITY indicator light goes off, turn ignition off for 30 seconds.

4) Attempt to start engine and then leave ignition on. After engine has stalled, leave ignition on for 10 minutes. SECURITY indicator light will come on for 10 minutes and then go off or until DTC 1630 is set in VCM.

5) Turn ignition off for 30 seconds. Turn ignition on and wait 30 seconds. Attempt to start engine. If engine starts, password learn procedure is complete. Ensure DTC 1630 is cleared from VCM by turning ignition off for 30 seconds and then turning ignition on again. If DTC 1630 is not cleared from VCM, perform test procedures for DTC 1630 and repair as necessary. See appropriate SELF-DIAGNOSTICS article in ENGINE PERFORMANCE.

NOTE: *DTC 1630 will be set in VCM as result of this procedure. DTC P1630 may be cleared from VCM by turning ignition off for 30 seconds and then turning ignition on again.*

6) If engine does not start, ensure procedure was properly followed. If procedure was properly followed, check for any DTCs. If any DTCs exist, perform test procedures for specified DTC and repair as necessary. See appropriate SELF-DIAGNOSTICS article in ENGINE PERFORMANCE.

Password Learn Procedure For Anti-Theft System (6.5L Diesel) – 1) Password learn procedure must be performed if Powertrain Control Module (PCM), passlock module or passlock sensor is replaced. A password is communicated between PCM and passlock module to provide engine operation. If PCM is replaced, the PCM must learn the password from the passlock module.

2) Attempt to start engine. Engine will start and then stall. After engine stalls, leave ignition on for 10 minutes. After engine stalls, the SECURITY indicator light will come on for 10 minutes and then go off. SECURITY indicator light is located on upper right corner of instrument panel, just above battery charge indicator. After SECURITY indicator light goes off, turn ignition off for 30 seconds.

NOTE: *Ensure battery is fully charged before proceeding. Performing this procedure will cause a Diagnostic Trouble Code (DTC) P1630 to be set in the VCM. It will be necessary to use scan tool to check for DTC P1630 when performing this procedure. Ensure steps are followed in correct order, or procedure may need to be repeated.*

3) Attempt to start engine and then leave ignition on. After engine has stalled, leave ignition on for 10 minutes. SECURITY indicator light will come on for 10 minutes and then go off. After SECURITY indicator light goes off, turn ignition off for 30 seconds.

4) Attempt to start engine and then leave ignition on. After engine has stalled, leave ignition on for 10 minutes. SECURITY indicator light will come on for 10 minutes and then go off or until DTC 1630 is set in PCM.

5) Turn ignition off for 30 seconds. Turn ignition on and wait 30 seconds. Attempt to start engine. If engine starts, password learn procedure is complete. Ensure DTC 1630 is cleared from PCM by turning ignition off for 30 seconds and then turning ignition on again. If DTC 1630 is not cleared from PCM, perform test procedures for DTC 1630 and repair as necessary. See appropriate SELF-DIAGNOSTICS article in ENGINE PERFORMANCE.

NOTE: *DTC 1630 will be set in PCM as result of this procedure. DTC P1630 may be cleared from PCM by turning ignition off for 30 seconds and then turning ignition on again.*

6) If engine does not start, ensure procedure was properly followed. If procedure was properly followed, check for any DTCs. If any DTCs exist, perform test procedures for specified DTC and repair as necessary. See appropriate SELF-DIAGNOSTICS article in ENGINE PERFORMANCE.

Vehicle Driveability Computer Relearn Procedure (4.8L, 5.3L & 6.0L) – 1) On manual transmission vehicles, go to next step. On automatic transmission vehicles, turn ignition off. Reconnect PCM battery connection. Turn A/C off. Set parking brake and block drive wheels. Start and run engine so coolant reaches 176°F (80°C). Shift transmission into Drive. Idle engine for 5 minutes. Shift transmission into Park. Idle engine another 5 minutes. Turn engine off for 30 seconds. PCM relearn procedure is completed.

2) On manual transmission vehicles, turn ignition off. Reconnect PCM battery connection. Turn A/C off. Set parking brake and block drive wheels. Shift transmission into Neutral. Start and run engine so coolant reaches 176°F (80°C). Idle engine for 5 minutes. Turn engine off for 30 seconds. PCM relearn procedure is completed.

Vehicle Driveability Computer Relearn Procedure (4.3L, 5.0L, 5.7L & 7.4L) – Manufacturer does not provide a specified computer relearn procedure for obtaining proper driveability. If vehicle battery was disconnected or Vehicle Control Module (VCM) was replaced, driving the vehicle will enable the VCM to perform a computer relearn procedure for obtaining proper driveability. Inform customer that driveability may differ from what they are accustomed to until the VCM completes the computer relearn procedure.

Vehicle Driveability Computer Relearn Procedure (6.5L Diesel) – Manufacturer does not provide a specified computer relearn procedure for obtaining proper driveability. If vehicle battery was disconnected or Powertrain Control Module (PCM) was replaced, driving the vehicle will enable the PCM to perform a computer relearn procedure for obtaining proper driveability. Inform customer that driveability may differ from what they are accustomed to until the PCM completes the computer relearn procedure.

FORWARD CONTROL & MOTORHOME CHASSIS

NOTE: *Read all procedures listed to determine why and when each procedure is to be performed before proceeding.*

NOTE: *References to California models apply to California emission vehicles, which may be verified by underhood Emission Control label. California emissions may be available in other states.*

Electronically Erasable Programmable Read Only Memory (EEPROM) Programming (4.3L & 5.7L) – 1) If Vehicle Control Module (VCM) was replaced, the EEPROM in the VCM must be programmed. If EEPROM is not programmed, a Diagnostic Trouble Code (DTC) will be set in the VCM.

2) Ensure battery is fully charged. Ensure cable is properly connected on Data Link Connector (DLC). Turn ignition on. Perform EEPROM programming using the Techline equipment manufacturer's instructions and latest software applicable for the vehicle model.

NOTE: *If EEPROM programming fails, ensure all electrical connections on VCM are okay. Check Techline for latest software. If EEPROM programming still fails, replace VCM.*

3) Once EEPROM has been reprogrammed, Crankshaft Position (CKP) sensor variation learn procedure must be performed using proper procedure. Once Crankshaft Position (CKP) sensor variation learn procedure has been performed, perform powertrain On-Board Diagnostic (OBD) system check. See POWERTRAIN ON-BOARD DIAGNOS-

GENERAL INFORMATION
Computer Relearn Procedures (Cont.)

TIC (OBD) SYSTEM CHECK in appropriate SELF-DIAGNOSTICS article in ENGINE PERFORMANCE.

Electronically Erasable Programmable Read Only Memory (EEPROM) Programming (7.4L) – 1) If Vehicle Control Module (VCM) was replaced, the EEPROM in the VCM must be programmed. If EEPROM is not programmed, a Diagnostic Trouble Code (DTC) will be set in the VCM.

2) Ensure battery is fully charged. Ensure cable is properly connected on Data Link Connector (DLC). Turn ignition on. Perform EEPROM programming using the Techline equipment manufacturer's instructions and latest software applicable for the vehicle model.

3) Once EEPROM has been reprogrammed, use scan tool to reset Idle Air Control (IAC) valve. On Calif. models, go to next step. On Except Calif. models, go to step **5)**.

NOTE: If EEPROM programming fails, ensure all electrical connections on VCM are okay. Check Techline for latest software. If EEPROM programming still fails, replace VCM.

NOTE: Crankshaft Position (CKP) sensor variation learn procedure should ONLY be performed on Except Calif. models. DO NOT perform CKP sensor variation learn procedure on Calif. models. Verify vehicle application by using underhood Emission Control label.

4) Once EEPROM has been reprogrammed, perform powertrain On-Board Diagnostic (OBD) system check. See POWERTRAIN ON-BOARD DIAGNOSTIC (OBD) SYSTEM CHECK in appropriate SELF-DIAGNOSTICS article in ENGINE PERFORMANCE.

5) Once EEPROM has been reprogrammed, Crankshaft Position (CKP) sensor variation learn procedure must be performed using proper procedure. Once Crankshaft Position (CKP) sensor variation learn procedure has been completed, perform powertrain On-Board Diagnostic (OBD) system check. See POWERTRAIN ON-BOARD DIAGNOSTIC (OBD) SYSTEM CHECK in appropriate SELF-DIAGNOSTICS article in ENGINE PERFORMANCE.

Powertrain Control Module (PCM) Programming (6.5L Non-Turbo Diesel With Electronic Fuel Injection (EFI) & 6.5L Turbo Diesel) – 1) If PCM was replaced, the PCM must be programmed. If PCM is not programmed, a Diagnostic Trouble Code (DTC) will be set in the PCM.

2) Ensure battery is fully charged. Ensure cable at Data Link Connector (DLC) and power supply for scan tool are properly connected. Turn ignition on. Perform EEPROM programming using the Techline equipment manufacturer's instructions and latest software applicable for the vehicle model.

3) Once PCM has been programmed, if only the PCM was replaced, go to next step. If the crankshaft position sensor, engine or PCM with fuel injection pump were replaced, perform TDC offset learn procedure.

NOTE: If PCM programming fails, ensure all electrical connections on PCM are okay. Check Techline for latest software. If EEPROM programming still fails, replace PCM.

4) Start engine and warm engine until engine coolant temperature is at least 170°F (77°C). This will allow TDC offset to be programmed into the PCM if necessary. The PCM has the ability to determine the amount of offset required to bring the engine to TDC. PCM uses the TDC offset to determine proper fuel injection pump timing. If TDC offset is not programmed, a Diagnostic Trouble Code (DTC) P1214 will be set in the PCM.

NOTE: PCM will only perform an auto learn when a TDC offset is not present (new or reprogrammed PCM).

TDC Offset Learn Procedure (6.5L Diesel) – PCM will automatically activate TDC offset program when engine coolant is greater than 170°F (77°C) and engine speed is 900 RPM or less. A momentary engine stumble will occur once engine has reached desired temperature and RPM. This is an indication that PCM auto learn function has been activated. If offset is programmed out of range, DTC P1214 will set.

Crankshaft Position (CKP) Sensor Variation Learn Procedure (4.3L, 5.7L & 7.4L Except Calif.) – 1) Procedure must be performed if any of the following have been done:

- EEPROM was reprogrammed.
- If crankshaft position sensor was removed or replaced.
- Vehicle Control Module (VCM) was replaced.

2) Install scan tool on Data Link Connector (DLC). Apply parking brake. Block rear wheels. Ensure hood is closed.

3) Place transmission in Park (A/T models) or Neutral (M/T models). Start engine and warm engine until engine coolant temperature is at least 150°F (65°C). Ensure all accessories are off.

4) Apply service brakes. With engine idling, use scan tool to select and enable CKP sensor variation learn procedure.

5) Gradually accelerate engine to 4000 RPM. Quickly release throttle to idle position once CKP sensor variation learn procedure is obtained and engine starts to decelerate. Once CKP sensor variation values are learned, the VCM will return engine control to the operator and engine will respond to throttle position.

CAUTION: Ensure throttle is quickly released to idle position once CKP sensor variation learn procedure fuel cut off is obtained and engine starts to decelerate.

6) If CKP sensor variation learn procedure was completed, turn ignition off for at least 15 seconds and remove scan tool. If CKP sensor variation learn procedure was not completed, a DTC P1336 should be stored in the VCM. Perform test procedures for DTC P1336 and repair as necessary. See appropriate SELF-DIAGNOSTICS article in ENGINE PERFORMANCE.

Vehicle Driveability Computer Relearn Procedure (4.3L, 5.7L & 7.4L) – Manufacturer does not provide a specified computer relearn procedure for obtaining proper driveability. If vehicle battery was disconnected or Vehicle Control Module (VCM) was replaced, driving the vehicle will enable the VCM to perform a computer relearn procedure for obtaining proper driveability. Inform customer that driveability may differ from what they are accustomed to until the VCM completes the computer relearn procedure.

Vehicle Driveability Computer Relearn Procedure (6.5L Diesel) – Manufacturer does not provide a specified computer relearn procedure for obtaining proper driveability. If vehicle battery was disconnected or Powertrain Control Module (PCM) was replaced, driving the vehicle will enable the PCM to perform a computer relearn procedure for obtaining proper driveability. Inform customer that driveability may differ from what they are accustomed to until the PCM completes the computer relearn procedure.

MONTANA, SILHOUETTE & VENTURE

NOTE: Read all procedures listed to determine why and when each procedure is to be performed before proceeding.

Electronically Erasable Programmable Read Only Memory (EEPROM) Programming – 1) If Powertrain Control Module (PCM) was replaced, the EEPROM in the PCM must be programmed. If EEPROM is not programmed, a Diagnostic Trouble Code (DTC) will be set in the PCM.

2) Ensure battery is fully charged. If battery is being charged, ensure battery charger is disconnected before performing EEPROM programming procedure.

3) Ensure cable is properly connected on Data Link Connector (DLC). Turn ignition on. Perform EEPROM programming using the Techline equipment manufacturer's instructions and latest software applicable for the vehicle model.

4) Once EEPROM has been reprogrammed, perform powertrain On-Board Diagnostic (OBD) system check. See POWERTRAIN ON-BOARD DIAGNOSTIC (OBD) SYSTEM CHECK in appropriate SELF-DIAGNOSTICS article in ENGINE PERFORMANCE. Ensure engine is idling for one minute before checking for DTCs when performing powertrain OBD system check. Also, after EEPROM has been repro-

Computer Relearn Procedures (Cont.)

grammed, the Crankshaft Position (CKP) sensor variation learn procedure must be performed using proper procedure.

NOTE: *If EEPROM programming fails, ensure all electrical connections on PCM are okay. Check Techline for latest software. If EEPROM programming still fails, replace PCM.*

Crankshaft Position (CKP) Sensor Variation Learn Procedure – 1) Procedure must be performed if any of the following have been done or exist:

- EEPROM was reprogrammed.
- If Diagnostic Trouble Code (DTC) P1336 exists.
- If crankshaft, crankshaft position sensor, engine, Powertrain Control Module (PCM) or vibration damper have been replaced.

2) CKP sensor variation compensating values are stored in Powertrain Control Module (PCM) after a learn procedure has been performed. If actual CKP sensor values are not within specification, Diagnostic Trouble Code (DTC) P0300 will be stored in the PCM.

3) Using scan tool, check for stored DTCs. See appropriate SELF-DIAGNOSTICS article in ENGINE PERFORMANCE. If no DTCs exist, or if DTC P1336 exists, go to next step. If any DTCs exist except for P1336, perform test procedures for specified DTC and repair as necessary. See appropriate SELF-DIAGNOSTICS article in ENGINE PERFORMANCE. Ensure all DTCs are learned from PCM. Go to next step.

4) Ensure ignition is off. Apply parking brake. Block front wheels. Ensure hood is closed. Start engine and warm engine until engine coolant temperature is at least 158°F (70°C). Turn ignition off.

NOTE: *Ensure engine coolant temperature is at least 158°F (70°C) before performing CKP sensor variation learn procedure.*

5) Using scan tool, select and enable CKP sensor variation learn procedure. Start engine. Apply service brakes. Ensure transaxle is in Park.

6) Accelerate engine until CKP sensor variation learn procedure fuel cut off is obtained at 5150 RPM. Quickly release throttle to idle position once CKP sensor variation learn procedure fuel cut off is obtained and engine starts to decelerate. Once CKP sensor variation values are learned, the PCM will return engine control to the operator and engine will respond to throttle position.

CAUTION: *Ensure throttle is quickly released to idle position once CKP sensor variation learn procedure fuel cut off is obtained.*

7) If CKP sensor variation learn procedure was not terminated, go to next step. If CKP sensor variation learn procedure was terminated, this may be caused by PCM detecting a problem in cam signal causing DTC P0341, 3X crank signal causing DTC P1374 3X, or 24X crank signal causing DTC P0336 24X. Using scan tool, check for stored DTCs. Perform test procedures for specified DTCs and repair as necessary. See appropriate SELF-DIAGNOSTICS article in ENGINE PERFORMANCE.

8) Check scan tool for status of DTC P1336. If scan tool indicates DTC P1336 ran and passed, CKP sensor variation learn procedure is complete. If scan tool indicates DTC P1336 failed or was not run, check for any other DTCs. See appropriate SELF-DIAGNOSTICS article in ENGINE PERFORMANCE. If any other DTCs exist, perform test procedures for specified DTC and repair as necessary. If no other DTCs exist, repeat CKP sensor variation learn procedure.

Vehicle Driveability Computer Relearn Procedure – Manufacturer does not provide a specified computer relearn procedure for obtaining proper driveability. If vehicle battery was disconnected or Powertrain Control Module (PCM) was replaced, driving the vehicle will enable the PCM to perform a computer relearn procedure for obtaining proper driveability. Inform customer that driveability may differ from what they are accustomed to until the PCM completes the computer relearn procedure.

TRACKER

NOTE: *Powertrain Control Module (PCM) does not have an reprogrammable EEPROM. No special procedures are required for programming the PCM.*

Vehicle Driveability Computer Relearn Procedure – Manufacturer does not provide a specified computer relearn procedure for obtaining proper driveability. If vehicle battery was disconnected or Powertrain Control Module (PCM) was replaced, driving the vehicle will enable the PCM to perform a computer relearn procedure for obtaining proper driveability. Inform customer that driveability may differ from what they are accustomed to until the PCM completes the computer relearn procedure.

GENERAL INFORMATION
Parasitic Load Explanation & Test Procedures

GENERAL INFORMATION

The term Parasitic Load refers to electrical devices that continue to use or draw current after the ignition switch is turned to OFF position. This small amount of continuous battery draw is expressed in milliamps (mA). On Ford Motor Co. and General Motors vehicles produced after 1980, a typical Parasitic Load should be no more than 50 milliamps (0.050 amps).

Vehicles produced since 1980 have memory devices that draw current with ignition off for as long as 20 minutes before shutting down the Parasitic Drain. When Parasitic Load exceeds normal specifications, the vehicle may exhibit dead battery and no-start condition.

Follow test procedure for checking Parasitic Loads to completion. A brief overview of a suggested test procedure is included along with some typical Parasitic Load specifications. Refer to GENERAL MOTORS PARASITIC LOAD TABLE chart.

TESTING FOR PARASITIC LOAD

CAUTION: Always turn ignition off when connecting or disconnecting battery cables, battery chargers or jumper cables. DO NOT turn test switch to OFF position (which causes current to run through ammeter or vehicle electrical system).

NOTE: Memory functions of various accessories must be reset after the battery is reconnected.

The battery circuit must be opened to connect test switch (shunt) and ammeter into the circuit. When a battery cable is removed, timer circuits within the vehicle computer are interrupted and immediately begin to discharge. If in doubt about the condition of the ammeter fuse, test it with an ohmmeter prior to beginning test. An open fuse will show the same reading (00.00) as no parasitic drain. Begin test sequence with the meter installed and on the 10-amp scale. Select lower scale to read parasitic draw.

TEST PROCEDURE USING TEST SWITCH

1) Turn ignition off. Remove negative battery terminal cable. Install Disconnect Tool (J-38758) test switch male end to negative battery cable. Turn test switch knob to OFF position (current through meter). Install negative battery cable to the female end of test switch.

2) Turn test switch knob to ON position (current through switch). Road test vehicle with vehicle accessories on (radio, air conditioner, etc). After road test, turn ignition switch to LOCKED position and remove key. Connect ammeter terminals to test switch terminals. *See Fig. 1.* Select 10-amp scale.

3) Turn off all electrical accessories. Turn off interior lights, underhood lamp, trunk light, illuminated entry, etc. To avoid damaging ammeter or obtaining a false meter reading, all accessories must be off before turning test switch knob to OFF position.

4) Turn test switch knob to OFF position to allow current to flow through ammeter. If meter reads wrong polarity, turn test switch to ON position

and reverse leads. Turn test switch to OFF position. Observe current reading. If reading is less than 2 amps, turn test switch to ON position to keep electrical circuits powered-up.

5) Select low amp scale. Switch lead to the correct meter position. Turn test switch to OFF position and compare results to normal current draw. See GENERAL MOTORS PARASITIC LOAD TABLE (MILLIAMPS). If current draw is unusually high for the vehicle's overall electrical system, remove system fuses one at a time until current draw returns to normal.

6) Turn test switch to ON position each time door is opened or fuse is removed. Turn switch to OFF position to read current draw value through meter. When the cause of excessive current drain has been located and repaired, remove test switch and reconnect negative battery cable to the negative battery terminal.

INTERMITTENT PARASITIC LOAD PROBLEMS

Intermittent parasitic load can occur because of a memory device that does not power down with ignition off. With an intermittent parasitic load, battery draw can be greater than 1.0 amp.

To find an intermittent problem requires that an ammeter and Disconnect Tool (J-38758) test switch be connected and left in the circuit. *See Fig. 1.* Road test vehicle. After road test, turn ignition off and remove key.

Monitor the milliamps scale for 15-20 minutes after ignition is turned off. This allows monitoring memory devices to determine if they time out and stop drawing memory current. The test switch is needed to protect ammeter when the vehicle is started.

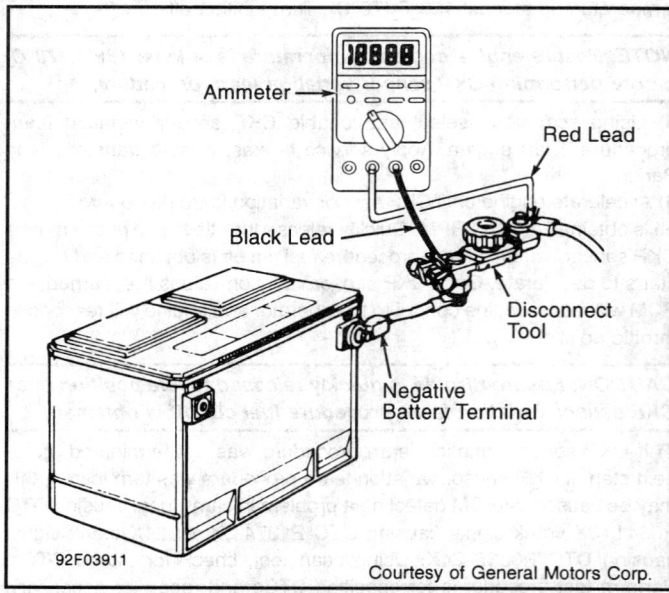

92F03911   Courtesy of General Motors Corp.

Fig. 1: Connecting Kent-Moore Disconnect Tool (J-38758)

GENERAL MOTORS PARASITIC LOAD

Component	Normal Draw	Maximum Draw	Time-Out (Minutes)
Anti-Theft System	0.4	1.0	
Auto Door Lock	1.0	1.0	
Body Control Module	3.6	12.4	20
Central Processing System	1.6	2.7	20
Electronic Control Module	5.6	10.0	
Electronic Level Control	2.0	3.3	20
Heated Windshield Module	0.3	0.4	
HVAC Power Module	1.0	1.0	
Illuminated Entry	1.0	1.0	1
Light Control Module	0.5	1.0	
Oil Level Module	0.1	0.1	
Multi-Function Chime	1.0	1.0	

Parasitic Load Explanation & Test Procedures (Cont.)

GENERAL MOTORS PARASITIC LOAD (Cont.)

Component	Normal Draw	Maximum Draw	Time-Out (Minutes)
Pass Key Decoder Module	0.75	1.0	
Power Control Module	5.0	7.0	
Retained Accessory Power	3.8	3.8	
Radio	7.0	8.0	15
Twilight Sentinel Module	1.0	1.0	
Voltage Regulator	1.4	2.0	

DIODE CHECK & SOLENOID TEST

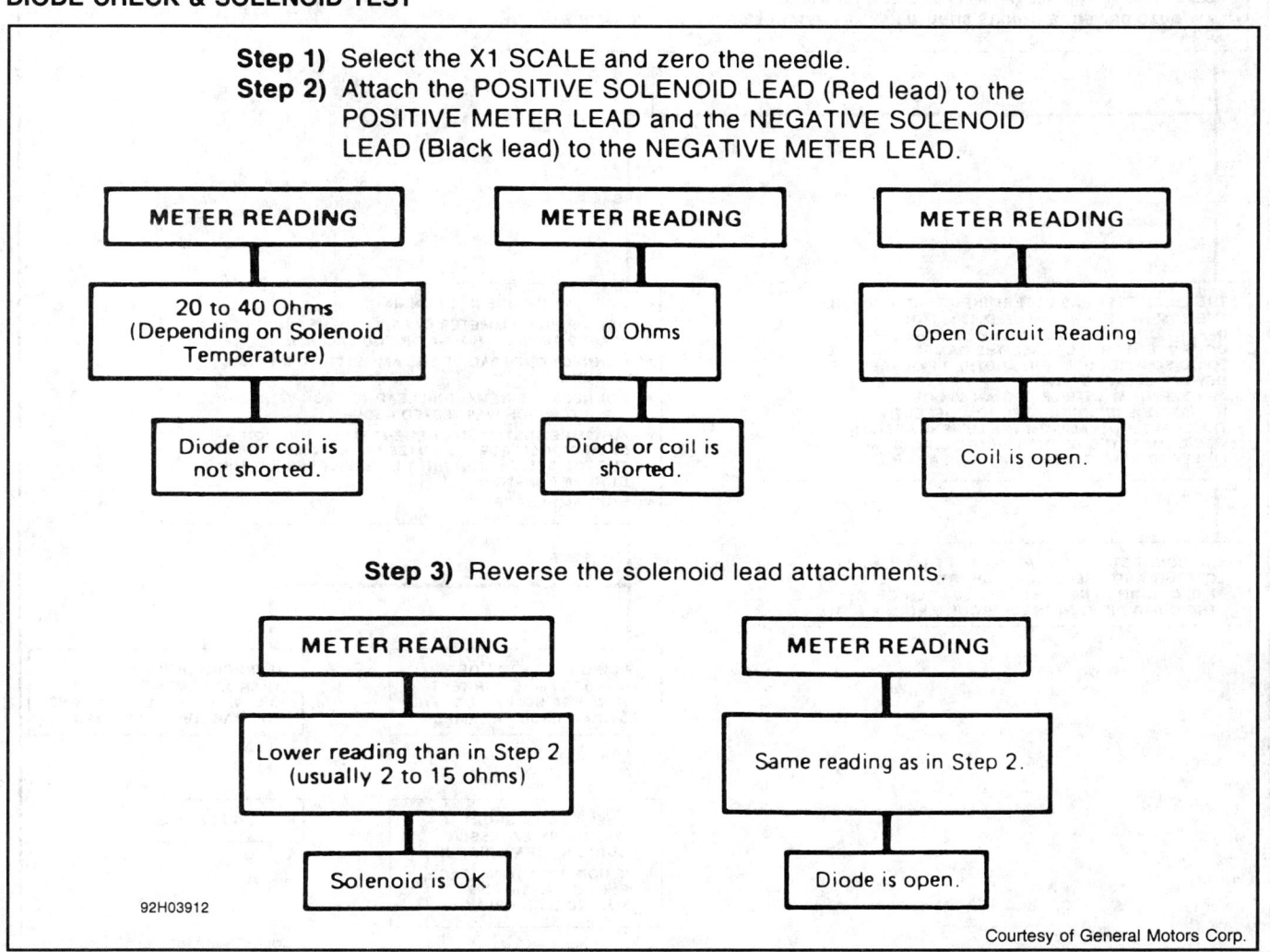

Step 1) Select the X1 SCALE and zero the needle.

Step 2) Attach the POSITIVE SOLENOID LEAD (Red lead) to the POSITIVE METER LEAD and the NEGATIVE SOLENOID LEAD (Black lead) to the NEGATIVE METER LEAD.

METER READING — 20 to 40 Ohms (Depending on Solenoid Temperature) — Diode or coil is not shorted.

METER READING — 0 Ohms — Diode or coil is shorted.

METER READING — Open Circuit Reading — Coil is open.

Step 3) Reverse the solenoid lead attachments.

METER READING — Lower reading than in Step 2 (usually 2 to 15 ohms) — Solenoid is OK

METER READING — Same reading as in Step 2. — Diode is open.

92H03912

Courtesy of General Motors Corp.

Fig. 2: Diode Check & Solenoid Test

GENERAL INFORMATION
Parasitic Load Explanation & Test Procedures (Cont.)

QUAD DRIVER TEST

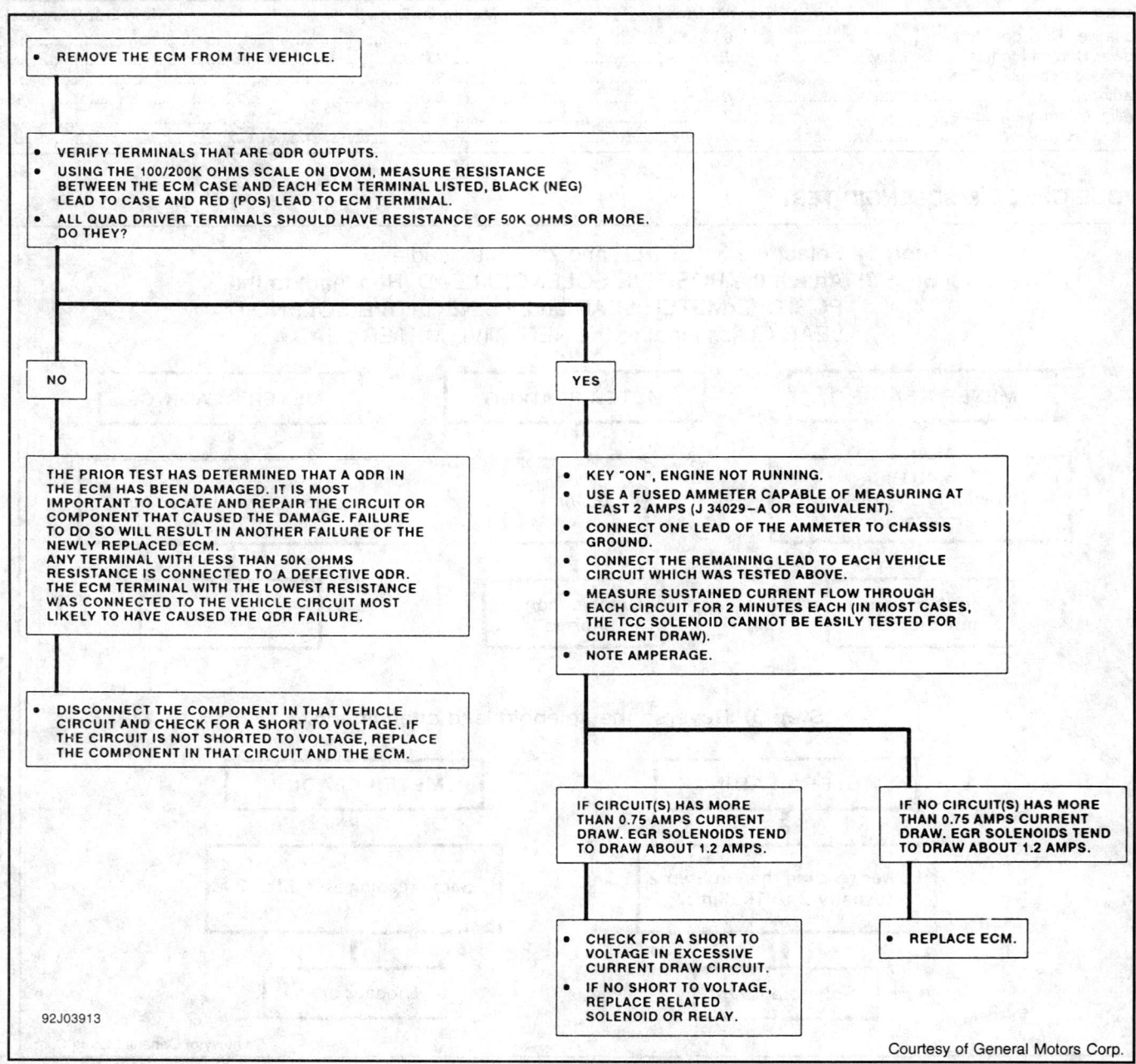

- REMOVE THE ECM FROM THE VEHICLE.

- VERIFY TERMINALS THAT ARE QDR OUTPUTS.
- USING THE 100/200K OHMS SCALE ON DVOM, MEASURE RESISTANCE BETWEEN THE ECM CASE AND EACH ECM TERMINAL LISTED, BLACK (NEG) LEAD TO CASE AND RED (POS) LEAD TO ECM TERMINAL.
- ALL QUAD DRIVER TERMINALS SHOULD HAVE RESISTANCE OF 50K OHMS OR MORE. DO THEY?

NO

YES

THE PRIOR TEST HAS DETERMINED THAT A QDR IN THE ECM HAS BEEN DAMAGED. IT IS MOST IMPORTANT TO LOCATE AND REPAIR THE CIRCUIT OR COMPONENT THAT CAUSED THE DAMAGE. FAILURE TO DO SO WILL RESULT IN ANOTHER FAILURE OF THE NEWLY REPLACED ECM.
ANY TERMINAL WITH LESS THAN 50K OHMS RESISTANCE IS CONNECTED TO A DEFECTIVE QDR. THE ECM TERMINAL WITH THE LOWEST RESISTANCE WAS CONNECTED TO THE VEHICLE CIRCUIT MOST LIKELY TO HAVE CAUSED THE QDR FAILURE.

- KEY "ON", ENGINE NOT RUNNING.
- USE A FUSED AMMETER CAPABLE OF MEASURING AT LEAST 2 AMPS (J 34029–A OR EQUIVALENT).
- CONNECT ONE LEAD OF THE AMMETER TO CHASSIS GROUND.
- CONNECT THE REMAINING LEAD TO EACH VEHICLE CIRCUIT WHICH WAS TESTED ABOVE.
- MEASURE SUSTAINED CURRENT FLOW THROUGH EACH CIRCUIT FOR 2 MINUTES EACH (IN MOST CASES, THE TCC SOLENOID CANNOT BE EASILY TESTED FOR CURRENT DRAW).
- NOTE AMPERAGE.

- DISCONNECT THE COMPONENT IN THAT VEHICLE CIRCUIT AND CHECK FOR A SHORT TO VOLTAGE. IF THE CIRCUIT IS NOT SHORTED TO VOLTAGE, REPLACE THE COMPONENT IN THAT CIRCUIT AND THE ECM.

IF CIRCUIT(S) HAS MORE THAN 0.75 AMPS CURRENT DRAW. EGR SOLENOIDS TEND TO DRAW ABOUT 1.2 AMPS.

IF NO CIRCUIT(S) HAS MORE THAN 0.75 AMPS CURRENT DRAW. EGR SOLENOIDS TEND TO DRAW ABOUT 1.2 AMPS.

- CHECK FOR A SHORT TO VOLTAGE IN EXCESSIVE CURRENT DRAW CIRCUIT.
- IF NO SHORT TO VOLTAGE, REPLACE RELATED SOLENOID OR RELAY.

- REPLACE ECM.

92J03913

Courtesy of General Motors Corp.

Fig. 3: Quad Driver Test

Wiring Diagram Component Locations

When trying to locate a component in a wiring diagram and you don't know the specific system where it is located, use this handy component locator to find the system wiring diagram in which the component is located. Then, go to that system and locate the component within the wiring diagram.

For example, if you don't know the specific system in which the ignition switch is located, look up ignition switch in the wiring diagram component location tables and go to the appropriate wiring diagram(s) which contain either full or partial views of the ignition switch. The full view of the ignition switch is located in Power Distribution.

The first listing for the component will be the full or most complete view of the component. Additional listings will be partial views of the component. Not all components are used on all models.

All components will have a partial view in Ground Distribution and Power Distribution. Data Link Connectors show connecting circuits between modules. Alternate names for components may be listed in wiring diagram component locations tables.

WIRING DIAGRAM COMPONENT LOCATIONS

Component	Wiring Diagram
ABS Electronic Control Unit	Anti-Lock Brakes
	Data Link Connectors
ABS Hydraulic Unit	Anti-Lock Brakes
Acceleration Sensor	Anti-Lock Brakes
Accessory Delay Relay	Power Windows
A/C Compressor Clutch Relay	Engine Performance
A/C Sensor	Engine Performance
A/C Pressure Switch	Engine Performance
Adaptive Lamp Control Module	Exterior Lights
Air Bag(s)	Air Bag Restraint System
Air Bag Module	Air Bag Restraint System
Air Bag Sensor(s)	Air Bag Restraint System
Air Injection Pump Relay	Engine Performance
Air Temperature Sensor	Overhead Console
Alternator (Generator)	Generators & Regulators
Anti-Theft Control Module	Anti-Theft System
	Starters
Autolamp Control Relay	Headlight Systems
	Daytime Running Lights
Automatic Shutdown (ASD) Relay	Engine Performance
	Generators & Regulators
Autostick Switch	Engine Performance
Auxiliary Battery Relay	Generators & Regulators
Back-Up Lights	Back-Up Lights
	Exterior Lights
Barometric (BARO) Pressure Sensor	Engine Performance
Battery	Power Distribution
Battery Temperature Sensor	Engine Performance
Body Control Module	Body Control Computer
	Anti-Theft System
	Daytime Running Lights
	Engine Performance
	Headlight Systems
	Warning Systems
Boost Control Solenoid	Engine Performance
Boost Sensor	Engine Performance
Brake Fluid Level Switch	Analog Instrument Panels
Brake On/Off (BOO) Switch	Cruise Control Systems
	Engine Performance
	Shift Interlock Systems
Buzzer Module	Warning Systems
Camshaft Position (CMP) Sensor	Engine Performance
Central Control Module	Anti-Theft System
Clockspring	Air Bag Restraint System
	Cruise Control Systems
	Steering Column Switches
Clutch Pedal Position Switch	Starters
Clutch Start Switch	Starters
Combination Meter	Analog Instrument Panels

WIRING DIAGRAM COMPONENT LOCATIONS (Cont.)

Component	Wiring Diagram
Constant Control Relay Module (CCRM)	Engine Performance
	Electric Cooling Fans
Convenience Center	Power Distribution
	Illumination/Interior Lights
Convertible Top Motor	Power Convertible Top
Convertible Top Switch	Power Convertible Top
Crankshaft Position (CKP) Sensor	Engine Performance
Cruise Control Module	Cruise Control Systems
Cruise Control Switch	Cruise Control Systems
Condenser Fan Relay(s)	Electric Cooling Fans
Data Link Connector (DLC)	Engine Performance
Daytime Running Lights Module	Daytime Running Lights
	Exterior Lights
Defogger Relay	Rear Window Defogger
Diagnostic Energy Reserve Module (DERM)	Air Bag Restraint System
Discriminating Sensor (Air Bag)	Air Bag Restraint System
Distributor	Engine Performance
Door Lock Actuators	Power Door Locks
	Remote Keyless Entry
Door Lock Relay(s)	Power Door Locks
Electrochromic Mirror	Power Mirrors
Electronic Level Control (ELC) Height Sensor	Electronic Suspension
Electronic Level Control (ELC) Module	Electronic Suspension
Engine Coolant Temperature (ECT) Sending Unit	Analog Instrument Panels
Engine Coolant Temperature (ECT) Sensor	Engine Performance
Engine Control Module	Engine Performance
	Generators & Regulators
	Starters
ETACS ECU	Warning Systems
	Power Windows
	Remote Keyless Entry
Evaporative (EVAP) Emissions Canister	Engine Performance
EVAP Canister Purge Solenoid	Engine Performance
EVAP Canister Vent Solenoid	Engine Performance
Exhaust Gas Recirculation (EGR) Valve	Engine Performance
Fuel Tank Vacuum Sensor	Engine Performance
Fog Lights	Headlight Systems
	Daytime Running Lights
Fog Light Relay	Headlight Systems
	Daytime Running Lights
Fuel Door Release Solenoid	Power Fuel Door Release
Fuel Gauge Sending Unit	Analog Instrument Panels
Fuel Injectors	Engine Performance
Fuel Pump	Engine Performance
Fuel Pump Relay	Engine Performance
	Power Distribution
Fuse/Relay Block	Power Distribution
Fusible Links	Power Distribution
	Generators & Regulators
	Starters
Generator	Generators & Regulators
	Engine Performance
	Power Distribution
Generic Electronic Module (GEM)	Body Control Modules
	Electronic Suspension
Glow Plug Relay	Engine Performance
Glow Plugs	Engine Performance
Grounds	Ground Distribution
Headlight Door Module	Headlight Doors
Headlight Relay	Headlight Systems
	Daytime Running Lights
Headlights	Headlight Systems
	Daytime Running Lights
Heated Oxygen Sensor(s) (HO2S)	Engine Performance

GENERAL INFORMATION
Wiring Diagram Component Locations (Cont.)

WIRING DIAGRAM COMPONENT LOCATIONS (Cont.)

Component	Wiring Diagram
Heated Windshield Control Module	Heated Windshields
Height Sensor	Electronic Suspension
Horns	Steering Column Switches
Horn Relay	Steering Column Switches
Idle Air Control (IAC) Motor/Valve	Engine Performance
Ignition Coil(s)	Engine Performance
Ignition Key Lock Cylinder	Anti-Theft System
Ignition Module	Engine Performance
Ignition Switch	Power Distribution
	Engine Performance
	Generators & Regulators
	Starters
Illuminated Entry Module	Illumination/Interior Lights
Illumination Lights	Illumination/Interior Lights
Impact Sensor	Air Bag Restraint System
Inertia Fuel Shutoff Switch	Engine Performance
Inhibit Relay	Starters
Instrument Cluster	Analog Instrument Panels
Intake Air Temperature (IAT) Sensor	Engine Performance
Interior Lights	Illumination/Interior Lights
Interlock Switch	Starters
Junction Block	Power Distribution
Keyless Entry Receiver	Remote Keyless Entry
Key Reminder Switch	Starters
Knock Sensor	Engine Performance
Lamp Control Module	Exterior Lights
Leak Detection Pump	Engine Performance
License Plate Lamp	Exterior Lights
Lighting Control Module	Lighting Control Modules
	Anti-Theft System
	Daytime Running Lights
	Headlight Systems
Lower Relay	Power Convertible Top
Malfunction Indicator Light (MIL)	Engine Performance
	Instrument Panels
Manifold Absolute Pressure (MAP) Sensor	Engine Performance
Mass Airflow (MAF) Sensor	Engine Performance
Mega Fuse	Generators & Regulators
Memory Seat/Mirror Module	Memory Systems
Mirror Defogger	Rear Window Defogger
Moon Roof Motor	Power Moon Roof
Moon Roof Relay	Power Moon Roof
Multi-Function Control Module	Warning Systems
Neutral Safety Switch	Starters
Oil Level Switch	Engine Performance
Oil Pressure Switch/Sending Unit	Analog Instrument Panels
	Engine Performance
Overhead Console	Overhead Console
Oxygen Sensor(s) (O2S)	Engine Performance
Parking Brake Switch	Analog Instrument Panels
Park Lights	Exterior Lights
Park/Neutral Position Switch	Starters
	Engine Performance
	Anti-Theft System
	Body Control Module
Perimeter Lighting Control Relay	Exterior Lights
Power Amplifier	Power Antennas
Power Antenna Module	Power Antennas
Power Antenna Motor	Power Antennas
Power Distribution Center	Power Distribution
	Generators & Regulators
	Starters
Power Door Lock Motors	Power Door Locks
Power Mirror Motors	Power Mirrors
	Memory Systems
Power Sliding Door Controller	Power Sliding Side Door
Power Seat Motors	Power Seats
	Memory Systems

WIRING DIAGRAM COMPONENT LOCATIONS (Cont.)

Component	Wiring Diagram
Power Steering Pressure Switch	Engine Performance
Power Top Motor	Power Convertible Top
Power Top Relay(s)	Power Convertible Top
Powertrain Control Module	Engine Performance
	Analog Instrument Panels
	Cruise Control Systems
	Data Link Connectors
	Generators & Regulators
	Starters
Power Window Motors	Power Windows
Power Window Relay(s)	Power Windows
Radiator Fan Motor(s)	Electric Cooling Fans
Radiator Fan Relay(s)	Engine Performance
	Electric Cooling Fans
Rainsense Module	Wiper/Washer Systems
Raise Relay	Power Convertible Top
Remote Anti-Theft Personality (RAP) Module	Anti-Theft System
	Starters
	Warning Systems
Seat Belt Pretensioners	Air Bag Restraint System
Seat Belt Retractor Solenoid	Passive Restraints
Seat Belt Switch	Air Bag Restraint System
	Passive Restraints
Shift Interlock Solenoid	Shift Interlock Systems
Shift Lock Actuator	Shift Interlock Systems
Side Marker Lights	Exterior Lights
SIR Coil Assembly (Clockspring)	Air Bag Restraint System
Slip Ring (Clockspring)	Air Bag Restraint System
	Steering Column Switches
SRS Control Module	Air Bag Restraint System
Starter Motor	Starters
Starter Interrupt Relay	Starters
Starter Solenoid	Starters
Starter Relay	Starters
Steering Wheel Position Sensor	Anti-Lock Brakes
Stoplights	Exterior Lights
Stoplight Switch	Engine Performance
	Cruise Control Systems
	Anti-Lock Brakes
Sun Roof ECU	Power Sun Roof
Sun Roof Motor	Power Sun Roof
Sun Roof Position Sensor	Power Sun Roof
Taillights	Exterior Lights
Throttle Position (TP) Sensor	Engine Performance
Torque Converter Clutch Solenoid/Switch	Engine Performance
Traction Control Switch	Anti-Lock Brakes
Trailer Tow Connector	Exterior Lights
Trailer Tow Relay	Exterior Lights
Transmission/Transaxle	Engine Performance
Transmission Control Module (TCM)	Engine Performance
	Starters
Transmission Range Sensor	Starters
	Back-Up Lights
	Engine Performance
Transmission Range Switch	Back-Up Lights
	Engine Performance
	Anti-Theft System
Turn Signal Flasher	Exterior Lights
Turn Signal Lights	Exterior Lights
Twilight Sentinel Switch	Headlight Systems
	Daytime Running Lights
Vapor Canister Leak Detection Pump	Engine Performance
Vehicle Control Module (VCM)	Engine Performance
Vehicle Dynamic Module	Electronic Suspension
Vehicle Speed Control Servo	Cruise Control Systems

Wiring Diagram Component Locations (Cont.)

WIRING DIAGRAM COMPONENT LOCATIONS (Cont.)

Component	Wiring Diagram
Vehicle Speed Sensor	Data Link Connectors
	Analog Instrument Panels
	Cruise Control Systems
	Electronic Suspension
Voltage Regulator	Generators & Regulators
Water-In-Fuel Sensor	Engine Performance
	Analog Instrument Panels
Wheel Speed Sensors	Anti-Lock Brakes
Window Timer Module	Power Convertible Top
Windshield Intermittent Wiper Relay	Wiper/Washer Systems
Windshield Washer Motor	Wiper/Washer Systems
Wiper Motor	Wiper/Washer Systems

GENERAL INFORMATION
Using Mitchell's Wiring Diagrams

INTRODUCTION

Mitchell® obtains wiring diagrams and technical service bulletins, containing wiring diagram changes, from the domestic and import manufacturers. These are checked for accuracy and are all redrawn into a consistent format for easy use.

In the past, when cars were simpler, diagrams were simpler. All components were connected by wires, and diagrams seldom exceeded 4 pages in length. Today, some wiring diagrams require more than 16 pages. It would be impractical to expect a service technician to trace a wire from page 1 across every page to page 16.

Removing some of the wiring maze reduces eyestrain and time wasted searching across several pages. Today, the majority of Mitchell® diagrams follow a much improved format, which permits space for internal switch details, and component and ground locations.

Today, the wiring diagram necessary to support a given repair procedure is included within that article. For example, the wiring diagram for a Ford EEC-IV system is included in ENGINE PERFORMANCE and WIRING DIAGRAMS sections for Ford Motor Co. The wiring diagram for a cruise control system is included in ACCESSORIES & EQUIPMENT section for the specific vehicle manufacturer, and the wiring diagram for an anti-lock brake system is included in BRAKES and WIRING DIAGRAMS sections for the specific manufacturer.

WIRING DIAGRAMS section contains all wiring diagrams not included in STARTING & CHARGING SYSTEMS and ACCESSORIES & EQUIPMENT. This includes: Data Link Connectors, Ground Distribution, Power Distribution, Engine Performance, Electric Cooling Fans, Anti-Lock Brakes, Electronic Suspension and Electronic Steering wiring diagrams. The Data Link Connectors wiring diagrams show the circuits by which the various on-board computers exchange information, and the diagnostic connectors used for diagnosis and their location. The Ground Distribution wiring diagrams show all vehicle ground points, their location, and the components common to those ground points. The Power Distribution wiring diagrams show the power feed circuits and the components common to those power feeds.

Wiring diagrams used to support the information in ACCESSORIES & EQUIPMENT are drawn in a "top-down" format. The diagrams are drawn with the power source at the top of the diagram and the ground point at the bottom of the diagram. Component locations are identified on the wiring diagrams. Any wires that do not connect directly to a component are identified on the diagram to indicate where they go.

COLOR ABBREVIATIONS

Color	Normal	Optional
Black	BLK	BK
Blue	BLU	BU
Brown	BRN	BN
Clear	CLR	CR
Dark Blue	DK BLU	DK BU
Dark Green	DK GRN	DK GN
Green	GRN	GN
Gray	GRY	GY
Light Blue	LT BLU	LT BU
Light Green	LT GRN	LT GN
Orange	ORG	OG
Pink	PNK	PK
Purple	PPL	PL
Red	RED	RD
Tan	TAN	TN
Violet	VIO	VI
White	WHT	WT
Yellow	YEL	YL

IDENTIFYING WIRING DIAGRAM ABBREVIATIONS

NOTE: Abbreviations used on Mitchell® diagrams are normally self-explanatory. To assist you, however, we have included a 2-page list of abbreviations. See the COMMONLY USED ABBREVIATIONS article.

GENERAL INFORMATION
Using Mitchell's Wiring Diagrams (Cont.)

IDENTIFYING WIRING DIAGRAM SYMBOLS

NOTE: Standard wiring symbols are used on MITCHELL® diagrams. The list below will help clarify any symbols that are not easily understood at a glance. Most components are labeled "Motor", "Switch" or "Relay" in addition to being drawn with the standard symbol.

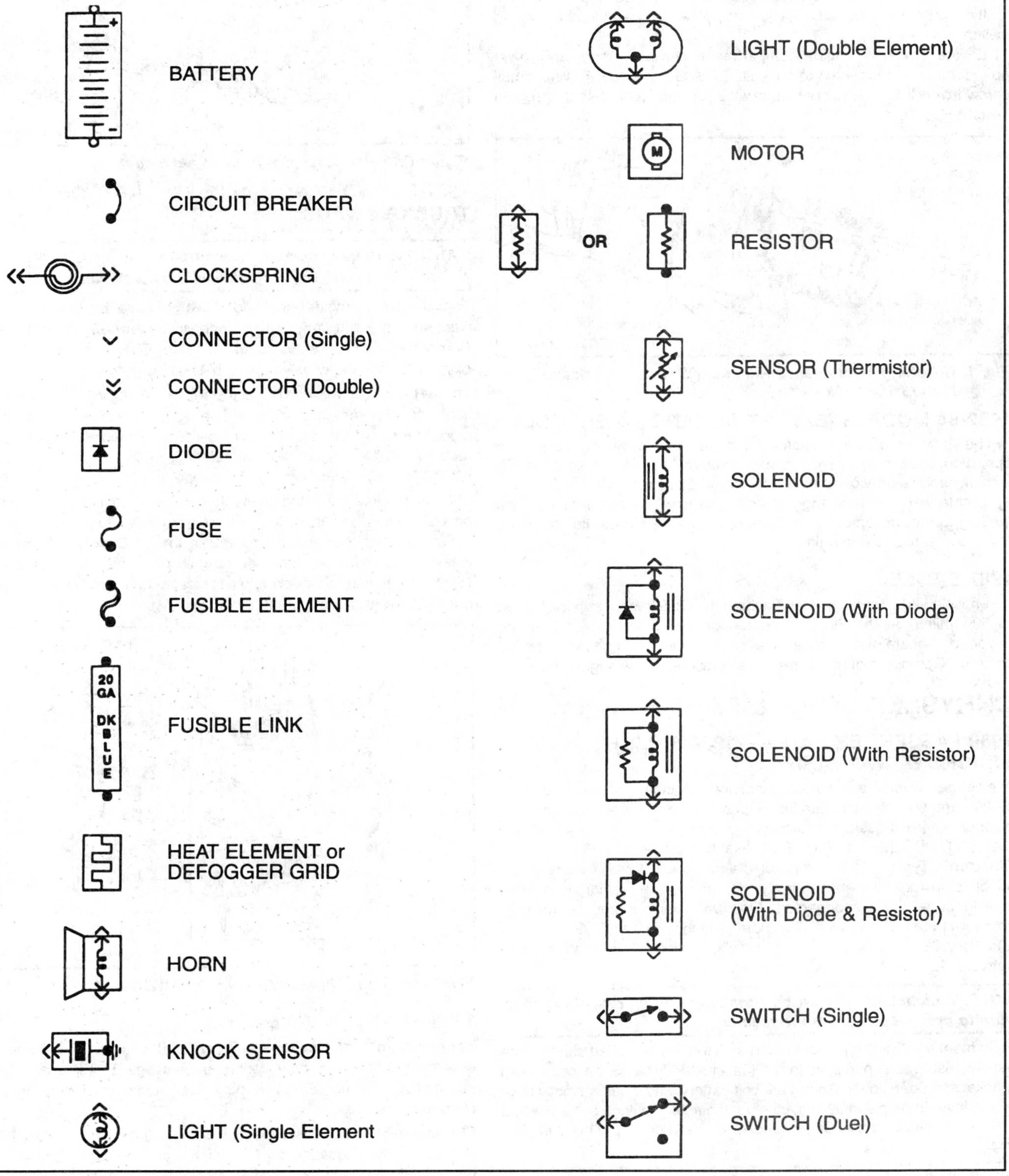

BATTERY
CIRCUIT BREAKER
CLOCKSPRING
CONNECTOR (Single)
CONNECTOR (Double)
DIODE
FUSE
FUSIBLE ELEMENT
20 GA DK BLUE
FUSIBLE LINK
HEAT ELEMENT or DEFOGGER GRID
HORN
KNOCK SENSOR
LIGHT (Single Element
LIGHT (Double Element)
MOTOR
OR
RESISTOR
SENSOR (Thermistor)
SOLENOID
SOLENOID (With Diode)
SOLENOID (With Resistor)
SOLENOID (With Diode & Resistor)
SWITCH (Single)
SWITCH (Duel)

1999 GENERAL INFORMATION
Service Reminder Indicators
1980-99 Domestic Cars & Trucks

AMERICAN MOTORS

1980-81 MODELS

1) Every 30,000 miles, a service reminder indicator will illuminate on the instrument panel, indicating oxygen sensor requires service. If sensor is faulty, it must be replaced. After servicing sensor, reset light activating switch.

2) Locate switch in engine compartment, between upper and lower speedometer cables, next to firewall. Slide rubber boot up. With small screwdriver, turn reset screw clockwise 1/4 turn until detent resets in switch. See Fig. 1.

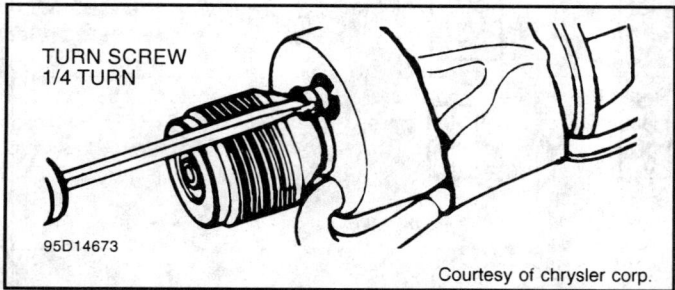

Fig. 1: Resetting Maintenance Reminder Switch (American Motors 1980-81 Models)

1982-84 MODELS (EXCEPT ALLIANCE & ENCORE)

1) The service reminder indicator illuminates after 1000 hours of engine operation, indicating oxygen sensor requires service. After servicing sensor, replace service reminder indicator E-cell timer.

2) Locate timer in passenger compartment within the wire harness leading to the microprocessor. Remove E-cell timer from its enclosure and insert a replacement timer.

1987 EAGLE

An emission light timer will start flashing the O2S sensor service light at 82,500 miles. At this time, O2S sensor and timer should both be replaced. Locate timer under the dash panel (to right of steering column). Remove mounting screws and disconnect wiring.

CHRYSLER CORP. & EAGLE

1980 PASSENGER CARS, & 1980-87 LIGHT DUTY TRUCKS & RWD VANS

A mileage counter activates the service reminder indicator between 12,000 and 30,000 mile intervals, depending on whether mechanical or electronic type is used. If equipped with mechanical type, see AMERICAN MOTORS 1980-81 MODELS reset procedure. See Fig. 1.

Electronic Type – 1) The electronic type uses a 9-volt battery which supplies power to the electronic counter, preventing memory loss when vehicle battery is disconnected. On 1987 Dakota models, mileage counter in the odometer will illuminate reminder light at 52,500, 82,500 and 105,000 miles. On all other models, reminder light will illuminate between 12,000 and 30,000 mile intervals.

NOTE: Vehicle battery must be connected during resetting procedure to prevent power loss to memory.

2) To reset electronic type, locate Green, Red, White or Tan plastic case behind instrument panel in lower left cluster area. Slide case from bracket and open cover. Remove 9-volt battery, and insert a small rod or screwdriver into hole in switch, closing contacts. Replace battery with a new 9-volt alkaline type. Close case. Slide case back into bracket. See Fig. 2.

NOTE: Some models use a non-resettable mileage counter. Replace it with a resettable type.

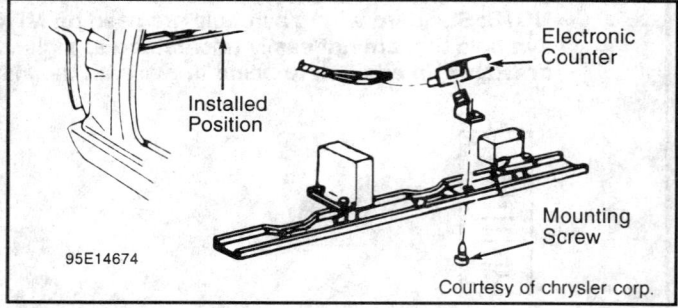

Fig. 2: Chrysler Corp. Electronic-Type Switch

1987-88 FWD VANS & ALL 1988 LIGHT DUTY TRUCKS & VANS

CAUTION: There is no test procedure for this system. Any attempt to test this system will damage system components.

The Service Reminder Indicator (SRI) module is not an emissions warning system. It is only a reminder to perform emissions servicing. Components to be serviced include the EGR system, PCV valve, oxygen sensor, delay valves, and bi-level purge valve.

The SRI module will illuminate the MAINT REQD/CHECK EGR dash light after a predetermined time. The light will remain on until the SRI module is reset by inserting a small screwdriver into the hole in the module (RWD only) and/or depressing the reset switch (FWD and RWD). Replace 9-volt battery (if equipped).

The SRI module is located on steering column, behind instrument panel on RWD vans and in instrument cluster, under fuel gauge, on FWD vans. See Fig. 3 or 4. On light trucks except Dakota, SRI module is located behind the far right side of dash panel next to glove box. See Fig. 5. On Dakota models, module is located on bracket below headlight switch, on rear of instrument panel. See Fig. 6.

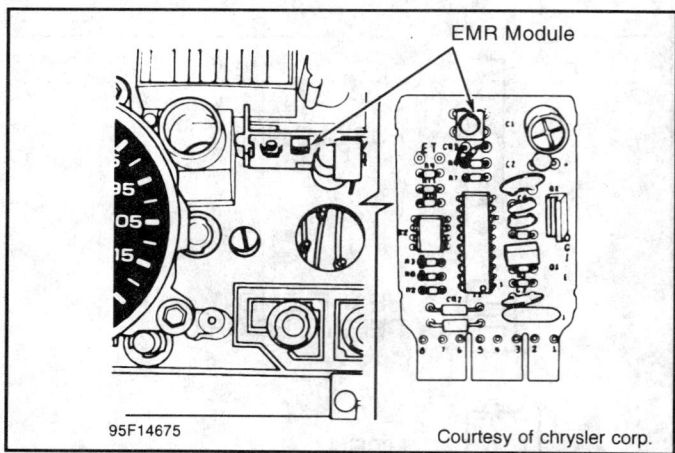

Fig. 3: Locating SRI Module (1987-88 FWD Vans)

1988-89 NEW YORKER

Service Reminder Message – Every 7500 miles or 12 months which ever comes first, a service reminder message on Electronic Vehicle Information Center (EVIC) display will illuminate, indicating an oil change is due.

Pressing INFO button with the ignition on will activate a MONITORED SYSTEMS OK message on the display if all systems are operating properly. If service is required, SERVICE REMINDER message will be displayed. Pressing the RESET button after message has been displayed will clear the message.

Service Reminder Indicators
1980-99 Domestic Cars & Trucks (Cont.)

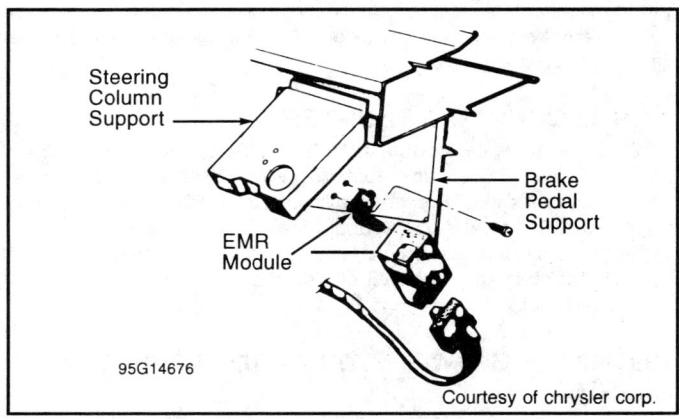

Fig. 4: Locating SRI Module (1988 RWD Vans)

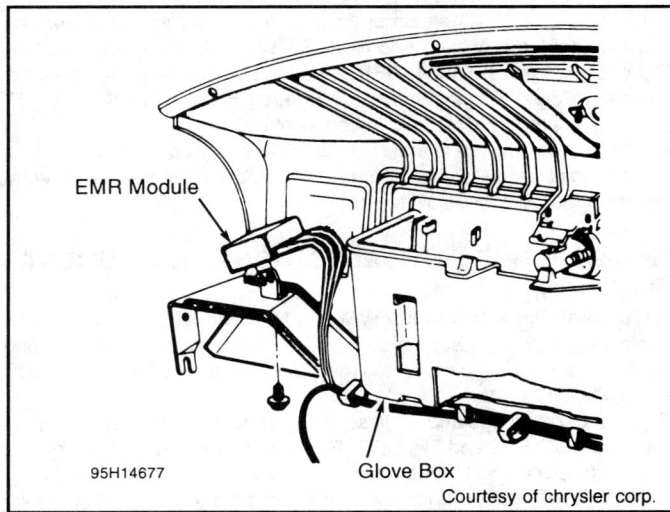

Fig. 5: Locating SRI Module (1988 Light Trucks Except Dakota)

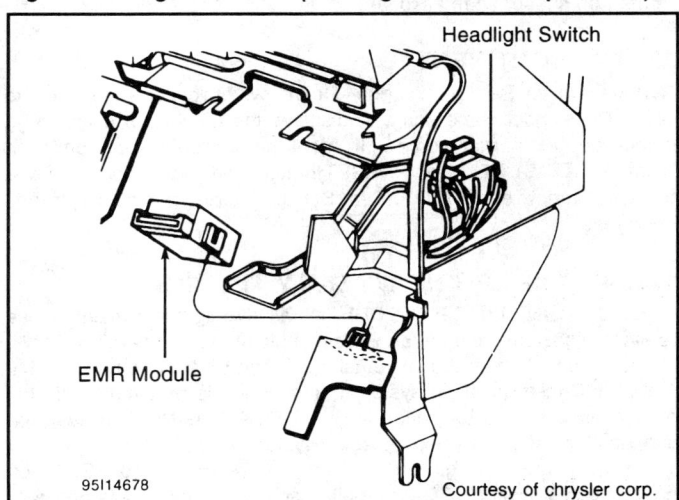

Fig. 6: Locating SRI Module (1988 Dakota)

1988-92 PREMIER & 1990-92 MONACO

Service Interval Reminder Light – Every 7500 miles, a Vehicle Maintenance Monitor (VMM) will illuminate a SERVICE interval reminder light. This indicates regular maintenance is due. After required service is performed, press RESET button on dash below VMM display. Hold button until a beep is heard. VMM display will now be clear.

1989-92 LIGHT DUTY TRUCKS & VANS

Emission Maintenance Reminder (EMR) Light – The EMR light is designed to be a reminder to service the vehicle emissions control system. It is not an emissions warning system, only a reminder to perform emissions servicing.

The components to be serviced include the EGR system, PCV valve, oxygen sensor and some vacuum-operated components. EMR light will illuminate after a predetermined mileage. To reset EMR light, a Chrysler Diagnostic Readout Box (DRB-II) Tester (C-4805) or suitable scan tool is required.

NOTE: If DRB-II scan tool is used, go to RESET PROCEDURE. If any other scan tool is used, use procedure provided by scan tool manufacturer.

Reset Procedure – Attach DRB-II tester to diagnostic connector. Turn ignition on but do not start engine. Access SELECT SYSTEMS function of DRB-II tester. Select appropriate engine. Select with or without A/C. Select FUEL & IGNITION. Select ADJUSTMENTS. Select RESET EMR LIGHT. Reset EMR light. When DRB-II is finished resetting light, DRB-II display will read EMR LIGHT IS RESET.

NOTE: If Single Module Engine Controller (SMEC) or Single Board Engine Controller (SBEC) is replaced, vehicle mileage must be programmed back into the SMEC/SBEC. DRB-II tester MUST be used for this procedure. If the following procedure is not performed, EMR light will not turn on at the proper mileage intervals.

EMR Mileage Reset – **1)** Using DRB-II tester, select EMR MEMORY CHECK. DRB-II display will read, EMR MEMORY CHECK ARE YOU SURE?. Press YES key.
2) Display will read, WRITE TEST. Display will read, IS INSTRUMENT PANEL MILEAGE BETWEEN XXXXXX AND XXXXXX? If odometer mileage on vehicle is within specification, press YES key. DRB-II will display EMR MEMORY CHECK TEST COMPLETE.

NOTE: DRB-II may display EMR MEMORY WRITE FAILURE or EMR MEMORY CHECK WRITE REFUSED if there is a problem with SMEC/SBEC.

3) If odometer mileage on vehicle is not within specification shown on DRB-II, press NO key. DRB-II will read DO YOU WANT TO CORRECT EMR MILEAGE?. Press YES key on DRB-II. DRB-II will display ENTER MILEAGE SHOWN ON INSTRUMENT PANEL.
4) Enter mileage shown on instrument panel. DO NOT enter tenths. Press ENTER key on DRB-II. DRB-II will ask for verification of entry. If mileage entry was correct, DRB-II will display SETTING ENGINE DATA and EMR MEMORY CHECK TEST COMPLETE. Vehicle must be driven for at least 8 miles for mileage reset to be accepted.

1990 FIFTH AVENUE, LEBARON, IMPERIAL & NEW YORKER

Service Reminder Message – Every 7500 miles or 12 months which ever comes first, a service reminder message on Electronic Vehicle Information Center (EVIC) display will illuminate, indicating an oil change is due.

Pressing INFO button with the ignition on will activate a MONITORED SYSTEMS OK message on the display if all systems are operating properly. If service is required, SERVICE REMINDER message will be displayed. To clear message, press INFO button and within 5 seconds, press SET button.

1993 LIGHT DUTY TRUCKS & VANS

Service Reminder Indicator (SRI) Light – The SRI is designed to be a reminder to service the vehicle emissions control system. It is not an emissions warning system, only a reminder to perform emissions servicing.

The components to be serviced include the EGR system, PCV valve, oxygen sensor and some vacuum-operated components. SRI will

1999 GENERAL INFORMATION
Service Reminder Indicators
1980-99 Domestic Cars & Trucks (Cont.)

illuminate after a predetermined mileage. To reset SRI, a Chrysler Diagnostic Readout Box (DRB) Tester or suitable scan tool is required.

NOTE: *If DRB tester is used, go to RESET PROCEDURE. If any other scan tool is used, use procedure provided by scan tool manufacturer.*

Reset Procedure – 1) Attach DRB tester to diagnostic connector. Turn ignition on but do not start engine. Using DRB, perform Service Reminder Indicator (SRI) memory test. If DRB displays WRITE FAILURE, replace Powertrain Control Module (PCM).

2) If DRB displays WRITE REFUSED, go to step **4)**. If DRB displays SRI MILEAGE INVALID, update mileage and retest SRI memory. If DRB does not display SRI MILEAGE INVALID, compare SRI mileage stored with instrument panel odometer.

3) If mileage is same, retest SRI memory. If mileage is not same, update mileage and retest SRI memory.

4) PCM was busy. Using DRB, perform SRI memory test. Retest SRI memory 2 or more times, if necessary. If WRITE REFUSED trouble code returns, replace PCM. If WRITE REFUSED does not return, procedure is complete.

1994-99 RAM PICKUP

Service Reminder Indicator (SRI) Light – The SRI is designed to be a reminder to service the vehicle emissions control system. It is not an emissions warning system, only a reminder to perform emissions servicing.

The components to be serviced include the EGR system, PCV valve, oxygen sensor and some vacuum-operated components. SRI will illuminate after a predetermined mileage. To reset SRI, a Chrysler Diagnostic Readout Box (DRB) Tester or suitable scan tool is required. Use scan tool manufacturer's information to reset SRI.

FORD MOTOR CO.

1985-87 LIGHT DUTY TRUCKS, 1988 NON-EEC LIGHT DUTY TRUCKS & 1989-92 HEAVY-DUTY TRUCKS

NOTE: *1980-84 trucks do not use a Service Reminder Indicator (SRI). Non-EEC vehicles for 1988 are the 2.0L Ranger, 2.3L Ranger, 6.1L and 7.0L gasoline trucks.*

Service Reminder Indicator (SRI) – A SRI is used to indicate emission system maintenance is required. Control unit (timer) for maintenance light is located under dash, near steering column or behind glove box. Some models use a non-resettable control unit. Replace it with a resettable type. After servicing emission system, reset SRI.

1) To reset SRI, turn ignition off. Remove tape over reset hole in timer. Lightly push a small Phillips screwdriver into hole in timer unit marked RESET. With light pressure on screwdriver, turn ignition switch to RUN position.

2) Light should stay on while screwdriver is pressed down. Hold screwdriver down for approximately 5 seconds. Remove screwdriver. Light should go out within 2-5 seconds. If light does not go out, repeat steps **1)** and **2)**.

3) Cycle ignition from OFF to RUN position. Light should glow for 2-5 seconds. This verifies proper reset of maintenance reminder light.

1985-89 PASSENGER CARS

Service Interval Reminder Light – Every 5000 or 7500 miles, depending upon engine application, a SERVICE interval reminder light on the dash will illuminate (for approximately 30 seconds), or begin flashing, indicating an oil change is due.

To reset reminder light, turn ignition on. Simultaneously depress and hold TRIP (ODO SEL on Taurus and Sable, SYSTEM CHECK or CHECK OUT on Continental) and RESET or TRIP RESET buttons. On

Probe models, depress and hold SERVICE RESET button, located on speed alarm keyboard. On all models, 3 beeps will verify that reminder light has been reset.

1989-92 COUGAR & THUNDERBIRD

Vehicle Maintenance Monitor (VMM) – 1) Turn ignition switch to ON position. Within 16 seconds of turning ignition on, insert small diameter shank into reset switch hole, and firmly push in switch. Reset switch hole is located on left side of VMM panel.

2) Keep switch depressed until left side of display stops flashing. If switch is not kept depressed until left side of display stops flashing, VMM will not be reset.

1990-92 PROBE (WITH STANDARD INSTRUMENT CLUSTER)

Vehicle Maintenance Monitor (VMM) – 1) The SERVICE light will come on approximately every 7500 miles, indicating routine service is required. The light will remain on for 3 minutes after vehicle is started.

2) To cancel the message and reset SERVICE light on 1990 models, depress and hold SERVICE RESET button until 3 beeps are sounded. This will verify that reminder light has been reset. SERVICE RESET button is located in VMM unit, in center of overhead console.

3) To cancel the message and reset SERVICE light on 1991-92 models, insert a small diameter shank into hole centered directly above VMM display lights, and press switch once.

1990-92 PROBE (WITH ELECTRONIC INSTRUMENT CLUSTER)

Vehicle Maintenance Monitor (VMM) – 1) SERVICE INTERVAL will be displayed on system scanner every 7500 miles, indicating that routine service is due. At 7500 miles, the message will remain on for 3 minutes after vehicle is started.

2) To cancel message and reset service interval on 1990 models, press and hold ODO SEL and TRIP RESET buttons until 3 beeps are heard. Buttons are located on speed alarm keyboard.

3) To cancel message and reset service interval on 1991-92 models, press and hold SERV button until 3 tones are heard. SERV button is located on speed alarm keyboard.

1990-94 CONTINENTAL

Service Interval Reminder Light – During system check sequence, the SERVICE symbol comes on and displays the number of miles to go before the next normal service. To reset the service interval reminder, press SYSTEM CHECK and RESET buttons simultaneously. The display should now show 7200 miles. Service interval reminder light has been reset.

1993-94 7.0L LPG HEAVY DUTY TRUCKS

CHECK ENGINE Light – The CHECK ENGINE light is a maintenance reminder light connected to an Emission Maintenance Warning (EMW) module, located under the instrument panel and is used to indicate that the 60,000 mile emission system maintenance is required. Emission maintenance should be performed if CHECK ENGINE light stays on continuously. After servicing emission system, reset light.

1) To reset light, turn ignition off. Remove sticker labeled RESET on EMW module. Using a 7/32" drill bit, insert and lightly press and hold down drill bit in reset hole.

2) Still pressing down on drill bit, turn ignition to RUN position. Light should stay on while drill bit is pressed down. Hold drill bit down for approximately 5 seconds.

3) Remove drill bit. Light should go out within 2-5 seconds. If light does not go out, repeat steps **1)**, **2)** and **3)**.

4) Cycle ignition from OFF to RUN position. CHECK ENGINE light should illuminate for 2-5 seconds. This verifies proper reset of EMW module.

1999 GENERAL INFORMATION
Service Reminder Indicators
1980-99 Domestic Cars & Trucks (Cont.)

GENERAL INFO.
49

1993-98 LINCOLN MARK VIII

Electronic Message Center, "CHANGE OIL SOON/OIL CHANGE REQUIRED" – **1)** The "CHANGE OIL SOON" warning will display on the message center when remaining engine oil life is 5 or less. The "OIL CHANGE REQUIRED" will display when engine oil life is 0.

2) To reset display after oil change, press "VEHICLE SETTINGS" control until "OIL CHANGE RESET" display appears. On 1993-96 models, press "OIL CHANGE RESET" switch and hold for 5 seconds as message center display counts down to trigger an oil change reset. On 1997-98 models, press "RESET" switch for 5 seconds to reset display.

3) After a successful reset, the message center will display "OIL LIFE RESET TO 100."

GENERAL MOTORS (CADILLAC)

NOTE: Most General Motors 1981-88 vehicles do not use a Service Reminder Indicator (SRI).

1980 CADILLAC

1) Every 15,000 miles, a reminder flag appears in speedometer face, indicating service of oxygen sensor is necessary. Inspect and service oxygen sensor as necessary and reset flag.

2) To reset flag, remove lower steering column cover. Sensor reset cable is located to the left of the speedometer cluster. Pull cable lightly (maximum 2 lbs. force). Reinstall lower steering column cover.

1989-93 CADILLAC ALLANTE

Engine Data Display – **1)** An OIL LIFE INDEX is one of the displays on Driver Information Center (DIC). It will display remaining oil life as a percentage estimate of the useful life of oil.

2) It will show 100 percent when the system is reset. When the oil life is 0 percent, the display will show CHANGE ENGINE OIL. After changing oil, reset oil life display.

3) To reset service reminder on 1989 models, press RANGE button until OIL LIFE INDEX appears on display. Depress and hold in AVG ECON and RANGE buttons for more than 5 seconds or until 100 is displayed. This will reset remaining oil life to 100 percent.

4) On 1990-93 models, press RANGE button until OIL LIFE INDEX appears on DIC display. Depress and hold in AVG SPEED and RANGE buttons for more than 5 seconds or until 100 is displayed. This will reset remaining oil life to 100 percent.

1989-91 CADILLAC ELDORADO & SEVILLE

Engine Data Display – **1)** An OIL LIFE INDEX is one of 4 displays on Driver Information Center (DIC). It will display remaining oil life as a percentage estimate of the useful life of oil.

2) Display will show 100 percent when the system is reset. When remaining oil life is 10 percent or less, the system will display CHANGE OIL SOON. When the oil life expires, the display will show CHANGE ENGINE OIL. After changing oil, reset oil life display.

3) To reset oil life display, press ENG DATA button until OIL LIFE INDEX appears on DIC display. Depress and hold in ENG DATA and RANGE buttons until 100 is displayed. This will reset remaining oil life to 100 percent.

1991-93 CADILLAC DEVILLE & 1991-92 FLEETWOOD

Engine Data Display – **1)** An OIL LIFE INDEX is one of the displays on Driver Information Center (DIC). It will display remaining oil life as a estimated percentage of the useful life of oil.

2) It will show 100 percent when the system is reset. When the oil life is 0 percent, the display will show CHANGE ENGINE OIL. After performing necessary services, reset service reminder.

3) To reset service reminder, depress and hold RANGE and FUEL USED buttons until OIL LIFE INDEX appears on DIC display. Depress and hold RANGE and RESET buttons for 5-60 seconds.

4) When CHANGE OIL SOON light flashes 4 times, remaining oil life index is reset to 100 percent. If CHANGE OIL SOON comes on and stays on for 5 seconds, display did not reset. Repeat step **3)**.

1992-93 CADILLAC ELDORADO & SEVILLE

Engine Data Display – **1)** Oil change reminder display is similar to 1990-91 models, but reset procedures are different. After changing oil, reset oil life display.

2) To reset, press INFORMATION button to display OIL LIFE INDEX. Press and hold STORE/RECALL button until 100 is displayed. This will reset oil life display to 100 percent.

1993 CADILLAC BROUGHAM & 1993-96 FLEETWOOD

Oil Life Indicator – **1)** Oil life indicator will display CHANGE OIL when oil change is needed, based upon engine oil temperatures and driving patterns. After changing oil, reset oil life indicator.

2) To reset, turn ignition switch to ON position. Do not start engine. Fully press and release accelerator pedal 3 times within 5 seconds. If CHANGE OIL light comes on and stays on for 5 seconds, it did not reset. Reset system again.

1992-99 CADILLAC DEVILLE, CONCOURS & ELDORADO, & 1992-97 CADILLAC SEVILLE

CHANGE TRANS FLUID Message – This message will appear on the Driver Information Center (DIC) when transaxle fluid change is due. To reset display, turn ignition key on with engine off. On the climate control panel, press and hold OFF and REAR DEFOG buttons until TRANS FLUID RESET message appears in DIC (about 5-20 seconds).

1994-96 CADILLAC CONCOURS, 1994-99 DEVILLE, 1994-97 ELDORADO & 1994-97 SEVILLE

CHANGE ENGINE OIL Display – **1)** The Driver Information Center (DIC) will display remaining oil life as a percentage estimate of the useful life of oil.

2) When remaining oil life is 10 percent or less, the system will display CHANGE OIL SOON. When oil life expires, display will show CHANGE ENGINE OIL. After changing oil, reset oil life display.

3) To reset oil life display, press INFORMATION button to display OIL LIFE LEFT. Press and hold RESET button until 100 OIL LIFE LEFT (0.0 OIL LIFE LEFT on some early models) is displayed.

1997-99 CADILLACE ELDORADO (ANALOG CONTROL BUTTONS) & 1997-99 CADILLAC CONCOURS

CHANGE ENGINE OIL Display – CHANGE ENGINE OIL message is displayed in The Driver Information Center (DIC) when oil change is due. To reset display, press the INFO button to display the OIL LIFE LEFT message. Press and hold the INFO RESET button until 100 OIL LIFE LEFT is displayed.

1998-99 CADILLAC SEVILLE

CHANGE ENGINE OIL Display – Drive Information Center (DIC) can display remaining oil life as a percentage estimate of the useful life of oil. CHANGE ENGINE OIL will display when oil change is due. To reset display, press INFO button to display ENGINE OIL LIFE. Press and hold INFO RESET button until 100 ENGINE OIL LIFE is displayed.

1998-99 CADILLAC SEVILLE

CHANGE TRANS FLUID Message – **1)** This message will appear on the Driver Information Center (DIC) when transaxle fluid change is due. To reset display, turn ignition key on with engine off.

2) Press the INFO button until TRANS FLUID LIFE message appears. Press and hold INFO RESET button until display shows "100".

GENERAL INFO.
50

1999 GENERAL INFORMATION
Service Reminder Indicators
1980-99 Domestic Cars & Trucks (Cont.)

GENERAL MOTORS (EXCEPT CADILLAC)

NOTE: Most General Motors 1981-88 vehicles do not use a Service Reminder Indicator (SRI).

1980 MODELS

1) Every 30,000 miles, a reminder flag appears in speedometer face, indicating service of oxygen sensor is necessary. See Fig. 7. Inspect and service oxygen sensor as necessary and reset flag.
2) To reset flag, remove instrument panel trim plate. Remove instrument cluster lens. Using pointed tool, apply light downward pressure on notches of flag until it is reset. An alignment mark will appear in left center of odometer window when flag is fully reset.

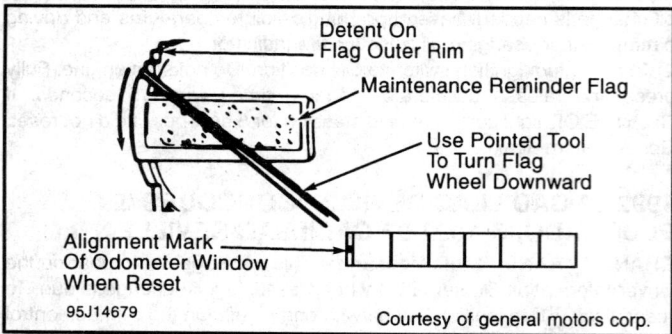

Fig. 7: Resetting Reminder Flag (1980 General Motors)

1988-89 PONTIAC BONNEVILLE & 1987-89 6000 STE

Service Interval Reminder Light – 1) SERVICE REMINDER light is used on models with a Driver Information Center (DIC). After performing necessary services, reset service reminder light.
2) To reset service reminder, push DIC button until desired service item is displayed. Press and hold down the DIC button. With button pressed, the distance display will decrease in increments of 500 miles. Release button when desired distance is displayed on the DIC.

1989-93 OLDSMOBILE TORONADO & TROFEO

Vehicles With Information Center Display – 1) OIL LIFE INDEX is one of 4 engine data displays used on models with Information Center display. It will display remaining oil life as estimated percentage of the useful life of oil. It will show 100 percent when the system is reset. After changing oil, reset oil life display.
2) To reset the display, press ENG DATA button (1989-90) or OPTIONS button (1991-93) until oil life index is displayed. Then, press and hold in ENG DATA and GAGE buttons (1989) or RESET/ENTER button (1990-93) for at least 5 seconds. This will reset remaining oil life to 100 percent.
Vehicles With Visual Information Center (VIC) – 1) OIL LIFE is one of the displays used on models with a VIC. It will display data regarding previous oil change. A bar graph display shows full when oil is changed. Bar graph will go down as vehicle is driven and oil ages. When bar graph reaches CHANGE OIL mark, oil should be changed. After changing oil, reset oil life display.
2) To reset the display, press INFO hard key and then OIL LIFE soft key to display oil life index. Press RESET soft key. A reset confirmation page will appear and ask if oil has been changed. Press YES soft key to reset bar graph, and update last oil change date and mileage information.

1990-91 CHEVROLET CORVETTE

Engine Oil Life Monitor – 1) Engine oil life monitor calculates engine oil temperature and RPM. It indicates when the oil is nearly worn out. A CHANGE OIL light on left side of instrument cluster is illuminated when it is time to change oil.

2) To reset oil life monitor, turn ignition on. Depress ENG MET button on trip monitor and release. Within 5 seconds, depress and release ENG MET button again. Within 5 seconds, depress and hold the RANGE button on trip monitor. The CHANGE OIL light should flash.
3) Hold the RANGE button depressed until the CHANGE OIL light stops flashing and goes out. When the light goes out, the engine oil life monitor is reset. This should take about 10 seconds. If the light does not reset, turn the ignition off and repeat the procedure.

1990-91 OLDSMOBILE CUTLASS CALAIS, CUTLASS SUPREME, CUTLASS CIERA, CUTLASS CRUISER, EIGHTY EIGHT, NINETY EIGHT & TOURING SEDAN

Engine Data Display – 1) An oil change reminder displays estimated percentage of the remaining useful life of the oil. When vehicle is started, a tone will sound and approximate distance to next oil change will be displayed.
2) When remaining oil life is 10 percent or less, the system will calculate distance to next oil change. When the oil life is 0 percent, the display will show CHANGE OIL NOW. After changing oil, reset oil life display.
3) To reset the display, press and hold in OIL button to select the oil life display. Then, press and hold in RESET and OIL buttons for at least 5 seconds. This will reset oil life display to 100 percent.

1990-91 PONTIAC BONNEVILLE

Service Interval Reminder Light – 1) SERVICE REMINDER light is used on models with a Driver Information Center (DIC). After performing necessary services, reset service reminder light.
2) To reset service reminder, push DIC button until service item preceding desired service item is displayed. Press and hold down the DIC button. This will advance display to desired service item and, with button pressed, the distance between service intervals will decrease in increments of 500 miles.
3) Release button when desired distance is displayed on the DIC. If the SERVICE REMINDER remains on after resetting, drive vehicle. Light should go out within 10 miles of driving.

1991-93 BUICK PARK AVENUE

CHANGE OIL SOON Light – 1) CHANGE OIL SOON light will come on when engine oil has broken down enough to require changing. After changing oil, reset oil life display.
2) To reset light, locate reset button hole under passenger side of dash. Use a pencil or similar object to push and hold button (inside hole) for 5 seconds. The CHANGE OIL SOON light will flash 4 times to indicate light has been reset.

1992-93 OLDSMOBILE EIGHTY EIGHT & NINETY EIGHT

Engine Data Display – 1) Oil change reminder display is similar to 1990-91 models, but reset procedures are different. After changing oil, reset oil life display.
2) To reset the display, press and release the TEST button. Press and release the OIL button. Press and hold the RESET button for at least 7 seconds. This will reset oil life display to 100 percent.

1992-96 CHEVROLET CORVETTE

Engine Oil Life Monitor – 1) The CHANGE OIL light, located on left side of instrument cluster is illuminated when its time to change oil. When engine oil is changed, reset CHANGE OIL indicator even if indicator did not illuminate. This ensures indicator accuracy for next oil change.
2) To reset oil life monitor, turn ignition on. Ensure DLC terminal No. 12 is not grounded. Press ENG MET button, located on the trip monitor, and release. Within 5 seconds, press and release ENG MET button again. Within another 5 seconds, press and hold the GAUGES button located on the trip monitor.

3) CHANGE OIL light will begin flashing. Hold GAUGES button pressed until CHANGE OIL light goes out. When light goes out, engine oil life monitor is reset. This should take about 10 seconds. If light does not reset, turn ignition off and repeat procedure.

1994-96 BUICK PARK AVENUE & 1996-98 BUICK LESABRE

CHANGE OIL SOON Light – 1) CHANGE OIL SOON light will come on when engine oil has broken down enough to require changing. After changing oil, reset oil life display.

2) To reset light, turn ignition on. Open glove box to access oil reset button. Press and hold oil reset button in glove box for at least 5 seconds, but not longer than 60 seconds. The CHANGE OIL SOON light will flash 4 times to indicate light has been reset.

1994 BUICK ROADMASTER, CHEVROLET CAPRICE & IMPALA SS

Engine Oil Life Monitor – 1) Engine oil life monitor calculates engine oil temperature and RPM. It indicates when the engine oil is nearly worn out. A CHANGE OIL light on the instrument cluster is illuminated when it is time to change the engine oil.

2) To reset CHANGE OIL light, press reset switch located behind fuse block access door.

1995-96 BUICK ROADMASTER, CHEVROLET CAPRICE & IMPALA SS

Engine Oil Life Monitor – 1) Engine oil life monitor calculates engine oil temperature and RPM. It indicates when the engine oil is nearly worn out. A CHANGE OIL light on the instrument cluster is illuminated when it is time to change the engine oil.

2) To reset oil life monitor and turn off CHANGE OIL light, turn ignition switch to ON position with engine off. Depress accelerator pedal to wide open throttle 3 times within 5 seconds. This throttle signal will inform the PCM to reset the oil life monitor and turn off the light. If light does not turn off, turn ignition off and repeat procedure.

1995-99 OLDSMOBILE AURORA

CHANGE OIL NOW or CHANGE TRNS FLUID NOW Display – 1) The Drive Information Center (DIC) displays estimated percentage of the remaining useful life of engine oil transaxle fluid. When remaining oil or fluid life is 0 percent, the display will show CHANGE OIL NOW or CHANGE TRNS FLUID NOW. After changing oil or transaxle fluid, reset oil life display.

2) To reset the display, turn ignition on with engine off. Press ENG button to select the OIL LIFE or TRNS FLUID LIFE percentage display. Then, press and hold in RESET for at least 5 seconds.

3) The word RESET will appear. Then, OIL LIFE 100 or TRNS FLUID 100 will be displayed.

1995-97 OLDSMOBILE EIGHTY EIGHT & NINETY EIGHT

Engine Data Display – 1) Oil change reminder display is similar to 1990-91 models, but reset procedures are different. After changing oil, reset oil life display.

2) To reset the display, press and release RESET button on Driver Information Center (DIC). Press SEL button (with down arrow) to select OIL. Press SEL button (with left and right arrows) to display oil life. Press and hold RESET button for about 5 seconds. A reset message will display, then oil life will display 100 percent.

1997-99 BUICK LESABRE

CHANGE OIL SOON Light – 1) CHANGE OIL SOON light will come on when engine oil has broken down enough to require changing. After changing oil, reset oil life display.

2) To reset light, turn ignition on. Open glove box to access oil reset button. Press and hold oil reset button in glove box for at least 5

seconds, but not longer than 60 seconds. The CHANGE OIL SOON light will flash 4 times to indicate light has been reset.

1997-99 BUICK PARK AVENUE

OIL LIFE INDEX CHANGE OIL Light – 1) To display this light press the GAUGE INFO or GAGES button on the Driver Information Center (DIC). When oil life index is less than 10 percent, display will show OIL LIFE INDEX CHANGE OIL. After changing oil, reset system.

2) To reset light, display OIL LIFE INDEX. Hold RESET button for more than 5 seconds. After reset, oil life will change to 100 percent.

1997-99 CHEVROLET CORVETTE

Engine Oil Life Monitor – 1) The CHANGE OIL light is illuminated when its time to change engine oil, usually between 3000 and 10,000 miles since last oil change. The Driver Information Center (DIC) will display CHANGE OIL NOW when an oil change is due.

2) To reset oil life monitor, turn ignition to RUN position. Press TRIP button, located on DIC switch to display OIL LIFE. Message will display percentage of oil life remaining.

3) Press and hold RESET button on DIC for at least 2 seconds. Word RESET will appear, then OIL LIFE 99. Turn ignition off.

1997-99 BUICK CENTURY & REGAL, CHEVROLET LUMINA & MONTE CARLO, OLDSMOBILE INTRIGUE & PONTIAC GRAND PRIX

CHANGE OIL SOON or CHANGE OIL Light – 1) Engine oil life monitor calculates engine oil temperature and RPM. It indicates when the engine oil is nearly worn out. A CHANGE OIL or CHANGE OIL SOON light on the instrument cluster is illuminated when it is time to change the engine oil.

2) To reset oil life monitor and turn off CHANGE OIL or CHANGE OIL SOON light, turn ignition switch to RUN position with engine off. Depress accelerator pedal to wide open throttle 3 times within 5 seconds. If the CHANGE OIL or CHANGE OIL SOON light flashes 2 times, the system is reset. If light comes on and stays on for 5 seconds, it did not reset. Repeat reset procedure again.

3) If vehicle is equipped with a Driver Information Center (DIC), system may be reset by pressing the DIC RESET button for 5 seconds while viewing the oil life display on the DIC.

1997 PONTIAC GRAND PRIX

CHECK TIRE PRESSURE Display – 1) If the Electronic Brake Control Module detects a tire with low pressure, it signals the Drive Information Center (DIC) to turn on the CHECK TIRE PRESSURE light. To reset the display, turn ignition on with engine off.

2) Press and hold calibrate tire pressure button for about 3 seconds. Button is under lower left part of instrument panel, to right of steering column. CHECK TIRE PRESSURE light will flash 3 times and go out.

JEEP

1988-90 CHEROKEE, COMANCHE, WAGONEER & WRANGLER

Service Reminder Indicator (SRI) – 1) Vehicles are equipped with SRI on instrument cluster. This light will come on one time at 82,500 miles to alert driver that emission service is required. At this time, oxygen sensor and PCV valve must be replaced and all other emission components should be inspected and serviced or replaced as necessary.

2) SRI timer is located under dash, near accelerator pedal or to right of steering column. Timer cannot be reset. To turn off light, timer must be replaced or disconnected. Since timer and sensor are interdependent, if timer should fail prematurely, oxygen sensor should be replaced at same time to preserve correct replacement interval.

3) To replace timer on Cherokee, Comanche and Wagoneer models, remove cruise control module (if equipped). Remove timer mounting

1999 GENERAL INFORMATION
Service Reminder Indicators
1980-99 Domestic Cars & Trucks (Cont.)

screws. Disconnect electrical connector. On Wrangler models, remove timer mounting screws. Disconnect electrical connector. To install, reverse removal procedure.

1991-92 CHEROKEE, COMANCHE & WRANGLER

Service Reminder Indicator (SRI) – Vehicles are equipped with SRI on instrument cluster. This light will come on one time at 82,500 miles to alert driver that emission service is required. At this time, oxygen sensor must be replaced and all other emission components should be inspected and serviced or replaced as necessary. Chrysler's Diagnostic Readout Box (DRB-II) tester is required to reset the SRI.

Reset Procedure – Using DRB-II tester, access SELECT SYSTEMS. Select appropriate engine. Select with or without A/C. Select FUEL & IGNITION. Select ADJUSTMENTS. Select RESET SRI LIGHT. Reset SRI light. When DRB-II is finished resetting light, DRB-II display will read SRI LIGHT IS RESET.

1993 CHEROKEE

Service Reminder Indicator (SRI) – Vehicles are equipped with SRI on instrument cluster. This light will come on one time at 82,500 miles to alert driver that emission service is required. At this time, oxygen sensor must be replaced and all other emission components should be inspected and serviced or replaced as necessary. Chrysler's Diagnostic Readout Box (DRB-II) tester is required to reset the SRI.

Reset Procedure – Using DRB-II tester, access SELECT SYSTEMS. Select appropriate engine. Select with or without A/C. Select FUEL & IGNITION. Select ADJUSTMENTS. Select RESET SRI LIGHT. Reset SRI light. When DRB-II is finished resetting light, DRB-II display will read SRI LIGHT IS RESET.

1994-98 GRAND CHEROKEE

Service Reminder Indicator (SRI) – Vehicle is equipped with a PERFORM SERVICE SRI. PERFORM SERVICE message is displayed when "miles/kms to service" is zero, indicating that regular service and maintenance is due. To reset counter, turn ignition on, press SELECT button momentarily, then press and hold SET button for at least 2 seconds.

CHARGING SYSTEM

CHARGING SYSTEM TROUBLE SHOOTING

Problem & Possible Cause	Action
NO START CONDITION	
Dead Or Weak Battery	Charge/Replace Battery
Bad Cable Connections	Clean/Replace Cables
Ignition Switch/Circuit Fault	Check Switch/Circuit
CHARGING SYSTEM WARNING LIGHT STAYS ON	
Loose/Worn Alternator Belt	Tighten/Replace Belt
Loose Alternator Connections	Check/Repair Connections
Warning Light Wiring	Check/Repair Wiring
Faulty Stator/Diodes	Test/Repair Alternator
Faulty Voltage Regulator	Test/Repair Regulator
WARNING LIGHT OFF WITH IGNITION SWITCH ON	
Blown Fuse	Check/Replace Fuse
Faulty Alternator	Test Alternator
Bad Warning Light Bulb	Test/Replace Bulb
WARNING LIGHT ON WITH IGNITION SWITCH OFF	
Alternator Wiring Short	Check/Repair Wiring
Faulty Rectifier Bridge	Test/Repair Alternator
AMMETER INDICATES DISCHARGE	
Loose/Worn Alternator Belt	Tighten/Replace Belt
Loose Alternator Connections	Check/Repair Connections
Faulty Ammeter	Test/Replace Ammeter
NOISY GENERATOR	
Loose Drive Pulley	Check/Tighten Pulley Nut
Loose Mounting Bolts	Tighten Mounting Bolts
Worn/Dirty Alternator Bearings	Clean/Replace Alternator Bearings
Faulty Diodes/Stator	Replace Diodes/Stator
BATTERY WON'T STAY CHARGED	
Defective Battery	Replace Battery
Accessories Left ON	Ensure Accessories Are OFF
Loose/Worn Alternator Belt	Tighten/Replace Belt
Loose Alternator Connections	Check/Repair Connections
Defective Alternator	Test/Repair Alternator
Short In System	Check/Repair Short
BATTERY OVERCHARGED	
Defective Battery	Replace Battery
Defective Alternator	Test/Repair Alternator
Defective Regulator	Test/Repair Regulator

STARTING SYSTEM

STARTING SYSTEM TROUBLE SHOOTING

Problem & Possible Cause	Action
STARTER FAILS TO OPERATE	
Dead Or Weak Battery	Charge/Replace Battery
Bad Connections/Wiring	Repair Connections/Wiring
Faulty Ignition Switch	Check Switch Circuit
Faulty Solenoid/Relay	Replace Solenoid/Relay
Faulty Ground	Check/Repair Ground
STARTER FAILS TO OPERATE – LIGHTS DIM	
Dead Or Weak Battery	Charge/Replace Battery
Bad Cable Connections	Check/Repair Connections
Grounded Starter Windings	Repair/Replace Starter
Faulty Bearing/Bushing	Repair/Replace Starter
Faulty Ground	Check/Repair Ground
Corroded Terminals	Clean/Replace Terminals
STARTER TURNS – ENGINE DOES NOT	
Faulty Starter Drive	Replace Starter Drive
Broken Drive Housing	Replace Starter
Faulty Pinion Shaft	Repair/Replace Shaft
Faulty Flywheel	Replace Flywheel

STARTING SYSTEM TROUBLE SHOOTING (Cont.)

Problem & Possible Cause	Action
STARTER DOES NOT CRANK ENGINE	
Faulty Starter Drive	Replace Starter
Broken Drive Housing	Replace Starter
Missing Flywheel Teeth	Replace Flywheel
Faulty Ground	Check/Repair Ground
Frozen Engine	Check Engine
Hydrostatically-Locked Engine	Check Cylinders
STARTER ROTATES ENGINE SLOWLY	
Dead Or Weak Battery	Charge/Replace Battery
Bad Connections/Wiring	Repair Connections/Wiring
Grounded Starter Windings	Repair/Replace Starter
Faulty Starter Bearings	Repair/Replace Starter
Faulty Ground	Check/Repair Ground
Engine Overheated	Check Cooling System
Broken Drive Housing	Repair/Replace Starter
Weak Starter Solenoid	Replace Starter Solenoid
STARTER DRIVE DOES NOT ENGAGE	
Bad Solenoid Contacts	Replace Solenoid
Bad Solenoid Ground	Test Solenoid Ground
SOLENOID/RELAY DOES NOT CLOSE	
Faulty Battery	Replace Battery
Bad Connections/Wiring	Repair Connections/Wiring
Faulty Safety Switch	Replace Safety Switch
Faulty Solenoid/Relay	Replace Solenoid/Relay
STARTER DRIVE WILL NOT DISENGAGE	
Loose Starter Bolts	Tighten Starter Bolts
Worn Drive End Bushing	Replace Drive End Bushing
Missing Flywheel Teeth	Check Flywheel/Drive
Faulty Ignition Switch	Replace Ignition Switch
SOLENOID CLICKS	
Dead Or Weak Battery	Charge/Replace Battery
Bad Solenoid Contacts	Replace Solenoid
Bad Connections/Wiring	Repair Connections/Wiring
Faulty Solenoid	Replace Solenoid
HIGH CURRENT DRAW	
Dragging Armature	Repair/Replace Starter
Shorted Armature Windings	Repair/Replace Starter
LOW CURRENT DRAW	
Worn Starter Brushes	Repair/Replace Starter
Weak Brush Springs	Replace Brush Springs
Faulty Engine Ground	Clean/Repair Ground Cable
High Resistance In Positive Battery Cable	Repair/Replace Cable
STARTER WHINES DURING CRANKING	
Starter Alignment	Check Starter Alignment
Too Much Distance Between Starter Drive & Flywheel	Ensure Flywheel is Okay
	Ensure Starter is Correct
STARTER WHINES AFTER STARTING	
Starter Alignment	Check Starter Alignment
Too Little Distance Between Starter Drive & Flywheel	Ensure Flywheel is Okay
	Ensure Starter is Correct

GENERAL INFORMATION
Commonly Used Abbreviations

"A"

A – Amperes
ABS – Anti-Lock Brakes
ABRS – Air Bag Restraint System
AC – Alternating Current
A/C – Air Conditioning
ACCS – A/C Cycling Switch
ACCUM – Accumulator
ACCY – Accessory
ACT – Air Charge Temperature Sensor
ADJ – Adjust or Adjustable
ADV – Advance
AFS – Airflow Sensor
AI – Air Injection
AIR or A.I.R. – Air Injection Reactor
AIS – Air Injection System
Alt. – Alternator or Altitude
Amp./amp/amps – Ampere
ASCS – Air Suction Control Solenoid
ASD – Auto Shutdown
ASDM – Air Bag System Diagnostic
Module
ASV – Air Suction Valve
A/T – Automatic Transmission/Transaxle
ATC – Automatic Temperature Control
ATDC – After Top Dead Center
ATF – Automatic Transmission Fluid
ATS – Air Temperature Sensor
Aux. – Auxiliary
Avg. – Average
AXOD – Automatic Transaxle Overdrive
(Ford Models Only)

"B"

BAC – By-Pass Air Control
BAP – Barometric Absolute Pressure
Sensor
BARO – Barometric
Batt. – Battery
Bbl. – Barrel (Example: 4-Bbl.)
BCM – Body Control Module
BHP – Brake Horsepower
BMAP – Barometric and Manifold
Absolute Pressure Sensor
BOO – Brake On-Off Switch
B/P – Backpressure
BPS – Barometric Pressure Sensor
BPT – Backpressure Transducer
BTDC – Before Top Dead Center
BTU – British Thermal Unit
BVSV – Bimetallic Vacuum Switching
Valve

"C"

° C – Celsius (Degrees)
Calif. – California
CANP – Canister Purge
CARB – California Air Resources Board
CAT – Catalytic Converter
CB – Circuit Breaker
CBD – Closed Bowl Distributor
cc – cubic centimeter
CCC – Computer Command Control
CCD – Computer Controlled Dwell
CCOT – Cycling Clutch Orifice Tube
CCW – Counterclockwise
CDI – Capacitor Discharge Ignition
CEC – Computerized Engine Control
CID – Cubic Inch Displacement
cm – Centimeter
CMP – Camshaft Position Sensor
CO – Carbon Monoxide
CO$_2$ – Carbon Dioxide
Cont. – Continued
CONV – Convertible
CP – Canister Purge
CKP – Crankshaft Position Sensor
CTS – Coolant Temperature Sensor
Cu. In. – Cubic Inch
CVC – Constant Vacuum Control
CV – Check Valve or Constant Velocity
CW – Clockwise
CYL or Cyl. – Cylinder
C^{3}I – Computer Controlled Coil Ignition
C^4 – Computer Controlled Catalytic
Converter

"D"

"D" – Drive
DC – Direct Current Or Discharge
DDD – Dual Diaphragm Distributor
Def. – Defrost
Defog. – Defogger
DERM – Diagnostic Energy Reserve
Module
DFI – Digital Fuel Injection
Diag. – Diagnostic
DTC – Diagnostic Trouble Code
DIC – Driver Information Center
DIS – Distributorless Ignition System
DIST – Distribution
DLC – Data Link Connector
DOHC – Double Overhead Cam
DOT – Department of Transportation
DRB-II – Diagnostic Readout Box
DVOM – Digital Volt-Ohmmeter

"E"

EACV – Electric Air Control Valve
EBCM – Electronic Brake Control Module
ECM – Engine Control Module
ECT – Engine Coolant Temperature
Sensor
EDIS – Electronic Distributorless Ignition
System
EEC – Electronic Engine Control
EECS – Evaporative Emission Control
System
EEPROM – Electronically Erasable
PROM
EFE – Early Fuel Evaporation
EGO – Exhaust Gas Oxygen Sensor
EGR – Exhaust Gas Recirculation
ESA – Electronic Spark Advance
ESC – Electronic Spark Control
EST – Electronic Spark Timing
EVAP – Fuel Evaporative System
EVIC – Electronic Vehicle Information
Center
EVP – EGR Valve Position Sensor
Exc. – Except

"F"

° F – Fahrenheit (Degrees)
F/B – Fuse Block
Fed. – Federal
FI – Fuel Injection
FIPL – Fuel Injector Pump Lever
FPR-VSV – Fuel Pressure Regulator
Vacuum Switching Valve
Ft. Lbs. – Foot Pounds
FWD – Front Wheel Drive

"G"

g – grams
Gals. – gallons
GND or GRND – Ground

"H"

HAC – High Altitude Compensation
HC – Hydrocarbons
H/D – Heavy Duty
HO2S – Heated Exhaust Gas Oxygen
Sensor
Hg – Mercury
Hgt. – Height
HLDT – Headlight
HO – High Output
HO2S – Heated Oxygen Sensor
HP – High Performance
HSC – High Swirl Combustion
HSO – High Specific Output
HTR – Heater
Hz – Hertz (Cycles Per Second)

"I"

IAC – Idle Air Control
IACV – Idle Air Control Valve
IAT – Intake Air Temperature
IC – Integrated Circuit
ID – Identification
I.D. – Inside Diameter
Ign. – Ignition
IMRC – Intake Manifold Runner Control
In. – Inches
INCH Lbs. – Inch Pounds
in. Hg – Inches of Mercury
Inj. – Injector
IP – Instrument Panel
ISC – Idle Speed Control
IVSV – Idle Vacuum Switching Valve

"J"

J/B – Junction Block

"K"

KAPWR – Keep Alive Power
k/ohms – kilo-ohms (1000 ohms)
kg – Kilograms (weight)
kg/cm² – Kilograms Per Square
    Centimeter
KM/H – Kilometers Per Hour
KOEO – Key On, Engine Off
KOER – Key On, Engine Running
KS – Knock Sensor
kW – Kilowatt
kV – Kilovolt

"L"

L – Liter
lbs. (Lbs. when used in table) – Pounds
LCD – Liquid Crystal Display
L/D – Light Duty
LED – Light Emitting Diode
LH – Left Hand

"M"

mA – Milliamps
MA or MAF – Mass Airflow
MAFS – Mass Airflow Sensor
MAP – Manifold Absolute Pressure
MAT – Manifold Air Temperature
Mem. – Memory
MEM-CAL – Memory Calibration Chip
mfd. – Microfarads
MFI – Multiport Fuel Injection
MIL – Malfunction Indicator Light
MPI – Multi-Point (Fuel) Injection
mm – Millimeters
MPH – Miles Per Hour
mV – Millivolts

"N"

NA – Not Available
NGS – New Generation Star
N.m – Newton Meter
No. – Number
Nos. – Numbers
NOx – Oxides of Nitrogen

"O"

O_2 – Oxygen
OBD – On-Board Diagnostics
OC – Oxidation Catalyst
OD – Overdrive
O.D. – Outside Diameter
OHC – Overhead Camshaft
O/S – Oversize
oz. – Ounce
ozs. – Ounces

"P"

"P" – Park
P/C – Printed Circuit
PCM – Powertrain Control Module
PCS – Purge Control Solenoid
PC-SOL – Purge Control Solenoid
PCV – Positive Crankcase Ventilation
PFI – Port Fuel Injection
PGM-FI – Programmed Fuel Injection
PID – Parameter Identification
PIP – Profile Ignition Pick-up
PNP – Park Neutral Position Switch
P/N – Park/Neutral
PRNDL – Park Reverse Neutral Drive
    Low
PROM – Programmable Read-Only
    Memory
psi – Pounds Per Square Inch
P/S – Power Steering
PSPS – Power Steering Pressure Switch
PTC – Positive Temperature Coefficient
PTO – Power Take-Off
Pts. – Pints
Pwr. – Power

"Q"

Qts. – Quarts

"R"

RABS – Rear Anti-Lock Brake System
RECIRC – Recirculation
RH – Right Hand
RPM – Revolutions Per Minute
RWAL – Rear Wheel Anti-Lock Brake
RWD – Rear Wheel Drive

"S"

SBC – Single Bed Converter
SBEC – Single Board Engine Controller
SES – Service Engine Soon
SFI – Sequential (Port) Fuel Injection
SIL – Shift Indicator Light
SIR – Supplemental Inflatable Restraint
SOHC – Single Overhead Cam
SOL or Sol. – Solenoid
SPFI – Sequential Port Fuel Injection
SPK – Spark Control
SPOUT – Spark Output
SRI – Service Reminder Indicator
SRS – Supplemental Restraint System
    (Air Bag)
STAR – Self-Test Automatic Readout
STO – Self-Test Output
SUB-O_2 – Sub Oxygen Sensor
Sw. – Switch
Sys. – System

"T"

TAB – Thermactor Air By-Pass
TAD – Thermactor Air Diverter
TBI – Throttle Body Injection
TCC – Torque Converter Clutch
TDC – Top Dead Center
Temp. – Temperature
TFI – Thick Film Ignition
THERMAC – Thermostatic Air Cleaner
TPS – Throttle Position Sensor/Switch
TS – Temperature Sensor
TV – Thermovalve
TWC – Three-Way Catalyst

"V"

V – Valve
Vac. – Vacuum
VAF – Vane Airflow
VAPS – Variable Assist Power Steering
VCC – Viscous Converter Clutch
VCRM – Variable Control Relay Module
VIN – Vehicle Identification Number
VM – Vacuum Modulator
Volt. – Voltage
VOM – Volt-Ohmmeter (Analog)
VRV – Vacuum Regulator Valve
VSS – Vehicle Speed Sensor
VSV – Vacuum Switching Valve

"W"

W/ – With
W/O – Without
WAC – Wide Open Throttle A/C Switch
WOT – Wide Open Throttle

GENERAL INFORMATION
English-Metric Conversion Chart

ENGLISH-METRIC CONVERSION CHART

Metric conversions are making life more difficult for the mechanic. In addition to increasing the number of tools required, metric-dimensioned nuts and bolts are used alongside English components in many new vehicles. The mechanic has to decide which tool to use, slowing down the job. The tool problem can be solved by trial and error, but some metric conversions aren't so simple.

Converting temperature, lengths or volumes requires a calculator and conversion charts, or else a very nimble mind. Conversion charts are only part of the answer though, because they don't help you "think" metric, or "visualize" what you are converting. The following examples are intended to help you "see" metric sizes:

LENGTH
Meters are the standard unit of length in the metric system. The smaller units are 10ths (decimeter), 100ths (centimeter), and 1000ths (millimeter) of a meter. These common examples might help you to visualize the metric units:
• A meter is slightly longer than a yard (about 40 inches).
• An aspirin tablet is about one centimeter across (.4 inches).
• A millimeter is about the thickness of a dime.

VOLUME
Cubic meters and centimeters are used to measure volume, just as we normally think of cubic feet and inches. Liquid volume measurements include the liter and milliliter, like the English quarts or ounces.
• One teaspoon is about 4 cubic centimeters.
• A liter is about one quart.
• A liter is about 61 cubic inches.

WEIGHT
The metric weight system is based on the gram, with the most common unit being the kilogram (1000 grams). Our comparable units are ounces and pounds.
• A kilogram is about 2.2 pounds.
• An ounce is about 28 grams.

TORQUE
Torque is somewhat complicated. The term describes the amount of effort exerted to turn something. A chosen unit of weight or force is applied to a lever of standard length. The resulting leverage is called torque. In our standard system, we use the weight of one pound applied to a lever a foot long, resulting in the unit called a foot-pound. A smaller unit is the inch-pound (the lever is one inch long). Metric units include the meter kilogram (lever one meter long with a kilogram of weight applied) and the Newton-meter (lever one meter long with

force of one Newton applied). Some conversions are:
• A meter kilogram is about 7.2 foot pounds.
• A foot pound is about 1.4 Newton-meters.
• A centimeter kilogram (cmkg) is equal to .9 inch pounds.

PRESSURE
Pressure is another complicated measurement. Pressure is described as a force or weight applied to a given area. Our common unit is pounds per square inch. Metric units can be expressed in several ways. One is the kilogram per square centimeter (kg/cm²). Another unit of pressure is the Pascal (force of one Newton on an area of one square meter), which equals about 4 ounces on a square yard. Since this is a very small amount of pressure, we usually see the kilo-Pascal, or kPa (1000 Pascals). Another common automotive term for pressure is the bar (used by German manufacturers), which equals 10 Pascals. Thoroughly confused? Try the examples below:
• Atmospheric pressure at sea level is about 14.7 psi.
• Atmospheric pressure at sea level is about 1 bar.
• Atmospheric pressure at sea level is about 1 kg/cm².
• One pound per square inch is about 7 kPa.

CONVERSION FACTORS

To Convert	To	Multiply By
LENGTH		
Millimeters	Inches	.03937
Inches	Millimeters	25.4
Meters	Feet	3.28084
Feet	Meters	.3048
Kilometers	Miles	.62137
Miles	Kilometers	1.60935
AREA		
Square Centimeters	Square Inches	.155
Square Inches	Square Centimeters	6.45159
VOLUME		
Cubic Centimeters	Cubic Inches	.06103
Cubic Inches	Cubic Centimeters	16.38703
Liters	Cubic Inches	61.025
Cubic Inches	Liters	.01639
Liters	Quarts	1.05672
Quarts	Liters	.94633
Liters	Pints	2.11344
Pints	Liters	.47317
Liters	Ounces	33.81497
Ounces	Liters	.02957
WEIGHT		
Grams	Ounces	.03527
Ounces	Grams	28.34953
Kilograms	Pounds	2.20462
Pounds	Kilograms	.45359
TORQUE		
Centimeter Kilograms	Inch Pounds	.8676
Inch Pounds	Centimeter Kilograms	1.15262
Meter Kilograms	Foot Pounds	7.23301
Foot Pounds	Meter Kilograms	.13826
PRESSURE		
Kilograms/ Sq. Centimeter	Pounds/Sq. Inch	14.22334
Pounds/Sq. Inch	Kilograms/Sq. Centimeter	.07031
Bar	Pounds/Sq. Inch	14.504
Pounds/Sq. Inch	Bar	.06895
Atmosphere	Pounds/Sq. Inch	14.696
Pounds/Sq. Inch	Atmosphere	.06805
TEMPERATURE		
Centigrade Degrees	Fahrenheit Degrees	(C°x⁹/₅) +32
Fahrenheit Degrees	Centigrade Degrees	(F°-32)x⁵/₉

Inches	Decimals	MM
1/64	.016	.397
1/32	.031	.794
3/64	.047	1.191
1/16	.063	1.588
5/64	.078	1.984
3/32	.094	2.381
7/64	.109	2.778
1/8	.125	3.175
9/64	.141	3.572
5/32	.156	3.969
11/64	.172	4.366
3/16	.188	4.763
13/64	.203	5.159
7/32	.219	5.556
15/64	.234	5.953
1/4	.250	6.350
17/64	.266	6.747
9/32	.281	7.144
19/64	.297	7.541
5/16	.313	7.938
21/64	.328	8.334
11/32	.344	8.731
23/64	.359	9.128
3/8	.375	9.525
25/64	.391	9.922
13/32	.406	10.319
27/64	.422	10.716
7/16	.438	11.113
29/64	.453	11.509
15/32	.469	11.906
31/64	.484	12.303
1/2	.500	12.700
33/64	.516	13.097
17/32	.531	13.494
35/64	.547	13.891
9/16	.563	14.288
37/64	.578	14.684
19/32	.594	15.081
39/64	.609	15.478
5/8	.625	15.875

Inches	Decimals	MM
41/64	.641	16.272
21/32	.656	16.669
43/64	.672	17.066
11/16	.687	17.463
45/64	.703	17.859
23/32	.719	18.256
47/64	.734	18.653
3/4	.750	19.050
49/64	.766	19.447
25/32	.781	19.844
51/64	.797	20.241
13/16	.813	20.638
53/64	.828	21.034
27/32	.844	21.431
55/64	.859	21.828
7/8	.875	22.225
57/64	.891	22.622
29/32	.906	23.019
59/64	.922	23.416
15/16	.938	23.813
61/64	.953	24.209
31/32	.969	24.606
63/64	.984	25.003
1	1.000	25.400

WE SUPPORT VOLUNTARY TECHNICIAN CERTIFICATION THROUGH
National Institute for AUTOMOTIVE SERVICE EXCELLENCE

Mitchell Repair Information Company also offers ASE Study Guides for mechanic training. For details on ordering please contact Mitchell at (888) 724-6742.

1999 CHRYSLER CORP.
Contents

1999 CHRYSLER CORP.
Contents (Cont.)

ACCESSORIES & EQUIPMENT (Cont.)

ACCESSORIES & EQUIPMENT (Cont.)

ACCESSORIES & EQUIPMENT (Cont.)

STEERING COLUMN SWITCHES (Cont.)

WIPER/WASHER SYSTEMS

ACCESSORIES & EQUIPMENT (Cont.)

WIPER/WASHER SYSTEMS (Cont.)

DESCRIPTION

Models equipped with V6 engine use a Mitsubishi reduction gear drive starter. Starter consists of a planetary gear drive and permanent magnets for current induction. Planetary gear drive is splined to both the armature shaft and overrunning clutch. Starter torque is transmitted to overrunning clutch pinion through planetary gears, which provide higher rotational speeds.

Models equipped with 4-cylinder engine use a conventional 12-volt, 4-pole brush type direct drive starter.

NOTE: For models not covered in this article, see STARTERS – EXCEPT AVENGER & SEBRING COUPE article.

CAUTION: Starters are extremely sensitive to hammering, shocks and external pressure which could result in damage to magnets.

TROUBLE SHOOTING

NOTE: See TROUBLE SHOOTING article in GENERAL INFORMATION.

ON-VEHICLE TESTING

CAUTION: When battery is disconnected, vehicle computer and memory systems may lose memory data. Driveability problems may exist until computer systems have completed a relearn cycle. See COMPUTER RELEARN PROCEDURES article in GENERAL INFORMATION before disconnecting battery.

CIRCUIT TEST

NOTE: Manufacturer recommends using Diagnostic Readout Box (DRB) to perform the following circuit tests. DRB is grounded through Data Link Connector (DLC), only one volt/ohmmeter test lead is required when using volt/ohmmeter mode option.

NOTE: Transmission Range (TR) sensor may be also known as Park/Neutral Position (PNP) switch or Park/Neutral switch.

A/T – 1) Ensure transmission gear selector is in Park or Neutral. Using scan tool, read TRANSAXLE RANGE SENSOR 1. If scan tool displays ON, go to next step. If scan tool does not display ON, inspect ground circuit. See WIRING DIAGRAMS.

2) Disconnect starter relay and ensure connector is clean and not damaged. *See Fig. 1.* Using scan tool in voltmeter mode, check voltage at starter relay connector terminal No. 2 (Red/Black wire). *See Fig. 2.* If voltage is more than 11.6 volts, go to next step. If voltage is 11.6 volts or less, repair open Red/Black wire.

3) Using scan tool in voltmeter mode, check voltage at starter relay connector terminal No. 3 (Black/Red wire). *See Fig. 2.* Check voltage with ignition switch in START position. If voltage is more than 10 volts, go to next step. If voltage is 10 volts or less, repair open Black/Red wire.

WARNING: Before performing next step, ensure transaxle selector is in Park and parking brake is set. Engine may crank in next step. Keep clear of any moving engine components.

4) Briefly connect a jumper wire between starter relay connector terminals No. 5 (Black/Yellow wire) and No. 2 (Red/Black wire). *See Fig. 2.* If starter cranks, go to step **7)** If starter does not crank and starter solenoid clicks, reinstall starter relay and go to step **6)**. If starter does not crank and starter solenoid does not click, disconnect jumper wire and go to next step.

5) Disconnect starter relay output wire connector from starter solenoid and ensure connector is clean and not damaged. Using an external ohmmeter, check resistance of Black/Yellow wire between solenoid and starter relay connector terminal No. 5. If resistance is less than 5 ohms,

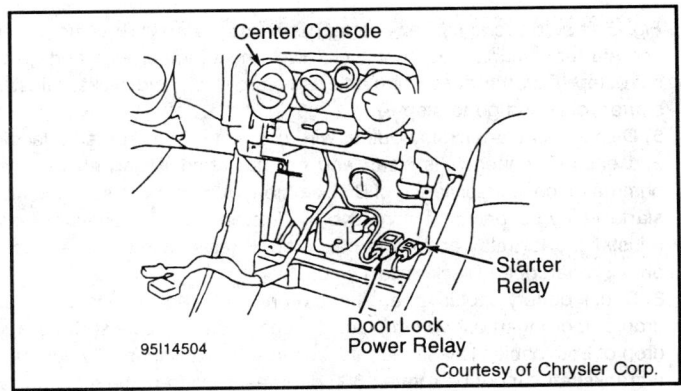

Fig. 1: Locating Starter Relay

reinstall starter relay and go to next step. If resistance is more than 5 ohms, repair open Black/Yellow wire.

6) Check battery cables for a voltage drop. If either cable has a voltage drop of more than 0.2 volt, replace or repair battery cable(s). If voltage drop of both cables is less than 0.2 volt, rotate crankshaft 360 degrees. If crankshaft cannot be rotated 360 degrees, repair engine mechanical problem. If crankshaft can be rotated 360 degrees, replace starter.

7) Using scan tool in ohmmeter mode, check resistance on starter relay connector terminal No. 5 (Black/Yellow wire). *See Fig. 2.* If resistance is less than 5 ohms, replace starter relay. If resistance is more than 5 ohms, repair open Black/Yellow wire.

M/T – 1) Disconnect starter relay and ensure connector is clean and not damaged. *See Fig. 1.* Using scan tool in ohmmeter mode, check resistance on starter relay connector terminal No. 1 (Green/Black wire). *See Fig. 3.* If resistance is less than 5 ohms, go to next step. If resistance is more than 5 ohms, repair open Green/Black wire.

2) Using scan tool in voltmeter mode, check voltage on starter relay connector terminal No. 2 (Black/Red wire). *See Fig. 3.* If voltage is more than 11.6 volts, go to next step. If voltage is 11.6 volts or less, repair open Black/Red wire.

3) Using an external voltmeter, check voltage between ground and starter relay connector terminal No. 3 (Black/Red wire). *See Fig. 3.* Check voltage with ignition switch in START position and clutch pedal depressed. If voltage is more than 10 volts, go to next step. If voltage is 10 volts or less, repair open Black/Red wire and/or ensure clutch switch is adjusted correctly and/or is operating properly.

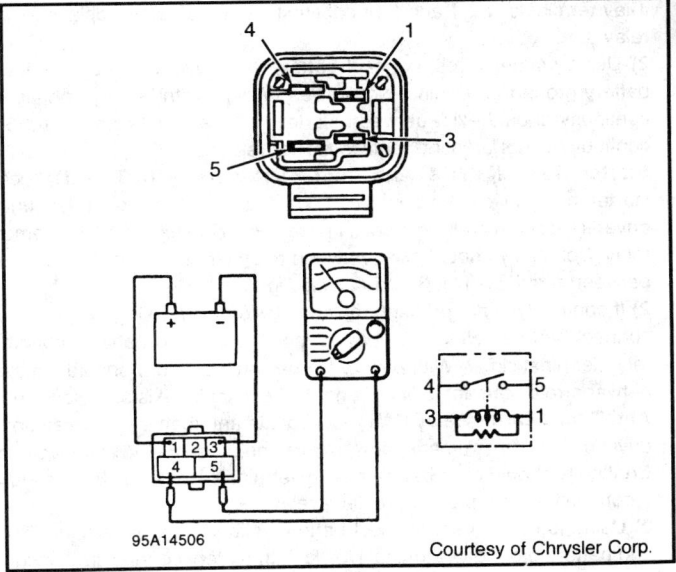

Fig. 2: Testing Starter Relay (A/T)

4) Briefly connect a jumper wire between starter relay connector terminals No. 4 (Black/Yellow wire) and No. 2 (Black/Red wire). *See*

Fig. 3. If starter cranks, replace starter relay. If starter does not crank and starter solenoid does not click, disconnect jumper wire and go to next step. If starter does not crank and starter solenoid clicks, reinstall starter relay and go to step **6**).

5) Disconnect starter relay output wire connector from starter solenoid and ensure connector is clean and not damaged. Using an external ohmmeter, check resistance of Black/Yellow wire between solenoid and starter relay connector terminal No. 4. If resistance is 5 ohms or less, reinstall starter relay and go to next step. If resistance is more than 5 ohms, repair open Black/Yellow wire.

6) Check battery cables for a voltage drop. If either cable has a voltage drop of more than 0.2 volt, replace or repair battery cable(s). If voltage drop of both cables is less than 0.2 volt, rotate crankshaft 360 degrees. If crankshaft cannot be rotated 360 degrees, repair engine mechanical problem. If crankshaft can be rotated 360 degrees, replace starter.

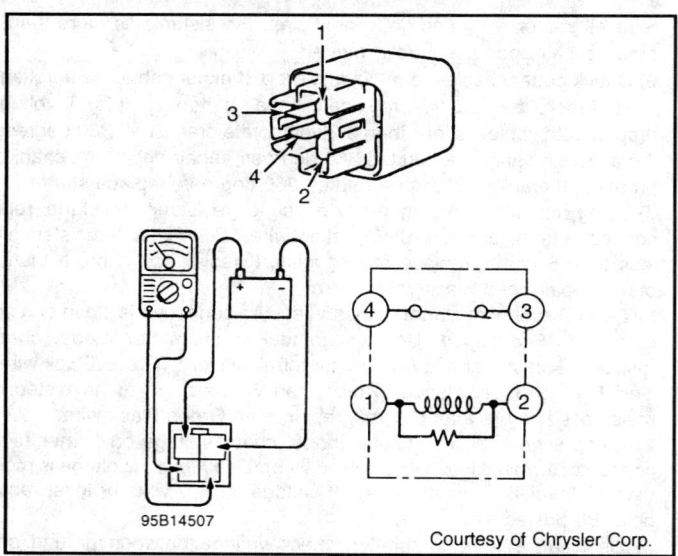

Fig. 3: Testing Starter Relay (M/T) & Anti-Theft Starter Relay (A/T)

RELAY TEST

Starter Relay (A/T) – 1) Locate starter relay in center console. *See Fig. 1.* Remove starter relay. Continuity should exist between starter relay terminals No. 1 and 3. If continuity is not present, replace starter relay.

2) Using jumper wires, connect battery voltage to terminal No. 1 and battery ground to terminal No. 3. *See Fig. 2.* With battery connected, continuity should exist between starter relay terminals No. 4 and 5. If continuity is not present, replace starter relay.

Starter Relay (M/T) & Anti-Theft Starter Relay (A/T) – 1) Locate starter relay in center console. Locate anti-theft starter relay under driver's side of instrument panel, in relay box. *See Figs. 1 and 4.* Remove relay. Continuity should exist between relay terminals No. 1 and 2, and between terminals No. 3 and 4. *See Fig. 3.*

2) If continuity is not present, replace starter relay. Using jumper wires, connect battery voltage to relay terminal No. 1 and battery ground to relay terminal No. 2. With battery connected, continuity should not exist between relay terminals No. 3 and 4. If continuity exists, replace relay.

Anti-Theft Starter Relay (M/T) – 1) Locate anti-theft starter relay under driver's side of instrument panel, in relay box. *See Fig. 4.* Remove relay. Continuity should exist between relay terminals No. 1 and 3. *See Fig. 5.* If continuity is not present, replace relay.

2) Using jumper wires, connect battery voltage to relay terminal No. 3 and battery ground to relay terminal No. 1. With battery connected, continuity should exist between relay terminals No. 2 and 5. If continuity does not exist, replace relay.

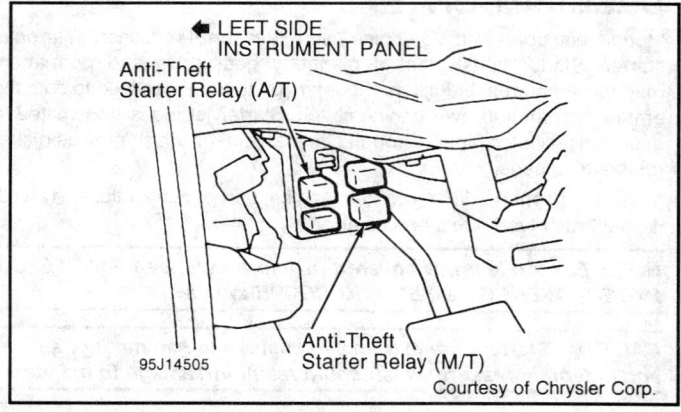

Fig. 4: Locating Anti-Theft Starter Relay

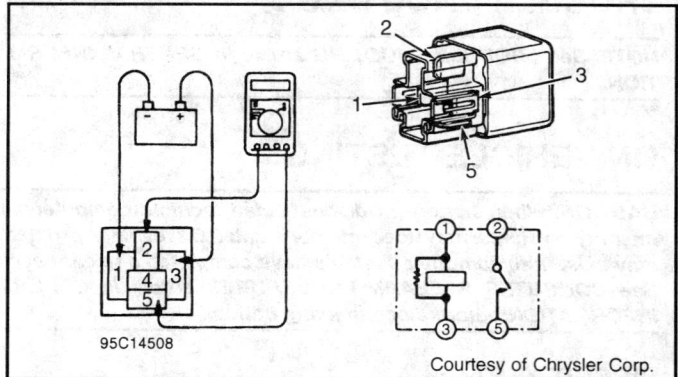

Fig. 5: Testing Anti-Theft Starter Relay (M/T)

IGNITION SWITCH TEST

WARNING: All models are equipped with Supplemental Restraint System (SRS). To avoid injury from accidental air bag deployment, read and carefully follow all WARNINGS and SERVICE PRECAUTIONS. See appropriate AIR BAG RESTRAINT SYSTEMS article in ACCESSORIES & EQUIPMENT. Failure to do so could result in accidental deployment of air bags and possible personal injury.

1) Disable air bag. See appropriate AIR BAG RESTRAINT SYSTEMS article in ACCESSORIES & EQUIPMENT. Remove instrument cluster undercover. Remove steering column covers to locate ignition switch 6-pin connector. Disconnect ignition switch 6-pin connector.

2) Place ignition switch in ON position. Using an ohmmeter, check continuity between switch terminals No. 1 (White wire), No. 2 (Black/White wire), No. 4 (Blue/Black wire) and No. 6 (Blue wire). If continuity is not present, replace ignition switch.

BENCH TESTING

CAUTION: DO NOT clamp starter in a vise by field housing. Damage to magnets could result. Starter may be clamped in vise by mounting flange. DO NOT operate starter for more than 10 seconds. Overheating, caused by excessive starter operation, will damage starter.

NO-LOAD TEST

Direct Drive Type Starter – 1) Clamp starter mounting flange in soft-jawed vise. Connect a carbon pile rheostat in series between battery positive terminal and starter terminal "M". *See Fig. 6.* An ammeter is not necessary.

2) Rotate carbon pile rheostat to maximum resistance position. Connect a cable from battery negative terminal to starter housing. Connect a voltmeter (set to 15-volt scale) between starter housing and starter terminal "M". Adjust carbon pile rheostat until voltmeter indicates approximately 11 volts.

3) Starter should turn smoothly and freely. If starter does not turn smoothly and freely, replace starter.

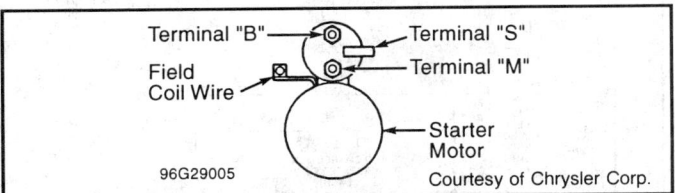

Fig. 6: Identifying Direct Drive Starter Solenoid Terminals (2.0L)

Reduction Gear Drive Starter – 1) Clamp starter mounting flange in soft-jawed vise. Connect an ammeter (set to 100-amp scale) and a carbon pile rheostat in series between battery positive terminal and starter "M" terminal. *See Fig. 7.*

2) Rotate carbon pile rheostat to maximum resistance position. Connect a cable from battery negative terminal to starter housing. Connect voltmeter (set to 15-volt scale) between starter housing and starter terminal "M". *See Fig. 7.*

3) Adjust carbon pile rheostat until voltmeter indicates approximately 11 volts. Starter should turn smoothly and freely. Maximum amperage should be 90 amps. Repair or replace starter if amperage is more than 90 amps.

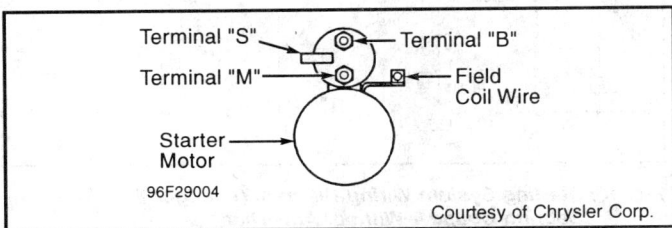

Fig. 7: Identifying Reduction Gear Drive Starter Solenoid Terminals (2.5L)

SOLENOID TESTS

Pull-In Coil Test (Reduction Gear Drive Starter) – 1) Disconnect field coil wire from terminal "M" at starter solenoid. *See Fig. 7.* Connect a jumper wire between positive battery terminal and terminal "S" of solenoid.

2) Connect a second jumper wire to negative battery terminal and touch terminal "M" of starter solenoid for no longer than 10 seconds. *See Fig. 7.* If pinion moves out, solenoid is good. If pinion does not move out, replace starter.

Hold-In Coil Test (Reduction Gear Drive Starter) – 1) Disconnect field coil wire from terminal "M" at starter solenoid. *See Fig. 7.* Connect jumper wire between positive battery terminal and terminal "S" of starter solenoid.

2) Connect a second jumper wire to negative battery terminal and touch starter housing for no longer than 10 seconds. If pinion remains out, hold-in coil is good. If pinion moves in, hold-in circuit is open. Replace starter.

Return Test (Reduction Gear Drive Starter) – 1) Disconnect field coil wire from terminal "M" at starter solenoid. *See Fig. 7.* Connect jumper wire between positive battery terminal and terminal "B" of starter solenoid.

2) Connect a second jumper wire from negative battery terminal and touch starter housing for no longer than 10 seconds. Manually, pull pinion outward and release. Pinion should retract. Replace solenoid if pinion remains extended.

Solenoid Continuity Test (Direct Drive Starter) – Disconnect field coil wire from terminal "M" at starter solenoid. Check for continuity between solenoid terminals "S" and "M". Check for continuity between solenoid terminal "S" and solenoid housing. *See Fig. 6.* If continuity is not present, solenoid has an open and is defective. If solenoid is defective, replace starter.

OVERHAUL

NOTE: Manufacturer does not recommend disassembling and servicing starters. If starter is found defective, a new unit must be installed.

STARTER SPECIFICATIONS

STARTER SPECIFICATIONS – DIRECT DRIVE

Application	Specification
Number Of Teeth	18
Rated Output At 12 Volts	1.95 Kw

STARTER SPECIFICATIONS – REDUCTION GEAR

Application	Specification
Carbon Brush	
Minimum Length	1
Commutator	
Diameter	
Standard	1.158" (29.4 mm)
Minimum	1.118" (28.4 mm)
Mica Undercut Depth	.020" (0.5 mm)
Runout	
Standard	.002" (.05 mm)
Maximum	.004" (.10 mm)
No-Load Test At 11 Volts	
Maximum Amps	90
Minimum RPM	3000
Number Of Teeth	
Non-Turbo	8
Turbo	8
Pinion Gap	.020-.079" (0.5-2.0 mm)
Rated Output At 12 Volts	
Canada	1.4 Kw
US	1.2 Kw

¹ – Replace brushes when worn to limit line.

TORQUE SPECIFICATIONS

TORQUE SPECIFICATIONS

Application	Ft. Lbs. (N.m)
DOHC	
Air Injection Valve	25 (34)
Starter Mounting Bolts	40 (54)
SOHC	
Front Exhaust Pipe	36 (49)
Starter Mounting Bolts	20-25 (27-34)
Starter Mounting Bolts	22 (30)

1999 STARTING & CHARGING SYSTEMS
Starters – Avenger & Sebring Coupe (Cont.)

WIRING DIAGRAMS

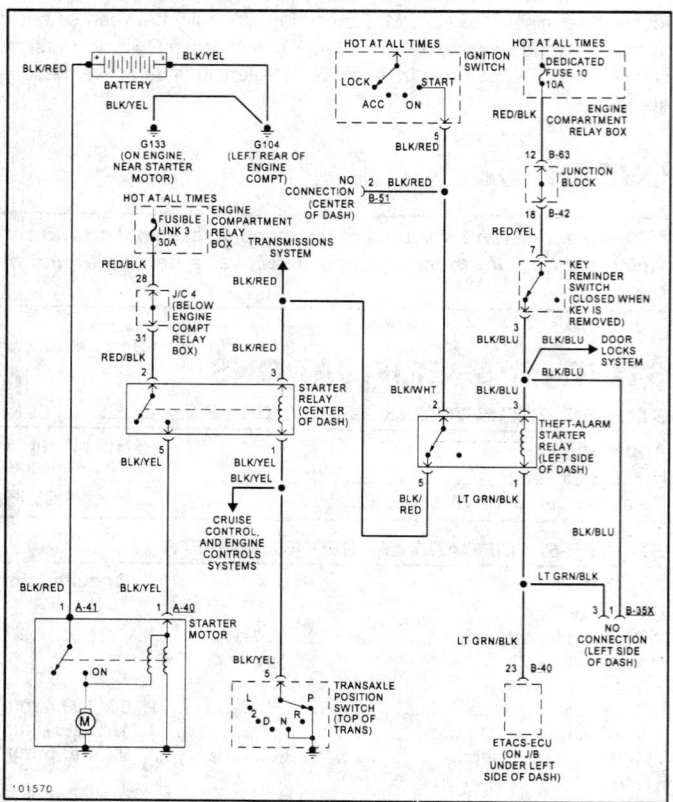

Fig. 8: Starting System Wiring Diagram (Avenger &
Sebring Coupe – A/T With Anti-Theft)

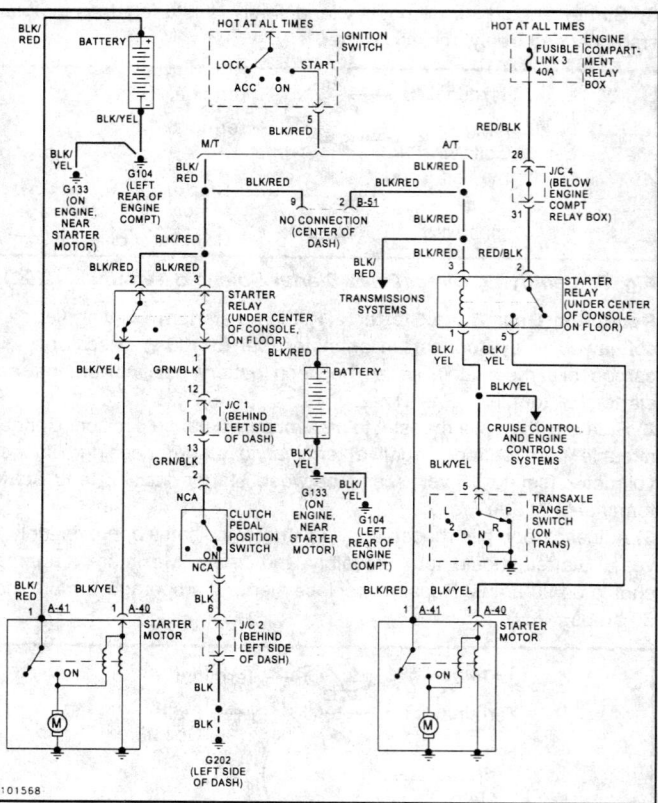

Fig. 10: Starting System Wiring Diagram (Avenger &
Sebring Coupe – Without Anti-Theft)

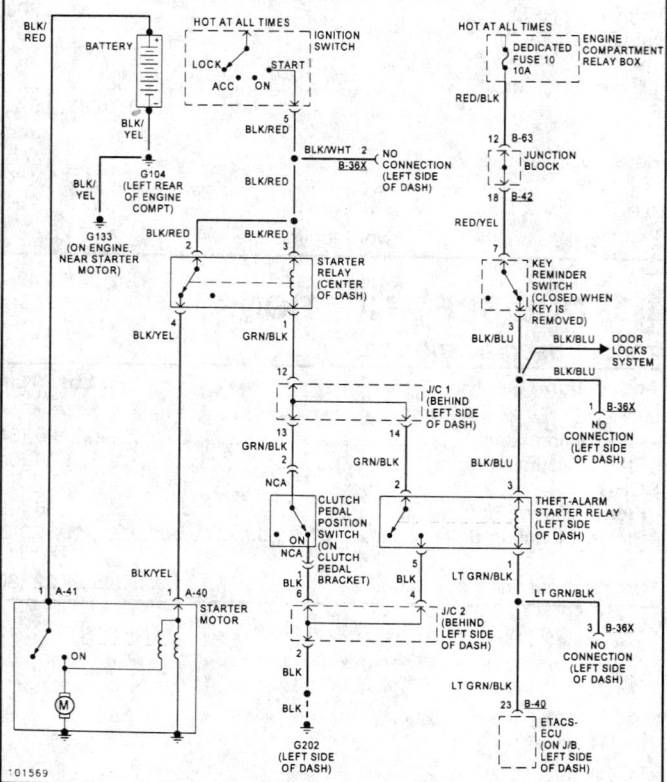

Fig. 9: Starting System Wiring Diagram (Avenger &
Sebring Coupe – M/T With Anti-Theft)

Breeze, Caravan, Cirrus, Concorde, Dakota, Durango, Intrepid, LHS, Neon, Ram Pickup, Ram Van, Ram Wagon, Sebring Convertible, Stratus, Town & Country, Voyager, 300M

NOTE: For models not covered in this article, see STARTERS – AVENGER, SEBRING COUPE & TALON article.

DESCRIPTION

Bosch, Melco and Mitsubishi starters use a planetary gear train that transmits power from starter motor to pinion shaft. Six permanent magnets (Bosch and Melco starters) or 4 permanent magnets (Mitsubishi starters) are used, eliminating potential field wire-to-frame short circuits.

Nippondenso starter is a 4-field, 4-brush, 12-volt motor with a solenoid mounted within the housing. The unit has a 2-to-1 reduction gear set in a die cast aluminum housing. Starter has serviceable gear and clutch assembly only. If starter solenoid fails, entire starter motor must be replaced.

All models use a starter relay in starter circuit between the battery and starter solenoid terminal. Automatic Transmission (A/T) equipped vehicles use a Park/Neutral Position (PNP) switch or a Transmission Range (TR) sensor to provide ground path for the starter relay. Manual Transmission (M/T) equipped vehicles use a clutch pedal position switch to provide battery voltage from ignition switch to the starter relay. See WIRING DIAGRAMS.

STARTER APPLICATIONS – CARS

Model	Type
Breeze & Stratus 2.0L .... Bosch	
Cirrus, Sebring Convertible & Stratus	
2.4L .... Nippondenso	
2.5L .... Melco	
Concorde, Intrepid, LHS & 300M	
2.7L .... Melco	
3.3L & 3.5L .... Nippondenso	
Neon .... Bosch	

STARTER APPLICATIONS – TRUCKS

Model	Type
Caravan, Town & Country, &	
Voyager .... Nippondenso	
Dakota & Durango	
2.5L .... Mitsubishi	
3.9L & 5.2L .... Nippondenso	
Ram Pickup, Ram Van &	
Ram Wagon .... Nippondenso	

TROUBLE SHOOTING

NOTE: See TROUBLE SHOOTING article in GENERAL INFORMATION.

ON-VEHICLE TESTING

CAUTION: When battery is disconnected, vehicle computer and memory systems may lose memory data. Driveability problems may exist until computer systems have completed a relearn cycle. See COMPUTER RELEARN PROCEDURES article in GENERAL INFORMATION before disconnecting battery.

DISABLING/ENABLING IGNITION & FUEL SYSTEMS

WARNING: To prevent engine from starting while performing tests, always disable ignition and fuel systems.

Disabling Ignition & Fuel Systems – Remove Automatic Shutdown Relay (ASD) located in Power Distribution Center (PDC). Refer to PDC cover for proper relay location. PDC is located in engine compartment. On 5.9L diesel engines, also disconnect fuel shutdown solenoid connector. Solenoid is located behind upper intake manifold. See appropriate SYSTEM & COMPONENT TESTING article in ENGINE PERFORMANCE in appropriate MITCHELL® manual.

Enabling Ignition & Fuel Systems – When testing and/or repairs have been completed, verify battery condition. Recharge battery as necessary, after starter tests have been completed. Disconnect all test equipment. Install ASD relay. On 5.9L diesel engines, reconnect fuel shutdown relay connector. On all models, start engine several times to verify malfunction has been corrected.

CRANKING TEST

NOTE: Ensure engine is at normal operating temperature. High viscosity oil, extreme cold temperatures, or tight engine will increase amperage draw.

1) Using a battery load tester, connect positive and negative leads to battery. Connect inductive ammeter pick-up to positive battery cable. Disable ignition and fuel systems. See DISABLING/ENABLING IGNITION & FUEL SYSTEMS.

2) Ensure all lights and accessories are off. Place A/T in Park position or M/T in Neutral position. Apply parking brake. Crank engine and observe voltmeter reading. If voltage is more than 9.6 volts and cranking amperage draw is more than specified amps, proceed to CIRCUIT RESISTANCE TESTS. See STARTER SPECIFICATIONS – CARS or STARTER SPECIFICATIONS – TRUCKS.

3) If voltage is 12.5 volts or more and cranking amperage draw is less than specified, check starter circuit components in the following order: starter solenoid, starter relay, starter relay circuit, park/neutral position switch or transmission range sensor (A/T), clutch pedal position switch (M/T), ignition switch, wiring harness and connections.

CIRCUIT RESISTANCE TESTS

NOTE: If excessive resistance is not found in circuits being tested, remove starter and proceed to BENCH TESTING.

Battery Connection Resistance Test – 1) Disable vehicle ignition and fuel systems. See DISABLING/ENABLING IGNITION & FUEL SYSTEMS. A voltmeter accurate to one tenth of a volt will be needed for the following tests.

2) Connect voltmeter positive lead to negative battery cable clamp. Connect voltmeter negative lead to negative battery post. Crank engine and observe voltmeter reading. If voltage is detected, repair poor contact between cable clamp and post. Perform same procedure to positive battery post and cable clamp.

Ground Connection Resistance Test – Connect voltmeter negative lead to negative battery post. Connect voltmeter positive lead to engine block, near negative battery cable grounding point. Crank engine and observe voltmeter reading. If voltmeter reading indicates more than 0.2 volt, repair poor ground connection or replace ground cable.

Starter Ground Connection Resistance Test – Connect voltmeter negative lead to negative battery post. Connect voltmeter positive lead to starter housing. Crank engine and observe voltmeter reading. If voltmeter reading indicates more than 0.2 volt, repair poor starter-to-ground connection.

Positive Battery Cable Resistance Test – 1) Remove starter heat shield (if equipped) to gain access to starter solenoid connections. Connect voltmeter negative lead to starter solenoid battery terminal and voltmeter positive lead to positive battery post.

2) Crank engine and observe voltmeter reading. If voltage reads more than 0.2 volt, correct poor connection between battery cable and starter solenoid or replace positive battery cable.

SOLENOID CIRCUIT TEST

NOTE: Perform SOLENOID CIRCUIT TEST before testing starter relay and starter relay circuit. Ensure A/T is in Park position or M/T is in Neutral position and parking brake is applied.

1) Disable vehicle ignition and fuel systems. See DISABLING/ENABLING IGNITION & FUEL SYSTEMS.

2) Ensure battery is fully charged. Ensure solenoid connections are not loose or corroded. Remove starter relay from Power Distribution Center (PDC). Refer to PDC cover for proper relay location. PDC is located in engine compartment.

3) Connect a remote starter switch or jumper wire between starter relay socket terminal No. 87 and positive battery post. *See Fig. 1 or 2.* If engine cranks, solenoid and starter are good. Go to STARTER RELAY TEST.

4) If engine fails to crank, or if solenoid chatters, check wiring and connectors from starter relay socket to starter solenoid terminal. Repair any loose or corroded connections. If engine still fails to crank, remove starter and proceed to SOLENOID TEST under BENCH TESTING.

STARTER RELAY TEST

NOTE: Perform SOLENOID CIRCUIT TEST before testing starter relay.

Remove starter relay from Power Distribution Center (PDC). Refer to PDC cover for proper relay location. PDC is located in engine compartment. Connect 12-volt power source to starter relay terminal No. 86 and ground terminal No. 85. *See Fig. 1 or 2.* Using ohmmeter, check continuity across starter relay terminals No. 30 and 87. If continuity is not present, replace starter relay.

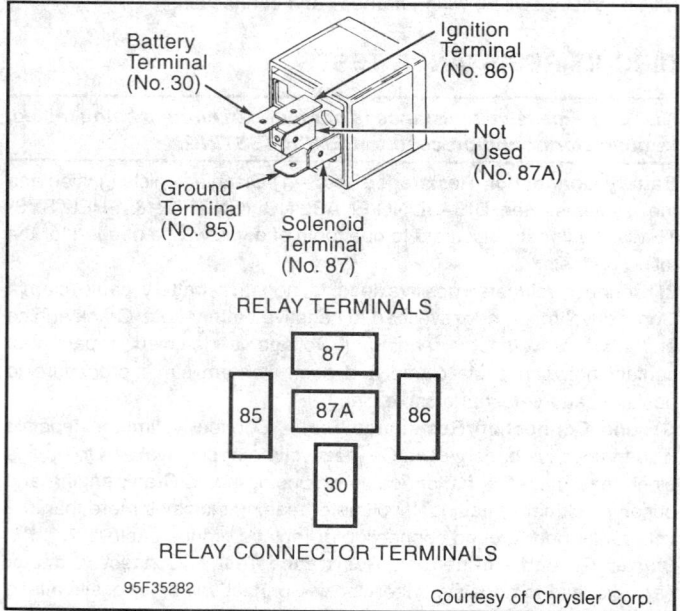

RELAY TERMINALS

RELAY CONNECTOR TERMINALS

95F35282   Courtesy of Chrysler Corp.

Fig. 1: Identifying Starter Relay Terminals (Except Concorde, Dakota, Durango, Intrepid, LHS, Ram Van, Ram Wagon & 300M)

STARTER RELAY CIRCUIT TEST

NOTE: Perform STARTER RELAY TEST before testing starter relay circuit.

1) Ensure battery is fully charged. Remove starter relay from Power Distribution Center (PDC). Refer to PDC cover for proper relay location. PDC is located in engine compartment.

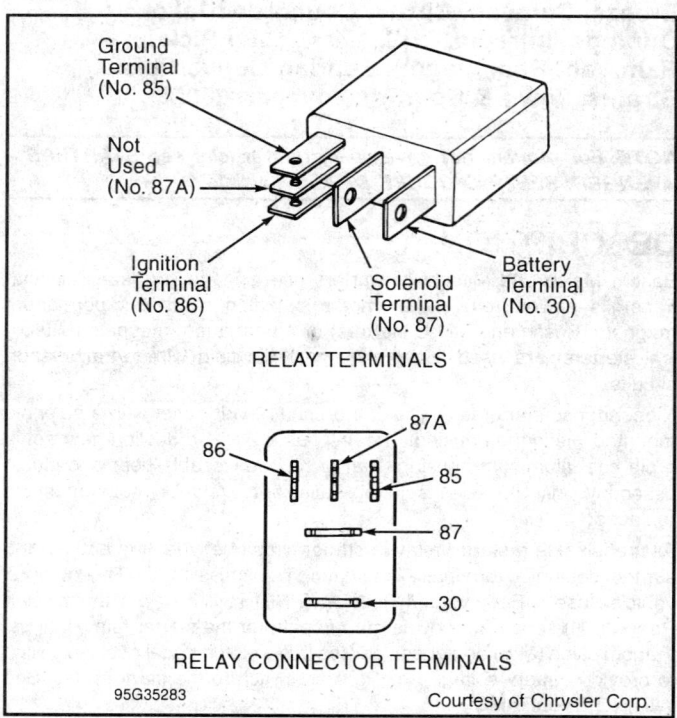

RELAY TERMINALS

RELAY CONNECTOR TERMINALS

95G35283   Courtesy of Chrysler Corp.

Fig. 2: Identifying Starter Relay Terminals (Concorde, Dakota, Durango, Intrepid, LHS, Ram Van, Ram Wagon & 300M)

2) Connect a jumper wire between starter relay socket terminal No. 30 and terminal No. 87. *See Fig. 1 or 2.* If engine does not crank, go to SOLENOID TEST under BENCH TESTING. If engine cranks, go to next step.

3) Turn ignition on. Check voltage between ground and starter relay socket terminal No. 30. If battery voltage is not present, repair open in circuit between starter relay socket and battery. If battery voltage is present, go to next step.

4) Check voltage between ground and starter relay socket terminal No. 86 with ignition switch in START position and clutch pedal depressed (if equipped with M/T). If battery voltage is present, circuit is okay. Go to step 6) if equipped with M/T or step 7) if equipped with A/T. If battery voltage is not present, repair open in circuit between ignition switch and starter relay socket (A/T) or go to next step (M/T).

5) Unplug wiring connector from clutch position switch mounted on clutch pedal bracket. Connect jumper wire between clutch position switch connector terminals. Recheck for voltage at starter relay socket terminal No. 86 with ignition switch in START position. If battery voltage is present, check clutch position switch adjustment (if applicable). Adjust switch as necessary. If switch adjustment is okay, check clutch position switch. See CLUTCH POSITION SWITCH TEST. If battery voltage is not present, repair wiring between ignition switch and starter relay socket as necessary.

6) On M/T models, connect voltmeter negative lead to starter relay socket terminal No. 85 and positive lead to terminal No. 86. Turn ignition switch to START position and depress clutch pedal. If battery voltage is present, starter relay socket ground circuit is good. Replace faulty starter relay. If battery voltage is not present, repair ground wire circuit.

7) On A/T models, connect voltmeter negative lead to starter relay socket terminal No. 85 and positive lead to terminal No. 86. Ensure transmission gear selector is in Park or Neutral position. Ground circuit runs through Park/Neutral Position (PNP) switch or Transmission Range (TR) sensor on transmission. Turn ignition switch to START position. If battery voltage is present, starter relay socket ground circuit is good. Replace faulty starter relay.

8) If battery voltage is not present, check PNP switch or TR sensor for loose or damaged connections. Also, check ground to PNP switch or TR sensor. Repair as necessary. If connections and ground are okay, check

1999 STARTING & CHARGING SYSTEMS
Starters – Except Avenger & Sebring Coupe (Cont.)

CHRY
2-7

PNP switch or TR sensor. See PARK/NEUTRAL POSITION (PNP) SWITCH & TRANSMISSION RANGE (TR) SENSOR TEST.

PARK/NEUTRAL POSITION (PNP) SWITCH & TRANSMISSION RANGE (TR) SENSOR TEST

NOTE: *Transmission Range (TR) sensor may be also known as Park/Neutral Position (PNP) switch or Park/Neutral switch.*

NOTE: *The following test is for Caravan, Ram Van, Ram Wagon and Voyager with 3-speed transmission. All other models are equipped with a Transmission Range (TR) sensor. If TR sensor or sensor circuit is defective, see appropriate NTC test in appropriate SELF-DIAGNOSTICS article in ENGINE PERFORMANCE in appropriate MITCHELL® manual.*

1) Place gear selector in Park. Disconnect negative battery cable. Raise and support vehicle. Disconnect PNP switch connector. Using an ohmmeter, check for continuity between ground and PNP switch center terminal. If continuity exists, go to next step. If continuity does not exist, replace PNP switch.

2) Place gear selector in Reverse. Check for continuity between ground and PNP switch center terminal. If continuity exists, PNP switch is okay. If continuity does not exist, replace PNP switch.

CLUTCH POSITION SWITCH TEST

Disconnect negative battery cable. Disconnect clutch position switch connector. Using an ohmmeter, check for continuity between clutch position switch terminals. With clutch pedal released, continuity should not exist. With clutch pedal depressed, continuity should exist. Replace clutch position switch if continuity is not as specified.

IGNITION SWITCH TEST

NOTE: *For ignition switch testing procedures, see appropriate STEERING COLUMN SWITCHES article in ACCESSORIES & EQUIPMENT.*

BENCH TESTING

SOLENOID TEST

1) With starter removed from vehicle, remove starter motor field coil wire from solenoid field coil terminal. Using an ohmmeter, check for continuity between solenoid terminal and field coil terminal of starter solenoid. Continuity should exist.

2) Check for continuity between solenoid terminal and solenoid housing. Continuity should exist. If continuity is not present in either test, replace starter and solenoid as an assembly.

OVERHAUL

NOTE: *Manufacturer does not recommend disassembling and servicing starters. If starter is found defective, a new unit must be installed.*

STARTER SPECIFICATIONS

STARTER SPECIFICATIONS – CARS

Application	Specification
Cranking Amperage Draw [1]	
Bosch 2.0L	150-280 Amps
Melco 2.5L & 2.7L	150-280 Amps
Nippondenso 2.4L, 3.2L & 3.5L	150-280 Amps
No-Load Test At 11 Volts	
Maximum Amps	
Bosch 2.0L	[2]
Melco 2.5L & 2.7L	[2]
Nippondenso 2.4L, 3.2L & 3.5L	[2]

STARTER SPECIFICATIONS – CARS (Cont.)

Application	Specification
No-Load Test At 11 Volts	
Minimum RPM	
Bosch 2.0L	[2]
Melco 2.5L & 2.7L	[2]
Nippondenso 2.4L, 2.7L & 3.5L	[2]
Power Rating	
Bosch 2.0L	0.95 Kw
Melco 2.5L & 2.7L	1.2 Kw
Nippondenso 2.4L, 2.7L & 3.5L	1.4 Kw

[1] – With engine at normal operating temperature. High viscosity oil, extreme cold temperatures, or tight engine will increase amperage draw.

[2] – Information is not available from manufacturer.

STARTER SPECIFICATIONS – TRUCKS

Application	Specification
Cranking Amperage Draw [1]	
Caravan, Town & Country & Voyager	150-200 Amps
Dakota & Durango	
2.5L	130 Amps
3.9L, 5.2L & 5.9L	125-250 Amps
Ram Pickup	
Diesel Engines	450-700 Amps
Gasoline Engines	125-250 Amps
Ram Van & Ram Wagon	125-250 Amps
No-Load Test At 11 Volts	
Maximum Amps	
Caravan, Town & Country & Voyager	73 Amps
Dakota & Durango	
2.5L	90 Amps
3.9L, 5.2L & 5.9L	73 Amps
Ram Pickup	
Gasoline	73 Amps
Diesel	200 Amps
Ram Van & Ram Wagon	73 Amps
Minimum RPM	
Caravan, Town & Country & Voyager	3401 RPM
Dakota & Durango	
2.5L	2600 RPM
3.9L, 5.2L & 5.9L	3601 RPM
Ram Pickup	
Gasoline	3601 RPM
Diesel	3000 RPM
Ram Van & Ram Wagon	3601 RPM
Power Rating	
Caravan, Town & Country & Voyager	1.2 Kw
Dakota & Durango	
2.5L	1.2 Kw
3.9L, 5.2L & 5.9L	1.4 Kw
Ram Pickup	
Gasoline	1.4 Kw
Diesel	2.7 Kw
Ram Van & Ram Wagon	1.4 Kw

[1] – With engine at normal operating temperature. High viscosity oil, extreme cold temperatures, or tight engine will increase amperage draw.

1999 Starting & Charging Systems
Starters – Except Avenger & Sebring Coupe (Cont.)

TORQUE SPECIFICATIONS

TORQUE SPECIFICATIONS – CARS & TRUCKS

Application	Ft. Lbs. (N.m)
Starter Mounting Bolts & Nuts	
All Except Dakota, Durango, Ram Pickup,	
Ram Van & Ram Wagon	40 (54)
Dakota & Durango	
2.5L	33 (45)
3.9L, 5.2L & 5.9L	50 (68)
Ram Pickup	
Diesel Engines	32 (43)
Gasoline Engines	50 (68)
Ram Van & Ram Wagon	50 (68)

WIRING DIAGRAMS

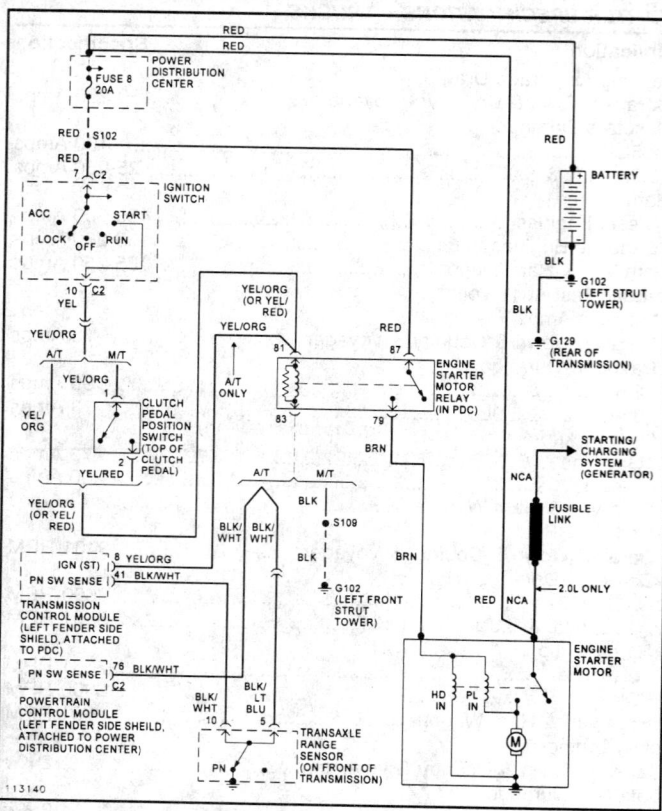

**Fig. 3: Starting System Wiring Diagram
(Breeze, Cirrus & Stratus)**

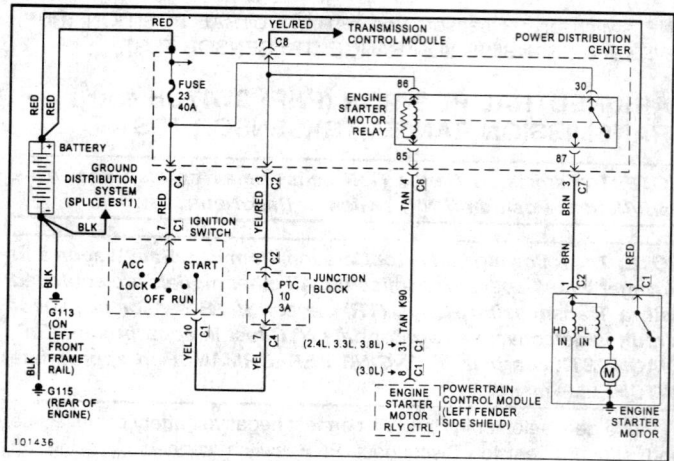

**Fig. 4: Starting System Wiring Diagram
(Caravan, Town & Country, & Voyager)**

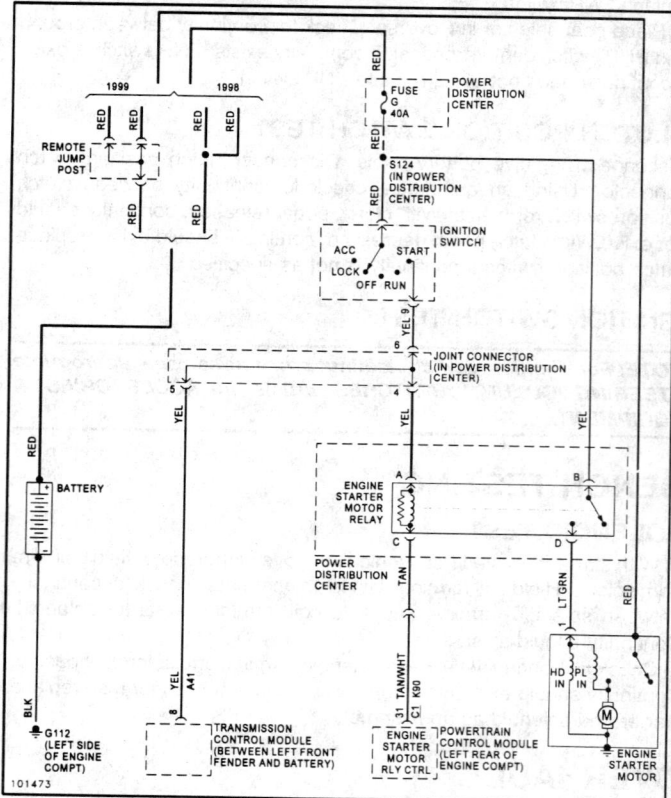

**Fig. 5: Starting System Wiring Diagram
(Concorde, Intrepid, LHS & 300M)**

1999 STARTING & CHARGING SYSTEMS
Starters — Except Avenger & Sebring Coupe (Cont.)

CHRY
2-9

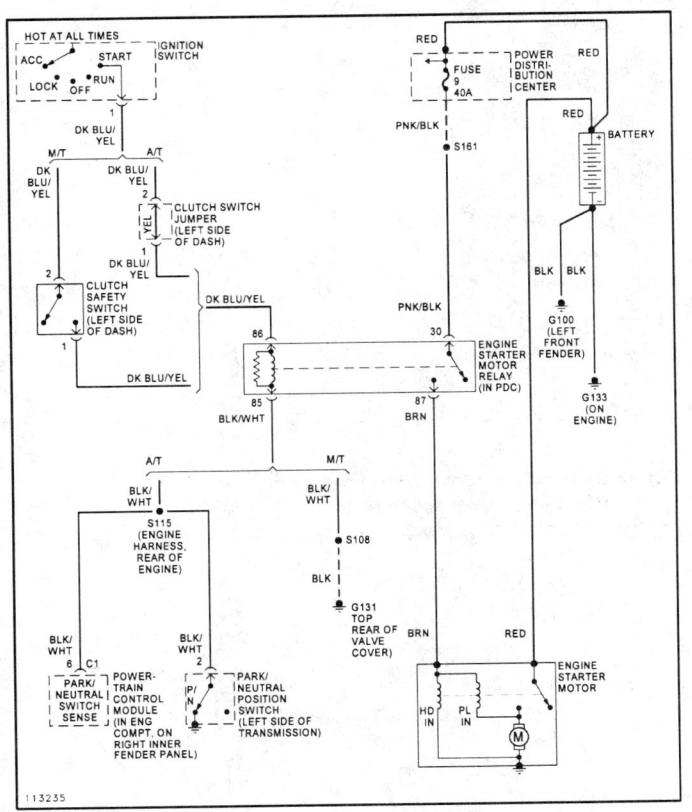

Fig. 6: Starting System Wiring Diagram (Dakota)

Fig. 8: Starting System Wiring Diagram (Neon)

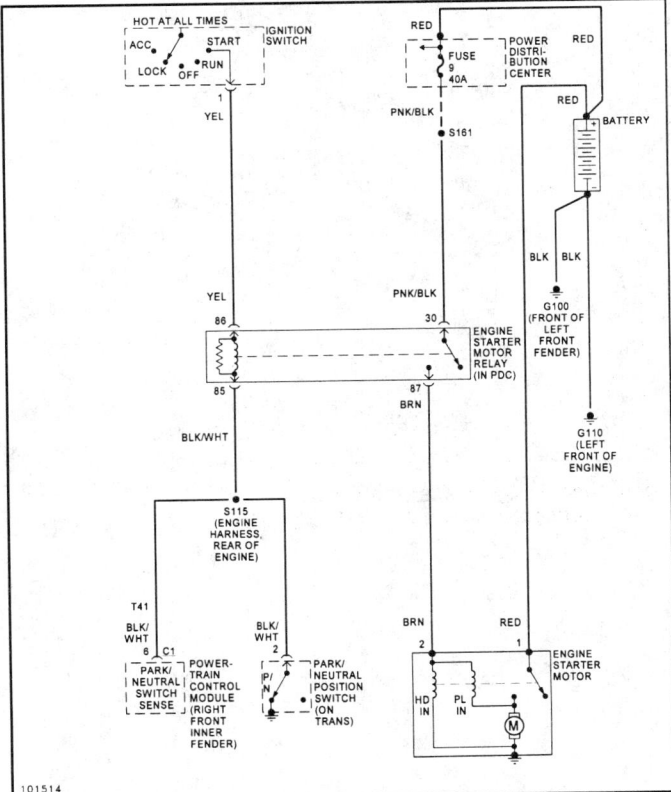

Fig. 7: Starting System Wiring Diagram (Durango)

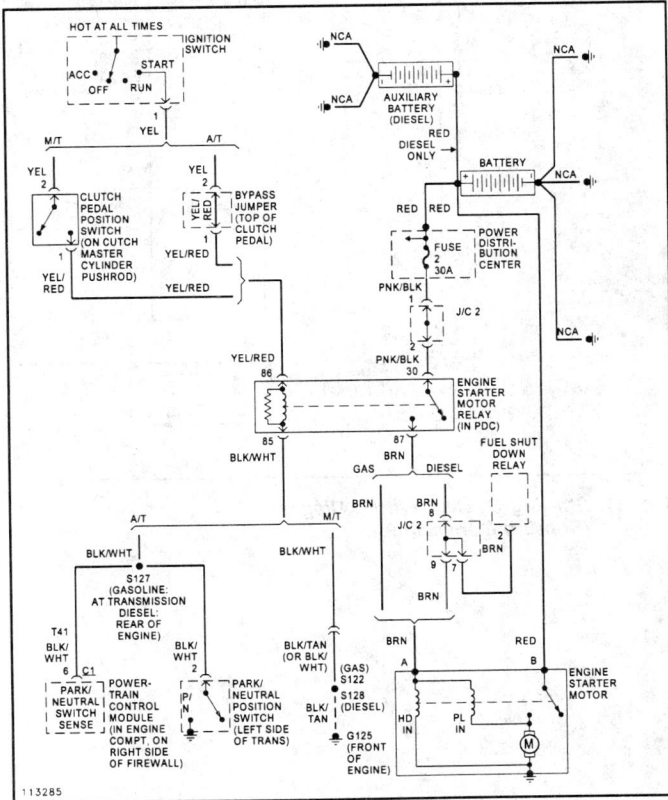

Fig. 9: Starting System Wiring Diagram (Ram Pickup)

CHRY
2-10

1999 STARTING & CHARGING SYSTEMS
Starters – Except Avenger & Sebring Coupe (Cont.)

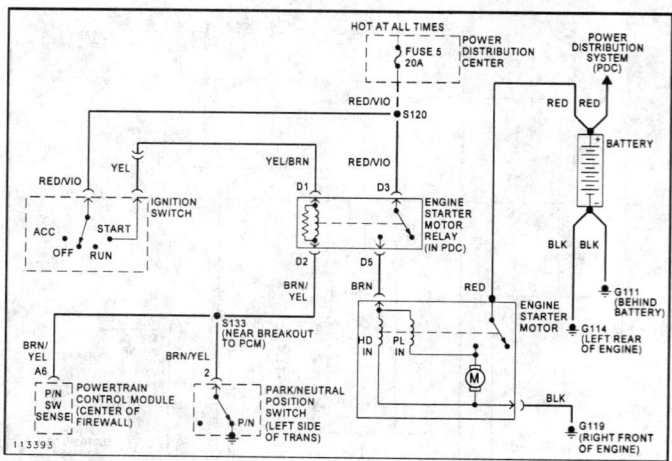

**Fig. 10: Starting System Wiring Diagram
(Ram Van & Ram Wagon)**

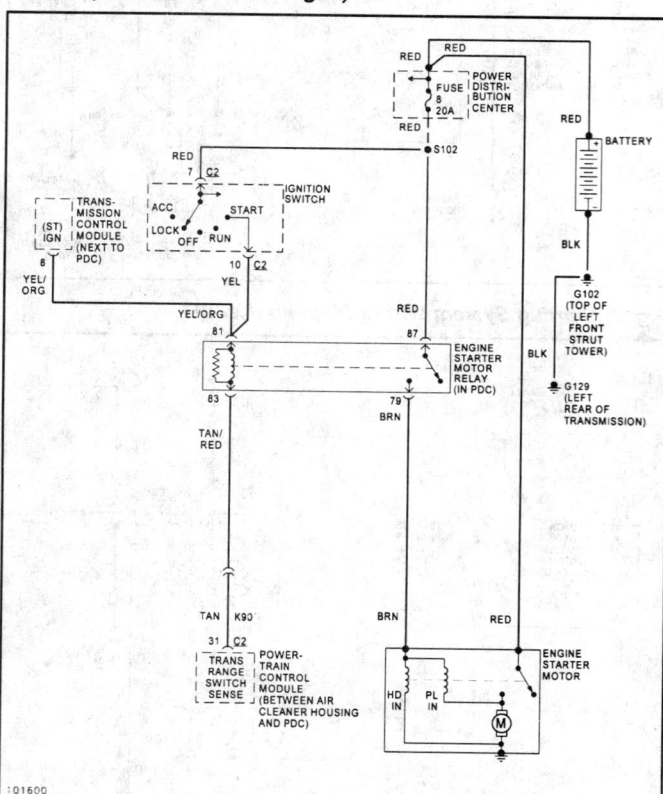

**Fig. 11: Starting System Wiring Diagram
(Sebring Convertible)**

Generators & Regulators – Cars

Avenger, Breeze, Cirrus, Concorde, Intrepid, LHS, Neon, Sebring Convertible, Sebring Coupe, Stratus, 300M

DESCRIPTION

Vehicles use either a Melco or Nippondenso generator. The generator contains a rotor, stator, rectifiers, front and rear covers and drive pulley. Generator is serviced as a complete unit only. Voltage regulation is controlled by the Powertrain Control Module (PCM). Electronic Voltage Regulator (EVR) is not a separate component, but a circuit located within the PCM. If EVR circuit is defective, PCM must be replaced.

OPERATION

The amount of amperage produced by the generator is controlled by Electronic Voltage Regulator (EVR) circuitry within the PCM. EVR circuity is connected in series with the generator field driver terminal and ground. A Battery Temperature Sensor (BTS) is located on rear of front bumper beam on all models except Avenger, Neon and Sebring Coupe is used to sense battery temperature. On Avenger and Sebring Coupe, BTS is located within PCM. On Neon, BTS is located on bottom of battery tray. Sensed battery temperature and data from monitored line voltage is used by PCM to adjust battery charging rate. This is accomplished by cycling the ground path to control the strength of generator rotor magnetic field. PCM then compensates and regulates generator amperage output accordingly. The PCM monitors critical input to control fuel injection, ignition, emission and other engine management functions. The PCM is also programmed to monitor charging system related circuits:

- Battery feed to PCM.
- Generator field control.
- Battery charging voltage (high & low).

If a problem is sensed in a monitored circuit, a Diagnostic Trouble Code (DTC) will be stored in PCM memory and Malfunction Indicator Light (MIL) will illuminate, provided specific criteria have been met. DTCs can be read using MIL or Chrysler's Diagnostic Readout Box (DRB-III).

NOTE: *DTC is erased from memory if failure does not reoccur after 50 engine starts.*

Certain DTCs cause MIL to illuminate and engine controller to enter limp-in mode. In limp-in mode, engine controller attempts to compensate for particular component failure by substituting information from other sources. This allows vehicle operation until proper repairs are made.

ADJUSTMENTS

BELT TENSION

BELT TENSION SPECIFICATIONS

Application	[1] Tension Lbs. (kg)
Avenger & Sebring Coupe	
2.0L	
New Belt	110-160 (50-73)
Used Belt	90-110 (41-50)
2.5L	
New Belt	143-187 (65-85)
Used Belt	99-121 (45-55)
Breeze, Cirrus, Sebring Convertible & Stratus	
2.0L, 2.4L & 2.5L	
New Belt	150 (68)
Used Belt	90 (41)
Concorde & Intrepid	
2.7L & 3.2L	
New Belt	180-200 (82-91)
Used Belt	120 (54)

BELT TENSION SPECIFICATIONS (Cont.)

Application	[1] Tension Lbs. (kg)
Neon	
2.0L	
New Belt	135 (61)
Used Belt	100 (45)

[1] – Measure tension using belt tension gauge.

TROUBLE SHOOTING

INITIAL CHECKS

Before proceeding with charging system diagnosis, ensure following conditions are met:

- Battery is fully charged and in good condition.
- Battery cables are in good condition with connections clean and secure.
- Generator belt is in good condition and properly tightened.
- Generator and PCM wiring harness connections are clean and tight.
- Engine ground strap is in place.

UNSTEADY OR LOW CHARGING

Check for loose generator belt, charging resistance too high, defective generator, loose generator ground wire, corroded battery terminals or faulty generator.

OVERCHARGING

Check for grounded generator field wiring or faulty generator.

NOISY GENERATOR

Check for worn or frayed drive belt, loose generator mounting, or faulty generator.

SELF-DIAGNOSTIC SYSTEM

If a problem is sensed in a monitored circuit, a Diagnostic Trouble Code (DTC) will be stored in PCM and Malfunction Indicator Light (MIL) will illuminate, provided specific criteria are met. PCM will then enter limp-in mode, substituting information from other sources to compensate for component failure. Vehicle is operational in limp-in mode, but driveability may not be optimal.

A specific DTC results from a particular system failure. DTC only indicates problem circuit. It does not identify specific component failure in the circuit.

If problem is repaired or ceases to exist, PCM automatically clears DTC after 50 ignition on-off cycles. DTCs can also be cleared using scan tool. See CLEARING DTCS.

PRECAUTIONS

Before proceeding with diagnosis, observe following precautions:

- Ensure battery is fully charged.
- Probe PCM connector from pin side. DO NOT backprobe PCM connector or probe wires through insulation.
- DO NOT cause short circuits when performing electrical tests. This will set additional DTCs, making diagnosis of original problem more difficult.
- DO NOT use a test light in place of a voltmeter.
- Always begin repair with lowest DTC number (MIL) or first DTC displayed (scan tool).
- Always perform verification test after repairs are made.
- Always disconnect scan tool after use.
- Always disconnect scan tool before charging battery.

ON-BOARD DIAGNOSTICS

CAUTION: Before entering on-board diagnostics, check charging system for other problems. See INITIAL CHECKS under TROUBLE SHOOTING. DO NOT connect scan tool to vehicle if battery charger is connected, scan tool damage will result.

NOTE: PCM cannot diagnose every charging system problem. If fault still exists after performing self-diagnostic procedures, proceed to ON- VEHICLE TESTING.

RETRIEVING DTCS

NOTE: Self-diagnostic tests are written specifically for Chrysler's Diagnostic Readout Box (DRB-III) scan tool, which will be referred to as scan tool during test procedures. A generic scan tool may also be used for system diagnostics, but may have limited diagnostic capability.

Using Scan Tool – 1) Ensure battery is fully charged. Connect scan tool to Data Link Connector (DLC). DLC is located below instrument panel, near steering column.

2) Using scan tool manufacturer's instructions, retrieve and record DTCs displayed on scan tool. Perform appropriate self-diagnostic test. See SELF-DIAGNOSTIC TESTS. Once repairs are made, clear DTCs from PCM memory. See CLEARING DTCS.

CLEARING DTCS

Powertrain Control Module (PCM) automatically clears DTC after 50 ignition on-off cycles. DTCs can also be cleared using scan tool. See scan tool manufacturer's instructions.

SCAN TOOL PROBLEMS & ERROR MESSAGES

NO RESPONSE Message – See appropriate NO-START TEST in appropriate SELF-DIAGNOSTICS article in ENGINE PERFORMANCE in appropriate MITCHELL® manual.

NOTE: For more information on scan tool and PCM diagnostics, see appropriate SELF-DIAGNOSTICS article in ENGINE PERFOR-MANCE in appropriate MITCHELL® manual.

SELF-DIAGNOSTIC TESTS

NOTE: When using diagnostic tests, DO NOT skip any steps or incorrect diagnosis may result. Ensure battery is fully charged.

NOTE: For connector terminal identification, see CONNECTOR IDENTIFICATION in appropriate SELF-DIAGNOSTICS article in ENGINE PERFORMANCE in appropriate MITCHELL® manual.

DTC TEST: CHECKING SYSTEM FOR DIAGNOSTIC TROUBLE CODES

NOTE: Ensure battery is fully charged before proceeding with test.

1) Attempt to start engine. Crank engine for up to 10 seconds (if necessary). Read and record DTCs. See RETRIEVING DTCS under SELF-DIAGNOSTIC SYSTEM. If scan tool displays NO RESPONSE, go to appropriate NO-START TEST in appropriate SELF-DIAGNOSTICS article in ENGINE PERFORMANCE in appropriate MITCHELL® manual.

2) If scan tool will not power up, check for loose cable connections or bad cable. If cable connections and cable are okay, check voltage at terminal No. 16 (Pink wire) on DLC. Voltage should be at least 11 volts. If voltage is not as specified, check wiring circuit and appropriate fuses. See WIRING DIAGRAMS.

3) If scan tool displays an error message, (i.e., USER-REQUESTED COLD BOOT or USER-REQUESTED WARM BOOT), follow scan tool manufacturer's instructions. If scan tool displays a BUS failure (i.e., SHORT TO BATTERY), this indicates either a scan tool failure or BUS failure. To diagnose and correct BUS failures, see appropriate BODY CONTROL COMPUTER – VEHICLE COMMUNICATIONS article.

4) If DTCs are displayed, see SCAN TOOL DTC MESSAGES table and perform appropriate test(s). Only DTCs relating to charging system are listed. For all other DTCs, see appropriate SELF-DIAGNOSTICS article. If no DTCs are displayed, go to TEST CH-1A: CHARGING SYSTEM NO CODE TEST.

SCAN TOOL DTC MESSAGES

Scan Tool Display	DTC
GENERATOR FIELD NOT SWITCHING PROPERLY	P0622
BATTERY TEMPERATURE SENSOR VOLTAGE TOO HIGH [1] [2]	P1492
BATTERY TEMPERATURE SENSOR VOLTAGE TOO LOW [1] [2]	P1493
CHARGING SYSTEM VOLTAGE TOO HIGH	P1594
CHARGING SYSTEM VOLTAGE TOO LOW	P1682

[1] – For Concorde, Intrepid, LHS and 300M, see OTIS TEST 3A in appropriate BODY CONTROL COMPUTER TESTS article in ACCESSORIES & EQUIPMENT.
[2] – On Avenger and Sebring Coupe, replace PCM. PCM is located in engine compartment, next to battery.

NOTE: For connector terminal identification, see CONNECTOR IDENTIFICATION in appropriate SELF-DIAGNOSTICS article in ENGINE PERFORMANCE.

DTC P0622: GENERATOR FIELD NOT SWITCHING PROPERLY

NOTE: DTC is set when PCM attempts to regulate generator field with no result during monitoring. Possible causes are Automatic Shut Down (ASD) relay output open circuit, generator field resistance greater than 5 ohms, open generator field driver circuit, generator field driver circuit shorted to ground, defective generator or PCM.

1) Using scan tool, erase trouble codes. Using scan tool, actuate generator field driver circuit. Using a voltmeter, backprobe generator field connector. Measure voltage between ground and ASD relay output circuit terminal. Generator field connector is located on back of generator. See WIRING DIAGRAMS. If voltage is more than 10 volts, go to next step. If voltage is 10 volts or less, repair open ASD relay output circuit. Perform TEST VER-3A.

2) Using a voltmeter, backprobe generator field connector generator field driver circuit. If voltage shifts from low to high, go to next step. If voltage does not shift from low to high, go to step **5)**.

3) Wiggle wiring harness from generator to PCM. Using scan tool, read DTCs with actuator test still running. If generator field driver circuit DTC sets, repair wiring harness as necessary where wiggling caused problem to appear. If DTC does not set, fault is currently not present. Test is complete. Perform TEST VER-3A.

4) Turn ignition off. Disconnect PCM harness connector. Disconnect field harness connector on rear of generator. Using an ohmmeter, measure resistance between generator field terminals on generator. If resistance is 5 ohms or more, repair or replace generator. Perform TEST VER-3A. If resistance is less than 5 ohms, go to next step.

5) Using an ohmmeter, check resistance of generator field driver circuit between generator field harness connector and PCM harness connector. See WIRING DIAGRAMS. If resistance is 5 ohms or more, repair open generator field driver circuit. Perform TEST VER-3A. If resistance is less than 5 ohms, go to next step.

6) With generator field connector disconnected, measure resistance from either generator field terminal (on back of generator) to ground. If resistance is less than 5 ohms, repair or replace shorted generator. If resistance is 5 ohms or more, replace PCM. Perform TEST VER-3A

DTC P1492/P1493: BATTERY TEMP SENSOR VOLTAGE TOO HIGH/BATTERY TEMP SENSOR VOLTAGE TOO LOW

NOTE: Battery Temperature Sensor (BTS) is also known as Ambient Temperature Sensor (ATS).

1) Read Battery Temperature Sensor (BTS) voltage using scan tool. If BTS voltage is .4 volt or more, go to next step. If BTS voltage is less than .4 volt, go to step **5)**.

2) Disconnect BTS connector. On Breeze, Cirrus, Sebring Convertible and Stratus, BTS is located on rear of front bumper beam. On Neon, BTS is located on bottom of battery tray. On all models, using scan tool, read BTS voltage. If BTS voltage is 4 volts or less, go to next step. If BTS voltage is more than 4 volts, replace BTS. Perform TEST VER-5A.

3) Turn ignition off. Disconnect Powertrain Control Module (PCM) connector. Using an ohmmeter, check resistance of BTS signal circuit between BTS connector and ground. See WIRING DIAGRAMS. If resistance is less than 5 ohms, repair short to ground on BTS signal circuit. Perform TEST VER-5A. If resistance is 5 ohms or more, replace PCM. Perform TEST VER-5A.

4) Condition to set trouble code is not present at this time. DTC P1492 or P1493 sets if BTS voltage is less than .5 volt or more than 4.9 volts for 3 seconds. Possible causes are: BTS failure, BTS signal circuit open, BTS signal circuit shorted, PCM failure, faulty connections or wiring.

5) Read Battery Temperature Sensor (BTS) voltage using scan tool. If BTS voltage is 4.9 volts or less, go to step **10)**. If BTS voltage is more than 4.9 volts, go to next step.

6) Turn ignition off. Disconnect BTS and PCM harness connectors. Using ohmmeter, measure resistance of sensor ground circuit between BTS harness connector and PCM harness connector. If resistance is less than 5 ohms, go to next step. If resistance is 5 ohms or greater, repair open circuit. Perform TEST VER-5A.

7) Connect PCM harness connector. Turn ignition on. Connect a jumper wire between BTS harness connector terminals. Using scan tool, read BTS voltage. If voltage is one volt or more, go to next step. If voltage is less than one volt, replace BTS. Perform TEST VER-5A.

8) Using a voltmeter, check voltage of BTS signal circuit between BTS connector and ground. If voltage is 5 volts or less, go to next step. If voltage is more than 5 volts, repair short to voltage on BTS signal circuit. Perform TEST VER-5A.

9) Turn ignition off. Disconnect BTS and PCM harness connectors. Using ohmmeter, measure resistance of sensor ground circuit between BTS harness connector and PCM harness connector. If resistance is less than 5 ohms, replace PCM. If resistance is 5 ohms or greater, repair open circuit. Perform TEST VER-5A.

10) While observing scan tool BTS voltage, wiggle wiring harness for BTS sensor. If voltage changes, repair wiring harness as necessary where wiggling caused problem to appear. Perform TEST VER-5A. If voltage does not change, go to next step.

11) Inspect all related wiring and connectors and repair as necessary. If no problems were found with wiring and connectors, test is complete. If related wiring and connectors were repaired, perform TEST VER-5A.

DTC P1594: CHARGING SYSTEM VOLTAGE TOO HIGH

NOTE: DTC is set when monitored battery voltage is one volt below charging system upper limit threshold for 25 seconds. PCM turns off field driver and monitors battery voltage. If voltage remains high, DTC P1594 is set. Possible causes are generator field driver circuit shorted to ground, shorted generator or Powertrain Control Module (battery temperature and/or charging voltage).

1) Ensure battery is fully charged, and generator belt tension and condition are okay. Using scan tool, actuate generator field driver. Using a voltmeter to ground, backprobe generator field connector, checking voltage on Dark Green wire. See WIRING DIAGRAMS. If voltage shifts from low to high, go to next step. If voltage does not shift from low to high, go to step **5)**.

2) Using scan tool, stop generator field driver actuation. Start engine. Using scan tool, read target charging voltage. If target charging voltage is more than 13 volts, go to step **4)**. If target charging voltage is 13 volts or less, go to next step.

3) On Avenger and Sebring, go to next step. On all other models, measure underhood temperature near PCM using scan tool temperature probe. Using scan tool, read battery temperature sensor temperature. If scan tool display is within 10 degrees of actual underhood temperature, go to next step. If scan tool display is not within 10 degrees of actual underhood temperature, replace BTS. Perform TEST VER-3A.

4) Start engine. Manually set engine speed to 1600 RPM. Using scan tool, read and compare voltage and target charging voltage. Observe voltage for up to 5 minutes (if necessary) for a one volt difference between voltage and target charging voltage. If difference between voltage and target charging voltage is one volt or less, go to TEST CH-1A: CHARGING SYSTEM NO CODE TEST. If difference between voltage and target charging voltage is more than one volt, replace Powertrain Control Module (PCM). Perform TEST VER-3A.

5) Turn ignition off. Disconnect PCM harness connector. Disconnect field harness connector on rear of generator. Using an ohmmeter, measure resistance of generator field driver circuit between PCM connector and ground. If resistance is 5 ohms or more, go to next step. If resistance is less than 5 ohms, repair short to ground on generator field driver circuit. Perform TEST VER-3A.

6) With generator field connector disconnected, measure resistance from either generator field terminal (on back of generator) to ground. If resistance is less than 5 ohms, repair or replace shorted generator. If resistance is 5 ohms or more, replace PCM. Perform TEST VER-3A.

DTC P1682: CHARGING SYSTEM VOLTAGE TOO LOW

NOTE: DTC is set when monitored battery voltage is one volt below charging system lower limit threshold for 25 seconds. PCM turns off field driver and monitors battery voltage. If voltage remains low, DTC P1682 is set. Possible causes are open ASD relay output circuit, high resistance in battery supply circuit between generator and battery, open driver circuit, high resistance in ground circuit, defective generator or defective battery temperature sensor.

1) Ensure battery is fully charged. Start engine. Using scan tool, read voltage goal. If voltage goal is more than 15.1 volts, go to next step. If voltage goal is 15.1 volts or less, go to step **6)**.

2) Manually set engine speed to 1600 RPM. Using scan tool, read and compare target voltage and charging voltage. If difference between target voltage and charging voltage is more than one volt, go to next step. If difference between target voltage and charging voltage is one volt or less, go to TEST CH-1A: CHARGING SYSTEM NO CODE TEST.

NOTE: Before starting engine, ensure all test equipment wires are clear of moving engine parts.

3) Connect an external voltmeter between generator B+ terminal and battery positive terminal. Start engine. If voltage is .4 volt or less, go to next step. If voltage is more than .4 volt, repair B+ circuit for high resistance between generator and battery. Perform TEST VER-3A.

4) Turn ignition off. Connect an external voltmeter between generator case and battery negative terminal. Start engine. If voltage is .1 volt or less, go to next step. If voltage is more than .1 volt, repair generator ground for high resistance between generator case and battery negative terminal. Perform TEST VER-3A.

5) Using scan tool, read Battery Temperature Sensor (BTS) temperature. On Avenger and Sebring Coupe, go to next step. On all other models, go to step **9)** if BTS temperature matches actual underhood temperature. If BTS temperature does not match actual underhood temperature, replace BTS temperature sensor. Perform TEST VER-2A.

6) Manually set engine speed to 1600 RPM. Using scan tool, read and compare target voltage and charging voltage. If difference between target voltage and charging voltage is more than one volt, go to next step. If difference between target voltage and charging voltage is one volt or less, go to TEST CH-1A: CHARGING SYSTEM NO CODE TEST.

> NOTE: *Before starting engine, ensure all test equipment wires are clear of moving engine parts.*

7) Connect an external voltmeter between generator B+ terminal and battery positive terminal. Start engine. If voltage is .4 volt or less, go to next step. If voltage is more than .4 volt, repair B+ circuit for high resistance between generator and battery. Perform TEST VER-3A.

8) Turn ignition off. Connect an external voltmeter between generator case and battery negative terminal. Start engine. If voltage is .1 volt or less, go to next step. If voltage is more than .1 volt, repair generator ground for high resistance between generator case and battery negative terminal. Perform TEST VER-3A.

9) Turn ignition off. Disconnect generator field connector. Ensure connector is clean. Disconnect Powertrain Control Module (PCM) connector. PCM is located next to underhood Power Distribution Center (PDC). Using external ohmmeter, measure resistance of circuit between ASD relay and generator field connector. See WIRING DIAGRAMS. If resistance is less than 5 ohms, go to next step. If resistance is 5 ohms or greater, repair open circuit. Perform TEST VER-3A.

10) Measure resistance of generator field driver circuit between PCM and generator field connector. See WIRING DIAGRAMS. If resistance is less than 5 ohms, go to next step. If resistance is 5 ohms or greater, repair open circuit. Perform TEST VER-3A.

11) If no problems were found, generator is assumed to be defective. Replace generator. Perform TEST VER-3A.

TEST CH-1A: CHARGING SYSTEM NO CODE TEST

1) Verify battery condition. Charge or replace battery as necessary. Inspect generator belt tension and condition. Replace generator belt as necessary. Start engine. Using scan tool, set engine speed to 1600 RPM for 30 seconds. Using scan tool, return engine to idle speed and read Diagnostic Trouble Codes (DTCs). If any charging system DTCs are set, see SCAN TOOL DTC MESSAGES table and perform appropriate test. If no charging system DTCs are set, go to next step.

2) Turn ignition on with engine off. Using scan tool, actuate generator field. Using scan tool in voltmeter mode, backprobe generator field terminals on back of generator. *See Fig. 1, 2 or 3.* Voltage should cycle from zero volts to battery voltage every 1.4 seconds at both terminals. While observing scan tool, wiggle field terminal wiring harness back to Powertrain Control Module (PCM). If any interruption of voltage cycling occurred, repair wiring harness where wiggling caused failure. Perform TEST VER-3A. If wiggling did not interrupt voltage cycling, go to next step.

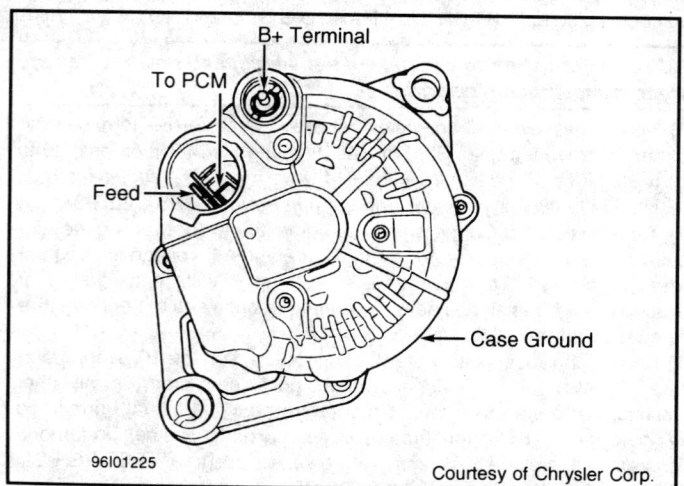

96I01225   Courtesy of Chrysler Corp.

Fig. 1: Identifying Generator Terminals (2.0L, 2.4L & 2.5L – Except Neon)

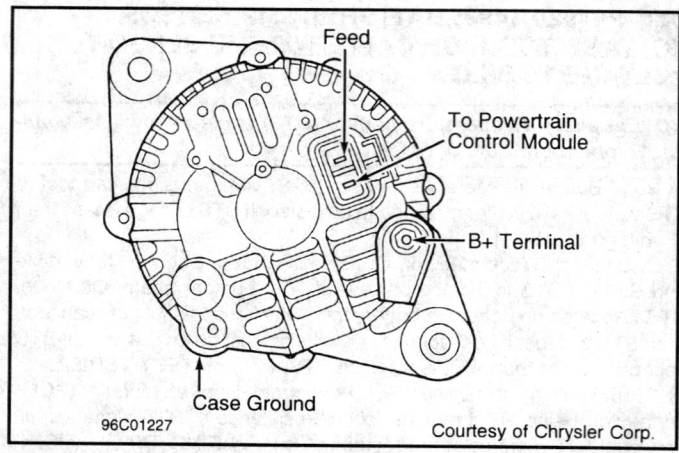

96C01227   Courtesy of Chrysler Corp.

Fig. 2: Identifying Generator Terminals (3.2L, 3.5L & Neon)

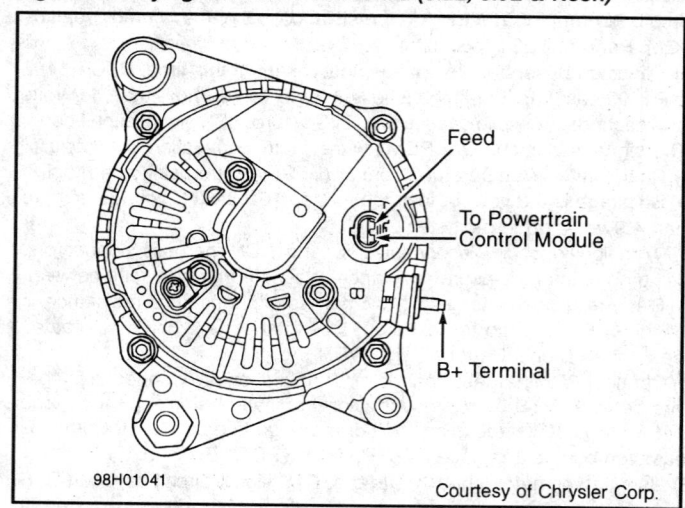

98H01041   Courtesy of Chrysler Corp.

Fig. 3: Identifying Generator Terminals (2.7L)

3) Using scan tool, read DTCs. If any charging system DTCs are set, see SCAN TOOL DTC MESSAGES table and perform appropriate test. If no charging system trouble codes are set, go to next step.

4) Turn ignition off. Using an external voltmeter, check voltage between generator case and battery negative terminal. Start engine. If voltage is greater than .1 volt, repair high resistance between generator battery negative terminal and battery negative terminal. Perform TEST VER-3A. If voltage is .1 volt or less, go to next step.

5) Using an external voltmeter, check voltage between generator B+ terminal located on rear of generator and battery positive terminal. *See Fig. 1, 2 or 3.* Ensure voltmeter wires are clear of moving engine parts. Start engine and observe voltmeter. If voltage is .4 volt or less, go to next step. If voltage is more than .4 volt, repair high resistance between generator B+ terminal and battery positive terminal. Perform TEST VER-3A.

6) With ignition on and engine off, read and record battery voltage using scan tool. Using voltmeter, measure and record voltage between battery terminals. If voltage difference is less than one volt, test is complete. If voltage difference is one volt or greater, go to next step.

7) With ignition on and engine off, read and record battery voltage using scan tool. Turn ignition off. Disconnect PCM connector. Turn ignition on. Using voltmeter, measure voltage between ground and terminal No. 46 on PCM connector. If voltage is within one volt of scan tool voltage, repair high resistance between PCM connector terminal No. 46 and battery positive terminal. Perform TEST VER-3A. If voltage is not within one volt of scan tool voltage, replace PCM. Perform TEST VER-3A.

TEST VER-2A: ROAD TEST VERIFICATION

CAUTION: If PCM is changed, correct VIN and mileage have to be programmed or ABS and SRS DTCs will be set. Also if vehicle is equipped with Smart Key Imbolizer Module (SKIM), secret key data must be updated to enable starting.

1) If PCM has been replaced, go to next step. If vehicle is equipped with SKIM system, go to step **3)**.

2) Connect scan tool to Data Link Connector (DLC). DLC is located below driver's side of instrument panel. Using scan tool, enter correct VIN and mileage into PCM. Using scan tool manufacturer's instructions, clear DTCs from ABS and SRS modules. Go to step **5)**.

3) Using scan tool, access THEFT ALARM, SKIM and then MISC menus. Place SKIM in SECURED ACCESS MODE by using appropriate Personal Identification Number (PIN) for vehicle. PIN may be vehicle's owner or manufacturer. Select UPDATE SECRET KEY DATA. Data will be transferred from SKIM to PCM.

4) If 3 attempts are made to enter SECURED ACCESS MODE using incorrect PIN, this scan tool mode will be locked out for one hour. To exit this locked out mode, leave ignition switch in ON position for one hour with all accessories turned off. If may be necessary to monitor battery state and connect a battery charger if necessary.

5) Inspect vehicle to ensure all engine components are connected. Reassemble and reconnect components as necessary.

6) Check if initial symptom still exists. If initial or another symptom exists, repair is not complete. Check for Technical Service Bulletins (TSBs) that apply to symptom.

7) If any DTCs have not been diagnosed, go to appropriate test and finish diagnosing remaining DTCs as necessary. If all DTCs have been diagnosed, go to next step.

8) Using scan tool, erase DTCs from PCM. Using scan tool, reset all values in adaptive memory. Disconnect scan tool. If no other DTCs remain, repair is now complete.

TEST VER-3A: CHARGING VERIFICATION

CAUTION: If PCM is changed, correct VIN and mileage have to be programmed or ABS and SRS DTCs will be set. Also if vehicle is equipped with Smart Key Imbolizer Module (SKIM), secret key data must be updated to enable starting.

1) If PCM has been replaced, go to next step. If vehicle is equipped with SKIM system, go to step **3)**.

2) Connect scan tool to Data Link Connector (DLC). DLC is located below driver's side of instrument panel. Using scan tool, enter correct VIN and mileage into PCM. Using scan tool manufacturer's instructions, clear DTCs from ABS and SRS modules.

3) Using scan tool, access THEFT ALARM, SKIM and then MISC menus. Place SKIM in SECURED ACCESS MODE by using appropriate Personal Identification Number (PIN) for vehicle. PIN may be vehicle's owner or manufacturer. Select UPDATE SECRET KEY DATA. Data will be transferred from SKIM to PCM.

4) If 3 attempts are made to enter SECURED ACCESS MODE using incorrect PIN, this scan tool mode will be locked out for one hour. To exit this locked out mode, leave ignition switch in ON position for one hour with all accessories turned off. If may be necessary to monitor battery state and connect a battery charger if necessary.

5) To ensure no charging system problem exists, start engine. Perform OUTPUT VOLTAGE TEST under ON-VEHICLE TESTING. Increase engine speed to 2000 RPM for at least 30 seconds. Allow engine to idle. Turn engine off.

6) Using scan tool, check for stored DTCs. If repaired DTC has reset, repair is not complete. Check for related Technical Service Bulletins (TSBs) and return to DTC TEST, if necessary. If another DTC exists, go to appropriate DTC test and follow specified procedure. If no other DTCs exist, repair is now complete.

TEST VER-5A: ROAD TEST VERIFICATION

CAUTION: If PCM is changed, correct VIN and mileage have to be programmed or ABS and SRS DTCs will be set. Also if vehicle is equipped with Smart Key Imbolizer Module (SKIM), secret key data must be updated to enable starting.

1) If PCM has been replaced, go to next step. If vehicle is equipped with SKIM system, go to step **3)**.

2) Connect scan tool to Data Link Connector (DLC). DLC is located below driver's side of instrument panel. Using scan tool, enter correct VIN and mileage into PCM. Using scan tool manufacturer's instructions, clear DTCs from ABS and SRS modules.

3) Using scan tool, access THEFT ALARM, SKIM and then MISC menus. Place SKIM in SECURED ACCESS MODE by using appropriate Personal Identification Number (PIN) for vehicle. PIN may be vehicle's owner or manufacturer. Select UPDATE SECRET KEY DATA. Data will be transferred from SKIM to PCM.

4) If 3 attempts are made to enter SECURED ACCESS MODE using incorrect PIN, this scan tool mode will be locked out for one hour. To exit this locked out mode, leave ignition switch in ON position for one hour with all accessories turned off. If may be necessary to monitor battery state and connect a battery charger if necessary.

5) Inspect vehicle to ensure all engine components are connected. Reassemble and reconnect components as necessary.

6) If any DTCs have not been diagnosed, go to appropriate test and finish diagnosing remaining DTCs as necessary. If all DTCs have been diagnosed, go to next step.

7) Connect scan tool to DLC connector. Ensure fuel tank is at least 25 percent full. Turn off all accessories.

8) Using scan tool OBDII monitor, verify DTC repair. See scan tool instructions. Allow PCM to run appropriate monitor(s) and increment a global good trip (drive cycle). Enabling conditions must be met before PCM will run OBDII monitor. Scan tool monitor pretest screen will display enabling conditions.

9) If repaired DTC has reset or was seen in OBDII monitor while on road test, repair is not complete. Check for any TSBs and return to appropriate test. Repair as needed.

10) If any other DTCs are set, repair as needed. If OBDII monitor is run and good trip counter is incremented and no new DTCs are set, repair is successful and complete. Erase DTCs. See CLEARING CODES.

ON-VEHICLE TESTING

CAUTION: When vehicle battery is disconnected, vehicle computer systems may lose memory data. Driveability problems may exist until computer systems have completed a relearn cycle. See COMPUTER RELEARN PROCEDURES article in GENERAL INFORMATION article.

OUTPUT VOLTAGE TEST

NOTE: OUTPUT VOLTAGE TEST determines if generator is capable of delivering its rated current output.

1) Before performing this test, ensure battery is fully charged. Connect voltmeter leads across battery terminals. Record voltage with ignition switch and all electrical loads off. Fully engage parking brake, and place gear selector in Park.

2) Start engine and operate at normal operating temperature. Record voltage with engine speed at 1500 RPM with no electrical loads. Voltage should not be greater than voltage recorded in step **1)** by more than 2.5 volts. If voltage is not as specified, go to DTC TEST: CHECKING SYSTEM FOR DIAGNOSTIC TROUBLE CODES.

3) Record voltage with engine speed at 2000 RPM, blower motor on high and headlights on high beam. Voltage should be more than 0.5 volt greater than battery voltage previously recorded in step **1)**. If voltage is less than 0.5 volt above previously recorded battery voltage, go to DTC TEST: CHECKING SYSTEM FOR DIAGNOSTIC TROUBLE CODES. If

1999 STARTING & CHARGING SYSTEMS
Generators & Regulators – Cars (Cont.)

voltage tests are satisfactory, reduce engine speed, and turn off blower motor, headlights and ignition switch.

AMPERAGE OUTPUT TEST

NOTE: A volt/amp tester equipped with both a battery load control (carbon pile) and an inductive-type pick-up clamp (ammeter probe) is necessary to perform following test procedure.

1) Start engine and run until normal operating temperature is reached. Ensure all accessories are off. Ensure tester battery load is off. Connect inductive ammeter probe. Connect voltmeter to positive and negative battery terminals.

2) Start engine. Raise and maintain engine speed at 2500 RPM. Slowly rotate battery load control until highest amperage reading is acheived. Record voltage reading and return load control to off position. Do not maintain load longer than 15 seconds. The amperage reading should meet minimum specification without battery voltage dropping below 12 volts. See GENERATOR SPECIFICATIONS table.

3) With load control off, maintain engine speed at 2500 RPM. Amperage should decrease to less than 15–20 amps within 2–3 minutes. If amperage does not significantly decrease, check battery. Also check if any DTCs are present. See SELF-DIAGNOSTIC SYSTEM.

GENERATOR SPECIFICATIONS

Application	[1] Minimum Output-Amps
Avenger & Sebring Coupe	
DOHC	63
SOHC	77
Concorde, Intrepid, LHS & 300M	
2.7L	105
3.2 & 3.5L	110
Breeze, Cirrus & Stratus	
2.0L, 2.4L & 2.5L	74
Neon	
2.0L	75
Sebring Convertible	
2.4L & 2.5L	74

[1] – At 2500 RPM.

VOLTAGE DROP TEST

NOTE: VOLTAGE DROP TEST determines amount of resistance in circuits between generator and battery.

1) Using external voltmeter, connect positive lead to generator B+ terminal stud (not the nut). *See Fig. 1, 2 or 3.* Connect voltmeter negative lead to positive battery cable. Connect tachometer to engine. Fully engage parking brake, and place gear selector in Neutral. Start engine and run for 2 minutes to allow for warm-up.

2) Turn A/C system on, A/C-heater blower motor to high speed and headlights on high beam. Increase engine speed to 2400 RPM. Voltmeter reading should not be more than 0.8 volt.

3) If voltage drop is more than 0.8 volt, inspect, clean and tighten all connections between generator B+ terminal and positive battery post. Voltage drop test may be performed at each connection to locate connection with excessive resistance. If resistance tests are satisfactory, reduce engine speed, turn off all electrical loads and ignition switch.

REMOVAL & INSTALLATION

CAUTION: When battery is disconnected, vehicle computer and memory systems may lose memory data. Driveability problems may exist until computer systems have completed a relearn cycle. See COMPUTER RELEARN PROCEDURES article in GENERAL INFORMATION before disconnecting battery.

GENERATOR

Removal & Installation (2.0L, 2.4L, 2.5L & 2.7L) – Disconnect negative battery cable. Disconnect generator field circuit connector. *See Fig. 1, 2 or 3.* Disconnect BAT terminal nut. Loosen, but DO NOT remove, adjusting "T" bolt. Loosen, but DO NOT remove, pivot bolt. Remove generator drive belt. Remove "T" bolt and pivot bolt. DO NOT lose pivot bolt spacer. Remove generator. To install, reverse removal procedure.

Removal & Installation (3.2L & 3.5L) – Disconnect negative battery cable. Loosen, but DO NOT remove, lower mounting bolt. Loosen, but DO NOT remove, pivot bolt. Loosen belt adjustment bolt. Remove generator drive belt. Remove bracket, lower mounting bolt and pivot bolt. Remove generator. Disconnect generator field circuit connector. *See Fig. 1, 2 or 3.* Disconnect BAT terminal nut. To install, reverse removal procedure.

TORQUE SPECIFICATIONS

TORQUE SPECIFICATIONS

Application	Ft. Lbs. (N.m)
Battery Hold-Down Bolt	10 (13.5)
Generator Mounting Bolts & Nuts	40 (54.0)
	INCH Lbs. (N.m)
Generator BAT Terminal Nut	75 (8.5)

WIRING DIAGRAMS

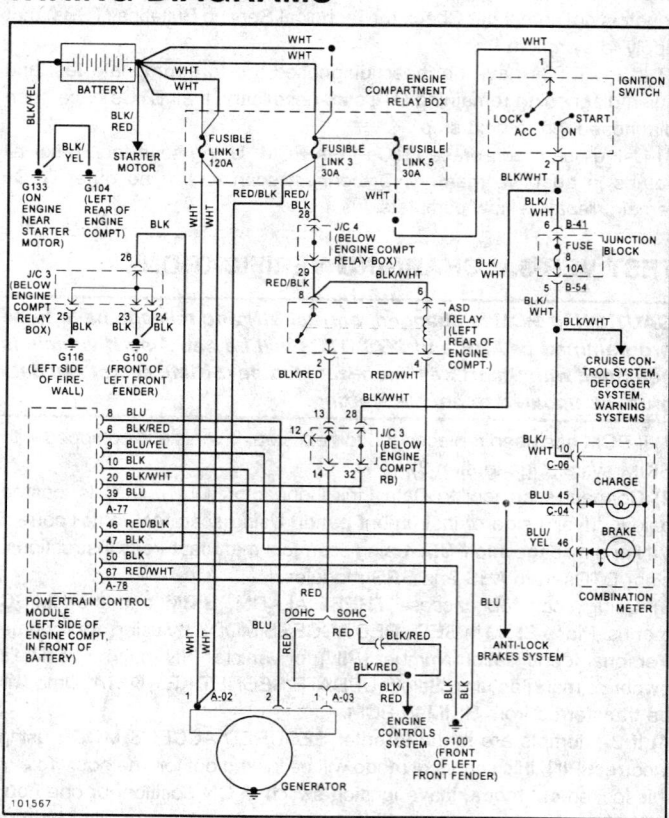

Fig. 4: Charging System Wiring Diagram (Avenger & Sebring Coupe)

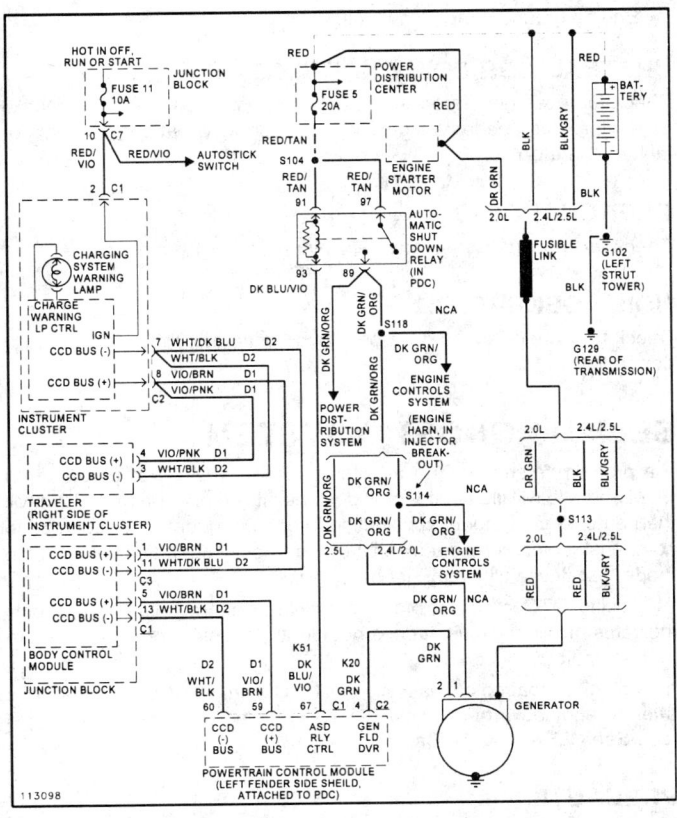

**Fig. 5: Charging System Wiring Diagram
(Breeze, Cirrus & Stratus)**

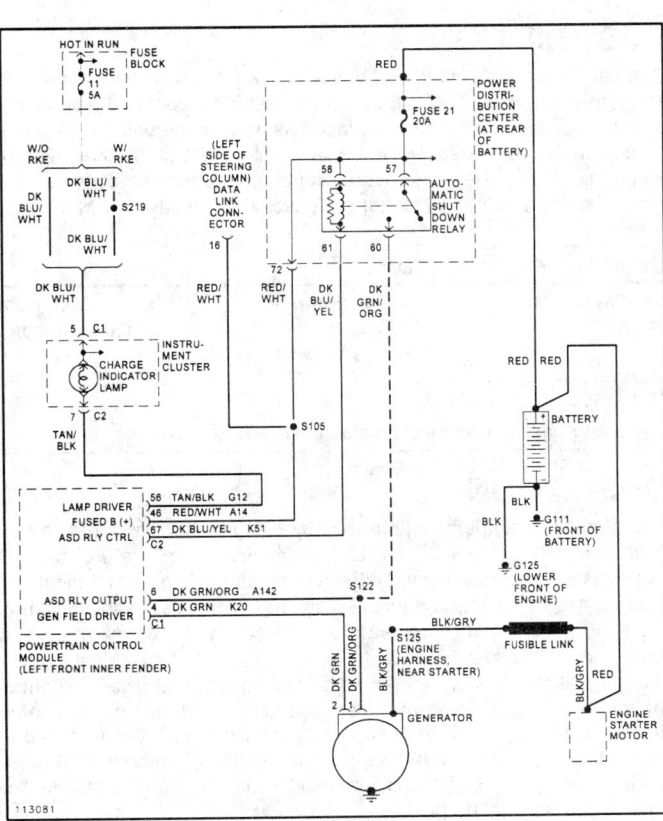

Fig. 7: Charging System Wiring Diagram (Neon)

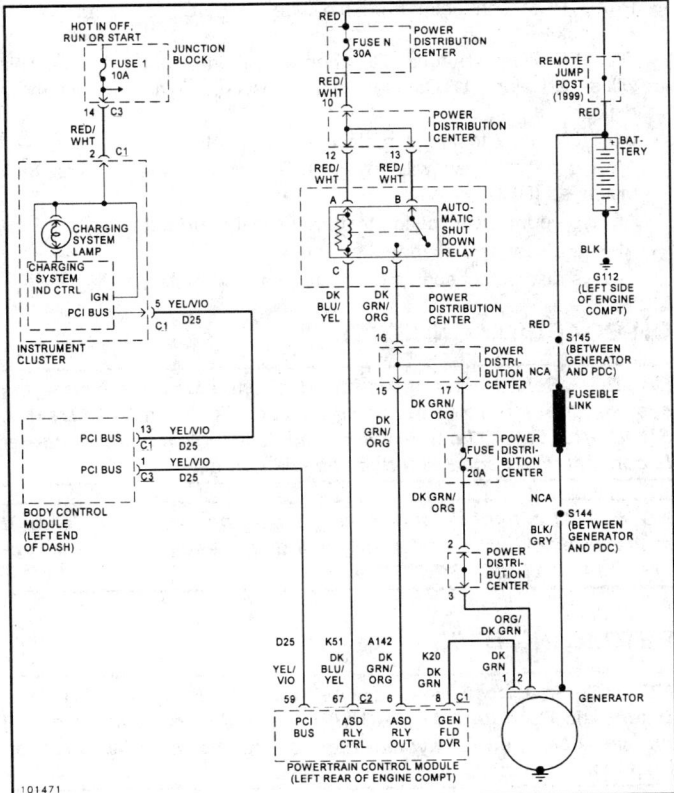

**Fig. 6: Charging System Wiring Diagram
(Concorde, Intrepid, LHS & 300M)**

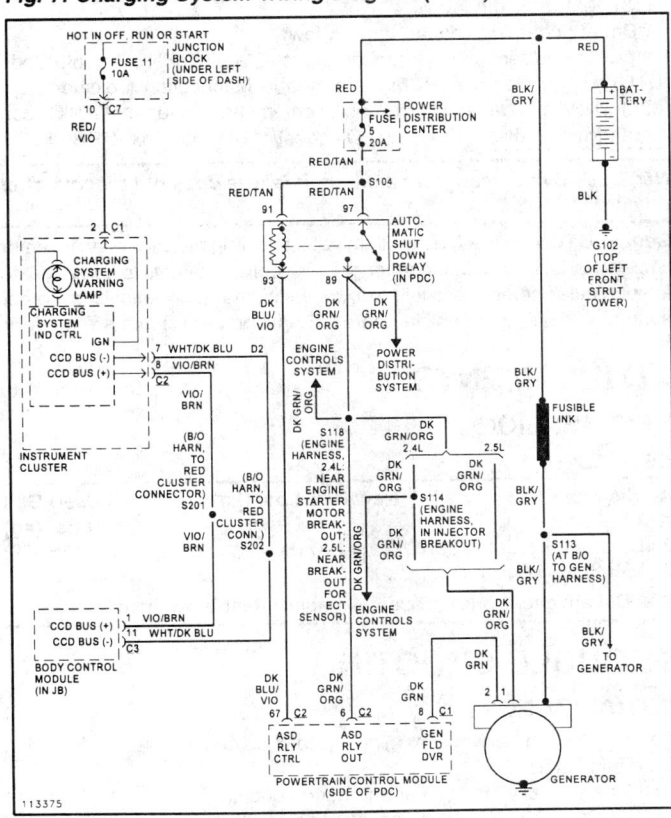

**Fig. 8: Charging System Wiring Diagram
(Sebring Convertible)**

1999 STARTING & CHARGING SYSTEMS
Generators & Regulators
Caravan, Town & Country, & Voyager

DESCRIPTION

Caravan, Town & Country, and Voyager use a Nippondenso generator. The generator consists of a rotor, stator, rectifiers, front and rear covers and drive pulley. Generator is serviced as a complete unit only. Voltage regulation is controlled by the Powertrain Control Module (PCM). Electronic Voltage Regulator (EVR) is not a separate component, but a circuit located within the PCM. If EVR circuit is defective, PCM must be replaced.

GENERATOR APPLICATION

Application	Case Number [1]	Minimum Output-Amps
90-Amp	4727220	86
120-Amp	4727325AA	98

[1] – Part number is located on side of generator case.

OPERATION

The amount of amperage produced by the generator is controlled by Electronic Voltage Regulator (EVR) circuitry within the PCM. EVR circuity is connected in series with the generator field driver terminal and ground. A Battery Temperature Sensor (BTS), located within PCM, is used to sense battery temperature. Sensed battery temperature and data from monitored line voltage is used by PCM to adjust battery charging rate. This is accomplished by cycling the ground path to control the strength of generator rotor magnetic field. PCM then compensates and regulates generator amperage output accordingly. The PCM monitors critical input to control fuel injection, ignition, emission and other engine management functions. The PCM is also programmed to monitor charging system related circuits:

- Battery feed to PCM.
- Generator field control.
- Battery charging voltage (high & low).

If a problem is sensed in a monitored circuit, a Diagnostic Trouble Code (DTC) will be stored in PCM memory and Malfunction Indicator Light (MIL) will illuminate, provided specific criteria have been met. DTCs can be read using MIL or Chrysler's Diagnostic Readout Box (DRB-III).

NOTE: DTC is erased from memory if failure does not reoccur after 50 engine starts.

Certain DTCs cause MIL to illuminate and engine controller to enter limp-in mode. In limp-in mode, engine controller attempts to compensate for particular component failure by substituting information from other sources. This allows vehicle operation until proper repairs are made.

ADJUSTMENTS

BELT TENSION

BELT TENSION

Application	New Belt Lbs. (kg)	Used Belt Lbs. (kg)
2.4L	190 (86)	115 (52)
3.0L, 3.3L & 3.8L	[1]	[1]

[1] – Dynamic tensioner is used. No adjustment is required.

TROUBLE SHOOTING

INITIAL CHECKS

Before proceeding with charging system diagnosis, ensure following conditions are met:

- Battery is fully charged and in good condition.
- Battery cables are in good condition with connections clean and secure.
- Generator belt is in good condition and properly tightened.
- Generator and PCM wiring harness connections are clean and tight.
- Engine ground strap is in place.

UNSTEADY OR LOW CHARGING

Check for loose generator belt, charging resistance too high, defective generator, loose generator ground wire, corroded battery terminals or faulty generator.

OVERCHARGING

Check for grounded generator field wiring or faulty generator.

NOISY GENERATOR

Check for worn or frayed drive belt, loose generator mounting, or faulty generator.

SELF-DIAGNOSTIC SYSTEM

If a problem is sensed in a monitored circuit, a DTC will be stored in PCM and MIL will illuminate, provided specific criteria are met. PCM will then enter limp-in mode, substituting information from other sources to compensate for component failure. Vehicle is operational in limp-in mode, but driveability may not be optimal.

A specific DTC results from a particular system failure. DTC only indicates problem circuit. It does not identify specific component failure in the circuit.

If problem is repaired or ceases to exist, PCM automatically clears DTCs after 40 engine warm-up cycles. DTCs can also be cleared using scan tool. See CLEARING DTCs.

PRECAUTIONS

Before proceeding with diagnosis, observe following precautions:

- Ensure battery is fully charged and charging system is functional.
- Probe PCM connector from pin side. DO NOT backprobe PCM connector.
- DO NOT cause short circuits when performing electrical tests. This will set additional DTCs, making diagnosis of original problem more difficult.
- DO NOT use a test light in place of a voltmeter.
- Always begin repair with lowest DTC number (MIL) or first fault displayed (DRB).
- Always perform verification test after repairs are made.
- Always disconnect scan tool after use.
- Always disconnect scan tool before charging battery.

ON-BOARD DIAGNOSTICS

CAUTION: Before entering on-board diagnostics, check charging system for other problems. See INITIAL CHECKS under TROUBLE SHOOTING. DO NOT connect scan tool to vehicle if battery charger is connected, as scan tool damage will result.

NOTE: PCM cannot diagnose every charging system problem. If fault still exists after performing self-diagnostic procedures, proceed to ON- VEHICLE TESTING.

RETRIEVING DTCS

NOTE: Self-diagnostic tests are written specifically for Chrysler's Diagnostic Readout Box (DRB-III) scan tool. A generic scan tool may also be used for system diagnostics, but may have limited diagnostic capability.

1) Ensure battery is fully charged. Connect scan tool to Data Link Connector (DLC). DLC is located below instrument panel, near steering column.

1999 STARTING & CHARGING SYSTEMS
Generators & Regulators
Caravan, Town & Country, & Voyager (Cont.)

CHRY
2-19

2) Using scan tool manufacturer's instructions, retrieve and record DTCs displayed on scan tool and proceed to SELF-DIAGNOSTIC TESTS. Once repairs are made, clear DTCs from PCM memory. See CLEARING DTCS.

CLEARING DTCS

PCM automatically clears DTCs from PCM memory after 40 engine warm-up cycles. DTCs can also be cleared using scan tool by following scan tool manufacturer's instructions.

SCAN TOOL PROBLEMS & ERROR MESSAGES

NO RESPONSE Message – See TEST NS-2A in appropriate SELF-DIAGNOSTICS article in ENGINE PERFORMANCE in appropriate MITCHELL® manual.

NOTE: For more information on scan tool and PCM diagnostics, see appropriate SELF-DIAGNOSTICS article in ENGINE PERFORMANCE.

SELF-DIAGNOSTIC TESTS

NOTE: When using diagnostic tests, DO NOT skip any steps or incorrect diagnosis may result. Ensure battery is fully charged.

DTC TEST: CHECKING FOR DTCS

NOTE: For connector terminal identification, see CONNECTOR IDENTIFICATION in appropriate SELF-DIAGNOSTICS article in ENGINE PERFORMANCE.

1) Attempt to start engine. If necessary, crank engine for up to 10 seconds. Connect scan tool to Data Link Connector (DLC). Record scan tool trouble codes. If scan tool screen shows no response, go to TEST NS-2A in appropriate SELF-DIAGNOSTICS TESTS article in ENGINE PERFORMANCE.

2) If DTCs are displayed, see SCAN TOOL DTC MESSAGES table. Only DTCs relating to charging system are listed. For all other DTCs, see appropriate SELF-DIAGNOSTICS article in ENGINE PERFORMANCE in appropriate MITCHELL® manual. If no DTCs are displayed, go to TEST CH-1A: CHARGING SYSTEM NO CODE TEST.

SCAN TOOL DTC MESSAGES

Scan Tool Display	DTC
GENERATOR FIELD NOT SWITCHING PROPERLY	P0622
BATTERY TEMPERATURE SENSOR VOLTAGE TOO HIGH [1]	P1492
BATTERY TEMPERATURE SENSOR VOLTAGE TOO LOW [1]	P1493
CHARGING SYSTEM VOLTAGE TOO HIGH	P1594
CHARGING SYSTEM VOLTAGE TOO LOW	P1682

[1] – Replace PCM. PCM is located next to battery. Perform TEST VER-5A.

DTC P0622: GENERATOR FIELD NOT SWITCHING PROPERLY

NOTE: DTC is set when PCM attempts to regulate generator field with no result during monitoring. Possible causes are ASD relay output open circuit, generator field resistance greater than 5 ohms, open generator field driver circuit, generator field driver circuit shorted to ground, defective generator or PCM.

1) Using scan tool, erase trouble codes. Using scan tool, actuate generator field driver circuit. Using a voltmeter, backprobe generator field connector. Measure voltage between ground and ASD relay output circuit terminal. Generator field connector is located on back of genera-

tor. See WIRING DIAGRAMS. If voltage is more than 10 volts, go to next step. If voltage is 10 volts or less, repair open ASD relay output circuit. Perform TEST VER-3A.

2) Using a voltmeter, backprobe generator field connector generator field driver circuit. If voltage shifts from low to high, go to next step. If voltage does not shift from low to high, go to step 4).

3) Wiggle wiring harness from generator to PCM. Using scan tool, read DTCs with actuator test still running. If generator field driver circuit DTC sets, repair wiring harness as necessary where wiggling caused problem to appear. If DTC does not set, fault is currently not present. Test is complete. Perform TEST VER-3A.

4) Turn ignition off. Disconnect PCM harness connector. Disconnect field harness connector on rear of generator. Using an ohmmeter, measure resistance between generator field terminals on generator. If resistance is 5 ohms or more, repair or replace generator. Perform TEST VER-3A. If resistance is less than 5 ohms, go to next step.

5) With generator field connector disconnected, measure resistance between ground and generator field driver terminal. If resistance is less than 5 ohms, repair generator field driver circuit for short to ground. Perform TEST VER-3A. If resistance is 5 ohms or more, go to next step.

6) Using an ohmmeter, check resistance of generator field driver circuit between generator field harness connector and PCM harness connector. See WIRING DIAGRAMS. If resistance is 5 ohms or more, repair open generator field driver circuit. Perform TEST VER-3A. If resistance is less than 5 ohms, replace PCM.

DTC P1594: CHARGING SYSTEM VOLTAGE TOO HIGH

NOTE: DTC is set when monitored battery voltage is one volt below charging system upper limit threshold for 25 seconds. PCM turns off field driver and monitors battery voltage. If voltage remains high, DTC P1594 is set. Possible causes are generator field driver circuit shorted to ground, shorted generator or Powertrain Control Module (battery temperature and/or charging voltage).

1) Ensure battery is fully charged, and generator belt tension and condition are okay. Using scan tool, actuate generator field driver. Using a voltmeter to ground, backprobe generator field connector, checking voltage on Dark Green wire. See WIRING DIAGRAMS. If voltage shifts from low to high, go to next step. If voltage does not shift from low to high, go to step 6).

2) Using scan tool, stop generator field driver actuation. Start engine. Using scan tool, read target charging voltage. If target charging voltage is more than 13 volts, go to step 4. If target charging voltage is 13 volts or less, go to next step.

3) Start engine. Manually set engine speed to 1600 RPM. Using scan tool, read and compare voltage and target charging voltage. Observe voltage for up to 5 minutes (if necessary) for a one volt difference between voltage and target charging voltage. If difference between voltage and target charging voltage is one volt or less, go to TEST CH-1A: CHARGING SYSTEM NO CODE TEST. If difference between voltage and target charging voltage is more than one volt, replace Powertrain Control Module (PCM). Perform TEST VER-3A.

4) Measure underhood temperature near PCM using scan tool temperature probe. Using scan tool, read battery temperature sensor temperature. If scan tool display is within 10 degrees of actual underhood temperature, go to next step. If scan tool display is not within 10 degrees of actual underhood temperature, replace BTS. Perform TEST VER-3A.

5) Turn ignition off. Allow engine to return to idle speed. Turn ignition off, then on. Erase DTCs. See CLEARING CODES. Go to TEST CH- 1A: CHARGING SYSTEM NO CODE TEST.

6) Turn ignition off. Disconnect PCM harness connector. Disconnect field harness connector on rear of generator. Using an ohmmeter, measure resistance of generator field driver circuit between PCM connector and ground. If resistance is 5 ohms or more, go to next step. If resistance is less than 5 ohms, repair short to ground on generator field driver circuit. Perform TEST VER-3A.

CHRY
2-20

1999 STARTING & CHARGING SYSTEMS
Generators & Regulators
Caravan, Town & Country, & Voyager (Cont.)

7) With generator field connector disconnected, measure resistance from either generator field terminal (on back of generator) to ground. If resistance is less than 5 ohms, repair or replace shorted generator. If resistance is 5 ohms or more, replace PCM. Perform TEST VER-3A.

DTC P1682: CHARGING SYSTEM VOLTAGE TOO LOW

NOTE: DTC is set when monitored battery voltage is one volt below charging system lower limit threshold for 25 seconds. PCM turns off field driver and monitors battery voltage. If voltage remains low, DTC P1682 is set. Possible causes are open ASD relay output circuit, high resistance in battery supply circuit between generator and battery, open driver circuit, high resistance in ground circuit, defective generator or defective battery temperature sensor.

1) Ensure battery is fully charged. Start engine. Using scan tool, read voltage goal. If voltage goal is more than 15.1 volts, go to next step. If voltage goal is 15.1 volts or less, go to step 5).

2) Using scan tool, read Battery Temperature Sensor (BTS) temperature. If BTS temperature matches actual underhood temperature, go to next step. If BTS temperature does not match actual underhood temperature, replace PCM. Perform TEST VER-3A.

3) Turn ignition off. Disconnect generator field connector. Ensure connector is clean. Disconnect Powertrain Control Module (PCM) connector. PCM is located next to battery. Using external ohmmeter, measure resistance of circuit between ASD relay and generator field connector. See WIRING DIAGRAMS. If resistance is less than 5 ohms, go to next step. If resistance is 5 ohms or greater, repair open circuit. Perform TEST VER-3A.

4) Measure resistance of generator field driver circuit between PCM and generator field connector. See WIRING DIAGRAMS. If resistance is less than 5 ohms, replace generator. If resistance is 5 ohms or greater, repair open circuit. Perform TEST VER-3A.

5) Disconnect generator field connector. Disconnect Powertrain Control Module (PCM) connector. PCM is located next to battery. Measure resistance of ASD output circuit between PCM connector and generator field connector. See WIRING DIAGRAMS. If resistance is less than 5 ohms, go to next step. If resistance is 5 ohms or greater, repair open ASD circuit. Perform TEST VER-3A.

6) Measure resistance of generator field driver circuit between PCM and generator field connector. See WIRING DIAGRAMS. If resistance is less than 5 ohms, replace generator. If resistance is 5 ohms or greater, repair open circuit. Perform TEST VER-3A.

TEST CH-1A: CHARGING SYSTEM NO CODE TEST

1) Verify battery condition. Charge or replace battery as necessary. Inspect generator belt tension and condition. Replace generator belt as necessary. Start engine. Using scan tool, set engine speed to 1600 RPM for 30 seconds. Using scan tool, return engine to idle speed and read Diagnostic Trouble Codes (DTCs). If any charging system DTCs are set, see SCAN TOOL DTC MESSAGES table and perform appropriate test. If no charging system DTCs are set, go to next step.

2) Turn ignition on with engine off. Using scan tool, actuate generator field. Using scan tool in voltmeter mode, backprobe generator field driver terminal on back of generator. *See Fig. 1.* Voltage should cycle from zero volts to battery voltage every 1.4 seconds at both terminals. While observing scan tool, wiggle field terminal wiring harness back to Powertrain Control Module (PCM). If any interruption of voltage cycling occurred, repair wiring harness where wiggling caused failure. Perform TEST VER-3A. If wiggling did not interrupt voltage cycling, go to next step.

3) Using scan tool, read DTCs. If any charging system DTCs are set, see SCAN TOOL DTC MESSAGES table and perform appropriate test. If no charging system trouble codes are set, go to next step.

4) Turn ignition off. Using an external voltmeter, check voltage between generator case and battery negative terminal. Start engine. If voltage is greater than .1 volt, repair high resistance between generator battery

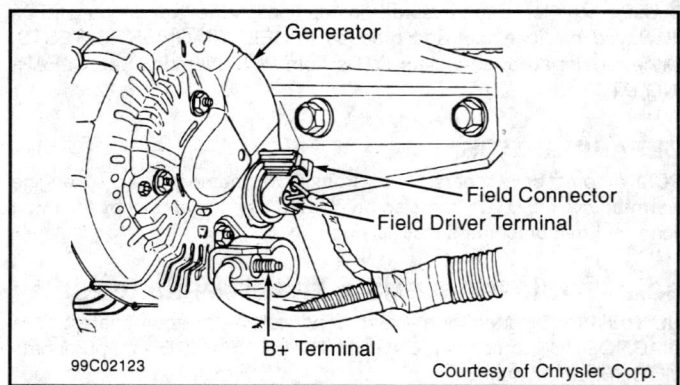

99C02123   Courtesy of Chrysler Corp.

Fig. 1: Identifying Generator Terminals

negative terminal and battery negative terminal. Perform TEST VER-3A. If voltage is .1 volt or less, go to next step.

5) Using an external voltmeter, check voltage between generator B+ terminal located on rear of generator and battery positive terminal. *See Fig. 1.* Ensure voltmeter wires are clear of moving engine parts. Start engine and observe voltmeter. If voltage is .4 volt or less, go to next step. If voltage is more than .4 volt, repair high resistance between generator B+ terminal and battery positive terminal. Perform TEST VER-3A.

6) With ignition on and engine off, read and record battery voltage using scan tool. Using voltmeter, measure and record voltage between battery terminals. If voltage difference is less than one volt, test is complete. If voltage difference is one volt or greater, go to next step.

7) With ignition on and engine off, read and record battery voltage using scan tool. Turn ignition off. Disconnect PCM connector. Turn ignition on. Using voltmeter, measure voltage between ground and terminal No. 46 on PCM connector. If voltage is within one volt of scan tool voltage, repair high resistance between PCM connector terminal No. 46 and battery positive terminal. Perform TEST VER-3A. If voltage is not within one volt of scan tool voltage, replace PCM. Perform TEST VER-3A.

TEST VER-2A: ROAD TEST VERIFICATION

CAUTION: If PCM is changed, correct VIN and mileage have to be programmed or ABS and SRS DTCs will be set.

1) Connect scan tool to Data Link Connector (DLC). DLC is located below driver's side of instrument panel. Using scan tool, enter correct VIN and mileage into PCM. Using scan tool manufacturer's instructions, clear DTCs from ABS and SRS modules.

2) Inspect vehicle to ensure all engine components are connected. Reassemble and reconnect components as necessary.

3) Check if initial symptom still exists. If initial or another symptom exists, repair is not complete. Check for Technical Service Bulletins (TSBs) that apply to symptom.

4) If any DTCs have not been diagnosed, go to appropriate test and finish diagnosing remaining DTCs as necessary. If all DTCs have been diagnosed, go to next step.

5) Using scan tool, erase DTCs from PCM. Using scan tool, reset all values in adaptive memory. Disconnect scan tool. If no other DTCs remain, repair is now complete.

TEST VER-3A: CHARGING VERIFICATION

CAUTION: If PCM is changed, correct VIN and mileage have to be programmed or ABS and SRS DTCs will be set.

1) Connect scan tool to Data Link Connector (DLC). DLC is located below driver's side of instrument panel. Using scan tool, enter correct VIN and mileage into PCM. Using scan tool manufacturer's instructions, clear DTCs from ABS and SRS modules.

2) To ensure no charging system problem exists, start engine. Perform OUTPUT VOLTAGE TEST under ON-VEHICLE TESTING. Increase engine speed to 2000 RPM for at least 30 seconds. Allow engine to idle. Turn engine off.

3) Using scan tool, check for stored DTCs. If repaired DTC has reset, repair is not complete. Check for related Technical Service Bulletins (TSBs) and return to DTC TEST, if necessary. If another DTC exists, go to appropriate DTC test and follow specified procedure. If no other DTCs exist, repair is now complete.

TEST VER-5A: ROAD TEST VERIFICATION

CAUTION: If PCM is changed, correct VIN and mileage have to be programmed or ABS and SRS DTCs will be set.

1) Connect scan tool to Data Link Connector (DLC). DLC is located below driver's side of instrument panel. Using scan tool, enter correct VIN and mileage into PCM. Using scan tool manufacturer's instructions, clear DTCs from ABS and SRS modules.

2) Inspect vehicle to ensure all engine components are connected. Reassemble and reconnect components as necessary.

3) If any DTCs have not been diagnosed, go to appropriate test and finish diagnosing remaining DTCs as necessary. If all DTCs have been diagnosed, go to next step.

4) Connect scan tool to DLC connector. Ensure fuel tank is at least 25 percent full. Turn off all accessories.

5) Using scan tool OBDII monitor, verify DTC repair. See scan tool instructions. Allow PCM to run appropriate monitor(s) and increment a global good trip (drive cycle). Enabling conditions must be met before PCM will run OBDII monitor. Scan tool monitor pretest screen will display enabling conditions.

6) If repaired DTC has reset or was seen in OBDII monitor while on road test, repair is not complete. Check for any TSBs and return to appropriate test. Repair as needed.

7) If any other DTCs are set, repair as needed. If OBDII monitor is run and good trip counter is incremented and no new DTCs are set, repair is successful and complete. Erase DTCs. See CLEARING CODES.

ON-VEHICLE TESTING

CAUTION: When battery is disconnected, vehicle computer and memory systems may lose memory data. Driveability problems may exist until computer systems have completed a relearn cycle. See COMPUTER RELEARN PROCEDURES article in GENERAL INFORMATION before disconnecting battery.

VOLTAGE DROP TEST

NOTE: VOLTAGE DROP TEST determines amount of resistance in circuits between generator and battery.

1) Ensure battery is in condition and is fully charged. Clean battery terminals (if necessary). Using external voltmeter, connect positive lead to generator B+ terminal stud (not the nut). Connect voltmeter negative lead to positive battery post. Connect tachometer to engine. Fully engage parking brake, and place gear selector in Neutral position. Start engine and run for 2 minutes to allow for warm-up.

2) Turn A/C system on, A/C-heater blower motor to high speed and headlights on high beam. Increase engine speed to 2400 RPM. Voltmeter reading should not be more than 0.6 volt.

3) If voltage drop is more than 0.6 volt, inspect, clean and tighten all connections between generator B+ terminal and positive battery post. Voltage drop test may be performed at each connection to locate connection with excessive resistance. If resistance tests are satisfactory, reduce engine speed, turn off all electrical loads and ignition switch.

CURRENT OUTPUT TEST

CAUTION: Generator has 2 field terminals: generator field driver (Dark Green wire) and ASD relay output (Dark Green/Orange wire). DO NOT connect generator ASD relay output terminal to ground.

NOTE: Perform VOLTAGE DROP TEST before continuing with this test. Perform test soon after starting engine, as charging amperage will drop quickly. A volt/amp tester equipped with both a battery load control (carbon pile rheostat) and an inductive type pick-up clamp is required to perform the following test.

1) Ensure battery is in good condition and is fully charged. Clean battery terminals (if necessary). Connect volt/amp tester leads to battery. Ensure carbon pile is in OFF position before connecting leads. Connect inductive pick-up clamp.

2) Connect tachometer to engine. Start engine and raise engine speed to 2500 RPM. Slowly adjust rheostat control (load) on volt/amp tester until highest amperage reading is obtained. DO NOT allow voltage to drop less than 12 volts.

NOTE: Depending on volt/amp tester manufacturer, load may be applied automatically. Refer to volt/amp tester manufacturer's instructions.

3) Note reading on ammeter. Generator amperage reading should be more than the minimum amperage rating specification. See GENERATOR APPLICATION table under DESCRIPTION. If amperage reading is less than minimum specification, go to step **5)**. If amperage reading is more than minimum specification, go to next step.

4) Rotate load control knob to OFF position. Continue to hold engine speed at 2500 RPM. Output amperage should change to less than 20-amps, indicating EVR circuity is okay and charging system is functioning properly. It may take several minutes for amperage to change. If output amperage does not change to less than 20-amps, go to SELF-DIAGNOSTIC TESTS.

5) Connect a jumper wire between ground and generator field driver terminal (Dark Green wire) on back of generator. *See Fig. 1.* Start engine, and immediately reduce engine speed to idle. Adjust carbon pile and engine speed in increments until engine speed is 1250 RPM and voltmeter reads 15 volts. DO NOT allow voltage to exceed 16 volts.

6) Note reading on volt/amp tester. Generator amperage reading should be more than the minimum amperage rating specification. See GENERATOR APPLICATION table under DESCRIPTION. If amperage reading is less than minimum specification, replace generator. If amperage reading is more than minimum specification, a fault exists in EVR circuitry. Go to SELF-DIAGNOSTIC TESTS.

REMOVAL & INSTALLATION

Removal & Installation (2.4L) – **1)** Disconnect negative battery cable. Remove accessory drive belt. Disconnect chassis wiring connector. Remove nut holding B+ cable to back of generator and disconnect B+ cable.

2) Remove generator mounting bolts. Remove generator. To install, reverse removal procedure. Tighten fasteners to specification. See TORQUE SPECIFICATIONS.

Removal & Installation (3.0L) – **1)** Disconnect negative battery cable. Remove windshield wiper housing. Remove accessory drive belt. Remove generator mounting bolts.

2) Disconnect chassis wiring connector. Remove B+ terminal nut and disconnect B+ cable. Remove wire connectors. Remove generator from vehicle. To install, reverse removal procedure. Tighten fasteners to specification. See TORQUE SPECIFICATIONS.

Removal & Installation (3.3L & 3.8L) – **1)** Disconnect negative battery cable. Remove windshield wiper housing. Remove accessory drive belt. Remove generator mounting bolts. Remove generator mount bracket.

1999 STARTING & CHARGING SYSTEMS
Generators & Regulators
Caravan, Town & Country, & Voyager (Cont.)

2) Disconnect chassis wiring connector. Remove B+ terminal nut and disconnect B+ cable. Remove generator. To install, reverse removal procedure. Tighten fasteners to specification. See TORQUE SPECIFICATIONS.

TORQUE SPECIFICATIONS

TORQUE SPECIFICATIONS

Application	Ft. Lbs. (N.m)
Generator Mounting Bolts	40 (54)

	INCH Lbs. (N.m)
Battery Hold-Down Bolt/Nut	125 (14)
Field Terminal Nuts	25 (3)
B+ & Ground Terminal Nuts	75 (9)

WIRING DIAGRAMS

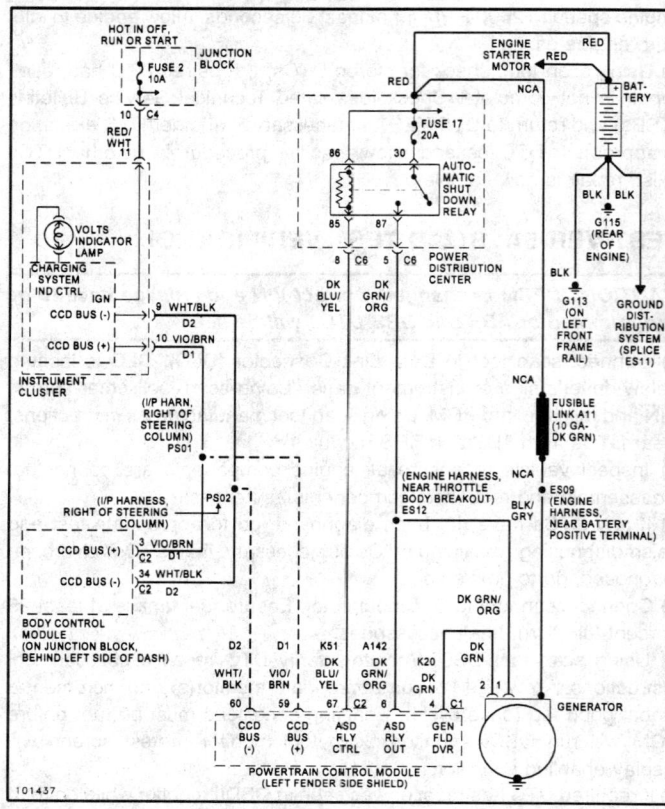

***Fig. 2: Charging System Wiring Diagram
(Caravan, Town & Country, & Voyager)***

Dakota, Durango, Pickup, Ram Van, Ram Wagon

MODEL IDENTIFICATION

Vehicle body codes are used throughout self-diagnostic tests. See BODY CODE DESIGNATION table for model identification.

BODY CODE DESIGNATION

Model Name	Body Type
Dakota	AN
Durango	DN
Ram Pickup	BR
Ram Van & Ram Wagon	AB

DESCRIPTION

Chrysler Corp. light trucks use a Denso generator. The generator consists of a rotor, stator, rectifiers, front and rear covers and drive pulley. Generator is serviced as a complete unit only. Voltage regulation is controlled by the Powertrain Control Module (PCM). Electronic Voltage Regulator (EVR) is not a separate component, but a circuit located within the PCM. If EVR circuit is defective, PCM must be replaced.

GENERATOR APPLICATION

Application	Minimum Output-Amps
Dakota & Durango	
2.5L	
117-Amp	88
136-Amp	95
3.9L, 5.2L & 5.9L	
117-Amp	90
136-Amp	100
Ram Pickup, Ram Van & Ram Wagon	
Gasoline	
3.9L, 5.2L, 5.9L & 8.0L	
117-Amp	90
136-Amp	100
Diesel	
5.9L	
136-Amp	120

OPERATION

The amount of amperage produced by the generator is controlled by Electronic Voltage Regulator (EVR) circuitry within the PCM. EVR circuity is connected in series with the generator field driver terminal and ground. A Battery Temperature Sensor (BTS), located in battery tray, is used to sense battery temperature. Sensed battery temperature and data from monitored line voltage is used by PCM to adjust battery charging rate. This is accomplished by cycling the ground path to control the strength of generator rotor magnetic field. PCM then compensates and regulates generator amperage output accordingly. The PCM monitors critical input to control fuel injection, ignition, emission and other engine management functions. The PCM is also programmed to monitor charging system related circuits:

- Battery feed to PCM.
- Generator field control.
- Battery charging voltage (high & low).

If a problem is sensed in a monitored circuit, a Diagnostic Trouble Code (DTC) will be stored in PCM memory and Malfunction Indicator Light (MIL) will illuminate, provided specific criteria have been met. DTCs can be read using Chrysler's Diagnostic Readout Box (DRB-III), or a generic scan tool.

NOTE: DTC is erased from memory if failure does not reoccur after 40 engine warm-up cycles.

Certain DTCs cause MIL to illuminate and PCM to enter limp-in mode. In limp-in mode, PCM attempts to compensate for particular component failure by substituting information from other sources. This allows vehicle operation until proper repairs are made.

ADJUSTMENTS

BELT TENSION

BELT TENSION

Application	New Belt Lbs. (kg)	Used Belt Lbs. (kg)
Dakota & Durango		
2.5L	180-200 (82-91)	140-160 (64-73)
3.9L & 5.2L	[1]	[1]
Ram Pickup, Ram Van &		
Ram Wagon	[1]	[1]

[1] – Dynamic tensioner is used. No adjustment is required.

TROUBLE SHOOTING

INITIAL CHECKS

Before proceeding with charging system diagnosis, ensure following conditions are met:

- Battery is fully charged and in good condition.
- Battery cables are in good condition with connections clean and secure.
- Generator belt is in good condition and properly tightened.
- Generator and PCM wiring harness connections are clean and tight.
- Engine ground strap is in place.

UNSTEADY OR LOW CHARGING

Check for loose generator belt, charging resistance too high, loose generator ground wire, corroded battery terminals or faulty generator.

OVERCHARGING

Check for grounded generator field wiring or faulty generator.

NOISY GENERATOR

Check for worn or frayed drive belt, loose generator mounting, or faulty generator.

SELF-DIAGNOSTIC SYSTEM

If a problem is sensed in a monitored circuit, a Diagnostic Trouble Code (DTC) will be stored in PCM and MIL will illuminate, provided specific criteria are met. PCM will then enter limp-in mode, substituting information from other sources to compensate for component failure. Vehicle is operational in limp-in mode, but driveability may not be optimal.

A specific DTC results from a particular system failure. DTC only indicates problem circuit. It does not identify specific component failure in the circuit.

If problem is repaired or ceases to exist, PCM automatically clears DTC after 40 engine warm-up cycles. DTCs can also be cleared using scan tool. See CLEARING DTCS.

PRECAUTIONS

Before proceeding with diagnosis, observe following precautions:

- Ensure battery is fully charged.
- Probe PCM connector from pin side. DO NOT backprobe PCM connector or probe wires through insulation.
- DO NOT cause short circuits when performing electrical tests. This will set additional DTCs, making diagnosis of original problem more difficult.
- DO NOT use a test light in place of a voltmeter.
- Always begin repair with lowest DTC number (MIL) or first DTC displayed (scan tool).
- Always perform verification (VER) test after repairs are made.
- Always disconnect scan tool after use.
- Always disconnect scan tool before charging battery.

CHRY
2-24

1999 STARTING & CHARGING SYSTEMS
Generators & Regulators – Trucks & RWD Vans (Cont.)

ON-BOARD DIAGNOSTICS

CAUTION: Before entering on-board diagnostics, check charging system for other problems. See INITIAL CHECKS under TROUBLE SHOOTING. DO NOT connect scan tool to vehicle if battery charger is connected, as scan tool damage will result.

NOTE: PCM cannot diagnose every charging system problem. If fault still exists after performing self-diagnostic procedures, proceed to ON- VEHICLE TESTING.

RETRIEVING DTCS

NOTE: Self-diagnostic tests are written specifically for Chrysler's Diagnostic Readout Box (DRB-III) scan tool. A generic scan tool may also be used for system diagnostics, but may have limited diagnostic capability.

1) Ensure battery is fully charged. Connect scan tool to Data Link Connector (DLC). DLC is located below instrument panel, near steering column.
2) Using scan tool manufacturer's instructions, retrieve and record DTCs displayed on scan tool and proceed to SELF-DIAGNOSTIC TESTS. Once repairs are made, clear DTCs from PCM memory. See CLEARING DTCS.

CLEARING DTCS

PCM automatically clears DTCs from PCM memory after 40 engine warm-up cycles. DTCs can also be cleared using scan tool by following scan tool manufacturer's instructions.

SCAN TOOL PROBLEMS & ERROR MESSAGES

Blank Message Screen – Check for loose cable connections or bad cable. If cable connections and cable are okay, check voltage at DLC terminal No. 16 (Pink wire). Voltage should be at least 11 volts. If voltage is not as specified, check wiring circuit and necessary fuses.
NO RESPONSE Message – See TEST NS-6A in appropriate SELF-DIAGNOSTICS article in ENGINE PERFORMANCE in appropriate MITCHELL® manual.

NOTE: For more information on scan tool and PCM diagnostics, see appropriate SELF-DIAGNOSTICS article in ENGINE PERFORMANCE.

SELF-DIAGNOSTIC TESTS

NOTE: When using diagnostic tests, DO NOT skip any steps in chart, or incorrect diagnosis may result. Ensure battery is fully charged.

DTC TEST: CHECKING SYSTEM FOR DIAGNOSTIC TROUBLE CODES

NOTE: For connector terminal identification, see CONNECTOR IDENTIFICATION in appropriate SELF-DIAGNOSTICS article in ENGINE PERFORMANCE.

1) Attempt to start engine. If necessary, crank engine for up to 10 seconds. Read and record DTCs. See RETRIEVING DTCS under SELF- DIAGNOSTIC SYSTEM. If scan tool screen is blank or displays NO RESPONSE, see SCAN TOOL PROBLEMS & ERROR MESSAGES under SELF-DIAGNOSTIC SYSTEM.
2) If DTCs are displayed, see SCAN TOOL DTC MESSAGES table. Only DTCs relating to charging system are listed. For all other DTCs, see appropriate SELF-DIAGNOSTICS article in ENGINE PERFORMANCE in appropriate MITCHELL® manual. If no DTCs are displayed, go to TEST CH-1A: CHARGING SYSTEM NO CODE TEST.

SCAN TOOL DTC MESSAGES

Scan Tool Display	DTC
CHARGING SYSTEM VOLTAGE TOO LOW [1]	P0562
GENERATOR FIELD NOT SWITCHING PROPERLY	P0622
BATTERY TEMPERATURE SENSOR VOLTAGE TOO HIGH	P1492
BATTERY TEMPERATURE SENSOR VOLTAGE TOO LOW	P1493
CHARGING SYSTEM VOLTAGE TOO HIGH	P1594
CHARGING SYSTEM VOLTAGE TOO LOW	P1682

[1] – Diesel only.

DTC P0562: CHARGING SYSTEM VOLTAGE TOO LOW

NOTE: DTC P0562 is set when battery voltage at Engine Control Module (ECM) is less than 6 volts. Possible causes are charging system malfunction, open ECM ground circuits, open fused B+ circuits, battery cable resistance, low battery charge, high resistance in battery supply circuit to ECM and/or defective ECM.

1) If DTC P1682 is also set with P0562, repair DTC P1682 first before proceeding with DTC P0562. If DTC P1682 is not set, go to next step.
2) Inspect condition of battery cables. Ensure battery cables do not have high resistance. Repair or replace as needed. Perform TEST VER-2A.
3) Ensure battery is fully charged. Charge as needed. Turn ignition off. Disconnect Engine Control Module (ECM) harness connector. ECM is attached to left side of engine behind fuel filter. Measure voltage between ground and terminals No. 48 and 50 on ECM harness connector. If battery voltage is present, go to next step. If battery voltage is not present, go to step 6).
4) Inspect starter current draw. See appropriate STARTERS article. If starter current draw is within specification, go to next step. If starter current draw is not within specification or battery voltage is low, repair as needed. Perform TEST VER-2A.
5) With ECM harness connector disconnected, measure voltage between terminal No. 48 and terminals No. 30 and 49 (ground circuits) on ECM harness connector. If battery voltage is present, replace ECM. Perform TEST VER-2A. If battery voltage is not present, inspect and repair ground circuits as needed.
6) Inspect starter current draw. See appropriate STARTERS article. If starter current draw is within specification, go to next step. If starter current draw is not within specification or battery voltage is low, repair as needed. Perform TEST VER-2A.
7) Turn ignition off. Remove fuse No. 3 from Power Distribution Center (PDC). Disconnect Engine Control Module (ECM) harness connector. ECM is attached to left side of engine behind fuel filter. Measure resistance between fuse No. 3 and terminals No. 48 and 50 on ECM harness connector. If resistance is less than 5 ohms, go to next step. If resistance is 5 ohms or greater, repair Red/White wire between PDC and ECM. Perform TEST VER-2A.
8) With fuse remove from PDC, measure voltage between ground and fuse No. 3 socket. If battery voltage is present, replace ECM. If battery voltage is not present, repair circuit between battery and fuse No. 3 socket. Perform TEST VER-2A.

DTC P0563: CHARGING SYSTEM VOLTAGE TOO HIGH

NOTE: DTC P0563 is set when battery supply voltage to Engine Control Module (ECM) is greater than 17 volts. Possible causes are charging system malfunction of open ground circuits at ECM.

1) Start engine. Backprobe ECM harness connector. ECM is attached to left side of engine behind fuel filter. Measure voltage between ground and terminals No. 48 and 50 on ECM harness connector. If voltage is less than 17 volts, go to next step. If voltage is 17 volts or greater, go to TEST CH-1A: CHARGING SYSTEM NO CODE TEST.
2) If DTC P1594 is also set with P0563, repair DTC P1594 first before proceeding with DTC P0563. If DTC P1594 is not set, go to next step.

1999 STARTING & CHARGING SYSTEMS
Generators & Regulators – Trucks & RWD Vans (Cont.)

CHRY
2-25

3) Ensure ignition is off. Backprobe ECM harness connector. Measure voltage between ground and terminals No. 48 and 50 on ECM harness connector. If voltage is less than 17 volts, go to next step. If voltage is 17 volts or greater, inspect battery installation. Correct as necessary. Perform TEST VER-2A.

4) Disconnect Engine Control Module (ECM) harness connector. Measure voltage between terminal No. 48 and terminals No. 30 and 49 (ground circuits) on ECM harness connector. If battery voltage is present, test is complete. If battery voltage is not present, inspect and repair ground circuits as needed. Perform TEST VER-2A.

DTC P0622: GENERATOR FIELD NOT SWITCHING PROPERLY

NOTE: DTC is set when PCM attempts to regulate generator field with no result during monitoring. Possible causes are generator field resistance greater than 5 ohms, open generator field driver circuit, generator field driver circuit shorted to ground, defective generator or PCM.

1) Record all DTC's and clear codes. Check all charging system related connectors for loose, corroded or damaged terminals. Repair as necessary. Using scan tool, actuate generator field driver circuit. Using a voltmeter, backprobe generator field connector generator field driver circuit. If voltage shifts from low to high, go to next step. If voltage does not shift from low to high, go to step 4).

NOTE: To identify field terminals, measure voltage between ground and each field terminal with engine running. Positive field terminal voltage should be 12.5–14.5 volts. Negative field terminal voltage should be 3-8 volts less than battery voltage.

2) Turn ignition on. Using scan tool, actuate generator field driver circuit. Using external voltmeter, measure voltage between ground and generator field source terminal (positive terminal) on 2-wire connector on rear of generator. See WIRING DIAGRAMS. If voltage is more than 10 volts, go to next step. If voltage is 10 volts or less, repair open in generator field source circuit between generator and PCM. Perform TEST VER-3A.

3) Wiggle wiring harness from generator to PCM. Using scan tool, read DTCs with actuator test still running. If generator field driver circuit DTC sets, repair wiring harness as necessary where wiggling caused problem to appear. If DTC does not set, fault is currently not present. Test is complete. Perform TEST VER-3A.

NOTE: To identify field terminals, measure voltage between ground and each field terminal with engine running. Positive field terminal voltage should be 12.5–14.5 volts. Negative field terminal voltage should be 3-8 volts less than battery voltage.

4) Turn ignition on. Using scan tool, actuate generator field driver circuit. Using external voltmeter, measure voltage between ground and generator field source terminal (positive terminal) on 2-wire connector on rear of generator. See WIRING DIAGRAMS. If voltage is more than 10 volts, go to next step. If voltage is 10 volts or less, repair open in generator field source circuit between generator and PCM. Perform TEST VER-3A.

5) Turn ignition off. Disconnect PCM harness connector. Disconnect field harness connector on rear of generator. Disconnect battery connections. Using an ohmmeter, measure resistance between generator field terminals on generator. If resistance is 5 ohms or more, repair or replace generator. Perform TEST VER-3A. If resistance is less than 5 ohms, go to next step.

6) Using an ohmmeter, check resistance of generator field driver circuit between generator field harness connector and PCM harness connector. See WIRING DIAGRAMS. If resistance is 5 ohms or more, repair open generator field driver circuit. Perform TEST VER-3A. If resistance is less than 5 ohms, go to next step.

7) With generator field connector disconnected, measure resistance from either generator field terminal (on back of generator) to ground. If resistance is less than 5 ohms, repair or replace shorted generator. If resistance is 5 ohms or more, replace PCM. Perform TEST VER-3A.

DTC P1492: BATTERY TEMP SENSOR VOLTAGE TOO HIGH

NOTE: Battery Temperature Sensor (BTS) is also known as Ambient Temperature Sensor (ATS).

1) Ensure ignition is on. Read Battery Temperature Sensor (BTS) voltage using scan tool. If BTS voltage is greater than 4.5 volts, go to next step. If BTS voltage is 4.5 volts or less, go to step 6).

2) Disconnect BTS connector. BTS is located in bottom of battery tray. Connect jumper wire between ground and terminal No. 2 (Pink/Yellow wire) on BTS harness connector. Turn ignition on. Using scan tool, read BTS voltage. If BTS voltage is less than one volt, go to next step. repair open BTS ground circuit. Perform TEST VER-5A. If BTS voltage is one volt or more, go to next step.

3) Turn ignition off. Move jumper wire between BTS harness connector terminals. Turn ignition on. Using scan tool, read BTS voltage. If BTS voltage is less than one volt, replace BTS. Perform TEST VER-5A. If BTS voltage is one volt or more, remove jumper wire and go to next step.

4) Measure voltage between ground and terminal No. 2 (Pink/Yellow wire) on BTS harness connector. If voltage is greater than 6 volts, repaie BTS sensor signal circuit for short to voltage. Perform TEST VER-5A. If voltage is 6 volts or less, go to next step.

5) Turn ignition off. Disconnect Powertrain Control Module (PCM) connector. Using an ohmmeter, check resistance of BTS signal circuit between ground and terminal No. 2 on BTS harness connector. See WIRING DIAGRAMS. If resistance is less than 5 ohms, replace PCM. Perform TEST VER-5A. If resistance is 5 ohms or greater, repair open BTS signal circuit. Perform TEST VER-5A.

6) While observing scan tool BTS voltage, wiggle wiring harness for BTS sensor. If voltage changes, repair wiring harness as necessary where wiggling caused problem to appear. Perform TEST VER-5A. If voltage does not change, inspect all related wiring and connectors and repair as necessary. If no problems were found with wiring and connectors, DTC may have been set by intermittent condition.

DTC P1493: BATTERY TEMP SENSOR VOLTAGE TOO LOW

NOTE: Battery Temperature Sensor (BTS) is also known as Ambient Temperature Sensor (ATS).

1) Ensure ignition is on. Using scan tool, read Battery Temperature Sensor (BTS) voltage. If BTS voltage is less than .5 volts, go to next step. If BTS voltage is .5 volts or greater, go to step 5).

2) Turn ignition off. Disconnect BTS connector. BTS is located in bottom of battery tray. Turn ignition on. Read Battery Temperature Sensor (BTS) voltage. If BTS voltage is greater than 4 volts, replace BTS. Perform TEST VER-5A. If BTS voltage is 4 volts or less, go to next step.

3) Ensure ignition is off and BTS is disconnected. Disconnect Powertrain Control Module (PCM) connector. Using an ohmmeter, measure resistance of BTS signal circuit between ground and terminal No. 2 on BTS harness connector. See WIRING DIAGRAMS. If resistance is less than 5 ohms, repair BTS signal circuit for short to ground. Perform TEST VER-5A. If resistance is 5 ohms or greater, go to next step.

4) Measure resistance between BTS harness connector terminals. See WIRING DIAGRAMS. If resistance is less than 5 ohms, repair BTS signal circuit shorted to sensor gound circuit. Perform TEST VER-5A. If resistance is 5 ohms or greater, replace PCM. Perform TEST VER- 5A.

5) While observing scan tool BTS voltage, wiggle wiring harness for BTS sensor. If voltage changes, repair wiring harness as necessary where wiggling caused problem to appear. Perform TEST VER-5A. If voltage does not change, inspect all related wiring and connectors and repair as necessary. If no problems were found with wiring and connectors, inspect all related wiring and connectors and repair as necessary. If no problems were found with wiring and connectors, DTC may have been set by intermittent condition.

CHRY
2-26

1999 STARTING & CHARGING SYSTEMS
Generators & Regulators – Trucks & RWD Vans (Cont.)

DTC P1594: CHARGING SYSTEM VOLTAGE TOO HIGH

NOTE: DTC is set when monitored battery voltage is one volt below charging system upper limit threshold for 25 seconds. PCM turns off field driver and monitors battery voltage. If voltage remains high, DTC P1594 is set. Possible causes are generator field driver circuit shorted to ground, shorted generator or Powertrain Control Module (battery temperature and/or charging voltage).

1) Ensure battery is fully charged, and generator belt tension and condition are okay. Using scan tool, actuate generator field driver. Using a voltmeter, backprobe generator field connector. Measure voltage between ground and terminal No. 1 (Dark Green or Dark Green/White wire) on generator field connector. See WIRING DIAGRAMS . If voltage shifts from low to high, go to next step. If voltage does not shift from low to high, go to step 6).

2) Using scan tool, stop generator field driver actuation. Start engine. Using scan tool, read target charging voltage. If target charging voltage is more than 13 volts, go to step 4). If target charging voltage is 13 volts or less, go to next step.

3) Measure underhood temperature near battery using scan tool temperature probe. Using scan tool, read battery temperature sensor temperature. If scan tool display is within 10 degrees of actual underhood temperature, go to next step. If scan tool display is not within 10 degrees of actual underhood temperature, replace BTS. Perform TEST VER-3A.

4) Start engine. Manually set engine speed to 1600 RPM. Using scan tool, read and compare voltage and target charging voltage. Observe voltage for up to 5 minutes (if necessary) for a one volt difference between voltage and target charging voltage. If difference between voltage and target charging voltage is one volt or less, go to TEST CH-1A. If difference between voltage and target charging voltage is more than one volt, replace Powertrain Control Module (PCM). Perform TEST VER-3A.

5) Turn ignition off. Disconnect PCM harness connector. Disconnect field harness connector on rear of generator. Using an ohmmeter, measure resistance of generator field driver circuit between PCM connector and ground. If resistance is 5 ohms or more, go to next step. If resistance is less than 5 ohms, repair short to ground on generator field driver circuit. Perform TEST VER-3A.

6) With generator field connector disconnected, measure resistance from either generator field terminal (on back of generator) to ground. If resistance is less than 5 ohms, repair or replace shorted generator. If resistance is 5 ohms or more, replace PCM. Perform TEST VER-3A.

DTC P1682: CHARGING SYSTEM VOLTAGE TOO LOW

NOTE: DTC is set when monitored battery voltage is one volt below charging system lower limit threshold for 25 seconds. PCM turns off field driver and monitors battery voltage. If voltage remains low, DTC P1682 is set. Possible causes are open high resistance in battery supply circuit between generator and battery, open field driver circuit, high resistance in ground circuit, defective generator or defective battery temperature sensor.

1) Ensure battery is fully charged. Start engine. Using scan tool, read voltage goal. If voltage goal is more than 15.1 volts, go to next step. If voltage goal is 15.1 volts or less, go to step 4).

2) Ensure engine is at normal operating temperature. Using scan tool, read Battery Temperature Sensor (BTS) temperature. Measure underhood temperature. If BTS temperature is within 10 degrees of actual underhood temperature, go to step 4). If BTS temperature is not within 10 degrees of actual underhood temperature, go to next step.

3) Turn ignition off. Disconnect BTS harness connector. BTS is mounted in bottom of battery tray. Connect jumper wire across BTS harness connector terminals. Turn ignition on. Using scan tool, read BTS voltage. If voltage is zero, replace BTS. Perform TEST VER-3A. If voltage is present, replace PCM. Perform TEST VER-3A.

4) Start engine and manually set engine speed to 1600 RPM. Using scan tool, read and compare target voltage and charging voltage. If difference between target voltage and charging voltage is more than one volt, go to next step. If difference between target voltage and charging voltage is one volt or less, go to step 12).

NOTE: Before starting engine, ensure all test equipment wires are clear of moving engine parts.

5) Connect an external voltmeter between generator B+ terminal and battery positive terminal. Start engine. If voltage is .4 volt or less, go to next step. If voltage is more than .4 volt, repair B+ circuit for high resistance between generator and battery. Perform TEST VER-3A.

6) Turn ignition off. Connect an external voltmeter between generator case and battery negative terminal. Start engine. If voltage is .1 volt or less, go to next step. If voltage is more than .1 volt, repair generator ground for high resistance between generator case and battery negative terminal. Perform TEST VER-3A.

7) With ignition on and engine not running, acutate generator field. Using voltmeter, measure voltage between ground and each generator field terminal. If voltage on both terminals is less than 3 volts, go to next step. If voltage for either terminal is 3 volts or greater, charging system is currently functioning correctly. Perform TEST VER-3A.

8) Turn ignition off. Disconnect Powertrain Control Module (PCM) harness connector. Using ohmmeter, measure resistance between ground and generator field driver terminal on PCM harness connector. See WIRING DIAGRAMS. If resistance is less than 5 ohms, repair field driver circuit for short to ground. Perform TEST VER-3A. If resistance is 5 ohms or greater, go to next step.

9) Disconnect generator field connector. Measure resistance of generator field driver circuit between PCM and generator field harness connector. See WIRING DIAGRAMS. If resistance is less than 5 ohms, go to next step. If resistance is 5 ohms or greater, repair open field driver circuit. Perform TEST VER-3A.

10) Using ohmmeter, measure resistance between ground and generator field source terminal on PCM harness connector. See WIRING DIAGRAMS. If resistance is less than 5 ohms, repair field source circuit for short to ground. Perform TEST VER-3A. If resistance is 5 ohms or greater, go to next step.

11) Disconnect generator field connector. Measure resistance of generator field source circuit between PCM and generator field harness connector. See WIRING DIAGRAMS. If resistance is less than 5 ohms, replace PCM. Perform TEST VER-3A. If resistance is 5 ohms or greater, repair open field source circuit. Perform TEST VER-3A.

NOTE: Before starting engine, ensure all test equipment wires are clear of moving engine parts.

12) Connect an external voltmeter between generator B+ terminal and battery positive terminal. Start engine. If voltage is .4 volt or less, go to next step. If voltage is more than .4 volt, repair B+ circuit for high resistance between generator and battery. Perform TEST VER-3A.

13) Turn ignition off. Connect an external voltmeter between generator case and battery negative terminal. Start engine. If voltage is .1 volt or less, test is complete. If voltage is more than .1 volt, repair generator ground for high resistance between generator case and battery negative terminal. Perform TEST VER-3A.

TEST CH-1A: CHARGING SYSTEM NO CODE TEST

1) Verify battery condition. Charge or replace battery as necessary. Inspect generator belt tension and condition. Replace generator belt as necessary. Start engine. Turn on all accessories. Set engine speed to 2000 RPM for 30 seconds, then return to idle. Read Diagnostic Trouble Codes (DTCs). See SCAN TOOL DTC MESSAGES table. If any charging system DTCs are set, perform appropriate test. If no charging system DTCs are set, go to next step.

2) With ignition on and engine off, read and record battery voltage using scan tool. Using voltmeter, measure and record voltage between battery posts. If voltage difference is less than one volt, test is complete. If voltage difference is one volt or greater, go to next step.

1999 STARTING & CHARGING SYSTEMS
Generators & Regulators – Trucks & RWD Vans (Cont.)

CHRY
2-27

3) Turn ignition on with engine off. Using scan tool, actuate generator field. Using voltmeter, backprobe generator field terminals on back of generator. Measure voltage between ground and each field terminal. *See Fig. 1 or 2.* Voltage should cycle from zero volts to battery voltage every 1.4 seconds at both terminals. While observing scan tool, wiggle field terminal wiring harness back to Powertrain Control Module (PCM). If any interruption of voltage cycling occurred, repair wiring harness where wiggling caused failure. Perform TEST VER-3A. If wiggling did not interrupt voltage cycling, go to next step.

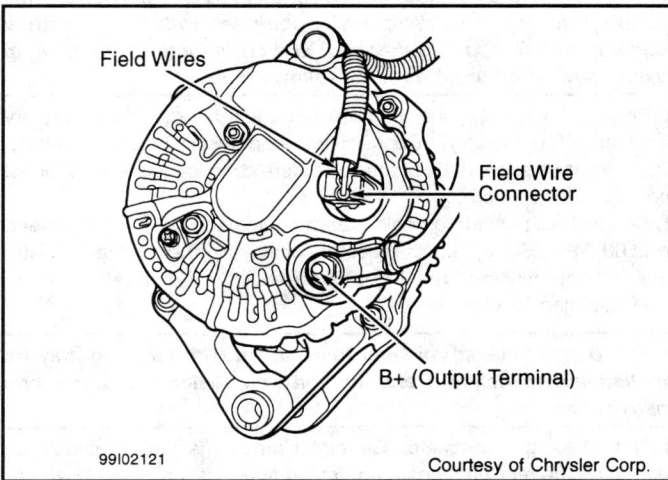

Fig. 1: Identifying Generator Terminals (Denso Generator)

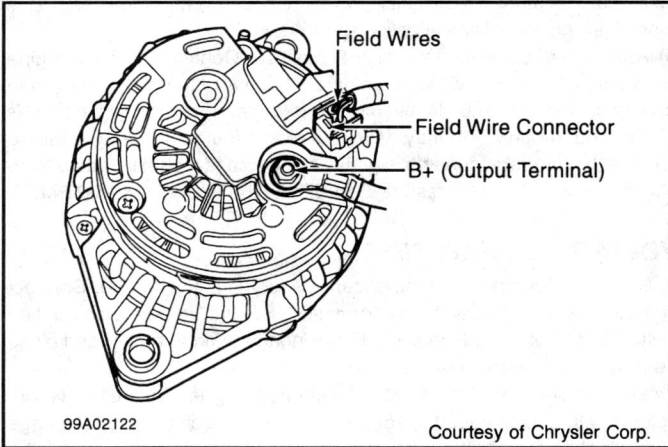

Fig. 2: Identifying Generator Terminals (Bosch Generator)

4) Using an external voltmeter, check voltage between generator B+ terminal located on rear of generator and battery positive terminal. *See Fig. 1 or 2.* Ensure voltmeter wires are clear of moving engine parts. Start engine and observe voltmeter. If voltage is .4 volt or less, go to next step. If voltage is more than .4 volt, repair high resistance between generator B+ terminal and battery positive terminal. Perform TEST VER-3A.

5) Using scan tool, read DTCs. If any charging system DTCs are set, see SCAN TOOL DTC MESSAGES table and perform appropriate test. If no charging system trouble codes are set, go to next step.

6) Turn ignition off. Using an external voltmeter, check voltage between generator case and battery negative terminal. Start engine. If voltage is greater than .1 volt, repair high resistance between generator battery negative terminal and battery negative terminal. Perform TEST VER-3A. If voltage is .1 volt or less, go to next step.

7) With ignition on and engine off, read and record battery voltage using scan tool. Turn ignition off. Disconnect PCM connector. Turn ignition on. Using voltmeter, measure voltage between ground and terminal No. 22 on PCM connector C1. If voltage is within one volt of scan tool voltage, repair high resistance between PCM connector terminal No. 22 and

battery positive terminal. Perform TEST VER-3A. If voltage is not within one volt of scan tool voltage, replace PCM. Perform TEST VER-3A.

TEST VER-2A: ROAD TEST VERIFICATION

CAUTION: If PCM is changed, correct VIN and mileage have to be programmed or ABS and SRS DTCs will be set.

1) If PCM has been replaced, go to next step. If ECM has been replaced or battery has been disconnected on diesel powered vehicles, go to step **3)**. If neither module has been replaced, go to step **4)**.

2) Connect scan tool to Data Link Connector (DLC). DLC is located below driver's side of instrument panel. Using scan tool, enter correct VIN and mileage into PCM. Using scan tool manufacturer's instructions, clear DTCs from ABS and SRS modules.

3) Programming of Accelerator Pedal Position Sensor (APPS) is necessary if ECM has been replaced or battery has been disconnected on diesel powered vehicles. Ensure all components are connected. Turn ignition on. Slowly depress accelerator pedal to floor, then slowly release. APPS is now programmed. Go to next step.

4) Inspect vehicle to ensure all engine components are connected. Reassemble and reconnect components as necessary.

5) Check if initial symptom still exists. If initial or another symptom exists, repair is not complete. Check for Technical Service Bulletins (TSBs) that apply to symptom.

6) If any DTCs have not been diagnosed, go to appropriate test and finish diagnosing remaining DTCs as necessary. If all DTCs have been diagnosed, go to next step.

7) Using scan tool, erase DTCs from PCM. Using scan tool, reset all values in adaptive memory. Disconnect scan tool. If no other DTCs remain, repair is now complete.

TEST VER-3A: CHARGING VERIFICATION

CAUTION: If PCM is changed, correct VIN and mileage have to be programmed or ABS and SRS DTCs will be set.

1) If PCM has been replaced, go to next step. If ECM has been replaced or battery has been disconnected on diesel powered vehicles, go to step **3)**. If neither module has been replaced, go to step **4)**.

2) Connect scan tool to Data Link Connector (DLC). DLC is located below driver's side of instrument panel. Using scan tool, enter correct VIN and mileage into PCM. Using scan tool manufacturer's instructions, clear DTCs from ABS and SRS modules.

3) Programming of Accelerator Pedal Position Sensor (APPS) is necessary if ECM has been replaced or battery has been disconnected on diesel powered vehicles. Ensure all components are connected. Turn ignition on. Slowly depress accelerator pedal to floor, then slowly release. APPS is now programmed. Go to next step.

4) Inspect vehicle to ensure all engine components are connected. Reassemble and reconnect components as necessary.

5) To ensure no charging system problem exists, start engine. Perform OUTPUT VOLTAGE TEST under ON-VEHICLE TESTING. Increase engine speed to 2000 RPM for at least 30 seconds. Allow engine to idle. Turn engine off.

6) Using scan tool, check for stored DTCs. If repaired DTC has reset, repair is not complete. Check for related Technical Service Bulletins (TSBs) and return to DTC TEST, if necessary. If another DTC exists, go to appropriate DTC test and follow specified procedure. If no other DTCs exist, repair is now complete.

TEST VER-5A: ROAD TEST VERIFICATION

CAUTION: If PCM is changed, correct VIN and mileage have to be programmed or ABS and SRS DTCs will be set.

1) If PCM has been replaced, go to next step. If ECM has been replaced or battery has been disconnected on diesel powered vehicles, go to step **3)**. If neither module has been replaced, go to step **4)**.

2) Connect scan tool to Data Link Connector (DLC). DLC is located below driver's side of instrument panel. Using scan tool, enter correct

CHRY
2-28

1999 STARTING & CHARGING SYSTEMS
Generators & Regulators – Trucks & RWD Vans (Cont.)

VIN and mileage into PCM. Using scan tool manufacturer's instructions, clear DTCs from ABS and SRS modules.

3) Programming of Accelerator Pedal Position Sensor (APPS) is necessary if ECM has been replaced or battery has been disconnected on diesel powered vehicles. Ensure all components are connected. Turn ignition on. Slowly depress accelerator pedal to floor, then slowly release. APPS is now programmed. Go to next step.

4) Connect scan tool to Data Link Connector (DLC). DLC is located below driver's side of instrument panel. Using scan tool, enter correct VIN and mileage into PCM. Using scan tool manufacturer's instructions, clear DTCs from ABS and SRS modules.

5) Inspect vehicle to ensure all engine components are connected. Reassemble and reconnect components as necessary.

6) If any DTCs have not been diagnosed, go to appropriate test and finish diagnosing remaining DTCs as necessary. If all DTCs have been diagnosed, go to next step.

7) Connect scan tool to DLC connector. Ensure fuel tank is at least 25 percent full. Turn off all accessories.

8) Using scan tool OBDII monitor, verify DTC repair. See scan tool instructions. Allow PCM to run appropriate monitor(s) and increment a global good trip (drive cycle). Enabling conditions must be met before PCM will run OBDII monitor. Scan tool monitor pretest screen will display enabling conditions.

9) If repaired DTC has reset or was seen in OBDII monitor while on road test, repair is not complete. Check for any TSBs and return to appropriate test. Repair as needed.

10) If any other DTCs are set, repair as needed. If OBDII monitor is run and good trip counter is incremented and no new DTCs are set, repair is successful and complete. Erase DTCs. See CLEARING CODES.

ON-VEHICLE TESTING

CAUTION: When battery is disconnected, vehicle computer and memory systems may lose memory data. Driveability problems may exist until computer systems have completed a relearn cycle. See COMPUTER RELEARN PROCEDURES article in GENERAL INFORMATION before disconnecting battery.

VOLTAGE DROP TEST

NOTE: VOLTAGE DROP TEST determines amount of resistance in circuits between generator and battery.

Testing Positive Circuit – 1) Ensure battery is in condition and is fully charged. Clean battery terminals (if necessary). Using external voltmeter, connect positive lead to generator B+ terminal stud (not the nut). Connect voltmeter negative lead to positive battery post. Connect tachometer to engine. Fully engage parking brake, and place gear selector in Neutral position. Start engine and run for 2 minutes to allow for warm-up.

2) Turn A/C system on, A/C-heater blower motor to high speed and headlights on high beam. Increase engine speed to 2400 RPM. Voltmeter reading should not be more than 0.6 volts.

3) If voltage drop is more than 0.6 volts, inspect, clean and tighten all connections between generator B+ terminal and positive battery post. Voltage drop test may be performed at each connection to locate connection with excessive resistance. If resistance tests are satisfactory, reduce engine speed, turn off all electrical loads and ignition switch.

Testing Negative Circuit – 1) Using external voltmeter, connect negative lead of voltmeter to negative battery post and postive lead to groung terminal stud on back of generator case. Voltmeter reading should not be more than 0.3 volts.

2) If voltage drop is more than 0.3 volts, inspect, clean and tighten all connections between generator ground terminal and negative battery post. Voltage drop test may be performed at each connection to locate connection with excessive resistance. If resistance tests are satisfactory, reduce engine speed, turn off all electrical loads and ignition switch.

CURRENT OUTPUT TEST

CAUTION: Generator has 2 field terminals: generator field driver (terminal No. 1) and generator field source (terminal No. 2). See WIRING DIAGRAMS. DO NOT connect generator field source terminal to ground.

NOTE: Perform VOLTAGE DROP TEST before continuing with this test. Perform test soon after starting engine, as charging amperage will drop quickly. A volt/amp tester equipped with both a battery load control (carbon pile rheostat) and an inductive type pick-up clamp is required to perform the following test.

1) Ensure battery is in good condition and is fully charged. Clean battery terminals (if necessary). Connect volt/amp tester leads to battery. Ensure carbon pile is in OFF position before connecting leads. Connect inductive pick-up clamp.

2) Connect tachometer to engine. Start engine and raise engine speed to 2500 RPM. Slowly adjust rheostat control (load) on volt/amp tester until highest amperage reading is obtained. DO NOT allow voltage to drop less than 12 volts.

NOTE: Depending on volt/amp tester manufacturer, load may be applied automatically. Refer to volt/amp tester manufacturer's instructions.

3) Note reading on ammeter. Generator amperage reading should be more than the minimum amperage rating specification. See GENERATOR APPLICATION table under DESCRIPTION. If amperage reading is less than minimum specification, go to step **5)**. If amperage reading is more than minimum specification, go to next step.

4) Rotate load control knob to OFF position. Continue to hold engine speed at 2500 RPM. Output amperage should change to less than 20-amps, indicating EVR circuity is okay and charging system is functioning properly. It may take several minutes for amperage to change. If amperage does not significantly decrease, check battery. Also check if any DTCs are present. See SELF-DIAGNOSTIC SYSTEM.

VOLTAGE OUTPUT TEST

1) Before performing this test, ensure battery is fully charged. Connect voltmeter leads across battery terminals. Record voltage with ignition switch and all electrical loads off. Fully engage parking brake, and place gear selector in Park position.

2) Start engine and operate at normal operating temperature. Record voltage with engine speed at 1500 RPM and no electrical loads. Voltage should not be greater than voltage recorded in step **1)** by more than 2.5 volts. If voltage is not as specified, check if any DTCs are present. See SELF-DIAGNOSTIC SYSTEM.

3) Record voltage with engine speed at 2000 RPM, blower motor on high and headlights on high beam. Voltage should be more than 0.5 volt above battery voltage previously recorded in step **1)**. If voltage is less than 0.5 volt above previously recorded battery voltage, check if any DTCs are present. See SELF-DIAGNOSTIC SYSTEM. If voltage tests are satisfactory, reduce engine speed, and turn off blower motor, headlights and ignition switch.

COMPONENT TESTING

BATTERY TEMPERATURE SENSOR

Disconnect and remove Battery Temperature Sensor (BTS) for battery tray (driver's side tray on diesel equipped vehicle). Using external ohmmeter, measure resistance across component connector terminals. Resistance at room temperature should be 9000-11,000 ohms. Replace sensor as needed.

1999 STARTING & CHARGING SYSTEMS
Generators & Regulators – Trucks & RWD Vans (Cont.)

CHRY
2-29

REMOVAL & INSTALLATION

CAUTION: When battery is disconnected, vehicle computer and memory systems may lose memory data. Driveability problems may exist until computer systems have completed a relearn cycle. See COMPUTER RELEARN PROCEDURES article in GENERAL INFORMATION before disconnecting battery.

Removal & Installation – 1) Disconnect negative battery cable. Remove generator drive belt and generator mounting bolts. Remove pivot bolt, and position generator aside to access wire connectors.
2) Remove B+ terminal nut, field terminal nuts and ground/wire harness hold-down nuts. Remove wire connectors. Remove generator from vehicle. To install, reverse removal procedure. Tighten fasteners to specification. See TORQUE SPECIFICATIONS.

TORQUE SPECIFICATIONS

TORQUE SPECIFICATIONS

Application	Ft. Lbs. (N.m)
Mounting Bolts	
Except Dakota 2.5L	30 (41)
Dakota 2.5L	41 (56)
	INCH Lbs. (N.m)
Field Terminal Nuts	25 (3)
Ground & B+ Terminal Nuts	75 (8)

WIRING DIAGRAMS

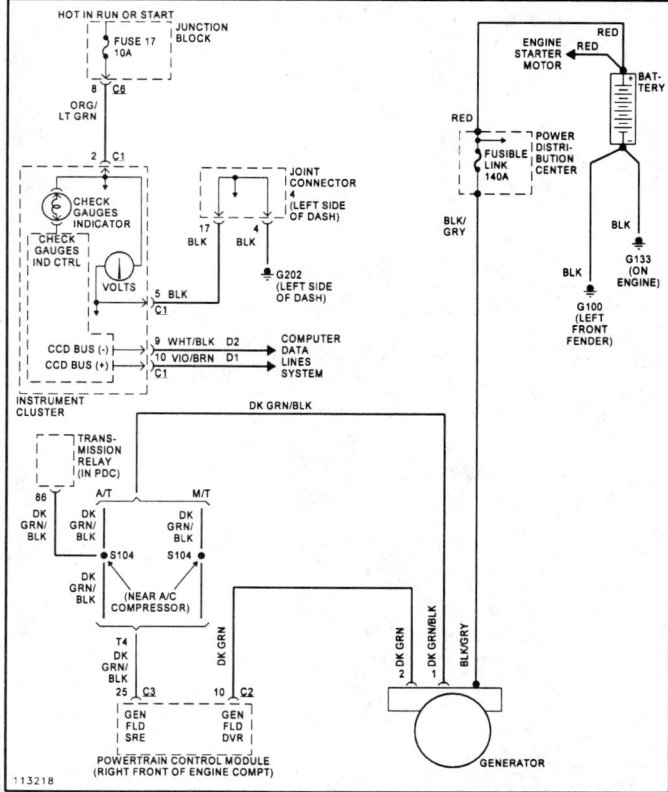

Fig. 3: Charging System Wiring Diagram (Dakota)

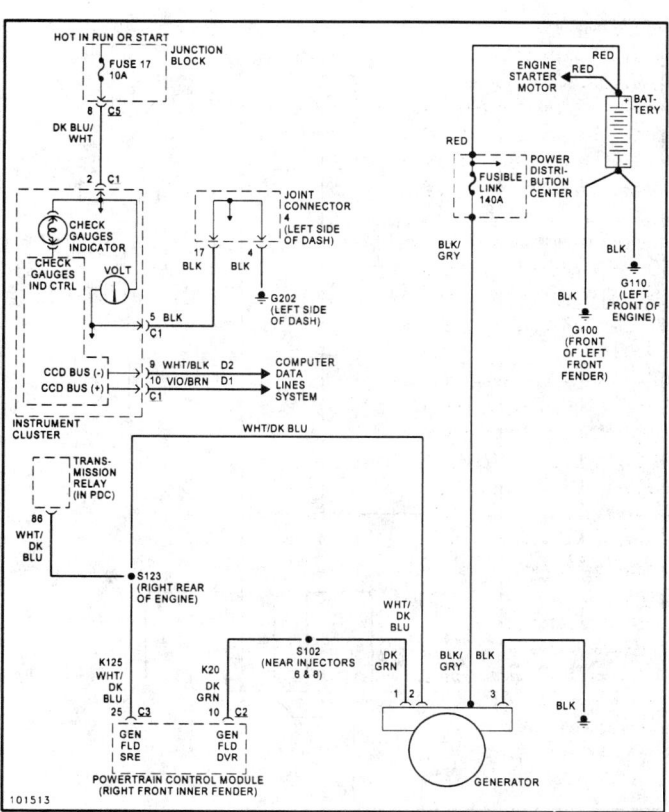

Fig. 4: Charging System Wiring Diagram (Durango)

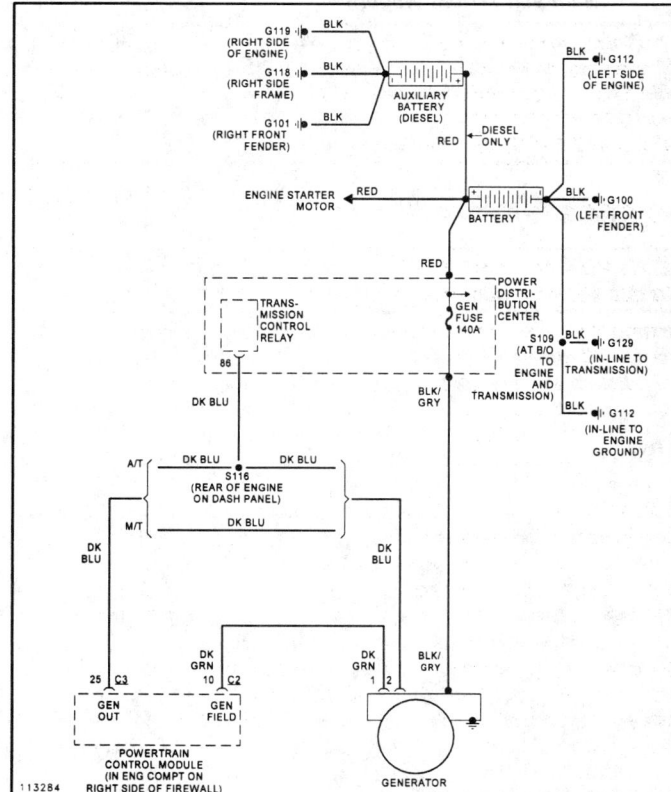

Fig. 5: Charging System Wiring Diagram (Ram Pickup)

1999 STARTING & CHARGING SYSTEMS
Generators & Regulators – Trucks & RWD Vans (Cont.)

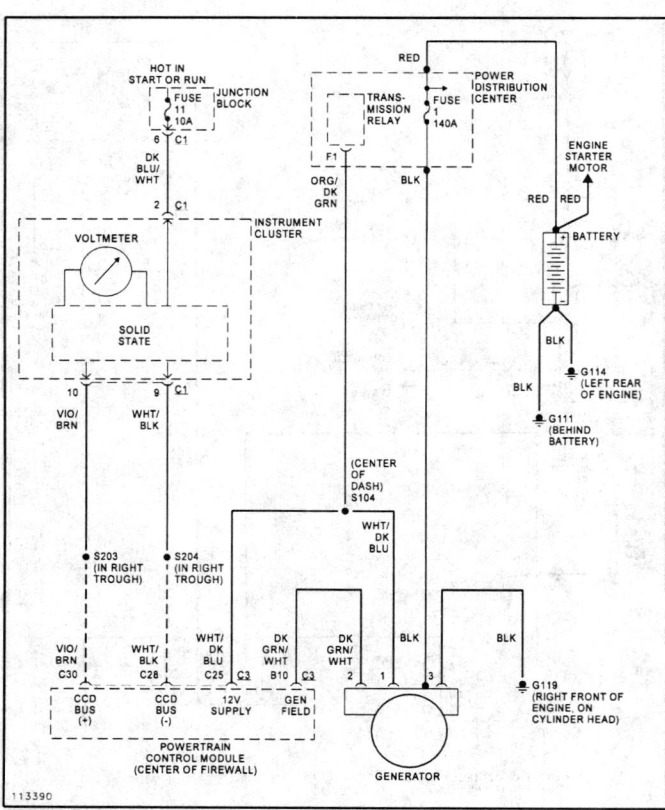

Fig. 6: Charging System Wiring Diagram
(Ram Van & Ram Wagon)

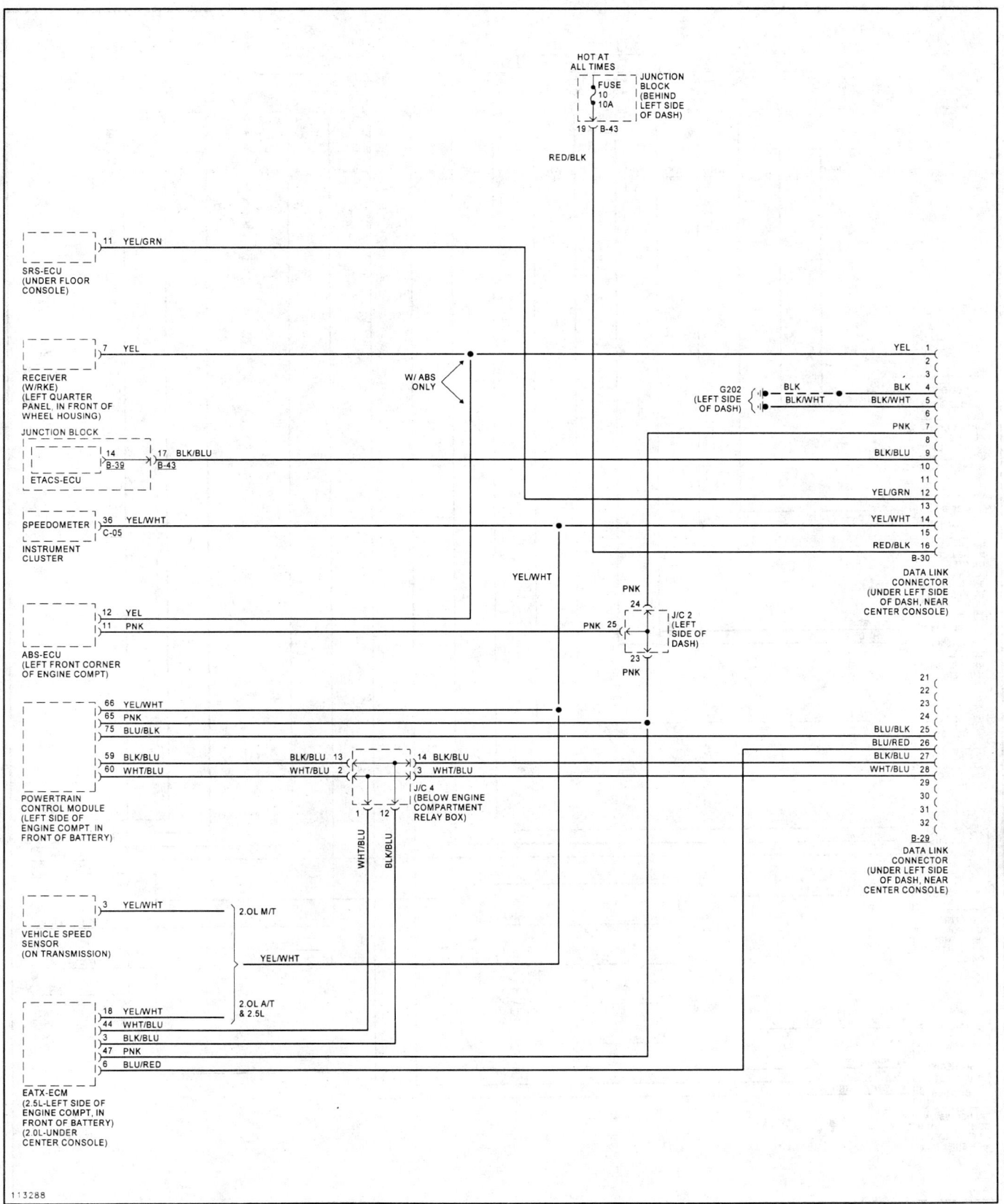

Fig. 1: Data Link Connectors Wiring Diagram (Avenger & Sebring Coupe)

1999 WIRING DIAGRAMS
Data Link Connectors (Cont.)

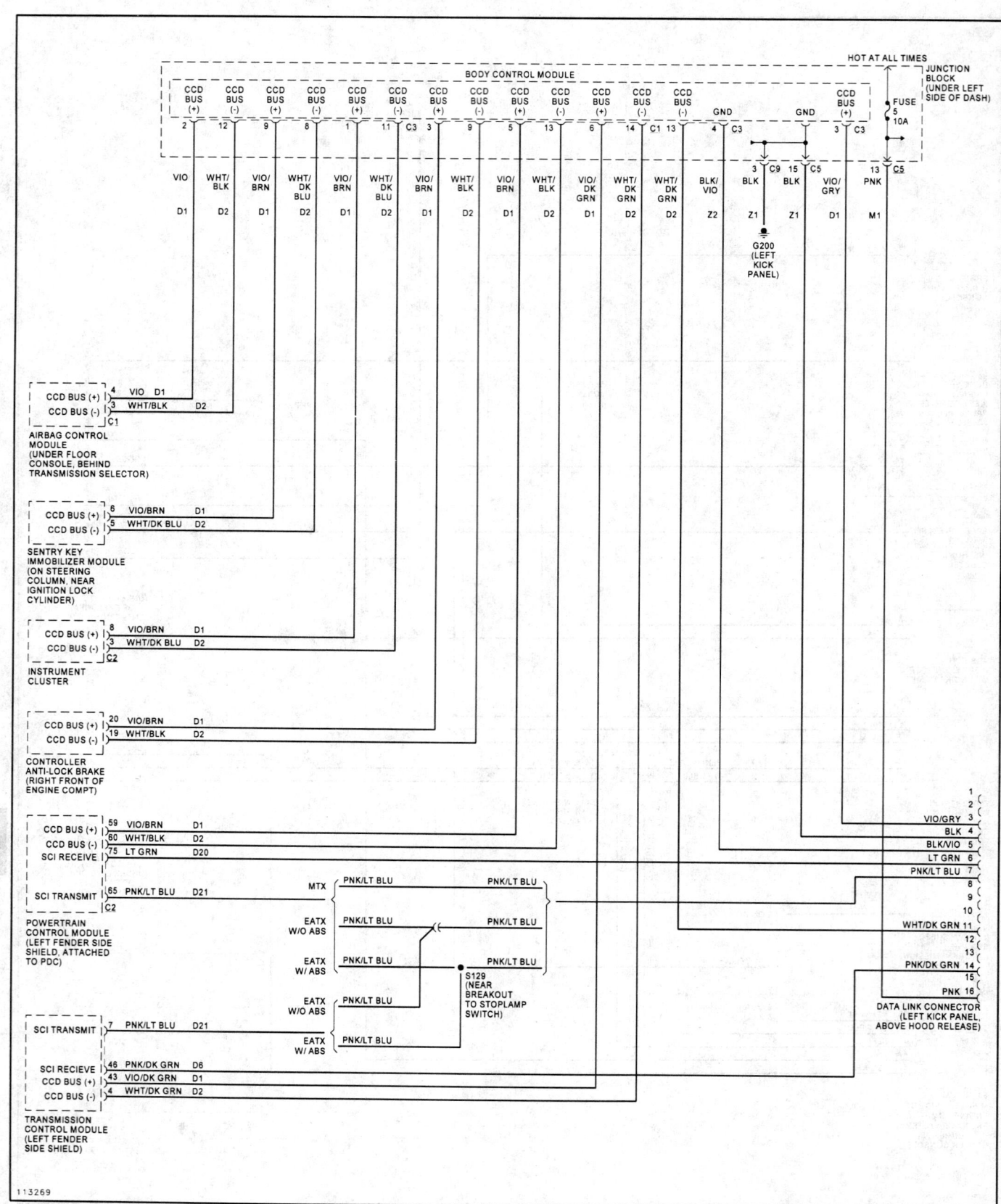

Fig. 2: Data Link Connectors Wiring Diagram (Breeze, Cirrus & Stratus)

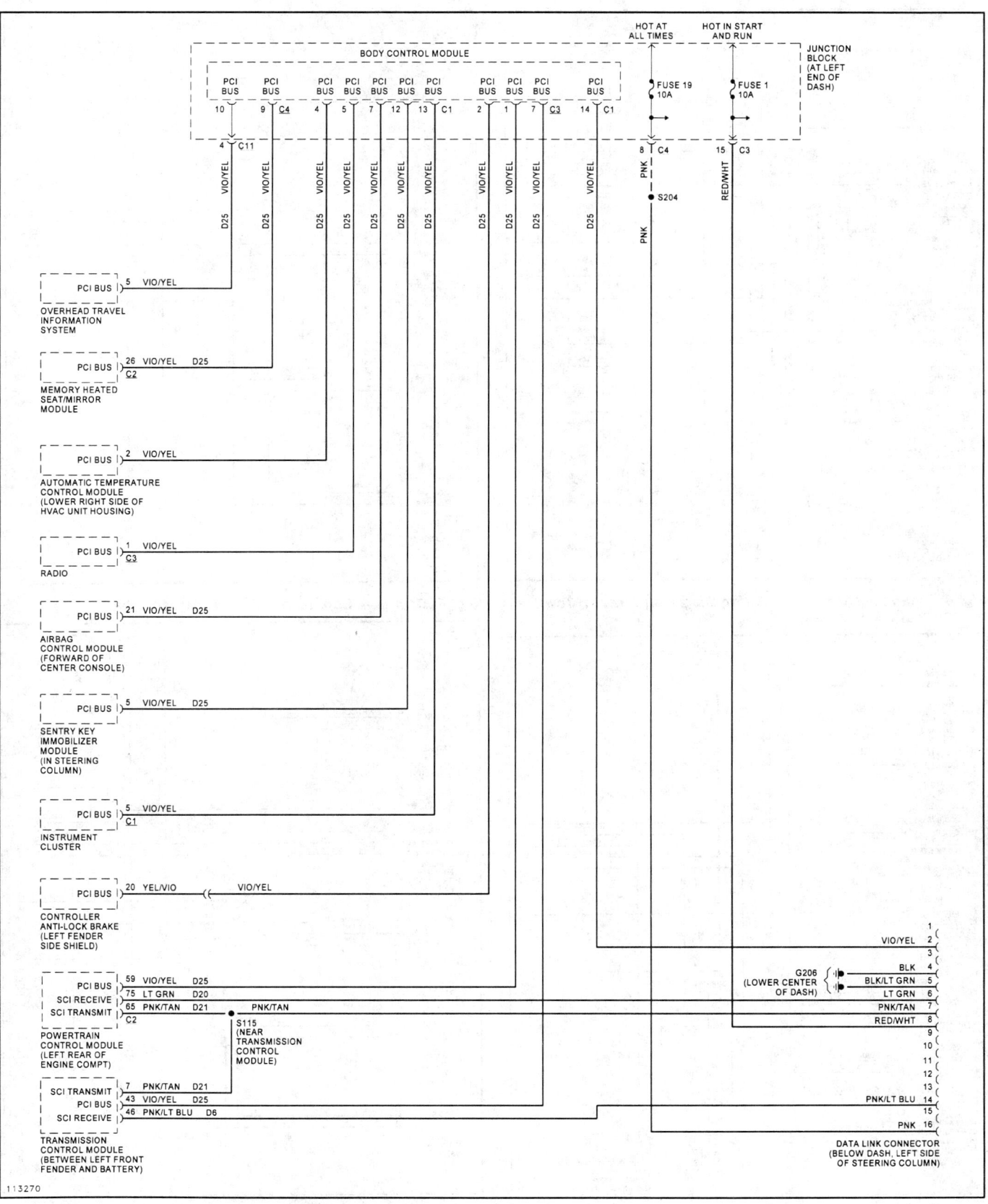

Fig. 3: Data Link Connectors Wiring Diagram (Concorde, Intrepid, LHS & 300M)

1999 WIRING DIAGRAMS
Data Link Connectors (Cont.)

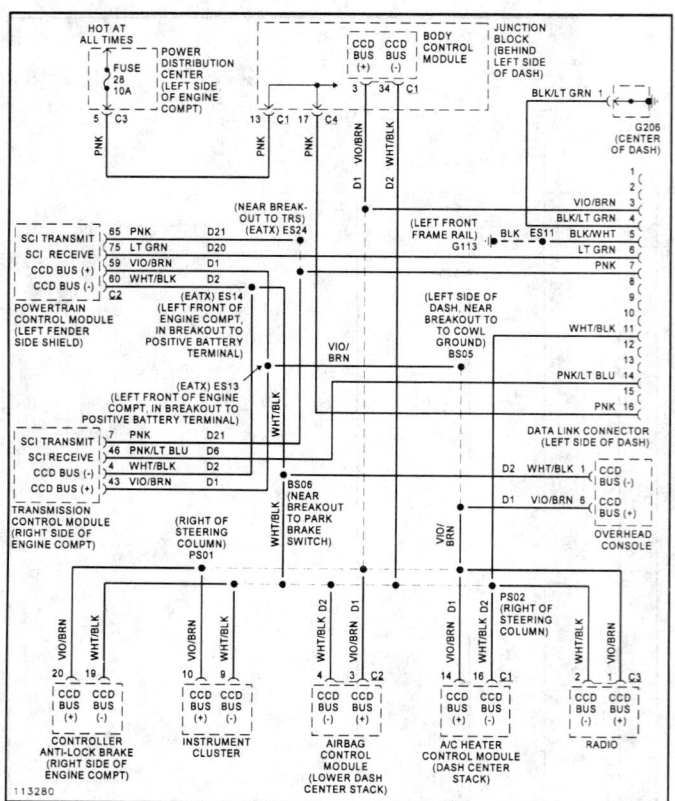

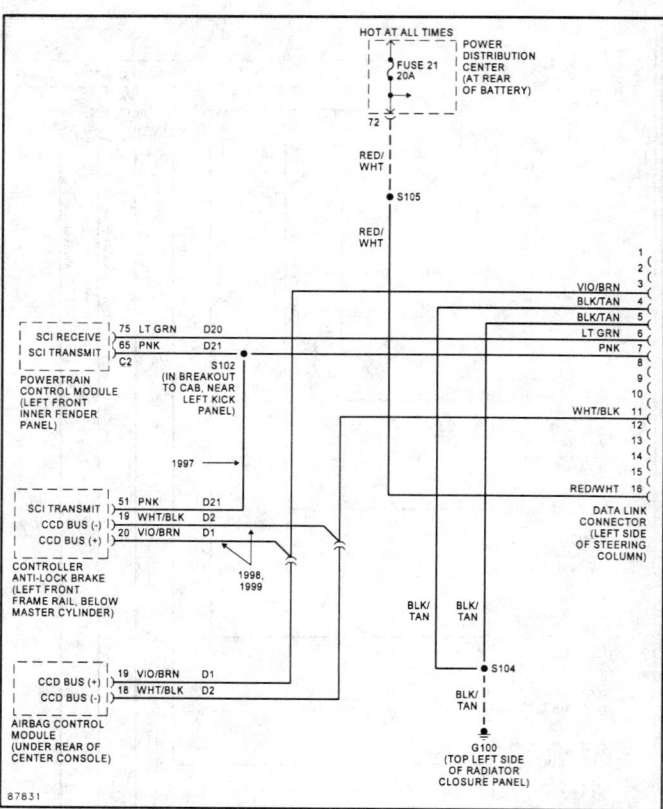

Fig. 4: Data Link Connectors Wiring Diagram (Caravan, Town & Country, & Voyager)

Fig. 6: Data Link Connectors Wiring Diagram (Neon)

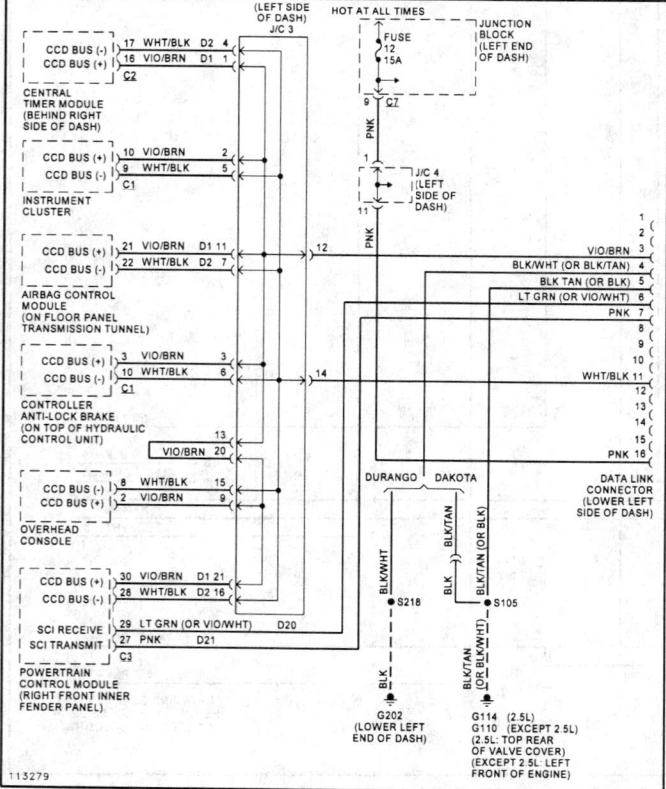

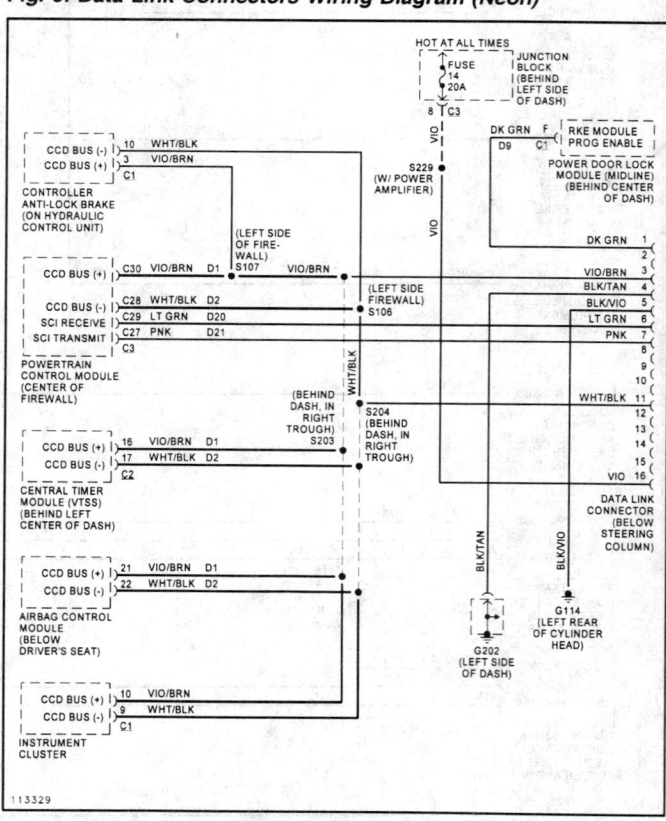

Fig. 5: Data Link Connectors Wiring Diagram (Dakota & Durango)

Fig. 7: Data Link Connectors Wiring Diagram (Ram Van & Ram Wagon)

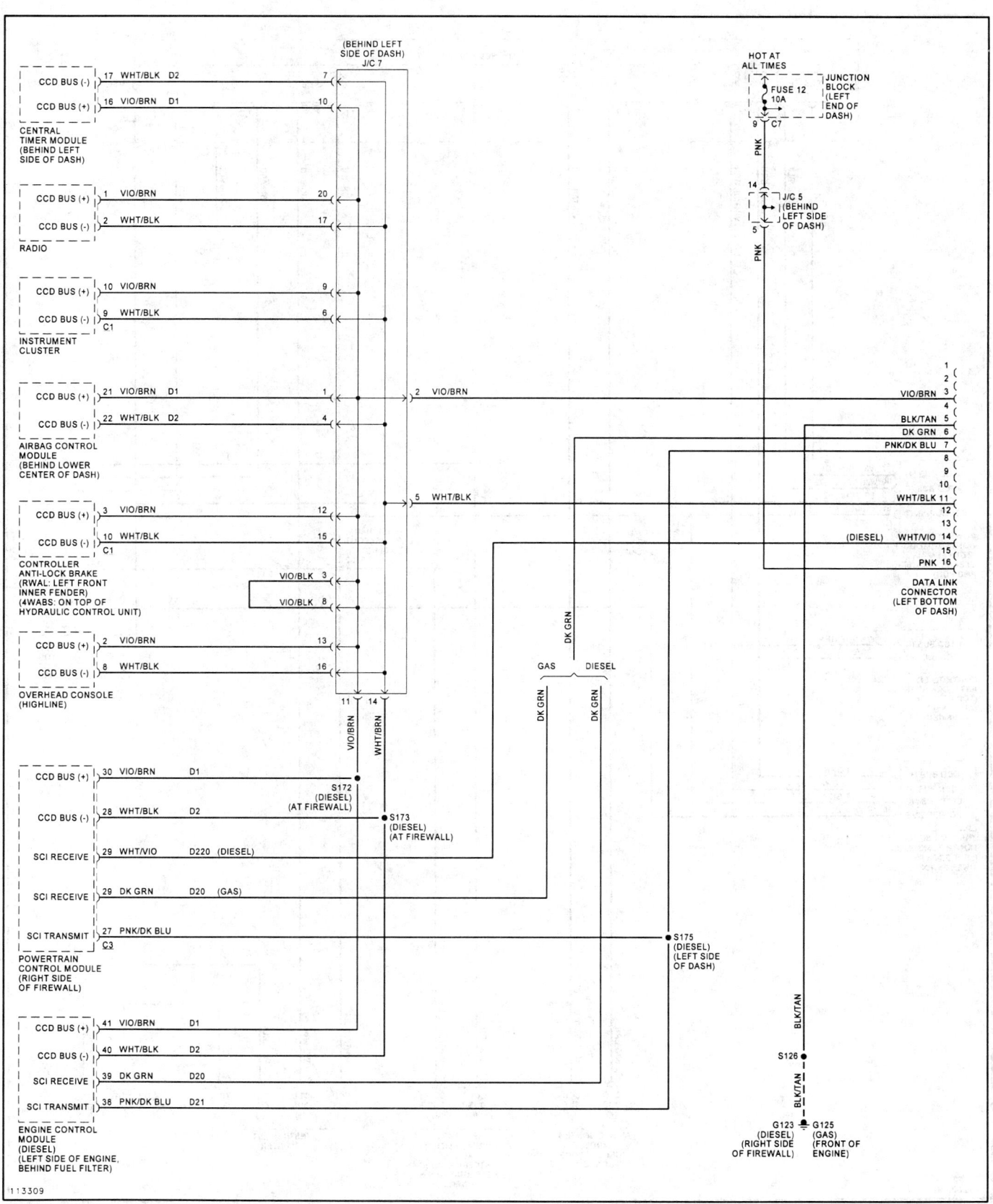

Fig. 8: Data Link Connectors Wiring Diagram (Ram Pickup)

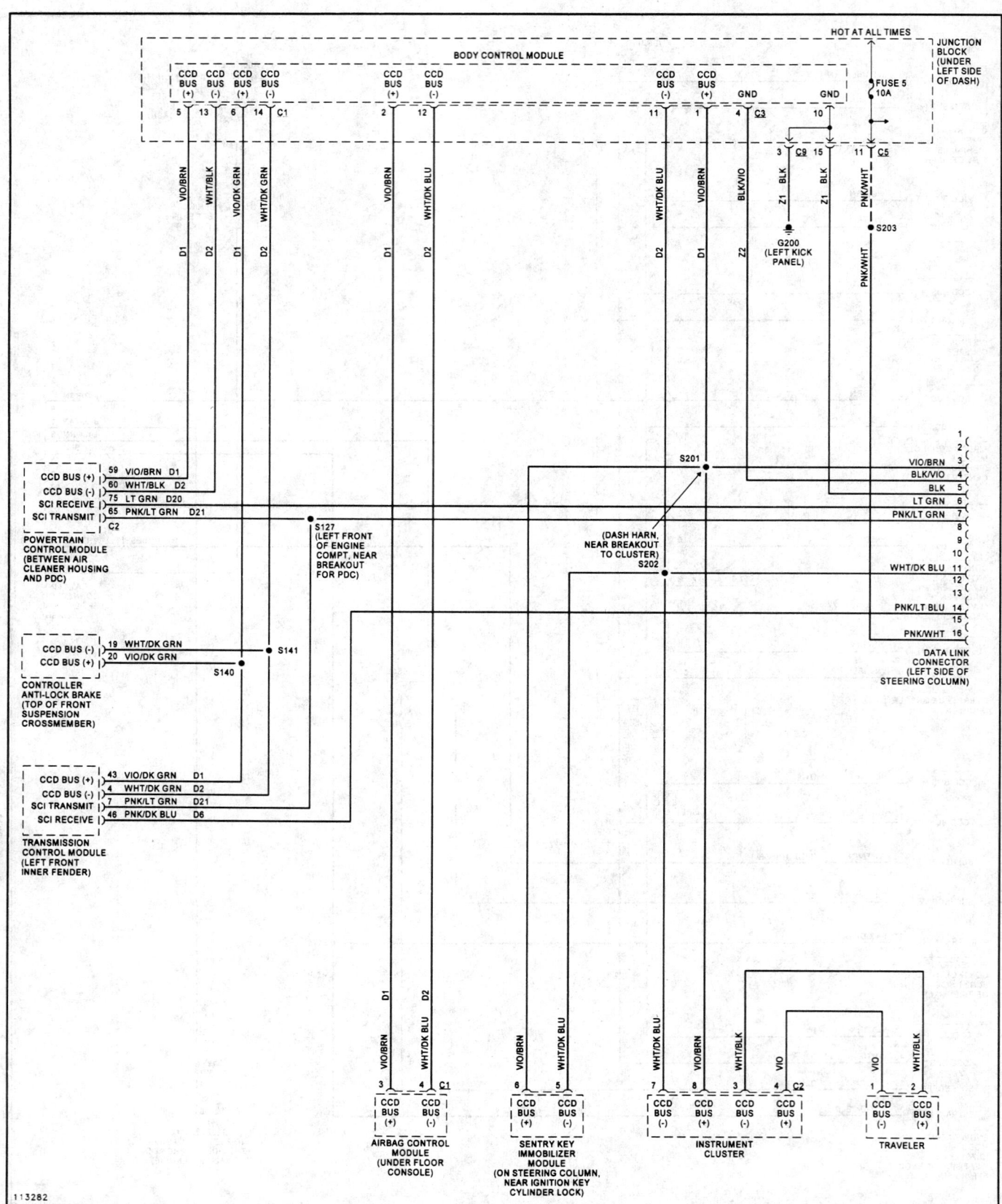

Fig. 9: Data Link Connectors Wiring Diagram (Sebring Convertible)

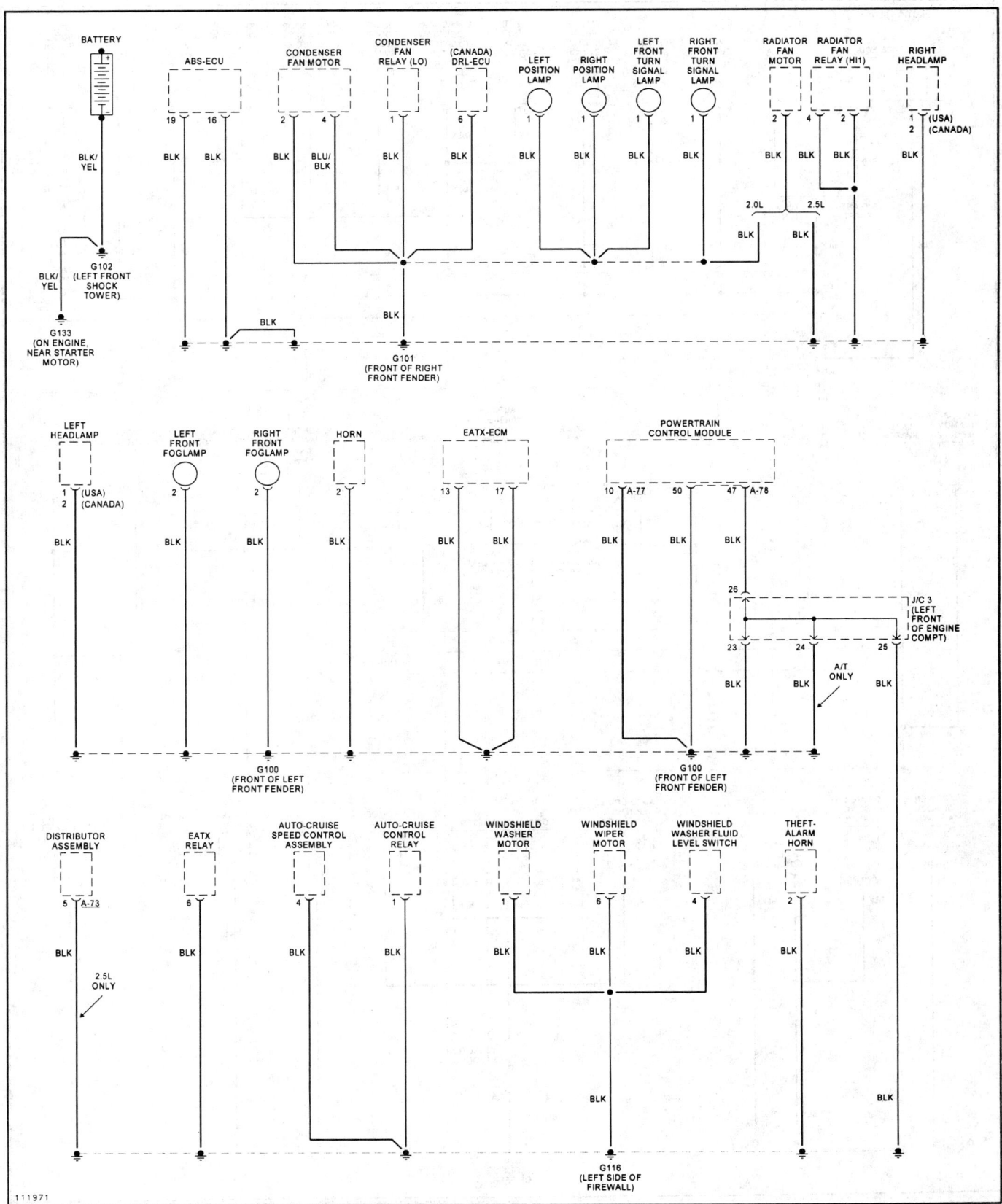

Fig. 1: Ground Distribution Wiring Diagram (Avenger & Sebring Coupe – 1 Of 3)

1999 WIRING DIAGRAMS
Ground Distribution (Cont.)

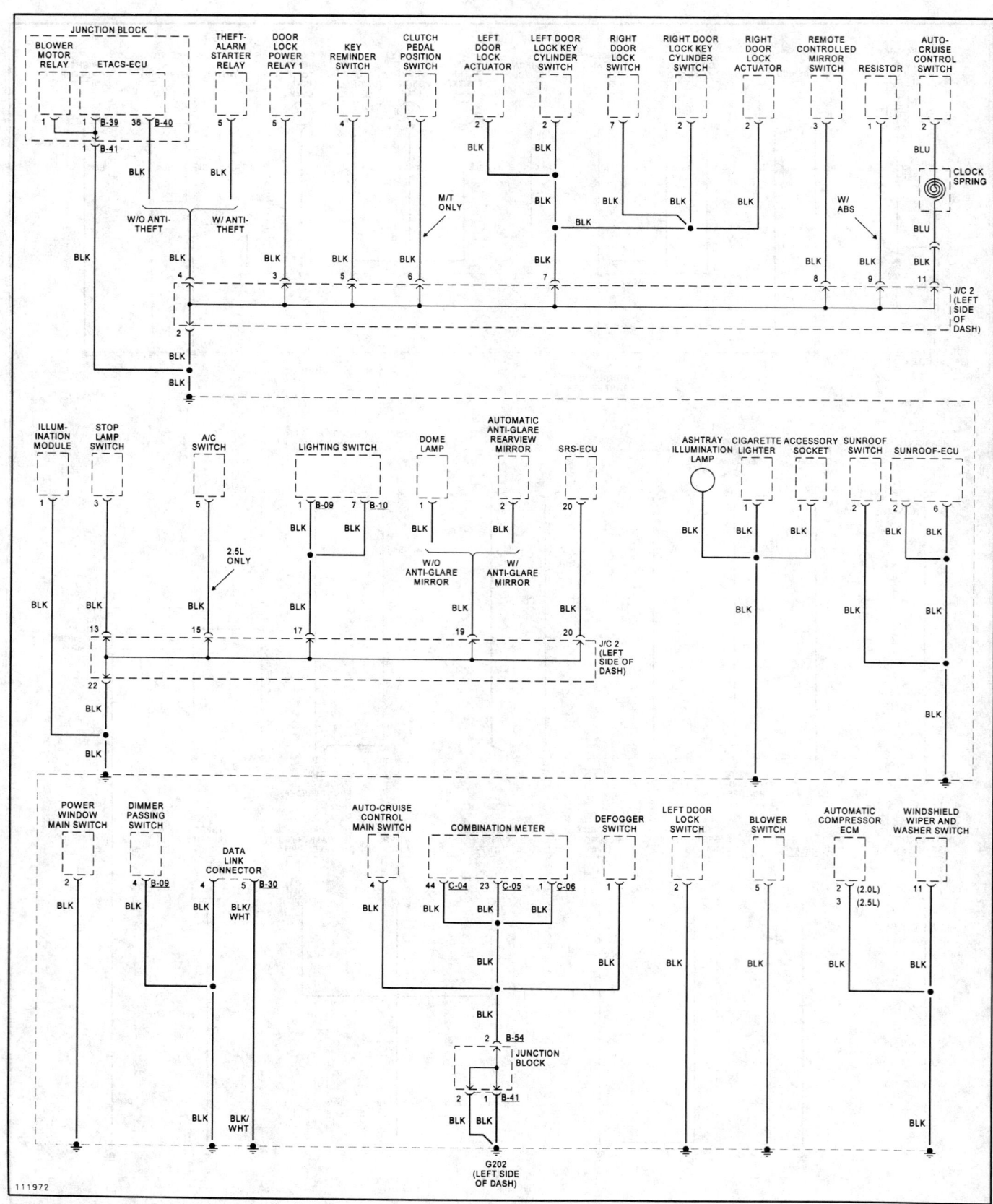

Fig. 2: Ground Distribution Wiring Diagram (Avenger & Sebring Coupe – 2 Of 3)

Ground Distribution (Cont.)

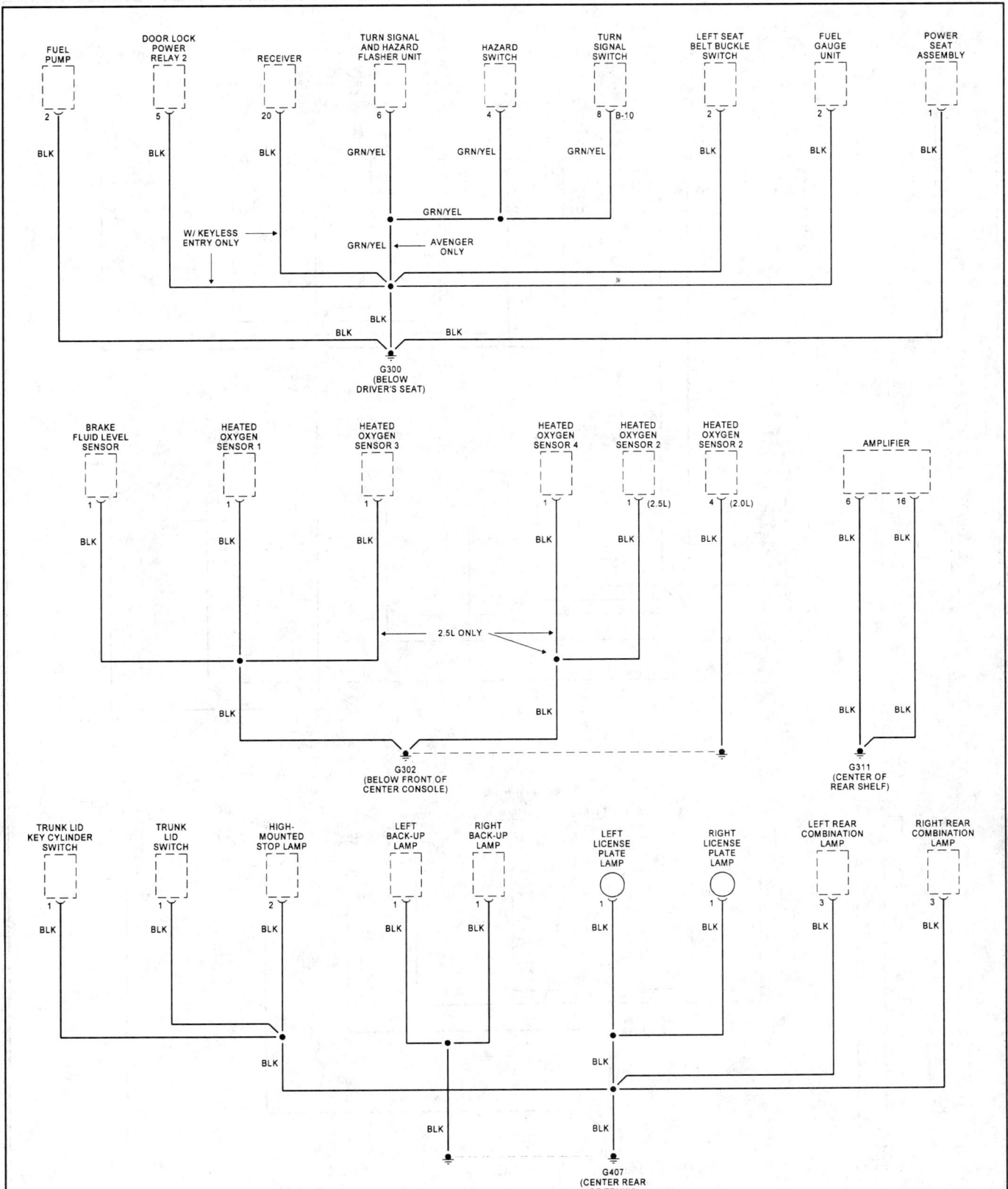

Fig. 3: Ground Distribution Wiring Diagram (Avenger & Sebring Coupe – 3 Of 3)

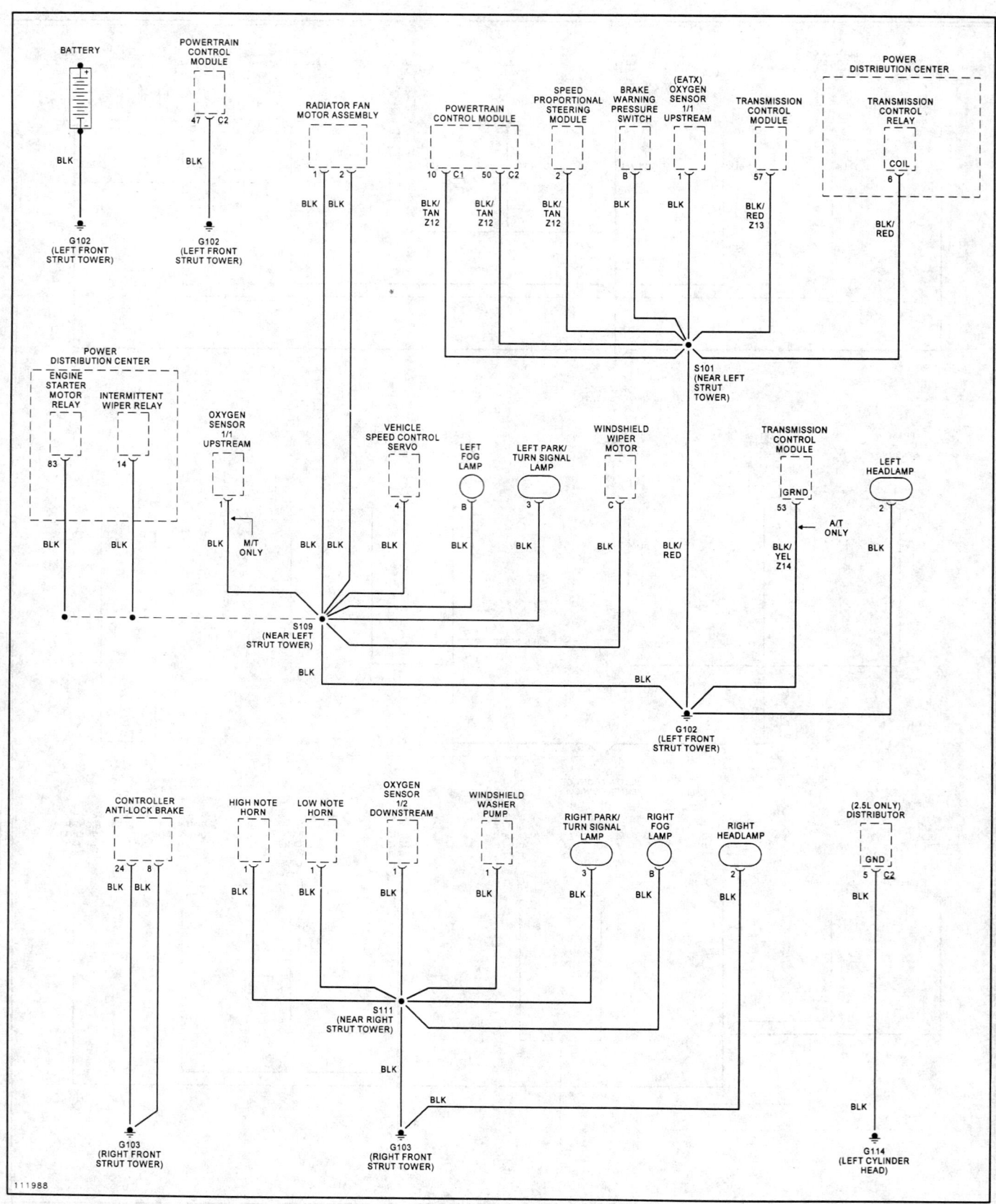

Fig. 4: Ground Distribution Wiring Diagram (Breeze, Cirrus & Stratus – 1 Of 2)

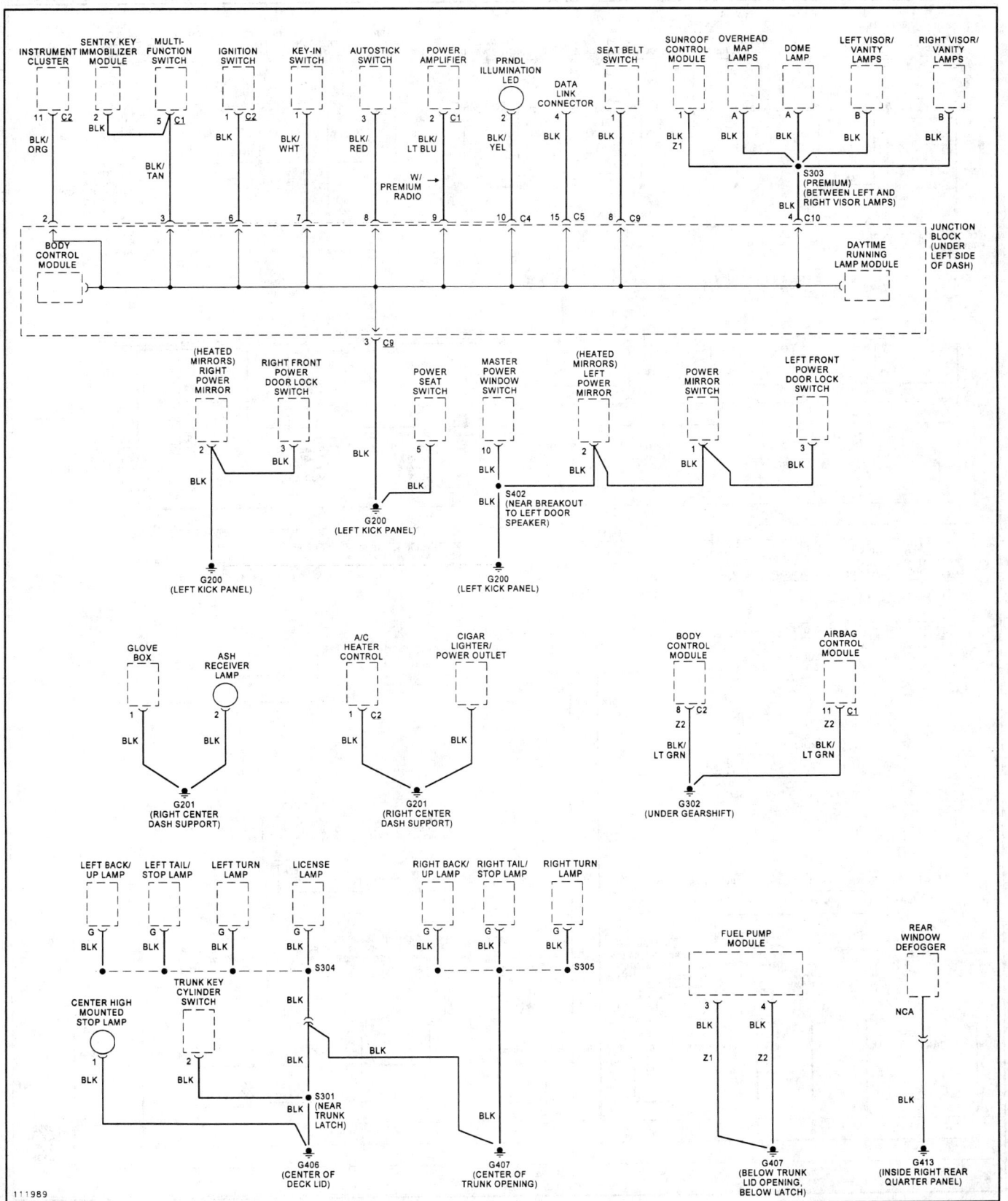

Fig. 5: Ground Distribution Wiring Diagram (Breeze, Cirrus & Stratus – 2 Of 2)

1999 WIRING DIAGRAMS
Ground Distribution (Cont.)

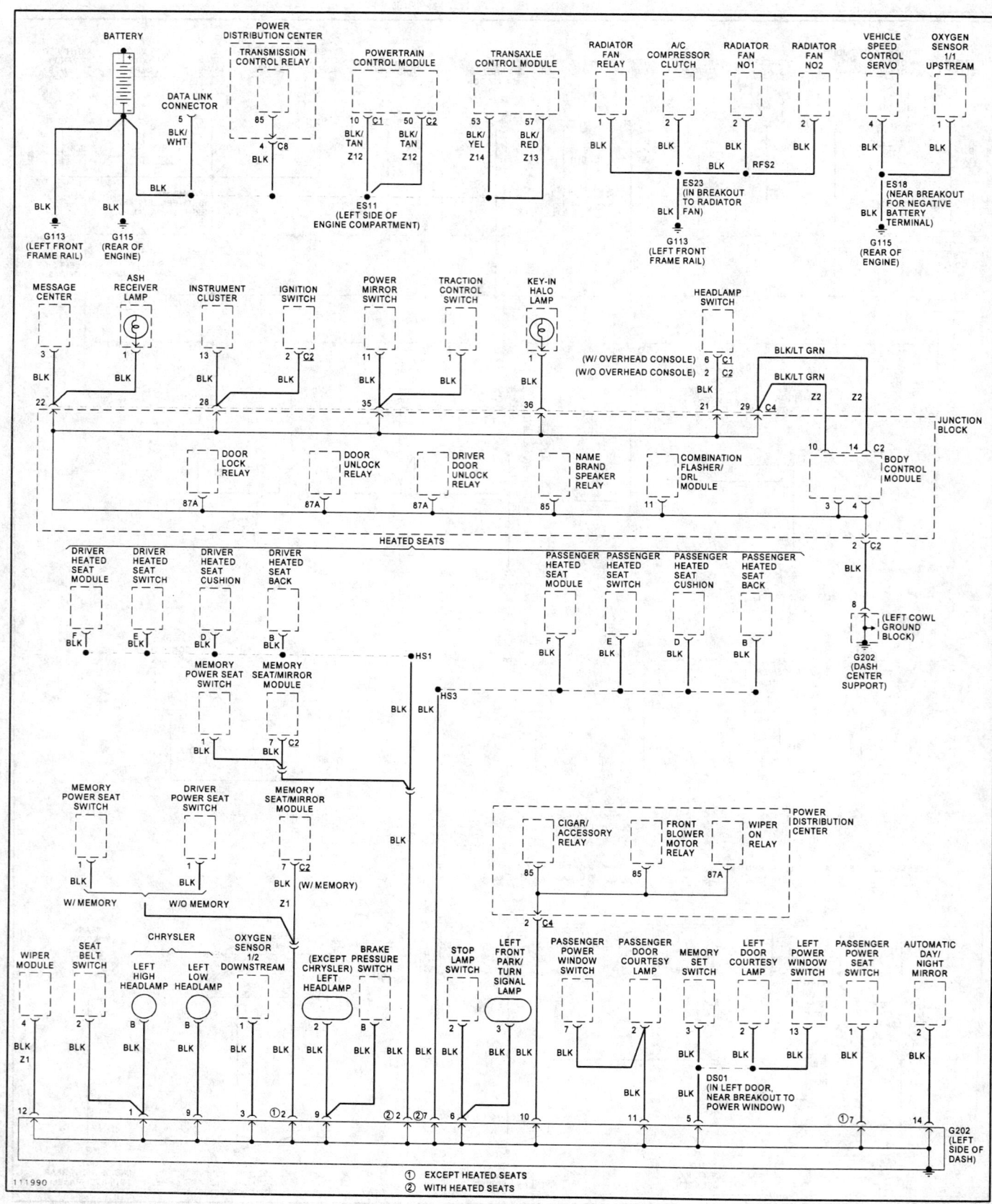

Fig. 6: Ground Distribution Wiring Diagram (Caravan, Town & Country, & Voyager – 1 Of 3)

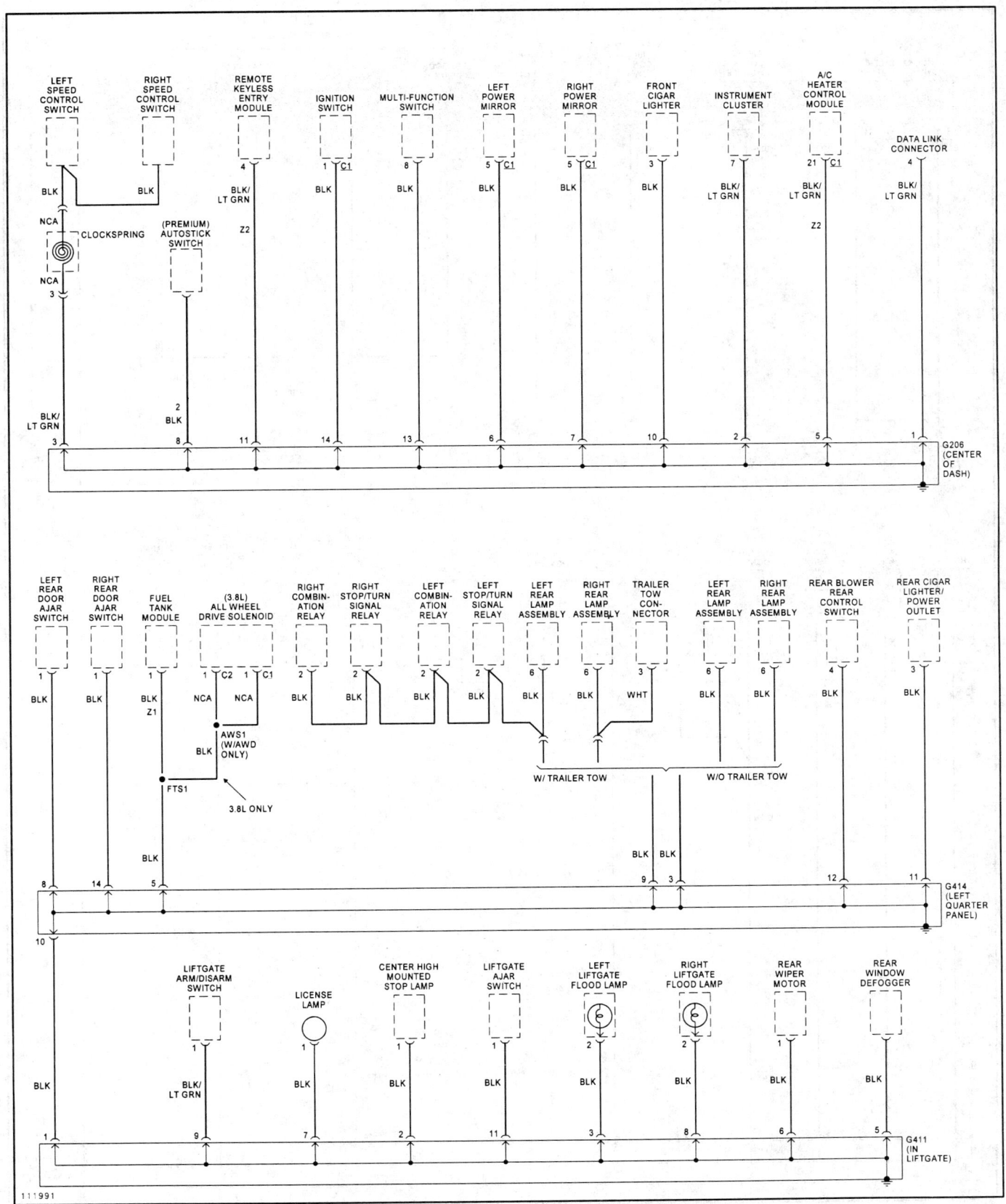

Fig. 7: Ground Distribution Wiring Diagram (Caravan, Town & Country, & Voyager – 2 Of 3)

1999 WIRING DIAGRAMS
Ground Distribution (Cont.)

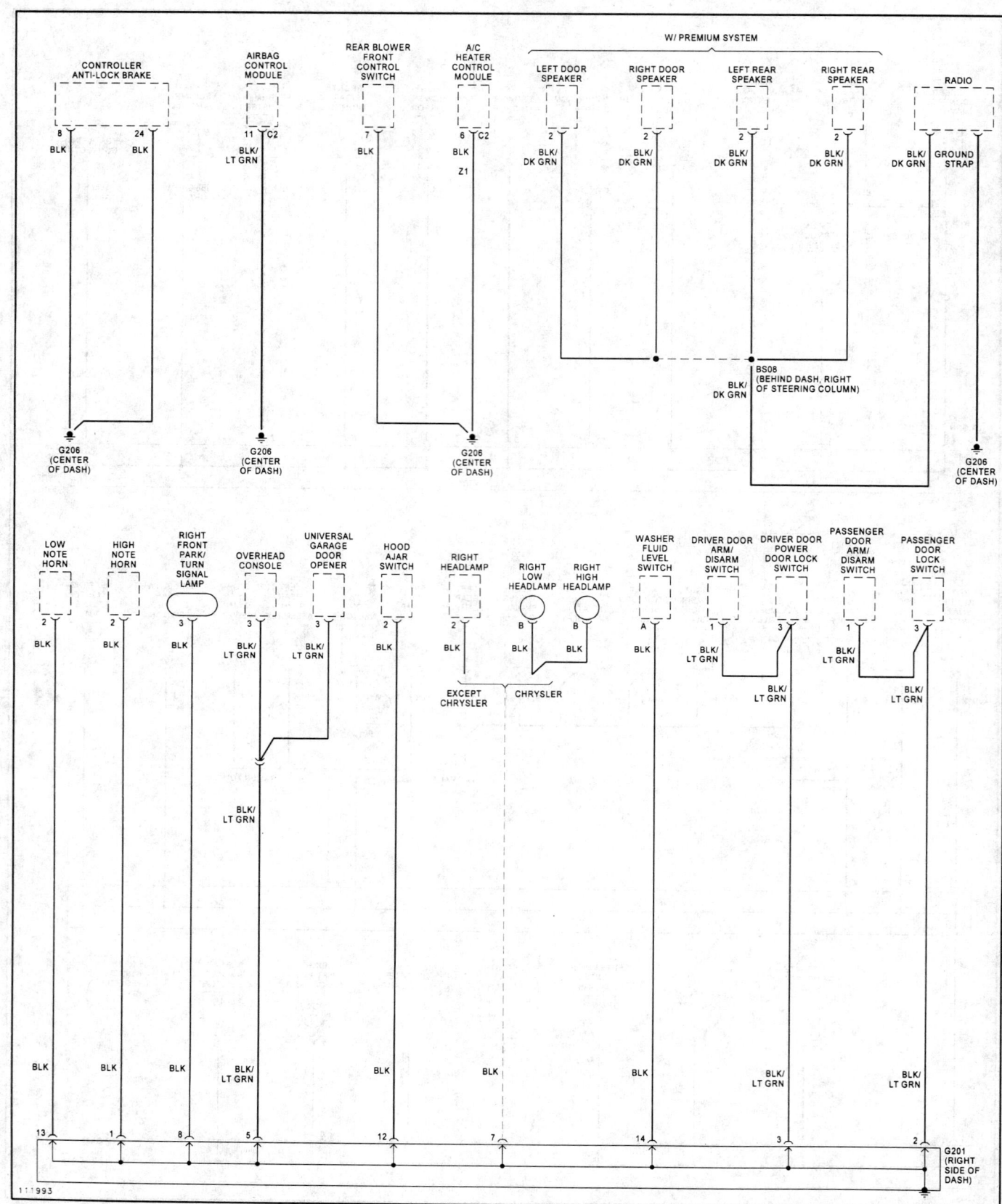

Fig. 8: Ground Distribution Wiring Diagram (Caravan, Town & Country, & Voyager – 3 Of 3)

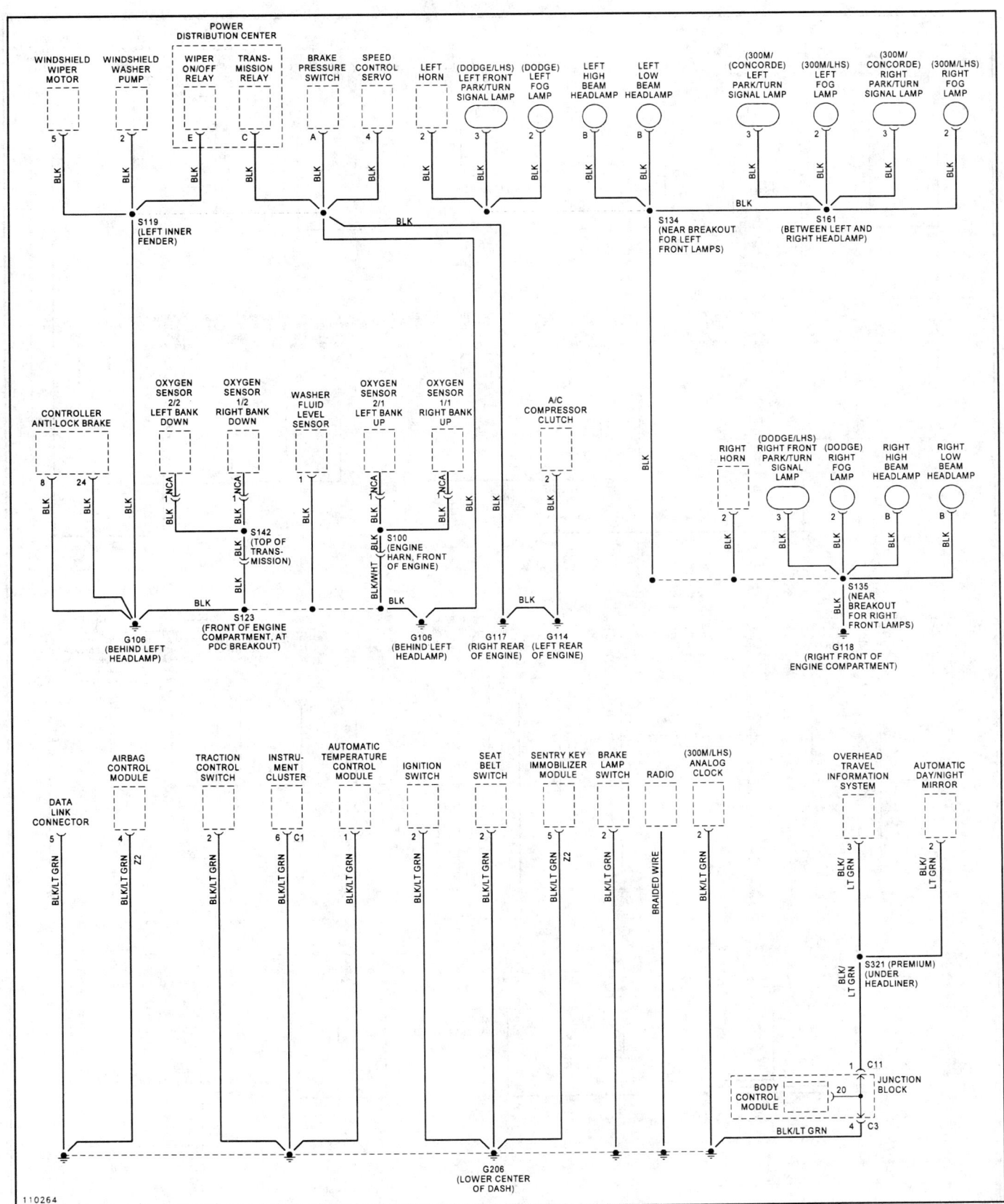

Fig. 9: Ground Distribution Wiring Diagram (Concorde, Intrepid, LHS & 300M – 1 Of 3)

1999 WIRING DIAGRAMS
Ground Distribution (Cont.)

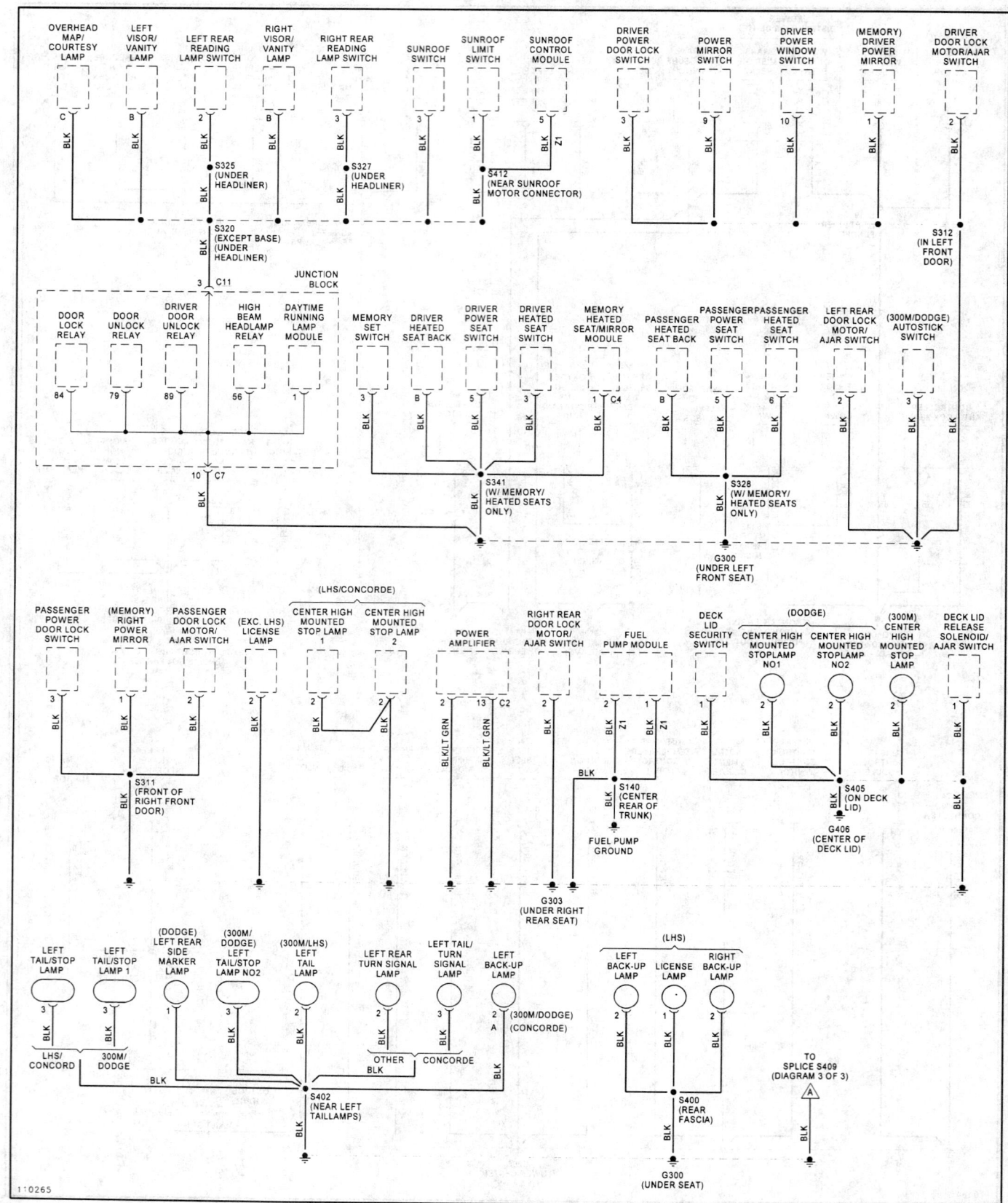

Fig. 10: Ground Distribution Wiring Diagram (Concorde, Intrepid, LHS & 300M – 2 Of 3)

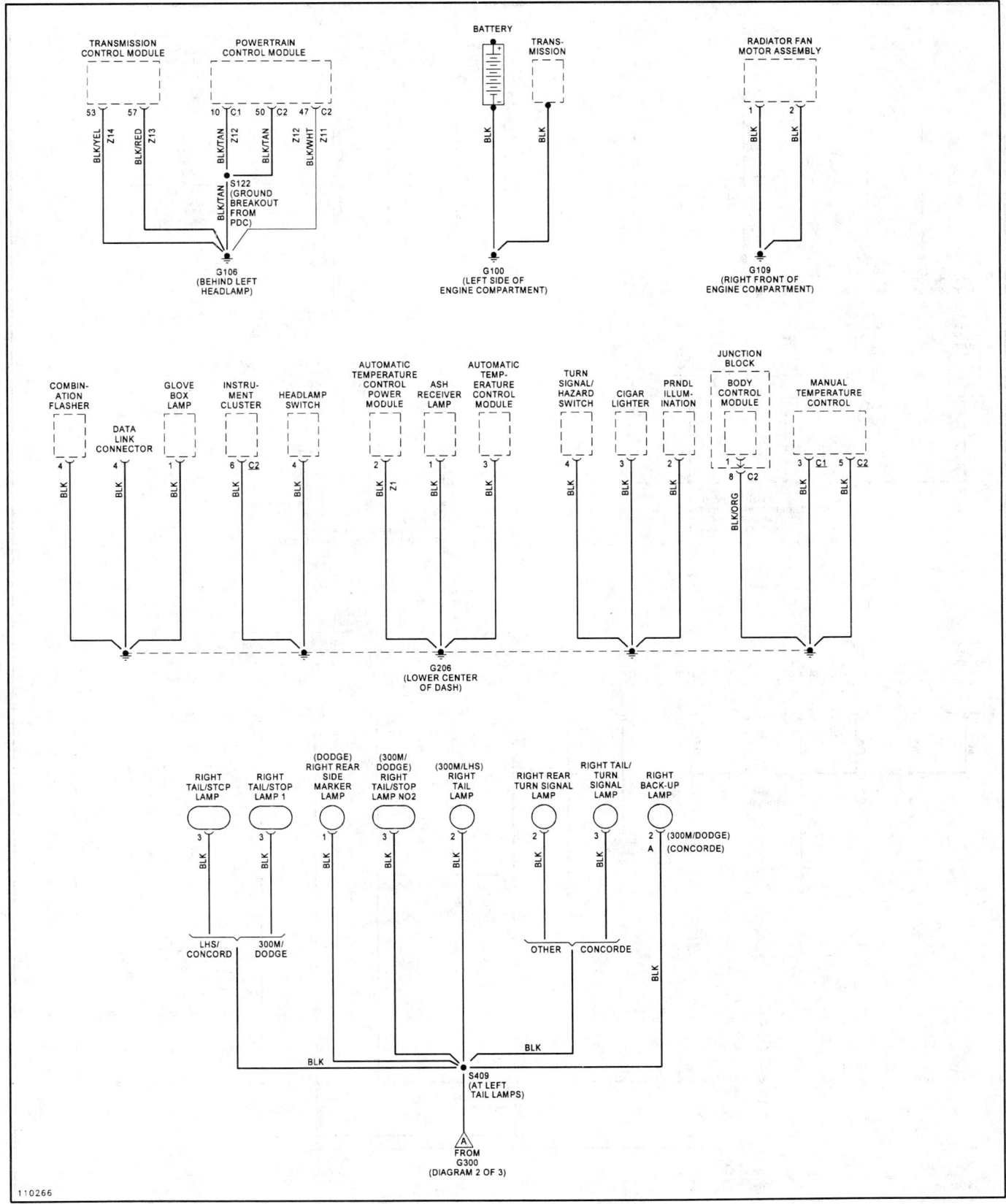

Fig. 11: Ground Distribution Wiring Diagram (Concorde, Intrepid, LHS & 300M – 3 Of 3)

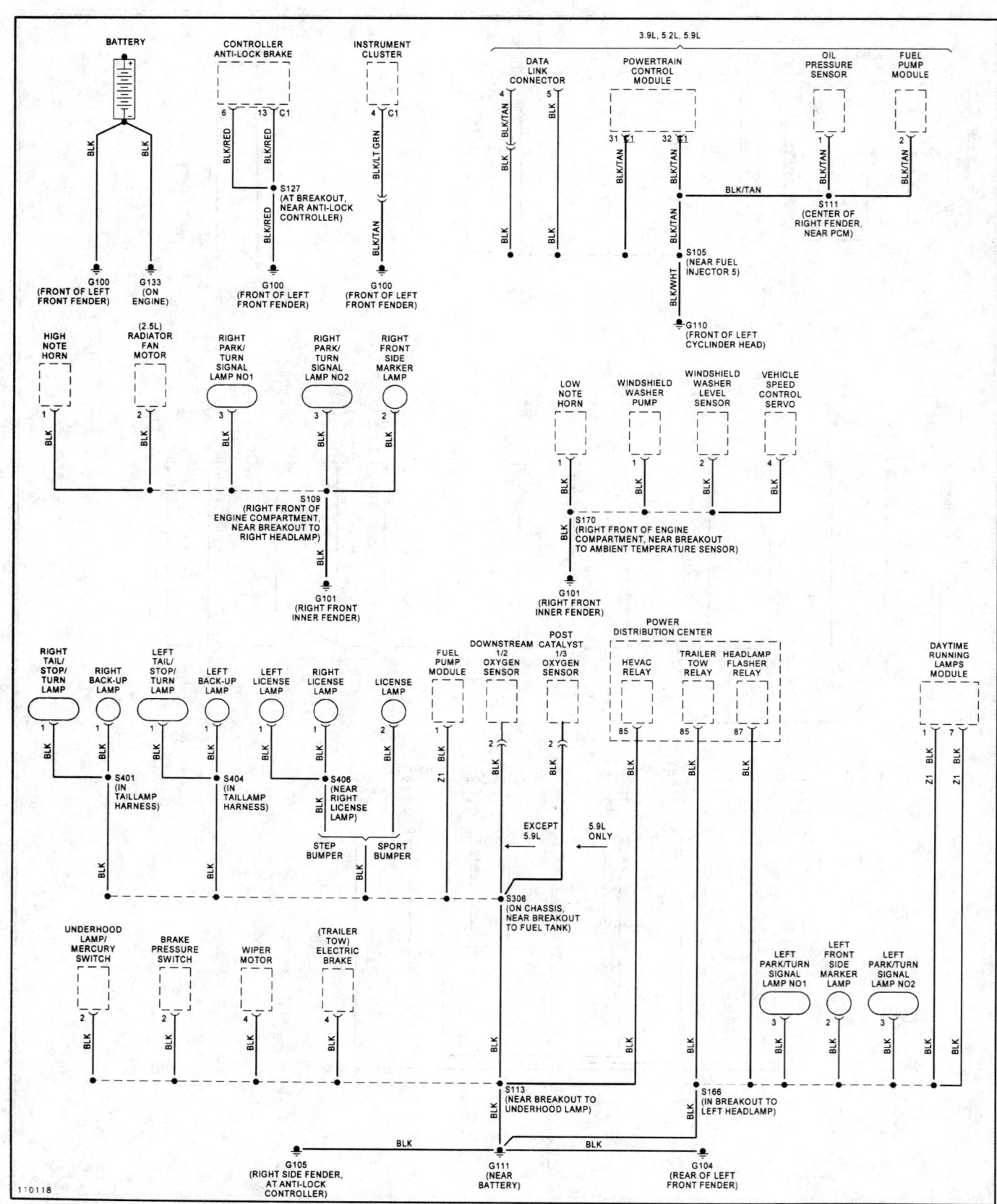

Fig. 12: Ground Distribution Wiring Diagram (Dakota – 1 Of 2)

110118

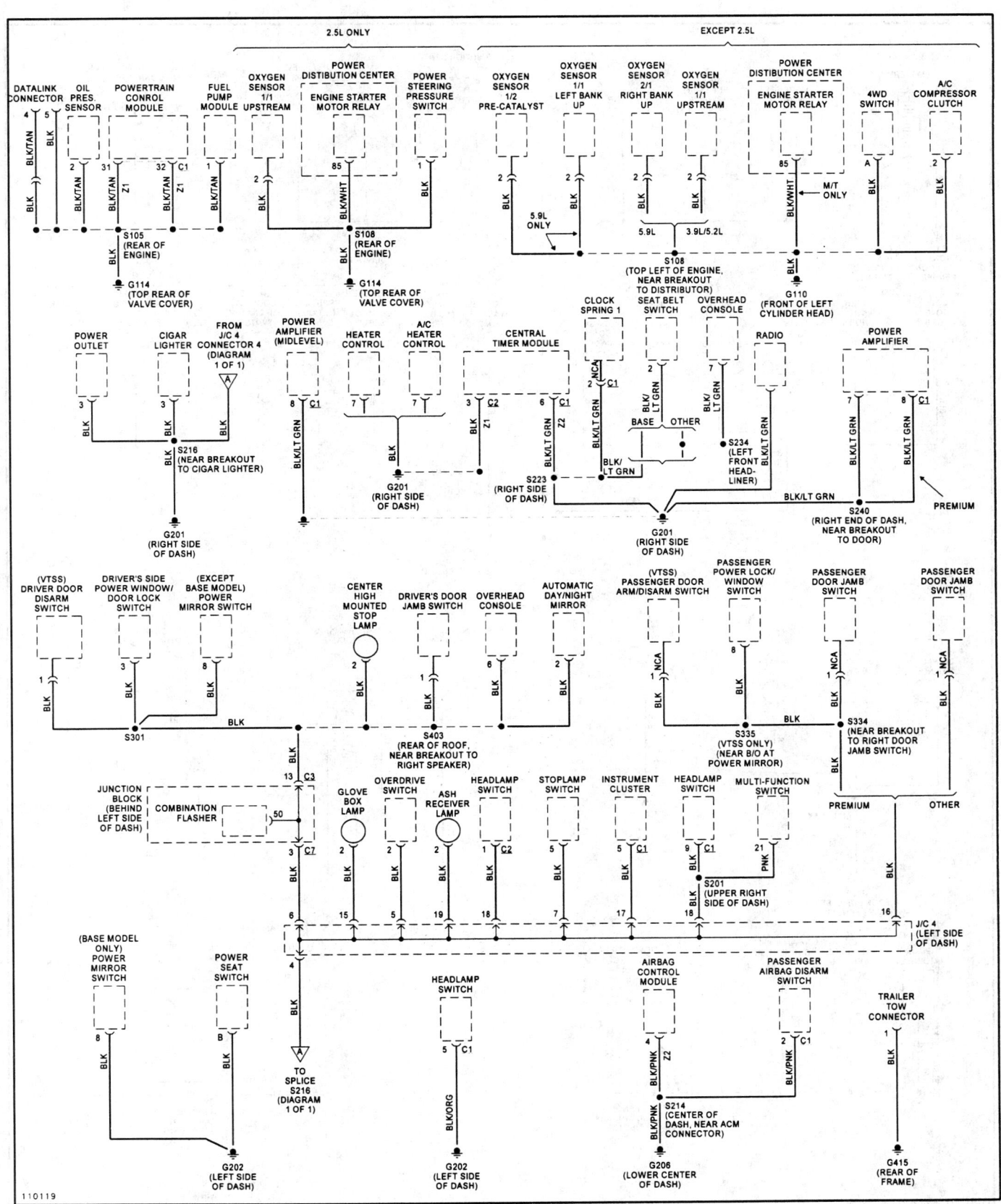

Fig. 13: Ground Distribution Wiring Diagram (Dakota – 2 Of 2)

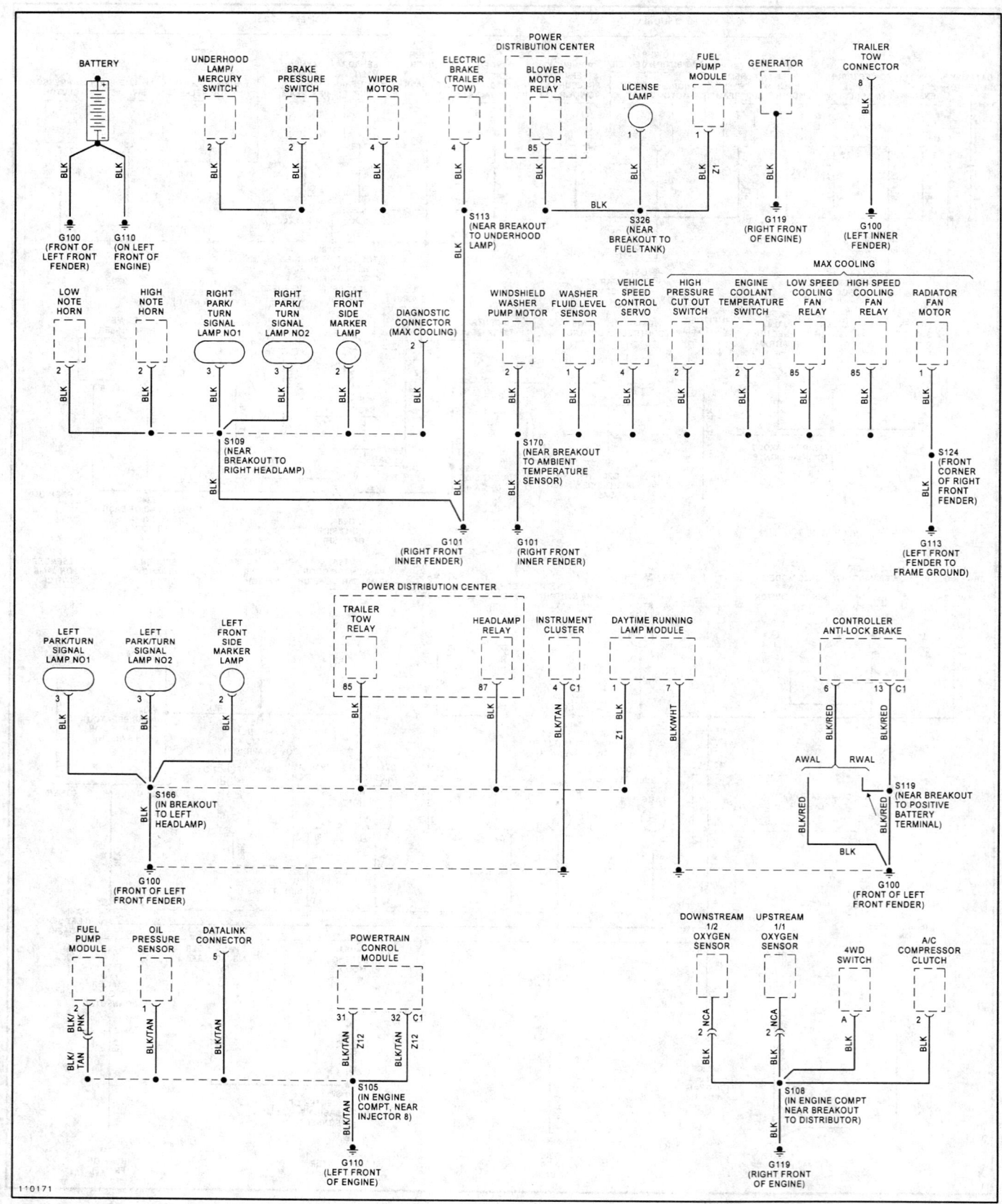

Fig. 14: Ground Distribution Wiring Diagram (Durango – 1 Of 2)

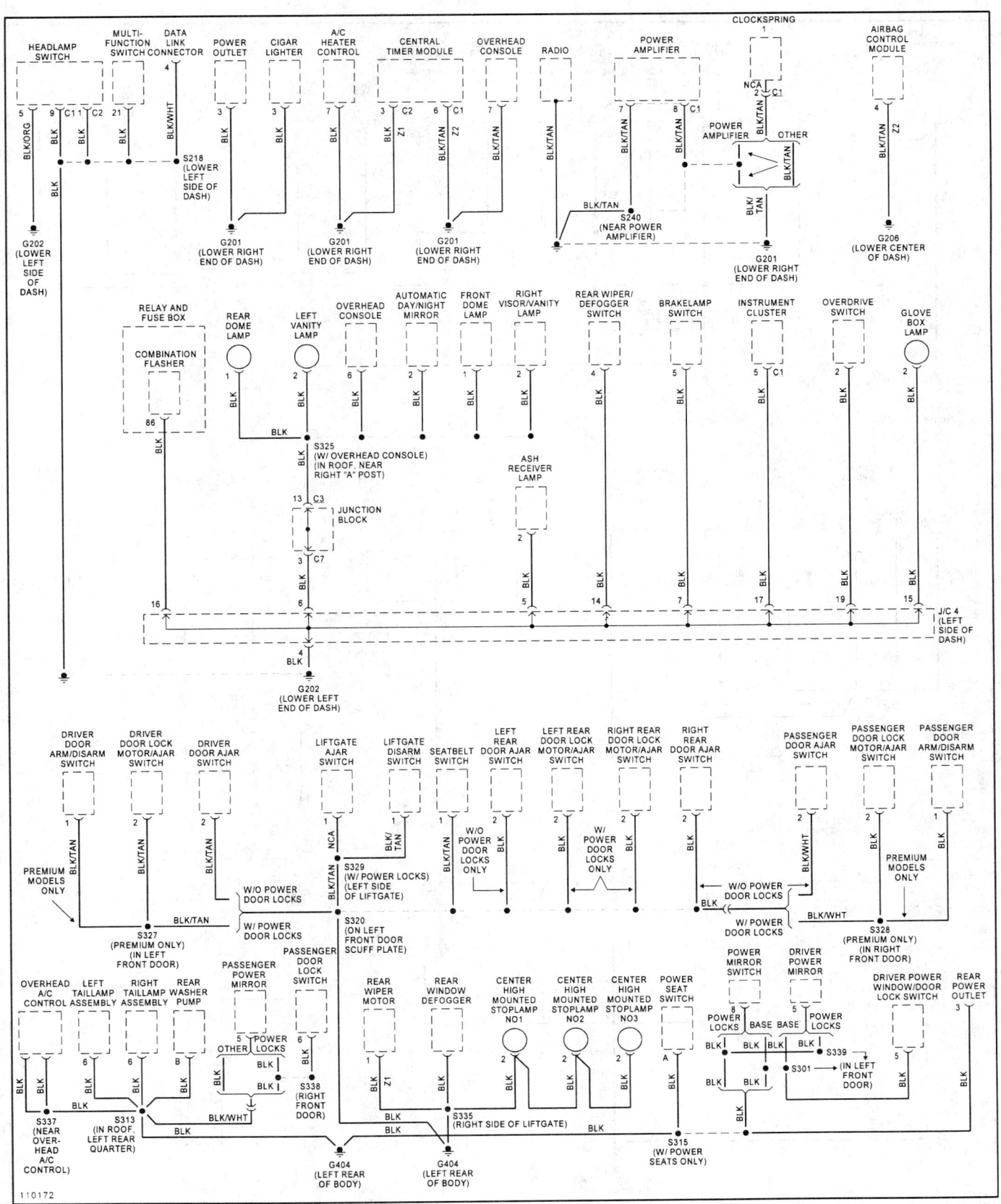

Fig. 15: Ground Distribution Wiring Diagram (Durango – 2 Of 2)

1999 WIRING DIAGRAMS
Ground Distribution (Cont.)

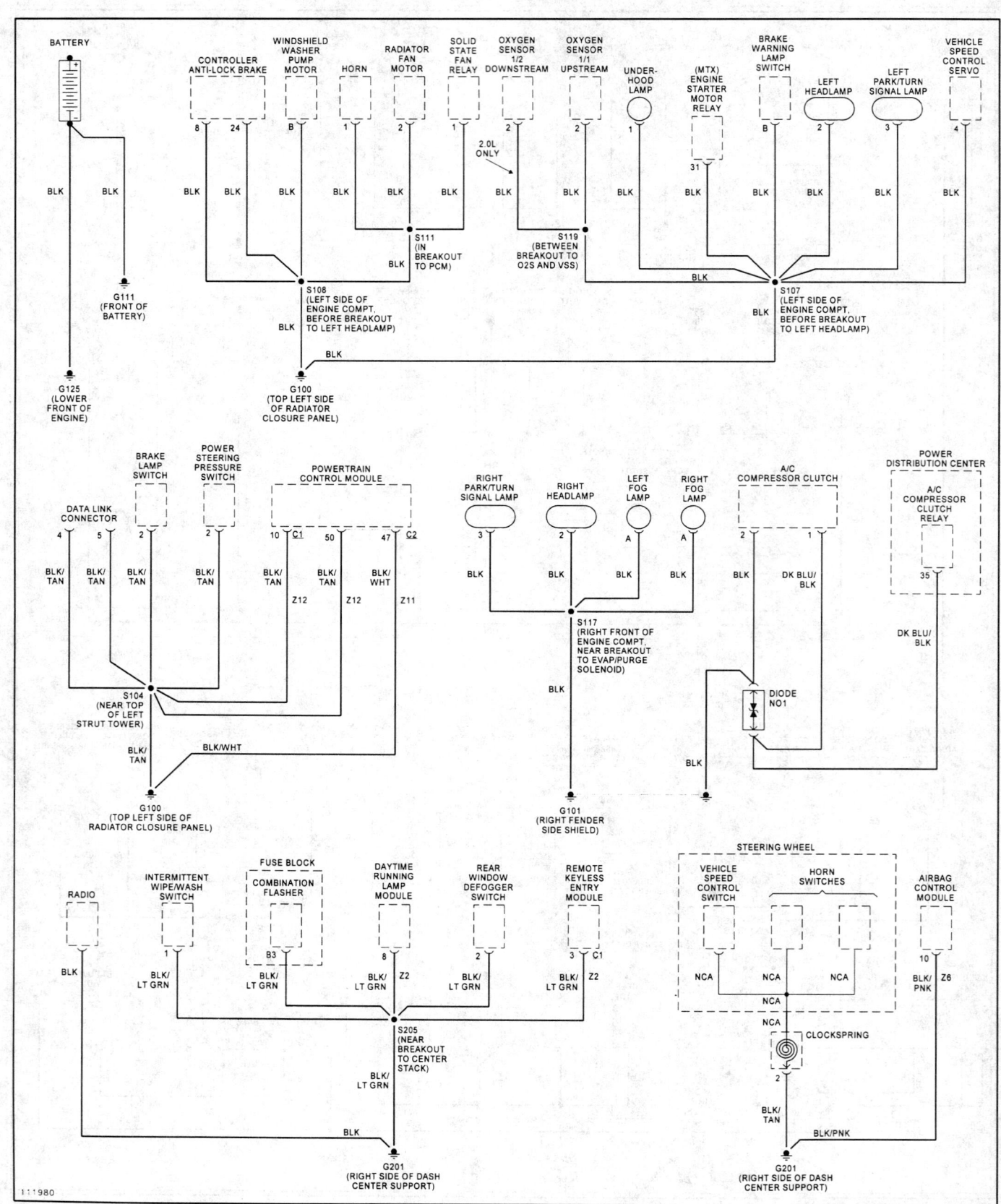

Fig. 16: Ground Distribution Wiring Diagram (Neon – 1 Of 2)

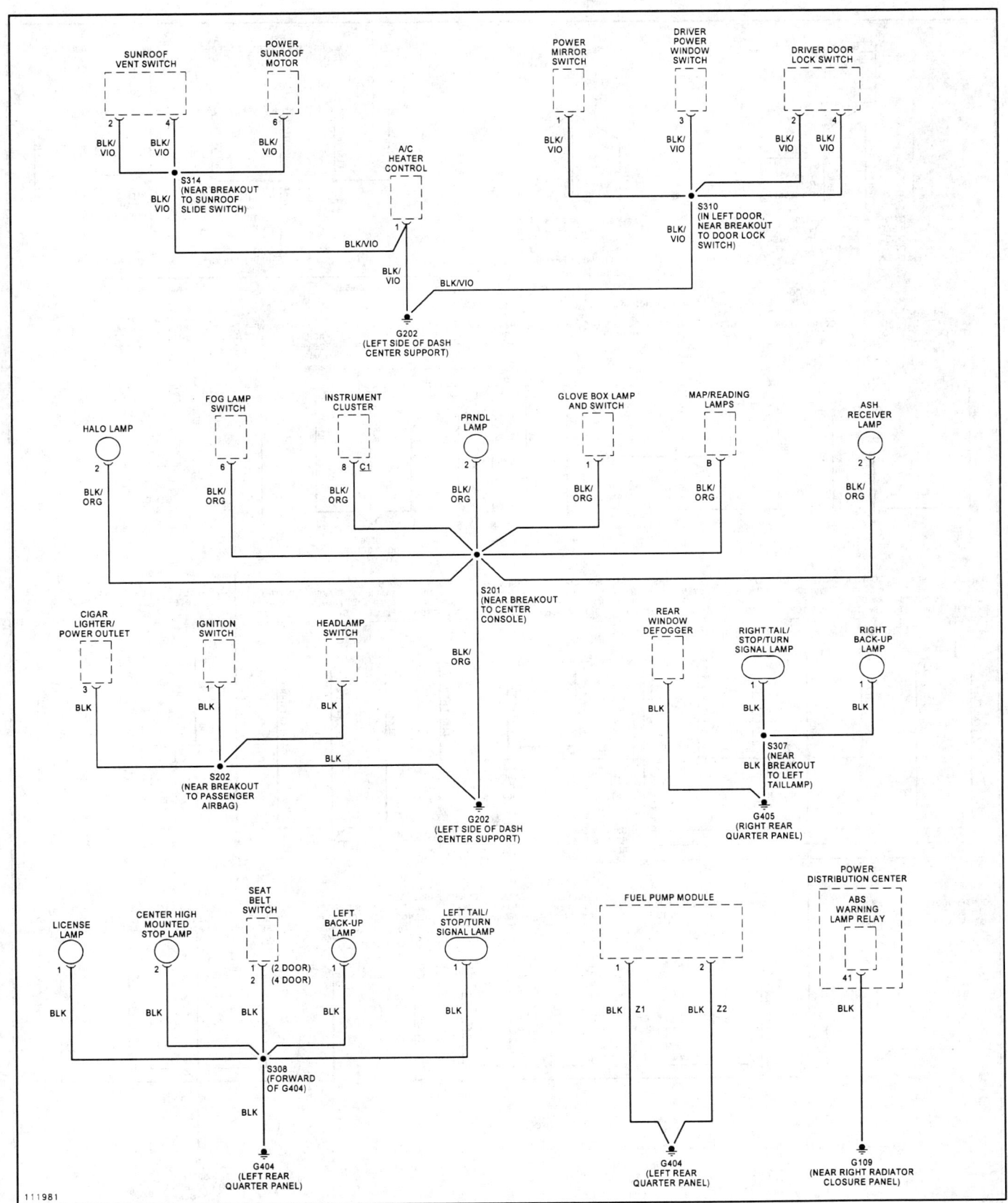

Fig. 17: Ground Distribution Wiring Diagram (Neon – 2 Of 2)

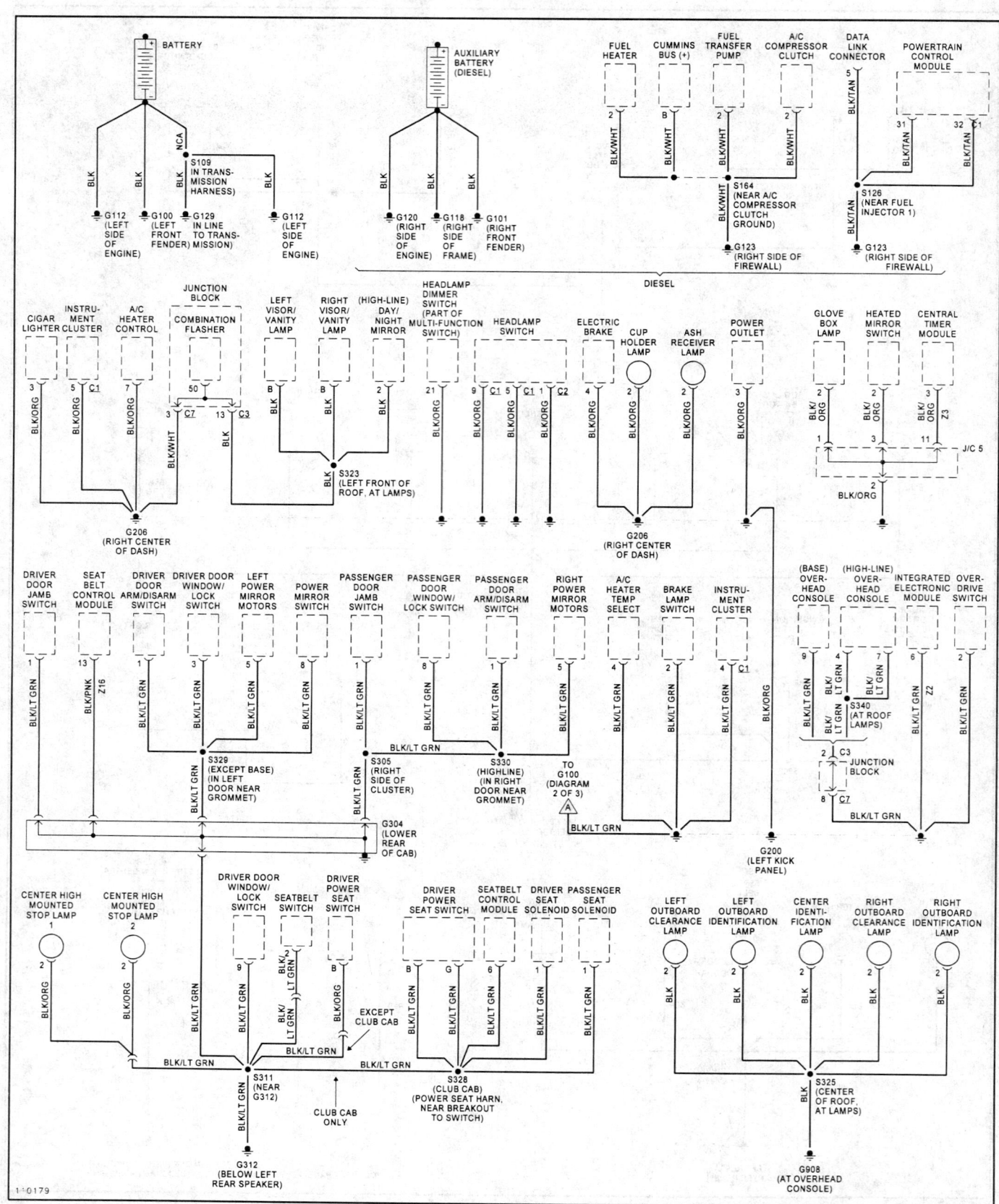

Fig. 18: Ground Distribution Wiring Diagram (Ram Pickup – 1 Of 3)

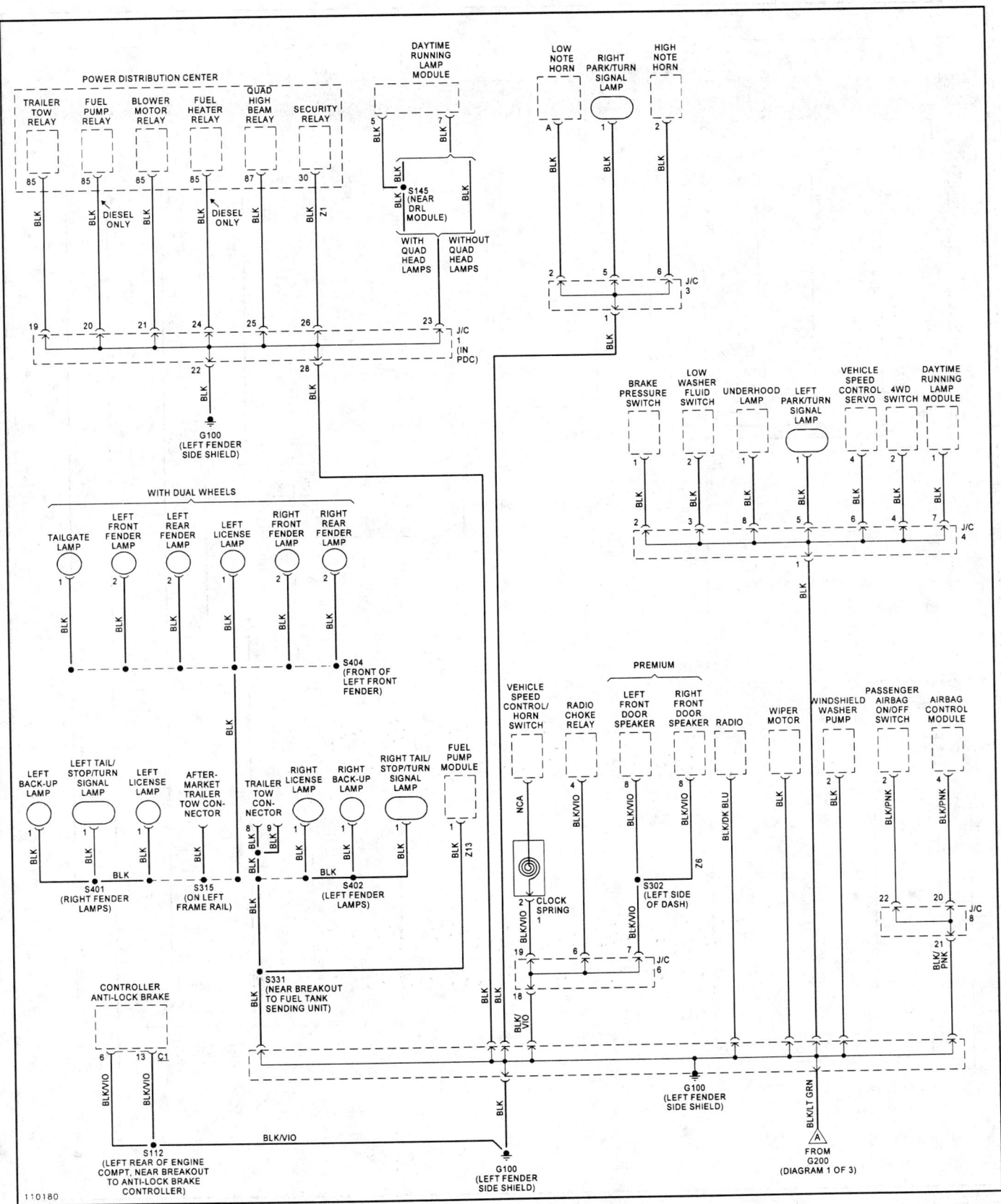

Fig. 19: Ground Distribution Wiring Diagram (Ram Pickup – 2 Of 3)

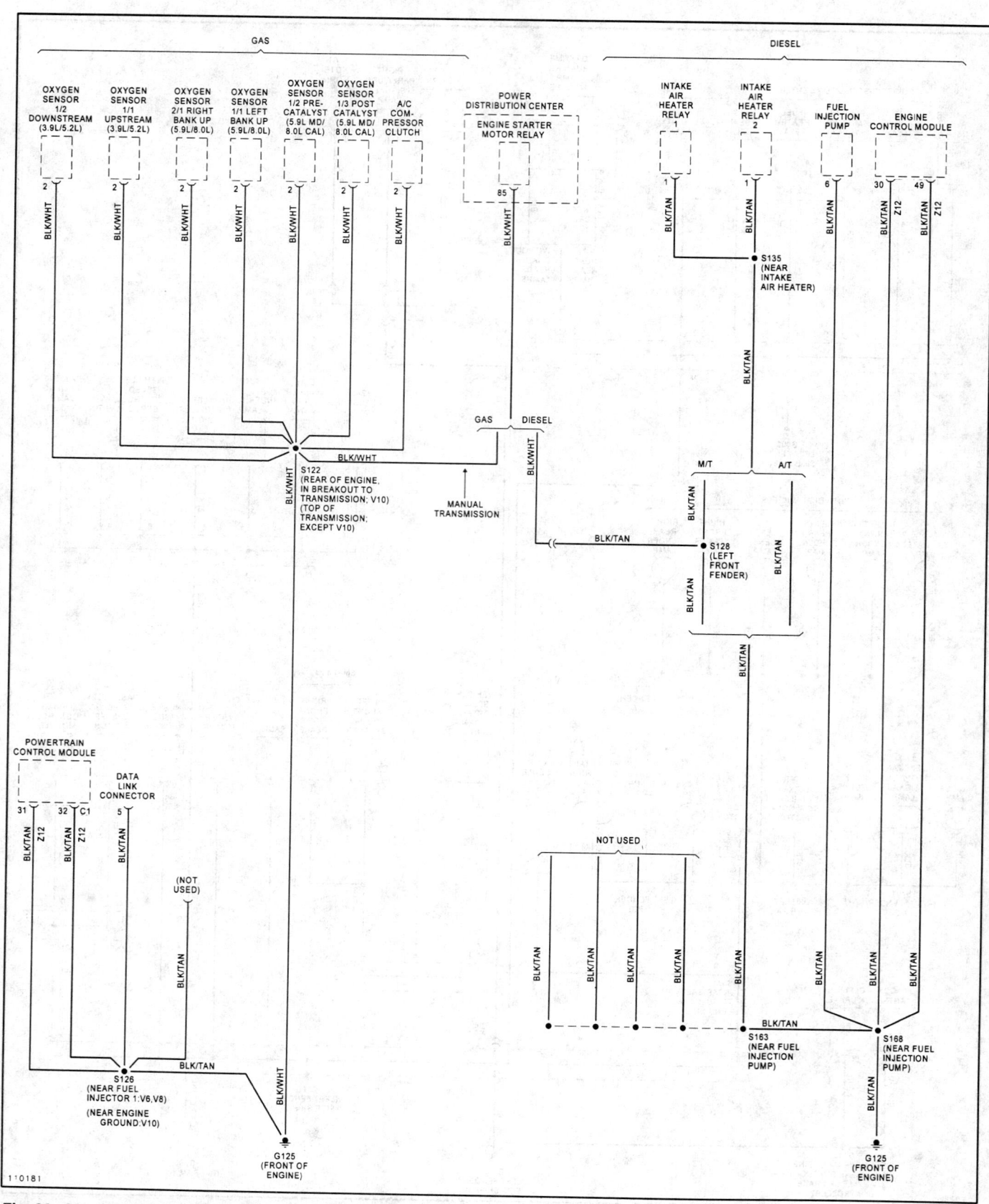

Fig. 20: Ground Distribution Wiring Diagram (Ram Pickup – 3 Of 3)

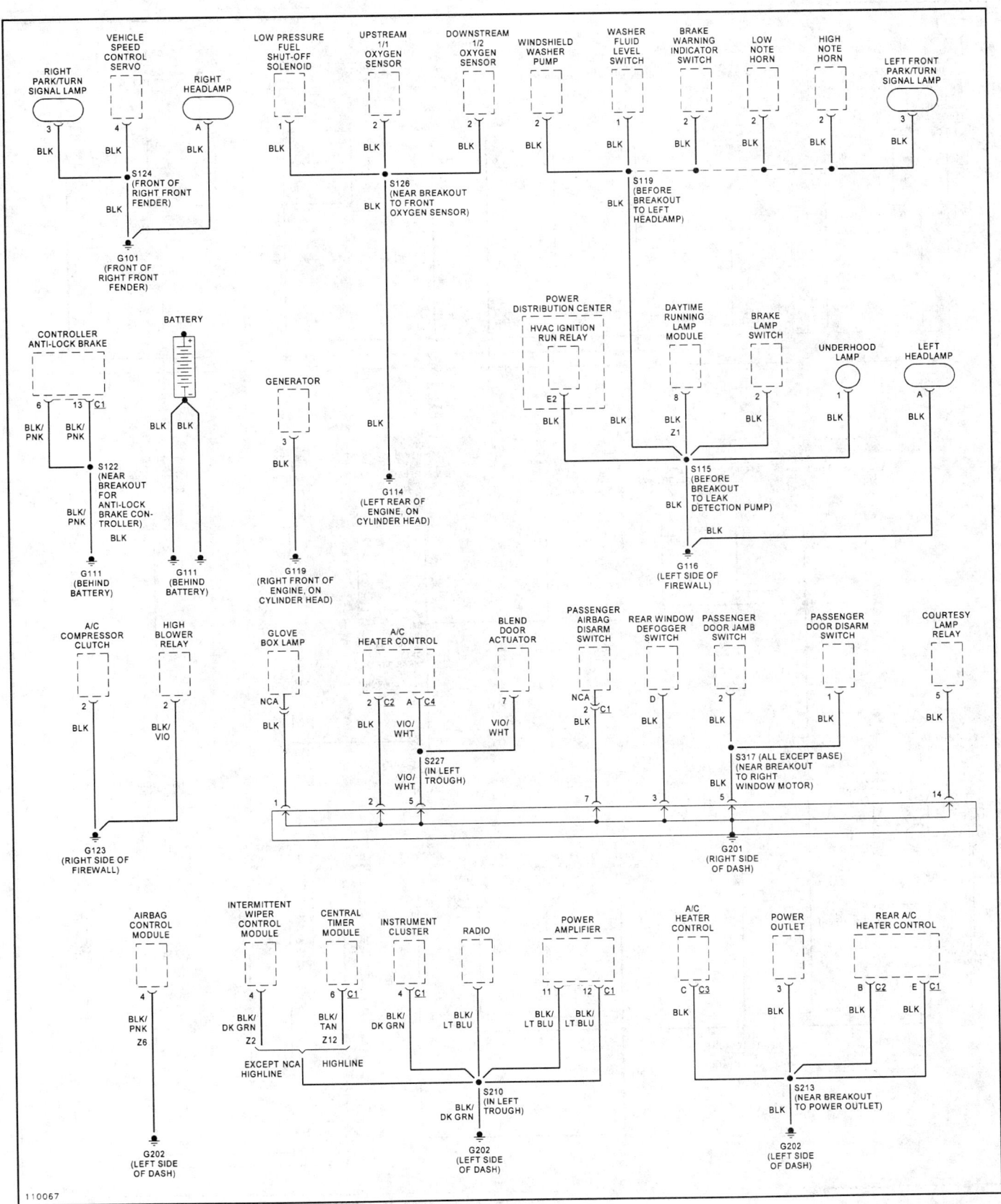

Fig. 21: Ground Distribution Wiring Diagram (Ram Van & Ram Wagon – 1 Of 2)

110067

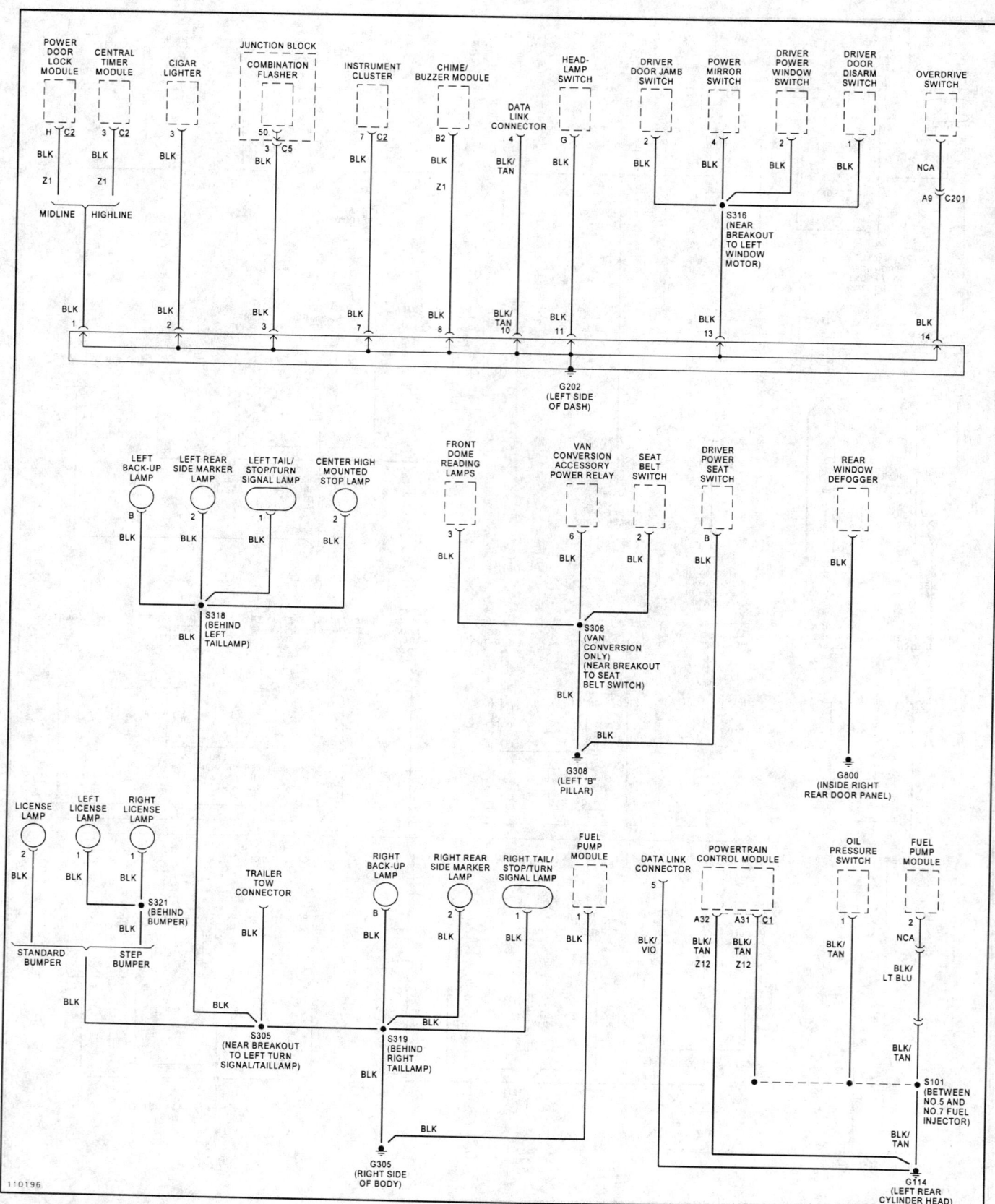

Fig. 22: Ground Distribution Wiring Diagram (Ram Van & Ram Wagon – 2 Of 2)

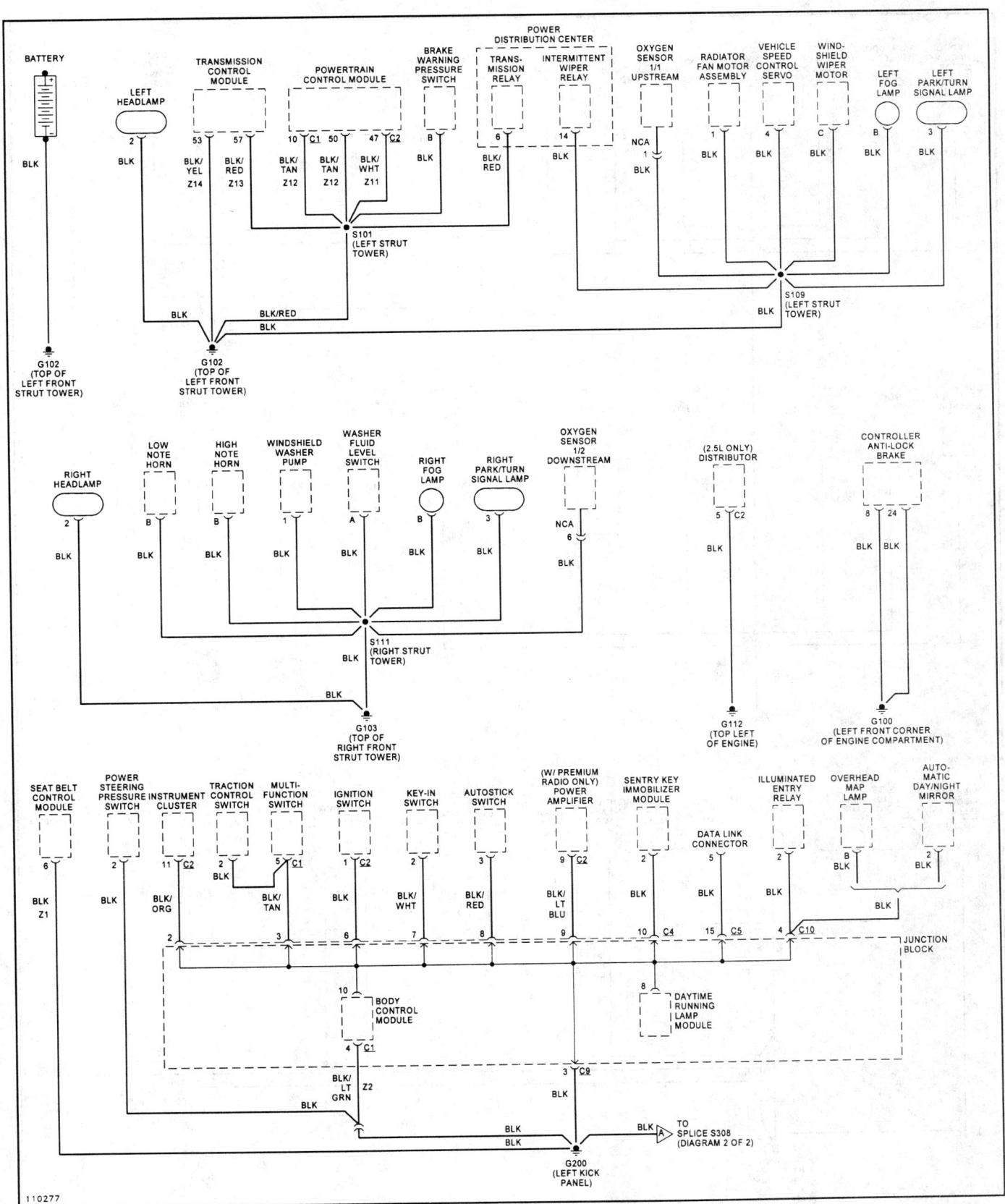

Fig. 23: Ground Distribution Wiring Diagram (Sebring Convertible – 1 Of 2)

1999 WIRING DIAGRAMS
Ground Distribution (Cont.)

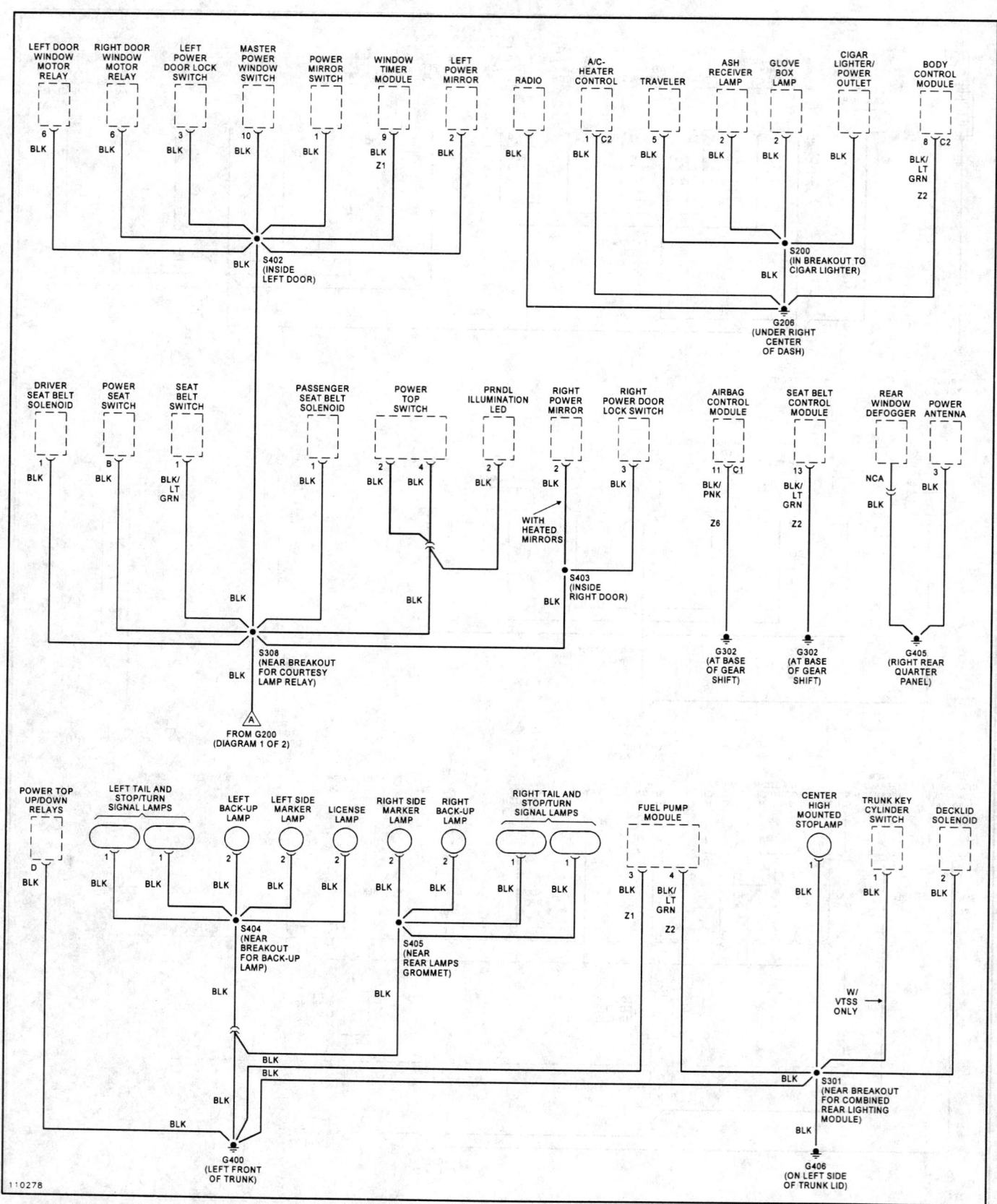

Fig. 24: Ground Distribution Wiring Diagram (Sebring Convertible – 2 Of 2)

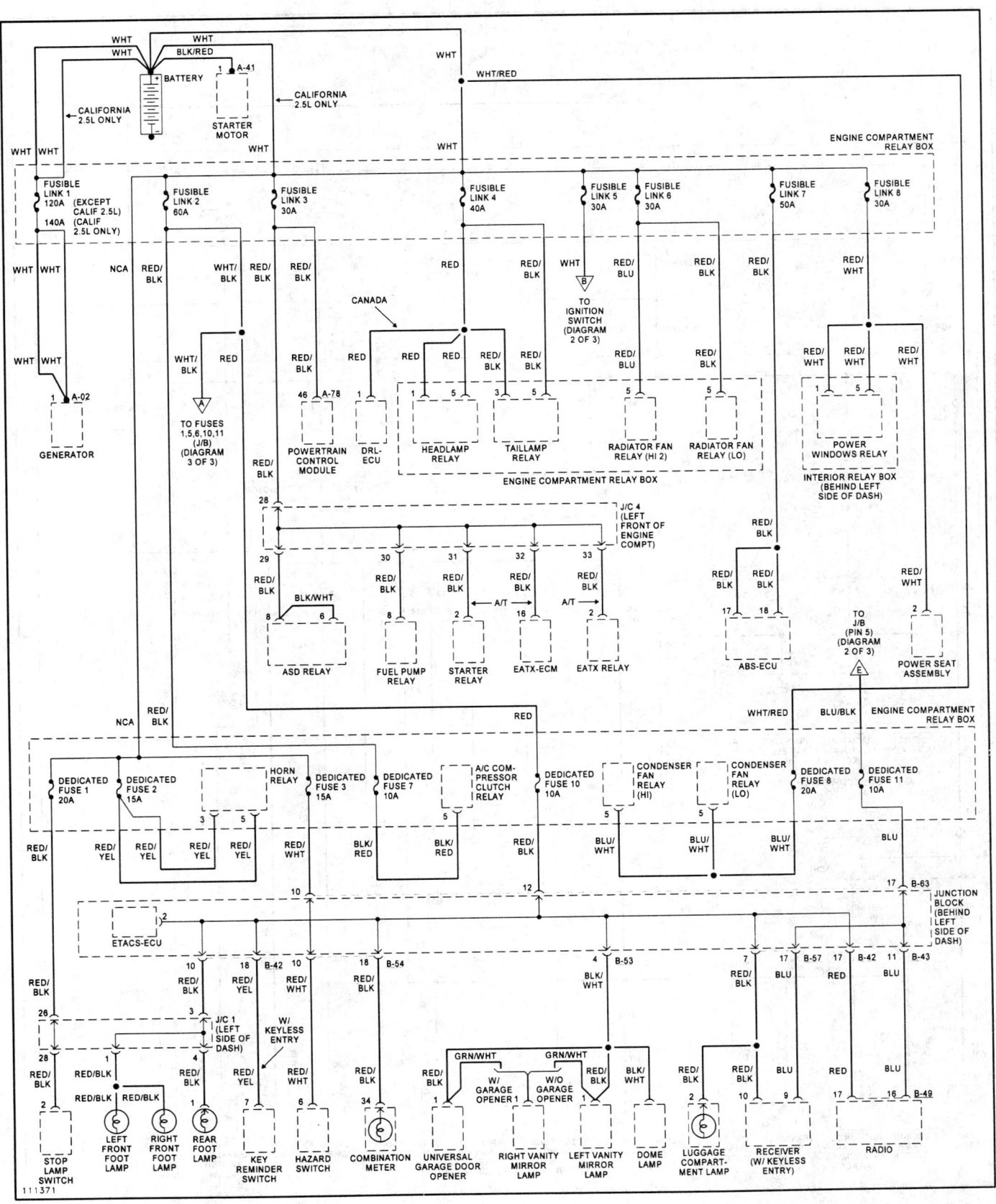

Fig. 1: Power Distribution Wiring Diagram (Avenger & Sebring Coupe – 1 Of 3)

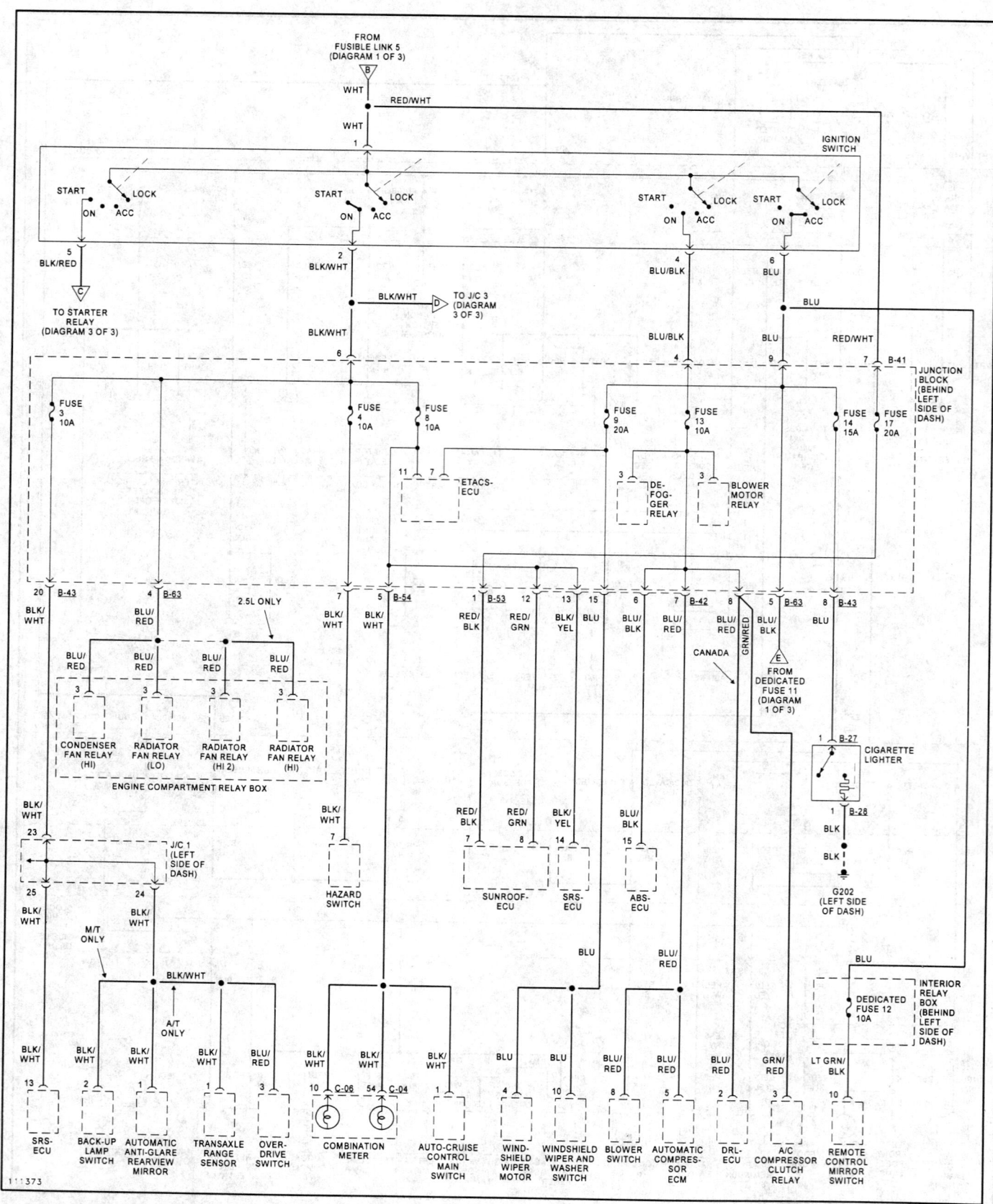

Fig. 2: Power Distribution Wiring Diagram (Avenger & Sebring Coupe – 2 Of 3)

111373

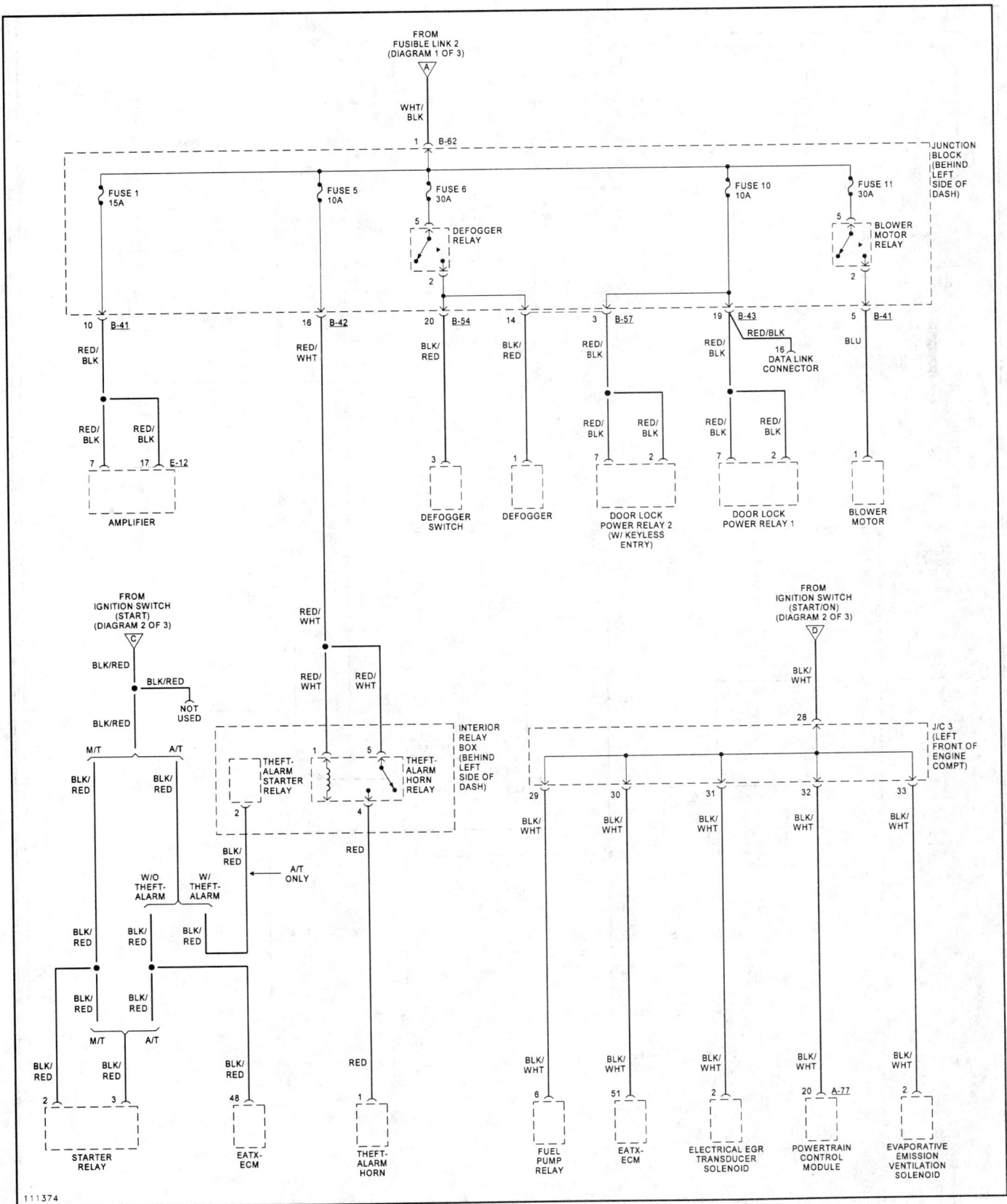

Fig. 3: Power Distribution Wiring Diagram (Avenger & Sebring Coupe – 3 Of 3)

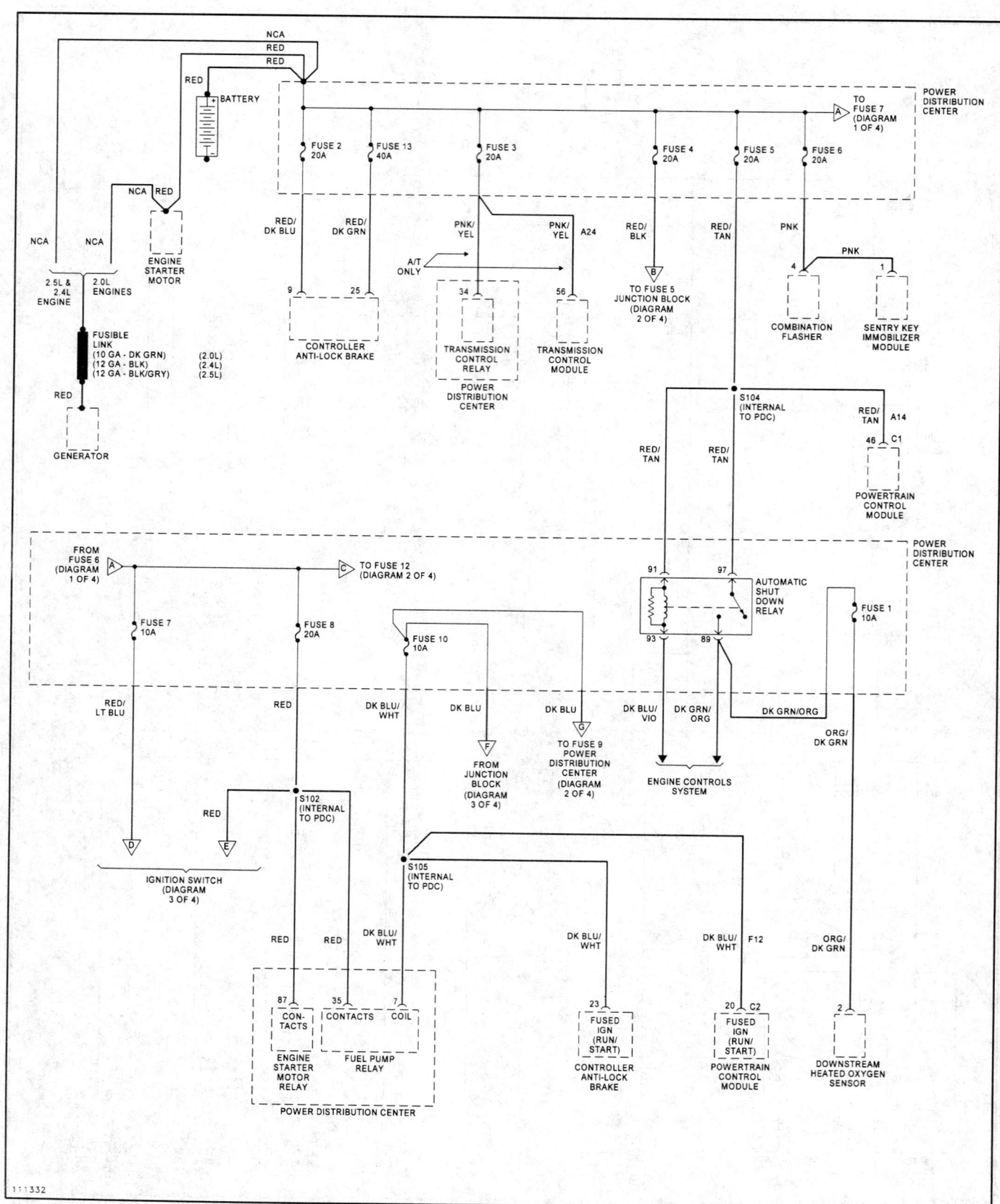

Fig. 4: Power Distribution Wiring Diagram (Breeze, Cirrus & Stratus – 1 Of 4)

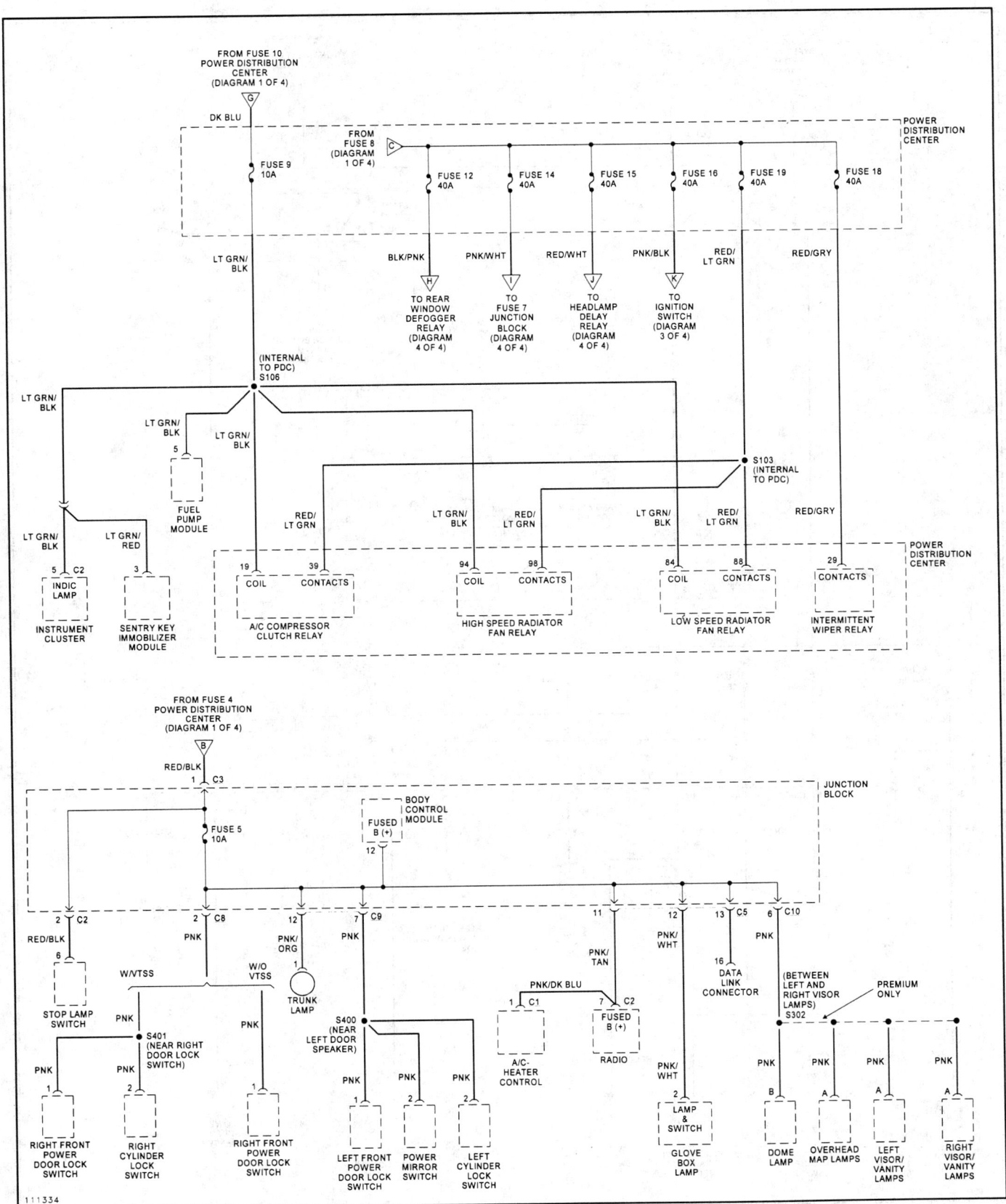

Fig. 5: Power Distribution Wiring Diagram (Breeze, Cirrus & Stratus – 2 Of 4)

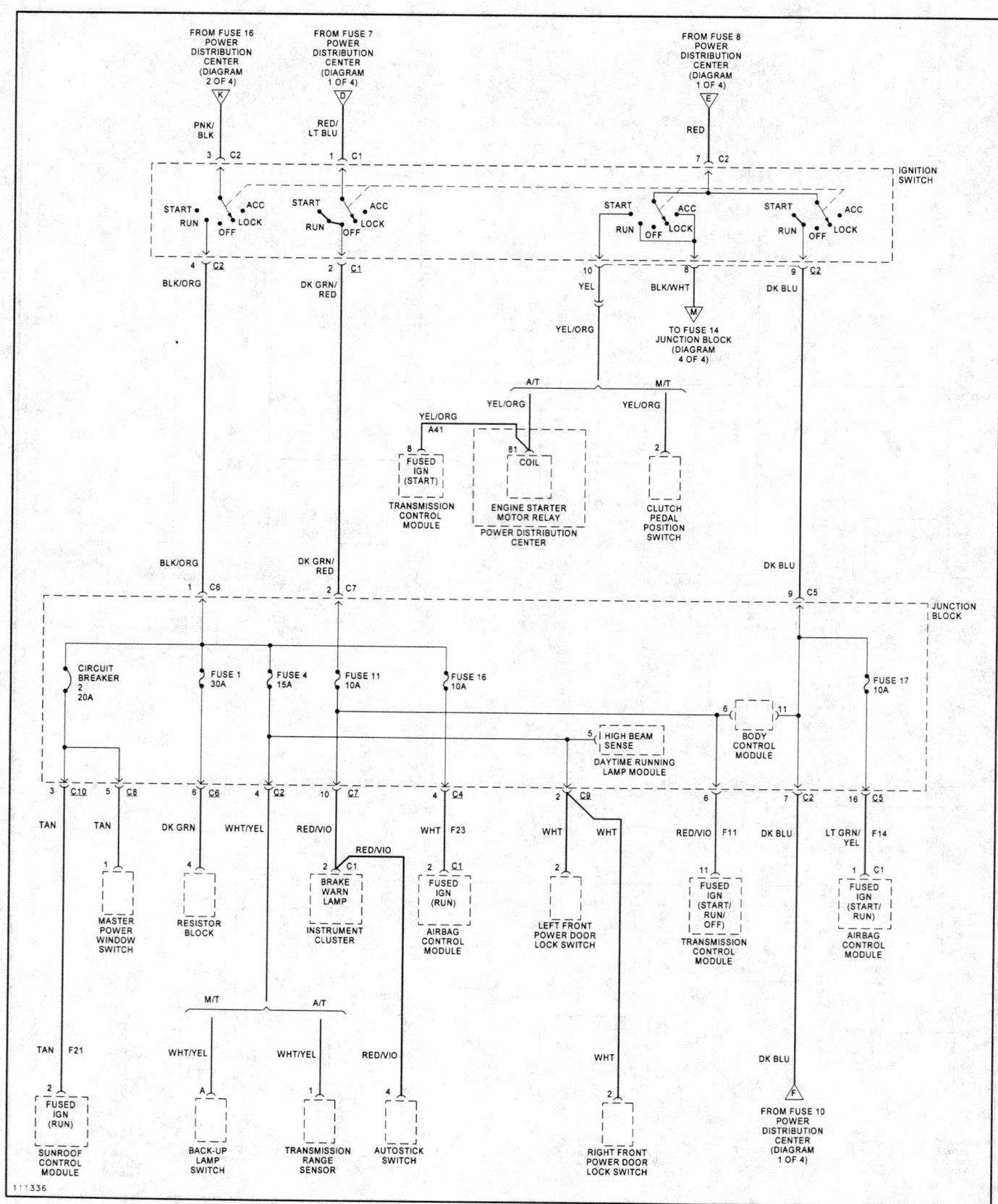

Fig. 6: Power Distribution Wiring Diagram (Breeze, Cirrus & Stratus – 3 Of 4)

111336

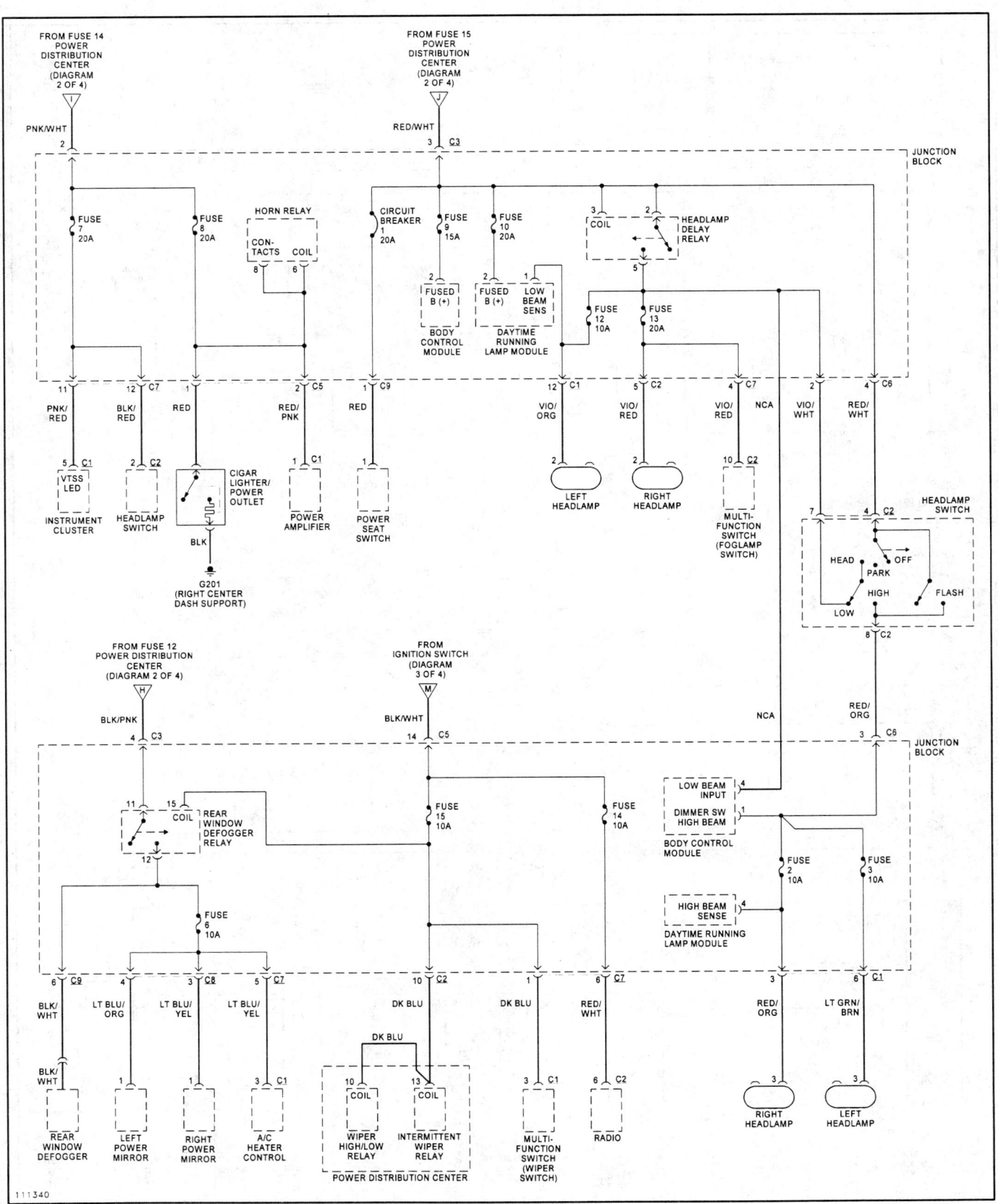

Fig. 7: Power Distribution Wiring Diagram (Breeze, Cirrus & Stratus – 4 Of 4)

111340

1999 WIRING DIAGRAMS
Power Distribution (Cont.)

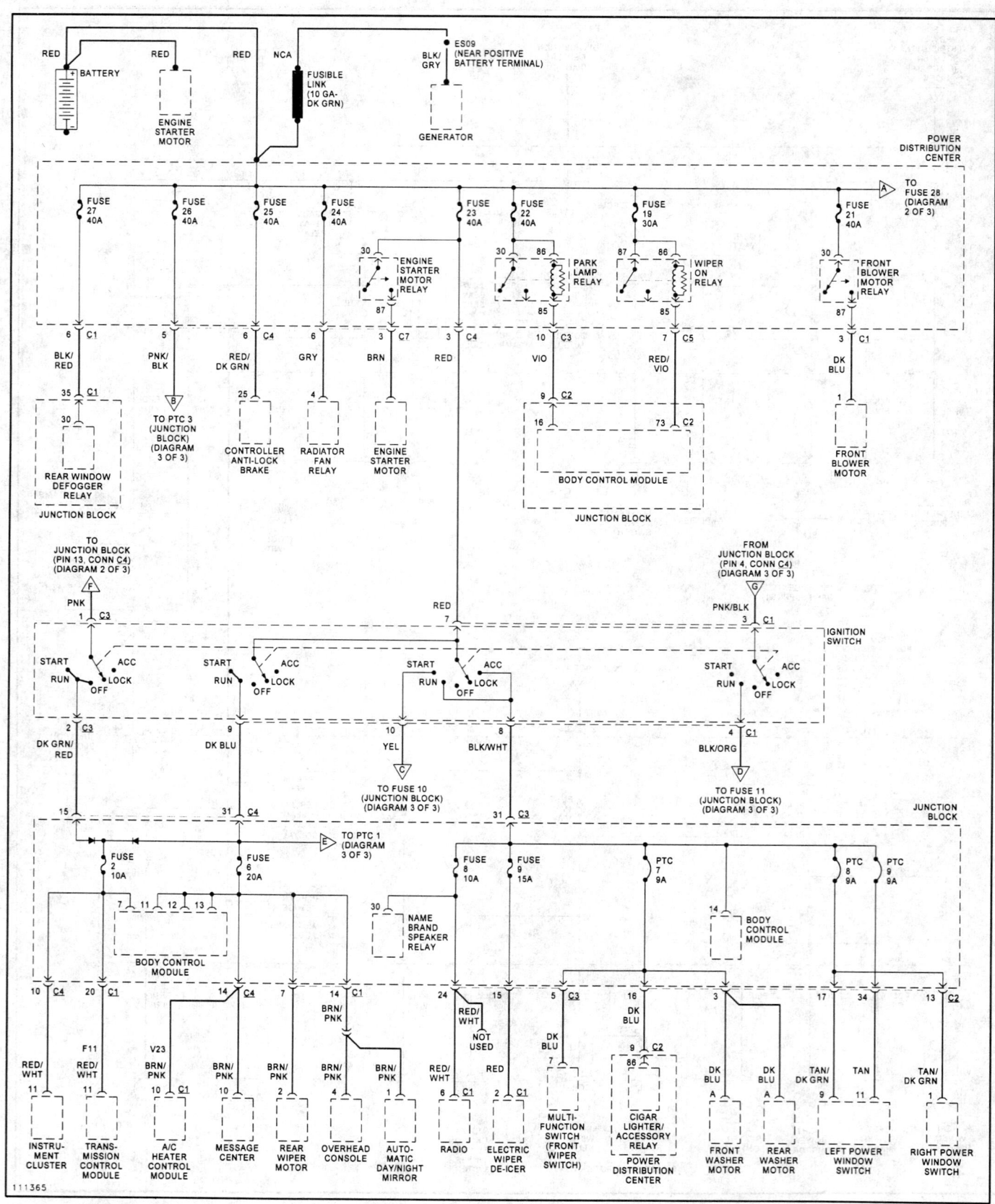

Fig. 8: Power Distribution Wiring Diagram (Caravan, Town & Country, & Voyager – 1 Of 3)

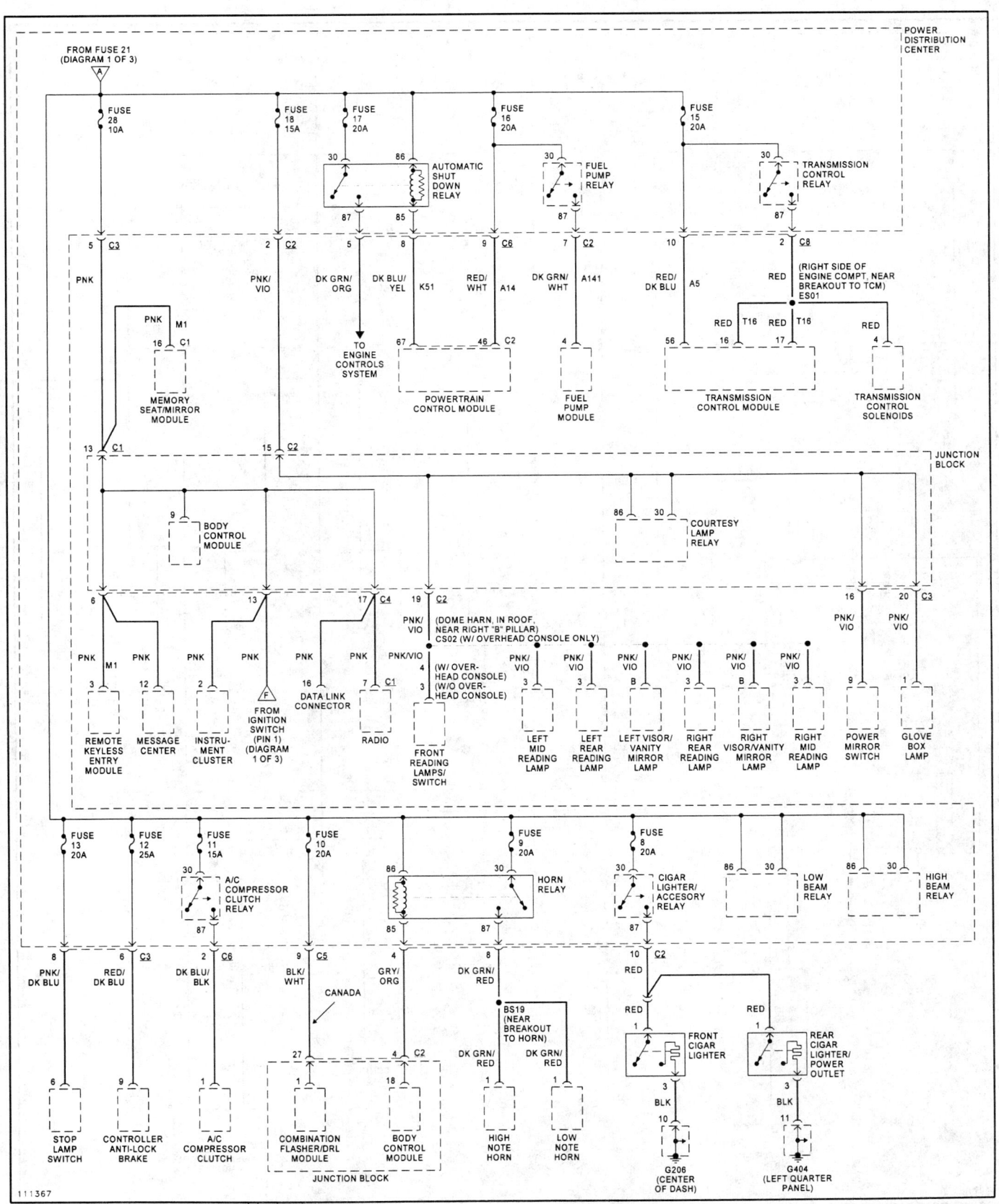

Fig. 9: Power Distribution Wiring Diagram (Caravan, Town & Country, & Voyager – 2 Of 3)

111367

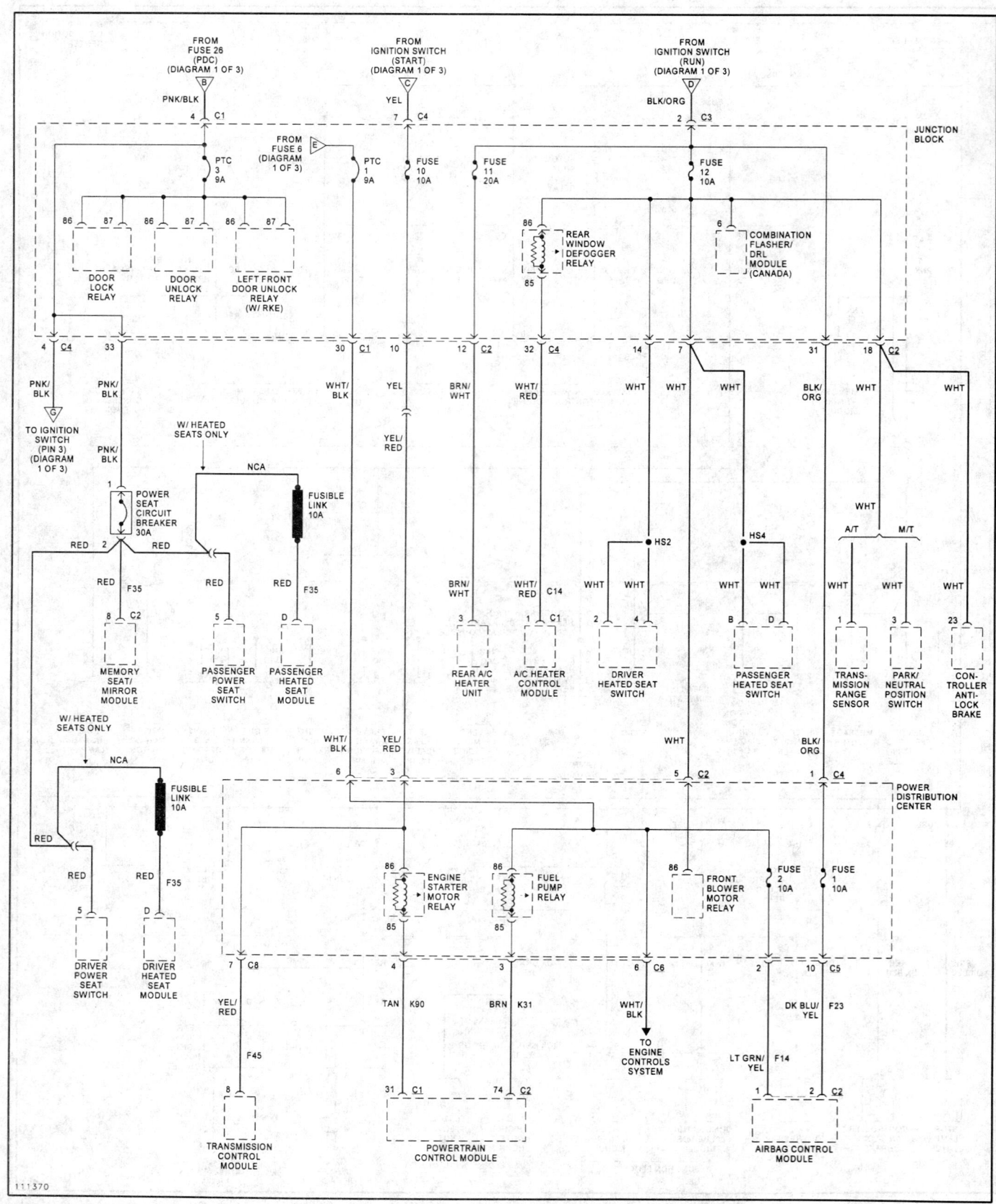

Fig. 10: Power Distribution Wiring Diagram (Caravan, Town & Country, & Voyager – 3 Of 3)

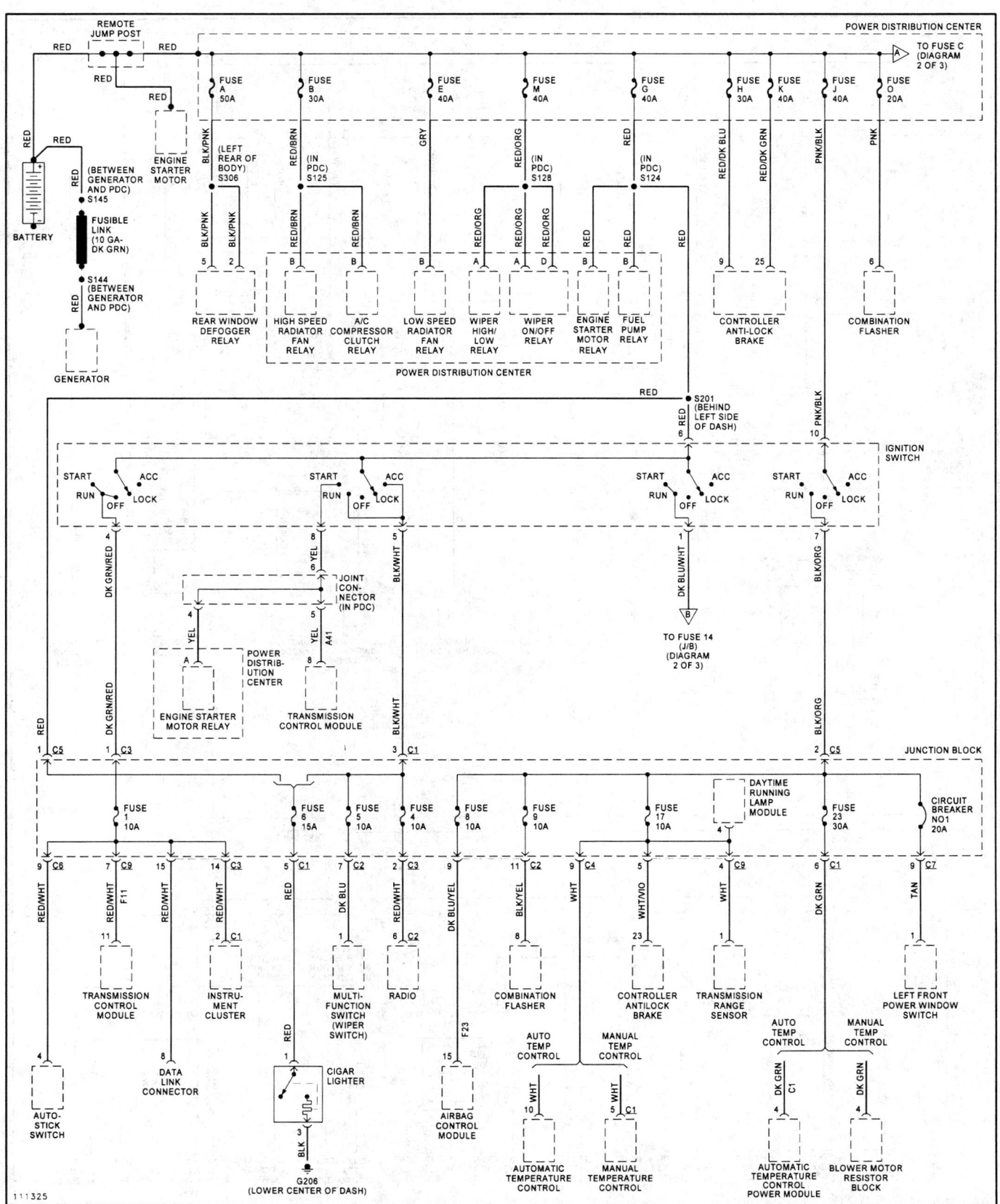

Fig. 11: Power Distribution Wiring Diagram (Concorde, Intrepid, LHS & 300M – 1 Of 3)

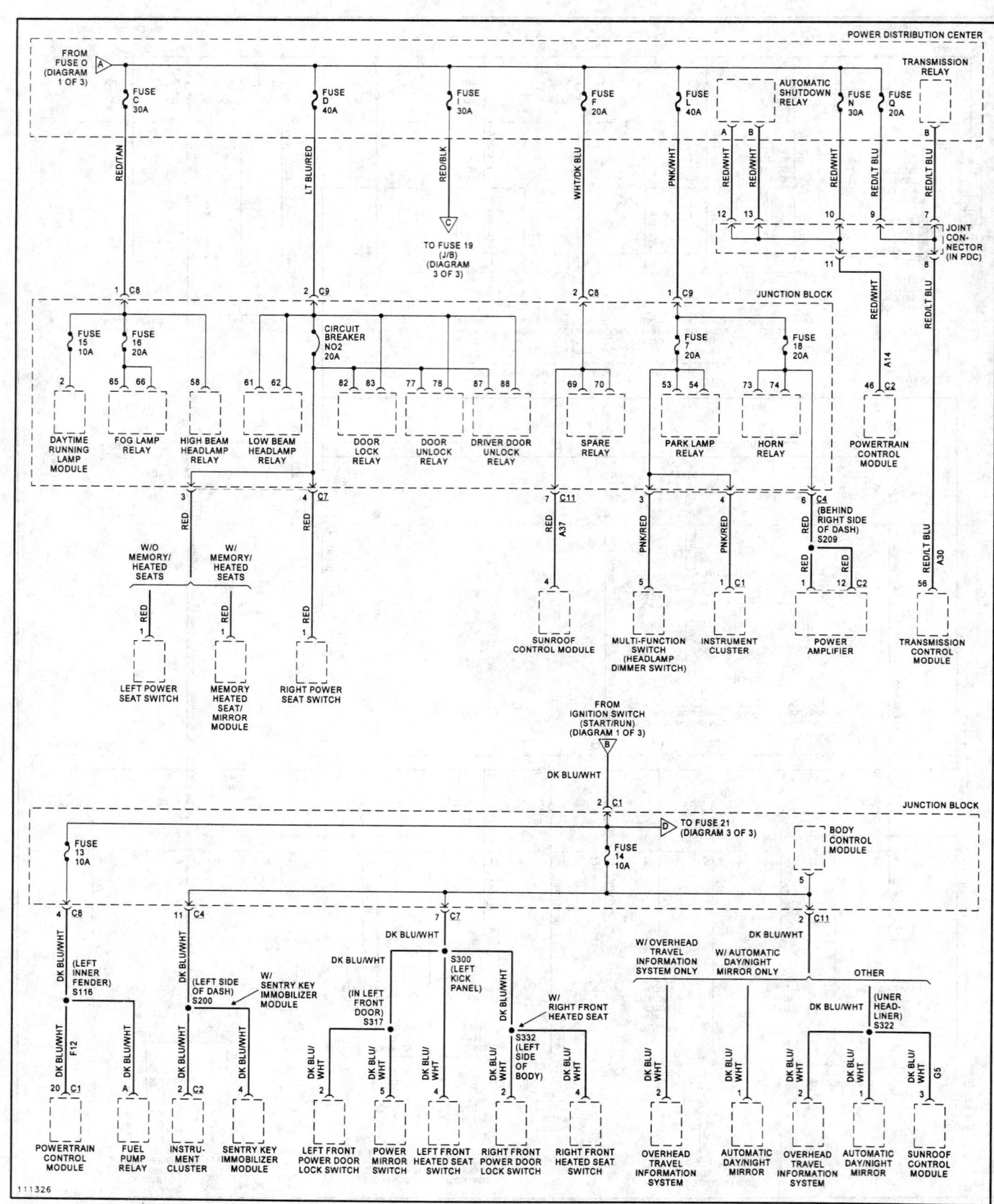

Fig. 12: Power Distribution Wiring Diagram (Concorde, Intrepid, LHS & 300M – 2 Of 3)

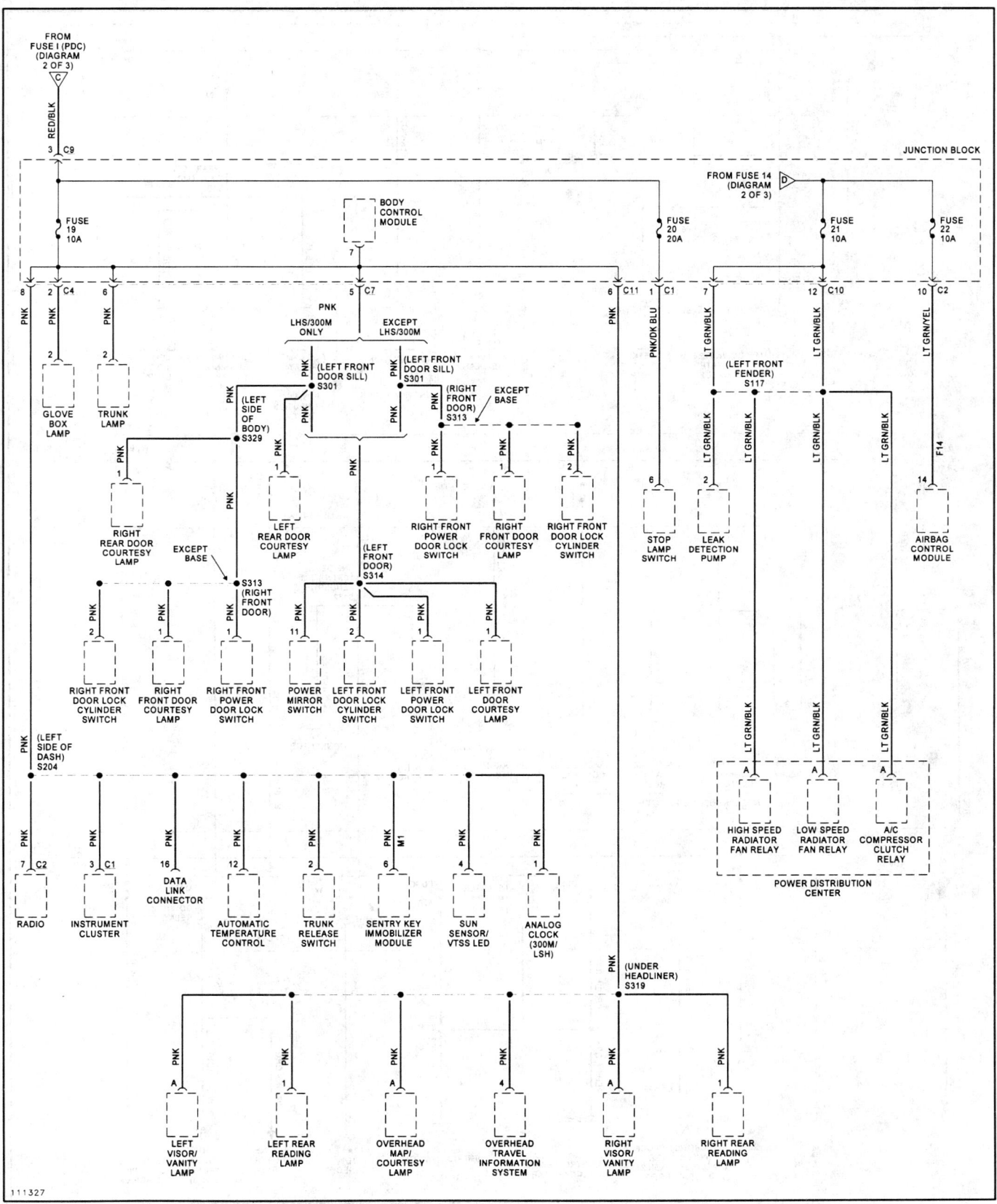

Fig. 13: Power Distribution Wiring Diagram (Concorde, Intrepid, LHS & 300M – 3 Of 3)

111327

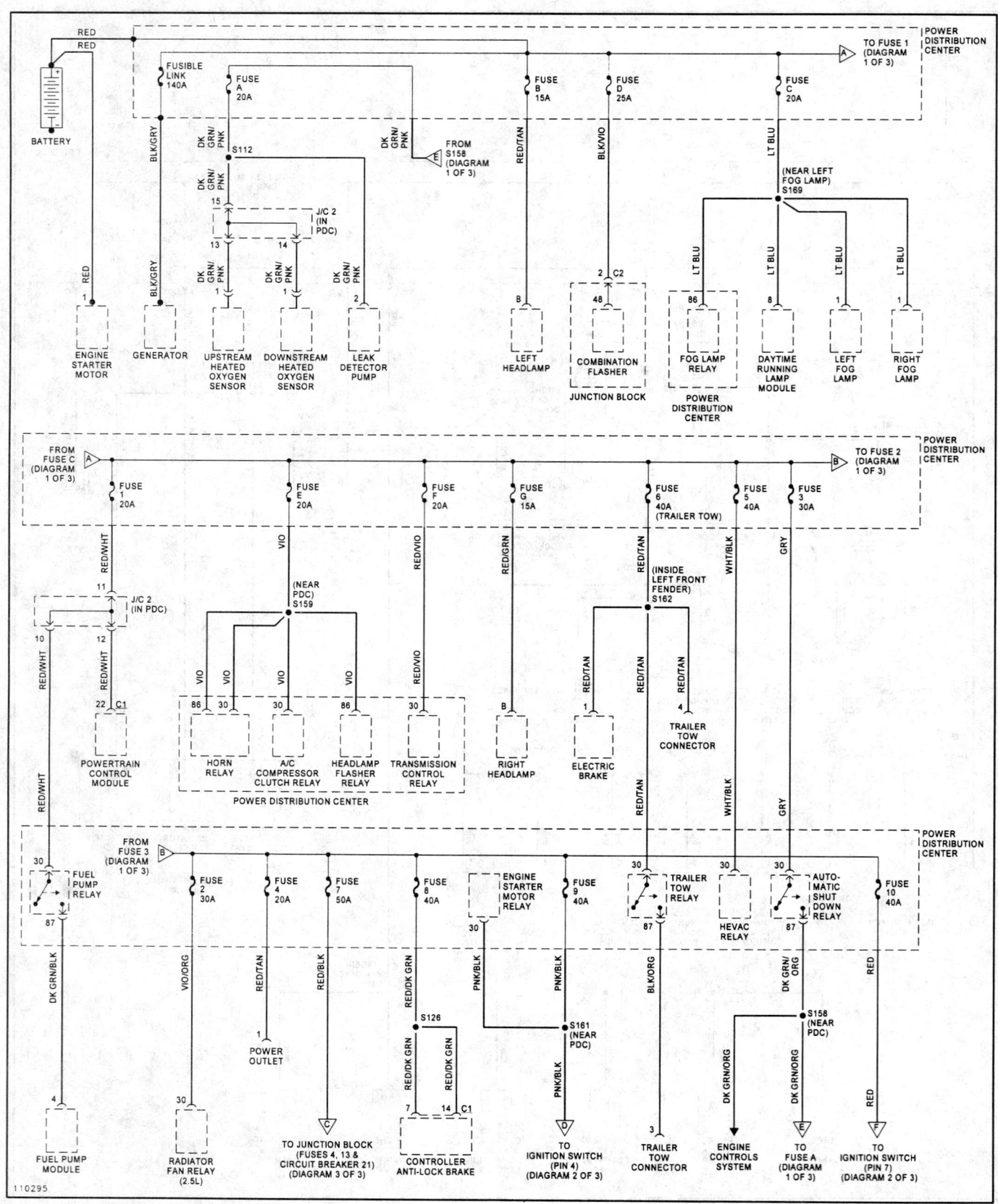

Fig. 14: Power Distribution Wiring Diagram (Dakota – 1 Of 3)

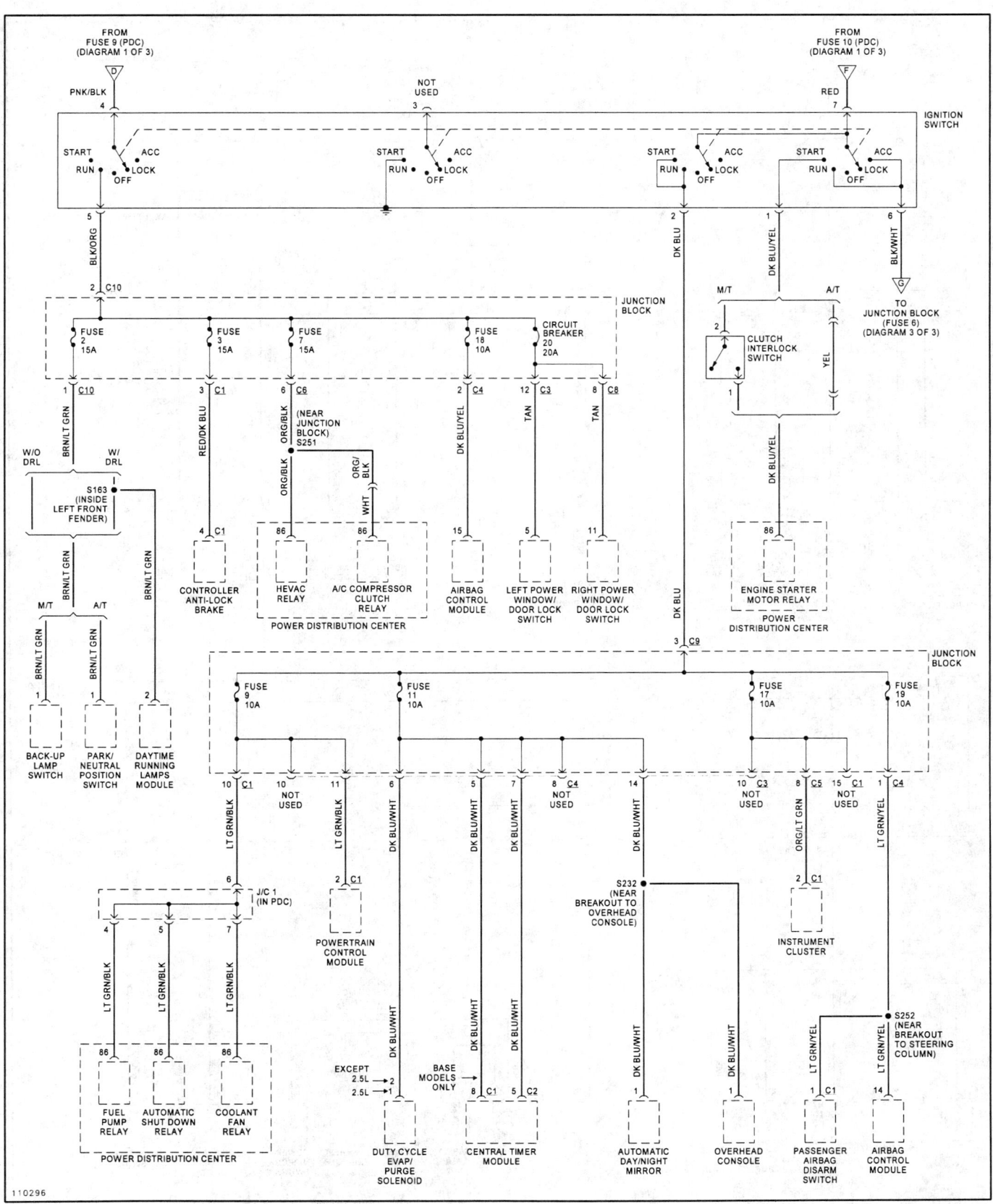

Fig. 15: Power Distribution Wiring Diagram (Dakota – 2 Of 3)

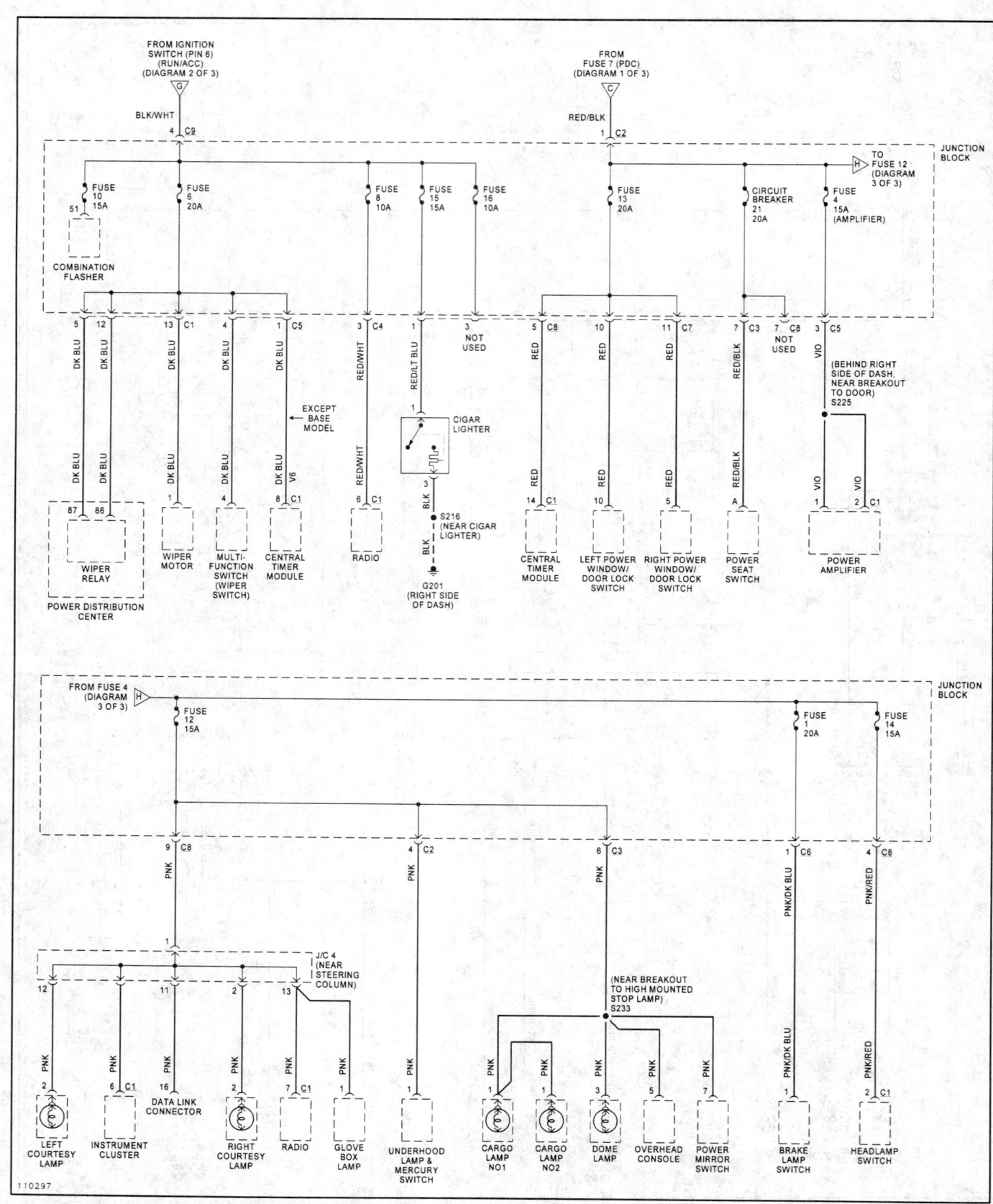

Fig. 16: Power Distribution Wiring Diagram (Dakota – 3 Of 3)

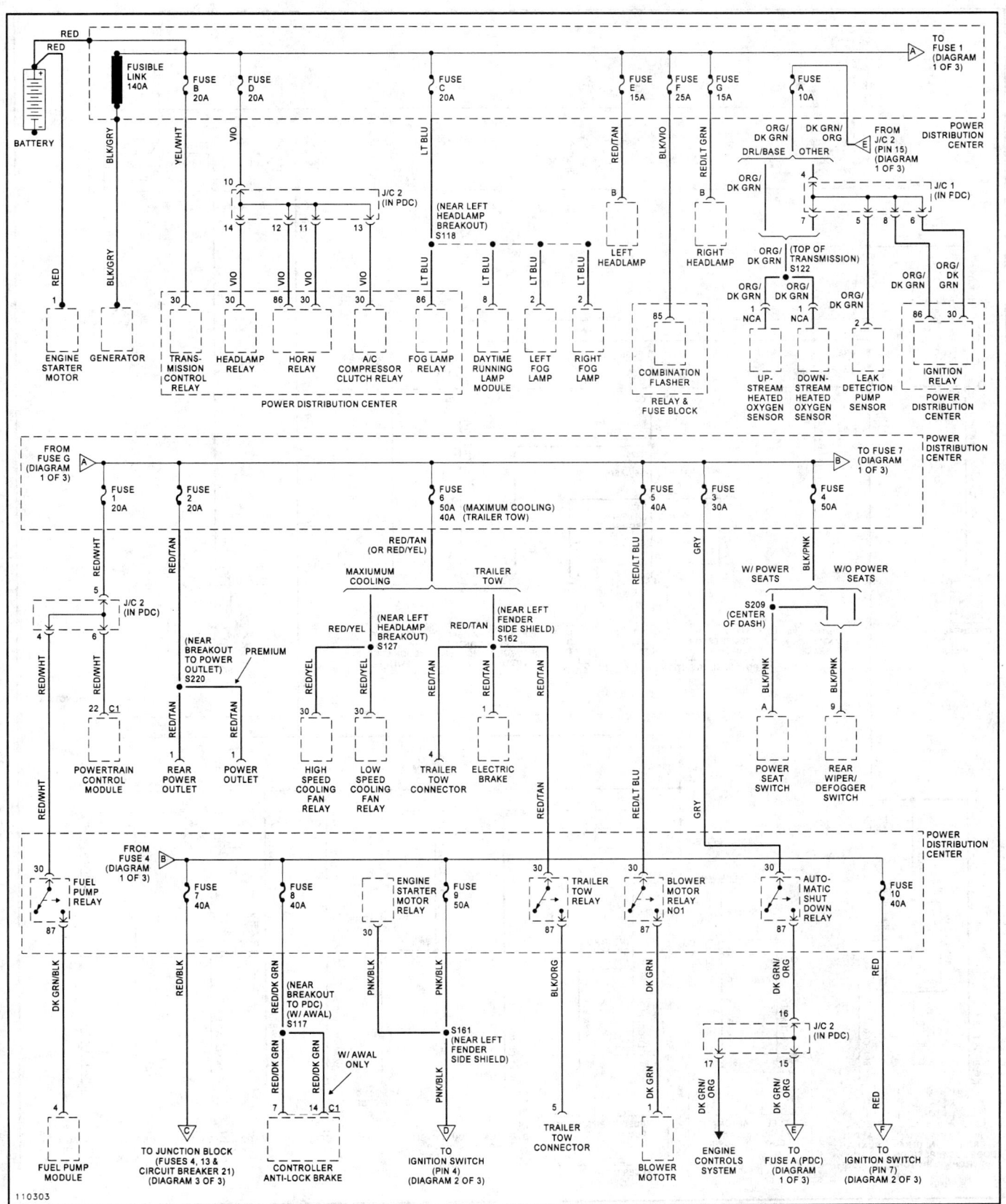

Fig. 17: Power Distribution Wiring Diagram (Durango – 1 Of 3)

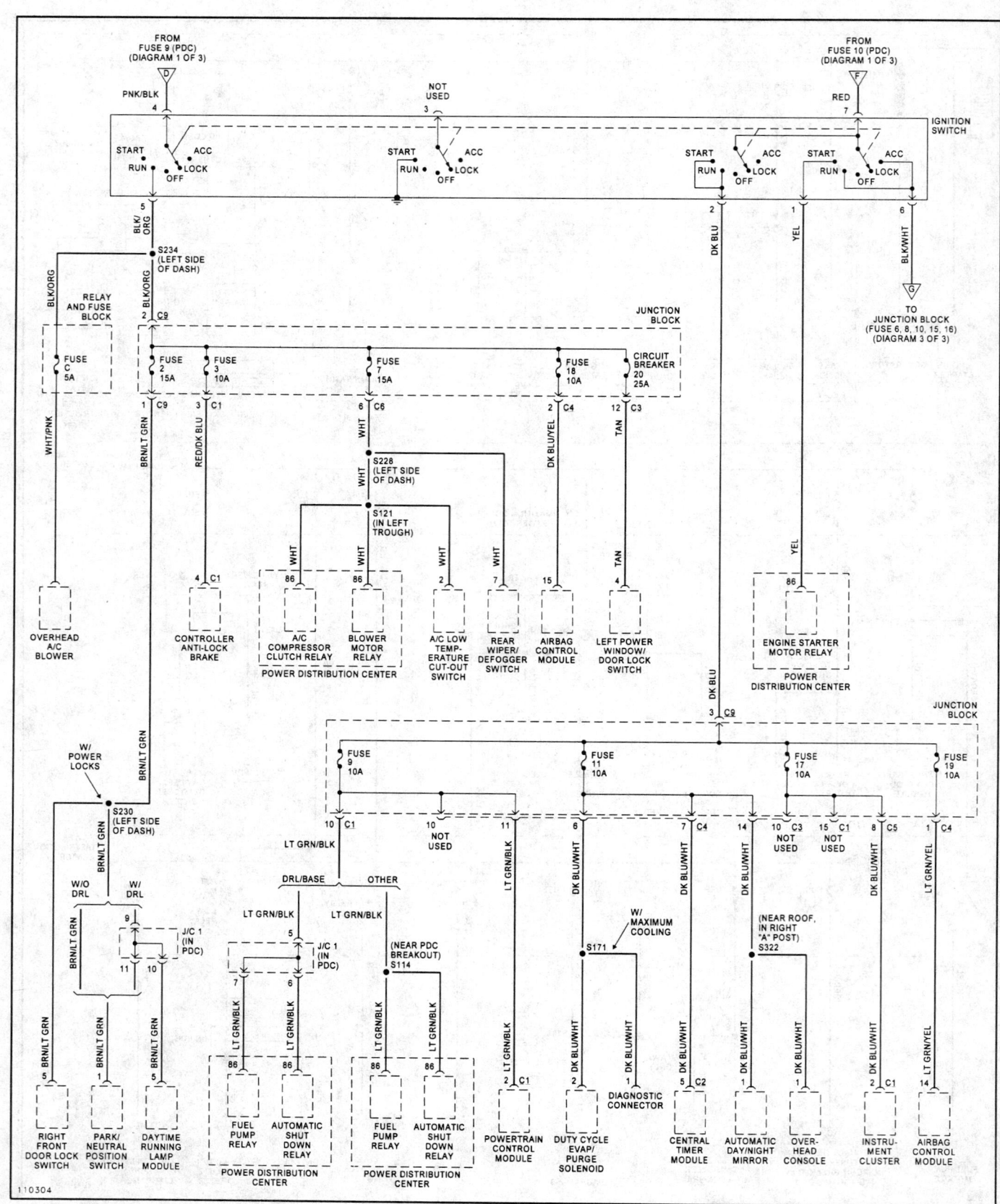

Fig. 18: Power Distribution Wiring Diagram (Durango – 2 Of 3)

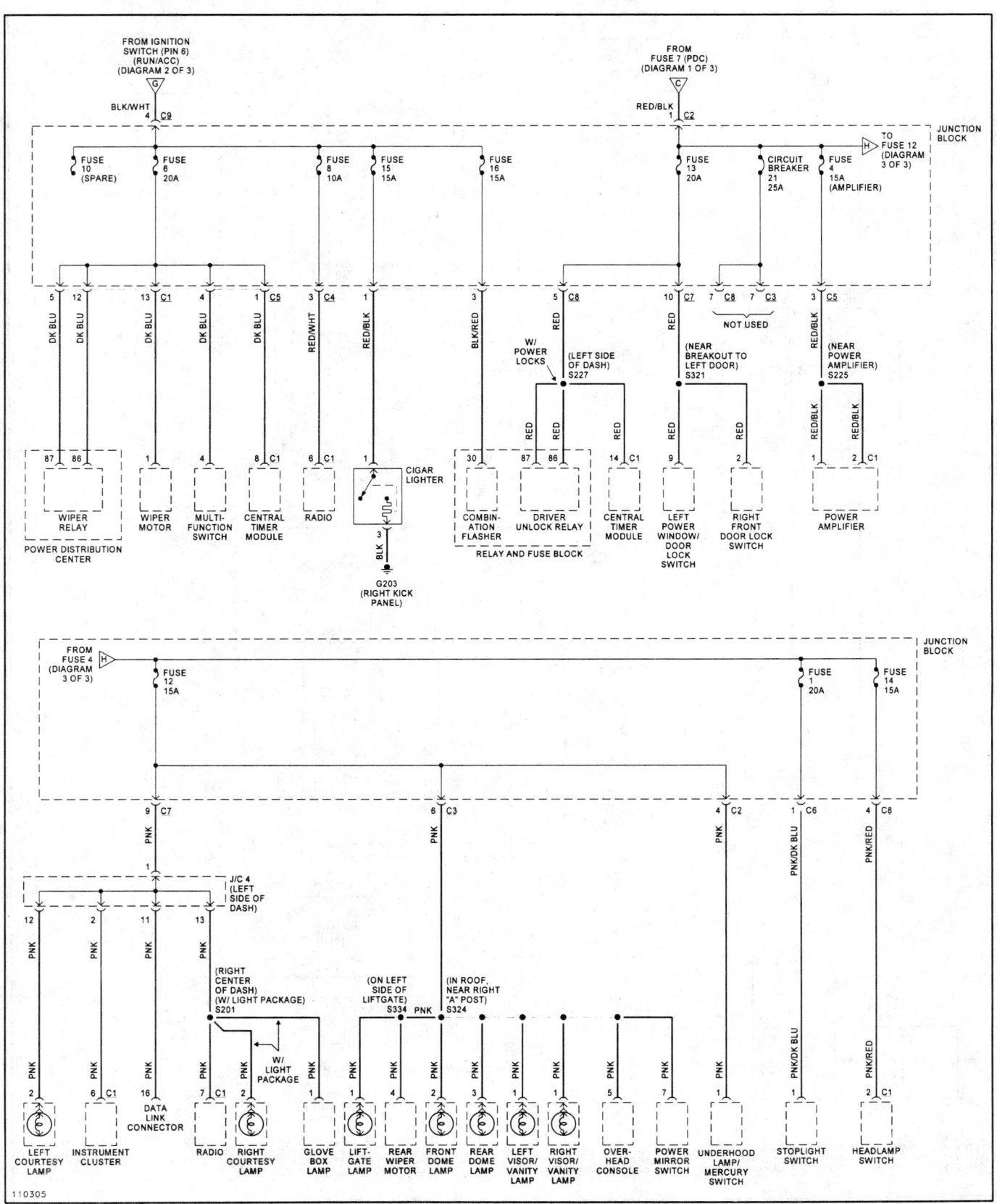

Fig. 19: Power Distribution Wiring Diagram (Durango – 3 Of 3)

110305

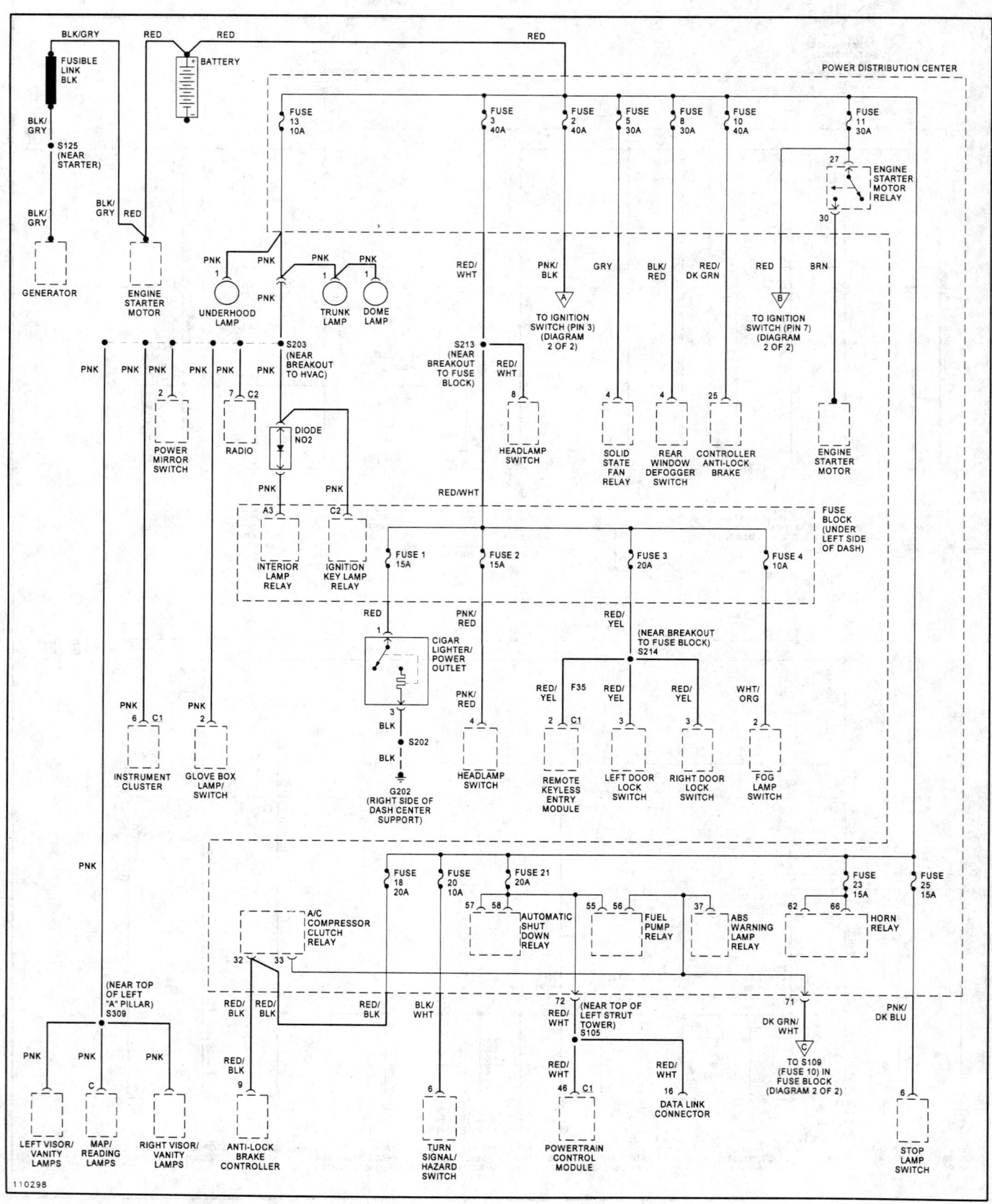

Fig. 20: Power Distribution Wiring Diagram (Neon – 1 Of 2)

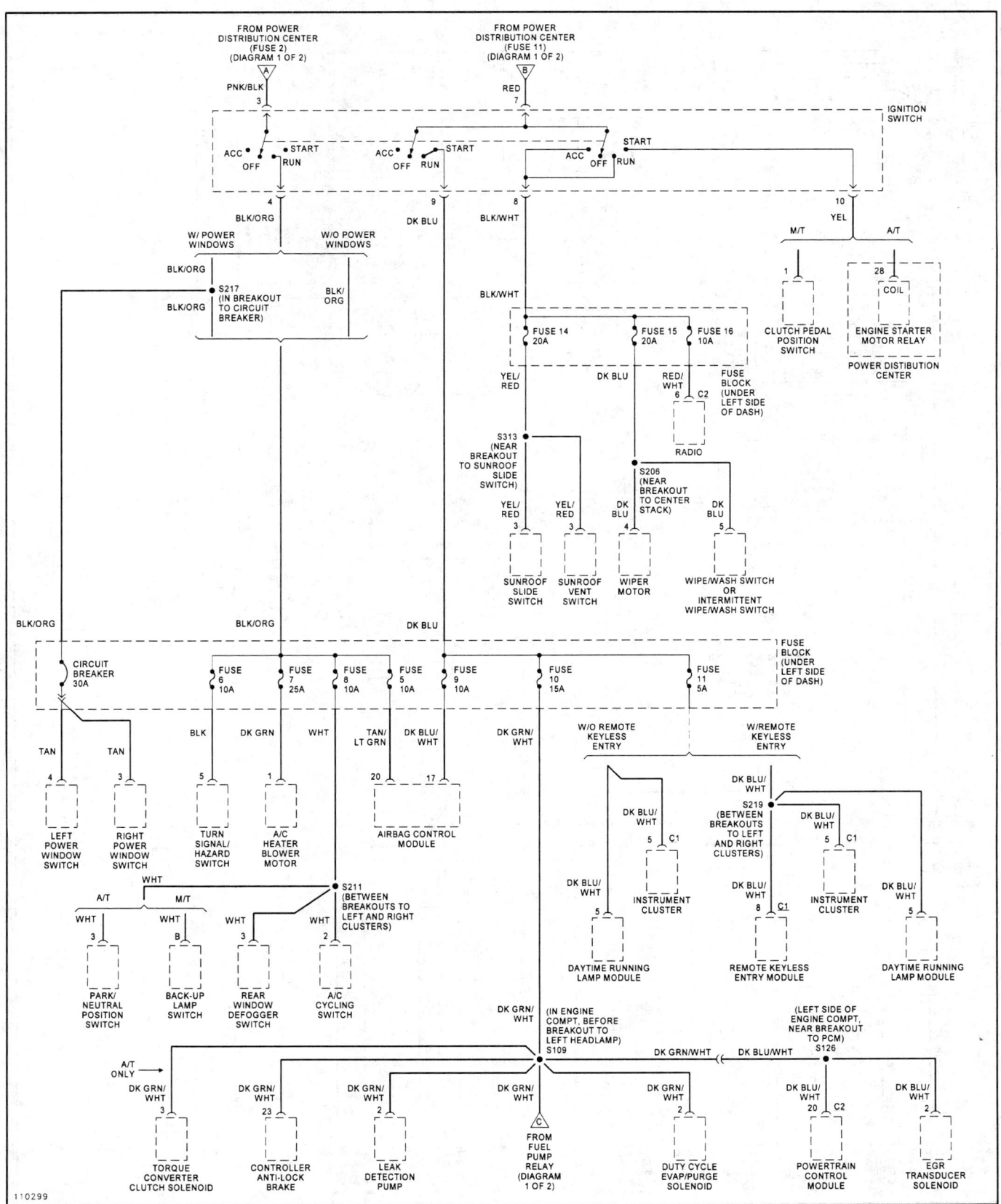

Fig. 21: Power Distribution Wiring Diagram (Neon – 2 Of 2)

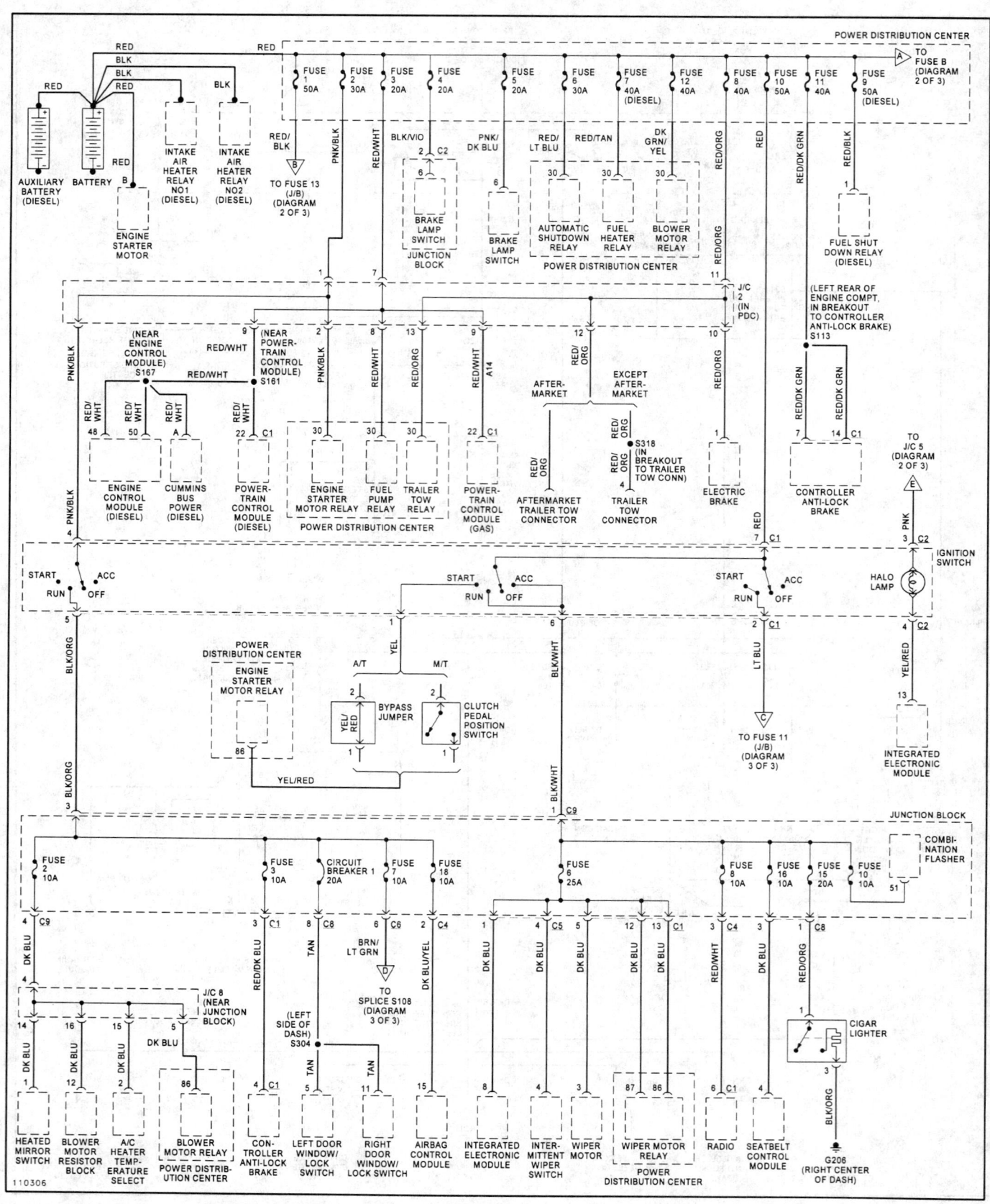

Fig. 22: Power Distribution Wiring Diagram (Ram Pickup – 1 Of 3)

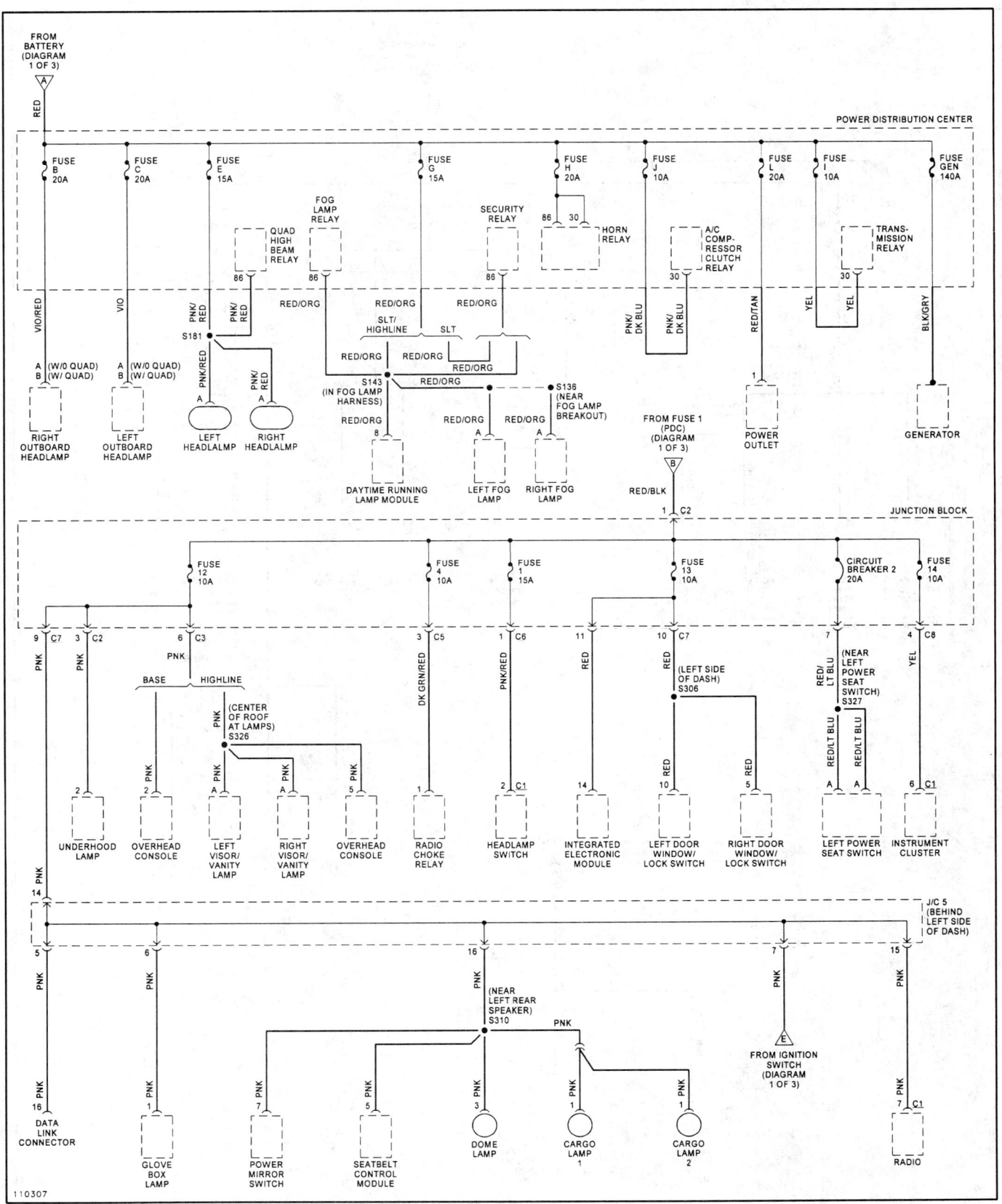

Fig. 23: Power Distribution Wiring Diagram (Ram Pickup – 2 Of 3)

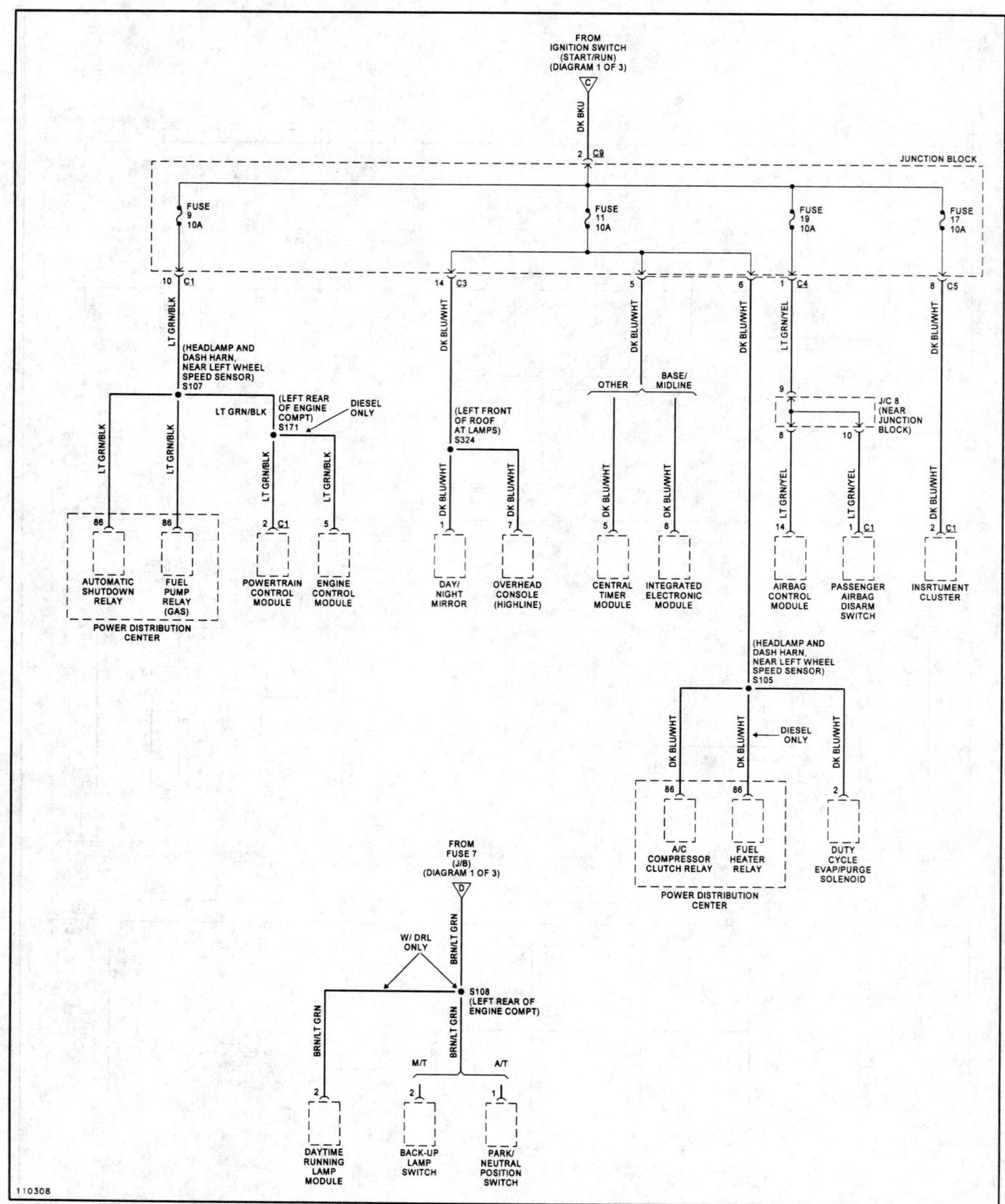

Fig. 24: Power Distribution Wiring Diagram (Ram Pickup – 3 Of 3)

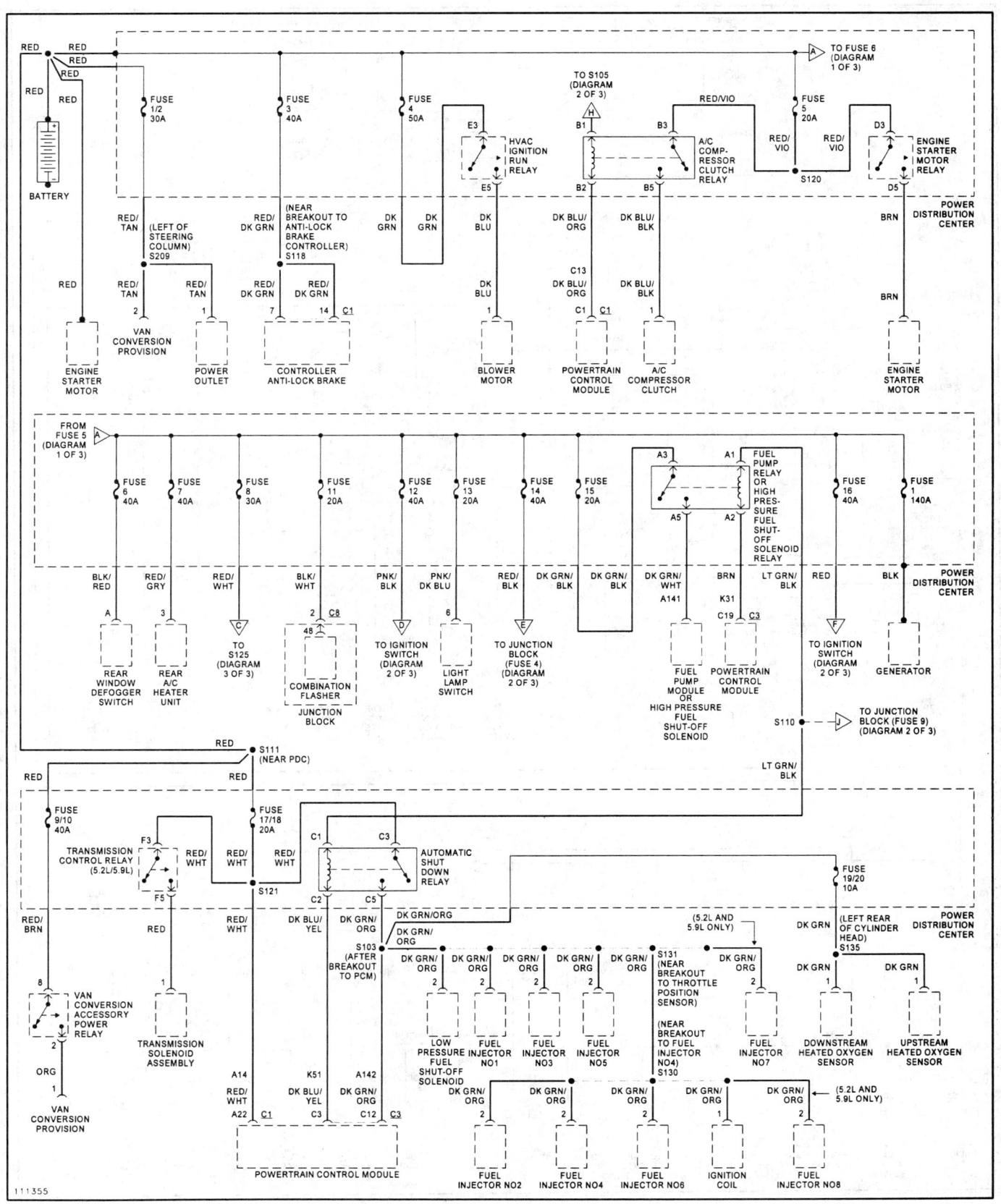

Fig. 25: Power Distribution Wiring Diagram (Ram Van & Ram Wagon – 1 Of 3)

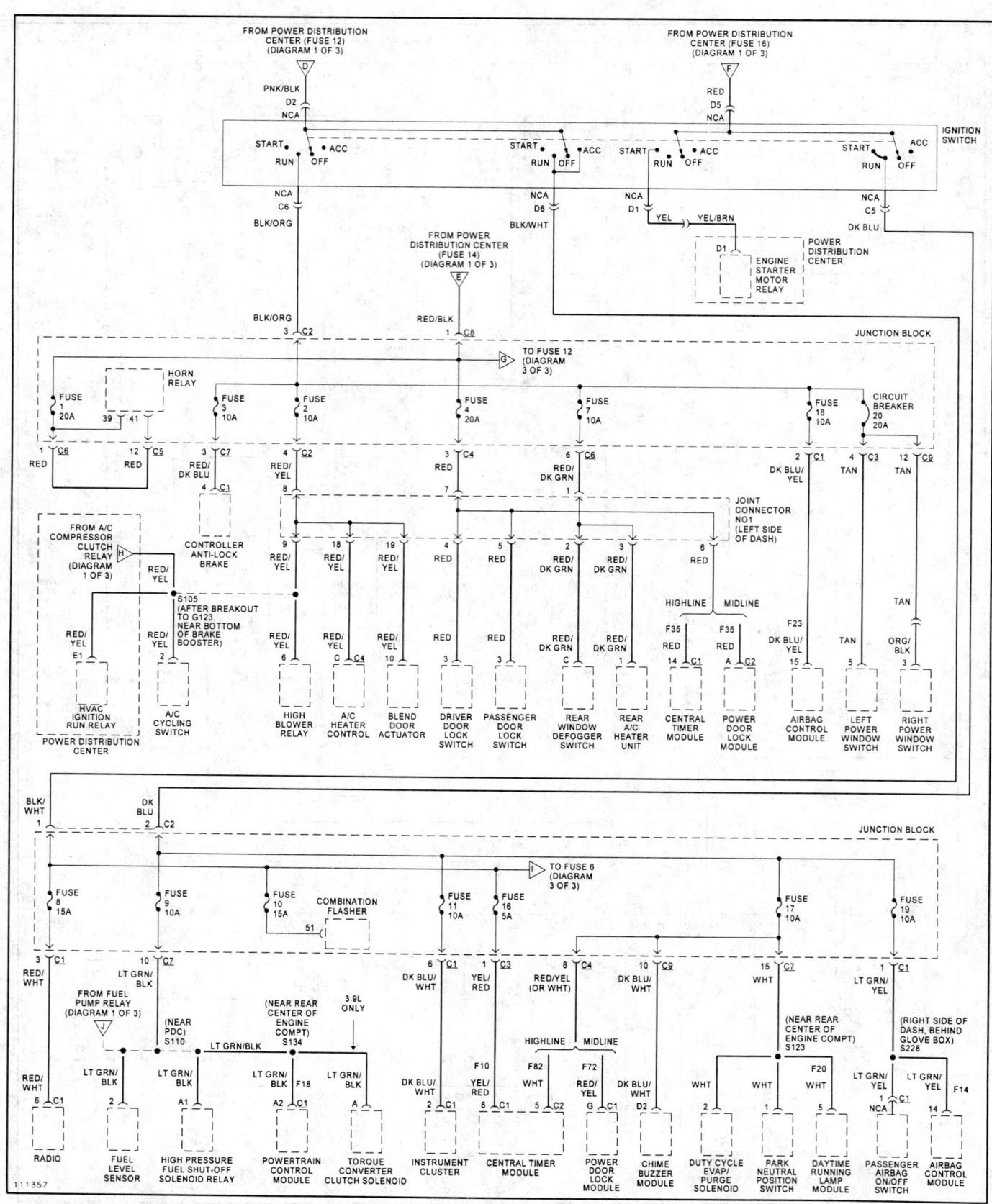

Fig. 26: Power Distribution Wiring Diagram (Ram Van & Ram Wagon – 2 Of 3)

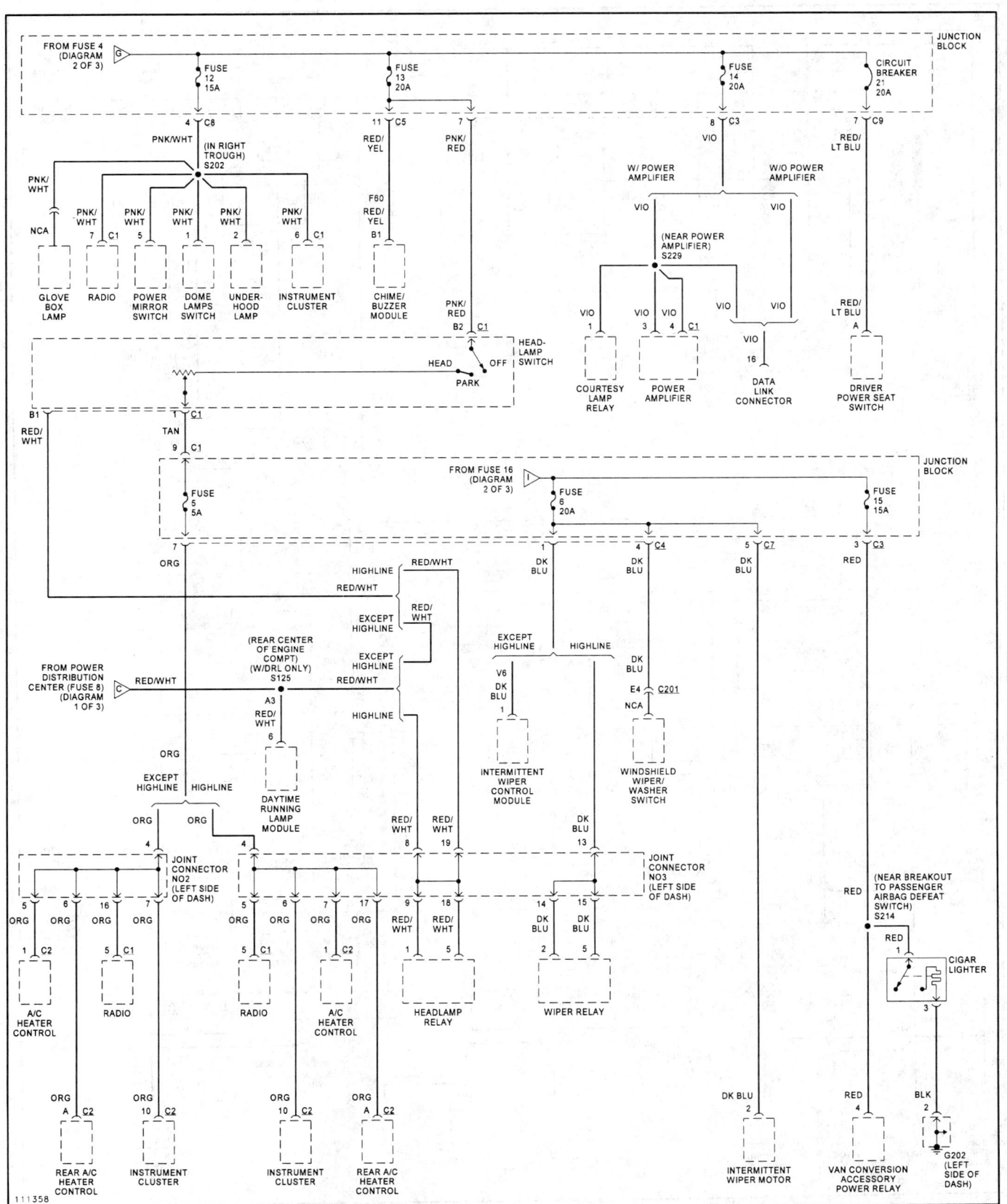

Fig. 27: Power Distribution Wiring Diagram (Ram Van & Ram Wagon – 3 Of 3)

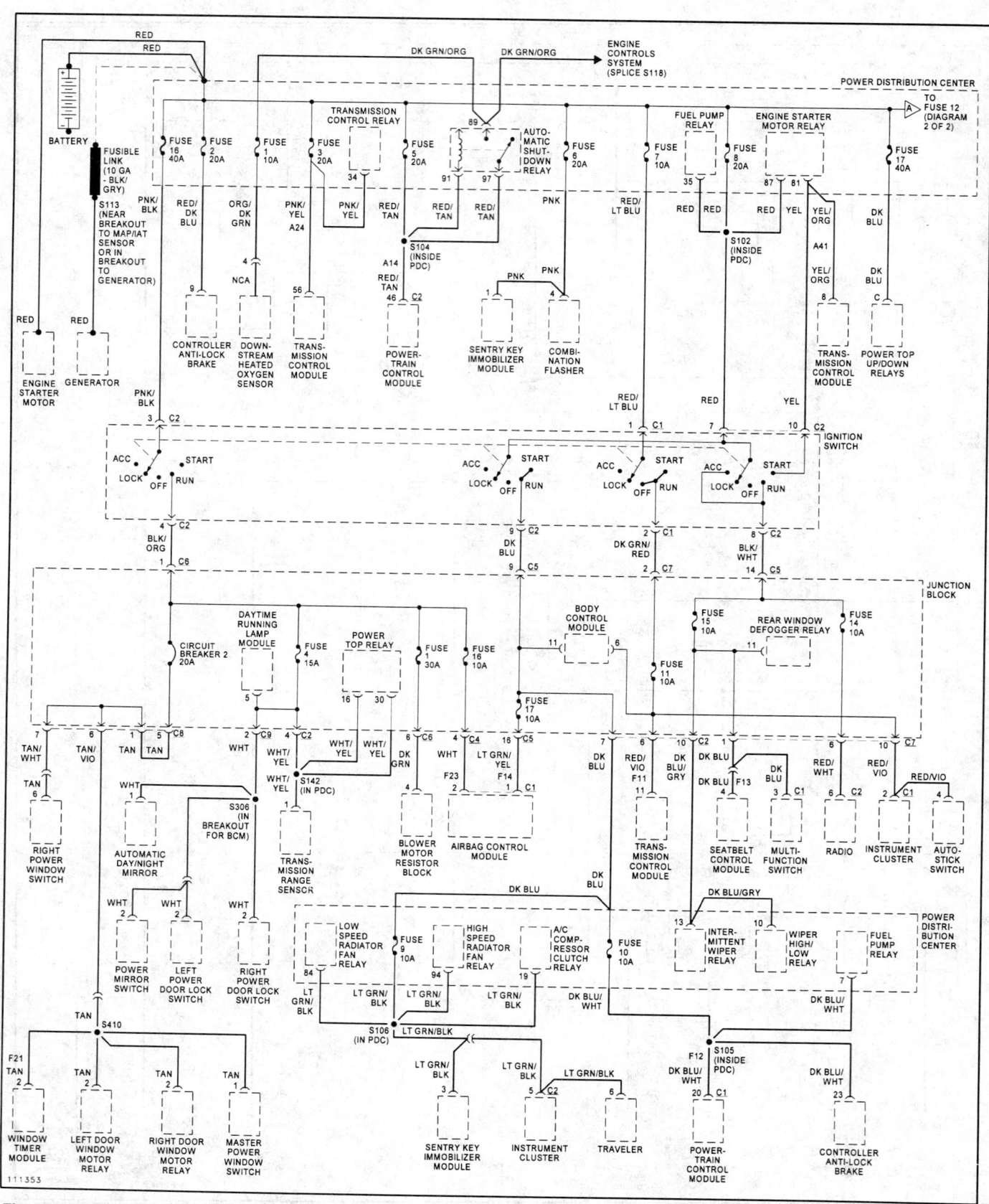

Fig. 28: Power Distribution Wiring Diagram (Sebring Convertible – 1 Of 2)

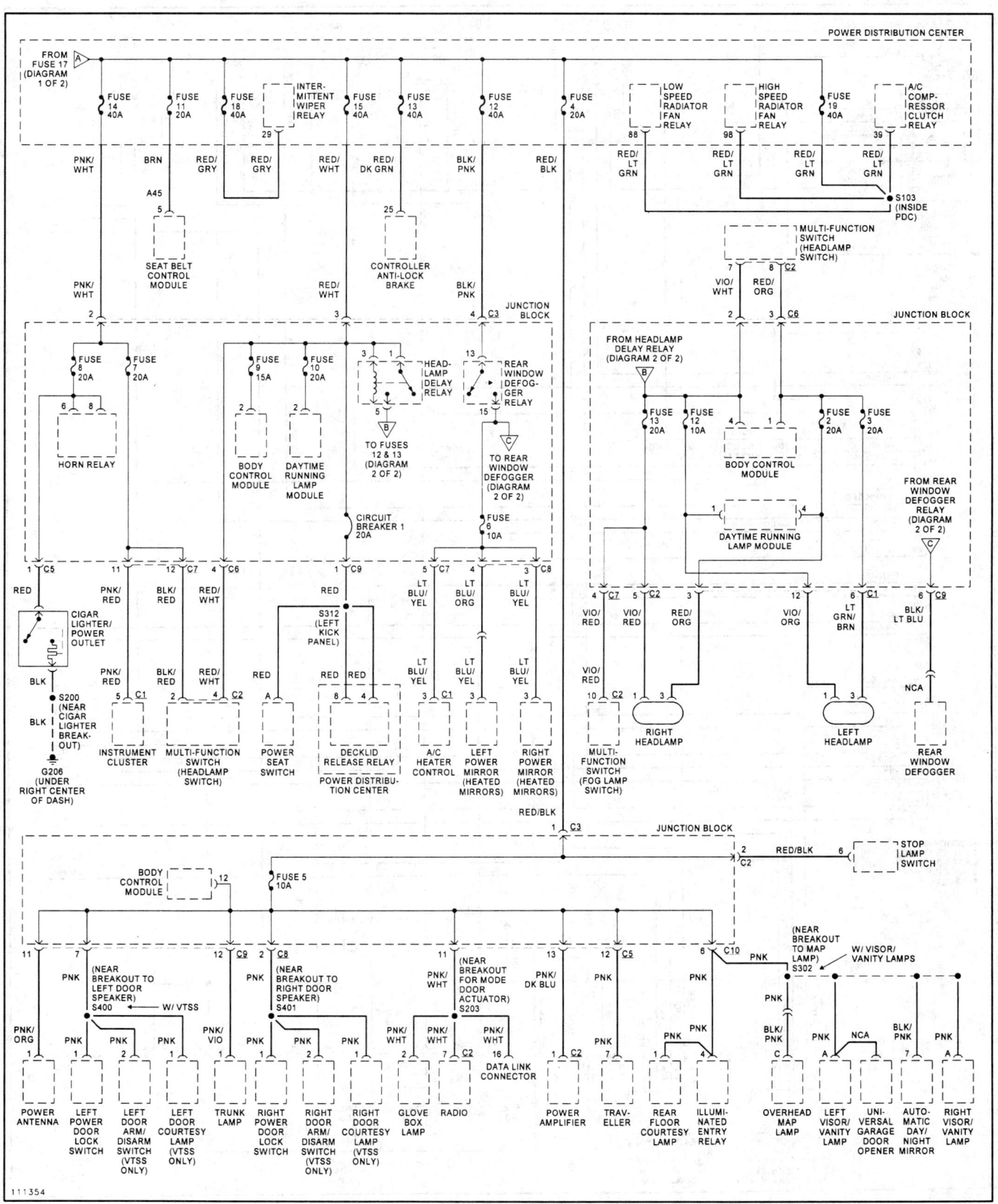

Fig. 29: Power Distribution Wiring Diagram (Sebring Convertible – 2 Of 2)

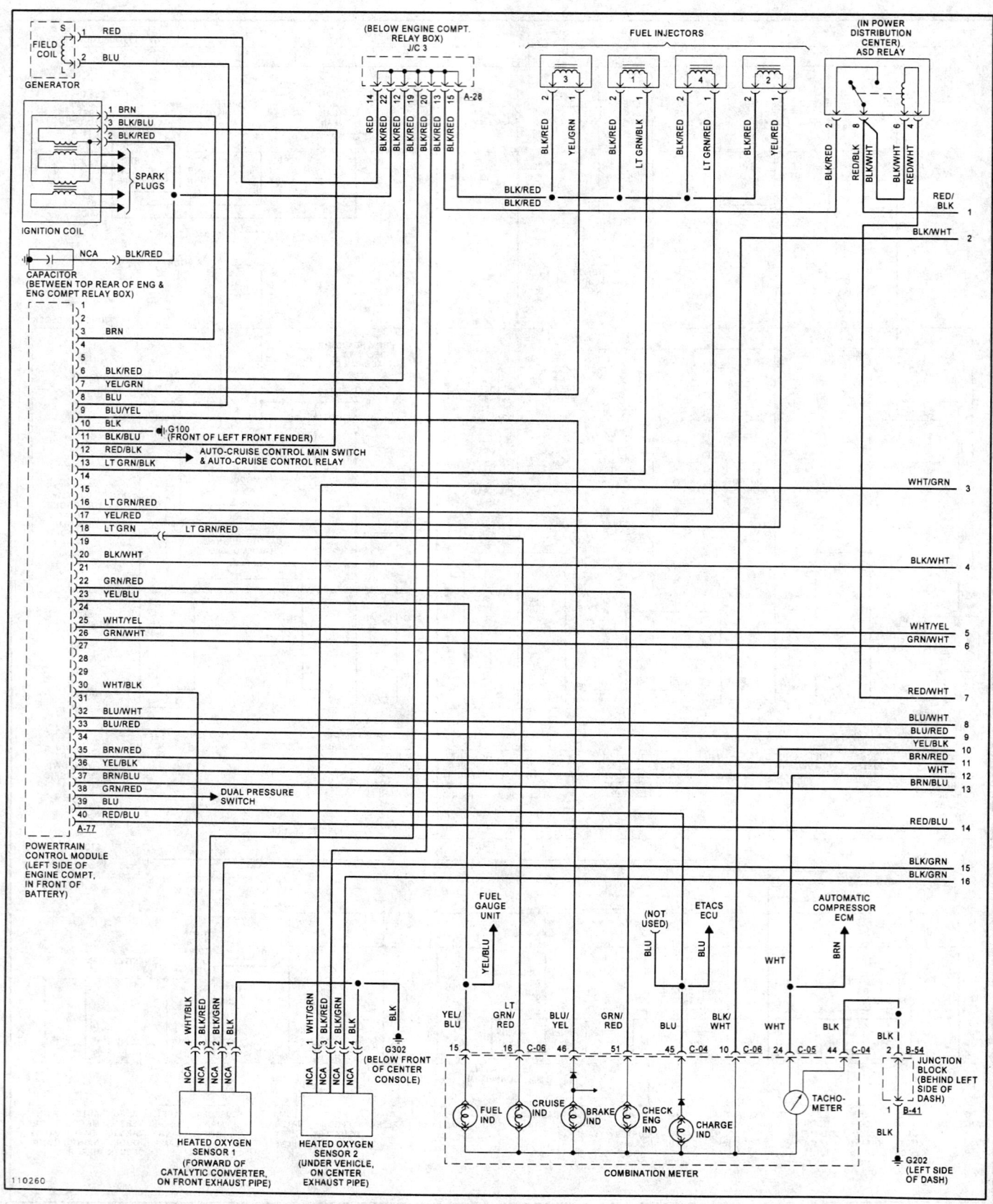

Fig. 1: PCM Wiring Diagram (Avenger & Sebring Coupe – 2.0L – 1 Of 3)

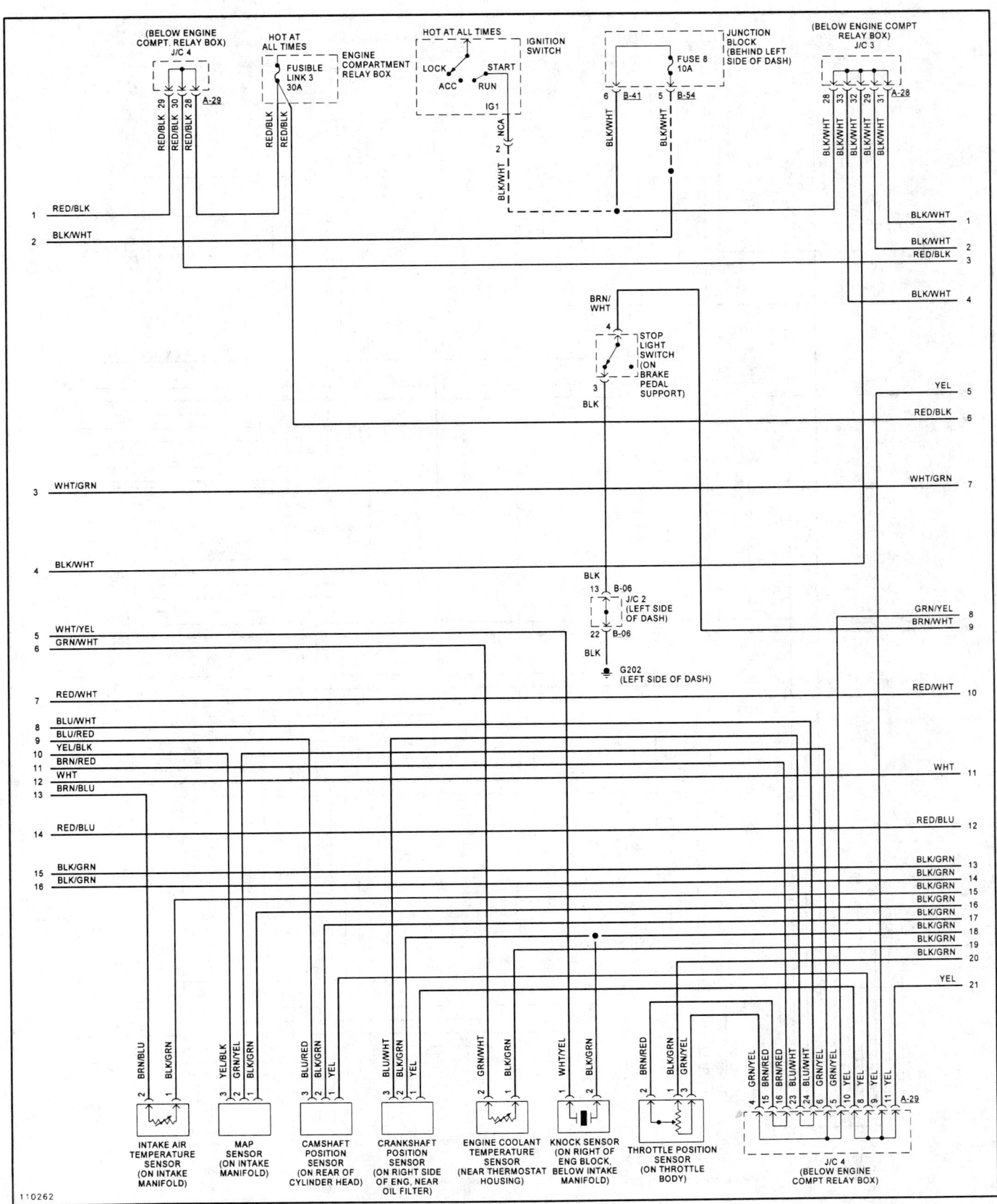

Fig. 2: PCM Wiring Diagram (Avenger & Sebring Coupe – 2.0L – 2 Of 3)

110262

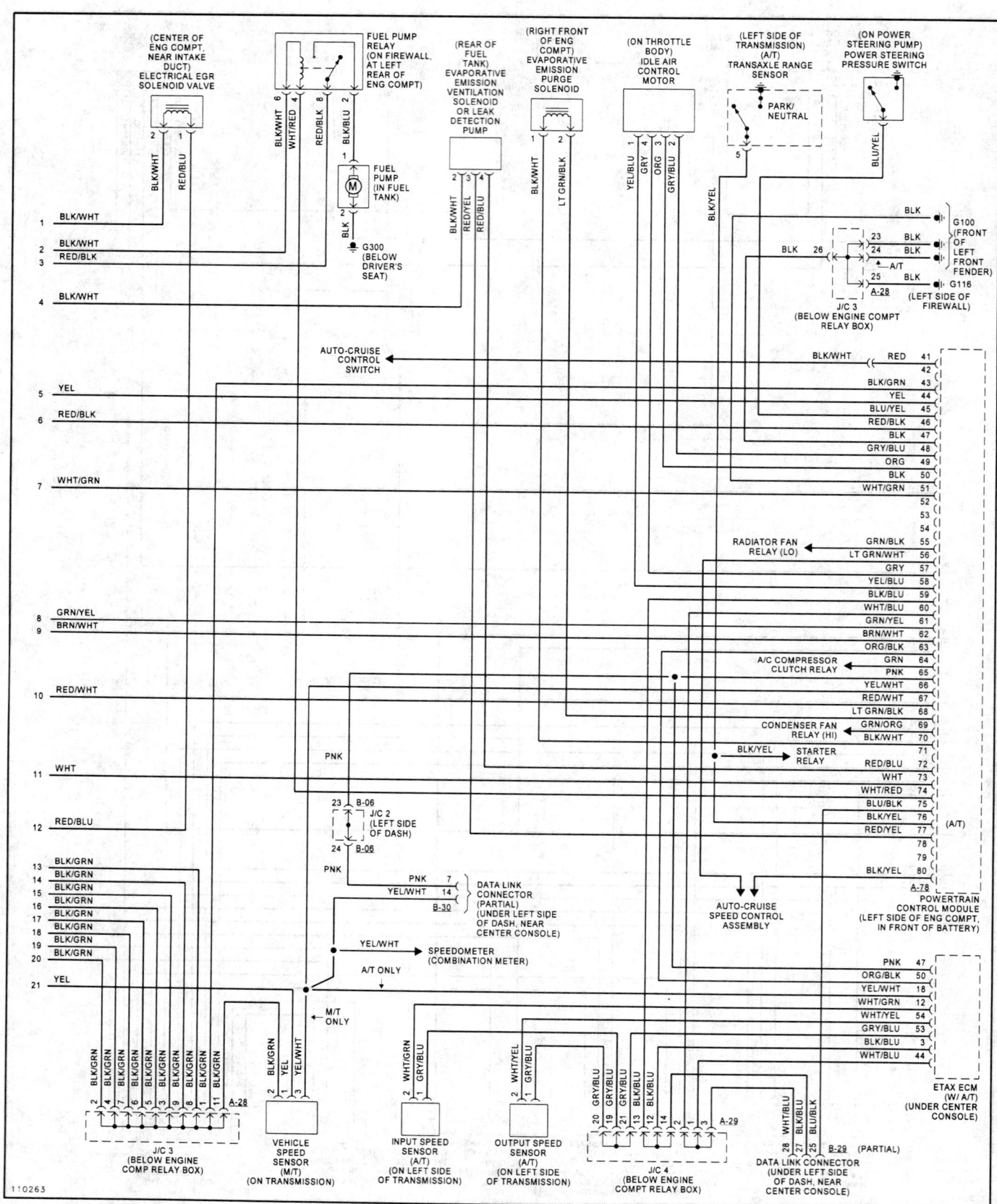

Fig. 3: PCM Wiring Diagram (Avenger & Sebring Coupe – 2.0L – 3 Of 3)

110263

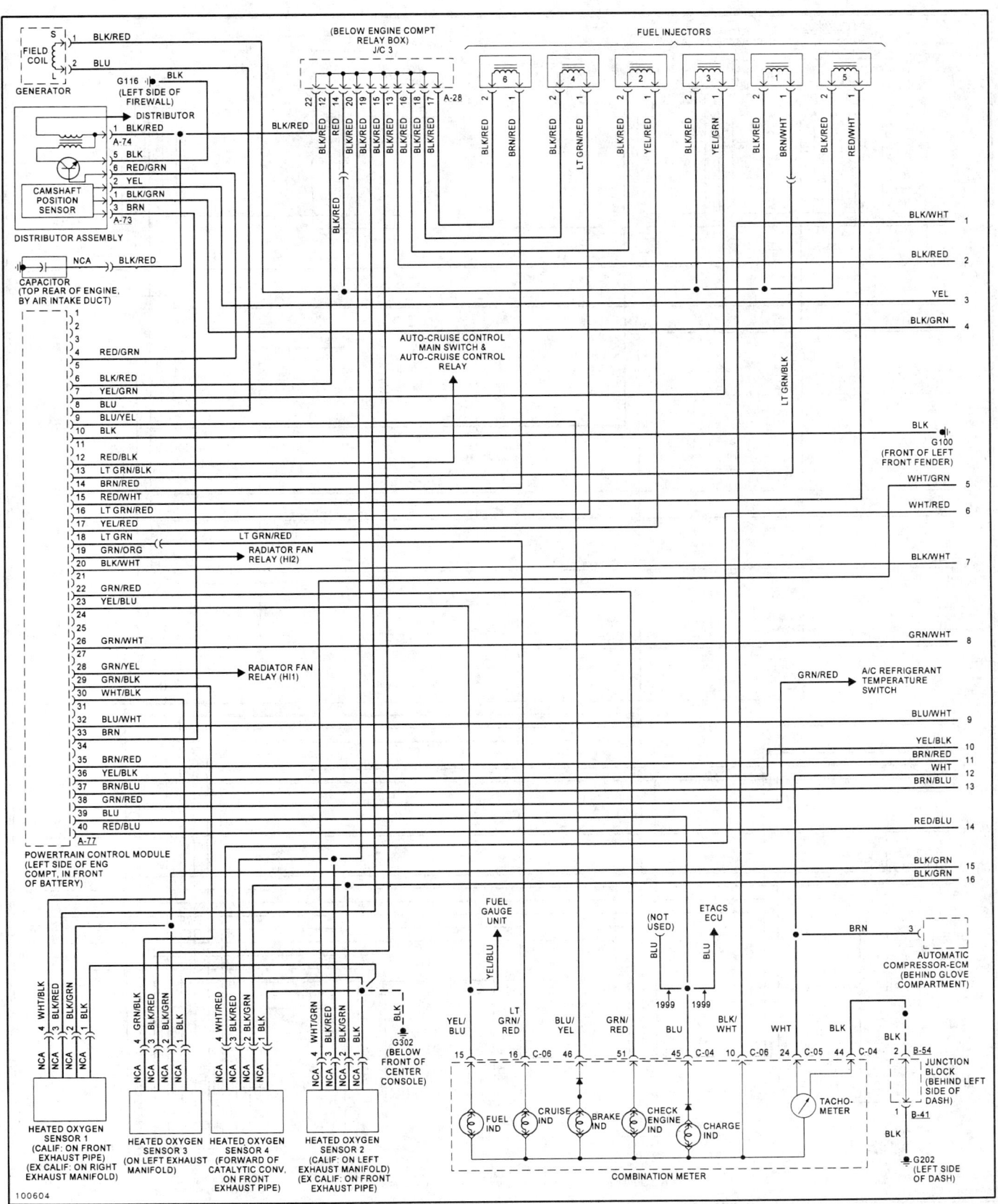

Fig. 4: PCM Wiring Diagram (Avenger & Sebring Coupe – 2.5L – 1 Of 3)

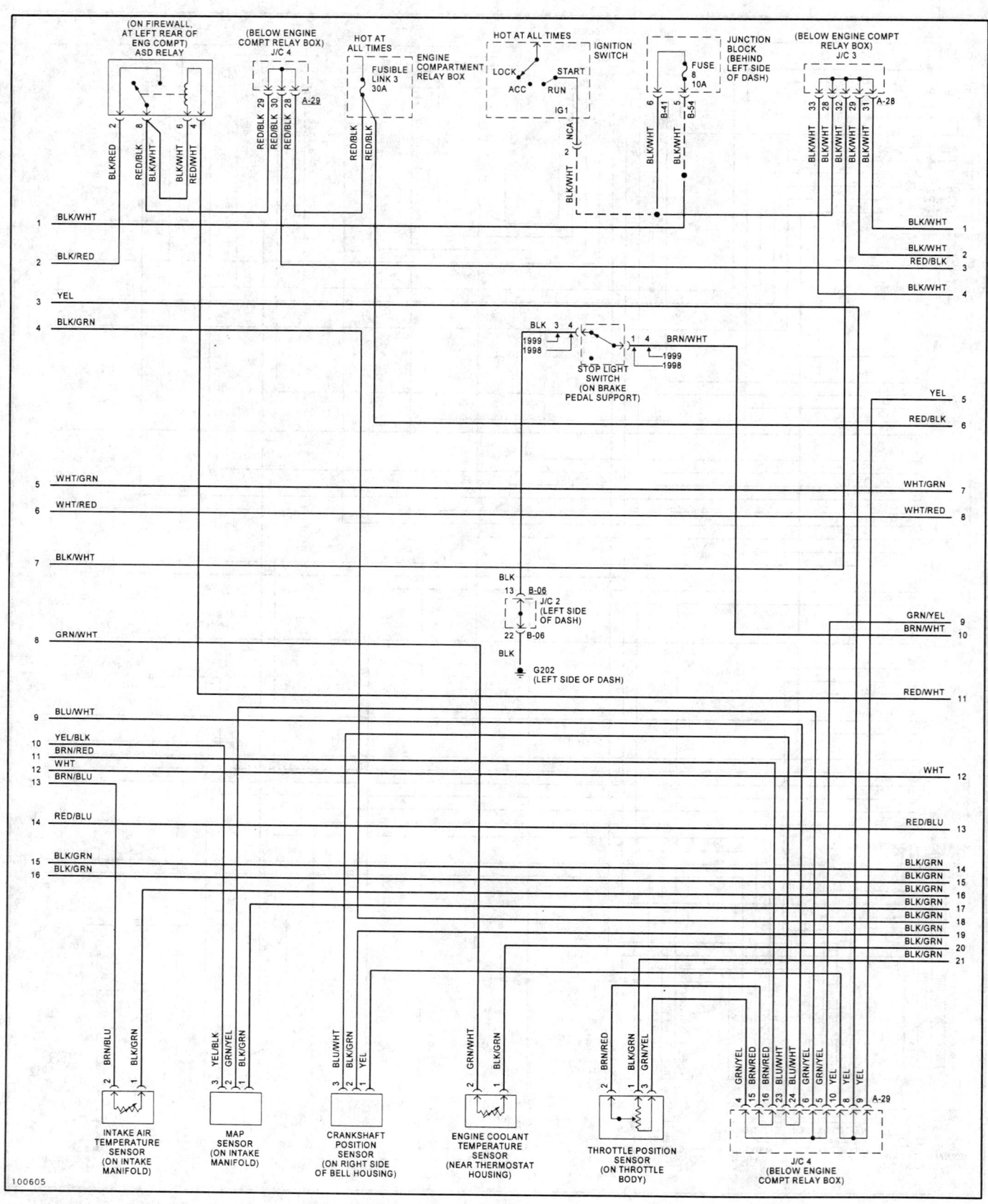

Fig. 5: PCM Wiring Diagram (Avenger & Sebring Coupe – 2.5L – 2 Of 3)

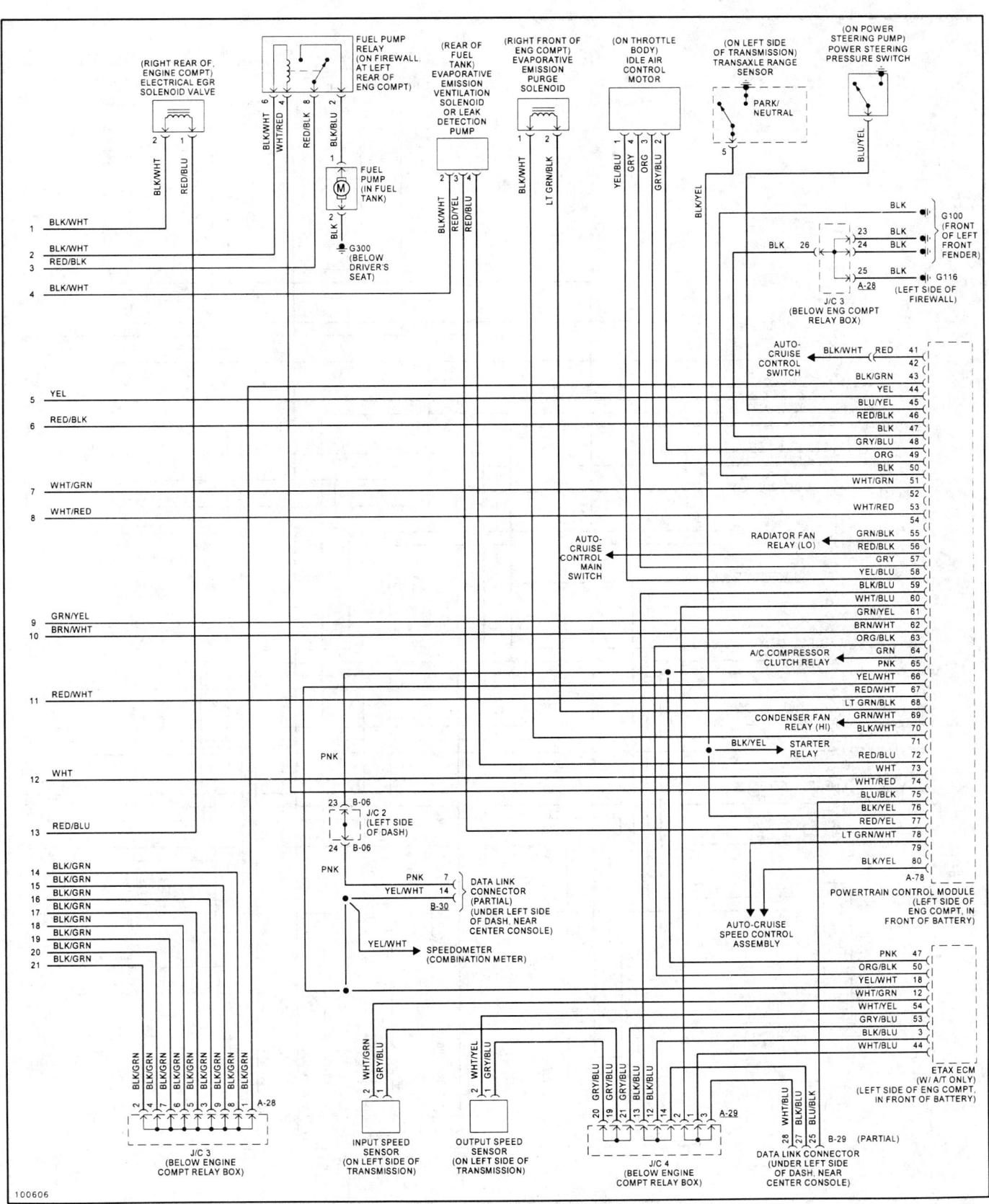

Fig. 6: PCM Wiring Diagram (Avenger & Sebring Coupe – 2.5L – 3 Of 3)

100606

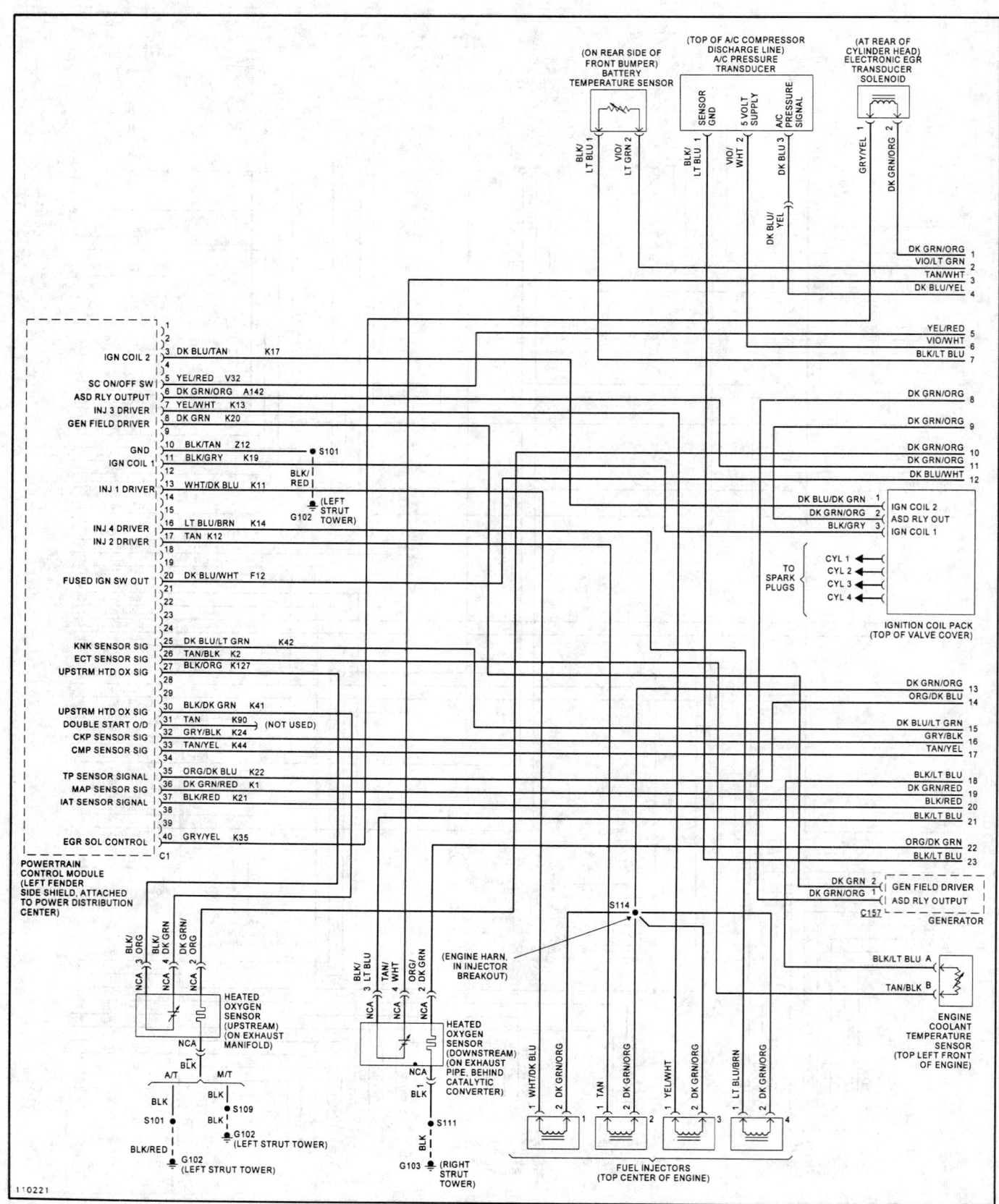

Fig. 7: PCM Wiring Diagram (Breeze & Stratus – 2.0L & 2.4L – 1 Of 3)

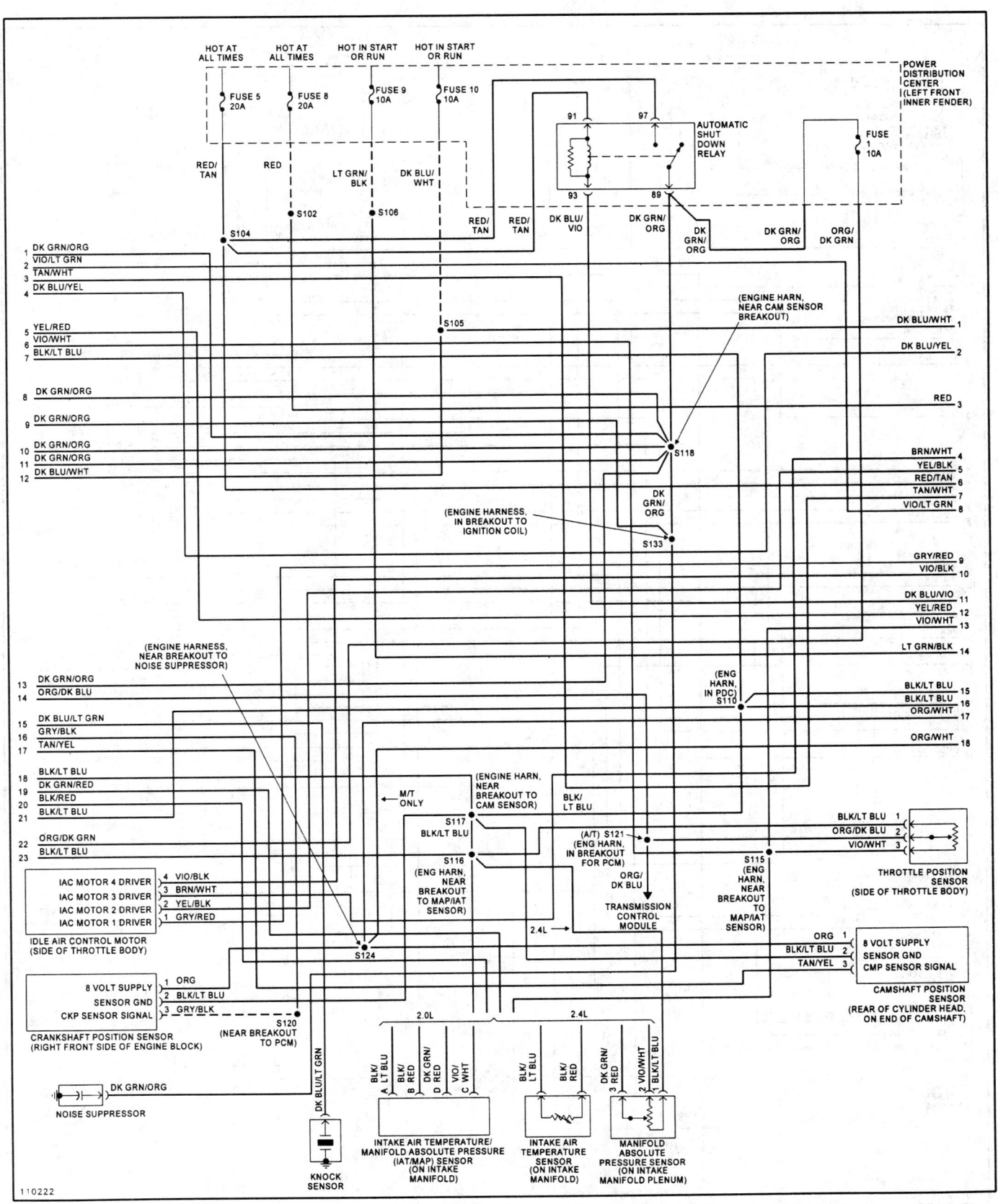

Fig. 8: PCM Wiring Diagram (Breeze & Stratus – 2.0L & 2.4L – 2 Of 3)

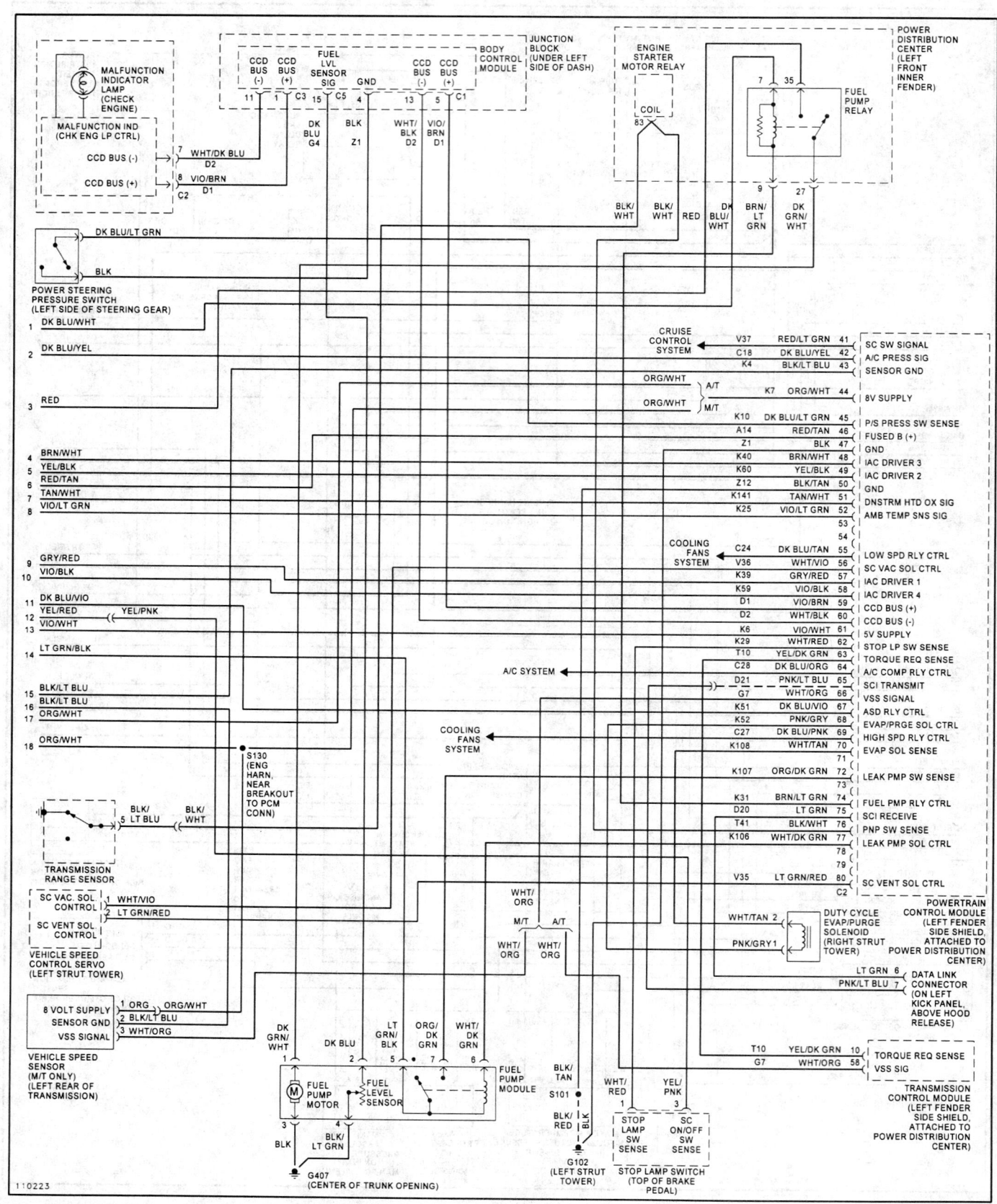

Fig. 9: PCM Wiring Diagram (Breeze & Stratus – 2.0L & 2.4L – 3 Of 3)

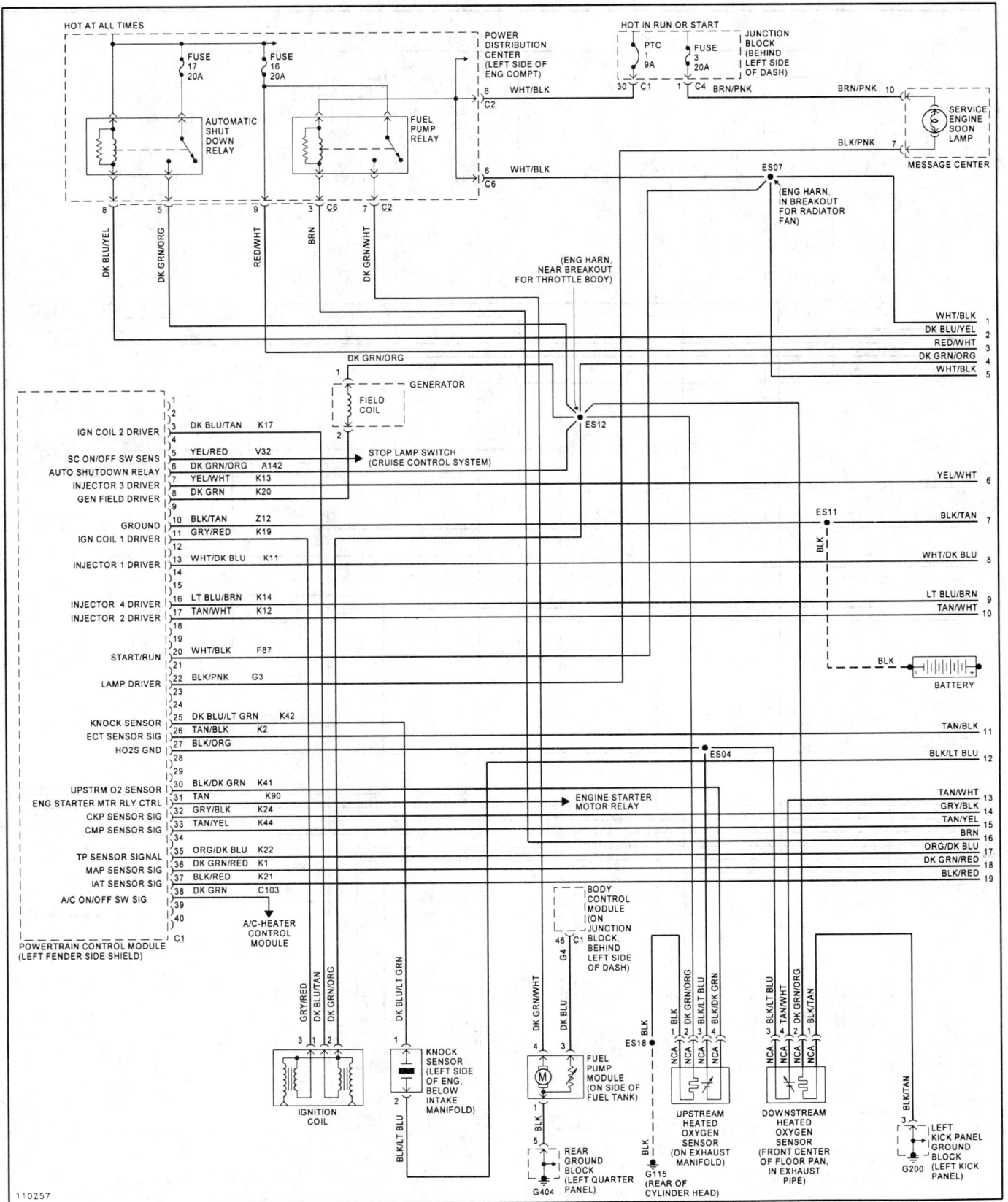

Fig. 10: PCM Wiring Diagram (Caravan & Voyager – 2.4L – 1 Of 3)

110257

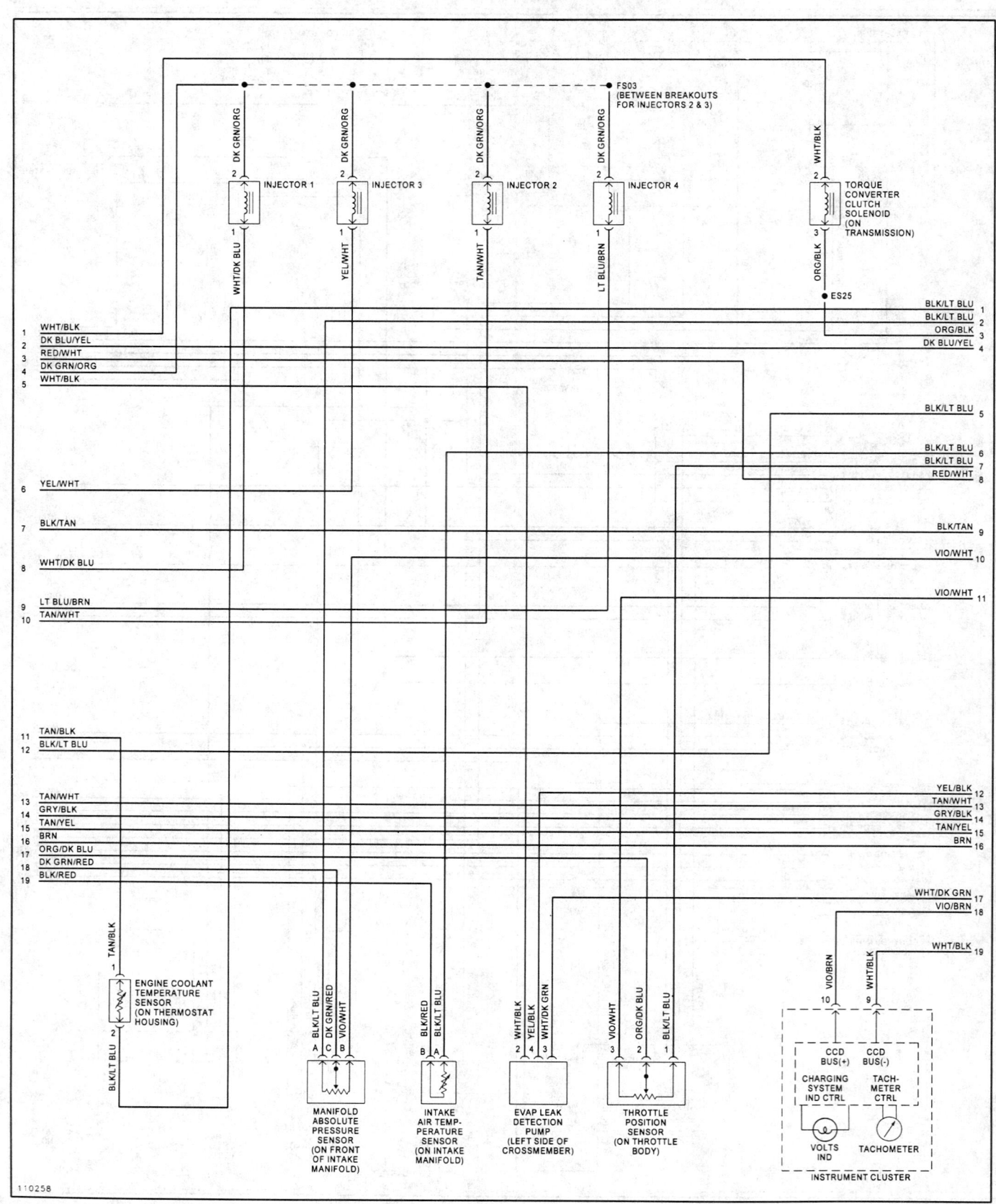

Fig. 11: PCM Wiring Diagram (Caravan & Voyager – 2.4L – 2 Of 3)

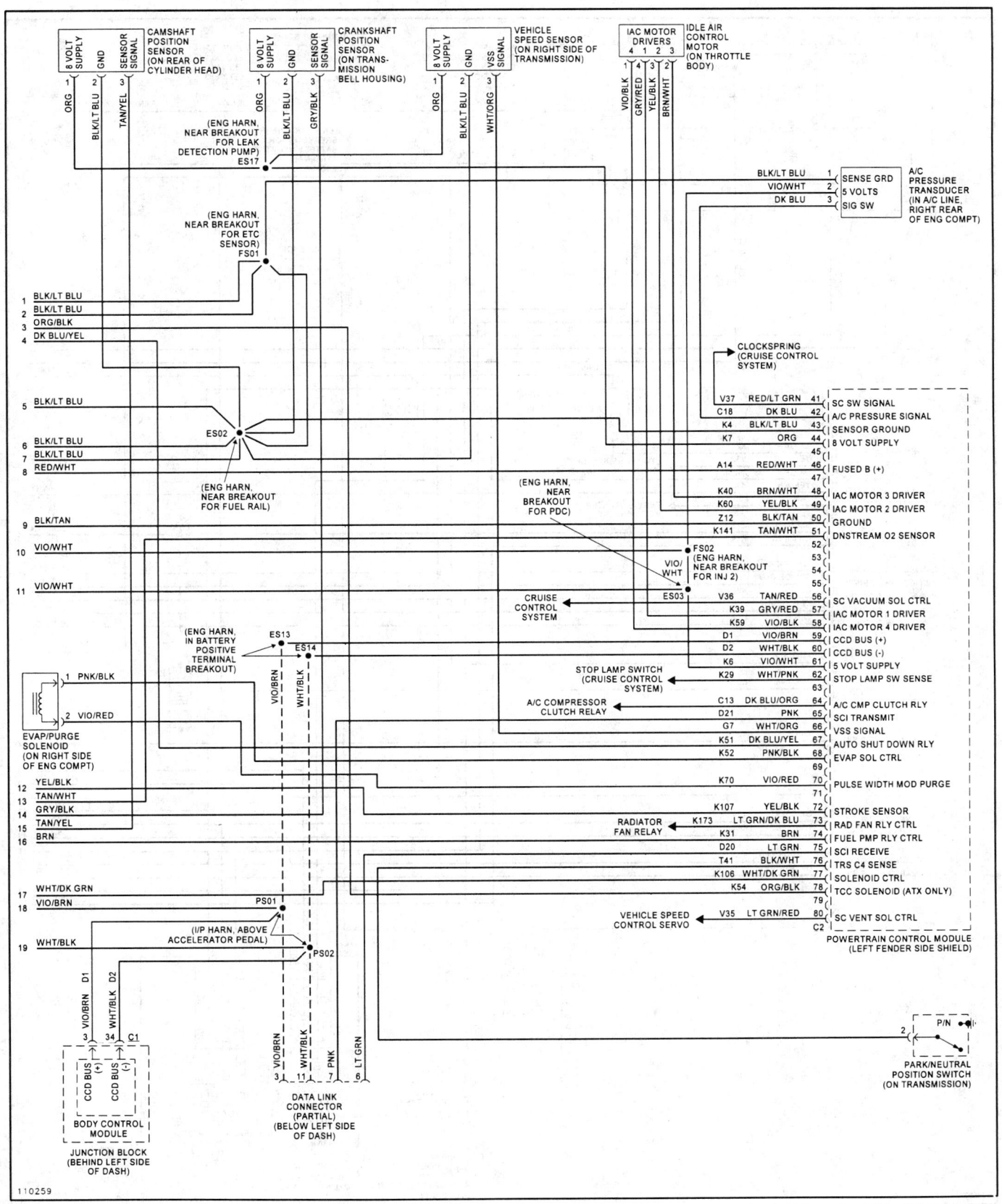

Fig. 12: PCM Wiring Diagram (Caravan & Voyager – 2.4L – 3 Of 3)

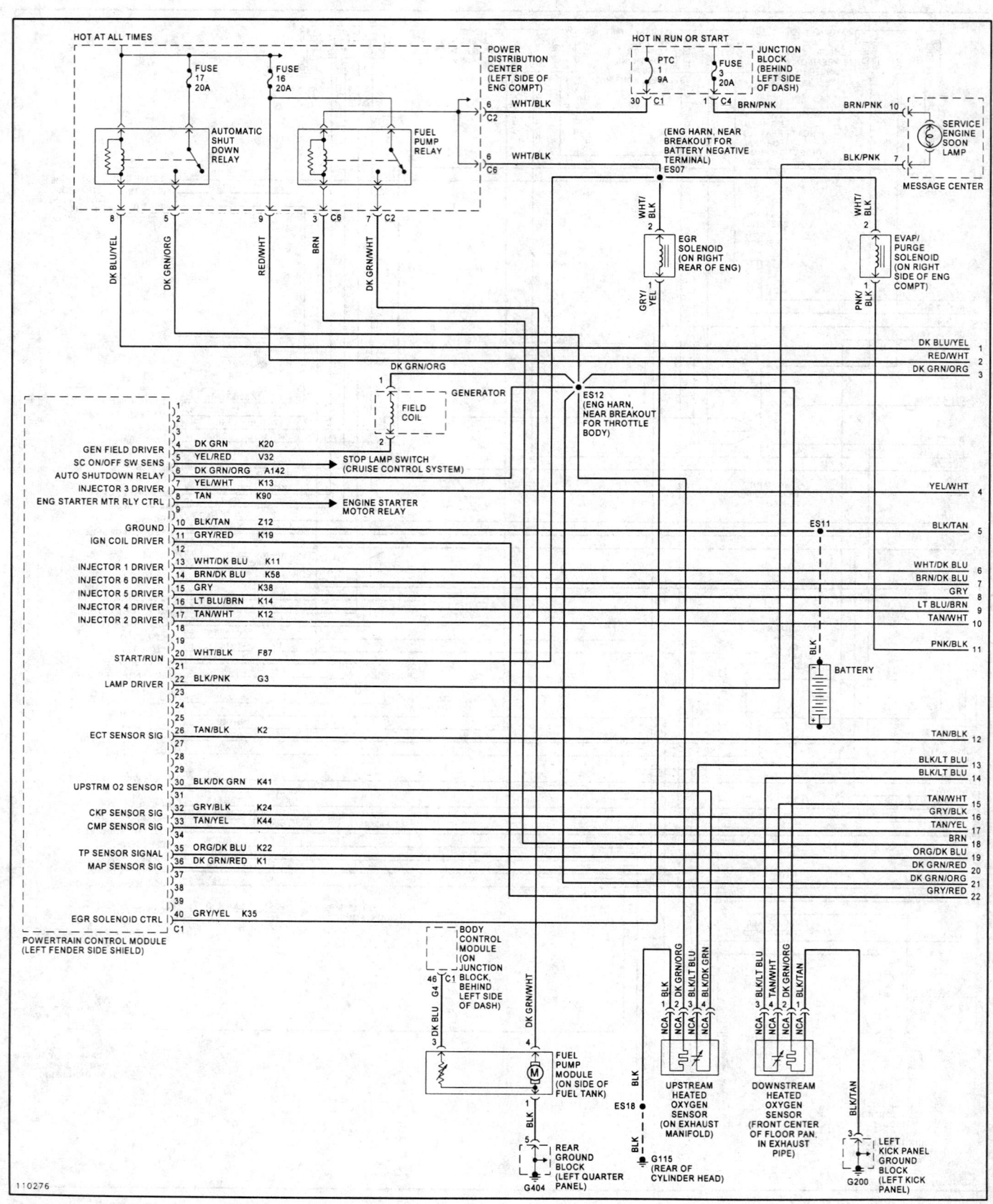

Fig. 13: PCM Wiring Diagram (Caravan & Voyager – 3.0L – 1 Of 3)

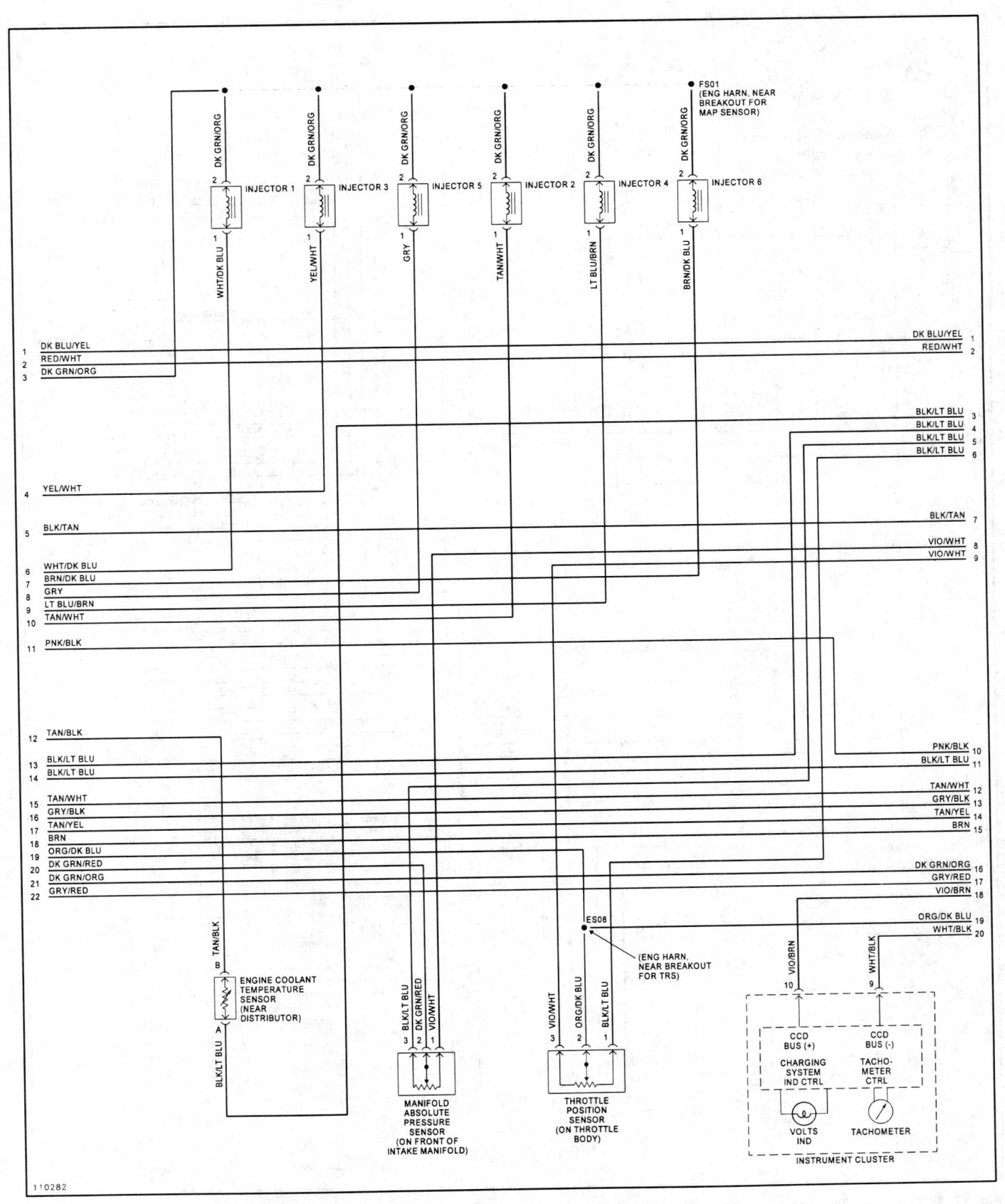

Fig. 14: PCM Wiring Diagram (Caravan & Voyager – 3.0L – 2 Of 3)

110282

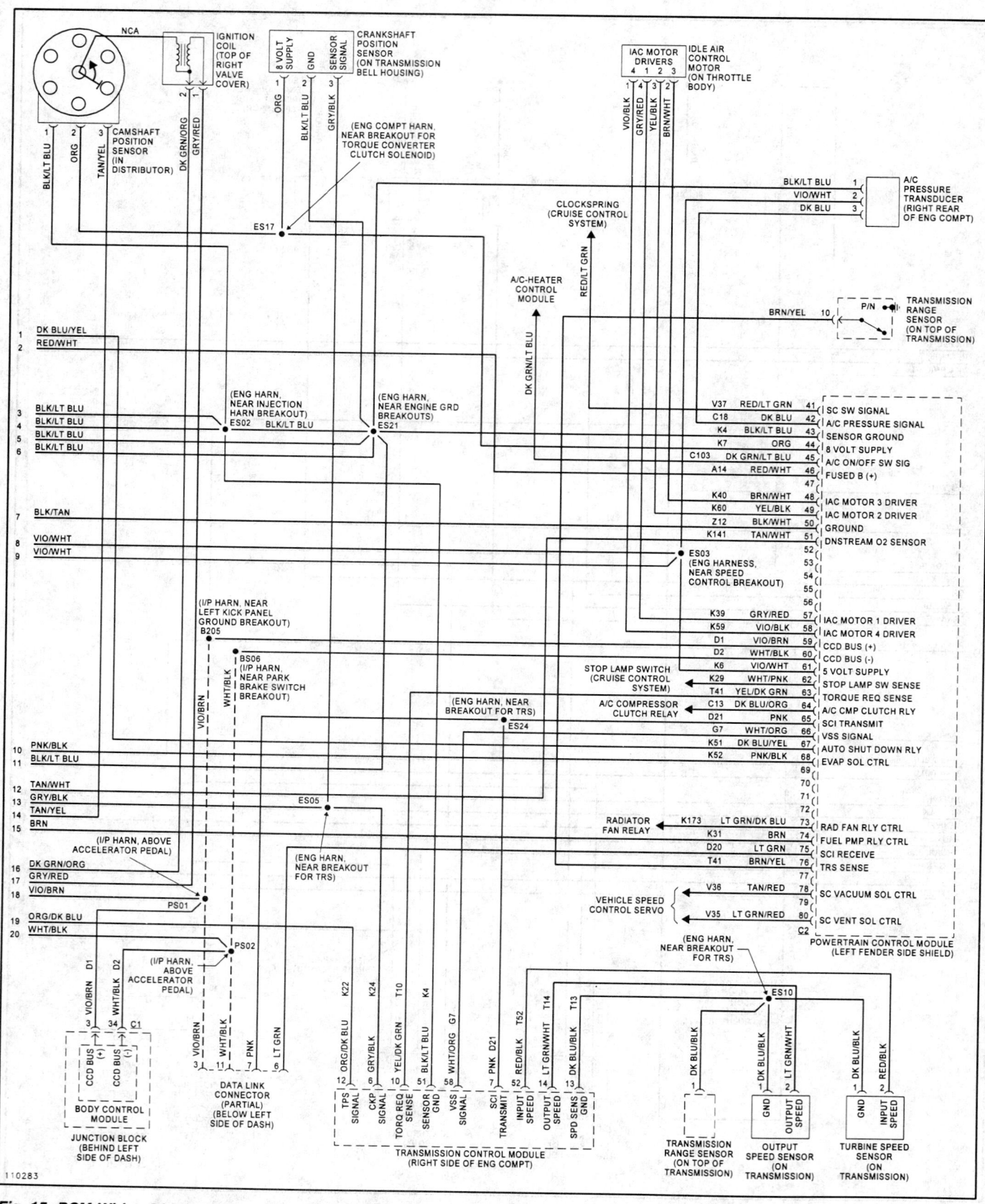

Fig. 15: PCM Wiring Diagram (Caravan & Voyager – 3.0L – 3 Of 3)

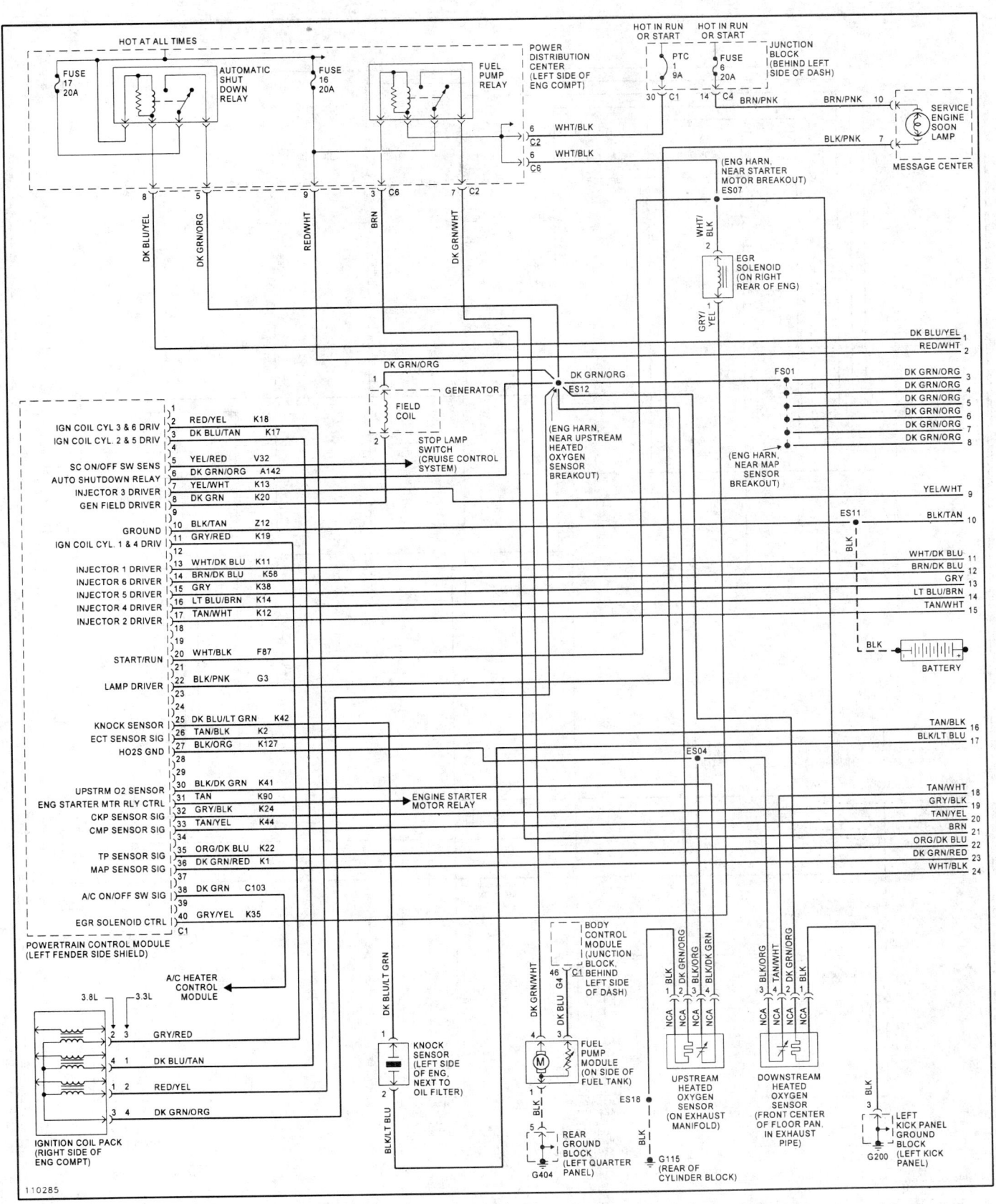

Fig. 16: PCM Wiring Diagram (Caravan, Town & Country, & Voyager – 3.3L, 3.3L Flex-Fuel & 3.8L – 1 Of 3)

1999 WIRING DIAGRAMS
Engine Performance (Cont.)

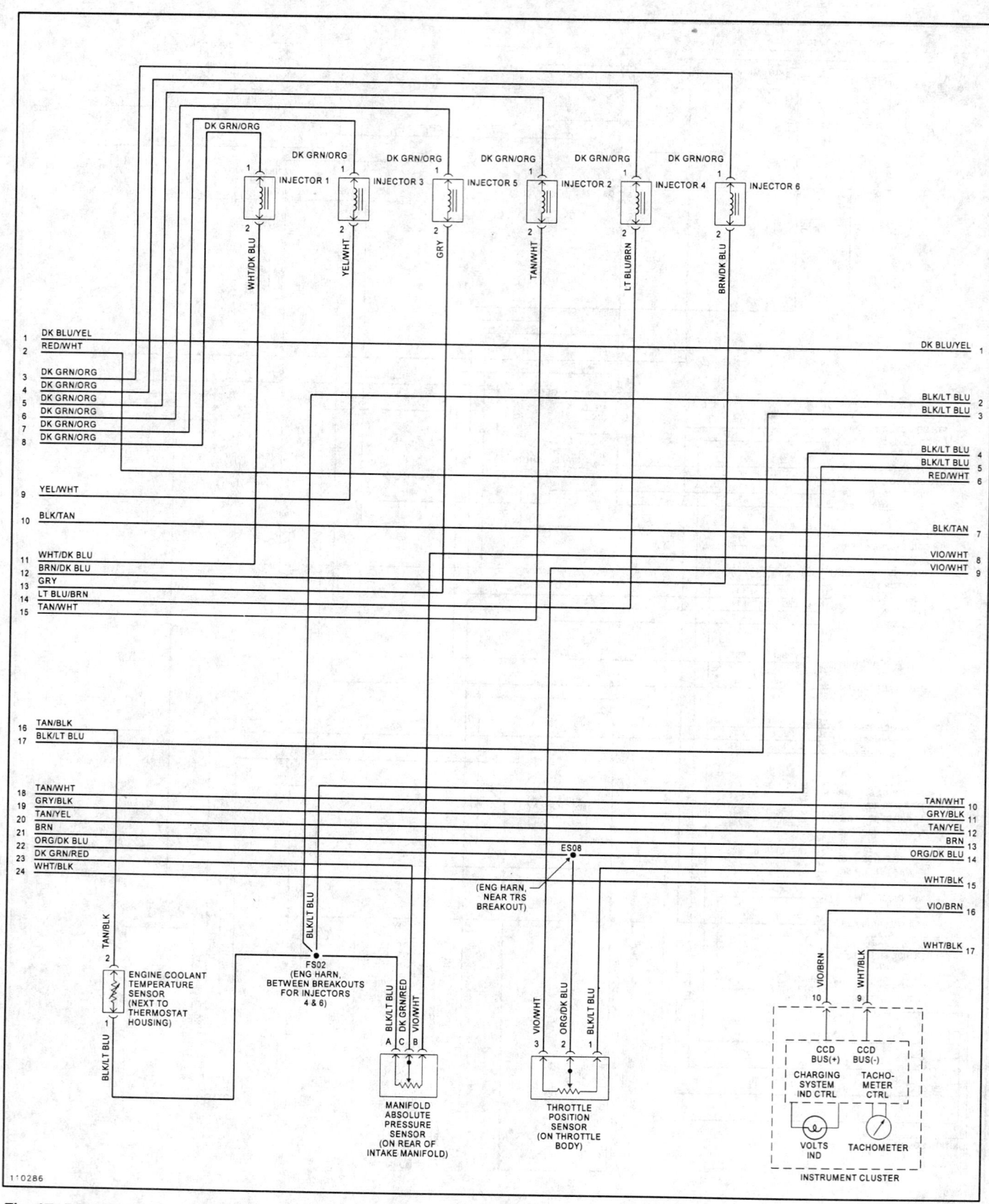

Fig. 17: PCM Wiring Diagram (Caravan, Town & Country, & Voyager – 3.3L, 3.3L Flex-Fuel & 3.8L – 2 Of 3)

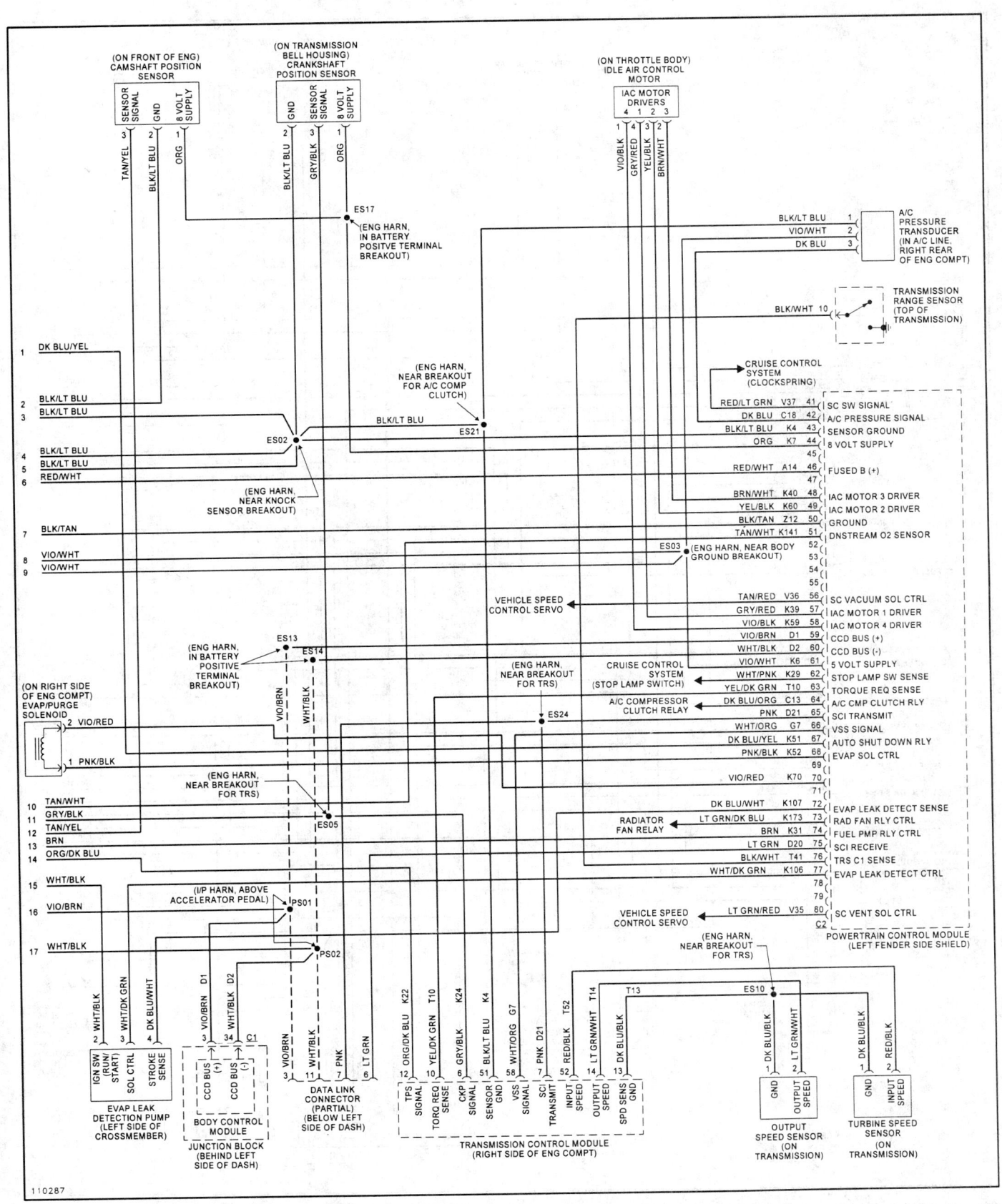

Fig. 18: PCM Wiring Diagram (Caravan, Town & Country, & Voyager – 3.3L, 3.3L Flex-Fuel & 3.8L – 3 Of 3)

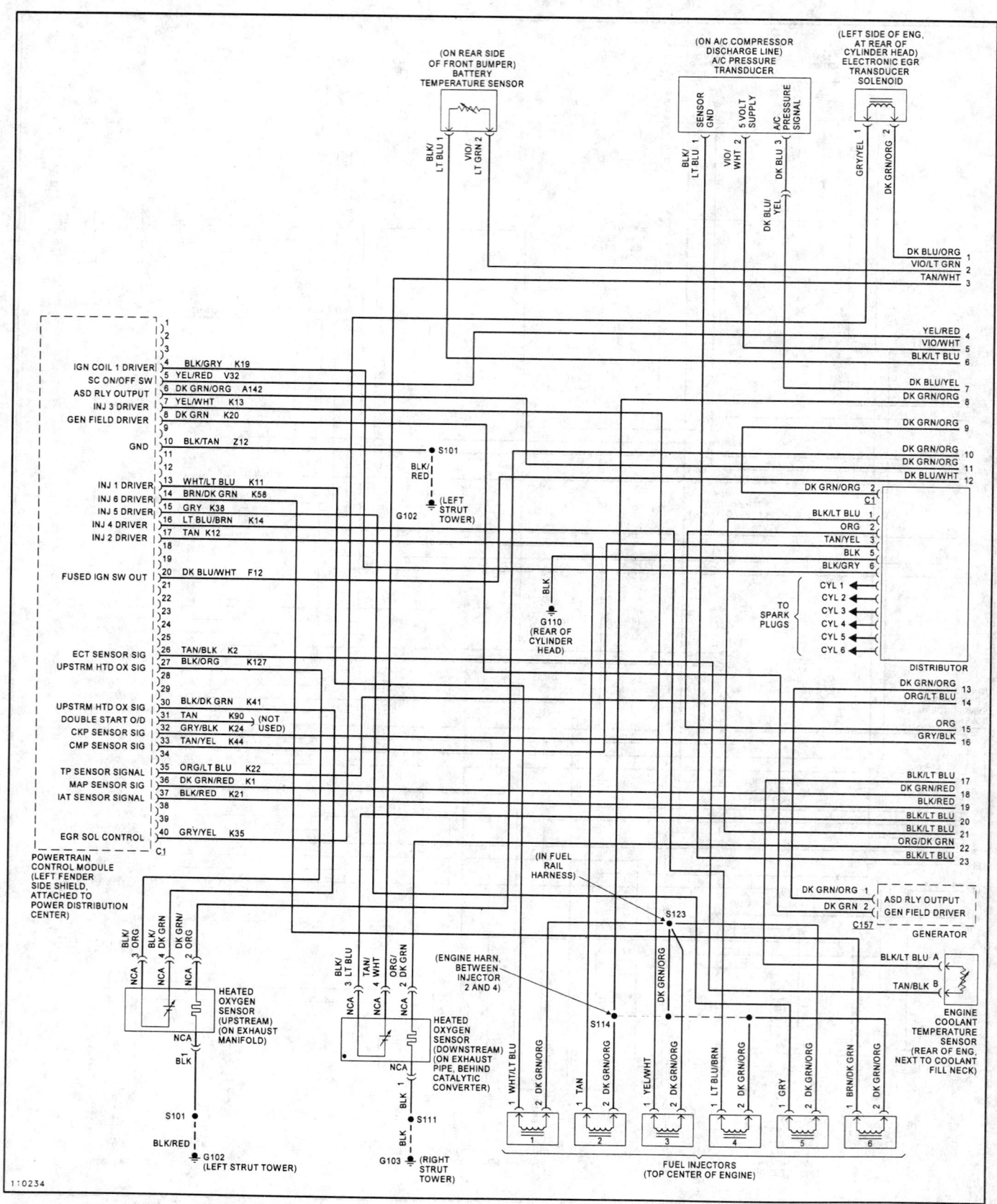

Fig. 19: PCM Wiring Diagram (Cirrus & Stratus – 2.5L – 1 Of 3)

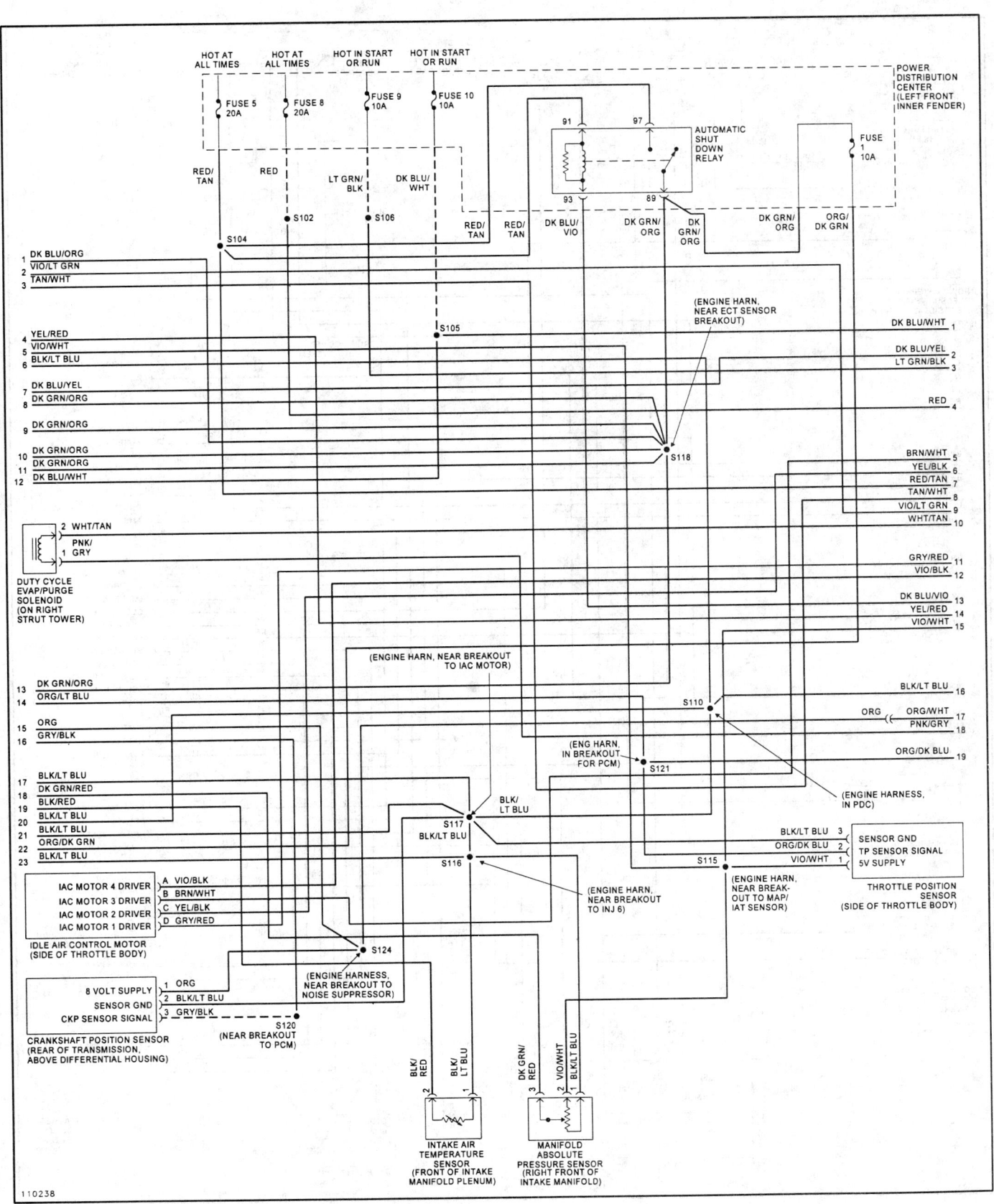

Fig. 20: PCM Wiring Diagram (Cirrus & Stratus – 2.5L – 2 Of 3)

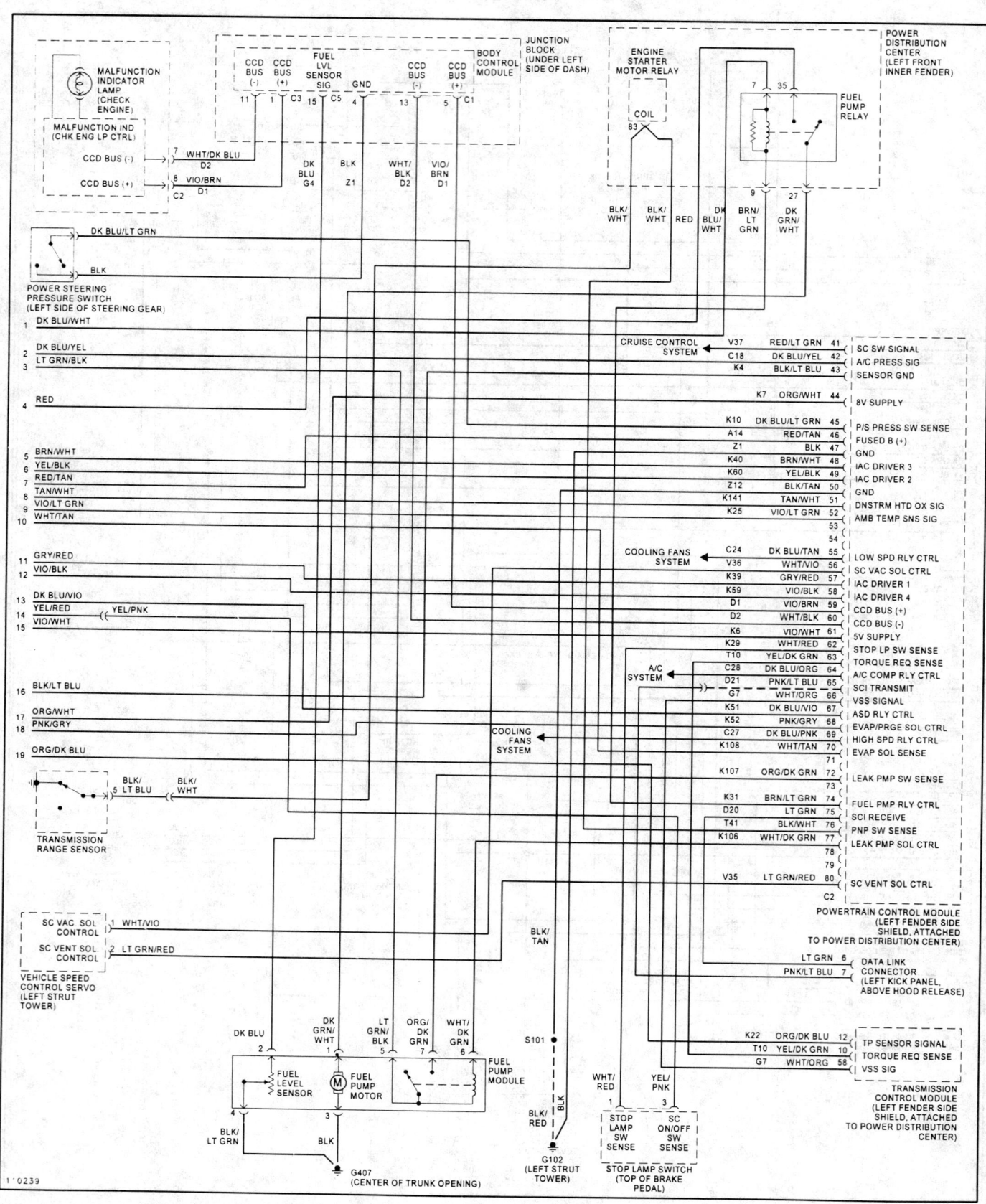

Fig. 21: PCM Wiring Diagram (Cirrus & Stratus – 2.5L – 3 Of 3)

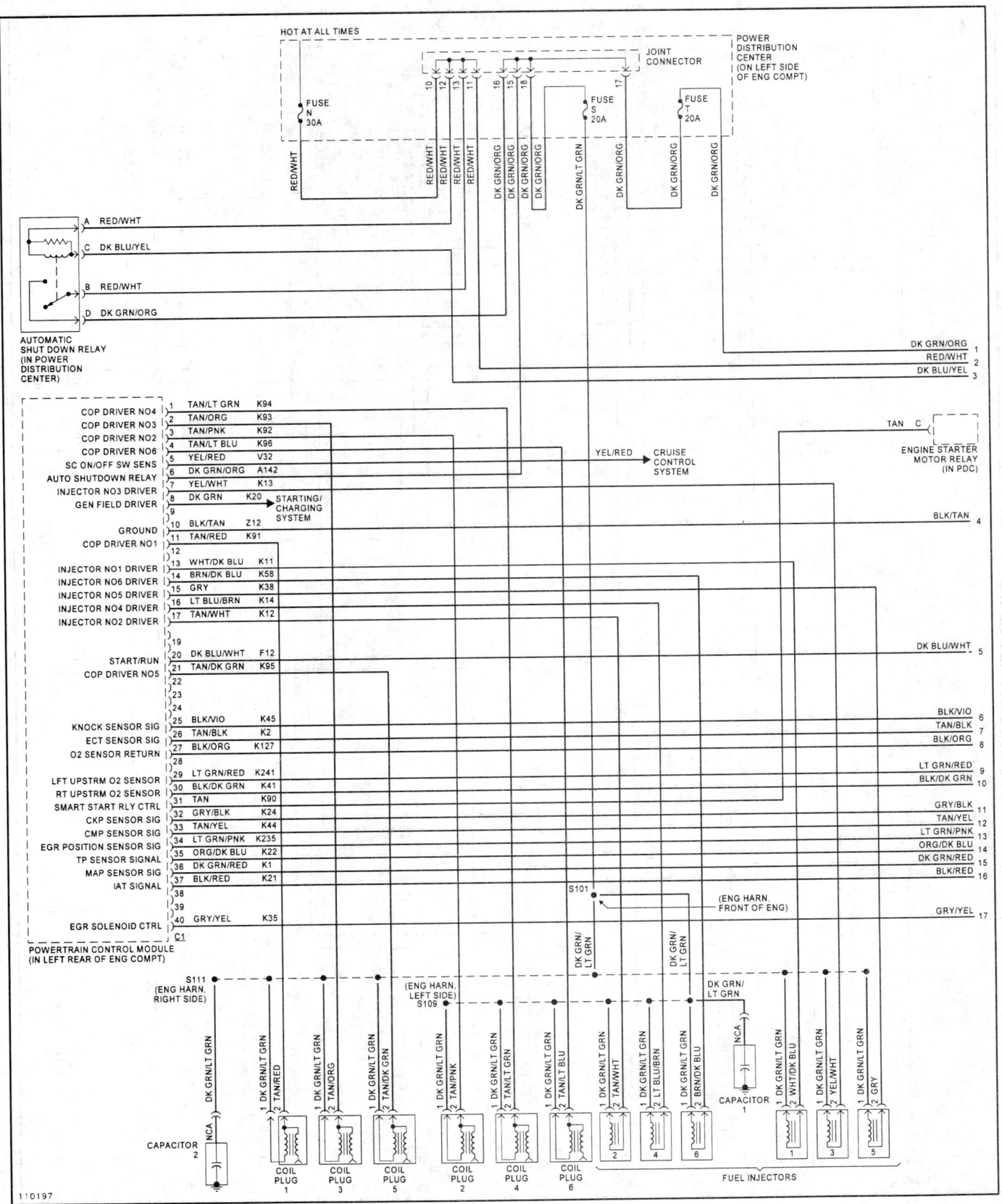

Fig. 22: PCM Wiring Diagram (Concorde & Intrepid – 2.7L – 1 Of 3)

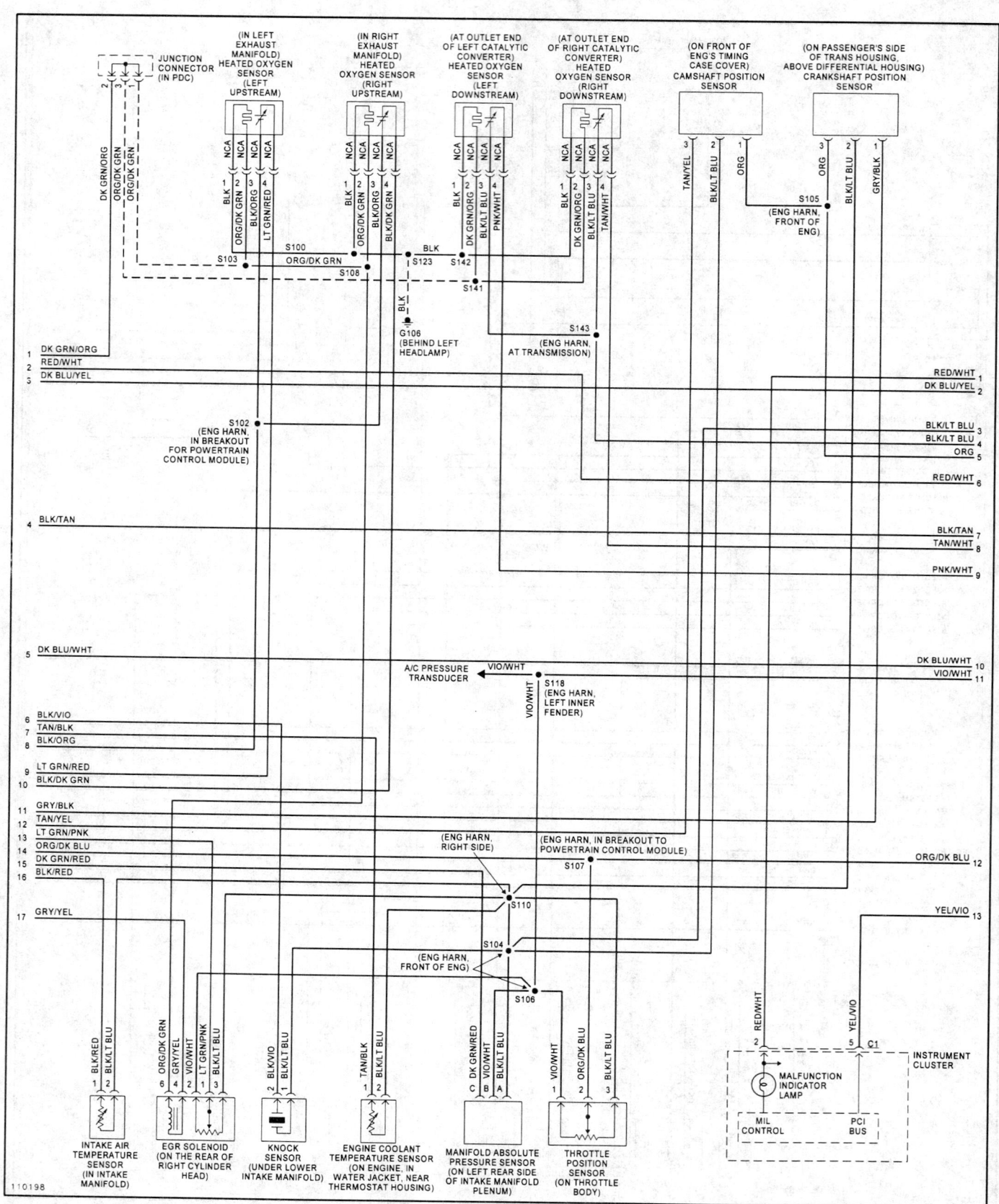

Fig. 23: PCM Wiring Diagram (Concorde & Intrepid – 2.7L – 2 Of 3)

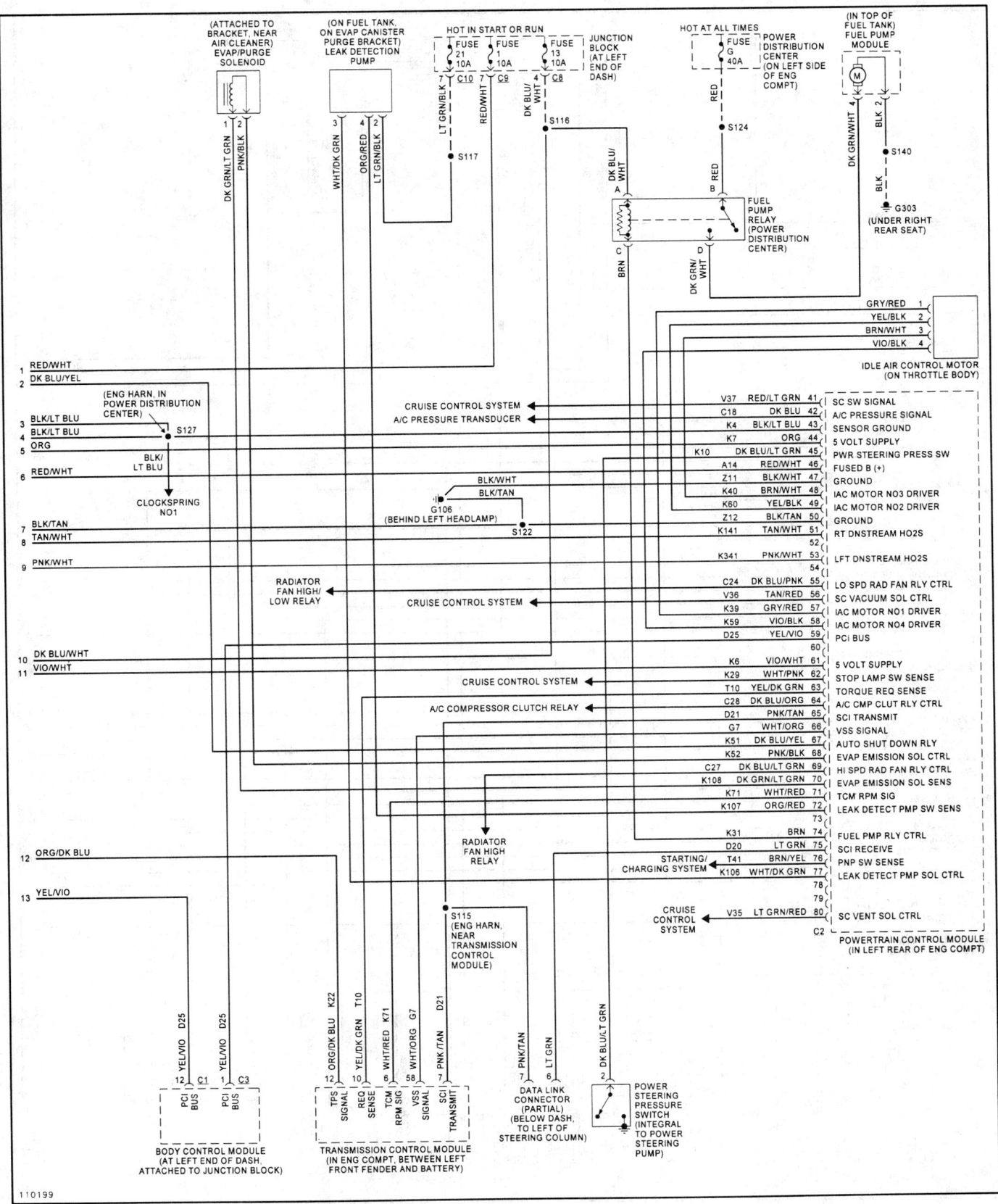

Fig. 24: PCM Wiring Diagram (Concorde & Intrepid – 2.7L – 3 Of 3)

110199

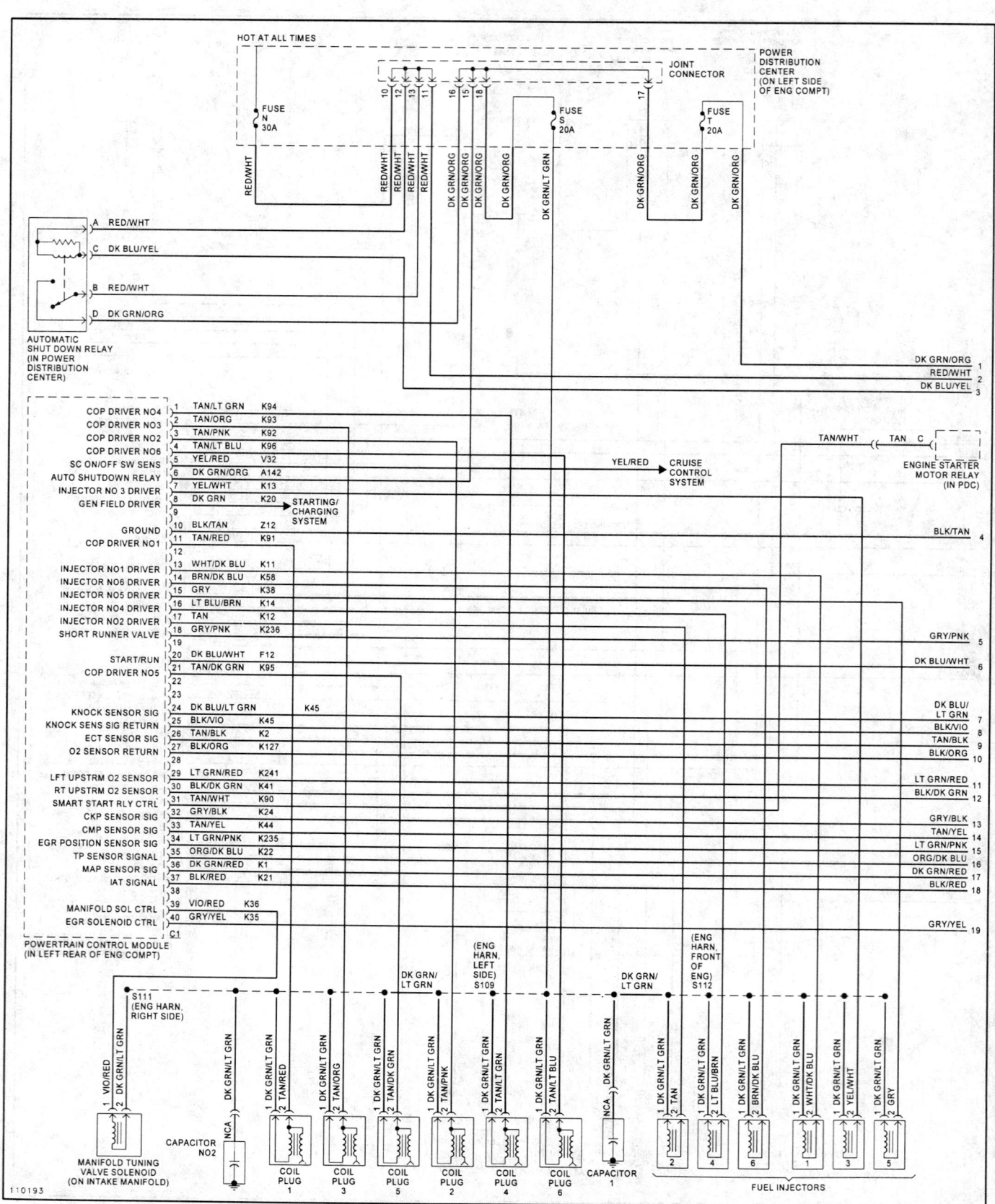

Fig. 25: PCM Wiring Diagram (Concorde & Intrepid – 3.2L, & LHS & 300M – 3.5L – 1 Of 3)

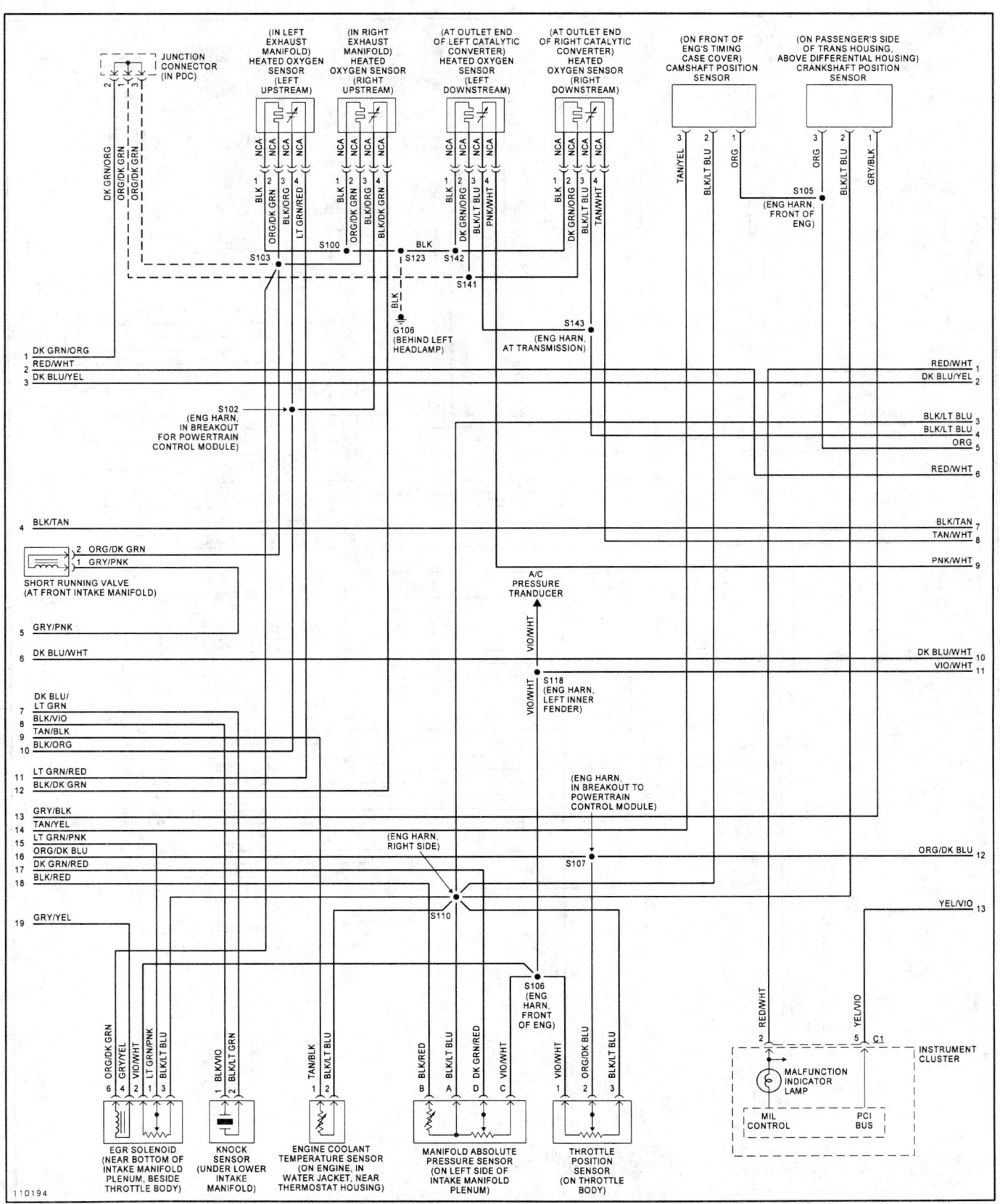

Fig. 26: PCM Wiring Diagram (Concorde & Intrepid – 3.2L, & LHS & 300M – 3.5L – 2 Of 3)

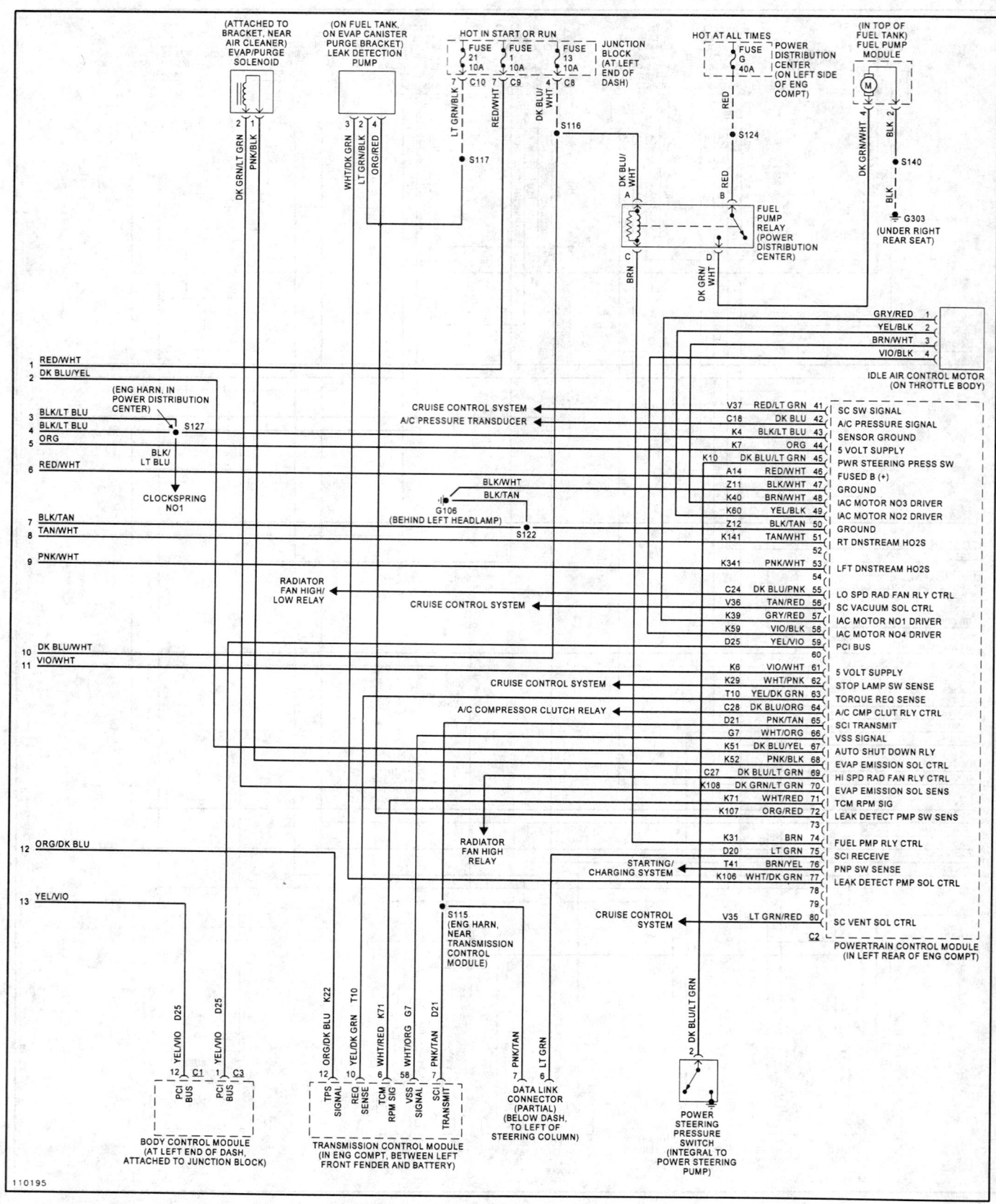

Fig. 27: PCM Wiring Diagram (Concorde & Intrepid – 3.2L, & LHS & 300M – 3.5L – 3 Of 3)

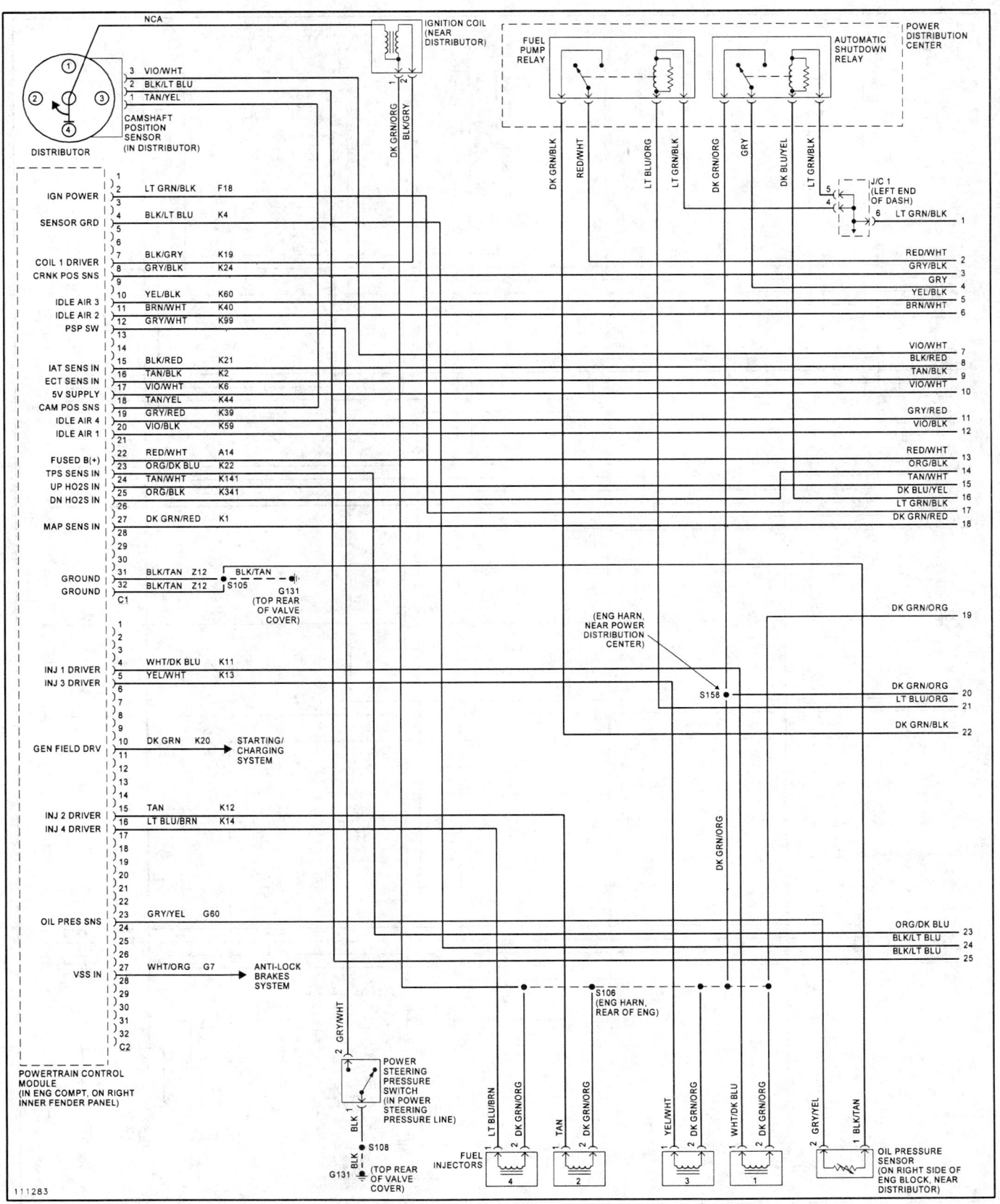

Fig. 28: PCM Wiring Diagram (Dakota – 2.5L – 1 Of 3)

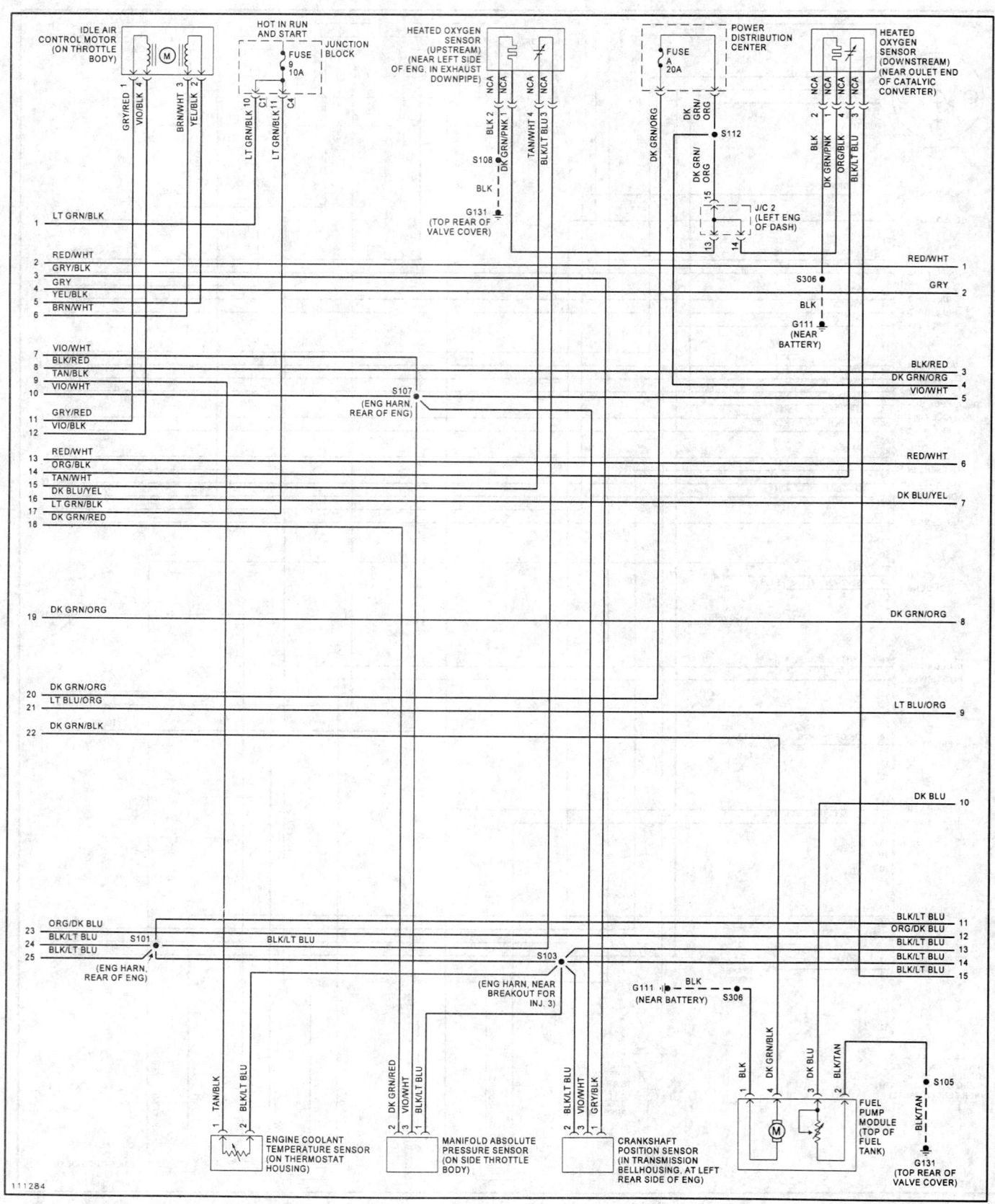

Fig. 29: PCM Wiring Diagram (Dakota – 2.5L – 2 Of 3)

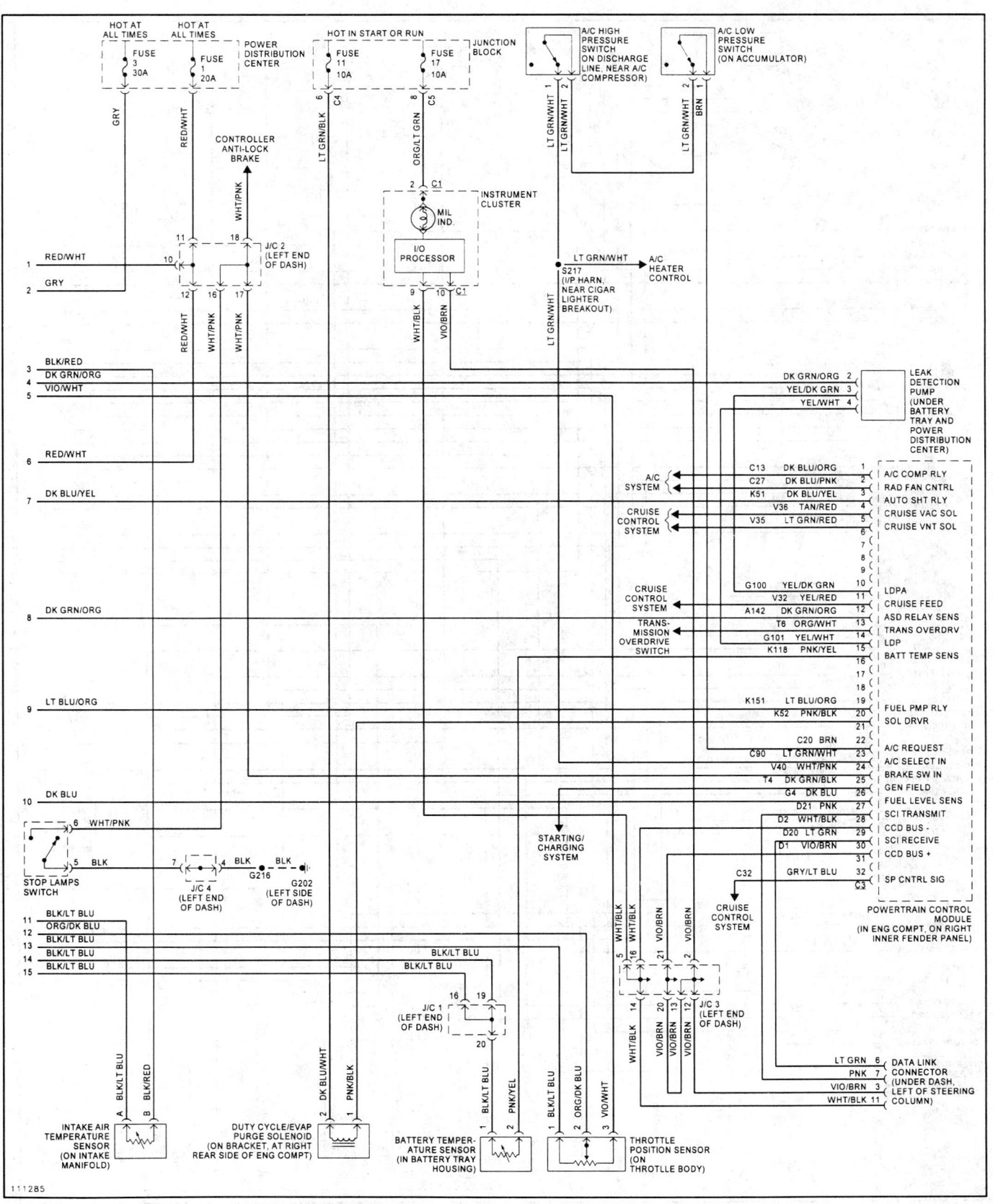

Fig. 30: PCM Wiring Diagram (Dakota – 2.5L – 3 Of 3)

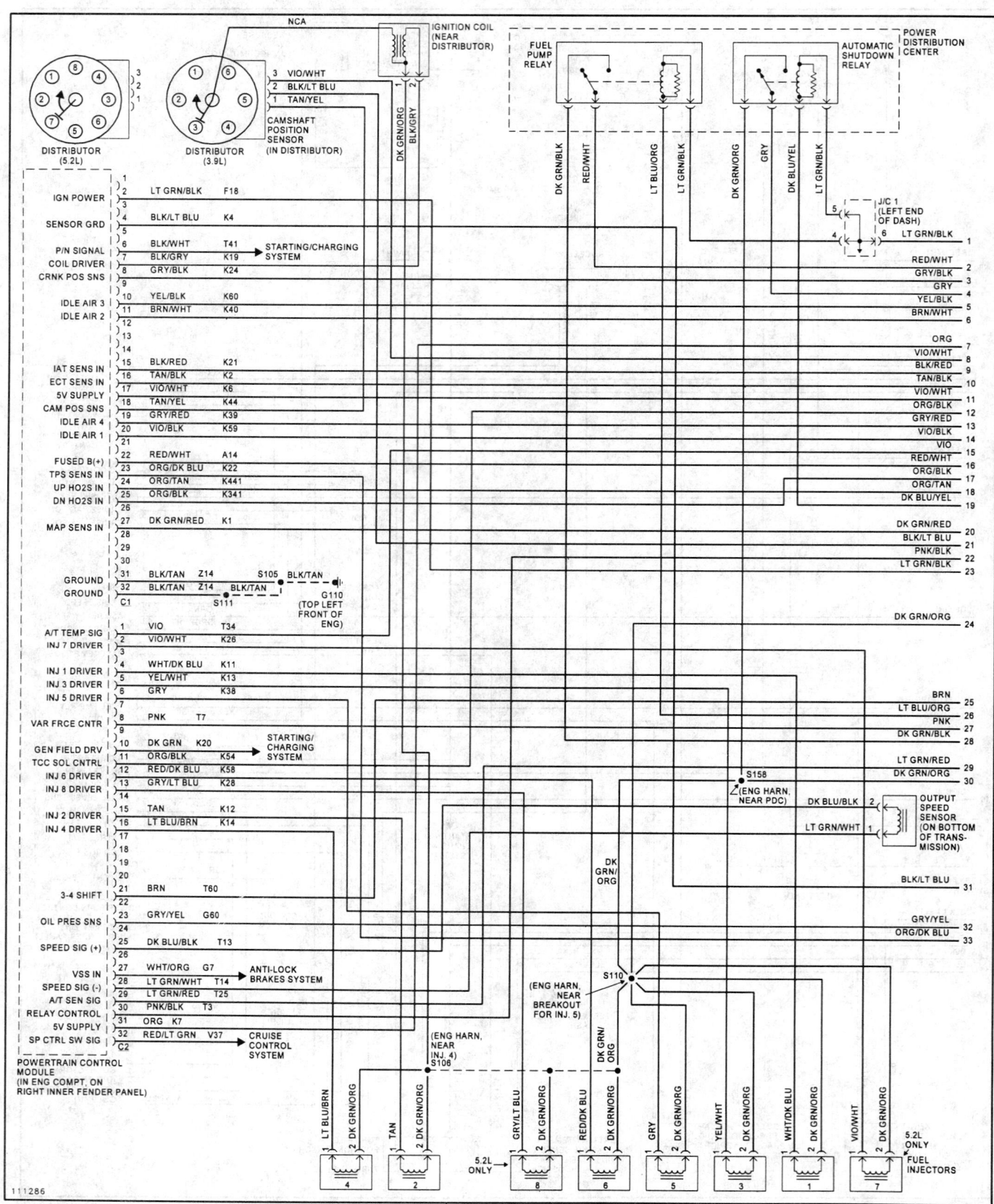

Fig. 31: PCM Wiring Diagram (Dakota – 3.9L & 5.2L – 1 Of 3)

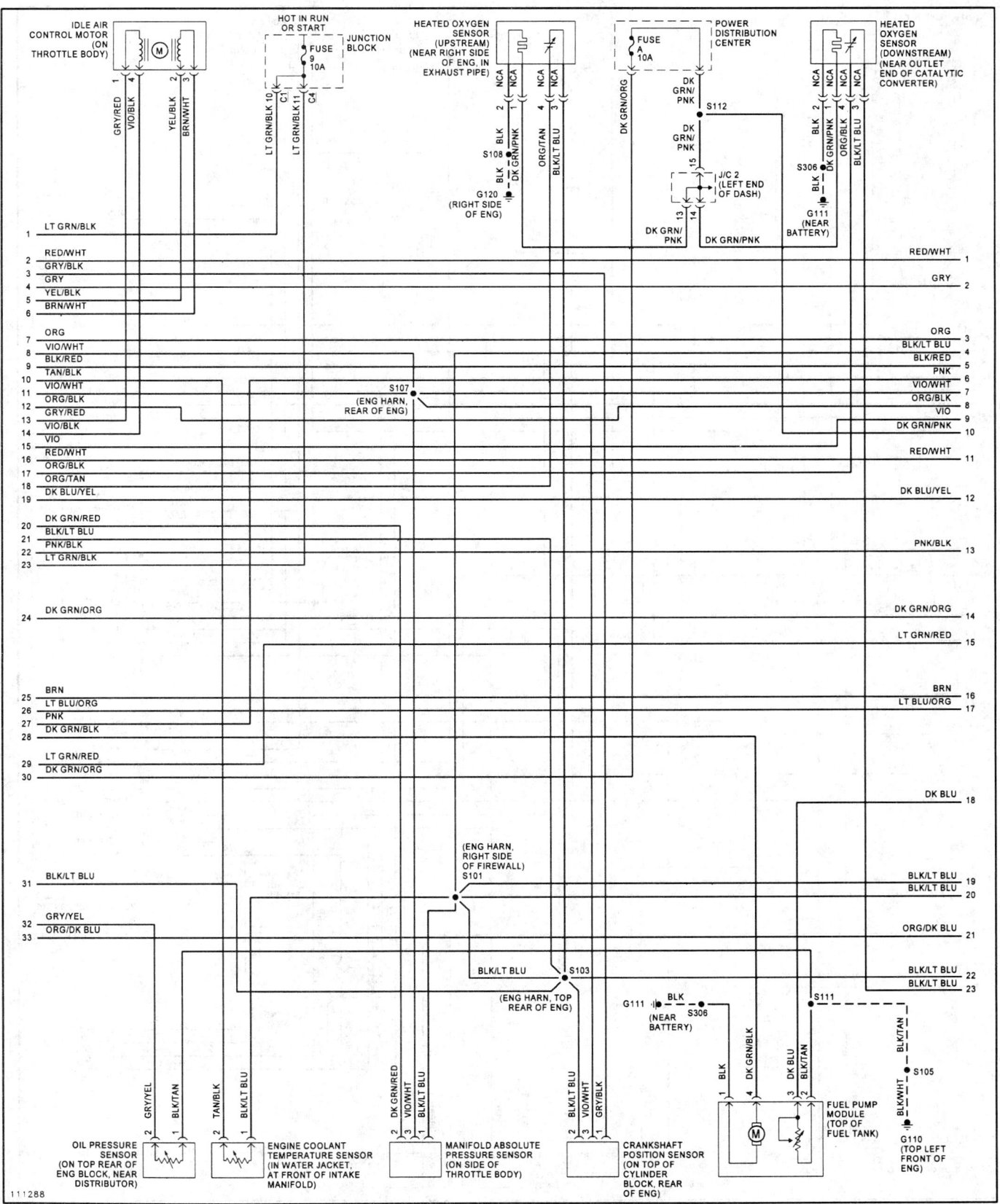

Fig. 32: PCM Wiring Diagram (Dakota – 3.9L & 5.2L – 2 Of 3)

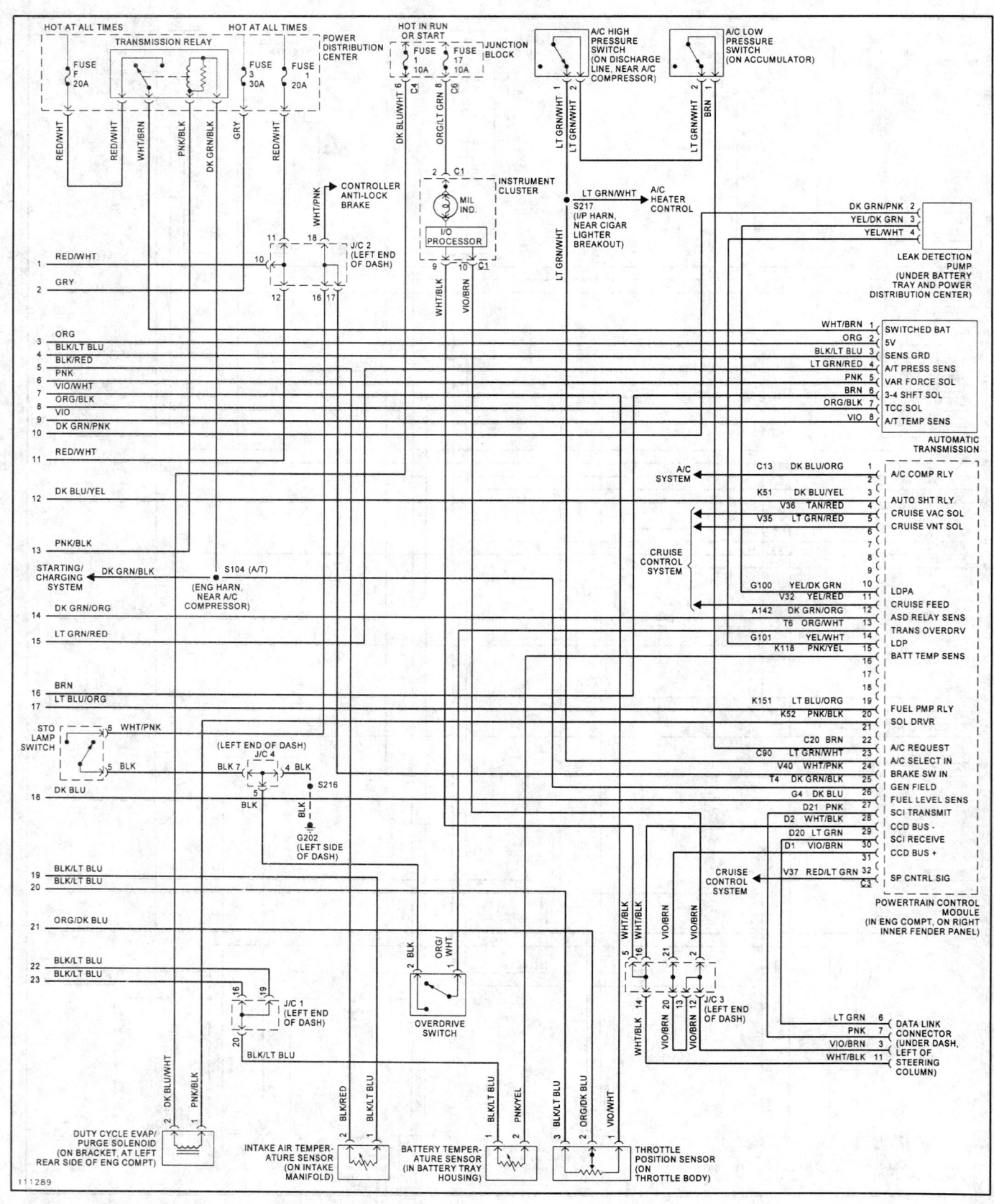

Fig. 33: PCM Wiring Diagram (Dakota – 3.9L & 5.2L – 3 Of 3)

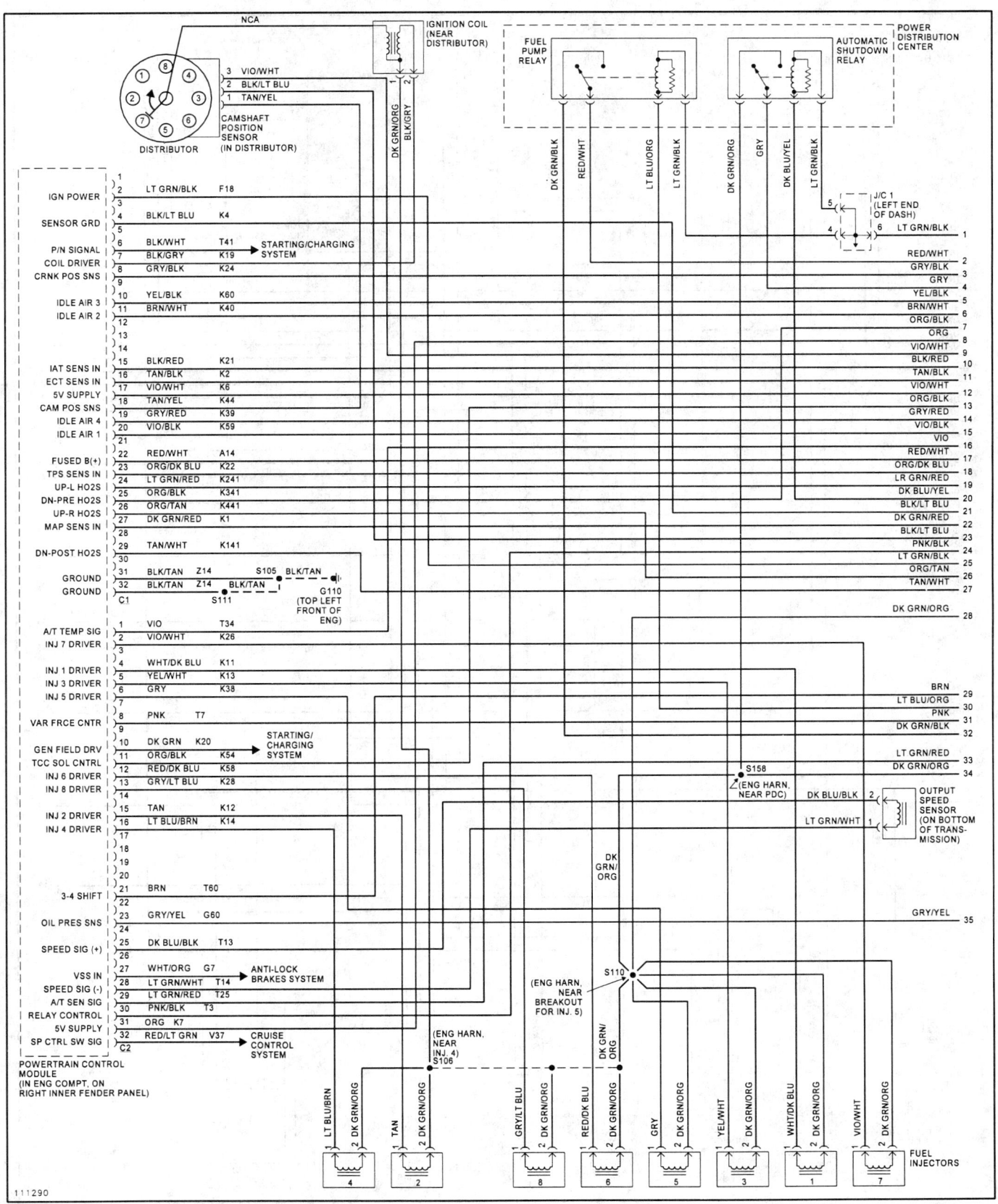

Fig. 34: PCM Wiring Diagram (Dakota – 5.9L – 1 Of 3)

111290

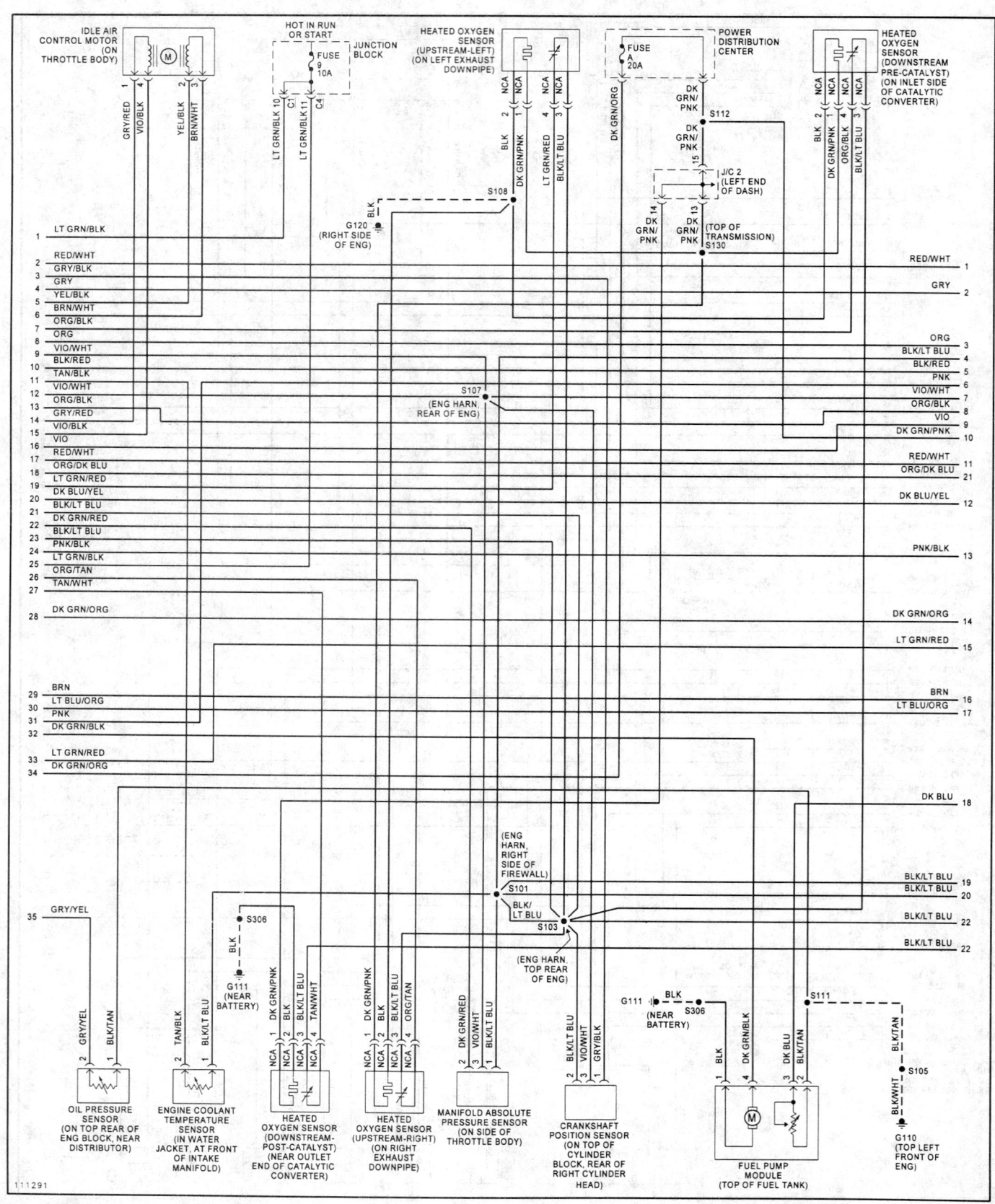

Fig. 35: PCM Wiring Diagram (Dakota – 5.9L – 2 Of 3)

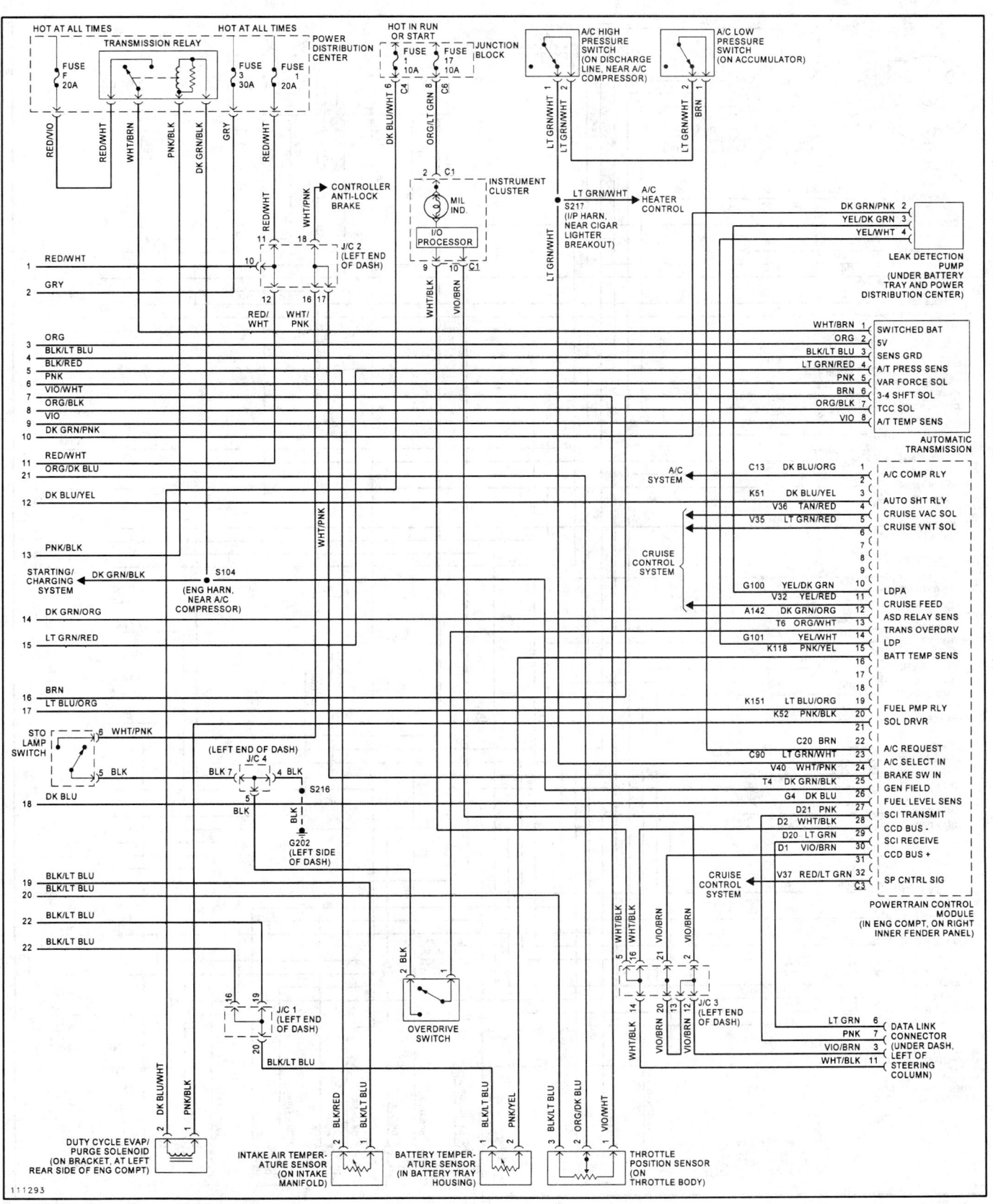

Fig. 36: PCM Wiring Diagram (Dakota – 5.9L – 3 Of 3)

111293

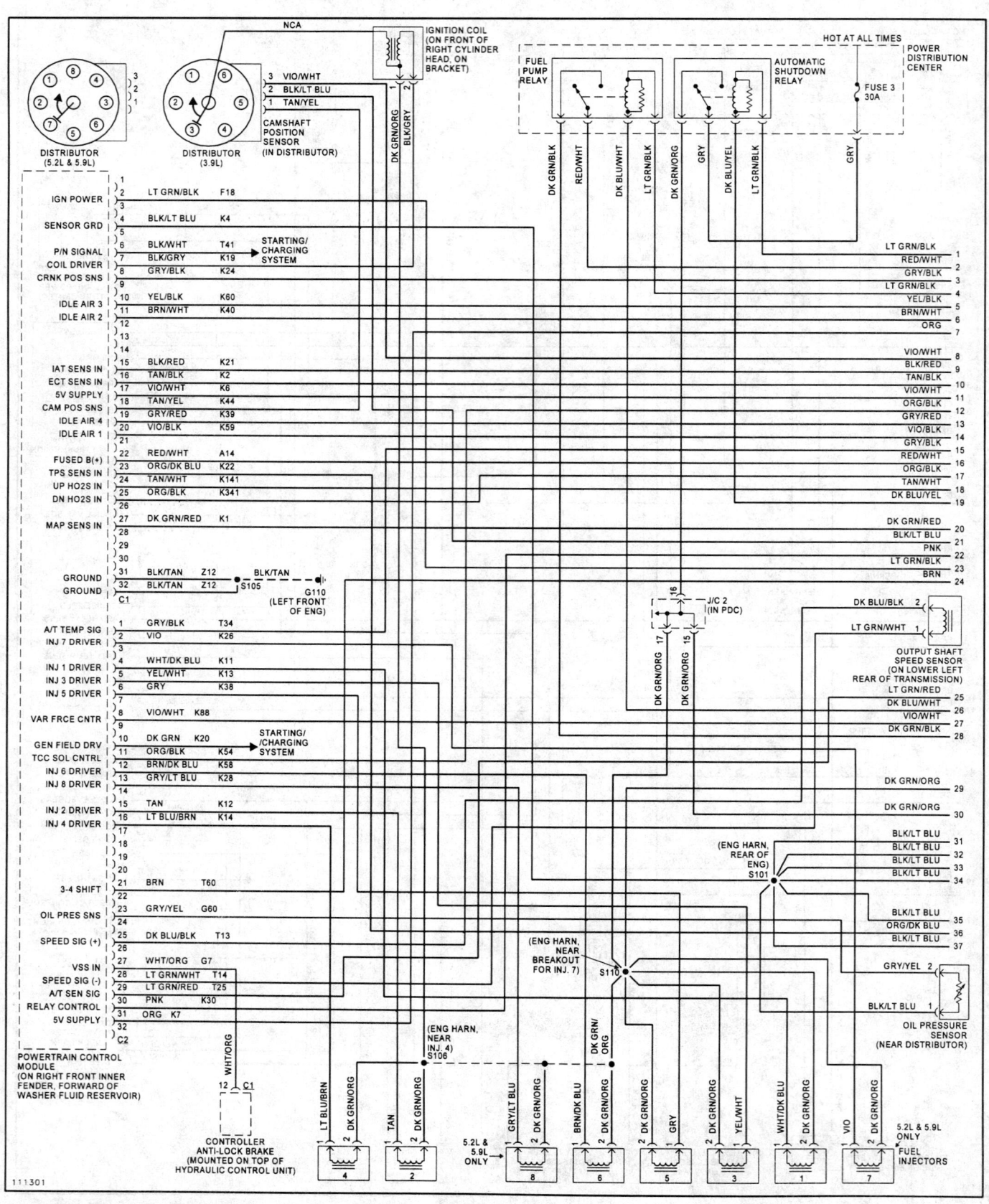

Fig. 37: PCM Wiring Diagram (Durango – 3.9L, 5.2L & 5.9L – 1 Of 3)

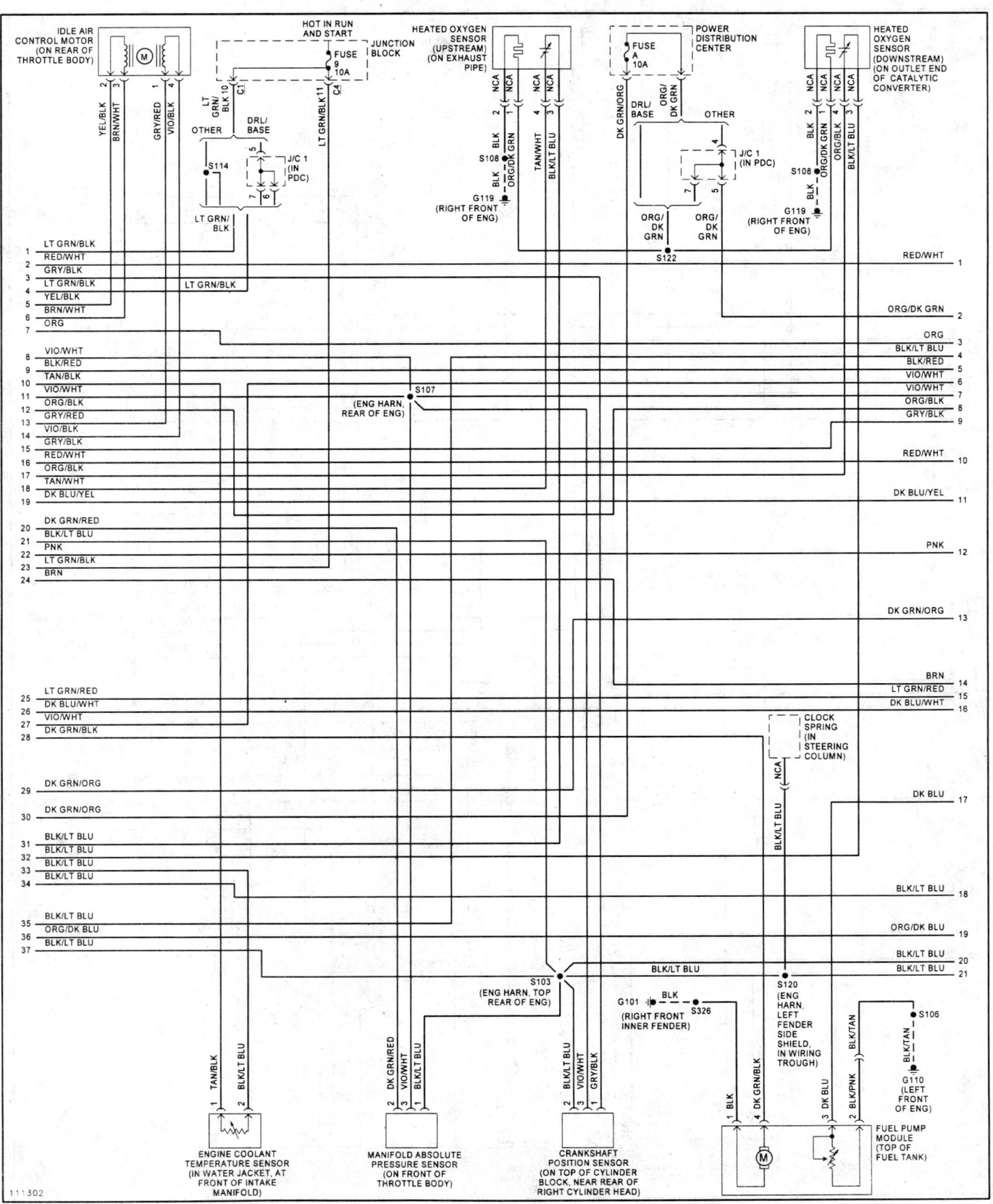

Fig. 38: PCM Wiring Diagram (Durango – 3.9L, 5.2L & 5.9L – 2 Of 3)

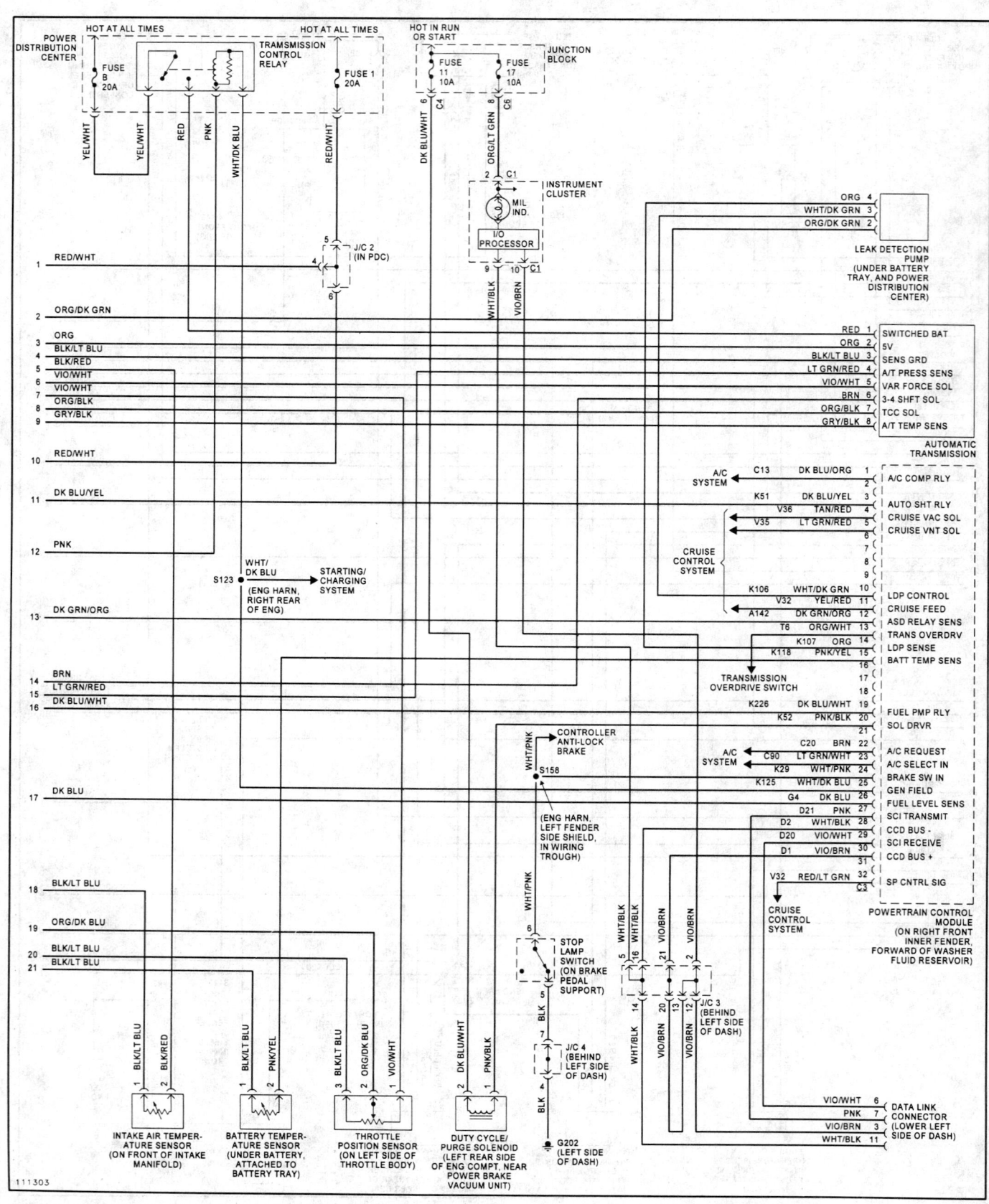

Fig. 39: PCM Wiring Diagram (Durango – 3.9L, 5.2L & 5.9L – 3 Of 3)

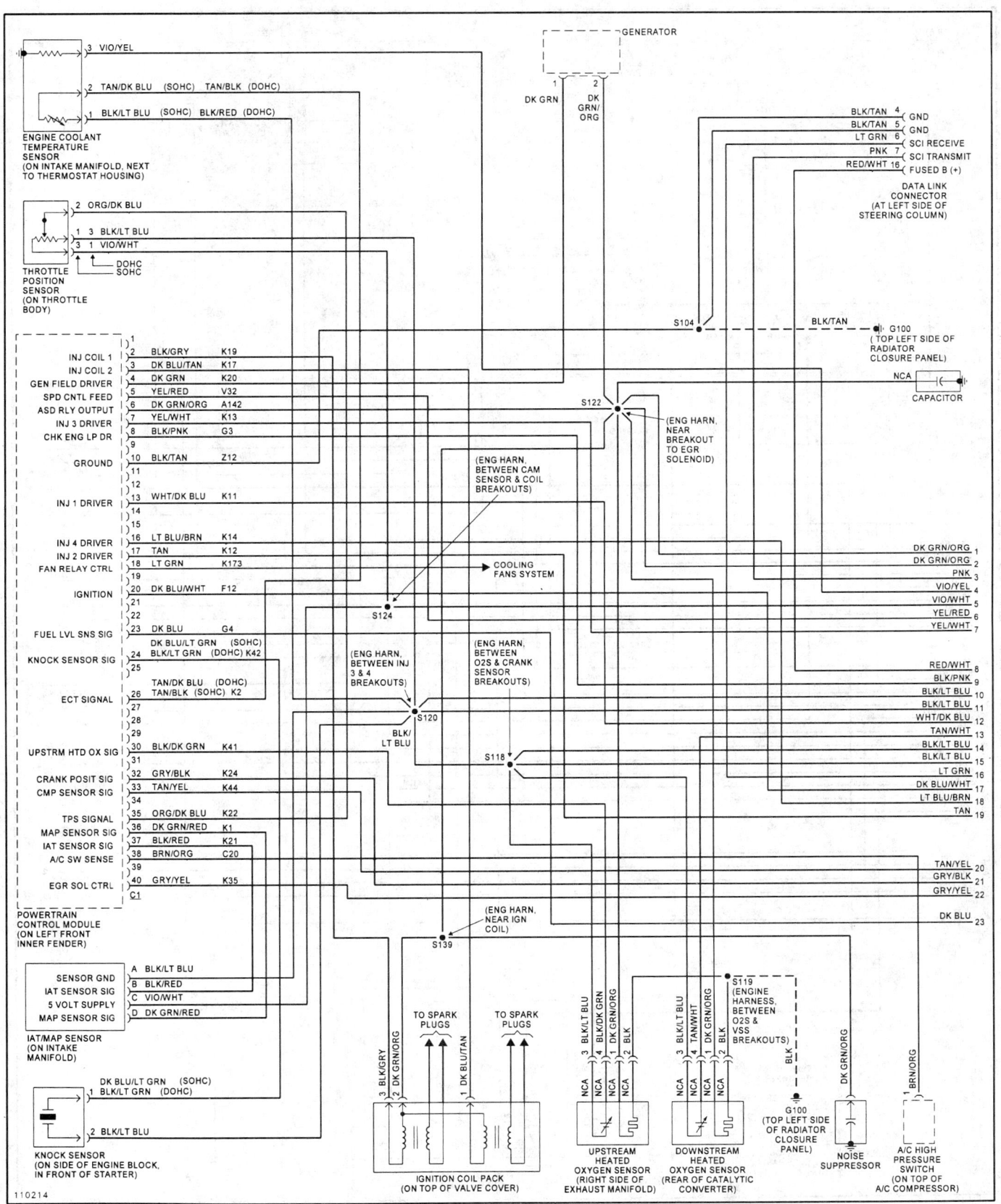

Fig. 40: PCM Wiring Diagram (Neon – 2.0L – 1 Of 3)

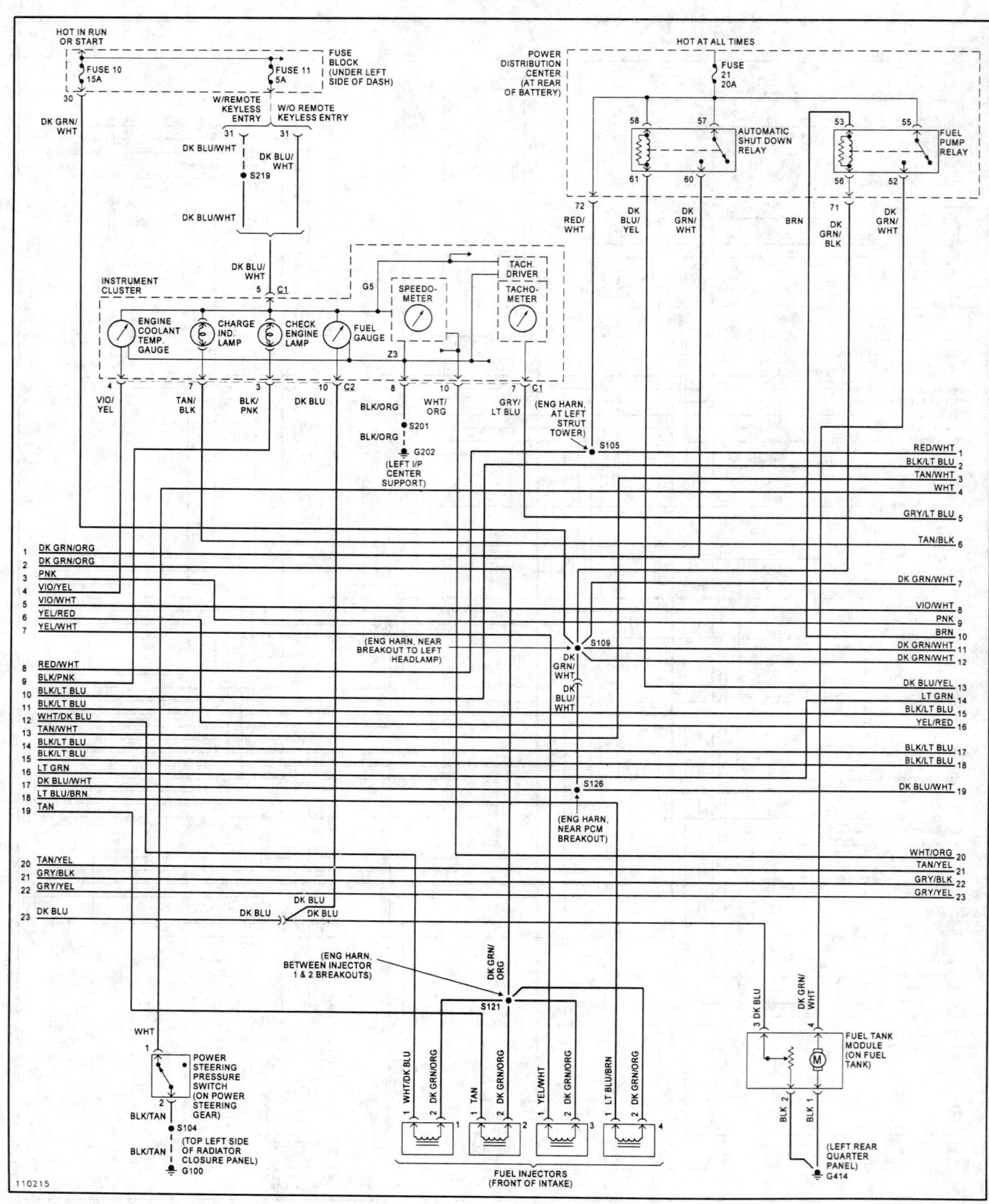

Fig. 41: PCM Wiring Diagram (Neon – 2.0L – 2 Of 3)

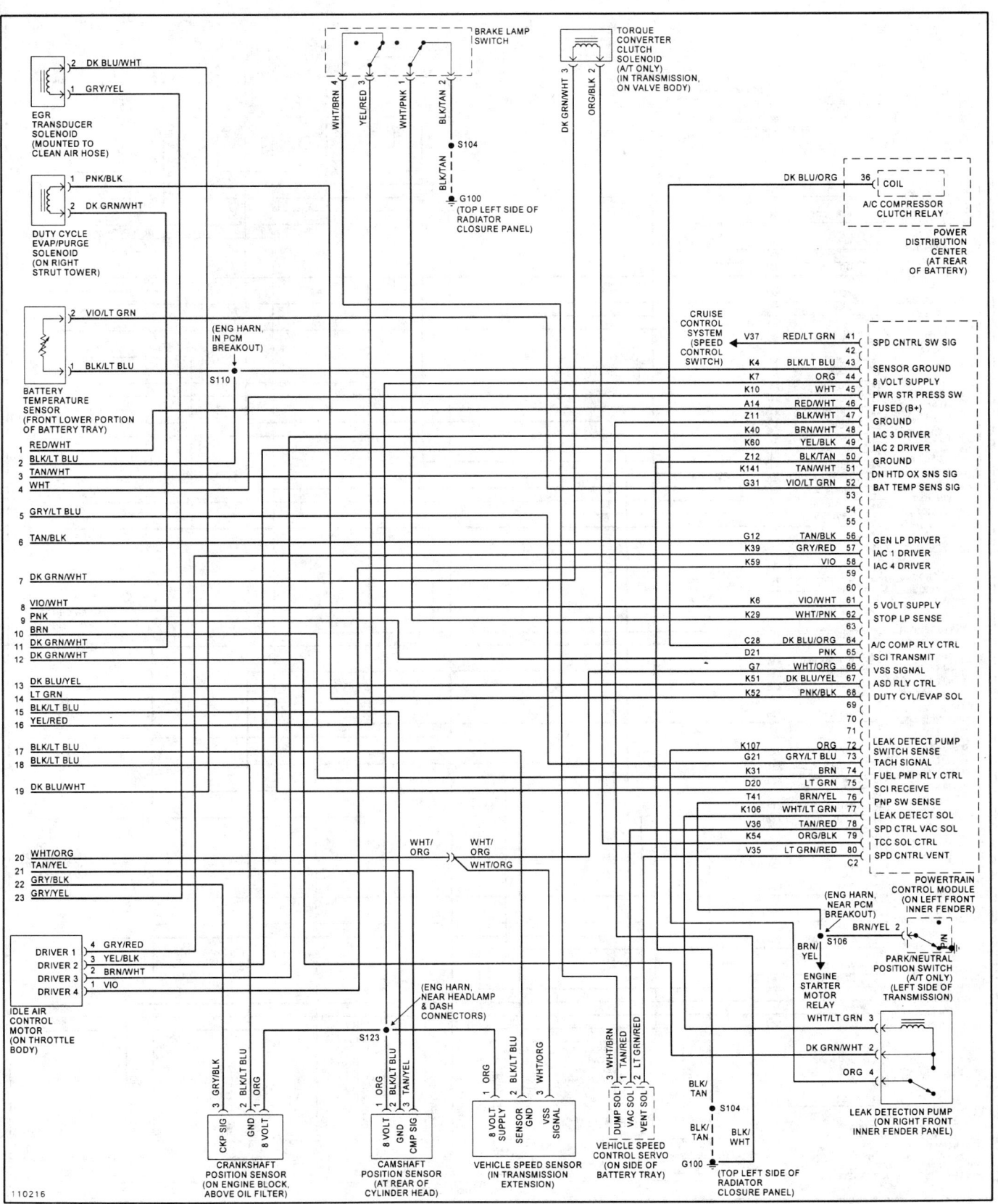

Fig. 42: PCM Wiring Diagram (Neon – 2.0L – 3 Of 3)

110216

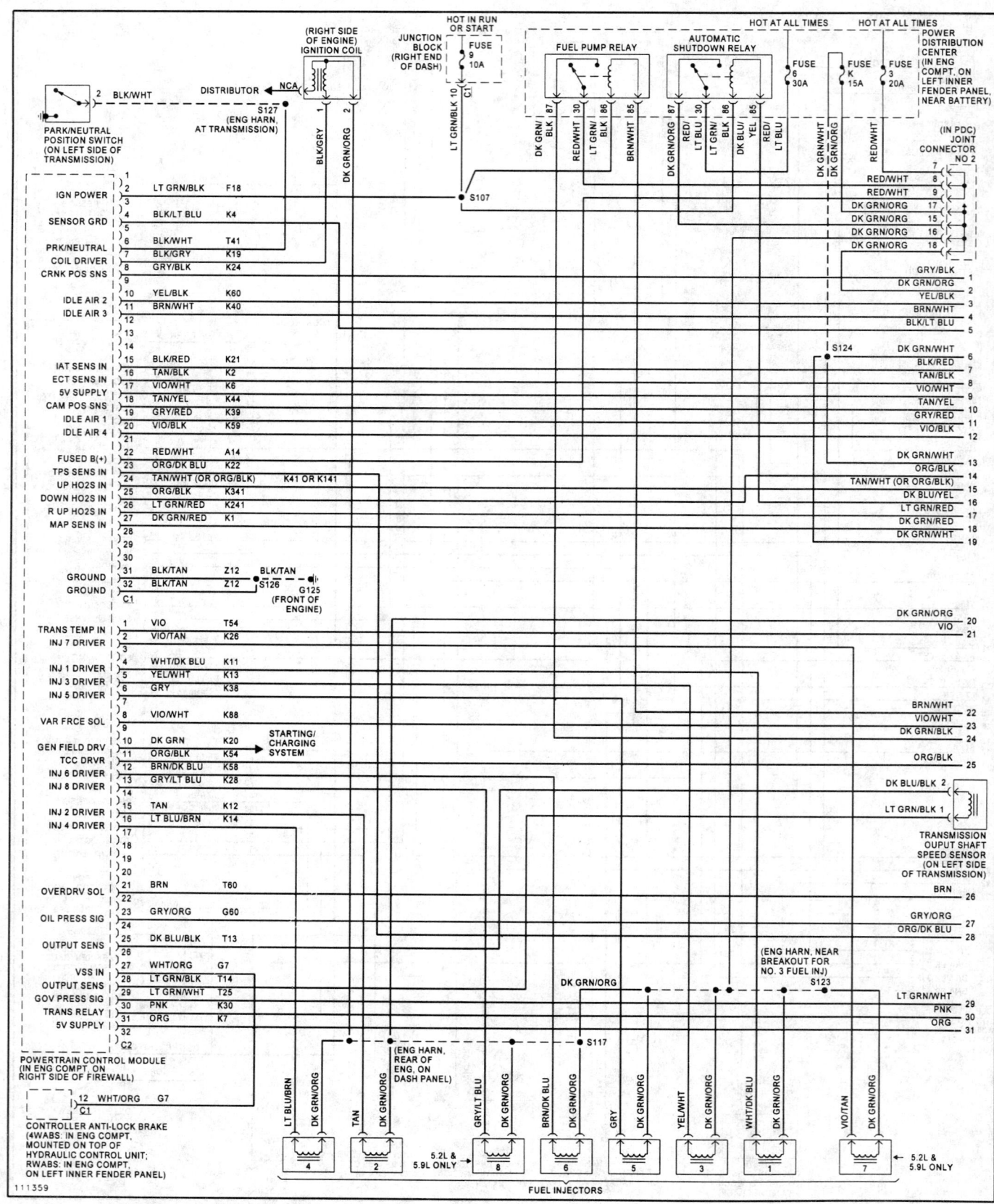

Fig. 43: PCM Wiring Diagram (Ram Pickup – 3.9L, 5.2L & 5.9L – 1 Of 3)

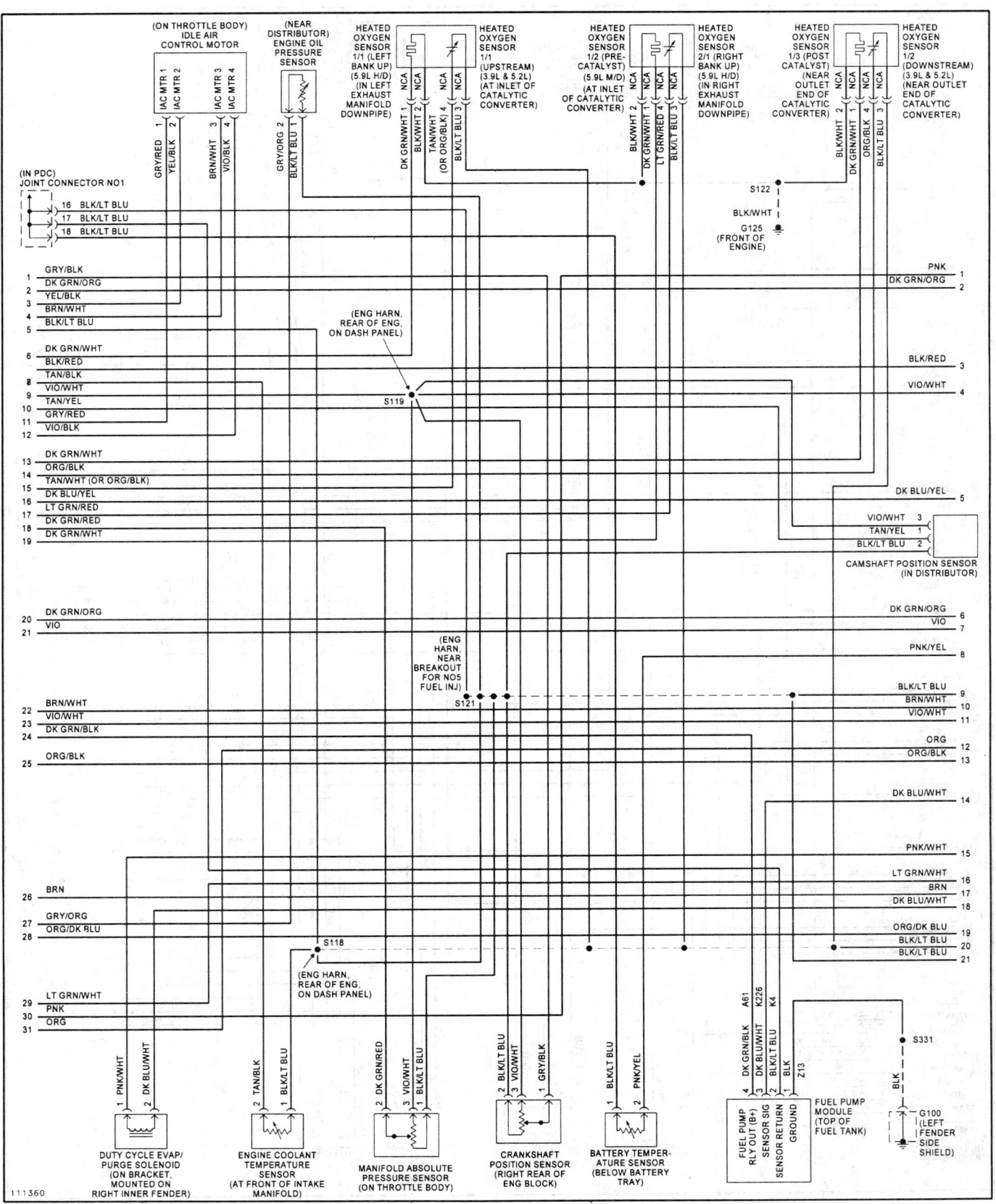

Fig. 44: PCM Wiring Diagram (Ram Pickup – 3.9L, 5.2L & 5.9L – 2 Of 3)

111360

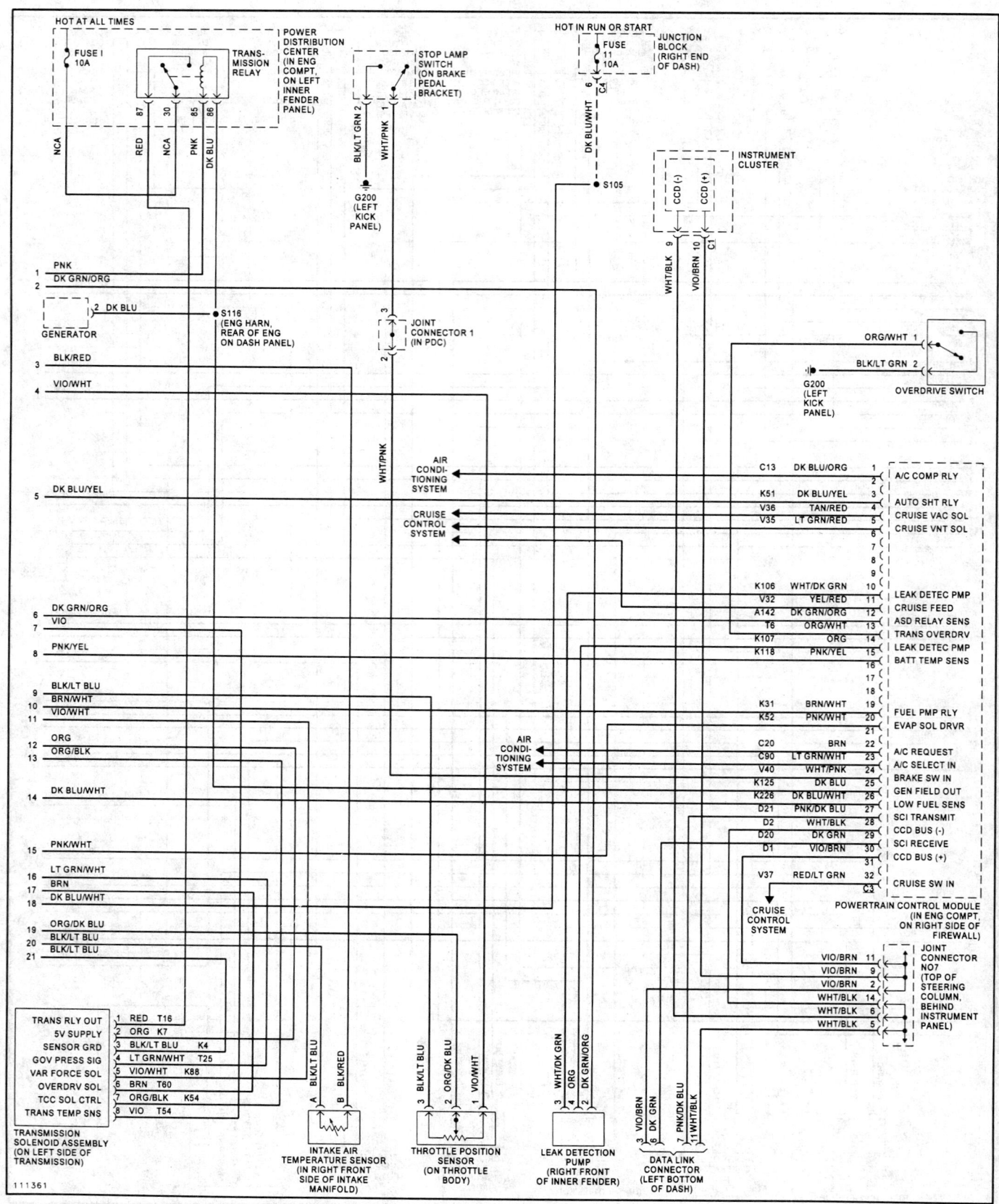

Fig. 45: PCM Wiring Diagram (Ram Pickup – 3.9L, 5.2L & 5.9L – 3 Of 3)

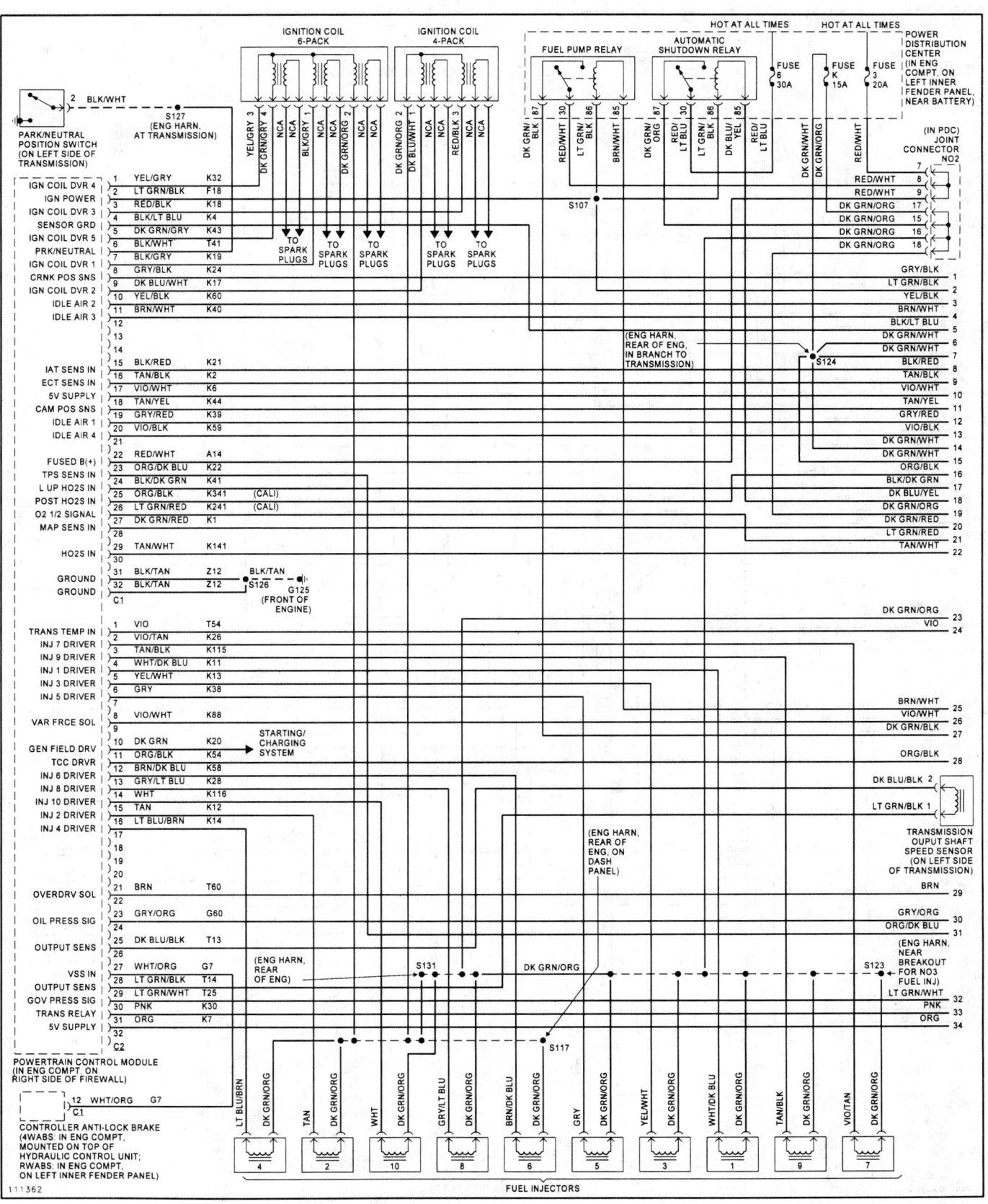

Fig. 46: PCM Wiring Diagram (Ram Pickup – 2500 & 3500 – 8.0L – 1 Of 3)

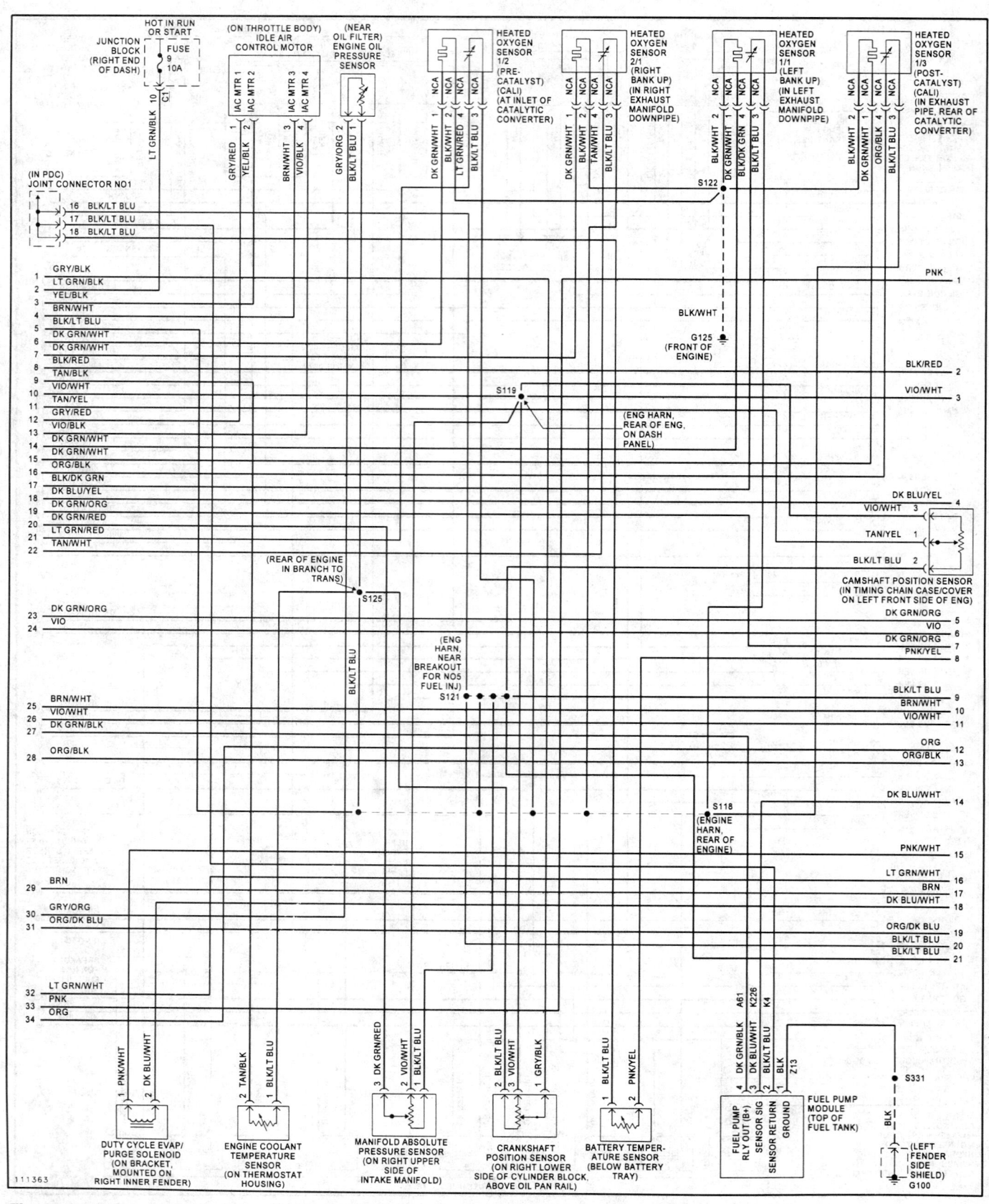

Fig. 47: PCM Wiring Diagram (Ram Pickup – 2500 & 3500 – 8.0L – 2 Of 3)

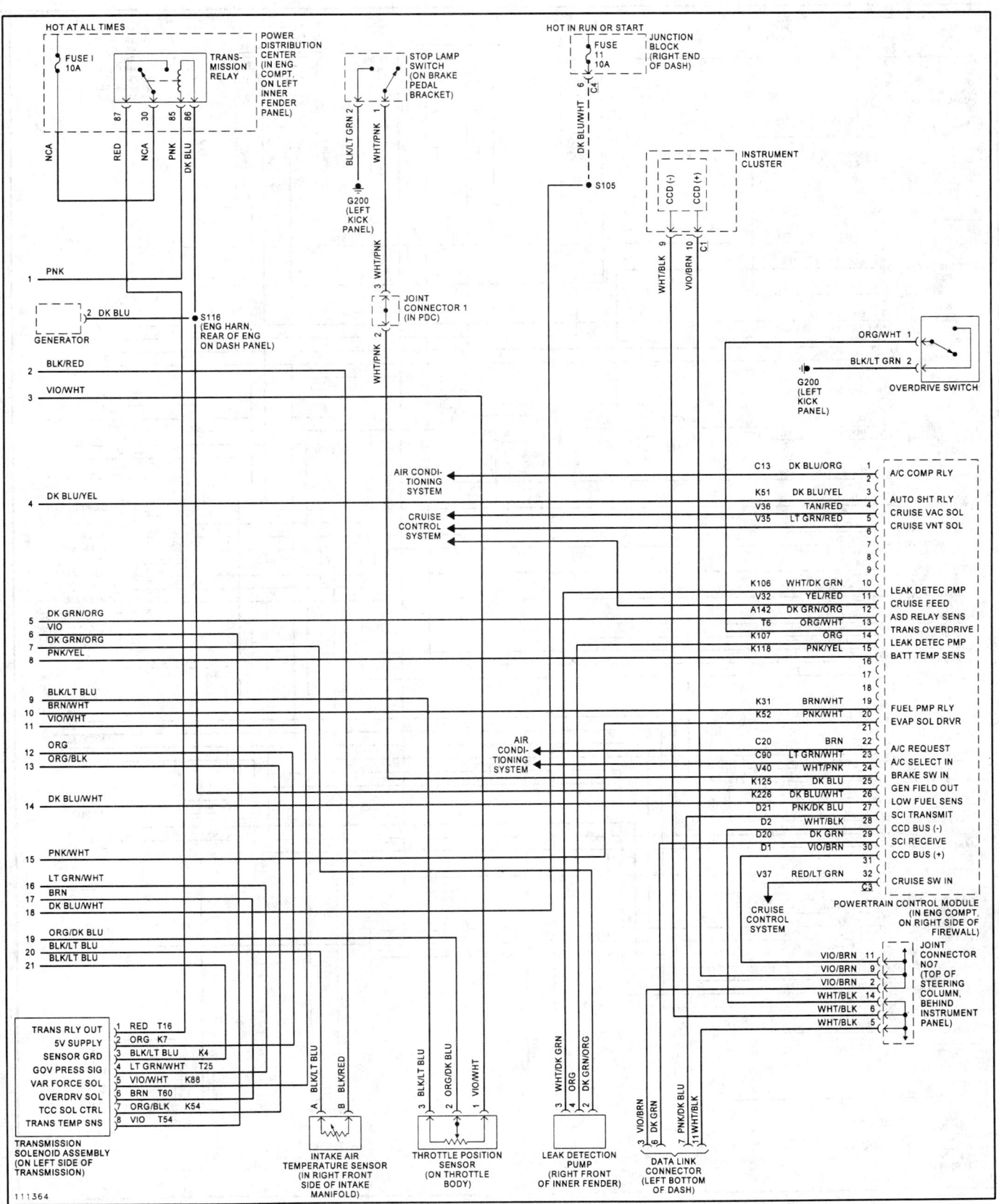

Fig. 48: PCM Wiring Diagram (Ram Pickup – 2500 & 3500 – 8.0L – 3 Of 3)

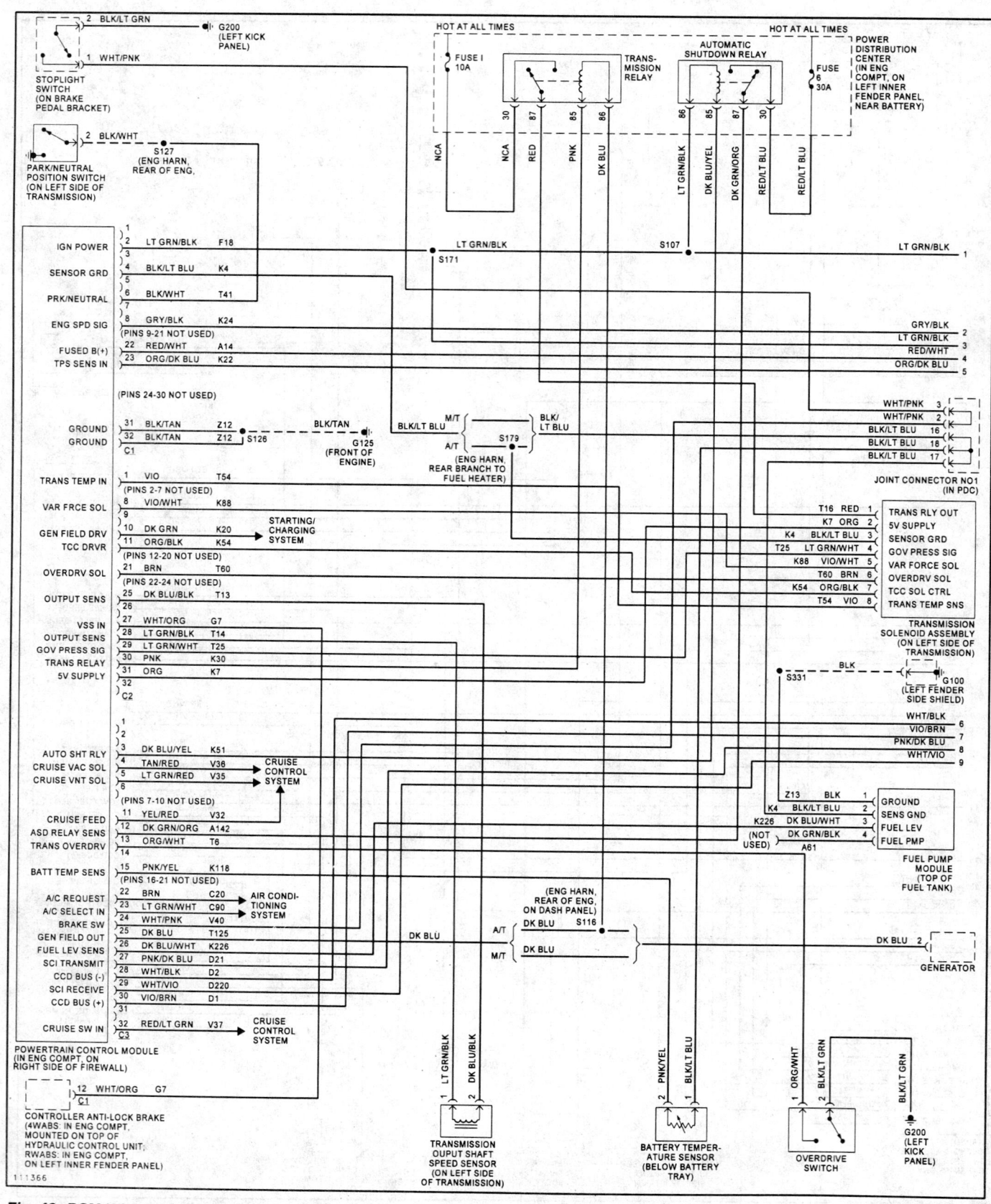

Fig. 49: PCM Wiring Diagram (Ram Pickup – 2500 & 3500 – 5.9L 24-Valve Diesel – 1 Of 3)

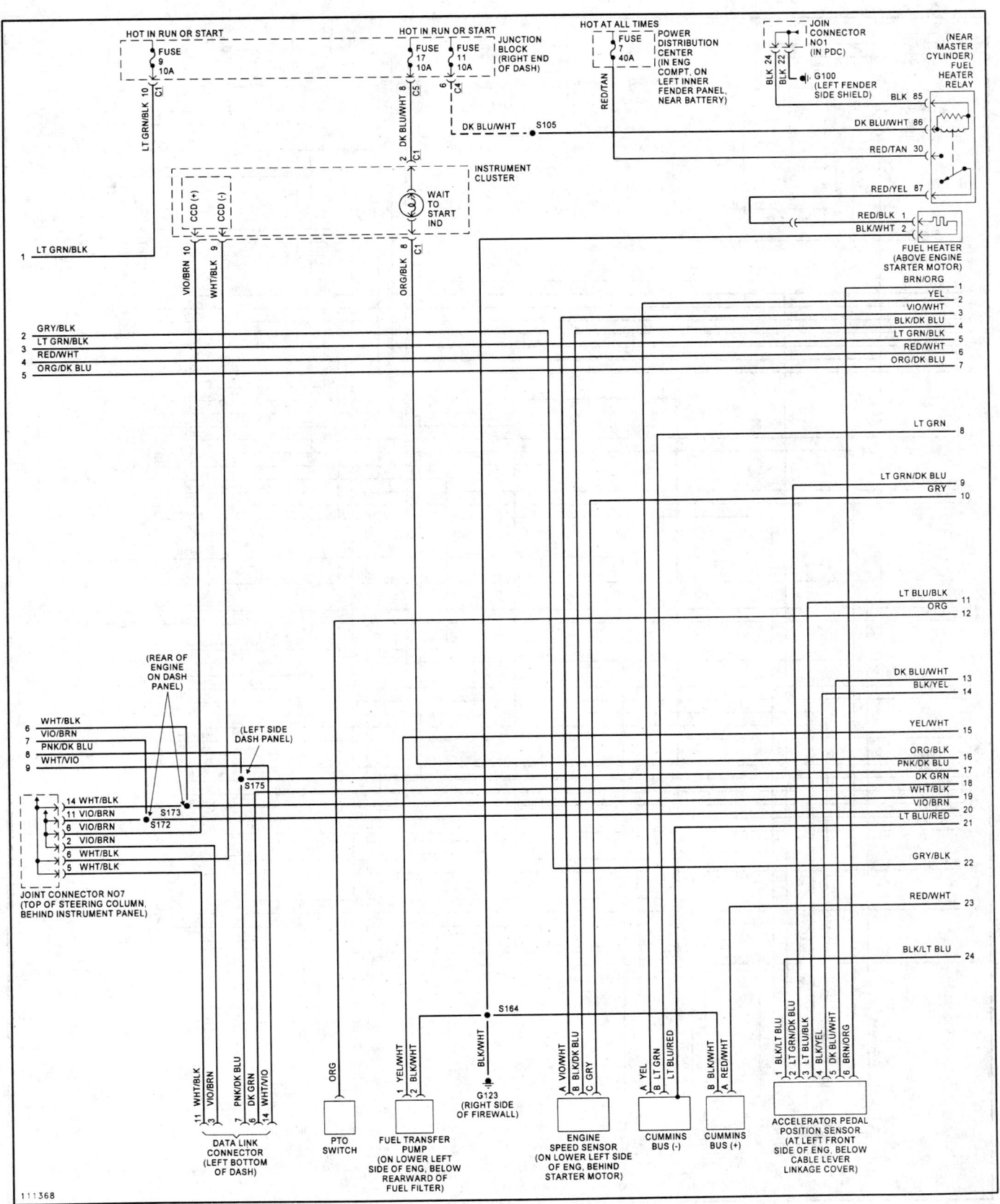

Fig. 50: PCM Wiring Diagram (Ram Pickup – 2500 & 3500 – 5.9L 24-Valve Diesel – 2 Of 3)

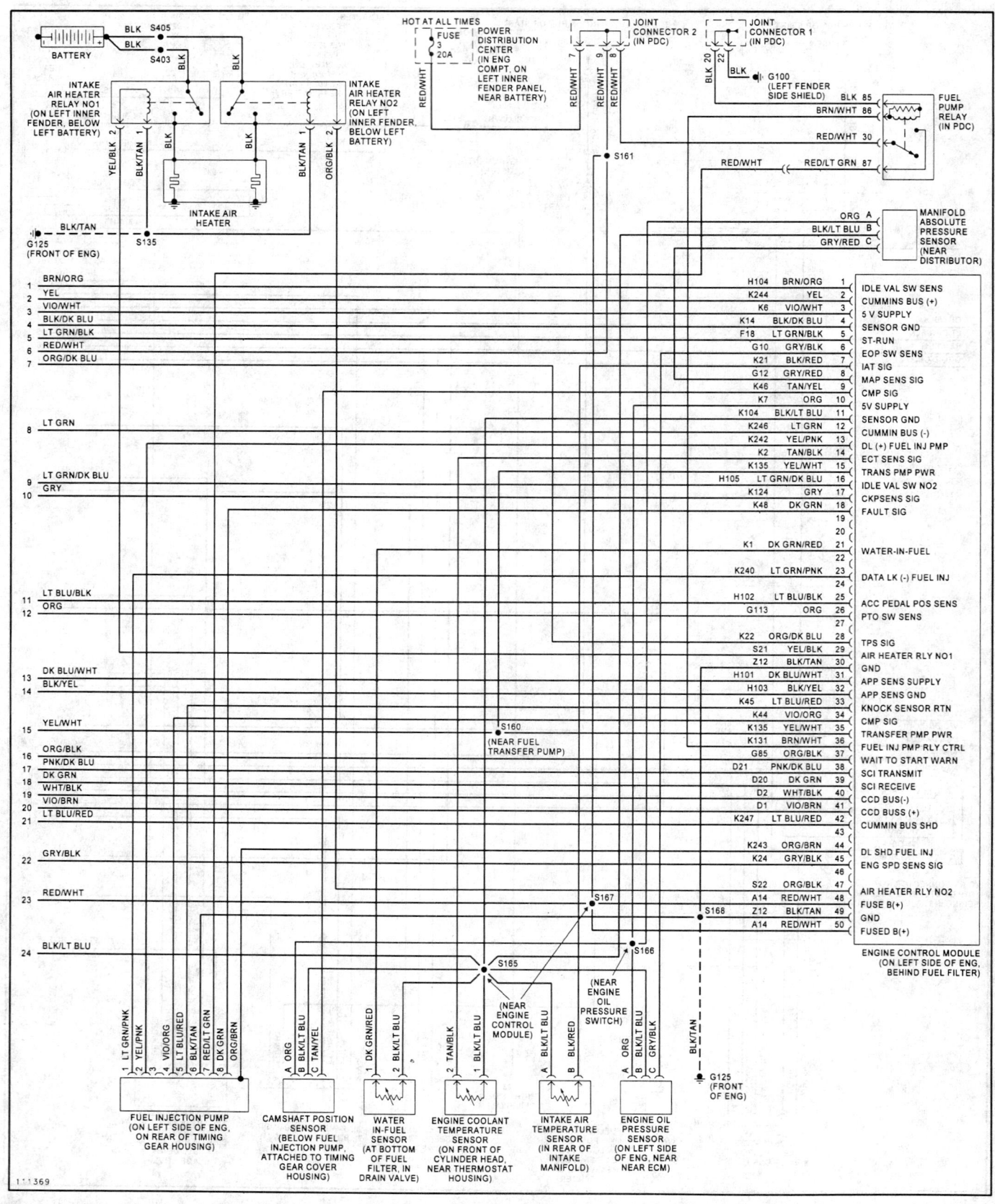

Fig. 51: PCM Wiring Diagram (Ram Pickup – 2500 & 3500 – 5.9L 24-Valve Diesel – 3 Of 3)

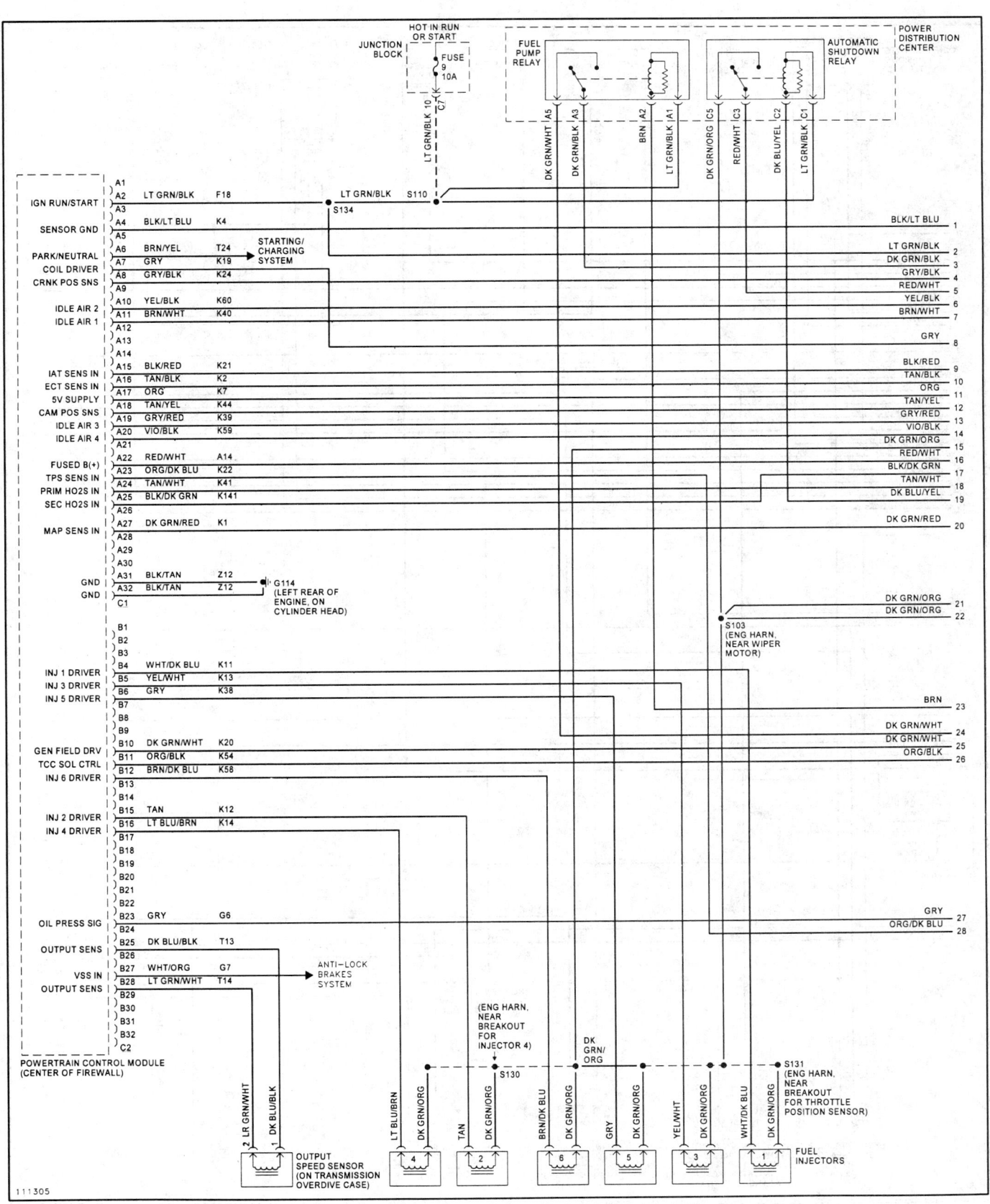

Fig. 52: PCM Wiring Diagram (Ram Van & Ram Wagon – 1500 – 3.9L – 1 Of 3)

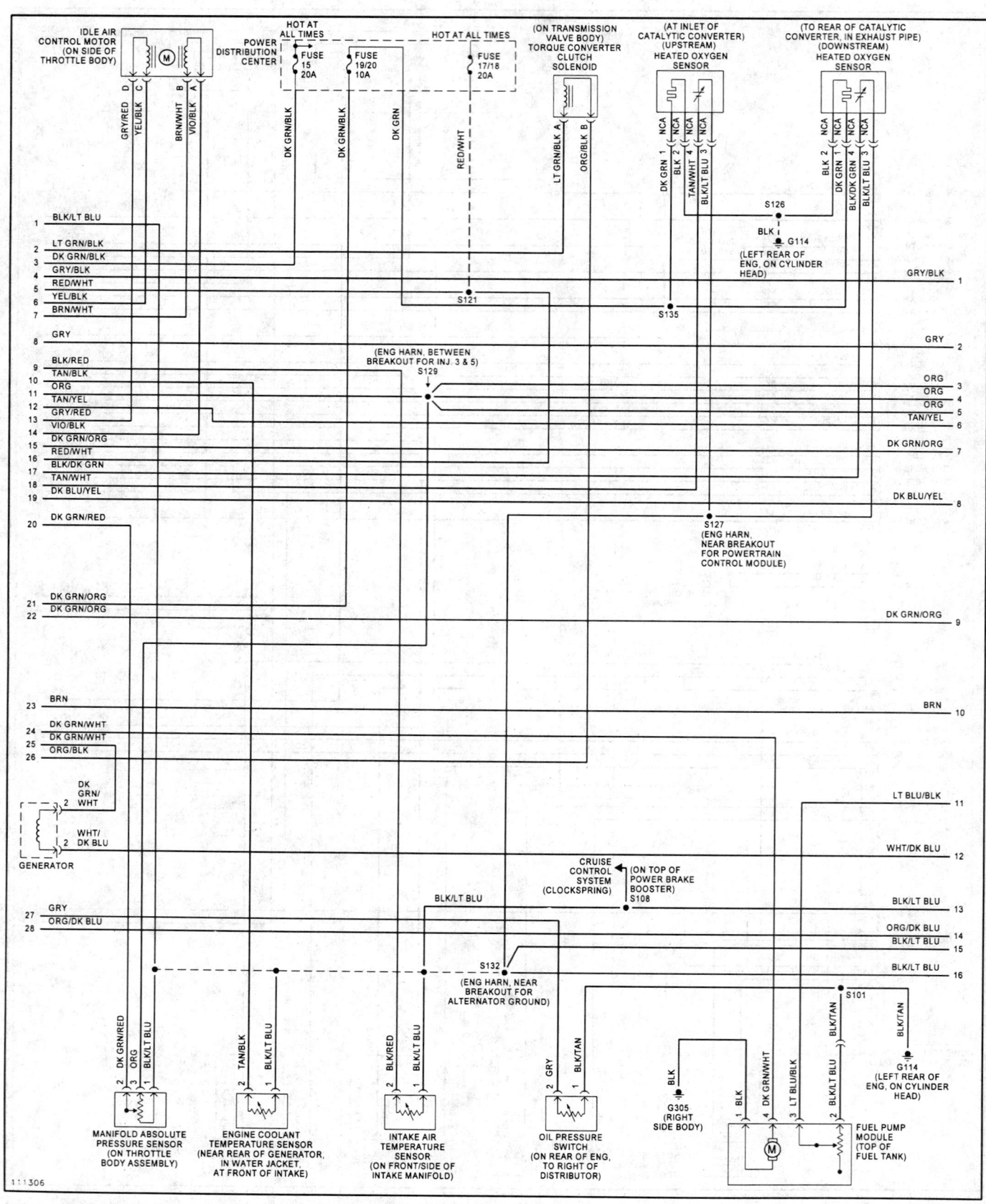

Fig. 53: PCM Wiring Diagram (Ram Van & Ram Wagon – 1500 – 3.9L – 2 Of 3)

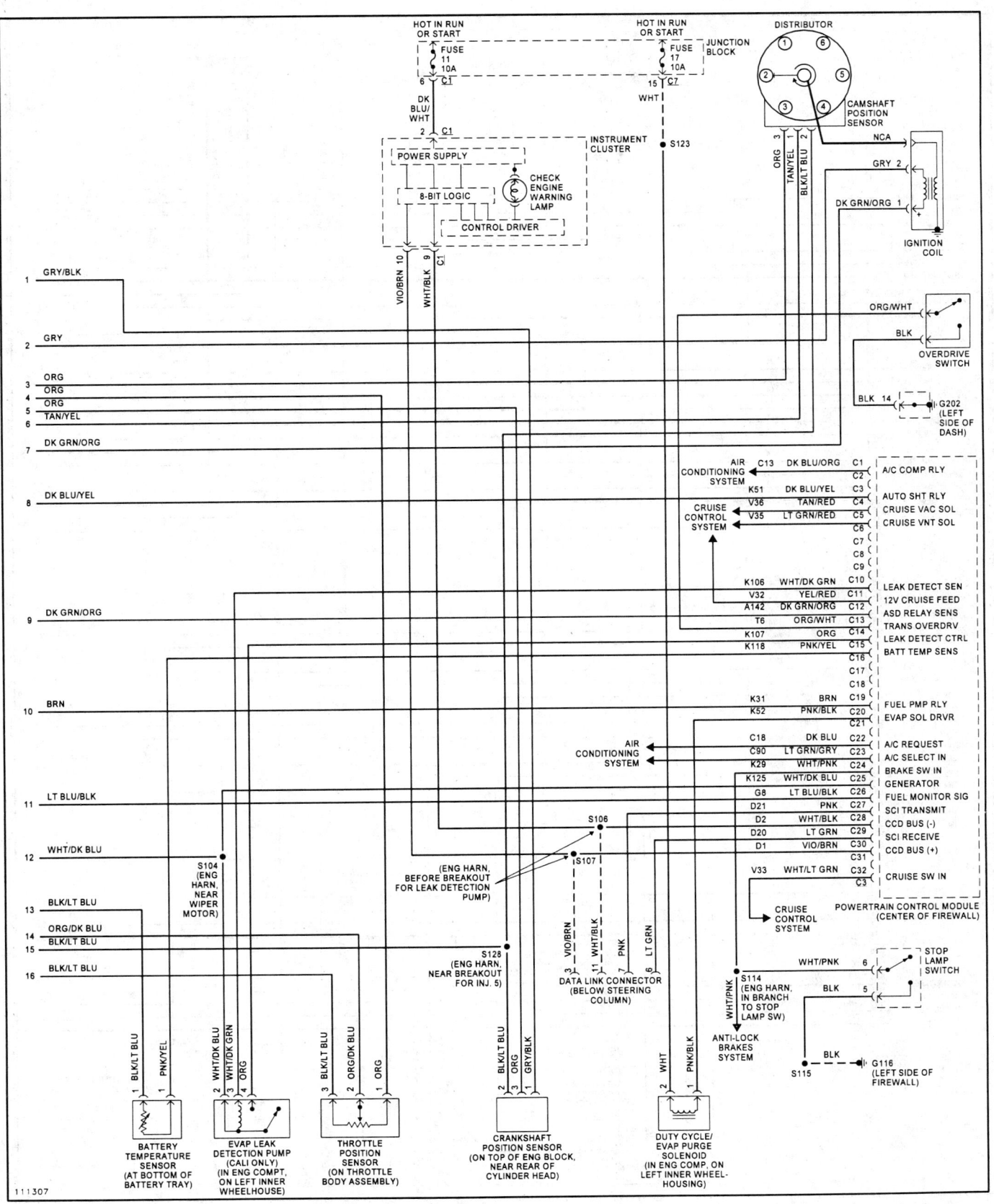

Fig. 54: PCM Wiring Diagram (Ram Van & Ram Wagon – 1500 – 3.9L – 3 Of 3)

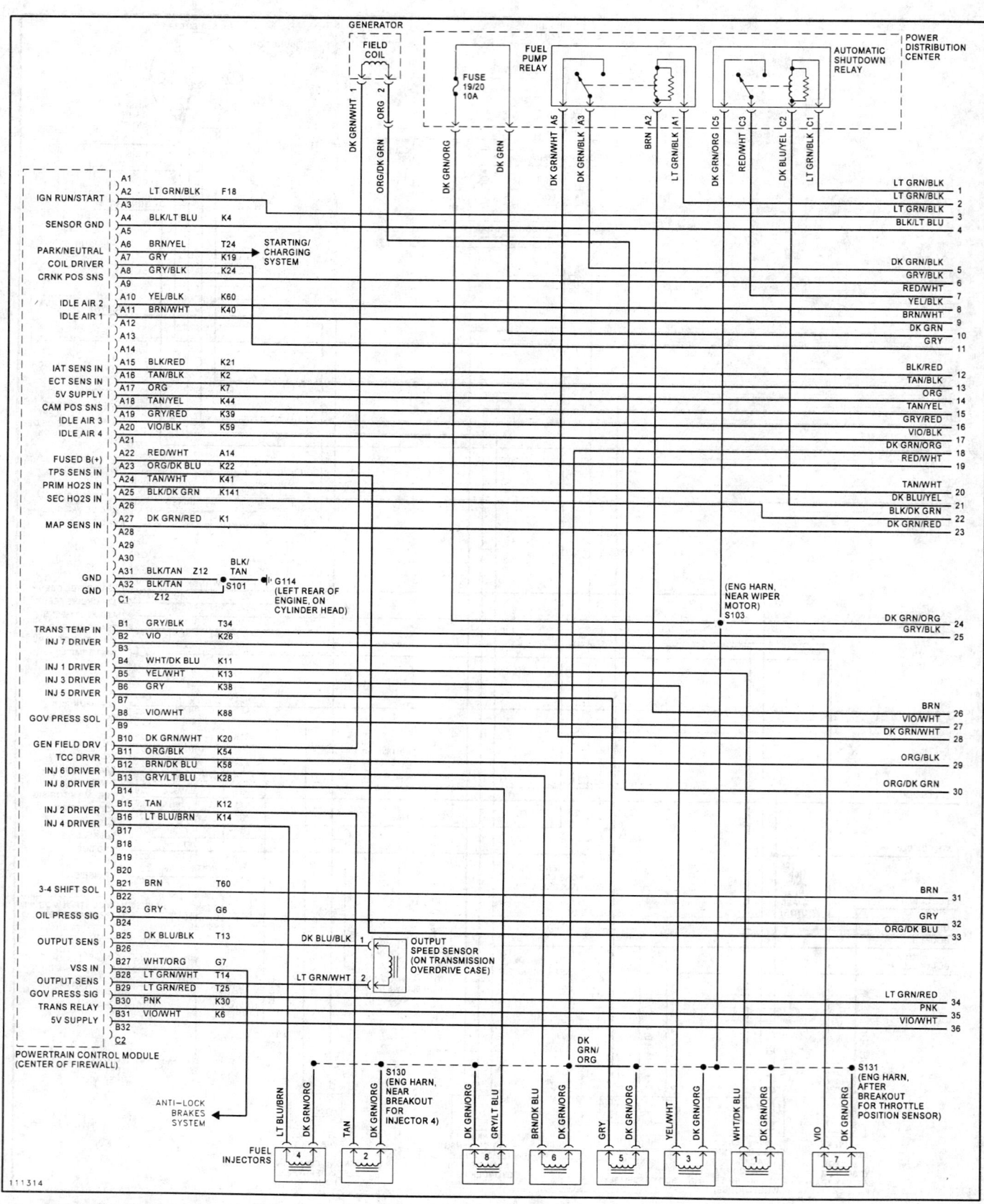

Fig. 55: PCM Wiring Diagram (Ram Van & Ram Wagon – 5.2L Gasoline & 5.9L – 1 Of 3)

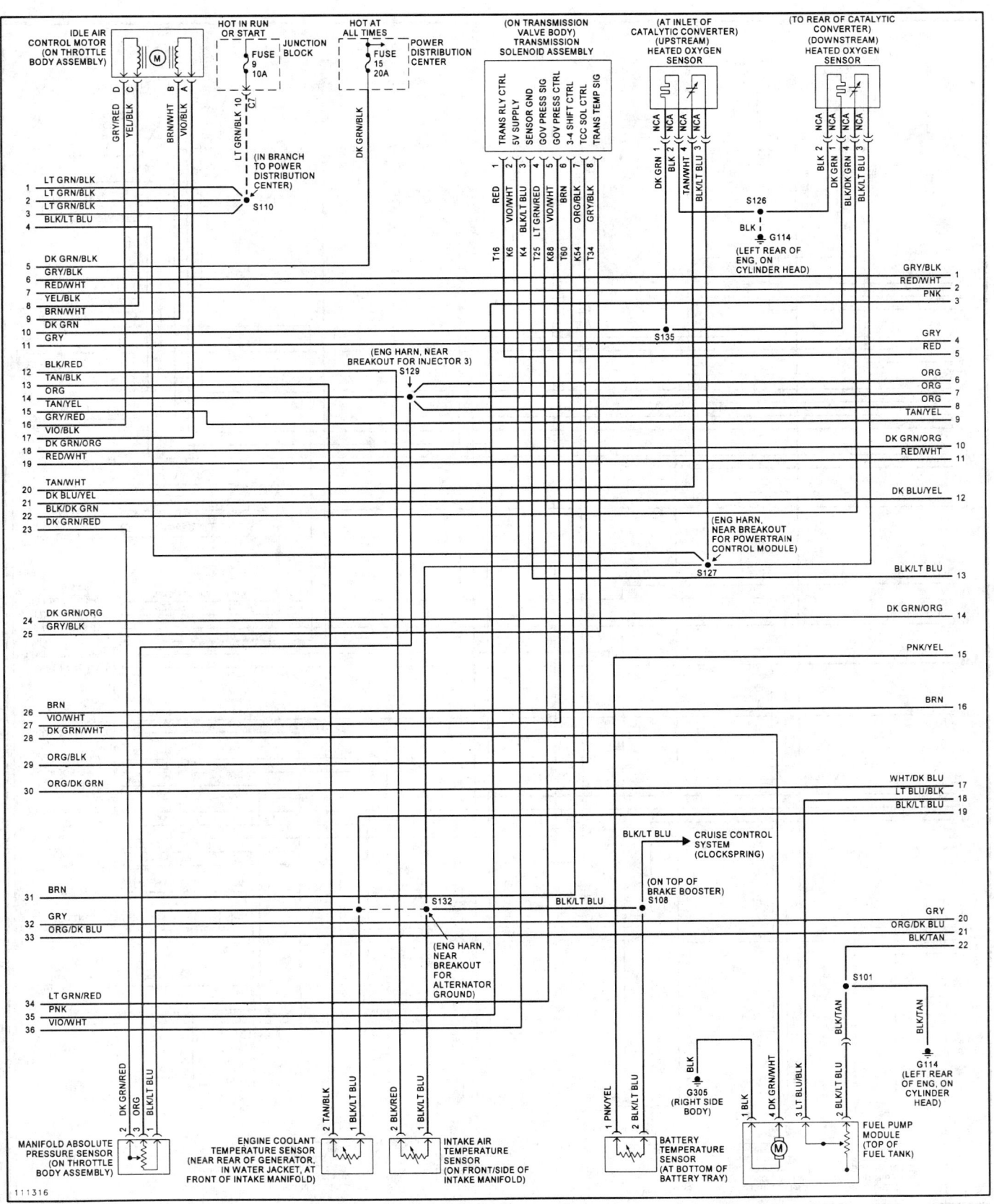

Fig. 56: PCM Wiring Diagram (Ram Van & Ram Wagon – 5.2L Gasoline & 5.9L – 2 Of 3)

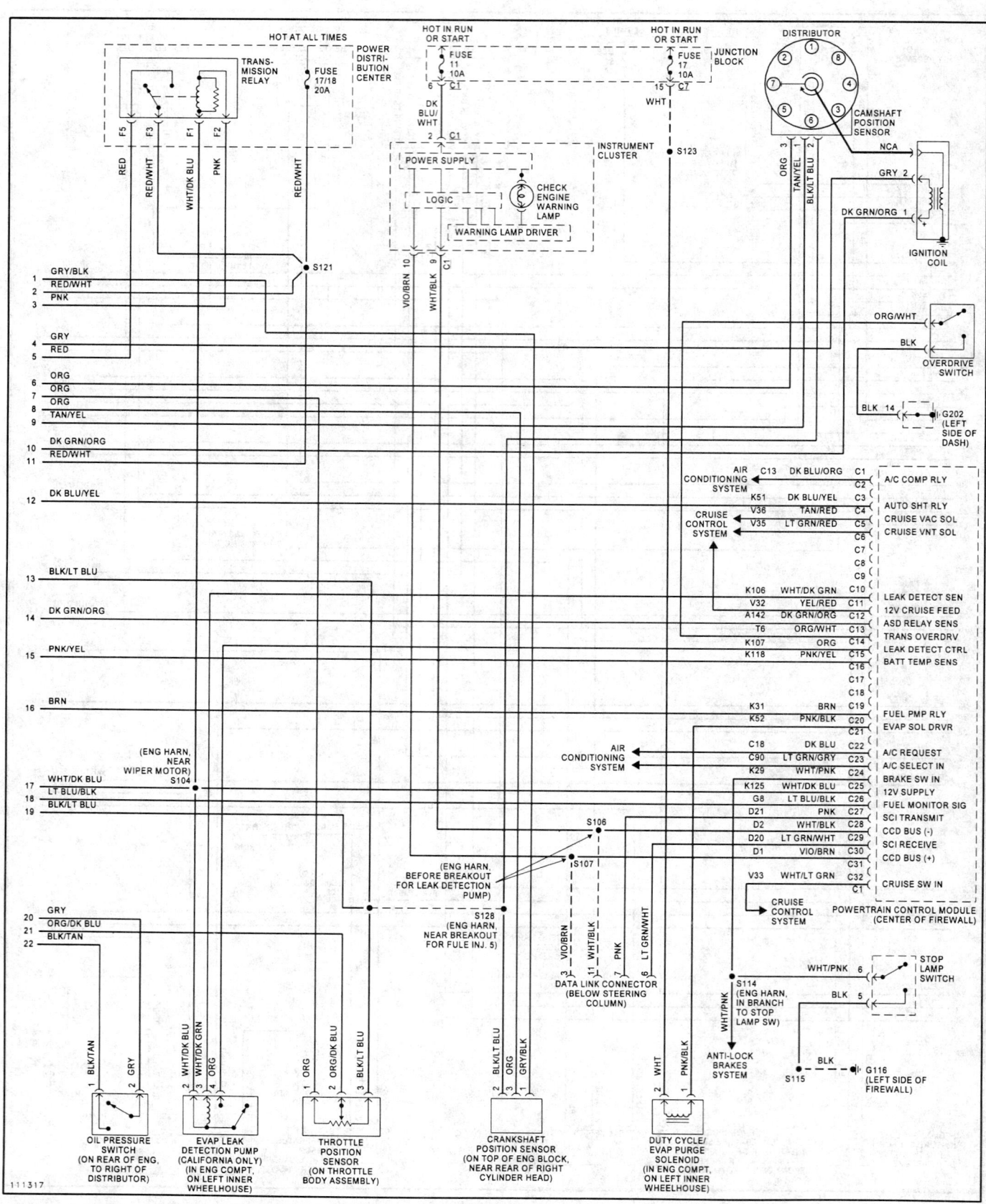

Fig. 57: PCM Wiring Diagram (Ram Van & Ram Wagon – 5.2L Gasoline & 5.9L – 3 Of 3)

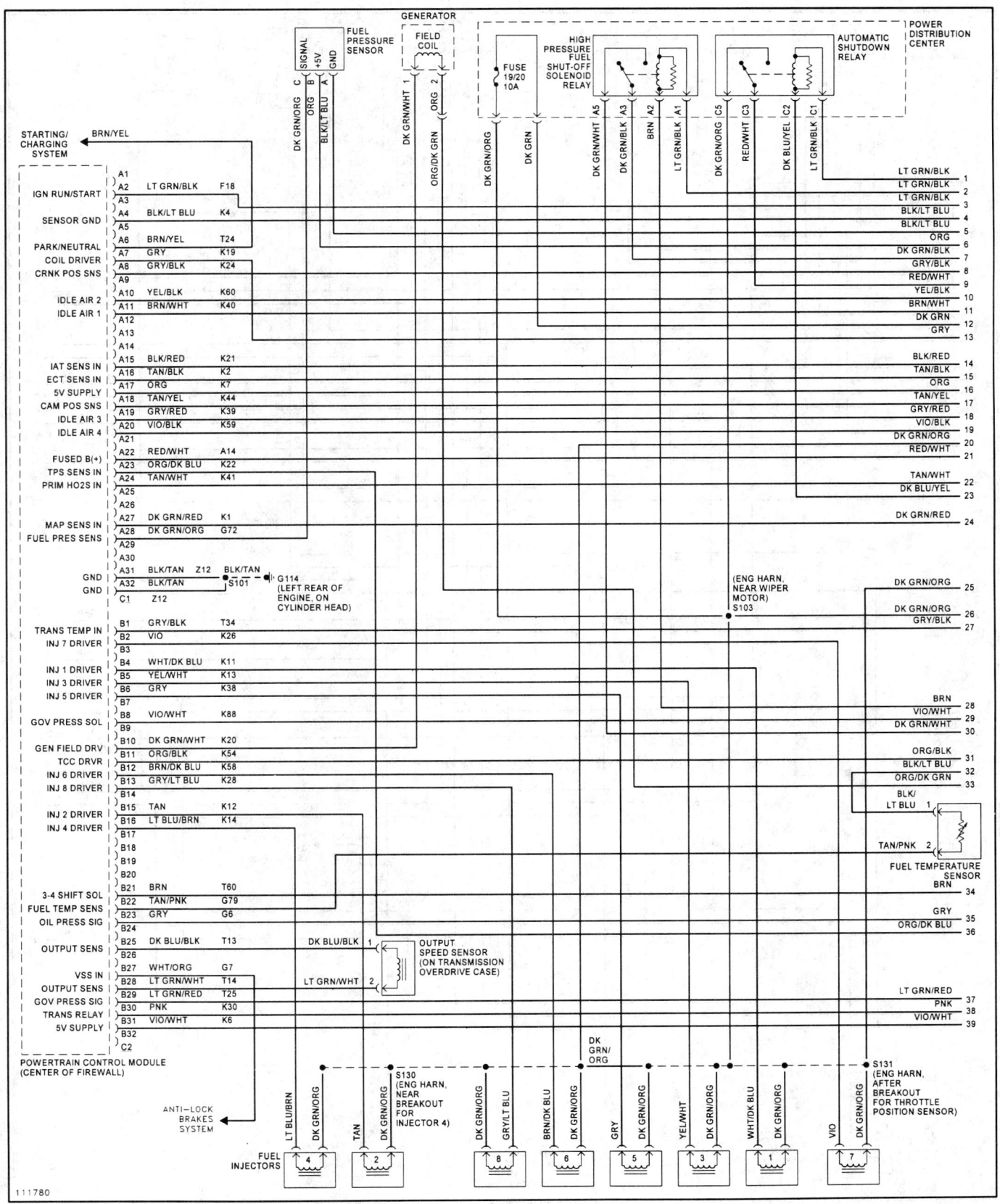

Fig. 58: PCM Wiring Diagram (Ram Van & Ram Wagon – 5.2L CNG – 1 Of 3)

111780

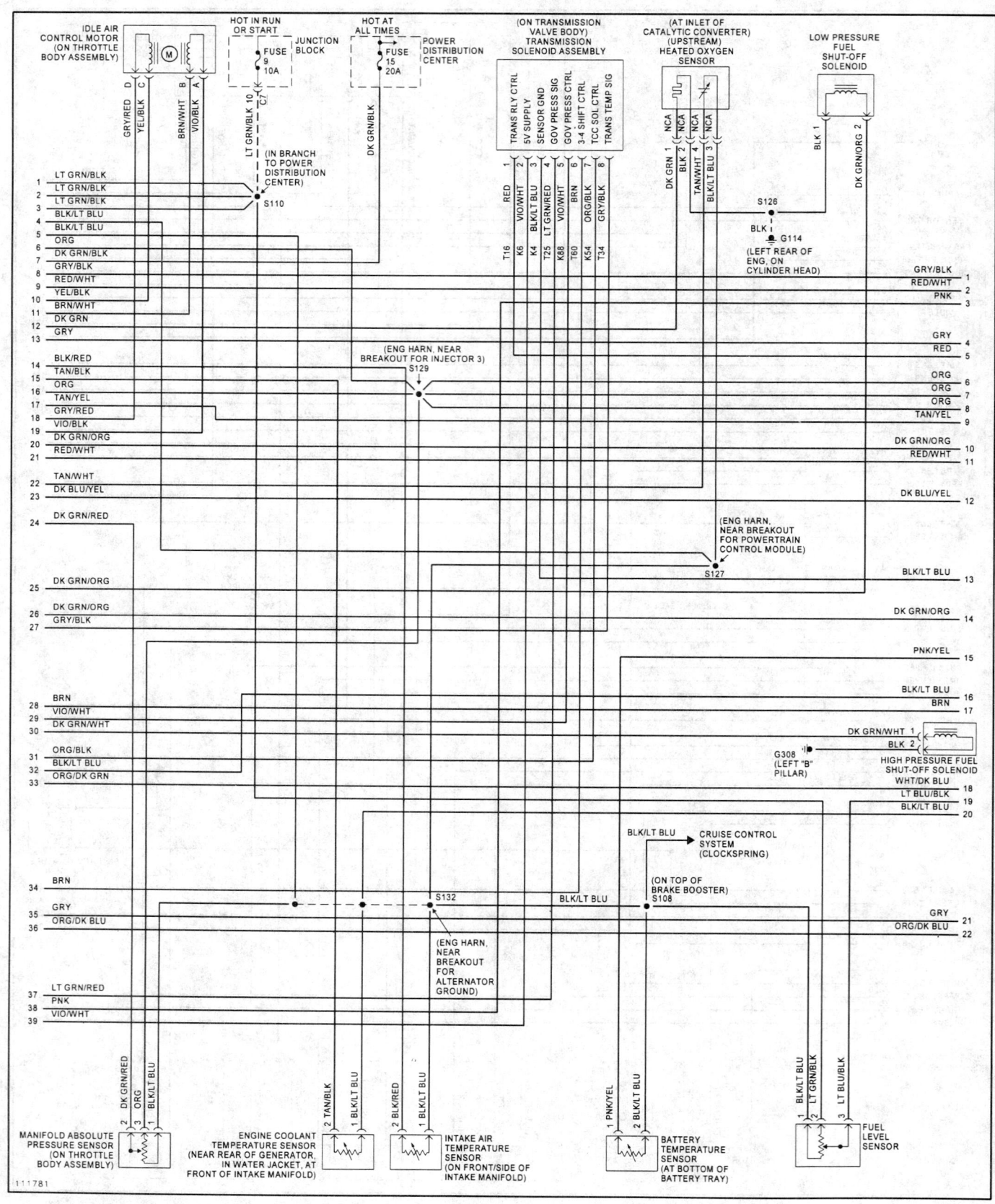

Fig. 59: PCM Wiring Diagram (Ram Van & Ram Wagon – 5.2L CNG – 2 Of 3)

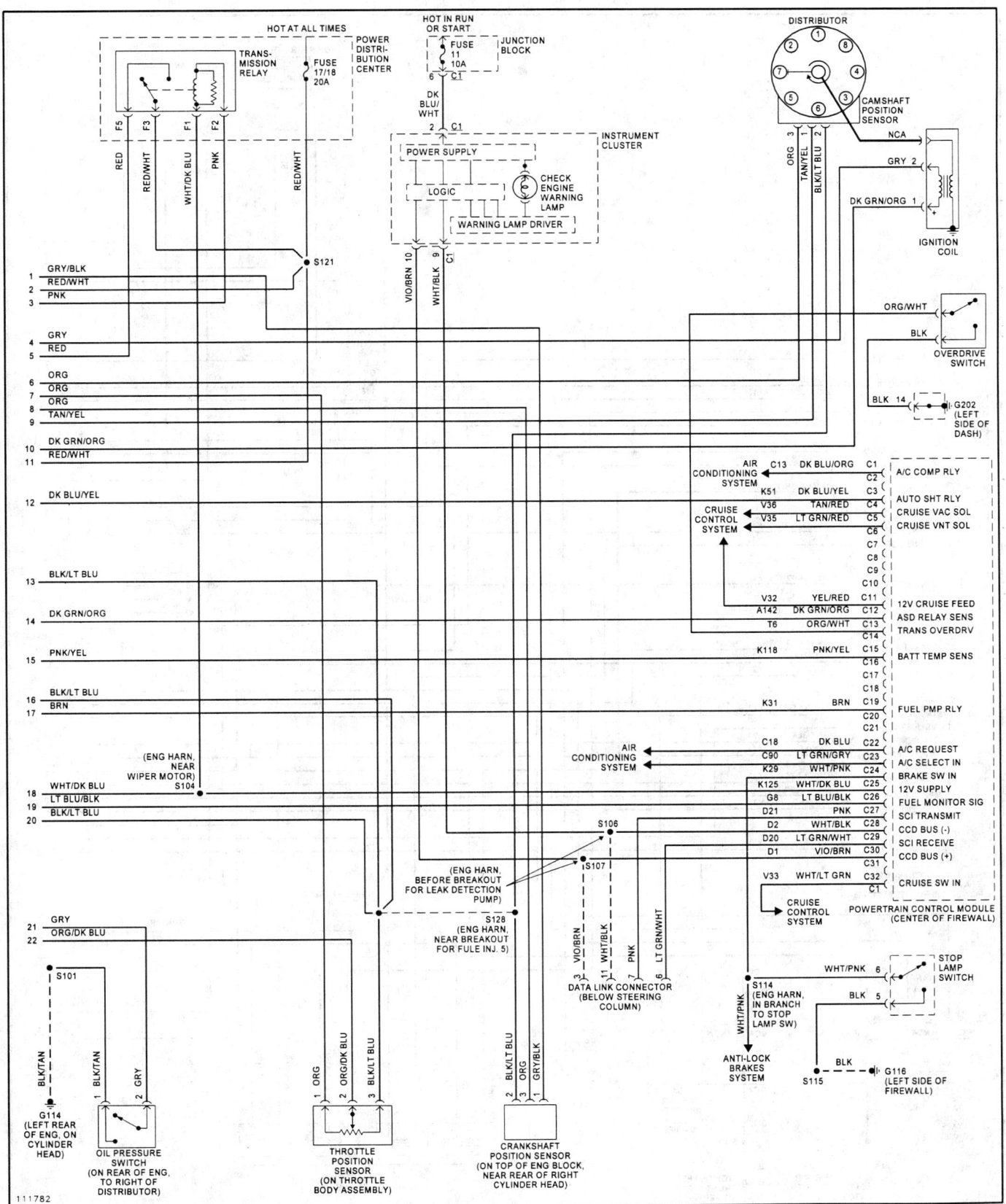

Fig. 60: PCM Wiring Diagram (Ram Van & Ram Wagon – 5.2L CNG – 3 Of 3)

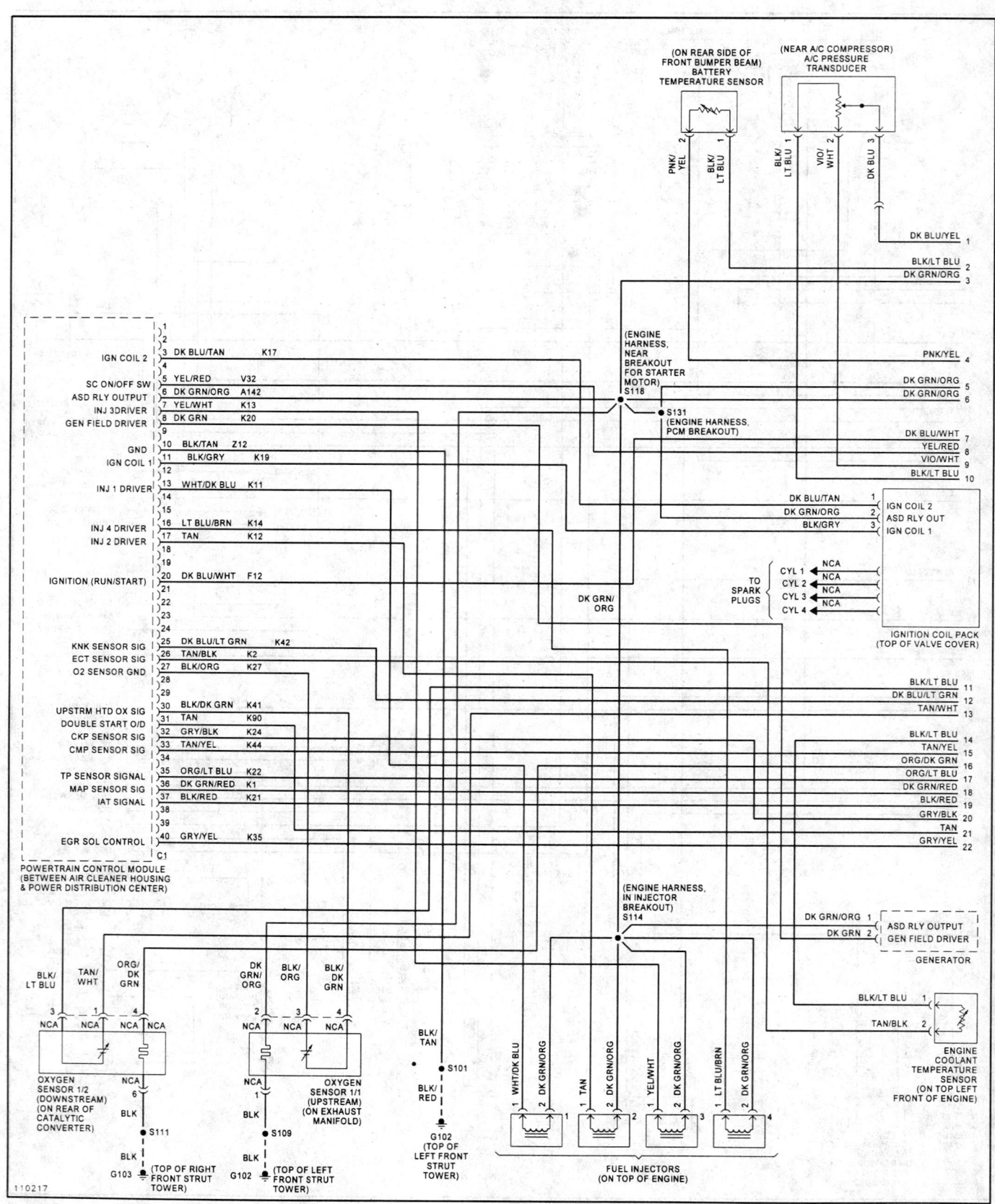

Fig. 61: PCM Wiring Diagram (Sebring Convertible – 2.4L – 1 Of 4)

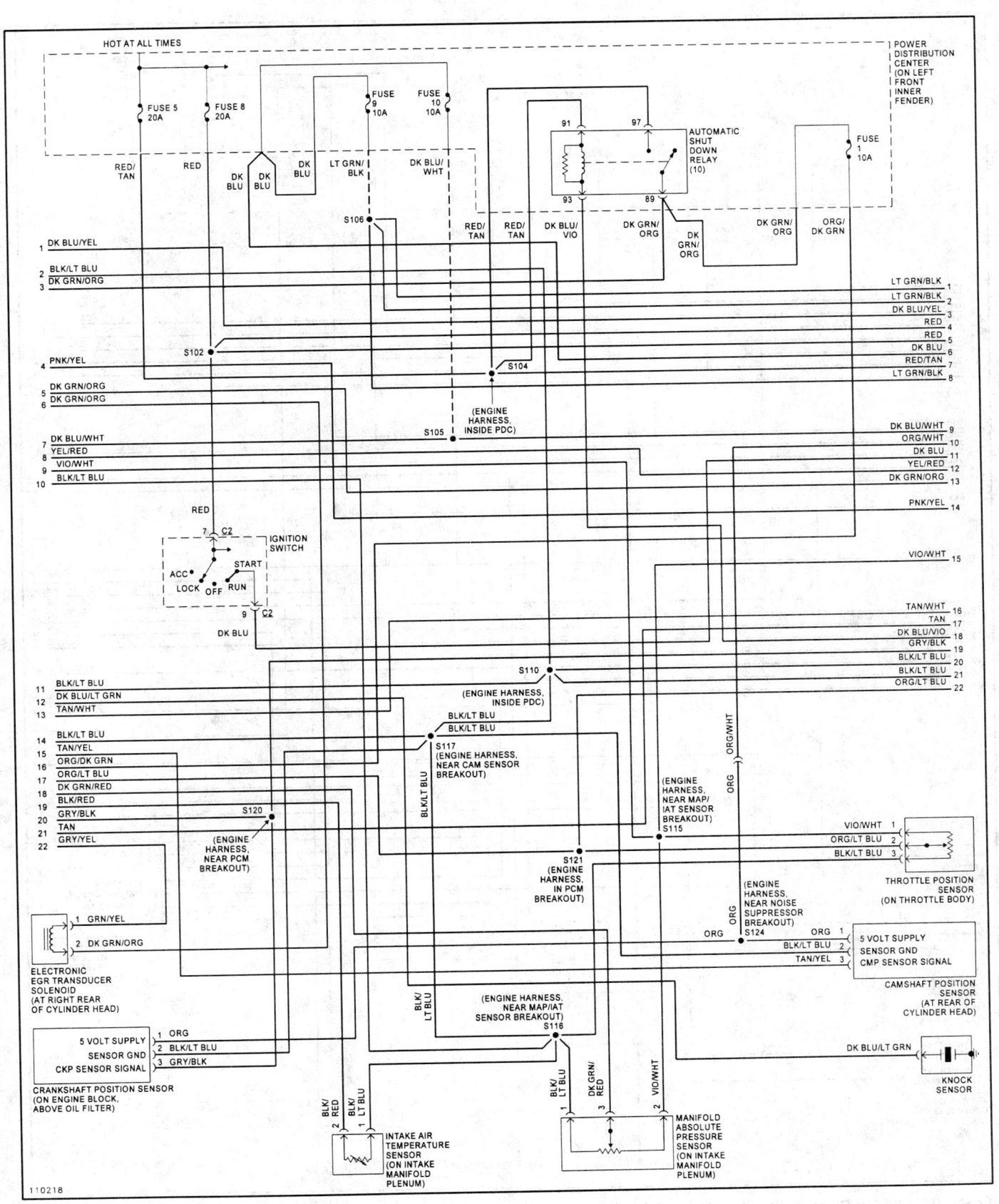

Fig. 62: PCM Wiring Diagram (Sebring Convertible – 2.4L – 2 Of 4)

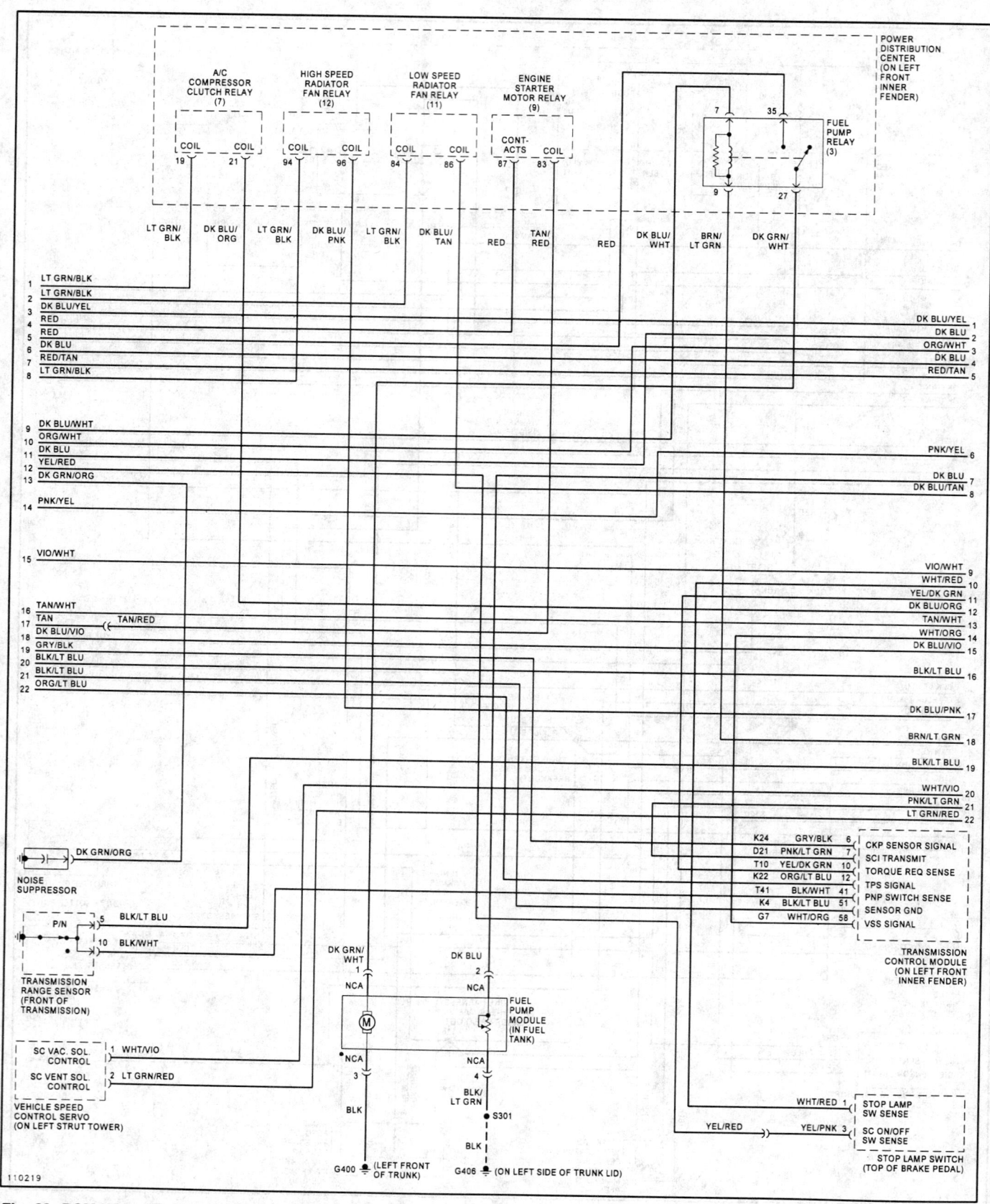

Fig. 63: PCM Wiring Diagram (Sebring Convertible – 2.4L – 3 Of 4)

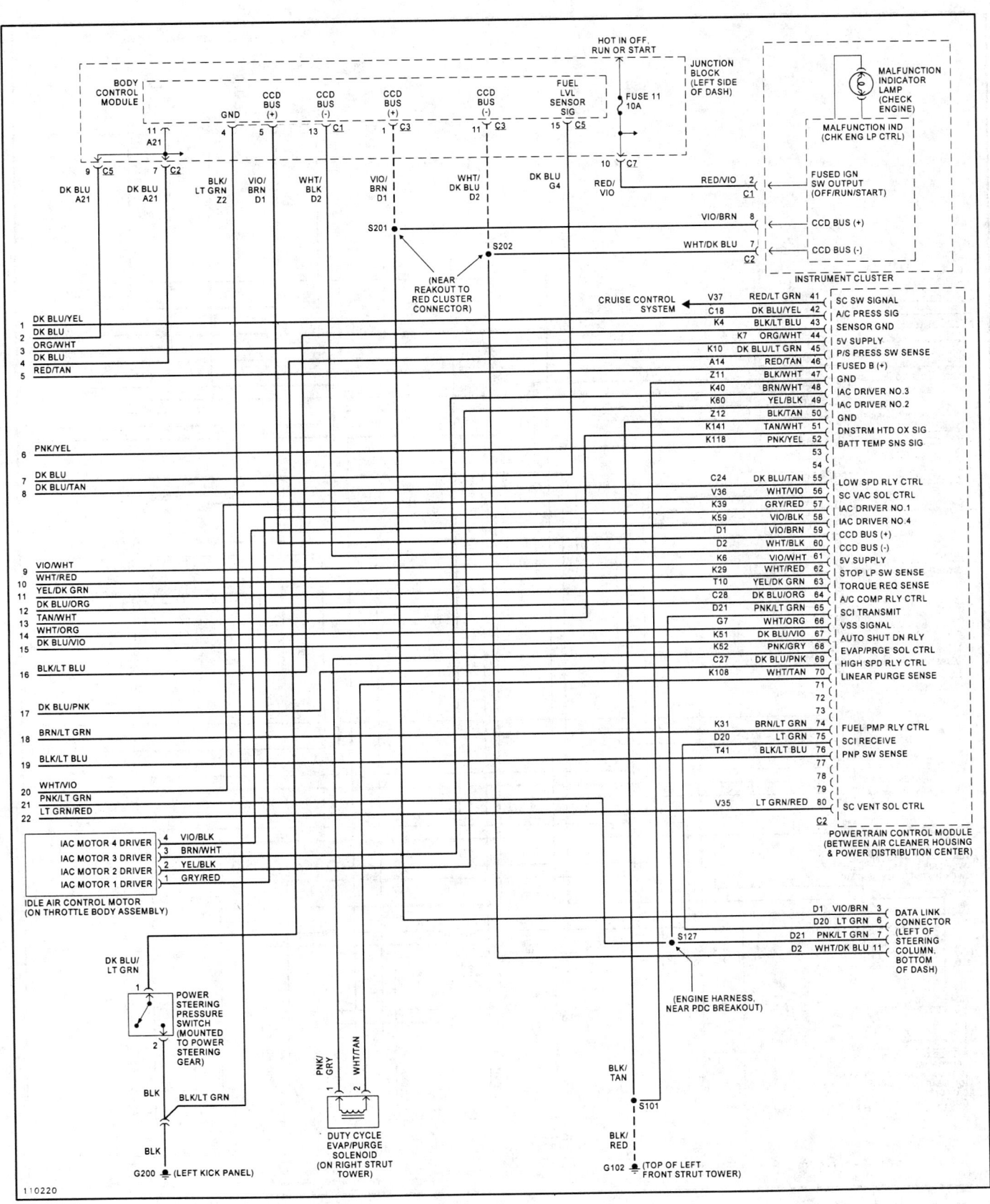

Fig. 64: PCM Wiring Diagram (Sebring Convertible – 2.4L – 4 Of 4)

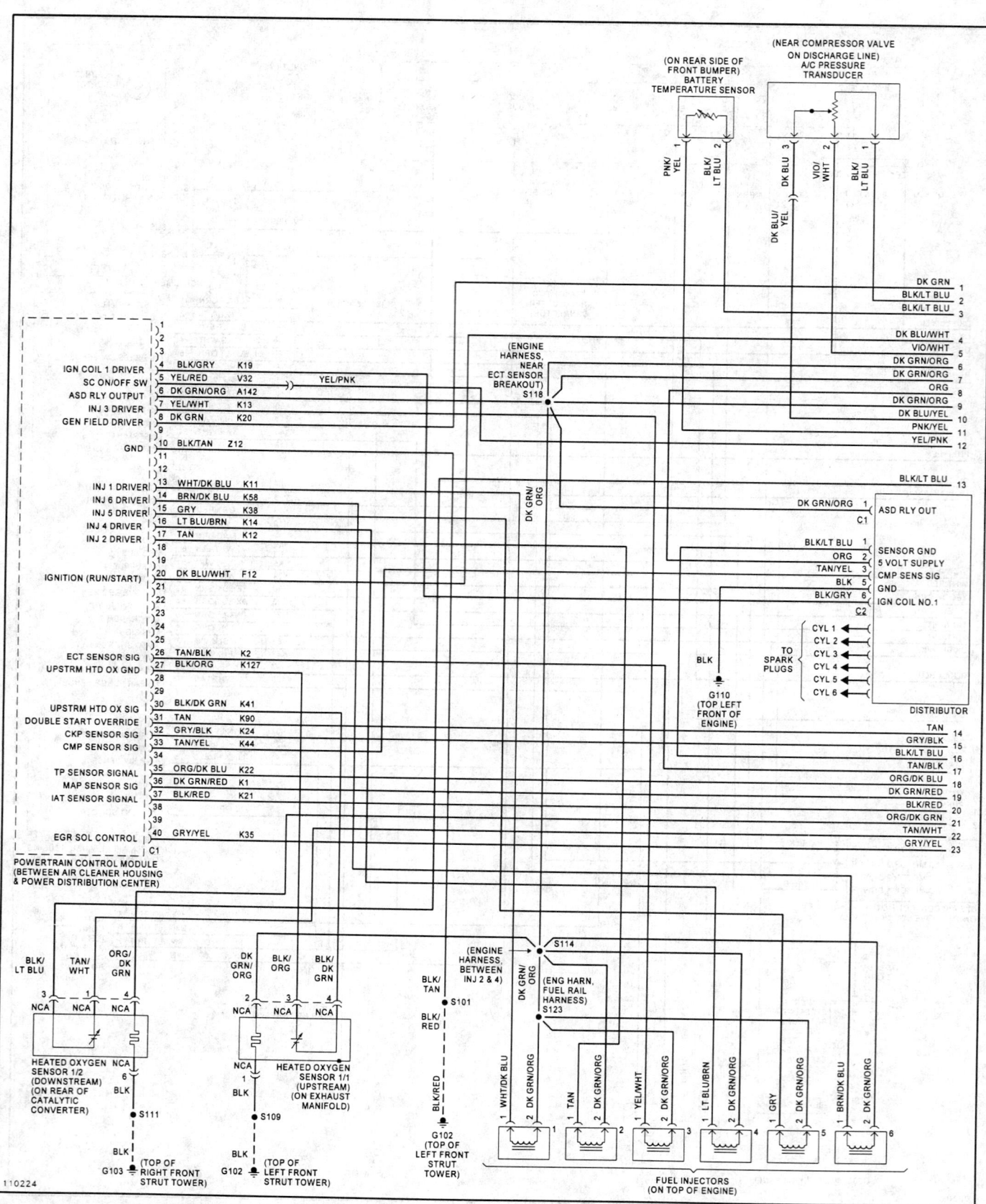

Fig. 65: PCM Wiring Diagram (Sebring Convertible – 2.5L – 1 Of 4)

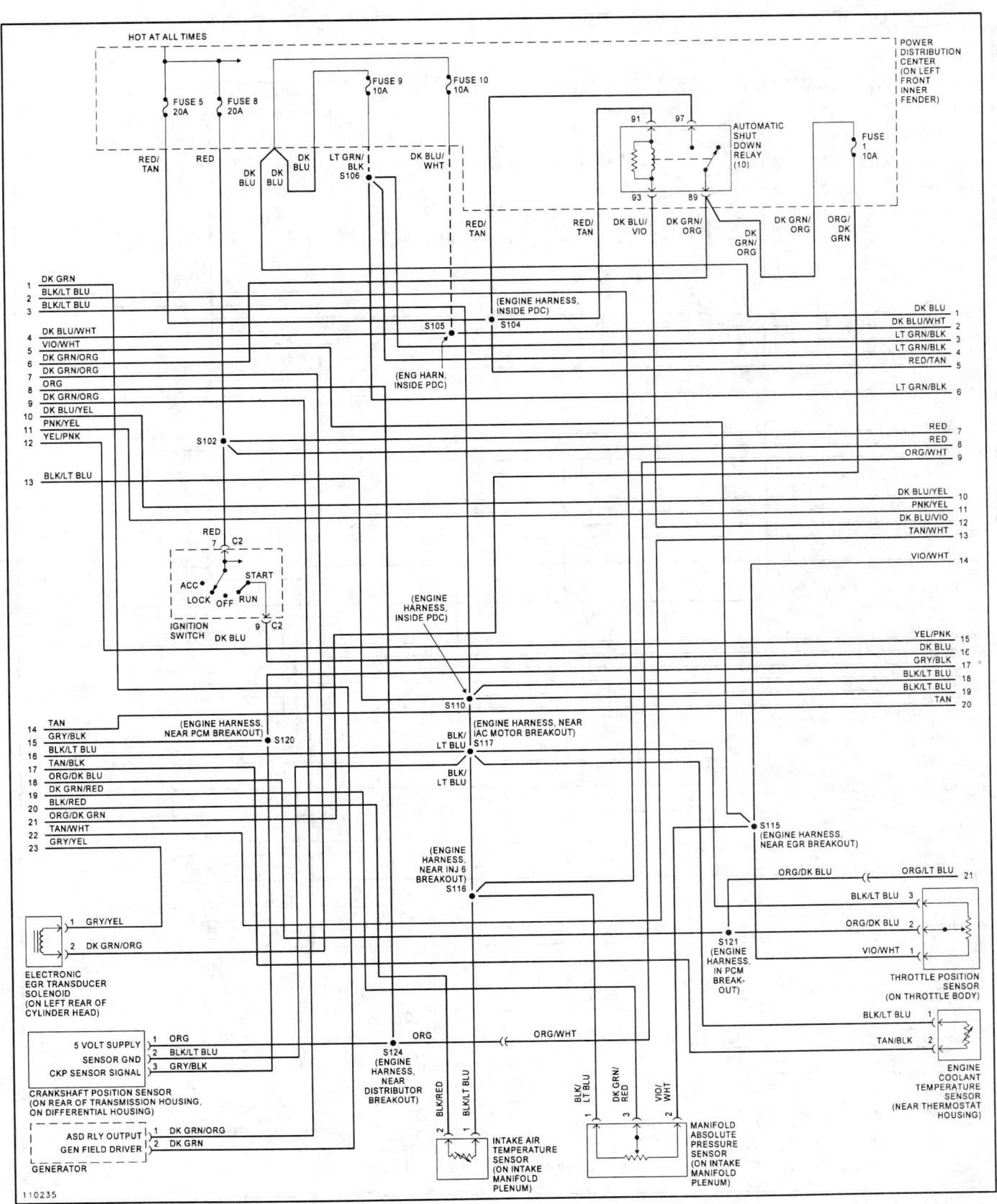

Fig. 66: PCM Wiring Diagram (Sebring Convertible – 2.5L – 2 Of 4)

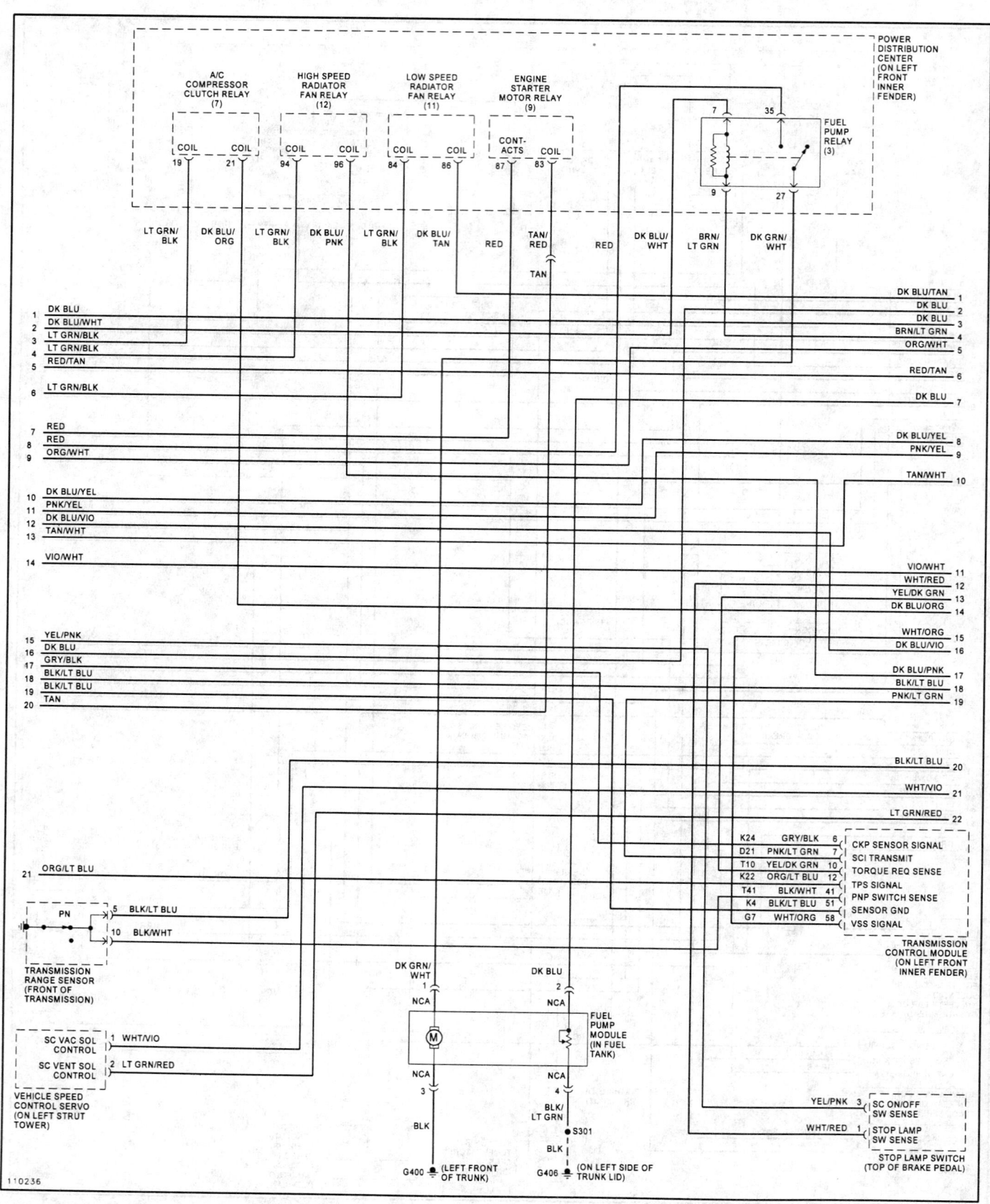

Fig. 67: PCM Wiring Diagram (Sebring Convertible – 2.5L – 3 Of 4)

110236

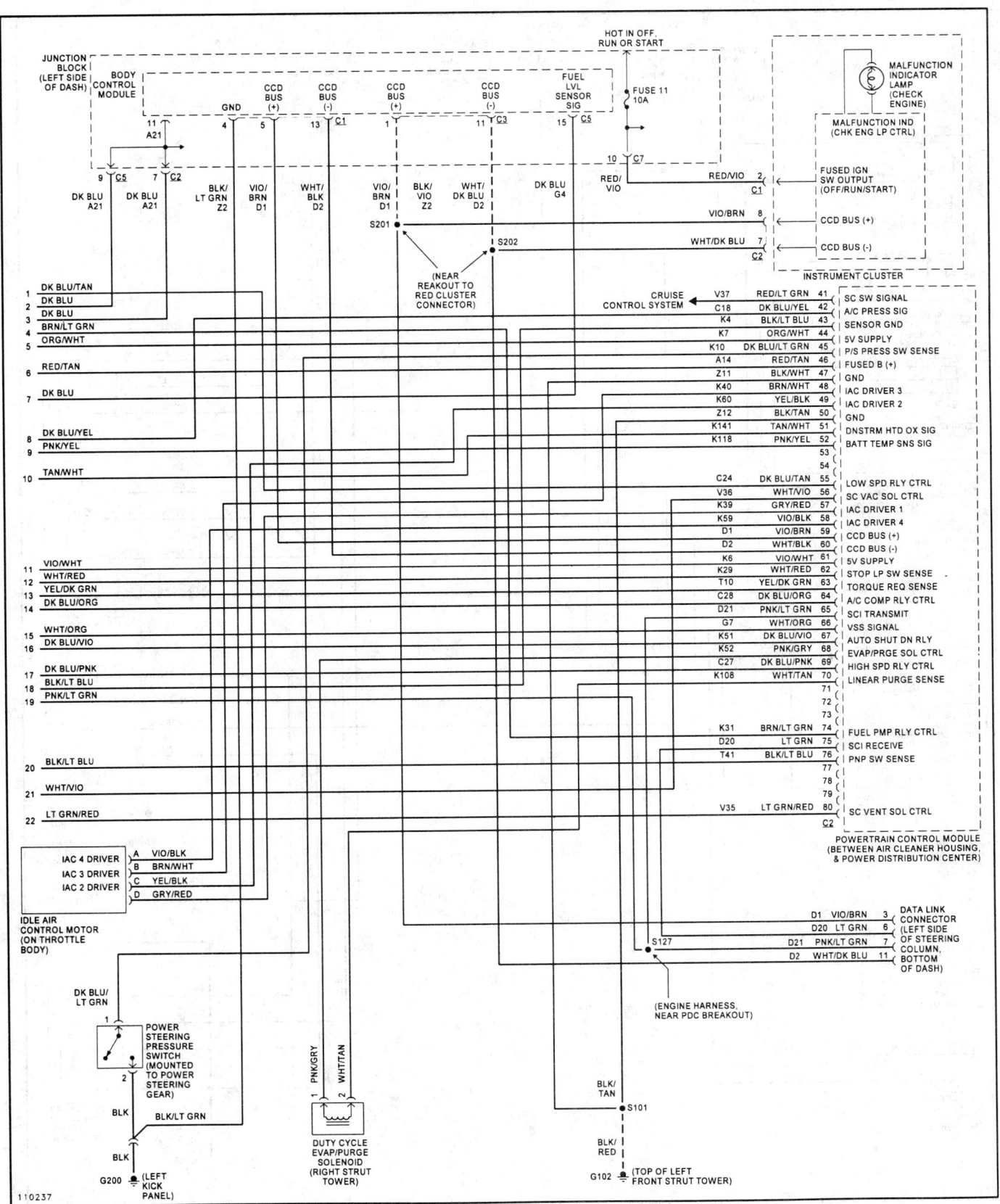

Fig. 68: PCM Wiring Diagram (Sebring Convertible – 2.5L – 4 Of 4)

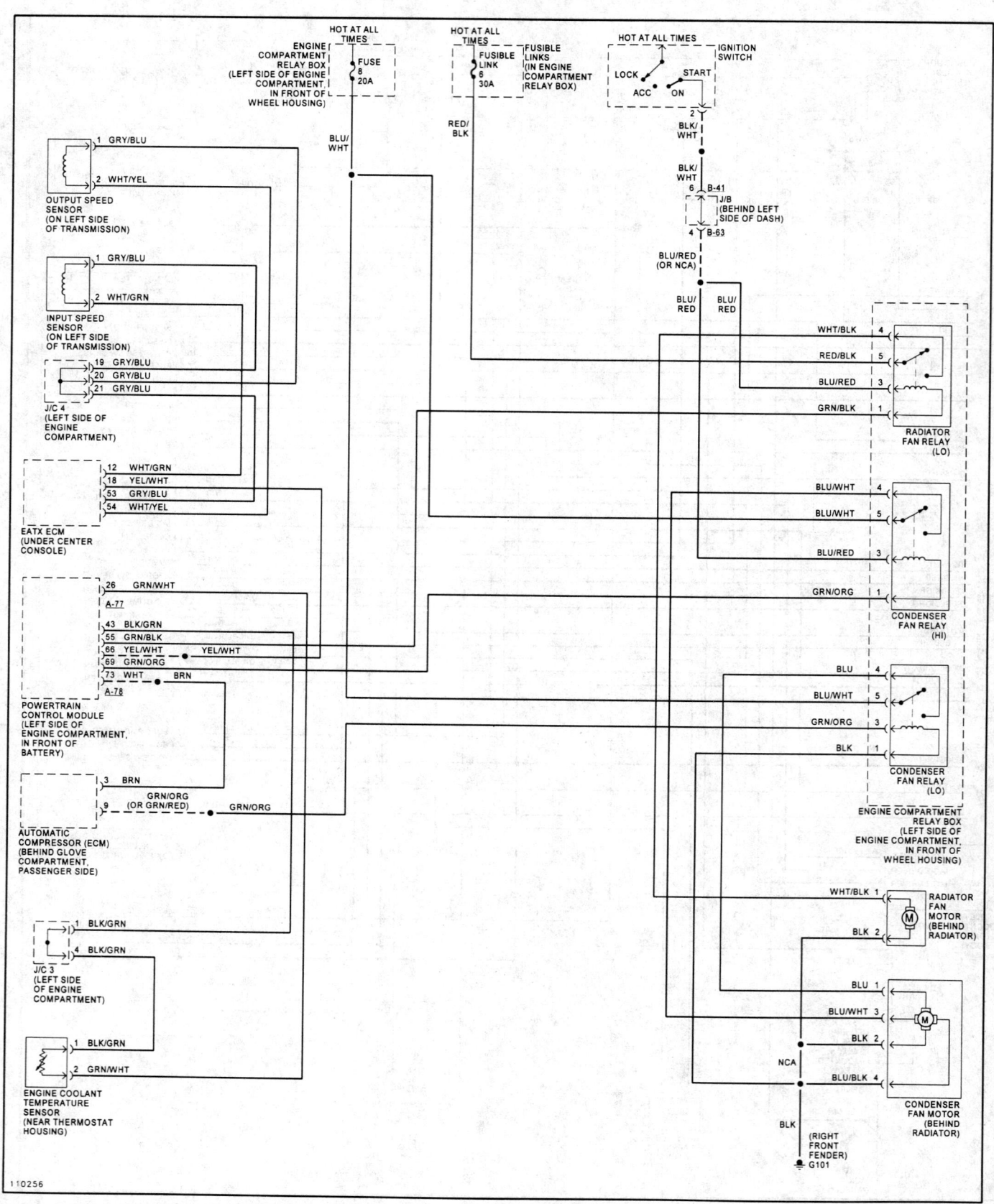

Fig. 1: Electric Cooling Fans Wiring Diagram (Avenger & Sebring Coupe – 2.0L With A/T)

110256

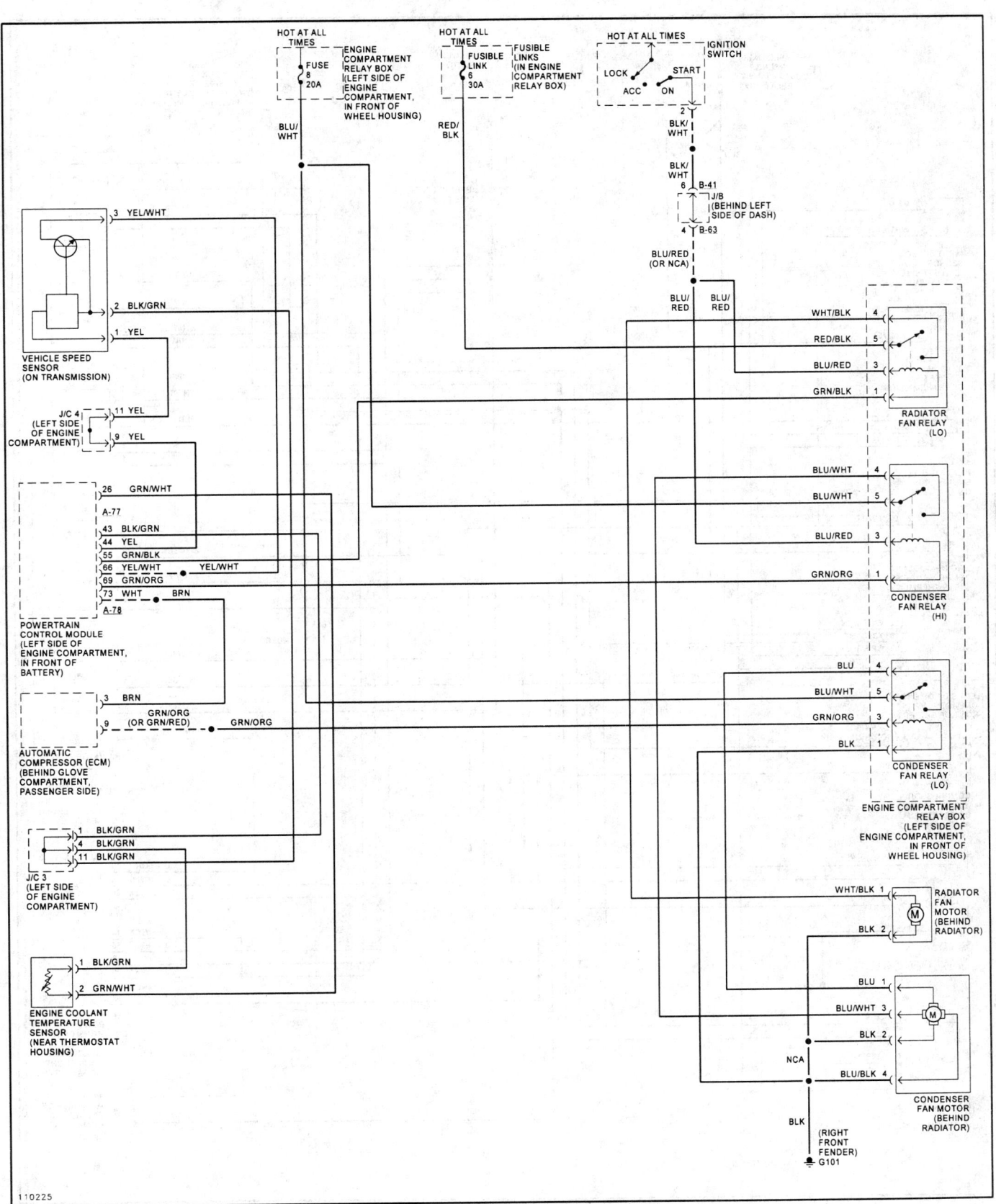

Fig. 2: Electric Cooling Fans Wiring Diagram (Avenger & Sebring Coupe – 2.0L With M/T)

110225

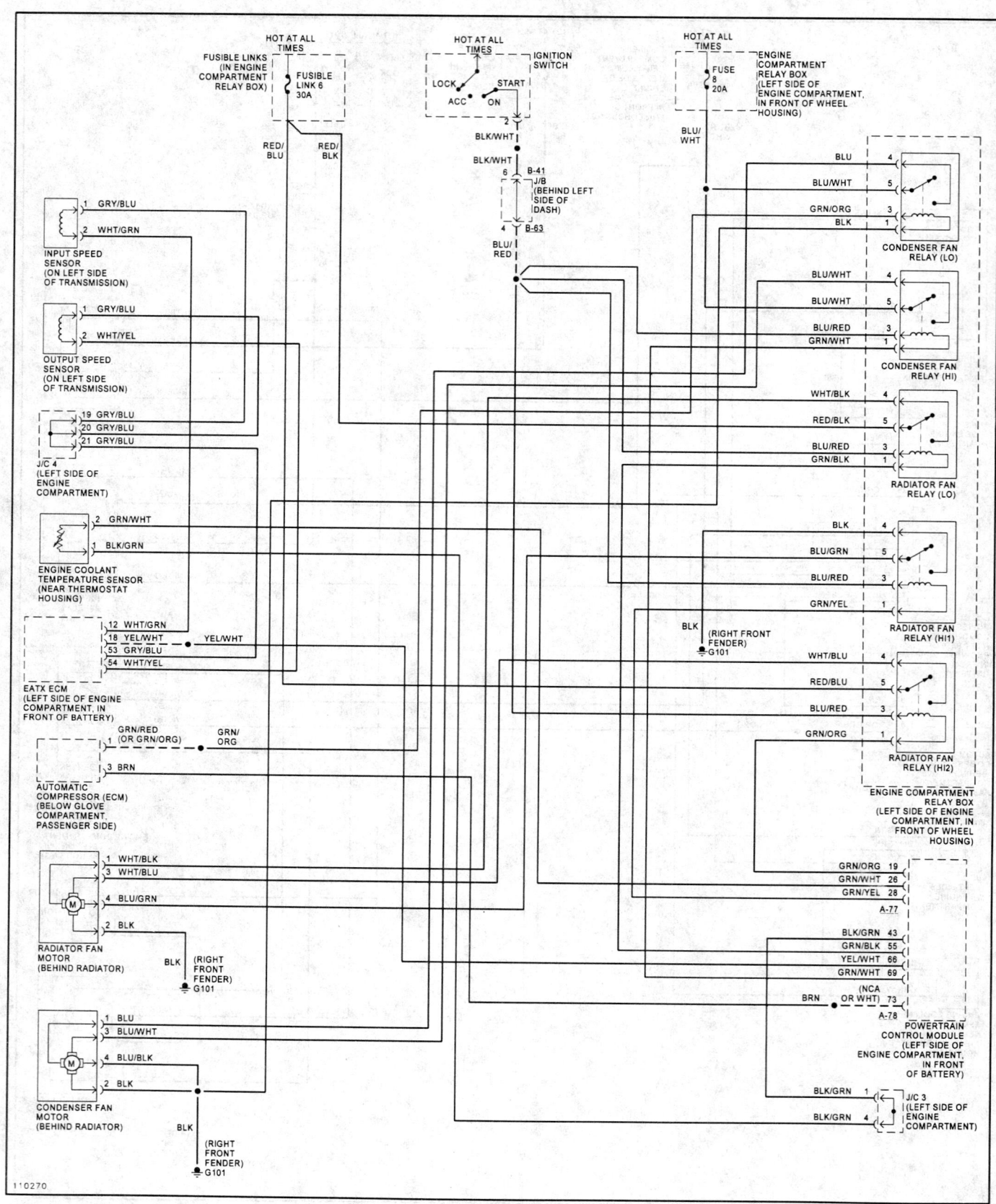

Fig. 3: Electric Cooling Fans Wiring Diagram (Avenger & Sebring Coupe – 2.5L)

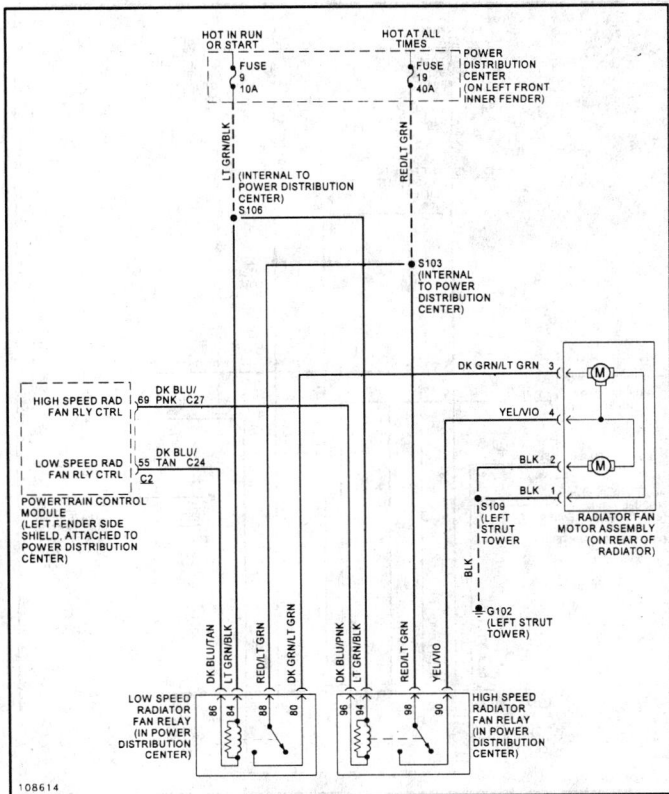

Fig. 4: Electric Cooling Fans Wiring Diagram (Breeze, Cirrus & Stratus)

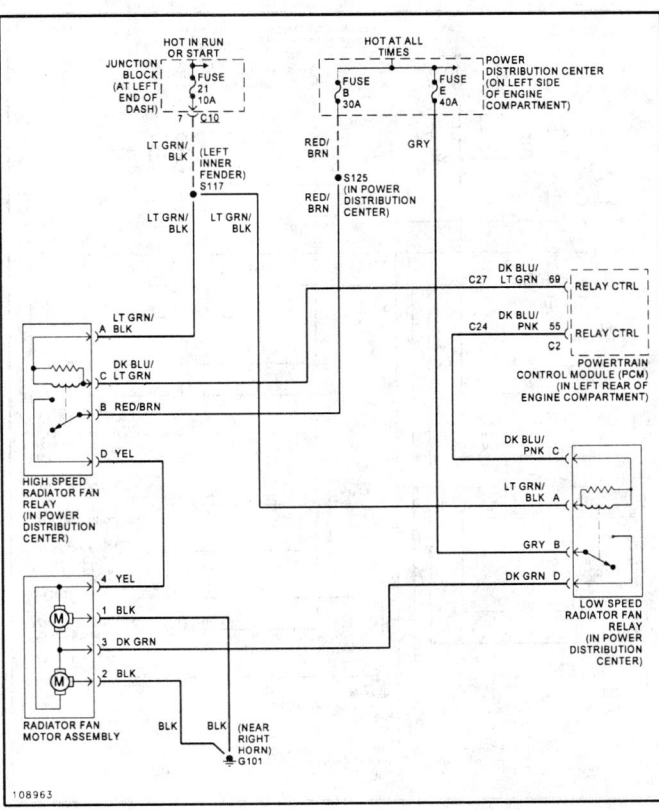

Fig. 6: Electric Cooling Fans Wiring Diagram (Concorde, Intrepid, LHS & 300M)

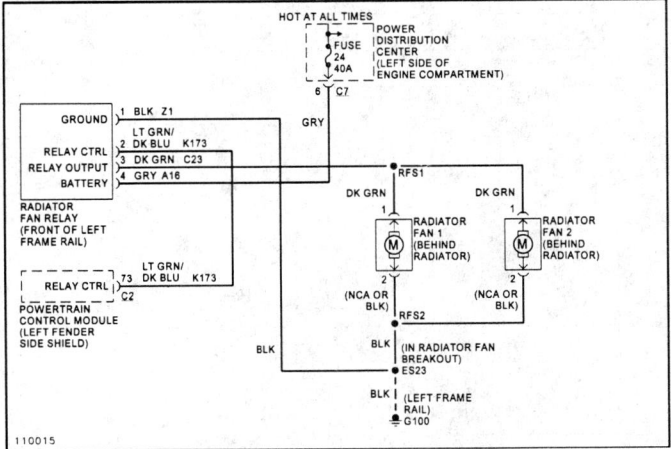

Fig. 5: Electric Cooling Fans Wiring Diagram (Caravan, Town & Country, & Voyager)

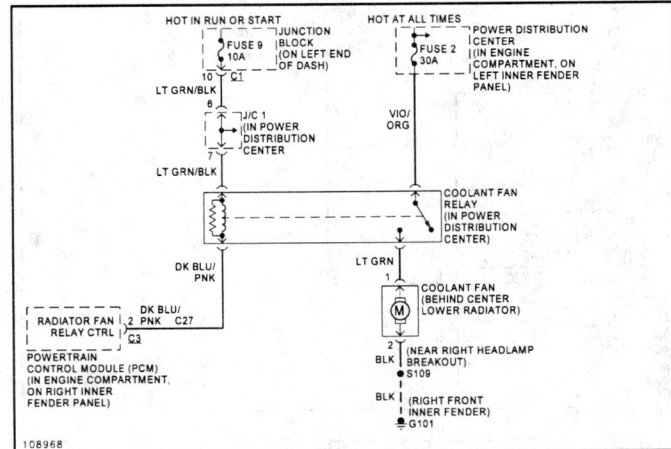

Fig. 7: Electric Cooling Fans Wiring Diagram (Dakota – 2.5L)

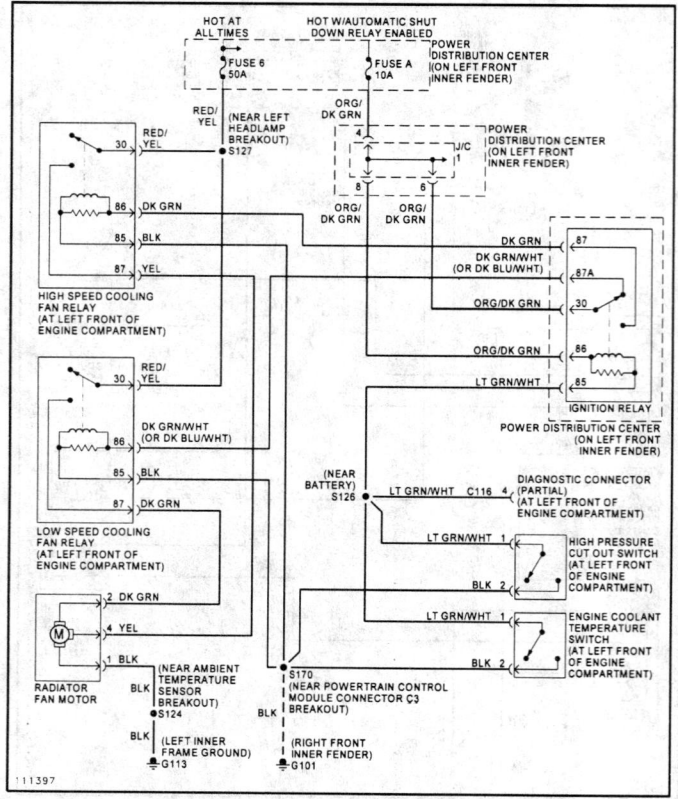

Fig. 8: Electric Cooling Fans Wiring Diagram (Durango)

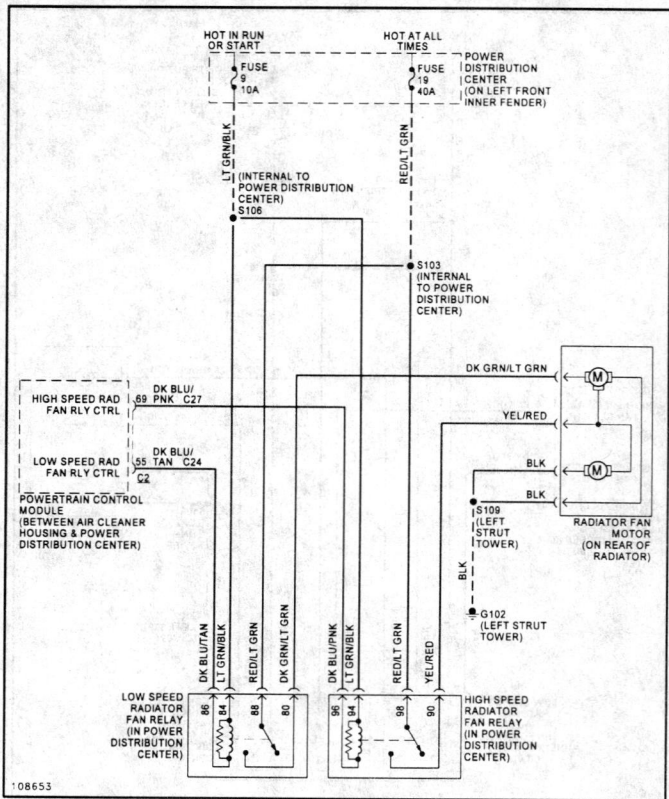

Fig. 10: Electric Cooling Fans Wiring Diagram (Sebring Convertible)

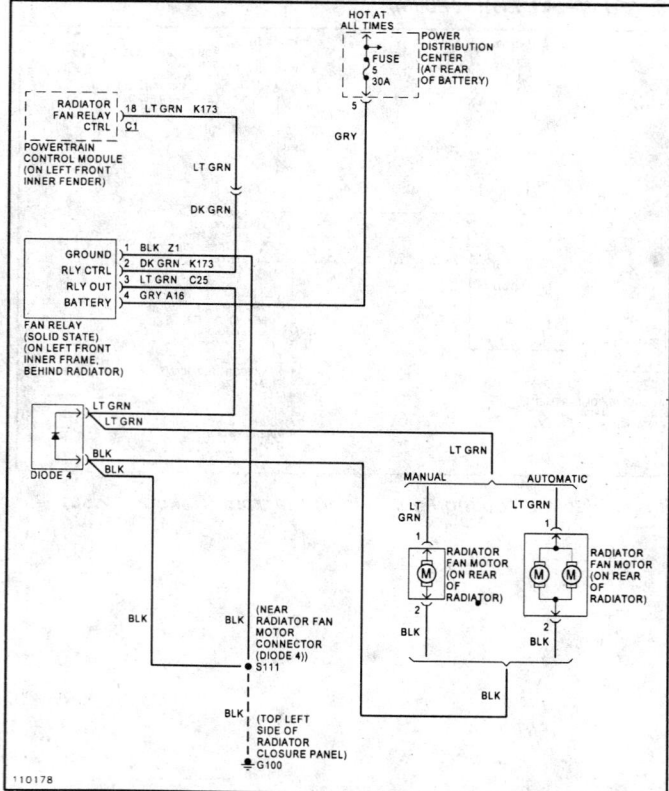

Fig. 9: Electric Cooling Fans Wiring Diagram (Neon)

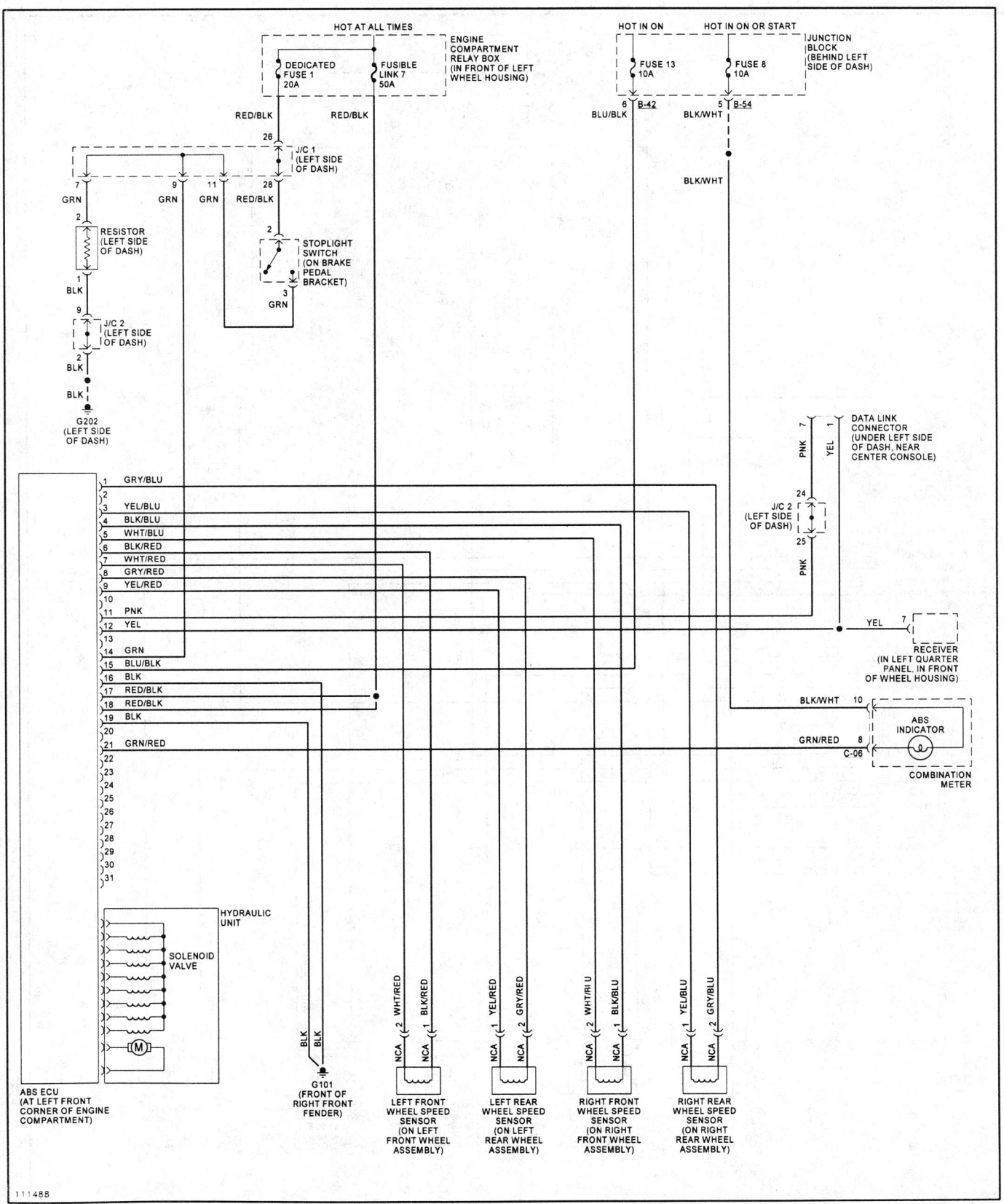

Fig. 1: Anti-Lock Brake System Wiring Diagram (Avenger & Sebring Coupe)

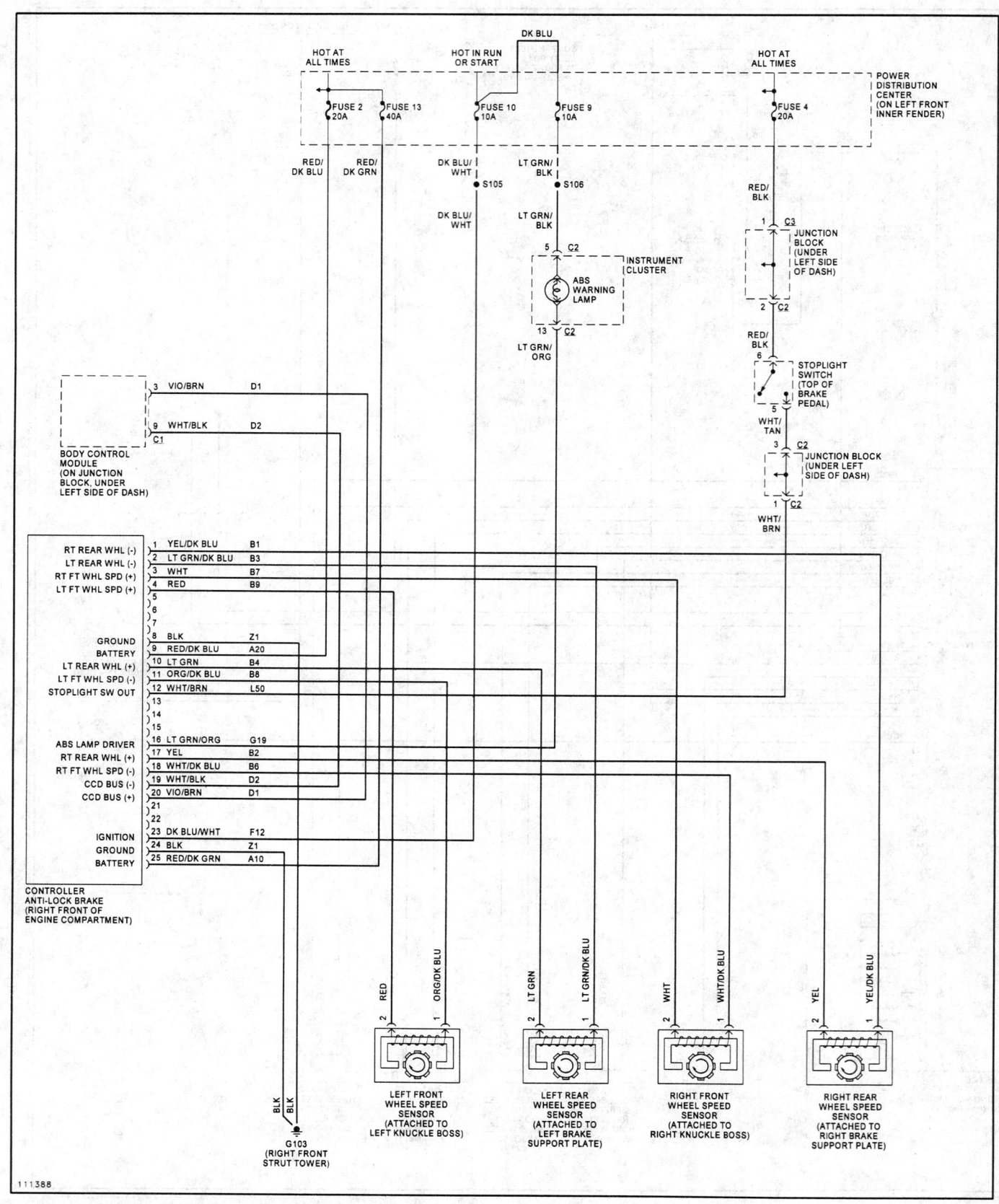

Fig. 2: Anti-Lock Brake System Wiring Diagram (Breeze, Cirrus & Stratus)

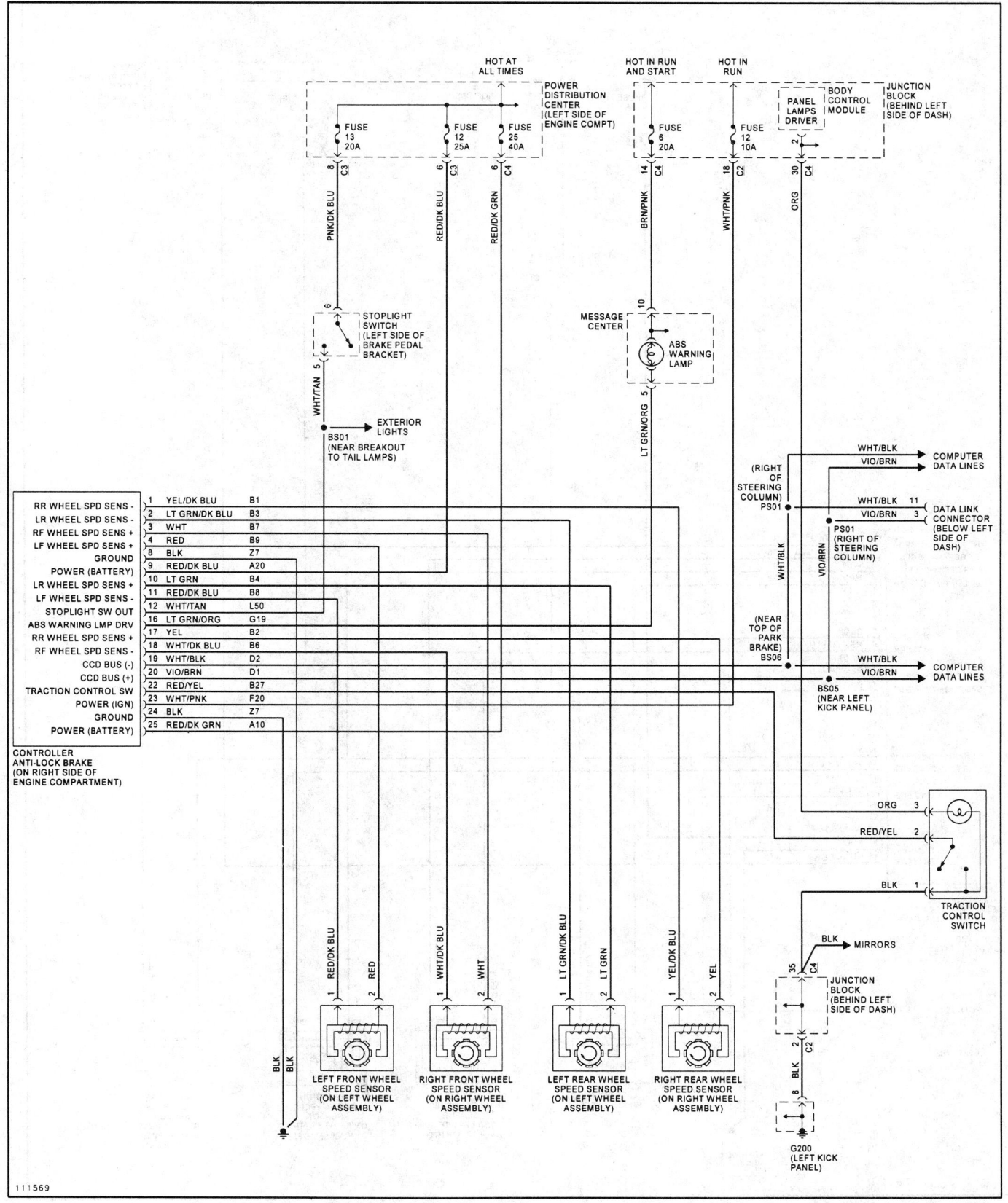

Fig. 3: Anti-Lock Brake System Wiring Diagram (Caravan, Town & Country, & Voyager)

1999 WIRING DIAGRAMS
Anti-Lock Brakes (Cont.)

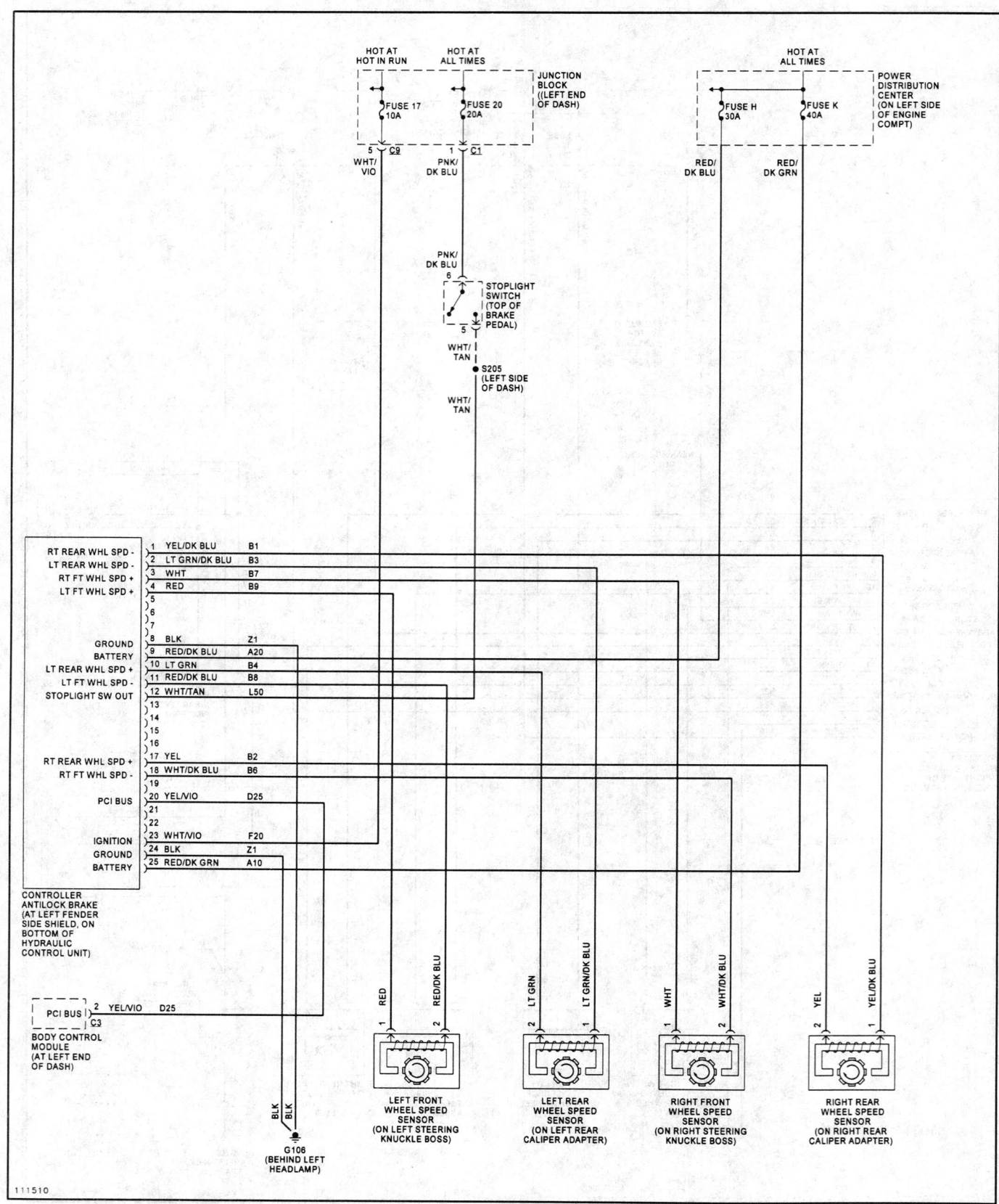

Fig. 4: Anti-Lock Brake System Wiring Diagram (Concorde, Intrepid, LHS & 300M)

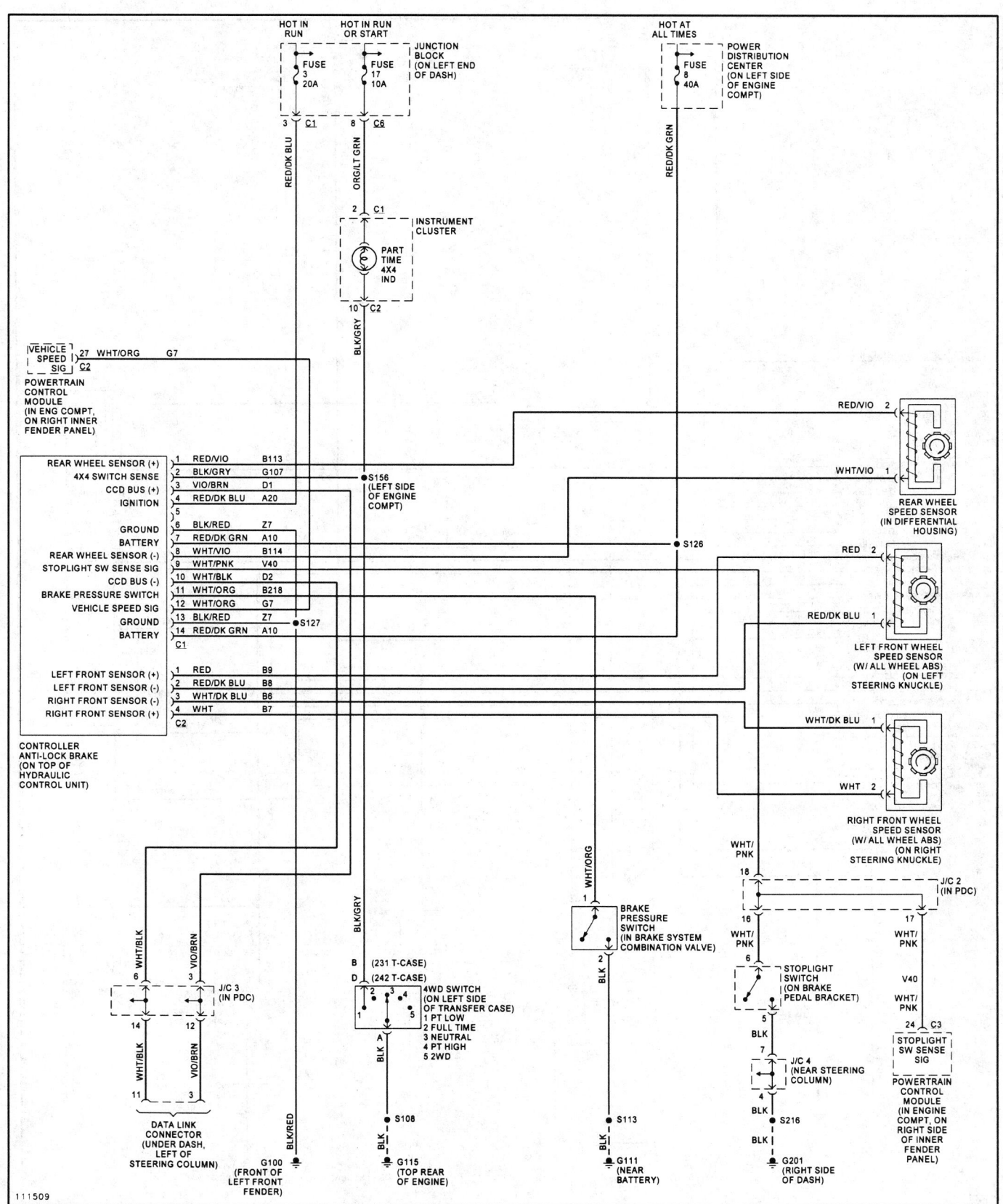

Fig. 5: Anti-Lock Brake System Wiring Diagram (Dakota)

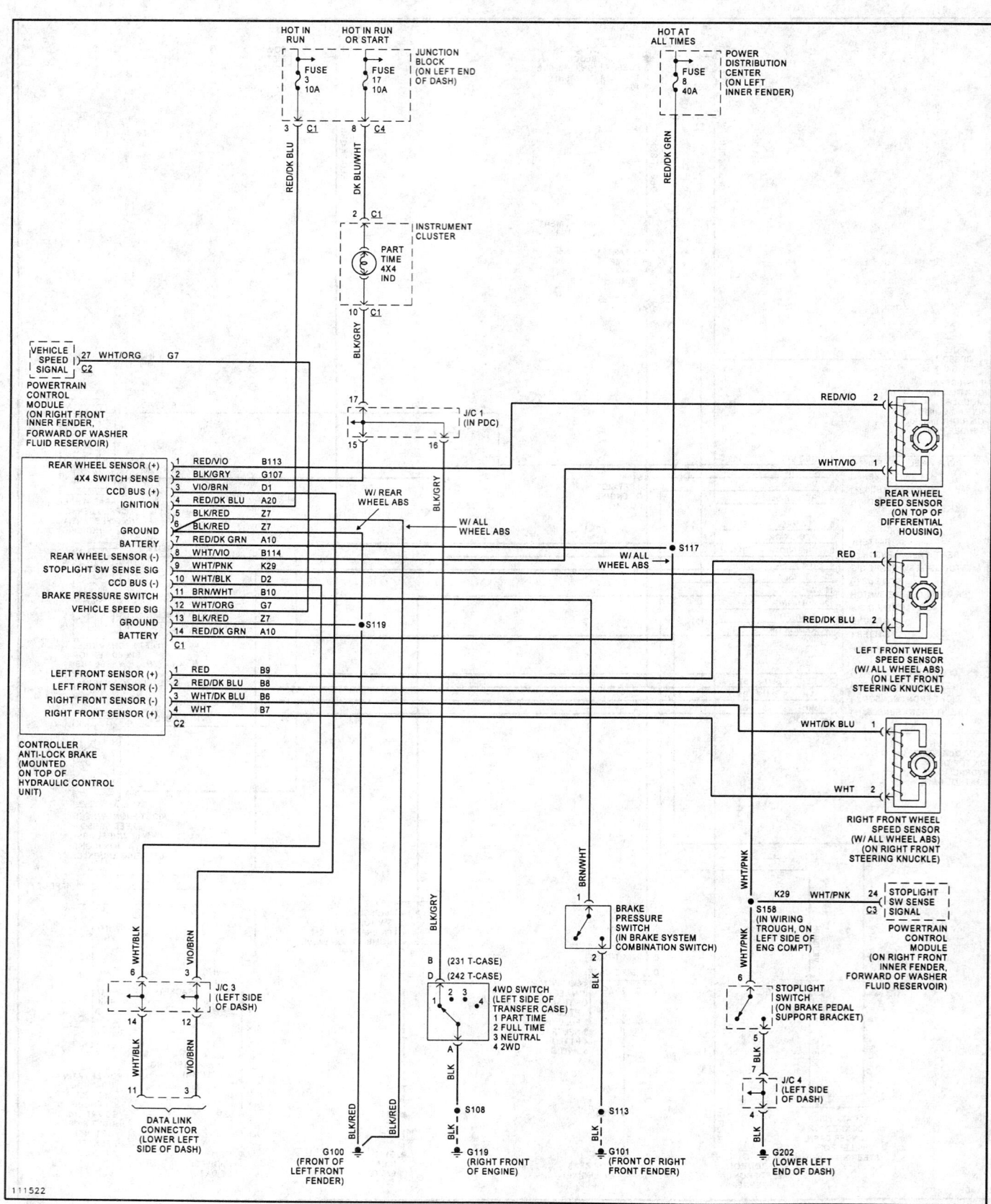

Fig. 6: Anti-Lock Brake System Wiring Diagram (Durango)

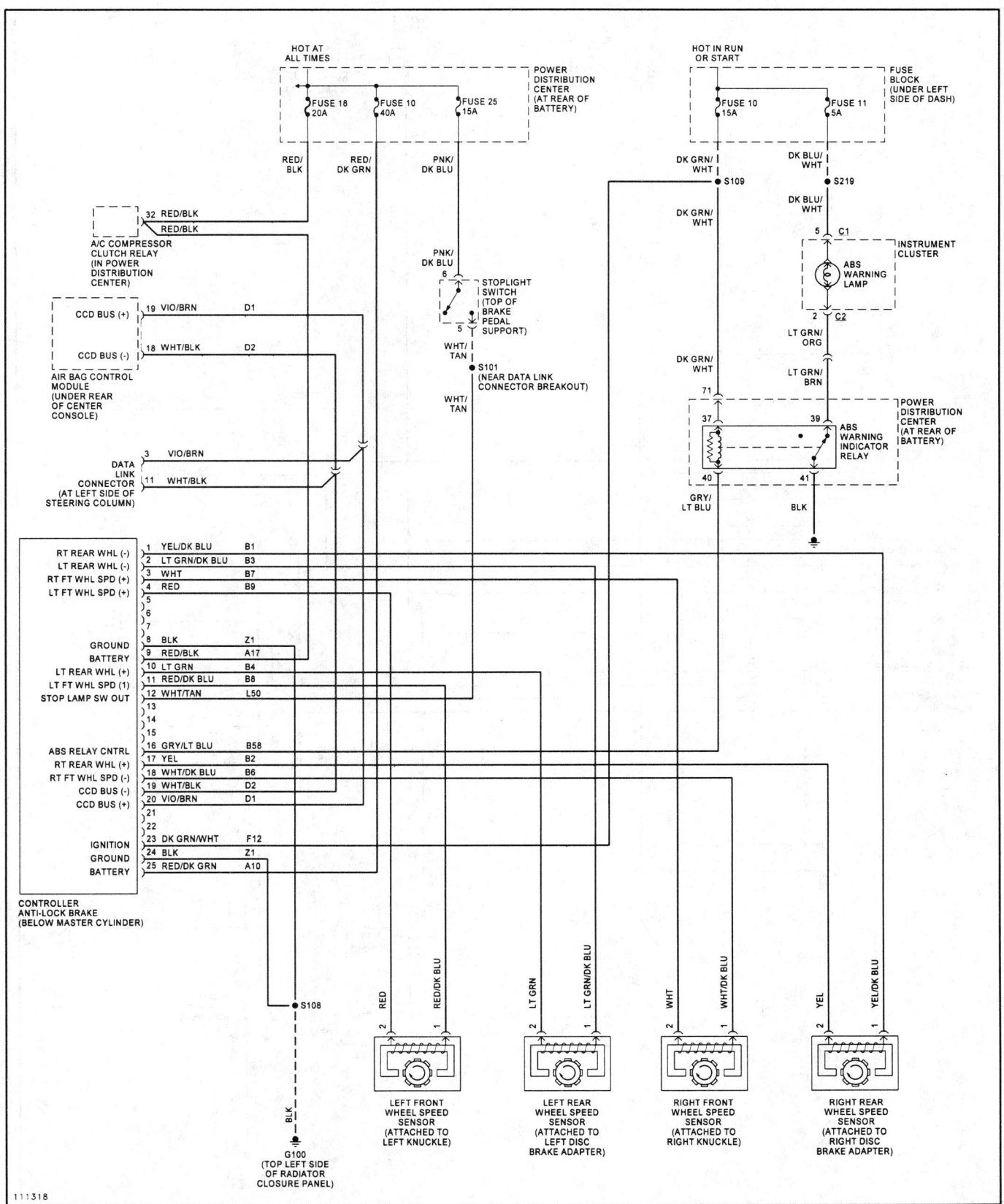

Fig. 7: Anti-Lock Brake System Wiring Diagram (Neon)

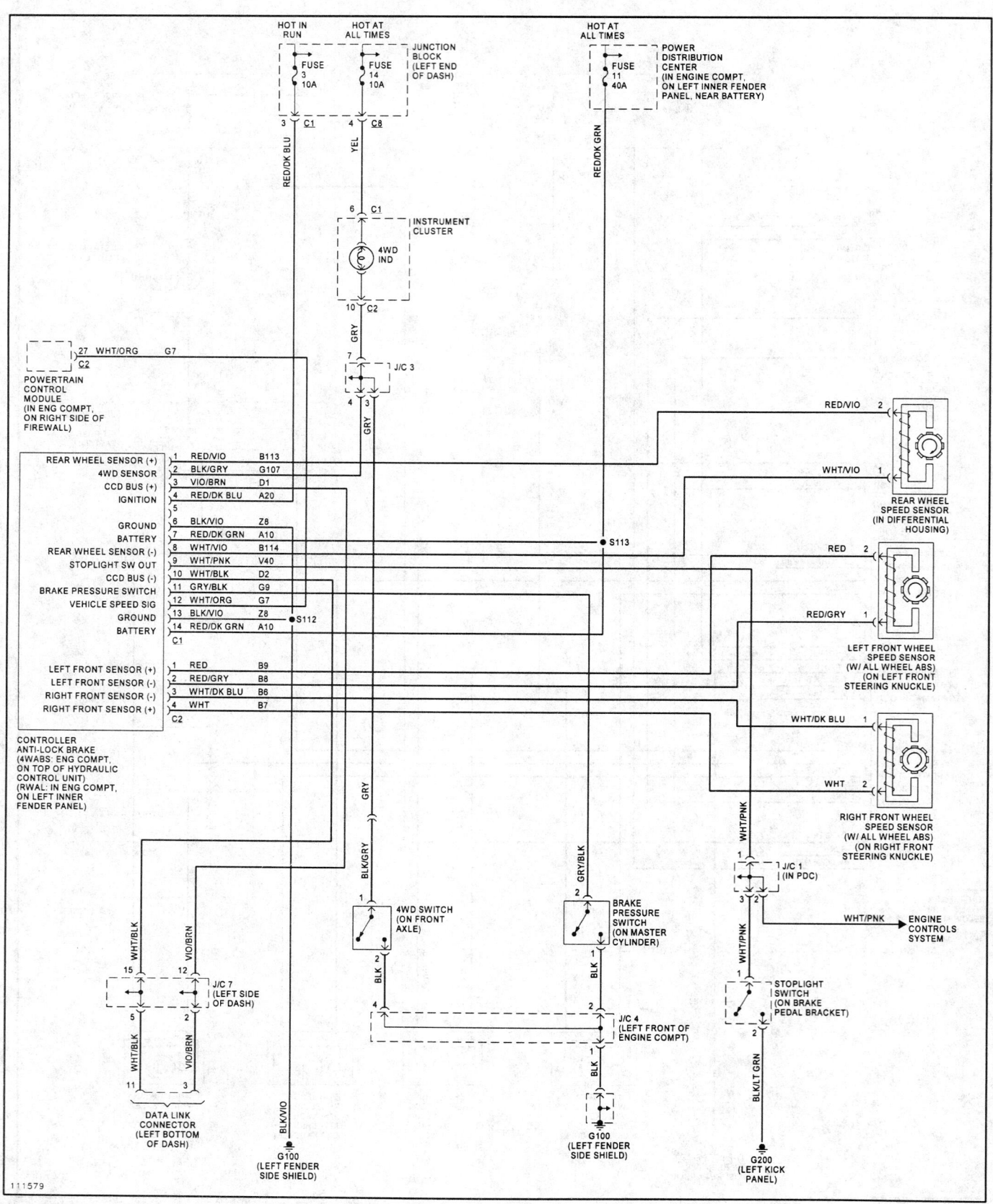

Fig. 8: Anti-Lock Brake System Wiring Diagram (Ram Pickup)

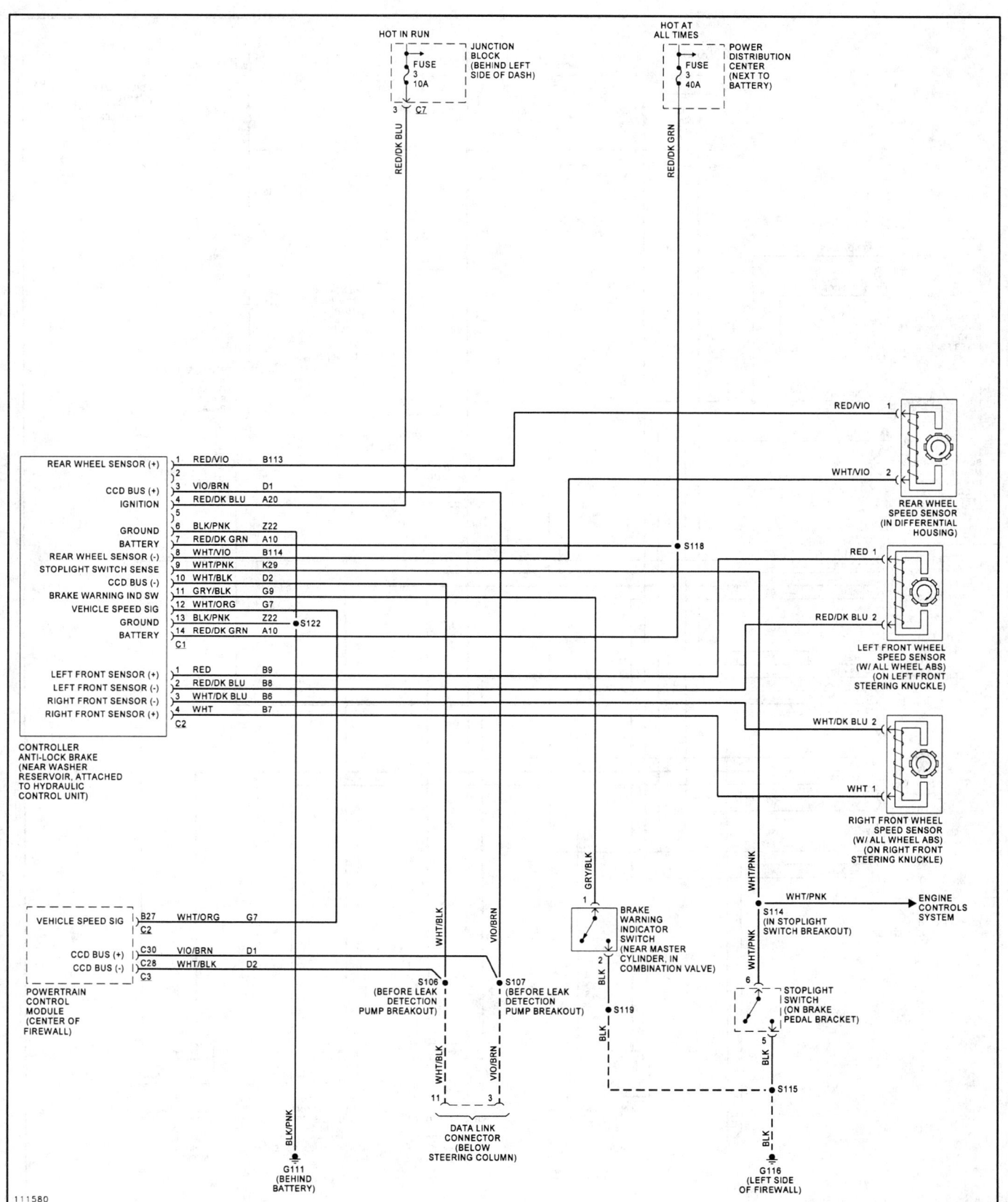

Fig. 9: Anti-Lock Brake System Wiring Diagram (Ram Van & Ram Wagon)

111580

1999 WIRING DIAGRAMS
Anti-Lock Brakes (Cont.)

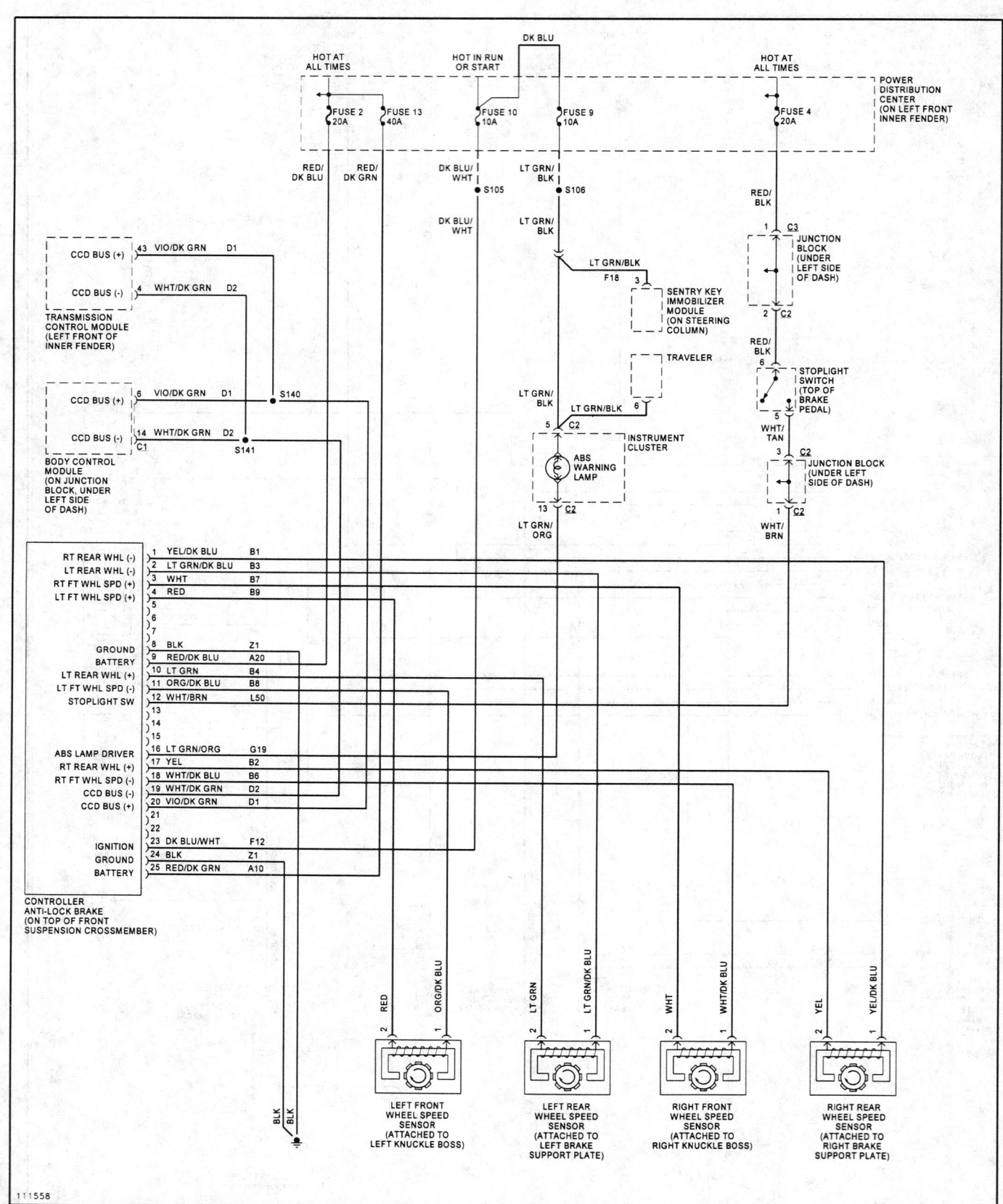

Fig. 10: Anti-Lock Brake System Wiring Diagram (Sebring Convertible)

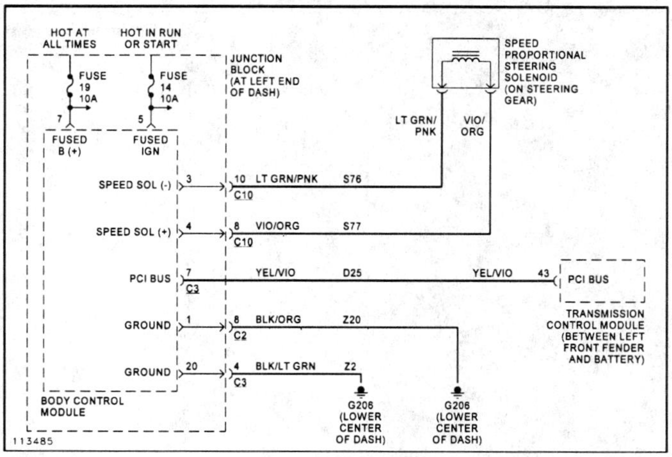

Fig. 1: Electronic Power Steering Wiring Diagram (Concorde, Intrepid, LHS & 300M)

Avenger, Breeze, Cirrus, Concorde, Intrepid, LHS, Neon, Sebring Convertible, Sebring Coupe, Stratus, 300M

WARNING: To avoid injury from accidental air bag deployment, read and carefully follow all WARNINGS and SERVICE PRECAUTIONS.

NOTE: For information on air bag DIAGNOSIS, TESTING or DISPOSAL PROCEDURES, see MITCHELL® AIR BAG SERVICE & REPAIR MANUAL, DOMESTIC & IMPORTED MODELS.

NOTE: References to SRS and SIR mean Supplemental Restraint Systems (SRS) and Supplemental Inflatable Restraints (SIR) respectively. The presence of an air bag system is identified by an SRS or SIR logo on the steering wheel pad and instrument panel pad.

DESCRIPTION

All models are equipped with a driver's and front passenger's Supplemental Restraint System (SRS). SRS is designed to supplement front seat belts. By inflating air bags, SRS helps to reduce the risk or severity of injury during a front-end collision. Driver's air bag is stored in a module within steering wheel pad. Passenger's air bag is stored above glove box, beneath instrument panel fascia on right side of vehicle.

Air bags are designed to inflate and deflate within 1/10th of a second once impact sensor(s) close. This creates a cushion of air between driver and steering wheel or passenger and instrument panel.

SRS consists of SRS/AIR BAG warning light, clockspring, air bag modules and Air Bag Control Module (ACM) containing an impact sensor. *See Fig. 1.*

The ACM monitors system and stores fault codes. The ACM provides information to SRS/AIR BAG warning light and diagnostic connector. A Diagnostic Trouble Code (DTC) will be stored when SRS/AIR BAG warning light is activated for more than 12 seconds.

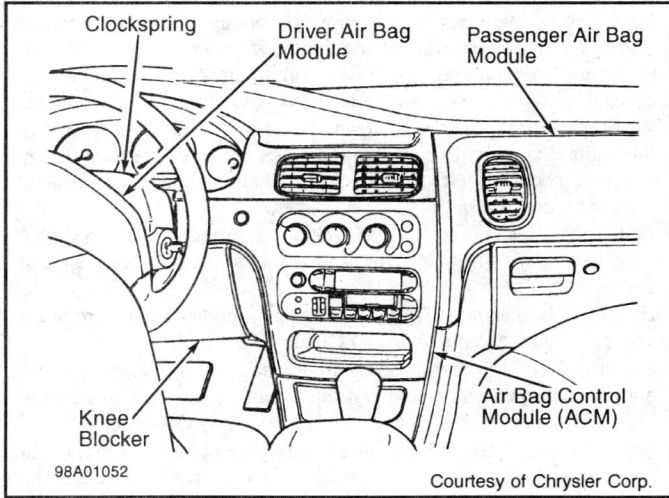

Clockspring   Driver Air Bag Module   Passenger Air Bag Module

Knee Blocker

Air Bag Control Module (ACM)

98A01052   Courtesy of Chrysler Corp.

Fig. 1: Locating SRS Components (Concorde, Intrepid, LHS & 300M Shown; Other Models Are Similar)

OPERATION

During a front-end collision severe enough to require air bag protection, impact sensor switch located within Air Bag Control Module (ACM) closes and a deployment signal is sent to each air bag module inflator. Inflators use electrical current from ACM capacitor to produce and release gas, which inflates air bags.

AIR BAG MODULES

Driver's air bag module is located in center of steering wheel. Passenger's air bag module is located under decorative cover of instrument panel facing the front passenger's seat. Air bag module inflator assembly produces nitrogen gas to fill air bag(s). When an electrical current from the Air Bag Control Module (ACM) capacitor is applied to module's ignitor assembly, ignitor starts a thermal reaction that spreads through a pellet-filled area to produce nitrogen gas. Ignitor assembly is referred to as a squib.

Gas pressure builds and discharges from module's inflator through a diffuser and screen assembly, forcing air bag module covers to burst along perforated seams and fully inflate air bags. Once air bags are full (within milliseconds), gas escapes from air bags through vents that are directed away from driver and passenger.

AIR BAG CONTROL MODULE (ACM)

NOTE: Impact sensor located inside ACM may also be known as a safing sensor or "G" sensor.

On all models except Concorde, Intrepid, LHS and 300M, ACM is located under center console. *See Fig. 2.* On Concorde, Intrepid, LHS and 300M, ACM is located under center of instrument panel. *See Fig. 1.* On all models, ACM contains a safing/impact sensor and energy reserve capacitor. ACM checks SRS readiness every time vehicle is started. If a fault is detected, ACM diagnostics will store a Diagnostic Trouble Code (DTC) and illuminate SRS/AIR BAG warning light. When a DTC is stored, warning light will be activated for at least 12 seconds.

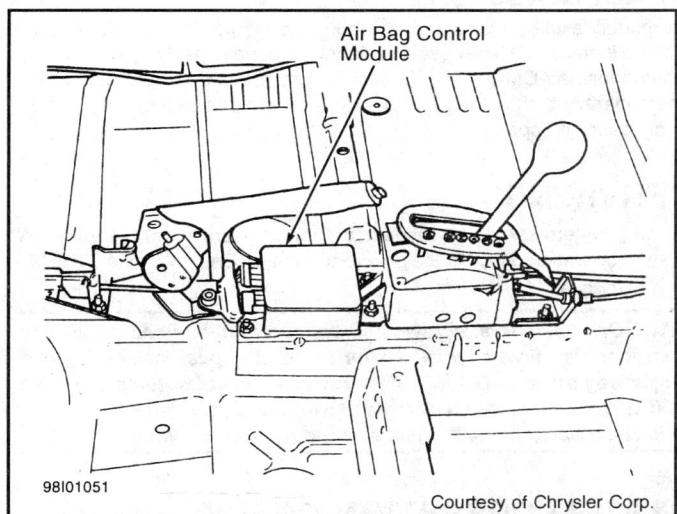

Air Bag Control Module

98I01051   Courtesy of Chrysler Corp.

Fig. 2: Locating Air Bag Control Module (Breeze, Cirrus, Sebring Convertible & Stratus Shown; Other Models Are Similar)

SRS/AIR BAG WARNING LIGHT

SRS/AIR BAG warning light is located in instrument cluster. Whenever ignition switch is in RUN or START position, SRS/AIR BAG warning light on instrument panel will illuminate for 6-8 seconds and then turn off. This signifies ACM has checked system and found it free of problems. If SRS/AIR BAG warning light blinks, stays on at all times or does not come on at all, a problem exists. For DIAGNOSIS & TESTING PROCEDURES, see MITCHELL® AIR BAG SERVICE & REPAIR MANUAL, DOMESTIC & IMPORTED MODELS.

CLOCKSPRING

NOTE: Clockspring MUST BE replaced whenever driver's air bag module deploys. These 2 components are designed for one deployment only and CANNOT be reused.

Clockspring is a rotating connection between system wiring harness and driver's air bag module, cruise control switch (if equipped) and horn switches. *See Fig. 3.* Clockspring is a flat, ribbon-like tape of conductive material, which winds and unwinds with steering wheel movement. It is the most fragile part of SRS. Clockspring MUST BE centered to allow for up to 2 1/2 steering wheel turns in either direction. If clockspring is not centered properly, it can break from stretching or fatigue. See CLOCK-SPRING CENTERING under ADJUSTMENTS.

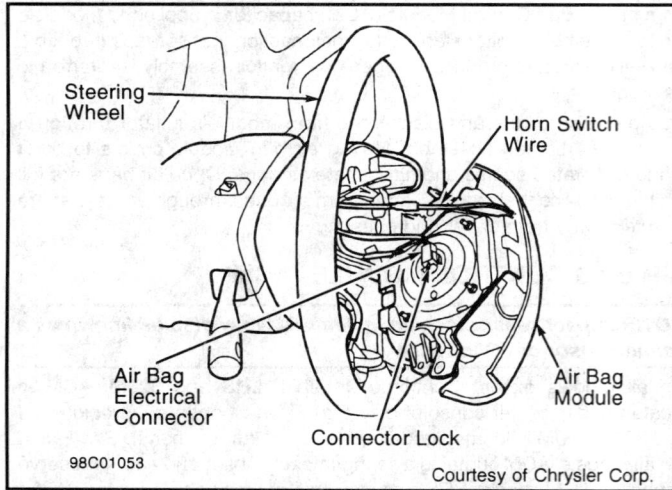

Fig. 3: Identifying Driver's Air Bag Module & Clockspring (Typical)

IMPACT SENSORS

All models except Avenger and Sebring Coupe use one impact sensor located inside ACM. Avenger and Sebring Coupe uses 2 impact sensors located inside ACM. All impact sensors provide verification of direction and severity of impact (except Neon). Neon models provide verification of direction of impact.

SERVICING

Air bag system should be inspected every 3 years or 30,000 miles. A system operation check is the only requirement. See SYSTEM OPERATION CHECK.

CAUTION: Fasteners, screws and bolts, originally used for air bag components, have special coatings and are specifically designed for air bag system. DO NOT replace with any substitutes. Anytime a NEW fastener is needed, replace with correct fasteners provided in service package or fasteners listed in parts books.

SYSTEM OPERATION CHECK

CAUTION: When battery is disconnected, vehicle computer and memory systems may lose memory data. Driveability problems may exist until computer systems have completed a relearn cycle. See COMPUTER RELEARN PROCEDURES article in GENERAL INFORMATION before disconnecting battery.

NOTE: On Breeze, Cirrus, Concorde, Intrepid, LHS, Sebring Convertible, Stratus and 300M, battery is located inside passenger's side wheel well. Disconnect and connect negative battery cable at point located on right front strut tower.

1) Disconnect negative battery cable. WAIT at least 2 minutes. Connect scan tool to Data Link Connector (DLC). DLC is located on underside of instrument panel, below steering column. Use latest version of scan tool cartridge.
2) Turn ignition switch to RUN position and exit vehicle with scan tool. Ensure no one is inside vehicle. Connect negative battery cable.
3) Using scan tool, read and record any active or stored Diagnostic Trouble Codes (DTCs). If DTCs are not active, erase all stored DTCs. If a SRS problem exists, DTCs will not erase. For diagnosis and testing

procedures, see MITCHELL® AIR BAG SERVICE & REPAIR MANUAL, DOMESTIC & IMPORTED MODELS.
4) Avoid being in line with air bag(s), then turn ignition switch to LOCK position, and then to RUN position. Observe SRS/AIR BAG warning light. SRS/AIR BAG warning light should illuminate on for 6-8 seconds and then go out, indicating system is functioning.
5) If SRS/AIR BAG warning light fails to illuminate, or illuminates and stays on, a system malfunction exists. For DIAGNOSIS & TESTING PROCEDURES, see MITCHELL® AIR BAG SERVICE & REPAIR MANUAL, DOMESTIC & IMPORTED MODELS.

SERVICE PRECAUTIONS

The following precautions should be observed when working with air bag systems:

- Disable air bag system before servicing any air bag system or steering column component. Failure to do this could result in accidental air bag deployment and possible personal injury. See DISABLING & ACTIVATING AIR BAG SYSTEM.
- Wait at least 2 minutes after disconnecting negative battery cable before servicing air bag system. Servicing air bag system before 2-minute period may cause accidental air bag deployment and possible personal injury.
- DO NOT use any electrical test equipment on or near SRS components unless specified to do so. DO NOT use an analog ohmmeter. Use a DVOM with a maximum test current of 2 milliamps or less, at minimum resistance measurement range.
- After deployment, air bag surface may contain sodium hydroxide deposits, which may irritate skin. Sodium hydroxide is a product of gas generant combustion. Always wear safety glasses, rubber gloves and a long-sleeved shirt during clean-up. Wash hands using mild soap and water. Follow correct disposal procedures. See MITCHELL® AIR BAG SERVICE & REPAIR MANUAL, DOMESTIC & IMPORTED MODELS.
- Because of critical system operating requirements, DO NOT try to service any air bag components. Defective components should always be replaced.
- Clockspring must be replaced if driver's air bag is deployed.
- Each time a connector is disconnected, ensure it is clean and not damaged. Always pay particular attention to circuit being tested. Dirt, water and corrosion are the most common problems in connectors, causing voltage drop, open circuits and other improper operations.
- When performing electrical tests, prevent accidental shorting of terminals. Such shorts can damage fuses or components and may cause a second fault code to set, making diagnosis of original problem more difficult.
- After repairs are complete and ignition is turned to RUN position, stay clear of air bag(s) to avoid injury in case of accidental air bag deployment.
- Ensure air bag warning light is operating properly and system faults are not indicated. See SYSTEM OPERATION CHECK.
- When placing a undeployed (live) air bag on a bench or other surface, always face air bag and trim cover up, away from surface. This will reduce motion of module if accidentally deployed.
- When carrying a undeployed (live) air bag module, point trim cover away from your body to minimize injury in case of accidental deployment.
- Air bag module must be stored in its original special container until used for service. It must be stored in a clean, dry place, away from sources of extreme heat, sparks and electrical energy.
- Electrical sources should never be allowed near connector on back of air bag module.
- If SRS is not fully functional for any reason, vehicle should not be driven until system is repaired and functions properly. DO NOT remove bulbs, modules, sensors or other components, or in any way disable system from operating normally.

DISABLING & ACTIVATING AIR BAG SYSTEM

CAUTION: When battery is disconnected, vehicle computer and memory systems may lose memory data. Driveability problems may exist until computer systems have completed a relearn cycle. See COMPUTER RELEARN PROCEDURES article in GENERAL INFORMATION before disconnecting battery.

WARNING: Wait at least 2 minutes after disconnecting negative battery cable before servicing air bag system. System reserve capacitor, integral to Air Bag Control Module (ACM), retains air bag system voltage for about 2 minutes after battery is disconnected. Servicing air bag system before 2 minutes may cause accidental air bag deployment and possible personal injury.

NOTE: On Breeze, Cirrus, Concorde, Intrepid, LHS, Sebring Convertible, Stratus and 300M, battery is located inside passenger's side wheel well. Disconnect and connect negative battery cable at point located on right front strut tower.

DISABLING SYSTEM

To disable air bag system for repairs, ensure ignition switch is in OFF position. Disconnect and shield negative battery cable. After disconnecting negative battery cable, wait at least 2 minutes for reserve capacitor to discharge before servicing air bag system.

ACTIVATING SYSTEM

Connect negative battery cable. From a position clear of air bag(s), turn ignition switch to RUN position. Observe SRS/AIR BAG warning light. Warning light should come on for 6-8 seconds and then go out, indicating system is functioning properly. If warning light fails to illuminate, or illuminates and stays on, a system malfunction exists. See SYSTEM OPERATION CHECK.

REMOVAL & INSTALLATION

WARNING: Failure to follow air bag service precautions may result in air bag deployment and personal injury. See SERVICE PRECAUTIONS. After component replacement, perform system operation check to ensure proper system operation. See SYSTEM OPERATION CHECK.

CAUTION: When battery is disconnected, vehicle computer and memory systems may lose memory data. Driveability problems may exist until computer systems have completed a relearn cycle. See COMPUTER RELEARN PROCEDURES article in GENERAL INFORMATION before disconnecting battery.

CAUTION: Fasteners, screws and bolts, originally used for air bag components, have special coatings and are specifically designed for air bag system. DO NOT replace fasteners with any substitutes. Anytime a NEW fastener is needed, replace with correct fasteners provided in service package or fasteners listed in parts books.

DRIVER'S AIR BAG MODULE & STEERING WHEEL

CAUTION: Before removing steering wheel, position front wheels in straight-ahead position, and lock steering column by removing ignition key. Failure to do so could damage clockspring or cause clockspring to be off-centered. DO NOT hammer on steering wheel during removal, or collapsible column could be damaged.

If driver's air bag is deployed in collision, manufacturer recommends that additional components be replaced. See RECOMMENDED AIR BAG REPLACEMENT COMPONENTS table. Ensure all SRS and other related components (i.e., steering column) are always inspected after air

bag deployment. Replace component(s) as needed.

RECOMMENDED AIR BAG REPLACEMENT COMPONENTS

Model	Description
Avenger & Sebring Coupe	Air Bag Control Module & Air Bag Module
Neon	Air Bag Module, Clockspring & Steering Column Assembly
All Other Models	Air Bag Module, Clockspring, Steering Wheel & Steering Column Assembly

Removal – 1) Before proceeding, follow air bag service precautions, and disable air bag system. See SERVICE PRECAUTIONS and DISABLING & ACTIVATING AIR BAG SYSTEM. Turn front wheels to straight-ahead position. Lock steering wheel in place by removing ignition key.

2) Remove cruise control switches (if equipped) and steering column covers (if necessary). Remove air bag module retaining bolts/nuts. Lift air bag module, and disconnect its connector by spreading apart latching arms and prying up on connector. Place air bag module on a clean, level surface with pad facing upward.

3) Remove steering wheel retaining nut. Using steering wheel puller, remove steering wheel. Note how wires are routed through steering wheel. While removing steering wheel, ensure module, horn, and cruise control wires (if equipped) are fed gently through holes in steering wheel. DO NOT turn clockspring.

Installation – 1) Ensure clockspring is centered. If front wheels are turned after steering wheel is removed, readjustment of clockspring is necessary. See CLOCKSPRING CENTERING under ADJUSTMENTS.

2) Noting wire positions made during removal procedure, carefully route wires through steering wheel. Position steering wheel to shaft. Ensure wires are not pinched behind steering wheel. Install steering wheel retaining nut and tighten to specification. See TORQUE SPECIFICATIONS.

3) To complete installation, reverse removal procedure. Before connecting negative battery cable, check system operation. See SYSTEM OPERATION CHECK.

PASSENGER'S AIR BAG MODULE

Removal & Installation (Avenger & Sebring Coupe) – 1) Before proceeding, follow air bag service precautions, and disable air bag system. See SERVICE PRECAUTIONS and DISABLING & ACTIVATING AIR BAG SYSTEM. Lower glove box door to access passenger's air bag module mounting bolts.

2) Disconnect air bag module connector. Remove air bag module. To install, reverse removal procedure. Before connecting negative battery cable, check system operation. See SYSTEM OPERATION CHECK

Removal & Installation (Breeze, Cirrus, Sebring Convertible & Stratus – Undeployed Air Bag) – 1) Before proceeding, follow air bag service precautions, and disable air bag system. See SERVICE PRECAUTIONS and DISABLING & ACTIVATING AIR BAG SYSTEM. Lower glove box door to access passenger's air bag module mounting bolts.

2) Disconnect air bag module connector. Remove air bag module. To install, reverse removal procedure. Before connecting negative battery cable, check system operation. See SYSTEM OPERATION CHECK

NOTE: On Breeze, Cirrus, Sebring Convertible and Stratus, instrument panel and pad are not reusable if passenger's air bag has deployed. Components that are not damaged should be transferred from old instrument panel to new instrument panel.

Removal & Installation (Breeze, Cirrus, Sebring Convertible & Stratus – Deployed Air Bag) – 1) Before proceeding, follow air bag service precautions, and disable air bag system. See SERVICE PRECAUTIONS and DISABLING & ACTIVATING AIR BAG SYSTEM. Rubber gloves, eye protection and a long sleeve shirt should be worn. There may be deposits on air bags which could cause skin and/or eye irritation.

2) Open both front doors, and remove left and right end covers from instrument panel. *See Fig. 4.* Carefully remove transmission range indicator bezel from floor console. Remove floor center console. Disconnect Air Bag Control Module (ACM). Remove 4 screws, pull on hood to disengage 8 clips, and remove instrument cluster hood. Remove cubby bin.

3) Remove knee bolster. Lower glove box door to access front of floor console. Remove 9 screws and one push pin from forward floor console. Pull driver's side underpanel outboard off distribution duct. Working from right to left, lift rear edge of top cover to disengage clips along rear edge. Lift rear edge, slide top cover rearward, and remove top cover.

4) Remove radio and A/C-heater control panel. Close glove box door. Remove 5 screws attaching instrument panel retainer to plenum. Remove steering column mounting bolts. Disconnect engine and body wiring harness from junction block and Body Control Module (BCM).

5) Remove the following fasteners:

- Four from left end and 3 from right end of car cross beam.
- Two at steering column plenum and one at glove box hinge to cowl.
- Two at center support to floor pan bracket.
- Remove 3 screws at bottom of A/C-heater control panel to instrument panel.

6) Lift instrument panel, move it rearward and remove. Disconnect passenger's air bag connector. Remove passenger's air bag. Install undamaged components from old instrument panel to a NEW instrument panel and pad.

7) Install passenger's air bag. Tighten nuts to 100 INCH lbs. (11 N.m) and screws to 20 INCH lbs. (2 N.m). To complete installation, reverse removal procedures. Before connecting negative battery cable, check system operation. See SYSTEM OPERATION CHECK.

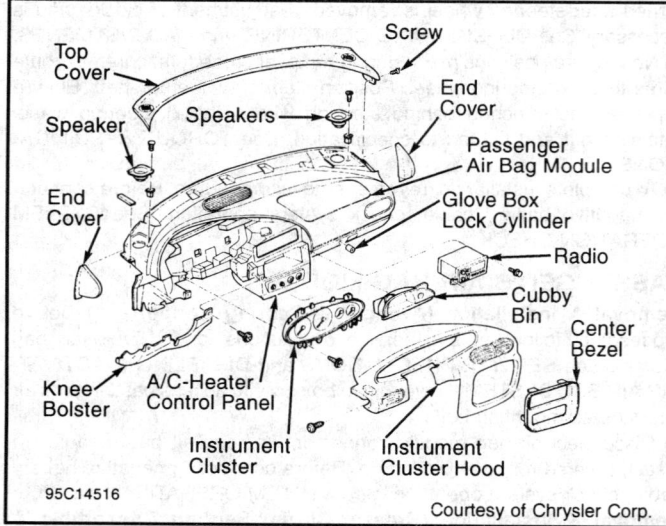

Fig. 4: Identifying Instrument Panel Components (Breeze, Cirrus, Sebring Convertible & Stratus)

NOTE: If passenger's air bag is deployed, replace instrument panel.

Removal & Installation (Concorde, Intrepid, LHS & 300M) – 1)
Before proceeding, follow air bag service precautions, and disable air bag system. See SERVICE PRECAUTIONS and DISABLING & ACTIVATING AIR BAG SYSTEM.

2) Remove shifter knob. Remove left and right instrument panel end covers. Using Trim Stick (C-4755), pry up on shifter bezel, disconnect connectors and remove. Remove 2 screws from outside end of lower instrument panel cover and disconnect trunk release switch.

3) Pull lower instrument panel cover rearward to release clips and remove parking brake release cable from handle. Continue pulling cover rearward and remove.

4) On 5-passenger models, remove instrument panel center bezel using trim stick and disconnect A/C-heater control and traction control switch wiring harnesses. On all models, remove instrument panel center bezel. Remove 2 left console side cover screws, pull outward and remove.

5) Lower glove box door. Remove 2 right console side cover screws, pull outward and remove. Remove console. Remove center lower instrument panel. Remove steel reinforcement from lower instrument panel cover and disconnect 16-pin Diagnostic Link Connector (DLC) from reinforcement.

6) Ensure front wheels are in a straight ahead position. Remove air bag module. Remove steering wheel. See DRIVER'S AIR BAG MODULE & STEERING WHEEL. Unsnap upper steering column cover from lower cover. Remove tilt lever. Remove lower cover. Remove clockspring. See CLOCKSPRING under REMOVAL & INSTALLATION. Remove multifunction switch from steering column. Remove ignition switch from steering column.

7) If vehicle is equipped with floor mounted shifter, depress locking tab on interlock cable and remove cable from key lock housing. *See Fig. 5.*

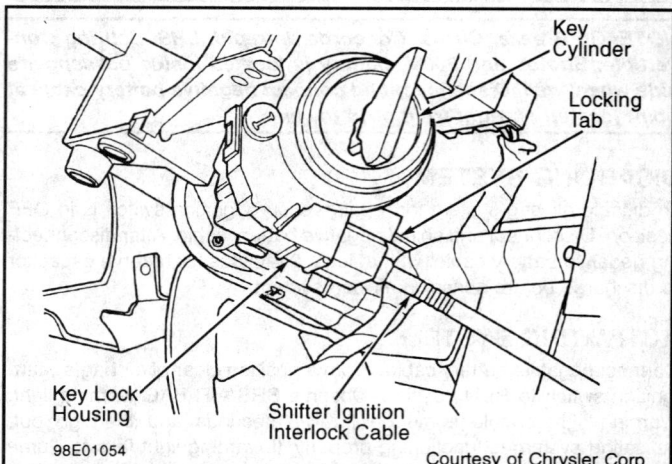

Fig. 5: Identifying Shifter/Ignition Interlock Cable (Concorde, Intrepid, LHS & 300M)

8) If vehicle is equipped steering column mounted shifter, remove shift cable from shifter mechanism. Unlock cable lock. Pry cable off pin. Remove shift cable mounting bracket from steering column.

9) Remove both air ducts from under steering column. Remove retaining pin in steering column flex coupler pinch bolt. Remove pinch bolt. Remove column upper mounting bracket-to-support bracket nuts. Loosen lower mounting bracket bolts. Pull steering column and remove from vehicle.

10) Remove under column duct section from vehicle. Remove left floor duct/silencer pad. Disconnect A/C-heater assembly and Air Bag Control Module (ACM) harness connectors and 3 ground connections left of floor tunnel.

11) Using a trim stick, remove left and right "A" pillar trim moldings. Using a trim stick, pry up on instrument panel top cover and remove towards rear of vehicle. Remove left and right cowl panels. Remove right side under dash silencer/pad. Disconnect radio antenna connectors and amplifier DIN cable.

12) Disconnect junction block and Body Control Module (BCM) harness connectors located on left side. Disconnect front wiper defrost grid wire connector. Remove 13 instrument panel retaining screws (one is located behind glove box). Pull instrument panel rearward and ensure all harnesses are free and clear from sagging. With assistance, remove instrument panel from vehicle and place on a clean bench.

13) On 6-passenger models, remove ashtray door. Remove 4 screws securing chin bezel and pull off instrument panel. Using trim stick, remove center bezel assembly. Disconnect power outlet and temperature control harness connectors. On all models, remove glove box assembly.

14) From rear of instrument panel, remove rod and boot assembly. Remove demister ducts. Remove center and right distribution ducts. Disconnect Yellow harness connector from passenger's air bag module.

Remove left and right pencil struts. Remove air bag module from instrument panel. Remove module from retainer. Remove reinforcement brace from module.

15) To install, reverse removal procedure. See TORQUE SPECIFICATIONS. Before connecting negative battery cable, check system operation. See SYSTEM OPERATION CHECK.

Removal & Installation (Neon) – 1) Before proceeding, follow air bag service precautions, and disable air bag system. See SERVICE PRECAUTIONS and DISABLING & ACTIVATING AIR BAG SYSTEM.

2) Remove instrument panel top cover and right trim bezel. Open glove box and push sides inward, allowing door bumper to pass and box to open. Remove air bag module mounting nuts. Lift air bag module until connector is accessible, and then disconnect connector.

3) To install, reverse removal procedure. Tighten module screws to specification. See TORQUE SPECIFICATIONS. Before connecting negative battery cable, check system operation. See SYSTEM OPERATION CHECK.

AIR BAG CONTROL MODULE (ACM)

WARNING: ACM contains impact sensor which enables SRS to activate air bags. To avoid accidental deployment, NEVER electrically connect ACM to system unless it is bolted to vehicle.

Removal (Avenger & Sebring Coupe) – Before proceeding, follow air bag service precautions, and disable air bag system. See SERVICE PRECAUTIONS and DISABLING & ACTIVATING AIR BAG SYSTEM. Remove radio/A/C control assembly trim panel. Lift center console lid and remove inner tray from console. On M/T models, remove shifter knob. On all models, remove console. Disconnect ACM connector and remove ACM.

Installation – Install ACM with top arrow pointing toward front of vehicle. Install ACM on center tunnel area mounting studs. Install and tighten ACM nuts to specification. See TORQUE SPECIFICATIONS. Connect ACM connector. To complete installation, reverse removal procedure. Before connecting negative battery cable, check system operation. See SYSTEM OPERATION CHECK.

Removal (Concorde & Intrepid – 5-Passenger Vehicle) – 1) Before proceeding, follow air bag service precautions, and disable air bag system. See SERVICE PRECAUTIONS and DISABLING & ACTIVATING AIR BAG SYSTEM. Remove ashtray. Remove shifter knob fastener, and remove shifter knob.

2) Remove 2 screws securing shifter bezel. Disconnect power output harness connector and remove bezel. Remove left instrument panel endcap. Remove lower steering column cover. Open glove box. Pull down on glove box door until glove box drops and screws in upper and lower left corner of glove box bin are visible.

3) Pull off right side console panel. Remove left side console panel. On exposed ACM, slide red tab out on harness connector. Press down on locking latch and disconnect ACM 23-pin connector. Unbolt and remove ACM.

Installation – 1) Position ACM with top arrow pointing toward front of vehicle. Install ACM into instrument panel bracket clip. Tighten mounting screws to specification. See TORQUE SPECIFICATIONS.

2) To complete installation, reverse removal procedure. Before connecting negative battery cable, check system operation. See SYSTEM OPERATION CHECK.

Removal (Concorde – 6-Passenger Vehicle) – 1) Before proceeding, follow air bag service precautions, and disable air bag system. See SERVICE PRECAUTIONS and DISABLING & ACTIVATING AIR BAG SYSTEM

2) Remove shift knob. Remove left and right instrument panel end covers. Using Trim Stick (C-4755), pry up on shifter bezel, disconnect connectors and remove. Remove 2 screws from outside end of lower instrument panel cover and disconnect trunk release switch.

3) Pull lower instrument panel cover rearward to release clips and remove parking brake release cable from handle. Continue pulling cover rearward and remove.

4) Remove instrument panel center bezel. Remove 2 left console side cover screws, pull outward and remove. Remove 2 right console side cover screws, pull outward and remove.

5) Remove console. Remove center lower instrument panel. Remove steel reinforcement from lower instrument panel cover and disconnect 16-pin Diagnostic Link Connector (DLC) from reinforcement.

6) Ensure front wheels are in a straight ahead position. Remove air bag module. Remove steering wheel. See DRIVER'S AIR BAG MODULE & STEERING WHEEL. Unsnap upper steering column cover from lower cover. Remove tilt lever. Remove lower cover. Remove clockspring. See CLOCKSPRING. Remove multifunction switch from steering column. Remove ignition switch from steering column.

7) If vehicle is equipped with floor mounted shifter, depress locking tab on interlock cable and remove cable from key lock housing. *See Fig. 5.*

8) If vehicle is equipped steering column mounted shifter, remove shift cable from shifter mechanism. Unlock cable lock. Pry cable off pin. Remove shift cable mounting bracket from steering column.

9) Remove both air ducts from under steering column. Remove retaining pin in steering column flex coupler pinch bolt. Remove pinch bolt. Remove column upper mounting bracket-to-support bracket nuts. Loosen lower mounting bracket bolts. Pull steering column and remove from vehicle.

10) Remove under column duct section from vehicle. Remove left floor duct/silencer pad. Disconnect A/C-heater assembly and Air Bag Control Module (ACM) harness connectors and 3 ground connections left of floor tunnel.

11) Using a trim stick, remove left and right "A" pillar trim moldings. Using a trim stick, pry up on instrument panel top cover and remove towards rear of vehicle. Remove left and right cowl panels. Remove right side under dash silencer/pad. Disconnect radio antenna connectors and amplifier DIN cable.

12) Disconnect junction block and Body Control Module (BCM) harness connectors located on left side. Disconnect front wiper defrost grid wire connector. Remove 13 instrument panel retaining screws (one is located behind glove box). Pull instrument panel rearward and ensure all harnesses are free and clear from sagging. With assistance, remove instrument panel from vehicle and place on a clean bench.

13) On exposed ACM, slide Red tab out on harness connector. Press down on locking latch and disconnect ACM 23-pin connector. Unbolt and remove ACM.

Installation – 1) Position ACM with top arrow pointing toward front of vehicle. Install ACM into instrument panel bracket clip. Tighten mounting screws to specification. See TORQUE SPECIFICATIONS.

2) To complete installation, reverse removal procedure. Before connecting negative battery cable, check system operation. See SYSTEM OPERATION CHECK.

Removal (Intrepid – 6-Passenger Vehicle) – 1) Before proceeding, follow air bag service precautions, and disable air bag system. See SERVICE PRECAUTIONS and DISABLING & ACTIVATING AIR BAG SYSTEM.

2) Open glove box door and release side tabs. Swing down door. Remove left instrument panel endcap. Remove lower steering column cover. Pull down on glove box door until glove box drops and screws in upper and lower left corner of glove box bin are visible.

3) Remove instrument panel center bezel with temperature control module, power outlet and traction control switch. Disconnect harness connectors. Remove 4 screws to chin bezel. Remove screw and push fastener retaining floor bin.

4) On exposed ACM, slide Red tab out on harness connector. Press down on locking latch and disconnect ACM 23-pin connector. Unbolt and remove ACM.

Installation – 1) Position ACM with top arrow pointing toward front of vehicle. Install ACM into instrument panel bracket clip. Tighten mounting screws to specification. See TORQUE SPECIFICATIONS.

2) To complete installation, reverse removal procedure. Before connecting negative battery cable, check system operation. See SYSTEM OPERATION CHECK.

Removal (Breeze, Cirrus & Stratus) – 1) Before proceeding, follow air bag service precautions, and disable air bag system. See SERVICE PRECAUTIONS and DISABLING & ACTIVATING AIR BAG SYSTEM **2)** Raise parking brake lever high as possible. On A/T models, loosen set screw on shifter knob and remove knob. Remove plastic plunger rod from shifter lever. Carefully pry up and remove shift range indicator bezel.

3) On M/T models, push shifter boot down to expose clips on gear shift knob and roll pin on shifter shaft. Using a small screwdriver, pry clips on shifter knob away from roll pin in shifter shaft. Pulling straight up, remove shifter knob. Remove shift boot.

4) On all models, remove center console retaining screws. Raise parking brake lever as high as necessary for required clearance, and remove center console. Remove ACM. Disconnect ACM connectors.

Installation – 1) Connect ACM connectors, and ensure all locking tabs are engaged. Install ACM with arrow pointing forward. Install and tighten ACM nuts to specification. See TORQUE SPECIFICATIONS. Install parking brake lever mechanism, and securely tighten nuts.

2) Raise parking brake lever, and install center console. To complete installation, reverse removal procedure. Before connecting negative battery cable, check system operation. See SYSTEM OPERATION CHECK.

Removal (Sebring Convertible) – 1) Before proceeding, follow air bag service precautions, and disable air bag system. See SERVICE PRECAUTIONS and DISABLING & ACTIVATING AIR BAG SYSTEM.

2) Raise parking brake lever high as possible. Loosen set screw on shifter knob and remove knob. Remove plastic plunger rod from shifter lever. Carefully pry up and remove shift range indicator bezel. Remove floor console retaining screws.

3) Disconnect accessory wiring harness connector from center console. Remove center console. Raise rear of center console. Disconnect center console wiring harness 10-pin connector. Remove center console.

4) Lower parking brake lever. Pull up parking brake output cable by hand. Pull cable until a 15/64" drill bit can be inserted into automatic adjuster mechanism. See Fig. 6. This will lock parking brake mechanism and remove tension from parking brake cables.

5) Remove rear parking brake cables from parking brake cable equalizer. Disconnect brake warning light connector at parking brake lever. Remove parking brake lever assembly. Remove ACM. Disconnect ACM connectors.

Installation – 1) Connect ACM connectors, and ensure all locking tabs are engaged. Install ACM with arrow pointing forward. Install and tighten ACM nuts to specification. See TORQUE SPECIFICATIONS. Install parking brake lever mechanism, and securely tighten nuts.

2) Ensure parking brake lever is in full down position. Install rear parking brake cable into equalizer on parking brake lever output cable. Ensure parking brake cable is correctly aligned with cable track. Pull up parking brake output cable by hand until all tension is removed from drill bit and remove drill bit.

3) Slowly release parking brake cable until all slack is removed from cable. Connect brake warning light connector. Cycle parking brake lever once to position parking brake cables. Ensure rear wheels rotate freely without dragging when parking brake lever is released.

4) Raise parking brake lever, and install center console. To complete installation, reverse removal procedure. Before connecting negative battery cable, check system operation. See SYSTEM OPERATION CHECK.

WARNING: On Neon, parking brake lever automatic adjusting mechanism contains a clockspring loaded to approximately 20 pounds. DO NOT release automatic adjuster lock-out device before installing cable into equalizer. Keep hands clear of automatic adjuster sector and pawl area. Failure to observe caution in handling automatic adjuster could result in serious injury and/or damage to mechanism.

Removal (Neon) – 1) Before proceeding, follow air bag service precautions, and disable air bag system. See SERVICE PRECAUTIONS and DISABLING & ACTIVATING AIR BAG SYSTEM. On M/T models,

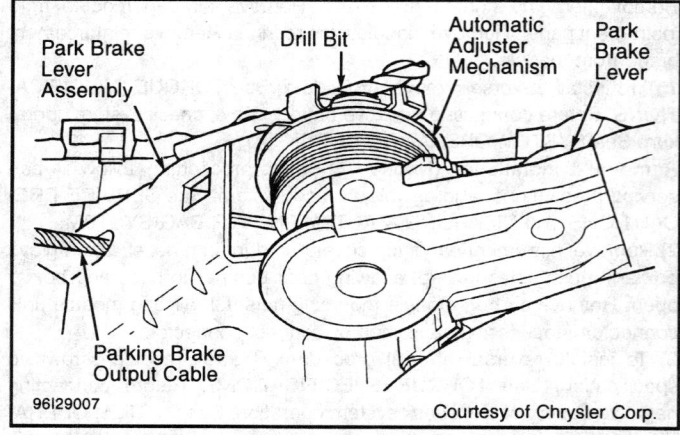

96I29007   Courtesy of Chrysler Corp.

Fig. 6: Identifying Parking Brake Components (Sebring Convertible)

remove shifter knob. On all models, remove screws from rear of console. Remove 2 screws located in cup holders at front of center console.

2) Raise parking brake lever as high as necessary for required clearance, and remove center console. Lower parking brake lever. Pull up parking brake output cable by hand. Pull cable until a 3/16" drill bit can be inserted into handle and sector gear of parking brake mechanism. See Fig. 7. This will lock parking brake mechanism and remove tension from parking brake cables.

3) Remove rear parking brake cables from parking brake cable equalizer. Disconnect brake warning light connector at parking brake lever. Remove parking brake mechanism. Remove ACM. Disconnect ACM 4-pin and 13-pin connectors.

Installation – 1) Connect ACM connectors, and ensure all locking tabs are engaged. Install ACM with arrow pointing forward. Install and tighten nuts to specification. See TORQUE SPECIFICATIONS. Install parking brake lever mechanism, and securely tighten nuts.

2) Install rear parking brake cable into equalizer on parking brake lever output cable. See Fig. 7. Ensure parking brake cable is correctly aligned with cable track. Pull parking brake lever all the way up. Quickly pull and remove drill bit from parking brake mechanism. This will allow parking brake lever mechanism to correctly adjust parking brake cables.

3) Connect brake warning light connector. Cycle parking brake lever once to position parking brake cables. Ensure rear wheels rotate freely without dragging when parking brake lever is released.

4) Raise parking brake lever, and install center console. Install shifter knob. Before connecting negative battery cable, see SYSTEM OPERATION CHECK.

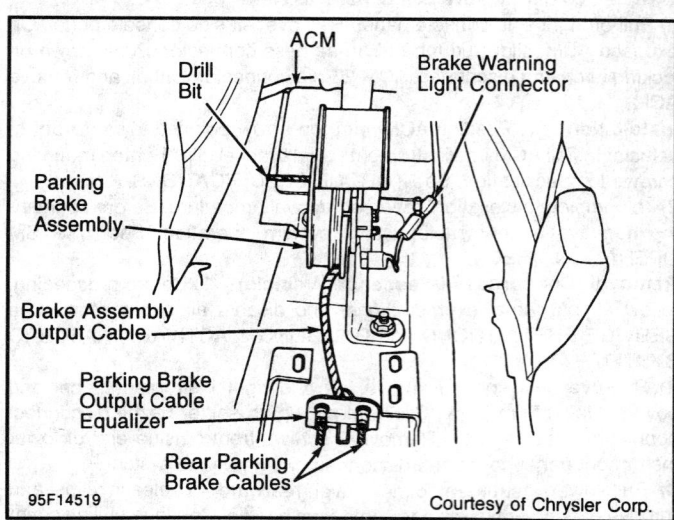

95F14519   Courtesy of Chrysler Corp.

Fig. 7: Parking Brake Components (Neon)

CLOCKSPRING

CAUTION: Before removing steering wheel, position front wheels in straight-ahead position, and lock steering column in place by removing ignition key. Failure to do so could damage clockspring or cause it to be off-centered.

Removal (Avenger & Sebring Coupe) – **1)** Before proceeding, follow air bag service precautions, and disable air bag system. See SERVICE PRECAUTIONS and DISABLING & ACTIVATING AIR BAG SYSTEM. Clockspring cannot be repaired and MUST be replaced if faulty or if air bag module has deployed.

2) Clockspring is located at top of steering column, behind steering wheel. Remove steering wheel and driver's air bag module. See DRIVER'S AIR BAG MODULE & STEERING WHEEL. Remove steering column lower cover. Disconnect clockspring connectors. *See Fig. 8.* Remove clockspring.

Installation – **1)** Align clockspring mating marks. *See Fig. 8.* Ensure front wheels are in straight-ahead position. Install clockspring to steering column switch. To complete installation, reverse removal procedures. Ensure wiring harness is not pinched behind steering wheel.

2) Turn steering wheel fully in both directions to confirm normal steering. Before connecting negative battery cable, check system operation. See SYSTEM OPERATION CHECK.

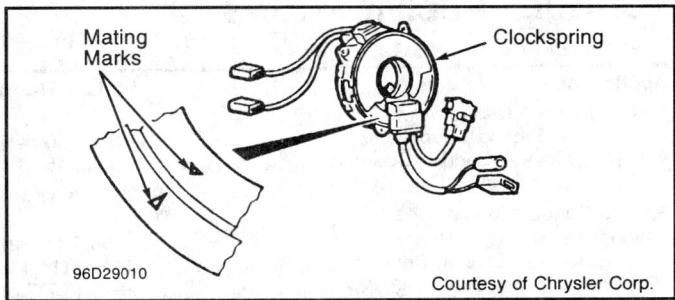

Fig. 8: Identifying Clockspring (Avenger & Sebring Coupe)

Removal (Breeze, Cirrus, Sebring Convertible & Stratus) – **1)** Before proceeding, follow air bag service precautions, and disable air bag system. See SERVICE PRECAUTIONS and DISABLING & ACTIVATING AIR BAG SYSTEM. Clockspring is located at top of steering column, behind steering wheel. Clockspring cannot be repaired and MUST be replaced if faulty or if air bag module has deployed.

2) Remove upper steering column cover. It may be necessary to loosen lower part of instrument cluster hood to remove steering column cover. Remove air bag module and steering wheel. See DRIVER'S AIR BAG MODULE & STEERING WHEEL.

3) Remove multifunction switch. Disconnect 2-pin and 4-pin connectors at base of clockspring. *See Fig. 9.* Release clockspring latch, and remove clockspring from steering shaft.

Installation – **1)** Ensure front wheels are in a straight-ahead position. Ensure clockspring Yellow indicator is centered in centering window. Place clockspring on lock housing and gently push into position.

2) Connect 2-pin and 4-pin clockspring connectors. To complete installation, reverse removal procedure. Before connecting negative battery cable, check system operation. See SYSTEM OPERATION CHECK.

Removal (Concorde & Intrepid) – **1)** Before proceeding, follow air bag service precautions, and disable air bag system. See SERVICE PRECAUTIONS and DISABLING & ACTIVATING AIR BAG SYSTEM. Clockspring cannot be repaired and MUST be replaced if faulty or if air bag module has deployed.

2) Clockspring is located at top of steering column, behind steering wheel. Rotate steering wheel half turn to right from straight-ahead position.

3) Remove air bag module and steering wheel. See DRIVER'S AIR BAG MODULE & STEERING WHEEL. Remove tilt wheel release lever. Remove upper and lower steering column covers.

4) Disconnect 2-pin and 4-pin connectors on bottom rear of clockspring. *See Fig. 10.* Remove clockspring from steering column.

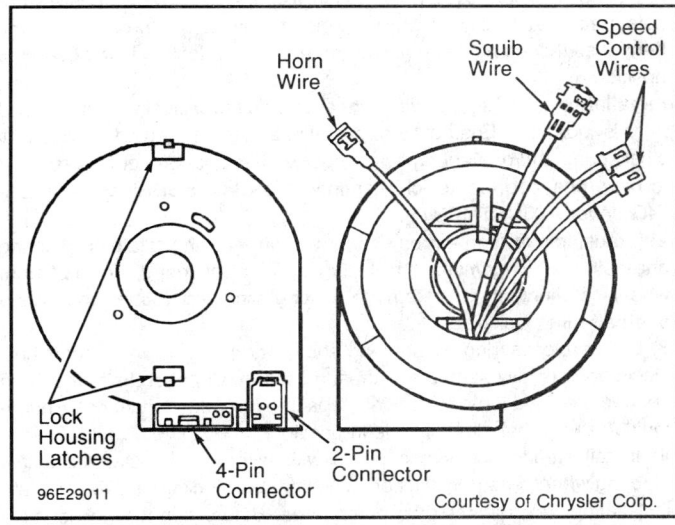

Fig. 9: Identifying Clockspring Components (Breeze, Cirrus, Sebring Convertible & Stratus Shown; Neon Is Similar)

Installation – **1)** Ensure steering wheel is half turn to right from straight ahead position. Position clockspring onto steering shaft with horn wire at the bottom and squib wire at the top. If horn and squib wires are not positioned as specified, go to CLOCKSPRING CENTERING under ADJUSTMENTS. *See Fig. 10.*

2) Connect clockspring wiring connector. Position steering wheel to shaft. Align flats on steering wheel hub with formations inside clockspring. Pull horn wire through small lower hole in steering wheel. Pull squib and cruise control wires through larger upper hole in steering wheel.

3) To complete installation, reverse removal procedure. Install all steering column covers. Before connecting negative battery cable, check system operation. See SYSTEM OPERATION CHECK.

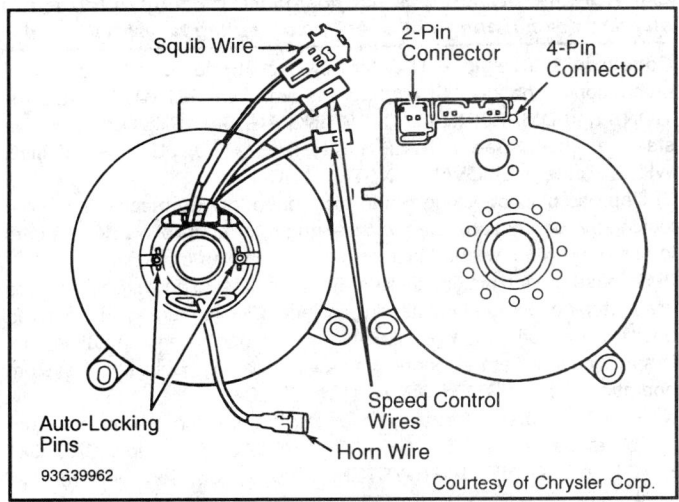

Fig. 10: Identifying Clockspring (Concorde & Intrepid)

Removal (Neon) – **1)** Before proceeding, follow air bag service precautions, and disable air bag system. See SERVICE PRECAUTIONS and DISABLING & ACTIVATING AIR BAG SYSTEM. Clockspring is located at top of steering column, behind steering wheel. Clockspring cannot be repaired and MUST be replaced if faulty or if air bag module has deployed.

2) Remove driver's air bag module and steering wheel. See DRIVER'S AIR BAG MODULE & STEERING WHEEL. Remove upper and lower steering column shrouds to access clockspring wiring. Disconnect 2-pin and 4-pin clockspring connectors. *See Fig. 9.* Release clockspring column latches, and remove clockspring from steering shaft.

3) Rotate clockspring rotor one-half turn counterclockwise. Locate small hole in rotor at 10 o'clock position. Insert a paper clip through hole and bend it so it does not fall out. Clockspring is now locked in the centered position.

Installation – 1) Turn steering wheel one-half turn clockwise and lock it in this position. Ensure turn signal stalk is in neutral position. If clockspring and/or steering wheel position has changed or is suspected to have changed, center clockspring. See CLOCKSPRING CENTER-ING under ADJUSTMENTS.

2) If reusing clockspring, remove paper clip wire and rotate clockspring one-half turn clockwise. If installing NEW clockspring, position front wheels straight ahead. Remove locking pin, and rotate clockspring one-half turn clockwise.

3) Locate clockspring on steering shaft, and push down on rotor until clockspring is fully seated on steering column. Connect 2-pin and 4-pin connectors, and ensure locking taps are properly engaged. Ensure ignition switch halo light wire is in position.

4) Install steering column shrouds with wires inside shrouds. Install steering wheel, ensuring flats on hub align with clockspring. To complete installation, reverse removal procedures. Before connecting negative battery cable, check system operation. See SYSTEM OPERATION CHECK.

IMPACT SENSORS

NOTE: *All models have impact sensor located within Air bag Control Module (ACM). If impact sensor is defective, ACM must be replaced. See AIR BAG CONTROL MODULE (ACM) under REMOVAL & INSTALLATION.*

ADJUSTMENTS
CLOCKSPRING CENTERING

CAUTION: *If clockspring is not positioned properly in relation to steering column and front wheels, clockspring failure will result.*

Concorde & Intrepid – 1) Before proceeding, follow air bag service precautions, and disable air bag system. See SERVICE PRECAU-TIONS and DISABLING & ACTIVATING AIR BAG SYSTEM. Remove steering wheel. See DRIVER'S AIR BAG MODULE & STEERING WHEEL under REMOVAL & INSTALLATION.

2) Depress plastic locking pin to disengage locking mechanism. With locking pin depressed, rotate clockspring rotor until yellow dot appears in centering window and black arrow lines up with drive pin.

3) Release locking pin. Install steering wheel upside down. Ensure wires are not pinched behind steering wheel. Clockspring is in centered position when steering wheel is a half turn to right. Tighten retaining nut to specification. Before connecting negative battery cable, check system operation. See SYSTEM OPERATION CHECK.

Neon – 1) Before proceeding, follow air bag service precautions, and disable air bag system. See SERVICE PRECAUTIONS and DISABLING & ACTIVATING AIR BAG SYSTEM. If not already removed, remove clockspring. See CLOCKSPRING under REMOVAL & INSTALLATION.

2) To center clockspring, depress and hold 2 plastic auto-locking pins in center of clockspring. Gently rotate clockspring rotor clockwise to end of its travel. Rotate clockspring rotor counterclockwise 2 1/2 turns from end of its travel.

3) Engage locking mechanism. Install clockspring. See CLOCKSPRING under REMOVAL & INSTALLATION. Before connecting negative battery cable, check system operation. See SYSTEM OPERATION CHECK.

Avenger & Sebring Coupe – 1) Follow air bag service precautions, and disable air bag system. See SERVICE PRECAUTIONS and DISABLING & ACTIVATING AIR BAG SYSTEM. If not already removed, remove clockspring. See CLOCKSPRING under REMOVAL & INSTALLATION.

2) To center clockspring, gently rotate clockspring rotor clockwise to end of its travel. Rotate clockspring rotor counterclockwise 3 1/8 turns from end of its travel. Align clockspring mating marks. *See Fig. 8.* Ensure front wheels are in straight-ahead position, and install clockspring.

Breeze, Cirrus, Sebring Convertible & Stratus – 1) Follow air bag service precautions, and disable air bag system. See SERVICE PRE-CAUTIONS and DISABLING & ACTIVATING AIR BAG SYSTEM. If not already removed, remove clockspring. See CLOCKSPRING under REMOVAL & INSTALLATION.

2) To center clockspring with steering wheel removed, depress and hold 2 plastic auto-locking pins. Rotate clockspring until Yellow mark appears in centering window. When clockspring is properly centered, arrow on rotor will point at the centering window.

3) Release auto-locking pins to engage locking pins. Before connecting negative battery cable, check system operation. See SYSTEM OPERA-TION CHECK.

TORQUE SPECIFICATIONS

TORQUE SPECIFICATIONS

Application	Ft. Lbs. (N.m)
Steering Wheel-To-Shaft Nut	
Avenger & Sebring Coupe	30 (41)
Except Avenger & Sebring Coupe	45 (61)

	INCH Lbs. (N.m)
Air Bag Control Module	
Avenger & Sebring Coupe	15-20 (1.7-2)
Breeze, Cirrus, Sebring Convertible & Stratus	125-170 (14-19)
Concorde, Intrepid, LHS & 300M	50-70 (5.7-7.9)
Neon	106-125 (12-14)
Air Bag Module	
Driver Side	
Avenger & Sebring Coupe	48 (5)
Breeze, Cirrus & Stratus	80-90 (9-10)
Concorde, Intrepid, LHS & 300M	62-80 (7-9)
Neon	90-100 (10-11)
Sebring Convertible	80-90 (9-10)
Passenger Side	
Avenger & Sebring Coupe	48 (5)
Breeze, Cirrus, Sebring Convertible & Stratus	
Nuts	100 (11)
Screws	20 (2)
Concorde, Intrepid, LHS & 300M	20 (2)
Neon	
Nuts	200-300 (23-34)
Screws	20 (2)

WIRING DIAGRAMS

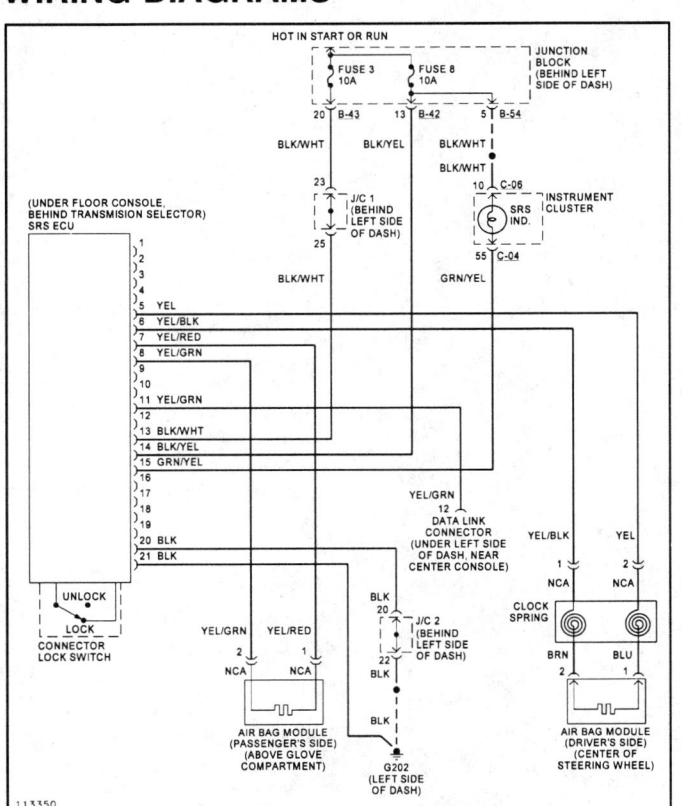

Fig. 11: Air Bag System Wiring Diagram (Avenger & Sebring Coupe)

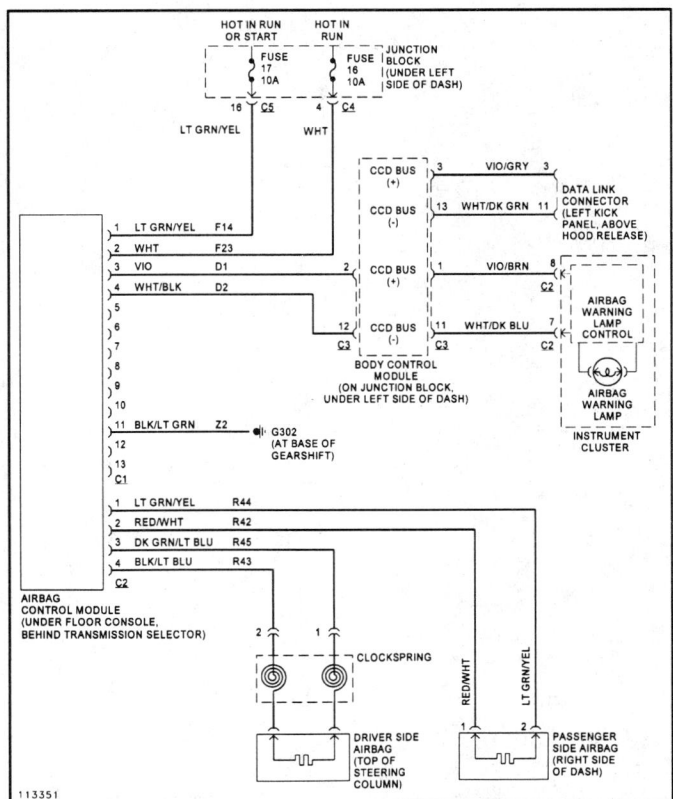

Fig. 12: Air Bag System Wiring Diagram (Breeze, Cirrus & Stratus)

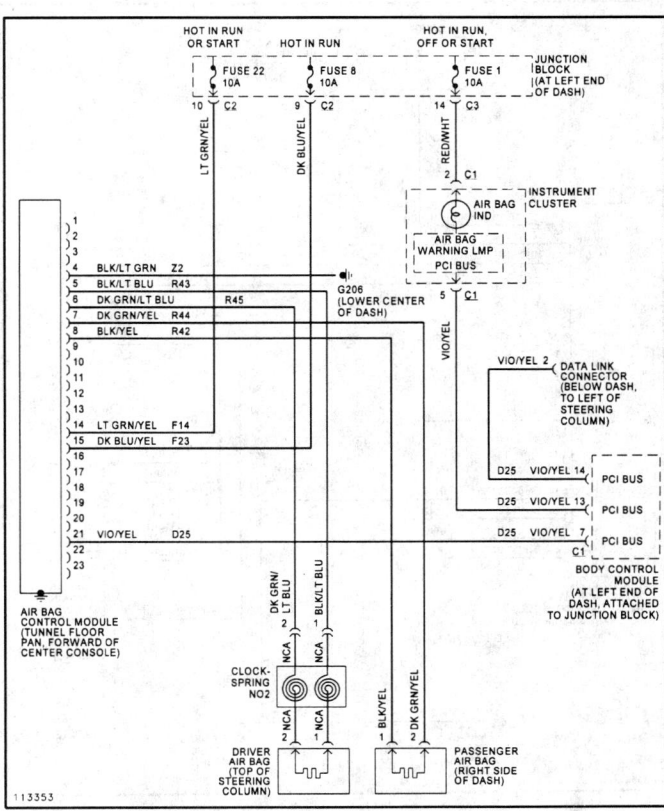

Fig. 13: Air Bag System Wiring Diagram (Concorde, Intrepid, LHS & 300M)

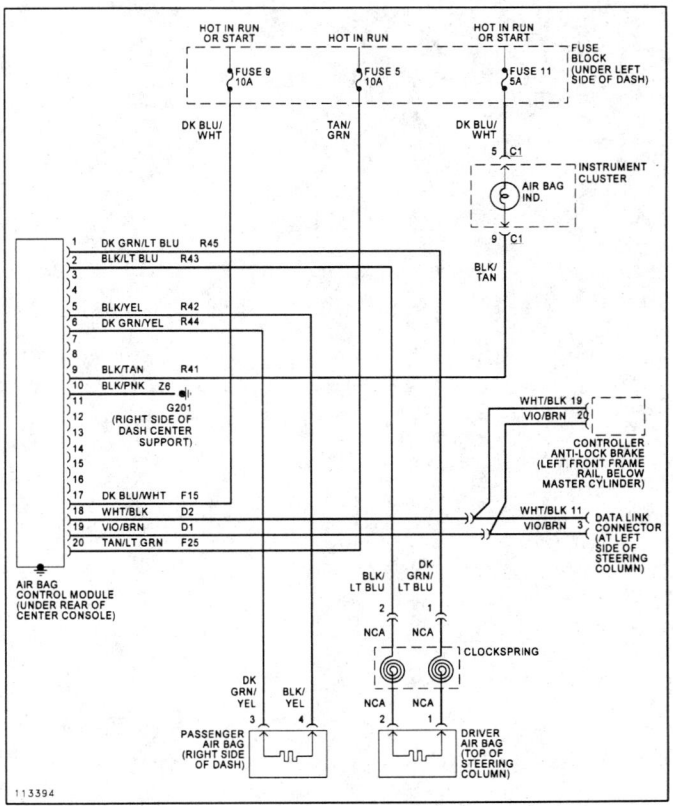

Fig. 14: Air Bag System Wiring Diagram (Neon)

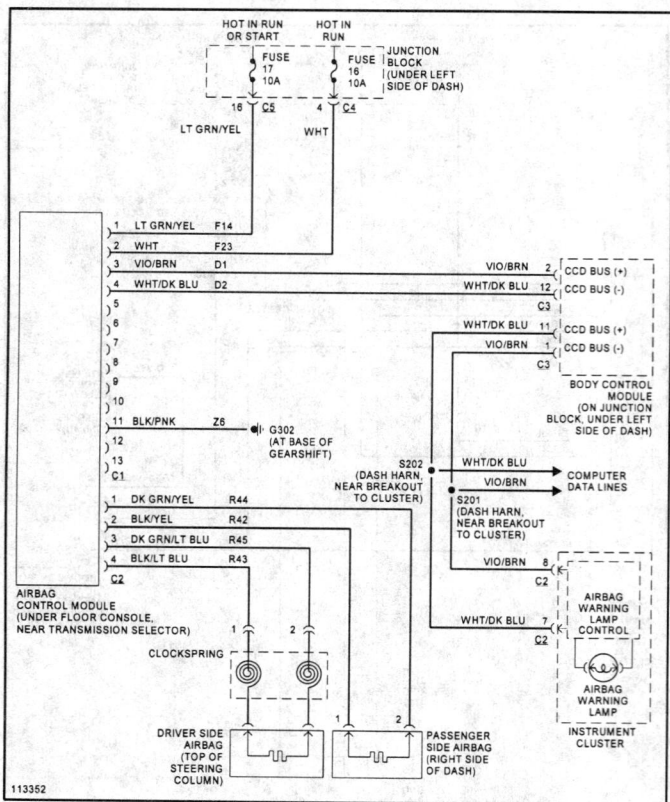

Fig. 15: Air Bag System Wiring Diagram (Sebring Convertible)

Caravan, Dakota, Durango, Ram Pickup, Ram Van, Ram Wagon, Town & Country, Voyager

NOTE: For information on air bag diagnosis & testing or disposal procedures, see MITCHELL® AIR BAG SERVICE & REPAIR MANUAL, DOMESTIC & IMPORTED MODELS.

WARNING: To avoid injury from accidental air bag deployment, read and carefully follow all WARNINGS and SERVICE PRECAUTIONS.

DESCRIPTION & OPERATION

Supplemental Restraint System (SRS) is designed to work in conjunction with seat belts. SRS helps to reduce the risk or severity of serious injury during a front-end collision. Driver's side air bag is stored in a module in steering wheel hub. All models are equipped with passenger's side air bags. Passenger's side air bag is stored in the instrument panel, above glove box. All air bags are covered by a pad bearing the air bag SRS logo.

Air bag(s) inflate and deflate within 1/10th of a second of impact sensor switches closing. This creates a cushion of air between driver and steering wheel and passenger and instrument panel.

System consists of an AIR BAG warning light, clockspring, driver's and passenger's side air bag modules, Air Bag Control Module (ACM), one impact sensor (located inside ACM) and an energy reserve capacitor. The ACM monitors system, stores fault codes (messages) and provides information to AIR BAG warning light and Data Link Connector (DLC). When a malfunction occurs, a fault code is stored and AIR BAG warning light is activated for more than 12 seconds.

When impact sensor registers sufficient deceleration force during a front-end collision, an electrical charge is sent from ACM to air bag module inflator via the clockspring. Inflator actuates and produces nitrogen gas, which inflates air bag(s).

AIR BAG WARNING LIGHT

Whenever ignition switch is in RUN or START position, AIR BAG warning light on instrument panel will illuminate for 6-8 seconds and then turn off. This signifies ACM has checked the system and found that it is functioning properly. If AIR BAG warning light illuminates for 12 seconds or more, stays on all the time or does not come on, a system malfunction exists and trouble code will be stored.

IMPACT SENSOR

All models have one impact sensor located inside ACM. Impact sensor is an accelerometer that measures deceleration. During a front-end collision, a signal is sent that completes an electrical circuit to inflators. Inflators actuate and produce nitrogen gas, which inflates each air bag. Impact sensors are calibrated for a specific vehicle and react to severity and direction of vehicle impact.

Impact sensors are threshold sensitive switches, which complete an electrical circuit when a front-end collision creates sufficient deceleration force to close switches. Impact sensors are calibrated for a specific vehicle and react to severity and direction of vehicle impact.

AIR BAG MODULE

WARNING: DO NOT attempt to disassemble air bag modules. Air bag modules are not serviceable.

Driver's Side – Driver's side air bag module is mounted on front face of steering wheel. A protective cover is fitted to front of air bag module bearing the SRS air bag logo. Air bag module contains air bag cushion, inflator and supporting components. Air bag module is a sealed unit and is not serviceable. The module inflator assembly produces nitrogen gas to fill air bag cushion when a small amount of current from ACM is applied to the ignitor assembly. Gas pressure builds and discharges from inflator through a diffuser and screen assembly, forcing steering wheel cover to burst along its seams until air bag is fully inflated. Once air bag cushion is fully inflated, gas escapes from bag through vents, away from driver.

Passenger's Side – Passenger's side air bag module is mounted to instrument panel mounting bracket. Module is covered by a protective door bearing the SRS air bag logo. When supplied an electrical signal, inflator will discharge nitrogen gas directly into air bag. When air bag inflates, protective door will pivot aside allowing air bag to deploy.

AIR BAG CONTROL MODULE (ACM)

Impact sensor, energy reserve capacitor and On-Board Diagnostics (OBD) are an integral part of ACM. ACM monitors critical input and output circuits within air bag system, ensuring they are operating correctly. Some circuits are tested continuously; others are checked only under certain conditions. ACM provides information about air bag system through AIR BAG warning light and Data Link Connector (DLC). When diagnostic trouble code (fault message) is stored, AIR BAG warning light will be activated for 12 seconds or more. For ACM location, see AIR BAG CONTROL MODULE LOCATION table.

AIR BAG CONTROL MODULE LOCATION

Application	Location
Caravan, Town & Country, & Voyager	Behind Center Console, At Center Of Lower Instrument Panel
Dakota, Durango & Ram Pickup	Under Instrument Panel, On Transmission Tunnel
Ram Van & Ram Wagon	Under Driver's Seat

DATA LINK CONNECTOR LOCATIONS

DATA LINK CONNECTOR LOCATIONS

Application	Location
Caravan, Dakota, Durango, Town & Country, & Voyager	Under Left Side Of Instrument Panel, Right Of Steering Column
Ram Pickup, Ram Van & Ram Wagon	Under Left Side Of Instrument Panel, Left Of Steering Column

CLOCKSPRING

Clockspring connects air bag module to steering column wiring, completing air bag system circuit. See Fig. 1. Inside clockspring is a flat, ribbon-like tape of conductive material, which winds and unwinds with steering wheel movement. Clockspring is the most fragile part of air bag system. Clockspring must be centered properly to allow 1 1/2 steering wheel turns in either direction. If clockspring is not centered properly, it can break from stretching or fatigue.

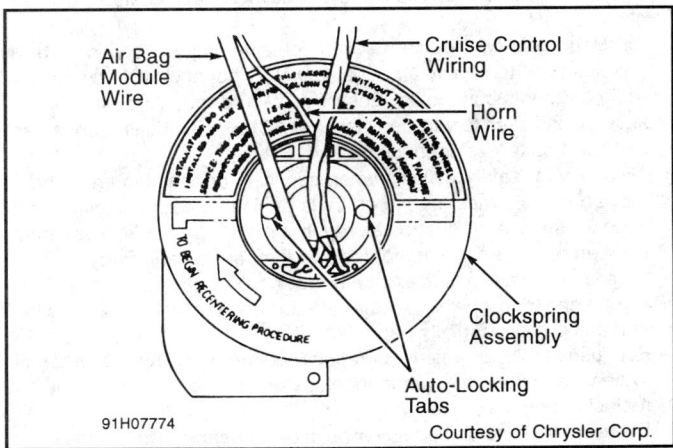

Air Bag Module Wire
Cruise Control Wiring
Horn Wire
Clockspring Assembly
Auto-Locking Tabs

91H07774

Courtesy of Chrysler Corp.

Fig. 1: Identifying Clockspring (Typical)

PASSENGER'S AIR BAG DISARM SWITCH (PADS)

On Dakota, Ram Pickup, Ram Van and Ram Wagon models, a Passenger's Air Bag Disarm Switch (PADS) is mounted on instrument panel. Switch allows passenger's side air bag module to be disarmed when rear facing child safety seats are being used. PADS is operated with ignition key.

SERVICING

Air bag system should be serviced every 3 years or 30,000 miles. The following items should be checked.
1) Check all air bag system components for damage or deterioration. Replace air bag module if air bag module housing shows signs of physical damage or abuse.
2) Check AIR BAG warning light for proper operation. Turn ignition switch to RUN position. AIR BAG warning light should illuminate for 6-8 seconds and go out.
3) If AIR BAG warning light does not illuminate or if AIR BAG warning light illuminates but fails to go out after 12 seconds or longer, a system malfunction exists. See SYSTEM OPERATION CHECK.

SYSTEM OPERATION CHECK

WARNING: To avoid possible injury from accidental air bag deployment after repairs, disconnect and isolate negative battery terminal. Turn ignition switch to RUN position. Ensure no one is inside vehicle and connect negative battery cable. Turn ignition switch to LOCK position.

Turn ignition switch to RUN position and observe AIR BAG warning light. AIR BAG warning light should come on for 6-8 seconds, then go out, indicating system is functioning properly. If AIR BAG warning light either fails to come on, blinks on and off, or comes on and stays on, a system malfunction exists. See MITCHELL® AIR BAG SERVICE & REPAIR MANUAL, DOMESTIC & IMPORTED MODELS. Repair as necessary.

SERVICE PRECAUTIONS

The following precautions should be observed when working with air bag systems:
• Disable air bag system before servicing any air bag system or steering column component. Failure to do this could result in accidental air bag deployment and possible personal injury. See DISABLING & ACTIVATING AIR BAG SYSTEM.
• To avoid possible injury from accidental air bag deployment after repairs, disconnect and isolate negative battery terminal. Turn ignition switch to RUN position. Ensure no one is inside vehicle and connect negative battery cable. Turn ignition switch to LOCK position. Ensure AIR BAG warning light is working properly and no system faults are indicated. See SYSTEM OPERATION CHECK.
• Before disconnecting Air Bag Control Module (ACM), ensure ignition switch is in LOCK position and negative battery cable is disconnected.
• Air Bag Control Module (ACM) contains impact sensor which enables SRS to deploy air bags. DO NOT connect ACM connector while battery is connected. Ensure ACM and mounting bracket are securely installed to vehicle whenever ACM is electrically connected SRS and battery is connected.
• Always wear safety glasses when servicing or handling an air bag.
• Air bag module must be stored in its original special container until used for service. It must be stored in a clean, dry place, away from sources of extreme heat, sparks and high electrical energy.
• When placing a live air bag on a bench or other surface, always face air bag and trim cover up, away from surface. This will reduce motion of module if accidentally deployed.
• Because of critical system operating requirements, DO NOT attempt to service any air bag components. Corrections are only made by replacing defective part.
• Electrical sources should never be allowed near inflator on the back of air bag module.

• DO NOT probe connectors with an ohmmeter unless specifically instructed to do so. Ohmmeters are self-powered and could deploy air bag(s).
• When carrying a live air bag module, trim cover should be pointed away from your body to minimize injury in case of accidental deployment.
• DO NOT probe any wire through insulator, as this will damage it and eventually cause failure due to corrosion.
• If air bag system is not fully functional for any reason, vehicle should not be driven until system is repaired and again becomes operational. DO NOT remove bulbs, modules, sensors or other components or in any way disable system from operating normally. If air bag system is not functional, park vehicle until it is repaired and functions properly.
• When battery is disconnected, vehicle computer and memory systems may lose memory data. Driveability problems may exist until computer systems have completed a relearn cycle. See COMPUTER RELEARN PROCEDURES in GENERAL INFORMATION before disconnecting battery.

DISABLING & ACTIVATING AIR BAG SYSTEM

WARNING: Wait at least 2 minutes after disconnecting negative battery cable before servicing air bag system. System reserve capacitor, integral to ACM, maintains air bag system voltage for about 2 minutes after battery is disconnected. Servicing air bag system before 2- minute period may cause accidental deployment of air bag(s) and possible personal injury. DO NOT use computer system memory saving devices. Enough voltage to deploy air bag(s) may be provided from device.

CAUTION: When battery is disconnected, vehicle computer and memory systems may lose memory data. Driveability problems may exist until computer systems have completed a relearn cycle. See COMPUTER RELEARN PROCEDURES article in GENERAL INFORMATION before disconnecting battery.

DISABLING SYSTEM

To disable air bag system for repairs, ensure ignition switch is in LOCK position. Disconnect and shield negative battery cable. After disconnecting negative battery cable, wait at least 2 minutes for reserve capacitor to discharge before servicing air bag system.

ACTIVATING SYSTEM

Reconnect negative battery cable. From a position clear of air bag(s), turn ignition switch to RUN position. Observe SRS/AIR BAG warning light. Warning light should illuminate for 6-8 seconds and then go out, indicating system is functioning properly. If warning light fails to illuminate, or illuminates and stays on, a system malfunction exists. See SYSTEM OPERATION CHECK.

REMOVAL & INSTALLATION

WARNING: *Failure to follow air bag service precautions may result in air bag deployment and personal injury. See SERVICE PRECAUTIONS. Air bag parts are not interchangeable between models. Always use NEW parts and correct part number for vehicle being worked on. After component replacement, always perform a system operation check to ensure proper system operation. See SYSTEM OPERATION CHECK.*

CAUTION: *When battery is disconnected, vehicle computer and memory systems may lose memory data. Driveability problems may exist until computer systems have completed a relearn cycle. DO NOT use computer system memory saving devices. Enough voltage to deploy air bag(s) may be provided from device. See COMPUTER RELEARN PROCEDURES in GENERAL INFORMATION before disconnecting battery.*

AIR BAG CONTROL MODULE (ACM)

WARNING: *ACM contains impact sensor, which enables SRS to activate air bag. To avoid accidental air bag deployment, DO NOT connect ACM electrically to system unless it is bolted to vehicle. DO NOT strike or kick ACM, as it may damage internal impact sensor or affect its calibration. If ACM is accidentally dropped during installation, it must be replaced.*

Removal (Caravan, Town & Country, & Voyager) – **1)** Before proceeding, follow air bag service precautions. See SERVICE PRECAUTIONS. Disable air bag system. See DISABLING & ACTIVATING AIR BAG SYSTEM.
2) ACM is located behind center console, at center of instrument panel. *See Fig. 2.* Remove forward lower console from instrument panel. Remove screw holding lower heater duct to instrument panel support. Remove heater duct from instrument panel. Remove bolts holding top of right support to instrument panel.
3) Remove bolts holding bottom of right support to floor pan. Separate right instrument panel support from vehicle. Disconnect ACM connectors. Remove ACM bracket assembly-to-floor bolts. Remove ACM.

CAUTION: *DO NOT remove bolts holding ACM to ACM bracket. Bracket is supplied with replacement ACM. Use correct screws when installing ACM.*

Installation – Using correct screws, install ACM with arrow pointing toward front of vehicle. Connect ACM connectors. Ensure connectors are locked into position. To complete installation, reverse removal procedure. Tighten mounting screws to 75-105 INCH lbs. (8.5-11.9 N.m). DO NOT connect negative battery cable at this time. See DISABLING & ACTIVATING AIR BAG SYSTEM.
Removal (Dakota & Durango) – **1)** Before proceeding, follow air bag service precautions. See SERVICE PRECAUTIONS. Disable air bag system. See DISABLING & ACTIVATING AIR BAG SYSTEM.
2) ACM is located under instrument panel, on transmission tunnel. *See Fig. 3.* Pull carpet back from front of transmission tunnel far enough to access center support bracket.
3) Remove center support bracket-to-lower instrument panel screws. Remove center support bracket-to-ACM bracket screws. Remove center support bracket. Disconnect instrument panel wiring harness ground eyelet at left side of transmission tunnel.
4) To disconnect ACM connector, remove Red Connector Position Assurance (CPA) lock from connector. Depress latch tab while pulling

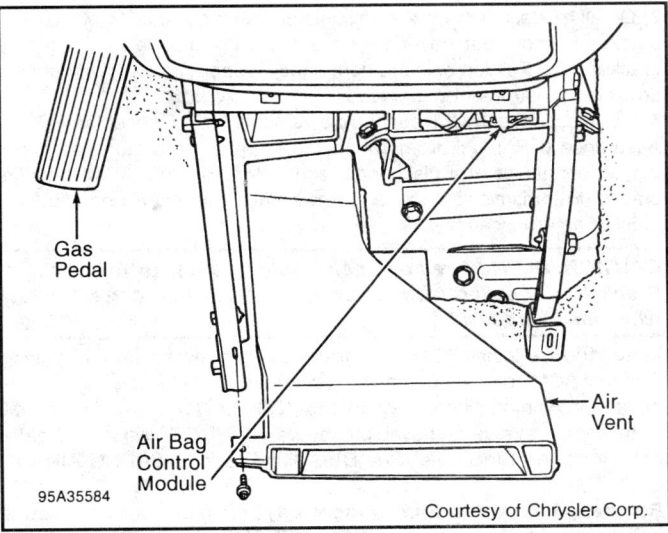

**Fig. 2: Removing Air Bag Control Module
(Caravan, Town & Country, & Voyager)**

out on connector and disconnect connector. Remove ACM mounting bracket-to-transmission tunnel screws. Remove ACM and mounting bracket as an assembly.

CAUTION: *DO NOT remove bolts holding ACM to ACM bracket. Bracket is supplied with replacement ACM. Use correct screws when installing ACM.*

Installation – **1)** Install ACM with arrow pointing toward front of vehicle. Tighten mounting screws to 105 INCH lbs. (11.9 N.m). Connect ACM connector, ensuring connector is locked into position.
2) To complete installation, reverse removal procedure. DO NOT connect negative battery cable at this time. See DISABLING & ACTIVATING AIR BAG SYSTEM.

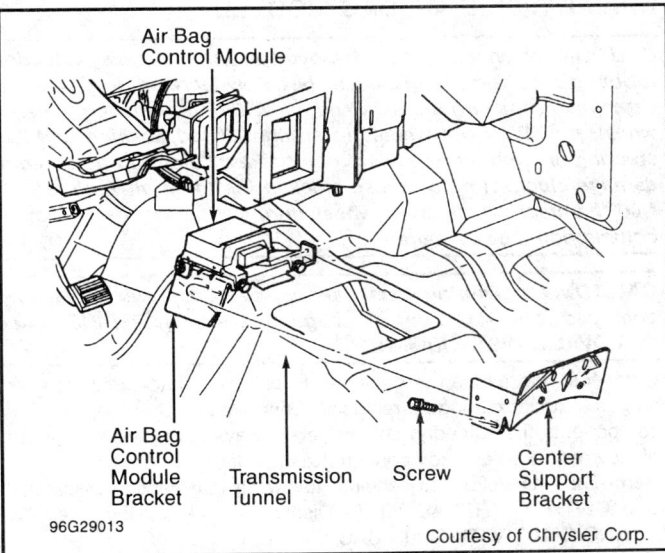

Fig. 3: Locating Air Bag Control Module (Dakota & Durango)

Removal (Ram Pickup) – **1)** Before proceeding, follow air bag service precautions. See SERVICE PRECAUTIONS. Disable air bag system. See DISABLING & ACTIVATING AIR BAG SYSTEM.
2) On M/T models, pry corner of shifter boot up and remove shifter boot from console. Remove cup holder, if equipped. Remove console mounting screws. Lift console upward and disconnect wire harness connector, if equipped. While removing console, route shifter boot through console.

3) On all models, remove 2 screws holding trim cover to ACM mounting bracket. Remove trim cover. Remove 2 instrument panel center support bracket nuts. Pull top of instrument panel support bracket rearward and down from instrument panel studs.

4) To disconnect ACM connector, remove Red Connector Position Assurance (CPA) lock from connector. Depress latch tab while pulling out on connector and disconnect connector. Remove ACM mounting bracket-to-transmission tunnel screws. Remove ACM and mounting bracket as an assembly.

CAUTION: DO NOT remove bolts holding ACM to ACM bracket. Bracket is supplied with replacement ACM. Use correct screws when installing ACM.

Installation – Install ACM with arrow pointing toward front of vehicle. Connect ACM connectors, ensuring connectors are locked into position. Tighten ACM mounting screws to 125 INCH lbs. (14 N.m). To complete installation, reverse removal procedure. DO NOT connect negative battery cable at this time. See DISABLING & ACTIVATING AIR BAG SYSTEM.

Removal (Ram Van & Ram Wagon) – 1) Before proceeding, follow air bag service precautions. See SERVICE PRECAUTIONS. Disable air bag system. See DISABLING & ACTIVATING AIR BAG SYSTEM.

2) To disconnect ACM connector, remove Red Connector Position Assurance (CPA) lock from connector. Depress latch tab while pulling out on connector and disconnect connector. Remove 3 screws holding ACM mounting bracket to floor. Remove ACM and mounting bracket as an assembly.

CAUTION: DO NOT remove bolts holding ACM to ACM bracket. Bracket is supplied with replacement ACM. Use correct screws when installing ACM.

Installation – Install ACM with arrow pointing toward front of vehicle. Tighten ACM mounting screws to 105 INCH lbs. (11.9 N.m). Connect ACM connectors, ensuring connectors are locked into position. DO NOT connect negative battery cable at this time. See DISABLING & ACTIVATING AIR BAG SYSTEM.

DRIVER'S SIDE AIR BAG MODULE

CAUTION: When removing a deployed air bag, wear eye protection, rubber gloves and a long-sleeve shirt. Powder residue from air bag deployment may irritate skin and eyes. Before removing steering wheel, position front wheels in straight-ahead position and lock steering column by removing ignition key. Failure to do so could damage clockspring or cause clockspring to be off-centered. DO NOT hammer on steering wheel during removal, or collapsible column could be damaged.

CAUTION: Clockspring must be replaced whenever replacing a deployed driver's side air bag. See CLOCKSPRING under REMOVAL & INSTALLATION.

If driver's side air bag is deployed in collision, manufacturer recommends that clockspring be replaced. Ensure all SRS and other related components (i.e., steering column) are always inspected after air bag deployment. Replace component(s) as needed.

Removal – 1) Before proceeding, follow air bag service precautions. See SERVICE PRECAUTIONS. Disable air bag system. See DISABLING & ACTIVATING AIR BAG SYSTEM.

2) Air bag module is mounted on face of steering wheel. *See Fig. 4.* Ensure wheels are pointed straight-ahead and steering wheel is locked.

3) Remove air bag module-to-steering wheel nuts/screws from back side of steering wheel. Lift air bag module and disconnect electrical connectors from rear of module.

Installation – 1) Connect air bag, cruise control and horn harness connectors to rear of air bag module. Secure module to steering wheel.

2) Tighten air bag module-to-steering wheel nuts/screws to specification. See TORQUE SPECIFICATIONS. DO NOT connect negative battery cable at this time. See DISABLING & ACTIVATING AIR BAG SYSTEM.

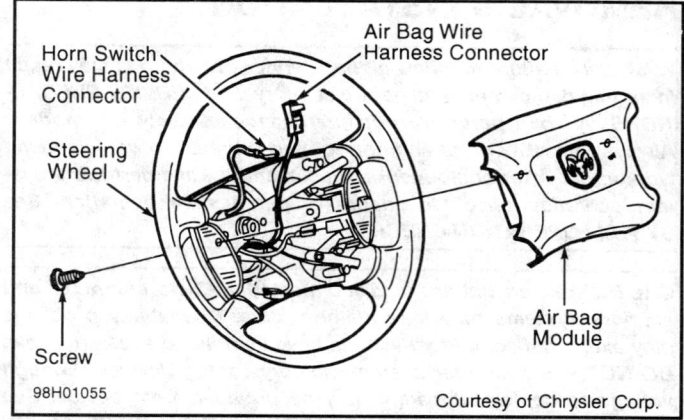

Fig. 4: Removing Driver's Side Air Bag Module (Ram Van & Ram Wagon Shown; All Others Are Similar)

PASSENGER'S SIDE AIR BAG MODULE

NOTE: On Caravan, Town & Country and Voyager, if passenger's side air bag has been deployed, instrument panel must be replaced.

Removal (Caravan, Town & Country, & Voyager – Deployed Air Bag) – 1) Before proceeding, follow air bag service precautions. See SERVICE PRECAUTIONS. Disable air bag system. See DISABLING & ACTIVATING AIR BAG SYSTEM.

2) Remove lower console. Remove instrument panel support bracket-to-lower heater duct screw. *See Fig. 5.* Remove lower heater duct. Remove instrument panel support brackets. Remove left and right instrument panel end covers.

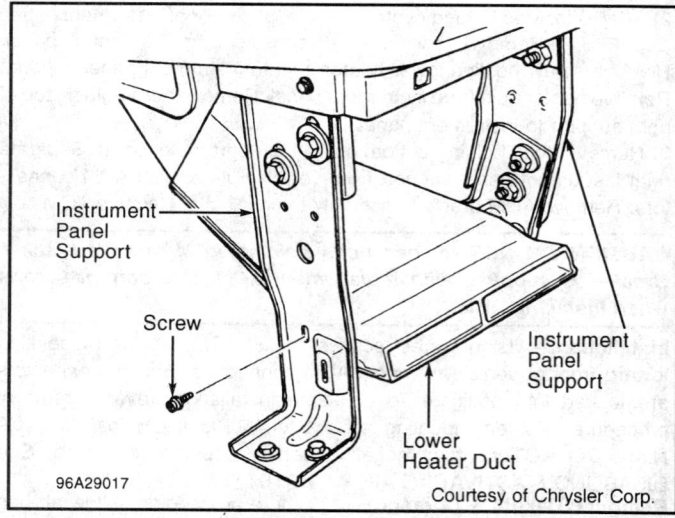

Fig. 5: Identifying Instrument Panel Lower Support Brackets (Caravan, Town & Country, & Voyager)

3) Disconnect passenger's side air bag module connector. Remove front door sill trim covers. Remove "A" pillar trim covers. Remove glove box. Disconnect antenna lead connector from behind glove box. Remove lower steering column cover.

4) Remove knee bolster. Disconnect lower two 40-pin wiring harness connectors from main junction block. *See Fig. 6.* Disconnect wiring harness connector from bottom of Body Control Module (BCM).

5) Disconnect two 40-pin wiring harness connectors from right side of steering column. *See Fig. 7.* Remove upper steering shaft-to-lower steering shaft pinch bolt. Separate upper shaft from lower shaft.

6) Remove instrument panel frame-to-brake pedal support nuts on each side of steering column. Disconnect gear shift cable from gear selector. Remove gear shift cable bracket-to-instrument panel frame nut and remove bracket.

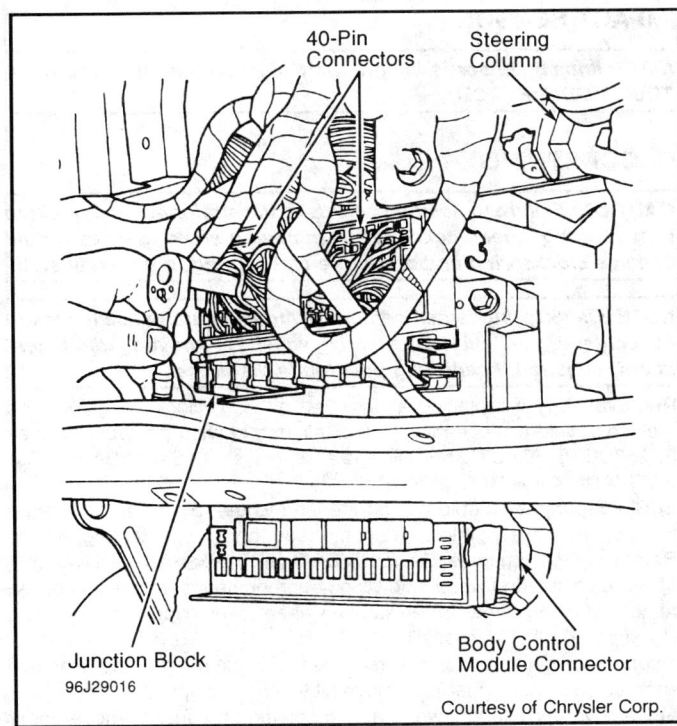

Fig. 6: Disconnecting Instrument Panel Wiring Harness Connectors (Caravan, Town & Country, & Voyager)

7) Disconnect hood release handle from instrument panel and position handle out of way. Remove instrument panel top cover. Disconnect heater-A/C wiring harness connector from behind glove box. Remove instrument panel frame-to-bracket bolts on cowl side panels.

8) Loosen, but DO NOT remove instrument panel-to-cowl panel pivot bolts. Remove bolts retaining instrument panel frame to dash panel below windshield opening. Ensure all wiring harnesses and connectors are positioned out of way and remove instrument panel.

Installation – Transfer all reusable components from old instrument panel to NEW instrument panel. Install NEW passenger's air bag module to instrument panel. To complete installation, reverse removal procedure. DO NOT connect negative battery cable at this time. See DISABLING & ACTIVATING AIR BAG SYSTEM.

Removal (Caravan, Town & Country, & Voyager – Undeployed Air Bag) – **1)** Before proceeding, follow air bag service precautions. See SERVICE PRECAUTIONS. Disable air bag system. See DISABLING & ACTIVATING AIR BAG SYSTEM.

2) Remove instrument panel top cover. Remove speaker from right front of instrument panel. Remove glove box. Disconnect Yellow wire connector from passenger's air bag.

3) Remove bolts retaining forward air bag mount to instrument panel. See Fig. 8. Working through access holes in instrument panel above glove box opening, remove screws holding air bag to back of panel. Remove screws holding air bag to instrument panel cover. Remove air bag from instrument panel.

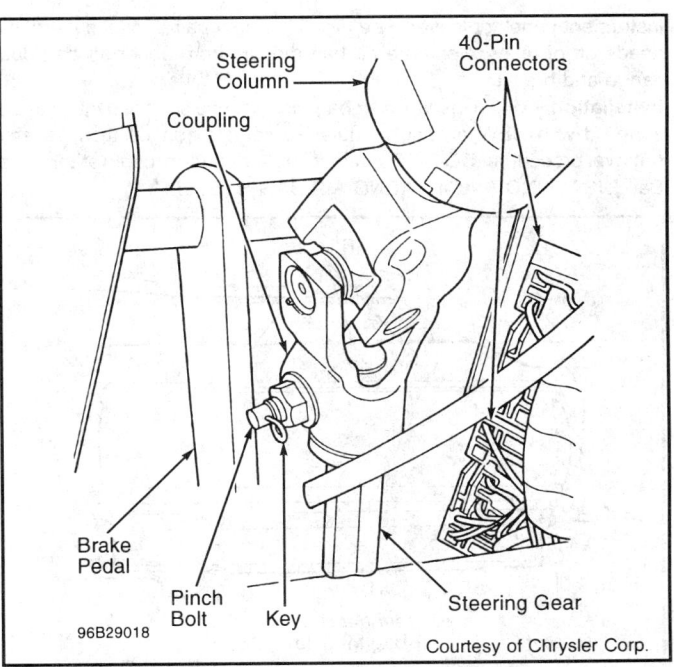

Fig. 7: Separating Upper & Lower Steering Shafts (Caravan, Town & Country, & Voyager)

Installation – To install, reverse removal procedure. Check module door for fit and trim while tightening module screws. DO NOT connect negative battery cable at this time. See DISABLING & ACTIVATING AIR BAG SYSTEM.

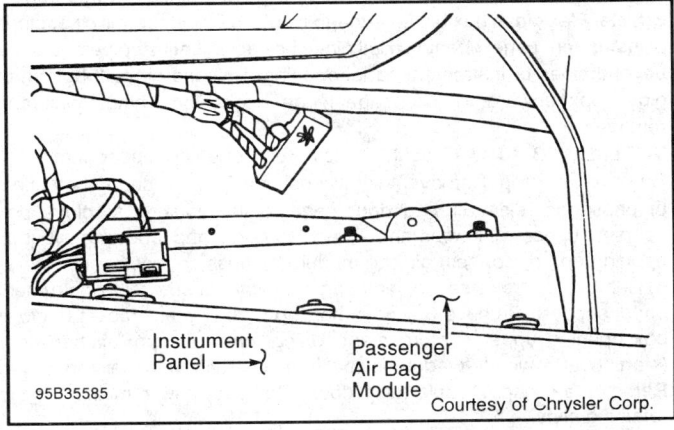

Fig. 8: Removing Passenger's Side Air Bag Module (Caravan, Town & Country, & Voyager)

WARNING: DO NOT use a drill to remove air bag module rivets. Sparks created when drilling could result in accidental air bag deployment.

NOTE: On Dakota and Durango, to replace passenger's side air bag, instrument panel and instrument panel top cover must be removed.

Removal (Dakota & Durango) – **1)** Before proceeding, follow air bag service precautions. See SERVICE PRECAUTIONS. Disable air bag system. See DISABLING & ACTIVATING AIR BAG SYSTEM.

2) Remove instrument panel and instrument panel top cover. See INSTRUMENT PANEL & TOP COVER. Cover air bag module vents with masking tape. Using a center punch, drive out mandrels from 4 rivets that secure air bag module to upper air bag door flange and bracket on instrument panel top cover. *See Fig. 9.* Using a pair of rivet cutters, cut heads off of rivets. Separate air bag module from upper air bag door flange and bracket.

Installation – When installing air bag module, use special rivets that are supplied with NEW air bag module. To complete installation, reverse removal procedure. DO NOT connect negative battery cable at this time. See DISABLING & ACTIVATING AIR BAG SYSTEM.

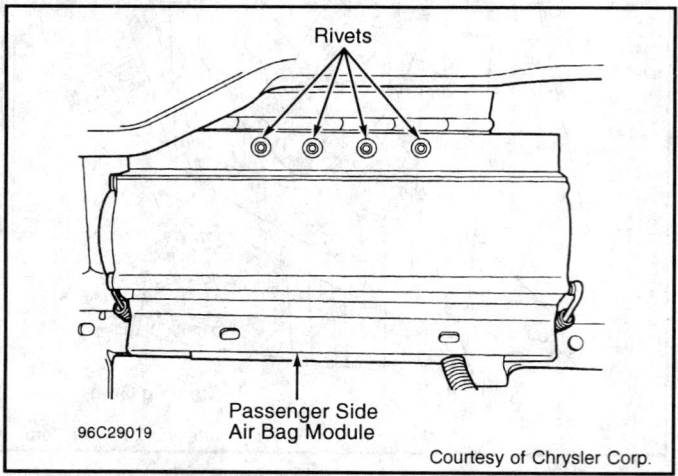

Fig. 9: Removing Passenger's Side Air Bag Module Rivets (Dakota & Durango)

Removal (Ram Pickup) – 1) Before proceeding, follow air bag service precautions. See SERVICE PRECAUTIONS. Disable air bag system. See DISABLING & ACTIVATING AIR BAG SYSTEM.

2) Holding glove box door, push center of glove box bin towards front of vehicle. Flex glove box bin far enough so glove box stops will clear sides of instrument panel opening. Roll glove box down until stop bumpers are beyond sides of instrument panel opening. Release bin. Lift bottom of glove box upward to disengage hinge hooks form hinge pins and remove.

3) Remove 3 screws securing glove box opening upper trim strip. Remove trim strip. Remove 4 screws holding 2 plastic support brackets of passenger side air bag door panel outlet housing to glove box opening upper reinforcement. Reach through and above glove box opening and disconnect air bag module harness connector.

4) Remove 2 screws securing air bag module front bracket to instrument panel support. Remove 3 screws holding air bag rear bracket to glove box opening upper reinforcement. Using trim stick, pry air bag door (starting at lower left edge) away from instrument panel top cover. Remove air bag module and door. Remove any remaining snap retaining clips.

Installation – To install, reverse removal procedure. Ensure air bag door is securely attached to instrument panel. Ensure air bag harness connector latches fully engaged. DO NOT connect negative battery cable at this time. See DISABLING & ACTIVATING AIR BAG SYSTEM.

Removal (Ram Van & Ram Wagon) – 1) Before proceeding, follow air bag service precautions. See SERVICE PRECAUTIONS. Disable air bag system. See DISABLING & ACTIVATING AIR BAG SYSTEM.

2) Open glove box. Push both sides of glove box bin inwards far enough so that glove box stops can be cleared and glove box rolled outward. Remove screws that secure air bag rear bracket and lower flange to glove box upper reinforcement. Reach through to access and unplug air bag harness connector.

3) Remove remaining screws that secure air bag to instrument panel. Using trim stick, pry air bag door (starting at lower left edge) away from instrument panel top cover. Remove air bag module and door. Remove any remaining snap retaining clips.

Installation – To install, reverse removal procedure. Ensure air bag door is securely attached to instrument panel. Ensure air bag harness connector latches fully engaged. DO NOT connect negative battery cable at this time. See DISABLING & ACTIVATING AIR BAG SYSTEM.

IMPACT SENSOR

NOTE: Impact sensor is integral part of ACM. See AIR BAG CONTROL MODULE (ACM).

CLOCKSPRING

CAUTION: Failure to position wheels in the straight-ahead position with steering wheel locked when removing steering wheel could damage clockspring and/or require clockspring to be readjusted.

NOTE: Clockspring is self-centering and will automatically lock in the centered position when steering wheel is removed. Adjustment is only required if centering position is disturbed.

Removal – 1) If replacing a deployed air bag, clockspring must be replaced. Before proceeding, follow air bag service precautions. See SERVICE PRECAUTIONS. Disable air bag system. See DISABLING & ACTIVATING AIR BAG SYSTEM.

2) Clockspring is located behind steering wheel. *See Fig. 10.* Ensure front wheels are pointed straight ahead and lock steering wheel. Remove air bag module. See DRIVER'S SIDE AIR BAG MODULE.

3) Remove steering wheel nut. Using appropriate steering wheel puller, remove steering wheel. When steering wheel is removed, self- centering clockspring will automatically lock in place. Remove upper and lower steering column shrouds to gain access to clockspring wiring. Remove knee bolster (if equipped). Remove tilt lever (if equipped).

4) Remove upper and lower steering column shrouds. Remove upper steering column wire harness tie straps. Disconnect Yellow 2-way clockspring (also known as squib or initiator) harness connector between clockspring and instrument panel wiring harness, at base of steering column. *See Fig. 11.*

5) On Ram Van and Ram Wagon, remove snap ring holding clockspring to upper steering column shaft. On all other models, carefully disengage plastic latches of clockspring from steering column lock housing. On all models, remove clockspring by carefully sliding it off steering column shaft. Clockspring cannot be repaired and must be replaced if faulty.

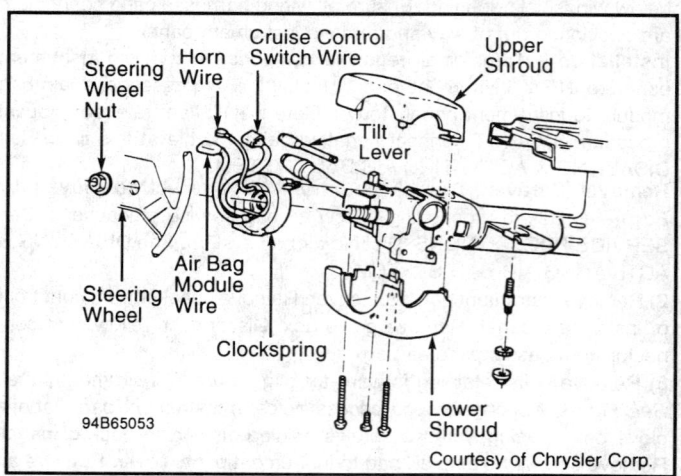

Fig. 10: Removing Clockspring (Typical)

Installation – 1) Snap clockspring onto steering column. If clockspring centering adjustment is disturbed, adjust clockspring before installing steering wheel. See CLOCKSPRING CENTERING under ADJUSTMENTS. Connect clockspring wiring connectors. Install steering column covers. Install knee bolster (if removed).

2) Position steering wheel on steering column. Ensure flats on steering wheel hub fit formations on inside of clockspring. Pull clockspring, cruise control switch (if equipped) and horn wires through lower large holes and upper small holes in steering wheel.

3) Install steering wheel retaining nut and tighten to 45 ft. lbs. (61 N.m). Connect horn and cruise control wires (if equipped). Connect clockspring wire to air bag module. To ensure complete connector connection, latching arms must be visible on top of connector housing. DO NOT connect negative battery cable at this time. See DISABLING & ACTIVATING AIR BAG SYSTEM.

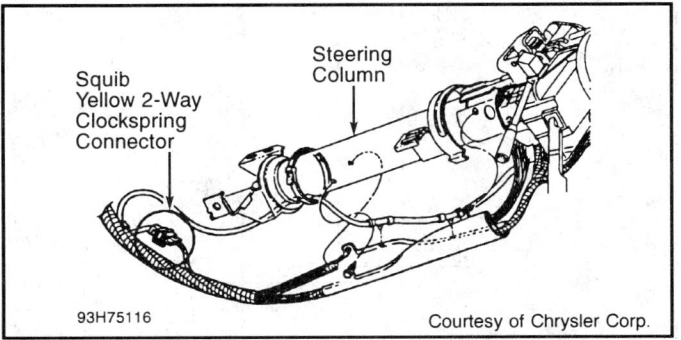

Fig. 11: Locating Yellow 2-Way Squib Connector (Typical)

INSTRUMENT PANEL & TOP COVER

Removal & Installation (Dakota & Durango) – 1) Place front wheels in strait ahead position. Disconnect negative battery cable. Remove sill trim from both doorways. Remove kick panel covers from both sides of vehicle. Remove mounting screws for hood release handle.

2) Remove steering column trim panel and support bracket. Remove tilt steering column lever (if equipped). Remove upper and lower shrouds from steering column. Unplug driver's side air bag module. Loosen multifunction switch wiring harness connector screw and disconnect from switch. Screw will remain in connector.

3) On A/T models, disconnect PRNDL cable. Disconnect shifter cable from steering column. On all models, remove steering coupler pinch bolt from upper shaft. Remove toe plate retaining screws. Remove steering column mounting bolts and remove steering column from vehicle.

4) Remove screw from bulk head wiring harness connector and disconnect connector. Disconnect 2 body wiring harness connectors located next to bulk head connector. Disconnect 3 wiring harness connectors located nearest to dash panel from junction block. Disconnect brakelight switch connector. Disconnect Rear Wheel Anti-Lock (RAWL) brake module (if equipped), located near steering column support brackets.

5) Disconnect plastic retainer clip from parking brake linkage rod, located at back of parking brake release handle. Remove rod end from parking brake handle. Remove instrument panel center support bracket. *See Fig. 13.* Unplug vacuum harness connector located at left end of A/C-heater housing. Disconnect Air Bag Control Module (ACM) connector.

6) Remove glove box. Reach through glove box opening and disconnect antenna coaxial cable connector. Disconnect blower motor connector located above glove box opening, near support brace for A/C-heater housing. Disconnect radio ground strap. Loosen instrument panel roll down bracket screws about 2 turns, located at lower corners on both sides of instrument panel. *See Fig. 12.* Remove 5 screws across top of dash panel at base of windshield, removing center screw last.

7) Roll down instrument panel and install a temporary support hook that is about 18 inches in length. Install hook from center hole in instrument panel to center hole of dash panel. Pull lower instrument panel outwards until both roll down bracket bolts are in slotted roll down position. Instrument panel should now be supported and away from firewall.

8) Disconnect 2 door jumper wiring harness connectors, located on a bracket near right end of instrument panel. Disconnect blower motor resistor. Disconnect temperature control cable from A/C-heater housing and remove from housing. Disconnect demister duct flex hose from A/C-heater housing.

9) Ensure instrument panel is free and clear for removal. With the aid of an assistant, remove temporary support hook. Lift instrument panel off of roll down bracket bolts and remove from vehicle.

10) Using a drill motor with a large drill bit, a high-speed grinder, or a soldering iron with a cutting tip, remove collapsed heat stakes from underside of 5 instrument panel-to-dash panel mounting screw holes at or below the cut line. *See Fig. 13.*

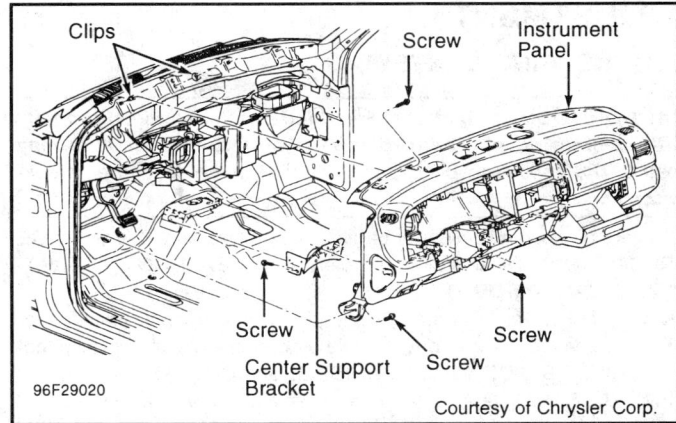

Fig. 12: Removing Instrument Panel (Dakota & Durango)

11) If instrument panel top cover is to be reused, use care not to drill through or to enlarge top cover screw holes. Using a trim stick, gently pry between top cover and instrument panel base bracket near the heat stake during removal process.

NOTE: NEW instrument panel top covers are supplied with heat stakes that have not been collapsed. Heat stakes must also be removed to install NEW top cover. Use a hack saw or razor blade to remove heat stakes.

---

12) This will cause panels to separate when collapsed heat stake has been removed and prevent removal of too much material. After removal, heat stakes should be flush with, or protruding no more than .188" (.47 mm) from lower surface of top cover. Remove instrument top panel-to-instrument panel base screws. Lift top cover off of instrument panel base.

13) To install, reverse removal procedure. Ensure all wiring and hoses are clear and not pinched. DO NOT connect negative battery cable at this time. See DISABLING & ACTIVATING AIR BAG SYSTEM.

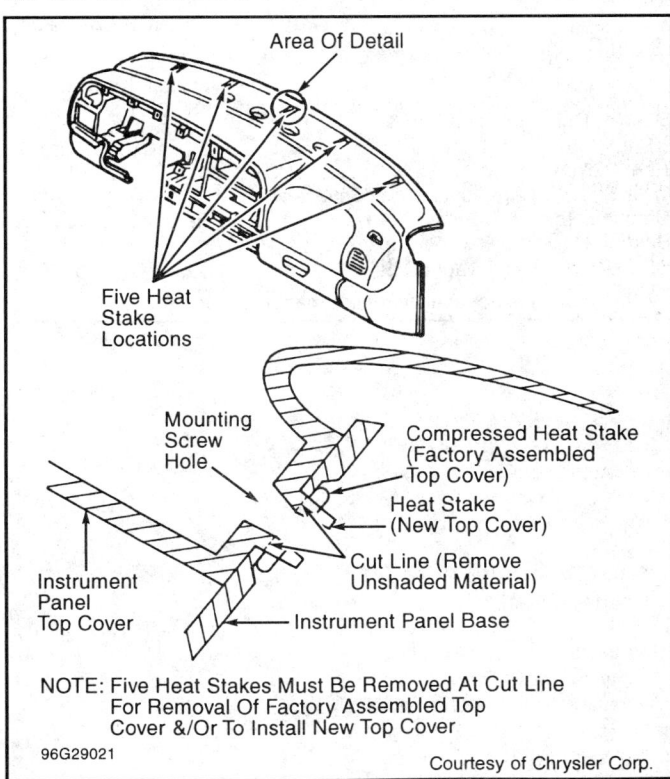

Fig. 13: Removing Top Cover Heat Stakes (Dakota & Durango)

1999 ACCESSORIES & EQUIPMENT
Air Bag Restraint Systems – Trucks (Cont.)

ADJUSTMENTS

CLOCKSPRING CENTERING

CAUTION: *If rotating part of clockspring is not positioned properly with steering column and front wheels, clockspring failure may result. The following procedure must be used to center clockspring.*

1) Before proceeding, follow air bag service precautions. See SERVICE PRECAUTIONS. Disable air bag system. See DISABLING & ACTIVATING AIR BAG SYSTEM.

2) Place front wheels in straight-ahead position. If clockspring is not already removed, remove driver's side air bag module and clockspring. See DRIVER'S SIDE AIR BAG MODULE and CLOCKSPRING under REMOVAL & INSTALLATION. Depress 2 plastic auto-locking tabs. *See Fig. 1.* Rotate clockspring rotor in clockwise direction to the end of its travel. DO NOT apply excessive torque.

3) From the end of its travel, rotate rotor 2 1/2 full turns (Dakota, Durango, Ram Pickup, Ram Van and Ram Wagon) or 3 full turns (Caravan, Town & Country, and Voyager) in counterclockwise direction.

4) On Caravan, Town & Country, and Voyager, wires should end up at top of clockspring. On Dakota, Durango, Ram Pickup, Ram Van and Ram Wagon, the horn wire should end up at the top and air bag module wire at the bottom.

5) On all models, install steering wheel. Tighten steering wheel retaining nut to 45 ft. lbs. (61 N.m). Install air bag module. Tighten air bag module nuts/screws to specification. See TORQUE SPECIFICATIONS. DO NOT connect negative battery cable at this time. See DISABLING & ACTIVATING AIR BAG SYSTEM.

TORQUE SPECIFICATIONS

TORQUE SPECIFICATIONS

Application	Ft. Lbs. (N.m)
Steering Wheel Nut	45 (61)
	INCH Lbs. (N.m)
Air Bag Control Module Screws	
Caravan, Town & Country, & Voyager	75-105 (8.5-11.9)
Dakota, Durango, Ram Van & Ram Wagon	105 (11.9)
Ram Pickup	125 (14)
Driver-Side Air Bag Module Nuts/Screws	
Caravan, Town & Country, & Voyager	1
Dakota, Durango, Ram Pickup, Ram Van & Ram Wagon	90 (10.2)

[1] – Information is not available from manufacturer.

WIRING DIAGRAMS

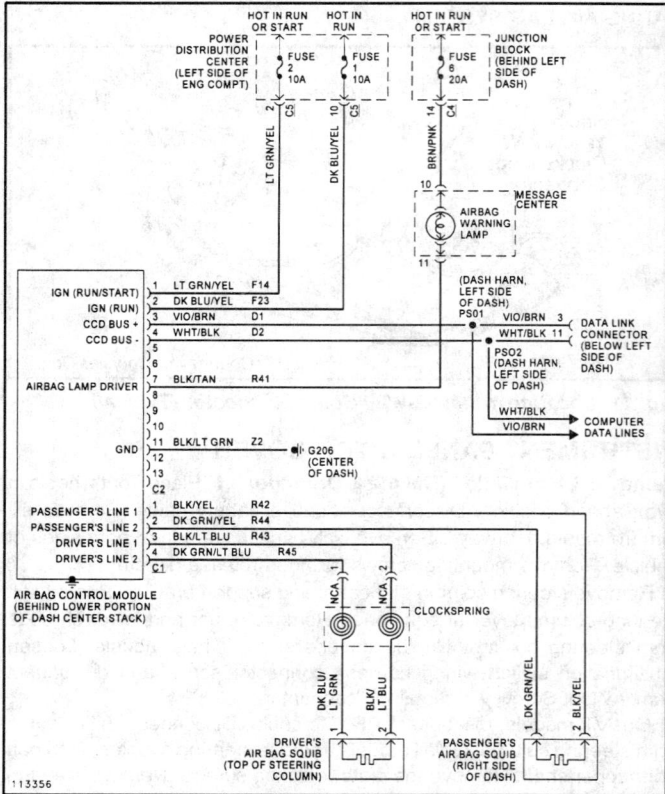

Fig. 14: Air Bag System Wiring Diagram (Caravan, Town & Country, & Voyager)

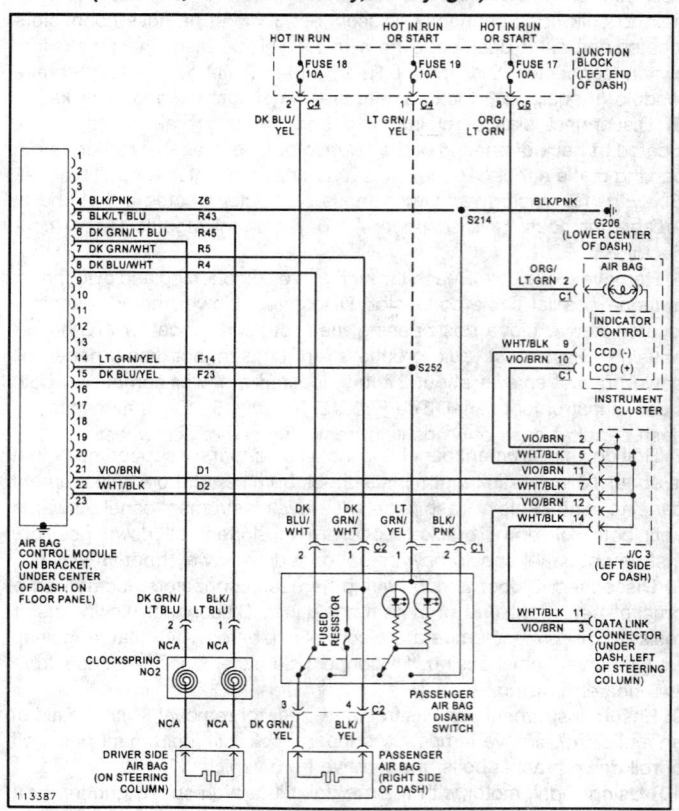

Fig. 15: Air Bag System Wiring Diagram (Dakota)

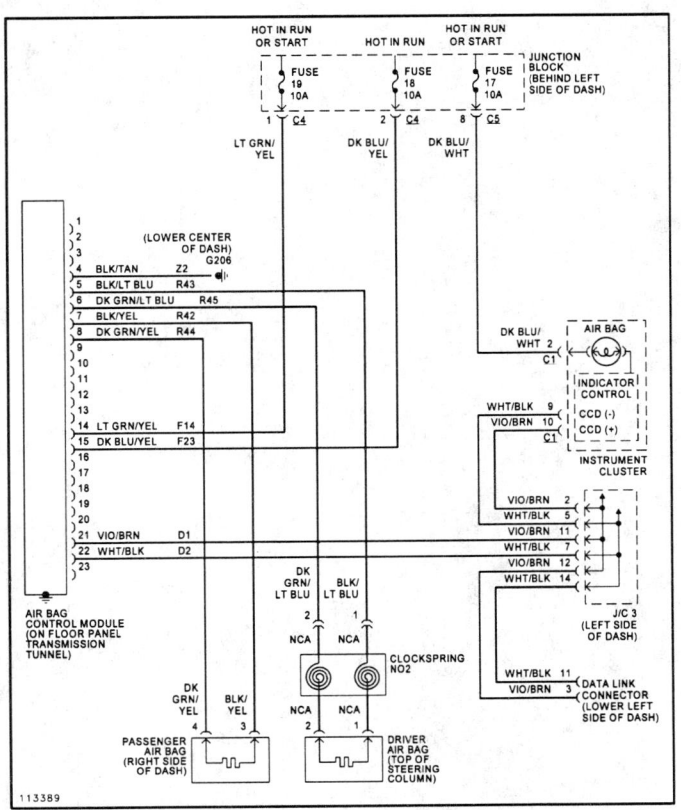

Fig. 16: Air Bag System Wiring Diagram (Durango)

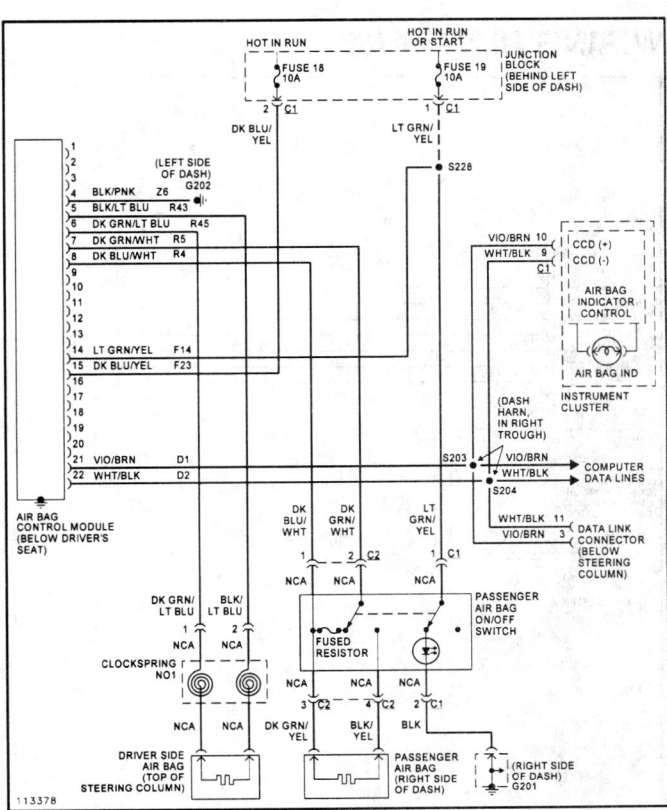

Fig. 18: Air Bag System Wiring Diagram (Ram Van & Ram Wagon)

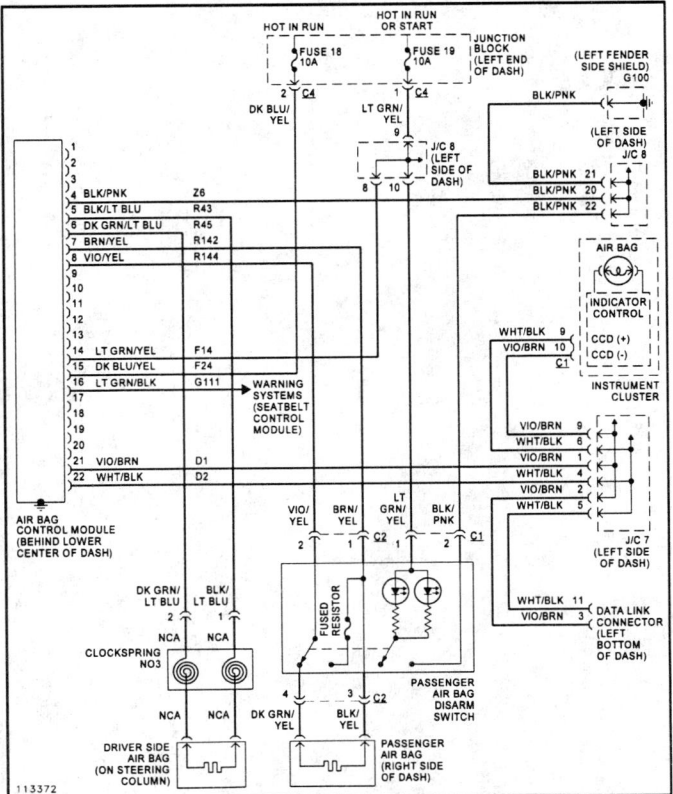

Fig. 17: Air Bag System Wiring Diagram (Ram Pickup)

WIRING DIAGRAMS

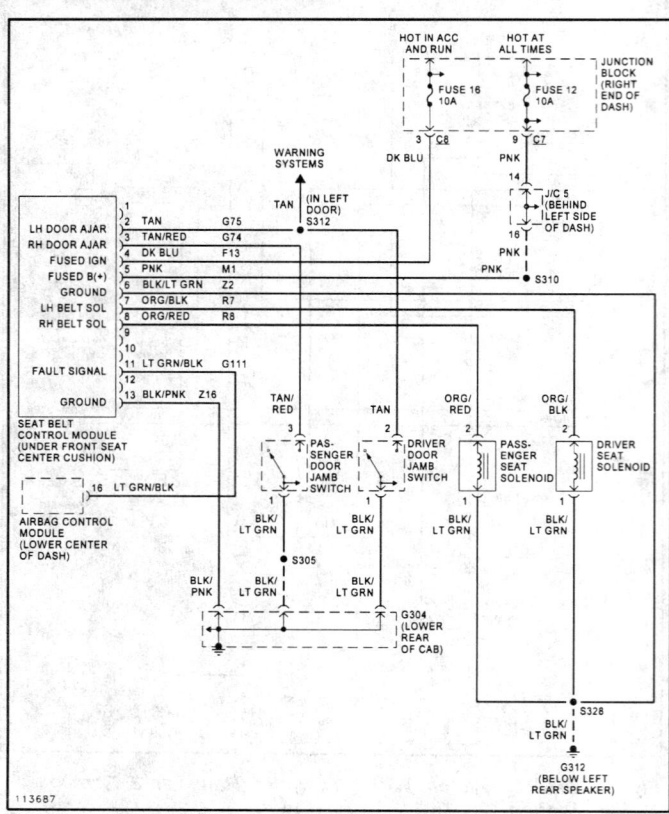

Fig. 1: Passive Restraint System Wiring Diagram (Ram Pickup)

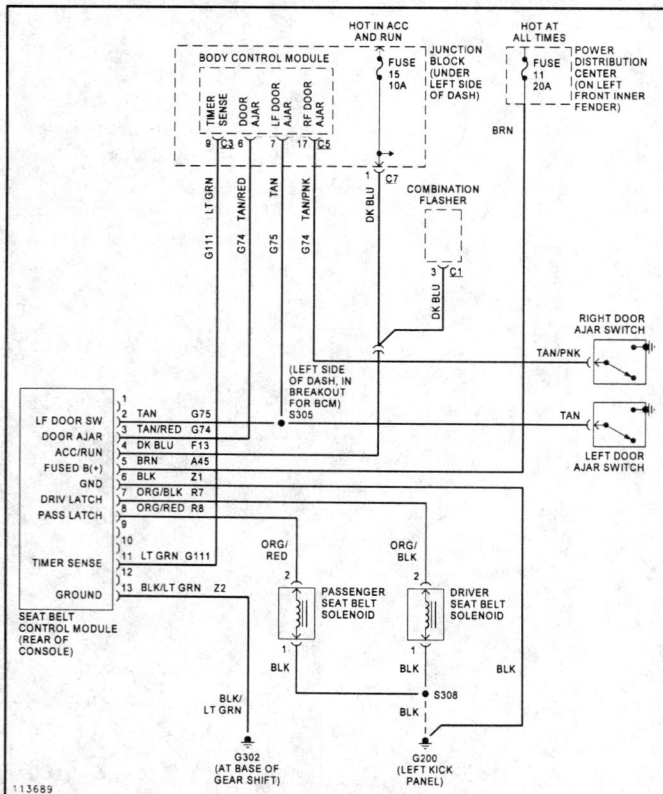

**Fig. 2: Passive Restraint System Wiring Diagram
(Sebring Convertible)**

Anti-Theft Systems – Avenger & Sebring Coupe

DESCRIPTION

Anti-theft system disables starter, flashes headlights and sounds horn if any doors, trunk, hatchback or hood is opened without using key or keyless entry controller. If battery cables are disconnected then reconnected when system is activated, alarm will sound.

Anti-theft system is controlled by Electronic Timer Alarm Control System Electronic Control Unit (ETACS-ECU). ETACS-ECU is located behind driver's side lower dash panel, to left side of steering column, on back of junction block.

OPERATION

SETTING ANTI-THEFT SYSTEM

NOTE: After setting anti-theft system, indicator light on instrument panel will light for approximately 20 seconds, then go out.

Close all doors, hood and trunk. Remove key from ignition switch. Lock vehicle using one of 2 methods: using key to lock vehicle at either front door or lock all doors using keyless entry system.

CANCELING ANTI-THEFT SYSTEM (SYSTEM SET, NO ALARM)

Cancel anti-theft system using one of 4 methods:
- Unlock either front door using key.
- Unlock all doors using remote keyless entry system.
- Turn ignition switch to ACC or ON position (this is operative only when anti-theft system has never been triggered).
- Using key, unlock trunk or hatchback. Anti-theft system is temporarily canceled only while trunk or hatchback door is open. Approximately 2 seconds after trunk or hatchback is closed, anti-theft system will reset.

CHECKING ANTI-THEFT SYSTEM OPERATION

Ensure anti-theft system is activated and indicator light is on for 20 seconds. Open hood or any door. Horn should sound and headlights should flash for approximately 3 minutes.

CANCELING ANTI-THEFT SYSTEM (SYSTEM SET, ALARM SOUNDING)

Anti-theft system can be shut off by performing one of 3 methods: unlock either front door with key, unlock trunk lid with key or unlock doors with remote keyless entry system.

TROUBLE SHOOTING

Check for possible cause by trouble symptom and then perform specified inspection procedure under SYMPTOM TESTS. See TROUBLE SYMPTOM INSPECTION table under SYMPTOM TESTS. If no problems are found, check ETACS-ECU inputs. See ETACS- ECU PIN VOLTAGES under SYSTEM TESTS.

COMPONENT TESTS

DOOR LOCK KEY CYLINDER SWITCH

Disconnect door lock key cylinder switch to be tested. Check continuity between specified terminals with key in appropriate position. See DOOR LOCK KEY CYLINDER SWITCH TEST table. *See Fig. 1.* Replace switch if continuity is not as specified.

DOOR LOCK KEY CYLINDER SWITCH TEST

Switch Position	Continuity Between Terminals
Driver's Side	
LOCK	2 & 3
UNLOCK	1 & 2
Passenger's Side	
LOCK	1 & 2
UNLOCK	2 & 3

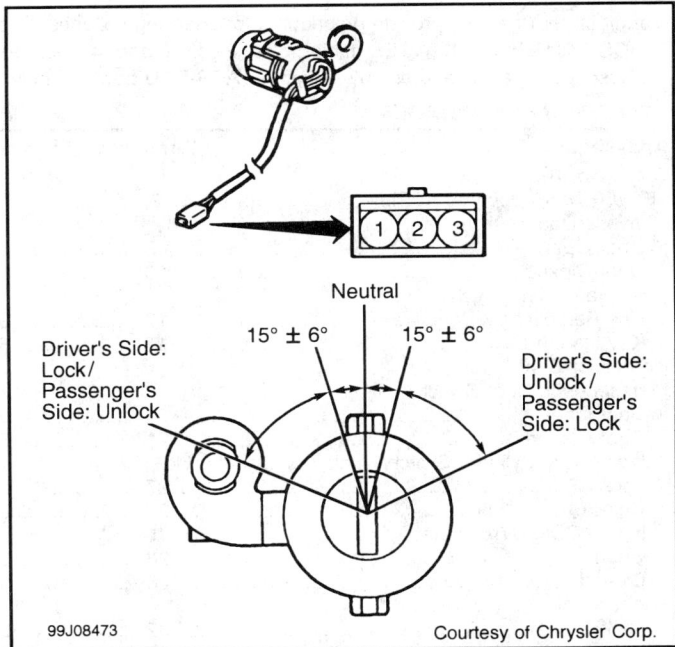

Fig. 1: Testing Door Lock Key Cylinder Switch

SYSTEM TESTS

KEY CYLINDER SWITCH INPUT CIRCUITS

1) Connect scan tool to DLC. Monitor door key cylinder switch input signals. If scan tool is not available, connect voltmeter to DLC terminal No. 9. *See Fig. 2.* If scan tool buzzer sounds once, or voltmeter deflects once when door key cylinder switch is turned from LOCK to UNLOCK, go to step **3)**. If scan tool buzzer does not sound, or voltmeter does not deflect, go to next step.

2) Test suspect door key cylinder switch. See DOOR LOCK KEY CYLINDER SWITCH under COMPONENT TESTS. Replace switch, if necessary. If door key cylinder switch is okay, check wiring and connectors between door key cylinder switch and ETACS-ECU. See WIRING DIAGRAMS. Repair as necessary. If wiring and connectors are okay, and symptom still exists, repair door key cylinder switch ground circuit.

3) Monitor trunk lid key cylinder switch input signals. If scan tool is not available, connect voltmeter to DLC terminal No. 9. *See Fig. 2.* If scan tool buzzer sounds once, or voltmeter deflects once, when trunk lid key cylinder switch is turned to UNLOCK position, replace ETACS-ECU. If scan tool buzzer does not sound, or voltmeter does not deflect, go to next step.

4) Disconnect trunk lid key cylinder switch. Check continuity between switch terminals. Continuity should exist when key cylinder is in LOCK position. Continuity should not exist when key cylinder is in UNLOCK position. If continuity is as specified, go to next step. If continuity is not as specified, replace key cylinder switch.

5) Check wiring and connectors between trunk lid key cylinder switch and ETACS-ECU. See WIRING DIAGRAMS. Repair as necessary. If wiring and connectors are okay, repair trunk lid key cylinder switch ground circuit.

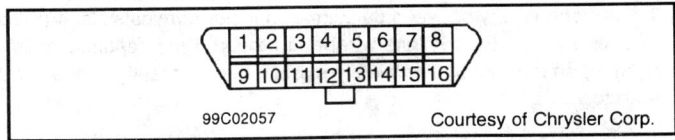

Fig. 2: Identifying DLC Connector Terminals

CHRY
4-22

1999 ACCESSORIES & EQUIPMENT
Anti-Theft Systems – Avenger & Sebring Coupe (Cont.)

ETACS-ECU PIN VOLTAGES

Manufacturer does not provide procedures for checking voltages. See ETACS-ECU PIN VOLTAGES table. See Figs. 3 and 4. Use an oscilloscope for all measurements except ETACS-ECU power supply.

ETACS-ECU PIN VOLTAGES

Application	Terminal	[1] Volts
Connector B-39 [2]		
ECU Power Supply At All Times	2	12
Driver's Door Switch		
Door Open	13	0
Door Closed	13	5
Key Reminder Switch		
Key Removed	17	0
Key Inserted	17	5
Connector B-40 [3]		
Passenger's Door Switch		
Door Open	21	0
Door Closed	21	5
Liftgate Key Cylinder Switch/Trunk Key Cylinder Lid		
Lock	27	5
Unlock	27	0
Liftgate Switch/Trunk Lid		
Open	28	0
Closed	28	5
Actuator Switch (LH)		
Lock	32	5
Unlock	32	0
Actuator Switch (RH)		
Lock	25	5
Unlock	25	0
Key Cylinder Switch (LH)		
Lock	33	0
Neutral	33	5
Key Cylinder Switch (LH)		
Unlock	38	0
Neutral	38	5
Key Cylinder Switch (RH)		
Lock	39	0
Neutral	39	5
Key Cylinder Switch (RH)		
Unlock	40	0
Neutral	40	5
Transmitter Switch		
On	34	0
Off	34	5

[1] – Oscilloscope must be used for measurements other than ECU power supply.
[2] – See Fig. 3.
[3] – See Fig. 4.

SYMPTOM TESTS

INSPECTION PROCEDURE NO. 1: COMMUNICATION WITH SCAN TOOL NOT POSSIBLE (ALL SYSTEMS)

1) Check for battery voltage at Data Link Connector (DLC) terminal No. 16 (Red/Black wire). See Fig. 2. If battery voltage does not exist, go to next step. If battery voltage exists, go to step 3).
2) Check for battery voltage at junction block fuse No. 10 (10-amp). If battery voltage exists and fuse is okay, repair open Red/Black wire between junction block and DLC. If battery voltage does not exist, repair open circuit to battery. See WIRING DIAGRAMS. If battery voltage exists and fuse is blown, repair short circuit and replace fuse.
3) Check continuity between data link connector terminals No. 4 (Black wire) and No. 5 (Black/White wire) and ground. If no continuity exists, repair open to ground. If continuity exists, check for faulty connector or scan tool.

INSPECTION PROCEDURE NO. 2: COMMUNICATION WITH SCAN TOOL NOT POSSIBLE (ONE-SHOT PULSE SIGNAL ONLY)

1) Disconnect junction block connector B-43. Check continuity between Data Link Connector (DLC) terminal No. 9 and junction block connector B-43 terminal No. 17 (Black/Blue wire). See Figs. 2 and 5. If continuity exists, go to next step. If continuity does not exist, repair open Black/Blue wire.
2) Remove ETACS-ECU from rear of junction block. Inspect DLC and junction block connectors for damage or corrosion. See Figs. 5 and 3. Repair as necessary. If connectors are okay, and symptom still exists, replace ETACS-ECU.

INSPECTION PROCEDURE NO. 3: ALARM SYSTEM INOPERATIVE

1) Check for battery voltage at relay box fuse No. 10 (10-amp). Relay box is located in engine compartment. If battery voltage exists and fuse is okay, go to next step. If battery voltage does not exist, check fusible link No. 2 (60-amp). If fusible link No. 2 is okay, repair open circuit to battery. If battery voltage exists and fuse is blown, repair short circuit and replace fuse.
2) Remove ETACS-ECU from rear of junction block. Measure voltage at ETACS-ECU connector B-39, terminal No. 2. See Fig. 3. If battery voltage exists, go to next step. If battery voltage does not exist, measure voltage at junction block connector B-63, terminal No. 12 (Red/Black wire). If battery voltage does not exist, repair open Red/Black wire to relay box. See WIRING DIAGRAMS. If battery voltage exists, repair open circuit in junction block.
3) Check continuity between ground and terminal No. 1 at ETACS-ECU connector B-39. See Fig. 3. If continuity exists, replace ETACS-ECU. If continuity does not exist, check continuity between ground and junction block connector B-41, terminal No. 1 (Black wire). If continuity does not exist, repair open Black wire. If continuity exists, repair open circuit in junction block.

1999 ACCESSORIES & EQUIPMENT
Anti-Theft Systems – Avenger & Sebring Coupe (Cont.)

CHRY
4-23

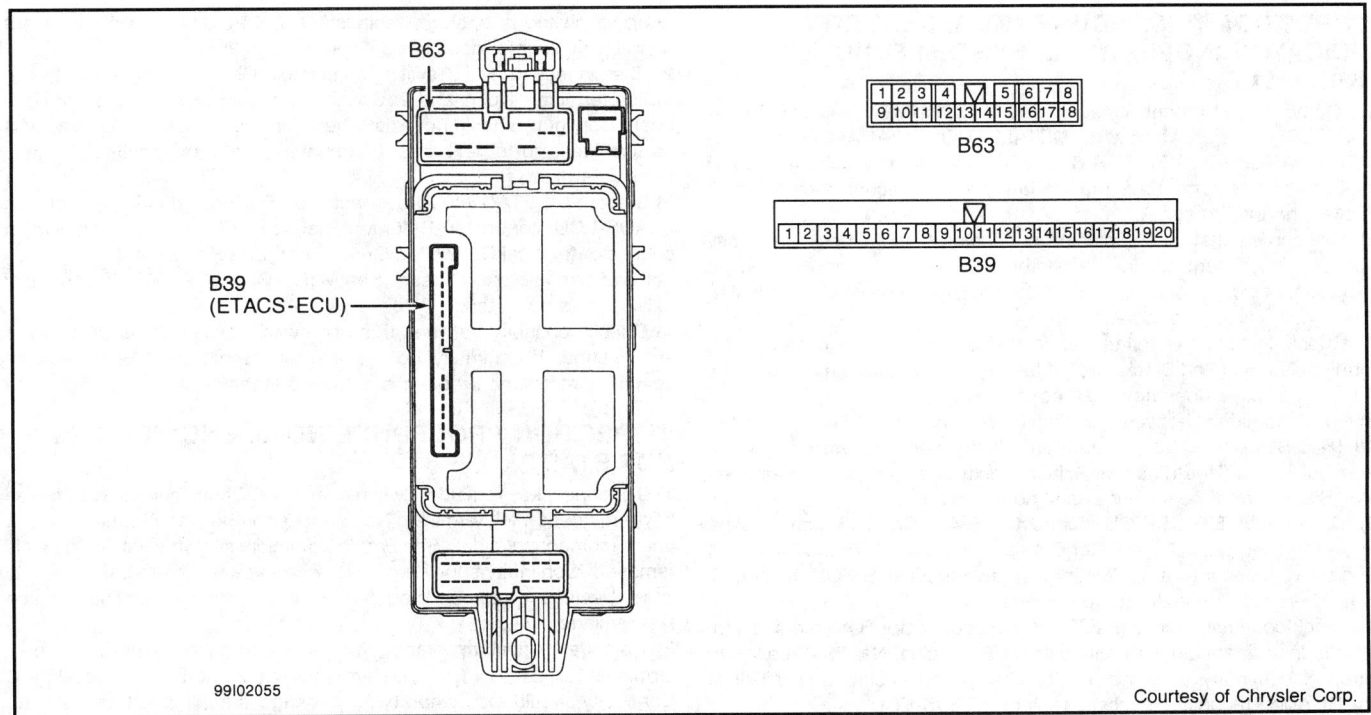

Fig. 3: Identifying Junction Block Connector Terminals (Rear View)

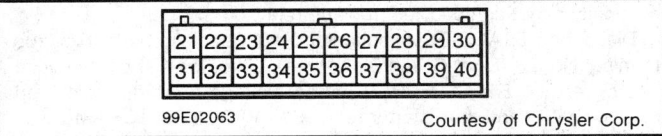

Fig. 4: Identifying ETACS-ECU Connector B-40 Terminals

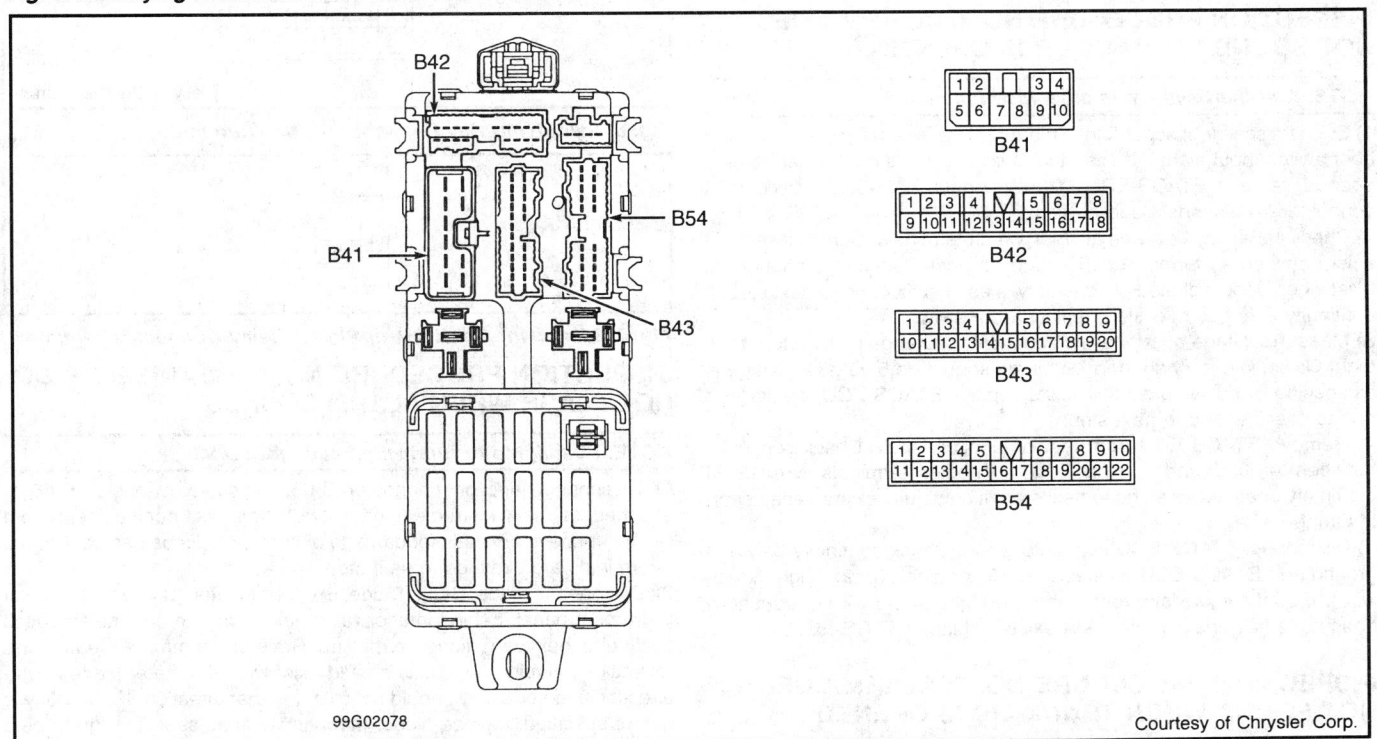

Fig. 5: Identifying Junction Block Connector Terminals (Front View)

CHRY
4-24

1999 ACCESSORIES & EQUIPMENT
Anti-Theft Systems – Avenger & Sebring Coupe (Cont.)

INSPECTION PROCEDURE NO. 4: SECURITY INDICATOR INOPERATIVE, SYSTEM FUNCTIONS NORMALLY

1) Remove instrument cluster. See INSTRUMENT CLUSTER & GAUGES under REMOVAL & INSTALLATION in ANALOG INSTRUMENT PANELS – AVENGER & SEBRING COUPE article. If security indicator bulb is burned out, replace faulty bulb. If security indicator bulb is okay, go to next step.

2) Disconnect instrument cluster connector C-05. Check continuity between instrument cluster connector C-05 terminals No. 33 and 34 (component side). If continuity does not exist, replace instrument cluster. If continuity exists, go to next step.

3) Check for battery voltage at instrument cluster connector C-05, terminal No. 34 (Red/Black wire). If battery voltage exists, go to step **5)**. If battery voltage does not exist, go to next step.

4) Check continuity between junction block connector B-54 terminal No. 18 (Red/Black wire) and instrument cluster security lamp connector terminal No. 34 (Red/Black wire). If continuity does not exist, repair open Red/Black wire. If continuity exists, go to next step.

5) Disconnect ETACS-ECU connector B-40. Connect jumper wire between ETACS-ECU connector B-40 terminal No. 31 (Blue/White wire) to ground. If security lamp illuminates, replace ETACS-ECU. If security lamp does not illuminate, go to next step.

6) Check continuity between ETACS-ECU connector B-40 terminal No. 31 and instrument cluster connector C-05, terminal No. 33 (Blue/White wire). If continuity does not exist, repair open circuit. See WIRING DIAGRAMS. If continuity exists, replace ETACS-ECU.

INSPECTION PROCEDURE NO. 5: ALARM SOUNDS WHEN SYSTEM IS DISARMED WITH KEY

NOTE: Anti-theft system is otherwise functional.

Check key cylinder switch inputs. See KEY CYLINDER SWITCH INPUT CIRCUITS under SYSTEM TESTS. Repair as necessary.

INSPECTION PROCEDURE NO. 6: ALARM DOES NOT SOUND WHEN DOOR IS OPENED

NOTE: Anti-theft system is otherwise functional.

1) Connect scan tool according to manufacturer's specifications. Monitor door switch input signal. If scan tool buzzer sounds once when door is opened, replace ETACS-ECU. If buzzer does not sound, disconnect connector from suspect door switch.

2) Check continuity between all door switch terminals. Continuity should exist between all terminals when door is open. Continuity should not exist when door is closed. If continuity is as specified, go to next step. If continuity is not as specified, replace door switch.

3) Measure voltage at door switch connector (Orange wire on left door; Light Green wire on right door). Voltage should be 5 volts. If voltage is as specified, and symptom still exists, replace ETACS-ECU. If voltage is not as specified, go to next step.

4) Remove ETACS-ECU from rear of junction block. Check continuity between ground and ETACS-ECU connector terminals No. 13. If continuity does not exist, go to next step. If continuity exists, repair short in Orange wire.

5) Disconnect ETACS-ECU connector B-40. Check continuity between ground and ETACS-ECU connector B-40, terminal No. 21 (Light Green wire). If continuity exists, repair short in Light Green wire. If continuity does not exist, and symptom still exists, replace ETACS-ECU.

INSPECTION PROCEDURE NO. 7: ALARM DOES NOT SOUND WHEN TRUNK LID IS OPENED

NOTE: Alarm is triggered when door is opened.

1) Connect scan tool to DLC. Monitor trunk lid switch input signals. If scan tool is not available, connect voltmeter to DLC terminal No. 9. *See Fig. 2.* If scan tool buzzer sounds once, or voltmeter deflects once when

trunk lid switch is opened, replace ETACS-ECU. If buzzer does not sound, or voltmeter does not deflect, go to next step.

2) Disconnect trunk lid switch connector. Check continuity between switch terminals No. 1 and 2. Continuity should exist when trunk lid is open. Continuity should not exist when trunk lid is closed. If continuity is as specified, go to next step. If continuity is not as specified, replace trunk lid switch.

3) Disconnect ETACS-ECU connector B-40. Check continuity between ETACS-ECU connector B-40 terminal No. 28 and trunk lid switch connector terminal No. 2 (Red/Green wire). *See Fig. 4.* If continuity does not exist, repair open circuit. See WIRING DIAGRAMS. If continuity exists, go to next step.

4) Check continuity between trunk lid switch connector terminal No. 1 and ground. If continuity does not exist, repair open Black wire. If continuity exists, no problem is indicated at this time.

INSPECTION PROCEDURE NO. 8: ENGINE DOES NOT START

1) Disconnect key reminder switch connector. Check continuity between key reminder switch terminals No. 3 and 7 and between terminals No. 4 and 6 (component side). *See Fig. 6.* Continuity should exist when key is removed. Continuity should not exist when key is inserted. If continuity is as specified, go to next step. If continuity is not as specified, replace key reminder switch.

2) Remove theft alarm starter relay. Check continuity between relay terminals No. 2 and 4 (M/T), or terminals No. 2 and 5 (A/T). *See Fig. 7.* Continuity should exist when battery voltage is applied to terminals No. 1 and 3. Continuity should not exist when battery voltage is not applied to terminals No. 1 and 3. If continuity is as specified, go to next step. If continuity is not as specified, replace relay.

3) Disconnect ETACS-ECU connector B-40. Check for battery voltage at terminal No. 23 (Light Green/Black wire). *See Fig. 4.* If battery voltage exists, replace ETACS-ECU. If battery voltage does not exist, repair open circuit to anti-theft starter relay. See WIRING DIAGRAMS.

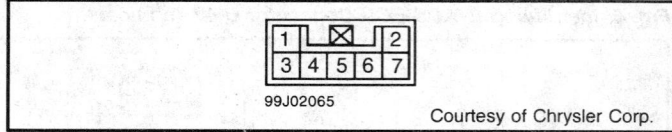

99J02065   Courtesy of Chrysler Corp.

Fig. 6: Identifying Key Reminder Switch Terminals

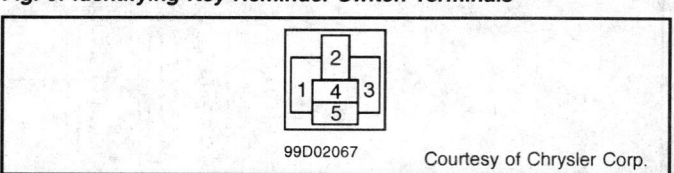

99D02067   Courtesy of Chrysler Corp.

Fig. 7: Identifying Theft Alarm Starter Relay Connector Terminals

INSPECTION PROCEDURE NO. 9: HEADLIGHTS DO NOT FLASH WHEN ALARM SOUNDS

NOTE: Headlights turn on with headlight switch.

1) Disconnect junction connector B-05. Junction connector B-05 is attached to main instrument panel wire harness, behind instrument cluster. Inspect terminals for damage or corrosion. Repair as necessary. If terminals are okay, go to next step.

2) Disconnect diode B-02. Diode B-02 is located under left side of instrument panel, behind interior relay box. Using an ohmmeter, check continuity between diode terminals. Reverse ohmmeter leads and recheck continuity. Continuity should exist with ohmmeter leads in one direction and continuity should not exist in other direction. If continuity is not as specified, replace diode. If continuity is as specified, go to next step.

3) Check continuity between junction connector B-05, terminal No. 33 (Red wire) and diode B-02. *See Fig. 8.* If continuity does not exist, repair open Red wire. If continuity exists, no problem is indicated at this time.

1999 ACCESSORIES & EQUIPMENT
Anti-Theft Systems – Avenger & Sebring Coupe (Cont.)

CHRY
4-25

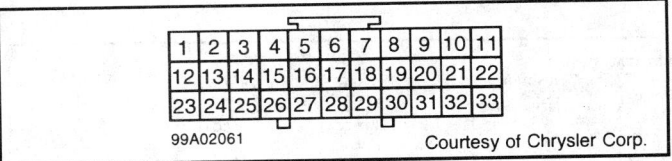

99A02061   Courtesy of Chrysler Corp.

Fig. 8: Identifying Junction Connector B-05 Terminals

INSPECTION PROCEDURE NO. 10: HEADLIGHTS FLASH, HORN DOES NOT SOUND

NOTE: Headlights flash and horn sounds if horn button is pressed.

1) Check fuse No. 5 (10-amp) in junction block. If fuse is okay, go to next step. If fuse is blown, repair short circuit and replace fuse.

2) Disconnect junction connector B-05. Junction connector B-05 is attached to main instrument panel wire harness, behind instrument cluster. Inspect terminals for damage or corrosion. Repair as necessary. If terminals are okay, go to next step.

3) Disconnect diode B-02. Diode B-02 is located under left side of instrument panel, behind interior relay box. Using an ohmmeter, check continuity between diode terminals. Reverse ohmmeter leads and recheck continuity. Continuity should exist with ohmmeter leads in one direction and continuity should not exist in other direction. If continuity is not as specified, replace diode. If continuity is as specified, go to next step.

4) Reconnect junction connector B-05 and diode B-02. Recheck system operation. If horn operates properly, go to next step. If horn still does not sound, check continuity of Red wire between junction connector B-05 and diode B-02. Repair as necessary. If wire is okay, no problem is indicated at this time. Test is complete.

5) Remove theft-alarm horn relay. Theft-alarm horn relay is located in interior relay box. Check continuity between terminals No. 4 and 5 (component side). *See Fig. 9.* Continuity should exist between when battery voltage is applied to terminals 1 and 3. Continuity should not exist when battery voltage is not applied. If continuity is not as specified, replace relay. If continuity is as specified, go to next step.

6) Measure voltage at theft-alarm horn relay terminals No. 1 and 5 in interior relay box. Battery voltage should exist. If battery voltage exists, go to next step. If battery voltage does not exist, disconnect junction block connector B-42. Measure voltage at junction block terminal No. 16. *See Fig. 5.* If battery voltage does not exist, repair open circuit in junction block. If battery voltage exists, repair open Red/White wire between junction block and theft-alarm horn relay.

7) Check wiring and connectors between theft-alarm horn relay and theft-alarm horn. See WIRING DIAGRAMS. Repair as necessary. If wiring and connectors are okay, replace theft-alarm horn.

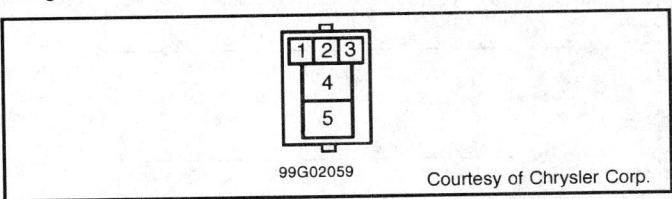

99G02059   Courtesy of Chrysler Corp.

Fig. 9: Identifying Headlight Relay, Horn Relay & Theft Alarm Horn Relay Connector Terminals

INSPECTION PROCEDURE NO. 11: SYSTEM WILL NOT DISARM

Check key cylinder switch inputs. See KEY CYLINDER SWITCH INPUT CIRCUITS under SYSTEM TESTS. Repair as necessary.

REMOVAL & INSTALLATION

Information is not available from manufacturer.

1999 ACCESSORIES & EQUIPMENT
Anti-Theft Systems – Avenger & Sebring Coupe (Cont.)

WIRING DIAGRAMS

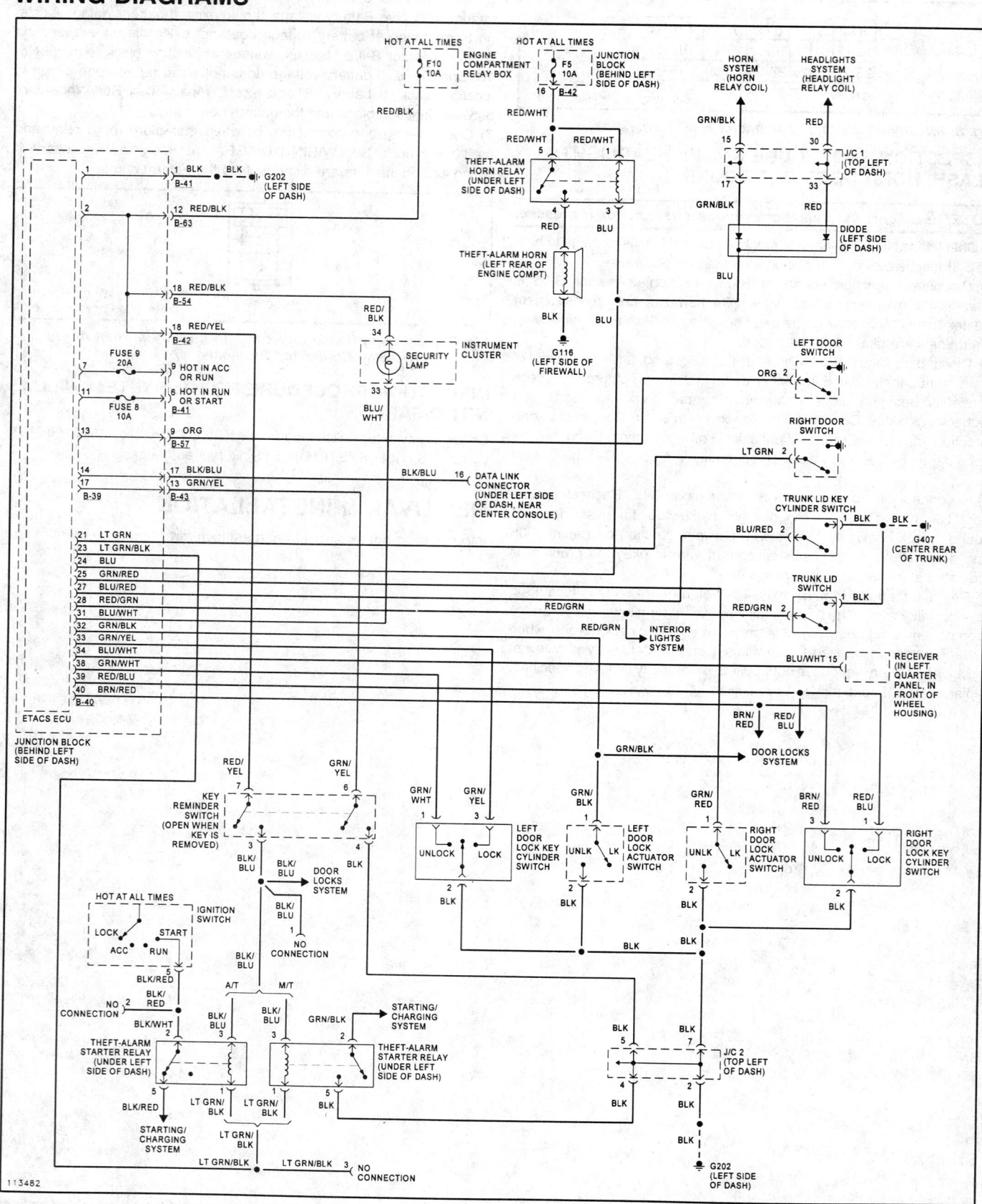

Fig. 10: Anti-Theft System Wiring Diagram

1999 ACCESSORIES & EQUIPMENT
Anti-Theft Systems
Breeze, Cirrus, Sebring Convertible & Stratus

DESCRIPTION

Vehicle Theft Security System (VTSS) monitors vehicle doors, ignition switch, power door lock circuits and trunk key cylinder to determine if Body Control Module (BCM) should sound horn, flash interior lights and headlights, and disable ignition system. BCM inputs for VTSS are divided into 2 sections: trunk area and passenger compartment.

VTSS incorporates Sentry Key Immobilizer Module (SKIM) system. SKIM system provides passive protection against theft. SKIM system sends a signal to PCM to disable engine operation if proper key is not used. Reprogramming or initialization must be performed if PCM, SKIM or ignition key is replaced.

VTSS deactivates garage door opener and trunk release button when armed. System is passively armed by opening door, locking door using power door locks and closing door. While system is arming, VTSS LED will flash rapidly for 15 seconds. Opening any door or turning the ignition key while light is flashing will abort arming process. After 15 second arming period VTSS LED will flash slowly to show system is armed. System can also be armed using Remote Keyless Entry (RKE) transmitter or locking doors with key. System will not arm if manual door lock knobs are used to lock door(s). VTSS system uses a Light Emitting Diode (LED) to indicate when the system is armed. VTSS LED is located in instrument cluster. VTSS LED is also used by SKIM to advise owner when system has been immobilized due to use of invalid ignition key. VTSS LED will stay on after restart if invalid ignition key is used.

VTSS is equipped with a tamper alert signal, indicating VTSS has been triggered (vehicle has been tampered with). When either front door is unlocked with key or RKE, the horn will sound 3 times.

OPERATION

Body Control Module (BCM) monitors driver's door on one circuit and all other doors on another circuit. Four door lock switches, one located at each door, are used for BCM DOOR OPEN input signal. Two arm/disarm switches are used in VTSS system. Arm/disarm switches are located in left and right front doors. These switches use internal resistors to send a signal to BCM when requested by the operator by selecting arm/disarm functions. A problem in any passenger compartment switch will not allow the system to arm.

BCM monitors trunk lock switch for a closed circuit. If switch circuit opens (trunk is opened or switch is removed), BCM triggers alarm. If there is a malfunction in trunk lock switch, system will arm, but switch will not be monitored. If switch becomes functional while system is armed, it will be used as an input to BCM.

SKIM system has 4 basic components; SKIM, sentry key transponder (key), VTSS light, and PCM. When ignition is turned on SKIM sends a Radio Frequency (RF) signal to transponder (key). RF signal excites transponder chip in ignition key and chip responds returning a RF signal with secret key code. SKIM compares code to information stored in memory to verify a valid key is being used. SKIM sends valid key signal to PCM. If wrong or new key is used, SKIM sends invalid key signal to PCM. PCM then disables engine operation. SKIM also sends signal to instrument cluster to illuminate VTSS light. Reprogramming or initialization must be performed if PCM, SKIM or ignition key is replaced. See SKIM INITIALIZATION PROCEDURE or PROGRAMMING BLANK SMART KEY USING SCAN TOOL under PROGRAMMING.

PROGRAMMING

SKIM INITIALIZATION PROCEDURE

General Information – If PCM is replaced, unique secret key data must be transferred from SKIM to PCM. This procedure requires SKIM to be placed in SECURED ACCESS mode using 4-digit PIN code. If 3 attempts are made to enter secured access mode using an incorrect PIN code, SECURED ACCESS mode will be locked out for one hour. To exit lock out mode, turn ignition switch to RUN/START position continuously for one hour. Ensure all accessories are turned off. Monitor battery state and connect battery charger is necessary.

To program smart keys using "customer programming method" requires 2 valid smart keys. See CUSTOMER LEARN PROGRAMMING METHOD.

Initialization Procedure – 1) Obtain vehicle's unique PIN code assigned to it's original SKIM module from vehicle owner or Chrysler's customer center. Using scan tool, select THEFT ALARM, then SKIM, then MISCELLANEOUS and then SKIM MODULE REPLACED function. **2)** Enter SECURED ACCESS mode using unique 4-digit PIN code. Program vehicle's VIN number into SKIM's memory. Program country code into SKIM's memory (U.S.).
3) Transfer vehicle's unique secret key data from PCM. This process will require SKIM module to be in SECURED ACCESS mode. The PIN code must be entered into scan tool before SKIM will enter SECURED ACCESS mode. Once SECURED ACCESS mode is active, SKIM will remain in that mode for 60 seconds.
4) Program all customer keys into SKIM's memory. This requires that SKIM be in SECURED ACCESS mode. The SKIM will immediately exit SECURED ACCESS mode after each key is programmed.

PROGRAMMING BLANK SENTRY KEY USING SCAN TOOL

Once key blank is cut, insert key into ignition switch. Turn ignition switch to RUN position. Using scan tool, select THEFT ALARM, then SKIM, then MISCELLANEOUS and then PROGRAM NEW KEY. Enter 4-digit PIN code. When programming is completed, SKIM will exit SECURED ACCESS mode and display status of key. One of five different status messages maybe displayed as follows:

* PROGRAMMING SUCCESSFUL is displayed if SKIM smart key programming succeeds.
* LEARNED KEY IN IGNITION is displayed if key in the ignition has already been programmed into vehicle's SKIM.
* 8 KEYS ALREADY LEARNED, PROGRAMMING NOT DONE is displayed if eight keys have already been programmed into SKIM. If a new key needs to be added due to a lost or defective key, the ERASE ALL KEYS function has to be performed. All keys to be used with vehicle will then need to be programmed into SKIM.
* PROGRAMMING NOT ATTEMPTED is displayed after an ERASE ALL KEYS function is executed.
* PROGRAMING KEY FAILED is displayed if further diagnosis is required. To program additional keys, turn ignition off. Remove current programmed key and insert next new blank key. Turn ignition switch to RUN position. Re-enter SECURED ACCESS function and repeat PROGRAM NEW KEY procedure.

CUSTOMER LEARN PROGRAMMING METHOD

NOTE: The following steps must be completed in proper order. SKIS will automatically exit CUSTOMER LEARN programming mode if time allotted is exceeded, or if 8 keys have already been programmed.

1) Once sentry key blank is cut, insert one of the 2 valid sentry keys into ignition. Turn ignition on.
2) After ignition has been on for 3 seconds, but no more than 15 seconds, turn ignition off. Remove key. Insert second valid sentry key. Turn ignition on. Both operations must be performed within 15 seconds.
3) About 10 seconds after completion of step 2, VTSS LED indicator will flash and a single tone will be heard. This indicates system has entered CUSTOMER LEARN programming mode.
4) Within 50 seconds, turn ignition off. Remove valid sentry key. Insert blank sentry key. Turn ignition on.
5) After about 10 seconds, a single tone will be heard. VTSS LED indicator will stop flashing and stay on for about 3 seconds to indicate sentry key has been successfully programmed.
6) SKIS will return to normal operation immediately following exit from CUSTOMER LEARN programming mode.

1999 ACCESSORIES & EQUIPMENT
Anti-Theft Systems
Breeze, Cirrus, Sebring Convertible & Stratus (Cont.)

7) Repeat procedure for each additional sentry key to be programmed.

SYSTEM TESTS

See appropriate BODY CONTROL COMPUTER TESTS article for VTSS and SKIS testing.

SYSTEM SELF-TESTS

NOTE: Vehicle Theft Security System (VTSS) and VTSS self-test mode will be inoperative if Powertrain Control Module (PCM) has been replaced within last 20 ignition switch cycles.

1) VTSS self-test mode is used to verify operation of all monitored switches or circuits and can only be activated with a scan tool. Connect scan tool to Data Link Connector (DLC). Using scan tool, select self-test mode. See appropriate BODY CONTROL COMPUTER TESTS article.
2) Once in self-test mode, horn will sound twice, indicating trunk key cylinder is positioned correctly. Place key in ignition. Warning light, headlights and interior lights will flash, indicating proper operation. If doors are not closed, interior lights will not flash. Remove key from ignition to check each door lock switch operation.
3) In the following self-test mode steps, there must be a one second delay between each action. While in self-test mode, horn should sound once at each of following steps, indicating proper operation:

* Activate power door locks in both LOCK and UNLOCK positions. Horn will sound after each activation.
* Open, then close each door, one at a time. Horn will sound when door lock switch closes, and then again when switch opens.
* Rotate key in both door lock cylinders to LOCK and UNLOCK positions. Horn will sound as switch closes, and again when it opens. Ensure there is a one second delay between changing switch positions or horn will not sound.
* Turn ignition switch to ON position. A single horn sound will indicate proper operation of ignition switch and take VTSS out of self-test mode. VTSS self-test mode can also be exited using scan tool.
* For any of these tests, if switch does not remain open or closed for at least one second, the horn will only sound once.
* If vehicle is equipped with Remote Keyless Entry (RKE) system, activating each RKE function will cause horn to sound.

4) Lack of a horn sound during any operation indicates a switch failure. Check for continuity at switch. If switch continuity is okay, check for an open or shorted circuit between switch and BCM. If there are no open or shorted circuits, failure could be a faulty horn or internal fault in BCM. See appropriate BODY CONTROL COMPUTER TESTS article.

REMOVAL & INSTALLATION

BODY CONTROL MODULE (BCM)

NOTE: If BCM is replaced, remote keyless entry transmitter codes must be programmed into replacement BCM memory (if equipped)

Removal & Installation – 1) Open driver's door and remove end cap from instrument panel. Remove scuff plate and center bezel. Remove instrument cluster hood. Remove left side knee bolster. Remove steering column cover. Remove silencer. Remove wiring harness connectors from junction block. Remove 3 junction block mounting screws.
2) Remove junction block/BCM assembly by pulling straight down from mounting bayonet. *See Fig. 1.* Disconnect BCM wiring connectors. Remove junction block/BCM assembly from vehicle. Remove 2 screws and 2 latches attaching BCM to junction block. Remove BCM. To install, reverse removal procedure.

DOOR LOCK CYLINDER SWITCH

Removal & Installation – 1) Lower door glass. Remove window crank (if equipped). Disengage clips holding speaker grille to trim panel. Remove door trim panel retaining screws from behind speaker grille. Remove screw cap and screw from bottom of armrest pull cup.

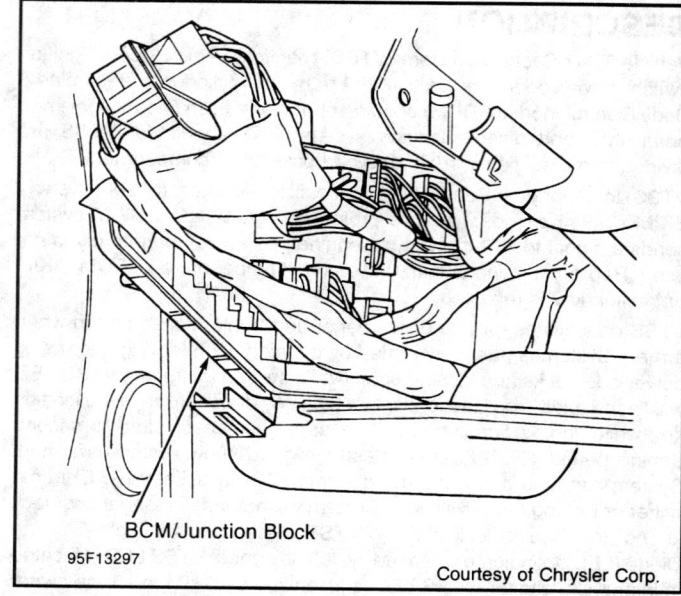

BCM/Junction Block
95F13297
Courtesy of Chrysler Corp.

Fig. 1: Locating BCM & Junction Block

2) Remove door latch screw cap and retaining screw. Disengage trim panel retaining clips from around edge of door. Tilt top of trim panel away from door. Disengage clip holding latch linkage to back of release handle. Remove door trim panel and water shield.
3) Remove clip from illuminated entry switch wiring and disconnect connector. Remove door lock switch from door handle. To install, reverse removal procedure.

SENTRY KEY IMMOBILIZER MODULE (SKIM)

Removal & Installation – 1) Disconnect negative battery cable. Remove knee bolster. Remove steering column shrouds. Disconnect steering column harness from SKIM.
2) Remove 2 screws holding SKIM to top of steering column. *See Fig. 2.* Rotate SKIM bracket to remove antenna ring from ignition key cylinder. Remove SKIM, bracket and antenna as an assembly. To install, reverse removal procedure. If new SKIM is being installed, ensure new SKIM is initialized. See SKIM INITIALIZATION PROCEDURE under PROGRAMMING.

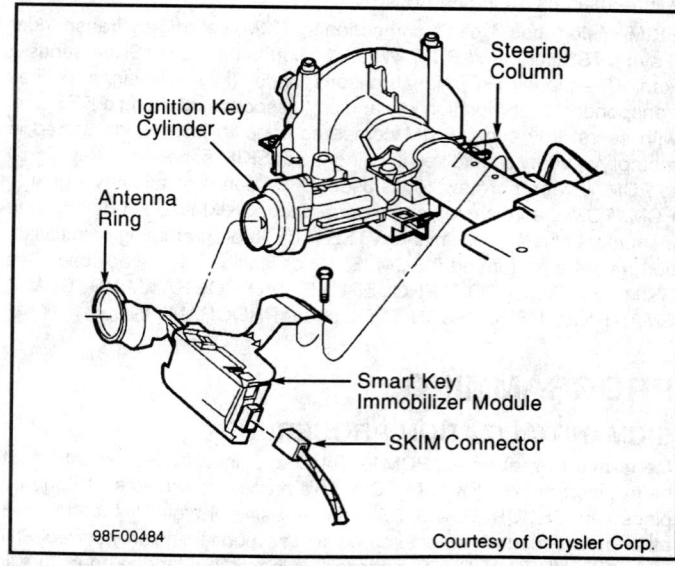

Steering Column
Ignition Key Cylinder
Antenna Ring
Smart Key Immobilizer Module
SKIM Connector
98F00484
Courtesy of Chrysler Corp.

Fig. 2: Identifying SKIM Components

Anti-Theft Systems
Breeze, Cirrus, Sebring Convertible & Stratus (Cont.)

VEHICLE THEFT SECURITY SYSTEM (VTSS) LED

Removal & Installation – Remove instrument cluster. Disconnect vehicle theft security system LED indicator connector from printed circuit board. Rotate LED socket counterclockwise and remove from printed circuit board. *See Fig. 3*. To install, reverse removal procedure. Align index on connector with latch on mating connector located on printed circuit board.

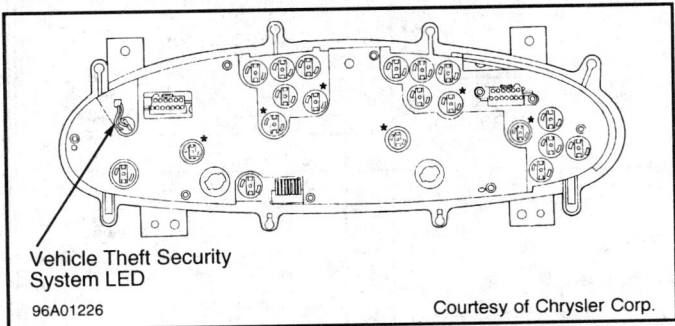

Vehicle Theft Security
System LED

96A01226   Courtesy of Chrysler Corp.

Fig. 3: Identifying Vehicle Theft Security System LED

CHRY
4-30

1999 ACCESSORIES & EQUIPMENT
Anti-Theft Systems
Breeze, Cirrus, Sebring Convertible & Stratus (Cont.)

WIRING DIAGRAMS

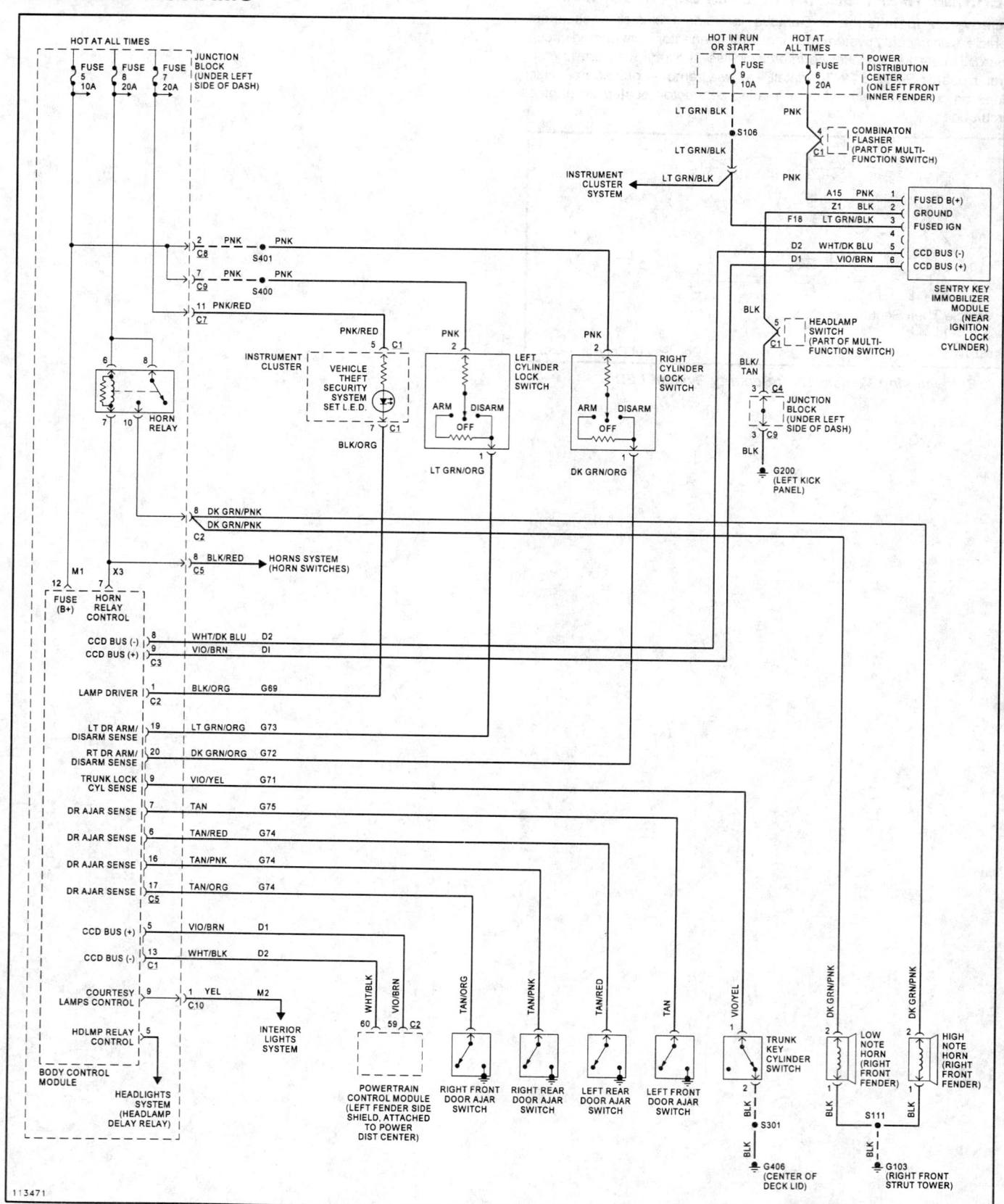

Fig. 4: Anti-Theft System Wiring Diagram (Breeze, Cirrus & Stratus)

1999 ACCESSORIES & EQUIPMENT
Anti-Theft Systems
Breeze, Cirrus, Sebring Convertible & Stratus (Cont.)

CHRY
4-31

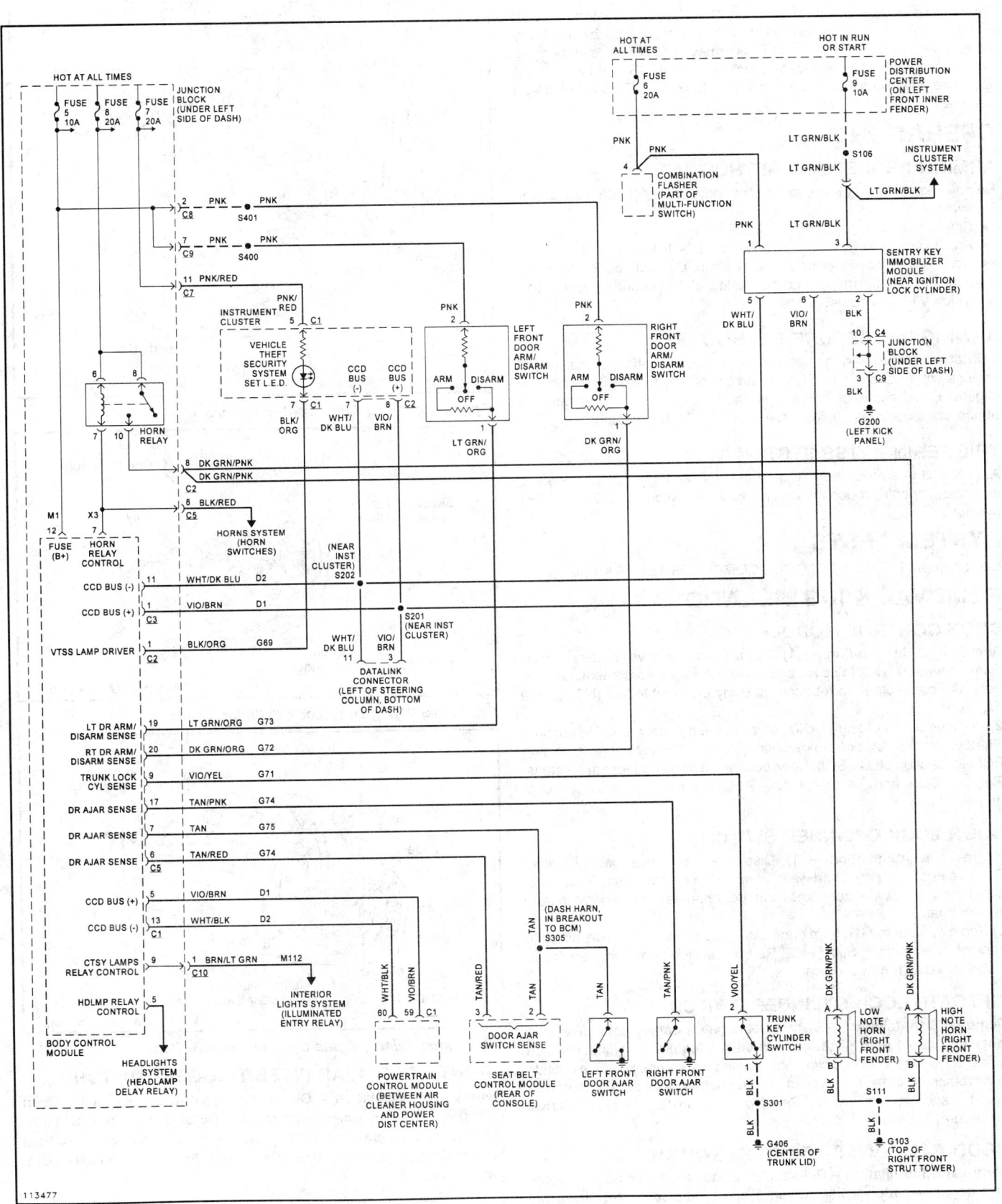

Fig. 5: Anti-Theft System Wiring Diagram (Sebring Convertible)

113477

1999 ACCESSORIES & EQUIPMENT
Anti-Theft Systems – Caravan, Town & Country, & Voyager

DESCRIPTION

On vehicles equipped with the Vehicle Theft Security System (VTSS), doors, liftgate, hood and ignition circuits are monitored by the Body Control Module (BCM) when system is armed. VTSS will prevent engine from starting until BCM receives disarm signal. If VTSS is triggered, horn will pulse, headlights and marker lights will flash and VTSS warning light will flash.

OPERATION

ARMING PROCEDURE METHOD "A"

Remove key from ignition, open any door and actuate one of the following:

- Power door lock button to LOCK.
- Press remote keyless entry transmitter LOCK button.
- Door lock key cylinder to locked position. Close all doors. After last door is closed, arming time-out period of 16 seconds begins, after which VTSS becomes armed.

ARMING PROCEDURE METHOD "B"

With doors closed and ignition switch in LOCK position, press remote keyless entry transmitter LOCK button or use key to lock front doors or liftgate. Once either of these 2 methods are used, arming time-out period of 16 seconds begins, after which VTSS becomes armed.

TRIGGERING VTSS SYSTEM

After VTSS is armed, the following actions will trigger alarm: opening any door, opening hood or turning ignition switch to ON or START position.

SYSTEM TESTS

See appropriate BODY CONTROL COMPUTER TESTS article.

REMOVAL & INSTALLATION

BODY CONTROL MODULE

Removal & Installation – 1) Disconnect negative battery cable. Remove left underdash cover and knee bolster reinforcement. Disconnect wire connectors from bottom of Body Control Module (BCM). *See Fig. 1.*

2) Remove bolts holding junction block to dash panel mounting bracket. Remove junction block from mounting bracket. Remove screws holding BCM to junction block. Slide BCM downward to disengage guide studs. Remove BCM from junction block. To install, reverse removal procedure.

DOOR LOCK CYLINDER SWITCH

Removal & Installation – 1) Disconnect negative battery cable. Remove door trim panel and water shield. Close door glass. Disconnect door lock cylinder wire connector from door harness and wiring clip from impact beam.

2) Remove outer handle from door. Disengage lock tab holding switch to back of lock cylinder. *See Fig. 2.* Remove switch from door handle. To install, reverse removal procedure.

LIFTGATE LOCK CYLINDER SWITCH

Removal & Installation – Disconnect negative battery cable. Remove inner trim panel from liftgate. Disconnect liftgate lock cylinder switch wiring connector. Remove clip from liftgate inner panel. Remove outside latch release handle. Disconnect lock tab holding switch to back of lock cylinder and remove switch. *See Fig. 3.* To install, reverse removal procedure.

HOOD AJAR (VTSS TRIGGER) SWITCH

Removal & Installation – Release hood latch and open hood. Disconnect negative battery cable. Using a small flat-blade screwdriver, pry trigger switch from top of radiator closure panel. Disconnect trigger switch from wire connector and remove switch. To install, reverse removal procedure.

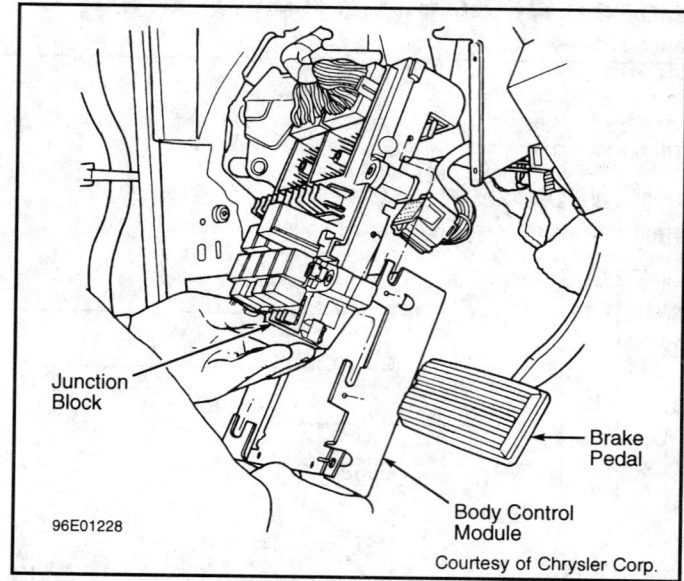

Fig. 1: Identifying Body Control Module

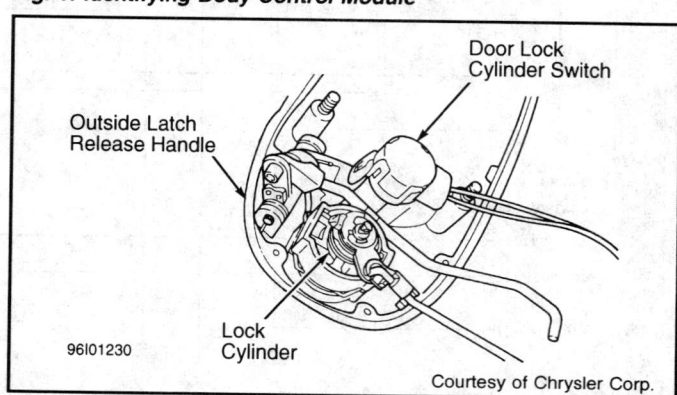

Fig. 2: Identifying Door Lock Cylinder Switch

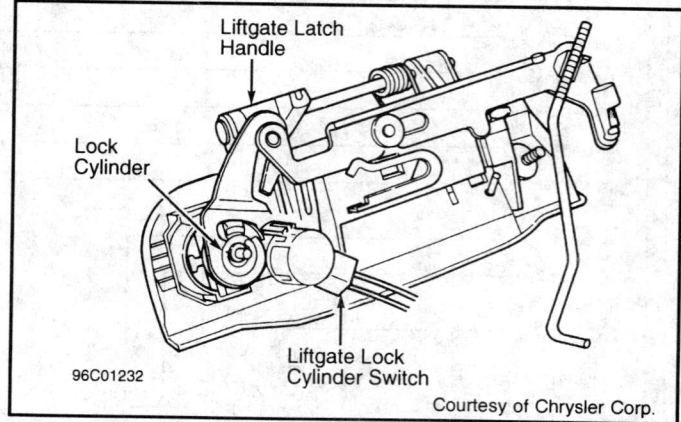

Fig. 3: Identifying Liftgate Cylinder Lock Switch

FRONT DOOR AJAR (VTSS TRIGGER) SWITCH

Removal & Installation – Disconnect negative battery cable. Open front door. Remove screw holding door ajar switch to door "B" pillar. Remove door ajar switch from "B" pillar. Disconnect wire connector from back of door ajar switch and remove switch. To install, reverse removal procedures.

SLIDING DOOR AJAR (VTSS TRIGGER) SWITCH

Removal & Installation – Disconnect negative battery cable. Release sliding door latch. Allow back of door to pop open. Through opening at rear edge of sliding door on outside of vehicle, pry door ajar switch from quarter panel opening. Disconnect wiring connector from back of switch. Remove sliding door ajar switch. To install, reverse removal procedure.

LIFTGATE AJAR (VTSS TRIGGER) SWITCH

Removal & Installation – Disconnect negative battery cable. Remove liftgate latch from vehicle. Disconnect wiring connector from liftgate ajar switch. Remove screw holding ajar switch to liftgate latch and remove switch. To install, reverse removal procedure.

CHRY
4-34

1999 ACCESSORIES & EQUIPMENT
Anti-Theft Systems – Caravan, Town & Country, & Voyager (Cont.)

WIRING DIAGRAMS

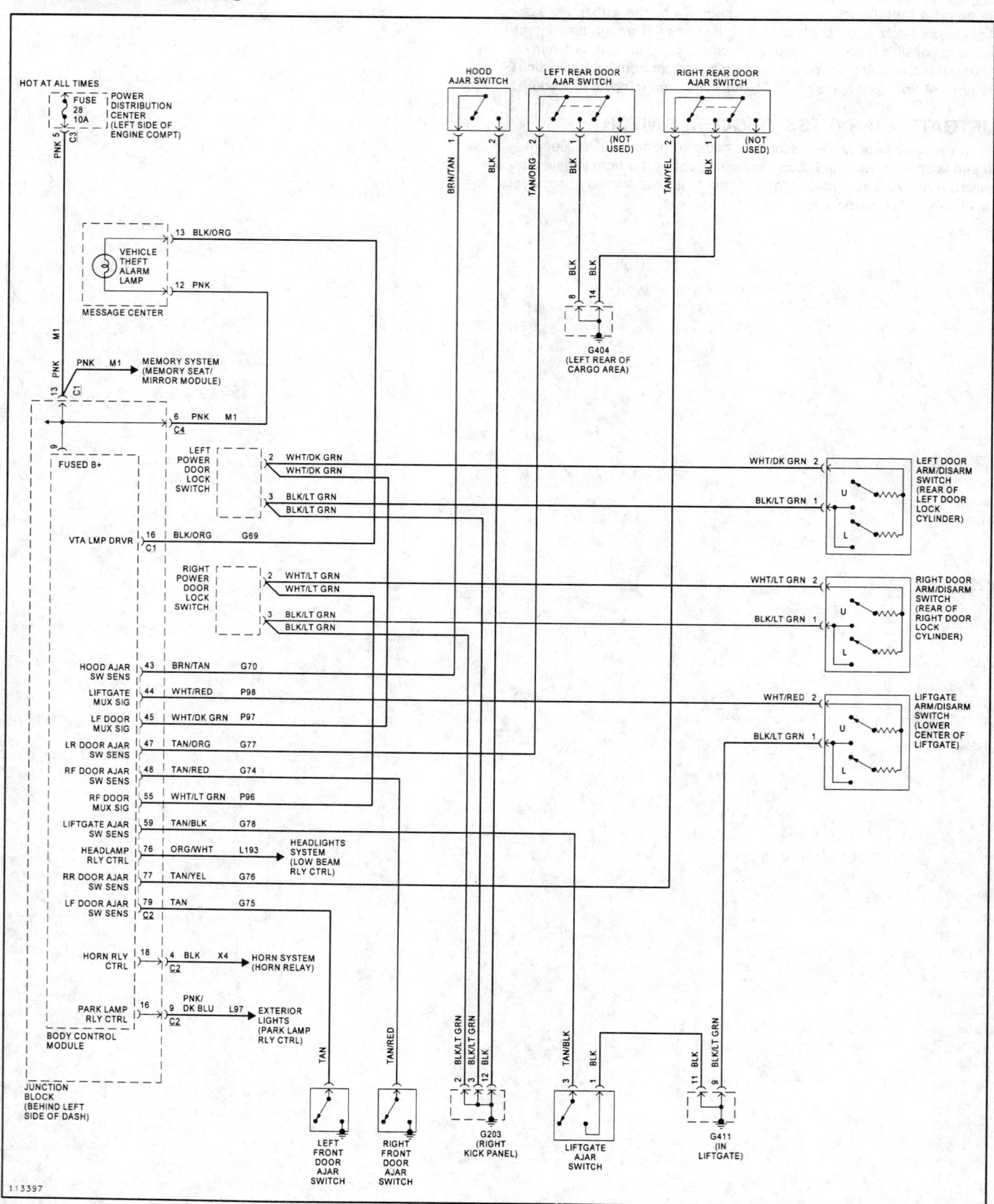

Fig. 4: Anti-Theft System Wiring Diagram (Caravan, Town & Country, & Voyager)

113397

Anti-Theft Systems – Concorde, Intrepid, LHS & 300M

DESCRIPTION & OPERATION

Vehicle Theft Security System (VTSS) is designed for entire vehicle theft protection. System monitors doors, deck lid lock cylinder and ignition switch for unauthorized operation. When system is triggered, horn will sound, and headlights, parking lights, taillights and VTSS indicator light will flash. After 3 minutes, horn will stop sounding, but lights will continue to flash for another 15 minutes. VTSS will reset after it has been triggered and system has timed out for 18 minutes. When unauthorized entry has occurred, VTSS activates an engine kill feature. Vehicle will not start until VTSS is disarmed using key or Remote Keyless Entry (RKE) system.

VTSS is equipped with a tamper alert signal, indicating VTSS has been triggered (vehicle has been tampered with). When either front door is unlocked with key or RKE, the horn will sound 3 times.

VTSS can be triggered from doors, trunk key cylinder and ignition switch. VTSS has a dash cover SET indicator light. SET indicator light flashes for 16 seconds during arming process. If indicator light comes on but does not flash, a problem exists in trunk circuit. VTSS is armed by locking doors using power lock button or RKE system. VTSS is disarmed through normal vehicle entry of unlocking door with key or RKE system. Whenever battery power is lost or disconnected, VTSS will prevent vehicle from starting. When battery power is restored, system must be disarmed before vehicle will start.

On vehicles equipped with Sentry Key Immobilizer System (SKIS), PCM will shut off fuel after 2 seconds of engine operation if proper communication has not been made from BCM and Sentry Key Immobilizer Module (SKIM). Engine will not re-crank until ignition is first turned off. After 6 consecutive fuel shut-offs, engine will no longer crank until failure is corrected and valid communication exists between PCM, BCM and SKIM.

PROGRAMMING

SKIM INITIALIZATION PROCEDURE

General Information – SECURED ACCESS mode is not required to check programmed status of key.

If PCM is replaced, unique secret key data must be transferred from SKIM to PCM. This procedure requires SKIM to be placed in SECURED ACCESS mode using 4-digit PIN code.

If 3 attempts are made to enter secured access mode using an incorrect PIN code, SECURED ACCESS mode will be locked out for one hour. To exit lock out mode, turn ignition switch to RUN/START position continuously for one hour. Ensure all accessories are turned off. Monitor battery state and connect battery charger is necessary.

To program smart keys using "customer programming method" requires 2 valid smart keys. See CUSTOMER LEARN PROGRAMMING METHOD.

Initialization Procedure – 1) Obtain vehicle's unique PIN code assigned to it's original SKIM module from vehicle owner or Chrysler's customer center. Using scan tool, select THEFT ALARM, SKIM, then MISCELLANEOUS. Select SKIM MODULE REPLACED function.

2) Enter SECURED ACCESS mode using unique 4-digit PIN code. Program vehicle's VIN into SKIM's memory. Program country code into SKIM's memory (U.S.).

3) Transfer vehicle's unique Secret Key data from PCM. This process will require SKIM module to be in SECURED ACCESS mode. The PIN code must be entered into scan tool before SKIM will enter SECURED ACCESS mode. Once SECURED ACCESS mode is active, SKIM will remain in that mode for 60 seconds.

4) Program all customer keys into SKIM's memory. This requires that SKIM be in SECURED ACCESS mode. The SKIM will immediately exit SECURED ACCESS mode after each key is programmed.

PROGRAMMING BLANK SENTRY KEY USING SCAN TOOL

Once key blank is cut, insert key into ignition switch. Turn ignition switch to RUN position. Using scan tool, select THEFT ALARM, then SKIM. Select MISCELLANEOUS, then PROGRAM NEW KEY. Enter 4-digit PIN code. When programming is completed, SKIM will exit SECURED ACCESS mode and display status of key. One of 5 different status messages maybe displayed as follows:

- PROGRAMMING SUCCESSFUL is displayed if SKIM smart key programming succeeds.
- LEARNED KEY IN IGNITION is displayed if key in the ignition has already been programmed into vehicle's SKIM.
- 8 KEYS ALREADY LEARNED, PROGRAMMING NOT DONE is displayed if eight keys have already been programmed into SKIM. If a new key needs to be added due to a lost or defective key, the ERASE ALL KEYS function has to be performed. Original 7 keys plus additional new key may then be reprogrammed into SKIM.
- PROGRAMMING NOT ATTEMPTED is displayed after an ERASE ALL KEYS function is executed.
- PROGRAMING KEY FAILED is displayed if further diagnosis is required. To program additional keys, turn ignition off. Remove current programmed key and insert next new blank key. Turn ignition switch to RUN position. Re-enter SECURED ACCESS mode function and repeat PROGRAM NEW KEY procedure.

CUSTOMER LEARN PROGRAMMING METHOD

NOTE: The following steps must be completed in proper order. SKIS will automatically exit CUSTOMER LEARN programming mode if time allotted is exceeded, or if 8 keys have already been programmed.

1) Once sentry key blank is cut, insert one of the 2 valid sentry keys into ignition. Turn ignition on.

2) After ignition has been on for 3 seconds, but no more than 15 seconds, turn ignition off. Remove key. Insert second valid sentry key. Turn ignition on. Both operations must be performed within 15 seconds.

3) About 10 seconds after completion of step 2, VTSS LED indicator will flash and a single tone will be heard. This indicates system has entered CUSTOMER LEARN programming mode.

4) Within 50 seconds, turn ignition off. Remove valid sentry key. Insert blank sentry key. Turn ignition on.

5) After about 10 seconds, a single tone will be heard. VTSS LED indicator will stop flashing and stay on for about 3 seconds to indicate sentry key has been successfully programmed.

6) SKIS will return to normal operation immediately following exit from CUSTOMER LEARN programming mode.

7) Repeat procedure for each additional sentry key to be programmed.

SYSTEM TESTS

SYSTEM SELF-TEST

1) System operation may be verified by entering self-test mode. Use scan tool to select self-test mode. See appropriate VEHICLE COMMUNICATIONS article.

NOTE: Vehicle Theft Security System (VTSS) or VTSS self-test will be inoperative if Powertrain Control Module (PCM) has been replaced within last 20 ignition switch cycles.

2) Once in self-test mode, parking lights and taillights will flash and horn will sound twice. Parking lights and taillights flashing verifies their operation, and horn sounding twice verifies proper trunk cylinder position.

3) Turn ignition switch to OFF position to stop lights from flashing, while keeping system in self-test. While in self-test mode, a horn pulse should occur at each of following steps, indicating proper operation:

- Ensure all doors are closed. Open, then close each door. Horn will sound when door ajar switch closes and opens. There must be a one-second delay between closing and opening switch.
- Activate power door locks in both LOCK and UNLOCK directions. Horn will sound after each activation.
- Rotate key in both door lock cylinders to unlock position. Horn will sound when switch closes and opens. Ensure there is a one-second delay between changing switch states, or horn will not sound.

CHRY
4-36

1999 ACCESSORIES & EQUIPMENT
Anti-Theft Systems – Concorde, Intrepid, LHS & 300M (Cont.)

- Using RKE system, activate locks in both LOCK and UNLOCK directions. Horn will sound after each activation.
- Cycle ignition switch to RUN position. A single horn pulse indicates proper operation of ignition input and take VTSS module out of self-test mode.
- For any of these tests, if switch does not remain open or closed for at least one second, the horn will only sound once.

4) Lack of horn pulse during any operation indicates a switch failure. Check for continuity at switch. If switch continuity is okay, check for open or shorted wire between switch and VTSS module.

5) Whenever a VTSS malfunction occurs, verify wiring harness is properly connected to all connectors before starting diagnosis and repair procedures.

REMOVAL & INSTALLATION
BODY CONTROL MODULE (BCM)

CAUTION: Always turn ignition switch to OFF position prior to disconnecting or connecting any module connector.

NOTE: After replacement of BCM, vehicle will not start until VTSS system is enabled. Use scan tool to enable VTSS system.

Removal & Installation – 1) Body Control Module (BCM) is attached to junction block. The junction block must be removed to enable removal of BCM. Junction block is located behind left kick panel below instrument panel. *See Fig. 1.*

2) Remove remote negative cable terminal. The remote negative battery cable terminal is located between right strut tower and air cleaner air intake hose. Open left front door. Pry off left dash end trim cap. Remove left side under dash cover. Remove trunk lid switch and wiring.

3) Disconnect harness connectors from junction block. Remove junction block by pulling straight down from mounting bayonet. Disconnect BCM and RKE module connectors. Remove 4 screws holding BCM to junction block and separate BCM from junction block.

4) To install, transfer RKE module to replacement BCM. To complete installation, reverse removal procedure. Using scan tool, enable VTSS system.

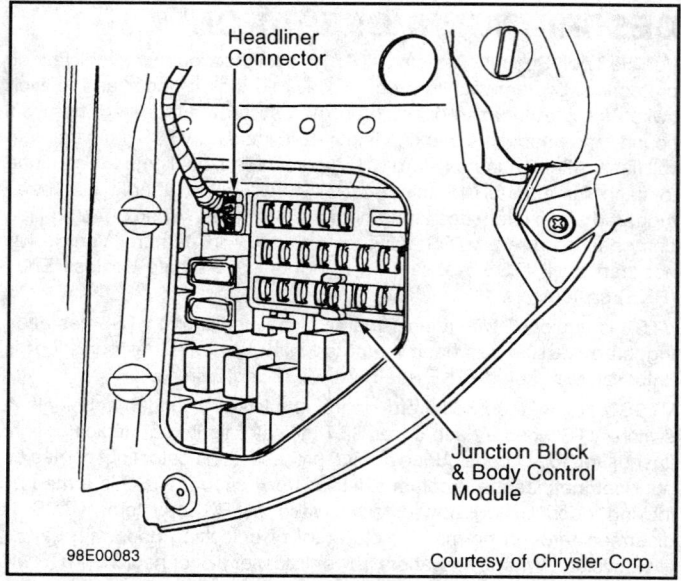

Fig. 1: Locating BCM

DOOR LOCK CYLINDER SWITCH

Removal & Installation – Remove door trim panel. Disconnect lock cylinder switch wire harness connector. Disconnect clip and remove lock cylinder switch. To install, reverse removal procedure.

TRUNK LID LOCK CYLINDER SWITCH

Removal & installation – Remove trunk lid lining as necessary to access trunk latch. Remove trunk lid latch mounting bolts. Disconnect wire connectors from latch. Remove trunk latch. Remove trunk lock cylinder from bracket. Remove switch. To install, reverse removal procedure.

SENTRY KEY IMMOBILIZER MODULE (SKIM)

Removal & Installation – 1) Remove negative battery cable. Remove knee bolster. Remove steering column shrouds. Disconnect steering column harness from SKIM.

2) Remove 1 screw holding SKIM to bottom of steering column. Slide SKIM away from steering column to clear antenna ring from ignition key cylinder. Remove SKIM. To install, reverse removal procedure. If new SKIM is being installed, ensure new SKIM is initialized. See SKIM INITIALIZATION PROCEDURE under PROGRAMMING.

1999 ACCESSORIES & EQUIPMENT
Anti-Theft Systems – Concorde, Intrepid, LHS & 300M (Cont.)

CHRY
4-37

WIRING DIAGRAMS

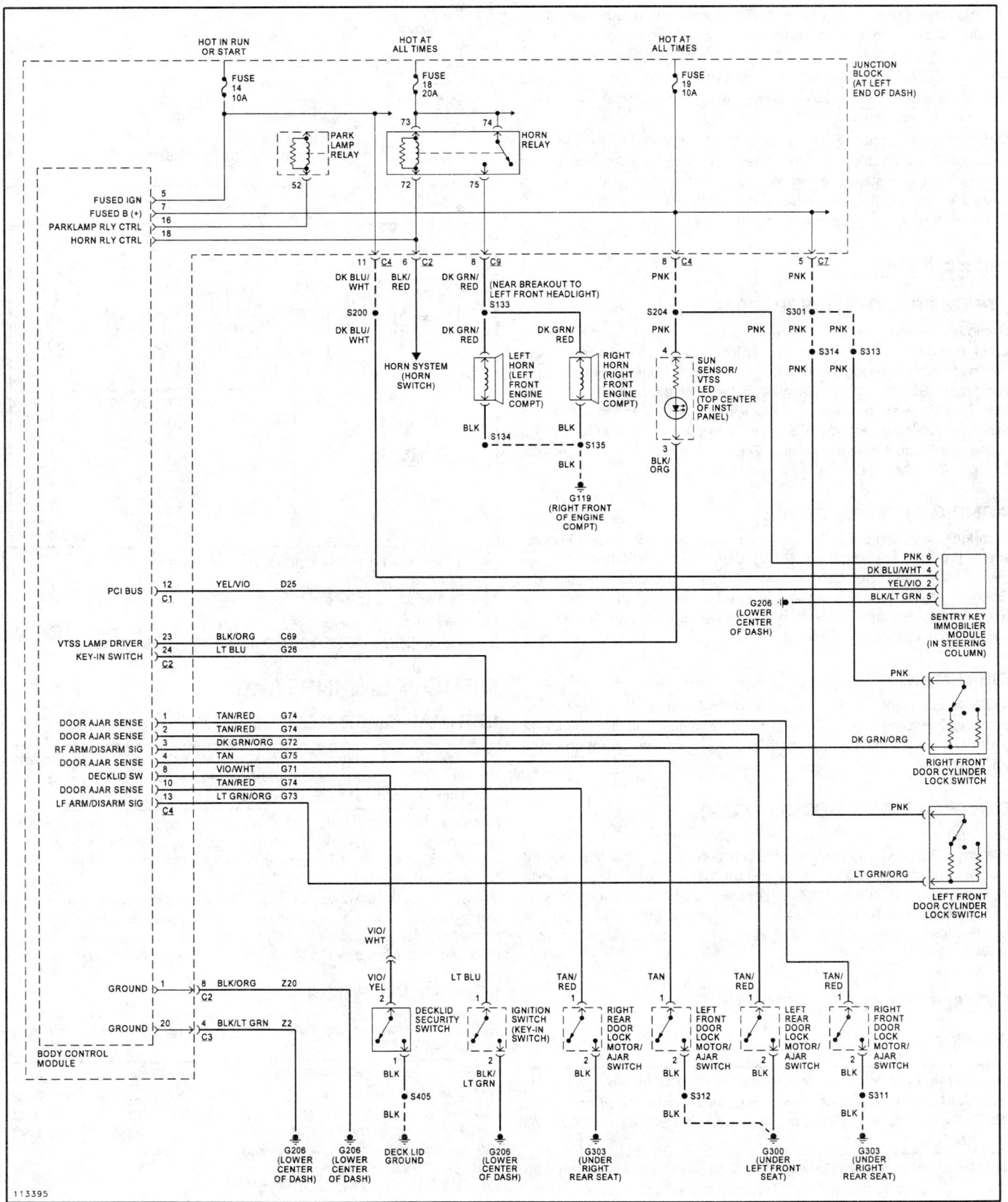

Fig. 2: Anti-Theft System Wiring Diagram (Concorde, Intrepid, LHS & 300M)

113395

DESCRIPTION

Vehicle Theft Security System (VTSS) provides an engine no-run feature, flashes headlights and sounds horn if any door or hood is opened without using key or remote keyless entry system.

VTSS is controlled by Central Timer Module (CTM). CTM is located behind right side of glove box. If CTM is faulty, CTM cannot be repaired and must be replaced.

VTSS is also equipped with a power-up mode. If battery is disconnected or looses power while VTSS is armed, VTSS system remains armed when power is restored. A temper alert signal is sounded on vehicle entry if VTSS was triggered while away from vehicle. Horn will sound 3 times, alerting owner VTSS was triggered.

OPERATION

ARMING PROCEDURE (PASSIVE)

Remove key from ignition. Ensure headlights are off. Lock doors while open, using power lock switch. Power lock switch will not operate with key in ignition or headlights on while door is open. Vehicle Theft Security System (VTSS) will not arm using key in lock cylinder or mechanical lock button. While system is arming, SECURITY light will flash rapidly for 15 seconds. Opening any door or turning key in ignition while light is flashing will abort arming process. Once arming process is complete, SECURITY light will flash at a slower rate.

ARMING PROCEDURE (ACTIVE)

Turn ignition switch to LOCK position, remove key and close all doors. Press Remote Keyless Entry (RKE) transmitter LOCK button. While system is arming, SECURITY light will flash rapidly for 15 seconds. Opening any door or turning key in ignition while light is flashing will abort arming process. Once arming process is complete, SECURITY light will flash at a slower rate.

DISARMING

VTSS can be disarmed 2 ways: unlock vehicle using key in any door or pressing Remote Keyless Entry (RKE) transmitter UNLOCK button. If alarm has been set off, either method can be used to disarm anti-theft system.

CENTRAL TIMER MODULE (CTM)

Central Timer Module (CTM) is processor for Vehicle Theft Security System (VTSS). CTM uses the data bus network to allow sharing and reporting of sensor information. if a door ajar sensor is opened while VTSS is set, a signal is sent to flash headlights and sound horn. PCM is also notified through bus network to enable engine no-run feature. CTM has Remote Keyless Entry (RKE) receiver and control logic incorporated.

COMPONENT TESTS

RELAYS

NOTE: *Headlight relay may also be referred to as the security relay. Headlight and horn relays are located in Power Distribution Center (PDC) in engine compartment. For circuit testing, see WIRING DIAGRAMS.*

Headlight Relay & Horn Relay – Remove relay to be tested. Measure resistance between appropriate relay terminals with relay de-energized and energized. See RELAY TEST SPECIFICATIONS table. See Fig. 1. If continuity or resistance is not as specified, replace relay.

RELAY TEST SPECIFICATIONS

Terminals	Condition
De-Energized	
87A & 30	Continuity
87 & 30	No Continuity
85 & 86	70-80 Ohms Resistance
Energized [1]	
87 & 30	Continuity
87A & 30	No Continuity

[1] – Apply position battery voltage to terminal No. 85 and ground terminal No. 86.

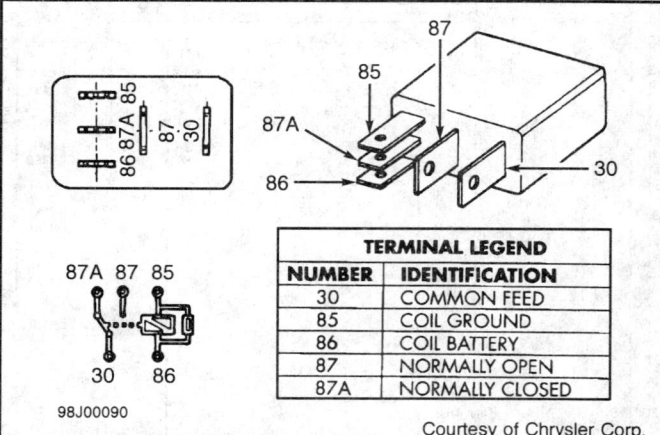

TERMINAL LEGEND	
NUMBER	IDENTIFICATION
30	COMMON FEED
85	COIL GROUND
86	COIL BATTERY
87	NORMALLY OPEN
87A	NORMALLY CLOSED

98J00090

Courtesy of Chrysler Corp.

Fig. 1: Identifying Relay Connector Terminals

SYSTEM TESTS

For Vehicle Theft Security System (VTSS) testing procedures, see appropriate BODY CONTROL COMPUTER TESTS article.

REMOVAL & INSTALLATION

CENTRAL TIMER MODULE (CTM)

NOTE: *Before removing Central Timer Module (CTM) use scan tool to view settings for programmable features. Use these settings to program replacement CTM.*

Removal & Installation – 1) Disconnect negative battery cable. Remove glove box. Remove right-side glove box bracket screws from instrument panel. Remove screws holding CTM bracket to right glove box bracket. See Fig. 2.

2) Remove right glove box bracket. Pull CTM (with bracket attached) into glove box opening and disconnect connectors. Remove CTM from instrument panel. To install CTM, reverse removal procedure. Ensure mounting tab is engaged in slot in instrument panel end bracket.

DOOR JAMB SWITCH

NOTE: *Door jamb switch may also be referred to as door ajar switch.*

Removal & Installation – On Durango, door jamb switches are part of latch assembly and are not serviced separately. On Dakota, disconnect negative battery cable. Using pliers, grasp body of door jamb switch and gently move back and forth while pulling switch from pillar. Disconnect wire connector. To install, reverse removal procedure.

DOOR LOCK CYLINDER SWITCH

Removal & Installation – Disconnect negative battery cable. Remove inside door panel. Remove door outside latch handle mounting hardware and linkage. Pull door outside handle away from door far enough to remove door lock cylinder switch from back of door lock cylinder. See

Fig. 3. Remove door lock cylinder switch pigtail retainers and remove door lock cylinder switch. To install, reverse removal procedure.

LIFTGATE AJAR SWITCH (DURANGO)

NOTE: Liftgate ajar switch is part of liftgate latch assembly. If liftgate ajar switch is defective, complete liftgate latch assembly must be replaced.

LIFTGATE LOCK CYLINDER SWITCH (DURANGO)

Removal & Installation – Disconnect negative battery cable. Remove inside liftgate panel. Reach through access hole and remove liftgate lock cylinder switch from back of liftgate lock cylinder. Disconnect liftgate lock cylinder switch harness connector, and remove liftgate lock cylinder switch. To install, reverse removal procedure.

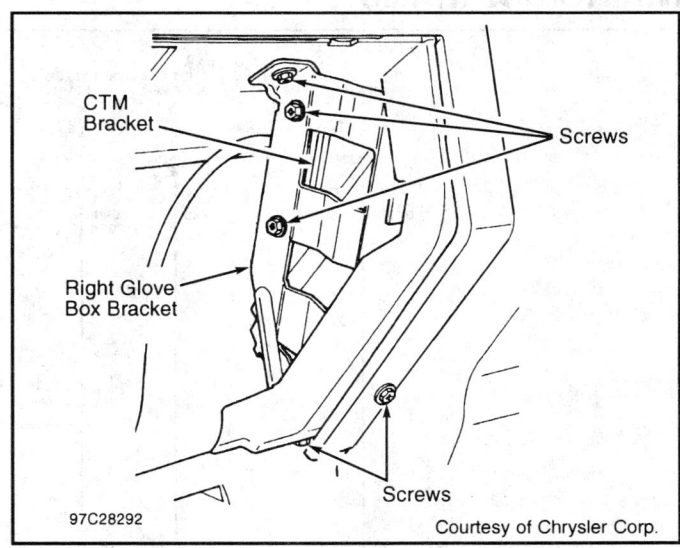

Fig. 2: Removing CTM From Instrument Panel

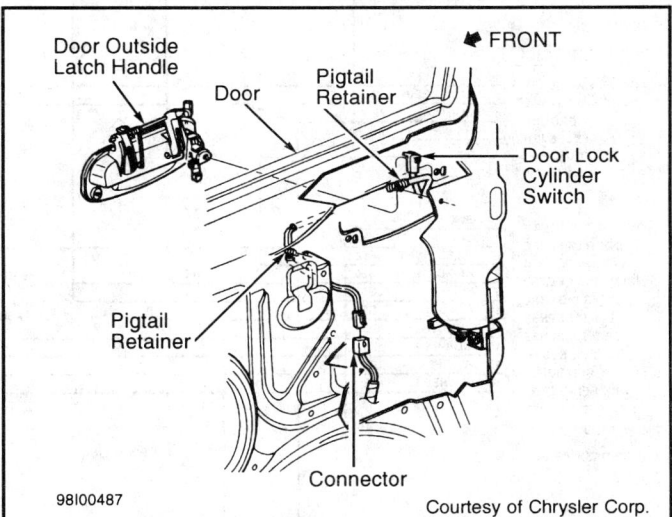

Fig. 3: Identifying Door Lock Cylinder Switch

1999 ACCESSORIES & EQUIPMENT
Anti-Theft Systems – Dakota & Durango (Cont.)

WIRING DIAGRAMS

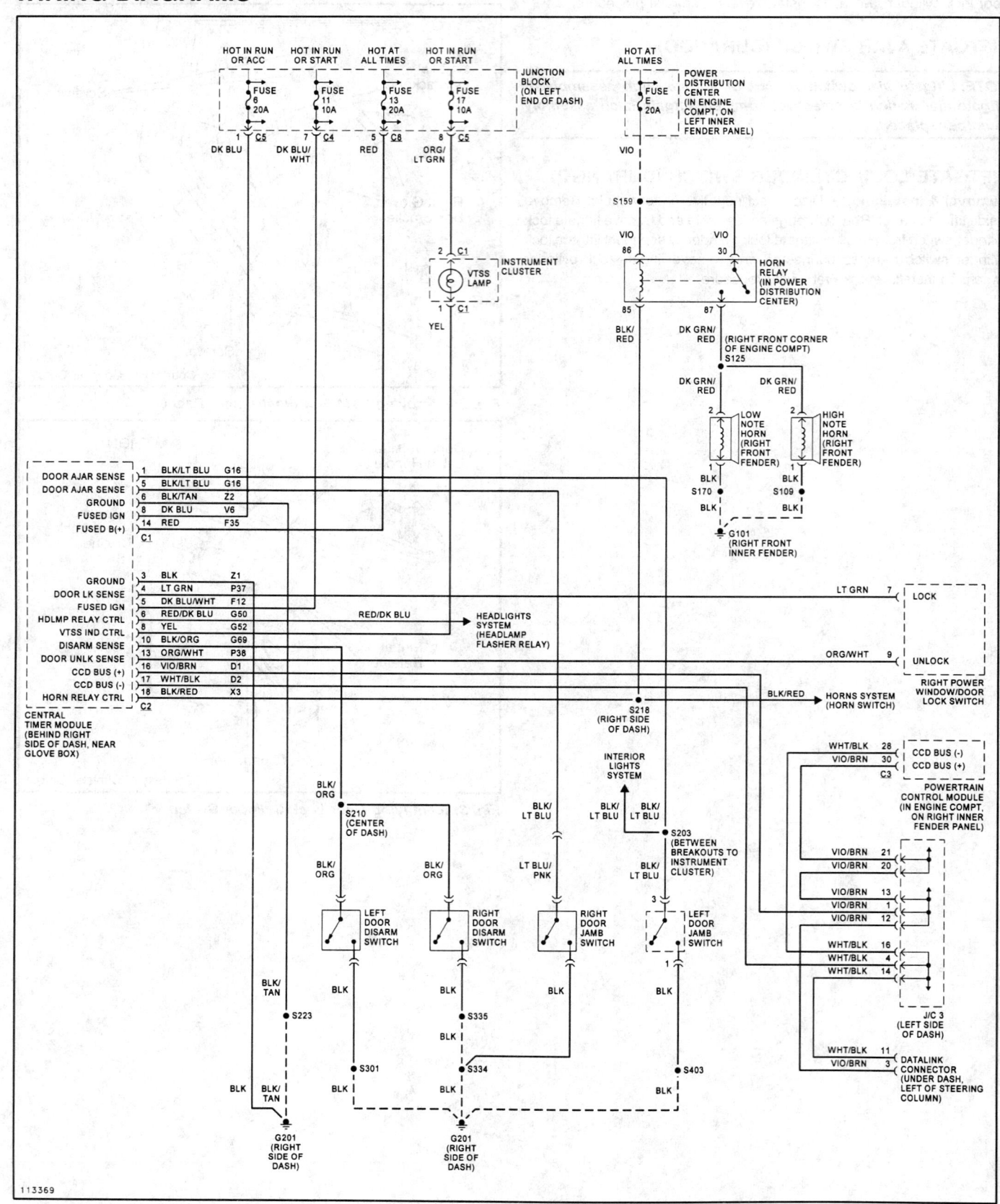

Fig. 4: Anti-Theft System Wiring Diagram (Dakota)

113369

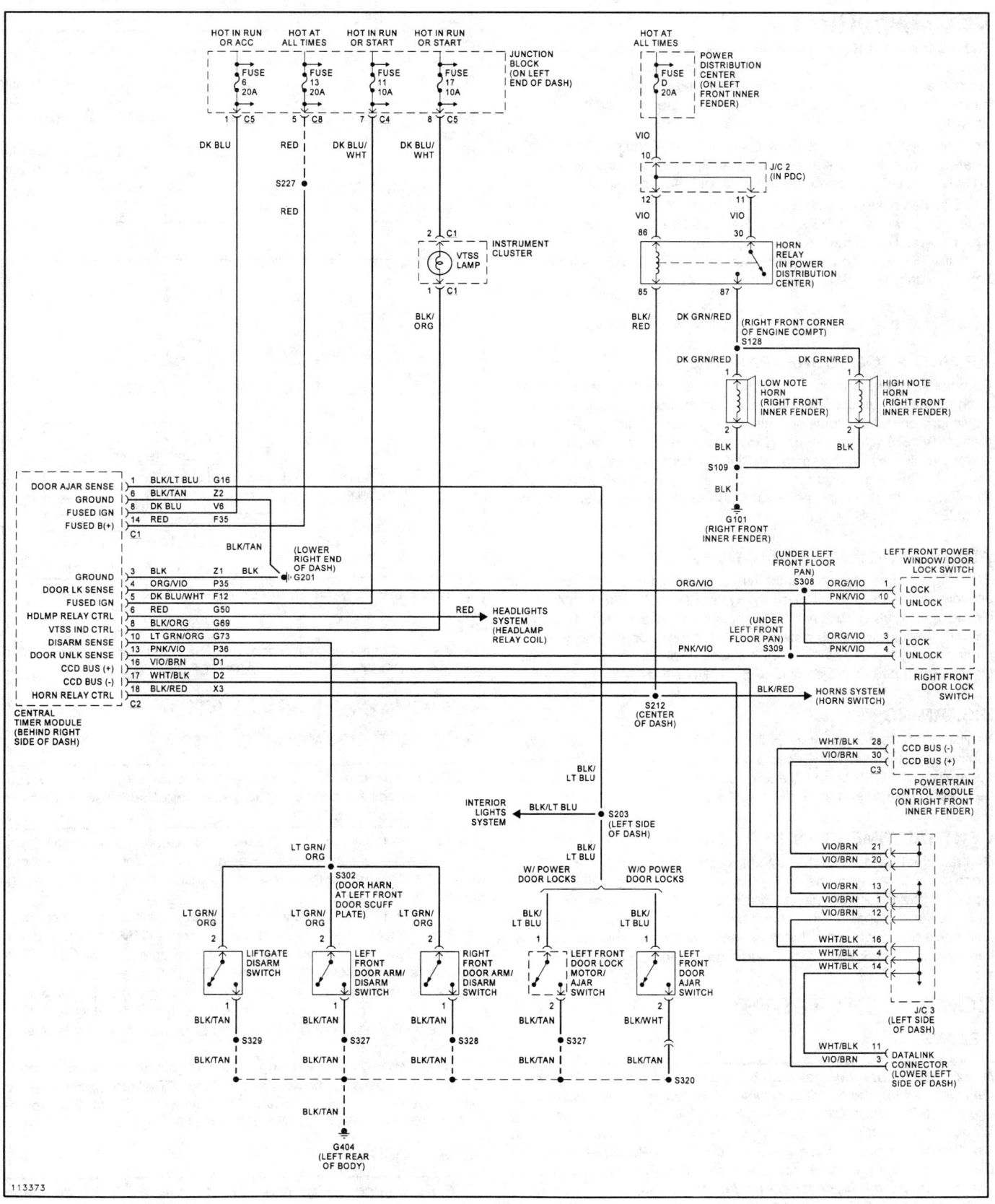

Fig. 5: Anti-Theft System Wiring Diagram (Durango)

DESCRIPTION

The Vehicle Theft Security System (VTSS) provides an engine no-run feature, flashes headlights and sounds horn if any door or hood is opened without using key or remote keyless entry transmitter, or if battery cables are disconnected then reconnected when system is activated.

Anti-theft system is controlled by Central Timer Module (CTM). CTM is located under driver's side of dash panel, right of steering column. If CTM is faulty, CTM cannot be repaired and must be replaced.

VTSS is also equipped with a power-up mode. If battery is disconnected or looses power while VTSS is armed, VTSS system remains armed when power is restored. A temper alert signal is sounded on vehicle entry if VTSS was triggered while away from vehicle. Horn will sound 3 times alerting owner VTSS was triggered.

OPERATION

ARMING PROCEDURE (PASSIVE)

Remove key from ignition. Ensure headlights are off. Lock doors while open, using power lock switch. Power lock switch will not operate with key in ignition or headlights on while door is open. Vehicle Theft Security System (VTSS) will not arm using key in lock cylinder or mechanical lock button. While system is arming, SECURITY light will flash rapidly for 15 seconds. Opening any door or turning the ignition key while light is flashing will abort arming process. Once arming process is complete, SECURITY light will go out.

ARMING PROCEDURE (ACTIVE)

Pressing Remote Keyless Entry (RKE) transmitter LOCK button will actively arm Vehicle Theft Security System (VTSS). All doors must be closed and ignition switch in OFF position. While system is arming, SECURITY light will flash rapidly for 15 seconds. Opening any door or turning the ignition key while light is flashing will abort arming process. Once arming process is complete, SECURITY light will go out.

DISARMING

Vehicle Theft Security System (VTSS) can be disarmed 2 ways: unlock vehicle using key in any door and pressing remote keyless entry transmitter UNLOCK button. If alarm has been set off, either method can be used to disarm and shut-off horn.

CENTRAL TIMER MODULE (CTM)

Central Timer Module (CTM) is Vehicle Theft Security System (VTSS) processor. CTM uses the data bus network to allow sharing and reporting of sensor information. If a door ajar sensor is opened while VTSS is set, a signal is sent to flash headlights and sound horn. PCM is also notified through bus network to enable engine no-run feature. CTM has remote keyless entry receiver and control logic incorporated.

COMPONENT TESTS

RELAYS

NOTE: Headlight relay may also be referred to as the security relay. On Ram Pickup, the headlight relay is located in Power Distribution Center (PDC) in engine compartment. On Ram Van and Ram Wagon, the headlight relay is taped to headlight switch harness. On Ram Pickup, the horn relay is located in Power Distribution Center (PDC) in engine compartment. On Ram Van and Ram Wagon, the horn relay is located in junction block under left side of instrument panel. For circuit testing, see WIRING DIAGRAMS.

Headlight Relay & Horn Relay – Remove relay to be tested. Measure resistance between appropriate relay terminals with relay de-energized and energized. See RELAY TEST SPECIFICATIONS table. *See Fig. 1.* If continuity or resistance is not as specified, replace relay.

RELAY TEST SPECIFICATIONS

Terminals	Condition
De-Energized	
87A & 30	Continuity
87 & 30	No Continuity
85 & 86	70-80 Ohms Resistance
Energized [1]	
87 & 30	Continuity
87A & 30	No Continuity

[1] – Apply position battery voltage to terminal No. 85 and ground terminal No. 86.

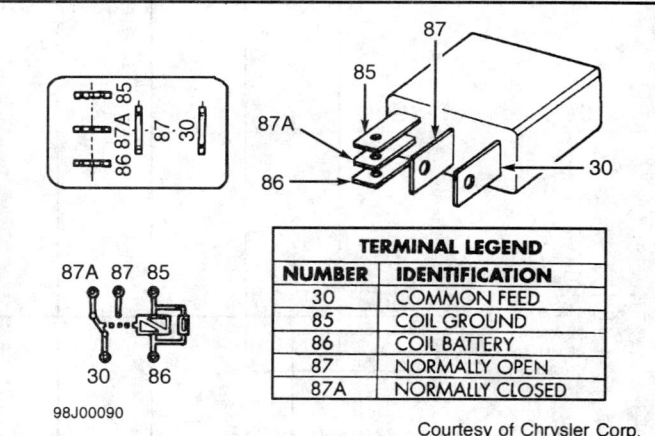

TERMINAL LEGEND	
NUMBER	**IDENTIFICATION**
30	COMMON FEED
85	COIL GROUND
86	COIL BATTERY
87	NORMALLY OPEN
87A	NORMALLY CLOSED

98J00090

Courtesy of Chrysler Corp.

Fig. 1: Identifying Relay Connector Terminals

SYSTEM TESTS

For Vehicle Theft Security System (VTSS) testing procedures, see appropriate BODY CONTROL COMPUTER TESTS article.

REMOVAL & INSTALLATION

CENTRAL TIMER MODULE (CTM)

NOTE: Before removing Central Timer Module (CTM), use scan tool to view settings for programmable features. Use these settings to program replacement CTM.

Removal & Installation (Ram Pickup) – 1) Disconnect negative battery cable. Remove left underdash cover and knee bolster reinforcement. Remove 2 CTM retaining screws at right side of underdash opening. *See Fig. 2.*

2) Slide CTM down into opening far enough to gain access to connectors. Disconnect harness connectors and remove CTM from underdash. To install, reverse removal procedure. Reprogram new CTM. See appropriate BODY CONTROL COMPUTER TESTS article.

Removal & Installation (Ram Van & Ram Wagon) – 1) Disconnect negative battery cable. Remove left underdash cover and knee bolster reinforcement. Remove 3 CTM retaining screws from left center instrument panel support. *See Fig. 3.*

2) Slide CTM away from mounting enough to gain access to connectors. Disconnect harness connectors and remove CTM from underdash. To install, reverse removal procedure. Reprogram new CTM. See appropriate BODY CONTROL COMPUTER TESTS article.

DOOR JAMB SWITCH

NOTE: Door jamb switch may also be referred to as door ajar switch. On Ram Van and Ram Wagon, front door jamb switches are part of latch assembly and are not serviced separately.

Removal & Installation – Disconnect negative battery cable. On Ram Van and Ram Wagon, unscrew door ajar switch from pillar. On Ram Pickup, using pliers, pull back and forth to slide switch from pillar. On all

1999 ACCESSORIES & EQUIPMENT

CHRY
4-43

Anti-Theft Systems – Ram Pickup, Ram Van & Ram Wagon (Cont.)

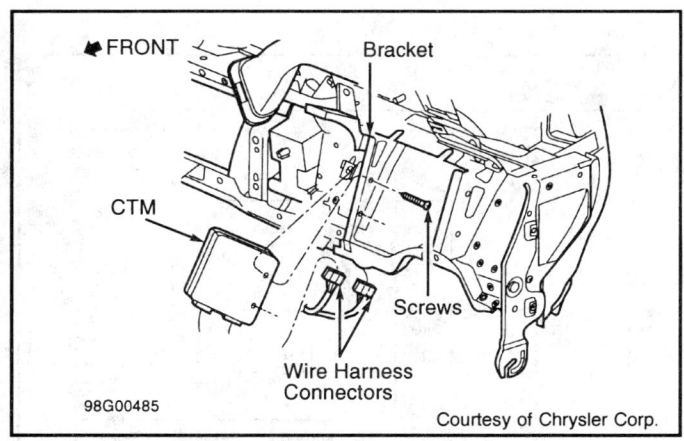

Fig. 2: Identifying CTM Location (Ram Pickup)

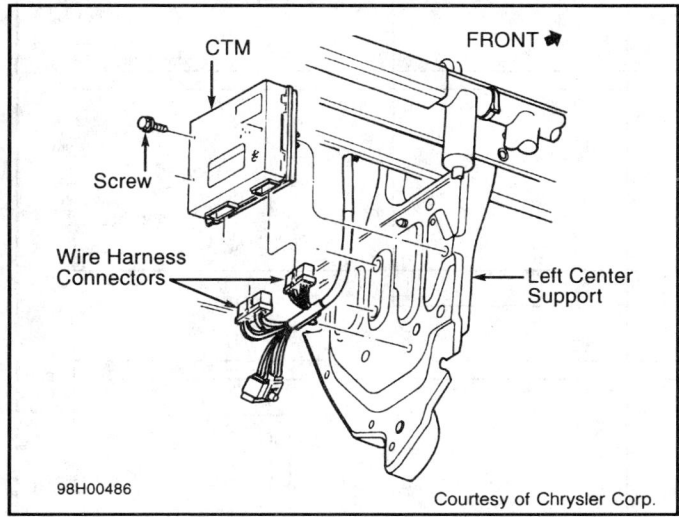

Fig. 3: Identifying CTM Location (Ram Van & Ram Wagon)

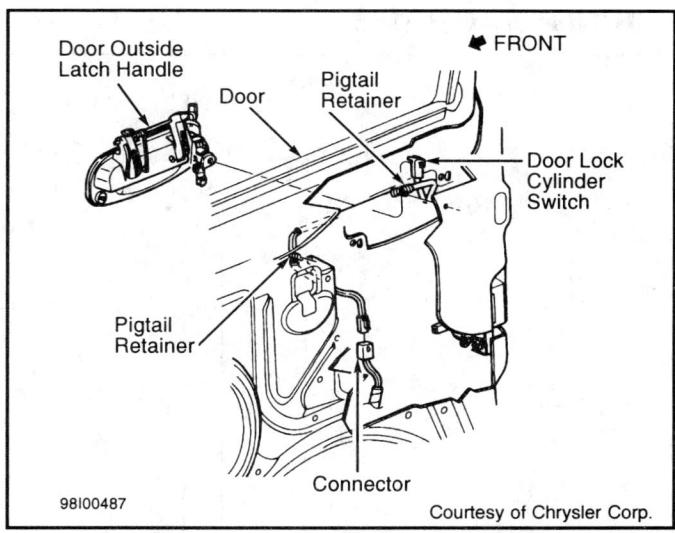

Fig. 4: Identifying Door Lock Cylinder Switch (Ram Pickup)

models, pull door jamb switch away from pillar enough to disconnect 2 harness connectors. To install, reverse removal procedure.

DOOR LOCK CYLINDER SWITCH

Removal & Installation (Ram Pickup) – Disconnect negative battery cable. Remove inside door panel. Remove door outside latch handle mounting hardware and linkage. Pull door outside handle away from door far enough to remove door lock cylinder switch from back of door lock cylinder. *See Fig. 4.* Remove door lock cylinder switch pigtail retainers and remove door lock cylinder switch. To install, reverse removal procedure.

Removal & Installation (Ram Van & Ram Wagon) – Disconnect negative battery cable. Remove inside door panel. Disconnect door lock cylinder harness connector. Disengage door lock cylinder switch from back of door lock cylinder. Remove door lock cylinder switch pigtail retainers and remove door lock cylinder switch. To install, reverse removal procedure.

1999 ACCESSORIES & EQUIPMENT
Anti-Theft Systems – Ram Pickup, Ram Van & Ram Wagon (Cont.)

WIRING DIAGRAMS

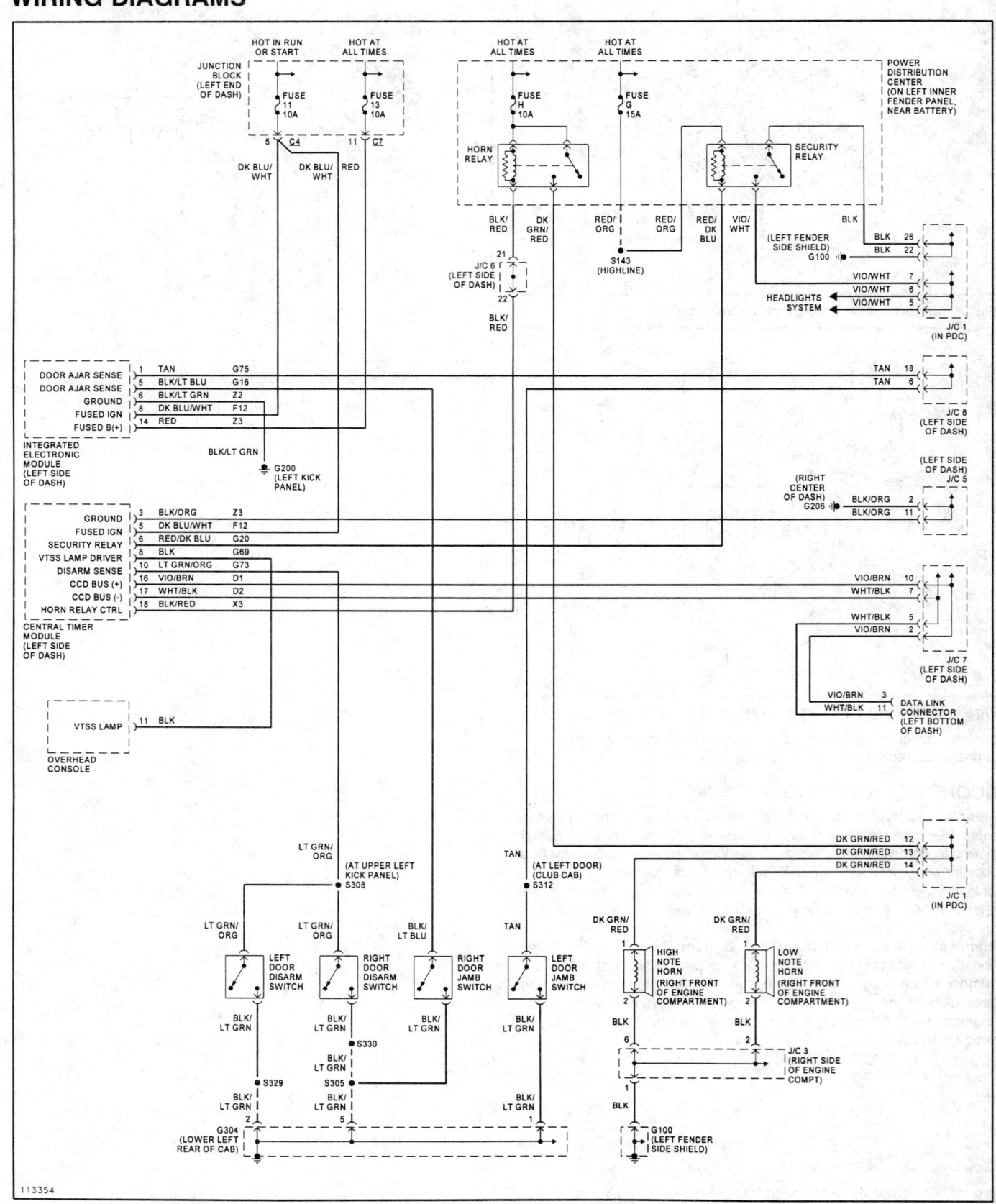

Fig. 5: Anti-Theft System Wiring Diagram (Ram Pickup)

1999 ACCESSORIES & EQUIPMENT
Anti-Theft Systems – Ram Pickup, Ram Van & Ram Wagon (Cont.)

CHRY
4-45

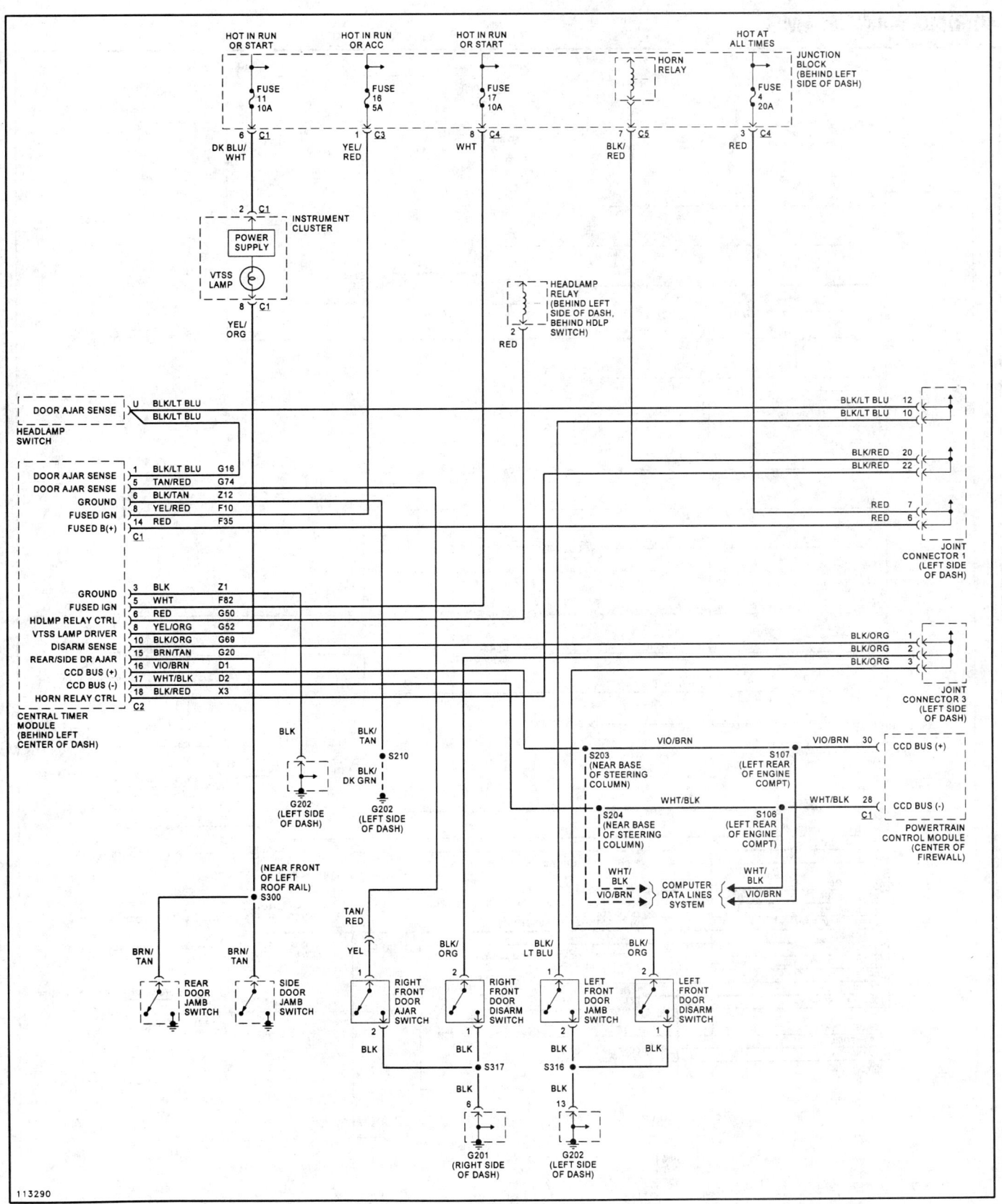

Fig. 6: Anti-Theft System Wiring Diagram (Ram Van & Ram Wagon)

113290

1999 ACCESSORIES & EQUIPMENT
Body Control Computer – Avenger & Sebring Coupe

WIRING DIAGRAMS

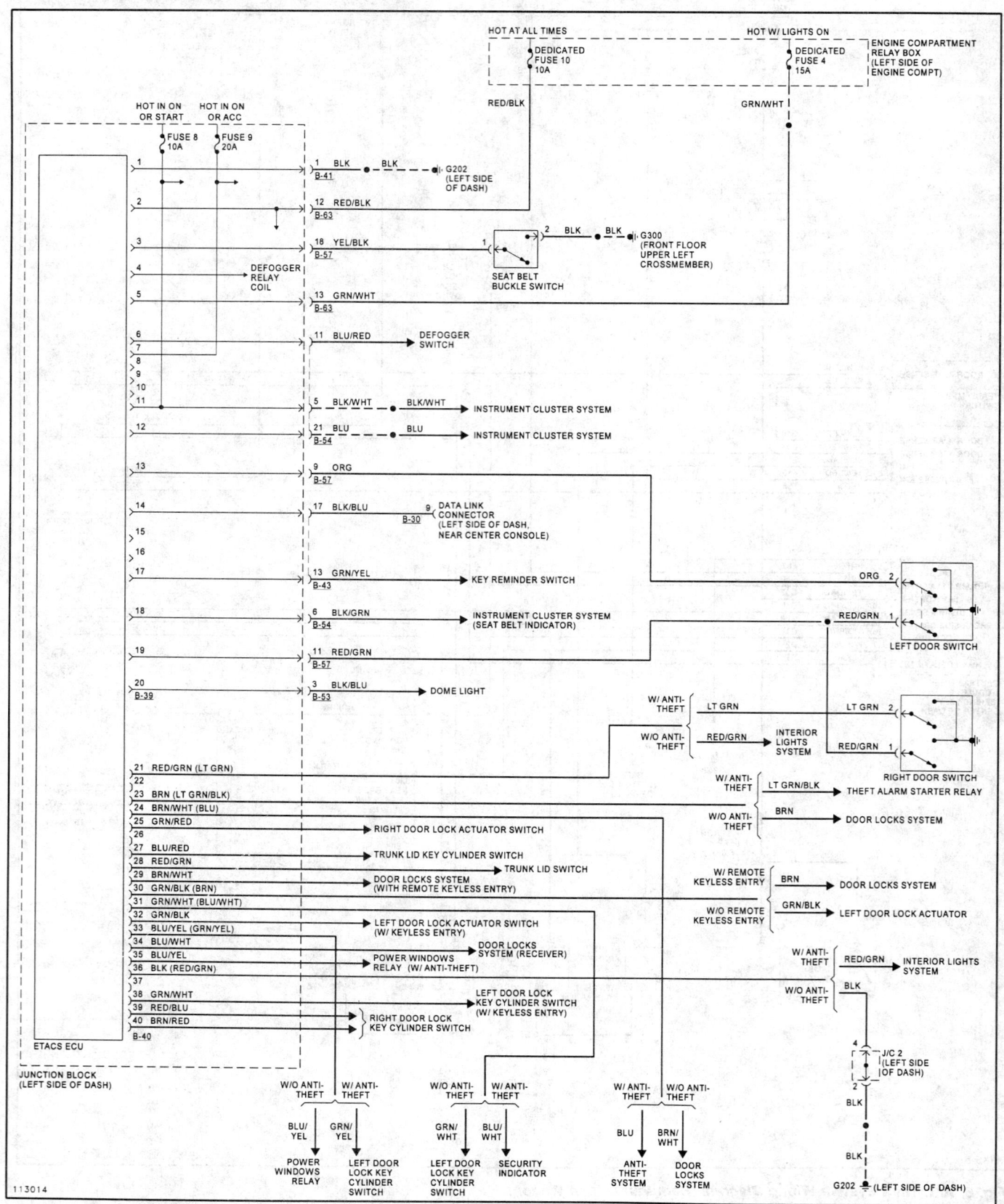

Fig. 1: BCM Wiring Diagram (Avenger & Sebring Coupe)

IDENTIFICATION

BODY IDENTIFICATION

Application	Body
Breeze, Cirrus & Stratus	JA
Caravan, Town & Country, & Voyager	NS
Concorde, Intrepid, LHS & 300M	LH
Dakota	AN
Durango	DN
Pickup	BR
Ram Van & Ram Wagon	AB
Sebring Convertible	JX

MODULE APPLICATIONS

Modules [1]	Body
Air Bag System Control Module (ABSCM)	All Models
Anti-Lock Brake Controller	JA, JX, LH & NS
Automatic Temperature Control (ATC) [2]	LH
Body Control Module (BCM)	JA, JX, LH & NS
Central Timer Module (CTM)	AB, AN, BR & DN
Compass/Mini-Trip Computer	AN, DN, JA, JX & NS
Mechanical Instrument Cluster (MIC)	All Models
Overhead Travel Information System (OTIS)	LH
Remote Keyless Entry (RKE)	BR, JA, JX, LH & NS
Smart Key Immobilizer Module	JX
Transmission Control Module (TCM)	JA, JX, LH & NS
Vehicle Information Center (VIC)	NS
Vehicle Theft Security System (VTSS)	BR, JA, JX, LH & NS

[1] – Modules or systems that communicate over CCD bus.

[2] – For Automatic Temperature Control (ATC) system and A/C-heater system diagnostic information, see appropriate AUTOMATIC A/C-HEATER SYSTEMS article in appropriate MITCHELL® AIR CONDITIONING & HEATING SERVICE & REPAIR manual.

DESCRIPTION

The body control computer system consists of a combination of modules that communicate over the Chrysler Collision Detection (CCD) bus system on all models except Concorde and Intrepid. Concorde and Intrepid communicate over the Programmable Communication Interface (PCI) bus system. Through the CCD or PCI bus, information related to the operation of vehicle components and circuits are relayed to the appropriate system module(s). This reduces the complexity of vehicle wiring and size of wiring harness.

Body control computer systems covered in BODY CONTROL COMPUTER TESTS article are as follows:

- Chime system
- Compass/Mini-Trip Computer (CMTC)
- Door ajar system
- Exterior lighting
- Instrument cluster
- Interior lighting
- Intermittent wipers
- Mechanical Instrument Cluster (MIC)
- Memory Heated Seat/Mirror System (MHSMS)
- Power door locks
- Power windows
- Remote keyless entry
- Sentry Key Immobilizer System (SKIS)
- Vehicle Information System (VIC)
- Vehicle Theft Security System (VTSS).

Body control computer fault messages are accessed through 16-pin Data Link Connector (DLC) using Chrysler's Diagnostic Readout Box (DRB) scan tool or generic scan tool. DLC is located on left side of steering column, above brake pedal.

NOTE: Self-diagnostic tests are written specifically for Chrysler's Diagnostic Readout Box (DRB) scan tool. A generic scan tool may not be capable of performing all necessary test functions.

OPERATION

BODY CONTROL COMPUTER

The Body Control Module (BCM) is part of junction block located under left side of instrument panel on JA, JX and NS models. On LH models, BCM is mounted to junction block located behind left end cap of instrument panel. BCM stores odometer information for electronic instrument cluster display and provides power and ground for a variety of systems.

The BCM on all models except Concorde, Intrepid, LHS and 300M is the only module that has the capability of providing both "bias" and "termination" on the CCD bus system. See CCD BUS SYSTEM. Systems are monitored by BCM through voltage drops.

Vehicle may be equipped with either a premium or base model BCM. Base body control computer is used on vehicles with a mechanical instrument cluster.

On JA body, premium BCM is used on vehicles with a trunk ajar switch. On LH body, premium BCM can be identified by the presence of either the Automatic Temperature Control (ATC) system, Overhead Travel Information System (OTIS), or both.

CCD BUS SYSTEM

The Chrysler Collision Detection (CCD) bus is a pair of twisted wires traveling from module-to-module receiving and delivering coded information. The code identifies the message and its importance. When multiple messages attempt to access CCD bus at once, code assigns priority ranking.

The 2 twisted wires used by the CCD bus system are called bus "+" (positive) and bus "-" (negative). Both wires carry approximately 2.5 volts. The network consists of some modules with "bias" and some with "termination".

Bias is the part of the voltage divider network which places both bus "+" and bus "-" at 2.5 volts. Termination is the part of the circuitry required to complete the voltage divider network and also provide some electromagnetic protection for the CCD bus. Terminations in all CCD applications have approximately 120 ohms resistance.

CENTRAL TIMER MODULE

The Central Timer Module (CTM) high line model only communicates over CCD bus line. CTM controls air bag, chime, courtesy lights, illuminated entry, power door locks, remote keyless entry, speed sensitive intermittent wipers and vehicle theft security system. For module location, see CTM MODULE LOCATION table.

CTM MODULE LOCATION

Model	Location
Dakota & Durango	Right Side Of Glove Box, Behind Metal Bracket
Ram Pickup	Right Side Of Steering Column, Behind Knee Bolster
Ram Van & Ram Wagon	Left Center Instrument Panel Support

COMPASS/MINI-TRIP COMPUTER (CMTC)

The CMTC is located in overhead console. This dual-function display provides a digital readout of ambient (outside) temperature and 8 primary compass readings to indicate the direction in which vehicle is facing.

The CMTC is self-calibrated and requires no adjustment. The word CAL will be displayed to indicate that the compass is in the fast calibrating mode. The CAL display may be turned off after the vehicle has completed 3 circles without stopping, in an area free of magnetic disturbance.

If the module displays ambient temperature while the compass display is blank, the vehicle must be demagnetized. If compass display still goes blank after the vehicle is demagnetized, the compass/temperature module must be replaced.

MECHANICAL INSTRUMENT CLUSTER (MIC)

Instrument cluster includes a speedometer, tachometer, fuel gauge, oil pressure gauge, water temperature gauge, voltmeter, Vacuum Fluorescent (VF) display and a series of warning lights.

Powertrain Control Module (PCM) sends signals necessary for the cluster to position gauges. Cluster receives these messages from CCD or PCI bus and translates them into gauge positions. BCM sends status of all indicator lights and dimming level to instrument cluster over CCD or PCI bus when ignition switch is in RUN or START positions. Malfunction (CHECK ENGINE) indicator light status is sent to BCM from PCM over CCD or PCI bus. Vacuum fluorescent odometer/trip display works when ignition switch is in RUN or START positions. BCM stores mileage information that odometer displays. If CCD bus is not functioning, odometer will display dashes instead of the mileage numbers. BCM sends mileage message and dimming level message to vacuum fluorescent display when ignition switch is in the ON position. All other instrument cluster features only work when the ignition switch is in the RUN position.

MEMORY HEATED SEAT & MIRROR SYSTEM

The Memory Heated Seat/Mirror Module (MHSMM) mounted under driver's seat, reads all seat switch, mirror switch and radio station preset inputs programmed by driver. Functionality includes memory preset capabilty for a second driver. Two stored sets of preferences can be recalled upon request.

The MHSMM monitors memory switches and stores desired positions in memory. MHSMM will activate seat and mirror motors in response to a recall request from individual memory switch or Remote Keyless Entry (RKE) fob.

OVERHEAD TRAVEL INFORMATION SYSTEM (OTIS)

The OTIS provides vehicle operator with supplementary information on a Vacuum Fluorescent (VF) display. The OTIS is located in overhead console. Vehicle operator selects and resets display functions through the use of 4 buttons (US/M, STEP, C/T and RESET). The OTIS obtains most of its information from the CCD or PCI bus.

The OTIS powers up when it senses vehicle (battery) voltage on the ignition input circuit. The OTIS blanks the display, then illuminates all segments of the VF display. During this time, the OTIS sends and receives information over CCD or PCI bus to determine what to display after its 2 second initialization. OTIS will display dashes (– –) for any of the screens for which it did not receive bus messages during the 2 second initialization. Dashes will be replaced by valid information if and when it is received.

PCI BUS SYSTEM (CONCORDE, INTREPID, LHS & 300M)

The Programmable Communication Interface multiplex system (PCI bus) consists of a single wire. The BCM acts as a splice to connect each module and DLC. Each module uses its local ground as bus reference. If more than one module is trying to access the PCI bus at one time, the code being sent determines which message has higher priority, and is then allowed to access bus first. Communication over the bus is essential to proper operation of vehicles on-board diagnostic systems and DRB. Problems with operation of bus or DRB must be corrected before proceeding with diagnostic testing. See appropriate VEHICLE COMMUNICATIONS article.

VEHICLE THEFT SECURITY SYSTEM (VTSS)

VTSS monitors vehicle doors, hood, trunk key cylinder and ignition for unauthorized operation/entry. When alarm is triggered, the horn will sound for 3 minutes and the parking lights will flash for 15-18 minutes.

When an unauthorized entry into vehicle occurs, the VTSS module signals Powertrain Control Module (PCM) via CCD or PCI bus that it is not okay to start the engine. The PCM then "zeros out" the pulse width of the fuel injectors, thus preventing the engine from starting (start/stall condition). The engine will NOT start until VTSS is disarmed.

Initialization & Verification – An initialization procedure, included in VTSS requires that vehicle record 20 engine cranking cycles before allowing VTSS module to function. For this reason, VTSS requires verification. To verify VTSS, perform the following: Open driver's door (all others closed). Remove ignition key. Lock doors with power door lock switch. Close driver's door. If VTSS SET light flashes, system is armed and operational. If VTSS SET light does not flash, 20 engine cranking cycles have not occurred or there is a problem with VTSS.

Manual Override Mode & Tamper Alert Mode – The VTSS will not arm if the doors are locked using the key or the manual lock control (manual override mode). If horn sounds 3 times when either front door is unlocked, the alarm was activated/triggered (tamper alert mode).

SELF-DIAGNOSTIC SYSTEM

CAUTION: When battery is disconnected, vehicle computer and memory systems may lose memory data. Driveability problems may exist until computer systems have completed a relearn cycle. See COMPUTER RELEARN PROCEDURES article in GENERAL INFORMATION before disconnecting battery.

PRETEST INSPECTION

Before proceeding with diagnosis, the following precautions must be followed:

- Vehicle must have a fully charged battery and functional charging system.
- Always start at SYMPTOM ID TEST 1A: IDENTIFYING VEHICLE EQUIPMENT & SYSTEM PROBLEMS. Starting with any other test may result in incorrect results.
- Only perform test steps indicated. It is NOT necessary to perform all steps in a test.
- VEHICLE COMMUNICATIONS article should only be used when instructed to do so by another test. Always start at SYMPTOM ID TEST 1A: IDENTIFYING VEHICLE EQUIPMENT & SYSTEM PROBLEMS.
- Turn ignition switch to OFF position before disconnecting or connecting components.
- Use extreme care when connecting or disconnecting wiring during testing to prevent accidental grounding or shorting.
- DO NOT use a test light in place of a voltmeter.
- Always disconnect scan tool after use.
- Always disconnect scan tool before charging battery.
- Always perform appropriate verification test after repairs are made.

DIAGNOSTIC PROCEDURE

NOTE: Before proceeding with diagnosis, certain precautions must be followed. See PRETEST INSPECTION under SELF-DIAGNOSTIC SYSTEM.

Diagnostic test procedures are designed to detect system faults as quickly as possible. Body Diagnostic Trouble Codes (DTCs) are accessed through Data Link Connector (DLC). Chrysler's Diagnostic Readout Box (DRB) scan tool or generic scan tool, is used to access information from DLC.

A 1999 diagnostic program cartridge (if applicable), scan tool, body diagnostics cable, hand-held oil pressure gauge, jumper wires, and digital volt-ohmmeter will be needed for testing. Proceed to SYMPTOM ID TEST 1A: IDENTIFYING VEHICLE EQUIPMENT & SYSTEM PROBLEMS in appropriate BODY CONTROL COMPUTER TESTS article.

GENERIC SCAN TOOL

Self-diagnostic tests are written specifically for Chrysler's Diagnostic Readout Box (DRB) scan tool. A generic scan tool can be used, but may not be capable of performing all necessary test functions.

DRB SCAN TOOL

Refer to DRB scan tool instructions to retrieve and clear fault messages, and when performing other scan tool function.

DRB scan tool is grounded through DLC connector. Only one volt/ohmmeter test lead is required when instructed by testing to measure voltage or resistance on specified circuit. DRB scan tool volt/ohmmeter mode should only be used when body control computer tests require the use of this option.

CONNECTOR IDENTIFICATION

NOTE: *For terminal identification of body control system connectors, use appropriate illustration(s). See CONNECTOR IDENTIFICATION DIRECTORY. Connector terminal numbers may be molded into connectors. If connector terminal identification differs from that shown in figure, use wire colors to ensure correct circuit is being tested. See WIRING DIAGRAMS.*

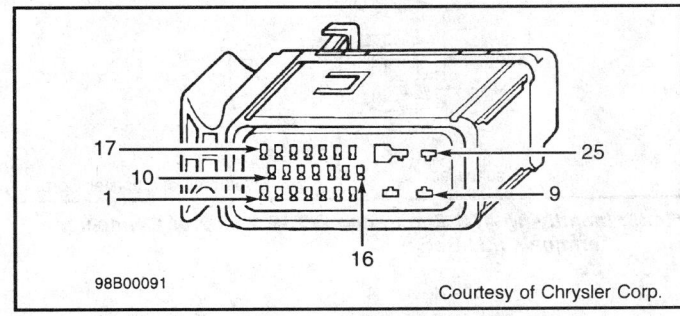

98B00091   Courtesy of Chrysler Corp.

Fig. 1: Identifying Anti-Lock Brake Controller Connector Terminals (JA, JX, LH & NS Bodies)

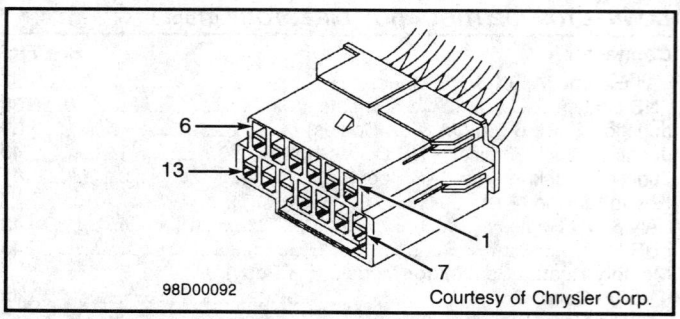

98D00092
Courtesy of Chrysler Corp.

Fig. 2: Identifying Air Bag Control Module Connector Terminals (JA, JX & NS Bodies)

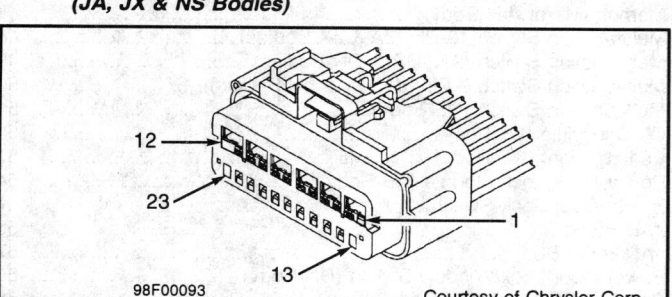

98F00093
Courtesy of Chrysler Corp.

Fig. 3: Identifying Air Bag Control Module Connector Terminals (AB, AN, BR, DN & LH Bodies)

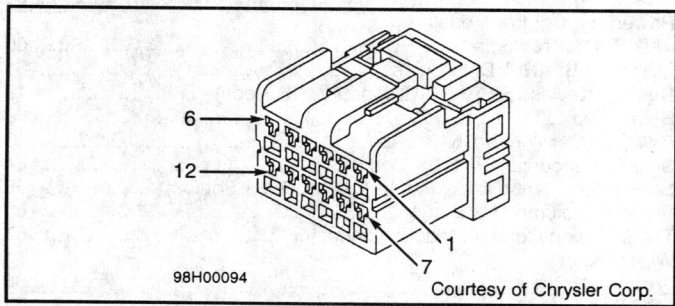

98H00094
Courtesy of Chrysler Corp.

Fig. 4: Identifying Automatic Temperature Control Module Connector Terminals (LH Body)

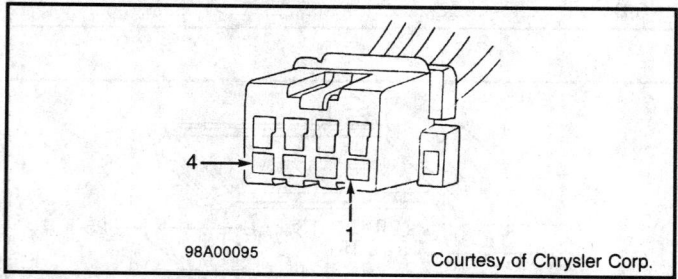

98A00095
Courtesy of Chrysler Corp.

Fig. 5: Identifying ATC Sun Sensor/VTSS Indicator Connector Terminals (LH Body)

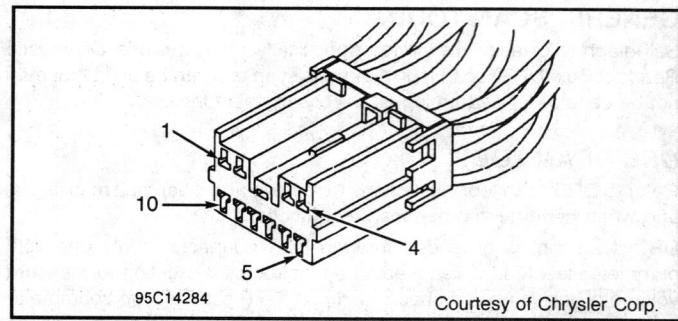

95C14284
Courtesy of Chrysler Corp.

Fig. 6: Identifying Body Control Module 10-Pin Connector Terminals (JA & JX Body)

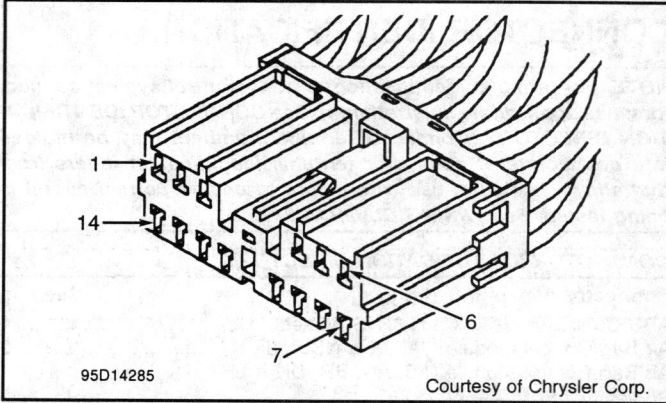

95D14285
Courtesy of Chrysler Corp.

Fig. 7: Identifying Body Control Module 14-Pin Connector Terminals (JA & JX Body)

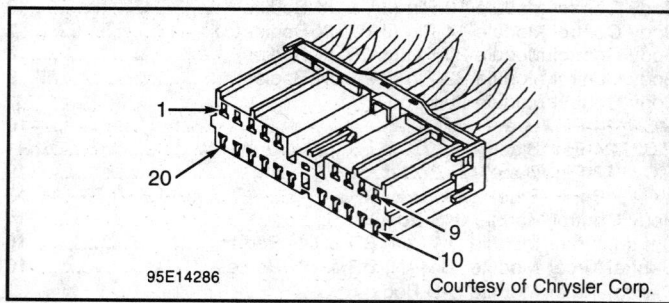

95E14286
Courtesy of Chrysler Corp.

Fig. 8: Identifying Body Control Module 20-Pin Connector Terminals (JA & JX Body)

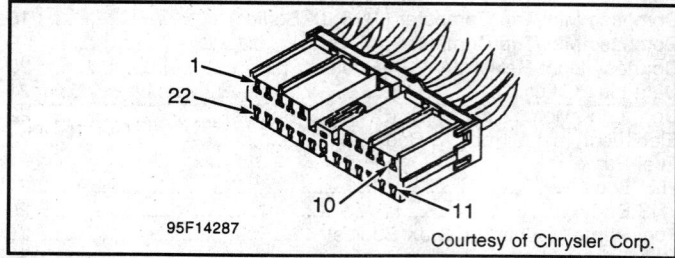

95F14287
Courtesy of Chrysler Corp.

Fig. 9: Identifying Body Control Module 22-Pin Connector Terminals (JA & JX Body)

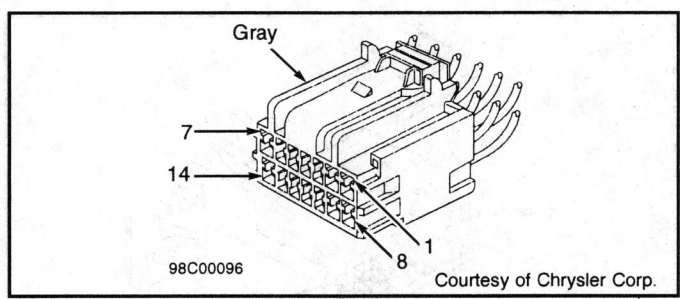

Fig. 10: Identifying Body Control Module 14-Pin "C1" Connector Terminals (LH Body)

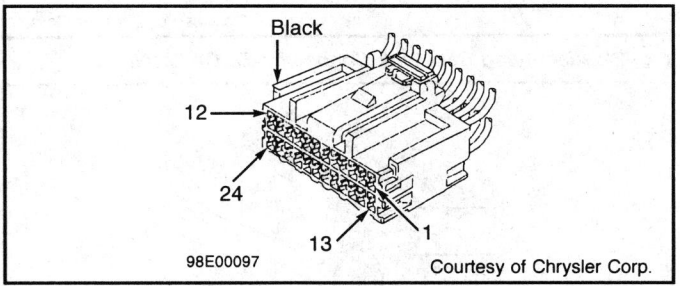

Fig. 11: Identifying Body Control Module 24-Pin "C2" Connector Terminals (LH Body)

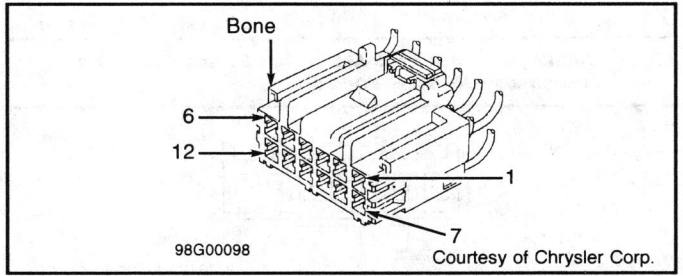

Fig. 12: Identifying Body Control Module 12-Pin "C3" Connector Terminals (LH Body)

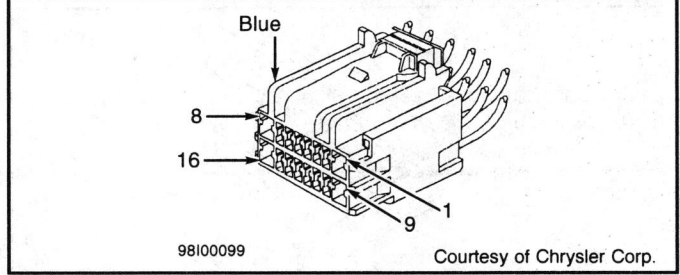

Fig. 13: Identifying Body Control Module 16-Pin "C4" Connector Terminals (LH Body)

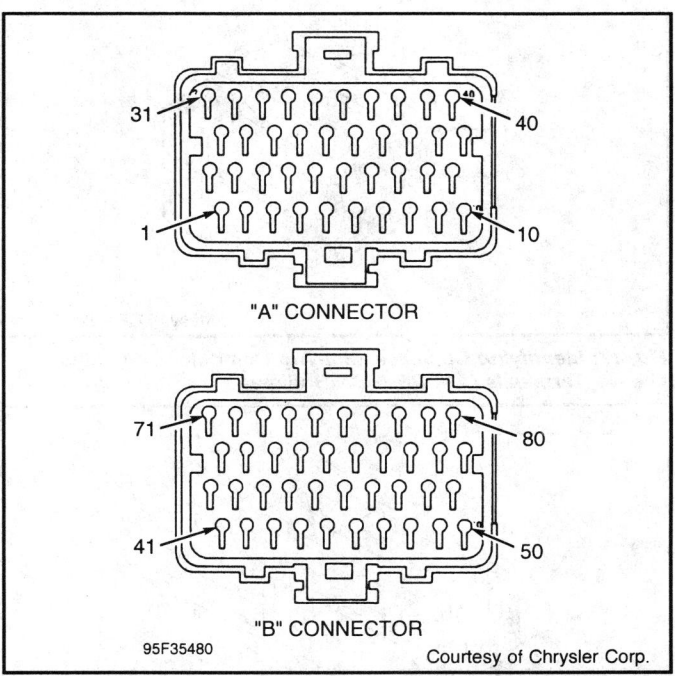

Fig. 14: Identifying Body Control Module Connector Terminals (NS Body)

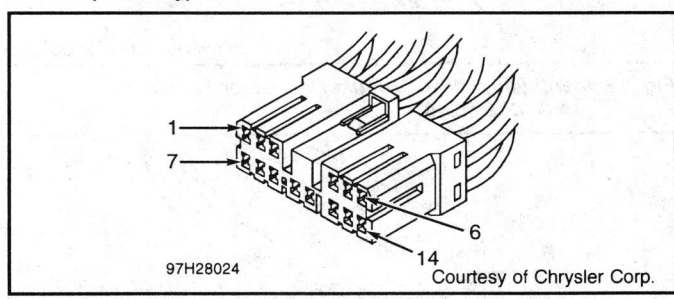

Fig. 15: Identifying Central Timer Module "A" (AN, BR & DN Bodies) or "C1" (AB Body) Connector Terminals

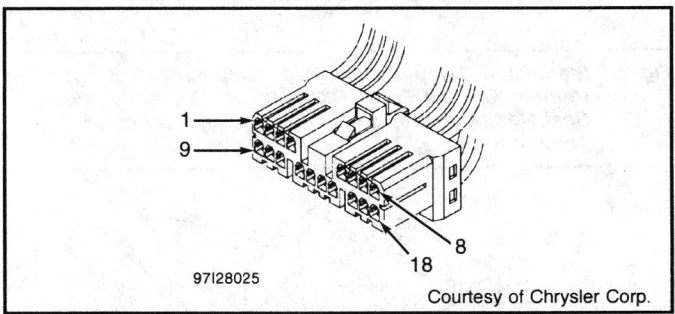

Fig. 16: Identifying Central Timer Module "B" (AN, BR & DN Bodies) or "C2" (AB Body) Connector Terminals

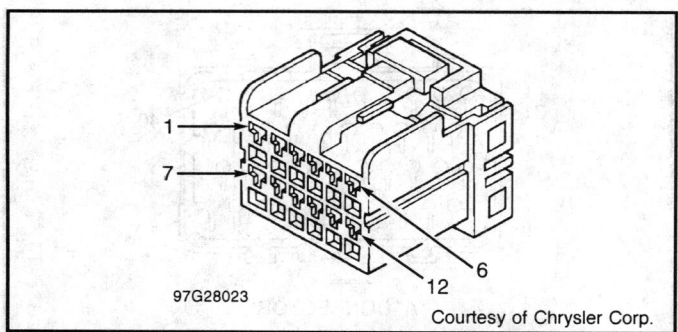

Fig. 17: Identifying Compass Mini-Trip Computer Connector Terminals (AN, BR & DN Bodies)

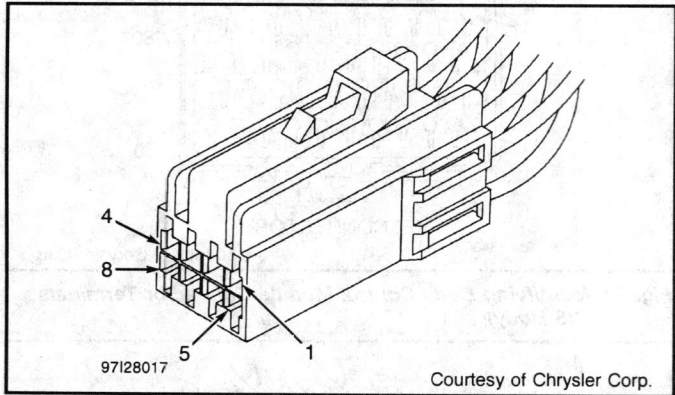

Fig. 18: Identifying CMTC Module Connector Terminals (JA & JX Bodies)

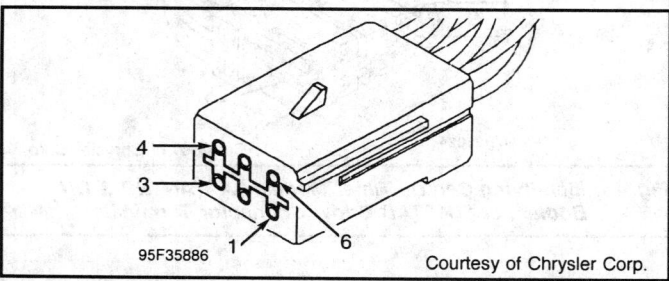

Fig. 19: Identifying Compass Mini-Trip Computer (NS Body), Remote Keyless Entry (RKE) Module (NS Body), Power Seat Memory/Heater Switch (LH Body) Connector Terminals

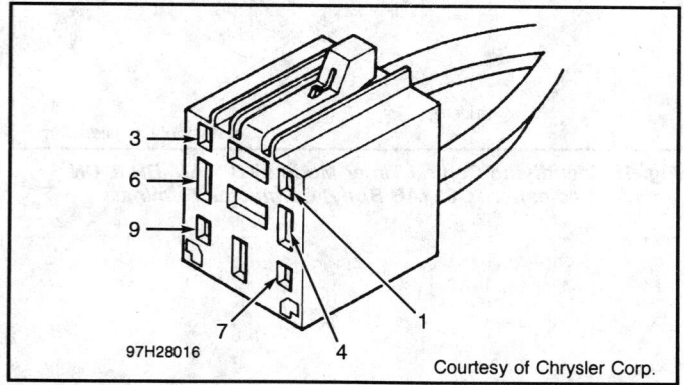

Fig. 20: Identifying Courtesy Light Relay Connector Terminals (JA & JX Bodies)

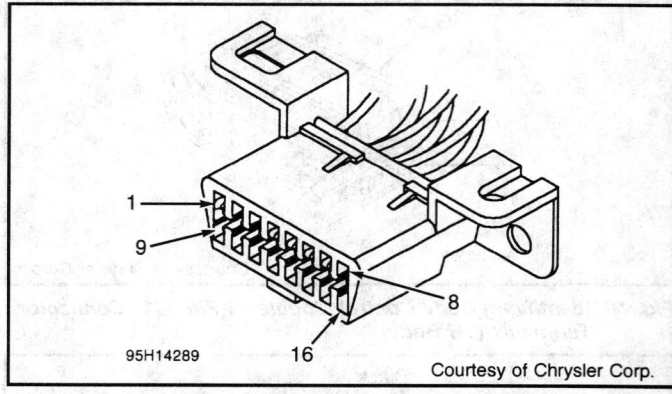

Fig. 21: Identifying Data Link Connector (DLC) Terminals

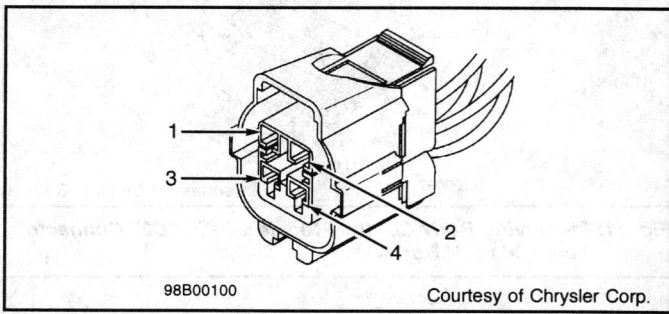

Fig. 22: Identifying Door Lock Motor/Ajar Switch Connector Terminals (DN & LH Bodies)

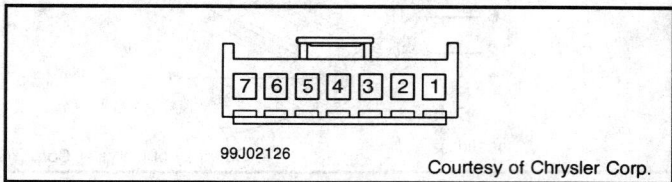

Fig. 23: Identifying Electrochromic Mirror Connector Terminals (NS Body)

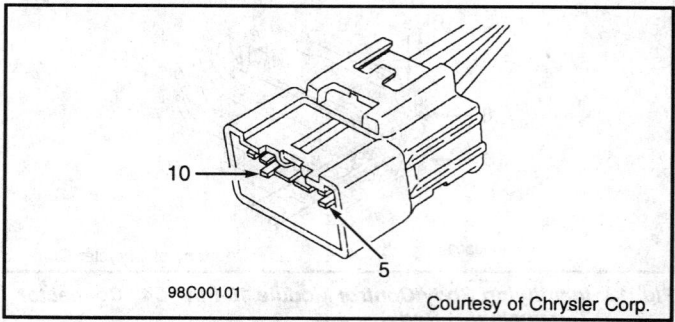

Fig. 24: Identifying Fuel Pump Connector Terminals (LH Body)

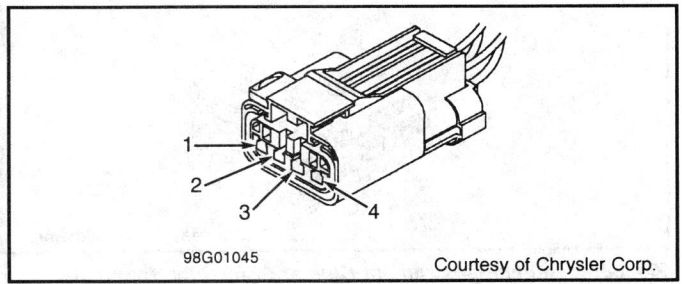

Fig. 25: Identifying Fuel Pump Motor Connector Terminals (NS Body)

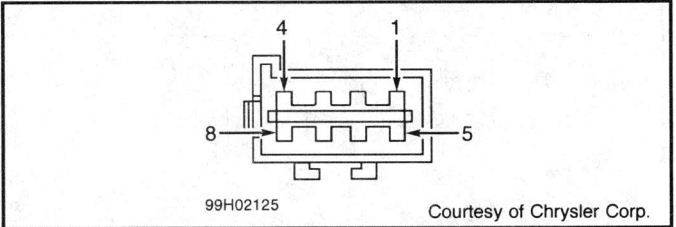

Fig. 26: Identifying Fuel Pump Module Connector Terminals (JA & JX Bodies)

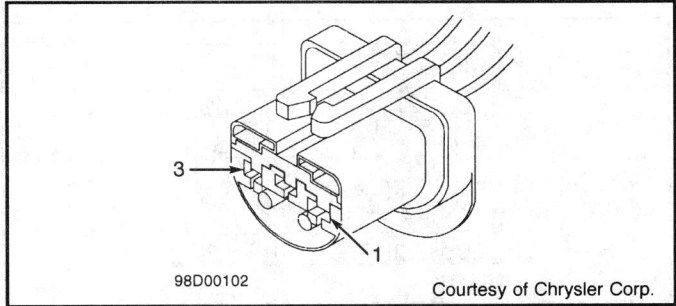

Fig. 27: Identifying Headlight Connector Terminals (Caravan & Voyager)

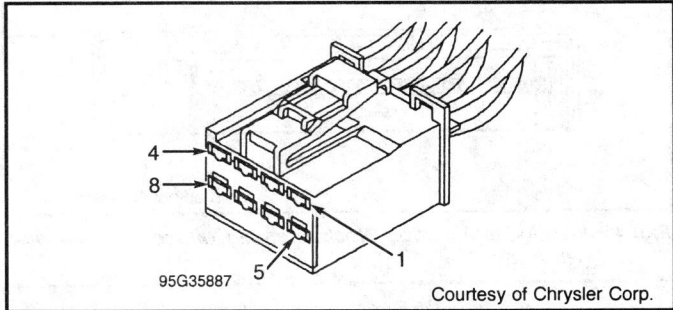

Fig. 28: Identifying Headlight 8-Pin Connector Terminals (NS Body)

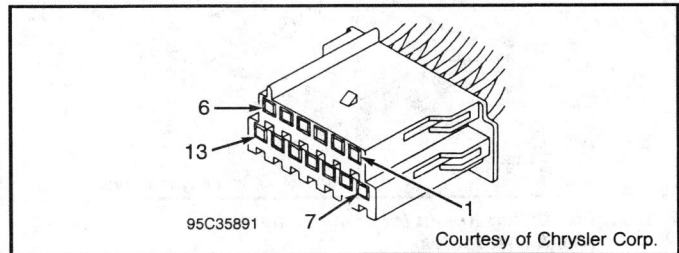

Fig. 29: Identifying Headlight Switch Connector Terminals (NS Body) & Information Center Connector Terminals (NS Body)

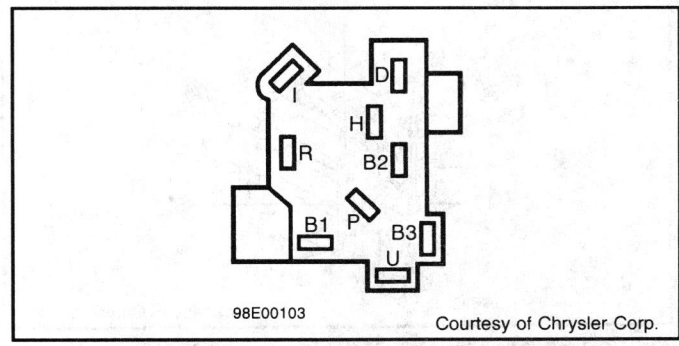

Fig. 30: Identifying Headlight Switch Connector Terminals (AB Body)

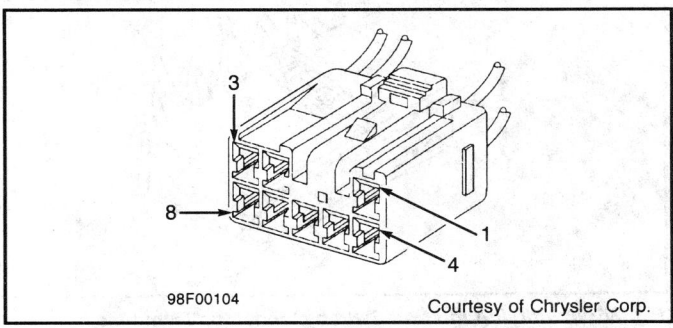

Fig. 31: Identifying Headliner Connector Terminals (LH Body)

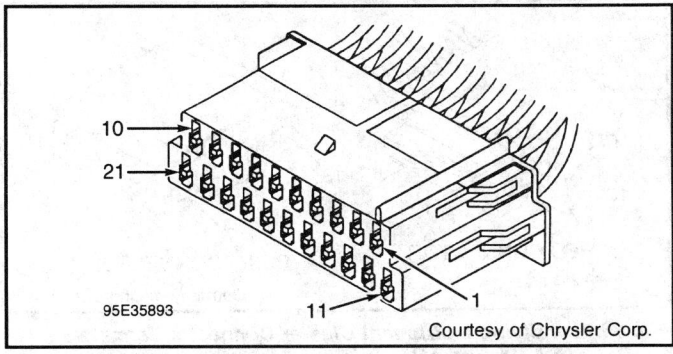

Fig. 32: Identifying HVAC Control Module Connector (Blue) Terminals (NS Body)

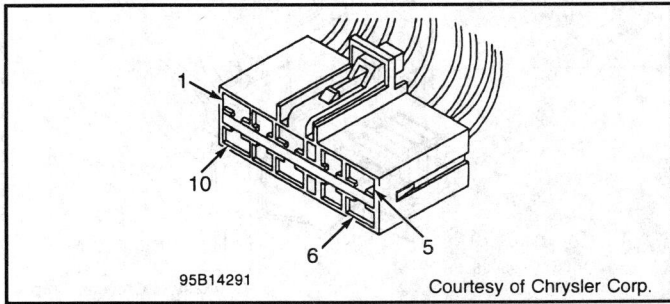

Fig. 33: Identifying Ignition Switch Connector Terminals (JA & JX Bodies)

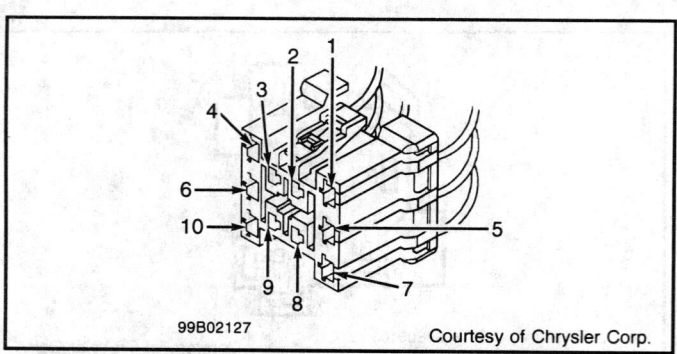

Fig. 34: Identifying Ignition Switch Connector Terminals (LH Body)

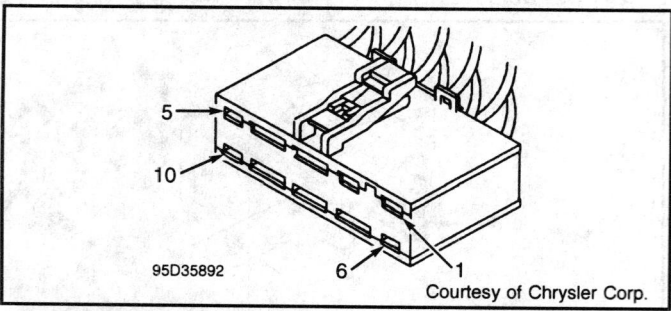

Fig. 35: Identifying Ignition Switch Connector Terminals (NS Body)

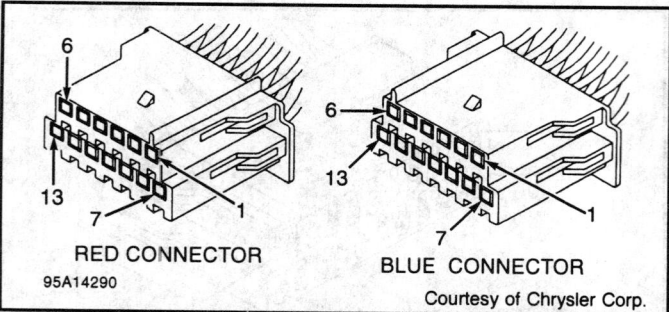

RED CONNECTOR

BLUE CONNECTOR

Fig. 36: Identifying Instrument Cluster Connector Terminals (JA & JX Bodies)

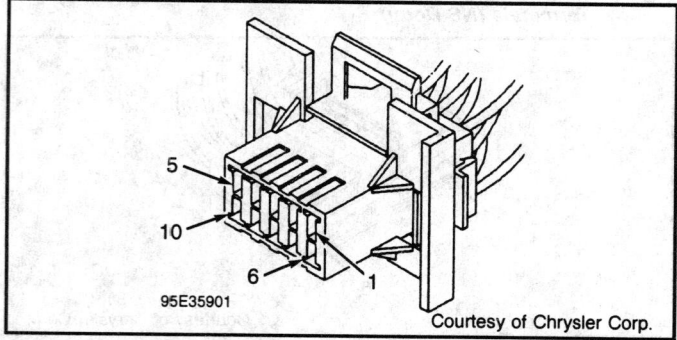

Fig. 37: Identifying Instrument Cluster Connector Terminals (All Except JA, JX & NS Bodies)

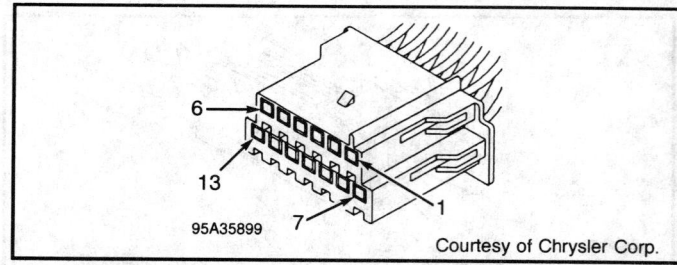

Fig. 38: Identifying Instrument Cluster Connector Terminals (NS Body)

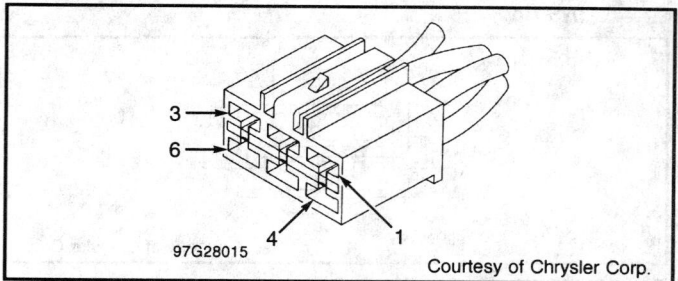

Fig. 39: Identifying Junction Block 6-Pin Connector Terminals (JA & JX Bodies)

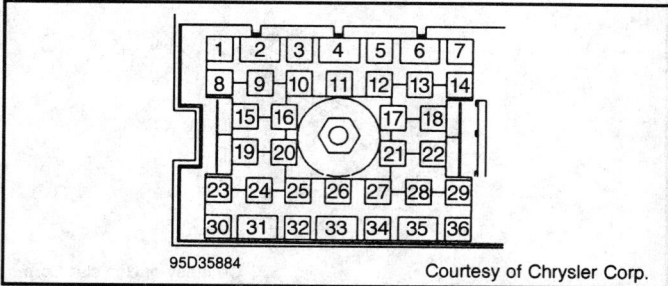

Fig. 40: Identifying Junction Block Connector Terminals (Typical) (NS Body)

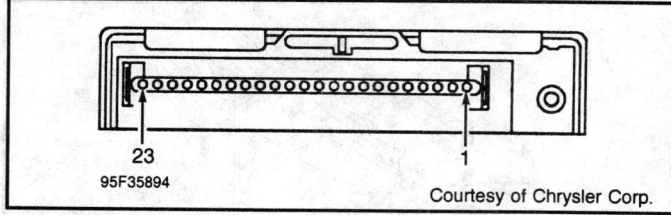

Fig. 41: Identifying Junction Block Internal Connector Terminals (NS Body)

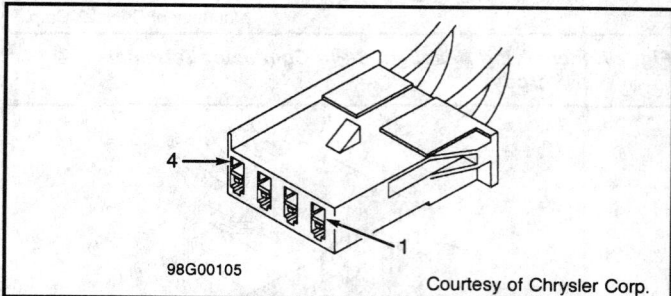

Fig. 42: Identifying Key-In Ignition Connector Terminals (AN & DN Bodies)

Courtesy of Chrysler Corp.

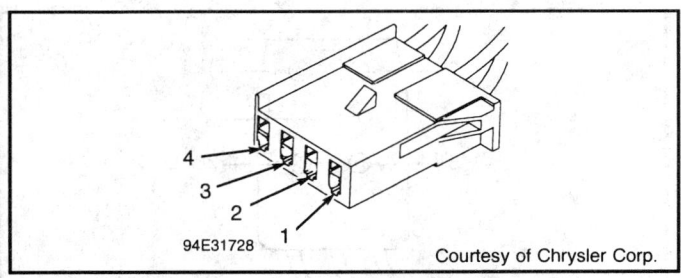

Fig. 43: Identifying Key-In Ignition Connector Terminals (BR Body)

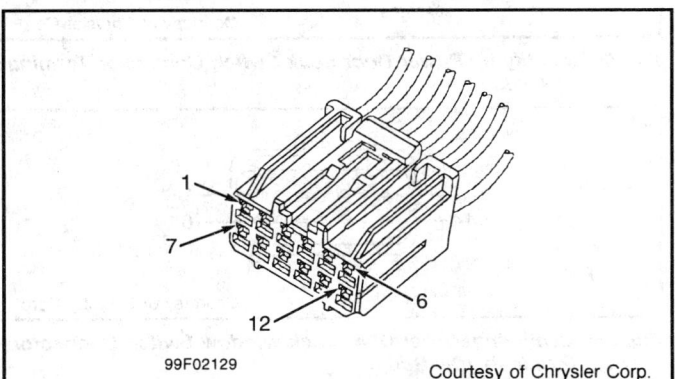

Fig. 44: Identifying Memory Heated Seat/Mirror Module (MHSMM) 12-Pin Connector Terminals (LH Body)

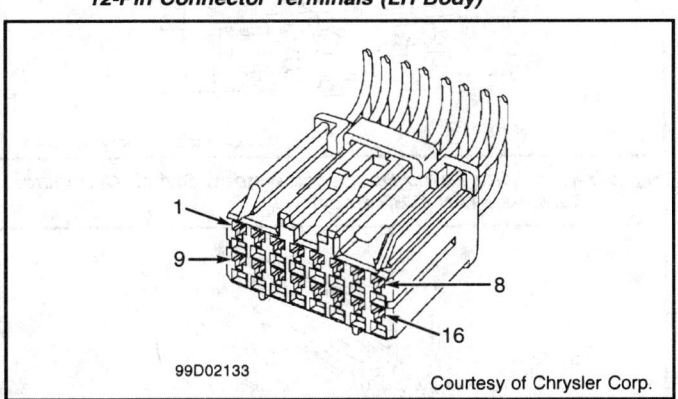

Fig. 45: Identifying Memory Heated Seat/Mirror Module (MHSMM) 16-Pin Connector Terminals (LH Body)

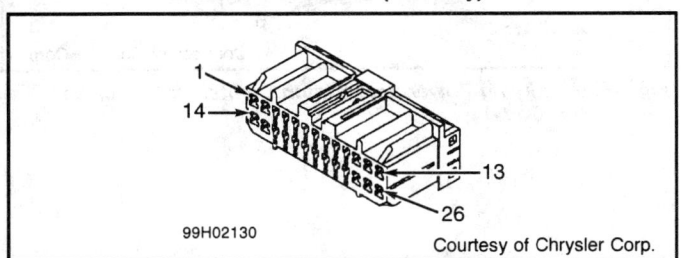

Fig. 46: Identifying Memory Heated Seat/Mirror Module (MHSMM) 26-Pin Connector Terminals (LH Body)

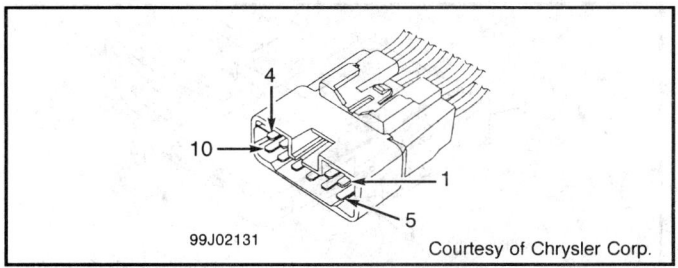

Fig. 47: Identifying Memory Mirror Connector Terminals (LH Body)

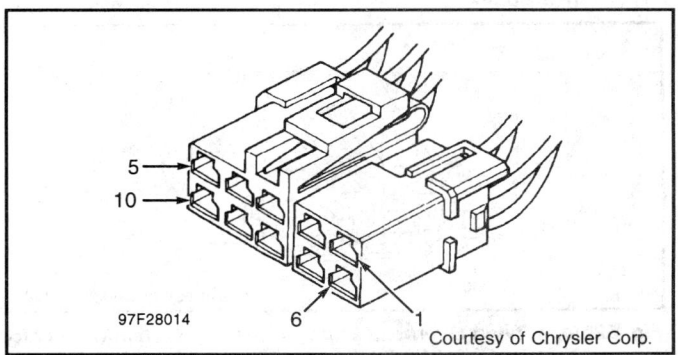

Fig. 48: Identifying Multifunction Switch 10-Pin Connector Terminals (JA & JX Bodies)

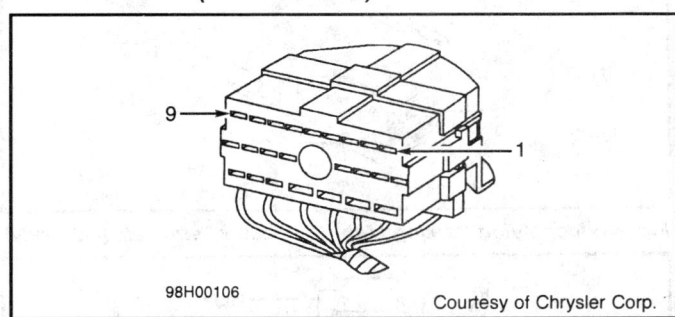

Fig. 49: Identifying Multifunction Switch Connector Terminals (AN, BR & DN Bodies)

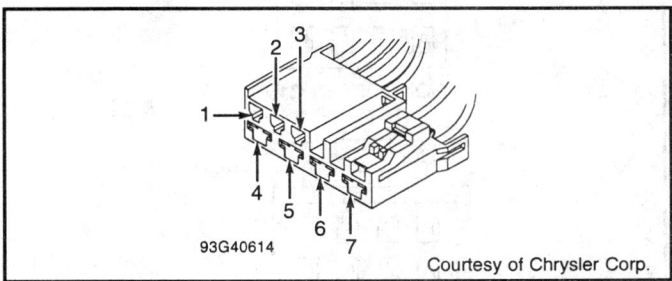

Fig. 50: Identifying Multifunction Switch 7-Pin Connector Terminals (JA, JX & LH Bodies)

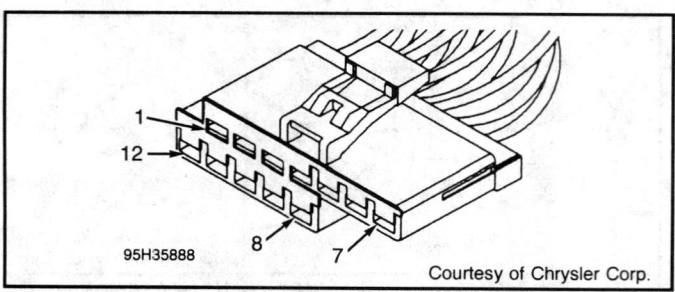

Fig. 51: Identifying Multifunction Switch Connector Terminals (NS Body)

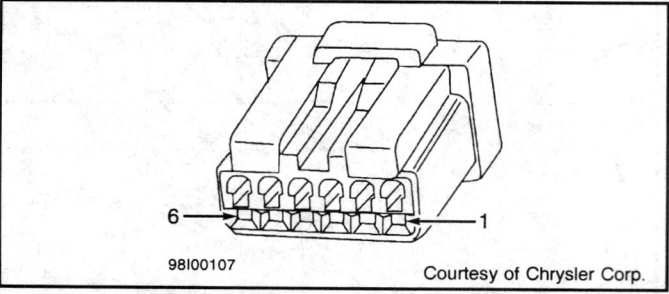

Fig. 52: Identifying Overhead Trip Information System Connector Terminals (LH Body)

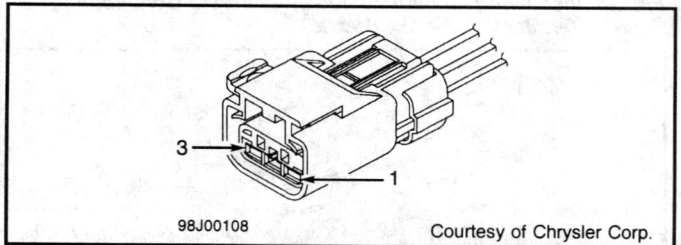

Fig. 53: Identifying Parking Light Connector Terminals (NS Body)

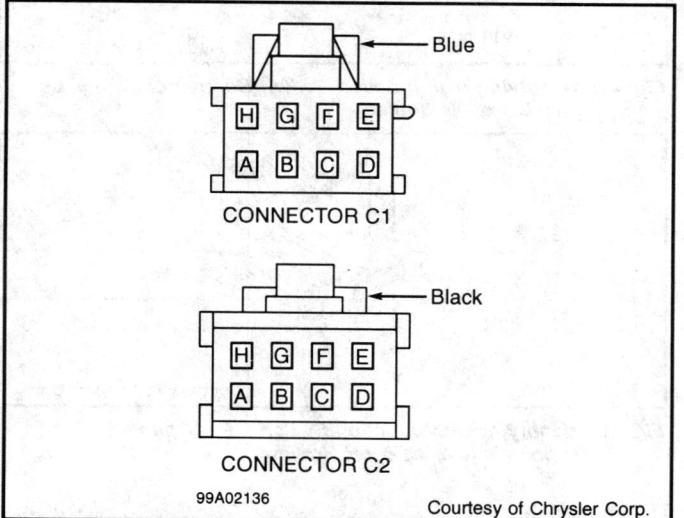

Fig. 54: Identifying Power Door Lock Module Connector Terminals (AB Body)

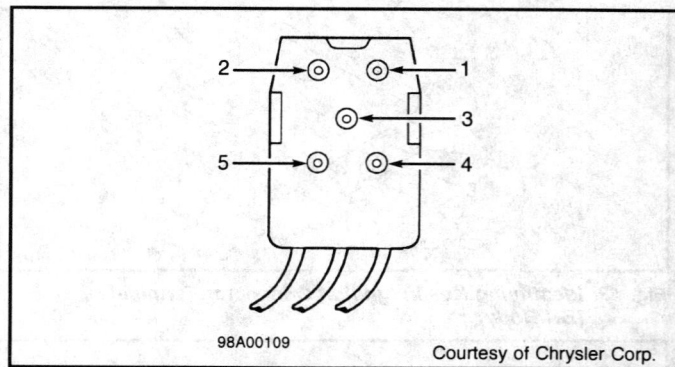

Fig. 55: Identifying Power Door Lock Switch Connector Terminals (AB Body)

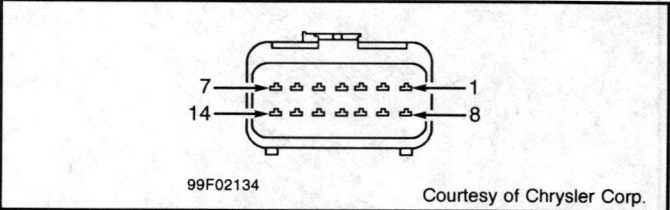

Fig. 56: Identifying Power Door Lock/Window Switch Connector Terminals (DN Body)

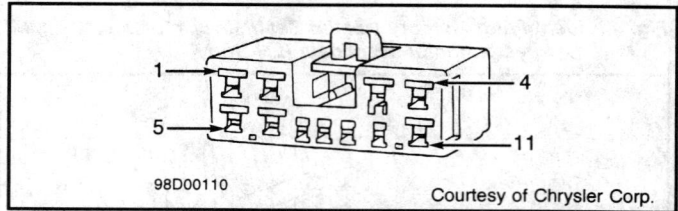

Fig. 57: Identifying Power Door Lock/Window Switch Connector Terminals (AN & BR Body)

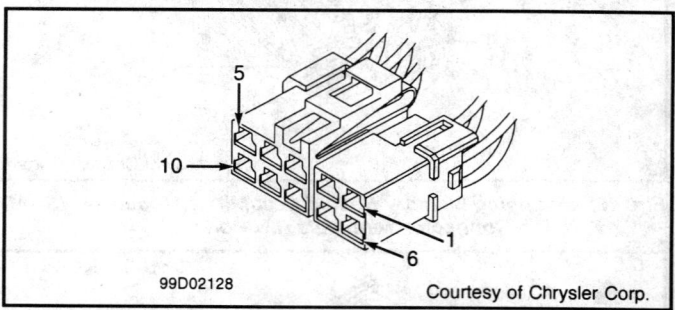

Fig. 58: Identifying Power Seat Switch Connector Terminals (LH Body)

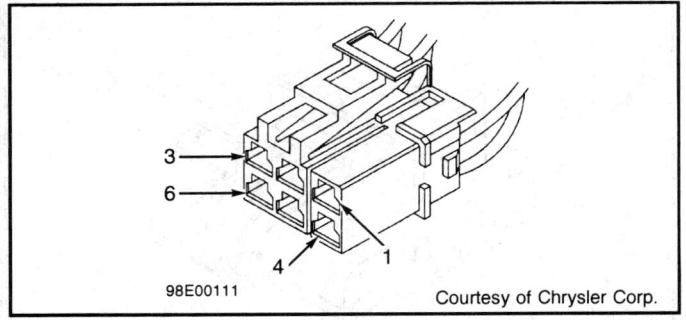

Fig. 59: Identifying Power Top Switch Connector Terminals (JX Body)

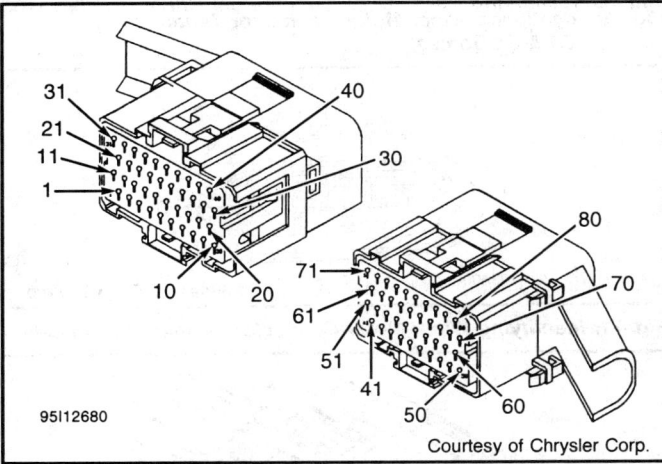

Fig. 60: Identifying Powertrain Control Module Connector Terminals (JA, JX, LH & NS Bodies)

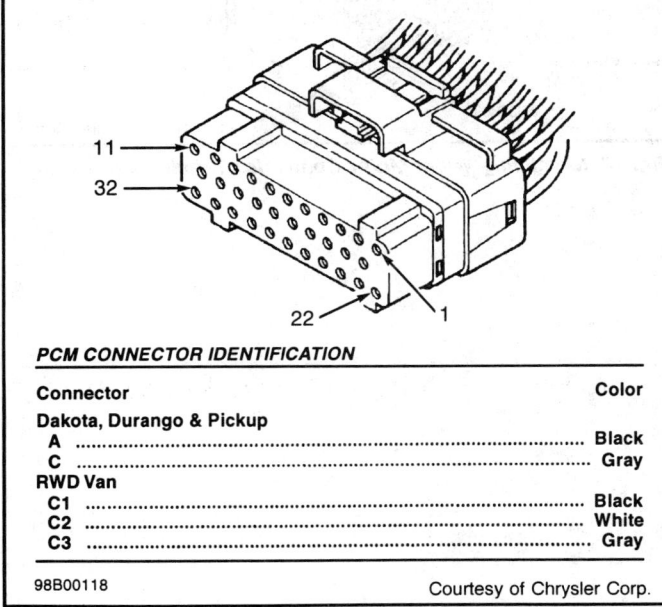

PCM CONNECTOR IDENTIFICATION

Connector	Color
Dakota, Durango & Pickup	
A	Black
C	Gray
RWD Van	
C1	Black
C2	White
C3	Gray
98B00118	Courtesy of Chrysler Corp.

Fig. 61: Identifying Powertrain Control Module Connector Terminals (AB, AN, BR & DN Bodies)

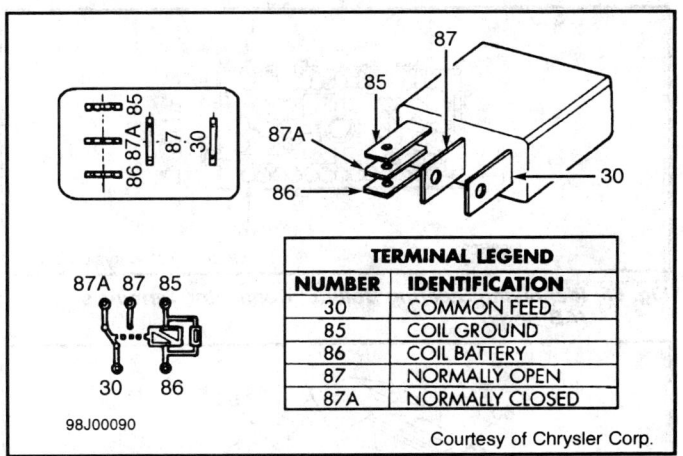

TERMINAL LEGEND	
NUMBER	**IDENTIFICATION**
30	COMMON FEED
85	COIL GROUND
86	COIL BATTERY
87	NORMALLY OPEN
87A	NORMALLY CLOSED

Fig. 62: Identifying Typical Relay

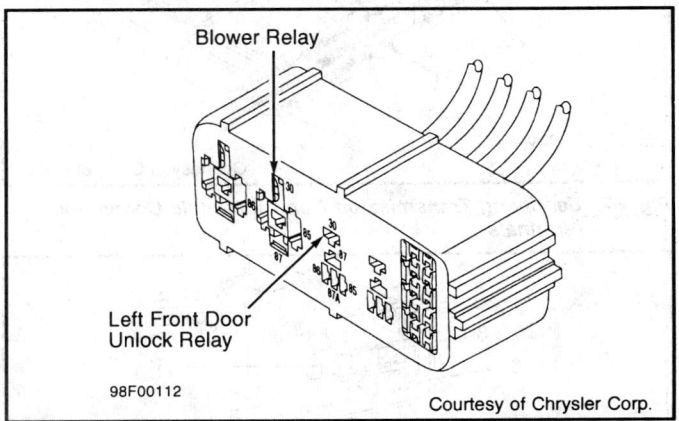

Fig. 63: Identifying Relay Center Connector (AN & DN Bodies)

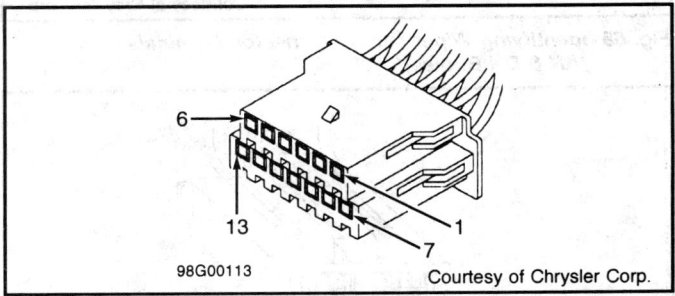

Fig. 64: Identifying Seat Belt Module (BR & JX Body)

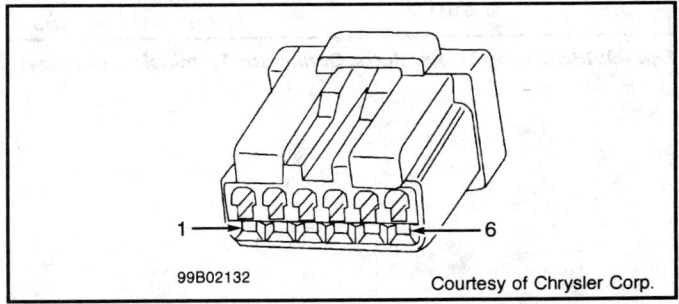

Fig. 65: Identifying Sentry Key Imobilizer Module (SKIM) Connector Terminals (JA, JX & LH Bodies)

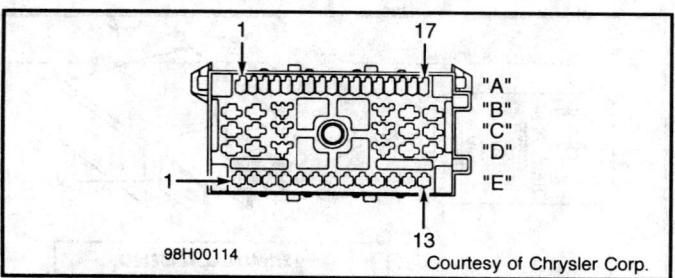

98H00114   Courtesy of Chrysler Corp.

Fig. 66: Identifying Steering Column Connector Terminals (AB Body)

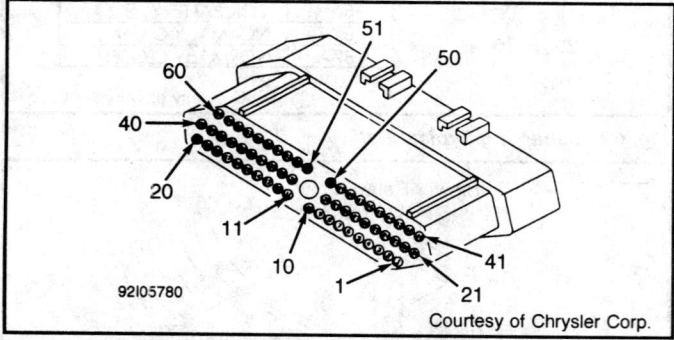

92I05780   Courtesy of Chrysler Corp.

Fig. 67: Identifying Transmission Control Module Connector Terminals

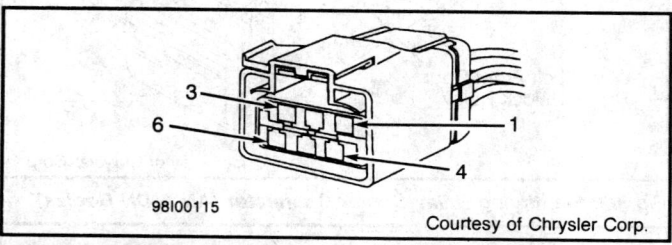

98I00115   Courtesy of Chrysler Corp.

Fig. 68: Identifying Wiper Motor Connector Terminals (AN & DN Bodies)

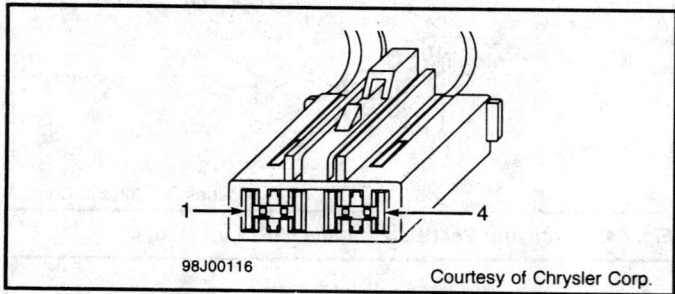

98J00116   Courtesy of Chrysler Corp.

Fig. 69: Identifying Wiper Motor Connector Terminals (BR Body)

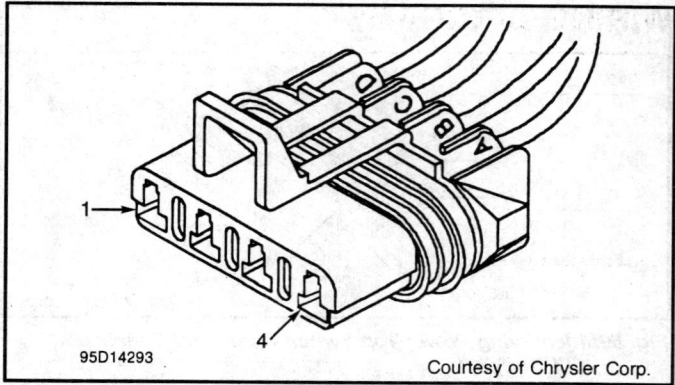

95D14293   Courtesy of Chrysler Corp.

Fig. 70: Identifying Wiper Motor Connector Terminals (JA & JX Bodies)

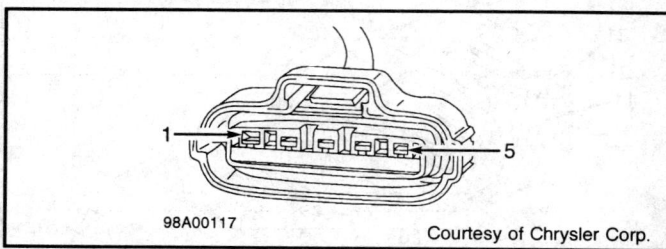

98A00117   Courtesy of Chrysler Corp.

Fig. 71: Identifying Wiper Motor Connector Terminals (LH Body)

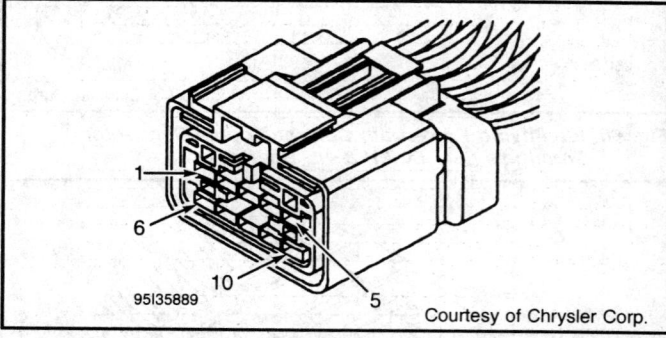

95I35889   Courtesy of Chrysler Corp.

Fig. 72: Identifying Wiper Motor Connector Terminals (NS Body)

WIRING DIAGRAMS

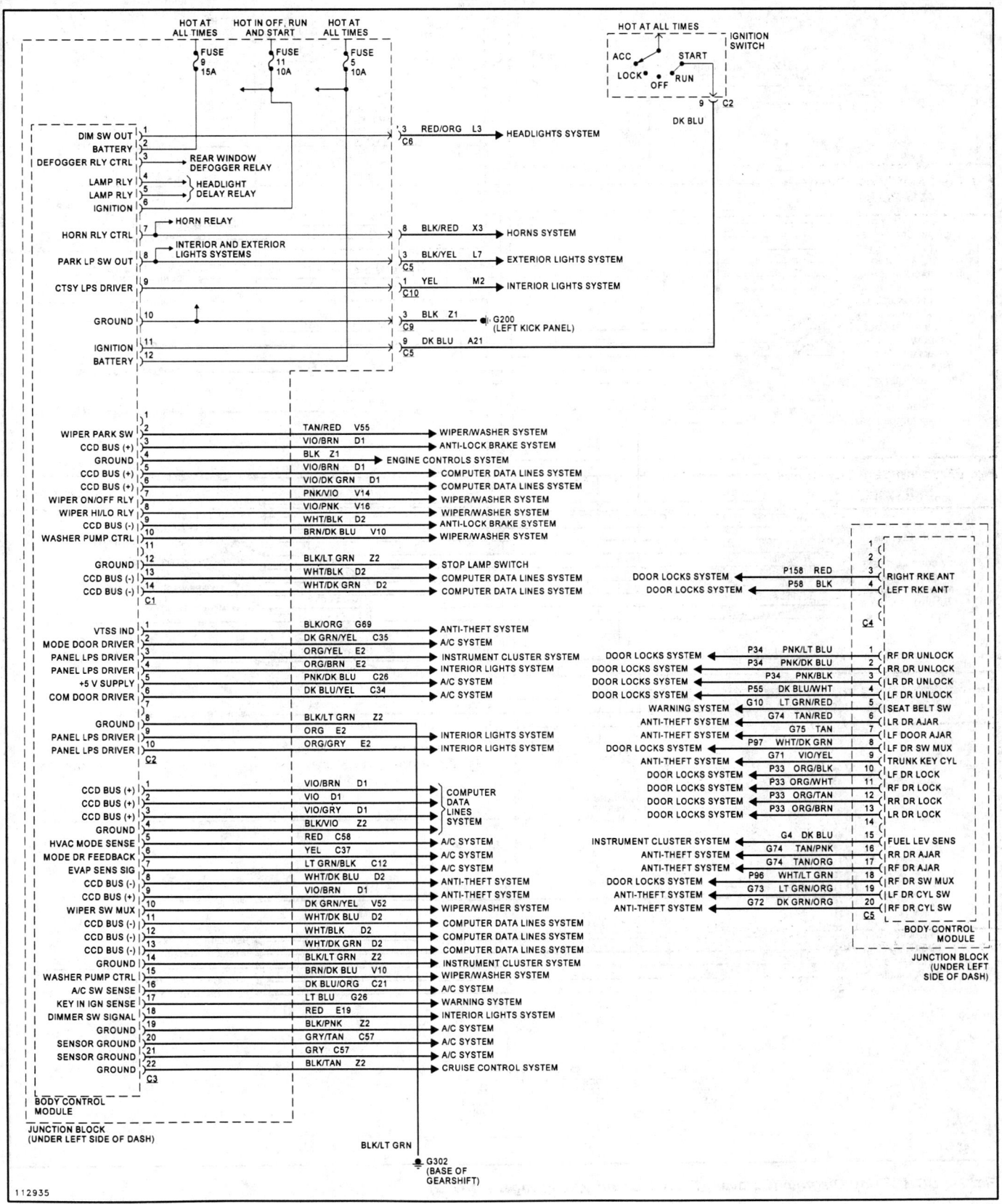

Fig. 73: BCM Wiring Diagram (Breeze, Cirrus & Stratus)

112935

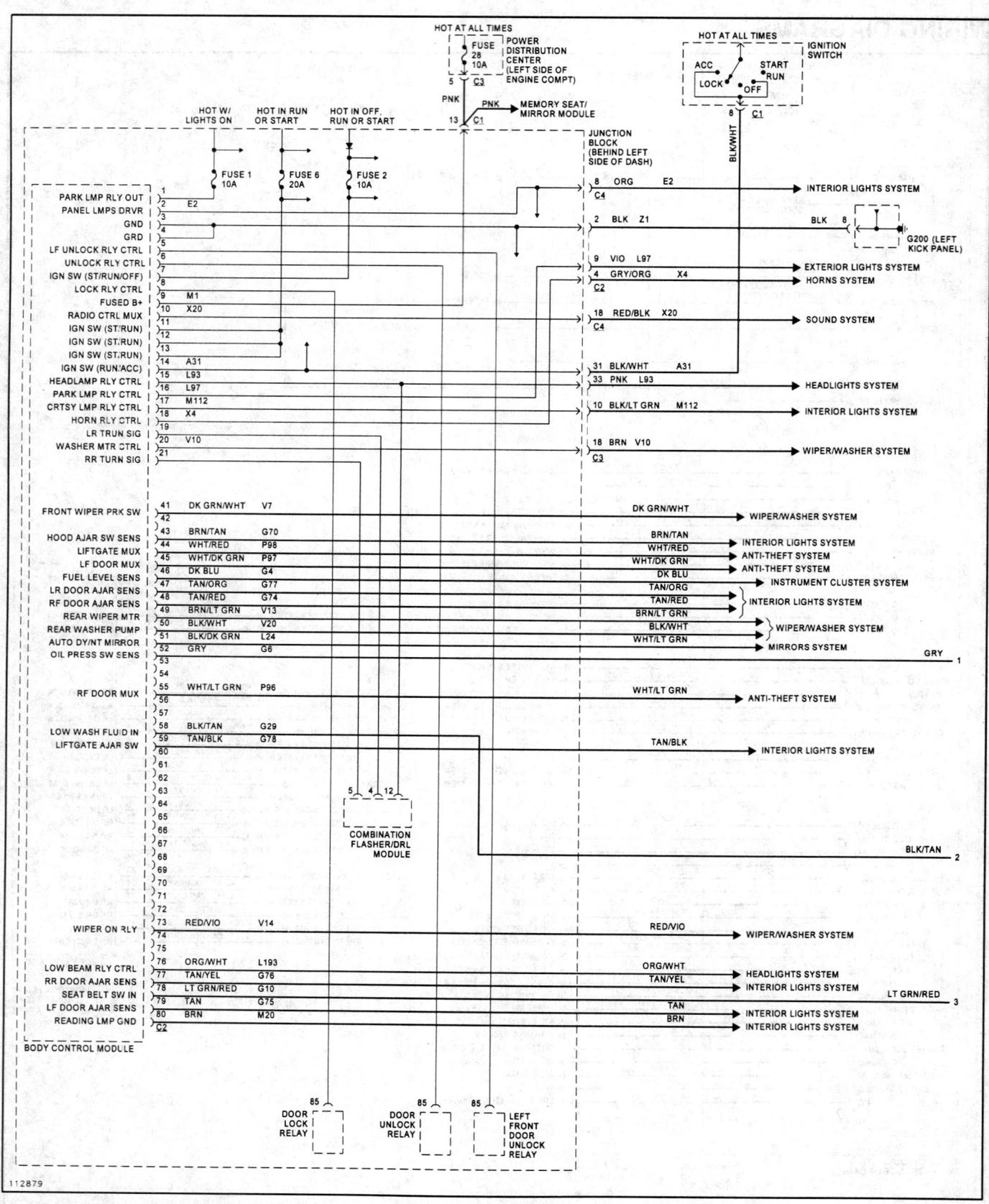

Fig. 74: BCM Wiring Diagram (Caravan, Town & Country, & Voyager – 1 Of 2)

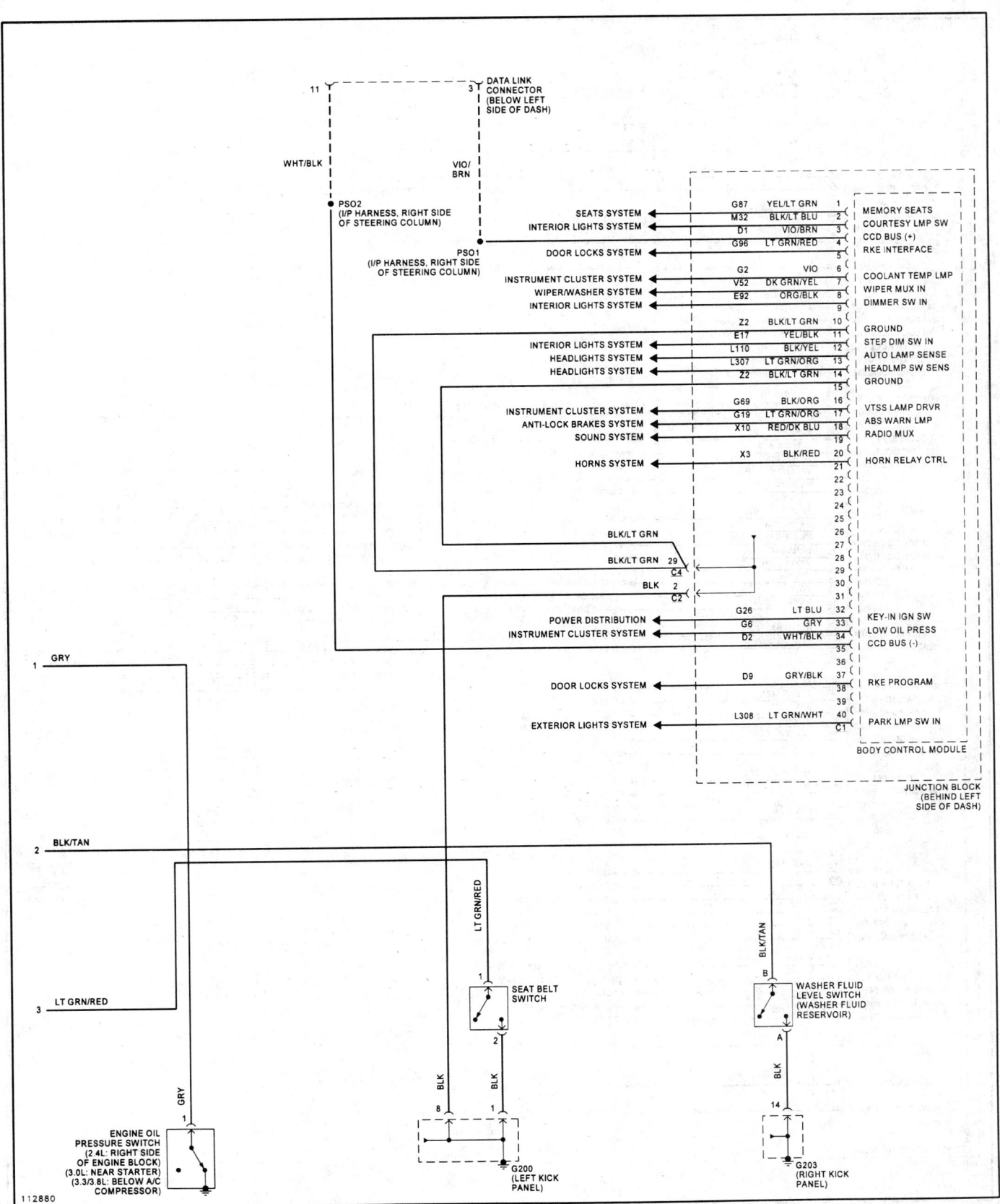

Fig. 75: BCM Wiring Diagram (Caravan, Town & Country, & Voyager – 2 Of 2)

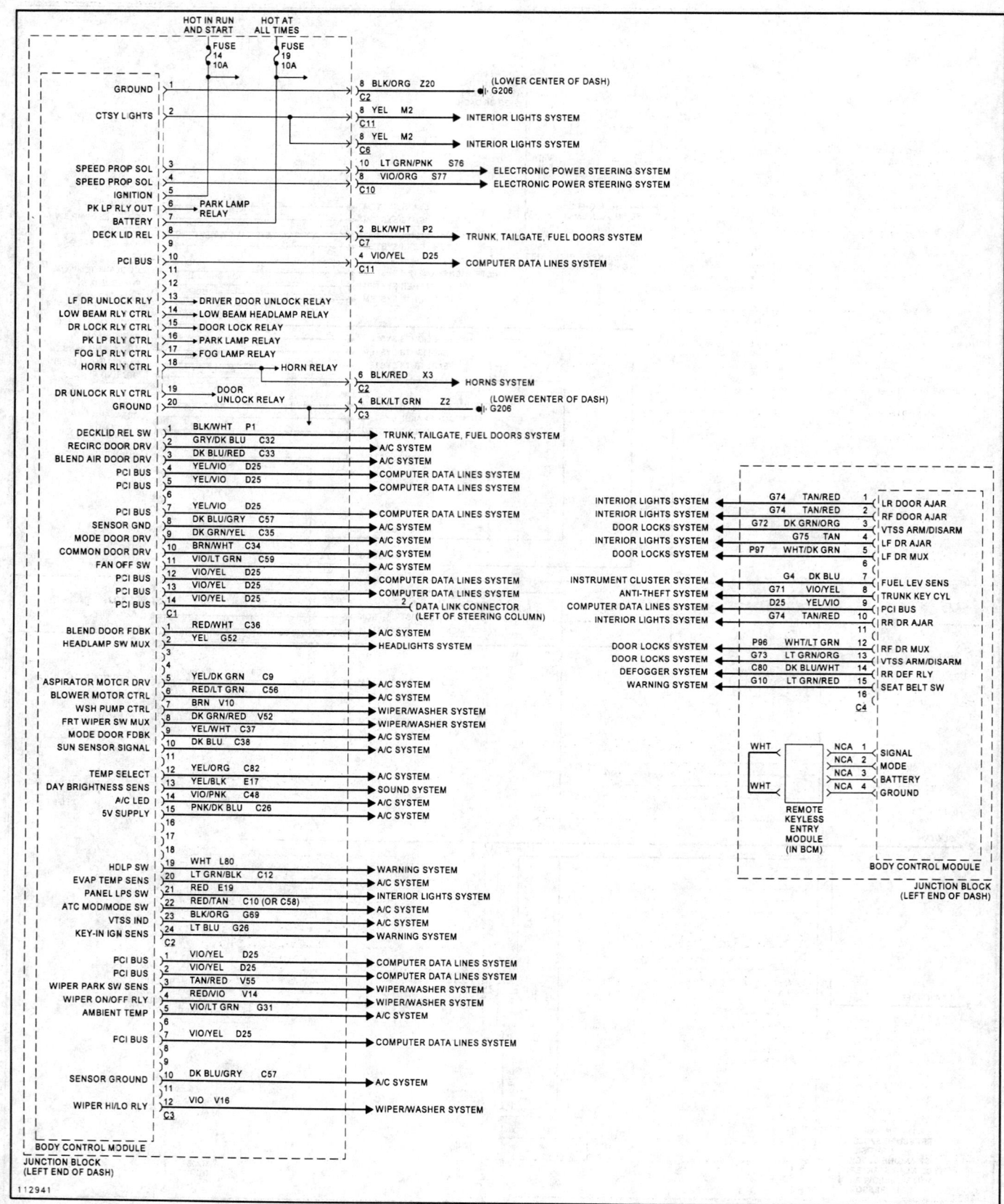

Fig. 76: BCM Wiring Diagram (Concorde, Intrepid, LHS & 300M)

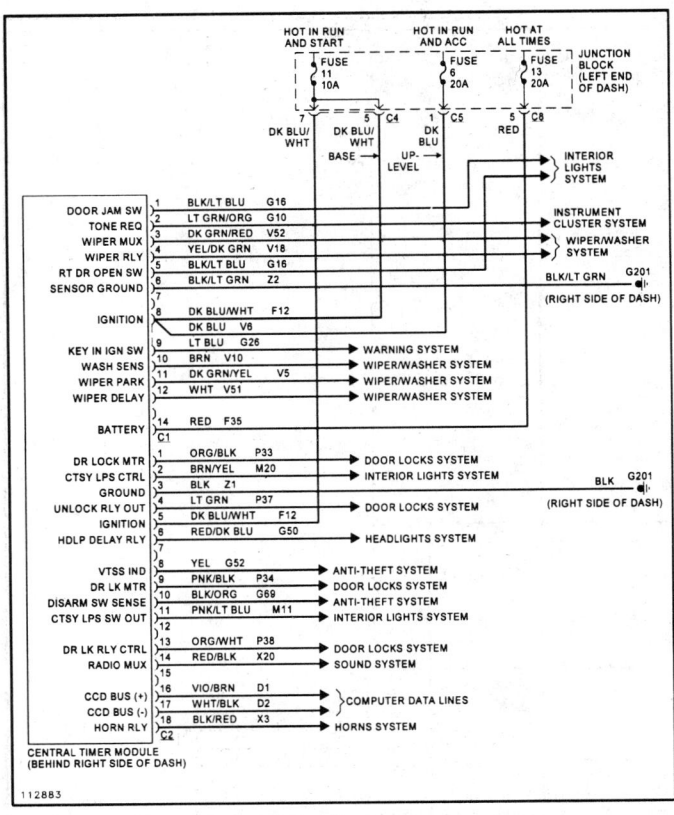

Fig. 77: BCM Wiring Diagram (Dakota)

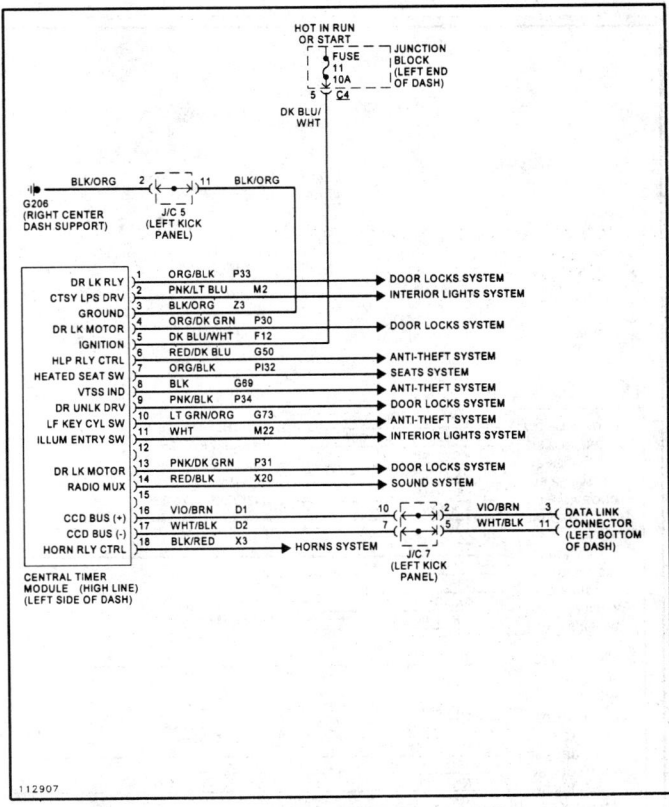

Fig. 79: BCM Wiring Diagram – Central Timer Module (Ram Pickup)

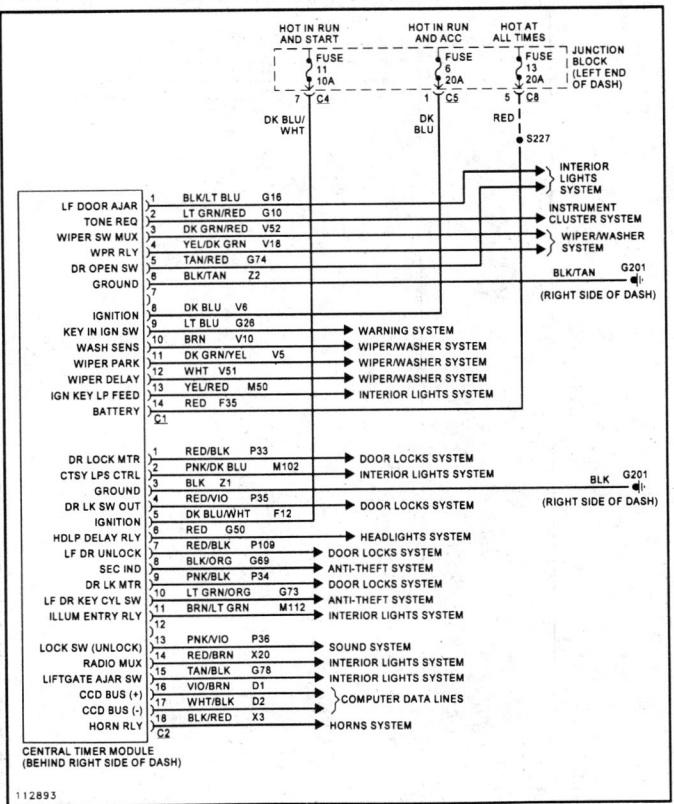

Fig. 78: BCM Wiring Diagram (Durango)

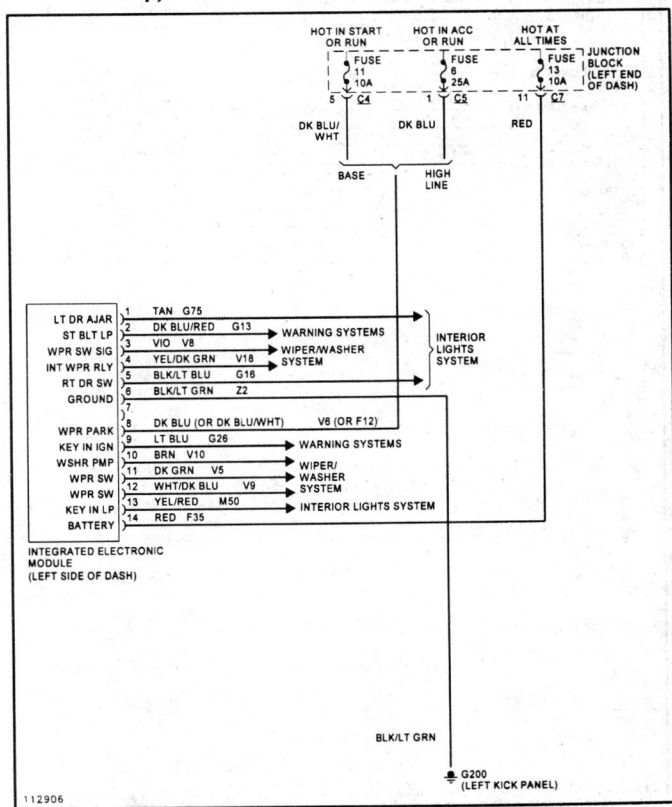

Fig. 80: BCM Wiring Diagram – Integrated Electronics Module (Ram Pickup)

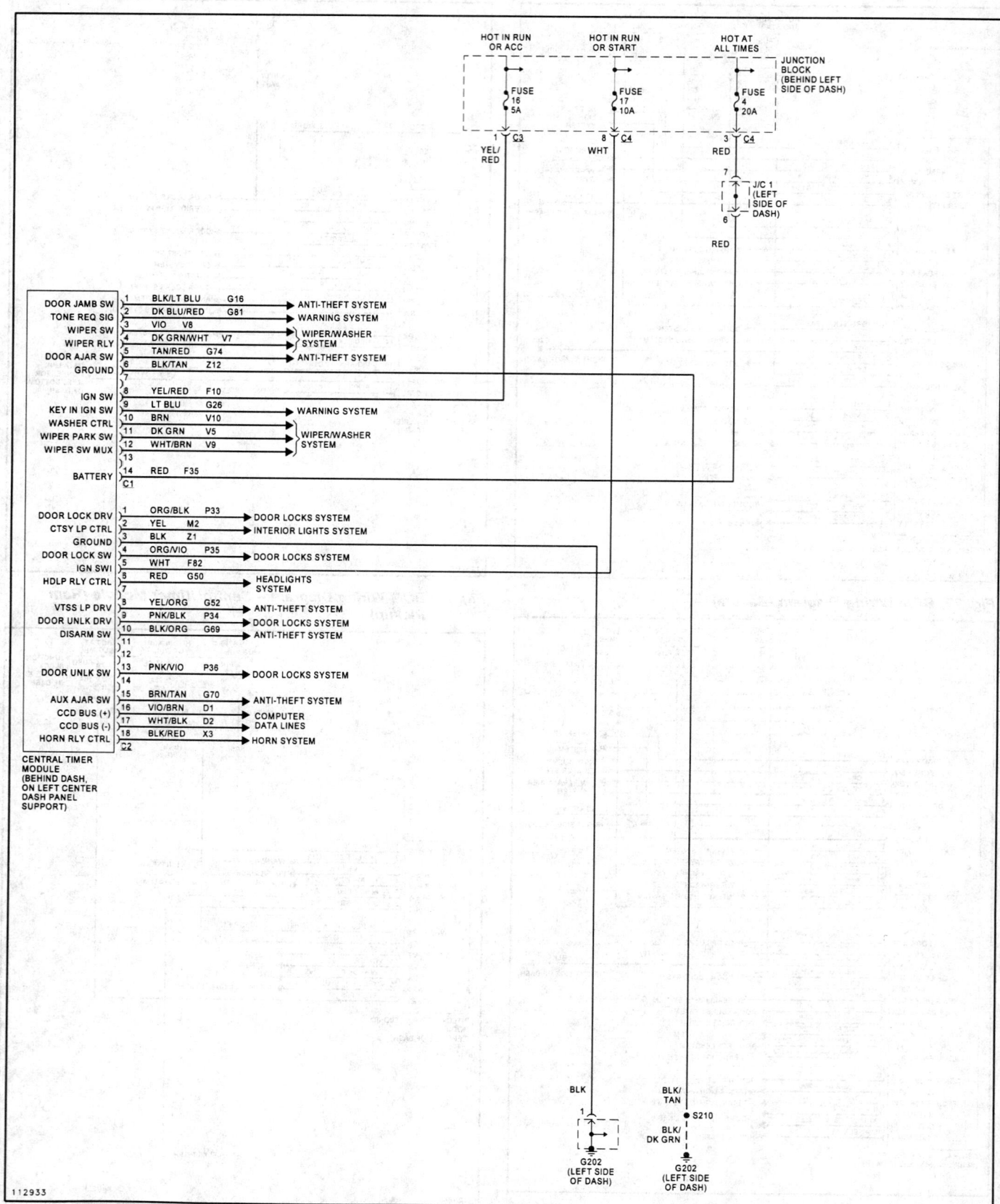

Fig. 81: BCM Wiring Diagram (Ram Van & Ram Wagon)

Body Control Computer – Introduction (Cont.)

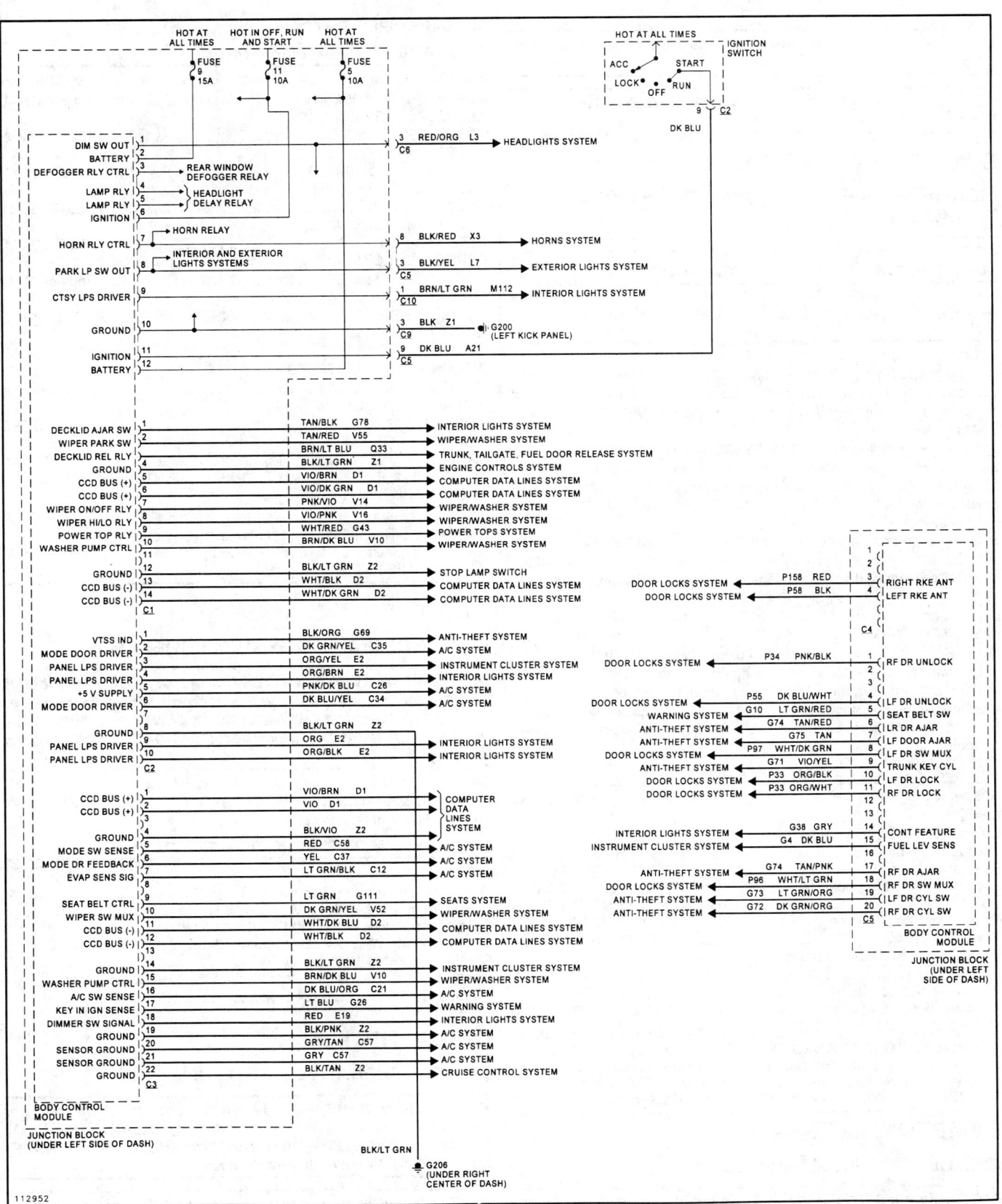

Fig. 82: BCM Wiring Diagram (Sebring Convertible)

112952

1999 ACCESSORIES & EQUIPMENT
Body Control Computer Tests
Breeze, Cirrus, Sebring Convertible & Stratus

NOTE: *Illustrations in following tests are Courtesy of Chrysler Corp.*

NOTE: *See BODY CONTROL COMPUTER – INTRODUCTION article before proceeding with following test.*

SYMPTOM ID TEST 1A

IDENTIFYING VEHICLE EQUIPMENT & SYSTEM PROBLEMS

NOTE: *For connector terminal identification wiring diagrams, see BODY CONTROL COMPUTER – INTRODUCTION article.*

NOTE: *Perform a visual inspection before proceeding with this test.*

1) Connect scan tool to Data Link Connector (DLC). DLC is a 16-pin connector located on left side kick panel, just above hood release. Turn ignition switch to ON position. If scan tool display is not blank, go to next step. If scan tool display is blank, see appropriate VEHICLE COMMUNICATIONS article.

2) Using scan tool, select BODY SYSTEM, then BODY COMPUTER. Scan tool will perform a CCD bus test. If scan tool displays BUS FAILED or NO RESPONSE, see appropriate VEHICLE COMMUNICATIONS article. If scan tool does not display BUS FAILED or NO RESPONSE, go to next step.

3) Using scan tool, select INPUT/OUTPUT and read IGN RUN/START status. If scan tool displays OPEN, see appropriate VEHICLE COMMUNICATIONS article. If scan tool does not display OPEN, go to next step.

4) Using scan tool, select READ DTCs. If any fault messages are present, go to SYMPTOM ID TEST 1B. If no messages are present, go to SYSTEM DIAGNOSTIC TEST DIRECTORY table for specific diagnosis. Problems listed are diagnosed using a scan tool. These problems may occur separately or in various combinations. When diagnosing a system with many apparent problems, a sequence of tests may be required. At the beginning of each test a note will indicate which test to perform first. After repairs, ensure problem(s) or failure(s) have been corrected.

SYSTEM DIAGNOSTIC TEST DIRECTORY [1]

Suspected System	Perform Test
Chime System	CHIME TEST 1
Compass/Mini-Trip Computer	CMTC TEST 1
Door Ajar System	DOOR AJAR TEST 1
Exterior Lighting System	EXTERIOR LIGHT TEST 1
Interior Lighting System	INTERIOR LIGHT TEST 1
Instrument Cluster	INSTRUMENT CLUSTER TEST 1
Power Door Lock System	POWER DOOR LOCK TEST 1
Power Top	POWER TOP TEST 1
Smart Key Immobilizer System (SKIS)	SKIS TEST 1
Vehicle Theft Security System	VTSS TEST 1
Windshield Wiper System	WINDSHIELD WIPER TEST 1

[1] – For problems or failures relating to A/C system, see appropriate MITCHELL® AIR CONDITIONING & HEATING SERVICE & REPAIR manual. For problems or failures relating to air bag system, see appropriate MITCHELL® AIR BAG SERVICE & REPAIR, DOMESTIC & IMPORTED MODELS manual.

SYMPTOM ID TEST 1B

IDENTIFYING FAULT MESSAGES

NOTE: *Perform SYMPTOM ID TEST 1A before proceeding with this test.*

If scan tool displays fault messages in SYMPTOM ID TEST 1A, record messages displayed and perform appropriate test(s). See SCAN TOOL MESSAGE DIRECTORY table.

SCAN TOOL MESSAGE DIRECTORY

Scan Tool Display	Perform Test
ABS MESSAGE MISMATCH	[1] VEHICLE COMM.
ABS MESSAGE NOT RECEIVED	[1] VEHICLE COMM.
BATTERY POWER TO MODULE DISCONNECTED	[1] VEHICLE COMM.
DRIVER DOOR DISARM SWITCH INPUT	VTSS TEST 11
EATX PRNDL MESSAGE TEST FAILED	[1] VEHICLE COMM.
EEPROM CHECKSUM FAILURE	[2] Replace BCM
FUEL LEVEL SENDING CIRCUIT ERROR	INSTRUMENT CLUSTER TEST 3
IGNITION VOLTAGE TOO LOW	[1] VEHICLE COMM.
INTERNAL MODULE TESTS FAILED	[1] Replace BCM
PASSENGER DOOR DISARM SWITCH INPUT	VTSS TEST 12
PCM MESSAGE NOT RECEIVED	[1] VEHICLE COMM.
SCTM FAILURE	INSTRUMENT CLUSTER TEST 11
WIPER PARK SWITCH FAILURE	WINDSHIELD WIPER TEST 6

[1] – See appropriate VEHICLE COMMUNICATIONS article.
[2] – After replacing Body Control Module (BCM), perform VERIFICATION TEST VER-1A.

CHIME TEST 1

IDENTIFYING CHIME SYSTEM PROBLEMS

NOTE: *Perform SYMPTOM ID TEST 1A before proceeding with this test. For connector terminal identification and wiring diagrams, see CONNECTOR IDENTIFICATION in BODY CONTROL COMPUTER – INTRODUCTION article. Perform VERIFICATION TEST VER-1A after each repair.*

Diagnosis of chime system is separated into 6 categories. Identify problem(s) listed in CHIME SYSTEM DIAGNOSTIC TEST DIRECTORY table and perform indicated test(s).

CHIME SYSTEM DIAGNOSTIC TEST DIRECTORY

Problem	CHIME TEST
Chime Inoperative At All Times	2
Chime Inoperative With Exterior Lights On	3
Chime Inoperative With Seat Belt Unfastened	4
Chime Sounds With Seat Belt Fastened	5
Chime Inoperative With Key In Ignition	6
Chime Sounds With Driver Door Open & Key Removed From Ignition	7

CHIME TEST 2

CHIME INOPERATIVE AT ALL TIMES

NOTE: *Perform CHIME TEST 1 before proceeding with this test. For connector terminal identification and wiring diagrams, see BODY CONTROL COMPUTER – INTRODUCTION article. Perform VERIFICATION TEST VER-1A after each repair.*

CAUTION: *Always turn ignition switch to OFF position prior to disconnecting any module connector.*

1) Turn ignition switch to ON position. Close all doors. Using scan tool, actuate chime test. If chime sounds, go to next step. If chime does not

1999 ACCESSORIES & EQUIPMENT
Body Control Computer Tests
Breeze, Cirrus, Sebring Convertible & Stratus (Cont.)

CHRY
4-67

sound, replace Body Control Module (BCM). BCM is located with junction block under driver's side instrument panel. *See Fig. 1.*

2) Using scan tool, stop chime test actuation. Read key-in ignition switch status. If scan tool displays KEY-IN IGN: CLOSED, go to next step. If scan tool does not display KEY-IN IGN: CLOSED, go to CHIME TEST 6.

3) Ensure left front seat belt is unfastened and fully retracted. Using scan tool, read seat belt switch status. If scan tool displays SEAT BELT: CLOSED, go to next step. If scan tool does not display SEAT BELT: CLOSED, go to CHIME TEST 4.

4) Turn parking lights on. Using scan tool, read parking lights status. If scan tool does not display PARK LAMPS: ON, go to CHIME TEST 3. If scan tool displays PARK LAMPS: ON, replace BCM.

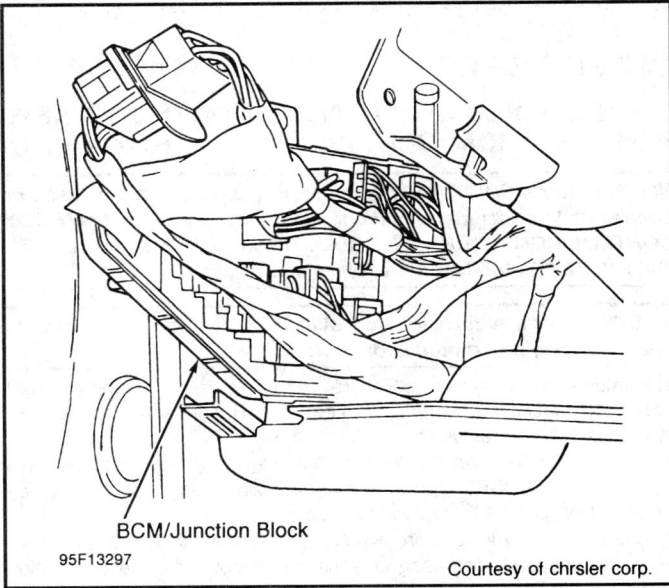

BCM/Junction Block

95F13297

Courtesy of chrsler corp.

Fig. 1: Locating BCM/Junction Block

CHIME TEST 3

CHIME INOPERATIVE WITH EXTERIOR LIGHTS ON

NOTE: Perform CHIME TEST 1 before proceeding with this test. For connector terminal identification and wiring diagrams, see BODY CONTROL COMPUTER – INTRODUCTION article. Perform VERIFICATION TEST VER-1A after each repair.

CAUTION: Always turn ignition switch to OFF position prior to disconnecting any module connector.

1) Turn headlights on. Using scan tool, read parking light status. If scan tool displays PARK LAMPS: ON, go to step 4). If scan tool does not display PARK LAMPS: ON, go to next step.

2) Turn headlights off. Locate junction block 16-pin connector on opposite side from BCM. *See Fig. 2.* DO NOT disconnect. Turn headlight switch on. Using scan tool in voltmeter mode, backprobe 16-pin connector terminal No. 4 (Black/Dark Green wire) and check voltage. If voltage is more than 10 volts, go to next step. If voltage is 10 volts or less, repair open in Black/Dark Green wire.

3) Turn ignition off and disconnect scan tool probe. Disconnect BCM from junction block and ensure connector is clean and not damaged. *See Figs. 1 and 3.* Using scan tool in voltmeter mode, measure voltage at connector No. 8 on BCM internal 12-pin connector. If voltage is more than 10 volts, replace BCM. If voltage is 10 volts or less, replace junction block.

4) Open left front door. Using scan tool, read left front door ajar switch status. If scan tool displays LF DOOR AJAR: CLOSED, replace BCM. If scan tool does not display LF DOOR AJAR: CLOSED, go to DOOR AJAR TEST 3.

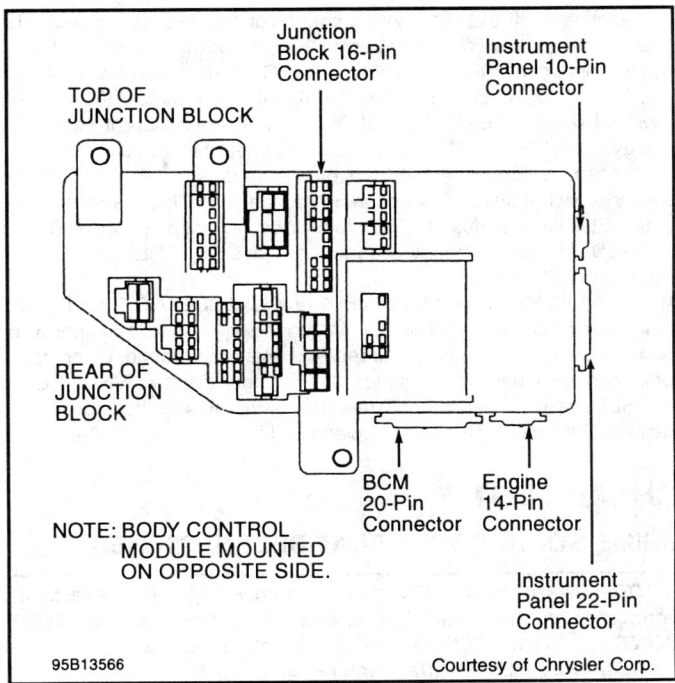

TOP OF JUNCTION BLOCK

Junction Block 16-Pin Connector

Instrument Panel 10-Pin Connector

REAR OF JUNCTION BLOCK

BCM 20-Pin Connector

Engine 14-Pin Connector

Instrument Panel 22-Pin Connector

NOTE: BODY CONTROL MODULE MOUNTED ON OPPOSITE SIDE.

95B13566

Courtesy of Chrysler Corp.

Fig. 2: Locating BCM/Junction Block Connectors

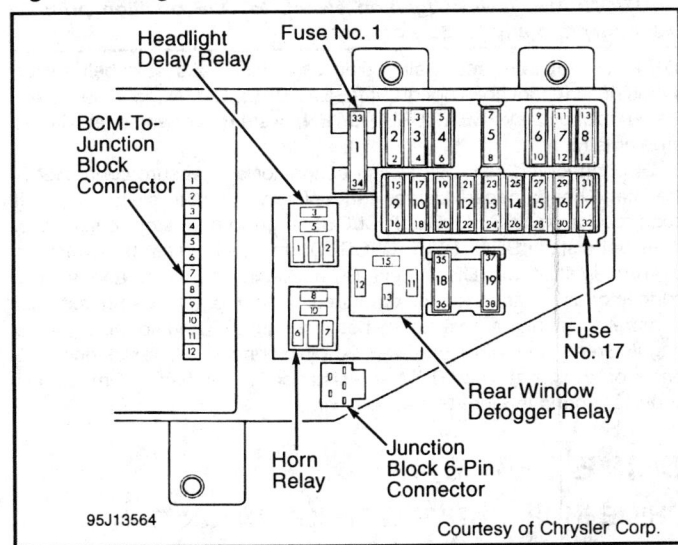

Headlight Delay Relay

Fuse No. 1

BCM-To-Junction Block Connector

Fuse No. 17

Rear Window Defogger Relay

Horn Relay

Junction Block 6-Pin Connector

95J13564

Courtesy of Chrysler Corp.

Fig. 3: Identifying BCM/Junction Block Components & Terminals

CHIME TEST 4

CHIME INOPERATIVE WITH SEAT BELT UNFASTENED

NOTE: Perform CHIME TEST 1 before proceeding with this test. For connector terminal identification and wiring diagrams, see BODY CONTROL COMPUTER – INTRODUCTION article. Perform VERIFICATION TEST VER-1A after each repair.

CAUTION: Always turn ignition switch to OFF position prior to disconnecting any module connector.

1) Ensure left front seat belt is unfastened and fully retracted. Using scan tool, read seat belt switch status. If scan tool does not display SEAT BELT: CLOSED, go to next step. If scan tool displays SEAT BELT: CLOSED, replace BCM.

CHRY
4-68

1999 ACCESSORIES & EQUIPMENT
Body Control Computer Tests
Breeze, Cirrus, Sebring Convertible & Stratus (Cont.)

2) Disconnect left seat belt switch connector and ensure connector is clean and not damaged. Connect a jumper wire between seat belt switch connector terminals No. 1 (Light Green/Red wire) and No. 2 (Black wire). Using scan tool, read seat belt switch status. If scan tool does not display SEAT BELT: CLOSED, go to next step. If scan tool displays SEAT BELT: CLOSED, replace left seat belt switch.

3) Connect jumper wire between ground and terminal No. 1 (Light Green/Red wire) on left seat belt switch connector. Using scan tool, read seat belt switch status. If scan tool does not display SEAT BELT: CLOSED, go to next step. If scan tool displays SEAT BELT: CLOSED, repair open Black wire.

4) Locate BCM 20-pin connector. *See Fig. 2.* DO NOT disconnect connector. Backprobing BCM 20- pin connector, connect a jumper wire between terminal No. 5 (Light Green/Red wire) and ground. Using scan tool, read seat belt switch status. If scan tool displays SEAT BELT: CLOSED, repair open Light Green/Red wire. If scan tool does not display SEAT BELT: CLOSED, replace BCM.

CHIME TEST 5

CHIME SOUNDS WITH SEAT BELT FASTENED

NOTE: Perform CHIME TEST 1 before proceeding with this test. For connector terminal identification and wiring diagrams, see BODY CONTROL COMPUTER – INTRODUCTION article. Perform VERIFICATION TEST VER-1A after each repair.

CAUTION: Always turn ignition switch to OFF position prior to disconnecting any module connector.

1) Fasten left front seat belt. Using scan tool, read seat belt switch status. If scan tool does not display SEAT BELT: OPEN, go to next step. If scan tool displays SEAT BELT: OPEN, system is operational with no problems found.

2) Disconnect left seat belt switch connector and ensure connector is clean and not damaged. Using scan tool, read seat belt switch status. If scan tool displays SEAT BELT: CLOSED, go to next step. If scan tool does not display SEAT BELT: CLOSED, replace left seat belt switch.

3) Turn ignition off. Disconnect BCM 20-pin connector and ensure connector is clean and not damaged. *See Fig. 2.* Using external ohmmeter, measure resistance between ground and terminal No. 5 (Light Green/Red wire) on BCM 20-pin connector. If resistance is 5 ohms or greater, replace BCM. If resistance is less than 5 ohms, repair short to ground in Light Green/Red wire.

CHIME TEST 6

CHIME INOPERATIVE WITH KEY IN IGNITION

NOTE: Perform CHIME TEST 1 before proceeding with this test. For connector terminal identification and wiring diagrams, see BODY CONTROL COMPUTER – INTRODUCTION article. Perform VERIFICATION TEST VER-1A after each repair.

CAUTION: Always turn ignition switch to OFF position prior to disconnecting any module connector.

1) Turn ignition on and open left front door. Using scan tool, read left front door ajar status. If scan tool does not display LF DOOR AJAR: CLOSED, go to DOOR AJAR TEST 3. If scan tool displays, LF DOOR AJAR: CLOSED, go to next step.

2) Using scan tool, read key-in ignition status. If scan tool does not display KEY-IN IGN: CLOSED, go to next step. If scan tool displays KEY-IN IGN: CLOSED, replace BCM.

3) Disconnect key-in ignition switch 2-pin connector and ensure connector is clean and not damaged. Locate 2-pin connector, next to ignition switch 10-pin connector, behind steering wheel. Using external ohmmeter, measure resistance between ground and terminal No. 2

(Black wire) on key-in ignition switch 2-pin connector. If resistance is less than 5 ohms, go to next step. If resistance is 5 ohms or greater, repair open Black wire.

4) Connect a jumper wire between key-in ignition switch 2-pin connector terminals. Using scan tool, read key-in ignition status. If scan tool does not display KEY-IN IGN: CLOSED, go to next step. If scan tool displays KEY-IN IGN: CLOSED, replace ignition switch.

5) Locate instrument panel 22-pin connector at BCM. *See Figs. 1 and 2.* DO NOT disconnect connector. Backprobe a jumper wire between ground and terminal No. 17 (Light Blue wire) on instrument panel 22-pin connector. Using scan tool, read key-in ignition status. If scan tool displays KEY-IN IGN: CLOSED, repair open Light Blue wire. If scan tool does not display KEY-IN IGN: CLOSED, replace BCM.

CHIME TEST 7

CHIME SOUNDS WITH DRIVER DOOR OPEN & KEY REMOVED FROM IGNITION

NOTE: Perform CHIME TEST 1 before proceeding with this test. For connector terminal identification and wiring diagrams, see BODY CONTROL COMPUTER – INTRODUCTION article. Perform VERIFICATION TEST VER-1A after each repair.

CAUTION: Always turn ignition switch to OFF position prior to disconnecting any module connector.

1) Remove key from ignition. Ensure exterior lights are off and left front door is open. If chime sounds, go to next step. If chime does not sound, system is operational with no problems found.

2) Using scan tool, read key-in ignition status. If scan tool displays KEY-IN IGN: CLOSED, go to next step. If scan tool does not display KEY-IN IGN: CLOSED, replace BCM.

3) Disconnect key-in ignition switch 2-pin connector and ensure connector is clean and not damaged. Locate 2-pin connector next to ignition switch 10-pin connector, behind steering wheel. Using scan tool, read key-in ignition status. If scan tool displays KEY-IN IGN: CLOSED, go to next step. If scan tool does not display KEY-IN IGN: CLOSED, replace ignition switch.

4) Disconnect instrument panel 22-pin connector at BCM. *See Fig. 2.* Ensure connector is clean and not damaged. Using external ohmmeter, measure resistance between ground and terminal No. 17 (Light Blue wire) on instrument panel 22- pin connector. If resistance is more than 5 ohms, replace BCM. If resistance is less than 5 ohms, repair short to ground in Light Blue wire.

CMTC TEST 1

IDENTIFYING COMPASS/MINI-TRIP PROBLEMS

NOTE: Perform SYMPTOM ID TEST 1A before proceeding with this test. For connector terminal identification and wiring diagrams, see BODY CONTROL COMPUTER – INTRODUCTION article. Perform VERIFICATION TEST VER-1A after each repair.

NOTE: For CMTC wiring diagram, see ANALOG INSTRUMENT PANELS – BREEZE, CIRRUS, SEBRING CONVERTIBLE & STRATUS article.

1) If Compass/Mini-Trip Computer (CMTC) display is blank or displays CCD, go to CMTC TEST 7.

2) Perform CMTC auto self test. Ensure ignition is off. Press and hold both CMTC buttons. Turn ignition on and release buttons. If any display segments fail to illuminate, replace CMTC module. If CMTC displays FAILED, replace CMTC module.

3) Diagnosis of CMTC system is separated into 10 faults. Identify fault(s) listed in CMTC SYSTEM DIAGNOSTIC TEST DIRECTORY table and perform indicated test(s).

1999 ACCESSORIES & EQUIPMENT
Body Control Computer Tests
Breeze, Cirrus, Sebring Convertible & Stratus (Cont.)

CHRY
4-69

CMTC SYSTEM DIAGNOSTIC TEST DIRECTORY

Problem	Perform
Outside Temperature	
CMTC Displays SC	CMTC TEST 2
CMTC Displays OC	CMTC TEST 3
Incorrect Reading (5 Degree Variation)	CMTC TEST 4
Average MPG Or Fuel Economy [1]	CMTC TEST 5
Trip Odometer Inoperative Or Wrong	CMTC TEST 5
Distance To Empty Inoperative Or Wrong	INSTRUMENT CLUSTER TEST 3
Elapsed Time Inoperative Or Wrong	CMTC TEST 6

[1] – Average MPG or fuel economy is inoperative or wrong. MPG calculations are only accurate to within 10 miles.

4) If CMTC fails to respond to instrument cluster dimming, replace CMTC module. If CMTC switch is inoperative, replace CMTC module. If compass is inoperative or wrong, locate open area away from large metal objects. Turn ignition on. Press and hold compass/temperature button until CAL is displayed. Driving slowly, perform 3 complete circles. CAL lamp will turn off and compass will be calibrated. If compass goes blank, replace CMTC module.

CMTC TEST 2

COMPASS/MINI-TRIP COMPUTER DISPLAYING "SC"

NOTE: Perform CMTC TEST 1 before proceeding with this test. For connector terminal identification and wiring diagrams, see BODY CONTROL COMPUTER – INTRODUCTION article. Perform VERIFICATION TEST VER-1A after each repair.

NOTE: For CMTC wiring diagram, see ANALOG INSTRUMENT PANELS – BREEZE, CIRRUS, SEBRING CONVERTIBLE & STRATUS article.

CAUTION: Always turn ignition switch to OFF position prior to disconnecting any module connector.

1) Disconnect ambient temperature/battery temperature sensor connector. Sensor is located behind front bumper (right center). Observe CMTC display. If CMTC displays OC, replace ambient temperature sensor. If CMTC does not display OC, go to next step.
2) Turn ignition off. Disconnect Powertrain Control Module (PCM) connector. Using external ohmmeter, measure resistance between ground and terminal No. 2 (Pink/Yellow wire) on ambient temperature/battery temperature sensor connector. If resistance is less than 5 ohms, repair Violet/Light Green wire between PCM and ambient temperature sensor for short to ground. If resistance is 5 ohms or greater, go to next step.
3) Using external ohmmeter, measure resistance between ambient temperature/battery temperature sensor connector terminals. If resistance is less than 1000 ohms, repair Pink/Yellow wire for short to Black/Light Blue wire. If resistance is 1000 ohms or greater, replace CMTC module.

CMTC TEST 3

COMPASS/MINI-TRIP COMPUTER DISPLAYING "OC"

NOTE: Perform CMTC TEST 1 before proceeding with this test. For connector terminal identification and wiring diagrams, see BODY CONTROL COMPUTER – INTRODUCTION article. Drive vehicle at least 3 miles (greater than 25 MPH) to update CMTC and perform VERIFICATION TEST VER-1A after each repair.

NOTE: For CMTC wiring diagram, see ANALOG INSTRUMENT PANELS – BREEZE, CIRRUS, SEBRING CONVERTIBLE & STRATUS article.

CAUTION: Always turn ignition switch to OFF position prior to disconnecting any module connector.

1) Disconnect ambient temperature/battery temperature sensor connector. Sensor is located behind front bumper (right center). Connect jumper wire between connector terminals. Turn ignition on. Observe CMTC display. If CMTC displays SC, replace ambient temperature/battery temperature sensor. If CMTC does not display SC, go to next step.
2) Turn ignition off. Disconnect jumper wire. Disconnect Powertrain Control Module (PCM) Gray connector. Connect jumper wires between ground and each terminal of ambient temperature/battery temperature sensor harness connector. Using scan tool in ohmmeter mode, measure resistance at terminal No. 52 (Pink/Yellow wire) on PCM harness connector. If resistance is less than 5 ohms, go to next step. If resistance is 5 ohms or greater, repair open sensor signal circuit between PCM and ambient temperature/battery temperature sensor.
3) With jumper wires still connected, measure resistance at terminal No. 43 (Black/Light Blue wire) on PCM connector. If resistance is less than 5 ohms, replace CMTC module. If resistance is 5 ohms or greater, repair open Black/Light Blue wire between PCM and ambient temperature/battery temperature sensor.

CMTC TEST 4

INCORRECT AMBIENT TEMPERATURE READING

NOTE: Perform CMTC TEST 1 before proceeding with this test. For connector terminal identification and wiring diagrams, see BODY CONTROL COMPUTER – INTRODUCTION article. Drive vehicle at least 3 miles (greater than 25 MPH) to update CMTC and perform VERIFICATION TEST VER-1A after each repair.

NOTE: For CMTC wiring diagram, see ANALOG INSTRUMENT PANELS – BREEZE, CIRRUS, SEBRING CONVERTIBLE & STRATUS article.

CAUTION: Always turn ignition switch to OFF position prior to disconnecting any module connector.

1) Using scan tool, select ENGINE, then SENSORS. Select AMBIENT/BAT TMP DEG. Compare scan tool reading with actual outside temperature. If temperature readings match, replace CMTC module. If temperature readings do not match, go to next step.
2) Disconnect and remove ambient temperature/battery temperature sensor. Sensor is located behind front bumper, right of center. Using external ohmmeter, measure resistance between sensor terminals and compare with AMBIENT TEMPERATURE SENSOR SPECIFICATIONS table. Go to next step.

CHRY
4-70

1999 ACCESSORIES & EQUIPMENT
Body Control Computer Tests
Breeze, Cirrus, Sebring Convertible & Stratus (Cont.)

AMBIENT TEMPERATURE SENSOR SPECIFICATIONS

Ambient Temperature	k/ohms
32°F (0°C)	29.3-36.0
50°F (10°C)	18.0-22.0
68°F (20°C)	11.4-13.6
77°F (25°C)	9.1-10.8
86°F (30°C)	7.4-8.7
104°F (40°C)	4.9-5.7
122°F (50°C)	3.3-3.8

3) If resistance measurement does not correspond with AMBIENT TEMPERATURE SENSOR SPECIFICATIONS table, replace sensor. If sensor is within specification, turn ignition off. Close all vehicle doors and ensure all lights are off. Wait one minute.

4) Using external ohmmeter, measure resistance between ground and terminal No. 1 (Black/Light Blue wire) on ambient temperature/battery temperature sensor connector. If resistance is less than 10 ohms, go to step 9). If resistance is 5 ohms or greater, go to next step.

5) Connect ambient temperature/battery temperature sensor. Disconnect Powertrain Control Module (PCM) Gray connector. Using external ohmmeter, measure resistance between terminals No. 43 and No. 52 on PCM harness connector.

6) Compare with AMBIENT TEMPERATURE SENSOR SPECIFICATIONS table. If resistance measurement does not correspond with AMBIENT TEMPERATURE SENSOR SPECIFICATIONS table, go to next step. If sensor is within specification, replace CMTC module.

7) Disconnect ambient temperature/battery temperature sensor. Using external ohmmeter, measure resistance between ground and terminal No. 1 (Black/Light Blue wire) on sensor connector. If resistance is less than 500 k/ohms, repair Black/Light Blue wire for partial short to ground. If resistance is 500 k/ohms or greater, go to next step.

8) Move ohmmeter lead to terminal No. 2 (Pink/Yellow wire) on sensor connector. If resistance is less than 500 k/ohms, repair Pink/Yellow wire for partial short to ground. If resistance is 500 k/ohms or greater, repair Pink/Yellow wire for short to Black/Light Blue wire.

9) Disconnect Powertrain Control Module (PCM) Gray connector. Using external ohmmeter, measure resistance of Black/Light Blue wire between terminal No. 43 on PCM connector and terminal No. 2 on ambient temperature/battery temperature sensor harness connector. If resistance is less than 5 ohms, replace PCM. If resistance is 5 ohms or greater, repair open Black/Light Blue wire.

CMTC TEST 5
INCORRECT MILEAGE OR DISTANCE PROBLEMS

NOTE: Perform CMTC TEST 1 before proceeding with this test. For connector terminal identification and wiring diagrams, see BODY CONTROL COMPUTER – INTRODUCTION article. Drive vehicle at least 3 miles (greater than 25 MPH) to update CMTC and perform VERIFICATION TEST VER-1A after each repair.

NOTE: For CMTC wiring diagram, see ANALOG INSTRUMENT PANELS – BREEZE, CIRRUS, SEBRING CONVERTIBLE & STRATUS article.

CAUTION: Always turn ignition switch to OFF position prior to disconnecting any module connector.

1) Turn ignition on. Using scan tool, read engine information under monitor display. If scan tool displays NO RESPONSE, see appropriate VEHICLE COMMUNICATIONS article. If scan tool does not display NO RESPONSE, go to next step.

2) Observe TP sensor while depressing accelerator pedal. If TP sensor percent does not increase while operating throttle, see appropriate SELF-DIAGNOSTICS article in ENGINE PERFORMANCE in appropriate MITCHELL® manual. If TP sensor percent does increase, go to next step.

3) Raise and support vehicle. Start vehicle and place transmission in Drive. Using scan tool, read vehicle speed signal. Increase vehicle speed and observe scan tool. If speed signal changes, system is currently operating correctly. If speed signal does not change, vehicle speed signal may be at fault. See appropriate SELF-DIAGNOSTICS article in ENGINE PERFORMANCE in appropriate MITCHELL® manual.

CMTC TEST 6
ELAPSED TIME INOPERATIVE OR WRONG

NOTE: Perform CMTC TEST 1 before proceeding with this test. For connector terminal identification and wiring diagrams, see BODY CONTROL COMPUTER – INTRODUCTION article. Perform VERIFICATION TEST VER-1A after each repair.

NOTE: For CMTC wiring diagram, see ANALOG INSTRUMENT PANELS – BREEZE, CIRRUS, SEBRING CONVERTIBLE & STRATUS article.

CAUTION: Always turn ignition switch to OFF position prior to disconnecting any module connector.

1) Cycle ignition switch off, then on. Observe instrument cluster warning lights. If lights illuminate, then go off, replace Body Control Module (BCM). BCM is located with junction block. See Fig. 1. If lights do not illuminate, go to next step.

2) Remove and inspect fuse No. 11 from junction block. See Fig. 3. If fuse is okay, go to next step. If fuse is open, go to step 7).

3) Turn ignition off. Install fuse No. 11. Disconnect Body Control Module (BCM). BCM is connected to junction block. Using external ohmmeter, measure resistance between ground and terminal No. 10 on junction block internal 12-pin connector. See Fig. 3. If resistance is 20 ohms or more, repair open ground circuit/junction block. If resistance is less than 20 ohms, go to next step.

4) Turn ignition on. Using external voltmeter, measure voltage between ground and terminal No. 12 on junction block internal 12-pin connector. If voltage is 10 volts or less, replace junction block. If voltage is more than 10 volts, go to next step.

5) Measure voltage between ground and terminal No. 6 on junction block internal 12-pin connector. If voltage is 10 volts or less, replace junction block. If voltage is more than 10 volts, go to next step.

6) Measure voltage between ground and terminal No. 11 on junction block internal 12-pin connector. If voltage is 10 volts or less, replace junction block. If voltage is more than 10 volts, replace BCM.

7) Turn ignition off. Using external ohmmeter, measure resistance between ground and component side (fused ignition output circuit) of fuse No. 11 (Red /Violet wire). If resistance is 5 ohms or more, replace fuse No. 11. If resistance is less than 5 ohms, go to next step.

8) Disconnect BCM. BCM is connect to junction block. Measure resistance between ground and component side (fused ignition output circuit) of fuse No. 11 (Red /Violet wire). If resistance is 5 ohms or more, replace fuse No. 11 and BCM. If resistance is less than 5 ohms, repair Red /Violet wire for short to ground. Replace fuse No. 11.

1999 ACCESSORIES & EQUIPMENT
Body Control Computer Tests
Breeze, Cirrus, Sebring Convertible & Stratus (Cont.)

CHRY
4-71

CMTC TEST 7

BLANK DISPLAY OR "CCD" DISPLAYED

NOTE: Perform CMTC TEST 1 before proceeding with this test. For connector terminal identification and wiring diagrams, see BODY CONTROL COMPUTER – INTRODUCTION article. Perform VERIFICATION TEST VER-1A after each repair.

NOTE: For CMTC wiring diagram, see ANALOG INSTRUMENT PANELS – BREEZE, CIRRUS, SEBRING CONVERTIBLE & STRATUS article.

CAUTION: Always turn ignition switch to OFF position prior to disconnecting any module connector.

1) Ensure ignition is off. Disconnect CMTC connector. Using scan tool in ohmmeter mode, measure resistance at terminal No. 5 (Black/Violet wire) on CMTC harness connector. If resistance is less than 10 ohms, go to next step. If resistance is 10 ohms or greater, repair open Black/Violet wire.

2) Turn ignition on. Using scan tool in voltmeter mode, measure voltage at terminal No. 6 (Light Green/Red wire) on CMTC harness connector. If voltage is 10 volts or less, repair open Light Green/Red wire between CMTC module and fuse No. 9 in Power Distribution Center (PDC). If voltage is greater than 10 volts, go to next step.

3) Using scan tool in voltmeter mode, measure voltage at terminal No. 7 (Pink/Dark Blue wire) on CMTC harness connector. If voltage is 10 volts or less, repair open Pink/Dark Blue wire between CMTC module and fuse No. 5 in junction block. If voltage is greater than 10 volts, go to next step.

4) Connect jumper wire between ground and terminal No. 2 (White/Black wire) on CMTC module connector. Using scan tool, read CCD bus status. If scan tool displays BUS SHORTED TO GROUND, go to next step. If scan tool does not display BUS SHORTED TO GROUND, repair open White/Black wire.

5) Move jumper wire to terminal No. 1 (Violet/Pink wire) on CMTC module connector. Using scan tool, read CCD bus status. If scan tool displays BUS SHORTED TO GROUND, replace CMTC module. If scan tool does not display BUS SHORTED TO GROUND, repair open Violet/Pink wire.

DOOR AJAR TEST 1

IDENTIFYING DOOR AJAR SYSTEM PROBLEM

NOTE: Perform SYMPTOM ID TEST 1A before proceeding with this test. For connector terminal identification and wiring diagrams, see BODY CONTROL COMPUTER – INTRODUCTION article. Perform VERIFICATION TEST VER-1A after each repair.

CAUTION: Always turn ignition switch to OFF position prior to disconnecting any module connector.

1) Body Control Module (BCM) monitors 2 or 4 door ajar switches (JX or JA models). When switch is closed (door open), BCM will sound chime once and display DOOR message in odometer Vacuum Fluorescent (VF) display. If all doors are closed and properly aligned, go to next step. If door(s) are out of alignment, repair door alignment and ensure door(s) close(s) properly.

2) If VF displays DECK, go to INSTRUMENT CLUSTER TEST 19A. Using scan tool, select BODY SYSTEM, and then INPUTS/OUTPUTS and read left front door ajar and door ajar switch status. Open and close each door one at a time. If switch status toggles from OPEN to CLOSED as each door is opened, door ajar circuits are operational with no problems found. If switch status does not toggle from OPEN to CLOSED as each door is opened, go to next step.

3) If door ajar switch status is CLOSED when door is closed, perform appropriate shorted circuit test. See DOOR AJAR SYSTEM DIAGNOSTIC TEST DIRECTORY table. If door ajar switch status is OPEN when door is open, perform appropriate open circuit test. See DOOR AJAR SYSTEM DIAGNOSTIC TEST DIRECTORY table.

NOTE: A shorted LF DOOR AJAR circuit will only affect left front door. One shorted passenger door ajar circuit will affect all passenger door circuits.

DOOR AJAR SYSTEM DIAGNOSTIC TEST DIRECTORY

Problem	DOOR AJAR TEST
Left Front Door Ajar Short Circuit	2
Left Front Door Ajar Open Circuit	3
Right Front Door Ajar Short Circuit	4
Right Front Door Ajar Open Circuit	5
Right Rear Door Ajar Open Circuit	6
Left Rear Door Ajar Open Circuit	7

DOOR AJAR TEST 2

LEFT FRONT DOOR AJAR SHORT CIRCUIT

NOTE: Perform DOOR AJAR TEST 1 before proceeding with this test. For connector terminal identification and wiring diagrams, see BODY CONTROL COMPUTER – INTRODUCTION article. Perform VERIFICATION TEST VER-1A after each repair.

CAUTION: Always turn ignition switch to OFF position prior to disconnecting any module connector.

1) Disconnect left front door ajar switch and ensure connector is clean and not damaged. Using scan tool, read left front door ajar switch status. If scan tool displays LF DOOR AJAR: CLOSED, go to next step. If scan tool does not display LF DOOR AJAR: CLOSED, replace left front door ajar switch.

2) On Sebring Convertible, disconnect Seat Belt Control Module (SBCM) connector under center console. *See Fig. 4.* Using scan tool, read left front door ajar switch status. If scan tool displays LF DOOR AJAR: CLOSED, go to next step. If scan tool does not display LF DOOR AJAR: CLOSED, replace SBCM.

3) On all models, disconnect BCM 20-pin connector at junction block and ensure connector is clean and not damaged. *See Fig. 2.* Using scan tool, read left front door ajar switch status. If scan tool displays LF DOOR AJAR: CLOSED, replace BCM. If scan tool does not display LF DOOR AJAR: CLOSED, repair short to ground in left front door ajar switch Tan wire.

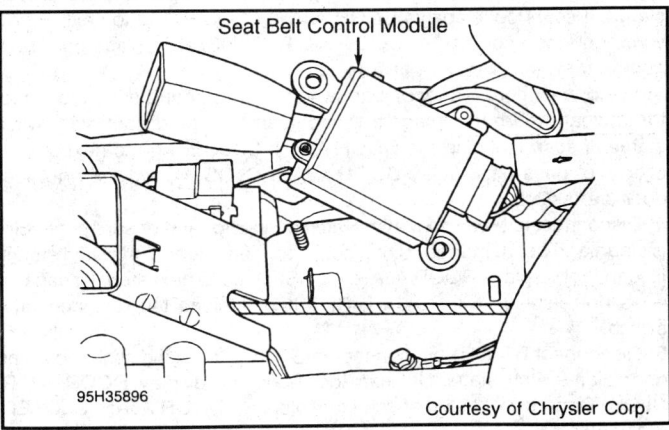

Seat Belt Control Module

95H35896

Courtesy of Chrysler Corp.

Fig. 4: Locating Seat Belt Control Module

CHRY
4-72

1999 ACCESSORIES & EQUIPMENT
Body Control Computer Tests
Breeze, Cirrus, Sebring Convertible & Stratus (Cont.)

DOOR AJAR TEST 3

LEFT FRONT DOOR AJAR OPEN CIRCUIT

NOTE: Perform DOOR AJAR TEST 1 before proceeding with this test. For connector terminal identification and wiring diagrams, see BODY CONTROL COMPUTER – INTRODUCTION article. Perform VERIFICATION TEST VER-1A after each repair.

CAUTION: Always turn ignition switch to OFF position prior to disconnecting any module connector.

1) Disconnect left front door ajar switch and ensure connector is clean and not damaged. Ensure left front door ajar switch ground strap is clean and not damaged. Repair or replace ground strap as necessary. If ground strap is okay, go to next step.

2) Connect a jumper wire between left front door ajar switch connector (Tan wire) and ground. Using scan tool, read left front door ajar switch status. If scan tool displays LF DOOR AJAR: CLOSED, replace left front door ajar switch. If scan tool does not display LF DOOR AJAR: CLOSED, go to next step.

3) Disconnect jumper wire. Locate BCM 20-pin connector at junction block. *See Fig. 2.* DO NOT disconnect connector. Backprobe a jumper wire between ground and terminal No. 7 (Tan wire) on BCM 20-pin connector. Using scan tool, read left front door ajar switch status. If scan tool displays LF DOOR AJAR: CLOSED, repair open in Tan wire between left front door ajar switch and BCM. If scan tool does not display LF DOOR AJAR: CLOSED, go to next step.

4) Turn ignition off. Disconnect BCM 20-pin connector at junction block. Inspect terminal No. 7. Repair as needed. If terminal is okay, replace BCM.

DOOR AJAR TEST 4

RIGHT FRONT DOOR AJAR SHORT CIRCUIT

NOTE: Perform DOOR AJAR TEST 1 before proceeding with this test. For connector terminal identification and wiring diagrams, see BODY CONTROL COMPUTER – INTRODUCTION article. Perform VERIFICATION TEST VER-1A after each repair.

CAUTION: Always turn ignition switch to OFF position prior to disconnecting any module connector.

1) On Sebring Convertible, go to step 8). On Breeze, Cirrus and Stratus, go to next step.

2) Disconnect right front door ajar switch connector and ensure connector is clean and not damaged. Using scan tool, read door ajar switch status. If scan tool displays DOOR AJAR: CLOSED, go to next step. If scan tool does not display DOOR AJAR: CLOSED, replace right front door ajar switch.

3) Disconnect right rear door ajar switch connector and ensure connector is clean and not damaged. Using scan tool, read door ajar switch status. If scan tool displays DOOR AJAR: CLOSED, go to next step. If scan tool does not display DOOR AJAR: CLOSED, replace right rear door ajar switch.

4) Disconnect left rear door ajar switch connector and ensure connector is clean and not damaged. Using scan tool, read door ajar switch status. If scan tool displays DOOR AJAR: CLOSED, go to next step. If scan tool does not display DOOR AJAR: CLOSED, replace left rear door ajar switch.

5) Disconnect BCM 20-pin connector. *See Fig. 2.* Using scan tool, read door ajar switch status. If scan tool does not display DOOR AJAR: CLOSED, go to next step. If scan tool displays DOOR AJAR: CLOSED, replace BCM.

6) Using external ohmmeter, measure resistance between ground and terminal No. 17 (Tan/Orange wire) on BCM 20-pin connector. If resistance is 5 ohms or greater, go to next step. If resistance is less than 5 ohms, repair Tan/Orange wire for short to ground.

7) Measure resistance between ground and terminal No. 16 (Tan/Pink wire) on BCM 20-pin connector. If resistance is 5 ohms or greater, repair Tan/Red wire (left rear door ajar switch sense circuit) for short to ground. If resistance is less than 5 ohms, repair Tan/Pink wire short to ground.

8) Disconnect right front door ajar switch connector. Using scan tool, read door ajar switch status. If scan tool displays DOOR AJAR: CLOSED, go to next step. If scan tool does not display DOOR AJAR: CLOSED, replace right front door ajar switch.

9) Disconnect Seat Belt Control Module (SBCM) connector under center console. *See Fig. 4.* Using scan tool, read door ajar switch status. If scan tool displays DOOR AJAR: CLOSED, go to next step. If scan tool does not display DOOR AJAR: CLOSED, replace SBCM.

10) Disconnect BCM 20-pin connector. *See Fig. 2.* Using scan tool, read door ajar switch status. If scan tool does not display DOOR AJAR: CLOSED, go to next step. If scan tool displays DOOR AJAR: CLOSED, replace BCM.

11) Using external ohmmeter, measure resistance between ground and terminal No. 17 (Tan/Pink wire) on BCM 20-pin connector. If resistance is 5 ohms or greater, repair Tan/Red wire between SBCM terminal No. 3 and BCM terminal No. 6 for short to ground. If resistance is less than 5 ohms, repair Tan/Pink wire short to ground.

DOOR AJAR TEST 5

RIGHT FRONT DOOR AJAR OPEN CIRCUIT

NOTE: Perform DOOR AJAR TEST 1 before proceeding with this test. For connector terminal identification and wiring diagrams, see BODY CONTROL COMPUTER – INTRODUCTION article. Perform VERIFICATION TEST VER-1A after each repair.

CAUTION: Always turn ignition switch to OFF position prior to disconnecting any module connector.

1) Disconnect right front door ajar switch and ensure connector is clean and not damaged. Ensure right front door ajar switch ground strap is clean and not damaged. Repair or replace ground strap as necessary. If ground strap is okay, go to next step.

2) Connect a jumper wire between right front door ajar switch connector Tan/Orange wire (Breeze, Cirrus and Stratus) or Tan/Pink wire (Sebring Convertible) and ground. Using scan tool, read door ajar switch status. If scan tool displays DOOR AJAR: CLOSED, replace right front door ajar switch. If scan tool does not display DOOR AJAR: CLOSED, go to next step.

3) Disconnect jumper wire. Locate BCM 20-pin connector at junction block. *See Fig. 2.* DO NOT disconnect connector. Connect jumper wire between ground and terminal No. 17 (Tan/Orange wire on Breeze, Cirrus and Stratus or Tan/Pink wire on Sebring Convertible) on BCM 20-pin connector. Using scan tool, read door ajar switch status. If scan tool does not display DOOR AJAR: CLOSED, go to next step. If scan tool displays DOOR AJAR: CLOSED, repair open in Tan/Orange wire or Tan/Pink.

4) Disconnect BCM 20-pin connector. Inspect terminal No. 17. Repair as needed. If terminal is okay, replace BCM.

DOOR AJAR TEST 6

RIGHT REAR DOOR AJAR OPEN CIRCUIT

NOTE: Perform DOOR AJAR TEST 1 before proceeding with this test. For connector terminal identification and wiring diagrams, see BODY CONTROL COMPUTER – INTRODUCTION article. Perform VERIFICATION TEST VER-1A after each repair.

CAUTION: Always turn ignition switch to OFF position prior to disconnecting any module connector.

1) Disconnect right rear door ajar switch and ensure connector is clean and not damaged. Ensure right rear door ajar switch ground strap is

clean and not damaged. Repair or replace ground strap as necessary. If ground strap is okay, go to next step.

2) Connect a jumper wire between right rear door ajar switch connector (Tan/Pink wire) and ground. Using scan tool, read door ajar switch status. If scan tool displays DOOR AJAR: CLOSED, replace right rear door ajar switch. If scan tool does not display DOOR AJAR: CLOSED, go to next step.

3) Disconnect jumper wire. Locate BCM 20-pin connector at junction block. *See Fig. 2.* DO NOT disconnect connector. Connect jumper wire between ground and terminal No. 16 (Tan/Pink wire) on BCM 20-pin connector. Using scan tool, read door ajar switch status. If scan tool does not display DOOR AJAR: CLOSED, go to next step. If scan tool displays DOOR AJAR: CLOSED, repair open in Tan/Pink wire.

4) Disconnect BCM 20-pin connector. Inspect terminal No. 16. Repair as needed. If terminal is okay, replace BCM.

DOOR AJAR TEST 7

LEFT REAR DOOR AJAR OPEN CIRCUIT

NOTE: Perform DOOR AJAR TEST 1 before proceeding with this test. For connector terminal identification and wiring diagrams, see BODY CONTROL COMPUTER – INTRODUCTION article. Perform VERIFICATION TEST VER-1A after each repair.

CAUTION: Always turn ignition switch to OFF position prior to disconnecting any module connector.

1) Disconnect left rear door ajar switch and ensure connector is clean and not damaged. Ensure left rear door ajar switch ground strap is clean and not damaged. Repair or replace ground strap as necessary. If ground strap is okay, go to next step.

2) Connect a jumper wire between left rear door ajar switch connector (Tan/Red wire) and ground. Using scan tool, read door ajar switch status. If scan tool displays DOOR AJAR: CLOSED, replace left rear door ajar switch. If scan tool does not display DOOR AJAR: CLOSED, go to next step.

3) Disconnect jumper wire. Locate BCM 20-pin connector at junction block. *See Fig. 2.* Connect jumper wire between ground and terminal No. 6 (Tan/Red wire) on BCM 20-pin connector. Using scan tool, read door ajar switch status. If scan tool does not display DOOR AJAR: CLOSED, go to next step. If scan tool displays DOOR AJAR: CLOSED, repair open in Tan/Red wire.

4) Disconnect BCM 20-pin connector. Inspect terminal No. 16. Repair as needed. If terminal is okay, replace BCM.

EXTERIOR LIGHT TEST 1

IDENTIFYING EXTERIOR LIGHTING SYSTEM PROBLEMS

NOTE: Perform SYMPTOM ID TEST 1A before proceeding with this test. For connector terminal identification, see CONNECTOR IDEN-TIFICATION in BODY CONTROL COMPUTER – INTRODUCTION article. For wiring diagrams, see WIRING DIAGRAMS in BODY CONTROL COMPUTER – INTRODUCTION article. Perform VERIFI-CATION TEST VER-1A after each repair.

CAUTION: Always turn ignition switch to OFF position prior to disconnecting or connecting any module connector.

Exterior lighting system uses a headlight time delay function. Identify problem(s) listed in EXTERIOR LIGHT SYSTEM DIAGNOSTIC TEST DIRECTORY table and perform indicated test(s).

NOTE: Headlight time delay will only operate when ignition switch is turned off, while headlights are still on and headlight switch is turned to OFF position within 45 seconds of ignition switch being turned off. Body Control Module (BCM) will provide a 90-second time delay before turning headlights off.

EXTERIOR LIGHT SYSTEM DIAGNOSTIC TEST DIRECTORY

Problem [1]	EXTERIOR LIGHT TEST
Headlights Will Not Turn Off	2
Headlight Time Delay Does Not Function	3

[1] – If headlights do not operate from headlight switch, see HEADLIGHT SYSTEMS article.

EXTERIOR LIGHT TEST 2

HEADLIGHTS WILL NOT TURN OFF

NOTE: Perform EXTERIOR LIGHT TEST 1 before proceeding with this test. For connector terminal identification, see CONNECTOR IDENTIFICATION in BODY CONTROL COMPUTER – INTRODUC-TION article. For wiring diagrams, see WIRING DIAGRAMS in BODY CONTROL COMPUTER – INTRODUCTION article. Perform VERIFI-CATION TEST VER-1A after each repair.

CAUTION: Always turn ignition switch to OFF position prior to disconnecting or connecting any module connector.

1) Disconnect headlight delay relay located in junction block. *See Fig. 3.* If headlights go off, go to next step. If headlights do not go off, repair short to battery voltage in Violet/White wire between ignition switch and junction block.

2) Using external ohmmeter, measure resistance between ground and terminal No. 2 on headlight delay relay socket. *See Fig. 3.* If resistance is less than 5 ohms, go to next step. If resistance is 5 ohms or greater, replace headlight delay relay.

3) Turn ignition off. Disconnect BCM from junction block and ensure connector is clean and not damaged. Leave BCM disconnected. Using external ohmmeter, measure resistance between ground and terminal No. 2 on headlight delay relay. *See Fig. 3.* If resistance is 5 ohms or greater, replace BCM. If resistance is less 5 ohms, replace junction block.

CHRY
4-74

1999 ACCESSORIES & EQUIPMENT
Body Control Computer Tests
Breeze, Cirrus, Sebring Convertible & Stratus (Cont.)

EXTERIOR LIGHT TEST 3

HEADLIGHT TIME DELAY DOES NOT FUNCTION

NOTE: *Perform EXTERIOR LIGHT TEST 1 before proceeding with this test. For connector terminal identification, see CONNECTOR IDENTIFICATION in BODY CONTROL COMPUTER – INTRODUCTION article. For wiring diagrams, see WIRING DIAGRAMS in BODY CONTROL COMPUTER – INTRODUCTION article. Perform VERIFICATION TEST VER-1A after each repair.*

CAUTION: *Always turn ignition switch to OFF position prior to disconnecting or connecting any module connector.*

1) Turn ignition on. Using scan tool, actuate headlight relay. If headlights toggle on and off, go to next step. If headlights do not toggle on and off, go to step 3).
2) Stop actuation of headlight relay and turn headlight switch to ON position. Using scan tool, read low beam sense status. Turn headlight switch OFF, and then to ON position. If scan tool displays LOW BEAM SENSE: OFF and then LOW BEAM SENSE: ON, replace BCM. If scan tool display does not match headlight switch positions, replace junction block.
3) Using scan tool, stop headlight relay actuation. Replace headlight delay relay with known good relay. Using scan tool, actuate headlight relay. If headlights toggle on and off, replace relay. If headlights do not toggle on and off, go to next step.
4) Using external voltmeter, measure voltage between ground and terminal No. 1 on headlight delay relay socket. See Fig. 3. If voltage is more than 10 volts, go to next step. If voltage is 10 volts or less, replace junction block.
5) Using external voltmeter, measure voltage between ground and terminal No. 3 on headlight delay relay socket. See Fig. 3. If voltage is more than 10 volts, go to next step. If voltage is 10 volts or less, replace junction block.
6) Connect a jumper wire between terminals No. 1 and 5 on headlight delay relay socket. See Fig. 3. If headlights illuminate, replace BCM. If headlights do not illuminate, replace junction block.

INSTRUMENT CLUSTER TEST 1A

IDENTIFYING INSTRUMENT CLUSTER PROBLEMS

NOTE: *Perform SYMPTOM ID TEST 1A before proceeding with this test. For connector terminal identification, see CONNECTOR IDENTIFICATION in BODY CONTROL COMPUTER – INTRODUCTION article. For wiring diagrams, see WIRING DIAGRAMS in BODY CONTROL COMPUTER – INTRODUCTION article. Perform VERIFICATION TEST VER-1A after each repair.*

CAUTION: *Always turn ignition switch to OFF position prior to disconnecting or connecting any module connector.*

1) Turn ignition on. Using scan tool, select MIC CLUSTER. If scan tool displays BUS OPERATIONAL, go to next step. If scan tool displays any other message, see appropriate VEHICLE COMMUNICATIONS article.
2) If scan tool displays NO RESPONSE or a false KEY MUST BE IN UNLOCK POSITION, see appropriate VEHICLE COMMUNICATIONS article. If Vacuum Fluorescent (VF) display is blank or displays NO BUS, see appropriate VEHICLE COMMUNICATIONS article. If scan tool display is other than described, go to next step.
3) Using scan tool, select MIC CLUSTER and then select READ DTCs. If scan tool displays RAM FAULT, replace Mechanical Instrument Cluster (MIC). If scan tool display is other than described, go to next step.
4) Using scan tool, select MIC CLUSTER and read cluster type. If cluster type matches vehicle equipment (US or Metric), go to next step. If cluster type does not match vehicle, replace MIC.

5) Using scan tool, select BODY COMPUTER systems test. If PCM status is INACTIVE ON THE BUS, see appropriate VEHICLE COMMUNICATIONS article. If scan tool display is other than described, go to next step.
6) Identify problems(s) listed in INSTRUMENT CLUSTER DIAGNOSTIC TEST DIRECTORY table and perform indicated test(s).

INSTRUMENT CLUSTER DIAGNOSTIC TEST DIRECTORY

Problem	INSTRUMENT CLUSTER TEST
All Gauges Do Not Operate	2A
Odometer Does Not Operate	Replace Odometer
One Gauge Not Operating Properly	
Fuel Gauge	3A
Speedometer	3B
Tachometer	3C
Temperature Gauge	3D
Identifying Warning Light Problems	4A
Cluster Illumination	5A
Gauges Not Going To Zero When Key Is Turned Off	6A
Trip Reset Button	1

1 – Using scan tool, read status of trip reset button switch (open or closed), and depress trip reset button. If status of trip reset button does not change, replace Mechanic Instrument Cluster (MIC).

INSTRUMENT CLUSTER TEST 2A

ALL GAUGES DO NOT OPERATE

NOTE: *Perform INSTRUMENT CLUSTER TEST 1A before proceeding with this test. For connector terminal identification, see CONNECTOR IDENTIFICATION in BODY CONTROL COMPUTER – INTRODUCTION article. For wiring diagrams, see WIRING DIAGRAMS in BODY CONTROL COMPUTER – INTRODUCTION article. Perform VERIFICATION TEST VER-1A after each repair.*

CAUTION: *Always turn ignition switch to OFF position prior to disconnecting or connecting any module connector.*

1) Turn ignition switch to OFF (UNLOCK) position. Using scan tool, select BODY, ELECTRO/MECH CLUSTER. Select ACTUATION TEST. If gauges move from lower to upper limits, go to next step. If gauges do not move, replace Mechanical Instrument Cluster (MIC).
2) Turn ignition on with engine off. Using scan tool, select BODY, then BODY CONTROL MODULE. Select INPUT/OUTPUT and read IGNITION SWITCH RUN/START status. If scan tool displays switch CLOSED, replace Body Control Module (BCM). BCM is mounted to junction block. See Fig. 1. If scan tool does not display switch CLOSED, see appropriate VEHICLE COMMUNICATIONS article.

INSTRUMENT CLUSTER TEST 3A

FUEL GAUGE NOT OPERATING PROPERLY

NOTE: *Perform INSTRUMENT CLUSTER TEST 1A before proceeding with this test. For connector terminal identification, see CONNECTOR IDENTIFICATION in BODY CONTROL COMPUTER – INTRODUCTION article. For wiring diagrams, see WIRING DIAGRAMS in BODY CONTROL COMPUTER – INTRODUCTION article. Perform VERIFICATION TEST VER-1A after each repair.*

CAUTION: *Always turn ignition switch to OFF position prior to disconnecting or connecting any module connector.*

1) Ensure there is fuel in fuel tank before proceeding with this test. If problem is only with fuel warning light, go to INSTRUMENT CLUSTER TEST 3G. If problem is with fuel gauge accuracy, go to INSTRUMENT CLUSTER TEST 3E. If problem is that fuel gauge always shows full, go to INSTRUMENT CLUSTER TEST 3F. If problem is other than those listed, go to next step.

1999 ACCESSORIES & EQUIPMENT
Body Control Computer Tests
Breeze, Cirrus, Sebring Convertible & Stratus (Cont.)

CHRY
4-75

2) Start engine. Using scan tool, select BODY COMPUTER. Read DTCs. If scan tool displays FUEL LEVEL SENDING CIRCUIT ERROR, go to step **5)**. If scan tool does not display FUEL LEVEL SENDING CIRCUIT ERROR, go to next step.

3) Turn ignition off. Disconnect fuel pump module 8-pin connector, located behind back seat, in trunk. Ensure connector is clean and not damaged. Using external voltmeter, measure voltage between ground and terminal No. 2 (Dark Blue wire) on fuel pump module 8-pin harness connector. If voltage is 9.5 volts or less, go to next step. If voltage is more than 9.5 volts, replace fuel tank sending unit.

4) Locate Body Control Module (BCM) 20-pin connector located at junction block. *See Fig. 2.* Do not disconnect connector. Using external voltmeter, backprobe BCM 20-pin connector. Measure voltage between ground and terminal No. 15 (Dark Blue wire). If voltage is more than 10 volts, repair open in Dark Blue wire. If voltage is 10 volts or less, replace BCM.

5) Turn ignition off. Disconnect fuel pump module 8-pin connector, located behind back seat, in trunk area. Ensure connector is clean and not damaged. Connect a jumper wire between terminals No. 4 (Black/Light Green wire) and No. 2 (Dark Blue wire) on fuel pump module 8-pin harness connector. Turn ignition on. Using scan tool, read fuel level voltage. If scan tool displays one volt or greater, go to next step. If scan tool displays less than one volt, replace fuel level sensor.

6) Disconnect jumper wire. Connect a jumper wire between ground and terminal No. 2 (Dark Blue wire) on fuel pump module 8-pin connector. Using scan tool, read fuel level voltage. If scan tool displays one volt or greater, go to next step. If scan tool displays less than one volt, repair open in Black/Light Green wire.

7) Disconnect jumper wire. Locate BCM 20-pin connector. Do not disconnect connector. Connect jumper wire between ground and terminal No. 15 (Dark Blue wire) on BCM 20-pin connector. Using scan tool, read fuel level voltage. If scan tool displays one volt or greater, replace BCM. If scan tool displays less than one volt, repair open Dark Blue wire between fuel pump module 8-pin connector and BCM 20-pin connector.

INSTRUMENT CLUSTER TEST 3B

SPEEDOMETER NOT OPERATING PROPERLY

NOTE: Perform INSTRUMENT CLUSTER TEST 3A before proceeding with this test. For connector terminal identification, see CONNECTOR IDENTIFICATION in BODY CONTROL COMPUTER – INTRODUCTION article. For wiring diagrams, see WIRING DIAGRAMS in BODY CONTROL COMPUTER – INTRODUCTION article. Perform VERIFICATION TEST VER-1A after each repair.

CAUTION: Always turn ignition switch to OFF position prior to disconnecting or connecting any module connector.

1) Using scan tool, read engine DTCs. If codes related to Vehicle Speed Sensor (VSS) are displayed, see appropriate SELF-DIAGNOSTICS article in ENGINE PERFORMANCE in appropriate MITCHELL® manual. If no VSS codes are displayed, go to next step.

2) Using scan tool, actuate instrument cluster gauges. Speedometer should move to 100 MPH mark, then in steps should move to 75, 55, 20, zero MPH marks. If speedometer functions as described, replace Body Control Module (BCM). *See Fig. 2.* If speedometer does not function correctly, go to next step.

3) Remove instrument cluster and access back of gauges. Using external ohmmeter, measure resistance diagonally across speedometer terminals. If resistance is 200-220 ohms, replace instrument cluster circuit board. If resistance is not 200-220 ohms, replace speedometer gauge pack.

INSTRUMENT CLUSTER TEST 3C

TACHOMETER NOT OPERATING PROPERLY

NOTE: Perform INSTRUMENT CLUSTER TEST 3A before proceeding with this test. For connector terminal identification, see CONNECTOR IDENTIFICATION in BODY CONTROL COMPUTER – INTRODUCTION article. For wiring diagrams, see WIRING DIAGRAMS in BODY CONTROL COMPUTER – INTRODUCTION article. Perform VERIFICATION TEST VER-1A after each repair.

CAUTION: Always turn ignition switch to OFF position prior to disconnecting or connecting any module connector.

1) Using scan tool, select ENGINE, then SENSOR DISPLAYS. Select ENGINE RPM. If tachometer reading is more than 100 RPM, go to next step. If tachometer reading is 100 RPM or less, see appropriate SELF-DIAGNOSTICS article in ENGINE PERFORMANCE in appropriate MITCHELL® manual.

2) Using scan tool, actuate instrument cluster gauges. Tachometer should move to 6000 RPM mark, then in steps should move to 3000, 1000, zero RPM marks. If tachometer functions as described, replace Body Control Module (BCM). *See Fig. 2.* If tachometer does not function correctly, go to next step.

3) Remove instrument cluster and access back of gauges. Using external ohmmeter, measure resistance diagonally across tachometer terminals. If resistance is 200-220 ohms, replace instrument cluster circuit board. If resistance is not 200-220 ohms, replace tachometer gauge pack.

INSTRUMENT CLUSTER TEST 3D

TEMPERATURE GAUGE NOT OPERATING PROPERLY

NOTE: Perform INSTRUMENT CLUSTER TEST 3A before proceeding with this test. For connector terminal identification, see CONNECTOR IDENTIFICATION in BODY CONTROL COMPUTER – INTRODUCTION article. For wiring diagrams, see WIRING DIAGRAMS in BODY CONTROL COMPUTER – INTRODUCTION article. Perform VERIFICATION TEST VER-1A after each repair.

CAUTION: Always turn ignition switch to OFF position prior to disconnecting or connecting any module connector.

1) Using scan tool, read engine trouble codes. If codes related to engine coolant temperature are displayed, see appropriate SELF-DIAGNOSTICS article in ENGINE PERFORMANCE in appropriate MITCHELL® manual. If no codes are displayed, go to next step.

2) Using scan tool, actuate instrument cluster gauges. Temperature gauge should move to HOT mark, then in steps should move to 1/2, COLD marks. If temperature gauge functions as described, replace BCM. If temperature gauge does not function correctly, go to next step.

3) Remove instrument cluster and access back of gauges. Using external ohmmeter, measure resistance across temperature gauge terminals at 12 and 6 o'clock (vertical), and 3 and 9 o'clock (horizontal). If resistance is 200-220 ohms, replace instrument cluster circuit board. If resistance is not 200-220 ohms, replace temperature gauge pack.

CHRY
4-76

1999 ACCESSORIES & EQUIPMENT
Body Control Computer Tests
Breeze, Cirrus, Sebring Convertible & Stratus (Cont.)

INSTRUMENT CLUSTER TEST 3E

CHECKING FUEL GAUGE ACCURACY

NOTE: Perform INSTRUMENT CLUSTER TEST 3A before proceeding with this test. For connector terminal identification, see CONNECTOR IDENTIFICATION in BODY CONTROL COMPUTER – INTRODUCTION article. For wiring diagrams, see WIRING DIAGRAMS in BODY CONTROL COMPUTER – INTRODUCTION article. Perform VERIFICATION TEST VER-1A after each repair.

CAUTION: Always turn ignition switch to OFF position prior to disconnecting or connecting any module connector.

1) Turn ignition off. Disconnect fuel pump module 8-pin connector, located behind back seat, in trunk. Ensure connector is clean and not damaged.
2) Using external ohmmeter, measure resistance between terminals No. 2 (Dark Blue wire) and No. 4 (Black/Light Green wire) on fuel pump module (component side) 8-pin connector. If resistance matches fuel gauge reading, go to next step. If resistance does not match fuel gauge reading, replace Body Control Module (BCM). *See Fig. 2.* See FUEL LEVEL SENDING UNIT RESISTANCE table.

FUEL LEVEL SENDING UNIT RESISTANCE

Fuel Level	Float Height In. (mm)	Resistance (Ohms)
Full	5.4-5.8 (137-147)	50-90
3/4	3.8 (97)	310-370
1/2	2.6 (66)	520-580
1/4	1.4 (35)	730-790
Empty	-.14-.18 (-3.5-4.6)	1020-1080

3) Remove fuel level sending unit from fuel tank. Inspect tank unit for foreign material and sending unit for bent, sticking or binding arm. If tank and sending unit are okay, system is operating properly. If tank and/or sending unit are not okay, repair or replace as necessary.

INSTRUMENT CLUSTER TEST 3F

REPAIRING FUEL GAUGE

NOTE: Perform INSTRUMENT CLUSTER TEST 3A before proceeding with this test. For connector terminal identification, see CONNECTOR IDENTIFICATION in BODY CONTROL COMPUTER – INTRODUCTION article. For wiring diagrams, see WIRING DIAGRAMS in BODY CONTROL COMPUTER – INTRODUCTION article. Perform VERIFICATION TEST VER-1A after each repair.

CAUTION: Always turn ignition switch to OFF position prior to disconnecting or connecting any module connector.

1) Turn ignition off. Disconnect fuel pump module 8-pin connector, located behind back seat, in trunk. Ensure connector is clean and not damaged. Ensure fuel tank has some fuel in it. Turn ignition on with engine off. If fuel gauge does not display empty, go to next step. If fuel gauge displays empty, go to step **3)**.
2) Turn ignition off. Disconnect Body Control Module (BCM) 20-pin connector located at junction block and ensure connector is clean and not damaged. *See Fig. 2.* Using external ohmmeter, measure resistance between ground and terminal No. 15 (Dark Blue wire) on BCM 20-pin connector. If resistance is less than 5 ohms, repair short to ground in Dark Blue wire. If resistance is 5 ohms or greater, replace BCM.
3) Remove fuel level sending unit from fuel tank. Inspect tank unit for foreign material and sending unit for bent, sticking or binding arm. If tank and sending unit are okay, system is operating properly. If tank and/or sending unit are not okay, repair or replace as necessary.

INSTRUMENT CLUSTER TEST 3G

REPAIRING LOW FUEL LIGHT

NOTE: Perform INSTRUMENT CLUSTER TEST 3A before proceeding with this test. For connector terminal identification, see CONNECTOR IDENTIFICATION in BODY CONTROL COMPUTER – INTRODUCTION article. For wiring diagrams, see WIRING DIAGRAMS in BODY CONTROL COMPUTER – INTRODUCTION article. Perform VERIFICATION TEST VER-1A after each repair.

CAUTION: Always turn ignition switch to OFF position prior to disconnecting or connecting any module connector.

1) Ensure fuel tank is more than 1/8 full, or low fuel light may illuminate. If low fuel light does illuminate, replace Body Control Module (BCM). *See Fig. 2.* If low fuel light does not illuminate, go to next step.
2) Using scan tool, actuate instrument cluster bulbs. If low fuel light illuminates, replace BCM. If low fuel light does not illuminate, remove instrument cluster and inspect low fuel light bulb. Replace as needed. If bulb is okay, replace instrument cluster circuit board.

INSTRUMENT CLUSTER TEST 4A

IDENTIFYING WARNING LIGHT PROBLEMS

NOTE: Perform INSTRUMENT CLUSTER TEST 1A before proceeding with this test. For connector terminal identification, see CONNECTOR IDENTIFICATION in BODY CONTROL COMPUTER – INTRODUCTION article. For wiring diagrams, see WIRING DIAGRAMS in BODY CONTROL COMPUTER – INTRODUCTION article. Perform VERIFICATION TEST VER-1A after each repair.

CAUTION: Always turn ignition switch to OFF position prior to disconnecting or connecting any module connector.

Ensure parking brake is completely released and place ignition switch in UNLOCK position. Using scan tool, select ELECTRO/MECH CLUSTER, then actuate ALL LAMPS, ODO/TRIP, and PRNDL LEDs. Identify problem(s) and perform indicated test(s) in WARNING LIGHT SYSTEM DIAGNOSTIC TEST DIRECTORY table.

NOTE: Brake warning light, fog light, oil warning light and turn signal indicator lights cannot be actuated using scan tool.

WARNING LIGHT SYSTEM DIAGNOSTIC TEST DIRECTORY

Problem	INSTRUMENT CLUSTER TEST
Vacuum Fluorescent Display	7A
Coolant Temperature Indicator Light	8A
Low Fuel Warning Light	9A
Oil Warning Light	10A
Seat Belt Warning Light	11A
Brake Warning Light	12A
High Beam Indicator Light	13A
Turn Signal Indicator Lights	14A
Alternator Indicator Light (Battery Symbol)	15A
Cruise Control Indicator Light	16A
Check Engine Light	17A
Fog Light Indicator	18A
Deck Ajar Message	19A
Low Wash Message	20A
Air Bag Warning Light	[1]
Amber ABS Warning Light	[2]
Traction Control Indicator	[2]

[1] – See MITCHELL® AIR BAG SERVICE & REPAIR MANUAL, DOMESTIC & IMPORTED MODELS.
[2] – See appropriate ANTI-LOCK article in BRAKES in appropriate MITCHELL® manual.

1999 ACCESSORIES & EQUIPMENT
Body Control Computer Tests
Breeze, Cirrus, Sebring Convertible & Stratus (Cont.)

CHRY
4-77

INSTRUMENT CLUSTER TEST 5A

CLUSTER ILLUMINATION

NOTE: *Perform INSTRUMENT CLUSTER TEST 1A before proceeding with this test. For connector terminal identification, see CONNECTOR IDENTIFICATION in BODY CONTROL COMPUTER – INTRODUCTION article. For wiring diagrams, see WIRING DIAGRAMS in BODY CONTROL COMPUTER – INTRODUCTION article. Perform VERIFICATION TEST VER-1 after each repair.*

CAUTION: *Always turn ignition switch to OFF position prior to disconnecting or connecting any module connector.*

1) Turn ignition on. Using scan tool, read Body Control Module (BCM) fault messages. If scan tool does not display PANEL LAMP PWM OUTPUT FAILURE, go to next step. If scan tool displays PANEL LAMP PWM OUTPUT FAILURE, go to INSTRUMENT CLUSTER TEST 5B.

2) Turn parking lights on. If parking lights illuminate, go to next step. If parking lights do not illuminate, repair parking lights as necessary.

3) Using scan tool, read parking light status. If scan tool displays PARK LAMPS: ON, go to next step. If scan tool does not display PARK LAMPS: ON, go to INSTRUMENT CLUSTER TEST 5F.

4) Using scan tool, read panel light sensor voltage. If scan tool displays zero volts, go to next step. If scan tool displays more than zero volts, go to step 6).

5) While using scan tool to read panel light sensor voltage, rotate dimmer control switch between high and low. If voltage changes, go to next step. If voltage does not change, go to INSTRUMENT CLUSTER TEST 5G.

6) Ensure parking lights are on and dimmer switch is at midway position. Locate instrument panel 10-pin connector at Body Control Module (BCM). See Fig. 2. Using scan tool in voltmeter mode, measure voltage at instrument panel 10-pin connector terminals No. 3 (Orange/Yellow wire), No. 4 (Orange/Brown wire), No. 9 (Orange wire) and No. 10 (Orange/Gray wire). As each terminal is backprobed, rotate dimmer switch from low to high. If voltage increases from zero volts to 12 volts at all terminals, go to next step. If voltage does not increase at any terminal, replace BCM.

7) Disconnect instrument cluster Blue 13-pin connector and ensure connector is clean and not damaged. Using scan tool in voltmeter mode, measure voltage at terminal No. 10 (Orange/Yellow wire) on instrument cluster Blue 13-pin connector. If voltage is more than 5 volts, replace instrument cluster. If voltage is 5 volts or less, repair open in Orange/Yellow wire between instrument cluster and BCM.

INSTRUMENT CLUSTER TEST 5B

PANEL LIGHTS POWER CIRCUIT

NOTE: *Perform INSTRUMENT CLUSTER TEST 5 before proceeding with this test. For connector terminal identification, see CONNECTOR IDENTIFICATION in BODY CONTROL COMPUTER – INTRODUCTION article. For wiring diagrams, see WIRING DIAGRAMS in BODY CONTROL COMPUTER – INTRODUCTION article. Perform VERIFICATION TEST VER-1A after each repair.*

CAUTION: *Always turn ignition switch to OFF position prior to disconnecting or connecting any module connector.*

1) Using scan tool, erase all BCM Diagnostic Trouble Codes (DTCs). Start engine, turn parking lights on and allow engine to run for at least 2 minutes. Turn parking lights off. Turn engine off. Turn ignition on. Using scan tool, read BCM DTCs. If PANEL LAMP PWM OUTPUT FAILURE trouble code is not present, system is operating properly. If PANEL LAMP PWM OUTPUT FAILURE trouble code is present, go to next step.

2) Turn ignition off. Disconnect instrument panel 10-pin connector at Body Control Module (BCM). See Fig. 2. Ensure connector is clean and not damaged. Using scan tool in ohmmeter mode, measure resistance at terminals No. 3 (Orange/Yellow wire), No. 4 (Orange/Brown wire), No. 9 (Orange wire) and No. 10 (Orange/Gray wire) instrument panel 10-pin connector. If resistance is less than 5 ohms at any connector terminal, go to next step. If resistance is 5 ohms or greater at any connector terminal, replace BCM.

3) If resistance is less than 5 ohms at terminal No. 4, go to INSTRUMENT CLUSTER TEST 5C. If resistance is less than 5 ohms at terminal No. 3, go to INSTRUMENT CLUSTER TEST 5D. If resistance is less than 5 ohms at terminal No. 9, go to INSTRUMENT CLUSTER TEST 5E. If resistance is less than 5 ohms on connector terminal No. 10, go to next step.

4) Remove shifter illumination light (automatic transaxle equipped only). If light is not okay, replace light. If light is okay, go to next step.

5) Using scan tool in ohmmeter mode, measure resistance at terminal No. 10 (Orange/Gray wire) on instrument panel 10-pin connector. If resistance is less than 5 ohms, repair short to ground in Orange/Gray wire. If resistance is 5 ohms or greater, there is an intermittent short. Check for a pinched harness or a wire exposed to ground.

INSTRUMENT CLUSTER TEST 5C

PANEL LIGHTS POWER CIRCUIT

NOTE: *Perform INSTRUMENT CLUSTER TEST 5A before proceeding with this test. For connector terminal identification, see CONNECTOR IDENTIFICATION in BODY CONTROL COMPUTER – INTRODUCTION article. For wiring diagrams, see WIRING DIAGRAMS in BODY CONTROL COMPUTER – INTRODUCTION article. Perform VERIFICATION TEST VER-1A after each repair.*

CAUTION: *Always turn ignition switch to OFF position prior to disconnecting or connecting any module connector.*

Disconnect radio connectors and ensure connectors are clean and not damaged. Using external ohmmeter, measure resistance between ground and terminal No. 4 (Orange/Brown wire) on instrument panel 10-pin connector at Body Control Module (BCM). If resistance is less than 5 ohms, repair short to ground in Orange/Brown wire. If resistance is more than 5 ohms, replace radio.

INSTRUMENT CLUSTER TEST 5D

PANEL LIGHTS POWER CIRCUIT

NOTE: *Perform INSTRUMENT CLUSTER TEST 5A before proceeding with this test. For connector terminal identification, see CONNECTOR IDENTIFICATION in BODY CONTROL COMPUTER – INTRODUCTION article. For wiring diagrams, see WIRING DIAGRAMS in BODY CONTROL COMPUTER – INTRODUCTION article. Perform VERIFICATION TEST VER-1A after each repair.*

CAUTION: *Always turn ignition switch to OFF position prior to disconnecting or connecting any module connector.*

Disconnect instrument cluster connectors. Ensure connectors are clean and not damaged. Using external ohmmeter, measure resistance between ground and terminal No. 3 (Orange/Yellow wire) on instrument panel 10-pin connector at Body Control Module (BCM). If resistance is less than 5 ohms, repair short to ground in Orange/Yellow wire. If resistance is 5 ohms or greater, inspect instrument cluster lights and printed circuit board. If lights and printed circuit board are okay, replace Mechanical Instrument Cluster (MIC). If lights and printed circuit board are not okay, repair or replace as necessary.

CHRY
4-78

1999 ACCESSORIES & EQUIPMENT
Body Control Computer Tests
Breeze, Cirrus, Sebring Convertible & Stratus (Cont.)

INSTRUMENT CLUSTER TEST 5E

PANEL LIGHTS POWER CIRCUIT

NOTE: Perform INSTRUMENT CLUSTER TEST 5A before proceeding with this test. For connector terminal identification, see CONNECTOR IDENTIFICATION in BODY CONTROL COMPUTER – INTRODUCTION article. For wiring diagrams, see WIRING DIAGRAMS in BODY CONTROL COMPUTER – INTRODUCTION article. Perform VERIFICATION TEST VER-1A after each repair.

CAUTION: Always turn ignition switch to OFF position prior to disconnecting or connecting any module connector.

Disconnect Heater Ventilation Air Conditioning (HVAC) control panel. Ensure connectors are clean and not damaged. Using scan tool in ohmmeter mode, measure resistance at terminal No. 9 (Orange wire) on instrument panel 10-pin connector at Body Control Module (BCM). If resistance is 5 ohms or greater, replace HVAC control panel. If resistance is less than 5 ohms, inspect ashtray light. If ashtray light is okay, repair short to ground Orange wire. If ashtray light is not okay, replace light.

INSTRUMENT CLUSTER TEST 5F

PARKING LIGHT SWITCH OUTPUT CIRCUIT TO BCM

NOTE: Perform INSTRUMENT CLUSTER TEST 5A before proceeding with this test. For connector terminal identification, see CONNECTOR IDENTIFICATION in BODY CONTROL COMPUTER – INTRODUCTION article. For wiring diagrams, see WIRING DIAGRAMS in BODY CONTROL COMPUTER – INTRODUCTION article. Perform VERIFICATION TEST VER-1A after each repair.

CAUTION: Always turn ignition switch to OFF position prior to disconnecting or connecting any module connector.

Turn ignition and parking lights off. Remove Body Control Module (BCM) from junction block. *See Figs. 5 and 3.* Turn parking lights on. Using external voltmeter, measure voltage between ground and terminal No. 8 on junction block 12-pin internal connector. If voltage is more than 10 volts, replace BCM. If voltage is 10 volts or less, repair Black/Yellow wire between parking light switch and junction block.

INSTRUMENT CLUSTER TEST 5G

DIMMER SWITCH SIGNAL CIRCUIT

NOTE: Perform INSTRUMENT CLUSTER TEST 5A before proceeding with this test. For connector terminal identification, see CONNECTOR IDENTIFICATION in BODY CONTROL COMPUTER – INTRODUCTION article. For wiring diagrams, see WIRING DIAGRAMS in BODY CONTROL COMPUTER – INTRODUCTION article. Perform VERIFICATION TEST VER-1A after each repair.

CAUTION: Always turn ignition switch to OFF position prior to disconnecting or connecting any module connector.

1) Turn parking lights on. While using scan tool to read panel light sensor voltage, rotate dimmer control switch between high and low. If voltage does not change and remains low, go to next step. If voltage does not change and remains high, go to step 4).

2) Locate instrument panel 22-pin connector at Body Control Module (BCM). Do not disconnect connector. *See Fig. 2.* Using scan tool in voltmeter mode, backprobe connector. Measure voltage at terminal No. 18 (Red wire) on instrument panel 22-pin connector. While checking voltage, rotate dimmer switch. If voltage changes from zero to more than 10 volts, replace BCM. If voltage does not change, go to next step.

3) Gain access to left side multifunction switch 10-pin connector, under steering wheel. *See Figs. 5 and 6.* Using external voltmeter, backprobe connector. Measure voltage at terminal No. 6 (Red wire) on multifunction switch 10-pin connector. Rotate dimmer switch from high to low. If voltage changes from zero to more than 10 volts, repair open in Red wire. If voltage does not change, replace multifunction switch.

4) Disconnect left side multifunction switch 10-pin connector and ensure connector is clean and not damaged. Using scan tool, read panel light sensor voltage. If voltage is more than 8 volts, go to next step. If voltage is 8 volts or less, replace multifunction switch.

5) Turn ignition off. Disconnect instrument panel 22-pin connector at BCM. *See Fig. 2.* Turn ignition on with engine off. Using external voltmeter, measure voltage at terminal No. 18 (Red wire) on instrument panel 22-pin connector. If voltage is more than 0.3 volt, repair short to voltage on Red wire. If voltage is 0.3 volt or less, replace BCM.

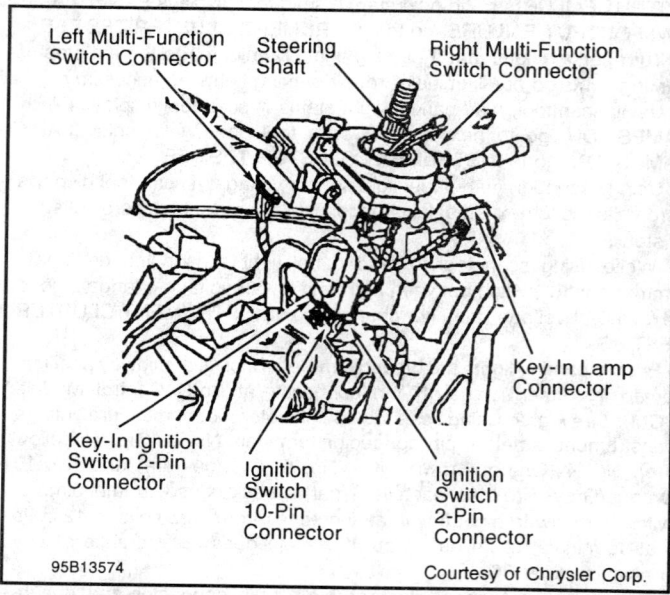

Left Multi-Function Switch Connector

Steering Shaft

Right Multi-Function Switch Connector

Key-In Lamp Connector

Key-In Ignition Switch 2-Pin Connector

Ignition Switch 10-Pin Connector

Ignition Switch 2-Pin Connector

95B13574

Courtesy of Chrysler Corp.

Fig. 5: Locating Steering Column Switches

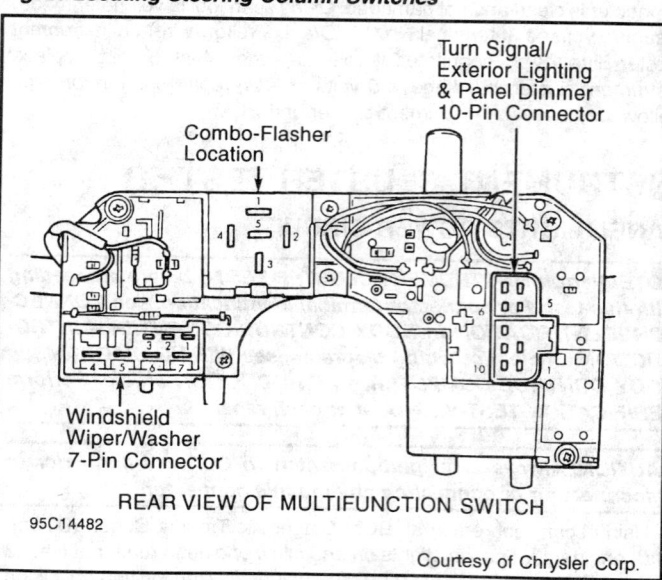

Turn Signal/ Exterior Lighting & Panel Dimmer 10-Pin Connector

Combo-Flasher Location

Windshield Wiper/Washer 7-Pin Connector

REAR VIEW OF MULTIFUNCTION SWITCH

95C14482

Courtesy of Chrysler Corp.

Fig. 6: Locating Multifunction Connectors

INSTRUMENT CLUSTER TEST 6A

GAUGES NOT GOING TO ZERO WHEN KEY IS TURNED OFF

NOTE: Perform INSTRUMENT CLUSTER TEST 1A before proceeding with this test. For connector terminal identification, see CONNECTOR IDENTIFICATION in BODY CONTROL COMPUTER – INTRODUCTION article. For wiring diagrams, see WIRING DIAGRAMS in BODY CONTROL COMPUTER – INTRODUCTION article. Perform VERIFICATION TEST VER-1A after each repair.

CAUTION: Always turn ignition switch to OFF position prior to disconnecting or connecting any module connector.

1) Turn ignition off. Remove and inspect junction block fuse No. 7. If fuse is blown, go to INSTRUMENT CLUSTER TEST 6B. If fuse is okay, go to next step.

2) Disconnect instrument cluster Red connector and ensure connector is clean and not damaged. *See Fig. 6.* Using external voltmeter, measure voltage at terminal No. 5 (Pink/Red wire) on instrument cluster Red 13-pin connector. If voltage is 10 volts or less, repair open Pink/Red wire. If voltage is more than 10 volts, replace instrument cluster.

INSTRUMENT CLUSTER TEST 6B

GAUGES NOT GOING TO ZERO WHEN KEY IS TURNED OFF

NOTE: Perform INSTRUMENT CLUSTER TEST 6A before proceeding with this test. For connector terminal identification, see CONNECTOR IDENTIFICATION in BODY CONTROL COMPUTER – INTRODUCTION article. For wiring diagrams, see WIRING DIAGRAMS in BODY CONTROL COMPUTER – INTRODUCTION article. Perform VERIFICATION TEST VER-1A after each repair.

CAUTION: Always turn ignition switch to OFF position prior to disconnecting or connecting any module connector.

Using external ohmmeter, measure resistance at component side terminal (Pink/Red wire) on fuse No. 7 socket in junction block. If resistance is less than 5 ohms, repair short to ground in Pink/Red wire. If resistance is 5 ohms or greater, replace fuse.

INSTRUMENT CLUSTER TEST 7A

VACUUM FLUORESCENT (VF) DISPLAY

NOTE: Perform INSTRUMENT CLUSTER TEST 4A before proceeding with this test. For connector terminal identification, see CONNECTOR IDENTIFICATION in BODY CONTROL COMPUTER – INTRODUCTION article. For wiring diagrams, see WIRING DIAGRAMS in BODY CONTROL COMPUTER – INTRODUCTION article. Perform VERIFICATION TEST VER-1A after each repair.

CAUTION: Always turn ignition switch to OFF position prior to disconnecting or connecting any module connector.

1) Turn ignition switch to UNLOCK position. Using scan tool, select PRND3L LED'S under ELECTRO/MECH actuators. If all of PRND3L characters and segments illuminate, stop actuation and go to next step. If all PRND3L characters and segments do not illuminate, replace vacuum fluorescent display module.

2) Using scan tool, select ODO/TRIP under ELECTRO/MECH actuators vacuum fluorescent display. If all odometer/trip characters and segments illuminate, stop actuation and go to next step. If all odometer/trip characters and segments do not illuminate, replace vacuum fluorescent display module.

3) Turn ignition on with engine off. Using scan tool, select TRANS TYPE from vehicle status monitor under BCM monitor displays. If transaxle status is MANUAL, go to step 5). If transaxle status is not MANUAL, go to next step.

4) Using scan tool, read BCM fault messages. If ETAX PRNDL MESSAGE is present, go to appropriate VEHICLE COMMUNICATIONS article. If ETAX PRNDL MESSAGE is not present, odometer vacuum fluorescent display is operating properly.

5) If transaxle status is MANUAL, PCM is for a manual transaxle. If vehicle is equipped with a manual transaxle, vacuum fluorescent display is operating properly. If vehicle is equipped with an automatic transaxle, install a PCM for an automatic transaxle.

INSTRUMENT CLUSTER TEST 8A

COOLANT TEMPERATURE LIGHT

NOTE: Perform INSTRUMENT CLUSTER TEST 4A before proceeding with this test. For connector terminal identification, see CONNECTOR IDENTIFICATION in BODY CONTROL COMPUTER – INTRODUCTION article. For wiring diagrams, see WIRING DIAGRAMS in BODY CONTROL COMPUTER – INTRODUCTION article. Perform VERIFICATION TEST VER-1A after each repair.

CAUTION: Always turn ignition switch to OFF position prior to disconnecting or connecting any module connector.

1) Turn ignition switch from OFF position to ON/RUN position. If coolant temperature light illuminates, go to next step. If coolant temperature light does not illuminate, go to step 3).

2) Using scan tool, select LIMP-IN MONITOR under body monitors and read ECT SENSOR LIMP-IN status. If scan tool displays ECT SENSOR LIMP-IN: YES, see appropriate SELF-DIAGNOSTICS article in ENGINE PERFORMANCE in appropriate MITCHELL® manual. If scan tool does not display YES and coolant temperature light does not remain illuminated, light is operating properly. If coolant temperature light remains illuminated, repair or replace Mechanical Instrument Cluster (MIC).

3) Turn ignition switch to UNLOCK position. Using scan tool, actuate ALL LAMPS. If coolant temperature light illuminates, light is operating properly. If coolant temperature light does not illuminate, go to next step.

4) Turn ignition off. Disconnect instrument cluster and ensure connectors are clean and not damaged. Remove and inspect coolant temperature bulb. *See Fig. 7.* If bulb is okay, go to next step. If bulb is defective, replace bulb.

5) Inspect instrument cluster and ensure bulb socket is clean and not damaged. If instrument cluster is okay, replace Body Control Module (BCM). If instrument cluster is defective, repair or replace as necessary.

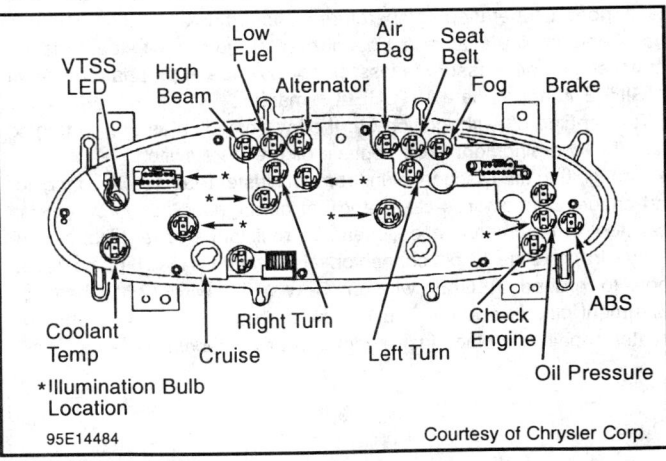

Fig. 7: Locating Instrument Cluster Light Bulbs

1999 ACCESSORIES & EQUIPMENT
Body Control Computer Tests
Breeze, Cirrus, Sebring Convertible & Stratus (Cont.)

INSTRUMENT CLUSTER TEST 9A

LOW FUEL WARNING LIGHT

NOTE: *Perform INSTRUMENT CLUSTER TEST 4A before proceeding with this test. For connector terminal identification, see CONNECTOR IDENTIFICATION in BODY CONTROL COMPUTER – INTRODUCTION article. For wiring diagrams, see WIRING DIAGRAMS in BODY CONTROL COMPUTER – INTRODUCTION article. Perform VERIFICATION TEST VER-1A after each repair.*

CAUTION: *Always turn ignition switch to OFF position prior to disconnecting or connecting any module connector.*

1) If low fuel light is illuminated when it should be off, replace Body Control Module (BCM). If low fuel light appears to operate correctly, go to next step.

2) Turn ignition switch to UNLOCK position. Using scan tool, actuate ALL LAMPS. If low fuel light illuminates and then goes off, replace BCM. If low fuel light does not illuminate, go to next step.

3) Disconnect instrument cluster and ensure connectors are clean and not damaged. Remove low fuel warning bulb and replace if defective. *See Fig. 7.* Inspect instrument cluster and ensure bulb socket is clean and not damaged. Repair or replace instrument cluster as necessary.

INSTRUMENT CLUSTER TEST 10A

OIL WARNING LIGHT

NOTE: *Perform INSTRUMENT CLUSTER TEST 4A before proceeding with this test. For connector terminal identification, see CONNECTOR IDENTIFICATION in BODY CONTROL COMPUTER – INTRODUCTION article. For wiring diagrams, see WIRING DIAGRAMS in BODY CONTROL COMPUTER – INTRODUCTION article. Perform VERIFICATION TEST VER-1A after each repair.*

CAUTION: *Always turn ignition switch to OFF position prior to disconnecting or connecting any module connector.*

1) Turn ignition off and ensure engine oil level is within specification. If engine oil level is within specification, go to next step.

2) Turn ignition on with engine off. If oil warning light (oil can indicator) did not illuminate, go to INSTRUMENT CLUSTER TEST 10B. If oil warning light did illuminate, turn ignition off and go to next step.

3) Locate oil pressure switch at right rear of 2.0L and 2.4L engines, or front of 2.5L engine and remove switch. Connect an external oil pressure gauge in place of oil pressure switch. Start engine and allow engine to reach normal operating temperature. If external oil pressure gauge shows engine oil pressure is 4 psi or greater, go to next step. If gauge shows engine oil pressure is less than 4 psi, see appropriate article in ENGINES in appropriate MITCHELL® manual.

4) Turn engine off with ignition on. If oil warning light is on, go to next step. If oil warning light is off, replace oil pressure switch.

5) Turn ignition off. Disconnect instrument cluster Blue 13-pin connector and ensure connector is clean and not damaged. *See Fig. 7.* Using scan tool in ohmmeter mode, measure resistance at terminal No. 12 (Gray wire) on Blue 13-pin connector. If resistance is less 5 ohms, repair short to ground in Gray wire or Gray/White wire (2.5L) between instrument cluster and oil pressure switch. If resistance is 5 ohms or greater, repair or replace instrument cluster as necessary.

INSTRUMENT CLUSTER TEST 10B

OIL WARNING LIGHT

NOTE: *Perform INSTRUMENT CLUSTER TEST 10A before proceeding with this test. For connector terminal identification, see CONNECTOR IDENTIFICATION in BODY CONTROL COMPUTER – INTRODUCTION article. For wiring diagrams, see WIRING DIAGRAMS in BODY CONTROL COMPUTER – INTRODUCTION article. Perform VERIFICATION TEST VER-1A after each repair.*

CAUTION: *Always turn ignition switch to OFF position prior to disconnecting or connecting any module connector.*

1) Locate oil pressure switch at right rear of 2.0L and 2.4L engines, or front of 2.5L engine and disconnect switch 2-pin connector. Connect a jumper wire between oil pressure switch 2-pin connector terminal No. 2 (Gray or Gray/White wire) and ground. If oil warning light (oil can indicator) does not illuminate, leave jumper wire connected and go to next step. If oil warning light illuminates, replace oil pressure switch.

2) Disconnect instrument cluster Blue 13-pin connector and ensure connector is clean and not damaged. Turn ignition on with engine off. Using external voltmeter, measure voltage between ground and terminal No. 5 (Light Green/Black wire) on instrument cluster Blue 13-pin connector. If voltage is more than 10 volts, go to next step. If voltage is 10 volts or less, repair open in Light Green/Black wire.

3) Turn ignition off. Ensure jumper wire is still connected between ground and terminal No. 2 (Gray wire) on oil pressure switch 2-pin connector. Using external ohmmeter, measure resistance between ground and terminal No. 12 (Gray wire) on instrument cluster Blue 13-pin connector. If resistance is less than 5 ohms, go to next step. If resistance is 5 ohms or more, repair open in Gray wire between instrument cluster and oil pressure switch.

4) Remove oil warning bulb (oil can indicator) from instrument cluster. *See Fig. 7.* If bulb is defective, replace light bulb. If bulb is okay, repair or replace instrument cluster as necessary.

INSTRUMENT CLUSTER TEST 11A

SEAT BELT WARNING LIGHT

NOTE: *Perform INSTRUMENT CLUSTER TEST 4A before proceeding with this test. For connector terminal identification, see CONNECTOR IDENTIFICATION in BODY CONTROL COMPUTER – INTRODUCTION article. For wiring diagrams, see WIRING DIAGRAMS in BODY CONTROL COMPUTER – INTRODUCTION article. Perform VERIFICATION TEST VER-1A after each repair.*

CAUTION: *Always turn ignition switch to OFF position prior to disconnecting or connecting any module connector.*

1) Turn ignition switch from OFF position to ON (RUN) position. If seat belt warning light illuminates and then goes off, system is operating properly. If seat belt warning light does not illuminate, go to next step.

2) Turn ignition switch to UNLOCK position. Using scan tool, actuate ALL LAMPS. If seat belt warning light does not illuminate, go to next step. If seat belt warning light illuminates, replace Body Control Module (BCM) on Breeze, Cirrus or Stratus models. On Sebring Convertible, go to step **4)**.

3) Turn ignition off. Disconnect instrument cluster and ensure connectors are clean and not damaged. Remove and inspect seat belt warning light bulb. *See Fig. 7.* If bulb is defective, replace bulb. If bulb is okay, repair or replace instrument cluster as necessary.

4) Disconnect seat belt control module (SBCM) connector under center console. *See Fig. 4.* Connect jumper wire between ground and terminal No. 11 (Light Green wire) on SBCM harness connector. If seat belt warning light goes out, see appropriate wiring diagram in PASSIVE RESTRAINT SYSTEMS article for futher diagnosis. If seat belt warning light is still illuminated, go to next step.

1999 ACCESSORIES & EQUIPMENT
Body Control Computer Tests
Breeze, Cirrus, Sebring Convertible & Stratus (Cont.)

CHRY
4-81

5) Disconnect instrument panel 22-pin connector at Body Control Module (BCM). *See Fig. 2.* Using external ohmmeter, measure resistance between ground and terminal No. 9 (Light Green wire) on 22-pin harness connector. If resistance is less than 5 ohms, go to next step. If resistance is 5 ohms or greater, repair open Light Green wire.

6) Disconnect jumper wire. Using external ohmmeter, measure resistance between ground and terminal No. 9 (Light Green wire) on 22-pin harness connector. If resistance is less than 5 ohms, repair Light Green wire for short to ground. If resistance is 5 ohms or greater, replace Body Control Module (BCM).

INSTRUMENT CLUSTER TEST 12A

BRAKE WARNING LIGHT

NOTE: Perform INSTRUMENT CLUSTER TEST 4A before proceeding with this test. For connector terminal identification, see CONNECTOR IDENTIFICATION in BODY CONTROL COMPUTER – INTRODUCTION article. For wiring diagrams, see WIRING DIAGRAMS in BODY CONTROL COMPUTER – INTRODUCTION article. Perform VERIFICATION TEST VER-1A after each repair.

CAUTION: Always turn ignition switch to OFF position prior to disconnecting or connecting any module connector.

1) If vehicle is equipped with anti-lock brakes, see appropriate ANTI-LOCK article in BRAKES in appropriate MITCHELL® manual. If vehicle is not equipped with anti-lock brakes, go to next step.

2) Ensure parking brake lever is fully released and operates smoothly and does not bind. If parking brake lever does not operate properly, repair as necessary. If parking brake operates properly, go to next step.

3) Turn ignition on with engine off. If brake warning light is not on, go to next step. If brake warning light is on, go to INSTRUMENT CLUSTER TEST 12B.

4) Crank engine and monitor brake warning light. If brake warning light illuminates as engine is cranking, go to next step. If brake warning light does not illuminate while engine is cranking, go to INSTRUMENT CLUSTER TEST 12C.

5) Apply parking brake lever. If brake warning light does not illuminate, go to INSTRUMENT CLUSTER TEST 12D. If brake warning light illuminates, release parking brake lever and go to INSTRUMENT CLUSTER TEST 12E.

INSTRUMENT CLUSTER TEST 12B

BRAKE WARNING LIGHT

NOTE: Perform INSTRUMENT CLUSTER TEST 12A before proceeding with this test. For connector terminal identification, see CONNECTOR IDENTIFICATION in BODY CONTROL COMPUTER – INTRODUCTION article. For wiring diagrams, see WIRING DIAGRAMS in BODY CONTROL COMPUTER – INTRODUCTION article. Perform VERIFICATION TEST VER-1A after each repair.

CAUTION: Always turn ignition switch to OFF position prior to disconnecting or connecting any module connector.

1) Inspect brake fluid reservoir level. If brake fluid level is low, fill to proper level and perform VERIFICATION TEST VER-1A. If brake fluid reservoir level is okay, go to next step.

2) Disconnect brake fluid level switch 2-pin connector and ensure connector is clean and not damaged. If brake warning light goes out, replace brake fluid level switch. If brake warning light does not go out, go to next step.

3) Disconnect parking brake switch connector. If brake warning light goes out, replace parking brake switch. If brake warning light does not go out, go to next step.

4) Turn ignition off. Disconnect instrument cluster and ensure connectors are clean and not damaged. *See Fig. 7.* Turn ignition on. Using

scan tool in ohmmeter mode, measure resistance at terminal No. 6 (Gray/Dark Blue wire) on instrument cluster Blue 13-pin connector. If resistance is less than 5 ohms, go to next step. If resistance is 5 ohms or greater, repair or replace instrument cluster as necessary.

5) Disconnect ignition switch 10-pin connector and ensure connector is clean and not damaged. *See Fig. 5.* Using scan tool in ohmmeter mode, measure resistance at terminal No. 6 (Gray/Dark Blue wire) on instrument cluster Blue 13-pin connector. If resistance is less than 5 ohms, repair short to ground in Gray/Dark Blue wire. If resistance is 5 ohms or greater, replace ignition switch.

INSTRUMENT CLUSTER TEST 12C

BRAKE WARNING LIGHT

NOTE: Perform INSTRUMENT CLUSTER TEST 12A before proceeding with this test. For connector terminal identification, see CONNECTOR IDENTIFICATION in BODY CONTROL COMPUTER – INTRODUCTION article. For wiring diagrams, see WIRING DIAGRAMS in BODY CONTROL COMPUTER – INTRODUCTION article. Perform VERIFICATION TEST VER-1A after each repair.

CAUTION: Always turn ignition switch to OFF position prior to disconnecting or connecting any module connector.

1) Turn ignition off. Disconnect ignition switch 10-pin connector. *See Fig. 5.* Using external ohmmeter, measure resistance between ground and terminal No. 5 (Black wire) on ignition switch 10-pin connector. If resistance is less than 5 ohms, go to next step. If resistance is 5 ohms or greater, repair open in Black wire.

2) Reconnect ignition switch 10-pin connector. Turn ignition on with engine off. Using a jumper wire, backprobe ignition switch 10-pin connector between terminal No. 2 (Gray/Dark Blue wire) and ground. If brake warning light does not illuminate, go to next step. If brake warning light illuminates, replace ignition switch.

3) Disconnect instrument cluster and ensure connectors are clean and not damaged. DO NOT disconnect jumper wire from ignition switch 10-pin connector. Using external ohmmeter, measure resistance between ground and terminal No. 6 (Gray/Dark Blue wire) on instrument cluster Blue 13-pin connector. If resistance is less than 5 ohms, go to next step. If resistance is 5 ohms or greater, repair open in Gray/Dark Blue wire between instrument cluster and ignition switch.

4) Remove and inspect Red brake warning light bulb. *See Fig. 7.* If bulb is defective, replace bulb. If bulb is okay, replace instrument cluster.

INSTRUMENT CLUSTER TEST 12D

BRAKE WARNING LIGHT

NOTE: Perform INSTRUMENT CLUSTER TEST 12A before proceeding with this test. For connector terminal identification, see CONNECTOR IDENTIFICATION in BODY CONTROL COMPUTER – INTRODUCTION article. For wiring diagrams, see WIRING DIAGRAMS in BODY CONTROL COMPUTER – INTRODUCTION article. Perform VERIFICATION TEST VER-1A after each repair.

Disconnect parking brake switch connector and ensure connector is clean and not damaged. Connect a jumper wire between parking brake switch connector and ground. If brake warning light illuminates, replace parking brake switch. If brake warning light does not illuminate, repair open Gray wire between parking brake switch and instrument cluster.

1999 ACCESSORIES & EQUIPMENT
Body Control Computer Tests
Breeze, Cirrus, Sebring Convertible & Stratus (Cont.)

INSTRUMENT CLUSTER TEST 12E

BRAKE WARNING LIGHT

NOTE: *Perform INSTRUMENT CLUSTER TEST 12A before proceeding with this test. For connector terminal identification, see CONNECTOR IDENTIFICATION in BODY CONTROL COMPUTER – INTRODUCTION article. For wiring diagrams, see WIRING DIAGRAMS in BODY CONTROL COMPUTER – INTRODUCTION article. Perform VERIFICATION TEST VER-1A after each repair.*

CAUTION: *Always turn ignition switch to OFF position prior to disconnecting or connecting any module connector.*

1) Turn ignition off. Disconnect brake fluid level switch 2-pin connector at master cylinder and ensure connector is clean and not damaged. Connect a jumper wire between brake fluid level switch connector terminals. Turn ignition on with engine off. If brake warning light does not illuminate, disconnect jumper wire and go to next step. If brake warning light illuminates, replace brake fluid level switch.
2) Connect a jumper wire between ground and terminal No. 2 (Gray/Dark Blue wire) on brake fluid level switch connector. If brake warning light comes on, repair open in Black wire. If parking brake light does not illuminate and testing was because light did not illuminate when brake fluid reservoir was empty, replace low brake fluid switch. If parking brake light does not illuminate and brake fluid level was okay, system is operating properly.

INSTRUMENT CLUSTER TEST 13A

HIGH BEAM INDICATOR LIGHT

NOTE: *Perform INSTRUMENT CLUSTER TEST 4A before proceeding with this test. For connector terminal identification, see CONNECTOR IDENTIFICATION in BODY CONTROL COMPUTER – INTRODUCTION article. For wiring diagrams, see WIRING DIAGRAMS in BODY CONTROL COMPUTER – INTRODUCTION article. Perform VERIFICATION TEST VER-1A after each repair.*

CAUTION: *Always turn ignition switch to OFF position prior to disconnecting or connecting any module connector.*

1) Turn ignition on with engine off. Turn headlights high beam on. If headlights high beam illuminate, go to next step. If headlights high beam do not illuminate, see HEADLIGHT SYSTEMS article.
2) Using scan tool, read HI BEAM SENSE. If high beam sense is ON, go to next step. If high beam sense is not ON, go to step 5).
3) Turn ignition switch to UNLOCK position. Using scan tool, actuate ALL LAMPS. If high beam indicator light illuminates, system is operating properly. If high beam indicator light does not illuminate, go to next step.
4) Disconnect instrument cluster and ensure connectors are clean and not damaged. *See Fig. 7.* Remove and inspect high beam indicator bulb. If bulb is defective, replace bulb. If bulb is okay, repair or replace instrument cluster.
5) Turn headlights and ignition off. Disconnect BCM from junction block. Turn headlights high beam on. Turn ignition on with engine off. Using scan tool in voltmeter mode, measure voltage at terminal No. 1 on junction block 12-pin internal connector. *See Fig. 3.* If voltage is 10 volts or less, replace junction block. If voltage is more than 10 volts, replace BCM.

INSTRUMENT CLUSTER TEST 14A

TURN SIGNAL INDICATOR LIGHTS

NOTE: *Perform INSTRUMENT CLUSTER TEST 4A before proceeding with this test. For connector terminal identification, see CONNECTOR IDENTIFICATION in BODY CONTROL COMPUTER – INTRODUCTION article. For wiring diagrams, see WIRING DIAGRAMS in BODY CONTROL COMPUTER – INTRODUCTION article. Perform VERIFICATION TEST VER-1A after each repair.*

CAUTION: *Always turn ignition switch to OFF position prior to disconnecting or connecting any module connector.*

1) Ensure parking lights operate properly. If parking lights operate correctly, go to next step. If parking lights do not operate correctly, see HEADLIGHT SYSTEMS article.
2) Disconnect instrument cluster. Ensure connectors are clean and not damaged. *See Fig. 7.* Remove and inspect both turn signal light bulbs. If bulbs are okay, go to next step. If bulbs are defective, replace bulbs.
3) Using external voltmeter, measure voltage between ground and terminal No. 1 (Tan/Brown wire) on instrument cluster Red 13-pin connector. Turn ignition on. Turn right turn signal on. If voltage increases to more than 10 volts, go to next step. If voltage does not increase to more than 10 volts, repair open in Tan/Brown wire.
4) Using external voltmeter, measure voltage between ground and terminal No. 2 (Light Green/Tan wire) on instrument cluster Blue 13-pin connector. Turn ignition on. Turn left turn signal on. If voltage increases to more than 10 volts, repair or replace instrument cluster. If voltage does not increase to more than 10 volts, repair open in Light Green/Tan wire.

INSTRUMENT CLUSTER TEST 15A

ALTERNATOR LIGHT (BATTERY SYMBOL)

NOTE: *Perform INSTRUMENT CLUSTER TEST 4A before proceeding with this test. For connector terminal identification, see CONNECTOR IDENTIFICATION in BODY CONTROL COMPUTER – INTRODUCTION article. For wiring diagrams, see WIRING DIAGRAMS in BODY CONTROL COMPUTER – INTRODUCTION article. Perform VERIFICATION TEST VER-1A after each repair.*

CAUTION: *Always turn ignition switch to OFF position prior to disconnecting or connecting any module connector.*

1) Start engine. Using scan tool, read CHARGING LIMP-IN status. If status is YES, see appropriate SELF-DIAGNOSTICS article in ENGINE PERFORMANCE in appropriate MITCHELL® manual. If status is not YES, go to next step.
2) Turn ignition off. Turn ignition switch from OFF position to ON/RUN position and observe alternator light (battery symbol). If alternator light does not illuminate, go to next step. If alternator light illuminates, system is operating properly.
3) Turn ignition switch to UNLOCK position. Using scan tool, actuate ALL LAMPS. If alternator light does not illuminate, go to next step. If alternator light illuminates, replace BCM.
4) Turn ignition off. Disconnect instrument cluster. Ensure connectors are clean and not damaged. *See Fig. 7.* Remove and inspect alternator light bulb. Ensure bulb socket is clean and not damaged. If bulb is defective, replace bulb. If bulb is okay, repair or replace instrument cluster as necessary.

Body Control Computer Tests
Breeze, Cirrus, Sebring Convertible & Stratus (Cont.)

INSTRUMENT CLUSTER TEST 16A

CRUISE CONTROL LIGHT

NOTE: Perform INSTRUMENT CLUSTER TEST 4A before proceeding with this test. For connector terminal identification, see CONNECTOR IDENTIFICATION in BODY CONTROL COMPUTER – INTRODUCTION article. For wiring diagrams, see WIRING DIAGRAMS in BODY CONTROL COMPUTER – INTRODUCTION article. Perform VERIFICATION TEST VER-1A after each repair.

CAUTION: Always turn ignition switch to OFF position prior to disconnecting or connecting any module connector.

1) If cruise control light is the only problem with cruise control system, go to next step. If there are more problems than just cruise control light, see appropriate CRUISE CONTROL SYSTEMS article.
2) Turn ignition switch from OFF position to ON/RUN position. If cruise control light does not illuminate and then go off, go to next step. If cruise control light illuminates and then goes off, system is operating properly.
3) Turn ignition switch to UNLOCK position. Using scan tool, actuate ALL LAMPS. If cruise control light does not illuminate, go to next step. If cruise control light illuminates and then goes off, replace BCM.
4) Disconnect instrument cluster. Ensure connectors are clean and not damaged. *See Fig. 7.* Remove and inspect cruise control light bulb. Ensure bulb socket is clean and not damaged. If bulb is defective, replace bulb. If bulb is okay, repair or replace instrument cluster as necessary.

INSTRUMENT CLUSTER TEST 17A

CHECK ENGINE LIGHT

NOTE: Perform INSTRUMENT CLUSTER TEST 4A before proceeding with this test. For connector terminal identification, see CONNECTOR IDENTIFICATION in BODY CONTROL COMPUTER – INTRODUCTION article. For wiring diagrams, see WIRING DIAGRAMS in BODY CONTROL COMPUTER – INTRODUCTION article. Perform VERIFICATION TEST VER-1A after each repair.

CAUTION: Always turn ignition switch to OFF position prior to disconnecting or connecting any module connector.

1) Start engine. Using scan tool, select vehicle status monitor under body monitor. Read CHECK ENGINE LAMP STATUS. If check engine lamp status is not ON, go to next step. If check engine lamp status is ON, see appropriate SELF-DIAGNOSTICS article in ENGINE PERFORMANCE in appropriate MITCHELL® manual.
2) Turn ignition switch from OFF position to ON/RUN position. If check engine light does not illuminate, go to next step. If check engine light illuminates and then goes off, system is operating properly.
3) Turn ignition switch to UNLOCK position. Using scan tool, actuate ALL LAMPS. If check engine light does not illuminate, go to next step. If check engine light illuminates, replace BCM.
4) Turn ignition off. Disconnect instrument cluster. Ensure connectors are clean and not damaged. *See Fig. 7.* Remove and inspect check engine light bulb. Ensure bulb socket is clean and not damaged. If bulb is defective, replace bulb. If bulb is okay, repair or replace instrument cluster as necessary.

INSTRUMENT CLUSTER TEST 18A

FOG LIGHT INDICATOR

NOTE: Perform INSTRUMENT CLUSTER TEST 4A before proceeding with this test. For connector terminal identification, see CONNECTOR IDENTIFICATION in BODY CONTROL COMPUTER – INTRODUCTION article. For wiring diagrams, see WIRING DIAGRAMS in BODY CONTROL COMPUTER – INTRODUCTION article. Perform VERIFICATION TEST VER-1A after each repair.

CAUTION: Always turn ignition switch to OFF position prior to disconnecting or connecting any module connector.

1) Turn headlight on low beam. Ensure headlight low beam is operating properly. Turn fog lights on. If headlights and fog lights are not operating properly, repair lights as necessary. If headlights and fog lights are operating properly, go to next step.
2) Disconnect instrument cluster. Ensure connectors are clean and not damaged. *See Fig. 7.* Remove and inspect fog light indicator light bulb. If bulb is okay, go to next step. If bulb is defective, replace fog light indicator light bulb.
3) Using scan tool in voltmeter mode, measure voltage at terminal No. 1 (Light Blue/Orange wire) on instrument cluster Blue 13-pin connector. Turn ignition and fog lights on. If voltage is 10 volts or less, repair Light Blue/Orange wire. If voltage is more than 10 volts, repair or replace instrument cluster.

INSTRUMENT CLUSTER TEST 19A

DECK AJAR MESSAGE

NOTE: Perform INSTRUMENT CLUSTER TEST 4A before proceeding with this test. For connector terminal identification, see CONNECTOR IDENTIFICATION in BODY CONTROL COMPUTER – INTRODUCTION article. For wiring diagrams, see WIRING DIAGRAMS in BODY CONTROL COMPUTER – INTRODUCTION article. Perform VERIFICATION TEST VER-1A after each repair.

CAUTION: Always turn ignition switch to OFF position prior to disconnecting or connecting any module connector.

1) Turn ignition on with engine off. Ensure both doors are closed. Monitor odometer on instrument cluster. If DECK message is displayed, go to step **6)**. If deck message is not displayed, go to next step.
2) Open trunk. If DECK message is displayed, system is currently operating correctly. If deck message is not displayed, go to next step.
3) Disconnect wire from trunk latch. Connect jumper wire between latch ajar connector and ground. Observe odometer display. If display changed from MILES to DECK, replace trunk latch assembly. If display did not change, go to next step.
4) With jumper wire connected, disconnect BCM 14-pin connector. *See Fig. 2.* Using external ohmmeter, measure resistance between ground and terminal No. 1 (Tan/Black wire) on 14-pin harness connector. If resistance is 5 ohms or greater, repair open Tan/Black wire. If resistance is less than 5 ohms, go to next step.
5) Using scan tool, select PRND3L LED'S under ELECTRO/MECH actuators. If all of PRND3L characters and segments illuminate, stop actuation and replace MIC circuit board. If all PRND3L characters and segments do not illuminate, replace vacuum fluorescent display module.
6) Ensure trunk lid is correctly adjusted. Repair as needed. Open trunk. Disconnect wire from trunk latch. If DECK message is no longer displayed, replace latch assembly. If DECK message is displayed, go to next step.
7) Disconnect BCM 14-pin connector. *See Fig. 2.* Using external ohmmeter, measure resistance between ground and terminal No. 1 (Tan/Black wire) on 14-pin harness connector. If resistance is 100 ohms or greater, replace Body Control Module (BCM). If resistance is less than 100 ohms, repair Tan/Black wire for short to ground.

CHRY
4-84

1999 ACCESSORIES & EQUIPMENT
Body Control Computer Tests
Breeze, Cirrus, Sebring Convertible & Stratus (Cont.)

INSTRUMENT CLUSTER TEST 20A

LO WASH MESSAGE

NOTE: Perform INSTRUMENT CLUSTER TEST 4A before proceeding with this test. For connector terminal identification, see CONNECTOR IDENTIFICATION in BODY CONTROL COMPUTER – INTRODUCTION article. For wiring diagrams, see WIRING DIAGRAMS in BODY CONTROL COMPUTER – INTRODUCTION article. Perform VERIFICATION TEST VER-1A after each repair.

CAUTION: Always turn ignition switch to OFF position prior to disconnecting or connecting any module connector.

1) Disconnect washer level sensor connector. Connect jumper wire between connector terminals. Turn ignition on. Observe odometer display. If display changed from MILES to LO WASH, replace level sensor inside washer reservoir. If display did not change, go to next step.

2) Remove jumper wire. Connect jumper wire between ground and terminal No. 2 (Black/Tan wire) on washer level sensor connector. Observe odometer display. If display changed from MILES to LO WASH, repair open Black wire to wash level sensor. If display did not change, go to next step.

3) With jumper wire connected, remove instrument cluster. Disconnect instrument cluster Red connector. Using external ohmmeter, measure resistance between ground and terminal No. 8 (Black/Tan wire) on Red connector. If resistance is less than 5 ohms, repair open Black/Tan wire. If resistance is 5 ohms or greater, go to next step.

4) Disconnect jumper wire. Connect instrument cluster connectors. Using scan tool, select PRND3L LED'S under ELECTRO/MECH actuators. If all of PRND3L characters and segments illuminate, stop actuation and replace MIC circuit board. If all PRND3L characters and segments do not illuminate, replace vacuum fluorescent display module.

INTERIOR LIGHT TEST 1

IDENTIFYING INTERIOR LIGHTING SYSTEM PROBLEMS

NOTE: Perform SYMPTOM ID TEST 1A before proceeding with this test. For connector terminal identification, see CONNECTOR IDENTIFICATION in BODY CONTROL COMPUTER – INTRODUCTION article. For wiring diagrams, see WIRING DIAGRAMS in BODY CONTROL COMPUTER – INTRODUCTION article. Perform VERIFICATION TEST VER-1A after each repair.

CAUTION: Always turn ignition switch to OFF position prior to disconnecting or connecting any module connector.

Interior lighting system consists of courtesy lights, illuminated entry, and key-in light. Identify problem(s) listed in INTERIOR LIGHT SYSTEM DIAGNOSTIC TEST DIRECTORY table and perform indicated test(s).

INTERIOR LIGHT SYSTEM DIAGNOSTIC TEST DIRECTORY

Problem	INTERIOR LIGHT TEST
Courtesy Light Inoperative With Any Door	2
Courtesy Light On At All Times	3
Courtesy Light Inoperative With Dome Light Switch	4
Illuminated Entry Inoperative	5

	DOOR AJAR TEST
Courtesy Light Inoperative With LF Door	3
Courtesy Light Inoperative With RF Door	5
Courtesy Light Inoperative With RR Door	6
Courtesy Light Inoperative With LR Door	7

INTERIOR LIGHT TEST 2

COURTESY LIGHT INOPERATIVE WITH ANY DOOR

NOTE: Perform INTERIOR LIGHT TEST 1 before proceeding with this test. For connector terminal identification, see CONNECTOR IDENTIFICATION in BODY CONTROL COMPUTER – INTRODUCTION article. For wiring diagrams, see WIRING DIAGRAMS in BODY CONTROL COMPUTER – INTRODUCTION article. Perform VERIFICATION TEST VER-1A after each repair.

CAUTION: Always turn ignition switch to OFF position prior to disconnecting or connecting any module connector.

1) If vehicle is Sebring Convertible, go to step 8). If vehicle is Breeze, Cirrus and Stratus, ensure dome light switch is in the middle position before proceeding. Using scan tool, actuate courtesy light. If courtesy light illuminates, go to step 6). If courtesy light does not illuminate, go to next step.

2) Stop courtesy light actuation. Locate junction block 6-pin connector below horn relay. Do not disconnect connector. See Fig. 3. Using external voltmeter, measure voltage between ground and terminal No. 6 (Pink wire) on junction block 6-pin connector. If voltage is more than 10 volts, go to next step. If voltage is 10 volts or less, replace junction block.

3) Using external voltmeter, measure voltage between ground and terminal No. 3 (Yellow wire) on junction block 6-pin connector. If voltage is more than 10 volts, go to step 7). If voltage is 10 volts or less, go to next step.

4) Disconnect dome light 3-pin connector and ensure connector is clean and not damaged. Inspect dome light bulb. Replace as needed. If dome light bulb is okay, go to next step.

5) Using external voltmeter, measure voltage between ground and terminal No. 2 (Pink wire) on dome light 3-pin connector. If voltage is 10 volts or less, repair open in Pink wire. If voltage is more than 10 volts, repair open in Yellow wire (terminal No. 3).

6) Stop courtesy light actuation. Open left front door. Using scan tool, read left front door ajar switch status. If scan tool displays LF DOOR AJAR: CLOSED, replace BCM. If scan tool does not display LF DOOR AJAR: CLOSED, go to DOOR AJAR TEST 3.

7) Disconnect probe from junction block 6-pin connector. Turn ignition off. Disconnect BCM from junction block and ensure connector is clean and not damaged. Using external voltmeter, measure voltage between ground and terminal No. 9 on junction block BCM connector. If voltage is more than 10 volts, replace BCM. If voltage is 10 volts or less, replace junction block.

8) Using scan tool, actuate courtesy lights. If courtesy lights illuminate, go to step 14). If courtesy lights do not illuminate, go to next step.

9) Stop actuation. Remove courtesy light relay harness connector. Relay is located above brake pedal. Using voltmeter, measure voltage between ground and terminal No. 4 (Pink wire) on courtesy light relay harness connector. If voltage is more than 10 volts, go to next step. If voltage is 10 volts or less, repair open Pink wire between relay and junction block.

10) Using voltmeter, measure voltage between ground and terminal No. 8 (Yellow wire) on courtesy light relay harness connector. If voltage is more than 9 volts, go to next step. If voltage is 9 volts or less, repair open Yellow wire.

11) Using external ohmmeter, measure resistance between ground and terminal No. 2 (Black wire) on courtesy light relay harness connector. If resistance is less than 10 ohms, go to next step. If resistance is 10 ohms or greater, repair open Black wire.

12) Connect test light between terminals No. 4 and 6 on courtesy light relay harness connector. Using scan tool, actuate courtesy lights. If test light illuminates, replace courtesy light relay. If test light does not illuminate, go to next step.

13) Connect courtesy light relay. Using external voltmeter, backprobe junction block 6-pin connector. See Fig. 3. Measure voltage between ground and terminal No. 1 (Brown/Light Green wire). If voltage is 9 volts

1999 ACCESSORIES & EQUIPMENT
Body Control Computer Tests
Breeze, Cirrus, Sebring Convertible & Stratus (Cont.)

CHRY
4-85

or less, repair open Brown/Light Green wire. If voltage is greater than 9 volts, replace Body Control Module (BCM). BCM is mounted to junction block. *See Fig. 1.*

14) Stop courtesy light actuation. Open left front door. Using scan tool, read left front door ajar switch status. If scan tool displays LFDOOR AJAR: CLOSED, replace Body Control Module (BCM). BCM is mounted to junction block. *See Fig. 1.* If scan tool does not display LFDOOR AJAR: CLOSED, go to DOOR AJAR TEST 3.

INTERIOR LIGHT TEST 3
COURTESY LIGHT ON AT ALL TIMES

NOTE: Perform INTERIOR LIGHT TEST 1 before proceeding with this test. For connector terminal identification, see CONNECTOR IDENTIFICATION in BODY CONTROL COMPUTER – INTRODUCTION article. For wiring diagrams, see WIRING DIAGRAMS in BODY CONTROL COMPUTER – INTRODUCTION article. Perform VERIFICATION TEST VER-1A after each repair.

CAUTION: Always turn ignition switch to OFF position prior to disconnecting or connecting any module connector.

1) Ensure dome light switch is in the middle position and all doors are aligned correctly before proceeding. Close all doors. Using scan tool, read left front door ajar switch status. If scan tool does not display LF DOOR AJAR: CLOSED, go to next step. If scan tool displays, LF DOOR AJAR: CLOSED, go to DOOR AJAR TEST 2.

2) Using scan tool, read door ajar switch status. If scan tool does not display DOOR AJAR: CLOSED, go to next step. If scan tool displays DOOR AJAR: CLOSED, go to DOOR AJAR TEST 4.

3) If vehicle is Sebring Convertible, go to step **5)**. If vehicle is Breeze, Cirrus and Stratus, locate junction block 6-pin connector below horn relay. *See Fig. 3.* Disconnect junction block 6-pin connector and ensure connector is clean and not damaged. Using external ohmmeter, measure resistance between ground and terminal No. 1 (Yellow wire) on 6-pin connector. If resistance is 10 ohms or greater, go to next step. If resistance is less than 10 ohms, repair short to ground in Yellow wire.

4) Turn ignition off. Disconnect Body Control Module (BCM) from junction block and ensure connector is clean and not damaged. Reconnect junction block 6-pin connector. If dome light illuminates, replace junction block. If dome light does not illuminate, replace BCM.

5) Disconnect courtesy light relay located above brake pedal. If courtesy lights are not illuminated, go to next step. If courtesy lights remain illuminated, repair courtesy light driver circuit (Yellow wire) for short to ground.

6) Disconnect junction block 6-pin connector. *See Fig. 3.* Ensure connector is clean and not damaged. Using external ohmmeter, measure resistance between ground and terminal No. 1 (Yellow wire) on 6-pin connector. If resistance is 500 ohms or greater, replace courtesy light relay. If resistance is less than 500 ohms, repair short to ground in Brown/Light Green wire between junction block and courtesy light relay.

INTERIOR LIGHT TEST 4
COURTESY LIGHT INOPERATIVE WITH DOME LIGHT SWITCH

NOTE: Perform INTERIOR LIGHT TEST 1 before proceeding with this test. For connector terminal identification, see CONNECTOR IDENTIFICATION in BODY CONTROL COMPUTER – INTRODUCTION article. For wiring diagrams, see WIRING DIAGRAMS in BODY CONTROL COMPUTER – INTRODUCTION article. Perform VERIFICATION TEST VER-1A after each repair.

CAUTION: Always turn ignition switch to OFF position prior to disconnecting or connecting any module connector.

1) Ensure dome light switch is in the middle position before proceeding. Locate junction block 6-pin connector below horn relay. *See Fig. 3.* Backprobing junction block 6-pin connector, connect jumper wire between terminal No. 4 (Black wire) and ground. If dome light does not illuminate, leave jumper wire connected and go to next step. If dome light illuminates, replace junction block.

2) Disconnect dome light 3-pin connector and ensure connector is clean and not damaged. Using external ohmmeter, measure resistance of dome light 3-pin connector terminal No. 1 (Black wire). If resistance is less than 20 ohms, replace dome light assembly. If resistance is 20 ohms or greater, repair open Black wire.

INTERIOR LIGHT TEST 5
ILLUMINATED ENTRY INOPERATIVE

NOTE: Perform INTERIOR LIGHT TEST 1 before proceeding with this test. For connector terminal identification, see CONNECTOR IDENTIFICATION in BODY CONTROL COMPUTER – INTRODUCTION article. For wiring diagrams, see WIRING DIAGRAMS in BODY CONTROL COMPUTER – INTRODUCTION article. Perform VERIFICATION TEST VER-1A after each repair.

CAUTION: Always turn ignition switch to OFF position prior to disconnecting or connecting any module connector.

NOTE: Illuminated entry will only operate when activated by Remote Keyless Entry (RKE) transmitter.

Ensure dome light switch is in the middle position before proceeding (if applicable). Using scan tool, actuate courtesy light. If dome light does not illuminate, go to INTERIOR LIGHT TEST 2. If dome light illuminates, stop actuation. If RKE is not operating properly, go to POWER DOOR LOCK TEST 8. If RKE is operating properly, replace Body Control Module (BCM). BCM is mounted to junction block. *See Fig. 1.*

POWER DOOR LOCK TEST 1
IDENTIFYING POWER DOOR LOCK PROBLEMS

NOTE: Perform SYMPTOM ID TEST 1A before proceeding with this test. For connector terminal identification and wiring diagrams, see BODY CONTROL COMPUTER – INTRODUCTION article. Perform VERIFICATION TEST VER-1A after each repair.

CAUTION: Always turn ignition switch to OFF position prior to disconnecting or connecting any module connector.

1) Lower both front windows. Close all doors and turn ignition off. Lock and unlock door from all front door switches, including key lock cylinders if vehicle is equipped with Vehicle Theft Security System (VTSS). If door locks operate properly, go to next step. If any door(s) fail to lock or unlock properly, go to appropriate test. See POWER DOOR LOCK SYSTEM DIAGNOSTIC TEST DIRECTORY table.

CHRY
4-86

1999 ACCESSORIES & EQUIPMENT
Body Control Computer Tests
Breeze, Cirrus, Sebring Convertible & Stratus (Cont.)

2) Turn ignition off and leave key in ignition switch. Open left front door. Using either switch, lock doors. If doors did not lock, go to next step. If doors lock (with key in ignition switch and left front door open), go to POWER DOOR LOCK TEST 6.

3) Close and unlock all doors. Drive vehicle at a speed greater than 15 MPH. If doors do not lock, go to POWER DOOR LOCK TEST 7. If doors lock, system is functioning properly.

POWER DOOR LOCK SYSTEM DIAGNOSTIC TEST DIRECTORY

Problem	POWER DOOR LOCK TEST
All Doors Fail To Lock & Unlock From Any Switch	2
All Doors Fail To Lock & Unlock From One Switch	3
One Door Fails To Lock & Unlock From Any Switch	4
Doors Fail To Lock From Any Switch	5
Doors Fail To Lock From One Switch	1
Doors Fail To Unlock From Any Switch	2
Doors Fail To Unlock From One Switch	1
Inoperative Door Lock Inhibit Circuit	6
Automatic (While Moving) Door Locks	7
Remote Keyless Entry (RKE)	8

[1] – Replace defective switch.
[2] – Replace defective Body Control Module (BCM).

POWER DOOR LOCK TEST 2

ALL DOORS FAIL TO LOCK & UNLOCK FROM ANY SWITCH

NOTE: Perform POWER DOOR LOCK TEST 1 before proceeding with this test. For connector terminal identification and wiring diagrams, see BODY CONTROL COMPUTER – INTRODUCTION article. Perform VERIFICATION TEST VER-1A after each repair.

CAUTION: Always turn ignition switch to OFF position prior to disconnecting or connecting any module connector.

NOTE: Door lock driver terminals No. 12 and 13 on BCM 20-pin connector do not apply to Sebring Convertible.

1) Ensure windows are down, key is removed from ignition and doors are unlocked. Using scan tool, actuate door locks. If door locks operate, go to next step. If door locks did not operate, go to step **7)**.

2) Using scan tool, read door lock switch voltage. If voltage is 0.5 volt or less, go to next step. If voltage is more than 0.5 volt, repair short to battery voltage in circuit between left or right door lock switch and Body Control Module (BCM).

3) Hold left door lock switch in lock position. Using scan tool, read door lock switch voltage. If voltage is more than 10 volts, replace BCM. If voltage is 10 volts or less, go to next step.

4) Disconnect left front door lock switch White 4-pin connector and ensure connector is clean and not damaged. Using external voltmeter, measure voltage on switch connector terminal No. 1 (Pink wire). If voltage is more than 10 volts, go to next step. If voltage is 10 volts or less, repair open in Pink wire.

5) Disconnect BCM 20-pin connector located at junction block and ensure connector is clean and not damaged. *See Figs. 1 and 3.* Using an external ohmmeter, measure resistance between terminal No. 8 (White/Dark Green wire) on BCM 20-pin connector and terminal No. 4 (White/Dark Green wire) on left door lock switch White 4-pin connector. If resistance is less than 5 ohms, go to next step. If resistance is 5 ohms or greater, repair open in White/Dark Green wire.

6) Reconnect left front door lock switch White 4-pin connector. Using external voltmeter, measure voltage between ground and terminal No. 8 (White/Dark Green wire) on BCM 20-pin connector. Depress left front door lock switch to LOCK position and measure voltage. If voltage is 10 volts or less, replace both door lock switches. If voltage is more than 10 volts, replace BCM.

7) Using scan tool, read door lock switch voltage. If voltage is 0.5 volt or less, go to next step. If voltage is more than 0.5 volt, repair short to battery voltage in White/Dark Green wire (terminal No. 8) or White/Light Green wire (terminal No. 18) at BCM 20-pin connector.

8) Remove and inspect fuse No. 9 (15-amp), located in junction block. *See Fig. 3.* If fuse is okay, reinstall fuse and go to next step. If fuse is open, go to step **12)**.

9) Using external voltmeter, measure voltage on battery voltage side (Red/White wire) of fuse No. 9. If voltage is more than 10 volts, go to next step. If voltage is 10 volts or less, repair open Red/White wire between junction block and Power Distribution Center (PDC).

10) Disconnect and remove BCM from junction block. Ensure 12-pin internal connector is clean and not damaged. Using scan tool in voltmeter mode, measure voltage at terminals No. 2 and No. 12 on BCM 12-pin internal connector. *See Fig. 3.* If voltage is more than 10 volts, go to next step. If voltage is 10 volts or less, replace junction block.

11) Using external ohmmeter, measure resistance between ground and terminal No. 10 on BCM 12-pin internal connector. If resistance is 5 ohms or more, repair open in Black (ground) wire. If resistance is less than 5 ohms, replace BCM.

12) Turn ignition off. Using external ohmmeter, measure resistance between ground and fused battery voltage terminal (internal circuit) on fuse No. 9. If resistance is less than 5 ohms, go to next step. If resistance is 5 ohms or greater, replace fuse No. 9 and press door lock switch to LOCK position. If fuse blows, go to step **15)**. If fuse does not blow, press door lock switch to UNLOCK position. If fuse blows, go to step **17)**. If fuse did not blow, system is operating properly.

13) Remove BCM and ensure connectors are clean and no terminals are pushed out. Repair as necessary and replace fuse No. 9. If connectors are okay, go to next step.

NOTE: Door lock and unlock driver terminals No. 2, 3, 12 and 13 on BCM 20-pin connector do not apply to Sebring Convertible.

14) Using external voltmeter, measure voltage between ground and each door unlock and lock driver (No. 1-4 and 10-13) terminals on BCM 20-pin harness connector. If voltage at any terminal is greater than .5 volts, repair driver suspect circuit(s) for short to voltage. Replace BCM and fuse No. 9. If voltage at all terminals is .5 volts or less, replace BCM and fuse No. 9.

15) Disconnect BCM 20-pin connector located at junction block and ensure connector is clean and not damaged. *See Fig. 2.* Using scan tool in ohmmeter mode, measure resistance at terminals No. 10 (Orange/Black wire), No. 11 (Orange/White wire), No. 12 (Orange/Tan wire) and No. 13 (Orange/Brown wire) on BCM 20-pin connector.

16) If resistance is less than 5 ohms, repair shorted door lock driver circuit, replace fuse No. 9 and BCM (relay in BCM will be damaged). If resistance 5 ohms or greater, replace BCM and replace fuse No. 9.

17) Disconnect BCM 20-pin connector located at junction block and ensure connector is clean and not damaged. *See Fig. 2.* Using external ohmmeter, measure resistance between ground and terminals No. 1 (Pink/Light Blue wire), No. 2 (Pink/Dark Blue wire), No. 3 (Pink/Black wire) and No. 4 (Dark Blue/White wire) on BCM 20-pin connector.

18) If resistance is less than 5 ohms, repair shorted door unlock driver circuit, replace fuse No. 9 in junction block and replace BCM (relay in BCM will be damaged). If resistance is 5 ohms or greater on any of tested circuits, replace BCM and fuse No. 9.

1999 ACCESSORIES & EQUIPMENT
Body Control Computer Tests
Breeze, Cirrus, Sebring Convertible & Stratus (Cont.)

CHRY
4-87

POWER DOOR LOCK TEST 3

ALL DOORS FAIL TO LOCK & UNLOCK FROM ONE SWITCH

NOTE: Perform POWER DOOR LOCK TEST 1 before proceeding with this test. For connector terminal identification, see CONNECTOR IDENTIFICATION in BODY CONTROL COMPUTER – INTRODUCTION article. For wiring diagrams, see WIRING DIAGRAMS in BODY CONTROL COMPUTER – INTRODUCTION article. Perform VERIFICATION TEST VER-1A after each repair.

CAUTION: Always turn ignition switch to OFF position prior to disconnecting or connecting any module connector.

1) If vehicle is not equipped with Vehicle Theft Security System (VTSS), go to next step. If vehicle is equipped with VTSS and problem is with either front door lock cylinder switch, go to VTSS TEST 11 (left door) or VTSS TEST 12 (right door).

2) Using scan tool, read door lock switch voltage while holding suspect door lock switch in LOCK position. If voltage is 9 volts or less, go to next step. If voltage is more than 9 volts, replace BCM.

3) Disconnect BCM 20-pin connector located at junction block and ensure connector is clean and not damaged. *See Fig. 2.* Using scan tool in voltmeter mode, measure voltage at either terminal No. 8 (White/Dark Green wire) for left front door or terminal No. 18 (White/Light Green wire) for right front door on BCM 20-pin connector. Hold suspect door lock switch in LOCK position and measure voltage. If voltage is 9 volts or less, go to next step. If voltage is more than 9 volts, replace BCM.

4) Disconnect suspect door lock switch connector and ensure connector is clean and not damaged. Using scan tool in voltmeter mode, measure voltage at terminal No. 1 (Pink wire) on suspect door switch connector. If voltage is more than 10 volts, go to next step. If voltage is 10 volts or less, repair open in Pink wire circuit.

5) Using an external ohmmeter, measure resistance of White/Dark Green wire between terminal No. 4 on left door switch connector and terminal No. 8 on BCM 20-pin connector. If resistance is more than 5 ohms, repair open in left door lock switch circuit. If resistance is less than 5 ohms, replace left door lock switch.

6) Using an external ohmmeter, measure resistance of White/Light Green wire between terminal No. 4 on right door switch connector and terminal No. 18 on BCM 20-pin connector. If resistance is more than 5 ohms, repair open in right door lock switch circuit. If resistance is less than 5 ohms, replace right door lock switch.

POWER DOOR LOCK TEST 4

ONE DOOR FAILS TO LOCK & UNLOCK FROM ANY SWITCH

NOTE: Perform POWER DOOR LOCK TEST 1 before proceeding with this test. For connector terminal identification, see CONNECTOR IDENTIFICATION in BODY CONTROL COMPUTER – INTRODUCTION article. For wiring diagrams, see WIRING DIAGRAMS in BODY CONTROL COMPUTER – INTRODUCTION article. Perform VERIFICATION TEST VER-1A after each repair.

CAUTION: Always turn ignition switch to OFF position prior to disconnecting or connecting any module connector.

1) Remove suspect door trim panel and inspect door lock motor-to-door latch linkage. If linkage is okay, go to next step. If linkage is not okay, repair and/or replace as needed.

2) Disconnect suspect door lock motor connector and ensure connector is clean and not damaged. Connect a test light between ground and terminal No. 2 (Orange/Black wire) on door lock motor harness connector. Turn ignition switch to ON position with engine off. Using scan tool,

actuate door locks while observing test light. If test light illuminates when door locks are actuated, go to next step. If test light does not illuminate, go to step 4).

3) Connect test light between ground and terminal No. 1 (Dark Blue/White wire on left front door; Pink/Black wire on all others) on door lock motor harness connector. Using scan tool, actuate door unlock relay while observing test light. On vehicles equipped with Remote Keyless Entry (RKE), if left front door is suspect, actuate left front door unlock relay. On all vehicles, if test light did not illuminate, go to step 6). If test light did illuminate, replace door lock motor.

4) Locate, but do not disconnect BCM 20-pin connector located at junction block. *See Fig. 2.* Using a test light, backprobe suspect terminal on BCM 20-pin connector. Left front door lock is terminal No. 10 (Orange/Black wire), right front door lock is terminal No. 11 (Orange/White wire), right rear door lock is terminal No. 12 (Orange/Tan wire) and left rear door lock is terminal No. 13 (Orange/Brown wire).

5) Using scan tool, actuate door locks while observing test light. If test light does not illuminate, replace BCM. If test light illuminates, repair open in wire between suspect door lock motor connector and BCM 20-pin connector.

6) Locate, but do not disconnect BCM 20-pin connector located at junction block. *See Fig. 2.* Using a test light, backprobe suspect terminal on BCM 20-pin connector. Left front door lock is terminal No. 4 (Dark Blue/White wire), right front door lock is terminal No. 1 (Pink/Light Blue wire), right rear door lock is terminal No. 2 (Pink/Dark Blue wire) and left rear door lock is terminal No. 3 (Pink/Black wire).

7) Using scan tool, actuate door unlock while observing test light. On vehicles equipped with Remote Keyless Entry (RKE), if left front door is suspect, actuate left front door unlock relay. On all vehicles, if test light does not illuminate, replace BCM. If test light illuminates, repair open in wire between suspect door lock motor connector and BCM 20-pin connector.

POWER DOOR LOCK TEST 5

DOORS FAIL TO LOCK FROM ANY SWITCH

NOTE: Perform POWER DOOR LOCK TEST 1 before proceeding with this test. For connector terminal identification, see CONNECTOR IDENTIFICATION in BODY CONTROL COMPUTER – INTRODUCTION article. For wiring diagrams, see WIRING DIAGRAMS in BODY CONTROL COMPUTER – INTRODUCTION article. Perform VERIFICATION TEST VER-1A after each repair.

CAUTION: Always turn ignition switch to OFF position prior to disconnecting or connecting any module connector.

1) Using scan tool, actuate door locks. If door locks operate, go to next step. If door locks do not operate, replace BCM.

2) Using scan tool, read left front door ajar status and close left front door. If scan tool displays, LF DOOR: OPEN, replace BCM. If scan tool does not display, LF DOOR: OPEN, go to DOOR AJAR TEST 2.

1999 ACCESSORIES & EQUIPMENT
Body Control Computer Tests
Breeze, Cirrus, Sebring Convertible & Stratus (Cont.)

POWER DOOR LOCK TEST 6

INOPERATIVE DOOR LOCK INHIBIT CIRCUIT

NOTE: *Perform POWER DOOR LOCK TEST 1 before proceeding with this test. For connector terminal identification, see CONNECTOR IDENTIFICATION in BODY CONTROL COMPUTER – INTRODUCTION article. For wiring diagrams, see WIRING DIAGRAMS in BODY CONTROL COMPUTER – INTRODUCTION article. Perform VERIFICATION TEST VER-1A after each repair.*

CAUTION: *Always turn ignition switch to OFF position prior to disconnecting or connecting any module connector.*

1) Open left front door and read left front door ajar status. If scan tool displays LF DOOR: CLOSED, go to next step. If scan tool does not display LF DOOR: CLOSED, go to DOOR AJAR TEST 3.
2) Remove key from ignition switch. Using scan tool, read key-in ignition status. If scan tool does not display KEY-IN IGN: CLOSED, go to next step. If scan tool displays KEY-IN IGN: CLOSED, go to CHIME TEST 7.
3) Insert key in ignition switch. Using scan tool, read key-in ignition status. If scan tool displays KEY-IN IGN: CLOSED, replace Body Control Module (BCM). If scan tool does not display KEY-IN IGN: CLOSED, go to CHIME TEST 6.

POWER DOOR LOCK TEST 7

AUTOMATIC (WHILE MOVING) DOOR LOCKS

NOTE: *Perform POWER DOOR LOCK TEST 1 before proceeding with this test. For connector terminal identification, see CONNECTOR IDENTIFICATION in BODY CONTROL COMPUTER – INTRODUCTION article. For wiring diagrams, see WIRING DIAGRAMS in BODY CONTROL COMPUTER – INTRODUCTION article. Perform VERIFICATION TEST VER-1A after each repair.*

CAUTION: *Always turn ignition switch to OFF position prior to disconnecting or connecting any module connector.*

1) Using scan tool, read auto door lock status. If scan tool displays AUTO DOOR LOCKS ARE ENABLED, go to next step. If scan tool does not display AUTO DOOR LOCKS ARE ENABLED, use scan tool to enable auto door locks.
2) Close all doors. Using scan tool, read left front door ajar status. If scan tool displays LF DOOR AJAR: CLOSED, go to DOOR AJAR TEST 2. If scan tool does not display LF DOOR AJAR: CLOSED, go to next step.
3) Using scan tool, read door ajar status. If scan tool displays DOOR AJAR: CLOSED, go to DOOR AJAR TEST 4. If scan tool does not display DOOR AJAR: CLOSED, go to next step.
4) Turn ignition on with engine off. Using scan tool, select SYSTEM TEST. If scan tool displays, POWERTRAIN CONTROL MODULE: INACTIVE ON BUS, go to appropriate VEHICLE COMMUNICATIONS article. If scan tool does not display, POWERTRAIN CONTROL MODULE: INACTIVE ON BUS, go to next step.
5) Using scan tool, read ENGINE INFO and observe Throttle Position (TP) sensor while depressing throttle. If TP sensor percentage increases as throttle is opened, go to next step. If TP percentage does not increase as throttle is opened, TP sensor is faulty. See appropriate SELF-DIAGNOSTICS article in ENGINE PERFORMANCE in appropriate MITCHELL® manual.
6) Raise and properly support vehicle drive wheels. Close all doors, start engine, apply brakes and put transmission into drive. Using scan tool, read ENGINE INFO and observe Vehicle Speed Sensor (VSS) when wheels rotate. Release brakes and carefully open throttle. If MPH increased as throttle is opened slightly for 15 seconds, go to next step. If MPH did not increase as throttle is opened slightly for 15 seconds, VSS is faulty. See appropriate SELF-DIAGNOSTICS article in ENGINE PERFORMANCE in appropriate MITCHELL® manual.

7) If doors locked automatically when MPH increased to more than 15 MPH, system is operating properly. If doors did not lock automatically when MPH increased to more than 15 MPH, replace BCM.

POWER DOOR LOCK TEST 8

IDENTIFYING RKE PROBLEMS

NOTE: *Perform POWER DOOR LOCK TEST 1 before proceeding with this test. For connector terminal identification, see CONNECTOR IDENTIFICATION in BODY CONTROL COMPUTER – INTRODUCTION article. For wiring diagrams, see WIRING DIAGRAMS in BODY CONTROL COMPUTER – INTRODUCTION article. Perform VERIFICATION TEST VER-1A after each repair.*

CAUTION: *Always turn ignition switch to OFF position prior to disconnecting or connecting any module connector.*

Remote Keyless Entry (RKE) Does Not Operate – 1) Ensure Body Control Module (BCM) is ACTIVE ON THE BUS. Go to SYMPTOM ID TEST 1A.
2) Using scan tool, select READ DTCs and look for NO POWER TO MODULE fault message. If NO POWER TO MODULE message is present, see appropriate VEHICLE COMMUNICATIONS article.
3) Check RKE transmitter battery voltage. If battery voltage is less than 3 volts, replace battery.
4) Substitute a known good RKE transmitter from another JA body vehicle. Using scan tool, select PROGRAM RKE and reprogram RKE transmitter according to scan tool instructions. If RKE system still does not operate, replace BCM.

NOTE: *If vehicle is equipped with Remote Keyless Entry (RKE), there will be a RKE antenna terminal at back of BCM. Antenna connector will have a single White wire terminal above instrument panel 10-pin connector.*

Remote Keyless Entry (RKE) Does Not Operate Properly (Must Be Held Very Close To Vehicle) – Locate RKE antenna wire at back of BCM, above instrument panel 10-pin connector. *See Fig. 2.* Ensure antenna wire is properly connected to BCM. Check RKE transmitter battery voltage. If battery voltage is less than 3 volts, replace battery. If antenna is properly connected and RKE transmitter battery voltage is more than 3 volts, replace BCM. For wiring diagrams, see WIRING DIAGRAMS in BODY CONTROL COMPUTER – INTRODUCTION article. Perform VERIFICATION TEST VER-1A.

POWER TOP TEST 1

IDENTIFYING POWER TOP PROBLEMS

NOTE: *Perform SYMPTOM ID TEST 1A before proceeding with this test. For connector terminal identification, see CONNECTOR IDENTIFICATION in BODY CONTROL COMPUTER – INTRODUCTION article. For wiring diagrams, see WIRING DIAGRAMS in BODY CONTROL COMPUTER – INTRODUCTION article. Perform VERIFICATION TEST VER-1A after each repair.*

The Body Control Module (BCM) interrupts power feed circuit to power top switch/ The BCM will open power top inhibit relay when vehicle speed is greater than 10 MPH. If power top motor is suspect, go to POWER TOPTEST 2. If further testing of power top system is needed, go to POWER CONVERTIBLE TOP article.

1999 ACCESSORIES & EQUIPMENT
Body Control Computer Tests
Breeze, Cirrus, Sebring Convertible & Stratus (Cont.)

CHRY
4-89

POWER TOP TEST 2

INOPERATIVE POWER TOP MOTOR

NOTE: Perform POWER TOP TEST 1 before proceeding with this test. For connector terminal identification, see CONNECTOR IDENTIFICATION in BODY CONTROL COMPUTER – INTRODUCTION article. For wiring diagrams, see WIRING DIAGRAMS in BODY CONTROL COMPUTER – INTRODUCTION article. Perform VERIFICATION TEST VER-1A after each repair.

CAUTION: Always turn ignition switch to OFF position prior to disconnecting or connecting any module connector.

1) Remove power top inhibit relay from Power Distribution Center (PDC). Turn ignition on. Using external voltmeter, measure voltage between ground and power top inhibit relay terminal No. 30 (White/Yellow wire) on PDC. If voltage is more than 10 volts, go to next step. If voltage is 10 volts or less, repair open White/Yellow wire.

2) Connect jumper wire between power top inhibit relay terminals No. 30 and 38 on PDC. Operate power convertible top. If power top operates correctly, go to next step. If power top does not operate correctly, go to step **6)**.

3) Using external voltmeter, measure voltage between ground and power top inhibit relay terminal No. 18 (White/Red wire) on PDC. If voltage is more than 10 volts, go to next step. If voltage is 10 volts or less, replace PDC.

4) Using test light, connect one lead to power top inhibit relay terminal No. 18 and other lead to terminal No. 16 on PDC. If test light illuminates, replace power top inhibit relay. If test light does not illuminate, go to next step.

5) Connect jumper wire between ground and power top inhibit relay terminal No. 18 on PDC. Turn ignition off. Disconnect BCM 14-pin connector located at junction block and ensure connector is clean and not damaged. *See Figs. 1 and 3.* Using external ohmmeter, measure resistance between ground and terminal No. 9 (White/Red wire) on 14-pin connector. If resistance is less than 5 ohms, replace BCM. If resistance is 5 ohms or greater, repair open White/Red wire.

6) Disconnect power top switch connector. Ensure ignition is on. Do not disconnect jumper wire. Using external voltmeter, measure voltage between ground and terminal No. 6 (White/Black wire) on power top switch connector. If voltage is more than 10 volts, problem is not with feed circuit to power top switch. Go to POWER CONVERTIBLE TOP article for further diagnosis. If voltage is 10 volts or less, repair open White/Black wire.

SKIS TEST 1

IDENTIFYING SMART KEY IMMOBILIZER SYSTEM (SKIS) PROBLEMS

NOTE: Perform SYMPTOM ID TEST 1A before proceeding with this test. For connector terminal identification, see CONNECTOR IDENTIFICATION in BODY CONTROL COMPUTER – INTRODUCTION article. For wiring diagrams, see WIRING DIAGRAMS in BODY CONTROL COMPUTER – INTRODUCTION article. Perform VERIFICATION TEST VER-1A after each repair.

CAUTION: Always turn ignition switch to OFF position prior to disconnecting or connecting any module connector.

1) Ensure that all customer's vehicle keys are present before beginning diagnosis and repair of SKIS. Ensure battery is fully charged. Using scan tool, select THEFT ALARM, then SKIM. If scan tool displays NO RESPONSE, go to appropriate VEHICLE COMMUNICATIONS article.

2) Using scan tool, read and record SKIM DTCs. Erase DTCs. Cycle ignition off, and then on. Allow ignition to be on for at least 90 seconds before retrieving DTCs. Read SKIM DTCs. Go to CURRENT SKIM

DTCS DISPLAYED table. If no DTCs are present, see PRE-EXISTING SKIM DTCS DISPLAYED table.

CURRENT SKIM DTCS DISPLAYED

Problem	SKIS TEST
Antenna Failure	1
Transponder Communication Failure	2
Transponder CRC Failure	2
Transponder ID Mismatch	3
Transponder ID Mismatch & EEPROM Failure	1
Transponder Response Mismatch	3
Transponder Response Mismatch & EEPROM Failure	1
VIN Mismatch	4
VIN Mismatch & PCM EEPROM Failure	2
VIN Mismatch & Rolling Code Failure With Or Without An EEPROM Failure	4
EEPROM Failure	1
Internal SKIM Failure	1
Serial Link External Failure [3]	9
Serial Link External Failure	10
PCM Status Failure	10
Rolling Code Failure	10

[1] – Replace smart key immobolizer module. Perform SKIM INITIALIZATION PROCEDURE.
[2] – For PCM EEPROM fault diagnosis, see appropriate SELF-DIAGNOSTICS article in ENGINE PERFORMANCE in appropriate MITCHELL® manual. Go to SKIS TEST 4.
[3] – When attempting to send secret key to PCM.

PRE-EXISTING SKIM DTCS DISPLAYED

Problem	SKIS TEST
Antenna Failure	1
VIN Mismatch & EEPROM Failure	5
VIN Mismatch & Rolling Code Failure With An EEPROM Failure	4
EEPROM Failure	6
Internal SKIM Failure	7
Serial Link External Failure	8
PCM Status Failure	8
Rolling Code Failure	8
Transponder ID Mismatch & EEPROM Failure	11
Transponder Response Mismatch & EEPROM Failure	11
Transponder ID Mismatch	12
Transponder Response Mismatch	12
Transponder Communication Failure	12
Transponder CRC Failure	12

[1] – Replace smart key immobolizer module. Perform SKIM INITIALIZATION PROCEDURE.

SKIS TEST 2

TRANSPONDER CRC FAILURE

NOTE: Perform SKIS TEST 1 before proceeding with this test. For connector terminal identification, see CONNECTOR IDENTIFICATION in BODY CONTROL COMPUTER – INTRODUCTION article. For wiring diagrams, see WIRING DIAGRAMS in BODY CONTROL COMPUTER – INTRODUCTION article. Perform VERIFICATION TEST VER-1A after each repair.

CAUTION: Always turn ignition switch to OFF position prior to disconnecting or connecting any module connector.

1) If a transponder GO/NO-GO tester is not available, go to next step. Place key in transponder GO/NO-GO tester. If transponder passes test, replace smart key immobilizer module. Perform SKIM INITIALIZATION PROCEDURE. If transponder does not pass test, erase SKIM DTCs. Replace and program new key.

2) Using another vehicle key, place key in ignition and turn ignition on. Using scan tool, erase DTCs. Cycle ignition off, and then on. Allow

CHRY
4-90

1999 ACCESSORIES & EQUIPMENT
Body Control Computer Tests
Breeze, Cirrus, Sebring Convertible & Stratus (Cont.)

ignition to be on for at least 90 seconds before retrieving DTCs. Read SKIM DTCs. If original DTC reoccurs, replace replace smart key immobolizer module. Perform SKIM INITIALIZATION PROCEDURE. If DTC is no longer present, erase SKIM DTCs. Replace and program new key.

SKIS TEST 3

TRANSPONDER ID MISMATCH OR TRANSPONDER RESPONSE MISMATCH

NOTE: Perform SKIS TEST 1 before proceeding with this test. For connector terminal identification, see CONNECTOR IDENTIFICATION in BODY CONTROL COMPUTER – INTRODUCTION article. For wiring diagrams, see WIRING DIAGRAMS in BODY CONTROL COMPUTER – INTRODUCTION article. Perform VERIFICATION TEST VER-1A after each repair.

CAUTION: Always turn ignition switch to OFF position prior to disconnecting or connecting any module connector.

1) If a transponder GO/NO-GO tester is not available, go to next step. Place key in transponder GO/NO-GO tester. If transponder passes test, go to step **3)**. If transponder does not pass test, erase SKIM DTCs. Replace and program new key.

2) Obtain another vehicle key from customer. If additonal key was not available, go to step **6)**. Place additional key in ignition and turn ignition on. Using scan tool, erase DTCs. Cycle ignition off, and then on. Allow ignition to be on for at least 90 seconds before retrieving DTCs. Read SKIM DTCs. If original DTC reoccurs, replace replace smart key immobolizer module. Perform SKIM INITIALIZATION PROCEDURE. If DTC is no longer present, erase SKIM DTCs. Replace and program new key.

3) Place key in ignition switch. Turn ignition switch to RUN position. Using scan tool, select MISCELLANOUS, then PROGRAM NEW KEY. Read CURRENT KEY status. If PROGRAMMING SUCCESSFUL is displayed, erase DTCs. Testing is complete. If PROGRAMMING SUCCESSFUL is not displayed, go to next step.

4) If PROGRAMING FAILED is displayed, replace smart key immobolizer module. Perform SKIM INITIALIZATION PROCEDURE. If PROGRAMING FAILED is not displayed, go to next step.

5) If MAXIMUM KEY LIMIT is displayed, no additional keys can be programmed. If MAXIMUM KEY LIMIT is not displayed, replace smart key immobilizer module. Perform SKIM INITIALIZATION PROCEDURE.

6) Place key in ignition switch. Turn ignition switch to RUN position. Using scan tool, select MISCELLANOUS, then PROGRAM NEW KEY. Read CURRENT KEY status. If MAXIMUM KEY LIMIT is displayed, no additional keys can be programmed. If MAXIMUM KEY LIMIT is not displayed, go to next step.

7) If PROGRAMING FAILED is displayed, replace smart key immobilizer module. Perform SKIM INITIALIZATION PROCEDURE. If PROGRAMING FAILED is not displayed, go to next step.

8) If PROGRAMMING SUCCESSFUL is displayed, erase DTCs. Replace original defective key. Perform PROGRAMMING BLANK SMART KEY. If PROGRAMMING SUCCESSFUL is not displayed, go to next step.

9) If PROGRAMMING NOT ATTEMPTED is displayed, repeat steps **6)**–**9)**. If PROGRAMMING NOT ATTEMPTED is displayed, replace smart key immobilizer module. Perform SKIM INITIALIZATION PROCEDURE.

SKIS TEST 4

VIN MISMATCH

NOTE: Perform SKIS TEST 1 before proceeding with this test. For connector terminal identification, see CONNECTOR IDENTIFICATION in BODY CONTROL COMPUTER – INTRODUCTION article. For wiring diagrams, see WIRING DIAGRAMS in BODY CONTROL COMPUTER – INTRODUCTION article. Perform VERIFICATION TEST VER-1A after each repair.

CAUTION: Always turn ignition switch to OFF position prior to disconnecting or connecting any module connector.

1) Using scan tool, read VIN from Powertrain Control Module (PCM). If VIN displayed by scan tool does not match vehicle VIN, go to step **4)**. If VIN displayed by scan tool matches vehicle VIN, go to next step.

2) Read VIN stored in Smart Key Immobilizer Module (SKIM) memory. If VIN stored by SKIM memory does not match vehicle VIN, replace smart key immobilizer module. Perform SKIM INITIALIZATION PROCEDURE. If VIN stored by SKIM memory matches vehicle VIN, go to next step.

3) Start and run engine for at least 90 seconds. Using scan tool, read SKIM DTCs. If VIN mismatch code is still present, replace smart key immobilizer module. Perform SKIM INITIALIZATION PROCEDURE. If VIN mismatch code is no longer present, system is currently operating correctly.

4) Using scan tool, re-program correct VIN into PCM memory. Erase SKIM DTCs. Verify DTC's are correctly erased. Start and run engine for at least 90 seconds. Using scan tool, read SKIM DTCs. If VIN mismatch code is still present, replace smart key immobilizer module. Perform SKIM INITIALIZATION PROCEDURE. If VIN mismatch code is no longer present, system is currently operating correctly.

SKIS TEST 5

VIN MISMATCH & EEPROM FAILURE

NOTE: Perform SKIS TEST 1 before proceeding with this test. For connector terminal identification, see CONNECTOR IDENTIFICATION in BODY CONTROL COMPUTER – INTRODUCTION article. For wiring diagrams, see WIRING DIAGRAMS in BODY CONTROL COMPUTER – INTRODUCTION article. Perform VERIFICATION TEST VER-1A after each repair.

CAUTION: Always turn ignition switch to OFF position prior to disconnecting or connecting any module connector.

1) Using scan tool, erase SKIM DTCs. Start engine 20 consecutive times. Using scan tool, read SKIM DTCs. If scan tool displays EEPROM FAILURE, replace smart key immobilizer module. Perform SKIM INITIALIZATION PROCEDURE. If scan tool does not display EEPROM FAILURE, go to next step.

2) Start and run engine for at least 90 seconds. Using scan tool, read SKIM DTCs. If VIN MISMATCH DTC is present, go to SKIS TEST 4. If VIN MISMATCH DTC is not present, go to next step.

3) If scan tool displays ROLLING CODE DTC, go to SKIS TEST 10. If scan tool does not display ROLLING CODE DTC, system is currently operating correctly.

1999 ACCESSORIES & EQUIPMENT
Body Control Computer Tests
Breeze, Cirrus, Sebring Convertible & Stratus (Cont.)

CHRY
4-91

SKIS TEST 6

VIN MISMATCH & EEPROM FAILURE

NOTE: Perform SKIS TEST 1 before proceeding with this test. For connector terminal identification, see CONNECTOR IDENTIFICATION in BODY CONTROL COMPUTER – INTRODUCTION article. For wiring diagrams, see WIRING DIAGRAMS in BODY CONTROL COMPUTER – INTRODUCTION article. Perform VERIFICATION TEST VER-1A after each repair.

CAUTION: Always turn ignition switch to OFF position prior to disconnecting or connecting any module connector.

Using scan tool, erase SKIM DTCs. Wait 10 seconds. Start engine 20 consecutive times. Using scan tool, read SKIM DTCs. If scan tool displays EEPROM FAILURE, replace smart key immobilizer module. Perform SKIM INITIALIZATION PROCEDURE. If scan tool does not display EEPROM FAILURE, system is currently operating correctly.

SKIS TEST 7

VIN MISMATCH & EEPROM FAILURE

NOTE: Perform SKIS TEST 1 before proceeding with this test. For connector terminal identification, see CONNECTOR IDENTIFICATION in BODY CONTROL COMPUTER – INTRODUCTION article. For wiring diagrams, see WIRING DIAGRAMS in BODY CONTROL COMPUTER – INTRODUCTION article. Perform VERIFICATION TEST VER-1A after each repair.

CAUTION: Always turn ignition switch to OFF position prior to disconnecting or connecting any module connector.

Using scan tool, erase SKIM DTCs. Wait 10 seconds. Start engine 20 consecutive times. Using scan tool, read SKIM DTCs. If scan tool displays INTERNAL SKIM FAILURE, replace smart key immobilizer module. Perform SKIM INITIALIZATION PROCEDURE. If scan tool does not display INTERNAL SKIM FAILURE, system is currently operating correctly.

SKIS TEST 8

SERIAL LINK EXTERNAL FAILURE, PCM STATUS FAILURE OR ROLLING CODE FAILURE

NOTE: Perform SKIS TEST 1 before proceeding with this test. For connector terminal identification, see CONNECTOR IDENTIFICATION in BODY CONTROL COMPUTER – INTRODUCTION article. For wiring diagrams, see WIRING DIAGRAMS in BODY CONTROL COMPUTER – INTRODUCTION article. Perform VERIFICATION TEST VER-1A after each repair.

CAUTION: Always turn ignition switch to OFF position prior to disconnecting or connecting any module connector.

1) Using scan tool, erase SKIM DTCs. Wait 10 seconds. Start engine 20 consecutive times. Using scan tool, read SKIM DTCs. If scan tool displays a SKIM related DTC, go to next step. If scan tool does not display a SKIM related DTC, system is currently operating correctly.
2) Using scan tool, select THEFT ALARM, then SKIM. If scan tool displays NO RESPONSE, see appropriate VEHICLE COMMUNICATIONS article. If scan tool does not display NO RESPONSE, go to next step.
3) Using scan tool, select BODY, then BODY COMPUTER. Select SYSTEM TEST, then PCM MONITOR. If scan tool displays PCM ACTIVE ON THE BUS, go to next step. If scan tool does not display PCM ACTIVE ON THE BUS, see appropriate VEHICLE COMMUNICATIONS article.

4) Using scan tool, select ENGINE, then read DTCs. If scan tool displays any PCM related DTCs, see appropriate SELF-DIAGNOSTICS article in ENGINE PERFORMANCE in appropriate MITCHELL® manual. If scan tool does not display any PCM related DTCs, replace smart key immobilizer module. Perform SKIM INITIALIZATION PROCEDURE.

SKIS TEST 9

SERIAL LINK EXTERNAL FAILURE

NOTE: Perform SKIS TEST 1 before proceeding with this test. For connector terminal identification, see CONNECTOR IDENTIFICATION in BODY CONTROL COMPUTER – INTRODUCTION article. For wiring diagrams, see WIRING DIAGRAMS in BODY CONTROL COMPUTER – INTRODUCTION article. Perform VERIFICATION TEST VER-1A after each repair.

CAUTION: Always turn ignition switch to OFF position prior to disconnecting or connecting any module connector.

1) Using scan tool, erase SKIM DTCs. Attempt another secret key transfer to Powertrain Control Module (PCM). Using scan tool, read SKIM DTCs. If scan tool displays SERIAL LINK EXTERNAL DTC, go to next step. If scan tool does not display SERIAL LINK EXTERNAL DTC, system is currently operating correctly.
2) Using scan tool, select THEFT ALARM, then SKIM. If scan tool displays NO RESPONSE, see appropriate VEHICLE COMMUNICATIONS article. If scan tool does not display NO RESPONSE, go to next step.
3) Using scan tool, select BODY, then BODY COMPUTER. Select SYSTEM TEST, then PCM MONITOR. If scan tool displays PCM ACTIVE ON THE BUS, go to next step. If scan tool does not display PCM ACTIVE ON THE BUS, see appropriate VEHICLE COMMUNICATIONS article.
4) Using scan tool, select ENGINE, then read DTCs. If scan tool displays any PCM related DTCs, see appropriate SELF-DIAGNOSTICS article in ENGINE PERFORMANCE in appropriate MITCHELL® manual. If scan tool does not display any PCM related DTCs, replace smart key immobilizer module. Perform SKIM INITIALIZATION PROCEDURE.

SKIS TEST 10

SERIAL LINK EXTERNAL FAILURE, PCM STATUS FAILURE OR ROLLING CODE FAILURE

NOTE: Perform SKIS TEST 1 before proceeding with this test. For connector terminal identification, see CONNECTOR IDENTIFICATION in BODY CONTROL COMPUTER – INTRODUCTION article. For wiring diagrams, see WIRING DIAGRAMS in BODY CONTROL COMPUTER – INTRODUCTION article. Perform VERIFICATION TEST VER-1A after each repair.

CAUTION: Always turn ignition switch to OFF position prior to disconnecting or connecting any module connector.

1) Using scan tool, erase SKIM DTCs. Using scan tool, select THEFT ALARM, then SKIM. If scan tool displays NO RESPONSE, see appropriate VEHICLE COMMUNICATIONS article. If scan tool does not display NO RESPONSE, go to next step.
2) Using scan tool, select BODY, then BODY COMPUTER. Select SYSTEM TEST, then PCM MONITOR. If scan tool displays PCM ACTIVE ON THE BUS, go to next step. If scan tool does not display PCM ACTIVE ON THE BUS, see appropriate VEHICLE COMMUNICATIONS article.
3) Using scan tool, select ENGINE, then read DTCs. If scan tool displays any PCM related DTCs, see appropriate SELF-DIAGNOSTICS article in ENGINE PERFORMANCE in appropriate MITCHELL® manual. If scan tool does not display any PCM related DTCs, replace smart key immobilizer module. Perform SKIM INITIALIZATION PROCEDURE.

CHRY
4-92

1999 ACCESSORIES & EQUIPMENT
Body Control Computer Tests
Breeze, Cirrus, Sebring Convertible & Stratus (Cont.)

SKIS TEST 11

TRANSPONDER ID MISMATCH, TRANSPONDER RESPONSE MISMATCH OR EEPROM FAILURE

NOTE: *Perform SKIS TEST 1 before proceeding with this test. For connector terminal identification, see CONNECTOR IDENTIFICATION in BODY CONTROL COMPUTER – INTRODUCTION article. For wiring diagrams, see WIRING DIAGRAMS in BODY CONTROL COMPUTER – INTRODUCTION article. Perform VERIFICATION TEST VER-1A after each repair.*

CAUTION: *Always turn ignition switch to OFF position prior to disconnecting or connecting any module connector.*

Using scan tool, erase SKIM DTCs. Turn ignition off. Wait 10 seconds. Start engine 20 consecutive times. Using scan tool, read SKIM DTCs. If scan tool displays EEPROM FAILURE and TRANSPONDER DTCs, replace smart key immobilizer module. Perform SKIM INITIALIZATION PROCEDURE. If scan tool displays EEPROM FAILURE DTC, go to SKIS TEST 6. If scan tool displays TRANSPONDER DTC, go to SKIS TEST 3. If scan tool does not display either EEPROM FAILURE and TRANSPONDER DTCs, system is currently operating correctly.

SKIS TEST 12

TRANSPONDER CRC FAILURE OR TRANSPONDER COMMUNICATION FAILURE

NOTE: *Perform SKIS TEST 1 before proceeding with this test. For connector terminal identification, see CONNECTOR IDENTIFICATION in BODY CONTROL COMPUTER – INTRODUCTION article. For wiring diagrams, see WIRING DIAGRAMS in BODY CONTROL COMPUTER – INTRODUCTION article. Perform VERIFICATION TEST VER-1A after each repair.*

CAUTION: *Always turn ignition switch to OFF position prior to disconnecting or connecting any module connector.*

Start engine several times using each of vehicle's keys. Using scan tool, read SKIM DTCs. If scan tool displays TRANSPONDER DTCs, replace smart key immobilizer module. Perform SKIM INITIALIZATION PROCEDURE. If scan tool does not display TRANSPONDER DTCs, system is currently operating correctly.

VTSS TEST 1

IDENTIFYING VEHICLE THEFT SECURITY SYSTEM (VTSS) PROBLEMS

NOTE: *Perform SYMPTOM ID TEST 1A before proceeding with this test. For connector terminal identification, see CONNECTOR IDENTIFICATION in BODY CONTROL COMPUTER – INTRODUCTION article. For wiring diagrams, see WIRING DIAGRAMS in BODY CONTROL COMPUTER – INTRODUCTION article. Perform VERIFICATION TEST VER-1A after each repair.*

CAUTION: *Always turn ignition switch to OFF position prior to disconnecting or connecting any module connector.*

NOTE: *If complaint is: VTSS indicator lamps stay on constantly (30 seconds after key is turned on) or while driving vehicle, see TEST 13A in appropriate VEHICLE COMMUNICATIONS article.*

1) Connect scan tool to Data Link Connector (DLC) and select THEFT ALARM. If scan tool displays NO RESPONSE, perform VTSS TEST 2. If scan tool reports a bus failure message, see appropriate VEHICLE COMMUNICATIONS article.

2) Using scan tool, select BODY. Select BODY COMPUTER and then READ DTCs. If BATTERY POWER TO MODULE fault message is present, see appropriate VEHICLE COMMUNICATIONS article. If DRIVER DOOR DISARM SWITCH INPUT is present, see VTSS TEST 11. If PASSENGER DOOR DISARM SWITCH INPUT is present, see VTSS TEST 12. Go to next step.

3) Using scan tool, select THEFT ALARM. Select MONITOR DISPLAY and read VTSS status. If VTSS mode is not disarmed, go to step 12). If VTSS mode is disarmed, go to next step.

4) Turn ignition on. Using scan tool, select THEFT ALARM. Select MISCELLANEOUS and CHANGE MODE. Select DIAGNOSTICS to put VTSS in diagnostics mode. Follow instructions displayed by scan tool. If PUT IGNITION IN OFF POSITION displays, go to next step (VTSS is in diagnostics mode). IF PUT IGNITION IN OFF POSITION does not display, perform VTSS TEST 3.

5) When VTSS is put into diagnostics mode, horn should sound 2 times and headlights and VTSS indicator light should flash. If horn sounds 2 times and headlights and VTSS indicator light flash, go to next step. If horn does not sound, perform VTSS TEST 4. If VTSS indicator light does not flash, perform VTSS TEST 5. If headlights do not flash, perform VTSS TEST 6.

6) With scan tool still connected to DLC, remove key from ignition switch. Open and close each door, then use key to turn each front door from lock to unlock position. If horn sounds after each action, go to step 8). If horn does not sound after each action, perform test indicated. See VEHICLE THEFT SECURITY SYSTEM DIAGNOSTIC TEST DIRECTORY table.

VEHICLE THEFT SECURITY SYSTEM DIAGNOSTIC TEST DIRECTORY

Problem	VTSS TEST
Left Front Door	7
Right Front Door	8
Right Rear Door	9
Left Rear Door	10
Left Front Door Key Cylinder (Disarm Circuit)	11
Right Front Door Key Cylinder (Disarm Circuit)	12

7) Turn ignition switch to ON position. If horn sounds, go to next step. If horn does not sound, perform VTSS TEST 3.

8) Using scan tool, select THEFT ALARM. Select MONITOR DISPLAY and read VTSS status. If VTSS status is not DISARMED, or PCM is not OK TO ARM/OK TO RUN ENGINE, go to next step. If VTSS status is DISARMED and PCM is OK TO ARM/OK TO RUN ENGINE, system is functioning properly.

9) If VTSS status is other than DISARMED, go to step 12). If PCM status is 1) NO RESPONSE, 2) NO RESPONSE, go to appropriate VEHICLE COMMUNICATIONS article. If PCM status is 1) OK TO ARM VTSS, 2) NOT OK TO RUN ENGINE, replace Powertrain Control Module (PCM). If there is a problem with RKE arm/disarm function, see VTSS TEST 8.

10) If VTSS light stays on constantly during arming process (15 seconds) but flashes properly when armed, go to step 12) in VTSS TEST 4. If RKE arm/disarm function is not operating correctly, go to POWER DOOR LOCK TEST 8.

11) On JX models, if garage door opener and decklid release lockout does not function correctly, go to VTSS TEST 13. If decklid release does not function using RKE transmitter, go to VTSS TEST 14.

12) Turn ignition off. Put key in left front door and turn to UNLOCK position. Using key, turn ignition on. Using scan tool, read VTSS status. If scan tool displays CURRENT MODE DISARMED, system is functioning properly. Return to VTSS TEST 1. If scan tool does not display CURRENT MODE DISARMED, perform VTSS TEST 11.

1999 ACCESSORIES & EQUIPMENT
Body Control Computer Tests
Breeze, Cirrus, Sebring Convertible & Stratus (Cont.)

CHRY
4-93

VTSS TEST 2

VTSS MODULE – NO RESPONSE

NOTE: Perform VTSS TEST 1 before proceeding with this test. For connector terminal identification, see CONNECTOR IDENTIFICATION in BODY CONTROL COMPUTER – INTRODUCTION article. For wiring diagrams, see WIRING DIAGRAMS in BODY CONTROL COMPUTER – INTRODUCTION article. Perform VERIFICATION TEST VER-1A after each repair.

CAUTION: Always turn ignition switch to OFF position prior to disconnecting or connecting any module connector.

1) Open trunk and inspect area around trunk cylinder. If key cylinder is equipped with a trunk cylinder knock out switch, go to next step. If key cylinder is not equipped with a trunk cylinder knock out switch, system is not equipped with VTSS.
2) Turn ignition on. Using scan tool, select SENSORS. Read ignition off/run voltage. If scan tool displays voltage more than 11 volts, go to next step. If scan tool displays 11 volts or less, go to VTSS TEST 3.
3) Access Body Control Module (BCM) 22-pin connector. *See Fig. 3.* Do not disconnect connector. Connect jumper wire between ground and terminal No. 9 (Violet/Yellow wire) on 22-pin connector. Go to next step.
4) Using scan tool, select BODY, then BODY COMPUTER. Select MISCELLANEOUS, then ENABLE THE VTSS. If system does not enable, replace BCM. If system does enable, remove jumper wire. Repair open trunk cylinder switch circuit (Violet/Yellow wire).

VTSS TEST 3

FUSED IGNITION SWITCH OUTPUT CIRCUIT TO BCM

NOTE: Perform VTSS TEST 2 before proceeding with this test. For connector terminal identification, see CONNECTOR IDENTIFICATION in BODY CONTROL COMPUTER – INTRODUCTION article. For wiring diagrams, see WIRING DIAGRAMS in BODY CONTROL COMPUTER – INTRODUCTION article. Perform VERIFICATION TEST VER-1A after each repair.

CAUTION: Always turn ignition switch to OFF position prior to disconnecting or connecting any module connector.

1) Remove and inspect fuse No. 11 (10-amp) located in junction block. *See Fig. 3.* If fuse is okay, go to step 4). If fuse is open, turn ignition off and go to next step.
2) Using external ohmmeter, measure resistance between ground and terminal No. 19 (Red/Violet wire) on fuse No. 11 socket. *See Fig. 3.* If resistance is less than 5 ohms, go to next step. If resistance is 5 ohms or greater, replace fuse No. 11.
3) Turn ignition off. Remove BCM from junction block and ensure connector is clean and not damaged. *See Figs. 1 and 3.* Using external ohmmeter, measure resistance between ground and terminal No. 19 (Red/Violet wire) on fuse No. 11 socket. If resistance is less than 5 ohms, repair ignition switch side (terminal No. 20) of fuse No. 11 and replace fuse. If resistance is 5 ohms or greater, replace Body Control Module (BCM) and fuse No. 11.
4) If fuse No. 11 is okay, turn ignition on. Using external voltmeter, measure voltage between ground and terminal No. 20 (Dark Green/Red wire) on fuse No. 11 socket. *See Fig. 3.* If voltage is greater than 10 volts, reinstall fuse No. 11 and go to next step. If voltage is 10 volts or less, repair open in Dark Green/Red wire between junction block and ignition switch.
5) Turn ignition off. Remove Body Control Module (BCM) from junction block and ensure connectors are clean and not damaged. Turn ignition on with engine off. Using external voltmeter, measure voltage between ground and terminal No. 6 on junction block internal 12-pin connector.

See Fig. 3. If voltage is 10 volts or less, replace junction block. If voltage is greater than 10 volts, replace BCM.

VTSS TEST 4

HORN CIRCUITS

NOTE: Perform VTSS TEST 1 before proceeding with this test. For connector terminal identification, see CONNECTOR IDENTIFICATION in BODY CONTROL COMPUTER – INTRODUCTION article. For wiring diagrams, see WIRING DIAGRAMS in BODY CONTROL COMPUTER – INTRODUCTION article. Perform VERIFICATION TEST VER-1A after each repair.

CAUTION: Always turn ignition switch to OFF position prior to disconnecting or connecting any module connector.

1) Depress horn button on steering wheel. If horn sounds, go to next step. If horn does not sound, go to step 4).
2) Using scan tool, read trunk key cylinder switch status. If scan tool displays SWITCH: CLOSED, go to next step. If scan tool does not display SWITCH: CLOSED, go to step 12).
3) Turn ignition off. Remove Body Control Module (BCM) from junction block and ensure connectors are clean and not damaged. Using external voltmeter, measure voltage between ground and terminal No. 7 on junction block internal 12-pin connector. *See Fig. 3.* If voltage is 10 volts or less, replace junction block. If voltage is greater than 10 volts, replace BCM.
4) Remove horn relay located in junction block. *See Fig. 3.* Using external voltmeter, measure voltage between ground and terminal No. 8 on horn relay socket. If voltage is greater than 10 volts, go to next step. If voltage is less than 10 volts, go to step 9).
5) Using external voltmeter, measure voltage between ground and terminal No. 6 on horn relay socket. *See Fig. 3.* If voltage is greater than 10 volts, go to next step. If voltage is 10 volts or less, replace junction block.
6) Connect a jumper wire between terminals No. 8 and 10 on horn relay socket. *See Fig. 3.* If horns sound, go to next step. If horns do not sound, repair open in Dark Green/Pink wire between junction block and horn(s).
7) Turn ignition off. Remove Body Control Module (BCM) from junction block and ensure connector is clean and not damaged. Using external ohmmeter, measure resistance between terminal No. 7 on BCM 12-pin connector and terminal No. 7 on horn relay socket. *See Fig. 3.* If resistance is less than 5 ohms, reinstall horn relay and go to next step. If resistance is 5 ohms or greater, replace junction block.
8) Using external voltmeter, measure voltage between ground and terminal No. 7 on junction block internal 12-pin connector. If voltage is 10 volts or less, replace horn relay. If voltage is greater than 10 volts, replace BCM.
9) Remove and inspect fuse No. 8 (20-amp), located in junction block. *See Fig. 3.* If fuse is okay, go to next step. If fuse is open, go to step 11).
10) Using external voltmeter, measure voltage between ground and terminal No. 14 (Pink/White wire) on fuse No. 8 socket. If voltage is 10 volts or less, repair open in Pink/White wire between junction block and Power Distribution Center (PDC). If voltage is greater than 10 volts, replace junction block.
11) Disconnect horns and remove horn relay. *See Fig. 3.* Using scan tool in ohmmeter mode, measure resistance at terminal No. 10 on horn relay socket. If resistance is less than 5 ohms, repair short to ground in Dark Green/Pink wire between junction block and horn(s). If resistance is 5 ohms or greater, replace fuse No. 8.
12) Disconnect trunk key cylinder switch 2-pin connector. Ensure connector is clean and not damaged. Connect a jumper wire between cylinder switch harness connector terminals. Using scan tool, read trunk key cylinder switch status. If scan tool does not display SWITCH: CLOSED, go to next step. If scan tool displays SWITCH: CLOSED, replace trunk key cylinder switch.

CHRY
4-94

1999 ACCESSORIES & EQUIPMENT
Body Control Computer Tests
Breeze, Cirrus, Sebring Convertible & Stratus (Cont.)

13) Connect jumper wire between ground and terminal No. 1 (Violet/Yellow wire) on trunk key cylinder switch connector. If scan tool does not display SWITCH: CLOSED, go to next step. If scan tool displays SWITCH: CLOSED, repair open in Black wire between 2-pin connector and ground.

14) Locate Body Control Module (BCM) 20-pin connector at junction block. *See Figs. 1 and 3.* Do not disconnect connector. Backprobe jumper wire between terminal No. 1 (Violet/Yellow wire) on BCM 20-pin connector and ground. If scan tool displays trunk key cylinder SWITCH: CLOSED, repair open in Violet/Yellow wire between BCM 20-pin connector and trunk key cylinder 2-pin connector. If scan tool does not display trunk key cylinder SWITCH: CLOSED, replace BCM.

VTSS TEST 5

VTSS INDICATOR LIGHT

NOTE: Perform VTSS TEST 1 before proceeding with this test. For connector terminal identification, see CONNECTOR IDENTIFICATION in BODY CONTROL COMPUTER – INTRODUCTION article. For wiring diagrams, see WIRING DIAGRAMS in BODY CONTROL COMPUTER – INTRODUCTION article. Perform VERIFICATION TEST VER-1A after each repair.

CAUTION: Always turn ignition switch to OFF position prior to disconnecting or connecting any module connector.

1) Using scan tool, select THEFT ALARM, then MONITOR DISPLAY. Read VTSS status. If scan tool displays PCM status as 1) NO RESPONSE, 2) NO RESPONSE, see appropriate VEHICLE COMMUNICATIONS article. If scan tool does not display PCM status as 1) NO RESPONSE, 2) NO RESPONSE and VTSS indicator light is on constantly, go to step **5)**. If scan tool does not display PCM status as 1) NO RESPONSE, 2) NO RESPONSE and VTSS indicator light is not on constantly, go to next step.

2) Turn ignition off. Locate instrument panel 10-pin connector at BCM/junction block. Disconnect connector. Ensure connector is clean and not damaged. Connect a jumper wire between ground and terminal No. 1 (Black/Orange wire) on BCM 10-pin connector. If VTSS indicator light does not illuminate, go to next step. If VTSS indicator light illuminates, replace Body Control Module (BCM).

3) Locate and disconnect instrument cluster Red 13-pin connector behind instrument cluster. *See Fig. 7.* Ensure connector is clean and not damaged. Using scan tool in voltmeter mode, measure voltage at terminal No. 5 (Pink/Red wire) on instrument cluster Red 13-pin connector. If voltage is greater than 10 volts, go to next step. If voltage is 10 volts or less, repair open in Pink/Red wire circuit.

4) Using an external ohmmeter, measure resistance between terminal No. 7 (Black/Orange wire) on instrument cluster Red 13-pin connector and terminal No. 4 (Black/Orange wire) instrument panel 10-pin connector at BCM. If resistance is 5 ohms or greater, repair open in Black/Orange wire circuit. If resistance is less than 5 ohms, replace VTSS indicator light.

5) Disconnect Body Control Module (BCM) instrument panel 10-pin connector and ensure connector is clean and not damaged. *See Fig. 2.* If VTSS indicator light goes off, replace BCM. If VTSS indicator light stays on, repair short to ground in Black/Orange wire circuit between BCM and VTSS indicator light.

VTSS TEST 6

HEADLIGHT CIRCUIT

NOTE: Perform VTSS TEST 1 before proceeding with this test. For connector terminal identification, see CONNECTOR IDENTIFICATION in BODY CONTROL COMPUTER – INTRODUCTION article. For wiring diagrams, see WIRING DIAGRAMS in BODY CONTROL COMPUTER – INTRODUCTION article. Perform VERIFICATION TEST VER-1A after each repair.

CAUTION: Always turn ignition switch to OFF position prior to disconnecting or connecting any module connector.

1) Turn low beam headlights on. If headlights do not illuminate, check headlight power and ground circuits, headlight and dimmer switches, and/or broken headlight circuit connectors or splices. If headlights illuminate, turn headlights off. Turn ignition on. Using scan tool, select BODY COMPUTER INPUT/OUTPUT display. Read KEY-IN IGNITION SW status. If scan tool displays SWITCH: CLOSED, go to next step. If scan tool does not display SWITCH: CLOSED, go to step **8)**.

2) Using scan tool, actuate headlight relay. If headlights toggle on and off, replace Body Control Module (BCM). If headlights do not toggle on and off, locate headlight delay relay in junction block. *See Fig. 3.* Remove headlight delay relay and ensure connector is clean and not damaged. Turn headlights on and go to next step.

3) Using external voltmeter, measure voltage between ground and terminal No. 5 on headlight delay relay socket. *See Fig. 3.* If voltage is greater than 10 volts, go to next step. If voltage is 10 volts or less, repair open in headlight switch output circuit between junction block and splice.

4) Turn headlights off. Using external voltmeter, measure voltage between ground and terminal No. 3 on headlight delay relay socket. *See Fig. 3.* If voltage is greater than 10 volts, go to next step. If voltage is less than 10 volts, repair Red/White wire between Power Distribution Center (PDC) and junction block.

5) Using external voltmeter, measure voltage between ground and terminal No. 1 on headlight delay relay socket. *See Fig. 3.* If voltage is greater than 10 volts, go to next step. If voltage is 10 volts or less, replace junction block.

6) Turn ignition off and disconnect Body Control Module (BCM). Using external ohmmeter, measure resistance between terminal No. 5 and terminal No. 2 on headlight delay relay socket. *See Fig. 3.* If resistance is less than 5 ohms, go to next step. If resistance is 5 ohms or greater, replace junction block.

7) Install headlight delay relay. Using external voltmeter, measure voltage between ground and terminal No. 5 on junction block internal 12-pin connector. *See Fig. 3.* If voltage is greater than 10 volts, replace BCM. If voltage is 10 volts or less, replace headlight delay relay.

8) Locate and disconnect key-in ignition switch 2-pin connector in ignition switch. *See Fig. 5.* Ensure connector is clean and not damaged. Using external ohmmeter, measure resistance between ground and terminal No. 2 (Black/White wire) on 2-pin connector. If resistance is less than 5 ohms, go to next step. If resistance is 5 ohms or greater, repair open in Black/White wire.

9) Connect a jumper wire between key-in ignition 2-pin connector terminals. Using scan tool, read key-in ignition status. If scan tool does not display KEY-IN IGN: CLOSED, go to next step. If scan tool displays KEY-IN IGN: CLOSED, replace ignition switch. See appropriate STEERING COLUMN SWITCHES article.

10) Locate instrument panel 22-pin connector at BCM/junction block. *See Fig. 3.* DO NOT disconnect connector. Backprobe jumper wire between terminal No. 17 (Light Blue wire) on instrument panel 22-pin connector and ground. Using scan tool, read key-in ignition status. If scan tool displays KEY-IN IGN: CLOSED, repair open in Light Blue wire circuit between BCM 22-pin connector and key-in ignition switch 2-pin connector. If scan tool does not display KEY-IN IGN: CLOSED, replace BCM.

1999 ACCESSORIES & EQUIPMENT
Body Control Computer Tests
Breeze, Cirrus, Sebring Convertible & Stratus (Cont.)

CHRY
4-95

VTSS TEST 7

LEFT FRONT DOOR AJAR

NOTE: Perform VTSS TEST 1 before proceeding with this test. For connector terminal identification, see CONNECTOR IDENTIFICATION in BODY CONTROL COMPUTER – INTRODUCTION article. For wiring diagrams, see WIRING DIAGRAMS in BODY CONTROL COMPUTER – INTRODUCTION article. Perform VERIFICATION TEST VER-1A after each repair.

Ensure door is closed. Using scan tool, read left front door ajar switch status. If scan tool displays LF DOOR AJAR: CLOSED, perform DOOR AJAR TEST 2. If scan tool does not display LF DOOR AJAR: CLOSED, perform DOOR AJAR TEST 3.

VTSS TEST 8

RIGHT FRONT DOOR AJAR

NOTE: Perform VTSS TEST 1 before proceeding with this test. For connector terminal identification, see CONNECTOR IDENTIFICATION in BODY CONTROL COMPUTER – INTRODUCTION article. For wiring diagrams, see WIRING DIAGRAMS in BODY CONTROL COMPUTER – INTRODUCTION article. Perform VERIFICATION TEST VER-1A after each repair.

Ensure all doors are closed. Using scan tool read door ajar switch status. If scan tool displays DOOR AJAR: CLOSED, perform DOOR AJAR TEST 4. If scan tool does not display DOOR AJAR: CLOSED, perform DOOR AJAR TEST 5.

VTSS TEST 9

RIGHT REAR DOOR AJAR

NOTE: Perform VTSS TEST 1 before proceeding with this test. For connector terminal identification, see CONNECTOR IDENTIFICATION in BODY CONTROL COMPUTER – INTRODUCTION article. For wiring diagrams, see WIRING DIAGRAMS in BODY CONTROL COMPUTER – INTRODUCTION article. Perform VERIFICATION TEST VER-1A after each repair.

Ensure all doors are closed. Using scan tool read door ajar switch status. If scan tool displays DOOR AJAR: CLOSED, perform DOOR AJAR TEST 4. If scan tool does not display DOOR AJAR: CLOSED, perform DOOR AJAR TEST 6.

VTSS TEST 10

LEFT REAR DOOR AJAR

NOTE: Perform VTSS TEST 1 before proceeding with this test. For connector terminal identification, see CONNECTOR IDENTIFICATION in BODY CONTROL COMPUTER – INTRODUCTION article. For wiring diagrams, see WIRING DIAGRAMS in BODY CONTROL COMPUTER – INTRODUCTION article. Perform after each repair.

NOTE: VERIFICATION TEST VER-1A

Ensure all doors are closed. Using scan tool read door ajar switch status. If scan tool displays DOOR AJAR: CLOSED, perform DOOR AJAR TEST 4. If scan tool does not display DOOR AJAR: CLOSED, perform DOOR AJAR TEST 7.

VTSS TEST 11

LEFT VTSS DISARM MALFUNCTION

NOTE: Perform VTSS TEST 1 before proceeding with this test. For connector terminal identification, see CONNECTOR IDENTIFICATION in BODY CONTROL COMPUTER – INTRODUCTION article. For wiring diagrams, see WIRING DIAGRAMS in BODY CONTROL COMPUTER – INTRODUCTION article. Perform VERIFICATION TEST VER-1A after each repair.

CAUTION: Always turn ignition switch to OFF position prior to disconnecting or connecting any module connector.

1) Turn ignition on with engine off. Using scan tool, select THEFT ALARM, SENSOR DISPLAY and read LF DR DISARM voltage. If no voltage is displayed, go to step **4)**. If voltage is displayed, access driver's door key lock cylinder harness. Go to next step.

2) Disconnect lock cylinder connector. Using scan tool, read LF DR DISARM voltage. If no voltage is displayed, replace driver's door key lock cylinder. If voltage is displayed, disconnect Body Control Module (BCM) 20-pin connector located at junction block and ensure connector is clean and not damaged. *See Fig. 2.* Go to next step.

3) Using external voltmeter, measure voltage between ground and terminal No. 19 (Light Green/Orange wire) on BCM 20-pin connector. If voltage is .5 volt or less, replace BCM. If voltage is .5 volt or more, repair Light Green/Orange wire for short to voltage.

4) Remove key from ignition switch. Open driver's door. Place key in driver's door key lock cylinder. Rotate key to UNLOCK position and hold. Using scan tool, read LF DR DISARM voltage. If voltage is more than 9 volts, go to next step. If voltage is 9 volts or less, go to step **6)**.

5) Rotate key to LOCK position and hold. Using scan tool, read LF DR DISARM voltage. If voltage is more than 6.8 volts, replace Body Control Module (BCM). If voltage is 6.8 volts or less, replace driver's door key lock cylinder switch.

6) Access driver's door key lock cylinder harness. Disconnect lock cylinder connector. Using external voltmeter, measure voltage between ground and terminal No. 1 (Pink wire) on key cylinder switch connector. If voltage is 10 volts or less, repair open Pink wire. If voltage is more than 10 volts, go to next step.

7) Using external ohmmeter, measure resistance between ground and terminal No. 2 (Light Green/Orange wire) on key cylinder switch connector. If resistance is less than 5 ohms, repair Light Green/Orange wire for short to ground. If resistance is 5 ohms or greater, go to next step.

8) Connect jumper wire between key cylinder lock switch connector terminals. Using scan tool, read LF DR DISARM voltage. If voltage displayed is more than 9.5 volts, replace driver's door key lock cylinder switch. If voltage is 9.5 volts or less, go to next step.

9) Access Body Control Module (BCM) 20-pin connector located at junction block. *See Fig. 2.* Do not disconnect connector. Using external voltmeter, measure voltage between ground and terminal No. 19 (Light Green/Orange wire) 20-pin connector. If voltage is more than 10 volts, replace BCM. If voltage is 10 volts or less, repair open Light Green/Orange wire.

1999 ACCESSORIES & EQUIPMENT
Body Control Computer Tests
Breeze, Cirrus, Sebring Convertible & Stratus (Cont.)

VTSS TEST 12

RIGHT VTSS DISARM MALFUNCTION

NOTE: Perform VTSS TEST 1 before proceeding with this test. For connector terminal identification, see CONNECTOR IDENTIFICATION in BODY CONTROL COMPUTER – INTRODUCTION article. For wiring diagrams, see WIRING DIAGRAMS in BODY CONTROL COMPUTER – INTRODUCTION article. Perform VERIFICATION TEST VER-1A after each repair.

CAUTION: Always turn ignition switch to OFF position prior to disconnecting or connecting any module connector.

1) Turn ignition on with engine off. Using scan tool, select THEFT ALARM, SENSOR DISPLAY and read RF DR DISARM voltage. If no voltage is displayed, go to step 4). If voltage is displayed, access passenger's door key lock cylinder harness. Go to next step.
2) Disconnect lock cylinder connector. Using scan tool, read RF DR DISARM voltage. If no voltage is displayed, replace passenger's door key lock cylinder. If voltage is displayed, disconnect Body Control Module (BCM) 20-pin connector located at junction block and ensure connector is clean and not damaged. *See Fig. 2.* Go to next step.
3) Using external voltmeter, measure voltage between ground and terminal No. 20 (Dark Green/Orange wire) on BCM 20-pin connector. If voltage is .5 volt or less, replace BCM. If voltage is .5 volt or more, repair Dark Green/Orange wire for short to voltage.
4) Remove key from ignition switch. Open passenger's door. Place key in passenger's door key lock cylinder. Rotate key to UNLOCK position and hold. Using scan tool, read RF DR DISARM voltage. If voltage is more than 9 volts, go to next step. If voltage is 9 volts or less, go to step 6).
5) Rotate key to LOCK position and hold. Using scan tool, read RF DR DISARM voltage. If voltage is more than 6.8 volts, replace BCM. If voltage is 6.8 volts or less, replace passenger's door key lock cylinder switch.
6) Access passenger's door key lock cylinder harness. Disconnect lock cylinder connector. Using external voltmeter, measure voltage between ground and terminal No. 1 (Pink wire) on key cylinder switch connector. If voltage is 10 volts or less, repair open Pink wire. If voltage is more than 10 volts, go to next step.
7) Using external ohmmeter, measure resistance between ground and terminal No. 2 (Dark Green/Orange wire) on key cylinder switch connector. If resistance is less than 5 ohms, repair Dark Green/Orange wire for short to ground. If resistance is 5 ohms or greater, go to next step.
8) Connect jumper wire between key cylinder lock switch connector terminals. Using scan tool, read RF DR DISARM voltage. If voltage displayed is more than 9.5 volts, replace passenger's door key lock cylinder switch. If voltage is 9.5 volts or less, go to next step.
9) Access BCM 20-pin connector located at junction block. *See Fig. 2.* Do not disconnect connector. Using external voltmeter, measure voltage between ground and terminal No. 20 (Dark Green/Orange wire) on 20-pin connector. If voltage is more than 10 volts, replace BCM. If voltage is 10 volts or less, repair open Light Green/Orange wire.

VTSS TEST 13

GARAGE DOOR OPENER & DECKLID RELEASE MALFUNCTION

NOTE: Perform VTSS TEST 1 before proceeding with this test. For connector terminal identification, see CONNECTOR IDENTIFICATION in BODY CONTROL COMPUTER – INTRODUCTION article. For wiring diagrams, see WIRING DIAGRAMS in BODY CONTROL COMPUTER – INTRODUCTION article. Perform VERIFICATION TEST VER-1A after each repair.

CAUTION: Always turn ignition switch to OFF position prior to disconnecting or connecting any module connector.

Disconnect BCM 20-pin connector located at junction block. *See Fig. 2.* Using external voltmeter, measure voltage between ground and terminal No. 14 (Gray wire) on 20-pin connector. If voltage is 6 volts or less, repair open Gray wire. If voltage is greater than 6 volts, replace Body Control Module (BCM).

VTSS TEST 14

DECKLID RELEASE INOPERATIVE FROM RKE

NOTE: Perform VTSS TEST 1 before proceeding with this test. For connector terminal identification, see CONNECTOR IDENTIFICATION in BODY CONTROL COMPUTER – INTRODUCTION article. For wiring diagrams, see WIRING DIAGRAMS in BODY CONTROL COMPUTER – INTRODUCTION article. Perform VERIFICATION TEST VER-1A after each repair.

CAUTION: Always turn ignition switch to OFF position prior to disconnecting or connecting any module connector.

Disconnect BCM 14-pin connector located at junction block. *See Fig. 2.* Using external voltmeter, measure voltage between ground and terminal No. 3 (Brown/Light Blue wire) on 20-pin connector. If voltage is greater than 6 volts, replace Body Control Module (BCM). If voltage is 6 volts or less, repair open Brown/Light Blue wire.

WINDSHIELD WIPER TEST 1

IDENTIFYING WINDSHIELD WIPER SYSTEM PROBLEMS

NOTE: Perform SYMPTOM ID TEST 1A before proceeding with this test. For connector terminal identification, see CONNECTOR IDENTIFICATION in BODY CONTROL COMPUTER – INTRODUCTION article. For wiring diagrams, see WIRING DIAGRAMS in BODY CONTROL COMPUTER – INTRODUCTION article. Perform VERIFICATION TEST VER-1A after each repair.

CAUTION: Always turn ignition switch to OFF position prior to disconnecting or connecting any module connector.

Turn ignition on and verify windshield wiper operation. Operate windshield wiper system in high speed mode, low speed mode, intermittent mode and wash mode (with wipers off). If wiper system does not operate properly, perform indicated test. See WINDSHIELD WIPER SYSTEM DIAGNOSTIC TEST DIRECTORY table.

Body Control Computer Tests
Breeze, Cirrus, Sebring Convertible & Stratus (Cont.)

WINDSHIELD WIPER TEST 2

WIPERS NOT WORKING AT ALL

NOTE: Perform WINDSHIELD WIPER TEST 1 before proceeding with this test. For connector terminal identification, see CONNECTOR IDENTIFICATION in BODY CONTROL COMPUTER – INTRODUCTION article. For wiring diagrams, see WIRING DIAGRAMS in BODY CONTROL COMPUTER – INTRODUCTION article. Perform VERIFICATION TEST VER-1A after each repair.

CAUTION: Always turn ignition switch to OFF position prior to disconnecting or connecting any module connector.

1) Using scan tool, actuate wipers in low speed mode. If wiper motor does not operate in low speed mode, go to next step. If wiper motor operates in low speed mode, go to step **10)**.

2) Using scan tool, stop wipers low speed actuation and actuate wipers in high speed mode. If wiper motor does not operate in high speed mode, stop wipers actuation and go to next step. If wiper motor operates in high speed mode, go to step **10)**.

3) Using scan tool, read intermittent wipe sensor. While observing scan tool, move wiper switch from OFF position to HI position. If scan tool displays INTRMT WIPE: 0V, go to next step. If scan tool displays INTRMT WIPE: with voltage reading, go to step **19)**.

4) Locate Power Distribution Center (PDC) on left front fender. Remove and inspect wiper fuse No. 14 (40-amp). *See Fig. 8.* If fuse is okay, go to next step. If fuse is open, go to step **15)**.

5) Using external voltmeter, measure voltage between ground and terminal No. 47 on fuse No. 14 socket. If voltage is more than 10 volts, go to next step. If voltage is 10 volts or less, repair open Red wire between battery and wiper fuse No. 14.

6) Reinstall wiper fuse No. 14. Disconnect intermittent wiper relay and ensure connector is clean and not damaged. Using external voltmeter, measure voltage between ground and terminal "B" (Red/Gray wire) on intermittent wiper relay socket. *See Fig. 8.* If voltage is more than 10 volts, go to next step. If voltage is 10 volts or less, repair open in Red/Gray wire between wiper fuse No. 14 and intermittent wiper relay.

7) Connect a jumper wire between intermittent wiper relay socket terminals "A" and "B". *See Fig. 8.* If wiper motor operates, disconnect jumper wire and go to step **19)**. If wiper motor does not operate, go to next step.

8) Disconnect wiper HI/LO relay, located in PDC. Ensure connector is clean and not damaged. Ensure jumper wire is still connected between intermittent wiper relay terminals "A" and "B". Using external voltmeter, measure voltage between ground and terminal "A" (Dark Green/Violet wire) on wiper HI/LO relay. If voltage is more than 10 volts, go to next step. If voltage is 10 volts or less, repair open in Dark Green/Violet wire between intermittent and HI/LO relays.

9) Disconnect jumper wire in intermittent relay terminal. Connect a jumper wire between terminal "B" (Red/Gray wire) on intermittent relay and terminal "D" (Brown/Orange wire) on wiper HI/LO relay. If wiper motor operates in low speed mode, replace wiper HI/LO relay. If wiper motor does not operate in low speed mode, go to step **22)**.

10) Stop low speed wiper motor actuation. Using scan tool, read intermittent wipe sensor voltage. Observe scan tool and move wiper switch from OFF position to HI position. If scan tool displays INTRMT WIPE: 0V, go to next step. If scan tool displays INTRMT WIPE:, with voltage present, replace BCM.

11) Disconnect right multifunction switch 7-pin connector. *See Fig. 5.* Ensure connector is clean and not damaged. Using external voltmeter, measure voltage between ground and terminal No. 1 (Dark Blue wire) on right multifunction switch 7-pin connector. If voltage is more than 10 volts, go to next step. If voltage is 10 volts or less, repair open in Dark Blue wire between multifunction switch and fuse No. 15.

12) Disconnect instrument panel 22-pin connector at Body Control Module (BCM). *See Fig. 2.* Ensure connector is clean and not damaged. Using external ohmmeter, measure resistance between ground and terminal No. 1 (Dark Green/Yellow wire) on instrument panel 22-pin connector. If resistance is 5 ohms or greater, go to next step. If resistance is less than 5 ohms, repair short to ground in Dark Green/Yellow wire.

13) Using an external ohmmeter, measure resistance between terminal No. 2 (Dark Green/Yellow wire) on right multifunction switch 7-pin connector and terminal No. 1 on instrument panel 22-pin connector. If resistance is less than 5 ohms, go to next step. If resistance is 5 ohms or greater, repair open in Dark Green/Yellow wire between multifunction switch and BCM.

14) Reconnect right multifunction switch 7-pin connector. Turn wiper switch to LO or HI position. Using external voltmeter, measure voltage between ground and terminal No. 1 (Dark Green/Yellow wire) on instrument panel 22-pin connector. If voltage is more than 10 volts, replace BCM. If voltage is 10 volts or less, replace multifunction switch.

15) Remove intermittent wiper relay from Power Distribution Center (PDC). Ensure connector is clean and not damaged. *See Fig. 8.* Remove HI/LO wiper relay and ensure connector is clean and not damaged. Using external ohmmeter, measure resistance between ground and terminal "B" (Red/Gray wire) on intermittent wiper relay socket. If resistance is 5 ohms or greater, go to next step. If resistance is less than 5 ohms, repair short to ground in Red/Gray wire and replace wiper fuse No. 14 (40-amp).

16) Using external ohmmeter, measure resistance between ground and terminal "A" (Dark Green/Violet wire) on intermittent relay socket. If resistance is more than 5 ohms, go to next step. If resistance is less than 5 ohms, repair short to ground in Dark Green/Violet wire between intermittent wiper relay and HI/LO wiper relay, and replace wiper fuse No. 14 (40-amp).

17) Disconnect wiper motor Light Gray 4-pin connector. Ensure connector is clean and not damaged. Using scan tool in ohmmeter mode, measure resistance between terminal "D" (Brown/Orange wire) on HI/LO wiper relay. If resistance is more than 5 ohms, go to next step. If resistance is less than 5 ohms, repair short to ground in Brown/Orange wire between wiper motor 4-pin connector and HI/LO wiper relay. Replace wiper fuse No. 14 (40-amp).

18) Using scan tool in ohmmeter mode, measure resistance at terminal "B" (Red/Yellow wire) on HI/LO wiper relay. If resistance is less than 5 ohms, repair short to ground in Red/Yellow wire between HI/LO wiper relay and wiper motor 4-pin connector. If resistance is more than 5 ohms, replace wiper motor and wiper fuse No. 14 (40-amp).

19) Remove intermittent wiper relay from Power Distribution Center (PDC). Ensure connector is clean and not damaged. *See Fig. 8.* Using external voltmeter, measure voltage between ground and terminal "E" (Pink/Violet wire) on intermittent relay socket. If voltage is more than 10 volts, go to next step. If voltage is 10 volts or less, go to step **27)**.

20) Reinstall intermittent wiper relay. Locate engine 14-pin connector at BCM. *See Fig. 2.* Do not disconnect connector. Backprobe jumper wire between terminal No. 7 (Pink/Violet wire) on engine 14-pin connector and ground. If wiper motor does not operate, go to next step. If wiper motor operates, replace BCM.

21) Remove intermittent wiper relay from PDC. Do not disconnect jumper wire. Using an external ohmmeter, measure resistance between ground and terminal "E" (Pink/Violet wire) on intermittent wiper relay socket. If resistance is less than 5 ohms, replace intermittent wiper relay.

CHRY
4-98

1999 ACCESSORIES & EQUIPMENT
Body Control Computer Tests
Breeze, Cirrus, Sebring Convertible & Stratus (Cont.)

If resistance is 5 ohms or greater, repair open Pink/Violet wire between engine 14-pin connector at BCM and intermittent wiper relay in PDC.

22) Disconnect wiper motor Light Gray 4-pin connector and ensure connector is clean and not damaged. Ensure jumper wire between terminal "B" (Red/Gray wire) on intermittent wiper relay and terminal "D" (Brown/Orange wire) on HI/LO wiper relay is connected. *See Fig. 8.*

23) Using external voltmeter, measure voltage between ground and terminal No. 3 (Brown/Orange wire) on wiper motor 4-pin connector. If voltage is more than 10 volts, go to next step. If voltage is 10 volts or less, repair open in Brown/Orange wire between HI/LO relay and wiper motor.

24) Using external ohmmeter, measure resistance between ground and terminal No. 2 (Black wire) on wiper motor 4-pin connector. If resistance is less than 5 ohms, replace wiper motor. If resistance is 5 ohms or greater, repair open in Black wire between wiper motor 4-pin connector terminal and ground.

25) Remove and inspect fuse No. 15 (10-amp) in junction block. *See Fig. 3.* If fuse is open, go to step **27)**. If fuse is okay, go to next step.

26) Using external voltmeter, measure voltage between ground and terminal No. 28 (Black/White wire) on fuse No. 15 socket. *See Fig. 3.* If voltage is 10 volts or less, repair open in Black/White wire between ignition switch and junction block. If voltage is more than 10 volts, repair open in Dark Blue/Gray wire between junction block and intermittent wiper relay.

27) Remove HI/LO relay. Using an external ohmmeter, measure resistance between component terminals "C" and "E" on HI/LO wiper relay. *See Fig. 8.* If resistance is 65-90 ohms, go to next step. If resistance is not 65-90 ohms, replace HI/LO wiper relay and replace fuse No. 15.

28) Using an external ohmmeter, measure resistance between component terminals "C" and "E" on intermittent wiper relay. *See Fig. 8.* If resistance is not 65-90 ohms, replace intermittent wiper relay and replace fuse No. 15. If resistance is 65-90 ohms, go to next step.

29) Disconnect right multifunction switch 7-pin connector. *See Fig. 5.* Using external ohmmeter, measure resistance between ground and terminal No. 1 (Dark Blue wire) on right multifunction switch 7-pin connector. If resistance is 5 ohms or greater, replace multi-function switch and fuse No. 15. If resistance is less than 5 ohms, repair short to ground in Dark Blue wire between fuse No. 15 (10-amp) and terminal No. 1 on right multifunction switch 7-pin connector. Replace fuse No. 15.

WINDSHIELD WIPER TEST 3

WIPERS NOT WORKING IN HIGH SPEED MODE

NOTE: Perform WINDSHIELD WIPER TEST 1 before proceeding with this test. For connector terminal identification, see CONNECTOR IDENTIFICATION in BODY CONTROL COMPUTER – INTRODUCTION article. For wiring diagrams, see WIRING DIAGRAMS in BODY CONTROL COMPUTER – INTRODUCTION article. Perform VERIFICATION TEST VER-1A after each repair.

CAUTION: Always turn ignition switch to OFF position prior to disconnecting or connecting any module connector.

1) Using scan tool, actuate wipers in high speed mode. If wiper motor operates in high speed mode, go to next step. If wiper motor does not operate in high speed mode, go to step **3)**.

2) Stop wiper actuation. Using scan tool, read intermittent wipe sensor voltage. While observing scan tool, turn wiper switch to high position. If scan tool displays intermittent wiper voltage 6.5 volts or less, replace multifunction switch. If scan tool displays intermittent wiper voltage more than 6.5 volts, replace Body Control Module (BCM).

3) Stop wiper actuation. Disconnect HI/LO wiper relay and ensure connector is clean and not damaged. *See Fig. 8.* Using external voltmeter, measure voltage between ground and terminal "C" (Dark Blue/Gray wire) on HI/LO wiper relay. If voltage is more than 10 volts, go

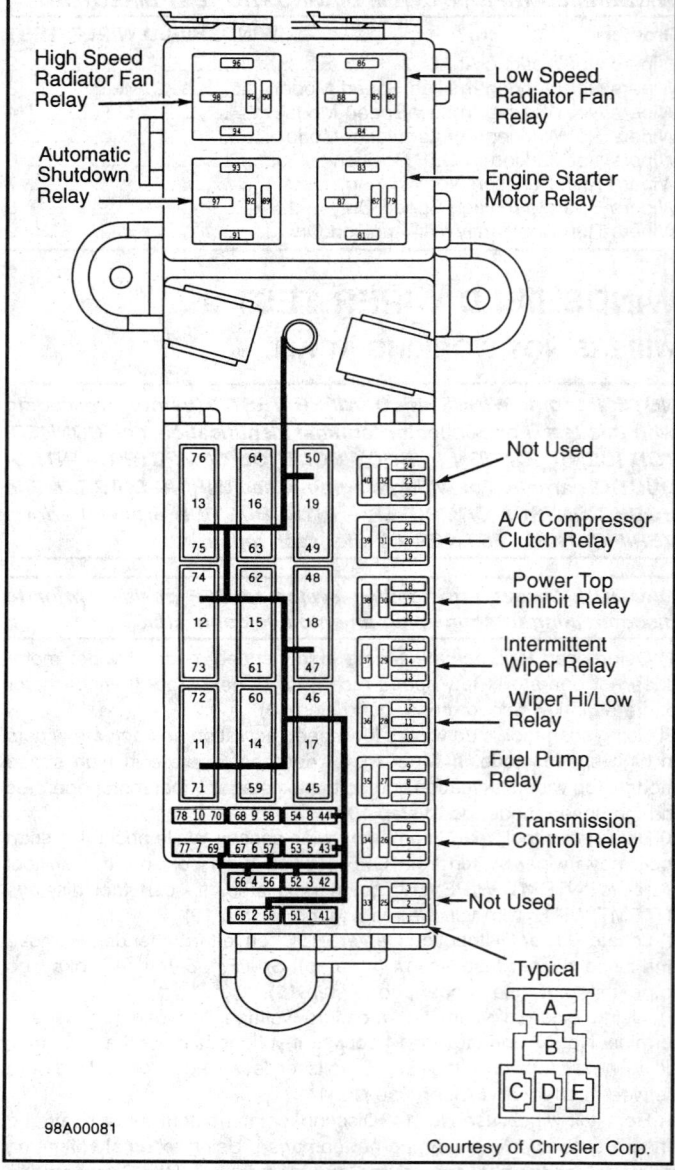

98A00081

Fig. 8: Locating Power Distribution Components & Terminals

to next step. If voltage is 10 volts or less, repair open Dark Blue/Gray wire between HI/LO wiper relay and fuse No. 15 (10-amp).

4) Connect a jumper wire between terminals "B" and "C" on HI/LO wiper relay socket. *See Fig. 8.* If wiper motor does not operate in high speed, disconnect jumper wire and go to next step. If wiper motor operates in high speed, go to step **6)**.

5) Disconnect wiper motor Light Gray 4-pin connector. Ensure connector is clean and not damaged. Using external voltmeter, measure voltage on wiper motor connector terminal "A" (Red/Yellow wire). If voltage is more than 10 volts, replace wiper motor. If voltage is 10 volts or less, repair open in Red/Yellow wire.

6) Disconnect jumper wire. Connect test light between ground and terminal "E" on HI/LO wiper relay socket. *See Fig. 8.* Using scan tool, actuate wipers in high speed mode and observe test light. If test light pulses on and off, replace HI/LO wiper relay. If test light does not pulse on and off, disconnect test light and go to next step.

7) Turn ignition off and stop high speed wiper actuation. Disconnect engine 14-pin connector at BCM. Ensure connector is clean and not damaged. Connect a jumper wire between ground and terminal No. 8 (Violet/Pink wire) on engine 14-pin connector. Go to next step.

1999 ACCESSORIES & EQUIPMENT

CHRY
4-99

Body Control Computer Tests
Breeze, Cirrus, Sebring Convertible & Stratus (Cont.)

8) Connect test light between terminals "C" and "E" on HI/LO wiper relay socket. Turn ignition on. If test light illuminates, replace BCM. If test light does not illuminate, repair open in Violet/Pink wire.

WINDSHIELD WIPER TEST 4

WIPERS NOT WORKING IN LOW SPEED MODE

NOTE: Perform WINDSHIELD WIPER TEST 1 before proceeding with this test. For connector terminal identification, see CONNECTOR IDENTIFICATION in BODY CONTROL COMPUTER – INTRODUCTION article. For wiring diagrams, see WIRING DIAGRAMS in BODY CONTROL COMPUTER – INTRODUCTION article. Perform VERIFICATION TEST VER-1A after each repair.

CAUTION: Always turn ignition switch to OFF position prior to disconnecting or connecting any module connector.

1) Using scan tool, actuate wiper motor in low speed. If wiper motor does not operate in low speed mode, go to next step. If wiper motor operates is low speed, go to step **4)**.

2) Disconnect HI/LO wiper relay and ensure connector is clean and not damaged. Connect a jumper wire between terminals "C" (Dark Blue/Gray wire) and "D" (Brown/Orange wire) on HI/LO wiper relay. *See Fig. 8.* If wiper motor does not operate in low speed, disconnect jumper wire and go to next step. If wiper motor operates in low speed, replace HI/LO wiper relay.

3) Disconnect wiper motor Light Gray 4-pin connector and ensure connector is clean and not damaged. Reconnect jumper wire as in step **2)**. Using external voltmeter, measure voltage on wiper motor 4-pin connector terminal "B" (Brown/Orange wire). If voltage is more than 10 volts, replace wiper motor. If voltage is 10 volts or less, repair open in Brown/Orange wire.

4) Using scan tool, stop wiper motor actuation. Using scan tool, read intermittent wipe sensor. While observing scan tool display, move wiper switch to low speed position. If scan tool displays an intermittent wiper voltage of approximately 5.5 volts, replace BCM. If scan tool does not display a voltage of approximately 5.5 volts, replace multifunction switch.

WINDSHIELD WIPER TEST 5

WIPERS NOT WORKING IN INTERMITTENT MODE

NOTE: Perform WINDSHIELD WIPER TEST 1 before proceeding with this test. For connector terminal identification, see CONNECTOR IDENTIFICATION in BODY CONTROL COMPUTER – INTRODUCTION article. For wiring diagrams, see WIRING DIAGRAMS in BODY CONTROL COMPUTER – INTRODUCTION article. Perform VERIFICATION TEST VER-1A after each repair.

CAUTION: Always turn ignition switch to OFF position prior to disconnecting or connecting any module connector.

1) Operate wipers in intermittent mode. If wiper delay times are okay, go to next step. If wiper delay times are inconsistent, reset wiper switch minimum using scan tool. Retest intermittent wiper operation.

2) Turn ignition on. Using scan tool, observe wiper voltage while moving stalk switch through all intermittent wiper positions. If voltage does not change, replace multifunction switch. Reset wiper switch minimum. If voltage does change, replace BCM. Reset wiper switch minimum.

WINDSHIELD WIPER TEST 6

WIPERS NOT PARKING IN OFF POSITION

NOTE: Perform WINDSHIELD WIPER TEST 1 before proceeding with this test. For connector terminal identification, see CONNECTOR IDENTIFICATION in BODY CONTROL COMPUTER – INTRODUCTION article. For wiring diagrams, see WIRING DIAGRAMS in BODY CONTROL COMPUTER – INTRODUCTION article. Perform VERIFICATION TEST VER-1A after each repair.

CAUTION: Always turn ignition switch to OFF position prior to disconnecting or connecting any module connector.

1) Operate wiper in intermittent mode. Using scan tool, observe wiper park switch. If wiper park switch does not toggle from closed to open, turn wipers off and go to next step. If wiper park switch toggles from closed to open, system is operating properly. Using scan tool, clear trouble codes, and try to reproduce fault.

2) Disconnect wiper motor Light Gray 4-pin connector and ensure connector is clean and not damaged. Using scan tool, continue observing wiper park switch and go to next step.

3) Connect a jumper wire between terminal "D" (White/Gray wire) and ground on wiper motor 4-pin connector. If scan tool does not display, SWITCH: CLOSED, go to next step. If scan tool display, SWITCH: CLOSED, replace wiper motor.

4) Locate engine 14-pin connector at Body Control Module (BCM). *See Fig. 3.* Using a jumper wire, backprobe between terminal No. 5 (White/Gray wire) on 14-pin connector and ground. If scan tool displays SWITCH: CLOSED, repair open in White/Gray wire. If scan tool does not display SWITCH: CLOSED, replace BCM.

WINDSHIELD WIPER TEST 7

WIPER WASH FUNCTION NOT WORKING PROPERLY

NOTE: Perform WINDSHIELD WIPER TEST 1 before proceeding with this test. For connector terminal identification, see CONNECTOR IDENTIFICATION in BODY CONTROL COMPUTER – INTRODUCTION article. For wiring diagrams, see WIRING DIAGRAMS in BODY CONTROL COMPUTER – INTRODUCTION article. Perform VERIFICATION TEST VER-1A after each repair.

CAUTION: Always turn ignition switch to OFF position prior to disconnecting or connecting any module connector.

1) Ensure windshield washer fluid reservoir is full. Momentarily pull and release wash button. If washer pump did not operate, but wipers did operate, go to next step. If washer pump and wipers did not operate, go to step **5)**. If washer pump operated without wiper operation, replace BCM. If washer pump and wipers operated, system is operating properly.

2) Locate and disconnect washer pump 2-pin connector at bottom of washer fluid reservoir. Ensure connector is clean and not damaged. Using external ohmmeter, measure resistance between ground and terminal "A" (Black wire) on washer pump connector. If resistance is less than 5 ohms, go to next step. If resistance is 5 ohms or greater, repair open in Black wire.

3) Activate washer pump switch. Using external voltmeter, measure voltage on washer pump 2-pin connector terminal "B" (Brown/Dark Blue wire). If voltage is 10 volts or less, go to next step. If voltage is more than 10 volts, replace washer pump.

4) Locate engine 14-pin connector at BCM. *See Fig. 3.* Do not disconnect connector. Activate washer pump switch. Using external voltmeter, measure voltage backprobing between terminal No. 10 (Brown/Dark Blue wire) on engine 14-pin connector and ground. If voltage is more than 10 volts, repair open Brown/Dark Blue wire. If voltage is 10 volts or less, replace BCM.

CHRY
4-100

1999 ACCESSORIES & EQUIPMENT
Body Control Computer Tests
Breeze, Cirrus, Sebring Convertible & Stratus (Cont.)

5) Using scan tool, read washer switch status while pulling washer switch. If scan tool does not display WASHER SW: CLOSED, go to next step. If scan tool displays WASHER SW: CLOSED, replace Body Control Module (BCM).

6) Locate and disconnect right multifunction switch 7-pin connector. *See Fig. 5.* Connect a jumper wire between terminals No. 1 (Dark Blue wire) and No. 3 (Brown/Dark Blue wire) on multifunction switch 7-pin connector. Using scan tool, read washer switch status while pulling washer switch. If scan tool does not display WASHER SW: CLOSED, go to next step. If scan tool displays WASHER SW: CLOSED, replace multifunction switch.

7) Disconnect instrument panel 22-pin connector at BCM. *See Fig. 2.* Ensure connector is clean and not damaged. Using external voltmeter, measure voltage between ground and terminal No. 15 (Brown/Dark Blue wire) on instrument panel 22-pin connector. If voltage is more than 10 volts, replace BCM. If voltage is less than 10 volts, repair open in Brown/Dark Blue wire.

WINDSHIELD WIPER TEST 8

WIPERS OPERATE IN HIGH SPEED ONLY

NOTE: Perform WINDSHIELD WIPER TEST 1 before proceeding with this test. For connector terminal identification, see CONNECTOR IDENTIFICATION in BODY CONTROL COMPUTER – INTRODUCTION article. For wiring diagrams, see WIRING DIAGRAMS in BODY CONTROL COMPUTER – INTRODUCTION article. Perform VERIFICATION TEST VER-1A after each repair.

CAUTION: Always turn ignition switch to OFF position prior to disconnecting or connecting any module connector.

1) Disconnect HI/LO wiper relay. *See Fig. 8.* Replace original HI/LO wiper relay with a known good relay. Turn ignition on and activate wipers. If wipers do not operate properly in low and high speed modes, go to next step. If wiper operate properly in low and high speed modes, replace original HI/LO wiper relay.

2) Turn ignition off. Disconnect engine 14-pin connector at BCM. *See Fig. 2.* Ensure connector is clean and not damaged. Remove substitute HI/LO wiper relay. Using external ohmmeter, measure resistance between ground and terminal No. 8 (Violet/Pink wire) on engine 14-pin connector. If resistance is 5 ohms or greater, replace BCM. If resistance is less than 5 ohms, repair short to ground in Violet/Pink wire.

WINDSHIELD WIPER TEST 9

WIPERS RUN CONSTANTLY WITH IGNITION ON

NOTE: Perform WINDSHIELD WIPER TEST 1 before proceeding with this test. For connector terminal identification, see CONNECTOR IDENTIFICATION in BODY CONTROL COMPUTER – INTRODUCTION article. For wiring diagrams, see WIRING DIAGRAMS in BODY CONTROL COMPUTER – INTRODUCTION article. Perform VERIFICATION TEST VER-1A after each repair.

CAUTION: Always turn ignition switch to OFF position prior to disconnecting or connecting any module connector.

1) Ensure ignition is on and wiper switch is off. Using scan tool, read intermittent wiper voltage. If scan tool displays a voltage of more than 9 volts, go to next step. If scan tool displays a voltage less than 9 volts, go to step **4)**.

2) Turn ignition off. Disconnect instrument panel 22-pin connector at BCM. *See Fig. 2.* Ensure connector is clean and not damaged. Using external voltmeter, measure voltage between ground and terminal No. 10 (Dark Green/Yellow wire) on instrument panel 22-pin connector. Turn ignition on with engine off. If voltage is more than .5 volt, go to next step. If voltage is .5 volt or less, replace BCM.

3) Turn ignition off. Disconnect right multifunction switch 7-pin connector. *See Fig. 5.* Using scan tool in voltmeter mode, measure voltage between ground and terminal No. 10 (Dark Green/Yellow wire) on instrument panel 22-pin connector. Turn ignition on with engine off. If voltage is more than .5 volt, repair short to battery voltage on Dark Green/Yellow wire. If voltage is .5 volt or less, replace multifunction switch.

4) Turn ignition off. Remove intermittent wiper relay and replace original wiper relay with a known good relay. *See Fig. 8.* Turn ignition on with engine off. If wipers still run constantly, go to next step. If wipers do not run constantly, replace intermittent wiper relay.

5) Turn ignition off. Disconnect engine 14-pin connector at BCM. Ensure connector is clean and not damaged. Turn ignition on with engine off. If wipers still run constantly, go to next step. If wipers do not run constantly, replace Body Control Module (BCM).

6) Turn ignition off. Remove substitute intermittent wiper relay. Using scan tool in ohmmeter mode, measure resistance at terminal No. 7 (Pink/Violet wire) on engine 14-pin connector. If resistance is less than 100 ohms, repair short to ground in Pink/Violet wire. If resistance is 100 ohms or greater, replace BCM.

SKIM INITIALIZATION PROCEDURE

General Information – SECURED ACCESS mode is not required to check programmed status of key.

If PCM is replaced, unique secret key data must be transferred from SKIM to PCM. This procedure requires SKIM to be placed in SECURED ACCESS mode using 4-digit PIN code.

If 3 attempts are made to enter secured access mode using an incorrect PIN, SECURED ACCESS mode will be locked out for one hour. To exit lock out mode, turn ignition switch to RUN/START position continuously for one hour. Ensure all accessories are turned off. Monitor battery state and connect battery charger is necessary.

To program smart keys using "customer programming method" requires 2 valid smart keys. See owner's manual.

Initialization Procedure – **1)** Obtain vehicle's unique PIN number assigned to it's original SKIM module from vehicle owner or Chrysler's customer center.

2) Using scan tool, select THEFT ALARM, SKIM, then MISCELLANEOUS. Select SKIM MODULE REPLACED function.

3) Enter SECURED ACCESS mode using unique 4-digit PIN number.

4) Program vehicle's VIN number into SKIM's memory.

5) Program country code into SKIM's memory (U.S.).

6) Transfer vehicle's unique Secret Key data from PCM. This process will require SKIM module to be in SECURED ACCESS mode. The PIN number must be entered into scan tool before SKIM will enter SECURED ACCESS mode. Once SECURED ACCESS mode is active, SKIM will remain in that mode for 60 seconds.

7) Program all customer keys into SKIM's memory. This requires that SKIM be in SECURED ACCESS mode. The SKIM will immediately exit SECURED ACCESS mode after each key is programmed.

PROGRAMMING BLANK SMART KEY USING SCAN TOOL

1) Once key blank is cut, insert key into ignition switch. Turn ignition switch to RUN position. Using scan tool, select THEFT ALARM, then SKIM. Select MISCELLANEOUS, then PROGRAM NEW KEY. Enter 4-digit PIN code. When programming is completed, SKIM will exit SECURED ACCESS mode and display status of key. One of five different status messages maybe displayed as follows:

- PROGRAMMING SUCCESSFUL is displayed if SKIM smart key programming succeeds.
- LEARNED KEY IN IGNITION is displayed if key in the ignition has already been programmed into vehicle's SKIM.
- 8 KEYS ALREADY LEARNED, PROGRAMMING NOT DONE is displayed if eight keys have already been programmed into SKIM. If

a new key needs to be added due to a lost or defective key, the ERASE ALL KEYS function has to be performed. Original 7 keys plus additional new key may then be reprogrammed into SKIM.

- PROGRAMMING NOT ATTEMPTED is displayed after an ERASE ALL KEYS function is executed.
- PROGRAMING KEY FAILED is displayed if further diagnosis is required.

2) To program additional keys, turn ignition off. Remove current programmed key and insert next new blank key. Turn ignition switch to RUN position. Re-enter SECURED ACCESS mode function and repeat PROGRAM NEW KEY procedure.

VERIFICATION TEST VER-1A

VERIFICATION PROCEDURE

1) Reconnect all previously disconnected components and wiring. If Sentry Key Immobilizer Module (SKIM) was replaced, go to SKIM INITIALIZATION PROCEDURE. If battery or BCM has been disconnected, or any work has been performed on A/C system, A/C mode doors must be calibrated. Start engine and use scan tool to calibrate A/C mode doors. Do not allow vehicle to move during calibration. When calibration is complete, turn engine off and ignition on. Use scan tool to erase trouble codes.

2) Turn ignition off and wait at least 5 seconds and then turn ignition on (engine off). Operate system that was malfunctioning to verify correct operation. If system operates properly, repair is complete. If system does not operate properly, go to SYMPTOM ID TEST 1A.

1999 ACCESSORIES & EQUIPMENT
Body Control Computer Tests
Caravan, Town & Country & Voyager

NOTE: See BODY CONTROL COMPUTER – INTRODUCTION article before proceeding with following test.

SYMPTOM IDENTIFICATION

IDENTIFYING VEHICLE EQUIPMENT & SYSTEM PROBLEMS

NOTE: For connector terminal identification and wiring diagrams, see BODY CONTROL COMPUTER – INTRODUCTION article. When directed to go to next step, disregard step if vehicle is not equipped with module being tested.

NOTE: Perform a visual inspection before proceeding with this test.

1) Connect scan tool to Data Link Connector (DLC). DLC is a 16-pin connector located on left side of steering column. Turn ignition switch to ON position. If scan tool display is not blank, go to next step. If scan tool display is blank, see appropriate VEHICLE COMMUNICATIONS article.
2) Using scan tool, select BODY SYSTEM, then BODY COMPUTER. Scan tool will perform a CCD bus test. If scan tool displays BUS FAILED or NO RESPONSE, see appropriate VEHICLE COMMUNICATIONS article. If scan tool does not display BUS FAILED or NO RESPONSE, go to next step.
3) Using scan tool, select SENSOR DISPLAY and read IGNITION VOLTAGE. If scan tool displays less than 10 volts, see appropriate VEHICLE COMMUNICATIONS article. If scan tool displays 10 volts or more, go to next step.
4) Using scan tool, select READ DTCs. If any Diagnostic Trouble Codes (fault messages) are present, go to appropriate fault message. If no fault messages are present, identify customer complaint. See following list for possible fault messages and customer complaint symptoms. Systems listed are diagnosed using a scan tool. Malfunctions in these systems may occur separately or in various combinations. When diagnosing a system with many apparent problems, a sequence of tests may be required. At the beginning of each test, a note will indicate which test to perform first. After repairs, ensure problem(s) or failure(s) have been corrected.

CHIME SYSTEM
- CHIME INOPERATIVE AT ALL TIMES
- CHIME INOPERATIVE WITH DRIVER SEAT BELT UNFASTENED
- CHIME INOPERATIVE WITH ENGINE TEMPERATURE CRITICAL (LOW OIL PRESSURE)
- CHIME INOPERATIVE WITH EXTERIOR LIGHTS ON
- CHIME INOPERATIVE WITH TURN SIGNAL ON
- CHIME INOPERATIVE WITH DOME LIGHTS ON
- CHIME INOPERATIVE WITH KEY IN IGNITION & DRIVER DOOR OPEN
- CHIME INOPERATIVE WITH DRIVER DOOR OPEN & KEY OUT
- CHIME SOUNDS WITH DRIVER'S SEAT BELT FASTENED

EXTERIOR LIGHTING SYSTEM
- AUTOMATIC HEADLIGHTS SIGNAL CIRCUIT OPEN
- AUTOMATIC HEADLIGHTS WILL NOT TURN OFF
- AUTOMATIC HEADLIGHTS WILL NOT TURN ON
- FOG LIGHTS WILL NOT TURN OFF
- FOG LIGHTS WILL NOT TURN ON
- HEADLIGHTS WILL NOT TURN OFF
- HEADLIGHTS WILL NOT TURN ON
- PARK LIGHTS WILL NOT TURN OFF
- PARK LIGHTS WILL NOT TURN ON

INFORMATION CENTER
- ABS WARNING LIGHT CONCERNS
- ALL WARNING LIGHTS INOPERATIVE
- ENGINE TEMPERATURE WARNING LIGHT CONCERNS
- HIGH BEAM INDICATOR LIGHT CONCERNS
- LOW OIL PRESSURE WARNING LIGHT CONCERNS
- RED BRAKE WARNING LIGHT MALFUNCTION
- SERVICE ENGINE SOON INDICATOR LIGHT CONCERNS
- TURN SIGNAL INDICATOR LIGHT CONCERNS

INSTRUMENT CLUSTER
- FUEL LEVEL SENDING CIRCUIT ERROR
- ALL GAUGES DO NOT OPERATE
- INSTRUMENT CLUSTER ILLUMINATION CONCERN
- INSTRUMENT CLUSTER WARNING LIGHTS, ODOMETER & PRNDL DISPLAY CONCERN
- GAUGES DO NOT ZERO WHEN KEY IS TURNED OFF
- ONE GAUGE NOT OPERATING PROPERLY
- TRIP & RESET BUTTON CONCERN

INTERIOR LIGHTING SYSTEM
- COURTESY LIGHTS INOPERATIVE WITH DOME LIGHT SWITCH
- COURTESY LIGHTS INOPERATIVE WITH ANY DOOR
- COURTESY LIGHTS INOPERATIVE WITH DRIVER DOOR (OPEN DRIVER DOOR AJAR CIRCUIT)
- COURTESY LIGHTS INOPERATIVE WITH LEFT SLIDING DOOR (OPEN LEFT SLIDING DOOR AJAR CIRCUIT)
- COURTESY LIGHTS INOPERATIVE WITH LIFTGATE (OPEN LIFTGATE AJAR CIRCUIT)
- COURTESY LIGHTS INOPERATIVE WITH PASSENGER DOOR (OPEN PASSENGER DOOR AJAR CIRCUIT)
- COURTESY LIGHTS INOPERATIVE WITH RIGHT SLIDING DOOR (OPEN RIGHT SLIDING DOOR AJAR CIRCUIT)
- COURTESY LIGHTS ON AT ALL TIMES
- ILLUMINATED ENTRY INOPERATIVE WITH DRIVER DOOR KEY (LEFT DOOR KEY CYLINDER DISARM SW FAILURE)
- ILLUMINATED ENTRY INOPERATIVE WITH RKE TRANSMITTER
- SHORTED DRIVER DOOR AJAR CIRCUIT
- SHORTED LEFT SLIDING DOOR AJAR CIRCUIT
- SHORTED LIFTGATE AJAR CIRCUIT
- SHORTED PASSENGER DOOR AJAR CIRCUIT
- SHORTED RIGHT SLIDING DOOR AJAR CIRCUIT

OVERHEAD CONSOLE CONCERNS
- COMPASS MINI-TRIP COMPUTER (CMTC) ELAPSED TIME INOPERATIVE OR WRONG
- COMPASS MINI-TRIP COMPUTER (CMTC) AVG MPH OR FUEL ECONOMY INOPERATIVE OR WRONG
- COMPASS MINI-TRIP COMPUTER (CMTC) DISPLAYING "OC"
- COMPASS MINI-TRIP COMPUTER (CMTC) DISPLAYING SC"
- COMPASS MINI-TRIP COMPUTER (CMTC) DOES NOT RESPOND TO INSTRUMENT CLUSTER DIMMING (COMPASS MINI-TRIP COMPUTER SWITCH INOPERATIVE)
- COMPASS MINI-TRIP COMPUTER (CMTC) SEGMENTS INOPERATIVE
- COMPASS MINI-TRIP COMPUTER (CMTC) SHOWS FAILED
- INCORRECT AMBIENT TEMPERATURE READINGS

POWER DOOR LOCK SYSTEM
- ALL DOORS (EXCEPT DRVR W/RKE) FAIL LCK/UNLCK FROM ANY SWITCH
- ALL DOORS FAIL TO LOCK & UNLOCK FROM ANY SWITCH
- ALL DOORS FAIL TO LOCK & UNLOCK FROM ONE SWITCH
- ALL DOORS FAILING TO LOCK FROM ANY SWITCH
- ALL DOORS (EXCEPT DRIVER W/RKE) FAIL TO UNLOCK
- DRIVER DOOR (W/RKE) FAILING TO UNLOCK FROM ANY SWITCH
- ONE DOOR FAILS TO LOCK & UNLOCK FROM ANY SWITCH
- LEFT DOOR KEY CYL ARM SW FAILURE

1999 ACCESSORIES & EQUIPMENT
Body Control Computer Tests
Caravan, Town & Country & Voyager (Cont.)

CHRY
4-103

- LEFT DOOR LOCK SWITCH FAILURE
- LEFT DOOR UNLOCK SWITCH FAILURE
- LIFTGATE DOOR MUX CKT SHORT TO GND
- LIFTGATE KEY CYL ARM SW FAILURE
- LIFTGATE KEY CYL DISARM SW FAILURE
- LT FRONT DOOR MUX CKT SHORT TO GND
- RIGHT DOOR KEY CYL ARM SW FAILURE
- RIGHT DOOR KEY CYL ARM SW FAILURE
- RIGHT DOOR LOCK SWITCH FAILURE
- RIGHT DOOR UNLOCK SWITCH FAILURE
- RT FRONT DOOR MUX CKT SHORT TO GND
- ALL DOORS (EXCEPT DRVR W/RKE) FAIL LCK/UNLCK FROM ANY SWITCH (ALL DOORS FAIL TO LOCK & UNLOCK FROM ONE SWITCH, ALL DOORS FAILING TO LOCK FROM ANY SWITCH OR ONE SWITCH, ALL DOORS FAILING TO UNLOCK FROM ONE SWITCH, DRIVER DOOR (W/RKE) FAILING TO UNLOCK FROM ANY SWITCH, ONE DOOR FAILS TO LOCK & UNLOCK FROM ANY SWITCH)
- ALL DOORS FAIL TO LOCK & UNLOCK FROM ANY SWITCH
- ALL DOORS (EXCEPT DRIVER W/RKE) FAIL TO UNLOCK
- AUTOMATIC DOOR LOCKS FAIL TO LOCK OVER 15 MPH
- DOORS LOCK WITH KEY IN IGNITION & LEFT DOOR OPEN
- REMOTE KEYLESS ENTRY PROBLEM

VEHICLE THEFT SECURITY SYSTEM (VTSS)

- VTSS SYSTEM CONCERNS

WINDSHIELD WIPER SYSTEM

- FRONT WIPER PARK SWITCH CIRCUIT OPEN (FRONT WIPER PARK SWITCH CIRCUIT SHORTED, FRONT WIPERS NOT PARKING IN OFF POSITION)
- REAR WIPER MUX CIRCUIT ERROR
- WIPER CONSTANTLY OPERATING WITH SWITCH IN OFF POSITION
- FRONT WIPERS NOT WORKING AT ALL
- WIPERS NOT WORKING IN INTERMITTENT MODE
- WIPERS NOT WORKING IN LOW SPEED MODE
- REAR WASHER MOTOR INOPERATIVE
- REAR WIPER NOT PARKING IN OFF POSITION
- REAR WIPER INOPERATIVE
- REAR WIPER/WASHER ON CONSTANTLY
- WIPER WASH FUNCTION NOT WORKING PROPERLY
- WIPERS NOT WORKING IN HIGH SPEED MODE

CHIME SYSTEM

CHIME INOPERATIVE AT ALL TIMES

NOTE: For connector terminal identification and wiring diagrams, see BODY CONTROL COMPUTER – INTRODUCTION article. Perform VERIFICATION TEST VER-1A after each repair.

CAUTION: Always turn ignition switch to OFF position prior to disconnecting any module connector.

Ensure all doors are closed. Turn ignition switch to ON position. Using scan tool, actuate chime test. If chime sounds, system is functional. If chime does not sound, replace Body Control Module (BCM). BCM is located with junction block under driver's side instrument panel. *See Fig. 1.*

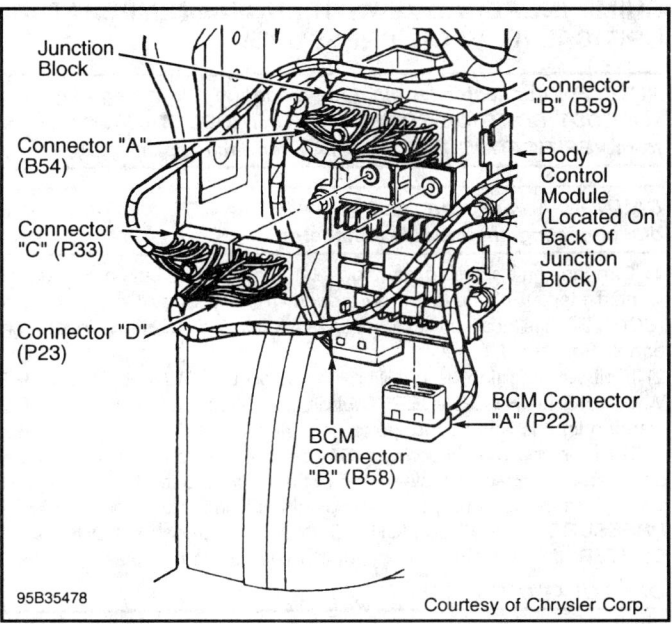

95B35478   Courtesy of Chrysler Corp.

Fig. 1: Identifying Junction Block/BCM Connectors

CHIME INOPERATIVE WITH DRIVER'S SEAT BELT UNFASTENED

NOTE: For connector terminal identification and wiring diagrams, see BODY CONTROL COMPUTER – INTRODUCTION article. Perform VERIFICATION TEST VER-1A after each repair.

CAUTION: Always turn ignition switch to OFF position prior to disconnecting any module connector.

1) Turn ignition off. Ensure driver's seat belt is unfastened and driver's door is closed. Turn ignition on. If chime sounds, system is currently functioning correctly. If chime does not sound, go to next step.

2) Using scan tool, read seat belt switch status. If scan tool does not display SEAT BELT SWITCH: CLOSED, go to next step. If scan tool displays SEAT BELT SWITCH: CLOSED, replace Body Control Module (BCM). BCM is located with junction block under driver's side instrument panel. *See Fig. 1.*

3) Disconnect driver's seat belt switch connector and ensure connector is clean and not damaged. Connect a jumper wire between harness connector terminals. Using scan tool, read seat belt switch status. If scan tool does not display SEAT BELT SWITCH: CLOSED, go to next step. If scan tool displays SEAT BELT SWITCH: CLOSED, replace driver's seat belt switch.

4) Connect jumper wire between ground and driver's seat belt switch harness connector terminal No. 1 (Light Green/Red wire). Using scan tool, read seat belt switch status. If scan tool does not display SEAT BELT SWITCH: CLOSED, go to next step. If scan tool displays SEAT BELT SWITCH: CLOSED, repair open ground (Black wire).

5) Access Body Control Module (BCM) connector "B". BCM is located with junction block under driver's side instrument panel. *See Fig. 1.* Remove connector cover. Do not disconnect connector. Connect a backprobe jumper wire between BCM connector "B" terminal No. 78 (Light Green/Red wire) and ground. Using scan tool, read seat belt switch status. If scan tool displays SEAT BELT: CLOSED, repair open Light Green/Red wire between driver's seat belt switch and BCM. If scan tool does not display SEAT BELT: CLOSED, replace BCM.

CHRY
4-104

1999 ACCESSORIES & EQUIPMENT
Body Control Computer Tests
Caravan, Town & Country & Voyager (Cont.)

CHIME INOPERATIVE WITH ENGINE TEMPERATURE CRITICAL (LOW OIL PRESSURE)

NOTE: For connector terminal identification and wiring diagrams, see BODY CONTROL COMPUTER – INTRODUCTION article. Perform VERIFICATION TEST VER-1A after each repair.

CAUTION: Always turn ignition switch to OFF position prior to disconnecting any module connector.

1) Turn ignition on. Using scan tool, actuate chime. If chime sounds, go to next step. If chime does not sound, replace Body Control Module (BCM). BCM is located with junction block under driver's side instrument panel. *See Fig. 1.*
2) If oil warning light is not illuminated, go to LOW OIL PRESSURE WARNING LIGHT CONCERNS under INFORMATION CENTER. If oil warning light is illuminated, go to next step.
3) Turn ignition off. Disconnect Oil Pressure Switch (OPS) connector and ensure connector is clean and not damaged. See OPS LOCATION table. Turn ignition on. If oil warning light is illuminated, go to LOW OIL PRESSURE WARNING LIGHT CONCERNS under INFORMATION CENTER. If oil warning light is not illuminated, go to next step.

OPS LOCATION

Engine	Location
2.4L	Side Of Block, Near Transaxle
3.0L	Next To Oil Filter
3.3L & 3.8L	Below A/C Compressor

4) Connect jumper wire between oil pressure switch terminal and ground. Start engine and idle for 20 seconds. Raise engine speed to 1600 RPM. If chime sounds, system is currently functioning correctly. If chime does not sound, replace BCM. BCM is located with junction block under driver's side instrument panel. *See Fig. 1.*

CHIME INOPERATIVE WITH EXTERIOR LIGHTS ON

NOTE: For connector terminal identification and wiring diagrams, see BODY CONTROL COMPUTER – INTRODUCTION article. Perform VERIFICATION TEST VER-1A after each repair.

CAUTION: Always turn ignition switch to OFF position prior to disconnecting any module connector.

1) Ensure headlights and all exterior lights are functioning properly. If any exterior lights do not illuminate, go to EXTERIOR LIGHTING SYSTEM. If all lights are functioning, go to next step.
2) Open driver's door. Using scan tool, read door ajar status. If scan tool displays DRDOOR AJAR SWITCH: CLOSED, go to next step. If scan tool does not display DRDOOR AJAR SWITCH: CLOSED, go to COURTESY LIGHTS INOPERATIVE WITH DRIVER DOOR (OPEN DRIVER DOOR AJAR CIRCUIT) under INTERIOR LIGHTING SYSTEM.
3) Remove ignition key. Using scan tool, read key-in ignition switch status. If scan tool does not display KEY-IN IGNITION SW: OPEN, go to step **6)**. If scan tool displays KEY-IN IGNITION SW: OPEN, go to next step.
4) Open driver's door. Turn on park lights. If chime does not sound, replace Body Control Module (BCM). BCM is located with junction block under driver's side instrument panel. *See Fig. 1.*
5) Turn on headlights. If chime sounds, system is currently functioning correctly. If chime does not sound, replace BCM. BCM is located with junction block under driver's side instrument panel. *See Fig. 1.*
6) Disconnect key-in ignition switch connector. *See Fig. 2.* Using scan tool, read key-in ignition switch status. If scan tool displays KEY-IN IGNITION SW: CLOSED, go to next step. If scan tool does not display KEY-IN IGNITION SW: CLOSED, replace ignition switch. See appropriate STEERING COLUMN SWITCHES article.

7) Disconnect BCM connector "A" and ensure connector is clean and not damaged. BCM is located with junction block under driver's side instrument panel. *See Fig. 1.* Ensure all lights and accessories are off. Close all doors. Using external ohmmeter, measure resistance between ground and BCM connector "A" terminal No. 32 (Light Blue wire). If resistance is less than 10 ohms, repair Light Blue wire between BCM and ignition switch for short to ground. If resistance is 10 ohms or more, replace BCM.

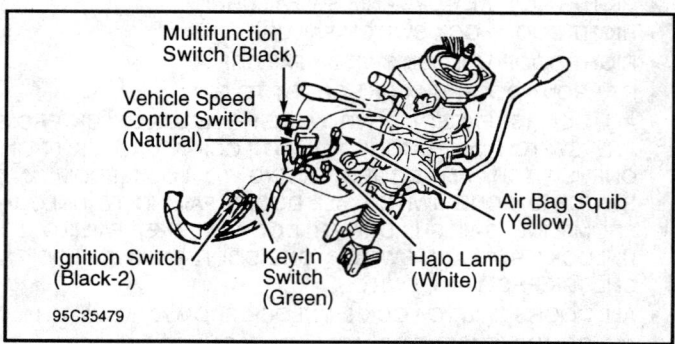

Fig. 2: Identifying Steering Column Harness Connector Locations

CHIME INOPERATIVE WITH TURN SIGNAL ON

NOTE: For connector terminal identification and wiring diagrams, see BODY CONTROL COMPUTER – INTRODUCTION article. Perform VERIFICATION TEST VER-1A after each repair.

CAUTION: Always turn ignition switch to OFF position prior to disconnecting any module connector.

1) Test drive vehicle. If speedometer is not functioning properly, go to INSTRUMENT CLUSTER. If speedometer is functioning, go to next step.

NOTE: Turn signals must be operating properly for chime to work. Operate turn signal in both directions. If turn signals do not function correctly, repair as needed.

2) Turn ignition on. Operate left turn signal. Using scan tool, read turn signal state in BODY, INPUTS/OUTPUTS. If scan tool displays OPEN, then CLOSED, go to next step. If scan tool does not display OPEN, then CLOSED, go to step **6)**.
3) Operate right turn signal. Using scan tool, read turn signal state. If scan tool displays OPEN, then CLOSED, go to next step. If scan tool does not display OPEN, then CLOSED, go to step **6)**.
4) Using scan tool, read turn signal status in CHIME MONITORS. If scan tool displays ENABLED, go to next step. If scan tool does not display ENABLED, go to step **6)**.
5) Using scan tool, enable turn signal chime. Raise and support vehicle. Start engine and move shift selector lever to "D" position. Turn on left turn signal. Increase vehicle speed to more than 20 MPH. Maintain speed for one mile. If chime sounds, system is currently functioning properly. If chime does not sound, replace Body Control Module (BCM). BCM is located with junction block under driver's side instrument panel. *See Fig. 1.*
6) Turn ignition off. Disconnect Body Control Module (BCM). BCM is located with junction block under driver's side instrument panel. *See Fig. 1.* Gain access to junction block/BCM internal 23-pin connector. Turn ignition on. Operate left turn signal. Using a test light, probe internal connector terminal No. 19. If test light flashes, go to next step. If test light does not flash, replace junction block.
7) Operate right turn signal. Move test light probe to terminal No. 21. If test light flashes, replace BCM. If test light does not flash, replace junction block.

CHIME INOPERATIVE WITH DOME LIGHTS ON

NOTE: For connector terminal identification and wiring diagrams, see BODY CONTROL COMPUTER – INTRODUCTION article. Perform VERIFICATION TEST VER-1A after each repair.

CAUTION: Always turn ignition switch to OFF position prior to disconnecting any module connector.

1) Open driver's door. Using scan tool, read door ajar status. If scan tool displays DRDOOR AJAR SWITCH: CLOSED, go to next step. If scan tool does not display DRDOOR AJAR SWITCH: CLOSED, go to COURTESY LIGHTS INOPERATIVE WITH DRIVER DOOR (OPEN DRIVER DOOR AJAR CIRCUIT) under INTERIOR LIGHTING SYSTEM.

2) Remove ignition key. Using scan tool, read key-in ignition switch status. If scan tool displays KEY-IN IGNITION SW: CLOSED, go to next step. If scan tool does not display KEY-IN IGNITION SW: CLOSED, go to step **5)**.

3) Disconnect key-in ignition switch connector. *See Fig. 2.* Using scan tool, read key-in ignition switch status. If scan tool displays KEY-IN IGNITION SW: CLOSED, go to next step. If scan tool does not display KEY-IN IGNITION SW: CLOSED, replace ignition switch. See appropriate STEERING COLUMN SWITCHES article.

4) Disconnect BCM connector "A" and ensure connector is clean and not damaged. BCM is located with junction block under driver's side instrument panel. *See Fig. 1.* Ensure all lights and accessories are off. Close all doors. Using external ohmmeter, measure resistance between ground and BCM connector "A" terminal No. 32 (Light Blue wire). If resistance is less than 10 ohms, repair Light Blue wire between BCM and ignition switch for short to ground. If resistance is 10 ohms or more, replace BCM.

5) Turn dome lights on. If dome lights do not illuminate, go to COURTESY LIGHTS INOPERATIVE WITH DOME LIGHT SWITCH under INTERIOR LIGHTING SYSTEMS. If dome lights illuminate, determine if chime sounds. If chime does not sound, replace Body Control Module (BCM). BCM is located with junction block under driver's side instrument panel. *See Fig. 1.* If chime sounds, system is currently functioning correctly.

CHIME INOPERATIVE WITH KEY IN IGNITION & DRIVER DOOR OPEN

NOTE: For connector terminal identification and wiring diagrams, see BODY CONTROL COMPUTER – INTRODUCTION article. Perform VERIFICATION TEST VER-1A after each repair.

CAUTION: Always turn ignition switch to OFF position prior to disconnecting any module connector.

1) Turn ignition off. Open driver's door. If chime does not sound, go to next step. If chime sounds, system is currently functioning correctly.

2) Using scan tool, read driver's door ajar switch status. If scan tool displays DRDOOR AJAR SWITCH: CLOSED, go to next step. If scan tool does not display DRDOOR AJAR SWITCH: CLOSED, go to COURTESY LIGHTS INOPERATIVE WITH DRIVER DOOR (OPEN DRIVER DOOR AJAR CIRCUIT) under INTERIOR LIGHTING SYSTEMS.

3) Ensure key is in ignition switch. Using scan tool, read key-in ignition switch status. If scan tool does not display KEY-IN IGNITION SW: CLOSED, go to next step. If scan tool displays KEY-IN IGNITION SW: CLOSED, replace Body Control Module (BCM). BCM is located with junction block under driver's side instrument panel. *See Fig. 1.*

4) Disconnect key-in ignition switch connector. *See Fig. 2.* Connect jumper wire between key-in ignition switch connector terminals. Using scan tool, read key-in ignition switch status. If scan tool does not display KEY-IN IGNITION SW: CLOSED, go to next step. If scan tool displays

KEY-IN IGNITION SW: CLOSED, replace ignition switch. See appropriate STEERING COLUMN SWITCHES article.

5) Connect jumper wire between ground and terminal No. 1 (Light Blue wire) on key-in ignition switch connector. Using scan tool, read key-in ignition switch status. If scan tool does not display KEY-IN IGNITION SW: CLOSED, go to next step. If scan tool displays KEY-IN IGNITION SW: CLOSED, repair open ground (Black wire) circuit.

6) Access Body Control Module (BCM) connector "A". BCM is located with junction block under driver's side instrument panel. *See Fig. 1.* Remove connector cover. Do not disconnect connector. Connect a backprobe jumper wire between BCM connector "A" terminal No. 4 (Light Blue wire) and chassis ground. Using scan tool, read key-in ignition switch status. If scan tool does not display KEY-IN IGNITION SW: CLOSED, replace BCM. If scan tool displays KEY-IN IGNITION SW: CLOSED, repair open Light Blue wire between BCM and ignition switch.

CHIME INOPERATIVE WITH DRIVER DOOR OPEN & KEY OUT

NOTE: For connector terminal identification and wiring diagrams, see BODY CONTROL COMPUTER – INTRODUCTION article. Perform VERIFICATION TEST VER-1A after each repair.

CAUTION: Always turn ignition switch to OFF position prior to disconnecting any module connector.

1) Ensure all interior and exterior lights are off. Turn ignition off and remove key from ignition. Open driver's door. If chime sounds, go to next step. If chime does not sound, system is currently functioning correctly.

2) Using scan tool, read key-in ignition switch status. If scan tool does not display KEY-IN IGNITION SW: CLOSED, replace Body Control Module (BCM). BCM is located with junction block under driver's side instrument panel. *See Fig. 1.* If scan tool displays KEY-IN IGNITION SW: CLOSED, go to next step.

3) Disconnect key-in ignition switch connector. *See Fig. 2.* Using scan tool, read key-in ignition switch status. If scan tool does not display KEY-IN IGNITION SW: CLOSED, replace ignition switch. See appropriate STEERING COLUMN SWITCHES article. If scan tool displays KEY-IN IGNITION SW: CLOSED, go to next step.

4) Ensure all lights and accessories are off. Close all doors. Using external ohmmeter, measure resistance between ground and BCM connector "A" terminal No. 32 (Light Blue wire). If resistance is less than 10 ohms, repair Light Blue wire between BCM and ignition switch for short to ground. If resistance is 10 ohms or more, replace BCM. BCM is located with junction block under driver's side instrument panel. *See Fig. 1.*

CHIME SOUNDS WITH DRIVER'S SEAT BELT FASTENED

NOTE: For connector terminal identification and wiring diagrams, see BODY CONTROL COMPUTER – INTRODUCTION article. Perform VERIFICATION TEST VER-1A after each repair.

CAUTION: Always turn ignition switch to OFF position prior to disconnecting any module connector.

1) Ensure ignition is off. Fasten driver's seat belt. Turn ignition on. If chime does not sound, chime system is currently functioning correctly. If chime sounds, go to next step.

2) Turn ignition on. Using scan tool, read seat belt switch status. If scan tool does not display SEAT BELT SWITCH: CLOSED, replace Body Control Module (BCM). BCM is located with junction block under driver's side instrument panel. *See Fig. 1.* If scan tool displays SEAT BELT SWITCH: CLOSED, go to next step.

3) Disconnect driver's seat belt switch connector and ensure connector is clean and not damaged. Using scan tool, read seat belt switch status.

CHRY
4-106

1999 ACCESSORIES & EQUIPMENT
Body Control Computer Tests
Caravan, Town & Country & Voyager (Cont.)

If scan tool displays SEAT BELT SWITCH: CLOSED, go to next step. If scan tool does not display SEAT BELT SWITCH: CLOSED, replace driver's seat belt switch.

4) Turn ignition off. Disconnect BCM connector "B" and ensure connector is clean and not damaged. Turn ignition on. Using scan tool, read seat belt switch status. If scan tool displays SEAT BELT SWITCH: CLOSED, replace BCM. If scan tool does not display SEAT BELT SWITCH: CLOSED, repair Light Green/Red wire between driver's seat belt switch and BCM "B" connector for short to ground.

EXTERIOR LIGHTING SYSTEM

AUTOMATIC HEADLIGHTS SIGNAL CIRCUIT OPEN

NOTE: For connector terminal identification and wiring diagrams, see BODY CONTROL COMPUTER – INTRODUCTION article. Perform VERIFICATION TEST VER-1A after each repair.

CAUTION: Always turn ignition switch to OFF position prior to disconnecting or connecting any module connector.

1) Using scan tool, select BODY CONTROL MODULE. If scan tool displays NO RESPONSE or CCD BUS FAILURE, go to appropriate VEHICLE COMMUNICATIONS article. If scan tool does not display NO RESPONSE or CCD BUS FAILURE, go to next step.

2) Using scan tool, select POWERTRAIN CONTROL MODULE. If scan tool displays NO RESPONSE or CCD BUS FAILURE, go to appropriate VEHICLE COMMUNICATIONS article. If scan tool does not display NO RESPONSE or CCD BUS FAILURE, go to next step.

3) Using scan tool, select BODY, BODY COMPUTER then SENSORS. Using scan tool, read AUTO HEADLAMP SENS VOLTS. If voltage is .6–4.8 volts, replace Body Control Module (BCM). BCM is located with junction block under driver's side instrument panel. *See Fig. 1.* If voltage is not .6–4.8 volts, go to next step.

4) Turn ignition off. Disconnect BCM connector "B" and ensure connector is clean and not damaged. Turn ignition on. Connect jumper wire between chassis ground and BCM connector "B" terminal No. 51 (White/Light Green wire). Disconnect interior electrochromic mirror connector and ensure connector is clean and not damaged. Using external ohmmeter, measure resistance between ground and interior electrochromic mirror connector terminal No. 7 (Black/Dark Green wire). If resistance is less than 5 ohms, go to next step. If resistance is 5 ohms or more, repair open Black/Dark Green wire between inside mirror connector and BCM.

5) Remove jumper wire. Measure resistance between ground and interior electrochromic mirror connector terminal No. 7 (Black/Dark Green wire). If resistance is less than 1000 ohms, repair short to ground in Black/Dark Green wire between inside mirror connector and BCM. If resistance is 1000 ohms or more, replace interior electrochromic mirror.

AUTOMATIC HEADLIGHTS WILL NOT TURN OFF

NOTE: For connector terminal identification and wiring diagrams, see BODY CONTROL COMPUTER – INTRODUCTION article. Perform VERIFICATION TEST VER-1A after each repair.

CAUTION: Always turn ignition switch to OFF position prior to disconnecting or connecting any module connector.

1) Using scan tool, select BODY CONTROL MODULE. If scan tool displays NO RESPONSE or CCD BUS FAILURE, go to appropriate VEHICLE COMMUNICATIONS article. If scan tool does not display NO RESPONSE or CCD BUS FAILURE, go to next step.

2) Using scan tool, select POWERTRAIN CONTROL MODULE. If scan tool displays NO RESPONSE or CCD BUS FAILURE, go to appropriate VEHICLE COMMUNICATIONS article. If scan tool does not display NO RESPONSE or CCD BUS FAILURE, go to next step.

3) Using scan tool, select BODY, BODY COMPUTER, then SENSORS. Read AUTO HEADLAMP SENS VOLTS. If voltage reading is 0.6- 4.8

volts, replace Body Control Module (BCM). BCM is located with junction block under driver's side instrument panel. *See Fig. 1.* If voltage reading is not 0.6-4.8 volts, go to next step.

4) Disconnect BCM "B" connector. Connect jumper wire between ground and BCM "B" connector terminal No. 51 (White/Light Green wire). Disconnect interior electrochromic mirror connector. Using external ohmmeter, measure resistance between ground and terminal No. 7 (White/Light Green wire) on mirror harness connector. If resistance is less than 5 ohms, go to next step. If resistance is 5 ohms or more, repair open White/Light Green wire.

5) Remove jumper wire. Using external ohmmeter, measure resistance between ground and interior electrochromic mirror connector terminal No. 7 (White/Light Green wire). If resistance is less than 1000 ohms, repair White/Light Green wire for short to ground. If resistance is 1000 ohms or more, replace interior electrochromic mirror.

AUTOMATIC HEADLIGHTS WILL NOT TURN ON

NOTE: For connector terminal identification and wiring diagrams, see BODY CONTROL COMPUTER – INTRODUCTION article. Perform VERIFICATION TEST VER-1A after each repair.

CAUTION: Always turn ignition switch to OFF position prior to disconnecting or connecting any module connector.

1) Using scan tool, select BODY CONTROL MODULE. If scan tool displays NO RESPONSE or CCD BUS FAILURE, go to appropriate VEHICLE COMMUNICATIONS article. If scan tool does not display NO RESPONSE or CCD BUS FAILURE, go to next step.

2) Using scan tool, select POWERTRAIN CONTROL MODULE. If scan tool displays NO RESPONSE or CCD BUS FAILURE, go to appropriate VEHICLE COMMUNICATIONS article. If scan tool does not display NO RESPONSE or CCD BUS FAILURE, go to next step.

3) Using scan tool, select SENSOR DISPLAY. Read IGNITION VOLTAGE. If voltage is less than 10 volts, go to appropriate VEHICLE COMMUNICATIONS article. If voltage is 10 volts or more, go to next step.

4) Using scan tool, select READ DTCs. If AUTO HEADLIGHTS SIGNAL CIRCUIT OPEN is present, go to AUTOMATIC HEADLIGHTS SIGNAL CIRCUIT OPEN. If AUTO HEADLIGHTS SIGNAL CIRCUIT OPEN is not present, go to next step.

5) Turn ignition on. Turn headlight switch to AUTO position. Cover sensor on back of interior electrochromic mirror. If headlights illuminate, system is currently operating correctly. If headlights do not illuminate, go to next step.

6) Ensure cover is installed on mirror. Using scan tool, select BODY, BODY COMPUTER, then SENSORS. Read AUTO HEADLAMP SENS VOLTS. If voltage reading is 0.0-0.5 volts, replace Body Control Module (BCM). BCM is located with junction block under driver's side instrument panel. *See Fig. 1.* If voltage reading is not 0.0-0.5 volts, go to next step.

7) Disconnect BCM "B" connector. Connect jumper wire between ground and terminal No. 51 (White/Light Green wire) on "B" connector. Disconnect interior electrochromic mirror connector. Using external ohmmeter, measure resistance between ground and terminal No. 7 (White/Light Green wire) on interior electrochromic mirror harness connector. If resistance is less than 5 ohms, replace interior electrochromic mirror. If resistance is 5 ohms or more, repair open White/Light Green wire.

FOG LIGHTS WILL NOT TURN OFF

NOTE: For connector terminal identification and wiring diagrams, see BODY CONTROL COMPUTER – INTRODUCTION article. Perform VERIFICATION TEST VER-1A after each repair.

1) Using scan tool, select BODY CONTROL MODULE. If scan tool displays NO RESPONSE or CCD BUS FAILURE, go to appropriate VEHICLE COMMUNICATIONS article. If scan tool does not display NO RESPONSE or CCD BUS FAILURE, go to next step.

Body Control Computer Tests
Caravan, Town & Country & Voyager (Cont.)

2) Turn headlight switch to OFF position. Disconnect headlight switch 13-pin connector. Using external ohmmeter, measure resistance between ground and headlight switch 13-pin connector terminal No. 6 (Black wire). If resistance is less than 100 ohms, repair Black wire for short to ground. If resistance is 100 ohms or more, replace headlight switch.

FOG LIGHTS WILL NOT TURN ON

NOTE: For connector terminal identification and wiring diagrams, see BODY CONTROL COMPUTER – INTRODUCTION article. Perform VERIFICATION TEST VER-1A after each repair.

CAUTION: Always turn ignition switch to OFF position prior to disconnecting or connecting any module connector.

1) Using scan tool, select BODY CONTROL MODULE. If scan tool displays NO RESPONSE or CCD BUS FAILURE, go to appropriate VEHICLE COMMUNICATIONS article. If scan tool does not display NO RESPONSE or CCD BUS FAILURE, go to next step.
2) Turn on low beam headlights. Turn on fog lights. If low beam headlights operate correctly, go to next step. If low beam headlights do not operate correctly, go to HEADLIGHTS WILL NOT TURN ON.
3) Remove fog light relay from junction block. *See Fig. 3.* Connect jumper wire between terminals 30 and 87 on relay connector. If fog lights illuminate, go to step **8)**. If fog lights do not illuminate, go to next step.
4) Install a known good relay. All relays in bottom row use same configuration as fog light relay. If fog lights illuminate, replace fog light relay. If fog lights do not illuminate, go to next step.
5) Gain access to junction block connector C3. Do not disconnect connector. Connect a backprobe jumper wire between ground and junction block connector C3 terminal No. 33 (Pink wire). If fog lights illuminate, replace Body Control Module (BCM). BCM is located with junction block under driver's side instrument panel. *See Fig. 1.* If fog lights do not illuminate, go to next step.
6) With jumper connected, disconnect multifunction switch connector. Using external ohmmeter, measure resistance between ground and multifunction switch connector terminal No. 9 (Pink wire). If resistance is less than 5 ohms, go to next step. If resistance is 5 ohms or more, repair open Pink wire.
7) Disconnect jumper wire. Connect jumper wire between ground and multifunction switch connector terminal No. 10 (Orange/White wire). If fog lights illuminate, replace multifunction switch. If fog lights do not illuminate, repair open Orange/White wire between multifunction switch connector and power distribution center.
8) Disconnect one foglight connector. Disconnect headlight switch connector. Connect jumper wire between ground and headlight switch 8-pin connector terminal No. 6 (Black wire). Using external ohmmeter, measure resistance between ground and fog light harness connector Black wire. If resistance is less than 5 ohms, go to next step. If resistance is 5 ohms or more, repair open Black wire.
9) Turn headlights on. Remove jumper wire. Remove fog light relay from junction block. Turn fog light switch on. Connect jumper wire between terminals 30 and 87 on relay connector. Using an external voltmeter, measure voltage between ground and fog light harness connector Black wire. If voltage is more than 10 volts, go to next step. If voltage is 10 volts or less, repair open Blue wire between fog light relay and fog light.
10) Using external ohmmeter, measure resistance between ground and fog light harness connector Blue wire. If resistance is less than 50 ohms, replace foglight bulbs. If resistance is 50 ohms or more, replace multifunction switch.

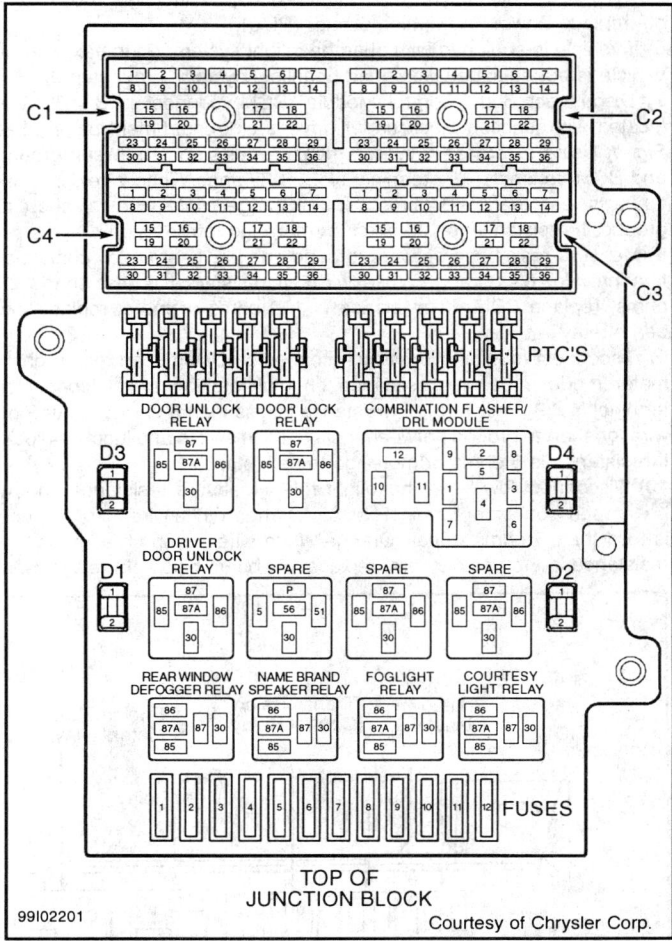

Fig. 3: Identifying Junction Block Relays & Connectors

HEADLIGHTS WILL NOT TURN OFF

NOTE: For connector terminal identification and wiring diagrams, see BODY CONTROL COMPUTER – INTRODUCTION article. Perform VERIFICATION TEST VER-1A after each repair.

CAUTION: Always turn ignition switch to OFF position prior to disconnecting or connecting any module connector.

1) Using scan tool, select BODY CONTROL MODULE. If scan tool displays NO RESPONSE or CCD BUS FAILURE, go to appropriate VEHICLE COMMUNICATIONS article. If scan tool does not display NO RESPONSE or CCD BUS FAILURE, go to next step.
2) Using scan tool, read headlight switch sense. If scan tool displays HEADLAMP SW: CLOSED, go to next step. If scan tool does not display HEADLAMP SW: CLOSED, go to step **5)**.
3) Disconnect headlight switch. Read headlight switch sense. If scan tool displays HEADLAMP SW: CLOSED, go to next step. If scan tool does not display HEADLAMP SW: CLOSED, replace headlight switch.
4) Disconnect Body Control Module (BCM) connector "A". BCM is located with junction block under driver's side instrument panel junction block connector "A". *See Fig. 1.* Using scan tool in ohmmeter mode, measure resistance on headlight switch 8-pin connector terminal No. 3 (Light Green/Orange wire). If resistance is less than 5 ohms, repair Light Green/Orange wire for short to ground. If resistance is 5 ohms or more, replace Body Control Module (BCM).
5) Disconnect low beam headlight relay. Low beam headlight relay is located in Power Distribution Center located under hood next to battery.

CHRY
4-108

1999 ACCESSORIES & EQUIPMENT
Body Control Computer Tests
Caravan, Town & Country & Voyager (Cont.)

See Fig. 4. If headlights turn off, go to next step. If headlights do not turn off, replace Power Distribution Center (PDC).

6) If vehicle is equipped with quad headlight system, go to next step. If vehicle is not equipped with quad headlight system, go to step **9)**.

7) Disconnect Body Control Module (BCM) connector "B". BCM is located with junction block under driver's side instrument panel. *See Fig. 1*. Using external ohmmeter, measure resistance between ground and BCM connector "B" terminal No. 78 (Orange/White wire). If resistance is less than 100 ohms, repair Orange/White wire for short to ground. If resistance is 100 ohms or more, go to next step.

8) Measure resistance between ground and low beam relay connector terminal No. 85 (Orange/White wire). If resistance is less than 100 ohms, replace BCM. If resistance is 100 ohms or more, replace low beam relay.

9) Disconnect multifunction switch connector. Using scan tool in ohmmeter mode, measure resistance on multifunction switch connector terminal No. 9 (Pink wire). If resistance is less than 5 ohms, repair Pink wire for short to ground between multifunction switch and junction block. If resistance is 5 ohms or more, go to next step.

10) Disconnect low beam headlight relay. Measure resistance on low beam relay connector terminal No. 85 (Orange/White wire). If resistance is less than 5 ohms, repair Orange/White wire for short to ground. If resistance is 5 ohms or more, replace low beam headlight relay.

bution Center (PDC). Inspect fuse No. 6 for left headlight or fuse No. 7 for right headlight. *See Fig. 4*. Replace fuse as needed. If fuse is okay, go to next step.

3) Reinstall fuse. Disconnect inoperative headlight connector. Turn headlight switch on. Using scan tool in voltmeter mode, measure voltage on terminal No. 3 (Violet wire (left), Violet/Red wire (right). If voltage is more than 10 volts, replace headlight. If voltage is 10 volts or less, repair open Violet or Violet/Red wire.

4) Using scan tool, actuate headlight relay. If headlights do not illuminate, go to step **9)**. If headlights illuminate, go to next step.

5) Stop headlight actuation. Turn on headlight switch. Using scan tool, read HEADLAMP SWITCH SENSE. If scan tool displays HEADLAMP SWITCH: CLOSED, replace Body Control Module (BCM). BCM is located with junction block under driver's side instrument panel. *See Fig. 1*. If scan tool does not display HEADLAMP SWITCH: CLOSED, go to next step.

6) Disconnect headlight switch connectors. Connect jumper wire between ground and headlight switch 8-pin connector terminal No. 3 (Light Green/Orange wire). Using scan tool, read HEADLAMP SWITCH SENSE. If scan tool displays HEADLAMP SWITCH: CLOSED, go to next step. If scan tool does not display HEADLAMP SWITCH: CLOSED, repair open Light Green/Orange wire.

7) Disconnect jumper wire. Access BCM connector "A". Remove con-

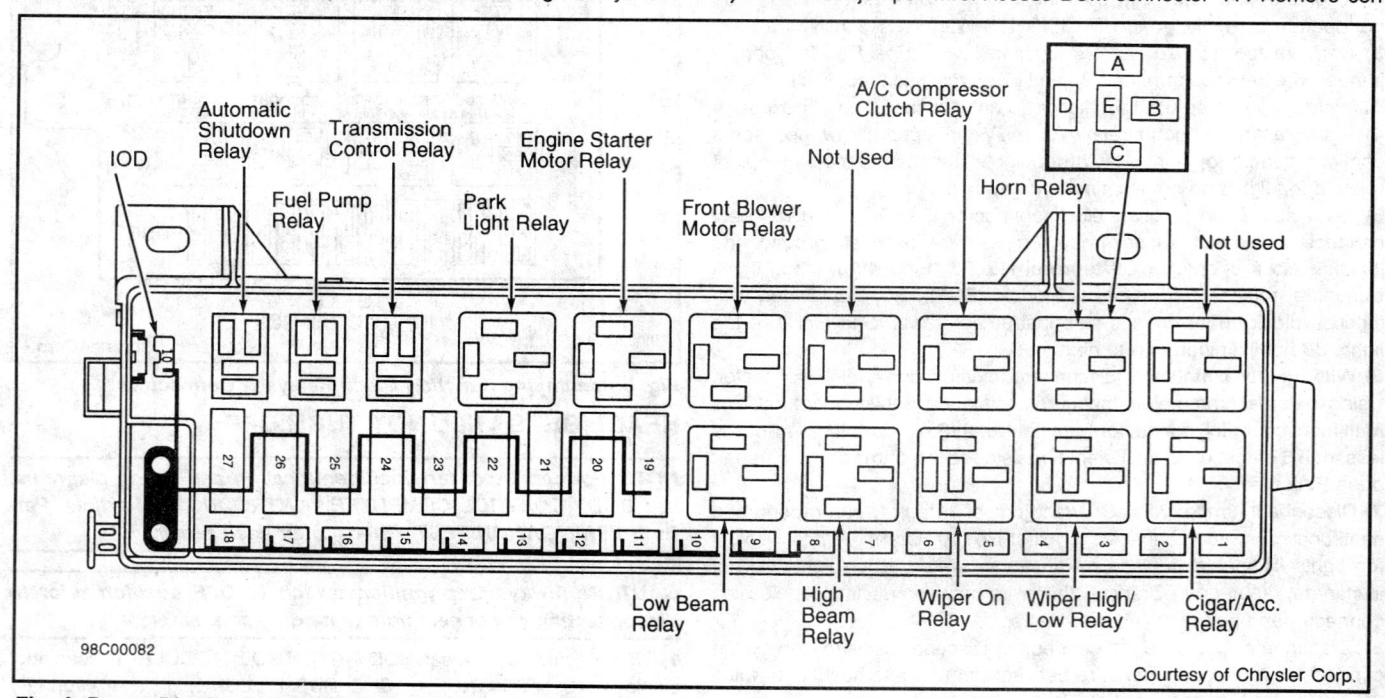

Fig. 4: Power Distribution Center Components

Fig. 4: Power Distribution Center Components

HEADLIGHTS WILL NOT TURN ON

NOTE: For connector terminal identification and wiring diagrams, see BODY CONTROL COMPUTER – INTRODUCTION article. Perform VERIFICATION TEST VER-1A after each repair.

CAUTION: Always turn ignition switch to OFF position prior to disconnecting or connecting any module connector.

1) Using scan tool, select BODY CONTROL MODULE. If scan tool displays NO RESPONSE or CCD BUS FAILURE, go to appropriate VEHICLE COMMUNICATIONS article. If scan tool does not display NO RESPONSE or CCD BUS FAILURE, go to next step.

2) If both headlights do not illuminate, go to next step. If only one headlight does not illuminate, inspect appropriate fuse in Power Distri-

nector cover. Do not disconnect connector. Connect a backprobe jumper wire between chassis ground and BCM connector "A" terminal No. 13 (Light Green/Orange wire). Using scan tool, read HEADLAMP SWITCH SENSE. If scan tool displays HEADLAMP SWITCH: CLOSED, go to next step. If scan tool does not display HEADLAMP SWITCH: CLOSED, replace BCM.

8) Disconnect jumper wire. Using an external ohmmeter, measure resistance between ground and headlight switch 8-pin connector terminal No. 2 (Black wire). If resistance is less than 5 ohms, replace headlight switch. If resistance is 5 ohms or more, repair open Black wire.

9) Stop headlight relay actuation. Remove and inspect fuses No. 6 and 7 in junction block. *See Fig. 3*. Replace as needed. Reinstall fuses. If fuses are okay, go to next step.

10) Disconnect headlight low beam relay. Using scan tool in voltmeter mode, measure voltage on relay socket terminal No. 86 (Red wire). If

1999 ACCESSORIES & EQUIPMENT
Body Control Computer Tests
Caravan, Town & Country & Voyager (Cont.)

CHRY
4-109

voltage is 10 volts or less, replace Power Distribution Center (PDC). If voltage is more than 10 volts, go to next step.

11) Using scan tool in voltmeter mode, measure voltage on relay socket terminal No. 30 (Red wire). If voltage is 10 volts or less, replace Power Distribution Center (PDC). If voltage is more than 10 volts, go to next step.

12) Connect jumper wire between low beam relay socket terminals No. 86 (Red wire) and 87 (Internal). If headlights do not illuminate, go to step **19)**. If headlights illuminate, go to next step.

13) Remove jumper wire. Install low beam headlight relay. If vehicle is equipped with quad headlights, go to next step. If vehicle is not equipped with quad headlights, go to step **16)**.

14) Disconnect BCM connector "B". Connect jumper wire between ground and BCM connector "B" terminal No. 76 (Orange/White wire). If headlights illuminate, replace BCM. If headlights do not illuminate, go to next step.

15) With jumper wire still connected, remove low beam relay. Using an external ohmmeter, measure resistance between ground and low beam relay connector terminal No. 85 (Orange/White wire). If resistance is less than 5 ohms, replace low beam relay. If resistance is 5 ohms or more, repair open Orange/White wire.

16) Disconnect multifunction switch connector. See Fig. 2. Connect jumper wire between ground and multifunction switch connector terminal No. 10 (Orange/White wire). If headlights illuminate, go to next step. If headlights do not illuminate, go to step **18)**.

17) Remove jumper wire. Connect jumper wire between multifunction switch connector terminal No. 9 (Pink wire) and chassis ground. Access junction block connector "D". See Fig. 1. Using scan tool in ohmmeter mode, measure resistance at junction block connector "D" terminal No. 33. If resistance is less than 5 ohms, replace multifunction switch. If resistance is 5 ohms or more, repair open Pink wire (low beam relay control circuit) between junction block and multifunction switch.

18) Disconnect multifunction switch connector. See Fig. 2. Connect jumper wire between ground and multifunction switch connector terminal No. 8 (Black wire). Disconnect low beam headlight relay. Using scan tool in ohmmeter mode, measure resistance at low beam relay connector terminal No. 85 (Orange/White wire). If resistance is less than 5 ohms, replace low beam relay. If resistance is 5 ohms or more, repair open Orange/White wire.

19) Disconnect low beam headlight relay. Connect jumper wire across low beam headlight relay coil terminals No. 85 and 86. Disconnect one low beam headlight fuse. Using scan tool in voltmeter mode, probe low beam headlight relay connector terminal No. 86 (Red wire). If voltage is less than 10 volts, replace Power Distribution Center (PDC). If voltage is 10 volts or more, go to next step.

20) Reconnect low beam headlight fuse. Disconnect one low beam headlight. Using scan tool in voltmeter mode, probe low beam headlight relay connector terminal No. 87. If voltage is less than 10 volts, replace headlight(s). If voltage is 10 volts or more, repair open Violet or Violet/Red wire between headlight fuse and headlight.

PARK LIGHTS WILL NOT TURN OFF

NOTE: For connector terminal identification and wiring diagrams, see BODY CONTROL COMPUTER – INTRODUCTION article. Perform VERIFICATION TEST VER-1A after each repair.

CAUTION: Always turn ignition switch to OFF position prior to disconnecting or connecting any module connector.

1) Using scan tool, select BODY CONTROL MODULE. If scan tool displays NO RESPONSE or CCD BUS FAILURE, go to appropriate VEHICLE COMMUNICATIONS article. If scan tool does not display NO RESPONSE or CCD BUS FAILURE, go to next step.

2) Using scan tool, read PARK LAMP SWITCH SENSE. If scan tool displays PARK LAMP SW: CLOSED, go to next step. If scan tool does not display PARK LAMP SW: CLOSED, go to step **5)**.

3) Disconnect headlight switch. Disconnect junction block connector "A". See Fig. 1. Using scan tool in ohmmeter mode, measure resistance on headlight switch 8-pin connector terminal No. 8 (Light Green/White wire). If resistance is less than 5 ohms, repair Light Green/White wire for short to ground. If resistance is 5 ohms or more, go to next step.

4) Using scan tool, read PARK LAMP SWITCH SENSE. If scan tool displays PARK LAMP SW: CLOSED, replace Body Control Module (BCM). BCM is located with junction block under driver's side instrument panel. If scan tool does not display PARK LAMP SW: CLOSED, replace headlight switch.

5) Disconnect park lamp relay. See Fig. 4. If park lights turn off, go to next step. If park lights do not turn off, repair park lamp relay output circuit for short to voltage.

6) Using external ohmmeter, measure resistance between ground and park lamp relay socket terminal No. 85 (Violet wire). If resistance is 100 ohms or more, replace park lamp relay. If resistance is less than 100 ohms, repair Violet wire between park lamp relay and junction block for short to ground.

PARK LIGHTS WILL NOT TURN ON

NOTE: For connector terminal identification and wiring diagrams, see BODY CONTROL COMPUTER – INTRODUCTION article. Perform VERIFICATION TEST VER-1A after each repair.

CAUTION: Always turn ignition switch to OFF position prior to disconnecting or connecting any module connector.

1) Using scan tool, select BODY CONTROL MODULE. If scan tool displays NO RESPONSE or CCD BUS FAILURE, go to appropriate VEHICLE COMMUNICATIONS article. If scan tool does not display NO RESPONSE or CCD BUS FAILURE, go to next step.

2) If both park lights are inoperative, go to next step. If only one park light is inoperative, go to step **15)**.

3) Using scan tool, actuate park lamp relay. If park lights do not illuminate, go to step **8)**. If park lights illuminate, go to next step.

4) Stop park lamp relay actuation. Access BCM connector "A". See Fig. 1. Remove connector cover. Do not disconnect connector. Connect jumper wire between ground and BCM connector "A" terminal No. 40 (Light Green/White wire). Read PARK LAMP SWITCH SENSE. If scan tool displays PARK LAMP SWITCH: CLOSED, go to next step. If scan tool does not display PARK LAMP SWITCH: CLOSED, replace Body Control Module (BCM).

5) Disconnect jumper wire. Disconnect headlight switch connector. Connect jumper wire between ground and headlight switch 8-pin connector terminal No. 8 (Light Green/White wire). If scan tool does not display PARK LAMP SWITCH: CLOSED, repair open Light Green/White wire. If scan tool displays PARK LAMP SWITCH: CLOSED, go to next step.

6) Using external ohmmeter, measure resistance between ground and headlight switch 8-pin connector terminal No. 2 (Black wire). If resistance is less than 5 ohms, go to next step. If resistance is 5 ohms or more, repair open Black wire.

7) Turn on headlight switch. Using scan tool, read PARK LAMP SWITCH SENSE. If scan tool displays PARK LAMP SWITCH: CLOSED, replace Body Control Module (BCM). BCM is located with junction block under driver's side instrument panel. See Fig. 1. If scan tool does not display PARK LAMP SWITCH: CLOSED, replace headlight switch.

8) Stop park lamp relay actuation. Remove and inspect park light fuses in junction block. Inspect fuse No. 3 for right light, fuse No. 5 for left light. Replace fuse as needed. If fuse is okay, go to next step.

9) Remove park lamp relay from Power Distribution Center (PDC). Using scan tool in voltmeter mode, measure voltage on park lamp relay connector terminal No. 30 (Red wire). If voltage is 10 volts or less, go to step **14)**. If voltage is more than 10 volts, go to next step.

10) Using scan tool in voltmeter mode, measure voltage on park lamp relay connector terminal No. 86 (Red wire). If voltage is 10 volts or less, repair or replace PDC. If voltage is more than 10 volts, go to next step.

CHRY
4-110

1999 ACCESSORIES & EQUIPMENT
Body Control Computer Tests
Caravan, Town & Country & Voyager (Cont.)

11) Connect jumper wire between park lamp relay connector terminals No. 86 (Red wire) and No. 87 (Black/Yellow wire). If park lights illuminate, go to next step. If park lights do not illuminate, repair open park lamp relay output circuit (Black/Yellow wire).

12) Connect test light between park lamp relay connector terminals No. 30 (Red wire) and No. 85 (Violet wire). Using scan tool, actuate park lamp relay. If test light flashes when relay is actuated, replace park lamp relay. If test light does not flash when relay is actuated, got to next step.

13) Do not disconnect test light. Access junction block connector "B". *See Fig. 1.* Do not disconnect connector. Connect jumper wire between ground and junction block connector "B" terminal No. 9 (Violet wire). If test light illuminates, replace Body Control Module (BCM). BCM is located with junction block under driver's side instrument panel. If test light does not illuminate, repair open Violet wire between junction block and park lamp relay control relay.

14) Inspect fuse No. 22 in PDC. *See Fig. 4.* If fuse is blown, check for shorted supply circuit to PDC. If fuse is okay, replace PDC.

15) Remove and inspect inoperative park light fuse in junction block. Inspect fuse No. 3 for right light, fuse No. 5 for left light. Repair appropriate shorted circuit. Replace fuse as needed. If fuse is okay, go to next step.

16) Reinstall fuse, if removed. Disconnect inoperative park light connector. Using scan tool in voltmeter mode, measure voltage on terminal No. 2 (middle terminal). If voltage is more than 10 volts, replace bulb. If voltage is 10 volts or less, repair open Brown/Yellow wire for left park light or Dark Green/Yellow wire for right park light.

INFORMATION CENTER

ABS WARNING LIGHT CONCERNS

NOTE: *For connector terminal identification and wiring diagrams, see BODY CONTROL COMPUTER – INTRODUCTION article. Perform VERIFICATION TEST VER-1A after each repair.*

CAUTION: *Always turn ignition switch to OFF position prior to disconnecting or connecting any module connector.*

NOTE: *If any trouble codes are present, repair prior to performing this test.*

1) Turn ignition on. Observe ABS warning light in message center. If ABS warning light stays on for several seconds and then goes out, warning light system is functioning properly at this time. If ABS warning light does not stay on for several seconds and then goes out, go to next step.

2) Observe ABS warning light in message center. If ABS warning light is on steady, go to next step. If ABS warning light is on steady, go to step 7).

3) Turn ignition off. Disconnect Body Control Module (BCM). BCM is located with junction block under driver's side instrument panel. *See Fig. 1.* Inspect connector for damaged, pushed out or crossed terminals. Repair as necessary. If terminals are okay, go to next step.

4) Disconnect anti-lock brake controller module connector. Inspect connector for damaged, pushed out or crossed terminals. Repair as necessary. If terminals are okay, go to next step.

5) Close connector release on anti-lock brake controller module connector. DO NOT reconnect connector. Using an external ohmmeter, measure resistance between ground and anti-lock brake controller module connector Terminal No. 16 (Gray wire). If resistance is less than 5 ohms, repair short to ground in Gray wire. If resistance is 5 ohms or more, go to next step.

6) Reconnect anti-lock brake controller module connector. Turn ignition on. Using scan tool, erase all DTCs. Observe ABS warning light. If ABS warning light is on steady, replace anti-lock brake controller module. If ABS warning light is not on steady, replace BCM.

7) Turn ignition. Set parking brake. If Red BRAKE warning light is illuminated, go to next step. If Red BRAKE warning light is not illuminated, repair open Brown/Pink wire between message center and fuse No. 6 in junction block.

8) Turn ignition off. Inspect ABS warning light bulb in message center. Replace as necessary. If bulb is okay, repair open Light Green/Orange wire between message center and anti-lock brake controller module or BCM.

ALL WARNING LIGHTS INOPERATIVE

NOTE: *For connector terminal identification and wiring diagrams, see BODY CONTROL COMPUTER – INTRODUCTION article. Perform VERIFICATION TEST VER-1A after each repair.*

CAUTION: *Always turn ignition switch to OFF position prior to disconnecting any module connector.*

1) Turn ignition off. Disconnect information center connector. Turn ignition on. Using external voltmeter, measure voltage between ground and information center connector terminal No. 10 (Brown/Pink wire). If voltage is 10 volts or less, repair open Brown/Pink wire. If voltage is more than 10 volts, go to next step.

2) Using external voltmeter, measure voltage between ground and information center connector terminal No. 12 (Pink wire) on. If voltage is 10 volts or less, repair open Pink wire. If voltage is more than 10 volts, go to next step.

3) Remove ignition key. Turn off all lights and accessories. Close all doors. Using external ohmmeter, measure resistance between ground and information center connector terminal No. 3 (Black wire). If resistance is 5 ohms or more, repair open Black wire. If resistance is less than 5 ohms, replace information center.

ENGINE TEMPERATURE WARNING LIGHT CONCERNS

NOTE: *For connector terminal identification and wiring diagrams, see BODY CONTROL COMPUTER – INTRODUCTION article. Perform VERIFICATION TEST VER-1A after each repair.*

CAUTION: *Always turn ignition switch to OFF position prior to disconnecting any module connector.*

1) Start engine. If engine temperature light is illuminated, go to next step. If engine temperature light is not illuminated, go to step 5).

2) Using scan tool, select BODY SYSTEMS. Read CHIME MONITOR. If ENGINE TEMPERATURE LIGHT is ON, see appropriate INSTRUMENT PANELS article. If engine temperature light is not illuminated, go to next step.

3) Turn engine off. Turn ignition switch to ON position. Disconnect Body Control Module (BCM) connector "A". BCM is located with junction block under driver's side instrument panel. *See Fig. 1.* If engine temperature light is not illuminated, replace BCM. If engine temperature light is illuminated, go to next step.

4) Disconnect information center connector. Remove ignition key. Turn off all lights and accessories. Close all doors. Using external ohmmeter, measure resistance between ground and information center connector terminal No. 6 (Violet wire). If resistance is 10 ohms or more, replace information center. If resistance is less than 10 ohms, repair Violet wire for short to ground.

5) Turn engine off and leave ignition on. Using scan tool, actuate engine temperature light. If engine temperature light illuminates, warning light system is currently functioning correctly. If engine temperature light does not illuminate, go to next step.

6) Disconnect information center connector. Using external voltmeter, measure voltage between ground and information center connector terminal No. 10 (Brown/Pink wire). If voltage is 10 volts or less, repair open Brown/Pink wire between junction block and information center. If voltage is more than 10 volts, go to next step.

1999 ACCESSORIES & EQUIPMENT
Body Control Computer Tests
Caravan, Town & Country & Voyager (Cont.)

CHRY
4-111

7) Remove and inspect engine temperature warning light bulb. Replace as needed. If bulb is okay, go to next step.

8) Reinstall bulb and reconnect information center connector. Back-probe information center connector with jumper wire. Connect jumper between ground and information center connector terminal No. 6 (Violet wire). If engine temperature warning light does not illuminate, replace information center. If engine temperature warning light illuminates, go to next step.

9) Gain access to Body Control Module (BCM) connector "A". BCM is located with junction block under driver's side instrument panel. *See Fig. 1.* Remove cover from connector "A". Connect jumper wire between ground and BCM connector "A" terminal No. 6 (Violet wire). If engine temperature warning light does not illuminate, repair open Violet wire. If engine temperature warning light illuminates, replace BCM.

HIGH BEAM INDICATOR LIGHT CONCERNS

NOTE: For connector terminal identification and wiring diagrams, see BODY CONTROL COMPUTER – INTRODUCTION article. Perform VERIFICATION TEST VER-1A after each repair.

CAUTION: Always turn ignition switch to OFF position prior to disconnecting any module connector.

1) Turn ignition on. Turn high beam headlights on. Ensure turn signals are off. If high beam headlights do not illuminate, go to EXTERIOR LIGHTING SYSTEM. If high beam headlights illuminate, go to next step.

2) Remove ignition key. Turn off all lights and accessories. Close all doors. Using external ohmmeter, measure resistance between ground and information center connector terminal No. 3 (Black wire). If resistance is 10 ohms or more, repair open Black wire. If resistance is less than 10 ohms, go to next step.

3) Disconnect information center. Remove and inspect high beam indicator light bulb. Replace as needed. If bulb is okay, go to next step.

4) Using external voltmeter, measure voltage between ground and information center connector terminal No. 1 (Red/Orange wire). If voltage is 10 volts or less, repair open Red/Orange wire. If voltage is more than 10 volts, replace information center.

LOW OIL PRESSURE WARNING LIGHT CONCERNS

NOTE: For connector terminal identification and wiring diagrams, see BODY CONTROL COMPUTER – INTRODUCTION article. Perform VERIFICATION TEST VER-1A after each repair.

CAUTION: Always turn ignition switch to OFF position prior to disconnecting any module connector.

1) Turn ignition off. Inspect engine oil level. Adjust as needed. Turn ignition on. If oil warning light does not illuminate, go to step **7)**. If oil warning light illuminates, go to next step.

2) Turn ignition off. Remove Oil Pressure Switch (OPS). See OPS LOCATION table. Connect oil pressure gauge. Start engine and run until normal operating temperature is reached. If oil pressure at idle is less than 4 psi, service engine mechanical condition for cause of low oil pressure. If oil pressure at idle is more than 4 psi, go to next step.

3) Turn engine off, ignition on. If oil warning light is not illuminated, replace OPS. If oil warning light is illuminated, go to next step.

4) Access Body Control Module (BCM). BCM is located with junction block under driver's side instrument panel. *See Fig. 1.* Disconnect BCM connector "B". If oil warning light is not illuminated, repair Gray wire between OPS and BCM connector "B" for short to ground. If warning light is illuminated, go to next step.

5) Disconnect BCM connector "A". If oil warning light is not illuminated, replace BCM. If warning light is illuminated, go to next step.

6) Turn ignition off. Disconnect information center connector. Remove ignition key. Turn off all lights and accessories. Close all doors. Using external ohmmeter, measure resistance between ground and informa-

tion center connector terminal No. 8 (Gray wire) . If resistance is 5 ohms or more, replace information center. If resistance is less than 5 ohms, repair Gray wire between information center and BCM connector "A".

7) Disconnect OPS connector. See OPS LOCATION table. Connect jumper wire between ground and OPS connector terminal No. 1 (Gray wire). If oil warning light illuminates, replace OPS. If oil warning light does not illuminate, go to next step.

8) Access Body Control Module (BCM). BCM is located with junction block under driver's side instrument panel. *See Fig. 1.* Remove BCM connector "B" cover. Do not disconnect connector. Connect a backprobe jumper wire between ground and BCM connector "B" terminal No. 52 (Gray wire). If oil warning light illuminates, repair open Gray wire. If oil warning light does not illuminate, go to next step.

9) Disconnect BCM connector "A". Connect jumper wire between ground and BCM connector "A" terminal No. 33 (Gray wire). If oil warning light illuminates, replace BCM. If oil warning light does not illuminate, go to next step.

10) Access information center connector. Do not disconnect connector. Connect a backprobe jumper wire between ground and information center connector terminal No. 8 (Gray wire). If oil warning light illuminates, repair open Gray wire. If oil warning light does not illuminate, go to next step.

11) Disconnect information center connector. Remove and inspect oil warning light bulb from information center. Replace as needed. If light bulb is okay, replace information center.

RED BRAKE WARNING LIGHT MALFUNCTION

NOTE: For connector terminal identification and wiring diagrams, see BODY CONTROL COMPUTER – INTRODUCTION article. Perform VERIFICATION TEST VER-1A after each repair.

CAUTION: Always turn ignition switch to OFF position prior to disconnecting any module connector.

1) If vehicle is equipped with ABS, see appropriate ANTI-LOCK article in BRAKES in appropriate MITCHELL® manual. On non-ABS vehicles, ensure park brake pedal is fully released. If park brake will not release, repair as needed. Turn ignition on. If brake warning light is illuminated, go to next step. If brake warning light is not illuminated, go to step **6)**.

2) Ensure brake fluid reservoir is full. Disconnect brake fluid level switch connector and observe brake warning light. If brake warning light is not illuminated, replace brake fluid level switch. If brake warning light is illuminated, go to next step.

3) Disconnect park brake switch connector located on park brake pedal bracket. If brake warning light is not illuminated, replace park brake switch. If brake warning light is illuminated, go to next step.

4) Turn ignition off. Disconnect information center connector. Remove ignition key. Turn off all lights and accessories. Close all doors. Using external ohmmeter, measure resistance between ground and at information center connector terminal No. 9 (Gray/Black wire). If resistance is 5 ohms or more, replace information center. If resistance is less than 5 ohms, go to next step.

5) Disconnect ignition switch connector. *See Fig. 2.* Using external ohmmeter, measure resistance between ground and at information center connector terminal No. 9 (Gray/Black wire). If resistance is 5 ohms or more, replace ignition switch. If resistance is less than 5 ohms, repair Gray/Black wire for short to ground.

6) Crank engine and observe brake warning light. If brake warning light does not illuminate, go to step **11)**. If brake warning light illuminates, go to next step.

7) Apply park brake. If brake warning light does not illuminate, go to step **10)**. If brake warning light illuminates, go to next step.

8) Turn ignition off. Disconnect brake fluid level switch connector. Connect jumper wire between switch connector terminals. Turn ignition on. If brake warning light illuminates, replace brake fluid level switch. If brake warning light does not illuminate, go to next step.

CHRY
4-112

1999 ACCESSORIES & EQUIPMENT
Body Control Computer Tests
Caravan, Town & Country & Voyager (Cont.)

9) Disconnect jumper wire. Connect jumper wire between chassis ground and brake fluid level switch connector terminal No. 2 (Gray/Black wire). If brake warning light does not illuminate, repair open Gray/Black wire. If brake warning light illuminates, repair open brake fluid level switch ground circuit (Black wire).

10) Disconnect parking brake switch connector located on parking brake pedal bracket. Connect jumper wire between chassis ground and switch connector. If brake warning light illuminates, replace parking brake switch. If brake warning light does not illuminate, repair open Gray/Black wire between parking brake switch and junction block.

11) Turn ignition off. Disconnect ignition switch connector. *See Fig. 2.* Using external ohmmeter, measure resistance between ground and ignition switch connector terminal No. 1 (Black wire). If resistance is 5 ohms or more, repair open Black wire. If resistance is less than 5 ohms, go to next step.

12) Reconnect ignition switch connector. Turn ignition on. Backprobing ignition switch connector, connect jumper wire between ground and ignition switch connector terminal No. 2 (Gray/Black wire). If brake warning light illuminates, replace ignition switch. If brake warning light does not illuminate, go to next step.

13) With jumper wire connected, disconnect information center connector. Remove ignition key. Turn off all lights and accessories. Close all doors. Using external ohmmeter, measure resistance at terminal No. 9 (Gray/Black wire) on information center connector. If resistance is 5 ohms or more, repair open Gray/Black wire. If resistance is less than 5 ohms, go to next step.

14) Remove and inspect red brake warning light bulb. Replace as needed. If bulb is okay, replace information center.

SERVICE ENGINE SOON INDICATOR LIGHT CONCERNS

NOTE: For connector terminal identification and wiring diagrams, see BODY CONTROL COMPUTER – INTRODUCTION article. Perform VERIFICATION TEST VER-1A after each repair.

NOTE: The SERVICE ENGINE SOON light may also be referred to as the MIL. MIL is located in the message center on top of driver's side of instrument panel.

CAUTION: Always turn ignition switch to OFF position prior to disconnecting any module connector.

1) Using scan tool, check for DTCs. If DTCs exist, proceed with testing as indicated in DTC test. If no DTCs exist, go to next step.

2) If MIL does not remain on steady with no DTCs present, go to step **5)**. If MIL remains on steady with no DTCs present, ensure ignition is off. Disconnect connectors from Powertrain Control Module (PCM). The PCM is located between driver's side front fender and power distribution center, near battery.

3) Turn ignition on with engine off and note operation of the MIL. If the MIL remains on, go to the next step. If the MIL goes off, replace PCM.

4) Disconnect connector from rear of the message center. Using ohmmeter, check resistance between ground and terminal No. 7 (Black/Pink wire) on connector for message center. If resistance is 100 ohms or more, replace circuit board in the message center. If resistance is less than 100 ohms, repair short to ground in Black/Pink wire between PCM and MIL in the message center.

5) Ensure ignition is off. Disconnect connectors from Powertrain Control Module (PCM). The PCM is located between driver's side front fender and power distribution center, near battery. Inspect connectors. Clean and/or repair connectors as necessary.

6) Turn ignition on with engine off. Connect jumper wire between ground and PCM connector terminal No. 22 (Black/Pink wire) and note operation of MIL. If MIL does not come on with jumper wire connected, go to next step. If MIL comes on with jumper wire connected, replace PCM.

7) Disconnect connector from rear of the message center. Inspect connector. Clean and/or repair connector as necessary. Remove and inspect the bulb and socket for the MIL in the message center. If bulb and socket are okay, go to next step. If bulb or socket is defective, replace as necessary.

8) Ensure jumper wire is still connected between ground and PCM connector terminal No. 22 (Black/Pink wire). Ensure connector is still disconnected from rear of the message center.

9) Using ohmmeter, check resistance between ground and terminal No. 7 (Black/Pink wire) on connector for message center. If resistance is less than 5 ohms, replace circuit board in the message center. If resistance is 5 ohms or more, repair open circuit in the Black/Pink wire between PCM and MIL in the message center.

TURN SIGNAL INDICATOR LIGHT CONCERNS

NOTE: For connector terminal identification and wiring diagrams, see BODY CONTROL COMPUTER – INTRODUCTION article. Perform VERIFICATION TEST VER-1A after each repair.

CAUTION: Always turn ignition switch to OFF position prior to disconnecting any module connector.

1) Turn ignition on. Turn on each individual turn signal. If turn signal(s) is not working, see EXTERIOR LIGHTS article. If turn signals are operating correctly, go to next step.

2) Using scan tool, read turn signal status. Turn on right turn signal. If scan tool does not display TURN SIGNAL status changing from OPEN to CLOSED, go to step **7)**. If scan tool displays TURN SIGNAL status changing from OPEN to CLOSED, go to next step.

3) Turn on left turn signal. If scan tool does not display TURN SIGNAL status changing from OPEN to CLOSED, go to step **7)**. If scan tool displays TURN SIGNAL status changing from OPEN to CLOSED, go to next step.

4) Turn ignition off. Disconnect information center connector. Remove ignition key. Turn off all lights and accessories. Close all doors. Using external ohmmeter, measure resistance between ground and information center connector terminal No. 3 (Black wire). If resistance is 10 ohms or more, repair open Black wire. If resistance is less than 10 ohms, go to next step.

5) Remove and inspect both information center turn signal bulbs. Replace as needed. Turn ignition on. Turn on right turn signal. Connect test light to between ground and information center connector terminal No. 4 (Brown/Red wire). If test light does not flash, repair open Brown/Red wire. If test light flashes, go to next step.

6) Turn on left turn signal. Connect test light to information center terminal No. 2 (Dark Green/Red wire). If test light does not flash, repair open Dark Green/Red wire. If test light flashes, replace information center.

7) Turn ignition off. Disconnect Body Control Module (BCM). BCM is located with junction block under driver's side instrument panel. *See Fig. 1.* Access junction block internal 23-pin connector. Turn ignition on. Turn on right turn signal. Using test light, probe internal connector, terminal No. 21. If test light does not flash, repair or replace junction block. If test light flashes, go to next step.

8) Turn on left turn signal. Using test light, probe internal connector, terminal No. 19. If test light does not flash, repair or replace junction block. If test light flashes, replace BCM.

Body Control Computer Tests
Caravan, Town & Country & Voyager (Cont.)

INSTRUMENT CLUSTER

FUEL LEVEL SENDING CIRCUIT ERROR

NOTE: For connector terminal identification and wiring diagrams, see BODY CONTROL COMPUTER – INTRODUCTION article. Perform VERIFICATION TEST VER-1A after each repair.

CAUTION: Always turn ignition switch to OFF position prior to disconnecting or connecting any module connector.

1) If fuel gauge has accuracy problem, go to next step. If fuel gauge does not have an accuracy problem, go to step **6)**.

2) Ensure there is fuel in fuel tank before proceeding with this test. If problem is only with fuel warning light, replace Body Control Module (BCM). BCM is located with junction block under driver's side instrument panel. *See Fig. 1.* If problem is other than with fuel warning light, go to next step.

3) Using scan tool, actuate gauges. Observe fuel gauge. If fuel gauge pointer sweeps and stops at E, 1/8, 1/4 and Full, go to next step. If fuel gauge does not operate correctly, recalibrate fuel gauge using scan tool.

4) Stop actuation. Inspect fuel tank for bowing on bottom of tank. Replace as needed. Turn ignition off. Disconnect Body Control Module (BCM) connector "B". Using scan tool in ohmmeter mode, measure resistance between chassis ground and BCM connector "B" terminal No. 46 (Dark Blue). Determine if ohmmeter reading matches fuel level. See FUEL LEVEL SENDING UNIT RESISTANCE table. If resistance matches fuel gauge reading, replace BCM. If resistance does not match fuel gauge reading, go to next step.

5) Remove fuel level sending unit from fuel tank. Inspect tank unit for foreign material. Replace as needed. If tank is okay, replace sending unit.

6) Ensure there is fuel in fuel tank before proceeding with this test. If problem is only with fuel warning light, replace Body Control Module (BCM). BCM is located with junction block under driver's side instrument panel. *See Fig. 1.* If problem is other than with fuel warning light, go to next step.

7) Turn ignition on. Using scan tool, read BCM DTCs. If scan tool displays FUEL LEVEL SENSOR CIRCUIT ERROR code, go to next step. If scan tool does not display FUEL LEVEL SENSOR CIRCUIT ERROR message, go to step **12)**.

8) Turn ignition off. Disconnect fuel tank sending unit 4-pin connector located next to fuel tank. Turn ignition on. Using scan tool in voltmeter mode, measure voltage at fuel pump harness connector terminal No. 3 (Dark Blue wire). If voltage is .5 volt or less, go to step **10)**. If voltage is more than .5 volt, go to next step.

9) Turn ignition off. Using scan tool in ohmmeter mode, measure resistance at fuel pump harness connector terminal No. 1 (Black wire). If resistance is less than 5 ohms, replace fuel level sending unit. If resistance is 5 ohms or more, repair open Black wire.

10) Turn ignition off. Using scan tool in ohmmeter mode, measure resistance at fuel pump harness connector terminal No. 3 (Dark Blue wire). If resistance is less than 5 ohms, repair Dark Blue wire for short to ground. If resistance is 5 ohms or more, go to next step.

11) Connect jumper wire between ground and fuel pump harness connector terminal No. 3 (Dark Blue wire). Disconnect BCM connector "B". Using an external ohmmeter, measure resistance between ground and BCM connector "B" terminal No. 46 (Dark Blue wire). If resistance is less than 5 ohms, replace BCM. If resistance is 5 ohms or more, repair open Dark Blue wire.

12) Turn ignition on. Using scan tool, read ignition voltage. If voltage is 11 volts or less, go to appropriate VEHICLE COMMUNICATIONS article. If voltage is more than 11 volts, go to next step.

13) Using scan tool, read fuel sensor voltage. If scan tool displays voltage of 1-10 volts, replace fuel level sensor. If scan tool does not display voltage of 1-10 volts, replace BCM.

FUEL LEVEL SENDING UNIT RESISTANCE

Float Position	Ohms
Full	50-90
3/4	310-370
1/2	520-580
1/4	730-790
Empty	1020-1080

ALL GAUGES DO NOT OPERATE

NOTE: For connector terminal identification and wiring diagrams, see BODY CONTROL COMPUTER – INTRODUCTION article. Perform VERIFICATION TEST VER-1A after each repair.

CAUTION: Always turn ignition switch to OFF position prior to disconnecting or connecting any module connector.

1) Turn ignition on. Using scan tool, select ELECTRO/MECHANICAL cluster. If scan tool displays NO RESPONSE or CCD BUS FAILURE, go to appropriate VEHICLE COMMUNICATIONS article. If scan tool does not display NO RESPONSE or CCD BUS FAILURE, go to next step.

2) Using scan tool, read DTCs. If scan tool displays ROM TEST FAILURE, recalibrate all gauges. If scan tool displays RAM TEST FAILURE, replace instrument cluster printed circuit. If scan tool displays BODY COMPUTER ODOMETER FAILURE, replace BCM. If scan tool displays NO MESSAGE FROM BCM, PCM or TCM, go to appropriate VEHICLE COMMUNICATIONS article. If scan tool does not display any of the listed messages, go to next step.

3) Using scan tool, select BODY, then BODY COMPUTER, then INPUT/OUTPUT. Read ignition unlock status. If scan tool displays IGNITION UNLOCK: CLOSED, go to next step. If scan tool does not display IGNITION UNLOCK: CLOSED, go to appropriate VEHICLE COMMUNICATIONS article.

4) Using scan tool, select BODY, then ELECTOR/MECH CLUSTER (MIC). Select ACTUATOR TEST, then actuate ALL GAUGES. If gauges move from lower to upper limits, replace Body Control Module (BCM). BCM is located with junction block under driver's side instrument panel. *See Fig. 1.* If gauges do not operate, replace instrument cluster circuit board. Using scan tool, recalibrate gauges.

INSTRUMENT CLUSTER ILLUMINATION CONCERN

NOTE: For connector terminal identification and wiring diagrams, see BODY CONTROL COMPUTER – INTRODUCTION article. Perform VERIFICATION TEST VER-1A after each repair.

CAUTION: Always turn ignition switch to OFF position prior to disconnecting or connecting any module connector.

1) Turn ignition on. Using scan tool, select ELECTRO/MECHANICAL cluster. If scan tool displays NO RESPONSE or CCD BUS FAILURE, go to appropriate VEHICLE COMMUNICATIONS article. If scan tool does not display NO RESPONSE or CCD BUS FAILURE, go to next step.

2) Using scan tool, read DTCs. If scan tool displays ROM TEST FAILURE, recalibrate all gauges. If scan tool displays RAM TEST FAILURE, replace instrument cluster printed circuit. If scan tool displays BODY COMPUTER ODOMETER FAILURE, replace BCM. If scan tool displays NO MESSAGE FROM BCM, PCM or TCM, go to appropriate VEHICLE COMMUNICATIONS article. If scan tool does not display any of the listed messages, go to next step.

3) Remove and inspect junction block fuse No. 2. *See Fig. 3.* If fuse is open, go to step **5)**. If fuse is okay, go to next step.

4) Replace fuse. Turn park lights on and rotate dimmer wheel to full intensity. If fuse No. 2 blows, repair short to ground in orange wire between junction block and instrument cluster connector terminal No. 6. If fuse No. 2 is okay, system is currently functioning correctly.

5) Turn park lights on. If park lights illuminate, go to next step. If park lights do not illuminate, go to EXTERIOR LIGHTING SYSTEM.

CHRY
4-114

1999 ACCESSORIES & EQUIPMENT
Body Control Computer Tests
Caravan, Town & Country & Voyager (Cont.)

6) Using scan tool, read park lamp switch status. If scan tool displays PARK LAMP ON, go to next step. If scan tool does not display PARK LAMP ON, go to step **19**).

7) Using scan tool, read panel lamp sensor voltage. If scan tool displays zero volts, go to next step. If scan tool displays voltage, go to step **15**).

8) While using scan tool to read panel light sensor voltage, rotate dimmer control switch between high and low. If voltage changes, go to step **15**). If voltage does not change, go to next step.

9) Using scan tool, read panel lamp sensor voltage. Rotate dimmer switch between high and low. If voltage remains high, go to next step. If voltage does not remain high, go to step **12**).

10) Ensure park lights are on. Rotate dimmer switch to high position. Access headlight switch connector. Do not disconnect connector. Using scan tool in voltmeter mode, backprobe connector. Measure voltage on headlight switch 13-pin connector terminal No. 6 (Black wire). If voltage is one volt or less, go to next step. If voltage is more than one volt, repair open Black wire.

11) Measure voltage on headlight switch 13-pin connector terminal No. 12 (Orange/Black wire). If voltage is .8 volt or less, repair open Orange/Black wire. If voltage is more than .8 volt, replace BCM.

12) Access Body Control Module (BCM) connector "A". BCM is located with junction block under driver's side instrument panel. *See Fig. 1.* Remove connector cover. Do not disconnect connector. Using scan tool in voltmeter mode, backprobe connector "A". Measure voltage on BCM connector "A" terminal No. 8 (Orange/Black wire) while rotating dimmer switch. If voltage varies from zero to 4 volts, replace BCM. If voltage does not vary from zero volts to 4 volts, go to next step.

13) Ensure park lights are still on. Disconnect headlight switch 13-pin connector. Using scan tool, read panel lamp sensor voltage. If voltage is more than 4 volts, replace headlight switch. If voltage is 4 volts or less, go to next step.

14) Turn park lights off. Using scan tool in ohmmeter mode, measure resistance at headlight switch 13-pin connector terminal No. 12 (Orange/Black wire). If resistance is 5 ohms or more, replace BCM. If resistance is less than 5 ohms, repair Orange/Black wire for short to ground.

15) Ensure park lights are on and dimmer switch is at midway position. Locate junction block 36-pin connectors "A" (Red) and "C" (Black). *See Fig. 1.* Using scan tool in voltmeter mode, measure voltage on each panel lamp driver terminal (Orange wire). See PANEL LAMP DRIVER TERMINAL IDENTIFICATION table. While backprobing each terminal, rotate dimmer switch from low to high. If voltage increases from zero volts to about 12 volts at all terminals, go to next step. If voltage does not increase at any terminal, replace junction block.

PANEL LAMP DRIVER TERMINAL IDENTIFICATION

Connector	Terminal
Connector "A"	1 & 8
Connector "C"	1, 8, 23 & 30

16) Disconnect instrument cluster 13-pin connector and ensure connector is clean and not damaged. Using scan tool in voltmeter mode, measure voltage at instrument cluster Blue 13-pin connector terminal No. 6 (Orange wire). If voltage is more than 5 volts, go to next step. If voltage is 5 volts or less, repair open Orange wire between instrument cluster and junction block.

17) Using scan tool in ohmmeter mode, measure resistance at instrument cluster 13-pin connector. terminal No. 13 (Black wire). If resistance is 20 ohms or more, repair open Black wire. If resistance is less than 5 ohms, system is currently functioning correctly.

18) If problem is only with instrument cluster illumination, replace instrument cluster circuit board. Recalibrate gauges using scan tool. If problem is with a specific light, inspect bulb. If bulb is okay, repair open in suspect indicator light driver and/or ground circuits.

19) Ensure park lights are on. Using scan tool in voltmeter mode, measure voltage on junction block fuse No. 2. If voltage is 10 volts or less, replace junction block. If voltage is more than 10 volts, replace

Body Control Module (BCM). BCM is located with junction block under driver's side instrument panel. *See Fig. 1.*

INSTRUMENT CLUSTER WARNING LIGHTS, ODOMETER & PRNDL DISPLAY CONCERN

NOTE: For connector terminal identification and wiring diagrams, see BODY CONTROL COMPUTER – INTRODUCTION article. Perform VERIFICATION TEST VER-1A after each repair.

CAUTION: Always turn ignition switch to OFF position prior to disconnecting or connecting any module connector.

1) Turn ignition on. Using scan tool, select ELECTRO/MECHANICAL cluster. If scan tool displays NO RESPONSE or CCD BUS FAILURE, go to appropriate VEHICLE COMMUNICATIONS article. If scan tool does not display NO RESPONSE or CCD BUS FAILURE, go to next step.

2) Using scan tool, read DTCs. If scan tool displays BODY COMPUTER ODOMETER FAILURE DTC, replace Body Control Module (BCM). BCM is located with junction block under driver's side instrument panel. *See Fig. 1.* If scan tool does not display BODY COMPUTER ODOMETER FAILURE DTC, go to next step.

3) Using scan tool, actuate ALL SEGMENTS test. If all segments fail to light, check connector between instrument cluster board and display. If any segments in odometer or PRNDL fail to illuminate, replace instrument cluster display. If any warning lights fail to illuminate, remove and inspect inoperative indicator light. Replace as needed. Visually inspect instrument cluster circuit board. Replace as needed. If circuit board is replaced, recalibrate gauges using scan tool. Identify problem(s) and perform indicated test(s) in WARNING LIGHT SYSTEM DIAGNOSTIC TEST DIRECTORY table.

WARNING LIGHT SYSTEM DIAGNOSTIC TEST DIRECTORY

Problem Circuit	Go To
Generator Indicator Light (Battery Symbol)	[1]
Door Ajar Light	Step **4**)
Liftgate Ajar Light	Step **4**)
Low Fuel Warning Light	[2]
Low Washer Fluid Light	Step **5**)

[1] – See appropriate GENERATORS & REGULATORS article in STARTING & CHARGING SYSTEMS.
[2] – See FUEL LEVEL SENDING CIRCUIT ERROR.

4) Ensure all doors are closed and properly aligned. Using scan tool, enter BODY SYSTEM, then BODY COMPUTER. Select INPUTS/OUTPUTS. Observe door and liftgate ajar switch status. If scan tool displays any ajar switch status CLOSED, perform appropriate test. See DOOR AJAR SYMPTOM DIRECTORY table. If scan tool does not display any ajar switch status CLOSED, system is currently functioning correctly.

DOOR AJAR SYMPTOM DIRECTORY

Problem Circuit	[1] Perform
Driver's Door Ajar	SHORTED DRIVER DOOR AJAR CIRCUIT
Passenger's Door Ajar	SHORTED PASSENGER DOOR AJAR CIRCUIT
Right Sliding Door Ajar	SHORTED RIGHT SLIDING DOOR AJAR CIRCUIT
Liftgate Ajar	SHORTED LIFTGATE AJAR CIRCUIT
Left Sliding Door Ajar	SHORTED LEFT SLIDING DOOR AJAR CIRCUIT

[1] – In INTERIOR LIGHTING SYSTEM.

5) Ensure washer fluid reservoir is not empty. Using scan tool, read washer fluid switch status. If scan tool displays CIRCUIT CLOSED, go to next step. If scan tool does not display CIRCUIT CLOSED, go to step **8**).

6) Disconnect washer fluid switch connector on bottom of reservoir. Using scan tool, read washer fluid switch status. If scan tool displays

1999 ACCESSORIES & EQUIPMENT
Body Control Computer Tests
Caravan, Town & Country & Voyager (Cont.)

CHRY
4-115

CIRCUIT CLOSED, go to next step. If scan tool does not display CIRCUIT CLOSED, replace washer fluid level switch.

7) Disconnect Body Control Module (BCM) connector "B". BCM is located with junction block under driver's side instrument panel. *See Fig. 1.* Using scan tool in ohmmeter mode, measure resistance at BCM connector "B" terminal No. 58 (Black/Tan wire). If resistance is less than 5 ohms, repair Black/Tan wire for short to ground. If resistance is 5 ohms or more, replace BCM.

8) Disconnect washer fluid switch connector on bottom of reservoir. Connect jumper wire between chassis ground and washer fluid level switch connector terminal "B" (Black/Tan wire). Using scan tool, read washer fluid switch status. If scan tool displays CIRCUIT CLOSED, repair open Black wire. If scan tool does not display CIRCUIT CLOSED, go to next step.

9) Remove jumper wire. Connect jumper wire between connector terminals. Using scan tool, read washer fluid switch status. If scan tool displays CIRCUIT CLOSED, replace washer fluid level switch. If scan tool does not display CIRCUIT CLOSED, go to next step.

10) Access Body Control Module (BCM) connector "B". BCM is located with junction block under driver's side instrument panel. Remove connector cover. Do not disconnect connector. Backprobing connector "B", connect jumper between terminal No. 58 (Black/Tan wire) and ground. Using scan tool read washer fluid switch status. If scan tool displays CIRCUIT CLOSED, repair open Black/Tan wire. If scan tool does not display CIRCUIT CLOSED, replace BCM.

GAUGES DO NOT ZERO WHEN KEY IS TURNED OFF

NOTE: For connector terminal identification and wiring diagrams, see BODY CONTROL COMPUTER – INTRODUCTION article. Perform VERIFICATION TEST VER-1A after each repair.

CAUTION: Always turn ignition switch to OFF position prior to disconnecting or connecting any module connector.

1) Turn ignition on. Using scan tool, select ELECTRO/MECHANICAL cluster. If scan tool displays NO RESPONSE or CCD BUS FAILURE, go to appropriate VEHICLE COMMUNICATIONS article. If scan tool does not display NO RESPONSE or CCD BUS FAILURE, go to next step.

2) Using scan tool, read DTCs. If scan tool displays ROM TEST FAILURE, recalibrate all gauges. If scan tool displays RAM TEST FAILURE, replace instrument cluster printed circuit. If scan tool displays BODY COMPUTER ODOMETER FAILURE, replace BCM. If scan tool displays NO MESSAGE FROM BCM, PCM or TCM, go to appropriate VEHICLE COMMUNICATIONS article. If scan tool does not display any of the listed messages, go to next step.

3) Turn ignition off. Disconnect instrument cluster and ensure connectors are clean and not damaged. Using scan tool in voltmeter mode, measure voltage at instrument cluster 13-pin connector terminal No. 2 (Pink wire). If voltage is 10 volts or less, repair open Pink wire. If voltage is more than 10 volts, replace instrument cluster circuit board. Recalibrate gauges using scan tool.

ONE GAUGE NOT OPERATING PROPERLY

NOTE: For connector terminal identification and wiring diagrams, see BODY CONTROL COMPUTER – INTRODUCTION article. Perform VERIFICATION TEST VER-1A after each repair.

CAUTION: Always turn ignition switch to OFF position prior to disconnecting or connecting any module connector.

1) Using scan tool, actuate gauges. If scan tool displays NO RESPONSE, go to appropriate VEHICLE COMMUNICATIONS article. If one gauge fails to actuate, go to next step. If all gauges fail to actuate, go to step **3)**. If none of the conditions listed occur, go to step **5)**.

2) Disconnect Mechanical Instrument Cluster (MIC) and ensure connectors are clean and not damaged. Remove inoperative gauge. Inspect printed circuit board and gauge connections. Repair printed circuit board as necessary. If printed circuit board is okay, replace inoperative gauge. Recalibrate gauge using scan tool.

3) Using scan tool, select BODY, then BODY COMPUTER, then INPUT/OUTPUT. Read ignition unlock status. If scan tool displays IGNITION UNLOCK: CLOSED, go to next step. If scan tool does not display IGNITION UNLOCK: CLOSED, go to appropriate VEHICLE COMMUNICATIONS article.

4) Using scan tool, select BODY, then ELECTOR/MECH CLUSTER (MIC). Select ACTUATOR TEST, then actuate ALL GAUGES. If gauges move from lower to upper limits, replace Body Control Module (BCM). BCM is located with junction block under driver's side instrument panel. *See Fig. 1.* If gauges do not operate, replace instrument cluster circuit board. Using scan tool, recalibrate gauges.

5) If problem is with fuel gauge, go to FUEL LEVEL SENDING CIRCUIT ERROR. If problem is with speedometer/odometer, go to next step. If problem is with tachometer, go to step **22)**. If problem is with temperature gauge, go to step **26)**. If problem is not listed, system is currently functioning correctly.

6) If problem is with odometer only, go to next step. If problem is not with odometer only, go to step **18)**.

7) If odometer fails to illuminate properly when key is turned on, go to next step. If odometer illuminates properly when key is turned on, go to step **16)**.

8) Using scan tool, actuate ALL SEGMENTS test. If all segments fail to light, check connector between instrument cluster board and display. If any segments in odometer or PRNDL fail to illuminate, replace instrument cluster display. If any warning lights fail to illuminate, remove and inspect inoperative indicator light. Replace as needed. Visually inspect instrument cluster circuit board. Replace as needed. If circuit board is replaced, recalibrate gauges using scan tool. Identify problem(s) and perform indicated test(s) in WARNING LIGHT FAILURE DIRECTORY table.

WARNING LIGHT FAILURE DIRECTORY

Problem Circuit	Go To
Generator Indicator Light (Battery Symbol)	[1]
Door Ajar Light	Step 9)
Liftgate Ajar Light	Step 9)
Low Fuel Warning Light	[2]
Low Washer Fluid Light	Step 10)

[1] – See appropriate GENERATORS & REGULATORS article in STARTING & CHARGING SYSTEMS.
[2] – See FUEL LEVEL SENDING CIRCUIT ERROR.

9) Ensure all doors are closed and properly aligned. Using scan tool, enter BODY SYSTEM, then BODY COMPUTER. Select INPUTS/OUTPUTS. Observe door and liftgate ajar switch status. If scan tool displays any ajar switch status CLOSED, perform appropriate test. See DOOR AJAR SYMPTOM DIRECTORY table under INSTRUMENT CLUSTER WARNING LIGHTS, ODOMETER & PRNDL DISPLAY CONCERN. If scan tool does not display any ajar switch status CLOSED, system is currently functioning correctly.

10) Ensure washer fluid reservoir is not empty. Using scan tool, read washer fluid switch status. If scan tool displays CIRCUIT CLOSED, go to next step. If scan tool does not display CIRCUIT CLOSED, go to step **13)**.

11) Disconnect washer fluid switch connector on bottom of reservoir. Using scan tool, read washer fluid switch status. If scan tool displays CIRCUIT CLOSED, go to next step. If scan tool does not display CIRCUIT CLOSED, replace washer fluid level switch.

12) Disconnect Body Control Module (BCM) connector "B". BCM is located with junction block under driver's side instrument panel. *See Fig. 1.* Using scan tool in ohmmeter mode, measure resistance at BCM connector "B" terminal No. 58 (Black/Tan wire). If resistance is less than 5 ohms, repair Black/Tan wire for short to ground. If resistance is 5 ohms or more, replace BCM.

CHRY
4-116

1999 ACCESSORIES & EQUIPMENT
Body Control Computer Tests
Caravan, Town & Country & Voyager (Cont.)

13) Disconnect washer fluid switch connector on bottom of reservoir. Connect jumper wire between chassis ground and washer fluid level switch connector terminal "B" (Black/Tan wire). Using scan tool, read washer fluid switch status. If scan tool displays CIRCUIT CLOSED, repair open Black wire. If scan tool does not display CIRCUIT CLOSED, go to next step.

14) Remove jumper wire. Connect jumper wire between connector terminals. Using scan tool, read washer fluid switch status. If scan tool displays CIRCUIT CLOSED, replace washer fluid level switch. If scan tool does not display CIRCUIT CLOSED, go to next step.

15) Access Body Control Module (BCM) connector "B". BCM is located with junction block under driver's side instrument panel. Remove connector cover. Do not disconnect connector. Backprobing connector "B", connect jumper between terminal No. 58 (Black/Tan wire) and ground. Using scan tool read washer fluid switch status. If scan tool displays CIRCUIT CLOSED, repair open Black/Tan wire. If scan tool does not display CIRCUIT CLOSED, replace BCM.

16) If odometer does not increment properly, recalibrate speedometer. If odometer increments properly, go to next step.

17) If odometer gains or looses mileage when ignition is turned on, check fuse No. 2 in junction block. If odometer does not gain or loose mileage when ignition is turned on, replace BCM. BCM is located with junction block under driver's side instrument panel. *See Fig. 1.*

18) Turn ignition on. Using scan tool, actuate gauges. If speedometer goes to 0, 20, 55, 75 MPH in steps, and then to zero, go to next step. If speedometer does not go to 0, 20, 55, 75 MPH in steps, and then to zero, recalibrate gauges using scan tool. If problem still exists, replace gauge pack and calibrate.

19) Using scan tool, read Powertrain Control Module (PCM) status. If scan tool displays, ACTIVE ON THE BUS, go to next step. If scan tool does not display ACTIVE ON THE BUS, go to appropriate VEHICLE COMMUNICATIONS article.

20) Using scan tool, read PCM DTCs. If a NO VEHICLE SPEED SENSOR SIGNAL message is not present, go to next step. If a NO VEHICLE SPEED SENSOR SIGNAL DTC is present, see appropriate SELF-DIAGNOSTICS article in ENGINE PERFORMANCE in appropriate MITCHELL® manual.

21) Raise and properly support vehicle. Start engine. Place transaxle in Drive and slowly allow drive wheels to turn. Using scan tool, observe vehicle speed under MONITORS. If scan tool speed display matches speedometer speed, check pinion factor using scan tool. If scan tool speed display does not match speedometer, replace Body Control Module (BCM). BCM is located with junction block under driver's side instrument panel. *See Fig. 1.*

22) Turn ignition on. Using scan tool, actuate gauges. If tachometer gradually steps up to 1000, 3000 then 6000 RPM and then returns to zero, go to next step. If tachometer does not go to 1000, 3000 then 6000 RPM, recalibrate gauges using scan tool. If tachometer still does not function correctly, replace gauge pack and recalibrate.

23) Using scan tool, read Powertrain Control Module (PCM) status. If scan tool displays ACTIVE ON THE BUS, go to next step. If scan tool does not display ACTIVE ON THE BUS, go to appropriate VEHICLE COMMUNICATIONS article.

24) Start and idle engine. Using scan tool, select MIC, then MONITORS, then ENG INFO. Read engine RPM. If scan tool RPM display matches tachometer RPM, tachometer is currently operating properly. If scan tool RPM display does not match tachometer RPM, replace Powertrain Control Module (PCM). PCM is located next to power distribution center.

25) Ensure cooling system is operating properly. If cooling system is operating properly, go to next step. If cooling system is not operating properly, repair as needed.

26) Turn ignition on. Using scan tool, actuate gauges. If temperature gauge gradually steps up from cold to hot, then back to cold, go to next step. If temperature gauge does not gradually steps up from cold to hot, replace temperature gauge. Recalibrate gauges using scan tool.

27) Using scan tool, read Powertrain Control Module (PCM) status. If scan tool displays ACTIVE ON THE BUS, go to next step. If scan tool does not display ACTIVE ON THE BUS, go to appropriate VEHICLE COMMUNICATIONS article.

28) Using scan tool, read PCM DTCs. If an engine COOLANT TEMPERATURE SENSOR DTC is not present, go to next step. If an engine COOLANT TEMPERATURE SENSOR DTC is present, see appropriate SELF-DIAGNOSTICS article in ENGINE PERFORMANCE in appropriate MITCHELL® manual.

29) Start and idle engine. Using scan tool, read engine temperature. If scan tool temperature display matches temperature gauge display, temperature gauge is operating properly. If scan tool display and temperature gauge do not match, replace Body Control Module (BCM). BCM is located with junction block under driver's side instrument panel. *See Fig. 1.*

TRIP & RESET BUTTON CONCERN

NOTE: For connector terminal identification and wiring diagrams, see BODY CONTROL COMPUTER – INTRODUCTION article. Perform VERIFICATION TEST VER-1A after each repair.

CAUTION: Always turn ignition switch to OFF position prior to disconnecting or connecting any module connector.

Turn ignition on. Using scan tool, read button state. Press trip and reset buttons while observing scan tool. If scan tool display does not change from PRESSED to RELEASED, replace VF display board. If scan tool display changes from PRESSED to RELEASED, system is currently functioning correctly.

INTERIOR LIGHTING SYSTEM
COURTESY LIGHTS INOPERATIVE WITH DOME LIGHT SWITCH

NOTE: For connector terminal identification and wiring diagrams, see BODY CONTROL COMPUTER – INTRODUCTION article. Perform VERIFICATION TEST VER-1A after each repair.

CAUTION: Always turn ignition switch to OFF position prior to disconnecting or connecting any module connector.

1) Rotate headlight switch to dome light position. Using scan tool, read dome lamp switch. If scan tool displays DOME LAMP SWITCH: CLOSED, replace Body Control Module (BCM). BCM is located with junction block under driver's side instrument panel. *See Fig. 1.* If scan tool does not display DOME LAMP SWITCH: CLOSED, go to next step.

2) Gain access to back of headlight switch. Do not disconnect connectors. Connect jumper wire between ground and headlight switch 13- pin connector terminal No. 4 (Black/Light Blue wire). If courtesy lights illuminate, replace headlight switch. If courtesy lights do not illuminate, go to next step.

3) Access junction block connector "A". Connect jumper wire between ground and junction block connector "A" terminal No. 2 (Black/Light Blue wire). If courtesy lights illuminate, repair open Black/Light Blue wire. If courtesy lights do not illuminate, replace BCM.

COURTESY LIGHTS INOPERATIVE WITH ANY DOOR

NOTE: For connector terminal identification and wiring diagrams, see BODY CONTROL COMPUTER – INTRODUCTION article. Perform VERIFICATION TEST VER-1A after each repair.

CAUTION: Always turn ignition switch to OFF position prior to disconnecting or connecting any module connector.

1) Using scan tool, select BODY CONTROL MODULE. If scan tool displays NO RESPONSE or CCD BUS FAILURE, go to appropriate

1999 ACCESSORIES & EQUIPMENT
Body Control Computer Tests
Caravan, Town & Country & Voyager (Cont.)

CHRY
4-117

VEHICLE COMMUNICATIONS article. If scan tool does not display NO RESPONSE or CCD BUS FAILURE, go to next step.

2) Ensure courtesy light switch on headlight switch is in middle position. Using scan tool, select BODY, BODY COMPUTER, then ACTUATOR TEST. Actuate COURTESY LMP RLY. If courtesy lights illuminate, go to next step. If courtesy lights do not illuminate, go to step **4)**.

3) Stop courtesy light actuation. Open driver's door. Using scan tool, read left front door ajar switch status. If scan tool displays DRDOOR AJAR: CLOSED, replace Body Control Module (BCM). BCM is located with junction block under driver's side instrument panel. See Fig. 1. If scan tool does not display DRDOOR AJAR: CLOSED, go to COURTESY LIGHTS INOPERATIVE WITH DRIVER DOOR (OPEN DRIVER DOOR AJAR CIRCUIT).

4) Disconnect courtesy light relay. See Fig. 3. Using scan tool in voltmeter mode, measure voltage at courtesy light relay socket terminal No. 30. If voltage is 10 volts or less, replace junction block. If voltage is more than 10 volts, go to next step.

5) Disconnect voltmeter probe. Connect jumper wire between courtesy light relay socket terminals No. 30 and 87. If courtesy lights illuminate, go to next step. If courtesy lights do not illuminate, replace junction block.

6) Using scan tool in voltmeter mode, measure voltage at courtesy light relay socket terminal No. 86. If voltage is 10 volts or less, replace junction block. If voltage is more than 10 volts, go to next step.

7) Disconnect jumper wire. Install courtesy light relay. Access junction block connector "D". See Fig. 1. Using scan tool in voltmeter mode, backprobe connector "D". Measure voltage on terminal No. 34 (Brown/White wire). If voltage is 10 volts or less, replace courtesy light relay. If voltage is more than 10 volts, go to next step.

8) Remove headlight switch from dash. Do not disconnect connectors. Using scan tool in voltmeter mode, backprobe headlight switch 13-pin connector terminal No. 9 (Brown/White wire). If voltage is 10 volts or less, repair open Brown/White wire. If voltage is more than 10 volts, go to next step.

9) Backprobe headlight switch 13-pin connector terminal No. 3 (Brown/Light Green wire) on switch connector. If voltage is 10 volts or less, replace headlight switch. If voltage is more than 10 volts, go to next step.

10) Access junction block connector "D". Using scan tool in voltmeter mode, backprobe connector "D". Measure voltage on terminal No. 10 (Brown/Light Green wire). If voltage is 10 volts or less, repair open Brown/Light Green wire. If voltage is more than 10 volts, replace Body Control Module (BCM). BCM is located with junction block under driver's side instrument panel.

COURTESY LIGHTS INOPERATIVE WITH DRIVER DOOR (OPEN DRIVER DOOR AJAR CIRCUIT)

NOTE: For connector terminal identification and wiring diagrams, see BODY CONTROL COMPUTER – INTRODUCTION article. Perform VERIFICATION TEST VER-1A after each repair.

CAUTION: Always turn ignition switch to OFF position prior to disconnecting any module connector.

1) Disconnect driver's door ajar switch and ensure connector is clean and not damaged. Ensure driver's door ajar switch ground strap is clean and not damaged. Repair or replace ground strap as necessary. If ground strap is okay, go to next step.

2) Connect a jumper wire between driver's door ajar switch connector (Tan wire) and chassis ground. Using scan tool, read driver's door ajar switch status. If scan tool displays DRDOOR AJAR SWITCH: CLOSED, replace driver's door ajar switch. If scan tool does not display DRDOOR AJAR SWITCH: CLOSED, go to next step.

3) Disconnect jumper wire. Locate Body Control Module (BCM) connector "B". BCM is located with junction block under driver's side instrument panel. See Fig. 1. Remove connector cover. Do not disconnect connector. Connect jumper wire between chassis ground and BCM connector "B" terminal No. 79 (Tan wire). Using scan tool, read driver's door ajar

switch status. If scan tool displays DRDOOR AJAR SWITCH: CLOSED, repair open in Tan wire between driver's door ajar switch and BCM. If scan tool does not display DRDOOR AJAR SWITCH: CLOSED, replace BCM.

COURTESY LIGHTS INOPERATIVE WITH LEFT SLIDING DOOR (OPEN LEFT SLIDING DOOR AJAR CIRCUIT)

NOTE: For connector terminal identification and wiring diagrams, see BODY CONTROL COMPUTER – INTRODUCTION article. Perform VERIFICATION TEST VER-1A after each repair.

CAUTION: Always turn ignition switch to OFF position prior to disconnecting any module connector.

1) Disconnect left sliding door ajar switch and ensure connector is clean and not damaged. Ensure door ajar switch ground strap is clean and not damaged. Repair or replace ground strap as necessary. If ground strap is okay, go to next step.

2) Connect a jumper wire between left sliding door ajar switch connector (Tan/Orange wire) and chassis ground. Using scan tool, read left sliding door ajar switch status. If scan tool displays LSLIDE DR AJAR: CLOSED, replace door ajar switch. If scan tool does not display LSLIDE DR AJAR: CLOSED, go to next step.

3) Disconnect jumper wire. Locate Body Control Module (BCM) connector "B". BCM is located with junction block under driver's side instrument panel. See Fig. 1. Remove connector cover. Do not disconnect connector. Connect jumper wire between chassis ground and BCM connector "B" terminal No. 47 (Tan/Orange wire). Using scan tool, read left front door ajar switch status. If scan tool displays LSLIDE DR AJAR SWITCH: CLOSED, repair open in Tan/Orange wire between left sliding door ajar switch and BCM. If scan tool does not display LSLIDE DR AJAR SWITCH: CLOSED, replace BCM.

COURTESY LIGHTS INOPERATIVE WITH LIFTGATE (OPEN LIFTGATE AJAR CIRCUIT)

NOTE: For connector terminal identification and wiring diagrams, see BODY CONTROL COMPUTER – INTRODUCTION article. Perform VERIFICATION TEST VER-1A after each repair.

CAUTION: Always turn ignition switch to OFF position prior to disconnecting any module connector.

1) Disconnect liftgate ajar switch and ensure connector is clean and not damaged. Ensure liftgate ajar switch ground strap is clean and not damaged. Repair or replace ground strap as necessary. If ground strap is okay, go to next step.

2) Connect a jumper wire between liftgate ajar switch connector (Tan/Black wire) and chassis ground. Using scan tool, read liftgate ajar switch status. If scan tool displays LIFTGATE AJAR SWITCH: CLOSED, replace left front door ajar switch. If scan tool does not display LIFTGATE AJAR SWITCH: CLOSED, go to next step.

3) Disconnect jumper wire. Locate Body Control Module (BCM) connector "B". BCM is located with junction block under driver's side instrument panel. See Fig. 1. Remove connector cover. Do not disconnect connector. Connect jumper wire between chassis ground and BCM connector "B" terminal No. 59 (Tan/Black wire). Using scan tool, read left front door ajar switch status. If scan tool displays LIFTGATE AJAR SWITCH: CLOSED, repair open in Tan/Black wire between liftgate ajar switch and BCM. If scan tool does not display LIFTGATE AJAR SWITCH: CLOSED, replace BCM.

1999 ACCESSORIES & EQUIPMENT
Body Control Computer Tests
Caravan, Town & Country & Voyager (Cont.)

COURTESY LIGHTS INOPERATIVE WITH PASSENGER DOOR (OPEN PASSENGER DOOR AJAR CIRCUIT)

NOTE: *For connector terminal identification and wiring diagrams, see BODY CONTROL COMPUTER – INTRODUCTION article. Perform VERIFICATION TEST VER-1A after each repair.*

CAUTION: *Always turn ignition switch to OFF position prior to disconnecting any module connector.*

1) Disconnect passengers door ajar switch and ensure connector is clean and not damaged. Ensure passengers door ajar switch ground strap is clean and not damaged. Repair or replace ground strap as necessary. If ground strap is okay, go to next step.
2) Connect a jumper wire between passengers door ajar switch connector (Tan/Red wire) and chassis ground. Using scan tool, read passengers door ajar switch status. If scan tool displays PASSDOOR AJAR SWITCH: CLOSED, replace passengers door ajar switch. If scan tool does not display PASSDOOR AJAR SWITCH: CLOSED, go to next step.
3) Disconnect jumper wire. Locate Body Control Module (BCM) connector "B". BCM is located with junction block under driver's side instrument panel. *See Fig. 1.* Remove connector cover. Do not disconnect connector. Connect jumper wire between chassis ground and BCM connector "B" terminal No. 48 (Tan/Red wire). Using scan tool, read passengers door ajar switch status. If scan tool displays PASSDOOR AJAR SWITCH: CLOSED, repair open in Tan/Red wire between right passengers ajar switch and BCM. If scan tool does not display PASSDOOR AJAR SWITCH: CLOSED, replace BCM.

COURTESY LIGHTS INOPERATIVE WITH RIGHT SLIDING DOOR (OPEN RIGHT SLIDING DOOR AJAR CIRCUIT)

NOTE: *For connector terminal identification and wiring diagrams, see BODY CONTROL COMPUTER – INTRODUCTION article. Perform VERIFICATION TEST VER-1A after each repair.*

CAUTION: *Always turn ignition switch to OFF position prior to disconnecting any module connector.*

1) Disconnect right sliding door ajar switch and ensure connector is clean and not damaged. Ensure door ajar switch ground strap is clean and not damaged. Repair or replace ground strap as necessary. If ground strap is okay, go to next step.
2) Connect a jumper wire between right sliding door ajar switch connector (Tan/Yellow wire) and chassis ground. Using scan tool, read right sliding door ajar switch status. If scan tool displays RSLIDE DR AJAR: CLOSED, replace door ajar switch. If scan tool does not display RSLIDE DR AJAR: CLOSED, go to next step.
3) Disconnect jumper wire. Locate Body Control Module (BCM) connector "B". BCM is located with junction block under driver's side instrument panel. *See Fig. 1.* Remove connector cover. Do not disconnect connector. Connect jumper wire between chassis ground and BCM connector "B" terminal No. 77 (Tan/Yellow wire). Using scan tool, read right front door ajar switch status. If scan tool displays RSLIDE DR AJAR SWITCH: CLOSED, repair open in Tan/Yellow wire between right sliding door ajar switch and BCM. If scan tool does not display RSLIDE DR AJAR SWITCH: CLOSED, replace BCM.

COURTESY LIGHTS ON AT ALL TIMES

NOTE: *For connector terminal identification and wiring diagrams, see BODY CONTROL COMPUTER – INTRODUCTION article. Perform VERIFICATION TEST VER-1A after each repair.*

CAUTION: *Always turn ignition switch to OFF position prior to disconnecting or connecting any module connector.*

1) Using scan tool, select BODY CONTROL MODULE. If scan tool displays NO RESPONSE or CCD BUS FAILURE, go to appropriate VEHICLE COMMUNICATIONS article. If scan tool does not display NO RESPONSE or CCD BUS FAILURE, go to next step.
2) Ensure all doors are closed and properly aligned. Using scan tool, enter BODY SYSTEM, then BODY COMPUTER. Select INPUTS/OUTPUTS. Observe door and liftgate ajar switch status. If scan tool displays any ajar switch status CLOSED, perform appropriate test. See DOOR AJAR SYMPTOM DIRECTORY table under INSTRUMENT CLUSTER. If scan tool does not display any ajar switch status CLOSED, go to next step.
3) Disconnect courtesy light relay. *See Fig. 3.* If courtesy lights are still illuminated, repair courtesy light relay output circuit (courtesy light relay terminal No. 87) for short to battery voltage. If courtesy lights are not illuminated, go to next step.
4) Disconnect headlight switch. Using scan tool in ohmmeter mode, measure resistance at courtesy light relay terminal No. 86. If resistance is 5 ohms or more, go to next step. If resistance is less than 5 ohms, repair short to ground in Brown/White wire between relay terminal No. 85 and headlight switch 13-pin connector terminal No. 9 (courtesy light relay control circuit).
5) Disconnect Body Control Module (BCM). BCM is located with junction block under driver's side instrument panel. *See Fig. 1.* Measure resistance at junction block connector "D" terminal No. 10 (Brown/Light Green wire). If resistance is less than 5 ohms, repair Brown/Light Green wire for short to ground. If resistance is 5 ohms or more, go to next step.
6) Measure resistance at courtesy light relay terminal No. 86. If resistance is less than 5 ohms, go to next step. If resistance is 5 ohms or more, replace courtesy light relay.
7) Measure resistance at courtesy light relay terminal No. 85. If resistance is 5 ohms or more, replace headlight switch. If resistance is less than 5 ohms, replace BCM.

ILLUMINATED ENTRY INOPERATIVE WITH DRIVER DOOR KEY (LEFT DOOR KEY CYLINDER DISARM SW FAILURE)

NOTE: *For connector terminal identification and wiring diagrams, see BODY CONTROL COMPUTER – INTRODUCTION article. Perform VERIFICATION TEST VER-1A after each repair.*

CAUTION: *Always turn ignition switch to OFF position prior to disconnecting or connecting any module connector.*

1) Clear trouble codes as needed. See BODY CONTROL COMPUTER – INTRODUCTION article. Using scan tool, read driver's door zone switch voltage. If LF DOOR ZONE SWITCH voltage is about 2 volts, inspect driver's door key lock. Replace key lock as needed. If LF DOOR ZONE SWITCH voltage is not about 2 volts, go to next step.
2) Turn driver's door key cylinder switch to unlock position and observe voltage on scan tool. Do not hold key in unlock position for more than 7 seconds or code will set. If LF DOOR ZONE SWITCH voltage is about 2 volts, go to next step. If LF DOOR ZONE SWITCH voltage is not about 2 volts, replace driver's door key cylinder switch.
3) Operate driver's door key lock cylinder several times from unlock to lock position. Release key lock cylinder. With key lock cylinder in neutral position, observe scan tool voltage. If LF DOOR ZONE SWITCH voltage is about 5 volts, system is currently functioning correctly. If LF DOOR ZONE SWITCH voltage is not about 5 volts, replace driver's door key

1999 ACCESSORIES & EQUIPMENT
Body Control Computer Tests
Caravan, Town & Country & Voyager (Cont.)

CHRY
4-119

cylinder switch.

POWER DOOR LOCK SYSTEM DIAGNOSTIC TEST DIRECTORY

Problem	[1] Perform
All Doors Fail To Lock/Unlock From Any Switch	ADDITIONAL ALL DOORS FAIL TO LOCK & UNLOCK FROM ANY SWITCH
All Doors Fail To Lock/Unlock From Any Switch [2]	ADDITIONAL ALL DOORS (EXCEPT DRVR W/RKE) FAIL LCK/UNLCK FROM ANY SWITCH
All Doors Fail To Lock/Unlock From One Switch	ADDITIONAL ALL DOORS FAIL TO LOCK & UNLOCK FROM ONE SWITCH
One Door Fails To Lock/Unlock From Any Switch	ADDITIONAL ONE DOOR FAILS TO LOCK & UNLOCK FROM ANY SWITCH
All Doors Fail To Lock From Any Switch	ADDITIONAL ALL DOORS FAILING TO LOCK FROM ANY SWITCH
All Doors Fail To Lock From One Switch	[3]
All Doors Fail To Unlock From Any Switch [2]	ADDITIONAL ALL DOORS (EXCEPT DRIVER W/RKE) FAIL TO UNLOCK
Left Front Door (W/RKE) Fails To Unlock	ADDITIONAL DRIVER DOOR (W/RKE) FAILING TO UNLOCK FROM ANY SWITCH
All Doors Fail To Unlock From One Switch	[3]

[1] – In POWER DOOR LOCK SYSTEM.
[2] – On systems with RKE, left front door is not included.
[3] – Replace defective switch.

ILLUMINATED ENTRY INOPERATIVE WITH RKE TRANSMITTER

NOTE: For connector terminal identification and wiring diagrams, see BODY CONTROL COMPUTER – INTRODUCTION article. Perform VERIFICATION TEST VER-1A after each repair.

CAUTION: Always turn ignition switch to OFF position prior to disconnecting or connecting any module connector.

1) Using scan tool, read diagnostic trouble codes. If any door lock code(s) are present, go to appropriate DTC message under POWER DOOR LOCK SYSTEM. If no codes are present, go to next step.

2) Lower both front windows. Remove key from ignition. Close all doors. Lock and unlock doors from all door switches. If door locks operate properly, go to next step. If any door(s) fail to lock or unlock properly, go to appropriate test. See POWER DOOR LOCK SYSTEM DIAGNOSTIC TEST DIRECTORY table.

3) Operate door locks using transmitter. If door locks when transmitter is actuated, system is currently functioning correctly. If doors do not lock when transmitter is actuated, go to next step.

4) Using scan tool, reprogram a known good transmitter: Ensure transmitter battery voltage is 3.2 volts. Turn ignition on. Place transmission in park and disarm anti-theft system. Select MISCELLANEOUS, then PROGRAM RKE. If BCM IS IN PROGRAMMING MODE does not appear, exit and select PROGRAM RKE again. Press any transmitter button. A single chime will announce RKE module accepted transmission. Repeat procedure for all transmitters used with vehicle. Operate door locks from reprogrammed transmitter. If door locks operate properly, system has been repaired. If door locks do not operate properly, go to next step.

5) Access RKE module under instrument panel cover. See Fig. 5. Turn ignition off. Disconnect RKE module connector. Using scan tool in ohmmeter mode, measure resistance at RKE module harness connector terminal No. 4 (Black/Light Green wire). If resistance is 5 ohms or more, repair open Black/Light Green wire. If resistance is less than 5 ohms, go to next step.

6) Using scan tool in voltmeter mode, measure voltage at RKE harness connector terminal No. 3 (Pink wire). If voltage is 10 volts or less, repair open Pink wire. If voltage is more than 10 volts, go to next step.

7) Using scan tool in ohmmeter mode, measure resistance at RKE module harness connector terminal No. 5 (Gray/Black wire). Grounding of circuit will cause RKE system to be inoperative. If resistance is less than 2000 ohms, repair Gray/Black wire for short to ground. If resistance is 2000 ohms or more, go to next step.

8) Ensure gear shift selector is in Park. Using an external voltmeter, measure voltage between ground and RKE module harness connector terminal No. 6 (Light Green/Red wire). If voltage is more than 4 volts, go to step 10). If voltage is 4 volts or less, go to next step.

9) Connect jumper wire between ground and RKE module harness connector terminal No. 5 (Gray/Black wire). Disconnect Body Control Module (BCM) connector "A". BCM is located with junction block under driver's side instrument panel. See Fig. 1. Using scan tool in ohmmeter mode, measure resistance at BCM connector "A" terminal No. 37 (Gray/Black wire). If resistance is 5 ohms or more, repair open Gray/Black wire. If resistance is less than 5 ohms, replace RKE module.

10) Move jumper wire from RKE module harness connector terminal No. 5 (Gray/Black wire) to terminal No. 6 (Light Green/Red wire). Using scan tool in ohmmeter mode, measure resistance at BCM connector "A" terminal No. 4 (Light Green/Red wire). If resistance is 5 ohms or more, repair open Light Green/Red wire. If resistance is less than 5 ohms, go to next step.

11) Remove jumper wire. Using an external ohmmeter, measure resistance between ground and BCM connector "A" terminal No. 4 (Light Green/Red wire). If resistance is 4800 ohms or more, replace BCM. If resistance is less than 4800 ohms, repair Light Green/Red wire for short to ground.

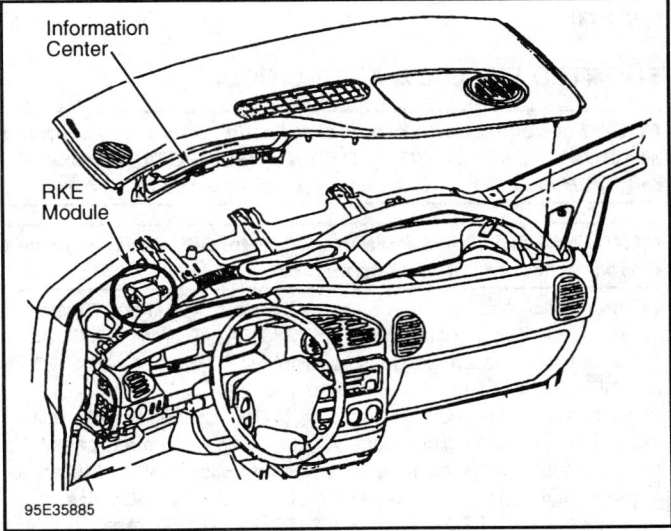

Fig. 5: Locating RKE Module

1999 ACCESSORIES & EQUIPMENT
Body Control Computer Tests
Caravan, Town & Country & Voyager (Cont.)

SHORTED DRIVER DOOR AJAR CIRCUIT

NOTE: For connector terminal identification and wiring diagrams, see BODY CONTROL COMPUTER – INTRODUCTION article. Perform VERIFICATION TEST VER-1A after each repair.

CAUTION: Always turn ignition switch to OFF position prior to disconnecting any module connector.

1) Disconnect driver's door ajar switch. Using scan tool, read left front door ajar switch status. If scan tool displays DRDOOR AJAR SWITCH: CLOSED, go to next step. If scan tool does not display DRDOOR AJAR SWITCH: CLOSED, replace door ajar switch.
2) Disconnect Body Control Module (BCM) connector "B". BCM is located with junction block under driver's side instrument panel. *See Fig. 1.* Using scan tool, read left front door ajar switch status. If scan tool displays DRDOOR AJAR SWITCH: CLOSED, replace BCM. If scan tool does not display DRDOOR AJAR SWITCH: CLOSED, repair Tan wire between driver's door ajar switch and BCM for short to ground.

SHORTED LEFT SLIDING DOOR AJAR CIRCUIT

NOTE: For connector terminal identification and wiring diagrams, see BODY CONTROL COMPUTER – INTRODUCTION article. Perform VERIFICATION TEST VER-1A after each repair.

CAUTION: Always turn ignition switch to OFF position prior to disconnecting any module connector.

1) Disconnect left sliding door ajar switch. Using scan tool, read left sliding door ajar switch status. If scan tool displays LSLIDE DR AJAR SWITCH: CLOSED, go to next step. If scan tool does not display LSLIDE DR AJAR SWITCH: CLOSED, replace door ajar switch.
2) Disconnect Body Control Module (BCM) connector "B". BCM is located with junction block under driver's side instrument panel. *See Fig. 1.* Using scan tool, read left sliding door ajar switch status. If scan tool displays LSLIDE DR AJAR SWITCH: CLOSED, replace BCM. If scan tool does not display LSLIDE DR AJAR SWITCH: CLOSED, repair Tan/Orange wire between left sliding door ajar switch and BCM for short to ground.

SHORTED LIFTGATE AJAR CIRCUIT

NOTE: For connector terminal identification and wiring diagrams, see BODY CONTROL COMPUTER – INTRODUCTION article. Perform VERIFICATION TEST VER-1A after each repair.

CAUTION: Always turn ignition switch to OFF position prior to disconnecting any module connector.

1) Disconnect liftgate ajar switch. Using scan tool, read liftgate ajar switch status. If scan tool displays LIFTGATE AJAR SWITCH: CLOSED, go to next step. If scan tool does not display LIFTGATE AJAR SWITCH: CLOSED, replace liftgate ajar switch.
2) Disconnect Body Control Module (BCM) connector "B". BCM is located with junction block under driver's side instrument panel. *See Fig. 1.* Using scan tool, read liftgate ajar switch status. If scan tool displays LIFTGATE AJAR SWITCH: CLOSED, replace BCM. If scan tool does not display LIFTGATE AJAR SWITCH: CLOSED, repair Tan/Black wire between liftgate ajar switch and BCM for short to ground.

SHORTED PASSENGER DOOR AJAR CIRCUIT

NOTE: For connector terminal identification and wiring diagrams, see BODY CONTROL COMPUTER – INTRODUCTION article. Perform VERIFICATION TEST VER-1A after each repair.

CAUTION: Always turn ignition switch to OFF position prior to disconnecting any module connector.

1) Disconnect passengers door ajar switch. Using scan tool, read right front door ajar switch status. If scan tool displays PASSDOOR AJAR SWITCH: CLOSED, go to next step. If scan tool does not display PASSDOOR AJAR SWITCH: CLOSED, replace door ajar switch.
2) Disconnect Body Control Module (BCM) connector "B". BCM is located with junction block under driver's side instrument panel. *See Fig. 1.* Using scan tool, read right front door ajar switch status. If scan tool displays PASSDOOR AJAR SWITCH: CLOSED, replace BCM. If scan tool does not display PASSDOOR AJAR SWITCH: CLOSED, repair Tan/Red wire between passengers door ajar switch and BCM for short to ground.

SHORTED RIGHT SLIDING DOOR AJAR CIRCUIT

NOTE: For connector terminal identification and wiring diagrams, see BODY CONTROL COMPUTER – INTRODUCTION article. Perform VERIFICATION TEST VER-1A after each repair.

CAUTION: Always turn ignition switch to OFF position prior to disconnecting any module connector.

1) Disconnect right sliding door ajar switch. Using scan tool, read right sliding door ajar switch status. If scan tool displays RSLIDE DR AJAR SWITCH: CLOSED, go to next step. If scan tool does not display RSLIDE DR AJAR SWITCH: CLOSED, replace door ajar switch.
2) Disconnect Body Control Module (BCM) connector "B". BCM is located with junction block under driver's side instrument panel. *See Fig. 1.* Using scan tool, read right sliding door ajar switch status. If scan tool displays RSLIDE DR AJAR SWITCH: CLOSED, replace BCM. If scan tool does not display RSLIDE DR AJAR SWITCH: CLOSED, repair Tan/Yellow wire between right sliding door ajar switch and BCM for short to ground.

OVERHEAD CONSOLE CONCERNS

COMPASS MINI-TRIP COMPUTER (CMTC) ELAPSED TIME INOPERATIVE OR WRONG

NOTE: For connector terminal identification and wiring diagrams, see BODY CONTROL COMPUTER – INTRODUCTION article. Perform VERIFICATION TEST VER-1A after each repair.

NOTE: For CMTC wiring diagram, see ANALOG INSTRUMENT PANELS – FWD VANS article.

CAUTION: Always turn ignition switch to OFF position prior to disconnecting any module connector.

Cycle ignition switch off, then on. Observe instrument cluster warning lights. If lights illuminate, then go off, replace Body Control Module (BCM). BCM is located with junction block under driver's side instrument panel. *See Fig. 1.* If lights do not illuminate, go to appropriate VEHICLE COMMUNICATIONS article.

1999 ACCESSORIES & EQUIPMENT
Body Control Computer Tests
Caravan, Town & Country & Voyager (Cont.)

CHRY
4-121

COMPASS MINI-TRIP COMPUTER (CMTC) AVG MPH OR FUEL ECONOMY INOPERATIVE OR WRONG

NOTE: For connector terminal identification and wiring diagrams, see BODY CONTROL COMPUTER – INTRODUCTION article. Perform VERIFICATION TEST VER-1A after each repair.

NOTE: For CMTC wiring diagram, see ANALOG INSTRUMENT PANELS – FWD VANS article.

CAUTION: Always turn ignition switch to OFF position prior to disconnecting any module connector.

1) Turn ignition on. Using scan tool, read engine information under monitor display. If scan tool displays NO RESPONSE FROM PCM, go to appropriate VEHICLE COMMUNICATIONS article. If scan tool does not display NO RESPONSE FROM PCM, go to next step.

2) Observe TP sensor reading on scan tool while depressing accelerator pedal. If TP sensor percent does not increase while operating throttle, see appropriate SELF-DIAGNOSTICS article in ENGINE PERFORMANCE in appropriate MITCHELL® manual. If TP sensor percent does increase, go to next step.

3) Raise and support vehicle. Start vehicle and place transmission in Drive. Using scan tool, read vehicle speed signal. Increase vehicle speed and observe scan tool. If speed signal changes, system is currently operating correctly. If speed signal does not change, vehicle speed signal may be at fault. See appropriate SELF-DIAGNOSTICS article in ENGINE PERFORMANCE in appropriate MITCHELL® manual.

COMPASS MINI-TRIP COMPUTER (CMTC) DISPLAYING "OC"

NOTE: For connector terminal identification and wiring diagrams, see BODY CONTROL COMPUTER – INTRODUCTION article. Perform VERIFICATION TEST VER-1A after each repair.

NOTE: For CMTC wiring diagram, see ANALOG INSTRUMENT PANELS – FWD VANS article.

CAUTION: Always turn ignition switch to OFF position prior to disconnecting any module connector.

1) Turn ignition off. Disconnect CMTC module connector. Disconnect ambient temperature sensor connector. Sensor is located behind front bumper (right center). Connect jumper wires between ground and each terminal of ambient temperature sensor harness connector. Using scan tool in ohmmeter mode, measure resistance at CMTC module harness connector terminal No. 2 (Black/Light Blue wire). If resistance is less than 5 ohms, go to next step. If resistance is 5 ohms or more, repair open Black/Light Blue wire between CMTC module and ambient temperature sensor.

2) Disconnect jumper wires. Connect jumper wire between ambient temperature sensor connector terminals. Turn ignition on. Observe CMTC display. If CMTC displays SC, replace ambient temperature sensor. If CMTC does not display SC, go to next step.

3) Connect jumper wires between ground and each terminal of ambient temperature sensor harness connector. Measure resistance at CMTC module connector terminal No. 5 (Violet/Light Green wire). If resistance is less than 5 ohms, replace CMTC module. If resistance is 5 ohms or more, repair open Violet/Light Green wire between CMTC module and ambient temperature sensor.

COMPASS MINI-TRIP COMPUTER (CMTC) DISPLAYING "SC"

NOTE: For connector terminal identification and wiring diagrams, see BODY CONTROL COMPUTER – INTRODUCTION article. Perform VERIFICATION TEST VER-1A after each repair.

NOTE: For CMTC wiring diagram, see ANALOG INSTRUMENT PANELS – FWD VANS article.

CAUTION: Always turn ignition switch to OFF position prior to disconnecting any module connector.

1) Disconnect ambient temperature sensor connector. Sensor is located behind front bumper (right center). Turn igniton on. Observe CMTC display. If CMTC displays OC, replace ambient temperature sensor. If CMTC does not display OC, go to next step.

2) Turn ignition off. Disconnect CMTC connector. Using external ohmmeter, measure resistance between CMTC harness connector terminals No. 2 (Black/Light Blue wire) and No. 5 (Violet/Light Green wire). If resistance is less than 1000 ohms, repair Violet/Light Green wire for short to Black/Light Blue wire. If resistance is 1000 ohms or more, go to next step.

3) Using scan tool ohmmeter mode, measure resistance at CMTC harness connector terminal No. 5 (Violet/Light Green wire). If resistance is less than 5 ohms, repair Violet/Light Green wire between CMTC module and ambient temperature sensor for short to ground. If resistance is 5 ohms or more, replace CMTC module.

COMPASS MINI-TRIP COMPUTER (CMTC) DOES NOT RESPOND TO INSTRUMENT CLUSTER DIMMING (COMPASS MINI- TRIP COMPUTER SWITCH INOPERATIVE)

NOTE: Perform VERIFICATION TEST VER-1A after each repair.

CAUTION: Always turn ignition switch to OFF position prior to disconnecting any module connector.

Replace Compass Mini-Trip Computer (CMTC). Retest system.

COMPASS MINI-TRIP COMPUTER (CMTC) SEGMENTS INOPERATIVE

NOTE: Perform VERIFICATION TEST VER-1A after each repair.

CAUTION: Always turn ignition switch to OFF position prior to disconnecting any module connector.

Replace Compass Mini-Trip Computer (CMTC). Retest system.

COMPASS MINI-TRIP COMPUTER (CMTC) SHOWS FAILED

NOTE: Perform VERIFICATION TEST VER-1A after each repair.

CAUTION: Always turn ignition switch to OFF position prior to disconnecting any module connector.

Using scan tool, perform AUTO SELF TEST. If CMTC shows failed, replace Compass Mini-Trip Computer (CMTC). If CMTC does not show failed, system is currently functioning correctly.

CHRY
4-122

1999 ACCESSORIES & EQUIPMENT
Body Control Computer Tests
Caravan, Town & Country & Voyager (Cont.)

INCORRECT AMBIENT TEMPERATURE READINGS

NOTE: For connector terminal identification and wiring diagrams, see BODY CONTROL COMPUTER – INTRODUCTION article. Drive vehicle at least 3 miles (more than 25 MPH) to update CMTC. Perform VERIFICATION TEST VER-1A after each repair.

NOTE: For CMTC wiring diagram, see ANALOG INSTRUMENT PANELS – FWD VANS article.

CAUTION: Always turn ignition switch to OFF position prior to disconnecting any module connector.

1) Disconnect and remove ambient temperature sensor. Sensor is located behind front bumper, right of center. Using external ohmmeter, measure resistance between sensor terminals and compare with AMBIENT TEMPERATURE SENSOR SPECIFICATIONS table. If resistance measurement does not correspond with specification, replace sensor. If sensor is within specification, go to next step.

AMBIENT TEMPERATURE SENSOR SPECIFICATIONS

Ambient Temperature	k/ohms
32°F (0°C)	29.3-36.0
50°F (10°C)	18.0-22.0
68°F (20°C)	11.4-13.6
77°F (25°C)	9.1-10.8
86°F (30°C)	7.4-8.7
104°F (40°C)	4.9-5.7
122°F (50°C)	3.3-3.8

2) Turn ignition off. Close all vehicle doors and ensure all lights are off. Using scan tool in ohmmeter mode, measure resistance at ambient temperature sensor connector terminal No. 1 (Black/Light Blue wire). If resistance is less than 5 ohms, go to step 6). If resistance is 5 ohms or more, go to next step.

3) Connect ambient temperature sensor. Disconnect CMTC module connector. Using external ohmmeter, measure resistance between terminals No. 2 (Black/Light Blue wire) and No. 5 (Violet/Light Green wire) on harness connector. Compare ohmmeter reading with AMBIENT TEMPERATURE SENSOR SPECIFICATIONS table. If resistance measurement corresponds with specification, replace CMTC module. If reading does not correspond, go to next step.

4) Disconnect ambient temperature sensor. Using scan tool in ohmmeter mode, measure resistance at ambient temperature sensor connector terminal No. 2 (Black/Light Blue wire). If resistance is less than 500 k/ohms, repair Black/Light Blue wire for partial short to ground. If resistance is 500 k/ohms or more, repair Violet/Light Green wire for short to Black/Light Blue wire.

5) Measure resistance at ambient temperature sensor connector terminal No. 1 (Violet/Light Green wire). If resistance is less than 500 k/ohms, repair Violet/Light Green wire for partial short to ground. If resistance is 500 k/ohms or more, go to next step.

6) Connect jumper wire between ground and ambient temperature sensor connector terminal No. 2 (Black/Light Blue wire). Disconnect CMTC module connector. Using scan tool in ohmmeter mode, measure resistance at terminal No. 2 (Black/Light Blue wire) on CMTC module connector. If resistance is less than 5 ohms, replace CMTC module. If resistance is 5 ohms or more, repair open Black/Light Blue wire between CMTC module and ambient temperature sensor.

POWER DOOR LOCK SYSTEM

ALL DOORS (EXCEPT DRVR W/RKE) FAIL LCK/UNLCK FROM ANY SWITCH

NOTE: For connector terminal identification and wiring diagrams, see BODY CONTROL COMPUTER – INTRODUCTION article. Perform VERIFICATION TEST VER-1A after each repair.

CAUTION: Always turn ignition switch to OFF position prior to disconnecting or connecting any module connector.

1) Remove door unlock relay. See 3). Using scan tool in ohmmeter mode, measure resistance at door unlock relay connector terminal No. 30. If resistance is less than 5 ohms, replace door unlock relay. If resistance is 5 ohms or more, go to next step.

2) Access junction block connector "A". Do not disconnect connector. Using scan tool in ohmmeter mode, backprobe connector "A". Measure resistance on specified terminal. See UNLOCK RELAY OUTPUT CIRCUITS table. If resistance is 5 ohms or more on any circuit, repair suspect output open circuit. If resistance is less than 5 ohms on all circuits, replace junction block.

UNLOCK RELAY OUTPUT CIRCUITS

Door	Terminal	Wire Color
Left Rear	15	Violet/White
Liftgate	15	Violet/White
Right Front	19	Violet/Yellow
Right Rear	19	Violet/Yellow

ALL DOORS FAIL TO LOCK & UNLOCK FROM ANY SWITCH

NOTE: For connector terminal identification and wiring diagrams, see BODY CONTROL COMPUTER – INTRODUCTION article. Perform VERIFICATION TEST VER-1A after each repair.

CAUTION: Always turn ignition switch to OFF position prior to disconnecting or connecting any module connector.

1) Using scan tool, actuate door lock relay. If doors lock, go to next step. If doors do not lock, go to step 6).

2) Disconnect Body Control Module (BCM) connector "B". BCM is located with junction block under driver's side instrument panel. *See Fig. 1.* Using scan tool in voltmeter mode, measure voltage at BCM connector "B" terminal No. 45 (White/Dark Green wire). If voltage is more than .5 volt, repair White/Dark Green wire for short to battery voltage. If voltage is .5 volt or less, go to next step.

3) Using scan tool in ohmmeter mode, measure resistance at BCM connector "B" terminal No. 45 (White/Dark Green wire). Hold driver's door lock switch in unlock position and observe resistance value. If resistance is 300 ohms or more, replace door lock switch and recheck power door system for additional codes or symptoms. If resistance is less than 300 ohms, go to next step.

4) Using scan tool in voltmeter mode, measure voltage at BCM connector "B" terminal No. 55 (White/Light Green wire). If voltage is more than .5 volt, repair White/Light Green wire for short to battery voltage. If voltage is .5 volt or less, go to next step.

5) Using scan tool in voltmeter mode, measure voltage at BCM connector "B" terminal No. 44 (White/Red wire). If voltage is more than .5 volt, repair White/Red wire for short to battery voltage. If voltage is .5 volt or less, replace BCM.

1999 ACCESSORIES & EQUIPMENT
Body Control Computer Tests
Caravan, Town & Country & Voyager (Cont.)

CHRY
4-123

6) Remove and inspect Power Distribution Center (PDC) fuse No. 26. *See Fig. 4*. If fuse is open, go to next step. If fuse is okay, go to step **8**).

NOTE: PDC fuse No. 26 also supplies voltage to power seat circuit. A short in power seat circuit can cause fuse to open when power door lock system is okay.

7) Using scan tool in ohmmeter mode, measure resistance at outside terminal of PDC fuse No. 26 (component side of circuit). If resistance is 5 ohms or more, replace fuse. If resistance is less than 5 ohms, repair component side of circuit for short to ground.

8) Install fuse No. 26. Remove door lock relay from junction block. See **3**). Using scan tool in voltmeter mode, measure voltage at door lock relay socket terminal No. 86. If voltage is 10 volts or less, repair open circuit between PDC and junction block. If voltage is more than 10 volts, go to next step.

9) Connect test light between door lock relay socket terminals No. 85 and 86. Using scan tool, actuate door lock relay. If test light flashes, go to next step. If test light does not flash, replace Body Control Module (BCM). BCM is located with junction block under driver's side instrument panel. *See Fig. 1*.

10) Turn ignition off. Turn off all lights. Using scan tool in ohmmeter mode, measure resistance at door lock relay socket terminal 87A. If resistance is 5 ohms or more, repair open ground circuit. If resistance is less than 5 ohms, go to next step.

11) Turn ignition on. Turn on all lights and accessories. Using scan tool in voltmeter mode, measure voltage at door lock relay socket terminal 87A. If voltage is more than one volt, repair open ground circuit. If voltage is one volt or less, replace door lock relay.

ALL DOORS FAIL TO LOCK & UNLOCK FROM ONE SWITCH

NOTE: For connector terminal identification and wiring diagrams, see BODY CONTROL COMPUTER – INTRODUCTION article. Perform VERIFICATION TEST VER-1A after each repair.

CAUTION: Always turn ignition switch to OFF position prior to disconnecting or connecting any module connector.

1) If complaint is not with an interior front door lock switch, go to step **6**). If complaint is with an interior front door lock switch, go to next step.

2) Disconnect inoperative front door lock switch connector. Using scan tool in voltmeter mode, measure voltage on switch connector middle terminal (White/Dark Green wire-left door, White/Light Green wire-right door). If voltage is more than 6 volts, repair White/Dark Green wire (left door) or White/Light Green wire (right door) for short to battery voltage. If voltage is 6 volts or less, go to next step.

3) If voltage measured is 4.5-6.0 volts, go to step **5**). If voltage measured is less than 4.5 volts, determine if vehicle is equipped with Vehicle Theft Security System (VTSS). If vehicle is not equipped with VTSS, go to step **11**). If vehicle is equipped with VTSS, go to next step.

4) Determine if door locks operate correctly from door key cylinder switch. If locks do not operate, go to step **11**). If door locks operate correctly from door key cylinder switch, repair open door lock switch MUX circuit (White/Dark Green wire-left door, White/Light Green wire-right door).

5) Turn ignition off. Turn off all lights and accessories. Using scan tool in ohmmeter mode, measure resistance at front door lock switch connector terminal No. 3 (Black/Light Green wire). If resistance is less than 5 ohms, replace door lock switch. If resistance is 5 ohms or more, repair open Black/Light Green.

6) Disconnect inoperative door key cylinder switch connector. Using scan tool in voltmeter mode, measure voltage at inoperative key cylinder switch connector terminal No. 1 (White/Dark Green – left door, White/Light Green wire – right door or White/Red – liftgate). If voltage is less than 4.5 volts, go to next step. If voltage is 4.5 volts or more, go to step **10**).

7) Turn ignition off. Turn off all lights and accessories. Using scan tool in ohmmeter mode, measure resistance at suspect key cylinder switch

connector terminal No. 2 (Black/Light Green wire). If resistance is 5 ohms or more, repair open Black/Light Green wire. If resistance is less than 5 ohms, go to next step.

8) If problem is not with liftgate key cylinder switch, replace suspect door lock switch. If liftgate key cylinder switch is suspect, go to next step.

9) Disconnect liftgate key cylinder switch connector. Using scan tool in voltmeter mode, measure voltage at liftgate key cylinder switch connector terminal No. 1 (White/Red wire). If voltage is more than 10 volts, repair White/Red wire for short to battery voltage. If voltage is 10 volts or less, replace liftgate key cylinder switch.

10) Determine if door locks operate properly when using interior door lock switch. If door lock does not operate properly, repair open in White/Dark Green – left door, White/Light Green – right door or White/Red – liftgate wire between key cylinder switch connector and BCM connector "B". If door lock operates properly, go to next step.

11) Access Body Control Module (BCM) connector "B". BCM is located with junction block under driver's side instrument panel. *See Fig. 1*. Remove connector cover. Do not disconnect connector. Using scan tool in voltmeter mode, backprobe connector "B". Measure voltage on terminal for suspect door or liftgate. See DOOR SWITCH MUX CIRCUITS table. If voltage is 4.5 volts or less, replace BCM. If voltage is more than 4.5 volts, repair open MUX circuit.

DOOR SWITCH MUX CIRCUITS

Door	Terminal	Wire Color
Left Front	45	White/Dark Green
Liftgate	44	White/Red
Right Front	55	White/Light Green

ALL DOORS FAILING TO LOCK FROM ANY SWITCH

NOTE: For connector terminal identification and wiring diagrams, see BODY CONTROL COMPUTER – INTRODUCTION article. Perform VERIFICATION TEST VER-1A after each repair.

CAUTION: Always turn ignition switch to OFF position prior to disconnecting or connecting any module connector.

1) Ensure ignition key is removed. Using scan tool, read key-in ignition status. If scan tool displays KEY IN IGNITION: OPEN, go to next step. If scan tool does not display KEY IN IGNITION: OPEN, go to step **6**).

2) Remove door lock relay from junction block. *See Fig. 3*. Using external ohmmeter, measure resistance between door lock relay terminals No. 85 and 86. If resistance is 60-80 ohms, go to next step. If resistance is not 60-80 ohms, replace door lock relay.

3) Using scan tool in voltmeter mode, measure voltage on door lock relay connector socket terminal No. 87A. If voltage is more than 10 volts, go to next step. If voltage is 10 volts or less, replace junction block.

4) Connect test light between door lock relay socket terminals No. 85 and 86. Using scan tool, actuate door lock relay. If test light illuminates, go to next step. If test light does not illuminate, replace Body Control Module (BCM). BCM is located with junction block under driver's side instrument panel. *See Fig. 1*.

5) Disconnect junction block "A" connector. Using external ohmmeter, measure resistance between ground and specified terminal. See LOCK RELAY OUTPUT CIRCUITS table. If resistance is less than 50 ohms, repair suspect output circuit for short to ground. If resistance is 50 ohms or more, replace door lock relay.

LOCK RELAY OUTPUT CIRCUITS

Door	Terminal	Wire Color
Driver's	32	Brown
Left Rear	26	Brown/Yellow
Liftgate	11	Brown/Red
Right Front	32	Brown
Right Rear	26	Brown/Yellow

6) Disconnect key-in ignition switch connector. *See Fig. 2*. Using scan tool, read key-in ignition switch status. If scan tool displays KEY-IN

CHRY
4-124

1999 ACCESSORIES & EQUIPMENT
Body Control Computer Tests
Caravan, Town & Country & Voyager (Cont.)

IGNITION SW: CLOSED, go to next step. If scan tool does not display KEY-IN IGNITION SW: CLOSED, replace ignition switch. See appropriate STEERING COLUMN SWITCHES article.

7) Turn ignition off. Disconnect Body Control Module (BCM) connector "A". BCM is located with junction block under driver's side instrument panel. *See Fig. 1.* Using scan tool in ohmmeter mode, measure resistance at BCM connector "A" terminal No. 4 (Light Blue wire). If resistance is less than 5 ohms, repair Light Blue wire for short to ground. If resistance is 5 ohms or more, replace BCM.

ALL DOORS (EXCEPT DRIVER W/RKE) FAIL TO UNLOCK

NOTE: For connector terminal identification and wiring diagrams, see BODY CONTROL COMPUTER – INTRODUCTION article. Perform VERIFICATION TEST VER-1A after each repair.

CAUTION: Always turn ignition switch to OFF position prior to disconnecting or connecting any module connector.

1) Remove door unlock relay from junction block. *See Fig. 3.* Using external ohmmeter, measure resistance between door unlock relay terminals No. 85 and 86. If resistance is 60-80 ohms, go to next step. If resistance is not 60-80 ohms, replace door unlock relay.

2) Using scan tool in voltmeter mode, measure voltage at door unlock relay socket terminal No. 87A. If voltage is more than 10 volts, go to next step. If voltage is 10 volts or less, replace junction block.

3) Connect test light between door lock relay socket terminals No. 85 and 86. Using scan tool, actuate door unlock relay. If test light illuminates, go to next step. If test light does not illuminate, replace Body Control Module (BCM). BCM is located with junction block under driver's side instrument panel. *See Fig. 1.*

4) Disconnect junction block "A" connector. Using external ohmmeter, measure resistance between ground and specified terminal. See UNLOCK RELAY OUTPUT CIRCUITS table. If resistance is less than 50 ohms, repair suspect output circuit for short to ground. If resistance is 50 ohms or more, replace door unlock relay.

UNLOCK RELAY OUTPUT CIRCUITS

Door	Terminal	Wire Color
Driver's	9	Black/Pink
Left Rear	15	Violet/White
Liftgate	15	Violet/White
Right Front	19	Violet/Yellow
Right Rear	19	Violet/Yellow

DRIVER DOOR (W/RKE) FAILING TO UNLOCK FROM ANY SWITCH

NOTE: For connector terminal identification and wiring diagrams, see BODY CONTROL COMPUTER – INTRODUCTION article. Perform VERIFICATION TEST VER-1A after each repair.

CAUTION: Always turn ignition switch to OFF position prior to disconnecting or connecting any module connector.

1) Remove driver door unlock relay from junction block. *See Fig. 3.* Using external ohmmeter, measure resistance between driver door unlock relay terminals No. 85 and 86. If resistance is 60-80 ohms, go to next step. If resistance is not 60-80 ohms, replace driver door unlock relay.

2) Using scan tool in voltmeter mode, measure voltage at driver door unlock relay socket terminal No. 87A. If voltage is more than 10 volts, go to next step. If voltage is 10 volts or less, replace junction block.

3) Connect test light between door lock relay socket terminals No. 85 and 86. Using scan tool, actuate driver door unlock relay. If test light illuminates, go to next step. If test light does not illuminate, replace Body Control Module (BCM). BCM is located with junction block under driver's side instrument panel. *See Fig. 1.*

4) Disconnect junction block "A" connector. Using external ohmmeter, measure resistance between ground and BCM connector "A" terminal No. 9 (Black/Pink wire). If resistance is less than 50 ohms, repair Black/Pink wire for short to ground. If resistance is 50 ohms or more, replace driver door unlock relay.

ONE DOOR FAILS TO LOCK & UNLOCK FROM ANY SWITCH

NOTE: For connector terminal identification and wiring diagrams, see BODY CONTROL COMPUTER – INTRODUCTION article. Perform VERIFICATION TEST VER-1A after each repair.

CAUTION: Always turn ignition switch to OFF position prior to disconnecting or connecting any module connector.

1) If driver's door lock is operational, go to step 5). If driver's door lock is not operational, go to next step.

2) Determine if vehicle is equipped with Remote Keyless Entry (RKE) system. If vehicle is equipped with RKE, go to next step. If vehicle is not equipped with RKE, ensure 30-amp jumper is installed in place of driver front door relay in junction block. *See Fig. 3.* Continue test, if necessary.

3) Remove driver door unlock relay from junction block. Ensure ignition and all lights are off. Using scan tool in ohmmeter mode, measure resistance at driver door unlock relay socket terminal No. 87A. If resistance is 5 ohms or more, replace junction block. If resistance is less than 5 ohms, go to next step.

4) Using external ohmmeter, measure resistance between driver door unlock relay terminals No. 30 and 87A. If resistance is 5 ohms or more, replace driver door unlock relay. If resistance is less than 5 ohms, go to next step.

5) Install driver door unlock relay in junction block. Disconnect inoperative door lock motor connector. If a sliding door lock is inoperative, ensure door is closed before proceeding with testing. Using scan tool in ohmmeter mode, measure resistance on lock relay output circuit at lock motor connector. See LOCK RELAY OUTPUT CIRCUIT IDENTIFICATION table. If resistance is 5 ohms or more, repair open lock output circuit. Ensure sliding door contacts are clean. If resistance is less than 5 ohms, go to next step.

LOCK RELAY OUTPUT CIRCUIT IDENTIFICATION

Door	Terminal	Wire Color
Left Front	1	Brown
Right Front	1	Brown
Sliding Door	1	Brown/Yellow
Liftgate	3	Brown/Red

6) Using scan tool in ohmmeter mode, measure resistance on unlock relay output circuit at lock motor connector. See UNLOCK RELAY OUTPUT CIRCUITS table. If resistance is 5 ohms or more, repair open unlock relay output circuit. Ensure sliding door contacts are clean. If resistance is less than 5 ohms, replace door lock motor.

LEFT DOOR KEY CYL ARM SW FAILURE

NOTE: For connector terminal identification and wiring diagrams, see BODY CONTROL COMPUTER – INTRODUCTION article. Perform VERIFICATION TEST VER-1A after each repair.

CAUTION: Always turn ignition switch to OFF position prior to disconnecting or connecting any module connector.

1) Clear trouble codes as needed. See BODY CONTROL COMPUTER – INTRODUCTION article. Using scan tool, read driver's door zone switch voltage. If DRIVER DOOR ZONE SWITCH voltage is about 4 volts, inspect driver's door key lock. Replace key lock as needed. If DRIVER DOOR ZONE SWITCH voltage is not about 4 volts, go to next step.

2) Turn driver's door key cylinder switch to lock position and observe voltage on scan tool. Do not hold key in lock position for more than 7

1999 ACCESSORIES & EQUIPMENT
Body Control Computer Tests
Caravan, Town & Country & Voyager (Cont.)

CHRY
4-125

seconds or code will set. If DRIVER DOOR ZONE SWITCH voltage is about 4 volts, go to next step. If DRIVER DOOR ZONE SWITCH voltage is not about 4 volts, replace driver's door key cylinder switch.

3) Operate driver's door key lock cylinder several times from unlock to lock position. Release key lock cylinder. With key lock cylinder in neutral position, observe scan tool voltage. If DRIVER DOOR ZONE SWITCH voltage is about 5 volts, system is currently functioning correctly. If DRIVER DOOR ZONE SWITCH voltage is not about 5 volts, replace driver's door key cylinder switch.

LEFT DOOR LOCK SWITCH FAILURE

NOTE: For connector terminal identification and wiring diagrams, see BODY CONTROL COMPUTER – INTRODUCTION article. Perform VERIFICATION TEST VER-1A after each repair.

CAUTION: Always turn ignition switch to OFF position prior to disconnecting or connecting any module connector.

1) Clear trouble codes as needed. See BODY CONTROL COMPUTER – INTRODUCTION article. Using scan tool, read driver's door zone switch voltage. If DRIVER DOOR ZONE SWITCH voltage is about 3 volts, replace driver's door lock switch. If DRIVER DOOR ZONE SWITCH voltage is not about 3 volts, go to next step.

2) Operate driver's door lock switch to lock position and observe voltage on scan tool. Do not hold switch in lock position for more than 7 seconds or code will set. If DRIVER DOOR ZONE SWITCH voltage is about 3 volts, go to next step. If DRIVER DOOR ZONE SWITCH voltage is not about 3 volts, replace driver's door lock switch.

3) Operate driver's door lock switch several times from unlock to lock position. Release switch. With switch in neutral position, observe scan tool voltage. If DRIVER DOOR ZONE SWITCH voltage is about 5 volts, system is currently functioning correctly. If DRIVER DOOR ZONE SWITCH voltage is not about 5 volts, replace driver's door lock switch.

LEFT DOOR UNLOCK SWITCH FAILURE

NOTE: For connector terminal identification and wiring diagrams, see BODY CONTROL COMPUTER – INTRODUCTION article. Perform VERIFICATION TEST VER-1A after each repair.

CAUTION: Always turn ignition switch to OFF position prior to disconnecting or connecting any module connector.

1) Clear trouble codes as needed. See BODY CONTROL COMPUTER – INTRODUCTION article. Using scan tool, read driver's door zone switch voltage. If DRIVER DOOR ZONE SWITCH voltage is about one volt, replace driver's door lock switch. If DRIVER DOOR ZONE SWITCH voltage is not about one volt, go to next step.

2) Operate driver's door lock switch to unlock position and observe voltage on scan tool. Do not hold switch in unlock position for more than 7 seconds or code will set. If DRIVER DOOR ZONE SWITCH voltage is about one volt, go to next step. If DRIVER DOOR ZONE SWITCH voltage is not about one volt, replace driver's door lock switch.

3) Operate driver's door lock switch several times from lock to unlock position. Release switch. With switch in neutral position, observe scan tool voltage. If DRIVER DOOR ZONE SWITCH voltage is about 5 volts, system is currently functioning correctly. If DRIVER DOOR ZONE SWITCH voltage is not about 5 volts, replace driver's door lock switch.

LIFTGATE DOOR MUX CKT SHORT TO GND

NOTE: For connector terminal identification and wiring diagrams, see BODY CONTROL COMPUTER – INTRODUCTION article. Perform VERIFICATION TEST VER-1A after each repair.

CAUTION: Always turn ignition switch to OFF position prior to disconnecting or connecting any module connector.

1) Clear trouble codes as needed. See BODY CONTROL COMPUTER – INTRODUCTION article. Turn ignition on. Wait 15 seconds. Using scan tool, read body control computer trouble codes (fault messages). If scan tool displays LIFTGATE DOOR MUX CKT SHORT TO GND, go to next step. If scan tool does not display LIFTGATE DOOR MUX CKT SHORT TO GND, system is currently operating correctly. Problem may be intermittent.

2) Disconnect Body Control Module (BCM) connector "B". BCM is located with junction block under driver's side instrument panel. *See Fig. 1.* Using scan tool in ohmmeter mode, measure resistance at BCM connector "B" terminal No. 44 (White/Red wire). If resistance is 100 ohms or more, replace BCM. If resistance is less than 100 ohms, repair White/Red wire for short to ground.

LIFTGATE KEY CYL ARM SW FAILURE

NOTE: For connector terminal identification and wiring diagrams, see BODY CONTROL COMPUTER – INTRODUCTION article. Perform VERIFICATION TEST VER-1A after each repair.

CAUTION: Always turn ignition switch to OFF position prior to disconnecting or connecting any module connector.

1) Clear trouble codes as needed. See BODY CONTROL COMPUTER – INTRODUCTION article. Using scan tool, read liftgate zone switch voltage. If LIFTGATE ZONE SWITCH voltage is about 4 volts, inspect liftgate key lock. Replace liftgate key lock as needed. If LIFTGATE ZONE SWITCH voltage is not about 4 volts, go to next step.

2) Turn liftgate key cylinder switch to lock position and observe voltage on scan tool. Do not hold key in lock position for more than 7 seconds or code will set. If LIFTGATE ZONE SWITCH voltage is about 4 volts, go to next step. If LIFTGATE ZONE SWITCH voltage is not about 4 volts, replace liftgate key cylinder switch.

3) Operate liftgate key lock cylinder several times from unlock to lock position. Release key lock cylinder. With key lock cylinder in neutral position, observe scan tool voltage. If LIFTGATE ZONE SWITCH voltage is about 5 volts, system is currently functioning correctly. If LIFTGATE ZONE SWITCH voltage is not about 5 volts, replace liftgate key cylinder switch.

LIFTGATE KEY CYL DISARM SW FAILURE

NOTE: For connector terminal identification and wiring diagrams, see BODY CONTROL COMPUTER – INTRODUCTION article. Perform VERIFICATION TEST VER-1A after each repair.

CAUTION: Always turn ignition switch to OFF position prior to disconnecting or connecting any module connector.

1) Clear trouble codes as needed. See BODY CONTROL COMPUTER – INTRODUCTION article. Using scan tool, read liftgate zone switch voltage. If LIFTGATE ZONE SWITCH voltage is about 2 volts, inspect liftgate key lock. Replace liftgate key lock as needed. If LIFTGATE ZONE SWITCH voltage is not about 2 volts, go to next step.

2) Turn liftgate key cylinder switch to unlock position and observe voltage on scan tool. Do not hold key in unlock position for more than 7 seconds or code will set. If LIFTGATE ZONE SWITCH voltage is about 2 volts, go to next step. If LIFTGATE ZONE SWITCH voltage is not about 2 volts, replace liftgate key cylinder switch.

3) Operate liftgate key lock cylinder several times from unlock to lock position. Release key lock cylinder. With key lock cylinder in neutral

CHRY
4-126

1999 ACCESSORIES & EQUIPMENT
Body Control Computer Tests
Caravan, Town & Country & Voyager (Cont.)

position, observe scan tool voltage. If LIFTGATE ZONE SWITCH voltage is about 5 volts, system is currently functioning correctly. If LIFTGATE ZONE SWITCH voltage is not about 5 volts, replace liftgate key cylinder switch.

LT FRONT DOOR MUX CKT SHORT TO GND

NOTE: For connector terminal identification and wiring diagrams, see BODY CONTROL COMPUTER – INTRODUCTION article. Perform VERIFICATION TEST VER-1A after each repair.

CAUTION: Always turn ignition switch to OFF position prior to disconnecting or connecting any module connector.

1) Clear trouble codes as needed. See BODY CONTROL COMPUTER – INTRODUCTION article. Turn ignition on. Wait 15 seconds. Using scan tool, read body control computer trouble codes (fault messages). If scan tool displays LT FRONT DOOR MUX CKT SHORT TO GND, go to next step. If scan tool does not display LT FRONT DOOR MUX CKT SHORT TO GND, system is currently operating correctly. Problem may be intermittent.
2) Disconnect Body Control Module (BCM) connector "B". BCM is located with junction block under driver's side instrument panel. *See Fig. 1.* Using scan tool in ohmmeter mode, measure resistance at BCM connector "B" terminal No. 45 (White/Dark Green wire) on connector. If resistance is 100 ohms or more, replace BCM. If resistance is less than 100 ohms, repair White/Dark Green wire for short to ground.

RIGHT DOOR KEY CYL ARM SW FAILURE

NOTE: For connector terminal identification and wiring diagrams, see BODY CONTROL COMPUTER – INTRODUCTION article. Perform VERIFICATION TEST VER-1A after each repair.

CAUTION: Always turn ignition switch to OFF position prior to disconnecting or connecting any module connector.

1) Clear trouble codes as needed. See BODY CONTROL COMPUTER – INTRODUCTION article. Using scan tool, read passengers door zone switch voltage. If PASSENGER DOOR ZONE SWITCH voltage is about 4 volts, inspect passengers door key lock. Replace key lock as needed. If PASSENGER DOOR ZONE SWITCH voltage is not about 4 volts, go to next step.
2) Turn passengers door key cylinder switch to lock position and observe voltage on scan tool. Do not hold key in lock position for more than 7 seconds or code will set. If PASSENGER DOOR ZONE SWITCH voltage is about 4 volts, go to next step. If PASSENGER DOOR ZONE SWITCH voltage is not about 4 volts, replace passengers door key cylinder switch.
3) Operate passengers door key lock cylinder several times from unlock to lock position. Release key lock cylinder. With key lock cylinder in neutral position, observe scan tool voltage. If PASSENGER DOOR ZONE SWITCH voltage is about 5 volts, system is currently functioning correctly. If PASSENGER DOOR ZONE SWITCH voltage is not about 5 volts, replace passengers door key cylinder switch.

RIGHT DOOR KEY CYLINDER DISARM SWITCH FAILURE

NOTE: For connector terminal identification and wiring diagrams, see BODY CONTROL COMPUTER – INTRODUCTION article. Perform VERIFICATION TEST VER-1A after each repair.

CAUTION: Always turn ignition switch to OFF position prior to disconnecting or connecting any module connector.

1) Clear trouble codes as needed. See BODY CONTROL COMPUTER – INTRODUCTION article. Using scan tool, read passenger door zone switch voltage. If PASSENGER DOOR ZONE SWITCH voltage is about

2 volts, inspect passengers door key lock. Replace key lock as needed. If PASSENGER DOOR ZONE SWITCH voltage is not about 2 volts, go to next step.
2) Turn passengers door key cylinder switch to unlock position and observe voltage on scan tool. Do not hold key in unlock position for more than 7 seconds or code will set. If PASSENGER DOOR ZONE SWITCH voltage is about 2 volts, go to next step. If PASSENGER DOOR ZONE SWITCH voltage is not about 2 volts, replace passengers door key cylinder switch.
3) Operate passengers door key lock cylinder several times from unlock to lock position. Release key lock cylinder. With key lock cylinder in neutral position, observe scan tool voltage. If PASSENGER DOOR ZONE SWITCH voltage is about 5 volts, system is currently functioning correctly. If PASSENGER DOOR ZONE SWITCH voltage is not about 5 volts, replace passengers door key cylinder switch.

RIGHT DOOR LOCK SWITCH FAILURE

NOTE: For connector terminal identification and wiring diagrams, see BODY CONTROL COMPUTER – INTRODUCTION article. Perform VERIFICATION TEST VER-1A after each repair.

CAUTION: Always turn ignition switch to OFF position prior to disconnecting or connecting any module connector.

1) Clear trouble codes as needed. See BODY CONTROL COMPUTER – INTRODUCTION article. Using scan tool, read passengers door zone switch voltage. If PASSENGER DOOR ZONE SWITCH voltage is about 3 volts, replace passengers door lock switch. If PASSENGER DOOR ZONE SWITCH voltage is not about 3 volts, go to next step.
2) Operate passengers door lock switch to lock position and observe voltage on scan tool. Do not hold switch in lock position for more than 7 seconds or code will set. If PASSENGER DOOR ZONE SWITCH voltage is about 3 volts, go to next step. If PASSENGER DOOR ZONE SWITCH voltage is not about 3 volts, replace passengers door lock switch.
3) Operate passengers door lock switch several times from unlock to lock position. Release switch. With switch in neutral position, observe scan tool voltage. If PASSENGER DOOR ZONE SWITCH voltage is about 5 volts, system is currently functioning correctly. If PASSENGER DOOR ZONE SWITCH voltage is not about 5 volts, replace passengers door lock switch.

RIGHT DOOR UNLOCK SWITCH FAILURE

NOTE: For connector terminal identification and wiring diagrams, see BODY CONTROL COMPUTER – INTRODUCTION article. Perform VERIFICATION TEST VER-1A after each repair.

CAUTION: Always turn ignition switch to OFF position prior to disconnecting or connecting any module connector.

1) Clear trouble codes as needed. See BODY CONTROL COMPUTER – INTRODUCTION article. Using scan tool, read passengers door zone switch voltage. If PASSENGER DOOR ZONE SWITCH voltage is about one volt, replace passengers door lock switch. If PASSENGER DOOR ZONE SWITCH voltage is not about one volt, go to next step.
2) Operate passengers door lock switch to unlock position and observe voltage on scan tool. Do not hold switch in unlock position for more than 7 seconds or code will set. If PASSENGER DOOR ZONE SWITCH voltage is about one volt, go to next step. If PASSENGER DOOR ZONE SWITCH voltage is not about one volt, replace passengers door lock switch.
3) Operate passengers door lock switch several times from lock to unlock position. Release switch. With switch in neutral position, observe scan tool voltage. If PASSENGER DOOR ZONE SWITCH voltage is about 5 volts, system is currently functioning correctly. If PASSENGER DOOR ZONE SWITCH voltage is not about 5 volts, replace passengers door lock switch.

RT FRONT DOOR MUX CKT SHORT TO GND

NOTE: For connector terminal identification and wiring diagrams, see BODY CONTROL COMPUTER – INTRODUCTION article. Perform VERIFICATION TEST VER-1A after each repair.

CAUTION: Always turn ignition switch to OFF position prior to disconnecting or connecting any module connector.

1) Clear trouble codes as needed. See BODY CONTROL COMPUTER – INTRODUCTION article. Turn ignition on. Wait 15 seconds. Using scan tool, read body control computer trouble codes (fault messages). If scan tool displays RT FRONT DOOR MUX CKT SHORT TO GND, go to next step. If scan tool does not display RT FRONT DOOR MUX CKT SHORT TO GND, system is currently operating correctly. Problem may be intermittent.
2) Disconnect Body Control Module (BCM) connector "B". BCM is located with junction block under driver's side instrument panel. *See Fig. 1.* Using scan tool in ohmmeter mode, measure resistance at BCM connector "B" terminal No. 55 (White/Light Green wire). If resistance is 100 ohms or more, replace BCM. If resistance is less than 100 ohms, repair White/Light Green wire for short to ground.

ALL DOORS (EXCEPT DRVR W/RKE) FAIL LCK/UNLCK FROM ANY SWITCH (ALL DOORS FAIL TO LOCK & UNLOCK FROM ONE SWITCH, ALL DOORS FAILING TO LOCK FROM ANY SWITCH OR ONE SWITCH, ALL DOORS FAILING TO UNLOCK FROM ONE SWITCH, DRIVER DOOR (W/RKE) FAILING TO UNLOCK FROM ANY SWITCH, ONE DOOR FAILS TO LOCK & UNLOCK FROM ANY SWITCH)

NOTE: Perform VERIFICATION TEST VER-1A after each repair.

1) Using scan tool, read DTCs. If any power door lock codes are present, go to appropriate DTC under POWER DOOR LOCK SYSTEM. If no power door lock codes are present, go to next step
2) Lower front door windows. Remove key from ignition. Close all doors. Lock and unlock doors from all switches and observe door locks. If all locks operate properly, system is currently functioning correctly. If all locks do not operate properly, see POWER DOOR LOCK SYSTEM under SYMPTOM IDENTIFICATION and proceed to appropriate test.

ALL DOORS FAILS TO LOCK & UNLOCK FROM ANY SWITCH

NOTE: For connector terminal identification and wiring diagrams, see BODY CONTROL COMPUTER – INTRODUCTION article. Perform VERIFICATION TEST VER-1A after each repair.

CAUTION: Always turn ignition switch to OFF position prior to disconnecting or connecting any module connector.

1) Using scan tool, select BODY SYSTEM, then BODY COMPUTER. Scan tool will perform a CCD bus test. If scan tool displays BUS FAILED or NO RESPONSE, see appropriate VEHICLE COMMUNICATIONS article. If scan tool does not display BUS FAILED or NO RESPONSE, go to next step.
2) Using scan tool, select SENSOR DISPLAY and read IGNITION VOLTAGE. If scan tool displays less than 10 volts, see appropriate VEHICLE COMMUNICATIONS article. If scan tool displays 10 volts or more, go to next step.
3) Using scan tool, select READ DTCs. If any Diagnostic Trouble Codes (DTC) are present, go to appropriate DTC under POWER DOOR LOCK SYSTEM. If no power door lock codes are present, go to next step
4) Lower front door windows. Remove key from ignition. Close all doors. Lock and unlock doors from all switches and observe door locks. If all

locks operate properly, system is currently functioning correctly. If all locks do not operate properly, see POWER DOOR LOCK SYSTEM under SYMPTOM IDENTIFICATION and proceed to appropriate test.

ALL DOORS (EXCEPT DRIVER W/RKE) FAIL TO UNLOCK

NOTE: For connector terminal identification and wiring diagrams, see BODY CONTROL COMPUTER – INTRODUCTION article. Perform VERIFICATION TEST VER-1A after each repair.

CAUTION: Always turn ignition switch to OFF position prior to disconnecting or connecting any module connector.

1) Using scan tool, read DTCs. If any power door lock codes are present, go to appropriate DTC under POWER DOOR LOCK SYSTEM. If no power door lock codes are present, go to next step
2) Lower front door windows. Remove key from ignition. Close all doors. Lock and unlock doors from all switches and observe door locks. If all locks operate properly, go to next step. If all locks do not operate properly, see POWER DOOR LOCK SYSTEM under SYMPTOM IDENTIFICATION and proceed to appropriate test.
3) Operate door locks using transmitter. If door locks when transmitter is actuated, system is currently functioning correctly. If doors do not lock when transmitter is actuated, go to next step.
4) Using scan tool, reprogram a known good transmitter: Ensure transmitter battery voltage is 3.2 volts. Turn ignition on. Place transmission in park and disarm anti-theft system. Select MISCELLANEOUS, then PROGRAM RKE. If BCM IS IN PROGRAMMING MODE does not appear, exit and select PROGRAM RKE again. Press any transmitter button. A single chime will announce RKE module accepted transmission. Repeat procedure for all transmitters used with vehicle. Operate door locks from reprogrammed transmitter. If door locks operate properly, system has been repaired. If door locks do not operate properly, go to next step.
5) Access RKE module under instrument panel cover. *See Fig. 5.* Turn ignition off. Disconnect RKE module connector. Using an external ohmmeter, measure resistance between ground and RKE module harness connector terminal No. 4 (Black/Light Green wire). If resistance is 5 ohms or more, repair open Black/Light Green wire. If resistance is less than 5 ohms, go to next step.
6) Using an external voltmeter, measure voltage between ground and RKE harness connector terminal No. 3 (Pink wire). If voltage is 10 volts or less, repair open Pink wire. If voltage is more than 10 volts, go to next step.
7) Using an external ohmmeter, measure resistance between ground and RKE module harness connector terminal No. 5 (Gray/Black wire). Grounding of circuit will cause RKE system to be inoperative. If resistance is less than 2000 ohms, repair Gray/Black wire for short to ground. If resistance is 2000 ohms or more, go to next step.
8) Ensure gear shift selector is in Park. Using an external voltmeter, measure voltage between ground and RKE module harness connector terminal No. 6 (Light Green/Red wire). If voltage is more than 4 volts, go to step 10). If voltage is 4 volts or less, go to next step.
9) Connect jumper wire between ground and RKE module harness connector terminal No. 5 (Gray/Black wire). Disconnect Body Control Module (BCM) connector "A". BCM is located with junction block under driver's side instrument panel. *See Fig. 1.* Using scan tool in ohmmeter mode, measure resistance at BCM connector "A" terminal No. 37 (Gray/Black wire). If resistance is 5 ohms or more, repair open Gray/Black wire. If resistance is less than 5 ohms, replace RKE module.
10) Move jumper wire from RKE module harness connector terminal No. 5 (Gray/Black wire) to terminal No. 6 (Light Green/Red wire). Using scan tool in ohmmeter mode, measure resistance at BCM connector "A" terminal No. 4 (Light Green/Red wire). If resistance is 5 ohms or more, repair open Light Green/Red wire. If resistance is less than 5 ohms, go to next step.

CHRY
4-128

1999 ACCESSORIES & EQUIPMENT
Body Control Computer Tests
Caravan, Town & Country & Voyager (Cont.)

11) Remove jumper wire. Using an external ohmmeter, measure resistance between ground and BCM connector "A" terminal No. 4 (Light Green/Red wire). If resistance is 4800 ohms or more, replace BCM. If resistance is less than 4800 ohms, repair Light Green/Red wire for short to ground.

AUTOMATIC DOOR LOCKS FAIL TO LOCK OVER 15 MPH

NOTE: For connector terminal identification and wiring diagrams, see BODY CONTROL COMPUTER – INTRODUCTION article. Perform VERIFICATION TEST VER-1A after each repair.

CAUTION: Always turn ignition switch to OFF position prior to disconnecting or connecting any module connector.

1) Using scan tool, select BODY SYSTEM, then BODY COMPUTER. Scan tool will perform a CCD bus test. If scan tool displays BUS FAILED or NO RESPONSE, see appropriate VEHICLE COMMUNICATIONS article. If scan tool does not display BUS FAILED or NO RESPONSE, go to next step.

2) Using scan tool, select SENSOR DISPLAY and read IGNITION VOLTAGE. If scan tool displays less than 10 volts, see appropriate VEHICLE COMMUNICATIONS article. If scan tool displays 10 volts or more, go to next step.

3) Drive vehicle over 15 MPH with all doors closed. If doors locked when speed reached 15 MPH, system is currently functioning correctly. If doors did not lock when speed reached 15 MPH, go to next step.

4) Using scan tool, read auto door lock status. If scan tool shows AUTO DOOR LOCKS ARE ENABLED, go to next step. If scan tool does not show AUTO DOOR LOCKS ARE ENABLED, using scan tool, enable door locks and retest system.

5) Ensure driver door is closed. Using scan tool, read DR DOOR AJAR SWITCH status. If scan tool shows, DR DOOR AJAR: OPEN, go to next step. If scan tool does not show DR DOOR AJAR: OPEN, go to SHORTED DRIVER DOOR AJAR CIRCUIT under INTERIOR LIGHTING SYSTEM.

6) Ensure passenger door is closed. Using scan tool, read PASS DOOR AJAR SWITCH status. If scan tool shows, PASS DOOR AJAR: OPEN, go to next step. If scan tool does not show PASS DOOR AJAR: OPEN, go to SHORTED PASSENGER DOOR AJAR CIRCUIT under INTERIOR LIGHTING SYSTEM.

7) Ensure left sliding door is closed. Using scan tool, read LEFT SLIDING DOOR AJAR SWITCH status. If scan tool shows, LEFT SLIDING DOOR AJAR: OPEN, go to next step. If scan tool does not show LEFT SLIDING DOOR AJAR: OPEN, go to SHORTED LEFT SLIDING DOOR AJAR CIRCUIT under INTERIOR LIGHTING SYSTEM.

8) Ensure right sliding door is closed. Using scan tool, read RIGHT SLIDING DOOR AJAR SWITCH status. If scan tool shows, RIGHT SLIDING DOOR AJAR: OPEN, go to next step. If scan tool does not show RIGHT SLIDING DOOR AJAR: OPEN, go to SHORTED RIGHT SLIDING DOOR AJAR CIRCUIT under INTERIOR LIGHTING SYSTEM.

9) Ensure liftgate door is closed. Using scan tool, read LIFTGATE DOOR AJAR SWITCH status. If scan tool shows, LIFTGATE DOOR AJAR: OPEN, go to next step. If scan tool does not show LIFTGATE DOOR AJAR: OPEN, go to SHORTED LIFTGATE DOOR AJAR CIRCUIT under INTERIOR LIGHTING SYSTEM.

10) Using scan tool, read CCD BUS INFO in BCM MONITORS. Observe TPS percentage while moving throttle. If TPS percentage increases while throttle is opened, go to next step. If TPS percentage does not increase while throttle is opened, TPS is inoperative. Repair as necessary.

11) Raise and support vehicle. If vehicle is equipped with AWD, ensure all wheels are supported. Start engine and place transmission in drive. Using scan tool, read ENGINE INFO in BCM MONITORS. Observe VSS while wheels rotate. If MPH increases when throttle is opened, system

is currently functioning correctly. If MPH does not increase when throttle is opened, VSS is inoperative. Repair as necessary.

DOORS LOCK WITH KEY IN IGNITION & LEFT DOOR OPEN

NOTE: For connector terminal identification and wiring diagrams, see BODY CONTROL COMPUTER – INTRODUCTION article. Perform VERIFICATION TEST VER-1A after each repair.

CAUTION: Always turn ignition switch to OFF position prior to disconnecting or connecting any module connector.

1) Using scan tool, select BODY SYSTEM, then BODY COMPUTER. Scan tool will perform a CCD bus test. If scan tool displays BUS FAILED or NO RESPONSE, see appropriate VEHICLE COMMUNICATIONS article. If scan tool does not display BUS FAILED or NO RESPONSE, go to next step.

2) Using scan tool, select SENSOR DISPLAY and read IGNITION VOLTAGE. If scan tool displays less than 10 volts, see appropriate VEHICLE COMMUNICATIONS article. If scan tool displays 10 volts or more, go to next step.

3) Place key in ignition. Open driver's door. Lock doors from interior lock switch. If doors locked, go to next step. If doors did not lock, system is currently functioning correctly.

4) Using scan tool, read driver door ajar status. If scan tool shows DR DOOR AJAR: CLOSED, go to next step. If scan tool does not show DR DOOR AJAR: CLOSED, go to COURTESY LIGHTS INOPERATIVE WITH DRIVER DOOR (OPEN DRIVER DOOR AJAR CIRCUIT) under INTERIOR LIGHTING SYSTEM.

5) Read key-in ignition status. If scan tool shows KEY-IN IGNITION: CLOSED, replace Body Control Module (BCM). BCM is located with junction block under driver's side instrument panel. *See Fig. 1.* If scan tool does not show KEY-IN IGNITION: CLOSED, go to next step.

6) Disconnect key-in ignition switch connector. *See Fig. 2.* Using scan tool in ohmmeter mode, measure resistance at key-in ignition switch connector terminal No. 2 (Black wire). If resistance is less than 5 ohms, go to next step. If resistance is 5 ohms or more, repair open Black wire.

7) Connect jumper wire between key-in ignition switch connector terminals. If scan tool shows KEY-IN IGNITION: CLOSED, replace ignition switch. If scan tool does not show KEY-IN IGNITION: CLOSED, go to next step.

8) Gain access to BCM connector "A". Do not disconnect connector. Connect a backprobe jumper between ground and BCM connector "A" terminal No. 32 (Light Blue wire). If scan tool shows KEY-IN IGNITION: CLOSED, repair open Light Blue wire. If scan tool does not show KEY-IN IGNITION: CLOSED, go to next step.

9) Disconnect BCM connector "A". Inspect connector for damaged, pushed out or crossed terminals. Repair as necessary. If terminals are okay, replace BCM.

REMOTE KEYLESS ENTRY PROBLEM

NOTE: For connector terminal identification and wiring diagrams, see BODY CONTROL COMPUTER – INTRODUCTION article. Perform VERIFICATION TEST VER-1A after each repair.

CAUTION: Always turn ignition switch to OFF position prior to disconnecting or connecting any module connector.

1) Using scan tool, select BODY SYSTEM, then BODY COMPUTER. Scan tool will perform a CCD bus test. If scan tool displays BUS FAILED or NO RESPONSE, see appropriate VEHICLE COMMUNICATIONS article. If scan tool does not display BUS FAILED or NO RESPONSE, go to next step.

2) Using scan tool, select SENSOR DISPLAY and read IGNITION VOLTAGE. If scan tool displays less than 10 volts, see appropriate VEHICLE COMMUNICATIONS article. If scan tool displays 10 volts or more, go to next step.

1999 ACCESSORIES & EQUIPMENT
Body Control Computer Tests
Caravan, Town & Country & Voyager (Cont.)

CHRY
4-129

3) Ensure RKE batteries are about 3.2 volts each. Operate door locks from RKE transmitter. If door locks lock when transmitter is actuated, system is currently functioning correctly. If door locks do not lock when transmitter is actuated, go to next step.

4) Using scan tool, reprogram a known good transmitter: Ensure transmitter battery voltage is 3.2 volts. Turn ignition on. Place transmission in park and disarm anti-theft system. Select MISCELLANEOUS, then PROGRAM RKE. If BCM IS IN PROGRAMMING MODE does not appear, exit and select PROGRAM RKE again. Press any transmitter button. A single chime will announce RKE module accepted transmission. Repeat procedure for all transmitters used with vehicle. Operate door locks from reprogrammed transmitter. If door locks operate properly, system has been repaired. If door locks do not operate properly, go to next step.

5) Access RKE module under instrument panel cover. *See Fig. 5.* Turn ignition off. Disconnect RKE module connector. Using scan tool in ohmmeter mode, measure resistance at RKE module harness connector terminal No. 4 (Black/Light Green wire). If resistance is 5 ohms or more, repair open Black/Light Green wire. If resistance is less than 5 ohms, go to next step.

6) Using scan tool in voltmeter mode, measure voltage at RKE harness connector terminal No. 3 (Pink wire). If voltage is 10 volts or less, repair open Pink wire. If voltage is more than 10 volts, go to next step.

7) Using scan tool in ohmmeter mode, measure resistance at RKE module harness connector terminal No. 5 (Gray/Black wire). Grounding of circuit will cause RKE system to be inoperative. If resistance is less than 2000 ohms, repair Gray/Black wire for short to ground. If resistance is 2000 ohms or more, go to next step.

8) Ensure gear shift selector is in Park. Using an external voltmeter, measure voltage between ground and RKE module harness connector terminal No. 6 (Light Green/Red wire). If voltage is more than 4 volts, go to step **10)**. If voltage is 4 volts or less, go to next step.

9) Connect jumper wire between ground and RKE module harness connector terminal No. 5 (Gray/Black wire). Disconnect Body Control Module (BCM) connector "A". BCM is located with junction block under driver's side instrument panel. *See Fig. 1.* Using scan tool in ohmmeter mode, measure resistance at BCM connector "A" terminal No. 37 (Gray/Black wire). If resistance is 5 ohms or more, repair open Gray/Black wire. If resistance is less than 5 ohms, replace RKE module.

10) Move jumper wire from RKE module harness connector terminal No. 5 (Gray/Black wire) to terminal No. 6 (Light Green/Red wire). Using scan tool in ohmmeter mode, measure resistance at BCM connector "A" terminal No. 4 (Light Green/Red wire). If resistance is 5 ohms or more, repair open Light Green/Red wire. If resistance is less than 5 ohms, go to next step.

11) Remove jumper wire. Using an external ohmmeter, measure resistance between ground and BCM connector "A" terminal No. 4 (Light Green/Red wire). If resistance is 4800 ohms or more, replace BCM. If resistance is less than 4800 ohms, repair Light Green/Red wire for short to ground.

VEHICLE THEFT SECURITY SYSTEM (VTSS)

VTSS SYSTEM CONCERNS

NOTE: For connector terminal identification and wiring diagrams, see BODY CONTROL COMPUTER – INTRODUCTION article. Perform VERIFICATION TEST VER-1A after each repair.

CAUTION: Always turn ignition switch to OFF position prior to disconnecting or connecting any module connector.

1) Using scan tool read body control module fault messages. If any power door lock codes are present, go to appropriate DTC under POWER DOOR LOCK SYSTEM. If no power door lock codes are present, go to next step.

2) Using scan tool, select THEFT ALARM, VTSS, then MONITOR DISPLAY. Read VTSS status. If scan tool displays NO RESPONSE, go to next step. If display is VTSS mode is ARMED, cycle key in door cylinder or push unlock button on RKE transmitter. If problem still exists, go to SYMPTOM IDENTIFICATION and continue diagnosis. If display is 1 NO RESPONSE/2 NO RESPONSE, go to step **6)**. If display is not listed, go to step **9)**.

3) Using scan tool, read body controller module information. If scan tool displays NS PREMIUM W/VTSS, see appropriate VEHICLE COMMUNICATIONS article. If scan tool does not display NS PREMIUM W/VTSS, go to next step.

4) Check if vehicle equipped with hood ajar switch. If switch is not present, vehicle is not equipped with VTSS. If switch is present, go to next step.

5) Close all doors and open hood. Insert key into liftgate key cylinder and turn to UNLOCK position. Using scan tool, read BCM controller information. If scan tool displays NS PREMIUM W/VTSS, system is currently functioning correctly. If scan tool does not display NS PREMIUM W/VTSS, replace Body Control Module (BCM). BCM is located with junction block under driver's side instrument panel. *See Fig. 1.*

6) If the engine runs, go to next step. If engine does not run, repair running problem and retest system.

7) Turn ignition off. Disconnect Powertrain Control Module (PCM) harness connectors. PCM is located between left inner fender and power distribution center. Inspect connector terminals No. 59 and 60. Repair as needed. Connect jumper wire between ground and PCM terminal No. 59 (Violet/Brown wire). Using scan tool, perform CCD BUS TEST. If scan tool shows SHORT TO GROUND, go to next step. If scan tool does not show SHORT TO GROUND, repair open Violet/Brown wire.

8) Move jumper wire from PCM terminal No. 59 (Violet/Brown wire) to terminal No. 60 (White/Black wire). Using scan tool, perform CCD BUS TEST. If scan tool shows SHORT TO GROUND, replace PCM. If scan tool does not show SHORT TO GROUND, repair open White/Black wire.

9) Using scan tool, actuate horn, headlights, park/tail lights and VTSS indicator light. If horn does not sound, go to next step. If horn sounds, go to next step. If headlights or park/tail lights do not flash, go to appropriate symptom under EXTERIOR LIGHTING SYSTEM. IF VTSS light does not flash, go to step **21)**. If all actuated (flashed), go to step **27)**.

10) Push horn button on steering wheel. If horn sounds, replace Body Control Module (BCM). BCM is located with junction block under driver's side instrument panel. *See Fig. 1.* If horn does not sound, go to next step.

11) Remove and inspect fuse No. 9 on Power Distribution Center (PDC). *See Fig. 4.* If fuse is open, go to next step. If fuse is okay, reinstall fuse and go to step **14)**.

12) Replace horn fuse (fuse No. 9). Depress horn button on steering wheel. Inspect horn fuse. If fuse is okay, system is currently functioning correctly. If fuse is blown, replace fuse and go to next step.

13) Disconnect horns. Remove horn relay from PDC. Using scan tool in ohmmeter mode, measure resistance at horn relay terminal No. 87. If resistance is less than 5 ohms, repair Dark Green/Red wires between horns and relay for short to ground. If resistance is 5 ohms or more, replace horns.

14) Remove horn relay from PDC. Using scan tool in voltmeter mode, measure voltage on horn relay socket terminal No. 86. If voltage is more than 10 volts, go to next step. If voltage is 10 volts or less, replace PDC.

15) Using scan tool in voltmeter mode, measure voltage on horn relay socket terminal No. 30. If voltage is more than 10 volts, go to next step. If voltage is 10 volts or less, replace PDC.

16) Connect jumper wire between relay socket terminals No. 30 and 87. If horn sounds, go to next step. If horn does not sound, go to step **19)**.

17) Connect test light between relay socket terminals No. 30 and 85. Using scan tool, actuate horn. If test light flashes, replace horn relay. If test light does not flash, go to next step.

CHRY
4-130

1999 ACCESSORIES & EQUIPMENT
Body Control Computer Tests
Caravan, Town & Country & Voyager (Cont.)

18) Install horn relay. Backprobing connector, jumper wire between ground and junction block connector "B" terminal No. 4 (Gray/Orange wire). *See Fig. 3.* If horn sounds, replace BCM. If does not sound, repair open Gray/Orange wire.

19) Ensure jumper wire is still connected. Disconnect horns. Using external ohmmeter, measure resistance between ground and terminal No. 2 (Black wire) on each horn harness connector. If resistance is less than 5 ohms, go to next step. If resistance is 5 ohms or more, repair open Black wire.

20) Using external voltmeter, measure voltage between ground and horn harness connector terminal No. 1 (Dark Green/Red wire). If voltage is more than 10 volts, replace horns. If voltage is 10 volts or less, repair open Dark Green/Red wire(s).

21) Turn ignition on. Once BCM has completed light check, determine if VTSS indicator light is illuminated constantly. If light is illuminated constantly, go to next step. If light is not illuminated constantly, go to step 24).

22) Using scan tool, read PCM status. If scan tool does not display ACTIVE ON THE BUS, see appropriate VEHICLE COMMUNICATIONS article. If scan tool displays ACTIVE ON THE BUS, go to next step.

23) Disconnect Body Control Module (BCM) connector "A". BCM is located with junction block under driver's side instrument panel. *See Fig. 1.* If VTSS indicator light is not illuminated, replace BCM. If VTSS indicator light is illuminated, repair VTSS indicator light driver circuit for short to ground. Circuit is between BCM connector "A" terminal No. 16 (Black/Orange wire) and junction block "C" connector terminal No. 16 (Pink wire).

24) Connect jumper wire between ground and BCM connector "A" terminal No. 16 (Black/Orange wire). If VTSS indicator light illuminates, replace BCM. If VTSS indicator light does not illuminate, go to next step.

25) Disconnect information center harness connector. Inspect circuit board. Replace as needed. Remove VTSS indicator light bulb. Replace bulb as needed. Go to next step.

26) Using scan tool in voltmeter mode, measure voltage at information center connector terminal No. 12 (Pink wire). If voltage is more than 10 volts, repair open Black/Orange wire between information center and BCM. If voltage is 10 volts or less, repair open Pink wire.

27) Using scan tool, select THEFT ALARM, then MISCELLANEOUS. Select CHANGE MODE, then DIAGNOSTICS. VTSS should now be in diagnostic mode. Follow instructions displayed by scan tool. If TURN KEY TO ACC POSITION is not displayed, go to step 64). If TURN KEY TO ACC POSITION for more than 15 seconds is displayed or NO RESPONSE once ignition is turned to ACC position, go to step 29). If no message is displayed, go to next step.

28) Access junction block connector "D". *See Fig. 3.* Do not disconnect connector. Ensure ignition is RUN position. Using scan tool in voltmeter mode, measure voltage on junction block connector "D" terminal No. 31 (Black/White wire) . If voltage is more than 10 volts, replace Body Control Module (BCM). BCM is located with junction block under driver's side instrument panel. *See Fig. 1.* If voltage is 10 volts or less, repair open Black/White wire.

NOTE: Do not rotate door or liftgate lock cylinder to UNLOCK position. This will cancel self-diagnostic test. If problem is with unlock function, replace lock cylinder switch.

29) Remove key from ignition switch. Wait 2 seconds after performing each of the following actions. Open, then close each door, liftgate and hood. Operate power door lock switch to lock, then unlock position. Rotate key to LOCK position only in each door and liftgate lock. Horn should sound after each action. If horn does not sound, see VTSS SYMPTOM DIRECTORY table. If horn sounds, go to step 62).

VTSS SYMPTOM DIRECTORY

VTSS SYMPTOM DIRECTORY (Cont.)

30) Ensure driver door is closed. Using scan tool, enter BODY SYSTEM, then BODY COMPUTER. Select INPUTS/OUTPUTS. Observe driver door ajar state. If driver door ajar state shows CLOSED, go to SHORTED DRIVER DOOR AJAR CIRCUIT under INTERIOR LIGHTING SYSTEM. If driver door ajar state does not show CLOSED, go to OPEN DRIVER DOOR AJAR CIRCUIT under INTERIOR LIGHTING SYSTEM.

31) Ensure passenger door is closed. Using scan tool, enter BODY SYSTEM, then BODY COMPUTER. Select INPUTS/OUTPUTS. Observe passenger door ajar state. If passenger door ajar state shows CLOSED, go to SHORTED PASSENGER DOOR AJAR CIRCUIT under INTERIOR LIGHTING SYSTEM. If passenger door ajar state does not show CLOSED, go to OPEN PASSENGER DOOR AJAR CIRCUIT under INTERIOR LIGHTING SYSTEM.

32) Ensure right sliding door is closed. Using scan tool, enter BODY SYSTEM, then BODY COMPUTER. Select INPUTS/OUTPUTS. Observe right sliding door ajar state. If right sliding door ajar state shows CLOSED, go to SHORTED RIGHT SLIDING DOOR AJAR CIRCUIT under INTERIOR LIGHTING SYSTEM. If right sliding door ajar state does not show CLOSED, go to OPEN RIGHT SLIDING DOOR AJAR CIRCUIT under INTERIOR LIGHTING SYSTEM.

33) Ensure left sliding door is closed. Using scan tool, enter BODY SYSTEM, then BODY COMPUTER. Select INPUTS/OUTPUTS. Observe left sliding door ajar state. If left sliding door ajar state shows CLOSED, go to SHORTED LEFT SLIDING DOOR AJAR CIRCUIT under INTERIOR LIGHTING SYSTEM. If left sliding door ajar state does not show CLOSED, go to OPEN LEFT SLIDING DOOR AJAR CIRCUIT under INTERIOR LIGHTING SYSTEM.

34) Ensure liftgate is closed. Using scan tool, enter BODY SYSTEM, then BODY COMPUTER. Select INPUTS/OUTPUTS. Observe liftgate ajar state. If liftgate ajar state shows CLOSED, go to SHORTED LIFTGATE AJAR CIRCUIT under INTERIOR LIGHTING SYSTEM. If liftgate ajar state does not show CLOSED, go to OPEN LIFTGATE AJAR CIRCUIT under INTERIOR LIGHTING SYSTEM.

35) Disconnect driver door lock switch connector. Using scan tool in voltmeter mode, measure voltage at driver door lock switch terminal No. 2 (White/Dark Green wire). If voltage is 6 volts or less, go to next step. If voltage is more than 6 volts, repair short to voltage in White/Dark Green wire.

36) If voltage is less than 4.5 volts, go to next step. If voltage is 4.5 volts or more, go to step 38).

37) If doors lock properly from door key cylinder, repair open White/Dark Green wire. If doors do not lock properly from door key cylinder, go to step 52).

38) Turn ignition off. Turn all lights and accessories off. Using scan tool in ohmmeter mode, measure resistance at driver door lock switch terminal No. 3 (Black/Light Green wire). If resistance is less than 5 ohms, replace driver door lock switch. If resistance is 5 ohms or more, repair open Black/Light Green wire.

39) Disconnect passenger door lock switch connector. Using scan tool in voltmeter mode, measure voltage at passenger door lock switch terminal No. 2 (White/Light Green wire). If voltage is 6 volts or less, go to next step. If voltage is more than 6 volts, repair short to voltage in White/Light Green wire.

40) If voltage is less than 4.5 volts, go to next step. If voltage is 4.5 volts or more, go to step 42).

1999 ACCESSORIES & EQUIPMENT
Body Control Computer Tests
Caravan, Town & Country & Voyager (Cont.)

CHRY
4-131

41) If doors lock properly from door key cylinder, repair open White/Light Green wire. If doors do not lock properly from door key cylinder, go to step **57**).

42) Turn ignition off. Turn all lights and accessories off. Using scan tool in ohmmeter mode, measure resistance at passenger door lock switch terminal No. 3 (Black/Light Green wire). If resistance is less than 5 ohms, replace passenger door lock switch. If resistance is 5 ohms or more, repair open Black/Light Green wire.

43) Ensure hood is closed and correctly aligned. Using scan tool, read hood ajar switch status. If scan tool displays CLOSED, go to next step. If scan tool does not display CLOSED, go to step **46**).

44) Disconnect hood ajar switch. Using scan tool, read hood ajar switch status. If scan tool displays CLOSED, go to next step. If scan tool does not display CLOSED, replace hood ajar switch.

45) Disconnect Body Control Module (BCM) connector "B". BCM is located with junction block under driver's side instrument panel. *See Fig. 1.* Using scan tool in ohmmeter mode, measure resistance at BCM connector "B" terminal No. 43 (Brown/Tan wire). If resistance is less than 5 ohms, repair Brown/Tan wire for short to ground. If resistance is 5 ohms or more, replace BCM.

46) Disconnect hood ajar switch connector. Connect jumper wire between ground and hood ajar switch connector terminal No. 1 (Brown/Tan wire). Using scan tool, read hood ajar switch status. If scan tool displays CLOSED, replace hood ajar switch. If scan tool does not display CLOSED, go to next step.

47) Access Body Control Module (BCM) connector "B". BCM is located with junction block under driver's side instrument panel. *See Fig. 1.* Remove connector cover. Do not disconnect connector. Connect a backprobe jumper wire between ground and BCM connector "B" terminal No. 43 (Brown/Tan wire). Using scan tool, read hood ajar switch status. If scan tool displays CLOSED, repair open Brown/Tan wire. If scan tool does not display CLOSED, replace BCM.

48) Disconnect driver door key cylinder switch connector. Using scan tool in voltmeter mode, measure voltage at driver door key cylinder switch connector terminal No. 2 (White/Dark Green wire). If voltage is 4.5 volts or less, go to step **51**). If voltage is more than 4.5 volts, go to next step.

49) Turn ignition off. Turn all lights and accessories off. Using scan tool in ohmmeter mode, measure resistance at driver door key cylinder switch connector terminal No. 1 (Black Light Green wire). If resistance is less than 5 ohms, go to next step. If resistance is 5 ohms or more, repair open in Black Light Green wire.

50) Measure voltage at driver door key cylinder switch connector terminal No. 2 (White/Dark Green wire). If voltage is more than 10 volts, repair short to battery in White/Dark Green wire. If voltage is 10 volts or less, replace driver door key cylinder switch.

51) If door locks operate properly from interior door lock switch, repair open White/Dark Green wire between driver door lock switch and driver door key cylinder switch. If door locks do not operate properly from interior door lock switch, go to next step.

52) Access Body Control Module (BCM) connector "B". BCM is located with junction block under driver's side instrument panel. *See Fig. 1.* Remove connector cover. Do not disconnect connector. Using scan tool in voltmeter mode, backprobe measure voltage at BCM connector "B" terminal No. 45 (White/Dark Green wire). If voltage is more than 4.5 volts, repair open White/Dark Green. If voltage is 4.5 volts or less, replace BCM.

53) Disconnect passenger door key cylinder switch connector. Using scan tool in voltmeter mode, measure voltage at passenger door key cylinder switch connector terminal No. 2 (White/Light Green wire). If voltage is 4.5 volts or less, go to step **56**). If voltage is more than 4.5 volts, go to next step.

54) Turn ignition off. Turn all lights and accessories off. Using scan tool in ohmmeter mode, measure resistance at passenger door key cylinder switch connector terminal No. 1 (Black/Light Green wire). If resistance is less than 5 ohms, go to next step. If resistance is 5 ohms or more, repair open in Black/Light Green wire.

55) Measure voltage at passenger door key cylinder switch connector terminal No. 2 (White/Light Green wire). If voltage is more than 10 volts, repair short to battery in White/Light Green wire. If voltage is 10 volts or less, replace passenger door key cylinder switch.

56) If door locks operate properly from interior door lock switch, repair open White/Light Green wire between passenger door lock switch and passenger door key cylinder switch. If door locks do not operate properly from interior door lock switch, go to next step.

57) Access Body Control Module (BCM) connector "B". BCM is located with junction block under passengers side instrument panel. *See Fig. 1.* Remove connector cover. Do not disconnect connector. Using scan tool in voltmeter mode, backprobe measure voltage at BCM connector "B" terminal No. 55 (White/Light Green wire). If voltage is more than 4.5 volts, repair open White/Light Green. If voltage is 4.5 volts or less, replace BCM.

58) Disconnect liftgate key cylinder switch connector. Using scan tool in voltmeter mode, measure voltage at liftgate key cylinder switch connector terminal No. 2 (White/Red wire). If voltage is 4.5 volts or less, go to step **61**). If voltage is more than 4.5 volts, go to next step.

59) Turn ignition off. Turn all lights and accessories off. Using scan tool in ohmmeter mode, measure resistance at liftgate key cylinder switch connector terminal No. 1 (Black/Light Green wire). If resistance is less than 5 ohms, go to next step. If resistance is 5 ohms or more, repair open in Black/Light Green wire.

60) Measure voltage at liftgate key cylinder switch connector terminal No. 2 (White/Red wire). If voltage is more than 10 volts, repair short to battery in White/Red wire. If voltage is 10 volts or less, replace liftgate key cylinder switch.

61) Access Body Control Module (BCM) connector "B". BCM is located with junction block under passengers side instrument panel. *See Fig. 1.* Remove connector cover. Do not disconnect connector. Using scan tool in voltmeter mode, backprobe measure voltage at BCM connector "B" terminal No. 44 (White/Red wire). If voltage is more than 4.5 volts, repair open White/Red. If voltage is 4.5 volts or less, replace BCM.

62) Insert key in ignition cylinder. Turn key to START position. If horn fails to sound, go to next step. If horn sounds, go to step **64**).

63) Turn ignition off. Remove Body Control Module (BCM) connector "B". BCM is located with junction block under passengers side instrument panel. *See Fig. 1.* Using an external voltmeter, measure voltage between ground and junction block internal connector terminals No. 11–13. If voltage is more than 10 volts at all terminal, replace BCM. If voltage is 10 volts or less at any terminals, repair open fused ignition switch output circuit to junction block.

64) Using scan tool, select THEFT ALARM, then MONITOR DISPLAY. Read VTSS status. If display is 1 NO RESPONSE/2 NO RESPONSE, go to appropriate VEHICLE COMMUNICATIONS article. If display is 1 NOT OK TO ARM VTSS/2 OK TO RUN ENGINE, 20 engine start cycles must be done before system is operational. If 1 NO RESPONSE/2 NO RESPONSE or 1 NOT OK TO ARM VTSS/2 OK TO RUN ENGINE is not displayed, system is currently functioning correctly.

WINDSHIELD WIPER SYSTEM

FRONT WIPER PARK SWITCH CIRCUIT OPEN (FRONT WIPER PARK SWITCH CIRCUIT SHORTED, FRONT WIPERS NOT PARKING IN OFF POSITION)

NOTE: For connector terminal identification and wiring diagrams, see BODY CONTROL COMPUTER – INTRODUCTION article. Perform VERIFICATION TEST VER-1A after each repair.

CAUTION: Always turn ignition switch to OFF position prior to disconnecting or connecting any module connector.

1) Turn ignition on. Operate wipers in intermittent mode. Using scan tool, observe wiper park switch. If wiper park switch does not toggle from CLOSED to OPEN, turn wipers off and go to next step. If wiper park

CHRY
4-132

1999 ACCESSORIES & EQUIPMENT
Body Control Computer Tests
Caravan, Town & Country & Voyager (Cont.)

switch toggles from CLOSED to OPEN, system is currently operating correctly. Using scan tool, clear trouble codes and attempt to reproduce fault.

2) Turn ignition off. Access Body Control Module (BCM) connector "B". BCM is located with junction block under driver's side instrument panel. *See Fig. 1.* Remove connector cover. Do not disconnect connector. Using scan tool in voltmeter mode, measure voltage on BCM connector "B" terminal No. 41 (Dark Green/White wire). Turn ignition on. Turn wiper switch to LOW speed position. Observe scan tool voltage reading. If voltage pulsates, replace BCM. If voltage does not pulsate, go to next step.

3) Turn ignition off. Disconnect scan tool voltmeter probe. Backprobing BCM connector "B", connect jumper wire between ground and terminal No. 41 (Dark Green/White wire). Disconnect wiper module connector. *See Fig. 6.* Using an external ohmmeter, measure resistance between chassis ground and wiper module connector, terminal No. 4 (Dark Green/White wire). If resistance is less than 5 ohms, replace wiper motor. If resistance is 5 ohms or more, repair open Dark Green/White wire between wiper motor and BCM.

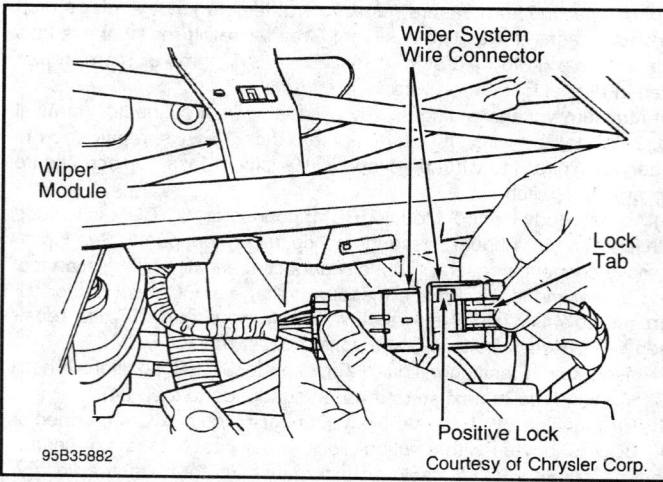

95B35882   Courtesy of Chrysler Corp.

Fig. 6: Locating Wiper Module Connector

REAR WIPER MUX CIRCUIT ERROR

NOTE: For connector terminal identification and wiring diagrams, see BODY CONTROL COMPUTER – INTRODUCTION article. Perform VERIFICATION TEST VER-1A after each repair.

CAUTION: Always turn ignition switch to OFF position prior to disconnecting or connecting any module connector.

1) Erase trouble code. Turn ignition on. Operate rear wiper for one minute (minimum). Using scan tool read DTCs (fault messages). If rear wiper MUX circuit error code is present, go to next step. If code is not present, system is currently functioning correctly.

2) Disconnect Heater, Ventilation and Air Conditioning (HVAC) control module 21-pin Blue connector (integral with instrument panel control). Using scan tool, monitor rear wiper switch voltage. Turn ignition on. If scan tool displays 5 volts, repair Yellow/White wire between Body Control Module (BCM) terminal No. 38 and HVAC Blue connector, terminal No. 2 for short to battery voltage. If scan tool does not display 5 volts, go to next step.

3) turn ignition off. Using scan tool in ohmmeter mode, measure resistance at HVAC connector terminal No. 21 (Black/Light Green wire). If resistance is less than 5 ohms, replace BCM. BCM is located with junction block under driver's side instrument panel. *See Fig. 1.* If resistance is 5 ohms or more, repair open Black/Light Green wire.

WIPER CONSTANTLY OPERATING WITH SWITCH IN OFF POSITION

NOTE: For connector terminal identification and wiring diagrams, see BODY CONTROL COMPUTER – INTRODUCTION article. Perform VERIFICATION TEST VER-1A after each repair.

CAUTION: Always turn ignition switch to OFF position prior to disconnecting or connecting any module connector.

1) Turn ignition on. Ensure wiper switch is in OFF position. Using scan tool, read intermittent wiper voltage. If voltage is .1 volts or less, go to next step. If voltage is more than .1 volts, replace multifunction switch.

2) Remove front wiper HI/LO relay in Power Distribution Center (PDC). *See Fig. 4.* If wipers stop operating, go to step 5). If wipers continue to operate, go to next step.

3) Reinstall front wiper HI/LO relay. Disconnect wiper module connector. *See Fig. 6.* Using external voltmeter, measure voltage between ground and wiper module harness connector terminal No. 1 (Brown/White wire). If voltage is more than .5 volts, repair Brown/White wire for short to voltage. If voltage is .5 volts or less, go to next step.

4) Measure voltage between ground and wiper module harness connector terminal No. 3 (Red/Yellow wire). If voltage is more than .5 volts, repair Red/Yellow wire for short to voltage. If voltage is .5 volts or less, system is currently functioning correctly.

5) Reinstall front wiper HI/LO relay. Replace front wiper ON relay in Power Distribution Center (PDC) with known good relay. If wipers stop operating, replace relay. If wipers continue to operate, go to next step.

6) Remove substitute wiper ON relay. Disconnect Body Control Module (BCM) connector "B". BCM is located with junction block under driver's side instrument panel. *See Fig. 1.* Using external ohmmeter, measure resistance between ground and wiper ON relay socket terminal No. 85. If resistance is less than 100 ohms, repair wiper ON relay control circuit (Red/Violet wire) for short to ground between relay and BCM. If resistance is 100 ohms or more, replace BCM.

FRONT WIPERS NOT WORKING AT ALL

NOTE: For connector terminal identification and wiring diagrams, see BODY CONTROL COMPUTER – INTRODUCTION article. Perform VERIFICATION TEST VER-1A after each repair.

CAUTION: Always turn ignition switch to OFF position prior to disconnecting or connecting any module connector.

1) Using scan tool, actuate front wiper relay. If wiper motor does not operate in low speed mode, go to step 7). If wiper motor operates in low speed mode, go to next step.

2) Stop wiper motor actuation. Ensure ignition is on. Turn wiper switch to LO position. Using scan tool, select SENSORS and read intermittent wiper voltage. If scan tool does displays INTRMT WIPE: 2.5V or less, go to next step. If scan tool displays more than INTRMT WIPE: 2.5V, replace Body Control Module (BCM). BCM is located with junction block under driver's side instrument panel. *See Fig. 1.*

3) Turn ignition off. Disconnect Body Control Module (BCM) connector "A". Using scan tool in voltmeter mode, measure voltage at BCM connector "A" terminal No. 7 (Dark Green/Yellow wire). If voltage is 10 volts or less, go to next step. If voltage is more than 10 volts, replace BCM.

4) Disconnect multifunction switch 12-pin connector. *See Fig. 2.* Ensure connector is clean and not damaged. Using an external voltmeter, measure voltage between ground and multifunction switch connector terminal No. 7 (Dark Blue wire). If voltage is 10 volts or less, repair open Dark Blue wire. If voltage is more than 10 volts, go to next step.

5) Turn ignition off. Using an external ohmmeter, measure resistance between ground and multifunction switch connector terminal No. 6 (Dark

1999 ACCESSORIES & EQUIPMENT
Body Control Computer Tests
Caravan, Town & Country & Voyager (Cont.)

CHRY
4-133

Green/Yellow wire). If resistance is less than 5 ohms, repair Dark Green/Yellow wire for short to ground. If resistance is 5 ohms or more, go to next step.

6) Turn ignition on. Connect jumper wire between multifunction switch connector terminals No. 6 and 7. Using an external voltmeter, measure voltage between ground and BCM connector "A" terminal No. 7 (Dark Green/Yellow wire). If voltage is 10 volts or less, repair open Dark Green/Yellow wire. If voltage is more than 10 volts, replace multifunction switch.

7) Using scan tool, stop front wiper low speed actuation. Locate Power Distribution Center (PDC) on left front fender next to battery. Remove and inspect wiper fuse No. 19 (30-amp). *See Fig. 4.* If fuse is okay, go to step **12)**. If fuse is open, go to next step.

8) Remove front wiper ON relay from Power Distribution Center (PDC). Ensure connector is clean and not damaged. Remove HI/LO wiper relay and ensure connector is clean and not damaged. Using an external ohmmeter, measure resistance between ground and front wiper ON relay socket terminal No. 87. If resistance is 5 ohms or more, go to next step. If resistance is less than 5 ohms, replace PDC.

9) Using an external ohmmeter, measure resistance between ground and front wiper ON relay socket terminal No. 30. If resistance is more than 5 ohms, go to next step. If resistance is less than 5 ohms, replace PDC.

10) Disconnect wiper module connector. *See Fig. 6.* Using an external ohmmeter, measure resistance between ground and wiper HI/LO relay socket terminal No. 87A. If resistance is 5 ohms or more, go to next step. If resistance is less than 5 ohms, repair short to ground in Brown/White wire between terminal No. 1 on wiper module connector and wiper HI/LO relay socket terminal No. 87A. Replace wiper fuse No. 19 (30-amp).

11) Using an external ohmmeter, measure resistance between ground and wiper HI/LO relay socket terminal No. 87. If resistance is less than 5 ohms, repair short to ground in Red/Yellow wire between wiper HI/LO relay socket terminal No. 87 and wiper module connector terminal No. 3. Replace wiper fuse No. 19 (30-amp). If resistance is 5 ohms or more, replace wiper motor and wiper fuse No. 19 (30-amp).

12) Using an external voltmeter, measure voltage between ground and outside terminal (fused B+) on fuse No. 19 socket. If voltage is more than 10 volts, go to next step. If voltage is 10 volts or less, repair or replace PDC.

13) Reinstall wiper fuse No. 19. Remove front wiper ON relay from PDC and ensure connector is clean and not damaged. Using an external voltmeter, measure voltage between ground and front wiper ON relay socket terminal No. 87. *See Fig. 4.* If voltage is more than 10 volts, go to next step. If voltage is 10 volts or less, repair or replace PDC.

14) Connect a jumper wire between wiper ON relay socket terminals No. 30 and 87. If wiper motor operates, disconnect jumper wire and go to next step. If wiper motor does not operate, go to step **18)**.

15) Using an external voltmeter, measure voltage between ground and front wiper ON relay socket terminal No. 86. If voltage is more than 10 volts, go to next step. If voltage is 10 volts or less, repair or replace Power Distribution Center (PDC).

16) Reinstall wiper ON relay. Access Body Control Module (BCM) connector "B". BCM is located with junction block under driver's side instrument panel. *See Fig. 1.* Remove connector cover. Do not disconnect connector. Connect jumper wire between ground and BCM connector "B" terminal No. 73 (Red/Violet wire). If wiper motor operates, replace BCM. If wiper motor does not operate, go to next step.

17) Remove wiper ON relay. Do not disconnect jumper wire. Using an external ohmmeter, measure resistance between ground and front wiper ON relay socket terminal No. 85. If resistance is less than 5 ohms, replace relay. If resistance is 5 ohms or more, repair open Red/Violet wire between BCM and front wiper ON relay socket.

18) Disconnect wiper HI/LO relay, located in PDC. Ensure connector is clean and not damaged. Ensure jumper wire is still connected between wiper ON relay socket terminals No. 30 and 87. Using an external voltmeter, measure voltage between ground and wiper HI/LO relay

socket terminal No. 30. If voltage is more than 10 volts, go to next step. If voltage is 10 volts or less, repair or replace PDC.

19) Disconnect jumper wire from front wiper ON relay socket. Connect a jumper wire between wiper ON relay socket terminal No. 87 and wiper HI/LO relay terminal No. No. 87A. If wiper motor operates in low speed mode, replace wiper HI/LO relay. If wiper motor does not operate in low speed mode, go to next step.

20) Disconnect wiper module connector. *See Fig. 6.* Ensure jumper wire between wiper ON relay socket terminals No. 30 and 87 is connected. Using an external voltmeter, measure voltage between ground and wiper module terminal No. 1 (Brown/White wire). If voltage is more than 10 volts, go to next step. If voltage is 10 volts or less, repair open in Brown/White wire between HI/LO wiper relay and wiper motor module.

21) Ensure ignition is off. Ensure all lights and accessories are off. Using an external ohmmeter, measure resistance between ground and wiper module terminal No. 4 (Black wire). If resistance is less than 5 ohms, replace wiper motor. If resistance is 5 ohms or more, repair open Black wire.

WIPERS NOT WORKING IN INTERMITTENT MODE

NOTE: For connector terminal identification and wiring diagrams, see BODY CONTROL COMPUTER – INTRODUCTION article. Perform VERIFICATION TEST VER-1A after each repair.

CAUTION: Always turn ignition switch to OFF position prior to disconnecting or connecting any module connector.

1) Turn ignition on. Move wiper switch through all 6 intermittent positions. If wipers were inoperative in all positions, go to next step. If wipers were only inoperative in some switch positions, replace multifunction switch.

2) Using scan tool, select SENSORS and monitor intermittent wiper voltage at each position of wiper switch. If voltage changes each time a different position is chosen, replace Body Control Module (BCM). BCM is located with junction block under driver's side instrument panel. *See Fig. 1.* If voltage does not change, replace multifunction switch.

WIPERS NOT WORKING IN LOW SPEED MODE

NOTE: For connector terminal identification and wiring diagrams, see BODY CONTROL COMPUTER – INTRODUCTION article. Perform VERIFICATION TEST VER-1A after each repair.

CAUTION: Always turn ignition switch to OFF position prior to disconnecting or connecting any module connector.

1) Disconnect HI/LO wiper relay from Power Distribution Center (PDC). *See Fig. 4.* Turn ignition off. Turn wiper switch to LO speed position. Using external ohmmeter, measure resistance between ground and HI/LO relay socket terminal No. 86. If resistance is less than 100 ohms, repair White wire for short to ground between PDC and multifunction switch. If resistance is 100 ohms or more, go to next step.

2) Connect a jumper wire between wiper HI/LO relay socket terminals No. 30 and 87A. Turn ignition on. Ensure wiper switch is in LO position. If wipers operate in low speed, replace wiper HI/LO relay. If wipers do not operate in low speed, go to next step.

3) Disconnect wiper module connector. *See Fig. 6.* Ensure jumper wire between wiper HI/LO relay socket terminals No. 30 and 87A is connected. Using external voltmeter, measure voltage between ground and terminal No. 1 (Brown/White wire) on wiper module connector. If voltage is 10 volts or less, repair open Brown/White wire. If voltage is more than 10 volts, repair wiper motor.

REAR WASHER MOTOR INOPERATIVE

NOTE: For connector terminal identification and wiring diagrams, see BODY CONTROL COMPUTER – INTRODUCTION article. Perform VERIFICATION TEST VER-1A after each repair.

CAUTION: Always turn ignition switch to OFF position prior to disconnecting or connecting any module connector.

1) Using scan tool, monitor rear wiper switch mux voltage. Press and hold rear washer switch. If voltage is not about 3.8 volts, replace Heating, Ventilation and Air Conditioning (HVAC) control module. If voltage is about 3.8 volts, go to next step.

2) Disconnect Body Control Module (BCM) connector "B". BCM is located with junction block under driver's side instrument panel. *See Fig. 1.* Connect jumper wire between ground and BCM connector "B" terminal No. 50 (Black/White wire). Disconnect rear washer pump connector at washer fluid reservoir in engine compartment. Using an external ohmmeter, measure resistance between ground and rear washer pump connector terminal "B" (Black/White wire). If resistance is less than 5 ohms, go to next step. If resistance is 5 ohms or more, repair open Black/White wire.

3) Using an external voltmeter, measure voltage between ground and rear washer pump connector terminal No. 1 (Dark Blue wire). If voltage is more than 10 volts, go to next step. If voltage is 10 volts or less, repair open Dark Blue wire.

4) Ensure BCM connector "B" is disconnected and jumper wire is connected. If rear washer motor operates, replace BCM. If rear washer does not operate, replace rear washer pump.

REAR WIPER NOT PARKING IN OFF POSITION

NOTE: For connector terminal identification and wiring diagrams, see BODY CONTROL COMPUTER – INTRODUCTION article. Perform VERIFICATION TEST VER-1A after each repair.

CAUTION: Always turn ignition switch to OFF position prior to disconnecting or connecting any module connector.

1) Turn ignition on. Ensure rear wiper switch is in OFF position. If any switch indicator light is illuminated, replace Heating, Ventilation and Air Conditioning (HVAC) control module. If all switch indicator lights are off, go to next step.

2) Using scan tool, monitor rear wiper switch voltage. If voltage is less than one volt, go to next step. If voltage is one volt or more, go to step 4).

3) Disconnect rear wiper motor connector. Connect test light between ground and rear wiper motor connector terminal No. 1 (Black wire). Turn intermittent switch to ON position. Monitor test light for 30 seconds (minimum). If test light cycles on, and then off, replace rear wiper motor. If test light does not illuminate, replace BCM. BCM is located with junction block under driver's side instrument panel. *See Fig. 1.*

4) Ensure rear wiper switch is off. Using scan tool, monitor rear wiper switch voltage. If voltage is more than 4.2 volts, replace Body Control Module (BCM). BCM is located with junction block under driver's side instrument panel. *See Fig. 1.* If voltage is 4.2 volts or less, go to next step.

5) Determine if washer motor runs for 10 seconds each time ignition switch is turned to ON position. If motor runs, replace BCM. If motor does not run, go to next step.

6) Disconnect rear wiper motor connector. Using an external voltmeter, measure voltage between ground and rear wiper motor connector, terminal No. 3 (Brown/Light Green wire). If no voltage is displayed, replace wiper motor. If any voltage is displayed, go to next step.

7) Disconnect Body Control Module (BCM) connector "B". *See Fig. 1.* Using an external voltmeter, measure voltage between ground and rear wiper motor connector, terminal No. 3 (Brown/Light Green wire). Turn ignition on. If no voltage is displayed, replace BCM. If any voltage is displayed, repair Brown/Light Green wire for short to battery voltage.

REAR WIPER INOPERATIVE

NOTE: For connector terminal identification and wiring diagrams, see BODY CONTROL COMPUTER – INTRODUCTION article. Perform VERIFICATION TEST VER-1A after each repair.

CAUTION: Always turn ignition switch to OFF position prior to disconnecting or connecting any module connector.

1) Turn ignition on. Depress rear wiper switch to ON position. If indicator light on switch illuminates, go to next step. If indicator light does not illuminate, go to step 7).

2) Using scan tool, read rear wiper switch voltage. If voltage is about 2.5 volts, go to next step. If voltage is not about 2.5 volts, check communications between Heater, Ventilation and Air Conditioning (HVAC) control module and Body Control Module (BCM). See appropriate VEHICLE COMMUNICATIONS article.

3) Turn ignition and all lights off. Disconnect rear wiper motor connector. Using external ohmmeter, measure resistance between ground and rear wiper motor connector terminal No. 3 (Black wire). If resistance is less than 10 ohms, go to next step. If resistance is 10 ohms or more, repair open Black wire.

4) Turn ignition on. Ensure rear wiper switch is still on. Using external voltmeter, measure voltage between ground and rear wiper motor connector terminal No. 2 (Brown/Pink wire). If voltage is more than 10 volts, go to next step. If voltage is 10 volts or less, repair open Brown/Pink wire or junction block fuse No. 6.

5) Move positive voltmeter probe to rear wiper motor connector terminal No. 3 (Brown/Light Green wire). If voltage is more than 10 volts, replace rear wiper motor. If voltage is 10 volts or less, go to next step.

6) Turn ignition off. Connect jumper wire between ground to rear wiper motor connector terminal No. 3 (Brown/Light Green wire). Disconnect Body Control Module (BCM) connector "B". BCM is located with junction block under driver's side instrument panel. *See Fig. 1.* Using external ohmmeter, measure resistance between ground and BCM connector "B" terminal No. 49 (Brown/Light Green wire). If resistance is less than 5 ohms, replace BCM. If resistance is 5 ohms or more, repair open Brown/Light Green wire.

7) Remove fuse No. 6 from junction block. *See Fig. 3.* If fuse is okay, go to next step. If fuse is open, go to step 8).

8) Disconnect Heater, Ventilation and Air Conditioning (HVAC) control module 21-pin Blue connector (integral with instrument panel unit). Using external ohmmeter, measure resistance between ground and HVAC connector terminal No. 10 (Brown/Pink wire). If resistance is less than 5 ohms, repair Brown/Pink wire for short to ground. If resistance is 5 ohms or more, replace HVAC module.

9) Disconnect Heater, Ventilation and Air Conditioning (HVAC) control module 21-pin Blue connector (integral with instrument panel unit). Using external voltmeter, measure voltage between ground and HVAC connector, terminal No. 10 (Brown/Pink wire). If voltage is more than 10 volts, replace HVAC module. If voltage is 10 volts or less, repair open Brown/Pink wire.

REAR WIPER/WASHER ON CONSTANTLY

NOTE: For connector terminal identification and wiring diagrams, see BODY CONTROL COMPUTER – INTRODUCTION article. Perform VERIFICATION TEST VER-1A after each repair.

CAUTION: Always turn ignition switch to OFF position prior to disconnecting or connecting any module connector.

1) Ensure rear wiper switch is off. Using scan tool, monitor rear wiper switch voltage. If voltage is more than 4.2 volts, replace Body Control Module (BCM). BCM is located with junction block under driver's side instrument panel. *See Fig. 1.* If voltage is 4.2 volts or less, go to next step.

1999 ACCESSORIES & EQUIPMENT
Body Control Computer Tests
Caravan, Town & Country & Voyager (Cont.)

CHRY
4-135

2) Determine if washer motor runs for 10 seconds each time ignition switch is turned to ON position. If motor runs, replace BCM. If motor does not run, go to next step.

3) Disconnect rear wiper motor connector. Using external voltmeter, measure voltage between ground and rear wiper motor connector, terminal No. 3 (Brown/Light Green wire). If no voltage is displayed, replace wiper motor. If any voltage is displayed, go to next step.

4) Disconnect Body Control Module (BCM) connector "B". Measure voltage between ground and rear wiper motor connector, terminal No. 3 (Brown/Light Green wire). Turn ignition on. If no voltage is displayed, replace BCM. If any voltage is displayed, repair Brown/Light Green wire for short to battery voltage.

WIPER WASH FUNCTION NOT WORKING PROPERLY

NOTE: For connector terminal identification and wiring diagrams, see BODY CONTROL COMPUTER – INTRODUCTION article. Perform VERIFICATION TEST VER-1A after each repair.

CAUTION: Always turn ignition switch to OFF position prior to disconnecting or connecting any module connector.

1) Ensure windshield washer fluid reservoir is full. Turn ignition on. Momentarily push and release wash button on stalk switch. If washer pump does not operate, go to step **3)**. If washer pump operates, but wipers do not operate, go to next step. If washer pump and wipers operate, system is currently operating correctly.

2) Turn ignition on. Using scan tool, monitor front washer switch while pushing switch. If front washer switch toggles from OFF to ON, replace Body Control Module (BCM). BCM is located with junction block under driver's side instrument panel. *See Fig. 1.* If front washer switch does not toggle from OFF to ON, got to next step.

3) Turn ignition off. Remove BCM from junction block. Using external ohmmeter, measure resistance between ground and terminal No. 20 on junction block internal 23-pin connector. Press wash button. If resistance is less than 5 ohms, replace BCM. If resistance is 5 ohms or more, replace junction block.

4) Locate and disconnect washer pump 2-pin connector at bottom of washer fluid reservoir. Ensure connector is clean and not damaged. Using external voltmeter, measure voltage between ground and washer pump connector terminal "A" (Dark Blue wire). If voltage is 10 volts or less, go to next step. If voltage is more than 10 volts, go to step **9)**.

5) Access junction block connector "B". *See Fig. 1.* Do not disconnect connector. Connect jumper wire between terminals No. 3 (Dark Blue wire) and No. 21 (Brown wire) on junction block "B" connector. Using external voltmeter, measure voltage between ground and terminal No. 3 (Dark Blue wire). If voltage is 10 volts or less, repair open Dark Blue wire. If voltage is more than 10 volts, go to next step.

6) Remove jumper wire and reconnect front washer pump connector. Connect jumper wire between ground and junction block connector "D", terminal No. 18 (Brown wire). If washer pump operates, go to next step. If washer pump does not operate, repair or replace junction block.

7) Move jumper from junction block connector "D", terminal No. 18 (Brown wire) to terminal No. 21 (Brown wire). If washer pump operates, go to next step. If washer pump does not operate, replace washer pump.

8) Disconnect jumper wire. Disconnect multifunction switch. *See Fig. 2.* Using external voltmeter, measure voltage between ground and multifunction switch connector terminal No. 11 (Brown wire). If voltage is 10 volts or less, repair open Brown wire. If voltage is more than 10 volts, replace multifunction switch.

9) Access junction block connector "B". *See Fig. 1.* Do not disconnect connector. Using external voltmeter, backprobe junction block connector "D". Measure voltage between ground and terminal No. 18 (Brown wire). If voltage is 10 volts or less, repair open Brown wire. If voltage is more than 10 volts, go to next step.

10) Disconnect junction block connector "B". Using external ohmmeter, measure resistance between ground and washer pump connector

terminal "A" (Dark Blue wire). If resistance is less than 5 ohms, repair Dark Blue wire for short to ground. If resistance is 5 ohms or more, repair or replace or junction block.

WIPERS NOT WORKING IN HIGH SPEED MODE

NOTE: For connector terminal identification and wiring diagrams, see BODY CONTROL COMPUTER – INTRODUCTION article. Perform VERIFICATION TEST VER-1A after each repair.

CAUTION: Always turn ignition switch to OFF position prior to disconnecting or connecting any module connector.

1) Disconnect wiper HI/LO relay from Power Distribution Center (PDC). *See Fig. 4.* Turn ignition on and wipers to LO speed setting. Using external voltmeter, measure voltage between ground and wiper HI/LO relay terminal No. 85. If voltage is more than 10 volts, go to next step. If voltage is 10 volts or less, repair or replace PDC.

2) Connect a jumper wire between wiper HI/LO relay socket terminals No. 30 and 87. If wiper motor does not operate, go to next step. If wiper motor operates in high speed, go to step **6)**.

3) Disconnect jumper wire. Turn ignition off. Using scan tool in ohmmeter mode, measure resistance at wiper HI/LO relay socket terminal No. 86. Move wiper switch to HI position. If resistance is less than 5 ohms, replace wiper HI/LO relay. If resistance is 5 ohms or more, go to next step.

4) Disconnect multifunction switch. *See Fig. 2.* Connect jumper wire between ground and multifunction switch connector terminal No. 5 (White wire). Using external ohmmeter, measure resistance between ground and wiper HI/LO relay socket terminal No. 86. If resistance is less than 5 ohms, go to next step. If resistance is 5 ohms or more, repair open White wire between PDC and multifunction switch.

5) Remove jumper wire. Using external ohmmeter, measure resistance between ground and multifunction switch connector terminal No. 8 (Black wire). If resistance is 5 ohms or more, repair open Black wire. If resistance is less than 5 ohms, replace multifunction switch.

6) Disconnect wiper module connector. *See Fig. 6.* Ensure connector is clean and not damaged. Connect a jumper wire between wiper HI/LO relay socket terminals No. 30 and 87. Using external voltmeter, measure voltage between ground and wiper module connector terminal No. 3 (Red/Yellow wire). If voltage is more than 10 volts, replace wiper motor. If voltage is 10 volts or less, repair open in Red/Yellow wire between HI/LO wiper relay and wiper motor module.

VERIFICATION TESTS

VERIFICATION TEST VER-1A

1) Reconnect all previously disconnected components and connectors. If Body Control Module (BCM) was replaced, you must enable the Vehicle Theft Security System (VTSS) or anti-theft system (if equipped) by using the key to unlock the liftgate while hood is open. If BCM was replaced you must program other options as necessary.

NOTE: To enable automatic headlight operation, vehicle must be driven over 3 miles and BCM must see one key transmission from the remote keyless entry transmitter.

2) Ensure ignition is on. Using scan tool, clears all DTCs. Turn ignition off and wait 5 seconds. Turn ignition on and fully operate system that was malfunctioning.

3) If the system is operating properly, continue to the next step. If system is not operating properly, check possible causes for the malfunction.

4) Using scan tool, read DTCs stored in the BCM. If no DTCs exist and customer's complaint cannot be duplicated, test is complete. If any DTCs exist, perform appropriate test for the DTC.

1999 ACCESSORIES & EQUIPMENT
Body Control Computer Tests
Concorde, Intrepid, LHS & 300M

NOTE: See BODY CONTROL COMPUTER – INTRODUCTION article before proceeding with following testing.

SYSTEM ID TEST 1A

IDENTIFYING VEHICLE EQUIPMENT & SYSTEM PROBLEMS

NOTE: For connector terminal identification, see CONNECTOR IDENTIFICATION in BODY CONTROL COMPUTER – INTRODUCTION article.

1) Connect scan tool to Data Link Connector (DLC). DLC is located under instrument cluster, right of steering column. If scan tool screen is blank, see appropriate VEHICLE COMMUNICATIONS article. If scan tool is not blank, go to next step.
2) Using scan tool, read body DTCs (fault messages). If any fault messages are displayed, go to SYSTEM ID TEST 1B. If no fault messages are displayed, see SYSTEM DIAGNOSTIC TEST DIRECTORY table for specific system diagnosis. When diagnosing a vehicle with many apparent failures, start at top of table and perform indicated tests. Failures may occur separately or in various combinations. After repairs, ensure specific failure or group of failures have been corrected.

SYSTEM ID TEST 1B

IDENTIFYING DIAGNOSTIC TROUBLE CODES

If scan tool displays fault messages in TEST 1A, record messages displayed and perform appropriate test(s) listed in SCAN TOOL MESSAGE DIRECTORY table.

SYSTEM DIAGNOSTIC TEST DIRECTORY [1]

Suspected System	Perform Test
Chime System	CHIME TEST 1A
Door Ajar Indicator System	DOOR AJAR TEST 1A
Exterior Lighting System	EXTERIOR LIGHT TEST 1A
Instrument Cluster	INSTRUMENT CLUSTER TEST 1A
Interior Lighting System	INTERIOR LIGHT TEST 1A
Memory System	MEMORY SYSTEM TEST 1A
Overhead Travel Information System (OTIS)	OTIS TEST 1A
PCI BUS Failures	[2] VEHICLE COMMUNICATIONS TEST 1A
Power Door Lock System	POWER DOOR LOCK TEST 1A
Remote Keyless Entry System	POWER DOOR LOCK TEST 1A
Sentry Key Immobilizer System	SKIS TEST 1A
Speed Proportional Steering System	SPEED PROPORTIONAL STEERING SYSTEM TEST 1A
Vehicle Communication System	[2] VEHICLE COMM. TEST 1A
Vehicle Theft Security System	VTSS TEST 1A
Windshield Wiper System	WIPER TEST 1A

[1] – For automatic or manual A/C-heater system test procedures, see appropriate MITCHELL® AIR CONDITIONING & HEATING SERVICE & REPAIR, DOMESTIC CARS, LIGHT TRUCKS & VANS manual. For testing information on air bag system, see appropriate MITCHELL® AIR BAG SERVICE & REPAIR, DOMESTIC & IMPORTED manual.
[2] – See appropriate BODY CONTROL COMPUTER TESTS or VEHICLE COMMUNICATIONS article.

SCAN TOOL MESSAGE DIRECTORY

Scan Tool Display	Perform Test
A/C Control A/C Switch Failure	1
A/C Control EBL Switch Failure	1
A/C Control Blend Door Input Open Or Shorted To Ground	1
A/C Control Blend Door Input Shorted To Battery	1
A/C Control Mode Door Input Open Or Shorted To Battery	1
A/C Control Mode Door Input Shorted To Ground	1
ABS Bus Communication Failure	[3] VEHICLE COMMUNICATIONS TEST 5A
Air Bag Bus Communication Failure	[3] VEHICLE COMMUNICATIONS TEST 2A
Ambient Temperature Sensor Failure	OTIS TEST 2A
ATC Messages Not Received	[3] VEHICLE COMMUNICATIONS TEST 3A
ATC Switch Failure	1
Battery Power To Module Disconnected	[3] VEHICLE COMMUNICATIONS TEST 4A
BCM Bus Communication Failure	[3] VEHICLE COMMUNICATIONS TEST 4A
Blend Door Feedback Failure	1
Blend Door Output Shorted To Battery	1
Blend Door Output Shorted To Ground	1
Blend Door Stall Test Failure	1
Bus Shorted To Battery	[3] VEHICLE COMMUNICATIONS TEST 13A
Bus Shorted To Ground	[3] VEHICLE COMMUNICATIONS TEST 14A
Common Output Shorted To Battery	1
Common Output Shorted To Ground	1
Courtesy Lamp Output Short To Battery	INTERIOR LIGHT TEST 2A
Decklid Release Motor Output Failure	POWER DOOR LOCK TEST 18A
Decklid Release Switch Failure	POWER DOOR LOCK TEST 17A
Dimming Level Switch Input Failure	INSTRUMENT CLUSTER TEST 3A
EATX Bus Comm Failure	[3] VEHICLE COMMUNICATIONS TEST 12A
EEPROM Constant Checksum Failure	1
Evaporator Temperature Sensor Failure	1
Fuel Level Sending Unit Failure	INSTRUMENT CLUSTER TEST 2A
Headlamp Switch Input Failure	EXTERIOR LIGHT TEST 2A
In-Car Temperature Sensor Failure	1
Internal Base/Premium Select Failure	2
I/P Illumination Failure	INSTRUMENT CLUSTER TEST 9A
Left Central Lock/Unlock Switch Failure	POWER DOOR LOCK TEST 13A

1999 ACCESSORIES & EQUIPMENT
Body Control Computer Tests
Concorde, Intrepid, LHS & 300M (Cont.)

CHRY
4-137

SCAN TOOL MESSAGE DIRECTORY (Cont.)

Scan Tool Display	Perform Test
MIC Messages Not Received	[3] VEHICLE COMMUNICATIONS TEST 6A
Mode Door Feedback Failure	[1]
Mode Door Output Shorted To Battery	[1]
Mode Door Output Shorted To Ground	[1]
Mode Door Stall Test Failure	[1]
OTIS Messages Not Received	[3] VEHICLE COMMUNICATIONS TEST 8A
Post Failure	[2]
Recirc Door Output Shorted To Ground	[1]
Recirc Door Output Shorted To Battery	[1]
Recirculation Door Test Failure	[1]
Right Central Lock/Unlock Switch Failure	POWER DOOR LOCK TEST 14A
RKE Unable To Enter Program Mode	POWER DOOR LOCK TEST 15A
RKE Program Mode Entered Without Program Request	POWER DOOR LOCK TEST 16A
SBEC Bus Communication Failure	[3] VEHICLE COMMUNICATIONS TEST 9A
Speed Proportional Steering Circuit Open Or Shorted To Ground	SPEED PROPORTIONAL STEERING TEST 2A
Speed Proportional Steering Circuit Shorted To Battery	SPEED PROPORTIONAL STEERING TEST 3A
Speed Proportional Steering Solenoid Over Temperature	SPEED PROPORTIONAL STEERING TEST 4A
Sun Load Sensor Failure	[1]
Wiper On/Off Relay Output Short High	WIPER TEST 4A
Wiper On/Off Relay Output Open Or Short Low	WIPER TEST 2A
Wiper Park Switch Failure	WIPER TEST 3A

[1] – See appropriate MITCHELL® AIR CONDITIONING & HEATING SERVICE & REPAIR, DOMESTIC CARS, LIGHT TRUCKS & VANS manual.
[2] – Replace body control module.
[3] – See appropriate BODY CONTROL COMPUTER TESTS or VEHICLE COMMUNICATIONS article.

CHIME TEST 1A

DIAGNOSING CHIME SYSTEM

Diagnosis of chime (warning) system is separated into 4 categories. Identify problem area(s) listed in CHIME TEST DIAGNOSTIC DIRECTORY table and perform the indicated test(s).

CHIME TEST DIAGNOSTIC DIRECTORY

Problem	CHIME TEST
Chime Inoperative At All Times	2A
Chime Inoperative With Exterior Lamps On	3A
Chime Inoperative With Driver's Seat Belt Unfastened	4A
Chime Inoperative With Key In Ignition Switch	5A
Chime Beep Request Inoperative [1]	6A

[1] – Chime will sound a short "beep" when request is received from Overhead Travel Information System (OTIS) or Automatic Temperature Control (ATC).

CHIME TEST 2A

CHIME INOPERATIVE AT ALL TIMES

NOTE: *Perform CHIME TEST 1A before proceeding with this test. For connector terminal identification and wiring diagrams, see BODY CONTROL COMPUTER – INTRODUCTION article. Perform VERIFICATION TEST: VER-2A after each repair.*

CAUTION: *Always turn ignition off prior to disconnecting any module connector.*

1) Turn ignition on. Ensure all doors are closed. Using scan tool, actuate chime. If chime does not sound, replace Body Control Module (BCM). BCM is mounted to junction block located behind left end cap of instrument panel. See Fig. 1. If chime sounds, go to next step.
2) Using scan tool, stop actuating chime. Turn ignition off. Remove key from ignition switch. Turn headlights on and open left front door. If chime does not sound, go to CHIME TEST 3A. If chime sounds, go to next step.
3) Turn headlights off. Ensure left front seat belt is unfastened. Close left front door. Insert key in ignition switch. Turn ignition on. If chime does not sound, go to CHIME TEST 4A. If chime sounds, go to next step.

4) Turn ignition off. Leave key in ignition switch. Open left front door. If chime does not sound, go to CHIME TEST 5A. If chime sounds, go to next step.
5) Turn ignition on. Press any key on Overhead Travel Information System (OTIS) and Automatic Temperature Control (ATC). If chime does not sound, go to CHIME TEST 6A. If chime sounds, system is currently operating properly.

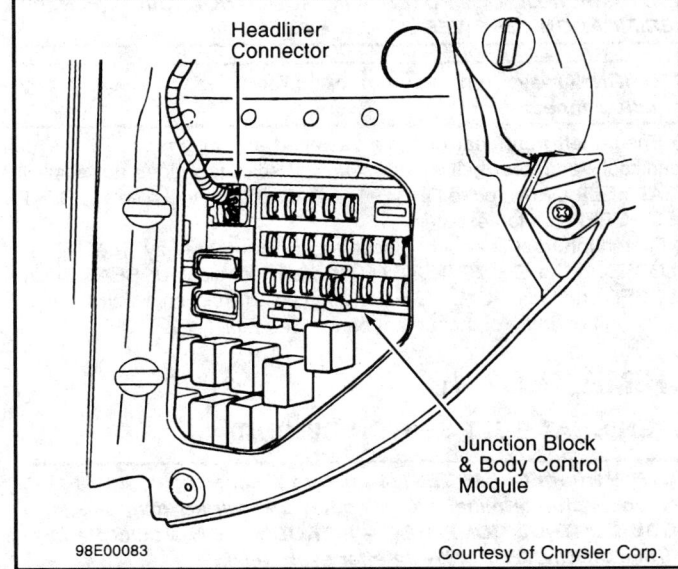

98E00083   Courtesy of Chrysler Corp.

Fig. 1: Identifying Junction Block/BCM Location

CHRY
4-138

1999 ACCESSORIES & EQUIPMENT
Body Control Computer Tests
Concorde, Intrepid, LHS & 300M (Cont.)

CHIME TEST 3A

CHIME INOPERATIVE WITH EXTERNAL LAMPS ON

NOTE: Perform CHIME TEST 1A before proceeding with this test. For connector terminal identification and wiring diagrams, see BODY CONTROL COMPUTER – INTRODUCTION article. Perform VERIFICATION TEST: VER-2A after each repair.

CAUTION: Always turn ignition off prior to disconnecting any module connector.

1) Turn headlights on. Using scan tool, read headlight status. If scan tool displays HEADLAMPS ON, go to step 3). If scan tool does not display HEADLAMPS ON, go to next step.
2) Turn headlights off. Turn ignition off. Disconnect Body Control Module (BCM) Black 24-pin connector. BCM is mounted to junction block located behind left end cap of instrument panel. *See Fig. 1.* Turn headlights on. Go to next step.
3) Using external ohmmeter, measure resistance between terminals No. 2 (Yellow wire) and 19 (White wire) on BCM Black harness connector. If resistance is 200-240 ohms, replace BCM. If resistance is not 200-240 ohms, go to EXTERIOR LIGHT TEST 1A.
4) Ensure left front door is open. Using scan tool, read left front door ajar switch status. If scan tool displays LFDOOR AJAR: CLOSED, replace BCM. If scan tool does not display LFDOOR AJAR: CLOSED, go to DOOR AJAR TEST 1A.

CHIME TEST 4A

CHIME INOPERATIVE WITH SEAT BELT UNFASTENED

NOTE: Perform CHIME TEST 1A before proceeding with this test. For connector terminal identification and wiring diagrams, see BODY CONTROL COMPUTER – INTRODUCTION article. Perform VERIFICATION TEST: VER-2A after each repair.

CAUTION: Always turn ignition off prior to disconnecting any module connector.

1) Ensure left front seat belt is unfastened and fully retracted. Using scan tool, read seat belt switch status. If scan tool does not display SEAT BELT: OPEN, go to CHIME TEST 4B. If scan tool displays SEAT BELT: OPEN, go to next step.
2) Fasten left front seat belt. If scan tool does not display SEAT BELT: CLOSED, go to CHIME TEST 4C. If scan tool displays SEAT BELT: CLOSED, replace BCM. BCM is mounted to junction block located behind left end cap of instrument panel. *See Fig. 1.*

CHIME TEST 4B

OPEN SEAT BELT SWITCH CIRCUIT

NOTE: Perform CHIME TEST 4A before proceeding with this test. For connector terminal identification and wiring diagrams, see BODY CONTROL COMPUTER – INTRODUCTION article. Perform VERIFICATION TEST: VER-2A after each repair.

CAUTION: Always turn ignition off prior to disconnecting any module connector.

1) Disconnect driver's seat belt switch connector. Connect jumper wire between harness connector terminals. Using scan tool, read seat belt switch status. If scan tool displays SEAT BELT: CLOSED, replace driver's seat belt switch. If scan tool does not display SEAT BELT: CLOSED, go to next step.
2) Move jumper wire lead from terminal No. 2 (Black wire) to chassis ground. Using scan tool, read seat belt switch status. If scan tool

displays SEAT BELT: CLOSED, repair open Black wire. If scan tool does not display SEAT BELT: CLOSED, go to next step.
3) Access Body Control Module (BCM). BCM is mounted to junction block located behind left end cap of instrument panel. *See Fig. 1.* Backprobe jumper wire between ground and terminal No. 15 (Light Green/Red wire) on BCM Blue 16-pin connector C4. Using scan tool, read seat belt switch status. If scan tool displays SEAT BELT: CLOSED, repair open Light Green/Red wire. If scan tool does not display SEAT BELT: CLOSED, replace BCM.

CHIME TEST 4C

OPEN SEAT BELT SWITCH CIRCUIT

NOTE: Perform CHIME TEST 4A before proceeding with this test. For connector terminal identification and wiring diagrams, see BODY CONTROL COMPUTER – INTRODUCTION article. Perform VERIFICATION TEST: VER-2A after each repair.

CAUTION: Always turn ignition off prior to disconnecting any module connector.

1) Turn ignition on. Ensure driver's seat belt is unfastened. Using scan tool, read seat belt switch status. If scan tool displays SEAT BELT: OPEN, go to next step. If scan tool does not display SEAT BELT: OPEN, go to CHIME TEST 4B.
2) Fasten driver's seat belt. Read seat belt switch status. If scan tool displays SEAT BELT: CLOSED, system is currently operating correctly. If scan tool does not display SEAT BELT: CLOSED, go to next step.
3) Disconnect driver's seat belt switch connector. Read seat belt switch status. If scan tool displays SEAT BELT: CLOSED, go to next step. If scan tool does not display SEAT BELT: CLOSED, replace driver's seat belt switch.
4) Turn ignition off. Disconnect Body Control Module (BCM) Blue 16-pin connector C4. BCM is mounted to junction block located behind left end cap of instrument panel. *See Fig. 1.* Using external ohmmeter, measure resistance between ground and terminal No. 15 (Light Green/Red wire) on BCM Blue harness connector. If resistance is less than 5 ohms, repair Light Green/Red wire for short to ground. If resistance is 5 ohms or greater, replace BCM.

CHIME TEST 5A

CHIME INOPERATIVE WITH KEY IN IGNITION

NOTE: Perform CHIME TEST 1A before proceeding with this test. For connector terminal identification and wiring diagrams, see BODY CONTROL COMPUTER – INTRODUCTION article. Perform VERIFICATION TEST: VER-2A after each repair.

CAUTION: Always turn ignition off prior to disconnecting any module connector.

1) Turn ignition on. Open driver's door. Using scan tool, read left front door ajar status. If scan tool does not display LF DOOR AJAR: CLOSED, go to DOOR AJAR TEST 1A. If scan tool displays LF DOOR AJAR: CLOSED, go to next step.
2) Using scan tool, read key-in ignition status. If scan tool displays KEY-IN IGN: CLOSED, replace Body Control Module (BCM). BCM is mounted to junction block located behind left end cap of instrument panel. *See Fig. 1.* If scan tool does not display KEY-IN IGN: CLOSE, go to next step.
3) Disconnect ignition switch connector. *See Fig. 2.* Using external ohmmeter, measure resistance between ground and terminal No. 3 (Black/Light Green wire) on ignition switch harness connector. If resistance is more than 5 ohms, repair open Black/Light Green wire. If resistance is 5 ohms or less, go to next step.
4) Connect jumper wire between terminals No. 2 (Light Blue wire) and No. 3 (Black/Light Green wire) on ignition switch connector. Using scan

1999 ACCESSORIES & EQUIPMENT
Body Control Computer Tests
Concorde, Intrepid, LHS & 300M (Cont.)

CHRY
4-139

tool, read KEY-IN ignition status. If scan tool displays KEY-IN IGN: CLOSED, replace ignition switch. If scan tool does not display KEY-IN IGN: CLOSED, go to next step.

5) Access BCM connectors. Do not disconnect connectors. Backprobe jumper wire between terminal No. 24 (Light Blue wire) on BCM Black 24-pin connector C2 and ground. Using scan tool, read KEY-IN ignition status. If scan tool displays KEY-IN IGN: CLOSED, repair open Light Blue wire. If scan tool does not display KEY-IN IGN: CLOSED, replace BCM.

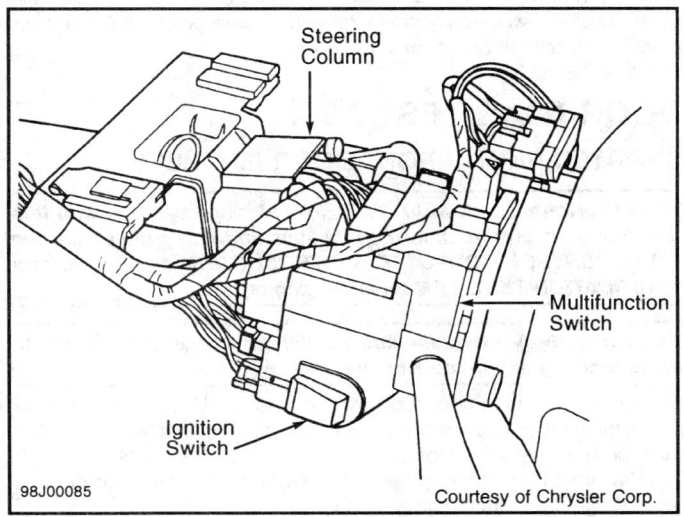

Fig. 2: Identifying Steering Column Component Connectors

CHIME TEST 6A

INOPERATIVE CHIME BEEP REQUEST

NOTE: Perform CHIME TEST 1A before proceeding with this test. For connector terminal identification and wiring diagrams, see BODY CONTROL COMPUTER – INTRODUCTION article. Perform VERIFICATION TEST: VER-2A after each repair.

CAUTION: Always turn ignition off prior to disconnecting any module connector.

1) Ensure vehicle is equipped with Overhead Travel Information System (OTIS) or Automatic Temperature Control (ATC). Turn ignition on. Using scan tool, check ID of Body Control Module (BCM). If communication with BCM is not possible, see appropriate VEHICLE COMMUNICATIONS article. If BCM communication is possible, go to next step.

2) Using scan tool, check ID of ATC and OTIS units. If communication with ATC and OTIS units is not possible, see appropriate VEHICLE COMMUNICATIONS article. If ATC and OTIS units communication is possible, go to next step.

3) Using scan tool, actuate chime test. If chime sounds, go to next step. If chime does not sound, replace BCM. BCM is mounted to junction block located behind left end cap of instrument panel. *See Fig. 1.*

4) Press any button on ATC or OTIS. If chime does not sound, replace ATC unit or OTIS unit (as applicable). If chime does sound, system is currently functioning correctly.

DOOR AJAR TEST 1A

IDENTIFYING DOOR AJAR PROBLEMS

NOTE: Perform SYMPTOM ID TEST 1A before proceeding with this test. For connector terminal identification and wiring diagrams, see BODY CONTROL COMPUTER – INTRODUCTION article. Perform VERIFICATION TEST: VER-2A after each repair.

CAUTION: Always turn ignition switch to OFF position prior to disconnecting any module connector.

1) Ensure all doors are closed and properly aligned. Using scan tool, enter BODY SYSTEM, then BODY COMPUTER. Select INPUTS/OUTPUTS. Observe door and decklid ajar switch status. Individually open and close all doors and decklid. Scan tool should display status opposite of actual door position.

2) If scan tool displays ajar switch status CLOSED when door is closed, perform appropriate SHORTED test. See DOOR AJAR SYMPTOM DIRECTORY table. If scan tool displays ajar switch status OPEN when door is open, perform appropriate OPEN test. See DOOR AJAR SYMPTOM DIRECTORY table.

DOOR AJAR SYMPTOM DIRECTORY

Problem Circuit	DOOR AJAR TEST
Open Driver's Door Ajar	2A
Shorted Driver's Door Ajar	3A
Open Left Rear Door Ajar	4A
Shorted Door Ajar [1]	5A
Open Right Front Door Ajar	6A
Open Right Rear Door Ajar	7A

[1] – All doors except driver's door.

DOOR AJAR TEST 2A

OPEN DRIVER'S DOOR AJAR CIRCUIT

NOTE: Perform DOOR AJAR TEST 1A before proceeding with this test. For connector terminal identification and wiring diagrams, see BODY CONTROL COMPUTER – INTRODUCTION article. Perform VERIFICATION TEST: VER-2A after each repair.

CAUTION: Always turn ignition switch to OFF position prior to disconnecting any module connector.

1) Disconnect driver's door ajar switch connector. Using external ohmmeter, measure resistance between ground and terminal No. 2 (Black wire) on harness connector. If resistance is less than 5 ohms, go to next step. If resistance is 5 ohms or greater, repair open Black wire.

2) Connect jumper wire between terminals No. 1 (Tan wire) and No. 2 (Black wire) on driver's door ajar switch harness connector. Using scan tool, read left front door ajar switch status. If scan tool displays LF DOOR AJAR SWITCH: CLOSED, replace driver's door latch assembly. If scan tool does not display LF DOOR AJAR SWITCH: CLOSED, go to next step.

3) Do not disconnect jumper wire. Disconnect Body Control Module (BCM) Blue 16-pin connector C4. BCM is mounted to junction block located behind left end cap of instrument panel. *See Fig. 1.* Using external ohmmeter, measure resistance between ground and terminal No. 4 (Tan wire) on BCM Blue connector. If resistance is less than 5 ohms, replace BCM. If resistance is 5 ohms or greater, repair open Tan wire.

CHRY
4-140

1999 ACCESSORIES & EQUIPMENT
Body Control Computer Tests
Concorde, Intrepid, LHS & 300M (Cont.)

DOOR AJAR TEST 3A

SHORTED LEFT REAR DOOR AJAR CIRCUIT

NOTE: Perform DOOR AJAR TEST 1A before proceeding with this test. For connector terminal identification and wiring diagrams, see BODY CONTROL COMPUTER – INTRODUCTION article. Perform VERIFICATION TEST: VER-2A after each repair.

CAUTION: Always turn ignition switch to OFF position prior to disconnecting any module connector.

1) Disconnect driver's door ajar switch connector. Using scan tool, read left front door ajar switch status. If scan tool displays LF DOOR AJAR SWITCH: CLOSED, go to next step. If scan tool does not display LF DOOR AJAR SWITCH: CLOSED, replace driver's door latch assembly.
2) Disconnect Body Control Module (BCM) Blue 16-pin connector C4. BCM is mounted to junction block located behind left end cap of instrument panel. *See Fig. 1.*

DOOR AJAR TEST 4A

OPEN LEFT REAR DOOR AJAR CIRCUIT

NOTE: Perform DOOR AJAR TEST 1A before proceeding with this test. For connector terminal identification and wiring diagrams, see BODY CONTROL COMPUTER – INTRODUCTION article. Perform VERIFICATION TEST: VER-2A after each repair.

CAUTION: Always turn ignition switch to OFF position prior to disconnecting any module connector.

1) Disconnect left rear door ajar switch connector. Using external ohmmeter, measure resistance between ground and terminal No. 2 (Black wire) on harness connector. If resistance is less than 5 ohms, go to next step. If resistance is 5 ohms or greater, repair open Black wire.
2) Connect jumper wire between terminals No. 1 (Tan/Red wire) and No. 2 (Black wire) on left rear door ajar switch harness connector. Using scan tool, read left rear door ajar switch status. If scan tool displays LR DOOR AJAR SWITCH: CLOSED, replace left rear door latch assembly. If scan tool does not display LR DOOR AJAR SWITCH: CLOSED, go to next step.
3) Do not disconnect jumper wire. Disconnect Body Control Module (BCM) Blue 16-pin connector C4. BCM is mounted to junction block located behind left end cap of instrument panel. *See Fig. 1.* Using external ohmmeter, measure resistance between ground and terminal No. 1 (Tan/Red wire) on BCM Blue connector. If resistance is less than 5 ohms, replace BCM. If resistance is 5 ohms or greater, repair open Tan/Red wire.

DOOR AJAR TEST 5A

SHORTED DOOR AJAR CIRCUIT

NOTE: Perform DOOR AJAR TEST 1A before proceeding with this test. For connector terminal identification and wiring diagrams, see BODY CONTROL COMPUTER – INTRODUCTION article. Perform VERIFICATION TEST: VER-2A after each repair.

CAUTION: Always turn ignition switch to OFF position prior to disconnecting any module connector.

1) Disconnect Body Control Module (BCM) Blue 16-pin connector C4. BCM is mounted to junction block located behind left end cap of instrument panel. *See Fig. 1.* Ensure all doors are closed. Using external ohmmeter, measure resistance between ground and terminal No. 2 (Tan/Red wire) on BCM Blue connector. If resistance is less than 5 ohms, go to DOOR AJAR TEST 5B. If resistance is 5 ohms of greater, go to next step.

2) Measure resistance between ground and terminal No. 10 (Tan/Red wire) on BCM Blue connector. If resistance is less than 5 ohms, go to DOOR AJAR TEST 5C. If resistance is 5 ohms or greater, go to next step.
3) Measure resistance between ground and terminal No. 1 (Tan/Red wire) on BCM Blue connector. If resistance is less than 5 ohms, go to next step. If resistance is 5 ohms or greater, replace BCM.
4) Disconnect left rear door ajar switch connector. Using external ohmmeter, measure resistance between ground and terminal No. 1 (Tan/Red wire) on harness connector. If resistance is less than 5 ohms, repair Tan/Red wire for short to ground. If resistance is 5 ohms or greater, replace left rear door latch assembly.

DOOR AJAR TEST 5B

SHORTED RIGHT FRONT DOOR AJAR CIRCUIT

NOTE: Perform DOOR AJAR TEST 5A before proceeding with this test. For connector terminal identification and wiring diagrams, see BODY CONTROL COMPUTER – INTRODUCTION article. Perform VERIFICATION TEST: VER-2A after each repair.

CAUTION: Always turn ignition switch to OFF position prior to disconnecting any module connector.

Disconnect right front door ajar switch connector. Using external ohmmeter, measure resistance between ground and terminal No. 1 (Tan/Red wire) on harness connector. If resistance is less than 5 ohms, repair Tan/Red wire for short to ground. If resistance is 5 ohms or greater, replace right front door latch assembly.

DOOR AJAR TEST 5C

SHORTED RIGHT REAR DOOR AJAR CIRCUIT

NOTE: Perform DOOR AJAR TEST 5A before proceeding with this test. For connector terminal identification and wiring diagrams, see BODY CONTROL COMPUTER – INTRODUCTION article. Perform VERIFICATION TEST: VER-2A after each repair.

CAUTION: Always turn ignition switch to OFF position prior to disconnecting any module connector.

Disconnect right rear door ajar switch connector. Using external ohmmeter, measure resistance between ground and terminal No. 1 (Tan/Red wire) on harness connector. If resistance is less than 5 ohms, repair Tan/Red wire for short to ground. If resistance is 5 ohms or greater, replace right rear door latch assembly.

DOOR AJAR TEST 6A

OPEN RIGHT FRONT DOOR AJAR CIRCUIT

NOTE: Perform DOOR AJAR TEST 1A before proceeding with this test. For connector terminal identification and wiring diagrams, see BODY CONTROL COMPUTER – INTRODUCTION article. Perform VERIFICATION TEST: VER-2A after each repair.

CAUTION: Always turn ignition switch to OFF position prior to disconnecting any module connector.

1) Disconnect right front door ajar switch connector. Using external ohmmeter, measure resistance between ground and terminal No. 2 (Black wire) on harness connector. If resistance is less than 5 ohms, go to next step. If resistance is 5 ohms or greater, repair open Black wire.
2) Connect jumper wire between terminals No. 1 (Tan/Red wire) and No. 2 (Black wire) on right front door ajar switch harness connector. Using scan tool, read right front door ajar switch status. If scan tool displays RF

1999 ACCESSORIES & EQUIPMENT
Body Control Computer Tests
Concorde, Intrepid, LHS & 300M (Cont.)

CHRY
4-141

DOOR AJAR SWITCH: CLOSED, replace right front door latch assembly. If scan tool does not display RF DOOR AJAR SWITCH: CLOSED, go to next step.

3) Do not disconnect jumper wire. Disconnect Body Control Module (BCM) Blue 16-pin connector C4. BCM is mounted to junction block located behind left end cap of instrument panel. *See Fig. 1.* Using external ohmmeter, measure resistance between ground and terminal No. 2 (Tan/Red wire) on BCM Blue connector. If resistance is less than 5 ohms, replace BCM. If resistance is 5 ohms or greater, repair open Tan/Red wire.

DOOR AJAR TEST 7A

OPEN RIGHT REAR DOOR AJAR CIRCUIT

NOTE: Perform DOOR AJAR TEST 1A before proceeding with this test. For connector terminal identification and wiring diagrams, see BODY CONTROL COMPUTER – INTRODUCTION article. Perform VERIFICATION TEST: VER-2A after each repair.

CAUTION: Always turn ignition switch to OFF position prior to disconnecting any module connector.

1) Disconnect right rear door ajar switch connector. Using external ohmmeter, measure resistance between ground and terminal No. 2 (Black wire) on harness connector. If resistance is less than 5 ohms, go to next step. If resistance is 5 ohms or greater, repair open Black wire.

2) Connect jumper wire between terminals No. 1 (Tan/Red wire) and No. 2 (Black wire) on right rear door ajar switch harness connector. Using scan tool, read right rear door ajar switch status. If scan tool displays RR DOOR AJAR SWITCH: CLOSED, replace right rear door latch assembly. If scan tool does not display RR DOOR AJAR SWITCH: CLOSED, go to next step.

3) Do not disconnect jumper wire. Disconnect Body Control Module (BCM) Blue 16-pin connector C4. BCM is mounted to junction block located behind left end cap of instrument panel. *See Fig. 1.* Using external ohmmeter, measure resistance between ground and terminal No. 10 (Tan/Red wire) on BCM Blue connector. If resistance is less than 5 ohms, replace BCM. If resistance is 5 ohms or greater, repair open Tan/Red wire.

EXTERIOR LIGHT TEST 1A

IDENTIFYING EXTERIOR LIGHTING SYSTEM PROBLEMS

NOTE: Perform SYMPTOM ID TEST 1A before proceeding with this test. For connector terminal identification and wiring diagrams, see BODY CONTROL COMPUTER – INTRODUCTION. Perform VERIFICATION TEST: VER-2A after each repair.

CAUTION: Always turn ignition switch to OFF position prior to disconnecting or connecting any module connector.

Using scan tool, select READ DTCs. If scan tool displays HEADLAMP SWITCH INPUT FAILURE, go to EXTERIOR LIGHT TEST 2A. If scan tool does not display HEADLAMP SWITCH INPUT FAILURE, go to EXTERIOR LIGHT SYSTEM DIAGNOSTIC TEST DIRECTORY.

EXTERIOR LIGHT SYSTEM DIAGNOSTIC TEST DIRECTORY

Problem	EXTERIOR LIGHT TEST
Low Beam Headlights Will Not Turn On	3A
Low Beam Headlights Will Not Turn Off	4A
Parking Lights Will Not Turn On	5A
Parking Lights Will Not Turn Off	6A
High Beam Headlights Will Not Turn On	7A
High Beam Headlights Will Not Turn Off	8A
Fog Lights Will Not Turn On	9A
Fog Lights Will Not Turn Off	10A
Headlight Time Delay	11A
Auto Headlights And/Or Fog Lights Not Operating Properly	12A

EXTERIOR LIGHT TEST 2A

HEADLIGHT SWITCH INPUT FAILURE

NOTE: Perform EXTERIOR LIGHT TEST 1A before proceeding with this test. For connector terminal identification and wiring diagrams, see BODY CONTROL COMPUTER – INTRODUCTION. Perform VERIFICATION TEST: VER-2A after each repair.

CAUTION: Always turn ignition switch to OFF position prior to disconnecting or connecting any module connector.

1) Ensure headlight switch is in OFF position. Using scan tool, select SENSORS. Read headlight switch voltage. If scan tool displays HEADLIGHT SWITCH VOLTAGE: 5 volts, go to next step. If scan tool does not display HEADLIGHT SWITCH VOLTAGE: 5 volts, go to EXTERIOR LIGHT TEST 2B.

2) Disconnect headlight switch 13-pin connector. Connect jumper wire between terminals No. 6 (White wire) and No. 12 (Yellow wire) on headlight switch harness connector. Read headlight switch voltage. If scan tool displays HEADLIGHT SWITCH VOLTAGE: 0.0 volts, replace headlight switch. If scan tool does not display HEADLIGHT SWITCH VOLTAGE: 0.0 volts, go to next step.

3) Remove jumper wire. Connect jumper wire between ground and terminal No. 12 (Yellow wire) on headlight switch 13-pin harness connector. Read headlight switch voltage. If scan tool displays HEADLIGHT SWITCH VOLTAGE: 0.0 volts, go to step **5)**. If scan tool does not display HEADLIGHT SWITCH VOLTAGE: 0.0 volts, go to next step.

4) Disconnect Body Control Module (BCM) Black 24-pin connector C2. BCM is mounted to junction block located behind left end cap of instrument panel. *See Fig. 1.*

5) Disconnect Body Control Module (BCM) Black 24-pin connector C2. BCM is mounted to junction block located behind left end cap of instrument panel. *See Fig. 1.*

6) Remove BCM from junction block. Inspect internal 20-pin connector. Repair as needed. If connector is okay, replace BCM.

EXTERIOR LIGHT TEST 2B

HEADLIGHT SWITCH INPUT FAILURE

NOTE: Perform EXTERIOR LIGHT TEST 2A before proceeding with this test. For connector terminal identification and wiring diagrams, see BODY CONTROL COMPUTER – INTRODUCTION. Perform VERIFICATION TEST: VER-2A after each repair.

CAUTION: Always turn ignition switch to OFF position prior to disconnecting or connecting any module connector.

1) Disconnect headlight switch 13-pin connector. Read headlight switch voltage. If scan tool displays HEADLIGHT SWITCH VOLTAGE: 5 volts, replace headlight switch. If scan tool does not display HEADLIGHT SWITCH VOLTAGE: 5 volts, go to next step.

2) Disconnect Body Control Module (BCM) Black 24-pin connector C2. BCM is mounted to junction block located behind left end cap of instrument panel. *See Fig. 1.*

CHRY
4-142

1999 ACCESSORIES & EQUIPMENT
Body Control Computer Tests
Concorde, Intrepid, LHS & 300M (Cont.)

EXTERIOR LIGHT TEST 3A

LOW BEAM HEADLIGHTS WILL NOT TURN ON

NOTE: *Perform EXTERIOR LIGHT TEST 1A before proceeding with this test. For connector terminal identification and wiring diagrams, see BODY CONTROL COMPUTER – INTRODUCTION. Perform VERIFICATION TEST: VER-2A after each repair.*

CAUTION: *Always turn ignition switch to OFF position prior to disconnecting or connecting any module connector.*

1) Turn on low beam headlights. If both headlights are not illuminated, go to EXTERIOR LIGHT TEST 3B. If one low beam headlight is not illuminated, go to next step.
2) Remove and inspect fuses No. 10 (right low beam headlight) and No. 12 (left low beam headlight) from junction block. *See Fig. 3*. Junction block is located behind left end cap of instrument panel. *See Fig. 1*. If fuse is open, go to step 5). If fuse is okay, install fuse and go to next step.
3) Disconnect inoperative headlight connector. Using external voltmeter, measure voltage between ground and terminal "A" (Violet or Violet/Red wire) on headlight harness connector. If voltage is 10 volts or less, repair open Violet or Violet/Red wire. If voltage is greater than 10 volts, go to next step.
4) Turn off headlights. Using external ohmmeter, measure resistance between ground and terminal "B" (Black wire) on headlight harness connector. If resistance is less than 5 ohms, replace headlight. If resistance is 5 ohms or greater, repair open Black wire.
5) Replace fuse. If headlight illuminates without blowing fuse, repair is complete. If fuse blows, go to next step.
6) Disconnect inoperative headlight connector. Using external ohmmeter, measure resistance between ground and terminal "A" (Violet or Violet/Red wire) on headlight harness connector. If resistance is less than 5 ohms, repair Violet or Violet/Red wire for short to ground. If resistance is 5 ohms or greater, replace headlight bulb.

EXTERIOR LIGHT TEST 3B

LOW BEAM HEADLIGHTS WILL NOT TURN ON

NOTE: *Perform EXTERIOR LIGHT TEST 3A before proceeding with this test. For connector terminal identification and wiring diagrams, see BODY CONTROL COMPUTER – INTRODUCTION. Perform VERIFICATION TEST: VER-2A after each repair.*

CAUTION: *Always turn ignition switch to OFF position prior to disconnecting or connecting any module connector.*

1) Turn headlights on. Ensure fog lights are off. Using scan tool, read headlight switch voltage. If scan tool does not display HEADLIGHT SWITCH VOLTAGE: 1.6 volts (approximately), replace headlight switch. If scan tool displays HEADLIGHT SWITCH VOLTAGE: 1.6 volts (approximately), go to next step.
2) Using scan tool, actuate headlight relay. If relay can be heard clicking during actuation, go to next step. If relay cannot be heard during actuation, go to EXTERIOR LIGHT TEST 3C.
3) Remove low beam relay from junction block. *See Fig. 3*. Using external voltmeter, measure voltage between ground and terminal "D" (fused B+ circuit) on relay socket. If voltage is 10 volts or less, repair open fused B+ circuit. If voltage is greater than 10 volts, go to next step.
4) Connect jumper wire between terminals "B" (low beam relay output circuit) and "D" on low beam relay socket. If headlights illuminate, replace low beam relay. If headlights do not illuminate, repair open low beam relay output circuit.

EXTERIOR LIGHT TEST 3C

LOW BEAM HEADLIGHTS WILL NOT TURN ON

NOTE: *Perform EXTERIOR LIGHT TEST 3A before proceeding with this test. For connector terminal identification and wiring diagrams, see BODY CONTROL COMPUTER – INTRODUCTION. Perform VERIFICATION TEST: VER-2A after each repair.*

CAUTION: *Always turn ignition switch to OFF position prior to disconnecting or connecting any module connector.*

1) Stop headlight actuation. Remove low beam relay from junction block. *See Fig. 3*. Using external voltmeter, measure voltage between ground and terminal "C" (fused B+ circuit) on relay socket. If voltage is 10 volts or less, repair open fused B+ circuit. If voltage is greater than 10 volts, go to next step.
2) Connect test light between terminals "A" (low beam relay control) and "C". Using scan tool, actuate low beam headlight relay. If test light flashes, replace low beam headlight relay. If test light does not flash, go to next step.
3) Remove Body Control Module (BCM) from junction block. BCM is mounted to junction block located behind left end cap of instrument panel. *See Fig. 1*.

EXTERIOR LIGHT TEST 4A

LOW BEAM HEADLIGHTS WILL NOT TURN OFF

NOTE: *Perform EXTERIOR LIGHT TEST 1A before proceeding with this test. For connector terminal identification and wiring diagrams, see BODY CONTROL COMPUTER – INTRODUCTION. Perform VERIFICATION TEST: VER-2A after each repair.*

CAUTION: *Always turn ignition switch to OFF position prior to disconnecting or connecting any module connector.*

1) Ensure headlight switch is in OFF position. Using scan tool, select SENSORS. Read headlight switch voltage. If scan tool does not display HEADLIGHT SWITCH VOLTAGE: 4.5 volts (approximately), replace headlight switch. If scan tool displays HEADLIGHT SWITCH VOLTAGE: 4.5 volts (approximately), go to next step.
2) Remove low beam relay from junction block. *See Fig. 3*. If low beam headlights are not illuminated, go to next step. If low beam headlights are illuminated, repair low beam relay output circuit for short to voltage.
3) Monitoring relay for clicking sound, install low beam relay in junction block. If clicking sound exists, replace Body Control Module (BCM). BCM is mounted to junction block located behind left end cap of instrument panel. *See Fig. 1*.

EXTERIOR LIGHT TEST 5A

PARKING LIGHTS WILL NOT TURN ON

NOTE: *Perform EXTERIOR LIGHT TEST 1A before proceeding with this test. For connector terminal identification and wiring diagrams, see BODY CONTROL COMPUTER – INTRODUCTION. Perform VERIFICATION TEST: VER-2A after each repair.*

CAUTION: *Always turn ignition switch to OFF position prior to disconnecting or connecting any module connector.*

1) Ensure headlight switch is in PARK position. Using scan tool, select SENSORS. Read headlight switch voltage. If scan tool does not display HEADLIGHT SWITCH VOLTAGE: .45 volts (approximately), replace headlight switch. If scan tool displays HEADLIGHT SWITCH VOLTAGE: .45 volts (approximately), go to next step.
2) Using scan tool, actuate parking light relay. If relay can be heard clicking during actuation, go to next step. If relay cannot be heard during actuation, go to step 5).

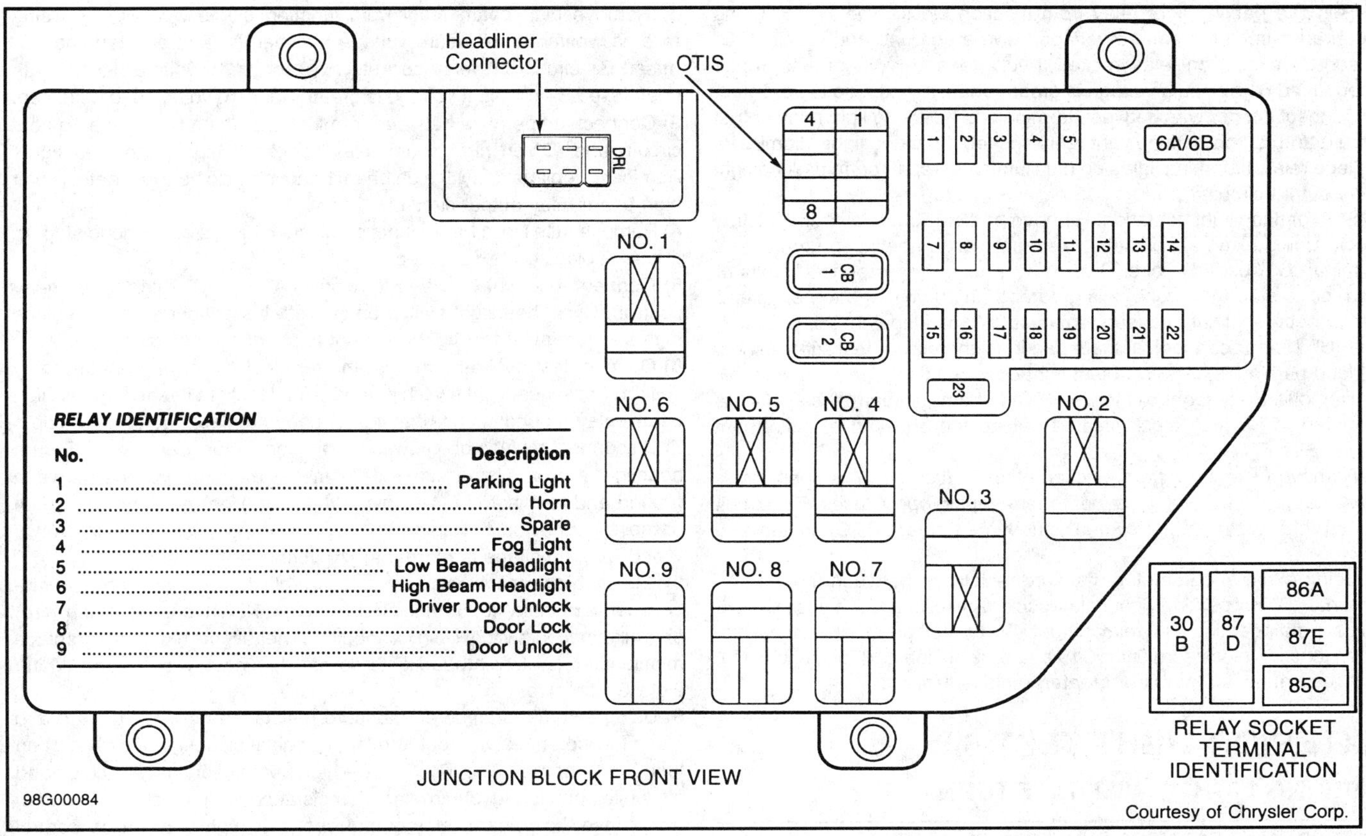

1999 ACCESSORIES & EQUIPMENT
Body Control Computer Tests
Concorde, Intrepid, LHS & 300M (Cont.)

CHRY
4-143

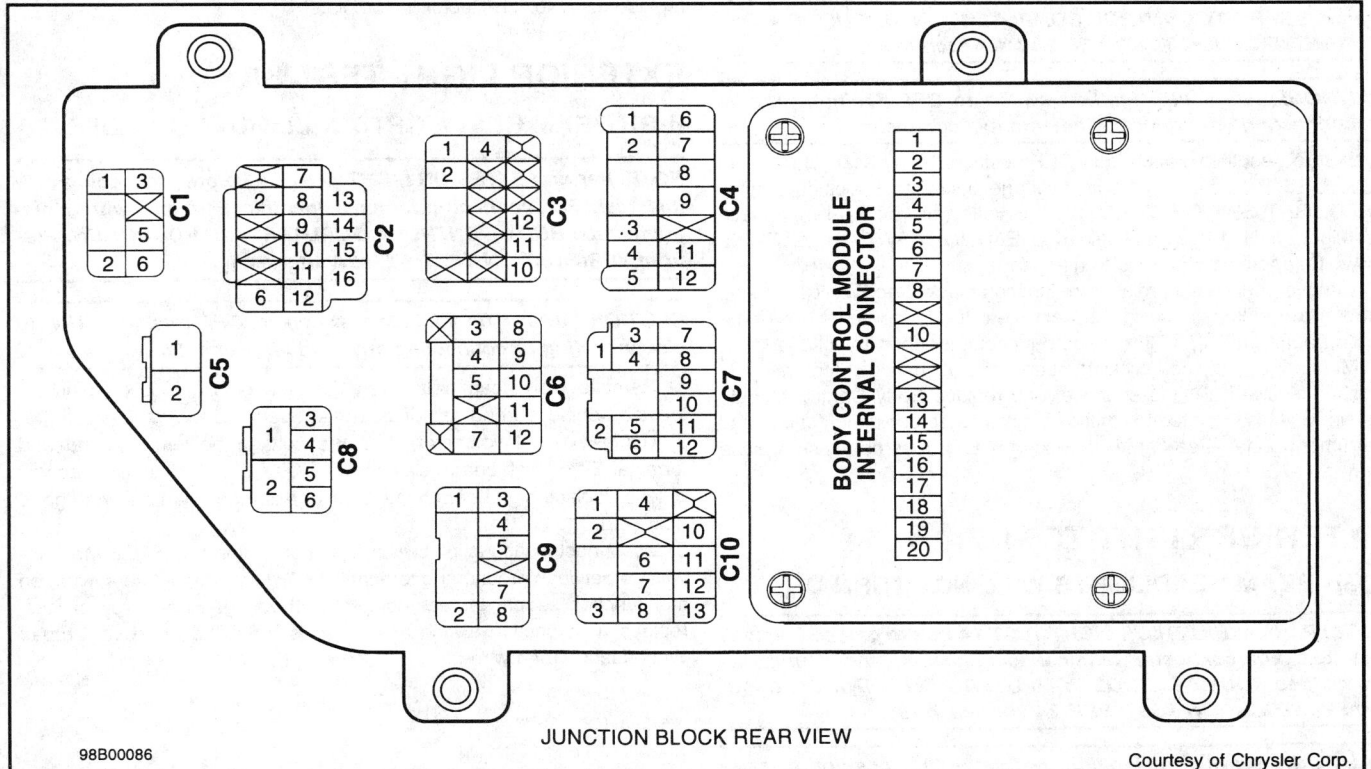

RELAY IDENTIFICATION

No.	Description
1	Parking Light
2	Horn
3	Spare
4	Fog Light
5	Low Beam Headlight
6	High Beam Headlight
7	Driver Door Unlock
8	Door Lock
9	Door Unlock

JUNCTION BLOCK FRONT VIEW

RELAY SOCKET TERMINAL IDENTIFICATION

98G00084

Courtesy of Chrysler Corp.

Fig. 3: Identifying BCM/Junction Block Components & Terminals

JUNCTION BLOCK REAR VIEW

98B00086

Courtesy of Chrysler Corp.

Fig. 4: Locating BCM/Junction Block Connectors

CHRY
4-144

1999 ACCESSORIES & EQUIPMENT
Body Control Computer Tests
Concorde, Intrepid, LHS & 300M (Cont.)

3) Remove parking light relay from junction block. *See Fig. 3.* Using external voltmeter, measure voltage between ground and terminal "D" (fused B+ circuit) on relay socket. If voltage is 10 volts or less, repair open fused B+ circuit. If voltage is greater than 10 volts, go to next step.

4) Connect jumper wire between terminals "B" (parking light relay output circuit) and "D" on parking light relay socket. If parking lights illuminate, replace relay. If parking lights do not illuminate, repair open parking light relay output circuit.

5) Stop parking light actuation. Remove parking light relay from junction block. Using external voltmeter, measure voltage between ground and terminal "C" (fused B+ circuit) on relay socket. If voltage is 10 volts or less, go to step **8)**. If voltage is greater than 10 volts, go to next step.

6) Connect test light between terminals "A" (parking light relay control) and "C". Using scan tool, actuate parking light relay. If test light flashes, replace parking light relay. If test light does not flash, go to next step.

7) Remove Body Control Module (BCM) from junction block. BCM is mounted to junction block located behind left end cap of instrument panel. *See Fig. 1.*

8) Remove fuse No. 7 from junction block. If fuse No. 7 is open, go to next step. If fuse No. 7 is not open, repair open fused B+ circuit (Pink/White wire) from Power Distribution Center (PDC) to junction block.

9) Using external ohmmeter, measure resistance between ground and terminal "B" on parking light relay socket. If resistance is less than 5 ohms, repair parking light relay output short circuit between terminal No. 11 on junction block connector C10 and parking lights. Replace fuse No. 7. If resistance is 5 ohms or greater, replace fuse No. 7.

EXTERIOR LIGHT TEST 6A

PARKING LIGHTS WILL NOT TURN OFF

NOTE: Perform EXTERIOR LIGHT TEST 1A before proceeding with this test. For connector terminal identification and wiring diagrams, see BODY CONTROL COMPUTER – INTRODUCTION. Perform VERIFICATION TEST: VER-2A after each repair.

CAUTION: Always turn ignition switch to OFF position prior to disconnecting or connecting any module connector.

1) Ensure headlight switch is in OFF position. Using scan tool, select SENSORS. Read headlight switch voltage. If scan tool does not display HEADLIGHT SWITCH VOLTAGE: 4.5 volts (approximately), replace headlight switch. If scan tool displays HEADLIGHT SWITCH VOLTAGE: 4.5 volts (approximately), go to next step.

2) Remove parking light relay from junction block. *See Fig. 3.* If parking lights are not illuminated, go to next step. If parking lights are illuminated, repair parking light relay output circuit for short to voltage.

3) Monitoring relay for clicking sound, install parking light relay in junction block. If clicking sound exists, replace Body Control Module (BCM). BCM is mounted to junction block located behind left end cap of instrument panel. *See Fig. 1.* If clicking sound does not exist, replace relay.

EXTERIOR LIGHT TEST 7A

HIGH BEAM HEADLIGHTS WILL NOT TURN ON

NOTE: Perform EXTERIOR LIGHT TEST 1A before proceeding with this test. For connector terminal identification and wiring diagrams, see BODY CONTROL COMPUTER – INTRODUCTION. Perform VERIFICATION TEST: VER-2A after each repair.

CAUTION: Always turn ignition switch to OFF position prior to disconnecting or connecting any module connector.

1) Access high beam headlight relay in junction block. Junction block is located behind left end cap of instrument panel. *See Fig. 1.*

2) Remove high beam relay from junction block. *See Fig. 3.* Using external voltmeter, measure voltage between ground and terminal "D" (fused B+ circuit) on relay socket. If voltage is 10 volts or less, repair open fused B+ circuit. If voltage is greater than 10 volts, go to next step.

3) Connect jumper wire between terminals "B" (high beam relay output circuit) and "D" on high beam relay socket. If high beam headlights illuminate, replace relay. If high beam headlights do not illuminate, repair high beam relay output circuit.

4) Remove fuse No. 11 from junction block. If fuse is open, go to step **9)**. If fuse is okay, go to next step.

5) Connect test light between terminals "A" and "C" (high beam relay control). Cycle headlight switch on and off. If test light flashes, replace high beam relay. If test light does not flash, go to next step.

6) Connect test between ground and terminal "C" on high beam relay socket. Cycle headlight switch on and off. If test light flashes, repair high beam relay ground circuit. If test light does not flash, go to next step.

7) Disconnect multifunction switch 7-pin connector. *See Fig. 2.* Ensure headlight are on. Using external voltmeter, measure voltage between ground and terminal No. 4 (Brown/White wire) on multifunction switch harness connector. If voltage is 10 volts or less, repair open Brown/White wire. If voltage is more than 10 volts, go to next step.

8) Install high beam relay in junction block. Connect jumper wire between terminals No. 5 (Pink/Red wire) and 7 (White/Light Green wire) on multifunction switch 7-pin connector. If headlights illuminate, replace multifunction switch. If headlights do not illuminate, repair open White/Light Green wire.

9) Using external ohmmeter, measure resistance between ground and fused low beam relay output terminal (terminal closest to fuse No. 5) on fuse No. 11 socket. *See Fig. 3.* Cycle high beam headlight switch on and off while monitoring ohmmeter. If resistance drops below 10 ohms, repair fused low beam relay output circuit or high beam relay control circuit for short to ground. If resistance does not drop below 10 ohms, replace fuse No. 11. Repair is complete.

EXTERIOR LIGHT TEST 8A

HIGH BEAM HEADLIGHTS WILL NOT TURN OFF

NOTE: Perform EXTERIOR LIGHT TEST 1A before proceeding with this test. For connector terminal identification and wiring diagrams, see BODY CONTROL COMPUTER – INTRODUCTION. Perform VERIFICATION TEST: VER-2A after each repair.

CAUTION: Always turn ignition switch to OFF position prior to disconnecting or connecting any module connector.

1) Remove high beam relay from junction block. Junction block is located behind left end cap of instrument panel. *See Fig. 1.*

2) Using external voltmeter, measure voltage between ground and terminal "C" on high beam relay socket. *See Fig. 3.* If voltage is one volt or less, replace high beam relay. If voltage is more than one volt, go to next step.

3) Disconnect multifunction switch 7-pin connector. *See Fig. 2.* Measure voltage between ground and terminal No. 7 (White/Light Green wire) on multifunction switch harness connector. If voltage is one volt or less, replace multifunction switch. If voltage is more than one volt, repair White/Light Green wire for short to voltage.

1999 ACCESSORIES & EQUIPMENT
Body Control Computer Tests
Concorde, Intrepid, LHS & 300M (Cont.)

CHRY
4-145

EXTERIOR LIGHT TEST 9A

FOG LIGHTS WILL NOT TURN ON

NOTE: Perform EXTERIOR LIGHT TEST 1A before proceeding with this test. For connector terminal identification and wiring diagrams, see BODY CONTROL COMPUTER – INTRODUCTION. Perform VERIFICATION TEST: VER-2A after each repair.

CAUTION: Always turn ignition switch to OFF position prior to disconnecting or connecting any module connector.

1) Turn fog light on with headlights on. Using scan tool, select SENSORS. Read headlight switch voltage. If scan tool does not display HEADLIGHT SWITCH VOLTAGE: 3.0 volts (approximately), replace headlight switch. If scan tool displays HEADLIGHT SWITCH VOLTAGE: 3.0 volts (approximately), go to next step.

2) Using scan tool, actuate fog light relay. If relay can be heard clicking during actuation, go to next step. If relay cannot be heard during actuation, go to step **5)**.

3) Remove fog light relay from junction block. *See Fig. 3.* Using external voltmeter, measure voltage between ground and terminal "D" (fused B+ circuit) on relay socket. If voltage is 10 volts or less, replace junction block. If voltage is greater than 10 volts, go to next step.

4) Connect jumper wire between terminals "B" (low beam relay output circuit) and "D" on fog light relay socket. If fog lights illuminate, replace relay. If fog lights do not illuminate, repair open fog light relay output circuit.

5) Stop fog light actuation. Turn on headlights and attempt to turn on high beam headlights. If high beam headlights operate, go to next step. If high beam headlights do not operate, repair open fused B+ circuit from Power Distribution Center fuse "C".

6) Inspect junction block fuse No. 16. If fuse is open, go to step **10)**. If fuse is okay, go to next step.

7) Remove fog light relay from junction block. Using external voltmeter, measure voltage between ground and terminal "C" (fused B+ circuit) on relay socket. If voltage is 10 volts or less, repair open fused B+ circuit. If voltage is more than 10 volts, go to next step.

8) Connect test light between terminals "A" and "C" on fog light relay socket. Using scan tool, actuate fog light relay. If test light flashes, replace relay. If test light does not flash, go to next step.

9) Remove Body Control Module (BCM) from junction block. BCM is mounted to junction block located behind left end cap of instrument panel. *See Fig. 1.*

10) Remove fog light relay. Using external ohmmeter, measure resistance between ground and terminal "B" on relay socket. If resistance is less than 10 ohms, repair shorted fused B+ circuit. Replace fuse No. 16. If resistance is 10 ohms or greater, replace fuse No. 16.

EXTERIOR LIGHT TEST 10A

FOG LIGHTS WILL NOT TURN OFF

NOTE: Perform EXTERIOR LIGHT TEST 1A before proceeding with this test. For connector terminal identification and wiring diagrams, see BODY CONTROL COMPUTER – INTRODUCTION. Perform VERIFICATION TEST: VER-2A after each repair.

CAUTION: Always turn ignition switch to OFF position prior to disconnecting or connecting any module connector.

1) Ensure headlight switch is in OFF position. Using scan tool, select SENSORS. Read headlight switch voltage. If scan tool displays HEADLAMP SWITCH VOLTAGE: 4.5 VOLTS, go to next step. If scan tool does not display HEADLAMP SWITCH VOLTAGE: 4.5 VOLTS, replace headlight switch.

2) Remove fog light relay from junction block. *See Fig. 3.* Junction block is located behind left end cap of instrument panel. *See Fig. 1.* If fog lights

are not illuminated, repair fog light relay output circuit for short to voltage. If fog lights are illuminated, go to next step.

3) Monitoring relay for clicking sound, install fog light relay in junction block. If clicking sound exists, replace Body Control Module (BCM). BCM is mounted to junction block located behind left end cap of instrument panel. *See Fig. 1.*

EXTERIOR LIGHT TEST 11A

HEADLIGHT TIME DELAY

NOTE: Perform EXTERIOR LIGHT TEST 1A before proceeding with this test. For connector terminal identification and wiring diagrams, see BODY CONTROL COMPUTER – INTRODUCTION. Perform VERIFICATION TEST: VER-2A after each repair.

CAUTION: Always turn ignition switch to OFF position prior to disconnecting or connecting any module connector.

If headlights do not operate correctly, go to EXTERIOR LIGHT TEST 1A. If headlights do operate correctly, turn ignition on. Using scan tool, select SENSORS. Read IGNITION VOLTAGE. If scan tool displays battery voltage, replace Body Control Module (BCM). BCM is mounted to junction block located behind left end cap of instrument panel. *See Fig. 1.*

EXTERIOR LIGHT TEST 12A

AUTO HEADLIGHTS AND/OR FOG LIGHTS NOT OPERATING PROPERLY

NOTE: Perform EXTERIOR LIGHT TEST 1A before proceeding with this test. For connector terminal identification and wiring diagrams, see BODY CONTROL COMPUTER – INTRODUCTION. Perform VERIFICATION TEST: VER-2A after each repair.

CAUTION: Always turn ignition switch to OFF position prior to disconnecting or connecting any module connector.

NOTE: Following test assumes that headlight and fog light systems are functioning correctly in manual mode.

1) Ensure headlight switch is in auto headlight IN position. Using scan tool, select BODY COMPUTER, then SENSORS. Read HEADLAMP SWITCH VOLTAGE. If voltage is about 2.3 volts, go to next step. If voltage is not about 2.3 volts, replace headlight switch.

2) Pull headlight switch knob out to fog light auto mode. Read HEADLAMP SWITCH VOLTAGE. If voltage is about 3.7 volts, go to next step. If voltage is not about 3.7 volts, replace

3) Shine light on sun sensor. Using scan tool, read AUTO HEADLAMP SENSOR volts. If AUTO HEADLAMP SENSOR voltage is about zero volts, go to next step. If AUTO HEADLAMP SENSOR voltage is not about zero volts, go to step **5)**.

4) Cover up sun sensor. Read AUTO HEADLAMP SENSOR volts. If AUTO HEADLAMP SENSOR voltage is about 5 volts, replace Body Control Module (BCM). BCM is mounted to junction block located behind left end cap of instrument panel. *See Fig. 1.* If AUTO HEADLAMP SENSOR voltage is not about 5 volts, go to step **5)**.

5) Disconnect sun sensor 4-pin connector. Read AUTO HEADLAMP SENSOR volts. If AUTO HEADLAMP SENSOR voltage is about 5 volts, go to next step. If AUTO HEADLAMP SENSOR voltage is not about 5 volts, go to step **8)**.

6) Connect jumper wire between terminals No. 3 and 4 on sun sensor harness connector. Read AUTO HEADLAMP SENSOR volts. If AUTO HEADLAMP SENSOR voltage is about zero volts, replace sun sensor. If AUTO HEADLAMP SENSOR voltage is not about zero volts, remove jumper wire and go to next step.

7) Connect jumper wire between ground and terminal No. 4 on sun sensor harness connector. Read AUTO HEADLAMP SENSOR volts. If

1999 ACCESSORIES & EQUIPMENT
Body Control Computer Tests
Concorde, Intrepid, LHS & 300M (Cont.)

AUTO HEADLAMP SENSOR voltage is about zero volts, repair open ground circuit. If AUTO HEADLAMP SENSOR voltage is not about zero volts, repair open sun sensor signal circuit.

8) Disconnect Body Control Module (BCM) 24-pin Black connector C2. BCM is mounted to junction block located behind left end cap of instrument panel. *See Fig. 1.* Using ohmmeter, measure resistance between ground and terminal No. 4 (Dark Blue wire) on sun sensor harness connector. If resistance is 5 ohms or greater, replace Body Control Module (BCM). BCM is mounted to junction block located behind left end cap of instrument panel. *See Fig. 1.* If resistance is less than 5 ohms, repair Dark Blue wire for short to ground.

INSTRUMENT CLUSTER TEST 1A

IDENTIFYING INSTRUMENT CLUSTER SYSTEM PROBLEMS

NOTE: Perform SYMPTOM ID TEST 1A before proceeding with this test. For connector terminal identification and wiring diagrams, see BODY CONTROL COMPUTER – INTRODUCTION. Perform VERIFICATION TEST: VER-2A after each repair.

CAUTION: Always turn ignition switch to OFF position prior to disconnecting or connecting any module connector.

1) Ensure scan tool can communicate with Body Control Module (BCM). If BCM communication is not possible, see appropriate VEHICLE COMMUNICATIONS article. Using scan tool, select BODY SYSTEM, BODY COMPUTER, then SENSORS. Read IGNITION VOLTAGE. If scan tool displays battery voltage, go to next step. If scan tool does not display battery voltage, go to TEST 16A in appropriate VEHICLE COMMUNICATIONS article.

2) Turn ignition on. Using scan tool, select ELECTRO/MECHANICAL cluster. If scan tool displays NO RESPONSE, go to TEST 6A in appropriate VEHICLE COMMUNICATIONS article. If scan tool does not display NO RESPONSE, go to next step.

3) Using scan tool, select MONITOR, then PCI BUS ENGINE INFO. If scan tool displays NO RESPONSE, go to TEST 9A in appropriate VEHICLE COMMUNICATIONS article. If scan tool does not display NO RESPONSE, go to next step.

4) Using scan tool, select INSTRUMENT CLUSTER. Read DTCs (fault messages). See INSTRUMENT CLUSTER FAULT MESSAGE DIRECTORY table. If none of the following messages are displayed, go to next step.

INSTRUMENT CLUSTER FAULT MESSAGE DIRECTORY

Message Displayed	[1] Go To Test
EATX BUS COMM FAILURE	10A
SBEC BUS COMM FAILURE	8A
AIR BAG BUS COMM FAILURE	2A
ABS BUS COMM FAILURE	11A
BCM BUS COMM FAILURE	4A

[1] – See test listed in appropriate VEHICLE COMMUNICATIONS article.

5) Using scan tool, select BODY CONTROL MODULE, then READ DTCs. If scan tool displays FUEL LEVEL SENDING UNIT FAILURE, go to INSTRUMENT CLUSTER TEST 2A. If scan tool does not display FUEL LEVEL SENDING UNIT FAILURE, go to next step.

6) If scan tool displays DIMMING LEVEL SWITCH FAILURE, go to INSTRUMENT CLUSTER TEST 3A. If scan tool does not display DIMMING LEVEL SWITCH FAILURE, go to next step.

7) Identify problem(s) listed in INSTRUMENT CLUSTER DIAGNOSTIC TEST DIRECTORY table and perform indicated test(s).

8) If speedometer, tachometer or temperature gauges intermittently go to zero or to lowest point, select MONITOR, then ENGINE INFO using scan tool. While wiggling wiring harness and connectors, monitor scan tool. If scan tool displays NO RESPONSE, disconnect appropriate

connectors and inspect terminals for corrosion or loose pushed out terminals. Repair as needed.

INSTRUMENT CLUSTER DIAGNOSTIC TEST DIRECTORY

Problem	INSTRUMENT CLUSTER TEST
All Gauges Not Operating	4A
One Gauge Not	5A
Odometer Malfunction	6A
Any Or All Warning Lights Malfunctioning	7A
PRNDL Not Malfunctioning	8A
Cluster And Panel Illumination Malfunction	9A

INSTRUMENT CLUSTER TEST 2A

FUEL LEVEL SENDING UNIT FAILURE

NOTE: Perform INSTRUMENT CLUSTER TEST 1A before proceeding with this test. For connector terminal identification and wiring diagrams, see BODY CONTROL COMPUTER – INTRODUCTION. Perform VERIFICATION TEST: VER-2A after each repair.

CAUTION: Always turn ignition switch to OFF position prior to disconnecting or connecting any module connector.

1) Disconnect Body Control Module (BCM) 16-pin Blue connector C4. BCM is mounted to junction block located behind left end cap of instrument panel. *See Fig. 1.*

2) Remove rear seat and disconnect left body harness connector. Using external voltmeter, measure voltage between ground and terminal No. 2 (Dark Blue wire) on body harness connector. If voltage is 5 volts or less, replace fuel sending unit. If voltage is more than 5 volts, repair Dark Blue wire for short to voltage.

INSTRUMENT CLUSTER TEST 3A

DIMMING LEVEL SWITCH FAILURE

NOTE: Perform INSTRUMENT CLUSTER TEST 1A before proceeding with this test. For connector terminal identification and wiring diagrams, see BODY CONTROL COMPUTER – INTRODUCTION. Perform VERIFICATION TEST: VER-2A after each repair.

CAUTION: Always turn ignition switch to OFF position prior to disconnecting or connecting any module connector.

1) Access Body Control Module (BCM) Black 24-pin connector C2. BCM is mounted to junction block located behind left end cap of instrument panel. *See Fig. 1.*

2) Disconnect BCM Black 24-pin connector. Using external voltmeter, measure voltage between ground and terminal No. 19 (White wire) on BCM Black connector. If voltage is 5 volts or less, go to next step. If voltage is more than 5 volts, repair White wire for short to voltage.

3) Using external ohmmeter, measure resistance between ground and terminal No. 19 (White wire) on BCM Black connector. If resistance is less than 5 ohms, repair White wire for short to ground. If resistance is 5 ohms or greater, go to next step.

4) Using external voltmeter, measure voltage between ground and terminal No. 21 (Red wire) on BCM Black connector. If voltage is 5 volts or less, go to next step. If voltage is more than 5 volts, repair Red wire for short to battery voltage.

5) Using external ohmmeter, measure resistance between ground and terminal No. 21 (Red wire) on BCM Black connector. If resistance is less than 5 ohms, repair Red wire for short to ground. If resistance is 5 ohms or greater, go to next step.

6) Disconnect headlight switch connector. Using external ohmmeter, measure resistance between terminals No. 19 and 21 on BCM Black connector. If resistance is less than 5 ohms, repair short between White wire and Red wire. If resistance is 5 ohms or greater, go to next step.

1999 ACCESSORIES & EQUIPMENT
Body Control Computer Tests
Concorde, Intrepid, LHS & 300M (Cont.)

CHRY
4-147

7) Using external ohmmeter, measure resistance of White wire between terminal No. 19 on BCM Black connector and terminal No. 6 on headlight switch harness connector. If resistance is less than 5 ohms, go to next step. If resistance is 5 ohms or greater, repair open White wire.

8) Using external ohmmeter, measure resistance of Red wire between terminal No. 21 on BCM Black connector and terminal No. 3 on headlight switch harness connector. If resistance is less than 5 ohms, replace headlight switch. If resistance is 5 ohms or greater, repair open Red wire.

INSTRUMENT CLUSTER TEST 4A

ALL GAUGES NOT OPERATING CORRECTLY

NOTE: Perform INSTRUMENT CLUSTER TEST 1A before proceeding with this test. For connector terminal identification and wiring diagrams, see BODY CONTROL COMPUTER – INTRODUCTION. Perform VERIFICATION TEST: VER-2A after each repair.

CAUTION: Always turn ignition switch to OFF position prior to disconnecting or connecting any module connector.

1) Turn ignition off. Remove and inspect fuse No. 1 from junction block. Junction block is located behind left end cap of instrument panel. *See Fig. 1.*

2) Install fuse in junction block. Turn ignition on. Using external voltmeter, measure voltage between ground and fuse No. 1. If voltage is 10 volts or less, go to step **6)**. If voltage is more than 10 volts, go to next step.

3) Disconnect instrument cluster Green 10-pin connector C1. Using external voltmeter, measure voltage between ground and terminal No. 2 (Red/White wire) on instrument cluster Green harness connector. If voltage is 10 volts or less, repair open Red/White wire. If voltage is more than 10 volts, go to next step.

4) Connect jumper wire between ground and terminal No. 5 (Yellow/Violet wire) on instrument cluster Green harness connector. Using scan tool, perform PCI BUS test. If scan tool displays BUS SHORTED TO GROUND, go to next step. If scan tool does not display BUS SHORTED TO GROUND, repair open Yellow/Violet wire.

5) Close all doors. Remove key from ignition switch and wait 30 seconds. Using external ohmmeter, measure resistance between ground and terminal No. 6 (Black/Green wire) on instrument cluster Green harness connector. If resistance is less than 5 ohms, replace instrument cluster. If resistance is 5 ohms or greater, repair open Black/Green wire.

6) Disconnect ignition switch connector. *See Fig. 2.* Using external voltmeter, measure voltage between ground and terminal No. 5 (Red wire) on ignition switch harness connector. If voltage is 10 volts or less, repair open Red wire. If voltage is more than 10 volts, go to next step.

7) Using external ohmmeter, measure resistance between fuse No. 1 and terminal No. 1 (Dark Green/Red wire) on ignition switch harness connector. If resistance is less than 5 ohms, replace ignition switch. If resistance is 5 ohms or greater, repair open Dark Green/Red wire.

INSTRUMENT CLUSTER TEST 4B

ALL GAUGES NOT OPERATING CORRECTLY

NOTE: Perform INSTRUMENT CLUSTER TEST 4A before proceeding with this test. For connector terminal identification and wiring diagrams, see BODY CONTROL COMPUTER – INTRODUCTION. Perform VERIFICATION TEST: VER-2A after each repair.

CAUTION: Always turn ignition switch to OFF position prior to disconnecting or connecting any module connector.

1) Using external ohmmeter, measure resistance between ground and fuse No. 1 lower terminal (terminal closest to fuse No. 7). If resistance is less than 5 ohms, go to next step. If resistance is 5 ohms or greater, replace fuse No. 1.

2) Disconnect instrument clutch connectors. Using external ohmmeter, measure resistance between ground and fuse No. 1 lower terminal (terminal closest to fuse No. 7). *See Fig. 3.* If resistance is less than 5 ohms, go to next step. If resistance is 5 ohms or greater, replace instrument cluster and fuse No. 1.

3) Disconnect Transmission Control Module (TCM). *See Fig. 4.* Using external ohmmeter, measure resistance between ground and fuse No. 1 lower terminal (terminal closest to fuse No. 7). If resistance is less than 5 ohms, go to next step. If resistance is 5 ohms or greater, replace TCM and fuse No. 1.

4) Disconnect Body Control Module (BCM) harness connectors. BCM is mounted to junction block located behind left end cap of instrument panel. *See Fig. 5.*

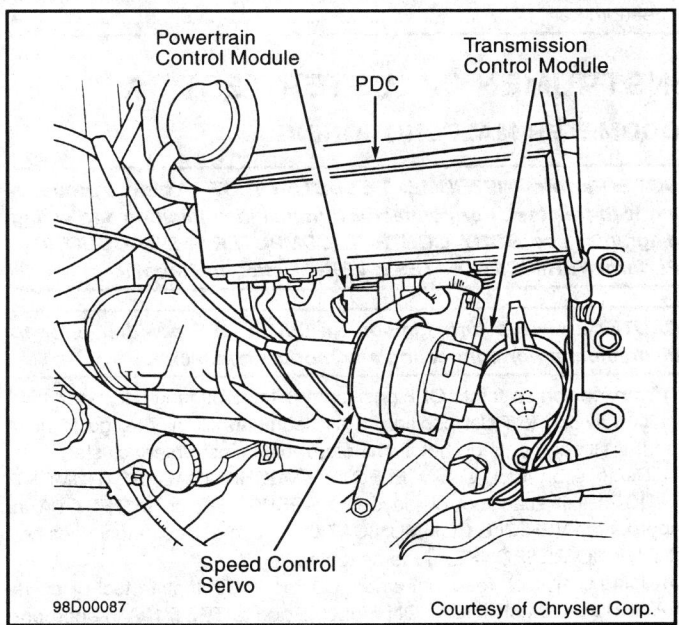

98D00087   Courtesy of Chrysler Corp.

Fig. 5: Locating Power Distribution Center, Powertrain Module & Transmission Control Module

CHRY
4-148

1999 ACCESSORIES & EQUIPMENT
Body Control Computer Tests
Concorde, Intrepid, LHS & 300M (Cont.)

INSTRUMENT CLUSTER TEST 5A

IDENTIFYING INOPERATIVE GAUGE

NOTE: Perform INSTRUMENT CLUSTER TEST 1A before proceeding with this test. For connector terminal identification and wiring diagrams, see BODY CONTROL COMPUTER – INTRODUCTION. Perform VERIFICATION TEST: VER-2A after each repair.

CAUTION: Always turn ignition switch to OFF position prior to disconnecting or connecting any module connector.

1) Turn ignition off. While holding TRIP reset button on instrument cluster, turn ignition switch to ON position. This will start Mechanical Instrument Cluster (MIC) self-test. This test actuates gauges through their full range. If each gauge passed the self-test, go to next step. If one or more gauges did not pass self-test, go to INSTRUMENT CLUSTER TEST 10A.

2) Cycle ignition switch to stop self-test. Go to appropriate test for malfunctioning gauge. See GAUGE TEST DIRECTORY table. If tachometer is only gauge malfunctioning, go to next step.

3) Start engine. Using scan tool, read engine RPM. If scan tool displays engine speed above 400 RPM, replace instrument cluster. If scan tool does not display engine speed above 400 RPM, go to TEST 8A in appropriate VEHICLE COMMUNICATIONS article.

GAUGE TEST DIRECTORY

Gauge	INSTRUMENT CLUSTER TEST
Temperature	11A
Fuel	12A
Speedometer	13A

INSTRUMENT CLUSTER TEST 6A

ODOMETER MALFUNCTIONING

NOTE: Perform INSTRUMENT CLUSTER TEST 1A before proceeding with this test. For connector terminal identification and wiring diagrams, see BODY CONTROL COMPUTER – INTRODUCTION. Perform VERIFICATION TEST: VER-2A after each repair.

CAUTION: Always turn ignition switch to OFF position prior to disconnecting or connecting any module connector.

1) Turn ignition switch to OFF position. While monitoring odometer, turn ignition switch to RUN position. If all segments illuminate, go to next step. If all segments do not illuminate, replace instrument cluster.

2) Using scan tool, select ELECTRO/MECHANICAL INSTRUMENT CLUSTER. If scan tool displays NO RESPONSE, go to TEST 6A in appropriate VEHICLE COMMUNICATIONS article. If scan tool does not display NO RESPONSE, go to next step.

3) Using scan tool, read instrument cluster DTCs. If scan tool displays EATX BUS COMMUNICATION FAILURE, go to TEST 10A in appropriate VEHICLE COMMUNICATIONS article. If scan tool does not display EATX BUS COMMUNICATION FAILURE, odometer is currently functioning correctly.

INSTRUMENT CLUSTER TEST 7A

IDENTIFYING WARNING LIGHT MALFUNCTION

NOTE: Perform INSTRUMENT CLUSTER TEST 1A before proceeding with this test. For connector terminal identification and wiring diagrams, see BODY CONTROL COMPUTER – INTRODUCTION. Perform VERIFICATION TEST: VER-2A after each repair.

CAUTION: Always turn ignition switch to OFF position prior to disconnecting or connecting any module connector.

Turn ignition switch to OFF position, then to RUN position. Observe all warning lights on instrument cluster. During self-test, brake warning light, oil warning light, high beam, trunk ajar and turn signal indicators can not be actuated. See WARNING LIGHT TEST DIRECTORY table. If charging, cruise control or MIL (Check Engine) warning lights are malfunctioning, go to appropriate SELF-DIAGNOSTICS article in ENGINE PERFORMANCE in appropriate MITCHELL® manual.

WARNING LIGHT TEST DIRECTORY

Description	INSTRUMENT CLUSTER TEST
PRND3L Light	14A
Coolant Temperature LED	11A
Low Fuel LED	12A
Oil Warning LED	15A
Seat Belt LED	16A
Park Brake Warning LED	17A
Air Bag Warning LED	[1]
Washer Fluid LED	18A
Door Ajar LED	19A
ABS LED	[2]
Traction Control Active Light	[2]
Traction Control OFF LED	[2]
Trunk Ajar LED	20A

[1] – See appropriate MITCHELL® AIR BAG SERVICE & REPAIR, DOMESTIC & IMPORTED manual.

[2] – See appropriate ANTI-LOCK article in BRAKES in appropriate MITCHELL® manual in appropriate MITCHELL® manual.

INSTRUMENT CLUSTER TEST 7B

INSTRUMENT CLUSTER PRINTED CIRCUIT BOARD WARNING LIGHT MALFUNCTION

NOTE: Perform INSTRUMENT CLUSTER TEST 7A before proceeding with this test. For connector terminal identification and wiring diagrams, see BODY CONTROL COMPUTER – INTRODUCTION. Perform VERIFICATION TEST: VER-2A after each repair.

CAUTION: Always turn ignition switch to OFF position prior to disconnecting or connecting any module connector.

Turn ignition off. Disconnect instrument cluster connectors. If malfunctioning light is CRUISE CONTROL or TRACTION CONTROL ACTIVE, replace instrument cluster. If malfunctioning light is not CRUISE CONTROL or TRACTION CONTROL ACTIVE, remove and inspect malfunctioning light. Replace as needed. If light is okay, replace instrument cluster.

1999 ACCESSORIES & EQUIPMENT
Body Control Computer Tests
Concorde, Intrepid, LHS & 300M (Cont.)

CHRY
4-149

INSTRUMENT CLUSTER TEST 8A

PRND3L LIGHT MALFUNCTIONING

NOTE: Perform INSTRUMENT CLUSTER TEST 1A before proceeding with this test. For connector terminal identification and wiring diagrams, see BODY CONTROL COMPUTER – INTRODUCTION. Perform VERIFICATION TEST: VER-2A after each repair.

CAUTION: Always turn ignition switch to OFF position prior to disconnecting or connecting any module connector.

1) While monitoring PRND3L indicator light, cycle ignition switch from OFF to RUN. If all indicator lights illuminate, go to next step. If all indicator lights do not illuminate, replace and recalibrate instrument cluster circuit board.
2) Engage parking brake. Using scan tool, select Transmission Control Module (TCM). Select MONITORS in status displays. Monitor SLP status of shift lever position. While monitoring scan tool, move shift lever through all positions. If scan tool display matches shift lever position, replace instrument cluster. If scan tool display does not match shift lever position, see appropriate MITCHELL® TRANSMISSION SERVICE & REPAIR, DOMESTIC VEHICLES manual.

INSTRUMENT CLUSTER TEST 9A

INSTRUMENT CLUSTER AND PANEL ILLUMINATION MALFUNCTIONS

NOTE: Perform INSTRUMENT CLUSTER TEST 1A before proceeding with this test. For connector terminal identification and wiring diagrams, see BODY CONTROL COMPUTER – INTRODUCTION. Perform VERIFICATION TEST: VER-2A after each repair.

CAUTION: Always turn ignition switch to OFF position prior to disconnecting or connecting any module connector.

1) Using scan tool, select BODY SENSORS. Read dimming level voltage. Rotate dimmer switch to low, then high position. If scan tool displays voltage change from 3 volts (approximately) to zero volts, go to next step. If scan tool does not display voltage change from 3 volts (approximately) to zero volts, go to INSTRUMENT CLUSTER TEST 3A.
2) While observing instrument panel lights, rotate dimmer switch from low to high position. If lights stay at full brightness, go to INSTRUMENT CLUSTER TEST 9B. If lights fail to illuminate, go to INSTRUMENT CLUSTER TEST 9C. If lights illuminate, but do not stay at full brightness, system is currently operating correctly.

INSTRUMENT CLUSTER TEST 9B

INSTRUMENT CLUSTER ILLUMINATION SHORTED TO BATTERY

NOTE: Perform INSTRUMENT CLUSTER TEST 9A before proceeding with this test. For connector terminal identification and wiring diagrams, see BODY CONTROL COMPUTER – INTRODUCTION. Perform VERIFICATION TEST: VER-2A after each repair.

CAUTION: Always turn ignition switch to OFF position prior to disconnecting or connecting any module connector.

NOTE: The following test covers all optional equipment. Skip any steps that do not apply.

1) Disconnect traction control switch connector. Monitor instrument panel lights while adjusting dimmer switch from low to high position. If lights function correctly, repair or replace traction control switch for short to battery voltage. If lights do not function correctly, go to next step.

2) Disconnect radio connectors. Monitor instrument panel lights while adjusting dimmer switch from low to high position. If lights function correctly, repair or replace radio for short to battery voltage. If lights do not function correctly, go to next step.
3) Disconnect ash tray illumination connector. Monitor instrument panel lights while adjusting dimmer switch from low to high position. If lights function correctly, repair or replace ash tray illumination for short to battery voltage. If lights do not function correctly, go to next step.
4) Disconnect Automatic Temperature Control (ATC) connector. Monitor instrument panel lights while adjusting dimmer switch from low to high position. If lights function correctly, repair or replace ATC for short to battery voltage. If lights do not function correctly, go to next step.
5) Disconnect PRND3L illumination connector. Monitor instrument panel lights while adjusting dimmer switch from low to high position. If lights function correctly, repair or replace PRND3L unit for short to battery voltage. If lights do not function correctly, go to next step.
6) Disconnect Overhead Traveler Information System (OTIS) connector. Monitor instrument panel lights while adjusting dimmer switch from low to high position. If lights function correctly, repair or replace OTIS unit for short to battery voltage. If lights do not function correctly, go to next step.
7) Disconnect headlight switch connector. Disconnect instrument cluster Green connector C1. Using external voltmeter, measure voltage between ground and terminal No. 4 (Orange wire) on Green connector. If voltage is 10 volts or less, repair or replace instrument cluster as needed. If voltage is greater than 10 volts, repair headlight switch for short to battery voltage.

INSTRUMENT CLUSTER TEST 9C

INSTRUMENT CLUSTER ILLUMINATION SHORTED TO BATTERY VOLTAGE

NOTE: PerformINSTRUMENT CLUSTER TEST 9A before proceeding with this test. For connector terminal identification and wiring diagrams, see BODY CONTROL COMPUTER – INTRODUCTION. Perform VERIFICATION TEST: VER-2A after each repair.

CAUTION: Always turn ignition switch to OFF position prior to disconnecting or connecting any module connector.

NOTE: The following test covers all optional equipment. Skip any steps that do not apply.

1) Using scan tool, check for instrument cluster DTCs. If scan tool displays PANEL LAMPS DRIVER OUTPUT CIRCUIT SHORTED, go to next step. If scan tool does not display PANEL LAMPS DRIVER OUTPUT CIRCUIT SHORTED, replace instrument cluster.
2) Disconnect traction control switch and instrument cluster Green connector C1. Using external ohmmeter, measure resistance between ground and terminal No. 4 (Orange wire). If resistance is less than 5 ohms, go to next step. If resistance is 5 ohms or greater, repair or replace traction control switch for short to ground.
3) Disconnect radio connectors. Using external ohmmeter, measure resistance between ground and terminal No. 4 (Orange wire) on instrument cluster Green connector C1. If resistance is less than 5 ohms, go to next step. If resistance is 5 ohms or greater, repair or replace radio for short to ground.
4) Disconnect ash tray illumination connector. Using external ohmmeter, measure resistance between ground and terminal No. 4 (Orange wire) on instrument cluster Green connector C1. If resistance is less than 5 ohms, go to next step. If resistance is 5 ohms or greater, repair ash tray illumination for short to ground.
5) Disconnect Automatic Temperature Control (ATC) connector. Using external ohmmeter, measure resistance between ground and terminal No. 4 (Orange wire) on instrument cluster Green connector C1. If resistance is less than 5 ohms, go to next step. If resistance is 5 ohms or greater, repair or replace ATC unit for short to ground.

CHRY
4-150

1999 ACCESSORIES & EQUIPMENT
Body Control Computer Tests
Concorde, Intrepid, LHS & 300M (Cont.)

6) Disconnect PRND3L illumination connector. Using external ohmmeter, measure resistance between ground and terminal No. 4 (Orange wire) on instrument cluster Green connector C1. If resistance is less than 5 ohms, go to next step. If resistance is 5 ohms or greater, repair or replace PRND3L unit for short to ground.

7) Disconnect headlight switch connector. Using external ohmmeter, measure resistance between ground and terminal No. 4 (Orange wire) on instrument cluster Green connector C1. If resistance is less than 5 ohms, replace instrument cluster. If resistance is 5 ohms or greater, repair or replace headlight switch for short to ground.

INSTRUMENT CLUSTER TEST 10A

MALFUNCTIONING GAUGE

NOTE: *Perform INSTRUMENT CLUSTER TEST 1A before proceeding with this test. For connector terminal identification and wiring diagrams, see BODY CONTROL COMPUTER – INTRODUCTION. Perform VERIFICATION TEST: VER-2A after each repair.*

Inspect printed circuit board on instrument cluster. If circuit board is okay, replace sub-dial assembly (4 gauges). If circuit appears faulty, replace circuit board and recalibrate gauges.

INSTRUMENT CLUSTER TEST 11A

TEMPERATURE GAUGE LED MALFUNCTION

NOTE: *Perform INSTRUMENT CLUSTER TEST 1A before proceeding with this test. For connector terminal identification and wiring diagrams, see BODY CONTROL COMPUTER – INTRODUCTION. Perform VERIFICATION TEST: VER-2A after each repair.*

CAUTION: *Always turn ignition switch to OFF position prior to disconnecting or connecting any module connector.*

1) Ensure engine cooling system is functioning correctly. Repair as needed. Using scan tool, select BODY SYSTEM TESTS, then PCM MONITOR. If scan tool displays ENGINE CONTROLLER ACTIVE ON THE BUS, go to next step. If scan tool does not display ENGINE CONTROLLER ACTIVE ON THE BUS, go to TEST 8A in appropriate VEHICLE COMMUNICATIONS article.

2) Using scan tool, select MODULE ENGINE CONTROLLER. Read Powertrain Control Module (PCM) DTCs. If scan tool displays ECT SENSOR VOLTAGE TOO HIGH, go to appropriate SELF-DIAGNOSTICS article in ENGINE PERFORMANCE in appropriate MITCHELL® manual. If scan tool does not display ECT SENSOR VOLTAGE TOO HIGH, go to next step.

3) If scan tool displays ECT SENSOR VOLTAGE TOO LOW, go to appropriate SELF-DIAGNOSTICS article in ENGINE PERFORMANCE in appropriate MITCHELL® manual. If scan tool does not display ECT SENSOR VOLTAGE TOO LOW, replace PCM. *See Fig. 5.*

INSTRUMENT CLUSTER TEST 12A

FUEL GAUGE LED MALFUNCTION

NOTE: *Perform INSTRUMENT CLUSTER TEST 1A before proceeding with this test. For connector terminal identification and wiring diagrams, see BODY CONTROL COMPUTER – INTRODUCTION. Perform VERIFICATION TEST: VER-2A after each repair.*

CAUTION: *Always turn ignition switch to OFF position prior to disconnecting or connecting any module connector.*

1) Ensure fuel tank is not empty. If fuel gauge always reads empty, go to INSTRUMENT CLUSTER TEST 12C. If fuel gauge reads between empty and full, go to INSTRUMENT CLUSTER TEST 12B. If fuel gauge always reads full, go to next step.

2) Turn ignition off. Remove rear seat cushion. Disconnect fuel pump harness connector. Using scan tool, select BODY, then SENSORS. Turn ignition on. Using scan tool, read fuel level voltage. If voltage is 9 volts or less, go to next step. If voltage is greater than 9 volts, replace fuel tank sending unit.

3) Turn ignition off. Disconnect Body Control Module (BCM) Blue connector C4. BCM is mounted to junction block located behind left end cap of instrument panel. *See Fig. 1.*

INSTRUMENT CLUSTER TEST 12B

INACCURATE FUEL GAUGE

NOTE: *Perform INSTRUMENT CLUSTER TEST 12A before proceeding with this test. For connector terminal identification and wiring diagrams, see BODY CONTROL COMPUTER – INTRODUCTION. Perform VERIFICATION TEST: VER-2A after each repair.*

CAUTION: *Always turn ignition switch to OFF position prior to disconnecting or connecting any module connector.*

1) Disconnect Body Control Module (BCM) Blue connector C4. BCM is mounted to junction block located behind left end cap of instrument panel. *See Fig. 1.*

2) Using external ohmmeter, measure and record resistance between ground and terminal No. 7 (Dark Blue wire) on Blue connector. Add or remove 5 gallons of gas. Measure and record resistance between ground and terminal No. 7 (Dark Blue wire). If resistance measurements match, repair or replace fuel tank sending unit. If resistance measurements do not match, system is currently operating correctly.

INSTRUMENT CLUSTER TEST 12C

FUEL GAUGE/LED FAULTY OPERATION

NOTE: *Perform INSTRUMENT CLUSTER TEST 12A before proceeding with this test. For connector terminal identification and wiring diagrams, see BODY CONTROL COMPUTER – INTRODUCTION. Perform VERIFICATION TEST: VER-2A after each repair.*

CAUTION: *Always turn ignition switch to OFF position prior to disconnecting or connecting any module connector.*

1) Ensure fuel tank is not empty. Turn ignition on. Using scan tool, read ignition voltage. If scan tool displays zero voltage, go to INSTRUMENT CLUSTER TEST 12D. If scan tool does not display zero voltage, go to next step.

2) Using scan tool, read fuel level voltage status. If scan tool displays one voltage, go to INSTRUMENT CLUSTER TEST 12E. If scan tool does not display one voltage, go to next step.

3) Remove rear seat cushion. Disconnect fuel pump 10-pin harness connector. Turn ignition on. Connect jumper wire between terminals No. 1 (Black wire) and No. 2 (Dark Blue wire) on harness side of connector. Using scan tool, read fuel level sensor voltage. If scan tool displays less than one volt, replace fuel level sensor. If scan tool displays one volt or greater, go to next step.

4) Disconnect jumper wire. Access Body Control Module (BCM). BCM is mounted to junction block located behind left end cap of instrument panel. *See Fig. 1.*

5) Turn ignition off. Disconnect BCM Blue 16-pin connector C4. Inspect harness connector. Repair as needed. If connector is okay, replace BCM.

1999 ACCESSORIES & EQUIPMENT
Body Control Computer Tests
Concorde, Intrepid, LHS & 300M (Cont.)

CHRY
4-151

INSTRUMENT CLUSTER TEST 12D

FUEL GAUGE/LED FAULTY OPERATION

NOTE: Perform INSTRUMENT CLUSTER TEST 12A before proceeding with this test. For connector terminal identification and wiring diagrams, see BODY CONTROL COMPUTER – INTRODUCTION. Perform VERIFICATION TEST: VER-2A after each repair.

CAUTION: Always turn ignition switch to OFF position prior to disconnecting or connecting any module connector.

Turn ignition off. Remove Body Control Module (BCM) from junction block. BCM is mounted to junction block located behind left end cap of instrument panel. *See Fig. 1.*

INSTRUMENT CLUSTER TEST 12E

FUEL LEVEL VOLTAGE BELOW ONE VOLT

NOTE: Perform INSTRUMENT CLUSTER TEST 12A before proceeding with this test. For connector terminal identification and wiring diagrams, see BODY CONTROL COMPUTER – INTRODUCTION. Perform VERIFICATION TEST: VER-2A after each repair.

CAUTION: Always turn ignition switch to OFF position prior to disconnecting or connecting any module connector.

1) Remove rear seat cushion. Disconnect fuel pump 10-pin harness connector. Using scan tool, read fuel level status. If scan tool displays less than one volt, go to next step. If scan tool displays one volt or greater, replace fuel level sending unit.
2) Disconnect Body Control Module (BCM) Blue 16-pin connector C4. BCM is mounted to junction block located behind left end cap of instrument panel. *See Fig. 1.*

INSTRUMENT CLUSTER TEST 13A

SPEEDOMETER MALFUNCTION

NOTE: Perform INSTRUMENT CLUSTER TEST 1A before proceeding with this test. For connector terminal identification and wiring diagrams, see BODY CONTROL COMPUTER – INTRODUCTION. Perform VERIFICATION TEST: VER-2A after each repair.

CAUTION: Always turn ignition switch to OFF position prior to disconnecting or connecting any module connector.

1) Using scan tool, select BODY SYSTEMS TESTS, then PCM MONITOR. If scan tool does not display ACTIVE ON THE BUS, go to TEST 8A in appropriate VEHICLE COMMUNICATIONS article. If scan tool displays ACTIVE ON THE BUS, go to next step.
2) Raise and support vehicle. Start engine. Ensure traction control system is off (if equipped). Place shift lever in Drive. Using scan tool, select MIC MONITORS. Read Vehicle Speed Signal (VSS). If vehicle speed increases proportionally as accelerator is depressed, replace instrument cluster. If vehicle speed does not increase, go to appropriate SELF-DIAGNOSTICS article in ENGINE PERFORMANCE in appropriate MITCHELL® manual.

INSTRUMENT CLUSTER TEST 14A

COMMUNICATION FAILURE WITH TRANSMISSION CONTROL MODULE

NOTE: Perform INSTRUMENT CLUSTER TEST 1A before proceeding with this test. For connector terminal identification and wiring diagrams, see BODY CONTROL COMPUTER – INTRODUCTION. Perform VERIFICATION TEST: VER-2A after each repair.

CAUTION: Always turn ignition switch to OFF position prior to disconnecting or connecting any module connector.

1) While monitoring PRND3L indicator lights, cycle ignition from OFF to RUN position. If all PRND3L indicator lights illuminate, go to next step. If all PRND3L indicator lights do not illuminate, replace instrument cluster.
2) Using scan tool, select TRANSMISSION CONTROL MODULE. Select MONITORS in status displays. Monitor SLP status of shift lever position. While monitoring scan tool, move shift lever through all positions. If scan tool display matches shift lever position, replace instrument cluster. If scan tool display does not match shift lever position, see appropriate MITCHELL® TRANSMISSION SERVICE & REPAIR, DOMESTIC VEHICLES manual.

INSTRUMENT CLUSTER TEST 15A

OIL PRESSURE SWITCH SENSE CIRCUIT SHORT TO GROUND

NOTE: Perform INSTRUMENT CLUSTER TEST 1A before proceeding with this test. For connector terminal identification and wiring diagrams, see BODY CONTROL COMPUTER – INTRODUCTION. Perform VERIFICATION TEST: VER-2A after each repair.

CAUTION: Always turn ignition switch to OFF position prior to disconnecting or connecting any module connector.

1) Turn ignition on. If oil warning light illuminates, go to next step. If oil warning light does not illuminate, go to INSTRUMENT CLUSTER TEST 15B. Turn ignition off.
2) Turn ignition off. Check engine oil level. Adjust as needed. Disconnect oil pressure switch. *See Fig. 6.* If oil pressure warning light is illuminated, go to step 5). If oil pressure warning light is not longer illuminated, go to next step.
3) Remove oil pressure switch. Using appropriate pressure gauge, start engine and read oil pressure. If oil pressure is 4 PSI or greater, go to next step. If oil pressure is less than 4 PSI, see appropriate article in ENGINES in appropriate MITCHELL® manual.
4) Allow engine to reach normal operating temperature. If oil pressure is 4 PSI or greater, replace oil pressure switch. If oil pressure is less than 4 PSI, see appropriate article in ENGINES in appropriate MITCHELL® manual.
5) Disconnect instrument cluster. Using external ohmmeter, measure resistance between ground and terminal No. 10 (Gray wire) on instrument cluster Blue 10-pin connector C2. If resistance is less than 5 ohms, repair Gray wire for short to ground. If resistance is 5 ohms or greater, repair or replace instrument cluster.

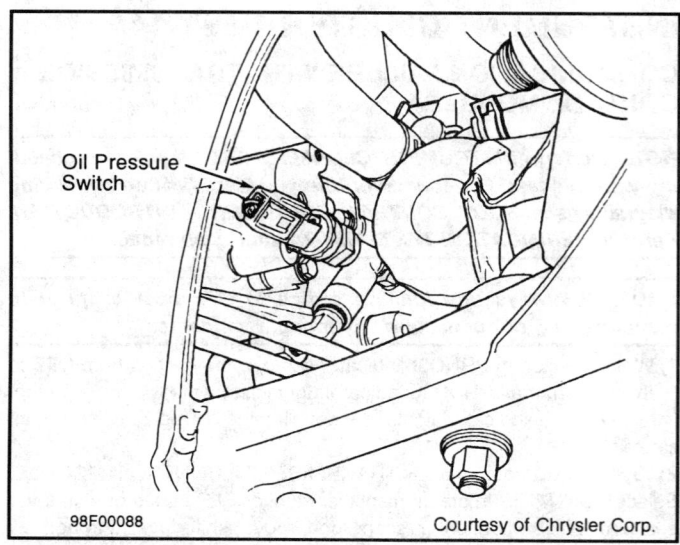

Oil Pressure Switch

98F00088   Courtesy of Chrysler Corp.

Fig. 6: Locating Oil Pressure Switch

INSTRUMENT CLUSTER TEST 15B

OIL PRESSURE SWITCH SENSE OPEN CIRCUIT

NOTE: Perform INSTRUMENT CLUSTER TEST 15A before proceeding with this test. For connector terminal identification and wiring diagrams, see BODY CONTROL COMPUTER – INTRODUCTION. Perform VERIFICATION TEST: VER-2A after each repair.

CAUTION: Always turn ignition switch to OFF position prior to disconnecting or connecting any module connector.

1) Disconnect oil pressure switch. *See Fig. 6.* Connect jumper wire between ground and terminal No. 1 (Gray wire) on oil pressure switch harness connector. If oil pressure warning light illuminated, replace oil pressure switch. If oil pressure warning light is not illuminated, go to next step.

2) Disconnect instrument cluster. Using scan tool in ohmmeter mode, measure resistance at terminal No. 10 (Gray wire) on instrument cluster Blue 10-pin connector C2. If resistance is less than 5 ohms, replace instrument cluster. If resistance is 5 ohms or greater, repair open Gray wire.

INSTRUMENT CLUSTER TEST 16A

SEAT BELT SWITCH CIRCUIT SHORT TO GROUND

NOTE: Perform INSTRUMENT CLUSTER TEST 1A before proceeding with this test. For connector terminal identification and wiring diagrams, see BODY CONTROL COMPUTER – INTRODUCTION. Perform VERIFICATION TEST: VER-2A after each repair.

While observing seat belt indicator, cycle key to OFF then ON position. If seat belt indicator is illuminated for 10 seconds, go to CHIME TEST 4B. If seat belt indicator is not illuminated for 10 seconds, replace instrument cluster.

INSTRUMENT CLUSTER TEST 17A

PARKING BRAKE WARNING LIGHT MALFUNCTION

NOTE: Perform INSTRUMENT CLUSTER TEST 1A before proceeding with this test. For connector terminal identification and wiring diagrams, see BODY CONTROL COMPUTER – INTRODUCTION. Perform VERIFICATION TEST: VER-2A after each repair.

1) If vehicle is equipped with anti-lock brakes, see appropriate ANTI-LOCK article in BRAKES in appropriate MITCHELL® manual. If vehicle is not equipped with anti-lock brakes, go to next step.

2) Ensure parking brake is released and operates correctly with no binding. Inspect brake pedal operation. If brake pedal does not operate correctly, see appropriate article in BRAKES in appropriate MITCHELL® manual. If brake pedal operates correctly, go to next step.

3) If brake warning light does not illuminate with empty brake fluid reservoir, go to INSTRUMENT CLUSTER TEST 17B. If brake warning light does illuminate with empty brake fluid reservoir, go to next step.

4) Turn ignition on. If parking brake warning light is illuminated, go to INSTRUMENT CLUSTER TEST 17D. If parking brake warning light is not illuminated, go to next step.

5) Depress parking brake. If parking brake warning light is illuminated, go to next step. If parking brake warning light is not illuminated, go to INSTRUMENT CLUSTER TEST 17C.

6) Release parking brake. Crank engine while monitoring parking brake warning light. If parking brake warning light is illuminated, system is currently operating correctly. If parking brake warning light is not illuminated, replace instrument cluster.

INSTRUMENT CLUSTER TEST 17B

BRAKE FLUID LEVEL SWITCH OPEN CIRCUIT

NOTE: Perform INSTRUMENT CLUSTER TEST 17A before proceeding with this test. For connector terminal identification and wiring diagrams, see BODY CONTROL COMPUTER – INTRODUCTION. Perform VERIFICATION TEST: VER-2A after each repair.

CAUTION: Always turn ignition switch to OFF position prior to disconnecting or connecting any module connector.

1) Disconnect brake fluid level switch connector. Connect jumper between connector terminals. Turn ignition on. If parking brake warning light is illuminated, replace brake fluid level switch. If parking brake warning light is not illuminated, go to next step.

2) Disconnect jumper wire. Connect jumper wire between ground and terminal No. 2 (Gray/Black wire) on brake fluid level switch harness connector. If parking brake warning light is illuminated, repair open ground circuit (terminal No. 1, Black wire). If parking brake warning light is not illuminated, go to next step.

3) With jumper wire connected, turn ignition off. Disconnect instrument cluster. Using external ohmmeter, measure resistance between ground and terminal No. 3 (Gray/Black wire) on instrument cluster Blue 10-pin connector C2. If resistance is less than 5 ohms, replace instrument cluster. If resistance is 5 ohms or greater, repair open Gray/Black wire.

INSTRUMENT CLUSTER TEST 17C

PARKING BRAKE SWITCH OPEN CIRCUIT

NOTE: Perform INSTRUMENT CLUSTER TEST 17A before proceeding with this test. For connector terminal identification and wiring diagrams, see BODY CONTROL COMPUTER – INTRODUCTION. Perform VERIFICATION TEST: VER-2A after each repair.

CAUTION: Always turn ignition switch to OFF position prior to disconnecting or connecting any module connector.

1) Disconnect parking brake switch connector. Connect jumper wire between ground and parking brake switch connector terminal. If parking brake light is illuminated, replace switch. If parking brake light is not illuminated, go to next step.

2) With jumper wire connected, turn ignition off. Disconnect instrument cluster. Using external ohmmeter, measure resistance between ground and terminal No. 3 (Gray/Black wire) on instrument cluster Blue 10-pin connector C2. If resistance is less than 5 ohms, replace instrument cluster. If resistance is 5 ohms or greater, repair open Gray/Black wire.

INSTRUMENT CLUSTER TEST 17D

PARKING BRAKE SWITCH CIRCUIT SHORT TO GROUND

NOTE: Perform INSTRUMENT CLUSTER TEST 17A before proceeding with this test. For connector terminal identification and wiring diagrams, see BODY CONTROL COMPUTER – INTRODUCTION. Perform VERIFICATION TEST: VER-2A after each repair.

CAUTION: Always turn ignition switch to OFF position prior to disconnecting or connecting any module connector.

1) Check brake fluid reservoir level. Fill as needed. Disconnect parking brake switch connector. If brake warning light is illuminated, go to next step. If brake warning light is not illuminated, replace parking brake switch.

2) Disconnect brake fluid level switch connector. If brake warning light is illuminated, go to next step. If brake warning light is not illuminated, replace brake fluid level switch.

3) Turn ignition off. Disconnect instrument cluster. Using external ohmmeter, measure resistance between ground and terminal No. 3 (Gray/Black wire). If resistance is less than 5 ohms, go to next step. If resistance is 5 ohms or greater, replace instrument cluster.

4) Disconnect ignition switch connector. *See Fig. 2.* Measure resistance between ground and terminal No. 3 (Gray/Black wire). If resistance is less than 5 ohms, repair Gray/Black wire for short to ground. If resistance is 5 ohms or greater, replace ignition switch.

INSTRUMENT CLUSTER TEST 18A

PARKING BRAKE SWITCH CIRCUIT SHORT TO GROUND

NOTE: Perform INSTRUMENT CLUSTER TEST 1A before proceeding with this test. For connector terminal identification and wiring diagrams, see BODY CONTROL COMPUTER – INTRODUCTION. Perform VERIFICATION TEST: VER-2A after each repair.

CAUTION: Always turn ignition switch to OFF position prior to disconnecting or connecting any module connector.

1) Turn ignition off. Wait 60 seconds. Check washer fluid reservoir level. Fill as needed. If low washer fluid light failed to illuminate when reservoir was low, go to INSTRUMENT CLUSTER TEST 18B. If low washer fluid light is illuminated when reservoir was low, go to next step.

2) Turn ignition on. Wait 60 seconds. Monitor instrument cluster. If low washer fluid light illuminated, go to next step. If low washer fluid light is not illuminated, system is currently operating correctly.

3) Using scan tool, read washer fluid status. If scan tool displays WASH FLUID: OPEN, replace instrument cluster. If scan tool does not display WASH FLUID: OPEN, go to next step.

4) Disconnect washer fluid switch connector. If scan tool displays WASH FLUID: OPEN, replace washer fluid level switch. If scan tool does not display WASH FLUID: OPEN, go to next step.

5) Turn ignition off. Disconnect instrument cluster Blue 10-pin connector C2. Using external ohmmeter, measure resistance between ground and terminal No. 4 (Black/Tan wire) on Blue connector. If resistance is less than 5 ohms, repair Black/Tan wire for short to ground. If resistance is 5 ohms or greater, replace instrument cluster.

INSTRUMENT CLUSTER TEST 18B

LOW WASHER FLUID INDICATOR OPEN CIRCUIT

NOTE: Perform INSTRUMENT CLUSTER TEST 18A before proceeding with this test. For connector terminal identification and wiring diagrams, see BODY CONTROL COMPUTER – INTRODUCTION. Perform VERIFICATION TEST: VER-2A after each repair.

CAUTION: Always turn ignition switch to OFF position prior to disconnecting or connecting any module connector.

1) While monitoring low washer fluid indicator light, cycle ignition switch from OFF to ON position. If indicator light toggles off and on, go to next step. If indicator light does not toggle off and on, replace instrument cluster.

2) Disconnect washer fluid level switch connector. Connect jumper wire between harness connector terminals. Using scan tool, read washer fluid switch status. If scan tool displays WASH FLUID: CLOSED, replace washer fluid level switch. If scan tool does not display WASH FLUID: CLOSED, go to next step.

3) Disconnect jumper wire. Connect jumper wire between ground and terminal No. 2 (Black/Tan wire) on washer fluid level switch harness connector. Read washer fluid switch status. If scan tool displays WASH FLUID: CLOSED, repair open ground circuit (terminal No. 1, Black/Gray wire). If scan tool does not display WASH FLUID: CLOSED, go to next step.

4) Access instrument cluster Blue 10-pin connector C2. Backprobe jumper wire between terminal No. 4 (Black/Tan wire) and ground. Read washer fluid switch status. If scan tool displays WASH FLUID: CLOSED, repair open Black/Tan wire. If scan tool does not display WASH FLUID: CLOSED, replace instrument cluster.

INSTRUMENT CLUSTER TEST 19A

DOOR AJAR INDICATOR CIRCUIT MALFUNCTION

NOTE: Perform INSTRUMENT CLUSTER TEST 1A before proceeding with this test. For connector terminal identification and wiring diagrams, see BODY CONTROL COMPUTER – INTRODUCTION. Perform VERIFICATION TEST: VER-2A after each repair.

CAUTION: Always turn ignition switch to OFF position prior to disconnecting or connecting any module connector.

1) Close all doors. Using scan tool, read door ajar status of each door. If scan tool displays CLOSED for any door, go to DOOR AJAR TEST 1A. If scan tool does not display CLOSED for any door, go to next step.

2) While monitoring scan tool, open and close each door. If scan tool display changes as door is opened and closed, go to next step. If scan tool display does not change as door is opened and closed, go to DOOR AJAR TEST 1A.

CHRY
4-154

1999 ACCESSORIES & EQUIPMENT
Body Control Computer Tests
Concorde, Intrepid, LHS & 300M (Cont.)

3) Ensure all doors are closed. If door ajar indicator light illuminated constantly, go to next step. If door ajar indicator light is not illuminated, go to step 5).

4) Disconnect Body Control Module (BCM) Gray 14-pin connector C1. BCM is mounted to junction block located behind left end cap of instrument panel. *See Fig. 1.*

5) Turn ignition switch to LOCK position. While observing door ajar indicator light, turn ignition switch to RUN position. If indicator light illuminates, go to DOOR AJAR TEST 1A. If indicator light does not illuminate, replace instrument cluster.

INSTRUMENT CLUSTER TEST 20A

PARKING BRAKE WARNING LIGHT MALFUNCTION

NOTE: Perform INSTRUMENT CLUSTER TEST 1A before proceeding with this test. For connector terminal identification and wiring diagrams, see BODY CONTROL COMPUTER – INTRODUCTION. Perform VERIFICATION TEST: VER-2A after each repair.

CAUTION: Always turn ignition switch to OFF position prior to disconnecting or connecting any module connector.

1) Turn ignition on. Ensure that trunk is aligned properly and fully closed. If trunk ajar indicator light is illuminated, go to step 6). If trunk ajar indicator light is not illuminated, go to next step.

2) Open trunk. If trunk ajar indicator light is illuminated, system is currently operating correctly. If trunk ajar indicator light is not illuminated, go to next step.

3) Disconnect decklid release solenoid/decklid ajar connector. Connect jumper wire between terminals No. 1 (Black wire) and 2 (Tan/Black wire) on harness connector. If trunk ajar indicator light is illuminated, replace trunk ajar switch. If trunk ajar indicator light is not illuminated, go to next step.

4) Disconnect instrument cluster Blue 10-pin connector C2. Using external ohmmeter, measure resistance between ground and terminal No. 9 (Tan/Black wire) on Blue harness connector. If resistance is less than 5 ohms, go to next step. If resistance is 5 ohms or greater, repair open Tan/Black wire.

5) Disconnect instrument cluster Green 10-pin connector C1. Using external voltmeter, measure voltage between ground and terminal No. 2 (Red/White wire) on Green harness connector. If voltage is 10 volts or less, repair open Red/White wire. If voltage is greater than 10 volts, replace instrument cluster.

6) Turn ignition on. Disconnect decklid release solenoid/decklid ajar connector. If trunk ajar indicator light is illuminated, go to next step. If trunk ajar indicator light is not illuminated, replace trunk ajar switch.

7) Disconnect instrument cluster Blue 10-pin connector C2. Using external ohmmeter, measure resistance between ground and terminal No. 9 (Tan/Black wire) on Blue harness connector. If resistance is less than 5 ohms, repair Tan/Black wire for short to ground. If resistance is 5 ohms or greater, replace instrument cluster.

INTERIOR LIGHT TEST 1A

IDENTIFYING INTERIOR LIGHT SYSTEM MALFUNCTIONS

NOTE: Perform SYSTEM ID TEST 1A before proceeding with this test. For connector terminal identification and wiring diagrams, see BODY CONTROL COMPUTER – INTRODUCTION. Perform VERIFICATION TEST: VER-2A after each repair.

CAUTION: Always turn ignition switch to OFF position prior to disconnecting or connecting any module connector.

1) Using scan tool, select BODY, then BODY COMPUTER. Verify communication with Body Control Module (BCM). If scan tool displays

NO RESPONSE, see appropriate VEHICLE COMMUNICATIONS article. If scan tool does not display NO RESPONSE, go to next step.

2) Using scan tool, select READ DTCS. If scan tool displays HEADLAMP SWITCH INPUT FAILURE, go to INTERIOR LIGHT TEST 2A. If HEADLAMP SWITCH INPUT FAILURE DTC is not displayed, identify problem(s) listed in INTERIOR LIGHT DIAGNOSTIC TEST DIRECTORY table and perform indicated test(s).

INTERIOR LIGHT DIAGNOSTIC TEST DIRECTORY

Problem	INTERIOR LIGHT TEST
Courtesy Light Output Short To Battery	2A
Courtesy Lights Inoperative From All Doors & Courtesy Light Switch	3A
Inoperative Courtesy Lights	4A
Courtesy Light Remain On	5A
Courtesy Light Switch Inoperative	6A
Illuminated Entry Inoperative	[1]

[1] – Courtesy lights and door locks operate properly. Replace Body Control Module (BCM).

INTERIOR LIGHT TEST 2A

COURTESY LIGHT OUTPUT SHORT TO BATTERY

NOTE: Perform INTERIOR LIGHT TEST 1A before proceeding with this test. For connector terminal identification and wiring diagrams, see BODY CONTROL COMPUTER – INTRODUCTION. Perform VERIFICATION TEST: VER-2A after each repair.

CAUTION: Always turn ignition switch to OFF position prior to disconnecting or connecting any module connector.

Disconnect driver's door courtesy light. Disconnect junction block fuse No. 19. Junction block is located behind left end cap of instrument panel. *See Fig. 1.*

INTERIOR LIGHT TEST 3A

COURTESY LIGHTS INOPERATIVE FROM ALL DOORS & COURTESY LIGHT SWITCH

NOTE: Perform INTERIOR LIGHT TEST 1A before proceeding with this test. For connector terminal identification and wiring diagrams, see BODY CONTROL COMPUTER – INTRODUCTION. Perform VERIFICATION TEST: VER-2A after each repair.

CAUTION: Always turn ignition switch to OFF position prior to disconnecting or connecting any module connector.

1) Using scan tool, actuate courtesy/dome lights. If lights illuminate, go to step 4). If lights do not illuminate, go to next step.

2) Access headliner connector at junction block. *See Fig. 4.* Junction block is located behind left end cap of instrument panel. *See Fig. 1.*

3) Backprobing headliner connector, measure voltage between ground and terminal No. 8 (Yellow wire). If voltage is 10 volts or less, go to next step. If voltage is greater than 10 volts, go to INTERIOR LIGHT TEST 3B.

4) Disconnect any courtesy light assembly. Using external voltmeter, measure voltage between ground and fused B+ circuit (Pink wire) on light socket. If voltage is 10 volts or less, repair open Pink wire. If voltage is greater than 10 volts, repair open courtesy light driver circuit (Yellow or Light Green wire).

5) Stop courtesy light actuation. Open driver's door. Using scan tool, read driver's door ajar switch status. If scan tool displays LFDOOR AJAR: CLOSED, replace Body Control Module (BCM). If scan tool does not display LFDOOR AJAR: CLOSED, go to .

Body Control Computer Tests
Concorde, Intrepid, LHS & 300M (Cont.)

INTERIOR LIGHT TEST 3B

COURTESY LIGHTS INOPERATIVE FROM ALL DOORS & COURTESY LIGHT SWITCH

NOTE: Perform INTERIOR LIGHT TEST 3A before proceeding with this test. For connector terminal identification and wiring diagrams, see BODY CONTROL COMPUTER – INTRODUCTION. Perform VERIFICATION TEST: VER-2A after each repair.

CAUTION: Always turn ignition switch to OFF position prior to disconnecting or connecting any module connector.

Remove BCM. Using external voltmeter, measure voltage between ground and terminal No. 2 (courtesy light driver circuit) on junction block internal 20-pin connector. If voltage is 10 volts or less, repair or replace junction block. If voltage is greater than 10 volts, replace BCM.

INTERIOR LIGHT TEST 4A

INOPERATIVE COURTESY LIGHTS

NOTE: Perform INTERIOR LIGHT TEST 1A before proceeding with this test. For connector terminal identification and wiring diagrams, see BODY CONTROL COMPUTER – INTRODUCTION. Perform VERIFICATION TEST: VER-2A after each repair.

CAUTION: Always turn ignition switch to OFF position prior to disconnecting or connecting any module connector.

Remove inoperative bulb. Replace as needed. If bulb is okay, disconnect inoperative light assembly. Using external voltmeter, measure voltage between ground and fused B+ circuit (Pink wire). If voltage is 10 volts or less, repair open Pink wire. If voltage is greater than 10 volts, repair open courtesy light driver circuit (Yellow or Light Green wire).

INTERIOR LIGHT TEST 5A

COURTESY LIGHTS REMAIN ON

NOTE: Perform INTERIOR LIGHT TEST 1A before proceeding with this test. For connector terminal identification and wiring diagrams, see BODY CONTROL COMPUTER – INTRODUCTION. Perform VERIFICATION TEST: VER-2A after each repair.

CAUTION: Always turn ignition switch to OFF position prior to disconnecting or connecting any module connector.

1) Ensure all doors are aligned properly and courtesy light switch is off. Adjust as needed. Close all doors. Using scan tool, read driver's door ajar switch status. If scan tool displays LFDOOR AJAR: CLOSED, go to DOOR AJAR TEST 3A. If scan tool does not display LFDOOR AJAR: CLOSED, go to next step.
2) Using scan tool, read door ajar switch status. If scan tool displays any (RF, LR, RR) DOOR AJAR: CLOSED, go to DOOR AJAR TEST 1A. If scan tool does not display any (RF, LR, RR) DOOR AJAR: CLOSED, go to next step.
3) Disconnect Body Control Module (BCM) from junction block. BCM is mounted to junction block located behind left end cap of instrument panel. *See Fig. 1.*

INTERIOR LIGHT TEST 6A

INOPERATIVE COURTESY LIGHT SWITCH

NOTE: Perform INTERIOR LIGHT TEST 1A before proceeding with this test. For connector terminal identification and wiring diagrams, see BODY CONTROL COMPUTER – INTRODUCTION. Perform VERIFICATION TEST: VER-2A after each repair.

CAUTION: Always turn ignition switch to OFF position prior to disconnecting or connecting any module connector.

Turn dash mounted courtesy light switch to ON position. Using scan tool, select INPUTS/OUTPUTS. Read courtesy light switch status. If scan tool displays ON, replace Body Control Module (BCM). BCM is mounted to junction block located behind left end cap of instrument panel. *See Fig. 1.* If scan tool does not display ON, replace headlight switch.

MEMORY SYSTEM TEST 1A

IDENTIFYING MEMORY SYSTEM MALFUNCTIONS

NOTE: Perform SYSTEM ID TEST 1A before proceeding with this test. For connector terminal identification and wiring diagrams, see BODY CONTROL COMPUTER – INTRODUCTION. Perform VERIFICATION TEST: VER-2A after each repair.

CAUTION: Always turn ignition switch to OFF position prior to disconnecting or connecting any module connector.

NOTE: If seat frame has been unbolted for accessability, frame must be connected to ground during testing.

1) Using scan tool, select BODY COMPUTER, then MEMORY SEAT MODULE. Read DTCs. If no codes are present, operate all seat and mirror switches while monitoring scan tool for DTCs. Operate seat heaters. Reset memory positions. If any codes are set, go to next step. If no codes are set, perform SWITCH SELF-TEST using scan tool.
2) Record DTC(s) that are set. Using scan tool, erase DTCs. operate all seat and mirror switches while monitoring scan tool for DTCs. Operate seat heaters. Reset memory positions. If original DTC(s) are set, see MEMORY SYSTEM DIAGNOSTIC TEST DIRECTORY table and perform indicated test(s). If no codes reset, see MEMORY SYSTEM SYMPTOM DIAGNOSTIC TEST DIRECTORY table.

MEMORY SYSTEM DIAGNOSTIC TEST DIRECTORY

Problem	Perform
EEPROM Refresh Failure	[1] Replace MHSMM
VEHICLE COMMUNICATION TEST	
Ignition Status Message Not Received	[2] 16A
PRNDL Display Message Not Received	[2] 12A
MEMORY SYSTEM TEST	
Front Riser Down Position Stuck	2A
Front Riser Up Position Stuck	3A
Front Riser Out Of Range Low	4A
Front Riser Out Of Range High	5A
Rear Riser Down Position Stuck	6A
Rear Riser Up Position Stuck	7A
Rear Riser Out Of Range Low	8A
Rear Riser Out Of Range High	9A
Horizontal Riser Down Position Stuck	10A
Horizontal Riser Up Position Stuck	11A
Horizontal Riser Out Of Range Low	12A
Horizontal Riser Out Of Range High	13A
Recliner Riser Down Position Stuck	14A
Recliner Riser Up Position Stuck	15A
Recliner Riser Out Of Range Low	16A
Recliner Riser Out Of Range High	17A

1999 ACCESSORIES & EQUIPMENT
Body Control Computer Tests
Concorde, Intrepid, LHS & 300M (Cont.)

MEMORY SYSTEM DIAGNOSTIC TEST DIRECTORY (Cont.)

Problem	MEMORY SYSTEM TEST
Memory Position No. 1 Stuck	18A
Memory Position No. 2 Stuck	19A
Memory Set "S" Position Stuck	20A
Left Seat Heat Output Open	21A
Left Seat Heat Output Shorted To Ground	22A
Left Heated Seat Switch Stuck In Low State	23A
Left Heated Seat Switch Stuck In High State	24A
Left Heated Seat Switch Open/shorted To Ground	25A
Left Thermistor Out Of Range Low	26A
Left Thermistor Out Of Range High	27A
Right Seat Heat Output Open	28A
Right Seat Heat Output Shorted To Ground	29A
Right Heated Seat Switch Stuck In Low State	30A
Right Heated Seat Switch Stuck In High State	31A
Right Heated Seat Switch Open/shorted To Ground	32A
Right Thermistor Out Of Range Low	33A
Right Thermistor Out Of Range High	34A
Left Mirror Horizontal sensor Out Of Range Low	35A
Left Mirror Horizontal sensor Out Of Range High	36A
Left Mirror Vertical Sensor Out Of Range Low	37A
Left Mirror Vertical Sensor Out Of Range High	38A
Right Mirror Horizontal sensor Out Of Range Low	39A
Right Mirror Horizontal sensor Out Of Range High	40A
Right Mirror Vertical Sensor Out Of Range Low	41A
Right Mirror Vertical Sensor Out Of Range High	42A

1 – Replace Memory Heated Seat/Mirror Module.
2 – See appropriate VEHICLE COMMUNICATIONS article.

MEMORY SEAT SYSTEM TEST DIRECTORY

Problem	PERFORM MEMORY SYSTEM TEST
Memory Switch Inoperative	43A
Left Mirror Inoperative From Memory	44A
Right Mirror Inoperative From Memory	45A

MEMORY SYSTEM TEST 2A

FRONT RISER DOWN POSITION STUCK

NOTE: Perform MEMORY SYSTEM TEST 1A before proceeding with this test. For connector terminal identification and wiring diagrams, see BODY CONTROL COMPUTER – INTRODUCTION. Perform VERIFICATION TEST: VER-4A after each repair.

CAUTION: Always turn ignition switch to OFF position prior to disconnecting or connecting any module connector.

1) Disconnect power seat switch 10-pin connector. Using voltmeter, measure voltage between ground and terminal No. 6 (Red/Light Green wire) on power seat switch harness connector. If voltage is .5 volts or less, replace power seat switch. If voltage is greater than .5 volts, go to next step.
2) Disconnect Memory Heated Seat/Mirror Module (MHSMM) 16-pin harness connector. MHSMM is located under front of seat. *See Fig. 7.* Measure voltage between ground and terminal No. 6 (Red/Light Green wire) on power seat switch harness connector. If voltrage is .5 volts or less, replace MHSMM. If voltage is greater than .5 volts, repair Red/Light Green wire for short to voltage.

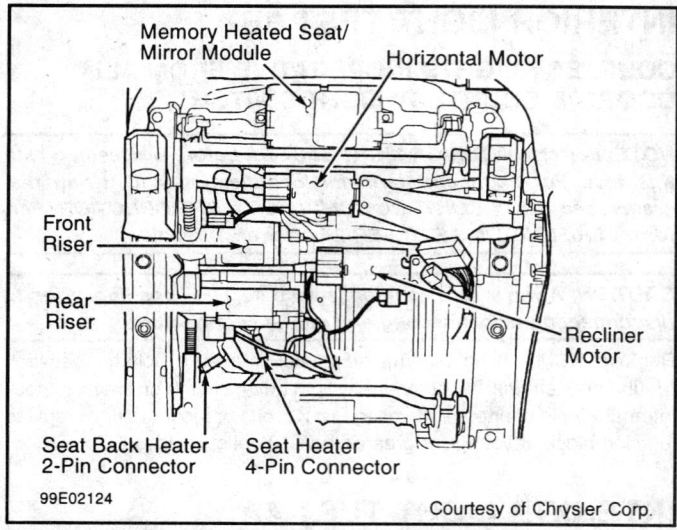

Fig. 7: Identifying Power Seat Components

MEMORY SYSTEM TEST 3A

FRONT RISER UP POSITION STUCK

NOTE: Perform MEMORY SYSTEM TEST 1A before proceeding with this test. For connector terminal identification and wiring diagrams, see BODY CONTROL COMPUTER – INTRODUCTION. Perform VERIFICATION TEST: VER-4A after each repair.

CAUTION: Always turn ignition switch to OFF position prior to disconnecting or connecting any module connector.

1) Disconnect power seat switch 10-pin connector. Using voltmeter, measure voltage between ground and terminal No. 9 (Yellow/Light Green wire) on power seat switch harness connector. If voltage is .5 volts or less, replace power seat switch. If voltage is greater than .5 volts, go to next step.
2) Disconnect Memory Heated Seat/Mirror Module (MHSMM) 16-pin harness connector. MHSMM is located under front of seat. *See Fig. 7.* Measure voltage between ground and terminal No. 9 (Yellow/Light Green wire) on power seat switch harness connector. If voltage is .5 volts or less, replace MHSMM. If voltage is greater than .5 volts, repair Yellow/Light Green wire for short to voltage.

MEMORY SYSTEM TEST 4A

FRONT RISER SENSOR OUT OF RANGE LOW

NOTE: Perform MEMORY SYSTEM TEST 1A before proceeding with this test. For connector terminal identification and wiring diagrams, see BODY CONTROL COMPUTER – INTRODUCTION. Perform VERIFICATION TEST: VER-4A after each repair.

CAUTION: Always turn ignition switch to OFF position prior to disconnecting or connecting any module connector.

1) Disconnect Memory Heated Seat/Mirror Module (MHSMM) 16-pin harness connector. MHSMM is located under front of seat. *See Fig. 7.* Using scan tool, select BODY MEMORY SEAT MODULE, then SENSORS. Read front riser position sensor voltage. If voltage is .7 volts or greater, replace MHSMM. If voltage is less than .7 volts, go to next step.
2) Disconnect front riser position sensor 3-pin connector. Using ohmmeter, measure resistance between ground and terminal "B" (Brown wire) on front riser position sensor harness connector. If resistance is less than 1000 ohms, repair Brown wire for short to ground. If resistance is 1000 ohms or greater, replace track assembly (includes front riser motor).

1999 ACCESSORIES & EQUIPMENT
Body Control Computer Tests
Concorde, Intrepid, LHS & 300M (Cont.)

CHRY
4-157

MEMORY SYSTEM TEST 5A

FRONT RISER SENSOR OUT OF RANGE HIGH

NOTE: Perform MEMORY SYSTEM TEST 1A before proceeding with this test. For connector terminal identification and wiring diagrams, see BODY CONTROL COMPUTER – INTRODUCTION. Perform VERIFICATION TEST: VER-4A after each repair.

CAUTION: Always turn ignition switch to OFF position prior to disconnecting or connecting any module connector.

1) Disconnect Memory Heated Seat/Mirror Module (MHSMM) 16-pin harness connector. MHSMM is located under front of seat. *See Fig. 7.* Using scan tool, select BODY MEMORY SEAT MODULE, then SENSORS. Read front riser position sensor voltage. If voltage is 4.5 volts or less, replace MHSMM. If voltage is greater than 4.5 volts, go to next step.

2) Disconnect front riser position sensor 3-pin connector. Using voltmeter, measure voltage between ground and terminal "B" (Brown wire) on front riser position sensor harness connector. If voltage is .2 volts or greater, repair Brown wire for short to voltage. If voltage is less than .2 volts, replace track assembly (includes front riser motor).

MEMORY SYSTEM TEST 6A

REAR RISER DOWN POSITION STUCK

NOTE: Perform MEMORY SYSTEM TEST 1A before proceeding with this test. For connector terminal identification and wiring diagrams, see BODY CONTROL COMPUTER – INTRODUCTION. Perform VERIFICATION TEST: VER-4A after each repair.

CAUTION: Always turn ignition switch to OFF position prior to disconnecting or connecting any module connector.

1) Disconnect power seat switch 10-pin connector. Using voltmeter, measure voltage between ground and terminal No. 7 (Red/White wire) on power seat switch harness connector. If voltage is .5 volts or less, replace power seat switch. If voltage is greater than .5 volts, go to next step.

2) Disconnect Memory Heated Seat/Mirror Module (MHSMM) 16-pin harness connector. MHSMM is located under front of seat. *See Fig. 7.* Measure voltage between ground and terminal No. 7 (Red/White wire) on power seat switch harness connector. If voltage is .5 volts or less, replace MHSMM. If voltage is greater than .5 volts, repair Red/White wire for short to voltage.

MEMORY SYSTEM TEST 7A

REAR RISER UP POSITION STUCK

NOTE: Perform MEMORY SYSTEM TEST 1A before proceeding with this test. For connector terminal identification and wiring diagrams, see BODY CONTROL COMPUTER – INTRODUCTION. Perform VERIFICATION TEST: VER-4A after each repair.

CAUTION: Always turn ignition switch to OFF position prior to disconnecting or connecting any module connector.

1) Disconnect power seat switch 10-pin connector. Using voltmeter, measure voltage between ground and terminal No. 8 (Yellow/White wire) on power seat switch harness connector. If voltage is .5 volts or less, replace power seat switch. If voltage is greater than .5 volts, go to next step.

2) Disconnect Memory Heated Seat/Mirror Module (MHSMM) 16-pin harness connector. MHSMM is located under front of seat. *See Fig. 7.* Measure voltage between ground and terminal No. 9 (Yellow/White wire)

on power seat switch harness connector. If voltage is .5 volts or less, replace MHSMM. If voltage is greater than .5 volts, repair Yellow/White wire for short to voltage.

MEMORY SYSTEM TEST 8A

REAR RISER SENSOR OUT OF RANGE LOW

NOTE: Perform MEMORY SYSTEM TEST 1A before proceeding with this test. For connector terminal identification and wiring diagrams, see BODY CONTROL COMPUTER – INTRODUCTION. Perform VERIFICATION TEST: VER-4A after each repair.

CAUTION: Always turn ignition switch to OFF position prior to disconnecting or connecting any module connector.

1) Disconnect Memory Heated Seat/Mirror Module (MHSMM) 16-pin harness connector. MHSMM is located under front of seat. *See Fig. 7.* Using scan tool, select BODY MEMORY SEAT MODULE, then SENSORS. Read rear riser position sensor voltage. If voltage is .7 volts or greater, replace MHSMM. If voltage is less than .7 volts, go to next step.

2) Disconnect rear riser position sensor 3-pin connector. Using ohmmeter, measure resistance between ground and terminal "B" (Light Blue/Red wire) on rear riser position sensor harness connector. If resistance is less than 1000 ohms, repair Light Blue/Red wire for short to ground. If resistance is 1000 ohms or greater, replace track assembly (includes rear riser motor).

MEMORY SYSTEM TEST 9A

REAR RISER SENSOR OUT OF RANGE HIGH

NOTE: Perform MEMORY SYSTEM TEST 1A before proceeding with this test. For connector terminal identification and wiring diagrams, see BODY CONTROL COMPUTER – INTRODUCTION. Perform VERIFICATION TEST: VER-4A after each repair.

CAUTION: Always turn ignition switch to OFF position prior to disconnecting or connecting any module connector.

1) Disconnect Memory Heated Seat/Mirror Module (MHSMM) 16-pin harness connector. MHSMM is located under front of seat. *See Fig. 7.* Using scan tool, select BODY MEMORY SEAT MODULE, then SENSORS. Read rear riser position sensor voltage. If voltage is 4.5 volts or less, replace MHSMM. If voltage is greater than 4.5 volts, go to next step.

2) Disconnect rear riser position sensor 3-pin connector. Using voltmeter, measure voltage between ground and terminal "B" (Light Blue/Red wire) on rear riser position sensor harness connector. If voltage is .2 volts or greater, repair Light Blue/Red wire for short to voltage. If voltage is less than .2 volts, replace track assembly (includes front riser motor).

MEMORY SYSTEM TEST 10A

HORIZONTAL FORWARD POSITION STUCK

NOTE: Perform MEMORY SYSTEM TEST 1A before proceeding with this test. For connector terminal identification and wiring diagrams, see BODY CONTROL COMPUTER – INTRODUCTION. Perform VERIFICATION TEST: VER-4A after each repair.

CAUTION: Always turn ignition switch to OFF position prior to disconnecting or connecting any module connector.

1) Disconnect power seat switch 10-pin connector. Using voltmeter, measure voltage between ground and terminal No. 10 (Yellow/Light Blue wire) on power seat switch harness connector. If voltage is .5 volts or less, replace power seat switch. If voltage is greater than .5 volts, go to next step.

CHRY
4-158

1999 ACCESSORIES & EQUIPMENT
Body Control Computer Tests
Concorde, Intrepid, LHS & 300M (Cont.)

2) Disconnect Memory Heated Seat/Mirror Module (MHSMM) 16-pin harness connector. MHSMM is located under front of seat. *See Fig. 7.* Measure voltage between ground and terminal No. 10 (Yellow/Light Blue wire) on power seat switch harness connector. If voltage is .5 volts or less, replace MHSMM. If voltage is greater than .5 volts, repair Yellow/Light Blue wire for short to voltage.

MEMORY SYSTEM TEST 11A

HORIZONTAL REARWARD POSITION STUCK

NOTE: Perform MEMORY SYSTEM TEST 1A before proceeding with this test. For connector terminal identification and wiring diagrams, see BODY CONTROL COMPUTER – INTRODUCTION. Perform VERIFICATION TEST: VER-4A after each repair.

CAUTION: Always turn ignition switch to OFF position prior to disconnecting or connecting any module connector.

1) Disconnect power seat switch 10-pin connector. Using voltmeter, measure voltage between ground and terminal No. 3 (Red/Light Blue wire) on power seat switch harness connector. If voltage is .5 volts or less, replace power seat switch. If voltage is greater than .5 volts, go to next step.
2) Disconnect Memory Heated Seat/Mirror Module (MHSMM) 16-pin harness connector. MHSMM is located under front of seat. *See Fig. 7.* Measure voltage between ground and terminal No. 9 (Red/Light Blue wire) on power seat switch harness connector. If voltage is .5 volts or less, replace MHSMM. If voltage is greater than .5 volts, repair Red/Light Blue wire for short to voltage.

MEMORY SYSTEM TEST 12A

HORIZONTAL SENSOR OUT OF RANGE LOW

NOTE: Perform MEMORY SYSTEM TEST 1A before proceeding with this test. For connector terminal identification and wiring diagrams, see BODY CONTROL COMPUTER – INTRODUCTION. Perform VERIFICATION TEST: VER-4A after each repair.

CAUTION: Always turn ignition switch to OFF position prior to disconnecting or connecting any module connector.

1) Disconnect Memory Heated Seat/Mirror Module (MHSMM) 16-pin harness connector. MHSMM is located under front of seat. *See Fig. 7.* Using scan tool, select BODY MEMORY SEAT MODULE, then SENSORS. Read horizontal position sensor voltage. If voltage is .6 volts or greater, replace MHSMM. If voltage is less than .6 volts, go to next step.
2) Disconnect horizontal position sensor 3-pin connector. Using ohmmeter, measure resistance between ground and terminal "B" (Violet/Red wire) on rear riser position sensor harness connector. If resistance is less than 1000 ohms, repair Violet/Red wire for short to ground. If resistance is 1000 ohms or greater, replace track assembly (includes horizontal motor).

MEMORY SYSTEM TEST 13A

HORIZONTAL SENSOR OUT OF RANGE HIGH

NOTE: Perform MEMORY SYSTEM TEST 1A before proceeding with this test. For connector terminal identification and wiring diagrams, see BODY CONTROL COMPUTER – INTRODUCTION. Perform VERIFICATION TEST: VER-4A after each repair.

CAUTION: Always turn ignition switch to OFF position prior to disconnecting or connecting any module connector.

1) Disconnect Memory Heated Seat/Mirror Module (MHSMM) 16-pin harness connector. MHSMM is located under front of seat. *See Fig. 7.*

Using scan tool, select BODY MEMORY SEAT MODULE, then SENSORS. Read horizontal position sensor voltage. If voltage is 4.8 volts or less, replace MHSMM. If voltage is greater than 4.8 volts, go to next step.
2) Disconnect horizontal position sensor 3-pin connector. Using voltmeter, measure voltage between ground and terminal "B" (Violet/Red wire) on horizontal position sensor harness connector. If voltage is .2 volts or greater, repair Violet/Red wire for short to voltage. If voltage is less than .2 volts, replace track assembly (includes horizontal motor).

MEMORY SYSTEM TEST 14A

RECLINER DOWN POSITION STUCK

NOTE: Perform MEMORY SYSTEM TEST 1A before proceeding with this test. For connector terminal identification and wiring diagrams, see BODY CONTROL COMPUTER – INTRODUCTION. Perform VERIFICATION TEST: VER-4A after each repair.

CAUTION: Always turn ignition switch to OFF position prior to disconnecting or connecting any module connector.

1) Disconnect power seat switch 10-pin connector. Using voltmeter, measure voltage between ground and terminal No. 2 (Gray/White wire) on power seat switch harness connector. If voltage is .5 volts or less, replace power seat switch. If voltage is greater than .5 volts, go to next step.
2) Disconnect Memory Heated Seat/Mirror Module (MHSMM) 16-pin harness connector. MHSMM is located under front of seat. *See Fig. 7.* Measure voltage between ground and terminal No. 2 (Gray/White wire) on power seat switch harness connector. If voltage is .5 volts or less, replace MHSMM. If voltage is greater than .5 volts, repair Gray/White wire for short to voltage.

MEMORY SYSTEM TEST 15A

RECLINER UP POSITION STUCK

NOTE: Perform MEMORY SYSTEM TEST 1A before proceeding with this test. For connector terminal identification and wiring diagrams, see BODY CONTROL COMPUTER – INTRODUCTION. Perform VERIFICATION TEST: VER-4A after each repair.

CAUTION: Always turn ignition switch to OFF position prior to disconnecting or connecting any module connector.

1) Disconnect power seat switch 10-pin connector. Using voltmeter, measure voltage between ground and terminal No. 4 (Gray/Light Blue wire) on power seat switch harness connector. If voltage is .5 volts or less, replace power seat switch. If voltage is greater than .5 volts, go to next step.
2) Disconnect Memory Heated Seat/Mirror Module (MHSMM) 16-pin harness connector. MHSMM is located under front of seat. *See Fig. 7.* Measure voltage between ground and terminal No. 4 (Gray/Light Blue wire) on power seat switch harness connector. If voltage is .5 volts or less, replace MHSMM. If voltage is greater than .5 volts, repair Gray/Light Blue wire for short to voltage.

1999 ACCESSORIES & EQUIPMENT
Body Control Computer Tests
Concorde, Intrepid, LHS & 300M (Cont.)

CHRY
4-159

MEMORY SYSTEM TEST 16A

RECLINER SENSOR OUT OF RANGE LOW

NOTE: *Perform MEMORY SYSTEM TEST 1A before proceeding with this test. For connector terminal identification and wiring diagrams, see BODY CONTROL COMPUTER – INTRODUCTION. Perform VERIFICATION TEST: VER-4A after each repair.*

CAUTION: *Always turn ignition switch to OFF position prior to disconnecting or connecting any module connector.*

1) Disconnect Memory Heated Seat/Mirror Module (MHSMM) 16-pin harness connector. MHSMM is located under front of seat. *See Fig. 7.* Using scan tool, select BODY MEMORY SEAT MODULE, then SENSORS. Read RECLINER POSITION SENSOR voltage. If voltage is .6 volts or greater, replace MHSMM. If voltage is less than .6 volts, go to next step.

2) Disconnect recliner position sensor 3-pin connector. Using ohmmeter, measure resistance between ground and terminal "B" (Light Blue wire) on recliner position sensor harness connector. If resistance is less than 1000 ohms, repair Light Blue wire for short to ground. If resistance is 1000 ohms or greater, replace track assembly (includes recliner motor).

MEMORY SYSTEM TEST 17A

RECLINER SENSOR OUT OF RANGE HIGH

NOTE: *Perform MEMORY SYSTEM TEST 1A before proceeding with this test. For connector terminal identification and wiring diagrams, see BODY CONTROL COMPUTER – INTRODUCTION. Perform VERIFICATION TEST: VER-4A after each repair.*

CAUTION: *Always turn ignition switch to OFF position prior to disconnecting or connecting any module connector.*

1) Disconnect Memory Heated Seat/Mirror Module (MHSMM) 16-pin harness connector. MHSMM is located under front of seat. *See Fig. 7.* Using scan tool, select BODY MEMORY SEAT MODULE, then SENSORS. Read RECLINER POSITION SENSOR voltage. If voltage is 4.8 volts or less, replace MHSMM. If voltage is greater than 4.8 volts, go to next step.

2) Disconnect horizontal position sensor 3-pin connector. Using voltmeter, measure voltage between ground and terminal "B" (Light Blue wire) on horizontal position sensor harness connector. If voltage is .2 volts or greater, repair Light Blue wire for short to voltage. If voltage is less than .2 volts, replace track assembly (includes recliner motor).

MEMORY SYSTEM TEST 18A

MEMORY POSITION NO. 1 STUCK

NOTE: *Perform MEMORY SYSTEM TEST 1A before proceeding with this test. For connector terminal identification and wiring diagrams, see BODY CONTROL COMPUTER – INTRODUCTION. Perform VERIFICATION TEST: VER-4A after each repair.*

CAUTION: *Always turn ignition switch to OFF position prior to disconnecting or connecting any module connector.*

1) Disconnect memory switch 6-pin connector. Using scan tool, select BODY MEMORY SEAT MODULE, then INPUT/OUTPUT. Read MEMORY POSITION NO. 1 status. If scan tool displays OPEN, replace memory switch. If scan tool does not display OPEN, go to next step.

2) Turn ignition off. Disconnect Memory Heated Seat/Mirror Module (MHSMM) 16-pin harness connector. MHSMM is located under front of seat. *See Fig. 7.* Using ohmmeter, measure resistance between ground and terminal No. 6 (Pink/Red wire) on memory switch harness connec-

tor. If resistance is less than 1000 ohms, repair Pink/Red wire for short to ground. If resistance is 1000 ohms or greater, replace MHSMM.

MEMORY SYSTEM TEST 19A

MEMORY POSITION NO. 2 STUCK

NOTE: *Perform MEMORY SYSTEM TEST 1A before proceeding with this test. For connector terminal identification and wiring diagrams, see BODY CONTROL COMPUTER – INTRODUCTION. Perform VERIFICATION TEST: VER-4A after each repair.*

CAUTION: *Always turn ignition switch to OFF position prior to disconnecting or connecting any module connector.*

1) Disconnect memory switch 6-pin connector. Using scan tool, select BODY MEMORY SEAT MODULE, then INPUT/OUTPUT. Read MEMORY POSITION NO. 2 status. If scan tool displays OPEN, replace memory switch. If scan tool does not display OPEN, go to next step.

2) Turn ignition off. Disconnect Memory Heated Seat/Mirror Module (MHSMM) 16-pin harness connector. MHSMM is located under front of seat. *See Fig. 7.* Using ohmmeter, measure resistance between ground and terminal No. 4 (Pink/White wire) on memory switch harness connector. If resistance is less than 1000 ohms, repair Pink/White wire for short to ground. If resistance is 1000 ohms or greater, replace MHSMM.

MEMORY SYSTEM TEST 20A

MEMORY SET "S" POSITION STUCK

NOTE: *Perform MEMORY SYSTEM TEST 1A before proceeding with this test. For connector terminal identification and wiring diagrams, see BODY CONTROL COMPUTER – INTRODUCTION. Perform VERIFICATION TEST: VER-4A after each repair.*

CAUTION: *Always turn ignition switch to OFF position prior to disconnecting or connecting any module connector.*

1) Disconnect memory switch 6-pin connector. Using scan tool, select BODY MEMORY SEAT MODULE, then INPUT/OUTPUT. Read MEMORY SET status. If scan tool displays OPEN, replace memory switch. If scan tool does not display OPEN, go to next step.

2) Turn ignition off. Disconnect Memory Heated Seat/Mirror Module (MHSMM) 16-pin harness connector. MHSMM is located under front of seat. *See Fig. 7.* Using ohmmeter, measure resistance between ground and terminal No. 5 (Pink/Black wire) on memory switch harness connector. If resistance is less than 1000 ohms, repair Pink/Black wire for short to ground. If resistance is 1000 ohms or greater, replace MHSMM.

MEMORY SYSTEM TEST 21A

LEFT SEAT HEAT OUTPUT OPEN

NOTE: *Perform MEMORY SYSTEM TEST 1A before proceeding with this test. For connector terminal identification and wiring diagrams, see BODY CONTROL COMPUTER – INTRODUCTION. Perform VERIFICATION TEST: VER-4A after each repair.*

CAUTION: *Always turn ignition switch to OFF position prior to disconnecting or connecting any module connector.*

1) Turn ignition off. Disconnect Memory Heated Seat/Mirror Module (MHSMM) 12-pin harness connector. MHSMM is located under front of seat. *See Fig. 7.* Using ohmmeter, measure resistance between ground and terminal No. 12 (Red/Dark Green wire) on 12-pin harness connector. If resistance is less than 8.5 ohms, replace MHSMM. If resistance is 8.5 ohms or greater, go to next step.

CHRY
4-160

1999 ACCESSORIES & EQUIPMENT
Body Control Computer Tests
Concorde, Intrepid, LHS & 300M (Cont.)

2) Disconnect left seat cushion heater 4-pin connector. Measure resistance of Red/Dark Green wire between terminal No. 12 on MHSMM 12-pin harness connector and terminal "A" on left seat cushion heater 4-pin harness connector. If resistance is 5 ohms or greater, repair open Red/Dark Green wire. If resistance is less than 5 ohms, go to next step.

3) Measure resistance between terminals "A" (Red/Dark Green wire) and "B" (Brown/Black wire) on left seat cushion heater component connector. If resistance is 2.5 ohms or greater, replace seat cushion. If resistance is less than 2.5 ohms, go to next step.

4) Disconnect seat back heater 2-pin connector. Measure resistance of Brown/Black wire between terminal "B" on seat cushion heater 4-pin component connector and terminal "A" on seat back heater 2-pin harness connector. If resistance is 5 ohms or greater, repair open Brown/Black wire. If resistance is less than 5 ohms, go to next step.

5) Measure resistance between seat back heater 2-pin component connector. If resistance is 2.5 ohms or greater, replace seat back. If resistance is 2.5 ohms or less, repair open Black wire (ground circuit).

MEMORY SYSTEM TEST 22A

LEFT SEAT HEAT OUTPUT SHORTED TO GROUND

NOTE: Perform MEMORY SYSTEM TEST 1A before proceeding with this test. For connector terminal identification and wiring diagrams, see BODY CONTROL COMPUTER – INTRODUCTION. Perform VERIFICATION TEST: VER-4A after each repair.

CAUTION: Always turn ignition switch to OFF position prior to disconnecting or connecting any module connector.

1) Disconnect left seat cushion heater 4-pin connector. Using scan tool, erase DTCs. Turn ignition off. Turn ignition on. Using scan tool, read DTCs. If LEFT SEAT HEAT OUTPUT OPEN fault message is present, go to step . If LEFT SEAT HEAT OUTPUT OPEN fault message is not present, go to next step.

2) Disconnect seat back heater 2-pin connector. Using ohmmeter, measure resistance between ground and terminal "A" (Red/Dark Green wire) on left seat cushion heater component connector. If resistance is less than 1000 ohms, replace seat cushion. If resistance is 1000 ohms or greater, go to next step.

3) Measure resistance between ground and terminal "A" (Brown/Black wire) on seat back heater component connector. If resistance is less than 1000 ohms, repair Brown/Black wire for short to ground. If resistance is 1000 ohms or greater, replace seat back.

4) Turn ignition off. Using ohmmeter, measure resistance between ground and terminal "A" (Red/Dark Green wire) on left seat cushion heater harness connector. If resistance is less than 1000 ohms, repair Red/Dark Green wire for short to ground. If resistance is 1000 ohms or greater, replace Memory Heated Seat/Mirror Module (MHSMM).

MEMORY SYSTEM TEST 23A

LEFT HEATED SEAT SWITCH STUCK IN LOW STATE

NOTE: Perform MEMORY SYSTEM TEST 1A before proceeding with this test. For connector terminal identification and wiring diagrams, see BODY CONTROL COMPUTER – INTRODUCTION. Perform VERIFICATION TEST: VER-4A after each repair.

CAUTION: Always turn ignition switch to OFF position prior to disconnecting or connecting any module connector.

1) Disconnect left seat heater switch 6-pin connector. Using scan tool, erase DTCs. Turn ignition off. Turn ignition on. Using scan tool, read DTCs. If LEFT HEATED SEAT SWITCH OPEN/SHORTED TO GROUND fault message is present, replace seat heater switch. If LEFT HEATED SEAT SWITCH OPEN/SHORTED TO GROUND fault message is not present, go to next step.

2) Disconnect Memory Heated Seat/Mirror Module (MHSMM) 16-pin harness connector. MHSMM is located under front of seat. *See Fig. 7.* Using voltmeter, measure voltage between ground and terminal No. 6 (Tan/Dark Green wire) on left seat heater switch harness connector. If voltage is greater than .2 volts, repair Tan/Dark Green wire for short to voltage. If voltage is .2 volts or less, replace MHSMM.

MEMORY SYSTEM TEST 24A

LEFT HEATED SEAT SWITCH STUCK IN HIGH STATE

NOTE: Perform MEMORY SYSTEM TEST 1A before proceeding with this test. For connector terminal identification and wiring diagrams, see BODY CONTROL COMPUTER – INTRODUCTION. Perform VERIFICATION TEST: VER-4A after each repair.

CAUTION: Always turn ignition switch to OFF position prior to disconnecting or connecting any module connector.

1) Disconnect left seat heater switch 6-pin connector. Using scan tool, erase DTCs. Turn ignition off. Turn ignition on. Using scan tool, read DTCs. If LEFT HEATED SEAT SWITCH OPEN/SHORTED TO GROUND fault message is present, replace seat heater switch. If LEFT HEATED SEAT SWITCH OPEN/SHORTED TO GROUND fault message is not present, go to next step.

2) Disconnect Memory Heated Seat/Mirror Module (MHSMM) 16-pin harness connector. MHSMM is located under front of seat. *See Fig. 7.* Using voltmeter, measure voltage between ground and terminal No. 6 (Tan/Dark Green wire) on left seat heater switch harness connector. If voltage is greater than .2 volts, repair Tan/Dark Green wire for short to voltage. If votlage is .2 volts or less, replace MHSMM.

MEMORY SYSTEM TEST 25A

LEFT HEATED SEAT SWITCH OPEN/SHORTED TO GROUND

NOTE: Perform MEMORY SYSTEM TEST 1A before proceeding with this test. For connector terminal identification and wiring diagrams, see BODY CONTROL COMPUTER – INTRODUCTION. Perform VERIFICATION TEST: VER-4A after each repair.

CAUTION: Always turn ignition switch to OFF position prior to disconnecting or connecting any module connector.

1) Disconnect Memory Heated Seat/Mirror Module (MHSMM) 26-pin harness connector. MHSMM is located under front of seat. *See Fig. 7.* Using voltmeter, measure voltage between ground and terminal No. 18 (Tan/Dark Green wire) on MHSMM harness connector. If voltage is greater than 10 volts, replace MHSMM. If voltage is 10 volts or less, go to next step.

2) Disconnect left seat heater switch 6-pin connector. Using ohmmeter, measure resistance between ground and terminal No. 6 (Tan/Dark Green wire) on left seat heater switch harness connector. If resistance is less than 100 ohms, repair Tan/Dark Green wire for short to ground. If resistance is 100 ohms or greater, go to next step.

3) Connect jumper wire between ground and terminal No. 18 (Tan/Dark Green wire) on on MHSMM harness connector. Measure resistance between ground and terminal No. 6 (Tan/Dark Green wire) on left seat heater switch harness connector. If resistance is less than 5 ohms, replace seat heater switch. If resistance is 100 ohms or greater, repair open Tan/Dark Green wire.

1999 ACCESSORIES & EQUIPMENT
Body Control Computer Tests
Concorde, Intrepid, LHS & 300M (Cont.)

CHRY
4-161

MEMORY SYSTEM TEST 26A

LEFT THERMISTOR OUT OF RANGE LOW

NOTE: Perform MEMORY SYSTEM TEST 1A before proceeding with this test. For connector terminal identification and wiring diagrams, see BODY CONTROL COMPUTER – INTRODUCTION. Perform VERIFICATION TEST: VER-4A after each repair.

CAUTION: Always turn ignition switch to OFF position prior to disconnecting or connecting any module connector.

1) Disconnect Memory Heated Seat/Mirror Module (MHSMM) 26-pin harness connector. MHSMM is located under front of seat. *See Fig. 7.* Using ohmmeter, measure resistance between ground and terminal No. 4 (Tan/Light Blue wire) on MHSMM harness connector. If resistance is 100 ohms or greater, replace MHSMM. If resistance is less than 100 ohms, go to next step.

2) Disconnect left seat cushion heater 4-pin connector. Measure resistance between ground and terminal "C" (Tan/Light Blue wire) on left seat cushion heater harness connector. If resistance is 1000 ohms or greater, replace left seat cushion. If resistance is less than 1000 ohms, repair Tan/Light Blue wire for short to ground.

MEMORY SYSTEM TEST 27A

LEFT THERMISTOR OUT OF RANGE HIGH

NOTE: Perform MEMORY SYSTEM TEST 1A before proceeding with this test. For connector terminal identification and wiring diagrams, see BODY CONTROL COMPUTER – INTRODUCTION. Perform VERIFICATION TEST: VER-4A after each repair.

CAUTION: Always turn ignition switch to OFF position prior to disconnecting or connecting any module connector.

1) Disconnect left seat cushion heater 4-pin connector. Turn ignition on. Turn left seat heater on. Using voltmeter, measure voltage between ground and terminal "D" (Black/Dark Green wire) on left seat cushion heater harness connector. If voltage is greater than 5.5 volts, go to step 3). If voltage is 5.5 volts or less, go to next step.

2) Measure voltage between ground and terminal "C" (Tan/Light Blue wire) on left seat cushion heater harness connector. If voltage is greater than .5 volts, repair (Tan/Light Blue wire) for short to voltage. If voltage is .5 volts or less, replace left seat cushion.

3) Disconnect Memory Heated Seat/Mirror Module (MHSMM) 26-pin harness connector. MHSMM is located under front of seat. *See Fig. 7.* Using voltmeter, measure measure voltage between ground and terminal "D" (Black/Dark Green wire) on left seat cushion heater harness connector. If voltage is greater than .3 volts, repair Black/Dark Green wire for short to voltage. If voltage is .3 volts or less, replace MHSMM.

MEMORY SYSTEM TEST 28A

RIGHT SEAT HEAT OUTPUT OPEN

NOTE: Perform MEMORY SYSTEM TEST 1A before proceeding with this test. For connector terminal identification and wiring diagrams, see BODY CONTROL COMPUTER – INTRODUCTION. Perform VERIFICATION TEST: VER-4A after each repair.

CAUTION: Always turn ignition switch to OFF position prior to disconnecting or connecting any module connector.

1) Turn ignition off. Disconnect Memory Heated Seat/Mirror Module (MHSMM) 12-pin harness connector. MHSMM is located under front of seat. *See Fig. 7.* Using ohmmeter, measure resistance between ground and terminal No. 6 (Red/Tan wire) on 12-pin harness connector. If resistance is less than 8.5 ohms, replace MHSMM. If resistance is 8.5 ohms or greater, go to next step.

2) Disconnect left seat cushion heater 4-pin connector. Measure resistance of Red/Tan wire between terminal No. 6 on MHSMM 12-pin harness connector and terminal "A" on left seat cushion heater 4-pin harness connector. If resistance is 5 ohms or greater, repair open Red/Tan wire. If resistance is less than 5 ohms, go to next step.

3) Measure resistance between terminals "A" (Red/Tan wire) and "B" (Brown/Black wire) on left seat cushion heater component connector. If resistance is 2.5 ohms or greater, replace seat cushion. If resistance is less than 2.5 ohms, go to next step.

4) Disconnect seat back heater 2-pin connector. Measure resistance of Brown/Black wire between terminal "B" on seat cushion heater 4-pin component connector and terminal "A" on seat back heater 2-pin harness connector. If resistance is 5 ohms or greater, repair open Brown/Black wire. If resistance is less than 5 ohms, go to next step.

5) Measure resistance between seat back heater 2-pin component connector. If resistance is 2.5 ohms or greater, replace seat back. If resistance is 2.5 ohms or less, repair open Black wire (ground circuit).

MEMORY SYSTEM TEST 29A

RIGHT SEAT HEAT OUTPUT SHORTED TO GROUND

NOTE: Perform MEMORY SYSTEM TEST 1A before proceeding with this test. For connector terminal identification and wiring diagrams, see BODY CONTROL COMPUTER – INTRODUCTION. Perform VERIFICATION TEST: VER-4A after each repair.

CAUTION: Always turn ignition switch to OFF position prior to disconnecting or connecting any module connector.

1) Disconnect right seat cushion heater 4-pin connector. Using scan tool, erase DTCs. Turn ignition off. Turn ignition on. Using scan tool, read DTCs. If RIGHT SEAT HEAT OUTPUT OPEN fault message is present, go to step 4). If RIGHT SEAT HEAT OUTPUT OPEN fault message is not present, go to next step.

2) Disconnect seat back heater 2-pin connector. Using ohmmeter, measure resistance between ground and terminal "A" (Red/Tan wire) on right seat cushion heater component connector. If resistance is less than 1000 ohms, replace seat cushion. If resistance is 1000 ohms or greater, go to next step.

3) Measure resistance between ground and terminal "A" (Brown/Black wire) on seat back heater component connector. If resistance is less than 1000 ohms, repair Brown/Black wire for short to ground. If resistance is 1000 ohms or greater, replace seat back.

4) Turn ignition off. Using ohmmeter, measure resistance between ground and terminal "A" (Red/Tan wire) on right seat cushion heater harness connector. If resistance is less than 1000 ohms, repair Red/Tan wire for short to ground. If resistance is 1000 ohms or greater, replace Memory Heated Seat/Mirror Module (MHSMM).

MEMORY SYSTEM TEST 30A

RIGHT HEATED SEAT SWITCH STUCK IN LOW STATE

NOTE: Perform MEMORY SYSTEM TEST 1A before proceeding with this test. For connector terminal identification and wiring diagrams, see BODY CONTROL COMPUTER – INTRODUCTION. Perform VERIFICATION TEST: VER-4A after each repair.

CAUTION: Always turn ignition switch to OFF position prior to disconnecting or connecting any module connector.

1) Disconnect right seat heater switch 6-pin connector. Using scan tool, erase DTCs. Turn ignition off. Turn ignition on. Using scan tool, read DTCs. If RIGHT HEATED SEAT SWITCH OPEN/SHORTED TO GROUND fault message is present, replace seat heater switch. If RIGHT HEATED SEAT SWITCH OPEN/SHORTED TO GROUND fault message is not present, go to next step.

CHRY
4-162

1999 ACCESSORIES & EQUIPMENT
Body Control Computer Tests
Concorde, Intrepid, LHS & 300M (Cont.)

2) Disconnect Memory Heated Seat/Mirror Module (MHSMM) 16-pin harness connector. MHSMM is located under front of seat. *See Fig. 7.* Using voltmeter, measure voltage between ground and terminal No. 6 (Tan/Light Green wire) on right seat heater switch harness connector. If voltage is greater than .2 volts, repair Tan/Light Green wire for short to voltage. If votlage is .2 volts or less, replace MHSMM.

MEMORY SYSTEM TEST 31A

RIGHT HEATED SEAT SWITCH STUCK IN HIGH STATE

NOTE: Perform MEMORY SYSTEM TEST 1A before proceeding with this test. For connector terminal identification and wiring diagrams, see BODY CONTROL COMPUTER – INTRODUCTION. Perform VERIFICATION TEST: VER-4A after each repair.

CAUTION: Always turn ignition switch to OFF position prior to disconnecting or connecting any module connector.

1) Disconnect right seat heater switch 6-pin connector. Using scan tool, erase DTCs. Turn ignition off. Turn ignition on. Using scan tool, read DTCs. If RIGHT HEATED SEAT SWITCH OPEN/SHORTED TO GROUND fault message is present, replace seat heater switch. If RIGHT HEATED SEAT SWITCH OPEN/SHORTED TO GROUND fault message is not present, go to next step.

2) Disconnect Memory Heated Seat/Mirror Module (MHSMM) 16-pin harness connector. MHSMM is located under front of seat. *See Fig. 7.* Using voltmeter, measure voltage between ground and terminal No. 6 (Tan/Light Green wire) on right seat heater switch harness connector. If voltage is greater than .2 volts, repair Tan/Light Green wire for short to voltage. If votlage is .2 volts or less, replace MHSMM.

MEMORY SYSTEM TEST 32A

RIGHT HEATED SEAT SWITCH OPEN/SHORTED TO GROUND

NOTE: Perform MEMORY SYSTEM TEST 1A before proceeding with this test. For connector terminal identification and wiring diagrams, see BODY CONTROL COMPUTER – INTRODUCTION. Perform VERIFICATION TEST: VER-4A after each repair.

CAUTION: Always turn ignition switch to OFF position prior to disconnecting or connecting any module connector.

1) Disconnect Memory Heated Seat/Mirror Module (MHSMM) 26-pin harness connector. MHSMM is located under front of seat. *See Fig. 7.* Using voltmeter, measure voltage between ground and terminal No. 5 (Tan/Light Green wire) on MHSMM harness connector. If voltage is greater than 10 volts, replace MHSMM. If voltage is 10 volts or less, go to next step.

2) Disconnect right seat heater switch 6-pin connector. Using ohmmeter, measure resistance between ground and terminal No. 6 (Tan/Light Green wire) on right seat heater switch harness connector. If resistance is less than 100 ohms, repair Tan/Dark Green wire for short to ground. If resistance is 100 ohms or greater, go to next step.

3) Connect jumper wire between ground and terminal No. 5 (Tan/Light Green wire) on on MHSMM harness connector. Measure resistance between ground and terminal No. 6 (Tan/Light Green wire) on right seat heater switch harness connector. If resistance is less than 5 ohms, replace seat heater switch. If resistance is 100 ohms or greater, repair open Tan/Light Green wire.

MEMORY SYSTEM TEST 33A

RIGHT THERMISTOR OUT OF RANGE LOW

NOTE: Perform MEMORY SYSTEM TEST 1A before proceeding with this test. For connector terminal identification and wiring diagrams, see BODY CONTROL COMPUTER – INTRODUCTION. Perform VERIFICATION TEST: VER-4A after each repair.

CAUTION: Always turn ignition switch to OFF position prior to disconnecting or connecting any module connector.

1) Disconnect Memory Heated Seat/Mirror Module (MHSMM) 26-pin harness connector. MHSMM is located under front of seat. *See Fig. 7.* Using ohmmeter, measure resistance between ground and terminal No. 17 (Tan/Dark Blue wire) on MHSMM harness connector. If resistance is 100 ohms or greater, replace MHSMM. If resistance is less than 100 ohms, go to next step.

2) Disconnect right seat cushion heater 4-pin connector. Measure resistance between ground and terminal "C" (Tan/Dark Blue wire) on right seat cushion heater harness connector. If resistance is 1000 ohms or greater, replace right seat cushion. If resistance is less than 1000 ohms, repair Tan/Dark Blue wire for short to ground.

MEMORY SYSTEM TEST 34A

RIGHT THERMISTOR OUT OF RANGE HIGH

NOTE: Perform MEMORY SYSTEM TEST 1A before proceeding with this test. For connector terminal identification and wiring diagrams, see BODY CONTROL COMPUTER – INTRODUCTION. Perform VERIFICATION TEST: VER-4A after each repair.

CAUTION: Always turn ignition switch to OFF position prior to disconnecting or connecting any module connector.

1) Disconnect right seat cushion heater 4-pin connector. Turn ignition on. Turn right seat heater on. Using voltmeter, measure voltage between ground and terminal "D" (Black/Light Green wire) on right seat cushion heater harness connector. If voltage is greater than 5.5 volts, go to step 3). If voltage is 5.5 volts or less, go to next step.

2) Measure voltage between ground and terminal "C" (Tan/Dark Blue wire) on right seat cushion heater harness connector. If voltage is greater than .5 volts, repair (Tan/Dark Blue wire) for short to voltage. If voltage is .5 volts or less, replace right seat cushion.

3) Disconnect Memory Heated Seat/Mirror Module (MHSMM) 26-pin harness connector. MHSMM is located under front of seat. *See Fig. 7.* Using voltmeter, measure measure voltage between ground and terminal "D" (Black/Light Green wire) on right seat cushion heater harness connector. If voltage is greater than .3 volts, repair Black/Light Green wire for short to voltage. If voltage is .3 volts or less, replace MHSMM.

MEMORY SYSTEM TEST 35A

LEFT MIRROR HORIZONTAL SENSOR OUT OF RANGE LOW

NOTE: Perform MEMORY SYSTEM TEST 1A before proceeding with this test. For connector terminal identification and wiring diagrams, see BODY CONTROL COMPUTER – INTRODUCTION. Perform VERIFICATION TEST: VER-4A after each repair.

CAUTION: Always turn ignition switch to OFF position prior to disconnecting or connecting any module connector.

1) Disconnect Memory Heated Seat/Mirror Module (MHSMM) 26-pin harness connector. MHSMM is located under front of seat. Using ohmmeter, measure resistance between ground and terminal No.

1999 ACCESSORIES & EQUIPMENT
Body Control Computer Tests
Concorde, Intrepid, LHS & 300M (Cont.)

CHRY
4-163

20 (Dark Blue/Yellow wire) on MHSMM harness connector. If resistance is .7 ohms or greater, replace MHSMM. If resistance is less than .7 ohms, go to next step.

2) Disconnect left memory mirror connector. Measure resistance between ground and terminal No. 9 (Dark Blue/Yellow wire) on left memory mirror harness connector. If resistance is less than 1000 ohms, repair Dark Blue/Yellow wire for short to ground. If resistance is 1000 ohms or greater, replace left memory mirror.

MEMORY SYSTEM TEST 36A

LEFT MIRROR HORIZONTAL SENSOR OUT OF RANGE HIGH

NOTE: *Perform MEMORY SYSTEM TEST 1A before proceeding with this test. For connector terminal identification and wiring diagrams, see BODY CONTROL COMPUTER – INTRODUCTION. Perform VERIFICATION TEST: VER-4A after each repair.*

CAUTION: *Always turn ignition switch to OFF position prior to disconnecting or connecting any module connector.*

1) Disconnect Memory Heated Seat/Mirror Module (MHSMM) 26-pin harness connector. MHSMM is located under front of seat. *See Fig. 7.* Using voltmeter, measure voltage between ground and terminal No. 20 (Dark Blue/Yellow wire) on MHSMM harness connector. If voltage is 4.5 volts or less, replace MHSMM. If voltage is greater than 4.5 ohms, go to next step.

2) Disconnect left memory mirror connector. Measure voltage between ground and terminal No. 9 (Dark Blue/Yellow wire) on left memory mirror harness connector. If voltage is .2 volts or less, repair Dark Blue/Yellow wire for short to voltage. If voltage is greater than .2 volts, replace left memory mirror.

MEMORY SYSTEM TEST 37A

LEFT MIRROR VERTICAL SENSOR OUT OF RANGE LOW

NOTE: *Perform MEMORY SYSTEM TEST 1A before proceeding with this test. For connector terminal identification and wiring diagrams, see BODY CONTROL COMPUTER – INTRODUCTION. Perform VERIFICATION TEST: VER-4A after each repair.*

CAUTION: *Always turn ignition switch to OFF position prior to disconnecting or connecting any module connector.*

1) Disconnect Memory Heated Seat/Mirror Module (MHSMM) 26-pin harness connector. MHSMM is located under front of seat. *See Fig. 7.* Using ohmmeter, measure resistance between ground and terminal No. 7 (Yellow/Orange wire) on MHSMM harness connector. If resistance is .7 ohms or greater, replace MHSMM. If resistance is less than .7 ohms, go to next step.

2) Disconnect left memory mirror connector. Measure resistance between ground and terminal No. 7 (Yellow/Orange wire) on left memory mirror harness connector. If resistance is less than 1000 ohms, repair Yellow/Orange wire for short to ground. If resistance is 1000 ohms or greater, replace left memory mirror.

MEMORY SYSTEM TEST 38A

LEFT MIRROR VERTICAL SENSOR OUT OF RANGE HIGH

NOTE: *Perform MEMORY SYSTEM TEST 1A before proceeding with this test. For connector terminal identification and wiring diagrams, see BODY CONTROL COMPUTER – INTRODUCTION. Perform VERIFICATION TEST: VER-4A after each repair.*

CAUTION: *Always turn ignition switch to OFF position prior to disconnecting or connecting any module connector.*

1) Disconnect Memory Heated Seat/Mirror Module (MHSMM) 26-pin harness connector. MHSMM is located under front of seat. *See Fig. 7.* Using voltmeter, measure voltage between ground and terminal No. 7 (Yellow/Orange wire) on MHSMM harness connector. If voltage is 4.5 volts or less, replace MHSMM. If voltage is greater than 4.5 ohms, go to next step.

2) Disconnect left memory mirror connector. Measure voltage between ground and terminal No. 7 (Yellow/Orange wire) on left memory mirror harness connector. If voltage is .2 volts or less, repair Yellow/Orange wire for short to voltage. If voltage is greater than .2 volts, replace left memory mirror.

MEMORY SYSTEM TEST 39A

RIGHT MIRROR HORIZONTAL SENSOR OUT OF RANGE LOW

NOTE: *Perform MEMORY SYSTEM TEST 1A before proceeding with this test. For connector terminal identification and wiring diagrams, see BODY CONTROL COMPUTER – INTRODUCTION. Perform VERIFICATION TEST: VER-4A after each repair.*

CAUTION: *Always turn ignition switch to OFF position prior to disconnecting or connecting any module connector.*

1) Disconnect Memory Heated Seat/Mirror Module (MHSMM) 26-pin harness connector. MHSMM is located under front of seat. *See Fig. 7.* Using ohmmeter, measure resistance between ground and terminal No. 19 (Dark Green/Red wire) on MHSMM harness connector. If resistance is .7 ohms or greater, replace MHSMM. If resistance is less than .7 ohms, go to next step.

2) Disconnect right memory mirror connector. Measure resistance between ground and terminal No. 9 (Dark Green/Red wire) on right memory mirror harness connector. If resistance is less than 1000 ohms, repair Dark Green/Red wire for short to ground. If resistance is 1000 ohms or greater, replace right memory mirror.

MEMORY SYSTEM TEST 40A

RIGHT MIRROR HORIZONTAL SENSOR OUT OF RANGE HIGH

NOTE: *Perform MEMORY SYSTEM TEST 1A before proceeding with this test. For connector terminal identification and wiring diagrams, see BODY CONTROL COMPUTER – INTRODUCTION. Perform VERIFICATION TEST: VER-4A after each repair.*

CAUTION: *Always turn ignition switch to OFF position prior to disconnecting or connecting any module connector.*

1) Disconnect Memory Heated Seat/Mirror Module (MHSMM) 26-pin harness connector. MHSMM is located under front of seat. *See Fig. 7.* Using voltmeter, measure voltage between ground and terminal No. 19 (Dark Green/Red wire) on MHSMM harness connector. If voltage is 4.5 volts or less, replace MHSMM. If voltage is greater than 4.5 ohms, go to next step.

CHRY
4-164

1999 ACCESSORIES & EQUIPMENT
Body Control Computer Tests
Concorde, Intrepid, LHS & 300M (Cont.)

2) Disconnect right memory mirror connector. Measure voltage between ground and terminal No. 9 (Dark Green/Red wire) on right memory mirror harness connector. If voltage is .2 volts or less, repair Dark Green/Red wire for short to voltage. If voltage is greater than .2 volts, replace right memory mirror.

MEMORY SYSTEM TEST 41A

RIGHT MIRROR VERTICAL SENSOR OUT OF RANGE LOW

NOTE: *Perform MEMORY SYSTEM TEST 1A before proceeding with this test. For connector terminal identification and wiring diagrams, see BODY CONTROL COMPUTER – INTRODUCTION. Perform VERIFICATION TEST: VER-4A after each repair.*

CAUTION: *Always turn ignition switch to OFF position prior to disconnecting or connecting any module connector.*

1) Disconnect Memory Heated Seat/Mirror Module (MHSMM) 26-pin harness connector. MHSMM is located under front of seat. See Fig. 7. Using ohmmeter, measure resistance between ground and terminal No. 6 (Yellow/Red wire) on MHSMM harness connector. If resistance is .7 ohms or greater, replace MHSMM. If resistance is less than .7 ohms, go to next step.

2) Disconnect right memory mirror connector. Measure resistance between ground and terminal No. 7 (Yellow/Red wire) on right memory mirror harness connector. If resistance is less than 1000 ohms, repair Yellow/Red wire for short to ground. If resistance is 1000 ohms or greater, replace right memory mirror.

MEMORY SYSTEM TEST 42A

RIGHT MIRROR VERTICAL SENSOR OUT OF RANGE HIGH

NOTE: *Perform MEMORY SYSTEM TEST 1A before proceeding with this test. For connector terminal identification and wiring diagrams, see BODY CONTROL COMPUTER – INTRODUCTION. Perform VERIFICATION TEST: VER-4A after each repair.*

CAUTION: *Always turn ignition switch to OFF position prior to disconnecting or connecting any module connector.*

1) Disconnect Memory Heated Seat/Mirror Module (MHSMM) 26-pin harness connector. MHSMM is located under front of seat. See Fig. 7. Using voltmeter, measure voltage between ground and terminal No. 6 (Yellow/Red wire) on MHSMM harness connector. If voltage is 4.5 volts or less, replace MHSMM. If voltage is greater than 4.5 ohms, go to next step.

2) Disconnect right memory mirror connector. Measure voltage between ground and terminal No. 7 (Yellow/Red wire) on right memory mirror harness connector. If voltage is .2 volts or less, repair Yellow/Red wire for short to voltage. If voltage is greater than .2 volts, replace right memory mirror.

MEMORY SYSTEM TEST 43A

INOPERATIVE MEMORY SWITCH

NOTE: *Perform MEMORY SYSTEM TEST 1A before proceeding with this test. For connector terminal identification and wiring diagrams, see BODY CONTROL COMPUTER – INTRODUCTION. Perform VERIFICATION TEST: VER-4A after each repair.*

CAUTION: *Always turn ignition switch to OFF position prior to disconnecting or connecting any module connector.*

1) Disconnect memory switch connector. Using ohmmeter, measure resistance between ground and terminal No. 3 (Black wire) on memory switch harness connector. If resistance is 5 ohms or greater, repair open ground circuit. If resistance is 5 ohms or less, go to next step.

2) Using voltmeter, measure voltage between ground and terminal No. 5 (Pink/Black wire) on memory switch harness connector. If voltage is .5 volts or less, go to step 5). If voltage is greater than .5 volts, go to next step.

3) Measure voltage between ground and terminal No. 6 (Pink/Red wire) on memory switch harness connector. If voltage is .5 volts or less, go to MEMORY SYSTEM TEST 43B. If voltage is greater than .5 volts, go to next step.

4) Measure voltage between ground and terminal No. 4 (Pink/White wire) on memory switch harness connector. If voltage is .5 volts or less, go to MEMORY SYSTEM TEST 43C. If voltage is greater than .5 volts, replace memory switch.

NOTE: *Ensure seat frame is connected to ground if seat is unbolted from vehicle.*

5) Disconnect Memory Heated Seat/Mirror Module (MHSMM) 26-pin harness connector. MHSMM is located under front of seat. See Fig. 7. Connect jumper wire between ground and terminal No. 5 (Pink/Black wire) on memory switch harness connector. Using ohmmeter, measure resistance between ground and terminal No. 13 (Pink/Black wire) on MHSMM harness connector. If resistance is 5 ohms or greater, repair open Pink/Black wire. If resistance is less than 5 ohms, replace MHSMM.

MEMORY SYSTEM TEST 43B

INOPERATIVE MEMORY SWITCH

NOTE: *Perform MEMORY SYSTEM TEST 43A before proceeding with this test. For connector terminal identification and wiring diagrams, see BODY CONTROL COMPUTER – INTRODUCTION. Perform VERIFICATION TEST: VER-4A after each repair.*

CAUTION: *Always turn ignition switch to OFF position prior to disconnecting or connecting any module connector.*

NOTE: *Ensure seat frame is connected to ground if seat is unbolted from vehicle.*

Disconnect Memory Heated Seat/Mirror Module (MHSMM) 26-pin harness connector. MHSMM is located under front of seat. See Fig. 7. Connect jumper wire between ground and terminal No. 6 (Pink/Red wire) on memory switch harness connector. Using ohmmeter, measure resistance between ground and terminal No. 12 (Pink/Red wire) on MHSMM harness connector. If resistance is 5 ohms or greater, repair open Pink/Red wire. If resistance is less than 5 ohms, replace MHSMM.

MEMORY SYSTEM TEST 43C

INOPERATIVE MEMORY SWITCH

NOTE: *Perform MEMORY SYSTEM TEST 43A before proceeding with this test. For connector terminal identification and wiring diagrams, see BODY CONTROL COMPUTER – INTRODUCTION. Perform VERIFICATION TEST: VER-4A after each repair.*

CAUTION: *Always turn ignition switch to OFF position prior to disconnecting or connecting any module connector.*

NOTE: *Ensure seat frame is connected to ground if seat is unbolted from vehicle.*

Disconnect Memory Heated Seat/Mirror Module (MHSMM) 26-pin harness connector. MHSMM is located under front of seat. See Fig. 7. Connect jumper wire between ground and terminal No. 4 (Pink/White wire) on memory switch harness connector. Using ohmmeter, measure

1999 ACCESSORIES & EQUIPMENT
Body Control Computer Tests
Concorde, Intrepid, LHS & 300M (Cont.)

CHRY
4-165

resistance between ground and terminal No. 25 (Pink/White wire) on MHSMM harness connector. If resistance is 5 ohms or greater, repair open Pink/White wire. If resistance is less than 5 ohms, replace MHSMM.

MEMORY SYSTEM TEST 44A

LEFT MIRROR INOPERATIVE FROM MEMORY

NOTE: Perform MEMORY SYSTEM TEST 1A before proceeding with this test. For connector terminal identification and wiring diagrams, see BODY CONTROL COMPUTER – INTRODUCTION. Perform VERIFICATION TEST: VER-4A after each repair.

CAUTION: Always turn ignition switch to OFF position prior to disconnecting or connecting any module connector.

NOTE: Ensure seat frame is connected to ground if seat is unbolted from vehicle.

1) Disconnect Memory Heated Seat/Mirror Module (MHSMM) 16-pin harness connector. MHSMM is located under front of seat. *See Fig. 7.* Using voltmeter, measure voltage between ground and terminal No. 4 (Black/White wire) on MHSMM harness connector. While monitoring voltmeter, press left mirror switch to left position. If voltage is 10 volts or less when switch is pressed, repair open Black/White wire. If voltage is greater than 10 volts when switch is pressed, go to next step.

2) Measure voltage between ground and terminal No. 5 (Yellow wire) on MHSMM harness connector. While monitoring voltmeter, press left mirror switch to up position. If voltage is 10 volts or less when switch is pressed, repair open Yellow wire. If voltage is greater than 10 volts when switch is pressed, go to next step.

3) Measure voltage between ground and terminal No. 3 (Yellow/Pink wire) on MHSMM harness connector. While monitoring voltmeter, press left mirror switch to down position. If voltage is 10 volts or less when switch is pressed, repair open Yellow/Pink wire. If voltage is greater than 10 volts when switch is pressed, repair MHSMM.

MEMORY SYSTEM TEST 45A

RIGHT MIRROR INOPERATIVE FROM MEMORY

NOTE: Perform MEMORY SYSTEM TEST 1A before proceeding with this test. For connector terminal identification and wiring diagrams, see BODY CONTROL COMPUTER – INTRODUCTION. Perform VERIFICATION TEST: VER-4A after each repair.

CAUTION: Always turn ignition switch to OFF position prior to disconnecting or connecting any module connector.

NOTE: Ensure seat frame is connected to ground if seat is unbolted from vehicle.

1) Disconnect Memory Heated Seat/Mirror Module (MHSMM) 16-pin harness connector. MHSMM is located under front of seat. *See Fig. 7.* Using voltmeter, measure voltage between ground and terminal No. 12 (Dark Blue wire) on MHSMM harness connector. While monitoring voltmeter, press right mirror switch to left position. If voltage is 10 volts or less when switch is pressed, repair open Dark Blue wire. If voltage is greater than 10 volts when switch is pressed, go to next step.

2) Measure voltage between ground and terminal No. 13 (Yellow/Black wire) on MHSMM harness connector. While monitoring voltmeter, press right mirror switch to up position. If voltage is 10 volts or less when switch is pressed, repair open Yellow/Black wire. If voltage is greater than 10 volts when switch is pressed, go to next step.

3) Measure voltage between ground and terminal No. 11 (White wire) on MHSMM harness connector. While monitoring voltmeter, press right mirror switch to down position. If voltage is 10 volts or less when switch

is pressed, repair open White wire. If voltage is greater than 10 volts when switch is pressed, repair MHSMM.

OTIS TEST 1A

IDENTIFYING OVERHEAD TRAVEL INFORMATION SYSTEM (OTIS) MALFUNCTIONS

NOTE: Perform SYSTEM ID TEST 1A before proceeding with this test. For connector terminal identification and wiring diagrams, see BODY CONTROL COMPUTER – INTRODUCTION. Perform VERIFICATION TEST: VER-2A after each repair.

CAUTION: Always turn ignition switch to OFF position prior to disconnecting or connecting any module connector.

1) Using scan tool, select BODY, then OTIS. If scan tool displays NO RESPONSE, go to TEST 8A in appropriate VEHICLE COMMUNICATIONS article. If any other communication problem exists, go to TEST 1A in appropriate VEHICLE COMMUNICATIONS article. If no communication problem exists, go to next step.

2) Select AUTO SELF TEST and observe OTIS screen. If any OTIS segments fail to illuminate, replace OTIS module. If OTIS screen displays FAIL, replace OTIS module. If OTIS screen does not show any communication, replace Body Control Module (BCM).

3) Diagnosis of OTIS system is separated into 9 faults. Identify fault(s) listed in OTIS SYSTEM DIAGNOSTIC TEST DIRECTORY table and perform indicated test(s)and perform indicated test(s).

4) If OTIS fails to respond to instrument cluster dimming, replace OTIS module. Calibrate compass if inoperative or wrong. See owner's manual. If compass goes blank, replace OTIS module.

OTIS SYSTEM DIAGNOSTIC TEST DIRECTORY

Problem	OTIS TEST
Outside Temperature	
OTIS Displays SC Or OC	2A
Sensor Failure	2A
Incorrect Reading (5 Degree Variation)	3A
Average MPG Or Fuel Economy [1]	4A
OTIS Switches	5A
	INSTRUMENT CLUSTER TEST
Distance To Empty Inoperative Or Wrong	12A
Elapsed Time Inoperative Or Wrong	Replace BCM

[1] – Average MPG or fuel economy is inoperative or wrong. MPG calculations are only accurate to within 10 miles.

OTIS TEST 2A

OTIS DISPLAYING "SC" Or "OC"

NOTE: Perform OTIS TEST 1A before proceeding with this test. For connector terminal identification and wiring diagrams, see BODY CONTROL COMPUTER – INTRODUCTION article. Perform VERIFICATION TEST: VER-2A after each repair. Drive vehicle at least 3 miles (greater than 25 MPH) to update OTIS and perform VERIFICATION TEST: VER-2A after each repair.

CAUTION: Always turn ignition switch to OFF position prior to disconnecting any module connector.

1) Using scan tool, select BODY CONTROLLER SENSORS. Read AMBIENT TEMPERATURE voltage. If scan tool displays AMBIENT TEMP. VOLTAGE (BELOW) or .5 VOLTS, go to next step. If scan tool does not display AMBIENT TEMP. VOLTAGE (BELOW) or .5 VOLTS, go to step 4).

2) Disconnect ambient temperature sensor connector. Sensor is located behind front bumper (right center). Read AMBIENT TEMPERATURE voltage. If voltage displayed increased to 5 volts (approximately),

CHRY
4-166

1999 ACCESSORIES & EQUIPMENT
Body Control Computer Tests
Concorde, Intrepid, LHS & 300M (Cont.)

replace ambient temperature sensor. If voltage displayed did not increase to 5 volts (approximately), go to next step.

3) Turn ignition off. Disconnect Body Control Module (BCM) Bone 12-pin connector C3. BCM is mounted to junction block located behind left end cap of instrument panel. *See Fig. 1.* Using external ohmmeter, measure resistance between ground and terminal No. 5 (Violet/Light Green wire) on Bone harness connector. If resistance is less than 300 ohms, repair Violet/Light Green wire for short to ground. If resistance is 300 ohms or greater, replace BCM.

4) Disconnect ambient temperature sensor connector. Sensor is located behind front bumper (right center). Read AMBIENT TEMPERATURE voltage. If voltage displayed is 5 volts (approximately), go to next step. If voltage displayed is not 5 volts (approximately), go to OTIS TEST 3A.

5) Connect jumper wire between ambient temperature sensor harness connector terminals. Read AMBIENT TEMPERATURE voltage. If voltage displayed is 0 volts (approximately), replace ambient temperature sensor. If voltage displayed is not 0 volts (approximately), go to next step.

6) Remove jumper wire. Connect jumper wire between ground and terminal No. 2 (Violet/Light Green wire) on ambient temperature sensor harness connector. Read AMBIENT TEMPERATURE voltage. If voltage displayed is 0 volts (approximately), go to step **8)**. If voltage displayed is not 0 volts (approximately), go to next step.

7) With jumper wire connected, turn ignition off. Disconnect Body Control Module (BCM) Bone 12-pin connector C3. BCM is mounted to junction block located behind left end cap of instrument panel. *See Fig. 1.*

8) Disconnect jumper wire. Connect jumper wire between ground and terminal No. 1 (Dark Blue/Gray wire) on ambient temperature sensor harness connector. Using external ohmmeter, measure resistance between ground and terminal No. 10 (Dark Blue/Gray wire) on Bone harness connector. If resistance is less than 5 ohms, replace BCM. If resistance is 5 ohms or greater, repair open Dark Blue/Gray wire.

OTIS TEST 3A

INCORRECT AMBIENT TEMPERATURE READING

NOTE: Perform OTIS TEST 1A before proceeding with this test. For connector terminal identification and wiring diagrams, see BODY CONTROL COMPUTER – INTRODUCTION article. Perform VERIFICATION TEST: VER-2A after each repair. Drive vehicle at least 3 miles (greater than 25 MPH) to update OTIS and perform VERIFICATION TEST: VER-2A after each repair.

CAUTION: Always turn ignition switch to OFF position prior to disconnecting any module connector.

1) Disconnect and remove ambient temperature sensor. Sensor is located behind front bumper, right of center. Using external ohmmeter, measure resistance between sensor terminals and compare with AMBIENT TEMPERATURE SENSOR SPECIFICATIONS table. Go to next step.

AMBIENT TEMPERATURE SENSOR SPECIFICATIONS

Ambient Temperature	k/ohms
32°F (0°C)	29.3-36.0
50°F (10°C)	18.0-22.0
68°F (20°C)	11.4-13.6
77°F (25°C)	9.1-10.8
86°F (30°C)	7.4-8.7
104°F (40°C)	4.9-5.7
122°F (50°C)	3.3-3.8

2) If resistance measurement does not correspond with AMBIENT TEMPERATURE SENSOR SPECIFICATIONS table, replace sensor. If sensor is within specification, turn ignition off. Close all vehicle doors and ensure all lights are off. Wait one minute.

3) Using external ohmmeter, measure resistance between ground and terminal No. 1 (Dark Blue/Gray wire) on ambient temperature sensor harness connector. If resistance is less than 30 ohms, go to OTIS TEST 3B. If resistance is 30 ohms or greater, go to next step.

4) Connect jumper wire between ground and terminal No. 1 (Dark Blue/Gray wire) on sensor connector. Disconnect Body Control Module (BCM) Bone 12-pin connector C3. BCM is mounted to junction block located behind left end cap of instrument panel. *See Fig. 1.*

5) Using external ohmmeter, measure resistance between ground and terminal No. 10 (Dark Blue/Gray wire) on Bone harness connector. If resistance is less than 5 ohms, replace BCM. If resistance is 5 ohms or greater, repair open Dark Blue/Gray wire.

OTIS TEST 3B

INCORRECT AMBIENT TEMPERATURE READING

NOTE: Perform OTIS TEST 1A before proceeding with this test. For connector terminal identification and wiring diagrams, see BODY CONTROL COMPUTER – INTRODUCTION article. Perform VERIFICATION TEST: VER-2A after each repair. Drive vehicle at least 3 miles (greater than 25 MPH) to update OTIS and perform VERIFICATION TEST: VER-2A after each repair.

CAUTION: Always turn ignition switch to OFF position prior to disconnecting any module connector.

1) Disconnect Body Control Module (BCM) Bone 12-pin connector C3. BCM is mounted to junction block located behind left end cap of instrument panel. *See Fig. 1.*

2) Measure resistance between ground and terminal No. 5 (Violet/Dark Green wire) on Bone connector. If resistance is less than 50 k/ohms, repair Violet/Dark Green wire for partial short to ground. If resistance is 50 k/ohms or greater, go to next step.

3) Measure resistance between terminals No. 5 and 10 on Bone connector. If resistance is less than 50 k/ohms, repair Violet/Dark Green wire for partial short to Dark Blue/Gray wire. If resistance is 50 k/ohms or greater, replace BCM.

OTIS TEST 4A

OTIS MILEAGE AND DISTANCE FUNCTION MALFUNCTION

NOTE: Perform OTIS TEST 1A before proceeding with this test. For connector terminal identification and wiring diagrams, see BODY CONTROL COMPUTER – INTRODUCTION article. Perform VERIFICATION TEST: VER-2A after each repair. Drive vehicle at least 3 miles (greater than 25 MPH) to update OTIS and perform VERIFICATION TEST: VER-2A after each repair.

CAUTION: Always turn ignition switch to OFF position prior to disconnecting any module connector.

1) If all other OTIS functions operating properly, go to next step. If any other OTIS functions are not working, replace OTIS unit.

2) Using scan tool, select engine controller. Read PCM DTCs. If any DTCs exist, go to appropriate SELF-DIAGNOSTICS article in ENGINE PERFORMANCE in appropriate MITCHELL® manual. If no DTCs exist, check for correct tire size.

1999 ACCESSORIES & EQUIPMENT
Body Control Computer Tests
Concorde, Intrepid, LHS & 300M (Cont.)

CHRY
4-167

OTIS TEST 5A

REPAIRING OTIS SWITCHES

NOTE: Perform OTIS TEST 1A before proceeding with this test. For connector terminal identification and wiring diagrams, see BODY CONTROL COMPUTER – INTRODUCTION article. Perform VERIFICATION TEST: VER-2A after each repair. Drive vehicle at least 3 miles (greater than 25 MPH) to update OTIS and perform VERIFICATION TEST: VER-2A after each repair.

CAUTION: Always turn ignition switch to OFF position prior to disconnecting any module connector.

1) Turn ignition off and leave key in ignition. Open driver's door. If chime sounds, go to next step. If chime does not sound, go to CHIME TEST 5A.

2) Turn ignition on and close driver's door. Press each button on OTIS unit and listen for audible beep at Body Control Module (BCM). If beep was heard each time a button is pressed, OTIS is currently operating correctly. If beep was not heard each time a button was pressed, replace OTIS unit.

POWER DOOR LOCK TEST 1A

IDENTIFYING POWER DOOR LOCK PROBLEMS

NOTE: Perform SYMPTOM ID TEST 1A before proceeding with this test. For connector terminal identification and wiring diagrams, see BODY CONTROL COMPUTER – INTRODUCTION article. Perform VERIFICATION TEST: VER-2A after each repair.

CAUTION: Always turn ignition switch to OFF position prior to disconnecting or connecting any module connector.

Using scan tool, read body DTCs. If any power door lock DTCs are present, see POWER DOOR LOCK FAULT MESSAGE DIRECTORY table. If no DTCs are present, see POWER DOOR LOCK SYMPTOM TEST DIRECTORY table.

POWER DOOR LOCK MESSAGE DIRECTORY

Scan Tool Display	POWER DOOR LOCK TEST
LEFT CENTRAL LOCK/UNLOCK SWITCH FAILURE	13A
RIGHT CENTRAL LOCK/UNLOCK SWITCH FAILURE	14A
RKE UNABLE TO ENTER PROGRAM MODE	15A
RKE PROGRAM MODE ENTERED W/O PROGRAM REQUEST	16A
DECKLID RELEASE SWITCH FAILURE	17A
DECKLID RELEASE MOTOR FAILURE	18A

POWER DOOR LOCK SYMPTOM TEST DIRECTORY

Problem	POWER DOOR LOCK TEST
All Doors Fail To Lock/Unlock From Any Switch	2A
One Door Fail To Lock/Unlock From Any Switch	3A
All Doors Fail To Lock/Unlock From One Switch	4A
All Doors Fail To Lock From Any Switch	5A
Driver's Door Failing To Lock From Any Switch	6A
All Doors Failing To unlock From One Switch	[1]
All Doors Failing To Unlock From Any Switch	7A
Driver's Door Failing To Unlock From Any Switch	8A
All Doors Failing To Unlock From One Switch	[1]
Door Lock Inhibit Inoperative	9A
Test Automatic (Rolling) Door Locks	10A
Remote Keyless Entry Problems & Options	11A
Decklid Release Inoperative	12A

[1] – Replace defective switch.

POWER DOOR LOCK TEST 2A

ALL DOORS FAIL TO LOCK/UNLOCK FROM ANY SWITCH

NOTE: Perform POWER DOOR LOCK TEST 1A before proceeding with this test. For connector terminal identification and wiring diagrams, see BODY CONTROL COMPUTER – INTRODUCTION article. Perform VERIFICATION TEST: VER-2A after each repair.

CAUTION: Always turn ignition switch to OFF position prior to disconnecting or connecting any module connector.

1) Using scan tool, actuate door lock relay. If all doors lock, go to next step. If all doors do not lock, go to POWER DOOR LOCK TEST 2B.

2) Using scan tool, read door lock switch voltage. If scan tool displays voltage greater than .2 volts, go to POWER DOOR LOCK TEST 2C. If scan tool displays voltage of .2 volts or less, go to next step.

3) Using scan tool, read door lock switch voltage. Press door lock switch to LOCK position. If scan tool displays voltage greater than 1.7 volts, replace Body Control Module (BCM). BCM is mounted to junction block located behind left end cap of instrument panel. See Fig. 1.

4) Remove right front door trim panel. Disconnect door lock switch connector. Using external voltmeter, measure voltage between ground and terminal No. 1 (Pink wire) on door lock harness connector. If voltage is 10 volts or less, repair open Pink wire. If voltage is greater than 10 volts, go to next step.

5) Measure voltage between ground and terminal No. 4 (White/Light Green wire) on door lock harness connector. If voltage is .3 volts or less, go to next step. If voltage is greater than .3 volts, repair White/Light Green wire for short to voltage.

6) Turn ignition off. Using external ohmmeter, measure resistance between ground and terminal No. 4 (White/Light Green wire) on door lock harness connector. If resistance is less than 100 ohms, repair White/Light Green wire for short to ground. If resistance is 100 ohms or greater, go to next step.

7) Connect jumper wire between terminals No. 1 and 4 on door lock harness connector. Using scan tool, read door lock switch voltage. If voltage is greater than 1.7 volts with door lock switch pressed, replace front door lock switches. If voltage is 1.7 volts or less with door lock switch pressed, go to next step.

8) Do not disconnect jumper wire. Disconnect BCM Blue 16-pin connector C4. Using external voltmeter, measure voltage between ground and terminal No. 12 (White/Light Green wire) on Blue connector. If voltage is 10 volts or less, repair open White/Light Green wire. If voltage is greater than 10 volts, replace BCM.

POWER DOOR LOCK TEST 2B

ALL DOORS FAIL TO LOCK/UNLOCK FROM ANY SWITCH

NOTE: Perform POWER DOOR LOCK TEST 2A before proceeding with this test. For connector terminal identification and wiring diagrams, see BODY CONTROL COMPUTER – INTRODUCTION article. Perform VERIFICATION TEST: VER-2A after each repair.

CAUTION: Always turn ignition switch to OFF position prior to disconnecting or connecting any module connector.

1) Using scan tool, read door lock switch voltage. If scan tool displays voltage greater than .2 volts, go to POWER DOOR LOCK TEST 2C. If scan tool displays voltage of .2 volts or less, go to next step.

2) Remove door unlock and lock relays from junction block. See Fig. 3. Junction block is located behind left end cap of instrument panel. See Fig. 1. Using external voltmeter, measure voltage between ground and terminal "D" (fused B+) on door lock relay socket. If voltage is 10 volts or less, repair open fused B+ circuit between Power Distribution Center (PDC) and lock relay. If voltage is more than 10 volts, go to next step.

CHRY
4-168

1999 ACCESSORIES & EQUIPMENT
Body Control Computer Tests
Concorde, Intrepid, LHS & 300M (Cont.)

3) Measure voltage between ground and terminal "C" (fused B+) on door lock relay socket. If voltage is 10 volts or less, repair open fused B+ circuit between PDC and lock relay. If voltage is more than 10 volts, go to next step.

4) Turn ignition off and ensure all lights are off. Using external ohmmeter, measure resistance between ground and terminal "E" (ground) on lock relay socket. If resistance is less than 10 ohms, go to next step. If resistance is 10 ohms or greater, repair open ground circuit.

5) Turn ignition off and ensure all lights are off. Using external ohmmeter, measure resistance between ground and terminal "E" (ground) on unlock relay socket. If resistance is less than 10 ohms, go to next step. If resistance is 10 ohms or greater, repair open ground circuit.

6) Using external ohmmeter, measure resistance between terminals "B" and "E" on lock relay. If resistance is less than 5 ohms, go to next step. If resistance is 5 ohms or greater, replace relay.

7) Using external ohmmeter, measure resistance between terminals "B" and "E" on unlock relay. If resistance is less than 5 ohms, go to next step. If resistance is 5 ohms or greater, replace relay.

8) Using external ohmmeter, measure resistance between terminals "A" and "C" on unlock relay. If resistance is 65-90 ohms, go to next step. If resistance is not 65-90 ohms, replace relay.

9) Using external ohmmeter, measure resistance between ground terminal "B" (lock relay output circuit) on lock relay socket. If resistance is less than 20 ohms, repair lock relay output circuit for short to ground. If resistance is 20 ohms or greater, go to next step.

10) Measure resistance between ground terminal "B" (unlock relay output circuit) on unlock relay socket. If resistance is less than 20 ohms, repair unlock relay output circuit for short to ground. If resistance is 20 ohms or greater, go to next step.

11) Install unlock relay in junction block. Measure resistance between ground terminal "B" (lock relay output circuit) on lock relay socket. If resistance is less than 10 ohms, go to next step. If resistance is 10 ohms or greater, repair open lock or unlock relay output circuit.

12) Connect test light between terminals "A" and "C" on lock relay socket. Using scan tool, actuate door lock relay. If test light flashes during actuation, replace relay. If test light does not flash during actuation, go to next step.

13) Stop actuation. Remove Body Control Module (BCM). BCM is mounted to junction block. Inspect junction block 20-pin internal connector. Repair as needed. If connector is okay, replace BCM.

POWER DOOR LOCK TEST 2C

ALL DOORS FAIL TO LOCK/UNLOCK FROM ANY SWITCH

NOTE: Perform POWER DOOR LOCK TEST 2A before proceeding with this test. For connector terminal identification and wiring diagrams, see BODY CONTROL COMPUTER – INTRODUCTION article. Perform VERIFICATION TEST: VER-2A after each repair.

CAUTION: Always turn ignition switch to OFF position prior to disconnecting or connecting any module connector.

1) Remove driver's door trim panel. See appropriate POWER WINDOWS article. Disconnect door lock switch connector. Using scan tool, read door lock switch voltage. If scan tool displays voltage greater than .2 volts, go to next step. If scan tool displays voltage than .2 volts or less, replace driver's door lock switch.

2) Remove right front door trim panel. Disconnect door lock switch connector. Using scan tool, read door lock switch voltage. If scan tool displays voltage greater than .2 volts, go to next step. If scan tool displays voltage than .2 volts or less, replace right front door lock switch.

3) Turn ignition off. Disconnect Body Control Module (BCM) Blue 16-pin connector C4. Using external voltmeter, measure voltage between ground and terminal No. 5 (White/Dark Green wire) on Blue connector. If voltage is .2 volts or less, go to next step. If voltage is more than .2 volts, repair White/Dark Green wire for short to voltage.

4) Measure voltage between ground and terminal No. 12 (White/Light Green wire) on Blue connector. If voltage is .2 volts or less, replace BCM. If voltage is more than .2 volts, repair White/Light Green wire for short to voltage.

POWER DOOR LOCK TEST 3A

ONE DOOR FAILS TO LOCK/UNLOCK FROM ANY SWITCH

NOTE: Perform POWER DOOR LOCK TEST 1A before proceeding with this test. For connector terminal identification and wiring diagrams, see BODY CONTROL COMPUTER – INTRODUCTION article. Perform VERIFICATION TEST: VER-2A after each repair.

CAUTION: Always turn ignition switch to OFF position prior to disconnecting or connecting any module connector.

1) If problem is with driver's door, go to step 4). If problem is not with driver's door, remove key from ignition switch. Remove appropriate door trim panel. Disconnect door lock motor connector.

2) Using external voltmeter, measure voltage between ground and terminal No. 4 (Orange wire) on door lock motor harness connector. Press door lock switch to LOCK position. If voltage is 10 volts or less, repair open Orange wire. If voltage is more than 10 volts, go to next step.

3) Measure voltage between ground and terminal No. 3 (Pink/Black wire) on door lock motor harness connector. Press door lock switch to UNLOCK position. If voltage is 10 volts or less, repair open Pink/Black wire. If voltage is more than 10 volts, replace door lock motor.

4) Remove driver's door unlock relay from junction block. *See Fig. 3.* Junction block is located behind left end cap of instrument panel. *See Fig. 1.* Connect jumper wire between terminals "B" and "E" on driver's unlock relay socket. Unlock driver's door. Press door lock switch to LOCK position. If driver's door locks, replace driver's door unlock relay. If driver's door does not lock, go to next step.

5) Do not disconnect jumper wire. Remove driver's door trim panel. See appropriate POWER WINDOWS article. Disconnect door lock motor connector. Using external ohmmeter, measure resistance between ground and terminal No. 3 (Dark Blue wire) on motor harness connector. If resistance is less than 5 ohms, go to next step. If resistance is 5 ohms or greater, repair open Dark Blue wire.

6) Using external voltmeter, measure voltage between ground and terminal No. 4 (Orange wire) on door lock motor harness connector. Press door lock switch to LOCK position. If voltage is 10 volts or less, repair open Orange wire. If voltage is more than 10 volts, replace door lock motor.

POWER DOOR LOCK TEST 4A

ALL DOORS FAIL TO LOCK/UNLOCK FROM ONE SWITCH

NOTE: Perform POWER DOOR LOCK TEST 1A before proceeding with this test. For connector terminal identification and wiring diagrams, see BODY CONTROL COMPUTER – INTRODUCTION article. Perform VERIFICATION TEST: VER-2A after each repair.

CAUTION: Always turn ignition switch to OFF position prior to disconnecting or connecting any module connector.

1) If problem is with door key cylinder switch on vehicle equipped with Vehicle Theft Security System (VTSS), go to step 4). Remove appropriate door trim panel. See appropriate POWER WINDOWS article. Disconnect door lock switch connector. Using external voltmeter, measure voltage between ground and terminal No. 1 (Pink wire) on harness connector. If voltage is 10 volts or less, repair open Pink wire. If voltage is more than 10 volts, go to next step.

2) Connect jumper wire between terminals No. 1 and 4 (White/Dark or Light Green wire) on door lock switch harness connector. Using scan

1999 ACCESSORIES & EQUIPMENT
Body Control Computer Tests
Concorde, Intrepid, LHS & 300M (Cont.)

CHRY
4-169

tool, read door lock switch voltage. If voltage is 8 volts or less, go to next step. If voltage is more than 8 volts, replace door lock switch.

3) Disconnect Body Control Module (BCM) Blue 16-pin connector C4. BCM is mounted to junction block located behind left end cap of instrument panel. See Fig. 1.

4) Remove appropriate door trim panel. See appropriate POWER WINDOWS article. Disconnect door key cylinder switch connector. Using external voltmeter, measure voltage between ground and terminal No. 2 (Pink wire) on harness connector. If voltage is 10 volts or less, repair open Pink wire. If voltage is more than 10 volts, go to next step.

5) Connect jumper wire between door key cylinder switch harness connector terminals. Using scan tool, read appropriate door arm/disarm switch voltage. If voltage is 8 volts or less, go to next step. If voltage is more than 8 volts, replace door key cylinder switch.

6) With jumper wire still connected, disconnect Body Control Module (BCM) Blue 16-pin connector C4. BCM is mounted to junction block located behind left end cap of instrument panel. See Fig. 1. Using voltmeter, measure voltage between ground and terminal No. 3 (Dark Green/Orange wire) or No. 13 (Light Green/Orange wire) on Blue BCM harness connector. If voltage is 10 volts or less, repair open Dark Green/Orange wire or Light Green/Orange wire. If voltage is greater than 10 volts, replace BCM.

POWER DOOR LOCK TEST 5A

ALL DOORS FAIL TO LOCK FROM ANY SWITCH

NOTE: Perform POWER DOOR LOCK TEST 1A before proceeding with this test. For connector terminal identification and wiring diagrams, see BODY CONTROL COMPUTER – INTRODUCTION article. Perform VERIFICATION TEST: VER-2A after each repair.

CAUTION: Always turn ignition switch to OFF position prior to disconnecting or connecting any module connector.

1) Using scan tool, monitor door lock switch voltage. If voltage is .2 volts or less, go to next step. If voltage is more than .2 volts, go to POWER DOOR LOCK TEST 2C.

2) Remove door lock relay from junction block. See Fig. 3. Junction block is located behind left end cap of instrument panel. See Fig. 1. Using external voltmeter, measure voltage between ground and terminals "D" and "C" (individually) on lock relay socket. If voltage is 10 volts or less, replace junction block. If voltage is more than 10 volts, go to next step.

3) Remove unlock relay. Using external ohmmeter, measure resistance between ground and terminal "B" on lock relay socket. If resistance is less than 50 ohms, repair unlock relay output circuit (terminal "B", unlock relay socket) for short to ground. If resistance is 50 ohms or greater, go to next step.

4) Connect test light between terminals "A" and "C" on lock relay socket. Using scan tool, actuate door lock relay. If test light flashes during actuation, go to next step. If test light does not flash, replace Body Control Module (BCM). BCM is mounted to junction block.

5) Stop actuation. Using external ohmmeter, measure resistance between ground and terminal "E" on unlock relay socket. If resistance is less than 5 ohms, go to next step. If resistance is 5 ohms or greater, replace junction block.

6) Using external ohmmeter, measure resistance between terminals "B" and "E" on unlock relay. If resistance is less than 5 ohms, replace lock relay. If resistance is 5 ohms or greater, replace unlock relay.

POWER DOOR LOCK TEST 6A

DRIVER'S DOOR FAILS TO LOCK FROM ANY SWITCH

NOTE: Perform POWER DOOR LOCK TEST 1A before proceeding with this test. For connector terminal identification and wiring diagrams, see BODY CONTROL COMPUTER – INTRODUCTION article. Perform VERIFICATION TEST: VER-2A after each repair.

CAUTION: Always turn ignition switch to OFF position prior to disconnecting or connecting any module connector.

Remove driver's door unlock relay from junction block. See Fig. 3. Junction block is located behind left end cap of instrument panel. See Fig. 1. Using external ohmmeter, measure resistance between ground and terminal "E" on relay socket. If resistance is less than 5 ohms, replace junction block. If resistance is 5 ohms or greater, replace driver's door unlock relay.

POWER DOOR LOCK TEST 7A

ALL DOORS FAIL TO UNLOCK FROM ANY SWITCH

NOTE: Perform POWER DOOR LOCK TEST 1A before proceeding with this test. For connector terminal identification and wiring diagrams, see BODY CONTROL COMPUTER – INTRODUCTION article. Perform VERIFICATION TEST: VER-2A after each repair.

CAUTION: Always turn ignition switch to OFF position prior to disconnecting or connecting any module connector.

1) Remove door unlock relay from junction block. See Fig. 3. Junction block is located behind left end cap of instrument panel.

2) Connect test light between terminals "A" and "C" on unlock relay socket. Using scan tool, actuate door unlock relay. If test light flashes during actuation, go to next step. If test light does not flash, go to step 5).

3) Stop actuation. Remove lock relay from junction block. Using external ohmmeter, measure resistance between ground and terminal "E" on relay socket. If resistance is less than 5 ohms, go to next step. If resistance is 5 ohms or greater, replace junction block.

4) Using external ohmmeter, measure resistance between terminals "B" and "E" on lock relay. If resistance is less than 5 ohms, replace unlock relay. If resistance is 5 ohms or greater, replace lock relay.

5) Using external voltmeter, measure voltage between ground and terminal "C" on unlock relay socket. If voltage is 10 volts or less, replace junction block. If voltage is greater than 10 volts, go to next step.

6) Remove Body Control Module (BCM) from junction block. Inspect junction block 20-pin internal connector. Repair as needed. If connector is okay, replace BCM.

POWER DOOR LOCK TEST 8A

DRIVER'S DOOR FAILS TO UNLOCK FROM ANY SWITCH

NOTE: Perform POWER DOOR LOCK TEST 1A before proceeding with this test. For connector terminal identification and wiring diagrams, see BODY CONTROL COMPUTER – INTRODUCTION article. Perform VERIFICATION TEST: VER-2A after each repair.

CAUTION: Always turn ignition switch to OFF position prior to disconnecting or connecting any module connector.

1) Remove driver's door unlock relay from junction block. See Fig. 3. Junction block is located behind left end cap of instrument panel.

2) Using external voltmeter, measure voltage between ground and terminal "C" on relay socket. If voltage is 10 volts or less, replace junction block. If voltage is greater than 10 volts, go to next step.

CHRY
4-170

1999 ACCESSORIES & EQUIPMENT
Body Control Computer Tests
Concorde, Intrepid, LHS & 300M (Cont.)

3) Connect test light between terminals "A" and "C" on driver's unlock relay socket. Using scan tool, actuate driver's door unlock relay. If test light flashes during actuation, replace driver's door unlock relay. If test light does not flash, go to next step.

4) Stop actuation. Remove Body Control Module (BCM) from junction block. Inspect junction block 20-pin internal connector. Repair or replace junction block as needed. If connector is okay, replace BCM.

POWER DOOR LOCK TEST 9A

DOOR LOCK INHIBIT MALFUNCTION

NOTE: *Perform POWER DOOR LOCK TEST 1A before proceeding with this test. For connector terminal identification and wiring diagrams, see BODY CONTROL COMPUTER – INTRODUCTION article. Perform VERIFICATION TEST: VER-2A after each repair.*

CAUTION: *Always turn ignition switch to OFF position prior to disconnecting or connecting any module connector.*

1) Open driver's door. Using scan tool, read driver's door ajar status. If scan tool displays LF DOOR AJAR: CLOSED, go to next step. If scan tool does not display LF DOOR AJAR: CLOSED, go to DOOR AJAR TEST 2A.

2) Ensure key is in ignition switch. Using scan tool, read key-in ignition status. If scan tool displays KEY-IN IGN: CLOSED, replace Body Control Module (BCM). BCM is mounted to junction block located behind left end cap of instrument panel. See Fig. 1. If scan tool does not display KEY-IN IGN: CLOSED, go to next step.

3) Disconnect ignition switch connector. See Fig. 2. Using external ohmmeter, measure resistance between ground and terminal No. 3 (Black/Light Green wire) on ignition switch harness connector. If resistance is less than 5 ohms, go to next step. If resistance is 5 ohms or greater, repair open Black/Light Green wire.

4) Connect jumper wire between terminals No. 2 (Light Blue wire) and 3 on ignition switch harness connector. Using scan tool, read key-in ignition status. If scan tool displays KEY-IN IGN: CLOSED, replace ignition switch. If scan tool does not display KEY-IN IGN: CLOSED, go to next step.

5) Do not disconnect jumper wire. Disconnect BCM Black 24-pin connector C2. Using external ohmmeter, measure resistance between ground and terminal No. 24 (Light Blue wire) on Black connector. If resistance is less than 5 ohms, replace BCM. If resistance is 5 ohms or greater, repair open Light Blue wire.

POWER DOOR LOCK TEST 10A

AUTOMATIC ROLLING DOOR LOCK MALFUNCTION

NOTE: *Perform POWER DOOR LOCK TEST 1A before proceeding with this test. For connector terminal identification and wiring diagrams, see BODY CONTROL COMPUTER – INTRODUCTION article. Perform VERIFICATION TEST: VER-2A after each repair.*

CAUTION: *Always turn ignition switch to OFF position prior to disconnecting or connecting any module connector.*

1) Using scan tool, select MISCELLANEOUS. Read auto door lock status. If scan tool displays AUTO DOOR LOCKS: ENABLED, go to next step. If scan tool does not display AUTO DOOR LOCKS: ENABLED, enable auto door locks.

2) Ensure all doors are closed. Using scan tool, read driver's door ajar status. If scan tool displays LF DOOR AJAR: CLOSED, perform DOOR AJAR TEST 3A. If scan tool does not display LF DOOR AJAR: CLOSED, go to next step.

3) Using scan tool, read door ajar switch status for remaining doors. If scan tool displays DOOR AJAR: CLOSED for any door, go to DOOR AJAR TEST 1A. If scan tool does not display DOOR AJAR: CLOSED for any door, go to next step.

4) Turn ignition on. Using scan tool, select MONITORS. Read PCI bus engine information. Monitor scan tool while depressing accelerator. If TP sensor status does not change, go to appropriate SELF-DIAGNOSTICS article in ENGINE PERFORMANCE in appropriate MITCHELL® manual. If TP sensor status does change, go to next step.

5) Raise and support vehicle. Ensure traction control is turned off (if equipped). Close all doors. Start engine and place shift lever in Drive position. Using scan tool, read PCI bus engine info. Monitor Vehicle Speed Sensor (VSS) while wheels are rotating.

6) If MPH does not increase while accelerator is depressed, go to appropriate SELF-DIAGNOSTICS article in ENGINE PERFORMANCE in appropriate MITCHELL® manual. If MPH increases while accelerator is depressed, determine if doors lock. If doors lock, system is currently operating correctly. If doors do not lock, replace Body Control Module (BCM). BCM is mounted to junction block located behind left end cap of instrument panel. See Fig. 1.

POWER DOOR LOCK TEST 11A

REMOTE KEYLESS ENTRY (RKE) MALFUNCTION

NOTE: *Perform POWER DOOR LOCK TEST 1A before proceeding with this test. For connector terminal identification and wiring diagrams, see BODY CONTROL COMPUTER – INTRODUCTION article. Perform VERIFICATION TEST: VER-2A after each repair.*

To test transmitter, obtain known good transmitter. Using scan tool, select BODY, then BODY COMPUTER. Select MISCELLANEOUS, then RKE FOB test. Press lock or unlock button on transmitter. If RKE responds correctly, replace and program new transmitter. If RKE is inoperative or does not operate correctly, replace RKE module and program all transmitters. To program transmitter, go to POWER DOOR LOCK TEST 11B. If horn chirp is inoperative, go to POWER DOOR LOCK TEST 11C. To cancel horn chirp or change decklid to single button operation, see vehicle owner's manual.

POWER DOOR LOCK TEST 11B

RKE TRANSMITTER PROGRAMMING

NOTE: *Perform POWER DOOR LOCK TEST 11A before proceeding with this test. For connector terminal identification and wiring diagrams, see BODY CONTROL COMPUTER – INTRODUCTION article. Perform VERIFICATION TEST: VER-2A after each repair.*

CAUTION: *Always turn ignition switch to OFF position prior to disconnecting or connecting any module connector.*

Ensure transmitter batteries are approximately 3.2 volts. Turn ignition on. Ensure shift lever is in Park position. Using scan tool, select MISCELLANEOUS, then PROGRAM RKE. Chime will sound. Press any button on transmitter. Chime will sound. Press any button on next transmitter. Chime will sound. Repeat procedure for additional transmitters. Exit PROGRAM RKE and turn ignition off. Chime will sound.

POWER DOOR LOCK TEST 11C

INOPERATIVE HORN CHIRP

NOTE: *Perform POWER DOOR LOCK TEST 11A before proceeding with this test. For connector terminal identification and wiring diagrams, see BODY CONTROL COMPUTER – INTRODUCTION article. Perform VERIFICATION TEST: VER-2A after each repair.*

CAUTION: *Always turn ignition switch to OFF position prior to disconnecting or connecting any module connector.*

1) Ensure horn operates correctly. Repair as needed. Using scan tool, select BODY COMPUTER, then MISCELLANEOUS. Ensure horn chirp

1999 ACCESSORIES & EQUIPMENT
Body Control Computer Tests
Concorde, Intrepid, LHS & 300M (Cont.)

CHRY
4-171

is ENABLED. Using scan tool, actuate horn relay. If horn sounds during actuation, replace Body Control Module (BCM). BCM is mounted to junction block located behind left end cap of instrument panel. *See Fig. 1*. If horn does not sound, go to next step.

2) Remove BCM from junction block. Inspect junction block internal 20-pin connector. Repair as needed. If connector is okay, go to next step.

3) Connect (momentarily) jumper wire between ground and terminal No. 18 (horn relay control) on junction block internal 20-pin connector. If horn sounds, replace BCM. If horn does not sound, replace junction block.

POWER DOOR LOCK TEST 12A
INOPERATIVE DECKLID RELEASE

NOTE: Perform POWER DOOR LOCK TEST 1A before proceeding with this test. For connector terminal identification and wiring diagrams, see BODY CONTROL COMPUTER – INTRODUCTION article. Perform VERIFICATION TEST: VER-2A after each repair.

CAUTION: Always turn ignition switch to OFF position prior to disconnecting or connecting any module connector.

1) Ensure no decklid release switch or decklid motor DTCs are present. Disconnect decklid release solenoid connector. Using external ohmmeter, measure resistance between ground and terminal No. 1 (Black wire) on solenoid harness connector. If resistance is less than 5 ohms, go to next step. If resistance is 5 ohms or greater, repair open Black wire.

2) Connect test light between terminals No. 1 and 3 (Black/White wire) on solenoid harness connector. Press decklid release switch. If test light illuminates when switch is pressed, replace decklid release motor. If test light does not illuminate, go to next step.

3) Do not disconnect test light. Disconnect decklid release switch. Using external voltmeter, measure voltage between ground and terminal No. 2 (Pink wire) on switch harness connector. If voltage is 10 volts or less, repair open Pink wire. If voltage is greater than 10 volts, go to next step.

4) Connect jumper wire between decklid release switch terminals. If test light illuminates, replace decklid release switch. If test light does not illuminate, go to next step.

5) Do not disconnect jumper wire. Disconnect Body Control Module (BCM) Gray 14-pin connector C1. BCM is mounted to junction block located behind left end cap of instrument panel. *See Fig. 1.* Using external voltmeter, measure voltage between ground and terminal No. 1 (Black/White wire) on Gray harness connector. If voltage is 10 volts or less, repair open Black/White wire. If voltage is greater than 10 volts, go to next step.

6) Disconnect jumper wire and test light. Connect jumper wire between terminals No. 1 and 3 on decklid release solenoid harness connector. Turn ignition off. Remove BCM from junction block. Connect test light between terminals No. 7 and 8 on junction block 20-pin internal connector. If test light illuminates, replace BCM. If test light does not illuminate, repair open Black/White wire (decklid release circuit) between decklid release solenoid and junction block.

POWER DOOR LOCK TEST 13A
LEFT CENTRAL LOCK/UNLOCK SWITCH FAILURE

NOTE: Perform POWER DOOR LOCK TEST 1A before proceeding with this test. For connector terminal identification and wiring diagrams, see BODY CONTROL COMPUTER – INTRODUCTION article. Perform VERIFICATION TEST: VER-2A after each repair.

CAUTION: Always turn ignition switch to OFF position prior to disconnecting or connecting any module connector.

1) Using scan tool, erase DTC. Using scan tool, select BODY, then BODY COMPUTER. Select SENSORS and monitor driver's door arm/

disarm switch. Insert key into driver's door lock and rotate switch from lock to unlock position. If lock or switch binds in either position, repair as needed. If lock or switch does not bind, go to next step.

2) Continue to slowly turn door lock and monitor scan tool voltage. If voltage displayed changes from zero to 2.4 volts to zero, system is currently operating correctly. If voltage displayed does not change from zero to 2.4 volts to zero, go to next step.

3) Remove driver's door trim panel. See appropriate POWER WINDOWS article. See appropriate POWER WINDOWS article. Disconnect door key cylinder switch. Using scan tool, read driver's door arm/disarm switch voltage. If scan tool displays zero volts, replace door key cylinder switch. If scan tool does not display zero volts, go to next step.

4) Disconnect Body Control Module (BCM) Gray 14-pin connector C1. BCM is mounted to junction block located behind left end cap of instrument panel. *See Fig. 1.* Using external voltmeter, measure voltage between ground and terminal No. 1 (Light Green/Orange wire) on driver's door key cylinder switch harness connector. If voltage is .1 volt or less, replace BCM. If voltage is greater than .1 volt, repair Light Green/Orange wire for short to voltage.

POWER DOOR LOCK TEST 14A
LEFT CENTRAL LOCK/UNLOCK SWITCH FAILURE

NOTE: Perform POWER DOOR LOCK TEST 1A before proceeding with this test. For connector terminal identification and wiring diagrams, see BODY CONTROL COMPUTER – INTRODUCTION article. Perform VERIFICATION TEST: VER-2A after each repair.

CAUTION: Always turn ignition switch to OFF position prior to disconnecting or connecting any module connector.

1) Using scan tool, erase DTCs. Using scan tool, select BODY, then BODY COMPUTER. Select SENSORS and monitor right door arm/disarm switch. Insert key into right door lock and rotate switch from lock to unlock position. If lock or switch binds in either position, repair as needed. If lock or switch does not bind, go to next step.

2) Continue to slowly turn door lock and monitor scan tool voltage. If voltage displayed changes from zero to 3 volts to zero, system is currently operating correctly. If voltage displayed does not change from zero to 3 volts to zero, go to next step.

3) Remove right door trim panel. See appropriate POWER WINDOWS article. See appropriate POWER WINDOWS article. Disconnect door key cylinder switch. Using scan tool, read right door arm/disarm switch voltage. If scan tool displays zero volts, replace door key cylinder switch. If scan tool does not display zero volts, go to next step.

4) Disconnect Body Control Module (BCM) Gray 14-pin connector C1. BCM is mounted to junction block located behind left end cap of instrument panel. *See Fig. 1.* Using external voltmeter, measure voltage between ground and terminal No. 1 (Dark Green/Orange wire) on right door key cylinder switch harness connector. If voltage is .1 volt or less, replace BCM. If voltage is greater than .1 volt, repair Dark Green/Orange wire for short to voltage.

POWER DOOR LOCK TEST 15A
RKE UNABLE TO ENTER PROGRAM MODE

NOTE: Perform POWER DOOR LOCK TEST 1A before proceeding with this test. For connector terminal identification and wiring diagrams, see BODY CONTROL COMPUTER – INTRODUCTION article. Perform VERIFICATION TEST: VER-2A after each repair.

CAUTION: Always turn ignition switch to OFF position prior to disconnecting or connecting any module connector.

DTC is set when there is lack of response from RKE module when attempting to enter program mode. Possible causes are failed RKE

CHRY
4-172

1999 ACCESSORIES & EQUIPMENT
Body Control Computer Tests
Concorde, Intrepid, LHS & 300M (Cont.)

module and failed Body Control Module (BCM). BCM is mounted to junction block located behind left end cap of instrument panel. *See Fig. 1.*

POWER DOOR LOCK TEST 16A

RKE PROGRAM MODE ENTERED WITHOUT PROGRAM REQUEST

NOTE: Perform POWER DOOR LOCK TEST 1A before proceeding with this test. For connector terminal identification and wiring diagrams, see BODY CONTROL COMPUTER – INTRODUCTION article. Perform VERIFICATION TEST: VER-2A after each repair.

CAUTION: Always turn ignition switch to OFF position prior to disconnecting or connecting any module connector.

DTC is set when Body Control Module (BCM) determines that RKE module without BCM request. Possible causes are failed RKE module and failed Body Control Module (BCM). BCM is mounted to junction block located behind left end cap of instrument panel. *See Fig. 1.*

POWER DOOR LOCK TEST 17A

DECKLID RELEASE SWITCH FAILURE

NOTE: Perform POWER DOOR LOCK TEST 1A before proceeding with this test. For connector terminal identification and wiring diagrams, see BODY CONTROL COMPUTER – INTRODUCTION article. Perform VERIFICATION TEST: VER-2A after each repair.

CAUTION: Always turn ignition switch to OFF position prior to disconnecting or connecting any module connector.

1) Disconnect decklid release switch connector. Using scan tool, erase DTCs. Cycle ignition switch off, then on. Wait 30 seconds. Using scan tool, read DTC's. If decklid release switch failure DTC reset, go to next step. If decklid release switch failure DTC is not reset, replace decklid release switch.

2) Disconnect Body Control Module (BCM) Gray 14-pin connector C1. BCM is mounted to junction block located behind left end cap of instrument panel. *See Fig. 1.* Using external voltmeter, measure voltage between ground and terminal No. 1 (Black/White wire) on decklid release switch harness connection. If voltage is .5 volts or less, replace BCM. If voltage is greater than .5 volts, repair Black/White wire for short to voltage.

POWER DOOR LOCK TEST 18A

DECKLID RELEASE MOTOR OUTPUT FAILURE

NOTE: Perform POWER DOOR LOCK TEST 1A before proceeding with this test. For connector terminal identification and wiring diagrams, see BODY CONTROL COMPUTER – INTRODUCTION article. Perform VERIFICATION TEST: VER-2A after each repair.

CAUTION: Always turn ignition switch to OFF position prior to disconnecting or connecting any module connector.

1) Disconnect decklid release motor connector. Using scan tool, erase DTCs. Cycle ignition switch off, then on. Using scan tool, read DTC's. Wait 30 seconds. While monitoring scan tool, press and hold decklid release switch for 30 seconds. If decklid release motor output DTC reset, go to next step. If decklid release motor output DTC is not reset, replace decklid release motor.

2) Remove Body Control Module (BCM) from junction block. BCM is mounted to junction block located behind left end cap of instrument panel. *See Fig. 1.*

SKIS TEST 1A

IDENTIFYING SENTRY KEY IMMOBILIZER SYSTEM (SKIS) PROBLEMS

NOTE: Ensure all of the customer's keys are obtained before beginning SKIS diagnosis and repair. If the Sentry Key Immobilizer Module (SKIM) requires replacing, all keys must be reprogrammed to new SKIM.

1) Ensure battery is fully charged. Using scan tool, select THEFT ALARM, then SKIM. If scan tool displays NO RESPONSE, go to TEST 16A in appropriate VEHICLE COMMUNICATIONS article.

2) Using scan tool, read and record SKIM DTCs (fault messages). Erase SKIM DTCs. Cycle ignition switch to OFF, then RUN/START position. Leave ignition in RUN/START position for 3 minutes. Read SKIM DTCs to verify that codes displayed are current faults. See SKIS DIAGNOSTIC TEST DIRECTORY table. If no codes (fault messages) are present, go to PRE-EXISTING FAULT MESSAGE TEST DIRECTORY table.

SKIS DIAGNOSTIC TEST DIRECTORY

Fault Message	SKIS TEST
Antenna Failure	1
EEPROM Failure	1
Transponder communication Failure	2A
Transponder Cyclic Redundancy Check (CRC) Failure	2A
Transponder ID Mismatched	3A
Transponder ID Mismatched & EEPROM Failure	1
Transponder Response Mismatch	3A
Transponder Response Mismatch & EEPROM Failure	1
VIN Mismatch	4A
VIN Mismatch & PCM Has An EEPROM DTC Stored In Memory	2
VIN Mismatch & Roll Code Failure With Or Without An EEPROM Failure	4A
Internal SKIM Failure	1
Serial Link External Failure [3]	9A
Serial Link External Failure	10A
Serial Link Internal Failure	1
PCM Status Failure [4]	10A
Rolling Code Failure [5]	10A

[1] – Replace SKIM and perform SKIM INITIALIZATION PROCEDURE.
[2] – See appropriate SELF-DIAGNOSTICS article in ENGINE PERFORMANCE in appropriate MITCHELL® manual. After repair, go to TEST 4A.
[3] – When attempting to send secret key to PCM.
[4] – Fault maturity time is approximately 20 seconds.
[5] – Fault maturity time is approximately 4 seconds.

PRE-EXISTING FAULT MESSAGE TEST DIRECTORY

Problem	SKIS TEST
Antenna Failure	1
VIN Mismatch & EEPROM Failure	5A
EEPROM Failure	6A
Internal SKIM Failure	7A
Serial Link External Failure	8A
Serial Link Internal Failure	1
PCM Status Failure	8A
Rolling Code Failure	8A
Transponder ID Mismatched & EEPROM Failure	11A
Transponder Response Mismatch & EEPROM failure	11A
Transponder ID Mismatched	12A
Transponder Response Mismatch	12A
Transponder Communication Failure	12A
Transponder Cyclic Redundancy Check (CRC) Failure	12A

[1] – Replace SKIM and perform SKIM INITIALIZATION PROCEDURE.

SKIS TEST 2A

TRANSPONDER COMMUNICATION FAILURE/TRANSPONDER CRC FAILURE

Using customer's extra key, insert key into ignition switch and turn switch to RUN position. Using scan tool, erase DTCs. Cycle ignition switch on, then off. Read DTCs. If DTC is reset, replace SKIM and perform SKIM INITIALIZATION PROCEDURE. If DTC is not reset, erase codes. Replace and program new key. See appropriate ANTI-THEFT SYSTEMS article.

SKIS TEST 3A

TRANSPONDER ID MISMATCH OR TRANSPONDER RESPONSE MISMATCH

NOTE: Perform SKIS TEST 1A before proceeding with this test. For connector terminal identification and wiring diagrams, see BODY CONTROL COMPUTER – INTRODUCTION article. Perform VERIFICATION TEST: VER-1A after each repair.

CAUTION: Always turn ignition switch to OFF position prior to disconnecting or connecting any module connector.

1) Obtain customer's extra key and go to next step. If no other key is available, have new key cut and go to SKIS TEST 3C.

2) Using customer's extra key, insert key into ignition switch and turn switch to RUN position. Using scan tool, erase DTCs. Cycle ignition switch on, then off. Read DTCs. If DTC is reset, replace SKIM and perform SKIM INITIALIZATION PROCEDURE. If DTC is not reset, erase codes. Replace and program new key. See appropriate ANTI-THEFT SYSTEM article.

SKIS TEST 3B

TRANSPONDER ID MISMATCH OR TRANSPONDER RESPONSE MISMATCH

NOTE: Perform SKIS TEST 3A before proceeding with this test. For connector terminal identification and wiring diagrams, see BODY CONTROL COMPUTER – INTRODUCTION article. Perform VERIFICATION TEST: VER-1A after each repair.

CAUTION: Always turn ignition switch to OFF position prior to disconnecting or connecting any module connector.

Place key in ignition switch and turn to RUN position.Using scan tool, select MISCELLANEOUS, then PROGRAM NEW KEY. Read CURRENT KEY STATUS. If status is PROGRAMING SUCCESSFUL, erase DTCs. Test is complete. If status is PROGRAMING FAILED, replace SKIM and perform SKIM INITIALIZATION PROCEDURE. If status is MAXIMUM KEY LIMIT, no additional keys can be programmed. See appropriate ANTI-THEFT SYSTEM article. If none of the above status messages are displayed, replace SKIM and perform SKIM INITIALIZATION PROCEDURE.

SKIS TEST 3C

TRANSPONDER ID MISMATCH OR TRANSPONDER RESPONSE MISMATCH

NOTE: Perform SKIS TEST 3A before proceeding with this test. For connector terminal identification and wiring diagrams, see BODY CONTROL COMPUTER – INTRODUCTION article. Perform VERIFICATION TEST: VER-1A after each repair.

CAUTION: Always turn ignition switch to OFF position prior to disconnecting or connecting any module connector.

Place key in ignition switch and turn to RUN position.Using scan tool, select MISCELLANEOUS, then PROGRAM NEW KEY. Read CURRENT KEY STATUS. If status is MAXIMUM KEY LIMIT, no additional keys can be programmed. See appropriate ANTI-THEFT SYSTEM article. If status is PROGRAMING FAILED, replace SKIM and perform SKIM INITIALIZATION PROCEDURE. If status is PROGRAMING SUCCESSFUL, erase DTCs. Replace original defective key. If status is PROGRAMING NOT ATTEMPTED, repeat procedure. If none of the above messages are displayed, replace SKIM and perform SKIM INITIALIZATION PROCEDURE.

SKIS TEST 4A

VIN MISMATCH

NOTE: Perform SKIS TEST 1A before proceeding with this test. For connector terminal identification and wiring diagrams, see BODY CONTROL COMPUTER – INTRODUCTION article. Perform VERIFICATION TEST: VER-1A after each repair.

CAUTION: Always turn ignition switch to OFF position prior to disconnecting or connecting any module connector.

1) Using scan tool, read VIN from Powertrain Control Module (PCM). If go to next step. If VIN displayed by scan tool does not match VIN on dash mounted plate, go to step **5)**.

2) Using scan tool, read VIN stored in SKIM's memory. If VIN displayed by scan tool matches VIN on dash mounted plate, go to next step. If VIN displayed by scan tool does not match VIN on dash mounted plate,

3) Using scan tool, erase VIN MISMATCH DTC. Verify that DTC has been cleared from memory. If VIN MISMATCH DTC no longer present, go to next step. If VIN MISMATCH DTC is still present in memory, replace SKIM and perform SKIM INITIALIZATION PROCEDURE.

4) Start engine and allow to idle for 3 minutes. Read SKIM DTCs. If VIN MISMATCH DTC resets, replace SKIM and perform SKIM INITIALIZATION PROCEDURE. If VIN MISMATCH DTC is no longer present, system is currently functioning correctly.

5) Using scan tool, reprogram correct VIN into PCM's memory following scan tool instruction manual. Using scan tool, erase VIN MISMATCH DTC. Verify that DTC has been cleared from memory. Using scan tool, read VIN stored in SKIM's memory. If VIN MISMATCH DTC resets, replace SKIM and perform SKIM INITIALIZATION PROCEDURE. If VIN MISMATCH DTC is no longer present, system is currently functioning correctly.

1999 ACCESSORIES & EQUIPMENT
Body Control Computer Tests
Concorde, Intrepid, LHS & 300M (Cont.)

SKIS TEST 5A

VIN MISMATCH, ROLLING CODE FAILURE & EEPROM FAILURE

NOTE: Perform SKIS TEST 1A before proceeding with this test. For connector terminal identification and wiring diagrams, see BODY CONTROL COMPUTER – INTRODUCTION article. Perform VERIFICATION TEST: VER-1A after each repair.

CAUTION: Always turn ignition switch to OFF position prior to disconnecting or connecting any module connector.

1) Using scan tool, erase SKIM DTCs. Start engine 20 times. Using scan tool, read DTCs. If EEPROM FAILURE DTC is present, replace SKIM and perform SKIM INITIALIZATION PROCEDURE. If EEPROM FAILURE DTC is not present, go to next step.
2) Start engine and allow to idle for 3 minutes. Read SKIM DTCs. If VIN MISMATCH DTC is set, go to SKIS TEST 4A. If ROLLING CODE DTC is set, go to SKIS TEST 10A. If neither of above DTCs are displayed, system is currently functioning correctly.

SKIS TEST 6A

EEPROM FAILURE

NOTE: Perform SKIS TEST 1A before proceeding with this test. For connector terminal identification and wiring diagrams, see BODY CONTROL COMPUTER – INTRODUCTION article. Perform VERIFICATION TEST: VER-1A after each repair.

CAUTION: Always turn ignition switch to OFF position prior to disconnecting or connecting any module connector.

Using scan tool, erase SKIM DTCs. Turn ignition off and wait 10 seconds. Start engine 20 times. Using scan tool, read DTCs. If EEPROM FAILURE DTC is present, replace SKIM and perform SKIM INITIALIZATION PROCEDURE. If EEPROM FAILURE DTC is not present, system is currently functioning correctly.

SKIS TEST 7A

INTERNAL SKIM FAILURE

NOTE: Perform SKIS TEST 1A before proceeding with this test. For connector terminal identification and wiring diagrams, see BODY CONTROL COMPUTER – INTRODUCTION article. Perform VERIFICATION TEST: VER-1A after each repair.

CAUTION: Always turn ignition switch to OFF position prior to disconnecting or connecting any module connector.

Using scan tool, erase SKIM DTCs. Turn ignition off and wait 10 seconds. Start engine 20 times. Using scan tool, read DTCs. If INTERNAL SKIM FAILURE DTC is present, replace SKIM and perform SKIM INITIALIZATION PROCEDURE. If INTERNAL SKIM FAILURE DTC is not present, system is currently functioning correctly.

SKIS TEST 8A

SERIAL LINK EXTERNAL FAILURE, PCM STATUS FAILURE OR ROLLING CODE FAILURE

NOTE: Perform SKIS TEST 1A before proceeding with this test. For connector terminal identification and wiring diagrams, see BODY CONTROL COMPUTER – INTRODUCTION article. Perform VERIFICATION TEST: VER-1A after each repair.

CAUTION: Always turn ignition switch to OFF position prior to disconnecting or connecting any module connector.

1) Using scan tool, erase SKIM DTCs. Turn ignition on and wait 10 seconds. Start engine 20 times. Using scan tool, read DTCs. If SKIM DTCs are present, go to next step. If no SKIM DTCs are present, system is currently functioning correctly.
2) Using scan tool, select THEFT ALARM, then SKIM. If scan tool displays NO RESPONSE, go to TEST 15A in appropriate VEHICLE COMMUNICATIONS article. If scan tool does not display NO RESPONSE, go to next step.
3) Using scan tool, select BODY, BODY COMPUTER, SYSTEM TEST and then PCM MONITOR. If scan tool displays PCM ACTIVE ON THE BUS, go to next step. If scan tool does not display PCM ACTIVE ON THE BUS, go to TEST 14A in appropriate VEHICLE COMMUNICATIONS article.
4) Using scan tool, select ENGINE. Read DTCs. If any engine related DTCs are present, go to appropriate SELF-DIAGNOSTICS article in ENGINE PERFORMANCE in appropriate MITCHELL® manual. If no engine related DTCs are present, replace SKIM and perform SKIM INITIALIZATION PROCEDURE.

SKIS TEST 9A

SERIAL LINK EXTERNAL FAILURE

NOTE: Perform SKIS TEST 1A before proceeding with this test. For connector terminal identification and wiring diagrams, see BODY CONTROL COMPUTER – INTRODUCTION article. Perform VERIFICATION TEST: VER-1A after each repair.

CAUTION: Always turn ignition switch to OFF position prior to disconnecting or connecting any module connector.

1) Using scan tool, erase SKIM DTCs. Attempt another secret key transfer to PCM. Read DTCs. If SERIAL LINK EXTERNAL DTC is present, go to next step. If SERIAL LINK EXTERNAL DTC is not present, system is currently functioning correctly.
2) Using scan tool, select THEFT ALARM, then SKIM. If scan tool displays NO RESPONSE, go to TEST 15A in appropriate VEHICLE COMMUNICATIONS article. If scan tool does not display NO RESPONSE, go to next step.
3) Using scan tool, select BODY, BODY COMPUTER, SYSTEM TEST and then PCM MONITOR. If scan tool displays PCM ACTIVE ON THE BUS, go to next step. If scan tool does not display PCM ACTIVE ON THE BUS, go to TEST 14A in appropriate VEHICLE COMMUNICATIONS article.
4) Using scan tool, select ENGINE. Read DTCs. If any engine related DTCs are present, go to appropriate SELF-DIAGNOSTICS article in ENGINE PERFORMANCE in appropriate MITCHELL® manual. If no engine related DTCs are present, replace SKIM and perform SKIM INITIALIZATION PROCEDURE.

1999 ACCESSORIES & EQUIPMENT
Body Control Computer Tests
Concorde, Intrepid, LHS & 300M (Cont.)

CHRY
4-175

SKIS TEST 10A

SERIAL LINK EXTERNAL FAILURE, PCM STATUS FAILURE OR ROLLING CODE FAILURE

NOTE: *Perform SKIS TEST 1A before proceeding with this test. For connector terminal identification and wiring diagrams, see BODY CONTROL COMPUTER – INTRODUCTION article. Perform VERIFICATION TEST: VER-1A after each repair.*

CAUTION: *Always turn ignition switch to OFF position prior to disconnecting or connecting any module connector.*

1) Using scan tool, select THEFT ALARM, then SKIM. If scan tool displays NO RESPONSE, go to TEST 15A in appropriate VEHICLE COMMUNICATIONS article. If scan tool does not display NO RESPONSE, go to next step.
2) Using scan tool, select BODY, BODY COMPUTER, SYSTEM TEST and then PCM MONITOR. If scan tool displays PCM ACTIVE ON THE BUS, go to next step. If scan tool does not display PCM ACTIVE ON THE BUS, go to TEST 14A in appropriate VEHICLE COMMUNICATIONS article.
3) Using scan tool, select ENGINE. Read DTCs. If any engine related DTCs are present, go to appropriate SELF-DIAGNOSTICS article in ENGINE PERFORMANCE in appropriate MITCHELL® manual. If no engine related DTCs are present, replace SKIM and perform SKIM INITIALIZATION PROCEDURE.

SKIS TEST 11A

TRANSPONDER ID MISMATCH OR TRANSPONDER RESPONSE MISMATCH & EEPROM FAILURE

NOTE: *Perform SKIS TEST 1A before proceeding with this test. For connector terminal identification and wiring diagrams, see BODY CONTROL COMPUTER – INTRODUCTION article. Perform VERIFICATION TEST: VER-1A after each repair.*

CAUTION: *Always turn ignition switch to OFF position prior to disconnecting or connecting any module connector.*

1) Using scan tool, erase SKIM DTCs. Turn ignition off and wait 10 seconds. Start engine 20 times. Using scan tool, read DTCs. If EEPROM FAILURE and TRANSPONDER DTCs are present, replace SKIM and perform SKIM INITIALIZATION PROCEDURE. If EEPROM FAILURE and TRANSPONDER DTCs are not present, go to next step.
2) If only EEPROM FAILURE DTC is present, go to SKIS TEST 6A. If EEPROM FAILURE DTC is not present but TRANSPONDER DTC is present, go to SKIS TEST 3A. If none of the above DTCs are present, system is currently functioning correctly.

SKIS TEST 12A

TRANSPONDER CRC FAILURE, TRANSPONDER COMMUNICATION, ID MISMATCH OR RESPONSE MISMATCH

NOTE: *Perform SKIS TEST 1A before proceeding with this test. For connector terminal identification and wiring diagrams, see BODY CONTROL COMPUTER – INTRODUCTION article. Perform VERIFICATION TEST: VER-1A after each repair.*

CAUTION: *Always turn ignition switch to OFF position prior to disconnecting or connecting any module connector.*

Using each of customer's keys, start vehicle. Using scan tool, read SKIM DTCs. If TRANSPONDER DTC is present, replace SKIM and perform SKIM INITIALIZATION PROCEDURE. If TRANSPONDER DTC is not present, system is currently functioning correctly.

SKIM INITIALIZATION PROCEDURE

GENERAL INFORMATION

SECURED ACCESS mode is not required to check programmed status of key.

If PCM is replaced, unique secret key data must be transferred from SKIM to PCM. This procedure requires SKIM to be placed in SECURED ACCESS mode using 4-digit PIN code.

If 3 attempts are made to enter secured access mode using an incorrect PIN, SECURED ACCESS mode will be locked out for one hour. To exit lock out mode, turn ignition switch to RUN/START position continuously for one hour. Ensure all accessories are turned off. Monitor battery state and connect battery charger is necessary.

To program smart keys using "customer programming method" requires 2 valid smart keys. See appropriate ANTI-THEFT SYSTEM article.

INITIALIZATION PROCEDURE

1) Obtain vehicle's unique PIN number assigned to it's original SKIM module from vehicle owner or Chrysler's customer center.
2) Using scan tool, select THEFT ALARM, SKIM, then MISCELLANEOUS. Select SKIM MODULE REPLACED function.
3) Enter SECURED ACCESS mode using unique 4-digit PIN number.
4) Program vehicle's VIN number into SKIM's memory.
5) Program country code into SKIM's memory (U.S.).
6) Transfer vehicle's unique Secret Key data from PCM. This process will require SKIM module to be in SECURED ACCESS mode. The PIN number must be entered into scan tool before SKIM will enter SECURED ACCESS mode. Once SECURED ACCESS mode is active, SKIM will remain in that mode for 60 seconds.
7) Program all customer keys into SKIM's memory. This requires that SKIM be in SECURED ACCESS mode. The SKIM will immediately exit SECURED ACCESS mode after each key is programmed.

SPEED PROPORTIONAL STEERING TEST 1A

IDENTIFYING SPEED PROPORTIONAL STEERING PROBLEMS

1) Conduct a thorough visual inspection of speed proportional steering system. Check for damaged components or disconnected harness connectors. Repair as needed.
2) Connect scan tool to DLC. Turn ignition on. Using scan tool, select BCM. Read and record all speed proportional steering system DTCs. If any DTCs (fault messages) are present, see SPEED PROPORTIONAL STEERING SYSTEM DIAGNOSTIC TEST DIRECTORY table. Proceed to appropriate test. If no DTCs are present, go to TEST 5A.

SPEED PROPORTIONAL STEERING SYSTEM DIAGNOSTIC TEST DIRECTORY

Fault Message	SPEED PROPORTIONAL STEERING TEST
Speed Proportional Steering Circuit Open Or Shorted To Ground	2A
Speed Proportional Steering Circuit Shorted To Voltage	3A
Speed Proportional Steering Solenoid Over-Temperature	4A

CHRY
4-176

1999 ACCESSORIES & EQUIPMENT
Body Control Computer Tests
Concorde, Intrepid, LHS & 300M (Cont.)

SPEED PROPORTIONAL STEERING TEST 2A

SPEED PROPORTIONAL STEERING CIRCUIT OPEN OR SHORTED TO GROUND

NOTE: Perform SPEED PROPORTIONAL STEERING TEST 1A before proceeding with this test. For connector terminal identification and wiring diagrams, see BODY CONTROL COMPUTER – INTRODUCTION article. Perform VERIFICATION TEST: VER-5A after each repair.

CAUTION: Always turn ignition switch to OFF position prior to disconnecting or connecting any module connector.

1) Start engine and turn steering wheel while monitoring amount of power steering assist. Using scan tool, de-activate Speed Proportional Steening (SPS) solenoid for 15 seconds. Turn steering wheel while monitoring amount of power steering assist. If steering has less power assist once SPS solenoid is de-activated, go to next step. If steering power assist is unchanged once SPS solenoid is de-activated, go to step **3)**.

2) System is currently operating correctly. Inspect condition of Body Control Module (BCM) internal 20-pin connector. Body Control Module (BCM). BCM is mounted to junction block located behind left end cap of instrument panel. *See Fig. 1.* Inspect SPS solenoid harness connector. Connector is located next to master cylinder. Clean and repair either connection as needed.

3) Turn ignition off. Inspect SPS solenoid harness connector. Connector is located next to master cylinder. Clean and repair either connection as needed. If connection is okay, go to next step.

4) Disconnect SPS solenoid connector. Using ohmmeter, measure resistance between SPS solenoid component connector terminals. If resistance is 5.7–6.3 ohms at 68° F (20° C), go to next step. If resistance is not 5.7–6.3 ohms at 68° F (20° C), replace SPS solenoid.

5) Turn ignition on. Using test light, probe terminal No. 2 (Violet/Orange wire) on SPS solenoid harness connector. If test light is brightly illuminated, repair Violet/Orange wire for short to ground. If test light is not brightly illuminated, go to next step.

6) Using test light, probe terminal No. 1 (Light Green/Pink wire) on SPS solenoid harness connector. If test light is illuminated, repair Light Green/Pink wire for short to ground. If test light is not illuminated, go to next step.

7) Disconnect Body Control Module (BCM) from junction block. BCM is mounted to junction block located behind left end cap of instrument panel. *See Fig. 1.* Inspect junction block 20-pin internal connector. Measure resistance between terminals No. 3 and 4 on junction block 20-pin internal connector. If resistance is less than 100 ohms, repair SPS negative (Light Green/Pink wire) circuit for short to positive (Violet/Orange wire) circuit. If resistance is 100 ohms or greater, go to next step.

8) Inspect continuity of both SPS solenoid circuits between harness connector and junction block 20-pin internal connector. If continuity is not present on either circuit, repair as needed. If both circuits are okay, replace BCM.

SPEED PROPORTIONAL STEERING TEST 3A

SPEED PROPORTIONAL STEERING CIRCUIT SHORTED TO VOLTAGE

NOTE: Perform SPEED PROPORTIONAL STEERING TEST 1A before proceeding with this test. For connector terminal identification and wiring diagrams, see BODY CONTROL COMPUTER – INTRODUCTION article. Perform VERIFICATION TEST: VER-5A after each repair.

CAUTION: Always turn ignition switch to OFF position prior to disconnecting or connecting any module connector.

1) Start engine and turn steering wheel while monitoring amount of power steering assist. Using scan tool, de-activate Speed Proportional Steening (SPS) solenoid for 15 seconds. Turn steering wheel while monitoring amount of power steering assist. If steering has less power assist once SPS solenoid is de-activated, go to next step. If steering power assist is unchanged once SPS solenoid is de-activated, go to step **3)**.

2) System is currently operating correctly. Inspect condition of Body Control Module (BCM) internal 20-pin connector. Body Control Module (BCM). BCM is mounted to junction block located behind left end cap of instrument panel. *See Fig. 1.* Inspect SPS solenoid harness connector. Connector is located next to master cylinder. Clean and repair either connection as needed.

3) Turn ignition off. Inspect SPS solenoid harness connector. Connector is located next to master cylinder. Clean and repair either connection as needed. If connection is okay, go to next step.

4) Disconnect SPS solenoid connector. Using ohmmeter, measure resistance between SPS solenoid component connector terminals. If resistance is 5.7–6.3 ohms at 68° F (20° C), go to next step. If resistance is not 5.7–6.3 ohms at 68° F (20° C), replace SPS solenoid.

5) Start engine and wait 10 seconds. Using voltmeter, measure voltage between ground and terminal No. 2 (Violet/Orange wire) on SPS solenoid harness connector. If voltage is greater than one volt, repair Violet/Orange wire for short to voltage. If voltage is one volt or less, go to next step.

6) Using voltmeter, measure voltage between ground and terminal No. 1 (Light Green/Pink wire) on SPS solenoid harness connector. If voltage is greater than one volt, repair Light Green/Pink wire for short to voltage. If voltage is one volt or less, go to next step.

7) Disconnect Body Control Module (BCM) from junction block. BCM is mounted to junction block located behind left end cap of instrument panel. *See Fig. 1.* Inspect junction block 20-pin internal connector. Measure resistance between terminals No. 3 and 4 on junction block 20-pin internal connector. If resistance is less than 5 ohms, repair SPS negative (Light Green/Pink wire) circuit for short to positive (Violet/Orange wire) circuit. If resistance is 5 ohms or greater, replace BCM.

1999 ACCESSORIES & EQUIPMENT
Body Control Computer Tests
Concorde, Intrepid, LHS & 300M (Cont.)

CHRY
4-177

SPEED PROPORTIONAL STEERING TEST 4A

SPEED PROPORTIONAL STEERING SOLENOID OVER-TEMPERATURE

NOTE: *Perform SPEED PROPORTIONAL STEERING TEST 1A before proceeding with this test. For connector terminal identification and wiring diagrams, see BODY CONTROL COMPUTER – INTRODUCTION article. Perform VERIFICATION TEST: VER-5A after each repair.*

CAUTION: *Always turn ignition switch to OFF position prior to disconnecting or connecting any module connector.*

1) Start engine and turn steering wheel while monitoring amount of power steering assist. Using scan tool, de-activate Speed Proportional Steering (SPS) solenoid for 15 seconds. Turn steering wheel while monitoring amount of power steering assist. If steering has less power assist once SPS solenoid is de-activated, go to next step. If steering power assist is unchanged once SPS solenoid is de-activated, go to step **3)**.

2) System is currently operating correctly. Inspect condition of Body Control Module (BCM) internal 20-pin connector. Body Control Module (BCM). BCM is mounted to junction block located behind left end cap of instrument panel. See Fig. 1. Inspect SPS solenoid harness connector. Connector is located next to master cylinder. Clean and repair either connection as needed.

3) Turn steering wheel from lock to lock position 10 times. Turn ignition off. Inspect SPS solenoid harness connector. Connector is located next to master cylinder. Clean and repair either connection as needed. If connection is okay, go to next step.

4) Disconnect SPS solenoid connector. Using ohmmeter, measure resistance between SPS solenoid component connector terminals. If resistance is 5.7–6.3 ohms at 68° F (20° C), go to next step. If resistance is not 5.7–6.3 ohms at 68° F (20° C), replace SPS solenoid.

5) Inspect both SPS solenoid circuits between harness connector and junction block 20-pin internal connector for intermittent short to ground. If short is not present on either circuit, repair as needed. If both circuits are okay, replace BCM.

SPEED PROPORTIONAL STEERING TEST 5A

SPEED PROPORTIONAL STEERING SYSTEM FUNCTIONAL TEST

NOTE: *Perform SPEED PROPORTIONAL STEERING TEST 1A before proceeding with this test. For connector terminal identification and wiring diagrams, see BODY CONTROL COMPUTER – INTRODUCTION article. Perform VERIFICATION TEST: VER-5A after each repair.*

CAUTION: *Always turn ignition switch to OFF position prior to disconnecting or connecting any module connector.*

1) Start engine and turn steering wheel while monitoring amount of power steering assist. Using scan tool, de-activate Speed Proportional Steering (SPS) solenoid for 15 seconds. Turn steering wheel while monitoring amount of power steering assist. If steering has less power assist once SPS solenoid is de-activated, go to next step. If steering power assist is unchanged once SPS solenoid is de-activated, go to appropriate STEERING article.

2) System is currently operating correctly. Inspect condition of Body Control Module (BCM) internal 20-pin connector. Body Control Module (BCM). BCM is mounted to junction block located behind left end cap of instrument panel. See Fig. 1. Inspect SPS solenoid harness connector. Connector is located next to master cylinder. Clean and repair either connection as needed.

VTSS TEST 1A

IDENTIFYING VEHICLE THEFT SECURITY SYSTEM PROBLEMS

NOTE: *Perform SYMPTOM ID TEST 1A before proceeding with this test. For connector terminal identification and wiring diagrams, see BODY CONTROL COMPUTER – INTRODUCTION article. Perform VERIFICATION TEST: VER-2A after each repair.*

CAUTION: *Always turn ignition switch to OFF position prior to disconnecting or connecting any module connector.*

1) If VTSS is operating without being tripped, select THEFT ALARM using scan tool. Select MONITOR DISPLAY and read ALARM TRIPPED BY status.

2) If VTSS indicator light is illuminated constantly 30 seconds after key is turned on or while driving, go to VTSS TEST 3A.

3) Using scan tool, select BODY SYSTEM, then BODY COMPUTER. Verify communication with Body Control Module (BCM). If scan tool displays NO RESPONSE, go to TEST 1A in appropriate VEHICLE COMMUNICATIONS article.

4) Using scan tool, select MONITOR DISPLAY. Read VTSS status. If VTSS mode is not DISARMED, go to VTSS TEST 2A. If VTSS mode is DISARMED, go to next step.

5) Using scan tool, select SENSORS. Read IGNITION VOLTAGE. If battery voltage is displayed with ignition on, go to next step. If battery voltage is not displayed with ignition on, go to TEST 16A in appropriate VEHICLE COMMUNICATIONS article.

6) Using scan tool, check KEY IN IGNITION SWITCH status. If scan tool displays CLOSED with key inserted, go to next step. If scan tool does not displayed CLOSED with key inserted, go to POWER DOOR LOCK TEST 9A.

7) Using scan tool, select MISCELLANEOUS, then CHANGE MODE. Select DIAGNOSTICS. VTSS is now in diagnostic mode. Follow scan tool directions. When entering diagnostic mode with key in ignition switch, horn should sound twice and headlights and VTSS indicator light should flash. If horn does not sound, go to VTSS TEST 4A. If VTSS indicator light does not illuminate, go to VTSS TEST 5A. If headlights do not illuminate, go to EXTERIOR LIGHTING TEST 1A.

8) Remove key from ignition switch. Open and close each door. Horn should sound after each action. If horn does not sound, go to DOOR AJAR TEST 1A. Rotate key in each front door key cylinder. Horn should sound. If horn does not sound, go to POWER DOOR LOCK TEST 1A.

9) Using scan tool, select MONITOR DISPLAY. Read VTSS status. If VTSS mode is other than DISARMED, go to VTSS TEST 2A. If engine controller is 1 NO RESPONSE/2 NO RESPONSE, go to TEST 9A in appropriate VEHICLE COMMUNICATIONS article. If engine controller is 1 NOT OK TO ARM VTSS/OK TO RUN ENGINE, replace Powertrain Control Module (PCM). See Fig. 5.

10) If problem is with Remote Keyless Entry (RKE) arm/disarm function, go to POWER DOOR LOCK TEST 11A.

CHRY
4-178

1999 ACCESSORIES & EQUIPMENT
Body Control Computer Tests
Concorde, Intrepid, LHS & 300M (Cont.)

VTSS TEST 2A

DISARMING VTSS SYSTEM

NOTE: Perform VTSS TEST 1A before proceeding with this test. For connector terminal identification and wiring diagrams, see BODY CONTROL COMPUTER – INTRODUCTION article. Perform VERIFICATION TEST: VER-2A after each repair.

CAUTION: Always turn ignition switch to OFF position prior to disconnecting or connecting any module connector.

1) Turn ignition off. Insert key into driver's door and turn lock to UNLOCK position. Turn ignition on. Using scan tool, select THEFT ALARM, then MONITORS. Read VTSS status. If scan tool displays CURRENT MODE DISARMED, go to VTSS TEST 1A. If scan tool does not display CURRENT MODE DISARMED, go to next step.
2) Turn ignition off. Insert key into right door and turn lock to UNLOCK position. Turn ignition on. Read VTSS status. If scan tool displays CURRENT MODE DISARMED, go to POWER DOOR LOCK TEST 14A. If scan tool does not display CURRENT MODE DISARMED, go to next step.
3) Using RKE transmitter, unlock doors. Read VTSS status. If scan tool displays CURRENT MODE DISARMED, go to POWER DOOR LOCK TEST 4A. If scan tool does not display CURRENT MODE DISARMED, replace Body Control Module (BCM). BCM is mounted to junction block located behind left end cap of instrument panel. *See Fig. 1.*

VTSS TEST 3A

VTSS INDICATOR LIGHT ON CONSTANTLY

NOTE: Perform VTSS TEST 1A before proceeding with this test. For connector terminal identification and wiring diagrams, see BODY CONTROL COMPUTER – INTRODUCTION article. Perform VERIFICATION TEST: VER-2A after each repair.

CAUTION: Always turn ignition switch to OFF position prior to disconnecting or connecting any module connector.

1) Using scan tool, select SYSTEM TEST, then PCM MONITOR. If scan tool displays PCM ACTIVE ON BUS, go to next step. If scan tool does not display PCM ACTIVE ON BUS, go to go to TEST 9A in appropriate VEHICLE COMMUNICATIONS article.
2) Using scan tool, select INPUTS/OUTPUTS. Read decklid cylinder switch status. If scan tool displays CLOSED, go to step 6). If scan tool does not display CLOSED, go to next step.
3) Disconnect decklid cylinder switch. Using external ohmmeter, measure resistance between ground and terminal No. 2 (Black wire) on cylinder switch harness connector. If resistance is less than 5 ohms, go to next step. If resistance is 5 ohms or greater, repair open Black wire.
4) Connect jumper wire across decklid cylinder switch harness connector terminals. Using scan tool, read decklid cylinder switch status. If scan tool displays CLOSED, replace decklid cylinder switch. If scan tool does not display CLOSED, go to next step.
5) Disconnect Body Control Module (BCM) Blue 16-pin connector C4. BCM is mounted to junction block located behind left end cap of instrument panel. *See Fig. 1.*
6) Disconnect Body Control Module (BCM) Blue 16-pin connector C4. BCM is mounted to junction block located behind left end cap of instrument panel. *See Fig. 1.*

VTSS TEST 4A

HORN CIRCUIT MALFUNCTION

NOTE: Perform VTSS TEST 1A before proceeding with this test. For connector terminal identification and wiring diagrams, see BODY CONTROL COMPUTER – INTRODUCTION article. Perform VERIFICATION TEST: VER-2A after each repair.

CAUTION: Always turn ignition switch to OFF position prior to disconnecting or connecting any module connector.

1) Press horn button on steering wheel. If horn does not sound, repair as needed. Using scan tool, select VEHICLE THEFT, then INPUTS/OUTPUTS. Read trunk key cylinder status. If scan tool displays CLOSED, go to next step. If scan tool does not display CLOSED, go to VTSS TEST 3A.
2) Disconnect Body Control Module (BCM) from junction block. BCM is mounted to junction block located behind left end cap of instrument panel. *See Fig. 1.*

VTSS TEST 5A

VTSS INDICATOR LIGHT DRIVER MALFUNCTION

NOTE: Perform VTSS TEST 1A before proceeding with this test. For connector terminal identification and wiring diagrams, see BODY CONTROL COMPUTER – INTRODUCTION article. Perform VERIFICATION TEST: VER-2A after each repair.

CAUTION: Always turn ignition switch to OFF position prior to disconnecting or connecting any module connector.

1) Disconnect Automatic Temperature Control (ATC) sun sensor/VTSS indicator connector. ATC sun sensor is located under instrument panel top cover. Using external voltmeter, measure voltage between terminals No. 1 (Pink wire) and 2 (Black/Orange wire) on ATC sun sensor/VTSS indicator harness connector. Using scan tool, actuate VTSS indicator light. If voltage toggles up to 10 volts, replace VTSS indicator light. If voltage does not toggle up to 10 volts, go to next step.
2) Measure voltage between ground and terminal No. 1 (Pink wire) on ATC sun sensor/VTSS indicator harness connector. If voltage is 10 volts or less, repair open Pink wire. If voltage is greater than 10 volts, go to next step.
3) Disconnect Body Control Module (BCM) Black 24-pin connector C2. BCM is mounted to junction block located behind left end cap of instrument panel. *See Fig. 1.*

WINDSHIELD WIPER TEST 1A

IDENTIFYING WINDSHIELD WIPER SYSTEM PROBLEMS

NOTE: Perform SYMPTOM ID TEST 1A before proceeding with this test. For connector terminal identification and wiring diagrams, see BODY CONTROL COMPUTER – INTRODUCTION article. Perform VERIFICATION TEST: VER-2A after each repair.

CAUTION: Always turn ignition switch to OFF position prior to disconnecting or connecting any module connector.

Turn ignition on and verify operation of windshield wipers. Operate windshield wiper system in high speed mode, low speed mode, intermittent mode and wash mode (with wipers off). Using scan tool, check DTC's. See WINDSHIELD WIPER SYSTEM DTC DIRECTORY table. If wiper system does not operate properly, perform indicated test. See WINDSHIELD WIPER SYSTEM DIAGNOSTIC TEST DIRECTORY table.

1999 ACCESSORIES & EQUIPMENT
Body Control Computer Tests
Concorde, Intrepid, LHS & 300M (Cont.)

CHRY
4-179

WINDSHIELD WIPER SYSTEM DTC DIRECTORY

Fault Message	WINDSHIELD WIPER TEST
Wiper ON/OFF Relay Control Open Or Short Circuit	2A
Wiper Park Switch Failure	3A
Wiper ON/OFF Relay Control Circuit Short High	4A

WINDSHIELD WIPER SYSTEM DIAGNOSTIC TEST DIRECTORY

Problem	WINDSHIELD WIPER TEST
Wipers Not Working At All	5A
Wipers Not Working In High Speed Mode	6A
Wipers Not Working In Low Speed Mode	7A
Wipers Not Working In Intermittent Mode	8A
Wipers Not Parking In Off Position	3A
Wash Function Not Operating	9A
Wipers Operate in High Speed Only	10A
Wiper Run Constantly With Ignition OFF	11A

WINDSHIELD WIPER TEST 2A

WIPER ON/OFF RELAY CONTROL OPEN OR SHORT CIRCUIT

NOTE: Perform WINDSHIELD WIPER TEST 1A before proceeding with this test. For connector terminal identification and wiring diagrams, see BODY CONTROL COMPUTER – INTRODUCTION article. Perform VERIFICATION TEST: VER-2A after each repair.

CAUTION: Always turn ignition switch to OFF position prior to disconnecting or connecting any module connector.

1) Remove wiper ON/OFF relay from Power Distribution Center (PDC). *See Fig. 8.* PDC is located in engine compartment. *See Fig. 5.* Turn ignition on. Using external voltmeter, measure voltage between ground and terminal "A" (Red wire) on wiper ON/OFF relay socket. If voltage is 10 volts or less, repair open Red wire. If voltage is greater than 10 volts, go to next step.

2) Install wiper ON/OFF relay in PDC. Disconnect Body Control Module (BCM) Bone 12-pin connector C3. BCM is mounted to junction block located behind left end cap of instrument panel. *See Fig. 1.* Using external voltmeter, measure voltage between ground and terminal No. 4 (Red/White wire) on Bone harness connector. If voltage is 8 volts or less, go to next step. If voltage is greater than 8 volts, replace BCM.

3) Disconnect wiper ON/OFF relay. Connect jumper wire between ground and terminal "C" on wiper ON/OFF relay. Using external ohmmeter, measure resistance between ground and terminal No. 4 (Red/White wire) on BCM Bone 12-pin connector C3. If resistance is less than 5 ohms, replace wiper ON/OFF relay. If resistance is 5 ohms or greater, repair open Red/White wire.

WINDSHIELD WIPER TEST 3A

WIPER PARK SWITCH FAILURE

NOTE: Perform WINDSHIELD WIPER TEST 1A before proceeding with this test. For connector terminal identification and wiring diagrams, see BODY CONTROL COMPUTER – INTRODUCTION article. Perform VERIFICATION TEST: VER-2A after each repair.

CAUTION: Always turn ignition switch to OFF position prior to disconnecting or connecting any module connector.

1) Operate windshield wipers in intermittent mode. Using scan tool, monitor wiper park switch. If scan tool displays wiper park switch toggle CLOSED to OPEN, system is currently operating correctly. If scan tool does not display wiper park switch toggle CLOSED to OPEN, go to next step.

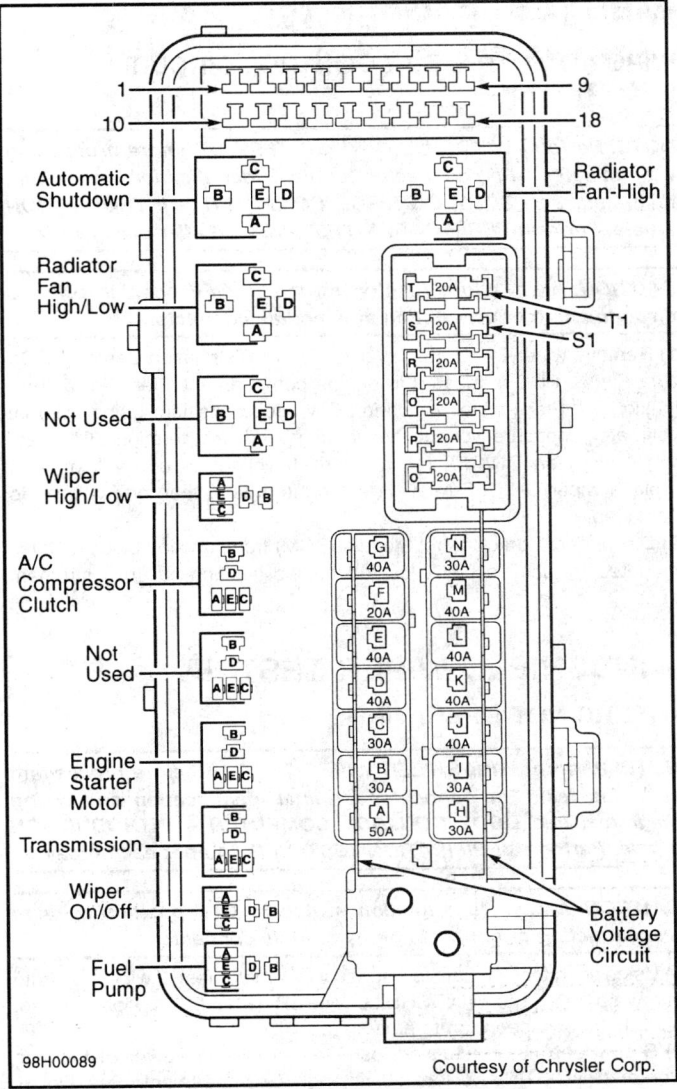

98H00089
Courtesy of Chrysler Corp.

Fig. 8: Identifying Power Distribution Center Components

2) Turn ignition off. Access Body Control Module (BCM). BCM is mounted to junction block located behind left end cap of instrument panel. *See Fig. 1.* Using external ohmmeter, backprobe BCM Bone 12-pin connector C3.

3) Measure resistance between ground and terminal No. 3 (Tan/Red wire). Turn ignition on. Place wiper switch in LOW speed position. If resistance pulsates, replace BCM. If resistance does not pulsate, go to next step.

4) Turn ignition off. Connect jumper wire between ground and terminal No. 3 (Tan/Red wire) on BCM Bone connector. Disconnect wiper motor connector. Using external ohmmeter, measure resistance between ground and terminal No. 4 (Tan/Red wire) on wiper motor harness connector. If resistance is less than 5 ohms, replace wiper motor. If resistance is 5 ohms or greater, repair open Tan/Red wire.

CHRY
4-180

1999 ACCESSORIES & EQUIPMENT
Body Control Computer Tests
Concorde, Intrepid, LHS & 300M (Cont.)

WINDSHIELD WIPER TEST 4A

WIPER ON/OFF RELAY CONTROL CIRCUIT SHORTED HIGH

NOTE: *Perform WINDSHIELD WIPER TEST 1A before proceeding with this test. For connector terminal identification and wiring diagrams, see BODY CONTROL COMPUTER – INTRODUCTION article. Perform VERIFICATION TEST: VER-2A after each repair.*

CAUTION: *Always turn ignition switch to OFF position prior to disconnecting or connecting any module connector.*

---

1) Remove wiper ON/OFF relay from Power Distribution Center (PDC). *See Fig. 8*. PDC is located in engine compartment. *See Fig. 5*. Turn ignition on. Place wiper switch in LOW speed position. Using external voltmeter, measure voltage between ground and terminal "C" (Red/White wire) on ON/OFF relay socket. If voltage is one volt or less, replace wiper ON/OFF relay. If voltage is greater than one volt, go to next step.

2) Disconnect Body Control Module (BCM) from junction block. BCM is mounted to junction block located behind left end cap of instrument panel. *See Fig. 1*.

WINDSHIELD WIPER TEST 5A

WIPERS NOT OPERATING

NOTE: *Perform WINDSHIELD WIPER TEST 1A before proceeding with this test. For connector terminal identification and wiring diagrams, see BODY CONTROL COMPUTER – INTRODUCTION article. Perform VERIFICATION TEST: VER-2A after each repair.*

CAUTION: *Always turn ignition switch to OFF position prior to disconnecting or connecting any module connector.*

---

1) Using scan tool, actuate low speed wiper motor test. If wipers operate in low speed, go to WINDSHIELD WIPER TEST 5B. If wipers do not operate in low speed, go to next step.

2) Stop wiper motor actuation test. Gain access to Power Distribution Center (PDC). PDC is located in engine compartment. *See Fig. 5*. Inspect fuse "M". If fuse is open, go to WINDSHIELD WIPER TEST 5C. If fuse is okay, go to next step.

3) Remove fuse "M". Using external voltmeter, measure voltage between ground and B+ circuit on fuse "M" socket. If voltage is 10 volts or less, repair open B+ circuit. If voltage is greater than 10 volts, go to next step.

4) Install fuse "M". Remove wiper ON/OFF relay from Power Distribution Center (PDC). *See Fig. 8*. Using external voltmeter, measure voltage between ground and terminal "D" (Red wire) on ON/OFF relay socket. If voltage is 10 volts or less, repair open Red wire circuit. If voltage is greater than 10 volts, go to next step.

5) Connect jumper wire between terminals "B" and "D" on ON/OFF relay socket. If wiper motor operates, go to WINDSHIELD WIPER TEST 5D. If wiper motor does not operate, go to next step.

6) Disconnect wiper HI/LO relay form PDC. Do not disconnect jumper wire. Using external voltmeter, measure voltage between ground and terminal "B" (Dark Green/Yellow wire) on HI/LO relay socket. If voltage is 10 volts or less, repair open Dark Green/Yellow wire between wiper ON/OFF and HI/LO relays. If voltage is greater than 10 volts, go to next step.

7) Disconnect jumper wire. Connect jumper wire between terminal "D" on wiper ON/OFF relay socket and terminal "E" on wiper HI/LO relay socket. If wiper motor operates in low speed, replace HI/LO relay. If wiper motor does not operate in low speed, go to WINDSHIELD WIPER TEST 5E.

WINDSHIELD WIPER TEST 5B

WIPERS NOT OPERATING

NOTE: *Perform WINDSHIELD WIPER TEST 5A before proceeding with this test. For connector terminal identification and wiring diagrams, see BODY CONTROL COMPUTER – INTRODUCTION article. Perform VERIFICATION TEST: VER-2A after each repair.*

CAUTION: *Always turn ignition switch to OFF position prior to disconnecting or connecting any module connector.*

---

1) Stop wiper motor actuation. Ensure ignition is on. Place wiper switch in LOW position. Using scan tool, read intermittent wiper switch voltage. If scan tool displays INTRMT WIPE: 2.5V or greater, replace Body Control Module (BCM). BCM is mounted to junction block located behind left end cap of instrument panel. *See Fig. 1*. If scan tool displays INTRMT WIPE: 2.4V or less, go to next step.

2) Remove and inspect fuse No. 5 in junction block. *See Fig. 3*. If fuse is open, go to step 5). If fuse is okay, go to next step.

3) Install fuse. Disconnect multifunction switch connector. *See Fig. 2*. Using external voltmeter, measure voltage between ground and terminal No. 1 (Dark Blue wire) on switch harness connector. If voltage is 10 volts or less, repair open Dark Blue wire. If voltage is greater than 10 volts, go to next step.

4) Turn ignition off. Disconnect BCM Black 24-pin connector C2. Using external ohmmeter, measure resistance of Dark Green/Red wire between terminal No. 3 on multifunction switch harness connector and terminal No. 8 on BCM Black harness connector. If resistance is less than 5 ohms, replace multifunction switch. If resistance is 5 ohms or greater, repair open Dark Green/Red wire.

5) Turn ignition on. Disconnect multifunction switch connector. *See Fig. 2*. Using external ohmmeter, measure resistance between ground and terminal No. 1 (Dark Blue wire) on switch harness connector. If resistance is less than 5 ohms, repair Dark Blue wire for short to ground. Replace fuse No. 5. If resistance is 5 ohms or greater, go to next step.

6) Using external ohmmeter, measure resistance between ground and terminal No. 3 (Dark Green/Red wire) on multifunction switch harness connector. If resistance is less than 5 ohms, repair Dark Green/Red wire for short to ground. Replace fuse No. 5. If resistance is 5 ohms or greater, replace multifunction switch. Replace fuse No. 5.

WINDSHIELD WIPER TEST 5C

WIPERS NOT OPERATING

NOTE: *Perform WINDSHIELD WIPER TEST 5A before proceeding with this test. For connector terminal identification and wiring diagrams, see BODY CONTROL COMPUTER – INTRODUCTION article. Perform VERIFICATION TEST: VER-2A after each repair.*

CAUTION: *Always turn ignition switch to OFF position prior to disconnecting or connecting any module connector.*

---

1) Turn ignition off. Disconnect wiper ON/OFF relay from PDC. Disconnect wiper HI/LO relay. Using external ohmmeter, measure resistance between ground and terminal "D" (Red wire) on ON/OFF relay socket. If resistance is less than 5 ohms, repair Red wire circuit for short to ground. Replace fuse "M". If resistance is 5 ohms or greater, go to next step.

2) Measure resistance between ground and terminal "B" (Dark Green/Yellow wire) on ON/OFF relay socket. If resistance is less than 5 ohms, repair Dark Green/Yellow wire for short to ground. Replace fuse "M". If resistance is 5 ohms or greater, go to next step.

3) Disconnect wiper motor connector. Using external ohmmeter, measure resistance between ground and terminal "E" (Brown/White wire) on HI/LO relay socket. If resistance is less than 5 ohms, repair Brown/White wire for short to ground. Replace fuse "M". If resistance is 5 ohms or greater, go to next step.

1999 ACCESSORIES & EQUIPMENT
Body Control Computer Tests
Concorde, Intrepid, LHS & 300M (Cont.)

CHRY
4-181

4) Using scan tool in ohmmeter mode, measure resistance at terminal "D" (Red/Yellow wire) on HI/LO relay socket. If resistance is less than 5 ohms, repair Red/Yellow wire for short to ground. Replace fuse "M". If resistance is 5 ohms or greater, replace wiper motor. Replace fuse "M".

WINDSHIELD WIPER TEST 5D

WIPERS NOT OPERATING

NOTE: Perform WINDSHIELD WIPER TEST 5A before proceeding with this test. For connector terminal identification and wiring diagrams, see BODY CONTROL COMPUTER – INTRODUCTION article. Perform VERIFICATION TEST: VER-2A after each repair.

CAUTION: Always turn ignition switch to OFF position prior to disconnecting or connecting any module connector.

1) Remove jumper wire. Turn ignition on. Using external voltmeter, measure voltage between ground and terminal "A" (Red wire) on wiper ON/OFF relay socket. If voltage is 10 volts or less, repair open Red wire. If voltage is greater than 10 volts, go to next step.
2) Install wiper ON/OFF relay. Disconnect Body Control Module (BCM) Bone 12-pin connector C3. BCM is mounted to junction block located behind left end cap of instrument panel. *See Fig. 1.* Connect jumper wire between ground and terminal No. 4 (Red/White wire) on BCM Bone connector. If wiper motor operates, replace BCM. If wiper motor does not operate, go to next step.
3) Turn ignition off. Remove wiper ON/OFF relay. Do not disconnect jumper wire. Using external ohmmeter, measure resistance between ground and terminal "C" (Red/White wire) on ON/OFF relay socket. If resistance is less than 5 ohms, replace wiper ON/OFF relay. If resistance is 5 ohms or greater, repair open Red/White wire.

WINDSHIELD WIPER TEST 5E

WIPERS NOT OPERATING

NOTE: Perform WINDSHIELD WIPER TEST 5A before proceeding with this test. For connector terminal identification and wiring diagrams, see BODY CONTROL COMPUTER – INTRODUCTION article. Perform VERIFICATION TEST: VER-2A after each repair.

CAUTION: Always turn ignition switch to OFF position prior to disconnecting or connecting any module connector.

1) Disconnect motor connector. Do not disconnect jumper wire. Using scan tool in voltmeter mode, measure voltage at terminal "E" (Brown/White wire) on wiper HI/LO relay socket. If voltage is 10 volts or less, repair open Brown/White wire. If voltage is greater than 10 volts, go to next step.
2) Ensure ignition, lights and accessories are off. Using scan tool in ohmmeter mode, measure resistance at "E" (Black wire) on wiper ON/OFF relay socket. If resistance is less than 5 ohms, replace wiper motor. If resistance is 5 ohms or greater, repair open Black wire.

WINDSHIELD WIPER TEST 6A

WIPERS NOT OPERATING IN HIGH SPEED MODE

NOTE: Perform WINDSHIELD WIPER TEST 1A before proceeding with this test. For connector terminal identification and wiring diagrams, see BODY CONTROL COMPUTER – INTRODUCTION article. Perform VERIFICATION TEST: VER-2A after each repair.

CAUTION: Always turn ignition switch to OFF position prior to disconnecting or connecting any module connector.

1) Disconnect wiper HI/LO relay from Power Distribution Center. Remove wiper ON/OFF relay from Power Distribution Center (PDC). *See Fig. 8.* PDC is located in engine compartment. *See Fig. 5.*

2) Turn ignition on. Place wiper switch on low speed position. Using external voltmeter, measure voltage between ground and terminal "A" (Red wire) on HI/LO relay socket. If voltage is 10 volts or less, repair open Red wire. If voltage is greater than 10 volts, go to next step.
3) Connect jumper wire between terminals "B" and "D" on HI/LO relay socket. If wiper motor operates, go to step 5). If wiper motor does not operate, go to next step.
4) Disconnect wiper motor connector. Do not disconnect jumper wire. Using external voltmeter, measure voltage between ground and terminal No. 1 (Red/Yellow wire) on wiper motor harness connector. If voltage is 10 volts or less, repair open Red/Yellow wire. If voltage is greater than 10 volts, replace wiper motor.
5) Remove jumper wire. Using external voltmeter, measure voltage between terminal "B" and "C" on HI/LO relay socket. Place wiper switch in high position. If voltage is 9 volts or less, go to next step. If voltage is greater than 9 volts, replace wiper HI/LO relay.
6) Turn ignition off. Disconnect Body Control Module (BCM) Bone 12-pin connector C3. BCM is mounted to junction block located behind left end cap of instrument panel. *See Fig. 1.* Connect jumper wire between ground and terminal No. 12 (Violet wire) on BCM Bone connector. Using external ohmmeter, measure resistance between ground and terminal "C" (Violet wire) on HI/LO relay socket. If resistance is less than 5 ohms, go to next step. If resistance is 5 ohms or greater, repair open Violet wire.
7) Disconnect BCM Black 24-pin connector C2. Turn ignition on. Place wiper switch on high speed position. Using external voltmeter, measure voltage between ground and terminal No. 8 (Dark Green/Red wire) on BCM Black harness connector. If voltage is 10 volts or less, replace multifunction switch. If voltage is greater than 10 volts, replace BCM.

WINDSHIELD WIPER TEST 7A

WIPERS NOT OPERATING IN LOW SPEED MODE

NOTE: Perform WINDSHIELD WIPER TEST 1A before proceeding with this test. For connector terminal identification and wiring diagrams, see BODY CONTROL COMPUTER – INTRODUCTION article. Perform VERIFICATION TEST: VER-2A after each repair.

CAUTION: Always turn ignition switch to OFF position prior to disconnecting or connecting any module connector.

1) Disconnect wiper HI/LO relay from Power Distribution Center. *See Fig. 8.* PDC is located in engine compartment. *See Fig. 5.*
2) Ensure ignition is off. Turn wiper switch to LOW speed position. Using external ohmmeter, measure resistance between ground and terminal "A" (Red wire) on HI/LO relay socket. If resistance is less than 100 ohms, repair Red wire for short to ground. If resistance is 100 ohms or greater, go to next step.
3) Connect jumper wire between terminals "B" and "E" on HI/LO relay socket. Turn ignition on. If wiper motor operates in low speed, replace HI/LO wiper relay. If wiper motor does not operate in low speed, go to next step.
4) Disconnect wiper motor connector. Do not disconnect jumper wire. Using external voltmeter, measure voltage between ground and terminal No. 2 (Brown/White wire) on wiper motor harness connector. If voltage is 10 volts or less, repair open Brown/White wire. If voltage is greater than 10 volts, replace wiper motor.

CHRY
4-182

1999 ACCESSORIES & EQUIPMENT
Body Control Computer Tests
Concorde, Intrepid, LHS & 300M (Cont.)

WINDSHIELD WIPER TEST 8A

WIPERS NOT OPERATING IN INTERMITTENT SPEED MODE

NOTE: Perform WINDSHIELD WIPER TEST 1A before proceeding with this test. For connector terminal identification and wiring diagrams, see BODY CONTROL COMPUTER – INTRODUCTION article. Perform VERIFICATION TEST: VER-2A after each repair.

CAUTION: Always turn ignition switch to OFF position prior to disconnecting or connecting any module connector.

1) Turn ignition on. Move wiper switch through all intermittent wiper positions. If wipers do not function in each position, go to next step. If wipers function in some positions, replace multifunction switch.

2) Using scan tool, select SENSORS. Monitor intermittent wiper voltage at each intermittent position. If voltage changes proportionally in each intermittent position, replace Body Control Module (BCM). BCM is mounted to junction block located behind left end cap of instrument panel. See Fig. 1.

WINDSHIELD WIPER TEST 9A

WIPER WASH FUNCTION NOT OPERATING

NOTE: Perform WINDSHIELD WIPER TEST 1A before proceeding with this test. For connector terminal identification and wiring diagrams, see BODY CONTROL COMPUTER – INTRODUCTION article. Perform VERIFICATION TEST: VER-2A after each repair.

CAUTION: Always turn ignition switch to OFF position prior to disconnecting or connecting any module connector.

1) Ensure washer fluid bottle is full. Turn ignition on. Momentarily push and then release wash button on stalk switch. If washer and wipers operate correctly, system is currently functioning correctly. If washer does not operate, go to step 3). If washer operates and wiper do not operate, go to next step.

2) Using scan tool, monitor front washer switch input while pushing wash button on stalk switch. If scan tool displays washer switch toggling from ON to OFF, replace Body Control Module (BCM). BCM is mounted to junction block located behind left end cap of instrument panel. See Fig. 1.

3) Turn ignition off. Disconnect washer pump connector. Using external ohmmeter, measure resistance between ground and terminal No. 1 (Black wire) on washer motor harness connector. If resistance is less than 5 ohms, go to next step. If resistance is 5 ohms or greater, replace washer motor.

4) Turn ignition on. Using external voltmeter, measure voltage between ground and terminal No. 2 (Brown wire) on washer motor harness connector. Press washer button on stalk switch. If voltage is 10 volts or less, go to next step. If voltage is greater than 10 volts, replace washer motor.

5) Disconnect multifunction switch. See Fig. 2. Connect jumper wire between ground and terminal No. 2 (Brown wire) on washer motor harness connector. Using external ohmmeter, measure resistance between ground and terminal No. 2 (Brown wire) on multifunction switch harness connector. If resistance is less than 5 ohms, go to next step. If resistance is 5 ohms or greater, repair open Brown wire.

6) Disconnect Body Control Module (BCM) Black 24-pin connector C2. BCM is mounted to junction block located behind left end cap of instrument panel. See Fig. 1.

WINDSHIELD WIPER TEST 10A

WIPERS OPERATE IN HIGH SPEED ONLY

NOTE: Perform WINDSHIELD WIPER TEST 1A before proceeding with this test. For connector terminal identification and wiring diagrams, see BODY CONTROL COMPUTER – INTRODUCTION article. Perform VERIFICATION TEST: VER-2A after each repair.

CAUTION: Always turn ignition switch to OFF position prior to disconnecting or connecting any module connector.

1) Remove HI/LO relay from Power Distribution Center (PDC). See Fig. 8. PDC is located in engine compartment. See Fig. 5. Using external voltmeter, measure voltage between terminals "B" and "C" on HI/LO relay socket. Turn ignition on. Turn wiper switch to LOW speed position. If voltage is 9 volts or less, replace HI/LO relay. If voltage is greater than 9 volts, go to next step.

2) Disconnect Body Control Module (BCM) Bone 12-pin connector C3. BCM is mounted to junction block located behind left end cap of instrument panel. See Fig. 1.

WINDSHIELD WIPER TEST 11A

WIPERS OPERATE IN WITH SWITCH IN OFF POSITION

NOTE: Perform WINDSHIELD WIPER TEST 1A before proceeding with this test. For connector terminal identification and wiring diagrams, see BODY CONTROL COMPUTER – INTRODUCTION article. Perform VERIFICATION TEST: VER-2A after each repair.

CAUTION: Always turn ignition switch to OFF position prior to disconnecting or connecting any module connector.

1) Disconnect Body Control Module (BCM) Black 24-pin connector C2. BCM is mounted to junction block located behind left end cap of instrument panel. See Fig. 1.

2) Disconnect BCM Bone 12-pin connector C3. If wipers stop, replace BCM. If wipers still operate, go to next step.

3) Disconnect wiper ON/OFF relay from Power Distribution Center (PDC). See Fig. 8. PDC is located in engine compartment. See Fig. 5. If wipers stop, repair Red/White wire (wiper ON/OFF relay control circuit) between ON/OFF relay and terminal No. 4 on BCM Bone 12-pin connector C3 for short to ground. If wipers still operate, repair Red/Yellow wire (wiper HI speed output circuit) or Brown/White wire (wiper LO speed output) between wiper HI/LO relay and wiper motor for short to battery voltage.

VERIFICATION TEST: VER-2A

BODY VERIFICATION TEST

1) Reconnect all previously disconnected components and connectors. If BCM was replaced, turn ignition on for at least 15 seconds. Program all RKE transmitters, recalibrate HVAC doors and program other options as necessary.

2) If vehicle is equipped with VTSS, select MISCELLANEOUS and ENABLE VTSS. If battery was disconnected, start engine and recalibrate HVAC doors using scan tool.

3) Ensure ignition is on. Erase all DTCs using scan tool. Turn ignition off and wait 5 seconds. Turn ignition on and fully operate system that was malfunctioning.

4) If system is not operating properly, go to SYMPTOM ID TEST 1A. Using scan tool, read Body DTCs. If any DTCs are present, go to SYMPTOM ID TEST 1B. If no DTCs are present, system is operating correctly and customer's complaint cannot be duplicated, repair is complete.

1999 ACCESSORIES & EQUIPMENT
Body Control Computer Tests
Concorde, Intrepid, LHS & 300M (Cont.)

CHRY
4-183

VERIFICATION TEST: VER-3A

VTSS VERIFICATION TEST

Ensure all doors, trunk and hood are closed. Open driver's door. Remove ignition key. Lock doors with power lock switch. Close driver's door. If instrument panel VTSS indicator light flashes, system is operational. If instrument panel VTSS indicator light does not flash, go to VTSS TEST 1A.

VERIFICATION TEST: VER-4A

MEMORY SYSTEM VERIFICATION TEST

Reconnect all previously disconnected components and connectors. Using scan tool, erase memory system DTCs. Operate power seat in all positions. Reset seat mirrors in both memory positions. Operate both seat heaters low and high. Using scan tool, read DTCs. If no DTCs are present, repair is complete. If any DTCs are present, go to MEMORY SYSTEM TEST 1A.

VERIFICATION TEST: VER-5A

SPEED PROPORTIONAL STEERING SYSTEM VERIFICATION TEST

Reconnect all previously disconnected components and connectors. Using scan tool, erase DTCs. Using scan tool, read DTCs. If any DTCs are present, go to SPEED PROPORTIONAL STEERING TEST 1A. If no DTCs are present, road test vehicle for at least 15 minutes. Perform several steering maneuvers at various speeds. Using scan tool, read DTCs. If any DTCs are present, go to SPEED PROPORTIONAL STEERING TEST 1A. If no DTCs are present, repair is complete.

NOTE: See BODY CONTROL COMPUTER – INTRODUCTION article before proceeding with following testing.

SYMPTOM IDENTIFICATION

IDENTIFYING VEHICLE EQUIPMENT & SYSTEM PROBLEMS

NOTE: For connector terminal identification wiring diagrams, see BODY CONTROL COMPUTER – INTRODUCTION article.

NOTE: Perform a visual inspection before proceeding with this test.

1) Connect scan tool to Data Link Connector (DLC). DLC is a 16-pin connector located under left side of dash, to left of steering wheel. Turn ignition switch to ON position. If scan tool display is not blank, go to next step. If scan tool display is blank, see appropriate VEHICLE COMMUNICATIONS article.

2) Using scan tool, select SYSTEM MONITORS, then CCD BUS TEST. Scan tool will perform a CCD bus test. If scan tool displays BUS OPERATIONAL, go to next step. If scan tool displays any message except BUS OPERATIONAL, see appropriate VEHICLE COMMUNICATIONS article.

3) Using scan tool, select READ DTCs. If any Diagnostic Trouble Codes (fault messages) are present, go to appropriate fault message. If no fault messages are present, identify customer complaint. See following list for possible fault messages and customer complaint symptoms. Problems listed are diagnosed using a scan tool. These problems may occur separately or in various combinations. When diagnosing a system with many apparent problems, a sequence of tests may be required. After repairs, ensure problem(s) or failure(s) have been corrected.

AUDIO SYSTEM

- CASS ERROR
- CD ERROR
- RADIO ERROR
- SHORTED FRONT CHANNEL
- SHORTED LEFT CHANNEL
- SHORTED REAR CHANNEL
- SHORTED RIGHT CHANNEL
- ANY RADIO FUNCTION SWITCH INOPERATIVE
- EXTERNAL CD CHANGER INOPERATIVE
- NO SOUND FROM ALL SPEAKERS
- NO SOUND FROM ONE SPEAKER
- POOR SOUND QUALITY ALL SPEAKERS
- POOR SOUND QUALITY FROM ONE SPEAKER
- REMOTE STEERING WHEEL SWITCHES INOPERATIVE

CHIME SYSTEM

- CHIME INOPERATIVE – ENGINE TEMPERATURE CRITICAL
- CHIME INOPERATIVE – KEY IN IGNITION & LF DOOR OPEN
- CHIME INOPERATIVE AT ALL TIMES
- CHIME INOPERATIVE WITH EXTERIOR LIGHTS ON
- CHIME INOPERATIVE WITH LOW OIL PRESSURE
- CHIME INOPERATIVE WITH DRIVER DOOR OPEN

DOOR AJAR SYSTEM

- OPEN DRIVER DOOR AJAR CIRCUIT
- OPEN GATE AJAR CIRCUIT (DURANGO)
- OPEN LEFT REAR DOOR AJAR CIRCUIT (DURANGO)
- OPEN RIGHT FRONT DOOR AJAR CIRCUIT
- OPEN RIGHT REAR DOOR AJAR CIRCUIT (DURANGO)
- SHORTED DRIVER DOOR AJAR CIRCUIT
- SHORTED GATE AJAR CIRCUIT (DURANGO)
- SHORTED PASSENGER DOOR AJAR CIRCUIT

INSTRUMENT CLUSTER

- ALL GAUGES INOPERATIVE
- ANY CCD CLUSTER LIGHT INOPERATIVE
- ANY HARD WIRED LIGHT INOPERATIVE
- ONE GAUGE NOT OPERATING PROPERLY

OVERHEAD CONSOLE CONCERNS

- AVERAGE MPH/FUEL ECON INOPERATIVE OR WRONG (CMTC FAILS TO RESPOND TO INSTRUMENT CLUSTER DIMMING, DISTANCE TO EMPTY INOPERATIVE OR WRONG, ELAPSED TIME INOPERATIVE OR WRONG, SWITCH ON CMTC INOPERATIVE, TRIP ODOMETER INOPERATIVE/WRONG)
- CMTC SHOWS FAILED
- CMTC SEGMENTS FAIL TO LIGHT UP
- INCORRECT READING BEYOND +/– 5
- REPAIRING "OC" IN CMTC DISPLAY
- REPAIRING "SC" IN CMTC DISPLAY

POWER DOOR LOCK SYSTEM

- DOOR LOCK SWITCH FAILURE (PDL)
- DOOR UNLOCK SWITCH FAILURE (PDL)
- AUTOMATIC (ROLLING) DOOR LOCKS INOPERATIVE
- DOORS LOCK WITH KEY IN IGNITION & LEFT DOOR OPEN
- ONE OR ALL DOORS FAILING TO LOCK FROM ONE SWITCH (ONE OR ALL DOORS FAILING TO UNLOCK FROM ONE SWITCH)
- REMOTE KEYLESS ENTRY PROBLEM

VEHICLE THEFT/SECURITY SYSTEM

- DOOR DISARM SWITCH FAILURE
- DOOR LOCK SWITCH FAILURE
- DOOR UNLOCK SWITCH FAILURE
- EEPROM CHECKSUM FAILURE
- INTERNAL ROM TEST FAILURE
- IDENTIFYING VTSS PROBLEMS

WINDSHIELD WIPER SYSTEM

- WIPER PARK SWITCH FAILURE
- INTERMITTENT WIPERS INOPERATIVE
- NO WIPE AFTER WASHERS ACTUATED
- WIPER SPEED SENSITIVE FEATURE INOPERATIVE

AUDIO SYSTEM

CASS ERROR, CD ERROR OR RADIO ERROR

NOTE: Perform VERIFICATION TEST VER-1A after each repair.

Radio is defective. Replace radio assembly.

SHORTED FRONT CHANNEL

NOTE: For connector terminal identification and wiring diagrams, see BODY CONTROL COMPUTER – INTRODUCTION article. Perform VERIFICATION TEST VER-1A after each repair.

1) Disconnect amplifier 10-pin connector C2. Amplifier is located under right side of instrument panel in cowl area. Turn radio on. Using an external voltmeter, measure voltage between ground and amplifier 10-pin connector C2 terminal No. 6 (Violet wire). If voltage is 4.5–5.5 volts, go to next step. If voltage is not 4.5–5.5 volts, repair ground in Violet wire.

2) Measure voltage between ground and amplifier 10-pin connector C2 terminal No. 5 (Dark Green wire). If voltage is 4.5–5.5 volts, go to next step. If voltage is not 4.5–5.5 volts, repair ground in Dark Green wire.

3) Measure voltage between ground and amplifier 10-pin connector C2 terminal No. 1 (Brown/Red wire). If voltage is 4.5–5.5 volts, go to next step. If voltage is not 4.5–5.5 volts, repair ground in Brown/Red wire.

1999 ACCESSORIES & EQUIPMENT
Body Control Computer Tests – Dakota & Durango (Cont.)

CHRY
4-185

4) Measure voltage between ground and amplifier 10-pin connector C2 terminal No. 2 (Dark Blue/Red wire). If voltage is 4.5–5.5 volts, replace radio. If voltage is not 4.5–5.5 volts, repair ground in Dark Blue/Red wire.

SHORTED LEFT CHANNEL

NOTE: For connector terminal identification and wiring diagrams, see BODY CONTROL COMPUTER – INTRODUCTION article. Perform VERIFICATION TEST VER-1A after each repair.

1) Disconnect amplifier 10-pin connector C2. Amplifier is located under right side of instrument panel in cowl area. Turn radio on. Using an external voltmeter, measure voltage between ground and amplifier 10-pin connector C2 terminal No. 7 (Brown/Yellow wire). If voltage is 4.5–5.5 volts, go to next step. If voltage is not 4.5–5.5 volts, repair ground in Brown/Yellow wire.

2) Measure voltage between ground and amplifier 10-pin connector C2 terminal No. 8 (Brown/Light Blue wire). If voltage is 4.5–5.5 volts, go to next step. If voltage is not 4.5–5.5 volts, repair ground in Brown/Light Blue wire.

3) Measure voltage between ground and amplifier 10-pin connector C2 terminal No. 5 (Dark Green wire). If voltage is 4.5–5.5 volts, go to next step. If voltage is not 4.5–5.5 volts, repair ground in Dark Green wire.

4) Measure voltage between ground and amplifier 10-pin connector C2 terminal No. 1 (Brown/Red wire). If voltage is 4.5–5.5 volts, replace radio. If voltage is not 4.5–5.5 volts, repair ground in Brown/Red wire.

SHORTED REAR CHANNEL

NOTE: For connector terminal identification and wiring diagrams, see BODY CONTROL COMPUTER – INTRODUCTION article. Perform VERIFICATION TEST VER-1A after each repair.

1) Disconnect amplifier 10-pin connector C2. Amplifier is located under right side of instrument panel in cowl area. Turn radio on. Using an external voltmeter, measure voltage between ground and amplifier 10-pin connector C2 terminal No. 7 (Brown/Yellow wire). If voltage is 4.5–5.5 volts, go to next step. If voltage is not 4.5–5.5 volts, repair ground in Brown/Yellow wire.

2) Measure voltage between ground and amplifier 10-pin connector C2 terminal No. 8 (Brown/Light Blue wire). If voltage is 4.5–5.5 volts, go to next step. If voltage is not 4.5–5.5 volts, repair ground in Brown/Light Blue wire.

3) Measure voltage between ground and amplifier 10-pin connector C2 terminal No. 9 (Dark Blue/White wire). If voltage is 4.5–5.5 volts, go to next step. If voltage is not 4.5–5.5 volts, repair ground in Dark Blue/White wire.

4) Measure voltage between ground and amplifier 10-pin connector C2 terminal No. 3 (Dark Blue/Orange wire). If voltage is 4.5–5.5 volts, replace radio. If voltage is not 4.5–5.5 volts, repair ground in Dark Blue/Orange wire.

SHORTED RIGHT CHANNEL

NOTE: For connector terminal identification and wiring diagrams, see BODY CONTROL COMPUTER – INTRODUCTION article. Perform VERIFICATION TEST VER-1A after each repair.

1) Disconnect amplifier 10-pin connector C2. Amplifier is located under right side of instrument panel in cowl area. Turn radio on. Using an external voltmeter, measure voltage between ground and amplifier 10-pin connector C2 terminal No. 9 (Dark Blue/White wire). If voltage is 4.5–5.5 volts, go to next step. If voltage is not 4.5–5.5 volts, repair ground in Dark Blue/White wire.

2) Measure voltage between ground and amplifier 10-pin connector C2 terminal No. 3 (Dark Blue/Orange wire). If voltage is 4.5–5.5 volts, go to next step. If voltage is not 4.5–5.5 volts, repair ground in Dark Blue/Orange wire.

3) Measure voltage between ground and amplifier 10-pin connector C2 terminal No. 6 (Violet wire). If voltage is 4.5–5.5 volts, go to next step. If voltage is not 4.5–5.5 volts, repair ground in Violet wire.

4) Measure voltage between ground and amplifier 10-pin connector C2 terminal No. 2 (Dark Blue/Red wire). If voltage is 4.5–5.5 volts, replace radio. If voltage is not 4.5–5.5 volts, repair ground in Dark Blue/Red wire.

ANY RADIO FUNCTION SWITCH INOPERATIVE

NOTE: Perform this test if any of the following symptoms are present:

* 1–5 Presets Inoperative
* AM/FM Switch Inoperative
* Balance Dial Inoperative
* CD Eject Switch Inoperative
* Equalizer Inoperative
* Fader Dial Inoperative
* FF/RW Switch Inoperative
* HOUR/MINUTE Inoperative
* PAUSE/PLAY Switch Inoperative
* PWR Switch Inoperative
* SCAN Switch Inoperative
* SEEK Switch Inoperative
* SET Switch Inoperative
* TAPE EJECT Switch Inoperative
* TUNE Switch Inoperative
* VOL/TIME Switch Inoperative

NOTE: For connector terminal identification and wiring diagrams, see BODY CONTROL COMPUTER – INTRODUCTION article. Perform VERIFICATION TEST VER-1A after each repair.

If radio function switch control radio properly, system is currently functioning correctly. If radio function switch does not control radio properly, replace radio.

EXTERNAL CD CHANGER INOPERATIVE

NOTE: For connector terminal identification and wiring diagrams, see BODY CONTROL COMPUTER – INTRODUCTION article. Perform VERIFICATION TEST VER-1A after each repair.

1) Using scan tool. read DTCs. If EXTERNAL CD CHANGER ERROR message is present, replace radio. If EXTERNAL CD CHANGER ERROR message is not present, go to next step.

2) Disconnect DIN cable between CD changer and radio. CD changer is located in trunk. Check continuity of DIN cable. If DIN cable continuity test is okay, replace CD changer. If DIN cable continuity test fails, replace DIN cable.

NO SOUND FROM ALL SPEAKERS

NOTE: For connector terminal identification and wiring diagrams, see BODY CONTROL COMPUTER – INTRODUCTION article. Perform VERIFICATION TEST VER-1A after each repair.

1) Using scan tool. read DTCs. If RADIO ERROR message is present, replace radio. If RADIO ERROR message is not present, go to next step.

2) Turn radio on. Gain access to radio Black connector. Do not disconnect. Using an external voltmeter, measure voltage connecting between ground and backprobe of radio Black connector terminal No. 2 (Brown/Yellow wire). If voltage is about 5.5 volts, go to next step. If voltage is not about 5.5 volts, replace radio.

3) Gain access to amplifier 14-pin connector C1. Measure voltage between ground and amplifier 14-pin connector C1 terminal No. 2 (Violet wire on Dakota or Red/Black wire on Durango). If voltage is 10 volts or less, repair open Violet or Red/Black wire. If voltage is more than 10 volts, go to next step.

4) Measure voltage between amplifier 14-pin connector C1 terminal No. 2 (Violet wire on Dakota or Red/Black wire on Durango) and terminal No. 8 (Black/Light Green wire on Dakota or Black/Tan wire on Durango). If voltage is 10 volts or less, repair open Black/Light Green or Black/Tan wire. If voltage is more than 10 volts, go to next step.

CHRY
4-186

1999 ACCESSORIES & EQUIPMENT
Body Control Computer Tests – Dakota & Durango (Cont.)

5) Gain access to amplifier 10-pin connector C2. Measure voltage between ground and amplifier 10-pin connector C2 terminal No. 4 (Dark Green/Red wire). If voltage is 10 volts or less, repair open Dark Green/Red wire. If voltage is more than 10 volts, go to next step.

6) Gain access to radio Black connector C2. Do not disconnect connector. Measure voltage between ground and backprobe radio Black connector C2 terminal No. 1 (Dark Green/Red wire). If voltage is about 10 volts, repair open Dark Green/Red wire. If voltage is not about 10 volts, replace radio.

NO SOUND FROM ONE SPEAKER

NOTE: For connector terminal identification and wiring diagrams, see BODY CONTROL COMPUTER – INTRODUCTION article. Perform VERIFICATION TEST VER-1A after each repair.

1) Using scan tool, read DTCs. If scan tool displays a specific shorted channel, go to that channel test. If scan tool does not display a specific shorted channel, go to next step.

2) If inoperative speaker is a pillar speaker, go to next step. If inoperative speaker is not a pillar speaker, go to step 5).

3) Ensure radio is off. Disconnect inoperative pillar and lower speaker from same side. Using an external ohmmeter, measure resistance between inoperative pillar (–) terminal and lower speaker (–) terminal. If resistance is less than 5 ohms, go to next step. If resistance is 5 ohms or more, repair open speaker (–) circuit.

4) Measure resistance between inoperative pillar (+) terminal and lower speaker (+) terminal. If resistance is less than 5 ohms, go to next step. If resistance is 5 ohms or more, repair open speaker (+) circuit.

5) Turn radio on. Disconnect inoperative speaker connector terminals. Using an external voltmeter, measure voltage between ground and inoperative speaker (+) terminal. If voltage is about 6 volts, go to next step. If voltage is not about 6 volts, go to step 8).

6) Measure voltage between ground and inoperative speaker (–) terminal. If voltage is about 6 volts, replace speaker. If voltage is not about 6 volts, go to next step.

7) Gain access to amplifier 14-pin connector C1. Do not disconnect connector. Measure voltage between ground and backprobe amplifier 14-pin connector C1 inoperative speaker ground circuit. See IDENTIFYING AMPLIFIER SPEAKER CIRCUITS table. If voltage is about 6 volts, repair open speaker (–) circuit. If voltage is not about 6 volts, replace amplifier.

IDENTIFYING AMPLIFIER SPEAKER CIRCUITS

Circuit	Terminal	Wire Color
Left Front (–)	1	Brown/Red
Left Rear (–)	8	Brown/Light Blue
Right Front (–)	2	Light Blue/Red
Right Rear (–)	3	Dark Blue/Orange
Left Front (+)	5	Dark Green
Left Rear (+)	7	Brown/Yellow
Right Front (+)	6	Violet
Right Rear (+)	9	Dark Blue/White

8) Ensure radio is on. Gain access to amplifier 14-pin connector C1. Do not disconnect connector. Measure voltage between ground and backprobe amplifier 14-pin connector C1 inoperative speaker (+) circuit. See IDENTIFYING AMPLIFIER SPEAKER CIRCUITS table. If voltage is about 6 volts, repair open speaker (+) circuit. If voltage is not about 6 volts, replace amplifier.

POOR SOUND QUALITY ALL SPEAKERS

NOTE: For connector terminal identification and wiring diagrams, see BODY CONTROL COMPUTER – INTRODUCTION article. Perform VERIFICATION TEST VER-1A after each repair.

1) Disconnect radio antenna connector. Inspect antenna connections and repair as necessary. If antenna connections are okay, go to next step.

2) Disconnect radio Gray connector. Inspect radio connector and repair as necessary. If radio connector is okay, go to next

3) Disconnect amplifier 14-pin connector C1. Inspect amplifier connector and repair as necessary. If amplifier connector is okay, go to next step.

4) Turn radio on. Gain access to radio Black connector. Do not disconnect connector. Using an external voltmeter, measure voltage between ground and backprobe radio Black connector terminal No. 2 (Brown/Yellow wire). If voltage is about 5.5 volts, go to next step. If voltage is not about 5.5 volts, replace radio.

5) Gain access to amplifier 14-pin connector C1. Do not disconnect connector. Measure voltage between ground and backprobe amplifier 14-pin connector C1 terminal No. 2 (Violet wire on Dakota or Red/Black wire on Durango). If voltage is 10 volts or less, repair open Violet or Red/Black wire. If voltage is more than 10 volts, go to next step.

6) Measure voltage between amplifier 14-pin connector C1 terminal No. 2 (Violet wire on Dakota or Red/Black wire on Durango) and terminal No. 8 (Black/Light Green wire on Dakota or Black/Tan wire on Durango). If voltage is 10 volts or less, repair open Black/Light Green or Black/Tan wire. If voltage is more than 10 volts, go to next step.

7) Gain access to amplifier 10-pin connector C2. Measure voltage between amplifier 10-pin connector C2 terminal No. 4 (Dark Green/Red wire). If voltage is more than 10 volts, system is functioning correctly. If voltage is 10 volts or less, go to next step.

8) Measure voltage between ground and backprobe radio Black connector terminal No. 1 (Dark Green/Red wire). If voltage is about 10 volts, repair open Dark Green/Red wire. If voltage is not about 10 volts, replace radio.

POOR SOUND QUALITY FROM ONE SPEAKER

NOTE: For connector terminal identification and wiring diagrams, see BODY CONTROL COMPUTER – INTRODUCTION article. Perform VERIFICATION TEST VER-1A after each repair.

1) Ensure radio is on. If speaker with poor quality is a pillar speaker, go to next step. If speaker with poor quality is not a pillar speaker, go to step 4).

2) Turn radio off. Disconnect poor quality pillar speaker and related lower speaker. Using external ohmmeter, measure resistance between poor quality pillar (–) terminal and lower speaker (–) terminal. If resistance is less than 5 ohms, go to next step. If resistance is 5 ohms or more, repair open speaker (–) circuit.

3) Measure resistance between poor quality pillar (+) terminal and lower speaker (+) terminal. If resistance is less than 5 ohms, go to next step. If resistance is 5 ohms or more, repair open speaker (+) circuit.

4) Turn radio on. Gain access to back of radio. Do not disconnect connectors. Measure voltage between ground and backprobe radio connector poor quality speaker ground circuit. See IDENTIFYING RADIO SPEAKER CIRCUITS table. If voltage is about 5 volts, repair open speaker (–) circuit. If voltage is not about 5 volts, replace radio.

IDENTIFYING RADIO SPEAKER CIRCUITS

Circuit/Connector	Terminal	Wire Color
Left Front (–)/Gray	2	Brown/Red
Left Rear (–)/Black	6	Brown/Light Blue
Right Front (–)/Gray	3	Light Blue/Red
Right Rear (–)/Black	7	Dark Blue/Orange
Left Front (+)/Black	4	Dark Green
Left Rear (+)/Black	2	Brown/Yellow
Right Front (+)/Black	5	Violet
Right Rear (+)/Black	3	Dark Blue/White

5) Measure voltage between ground and backprobe radio connector poor quality speaker (+) circuit. See IDENTIFYING RADIO SPEAKER CIRCUITS table. If voltage is about 5 volts, repair open speaker (+) circuit. If voltage is not about 5 volts, replace radio.

6) Turn radio on. Disconnect poor quality speaker connector terminals. Using an external voltmeter, measure voltage between ground and poor quality speaker (+) terminal. If voltage is more than 5 volts, replace poor quality speaker. If voltage is 5 volts or less, go to next step.

7) Measure voltage between ground and poor quality speaker (–) terminal. If voltage is less than 5 volts, repair open speaker circuit. If voltage is 5 volts or more, system is functioning correctly.

1999 ACCESSORIES & EQUIPMENT
Body Control Computer Tests – Dakota & Durango (Cont.)

CHRY
4-187

REMOTE STEERING WHEEL SWITCHES INOPERATIVE

NOTE: For connector terminal identification and wiring diagrams, see BODY CONTROL COMPUTER – INTRODUCTION article. Perform VERIFICATION TEST VER-1A after each repair.

1) Connect scan tool to Data Link Connector (DLC). DLC is a 16-pin connector located under left side of dash, to left of steering wheel. Turn ignition switch to ON position. If scan tool display is not blank or have a CCD bus failure message, go to next step. If scan tool display is blank or has a CCD bus failure message, see appropriate VEHICLE COMMUNICATIONS article.

2) Turn radio on. Operate all radio remote control functions in steering wheel. If one remote control function is inoperative, replace inoperative switch. If more than one remote control function is inoperative, go to next step.

3) Turn radio off. Disconnect battery and wait 2 minutes. Disconnect and remove air bag module from steering wheel. Disconnect inoperative radio control switch 2-pin connector. Turn ignition on and reconnect battery. Turn radio on. Connect jumper wire between ground and inoperative radio control switch 2-pin connector Red/Black wire. If radio changes stations, repair open ground circuit (Black/Light Green wire) between inoperative radio control switch and ground. If radio stations do not change, go to next step.

4) Move jumper wire to 4-pin connector Red/Black wire. If radio changes stations, repair open Red/Black wire between switch and 4-pin connector. If radio stations do not change, go to next step.

5) Using an external voltmeter, measure voltage between ground and inoperative radio control switch 2-pin connector Red/Black wire. If voltage is about 5 volts, replace radio. If voltage is not about 5 volts, go to next step.

6) Measure voltage between ground and 4-pin connector Red/Black wire. If voltage is about 5 volts, replace clockspring. If voltage is not about 5 volts, go to next step.

7) Gain access to Central Timer Module (CTM). CTM is located behind right kick panel. Do not disconnect connector. Measure voltage between ground and CTM 18-pin connector terminal No. 14 (Red/Black wire). If voltage is about 5 volts, repair open Red/Black wire between CTM and 4-pin connector. If voltage is not about 5 volts, replace CTM.

CHIME SYSTEM

CHIME INOPERATIVE – ENGINE TEMPERATURE CRITICAL

NOTE: For connector terminal identification and wiring diagrams, see BODY CONTROL COMPUTER – INTRODUCTION article. Perform VERIFICATION TEST VER-1A after each repair.

CAUTION: Always turn ignition switch to OFF position prior to disconnecting any module connector.

1) Turn ignition on. Using scan tool, actuate chime. If chime sounds, go to next step. If chime does not sound, replace Central Timer Module (CTM). CTM is located behind right kick panel.

2) Using scan tool, read PCM DTCs. If no engine coolant temperature related codes exist, go to next step. If engine coolant temperature related codes exist, see appropriate SELF-DIAGNOSTICS article in ENGINE PERFORMANCE in appropriate MITCHELL® manual.

3) Due to difficult access of coolant temperature sensor, Oil Pressure Switch (OPS) will be used to verify CCD bus message from PCM. Disconnect OPS connector. See OPS LOCATION table. Connect a jumper wire between OPS connector terminals. Start engine and allow to idle for 20 seconds. Increase engine speed to 1600 RPM. If chime sounds, system is currently functioning properly. If chime does not sound, go to next step.

OPS LOCATION

Engine	Location
2.5L	Side Of Block, Near Generator
3.9L, 5.2L & 5.9L	Bottom Of Distributor

4) Remove instrument cluster. See appropriate INSTRUMENT PANELS article. Disconnect Instrument cluster 10-pin Gray connector "B". Connect a jumper wire between ground and instrument cluster 10-pin Gray connector terminal No. 7 (Light Green/Orange wire). Turn ignition on. If chime sounds, replace instrument cluster. If chime does not sound, repair open Light Green/Orange wire.

CHIME INOPERATIVE – KEY IN IGNITION & LF DOOR OPEN

NOTE: For connector terminal identification and wiring diagrams, see BODY CONTROL COMPUTER – INTRODUCTION article. Perform VERIFICATION TEST VER-1A after each repair.

CAUTION: Always turn ignition switch to OFF position prior to disconnecting any module connector.

1) Turn ignition off leaving key in ignition. Open driver's door. If chime does not sound, go to next step. If chime sounds, system is currently functioning correctly.

2) Using scan tool, select BODY SYSTEM, INPUTS/OUTPUTS. Read driver's door ajar switch status. If scan tool displays LFDOOR AJAR SWITCH: CLOSED, go to next step. If scan tool does not display LFDOOR AJAR SWITCH: CLOSED, go to OPEN DRIVER'S DOOR AJAR CIRCUIT under DOOR AJAR SYSTEM.

3) Using scan tool, read key-in ignition switch status. If scan tool does not display KEY-IN IGNITION SW: KEY IN, go to next step. If scan tool displays KEY-IN IGNITION SW: KEY IN, replace Central Timer Module (CTM). CTM is located behind right kick panel.

4) Disconnect key-in ignition switch connector. *See Fig. 1.* Connect jumper wire between key-in ignition switch connector Black/Light Blue wire and ground. Using scan tool, read key-in ignition switch status. If scan tool does not display KEY-IN IGNITION SW: KEY IN, go to next step. If scan tool displays KEY-IN IGNITION SW: KEY IN, replace ignition switch. See appropriate STEERING COLUMN SWITCHES article.

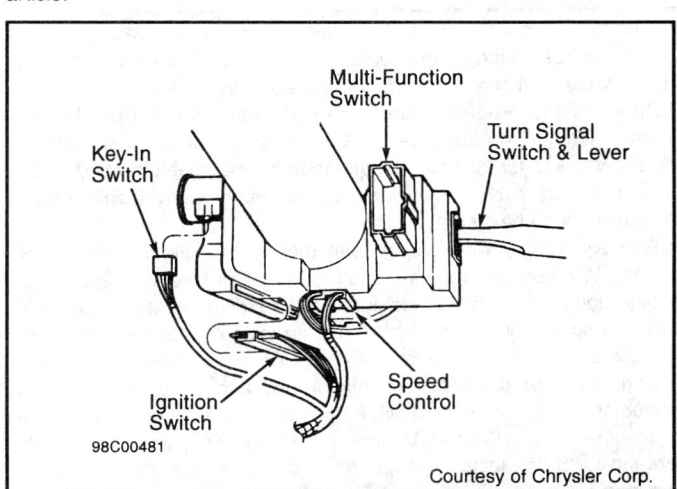

Fig. 1: Identifying Steering Column Harness Connector Locations

5) Access CTM 14-pin Green connector "A". Remove connector cover. Do not disconnect connector. Connect a backprobe jumper wire between terminal No. 9 (Light Blue wire) and chassis ground. Using scan tool, read key-in ignition switch status. If scan tool does not display KEY-IN IGNITION SW: KEY IN, replace CTM. If scan tool displays KEY-IN IGNITION SW: KEY IN, repair open Light Blue wire between CTM and ignition switch.

CHRY
4-188

1999 ACCESSORIES & EQUIPMENT
Body Control Computer Tests – Dakota & Durango (Cont.)

CHIME INOPERATIVE AT ALL TIMES

NOTE: *Perform VERIFICATION TEST VER-1A after each repair.*

Turn ignition on. Using scan tool, select BODY SYSTEM, BODY COMPUTER then ACTUATORS. Actuate chime. If chime sounds, system is currently functioning correctly. If chime does not sound, replace Central Timer Module (CTM). CTM is located behind right kick panel.

CHIME INOPERATIVE WITH EXTERIOR LIGHTS ON

NOTE: *For connector terminal identification and wiring diagrams, see BODY CONTROL COMPUTER – INTRODUCTION article. Perform VERIFICATION TEST VER-1A after each repair.*

CAUTION: *Always turn ignition switch to OFF position prior to disconnecting any module connector.*

1) Remove ignition key. Using scan tool, read key-in ignition switch status. If scan tool does not display KEY-IN IGNITION SW: KEY OUT, go to OPEN DRIVER'S DOOR AJAR CIRCUIT. If scan tool displays KEY-IN IGNITION SW: KEY OUT, go to next step.
2) Open driver's door. Using scan tool, read door ajar status. If scan tool displays LFDOOR AJAR SWITCH: CLOSED, go to next step. If scan tool does not display LFDOOR AJAR SWITCH: CLOSED, go to OPEN DRIVER'S DOOR AJAR CIRCUIT.
3) Turn on headlights. If chime does not sound, repair open headlight sense circuit between CTM and headlight switch. See appropriate wiring diagram in BODY CONTROL COMPUTER – INTRODUCTION article. If chime sounds, system is currently functioning correctly.

CHIME INOPERATIVE WITH LOW OIL PRESSURE

NOTE: *For connector terminal identification and wiring diagrams, see BODY CONTROL COMPUTER – INTRODUCTION article. Perform VERIFICATION TEST VER-1A after each repair.*

CAUTION: *Always turn ignition switch to OFF position prior to disconnecting any module connector.*

1) Turn ignition on. Using scan tool, actuate chime. If chime does not sound, replace Central Timer Module (CTM). CTM is located behind right kick panel. If chime sounds, go to next step.
2) Disconnect Oil Pressure Switch (OFS). See OPS LOCATION table. Connect a jumper wire between OPS connector terminals. Start engine and allow to idle for 20 seconds. increase engine speed to 1600 RPM. If chime sounds, system is currently functioning properly. If chime does not sound, go to next step.
3) Remove jumper wire. Using scan tool, access instrument cluster monitor. With engine running, read CCD oil pressure. If scan tool reading does not match instrument cluster reading, replace instrument cluster. If scan tool reading matches instrument cluster reading, go to next step.
4) Connect a jumper wire between ground and Gray wire on OPS connector. Start engine and allow to idle for 20 seconds. Increase engine speed to 1600 RPM. If chime sounds, repair open ground circuit between OPS connector and ground. If chime does not sound, go to next step.
5) Remove instrument cluster. See appropriate INSTRUMENT PANELS article. Disconnect CTM 14-pin Green connector "A". Using an external ohmmeter, measure resistance of Light Green/Orange wire on Dakota or Light Green/Red wire on Durango between CTM 14-pin Green connector "A" terminal No. 2 and instrument cluster 10-pin connector terminal No. 7. If resistance is less than 5 ohms, replace CTM. If resistance is 5 ohms or more, repair open Light Green/Orange or Light Green/Red wire.

CHIME SOUNDS WITH DRIVER DOOR OPEN

NOTE: *For connector terminal identification and wiring diagrams, see BODY CONTROL COMPUTER – INTRODUCTION article. Perform VERIFICATION TEST VER-1A after each repair.*

CAUTION: *Always turn ignition switch to OFF position prior to disconnecting any module connector.*

1) Ensure all interior and exterior lights are off. Remove ignition key and open driver's door. If chime does not sound, system is currently functioning correctly. If chime sounds, go to next step.
2) Using scan tool, select BODY SYSTEM, INPUTS/OUTPUTS. Read key-in ignition switch status. If scan tool displays KEY-IN IGNITION SW: KEY-IN, go to next step. If scan tool does not display KEY-IN IGNITION SW: KEY-IN, replace Central Timer Module (CTM). CTM is located behind right kick panel.
3) Disconnect key-in ignition switch connector. *See Fig. 1.* Using scan tool, read key-in ignition switch status. If scan tool displays KEY-IN IGNITION SW: KEY-IN, go to next step. If scan tool does not display KEY-IN IGNITION SW: KEY-IN, replace ignition switch. See appropriate STEERING COLUMN SWITCHES article.
4) Turn ignition off. Disconnect Central Timer Module (CTM). CTM is located behind right kick panel. Remove ignition key. Ensure all lights and accessories are off. Close all doors. Using external ohmmeter, measure resistance between ground and CTM connector "A" terminal No. 9 (Light Blue wire). If resistance is less than 10 ohms, repair short to ground in Light Blue wire between CTM and ignition switch. If resistance is 10 ohms or more, replace CTM.

DOOR AJAR SYSTEM
OPEN DRIVER'S DOOR AJAR CIRCUIT

NOTE: *For connector terminal identification and wiring diagrams, see BODY CONTROL COMPUTER – INTRODUCTION article. Perform VERIFICATION TEST VER-1A after each repair.*

CAUTION: *Always turn ignition switch to OFF position prior to disconnecting any module connector.*

1) Disconnect driver's door ajar switch connector and ensure connector is clean and not damaged. Connect a jumper wire between left front door ajar switch connector Black/Light Blue wire and Black wire on Dakota or Black/Tan wire on Durango. Using scan tool, read left front door ajar switch status. If scan tool displays DR DOOR AJAR SWITCH: CLOSED, replace left front door ajar switch. If scan tool does not display DR DOOR AJAR SW: CLOSED, go to next step.
2) Disconnect jumper wire from Black wire on Dakota or Black/Tan wire on Durango. Take jumper wire end removed from Black or Black/Tan wire and connect to ground. If scan tool displays DR DOOR AJAR SWITCH: CLOSED, repair open ground circuit. If scan tool does not display DR DOOR AJAR SW: CLOSED, go to next step.
3) Disconnect jumper wire. Locate Central Timer Module (CTM). CTM is located behind right kick panel. Access CTM 14-pin Green connector "A". Remove connector cover. Do not disconnect connector. Connect a backprobe jumper wire between chassis ground and CTM 14-pin Green connector "A" terminal No. 1 (Black/Light Blue wire). Using scan tool, read left front door ajar switch status. If scan tool displays DR DOOR AJAR SWITCH: CLOSED, repair open in Black/Light Blue wire between left front door ajar switch and CTM. If scan tool does not display DR DOOR AJAR SWITCH: CLOSED, replace CTM.

1999 ACCESSORIES & EQUIPMENT
Body Control Computer Tests – Dakota & Durango (Cont.)

CHRY
4-189

OPEN GATE AJAR CIRCUIT (DURANGO)

NOTE: For connector terminal identification and wiring diagrams, see BODY CONTROL COMPUTER – INTRODUCTION article. Perform VERIFICATION TEST VER-1A after each repair.

CAUTION: Always turn ignition switch to OFF position prior to disconnecting any module connector.

1) Disconnect GATE ajar switch connector and ensure connector is clean and not damaged. Connect a jumper wire between liftgate ajar switch connector Tan/Black wire and Black/Tan wire. Using scan tool, read liftgate ajar switch status. If scan tool displays GATE AJAR SWITCH: CLOSED, replace liftgate door ajar switch. If scan tool does not display GATE AJAR SWITCH: CLOSED, go to next step.
2) Disconnect jumper from Black/Tan wire. Take jumper wire end removed from Black/Tan wire and connect to ground. If scan tool displays GATE AJAR SWITCH: CLOSED, repair open ground circuit. If scan tool does not display GATE AJAR SWITCH: CLOSED, go to next step.
3) Disconnect jumper wire. Locate Central Timer Module (CTM). CTM is located behind right kick panel. Access CTM 18-pin connector "B". Remove connector cover. Do not disconnect connector. Connect a backprobe jumper wire between chassis ground and CTM 18- pin Green connector "B" terminal No. 15 (Tan/Black wire). If scan tool displays GATE AJAR SWITCH: CLOSED, repair open in Tan/Black wire between liftgate ajar switch and CTM. If scan tool does not display GATE AJAR SWITCH: CLOSED, replace CTM.

OPEN LEFT REAR DOOR AJAR CIRCUIT (DURANGO)

NOTE: For connector terminal identification and wiring diagrams, see BODY CONTROL COMPUTER – INTRODUCTION article. Perform VERIFICATION TEST VER-1A after each repair.

CAUTION: Always turn ignition switch to OFF position prior to disconnecting any module connector.

1) Disconnect left rear door ajar switch and ensure connector is clean and not damaged. Connect a jumper wire between left rear door ajar switch connector Tan/Red wire and Black wire. Using scan tool, read left rear door ajar switch status. If scan tool displays PASS DOOR AJAR SW: CLOSED, replace left rear door ajar switch. If scan tool does not display PASS DOOR AJAR SW: CLOSED, go to next step.
2) Disconnect jumper from Black wire. Take jumper wire end removed from Black wire and connect to ground. If scan tool displays PASS DOOR AJAR SW: CLOSED, repair open ground circuit. If scan tool does not display PASS DOOR AJAR SW: CLOSED, go to next step.
3) Disconnect jumper wire. Locate Central Timer Module (CTM). CTM is located behind right kick panel. Access CTM 14-pin Green connector "A". Remove connector cover. Do not disconnect connector. Connect a backprobe jumper wire between chassis ground and CTM 14-pin Green connector "A" terminal No. 5 (Tan/Red wire). If scan tool displays PASS DOOR AJAR SW: CLOSED, repair open Tan/Red wire between CTM and left rear door ajar switch. If scan tool does not display PASS DOOR AJAR SW: CLOSED, replace CTM.

OPEN RIGHT FRONT DOOR AJAR CIRCUIT

NOTE: For connector terminal identification and wiring diagrams, see BODY CONTROL COMPUTER – INTRODUCTION article. Perform VERIFICATION TEST VER-1A after each repair.

CAUTION: Always turn ignition switch to OFF position prior to disconnecting any module connector.

1) Disconnect right front door ajar switch connector and ensure connector is clean and not damaged. Connect a jumper wire between right front door ajar switch connector Light Blue/Pink and Black wire on Dakota or Tan/Red and Black/Tan wire on Durango. Using scan tool, read right front door ajar switch status. If scan tool displays PASS DOOR AJAR SW: CLOSED, replace right front door ajar switch. If scan tool does not display PASS DOOR AJAR SW: CLOSED, go to next step.
2) Disconnect jumper from Black or Black/Tan wire. Take jumper wire end removed from Black or Black/Tan wire and connect to ground. If scan tool displays PASS DOOR AJAR SWITCH: CLOSED, repair open ground circuit. If scan tool does not display PASS DOOR AJAR SW: CLOSED, go to next step.
3) Disconnect jumper wire. Locate Central Timer Module (CTM). CTM is located behind right kick panel. Access CTM 14-pin Green connector "A". Remove connector cover. Do not disconnect connector. Connect a backprobe jumper wire between chassis ground and terminal CTM 14-pin Green connector "A" No. 5 (Black/Light Blue wire on Dakota or Tan/Red wire on Durango). If scan tool displays PASS DOOR AJAR SW: CLOSED, repair open Black/Light Blue or Tan/Red wire between CTM and right front door ajar switch. If scan tool does not display PASS DOOR AJAR SW: CLOSED, replace CTM.

OPEN RIGHT REAR DOOR AJAR CIRCUIT (DURANGO)

NOTE: For connector terminal identification and wiring diagrams, see BODY CONTROL COMPUTER – INTRODUCTION article. Perform VERIFICATION TEST VER-1A after each repair.

CAUTION: Always turn ignition switch to OFF position prior to disconnecting any module connector.

1) Disconnect right rear door ajar switch connector and ensure connector is clean and not damaged. Connect a jumper wire between right rear door ajar switch connector Tan/Red wire and Black wire. Using scan tool, read right rear door ajar switch status. If scan tool displays PASS DOOR AJAR SW: CLOSED, replace right rear door ajar switch. If scan tool does not display PASS DOOR AJAR SW: CLOSED, go to next step.
2) Disconnect jumper from Black wire. Take jumper wire end removed from Black wire and connect to ground. If scan tool displays PASS DOOR AJAR SW: CLOSED, repair open ground circuit. If scan tool does not display PASS DOOR AJAR SW: CLOSED, go to next step.
3) Disconnect jumper wire. Locate Central Timer Module (CTM). CTM is located behind right kick panel. Access CTM 14-pin Green connector "A". Remove connector cover. Do not disconnect connector. Connect a backprobe jumper wire between chassis ground and terminal No. 5 (Tan/Red wire). If scan tool displays PASS DOOR AJAR SW: CLOSED, repair open Tan/Red wire between CTM and right rear door ajar switch. If scan tool does not display PASS DOOR AJAR SW: CLOSED, replace CTM.

SHORTED DRIVER DOOR AJAR CIRCUIT

NOTE: For connector terminal identification and wiring diagrams, see BODY CONTROL COMPUTER – INTRODUCTION article. Perform VERIFICATION TEST VER-1A after each repair.

CAUTION: Always turn ignition switch to OFF position prior to disconnecting any module connector.

1) Disconnect driver's door ajar switch connector. Using scan tool, read left front door ajar switch status. If scan tool displays DR DOOR AJAR SWITCH: CLOSED, go to next step. If scan tool does not display DR DOOR AJAR SWITCH: CLOSED, replace left front door ajar switch.
2) Disconnect Central Timer Module (CTM) 14-pin Green connector "A". CTM is located behind right kick panel. Using an external ohmmeter, measure resistance between ground and CTM 14-pin Green connector "A" terminal No. 1 (Black/Light Blue wire). If resistance is less than 5 ohms, repair short to ground in Black/Light Blue wire between CTM connector "A" and left front door ajar switch. If resistance is 5 ohms or more, replace CTM.

CHRY
4-190

1999 ACCESSORIES & EQUIPMENT
Body Control Computer Tests – Dakota & Durango (Cont.)

SHORTED GATE AJAR CIRCUIT (DURANGO)

NOTE: For connector terminal identification and wiring diagrams, see BODY CONTROL COMPUTER – INTRODUCTION article. Perform VERIFICATION TEST VER-1A after each repair.

CAUTION: Always turn ignition switch to OFF position prior to disconnecting any module connector.

1) Remove liftgate panel. Disconnect liftgate ajar switch connector. Using scan tool, read liftgate ajar switch status. If scan tool displays GATE AJAR SWITCH: CLOSED, go to next step. If scan tool does not display GATE AJAR SWITCH: CLOSED, replace liftgate ajar switch.

2) Disconnect Central Timer Module (CTM) 18-pin connector "B". CTM is located behind right kick panel. Using an external ohmmeter, measure resistance between ground and CTM 18-pin connector "B" terminal No. 15 (Tan/Black wire). If resistance is less than 5 ohms, repair short to ground in Tan/Black wire. If resistance is 5 ohms or more, replace CTM.

SHORTED PASSENGER DOOR AJAR CIRCUIT

NOTE: For connector terminal identification and wiring diagrams, see BODY CONTROL COMPUTER – INTRODUCTION article. Perform VERIFICATION TEST VER-1A after each repair.

CAUTION: Always turn ignition switch to OFF position prior to disconnecting any module connector.

1) Ensure all doors are closed. Open right front door and remove door panel. Disconnect right front door ajar switch connector. Using scan tool, read right front door ajar switch status. If scan tool displays PASS DOOR AJAR SW: CLOSED, on Dakota go to step 4) or on Durango go to next step. If scan tool does not display PASS DOOR AJAR SW: CLOSED, replace right front door ajar switch.

2) Close right front door. Open right rear door and remove door panel. Disconnect right rear door ajar switch. Using scan tool, read right rear door ajar switch status. If scan tool displays PASS DOOR AJAR SW: CLOSED, go to next step. If scan tool does not display PASS DOOR AJAR SW: CLOSED, replace right rear door ajar switch.

3) Close right rear door. Open left rear door and remove door panel. Disconnect left rear door ajar switch. Using scan tool, read left rear door ajar switch status. If scan tool displays PASS DOOR AJAR SW: CLOSED, go to next step. If scan tool does not display PASS DOOR AJAR SW: CLOSED, replace left rear door ajar switch.

4) Close all doors. Disconnect Central Timer Module (CTM) 14-pin Green connector "A". CTM is located behind right kick panel. Using an external ohmmeter, measure resistance between ground and CTM 14-pin Green connector "A" terminal No. 5 (Tan/Red wire). If resistance is less than 5 ohms, repair short to ground in Tan/Red wire. If resistance is 5 ohms or more, replace CTM.

INSTRUMENT CLUSTER

ALL GAUGES INOPERATIVE

NOTE: For connector terminal identification and wiring diagrams, see BODY CONTROL COMPUTER – INTRODUCTION article. Perform VERIFICATION TEST VER-1A after each repair.

CAUTION: Always turn ignition switch to OFF position prior to disconnecting or connecting any module connector.

1) Turn ignition on. Using scan tool, select ELECTRO/MECH CLUSTER (MIC). If scan tool displays NO RESPONSE, go to appropriate VEHICLE COMMUNICATIONS article. If scan tool display is a CCD bus failure, go to appropriate failure message. If scan tool display is other than described, go to next step.

2) Using scan tool, select SYSTEM TEST. If scan tool displays PCM INACTIVE ON BUS, go to appropriate VEHICLE COMMUNICATIONS article. If scan tool does not display PCM INACTIVE ON BUS, go to next step.

3) Remove and inspect junction block fuse No. 17. If fuse is blown, repair short to ground in fused ignition switch output circuit from junction block to instrument cluster (Dark Blue/White wire). If fuse is okay, go to next step.

4) Turn ignition off. Remove instrument cluster. See appropriate INSTRUMENT PANELS article. Turn ignition on. Using external voltmeter, measure voltage between ground and Blue instrument cluster connector terminal No. 2 (Dark Blue/White wire). If voltage is 10 volts or less, repair open Dark Blue/White wire. If voltage is more than 10 volts, replace instrument cluster.

ANY CCD CLUSTER LIGHT INOPERATIVE

NOTE: For connector terminal identification and wiring diagrams, see BODY CONTROL COMPUTER – INTRODUCTION article. Perform VERIFICATION TEST VER-1A after each repair.

CAUTION: Always turn ignition switch to OFF position prior to disconnecting or connecting any module connector.

1) Turn ignition on. Using scan tool, select ELECTRO/MECH CLUSTER (MIC). If scan tool displays NO RESPONSE, go to appropriate VEHICLE COMMUNICATIONS article. If scan tool display is a CCD bus failure, go to appropriate failure message. If scan tool display is other than described, go to next step.

2) Using scan tool, select SYSTEM TEST. If scan tool displays PCM INACTIVE ON BUS, go to appropriate VEHICLE COMMUNICATIONS article. If scan tool does not display PCM INACTIVE ON BUS, go to next step.

3) Push and hold RESET button while cycling ignition key. Observe inoperative light during self-test. If inoperative light did not illuminate during self-test, go to next step. If inoperative light illuminated during self-test, verify if light is controlled by an input to instrument cluster. See appropriate wiring diagram in BODY CONTROL COMPUTER – INTRODUCTION article. If light is controlled by an input to instrument cluster, go to appropriate circuits article or symptom test. See IDENTIFYING VEHICLE EQUIPMENT & SYSTEM PROBLEMS. If light is not controlled by an input to instrument cluster, system is currently functioning correctly.

4) Gain access to instrument cluster. See appropriate INSTRUMENT PANELS article. If defective light is a LED, replace instrument cluster. If defective light is a bulb, go to next step.

5) Remove and inspect defective bulb. If bulb is burned out, replace bulb. If bulb is not burned out, replace instrument cluster.

ANY HARD WIRED LIGHT INOPERATIVE

NOTE: For connector terminal identification and wiring diagrams, see BODY CONTROL COMPUTER – INTRODUCTION article. Perform VERIFICATION TEST VER-1A after each repair.

CAUTION: Always turn ignition switch to OFF position prior to disconnecting or connecting any module connector.

1) Remove instrument cluster. See appropriate INSTRUMENT PANELS article. Remove inoperative bulb. If bulb is burned out, replace bulb. If bulb is not burned out, go to next step.

2) Inspect wiring diagram and evaluate which instrument cluster provides; power or ground for inoperative bulb. See appropriate wiring diagram in BODY CONTROL COMPUTER – INTRODUCTION article. Using external ohmmeter or voltmeter, check appropriate power or ground circuit. If circuit is okay, replace instrument cluster. If power or ground is not available at appropriate circuit, repair open or shorted circuit.

1999 ACCESSORIES & EQUIPMENT
Body Control Computer Tests – Dakota & Durango (Cont.)

CHRY
4-191

ONE GAUGE NOT OPERATING PROPERLY

NOTE: For connector terminal identification and wiring diagrams, see BODY CONTROL COMPUTER – INTRODUCTION article. Perform VERIFICATION TEST VER-1A after each repair.

CAUTION: Always turn ignition switch to OFF position prior to disconnecting or connecting any module connector.

1) Push and hold RESET button while cycling ignition key; ON-OFF-ON. Instrument cluster self-test will start. If inoperative gauge reached proper calibration point, go to next step. If inoperative gauge did not reach proper calibration point, replace instrument cluster.

2) Stop instrument cluster self-test. If problem is with speedometer, go to next step. If problem is with oil pressure gauge, go to step 5). If problem is with temperature gauge, go to step 13). If problem is with fuel level gauge, go to appropriate SELF- DIAGNOSTICS article in ENGINE PERFORMANCE in appropriate MITCHELL® manual and review powertrain symptoms. Using scan tool, read PCM DTCs. If any DTCs are present relating to tachometer, volts or any unlisted gauge, go to appropriate SELF-DIAGNOSTICS article in ENGINE PERFORMANCE and repair DTC as necessary. If no PCM DTCs are present, go to appropriate TROUBLE SHOOTING – NO CODES article in ENGINE PERFORMANCE in appropriate MITCHELL® manual.

3) Using scan tool, select BODY, SYSTEMS TESTS then PCM MONITOR. If scan tool displays PCM ACTIVE ON BUS, go to next step. If scan tool does not display PCM ACTIVE ON BUS, go to appropriate VEHICLE COMMUNICATIONS article.

4) Raise and support all wheels. Start engine and place gear selector in drive. Using scan tool, select MIC, MONITORS then CCD BUS ENGINE INFO. Read VSS. If vehicle speed on scan tool matches speedometer, see appropriate ANTI-LOCK article in BRAKES in appropriate MITCHELL® manual. If vehicle speed on scan tool does not match speedometer, replace instrument cluster circuit board.

5) Turn ignition on. If CHECK GAUGES light illuminated, go to next step. If CHECK GAUGES light did not illuminate, go to step 11).

6) Turn ignition off. Inspect oil level. If oil level is within specification, go to next step. If oil level is not within specification, adjust oil level and retest.

7) Turn ignition on. Disconnect engine Oil Pressure Switch (OPS) connector. See OPS LOCATION table. If CHECK GAUGES light went out, go to next step. If CHECK GAUGES light did not go out, go to step 10).

8) Remove OPS. Connect mechanical oil pressure gauge to OPS port. Start engine. If engine oil pressure at idle is 4 psi or more, go to next step. If engine oil pressure at idle is less than 4 psi, repair mechanical engine problem.

9) Run engine to reach normal operating temperature. If engine oil pressure at idle is 4 psi or more, replace OPS. If engine oil pressure at idle is less than 4 psi, repair mechanical engine problem.

10) Turn ignition off. Disconnect PCM White connector. PCM is located in engine compartment on right inner fender. Using an external ohmmeter, measure resistance between ground and PCM White connector terminal No. 23 (Gray/Yellow wire). If resistance is less than 5 ohms, repair short to ground in Gray/Yellow wire. If resistance is 5 ohms or more, replace PCM.

11) Disconnect engine Oil Pressure Switch (OPS) connector. See OPS LOCATION table. Connect jumper wire between OPS connector terminals. If oil pressure warning indicator illuminates, replace OPS. If oil pressure warning indicator does not illuminate, go to next step.

12) Do not remove jumper wire. Disconnect PCM White connector. PCM is located in engine compartment on right inner fender. Using an external ohmmeter, measure resistance between ground and PCM White connector terminal No. 23 (Gray/Yellow wire). If resistance is less than 5 ohms, replace PCM. If resistance is 5 ohms or more, repair open Gray/Yellow wire.

13) Check cooling system operation. If cooling system is operating properly, go to next step. If cooling system is not operating properly, repair engine cooling problem.

14) Using scan tool, select PCM MONITOR under SYSTEM TESTS. If scan tool displays PCM ACTIVE ON BUS, go to next step. If scan tool does not display PCM ACTIVE ON BUS, go to appropriate VEHICLE COMMUNICATIONS article.

15) Using scan tool, select MODULE ENGINE CONTROLLER. Read PCM DTCs. If scan tool displays ECT VOLTAGE TOO HIGH, go to appropriate SELF-DIAGNOSTICS article in ENGINE PERFORMANCE in appropriate MITCHELL® manual and repair DTC as necessary. If scan tool does not display ECT VOLTAGE TOO HIGH, go to next step.

16) If scan tool displays ECT VOLTAGE TOO LOW, go to appropriate SELF-DIAGNOSTICS article in ENGINE PERFORMANCE in appropriate MITCHELL® manual and repair DTC as necessary. If scan tool does not display ECT VOLTAGE TOO LOW, replace PCM.

OVERHEAD CONSOLE CONCERNS

AVERAGE MPH/FUEL ECON INOPERATIVE OR WRONG (CMTC FAILS TO RESPOND TO INSTRUMENT CLUSTER DIMMING, DISTANCE TO EMPTY INOPERATIVE OR WRONG, ELAPSED TIME INOPERATIVE OR WRONG, SWITCH ON CMTC INOPERATIVE, TRIP ODOMETER INOPERATIVE/WRONG)

NOTE: If any listed symptoms exist, Compass Mini-Trip computer (CMTC) is defective. Replace CMTC. Perform VERIFICATION TEST VER- 1A after each repair.

CMTC SHOWS FAILED

NOTE: For connector terminal identification and wiring diagrams, see BODY CONTROL COMPUTER – INTRODUCTION article. Perform VERIFICATION TEST VER-1A after each repair.

Using scan tool, perform AUTO SELF TEST. If CMTC shows failed, replace CMTC. If CMTC does not show failed, system is currently functioning properly.

CMTC SEGMENTS FAIL TO LIGHT UP

NOTE: For connector terminal identification and wiring diagrams, see BODY CONTROL COMPUTER – INTRODUCTION article. Perform VERIFICATION TEST VER-1A after each repair.

Using scan tool, perform AUTO SELF TEST. If CMTC shows failed, replace CMTC. If CMTC does not show failed, system is currently functioning properly.

INCORRECT READING BEYOND +/– 5

NOTE: For connector terminal identification and wiring diagrams, see BODY CONTROL COMPUTER – INTRODUCTION article. Perform VERIFICATION TEST VER-1A after each repair.

If temperature reading is off by more than 5°F, ambient temperature sensor is defective. Replace ambient temperature sensor. Ambient temperature sensor is located to the right of condenser on radiator saddle.

REPAIRING "OC" IN CMTC DISPLAY

NOTE: For connector terminal identification and wiring diagrams, see BODY CONTROL COMPUTER – INTRODUCTION article. Drive vehicle at least 3 miles (greater than 25 MPH) to update CMTC and perform VERIFICATION TEST VER-1A after each repair.

CAUTION: Always turn ignition switch to OFF position prior to disconnecting any module connector.

1) Disconnect ambient temperature sensor connector. Sensor is located to the right of condenser on radiator saddle. Connect jumper wire

CHRY
4-192

1999 ACCESSORIES & EQUIPMENT
Body Control Computer Tests – Dakota & Durango (Cont.)

between sensor connector terminals. Turn ignition on. Observe CMTC display. If CMTC displays SC, replace ambient temperature sensor. If CMTC does not display SC, go to next step.

2) Turn ignition off. Disconnect jumper wire. Disconnect CMTC module connector. Connect a jumper wire between ground and ambient temperature sensor harness connector Violet/Light Green wire. If CMTC displays SC, repair open Black/Light Blue wire between ambient temperature sensor harness connector and ground. If CMTC does not display SC, go to next step.

3) Connect a backprobe jumper wire between ground and CMTC harness connector terminal No. 3 (Violet/Light Green wire). If CMTC displays SC, repair open Violet/Light Green wire between ambient temperature sensor harness connector and CMTC connector. If CMTC does not display SC, replace CMTC module.

REPAIRING "SC" IN CMTC DISPLAY

NOTE: *For connector terminal identification and wiring diagrams, see BODY CONTROL COMPUTER – INTRODUCTION article. Perform VERIFICATION TEST VER-1A after each repair.*

CAUTION: *Always turn ignition switch to OFF position prior to disconnecting any module connector.*

1) Disconnect ambient temperature sensor connector. Sensor is located to the right of condenser on radiator saddle. Observe CMTC display. If CMTC displays OC, replace ambient temperature sensor. If CMTC does not display OC, go to next step.

2) Turn ignition off. Disconnect CMTC connector. Using an external ohmmeter, measure resistance between ground and CMTC harness connector terminal No. 3 (Violet/Light Green wire). If resistance is less than 5 ohms, repair Violet/Light Green wire between CMTC module and ambient temperature sensor for short to ground. If resistance is 5 ohms or more, go to next step.

3) Measure resistance between terminals No. 9 (Black/Light Blue wire) and No. 3 (Violet/Light Green wire) on CMTC harness connector. If resistance is less than 1000 ohms, repair Violet/Light Green wire for short to Black/Light Blue wire. If resistance is 1000 ohms or more, replace CMTC module.

POWER DOOR LOCK SYSTEM

DOOR LOCK SWITCH FAILURE (PDL)

NOTE: *For connector terminal identification and wiring diagrams, see BODY CONTROL COMPUTER – INTRODUCTION article. Perform VERIFICATION TEST VER-1A after each repair.*

CAUTION: *Always turn ignition switch to OFF position prior to disconnecting or connecting any module connector.*

1) Clear trouble codes as needed. See BODY CONTROL COMPUTER – INTRODUCTION article. Using scan tool, read I/O's door lock switch status. If scan tool displays PRESSED, go to next step. If scan tool does not display PRESSED, system is currently functioning properly.

2) Disconnect left door lock switch connector. If scan tool displays PRESSED, go to next step. If scan tool does not display PRESSED, replace left door lock switch.

3) Disconnect right door lock switch connector. If scan tool displays PRESSED, go to next step. If scan tool does not display PRESSED, replace right door lock switch.

4) Locate Central Timer Module (CTM). CTM is located behind right kick panel. Disconnect CTM 18-pin connector "B". Using an external voltmeter, measure voltage between ground and CTM 18-pin connector "B" terminal No. 4 (Light Green wire on Dakota or Orange/Violet wire on Durango). If voltage is more than 1.5 volts, repair short to voltage in Light Green wire or Orange/Violet wire between CTM and door lock switch. If voltage is 1.5 volts or less, replace CTM.

DOOR UNLOCK SWITCH FAILURE (PDL)

NOTE: *For connector terminal identification and wiring diagrams, see BODY CONTROL COMPUTER – INTRODUCTION article. Perform VERIFICATION TEST VER-1A after each repair.*

CAUTION: *Always turn ignition switch to OFF position prior to disconnecting or connecting any module connector.*

1) Clear trouble codes as needed. See BODY CONTROL COMPUTER – INTRODUCTION article. Using scan tool, read I/O's door unlock switch status. If scan tool displays PRESSED, go to next step. If scan tool does not display PRESSED, system is currently functioning properly.

2) Disconnect left door lock switch connector. If scan tool displays PRESSED, go to next step. If scan tool does not display PRESSED, replace left door lock switch.

3) Disconnect right door lock switch connector. If scan tool displays PRESSED, go to next step. If scan tool does not display PRESSED, replace right door lock switch.

4) Locate Central Timer Module (CTM). CTM is located behind right kick panel. Disconnect CTM 18-pin connector "B". Using an external voltmeter, measure voltage between ground and CTM 18-pin connector "B" terminal No. 13 (Orange/White wire on Dakota or Pink/Violet wire on Durango). If voltage is more than 1.5 volts, repair short to voltage in Orange/White wire on Dakota or Pink/Violet wire on Durango between CTM and door lock switch. If voltage is 1.5 volts or less, replace CTM.

AUTOMATIC (ROLLING) DOOR LOCKS INOPERATIVE

NOTE: *For connector terminal identification and wiring diagrams, see BODY CONTROL COMPUTER – INTRODUCTION article. Perform VERIFICATION TEST VER-1A after each repair.*

1) Using scan tool select SYSTEM MONITORS, then CCD BUS TEST. If scan tool displays BUS OPERATIONAL, go to next step. If scan tool does not display BUS OPERATIONAL, go to appropriate VEHICLE COMMUNICATIONS article.

2) Using scan tool select BODY COMPUTER. If scan tool displays NO RESPONSE, go to appropriate VEHICLE COMMUNICATIONS article. If scan tool displays NO RESPONSE, go to next step.

3) This test is only for vehicles equipped with speed sensitive door locks. With doors closed and unlocked drive vehicle faster than 15 MPH. If doors lock, system is currently functioning properly. If doors do not lock, using scan tool select ROLLING LOCKS. Retest system.

DOORS LOCK WITH KEY IN IGNITION & LEFT DOOR OPEN

NOTE: *For connector terminal identification and wiring diagrams, see BODY CONTROL COMPUTER – INTRODUCTION article. Perform VERIFICATION TEST VER-1A after each repair.*

CAUTION: *Always turn ignition switch to OFF position prior to disconnecting or connecting any module connector.*

1) Using scan tool select SYSTEM MONITORS, then CCD BUS TEST. If scan tool displays BUS OPERATIONAL, go to next step. If scan tool does not display BUS OPERATIONAL, go to appropriate VEHICLE COMMUNICATIONS article.

2) Using scan tool select BODY COMPUTER. If scan tool displays NO RESPONSE, go to appropriate VEHICLE COMMUNICATIONS article. If scan tool displays NO RESPONSE, go to next step.

3) Place key in ignition. Open driver's door. Lock doors from interior lock switch. If doors locked, go to next step. If doors did not lock, system is currently functioning correctly.

4) Using scan tool, read driver's door ajar status. Open and close driver's door. If door ajar state changed from OPEN to CLOSED, go to

1999 ACCESSORIES & EQUIPMENT
Body Control Computer Tests – Dakota & Durango (Cont.)

CHRY
4-193

next step. If door ajar state did not change from OPEN to CLOSED, go to OPEN DRIVER'S DOOR AJAR CIRCUIT under DOOR AJAR SYSTEM.

5) Ensure driver's door is open. Read key-in ignition status. If scan tool shows KEY-IN, replace Central Timer Module (CTM). CTM is located behind right kick panel. If scan tool does not show KEY-IN, go to next step.

6) Gain access to CTM connector "A". Do not disconnect connector. Using an external voltmeter, measure voltage between ground and CTM 14-pin connector "A" terminal No. 9 (Light Blue wire). If voltage is more than 1.5 volts, repair open Light Blue wire. If voltage is 1.5 volts or less, go to next step.

7) Turn ignition off and remove key. Measure voltage between ground and CTM 14-pin connector "A" terminal No. 9 (Light Blue wire). If voltage is less than 1.5 volts, replace CTM. If voltage is 1.5 volts or more, replace ignition switch.

ONE OR ALL DOORS FAILING TO LOCK FROM ONE SWITCH (ONE OR ALL DOORS FAILING TO UNLOCK FROM ONE SWITCH)

NOTE: For connector terminal identification and wiring diagrams, see BODY CONTROL COMPUTER – INTRODUCTION article. Perform VERIFICATION TEST VER-1A after each repair.

CAUTION: Always turn ignition switch to OFF position prior to disconnecting or connecting any module connector.

1) Using scan tool select SYSTEM MONITORS, then CCD BUS TEST. If scan tool displays BUS OPERATIONAL, go to next step. If scan tool does not display BUS OPERATIONAL, go to appropriate VEHICLE COMMUNICATIONS article.

2) Using scan tool select BODY COMPUTER. If scan tool displays NO RESPONSE, go to appropriate VEHICLE COMMUNICATIONS article. If scan tool displays NO RESPONSE, go to next step.

3) Read DTCs. If no DTCs are displayed, go to next step. If DOOR LOCK SWITCH FAILURE is displayed, go to DOOR LOCK SWITCH FAILURE (PDL). If DOOR UNLOCK SWITCH FAILURE is displayed, go to DOOR UNLOCK SWITCH FAILURE (PDL).

4) Lower both front windows. Remove key from ignition switch and close all doors. Lock and unlock doors from all switches. If all doors lock and unlock properly, system is currently functioning properly. If one or all locks fail to lock from one switch, go to next step. If one or all locks fail to unlock from one switch, go to step **12)**.

5) Using scan tool, read I/O's door lock switch status. Press lock button on inoperative door. If scan tool does not display LOCK SW PRESSED while lock switch is pressed on inoperative door, go to step **10)**. If scan tool displays LOCK SW PRESSED while lock switch is pressed on inoperative door, go to next step.

6) Access door lock actuator inside inoperative door. Disconnect door lock actuator connector. Remove key from ignition and roll windows down. Connect test light between door lock actuator connector terminals. If test light illuminates while door lock switch is pressed, replace door lock actuator. If test light does not illuminate while door lock switch is pressed, go to next step.

7) Connect test light to ground and probe Orange/Black wire of door lock actuator connector. If test light illuminates while door lock switch is pressed, repair open Orange/Black wire between door lock actuator and Central Timer Module (CTM). CTM is located behind right kick panel. If test light does not illuminate while door lock switch is pressed, go to next step.

8) Access CTM 18-pin connector "B". Remove connector cover. Do not disconnect connector. Using an external voltmeter, measure voltage between ground and CTM 18-pin connector "B" terminal No. 1 (Orange/Black wire). If voltage is more than 9.5 volts while door lock switch is pressed, repair open Orange/Black wire. If voltage is 9.5 volts or less while door lock switch is pressed, replace CTM.

9) Disconnect inoperative lock switch connector. Using an external voltmeter, measure voltage between ground and Red wire of door lock

switch connector. If voltage is more than 9.5 volts, repair open Red wire between door lock switch connector and voltage source. If voltage is 9.5 volts or less, go to next step.

10) Reconnect door lock switch connector. Measure voltage between ground and backprobe Orange/Violet wire of door lock switch connector. If voltage is more than 9.5 volts while pressing lock switch, go to next step. If voltage is 9.5 volts or less while pressing lock switch, replace door lock switch.

11) Access CTM 18-pin connector "B". Remove connector cover. Do not disconnect connector. Using an external voltmeter, measure voltage between ground and CTM 18-pin connector "B" terminal No. 4 (Orange/Violet wire). If voltage is more than 9.5 volts while pressing lock switch, replace CTM. If voltage is 9.5 volts or less while pressing lock switch, repair open Orange/Violet wire between CTM and door lock switch.

12) Using scan tool, read I/O's door unlock switch status. If scan tool does not display UNLOCK SW PRESSED while unlock switch is pressed on inoperative door, go to step **16)**. If scan tool displays UNLOCK SW PRESSED while unlock switch is pressed on inoperative door, go to next step.

13) Access door lock actuator inside inoperative door. Disconnect door lock actuator connector. Remove key from ignition and roll windows down. Connect test light between door lock actuator connector terminals. If test light illuminates while door unlock switch is pressed, replace door lock actuator. If test light does not illuminate while door unlock switch is pressed, go to next step.

14) Connect test light to ground and probe Orange/Black wire of door lock actuator connector. If test light illuminates while door unlock switch is pressed, repair open Orange/Black wire between door lock actuator and Central Timer Module (CTM). CTM is located behind right kick panel. If test light does not illuminate while door unlock switch is pressed, go to next step.

15) Access CTM 18-pin connector "B". Remove connector cover. Do not disconnect connector. Using an external voltmeter, measure voltage between ground and CTM 18-pin connector "B" terminal No. 9 (Pink/Black wire). If voltage is more than 9.5 volts while door unlock switch is pressed, repair open Pink/Black wire. If voltage is 9.5 volts or less while door unlock switch is pressed, replace CTM.

16) Disconnect inoperative lock switch connector. Using an external voltmeter, measure voltage between ground and Red wire of door lock switch connector. If voltage is more than 9.5 volts, repair open Red wire between door lock switch connector and voltage source. If voltage is 9.5 volts or less, go to next step.

17) Reconnect door lock switch connector. Measure voltage between ground and backprobe Pink/Violet wire of door lock switch connector. If voltage is more than 9.5 volts, go to next step. If voltage is 9.5 volts or less, replace door lock switch.

18) Access CTM 18-pin connector "B". Remove connector cover. Do not disconnect connector. Using an external voltmeter, measure voltage between ground and CTM 18-pin connector "B" terminal No. 13 (Pink/Violet wire). If voltage is more than 9.5 volts, replace CTM. If voltage is 9.5 volts or less, repair open Pink/Violet wire between CTM and door lock switch.

REMOTE KEYLESS ENTRY PROBLEM

NOTE: For connector terminal identification and wiring diagrams, see BODY CONTROL COMPUTER – INTRODUCTION article. Perform VERIFICATION TEST VER-1A after each repair.

CAUTION: Always turn ignition switch to OFF position prior to disconnecting or connecting any module connector.

1) Using scan tool select SYSTEM MONITORS, then CCD BUS TEST. If scan tool displays BUS OPERATIONAL, go to next step. If scan tool does not display BUS OPERATIONAL, go to appropriate VEHICLE COMMUNICATIONS article.

2) Using scan tool select BODY COMPUTER. If scan tool displays NO RESPONSE, go to appropriate VEHICLE COMMUNICATIONS article. If scan tool displays NO RESPONSE, go to next step.

CHRY
4-194

1999 ACCESSORIES & EQUIPMENT
Body Control Computer Tests – Dakota & Durango (Cont.)

3) Operate door locks with Remote Keyless Entry (RKE) transmitter. If doors locked when transmitter was actuated, on Dakota go to step 5) or on Durango go to next step. If doors do not lock when transmitter was actuated, go to step 13).

4) Press RKE unlock button once. If driver's door unlocks, go to next step. If driver's door does not unlock, go to step 5).

5) Ensure transmitter battery voltage is 3.2 volts. Turn ignition on. Place transmission in park and disarm anti-theft system. Using scan tool, select MISCELLANEOUS, then PROGRAM RKE. If BCM IS IN PROGRAMMING MODE does not appear, exit and select PROGRAM RKE again. Press any transmitter button. A single chime will announce RKE module accepted transmission. Repeat procedure for all transmitters used with vehicle. Operate door locks from reprogrammed transmitter. If door locks operate properly, system has been repaired. If door locks do not operate properly, go to step 13).

6) Turn ignition off. Access Central Timer Module (CTM). CTM is located behind right kick panel. Disconnect CTM 18-pin connector "B". Using an external voltmeter, measure voltage between ground and CTM 18-pin connector "B" terminal No. 7 (Red/Black wire). If voltage is 10 volts or less, go to step 10). If voltage is more than 10 volts, go to next step.

7) Locate left front door unlock relay in fuse/relay panel under left side of dash. Connect a jumper wire to ground and touch CTM 18-pin connector "B" terminal No. 7 (Red/Black wire). If left front door unlock relay clicks, go to next step. If left front door unlock relay does not click, replace left front door unlock relay.

8) If left front door unlocks, replace CTM. If left front door does not unlock, go to next step.

9) Remove left front door unlock relay. Measure voltage between ground and left front door unlock relay terminal No. 87. If voltage is 10 volts or less, repair open Red wire between left front door unlock relay terminal No. 87 and junction block fuse No. 13. If voltage is more than 10 volts, replace left front door unlock relay.

10) Using an external ohmmeter, measure resistance between left front door unlock relay terminal No. 85 and 86. If resistance is not 60-80 ohms, replace left front door unlock relay. If resistance is 60-80 ohms, go to next step.

11) Remove left front door unlock relay. Measure voltage between ground and left front door unlock relay terminal No. 86. If voltage is 10 volts or less, repair open Red wire between left front door unlock relay terminal No. 86 and junction block fuse No. 13. If voltage is more than 10 volts, go to next step.

12) Measure resistance between left front door unlock relay terminal No. 85 and CTM 18-pin connector "B" terminal No. 7 (Red/Black wire). If resistance is less than 5 ohms, replace CTM. If resistance is 5 ohms or more, repair open Red/Black wire between CTM and left front door unlock relay.

13) Using scan tool, reprogram a known good transmitter: Operate door locks with reprogrammed transmitter. If doors locked properly, replace transmitter. If doors did not lock properly, replace CTM.

VEHICLE THEFT/SECURITY SYSTEM
DOOR DISARM SWITCH FAILURE

NOTE: For connector terminal identification and wiring diagrams, see BODY CONTROL COMPUTER – INTRODUCTION article. Perform VERIFICATION TEST VER-1A after each repair.

CAUTION: Always turn ignition switch to OFF position prior to disconnecting or connecting any module connector.

1) Using scan tool, read Vehicle Theft Security System (VTSS) inputs/outputs information. If scan tool displays door disarm switch state OPEN, system is currently functioning properly. If scan tool does not display door disarm switch state OPEN, go to next step.

2) Disconnect left door disarm switch. If scan tool displays door disarm switch state OPEN, replace left door disarm switch. If scan tool does not display door disarm switch state OPEN, go to next step.

3) Disconnect right door disarm switch. If scan tool displays door disarm switch state OPEN, replace right door disarm switch. If scan tool does not display door disarm switch state OPEN, go to next step.

4) Disconnect liftgate disarm switch, if equipped. If scan tool displays liftgate disarm switch state OPEN, replace liftgate disarm switch. If scan tool does not display liftgate disarm switch state OPEN, go to next step.

5) Access Central Timer Module (CTM). CTM is located behind right kick panel. Disconnect CTM 18-pin connector "B". Using an external ohmmeter, measure resistance between ground and CTM 18-pin connector "B" terminal No. 10 (Black/Orange wire on Dakota or Light Green/Orange wire on Durango). If resistance is less than 1000 ohms, repair short to ground in Black/Orange wire on Dakota or Light Green/Orange wire on Durango. If resistance is 1000 ohms or more, replace CTM.

DOOR LOCK SWITCH FAILURE

NOTE: For connector terminal identification and wiring diagrams, see BODY CONTROL COMPUTER – INTRODUCTION article. Perform VERIFICATION TEST VER-1A after each repair.

CAUTION: Always turn ignition switch to OFF position prior to disconnecting or connecting any module connector.

1) Clear trouble codes as needed. See BODY CONTROL COMPUTER – INTRODUCTION article. Using scan tool, read Vehicle Theft Security System (VTSS) inputs/outputs door lock switch status. If scan tool displays RELEASED, system is currently functioning properly. If scan tool does not display RELEASED, go to next step.

2) Disconnect left door lock switch connector. If scan tool displays RELEASED, replace left door lock switch. If scan tool does not display RELEASED, go to next step.

3) Disconnect right door lock switch connector. If scan tool displays RELEASED, replace right door lock switch. If scan tool does not display RELEASED, go to next step.

4) Locate Central Timer Module (CTM). CTM is located behind right kick panel. Disconnect CTM 18-pin connector "B". Using an external voltmeter, measure voltage between ground and CTM 18-pin connector "B" terminal No. 4 (Light Green wire on Dakota or Orange/Violet wire on Durango). If voltage is more than 1.5 volts, repair short to voltage in Light Green wire on Dakota or Orange/Violet wire on Durango between CTM and door lock switch. If voltage is 1.5 volts or less, replace CTM.

DOOR UNLOCK SWITCH FAILURE

NOTE: For connector terminal identification and wiring diagrams, see BODY CONTROL COMPUTER – INTRODUCTION article. Perform VERIFICATION TEST VER-1A after each repair.

CAUTION: Always turn ignition switch to OFF position prior to disconnecting or connecting any module connector.

1) Clear trouble codes as needed. See BODY CONTROL COMPUTER – INTRODUCTION article. Using scan tool, read Vehicle Theft Security System (VTSS) inputs/outputs door unlock switch status. If scan tool displays RELEASED, system is currently functioning properly. If scan tool does not display RELEASED, go to next step.

2) Disconnect left door lock switch connector. If scan tool displays RELEASED, replace left door lock switch. If scan tool does not display RELEASED, go to next step.

3) Disconnect right door lock switch connector. If scan tool displays RELEASED, replace right door lock switch. If scan tool does not display RELEASED, go to next step.

4) Locate Central Timer Module (CTM). CTM is located behind right kick panel. Disconnect CTM 18-pin connector "B". Using an external voltmeter, measure voltage between ground and CTM 18-pin connector "B" terminal No. 13 (Orange/White wire on Dakota or Pink/Violet wire on Durango). If voltage is more than 1.5 volts, repair short to voltage in Orange/White wire on Dakota or Pink/Violet wire on Durango between CTM and door lock switch. If voltage is 1.5 volts or less, replace CTM.

1999 ACCESSORIES & EQUIPMENT
Body Control Computer Tests – Dakota & Durango (Cont.)

CHRY
4-195

IDENTIFYING VTSS PROBLEMS

NOTE: For connector terminal identification and wiring diagrams, see BODY CONTROL COMPUTER – INTRODUCTION article. Perform VERIFICATION TEST VER-1A after each repair.

CAUTION: Always turn ignition switch to OFF position prior to disconnecting or connecting any module connector.

1) Using scan tool, select BODY SYSTEM then VTSS and read Central Timer Module (CTM) DTCs. If any VTSS DTCs are displayed, perform appropriate procedure. See VTSS DTC table. If no VTSS DTCs are displayed, go to next step.

VTSS DTC

DTC Message	Perform
DOOR DISARM SWITCH FAILURE	DOOR DISARM SWITCH FAILURE
DOOR LOCK SWITCH FAILURE	DOOR LOCK SWITCH FAILURE
DOOR UNLOCK SWITCH FAILURE	DOOR UNLOCK SWITCH FAILURE
EEPROM CHECKSUM FAILURE	Replace CTM
INTERNAL ROM TEST FAILURE	Replace CTM

2) Select VTSS then MONITORS. If scan tool displays, OK TO RUN, NOT OK TO ARM, PCM has not recorded more than 20 starts. Start engine 20 times and retest. If message does not change to OK TO ARM, replace PCM. If scan tool displays NO RESPONSE TO PCM, see appropriate VEHICLE COMMUNICATIONS article. If scan tool display OK TO RUN, NOT OK TO ARM or NO RESPONSE TO PCM, go to next step.

3) Using scan tool, actuate horn, headlights and VTSS light to flash. If horn does not sound, go to next step. If headlights do not flash, go to step 6). If VTSS light does not flash, go to step 9). If all function properly, go to step 11).

4) Press horn button. If horn does not sound, go to appropriate STEERING COLUMN SWITCHES article. If horn sounds, go to next step.

5) Locate Central Timer Module (CTM). CTM is located behind right kick panel. Disconnect CTM 18-pin connector "B". Turn ignition on. Using an external voltmeter, measure voltage between ground and CTM 18-pin connector "B" terminal No. 18 (Black/Red wire). If voltage is more than 9.5 volts, replace CTM. If voltage is 9.5 volts or less, repair open in Black/Red wire between CTM and horn relay.

6) Remove headlight relay from junction block. Turn ignition on. Using an external voltmeter, measure voltage between battery voltage and headlight relay connector terminal No. 86 on Dakota or terminal No. 85 on Durango (Violet wire). If voltage is more than 9.5 volts, go to next step. If voltage is 9.5 volts or less, repair open in Violet wire between battery source and headlight relay.

7) Connect a test light between battery source and headlight relay connector terminal No. 85 on Dakota or terminal No. 86 on Durango (Red/Dark Blue wire on Dakota or Red wire on Durango). If test light illuminates, go to next step. If test light does not illuminate, replace headlight relay.

8) Reinstall head light relay. Locate Central Timer Module (CTM). CTM is located behind right kick panel. Disconnect CTM 18-pin connector "B". Using an external voltmeter, measure voltage between ground and CTM 18-pin connector "B" terminal No. 6 (Red/Dark Blue wire on Dakota or Red wire on Durango). If voltage is more than 9.5 volts, replace CTM. If voltage is 9.5 volts or less, repair open in Red/Dark Blue wire on Dakota or Red wire on Durango between CTM and headlight relay.

9) Using scan tool, actuate VTSS indicator light. If VTSS indicator light is not illuminated, see appropriate INSTRUMENT PANELS article. If VTSS indicator light is illuminated, go to next step.

10) Locate Central Timer Module (CTM). CTM is located behind right kick panel. Disconnect CTM 18-pin connector "B". Using an external voltmeter, measure voltage between ground and CTM 18-pin connector "B" terminal No. 8 (Yellow wire on Dakota or Black/Orange wire on Durango). If voltage is more than 9.5 volts, replace CTM. If voltage is 9.5 volts or less, repair open in Yellow wire or Black/Orange wire between CTM and VTSS indicator light.

11) Using scan tool, place VTSS in diagnostic mode and follow directions on screen. If TURN KEY TO ACC POSITION is not displayed, go to step 23). If NO RESPONSE after turning key to accessory position or TURN KEY TO ACC POSITION is displayed longer than 15 seconds, go to next step. If neither response is received, go to step 13).

12) Locate Central Timer Module (CTM). CTM is located behind right kick panel. Gain access to CTM 18-pin connector "B". Ensure key is in accessory position. Using an external voltmeter, measure voltage between ground and backprobe of CTM 18-pin connector "B" terminal No. 5 (Dark Blue/White wire). If voltage is more than 10 volts, replace CTM. If voltage is 10 volts or less, repair open Dark Blue/White wire between CTM and junction block.

13) Remove key from ignition. Wait 2 seconds after performing each of the following actions. Open, then close both door. Operate power door lock switch to lock, then unlock position. Rotate key both directions in both doors. Ensure each operation is successful. If any operation is unsuccessful, see VTSS SYMPTOM DIRECTORY table for repair of failed operation. If all operations are successful, go to step 22).

VTSS SYMPTOM DIRECTORY

Problem Circuit	Go To
Driver's Door Open Or Close	Step 14)
Passenger's Door Open Or Close	Step 15)
Driver's Door Lock Switch	ONE OR ALL DOORS FAILING TO LOCK FROM ONE SWITCH
Passenger's Door Lock Switch	ONE OR ALL DOORS FAILING TO LOCK FROM ONE SWITCH
Driver's Key Cylinder	Step 16)
Passenger's Key Cylinder	Step 19)
Driver's Door Unlock Switch	ONE OR ALL DOORS FAILING TO UNLOCK FROM ONE SWITCH
Passenger's Door Unlock Switch	ONE OR ALL DOORS FAILING TO UNLOCK FROM ONE SWITCH

14) Ensure driver's door is closed. Using scan tool, read VTSS inputs/outputs door ajar status. If scan tool displays DR DOOR AJAR SWITCH: CLOSED, go to SHORTED DRIVER'S DOOR AJAR CIRCUIT under DOOR AJAR SYSTEM. If scan tool does not display DR DOOR AJAR SWITCH: CLOSED, go to OPEN DRIVER'S DOOR AJAR CIRCUIT under DOOR AJAR SYSTEM.

15) Ensure passenger's door is closed. Using scan tool, read VTSS inputs/outputs door ajar status. If scan tool displays DR DOOR AJAR SWITCH: CLOSED, go to SHORTED PASSENGER'S DOOR AJAR CIRCUIT under DOOR AJAR SYSTEM. If scan tool does not display DR DOOR AJAR SWITCH: CLOSED, go to OPEN DRIVER'S DOOR AJAR CIRCUIT under DOOR AJAR SYSTEM.

16) Using scan tool, monitor door disarm switch state. Disconnect left door disarm switch. Connect jumper wire between left door disarm switch connector terminals. If scan tool displays door disarm switch state CLOSED, replace left door disarm switch. If scan tool does not display door disarm switch state CLOSED, go to next step.

17) Disconnect jumper wire. Connect jumper wire between ground and left door disarm switch connector Black/Orange wire on Dakota or Light Green/Orange wire on Durrango. If scan tool displays door disarm switch state CLOSED, go to next step. If scan tool does not display door disarm switch state CLOSED, repair open left door disarm switch ground circuit (Black wire on Dakota or Black/Tan wire on Durango).

18) Access Central Timer Module (CTM). CTM is located behind right kick panel. Remove connector cover. Do not disconnect connector. Connect a jumper between ground and backprobe CTM 18-pin connector "B" terminal No. 10 (Black/Orange wire on Dakota or Light Green/Orange wire on Durango). If scan tool displays door disarm switch state CLOSED, repair open left door disarm switch sense circuit (Black/

CHRY
4-196

1999 ACCESSORIES & EQUIPMENT
Body Control Computer Tests – Dakota & Durango (Cont.)

Orange wire on Dakota or Light Green/Orange wire on Durango). If scan tool does not display door disarm switch state CLOSED, replace CTM.

19) Using scan tool, monitor door disarm switch state. Disconnect right door disarm switch. Connect jumper wire between right door disarm switch connector terminals. If scan tool displays door disarm switch state CLOSED, replace right door disarm switch. If scan tool does not display door disarm switch state CLOSED, go to next step.

20) Disconnect jumper wire. Connect jumper wire between ground and right door disarm switch connector Black/Orange wire on Dakota or Light Green/Orange wire on Durrango. If scan tool displays door disarm switch state CLOSED, go to next step. If scan tool does not display door disarm switch state CLOSED, repair open right door disarm switch ground circuit (Black wire on Dakota or Black/Tan wire on Durango) .

21) Access Central Timer Module (CTM). CTM is located behind right kick panel. Remove connector cover. Do not disconnect connector. Connect a jumper between ground and backprobe CTM 18-pin connector "B" terminal No. 10 (Black/Orange wire on Dakota or Light Green/Orange wire on Durango). If scan tool displays door disarm switch state CLOSED, repair open right door disarm switch sense circuit (Black/Orange wire on Dakota or Light Green/Orange wire on Durango). If scan tool does not display door disarm switch state CLOSED, replace CTM.

22) Turn ignition switch to START position. If horn does not sound, go to next step. If horn sounds, go to step 24).

23) Locate Central Timer Module (CTM). CTM is located behind right kick panel. Disconnect CTM 14-pin Green connector "A". Using an external voltmeter, measure voltage between ground and CTM 14-pin Green connector "A" terminal No. 8 (Dark Blue wire). If voltage is more than 10 volts, replace CTM. If voltage is 10 volts or less, repair open Dark Blue wire between CTM and RUN-ACC fuse in junction block.

24) Select VTSS then MONITORS. If scan tool displays NO RESPONSE TO PCM, see appropriate VEHICLE COMMUNICATIONS article. If scan tool displays, OK TO RUN, NOT OK TO ARM, go to next step. If scan tool display OK TO RUN, NOT OK TO ARM or NO RESPONSE TO PCM, system is currently functioning properly.

25) Start engine 20 times and retest. If message does not change to OK TO ARM, replace PCM. If message changes to OK TO ARM, test is complete. System is currently functioning properly.

WINDSHIELD WIPER SYSTEM

WIPER PARK SWITCH FAILURE

NOTE: For connector terminal identification and wiring diagrams, see BODY CONTROL COMPUTER – INTRODUCTION article. Perform VERIFICATION TEST VER-1A after each repair.

CAUTION: Always turn ignition switch to OFF position prior to disconnecting or connecting any module connector.

NOTE: It takes 8 seconds for wiper park switch failure DTC to set.

1) If low and high speed wipers work properly, go to next step. If low and high speed wipers do not work properly, see appropriate WIPER/WASHER SYSTEMS article.

2) Turn ignition on. Using scan tool, erase DTCs. See appropriate SELF-DIAGNOSTICS article. Operate wipers in low speed, then intermittent mode. Using scan tool, read DTCs. If WIPER PARK SWITCH FAILURE is displayed, go to next step. If WIPER PARK SWITCH FAILURE is not displayed, system is currently functioning properly.

3) Inspect wiper relay in Power Distribution Center (PDC). PDC is located on left inner fender well of engine compartment. If a wiper relay installed in wiper slot, go to next step. See Fig. 2. If a wiper relay is not installed in wiper slot, install wiper relay.

4) Swap starter relay and wiper relay. See Fig. 2 Using scan tool, clear and reread DTCs. Operate wipers in intermittent mode. Using scan tool, read DTCs. If WIPER PARK SWITCH FAILURE returned, go to next step. If WIPER PARK SWITCH FAILURE did not return, reinstall starter relay and replace wiper relay.

5) Reinstall starter relay. Using an external voltmeter, measure voltage between ground and wiper relay terminal No. 87 then terminal No. 86.

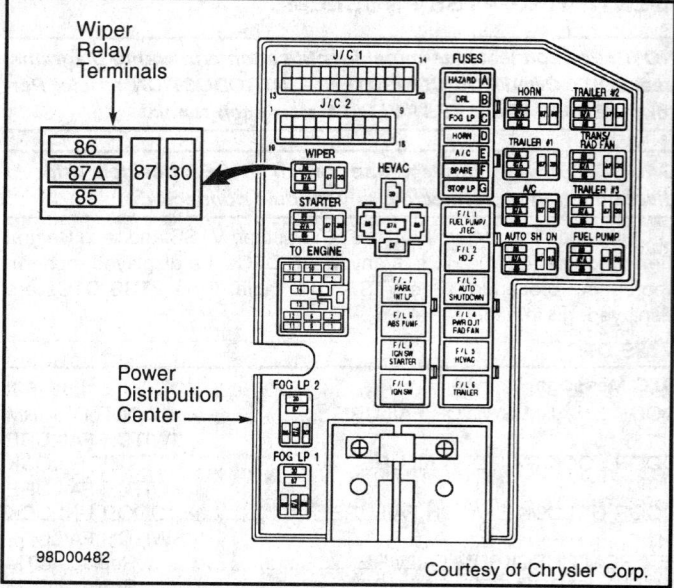

Fig. 2: Identifying PDC Components

See Fig. 2. If voltage at both terminals is more than 10 volts, go to next step. If voltage at either terminal is 10 volts or less, repair open Dark Blue wire between wiper relay and fuse in junction block.

6) Connect test light between battery voltage and wiper relay terminal No. 85. Using scan tool, actuate wiper relay. If test light flashes on and off, system is currently functioning properly. If test light does not flash on and off, go to next step.

7) Locate Central Timer Module (CTM). CTM is located behind right kick panel. Using an external voltmeter, measure voltage between ground and backprobe of CTM 14-pin Green connector "A" terminal No. 11 (Dark Green/Yellow wire). If voltage does not cycle between zero and 10 volts, replace CTM. If voltage cycles between zero and 10 volts, repair open Dark Green/Yellow wire between CTM and wiper relay or park switch.

INTERMITTENT WIPERS INOPERATIVE

NOTE: For connector terminal identification and wiring diagrams, see BODY CONTROL COMPUTER – INTRODUCTION article. Perform VERIFICATION TEST VER-1A after each repair.

CAUTION: Always turn ignition switch to OFF position prior to disconnecting or connecting any module connector.

1) Connect scan tool to Data Link Connector (DLC). DLC is a 16-pin connector located under left side of dash, to left of steering wheel. Turn ignition switch to ON position. If scan tool display is not blank or have a CCD bus failure message, go to next step. If scan tool display is blank or has a CCD bus failure message, see appropriate VEHICLE COMMUNICATIONS article.

2) If problem is wipers parking in wrong position, go to step 5). If problem is not wipers parking in wrong position, go to next step.

3) Gain access to wiper motor connector. Turn wipers on to low speed. Using an external voltmeter, measure voltage between ground and wiper motor switch terminal No. 2 (Dark Green/Yellow wire). If voltage does not cycle between zero and 12 volts, replace wiper motor. If voltage cycles between zero and 12 volts, go to next step.

4) Locate Central Timer Module (CTM). CTM is located behind right kick panel. Using an external voltmeter, measure voltage between ground and backprobe CTM 14-pin Green connector "A" terminal No. 11 (Dark Green/Yellow wire). Wipers should be operating at low speed. If voltage does not cycle between zero and 12 volts, repair open Dark Green/Yellow wire between CTM and wiper relay or park switch. If voltage cycles between zero and 10 volts, replace CTM.

1999 ACCESSORIES & EQUIPMENT
Body Control Computer Tests – Dakota & Durango (Cont.)

CHRY
4-197

5) Using scan tool, monitor intermittent wiper voltage level. Rotate wiper switch from low intermittent to high intermittent level. If voltage changes from approximately 2.5 to 12 volts, replace CTM. If voltage does not change from approximately 2.5 to 12 volts, go to next step.

6) Disconnect 24-pin multifunction switch connector. Using an external ohmmeter, measure resistance of White wire between multifunction switch connector terminal No. 1 and CTM 14-pin Green connector "A" terminal No. 12. if resistance is less than 5 ohms, replace multifunction switch. If resistance is 5 ohms or more, repair open White wire between multifunction switch and CTM.

NO WIPE AFTER WASHERS ACTUATED

NOTE: For connector terminal identification and wiring diagrams, see BODY CONTROL COMPUTER – INTRODUCTION article. Perform VERIFICATION TEST VER-1A after each repair.

CAUTION: Always turn ignition switch to OFF position prior to disconnecting or connecting any module connector.

1) Connect scan tool to Data Link Connector (DLC). DLC is a 16-pin connector located under left side of dash, to left of steering wheel. Turn ignition switch to ON position. If scan tool display is not blank or have a CCD bus failure message, go to next step. If scan tool display is blank or has a CCD bus failure message, see appropriate VEHICLE COMMUNICATIONS article.

2) Turn ignition on. If washer system works, go to next step. If washer system does not work, see appropriate WIPER/WASHER SYSTEMS article.

3) Using scan tool, actuate washer. If washer pump sense displays ON, replace CTM. If washer pump sense does not display ON, repair open Brown wire between CTM 14-pin Green connector "A" terminal No. 10 and multifunction switch.

WIPER SPEED SENSITIVE FEATURE INOPERATIVE

NOTE: For connector terminal identification and wiring diagrams, see BODY CONTROL COMPUTER – INTRODUCTION article. Perform VERIFICATION TEST VER-1A after each repair.

CAUTION: Always turn ignition switch to OFF position prior to disconnecting or connecting any module connector.

1) Connect scan tool to Data Link Connector (DLC). DLC is a 16-pin connector located under left side of dash, to left of steering wheel. Turn ignition switch to ON position. Using scan tool select Central timer module (CTM). If scan tool display is not blank or have a CCD bus failure message, go to next step. If scan tool display is blank or has a CCD bus failure message, see appropriate VEHICLE COMMUNICATIONS article.

2) Using scan tool, read Powertrain Control Module (PCM). If scan tool display is not blank or have a CCD bus failure message, go to next step. If scan tool display is blank or has a CCD bus failure message, see appropriate VEHICLE COMMUNICATIONS article.

3) Raise and support vehicle. Turn wipers on to lowest intermittent position. Time interval between wipes. Spin rear wheels to more than 15 MPH. If interval between wipes decreased to approximately 18 seconds, system is currently functioning properly. If interval between wipes did not decrease to approximately 18 seconds, replace CTM.

VERIFICATION TEST VER–1A

BODY VERIFICATION TEST

1) Reconnect all previously disconnected components and connectors. Turn ignition on. If entry module was replaced, program all RKE transmitters, recalibrate HVAC doors and program other options as necessary.

2) Ensure ignition is on. Erase all DTCs using scan tool. Turn ignition off and wait 5 seconds. Turn ignition on and fully operate system that was malfunctioning.

3) If system is not operating properly, go to SYMPTOM IDENTIFICATION. If system is operating correctly and customer's complaint cannot be duplicated, repair is complete.

NOTE: See BODY CONTROL COMPUTER – INTRODUCTION article before proceeding with following test. Body control computer in RWD trucks is the Central Timer Module (CTM).

SYMPTOM IDENTIFICATION

IDENTIFYING VEHICLE EQUIPMENT & SYSTEM PROBLEMS

NOTE: For connector terminal identification wiring diagrams, see BODY CONTROL COMPUTER – INTRODUCTION article.

NOTE: Perform a visual inspection before proceeding with this test. Ensure battery is fully charged.

1) Connect scan tool to Data Link Connector (DLC). DLC is a 16-pin connector located under left side of dash, to left of steering wheel. Turn ignition switch to ON position. If scan tool display is not blank, go to next step. If scan tool display is blank, see appropriate VEHICLE COMMUNICATIONS article.

2) Using scan tool, select SYSTEM MONITORS, then CCD BUS TEST. Scan tool will perform a CCD bus test. If scan tool displays BUS OPERATIONAL, go to next step. If scan tool displays any message except BUS OPERATIONAL, see appropriate VEHICLE COMMUNICATIONS article.

3) Using scan tool, select READ DTCs. If any Diagnostic Trouble Codes (fault messages) are present, go to appropriate fault message. If no fault messages are present, identify customer complaint. See following list for possible fault messages and customer complaint symptoms. Problems listed are diagnosed using a scan tool. These problems may occur separately or in various combinations. When diagnosing a system with many apparent problems, a sequence of tests may be required. After repairs, ensure problem(s) or failure(s) have been corrected.

CHIME SYSTEM

- CHIME INOPERATIVE – ENGINE TEMPERATURE CRITICAL
- CHIME INOPERATIVE – KEY IN IGNITION & LF DOOR OPEN
- CHIME INOPERATIVE AT ALL TIMES
- CHIME INOPERATIVE WITH EXTERIOR LIGHTS ON
- CHIME INOPERATIVE WITH LOW OIL PRESSURE
- CHIME INOPERATIVE WITH DRIVER DOOR OPEN

DOOR AJAR SYSTEM

- OPEN LEFT DOOR AJAR CIRCUIT
- OPEN RIGHT DOOR AJAR CIRCUIT
- SHORTED LEFT DOOR AJAR CIRCUIT
- SHORTED RIGHT DOOR AJAR CIRCUIT

INSTRUMENT CLUSTER

- ALL GAUGES INOPERATIVE
- ANY CCD CLUSTER WARNING LIGHT INOPERATIVE
- ANY HARD WIRED CLUSTER WARNING LIGHT INOPERATIVE
- ONE GAUGE NOT OPERATING PROPERLY

OVERHEAD CONSOLE CONCERNS

- AVERAGE MPH/FUEL ECON INOPERATIVE OR WRONG (CMTC FAILS TO RESPOND TO INSTRUMENT CLUSTER DIMMING, DISTANCE TO EMPTY INOPERATIVE OR WRONG, ELAPSED TIME INOPERATIVE/WRONG, SWITCH ON CMTC INOPERATIVE, TRIP ODOMETER INOPERATIVE/WRONG)
- CMTC DISPLAY SHOWS FAILED
- CMTC SEGMENTS FAIL TO LIGHT UP
- INCORRECT READING BEYOND +/- 5
- REPAIRING "OC" IN CMTC DISPLAY
- REPAIRING "SC" IN CMTC DISPLAY

POWER DOOR LOCK SYSTEM

- DOOR LOCK SWITCH FAILURE (PDL)
- DOOR UNLOCK SWITCH FAILURE (PDL)
- AUTOMATIC (ROLLING) DOOR LOCKS INOPERATIVE
- DOORS LOCK WITH KEY IN IGNITION & LEFT DOOR OPEN
- ONE OR ALL DOORS FAILING TO LOCK FROM ONE SWITCH (ONE OR ALL DOORS FAILING TO UNLOCK FROM ONE SWITCH)
- REMOTE KEYLESS ENTRY PROBLEM

VEHICLE THEFT/SECURITY SYSTEM

- DOOR DISARM SWITCH FAILURE
- DOOR LOCK SWITCH FAILURE
- DOOR UNLOCK SWITCH FAILURE
- EEPROM CHECKSUM FAILURE
- INTERNAL ROM TEST FAILURE
- IDENTIFYING VTSS PROBLEMS

WINDSHIELD WIPER SYSTEM

- WIPER PARK SWITCH FAILURE
- INTERMITTENT WIPERS INOPERATIVE
- NO WIPER ACTUATION AFTER WASH BUTTON PUSHED
- WIPER SPEED SENSITIVE FEATURE INOPERATIVE

CHIME SYSTEM

CHIME INOPERATIVE WITH EXTREME COOLANT TEMPERATURE

NOTE: For connector terminal identification and wiring diagrams, see BODY CONTROL COMPUTER – INTRODUCTION article. Perform VERIFICATION TEST VER-1A after each repair.

CAUTION: Always turn ignition switch to OFF position prior to disconnecting any module connector.

1) Using scan tool, actuate chime. If chime sounds, go to next step. If chime does not sound, replace Central Timer Module (CTM). CTM is located under left side of instrument panel.

2) Using scan tool, read Powertrain Control Module (PCM) DTCs. If no engine coolant temperature related codes exist, go to next step. If engine coolant temperature related codes exist, see appropriate SELF-DIAGNOSTICS article in ENGINE PERFORMANCE in appropriate MITCHELL® manual.

3) Due to difficult access of coolant temperature sensor, Oil Pressure Switch (OPS) will be used to verify CCD bus message from PCM. Disconnect OPS connector. OPS is located near bottom of distributor. Connect a jumper wire between OPS connector terminals. Start engine and allow to idle for 20 seconds. Increase engine speed to 1600 RPM. If chime sounds, system is currently functioning properly. If chime does not sound, go to next step.

4) Remove instrument cluster. See appropriate INSTRUMENT PANELS article. Disconnect Instrument cluster 10-pin Gray connector "B". Connect a jumper wire between ground and Dark Blue/Red wire of instrument cluster 10-pin Gray connector terminal No. 7. Turn ignition on. If chime sounds, replace instrument cluster. If chime does not sound, repair open Dark Blue/Red wire.

CHIME INOPERATIVE – KEY IN IGNITION & LF DOOR OPEN

NOTE: For connector terminal identification and wiring diagrams, see BODY CONTROL COMPUTER – INTRODUCTION article. Perform VERIFICATION TEST VER-1A after each repair.

CAUTION: Always turn ignition switch to OFF position prior to disconnecting any module connector.

1) Turn ignition off. Open driver's door. If chime does not sound, go to next step. If chime sounds, system is currently functioning correctly.

1999 ACCESSORIES & EQUIPMENT
Body Control Computer Tests – Ram Pickup (Cont.)

CHRY
4-199

2) Using scan tool, read driver's door ajar switch status. If scan tool displays LFDOOR AJAR SWITCH: CLOSED, go to next step. If scan tool does not display LFDOOR AJAR SWITCH: CLOSED, go to OPEN LEFT DOOR AJAR CIRCUIT.

3) Using scan tool, read key-in ignition chime state. If scan tool does not display KEY-IN IGNITION CHIME STATE: ON, go to next step. If scan tool displays KEY-IN IGNITION CHIME STATE: ON, replace Central Timer Module (CTM). CTM is located under left side of instrument panel.

4) Disconnect key-in ignition switch connector. *See Fig. 1.* Connect jumper wire between key-in ignition switch connector Light Blue wire and ground. Using scan tool, read key-in ignition chime state. If scan tool does not display KEY-IN IGNITION CHIME STATE: ON, go to next step. If scan tool displays KEY-IN IGNITION CHIME STATE: ON, replace ignition switch. See appropriate STEERING COLUMN SWITCHES article.

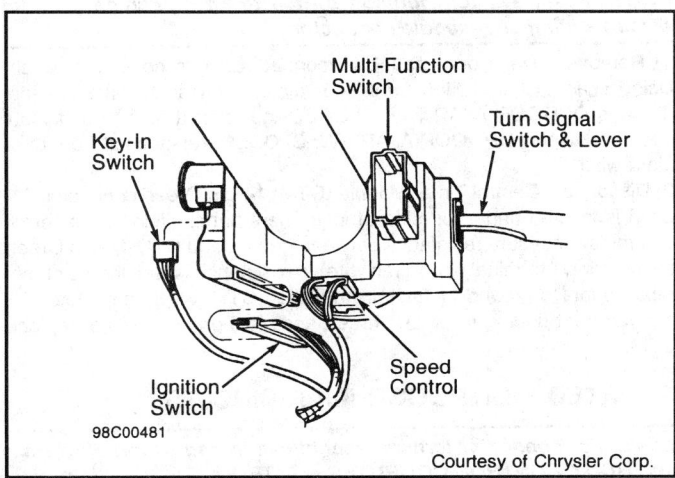

98C00481

Courtesy of Chrysler Corp.

Fig. 1: Identifying Steering Column Harness Connector Locations

5) Access CTM 14-pin Green connector C1. Remove connector cover. Do not disconnect connector. Connect a backprobe jumper wire between terminal No. 9 (Light Blue wire) and chassis ground. Using scan tool, read key-in ignition switch status. If scan tool does not display KEY-IN IGNITION CHIME STATE: ON, replace CTM. If scan tool displays KEY-IN IGNITION CHIME STATE: ON, repair open Light Blue wire between CTM and ignition switch.

CHIME INOPERATIVE AT ALL TIMES

NOTE: Perform VERIFICATION TEST VER-1A after each repair.

Turn ignition on. Using scan tool, select BODY SYSTEM, BODY COMPUTER then ACTUATORS. Actuate chime. If chime sounds, system is currently functioning correctly. If chime does not sound, replace Central Timer Module (CTM). CTM is located under left side of instrument panel.

CHIME INOPERATIVE WITH EXTERIOR LIGHTS ON

NOTE: For connector terminal identification and wiring diagrams, see BODY CONTROL COMPUTER – INTRODUCTION article. Perform VERIFICATION TEST VER-1A after each repair.

CAUTION: Always turn ignition switch to OFF position prior to disconnecting any module connector.

1) Remove ignition key. Using scan tool, read key-in ignition chime state. If scan tool does not display KEY-IN IGNITION CHIME STATE: OFF, go to step 4). If scan tool displays KEY-IN IGNITION CHIME STATE: OFF, go to next step.

2) Open driver's door. Using scan tool, read door ajar status. If scan tool displays LFDOOR AJAR SWITCH: CLOSED, go to next step. If scan tool does not display LFDOOR AJAR SWITCH: CLOSED, go to OPEN LEFT DOOR AJAR CIRCUIT.

3) Turn on headlights. If chime does not sound, repair open headlight sense circuit (Light Blue wire) between CTM and headlight switch. See appropriate wiring diagram in BODY CONTROL COMPUTER – INTRODUCTION article. If chime sounds, system is currently functioning correctly.

4) Open driver's door. Using scan tool, read door ajar status. If scan tool displays LFDOOR AJAR SWITCH: CLOSED, go to next step. If scan tool does not display LFDOOR AJAR SWITCH: CLOSED, go to OPEN LEFT DOOR AJAR CIRCUIT.

5) Disconnect key-in ignition switch connector. *See Fig. 1.* Using scan tool, read key-in ignition chime state. If scan tool displays KEY-IN IGNITION CHIME STATE: ON, go to next step. If scan tool does not display KEY-IN IGNITION CHIME STATE: ON, replace ignition switch. See appropriate STEERING COLUMN SWITCHES article.

6) Turn ignition off. Disconnect Central Timer Module (CTM). CTM is located under left side of instrument panel. Remove ignition key. Ensure all lights and accessories are off. Close all doors. Using external ohmmeter, measure resistance between ground and terminal No. 9 (Light Blue wire) on CTM Green connector "A". If resistance is less than 10 ohms, repair Light Blue wire between CTM and ignition switch for short to ground. If resistance is 10 ohms or more, replace CTM.

CHIME INOPERATIVE WITH LOW OIL PRESSURE

NOTE: For connector terminal identification and wiring diagrams, see BODY CONTROL COMPUTER – INTRODUCTION article. Perform VERIFICATION TEST VER-1A after each repair.

CAUTION: Always turn ignition switch to OFF position prior to disconnecting any module connector.

1) Disconnect Oil Pressure Switch (OPS). OPS is located near bottom of distributor. Connect a jumper wire between OPS connector terminals. Start engine and allow to idle for 20 seconds. Increase engine speed to 1600 RPM. If chime sounds, go to next step. If chime does not sound, go to step 3).

2) Turn ignition on. Using scan tool, actuate chime. If chime does not sound, replace Central Timer Module (CTM). CTM is located under left side of instrument panel. If chime sounds, system is currently functioning properly.

3) Using scan tool, access CLUSTER MONITOR. With engine running, read CCD oil pressure. If scan tool reading does not match instrument cluster reading, replace instrument cluster. If scan tool reading matches instrument cluster reading, go to next step.

4) Remove jumper wire. Connect a jumper wire between ground and OPS connector Gray wire. Start engine and allow to idle for 20 seconds. Increase engine speed to 1600 RPM. If chime sounds, repair open ground circuit between OPS connector and ground. If chime does not sound, go to next step.

5) Turn ignition on. Using scan tool, actuate chime. If chime does not sound, replace Central Timer Module (CTM). CTM is located under left side of instrument panel. If chime sounds, go to next step.

6) Remove instrument cluster. See appropriate INSTRUMENT PANELS article. Disconnect CTM 14-pin Green connector C1. Using an external ohmmeter, measure resistance of Dark Blue/Red wire between CTM 14-pin Green connector C1 terminal No. 2 and instrument cluster 10-pin connector C2 terminal No. 7. If resistance is less than 5 ohms, replace CTM. If resistance is 5 ohms or more, repair open Dark Blue/Red wire.

CHIME SOUNDS WITH DRIVER DOOR OPEN

NOTE: For connector terminal identification and wiring diagrams, see BODY CONTROL COMPUTER – INTRODUCTION article. Perform VERIFICATION TEST VER-1A after each repair.

CAUTION: Always turn ignition switch to OFF position prior to disconnecting any module connector.

1) Ensure all interior and exterior lights are off. Remove ignition key and open driver's door. If chime does not sound, system is currently functioning correctly. If chime sounds, go to next step.

CHRY
4-200

1999 ACCESSORIES & EQUIPMENT
Body Control Computer Tests – Ram Pickup (Cont.)

2) Using scan tool, read key-in ignition chime state. If scan tool displays KEY-IN IGNITION CHIME STATE: "ON/OFF", go to next step. If scan tool does not display KEY-IN IGNITION CHIME STATE: "ON/OFF", replace Central Timer Module (CTM). CTM is located under left side of instrument panel.

3) Disconnect key-in ignition switch connector. See Fig. 1. Using scan tool, read key-in ignition chime state. If scan tool displays KEY-IN IGNITION CHIME STATE: ON, go to next step. If scan tool does not display KEY-IN IGNITION CHIME STATE: ON, replace ignition switch. See appropriate STEERING COLUMN SWITCHES article.

4) Turn ignition off. Disconnect Central Timer Module (CTM). CTM is located under left side of instrument panel. Remove ignition key. Ensure all lights and accessories are off. Close all doors. Using external ohmmeter, measure resistance between ground and terminal No. 9 (Light Blue wire) on CTM Green connector "A". If resistance is less than 10 ohms, repair Light Blue wire between CTM and ignition switch for short to ground. If resistance is 10 ohms or more, replace CTM.

DOOR AJAR SYSTEM
OPEN LEFT DOOR AJAR CIRCUIT

NOTE: For connector terminal identification and wiring diagrams, see BODY CONTROL COMPUTER – INTRODUCTION article. Perform VERIFICATION TEST VER-1A after each repair.

CAUTION: Always turn ignition switch to OFF position prior to disconnecting any module connector.

1) Remove driver's door panel. Disconnect driver's door ajar switch and ensure connector is clean and not damaged. Connect a jumper wire between left front door ajar switch connector Tan wire and Black/Light Green wire. Using scan tool, read left front door ajar switch status. If scan tool displays DRDOOR AJAR SW: CLOSED, replace left front door ajar switch. If scan tool does not display DRDOOR AJAR SW: CLOSED, go to next step.

2) Disconnect jumper wire from Black/Light Green wire. Take jumper wire end removed from Black/Light Green wire and connect to ground. If scan tool displays DRDOOR AJAR SW: CLOSED, repair open ground circuit (Black/Light Green wire). If scan tool does not display DRDOOR AJAR SW: CLOSED, go to next step.

3) Disconnect jumper wire. Locate Central Timer Module (CTM). CTM is located under left side of instrument panel. Access CTM 14-pin Green connector C1. Remove connector cover. Do not disconnect connector. Connect a backprobe jumper wire between chassis ground and terminal No. 1 (Tan wire). Using scan tool, read left front door ajar switch status. If scan tool displays DRDOOR AJAR SW: CLOSED, repair open in Tan wire between left front door ajar switch and CTM. If scan tool does not display DRDOOR AJAR SW: CLOSED, replace CTM.

OPEN RIGHT DOOR AJAR CIRCUIT

NOTE: For connector terminal identification and wiring diagrams, see BODY CONTROL COMPUTER – INTRODUCTION article. Perform VERIFICATION TEST VER-1A after each repair.

CAUTION: Always turn ignition switch to OFF position prior to disconnecting any module connector.

1) Remove passenger's door panel. Disconnect right front door ajar switch and ensure connector is clean and not damaged. Connect a jumper wire between right front door ajar switch connector Black/Light Blue wire and Black/Light Green wire. Using scan tool, read right front door ajar switch status. If scan tool displays PASSDOOR AJAR SW: CLOSED, replace right front door ajar switch. If scan tool does not display PASSDOOR AJAR SW: CLOSED, go to next step.

2) Disconnect jumper from Black/Light Green wire. Take jumper wire end removed from Black/Light Green wire and connect to ground. If scan tool displays PASSDOOR AJAR SWITCH: CLOSED, repair open ground circuit (Black/Light Green wire). If scan tool does not display PASSDOOR AJAR SW: CLOSED, go to next step.

3) Disconnect jumper wire. Locate Central Timer Module (CTM). CTM is located under left side of instrument panel. Access CTM 14-pin Green connector C1. Remove connector cover. Do not disconnect connector. Connect a backprobe jumper wire between chassis ground and terminal No. 5 (Black/Light Blue wire). If scan tool displays PASS DOOR AJAR SW: CLOSED, repair open Black/Light Blue wire between CTM and right front door ajar switch. If scan tool does not display PASS DOOR AJAR SW: CLOSED, replace CTM.

SHORTED LEFT DOOR AJAR CIRCUIT

NOTE: For connector terminal identification and wiring diagrams, see BODY CONTROL COMPUTER – INTRODUCTION article. Perform VERIFICATION TEST VER-1A after each repair.

CAUTION: Always turn ignition switch to OFF position prior to disconnecting any module connector.

1) Remove driver's door panel. Disconnect driver's door ajar switch. Using scan tool, read left front door ajar switch status. If scan tool displays DRDOOR AJAR SW: CLOSED, go to next step. If scan tool does not display DRDOOR AJAR SW: CLOSED, replace left front door ajar switch.

2) Disconnect Central Timer Module (CTM) 14-pin Green connector C1. CTM is located under left side of instrument panel. Using an external ohmmeter, measure resistance between ground and CTM 14-pin Green connector C1 terminal No. 1 (Tan wire). If resistance is less than 5 ohms, repair short to ground in Tan wire between CTM 14-pin connector C1 and left front door ajar switch. If resistance is 5 ohms or more, replace CTM.

SHORTED RIGHT DOOR AJAR CIRCUIT

NOTE: For connector terminal identification and wiring diagrams, see BODY CONTROL COMPUTER – INTRODUCTION article. Perform VERIFICATION TEST VER-1A after each repair.

CAUTION: Always turn ignition switch to OFF position prior to disconnecting any module connector.

1) Ensure all doors are closed. Open right front door and remove door panel. Disconnect right front door ajar switch. Using scan tool, read right front door ajar switch status. If scan tool displays PASSDOOR AJAR SW: CLOSED, go to next step. If scan tool does not display PASSDOOR AJAR SW: CLOSED, replace right front door ajar switch.

2) Disconnect Central Timer Module (CTM) 14-pin Green connector C1. CTM is located under left side of instrument panel. Using an external ohmmeter, measure resistance between ground and CTM 14-pin Green connector C1 terminal No. 5 (Black/Light Blue wire). If resistance is less than 5 ohms, repair short to ground in Black/Light Blue wire. If resistance is 5 ohms or more, replace CTM.

INSTRUMENT CLUSTER
ALL GAUGES DO NOT OPERATE

NOTE: For connector terminal identification and wiring diagrams, see BODY CONTROL COMPUTER – INTRODUCTION article. Perform VERIFICATION TEST VER-1A after each repair.

CAUTION: Always turn ignition switch to OFF position prior to disconnecting or connecting any module connector.

1) Turn ignition on. Using scan tool, select ELECTRO/MECH CLUSTER. If scan tool displays BUS OPERATIONAL, go to next step. If scan tool does not display BUS OPERATIONAL, go to appropriate VEHICLE COMMUNICATIONS article and follow appropriate symptom diagnostics.

2) If scan tool displays NO RESPONSE, go to appropriate VEHICLE COMMUNICATIONS article. If scan tool does not display NO RESPONSE, go to next step.

1999 ACCESSORIES & EQUIPMENT
Body Control Computer Tests – Ram Pickup (Cont.)

CHRY
4-201

3) Using scan tool, select SYSTEM TEST. If scan tool displays PCM INACTIVE ON BUS, go to appropriate VEHICLE COMMUNICATIONS article. If scan tool does not display PCM INACTIVE ON BUS, go to next step.

4) Turn ignition off. Remove instrument cluster. See appropriate INSTRUMENT PANELS article. Turn ignition on. Using external voltmeter, measure voltage between ground and instrument cluster connector C1 terminal No. 6 (Yellow wire). If voltage is 10 volts or less, repair open Yellow wire. If voltage is more than 10 volts, replace instrument cluster.

ANY CCD CLUSTER LIGHT INOPERATIVE

NOTE: *For connector terminal identification and wiring diagrams, see BODY CONTROL COMPUTER – INTRODUCTION article. Perform VERIFICATION TEST VER-1A after each repair.*

CAUTION: *Always turn ignition switch to OFF position prior to disconnecting or connecting any module connector.*

1) Turn ignition on. Using scan tool, select ELECTRO/MECH CLUSTER. If scan tool displays BUS OPERATIONAL, go to next step. If scan tool does not display BUS OPERATIONAL, go to appropriate VEHICLE COMMUNICATIONS article and follow appropriate symptom diagnostics.

2) If scan tool displays NO RESPONSE, go to appropriate VEHICLE COMMUNICATIONS article. If scan tool does not display NO RESPONSE, go to next step.

3) Using scan tool, select SYSTEM TEST. If scan tool displays PCM INACTIVE ON BUS, go to appropriate VEHICLE COMMUNICATIONS article. If scan tool does not display PCM INACTIVE ON BUS, go to next step.

4) Push and hold RESET button while cycling ignition key. Release RESET button when CHEC appears in odometer display. Observe inoperative light during self-test. If inoperative light did not illuminate during self-test, go to next step. If inoperative light illuminated during self-test, verify if light is controlled by an input to instrument cluster. See appropriate wiring diagram in BODY CONTROL COMPUTER – INTRODUCTION article. If light is controlled by an input to instrument cluster, go to appropriate circuits article or symptom test. See IDENTIFYING VEHICLE EQUIPMENT & SYSTEM PROBLEMS. If light is not controlled by an input to instrument cluster, system is currently functioning correctly.

5) Gain access to instrument cluster. See appropriate INSTRUMENT PANELS article. If defective light is a LED, replace instrument cluster. If defective light is a bulb, go to next step.

6) Remove and inspect defective bulb. If bulb is burned out, replace bulb. If bulb is not burned out, replace instrument cluster.

ANY HARD WIRED CLUSTER WARNING LIGHT INOPERATIVE

NOTE: *For connector terminal identification and wiring diagrams, see BODY CONTROL COMPUTER – INTRODUCTION article. Perform VERIFICATION TEST VER-1A after each repair.*

CAUTION: *Always turn ignition switch to OFF position prior to disconnecting or connecting any module connector.*

1) Remove instrument cluster. See appropriate INSTRUMENT PANELS article. Remove inoperative bulb. If bulb is burned out, replace bulb. If bulb is not burned out, go to next step.

2) Inspect wiring diagram and evaluate which instrument cluster provides; power or ground for inoperative bulb. See appropriate wiring diagram in BODY CONTROL COMPUTER – INTRODUCTION article. Using external ohmmeter or voltmeter, check appropriate power or ground circuit. If circuit is okay, replace instrument cluster. If power or ground is not available at appropriate circuit, repair open circuit.

ONE GAUGE NOT OPERATING PROPERLY

NOTE: *For connector terminal identification and wiring diagrams, see BODY CONTROL COMPUTER – INTRODUCTION article. Perform VERIFICATION TEST VER-1A after each repair.*

CAUTION: *Always turn ignition switch to OFF position prior to disconnecting or connecting any module connector.*

1) Push and hold RESET button while cycling ignition key; ON-OFF-ON. Instrument cluster self-test will start. If inoperative gauge reached proper calibration point, go to next step. If inoperative gauge did not reach proper calibration point, replace instrument cluster.

2) Stop instrument cluster self-test. If problem is with speedometer, go to next step. If problem is with oil pressure gauge, go to step 5). If problem is with temperature gauge, go to step 14). If problem is with fuel level gauge, go to appropriate SELF-DIAGNOSTICS article in ENGINE PERFORMANCE in appropriate MITCHELL® manual and review powertrain symptoms. If problem is with volt gauge, go to step 16). If problem is with tachometer, go to step 18).

3) Using scan tool, select BODY, SYSTEMS TESTS then PCM MONITOR. If scan tool displays PCM ACTIVE ON BUS, go to next step. If scan tool does not display PCM ACTIVE ON BUS, go to appropriate VEHICLE COMMUNICATIONS article.

4) Raise and support all wheels. Start engine and place gear selector in drive. Using scan tool, select MIC, MONITORS then CCD BUS ENGINE INFO. Read VSS. If vehicle speed on scan tool matches speedometer, see appropriate ANTI-LOCK BRAKE article. If vehicle speed on scan tool does not match speedometer, replace instrument cluster circuit board.

5) Turn ignition on. If CHECK GAUGES light illuminated, go to next step. If CHECK GAUGES light did not illuminate, go to step 11).

6) Turn ignition off. Inspect oil level. If oil level is within specification, go to next step. If oil level is not within specification, adjust oil level and retest.

7) Turn ignition on. Disconnect engine Oil Pressure Switch (OPS) connector. OPS is located near bottom of distributor. If CHECK GAUGES light went out, go to next step. If CHECK GAUGES light did not go out, go to step 10).

8) Remove OPS. Connect mechanical oil pressure gauge to OPS port. Start engine. If engine oil pressure at idle is 4 psi or more, go to next step. If engine oil pressure at idle is less than 4 psi, repair mechanical engine problem.

9) Run engine to reach normal operating temperature. If engine oil pressure at idle is 4 psi or more, replace OPS. If engine oil pressure at idle is less than 4 psi, repair mechanical engine problem.

10) Turn ignition off. Disconnect PCM White connector C2. PCM is located in engine compartment on right inner fender. Using an external ohmmeter, measure resistance between ground and PCM Black connector terminal No. 23 (Gray/Orange wire). If resistance is less than 5 ohms, repair short to ground in Gray/Orange wire. If resistance is 5 ohms or more, replace PCM.

11) Disconnect engine Oil Pressure Switch (OPS) connector. OPS is located near bottom of distributor. Using an external ohmmeter, measure resistance between ground and OPS connector Black/Light Blue wire. If resistance is less than 5 ohms, go to next step. If resistance is 5 ohms or more, repair open Black/Light Blue wire. Black/Light Blue wire is a common sensor ground. If no other engine sensors are failed, repair ground between sensor and splice. If multiple engine sensors have failed, repair ground between splice and PCM.

12) Connect jumper wire between OPS connector terminals. If oil pressure warning indicator illuminates, replace OPS. If oil pressure warning indicator does not illuminate, go to next step.

13) Do not remove jumper wire. Disconnect PCM Black connector C2. PCM is located in engine compartment on right inner fender. Using an external ohmmeter, measure resistance between ground and PCM White connector C2 terminal No. 23 (Gray/Orange wire). If resistance is less than 5 ohms, replace PCM. If resistance is 5 ohms or more, repair open Gray/Orange wire.

CHRY
4-202

1999 ACCESSORIES & EQUIPMENT
Body Control Computer Tests – Ram Pickup (Cont.)

14) Check cooling system operation. If cooling system is operating properly, go to next step. If cooling system is not operating properly, repair engine cooling problem.

15) Using scan tool, select PCM MONITOR under SYSTEM TESTS. If scan tool displays PCM ACTIVE ON BUS, system is currently functioning properly. If scan tool does not display PCM ACTIVE ON BUS, go to appropriate VEHICLE COMMUNICATIONS article.

16) Using scan tool, select MODULE ENGINE CONTROLLER. Read PCM DTCs. If scan tool displays any charging system related DTCs, go to appropriate SELF-DIAGNOSTICS article in ENGINE PERFORMANCE in appropriate MITCHELL® manual and repair DTC as necessary. If scan tool does not display any charging system related DTCs, go to next step.

17) Check charging system operation. If charging system is operating properly, replace instrument cluster. If charging system is not operating properly, repair engine charging problem.

18) Using scan tool, select BODY COMPUTER MONITORS. Read CCD BUS ENGINE INFO. If scan tool displays engine RPM, replace instrument cluster. If scan tool does not display engine RPM, replace PCM.

OVERHEAD CONSOLE CONCERNS

AVERAGE MPH/FUEL ECON INOPERATIVE OR WRONG (CMTC FAILS TO RESPOND TO INSTRUMENT CLUSTER DIMMING, DISTANCE TO EMPTY INOPERATIVE OR WRONG, ELAPSED TIME INOPERATIVE/WRONG, SWITCH ON CMTC INOPERATIVE, TRIP ODOMETER INOPERATIVE/WRONG)

NOTE: If any listed symptoms exist, Compass Mini-Trip computer (CMTC) is defective. Replace CMTC. Perform VERIFICATION TEST VER-1A after each repair.

CMTC SHOWS FAILED

NOTE: For connector terminal identification and wiring diagrams, see BODY CONTROL COMPUTER – INTRODUCTION article. Perform VERIFICATION TEST VER-1A after each repair.

Using scan tool, perform AUTO SELF TEST. If CMTC shows failed, replace CMTC. If CMTC does not show failed, system is currently functioning properly.

CMTC SEGMENTS FAIL TO LIGHT UP

NOTE: For connector terminal identification and wiring diagrams, see BODY CONTROL COMPUTER – INTRODUCTION article. Perform VERIFICATION TEST VER-1A after each repair.

Using scan tool, perform AUTO SELF TEST. If CMTC segments fail to illuminate, replace CMTC. If CMTC segments all illuminate properly, system is currently functioning properly.

INCORRECT READING BEYOND +/– 5

NOTE: For connector terminal identification and wiring diagrams, see BODY CONTROL COMPUTER – INTRODUCTION article. Perform VERIFICATION TEST VER-1A after each repair.

If temperature reading is off by more than 5°F, ambient temperature sensor is defective. Replace ambient temperature sensor. Ambient temperature sensor is located on left radiator saddle.

REPAIRING "OC" IN CMTC DISPLAY

NOTE: For connector terminal identification and wiring diagrams, see BODY CONTROL COMPUTER – INTRODUCTION article. Drive vehicle at least 3 miles (greater than 25 MPH) to update CMTC and perform VERIFICATION TEST VER-1A after each repair.

CAUTION: Always turn ignition switch to OFF position prior to disconnecting any module connector.

1) Disconnect ambient temperature sensor connector. Sensor is located on left radiator saddle. Connect jumper wire between sensor connector terminals. Turn ignition on. Observe CMTC display. If CMTC displays SC, replace ambient temperature sensor. If CMTC does not display SC, go to next step.

2) Turn ignition off. Disconnect jumper wire. Disconnect CMTC module connector. Connect a jumper wire between ground and ambient temperature sensor harness connector Violet/Light Green wire. If CMTC displays SC, repair open Black/Violet wire between ambient temperature sensor harness connector and ground. If CMTC does not display SC, go to next step.

3) Connect a backprobe jumper wire between ground and CMTC harness connector terminal No. 3 (Violet/Light Green wire). If CMTC displays SC, repair open Violet/Light Green wire between ambient temperature sensor harness connector and CMTC connector. If CMTC does not display SC, replace CMTC module.

REPAIRING "SC" IN CMTC DISPLAY

NOTE: For connector terminal identification and wiring diagrams, see BODY CONTROL COMPUTER – INTRODUCTION article. Perform VERIFICATION TEST VER-1A after each repair.

CAUTION: Always turn ignition switch to OFF position prior to disconnecting any module connector.

1) Turn ignition off. Disconnect CMTC connector. Using an external ohmmeter, measure resistance between CMTC harness connector terminal No. 3 (Violet/Light Green wire) and terminal No. 7 (Black/Light Green wire). If resistance is less than 5 ohms, repair Violet/Light Green wire between CMTC module and ambient temperature sensor for short to ground. If resistance is 5 ohms or more, go to next step.

2) Measure resistance between CMTC harness connector terminal No. 9 (Black/Light Blue wire) and terminal No. 3 (Violet/Light Green wire). If resistance is less than 1000 ohms, repair Violet/Light Green wire for short to Black/Light Blue wire. If resistance is 1000 ohms or more, go to next step.

3) Disconnect ambient temperature sensor connector. Sensor is located on left radiator saddle. Observe CMTC display. If CMTC displays OC, replace ambient temperature sensor. If CMTC does not display OC, replace CMTC module.

POWER DOOR LOCK SYSTEM
DOOR LOCK SWITCH FAILURE (PDL)

NOTE: For connector terminal identification and wiring diagrams, see BODY CONTROL COMPUTER – INTRODUCTION article. Perform VERIFICATION TEST VER-1A after each repair.

CAUTION: Always turn ignition switch to OFF position prior to disconnecting or connecting any module connector.

1) Clear trouble codes as needed. See BODY CONTROL COMPUTER – INTRODUCTION article. Using scan tool, read I/O's door lock switch status. If scan tool displays PRESSED, go to next step. If scan tool does not display PRESSED, system is currently functioning properly.

2) Disconnect left door lock switch connector. If scan tool displays PRESSED, go to next step. If scan tool does not display PRESSED, replace left door lock switch.

1999 ACCESSORIES & EQUIPMENT
Body Control Computer Tests – Ram Pickup (Cont.)

CHRY
4-203

3) Disconnect right door lock switch connector. If scan tool displays PRESSED, go to next step. If scan tool does not display PRESSED, replace right door lock switch.

4) Locate Central Timer Module (CTM). CTM is located under left side of instrument panel. Disconnect CTM 18-pin connector C2. Using an external voltmeter, measure voltage between ground and CTM 18-pin connector C2 terminal No. 4 (Orange/Dark Green wire). If voltage is more than 1.5 volts, repair short to voltage in Orange/Dark Green wire. If voltage is 1.5 volts or less, replace CTM.

DOOR UNLOCK SWITCH FAILURE (PDL)

NOTE: For connector terminal identification and wiring diagrams, see BODY CONTROL COMPUTER – INTRODUCTION article. Perform VERIFICATION TEST VER-1A after each repair.

CAUTION: Always turn ignition switch to OFF position prior to disconnecting or connecting any module connector.

1) Clear trouble codes as needed. See BODY CONTROL COMPUTER – INTRODUCTION article. Using scan tool, read I/O's door unlock switch status. If scan tool displays PRESSED, go to next step. If scan tool does not display PRESSED, system is currently functioning properly.

2) Disconnect left door lock switch connector. If scan tool displays PRESSED, go to next step. If scan tool does not display PRESSED, replace left door lock switch.

3) Disconnect right door lock switch connector. If scan tool displays PRESSED, go to next step. If scan tool does not display PRESSED, replace right door lock switch.

4) Locate Central Timer Module (CTM). CTM is located under left side of instrument panel. Disconnect CTM 18-pin connector C2. Using an external voltmeter, measure voltage between ground and CTM 18-pin connector C2 terminal No. 13 (Pink/Dark Green wire). If voltage is more than 1.5 volts, repair short to voltage in Pink/Dark Green wire. If voltage is 1.5 volts or less, replace CTM.

AUTOMATIC (ROLLING) DOOR LOCKS INOPERATIVE

NOTE: For connector terminal identification and wiring diagrams, see BODY CONTROL COMPUTER – INTRODUCTION article. Perform VERIFICATION TEST VER-1A after each repair.

1) Using scan tool select SYSTEM MONITORS, then CCD BUS TEST. If scan tool displays BUS OPERATIONAL, go to next step. If scan tool does not display BUS OPERATIONAL, go to appropriate VEHICLE COMMUNICATIONS article.

2) Using scan tool select BODY COMPUTER. If scan tool displays NO RESPONSE, go to appropriate VEHICLE COMMUNICATIONS article. If scan tool does not displays NO RESPONSE, go to next step.

3) This test is only for vehicles equipped with speed sensitive door locks. With doors closed and unlocked drive vehicle faster than 15 MPH. If doors lock, system is currently functioning properly. If doors do not lock, using scan tool select ROLLING LOCKS. Retest system.

DOORS LOCK WITH KEY IN IGNITION & LEFT DOOR OPEN

NOTE: For connector terminal identification and wiring diagrams, see BODY CONTROL COMPUTER – INTRODUCTION article. Perform VERIFICATION TEST VER-1A after each repair.

CAUTION: Always turn ignition switch to OFF position prior to disconnecting or connecting any module connector.

1) Using scan tool select SYSTEM MONITORS, then CCD BUS TEST. If scan tool displays BUS OPERATIONAL, go to next step. If scan tool does not display BUS OPERATIONAL, go to appropriate VEHICLE COMMUNICATIONS article.

2) Using scan tool select BODY COMPUTER. If scan tool displays NO RESPONSE, go to appropriate VEHICLE COMMUNICATIONS article. If scan tool does not display NO RESPONSE, go to next step.

3) Place key in ignition. Open driver's door. Lock doors from interior lock switch. If doors locked, go to next step. If doors did not lock, system is currently functioning correctly.

4) Using scan tool, read left door ajar status. Open and close left door. If door ajar state changed from OPEN to CLOSED, go to next step. If door ajar state did not change from OPEN to CLOSED, go to OPEN LEFT DOOR AJAR CIRCUIT under DOOR AJAR SYSTEM.

5) Ensure driver's door is open. Read key-in ignition status. If scan tool shows KEY-IN, replace Central Timer Module (CTM). CTM is located behind right kick panel. If scan tool does not show KEY-IN, go to next step.

6) Gain access to CTM connector C1. Do not disconnect connector. Using an external voltmeter, measure voltage between ground and CTM 14-pin connector C1 terminal No. 9 (Light Blue wire). If voltage is more than 1.5 volts, repair open Light Blue wire. If voltage is 1.5 volts or less, go to next step.

7) Turn ignition off and remove key. Measure voltage between ground and CTM 14-pin connector C1 terminal No. 9 (Light Blue wire). If voltage is less than 1.5 volts, replace CTM. If voltage is 1.5 volts or more, replace ignition switch.

ONE OR ALL DOORS FAILING TO LOCK FROM ONE SWITCH (ONE OR ALL DOORS FAILING TO UNLOCK FROM ONE SWITCH)

NOTE: For connector terminal identification and wiring diagrams, see BODY CONTROL COMPUTER – INTRODUCTION article. Perform VERIFICATION TEST VER-1A after each repair.

CAUTION: Always turn ignition switch to OFF position prior to disconnecting or connecting any module connector.

1) Using scan tool select SYSTEM MONITORS, then CCD BUS TEST. If scan tool displays BUS OPERATIONAL, go to next step. If scan tool does not display BUS OPERATIONAL, go to appropriate VEHICLE COMMUNICATIONS article.

2) Using scan tool select BODY COMPUTER. If scan tool displays NO RESPONSE, go to appropriate VEHICLE COMMUNICATIONS article. If scan tool does not display NO RESPONSE, go to next step.

3) Read DTCs. If no DTCs are displayed, go to next step. If DOOR LOCK SWITCH FAILURE is displayed, go to DOOR LOCK SWITCH FAILURE (PDL). If DOOR UNLOCK SWITCH FAILURE is displayed, go to DOOR UNLOCK SWITCH FAILURE (PDL).

4) Lower both front windows. Remove key from ignition switch and close all doors. Lock and unlock doors from all switches. If all doors lock and unlock properly, system is currently functioning properly. If one or all locks fail to lock from one switch, go to next step. If one or all locks fail to unlock from one switch, go to step **12**).

5) Using scan tool, read I/O's door lock switch status. Press lock button on inoperative door. If scan tool does not display LOCK SW PRESSED while lock switch is pressed on inoperative door, go to step **9**). If scan tool displays LOCK SW PRESSED while lock switch is pressed on inoperative door, go to next step.

6) Access door lock actuator inside inoperative door. Disconnect door lock actuator connector. Remove key from ignition and roll windows down. Connect test light between door lock actuator connector terminals. If test light illuminates while door lock switch is pressed, replace door lock actuator. If test light does not illuminate while door lock switch is pressed, go to next step.

7) Connect test light to ground and probe Orange/Black wire of door lock actuator connector. If test light illuminates while door lock switch is pressed, repair open Orange/Black wire between door lock actuator and Central Timer Module (CTM). CTM is located behind right kick panel. If test light does not illuminate while door lock switch is pressed, go to next step.

8) Access CTM 18-pin connector C2. Remove connector cover. Do not disconnect connector. Using an external voltmeter, measure voltage

CHRY
4-204

1999 ACCESSORIES & EQUIPMENT
Body Control Computer Tests – Ram Pickup (Cont.)

between ground and CTM 18-pin connector C2 terminal No. 1 (Orange/Black wire). If voltage is more than 9.5 volts while door lock switch is pressed, repair open Orange/Black wire. If voltage is 9.5 volts or less while door lock switch is pressed, replace CTM.

9) Disconnect inoperative lock switch connector. Using an external voltmeter, measure voltage between ground and Red wire of door lock switch connector. If voltage is more than 9.5 volts, go to next step. If voltage is 9.5 volts or less, repair open Red wire between door lock switch connector and voltage source.

10) Reconnect door lock switch connector. Measure voltage between ground and backprobe Orange/Violet wire of door lock switch connector. If voltage is more than 9.5 volts while pressing lock switch, go to next step. If voltage is 9.5 volts or less while pressing lock switch, replace door lock switch.

11) Access CTM 18-pin connector C2. Remove connector cover. Do not disconnect connector. Using an external voltmeter, measure voltage between ground and CTM 18-pin connector C2 terminal No. 4 (Orange/Dark Green wire). If voltage is more than 9.5 volts while pressing lock switch, replace CTM. If voltage is 9.5 volts or less while pressing lock switch, repair open Orange/Dark Green wire between CTM and door lock switch.

12) Using scan tool, read I/O's door unlock switch status. If scan tool does not display UNLOCK SW PRESSED while unlock switch is pressed on inoperative door, go to step 16). If scan tool displays UNLOCK SW PRESSED while unlock switch is pressed on inoperative door, go to next step.

13) Access door lock actuator inside inoperative door. Disconnect door lock actuator connector. Remove key from ignition and roll windows down. Connect test light between door lock actuator connector terminals. If test light illuminates while door unlock switch is pressed, replace door lock actuator. If test light does not illuminate while door unlock switch is pressed, go to next step.

14) Connect test light to ground and probe Orange/Black wire of door lock actuator connector. If test light illuminates while door unlock switch is pressed, repair open Orange/Black wire between door lock actuator and Central Timer Module (CTM). CTM is located behind right kick panel. If test light does not illuminate while door unlock switch is pressed, go to next step.

15) Access CTM 18-pin connector C2. Remove connector cover. Do not disconnect connector. Using an external voltmeter, measure voltage between ground and CTM 18-pin connector C2 terminal No. 9 (Pink/Black wire). If voltage is more than 9.5 volts while door unlock switch is pressed, repair open Pink/Black wire. If voltage is 9.5 volts or less while door unlock switch is pressed, replace CTM.

16) Disconnect inoperative lock switch connector. Using an external voltmeter, measure voltage between ground and Red wire of door lock switch connector. If voltage is more than 9.5 volts, repair open Red wire between door lock switch connector and voltage source. If voltage is 9.5 volts or less, go to next step.

17) Reconnect door lock switch connector. Measure voltage between ground and backprobe Pink/Violet wire of door lock switch connector. If voltage is more than 9.5 volts, go to next step. If voltage is 9.5 volts or less, replace door lock switch.

18) Access CTM 18-pin connector "B". Remove connector cover. Do not disconnect connector. Using an external voltmeter, measure voltage between ground and CTM 18-pin connector "B" terminal No. 13 (Pink/Dark Green wire). If voltage is more than 9.5 volts, replace CTM. If voltage is 9.5 volts or less, repair open Pink/Dark Green wire between CTM and door lock switch.

REMOTE KEYLESS ENTRY PROBLEM

NOTE: For connector terminal identification and wiring diagrams, see BODY CONTROL COMPUTER – INTRODUCTION article. Perform VERIFICATION TEST VER-1A after each repair.

CAUTION: Always turn ignition switch to OFF position prior to disconnecting or connecting any module connector.

1) Using scan tool select SYSTEM MONITORS, then CCD BUS TEST. If scan tool displays BUS OPERATIONAL, go to next step. If scan tool does not display BUS OPERATIONAL, go to appropriate VEHICLE COMMUNICATIONS article.

2) Using scan tool select BODY COMPUTER. If scan tool displays NO RESPONSE, go to appropriate VEHICLE COMMUNICATIONS article. If scan tool does not display NO RESPONSE, go to next step.

3) Operate door locks with Remote Keyless Entry (RKE) transmitter. If doors locked when transmitter was actuated, system is currently functioning properly. If doors do not lock when transmitter was actuated, go to next step.

4) Ensure transmitter battery voltage is 3.2 volts. Turn ignition on. Place transmission in park and disarm anti-theft system. Using scan tool, select MISCELLANEOUS, then PROGRAM RKE. If BCM IS IN PROGRAMMING MODE does not appear, exit and select PROGRAM RKE again. Press any transmitter button. A single chime will announce RKE module accepted transmission. Repeat procedure for all transmitters used with vehicle. Operate door locks from reprogrammed transmitter. If door locks operate properly, system has been repaired. If door locks do not operate properly, go to next step.

5) Using scan tool, reprogram a known good transmitter: Operate door locks with reprogrammed transmitter. If doors locked properly, replace transmitter. If doors did not lock properly, replace CTM.

VEHICLE THEFT/SECURITY SYSTEM
DOOR DISARM SWITCH FAILURE

NOTE: For connector terminal identification and wiring diagrams, see BODY CONTROL COMPUTER – INTRODUCTION article. Perform VERIFICATION TEST VER-1A after each repair.

CAUTION: Always turn ignition switch to OFF position prior to disconnecting or connecting any module connector.

1) Using scan tool, read VTSS inputs/outputs information. If scan tool displays door disarm switch state OPEN, system is currently functioning properly. If scan tool does not display door disarm switch state OPEN, go to next step.

2) Disconnect left door disarm switch. If scan tool displays door disarm switch state OPEN, replace left door disarm switch. If scan tool does not display door disarm switch state OPEN, go to next step.

3) Disconnect right door disarm switch. If scan tool displays door disarm switch state OPEN, replace left door disarm switch. If scan tool does not display door disarm switch state OPEN, go to next step.

4) Access Central Timer Module (CTM). CTM is located under left side of instrument panel. Disconnect CTM 18-pin connector C2. Using an external ohmmeter, measure resistance between ground and CTM 18-pin connector C2 terminal No. 10 (Light Green/Orange wire). If resistance is less than 1000 ohms, repair short to ground in Light Green/Orange wire. If resistance is 1000 ohms or more, replace CTM.

DOOR LOCK SWITCH FAILURE

NOTE: For connector terminal identification and wiring diagrams, see BODY CONTROL COMPUTER – INTRODUCTION article. Perform VERIFICATION TEST VER-1A after each repair.

CAUTION: Always turn ignition switch to OFF position prior to disconnecting or connecting any module connector.

1) Clear trouble codes as needed. See BODY CONTROL COMPUTER – INTRODUCTION article. Using scan tool, read I/O's door lock switch

1999 ACCESSORIES & EQUIPMENT
Body Control Computer Tests – Ram Pickup (Cont.)

CHRY
4-205

status. If scan tool displays RELEASED, system is currently functioning properly. If scan tool does not display RELEASED, go to next step.

2) Disconnect left door lock switch connector. If scan tool displays RELEASED, replace left door lock switch. If scan tool does not display RELEASED, go to next step.

3) Disconnect right door lock switch connector. If scan tool displays RELEASED, replace right door lock switch. If scan tool does not display RELEASED, go to next step.

4) Locate Central Timer Module (CTM). CTM is located under left side of instrument panel. Disconnect CTM 18-pin connector C2. Using an external voltmeter, measure voltage between ground and CTM 18-pin connector C2 terminal No. 13 (Pink/Dark Green wire). If voltage is more than 1.5 volts, repair short to voltage in Pink/Dark Green wire between CTM and door lock switch. If voltage is 1.5 volts or less, replace CTM.

DOOR UNLOCK SWITCH FAILURE

NOTE: For connector terminal identification and wiring diagrams, see BODY CONTROL COMPUTER – INTRODUCTION article. Perform VERIFICATION TEST VER-1A after each repair.

CAUTION: Always turn ignition switch to OFF position prior to disconnecting or connecting any module connector.

1) Clear trouble codes as needed. See BODY CONTROL COMPUTER – INTRODUCTION article. Using scan tool, read I/O's door unlock switch status. If scan tool displays RELEASED, system is currently functioning properly. If scan tool does not display RELEASED, go to next step.

2) Disconnect left door lock switch connector. If scan tool displays RELEASED, replace left door lock switch. If scan tool does not display RELEASED, go to next step.

3) Disconnect right door lock switch connector. If scan tool displays RELEASED, replace right door lock switch. If scan tool does not display RELEASED, go to next step.

4) Locate Central Timer Module (CTM). CTM is located under left side of instrument panel. Disconnect CTM 18-pin connector C2. Using an external voltmeter, measure voltage between ground and CTM 18-pin connector C2 terminal No. 4 (Orange/Dark Green wire). If voltage is more than 1.5 volts, repair short to voltage in Orange/Dark Green wire between CTM and door lock switch. If voltage is 1.5 volts or less, replace CTM.

IDENTIFYING VTSS PROBLEMS

NOTE: For connector terminal identification and wiring diagrams, see BODY CONTROL COMPUTER – INTRODUCTION article. Perform VERIFICATION TEST VER-1A after each repair.

CAUTION: Always turn ignition switch to OFF position prior to disconnecting or connecting any module connector.

1) Using scan tool, select BODY SYSTEM then VTSS and read Central Timer Module (CTM) DTCs. If any VTSS DTCs are displayed, perform appropriate procedure. See VTSS DTC table. If no VTSS DTCs are displayed, go to next step.

VTSS DTC

DTC Message	Perform
DOOR DISARM SWITCH FAILURE	DOOR DISARM SWITCH FAILURE
DOOR LOCK SWITCH FAILURE	DOOR LOCK SWITCH FAILURE
DOOR UNLOCK SWITCH FAILURE	DOOR UNLOCK SWITCH FAILURE
EEPROM CHECKSUM FAILURE	Replace CTM
INTERNAL ROM TEST FAILURE	Replace CTM

2) Select VTSS then MONITORS. If scan tool displays, OK TO RUN, NOT OK TO ARM, PCM has not recorded more than 20 starts. Start engine 20 times and retest. If message does not change to OK TO ARM,

replace PCM. If scan tool displays NO RESPONSE TO PCM, see appropriate VEHICLE COMMUNICATIONS article. If scan tool does not display OK TO RUN, NOT OK TO ARM or NO RESPONSE TO PCM, go to next step.

3) Using scan tool, actuate horn, headlights and VTSS light to flash. If horn does not sound, go to next step. If headlights do not flash, go to step **6)**. If VTSS light does not flash, go to step **9)**. If all function properly, go to step **12)**.

4) Press horn button. If horn does not sound, go to appropriate STEERING COLUMN SWITCHES article. If horn sounds, go to next step.

5) Locate Central Timer Module (CTM). CTM is located behind right kick panel. Disconnect CTM 18-pin connector C2. Turn ignition on. Using an external voltmeter, measure voltage between ground and CTM 18-pin connector C2 terminal No. 18 (Black/Red wire). If voltage is more than 9.5 volts, replace CTM. If voltage is 9.5 volts or less, repair open in Black/Red wire between CTM and horn relay.

6) Remove security relay from Power Distribution Center (PDC). Turn ignition on. Connect a test light between battery source and headlight relay connector terminal No. 85 (Red/Dark Blue wire). Using scan tool, actuate relay. If test light illuminates, replace security relay. If test light does not illuminate, go to next step.

7) Using an external voltmeter, measure voltage between battery voltage and security relay connector terminal No. 86 (Red/Orange wire). If voltage is more than 9.5 volts, go to next step. If voltage is 9.5 volts or less, repair open in Red/Orange wire between battery source and security relay.

8) Reinstall security relay. Locate Central Timer Module (CTM). CTM is located behind right kick panel. Disconnect CTM 18-pin connector C2. Using an external voltmeter, measure voltage between ground and CTM 18-pin connector C2 terminal No. 6 (Red/Dark Blue wire). If voltage is more than 9.5 volts, replace CTM. If voltage is 9.5 volts or less, repair open in Red/Dark Blue wire between CTM and security relay.

9) Disconnect overhead console 12-pin connector. Using an external voltmeter, measure voltage between battery and overhead console 12-pin connector terminal No. 11 (Black wire). Using scan tool, actuate VTSS indicator light. If voltage is about 10 volts, replace overhead console. If voltage is not about 10 volts, go to next step.

10) Measure voltage between ground and overhead console 12-pin connector terminal No. 5 (Pink wire). Turn ignition on. If voltage is more than 10 volts, go to next step. If voltage is 10 volts or less, repair open Pink wire.

11) Locate Central Timer Module (CTM). CTM is located behind right kick panel. Disconnect CTM 18-pin connector C2. Turn ignition on. Using an external ohmmeter, measure resistance between ground and CTM 18-pin connector C2 terminal No. 8 (Black wire). If resistance is 5 ohms or more, replace CTM. If resistance is less than 5 ohms, repair open Black wire between CTM and VTSS indicator light.

12) Using scan tool, place VTSS in diagnostic mode and follow directions on screen. If TURN KEY TO ACC POSITION is not displayed, go to step **24)**. If NO RESPONSE after turning key to accessory position or TURN KEY TO ACC POSITION is displayed longer than 15 seconds, go to next step. If neither response is received, go to step **14)**.

13) Locate Central Timer Module (CTM). CTM is located behind right kick panel. Gain access to CTM 18-pin connector C2. Ensure key is in accessory position. Using an external voltmeter, measure voltage between ground and backprobe of CTM 18-pin connector C2 terminal No. 5 (Dark Blue/White wire). If voltage is more than 10 volts, replace CTM. If voltage is 10 volts or less, repair open Dark Blue/White wire between CTM and junction block.

14) Remove key from ignition. Wait 2 seconds after performing each of the following actions. Open, then close both door. Operate power door lock switch to lock, then unlock position. Rotate key both directions in both doors. Ensure each operation is successful. If any operation is unsuccessful, see VTSS SYMPTOM DIRECTORY table for repair of failed operation. If all operations are successful, go to step **22)**.

CHRY
4-206

1999 ACCESSORIES & EQUIPMENT
Body Control Computer Tests – Ram Pickup (Cont.)

VTSS SYMPTOM DIRECTORY

Problem Circuit	Go To
Driver's Door Open Or Close	Step 15
Passenger's Door Open Or Close	Step 16
Driver's Door Lock Switch .... ONE OR ALL DOORS FAILING TO LOCK FROM ONE SWITCH	
Passenger's Door Lock Switch .... ONE OR ALL DOORS FAILING TO LOCK FROM ONE SWITCH	
Driver's Key Cylinder	Step 17
Passenger's Key Cylinder	Step 20
Driver's Door Unlock Switch .... ONE OR ALL DOORS FAILING TO UNLOCK FROM ONE SWITCH	
Passenger's Door Unlock Switch .... ONE OR ALL DOORS FAILING TO UNLOCK FROM ONE SWITCH	

15) Ensure driver's door is closed. Using scan tool, read VTSS inputs/outputs door ajar status. If scan tool displays DR DOOR AJAR SWITCH: CLOSED, go to SHORTED LEFT DOOR AJAR CIRCUIT under DOOR AJAR SYSTEM. If scan tool does not display DR DOOR AJAR SWITCH: CLOSED, go to OPEN LEFT DOOR AJAR CIRCUIT under DOOR AJAR SYSTEM.

16) Ensure passenger's door is closed. Using scan tool, read VTSS inputs/outputs door ajar status. If scan tool displays DR DOOR AJAR SWITCH: CLOSED, go to SHORTED RIGHT DOOR AJAR CIRCUIT under DOOR AJAR SYSTEM. If scan tool does not display DR DOOR AJAR SWITCH: CLOSED, go to OPEN RIGHT DOOR AJAR CIRCUIT under DOOR AJAR SYSTEM.

17) Using scan tool, monitor door disarm switch state. Disconnect left door disarm switch. Connect jumper wire between left door disarm switch connector terminals. If scan tool displays door disarm switch state CLOSED, replace left door disarm switch. If scan tool does not display door disarm switch state CLOSED, go to next step.

18) Disconnect jumper wire. Connect jumper wire between ground and left door disarm switch connector Light Green/Orange wire. If scan tool displays door disarm switch state CLOSED, go to next step. If scan tool does not display door disarm switch state CLOSED, repair open left door disarm switch ground circuit (Black/Light Green wire).

19) Access Central Timer Module (CTM). CTM is located behind right kick panel. Remove connector cover. Do not disconnect connector. Connect a jumper between ground and backprobe CTM 18-pin connector C2 terminal No. 10 (Light Green/Orange wire). If scan tool displays door disarm switch state CLOSED, repair open left door disarm switch sense circuit (Light Green/Orange wire). If scan tool does not display door disarm switch state CLOSED, replace CTM.

20) Using scan tool, monitor door disarm switch state. Disconnect right door disarm switch. Connect jumper wire between right door disarm switch connector terminals. If scan tool displays door disarm switch state CLOSED, replace right door disarm switch. If scan tool does not display door disarm switch state CLOSED, go to next step.

21) Disconnect jumper wire. Connect jumper wire between ground and right door disarm switch connector Light Green/Orange wire. If scan tool displays door disarm switch state CLOSED, go to next step. If scan tool does not display door disarm switch state CLOSED, repair open right door disarm switch ground circuit (Black/Light Green wire).

22) Access Central Timer Module (CTM). CTM is located behind right kick panel. Remove connector cover. Do not disconnect connector. Connect a jumper between ground and backprobe CTM 18-pin connector C2 terminal No. 10 (Light Green/Orange wire). If scan tool displays door disarm switch state CLOSED, repair open right door disarm switch sense circuit (Light Green/Orange wire). If scan tool does not display door disarm switch state CLOSED, replace CTM.

23) Turn ignition switch to START position. If horn does not sound, go to next step. If horn sounds, go to step **24)**.

24) Locate Central Timer Module (CTM). CTM is located behind right kick panel. Disconnect CTM 14-pin connector C1. Using an external voltmeter, measure voltage between ground and CTM 14-pin connector

C1 terminal No. 8 (Dark Blue/White wire). If voltage is more than 10 volts, replace CTM. If voltage is 10 volts or less, repair open Dark Blue/White wire between CTM and RUN-ACC fuse in junction block.

WINDSHIELD WIPER SYSTEM

WIPER PARK SWITCH FAILURE

NOTE: For connector terminal identification and wiring diagrams, see BODY CONTROL COMPUTER – INTRODUCTION article. Perform VERIFICATION TEST VER-1A after each repair.

CAUTION: Always turn ignition switch to OFF position prior to disconnecting or connecting any module connector.

NOTE: It takes 8 seconds for wiper park switch failure DTC to set.

1) Using scan tool, clear DTCs. See appropriate SELF-DIAGNOSTICS article. Operate wipers in low speed, then intermittent mode. Reread DTCs. If WIPER PARK SWITCH FAILURE is displayed, go to next step. If WIPER PARK SWITCH FAILURE is not displayed, system is currently functioning properly.

2) Gain access to wiper motor connector. Using an external voltmeter, measure voltage between ground and wiper motor terminal No. 2 (Dark Green wire). If voltage is more than 9 volts, go to next step. If voltage is 9 volts or less, replace wiper motor.

3) Locate Central Timer Module (CTM). CTM is located under left side of instrument panel. Using an external voltmeter, measure voltage between ground and backprobe of CTM 14-pin Green connector C1 terminal No. 11 (Dark Green wire). If voltage is 9 volts or less, replace CTM. If voltage is more than 9 volts, repair short to voltage in Dark Green wire between CTM and wiper relay or wiper motor.

INTERMITTENT WIPERS INOPERATIVE

NOTE: For connector terminal identification and wiring diagrams, see BODY CONTROL COMPUTER – INTRODUCTION article. Perform VERIFICATION TEST VER-1A after each repair.

CAUTION: Always turn ignition switch to OFF position prior to disconnecting or connecting any module connector.

1) Using scan tool select CENTRAL TIMER MODULE. If scan tool displays NO RESPONSE, go to appropriate VEHICLE COMMUNICATIONS article. If scan tool displays any CCD bus failure message, go to SYMPTOM IDENTIFICATION. If scan tool does not display NO RESPONSE or any CCD bus failure message, go to next step.

2) If problem is wipers parking in wrong position, go to next step. If problem is not wipers parking in wrong position, go to step **5)**.

3) Gain access to wiper motor connector. Turn wipers on to low speed. Using an external voltmeter, measure voltage between ground and wiper motor switch terminal No. 2 (Dark Green wire). If voltage does not cycle between zero and 12 volts, replace wiper motor. If voltage cycles between zero and 12 volts, go to next step.

4) Locate Central Timer Module (CTM). CTM is located under left side of instrument panel. Using an external voltmeter, measure voltage between ground and backprobe of CTM 14-pin Green connector C1 terminal No. 11 (Dark Green wire). Wipers should be operating at low speed. If voltage does not cycle between zero and 12 volts, repair open Dark Green wire between CTM and wiper relay or wiper motor. If voltage cycles between zero and 10 volts, replace CTM.

5) Using scan tool, monitor intermittent wiper voltage level. Rotate wiper switch from low intermittent to high intermittent level. If voltage changes from approximately 2.5 to 12 volts, replace CTM. If voltage does not change from approximately 2.5 to 12 volts, go to next step.

6) Disconnect 24-pin multifunction switch connector. Using an external ohmmeter, measure resistance of White/Dark Blue wire between multifunction switch connector terminal No. 1 and CTM 14-pin Green connector C1 terminal No. 12. if resistance is less than 5 ohms, replace multifunction switch. If resistance is 5 ohms or more, repair open White/Dark Blue wire between multifunction switch and CTM.

1999 ACCESSORIES & EQUIPMENT
Body Control Computer Tests – Ram Pickup (Cont.)

CHRY
4-207

NO WIPER ACTUATION AFTER WASH BUTTON PUSHED

NOTE: For connector terminal identification and wiring diagrams, see BODY CONTROL COMPUTER – INTRODUCTION article. Perform VERIFICATION TEST VER-1A after each repair.

CAUTION: Always turn ignition switch to OFF position prior to disconnecting or connecting any module connector.

1) Using scan tool select Central Timer Module (CTM). If scan tool displays NO RESPONSE, go to appropriate VEHICLE COMMUNICATIONS article. If scan tool displays any CCD bus failure message, go to SYMPTOM IDENTIFICATION. If scan tool does not display NO RESPONSE or any CCD bus failure message, go to next step.

2) Turn ignition on. If washer system works, go to next step. If washer system does not work, see appropriate WIPER/WASHER SYSTEMS article.

3) Using scan tool, actuate washer. If washer pump sense displays ON, replace CTM. If washer pump sense does not display ON, repair open Brown wire between CTM 14-pin connector C1 terminal No. 10 and multifunction switch.

WIPER SPEED SENSITIVE FEATURE INOPERATIVE

NOTE: For connector terminal identification and wiring diagrams, see BODY CONTROL COMPUTER – INTRODUCTION article. Perform VERIFICATION TEST VER-1A after each repair.

CAUTION: Always turn ignition switch to OFF position prior to disconnecting or connecting any module connector.

1) Using scan tool select Central timer module (CTM). If scan tool display is not blank or have a CCD bus failure message, go to next step. If scan tool display is blank or has a CCD bus failure message, see appropriate VEHICLE COMMUNICATIONS article.

2) Using scan tool, select Powertrain Control Module (PCM). If scan tool display is not blank or have a CCD bus failure message, go to next step. If scan tool display is blank or has a CCD bus failure message, see appropriate VEHICLE COMMUNICATIONS article.

3) Raise and support vehicle. Turn wipers on to lowest intermittent position. Time interval between wipes. Spin rear wheels to more than 15 MPH. If interval between wipes decreased to approximately 18 seconds, system is currently functioning properly. If interval between wipes did not decrease to approximately 18 seconds, replace CTM.

VERIFICATION TEST VER-1A

BODY VERIFICATION TEST

1) Reconnect all previously disconnected components and connectors. Turn ignition on. If entry module was replaced, program all RKE transmitters and program other options as necessary.

2) Ensure ignition is on. Erase all DTCs using scan tool. Turn ignition off and wait 5 seconds. Turn ignition on and fully operate system that was malfunctioning.

3) If system is not operating properly, go to SYMPTOM IDENTIFICATION. If system is operating correctly and customer's complaint cannot be duplicated, repair is complete.

1999 ACCESSORIES & EQUIPMENT
Body Control Computer Tests – Ram Van & Ram Wagon

NOTE: See BODY CONTROL COMPUTER – INTRODUCTION article before proceeding with following test. Body control computer in Ram Van and Ram Wagon is the Central Timer Module (CTM).

SYMPTOM IDENTIFICATION

IDENTIFYING VEHICLE EQUIPMENT & SYSTEM PROBLEMS

NOTE: For connector terminal identification wiring diagrams, see BODY CONTROL COMPUTER – INTRODUCTION article.

NOTE: Perform a visual inspection before proceeding with this test. Ensure battery is fully charged.

1) Connect scan tool to Data Link Connector (DLC). DLC is a 16-pin connector located under left side of dash, to left of steering wheel. Turn ignition switch to ON position. If scan tool display is not blank, go to next step. If scan tool display is blank, see appropriate VEHICLE COMMUNICATIONS article.

2) Using scan tool, select SYSTEM MONITORS, then CCD BUS TEST. Scan tool will perform a CCD bus test. If scan tool displays BUS OPERATIONAL, go to next step. If scan tool displays any message except BUS OPERATIONAL, see appropriate VEHICLE COMMUNICATIONS article.

3) Using scan tool, select READ DTCs. If any Diagnostic Trouble Codes (fault messages) are present, go to appropriate fault message. If no fault messages are present, identify customer complaint. See following list for possible fault messages and customer complaint symptoms. Problems listed are diagnosed using a scan tool. These problems may occur separately or in various combinations. When diagnosing a system with many apparent problems, a sequence of tests may be required. After repairs, ensure problem(s) or failure(s) have been corrected.

CHIME SYSTEM
- CHIME INOPERATIVE AT ALL TIMES
- CHIME INOPERATIVE WITH ANY WARNING LIGHT ON
- CHIME INOPERATIVE WITH EXTERIOR LIGHTS ON
- CHIME INOPERATIVE – KEY IN IGNITION & DRIVER'S DOOR OPEN
- CHIME INOPERATIVE WITH ONLY ONE WARNING LIGHT CONDITION
- CHIME REMAINS ON WITH IGNITION ON
- CHIME SOUNDS WITH DRIVER DOOR OPEN

DOOR AJAR SYSTEM
- OPEN AUXILIARY DOOR (SIDE OR REAR) AJAR, (ILLUMINATED ENTRY INOPERATIVE FROM EITHER AUXILIARY DOOR)
- OPEN DRIVER DOOR AJAR CIRCUIT (COURTESY LIGHTS INOPERATIVE FROM LEFT FRONT DOOR)
- OPEN PASSENGER DOOR AJAR CIRCUIT (COURTESY LIGHTS INOPERATIVE FROM RIGHT FRONT DOOR)
- SHORTED AUXILIARY DOOR (SIDE OR REAR) AJAR
- SHORTED DRIVER DOOR AJAR CIRCUIT
- SHORTED PASSENGER DOOR AJAR CIRCUIT

INSTRUMENT CLUSTER
- ALL GAUGES INOPERATIVE
- ANY CCD CLUSTER LIGHT INOPERATIVE
- ANY HARD WIRED LIGHT INOPERATIVE
- ONE GAUGE NOT OPERATING PROPERLY

INTERIOR LIGHTING SYSTEM
- COURTESY LIGHTS INOPERATIVE FROM ALL DOORS & COURTESY LIGHT SWITCH
- COURTESY LIGHTS INOPERATIVE FROM BOTH FRONT DOORS (ILLUMINATED ENTRY INOPERATIVE)
- COURTESY LIGHTS INOPERATIVE FROM COURTESY LIGHT SWITCH
- COURTESY LIGHTS INOPERATIVE FROM EITHER AUXILIARY DOOR
- COURTESY LIGHTS ON AT ALL TIMES

POWER DOOR LOCKS/RKE SYSTEM
- DOOR LOCK SWITCH FAILURE (ALL DOORS FAILING TO LOCK & UNLOCK FROM ONE SWITCH, ALL DOORS FAILING TO LOCK FROM ONE SWITCH)
- DOOR UNLOCK SWITCH FAILURE (ALL DOORS FAILING TO UNLOCK FROM ONE SWITCH)
- ALL DOORS FAILING TO LOCK/UNLOCK FROM ANY SWITCH
- ALL DOORS FAILING TO LOCK FROM ANY SWITCH
- ALL DOORS FAILING TO UNLOCK FROM ANY SWITCH
- AUXILIARY DOORS FAIL TO LOCK
- CANCELLING HORN CHIRP
- CHANGING HORN CHIRP DURATION
- DOOR LOCK INHIBIT INOPERATIVE
- HORN CHIRP INOPERATIVE (W/CHIRP ENABLED)
- ONE DOOR FAILING TO LOCK/UNLOCK FROM ANY SWITCH
- PROGRAMMING A TRANSMITTER
- REMOTE KEYLESS ENTRY (RKE) INOPERATIVE
- TEST AUTOMATIC (ROLLING) DOOR LOCKS

VEHICLE THEFT/SECURITY SYSTEM
- DOOR DISARM SWITCH FAILURE
- DOOR LOCK SWITCH FAILURE
- DOOR UNLOCK SWITCH FAILURE
- IDENTIFYING VTSS PROBLEMS

WINDSHIELD WIPER SYSTEM
- WIPER PARK SWITCH FAILURE
- INTERMITTENT WIPERS INOPERATIVE OR ERRATIC
- NO WIPE AFTER WASHERS ACTUATED
- WIPER SPEED SENSITIVE INOPERATIVE

CHIME SYSTEM

CHIME INOPERATIVE AT ALL TIMES

NOTE: Perform VERIFICATION TEST VER-1A after each repair.

Turn ignition on. Using scan tool, select BODY SYSTEM, BODY COMPUTER then ACTUATORS. Actuate chime. Proceed to EXTERNAL CHIME. If both chimes sound, system is currently functioning correctly. If one or both chimes do not sound, replace Central Timer Module (CTM). CTM is located on left side of engine cover under dash.

CHIME INOPERATIVE WITH ANY WARNING LIGHT ON

NOTE: For connector terminal identification and wiring diagrams, see BODY CONTROL COMPUTER – INTRODUCTION article. Perform VERIFICATION TEST VER-1A after each repair.

CAUTION: Always turn ignition switch to OFF position prior to disconnecting or connecting any module connector.

1) Disconnect instrument cluster. Turn ignition on. Connect jumper wire between ground and instrument cluster Gray connector terminal No. 4 (Dark Blue/Red wire). If chime stays on, replace instrument cluster. If chime does not stay on, go to next step.

2) Ensure ignition is off. With jumper wire still connected. Disconnect Central Timer Module (CTM) Green connector C1. CTM is located on left side of engine cover under dash. Using external ohmmeter, measure resistance between ground and CTM Green connector C1 terminal No.

1999 ACCESSORIES & EQUIPMENT
Body Control Computer Tests – Ram Van & Ram Wagon (Cont.)

CHRY
4-209

2 (Dark Blue/Red wire). If resistance is more than 5 ohms, repair open Dark Blue/Red wire between CTM and instrument cluster. If resistance is 5 ohms or less, replace CTM.

CHIME INOPERATIVE WITH EXTERIOR LIGHTS ON

NOTE: *For connector terminal identification and wiring diagrams, see BODY CONTROL COMPUTER – INTRODUCTION article. Perform VERIFICATION TEST VER-1A after each repair.*

CAUTION: *Always turn ignition switch to OFF position prior to disconnecting any module connector.*

1) Turn on headlights. Open driver door. If chime does not sound, go to next step. If chime sounds, system is currently functioning correctly.
2) Place key in ignition switch in OFF position. Using scan tool, read key-in ignition chime state. If scan tool does not display KEY-IN IGNITION CHIME STATE: ON, go to CHIME INOPERATIVE – KEY IN IGNITION & DRIVER'S DOOR OPEN. If scan tool displays KEY-IN IGNITION CHIME STATE: ON, go to next step.
3) Using scan tool, read driver door ajar switch status. Open and close driver's door. If scan tool driver's door ajar switch status does not change from OPEN to CLOSED, go to OPEN DRIVER DOOR AJAR CIRCUIT (COURTESY LIGHTS INOPERATIVE FROM LEFT FRONT DOOR) under DOOR AJAR SYSTEM.

CHIME INOPERATIVE – KEY IN IGNITION & DRIVER'S DOOR OPEN

NOTE: *For connector terminal identification and wiring diagrams, see BODY CONTROL COMPUTER – INTRODUCTION article. Perform VERIFICATION TEST VER-1A after each repair.*

CAUTION: *Always turn ignition switch to OFF position prior to disconnecting any module connector.*

1) Turn ignition off. Open driver's door. If chime does not sound, go to next step. If chime sounds, system is currently functioning correctly.
2) Using scan tool, read driver's door ajar switch status. Open and close driver's door. If scan tool driver's door ajar switch status does not change from OPEN to CLOSED, go to DOOR AJAR SYSTEM and review symptoms and fault messages. If scan tool driver's door ajar switch status changes from OPEN to CLOSED, go to next step.
3) Using scan tool, read key-in ignition chime state. If scan tool does not display KEY-IN IGNITION CHIME STATE: ON, go to next step. If scan tool displays KEY-IN IGNITION CHIME STATE: ON, replace Central Timer Module (CTM). CTM is located on left side of engine cover under dash.
4) Ensure key is in ignition. Disconnect CTM Green connector C1. CTM is located on left side of engine cover under dash. Using external ohmmeter, measure resistance between ground and CTM Green connector C1 terminal No. 9 (Light Blue wire). If resistance is less than 5 ohms, replace CTM. If resistance is 5 ohms or more, go to next step.
5) Connect jumper wire between ground and CTM Green connector C1 terminal No. 9 (Light Blue wire). Disconnect steering column connector. Measure resistance between ground and steering column harness connector terminal No. B4 (Light Blue wire). If resistance is less than 5 ohms, replace ignition switch. If resistance is 5 ohms or more, repair open Light Blue wire between CTM and ignition switch.

CHIME INOPERATIVE WITH ONLY ONE WARNING LIGHT CONDITION

NOTE: *For connector terminal identification and wiring diagrams, see BODY CONTROL COMPUTER – INTRODUCTION article. Perform VERIFICATION TEST VER-1A after each repair.*

CAUTION: *Always turn ignition switch to OFF position prior to disconnecting any module connector.*

1) Identify inoperative chime circuit by identifying which light is on. See WARNING LIGHT CONDITION table. If warning light is not listed in WARNING LIGHT CONDITION table, system is currently functioning correctly.

WARNING LIGHT CONDITION

Light	Perform
Low Fuel	[1] ANY CCD CLUSTER LIGHT INOPERATIVE
Air Bag Warning	[1] ANY CCD CLUSTER LIGHT INOPERATIVE
Seat Belt Warning	[1] ANY HARD WIRED LIGHT INOPERATIVE
Anti Lock Brake System (ABS)	[1] ANY HARD WIRED LIGHT INOPERATIVE
Low Washer Fluid Warning	[1] ANY HARD WIRED LIGHT INOPERATIVE
CHECK ENGINE (MIL) W/Low Oil Pressure	Step **2)**
CHECK ENGINE (MIL) W/High Engine Temperature	Step **4)**
Transmission Temperature	[1] ANY HARD WIRED LIGHT INOPERATIVE

[1] – Under INSTRUMENT CLUSTER.

2) Disconnect Oil Pressure Switch (OPS). OPS is located near bottom of distributor. Connect a jumper wire between OPS connector terminals. If oil pressure warning light illuminated, replace oil pressure sensor. If oil pressure warning light did not illuminate, go to next step.
3) Turn ignition off. Disconnect PCM White connector C2. PCM is located in engine compartment on right inner fender. Using an external ohmmeter, measure resistance between ground and PCM White connector terminal No. 23 (Gray wire). If resistance is less than 5 ohms, replace PCM. If resistance is 5 ohms or more, repair short to ground in Gray wire.
4) Ensure cooling system is functioning correctly. If cooling system is functioning correctly, go to next step. If cooling system is not functioning correctly, repair cooling system as necessary.
5) Using scan tool, select BODY, SYSTEMS TESTS then PCM MONITOR. If scan tool displays PCM ACTIVE ON BUS, go to next step. If scan tool does not display PCM ACTIVE ON BUS, go to appropriate VEHICLE COMMUNICATIONS article.
6) Select MODULE ENGINE CONTROLLER. Read PCM DTCs. If scan tool displays ECT SENSOR VOLTAGE TOO HIGH, see appropriate SELF-DIAGNOSTICS article in ENGINE PERFORMANCE in appropriate MITCHELL® manual. If scan tool does not display ECT SENSOR VOLTAGE TOO HIGH, go to next step.
7) If scan tool displays ECT SENSOR VOLTAGE TOO LOW, see appropriate SELF-DIAGNOSTICS article in ENGINE PERFORMANCE in appropriate MITCHELL® manual. If scan tool does not display ECT SENSOR VOLTAGE TOO LOW, replace PCM.

CHIME REMAINS ON WITH IGNITION ON

NOTE: *For connector terminal identification and wiring diagrams, see BODY CONTROL COMPUTER – INTRODUCTION article. Perform VERIFICATION TEST VER-1A after each repair.*

CAUTION: *Always turn ignition switch to OFF position prior to disconnecting any module connector.*

1) Inspect instrument for any indicator lights or gauges showing a chime condition. If any indicator lights or gauges show a chime condition, diagnosis cause of light or gauge chime and repair as necessary. If no indicator lights or gauges show a chime condition, go to next step.
2) Using scan tool, read chime status. If scan tool does not display chime status OFF, go to next step. If scan tool displays chime status OFF, replace CTM. CTM is located on left side of engine cover.
3) Remove instrument cluster. See appropriate INSTRUMENT PANELS article. If chime stopped, replace instrument cluster. If chime did not stop, go to next step.
4) Disconnect CTM Green connector C1. Using external ohmmeter, measure resistance between ground and terminal No. 2 (Dark Blue/Red

CHRY
4-210

1999 ACCESSORIES & EQUIPMENT
Body Control Computer Tests – Ram Van & Ram Wagon (Cont.)

wire). If resistance is 1000 ohms or more, system is currently functioning correctly, retest system. If resistance is less than 1000 ohms, repair Dark Blue/Red wire between CTM and instrument cluster for short to ground.

CHIME SOUNDS WITH DRIVER DOOR OPEN

NOTE: *For connector terminal identification and wiring diagrams, see* BODY CONTROL COMPUTER – INTRODUCTION *article. Perform* VERIFICATION TEST VER-1A *after each repair.*

CAUTION: *Always turn ignition switch to OFF position prior to disconnecting any module connector.*

1) Ensure all interior and exterior lights are off. Remove ignition key and open driver's door. If chime does not sound, system is currently functioning correctly. If chime sounds, go to next step.
2) Using scan tool, read key-in ignition chime state. If scan tool displays KEY-IN IGNITION CHIME STATE: "ON", go to next step. If scan tool does not display KEY-IN IGNITION CHIME STATE: "ON", replace Central Timer Module (CTM). CTM is located under left center of instrument panel.
3) Turn ignition on. Using scan tool, rear DRDOOR AJAR SWITCH status. Open and close driver's door while monitoring scan tool. If DRDOOR AJAR SWITCH status changes from OPEN to CLOSED, go to next step. If DRDOOR AJAR SWITCH status does not change from OPEN to CLOSED, adjust door and retest. If DRDOOR AJAR SWITCH status does not change from OPEN to CLOSED, go to SHORTED DRIVER DOOR AJAR CIRCUIT.
4) Turn ignition off. Remove ignition key. Ensure all lights and accessories are off. Close all doors. Disconnect CTM Green connector C1. CTM is located on left side of engine cover under dash. Using external ohmmeter, measure resistance between ground and CTM Green connector C1 terminal No. 9 (Light Blue wire). If resistance is 150 ohms or less, repair short to ground in Light Blue wire. If resistance is more than 150 ohms, go to next step.
5) Measure resistance between ground and CTM Green connector C1 terminal No. 1 (Black/Light Blue wire). If resistance is 150 ohms or less, repair short to ground in Black/Light Blue wire. If resistance is more than 150 ohms, replace CTM.

DOOR AJAR SYSTEM

OPEN AUXILIARY DOOR (SIDE OR REAR) AJAR, (ILLUMINATED ENTRY INOPERATIVE FROM EITHER AUXILIARY DOOR)

NOTE: *For connector terminal identification and wiring diagrams, see* BODY CONTROL COMPUTER – INTRODUCTION *article. Perform* VERIFICATION TEST VER-1A *after each repair.*

CAUTION: *Always turn ignition switch to OFF position prior to disconnecting any module connector.*

1) Disconnect inoperative auxiliary door ajar switch and ensure connector is clean and not damaged. Connect a jumper wire between ground and auxiliary door ajar switch connector Brown/Tan wire. Using scan tool, read auxiliary door ajar switch status. If scan tool displays AUXILIARY DOOR SWITCH: CLOSED, replace auxiliary door ajar switch. If scan tool does not display AUXILIARY DOOR SWITCH: CLOSED, go to next step.
2) Do not remove jumper wire. Disconnect Central Timer Module (CTM) 18-pin White connector C2. CTM is located on left side of engine cover. Using an external ohmmeter, measure resistance between ground and CTM 18-pin White connector C2 terminal No. 15 (Brown/Tan wire). If resistance is less than 5 ohms, replace CTM. If resistance is 5 ohms or more, repair open Brown/Tan wire.

OPEN DRIVER DOOR AJAR CIRCUIT (COURTESY LIGHTS INOPERATIVE FROM LEFT FRONT DOOR)

NOTE: *For connector terminal identification and wiring diagrams, see* BODY CONTROL COMPUTER – INTRODUCTION *article. Perform* VERIFICATION TEST VER-1A *after each repair.*

CAUTION: *Always turn ignition switch to OFF position prior to disconnecting any module connector.*

1) Remove driver's door panel. Disconnect driver's door ajar switch and ensure connector is clean and not damaged. Connect a jumper wire between driver's door ajar switch connector Black wire and Black/Light Blue wire. Using scan tool, read left front door ajar switch status. If scan tool displays DRDOOR AJAR SW: CLOSED, replace driver's door ajar switch. If scan tool does not display DRDOOR AJAR SW: CLOSED, go to next step.
2) Disconnect jumper wire from Black wire. Take jumper wire end removed from Black wire and connect to ground. If scan tool displays DRDOOR AJAR SW: CLOSED, repair open ground circuit (Black wire). If scan tool does not display DRDOOR AJAR SW: CLOSED, go to next step.
3) Disconnect CTM Green connector C1. CTM is located on left side of engine cover under dash. Using an external ohmmeter, measure resistance between ground and CTM Green connector C1 terminal No. 1 (Black/Light Blue wire). If resistance is less than 5 ohms, replace CTM. If resistance is 5 ohms or more, repair open Black/Light Blue wire.

OPEN PASSENGER DOOR AJAR CIRCUIT (COURTESY LIGHTS INOPERATIVE FROM RIGHT FRONT DOOR)

NOTE: *For connector terminal identification and wiring diagrams, see* BODY CONTROL COMPUTER – INTRODUCTION *article. Perform* VERIFICATION TEST VER-1A *after each repair.*

CAUTION: *Always turn ignition switch to OFF position prior to disconnecting any module connector.*

1) Remove passenger's door panel. Disconnect passenger's door ajar switch and ensure connector is clean and not damaged. Connect a jumper wire between passenger's door ajar switch connector Yellow wire and Black wire. Using scan tool, read passenger's door ajar switch status. If scan tool displays PASSDOOR AJAR SW: CLOSED, replace passenger's door ajar switch. If scan tool does not display PASSDOOR AJAR SW: CLOSED, go to next step.
2) Disconnect jumper from Black wire. Take jumper wire end removed from Black wire and connect to ground. If scan tool displays PASSDOOR AJAR SWITCH: CLOSED, repair open ground circuit (Black wire). If scan tool does not display PASSDOOR AJAR SW: CLOSED, go to next step.
3) Locate Central Timer Module (CTM). CTM is located under left center of instrument panel. Disconnect CTM Green connector C1. Using an external ohmmeter, measure resistance between ground and CTM Green connector C1 terminal No. 5 (Tan/Red wire). If resistance is less than 5 ohms, replace CTM. If resistance is 5 ohms or more, repair open Tan/Red wire.

SHORTED AUXILIARY DOOR (SIDE OR REAR) AJAR

NOTE: *For connector terminal identification and wiring diagrams, see* BODY CONTROL COMPUTER – INTRODUCTION *article. Perform* VERIFICATION TEST VER-1A *after each repair.*

CAUTION: *Always turn ignition switch to OFF position prior to disconnecting any module connector.*

1) Remove side auxiliary door panel. Disconnect side auxiliary door ajar switch connector. Using scan tool, read auxiliary door ajar switch status. If scan tool displays AUXILIARY DOOR SWITCH: CLOSED, go to next

step. If scan tool does not display AUXILIARY DOOR SWITCH: CLOSED, replace side auxiliary door ajar switch.

2) Remove rear auxiliary door panel. Disconnect rear auxiliary door ajar switch connector. Using scan tool, read auxiliary door ajar switch status. If scan tool displays AUXILIARY DOOR SWITCH: CLOSED, go to next step. If scan tool does not display AUXILIARY DOOR SWITCH: CLOSED, replace rear auxiliary door ajar switch.

3) Disconnect Central Timer Module (CTM) 18-pin White connector C2. CTM is located on left side of engine cover. Using an external ohmmeter, measure resistance between ground and CTM 18-pin White connector C2 terminal No. 15 (Brown/Tan wire). If resistance is less than 5 ohms, repair short to ground in Brown/Tan wire. If resistance is 5 ohms or more, replace CTM.

SHORTED DRIVER DOOR AJAR CIRCUIT

NOTE: For connector terminal identification and wiring diagrams, see BODY CONTROL COMPUTER – INTRODUCTION article. Perform VERIFICATION TEST VER-1A after each repair.

CAUTION: Always turn ignition switch to OFF position prior to disconnecting any module connector.

1) Remove driver's door panel. Disconnect driver's door ajar switch. Using scan tool, read driver's door ajar switch status. If scan tool displays DRDOOR AJAR SW: CLOSED, go to next step. If scan tool does not display DRDOOR AJAR SW: CLOSED, replace driver's door ajar switch.

2) Disconnect Central Timer Module (CTM) 14-pin Green connector C1. CTM is located under left center of instrument panel. Using an external ohmmeter, measure resistance between ground and CTM 14-pin Green connector C1 terminal No. 1 (Black/Light Blue wire). If resistance is less than 5 ohms, repair short to ground in Black/Light Blue wire between CTM 14-pin connector C1 and driver's door ajar switch. If resistance is 5 ohms or more, replace CTM.

SHORTED PASSENGER DOOR AJAR CIRCUIT

NOTE: For connector terminal identification and wiring diagrams, see BODY CONTROL COMPUTER – INTRODUCTION article. Perform VERIFICATION TEST VER-1A after each repair.

CAUTION: Always turn ignition switch to OFF position prior to disconnecting any module connector.

1) Ensure all doors are closed. Open passenger's door and remove door panel. Disconnect passenger's door ajar switch. Using scan tool, read passenger's door ajar switch status. If scan tool displays PASSDOOR AJAR SW: CLOSED, go to next step. If scan tool does not display PASSDOOR AJAR SW: CLOSED, replace passenger's door ajar switch.

2) Disconnect Central Timer Module (CTM) 14-pin Green connector C1. CTM is located under left center of instrument panel. Using an external ohmmeter, measure resistance between ground and CTM 14-pin Green connector C1 terminal No. 5 (Tan/Red wire). If resistance is less than 5 ohms, repair short to ground in Tan/Red wire. If resistance is 5 ohms or more, replace CTM.

INSTRUMENT CLUSTER

ALL GAUGES INOPERATIVE

NOTE: For connector terminal identification and wiring diagrams, see BODY CONTROL COMPUTER – INTRODUCTION article. Perform VERIFICATION TEST VER-1A after each repair.

CAUTION: Always turn ignition switch to OFF position prior to disconnecting or connecting any module connector.

1) Turn ignition on. Using scan tool, select ELECTRO/MECH CLUSTER (MIC). If scan tool displays NO RESPONSE, go to appropriate VEHICLE COMMUNICATIONS article. If scan tool displays any bus failure mes-

sage, go to SYMPTOM IDENTIFICATION. If scan tool does not display NO RESPONSE or bus failure message, go to next step.

2) Using scan tool, select SYSTEM TEST. If scan tool displays PCM INACTIVE ON BUS, go to appropriate VEHICLE COMMUNICATIONS article. If scan tool does not display PCM INACTIVE ON BUS, go to next step.

3) Remove and inspect fuse No. 11. Fuse No. 11 is located in junction block behind left kick panel. If fuse is okay, go to next step. If fuse is open, go to appropriate VEHICLE COMMUNICATIONS article.

4) Disconnect scan tool from Data Link Connector (DLC). Ensure ground circuit has continuity at DLC terminal No. 4. Ensure 12 volts exists at DLC terminal No. 16. If 12 volts does not exist, check junction block fuse No. 14. If scan tool is still blank, try another scan tool and/or cable. If scan tool is not blank, go to next step.

5) Turn ignition off. Remove instrument cluster. See appropriate INSTRUMENT PANELS article. Turn ignition on. Using external voltmeter, measure voltage between ground and instrument cluster connector C1 terminal No. 2 (Dark Blue/White wire). If voltage is 10 volts or less, repair open Dark Blue/White wire. If voltage is more than 10 volts, replace instrument cluster.

ANY CCD CLUSTER LIGHT INOPERATIVE

NOTE: For connector terminal identification and wiring diagrams, see BODY CONTROL COMPUTER – INTRODUCTION article. Perform VERIFICATION TEST VER-1A after each repair.

CAUTION: Always turn ignition switch to OFF position prior to disconnecting or connecting any module connector.

1) Turn ignition on. Using scan tool, select ELECTRO/MECH CLUSTER (MIC). If scan tool displays NO RESPONSE, go to appropriate VEHICLE COMMUNICATIONS article. If scan tool displays any bus failure message, go to SYMPTOM IDENTIFICATION. If scan tool does not display NO RESPONSE or bus failure message, go to next step.

2) Using scan tool, select SYSTEM TEST. If scan tool displays PCM INACTIVE ON BUS, go to appropriate VEHICLE COMMUNICATIONS article. If scan tool does not display PCM INACTIVE ON BUS, go to next step.

3) Push and hold RESET button while cycling ignition key. Release RESET button when CHEC appears in odometer display. Observe inoperative light during self-test. If inoperative light did not illuminate during self-test, go to step 5). If inoperative light illuminated during self-test, go to next step.

4) Verify if light is controlled by an input to instrument cluster. See appropriate wiring diagram in BODY CONTROL COMPUTER – INTRODUCTION article. If light is controlled by an input to instrument cluster, go to appropriate circuits article or symptom test. See IDENTIFYING VEHICLE EQUIPMENT & SYSTEM PROBLEMS. If light is not controlled by an input to instrument cluster, system is currently functioning correctly.

5) Gain access to instrument cluster. See appropriate INSTRUMENT PANELS article. Remove and inspect defective bulb. If bulb is burned out, replace bulb. If bulb is not burned out, replace instrument cluster.

ANY HARD WIRED LIGHT INOPERATIVE

NOTE: For connector terminal identification and wiring diagrams, see BODY CONTROL COMPUTER – INTRODUCTION article. Perform VERIFICATION TEST VER-1A after each repair.

CAUTION: Always turn ignition switch to OFF position prior to disconnecting or connecting any module connector.

1) Remove instrument cluster. See appropriate INSTRUMENT PANELS article. Remove inoperative bulb. If bulb is burned out, replace bulb. If bulb is not burned out, go to next step.

2) Inspect wiring diagram and evaluate which instrument cluster provides; power or ground for inoperative bulb. See appropriate wiring diagram in BODY CONTROL COMPUTER – INTRODUCTION article.

CHRY
4-212

1999 ACCESSORIES & EQUIPMENT
Body Control Computer Tests – Ram Van & Ram Wagon (Cont.)

Using external ohmmeter or voltmeter, check appropriate power or ground circuit. If circuit is okay, replace instrument cluster. If power or ground is not available at appropriate circuit, repair open circuit.

ONE GAUGE NOT OPERATING PROPERLY

NOTE: For connector terminal identification and wiring diagrams, see BODY CONTROL COMPUTER – INTRODUCTION article. Perform VERIFICATION TEST VER-1A after each repair.

CAUTION: Always turn ignition switch to OFF position prior to disconnecting or connecting any module connector.

1) Push and hold RESET button while cycling ignition key; ON-OFF-ON. Instrument cluster self-test will start. If inoperative gauge reached proper calibration point, go to next step. If inoperative gauge did not reach proper calibration point, replace instrument cluster.
2) Stop instrument cluster self-test. If problem is with speedometer, go to next step. If problem is with oil pressure gauge, go to step 6). If problem is with temperature gauge, go to step 14). If problem is with fuel level gauge, go to appropriate SELF-DIAGNOSTICS article in ENGINE PERFORMANCE in appropriate MITCHELL® manual and review powertrain symptoms. If problem is with volt gauge, go to step 16). If gauge is not listed, system is currently functioning properly.
3) Using scan tool, select BODY--SYSTEMS TESTS then PCM MONI-TOR. If scan tool displays PCM ACTIVE ON BUS, go to next step. If scan tool does not display PCM ACTIVE ON BUS, go to appropriate VEHICLE COMMUNICATIONS article.
4) Using scan tool, read PCM DTCs. If any speedometer DTCs are present, go to appropriate SELF-DIAGNOSTICS article in ENGINE PERFORMANCE in appropriate MITCHELL® manual. If no speedometer DTCs are present, go to next step.
5) Raise and support all wheels. Start engine and place gear selector in drive. Using scan tool, select MIC, MONITORS then CCD BUS ENGINE INFO. Read VSS. If vehicle speed on scan tool matches speedometer, see appropriate ANTI-LOCK BRAKE article. If vehicle speed on scan tool does not match speedometer, replace instrument cluster circuit board.
6) Turn ignition on. If CHECK GAUGES light illuminated, go to next step. If CHECK GAUGES light did not illuminate, go to step 12).
7) Turn ignition off. Inspect oil level. If oil level is within specification, go to next step. If oil level is not within specification, adjust oil level and retest.
8) Turn ignition on. Disconnect engine Oil Pressure Switch (OPS) connector. OPS is located near bottom of distributor. If CHECK GAUGES light went out, go to next step. If CHECK GAUGES light did not go out, go to step 11).
9) Remove OPS. Connect mechanical oil pressure gauge to OPS port. Start engine. If engine oil pressure at idle is 4 psi or more, go to next step. If engine oil pressure at idle is less than 4 psi, repair mechanical engine problem.
10) Run engine to reach normal operating temperature. If engine oil pressure at idle is 4 psi or more, replace OPS. If engine oil pressure at idle is less than 4 psi, repair mechanical engine problem.
11) Turn ignition off. Disconnect PCM White connector C2. PCM is located in engine compartment on right inner fender. Using an external ohmmeter, measure resistance between ground and PCM Black connector terminal No. 23 (Gray wire). If resistance is less than 5 ohms, repair short to ground in Gray wire. If resistance is 5 ohms or more, replace PCM.
12) Disconnect engine Oil Pressure Switch (OPS) connector. OPS is located near bottom of distributor. Connect jumper wire between OPS connector terminals. If oil pressure warning indicator illuminates, replace OPS. If oil pressure warning indicator does not illuminate, go to next step.
13) Do not remove jumper wire. Disconnect PCM Black connector C2. PCM is located in engine compartment on right inner fender. Using an external ohmmeter, measure resistance between ground and PCM

White connector C2 terminal No. 23 (Gray wire). If resistance is less than 5 ohms, replace PCM. If resistance is 5 ohms or more, repair open Gray wire.
14) Check cooling system operation. If cooling system is operating properly, go to next step. If cooling system is not operating properly, repair engine cooling problem.
15) Using scan tool, select PCM MONITOR under SYSTEM TESTS. If scan tool displays PCM ACTIVE ON BUS, system is currently functioning properly. If scan tool does not display PCM ACTIVE ON BUS, go to appropriate VEHICLE COMMUNICATIONS article.
16) Select MODULE ENGINE CONTROLLER. Read PCM DTCs. If scan tool displays ECT SENSOR VOLTAGE TOO HIGH, see appropriate SELF-DIAGNOSTICS article in ENGINE PERFORMANCE in appropriate MITCHELL® manual. If scan tool does not display ECT SENSOR VOLTAGE TOO HIGH, go to next step.
17) Select MODULE ENGINE CONTROLLER. Read PCM DTCs. If scan tool displays ECT SENSOR VOLTAGE TOO LOW, see appropriate SELF-DIAGNOSTICS article in ENGINE PERFORMANCE in appropriate MITCHELL® manual. If scan tool does not display ECT SENSOR VOLTAGE TOO LOW, go to next step.
18) Using scan tool, read PCM DTCs. If any charging system or voltmeter DTCs are present, see appropriate SELF-DIAGNOSTICS article in ENGINE PERFORMANCE in appropriate MITCHELL® manual. If no charging system or voltmeter DTCs are present, go to next step.
19) Push and hold RESET button while cycling ignition key; ON-OFF-ON. Instrument cluster self-test will start. Observe volt gauge. Volt gauge should stop at 8, low end of normal, High end of normal and 18. If volt gauge responded as described, volt gauge is functioning properly. If volt gauge did not respond as described, replace instrument cluster.

INTERIOR LIGHTING SYSTEM

COURTESY LIGHTS INOPERATIVE FROM ALL DOORS & COURTESY LIGHT SWITCH

NOTE: For connector terminal identification and wiring diagrams, see BODY CONTROL COMPUTER – INTRODUCTION article. Perform VERIFICATION TEST VER-1A after each repair.

CAUTION: Always turn ignition switch to OFF position prior to disconnecting or connecting any module connector.

1) Using scan tool, select CENTRAL TIMER MODULE. If scan tool displays NO RESPONSE or CCD BUS FAILURE, go to appropriate VEHICLE COMMUNICATIONS article. If scan tool does not display NO RESPONSE or CCD BUS FAILURE, go to next step.
2) Ensure courtesy light switch on headlight switch is in middle position. Disconnect middle courtesy light 3-pin connector. Using external voltmeter, measure voltage between ground and middle courtesy light 3-pin connector terminal No. 2 (Black/Pink wire). If voltage is 10 volts or less, go to next step. If voltage is more than 10 volts, repair open Yellow wire between courtesy lights and headlight switch.
3) Disconnect courtesy light defeat switch (dome light switch) connector. Measure voltage between ground and defeat switch Pink/White wire. If voltage is 10 volts or less, repair open Pink/White wire between junction block fuse No. 12 and defeat switch. If voltage is more than 10 volts, go to next step.
4) Connect jumper wire between courtesy light defeat switch (dome light switch) connector Pink/White and Pink/Light Blue wire. If courtesy lights illuminate, replace headlight switch. Courtesy light defeat switch (dome light switch) is part of headlight switch. If courtesy lights do not illuminate, repair open output circuit between courtesy light defeat switch (dome light switch) Pink/Light Blue wire and any courtesy light Black/Pink wire.

1999 ACCESSORIES & EQUIPMENT
Body Control Computer Tests – Ram Van & Ram Wagon (Cont.)

CHRY
4-213

COURTESY LIGHTS INOPERATIVE FROM BOTH FRONT DOORS (ILLUMINATED ENTRY INOPERATIVE)

NOTE: *For connector terminal identification and wiring diagrams, see BODY CONTROL COMPUTER – INTRODUCTION article. Perform VERIFICATION TEST VER-1A after each repair.*

CAUTION: *Always turn ignition switch to OFF position prior to disconnecting or connecting any module connector.*

1) Using scan tool, read driver's door ajar switch status with driver's door open. If scan tool displays DRDOOR AJAR SW: CLOSED, go to next step. If scan tool does not display DRDOOR AJAR SW: CLOSED, go to OPEN DRIVER DOOR AJAR CIRCUIT (COURTESY LIGHTS INOPERATIVE FROM LEFT FRONT DOOR) under DOOR AJAR SYSTEM.
2) Disconnect Central Timer Module (CTM) 18-pin White connector C2. CTM is located on left side of engine cover. Connect jumper wire between ground and CTM 18-pin White connector C2 terminal No. 2 (Yellow wire). If courtesy lights illuminate, replace CTM. If courtesy lights do not illuminate, repair open courtesy light driver circuit (Yellow wire) between CTM and splice. See appropriate wiring diagram in BODY CONTROL COMPUTER – INTRODUCTION article.

COURTESY LIGHTS INOPERATIVE FROM COURTESY LIGHT SWITCH

NOTE: *For connector terminal identification and wiring diagrams, see BODY CONTROL COMPUTER – INTRODUCTION article. Perform VERIFICATION TEST VER-1A after each repair.*

CAUTION: *Always turn ignition switch to OFF position prior to disconnecting or connecting any module connector.*

1) Gain access to back of headlight switch. Disconnect 1-pin ground connector Black wire. Using an external ohmmeter, measure resistance between ground and headlight switch 1-pin connector Black wire. If resistance is less than 10 ohms, go to next step. If resistance is 10 ohms or more, repair open Black wire.
2) Disconnect headlight switch 9-pin connector. Connect jumper wire between ground and headlight switch 9-pin connector terminal "D". If courtesy lights illuminate, replace headlight switch. If courtesy lights do not illuminate, repair open courtesy light driver circuit (Yellow wire) between headlight switch and splice. See appropriate wiring diagram in BODY CONTROL COMPUTER – INTRODUCTION article.

COURTESY LIGHTS INOPERATIVE FROM EITHER AUXILIARY DOOR

NOTE: *For connector terminal identification and wiring diagrams, see BODY CONTROL COMPUTER – INTRODUCTION article. Perform VERIFICATION TEST VER-1A after each repair.*

CAUTION: *Always turn ignition switch to OFF position prior to disconnecting or connecting any module connector.*

1) Ensure courtesy light switch is in middle position. Disconnect inoperative auxiliary door ajar switch connector. Connect jumper wire between ground and auxiliary door ajar switch terminal (Yellow wire).
2) If courtesy lights illuminated, replace defective auxiliary door ajar switch. If courtesy lights did not illuminate, repair open courtesy light driver circuit (Yellow wire) between auxiliary door ajar switch and splice. See appropriate wiring diagram in BODY CONTROL COMPUTER – INTRODUCTION article.

COURTESY LIGHTS ON AT ALL TIMES

NOTE: *For connector terminal identification and wiring diagrams, see BODY CONTROL COMPUTER – INTRODUCTION article. Perform VERIFICATION TEST VER-1A after each repair.*

CAUTION: *Always turn ignition switch to OFF position prior to disconnecting or connecting any module connector.*

1) Using scan tool, select CENTRAL TIMER MODULE. If scan tool displays NO RESPONSE or CCD BUS FAILURE, go to appropriate VEHICLE COMMUNICATIONS article. If scan tool does not display NO RESPONSE or CCD BUS FAILURE, go to next step.
2) Ensure auxiliary door switches are properly adjusted. Ensure all doors are closed and courtesy light switch is in middle position. Using scan tool, read auxiliary door ajar switch status. If scan tool displays AUXILIARY DOOR SWITCH: CLOSED, go to SHORTED AUXILIARY DOOR (SIDE OR REAR) AJAR. If scan tool does not display AUXILIARY DOOR SWITCH: CLOSED, go to next step.
3) Read driver's door ajar switch status. If scan tool displays DRDOOR AJAR SW: CLOSED, go to SHORTED DRIVER DOOR AJAR CIRCUIT. If scan tool does not display DRDOOR AJAR CLOSED, go to next step.
4) Read passenger's door ajar switch status. If scan tool displays PASSDOOR AJAR SW: CLOSED, go to SHORTED PASSENGER DOOR AJAR CIRCUIT. If scan tool does not display PASSDOOR AJAR CLOSED, go to next step
5) Disconnect auxiliary door ajar switches one at a time while monitoring courtesy lights. If courtesy lights turned off after either auxiliary door ajar switch was disconnected, replace defective auxiliary door ajar switch. If courtesy lights remained on after both auxiliary door ajar switch was disconnected, go to next step.
6) Disconnect headlight switch 9-pin connector. If courtesy lights turned off after headlight switch was disconnected, replace defective headlight switch. If courtesy lights remained on after headlight switch was disconnected, go to next step.
7) Disconnect Central Timer Module (CTM) 18-pin White connector C2. CTM is located on left side of engine cover. If courtesy lights turned off after CTM was disconnected, replace defective CTM. If courtesy lights remained on after CTM was disconnected, repair short to ground in courtesy light driver circuit (Yellow wire) between CTM and splice. See appropriate wiring diagram in BODY CONTROL COMPUTER – INTRODUCTION article.

POWER DOOR LOCKS/RKE SYSTEM

DOOR LOCK SWITCH FAILURE (ALL DOORS FAILING TO LOCK & UNLOCK FROM ONE SWITCH, ALL DOORS FAILING TO LOCK FROM ONE SWITCH)

NOTE: *For connector terminal identification and wiring diagrams, see BODY CONTROL COMPUTER – INTRODUCTION article. Perform VERIFICATION TEST VER-1A after each repair.*

CAUTION: *Always turn ignition switch to OFF position prior to disconnecting or connecting any module connector.*

1) Clear trouble codes as needed. See BODY CONTROL COMPUTER – INTRODUCTION article. Using scan tool, read I/O's door lock switch status. If scan tool displays PRESSED, go to next step. If scan tool does not display PRESSED, go to step 5).
2) Disconnect left door lock switch connector. If scan tool displays PRESSED, go to next step. If scan tool does not display PRESSED, replace left door lock switch.
3) Disconnect right door lock switch connector. If scan tool displays PRESSED, go to next step. If scan tool does not display PRESSED, replace right door lock switch.
4) Locate Central Timer Module (CTM). CTM is located on left side of engine cover under dash. Disconnect CTM 18-pin White connector C2. Using an external voltmeter, measure voltage between ground and CTM

CHRY
4-214

1999 ACCESSORIES & EQUIPMENT
Body Control Computer Tests – Ram Van & Ram Wagon (Cont.)

18-pin connector C2 terminal No. 4 (Orange/Violet wire). If voltage is more than 1.5 volts, repair short to voltage in Orange/Violet wire. If voltage is 1.5 volts or less, replace CTM.

5) Erase all DTCs using scan tool. See BODY CONTROL COMPUTER – INTRODUCTION article. Using scan tool, read I/O's door lock switch status. Press door lock switch to lock. If scan tool displays PRESSED, system is currently functioning properly. If scan tool does not display PRESSED, go to next step.

6) Gain access to back of door lock switch. Using external voltmeter, measure voltage between ground and door lock switch connector terminal No. 3 (Red wire). If voltage is more than 10 volts, go to next step. If voltage is 10 volts or less, repair open Red wire between junction block and door lock switch.

7) Ensure door lock switch is connected. Measure voltage between ground and door lock switch connector terminal No. 1 (Orange/Violet wire). Press door lock switch to lock while monitoring voltmeter. If voltage is more than 10 volts while pressing door lock switch, go to next step. If voltage is 10 volts or less while pressing door lock switch, replace door lock switch.

8) Locate Central Timer Module (CTM). CTM is located on left side of engine cover under dash. Disconnect CTM 18-pin White connector C2. Using an external voltmeter, measure voltage between ground and CTM 18-pin connector C2 terminal No. 4 (Orange/Violet wire). If voltage is 10 volts or less, repair short to voltage in Orange/Violet wire. If voltage is more than 10 volts, replace CTM.

DOOR UNLOCK SWITCH FAILURE (ALL DOORS FAILING TO UNLOCK FROM ONE SWITCH)

NOTE: For connector terminal identification and wiring diagrams, see BODY CONTROL COMPUTER – INTRODUCTION article. Perform VERIFICATION TEST VER-1A after each repair.

CAUTION: Always turn ignition switch to OFF position prior to disconnecting or connecting any module connector.

1) Clear trouble codes as needed. See BODY CONTROL COMPUTER – INTRODUCTION article. Using scan tool, read I/O's door unlock switch status. If scan tool displays PRESSED, go to next step. If scan tool does not display PRESSED, go to step **5)**.

2) Disconnect left door lock switch connector. If scan tool displays PRESSED, go to next step. If scan tool does not display PRESSED, replace left door lock switch.

3) Disconnect right door lock switch connector. If scan tool displays PRESSED, go to next step. If scan tool does not display PRESSED, replace right door lock switch.

4) Locate Central Timer Module (CTM). CTM is located on left side of engine cover under dash. Disconnect CTM 18-pin connector C2. Using an external voltmeter, measure voltage between ground and CTM 18-pin connector C2 terminal No. 13 (Pink/Violet wire). If voltage is more than 1.5 volts, repair short to voltage in Pink/Violet wire. If voltage is 1.5 volts or less, replace CTM.

5) Erase all DTCs using scan tool. See BODY CONTROL COMPUTER – INTRODUCTION article. Using scan tool, read I/O's door lock switch status. Press door unlock switch to lock. If scan tool displays PRESSED, system is currently functioning properly. If scan tool does not display PRESSED, go to next step.

6) Gain access to back of door lock switch. Using external voltmeter, measure voltage between ground and door lock switch connector terminal No. 3 (Red wire). If voltage is more than 10 volts, go to next step. If voltage is 10 volts or less, repair open Red wire between junction block and door lock switch.

7) Ensure door lock switch is connected. Measure voltage between ground and door lock switch connector terminal No. 5 (Pink/Violet wire). Press door unlock switch to lock while monitoring voltmeter. If voltage is more than 10 volts while pressing door lock switch, go to next step. If voltage is 10 volts or less while pressing door lock switch, replace door lock switch.

8) Locate Central Timer Module (CTM). CTM is located on left side of engine cover under dash. Disconnect CTM 18-pin connector C2. Using

an external voltmeter, measure voltage between ground and CTM 18-pin connector C2 terminal No. 13 (Pink/Violet wire). If voltage is 10 volts or less, repair short to voltage in Pink/Violet wire. If voltage is more than 10 volts, replace CTM.

ALL DOORS FAILING TO LOCK/UNLOCK FROM ANY SWITCH

NOTE: For connector terminal identification and wiring diagrams, see BODY CONTROL COMPUTER – INTRODUCTION article. Perform VERIFICATION TEST VER-1A after each repair.

CAUTION: Always turn ignition switch to OFF position prior to disconnecting or connecting any module connector.

1) Using scan tool, select CENTRAL TIMER MODULE. If scan tool displays NO RESPONSE or CCD BUS FAILURE, go to appropriate VEHICLE COMMUNICATIONS article. If scan tool does not display NO RESPONSE or CCD BUS FAILURE, go to next step.

2) Using scan tool, select READ DTCs. If any Diagnostic Trouble Codes (fault messages) are present, go to appropriate fault message. If no fault messages are present, go to next step.

3) Ensure windows are down, ignition key is removed and doors are unlocked. Using scan tool, actuate door lock relay. If door locks operate, go to DOOR LOCK SWITCH FAILURE (ALL DOORS FAILING TO LOCK & UNLOCK FROM ONE SWITCH, ALL DOORS FAILING TO LOCK FROM ONE SWITCH). If door locks do not operate, go to next step.

4) Remove and inspect fuse No. 4 from junction block. Junction block is located behind left kick panel. If fuse is open, go to step **12)**. If fuse is okay, go to next step.

5) Replace fuse No. 4. Press door lock switch to lock position and inspect fuse No. 4. If fuse is okay, go to step **8)**. If fuse is blown, go to next step.

6) Turn ignition off. Using external ohmmeter, measure resistance between ground and fuse No. 4 (Red wire). If resistance is 5 ohms or more, repair short to ground in Red wire between junction block and battery source. See appropriate wiring diagram in BODY CONTROL COMPUTER – INTRODUCTION article. If resistance is less than 5 ohms, go to next step.

7) Locate Central Timer Module (CTM). CTM is located on left side of engine cover. Disconnect CTM 18-pin White connector C2. Using external ohmmeter, measure resistance between ground and CTM 18-pin White connector C2 terminal No. 1 (Orange/Black wire). If resistance is 5 ohms or more, replace fuse No. 4. If resistance is less than 5 ohms, repair short to ground in Orange/Black wire between CTM and door lock motors.

8) Press door lock switch to unlock position and inspect fuse No. 4. If fuse is okay, go to step **11)**. If fuse is blown, go to next step.

9) Turn ignition off. Using external ohmmeter, measure resistance between ground and fuse No. 4 (Red wire). If resistance is 5 ohms or more, repair short to ground in Red wire between junction block and battery source. See appropriate wiring diagram in BODY CONTROL COMPUTER – INTRODUCTION article. If resistance is less than 5 ohms, go to next step.

10) Locate Central Timer Module (CTM). CTM is located on left side of engine cover. Disconnect CTM 18-pin White connector C2. Using external ohmmeter, measure resistance between ground and CTM 18-pin White connector C2 terminal No. 9 (Pink/Black wire). If resistance is 5 ohms or more, replace fuse No. 4. If resistance is less than 5 ohms, repair short to ground in Pink/Black wire between CTM and door lock motors.

11) Turn ignition off. Using external ohmmeter, measure resistance between ground and fuse No. 4 (Red wire). If resistance is 5 ohms or more, repair short to ground in Red wire between junction block and battery source. See appropriate wiring diagram in BODY CONTROL COMPUTER – INTRODUCTION article. If resistance is less than 5 ohms, go to next step.

12) Reinstall fuse. Locate Central Timer Module (CTM). CTM is located on left side of engine cover. Disconnect CTM 14-pin Green connector

1999 ACCESSORIES & EQUIPMENT
Body Control Computer Tests – Ram Van & Ram Wagon (Cont.)

CHRY
4-215

C1. Using an external voltmeter, measure voltage between ground and CTM 14-pin Green connector C1 terminal No. 14 (Red wire). If voltage is more than 10 volts, go to next step. If voltage is 10 volts or less, repair open Red wire between fuse No. 4 and door lock switch.

13) Turn ignition off. Disconnect CTM 18-pin White connector C2. Using external ohmmeter, measure resistance between ground and CTM 18-pin White connector C2 terminal No. 3 (Black wire). If resistance is more than 5 ohms, repair open Black wire between CTM and ground. If resistance is 5 ohms or less, replace CTM.

14) Measure resistance between ground and CTM 18-pin White connector C2 terminal No. 3 (Black wire). If resistance is 5 ohms or more, repair open Black wire. If resistance is less than 5 ohms, replace CTM.

ALL DOORS FAILING TO LOCK FROM ANY SWITCH

NOTE: For connector terminal identification and wiring diagrams, see BODY CONTROL COMPUTER – INTRODUCTION article. Perform VERIFICATION TEST VER-1A after each repair.

CAUTION: Always turn ignition switch to OFF position prior to disconnecting or connecting any module connector.

1) Using scan tool, select CENTRAL TIMER MODULE, READ DTCs. If DOOR LOCK SWITCH FAILURE is displayed, go to DOOR LOCK SWITCH FAILURE (ALL DOORS FAILING TO LOCK & UNLOCK FROM ONE SWITCH, ALL DOORS FAILING TO LOCK FROM ONE SWITCH). If DOOR LOCK SWITCH FAILURE is not displayed, go to next step.

2) Ensure driver's door is closed. Using scan tool, read I/O's driver's door ajar switch status. If scan tool displays DRDOOR AJAR SW: CLOSED, go to next step. If scan tool does not display DRDOOR AJAR SW: CLOSED, go to step **4)**.

3) Ensure all doors are closed and properly aligned. Using scan tool, enter BODY SYSTEM, then BODY COMPUTER. Select INPUTS/OUTPUTS. Observe door ajar switch status. Open and close door in question. Scan tool should display status opposite of actual door position. If driver's door is properly aligned, go to SHORTED DRIVER DOOR AJAR CIRCUIT under DOOR AJAR SYSTEM. If driver's door is out of alignment, align door and retest.

4) Locate Central Timer Module (CTM). CTM is located on left side of engine cover. Disconnect CTM 18-pin White connector C2. Turn ignition on and check all fuses, replacing as necessary. Using external voltmeter, measure voltage between ground and CTM 18-pin White connector C2 terminal No. 9 (Pink/Black wire). If voltage is more than .1 volt, repair Pink/Black wire for short to voltage between CTM and door lock motor. If voltage is .1 volt or less, go to next step.

5) Turn ignition off. Using external ohmmeter, measure resistance between ground and CTM 18-pin White connector C2 terminal No. 1 (Orange/Black wire). If resistance is 100 ohms or more, repair short to ground in Orange/Black wire between CTM and door lock motors. If resistance is less than 100 ohms, replace CTM.

ALL DOORS FAILING TO UNLOCK FROM ANY SWITCH

NOTE: For connector terminal identification and wiring diagrams, see BODY CONTROL COMPUTER – INTRODUCTION article. Perform VERIFICATION TEST VER-1A after each repair.

CAUTION: Always turn ignition switch to OFF position prior to disconnecting or connecting any module connector.

1) Using scan tool, select CENTRAL TIMER MODULE, READ DTCs. If DOOR LOCK SWITCH FAILURE is displayed, go to DOOR UNLOCK SWITCH FAILURE (ALL DOORS FAILING TO UNLOCK FROM ONE SWITCH). If DOOR LOCK SWITCH FAILURE is not displayed, go to next step.

2) Locate Central Timer Module (CTM). CTM is located on left side of engine cover. Disconnect CTM 18-pin White connector C2. Turn ignition on and check all fuses, replacing as necessary. Using external voltme-

ter, measure voltage between ground and CTM 18-pin White connector C2 terminal No. 1 (Orange/Black wire). If voltage is more than .1 volt, repair Orange/Black wire for short to voltage between CTM and door lock motor. If voltage is .1 volt or less, go to next step.

3) Turn ignition off. Locate Central Timer Module (CTM). CTM is located on left side of engine cover. Using external ohmmeter, measure resistance between ground and CTM 18-pin White connector C2 terminal No. 9 (Pink/Black wire). If resistance is 100 ohms or more, repair short to ground in Orange/Black wire between CTM and door lock motors. If resistance is less than 100 ohms, replace CTM.

AUXILIARY DOORS FAIL TO LOCK

NOTE: For connector terminal identification and wiring diagrams, see BODY CONTROL COMPUTER – INTRODUCTION article. Perform VERIFICATION TEST VER-1A after each repair.

CAUTION: Always turn ignition switch to OFF position prior to disconnecting or connecting any module connector.

1) Using scan tool, read I/O's auxiliary door(s) ajar switch status. If scan tool displays OPEN, go to ONE DOOR FAILING TO LOCK/UNLOCK FROM ANY SWITCH. If scan tool does not display OPEN, go to next step.

2) Disconnect rear auxiliary door switch connector. If scan tool displays OPEN, replace rear auxiliary door switch. If scan tool does not display OPEN, go to next step.

3) Disconnect side auxiliary door switch connector. If scan tool displays OPEN, replace side auxiliary door switch. If scan tool does not display OPEN, go to next step.

4) Locate Central Timer Module (CTM). CTM is located on left side of engine cover. Disconnect CTM 18-pin White connector C2. Using external ohmmeter, measure resistance between ground and CTM 18-pin White connector C2 terminal No. 15 (Brown/Tan wire). If resistance is 5 ohms or more, replace CTM. If resistance is less than 5 ohms, repair short to ground in Brown/Tan wire between CTM and rear auxiliary door switch connector.

CANCELLING HORN CHIRP

NOTE: For connector terminal identification and wiring diagrams, see BODY CONTROL COMPUTER – INTRODUCTION article. Perform VERIFICATION TEST VER-1A after each repair.

Using scan tool, select CENTRAL TIMER MODULE. If scan tool displays NO RESPONSE or CCD BUS FAILURE, go to appropriate VEHICLE COMMUNICATIONS article. If scan tool does not display NO RESPONSE or CCD BUS FAILURE, using scan tool, select VEHICLE THEFT then MISCELLANEOUS. Follow scan tool prompts to cancel horn chirp.

CHANGING HORN CHIRP DURATION

NOTE: For connector terminal identification and wiring diagrams, see BODY CONTROL COMPUTER – INTRODUCTION article. Perform VERIFICATION TEST VER-1A after each repair.

Using scan tool, select CENTRAL TIMER MODULE. If scan tool displays NO RESPONSE or CCD BUS FAILURE, go to appropriate VEHICLE COMMUNICATIONS article. If scan tool does not display NO RESPONSE or CCD BUS FAILURE, using scan tool, select VEHICLE THEFT then MISCELLANEOUS. Follow scan tool prompts to change horn chirp duration.

CHRY
4-216

1999 ACCESSORIES & EQUIPMENT
Body Control Computer Tests – Ram Van & Ram Wagon (Cont.)

DOOR LOCK INHIBIT INOPERATIVE

NOTE: *For connector terminal identification and wiring diagrams, see BODY CONTROL COMPUTER – INTRODUCTION article. Perform VERIFICATION TEST VER-1A after each repair.*

CAUTION: *Always turn ignition switch to OFF position prior to disconnecting or connecting any module connector.*

1) Using scan tool, select CENTRAL TIMER MODULE. If scan tool displays NO RESPONSE or CCD BUS FAILURE, go to appropriate VEHICLE COMMUNICATIONS article. If scan tool does not display NO RESPONSE or CCD BUS FAILURE, go to next step.
2) Turn ignition on. Using scan tool, select BODY COMPUTER then I/O. Open and close driver's door and read driver's door ajar status. If scan tool driver's door ajar status changes from OPEN to CLOSED, go to next step. If scan tool driver's door ajar status does not change from OPEN to CLOSED, go to step 6).
3) Ensure key is in ignition. Using scan tool, read key-in ignition chime status. If scan tool does not display KEY-IN IGNITION CHIME STATE: ON, go to next step. If scan tool displays KEY-IN IGNITION CHIME STATE: ON, replace Central Timer Module (CTM). CTM is located on left side of engine cover.
4) Ensure key is in ignition. Disconnect CTM 14-pin Green connector C1. Using an external ohmmeter, measure resistance between ground and CTM 14-pin Green connector C1 terminal No. 9 (Light Blue wire). If resistance is 5 ohms or more, go to next step. If resistance is less than 5 ohms, replace CTM.
5) Connect jumper wire between ground and CTM 14-pin Green connector C1 terminal No. 9 (Light Blue wire). Disconnect steering column 48-pin connector. The steering column 48-pin connector is located near bottom of steering column. Measure resistance between ground and steering column 48-pin connector terminal B4 (Light Blue wire). If resistance is less than 5 ohms, replace ignition switch. If resistance is 5 ohms or more, repair open Light Blue wire between steering column 48-pin connector and CTM.
6) Ensure all doors are closed and properly aligned. Using scan tool, enter BODY SYSTEM, then BODY COMPUTER. Select INPUTS/OUTPUTS. Observe door ajar switch status. Open and close door in question. Scan tool should display status opposite of actual door position. If driver's door is properly aligned, go to SHORTED DRIVER DOOR AJAR CIRCUIT under DOOR AJAR SYSTEM. If driver's door is out of alignment, align door and retest.

HORN CHIRP INOPERATIVE (W/CHIRP ENABLED)

NOTE: *For connector terminal identification and wiring diagrams, see BODY CONTROL COMPUTER – INTRODUCTION article. Perform VERIFICATION TEST VER-1A after each repair.*

Locate Central Timer Module (CTM). CTM is located on left side of engine cover. Disconnect CTM 18-pin White connector C2. Using external ohmmeter, measure resistance between ground and CTM 18-pin White connector C2 terminal No. 18 (Black/Red wire). If horn sounds, replace CTM. If horn does not sound, repair open Black/Red wire between junction block and CTM.

ONE DOOR FAILING TO LOCK/UNLOCK FROM ANY SWITCH

NOTE: *For connector terminal identification and wiring diagrams, see BODY CONTROL COMPUTER – INTRODUCTION article. Perform VERIFICATION TEST VER-1A after each repair.*

CAUTION: *Always turn ignition switch to OFF position prior to disconnecting or connecting any module connector.*

1) Remove door panel from door failing to lock. Disconnect door lock motor connector. Connect test light between ground and Orange/Black wire of door lock motor connector. If an auxiliary door is being tested, door must be closed before ignition is turned on. Turn ignition on. Using scan tool, actuate door lock relay while monitoring test light. If test light illuminates, go to next step. If test light does not illuminate, repair open Orange/Black wire between CTM and door lock motor.
2) Move test light from Orange/Black wire to Pink/Black wire of door lock motor. Actuate door lock relay while monitoring test light. If test light illuminates, replace door lock motor. If test light does not illuminate, repair open Pink/Black wire between CTM and door lock motor.

PROGRAMMING A TRANSMITTER

NOTE: *For connector terminal identification and wiring diagrams, see BODY CONTROL COMPUTER – INTRODUCTION article. Perform VERIFICATION TEST VER-1A after each repair.*

Using scan tool, select CENTRAL TIMER MODULE. If scan tool displays NO RESPONSE or CCD BUS FAILURE, go to appropriate VEHICLE COMMUNICATIONS article. If scan tool does not display NO RESPONSE or CCD BUS FAILURE, using scan tool, select MISCELLANEOUS then PROGRAM RKE. Follow scan tool prompts to program transmitter.

REMOTE KEYLESS ENTRY (RKE) INOPERATIVE

NOTE: *For connector terminal identification and wiring diagrams, see BODY CONTROL COMPUTER – INTRODUCTION article. Perform VERIFICATION TEST VER-1A after each repair.*

CAUTION: *Always turn ignition switch to OFF position prior to disconnecting or connecting any module connector.*

1) Using scan tool, select CENTRAL TIMER MODULE. If scan tool displays NO RESPONSE or CCD BUS FAILURE, go to appropriate VEHICLE COMMUNICATIONS article. If scan tool does not display NO RESPONSE or CCD BUS FAILURE, go to next step.
2) Ensure transmitter battery voltage is 3.2 volts. Turn ignition on. Place transmission in park and disarm anti-theft system. Secure known good transmitter. Using scan tool, select MISCELLANEOUS, then PROGRAM RKE. Press any transmitter button. A single chime will announce RKE module accepted transmission. Repeat procedure for all transmitters used with vehicle. Operate door locks from reprogrammed transmitter. If door locks operate properly, system has been repaired. If doors did not lock properly, replace CTM.

TEST AUTOMATIC (ROLLING) DOOR LOCKS

NOTE: *For connector terminal identification and wiring diagrams, see BODY CONTROL COMPUTER – INTRODUCTION article. Perform VERIFICATION TEST VER-1A after each repair.*

1) Using scan tool, select CENTRAL TIMER MODULE. If scan tool displays NO RESPONSE or CCD BUS FAILURE, go to appropriate VEHICLE COMMUNICATIONS article. If scan tool does not display NO RESPONSE or CCD BUS FAILURE, go to next step.
2) Using scan tool select POWERTRAIN CONTROLLER. If scan tool displays NO RESPONSE or CCD BUS FAILURE, go to appropriate VEHICLE COMMUNICATIONS article. If scan tool does not display NO RESPONSE or CCD BUS FAILURE, go to next step.
3) Ensure all doors are closed. Using scan tool, read auxiliary door(s) ajar status. If scan tool displays AUXILIARY DOOR(S) AJAR: CLOSED, go to SHORTED AUXILIARY DOOR (SIDE OR REAR) AJAR under DOOR AJAR SYSTEM. If scan tool does not display AUXILIARY DOOR(S) AJAR: CLOSED, go to next step.
4) Ensure driver's door is closed. Using scan tool, read driver's door ajar status. If scan tool displays DR DOOR AJAR SWITCH: CLOSED, go to SHORTED DRIVER DOOR AJAR CIRCUIT under DOOR AJAR SYSTEM. If scan tool does not display DR DOOR AJAR SWITCH: CLOSED, go to next step.
5) Using scan tool, select ENGINE. Read DTCs. If any Throttle position Sensor (TPS) or Vehicle Speed Sensor (VSS) DTCs are present, see

1999 ACCESSORIES & EQUIPMENT
Body Control Computer Tests – Ram Van & Ram Wagon (Cont.)

CHRY
4-217

appropriate SELF-DIAGNOSTICS article in ENGINE PERFORMANCE in appropriate MITCHELL® manual. If no TPS or VSS DTCs are present, go to next step.

6) Ensure passenger's door is closed. Using scan tool, read passenger's door ajar status. If scan tool displays PASSENGER DOOR AJAR SWITCH: CLOSED, go to SHORTED PASSENGER DOOR AJAR CIRCUIT under DOOR AJAR SYSTEM. If scan tool does not display PASSENGER DOOR AJAR SWITCH: CLOSED, go to next step.

7) Turn ignition on with engine off. Using scan tool, select SYSTEM TEST then PCM MONITOR. If scan tool displays, POWERTRAIN CONTROL MODULE: ACTIVE ON BUS, go to next step. If scan tool does not display, POWERTRAIN CONTROL MODULE: ACTIVE ON BUS, go to appropriate VEHICLE COMMUNICATIONS article.

8) Using scan tool, select MISCELLANEOUS. Read AUTO DOOR LOCK status. If scan tool displays, AUTO DOOR LOCKS: ENABLED, go to next step. If scan tool does not display, AUTO DOOR LOCKS: ENABLED, using scan tool, enable door locks.

9) Raise and properly support vehicle drive wheels. Close all doors, start engine, apply brakes and put transmission into drive. release brake and raise vehicle speed to 20 MPH. If doors locked automatically when MPH increased to 20 MPH, system is operating properly. If doors did not lock automatically when MPH increased 20 MPH, replace CTM.

VEHICLE THEFT/SECURITY SYSTEM

DOOR DISARM SWITCH FAILURE

NOTE: For connector terminal identification and wiring diagrams, see BODY CONTROL COMPUTER – INTRODUCTION article. Perform VERIFICATION TEST VER-1A after each repair.

CAUTION: Always turn ignition switch to OFF position prior to disconnecting or connecting any module connector.

1) Using scan tool, read VTSS inputs/outputs information. If scan tool displays door disarm switch state OPEN, go to next step. If scan tool does not display door disarm switch state OPEN, go to step **4)**.

2) Using door key, lock and unlock door several times. If door switch moves freely, go to next step. If door switch does not move freely, repair or replace lock assembly.

3) Using scan tool, read VTSS inputs/outputs information. If scan tool displays proper door disarm switch state, system is currently functioning properly. If scan tool does not display proper door disarm switch state, replace disarm switch.

4) Disconnect left door disarm switch. If scan tool displays door disarm switch state OPEN, replace left door disarm switch. If scan tool does not display door disarm switch state OPEN, go to next step.

5) Disconnect right door disarm switch. If scan tool displays door disarm switch state OPEN, replace left door disarm switch. If scan tool does not display door disarm switch state OPEN, go to next step.

6) Access Central Timer Module (CTM). CTM is located on left side of engine cover under dash. Disconnect CTM 18-pin connector C2. Using an external ohmmeter, measure resistance between ground and CTM 18-pin connector C2 terminal No. 10 (Black/Orange wire). If resistance is less than 1000 ohms, repair short to ground in Black/Orange wire. If resistance is 1000 ohms or more, replace CTM.

DOOR LOCK SWITCH FAILURE

NOTE: For connector terminal identification and wiring diagrams, see BODY CONTROL COMPUTER – INTRODUCTION article. Perform VERIFICATION TEST VER-1A after each repair.

CAUTION: Always turn ignition switch to OFF position prior to disconnecting or connecting any module connector.

1) Clear trouble codes as needed. See BODY CONTROL COMPUTER – INTRODUCTION article. Using scan tool, read I/O's door lock switch status. If scan tool displays RELEASED, system is currently functioning properly. If scan tool does not display RELEASED, go to next step.

2) Disconnect left door lock switch connector. If scan tool displays RELEASED, replace left door lock switch. If scan tool does not display RELEASED, go to next step.

3) Disconnect right door lock switch connector. If scan tool displays RELEASED, replace right door lock switch. If scan tool does not display RELEASED, go to next step.

4) Locate Central Timer Module (CTM). CTM is located on left side of engine cover under dash. Disconnect CTM 18-pin connector C2. Using an external voltmeter, measure voltage between ground and CTM 18-pin connector C2 terminal No. 13 (Pink/Violet wire). If voltage is more than 1.5 volts, repair short to voltage in Pink/Violet wire between CTM and door lock switch. If voltage is 1.5 volts or less, replace CTM.

DOOR UNLOCK SWITCH FAILURE

NOTE: For connector terminal identification and wiring diagrams, see BODY CONTROL COMPUTER – INTRODUCTION article. Perform VERIFICATION TEST VER-1A after each repair.

CAUTION: Always turn ignition switch to OFF position prior to disconnecting or connecting any module connector.

1) Clear trouble codes as needed. See BODY CONTROL COMPUTER – INTRODUCTION article. Using scan tool, read I/O's door unlock switch status. If scan tool displays RELEASED, system is currently functioning properly. If scan tool does not display RELEASED, go to next step.

2) Disconnect left door lock switch connector. If scan tool displays RELEASED, replace left door lock switch. If scan tool does not display RELEASED, go to next step.

3) Disconnect right door lock switch connector. If scan tool displays RELEASED, replace right door lock switch. If scan tool does not display RELEASED, go to next step.

4) Locate Central Timer Module (CTM). CTM is located on left side of engine cover under dash. Disconnect CTM 18-pin connector C2. Using an external voltmeter, measure voltage between ground and CTM 18-pin connector C2 terminal No. 4 (Orange/Violet wire). If voltage is more than 1.5 volts, repair short to voltage in Orange/Violet wire between CTM and door lock switch. If voltage is 1.5 volts or less, replace CTM.

IDENTIFYING VTSS PROBLEMS

NOTE: For connector terminal identification and wiring diagrams, see BODY CONTROL COMPUTER – INTRODUCTION article. Perform VERIFICATION TEST VER-1A after each repair.

CAUTION: Always turn ignition switch to OFF position prior to disconnecting or connecting any module connector.

1) Using scan tool, select BODY SYSTEM then VTSS and read Central Timer Module (CTM) DTCs. If any VTSS DTCs are displayed, perform appropriate procedure. See VTSS DTC table. If no VTSS DTCs are displayed, go to next step.

VTSS DTC

DTC Message	Perform
DOOR DISARM SWITCH FAILURE	DOOR DISARM SWITCH FAILURE
DOOR LOCK SWITCH FAILURE	DOOR LOCK SWITCH FAILURE
DOOR UNLOCK SWITCH FAILURE	DOOR UNLOCK SWITCH FAILURE
EEPROM CHECKSUM FAILURE	Replace CTM
INTERNAL ROM TEST FAILURE	Replace CTM

2) Select VTSS then MONITORS. If scan tool displays, OK TO RUN, NOT OK TO ARM, PCM has not recorded more than 20 starts. Start engine 20 times and retest. If message does not change to OK TO ARM, replace PCM. If scan tool displays 1 NO RESPONSE/2 NO RESPONSE, see appropriate VEHICLE COMMUNICATIONS article. If

CHRY
4-218

1999 ACCESSORIES & EQUIPMENT
Body Control Computer Tests – Ram Van & Ram Wagon (Cont.)

scan tool does not display OK TO RUN, NOT OK TO ARM or 1 NO RESPONSE/2 NO RESPONSE, go to next step.

3) Using scan tool, actuate horn, headlights and VTSS light to flash. If horn does not sound, go to next step. If headlights do not flash, go to step **5)**. If VTSS light does not flash, go to step **9)**. If all function properly, go to step **11)**.

4) Locate Central Timer Module (CTM). CTM is located on left side of engine cover under dash. Disconnect CTM 18-pin connector C2. Connect jumper wire between ground and CTM 18-pin connector C2 terminal No. 18 (Black/Red wire). If horn sounds, replace CTM. If horn does not sound, repair open in Black/Red wire between CTM and horn relay.

5) Remove headlight relay. Headlight relay is taped into harness behind headlight switch. *See Fig. 1.* Using an external voltmeter, measure voltage between ground and headlight relay connector terminal No. 3 (Violet/White wire). Turn low beam headlights on. If voltage is more than 10 volts, go to next step. If voltage is 10 volts or less, repair open Violet/White wire between splice and headlight relay. See appropriate wiring diagram in BODY CONTROL COMPUTER – INTRODUCTION article.

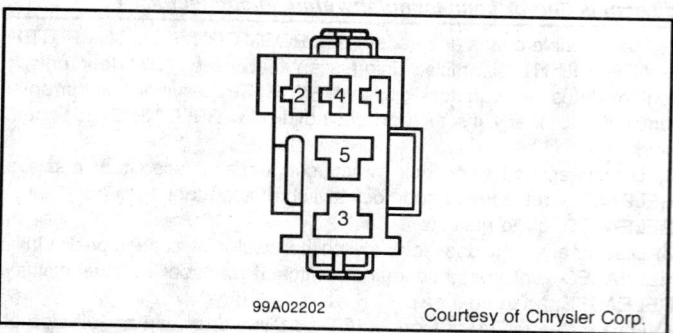

99A02202   Courtesy of Chrysler Corp.

***Fig. 1: Identifying Headlight & Intermittent Wiper Relay
Connector Terminals***

6) Measure voltage between ground and headlight relay connector No. 1 and No. 5 (Red/White wires). If voltage is more than 10 volts at both terminals, go to next step. If voltage is 10 volts or less at either terminal, repair open in appropriate Red/White wire between fuse No. 8 30-amp and headlight relay.

7) Connect a test light between headlight relay connector terminals No. 1 (Red/White wire) and terminal No. 2 (Red wire). Using scan tool, actuate relay. If test light illuminates, replace headlight relay. If test light does not illuminate, go to next step.

8) Locate Central Timer Module (CTM). CTM is located on left side of engine cover under dash. Disconnect CTM 18-pin connector C2. Connect jumper wire between ground and CTM 18-pin connector C2 terminal No. 6 (Red wire). If test light illuminates, replace CTM. If test light does not illuminate, repair open in Red wire between CTM and headlight relay.

9) Using scan tool, actuate VTSS indicator light. If VTSS light illuminates, go to next step. If test light does not illuminate, go to ANY CCD CLUSTER LIGHT INOPERATIVE under INSTRUMENT CLUSTER.

10) Locate Central Timer Module (CTM). CTM is located on left side of engine cover under dash. Disconnect CTM 18-pin connector C2. Connect jumper wire between ground and CTM 18-pin connector C2 terminal No. 8 (Yellow/Orange wire). If VTSS indicator light illuminates, replace CTM. If VTSS indicator light does not illuminate, repair open Yellow/Orange wire between CTM and VTSS indicator light.

11) Using scan tool, select VTSS then CHANGE MODE. Place VTSS in diagnostic mode and follow directions on screen. If TURN KEY TO ACC POSITION is not displayed, go to step **27)**. If NO RESPONSE after turning key to accessory position or TURN KEY TO ACC POSITION is displayed longer than 15 seconds, go to next step. If neither response is received, go to step **15)**.

12) Inspect junction block fuse No. 16. Junction block is located behind left kick panel. If fuse is okay, go to step **14)**. If fuse is blown, go to next step.

13) Turn ignition off. Using an external ohmmeter, measure resistance between ground and fuse No. 16 Yellow/Red wire terminal. If resistance is less than 5 ohms, repair Yellow/Red wire between junction block and CTM for short to ground and replace fuse No. 16. If resistance is 5 ohms or more, replace fuse No. 16.

14) Locate Central Timer Module (CTM). CTM is located on left side of engine cover under dash. Disconnect CTM 18-pin connector C2. Ensure key is in accessory position. Using an external voltmeter, measure voltage between ground and backprobe of CTM 18-pin connector C2 terminal No. 5 (White wire). If voltage is more than 10 volts, replace CTM. If voltage is 10 volts or less, repair open White wire between CTM and junction block.

15) Remove key from ignition. Wait 2 seconds after performing each of the following actions. Open, then close both door. Operate power door lock switch to lock, then unlock position. Rotate key both directions in both doors. Ensure each operation is successful. If any operation is unsuccessful, see VTSS SYMPTOM DIRECTORY table for repair of failed operation. If all operations are successful, go to step **26)**.

VTSS SYMPTOM DIRECTORY

Problem Circuit	Go To
Driver's Door Open Or Close	Step **16**
Passenger's Door Open Or Close	Step **17**
Side Auxiliary Door Open Or Close	Step **18**
Rear Auxiliary Door Open Or Close	Step **19**
Driver's Door Lock Or Unlock Switch	ALL DOORS FAILING TO LOCK & UNLOCK FROM ONE SWITCH
Passenger's Door Lock Or Unlock Switch	ALL DOORS FAILING TO LOCK & UNLOCK FROM ONE SWITCH
Driver's Key Cylinder	Step **20)**
Passenger's Key Cylinder	Step **23)**

16) Ensure driver's door is closed. Using scan tool, read VTSS inputs/outputs door ajar status. If scan tool displays DR DOOR AJAR SWITCH: CLOSED, go to SHORTED DRIVER DOOR AJAR CIRCUIT under DOOR AJAR SYSTEM. If scan tool does not display DR DOOR AJAR SWITCH: CLOSED, go to OPEN DRIVER DOOR AJAR CIRCUIT under DOOR AJAR SYSTEM.

17) Ensure passenger's door is closed. Using scan tool, read VTSS inputs/outputs door ajar status. If scan tool displays DR DOOR AJAR SWITCH: CLOSED, go to SHORTED PASSENGER DOOR AJAR CIRCUIT under DOOR AJAR SYSTEM. If scan tool does not display DR DOOR AJAR SWITCH: CLOSED, go to OPEN PASSENGER DOOR AJAR CIRCUIT under DOOR AJAR SYSTEM.

18) Ensure auxiliary doors are closed. Using scan tool, read VTSS inputs/outputs door ajar status. If scan tool displays AUXILIARY DOOR SWITCH: CLOSED, go to SHORTED AUXILIARY DOOR (SIDE OR REAR) AJAR under DOOR AJAR SYSTEM. If scan tool does not display AUXILIARY DOOR SWITCH: CLOSED, go to OPEN AUXILIARY DOOR (SIDE OR REAR) AJAR under DOOR AJAR SYSTEM.

19) Ensure auxiliary doors are closed. Using scan tool, read VTSS inputs/outputs door ajar status. If scan tool displays AUXILIARY DOOR SWITCH: CLOSED, go to SHORTED AUXILIARY DOOR (SIDE OR REAR) AJAR under DOOR AJAR SYSTEM. If scan tool does not display AUXILIARY DOOR SWITCH: CLOSED, go to OPEN AUXILIARY DOOR (SIDE OR REAR) AJAR under DOOR AJAR SYSTEM.

20) Using scan tool, monitor door disarm switch state. Disconnect left door disarm switch. Connect jumper wire between left door disarm switch connector terminals. If scan tool displays door disarm switch state CLOSED, replace left door disarm switch. If scan tool does not display door disarm switch state CLOSED, go to next step.

21) Disconnect jumper wire. Connect jumper wire between ground and left door disarm switch connector Black/Orange wire. If scan tool displays door disarm switch state CLOSED, go to next step. If scan tool does not display door disarm switch state CLOSED, repair open left door disarm switch ground circuit (Black wire).

22) Access Central Timer Module (CTM). CTM is located on left side of engine cover under dash. Using an external ohmmeter, measure

1999 ACCESSORIES & EQUIPMENT
Body Control Computer Tests – Ram Van & Ram Wagon (Cont.)

CHRY
4-219

resistance between ground and CTM 18-pin connector C2 terminal No. 10 (Black/Orange wire). If resistance is less than 5 ohms, replace CTM. If resistance is 5 ohms or more, repair open left door disarm switch sense circuit (Black/Orange wire).

23) Using scan tool, monitor door disarm switch state. Disconnect right door disarm switch. Connect jumper wire between right door disarm switch connector terminals. If scan tool displays door disarm switch state CLOSED, replace right door disarm switch. If scan tool does not display door disarm switch state CLOSED, go to next step.

24) Disconnect jumper wire. Connect jumper wire between ground and right door disarm switch connector Black/Orange wire. If scan tool displays door disarm switch state CLOSED, go to next step. If scan tool does not display door disarm switch state CLOSED, repair open right door disarm switch ground circuit (Black wire).

25) Access Central Timer Module (CTM). CTM is located on left side of engine cover under dash. Using an external ohmmeter, measure resistance between ground and CTM 18-pin connector C2 terminal No. 10 (Black/Orange wire). If resistance is less than 5 ohms, replace CTM. If resistance is 5 ohms or more, repair open left door disarm switch sense circuit (Black/Orange wire).

26) Turn ignition switch to START position. If horn does not sound, go to next step. If horn sounds, system is currently functioning properly.

27) Inspect junction block fuse No. 17. Junction block is located behind left kick panel. If fuse is okay, go to step **29)**. If fuse is blown, go to next step.

28) Using an external ohmmeter, measure resistance between ground and fuse No. 17 White wire terminal. If resistance is less than 5 ohms, repair White wire between junction block and CTM for short to ground and replace fuse No. 17. If resistance is 5 ohms or more, replace fuse No. 17.

29) Locate Central Timer Module (CTM). CTM is located on left side of engine cover under dash. Disconnect CTM 14-pin connector C1. Using an external voltmeter, measure voltage between ground and CTM 14-pin connector C1 terminal No. 8 (Yellow/Red wire). If voltage is more than 10 volts, replace CTM. If voltage is 10 volts or less, repair open Yellow/Red wire between CTM and RUN-ACC fuse in junction block.

WINDSHIELD WIPER SYSTEM

WIPER PARK SWITCH FAILURE

NOTE: For connector terminal identification and wiring diagrams, see BODY CONTROL COMPUTER – INTRODUCTION article. Perform VERIFICATION TEST VER-1A after each repair.

CAUTION: Always turn ignition switch to OFF position prior to disconnecting or connecting any module connector.

NOTE: It takes 8 seconds for wiper park switch failure DTC to set.

1) Using scan tool, clear DTCs. See appropriate SELF-DIAGNOSTICS article. Turn ignition on. Turn wipers switch to all positions including off. Reread DTCs. If WIPER PARK SWITCH FAILURE is displayed, go to next step. If WIPER PARK SWITCH FAILURE is not displayed, system is currently functioning properly.

2) If wipers work properly in all positions, replace Central Timer Module (CTM). CTM is located on left side of engine cover. If wipers do not work properly in all positions, go to next step.

3) If intermittent wipers work erratic or wipers stop in up position, go to next step. If intermittent wipers do not work erratic or wipers do not stop in up position, go to step **6)**.

4) Using an external voltmeter, measure voltage between ground and backprobe of steering column 48-pin connector terminal A15 (White/Brown wire). The steering column 48-pin connector is located near bottom of steering column. Monitor voltmeter while turning wiper switch to each intermittent position. If voltage is more than 2 volts in each position, go to next step. If voltage is 2 volts or less in each position, replace wiper switch.

5) Measure voltage between ground and backprobe of CTM 14-pin Green connector C1 terminal No. 12 (White/Brown wire). If voltage is more than 2 volts in each position, replace CTM. If voltage is 2 volts or less in each position, repair open White/Brown wire between CTM and steering column 48-pin connector.

6) If wipers do not park in low and hi positions, go to next step. If wipers park in low and hi positions, replace CTM.

7) Place wipers in up position with wiper switch off. Gain access to intermittent wiper relay. Intermittent wiper relay is located behind glove box. Do not remove relay. Connect jumper wire between ground and backprobe of intermittent wiper relay terminal No. 3 (Black/Tan wire). *See Fig. 1.* If wipers moved to park position, replace intermittent wiper relay. If wipers did not move to park position, repair open Black/Tan wire between intermittent wiper relay and multifunction switch.

INTERMITTENT WIPERS INOPERATIVE OR ERRATIC

NOTE: For connector terminal identification and wiring diagrams, see BODY CONTROL COMPUTER – INTRODUCTION article. Perform VERIFICATION TEST VER-1A after each repair.

CAUTION: Always turn ignition switch to OFF position prior to disconnecting or connecting any module connector.

1) Using scan tool select CENTRAL TIMER MODULE. If scan tool displays NO RESPONSE, go to appropriate VEHICLE COMMUNICATIONS article. If scan tool displays any CCD bus failure message, go to SYMPTOM IDENTIFICATION. If scan tool does not display NO RESPONSE or any CCD bus failure message, go to next step.

2) If wipers run constantly in intermittent mode, go to step **5)**. If wipers do not run constantly in intermittent mode, go to next step.

3) Gain access to steering column 48-pin connector. The steering column 48-pin connector is located near bottom of steering column. Do not disconnect. Using an external voltmeter, measure voltage between ground and backprobe of steering column 48-pin connector terminal A15 (White/Brown wire). monitor voltmeter while turning wipers to each intermittent speed. If voltage is more than 2 volts in each position, go to next step. If voltage is 2 volts or less in each position, replace wiper switch.

4) Locate Central Timer Module (CTM). CTM is located on left side of engine cover. Measure voltage between ground and backprobe of CTM 14-pin Green connector C1 terminal No. 12 (White/Brown wire). If voltage is more than 2 volts in each position, replace CTM. If voltage is 2 volts or less in each position, repair open White/Brown wire between CTM and steering column 48-pin connector.

5) Gain access to steering column 48-pin connector. The steering column 48-pin connector is located near bottom of steering column. Do not disconnect. Using an external voltmeter, measure voltage between ground and backprobe of steering column 48-pin connector terminal A14 (Violet wire). Turn wiper switch to intermittent position. If voltage is more than 10 volts, go to next step. If voltage is 10 volts or less, replace wiper switch.

6) Locate Central Timer Module (CTM). CTM is located on left side of engine cover. Measure voltage between ground and backprobe of CTM 14-pin Green connector C1 terminal No. 3 (Violet wire). Turn wiper switch to intermittent position. If voltage is more than 10 volts, replace CTM. If voltage is 10 volts or less, repair open Violet wire between CTM and steering column 48-pin connector.

NO WIPE AFTER WASHERS ACTUATED

NOTE: For connector terminal identification and wiring diagrams, see BODY CONTROL COMPUTER – INTRODUCTION article. Perform VERIFICATION TEST VER-1A after each repair.

CAUTION: Always turn ignition switch to OFF position prior to disconnecting or connecting any module connector.

1) Using scan tool select Central Timer Module (CTM). If scan tool displays NO RESPONSE, go to appropriate VEHICLE COMMUNICATIONS article. If scan tool displays any CCD bus failure message, go to SYMPTOM IDENTIFICATION. If scan tool does not display NO RESPONSE or any CCD bus failure message, go to next step.

CHRY
4-220

1999 ACCESSORIES & EQUIPMENT
Body Control Computer Tests – Ram Van & Ram Wagon (Cont.)

2) Turn ignition on. If washer system works, go to next step. If washer system does not work, see appropriate WIPER/WASHER SYSTEMS article.

3) If wipers function properly, go to next step. If wipers do not function properly, see appropriate WIPER/WASHER SYSTEMS article.

4) Using scan tool, select WIPER MONITORS. Observe washer switch status. If washer switch status changes from OFF to ON, replace CTM. If washer switch status changes from OFF to ON, repair open Brown wire between CTM 14-pin Green connector C1 terminal No. 10 and multifunction switch.

WIPER SPEED SENSITIVE INOPERATIVE

NOTE: *For connector terminal identification and wiring diagrams, see BODY CONTROL COMPUTER – INTRODUCTION article. Perform VERIFICATION TEST VER-1A after each repair.*

CAUTION: **Always turn ignition switch to OFF position prior to disconnecting or connecting any module connector.**

1) Using scan tool select Central timer module (CTM). If scan tool display is not blank or have a CCD bus failure message, go to next step. If scan tool display is blank or has a CCD bus failure message, see appropriate VEHICLE COMMUNICATIONS article.

2) Using scan tool, select Powertrain Control Module (PCM). If scan tool display is not blank or have a CCD bus failure message, go to next step. If scan tool display is blank or has a CCD bus failure message, see appropriate VEHICLE COMMUNICATIONS article.

3) Raise and support vehicle. Turn wipers on to lowest intermittent position. Time interval between wipes. Spin rear wheels to more than 15 MPH. If interval between wipes decreased, system is currently functioning properly. If interval between wipes did not decrease, go to next step.

4) Using scan tool, access wiper system monitor. If vehicle speed signal on scan tool matches speedometer, replace CTM. If vehicle speed signal on scan tool does not match speedometer, go to ONE GAUGE NOT OPERATING PROPERLY under INSTRUMENT CLUSTER.

VERIFICATION TEST VER–1A

BODY VERIFICATION TEST

1) Reconnect all previously disconnected components and connectors. Turn ignition on. If Central Timing Module (CTM) was replaced, program all RKE transmitters and program other options as necessary.

2) Ensure ignition is on. Erase all DTCs using scan tool. Turn ignition off and wait 5 seconds. Turn ignition on and fully operate system that was malfunctioning.

3) If system is not operating properly, go to SYMPTOM IDENTIFICATION. If system is operating correctly and customer's complaint cannot be duplicated, repair is complete.

IDENTIFYING VEHICLE COMMUNICATION PROBLEMS

Connect scan tool to Data Link Connector (DLC) to retrieve messages. If scan tool message is blank, see DRB BLANK SCREEN test. Disconnect scan tool. Ensure ground circuit has continuity at DLC terminal No. 4. Ensure 12 volts is present at DLC terminal No. 16. Try another scan tool and/or cable. See following bus fault messages list and proceed to appropriate DTC or fault message. If EEPROM CHECKSUM FAILURE or INTERNAL MODULE TESTS FAILURE message is received, replace BCM.

- ABS MESSAGE MISMATCH (ABS MESSAGE NOT RECEIVED; NO RESP CONTROLLER ANTILOCK BRAKE)
- BATTERY POWER TO MODULE DISCONNECT (NO RESPONSE FROM BCM, (BAT PWR DISCON'D) BATTERY POWER TO MODULE)
- EATX PRNDL MESSAGE TEST FAILED (NO RESPONSE FROM TCM)
- EEPROM CHECKSUM FAILURE (INTERNAL MODULE TESTS FAILURE). Replace BCM.
- PCM MESSAGE NOT RECEIVED (NO RESPONSE FROM PCM)
- BUS (+) & (–) OPEN (BUS (+) OPEN, BUS (–) OPEN, NO BUS BIAS)
- BUS (+) & BUS (–) SHORTED TOGETHER
- BUS BIAS LEVEL TOO HIGH (BUS BIAS LEVEL TOO LOW)
- CCD SHORT TO 5 VOLTS
- CCD SHORT TO BATTERY
- CCD SHORT TO GROUND
- DRB BLANK SCREEN
- NO RESPONSE FROM ACM
- NO RESPONSE FROM SKIM
- NO RESPONSE INSTRUMENT CLUSTER
- NO TERMINATION
- NOT RECEIVING BUS MESSAGES PROPERLY

ABS MESSAGE MISMATCH (ABS MESSAGE NOT RECEIVED, NO RESP CONTROLLER ANTILOCK BRAKE)

NOTE: For connector terminal identification and wiring diagrams, see BODY CONTROL COMPUTER – INTRODUCTION article. Perform VERIFICATION TEST VER-1 after each repair.

CAUTION: Always turn ignition off prior to disconnecting any module connector.

1) Turn ignition off. Disconnect anti-lock brake controller module. Anti-lock brake controller module is mounted on right inner fender panel of engine compartment. Turn ignition on. Using external voltmeter, measure voltage between ground and anti-lock brake controller module 25- pin connector terminal No. 23 (Dark Blue/White wire). If voltage is 10 volts or less, repair open Dark Blue/White wire. If voltage is more than 10 volts, go to next step.
2) Measure voltage between ground and anti-lock brake controller module 25-pin connector terminal No. 25 (Red/Dark Green wire). If voltage is 10 volts or less, repair open Red/Dark Green wire. If voltage is more than 10 volts, go to next step.
3) Turn ignition off. Using external ohmmeter, measure resistance between ground and anti-lock brake controller module 25-pin connector terminal No. 24 (Black wire). If resistance is 10 ohms or more, repair open Black wire. If resistance is less than 10 ohms, go to next step.
4) Connect jumper wire between ground and anti-lock brake controller module 25-pin connector terminal No. 20 (Violet/Brown wire). Using scan tool, select BODY, BODY COMPUTER, then SYSTEM TEST. Perform CCD BUS test. If scan tool does not display BUS SHORT TO GROUND, repair open Violet/Brown wire. If scan tool displays BUS SHORT TO GROUND, go to next step.

5) Move jumper wire to terminal No. 19 (White/Black wire). Perform CCD BUS test. If scan tool does not display BUS SHORT TO GROUND, repair open White/Black wire. If scan tool displays BUS SHORT TO GROUND, replace anti-lock brake controller module.

BATTERY POWER TO MODULE DISCONNECT (NO RESPONSE FROM BCM, (BAT PWR DISCON'D) BATTERY POWER TO MODULE)

NOTE: For connector terminal identification and wiring diagrams, see BODY CONTROL COMPUTER – INTRODUCTION article. Perform VERIFICATION TEST VER-1 after each repair.

CAUTION: Always turn ignition off prior to disconnecting any module connector.

1) Remove and inspect fuse No. 11. If fuse is blown, go to next step. If fuse is okay, go to step 4).
2) Turn ignition off. Using external ohmmeter, measure resistance between ground and component side of fuse No. 11 terminal No. 19. See Fig. 1. If resistance is 5 ohms or more, replace fuse No. 11. If resistance is less than 5 ohms, go to next step.

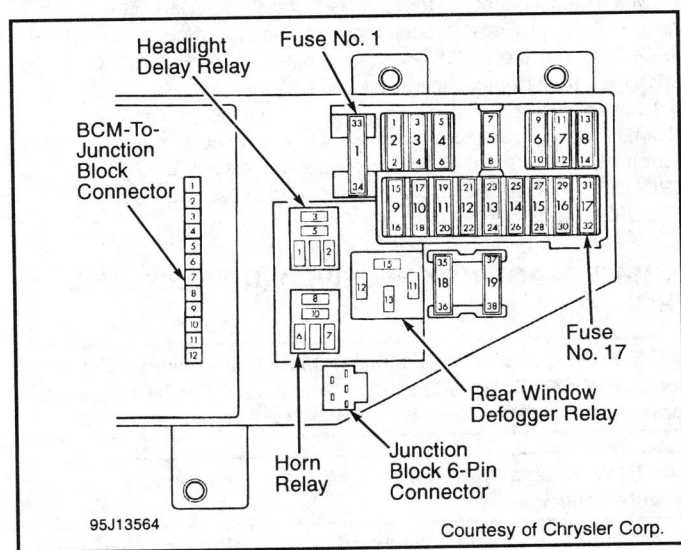

Fig. 1: Locating BCM/Junction Block Connector Terminals

3) Disconnect BCM. BCM is connected to junction block. Measure resistance between ground and component side of fuse No. 11 terminal No. 19. If resistance is 5 ohms or more, replace BCM and fuse No. 11. If resistance is less than 5 ohms, replace junction block.
4) Turn ignition off. Install fuse No. 11. Disconnect Body Control Module (BCM). BCM is connected to junction block. Using external ohmmeter, measure resistance between ground and junction block internal 12-pin connector terminal No. 10. See Fig. 1. If resistance is 20 ohms or more, repair open ground circuit/junction block. If resistance is less than 20 ohms, go to next step.
5) Turn ignition on. Using external voltmeter, measure voltage between ground and junction block internal 12-pin connector terminal No. 12. If voltage is 10 volts or less, replace junction block. If voltage is more than 10 volts, go to next step.
6) Measure voltage between ground and junction block internal 12-pin connector terminal No. 6. If voltage is 10 volts or less, replace junction block. If voltage is more than 10 volts, go to next step.
7) Measure voltage between ground and junction block internal 12-pin connector terminal No. 11. If voltage is 10 volts or less, replace junction block. If voltage is more than 10 volts, replace BCM.

CHRY
4-222

1999 ACCESSORIES & EQUIPMENT
Vehicle Communications
Breeze, Cirrus, Sebring Convertible & Stratus (Cont.)

EATX PRNDL MESSAGE TEST FAILED (NO RESPONSE FROM TCM)

NOTE: For connector terminal identification and wiring diagrams, see BODY CONTROL COMPUTER – INTRODUCTION article. Perform VERIFICATION TEST VER-1 after each repair.

CAUTION: Always turn ignition off prior to disconnecting any module connector.

1) Disconnect Transmission Control Module (TCM). TCM is located at left fenderwell, next to power distribution center. Turn ignition on. Connect jumper wire between ground and TCM connector terminal No. 43 (Violet/Dark Green wire). Using scan tool, select BODY, BODY COMPUTER, then SYSTEM TEST. Perform CCD BUS test. If scan tool does not display BUS SHORT TO GROUND, go to step **4)**. If scan tool displays BUS SHORT TO GROUND, go to next step.

2) Move jumper wire to terminal No. 4 (White/Dark Green wire). Perform CCD BUS test. If scan tool displays BUS SHORT TO GROUND, replace TCM. If scan tool does not display BUS SHORT TO GROUND, go to next step.

3) Connect jumper wire to ground and backprobe Body Control Module (BCM) 14-pin connector terminal No. 14 (White/Dark Green wire). Perform CCD BUS test. If scan tool does not display BUS SHORT TO GROUND, replace BCM. If scan tool displays BUS SHORT TO GROUND, repair open White/Dark Green wire.

4) Connect jumper wire between ground and Body Control Module (BCM) 14-pin connector, terminal No. 6 (Violet/Dark Green wire). Perform CCD BUS test. If scan tool does not display BUS SHORT TO GROUND, replace BCM. If scan tool displays BUS SHORT TO GROUND, repair open Violet/Dark Green wire.

PCM MESSAGE NOT RECEIVED (NO RESPONSE FROM PCM)

NOTE: For connector terminal identification and wiring diagrams, see BODY CONTROL COMPUTER – INTRODUCTION article. Perform VERIFICATION TEST VER-1 after each repair.

CAUTION: Always turn ignition off prior to disconnecting any module connector.

1) Disconnect Powertrain Control Module (PCM). PCM is located next to air cleaner. Turn ignition on. Connect jumper wire between ground and PCM connector terminal No. 59 (Violet/Brown wire). Using scan tool, select BODY, BODY COMPUTER, then SYSTEM TEST. Perform CCD BUS test. If scan tool does not display BUS SHORT TO GROUND, go to step **4)**. If scan tool displays BUS SHORT TO GROUND, go to next step.

2) Move jumper wire to terminal No. 60 (White/Black wire). Perform CCD BUS test. If scan tool displays BUS SHORT TO GROUND, replace PCM. If scan tool does not display BUS SHORT TO GROUND, go to next step.

3) Using jumper wire, backprobe BCM 14-pin connector between terminal No. 13 (White/Dark Green wire) and ground. Do not disconnect connector. Perform CCD BUS test. If scan tool does not display BUS SHORT TO GROUND, replace BCM. If scan tool displays BUS SHORT TO GROUND, repair open White/Dark Green wire.

4) Using jumper wire, backprobe BCM 14-pin connector between terminal No. 5 (Violet/Brown wire) and ground. Perform CCD BUS test. If scan tool does not display BUS SHORT TO GROUND, replace BCM. If scan tool displays BUS SHORT TO GROUND, repair open Violet/Brown wire.

BUS (+) & (−) OPEN (BUS (+) OPEN, BUS (−) OPEN, NO BUS BIAS)

NOTE: For connector terminal identification and wiring diagrams, see BODY CONTROL COMPUTER – INTRODUCTION article. Perform VERIFICATION TEST VER-1 after each repair.

CAUTION: Always turn ignition off prior to disconnecting any module connector.

NOTE: Ignition off during bus test is most common cause for this message.

1) If ignition was off during BUS test, turn ignition on. If ignition was on during BUS test, turn ignition on, engine off. Do not disconnect scan tool. Using an external voltmeter, backprobe DLC connector terminals. Measure voltage between ground and DLC terminal No. 3 (Violet/Gray wire on Breeze, Cirrus and Stratus, or Violet/Brown wire on Sebring Convertible). If voltage is not 2.3-2.6 volts, go to step **3)**. If voltage is 2.3-2.6 volts, go to next step.

2) Measure voltage between ground and DLC terminal No. 11 (White/Dark Green wire on Breeze, Cirrus and Stratus, or White/Dark Blue wire on Sebring Convertible). If voltage is not 2.3-2.6 volts, go to next step. If voltage is 2.3-2.6 volts, replace scan tool cable or scan tool.

3) Access Body Control Module (BCM) connectors. BCM is connected to junction block. Using jumper wire, backprobe BCM 22-pin connector between terminal No. 3 (Violet/Gray wire) on Breeze, Cirrus and Stratus or terminal No. 1 (Violet/Brown wire) on Sebring Convertible and ground. Using scan tool, select BODY, BODY COMPUTER, then SYSTEM TEST. Perform CCD BUS test. If scan tool does not display BUS SHORT TO GROUND, repair open Violet/Gray or Violet/Brown wire. If scan tool displays BUS SHORT TO GROUND, go to next step.

4) Move jumper wire to BCM 22-pin connector, terminal No. 13 (White/Dark Green wire) on Breeze, Cirrus and Stratus or terminal No. 11 (White/Dark Blue wire) on Sebring Convertible. Perform CCD BUS test. If scan tool does not display BUS SHORT TO GROUND, repair open White/Dark Green or White/Dark Blue wire. If scan tool displays BUS SHORT TO GROUND, go to next step.

NOTE: The resistance measurement in next 2 steps are performed at BCM, not at connectors.

5) Turn ignition off. Disconnect BCM from junction block. Using an external ohmmeter, measure resistance between BCM pins CCD BUS (+) and (−) terminals for 22-pin connector. See CCD BUS CIRCUIT IDENTIFICATION table. If resistance is not 100-140 ohms on all circuits, replace BCM. If resistance is 100-140 ohms on all circuits, go to next step.

CCD BUS CIRCUIT IDENTIFICATION

Terminal	Wire Color
Breeze, Cirrus & Stratus	
BCM 14-Pin Connector Bus (+)	
3	Violet/Brown
5	Violet/Brown
6	Violet/Dark Green
BCM 14-Pin Connector Bus (−)	
9	White/Black
13	White/Black
14	White/Dark Green
BCM 22-Pin Connector Bus (+)	
1	Violet/Brown
2	Violet
3	Violet/Gray
BCM 22-Pin Connector Bus (−)	
11	White/Dark Blue
12	White/Black
13	White/Dark Green
Sebring Convertible	

1999 ACCESSORIES & EQUIPMENT
Vehicle Communications
Breeze, Cirrus, Sebring Convertible & Stratus (Cont.)

CHRY
4-223

CCD BUS CIRCUIT IDENTIFICATION (Cont.)

Terminal	Wire Color
BCM 14-Pin Connector Bus (+)	
5	Violet/Brown
6	Violet/Dark Green
BCM 14-Pin Connector Bus (−)	
13	White/Black
14	White/Dark Green
BCM 22-Pin Connector Bus (+)	
1	Violet/Brown
2	Violet/Brown
BCM 22-Pin Connector Bus (−)	
11	White/Dark Blue
12	White/Dark Blue

6) Measure resistance between BCM pins CCD BUS (+) and (−) terminals for 14-pin connector. See CCD BUS CIRCUIT IDENTIFICATION table. If resistance is not 100-140 ohms on all circuits, replace BCM. If resistance is 100-140 ohms on all circuits, go to next step.

7) Turn ignition on. Using external voltmeter, measure voltage between ground and junction block internal 12-pin connector terminals No. 2 and 12. *See Fig. 1.* If voltage is 10 volts or less, repair fused B+ circuit/junction block as needed. See appropriate wiring diagram in BODY CONTROL COMPUTER – INTRODUCTION article. If voltage is more than 10 volts, go to next step.

8) Using external voltmeter, measure voltage between ground and junction block internal 12-pin connector terminal No. 6. If voltage is 10 volts or less, repair fused ignition switch output circuit as needed. See appropriate wiring diagram in BODY CONTROL COMPUTER – INTRODUCTION article. If voltage is more than 10 volts, go to next step.

9) Turn ignition off. Using external ohmmeter, measure resistance between ground and junction block internal 12-pin connector terminal No. 10. If resistance is 15 ohms or more, repair open ground circuit/junction block. See appropriate wiring diagram in BODY CONTROL COMPUTER – INTRODUCTION article. If resistance is less than 15 ohms, replace BCM.

BUS (+) & BUS (−) SHORTED TOGETHER

NOTE: For connector terminal identification and wiring diagrams, see BODY CONTROL COMPUTER – INTRODUCTION article. Perform VERIFICATION TEST VER-1 after each repair.

CAUTION: Always turn ignition off prior to disconnecting any module connector.

1) Turn ignition off. Disconnect Transmission Control Module (TCM), if equipped. TCM is located in left front corner of engine compartment, next to power distribution center. Turn ignition on. If scan tool does not display BUS (+) & BUS (−) SHORTED TOGETHER, replace TCM. If scan tool displays BUS (+) & BUS (−) SHORTED TOGETHER, go to next step.

2) Turn ignition off. Disconnect Powertrain Control Module (PCM). PCM is located next to air cleaner. Turn ignition on. If scan tool does not display BUS (+) & BUS (−) SHORTED TOGETHER, replace PCM. If scan tool displays BUS (+) & BUS (−) SHORTED TOGETHER, go to next step.

3) Turn ignition off. Disconnect instrument cluster. Turn ignition on. If scan tool does not display BUS (+) & BUS (−) SHORTED TOGETHER, replace instrument cluster. If scan tool displays BUS (+) & BUS (−) SHORTED TOGETHER, go to next step.

4) Turn ignition off. Disconnect Smart Key Immobilizer Module (SKIM), if equipped. SKIM is located at ignition lock cylinder. Turn ignition on. If scan tool does not display BUS (+) & BUS (−) SHORTED TOGETHER, replace SKIM. If scan tool displays BUS (+) & BUS (−) SHORTED TOGETHER, go to next step.

5) Turn ignition off. Disconnect anti-lock brake controller module. Anti-lock brake controller module is mounted on right inner fender panel of engine compartment. Turn ignition on. If scan tool does not display

BUS (+) & BUS (−) SHORTED TOGETHER, replace anti-lock brake controller module. If scan tool displays BUS (+) & BUS (−) SHORTED TOGETHER, go to next step.

6) Turn ignition off and wait 5 minutes. Disconnect Air Bag Control Module (ACM) 13-pin connector. ACM is located under center console. Turn ignition on. Open driver's door or turn on courtesy light. If scan tool does not display BUS (+) & BUS (−) SHORTED TOGETHER, replace ACM. If scan tool displays BUS (+) & BUS (−) SHORTED TOGETHER, go to next step.

7) Disconnect Body Control Module (BCM) 14-pin and 22-pin connectors. BCM is connected to junction block. Disconnect scan tool from Data Link Connector (DLC). Using an external ohmmeter, measure resistance between DLC bus (+) and related bus (−) terminals on BCM 14-pin and 22-pin connectors. See CCD BUS CIRCUIT IDENTIFICATION table. If resistance is less than 1000 ohms, repair short between applicable circuits. If resistance is 1000 ohms or more, go to next step.

8) Reconnect scan tool. Turn ignition on. Using scan tool, perform CCD bus test. If scan tool displays BUS (+) & BUS (−) SHORTED TOGETHER, replace scan tool cable or scan tool as necessary. If scan tool does not display BUS (+) & BUS (−) SHORTED TOGETHER, replace BCM.

BUS BIAS TO HIGH/LOW LEVEL

NOTE: For connector terminal identification and wiring diagrams, see BODY CONTROL COMPUTER – INTRODUCTION article. Perform VERIFICATION TEST VER-1 after each repair.

CAUTION: Always turn ignition off prior to disconnecting any module connector.

NOTE: Ignition off during bus test is most common cause for this trouble code.

1) Turn ignition off. Disconnect Transmission Control Module (TCM), if equipped. TCM is located at left front corner of engine compartment, next to power distribution center. Turn ignition on. If scan tool does not display BUS BIAS TOO HIGH/LOW, replace TCM. If scan tool displays BUS BIAS TOO HIGH/LOW, go to next step.

2) Turn ignition off. Disconnect Powertrain Control Module (PCM). PCM is located next to air cleaner. Turn ignition on. If scan tool does not display BUS BIAS TOO HIGH/LOW, replace PCM. If scan tool displays BUS BIAS TOO HIGH/LOW, go to next step.

3) Turn ignition off. Disconnect instrument cluster. Turn ignition on. If scan tool does not display BUS BIAS TOO HIGH/LOW, replace instrument cluster. If scan tool displays BUS BIAS TOO HIGH/LOW, go to next step.

4) Turn ignition off. Disconnect Smart Key Immobilizer Module (SKIM), if equipped. SKIM is located at ignition lock cylinder. Turn ignition on. If scan tool does not display BUS BIAS TOO HIGH/LOW, replace SKIM. If scan tool displays BUS BIAS TOO HIGH/LOW, go to next step.

5) Turn ignition off. Disconnect anti-lock brake controller module. Anti-lock brake controller module is mounted on right inner fender panel of engine compartment. Turn ignition on. If scan tool does not display BUS BIAS TOO HIGH/LOW, replace anti-lock brake controller module. If scan tool displays BUS BIAS TOO HIGH/LOW, go to next step.

6) Turn ignition off and wait 5 minutes. Disconnect Air Bag Control Module (ACM) 13-pin connector. ACM is located under center console. Turn ignition on. If scan tool does not display BUS BIAS TOO HIGH/LOW, replace ACM. If scan tool displays BUS BIAS TOO HIGH/LOW, go to next step.

7) Disconnect Body Control Module (BCM) 14-pin and 22-pin connectors. BCM is connected to junction block. Turn ignition on. If scan tool displays BUS BIAS TOO HIGH, go to step **10)**. If scan tool does not display BUS BIAS TOO HIGH, go to next step.

8) Turn ignition off. Using external ohmmeter, measure resistance between each CCD BUS (+) terminals on BCM 14-pin and 22-pin connectors and ground. See CCD BUS CIRCUIT IDENTIFICATION

CHRY
4-224

1999 ACCESSORIES & EQUIPMENT
Vehicle Communications
Breeze, Cirrus, Sebring Convertible & Stratus (Cont.)

table. If resistance is less than 17 k/ohms, repair appropriate circuit for partial short to ground. If resistance is 17 k/ohms or more, go to next step.

9) Measure resistance between each CCD BUS (–) terminals on BCM 14-pin and 22-pin connectors and ground. See CCD BUS CIRCUIT IDENTIFICATION table. If resistance is less than 17 k/ohms, repair appropriate circuit for partial short to ground. If resistance is 17 k/ohms or more, replace BCM.

10) Using external voltmeter, measure voltage between each CCD BUS (+) terminals on BCM 14-pin and 22-pin connectors and ground. See CCD BUS CIRCUIT IDENTIFICATION table. If voltage is more than 0.2 volt, repair appropriate circuit for partial short to voltage. If voltage is 0.2 volt or less, go to next step.

11) Measure voltage between each CCD BUS (–) terminals on BCM 14-pin and 22-pin connectors and ground. See CCD BUS CIRCUIT IDENTIFICATION table. If voltage is more than 0.2 volt, repair appropriate circuit for partial short to voltage. If voltage is 0.2 volt or less, replace BCM.

CCD SHORT TO 5 VOLTS

NOTE: For connector terminal identification and wiring diagrams, see BODY CONTROL COMPUTER – INTRODUCTION article. Perform VERIFICATION TEST VER-1 after each repair.

CAUTION: Always turn ignition off prior to disconnecting any module connector.

1) Turn ignition off. Disconnect Transmission Control Module (TCM), if equipped. TCM is located next to power distribution center in left front corner of engine compartment. Turn ignition on. If scan tool does not display BUS SHORT TO 5 VOLTS, replace TCM. If scan tool displays BUS SHORT TO 5 VOLTS, go to next step.

2) Turn ignition off. Disconnect Powertrain Control Module (PCM). PCM is located next to air cleaner. Turn ignition on. If scan tool does not display BUS SHORT TO 5 VOLTS, go to step **16)**. If scan tool displays BUS SHORT TO 5 VOLTS, go to next step.

3) Turn ignition off. Disconnect instrument cluster. Turn ignition on. If scan tool does not display BUS SHORT TO 5 VOLTS, go to step **14)**. If scan tool displays BUS SHORT TO 5 VOLTS, go to next step.

4) Turn ignition off. Disconnect Smart Key Immobilizer Module (SKIM), if equipped. SKIM is located at ignition lock cylinder. Turn ignition on. If scan tool does not display BUS SHORT TO 5 VOLTS, replace SKIM. If scan tool displays BUS SHORT TO 5 VOLTS, go to next step.

5) Turn ignition off. Disconnect anti-lock brake controller module. Anti-lock brake controller module is mounted on right inner fender panel of engine compartment. Turn ignition on. If scan tool does not display BUS SHORT TO 5 VOLTS, replace anti-lock brake controller module. If scan tool displays BUS SHORT TO 5 VOLTS, go to next step.

6) Turn ignition off and wait 5 minutes. Disconnect Air Bag Control Module (ACM) connector. ACM is located under center console. Turn ignition on. If scan tool does not display BUS SHORT TO 5 VOLTS, replace ACM. If scan tool displays BUS SHORT TO 5 VOLTS, go to next step.

7) Disconnect scan tool from Data Link Connector (DLC). Disconnect Body Control Module (BCM) 22-pin connector. Turn ignition on. Using an external voltmeter, measure voltage between ground and DLC terminal No. 3 (Violet/Gray wire on Breeze, Cirrus and Stratus and Violet/Brown wire on Sebring Convertible). If voltage is more than .5 volt, repair Violet/Gray or Violet/Brown wire for short to voltage. If voltage is .5 volt or less, go to next step.

8) Measure voltage between ground and DLC terminal No. 11 (White/Dark Green on Breeze, Cirrus and Stratus and White/Dark Blue wire on Sebring Convertible). If voltage is more than .5 volt, repair White/Dark Green wire or White/Dark Blue wire for short to voltage. If voltage is less than .5 volt, go to next step.

9) Turn ignition off. Using an external ohmmeter, measure resistance between Body Control Module (BCM) 22-pin connector terminal No. 7

(Light Green/Black wire) and each CCD BUS (+) terminals on BCM 22-pin connector. See CCD BUS CIRCUIT IDENTIFICATION table. If resistance between any terminals is less than 5 ohms, repair appropriate wire for short to Light Green/Black wire. If resistance of all terminals are 5 ohms or more, go to next step.

10) Measure resistance between BCM 22-pin connector terminal No. 7 (Light Green/Black wire) and each CCD BUS (–) terminals on BCM 22-pin connector. See CCD BUS CIRCUIT IDENTIFICATION table. If resistance between any terminals is less than 5 ohms, repair appropriate wire for short to Light Green/Black wire. If resistance of all terminals are 5 ohms or more, go to next step.

11) Measure resistance between BCM 22-pin connector terminal No. 17 (Light Blue wire) and each CCD BUS (+) terminals on BCM 22-pin connector. See CCD BUS CIRCUIT IDENTIFICATION table. If resistance between any terminals is less than 5 ohms, repair appropriate wire for short to Light Blue wire. If resistance of all terminals are 5 ohms or more, go to next step.

12) Measure resistance between BCM 22-pin connector terminal No. 17 (Light Blue wire) and each CCD BUS (–) terminals on BCM 22-pin connector. See CCD BUS CIRCUIT IDENTIFICATION table. If resistance between any terminals is less than 5 ohms, repair appropriate wire for short to Light Blue wire. If resistance of all terminals are 5 ohms or more, go to next step.

13) Reconnect scan tool from DLC. Using scan tool, perform CCD bus test. If scan tool does not display BUS SHORT TO 5 VOLTS, replace BCM. If scan tool displays BUS SHORT TO 5 VOLTS, replace scan tool cable or scan tool as necessary.

14) Turn ignition off. Using external ohmmeter, measure resistance between ground and instrument cluster Red connector terminal No. 4 (Black/Light Green wire). If resistance is 5 ohms or more, repair open Black/Light Green wire. If resistance is less than 5 ohms, go to next step.

15) Measure resistance of instrument cluster Blue connector, terminal No. 11 (Black/Orange wire) circuit. If resistance is 5 ohms or more, repair open Black/Orange wire. If resistance is less than 5 ohms, replace instrument cluster circuit board.

16) Turn ignition off. Using an external ohmmeter, measure resistance between PCM connector terminals No. 59 (Violet/Brown wire) and No. 61 (Violet/White wire). If resistance is less than 5 ohms, repair short between Violet/Brown wire and Violet/White wire. If resistance is 5 ohms or more, go to next step.

17) Measure resistance between PCM connector terminals No. 60 (White/Black wire) and No. 61 (Violet/White wire). If resistance is less than 5 ohms, repair short between White/Black wire and Violet/White wire. If resistance is 5 ohms or more, replace PCM.

CCD SHORT TO BATTERY

NOTE: For connector terminal identification and wiring diagrams, see BODY CONTROL COMPUTER – INTRODUCTION article. Perform VERIFICATION TEST VER-1 after each repair.

CAUTION: Always turn ignition off prior to disconnecting any module connector.

1) Turn ignition off. Disconnect Transmission Control Module (TCM), if equipped. TCM is located next to power distribution center in left front corner of engine compartment. Turn ignition on. If scan tool does not display BUS SHORT TO BATTERY, replace TCM. If scan tool displays BUS SHORT TO BATTERY, go to next step.

2) Turn ignition off. Disconnect Powertrain Control Module (PCM). PCM is located next to air cleaner. Turn ignition on. If scan tool does not display BUS SHORT TO BATTERY, go to step **14)**. If scan tool displays BUS SHORT TO BATTERY, go to next step.

3) Turn ignition off. Disconnect instrument cluster. Turn ignition on. If scan tool does not display BUS SHORT TO BATTERY, go to step **12)**. If scan tool displays BUS SHORT TO BATTERY, go to next step.

4) Turn ignition off and wait 5 minutes. Disconnect Air Bag Control Module (ACM) connector. ACM is located under center console. Turn

1999 ACCESSORIES & EQUIPMENT
Vehicle Communications
Breeze, Cirrus, Sebring Convertible & Stratus (Cont.)

CHRY
4-225

ignition on. If scan tool does not display BUS SHORT TO BATTERY, replace ACM. If scan tool displays BUS SHORT TO BATTERY, go to next step.

5) Turn ignition off. Disconnect Smart Key Immobilizer Module (SKIM), if equipped. SKIM is located at ignition lock cylinder. Turn ignition on. If scan tool does not display BUS SHORT TO BATTERY, replace SKIM. If scan tool displays BUS SHORT TO BATTERY, go to next step.

6) Turn ignition off. Disconnect anti-lock brake controller module. Anti-lock brake controller module is mounted on right inner fender panel of engine compartment. Turn ignition on. If scan tool does not display BUS SHORT TO BATTERY, replace anti-lock brake controller module. If scan tool displays BUS SHORT TO BATTERY, go to next step.

7) Turn ignition off. Disconnect Body Control Module (BCM) 22-pin connector. BCM is located on back of junction block. Turn ignition on. If scan tool does not display BUS SHORT TO BATTERY, go to step **10)**. If scan tool displays BUS SHORT TO BATTERY, go to next step.

8) Disconnect scan tool from Data Link Connector (DLC). Disconnect BCM 22-pin connector. Turn ignition on. Using an external voltmeter, measure voltage between ground and DLC terminal No. 3 (Violet/Gray wire on Breeze, Cirrus and Stratus or Violet/Brown wire on Sebring Convertible). If voltage is more than .5 volt, repair Violet/Gray or Violet/Brown wire for short to voltage. If voltage is .5 volt or less, go to next step.

9) Measure voltage between ground and DLC terminal No. 11 (White/Dark Green on Breeze, Cirrus and Stratus or White/Dark Blue wire on Sebring Convertible). If voltage is more than .5 volt, repair White/Dark Green wire or White/Dark Blue wire for short to voltage. If voltage is less than .5 volt, go to next step.

10) Reconnect scan tool from DLC. Ensure ignition is on. If scan tool does not display BUS SHORT TO BATTERY, replace BCM. If scan tool displays BUS SHORT TO BATTERY, replace scan tool cable or scan tool as necessary.

11) Turn ignition on. Using external voltmeter, measure voltage between ground and each CCD BUS (+) terminals on BCM 22-pin connector. See CCD BUS CIRCUIT IDENTIFICATION table. If voltage of any terminal is more than .5 volt, repair short to voltage in appropriate circuit. If voltage of all terminals are .5 volt or less, go to next step.

12) Measure voltage between ground and each CCD BUS (–) terminals on BCM 22-pin connector. See CCD BUS CIRCUIT IDENTIFICATION table. If voltage of any terminal is more than .5 volt, repair short to voltage in appropriate circuit. If voltage of all terminals are .5 volt or less, replace BCM.

13) Turn ignition off. Using external ohmmeter, measure resistance between ground and instrument cluster Red connector, terminal No. 4 (Black/Light Green wire). If resistance is 5 ohms or more, repair open Black/Light Green wire. If resistance is less than 5 ohms, go to next step.

14) Measure resistance between ground and instrument cluster Blue connector, terminal No. 11 (Black/Orange wire). If resistance is 5 ohms or more, repair open Black/Orange wire. If resistance is less than 5 ohms, replace instrument cluster circuit board.

15) Turn ignition off. Using an external ohmmeter, measure resistance between PCM connector terminals No. 44 (Orange/White wire) and No. 59 (Violet/Brown wire). If resistance is less than 5 ohms, repair short between Orange/White wire and Violet/Brown wire. If resistance is 5 ohms or more, go to next step.

16) Measure resistance between PCM connector terminals No. 44 (Orange/White wire) and No. 60 (White/Black wire). If resistance is less than 5 ohms, repair short between Orange/White wire and White/Black wire. If resistance is 5 ohms or more, replace PCM.

CCD SHORT TO GROUND

NOTE: For connector terminal identification and wiring diagrams, see BODY CONTROL COMPUTER – INTRODUCTION article. Perform VERIFICATION TEST VER-1 after each repair.

CAUTION: Always turn ignition off prior to disconnecting any module connector.

NOTE: For appropriate wire color tracers (i.e., Black/*), see appropriate wiring diagram in BODY CONTROL COMPUTER – INTRODUCTION article.

1) Connect backprobe jumper wire between Data Link Connector (DLC) ground terminals No. 4 (Black/* wire) and No. 5 (Black/* wire). If scan tool does not display BUS SHORT TO GROUND, repair open ground wire. See appropriate wiring diagram in BODY CONTROL COMPUTER – INTRODUCTION article. If scan tool displays BUS SHORT TO GROUND, go to next step.

2) Turn ignition off. Disconnect Transmission Control Module (TCM), if equipped. TCM is located at left front corner of engine compartment, next to power distribution center. Turn ignition on. If scan tool does not display BUS SHORT TO GROUND, replace TCM. If scan tool displays BUS SHORT TO GROUND, go to next step.

3) Turn ignition off. Disconnect Powertrain Control Module (PCM). PCM is located next to air cleaner. Turn ignition on. If scan tool does not display BUS SHORT TO GROUND, replace PCM. If scan tool displays BUS SHORT TO GROUND, go to next step.

4) Turn ignition off. Disconnect instrument cluster. Turn ignition on. If scan tool does not display BUS SHORT TO GROUND, replace instrument cluster. If scan tool displays BUS SHORT TO GROUND, go to next step.

5) Turn ignition off. Disconnect Smart Key Immobilizer Module (SKIM), if equipped. SKIM is located at ignition lock cylinder. Turn ignition on. If scan tool does not display BUS SHORT TO GROUND, replace SKIM. If scan tool displays BUS SHORT TO GROUND, go to next step.

6) Turn ignition off. Disconnect anti-lock brake controller module. Anti-lock brake controller module is mounted on right inner fender panel of engine compartment. Turn ignition on. If scan tool does not display BUS SHORT TO GROUND, replace anti-lock brake controller module. If scan tool displays BUS SHORT TO GROUND, go to next step.

7) Turn ignition off and wait 5 minutes. Disconnect Air Bag Control Module (ACM) 13-pin connector. ACM is located under center console. Turn ignition on. If scan tool does not display BUS SHORT TO GROUND, replace ACM. If scan tool displays BUS SHORT TO GROUND, go to next step.

8) Disconnect Body Control Module (BCM) 22-pin connector. BCM is connected to junction block. Turn ignition on. If scan tool does not display BUS SHORT TO GROUND, go to step **12)**. If scan tool displays BUS SHORT TO GROUND, go to next step.

9) Disconnect BCM 10-pin instrument panel connector. Measure resistance between ground and BCM 10-pin connector terminal No. 8 (Black/Light Green wire). If resistance is less than 5 ohms, repair short to ground in Black/Light Green wire. If resistance is 5 ohms or more, go to next step.

10) Disconnect scan tool from DLC. Measure resistance between ground and DLC terminal No. 3 (Violet/Gray wire on Breeze, Cirrus and Stratus and Violet/Brown wire on Sebring Convertible). If resistance is less than 5 ohms, repair Violet/Gray or Violet/Brown wire for short to ground. If resistance is 5 ohms or more, go to next step.

11) Measure resistance between ground and DLC terminal No. 11 (White/Dark Green on Breeze, Cirrus and Stratus and White/Dark Blue wire on Sebring Convertible). If resistance is less than 5 ohms, repair White/Dark Green wire or White/Dark Blue wire for short to ground. If resistance is 5 ohms or more, replace scan tool cable or scan tool as necessary.

CHRY
4-226

1999 ACCESSORIES & EQUIPMENT
Vehicle Communications
Breeze, Cirrus, Sebring Convertible & Stratus (Cont.)

12) Turn ignition off. Using an external ohmmeter, measure resistance between ground and each CCD BUS (+) terminals on BCM 22-pin connector. See CCD BUS CIRCUIT IDENTIFICATION table. If resistance of any terminals are less than 5 ohms, repair short to ground in appropriate circuit. If resistance of all terminals are 5 ohms or more, go to next step.

13) Measure resistance between ground and each CCD BUS (−) terminals on BCM 22-pin connector. See CCD BUS CIRCUIT IDENTIFICATION table. If resistance of any terminals are less than 5 ohms, repair short to ground in appropriate circuit. See appropriate wiring diagram in BODY CONTROL COMPUTER – INTRODUCTION article. If resistance of all terminals are 5 ohms or more, replace BCM.

DRB BLANK SCREEN

NOTE: *For connector terminal identification and wiring diagrams, see BODY CONTROL COMPUTER – INTRODUCTION article. Perform VERIFICATION TEST VER-1 after each repair.*

CAUTION: *Always turn ignition off prior to disconnecting any module connector.*

Disconnect scan tool from DLC. Ensure ground circuit has continuity at DLC terminal No. 4. Ensure 12 volts is present at DLC terminal No. 16. If voltage is not present at DLC terminal No. 16, inspect junction block fuse No. 5 and Power Distribution Center fuse No. 4. Try another scan tool and/or cable.

NO RESPONSE FROM AIR BAG CONTROL MODULE (ACM)

NOTE: *For connector terminal identification and wiring diagrams, see BODY CONTROL COMPUTER – INTRODUCTION article. Perform VERIFICATION TEST VER-1 after each repair.*

CAUTION: *Always turn ignition off prior to disconnecting any module connector.*

1) Remove and inspect fuse No. 17. If fuse is blown, go to next step. If fuse is okay, go to step **3)**.

2) Disconnect battery and wait 2 minutes. Disconnect Air Bag Control Module (ACM) 13-pin connector. ACM is located under center console. Remove fuse No. 16. Using external ohmmeter, measure resistance between ground and component side of fuse No. 17 (Light Green/Yellow wire). If resistance is less than 5 ohms, repair Light Green/Yellow wire between fuse and Air Bag Control Module (ACM) for short to ground. If resistance is 5 ohms or more, replace fuse.

3) Turn ignition on. Using external voltmeter, measure voltage between ground and feed side of fuse No. 17 (Dark Blue wire). If voltage is 10 volts or less, repair open Dark Blue wire between ignition switch and junction block. If voltage is more than 10 volts, go to next step.

4) Disconnect battery and wait 2 minutes. Disconnect Air Bag Control Module (ACM) 13-pin connector. ACM is located under center console. Reinstall fuse No. 17. Reconnect battery. Turn ignition on. Using external voltmeter, measure voltage between ground and ACM connector terminal No. 1 (Light Green/Yellow wire). If voltage is 10 volts or less, repair open Light Green/Yellow wire. If voltage is more than 10 volts, go to next step.

5) Turn ignition off. Using ohmmeter, measure resistance between ground and ACM connector terminal No. 11 (Black/Light Green wire on Breeze, Cirrus and Stratus or Black/Pink wire on Sebring Convertible). If resistance is 5 ohms or more, repair open Black/Light Green wire or Black/Pink wire. If resistance is less than 5 ohms, go to next step.

6) Connect jumper between ground and ACM 13-pin connector terminal No. 3 (Violet wire on Breeze, Cirrus and Stratus or Violet/Brown wire on Sebring Convertible). Using scan tool, select BODY, BODY COMPUTER, then SYSTEM TEST. Perform CCD BUS test. If scan tool does not display BUS SHORT TO GROUND, repair open Violet or Violet/Brown wire. If scan tool displays BUS SHORT TO GROUND, go to next step.

7) Move jumper wire to ACM 13-pin terminal No. 4 (White/Black wire on Breeze, Cirrus and Stratus and White/Dark Blue wire on Sebring Convertible). Perform CCD BUS test. If scan tool does not display BUS SHORT TO GROUND, repair open White/Black or White/Dark Blue wire. If scan tool displays BUS SHORT TO GROUND, replace ACM.

NO RESPONSE FROM SMART KEY IMMOBILIZER MODULE (SKIM)

NOTE: *For connector terminal identification and wiring diagrams, see BODY CONTROL COMPUTER – INTRODUCTION article. Perform VERIFICATION TEST VER-1 after each repair.*

CAUTION: *Always turn ignition off prior to disconnecting any module connector.*

1) Using scan tool select BODY COMPUTER, SYSTEM TEST then PCM MONITOR. If scan tool does not display PCM ACTIVE ON THE BUS, go to PCM MESSAGE NOT RECEIVED (NO RESPONSE FROM PCM). If scan tool displays PCM ACTIVE ON THE BUS, go to next step.

2) Disconnect Smart Key Immobilizer Module (SKIM). SKIM is located at ignition lock cylinder. Turn ignition off. Using external ohmmeter, measure resistance between ground and SKIM connector terminal No. 2 (Black wire). If resistance is 5 ohms or more, repair open Black wire. If resistance is less than 5 ohms, go to next step.

3) Using an external voltmeter, measure voltage between ground and SKIM connector terminal No. 1 (Pink wire). If voltage is 10 volts or less, repair open Pink wire. If voltage is more than 10 volts, go to next step.

4) Turn ignition on. Measure voltage between ground and SKIM connector terminal No. 3 (Light Green/Black wire). If voltage is 10 volts or less, repair open Light Green/Black wire. If voltage is more than 10 volts, go to next step.

5) Connect jumper wire between ground and SKIM connector terminal No. 5 (White/Dark Blue wire). Using scan tool, select BODY, BODY COMPUTER, then SYSTEM TEST. Perform CCD BUS test. If scan tool does not display BUS SHORT TO GROUND, repair open White/Dark Blue wire. If scan tool displays BUS SHORT TO GROUND, go to next step.

6) Move jumper wire to terminal No. 6 (Violet/Brown wire). Perform CCD BUS test. If scan tool does not display BUS SHORT TO GROUND, repair open Violet/Brown wire. If scan tool displays BUS SHORT TO GROUND, replace SKIM.

NO RESPONSE FROM INSTRUMENT CLUSTER

NOTE: *For connector terminal identification and wiring diagrams, see BODY CONTROL COMPUTER – INTRODUCTION article. Perform VERIFICATION TEST VER-1 after each repair.*

CAUTION: *Always turn ignition off prior to disconnecting any module connector.*

1) Turn ignition off. Remove and inspect fuse No. 7. If fuse No. 7 is blown, go to next step. If fuse No. 7 is okay, go to step **3)**.

2) Using external ohmmeter, measure resistance between ground and component side of fuse No. 7 (Pink/Red wire). If resistance is less than 5 ohms, repair Pink/Red wire for short to ground and replace fuse No. 7. If resistance is 5 ohms or more, replace fuse.

3) Turn ignition off. Remove and inspect fuse No. 11. If fuse No. 11 is blown, go to next step. If fuse No. 11 is okay, go to step **5)**.

4) Using external ohmmeter, measure resistance between ground and component side of fuse No. 11 (Red/Violet wire). If resistance is less than 5 ohms, repair Red/Violet wire for short to ground and replace fuse No. 11. If resistance is 5 ohms or more, replace fuse.

5) Install both fuses. Disconnect instrument cluster connectors. Turn ignition on. Using external voltmeter, measure voltage between ground

1999 ACCESSORIES & EQUIPMENT
Vehicle Communications
Breeze, Cirrus, Sebring Convertible & Stratus (Cont.)

CHRY
4-227

and Red instrument cluster connector terminal No. 2 (Red/Violet wire). If voltage is 10 volts or less, repair open Red/Violet wire. If voltage is more than 10 volts, go to next step.

6) Measure voltage between ground and Red instrument cluster connector terminal No. 5 (Pink/Red wire). If voltage is 10 volts or less, repair open Pink/Red wire. If voltage is more than 10 volts, go to next step.

7) Turn ignition off. Using external ohmmeter, measure resistance between ground and Red instrument cluster connector, terminal No. 4 (Black/Light Green wire). If resistance is 10 ohms or more, repair open Black/Light Green wire. If resistance is less than 10 ohms, go to next step.

8) Turn ignition on. Connect jumper between instrument cluster Blue connector, terminal No. 8 (Violet/Brown wire) and ground. Using scan tool, select BODY, BODY COMPUTER, then SYSTEM TEST. Perform CCD BUS test. If scan tool does not display BUS SHORT TO GROUND, go to step 11). If scan tool displays BUS SHORT TO GROUND, go to next step.

9) Move jumper wire to terminal No. 7 (White/Dark Blue wire). Perform CCD BUS test. If scan tool displays BUS SHORT TO GROUND, replace instrument cluster. If scan tool does not display BUS SHORT TO GROUND, go to next step.

10) Using jumper wire, backprobe BCM 22-pin connector between terminal No. 11 (White/Dark Blue wire) and ground. Do not disconnect connector. Perform CCD BUS test. If scan tool does not display BUS SHORT TO GROUND, replace BCM. If scan tool displays BUS SHORT TO GROUND, repair open White/Dark Blue wire.

11) Using jumper wire, backprobe BCM 22-pin connector between terminal No. 1 (Violet/Brown wire) and ground. Do not disconnect connector. Perform CCD BUS test. If scan tool does not display BUS SHORT TO GROUND, replace BCM. If scan tool displays BUS SHORT TO GROUND, repair open Violet/Brown wire.

NO TERMINATION

NOTE: For connector terminal identification and wiring diagrams, see BODY CONTROL COMPUTER – INTRODUCTION article. Perform VERIFICATION TEST VER-1 after each repair.

CAUTION: Always turn ignition off prior to disconnecting any module connector.

NOTE: Ignition off during bus test is most common cause for this trouble code.

1) Turn ignition off. Access Body Control Module (BCM) 22-pin connector. BCM is connected to junction block. Do not disconnect connector. Using jumper wire connected to ground, backprobe BCM 22-pin connector between terminal No. 3 (Violet/Gray wire) on Breeze, Cirrus and Stratus or terminal No. 1 (Violet/Brown wire) on Sebring Convertible. Using scan tool, select BODY, BODY COMPUTER, then SYSTEM TEST. Perform CCD BUS test. If scan tool does not display BUS SHORT TO GROUND, repair open Violet/Gray or Violet/Brown wire. If scan tool displays BUS SHORT TO GROUND, go to next step.

2) Move jumper wire to BCM 22-pin connector, terminal No. 13 (White/Dark Green wire) on Breeze, Cirrus and Stratus or terminal No. 11 (White/Dark Blue wire) on Sebring Convertible. Perform CCD BUS test. If scan tool does not display BUS SHORT TO GROUND, repair open White/Dark Green or White/Dark Blue wire. If scan tool displays BUS SHORT TO GROUND, go to next step.

NOTE: The resistance measurement in next 2 steps are performed at BCM, not at connectors.

3) Turn ignition off. Disconnect scan tool from DLC. Disconnect BCM from junction block. Using an external ohmmeter, measure resistance between BCM pins CCD BUS (+) and (–) terminals for 22-pin connector. See CCD BUS CIRCUIT IDENTIFICATION table. If resistance is not 100-140 ohms on all circuits, replace BCM. If resistance is 100-140 ohms on all circuits, go to next step.

4) Measure resistance between BCM pins CCD BUS (+) and (–) terminals for 14-pin connector. See CCD BUS CIRCUIT IDENTIFICATION table. If resistance is not 100-140 ohms on all circuits, replace BCM. If resistance is 100-140 ohms on all circuits, replace scan tool cable or scan tool.

NOT RECEIVING BUS MESSAGES CORRECTLY

NOTE: For connector terminal identification and wiring diagrams, see BODY CONTROL COMPUTER – INTRODUCTION article. Perform VERIFICATION TEST VER-1 after each repair.

CAUTION: Always turn ignition off prior to disconnecting any module connector.

1) Turn ignition off. Disconnect Transmission Control Module (TCM), if equipped. TCM is located in left front corner of engine compartment, next to power distribution center. Turn ignition on. If scan tool does not display NOT RECEIVING BUS MESSAGES CORRECTLY, replace TCM. If scan tool displays NOT RECEIVING BUS MESSAGES CORRECTLY, go to next step.

2) Turn ignition off and reconnect TCM. Disconnect Powertrain Control Module (PCM). PCM is located next to air cleaner. Turn ignition on. If scan tool does not display NOT RECEIVING BUS MESSAGES CORRECTLY, replace PCM. If scan tool displays NOT RECEIVING BUS MESSAGES CORRECTLY, go to next step.

3) Turn ignition off and reconnect PCM. Disconnect instrument cluster. Turn ignition on. If scan tool does not display NOT RECEIVING BUS MESSAGES CORRECTLY, replace instrument cluster. If scan tool displays NOT RECEIVING BUS MESSAGES CORRECTLY, go to next step.

4) Turn ignition off and wait 5 minutes. Reconnect instrument cluster. Disconnect Air Bag Control Module (ACM) 13-pin connector. ACM is located under center console. Turn ignition on. If scan tool does not display NOT RECEIVING BUS MESSAGES CORRECTLY, replace ACM. If scan tool displays NOT RECEIVING BUS MESSAGES CORRECTLY, go to next step.

5) Turn ignition off and reconnect ACM. Disconnect Smart Key Immobilizer Module (SKIM), if equipped. SKIM is located at ignition lock cylinder. Turn ignition on. If scan tool does not display NOT RECEIVING BUS MESSAGES CORRECTLY, replace SKIM. If scan tool displays NOT RECEIVING BUS MESSAGES CORRECTLY, go to next step.

6) Turn ignition off and reconnect SKIM. Disconnect anti-lock brake controller module. Anti-lock brake controller module is mounted on right inner fender panel of engine compartment. Turn ignition on. If scan tool does not display NOT RECEIVING BUS MESSAGES CORRECTLY, replace anti-lock brake controller module. If scan tool displays NOT RECEIVING BUS MESSAGES CORRECTLY, go to next step.

7) Disconnect Body Control Module (BCM) 14-pin and 22-pin connectors. BCM is connected to junction block. If scan tool does not display NOT RECEIVING BUS MESSAGES CORRECTLY, replace BCM. If scan tool displays NOT RECEIVING BUS MESSAGES CORRECTLY, replace scan tool cable or scan tool.

VERIFICATION TEST VER-1A

1) Reconnect all previously disconnected components and wiring. Turn ignition on. Use scan tool to erase trouble codes. Turn ignition off and wait at least 5 seconds and then turn ignition on (engine off).

2) Operate system that was malfunctioning to verify correct operation. If system does not operate properly, go to SYMPTOM IDENTIFICATION TEST 1A in BODY CONTROL COMPUTER TESTS – BREEZE, CIRRUS, SEBRING CONVERTIBLE, STRATUS article. If system operates properly, read fault messages using scan tool. If any codes are present, go to SYMPTOM IDENTIFICATION TEST 1A in BODY CONTROL COMPUTER TESTS – BREEZE, CIRRUS, SEBRING CONVERTIBLE, STRATUS article. If no codes are present, repair is complete.

IDENTIFYING VEHICLE COMMUNICATION PROBLEMS

Connect scan tool to Data Link Connector (DLC) to retrieve messages. If scan tool message is blank, disconnect scan tool. Ensure ground circuit has continuity at DLC terminal No. 4. Ensure 12 volts is present at DLC terminal No. 16. Try another scan tool and/or cable. See following bus fault messages list and proceed to appropriate DTC or fault message.

- ABS MESSAGE NOT RECEIVED (NO RESPONSE FROM CAB)
- AIR BAG MESSAGE NOT RECEIVED (NO RESPONSE FROM ACM)
- BATTERY POWER TO MODULE DISCONNECT (NO RESPONSE FROM BCM)
- EATX PRNDL MESSAGE TEST FAILED
- NO CCD MESSAGE FROM PCM
- BUS (+) & BUS (−) SHORTED TOGETHER
- BUS (+) OPEN (BUS (−) OPEN, BUS BIAS LEVEL TOO HIGH, BUS BIAS LEVEL TOO LOW)
- NO BUS BIAS
- NO RESPONSE FROM CMTC (NO DISPLAY ON CMTC EXCEPT DIRECTION & TEMPERATURE)
- NO RESPONSE FROM HVAC
- NO RESPONSE FROM INSTRUMENT CLUSTER
- NO RESPONSE FROM PCM
- NO RESPONSE FROM RADIO
- NO RESPONSE FROM TCM
- NO TERMINATION
- NOT RECEIVING MESSAGES CORRECTLY
- SHORT TO 5 VOLTS
- SHORT TO BATTERY
- SHORT TO GROUND

ABS MESSAGE NOT RECEIVED (NO RESPONSE FROM CAB)

NOTE: For connector terminal identification and wiring diagrams, see BODY CONTROL COMPUTER – INTRODUCTION article. Perform VERIFICATION TEST VER-1A after each repair. Controller Anti-Lock Brake (CAB) module will be referred to as anti-lock brake controller module.

CAUTION: Always turn ignition off prior to disconnecting any module connector.

1) Turn ignition off. Disconnect anti-lock brake controller module connector. Anti-lock brake controller module is located under left front of vehicle, behind transaxle. Using an external ohmmeter, measure resistance between anti-lock brake controller module connector terminal No. 24 (Black wire) and ground. If resistance is 10 ohms or more, repair open Black wire. If resistance is less than 10 ohms, go to next step.
2) Connect jumper wire between ground and anti-lock brake controller module connector terminal No. 20 (Violet/Brown wire). Turn ignition on. Using scan tool, select BODY, BODY COMPUTER, then SYSTEM TEST. Perform CCD BUS test. If scan tool does not display BUS SHORT TO GROUND, repair open Violet/Brown wire. If scan tool displays BUS SHORT TO GROUND, go to next step.
3) Move jumper wire to anti-lock brake controller module connector terminal No. 19 (White/Black wire). Perform CCD BUS test. If scan tool does not display BUS SHORT TO GROUND, repair open White/Black wire. If scan tool displays BUS SHORT TO GROUND, go to next step.
4) Measure voltage between ground and anti-lock brake controller module connector terminal No. 25 (Red/Dark Green wire). If voltage is 10 volts or less, repair open Red/Dark Green wire. If voltage is more than 10 volts, go to next step.
5) Turn ignition on. Using an external voltmeter, measure voltage between ground and anti-lock brake controller module connector termi-

nal No. 23 (White wire). If voltage is 10 volts or less, repair open White wire. If voltage is more than 10 volts, replace anti-lock brake controller module.

AIR BAG MESSAGE NOT RECEIVED (NO RESPONSE FROM ACM)

NOTE: For connector terminal identification and wiring diagrams, see BODY CONTROL COMPUTER – INTRODUCTION article. Perform VERIFICATION TEST VER-1A after each repair.

CAUTION: Always turn ignition off prior to disconnecting any module connector.

1) Remove Power Distribution Center (PDC) fuse No. 2. Using external voltmeter, measure voltage between ground and Air Bag Control Module (ACM) side of PDC fuse No. 2 (Light Green/Yellow wire). If voltage is 10 volts or less, go to step 6). If voltage is more than 10 volts, go to next step.
2) Disconnect battery and wait 2 minutes. Disconnect ACM connector. ACM is located under center of instrument panel. Using an external ohmmeter, measure resistance between ground and ACM connector terminal No. 11 (Black/Light Green wire). If resistance is 15 ohms or more, repair open Black/Light Green wire. If resistance is less than 15 ohms, go to next step.
3) Connect battery. Turn ignition on. Measure voltage between ground and ACM connector terminal No. 1 (Light Green/Yellow wire). If voltage is 10 volts or less, go to next step. If voltage is more than 10 volts, repair open Light Green/Yellow wire.
4) Measure voltage between ground and ACM connector terminal No. 3 (Violet/Brown wire). If voltage is more than 1.5 volts, go to next step. If voltage is less than 1.5 volts, repair open Violet/Brown wire.
5) Measure voltage between ground and ACM connector terminal No. 4 (White/Black wire). If voltage is more than 1.5 volts, replace ACM. If voltage is less than 1.5 volts, repair open White/Black wire.
6) Using external voltmeter, measure voltage between ground and junction block side of PDC fuse No. 2 (White/Black wire). If voltage is 10 volts or less, repair open ignition switch output circuit between fuse and junction block. If voltage is more than 10 volts, go to next step.
7) Turn ignition off. Remove PDC fuse No. 2. Using external ohmmeter, measure resistance between ground and ACM side of PDC fuse No. 2 (Light Green/Yellow wire). If resistance is 5 ohms or more, replace fuse No. 2. If resistance is less than 5 ohms, go to next step.
8) Disconnect battery and wait 2 minutes. Disconnect ACM 13-pin connector. Measure resistance between ground and ACM connector terminal No. 1 (Light Green/Yellow wire). If resistance is less than 5 ohms, repair Light Green/Yellow wire for short to ground and replace PDC fuse No. 2. If resistance is 5 ohms or more, replace ACM and fuse No. 2.

BATTERY POWER TO MODULE DISCONNECT (NO RESPONSE FROM BCM)

NOTE: For connector terminal identification and wiring diagrams, see BODY CONTROL COMPUTER – INTRODUCTION article. Perform VERIFICATION TEST VER-1A after each repair.

CAUTION: Always turn ignition off prior to disconnecting any module connector.

1) If fault message is BATTERY POWER TO MODULE DISCONNECTED, go to next step. If fault message is not BATTERY POWER TO MODULE DISCONNECTED, go to step 3).
2) Turn ignition off. Remove Body Control Module (BCM) from junction block. Junction block is located under left side of instrument panel. Turn ignition on. Using external voltmeter, measure voltage between ground and junction block internal connector, terminal No. 9. If voltage is more than 10 volts, replace BCM. If voltage is 10 volts or less, replace junction block.

1999 ACCESSORIES & EQUIPMENT
Vehicle Communications
Caravan, Town & Country, & Voyager (Cont.)

CHRY
4-229

3) Remove and inspect junction block fuses No. 2 and No. 6. If neither fuse is blown, go to step 9). If both fuses are blown, go to step 6). If junction block fuse No. 2 (gauge) is blown, go to next step. If junction block fuse No. 6 (rear wiper) is blown, go to step 7).

4) Turn ignition off. Replace fuse. Turn ignition on. Inspect junction block fuse No. 2. If fuse is blown, go to next step. If fuse is okay, circuit is currently operating correctly.

5) Turn ignition off. Remove Body Control Module (BCM) from junction block. Junction block is located under left side of instrument panel. Replace junction block fuse No. 2. Turn ignition on. Inspect junction block fuse No. 2. If fuse is okay, replace BCM. If fuse is blown, repair fused ignition switch output circuit for short to ground. See appropriate wiring diagram in BODY CONTROL COMPUTER – INTRODUCTION article. Replace fuse.

6) Turn ignition off. Replace junction block fuse No. 2. Turn ignition on. Inspect junction block fuse No. 2. If fuse is blown, go to next step. If fuse is okay, circuit is currently operating correctly.

7) Turn ignition off. Replace junction block fuse No. 6 (rear wiper). Turn ignition on. Inspect junction block fuse No. 6. If fuse is okay, circuit is currently operating correctly. If fuse is blown, go to next step.

8) Turn ignition off. Remove BCM from junction block. Replace junction block fuse No. 6. Turn ignition on. Inspect junction block fuse No. 6. If fuse is okay, replace BCM. If fuse is blown, repair fused ignition switch output circuit for short to ground. See appropriate wiring diagram in BODY CONTROL COMPUTER – INTRODUCTION article. Replace fuse.

9) Turn ignition off. Disconnect Body Control Module (BCM) connectors. BCM is connected to junction block. Connect jumper wire between ground and BCM Black connector "A" terminal No. 3 (Violet/Brown wire). Turn ignition on. Using scan tool, select BODY, BODY COMPUTER, then SYSTEM TEST. Perform CCD BUS test. If scan tool does not display BUS SHORT TO GROUND, repair open Violet/Brown wire. If scan tool displays BUS SHORT TO GROUND, go to next step.

10) Move jumper wire to BCM Black connector "A" terminal No. 34 (White/Black wire). Perform CCD BUS test. If scan tool does not display BUS SHORT TO GROUND, repair open White/Black wire. If scan tool displays BUS SHORT TO GROUND, go to next step.

11) Remove jumper wire. Turn ignition off. Using external ohmmeter, measure resistance between ground and BCM Black connector "A" terminal No. 10 (Black/Light Green wire). If resistance is 15 ohms or more, repair open Black/Light Green wire. If resistance is less than 15 ohms, go to next step.

12) Disconnect BCM from junction block. Turn ignition on. Using external voltmeter, measure voltage between ground and junction block internal 23-pin connector terminal No. 11. If voltage is more than 10 volts, replace BCM. If voltage is 10 volts or less, go to next step.

13) Measure voltage between ground and junction block Black connector "C" terminal No. 15 (Dark Green/Red wire). If voltage is more than 10 volts, replace junction block. If voltage is 10 volts or less, repair open Dark Green/Red wire.

EATX PRNDL MESSAGE TEST FAILED

NOTE: For connector terminal identification and wiring diagrams, see BODY CONTROL COMPUTER – INTRODUCTION article. Perform VERIFICATION TEST VER-1A after each repair.

CAUTION: Always turn ignition off prior to disconnecting any module connector.

1) If transaxle operates properly, go to next step. If transaxle does not operate properly, go to appropriate TRANSMISSION SERVICE & REPAIR article.

2) Turn ignition off. Disconnect Transmission Control Module (TCM). TCM is located on right fenderwell, next to washer reservoir. Turn ignition on. Connect jumper wire between ground and TCM connector terminal No. 43 (Violet/Brown wire). Using scan tool, select BODY, BODY COMPUTER, then SYSTEM TEST. Perform CCD BUS test. If

scan tool does not display BUS SHORT TO GROUND, repair open Violet/Brown wire. If scan tool displays BUS SHORT TO GROUND, go to next step.

3) Move jumper wire to TCM connector terminal No. 4 (White/Black wire). Perform CCD BUS test. If scan tool does not display BUS SHORT TO GROUND, repair open White/Black wire. If scan tool displays BUS SHORT TO GROUND, replace TCM.

NO CCD MESSAGE FROM PCM

NOTE: For connector terminal identification and wiring diagrams, see BODY CONTROL COMPUTER – INTRODUCTION article. Perform VERIFICATION TEST VER-1A after each repair.

CAUTION: Always turn ignition off prior to disconnecting any module connector.

1) If engine does not run, see appropriate BASIC DIAGNOSTIC PROCEDURES article in ENGINE PERFORMANCE in appropriate MITCHELL® manual. If engine runs, go to next step.

2) Turn ignition off. Disconnect Powertrain Control Module (PCM). PCM is located in engine compartment on left fenderwell, next to power distribution center. Turn ignition on. Connect jumper wire between ground and PCM connector terminal No. 59 (Violet/Brown wire). Using scan tool, select BODY, BODY COMPUTER, then SYSTEM TEST. Perform CCD BUS test. If scan tool does not display BUS SHORT TO GROUND, repair open Violet/Brown wire. If scan tool displays BUS SHORT TO GROUND, go to next step.

3) Move jumper wire to terminal No. 60 (White/Black wire). Perform CCD BUS test. If scan tool does not display BUS SHORT TO GROUND, repair open White/Black wire. If scan tool displays BUS SHORT TO GROUND, replace PCM.

BUS (+) & BUS (–) SHORTED TOGETHER

NOTE: For connector terminal identification and wiring diagrams, see BODY CONTROL COMPUTER – INTRODUCTION article. Perform VERIFICATION TEST VER-1A after each repair.

CAUTION: Always turn ignition off prior to disconnecting any module connector.

1) Turn ignition off. Disconnect Transmission Control Module (TCM), if equipped. TCM is located on right fenderwell, next to washer reservoir. Turn ignition on. If scan tool does not display BUS (+) & BUS (–) SHORTED TOGETHER, replace TCM. If scan tool displays BUS (+) & BUS (–) SHORTED TOGETHER, go to next step.

2) Turn ignition off and disconnect Powertrain Control Module (PCM). PCM is located next power distribution center, on left inner fender panel. Turn ignition on. If scan tool does not display BUS (+) & BUS (–) SHORTED TOGETHER, replace PCM. If scan tool displays BUS (+) & BUS (–) SHORTED TOGETHER, go to next step.

3) Turn ignition off and disconnect CCD radio 2-pin connector. Turn ignition on. If scan tool does not display BUS (+) & BUS (–) SHORTED TOGETHER, replace radio. If scan tool displays BUS (+) & BUS (–) SHORTED TOGETHER, go to next step.

4) Turn ignition off. Disconnect compass/mini-trip module. Turn ignition on. If scan tool does not display BUS (+) & BUS (–) SHORTED TOGETHER, replace compass/mini-trip module. If scan tool displays BUS (+) & BUS (–) SHORTED TOGETHER, go to next step.

5) Turn ignition off. Disconnect anti-lock brake controller module. Turn ignition on. If scan tool does not display BUS (+) & BUS (–) SHORTED TOGETHER, replace anti-lock brake controller module. If scan tool displays BUS (+) & BUS (–) SHORTED TOGETHER, go to next step.

6) Turn ignition off. Disconnect instrument cluster. Turn ignition on. If scan tool does not display BUS (+) & BUS (–) SHORTED TOGETHER, replace instrument cluster. If scan tool displays BUS (+) & BUS (–) SHORTED TOGETHER, go to next step.

CHRY
4-230

1999 ACCESSORIES & EQUIPMENT
Vehicle Communications
Caravan, Town & Country, & Voyager (Cont.)

7) Turn ignition off. Disconnect HVAC module. Turn ignition on. If scan tool does not display BUS (+) & BUS (−) SHORTED TOGETHER, replace HVAC module. If scan tool displays BUS (+) & BUS (−) SHORTED TOGETHER, go to next step.

8) Turn ignition off. Disconnect Body Control Module (BCM) connectors. BCM is located on back of junction block, under left side of instrument panel. Turn ignition on. If scan tool does not display BUS (+) & BUS (−) SHORTED TOGETHER, replace BCM. If scan tool displays BUS (+) & BUS (−) SHORTED TOGETHER, go to next step.

9) Turn ignition off and wait 5 minutes. Disconnect Air Bag Control Module (ACM) connector. ACM is located under center of instrument panel. Turn ignition on. If scan tool does not display BUS (+) & BUS (−) SHORTED TOGETHER, replace ACM. If scan tool displays BUS (+) & BUS (−) SHORTED TOGETHER, go to next step.

10) Turn ignition off. Using external ohmmeter, measure resistance between BCM Black connector "A" terminals No. 3 (Violet/Brown wire) and No. 34 (White/Black wire). If resistance is 500 ohms or more, replace scan tool cable or scan tool. If resistance is less than 500 ohms, repair Violet/Brown wire for short to White/Black wire ground.

BUS (+) OPEN (BUS (−) OPEN, BUS BIAS LEVEL TOO HIGH, BUS BIAS LEVEL TOO LOW)

NOTE: For connector terminal identification and wiring diagrams, see BODY CONTROL COMPUTER – INTRODUCTION article. Perform VERIFICATION TEST VER-1A after each repair.

CAUTION: Always turn ignition off prior to disconnecting any module connector.

NOTE: Ignition off during bus test is most common cause for this trouble code.

1) If ignition was off during BUS test, turn ignition on. If ignition was on during BUS test, turn ignition on, engine off. Disconnect scan tool from Data Link Connector (DLC). Using an external voltmeter, measure voltage between ground and DLC terminal No. 3 (Violet/Brown wire). If voltage is not 2.3-2.6 volts, go to step 3). If voltage is 2.3-2.6 volts, go to next step.

2) Measure voltage between ground and DLC terminal No. 11 (White/Black wire). If voltage is not 2.3-2.6 volts, go to next step. If voltage is 2.3-2.6 volts, replace scan tool cable or scan tool.

3) Connect scan tool to DLC. Disconnect Body Control Module (BCM) connectors. BCM is connected to junction block, under left side of instrument panel. Using an external ohmmeter, measure resistance between BCM component terminals No. 3 and No. 34. If resistance is not 100-140 ohms, replace BCM. If resistance is 100-140 ohms, go to next step.

4) Connect jumper wire between ground and BCM Black connector "A" terminal No. 3 (Violet/Brown wire). Using scan tool, select BODY, BODY COMPUTER, then SYSTEM TEST. Perform CCD BUS test. If scan tool does not display BUS SHORT TO GROUND, repair open Violet/Brown wire. If scan tool displays BUS SHORT TO GROUND, go to next step.

5) Move jumper wire to BCM Black connector "A", terminal No. 34 (White/Black wire). Perform CCD BUS test. If scan tool does not display BUS SHORT TO GROUND, repair open White/Black wire. If scan tool displays BUS SHORT TO GROUND, go to next step.

6) Disconnect Powertrain Control Module (PCM) connectors. PCM is located next to power distribution center, on left inner fender panel. Using an external ohmmeter, measure resistance between PCM component terminals No. 59 and No. 60. If resistance is not 100-140 ohms, replace PCM. If resistance is 100-140 ohms, go to next step.

7) Connect jumper wire between ground and PCM connector terminal No. 59 (Violet/Brown wire). Using scan tool, select BODY, BODY COMPUTER, then SYSTEM TEST. Perform CCD BUS test. If scan tool does not display BUS SHORT TO GROUND, repair open Violet/Brown wire. If scan tool displays BUS SHORT TO GROUND, go to next step.

8) Move jumper wire to PCM connector, terminal No. 60 (White/Black wire). Perform CCD BUS test. If scan tool does not display BUS SHORT TO GROUND, repair open White/Black wire. If scan tool displays BUS SHORT TO GROUND, go to next step.

9) Disconnect jumper wire. Using an external ohmmeter, measure resistance between ground and BCM connector terminal No. 3 (Violet/Brown wire). If resistance is less than 50 ohms, repair Violet/Brown wire for short to ground. If resistance is 50 ohms or more, go to next step.

10) Measure resistance between ground and BCM connector terminal No. 34 (White/Black wire). If resistance is less than 50 ohms, repair White/Black wire for short to ground. If resistance is 50 ohms or more, replace BCM.

NO BUS BIAS

NOTE: For connector terminal identification and wiring diagrams, see BODY CONTROL COMPUTER – INTRODUCTION article. Perform VERIFICATION TEST VER-1A after each repair.

CAUTION: Always turn ignition off prior to disconnecting any module connector.

NOTE: Ignition off during bus test is most common cause for this trouble code.

1) If ignition was off during BUS test, turn ignition on. If ignition was on during BUS test, turn ignition on, engine off. Disconnect scan tool. Using an external voltmeter, measure voltage between ground and Data Link Connector (DLC) terminal No. 3 (Violet/Brown wire). If voltage is not 2.3-2.6 volts, go to step 3). If voltage is 2.3-2.6 volts, go to next step.

2) Measure voltage between ground and DLC terminal No. 11 (White/Black wire). If voltage is not 2.3-2.6 volts, go to next step. If voltage is 2.3-2.6 volts, replace scan tool cable or scan tool.

3) Turn ignition off. Disconnect Body Control Module (BCM) connectors. Using external ohmmeter, measure resistance between BCM component terminals No. 3 and No. 34. If resistance is not 100-140 ohms, replace BCM. If resistance is 100-140 ohms, go to next step.

4) Connect jumper wire between ground and BCM Black connector "A" terminal No. 3 (Violet/Brown wire). Using scan tool, select BODY, BODY COMPUTER, then SYSTEM TEST. Perform CCD BUS test. If scan tool does not display BUS SHORT TO GROUND, repair open Violet/Brown wire. If scan tool displays BUS SHORT TO GROUND, go to next step.

5) Move jumper wire to BCM Black connector "A" terminal No. 34 (White/Black wire). Perform CCD BUS test. If scan tool does not display BUS SHORT TO GROUND, repair open White/Black wire. If scan tool displays BUS SHORT TO GROUND, go to next step.

6) Disconnect Powertrain Control Module (PCM) connectors. PCM is located next to power distribution center, on left inner fender panel. Using external ohmmeter, measure resistance between PCM component terminals No. 59 and No. 60. If resistance is not 100-140 ohms, replace PCM. If resistance is 100-140 ohms, go to next step.

7) Turn ignition on. Using external voltmeter, measure voltage between ground and junction block internal 23-pin connector terminal No. 9, located under left side of instrument panel. If voltage is 10 volts or less, repair fused B+ circuit as needed. See appropriate wiring diagram in BODY CONTROL COMPUTER – INTRODUCTION article. If voltage is more than 10 volts, go to next step.

8) Measure voltage between ground and junction block internal 23-pin connector terminal No. 11. If voltage is 10 volts or less, repair fused ignition switch output as needed. See appropriate wiring diagram in BODY CONTROL COMPUTER – INTRODUCTION article. If voltage is more than 10 volts, go to next step.

9) Turn ignition off. Using external ohmmeter, measure resistance between ground and BCM Black connector "A" terminal No. 10 (Black/Light Green wire). If resistance is 5 ohms or more, repair open Black/Light Green wire. If resistance is less than 5 ohms, replace BCM.

NO RESPONSE FROM CMTC (NO DISPLAY ON CMTC EXCEPT DIRECTION & TEMPERATURE)

NOTE: For connector terminal identification and wiring diagrams, see BODY CONTROL COMPUTER – INTRODUCTION article. Perform VERIFICATION TEST VER-1A after each repair.

CAUTION: Always turn ignition off prior to disconnecting any module connector.

1) Move jumper wire to terminal No. 6 (Violet/Brown wire). Perform CCD BUS test. If scan tool does not display BUS SHORT TO GROUND, repair open Violet/Brown wire. If scan tool displays BUS SHORT TO GROUND, go to next step.

2) Connect jumper wire between compass/mini trip module 6-pin connector terminal No. 1 (White/Black wire) and ground. Using scan tool, select BODY, BODY COMPUTER, then SYSTEM TEST. Perform CCD BUS test. If scan tool does not display BUS SHORT TO GROUND, repair open White/Black wire. If scan tool displays BUS SHORT TO GROUND, go to next step.

3) Turn ignition on. Using external voltmeter, measure voltage between ground and terminal No. 4 (Brown/Pink wire). If voltage is 10 volts or less, repair open Brown/Pink wire. If voltage is more than 10 volts, go to next step.

4) Turn ignition off. Disconnect compass/mini trip module 6-pin connector. Using external ohmmeter, measure resistance between ground and terminal No. 3 (Black/Light Green wire). If resistance is 5 ohms or more, repair open Black/Light Green wire. If resistance is less than 5 ohms, replace compass/mini trip module.

NO RESPONSE FROM HVAC

NOTE: For connector terminal identification and wiring diagrams, see BODY CONTROL COMPUTER – INTRODUCTION article. Perform VERIFICATION TEST VER-1A after each repair.

CAUTION: Always turn ignition off prior to disconnecting any module connector.

1) Turn ignition off. Disconnect HVAC control module connector. HVAC control module is part of heater-A/C control head. Using an external ohmmeter, measure resistance between HVAC control module connector terminal No. 21 (Black/Light Green wire) and ground. If resistance is 5 ohms or more, repair open Black/Light Green wire. If resistance is less than 5 ohms, go to next step.

2) Turn ignition on. Using an external voltmeter, measure voltage between ground and HVAC control module connector terminal No. 10 (Brown/Pink wire). If voltage is 10 volts or less, repair open Brown/Pink wire. If voltage is more than 10 volts, go to next step.

3) Connect jumper wire between ground and HVAC control module connector terminal No. 14 (Violet/Brown wire). Turn ignition on. Using scan tool, select BODY, BODY COMPUTER, then SYSTEM TEST. Perform CCD BUS test. If scan tool does not display BUS SHORT TO GROUND, repair open Violet/Brown wire. If scan tool displays BUS SHORT TO GROUND, go to next step.

4) Move jumper wire to HVAC control module connector terminal No. 16 (White/Black wire). Perform CCD BUS test. If scan tool does not display BUS SHORT TO GROUND, repair open White/Black wire. If scan tool displays BUS SHORT TO GROUND, replace HVAC control module.

NO RESPONSE FROM INSTRUMENT CLUSTER

NOTE: For connector terminal identification and wiring diagrams, see BODY CONTROL COMPUTER – INTRODUCTION article. Perform VERIFICATION TEST VER-1A after each repair.

CAUTION: Always turn ignition off prior to disconnecting any module connector.

1) Disconnect instrument cluster 13-pin connector. Turn ignition on. Using external voltmeter, measure voltage between ground and terminal No. 11 (Red/White wire). If voltage is 10 volts or less, repair open Red/White wire. If voltage is more than 10 volts, go to next step.

2) Measure voltage between ground and terminal No. 2 (Pink wire). If voltage is 10 volts or less, repair open Pink wire. If voltage is more than 10 volts, go to next step.

3) Connect jumper wire between instrument cluster 13-pin connector terminal No. 10 (Violet/Brown wire) and ground. Using scan tool, select BODY, BODY COMPUTER, then SYSTEM TEST. Perform CCD BUS test. If scan tool does not display BUS SHORT TO GROUND, repair open Violet/Brown wire. If scan tool displays BUS SHORT TO GROUND, go to next step.

4) Move jumper to instrument cluster 13-pin connector terminal No. 9 (White/Black wire). Perform CCD BUS test. If scan tool does not display BUS SHORT TO GROUND, repair open White/Black wire. If scan tool displays BUS SHORT TO GROUND, replace instrument cluster circuit board. Using scan tool, recalibrate gauges.

NO RESPONSE FROM PCM

NOTE: For connector terminal identification and wiring diagrams, see BODY CONTROL COMPUTER – INTRODUCTION article. Perform VERIFICATION TEST VER-1A after each repair.

CAUTION: Always turn ignition off prior to disconnecting any module connector.

1) If engine does not run, see appropriate BASIC DIAGNOSTIC PROCEDURES article in ENGINE PERFORMANCE in appropriate MITCHELL® manual. If engine runs, turn ignition off. Disconnect Powertrain Control Module (PCM). PCM is located on left fenderwell, next to power distribution center. Turn ignition on. Connect jumper wire between ground and PCM connector terminal No. 59 (Violet/Brown wire).

2) Using scan tool, select BODY, BODY COMPUTER, then SYSTEM TEST. Perform CCD BUS test. If scan tool does not display BUS SHORT TO GROUND, repair open Violet/Brown wire. If scan tool displays BUS SHORT TO GROUND, go to next step.

3) Move jumper wire to terminal No. 60 (White/Black wire). Perform CCD BUS test. If scan tool does not display BUS SHORT TO GROUND, repair open White/Black wire. If scan tool displays BUS SHORT TO GROUND, replace PCM.

NO RESPONSE FROM RADIO

NOTE: For connector terminal identification and wiring diagrams, see BODY CONTROL COMPUTER – INTRODUCTION article. Perform VERIFICATION TEST VER-1A after each repair.

CAUTION: Always turn ignition off prior to disconnecting any module connector.

1) If radio screen is not blank, go to step **7)**. If radio screen is blank, go to next step.

2) Remove and inspect junction block fuse No. 8 (radio). If fuse is blown, go to next step. If fuse is okay, go to step **4)**.

3) Turn ignition off. Disconnect radio Gray connector. Using external ohmmeter, measure resistance between ground and terminal No. 6 (Red/White wire). If resistance is less than 5 ohms, repair Red/White

CHRY
4-232

1999 ACCESSORIES & EQUIPMENT
Vehicle Communications
Caravan, Town & Country, & Voyager (Cont.)

wire for short to ground. Replace junction block fuse No. 8. If resistance is 5 ohms or more, replace radio. Replace junction block fuse No. 8.

4) Inspect ground strap and antenna for correct installation. Repair as needed. If ground strap and antenna are okay, go to next step.

5) Install fuse. Disconnect radio Gray connector. Using external voltmeter, measure voltage between ground and terminal No. 6 (Red/White wire). If voltage is 10 volts or less, repair open Red/White wire. If voltage is more than 10 volts, go to next step.

6) Turn ignition on. Measure voltage between ground and terminal No. 7 (Pink wire). If voltage is 10 volts or less, repair open Pink wire. If voltage is more than 10 volts, replace radio.

7) Disconnect 2-pin CCD BUS connector on back of radio. Connect jumper wire between terminal No. 2 (White/Black wire) and ground. Using scan tool, select BODY, BODY COMPUTER, then SYSTEM TEST. Perform CCD BUS test. If scan tool does not display BUS SHORT TO GROUND, repair open White/Black wire. If scan tool displays BUS SHORT TO GROUND, go to next step.

8) Move jumper wire to terminal No. 1 (Violet/Brown wire). Perform CCD BUS test. If scan tool does not display BUS SHORT TO GROUND, repair open Violet/Brown wire. If scan tool displays BUS SHORT TO GROUND, replace radio.

NO RESPONSE FROM TCM

NOTE: For connector terminal identification and wiring diagrams, see BODY CONTROL COMPUTER – INTRODUCTION article. Perform VERIFICATION TEST VER-1A after each repair.

CAUTION: Always turn ignition off prior to disconnecting any module connector.

1) If transmission is operating correctly, go to next step. If transmission is not operating correctly, see appropriate AUTOMATIC TRANSMISSIONS article in MITCHELL® TRANSMISSION SERVICE & REPAIR manual as needed.

2) Turn ignition off. Disconnect Transmission Control Module (TCM). TCM is located on right fenderwell, next to washer reservoir. Turn ignition on. Connect jumper wire between ground and TCM connector terminal No. 43 (Violet/Brown wire). Using scan tool, select BODY, BODY COMPUTER, then SYSTEM TEST. Perform CCD BUS test. If scan tool does not display BUS SHORT TO GROUND, repair open Violet/Brown wire. If scan tool displays BUS SHORT TO GROUND, go to next step.

3) Move jumper wire to TCM connector terminal No. 4 (White/Black wire). Perform CCD BUS test. If scan tool does not display BUS SHORT TO GROUND, repair open White/Black wire. If scan tool displays BUS SHORT TO GROUND, replace TCM.

NO TERMINATION

NOTE: For connector terminal identification and wiring diagrams, see BODY CONTROL COMPUTER – INTRODUCTION article. Perform VERIFICATION TEST VER-1A after each repair.

CAUTION: Always turn ignition off prior to disconnecting any module connector.

1) Turn ignition off. Disconnect Powertrain Control Module (PCM) connectors. PCM is located next to power distribution center, on left inner fender panel. Connect jumper wire between ground and PCM connector terminal No. 59 (Violet/Brown wire). Using scan tool, select BODY, BODY COMPUTER, then SYSTEM TEST. Perform CCD BUS test. If scan tool does not display BUS SHORT TO GROUND, repair open Violet/Brown wire. If scan tool displays BUS SHORT TO GROUND, go to next step.

2) Move jumper wire to PCM connector, terminal No. 60 (White/Black wire). Perform CCD BUS test. If scan tool does not display BUS SHORT TO GROUND, repair open White/Black wire. If scan tool displays BUS SHORT TO GROUND, go to next step.

3) Turn ignition off. Disconnect Body Control Module (BCM). BCM is connected to junction block, under left side of instrument panel. Disconnect BCM connectors and remove from junction block. Connect jumper wire between ground and BCM Black connector "A" terminal No. 3 (Violet/Brown wire). Perform CCD BUS test. If scan tool does not display BUS SHORT TO GROUND, repair open Violet/Brown wire. If scan tool displays BUS SHORT TO GROUND, go to next step.

4) Move jumper wire to BCM Black connector "A" terminal No. 34 (White/Black wire). Perform CCD BUS test. If scan tool does not display BUS SHORT TO GROUND, repair open White/Black wire. If scan tool displays BUS SHORT TO GROUND, go to next step.

5) Using an external ohmmeter, measure resistance between PCM component terminals No. 59 and No. 60. If resistance is not 100-140 ohms, replace PCM. If resistance is 100-140 ohms, go to next step.

6) Using an external ohmmeter, measure resistance between BCM component terminals No. 3 and No. 34. If resistance is not 100-140 ohms, replace BCM. If resistance is 100-140 ohms, replace scan tool cable or scan tool.

NOT RECEIVING BUS MESSAGE CORRECTLY

NOTE: For connector terminal identification and wiring diagrams, see BODY CONTROL COMPUTER – INTRODUCTION article. Perform VERIFICATION TEST VER-1A after each repair.

CAUTION: Always turn ignition off prior to disconnecting any module connector.

1) Turn ignition off. Disconnect anti-lock brake controller module. Turn ignition on. If scan tool does not display NOT RECEIVING BUS MESSAGE CORRECTLY, replace anti-lock brake controller module. If scan tool displays NOT RECEIVING BUS MESSAGE CORRECTLY, go to next step.

2) Turn ignition off and wait 5 minutes. Disconnect Air Bag Control Module (ACM) 13-pin connector. ACM is located under center of instrument panel. Turn ignition on. If scan tool does not display NOT RECEIVING BUS MESSAGE CORRECTLY, replace ACM. If scan tool displays NOT RECEIVING BUS MESSAGE CORRECTLY, go to next step.

3) Turn ignition off. Disconnect compass/mini-trip module. Turn ignition on. If scan tool does not display NOT RECEIVING BUS MESSAGE CORRECTLY, replace compass/mini-trip module. If scan tool displays NOT RECEIVING BUS MESSAGE CORRECTLY, go to next step.

4) Turn ignition off. Disconnect instrument cluster. Turn ignition on. If scan tool does not display NOT RECEIVING BUS MESSAGE CORRECTLY, replace instrument cluster. If scan tool displays NOT RECEIVING BUS MESSAGE CORRECTLY, go to next step.

5) Turn ignition off. Disconnect Transmission Control Module (TCM), if equipped. TCM is located on right fenderwell, next to washer reservoir. Turn ignition on. If scan tool does not display NOT RECEIVING BUS MESSAGE CORRECTLY, replace TCM. If scan tool displays NOT RECEIVING BUS MESSAGE CORRECTLY, go to next step.

6) Turn ignition off and disconnect CCD radio 2-pin connector. Turn ignition on. If scan tool does not display NOT RECEIVING BUS MESSAGE CORRECTLY, replace radio. If scan tool displays NOT RECEIVING BUS MESSAGE CORRECTLY, go to next step.

7) Turn ignition off and disconnect Powertrain Control Module (PCM). PCM is located next power distribution center, on left inner fender panel. Turn ignition on. If scan tool does not display NOT RECEIVING BUS MESSAGE CORRECTLY, replace PCM. If scan tool displays NOT RECEIVING BUS MESSAGE CORRECTLY, go to next step.

8) Turn ignition off. Disconnect HVAC module. Turn ignition on. If scan tool does not display NOT RECEIVING BUS MESSAGE CORRECTLY, replace HVAC module. If scan tool displays NOT RECEIVING BUS MESSAGE CORRECTLY, go to next step.

9) Turn ignition off. Disconnect Body Control Module (BCM) connectors. BCM is located on back of junction block, under left side of instrument panel. Turn ignition on. If scan tool does not display NOT RECEIVING

1999 ACCESSORIES & EQUIPMENT
Vehicle Communications
Caravan, Town & Country, & Voyager (Cont.)

CHRY
4-233

BUS MESSAGE CORRECTLY, replace BCM. If scan tool displays NOT RECEIVING BUS MESSAGE CORRECTLY, replace scan tool cable or scan tool.

BUS SHORT TO 5 VOLTS

NOTE: For connector terminal identification and wiring diagrams, see BODY CONTROL COMPUTER – INTRODUCTION article. Perform VERIFICATION TEST VER-1A after each repair.

CAUTION: Always turn ignition off prior to disconnecting any module connector.

1) Turn ignition off. Disconnect Transmission Control Module (TCM), if equipped. TCM is located on right fenderwell, next to washer reservoir. Turn ignition on. If scan tool does not display BUS SHORT TO 5 VOLTS, replace TCM. If scan tool displays BUS SHORT TO 5 VOLTS, go to next step.

2) Turn ignition off and disconnect Powertrain Control Module (PCM). PCM is located next power distribution center on left inner fenderwell. Turn ignition on. If scan tool does not display BUS SHORT TO 5 VOLTS, go to step 20). If scan tool displays BUS SHORT TO 5 VOLTS, go to next step.

3) Turn ignition off and disconnect CCD radio 2-pin connector. Turn ignition on. If scan tool does not display BUS SHORT TO 5 VOLTS, replace radio. If scan tool displays BUS SHORT TO 5 VOLTS, go to next step.

4) Turn ignition off. Disconnect compass/mini-trip module. Turn ignition on. If scan tool does not display BUS SHORT TO 5 VOLTS, replace compass/mini-trip module. If scan tool displays BUS SHORT TO 5 VOLTS, go to next step.

5) Turn ignition off. Disconnect anti-lock brake controller module. Turn ignition on. If scan tool does not display BUS SHORT TO 5 VOLTS, replace anti-lock brake controller module. If scan tool displays BUS SHORT 5 VOLTS, go to next step.

6) Turn ignition off. Disconnect instrument cluster. Turn ignition on. If scan tool does not display BUS SHORT TO 5 VOLTS, replace instrument cluster. If scan tool displays BUS SHORT TO 5 VOLTS, go to next step.

7) Turn ignition off. Disconnect HVAC module. Turn ignition on. If scan tool does not display BUS SHORT TO 5 VOLTS, replace HVAC module. If scan tool displays BUS SHORT TO 5 VOLTS, go to next step.

8) Turn ignition off. Disconnect Body Control Module (BCM) connectors. BCM is located on back of junction block under left side of instrument panel. Turn ignition on. If scan tool does not display BUS SHORT TO 5 VOLTS, go to step 12). If scan tool displays BUS SHORT TO 5 VOLTS, go to next step.

9) Turn ignition off and wait 5 minutes. Disconnect Air Bag Control Module (ACM) 13-pin connector. ACM is located under center of instrument panel. Turn ignition on. If scan tool does not display BUS SHORT TO 5 VOLTS, replace ACM. If scan tool displays BUS SHORT TO 5 VOLTS, go to next step.

10) Using external voltmeter, measure voltage between ground and BCM Connector "A" terminal No. 3 (Violet/Brown wire). If voltage is more than 4 volts, repair Violet/Brown wire for short to voltage. If voltage is 4 volts or less, go to next step.

11) Measure voltage between ground and terminal No. 34 (White/Black wire). If voltage is more than 4 volts, repair White/Black wire for short to voltage. If voltage is less than 4 volts, replace scan tool cable or scan tool as necessary.

12) Turn ignition off. Using external ohmmeter, measure resistance between Body Control Module (BCM) Black connector "A" terminal No. 3 (Violet/Brown wire) and Gray connector "B" terminal No. 78 (Light Green/Red wire). If resistance is less than 5 ohms, repair short between Violet/Brown wire and Light Green/Red wire. If resistance is 5 ohms or more, go to next step.

13) Measure resistance between BCM Black connector "A" terminal No. 34 (White/Black wire) and Gray connector "B" terminal No. 78 (Light Green/Red wire). If resistance is less than 5 ohms, repair short between White/Black wire and Light Green/Red wire. If resistance is 5 ohms or more, go to next step.

14) Measure resistance between BCM Black connector "A" terminals No. 3 (Violet/Brown wire) and No. 32 (Light Blue wire). If resistance is less than 5 ohms, repair short between Violet/Brown wire and Light Blue wire. If resistance is 5 ohms or more, go to next step.

15) Measure resistance between BCM Black connector "A" terminals No. 32 (Light Blue wire) and No. 34 (White/Black wire). If resistance is less than 5 ohms, repair short between Light Blue wire and White/Black wire. If resistance is 5 ohms or more, go to next step.

16) Measure resistance between BCM Black connector "A" terminal No. 3 (Violet/Brown wire) and Gray connector "B" terminal No. 79 (Tan wire). If resistance is less than 5 ohms, repair short between Violet/Brown wire and Tan wire. If resistance is 5 ohms or more, go to next step.

17) Measure resistance between BCM Black connector "A" terminal No. 34 (White/Black wire) and Gray connector "B" terminal No. 79 (Tan wire). If resistance is less than 5 ohms, repair short between White/Black wire and Tan wire. If resistance is 5 ohms or more, go to next step.

18) Measure resistance between BCM Black connector "A" terminal No. 3 (Violet/Brown wire) and Gray connector "B" terminal No. 48 (Tan/Red wire). If resistance is less than 5 ohms, repair short between Violet/Brown wire and Tan/Red wire. If resistance is 5 ohms or more, go to next step.

19) Measure resistance between BCM Black connector "A" terminal No. 34 (White/Black wire) and Gray connector "B" terminal No. 48 (Tan/Red wire). If resistance is less than 5 ohms, repair short between White/Black wire and Tan/Red wire. If resistance is 5 ohms or more, replace BCM.

20) Turn ignition off. Using external ohmmeter, measure resistance between Powertrain Control Module (PCM) connector terminals No. 59 (Violet/Brown wire) and No. 61 (Violet/White wire). If resistance is less than 5 ohms, repair short between Violet/Brown and Violet/White wire. If resistance is 5 ohms or more, go to next step.

21) Measure resistance between PCM connector terminals No. 60 (White/Black wire) and No. 61 (Violet/White wire). If resistance is less than 5 ohms, repair short between White/Black wire and Violet/White wire. If resistance is 5 ohms or more, replace PCM.

BUS SHORT TO BATTERY

NOTE: For connector terminal identification and wiring diagrams, see BODY CONTROL COMPUTER – INTRODUCTION article. Perform VERIFICATION TEST VER-1A after each repair.

CAUTION: Always turn ignition off prior to disconnecting any module connector.

1) Turn ignition off. Disconnect Transmission Control Module (TCM), if equipped. TCM is located on right fenderwell, next to washer reservoir. Turn ignition on. If scan tool does not display BUS SHORT TO BATTERY, replace TCM. If scan tool displays BUS SHORT TO BATTERY, go to next step.

2) Turn ignition off and disconnect Powertrain Control Module (PCM). PCM is located next power distribution center. Turn ignition on. If scan tool does not display BUS SHORT TO BATTERY, go to step 15). If scan tool displays BUS SHORT TO BATTERY, go to next step.

3) Turn ignition off and disconnect CCD radio 2-pin connector. Turn ignition on. If scan tool does not display BUS SHORT TO BATTERY, replace radio. If scan tool displays BUS SHORT TO BATTERY, go to next step.

4) Turn ignition off. Disconnect compass/mini-trip module. Turn ignition on. If scan tool does not display BUS SHORT TO BATTERY, go to step 14). If scan tool displays BUS SHORT TO BATTERY, go to next step.

5) Turn ignition off. Disconnect anti-lock brake controller module. Turn ignition on. If scan tool does not display BUS SHORT TO BATTERY, replace anti-lock brake controller module. If scan tool displays BUS SHORT TO BATTERY, go to next step.

CHRY
4-234

1999 ACCESSORIES & EQUIPMENT
Vehicle Communications
Caravan, Town & Country, & Voyager (Cont.)

6) Turn ignition off. Disconnect instrument cluster. Turn ignition on. If scan tool does not display BUS SHORT TO BATTERY, go to step 13). If scan tool displays BUS SHORT TO BATTERY, go to next step.

7) Turn ignition off. Disconnect HVAC module. Turn ignition on. If scan tool does not display BUS SHORT TO BATTERY, replace HVAC module. If scan tool displays BUS SHORT TO BATTERY, go to next step.

8) Turn ignition off. Disconnect Body Control Module (BCM) connectors. BCM is located on back of junction block. Junction block is located under left side of instrument panel. Turn ignition on. If scan tool does not display BUS SHORT TO BATTERY, go to step 12). If scan tool displays BUS SHORT TO BATTERY, go to next step.

9) Turn ignition off and wait 5 minutes. Disconnect Air Bag Control Module (ACM) 13-pin connector. ACM is located under center of instrument panel. Turn ignition on. If scan tool does not display BUS SHORT TO BATTERY, replace ACM. If scan tool displays BUS SHORT TO BATTERY, go to next step.

10) Turn ignition off. Using external voltmeter, measure voltage between ground and BCM Connector "A", terminal No. 3 (Violet/Brown wire). If voltage is more than 8 volts, repair Violet/Brown wire for short to voltage. If voltage is 8 volts or less, go to next step.

11) Measure voltage between ground and terminal No. 34 (White/Black wire). If voltage is more than 8 volts, repair White/Black wire for short to voltage. If voltage is less than 8 volts, replace scan tool cable or scan tool as necessary.

12) Using external ohmmeter, measure resistance between ground and BCM connector "A" terminal No. 10 (Black/Light Green wire). If resistance is 5 ohms or more, repair open Black/Light Green wire. If resistance is less than 5 ohms, replace BCM.

13) Turn ignition off. Using external ohmmeter, measure resistance between ground and instrument cluster 13-pin connector terminal No. 7 (Black/Light Green wire). If resistance is 5 ohms or more, repair open Black/Light Green wire circuit. If resistance is less than 5 ohms, replace instrument cluster.

14) Turn ignition off. Using external ohmmeter, measure resistance between ground and compass/mini-trip computer connector terminal No. 3 (Black/Light Green wire). If resistance is 5 ohms or more, repair open Black/Light Green wire circuit. If resistance is less than 5 ohms, replace compass/mini-trip computer.

15) Turn ignition off. Using external ohmmeter, measure resistance between Powertrain Control Module (PCM) connector terminals No. 44 (Orange wire) and No. 59 (Violet/Brown wire). PCM is located on left inner fenderwell, near battery. If resistance is less than 5 ohms, repair short between Orange wire and Violet/Brown wire. If resistance is 5 ohms or more, go to next step.

16) Measure resistance between PCM connector terminals No. 44 (Orange wire) and No. 60 (White/Black wire). If resistance is less than 5 ohms, repair short between Orange wire and White/Black wire. If resistance is 5 ohms or more, replace PCM.

BUS SHORT TO GROUND

NOTE: For connector terminal identification and wiring diagrams, see BODY CONTROL COMPUTER – INTRODUCTION article. Perform VERIFICATION TEST VER-1A after each repair.

CAUTION: Always turn ignition off prior to disconnecting any module connector.

1) Connect scan tool to Data Link Connector (DLC). Connect backprobe jumper wire between DLC ground terminals No. 4 (Black/Light Green wire) and No. 5 (Black/White wire). If scan tool does not display BUS SHORT TO GROUND, repair open ground wire. If scan tool displays BUS SHORT TO GROUND, go to next step.

2) Turn ignition off. Disconnect Transmission Control Module (TCM), if equipped. TCM is located on right fenderwell, next to washer reservoir.

Turn ignition on. If scan tool does not display BUS SHORT TO GROUND, replace TCM. If scan tool displays BUS SHORT TO GROUND, go to next step.

3) Turn ignition off and disconnect Powertrain Control Module (PCM). PCM is located next power distribution center on left inner fenderwell. Turn ignition on. If scan tool does not display BUS SHORT TO GROUND, replace PCM. If scan tool displays BUS SHORT TO GROUND, go to next step.

4) Turn ignition off and disconnect CCD radio 2-pin connector. Turn ignition on. If scan tool does not display BUS SHORT TO GROUND, replace radio. If scan tool displays BUS SHORT TO GROUND, go to next step.

5) Turn ignition off. Disconnect compass/mini-trip module. Turn ignition on. If scan tool does not display BUS SHORT TO GROUND, replace compass/mini-trip module. If scan tool displays BUS SHORT TO GROUND, go to next step.

6) Turn ignition off. Disconnect instrument cluster. Turn ignition on. If scan tool does not display BUS SHORT TO GROUND, replace instrument cluster. If scan tool displays BUS SHORT TO GROUND, go to next step.

7) Turn ignition off. Disconnect anti-lock brake controller module. Turn ignition on. If scan tool does not display BUS SHORT TO GROUND, replace anti-lock brake controller module. If scan tool displays BUS SHORT TO GROUND, go to next step.

8) Turn ignition off. Disconnect HVAC module. Turn ignition on. If scan tool does not display BUS SHORT TO GROUND, replace HVAC module. If scan tool displays BUS SHORT TO GROUND, go to next step.

9) Turn ignition off. Disconnect Body Control Module (BCM) connectors. BCM is located on back of junction block, under left side of instrument panel. Turn ignition on. If scan tool does not display BUS SHORT TO GROUND, replace BCM. If scan tool displays BUS SHORT TO GROUND, go to next step.

10) Turn ignition off and wait 5 minutes. Disconnect Air Bag Control Module (ACM) 13-pin connector. ACM is located under center of instrument panel. Turn ignition on. If scan tool does not display BUS SHORT TO GROUND, replace ACM. If scan tool displays BUS SHORT TO GROUND, go to next step.

11) Disconnect scan tool from DLC. Using external ohmmeter, measure resistance between BCM Black connector "A" terminal No. 3 (Violet/Brown wire) and ground. If resistance is 5 ohms or more, go to next step. If resistance is less than 5 ohms, repair Violet/Brown wire for short to ground.

12) Measure resistance between BCM Black connector "A" terminal No. 34 (White/Black wire) and ground. If resistance is 5 ohms or more, replace scan tool cable or scan tool as necessary. If resistance is less than 5 ohms repair White/Black wire for short to ground.

VERIFICATION TEST VER-1A

1) Reconnect all previously disconnected components and connectors. If Body Control Module (BCM) was replaced, you must enable the Vehicle Theft Security System (VTSS) or anti-theft system (if equipped) by using the key to unlock the liftgate while hood is open. If BCM was replaced you must program other options as necessary.

NOTE: To enable automatic headlight operation, vehicle must be driven over 3 miles and BCM must see one key transmission from the remote keyless entry transmitter.

2) Ensure ignition is on. Using scan tool, clears all DTCs. Turn ignition off and wait 5 seconds. Turn ignition on and fully operate system that was malfunctioning.

3) If the system is operating properly, continue to the next step. If system is not operating properly, check possible causes for the malfunction.

4) Using scan tool, read DTCs stored in the BCM. If no DTCs exist and customer's complaint cannot be duplicated, test is complete. If any DTCs exist, perform appropriate test for the DTC.

SYMPTOM ID TESTS

TEST 1A: IDENTIFYING VEHICLE COMMUNICATION PROBLEMS

Connect scan tool to Data Link Connector (DLC) to retrieve Diagnostic Trouble Codes (DTC) and bus failure messages. If scan tool message is blank, see NO RESPONSE DIAGNOSIS table and proceed to appropriate test number. Disconnect scan tool. Ensure ground circuit has continuity at DLC terminals No. 4 and 5. Ensure 12 volts is present at DLC terminal No. 16. Try another scan tool and/or cable. See NO RESPONSE DIAGNOSIS, BUS FAULT MESSAGES and BUS SYMPTOMS tables and proceed to appropriate test number.

NO RESPONSE DIAGNOSIS

Problem Module	Test
Air Bag Control Module (ACM)	2A
Automatic Temperature Control (ATC)	3A
Body Control Module (BCM) [1]	4A
Anti-Lock Brake Module	5A
Mechanical Instrument Cluster (MIC)	6A
Memory Heated Seats (MHS)	7A
Overhead Traveler Information System (OTIS)	8A
Powertrain Control Module (PCM)	9A
Radio	10A
Sentry Key Immobilizer (SKIM)	11A
Transmission Control Module (TCM)	12A

[1] – Battery power to module disconnected.

BUS FAULT MESSAGES

Fault Messages	Test
BUS SHORT TO BATTERY	13A
BUS SHORT TO GROUND	14A

BUS SYMPTOMS

Symptom Messages	Test
Odometer Displays NO BUS	15A
No Fused Ignition Switch Output To BCM	16A

TEST 2A: NO RESPONSE FROM AIR BAG CONTROL MODULE

NOTE: For connector terminal identification and wiring diagrams, see BODY CONTROL COMPUTER – INTRODUCTION article. Perform VERIFICATION TEST VER-1 after each repair.

CAUTION: Always turn ignition off prior to disconnecting any module connector.

1) Remove and inspect fuse No. 22. If fuse is open, go to TEST 2B. If fuse is okay, go to next step.
2) Using external voltmeter, measure voltage between ground and feed side of fuse No. 22 (Dark Blue/White wire). If voltage is 10 volts or less, repair open Dark Blue/White wire. If voltage is more than 10 volts, go to next step.
3) Disconnect battery and wait 2 minutes. Disconnect 13-pin connector. ACM is located under center of instrument panel. Reinstall fuse No. 22. Reconnect battery. Turn ignition on.
4) Using external voltmeter, measure voltage between ground and ACM connector terminal No. 14 (Light Green/Yellow wire). If voltage is 10 volts or less, repair open Light Green/Yellow wire. If voltage is more than 10 volts, go to next step.
5) Turn ignition off. Using an external ohmmeter, measure resistance between ground and ACM connector terminal No. 4 (Black/Light Green wire). If resistance is 5 ohms or more, repair open Black/Light Green wire. If resistance is less than 5 ohms, go to next step.
6) Turn ignition on. Open all doors. Using external voltmeter, measure voltage between ground and ACM connector terminal No. 21 (Violet/Yellow wire). If voltage is less than .5 volt, go to next step. If voltage is .5 volt or more, replace ACM.

7) Disconnect battery cables. Using an external ohmmeter, measure resistance of Violet/Yellow wire between DLC terminal No. 2 and ACM connector terminal No. 21. If resistance is 5 ohms or more, repair open Violet/Yellow wire. If resistance is less than 5 ohms, replace ACM.

TEST 2B: NO RESPONSE FROM AIR BAG CONTROL MODULE

NOTE: For connector terminal identification and wiring diagrams, see BODY CONTROL COMPUTER – INTRODUCTION article. Perform VERIFICATION TEST VER-1 after each repair.

CAUTION: Always turn ignition off prior to disconnecting any module connector.

1) Turn ignition on. Using external voltmeter, measure voltage between ground and fuse No. 22 (Dark Blue/White wire). If voltage is 10 volts or less, repair open Dark Blue/White wire between ignition switch and fuse No. 22. If voltage is more than 10 volts, go to next step.
2) Disconnect battery and wait 2 minutes. Using external ohmmeter, measure resistance between ground and component side of fuse No. 22 (Light Green/Yellow wire). If resistance is 5 ohms or more, go to step **4)**. If resistance is less than 5 ohms, go to next step.
3) Disconnect Air Bag Control Module (ACM) 23-pin connector. Measure resistance between ground and fuse No. 22 (Light Green/Yellow wire). If resistance is 5 ohms or more, replace fuse and ACM. If resistance is less than 5 ohms, repair Light Green/Yellow wire between fuse and ACM for short to ground and replace fuse.
4) Disconnect battery and wait 2 minutes. Disconnect ACM 23-pin connector. Using external ohmmeter, measure resistance of Light Green/Yellow wire between fuse No. 22 and ACM 23-pin connector terminal No. 14. If resistance is 5 ohms or more, replace fuse and repair open Light Green/Yellow wire. If resistance is less than 5 ohms, go to next step.
5) Reconnect ACM connector. Turn ignition on. Replace fuse No. 22. Go to TEST 1A of appropriate Chrysler Corp. & MITSUBISHI article in appropriate MITCHELL® AIR BAG SERVICE & REPAIR, DOMESTIC CARS, LIGHT TRUCKS & VANS for further testing.

TEST 3A: NO RESPONSE FROM AUTOMATIC TEMPERATURE CONTROL (ATC) MODULE

NOTE: For connector terminal identification and wiring diagrams, see BODY CONTROL COMPUTER – INTRODUCTION article. Perform VERIFICATION TEST VER-1 after each repair.

CAUTION: Always turn ignition off prior to disconnecting any module connector.

1) Ensure ignition is off. Remove and inspect fuse No. 17. If fuse is okay, go to step **4)**. If fuse is open, go to next step.
2) Using external ohmmeter, measure resistance between ground and fuse No. 17 (White wire). If resistance is 5 ohms or more, replace fuse No. 17. If resistance is less than 5 ohms, go to next step.
3) Disconnect Automatic Temperature Control (ATC) head. Measure resistance between ground and ATC connector terminal No. 10 (White wire). If resistance is 5 ohms or more, replace fuse No. 17 and ATC head. If resistance is less than 5 ohms, replace fuse and repair short to ground in White wire between ATC head and fuse No. 17.
4) Reinstall fuse No. 17. Turn ignition on. Using external voltmeter, measure voltage between ground and output side of fuse No. 17 (White wire). If voltage is 10 volts or less, repair open Black/Orange wire between ignition switch and junction block. If voltage is more than 10 volts, go to next step.
5) Turn ignition off. Disconnect Automatic Temperature Control (ATC) head. Measure voltage between ground and ATC connector terminal No. 10 (White wire). If voltage is 10 volts or less, repair open White wire between fuse No. 17 and ATC head. If voltage is more than 10 volts, go to next step.
6) Turn ignition off. Close all doors and ensure all courtesy lights are off. Using an external ohmmeter, measure **resistance between ground and**

CHRY
4-236

1999 ACCESSORIES & EQUIPMENT
Vehicle Communications – Concorde, Intrepid, LHS & 300M (Cont.)

ATC connector terminals No. 1 (Black/Light Green wire) and terminal No. 3 (Black wire). If resistance in either circuit is 5 ohms or more, repair open Black/Light Green or Black wire. If resistance in both circuits is less than 5 ohms, go to next step.

7) Measure voltage between ground and ATC connector terminal No. 2 (Violet/Yellow wire). Turn headlights on and observe voltmeter. If voltage does not modulate above .6 volt, repair open Violet/Yellow wire. If voltage modulates above .6 volt, replace ATC head.

TEST 4A: NO RESPONSE FROM BODY CONTROL MODULE

NOTE: For connector terminal identification and wiring diagrams, see BODY CONTROL COMPUTER – INTRODUCTION article. Perform VERIFICATION TEST VER-1 after each repair.

CAUTION: Always turn ignition off prior to disconnecting any module connector.

1) Turn ignition on. Using scan tool, read BCM DTCs. If scan tool does not display BATTERY POWER TO MODULE DISCONNECTED, go to step **3)**. If scan tool displays BATTERY POWER TO MODULE DISCONNECTED, go to next step.

2) Turn ignition off. Disconnect Body Control Module (BCM). BCM is connected to junction block. Turn ignition on. Using external voltmeter, measure voltage between ground and junction block internal 20-pin connector terminal No. 7. *See Fig. 1.* If voltage is 10 volts or less, replace junction block. If voltage is more than 10 volts, replace BCM.

junction block internal 20-pin connector terminal No. 7. *See Fig. 1.* If voltage is 10 volts or less, replace junction block. If voltage is more than 10 volts, go to next step.

5) Turn ignition off. Using external ohmmeter, measure resistance between ground and junction block internal 20-pin connector terminal No. 1. If resistance is 5 ohms or more, repair open ground circuit. See appropriate wiring diagram in BODY CONTROL COMPUTER – INTRODUCTION article. If resistance is less than 5 ohms, go to next step.

6) Measure resistance between ground and junction block internal 20-pin connector terminal No. 20. If resistance is 100 ohms or more, repair open ground circuit. See appropriate wiring diagram in BODY CONTROL COMPUTER – INTRODUCTION article. If resistance is less than 100 ohms, replace BCM.

TEST 5A: NO RESPONSE FROM ANTI-LOCK BRAKE CONTROLLER MODULE

NOTE: For connector terminal identification and wiring diagrams, see BODY CONTROL COMPUTER – INTRODUCTION article. Perform VERIFICATION TEST VER-1 after each repair.

CAUTION: Always turn ignition off prior to disconnecting any module connector.

1) Turn ignition off. Disconnect anti-lock brake controller module. Anti-lock brake controller module is mounted on left inner fender panel. Inspect terminals and repair as necessary. Using external ohmmeter, measure resistance between ground and anti-lock brake controller

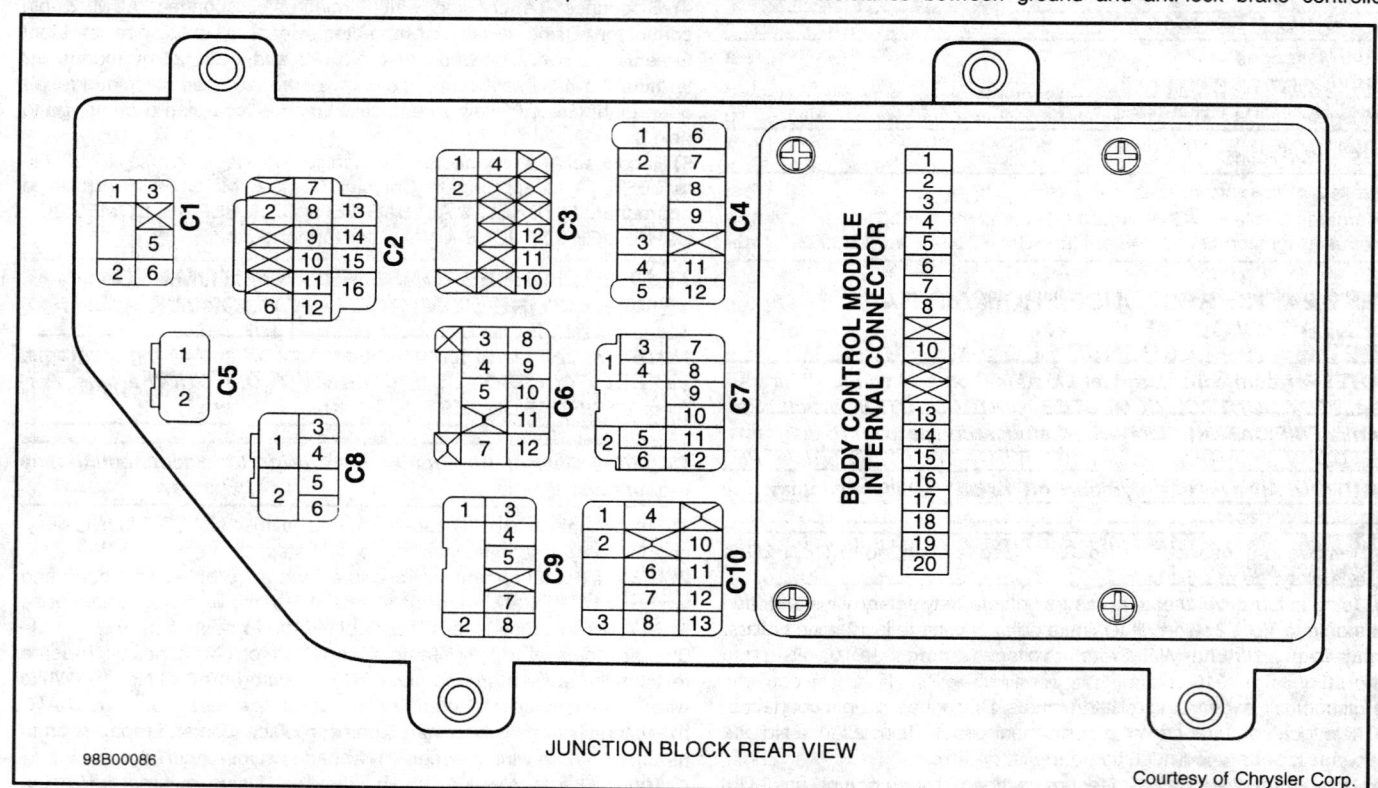

JUNCTION BLOCK REAR VIEW

98B00086

Courtesy of Chrysler Corp.

Fig. 1: Locating BCM/Junction Block Connector Terminals (Rear View)

3) Disconnect scan tool from DLC. Using external voltmeter, measure voltage between ground and DLC terminal No. 2 (Violet/Yellow wire). If voltage is .5-8 volts, go to TEST 12A. If voltage is more than 8 volts, go to TEST 13A. If voltage is less than .5 volt, go to next step.

4) Turn ignition off. Disconnect Body Control Module (BCM). BCM is connected to junction block. Ensure all junction block connectors are connected. Turn ignition on. Measure voltage between ground and

module 25-pin connector terminals No. 8 (Black wire) and No. 24 (Black wire). If resistance of either circuit is 10 ohms or more, repair appropriate open Black wire. If resistance of both circuits is less than 10 ohms, go to next step.

2) Turn ignition on. Using external voltmeter, measure voltage between ground and anti-lock brake controller module 25-pin connector terminal No. 9 (Red/Dark Blue wire). If voltage is 10 volts or less, go to TEST 5B. If voltage is more than 10 volts, go to next step.

3) Measure voltage between ground and anti-lock brake controller module 25-pin connector terminal No. 23 (White/Violet wire). If voltage is 10 volts or less, go to step 6). If voltage is more than 10 volts, go to next step.

4) Inspect fuse No. 17 in junction block. If fuse is okay, repair open White/Violet wire between fuse No. 17 and anti-lock brake controller module 25-pin connector. If fuse is blown, go to next step.

5) Turn ignition off. Using external ohmmeter, measure resistance between ground and anti-lock brake controller module 25-pin connector terminal No. 23 (White/Violet wire). If resistance is 5 ohms or more, replace fuse. If resistance is less than 5 ohms, repair short to ground in White/Violet wire between fuse No. 17 and anti-lock brake controller module 25-pin connector.

6) Turn ignition off. Using external ohmmeter, measure resistance of Violet/Yellow wire between BCM 12-pin White connector terminal No. 2 and anti-lock brake controller module 25-pin connector terminal No. 20. If resistance is 5 ohms or more, repair open Violet/Yellow wire. If resistance is less than 5 ohms, replace anti-lock brake controller module.

TEST 5B: NO RESPONSE FROM ANTI-LOCK BRAKE CONTROLLER MODULE

NOTE: For connector terminal identification and wiring diagrams, see BODY CONTROL COMPUTER – INTRODUCTION article. Perform VERIFICATION TEST VER-1 after each repair.

CAUTION: Always turn ignition off prior to disconnecting any module connector.

1) Inspect fuse "K" in Power Distribution Center (PDC). PDC is located in engine compartment. If fuse is okay, repair open Red/Dark Green wire between PDC and anti-lock brake controller module 25-pin connector. If fuse is blown, go to next step.

2) Using external ohmmeter, measure resistance between battery ground and PDC fuse "K" (Red/Dark Green wire). If resistance is less than 20 ohms, repair Red/Dark Green wire for short to ground. If resistance is 20 ohms or more, replace fuse.

TEST 6A: NO RESPONSE FROM MECHANICAL INSTRUMENT CLUSTER (MIC)

NOTE: For connector terminal identification and wiring diagrams, see BODY CONTROL COMPUTER – INTRODUCTION article. Perform VERIFICATION TEST VER-1 after each repair.

CAUTION: Always turn ignition off prior to disconnecting any module connector.

1) Turn ignition off. Disconnect Mechanical Instrument Cluster (MIC) connectors. Turn ignition on. Using external voltmeter, measure voltage between ground and MIC Green connector terminal No. 1 (Pink/Red wire). If voltage is 10 volts or less, repair open Pink/Red wire between junction block and MIC. If voltage is more than 10 volts, go to next step.

2) Turn ignition off. Using external ohmmeter, measure resistance between ground and MIC Green connector terminal No. 6 (Black/Light Green wire). If resistance is 20 ohms or more, repair open Black/Light Green wire. If resistance is less than 20 ohms, go to next step.

3) Measure resistance between ground and MIC Blue connector terminal No. 6 (Black wire). If resistance is 20 ohms or more, repair open Black wire. If resistance is less than 20 ohms, go to next step.

4) Disconnect scan tool from DLC. Open left front door. Turn ignition on. Using an external voltmeter, measure voltage between ground and MIC Green connector terminal No. 5 (Violet/Yellow wire). If voltage is .5 volt or less, repair short to ground in Violet/Yellow wire. If voltage is more than .5 volt, go to next step.

5) If voltage is more than 8 volts, replace MIC. If voltage is .5-8 volts repair short to voltage in Violet/Yellow wire.

TEST 7A: NO RESPONSE FROM MEMORY HEATED SEAT/ MIRROR MODULE (MHSMM)

NOTE: For connector terminal identification and wiring diagrams, see BODY CONTROL COMPUTER – INTRODUCTION article. Perform VERIFICATION TEST VER-1 after each repair.

CAUTION: Always turn ignition off prior to disconnecting any module connector.

1) Turn ignition off. Disconnect Memeoy Heated Seat/Mirror Module (MHSMM) 2-pin connector. Turn ignition on. Using external voltmeter, measure voltage between ground and MHSMM 2-pin connector terminal No. 2 (Red wire). If voltage is 11 volts or less, repair open Red wire between junction block and MHSMM. If voltage is more than 11 volts, go to next step.

2) Turn ignition off. Ensure all accessories and courtesy lights are off. Using external ohmmeter, measure resistance between ground and MHSMM 2-pin connector terminal No. 1 (Black wire). If resistance is 5 ohms or more, repair open Black wire. If resistance is less than 5 ohms, go to next step.

3) Disconnect MHSMM 26-pin connector. Turn ignition, headlights and courtesy lihgts on. Using external voltmeter, measure voltage between ground and MHSMM 26-pin connector terminal No. 26 (Violet/Yellow wire). If voltage is .6 volt or less, go to next step. If voltage is more than .6 volt, replace MHSMM.

4) Disconnect Body Control Module (BCM) Blue 16-pin connector. Connect jumper wire between ground and BCM Blue 16-pin connector terminal No. 9 (Violet/Yellow wire). Turn ignition off. Using an external ohmmeter, measure resistance between ground and MHSMM 26-pin connector terminal No. 26 (Violet/Yellow wire). If resistance is less than 5 ohms, replace BCM. If resistance is 5 ohms or more, repair open Violet/Yellow wire.

TEST 8A: NO RESPONSE FROM OTIS MODULE

NOTE: For connector terminal identification and wiring diagrams, see BODY CONTROL COMPUTER – INTRODUCTION article. Perform VERIFICATION TEST VER-1 after each repair.

CAUTION: Always turn ignition off prior to disconnecting any module connector.

1) Turn ignition off. Disconnect Overhead Travel Information System (OTIS) module 6-pin connector. OTIS module is mounted to headliner. Using external ohmmeter, measure resistance between ground and OTIS module 6-pin connector terminal No. 3 (Black/Light Green wire). If resistance is 10 ohms or more, repair open Black/Light Green wire. If resistance is less than 10 ohms, go to next step.

2) Turn ignition on. Using external voltmeter, measure voltage between ground and OTIS module 6-pin connector terminal No. 2 (Dark Blue/White wire). If voltage is 10 volts or less, repair open Dark Blue/White wire. If voltage is more than 10 volts, go to next step.

3) Measure voltage between ground and OTIS module 6-pin connector terminal No. 5 (Violet/Yellow wire). If voltage is more than .5 volt, replace OTIS module. If voltage is .5 volt or less, go to next step.

4) Disconnect junction block headliner connector C11. *See Fig. 2.* Measure voltage between ground and junction block headliner connector C11 terminal No. 4 (Violet/Yellow wire). If voltage is .5 volt or less, repair open Violet/Yellow wire between junction block and OTIS module. If voltage is more than .5 volt, go to next step.

CHRY
4-238

1999 ACCESSORIES & EQUIPMENT
Vehicle Communications – Concorde, Intrepid, LHS & 300M (Cont.)

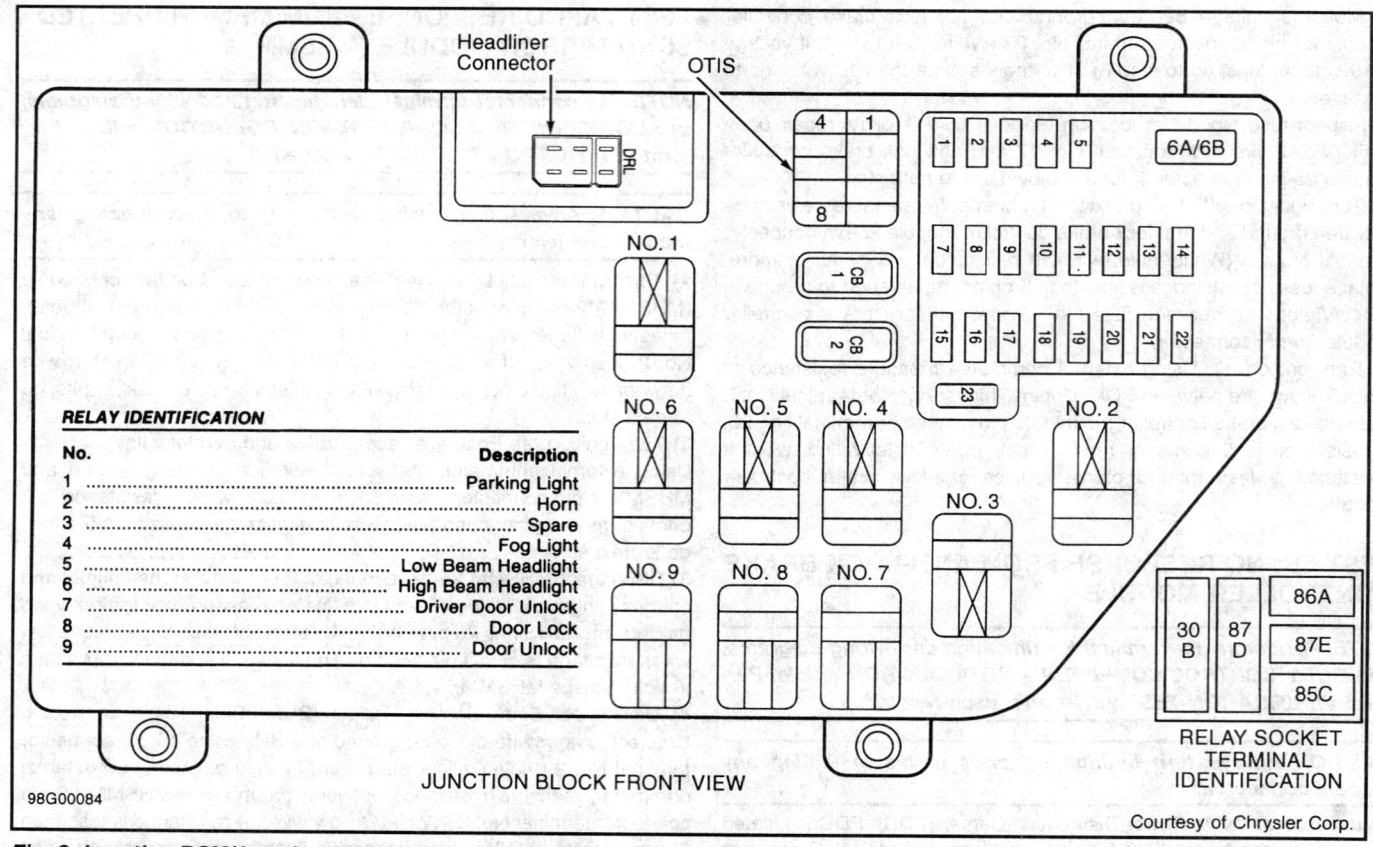

Fig. 2: Locating BCM/Junction Block Connector Terminals (Rear View)

5) Disconnect Body Control Module (BCM). BCM is connected to junction block. Ensure junction block 20-pin internal connector pins are not damaged, repair as necessary. If 20-pin internal connector is okay, replace BCM.

TEST 9 A: NO RESPONSE FROM POWERTRAIN CONTROL MODULE

NOTE: For connector terminal identification and wiring diagrams, see BODY CONTROL COMPUTER – INTRODUCTION article. Perform VERIFICATION TEST VER-1 after each repair.

CAUTION: Always turn ignition off prior to disconnecting any module connector.

1) Using scan tool, select ENGINE and read PCM DTCs. If scan tool displays NO RESPONSE, go to TEST NS–6A in appropriate SELF-DIAGNOSTICS article in ENGINE PERFORMANCE in appropriate MITCHELL® manual in appropriate MITCHELL® manual. If scan tool does not display NO RESPONSE, go to next step.

2) Turn ignition off and disconnect both battery cables. Disconnect Powertrain Control Module (PCM). PCM is located next to air cleaner. Using external ohmmeter, measure resistance of Violet/Yellow wire between PCM Gray 80-pin connector C2 terminal No. 59 and DLC terminal No. 2. If resistance is 320-2000 ohms, replace PCM. If resistance is not 320-2000 ohms, repair open Violet/Yellow wire.

TEST 10A: NO RESPONSE FROM RADIO

NOTE: For connector terminal identification and wiring diagrams, see BODY CONTROL COMPUTER – INTRODUCTION article. Perform VERIFICATION TEST VER-1 after each repair.

CAUTION: Always turn ignition off prior to disconnecting any module connector.

1) If radio screen is not blank, go to step 5). If radio screen is blank, remove and inspect fuse No. 4. If fuse is open, go to TEST 10B. If fuse is okay, go to next step.

2) Reinstall fuse. Access back of radio. Disconnect radio Gray 7-pin connector. Turn ignition on. Using external voltmeter, measure voltage between ground and radio Gray connector terminal No. 7 (Pink wire). If voltage is 10 volts or less, repair open Pink wire. If voltage is more than 10 volts, go to next step.

3) Measure voltage between ground and radio Gray 7-pin connector terminal No. 6 (Red wire). If voltage is 10 volts or less, repair open Red wire. If voltage is more than 10 volts, go to next step.

4) Ensure radio ground circuit and antenna are correctly installed. Repair as needed. If radio ground circuit and antenna were correctly installed, replace radio.

5) Disconnect radio PCI 2-pin connector. Turn ignition on and open all doors. Using external voltmeter, measure voltage between ground and PCI 2-pin connector, terminal No. 1 (Violet/Yellow wire). If voltage is more than .5 volt, replace radio. If voltage is .5 volt or less, go to next step.

6) Disconnect Body Control Module (BCM) Gray 14-pin connector. BCM is connected to junction block. Using external ohmmeter, measure resistance of Violet/Yellow wire between BCM Gray 14-pin connector terminal No. 5 and radio PCI connector terminal No. 1. If resistance is less than 5 ohms, replace radio. If resistance is 5 ohms or more, repair open Violet/Yellow wire.

1999 ACCESSORIES & EQUIPMENT

CHRY
4-239
Vehicle Communications – Concorde, Intrepid, LHS & 300M (Cont.)

TEST 10B: NO RESPONSE FROM RADIO

NOTE: For connector terminal identification and wiring diagrams, see BODY CONTROL COMPUTER – INTRODUCTION article. Perform VERIFICATION TEST VER-1 after each repair.

CAUTION: Always turn ignition off prior to disconnecting any module connector.

Turn ignition off. Disconnect radio Gray 7-pin connector. Using external ohmmeter, measure resistance between ground and terminal No. 7 (Pink wire). If resistance is less than 5 ohms, repair Pink wire for short to ground and replace fuse. If resistance is 5 ohms or greater, replace radio and fuse.

TEST 11A: NO RESPONSE FROM SENTRY KEY IMMOBILIZER MODULE (SKIM)

NOTE: For connector terminal identification and wiring diagrams, see BODY CONTROL COMPUTER – INTRODUCTION article. Perform VERIFICATION TEST VER-1 after each repair.

CAUTION: Always turn ignition off prior to disconnecting any module connector.

1) Turn ignition off. Disconnect Sentry Key Immobilizer Module (SKIM) connector. Turn ignition on. Using external ohmmeter, measure resistance between ground and SKIM connector terminal No. 2 (Black/Light Green wire). If resistance is 5 ohms or more, repair open Black/Light Green wire. If resistance is less than 5 ohms, go to next step.
2) Using external voltmeter, measure voltage between ground and SKIM connector terminal No. 1 (Pink wire). If voltage is 10 volts or less, repair open Pink wire between junction block and SKIM. If voltage is more than 10 volts, go to next step.
3) Turn ignition on. Measure voltage between ground and SKIM connector terminal No. 3 (Dark Blue/White wire). If voltage is .10 volts or less, repair open Dark Blue/White wire between junction block and SKIM. If voltage is more than 10 volts, go to next step.
4) Open and close drivers door. Measure voltage between ground and SKIM connector terminal No. 5 (Violet/Yellow wire). If voltage is more than .5 volt, replace SKIM and reprogram keys. If voltage is .5 volt or less, repair open Violet/Yellow wire.

TEST 12A: NO RESPONSE FROM TRANSMISSION CONTROL MODULE

NOTE: For connector terminal identification and wiring diagrams, see BODY CONTROL COMPUTER – INTRODUCTION article. Perform VERIFICATION TEST VER-1 after each repair.

CAUTION: Always turn ignition off prior to disconnecting any module connector.

1) Disconnect Transmission Control Module (TCM). TCM is located at left fenderwell, next to power distribution center in engine compartment. Turn ignition on. Using external voltmeter, measure voltage between ground and TCM connector terminal No. 11 (Red/White wire). If voltage is 10 volts or less, repair open Red/White wire. If voltage is more than 10 volts, go to next step.
2) Measure voltage between ground and TCM connector terminal No. 56 (Red/Light Blue wire). If voltage is 10 volts or less, repair open Red/Light Blue wire. If voltage is more than 10 volts, go to next step.
3) Turn ignition off. Using external ohmmeter, measure resistance between ground and TCM connector terminals No. 53 (Black wire) and No. 57 (Black/Red wire). If resistance of either circuit is 5 ohms or more, repair open Black or Black/Red wire. If resistance of both circuits is less than 5 ohms, go to next step.
4) Turn ignition on. Using external voltmeter, measure voltage between ground and TCM connector terminal No. 43 (Violet/Yellow wire). If voltage is .5 volt or less, repair open Violet/Yellow wire. If voltage is more than 10 volts, replace TCM.

TEST 13A: BUS SHORT TO BATTERY

NOTE: For connector terminal identification and wiring diagrams, see BODY CONTROL COMPUTER – INTRODUCTION article. Perform VERIFICATION TEST VER-1 after each repair.

CAUTION: Always turn ignition off prior to disconnecting any module connector.

1) Turn ignition on. Use scan tool to erase BCM DTCs. Using scan tool, read BCM DTCs. If scan tool does not display BUS SHORT TO BATTERY, go to next step. If scan tool displays BUS SHORT TO BATTERY, go to step 3).
2) Monitor the odometer display while performing wiggle test on BCM harness. Inspect all BCM connectors and terminals for damage. Repair as necessary. If odometer does not display NO BUS, perform TEST 15A. If odometer displays NO BUS, replace BCM.
3) If odometer does not display NO BUS, perform TEST 1A. If odometer displays NO BUS, replace BCM.

TEST 14A: BUS SHORT TO GROUND

NOTE: For connector terminal identification and wiring diagrams, see BODY CONTROL COMPUTER – INTRODUCTION article. Perform VERIFICATION TEST VER-1 after each repair.

CAUTION: Always turn ignition off prior to disconnecting any module connector.

1) Turn ignition on. Use scan tool to erase BCM DTCs. Using scan tool, read BCM DTCs. If scan tool does not display BUS SHORT TO GROUND, go to next step. If scan tool displays BUS SHORT TO GROUND, go to step 3).
2) Monitor the odometer display while performing wiggle test on BCM harness. Inspect all BCM connectors and terminals for damage. Repair as necessary. If odometer does not display NO BUS, perform TEST 15A. If odometer displays NO BUS, replace BCM.
3) If odometer does not display NO BUS, perform TEST 1A. If odometer displays NO BUS, replace BCM.

TEST 15A: ODOMETER NO BUS MESSAGE

NOTE: For connector terminal identification and wiring diagrams, see BODY CONTROL COMPUTER – INTRODUCTION article. Perform VERIFICATION TEST VER-1 after each repair.

CAUTION: Always turn ignition off prior to disconnecting any module connector.

1) Using an external voltmeter, measure voltage between ground and backprobe of DLC terminal No. 2 (Violet/Yellow wire). Turn ignition on. Open all doors and turn on A/C. If voltage is more than 8 volts, go to TEST 15D. If voltage is less than .5 volt, go to step 3). If voltage is .5-8 volts, go to next step.
2) Disconnect both battery cables. Using external ohmmeter, measure resistance between ground and DLC terminal No. 2 (Violet/Yellow wire). If resistance is more than 2000 ohms, go to next step. If resistance is less than 320 ohms, go to TEST 15E. If resistance is 320-2000 ohms and odometer displays NO BUS, go to TEST 15C. If resistance is 320-2000 ohms and odometer does not display NO BUS, go to next step.
3) Turn ignition off. Disconnect both battery cables. Disconnect Overhead Travel Information System (OTIS) module headliner connector at junction block (junction block C11). See Fig. 3. Using external ohmmeter, measure resistance between ground and junction block connector C11 terminal No. 4 (Violet/Yellow wire). If resistance is 9-11 k/ohms, go to next step. If resistance is not 9-11 k/ohms, go to TEST 15B.
4) Disconnect BCM White 12-pin connector. Measure resistance between ground and BCM White 12-pin connector terminal No. 1 (Violet/Yellow wire). If resistance is 900-1100 ohms, go to next step. If resistance is not 900-1100 ohms, go to TEST 15B.

CHRY
4-240

1999 ACCESSORIES & EQUIPMENT
Vehicle Communications – Concorde, Intrepid, LHS & 300M (Cont.)

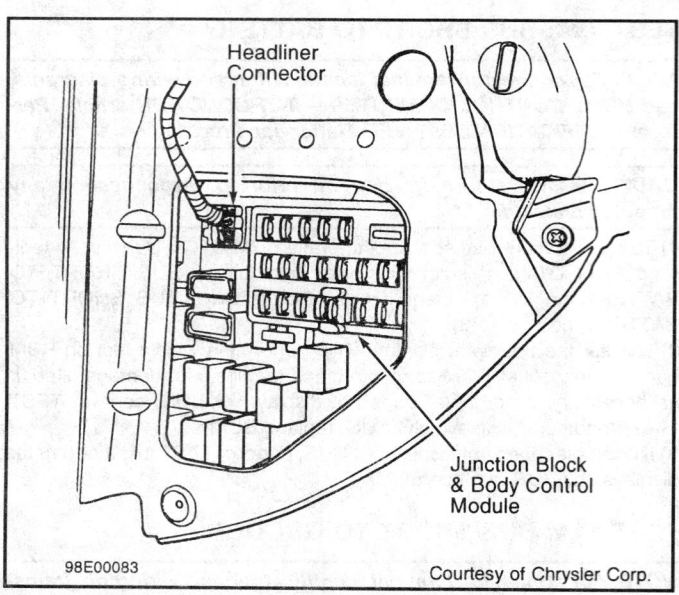

Headliner Connector

Junction Block & Body Control Module

98E00083
Courtesy of Chrysler Corp.

Fig. 3: Locating Headliner Connector

5) Measure resistance between ground and BCM White 12-pin connector terminal No. 2 (Violet/Yellow wire). If resistance is 9-11 k/ohms, go to next step. If resistance is not 9-11 k/ohms, go to TEST 15B.

6) Measure resistance between ground and BCM White 12-pin connector terminal No. 7 (Violet/Yellow wire). If resistance is 9-11 k/ohms, go to next step. If resistance is not 9-11 k/ohms, go to TEST 15B.

7) Disconnect BCM Blue 16-pin connector. Measure resistance between ground and BCM Blue 16-pin connector terminal No. 9 (Violet/Yellow wire). If resistance is 9-11 k/ohms, go to next step. If resistance is not 9-11 k/ohms, go to TEST 15B.

8) Disconnect BCM Gray 14-pin connector. Measure resistance between ground and BCM Gray 14-pin connector terminal No. 14 (Violet/Yellow wire). If resistance is less than 5 ohms, repair open Violet/Yellow wire. If resistance is 5 ohms or more, go to next step.

9) Measure resistance between ground and BCM Gray 14-pin connector terminal No. 4 (Violet/Yellow wire). If resistance is 9-11 k/ohms, go to next step. If resistance is not 9-11 k/ohms, go to TEST 15B.

10) Measure resistance between ground and BCM Gray 14-pin connector terminal No. 5 (Violet/Yellow wire). If resistance is 9-11 k/ohms, go to next step. If resistance is not 9-11 k/ohms, go to TEST 15D.

11) Measure resistance between ground and BCM Gray 14-pin connector terminal No. 7 (Violet/Yellow wire). If resistance is 9-11 k/ohms, go to next step. If resistance is not 9-11 k/ohms, go to TEST 15B.

12) Measure resistance between ground and BCM Gray 14-pin connector terminal No. 12 (Violet/Yellow wire). If resistance is 9-11 k/ohms, go to next step. If resistance is not 9-11 k/ohms, go to TEST 15B.

13) Measure resistance between ground and BCM Gray 14-pin connector terminal No. 13 (Violet/Yellow wire). If resistance is 9-11 k/ohms, go to TEST 13C. If resistance is not 9-11 k/ohms, go to TEST 15B.

14) Remove BCM from junction block. Measure resistance between ground and junction block 20-pin internal connector. *See Fig. 1.* If resistance is less than one ohm, replace BCM. If resistance is more than one ohm, replace junction block.

TEST 15B: ODOMETER NO BUS MESSAGE

NOTE: For connector terminal identification and wiring diagrams, see BODY CONTROL COMPUTER – INTRODUCTION article. Perform VERIFICATION TEST VER-1 after each repair.

CAUTION: Always turn ignition off prior to disconnecting any module connector.

1) Disconnect appropriate module from defective circuit. Using an external ohmmeter, measure resistance between ground and appropriate terminal of BCM connector (Violet/Yellow wire), as specified in TEST

15A. If resistance is less than 5 ohms, repair Violet/Yellow wire for short to ground. If resistance is 5 ohms or more, go to next step.

2) Connect jumper wire between ground and Violet/Yellow wire of appropriate module. Measure resistance between ground and appropriate terminal of BCM connector (Violet/Yellow wire), as specified in TEST 15A. If resistance is less than 5 ohms, repair open Violet/Yellow wire between BCM and appropriate module. If resistance is 5 ohms or more, replace appropriate module.

TEST 15C: ODOMETER NO BUS MESSAGE

NOTE: For connector terminal identification and wiring diagrams, see BODY CONTROL COMPUTER – INTRODUCTION article. Perform VERIFICATION TEST VER-1 after each repair.

CAUTION: Always turn ignition off prior to disconnecting any module connector.

1) Disconnect Overhead Travel Information System (OTIS) module, if equipped. OTIS module is mounted to headliner. Turn ignition on. If odometer does not display NO BUS, replace OTIS module. If odometer displays NO BUS, go to next step.

2) Turn ignition off. Disconnect Memory Heated Seat/Mirror Module (MHSMM), if equipped. MHSMM is located under drivers seat. Turn ignition on. If odometer does not display NO BUS, replace MHSMM module. If odometer displays NO BUS, go to next step.

3) Turn ignition off. Disconnect Transmission Control Module (TCM), if equipped. TCM is located at left fenderwell, next to power distribution center in engine compartment. Turn ignition on. If odometer does not display NO BUS, replace TCM module. If odometer displays NO BUS, go to next step.

4) Turn ignition off and disconnect Powertrain Control Module (PCM). PCM is located next to air cleaner. Turn ignition on. If odometer does not display NO BUS, replace PCM module. If odometer displays NO BUS, go to next step.

5) Turn ignition off. Disconnect anti-lock brake controller module. Anti-lock brake controller module is mounted on left inner fender panel. Turn ignition on. If odometer does not display NO BUS, replace anti-lock brake controller module. If odometer displays NO BUS, go to next step.

6) Turn ignition off. Disconnect Automatic Temperature Control (ATC) head. Turn ignition on. If odometer does not display NO BUS, replace ATC head. If odometer displays NO BUS, go to next step.

7) Turn ignition off and wait 5 minutes. Disconnect Air Bag Control Module (ACM) 23-pin connector. ACM is located under center console. Turn ignition on. If odometer does not display NO BUS, replace ACM module. If odometer displays NO BUS, go to next step.

8) Disconnect audio CD player connector, if equipped. Turn ignition on. If odometer does not display NO BUS, replace audio CD player . If odometer displays NO BUS, go to next step.

9) Disconnect radio connector, if equipped. Turn ignition on. If odometer does not display NO BUS, replace radio. If odometer displays NO BUS, go to next step.

10) Disconnect Sentry Key Immobilizer Module (SKIM) connector. SKIM is located at ignition switch. Turn ignition on. If odometer does not display NO BUS, replace SKIM. If odometer displays NO BUS, go to next step.

11) Disconnect BCM Gray 14-pin connector. Connect jumper wire between BCM Gray 14-pin connector terminals No. 13 and No. 14. Using scan tool, select MIC CLUSTER. If odometer does not display NO BUS, replace BCM. If odometer displays NO BUS, replace instrument cluster.

TEST 15D: BUS SHORT TO BATTERY

NOTE: For connector terminal identification and wiring diagrams, see BODY CONTROL COMPUTER – INTRODUCTION article. Perform VERIFICATION TEST VER-1 after each repair.

CAUTION: Always turn ignition off prior to disconnecting any module connector.

1) Ensure voltmeter is still connected from TEST 15A. Turn ignition off. Disconnect Overhead Travel Information System (OTIS) module, if equipped. OTIS module is mounted to headliner. Turn ignition on. If voltage is more than 8 volts, go to next step. If voltage is 8 volts or less, replace OTIS module..

2) Turn ignition off. Disconnect OTIS harness at junction block. Turn ignition on. If voltage is more than 8 volts, go to next step. If voltage is 8 volts or less, repair short to battery in OTIS harness.

3) Turn ignition off. Disconnect Transmission Control Module (TCM), if equipped. TCM is located at left fenderwell, next to power distribution center in engine compartment. Turn ignition on. If voltage is 8 volts or less, replace TCM. If voltage is more than 8 volts, go to next step.

4) Turn ignition off and disconnect Powertrain Control Module (PCM). PCM is located next to air cleaner. Turn ignition on. If voltage is 8 volts or less, replace PCM. If voltage is more than 8 volts, go to next step.

5) Turn ignition off. Disconnect anti-lock brake controller module. Anti-lock brake controller module is mounted on left inner fender panel. Turn ignition on. If voltage is 8 volts or less, replace anti-lock brake controller module. If voltage is more than 8 volts, go to next step.

6) Turn ignition off. Disconnect Body Control Module (BCM) White 12-pin connector. BCM is located on back of junction block. Turn ignition on. If voltage is 8 volts or less, repair short to battery in BCM White 12-pin connector bus circuits. See BODY CONTROL COMPUTER – INTRODUCTION article. If voltage is more than 8 volts, go to next step.

7) Turn ignition off. Disconnect Memory Heated Seat/Mirror Module (MHSMM), if equipped. MHSMM is located under drivers seat. Turn ignition on. If voltage is 8 volts or less, replace MHSMM module. If voltage is more than 8 volts, go to next step.

8) Turn ignition off. Disconnect Body Control Module (BCM) Blue 16-pin connector. BCM is located on back of junction block. Turn ignition on. If voltage is 8 volts or less, repair short to battery in BCM Blue 16-pin connector bus circuits. See BODY CONTROL COMPUTER – INTRODUCTION article. If voltage is more than 8 volts, go to next step.

9) Turn ignition off. Disconnect Automatic Temperature Control (ATC) head. Turn ignition on. If voltage is 8 volts or less, replace ATC head. If voltage is more than 8 volts, go to next step.

10) Disconnect audio CD player connectors and cable, if equipped. Turn ignition on. If voltage is 8 volts or less, replace audio CD player. If voltage is more than 8 volts, go to next step.

11) Disconnect audio CD player cable, if equipped. Turn ignition on. If voltage is 8 volts or less, replace audio CD player cable. If voltage is more than 8 volts, go to next step.

12) Disconnect radio connector, if equipped. Turn ignition on. If voltage is 8 volts or less, replace radio. If voltage is more than 8 volts, go to next step.

13) Turn ignition off and wait 5 minutes. Disconnect Air Bag Control Module (ACM) 23-pin connector. ACM is located under center console. Turn ignition on. If voltage is 8 volts or less, replace ACM. If voltage is more than 8 volts, go to next step.

14) Disconnect Sentry Key Immobilizer Module (SKIM) connector. SKIM is located at ignition switch. Turn ignition on. If voltage is 8 volts or less, replace SKIM. If voltage is more than 8 volts, go to next step.

15) Turn ignition off. Disconnect Mechanical Instrument Cluster (MIC). Turn ignition on. If voltage is 8 volts or less, replace MIC. If voltage is more than 8 volts, go to next step.

16) Turn ignition off. Disconnect Body Control Module (BCM) Gray 14-pin connector. BCM is located on back of junction block. Turn ignition on. If no voltage exists bus, repair short to battery in BCM Gray 14-pin connector bus circuits. See BODY CONTROL COMPUTER – INTRODUCTION article. If any voltage exists bus, replace BCM.

TEST 15E: BUS SHORT TO GROUND

NOTE: For connector terminal identification and wiring diagrams, see BODY CONTROL COMPUTER – INTRODUCTION article. Perform VERIFICATION TEST VER-1 after each repair.

CAUTION: Always turn ignition off prior to disconnecting any module connector.

1) Using external ohmmeter, measure resistance between ground and Data Link Connector (DLC) terminal No. 2 (Violet/Yellow wire). Turn ignition off and disconnect Powertrain Control Module (PCM). PCM is located next to air cleaner. If resistance is 9-11 k/ohms, replace PCM. If resistance is not 9-11 k/ohms, go to next step.

2) Turn ignition off. Disconnect Transmission Control Module (TCM), if equipped. TCM is located at left fenderwell, next to power distribution center in engine compartment. If resistance is 9-11 k/ohms, replace TCM. If resistance is not 9-11 k/ohms, go to next step.

3) Turn ignition off. Disconnect anti-lock brake controller module. Anti-lock brake controller module is mounted on left inner fender panel. If resistance is 9-11 k/ohms, replace anti-lock brake controller module. If resistance is not 9-11 k/ohms, go to next step.

4) Turn ignition off. Disconnect Overhead Travel Information System (OTIS) module 6-pin connector. OTIS module is mounted to headliner. If resistance is 9-11 k/ohms, go to next step. If resistance is not 9-11 k/ohms, replace OTIS module.

5) Turn ignition off. Disconnect Memory Heated Seat/Mirror Module (MHSMM), if equipped. MHSMM is located under drivers seat. If resistance is 9-11 k/ohms, go to next step. If resistance is not 9-11 k/ohms, replace MHSMM.

6) Turn ignition off. Disconnect Mechanical Instrument Cluster (MIC). If resistance is 9-11 k/ohms, replace MIC. If resistance is not 9-11 k/ohms, go to next step.

7) Turn ignition off and wait 5 minutes. Disconnect Air Bag Control Module (ACM) 23-pin connector. ACM is located under center console. If resistance is 9-11 k/ohms, replace ACM. If resistance is not 9-11 k/ohms, go to next step.

8) Disconnect Sentry Key Immobilizer Module (SKIM) connector. SKIM is located at ignition switch. If resistance is 9-11 k/ohms, replace SKIM. If resistance is not 9-11 k/ohms, go to next step.

9) Disconnect audio CD player connectors and cable, if equipped. If resistance is 9-11 k/ohms, replace audio CD player. If resistance is not 9-11 k/ohms, go to next step.

10) Disconnect audio CD player cable, if equipped. If resistance is 9-11 k/ohms, replace audio CD player cable. If resistance is not 9-11 k/ohms, go to next step.

11) Disconnect radio connector, if equipped. If resistance is 9-11 k/ohms, replace radio. If resistance is not 9-11 k/ohms, go to next step.

12) Turn ignition off. Disconnect Automatic Temperature Control (ATC) head. If resistance is 9-11 k/ohms, replace ATC. If resistance is not 9- 11 k/ohms, go to next step.

13) Disconnect Body Control Module (BCM) connectors. BCM is connected to junction block. If resistance is 2 k/ohms ohms or more, go to next step. If resistance is less than 2 k/ohms, repair short to ground in bus circuit between BCM Gray 14-pin connector and DLC. See BODY CONTROL COMPUTER – INTRODUCTION article.

14) Using external ohmmeter, measure resistance between ground and each BCM and junction block connector Violet/Yellow wire. If resistance in any circuit is less than 2 k/ohms, repair appropriate Yellow/Violet wire for short to ground. If resistance in all circuits is 2 k/ohms or more, replace BCM.

CHRY
4-242

1999 ACCESSORIES & EQUIPMENT
Vehicle Communications – Concorde, Intrepid, LHS & 300M (Cont.)

TEST 15F: ODOMETER NO BUS MESSAGE

NOTE: For connector terminal identification and wiring diagrams, see BODY CONTROL COMPUTER – INTRODUCTION article. Perform VERIFICATION TEST VER-1 after each repair.

CAUTION: Always turn ignition off prior to disconnecting any module connector.

1) Disconnect audio CD player. Using externnal ohmmeter, measure resistance between ground and Body Control Module (BCM) Gray 14-pin connector terminal No. 5 (Violet/Yellow wire). If resistance is 9-11 k/ohms, replace audio CD player. If resistance is not 9-11 k/ohms, go to next step.

2) Disconnect audio CD player bus wire from radio (Violet/Yellow wire). If resistance is 9-11 k/ohms, repair short to ground in Violet/Yellow wire. If resistance is not 9-11 k/ohms, go to next step.

3) Disconnect radio connectors. If resistance is 9-11 k/ohms, replace radio. If resistance is not 9-11 k/ohms, repair short to ground in Violet/Yellow wire between BCM and radio.

TEST 16A: NO FUSED IGNITION SWITCH OUTPUT TO BCM

NOTE: For connector terminal identification and wiring diagrams, see BODY CONTROL COMPUTER – INTRODUCTION article. Perform VERIFICATION TEST VER-1 after each repair.

CAUTION: Always turn ignition off prior to disconnecting any module connector.

1) Remove and inspect fuse No. 14. If fuse is okay, go to step **6)**. If fuse is blown, go to next step.

2) turn ignition off. Using an external ohmmeter, measure resistance between ground and fuse No. 14 (Dark Blue/White wire closest to top of junction block). If resistance is 5 ohms or more, replace fuse No. 14. If resistance is less than 5 ohms, go to next step.

3) Disconnect headliner connector at junction block. *See Fig. 3.* Measure resistance between ground and fuse No. 14 (Dark Blue/White wire closest to bottom of junction block). If resistance is 5 ohms or more, go to TEST 8A. If resistance is less than 5 ohms, go to next step.

4) Disconnect junction block connector C7. Measure resistance between ground and junction block connector C7 terminal No. 5 (Dark Blue/White wire). If resistance is 5 ohms or more, repair short to ground in Dark Blue/White wire. See appropriate wiring diagram in BODY CONTROL COMPUTER – INTRODUCTION article. If resistance is less than 5 ohms, go to next step.

5) Disconnect BCM from junction block. Measure resistance between ground and junction block internal 20-pin connector terminal No. 5. *See Fig. 1.* If resistance is 5 ohms or more, replace junction block and fuse No. 14. If resistance is less than 5 ohms, replace BCM and fuse No. 14.

6) Turn ignition on. Using an external voltmeter, measure voltage between ground and fuse No. 14 (Dark Blue/White wire closest to bottom of junction block). If voltage is 10 volts or less, repair open Dark Blue/White wire between ignition switch and junction block. If voltage is more than 10 volts, go to next step.

7) Turn ignition off. Reinstall fuse No. 14. Disconnect BCM from junction block. Ensure all junction block connectors are connected. Turn ignition on. Measure voltage between ground and junction block internal 20-pin connector terminal No. 5. *See Fig. 1.* If voltage is 10 volts or less, replace junction block. If voltage is more than 10 volts, replace BCM.

VERIFICATION TEST VER-1A

1) Reconnect all previously disconnected components and connectors. If BCM was replaced, turn ignition on for at least 15 seconds. Program all RKE transmitters, recalibrate HVAC doors and program other options as necessary.

2) If vehicle is equipped with VTSS, select MISCELLANEOUS and ENABLE VTSS. If battery was disconnected, start engine and recalibrate HVAC doors using scan tool.

3) Ensure ignition is on. Erase all DTCs using scan tool. Turn ignition off and wait 5 seconds. Turn ignition on and fully operate system that was malfunctioning.

4) If system does not operate properly, go to SYMPTOM IDENTIFICATION TEST 1A in BODY CONTROL COMPUTER TESTS – CONCORDE, INTREPID, LHS & 300M article. If system operates properly, read fault messages using scan tool. If any codes are present, go to SYMPTOM IDENTIFICATION TEST 1B in BODY CONTROL COMPUTER TESTS – CONCORDE, INTREPID, LHS & 300M article. If no DTCs are present, system is operating correctly and customer's complaint cannot be duplicated, repair is complete.

IDENTIFYING VEHICLE COMMUNICATION PROBLEMS

Connect scan tool to Data Link Connector (DLC) to retrieve messages. If scan tool message is blank, disconnect scan tool. Ensure ground circuit has continuity at DLC terminal No. 4. Ensure 12 volts exists at DLC terminal No. 16. Check power to DLC terminal No. 16 from Power Distribution Center (PDC) fuse No. 12. Try another scan tool and/or cable. If scan tool DTC or fault message is present, see following bus fault messages list and proceed to appropriate DTC or fault message:

- BUS (+) & BUS (–) OPEN
- BUS (+) OPEN
- BUS (–) OPEN
- BUS (+) & BUS (–) SHORTED TOGETHER
- BUS BIAS LEVEL TOO HIGH
- BUS BIAS LEVEL TOO LOW
- NO BUS BIAS
- NO RESPONSE AIR BAG CONTROL MODULE
- NO RESPONSE CENTRAL TIMER MODULE
- NO RESPONSE COMPASS/MINI-TRIP SYSTEM
- NO RESPONSE POWERTRAIN CONTROL MODULE
- NO RESPONSE CCD RADIO
- NO RESPONSE INSTRUMENT CLUSTER
- NO TERMINATION
- NOT RECEIVING BUS MESSAGES CORRECTLY
- BUS SHORT TO 5 VOLTS
- BUS SHORT TO BATTERY
- BUS SHORT TO GROUND

BUS (+) & BUS (–) OPEN, (BUS (+) OPEN OR BUS (–) OPEN)

NOTE: For connector terminal identification and wiring diagrams, see BODY CONTROL COMPUTER – INTRODUCTION article. Perform VERIFICATION TEST VER-1 after each repair.

CAUTION: Always turn ignition off prior to disconnecting any module connector.

1) Disconnect scan tool. Ensure ignition is on. Using an external voltmeter, measure voltage between ground and DLC terminal No. 3 (Violet/Brown wire). If voltage is not 1.8-2.3 volts, go to step 3). If voltage is 1.8-2.3 volts, go to next step.
2) Measure voltage between ground and DLC terminal No. 11 (White/Black wire). If voltage is not 1.8-2.3 volts, go to next step. If voltage is 1.8-2.3 volts, replace scan tool cable or scan tool.
3) Connect jumper wire between ground and DLC connector terminal No. 11 (White/Black wire). Turn ignition off. Remove instrument cluster. Using external ohmmeter, measure resistance between ground and oil pressure gauge side instrument cluster connector terminal No. 9 (White/Black wire). If resistance is less than 5 ohms, go to next step. If resistance is 5 ohms or more, repair open White/Black wire.
4) Disconnect jumper wire. Connect jumper wire between ground and DLC connector terminal No. 3 (White/Black wire). Measure resistance between ground and oil pressure gauge side instrument cluster connector terminal No. 10 (Violet/Brown wire). If resistance is less than 5 ohms, replace instrument cluster. If resistance is 5 ohms or more, repair open Violet/Brown wire.

BUS (+) & BUS (–) SHORTED TOGETHER

NOTE: For connector terminal identification and wiring diagrams, see BODY CONTROL COMPUTER – INTRODUCTION article. Perform VERIFICATION TEST VER-1 after each repair.

CAUTION: Always turn ignition off prior to disconnecting any module connector.

1) Turn ignition off. Disconnect Powertrain Control Module (PCM). PCM is mounted to right inner fender. Turn ignition on. If scan tool does not display BUS (+) & BUS (–) SHORTED TOGETHER, replace PCM. If scan tool displays BUS (+) & BUS (–) SHORTED TOGETHER, go to next step.
2) Turn ignition off. Disconnect anti-lock brake controller module. Controller is mounted to top of ABS hydraulic unit. Turn ignition on. If scan tool does not display BUS (+) & BUS (–) SHORTED TOGETHER, replace anti-lock brake controller module. If scan tool displays BUS (+) & BUS (–) SHORTED TOGETHER, go to next step.
3) Turn ignition off. Disconnect instrument cluster. Turn ignition on. If scan tool does not display BUS (+) & BUS (–) SHORTED TOGETHER, replace instrument cluster circuit board. If scan tool displays BUS (+) & BUS (–) SHORTED TOGETHER, go to next step.
4) Turn ignition off. Disconnect compass mini-trip computer. Turn ignition on. If scan tool does not display BUS (+) & BUS (–) SHORTED TOGETHER, replace compass mini-trip computer. If scan tool displays BUS (+) & BUS (–) SHORTED TOGETHER, go to next step.
5) Turn ignition off. Disconnect radio connector. Turn ignition on. If scan tool does not display BUS (+) & BUS (–) SHORTED TOGETHER, replace radio. If scan tool displays BUS (+) & BUS (–) SHORTED TOGETHER, go to next step.
6) Turn ignition off and wait 2 minutes. Disconnect Air Bag Control Module (ACM). ACM is located under front of center console. Turn ignition on. If scan tool does not display BUS (+) & BUS (–) SHORTED TOGETHER, replace ACM. If scan tool displays BUS (+) & BUS (–) SHORTED TOGETHER, go to next step.
7) Turn ignition off. Disconnect Central Timer Module (CTM). CTM is behind right corner of dash, behind glove box. Turn ignition on. If scan tool does not display BUS (+) & BUS (–) SHORTED TOGETHER, replace CTM. If scan tool displays BUS (+) & BUS (–) SHORTED TOGETHER, go to next step.
8) Disconnect scan tool from DLC. Using external ohmmeter, measure resistance between terminals No. 3 (Violet/Brown wire) and No. 11 (White/Black wire) on DLC connector. If resistance is less than 5 ohms, repair short between Violet/Brown wire and White/Dark Green wire. If resistance is 5 ohms or more, replace scan tool cable or scan tool as necessary.

BUS BIAS LEVEL TOO LOW (BUS BIAS LEVEL TOO HIGH)

NOTE: For connector terminal identification and wiring diagrams, see BODY CONTROL COMPUTER – INTRODUCTION article. Perform VERIFICATION TEST VER-1 after each repair.

CAUTION: Always turn ignition off prior to disconnecting any module connector.

1) Disconnect scan tool. Using an external voltmeter, measure voltage between ground and DLC connector terminal No. 3 (Violet/Brown wire). If voltage is not 1.8-2.8 volts, go to step 3). If voltage is 1.8-2.8 volts, go to next step.
2) Measure voltage between ground and DLC connector terminal No. 11 (White/Black wire). If voltage is not 1.8-2.8 volts, go to next step. If voltage is 1.8-2.8 volts, replace scan tool cable or scan tool.
3) Turn ignition off. Disconnect instrument cluster. Ensure interior lights are off. Using external ohmmeter, measure resistance between ground and oil pressure gauge side instrument cluster connector terminal No. 4 (Black/Light Green wire on Dakota or Black/Tan wire on Durango). If resistance is 5 ohms or less, repair open Black/Light Green or Black/Tan wire. If resistance is more than 5 ohms, go to next step.
4) Measure resistance between ground and oil pressure gauge side instrument cluster connector terminal No. 5 (Black wire). If resistance is 5 ohms or less, repair open Black wire. If resistance is more than 5 ohms, go to next step.
5) Connect jumper wire between ground and DLC connector terminal No. 11 (White/Black wire). Measure resistance between ground and oil pressure gauge side instrument cluster connector terminal No. 9 (White/Black wire). If resistance is less than 5 ohms, go to next step. If resistance is 5 ohms or more, repair open White/Black wire.

6) Disconnect jumper wire. Measure resistance between ground and oil pressure gauge side instrument cluster connector terminal No. 9 (White/Black wire). If resistance is less than 1000 ohms, repair White/Black wire for short to ground. If resistance is 1000 ohms or more, go to next step.

7) Connect jumper wire between ground and DLC connector terminal No. 3 (White/Black wire). Measure resistance between ground and right instrument cluster connector terminal No. 10 (Violet/Brown wire). If resistance is less than 5 ohms, go to next step. If resistance is 5 ohms or more, repair open Violet/Brown wire.

8) Disconnect jumper wire. Measure resistance between ground and oil pressure gauge side instrument cluster connector terminal No. 10 (Violet/Brown wire). If resistance is less than 1000 ohms, repair Violet/Brown wire for short to ground. If resistance is 1000 ohms or more, replace instrument cluster.

NO BUS BIAS

NOTE: For connector terminal identification and wiring diagrams, see BODY CONTROL COMPUTER – INTRODUCTION article. Perform VERIFICATION TEST VER-1 after each repair.

CAUTION: Always turn ignition off prior to disconnecting any module connector.

1) Remove and inspect fuse No. 11 from junction block. Junction block is on left side of instrument panel. If fuse is open, go to next step. If fuse is okay, go to step 4).

2) Turn ignition off. Using external ohmmeter, measure resistance between ground and fused ignition switch output run/start terminal (Dark Blue/White wire) on fuse No. 11 socket. If resistance is less than 5 ohms, repair Dark Blue/White wire for short to ground. Replace fuse No. 11. If resistance is 5 ohms or more, replace fuse No. 11.

3) Turn ignition on. Using an external voltmeter, measure voltage between ground and fuse No. 11 Dark Blue wire terminal. If voltage is more than 10 volts, go to next step. If voltage is 10 volts or less, repair open Dark Blue wire.

4) Disconnect scan tool. Turn ignition on. Using an external voltmeter, measure voltage between ground and DLC terminal No. 3 (Violet/Brown wire). If voltage is not 1.8-2.3 volts, go to step 6). If voltage is 1.8-2.3 volts, go to next step.

5) Measure voltage between ground and DLC terminal No. 11 (White/Black wire). If voltage is not 1.8-2.3 volts, go to next step. If voltage is 1.8-2.3 volts, replace scan tool cable or scan tool.

6) Connect jumper wire between ground and DLC connector terminal No. 11 (White/Black wire). Turn ignition off. Remove instrument cluster. Using external ohmmeter, measure resistance between ground and oil pressure gauge side instrument cluster connector terminal No. 9 (White/Black wire). If resistance is less than 5 ohms, go to next step. If resistance is 5 ohms or more, repair open White/Black wire.

7) Disconnect jumper wire. Measure resistance between ground and oil pressure gauge side instrument cluster connector terminal No. 9 (White/Black wire). If resistance is less than 1000 ohms, repair White/Black wire for short to ground. If resistance is 1000 ohms or more, go to next step.

8) Connect jumper wire between ground and DLC connector terminal No. 3 (White/Black wire). Measure resistance between ground and oil pressure gauge side instrument cluster connector terminal No. 10 (Violet/Brown wire). If resistance is less than 5 ohms, go to next step. If resistance is 5 ohms or more, repair open Violet/Brown wire.

9) Disconnect jumper wire. Measure resistance between ground and oil pressure gauge side instrument cluster connector terminal No. 10 (Violet/Brown wire). If resistance is less than 1000 ohms, repair Violet/Brown wire for short to ground. If resistance is 1000 ohms or more, go to next step.

10) Turn ignition on. Using external voltmeter, measure voltage between ground and oil pressure gauge side instrument cluster connector terminal No. 2 (Dark Blue/White wire). If voltage is 9.5 volts or less, repair open Dark Blue/White wire. If voltage is more than 9.5 volts, go to next step.

11) Turn ignition off. Using external ohmmeter, measure resistance between ground and oil pressure gauge side instrument cluster connec-tor terminal No. 4 (Black/Tan wire). If resistance is 5 ohms or less, go to next step. If resistance is more than 5 ohms, repair open Black/Tan wire.

12) Measure resistance between ground and oil pressure gauge side instrument cluster connector terminal No. 5 (Black wire). If resistance is 5 ohms or less, replace instrument cluster. If resistance is more than 5 ohms, repair open Black wire.

NO RESPONSE AIR BAG CONTROL MODULE

NOTE: For connector terminal identification and wiring diagrams, see BODY CONTROL COMPUTER – INTRODUCTION article. Perform VERIFICATION TEST VER-1 after each repair.

CAUTION: Always turn ignition off prior to disconnecting any module connector.

1) Remove and inspect fuse No. 19 from junction block. Junction block is on left side of instrument panel. If fuse is open, go to next step. If fuse is okay, go to next step 6).

2) Using external voltmeter, measure voltage between ground and fused ignition switch output run/start terminal (Light Green/Yellow wire) on fuse No. 19 socket. If voltage is 10 volts or less, repair open Light Green/Yellow wire. If voltage is more than 10 volts, go to next step.

3) Turn ignition off and wait 2 minutes. Using external ohmmeter, measure resistance between ground and fused ignition switch output run/start terminal (Light Green/Yellow wire) on fuse No. 19 socket. If resistance is less than 5 ohms, go to next step. If resistance is 5 ohms or more, go to step 5).

4) Disconnect Air Bag Control Module (ACM) connector. ACM is located under front of center console. Turn ignition on. Measure resistance between ground and fused ignition switch output run/start terminal (Light Green/Yellow wire) on fuse No. 19 socket. If resistance is less than 5 ohms, repair Light Green/Yellow wire for short to ground. Replace fuse No. 19. If resistance is 5 ohms or more, replace air bag control module and fuse No. 19.

5) Turn ignition off and wait 2 minutes. Disconnect Air Bag Control Module (ACM) connector. ACM is located under front of center console. Using external ohmmeter, measure resistance between terminal No. 17 (Light Green/Yellow wire) on ACM connector and fused ignition switch output run/start terminal (Light Green/Yellow wire) on fuse No. 19 socket. If resistance is less than 5 ohms, connect ACM connector. Turn ignition on. Replace fuse No. 19 in junction block. Go to appropriate MITCHELL® AIR BAG SERVICE & REPAIR, DOMESTIC CARS, LIGHT TRUCKS & VANS for further testing. If resistance is 5 ohms or more, repair open Light Green/Yellow wire. Replace fuse No. 19.

6) Using external voltmeter, measure voltage between ground and voltage input side of fuse No. 19 socket. If voltage is 10 volts or less, repair open ignition switch output circuit (Dark Blue wire between ignition switch and junction block). If voltage is more than 10 volts, go to next step.

7) Turn ignition off and wait 2 minutes. Install fuse No. 19. Disconnect Air Bag Control Module (ACM) connector. ACM is located under front of center console. Turn ignition on. Using external voltmeter, measure voltage between ground and terminal No. 14 (Light Green/Yellow wire) on ACM connector. If voltage is 10 volts or less, repair open Light Green/Yellow wire. If voltage is more than 10 volts, go to next step.

8) Turn ignition off. Using external ohmmeter, measure resistance between ground and ACM connector terminal No. 4 (Black/Pink wire on Dakota or Black/Tan wire Durango). If resistance is 5 ohms or more, repair open Black/Pink or Black/Tan wire. If resistance is less than 5 ohms, go to next step.

9) Turn ignition on. Using external voltmeter, measure voltage between ground and ACM connector terminal No. 19 (Violet/Brown wire). If voltage is not 1.8-2.6 volts, repair open Violet/Brown wire. If voltage is 1.8-2.6 volts, go to next step.

10) Using external voltmeter, measure voltage between ground and ACM connector terminal No. 18 (White/Black wire). If voltage is not 1.8-2.6 volts, repair White/Black wire. If voltage is 1.8-2.6 volts, replace ACM.

NO RESPONSE CENTRAL TIMER MODULE

NOTE: For connector terminal identification and wiring diagrams, see BODY CONTROL COMPUTER – INTRODUCTION article. Perform VERIFICATION TEST VER-1 after each repair.

CAUTION: Always turn ignition off prior to disconnecting any module connector.

1) Remove and inspect fuse No. 11 from junction block. Junction block is on left side of instrument panel. If fuse is open, go to next step. If fuse is okay, go to step **3**).

2) Using external ohmmeter, measure resistance between ground and fused ignition switch output run/start terminal (Dark Blue/White wire) on fuse No. 11 socket. If resistance is less than 5 ohms, repair short to ground in Dark Blue/White wire. Replace fuse No. 11. If resistance is 5 ohms or more, replace fuse No. 11.

3) Install fuse No. 11. Remove and inspect fuse No. 6 from junction block. If fuse is open, next step. If fuse is okay, go to step **5**).

4) Using external ohmmeter, measure resistance between ground and fused ignition switch output run/accy terminal (Dark Blue wire) on fuse No. 6 socket. If resistance is less than 5 ohms, repair short to ground in Dark Blue wire. Replace fuse No. 6. If resistance is 5 ohms or more, replace fuse No. 6.

5) Install fuse No. 6. Disconnect Central Timer Module (CTM). CTM is located behind right corner of dash, behind glove box. Using external ohmmeter, measure resistance between ground and CTM 18-pin connector terminal No. 3 (Black wire). If resistance is more than 5 ohms, repair open Black wire. If resistance is 5 ohms or less, go to next step.

6) Measure resistance between ground and CTM 14-pin connector terminal No. 6 (Black/Light Green wire on Dakota or Black/Tan wire on Durango). If resistance is more than 5 ohms, repair open Black/Light Green wire or Black/Tan wire. If resistance is 5 ohms or less, go to next step.

7) Turn ignition on. Using scan tool, perform CCD Bus test. Connect jumper wire between ground and CTM 18-pin connector terminal No. 16 (Violet/Brown wire). If scan tool does not display BUS SHORT TO GROUND, repair open Violet/Brown wire. If scan tool displays BUS SHORT TO GROUND, go to next step.

8) Disconnect jumper wire. Connect jumper wire between ground and CTM 18-pin connector terminal No. 17 (White/Black wire). If scan tool does not display BUS SHORT TO GROUND, repair open White/Black wire. If scan tool displays BUS SHORT TO GROUND, replace CTM.

NO RESPONSE COMPASS/MINI-TRIP SYSTEM

NOTE: For connector terminal identification and wiring diagrams, see BODY CONTROL COMPUTER – INTRODUCTION article. Perform VERIFICATION TEST VER-1 after each repair.

CAUTION: Always turn ignition off prior to disconnecting any module connector.

1) Remove and inspect fuse No. 11 from junction block. Junction block is on left side of instrument panel. If fuse is open, go to next step. If fuse is okay, go to step **3**).

2) Using external ohmmeter, measure resistance between ground and fused ignition switch output run/start terminal (Dark Blue/White wire) on fuse No. 11 socket. If resistance is less than 5 ohms, repair Dark Blue/White wire for short to ground. Replace fuse No. 11. If resistance is 5 ohms or more, replace fuse No. 11.

3) Reinstall fuse. Disconnect CMTC 12-pin connector. Turn ignition on. Using external voltmeter, measure voltage between ground and CMTC connector terminal No. 1 (Dark Blue/White wire). If voltage is less than 9.5 volts, repair open Dark Blue/White wire. If voltage is 9.5 volts or more, go to next step.

4) Using external voltmeter, measure voltage between ground and CMTC connector terminal No. 5 (Pink wire). If voltage is less than 9.5 volts, repair open Pink wire. If voltage is 9.5 volts or more, go to next step.

5) Turn ignition off. Using external ohmmeter, measure resistance between ground and CMTC connector terminal No. 7 (Black/Light Green wire on Dakota or Black/Tan wire on Durango). If resistance is 5 ohms or less, go to next step. If resistance is more than 5 ohms, repair open Black/Light Green or Black/Tan wire.

6) Using scan tool, perform CCD bus test. Connect jumper wire between ground and CMTC connector terminal No. 2 (Violet/Brown wire). If scan tool displays BUS (+) SHORTED TO GROUND, go to next step. If scan tool does not display BUS (+) SHORTED TO GROUND, repair open Violet/Brown wire.

7) Move jumper wire to CMTC connector terminal No. 8 (White/Black wire). If scan tool displays BUS (+) SHORTED TO GROUND, replace CMTC. If scan tool does not display BUS (+) SHORTED TO GROUND, repair open White/Black wire.

NO RESPONSE POWERTRAIN CONTROL MODULE

NOTE: For connector terminal identification and wiring diagrams, see BODY CONTROL COMPUTER – INTRODUCTION article. Perform VERIFICATION TEST VER-1 after each repair.

CAUTION: Always turn ignition off prior to disconnecting any module connector.

1) If engine does not run, see appropriate BASIC DIAGNOSTIC PROCEDURES article in ENGINE PERFORMANCE in appropriate MITCHELL® manual. If engine runs, go to next step.

2) Turn ignition off. Disconnect Powertrain Control Module (PCM). PCM is mounted to right inner fender. Turn ignition on. Connect jumper wire between ground and PCM Gray connector C3 terminal. No. 30 (Violet/Brown wire) PCM connector. Using scan tool, perform CCD BUS test. If scan tool does not display SHORT TO GROUND, repair open Violet/Brown wire. If scan tool displays SHORT TO GROUND, go to next step.

3) Move jumper wire to PCM Gray connector C3 terminal No. 28 (White/Black wire). Perform CCD BUS test. If scan tool does not display SHORT TO GROUND, repair open White/Black wire. If scan tool displays SHORT TO GROUND, replace PCM.

NO RESPONSE CCD RADIO

NOTE: For connector terminal identification and wiring diagrams, see BODY CONTROL COMPUTER – INTRODUCTION article. Perform VERIFICATION TEST VER-1A after each repair.

CAUTION: Always turn ignition off prior to disconnecting any module connector.

1) If radio screen is not blank, go to step **7**). If radio screen is blank, go to next step.

2) Remove and inspect junction block fuse No. 8 (radio). If fuse is blown, go to next step. If fuse is okay, go to step **4**).

3) Turn ignition off. Disconnect radio Gray connector. Using external ohmmeter, measure resistance between ground and terminal No. 6 (Red/White wire). If resistance is less than 5 ohms, repair Red/White wire for short to ground. Replace junction block fuse No. 8. If resistance is 5 ohms or more, replace radio. Replace junction block fuse No. 8.

4) Turn ignition on. Measure voltage between ground and terminal No. 7 (Pink wire). If voltage is 10 volts or less, repair open Pink wire. If voltage is more than 10 volts, go to next step.

5) Install fuse. Disconnect radio Gray connector. Using external voltmeter, measure voltage between ground and terminal No. 6 (Red/White wire). If voltage is 10 volts or less, repair open Red/White wire. If voltage is more than 10 volts, go to next step.

6) Inspect ground strap and antenna for correct installation. Repair as needed. If ground strap and antenna are okay, replace radio.

7) Disconnect 2-pin CCD BUS connector on back of radio. Connect jumper wire between terminal No. 2 (White/Black wire) and ground. Using scan tool, select BODY, BODY COMPUTER, then SYSTEM TEST. Perform CCD BUS test. If scan tool does not display BUS SHORT TO GROUND, repair open White/Black wire. If scan tool displays BUS SHORT TO GROUND, go to next step.

8) Move jumper wire to terminal No. 1 (Violet/Brown wire). Perform CCD BUS test. If scan tool does not display BUS SHORT TO GROUND, repair open Violet/Brown wire. If scan tool displays BUS SHORT TO GROUND, replace radio.

NO RESPONSE INSTRUMENT CLUSTER

NOTE: For connector terminal identification and wiring diagrams, see BODY CONTROL COMPUTER – INTRODUCTION article. Perform VERIFICATION TEST VER-1A after each repair.

CAUTION: Always turn ignition off prior to disconnecting any module connector.

1) Turn ignition on. Using scan tool, select BODY CONTROL MODULE. If scan tool displays NO RESPONSE, go to NO RESPONSE CENTRAL TIMER MODULE. If scan tool does not display NO RESPONSE, go to next step.

2) Using scan tool, select SYSTEM TEST. If scan tool displays PCM ACTIVE ON THE BUS, go to next step. If scan tool does not display PCM ACTIVE ON THE BUS, go to NO RESPONSE POWERTRAIN CONTROL MODULE.

3) Turn ignition off. Remove instrument cluster. Turn ignition on. Using scan tool, turn on CCD bus bias under SYSTEM MONITORS, then CCD BUS VOLTAGE. Connect jumper wire between ground and instrument cluster connector terminal No. 10 (Violet/Brown wire). If scan tool voltage did not drop to about zero volts, repair open Violet/Brown wire. If scan tool voltage dropped to about zero volts, go to next step.

4) Move jumper to instrument cluster connector terminal No. 9 (White/Black wire). Monitor CCD BUS VOLTAGE. If scan tool voltage did not drop to about zero volts, repair open White/Black wire. If scan tool voltage did not drop to about zero volts, replace instrument cluster.

NO TERMINATION

NOTE: For connector terminal identification and wiring diagrams, see BODY CONTROL COMPUTER – INTRODUCTION article. Perform VERIFICATION TEST VER-1 after each repair.

CAUTION: Always turn ignition off prior to disconnecting any module connector.

1) Disconnect Powertrain Control Module (PCM) connectors. PCM is mounted to right inner fender. Connect jumper wire between ground and PCM Gray connector C3 terminal No. 30 (Violet/Brown wire). Using scan tool, select SYSTEM MONITORS. Perform CCD BUS test. If scan tool does not display BUS SHORT TO GROUND, repair open Violet/Brown wire. If scan tool displays BUS SHORT TO GROUND, go to next step.

2) Move jumper wire to PCM Gray connector C3 terminal No. 28 (White/Black wire). Perform CCD BUS test. If scan tool does not display BUS SHORT TO GROUND, repair open White/Black wire. If scan tool displays BUS SHORT TO GROUND, replace PCM.

NOT RECEIVING BUS MESSAGES CORRECTLY

NOTE: For connector terminal identification and wiring diagrams, see BODY CONTROL COMPUTER – INTRODUCTION article. Perform VERIFICATION TEST VER-1 after each repair.

CAUTION: Always turn ignition off prior to disconnecting any module connector.

1) Disconnect anti-lock brake controller module. Controller module is mounted to top of ABS hydraulic unit. Turn ignition on. If scan tool displays BUS OPERATIONAL, replace anti-lock brake controller module. If scan tool does not display BUS OPERATIONAL, go to next step.

2) Disconnect compass mini-trip computer. Turn ignition on. If scan tool displays BUS OPERATIONAL, replace compass mini-trip computer. If scan tool does not display BUS OPERATIONAL, go to next step.

3) Turn ignition off and wait 2 minutes. Disconnect Air Bag Control Module (ACM). ACM is located under front of center console. Turn ignition on. If scan tool displays BUS OPERATIONAL, replace ACM. If scan tool does not display BUS OPERATIONAL, go to next step.

4) Disconnect Central Timer Module (CTM). CTM is located behind right corner of dash, behind glove box. Turn ignition on. If scan tool displays BUS OPERATIONAL, replace CTM. If scan tool does not display BUS OPERATIONAL, replace scan tool cable or scan tool.

BUS SHORT TO 5 VOLTS

NOTE: For connector terminal identification and wiring diagrams, see BODY CONTROL COMPUTER – INTRODUCTION article. Perform VERIFICATION TEST VER-1 after each repair.

CAUTION: Always turn ignition off prior to disconnecting any module connector.

1) Turn ignition off. Disconnect Powertrain Control Module (PCM). PCM is mounted to right inner fender. Turn ignition on. If scan tool does not display BUS SHORT TO 5 VOLTS, go to step 10). If scan tool displays BUS SHORT TO 5 VOLTS, go to next step.

2) Turn ignition off. Disconnect anti-lock brake controller module. Controller module is mounted to top of ABS hydraulic unit. Turn ignition on. If scan tool does not display BUS SHORT TO 5 VOLTS, replace anti-lock brake controller module. If scan tool displays BUS SHORT TO 5 VOLTS, go to next step.

3) Turn ignition off. Disconnect instrument cluster. Turn ignition on. If scan tool does not display BUS SHORT TO 5 VOLTS, replace instrument cluster circuit board. If scan tool displays BUS SHORT TO 5 VOLTS, go to next step.

4) Turn ignition off. Disconnect compass mini-trip computer. Turn ignition on. If scan tool does not display BUS SHORT TO 5 VOLTS, replace compass mini-trip computer. If scan tool displays BUS SHORT TO 5 VOLTS, go to next step.

5) Turn ignition off. Disconnect CCD radio. Turn ignition on. If scan tool does not display BUS SHORT TO 5 VOLTS, replace radio. If scan tool displays BUS SHORT TO 5 VOLTS, go to next step.

6) Turn ignition off and wait 2 minutes. Disconnect Air Bag Control Module (ACM). ACM is located under front of center console. Turn ignition on. If scan tool does not display BUS SHORT TO 5 VOLTS, replace ACM. If scan tool displays BUS SHORT TO 5 VOLTS, go to next step.

7) Turn ignition off. Disconnect Central Timer Module (CTM). CTM is mounted behind right corner of dash, beside glove box. Turn ignition on. If scan tool does not display BUS SHORT TO 5 VOLTS, replace CTM. If scan tool displays BUS SHORT TO 5 VOLTS, go to next step.

8) Disconnect scan tool from DLC. Using external voltmeter, measure voltage between ground and DLC connector terminal No. 3 (Violet/Brown wire). If voltage is more than 4 volts, repair Violet/Brown wire for short to voltage. If voltage is 4 volts or less, go to next step.

9) Measure voltage between ground and DLC connector terminal No. 11 (White/Black wire). If voltage is more than 4 volts, repair White/Black wire for short to voltage. If voltage is less than 4 volts, replace scan tool cable or scan tool as necessary.

10) Turn ignition off. Using external ohmmeter, measure resistance between Powertrain Control Module (PCM) Gray connector C3 terminal No. 30 (Violet/Brown wire) and Black connector C1 terminal No. 17 (Violet/Black wire). PCM is located at right inner fender. If resistance is less than 800 ohms, repair short between Violet/Brown wire and Violet/Black wire. If resistance is 800 ohms or more, go to next step.

11) Measure resistance between PCM Gray connector C3 terminal No. 28 (White/Black wire) and PCM Black connector C1 terminal No. 17 (Violet/Black wire). If resistance is less than 800 ohms, repair short between Violet/Black and White/Black wires of both connectors. See wiring diagram for clarification. If resistance is 800 ohms or more, replace PCM.

BUS SHORT TO BATTERY

NOTE: For connector terminal identification and wiring diagrams, see BODY CONTROL COMPUTER – INTRODUCTION article. Perform VERIFICATION TEST VER-1 after each repair.

CAUTION: Always turn ignition off prior to disconnecting any module connector.

1) Turn ignition off. Disconnect Powertrain Control Module (PCM). PCM is mounted to right inner fender. Turn ignition on. If scan tool does not display BUS SHORT TO BATTERY, go to step 10). If scan tool displays BUS SHORT TO BATTERY, go to next step.

2) Turn ignition off. Disconnect instrument cluster. Turn ignition on. If scan tool does not display BUS SHORT TO BATTERY, replace instrument cluster. If scan tool displays BUS SHORT TO BATTERY, go to next step.

3) Turn ignition off. Disconnect compass mini-trip computer. Turn ignition on. If scan tool does not display BUS SHORT TO BATTERY, replace compass mini-trip computer. If scan tool displays BUS SHORT TO BATTERY, go to next step.

4) Turn ignition off. Disconnect CCD radio. Turn ignition on. If scan tool does not display BUS SHORT TO BATTERY, replace radio. If scan tool displays BUS SHORT TO BATTERY, go to next step.

5) Turn ignition off and wait 2 minutes. Disconnect Air Bag Control Module (ACM). ACM is located under front of center console. Turn ignition on. If scan tool does not display BUS SHORT TO BATTERY, replace ACM. If scan tool displays BUS SHORT TO BATTERY, go to next step.

6) Turn ignition off. Disconnect Central Timer Module (CTM). CTM is located behind right kick panel. Turn ignition on. If scan tool does not display BUS SHORT TO BATTERY, replace CTM. If scan tool displays BUS SHORT TO BATTERY, go to next step.

7) Turn ignition off. Disconnect anti-lock brake controller module. Controller module is mounted to top of ABS hydraulic unit. Turn ignition on. If scan tool does not display BUS SHORT TO BATTERY, replace anti-lock brake controller module. If scan tool displays BUS SHORT TO BATTERY, go to next step.

8) Disconnect scan tool from DLC. Using external voltmeter, measure voltage between ground and DLC connector terminal No. 3 (Violet/Brown wire). If voltage is more than .2 volt, repair Violet/Brown wire for short to voltage. If voltage is .2 volt or less, go to next step.

9) Measure voltage between ground and DLC connector terminal No. 11 (White/Black wire). If voltage is more than .2 volt, repair White/Black wire for short to voltage. If voltage is less than .2 volt, replace scan tool cable or scan tool as necessary.

10) Turn ignition off. Using external ohmmeter, measure resistance between ground and Powertrain Control Module (PCM) Black connector C1 terminal No. 31 (Black wire). PCM is located at right inner fender, at corner of firewall. If resistance is less than 10 ohms, go to next step. If resistance is 10 ohms or more, repair open Black wire.

11) Measure resistance between ground and PCM Black connector C1 terminal No. 32 (Black wire). If resistance is less than 5 ohms, replace PCM. If resistance is 5 ohms or more, repair open Black wire.

BUS SHORT TO GROUND

NOTE: For connector terminal identification and wiring diagrams, see BODY CONTROL COMPUTER – INTRODUCTION article. Perform VERIFICATION TEST VER-1 after each repair.

CAUTION: Always turn ignition off prior to disconnecting any module connector.

1) Turn ignition off. Disconnect Powertrain Control Module (PCM). PCM is mounted to right inner fender. Turn ignition on. If scan tool does not display BUS SHORT TO GROUND, replace PCM. If scan tool displays BUS SHORT TO GROUND, go to next step.

2) Turn ignition off. Disconnect anti-lock brake controller module. Controller module is mounted to top of ABS hydraulic unit. Turn ignition on. If scan tool does not display BUS SHORT TO GROUND, replace anti-lock brake controller module. If scan tool displays BUS SHORT TO GROUND, go to next step.

3) Turn ignition off. Disconnect instrument cluster. Turn ignition on. If scan tool does not display BUS SHORT TO GROUND, replace instrument cluster circuit board. If scan tool displays BUS SHORT TO GROUND, go to next step.

4) Turn ignition off. Disconnect compass mini-trip computer. Turn ignition on. If scan tool does not display BUS SHORT TO GROUND, replace compass mini-trip computer. If scan tool displays BUS SHORT TO GROUND, go to next step.

5) Turn ignition off. Disconnect CCD radio. Turn ignition on. If scan tool does not display BUS SHORT TO GROUND, replace radio. If scan tool displays BUS SHORT TO GROUND, go to next step.

6) Turn ignition off and wait 2 minutes. Disconnect Air Bag Control Module (ACM). ACM is located under front of center console. Turn ignition on. If scan tool does not display BUS SHORT TO GROUND, replace ACM. If scan tool displays BUS SHORT TO GROUND, go to next step.

7) Turn ignition off. Disconnect Central Timer Module (CTM). CTM is located behind right corner of dash, beside glove box. Turn ignition on. If scan tool does not display BUS SHORT TO GROUND, replace CTM. If scan tool displays BUS SHORT TO GROUND, go to next step.

8) Disconnect scan tool from DLC. Using external ohmmeter, measure resistance between ground and DLC connector terminal No. 3 (Violet/Brown wire). If resistance is less than 700 ohms, repair Violet/Brown wire for short to ground. If resistance is 700 ohms or more, go to next step.

9) Measure resistance between ground and DLC connector terminal No. 11 (White/Black wire). If resistance is less than 700 ohms, repair White/Dark Green wire for short to ground. If resistance is 700 ohms or more, replace scan tool cable or scan tool as necessary.

VERIFICATION TEST VER-1A

VERIFICATION PROCEDURE

1) Reconnect all previously disconnected components and connectors. Turn ignition on. If entry module was replaced, program all RKE transmitters, recalibrate HVAC doors and program other options as necessary.

2) Ensure ignition is on. Erase all DTCs using scan tool. Turn ignition off and wait 5 seconds. Turn ignition on and fully operate system that was malfunctioning.

3) If system is not operating properly, go to SYMPTOM IDENTIFICATION in BODY CONTROL COMPUTER TESTS – DAKOTA & DURANGO. If system is operating correctly and customer's complaint cannot be duplicated, repair is complete.

IDENTIFYING VEHICLE COMMUNICATION PROBLEMS

Connect scan tool to Data Link Connector (DLC) to retrieve messages. If scan tool message is blank, disconnect scan tool. Ensure ground circuit has continuity at DLC terminal No. 4. Ensure 12 volts exists at DLC terminal No. 16. Check power to DLC terminal No. 16 from Power Distribution Center (PDC) fuse No. 12. Try another scan tool and/or cable. If scan tool DTC or fault message is present, see following bus fault messages list and proceed to appropriate DTC or fault message:

- BUS (+) & BUS (−) OPEN
- BUS (+) OPEN
- BUS (−) OPEN
- BUS (+) & BUS (−) SHORTED TOGETHER
- BUS BIAS LEVEL TOO HIGH
- BUS BIAS LEVEL TOO LOW
- NO BUS BIAS
- NO RESPONSE AIR BAG CONTROL MODULE
- NO RESPONSE CENTRAL TIMER MODULE
- NO RESPONSE INSTRUMENT CLUSTER
- NO RESPONSE POWERTRAIN CONTROL MODULE
- NO RESPONSE COMPASS/MINI-TRIP SYSTEM
- NO RESPONSE RADIO
- NO TERMINATION
- NOT RECEIVING BUS MESSAGES CORRECTLY
- BUS SHORT TO 5 VOLTS
- BUS SHORT TO BATTERY
- BUS SHORT TO GROUND

BUS (+) & BUS (−) OPEN, (BUS (+) OPEN OR BUS (−) OPEN)

NOTE: For connector terminal identification and wiring diagrams, see BODY CONTROL COMPUTER – INTRODUCTION article. Perform VERIFICATION TEST VER-1 after each repair.

CAUTION: Always turn ignition off prior to disconnecting any module connector.

1) Disconnect scan tool. Ensure ignition is on. Using an external voltmeter, measure voltage between ground and DLC terminal No. 3 (Violet/Brown wire). If voltage is not 1.8-2.3 volts, go to step 3). If voltage is 1.8-2.3 volts, go to next step.
2) Measure voltage between ground and DLC terminal No. 11 (White/Black wire). If voltage is not 1.8-2.3 volts, go to next step. If voltage is 1.8-2.3 volts, replace scan tool cable or scan tool.
3) Connect jumper wire between ground and DLC connector terminal No. 11 (White/Black wire). Turn ignition off. Remove instrument cluster. Using external ohmmeter, measure resistance between ground and instrument cluster connector C1 terminal No. 9 (White/Black wire). If resistance is less than 5 ohms, go to next step. If resistance is 5 ohms or more, repair open White/Black wire.
4) Disconnect jumper wire. Connect jumper wire between ground and DLC connector terminal No. 3 (White/Black wire). Measure resistance between ground and instrument cluster connector C1 terminal No. 10 (Violet/Brown wire). If resistance is less than 5 ohms, replace instrument cluster. If resistance is 5 ohms or more, repair open Violet/Brown wire.

BUS (+) & BUS (−) SHORTED TOGETHER

NOTE: For connector terminal identification and wiring diagrams, see BODY CONTROL COMPUTER – INTRODUCTION article. Perform VERIFICATION TEST VER-1 after each repair.

CAUTION: Always turn ignition off prior to disconnecting any module connector.

1) Turn ignition off. Disconnect Powertrain Control Module (PCM). PCM is mounted in right side of firewall. Turn ignition on. If scan tool does not

display BUS (+) & BUS (−) SHORTED TOGETHER, replace PCM. If scan tool displays BUS (+) & BUS (−) SHORTED TOGETHER, go to next step.
2) Turn ignition off. Disconnect anti-lock brake controller module. Controller is mounted to top of ABS hydraulic unit. Turn ignition on. If scan tool does not display BUS (+) & BUS (−) SHORTED TOGETHER, replace anti-lock brake controller module. If scan tool displays BUS (+) & BUS (−) SHORTED TOGETHER, go to next step.
3) Turn ignition off. Disconnect instrument cluster. Turn ignition on. If scan tool does not display BUS (+) & BUS (−) SHORTED TOGETHER, replace instrument cluster circuit board. If scan tool displays BUS (+) & BUS (−) SHORTED TOGETHER, go to next step.
4) Turn ignition off. Disconnect compass mini-trip computer. Turn ignition on. If scan tool does not display BUS (+) & BUS (−) SHORTED TOGETHER, replace compass mini-trip computer. If scan tool displays BUS (+) & BUS (−) SHORTED TOGETHER, go to next step.
5) Turn ignition off. Disconnect radio connector. Turn ignition on. If scan tool does not display BUS (+) & BUS (−) SHORTED TOGETHER, replace radio. If scan tool displays BUS (+) & BUS (−) SHORTED TOGETHER, go to next step.
6) Turn ignition off and wait 2 minutes. Disconnect Air Bag Control Module (ACM). ACM is located under center of instrument panel. Turn ignition on. If scan tool does not display BUS (+) & BUS (−) SHORTED TOGETHER, replace ACM. If scan tool displays BUS (+) & BUS (−) SHORTED TOGETHER, go to next step.
7) Turn ignition off. Disconnect Central Timer Module (CTM). CTM is located under left side of instrument panel. Turn ignition on. If scan tool does not display BUS (+) & BUS (−) SHORTED TOGETHER, replace CTM. If scan tool displays BUS (+) & BUS (−) SHORTED TOGETHER, go to next step.
8) Disconnect scan tool from DLC. Using external ohmmeter, measure resistance between terminals No. 3 (Violet/Brown wire) and No. 11 (White/Black wire) on DLC connector. If resistance is less than 5 ohms, repair short between Violet/Brown wire and White/Dark Green wire. If resistance is 5 ohms or more, replace scan tool cable or scan tool as necessary.

BUS BIAS LEVEL TOO LOW (BUS BIAS LEVEL TOO HIGH)

NOTE: For connector terminal identification and wiring diagrams, see BODY CONTROL COMPUTER – INTRODUCTION article. Perform VERIFICATION TEST VER-1 after each repair.

CAUTION: Always turn ignition off prior to disconnecting any module connector.

1) Disconnect scan tool. Using an external voltmeter, measure voltage between ground and DLC connector terminal No. 3 (Violet/Brown wire). If voltage is not 1.8-2.8 volts, go to step 9). If voltage is 1.8-2.8 volts, go to next step.
2) Measure voltage between ground and DLC connector terminal No. 11 (White/Black wire). If voltage is not 1.8-2.8 volts, go to next step. If voltage is 1.8-2.8 volts, replace scan tool cable or scan tool.
3) Turn ignition off. Disconnect instrument cluster. Ensure interior lights are off. Using external ohmmeter, measure resistance between ground and instrument cluster connector C1 terminal No. 10 (Violet/Brown wire). If resistance is less than 1000 ohms, repair Violet/Brown wire for short to ground. If resistance is 1000 ohms or more, go to next step.
4) Measure resistance between ground and instrument cluster connector C1 terminal No. 9 (White/Black wire). If resistance is less than 1000 ohms, repair White/Black wire for short to ground. If resistance is 1000 ohms or more, go to next step.
5) Connect jumper wire between ground and DLC connector terminal No. 3 (White/Black wire). Measure resistance between ground and instrument cluster connector C1 terminal No. 10 (Violet/Brown wire). If resistance is less than 5 ohms, go to next step. If resistance is 5 ohms or more, repair open Violet/Brown wire.
6) Disconnect jumper wire. Connect jumper wire between ground and DLC connector terminal No. 11 (White/Black wire). Measure resistance

between ground and instrument cluster connector C1 terminal No. 9 (White/Black wire). If resistance is less than 5 ohms, go to next step. If resistance is 5 ohms or more, repair open White/Black wire.

7) Disconnect jumper wire. Measure resistance between ground and instrument cluster connector C1 terminal No. 4 (Black/Light Green wire). If resistance is 5 ohms or less, repair open Black/Light Green wire. If resistance is more than 5 ohms, go to next step.

8) Measure resistance between ground and instrument cluster connector C1 terminal No. 5 (Black wire). If resistance is 5 ohms or less, repair open Black wire. If resistance is more than 5 ohms, replace instrument cluster.

9) Turn ignition off. Disconnect instrument cluster. Ensure interior lights are off. Measure resistance between ground and instrument cluster connector C1 terminal No. 4 (Black/Light Green wire). If resistance is 5 ohms or less, repair open Black/Light Green wire. If resistance is more than 5 ohms, go to next step.

10) Measure resistance between ground and instrument cluster connector C1 terminal No. 5 (Black wire). If resistance is 5 ohms or less, repair open Black wire. If resistance is more than 5 ohms, replace instrument cluster.

11) Connect jumper wire between ground and DLC connector terminal No. 11 (White/Black wire). Measure resistance between ground and instrument cluster connector C1 terminal No. 9 (White/Black wire). If resistance is less than 5 ohms, go to next step. If resistance is 5 ohms or more, repair open White/Black wire.

12) Disconnect jumper wire. Measure resistance between ground and instrument cluster connector C1 terminal No. 9 (White/Black wire). If resistance is less than 1000 ohms, repair White/Black wire for short to ground. If resistance is 1000 ohms or more, go to next step.

13) Connect jumper wire between ground and DLC connector terminal No. 3 (White/Black wire). Measure resistance between ground and instrument cluster connector C1 terminal No. 10 (Violet/Brown wire). If resistance is less than 5 ohms, go to next step. If resistance is 5 ohms or more, repair open Violet/Brown wire.

14) Using external ohmmeter, measure resistance between ground and instrument cluster connector C1 terminal No. 10 (Violet/Brown wire). If resistance is less than 1000 ohms, repair Violet/Brown wire for short to ground. If resistance is 1000 ohms or more, replace instrument cluster.

NO BUS BIAS

NOTE: For connector terminal identification and wiring diagrams, see BODY CONTROL COMPUTER – INTRODUCTION article. Perform VERIFICATION TEST VER-1 after each repair.

CAUTION: Always turn ignition off prior to disconnecting any module connector.

1) Disconnect scan tool. Turn ignition on. Using an external voltmeter, measure voltage between ground and DLC terminal No. 3 (Violet/Brown wire). If voltage is not 1.8-2.3 volts, go to step 3). If voltage is 1.8-2.3 volts, go to next step.

2) Measure voltage between ground and DLC terminal No. 11 (White/Black wire). If voltage is not 1.8-2.3 volts, go to next step. If voltage is 1.8-2.3 volts, replace scan tool cable or scan tool.

3) Connect jumper wire between ground and DLC connector terminal No. 11 (White/Black wire). Turn ignition off. Remove instrument cluster. Using external ohmmeter, measure resistance between ground and instrument cluster connector C1 terminal No. 9 (White/Black wire). If resistance is less than 5 ohms, go to next step. If resistance is 5 ohms or more, repair open White/Black wire.

4) Disconnect jumper wire. Measure resistance between ground and instrument cluster connector C1 terminal No. 9 (White/Black wire). If resistance is less than 1000 ohms, repair White/Black wire for short to ground. If resistance is 1000 ohms or more, go to next step.

5) Connect jumper wire between ground and DLC connector terminal No. 3 (White/Black wire). Measure resistance between ground and instrument cluster connector C1 terminal No. 10 (Violet/Brown wire). If resistance is less than 5 ohms, go to next step. If resistance is 5 ohms or more, repair open Violet/Brown wire.

6) Disconnect jumper wire. Measure resistance between ground and instrument cluster connector C1 terminal No. 10 (Violet/Brown wire). If resistance is less than 1000 ohms, repair Violet/Brown wire for short to ground. If resistance is 1000 ohms or more, go to next step.

7) Turn ignition on. Using external voltmeter, measure voltage between ground and instrument cluster connector C1 terminal No. 2 (Dark Blue/White wire). If voltage is 9.5 volts or less, repair open Dark Blue/White wire. If voltage is more than 9.5 volts, go to next step.

8) Turn ignition off. Using external ohmmeter, measure resistance between ground and instrument cluster connector C1 terminal No. 4 (Black/Light Green wire). If resistance is 5 ohms or less, go to next step. If resistance is more than 5 ohms, repair open Black/Light Green wire.

9) Measure resistance between ground and instrument cluster connector C1 terminal No. 5 (Black/Orange wire). If resistance is 5 ohms or less, replace instrument cluster. If resistance is more than 5 ohms, repair open Black/Orange wire.

NO RESPONSE AIR BAG CONTROL MODULE

NOTE: For connector terminal identification and wiring diagrams, see BODY CONTROL COMPUTER – INTRODUCTION article. Perform VERIFICATION TEST VER-1 after each repair.

CAUTION: Always turn ignition off prior to disconnecting any module connector.

1) Remove and inspect fuse No. 19 from junction block. Junction block is on left side of instrument panel. If fuse is open, go to next step. If fuse is okay, go to step 6).

2) Using external voltmeter, measure voltage between ground and voltage input side of fuse No. 19 socket. If voltage is 10 volts or less, repair open ignition switch output circuit (Dark Blue wire between ignition switch and junction block). If voltage is more than 10 volts, go to next step.

3) Turn ignition off and wait 2 minutes. Using external ohmmeter, measure resistance between ground and fused ignition switch output run/start terminal (Light Green/Yellow wire) on fuse No. 19 socket. If resistance is less than 5 ohms, go to next step. If resistance is 5 ohms or more, go to step 5).

4) Disconnect Air Bag Control Module (ACM) connector. ACM is located under center of instrument panel. Turn ignition on. Measure resistance between ground and fused ignition switch output run/start terminal (Light Green/Yellow wire) on fuse No. 19 socket. If resistance is less than 5 ohms, repair Light Green/Yellow wire for short to ground. Replace fuse No. 19. If resistance is 5 ohms or more, replace air bag control module and fuse No. 19.

5) Turn ignition off and wait 2 minutes. Disconnect Air Bag Control Module (ACM) connector. ACM is located under center of instrument panel. Using external ohmmeter, measure resistance of Light Green/Yellow wire between ACM connector terminal No. 14 and fused ignition switch output run/start terminal on fuse No. 19 socket. If resistance is less than 5 ohms, connect ACM connector. Turn ignition on. Replace fuse No. 19 in junction block. Go to appropriate MITCHELL® AIR BAG SERVICE & REPAIR, DOMESTIC CARS, LIGHT TRUCKS & VANS for further testing. If resistance is 5 ohms or more, repair open Light Green/Yellow wire. Replace fuse No. 19.

6) Using external voltmeter, measure voltage between ground and voltage input side of fuse No. 19 socket. If voltage is 10 volts or less, repair open ignition switch output circuit (Dark Blue wire between ignition switch and junction block). If voltage is more than 10 volts, go to next step.

7) Turn ignition off and wait 2 minutes. Install fuse No. 19. Disconnect Air Bag Control Module (ACM) connector. ACM is located under center of instrument panel. Turn ignition on. Using external voltmeter, measure voltage between ground and ACM connector terminal No. 14 (Light Green/Yellow wire). If voltage is 10 volts or less, repair open Light Green/Yellow wire. If voltage is more than 10 volts, go to next step.

8) Turn ignition off. Using external ohmmeter, measure resistance between ground and ACM connector terminal No. 4 (Black/Pink). If resistance is 5 ohms or more, repair open Black/Pink wire. If resistance is less than 5 ohms, go to next step.

9) Turn ignition on. Using external voltmeter, measure voltage between ground and ACM connector terminal No. 21 (Violet/Brown wire). If voltage is not 1.8-2.6 volts, repair open Violet/Brown wire. If voltage is 1.8-2.6 volts, go to next step.

10) Turn ignition off. Using external ohmmeter, measure resistance between ground and ACM connector terminal No. 4 (Black/Pink wire). If resistance is 5 ohms or more, repair open Black/Pink wire. If resistance is less than 5 ohms, go to next step.

11) Using external voltmeter, measure voltage between ground and ACM connector terminal No. 22 (White/Black wire). If voltage is not 1.8-2.6 volts, repair open White/Black wire. If voltage is 1.8-2.6 volts, replace ACM.

NO RESPONSE CENTRAL TIMER MODULE

NOTE: *For connector terminal identification and wiring diagrams, see BODY CONTROL COMPUTER – INTRODUCTION article. Perform VERIFICATION TEST VER-1 after each repair.*

CAUTION: *Always turn ignition off prior to disconnecting any module connector.*

1) Remove and inspect fuse No. 11 from junction block. Junction block is on left side of instrument panel. If fuse is open, go to next step. If fuse is okay, go to step 3).

2) Using external ohmmeter, measure resistance between ground and fused ignition switch output run/start terminal (Dark Blue/White wire) on fuse No. 11 socket. If resistance is less than 5 ohms, repair short to ground in Dark Blue/White wire. Replace fuse No. 11. If resistance is 5 ohms or more, replace fuse No. 11.

3) Install fuse No. 11. Remove and inspect fuse No. 6 from junction block. If fuse is open, next step. If fuse is okay, go to step 5).

4) Using external ohmmeter, measure resistance between ground and fused ignition switch output run/accy terminal (Dark Blue wire) on fuse No. 6 socket. If resistance is less than 5 ohms, repair short to ground in Dark Blue wire. Replace fuse No. 6. If resistance is 5 ohms or more, replace fuse No. 6.

5) Install fuse No. 6. Disconnect Central Timer Module (CTM). CTM is located under left side of instrument panel. Using external ohmmeter, measure resistance between ground and CTM 18-pin connector terminal No. 3 (Black/Orange wire). If resistance is more than 5 ohms, repair open Black/Orange wire. If resistance is 5 ohms or less, go to next step.

6) Measure resistance between ground and CTM 14-pin connector terminal No. 6 (Black/Light Green wire). If resistance is more than 5 ohms, repair open Black/Light Green wire. If resistance is 5 ohms or less, go to next step.

7) Turn ignition on. Using scan tool, perform CCD Bus test. Connect jumper wire between ground and CTM 18-pin connector terminal No. 16 (Violet/Brown wire). If scan tool does not display BUS SHORT TO GROUND, repair open Violet/Brown wire. If scan tool displays BUS SHORT TO GROUND, go to next step.

8) Disconnect jumper wire. Connect jumper wire between ground and CTM 18-pin connector terminal No. 17 (White/Black wire). If scan tool does not display BUS SHORT TO GROUND, repair open White/Black wire. If scan tool displays BUS SHORT TO GROUND, replace CTM.

NO RESPONSE INSTRUMENT CLUSTER

NOTE: *For connector terminal identification and wiring diagrams, see BODY CONTROL COMPUTER – INTRODUCTION article. Perform VERIFICATION TEST VER-1A after each repair.*

CAUTION: *Always turn ignition off prior to disconnecting any module connector.*

1) Turn ignition on. Using scan tool, select BODY CONTROL MODULE. If scan tool displays NO RESPONSE, go to NO RESPONSE CENTRAL TIMER MODULE. If scan tool does not display NO RESPONSE, go to next step.

2) Using scan tool, select SYSTEM TEST. If scan tool displays PCM ACTIVE ON THE BUS, go to next step. If scan tool does not display PCM ACTIVE ON THE BUS, go to NO RESPONSE POWERTRAIN CONTROL MODULE.

3) Turn ignition off. Remove instrument cluster. Turn ignition on. Using scan tool, turn on CCD bus bias under SYSTEM MONITORS, then CCD BUS VOLTAGE. Connect jumper wire between ground and instrument cluster connector C1 terminal No. 10 (Violet/Brown wire). If scan tool voltage did not drop to about zero volts, repair open Violet/Brown wire. If scan tool voltage dropped to about zero volts, go to next step.

4) Move jumper to instrument cluster connector C1 terminal No. 9 (White/Black wire). Monitor CCD BUS VOLTAGE. If scan tool voltage did not drop to about zero volts, repair open White/Black wire. If scan tool voltage did not drop to about zero volts, replace instrument cluster.

NO RESPONSE POWERTRAIN CONTROL MODULE

NOTE: *For connector terminal identification and wiring diagrams, see BODY CONTROL COMPUTER – INTRODUCTION article. Perform VERIFICATION TEST VER-1 after each repair.*

CAUTION: *Always turn ignition off prior to disconnecting any module connector.*

1) If engine does not run, see appropriate BASIC DIAGNOSTIC PROCEDURES article in ENGINE PERFORMANCE in appropriate MITCHELL® manual. If engine runs, go to next step.

2) Turn ignition off. Disconnect Powertrain Control Module (PCM). PCM is mounted in right side of firewall. Turn ignition on. Connect jumper wire between ground and PCM connector C3 terminal. No. 30 (Violet/Brown wire). Using scan tool, perform CCD BUS test. If scan tool does not display SHORT TO GROUND, repair open Violet/Brown wire. If scan tool displays SHORT TO GROUND, go to next step.

3) Move jumper wire to PCM connector C3 terminal No. 28 (White/Black wire). Perform CCD BUS test. If scan tool does not display SHORT TO GROUND, repair open White/Black wire. If scan tool displays SHORT TO GROUND, replace PCM.

NO RESPONSE COMPASS/MINI-TRIP SYSTEM

NOTE: *For connector terminal identification and wiring diagrams, see BODY CONTROL COMPUTER – INTRODUCTION article. Perform VERIFICATION TEST VER-1 after each repair.*

CAUTION: *Always turn ignition off prior to disconnecting any module connector.*

1) Remove and inspect fuse No. 11 from junction block. Junction block is on left side of instrument panel. If fuse is open, go to next step. If fuse is okay, go to step 3).

2) Using external ohmmeter, measure resistance between ground and fused ignition switch output run/start terminal (Dark Blue/White wire) on fuse No. 11 socket. If resistance is less than 5 ohms, repair Dark Blue/White wire for short to ground. Replace fuse No. 11. If resistance is 5 ohms or more, replace fuse No. 11.

3) Reinstall fuse. Disconnect CMTC 12-pin connector. Turn ignition on. Using external voltmeter, measure voltage between ground and CMTC connector terminal No. 1 (Dark Blue/White wire). If voltage is less than 9.5 volts, repair open Dark Blue/White wire. If voltage is 9.5 volts or more, go to next step.

4) Using external voltmeter, measure voltage between ground and CMTC connector terminal No. 5 (Pink wire). If voltage is less than 9.5 volts, repair open Pink wire. If voltage is 9.5 volts or more, go to next step.

5) Turn ignition off. Using external ohmmeter, measure resistance between ground and CMTC connector terminal No. 7 (Black/Light Green wire). If resistance is 5 ohms or less, go to next step. If resistance is more than 5 ohms, repair open Black/Light Green wire.

6) Using scan tool, perform CCD bus test. Connect jumper wire between ground and CMTC connector terminal No. 2 (Violet/Brown wire). If scan

tool displays BUS (+) SHORTED TO GROUND, go to next step. If scan tool does not display BUS (+) SHORTED TO GROUND, repair open Violet/Brown wire.

7) Move jumper wire to CMTC connector terminal No. 8 (White/Black wire). If scan tool displays BUS (+) SHORTED TO GROUND, replace CMTC. If scan tool does not display BUS (+) SHORTED TO GROUND, repair open White/Black wire.

NO RESPONSE RADIO

NOTE: For connector terminal identification and wiring diagrams, see BODY CONTROL COMPUTER – INTRODUCTION article. Perform VERIFICATION TEST VER-1A after each repair.

CAUTION: Always turn ignition off prior to disconnecting any module connector.

1) If radio screen is not blank, go to step **7)**. If radio screen is blank, go to next step.

2) Remove and inspect junction block fuse No. 8 (radio). If fuse is blown, go to next step. If fuse is okay, go to step **4)**.

3) Turn ignition off. Disconnect radio Gray connector. Using external ohmmeter, measure resistance between ground and radio Gray connector terminal No. 6 (Red/White wire). If resistance is less than 5 ohms, repair Red/White wire for short to ground. Replace junction block fuse No. 8. If resistance is 5 ohms or more, replace radio. Replace junction block fuse No. 8.

4) Turn ignition on. Measure voltage between ground and terminal No. 7 (Pink wire). If voltage is 10 volts or less, repair open Pink wire. If voltage is more than 10 volts, go to next step.

5) Install fuse. Disconnect radio Gray connector. Using external voltmeter, measure voltage between ground and radio Gray terminal No. 6 (Red/White wire). If voltage is 10 volts or less, repair open Red/White wire. If voltage is more than 10 volts, go to next step.

6) Inspect ground strap and antenna for correct installation. Repair as needed. If ground strap and antenna are okay, replace radio.

7) Disconnect 2-pin CCD BUS connector on back of radio. Connect jumper wire between terminal No. 2 (White/Black wire) and ground. Using scan tool, select BODY, BODY COMPUTER, then SYSTEM TEST. Perform CCD BUS test. If scan tool does not display BUS SHORT TO GROUND, repair open White/Black wire. If scan tool displays BUS SHORT TO GROUND, go to next step.

8) Move jumper wire to terminal No. 1 (Violet/Brown wire). Perform CCD BUS test. If scan tool does not display BUS SHORT TO GROUND, repair open Violet/Brown wire. If scan tool displays BUS SHORT TO GROUND, replace radio.

NO TERMINATION

NOTE: For connector terminal identification and wiring diagrams, see BODY CONTROL COMPUTER – INTRODUCTION article. Perform VERIFICATION TEST VER-1 after each repair.

CAUTION: Always turn ignition off prior to disconnecting any module connector.

1) Disconnect Powertrain Control Module (PCM) connectors. PCM is mounted in right side of firewall. Connect jumper wire between ground and PCM connector C3 terminal No. 30 (Violet/Brown wire). Using scan tool, select SYSTEM MONITORS. Perform CCD BUS test. If scan tool does not display BUS SHORT TO GROUND, repair open Violet/Brown wire. If scan tool displays BUS SHORT TO GROUND, go to next step.

2) Move jumper wire to PCM connector C3 terminal No. 28 (White/Black wire). Perform CCD BUS test. If scan tool does not display BUS SHORT TO GROUND, repair open White/Black wire. If scan tool displays BUS SHORT TO GROUND, replace PCM.

NOT RECEIVING BUS MESSAGES CORRECTLY

NOTE: For connector terminal identification and wiring diagrams, see BODY CONTROL COMPUTER – INTRODUCTION article. Perform VERIFICATION TEST VER-1 after each repair.

CAUTION: Always turn ignition off prior to disconnecting any module connector.

1) Disconnect anti-lock brake controller module. Controller module is mounted to top of ABS hydraulic unit. Turn ignition on. If scan tool displays BUS OPERATIONAL, replace anti-lock brake controller module. If scan tool does not display BUS OPERATIONAL, go to next step.

2) Turn ignition off and wait 2 minutes. Disconnect Air Bag Control Module (ACM). ACM is located under center of instrument panel. Turn ignition on. If scan tool displays BUS OPERATIONAL, replace ACM. If scan tool does not display BUS OPERATIONAL, go to next step.

3) Disconnect Central Timer Module (CTM). CTM is located under left side of instrument panel. Turn ignition on. If scan tool displays BUS OPERATIONAL, replace CTM. If scan tool does not display BUS OPERATIONAL, replace scan tool cable or scan tool.

BUS SHORT TO 5 VOLTS

NOTE: For connector terminal identification and wiring diagrams, see BODY CONTROL COMPUTER – INTRODUCTION article. Perform VERIFICATION TEST VER-1 after each repair.

CAUTION: Always turn ignition off prior to disconnecting any module connector.

1) Turn ignition off. Disconnect Powertrain Control Module (PCM). PCM is mounted in right side of firewall. Turn ignition on. If scan tool does not display BUS SHORT TO 5 VOLTS, go to step **10)**. If scan tool displays BUS SHORT TO 5 VOLTS, go to next step.

2) Turn ignition off. Disconnect anti-lock brake controller module. Controller module is mounted to top of ABS hydraulic unit. Turn ignition on. If scan tool does not display BUS SHORT TO 5 VOLTS, replace anti-lock brake controller module. If scan tool displays BUS SHORT TO 5 VOLTS, go to next step.

3) Turn ignition off. Disconnect instrument cluster. Turn ignition on. If scan tool does not display BUS SHORT TO 5 VOLTS, replace instrument cluster circuit board. If scan tool displays BUS SHORT TO 5 VOLTS, go to next step.

4) Turn ignition off. Disconnect compass mini-trip computer. Turn ignition on. If scan tool does not display BUS SHORT TO 5 VOLTS, replace compass mini-trip computer. If scan tool displays BUS SHORT TO 5 VOLTS, go to next step.

5) Turn ignition off. Disconnect CCD radio. Turn ignition on. If scan tool does not display BUS SHORT TO 5 VOLTS, replace radio. If scan tool displays BUS SHORT TO 5 VOLTS, go to next step.

6) Turn ignition off and wait 2 minutes. Disconnect Air Bag Control Module (ACM). ACM is located under center of instrument panel. Turn ignition on. If scan tool does not display BUS SHORT TO 5 VOLTS, replace ACM. If scan tool displays BUS SHORT TO 5 VOLTS, go to next step.

7) Turn ignition off. Disconnect Central Timer Module (CTM). CTM is mounted behind right corner of dash, beside glove box. Turn ignition on. If scan tool does not display BUS SHORT TO 5 VOLTS, replace CTM. If scan tool displays BUS SHORT TO 5 VOLTS, go to next step.

8) Disconnect scan tool from DLC. Using external voltmeter, measure voltage between ground and DLC connector terminal No. 3 (Violet/Brown wire). If voltage is more than 4 volts, repair Violet/Brown wire for short to voltage. If voltage is 4 volts or less, go to next step.

9) Measure voltage between ground and DLC connector terminal No. 11 (White/Black wire). If voltage is more than 4 volts, repair White/Black wire for short to voltage. If voltage is less than 4 volts, replace scan tool cable or scan tool as necessary.

10) Turn ignition off. Using external ohmmeter, measure resistance between Powertrain Control Module (PCM) connector C3 terminal No.

30 (Violet/Brown wire) and connector C1 terminal No. 17 (Violet/Black wire). PCM is located at right inner fender. If resistance is less than 800 ohms, repair short between Violet/Brown wire and Violet/Black wire. If resistance is 800 ohms or more, go to next step.

11) Measure resistance between PCM connector C3 terminal No. 28 (White/Black wire) and PCM connector C1 terminal No. 17 (Violet/Black wire). If resistance is less than 800 ohms, repair short between Violet/Black and White/Black wires of both connectors. See wiring diagram for clarification. If resistance is 800 ohms or more, replace PCM.

BUS SHORT TO BATTERY

NOTE: *For connector terminal identification and wiring diagrams, see BODY CONTROL COMPUTER – INTRODUCTION article. Perform VERIFICATION TEST VER-1 after each repair.*

CAUTION: *Always turn ignition off prior to disconnecting any module connector.*

1) Turn ignition off. Disconnect Powertrain Control Module (PCM). PCM is mounted in right side of firewall. Turn ignition on. If scan tool does not display BUS SHORT TO BATTERY, go to step 10). If scan tool displays BUS SHORT TO BATTERY, go to next step.

2) Turn ignition off. Disconnect instrument cluster. Turn ignition on. If scan tool does not display BUS SHORT TO BATTERY, replace instrument cluster. If scan tool displays BUS SHORT TO BATTERY, go to next step.

3) Turn ignition off. Disconnect compass mini-trip computer. Turn ignition on. If scan tool does not display BUS SHORT TO BATTERY, replace compass mini-trip computer. If scan tool displays BUS SHORT TO BATTERY, go to next step.

4) Turn ignition off. Disconnect CCD radio. Turn ignition on. If scan tool does not display BUS SHORT TO BATTERY, replace radio. If scan tool displays BUS SHORT TO BATTERY, go to next step.

5) Turn ignition off and wait 2 minutes. Disconnect Air Bag Control Module (ACM). ACM is located under center of instrument panel. Turn ignition on. If scan tool does not display BUS SHORT TO BATTERY, replace ACM. If scan tool displays BUS SHORT TO BATTERY, go to next step.

6) Turn ignition off. Disconnect Central Timer Module (CTM). CTM is located under left side of instrument panel. Turn ignition on. If scan tool does not display BUS SHORT TO BATTERY, replace CTM. If scan tool displays BUS SHORT TO BATTERY, go to next step.

7) Turn ignition off. Disconnect anti-lock brake controller module. Controller module is mounted to top of ABS hydraulic unit. Turn ignition on. If scan tool does not display BUS SHORT TO BATTERY, replace anti-lock brake controller module. If scan tool displays BUS SHORT TO BATTERY, go to next step.

8) Disconnect scan tool from DLC. Using external voltmeter, measure voltage between ground and DLC connector terminal No. 3 (Violet/Brown wire). If voltage is more than .2 volt, repair Violet/Brown wire for short to voltage. If voltage is .2 volt or less, go to next step.

9) Measure voltage between ground and DLC connector terminal No. 11 (White/Black wire). If voltage is more than .2 volt, repair White/Black wire for short to voltage. If voltage is less than .2 volt, replace scan tool cable or scan tool as necessary.

10) Turn ignition off. Using external ohmmeter, measure resistance between ground and Powertrain Control Module (PCM) connector C1 terminal No. 31 (Black/Tan wire). PCM is located at right inner fender, at corner of firewall. If resistance is less than 10 ohms, go to next step. If resistance is 10 ohms or more, repair open Black/Tan wire.

11) Measure resistance between ground and PCM connector C1 terminal No. 32 (Black/Tan wire). If resistance is less than 10 ohms, replace PCM. If resistance is 5 ohms or more, repair open Black/Tan wire.

BUS SHORT TO GROUND

NOTE: *For connector terminal identification and wiring diagrams, see BODY CONTROL COMPUTER – INTRODUCTION article. Perform VERIFICATION TEST VER-1 after each repair.*

CAUTION: *Always turn ignition off prior to disconnecting any module connector.*

1) Turn ignition off. Disconnect Powertrain Control Module (PCM). PCM is mounted in right side of firewall. Turn ignition on. If scan tool does not display BUS SHORT TO GROUND, replace PCM. If scan tool displays BUS SHORT TO GROUND, go to next step.

2) Turn ignition off. Disconnect anti-lock brake controller module. Controller module is mounted to top of ABS hydraulic unit. Turn ignition on. If scan tool does not display BUS SHORT TO GROUND, replace anti-lock brake controller module. If scan tool displays BUS SHORT TO GROUND, go to next step.

3) Turn ignition off. Disconnect instrument cluster. Turn ignition on. If scan tool does not display BUS SHORT TO GROUND, replace instrument cluster circuit board. If scan tool displays BUS SHORT TO GROUND, go to next step.

4) Turn ignition off. Disconnect compass mini-trip computer. Turn ignition on. If scan tool does not display BUS SHORT TO GROUND, replace compass mini-trip computer. If scan tool displays BUS SHORT TO GROUND, go to next step.

5) Turn ignition off. Disconnect CCD radio. Turn ignition on. If scan tool does not display BUS SHORT TO GROUND, replace radio. If scan tool displays BUS SHORT TO GROUND, go to next step.

6) Turn ignition off and wait 2 minutes. Disconnect Air Bag Control Module (ACM). ACM is located under center of instrument panel. Turn ignition on. If scan tool does not display BUS SHORT TO GROUND, replace ACM. If scan tool displays BUS SHORT TO GROUND, go to next step.

7) Turn ignition off. Disconnect Central Timer Module (CTM). CTM is located under left side of instrument panel. Turn ignition on. If scan tool does not display BUS SHORT TO GROUND, replace CTM. If scan tool displays BUS SHORT TO GROUND, go to next step.

8) Disconnect scan tool from DLC. Using external ohmmeter, measure resistance between ground and DLC connector terminal No. 3 (Violet/Brown wire). If resistance is less than 700 ohms, repair Violet/Brown wire for short to ground. If resistance is 700 ohms or more, go to next step.

9) Measure resistance between ground and DLC connector terminal No. 11 (White/Black wire). If resistance is less than 700 ohms, repair White/Dark Green wire for short to ground. If resistance is 700 ohms or more, replace scan tool cable or scan tool as necessary.

VERIFICATION TEST VER-1

1) Reconnect all previously disconnect connectors. Turn ignition on, engine off. Using scan tool, erase all fault messages. Turn ignition off. Wait 10 seconds. Turn ignition on, engine off. Operate system that is malfunctioning. If system does not operate properly, perform SYMPTOM IDENTIFICATION of BODY CONTROL COMPUTER TESTS – RAM PICKUP article. If system operates properly, go to next step.

2) Using scan tool, read fault messages. If fault messages exist, perform SYMPTOM IDENTIFICATION of BODY CONTROL COMPUTER TESTS – RAM PICKUP article. If fault messages do not exist, repair is complete.

IDENTIFYING VEHICLE COMMUNICATION PROBLEMS

Connect scan tool to Data Link Connector (DLC) to retrieve messages. If scan tool message is blank, disconnect scan tool. Ensure ground circuit has continuity at DLC terminal No. 4. Ensure 12 volts exists at DLC terminal No. 16. Check power to DLC terminal No. 16 from junction block fuse No. 14. Try another scan tool and/or cable. If scan tool DTC or fault message is present, see following bus fault messages list and proceed to appropriate DTC or fault message:

- BUS (+) & BUS (–) OPEN
- BUS (+) OPEN
- BUS (–) OPEN
- BUS BIAS LEVEL TOO HIGH
- BUS BIAS LEVEL TOO LOW
- BUS (+) & BUS (–) SHORTED TOGETHER
- NO TERMINATION
- BUS SHORT TO 5 VOLTS
- BUS SHORT TO BATTERY
- BUS SHORT TO GROUND
- NO BUS BIAS
- NO RESPONSE FROM AIR BAG CONTROL MODULE
- NO RESPONSE FROM CENTRAL TIMER MODULE
- NO RESPONSE FROM INSTRUMENT CLUSTER
- NO RESPONSE FROM POWERTRAIN CONTROL MODULE
- NOT RECEIVING BUS MESSAGES CORRECTLY

BUS (+) & BUS (–) OPEN; (BUS (+) OPEN OR BUS (–) OPEN)

NOTE: For connector terminal identification and wiring diagrams, see BODY CONTROL COMPUTER – INTRODUCTION article. Perform VERIFICATION TEST VER-1 after each repair.

CAUTION: Always turn ignition off prior to disconnecting any module connector.

1) Disconnect scan tool. Ensure ignition is on. Using an external voltmeter, measure voltage between ground and DLC terminal No. 3 (Violet/Brown wire). If voltage is not 1.8-2.3 volts, go to step 3). If voltage is 1.8-2.3 volts, go to next step.
2) Measure voltage between ground and DLC terminal No. 11 (White/Black wire). If voltage is not 1.8-2.3 volts, go to next step. If voltage is 1.8-2.3 volts, replace scan tool cable or scan tool.
3) Connect jumper wire between ground and DLC connector terminal No. 11 (White/Black wire). Turn ignition off. Remove instrument cluster. Using external ohmmeter, measure resistance between ground and instrument cluster Black connector C1 terminal No. 9 (White/Black wire). If resistance is less than 5 ohms, go to next step. If resistance is 5 ohms or more, repair open White/Black wire.
4) Disconnect jumper wire. Connect jumper wire between ground and DLC connector terminal No. 3 (White/Black wire). Measure resistance between ground and instrument cluster Black connector C1 terminal No. 10 (Violet/Brown wire). If resistance is less than 5 ohms, replace instrument cluster. If resistance is 5 ohms or more, repair open Violet/Brown wire.

BUS BIAS LEVEL TOO HIGH (BUS BIAS LEVEL TOO LOW)

NOTE: For connector terminal identification and wiring diagrams, see BODY CONTROL COMPUTER – INTRODUCTION article. Perform VERIFICATION TEST VER-1 after each repair.

CAUTION: Always turn ignition off prior to disconnecting any module connector.

1) Disconnect scan tool. Using an external voltmeter, measure voltage between ground and Data Link Connector (DLC) connector terminal No.

3 (Violet/Brown wire). If voltage is not 1.8-2.8 volts, go to step 3). If voltage is 1.8-2.8 volts, go to next step.
2) Measure voltage between ground and DLC connector terminal No. 11 (White/Black wire). If voltage is not 1.8-2.8 volts, go to next step. If voltage is 1.8-2.8 volts, replace scan tool cable or scan tool.
3) Turn ignition off. Disconnect instrument cluster. Ensure interior lights are off. Using external ohmmeter, measure resistance between ground and instrument cluster Black connector C1 terminal No. 4 (Black/Dark Green wire). If resistance is 5 ohms or less, repair open Black/Dark Green wire. If resistance is more than 5 ohms, go to next step.
4) Connect jumper wire between ground and DLC connector terminal No. 11 (White/Black wire). Measure resistance between ground and instrument cluster Black connector C1 terminal No. 9 (White/Black wire). If resistance is less than 5 ohms, go to next step. If resistance is 5 ohms or more, repair open White/Black wire.
5) Disconnect jumper wire. Measure resistance between ground and instrument cluster Black connector C1 terminal No. 9 (White/Black wire). If resistance is less than 1000 ohms, repair White/Black wire for short to ground. If resistance is 1000 ohms or more, go to next step.
6) Connect jumper wire between ground and DLC connector terminal No. 3 (White/Black wire). Measure resistance between ground and instrument cluster Black connector C1 terminal No. 10 (Violet/Brown wire). If resistance is 1000 ohms or more, go to next step. If resistance is less than 1000 ohms, repair open Violet/Brown wire.
7) Measure resistance between ground and instrument cluster Black connector C1 terminal No. 10 (Violet/Brown wire). If resistance is less than 1000 ohms, repair Violet/Brown wire for short to ground. If resistance is 1000 ohms or more, replace instrument cluster.

BUS (+) & BUS (–) SHORTED TOGETHER

NOTE: For connector terminal identification and wiring diagrams, see BODY CONTROL COMPUTER – INTRODUCTION article. Perform VERIFICATION TEST VER-1 after each repair.

CAUTION: Always turn ignition off prior to disconnecting any module connector.

1) Turn ignition off. Disconnect Powertrain Control Module (PCM). PCM is mounted in center of firewall. Turn ignition on. If scan tool does not display BUS (+) & BUS (–) SHORTED TOGETHER, replace PCM. If scan tool displays BUS (+) & BUS (–) SHORTED TOGETHER, go to next step.
2) Turn ignition off. Disconnect anti-lock brake controller module. Controller is mounted to top of ABS hydraulic unit. Turn ignition on. If scan tool does not display BUS (+) & BUS (–) SHORTED TOGETHER, replace anti-lock brake controller module. If scan tool displays BUS (+) & BUS (–) SHORTED TOGETHER, go to next step.
3) Turn ignition off. Disconnect instrument cluster. Turn ignition on. If scan tool does not display BUS (+) & BUS (–) SHORTED TOGETHER, replace instrument cluster circuit board. If scan tool displays BUS (+) & BUS (–) SHORTED TOGETHER, go to next step.
4) Turn ignition off and wait 2 minutes. Disconnect Air Bag Control Module (ACM). ACM is located under driver's seat. Turn ignition on. If scan tool does not display BUS (+) & BUS (–) SHORTED TOGETHER, replace ACM. If scan tool displays BUS (+) & BUS (–) SHORTED TOGETHER, go to next step.
5) Turn ignition off. Disconnect Central Timer Module (CTM). CTM is located under left center of instrument panel. Turn ignition on. If scan tool does not display BUS (+) & BUS (–) SHORTED TOGETHER, replace CTM. If scan tool displays BUS (+) & BUS (–) SHORTED TOGETHER, go to next step.
6) Disconnect scan tool from Data Link Connector (DLC). Using external ohmmeter, measure resistance between DLC connector terminals No. 3 (Violet/Brown wire) and No. 11 (White/Black wire). If resistance is less than 5 ohms, repair short between Violet/Brown wire and White/Dark Green wire. If resistance is 5 ohms or more, replace scan tool cable or scan tool as necessary.

CHRY
4-254

1999 ACCESSORIES & EQUIPMENT
Vehicle Communications – Ram Van & Ram Wagon (Cont.)

NO TERMINATION

NOTE: *For connector terminal identification and wiring diagrams, see BODY CONTROL COMPUTER – INTRODUCTION article. Perform VERIFICATION TEST VER-1 after each repair.*

CAUTION: *Always turn ignition off prior to disconnecting any module connector.*

1) Disconnect Powertrain Control Module (PCM) connectors. PCM is mounted in right side of firewall. Connect jumper wire between ground and PCM connector C3 terminal No. 30 (Violet/Brown wire). Using scan tool, select SYSTEM MONITORS. Perform CCD BUS test. If scan tool does not display BUS SHORT TO GROUND, repair open Violet/Brown wire. If scan tool displays BUS SHORT TO GROUND, go to next step.
2) Move jumper wire to PCM connector C3 terminal No. 28 (White/Black wire). Perform CCD BUS test. If scan tool does not display BUS SHORT TO GROUND, repair open White/Black wire. If scan tool displays BUS SHORT TO GROUND, replace PCM.

BUS SHORT TO 5 VOLTS

NOTE: *For connector terminal identification and wiring diagrams, see BODY CONTROL COMPUTER – INTRODUCTION article. Perform VERIFICATION TEST VER-1 after each repair.*

CAUTION: *Always turn ignition off prior to disconnecting any module connector.*

1) Turn ignition off. Disconnect Powertrain Control Module (PCM). PCM is mounted in center of firewall. Turn ignition on. If scan tool does not display BUS SHORT TO 5 VOLTS, go to step **8)**. If scan tool displays BUS SHORT TO 5 VOLTS, go to next step.
2) Turn ignition off. Disconnect anti-lock brake controller module. Controller module is mounted to top of ABS hydraulic unit. Turn ignition on. If scan tool does not display BUS SHORT TO 5 VOLTS, replace anti-lock brake controller module. If scan tool displays BUS SHORT TO 5 VOLTS, go to next step.
3) Turn ignition off. Disconnect instrument cluster. Turn ignition on. If scan tool does not display BUS SHORT TO 5 VOLTS, replace instrument cluster circuit board. If scan tool displays BUS SHORT TO 5 VOLTS, go to next step.
4) Turn ignition off and wait 2 minutes. Disconnect Air Bag Control Module (ACM). ACM is located under driver's seat. Turn ignition on. If scan tool does not display BUS SHORT TO 5 VOLTS, replace ACM. If scan tool displays BUS SHORT TO 5 VOLTS, go to next step.
5) Turn ignition off. Disconnect Central Timer Module (CTM). CTM is located under left center of instrument panel. Turn ignition on. If scan tool does not display BUS SHORT TO 5 VOLTS, replace CTM. If scan tool displays BUS SHORT TO 5 VOLTS, go to next step.
6) Disconnect scan tool from Data Link Connector (DLC). Using external voltmeter, measure voltage between ground and DLC connector terminal No. 3 (Violet/Brown wire). If voltage is more than 4 volts, repair Violet/Brown wire for short to voltage. If voltage is 4 volts or less, go to next step.
7) Measure voltage between ground and DLC connector terminal No. 11 (White/Black wire). If voltage is more than 4 volts, repair White/Black wire for short to voltage. If voltage is less than 4 volts, replace scan tool cable or scan tool as necessary.
8) Turn ignition off. Using external ohmmeter, measure resistance between PCM connector C3 terminal No. 30 (Violet/Brown wire) and connector C1 terminal No. 17 (Violet/Black wire). If resistance is less than 800 ohms, repair short between Violet/Brown wire and Violet/Black wire. If resistance is 800 ohms or more, go to next step.
9) Measure resistance between PCM connector C3 terminal No. 30 (Violet/Brown wire) PCM connector C2 terminal No. 31 (Violet/White wire). If resistance is less than 800 ohms, repair short to 5 volts in Violet/Brown wire. If resistance is 800 ohms or greater, go to next step.
10) Measure resistance between PCM connector C3 terminal No. 28 (White/Black wire) and PCM connector C1 terminal No. 17 (Violet/Black

wire). If resistance is less than 800 ohms, repair short between Violet/Black and White/Black wires of both connectors. See wiring diagram for clarification. If resistance is 800 ohms or more, go to next step.
11) Measure resistance between PCM connector C3 terminal No. 28 (White/Black wire) PCM connector C2 terminal No. 31 (Violet/White wire) . If resistance is less than 800 ohms, repair short to 5 volts in White/Black wire. If resistance is 800 ohms or greater, replace PCM.

BUS SHORT TO BATTERY

NOTE: *For connector terminal identification and wiring diagrams, see BODY CONTROL COMPUTER – INTRODUCTION article. Perform VERIFICATION TEST VER-1 after each repair.*

CAUTION: *Always turn ignition off prior to disconnecting any module connector.*

1) Turn ignition off. Disconnect Powertrain Control Module (PCM). PCM is mounted in center of firewall. Turn ignition on. If scan tool does not display BUS SHORT TO BATTERY, go to step **12)**. If scan tool displays BUS SHORT TO BATTERY, go to next step.
2) Turn ignition off. Disconnect instrument cluster. Turn ignition on. If scan tool does not display BUS SHORT TO BATTERY, go to step **10)**. If scan tool displays BUS SHORT TO BATTERY, go to next step.
3) Turn ignition off and wait 2 minutes. Disconnect Air Bag Control Module (ACM). ACM is located under driver's seat. Turn ignition on. If scan tool does not display BUS SHORT TO BATTERY, replace ACM. If scan tool displays BUS SHORT TO BATTERY, go to next step.
4) Turn ignition off. Disconnect Central Timer Module (CTM). CTM is located under left center of instrument panel. Turn ignition on. If scan tool does not display BUS SHORT TO BATTERY, go to step **8)**. If scan tool displays BUS SHORT TO BATTERY, go to next step.
5) Turn ignition off. Disconnect anti-lock brake controller module. Controller module is mounted to top of ABS hydraulic unit. Turn ignition on. If scan tool does not display BUS SHORT TO BATTERY, replace anti-lock brake controller module. If scan tool displays BUS SHORT TO BATTERY, go to next step.
6) Disconnect scan tool from Data Link Connector (DLC). Using external voltmeter, measure voltage between ground and DLC connector terminal No. 3 (Violet/Brown wire). If voltage is more than .2 volt, repair Violet/Brown wire for short to voltage. If voltage is .2 volt or less, go to next step.
7) Measure voltage between ground and DLC connector terminal No. 11 (White/Black wire). If voltage is more than .2 volt, repair White/Black wire for short to voltage. If voltage is less than .2 volt, replace scan tool cable or scan tool as necessary.
8) Turn ignition off. Using external ohmmeter, measure resistance between ground and CTM 14-pin Green connector C1 terminal No. 6 (Black/Tan wire). If resistance is less than 5 ohms, go to next step. If resistance is 5 ohms or greater, repair open Black/Tan wire.
9) Measure resistance between ground and CTM 18-pin White connector C2 terminal No. 3 (Black wire). If resistance is less than 5 ohms, replace CTM. If resistance is 5 ohms or greater, repair open Black wire.
10) Turn ignition off. Using external ohmmeter, measure resistance between ground and instrument cluster Black connector C1 terminal No. 4 (Black/Dark Green wire). If resistance is less than 5 ohms, go to next step. If resistance is 5 ohms or greater, repair open Black/Dark Green wire.
11) Measure resistance between ground and instrument cluster Gray connector C2 terminal No. 7 (Black wire). If resistance is less than 5 ohms, replace instrument cluster. If resistance is 5 ohms or greater, repair open Black wire.
12) Turn ignition off. Using external ohmmeter, measure resistance between ground and PCM connector C1 terminal No. 31 (Black/Tan wire). PCM is located at right inner fender, at corner of firewall. If resistance is less than 10 ohms, go to next step. If resistance is 10 ohms or more, repair open Black/Tan wire.

1999 ACCESSORIES & EQUIPMENT
Vehicle Communications – Ram Van & Ram Wagon (Cont.)

CHRY
4-255

13) Measure resistance between ground and PCM connector C1 terminal No. 32 (Black/Tan wire). If resistance is less than 10 ohms, replace PCM. If resistance is 5 ohms or more, repair open Black/Tan wire.

BUS SHORT TO GROUND

NOTE: For connector terminal identification and wiring diagrams, see BODY CONTROL COMPUTER – INTRODUCTION article. Perform VERIFICATION TEST VER-1 after each repair.

CAUTION: Always turn ignition off prior to disconnecting any module connector.

1) Connect backprobe jumper between DLC connector terminal No. 4 and No. 5. If scan tool does not display BUS SHORT TO GROUND, repair open ground wire between DLC terminal No. 5 and ground. If scan tool displays BUS SHORT TO GROUND, go to next step.

2) Turn ignition off. Disconnect Powertrain Control Module (PCM). PCM is mounted in center of firewall. Turn ignition on. If scan tool does not display BUS SHORT TO GROUND, replace PCM. If scan tool displays BUS SHORT TO GROUND, go to next step.

3) Turn ignition off. Disconnect anti-lock brake controller module. Controller module is mounted to top of ABS hydraulic unit. Turn ignition on. If scan tool does not display BUS SHORT TO GROUND, replace anti-lock brake controller module. If scan tool displays BUS SHORT TO GROUND, go to next step.

4) Turn ignition off. Disconnect instrument cluster. Turn ignition on. If scan tool does not display BUS SHORT TO GROUND, replace instrument cluster circuit board. If scan tool displays BUS SHORT TO GROUND, go to next step.

5) Turn ignition off and wait 2 minutes. Disconnect Air Bag Control Module (ACM). ACM is located under driver's seat. Turn ignition on. If scan tool does not display BUS SHORT TO GROUND, replace ACM. If scan tool displays BUS SHORT TO GROUND, go to next step.

6) Turn ignition off. Disconnect Central Timer Module (CTM). CTM is located under left center of instrument panel. Turn ignition on. If scan tool does not display BUS SHORT TO GROUND, replace CTM. If scan tool displays BUS SHORT TO GROUND, go to next step.

7) Disconnect scan tool from Data Link Connector (DLC). Using external ohmmeter, measure resistance between ground and DLC connector terminal No. 3 (Violet/Brown wire). If resistance is less than 700 ohms, repair Violet/Brown wire for short to ground. If resistance is 700 ohms or more, go to next step.

8) Measure resistance between ground and DLC connector terminal No. 11 (White/Black wire). If resistance is less than 700 ohms, repair White/Dark Green wire for short to ground. If resistance is 700 ohms or more, replace scan tool cable or scan tool as necessary.

NO BUS BIAS

NOTE: For connector terminal identification and wiring diagrams, see BODY CONTROL COMPUTER – INTRODUCTION article. Perform VERIFICATION TEST VER-1 after each repair.

CAUTION: Always turn ignition off prior to disconnecting any module connector.

1) Remove and inspect fuse No. 11 from junction block. Junction block is behind left kick panel. If fuse is open, go to next step. If fuse is okay, go to step **3)**.

2) Using external ohmmeter, measure resistance between ground and fused ignition switch output run/start terminal (Dark Blue/White wire) on fuse No. 11 socket. If resistance is less than 5 ohms, repair Dark Blue/White wire for short to ground. Replace fuse No. 11. If resistance is 5 ohms or greater, replace fuse No. 11.

3) Turn ignition on. Using an external voltmeter, measure voltage between ground and ignition switch output run/start terminal (Dark Blue wire) on fuse No. 11 socket. If voltage is 10 volts or less, repair open Dark Blue wire between junction block and ignition switch. If voltage is more than 10 volts, go to next step.

4) Disconnect scan tool. Turn ignition on. Using an external voltmeter, measure voltage between ground and DLC terminal No. 3 (Violet/Brown wire). If voltage is not 1.8-2.3 volts, go to step **6)**. If voltage is 1.8-2.3 volts, go to next step.

5) Measure voltage between ground and DLC terminal No. 11 (White/Black wire). If voltage is not 1.8-2.3 volts, go to next step. If voltage is 1.8-2.3 volts, replace scan tool cable or scan tool.

6) Connect jumper wire between ground and DLC connector terminal No. 11 (White/Black wire). Turn ignition off. Remove instrument cluster. Using external ohmmeter, measure resistance between ground and instrument cluster Black connector C1 terminal No. 9 (White/Black wire). If resistance is less than 5 ohms, go to next step. If resistance is 5 ohms or more, repair open White/Black wire.

7) Disconnect jumper wire. Measure resistance between ground and instrument cluster Black connector C1 terminal No. 9 (White/Black wire). If resistance is less than 1000 ohms, repair White/Black wire for short to ground. If resistance is 1000 ohms or more, go to next step.

8) Connect jumper wire between ground and DLC connector terminal No. 3 (White/Black wire). Measure resistance between ground and instrument cluster Black connector C1 terminal No. 10 (Violet/Brown wire). If resistance is less than 5 ohms, go to next step. If resistance is 5 ohms or more, repair open Violet/Brown wire.

9) Disconnect jumper wire. Measure resistance between ground and instrument cluster Black connector C1 terminal No. 10 (Violet/Brown wire). If resistance is less than 1000 ohms, repair Violet/Brown wire for short to ground. If resistance is 1000 ohms or more, go to next step.

10) Turn ignition on. Using external voltmeter, measure voltage between ground and instrument cluster Black connector C1 terminal No. 2 (Dark Blue/White wire). If voltage is 9.5 volts or less, repair open Dark Blue/White wire. If voltage is more than 9.5 volts, go to next step.

11) Turn ignition off. Using external ohmmeter, measure resistance between ground and instrument cluster Black connector C1 terminal No. 4 (Black/Light Green wire). If resistance is 5 ohms or less, go to next step. If resistance is more than 5 ohms, repair open Black/Light Green wire.

12) Measure resistance between ground and instrument cluster Gray connector C2 terminal No. 7 (Black wire). If resistance is 5 ohms or less, replace instrument cluster. If resistance is more than 5 ohms, repair open Black wire.

NO RESPONSE AIR BAG CONTROL MODULE

NOTE: For connector terminal identification and wiring diagrams, see BODY CONTROL COMPUTER – INTRODUCTION article. Perform VERIFICATION TEST VER-1 after each repair.

CAUTION: Always turn ignition off prior to disconnecting any module connector.

1) Remove and inspect fuse No. 19 from junction block. Junction block is on left side of instrument panel. If fuse is open, go to next step. If fuse is okay, go to step **6)**.

2) Using external voltmeter, measure voltage between ground and voltage input side of fuse No. 19 socket. If voltage is 10 volts or less, repair open ignition switch output circuit (Dark Blue wire between ignition switch and junction block). If voltage is more than 10 volts, go to next step.

3) Turn ignition off and wait 2 minutes. Using external ohmmeter, measure resistance between ground and fused ignition switch output run/start terminal of fuse No. 19 socket (Light Green/Yellow wire). If resistance is less than 5 ohms, go to next step. If resistance is 5 ohms or more, go to step **5)**.

4) Disconnect Air Bag Control Module (ACM) connector. ACM is located under driver's seat. Turn ignition on. Measure resistance between ground and fused ignition switch output run/start terminal of fuse No. 19 socket (Light Green/Yellow wire). If resistance is less than 5 ohms, repair Light Green/Yellow wire for short to ground. Replace fuse No. 19. If resistance is 5 ohms or more, replace air bag control module and fuse No. 19.

CHRY
4-256

1999 ACCESSORIES & EQUIPMENT
Vehicle Communications – Ram Van & Ram Wagon (Cont.)

5) Turn ignition off and wait 2 minutes. Disconnect Air Bag Control Module (ACM) connector. ACM is located under driver's seat. Using external ohmmeter, measure resistance of Light Green/Yellow wire between ACM connector terminal No. 14 and fused ignition switch output run/start terminal on fuse No. 19 socket. If resistance is less than 5 ohms, connect ACM connector. Turn ignition on. Replace junction block fuse No. 19. Go to appropriate MITCHELL® AIR BAG SERVICE & REPAIR, DOMESTIC CARS, LIGHT TRUCKS & VANS article for further testing. If resistance is 5 ohms or more, repair open Light Green/Yellow wire. Replace fuse No. 19.

6) Using external voltmeter, measure voltage between ground and voltage input side of fuse No. 19 socket (Dark Blue wire). If voltage is 10 volts or less, repair open ignition switch output circuit (Dark Blue wire between ignition switch and junction block). If voltage is more than 10 volts, go to next step.

7) Turn ignition off and wait 2 minutes. Install fuse No. 19. Disconnect Air Bag Control Module (ACM) connector. ACM is located under driver's seat. Turn ignition on. Using external voltmeter, measure voltage between ground and ACM connector terminal No. 14 (Light Green/Yellow wire). If voltage is 10 volts or less, repair open Light Green/Yellow wire. If voltage is more than 10 volts, go to next step.

8) Turn ignition off. Using external ohmmeter, measure resistance between ground and ACM connector terminal No. 4 (Black/Pink). If resistance is 5 ohms or more, repair open Black/Pink wire. If resistance is less than 5 ohms, go to next step.

9) Turn ignition on. Using external voltmeter, measure voltage between ground and ACM connector terminal No. 21 (Violet/Brown wire). If voltage is not 1.8-2.6 volts, repair open Violet/Brown wire. If voltage is 1.8-2.6 volts, go to next step.

10) Using external voltmeter, measure voltage between ground and ACM connector terminal No. 22 (White/Black wire). If voltage is not 1.8-2.6 volts, repair open White/Black wire. If voltage is 1.8-2.6 volts, replace ACM.

NO RESPONSE CENTRAL TIMER MODULE

NOTE: For connector terminal identification and wiring diagrams, see BODY CONTROL COMPUTER – INTRODUCTION article. Perform VERIFICATION TEST VER-1 after each repair.

CAUTION: Always turn ignition off prior to disconnecting any module connector.

1) Remove and inspect junction block fuse No. 17. Junction block is on left side of instrument panel. If fuse is open, go to next step. If fuse is okay, go to step **3)**.

2) Using external ohmmeter, measure resistance between ground and fused ignition switch output run/start terminal of fuse No. 17 socket (White wire). If resistance is less than 5 ohms, repair short to ground in White wire. Replace fuse No. 17. If resistance is 5 ohms or more, replace fuse No. 17.

3) Install fuse No. 17. Remove and inspect junction block fuse No. 16. If fuse is open, next step. If fuse is okay, go to step **5)**.

4) Using external ohmmeter, measure resistance between ground and fused ignition switch output run/acc terminal of fuse No. 16 socket (Yellow/Red wire). If resistance is less than 5 ohms, repair short to ground in Yellow/Red wire. Replace fuse No. 16. If resistance is 5 ohms or more, replace fuse No. 16.

5) Install fuse No. 16. Disconnect Central Timer Module (CTM). CTM is located on left side of engine cover under dash. Using external ohmmeter, measure resistance between ground and CTM 18-pin connector terminal No. 3 (Black wire). If resistance is more than 5 ohms, repair open Black wire. If resistance is 5 ohms or less, go to next step.

6) Measure resistance between ground and CTM 14-pin connector terminal No. 6 (Black/Tan wire). If resistance is more than 5 ohms, repair open Black/Tan wire. If resistance is 5 ohms or less, go to next step.

7) Turn ignition on. Using scan tool, perform CCD Bus test. Connect jumper wire between ground and CTM 18-pin connector terminal No. 16 (Violet/Brown wire). If scan tool does not display BUS SHORT TO

GROUND, repair open Violet/Brown wire. If scan tool displays BUS SHORT TO GROUND, go to next step.

8) Disconnect jumper wire. Connect jumper wire between ground and CTM 18-pin connector terminal No. 17 (White/Black wire). If scan tool does not display BUS SHORT TO GROUND, repair open White/Black wire. If scan tool displays BUS SHORT TO GROUND, replace CTM.

NO RESPONSE INSTRUMENT CLUSTER

NOTE: For connector terminal identification and wiring diagrams, see BODY CONTROL COMPUTER – INTRODUCTION article. Perform VERIFICATION TEST VER-1A after each repair.

CAUTION: Always turn ignition off prior to disconnecting any module connector.

1) Turn ignition off. Remove instrument cluster. Turn ignition on. Using scan tool, turn on internal CCD bus bias under SYSTEM MONITORS, then CCD BUS VOLTAGE. Connect jumper wire between ground and instrument cluster connector C1 terminal No. 10 (Violet/Brown wire). If scan tool voltage did not drop to about zero volts, repair open Violet/Brown wire. If scan tool voltage dropped to about zero volts, go to next step.

2) Move jumper to instrument cluster connector C1 terminal No. 9 (White/Black wire). Monitor CCD BUS VOLTAGE. If scan tool voltage did not drop to about zero volts, repair open White/Black wire. If scan tool voltage did not drop to about zero volts, replace instrument cluster.

NO RESPONSE POWERTRAIN CONTROL MODULE

NOTE: For connector terminal identification and wiring diagrams, see BODY CONTROL COMPUTER – INTRODUCTION article. Perform VERIFICATION TEST VER-1 after each repair.

CAUTION: Always turn ignition off prior to disconnecting any module connector.

1) If engine does not run, see appropriate BASIC DIAGNOSTIC PROCEDURES article in ENGINE PERFORMANCE in appropriate MITCHELL® manual. If engine runs, go to next step.

2) Turn ignition off. Disconnect Powertrain Control Module (PCM). PCM is mounted in center of firewall. Turn ignition on. Connect jumper wire between ground and PCM connector C3 terminal. No. 30 (Violet/Brown wire). Using scan tool, perform CCD BUS test. If scan tool does not display SHORT TO GROUND, repair open Violet/Brown wire. If scan tool displays SHORT TO GROUND, go to next step.

3) Move jumper wire to PCM connector C3 terminal No. 28 (White/Black wire). Perform CCD BUS test. If scan tool does not display SHORT TO GROUND, repair open White/Black wire. If scan tool displays SHORT TO GROUND, replace PCM.

NOT RECEIVING BUS MESSAGES CORRECTLY

NOTE: For connector terminal identification and wiring diagrams, see BODY CONTROL COMPUTER – INTRODUCTION article. Perform VERIFICATION TEST VER-1 after each repair.

CAUTION: Always turn ignition off prior to disconnecting any module connector.

1) Disconnect anti-lock brake controller module. Controller module is mounted to top of ABS hydraulic unit. Turn ignition on. If scan tool displays BUS OPERATIONAL, replace anti-lock brake controller module. If scan tool does not display BUS OPERATIONAL, go to next step.

2) Turn ignition off and wait 2 minutes. Disconnect Air Bag Control Module (ACM). ACM is located under driver's seat. Turn ignition on. If scan tool displays BUS OPERATIONAL, replace ACM. If scan tool does not display BUS OPERATIONAL, go to next step.

3) Disconnect Central Timer Module (CTM). CTM is located on left side of engine cover under dash. Turn ignition on. If scan tool displays BUS

1999 ACCESSORIES & EQUIPMENT
Vehicle Communications – Ram Van & Ram Wagon (Cont.)

CHRY
4-257

OPERATIONAL, replace CTM. If scan tool does not display BUS OPERATIONAL, replace scan tool cable or scan tool.

VERIFICATION TEST VER-1A

VERIFICATION PROCEDURE

1) Reconnect all previously disconnected components and connectors. Turn ignition on. If Central Timing Module (CTM) was replaced, program all RKE transmitters and program other options as necessary.

2) Ensure ignition is on. Erase all DTCs using scan tool. Turn ignition off and wait 5 seconds. Turn ignition on and fully operate system that was malfunctioning.

3) If system is not operating properly, go to SYMPTOM IDENTIFICATION in BODY CONTROL COMPUTER TESTS – RAM VAN & RAM WAGON. If system is operating correctly and customer's complaint cannot be duplicated, repair is complete.

1999 ACCESSORIES & EQUIPMENT
Cruise Control Systems – Avenger & Sebring Coupe

CAUTION: *When battery is disconnected, vehicle computer and memory systems may lose memory data. Driveability problems may exist until computer systems have completed a relearn cycle. See COMPUTER RELEARN PROCEDURES article in GENERAL INFORMATION before disconnecting battery.*

DESCRIPTION

The speed (cruise) control system is electronically controlled and vacuum operated. The electronic control is integrated into the Powertrain Control Module (PCM) located in left front corner of engine compartment. System consists of the following components: PCM, servo, speed control switches, vacuum reservoir, vehicle speed sensor, speed control relay and brakelight switch.

System controls are located on left side of instrument panel (main speed control switch – OFF/ON) and on right stalk under air bag module and consist of ACC/RES, CANCEL and COAST/SET positions.

OPERATION

SYSTEM CONTROLS

To Set Speed Control – Press ON/OFF button to turn speed control system on. CRUISE indicator will illuminate. Accelerate to desired speed (minimum of 25 MPH) and pull SET/COAST switch. Vehicle speed will be maintained.

NOTE: *Speed control system will automatically disengage when vehicle speed decreases to less than 25 MPH or increases to more than 85 MPH.*

To Disengage Speed Control – Press brake pedal. Press clutch pedal. Pull CANCEL switch. Press ON/OFF button. If ON/OFF button is used, set speed will be erased from memory.

To Resume Previous Speed – If set speed has not been erased from memory and vehicle speed is more than 35 MPH, pull RES/ACCEL switch.

To Increase Speed – With speed control system on, increase set speed by holding RES/ACCEL switch upward. Speed will increase gradually. When button is released, new set speed will be maintained. To increase speed quickly, use accelerator pedal to reach desired speed. Pull down SET switch.

To Decrease Speed – With speed control system on, decrease set speed by pulling SET/COAST switch. Vehicle speed will gradually decrease. Releasing button will set a new speed as long as vehicle speed is still more than 25 MPH. To decrease speed quickly, use brake pedal. Pull down SET switch.

COMPONENT LOCATIONS

COMPONENT LOCATIONS

Component	Location
Powertrain Control Module (PCM)	Left Front Of Engine Compartment
Speed Control Servo	Right Rear Corner Of Engine Compartment
Transmission Control Module (TCM)	In Front Of Left Front Strut Tower
Vehicle Speed Sensor (VSS)	Top Of Transaxle, Near Right Axle Shaft

TROUBLE SHOOTING

PRELIMINARY INSPECTION

Inspect vacuum hoses and throttle cables. Ensure linkage and cables operate smoothly. Ensure cables are adjusted properly. To diagnose speed control system, operate cruise control system to verify customer complaint. Check for DTCs. See SELF-DIAGNOSTIC SYSTEM. If no DTCs are stored, go to SYSTEM TESTS.

COMPONENT TESTS

WARNING: *Vehicle is equipped with an air bag. Air bag must be deactivated before servicing speed control components on or around steering column. See AIR BAG RESTRAINT SYSTEMS – CARS article.*

BRAKE SWITCH

Disconnect brake switch connector. Using an ohmmeter, check for continuity at brake switch. *See Fig. 1.* If continuity is not as specified in BRAKE SWITCH CONTINUITY table, check brake switch adjustment. See BRAKE SWITCH under REMOVAL & INSTALLATION. If brake switch adjustment is okay, replace defective brake switch.

BRAKE SWITCH CONTINUITY

Switch Plunger Position	Check Between Terminals	Continuity
Released	3 & 4	Yes
	1 & 2	No
Depressed	3 & 4	No
	1 & 2	Yes

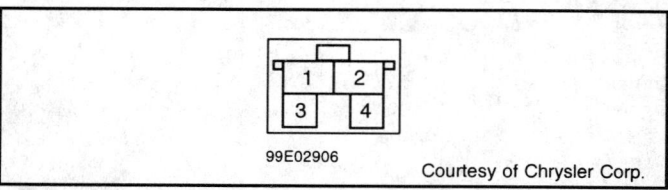

99E02906   Courtesy of Chrysler Corp.

Fig. 1: Identifying Brake Switch Terminals

CLOCKSPRING

1) Gain access to clockspring connectors. See CLOCKSPRING under REMOVAL & INSTALLATION. Check clockspring connectors and protective tube for wear or damage. Using an ohmmeter, check for continuity between clockspring connector No. 1, terminal No. 1 and connector No. 4, terminal No. 2. *See Fig. 2.*

2) Check for continuity between clockspring connector No. 1, terminal No. 2 and connector No. 4, terminal No. 1. Check for continuity between clockspring connector No. 1, terminal No. 3 and connector No. 3. Continuity should exist in all tests. If continuity does not exist in any test, replace clockspring.

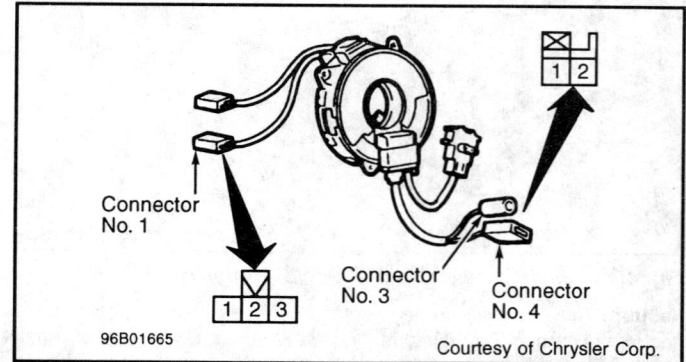

Connector No. 1

Connector No. 3

Connector No. 4

96B01665   Courtesy of Chrysler Corp.

Fig. 2: Identifying Clockspring Connectors & Terminals

SPEED CONTROL RELAY

1) Disconnect and remove speed control relay. Relay is attached to speed control servo assembly located at right rear of engine compartment. Using an ohmmeter, check for continuity between relay terminals No. 1 and 2 and terminals No. 3 and 4. Continuity should exist. If continuity does not exist in both tests, replace speed control relay.

2) If continuity exists in both tests, apply battery voltage to relay terminal No. 1. Apply ground to relay terminal No. 2 using jumper wires. *See*

1999 ACCESSORIES & EQUIPMENT
Cruise Control Systems – Avenger & Sebring Coupe (Cont.)

CHRY
4-259

Fig. 3. Using an ohmmeter, check for continuity between relay terminals No. 3 and 4. Continuity should not exist. If continuity exists, replace speed control relay.

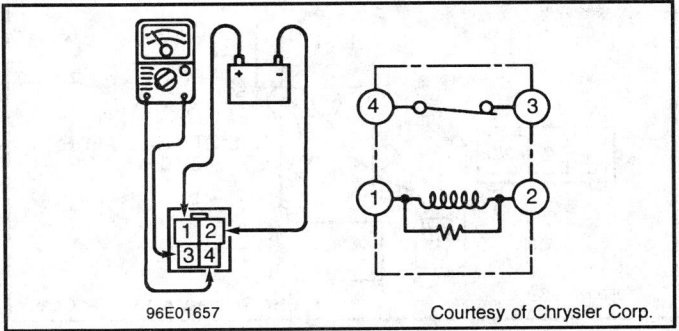

96E01657   Courtesy of Chrysler Corp.

Fig. 3: Testing Speed Control Relay

SPEED CONTROL SERVO

Electrical Test – 1) Turn ignition and speed control main switch on. Disconnect speed control servo 4-pin connector. Using a voltmeter, measure voltage between ground and servo harness connector terminal No. 3 (Blue/White wire). *See Fig. 4*. Battery voltage should exist. If battery voltage does not exist, check power supply circuit. See WIRING DIAGRAMS.

2) If battery voltage is present, connect a jumper wire between servo harness connector terminal No. 3 (Blue/White wire) and servo connector terminal No. 3. Using a voltmeter check for voltage at remaining 3 servo connector terminals. If voltage is not present at all 3 remaining servo connector terminals, replace speed control servo.

3) If voltage is present at all 3 remaining servo connector terminals, turn ignition off and remove jumper wire. Using an ohmmeter, check for continuity between ground and servo harness connector terminal No. 4 (Black wire). *See Fig. 4*. Continuity should exist. If continuity does not exist, repair open in speed control servo ground circuit. See WIRING DIAGRAMS.

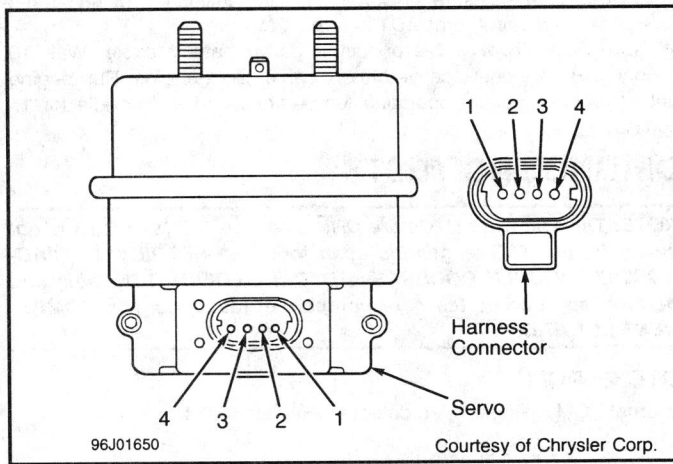

96J01650   Courtesy of Chrysler Corp.

Fig. 4: Identifying Speed Control Servo Terminals

Vacuum Test – Remove speed control cable at throttle body. Disconnect 4-pin connector and vacuum hoses at servo. Using jumper wires, connect battery voltage to servo pin No. 3 and ground pins No. 1, 2 and 4. Using a hand-held vacuum pump, apply 10-15 in. Hg of vacuum to servo. Cable should retract and hold as long as vacuum is applied.

SPEED CONTROL SWITCHES

Main Switch – 1) Remove speed control main switch from instrument panel and disconnect harness connector. Using an ohmmeter, check speed control main switch. If speed control main switch does not test as specified, replace switch. See SPEED CONTROL MAIN SWITCH CONTINUITY table. *See Fig. 5*.

2) Using jumper wires, apply battery voltage to main switch terminal No. 1 and ground to terminal No. 4. Using a voltmeter, measure voltage on switch terminal No. 5. Voltage should be present with switch in ON position. Voltage should not be present when switch is in OFF position. If switch does not function as described, replace speed control master switch.

SPEED CONTROL MAIN SWITCH CONTINUITY

Switch Position	Check Between Terminals	Continuity
OFF	2 & 7	Yes
	All Other Terminals	No
Neutral	4 & 5	Yes
	2 & 7	Yes
	All Other Terminals	No
On	1 & 4	Yes
	1 & 5	Yes
	2 & 7	Yes

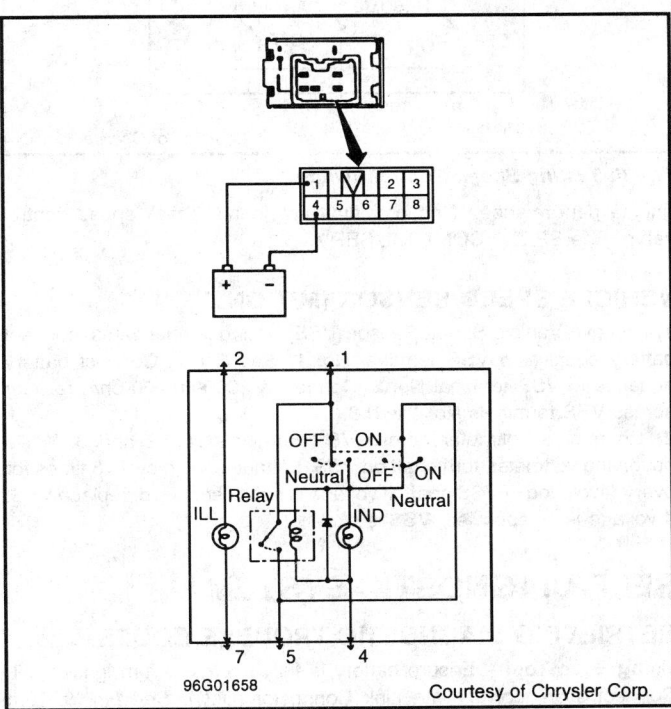

96G01658   Courtesy of Chrysler Corp.

Fig. 5: Testing Speed Control Main Switch

Control Switch – Access speed control switch. Disconnect speed control switch 2-pin connector. Using an ohmmeter, check speed control switch resistance. If speed control switch does not test as specified, replace speed control switch. *See Fig. 6*. See SPEED CONTROL SWITCH RESISTANCE table.

SPEED CONTROL SWITCH RESISTANCE

Switch Position	Resistance (Ohms)
Switch OFF	Infinity
CANCEL Switch ON	0
RESUME Switch ON	820
SET Switch ON	2700

VACUUM SUPPLY

1) Disconnect vacuum hose at speed control servo. Install vacuum gauge to disconnected vacuum hose. Start engine and observe gauge. Vacuum reading should be a minimum of 10 in. Hg. Turn engine off. Vacuum should continue to hold at a minimum of 10 in. Hg.

2) If vacuum is not as specified, check for kinked or leaking vacuum lines, defective check valve, defective vacuum reservoir and/or poor

CHRY
4-260

1999 ACCESSORIES & EQUIPMENT
Cruise Control Systems – Avenger & Sebring Coupe (Cont.)

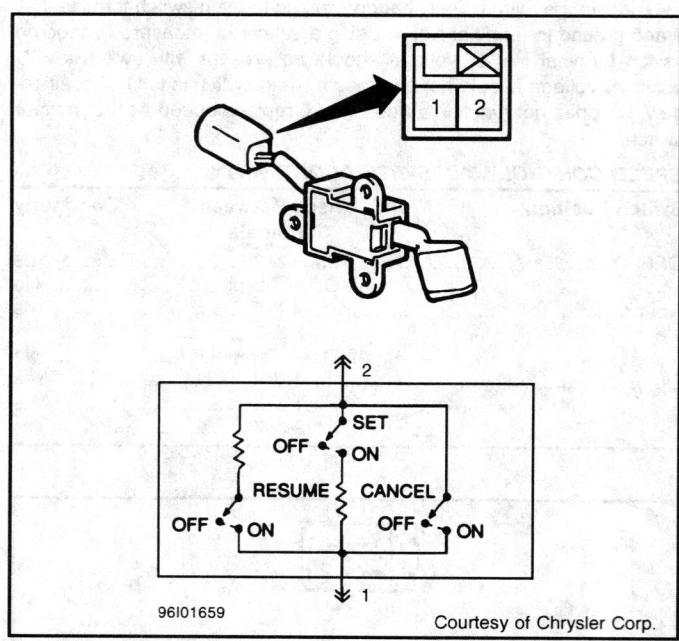

Fig. 6: Testing Speed Control Switch

engine performance. If no problems are found, check speed control servo. See SPEED CONTROL SERVO.

VEHICLE SPEED SENSOR (M/T ONLY)

1) Remove Vehicle Speed Sensor (VSS). Using jumper wires, connect battery positive to VSS terminal No. 1. *See Fig. 7.* Connect battery negative to VSS terminal No. 3. Connect a 3000-10,000 ohm resistor across VSS terminals No. 1 and 3.

2) Connect a voltmeter across VSS terminals No. 2 and 3. While observing voltmeter, turn shaft on VSS. Voltage should cycle 8 times for every revolution of VSS shaft. If voltage is not as specified, replace VSS. If voltage is as specified, VSS is okay.

SELF-DIAGNOSTIC SYSTEM

RETRIEVING DIAGNOSTIC TROUBLE CODES

Using Scan Tool – Ensure battery is fully charged. Turn ignition off. Connect scan tool to Data Link Connector (DLC). *See Fig. 8.* Turn ignition on. Read DTCs. See DTC IDENTIFICATION table and perform appropriate DTC test.

Using MIL – Cycle ignition key On-Off-On-Off-On within 5 seconds. Record number of times MIL flashes. There is a slight pause between flashes to separate first and second digits of DTC. Longer pauses between flashes indicate individual DTCs. See DTC IDENTIFICATION table and perform appropriate DTC test.

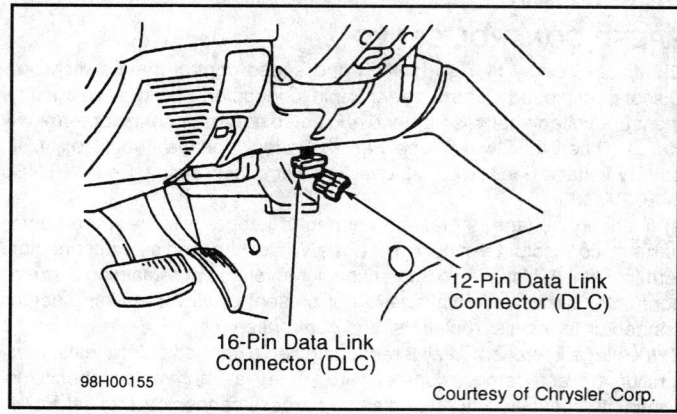

Fig. 7: Testing Vehicle Speed Sensor (M/T Only)

Fig. 8: Locating Data Link Connector

CLEARING DIAGNOSTIC TROUBLE CODES

With Scan Tool – Ensure ignition is off. Turn ignition on. Using screen prompts on scan tool, erase DTC from PCM.

Without Scan Tool – Disconnect negative battery cable. Wait 10 seconds. Reconnect negative battery cable. Start engine. Run engine until it reaches normal operating temperature. Let engine idle for 15 minutes.

DIAGNOSTIC TESTS

NOTE: The following DTCs are DRB scan tool DTCs. If DRB is not available, use MIL or generic scan tool. See RETRIEVING DIAGNOSTIC TROUBLE CODES. See DTC IDENTIFICATION table and perform appropriate test. For component locations, see COMPONENT LOCATIONS.

DTC 2: PCM

Internal PCM malfunction is detected. Replace PCM

DTC IDENTIFICATION

DRB Scan Tool DTC	Generic Scan Tool DTC	MIL DTC	Probable Cause	Perform Test
2	P0605	53	PCM	DTC 2: PCM
15		34	Speed Control Servo	DTC 15: SPEED CONTROL SERVO
35	P0500	15	Vehicle Speed Sensor	DTC 35: NO VEHICLE SPEED SENSOR SIGNAL
82		77	Speed Control Relay	DTC 82: SPEED CONTROL RELAY
86		34	Speed Control Switch	DTC 86: SPEED CONTROL SWITCH
87		34	Speed Control Switch	DTC 87: SPEED CONTROL SWITCH

1999 ACCESSORIES & EQUIPMENT
Cruise Control Systems – Avenger & Sebring Coupe (Cont.)

CHRY
4-261

DTC 15: SPEED CONTROL SERVO

Speed control vacuum or vent solenoid control circuit is open or shorted.

Possible Causes:
- Speed control servo defective
- Wiring open or shorted.
- PCM defective.

1) Check speed control servo. See SPEED CONTROL SERVO under COMPONENT TESTS. Replace if necessary. If speed control servo is okay, go to next step.

2) Turn ignition off. Disconnect PCM. Check for battery voltage at PCM connector A78, terminals No. 78 (Light Green/White wire) and 80 (Black/Yellow wire). If battery voltage does not exist, check wiring between speed control servo and PCM. Repair as necessary. If wiring is okay, replace PCM.

DTC 35: NO VEHICLE SPEED SENSOR SIGNAL

DTC 35 will set if PCM senses vehicle speed less than one MPH for 11 seconds under the following conditions:
- Engine coolant temperature 180°F (83°C) or more
- Transmission NOT in Park or Neutral (A/T only).
- Engine has been running for more than 31 seconds.
- Brakes not applied.
- Throttle open.
- Engine speed 1800 RPM or more.
- Intake manifold vacuum 10 in. Hg. or more.

Possible Causes:
- VSS signal circuit open or shorted.
- Speedometer pinion damaged.
- VSS 9-volt supply circuit open.
- VSS sensor ground circuit open.
- VSS defective.
- PCM defective.

M/T Models – 1) Using scan tool, go to SENSOR READ TESTS. While observing vehicle speed on scan tool, drive vehicle at a speed grater than 10 MPH. If scan tool does not display actual speed, go to next step. If scan tool displays actual speed, problem is intermittent. Try to duplicate conditions that caused DTC to set.

2) Disconnect Vehicle Speed Sensor (VSS). Turn ignition on. Using a voltmeter, measure voltage at VSS connector terminal No. 1 (Yellow wire). If voltage is not 8.5-9.5 volts, check circuit between VSS and PCM connector A78, terminal No. 44. See WIRING DIAGRAMS. Repair as necessary. If voltage is 8.5-9.5 volts, go to next step.

3) Check for continuity between ground and VSS connector terminal No. 2 (Black/Green wire). Continuity should exist. If continuity does not exist, repair open circuit. See WIRING DIAGRAMS. If continuity exists, replace VSS.

A/T Models – 1) Using scan tool, go to SENSOR READ TESTS. While observing vehicle speed on scan tool, drive vehicle at a speed grater than 10 MPH. If scan tool does not display actual speed, go to next step. If scan tool displays actual speed, problem is intermittent. Try to duplicate conditions that caused DTC to set.

2) Inspect wiring between PCM and Transmission Control Module (TCM). Repair as necessary. If wiring is okay, check for transmission DTCs. See 41TE/AE ELECTRONIC CONTROLS article in AUTOMATIC TRANSMISSIONS in appropriate MITCHELL® TRANSMISSION SERVICE & REPAIR manual.

DTC 82: SPEED CONTROL RELAY

Speed control power relay control circuit is open or shorted.

Possible Causes:
- Speed control servo defective.
- Speed control relay defective.
- PCM defective.
- Wiring open or shorted.

1) Check speed control servo. See SPEED CONTROL SERVO under COMPONENT TESTS. Replace if necessary. If speed control servo is okay, go to next step.

2) Turn ignition off. Disconnect PCM. Turn ignition on. Check for battery voltage at PCM connector A78, terminals No. 78 (Light Green/White wire) and 80 (Black/Yellow wire). If battery voltage exists, inspect PCM connector A78. Repair as necessary. If connector A78 is okay, replace PCM. If battery voltage does not exist, go to next step.

3) Disconnect speed control relay. Check for battery voltage at speed control relay connector terminal No. 4 (Red/Black wire). If battery voltage exists, go to next step. If battery voltage does not exist, check wiring between speed control main switch and speed control relay. Repair as necessary.

4) Check speed control relay. See SPEED CONTROL RELAY under COMPONENT TESTS. Replace if necessary. If speed control relay is okay, check wiring between speed control relay, speed control servo and PCM. Repair as necessary.

DTC 86: SPEED CONTROL SWITCH

Speed control switch voltage is more than maximum voltage. Replace speed control switch.

DTC 87: SPEED CONTROL SWITCH

Speed control switch voltage is less than minimum voltage. Replace speed control switch.

SYSTEM TESTS

NOTE: For component locations, see COMPONENT LOCATIONS.

COMMUNICATION WITH SCAN TOOL NOT POSSIBLE

Scan Tool Communication With All Systems Not Possible – 1) Measure voltage at Data Link Connector (DLC) terminal No. 16 (Red/Black wire). If battery voltage does not exist, go to next step. If battery voltage exists, go to step **3)**.

2) Check fuse and connections in engine compartment relay box. See WIRING DIAGRAMS. Repair as necessary. If fuse and connections are okay, repair open Red/Black wire.

3) Check for continuity between ground and DLC terminals No. 4 (Black wire) and No. 5 (Black/White wire). If continuity does not exist, repair open ground circuit. If continuity exists, replace scan tool.

Scan Tool Communication With PCM Not Possible – Check power supply and ground circuits to Powertrain Control Module (PCM). See WIRING DIAGRAMS. Check circuits between PCM and DLC. Repair as necessary. If circuits are okay, replace PCM.

SPEED CONTROL DOES NOT CANCEL WHEN ENGINE SPEED RISES SUDDENLY

Replace PCM.

SPEED CONTROL DOES NOT CANCEL WHEN BRAKE PEDAL IS DEPRESSED

1) Check brake switch. See BRAKE SWITCH under COMPONENT TESTS. Replace if necessary. If brake switch is okay, go to next step.

2) Measure voltage at brake switch connector terminal No. 4 (Brown/White wire). If battery voltage exists, go to next step. If battery voltage does not exist, check wiring and connectors between PCM and brake switch connector terminal No. 4 (Brown/White wire). See WIRING DIAGRAMS. Repair as necessary.

3) Check wiring and connectors between ground and brake switch connector terminal No. 3 (Black wire). See WIRING DIAGRAMS. Repair as necessary. If wiring and connectors are okay, replace PCM.

SPEED CONTROL DOES NOT CANCEL WHEN TRANSMISSION IS SHIFTED INTO NEUTRAL (A/T ONLY)

Check wiring and connectors between Park/Neutral Position (PNP) switch and PCM. See WIRING DIAGRAMS. Repair as necessary. If wiring and connectors are okay, replace PCM.

SPEED CONTROL CAN NOT BE SET

1) Check speed control switches. See SPEED CONTROL SWITCHES under COMPONENT TESTS. Replace if necessary. If speed control switches are okay, check clockspring. See CLOCKSPRING under COMPONENT TESTS. Replace if necessary. If clockspring is okay, go to next step.

2) Disconnect clockspring connector located under steering column. Turn ignition on. Measure voltage between ground and Red wire at clockspring harness connector. Voltage should be 5 volts. If voltage is not as specified, check wiring and connectors between clockspring and PCM. See WIRING DIAGRAMS. Repair as necessary. If voltage is as specified, repair circuit between clockspring connector Blue wire and ground.

HUNTING OCCURS AT SET SPEED

1) On M/T models, check Vehicle Speed Sensor (VSS). See VEHICLE SPEED SENSOR (M/T ONLY) under COMPONENT TESTS. Replace VSS as necessary. If VSS is okay, go to next step. On A/T models, disconnect Input Speed Sensor (ISS) and Output Speed Sensor (OSS). Measure resistance across ISS and OSS terminals. Resistance should be 300-1200 ohms. If resistance is not as specified, replace faulty sensor. If resistance is as specified, go to next step.

2) On all models, check speed control servo. See SPEED CONTROL SERVO under COMPONENT TESTS. Replace if necessary. If speed control servo is okay, check vacuum supply. See VACUUM SUPPLY under COMPONENT TESTS. Repair as necessary. If vacuum supply is okay, replace PCM.

SPEED CONTROL MAIN SWITCH ILLUMINATION LIGHT INOPERATIVE

1) Check speed control main switch. See SPEED CONTROL SWITCHES under COMPONENT TESTS. Replace if necessary. If speed control main switch is okay, go to next step.

2) Disconnect speed control main switch. Measure voltage at speed control main switch connector terminal No. 2 (Green/White wire). If battery voltage does not exist, go to next step. Repair as necessary. If battery voltage exists, go to step 4).

3) Check wiring and connectors between speed control main switch and engine compartment relay box. See WIRING DIAGRAMS. Repair as necessary.

4) Check wiring between speed control main switch and rheostat. See WIRING DIAGRAMS. Repair as necessary.

CRUISE CONTROL INDICATOR LIGHT ON MAIN SWITCH INOPERATIVE, BUT SPEED CONTROL OPERATES NORMALLY

Replace speed control main switch.

CRUISE CONTROL INDICATOR ON INSTRUMENT CLUSTER INOPERATIVE, BUT SPEED CONTROL OPERATES NORMALLY

1) Remove Instrument cluster. See INSTRUMENT CLUSTER. Check for continuity between instrument cluster 17-pin connector terminals No. 10 and 16. See Fig. 9. If continuity does not exist, indicator bulb is faulty or open circuit exists in instrument cluster. Repair as necessary. If continuity exists, go to next step.

2) Install instrument cluster. Disconnect PCM. Turn ignition on. Turn speed control main switch on. Using a jumper wire, ground PCM connector A77, terminal No. 18 (Light Green wire). If cruise control indicator does not illuminate, check wiring and connectors between instrument cluster and PCM. Repair as necessary. If cruise control indicator illuminates, replace PCM.

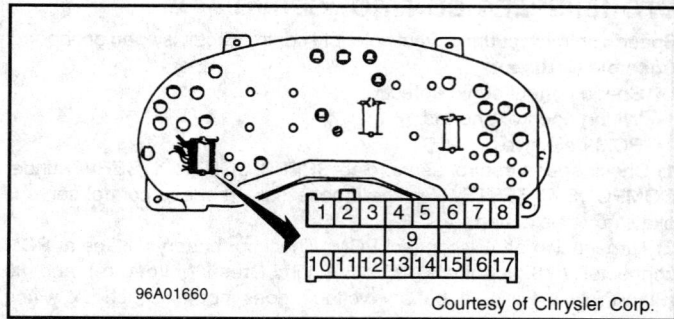

96A01660   Courtesy of Chrysler Corp.

Fig. 9: Identifying Instrument Cluster Terminals

REMOVAL & INSTALLATION

WARNING: *Vehicle is equipped with an air bag. Air bag must be deactivated before servicing speed control components on or around steering column. See AIR BAG RESTRAINT SYSTEMS – CARS article.*

CAUTION: *When battery is disconnected, vehicle computer and memory systems may lose memory data. Driveability problems may exist until computer systems have completed a relearn cycle. See COMPUTER RELEARN PROCEDURES in GENERAL INFORMATION before disconnecting battery.*

BRAKE SWITCH

Removal & Installation – Disconnect brake switch harness connector. Loosen brake switch lock nut and unscrew switch from bracket. To install, screw in brake switch until it contacts brake pedal stopper (just before the brake pedal is caused to move). Back out brake switch 1/2-1 turn and tighten lock nut and reconnect harness connector.

CLOCKSPRING

Removal & Installation – Turn ignition switch to OFF position. Deactivate air bag. See AIR BAG RESTRAINT SYSTEMS – CARS article. Remove air bag module. Remove steering wheel and speed control switch. Remove steering column lower cover. Disconnect clockspring connectors and remove clockspring assembly. To install, reverse removal procedure.

SPEED CONTROL SERVO

Removal – Remove speed control cable mounting bracket from servo. Remove servo mounting bracket. Disconnect wiring harness connector and vacuum hose from servo. Pull cable away from servo to expose retaining clip. Remove retaining clip and cable. Remove servo.

Installation – With throttle in full open position, align hole in speed control cable sleeve with hole in servo pin. Install retaining clip. To complete installation, reverse removal procedure.

SPEED CONTROL SWITCH

Removal & Installation (Main Switch) – Using Ornament Remover (MB990784), remove left instrument switch assembly. Separate speed control main switch from switch assembly. To install, reverse removal procedure.

Removal & Installation (Control Switch) – Turn ignition switch to OFF position. Deactivate air bag. See AIR BAG RESTRAINT SYSTEMS – CARS article. Remove air bag module. Remove speed control switch. To install, reverse removal procedure.

INSTRUMENT CLUSTER

Removal & Installation – Disconnect negative battery cable. Remove 2 instrument cluster bezel screws and remove bezel. Remove 4 instrument cluster screws. Disconnect necessary electrical connectors and remove instrument cluster. To install, reverse removal procedure.

1999 ACCESSORIES & EQUIPMENT
Cruise Control Systems – Avenger & Sebring Coupe (Cont.)

CHRY
4-263

WIRING DIAGRAMS

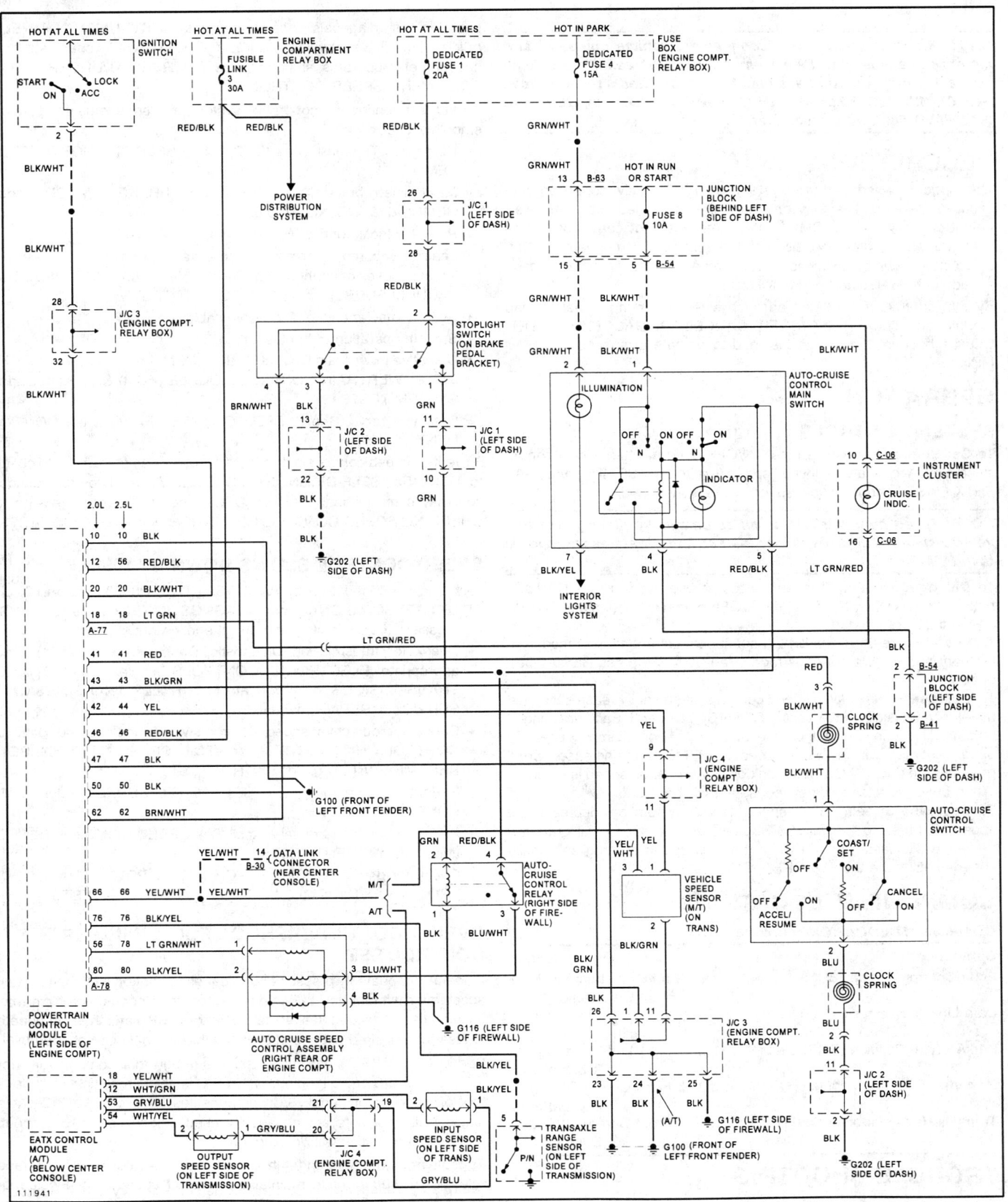

Fig. 10: Cruise Control System Wiring Diagram (Avenger & Sebring Coupe)

1999 ACCESSORIES & EQUIPMENT
Cruise Control Systems
Breeze, Cirrus, Sebring Convertible & Stratus

CAUTION: *When battery is disconnected, vehicle computer and memory systems may lose memory data. Driveability problems may exist until computer systems have completed a relearn cycle. See COMPUTER RELEARN PROCEDURES article in GENERAL INFORMATION before disconnecting battery.*

DESCRIPTION

The speed (cruise) control system is electronically controlled and vacuum operated. The electronic control is integrated into the Powertrain Control Module (PCM) located near left front corner of engine compartment. System consists of the following components: PCM, servo, speed control switches, vacuum reservoir, vehicle speed sensor, speed control relay and brake switch.

System controls are located on each side of steering wheel air bag module and consist of ON/OFF, CANCEL, RES/ACCEL and SET/COAST buttons. System is designed to operate at speeds above 30 MPH.

OPERATION

SYSTEM CONTROLS

To Set Speed Control – Press ON/OFF button to turn speed control system on. Accelerate to desired speed (minimum of 35 MPH) and press SET/COAST button. Vehicle speed will be maintained.

NOTE: *Speed control system will automatically disengage when vehicle speed decreases to less than 35 MPH or increases to more than 85 MPH.*

To Disengage Speed Control – Press brake pedal. Press CANCEL button. Press ON/OFF button. If ON/OFF button is used, set speed will be erased from memory.
To Resume Previous Speed – If set speed has not been erased from memory and vehicle speed is more than 35 MPH, press RES/ACCEL button.
To Increase Speed – With speed control system on, increase set speed by rapidly pressing and releasing RES/ACCEL button. Each pressing of button will cause speed increase of 2 MPH. For example, pressing button 3 times will increase speed by 6 MPH. To increase speed gradually, hold RES/ACCEL button down until desired speed is reached. When button is released, new set speed will be maintained.
To Decrease Speed – With speed control system on, decrease set speed by pressing SET/COAST button. Vehicle speed will gradually decrease. Releasing button will set a new speed as long as vehicle speed is still more than 35 MPH.

COMPONENT LOCATIONS

COMPONENT LOCATIONS

Component	Location
Body Control Module (BCM)	Left End Of Instrument Panel On Junction Block
Data Link Connector (DLC)	Lower Left Side Of Instrument Panel
Park/Neutral Position (PNP) Switch	Left Front Side Of Transmission
Powertrain Control Module (PCM)	Left Front Corner Of Engine Compartment
Transmission Control Module (TCM)	Left Front Corner Of Engine Compartment

TROUBLE SHOOTING

ROAD TEST

Perform a road test to verify speed control malfunctions. Ensure speedometer operation is smooth without flutter at all speeds. Speedometer fluttering may cause surging in speed control system. For speedometer diagnosis, see appropriate INSTRUMENT PANELS article. If road test verifies a surge following speed control set and speedometer operates smoothly, see OVERSHOOT/UNDERSHOOT FOLLOWING SPEED CONTROL SET.

If road test verifies an inoperative system, and speedometer operates smoothly, check for:

- Diagnostic Trouble Codes (DTCs). See SELF-DIAGNOSTIC SYSTEM.
- Misadjusted brake lamp switch. See BRAKE SWITCH under REMOVAL & INSTALLATION.
- Poor electrical connections at servo.
- Leaking vacuum reservoir, defective vacuum check valve, leaking vacuum hoses or connections. Perform VACUUM SUPPLY test. See VACUUM SUPPLY under COMPONENT TESTS.
- Secure attachments of S/C servo cable.
- Smooth operation of throttle linkage.
- Defective Powertrain Control Module (PCM) or wiring. See CHECKING POWERTRAIN CONTROL MODULE (PCM) & WIRING under SYSTEM TESTS.
- Defective servo. See SPEED CONTROL SERVO under COMPONENT TESTS.

To verify a speed control electronic malfunction, use a scan tool to check for DTCs. See SELF-DIAGNOSTIC SYSTEM. A speed control malfunction may occur without setting a DTC. If no DTCs are stored, go to CHECKING SPEED CONTROL OPERATION under SYSTEM TESTS.

SPEED CONTROL SLOWS DOWN BY ITSELF

Test Vehicle Speed Sensor (VSS). See DTC P0500: NO VEHICLE SPEED SENSOR SIGNAL under DIAGNOSTIC TESTS. Replace VSS if necessary. If VSS is okay, perform the following:

- Check for transmission Diagnostic Trouble Codes (DTCs). See appropriate ELECTRONIC CONTROLS article in AUTOMATIC TRANSMISSIONS in appropriate MITCHELL® TRANSMISSION SERVICE & REPAIR manual.
- Check for defective speed control switch. See NTC-4: SPEED CONTROL ON/OFF SWITCH or NTC-5: SPEED CONTROL SET/RESUME SWITCH under SYSTEM TESTS.
- Perform vacuum supply test. See VACUUM SUPPLY under COMPONENT TESTS.
- Perform speed control servo test. See SPEED CONTROL SERVO under COMPONENT TESTS.
- Check for defective PCM. See CHECKING POWERTRAIN CONTROL MODULE (PCM) & WIRING under SYSTEM TESTS.

OVERSHOOT/UNDERSHOOT FOLLOWING SPEED CONTROL SET

If operator repeatedly presses and releases set button with their foot off accelerator (lift foot set) to begin speed control operation, vehicle may accelerate and exceed desired set speed by 5 MPH and then decelerate to less than desired set speed before achieving desired set speed.

Speed Control (S/C) has as adaptive strategy that compensates for variations in S/C cable lengths. When S/C is set with vehicle operator's foot off accelerator pedal, S/C compensates for excessive S/C cable slack. If lift foot sets are continually used, speed control overshoot/undershoot condition will develop.

To "unlearn" overshoot/undershoot condition, operator must press and release set button while maintaining desired speed with accelerator pedal, then turn S/C switch to OFF position after waiting 10 seconds. This procedure must be repeated 10-15 times to completely unlearn overshoot/undershoot condition.

Cruise Control Systems
Breeze, Cirrus, Sebring Convertible & Stratus (Cont.)

COMPONENT TESTS

WARNING: Vehicle is equipped with an air bag. Air bag must be deactivated before servicing speed control components on or around steering column. See appropriate AIR BAG RESTRAINT SYSTEMS article.

NOTE: For component locations, See COMPONENT LOCATIONS. For connector terminal identification, see CONNECTOR IDENTIFICATION. For wiring diagram, see WIRING DIAGRAMS.

BRAKE SWITCH

Disconnect brake switch 6-pin connector. Using an ohmmeter, check for continuity at brake switch. *See Fig. 1.* If continuity is not as specified in BRAKE SWITCH CONTINUITY table, check brake switch adjustment. See BRAKE SWITCH under REMOVAL & INSTALLATION. If brake switch adjustment is okay, replace defective brake switch.

BRAKE SWITCH CONTINUITY

Switch Plunger Position	Check Between Terminals	Continuity
Released	5 & 6	Yes
Depressed	1 & 2	Yes
	3 & 4	Yes

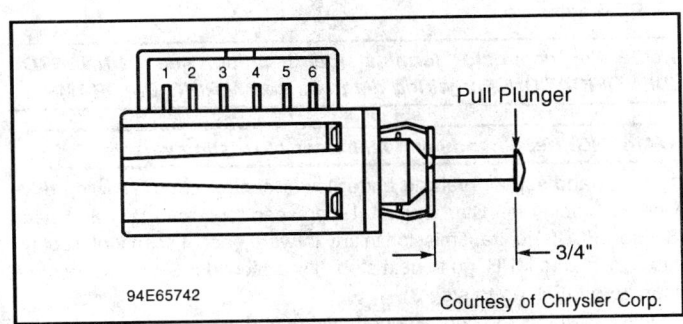

Fig. 1: Identifying Brake Switch Terminals

SPEED CONTROL SERVO

1) Turn ignition switch and speed control switch to ON position, but do not start engine. Disconnect speed control servo 4-pin connector. Connect a jumper wire between Speed Control (S/C) servo harness connector terminal No. 3 and S/C servo terminal No. 3. *See Fig. 5.* Using jumper wires, connect S/C servo terminals No. 2 and No. 4 to ground.

2) Using a hand-held vacuum pump, apply 10-15 in. Hg of vacuum to S/C servo vacuum nipple. Throttle cable should not retract. If throttle cable retracts, replace S/C servo. If throttle cable does not retract, connect servo S/C terminal No. 1 to ground. Throttle cable should now retract and hold position for at least one minute.

3) If throttle cable does not remain retracted, replace servo. If throttle cable remains retracted, remove jumper wire from S/C servo terminal No. 3. Throttle cable should return to released position. If throttle cable does not return to released position, replace S/C servo. If S/C servo functions as described, no problem is indicated at this time.

VACUUM SUPPLY

1) Disconnect vacuum hose at speed control servo. Install vacuum gauge to disconnected vacuum hose. Start engine and observe gauge. Vacuum reading should be a minimum of 10 in. Hg. Turn engine off. Vacuum should continue to hold at a minimum of 10 in. Hg.

2) If vacuum is not as specified, check for kinked or leaking vacuum lines, defective check valve, defective vacuum reservoir and/or poor engine performance. If no problems are found, check speed control servo. See SPEED CONTROL SERVO.

CONNECTOR IDENTIFICATION

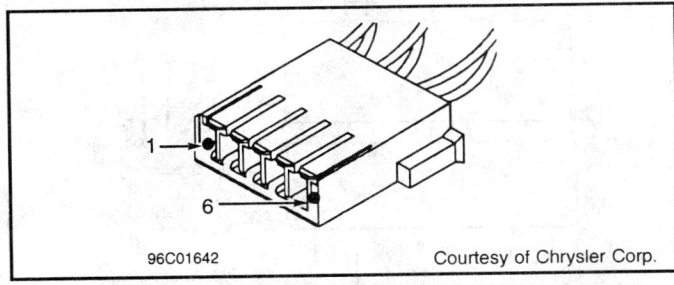

Fig. 2: Identifying Brake Switch Harness Connector Terminals

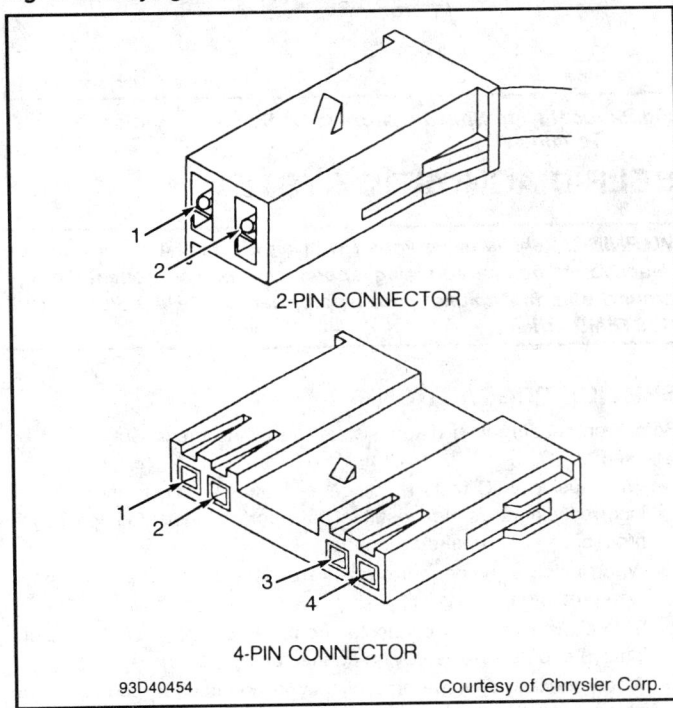

Fig. 3: Identifying Clockspring Connector Terminals

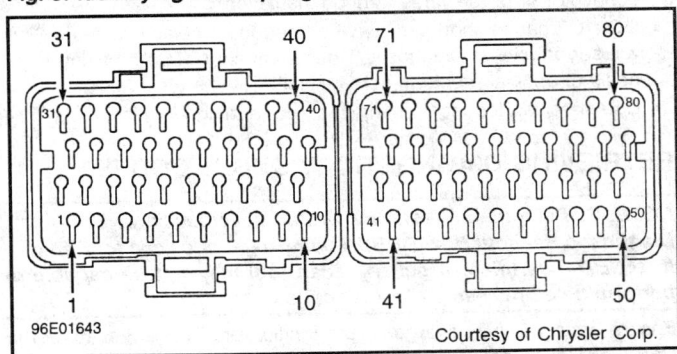

Fig. 4: Identifying Powertrain Control Module (PCM) Connector Terminals

1999 ACCESSORIES & EQUIPMENT
Cruise Control Systems
Breeze, Cirrus, Sebring Convertible & Stratus (Cont.)

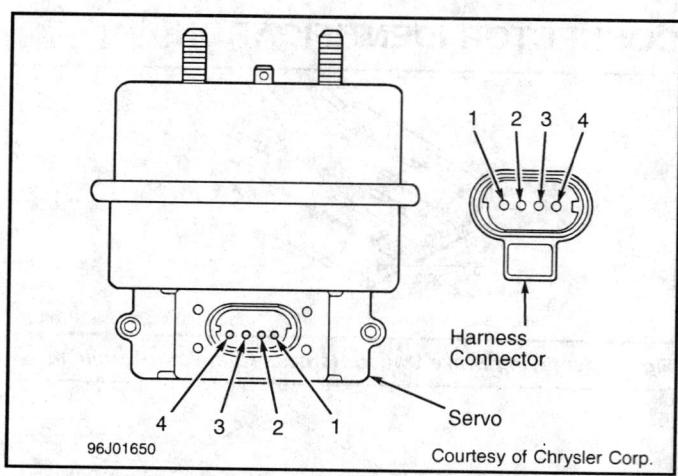

Fig. 5: Identifying Speed Control (S/C) Servo Connector Terminals

SELF-DIAGNOSTIC SYSTEM

WARNING: Vehicle is equipped with an air bag. Air bag must be deactivated before servicing speed control components on or around steering column. See appropriate AIR BAG RESTRAINT SYSTEMS article.

SERVICE PRECAUTIONS

Before proceeding with diagnosis, the following precautions must be followed:

- When using DTC tests for diagnosis, DO NOT skip any steps, or incorrect diagnosis may result. Always perform indicated verification procedure after repairs are made.
- When using a jumper wire, ensure either jumper wire or circuit is fuse-protected.
- Before disconnecting connector from any control module, ensure ignition is off before removing connector.
- When checking voltage or continuity at any control module, probe connector for control module from pin side. DO NOT backprobe connector or probe wires through insulation.
- DO NOT cause short circuits when performing electrical tests. This will set additional Diagnostic Trouble Codes (DTCs), making diagnosis of original problem more difficult.
- Use specified test equipment when performing electrical tests.

RETRIEVING DIAGNOSTIC TROUBLE CODES

NOTE: Self-diagnostic tests are written specifically for Chrysler's Diagnostic Readout Box (DRB). If using a generic scan tool, ensure it is OBD-II certified. A generic scan tool may not be capable of performing all necessary test functions.

Ensure battery is fully charged. Turn ignition off. Connect scan tool to Data Link Connector (DLC). *See Fig. 6.* Turn ignition on. Using scan tool manufacturer's instructions, record all DTCs displayed on scan tool. If any DTCs are retrieved, perform appropriate test under DIAGNOSTIC TESTS. Once all repairs are made, clear DTCs. See CLEARING DIAGNOSTIC TROUBLE CODES. If no DTCs are retrieved and fault still exists, go to CHECKING SPEED CONTROL OPERATION under SYSTEM TESTS.

CLEARING DIAGNOSTIC TROUBLE CODES

Ensure ignition is off. Turn ignition on. Using screen prompts on scan tool, erase DTC from PCM.

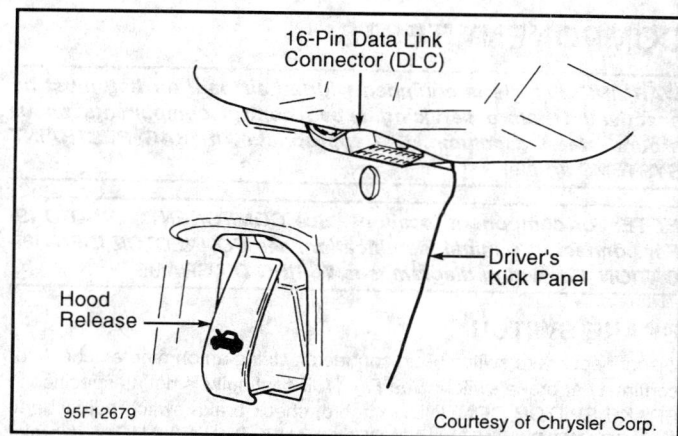

Fig. 6: Locating Engine Data Link Connector

DIAGNOSTIC TESTS

DTC P0500: NO VEHICLE SPEED SENSOR SIGNAL

Possible Causes:

- VSS defective.
- VSS circuit open or shorted.
- Speedometer pinion gear defective.
- PCM defective.

NOTE: For connector terminal identification, see CONNECTOR IDENTIFICATION. For wiring diagram, see WIRING DIAGRAMS.

WARNING: Keep hands and feet clear of rotating wheels.

1) Raise and support vehicle under lower control arms, allowing drive wheels to spin free. Start engine. Using scan tool, read Vehicle Speed Sensor (VSS). Put transmission in any forward gear. If scan tool displays more than zero MPH, go to next step. If scan tool does not display more than zero MPH, go to step **3)**.

2) Inspect wiring and connectors. If wiring and connectors are okay, go to next step. If wiring or connector problems exist, repair as necessary. Perform TEST VER-5A under VERIFICATION TESTS. If wiring is okay, no problem is indicated at this time.

3) If vehicle is equipped with a 4-speed automatic transmission, go to next step. If vehicle is equipped with a 3-speed automatic transmission, go to step **8)**.

4) Using scan tool, read transmission DTCs. If DTC P0731-P0736, P0720 or P1794 is present or pinion factor is not programmed, repair transmission as required. See appropriate ELECTRONIC CONTROLS article in AUTOMATIC TRANSMISSIONS in appropriate MITCHELL® TRANSMISSION SERVICE & REPAIR manual. If DTC P0731-P0736, P0720 or P1794 is not present or pinion factor is programmed, go to next step.

5) Turn ignition off. Disconnect Transmission Control Module (TCM) harness connector. Inspect connector. Clean or repair as necessary. Connect one end of jumper wire to terminal No. 58 (White/Orange wire). Turn ignition on. Using scan tool, read VSS signal. While observing scan tool display, quickly and repeatedly tap other end of jumper wire to ground. If scan tool does not display more than zero MPH, go to next step. If scan tool displays more than zero MPH, repair transmission as required. See appropriate article in TRANSMISSIONS in appropriate MITCHELL® TRANSMISSION SERVICE & REPAIR manual.

6) Turn ignition off. Disconnect PCM connector. Using an ohmmeter, check resistance of VSS signal circuit between PCM connector terminal No. 66 and TCM connector terminal No. 58 (White/Orange wire). If resistance is less than 5 ohms, go to next step. If resistance is 5 ohms or more, repair open VSS signal circuit. Perform TEST VER-5A under VERIFICATION TESTS.

1999 ACCESSORIES & EQUIPMENT
Cruise Control Systems
Breeze, Cirrus, Sebring Convertible & Stratus (Cont.)

CHRY
4-267

7) Using an ohmmeter, check resistance of VSS signal circuit between TCM connector terminal No. 58 and ground (White/Orange wire). If resistance is less than 5 ohms, repair short to ground on VSS signal circuit. Perform TEST VER-5A under VERIFICATION TESTS. If resistance is 5 ohms or more, replace PCM. Perform TEST VER-5A under VERIFICATION TESTS.

8) Turn ignition off. Disconnect 3-pin Vehicle Speed Sensor (VSS) connector. Turn ignition on. Using a voltmeter, check voltage of 8-volt power supply circuit on VSS connector terminal No. 1 (Orange wire). If voltage is more than 7 volts, go to next step. If voltage is 7 volts or less, repair open 8-volt power supply circuit. Perform TEST VER-5A under VERIFICATION TESTS.

9) Using a voltmeter, check voltage of VSS connector signal circuit at VSS connector terminal No. 3 (White/Orange wire). If voltage is more than 4 volts, go to next step. If voltage is 4 volts or less, go to step **13)**.

10) Connect a jumper wire to VSS connector signal circuit at VSS connector terminal No. 3 (White/Orange wire). Using scan tool, read VSS signal. While observing scan tool, quickly and repeatedly tap other end of jumper wire to VSS connector ground circuit at VSS connector. If scan tool displays more than zero MPH, go to next step. If scan tool does not display more than zero MPH, go to step **12)**.

11) Remove VSS sensor from transmission. Inspect speedometer pinion gear. If speedometer pinion gear is okay, replace VSS. Perform TEST VER-5A under VERIFICATION TESTS. If speedometer pinion gear is not okay, repair or replace as necessary. Perform TEST VER-5A under VERIFICATION TESTS.

12) Disconnect VSS connector. Using an ohmmeter, check resistance between ground and VSS ground circuit at VSS connector terminal No. 2 (Black/Light Blue wire). If resistance is less than 5 ohms, go to next step. If resistance is 5 ohms or more, repair VSS ground circuit.

13) Turn ignition off. Disconnect VSS connector. and PCM connector. Inspect connectors. Clean or repair as necessary. Using an ohmmeter, check resistance of VSS signal circuit between VSS connector and PCM connector terminal No. 66 (White/Orange wire). If resistance is less than 5 ohms, replace PCM. Perform TEST VER-5A under VERIFICATION TESTS. If resistance is 5 ohms or more, repair open VSS signal circuit. Perform TEST VER-5A under VERIFICATION TESTS.

14) Disconnect VSS connector. Using an ohmmeter, check resistance of VSS signal circuit between PCM connector terminal No. 66 and ground. If resistance is less than 5 ohms, repair short to ground in VSS signal circuit. Perform TEST VER-5A under VERIFICATION TESTS. If resistance is 5 ohms or more, replace PCM. Perform TEST VER-5A under VERIFICATION TESTS.

DTC P1595: SPEED CONTROL SOLENOID CIRCUITS

DTC P1595 will set if vacuum and vent solenoids do not respond when actuated by PCM.

Possible Causes:

- Ground circuit open.
- Speed Control (S/C) brake switch output circuit open.
- S/C power supply circuit open or shorted.
- S/C servo defective.
- S/C vacuum solenoid control circuit open or shorted.
- S/C vent solenoid control circuit open or shorted.
- Brake switch defective or out of adjustment.
- Defective PCM.

NOTE: *For component locations, see COMPONENT LOCATIONS. For connector terminal identification, see CONNECTOR IDENTIFICATION. For wiring diagram, see WIRING DIAGRAMS.*

Breeze, Cirrus & Stratus – 1) Turn ignition on. Turn S/C on. Using scan tool, actuate S/C vent solenoid. If S/C servo clicks, go to next step. If S/C servo does not click, go to step **13)**.

2) Using scan tool, actuate S/C vacuum solenoid. If S/C servo clicks, go to next step. If S/C servo does not click, go to step **6)**.

3) Inspect S/C wiring and connectors. Clean or repair as necessary. Perform TEST VER-4A under VERIFICATION TESTS. If wiring and connectors are okay, go to next step.

4) Using scan tool, actuate S/C vent solenoid. Wiggle wiring harness between S/C servo and brake switch to PCM while scan tool is still actuating speed control vent solenoid. If wiggling did not cause interruption of S/C servo actuation, go to next step. If wiggling caused interruption of S/C servo actuation, repair wiring harness as necessary. Perform TEST VER-4A under VERIFICATION TESTS.

5) Using scan tool, actuate S/C vacuum solenoid. Wiggle wiring harness between S/C servo and brake switch to PCM while scan tool is still actuating speed control vacuum solenoid. If wiggling did not cause an interruption of S/C servo actuation, test is complete. If wiggling caused an interruption of S/C servo actuation, repair wiring harness as necessary. Perform TEST VER-4A under VERIFICATION TESTS.

NOTE: *Ensure brake pedal is NOT depressed during the following steps.*

6) Turn ignition off. Disconnect S/C servo 4-pin connector. Inspect all related wiring and connectors and repair as necessary. Turn ignition on. Turn S/C switch on. Using voltmeter, check voltage of brake switch output circuit at S/C servo connector terminal No. 3 (Dark Blue/Red wire). If voltage is 10 volts or less, go to next step. If voltage is more than 10 volts, go to step **14)**.

7) Disconnect brake switch connector. Inspect all related wiring and connectors and repair as necessary. Turn ignition on. Using voltmeter, check voltage of S/C power supply circuit at brake switch connector terminal No. 3 (Yellow/Pink wire). If voltage is more than 10 volts, go to next step. If voltage is 10 volts or less, go to step **10)**.

8) Check brake switch adjustment. See BRAKE SWITCH under REMOVAL & INSTALLATION. Adjust as necessary. Perform TEST VER-4A under VERIFICATION TESTS. If brake switch adjustment is okay, go to next step.

9) Turn ignition off. Disconnect brake switch connector and S/C servo connector. Using an ohmmeter, check resistance between ground and brake switch output circuit at S/C servo connector No. 3 (Dark Blue/Red wire). If resistance is 5 ohms or more, go to step **22)**. If resistance is less than 5 ohms, repair short to ground. Perform TEST VER-4A under VERIFICATION TESTS.

10) Turn ignition off. Disconnect brake switch connector and S/C servo connector. Using ohmmeter, check resistance between ground and brake switch output circuit at S/C servo connector No. 3 (Dark Blue/Red wire). If resistance is 5 ohms or more, go to next step. If resistance is less than 5 ohms, repair short to ground. Perform TEST VER-4A under VERIFICATION TESTS.

11) Using an ohmmeter, check resistance of S/C power supply circuit between brake switch connector terminal No. 3 (Yellow/Pink wire) and PCM connector C1, terminal No. 5 (Yellow/Red wire). If resistance is less than 5 ohms, go to next step. If resistance is 5 ohms or more, repair open S/C power supply circuit. See WIRING DIAGRAMS. Perform TEST VER-4A under VERIFICATION TESTS.

12) Turn ignition on. Turn S/C on. Using scan tool, actuate S/C vent solenoid. Wiggle wiring harness between S/C servo and brake switch to PCM. If wiggling interrupts S/C servo actuation, repair wiring as necessary. If wiggling does not interrupt S/C servo actuation, replace PCM. Perform TEST VER-4A under VERIFICATION TESTS.

13) Turn ignition off. Disconnect S/C servo connector. Turn ignition on. Turn S/C switch on. Using voltmeter, check voltage on brake switch output circuit at S/C servo connector terminal No. 3 (Dark Blue/Red wire). If voltage is more than 10 volts, go to next step. If voltage is 10 volts or less, go to step **19)**.

14) Using an ohmmeter, check resistance of ground circuit at S/C servo connector terminal No. 4 (Black wire). If resistance is less than 5 ohms, go to next step. If resistance is 5 ohms or more, repair open ground circuit. Perform TEST VER-4A under VERIFICATION TESTS.

15) Disconnect PCM connector C2. Using an ohmmeter, check resistance of S/C vacuum solenoid control circuit between PCM connector

CHRY
4-268

1999 ACCESSORIES & EQUIPMENT
Cruise Control Systems
Breeze, Cirrus, Sebring Convertible & Stratus (Cont.)

C2, terminal No. 56 and S/C servo connector terminal No. 1 (White/Violet wire). If resistance is less than 5 ohms, go to next step. If resistance is 5 ohms or more, repair open circuit. Perform TEST VER-4A under VERIFICATION TESTS.

16) Using an ohmmeter, check resistance of S/C vacuum solenoid control circuit between ground and S/C servo connector terminal No. 1 (White/Violet wire). If resistance is less than 5 ohms, repair short to ground. Perform TEST VER-4A under VERIFICATION TESTS. If resistance is 5 ohms or more, go to next step.

17) Using an ohmmeter, check resistance of S/C vent solenoid control circuit between S/C servo connector terminal No. 2 and PCM connector C2, terminal No. 80 (Light Green/Red wire). If resistance is less than 5 ohms, go to next step. If resistance is 5 ohms or more, repair open circuit. Perform TEST VER-2A under VERIFICATION TESTS.

18) Using an ohmmeter, check resistance of S/C vent solenoid control circuit between ground and S/C servo connector terminal No. 2 (Light Green/Red wire). If resistance is less than 5 ohms, repair short to ground. Perform TEST VER-2A under VERIFICATION TESTS. If resistance is 5 ohms or more, replace S/C servo. Perform TEST VER-4A under VERIFICATION TESTS.

19) Disconnect brake switch connector. Turn ignition on. Using voltmeter, check voltage on S/C power supply circuit at brake switch connector terminal No. 3 (Yellow/Pink wire). If voltage is more than 10 volts, go to next step. If voltage is 10 volts or less, go to step **23)**.

20) Disconnect S/C servo connector. Using an ohmmeter, check resistance of S/C brake switch output circuit on S/C servo connector terminal No. 3 (Dark Blue/Red wire). If resistance is less than 5 ohms, repair short to ground. Perform TEST VER-4A under VERIFICATION TESTS. If resistance is 5 ohms or more, go to next step.

21) Check brake switch adjustment. See BRAKE SWITCH under REMOVAL & INSTALLATION. Adjust as necessary. Perform TEST VER-4A under VERIFICATION TESTS. If brake switch adjustment is okay, go to next step.

22) Using an ohmmeter, check resistance of brake switch output circuit between brake switch connector and servo connector terminal No. 3 (Dark Blue/Red wire). If resistance is less than 5 ohms, replace brake switch. Perform TEST VER-4A under VERIFICATION TESTS. If resistance is 5 ohms or more, repair open circuit. Perform TEST VER-4A under VERIFICATION TESTS.

23) Using an ohmmeter, check resistance between ground and S/C servo connector terminal No. 3 (Dark Blue/Red wire). If resistance 5 ohms or more, go to next step. If resistance is less than 5 ohms, repair short to ground. Perform TEST VER-4A under VERIFICATION TESTS.

24) Using an ohmmeter, check resistance of S/C power supply circuit between brake switch connector terminal No. 3 (Yellow/Pink wire) and PCM connector C1, terminal No. 5 (Yellow/Red wire). If resistance is less than 5 ohms, replace PCM. Perform TEST VER-4A under VERIFICATION TESTS. If resistance is 5 ohms or more, repair open circuit. Perform TEST VER-4A under VERIFICATION TESTS.

Sebring Convertible – 1) Turn ignition on. Turn S/C on. Using scan tool, actuate S/C vent solenoid. If S/C servo clicks, go to next step. If S/C servo does not click, go to step **6)**.

2) Turn ignition off. Inspect wiring and connectors in S/C circuit. See WIRING DIAGRAMS. Repair as necessary. Perform TEST VER-4A under VERIFICATION TESTS. If wiring and connectors are okay, go to next step.

3) Turn ignition and S/C on. Using scan tool, actuate S/C vacuum solenoid. If S/C servo clicks, go to next step. If S/C servo does not click, go to step **5)**.

4) Using scan tool, actuate S/C vacuum solenoid. Wiggle wiring harness between S/C servo, brake switch and PCM. If wiggling interrupted S/C servo actuation, repair wiring where wiggling caused interruption. Perform TEST VER-4A under VERIFICATION TESTS. If wiggling did not interrupt S/C servo actuation, go to next step.

5) Using scan tool, actuate S/C vent solenoid. Wiggle wiring harness between S/C servo, brake switch and PCM. If wiggling interrupted S/C servo actuation, repair wiring where wiggling caused interruption. Per-

form TEST VER-4A under VERIFICATION TESTS. If wiggling did not interrupt S/C servo actuation, go to next step.

6) Turn ignition off. Disconnect S/C servo connector. Inspect connectors. Clean or repair as necessary. Turn ignition and S/C on. Using a voltmeter, check voltage on S/C brake switch output circuit at S/C servo connector terminal No. 3 (Dark Blue/Red wire). If voltage is more than 10 volts, go to next step. If voltage is 10 volts or less, go to step **12)**.

7) Turn ignition off. Using an ohmmeter, check resistance of ground circuit at S/C servo connector terminal No. 4 (Black wire). If resistance is 5 ohms or more, repair open circuit. Perform TEST VER-4A under VERIFICATION TESTS. If resistance is less than 5 ohms, go to next step.

8) Disconnect PCM connectors. Inspect connectors. Clean or repair as necessary. Using an ohmmeter, check resistance of S/C vacuum solenoid control circuit between PCM connector C2, terminal No. 56 and S/C servo connector terminal No. 1 (White/Violet wire). If resistance is 5 ohms or more, repair open circuit. Perform TEST VER-4A under VERIFICATION TESTS. If resistance is less than 5 ohms, go to next step.

9) Using an ohmmeter, check resistance between ground and S/C vacuum solenoid control circuit at S/C servo connector terminal No. 1 (White/Violet wire). If resistance is less than 5 ohms, repair short to ground. Perform TEST VER-4A under VERIFICATION TESTS. If resistance is 5 ohms or more, go to next step.

10) Using an ohmmeter, check resistance of S/C vent solenoid control circuit between PCM connector C2, terminal No. 80 and S/C servo connector terminal No. 2 (Light Green/Red wire). If resistance is 5 ohms or more, repair open circuit. Perform TEST VER-2A under VERIFICATION TESTS. If resistance is less than 5 ohms, go to next step.

11) Using an ohmmeter, check resistance between ground and S/C vent solenoid control circuit at S/C servo connector terminal No. 2 (Light Green/Red wire). If resistance is less than 5 ohms, repair short to ground. Perform TEST VER-2A under VERIFICATION TESTS. If resistance is 5 ohms or more, replace S/C servo. Perform TEST VER-4A under VERIFICATION TESTS.

12) Turn ignition off. Disconnect brake switch connector. Inspect connector. Clean or repair as necessary. Turn ignition on. Using a voltmeter, check voltage on S/C power supply circuit at brake switch connector terminal No. 3 (Yellow/Pink wire). If voltage is more than 10 volts, go to next step. If voltage is 10 volts or less, go to step **16)**.

13) Turn ignition off. Using an ohmmeter, check resistance between ground and S/C power supply circuit at brake switch connector terminal No. 3 (Yellow/Pink wire). If resistance is less than 5 ohms, repair short to ground. Perform TEST VER-4A under VERIFICATION TESTS. If resistance is 5 ohms or more, go to next step.

14) Check brake switch adjustment. See BRAKE SWITCH under REMOVAL & INSTALLATION. Adjust as necessary. Perform TEST VER-4A under VERIFICATION TESTS. If brake switch adjustment is okay, go to next step.

15) Using an ohmmeter, check resistance of S/C brake switch output circuit between brake switch connector terminal No. 4 and S/C servo connector terminal No. 3 (Dark Blue/Red wire). If resistance is more than 5 ohms, repair open circuit. Perform TEST VER-4A under VERIFICATION TESTS. If resistance is 5 ohms or less, replace brake switch. Perform TEST VER-4A under VERIFICATION TESTS.

16) Turn ignition off. Using an ohmmeter, check resistance between ground and S/C power supply circuit at brake switch connector terminal No. 3 (Yellow/Pink wire). If resistance is less than 5 ohms, repair short to ground. Perform TEST VER-4A under VERIFICATION TESTS. If resistance is 5 ohms or more, go to next step.

17) Disconnect PCM connectors. Inspect connectors. Clean or repair as necessary. Using an ohmmeter, check resistance of S/C power supply circuit between PCM connector C1, terminal No. 5 (Yellow/Red wire) and brake switch connector terminal No. 3 (Yellow/Pink wire). If resistance is 5 ohms or more, repair open circuit. Perform TEST VER-4A under VERIFICATION TESTS. If resistance is less than 5 ohms, replace PCM. Perform TEST VER-4A under VERIFICATION TESTS.

1999 ACCESSORIES & EQUIPMENT
Cruise Control Systems
Breeze, Cirrus, Sebring Convertible & Stratus (Cont.)

CHRY
4-269

DTC P1596: SPEED CONTROL SWITCH ALWAYS HIGH

DTC P1596 will set if open circuit is detected in Speed Control (S/C) ON/OFF switch circuit.

Possible Causes:

- Intermittent wiring harness defect.
- S/C switch ground circuit open.
- S/C switch signal circuit shorted to voltage.
- Defective PCM.
- Defective S/C ON/OFF switch.
- Defective clockspring.

NOTE: For connector terminal identification, see CONNECTOR IDENTIFICATION. For wiring diagram, see WIRING DIAGRAMS. Speed control switch wire colors are not available from manufacturer.

1) Using scan tool, read speed control inputs. While observing scan tool display, push S/C ON/OFF switch several times and leave on. If scan tool displays speed control switch off and on, go to next step. If scan tool does not display speed control switch off and on, go to step **3**).

2) Using scan tool, monitor switch voltage while wiggling wiring between PCM and S/C ON/OFF switch. If voltage was more than 4.9 volts at any time while wiggling, repair wiring. Perform TEST VER-4A under VERIFICATION TESTS. If voltage was 4.9 volts or less while wiggling, no problem is indicated at this time.

3) Turn ignition off. Disconnect S/C ON/OFF switch connector (located behind S/C switch). Using an ohmmeter, check resistance between ground and S/C ON/OFF switch connector ground circuit. See WIRING DIAGRAMS. If resistance is less than 5 ohms, go to next step. If resistance is 5 ohms or more, repair open ground circuit. Perform TEST VER-4A under VERIFICATION TESTS.

4) Turn ignition on. Using a voltmeter, check voltage on S/C switch signal circuit on S/C ON/OFF switch connector. See WIRING DIAGRAMS. On Breeze, Cirrus or Stratus, if voltage is 4.8 volts or less, go to next step. If voltage is more than 4.8 volts, repair short to voltage on signal circuit. Perform TEST VER-4A under VERIFICATION TESTS. On Sebring Convertible, if voltage is 5.5 volts or less, go to next step. If voltage is 5.5 volts or more, repair short to voltage. Perform TEST VER-4A under VERIFICATION TESTS.

5) On all models, turn ignition off. Disconnect PCM connectors. Inspect connectors. Clean or repair as necessary. Using an ohmmeter, check resistance of S/C switch signal circuit between S/C ON/OFF switch and PCM connector C2, terminal No. 41 (Red/Light Green or Pink/Light Green wire). If resistance is less than 5 ohms, go to next step. If resistance is 5 ohms or more, go to step **7**).

6) Using an ohmmeter, check resistance across S/C switch terminals. If resistance is 25,000 ohms or more, replace S/C switch. Perform TEST VER-4A under VERIFICATION TESTS. If resistance is less than 25,000 ohms, replace PCM. Perform TEST VER-4A under VERIFICATION TESTS.

7) Disconnect 4-pin clockspring connector located behind lower steering column shroud. Using an ohmmeter, check resistance of S/C switch signal circuit between 4-pin clockspring connector terminal No. 2 and PCM connector terminal No. 41 (Red/Light Green or Pink/Light Green wire). If resistance is 5 ohms or more, repair open signal circuit between 4-pin clockspring connector and PCM connector terminal No. 41. Perform TEST VER-4A under VERIFICATION TESTS. If resistance is less than 5 ohms, replace clockspring. See appropriate AIR BAG RESTRAINT SYSTEMS article. Perform TEST VER-4A under VERIFICATION TESTS.

DTC P1597: SPEED CONTROL SWITCH ALWAYS LOW

DTC P1597 will set if Speed Control (S/C) switch voltage is less than 4.5 volts for 2 minutes while battery voltage is more than 10.4 volts.

Possible Causes:

- S/C switch signal circuit shorted to ground or sensor ground.
- Defective S/C ON/OFF switch.
- Defective PCM.

NOTE: For connector terminal identification, see CONNECTOR IDENTIFICATION. For wiring diagram, see WIRING DIAGRAMS.

NOTE: Speed control switch wire colors are not available from manufacturer.

1) Using scan tool, record all DTCs and freeze frame data. Erase DTCs. Read speed control switch voltage. If voltage is less than one volt, go to next step. If voltage is one volt or more, test is complete.

2) Turn ignition off. Disconnect S/C ON/OFF switch. Inspect connectors. Clean or repair as necessary. Using an ohmmeter, check resistance between S/C switch signal circuit and sensor ground circuit across S/C ON/OFF switch connector terminals. If resistance is less than 5 ohms, repair short to sensor ground on speed control switch signal circuit. Perform TEST VER-4A under VERIFICATION TESTS. If resistance is 5 ohms or more, go to next step.

3) Turn ignition on. Using scan tool, read S/C switch volts. If voltage is 5 volts, replace S/C ON/OFF switch. Perform TEST VER-4A under VERIFICATION TESTS. If voltage is less than 5 volts, go to next step.

4) Disconnect PCM connector C2. Inspect connector. Clean or repair as necessary. Using an ohmmeter, check resistance between ground and S/C switch signal circuit at PCM connector C2, terminal No. 41 (Red/Light Green wire). If resistance is less than 5 ohms, repair short to ground. Perform TEST VER-4A under VERIFICATION TESTS. If resistance is 5 ohms or more, replace PCM. Perform TEST VER-4A under VERIFICATION TESTS.

SYSTEM TESTS

NOTE: For component locations, See COMPONENT LOCATIONS. For connector terminal identification, see CONNECTOR IDENTIFICATION. For wiring diagram, see WIRING DIAGRAMS.

CHECKING POWERTRAIN CONTROL MODULE (PCM) & WIRING

1) Disconnect PCM connector C2. Remove both Speed Control (S/C) switches and disconnect connectors. Using an ohmmeter, check for continuity between PCM connector C2, terminal No. 41 (Red/Light Green wire) and terminal No. 1 of each S/C switch connector. *See Fig. 4.* If continuity exists, go to next step. If continuity does not exist, repair open circuit.

2) Using an ohmmeter, check for continuity between ground and PCM connector C2, terminal No. 41 (Red/Light Green wire). *See Fig. 4.* If continuity exists, repair short circuit. If continuity does not exist, test switches. See appropriate NTC TEST.

3) Reconnect S/C switches and PCM connector C2. Disconnect S/C servo connector. Turn ignition on. Turn S/C switch On. Using a voltmeter, check voltage at S/C servo connector terminal 3 (Dark Blue/Red wire). Battery voltage should exist. If battery voltage exists, go to next step. If battery voltage does not exist, go to step **16**).

4) Turn S/C and ignition off. Using an ohmmeter, place positive lead on S/C servo terminal No. 3 and negative lead on terminal No. 4. If continuity does not exist, replace S/C servo. If resistance is 50 ohms or more, clean terminals and retest. If resistance is less than 50 ohms, go to next step.

5) Using an ohmmeter, place positive lead on S/C servo terminal No. 3 and negative lead on terminal No. 2. If continuity does not exist, replace S/C servo. If resistance is 50 ohms or more, clean terminals and retest. If resistance is less than 50 ohms, go to next step.

6) Using an ohmmeter, place positive lead on S/C servo terminal No. 3 and negative lead on terminal No. 1. If continuity does not exist, replace S/C servo. If resistance is 50 ohms or more, clean terminals and retest. If resistance is less than 50 ohms, go to next step.

1999 ACCESSORIES & EQUIPMENT
Cruise Control Systems
Breeze, Cirrus, Sebring Convertible & Stratus (Cont.)

7) Using an ohmmeter, check for continuity between ground and S/C servo connector terminal No. 4 (Black wire). If continuity does not exist, repair open ground circuit. If continuity exists, go to next step.

8) Disconnect PCM connectors. Using an ohmmeter, check for continuity between S/C servo connector terminal No. 1 and PCM connector C2, terminal No. 56 (White/Violet wire). If continuity does not exist, repair open circuit. If continuity exists, go to next step.

9) Using an ohmmeter, check for continuity between ground and S/C servo connector terminal No. 1 (White/Violet wire). If continuity exists, repair short circuit. If continuity does not exist, go to next step.

10) Using an ohmmeter, check for continuity between S/C servo connector terminal No. 2 and PCM connector C2, terminal No. 80 (Light Green/Red wire). If continuity does not exist, repair open circuit. If continuity exists, go to next step.

11) Using an ohmmeter, check for continuity between ground and S/C servo connector terminal No. 2 (Light Green/Red wire). If continuity exists, repair short circuit. If continuity does not exist, go to next step.

12) Using an ohmmeter, check for continuity between S/C servo connector terminals No. 1 and 2. If continuity exists, repair short circuit. If continuity does not exist, go to next step.

13) Reconnect S/C servo connector. Ensure brake pedal is not pressed. Using an ohmmeter, check for continuity between ground and PCM connector C2, terminal No. 62 (White/Red wire). If continuity exists, go to step 15). If continuity does not exist, test brake switch. See BRAKE SWITCH under COMPONENT TESTS. If brake switch is okay, go to next step.

14) Using an ohmmeter, check for continuity between PCM connector C2, terminal No. 62 and brake switch connector terminal No. 1 (White/Red wire). If continuity does not exist, repair open circuit. If continuity exists, repair open circuit between brake switch connector terminal No. 2 and ground (Black/Light Green wire).

15) Ensure transmission is in Park or Neutral. Using an ohmmeter, check for continuity between ground and PCM connector C2, terminal No. 76 (Black/White or Black/Light Blue wire). If continuity does not exist, test Park/Neutral Position (PNP) switch and wiring. See NTC-2: PARK/NEUTRAL POSITION (PNP) SWITCH. If continuity exists, go to next step.

16) Turn S/C and ignition off. Using an ohmmeter, check for continuity between S/C servo connector terminal No. 3 (Dark Blue/Red wire) and PCM connector C1, terminal No. 5 (Yellow/Red wire). If continuity exists, go to next step. If continuity does not exist, test brake switch. See BRAKE SWITCH under COMPONENT TESTS. If brake switch is okay, go to step 18).

17) Using an ohmmeter, check for continuity between ground and S/C servo connector terminal No. 3 (Dark Blue/Red wire). If continuity exists, repair short circuit. If continuity does not exist, replace PCM.

18) Using an ohmmeter, check for continuity between S/C servo connector terminal No. 3 and brake switch connector terminal No. 4 (Dark Blue/Red wire). If continuity does not exist, repair open circuit. If continuity exists, go to next step.

19) Using an ohmmeter, check for continuity between brake switch terminal No. 3 (Yellow/Pink wire) to PCM connector C1, terminal No. 5 (Yellow/Red wire). If continuity does not exist, repair open circuit. If continuity exists, no problem is indicated at this time.

CHECKING SPEED CONTROL OPERATION

NOTE: *Perform this test only if there are no DTCs.*

1) Turn ignition on. Using scan tool, monitor Speed Control (S/C) switch inputs. Turn S/C on. If scan tool displays S/C switch ON, go to next step. If scan tool does not display S/C switch ON, go to NTC-4: SPEED CONTROL ON/OFF SWITCH.

2) While observing scan tool, press SET switch several times. If scan tool displays PRESSED and RELEASED, go to next step. If scan tool does not display PRESSED and RELEASED, go to NTC-5: SPEED CONTROL SET/RESUME SWITCH.

3) While observing scan tool, press brake pedal several times. If scan tool displays brake pedal PRESSED and RELEASED, go to next step. If scan tool does not display brake pedal PRESSED and RELEASED, go to NTC-1: BRAKE SWITCH SENSE.

4) While observing scan tool, move gear selector to Drive. If scan tool displays park neutral switch D/R, go to next step. If scan tool does not display park neutral switch D/R, go to NTC-2: PARK/NEUTRAL POSITION (PNP) SWITCH.

5) While observing scan tool, press cancel switch several times. If scan tool displays cancel switch PRESSED or RELEASED, go to next step. If scan tool does not display cancel switch PRESSED or RELEASED, replace cancel switch. Perform TEST VER-4A under VERIFICATION TESTS.

6) While observing scan tool, press resume switch several times. If scan tool displays resume switch PRESSED or RELEASED, go to next step. If scan tool does not display resume switch PRESSED or RELEASED, replace SET/RESUME switch. Perform TEST VER-4A under VERIFICATION TESTS.

7) Turn ignition off. Disconnect S/C servo connector. Inspect connector. Clean or repair as necessary. Turn ignition on. Using scan tool, actuate S/C vent solenoid. Using voltmeter, check voltage on S/C brake switch circuit at S/C servo connector terminal No. 3 (Dark Blue/Red wire). If voltage is more than 10 volts, go to next step. If voltage is 10 volts or less, go to step 17).

8) Start engine and let idle for one minute. Turn engine off. Turn ignition on (engine off). Using scan tool, actuate S/C servo solenoids. If throttle opens and closes, go to NTC-3: CHECKING FOR SPEED CONTROL DENIED MESSAGE. If throttle does not open and close, go to next step.

9) Turn ignition off. Disconnect S/C servo connector. Using an ohmmeter, check resistance of S/C servo ground circuit at S/C servo connector terminal No. 4 (Black wire). If resistance is less than 5 ohms, go to next step. If resistance is 5 ohms or more, repair open ground circuit. Perform TEST VER-4A under VERIFICATION TESTS.

10) Disconnect vacuum supply hose from S/C servo. Connect vacuum gauge to supply hose. Start engine. If vacuum gauge does not read manifold vacuum, repair vacuum supply leak or restriction. Perform TEST VER-4A under VERIFICATION TESTS. If vacuum gauge reads manifold vacuum, turn engine off. Observe vacuum gauge for 10 seconds. If vacuum gauge holds for at least 10 seconds, go to next step. If vacuum gauge does not hold, replace vacuum reservoir. Perform TEST VER-4A under VERIFICATION TESTS.

11) Turn ignition off. Disconnect S/C servo connector. Inspect terminals. If any terminal is damaged, pushed out or miswired, repair as necessary. Perform TEST VER-4A under VERIFICATION TESTS. If terminals are okay, go to next step.

12) Using an ohmmeter, check resistance of S/C brake switch output circuit between S/C servo connector terminal No. 3 (Dark Blue/Red wire) and ground. If resistance is less than 5 ohms, repair short to ground. Perform TEST VER-4A under VERIFICATION TESTS. If resistance is 5 ohms or more, go to next step.

13) Disconnect brake switch connector. Turn ignition on. Using scan tool, actuate S/C vent solenoid. Using a voltmeter, check voltage on S/C power supply circuit at brake switch connector terminal No. 3 (Yellow/Pink wire). If voltage is more than 10 volts, go to next step. If voltage is 10 volts or less, go to step 16).

14) Check brake switch adjustment. See BRAKE SWITCH under REMOVAL & INSTALLATION. If brake switch is adjusted properly, go to next step. If brake switch is not adjusted properly, adjust brake switch. Perform TEST VER-4A under VERIFICATION TESTS.

15) Inspect brake switch connector. If any terminal is damaged, pushed out or miswired, repair as necessary. Perform TEST VER-4A under VERIFICATION TESTS. If terminals are okay, replace brake switch. Perform TEST VER-4A under VERIFICATION TESTS.

16) Inspect brake switch connector. If any terminal is damaged, pushed out or miswired, repair as necessary. Perform TEST VER-4A under VERIFICATION TESTS. If connector is okay, go to step 25).

1999 ACCESSORIES & EQUIPMENT
Cruise Control Systems
Breeze, Cirrus, Sebring Convertible & Stratus (Cont.)

CHRY
4-271

17) Turn ignition off. Using an ohmmeter, check resistance between ground and S/C brake switch output circuit at S/C servo connector terminal No. 3 (Dark Blue/Red wire). If resistance is less than 5 ohms, repair short to ground. Perform TEST VER-4A under VERIFICATION TESTS. If resistance is 5 ohms or more, go to next step.

18) Using an ohmmeter, check resistance of S/C servo ground circuit between ground and S/C servo connector terminal No. 4 (Black wire). If resistance is less than 5 ohms, go to next step. If resistance is 5 ohms or more, repair open ground circuit. Perform TEST VER-4A under VERIFICATION TESTS.

19) Turn ignition off. Disconnect brake switch connector. Inspect connector. Clean or repair as necessary. Turn ignition on. Using scan tool, actuate S/C vent solenoid. Using a voltmeter, check voltage on S/C power supply circuit at brake switch connector terminal No. 3 (Yellow/Pink wire). If voltage is more than 10 volts, go to next step. If voltage is 10 volts or less, go to step **23)**.

20) Turn ignition off. Check brake switch adjustment. If brake switch adjustment is okay, go to next step. If brake switch adjustment is not okay, adjust brake switch. See BRAKE SWITCH under REMOVAL & INSTALLATION. Perform TEST VER-4A under VERIFICATION TESTS.

21) Inspect brake switch connector terminals. If any terminals are damaged, pushed out or miswired, repair as necessary. Perform TEST VER-4A under VERIFICATION TESTS. If terminals are okay, go to next step.

22) Inspect S/C servo connector terminals. If any terminals are damaged, pushed out or miswired, repair as necessary. Perform TEST VER-4A under VERIFICATION TESTS. If terminals are okay, replace brake switch. Perform TEST VER-4A under VERIFICATION TESTS.

23) Turn ignition off. Disconnect brake switch connector. Inspect terminals. If any terminals are damaged, pushed out or miswired, repair as necessary. Perform TEST VER-4A under VERIFICATION TESTS. If terminals are okay, go to next step.

24) Disconnect S/C servo connector. Inspect terminals. If any terminals are damaged, pushed out or miswired, repair as necessary. Perform TEST VER-4A under VERIFICATION TESTS. If terminals are okay, go to next step.

25) Disconnect brake switch connector. Disconnect PCM connectors. Inspect connectors. Clean or repair as necessary. Using an ohmmeter, check resistance of S/C power supply circuit between PCM connector C1, terminal No. 5 (Yellow/Red wire) and brake switch connector terminal No. 3 (Yellow/Pink wire). If resistance is 5 ohms or more, repair open circuit. Perform TEST VER-4A under VERIFICATION TESTS. If resistance is less than 5 ohms, replace PCM. Perform TEST VER-4A under VERIFICATION TESTS.

NTC-1: BRAKE SWITCH SENSE

Possible Causes:
- Ground circuit open.
- Defective brake switch.
- Brake switch sense circuit open or shorted.
- Defective PCM.

1) Turn ignition off. Disconnect brake switch connector. Inspect connector. Clean or repair as necessary. Turn ignition on. Using a voltmeter, check voltage of brake switch sense circuit at brake switch connector terminal No. 1 (White/Red wire). If voltage is more than 10 volts, go to next step. If voltage is 10 volts or less, go to step **3)**.

2) Connect a jumper wire between ground and brake switch connector terminal No. 1 (White/Red wire). Using scan tool, read brake switch input status. If scan tool displays brake switch RELEASED, replace brake switch. Perform TEST VER-4A under VERIFICATION TESTS. If scan tool does not display brake switch RELEASED, repair open ground circuit. Perform TEST VER-4A under VERIFICATION TESTS.

3) Turn ignition off. Disconnect PCM connectors. Inspect connector terminals. If any terminal is damaged, pushed out or miswired, repair as necessary. Perform TEST VER-4A under VERIFICATION TESTS. If terminals are okay, go to next step.

4) Disconnect brake switch connector. Disconnect PCM connectors. Using an ohmmeter, check resistance between ground and brake switch sense circuit at PCM connector C2, terminal No. 62 (White/Red wire). If resistance less than 5 ohms, repair short to ground. Perform TEST VER-4A under VERIFICATION TESTS. If resistance is 5 ohms or more, go to next step.

5) Using an ohmmeter, check resistance of brake switch sense circuit between PCM connector C2, terminal No. 62 and brake switch terminal No. 1 (White/Red wire). If resistance is 5 ohms or more, repair open brake switch sense circuit. Perform TEST VER-4A under VERIFICATION TESTS. If resistance is less than 5 ohms, replace PCM. Perform TEST VER-4A under VERIFICATION TESTS.

NTC-2: PARK/NEUTRAL POSITION (PNP) SWITCH

NOTE: PNP switch is incorporated with Transmission Range Sensor (TRS).

Possible Causes:
- PNP switch sense circuit shorted to ground.
- Defective PNP switch.
- Defective PCM.

1) Disconnect PCM connectors. Disconnect Transmission Range Sensor (TRS) connector. Inspect connector. Clean or repair as necessary. Using an ohmmeter, check resistance between ground and PNP sense circuit at PCM connector C2, terminal No. 76 (Black/White or Black/Light Blue wire). If resistance is less than 5 ohms, repair short to ground. Perform TEST VER-4A under VERIFICATION TESTS. If resistance is 5 ohms or more, go to next step.

2) Connect TRS connector. Place transmission in Drive. Using an ohmmeter, check resistance between ground and PNP sense circuit at PCM connector C2, terminal No. 76 (Black/White or Black/Light Blue wire). If resistance is less than 5 ohms, replace TRS. Perform TEST VER-4A under VERIFICATION TESTS. If resistance is 5 ohms or more, replace PCM. Perform TEST VER-4A under VERIFICATION TESTS.

NTC-3: CHECKING FOR SPEED CONTROL DENIED MESSAGE

At this time speed control switch and servo functions appear to operate properly. Using scan tool, monitor speed control output status. Road test vehicle at speeds more than 35 MPH. Attempt to set speed control. See SCAN TOOL DENIED STATUS table. Items listed in table will not allow speed control to set. The last or most recent cause for speed control not to set is indicated by denied status. Correct fault and recheck system operation.

SCAN TOOL DENIED STATUS

Denied Message	Reason
ON/OFF	PCM Does Not See An ON Signal From Switch At PCM Terminal No. 41
SPEED	Vehicle Speed As Seen By PCM Terminal No. 66 Is Not Greater Than 30 MPH
RPM	Engine RPM Is Excessively High
BRAKE	Brake Switch Sense Circuit Is Open Indicating That Brakes Are Applied
P/N	Park/Neutral Switch Sense Circuit Is Grounded Indicating That Transmission Is In Park Or Neutral
RPM/SPD	PCM Senses Excessive Engine RPM For A Given Vehicle Speed
SOL FLT	PCM Senses A Servo Solenoid Circuit Trouble Code That Is Maturing Or Set In Memory

NTC-4: SPEED CONTROL ON/OFF SWITCH

Possible Causes:
- Ground circuit open.
- Speed Control (S/C) SET/RESUME switch voltage more than 4 volts.
- S/C switch signal circuit shorted to voltage or ground.

CHRY
4-272

1999 ACCESSORIES & EQUIPMENT
Cruise Control Systems
Breeze, Cirrus, Sebring Convertible & Stratus (Cont.)

- S/C ON/OFF switch voltage less than 1 volt or more than 4 volts.
- Defective PCM.

NOTE: Speed control switch wire colors are not available from manufacturer.

1) Using scan tool, read S/C switch voltage. If voltage is more than 4 volts, go to next step. If voltage is 4 volts or less, go to step **5**).

2) Turn ignition off. Disconnect S/C ON/OFF switch. Inspect connector. Clean or repair as necessary. Turn ignition on. Using a voltmeter, check voltage across S/C ON/OFF switch connector terminals. If voltage is more than 4 volts, repair open ground circuit. Perform TEST VER-4A under VERIFICATION TESTS. If voltage is 4 volts or less, go to next step.

3) Using a voltmeter, check voltage on S/C ON/OFF switch signal circuit at S/C ON/OFF switch connector. See WIRING DIAGRAMS. If voltage is more than 6 volts, repair short to voltage. Perform TEST VER-4A under VERIFICATION TESTS. If voltage is 6 volts or less, go to next step.

4) Turn ignition off. Connect a jumper wire between S/C ON/OFF switch signal circuit at S/C ON/OFF switch connector and ground. See WIRING DIAGRAMS. Turn ignition on. Using scan tool, read S/C switch voltage. If voltage is less than one volt, replace S/C ON/OFF switch. Perform TEST VER-4A under VERIFICATION TESTS. If voltage is one volt or more, replace PCM. Perform TEST VER-4A under VERIFICATION TESTS.

5) Turn ignition off. Disconnect S/C SET/RESUME switch. Inspect connector. Clean or repair as necessary. Turn ignition on. Using scan tool, read S/C switch voltage. If voltage is more than 4 volts, replace S/C SET/RESUME switch. Perform TEST VER-4A under VERIFICATION TESTS. If voltage is 4 volts or less, go to next step.

6) Turn ignition off. Disconnect S/C ON/OFF switch. Inspect connector. Clean or repair as necessary. Turn ignition on. Using scan tool, read S/C switch voltage. If voltage is more than 4 volts, replace S/C ON/OFF switch. Perform TEST VER-4A under VERIFICATION TESTS. If voltage is 4 volts or less, go to next step.

7) Turn ignition off. Disconnect PCM. Inspect connectors. Clean or repair as necessary. Using an ohmmeter, check resistance between ground and S/C switch signal circuit from PCM connector C2, terminal No. 41 (Red/Light Green wire). If resistance is less than 5100 ohms, repair short to ground. Perform TEST VER-4A under VERIFICATION TESTS. If resistance is 5100 ohms or more, replace PCM. Perform TEST VER-4A under VERIFICATION TESTS.

NTC-5: SPEED CONTROL SET/RESUME SWITCH
Possible Causes:
- Open circuit.
- Defective Speed Control (S/C) SET/RESUME switch.

NOTE: Speed control switch wire colors are not available from manufacturer.

1) Disconnect S/C SET/RESUME switch connector. Connect a jumper wire between S/C switch signal circuit at S/C SET/RESUME switch connector and ground. See WIRING DIAGRAMS. Using scan tool, read S/C switch voltage. If voltage is less than one volt, replace S/C SET/RESUME switch. Perform TEST VER-4A under VERIFICATION TESTS. If voltage is one volt or more, go to next step.

2) Turn ignition off. Disconnect S/C SET/RESUME switch. Inspect connector. Clean or replace as necessary. Using an ohmmeter, check resistance of ground circuit between S/C SET/RESUME switch connector and ground. See WIRING DIAGRAMS. If resistance is less than 5 ohms, repair open S/C switch signal circuit. Perform TEST VER-4A under VERIFICATION TESTS. If resistance is 5 ohms or more, repair open ground circuit. Perform TEST VER-4A under VERIFICATION TESTS.

VERIFICATION TESTS
TEST VER-2A

NOTE: If PCM has been replaced and correct VIN and mileage have not been programmed, a DTC will be set in ABS and air bag modules. If vehicle is equipped with a Sentry Key Immobilizer Module (SKIM), sentry key data must be updated to enable starting. See COMPUTER RELEARN PROCEDURES article in GENERAL INFORMATION.

1) Inspect vehicle to ensure all engine components are connected. Reassemble and reconnect components as necessary. If any DTCs have not been repaired, go to SELF-DIAGNOSTIC SYSTEM. If all DTCs have been repaired, perform appropriate verification test.

2) If this verification procedure is being performed following a No Trouble Code (NTC) test, check if initial symptom still exists. If initial or another symptom exists, repair is not complete. Check for Technical Service Bulletins (TSBs) or flash updates and return to TROUBLE SHOOTING.

3) Using scan tool, erase DTCs and reset all values in PCM. Disconnect scan tool. Road test vehicle. Use all accessories related to repair. Ensure initial symptom does not exist.

4) Using scan tool, read Global Good Trips. If Global Good Trips is zero, repair is not complete. Check for related TSBs or flash updates and return to TROUBLE SHOOTING.

5) Using scan tool, check for stored DTCs. If repaired DTC or another DTC has set, repair is not complete. Check for related TSBs and return to TROUBLE SHOOTING. If no other DTCs exist, and Global Good Trips is more than zero, repair is complete.

TEST VER-4A

NOTE: If PCM has been replaced and correct VIN and mileage have not been programmed, a DTC will be set in ABS and air bag modules. If vehicle is equipped with a Sentry Key Immobilizer Module (SKIM), sentry key data must be updated to enable starting. See COMPUTER RELEARN PROCEDURES article in GENERAL INFORMATION.

1) If vehicle is equipped with ABS or air bag, enter correct VIN and mileage in PCM. Erase DTCs in ABS and air bag modules. Inspect vehicle to ensure all engine and speed control system components are connected. Reassemble and reconnect components as necessary. Using scan tool, erase DTCs from PCM.

2) Road test vehicle at a speed greater than 30 MPH. Turn S/C switch on. Press and release SET button. If S/C does not engage, repair is not complete. Check for related TSBs and return to TROUBLE SHOOTING, if necessary. If speed control engages, go to next step

3) Quickly depress and release RESUME/ACCEL switch. If vehicle speed increases by 2 MPH, go to next step. If vehicle speed does not increase by 2 MPH, repair is not complete. Return to test that directed you here or perform appropriate test under SYSTEM TESTS.

4) Press and hold COAST switch. Vehicle speed should decrease. If vehicle speed decreases, go to next step. If vehicle speed does not decrease, repair is not complete. Return to test that directed you here or perform appropriate test under SYSTEM TESTS.

5) Using caution, depress and release brake pedal. If S/C disengages, go to next step. If S/C does not disengage, repair is not complete. Return to test that directed you here or perform appropriate test under SYSTEM TESTS.

6) Bring vehicle speed to 25 MPH. Depress speed control RESUME/ACCEL switch. If vehicle resumes to previously set speed, go to next step. If vehicle does not resume to previously set speed, repair is not complete. Return to test that directed you here or perform appropriate test under SYSTEM TESTS.

7) Hold down SET switch. Vehicle speed should decrease. If vehicle speed decreases, go to next step. If vehicle speed did not decrease, repair is not complete. Return to test that directed you here or perform appropriate test under SYSTEM TESTS.

1999 ACCESSORIES & EQUIPMENT
Cruise Control Systems
Breeze, Cirrus, Sebring Convertible & Stratus (Cont.)

CHRY
4-273

8) Ensure vehicle speed is more than 30 MPH and release SET switch. If vehicle sets a new speed, go to next step. If vehicle did not set a new speed, repair is not complete. Return to test that directed you here or perform appropriate test under SYSTEM TESTS.

9) Depress and release CANCEL switch. If S/C disengages, go to next step. If S/C did not disengage, repair is not complete. Return to test that directed you here or perform appropriate test under SYSTEM TESTS.

10) Ensure vehicle speed is greater than 35 MPH. Engage speed control. Turn S/C off. If speed control disengages, system is operating correctly. Repair is complete. If speed control does not disengage, repair is not complete. Return to test that directed you here or perform appropriate test under SYSTEM TESTS.

TEST VER-5A

NOTE: If PCM has been replaced and correct VIN and mileage have not been programmed, a DTC will be set in ABS and air bag modules. If vehicle is equipped with a Sentry Key Immobilizer Module (SKIM), sentry key data must be updated to enable starting. See COMPUTER RELEARN PROCEDURES article in GENERAL INFORMATION.

1) If vehicle is equipped with ABS or air bag, enter correct VIN and mileage in PCM. Erase DTCs in ABS and air bag modules. Inspect vehicle to ensure all engine and speed control system components are connected.

2) If there are any DTCs that have not been repaired, go to SELF-DIAGNOSTIC SYSTEM. After all DTCs have been repaired, run appropriate monitor for previously repaired DTC.

3) Connect scan tool to DLC. Ensure fuel tank is at least 1/4 full. Turn off all accessories. Allow PCM to run appropriate monitor(s).

4) Enabling conditions must be met before PCM will run monitor. Using scan tool, monitor pretest enabling conditions until all conditions have been met. Once enabling conditions have been met, monitor appropriate monitor.

5) If repaired DTC has reset or was seen in monitor while on road test, repair is not complete. Check for TSBs or flash updates and return to TROUBLE SHOOTING.

6) If appropriate monitor ran, good trip counter incremented and no DTCs have been set, repair is complete.

REMOVAL & INSTALLATION

WARNING: Vehicle is equipped with an air bag. Air bag must be deactivated before servicing speed control components on or around steering column. See appropriate AIR BAG RESTRAINT SYSTEMS article.

CAUTION: When battery is disconnected, vehicle computer and memory systems may lose memory data. Driveability problems may exist until computer systems have completed a relearn cycle. See COMPUTER RELEARN PROCEDURES in GENERAL INFORMATION before disconnecting battery.

BRAKE SWITCH

Removal – Fully depress brake pedal and rotate brake switch counterclockwise approximately 30 degrees. Remove brake switch from bracket. Depress lock tabs holding brake switch mounting bracket and separate harness connector from brake switch.

Installation – 1) Before installing brake switch, reset adjustable plunger by pulling on plunger head until plunger reaches end of travel. Connect harness connector to brake switch. Depress brake pedal and insert brake switch into keyed hole in mounting bracket. Rotate brake switch clockwise into locked position.

2) Gently pull back on brake pedal until pedal will go no further. This causes the brake switch plunger to ratchet backward to the correct position. No further adjustment is required.

SPEED CONTROL SERVO

Removal & Installation – 1) Remove speed control cable mounting bracket from servo. Remove servo mounting bracket. Disconnect wiring harness connector and vacuum hose from servo. Pull cable away from servo to expose retaining clip. Remove retaining clip and cable. Remove servo.

2) To install, align hole in speed control cable sleeve with hole in servo pin with throttle in full open position. Install retaining clip. To complete installation, reverse removal procedure. Tighten retaining nuts to 60 INCH lbs. (7 N.m).

SPEED CONTROL SWITCH

Removal & Installation – 1) Speed control switches are mounted on steering wheel and wired through clockspring device under air bag module.

2) Turn ignition off. Deactivate air bag. See appropriate AIR BAG RESTRAINT SYSTEMS article. Remove 2 screws from side of each switch. Rock switch back and forth to remove switch from steering wheel. Disconnect speed control switch connector. To install switch, reverse removal procedure.

WIRING DIAGRAMS

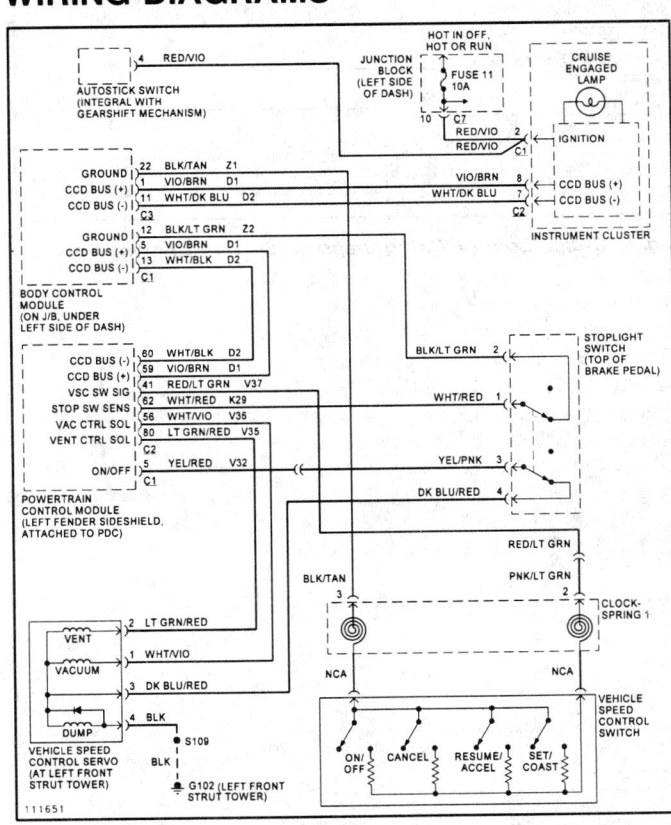

Fig. 7: Cruise Control Wiring Diagram (Breeze, Cirrus & Stratus)

1999 ACCESSORIES & EQUIPMENT
Cruise Control Systems
Breeze, Cirrus, Sebring Convertible & Stratus (Cont.)

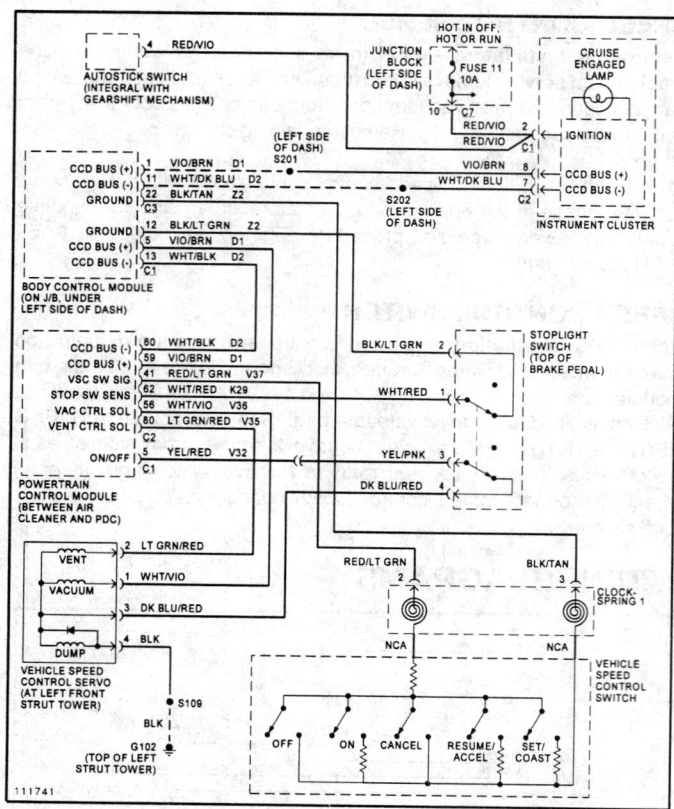

Fig. 8: Cruise Control Wiring Diagram (Sebring Convertible)

Cruise Control Systems
Caravan, Town & Country, & Voyager

CAUTION: When battery is disconnected, vehicle computer and memory systems may lose memory data. Driveability problems may exist until computer systems have completed a relearn cycle. See COMPUTER RELEARN PROCEDURES article in GENERAL INFORMATION before disconnecting battery.

DESCRIPTION

The speed (cruise) control system is electronically controlled and vacuum operated. The electronic control is integrated into the Powertrain Control Module (PCM) located on left front corner of engine compartment. System consists of the following components: Powertrain Control Module (PCM), servo, speed control switches, vacuum reservoir, vehicle speed sensor, speed control relay and brake switch.

System controls are located on each side of steering wheel air bag module and consist of ON/OFF, CANCEL, RES/ACCEL and SET/COAST buttons. System is designed to operate at speeds above 30 MPH.

OPERATION

SYSTEM CONTROLS

To Set Speed Control – Press ON/OFF button to turn speed control system on. Accelerate to desired speed (minimum of 35 MPH) and press SET/COAST button. Vehicle speed will be maintained.

NOTE: Speed control system will automatically disengage when vehicle speed decreases to less than 35 MPH or increases to more than 85 MPH.

To Disengage Speed Control – Press brake pedal. Press CANCEL button. Press ON/OFF button. If ON/OFF button is used, set speed will be erased from memory.

To Resume Previous Speed – If set speed has not been erased from memory and vehicle speed is more than 35 MPH, press RES/ACCEL button.

To Increase Speed – With speed control system on, increase set speed by rapidly pressing and releasing RES/ACCEL button. Each pressing of button will cause speed increase of 2 MPH. For example, pressing button 3 times will increase speed by 6 MPH. To increase speed gradually, hold RES/ACCEL button down until desired speed is reached. When button is released, new set speed will be maintained.

To Decrease Speed – With speed control system on, decrease set speed by pressing SET/COAST button. Vehicle speed will gradually decrease. Releasing button will set a new speed as long as vehicle speed is still more than 35 MPH.

COMPONENT LOCATIONS

COMPONENT LOCATIONS

Component	Location
Data Link Connector (DLC)	Lower Left Side Of Instrument Panel
Output Speed Sensor	Front Side Of Transmission Next To Manual Shift Lever
Powertrain Control Module (PCM)	Left Front Corner Of Engine Compartment
Transmission Control Module (TCM)	Right Front Corner Of Engine Compartment
Transmission Range Switch (TRS) Or Park/Neutral Position (PNP) Switch	Top Of Transmission
Vehicle Speed Sensor (VSS)	On Transmission Extension Housing

TROUBLE SHOOTING

ROAD TEST

Perform a road test to verify speed control malfunctions. Ensure speedometer operation is smooth without flutter at all speeds. Speedometer fluttering may cause surging in speed control system. For speedometer diagnosis, see appropriate INSTRUMENT PANELS article. If road test verifies a surge following speed control set and speedometer operates smoothly, see OVERSHOOT/UNDERSHOOT FOLLOWING SPEED CONTROL SET.

If road test verifies an inoperative system, and speedometer operates smoothly, check for:

- DTCs. See SELF-DIAGNOSTIC SYSTEM.
- Misadjusted brake switch. See BRAKE SWITCH under REMOVAL & INSTALLATION.
- Poor electrical connections at servo.
- Leaking vacuum reservoir, check valve, hoses or connections. See VACUUM SUPPLY under COMPONENT TESTS.
- Secure attachments of S/C servo cable.
- Smooth operation of throttle linkage.
- Defective PCM or wiring. See CHECKING POWERTRAIN CONTROL MODULE (PCM) & WIRING under SYSTEM TESTS.
- Defective servo. See SPEED CONTROL SERVO under COMPONENT TESTS.

To verify a speed control electronic malfunction, use a scan tool to check for DTCs. See SELF-DIAGNOSTIC SYSTEM. A speed control malfunction may occur without setting a DTC. If no DTCs are stored, go to CHECKING SPEED CONTROL OPERATION under SYSTEM TESTS.

SPEED CONTROL SLOWS DOWN BY ITSELF

Test Vehicle Speed Sensor (VSS). See DTC P0500: NO VEHICLE SPEED SENSOR SIGNAL under DIAGNOSTIC TESTS. Replace VSS, if necessary. If VSS is okay, perform the following:

- Check for transmission Diagnostic Trouble Codes (DTCs). See appropriate ELECTRONIC CONTROLS article in TRANSMISSIONS in appropriate MITCHELL® TRANSMISSION SERVICE & REPAIR manual.
- Check for defective speed control switch. See NTC-4: SPEED CONTROL ON/OFF SWITCH under SYSTEM TESTS.
- Perform vacuum supply test. See VACUUM SUPPLY under COMPONENT TESTS.
- Perform speed control servo test. See SPEED CONTROL SERVO under COMPONENT TESTS.
- Check for defective PCM. See CHECKING POWERTRAIN CONTROL MODULE (PCM) & WIRING under SYSTEM TESTS.

OVERSHOOT/UNDERSHOOT FOLLOWING SPEED CONTROL SET

If operator repeatedly presses and releases set button with their foot off accelerator (lift foot set) to begin speed control operation, vehicle may accelerate and exceed desired set speed by 5 MPH and then decelerate to less than desired set speed before achieving desired set speed.

Speed Control (S/C) has as adaptive strategy that compensates for variations in S/C cable lengths. When S/C is set with vehicle operator's foot off accelerator pedal, S/C compensates for excessive S/C cable slack. If lift foot sets are continually used, speed control overshoot/undershoot condition will develop.

To "unlearn" overshoot/undershoot condition, operator must press and release set button while maintaining desired speed with accelerator pedal, then turn S/C switch off after waiting 10 seconds. This procedure must be repeated 10-15 times to completely unlearn overshoot/undershoot condition.

CHRY
4-276

1999 ACCESSORIES & EQUIPMENT
Cruise Control Systems
Caravan, Town & Country, & Voyager (Cont.)

COMPONENT TESTS

WARNING: Vehicle is equipped with an air bag. Air bag must be deactivated before servicing speed control components on or around steering column. See AIR BAG RESTRAINT SYSTEMS – TRUCKS article.

NOTE: For component location, See COMPONENT LOCATIONS. For connector terminal identification, see CONNECTOR IDENTIFICATION. For wiring diagram, see WIRING DIAGRAMS.

BRAKE SWITCH

Disconnect brake switch 6-pin connector. Using an ohmmeter, check for continuity at brake switch. *See Fig. 1.* If continuity is not as specified in BRAKE SWITCH CONTINUITY table, check brake switch adjustment. See BRAKE SWITCH under REMOVAL & INSTALLATION. If brake switch adjustment is okay, replace defective brake switch.

BRAKE SWITCH CONTINUITY

Switch Plunger Position	Check Between Terminals	Continuity
Released	5 & 6	Yes
Depressed	1 & 2	Yes
	3 & 4	Yes

SPEED CONTROL SERVO

1) Turn ignition switch and speed control switch on, but do not start engine. Disconnect Speed Control (S/C) servo 4-pin connector. Connect a jumper wire between S/C servo harness connector terminal No. 3 and S/C servo terminal No. 3. Using jumper wires, connect S/C servo terminals No. 2 and No. 4 to ground.

2) Using a hand-held vacuum pump, apply 10-15 in. Hg of vacuum to S/C servo vacuum nipple. Throttle cable should not retract. If throttle cable retracts, replace S/C servo. If throttle cable does not retract, connect S/C servo terminal No. 1 to ground. Throttle cable should now retract and hold position for at least one minute.

3) If throttle cable does not remain retracted, replace S/C servo. If throttle cable remains retracted, remove jumper wire from S/C servo terminal No. 3. Throttle cable should return to released position. If throttle cable does not return to released position, replace S/C servo. If servo functions as described, no problem is indicated at this time.

VACUUM SUPPLY

1) Disconnect vacuum hose at speed control servo. Install vacuum gauge to disconnected vacuum hose. Start engine and observe gauge. Vacuum reading should be a minimum of 10 in. Hg. Turn engine off. Vacuum should continue to hold at a minimum of 10 in. Hg.

2) If vacuum is not as specified, check for kinked or leaking vacuum lines, defective check valve, defective vacuum reservoir and/or poor engine performance. If no problems are found, check speed control servo. See SPEED CONTROL SERVO.

CONNECTOR IDENTIFICATION

SELF-DIAGNOSTIC SYSTEM

WARNING: Vehicle is equipped with an air bag. Air bag must be deactivated before servicing speed control components on or around steering column. See AIR BAG RESTRAINT SYSTEMS – TRUCKS article.

SERVICE PRECAUTIONS

Before proceeding with diagnosis, the following precautions must be followed:

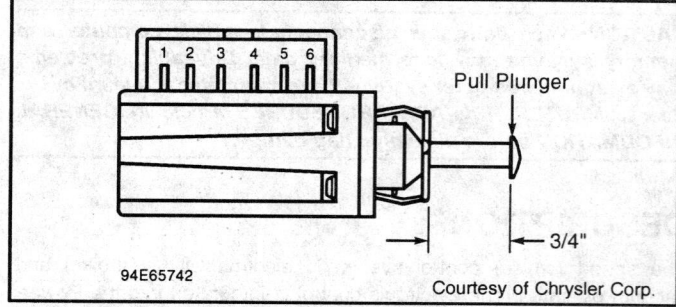

Fig. 1: Identifying Brake Switch Terminals

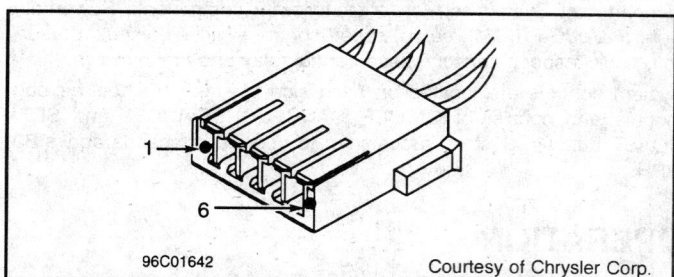

Fig. 2: Identifying Brake Switch Harness Connector Terminals

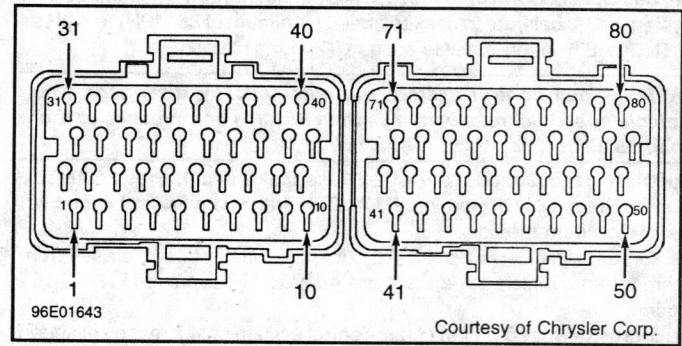

Fig. 3: Identifying Powertrain Control Module (PCM) Connector Terminals

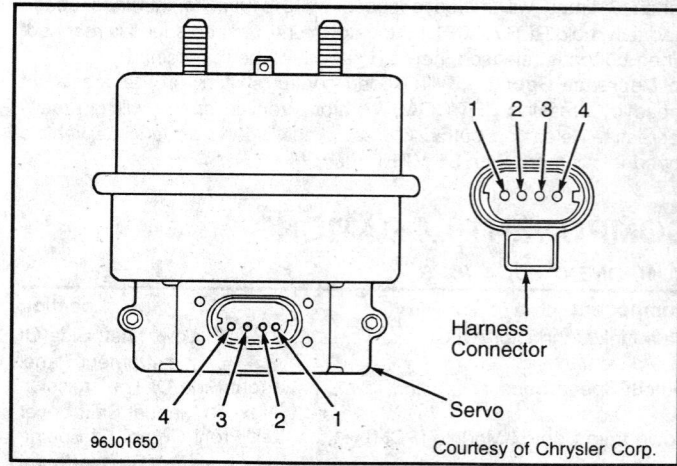

Fig. 4: Identifying Speed Control (S/C) Servo Connector Terminals

- When using Diagnostic Trouble Code (DTC) tests for diagnosis, DO NOT skip any steps, or incorrect diagnosis may result. Always perform indicated verification procedure after repairs are made.
- When using a jumper wire, ensure either jumper wire or circuit is fuse-protected.

Cruise Control Systems
Caravan, Town & Country, & Voyager (Cont.)

- Before disconnecting connector from any control module, ensure ignition is off before removing connector.
- When checking voltage or continuity at any control module, probe connector for control module from pin side. DO NOT backprobe connector or probe wires through insulation.
- DO NOT cause short circuits when performing electrical tests. This will set additional DTCs, making diagnosis of original problem more difficult.
- Use specified test equipment when performing electrical tests.

RETRIEVING DIAGNOSTIC TROUBLE CODES

NOTE: Self-diagnostic tests are written specifically for Chrysler's Diagnostic Readout Box (DRB). If using a generic scan tool, ensure it is OBD-II certified. A generic scan tool may not be capable of performing all necessary test functions.

Ensure battery is fully charged. Turn ignition off. Connect scan tool to Data Link Connector (DLC). *See Fig. 5.* Turn ignition on. Using scan tool manufacturer's instructions, record all DTCs displayed on scan tool. If any DTCs are retrieved, perform appropriate test under DIAGNOSTIC TESTS. Once all repairs are made, clear DTCs. See CLEARING DIAGNOSTIC TROUBLE CODES. If no DTCs are retrieved and fault still exists, go to CHECKING SPEED CONTROL OPERATION under SYSTEM TESTS.

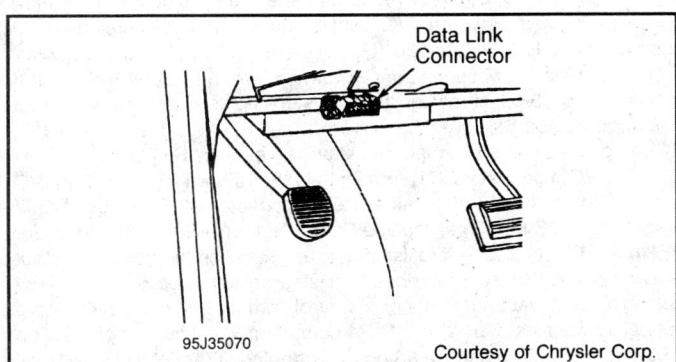

95J35070   Courtesy of Chrysler Corp.

Fig. 5: Locating Data Link Connector

CLEARING DIAGNOSTIC TROUBLE CODES

Ensure ignition is off. Turn ignition on. Using screen prompts on scan tool, erase DTCs from PCM.

DIAGNOSTIC TESTS

DTC P0500: NO VEHICLE SPEED SENSOR SIGNAL

Vehicle Speed Sensor (VSS) is monitored with engine running, transmission not in Park or Neutral, brakes not applied and engine speed more than 1500 RPM. On 3-speed transmission, DTC P0500 will set if there is no signal from VSS for more than 11 seconds on 2 consecutive trips. On 4-speed transmission, DTC P0500 will set if there is no VSS signal from Transmission Control Module (TCM) for more than 11 seconds on 2 consecutive trips.

Possible Causes:
- VSS defective.
- VSS circuit open or shorted.
- Speedometer pinion gear defective.
- PCM defective.

NOTE: For connector terminal identification, see CONNECTOR IDENTIFICATION. For wiring diagram, see WIRING DIAGRAMS.

3-Speed Transmission – 1) Raise drive wheels to spin free. Start engine. Using scan tool, read Vehicle Speed Sensor (VSS). Put transmission in any forward gear. If scan tool displays more than zero MPH, go to next step. If scan tool does not display more than zero MPH, go to step **3)**.

2) Inspect wiring and connectors. If wiring and connectors are okay, go to next step. If wiring or connector problems exist, repair as necessary. Perform TEST VER-5A under VERIFICATION TESTS. If wiring is okay, test is complete.

3) Disconnect VSS connector. Inspect connectors. Clean or repair as necessary. Turn ignition on. Using a voltmeter, check voltage on 8-volt power supply circuit at VSS connector terminal No. 1 (Orange wire). If voltage is more than 7 volts, go to next step. If voltage is 7 volts or less, repair open circuit. Perform TEST VER-5A under VERIFICATION TESTS.

4) Using a voltmeter, check voltage on VSS signal circuit at VSS connector terminal No. 3 (White/Orange wire). If voltage is more than 4 volts, go to next step. If voltage is 4 volts or less, go to step **9)**.

5) Connect a jumper wire between VSS signal circuit and VSS ground circuit at VSS connector terminals No. 2 and 3 (White/Orange wire and Black/Light Blue wire). Using scan tool, read VSS signal. While observing display, quickly and repeatedly disconnect and reconnect jumper wire. If display shows more than zero MPH, go to next step. If display shows zero MPH, go to step **7)**.

6) Turn ignition off. Remove VSS. Inspect speedometer pinion gear. Repair as necessary. Perform TEST VER-5A under VERIFICATION TESTS. If pinion gear is okay, replace VSS. Perform TEST VER-5A under VERIFICATION TESTS.

7) Turn ignition off. Using an ohmmeter, check resistance between engine ground and sensor ground circuit at VSS connector terminal No. 2 (Black/Light Blue wire). If resistance is 5 ohms or more, repair open ground circuit. Perform TEST VER-5A under VERIFICATION TESTS. If resistance is less than 5 ohms, go to next step.

8) Disconnect PCM connectors. Inspect connectors. Clean or repair as necessary. If any terminal is damaged, pushed out or miswired, repair as necessary. Perform TEST VER-5A under VERIFICATION TESTS. If terminals are okay, replace PCM. Perform TEST VER-5A under VERIFICATION TESTS.

9) Turn ignition off. Disconnect PCM connectors. Inspect connectors. Clean or repair as necessary. Using an ohmmeter, check resistance of VSS signal circuit between VSS connector terminal No. 3 and PCM connector C2, terminal No. 66 (White/Orange wire). If resistance is 5 ohms or more, repair open circuit. Perform TEST VER-5A under VERIFICATION TESTS. If resistance is less than 5 ohms, go to next step.

10) Using scan tool in ohmmeter mode, check resistance between ground and VSS signal circuit at PCM connector C2, terminal No. 66 (White/Orange wire). If resistance is less than 5 ohms, repair short to ground. Perform TEST VER-5A under VERIFICATION TESTS. If resistance is 5 ohms or more, replace PCM. Perform TEST VER-5A under VERIFICATION TESTS.

4-Speed Transmission – 1) Raise drive wheels to spin free. Start engine. Using scan tool, read Vehicle Speed Sensor (VSS). Put transmission in any forward gear. If scan tool displays more than zero MPH, go to next step. If scan tool does not display more than zero MPH, go to step **3)**.

2) Turn ignition off. Inspect wiring and connectors. If wiring and connectors are okay, go to next step. If wiring or connector problems exist, repair as necessary. Perform TEST VER-5A under VERIFICATION TESTS. If wiring is okay, test is complete.

3) Using scan tool, read transmission DTCs. If DTC P0731, P0734, P0736, P0715, P0720 or P1794 is present or pinion factor is not programmed, repair transmission as required. See appropriate article in AUTOMATIC TRANSMISSIONS in appropriate MITCHELL® TRANSMISSION SERVICE & REPAIR manual. If DTC P0731, P0734, P0736, P0715, P0720 or P1794 DTCs is not present and pinion factor is programmed, go to next step.

4) Turn ignition off. Disconnect Transmission Control Module (TCM) harness connector. Inspect connectors. Clean or repair as necessary. Connect one end of jumper wire to terminal No. 58 (White/Orange wire). Turn ignition on. Using scan tool, read VSS signal. While observing scan tool display, quickly and repeatedly tap other end of jumper wire to

CHRY
4-278

1999 ACCESSORIES & EQUIPMENT
Cruise Control Systems
Caravan, Town & Country, & Voyager (Cont.)

ground. If scan tool displays more than zero MPH, go to next step. If scan tool does not display more than zero MPH, go to step 10).

5) Turn ignition off. Disconnect PCM connector. Using an ohmmeter, check resistance of VSS signal circuit between PCM connector terminal No. 66 and TCM connector terminal No. 58 (White/Orange wire). If resistance is less than 5 ohms, go to next step. If resistance is 5 ohms or more, go to step 7).

6) Disconnect Output Speed Sensor (OSS) connector. Inspect connectors. Clean or repair as necessary. Using an ohmmeter, check resistance between ground and OSS signal circuit at TCM connector terminal No. 14 (Light Green/White wire). If resistance is less than 5 ohms, repair short to ground. Perform TEST VER-5A under VERIFICATION TESTS. If resistance is 5 ohms or more, replace OSS. Perform TEST VER-5A under VERIFICATION TESTS.

7) Turn ignition off. Using an ohmmeter, check resistance between OSS ground circuit at TCM connector terminal No. 13 (Dark Blue/Black wire) and OSS signal circuit at TCM connector terminal No. 14 (Light Green/White wire). If resistance is 300-1200 ohms, replace TCM. Perform TEST VER-5A under VERIFICATION TESTS. If resistance is not 300-1200 ohms, go to next step.

8) Disconnect Output Speed Sensor (OSS) connector. Inspect connectors. Clean or repair as necessary. Using an ohmmeter, check resistance of OSS ground circuit between TCM connector terminal No. 13 and OSS connector terminal No. 1 (Dark Blue/Black wire). If resistance is 5 ohms or more, repair open circuit. Perform TEST VER-5A under VERIFICATION TESTS. If resistance is less than 5 ohms, go to next step.

9) Using an ohmmeter, check resistance of OSS signal circuit between TCM connector terminal No. 14 and OSS connector terminal No. 2 (Light Green/White wire). If resistance is 5 ohms or more, repair open circuit. Perform TEST VER-5A under VERIFICATION TESTS. If resistance is less than 5 ohms, replace OSS. Perform TEST VER-5A under VERIFICATION TESTS.

10) Turn ignition off. Disconnect PCM connectors. Inspect connectors. Clean or repair as necessary. Using an ohmmeter, check resistance between ground and VSS signal circuit at PCM connector C2, terminal No. 66 (White/Orange wire). If resistance is less than 5 ohms, repair short to ground. Perform TEST VER-5A under VERIFICATION TESTS. If resistance is 5 ohms or more, go to next step.

11) Using an ohmmeter, check resistance of VSS signal circuit between PCM connector C2, terminal No. 66 and TCM connector terminal No. 58 (White/Orange wire). If resistance is 5 ohms or more, repair open circuit. Perform TEST VER-5A under VERIFICATION TESTS. If resistance is less than 5 ohms, replace PCM. Perform TEST VER-5A under VERIFICATION TESTS.

DTC P1595: SPEED CONTROL SOLENOID CIRCUITS OR DTC P1683: SPEED CONTROL POWER RELAY

DTC P1595 or P1683 will set if vacuum and vent solenoids do not respond when actuated by PCM.

Possible Causes:
- Ground circuit open.
- S/C brake switch output circuit open.
- S/C power supply circuit open or shorted.
- S/C servo defective.
- S/C vacuum solenoid control circuit open or shorted.
- S/C vent solenoid control circuit open or shorted.
- Brake switch defective or out of adjustment.

- Defective PCM.

NOTE: For component location, see COMPONENT LOCATIONS. For connector terminal identification, see CONNECTOR IDENTIFICATION. For wiring diagram, see WIRING DIAGRAMS.

1) Check brake switch adjustment. See BRAKE SWITCH under REMOVAL & INSTALLATION. Adjust as necessary. Perform TEST VER-4A under VERIFICATION TESTS. If brake switch adjustment is okay, go to next step.

NOTE: Ensure brake pedal is not depressed during the following steps.

2) Turn ignition off. Disconnect S/C servo connector. Inspect connectors. Clean or repair as necessary. Turn ignition and S/C on. Using a voltmeter, check voltage on brake switch output circuit at S/C servo connector terminal No. 3 (Dark Blue/Red wire). If voltage is more than 10 volts, go to next step. If voltage is 10 volts or less, go to step 8).

3) Turn ignition off. Using an ohmmeter, check resistance of ground circuit at S/C servo connector terminal no. 4 (Black wire). If resistance is 5 ohms or more, repair open ground circuit. Perform TEST VER-4A under VERIFICATION TESTS. If resistance is less than 5 ohms, go to next step.

4) Reconnect S/C servo connector. Disconnect PCM connectors. Inspect connectors. Clean or repair as necessary. Using an ohmmeter, check resistance between S/C vent solenoid control circuit at PCM connector C2, terminal No. 80 (Light Green/Red wire) and S/C power supply circuit at PCM connector C1, terminal No. 5 (Yellow/Red wire). If resistance is 35-55 ohms, go to next step. If resistance is not 35-55 ohms, go to step 6).

5) Using an ohmmeter, check resistance between S/C power supply circuit at PCM connector C1, terminal No. 5 (Yellow/Red wire) and S/C vacuum solenoid control circuit at PCM connector C2, Tan/Red wire. If resistance is 35-55 ohms, replace PCM. Perform TEST VER-4A under VERIFICATION TESTS. If resistance is not 35-55 ohms, go to next step.

6) Disconnect S/C servo connector. Using an ohmmeter, check resistance of S/C vacuum solenoid control circuit between S/C servo connector terminal No. 1 and PCM connector C2, terminal No. 78 on 3.0L engine, or terminal No. 56 on other engines (Tan/Red wire). On all applications, if resistance is 5 ohms or more, repair open circuit. Perform TEST VER-4A under VERIFICATION TESTS. If resistance is less than 5 ohms, go to next step.

7) Using an ohmmeter, check resistance of S/C vent solenoid control circuit between S/C servo connector terminal No. 2 and PCM connector C2, terminal No. 80 (Light Green/red wire). If resistance is 5 ohms or more, repair open circuit. Perform TEST VER-4A under VERIFICATION TESTS. If resistance is less than 5 ohms, replace S/C servo. Perform TEST VER-4A under VERIFICATION TESTS.

8) Turn ignition and speed control off. Disconnect brake switch connector. Inspect connectors. Clean or repair as necessary. Turn ignition and speed control on. Using a voltmeter, check voltage on S/C power supply circuit at brake switch connector terminal No. 3 (Yellow/Red wire). If voltage is more than 10 volts, go to next step. If voltage is 10 volts or less, go to step 11).

9) Turn ignition off. Using an ohmmeter, check resistance between ground and S/C brake switch output circuit at S/C servo connector terminal No. 3 (Dark Blue/red wire). If resistance is less than 5 ohms, repair short to ground. Perform TEST VER-4A under VERIFICATION TESTS. If resistance is 5 ohms or more, go to next step.

10) Using an ohmmeter, check resistance of S/C brake switch output circuit between S/C servo connector terminal No. 3 and brake switch connector terminal No. 4 (Dark Blue/Red wire). If resistance is 5 ohms or more, repair open circuit. Perform TEST VER-4A under VERIFICATION TESTS. If resistance is less than 5 ohms, replace brake switch. Perform TEST VER-4A under VERIFICATION TESTS.

11) Turn ignition off. Using an ohmmeter, check resistance between ground and S/C brake switch output circuit at S/C servo connector terminal No. 3 (Dark Blue/Red wire). If resistance is less than 5 ohms,

1999 ACCESSORIES & EQUIPMENT
Cruise Control Systems
Caravan, Town & Country, & Voyager (Cont.)

CHRY
4-279

repair short to ground. Perform TEST VER-4A under VERIFICATION TESTS. If resistance is 5 ohms or more, go to next step.

12) Disconnect PCM connectors. Inspect connectors. Clean or repair as necessary. Using an ohmmeter, check resistance of S/C power supply circuit between PCM connector C1, terminal No. 5 and brake switch connector terminal No. 3 (Yellow/Red wire). If resistance is 5 ohms or more, repair open circuit. Perform TEST VER-4A under VERIFICATION TESTS. If resistance is less than 5 ohms, replace PCM. Perform TEST VER-4A under VERIFICATION TESTS.

SYSTEM TESTS

NOTE: For component location, See COMPONENT LOCATIONS. For connector terminal identification, see CONNECTOR IDENTIFICATION. For wiring diagram, see WIRING DIAGRAMS.

CHECKING POWERTRAIN CONTROL MODULE (PCM) & WIRING

1) Disconnect PCM connector C2. Remove both Speed Control (S/C) switches and disconnect wire connectors. Using an ohmmeter, check for continuity between PCM connector C2, terminal No. 41 (Red/Light Green wire) and terminal No. 1 of each S/C switch connector. If continuity exists, go to next step. If continuity does not exist, repair open circuit.

2) Using an ohmmeter, check for continuity between ground and PCM connector C2, terminal No. 41 (Red/Light Green wire). If continuity exists, repair short circuit. If continuity does not exist, test switches. See appropriate NTC TEST.

3) Reconnect S/C switches and PCM connector C2. Disconnect S/C servo connector. Turn ignition on. Turn S/C switch on. Using a voltmeter, check voltage at S/C servo connector terminal 3 (Dark Blue/Red wire). Battery voltage should exist. If battery voltage exists, go to next step. If battery voltage does not exist, go to step 16).

4) Turn S/C and ignition off. Using an ohmmeter, place positive lead on S/C servo terminal No. 3 and negative lead on terminal No. 4. If continuity does not exist, replace S/C servo. If resistance is 50 ohms or more, clean terminals and retest. If resistance is less than 50 ohms, go to next step.

5) Using an ohmmeter, place positive lead on S/C servo terminal No. 3 and negative lead on terminal No. 2. If continuity does not exist, replace S/C servo. If resistance is 50 ohms or more, clean terminals and retest. If resistance is less than 50 ohms, go to next step.

6) Using an ohmmeter, place positive lead on S/C servo terminal No. 3 and negative lead on terminal No. 1. If continuity does not exist, replace S/C servo. If resistance is 50 ohms or more, clean terminals and retest. If resistance is less than 50 ohms, go to next step.

7) Using an ohmmeter, check for continuity between ground and S/C servo connector terminal No. 4 (Black wire). If continuity does not exist, repair open ground circuit. If continuity exists, go to next step.

8) Disconnect PCM connectors. Using an ohmmeter, check for continuity between S/C servo connector terminal No. 1 and PCM connector C2, Tan/Red wire (terminal No. 78 on 3.0L engine or terminal No. 56 on other engines). If continuity does not exist, repair open circuit. If continuity exists, go to next step.

9) Using an ohmmeter, check for continuity between ground and S/C servo connector terminal No. 1 (Tan/Red wire). If continuity exists, repair short circuit. If continuity does not exist, go to next step.

10) Using an ohmmeter, check for continuity between S/C servo connector terminal No. 2 and PCM connector C2, terminal No. 80 (Light Green/Red wire). If continuity does not exist, repair open circuit. If continuity exists, go to next step.

11) Using an ohmmeter, check for continuity between ground and S/C servo connector terminal No. 2 (Light Green/Red wire). If continuity exists, repair short circuit. If continuity does not exist, go to next step.

12) Using an ohmmeter, check for continuity between S/C servo connector terminals No. 1 and 2. If continuity exists, repair short circuit. If continuity does not exist, go to next step.

13) Reconnect S/C servo connector. Ensure brake pedal is not pressed. Using an ohmmeter, check for continuity between ground and PCM connector C2, terminal No. 62 (White/Pink wire). If continuity exists, go to step 15). If continuity does not exist, test brake switch. See BRAKE SWITCH under COMPONENT TESTS. If brake switch is okay, go to next step.

14) Using an ohmmeter, check for continuity between PCM connector C2, terminal No. 62 and brake switch connector terminal No. 1 (White/Pink wire). If continuity does not exist, repair open circuit. If continuity exists, repair open ground circuit at brake switch connector terminal No. 2 (Black wire).

15) Using an ohmmeter, check for continuity between ground and PCM connector C2, terminal No. 76 (Brown/Yellow wire) with transmission in Drive. If continuity exists, test Park/Neutral Position (PNP) switch and wiring. See NTC-2: PARK/NEUTRAL POSITION (PNP) SWITCH. If continuity does not exist, go to next step.

16) Turn S/C and ignition off. Using an ohmmeter, check for continuity between S/C servo connector terminal No. 3 and PCM connector C1, terminal No. 5 (Yellow/Red wire). If continuity exists, go to next step. If continuity does not exist, test brake switch. See BRAKE SWITCH under COMPONENT TESTS. If brake switch is okay, go to step 18).

17) Using an ohmmeter, check for continuity between ground and S/C servo connector terminal No. 3 (Yellow/Red wire). If continuity exists, repair short circuit. If continuity does not exist, replace PCM.

18) Using an ohmmeter, check for continuity between S/C servo connector terminal No. 3 and brake switch connector terminal No. 4 (Dark Blue/Red wire). If continuity does not exist, repair open circuit. If continuity exists, go to next step.

19) Using an ohmmeter, check for continuity between brake switch terminal No. 3 to PCM connector C1, terminal No. 5 (Yellow/Red wire). If continuity does not exist, repair open circuit. If continuity exists, no problem is indicated at this time.

CHECKING SPEED CONTROL OPERATION

NOTE: Perform this test only if there are no DTCs.

1) Turn ignition on. Using scan tool, monitor Speed Control (S/C) switch inputs. Turn S/C on. If scan tool displays speed control switch ON, go to next step. If scan tool does not display speed control switch ON, go to NTC-4: SPEED CONTROL ON/OFF SWITCH.

2) While observing scan tool, press ACCEL/RESUME/CANCEL and DECEL switches several times. If scan tool displays PRESSED and RELEASED for all switches, go to next step. If scan tool does not display PRESSED and RELEASED for all switches, go to step 21).

3) While observing scan tool, press SET switch several times. If scan tool displays PRESSED and RELEASED, go to next step. If scan tool does not display PRESSED and RELEASED, replace ON/OFF/SET switch. Perform TEST VER-4A under VERIFICATION TESTS.

4) While observing scan tool, press brake pedal several times. If scan tool displays brake pedal PRESSED and RELEASED, go to next step. If scan tool does not display brake pedal PRESSED and RELEASED, go to NTC-1: BRAKE SWITCH SENSE.

5) While observing scan tool, move gear selector to Drive. If scan tool displays park neutral switch D/R, go to next step. If scan tool does not display park neutral switch D/R, go to NTC-2: PARK/NEUTRAL POSITION (PNP) SWITCH.

6) Turn ignition off. Disconnect S/C servo connector. Inspect connectors. Clean or repair as necessary. Turn ignition and S/C on. Using a voltmeter, check voltage on S/C brake switch output circuit at S/C servo connector terminal No. 3 (Dark Blue/Red wire). If voltage is more than 10 volts, go to next step. If voltage is 10 volts or less, go to step 13).

7) Turn ignition off. Reconnect S/C servo connector. Start engine and let idle for one minute. Turn engine off. Turn ignition on (engine off). Using scan tool, actuate S/C servo solenoids. If throttle opens and closes, go to NTC-3: CHECKING FOR SPEED CONTROL DENIED MESSAGE. If throttle does not open and close, go to next step.

CHRY
4-280

1999 ACCESSORIES & EQUIPMENT
Cruise Control Systems
Caravan, Town & Country, & Voyager (Cont.)

8) Turn ignition off. Inspect S/C throttle cable. Reconnect or repair as necessary. Perform TEST VER-4A under VERIFICATION TESTS. If S/C throttle cable is okay, go to next step.

9) Turn ignition off. Disconnect vacuum supply hose from S/C servo. Attach vacuum gauge to disconnected hose. Start engine. If vacuum gauge does not read vacuum, repair vacuum leak or restriction. Perform TEST VER-4A under VERIFICATION TESTS. If vacuum gauge reads manifold vacuum, go to next step.

10) Turn ignition off. Disconnect S/C servo connector. Using an ohmmeter, check resistance between ground and S/C servo connector terminal No. 4 (Black wire). If resistance is 5 ohms or more, repair open ground circuit. Perform TEST VER-4A under VERIFICATION TESTS. If resistance is less than 5 ohms, go to next step.

11) Inspect S/C servo connector terminals. If any terminal is damaged, pushed out or miswired, repair as necessary. Perform TEST VER-4A under VERIFICATION TESTS. If terminals are okay, go to next step.

12) Reconnect S/C servo connector. Start engine and let idle for one minute with vacuum gauge still attached to S/C servo vacuum supply hose. Turn engine off. If vacuum does not hold for 10 seconds, replace vacuum reservoir. Perform TEST VER-4A under VERIFICATION TESTS. If vacuum holds for at least 10 seconds, replace S/C servo. Perform TEST VER-4A under VERIFICATION TESTS.

13) Turn ignition off. Using an ohmmeter, check resistance between ground and S/C servo connector terminal No. 4 (Black wire). If resistance is 5 ohms or more, repair open ground circuit. Perform TEST VER-4A under VERIFICATION TESTS. If resistance is less than 5 ohms, go to next step.

14) Using an ohmmeter, check resistance between ground and S/C brake switch output circuit at S/C servo connector terminal No. 3 (Dark Blue/Red wire). If resistance is less than 5 ohms, go to next step. If resistance is 5 ohms or more, go to step 17).

15) Inspect S/C servo connector. If any terminal is damaged, pushed out or miswired, repair as necessary. Perform TEST VER-4A under VERIFICATION TESTS. If terminals are okay, go to next step.

16) Disconnect brake switch connector. Using an ohmmeter, check resistance between ground and S/C brake switch output circuit at brake switch connector terminal No. 4 (Dark Blue/Red wire). If resistance is less than 5 ohms, repair short to ground. Perform TEST VER-4A under VERIFICATION TESTS. If resistance is 5 ohms or more, repair short to ground on S/C power supply circuit between PCM connector C1, terminal No. 5 and brake switch connector terminal No. 3 (Yellow/Red wire). Perform TEST VER-4A under VERIFICATION TESTS.

17) Inspect S/C servo connector. If any terminal is damaged, pushed out or miswired, repair as necessary. Perform TEST VER-4A under VERIFICATION TESTS. If terminals are okay, go to next step.

18) Disconnect brake switch connector. Turn ignition and S/C on. Using a voltmeter, check voltage on S/C power supply circuit at brake switch connector terminal No. 3 (Yellow/Red wire). If voltage is more than 10 volts, go to next step. If voltage is 10 volts or less, go to step 20).

19) Turn ignition off. Using an ohmmeter, check resistance of brake switch output circuit between brake switch connector terminal No. 4 and S/C servo connector terminal No. 3 (Dark Blue/Red wire). If resistance is 5 ohms or more, repair open circuit. Perform TEST VER-4A under VERIFICATION TESTS. If resistance is less than 5 ohms, replace brake switch. Perform TEST VER-4A under VERIFICATION TESTS.

20) Disconnect PCM connectors. Inspect connectors. Clean or repair as necessary. Using an ohmmeter, check resistance of S/C power supply circuit between PCM connector C1, terminal No. 5 and brake switch connector terminal No. 3 (Yellow/Red wire). If resistance is 5 ohms or more, repair open circuit. Perform TEST VER-4A under VERIFICATION TESTS. If resistance is less than 5 ohms, replace PCM. Perform TEST VER-4A under VERIFICATION TESTS.

21) Using scan tool, perform S/C switch test. Replace S/C switch as necessary. Perform TEST VER-4A under VERIFICATION TESTS. If S/C switch is okay, go to next step.

22) Using scan tool, monitor S/C switch inputs. While observing display, press SET switch several times. If scan tool does not display SET switch

PRESSED and RELEASED, replace ON/OFF/SET switch. Perform TEST VER-4A under VERIFICATION TESTS. If scan tool displays SET switch PRESSED and RELEASED, replace clockspring. See AIR BAG RESTRAINT SYSTEMS – TRUCKS article. Perform TEST VER-4A under VERIFICATION TESTS.

NTC-1: BRAKE SWITCH SENSE
Possible Causes:
- Ground circuit open.
- Defective brake switch.
- Brake switch sense circuit open or shorted.
- Defective PCM.

1) Turn ignition off. Disconnect brake switch connector. Inspect connector. Clean or repair as necessary. Turn ignition on. Using a voltmeter, check voltage of brake switch sense circuit at brake switch connector terminal No. 1 (White/Pink wire). If voltage is more than 10 volts, go to next step. If voltage is 10 volts or less, go to step 3).

2) Connect a jumper wire between ground and brake switch connector terminal No. 1 (White/Pink wire). Using scan tool, read brake switch input status. If scan tool displays brake switch released, replace brake switch. Perform TEST VER-4A under VERIFICATION TESTS. If scan tool does not display brake switch released, repair open ground circuit. Perform TEST VER-4A under VERIFICATION TESTS.

3) Turn ignition off. Disconnect PCM connectors. Inspect connector terminals. If any terminal is damaged, pushed out or miswired, repair as necessary. Perform TEST VER-4A under VERIFICATION TESTS. If terminals are okay, go to next step.

4) Using an ohmmeter, check resistance between ground and brake switch sense circuit at PCM connector C2, terminal No. 62 (White/Pink wire). If resistance less than 5 ohms, repair short to ground. Perform TEST VER-4A under VERIFICATION TESTS. If resistance is 5 ohms or more, go to next step.

5) Using an ohmmeter, check resistance of brake switch sense circuit between PCM connector C2, terminal No. 62 and brake switch terminal No. 1 (White/Pink wire). If resistance is 5 ohms or more, repair open brake switch sense circuit. Perform TEST VER-4A under VERIFICATION TESTS. If resistance is less than 5 ohms, replace PCM. Perform TEST VER-4A under VERIFICATION TESTS.

NTC-2: PARK/NEUTRAL POSITION (PNP) SWITCH

NOTE: PNP switch is incorporated with Transmission Range Switch (TRS).

Possible Causes:
- PNP switch sense circuit shorted to ground.
- Defective PNP switch.
- Defective PCM.

1) Disconnect PCM connectors. Disconnect Transmission Range Switch (TRS) connector. Inspect connectors. Clean or repair as necessary. Using an ohmmeter, check resistance between ground and PNP sense circuit at PCM connector C2, terminal No. 76 (Brown/Yellow wire). If resistance is less than 5 ohms, repair short to ground. Perform TEST VER-4A under VERIFICATION TESTS. If resistance is 5 ohms or more, go to next step.

2) Connect TRS connector. Place transmission in Drive. Using an ohmmeter, check resistance between ground and PNP sense circuit at PCM connector C2, terminal No. 76 (Brown/Yellow wire). If resistance is less than 5 ohms, replace TRS. Perform TEST VER-4A under VERIFICATION TESTS. If resistance is 5 ohms or more, replace PCM. Perform TEST VER-4A under VERIFICATION TESTS.

NTC-3: CHECKING FOR SPEED CONTROL DENIED MESSAGE
At this time speed control switch and servo functions appear to operate properly. Using scan tool, monitor speed control output status. Road test vehicle at speeds more than 30 MPH. Attempt to set speed control. See

1999 ACCESSORIES & EQUIPMENT
Cruise Control Systems
Caravan, Town & Country, & Voyager (Cont.)

CHRY
4-281

SCAN TOOL DENIED STATUS table. Items listed in table will not allow speed control to set. The last or most recent cause for speed control not to set is indicated by denied status. Correct fault and recheck system operation.

SCAN TOOL DENIED STATUS

Denied Message	Reason
ON/OFF	PCM Does Not See An ON Signal From Switch At PCM Terminal No. 41
SPEED	Vehicle Speed As Seen By PCM Terminal No. 66 Is Not Greater Than 36 MPH
RPM	Engine RPM Is Excessively High
BRAKE	Brake Switch Sense Circuit Is Open Indicating That Brakes Are Applied
P/N	Park/Neutral Switch Sense Circuit Is Grounded Indicating That Transmission Is In Park Or Neutral
RPM/SPD	PCM Senses Excessive Engine RPM For A Given Vehicle Speed
SOL FLT	PCM Senses A Servo Solenoid Circuit Trouble Code That Is Maturing Or Set In Memory

NTC-4: SPEED CONTROL ON/OFF SWITCH

Possible Causes:
- Ground circuit open.
- S/C SET/RESUME switch voltage more than 4 volts.
- S/C switch signal circuit shorted to voltage or ground.
- S/C ON/OFF switch voltage less than one volt or more than 4 volts.
- Defective PCM.
- Defective clockspring.

1) Turn ignition off. Disconnect PCM connectors. Disconnect clockspring 5-pin connector located behind steering wheel. Inspect connectors. Clean or repair as necessary. Using an ohmmeter, check resistance of S/C switch signal circuit between PCM connector C2, terminal No. 41 and clockspring 5-pin connector, terminal No. 4 (Red/Light Green wire). If resistance is 5 ohms or more, repair open circuit. Perform TEST VER-4A under VERIFICATION TESTS. If resistance is less than 5 ohms, go to next step.

2) Reconnect clockspring. Disconnect S/C ON/OFF switch connector. Inspect connector. Clean or repair as necessary. Using an ohmmeter, check resistance of S/C switch ground circuit at S/C ON/OFF switch connector Black wire. If resistance is 5 ohms or more, repair open ground circuit. Perform TEST VER-4A under VERIFICATION TESTS. If resistance is less than 5 ohms, go to next step.

3) Reconnect PCM. Connect a jumper wire across S/C ON/OFF switch terminals. Turn ignition on. Using scan tool, read S/C switch voltage. If scan tool displays zero volts or OFF, replace S/C ON/OFF switch. Perform TEST VER-4A under VERIFICATION TESTS. If scan tool does not display zero volts or OFF, go to next step.

4) Disconnect PCM connectors. Using an ohmmeter, check resistance of S/C switch signal circuit between S/C ON/OFF switch White wire and PCM connector C2, terminal No. 41 (Red/Light Green wire). If resistance is less than 5 ohms, replace PCM. Perform TEST VER-4A under VERIFICATION TESTS. If resistance is 5 ohms or more, go to next step.

5) Using an ohmmeter, check resistance between ground and S/C switch signal circuit at S/C ON/OFF switch White wire. If resistance is less than 5 ohms, repair short to ground. Perform TEST VER-4A under VERIFICATION TESTS. If resistance is 5 ohms or more, go to next step.

6) Inspect S/C ON/OFF switch connector. If any terminal is damaged, pushed out or miswired, repair as necessary. Perform TEST VER-4A under VERIFICATION TESTS. If terminals are okay, replace clockspring. See AIR BAG RESTRAINT SYSTEMS – TRUCKS article. Perform TEST VER-4A under VERIFICATION TESTS.

VERIFICATION TESTS

TEST VER-4A

NOTE: If PCM has been replaced and correct VIN and mileage have not been programmed, a DTC will be set in ABS and air bag modules.

1) If vehicle is equipped with ABS or air bag, enter correct VIN and mileage in PCM. Erase DTCs in ABS and air bag modules. Inspect vehicle to ensure all engine and speed control system components are connected. Reassemble and reconnect components as necessary. Using scan tool, erase DTCs from PCM.

2) Road test vehicle at a speed greater than 35 MPH. Turn S/C switch on. Press and release SET button. If S/C does not engage, repair is not complete. Check for related TSBs and return to TROUBLE SHOOTING, if necessary. If speed control engages, go to next step.

3) Quickly depress and release RESUME/ACCEL switch. If vehicle speed increases by 2 MPH, go to next step. If vehicle speed does not increase by 2 MPH, repair is not complete. Check for related TSBs and return to TROUBLE SHOOTING, if necessary.

4) Press and hold COAST switch. Vehicle speed should decrease. If vehicle speed decreases, go to next step. If vehicle speed does not decrease, repair is not complete. Check for related TSBs and return to TROUBLE SHOOTING, if necessary.

5) Using caution, depress and release brake pedal. If S/C disengages, go to next step. If S/C does not disengage, repair is not complete. Check for related TSBs and return to TROUBLE SHOOTING, if necessary.

6) Bring vehicle speed to 35 MPH. Depress speed control RESUME/ACCEL switch. If vehicle resumes to previously set speed, go to next step. If vehicle does not resume to previously set speed, repair is not complete. Check for related TSBs and return to TROUBLE SHOOTING, if necessary.

7) Hold down SET switch. Vehicle speed should decrease. If vehicle speed decreases, go to next step. If vehicle speed did not decrease, repair is not complete. Check for related TSBs and return to TROUBLE SHOOTING, if necessary.

8) Ensure vehicle speed is more than 35 MPH and release SET switch. Vehicle should set a new speed. If vehicle sets a new speed, go to next step. If vehicle did not set a new speed, repair is not complete. Check for related TSBs and return to TROUBLE SHOOTING, if necessary.

9) Depress and release CANCEL switch. If S/C disengages, go to next step. If S/C did not disengage, repair is not complete. Check for related TSBs and return to TROUBLE SHOOTING, if necessary.

10) Ensure vehicle speed is greater than 35 MPH. Engage speed control. Turn S/C ON/OFF switch to OFF position. If speed control disengages, system is operating correctly. Repair is complete. If speed control does not disengage, repair is not complete. Check for related TSBs and return to TROUBLE SHOOTING, if necessary.

TEST VER-5A

NOTE: If PCM has been replaced and correct VIN and mileage have not been programmed, a DTC will be set in ABS and air bag modules. If vehicle is equipped with a Sentry Key Immobilizer Module (SKIM), sentry key data must be updated to enable starting. See COMPUTER RELEARN PROCEDURES article in GENERAL INFORMATION.

1) If vehicle is equipped with ABS or air bag, enter correct VIN and mileage in PCM. Erase DTCs in ABS and air bag modules. Inspect vehicle to ensure all engine and speed control system components are connected.

2) If there are any DTCs that have not been repaired, go to SELF-DIAGNOSTIC SYSTEM. After all DTCs have been repaired, run appropriate monitor for previously repaired DTC.

3) Connect scan tool to DLC. Ensure fuel tank is at least 1/4 full. Turn off all accessories. Allow PCM to run appropriate monitor. Enabling conditions must be met before monitor will run.

CHRY
4-282

1999 ACCESSORIES & EQUIPMENT
Cruise Control Systems
Caravan, Town & Country, & Voyager (Cont.)

4) Using scan tool, monitor pretest enabling conditions until all conditions have been met. Once enabling conditions have been met, monitor appropriate monitor.

5) If repaired DTC has reset or was seen in monitor while on road test, repair is not complete. Check for TSBs or flash updates and return to TROUBLE SHOOTING.

6) If appropriate monitor ran, good trip counter incremented and no DTCs have been set, repair is complete.

REMOVAL & INSTALLATION

WARNING: Vehicle is equipped with an air bag. Air bag must be deactivated before servicing speed control components on or around steering column. See AIR BAG RESTRAINT SYSTEMS – TRUCKS article.

CAUTION: When battery is disconnected, vehicle computer and memory systems may lose memory data. Driveability problems may exist until computer systems have completed a relearn cycle. See COMPUTER RELEARN PROCEDURES in GENERAL INFORMATION before disconnecting battery.

BRAKE SWITCH

Removal – Fully depress brake pedal and rotate brake switch counterclockwise approximately 30 degrees. Remove brake switch from bracket. Depress lock tabs holding brake switch mounting bracket and separate harness connector from brake switch.

Installation – 1) Before installing brake switch, reset adjustable plunger by pulling on plunger head until plunger reaches end of travel. Connect harness connector to brake switch. Depress brake pedal and insert brake switch into keyed hole in mounting bracket. Rotate brake switch clockwise into locked position.

2) Gently pull back on brake pedal until pedal will go no further. This causes the brake switch plunger to ratchet backward to the correct position. No further adjustment is required.

SPEED CONTROL SERVO

Removal – 1) On 3.3L/3.8L, remove air cleaner resonator. On all models, disconnect throttle and speed control cable at throttle body. Depress lock tabs in speed control cable housing and remove cable housing from bracket.

2) Disconnect wiring harness connector and vacuum hose from servo. Remove bolt retaining speed control servo to battery tray and remove speed control servo. Pull cable away from servo to expose retaining clip. Remove retaining clip and cable.

Installation – With throttle in full open position, align hole in speed control cable sleeve with hole in servo pin. Install retaining clip. To complete installation, reverse removal procedure.

SPEED CONTROL SWITCHES

Removal & Installation – Turn ignition off. Disconnect negative battery cable. Wait 2 minutes for air bag system to discharge reserve voltage. Remove 3 screws holding air bag assembly to steering column. Separate air bag assembly from steering column and disconnect air bag, horn and speed control switch connectors. Remove screws securing speed control switch to air bag assembly. Separate speed control switch from air bag assembly. To install, reverse removal procedure.

WIRING DIAGRAMS

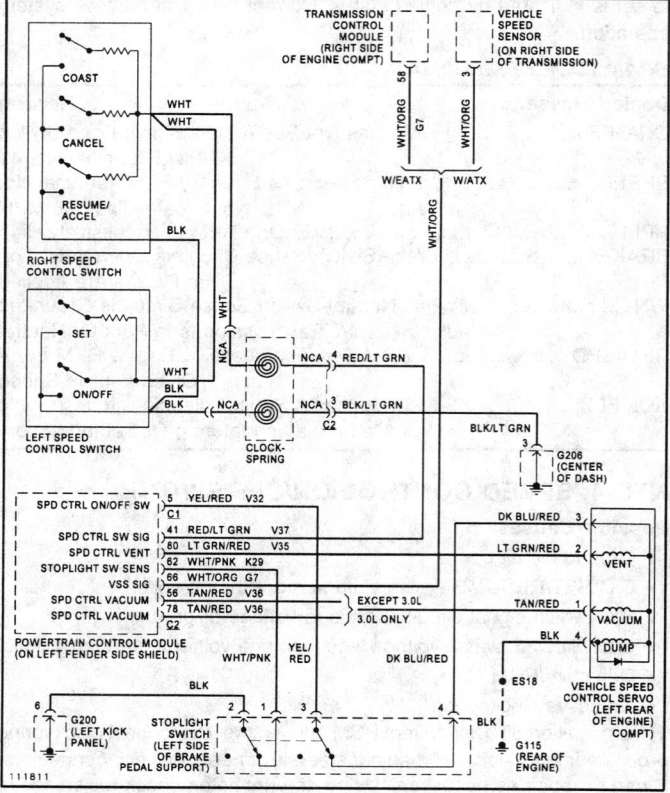

Fig. 6: Cruise Control System Wiring Diagram (Caravan, Town & Country, & Voyager)

DESCRIPTION

The speed (cruise) control system is electronically controlled and vacuum operated. The electronic control is integrated into the Powertrain Control Module (PCM) located under the air cleaner housing. System consists of the following components: Powertrain Control Module (PCM), servo, speed control switches, vacuum reservoir, vehicle speed sensor, speed control relay and brake switch. System controls are located on each side of steering wheel air bag module and consist of ON/OFF, CANCEL, RES/ACCEL and SET/COAST buttons.

OPERATION

SYSTEM CONTROLS

To Set Speed Control – Press ON/OFF button to turn speed control system on. Accelerate to desired (minimum of 30 MPH) and press SET/COAST button. Vehicle speed will be maintained.

To Disengage Speed Control – Press brake pedal. Press CANCEL button. Press ON/OFF button. If ON/OFF button is used, set speed will be erased from memory.

To Resume Previous Speed – If set speed has not been erased from memory and vehicle speed is more than 25 MPH, press RES/ACCEL button.

To Increase Speed – With speed control system on, increase set speed by rapidly pressing and releasing RES/ACCEL button. Each pressing of button will cause speed increase of 2 MPH. For example, pressing button 3 times will increase speed by 6 MPH. To increase speed gradually, hold RES/ACCEL button down until desired speed is reached. When button is released, new set speed will be maintained.

To Decrease Speed – With speed control system on, decrease set speed by pressing SET/COAST button. Vehicle speed will gradually decrease. Releasing button will set a new speed as long as vehicle speed is still more than 25 MPH.

COMPONENT LOCATION

COMPONENT LOCATION

Application	Location
Powertrain Control Module (PCM)	Driver's Side Front Corner Of Engine Compartment, Between Power Distribution Center & Transmission Control Module
Brake Switch	Near Top Of Brake Pedal
Transmission Control Module (TCM)	Left Side Of Engine Compartment Between Power Distribution Center & Headlight
Transmission Range Sensor (TRS)	Top Of Valve Body Inside Transmission

TROUBLE SHOOTING

WARNING: Vehicle is equipped with an air bag. Air bag must be deactivated before servicing speed control components on or around steering column. See AIR BAG RESTRAINT SYSTEMS – CARS article.

NO SPEED CONTROL WHEN SET BUTTON IS PRESSED & RELEASED

Check for blown fuse, no vacuum at servo and/or defective servo, disconnected speed control cable, brake switch out of adjustment, faulty electrical circuit, faulty Manual Valve Lever Position Switch (MVLPS) input to PCM and/or faulty PCM.

SPEED CONTROL ENGAGES WITHOUT ACTUATING SPEED SET BUTTON

Check for defective servo, faulty electrical circuit or control switch.

SPEED CONTROL ENGAGES WHEN ENGINE IS STARTED

Check for defective servo or faulty electrical circuit.

ERRATIC SPEED OR ENGINE SHUTS OFF

Check for poor engine performance (surge), defective vehicle speed sensor, vacuum leak, faulty servo or faulty PCM.

EXCESSIVE SAG ON HILLS OR IN TRAILER TOWING

Check for engine performance, vacuum leak or excessive load requiring manual assistance on hills.

SPEED CONTROL DISENGAGES ON ROUGH ROAD

Check for brake switch out of adjustment or faulty electrical circuit.

ENGINE DOES NOT RETURN TO NORMAL IDLE

Check for kinked and/or damaged speed control cable or faulty throttle linkage.

NO RESUME WHEN RESUME BUTTON IS PRESSED

Check for defective switch or faulty electrical circuit.

SPEED CONTROL DOES NOT DISENGAGE WITH BRAKE PEDAL DEPRESSED

Check for defective or improperly adjusted brake switch, kinked and/or damaged speed control cable or faulty electrical circuit.

COMPONENT TESTS

WARNING: Vehicle is equipped with an air bag. Air bag must be deactivated before servicing speed control components on or around steering column. See AIR BAG RESTRAINT SYSTEMS – CARS article.

BRAKE SWITCH

Disconnect brake switch 6-pin connector. Using an ohmmeter, check for continuity at brake switch. *See Fig. 1.* If continuity is not as specified in BRAKE SWITCH CONTINUITY table, check brake switch adjustment. See BRAKE SWITCH under REMOVAL & INSTALLATION. If brake switch adjustment is okay, replace defective brake switch.

BRAKE SWITCH CONTINUITY

Switch Plunger Position	Continuity Between Terminals
Released	5 & 6
Depressed	1 & 2
	3 & 4

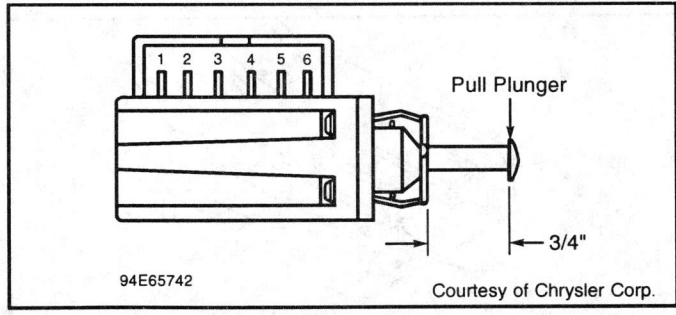

94E65742   Courtesy of Chrysler Corp.

Fig. 1: Identifying Brake Switch Terminals

SPEED CONTROL SERVO

1) Turn ignition switch and speed control switch to ON position, but do not start engine. Disconnect speed control servo 4-pin connector. Connect a jumper wire between servo harness connector terminal No. 3

CHRY
4-284

1999 ACCESSORIES & EQUIPMENT
Cruise Control Systems – Concorde, Intrepid, LHS & 300M (Cont.)

and speed control servo terminal No. 3. *See Fig. 2.* Using jumper wires, connect servo terminals No. 2 and No. 4 to ground.

2) Using a hand-held vacuum pump, apply 10-15 in. Hg of vacuum to servo vacuum nipple. Throttle cable should not retract. If throttle cable retracts, replace servo. If throttle cable does not retract, connect servo terminal No. 1 to ground. Throttle cable should now retract and hold position for at least one minute.

3) If throttle cable does not remain retracted, replace servo. If throttle cable remains retracted, remove jumper wire from servo terminal No. 3. Throttle cable should return to released position. If throttle cable does not return to released position, replace servo. If servo functions as described, no problem is indicated at this time.

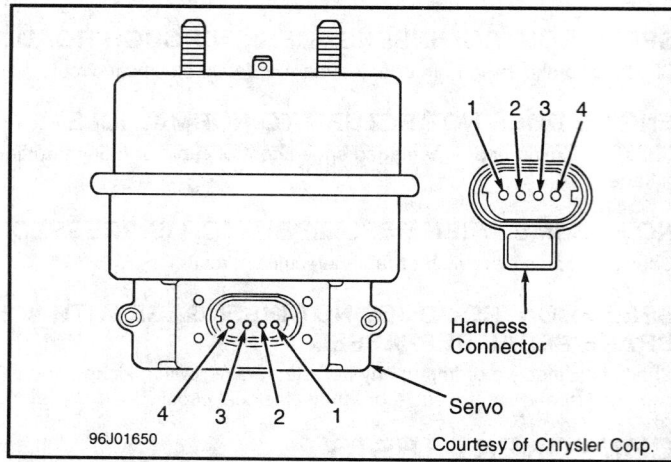

Fig. 2: Identifying Speed Control Servo Terminals

SPEED CONTROL SWITCHES

NOTE: For testing of speed control switches, see NTC-1A: CHECKING SPEED CONTROL OPERATION under DIAGNOSTIC TESTS

VACUUM SUPPLY

1) Disconnect vacuum hose at speed control servo. Install vacuum gauge to disconnected vacuum hose. Start engine and observe gauge. Vacuum reading should be a minimum of 10 in. Hg. Turn engine off. Vacuum should continue to hold at a minimum of 10 in. Hg.

2) If vacuum is not as specified, check for kinked or leaking vacuum lines, defective check valve, defective vacuum reservoir and/or poor engine performance. If no problems are found, check speed control servo. See SPEED CONTROL SERVO.

CONNECTOR IDENTIFICATION

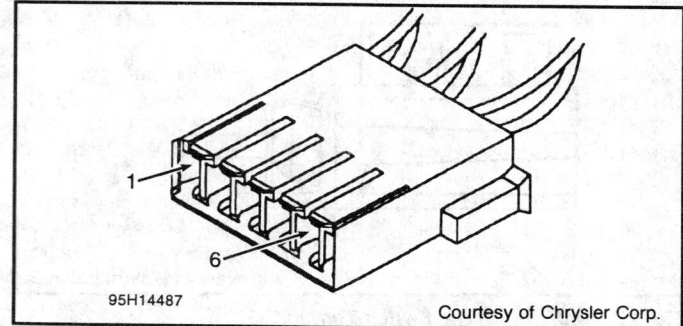

Fig. 3: Identifying Brake Switch Harness Connector

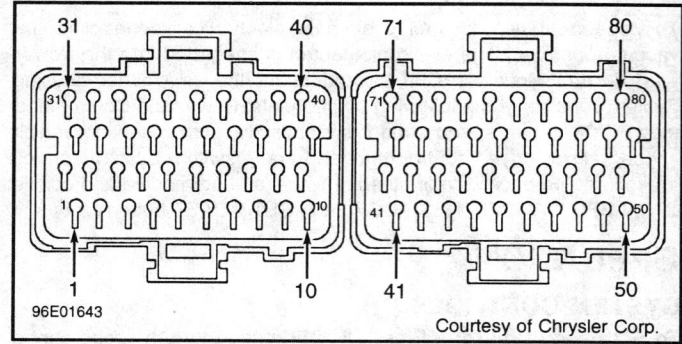

Fig. 4: Identifying Powertrain Control Module (PCM) Connectors

SELF-DIAGNOSTIC SYSTEM

SYSTEM DIAGNOSTICS

CAUTION: When battery is disconnected, vehicle computer and memory systems may lose memory data. Driveability problems may exist until computer systems have completed a relearn cycle. See COMPUTER RELEARN PROCEDURES article in GENERAL INFORMATION before disconnecting battery.

NOTE: Self-diagnostic tests are written specifically for Chrysler's Diagnostic Readout Box (DRB-III) scan tool, which will be referred to as scan tool during testing procedures. If using a generic scan tool, ensure scan tool is OBD-II certified. A generic scan tool may not be capable of performing all necessary test functions. Malfunction Indicator Light (MIL), also known as CHECK ENGINE light (located on instrument panel, just below fuel gauge) may also be used for system diagnostics, but has limited diagnostic capability.

SERVICE PRECAUTIONS

Before proceeding with diagnosis, the following precautions must be followed:

- When using DIAGNOSTIC TESTS for diagnosis, DO NOT skip any steps, or incorrect diagnosis may result. Always perform indicated verification procedure after repairs are made.
- When using a jumper wire, ensure either jumper wire or circuit is fuse-protected.
- Before disconnecting connector from any control module, ensure ignition is off before removing connector.
- When checking voltage or continuity at any control module, probe connector for control module from pin side. DO NOT backprobe connector or probe wires through insulation.
- DO NOT cause short circuits when performing electrical tests. This will set additional Diagnostic Trouble Codes (DTCs), making diagnosis of original problem more difficult.
- Use specified test equipment when performing electrical tests.

DIAGNOSTIC PROCEDURE

Always perform a visual inspection before attempting to diagnose engine control system problems. See VISUAL INSPECTION. Retrieve DTCs. See RETRIEVING DIAGNOSTIC TROUBLE CODES.

VISUAL INSPECTION

Most driveability problems in the engine control system result from faulty wiring, poor electrical connections, improper wire routing, or leaking air and vacuum hose connections. Inspect all engine control system components, hoses, connectors and wiring for damage before proceeding with system testing.

RETRIEVING DIAGNOSTIC TROUBLE CODES

NOTE: *Self-diagnostic tests are written specifically for Chrysler's Diagnostic Readout Box (DRB-III). If using a generic scan tool, ensure it is OBD-II certified. A generic scan tool may not be capable of performing all necessary test functions.*

For retrieving Diagnostic Trouble Codes (DTCs), perform DTC TEST: CHECKING SYSTEM FOR DIAGNOSTIC TROUBLE CODES under DIAGNOSTIC TESTS.

CLEARING DIAGNOSTIC TROUBLE CODES

Ensure ignition is off. Turn ignition on. Using screen prompts on scan tool, erase DTC from PCM.

INACTIVE TROUBLE CODE CONDITION

This procedure applies if you have been sent here from diagnostic tests and have just attempted to simulate the condition that initially set the Diagnostic Trouble Code (DTC). The following additional checks may assist in identifying a possible intermittent problem:

- Visually inspect related wiring harness connectors for broken, bent, pushed out or corroded terminals.
- Visually inspect related wiring harnesses for chafed, pierced or partially broken wires.
- Check for pertinent Technical Service Bulletins (TSBs) relating to the problem.

DIAGNOSTIC TESTS

NOTE: *For connector terminal identification, see CONNECTOR IDENTIFICATION.*

DTC TEST: CHECKING SYSTEM FOR DIAGNOSTIC TROUBLE CODES

NOTE: *Ensure battery is fully charged before proceeding with test.*

1) Attempt to start engine. Crank engine for up to 10 seconds (if necessary). Diagnostic Trouble Codes (DTCs) are retrieved using a scan tool.

2) Connect scan tool to Data Link Connector (DLC). DLC is located right of steering column next to center console. *See Fig. 5.* Using scan tool manufacturer's instructions, read DTC message and code.

3) If scan tool displays NO RESPONSE, go to TEST NS-6A in appropriate SELF-DIAGNOSTICS article in ENGINE PERFORMANCE in appropriate MITCHELL® manual. If scan tool will not power up, check for loose cable connections or bad cable. If cable connections and cable are okay, check voltage at cavity No. 16 on 16-pin DLC. Voltage should be at least 11 volts. If voltage is not as specified, check wiring circuit and necessary fuses. See WIRING DIAGRAMS.

4) If scan tool displays an error message, (i.e, USER-REQUESTED COLD BOOT or USER-REQUESTED WARM BOOT), follow scan tool manufacturer's instructions. If any other error message is displayed, contact scan tool manufacturer for further instructions.

5) If DTCs are displayed, see DTC MESSAGES & CODES table and perform appropriate test(s). If no DTCs are displayed, refer to one of the following:

- For driveability problems, see appropriate SELF-DIAGNOSTICS article in ENGINE PERFORMANCE in appropriate MITCHELL® manual.
- For no-start problems, see appropriate SELF-DIAGNOSTICS article in ENGINE PERFORMANCE in appropriate MITCHELL® manual.
- For speed (cruise) control problems, perform NTC-1A: CHECKING SPEED CONTROL OPERATION under SYSTEM TESTS.
- For charging system problems, see appropriate GENERATORS & REGULATORS article in STARTING & CHARGING SYSTEMS.

NOTE: *Testing procedures are specific for Diagnostic Readout Box (DRB-III) scan tool.*

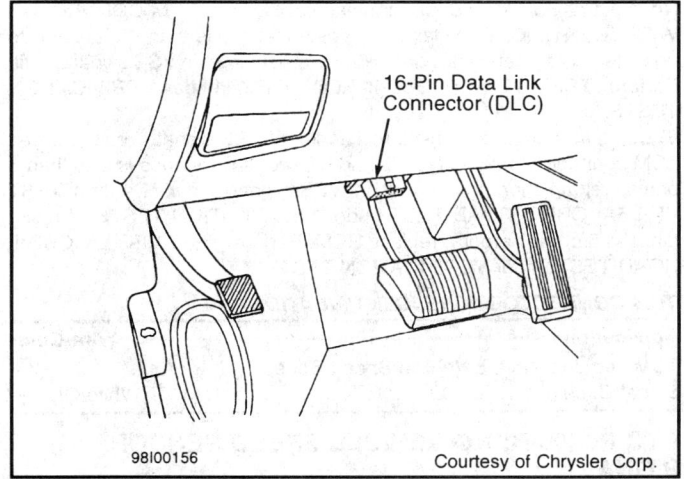

16-Pin Data Link Connector (DLC)

98I00156 — Courtesy of Chrysler Corp.

Fig. 5: Locating Data Link Connector (DLC)

DTC MESSAGES & CODES

Scan Tool Message	Scan Tool Code	DTC Test
NO VEHICLE SPEED SENSOR SIGNAL	P0500	P0500-A
BRAKE SWITCH STUCK PRESSED OR RELEASED	P0703	P0703-A
SPEED CONTROL SOLENOID CIRCUITS	P1595	P1595-A
SPEED CONTROL SWITCH ALWAYS LOW	P1597	P1597-A
SPEED CONTROL POWER RELAY CIRCUIT, OR 12V DRIVER CIRCUIT	P1683	P1683-A
PARK/NEUTRAL SWITCH STUCK IN PARK OR IN GEAR	P1899	P1899-A

DTC P0500-A: NO VEHICLE SPEED SENSOR SIGNAL

NOTE: *For connector terminal identification, see CONNECTOR IDENTIFICATION. For wiring diagram, see WIRING DIAGRAMS.*

1) Using scan tool, read DTCs. If Global Good Trips is displayed and equal to zero, go to next step. If Global Good Trips is not displayed or is equal to more than zero, go to DTC P0500-B: NO VEHICLE SPEED SENSOR SIGNAL.

2) Raise and support vehicle under lower control arms, allowing drive wheels to spin free. Start engine. Using scan tool, read Vehicle Speed Sensor (VSS). Put transmission in any forward gear. If scan tool displays more than zero MPH, go to DTC P0500-B: NO VEHICLE SPEED SENSOR SIGNAL. If scan tool does not display more than zero MPH, go to next step.

3) Using scan tool, read Electronic Automatic Transaxle (EATX) DTCs. If P0731-P0736, P0715, P0720, P0736 or PINION FACTOR NOT PROGRAMMED is displayed, repair transmission as required. See appropriate article in AUTOMATIC TRANSMISSIONS in appropriate MITCHELL® TRANSMISSION SERVICE & REPAIR manual. If P0731-P0736, P0715, P0720, P0736 or PINION FACTOR NOT PROGRAMMED is not displayed, go to next step.

4) Turn ignition off. Disconnect Transmission Control Module (TCM) connector. Connect one end of a jumper wire to TCM connector terminal No. 58. See TCM CONNECTOR WIRE IDENTIFICATION table. Turn ignition on. Using scan tool, read VSS signal. While observing scan tool display, quickly tap other end of jumper wire to ground. If scan tool does not display more than zero MPH, go to next step. If scan tool displays more than zero MPH, repair transmission as required. See appropriate article in AUTOMATIC TRANSMISSIONS in appropriate MITCHELL® TRANSMISSION SERVICE & REPAIR manual.

5) Turn ignition off. Disconnect PCM connector. Using an ohmmeter, check resistance of VSS signal circuit between PCM connector terminal

CHRY
4-286

1999 ACCESSORIES & EQUIPMENT
Cruise Control Systems – Concorde, Intrepid, LHS & 300M (Cont.)

No. 66 and TCM connector terminal No. 58. See TCM CONNECTOR WIRE IDENTIFICATION table. If resistance is less than 5 ohms, go to next step. If resistance is 5 ohms or more, repair open VSS signal circuit. Perform TEST VER-5A: OBD-II ROAD TEST under VERIFICATION TESTS.

6) Using an ohmmeter, check resistance of VSS signal circuit between TCM connector terminal No. 58 and ground. If resistance is less than 5 ohms, repair short to ground on VSS signal circuit. Perform TEST VER-5A: OBD-II ROAD TEST under VERIFICATION TESTS. If resistance is 5 ohms or more, replace PCM. Perform TEST VER-5A: OBD-II ROAD TEST under VERIFICATION TESTS.

TCM CONNECTOR WIRE IDENTIFICATION

Application	Wire Color
TCM Terminal No. 58 Vehicle Speed Sensor Signal Circuit	White/Orange

DTC P0500-B: NO VEHICLE SPEED SENSOR SIGNAL

1) Using scan tool, check freeze frame data to determine conditions when DTC set. Attempt to duplicate freeze frame data and set DTC again. Raise and support vehicle under lower control arms, allowing drive wheels to spin free. Start engine. Read Vehicle Speed Sensor (VSS). Put transmission in any forward gear. If scan tool displays zero MPH, go to DTC P0500-A: NO VEHICLE SPEED SENSOR SIGNAL. If scan tool displays more than zero MPH, go to next step.

2) Inspect wiring and connectors. Repair as necessary. Perform TEST VER-5A: OBD-II ROAD TEST under VERIFICATION TESTS. If wiring and connectors are okay, go to INACTIVE TROUBLE CODE CONDITION under SELF-DIAGNOSTIC SYSTEM.

DTC P0703-A: BRAKE SWITCH SENSE CIRCUIT

NOTE: For connector terminal identification, see CONNECTOR IDENTIFICATION. For wiring diagram, see WIRING DIAGRAMS.

1) Turn ignition off. Disconnect brake switch connector. Turn ignition on. Using a voltmeter, check voltage of brake switch sense circuit at brake switch connector. See BRAKE SWITCH CONNECTOR WIRE IDENTIFICATION table. If voltage is more than 9 volts, go to next step. If voltage is 9 volts or less, go to step 4).

2) Observe brake switch status on scan tool. Connect a jumper wire from brake switch sense circuit to brake switch ground circuit. If scan tool display changed from PRESSED to RELEASED, replace brake switch. Perform TEST VER-2A: ROAD TEST VERIFICATION under VERIFICATION TESTS. If scan tool display did not change, go to next step.

3) Using a ohmmeter, check resistance of ground circuit between brake switch connector and ground. See BRAKE SWITCH CONNECTOR WIRE IDENTIFICATION table. If resistance is less than 5 ohms, replace PCM. Perform TEST VER-2A: ROAD TEST VERIFICATION under VERIFICATION TESTS. If resistance is 5 ohms or more, repair open ground circuit. Perform TEST VER-2A: ROAD TEST VERIFICATION under VERIFICATION TESTS.

4) Turn ignition off. Disconnect Powertrain Control Module (PCM) connector. Inspect PCM connector for pushed out terminals or damage. Repair PCM connector as necessary. Perform TEST VER-2A: ROAD TEST VERIFICATION under VERIFICATION TESTS. If PCM connector is okay, go to next step.

5) Using a ohmmeter, check resistance of brake switch sense circuit between PCM connector terminal No. 62 and brake switch connector. See BRAKE SWITCH CONNECTOR WIRE IDENTIFICATION table and PCM CONNECTOR WIRE IDENTIFICATION table. If resistance is less than 5 ohms, go to next step. If resistance is 5 ohms or more, repair open brake switch sense circuit. Perform TEST VER-2A: ROAD TEST VERIFICATION under VERIFICATION TESTS.

6) Using a ohmmeter, check resistance of brake switch sense circuit between PCM connector terminal No. 62 and ground. See PCM CONNECTOR WIRE IDENTIFICATION table. If resistance is less than 5 ohms, repair short to ground on brake switch sense circuit. Perform

TEST VER-2A: ROAD TEST VERIFICATION under VERIFICATION TESTS. If resistance is 5 ohms or more, replace PCM. Perform TEST VER-2A: ROAD TEST VERIFICATION under VERIFICATION TESTS.

BRAKE SWITCH CONNECTOR WIRE IDENTIFICATION

Application	Wire Color
Brake Switch Sense Circuit	White/Pink
Brake Switch Ground Circuit	Black/Tan

PCM CONNECTOR WIRE IDENTIFICATION

Application	Wire Color
PCM Terminal No. 50 Ground Circuit	Black/Tan
PCM Terminal No. 62 Brake Switch Sense Circuit	White/Pink

DTC P1595-A: SPEED CONTROL SOLENOID CIRCUITS

NOTE: For connector terminal identification, see CONNECTOR IDENTIFICATION. For wiring diagram, see WIRING DIAGRAMS.

1) Turn speed control (cruise control) on. Using scan tool, actuate speed control vent solenoid. If speed control servo clicks, go to next step. If speed control servo does not click, go to step 7).

2) Scan tool should still be actuating speed control vent solenoid. Wiggle wiring harness between speed control servo, brake switch and Powertrain Control Module (PCM). If wiggling did not cause an interruption of speed control servo actuation, go to next step. If wiggling caused an interruption of speed control servo actuation, repair wiring harness as necessary where wiggling caused problem to appear. Perform TEST VER-4A: SPEED CONTROL VERIFICATION under VERIFICATION TESTS.

3) Using scan tool, actuate speed control vacuum solenoid. If speed control servo clicks, go to next step. If speed control vacuum solenoid does not click, go to step 7).

4) Scan tool should still be actuating speed control vent solenoid. Wiggle wiring harness between speed control servo and brake switch to PCM while scan tool is still actuating speed control vacuum solenoid. If wiggling did not cause an interruption of speed control servo actuation, go to next step. If wiggling caused an interruption of speed control servo actuation, repair wiring harness as necessary where wiggling caused problem to appear. Perform TEST VER-4A: SPEED CONTROL VERIFICATION under VERIFICATION TESTS.

5) Condition to set trouble code is not present at this time. SPEED CONTROL SOLENOID CIRCUITS DTC sets when PCM actuates vacuum and vent solenoids, but solenoids do not respond. Possible causes are: solenoid control circuit open or shorted, vacuum or vent solenoid shorted or open, open or shorted speed control power supply circuit or PCM failure. Go to next step.

6) Inspect all related wiring and connectors and repair as necessary. If related wiring and connectors were repaired, perform TEST VER-4A: SPEED CONTROL VERIFICATION under VERIFICATION TESTS. If no problems were found with wiring and connectors, test is complete. Perform TEST VER-4A: SPEED CONTROL VERIFICATION under VERIFICATION TESTS.

7) Disconnect speed control servo 4-pin connector. DO NOT depress brake pedal during testing. Turn ignition on with engine off. Turn speed control switch on. Using a 12-volt test light, probe brake switch output circuit at speed control servo connector. See SPEED CONTROL SERVO CONNECTOR WIRE IDENTIFICATION table. If test light is not illuminated or dim, go to next step. If test light is illuminated and bright, go to step 11).

8) Turn ignition off. Using an ohmmeter, check resistance of speed control servo 4-pin connector brake switch output circuit to ground. See SPEED CONTROL SERVO CONNECTOR WIRE IDENTIFICATION table. If resistance is 5 ohms or more, go to next step. If resistance is less than 5 ohms, repair short to ground on appropriate wire. Perform TEST VER-4A: SPEED CONTROL VERIFICATION under VERIFICATION TESTS.

9) Disconnect brake switch connector. Brake switch connector is located near top of brake pedal. Turn ignition on with engine off. Using a 12-volt test light, probe S/C power supply circuit at brake switch connector. See BRAKE SWITCH CONNECTOR WIRE IDENTIFICATION table. If test light is not illuminated or dim, go to next step. If test light is illuminated and bright, perform DTC P1595-B: SPEED CONTROL SOLENOID CIRCUITS.

10) Turn ignition off. Disconnect Powertrain Control Module (PCM) connector. Using an ohmmeter, check resistance of speed control power supply circuit between brake switch connector and PCM connector terminal No. 50. See BRAKE SWITCH CONNECTOR WIRE IDENTIFICATION table. If resistance is less than 5 ohms, replace PCM. Perform TEST VER-4A: SPEED CONTROL VERIFICATION under VERIFICATION TESTS. If resistance is 5 ohms or more, repair open speed control power supply circuit. Perform TEST VER-4A: SPEED CONTROL VERIFICATION under VERIFICATION TESTS.

11) Using an ohmmeter, check resistance of ground circuit between speed control servo 4-pin connector and ground. See BRAKE SWITCH CONNECTOR WIRE IDENTIFICATION table. If resistance is less than 5 ohms, go to next step. If resistance is 5 ohms or more, repair open ground circuit. Perform TEST VER-4A: SPEED CONTROL VERIFICATION under VERIFICATION TESTS.

12) Disconnect Powertrain Control Module (PCM) connectors. Using an ohmmeter, check resistance of speed control vacuum solenoid control circuit between speed control servo 4-pin connector and PCM connector terminal No. 56. See SPEED CONTROL SERVO CONNECTOR WIRE IDENTIFICATION table and PCM CONNECTOR WIRE IDENTIFICATION table. If resistance is less than 5 ohms, go to next step. If resistance is 5 ohms or more, repair open speed control vacuum solenoid control circuit. Perform TEST VER-4A: SPEED CONTROL VERIFICATION under VERIFICATION TESTS.

13) Using an ohmmeter, check resistance of speed control vent solenoid control circuit between PCM connector terminal No. 80 and speed control servo 4-pin connector. See SPEED CONTROL SERVO CONNECTOR WIRE IDENTIFICATION table and PCM CONNECTOR WIRE IDENTIFICATION table. If resistance is less than 5 ohms, go to next step. If resistance is 5 ohms or more, repair open speed control vent solenoid control circuit. Perform TEST VER-4A: SPEED CONTROL VERIFICATION under VERIFICATION TESTS.

14) Using an ohmmeter, check resistance of speed control vacuum solenoid control circuit between speed control servo 4-pin connector and ground. See SPEED CONTROL SERVO CONNECTOR WIRE IDENTIFICATION table. If resistance is 5 ohms or more, go to next step. If resistance is less than 5 ohms, repair short to ground on speed control vacuum solenoid control circuit. Perform TEST VER-4A: SPEED CONTROL VERIFICATION under VERIFICATION TESTS.

15) Using an ohmmeter, check resistance of speed control vent solenoid control circuit between speed control servo 4-pin connector and ground. See SPEED CONTROL SERVO CONNECTOR WIRE IDENTIFICATION table. If resistance is less than 5 ohms, repair short to ground on speed control vent solenoid control circuit. Perform TEST VER-4A: SPEED CONTROL VERIFICATION under VERIFICATION TESTS. If resistance is 5 ohms or more, replace speed control servo. Perform TEST VER-4A: SPEED CONTROL VERIFICATION under VERIFICATION TESTS.

SPEED CONTROL SERVO CONNECTOR WIRE IDENTIFICATION

Application	Wire Color
Brake Switch Output Circuit	Dark Blue/Red
Ground	Black
Vacuum Solenoid Control Circuit	Tan/Red
Vent Solenoid Control Circuit	Light Green/Red

BRAKE SWITCH CONNECTOR WIRE IDENTIFICATION

Application	Wire Color
Brake Switch Sense	White/Pink
Speed Control Brake Switch Output	Dark Blue/Red
Speed Control Power Supply Circuit Input	Yellow/Red

PCM CONNECTOR WIRE IDENTIFICATION

Application	Wire Color
PCM Terminal No. 50 Ground	Black/Tan
PCM Terminal No. 56 Speed Control Vacuum Solenoid Control Circuit	Tan/Red
PCM Terminal No. 80 Speed Control Vent Solenoid Control Circuit	Light Green/Red

DTC P1595-B: SPEED CONTROL SOLENOID CIRCUITS

NOTE: For connector terminal identification, see CONNECTOR IDENTIFICATION. For wiring diagram, see WIRING DIAGRAMS.

1) Using an ohmmeter, check resistance of speed control brake switch output circuit between brake switch connector and speed control servo 4-pin connector. See SPEED CONTROL SERVO CONNECTOR WIRE IDENTIFICATION table and BRAKE SWITCH CONNECTOR WIRE IDENTIFICATION table. If resistance is 5 ohms or less, go to next step. If resistance is more than 5 ohms, repair open brake switch output circuit. Perform TEST VER-4A: SPEED CONTROL VERIFICATION under VERIFICATION TESTS.

2) Check brake switch adjustment. See BRAKE SWITCH under REMOVAL & INSTALLATION. If brake switch adjustment is okay, replace brake switch. Perform TEST VER-4A: SPEED CONTROL VERIFICATION under VERIFICATION TESTS. If brake switch adjustment is not okay, adjust brake switch as necessary. Perform TEST VER-4A: SPEED CONTROL VERIFICATION under VERIFICATION TESTS.

DTC P1597-A: SPEED CONTROL SWITCH ALWAYS LOW

NOTE: For connector terminal identification, see CONNECTOR IDENTIFICATION. For wiring diagram, see WIRING DIAGRAMS.

1) Using scan tool, read speed control switch volts. If voltage is less than one volt, go to step **3)**. If voltage is one volt or more, go to next step.

2) Condition to set trouble code is not present at this time. SPEED CONTROL SWITCH ALWAYS LOW DTC sets if speed control switch voltage is less than 4.5 volts for 2 minutes. Possible causes are: speed control switch circuit shorted, Powertrain Control Module (PCM) failure, shorted speed control switch signal circuit, or shorted speed control switch. See INACTIVE TROUBLE CODE CONDITION under SELF-DIAGNOSTIC SYSTEM. Test is complete. Perform TEST VER-4A: SPEED CONTROL VERIFICATION under VERIFICATION TESTS.

3) Disconnect speed control on/off switch 2-pin connector. Observe scan tool voltage reading. If voltage changed to 5 volts, replace speed control on/off switch. Perform TEST VER-4A: SPEED CONTROL VERIFICATION under VERIFICATION TESTS. If voltage did not change to 5 volts, go to next step.

4) Disconnect speed control resume/accel switch. Observe scan tool voltage reading. If voltage changed to 5 volts, replace speed control resume/accel switch. Perform TEST VER-4A: SPEED CONTROL VERIFICATION under VERIFICATION TESTS. If voltage did not change to 5 volts, go to next step.

5) Turn ignition off. Using an ohmmeter, check resistance between speed control on/off switch 2-pin connector terminals. See SPEED CONTROL SWITCH CONNECTOR WIRE IDENTIFICATION table. If resistance is less than 5 ohms, repair short to ground. Perform TEST VER-4A: SPEED CONTROL VERIFICATION under VERIFICATION TESTS. If resistance is 5 ohms or more, go to next step.

6) Disconnect PCM connectors. Inspect connectors. Clean or repair as necessary. Using an ohmmeter, check resistance between ground and speed control switch signal circuit at speed control switch connector. See SPEED CONTROL SWITCH CONNECTOR WIRE IDENTIFICATION table. If resistance is less than 5 ohms, go to next step. If resistance is 5 ohms or more, replace PCM. Perform TEST VER-4A: SPEED CONTROL VERIFICATION under VERIFICATION TESTS.

CHRY
4-288

1999 ACCESSORIES & EQUIPMENT
Cruise Control Systems – Concorde, Intrepid, LHS & 300M (Cont.)

7) Disconnect clockspring 5-pin connector. Inspect connectors. Clean or repair as necessary. Using an ohmmeter, check resistance of speed control switch signal circuit between clockspring and speed control switch connector (Red/Light Green wire). If resistance is 5 ohms or more, replace clockspring. Perform TEST VER-4A: SPEED CONTROL VERIFICATION under VERIFICATION TESTS. If resistance is less than 5 ohms, repair short to ground. Perform TEST VER-4A: SPEED CONTROL VERIFICATION under VERIFICATION TESTS.

SPEED CONTROL SWITCH CONNECTOR WIRE IDENTIFICATION

Application	Wire Color
Ground Circuit	Black/Light Green
Speed Control Switch Signal Circuit	Red/Light Green

DTC P1683-A: SPEED CONTROL POWER RELAY CIRCUIT, OR 12V DRIVER CIRCUIT

NOTE: *For connector terminal identification, see CONNECTOR IDENTIFICATION. For wiring diagram, see WIRING DIAGRAMS.*

1) Disconnect speed control servo 4-pin connector. DO NOT depress brake pedal during testing. Turn ignition on with engine off. Using scan tool, actuate speed control relay. Using a 12-volt test light, probe speed control servo 4-pin connector brake switch output circuit. See SPEED CONTROL SERVO CONNECTOR WIRE IDENTIFICATION table. If test light is not illuminated or dim, go to next step. If test light is illuminated and bright, go to step 5).

2) Turn ignition off. Using an ohmmeter, check resistance of speed control servo 4-pin connector brake switch output circuit to ground. See SPEED CONTROL SERVO CONNECTOR WIRE IDENTIFICATION table. If resistance is 5 ohms or more, go to next step. If resistance is less than 5 ohms, repair short to ground on brake switch output circuit. Perform TEST VER-4A: SPEED CONTROL VERIFICATION under VERIFICATION TESTS.

3) Disconnect brake switch connector. Brake switch connector is located near top of brake pedal. Turn ignition on with engine off. Using scan tool, actuate speed control solenoid. Using a 12-volt test light, probe speed control power supply circuit at brake switch connector. See BRAKE SWITCH CONNECTOR WIRE IDENTIFICATION table. If test light is not illuminated or dim, go to next step. If test light is illuminated and bright, perform DTC P1683-B: SPEED CONTROL POWER RELAY CIRCUIT, OR S/C 12V DRIVER CIRCUIT. test

4) Turn ignition off. Disconnect Powertrain Control Module (PCM) connector. Using an ohmmeter, check resistance of speed control power supply circuit between brake switch connector and PCM connector terminal No. 5. See BRAKE SWITCH CONNECTOR WIRE IDENTIFICATION table and PCM CONNECTOR WIRE IDENTIFICATION table. If resistance is less than 5 ohms, replace PCM. Perform TEST VER-4A: SPEED CONTROL VERIFICATION under VERIFICATION TESTS. If resistance is 5 ohms or more. repair open speed control power supply circuit. Perform TEST VER-4A: SPEED CONTROL VERIFICATION under VERIFICATION TESTS.

5) Turn ignition off. Using an ohmmeter, check resistance of ground circuit at speed control servo 4-pin connector. See SPEED CONTROL SERVO CONNECTOR WIRE IDENTIFICATION table. If resistance is less than 5 ohms, go to next step. If resistance is 5 ohms or more, repair open ground circuit. Perform TEST VER-4A: SPEED CONTROL VERIFICATION under VERIFICATION TESTS.

6) Disconnect Powertrain Control Module (PCM) connectors. Using an ohmmeter, check resistance of speed control vacuum solenoid control circuit between speed control servo 4-pin connector and PCM connector terminal No. 56. See SPEED CONTROL SERVO CONNECTOR WIRE IDENTIFICATION table and PCM CONNECTOR WIRE IDENTIFICATION table. If resistance is less than 5 ohms, go to next step. If resistance is 5 ohms or more, repair open speed control vacuum solenoid control circuit. Perform TEST VER-4A: SPEED CONTROL VERIFICATION under VERIFICATION TESTS.

7) Using an ohmmeter, check resistance of speed control vent solenoid control circuit between PCM connector terminal No. 80 and speed control servo 4-pin connector. If resistance is less than 5 ohms, go to

next step. If resistance is 5 ohms or more, repair open speed control vent solenoid control circuit. Perform TEST VER-4A: SPEED CONTROL VERIFICATION under VERIFICATION TESTS.

8) Using an ohmmeter, check resistance of speed control vacuum solenoid control circuit between speed control servo 4-pin connector and ground. See SPEED CONTROL SERVO CONNECTOR WIRE IDENTIFICATION table. If resistance is 5 ohms or more, go to next step. If resistance is less than 5 ohms, repair short to ground on speed control vacuum solenoid control circuit. Perform TEST VER-4A: SPEED CONTROL VERIFICATION under VERIFICATION TESTS.

9) Using an ohmmeter, check resistance of speed control vent solenoid control circuit between speed control servo 4-pin connector and ground. If resistance is less than 5 ohms, repair short to ground on speed control vent solenoid control circuit. Perform TEST VER-4A: SPEED CONTROL VERIFICATION under VERIFICATION TESTS. If resistance is 5 ohms or more, replace speed control servo. Perform TEST VER-4A: SPEED CONTROL VERIFICATION under VERIFICATION TESTS.

SPEED CONTROL SERVO CONNECTOR WIRE IDENTIFICATION

Application	Wire Color
Brake Switch Output Circuit	Dark Blue/Red
Ground	Black
Speed Control Vacuum Solenoid Control Circuit	Tan/Red
Speed Control Vent Solenoid Control Circuit	Light Green/Red

BRAKE SWITCH CONNECTOR WIRE IDENTIFICATION

Application	Wire Color
Speed Control Power Supply Circuit	Yellow/Red

PCM CONNECTOR WIRE IDENTIFICATION

Application	Wire Color
PCM Terminal No. 5	
Speed Control Power Supply Circuit	Yellow/Red
PCM Terminal No. 56	
Speed Control Vacuum Solenoid Control Circuit	Tan/Red
PCM Terminal No. 80	
Speed Control Vent Solenoid Control Circuit	Light Green/Red

DTC P1683-B: SPEED CONTROL POWER RELAY CIRCUIT, OR S/C 12V DRIVER CIRCUIT

NOTE: *For connector terminal identification, see CONNECTOR IDENTIFICATION. For wiring diagram, see WIRING DIAGRAMS.*

1) Using an ohmmeter, check resistance of speed control brake switch output circuit between brake switch connector and speed control servo 4-pin connector. See SPEED CONTROL SERVO CONNECTOR WIRE IDENTIFICATION table and BRAKE SWITCH CONNECTOR WIRE IDENTIFICATION table. If resistance is 5 ohms or less, go to next step. If resistance is more than 5 ohms, repair open brake switch output circuit. Perform TEST VER-4A: SPEED CONTROL VERIFICATION under VERIFICATION TESTS.

2) Check brake switch adjustment. See BRAKE SWITCH under REMOVAL & INSTALLATION. If brake switch adjustment is okay, replace brake switch. Perform TEST VER-4A: SPEED CONTROL VERIFICATION under VERIFICATION TESTS. If brake switch adjustment is not okay, adjust brake switch as necessary. Perform TEST VER-4A: SPEED CONTROL VERIFICATION under VERIFICATION TESTS.

SPEED CONTROL SERVO CONNECTOR WIRE IDENTIFICATION

Application	Wire Color
Brake Switch Output Circuit	Dark Blue/Red

BRAKE SWITCH CONNECTOR WIRE IDENTIFICATION

Application	Wire Color
Brake Switch Output Circuit	Dark Blue/Red

DTC P1899-A: PARK/NEUTRAL SWITCH STUCK IN PARK OR IN GEAR

NOTE: DTC will set if PCM detects an incorrect P/N switch signal for given mode of operation.

1) Using scan tool, read DTCs. If Global Good Trips is displayed and equal to zero, go to next step. If Global Good Trips is not displayed or equal to zero, go to DTC P1899-B: PARK/NEUTRAL SWITCH STUCK IN PARK OR IN GEAR.

2) Using scan tool, read Park/Neutral (P/N) switch state while moving gear selector through all positions. If scan tool displays P/N and D/R, go to next step. If scan tool does not display P/N and D/R, go to DTC P1899-B: PARK/NEUTRAL SWITCH STUCK IN PARK OR IN GEAR.

3) Turn ignition off. Disconnect PCM connectors. Inspect connectors. Clean or repair as necessary. Using an ohmmeter, check resistance between ground and P/N switch sense circuit at PCM connector C2, terminal No. 76 (Black/Pink wire). Move gear selector through all positions. If resistance did not switch from less than 5 ohms to more than 5 ohms, go to step . If resistance was less than 5 ohms at all gear positions, go to next step. If resistance switched from less than 5 ohms to more than 5 ohms, replace PCM. Perform TEST VER-5A: OBD-II ROAD TEST under VERIFICATION TESTS.

4) Disconnect Transmission Range Sensor (TRS) connector. Inspect connectors. Clean or repair as necessary. If resistance is still less than 5 ohms, repair short to ground. Perform TEST VER-5A: OBD-II ROAD TEST under VERIFICATION TESTS. If resistance is 5 ohms or more, replace TRS. Perform TEST VER-5A: OBD-II ROAD TEST under VERIFICATION TESTS.

5) Disconnect Transmission Range Sensor (TRS) connector. Inspect connectors. Clean or repair as necessary. Using an ohmmeter, check resistance of P/N switch sense circuit between PCM connector C2, terminal No. 76 and TRS connector terminal No. 10 (Black/Pink wire). If resistance is 5 ohms or more, repair open circuit. Perform TEST VER-5A: OBD-II ROAD TEST under VERIFICATION TESTS. If resistance is less than 5 ohms, replace TRS. Perform TEST VER-5A: OBD-II ROAD TEST under VERIFICATION TESTS.

DTC P1899-B: PARK/NEUTRAL SWITCH STUCK IN PARK OR IN GEAR

1) Turn ignition off. Disconnect PCM connectors. Inspect connectors. Clean or repair as necessary. Using an ohmmeter, check resistance between ground and P/N switch sense circuit at PCM connector C2, terminal No. 76 (Black/Pink wire). While observing ohmmeter, wiggle wiring between TRS and PCM. If resistance changes while wiggling wires, repair wiring. Perform TEST VER-5A: OBD-II ROAD TEST under VERIFICATION TESTS. If resistance does not change while wiggling wires, go to next step.

2) Visually inspect wiring and connectors in P/N switch circuit. Repair as necessary. Perform TEST VER-5A: OBD-II ROAD TEST under VERIFICATION TESTS. If wiring and connectors are okay, go to INACTIVE TROUBLE CODE CONDITION under SELF-DIAGNOSTIC SYSTEM.

SYSTEM TESTS

NTC-1A: CHECKING SPEED CONTROL OPERATION

NOTE: Use this test only if no speed control trouble codes are set.

1) Turn ignition on. Using scan tool, monitor speed control switch inputs. While observing scan tool, press speed control ON switch several times. If scan tool does not display speed control switch ON and OFF, go to NTC-2A: CHECKING SPEED CONTROL ON/OFF SWITCH. If scan tool displays speed control switch ON and OFF, go to next step.

2) While observing scan tool, press SET switch several times. If scan tool does not display PRESSED and RELEASED, replace SET switch. Perform TEST VER-4A: SPEED CONTROL VERIFICATION under VERIFICATION TESTS. If scan tool displays PRESSED and RELEASED, go to next step.

3) While observing scan tool, press RESUME switch several times. If scan tool does not display PRESSED and RELEASED, go to NTC- 3A: CHECKING SPEED CONTROL RESUME SWITCH. Perform TEST VER-4A: SPEED CONTROL VERIFICATION under VERIFICATION TESTS. If scan tool displays PRESSED and RELEASED, go to next step.

4) While observing scan tool, press CANCEL switch several times. If scan tool does not display PRESSED and RELEASED, replace CANCEL switch. Perform TEST VER-4A: SPEED CONTROL VERIFICATION under VERIFICATION TESTS. If scan tool displays PRESSED and RELEASED, go to next step.

5) While observing scan tool, press COAST switch several times. If scan tool does not display PRESSED and RELEASED, replace COAST switch. Perform TEST VER-4A: SPEED CONTROL VERIFICATION under VERIFICATION TESTS. If scan tool displays PRESSED and RELEASED, go to next step.

6) While observing scan tool, press brake pedal several times. If scan tool does not display PRESSED and RELEASED, go to NTC-4A: CHECKING BRAKE SWITCH SENSE. If scan tool displays PRESSED and RELEASED, go to NTC-1B: CHECKING SPEED CONTROL OPERATION.

NTC-1B: CHECKING SPEED CONTROL OPERATION

NOTE: Perform NTC-1A: CHECKING SPEED CONTROL OPERATION before proceeding.

1) While observing scan tool, place transmission in Drive. If scan tool does not display P/N switch D/R, go to DTC P1899-A: PARK/NEUTRAL SWITCH STUCK IN PARK OR IN GEAR under DIAGNOSTIC TESTS. If scan tool displays P/N switch D/R, go to next step.

2) Turn ignition off. Disconnect speed control servo connector. Inspect speed control servo connector for damaged or pushed out terminals. Repair as necessary. Perform TEST VER-4A: SPEED CONTROL VERIFICATION under VERIFICATION TESTS. If wiring and connectors are okay, go to next step.

3) Using an external ohmmeter, measure resistance of ground circuit (Black wire) between speed control servo connector terminal No. 4 and ground. If resistance is 5 ohms or more, repair open ground circuit. Perform TEST VER-4A: SPEED CONTROL VERIFICATION under VERIFICATION TESTS. If resistance is less than 5 ohms, go to next step.

4) Reconnect S/C servo connector. Turn ignition on. Using scan tool, actuate speed control vent solenoid. Using a 12-volt test light, back-probe S/C brake switch output circuit at S/C servo connector terminal No. 3 (Dark Blue/Red wire). If test light is not on or dim, go to NTC-4A: CHECKING BRAKE SWITCH SENSE. If test light is bright, go to next step.

5) Start engine. Allow engine to idle for one minute. Turn engine off. Turn ignition on. Using scan tool, actuate speed control servo solenoids. If throttle opens and closes, go to NTC-5A: CHECKING PARK/NEUTRAL POSITION SWITCH SENSE. If throttle does not open and close, go to next step.

6) Turn ignition off. Disconnect vacuum supply from speed control servo. Attach a vacuum gauge to disconnected vacuum hose. Start engine. If vacuum gauge does not read manifold vacuum, repair vacuum supply hose for a leak or restriction. Perform TEST VER-4A: SPEED CONTROL VERIFICATION under VERIFICATION TESTS. If vacuum gauge reads manifold vacuum, go to NTC-1C: CHECKING SPEED CONTROL OPERATION.

NTC-1C: CHECKING SPEED CONTROL OPERATION

NOTE: Perform NTC-1A: CHECKING SPEED CONTROL OPERATION before proceeding.

1) Turn engine off. Observe vacuum gauge for 10 seconds. If vacuum holds for at least 10 seconds, go to next step. If vacuum does not hold for at least 10 seconds, replace vacuum check valve. Perform TEST VER-4A: SPEED CONTROL VERIFICATION under VERIFICATION TESTS.

CHRY
4-290

1999 ACCESSORIES & EQUIPMENT
Cruise Control Systems – Concorde, Intrepid, LHS & 300M (Cont.)

2) Inspect throttle cable. If throttle cable is damaged or misadjusted, repair as necessary. Perform TEST VER-4A: SPEED CONTROL VERIFICATION under VERIFICATION TESTS. If throttle cable is okay, go to next step.

3) Turn ignition off. Disconnect speed control servo connector. Disconnect Powertrain Control Module (PCM) connector. Inspect connectors. Clean or repair as necessary. Using an external ohmmeter, measure resistance of speed control vacuum solenoid control circuit between PCM connector terminal No. 56 (Tan/Red wire) and speed control servo connector terminal No. 1 (Tan/Red wire). If resistance is 5 ohms or more, repair open speed control vacuum solenoid control circuit. Perform TEST VER-4A: SPEED CONTROL VERIFICATION under VERIFICATION TESTS. If resistance is less than 5 ohms, go to next step.

4) Measure resistance of speed control vent solenoid control circuit (Light Green/White wire) between PCM connector terminal No. 80 and speed control servo connector terminal No. 2. If resistance is less than 5 ohms, replace speed control servo. Perform TEST VER-4A: SPEED CONTROL VERIFICATION under VERIFICATION TESTS. If resistance is 5 ohms or more, repair open speed control vent solenoid control circuit. Perform TEST VER-4A: SPEED CONTROL VERIFICATION under VERIFICATION TESTS.

NTC-2A: CHECKING SPEED CONTROL ON/OFF SWITCH

NOTE: Perform NTC-1A: CHECKING SPEED CONTROL OPERATION before proceeding.

1) Turn ignition on. Using scan tool, read speed control switch voltage. If voltage is more than 4 volts, go to step 6). If voltage is 4 volts or less, go to next step.

2) Disconnect 2-pin ON/OFF/SET switch connector (located behind speed control ON/OFF/SET switch). Inspect connectors. Clean or repair as necessary. Using scan tool, read speed control switch voltage. If voltage is more than 4 volts, replace speed control ON/OFF/SET switch. Perform TEST VER-4A: SPEED CONTROL VERIFICATION under VERIFICATION TESTS. If voltage is 4 volts or less, go to next step.

3) Disconnect 2-pin RESUME/CANCEL/COAST switch connector (located behind speed control RESUME/CANCEL/COAST switch). Inspect connectors. Clean or repair as necessary. Using scan tool, read speed control switch voltage. If voltage is more than 4 volts, replace speed control RESUME/CANCEL/COAST switch. Perform TEST VER-4A: SPEED CONTROL VERIFICATION under VERIFICATION TESTS. If voltage is 4 volts or less, go to next step.

4) Disconnect clockspring 5-pin connector located underneath steering column. Inspect connectors. Clean or repair as necessary. Using scan tool, read speed control switch voltage. If voltage is more than 4 volts, replace clockspring. Perform TEST VER-4A: SPEED CONTROL VERIFICATION under VERIFICATION TESTS. If voltage is 4 volts or less, go to next step.

5) Disconnect Powertrain Control Module (PCM) connector. Inspect connectors. Clean or repair as necessary. Using external ohmmeter, measure resistance of speed control switch signal circuit between PCM connector terminal No. 41 (Red/Light Green wire) and ground. If resistance is less than 5100 ohms, repair short to ground on speed control switch signal circuit (Red/Light Green wire). Perform TEST VER-4A: SPEED CONTROL VERIFICATION under VERIFICATION TESTS. If resistance is 5100 ohms or more, replace PCM. Perform TEST VER-4A: SPEED CONTROL VERIFICATION under VERIFICATION TESTS.

6) Disconnect 2-pin speed control ON/OFF/SET switch connector (located behind speed control ON/OFF/SET switch). Inspect connectors. Clean or repair as necessary. Using an external voltmeter, measure voltage of speed control switch signal circuit between 2-pin speed control ON/OFF/SET switch connector (Red/Light Green wire) and ground. If voltage is more than 6 volts, repair speed control switch circuit (Red/Light Green wire) for short to voltage. Perform TEST VER-4A: SPEED CONTROL VERIFICATION under VERIFICATION TESTS. If voltage is less than 4 volts, go to next step. If voltage is 4-6 volts, repair

open or high resistance in speed control switch signal circuit. Perform TEST VER-4A: SPEED CONTROL VERIFICATION under VERIFICATION TESTS.

7) Connect a jumper wire between ground and 2-pin speed control ON/OFF/SET switch connector Red/Light Green wire. Turn ignition on. Using scan tool, read speed control switch voltage. If voltage is less than one volt, replace speed control ON/OFF/SET switch. Perform TEST VER-4A: SPEED CONTROL VERIFICATION under VERIFICATION TESTS. If voltage is one volt or more, replace PCM. Perform TEST VER-4A: SPEED CONTROL VERIFICATION under VERIFICATION TESTS.

NTC-3A: CHECKING SPEED CONTROL RESUME SWITCH

NOTE: Perform NTC-1A: CHECKING SPEED CONTROL OPERATION before proceeding.

1) Disconnect 2-pin RESUME/ACCEL switch connector (located behind speed control RESUME/ACCEL switch). Inspect connectors. Clean or repair as necessary. Connect a jumper wire between ground and 2-pin speed control RESUME/ACCEL switch connector (Red/Light Green wire). Turn ignition on. Using scan tool, read speed control switch voltage. If voltage is less than one volt, replace speed control RESUME/ACCEL switch. Perform TEST VER-4A: SPEED CONTROL VERIFICATION under VERIFICATION TESTS. If voltage is one volt or more, go to next step.

2) Remove jumper wire from 2-pin speed control RESUME/ACCEL switch connector. Using external ohmmeter, measure resistance between speed control RESUME/ACCEL switch (Black/Light Green wire) and ground. If resistance is less than 5 ohms, repair open speed control switch signal circuit between RESUME/ACCEL switch and clockspring. Perform TEST VER-4A: SPEED CONTROL VERIFICATION under VERIFICATION TESTS. See WIRING DIAGRAMS. If resistance is 5 ohms or more, repair open ground circuit (Black/Light Green wire). Perform TEST VER-4A: SPEED CONTROL VERIFICATION under VERIFICATION TESTS.

NTC-4A: CHECKING BRAKE SWITCH SENSE

NOTE: Perform NTC-1A: CHECKING SPEED CONTROL OPERATION before proceeding.

1) Disconnect brake switch connector. Inspect connector. Clean or replace as necessary. Using a voltmeter, measure voltage on brake switch sense circuit at brake switch connector terminal No. 1 (White/Pink wire). If voltage is more than 10 volts, go to next step. If voltage is 10 volts or less, go to step .

2) Connect jumper wire between brake switch connector White/Pink wire and ground. Using scan tool, read brake switch input status. If scan tool displays brake switch RELEASED, replace brake switch. Perform TEST VER-4A: SPEED CONTROL VERIFICATION under VERIFICATION TESTS. If scan tool does not display brake switch RELEASED, repair open ground circuit. Perform TEST VER-4A: SPEED CONTROL VERIFICATION under VERIFICATION TESTS.

3) Turn ignition off. Disconnect PCM connectors. Inspect connector terminals. If any terminal is damaged, pushed out or miswired, repair as necessary. Perform TEST VER-4A: SPEED CONTROL VERIFICATION under VERIFICATION TESTS. If terminals are okay, go to next step.

4) Using an ohmmeter, check resistance between ground and brake switch sense circuit at PCM connector C2, terminal No. 62 (White/Pink wire). If resistance is less than 5 ohms, repair short to ground. Perform TEST VER-4A: SPEED CONTROL VERIFICATION under VERIFICATION TESTS. If resistance is 5 ohms or more, go to next step.

5) Using an ohmmeter, check resistance of brake switch sense circuit between brake switch connector terminal No. 1 and PCM connector C2, terminal No. 62 (White/Pink wire). If resistance is 5 ohms or more, repair open circuit. Perform TEST VER-4A: SPEED CONTROL VERIFICATION under VERIFICATION TESTS. If resistance is less than 5 ohms, replace PCM. Perform TEST VER-4A: SPEED CONTROL VERIFICATION under VERIFICATION TESTS.

1999 ACCESSORIES & EQUIPMENT
Cruise Control Systems – Concorde, Intrepid, LHS & 300M (Cont.)

CHRY
4-291

NTC-5A: CHECKING FOR A SPEED CONTROL DENIED MESSAGE

NOTE: Perform NTC-1A: CHECKING SPEED CONTROL OPERATION before proceeding.

1) At this time speed control switch and servo functions appear to operate properly. Using scan tool, monitor speed control output status. Road test vehicle at speeds of more than 35 MPH.

2) Attempt to set speed control. See SCAN TOOL DENIED STATUS table. Items listed in table will not allow speed control to set. The last or most recent cause for speed control not to set is indicated by denied status. Correct fault and recheck system operation.

SCAN TOOL DENIED STATUS

Denied Message	Reason
ON/OFF	PCM Does Not See An ON Signal From Switch At PCM Terminal No. 41.
SPEED	Vehicle Speed As Seen By PCM Terminal No. 66 Is Not Greater Than 30 MPH.
RPM	Engine RPM Is Excessively High.
BRAKE	Brake Switch Sense Circuit Is Open Indicating To PCM Brakes Are Applied. PCM Terminal No. 62 (Sense Circuit) Is Grounded Through Brake Pedal Switch When Brakes Are Released.
P/N	Park/Neutral Switch Sense Circuit Is Grounded Indicating To PCM Transmission Is Not In Gear. PCM Terminal No. 76 (Sense Circuit) Is Grounded Through Park/Neutral Switch When Transmission Is In Park Or Neutral.
RPM/SPD	PCM Senses Excessive Engine RPM For A Given Vehicle Speed.
SOL FLT	PCM Senses A Servo Solenoid Circuit Trouble Code That Is Maturing Or Set In Memory.

VERIFICATION TESTS

TEST VER-2A: ROAD TEST VERIFICATION

1) inspect vehicle to ensure that all engine components are connected. Connect all components as necessary. Using scan tool, erase DTCs. Reset all memory values.

2) Drive vehicle for at least 5 minutes. Accelerate to at least 40 MPH. Stop and turn engine off for 10 seconds. Restart vehicle and continue. Ensure transmission shifts through all gears.

3) After completion of road test, turn engine off. Using scan tool, read DTCs. If any DTCs exist, go to DTC TEST: CHECKING SYSTEM FOR DIAGNOSTIC TROUBLE CODES under DIAGNOSTIC TESTS. If there are no DTCs, repair was successful and is now complete.

TEST VER-4A: SPEED CONTROL VERIFICATION

1) If PCM has been replaced, and correct VIN and mileage have not been programmed, a DTC will be set in ABS, Air bag and SKIM modules. If vehicle is equipped with Sentry Key Immobilizer Module (SKIM), secret key data must be updated to enable starting. See PROGRAMMING in appropriate ANTI-THEFT SYSTEMS article.

2) For ABS and air bag systems, enter correct VIN and mileage in PCM. Erase DTCs in ABS and air bag modules. Inspect vehicle to ensure that all engine components are connected. Reassemble and connect components as necessary.

3) Using scan tool, erase DTCs in PCM. To ensure no other speed control problems exist, road test vehicle at a speed greater than 30 MPH. Turn speed control on. Depress and release SET switch. If speed control does not engage, repair is not complete. Check for related Technical Service Bulletins (TSBs) and return to DTC TEST: CHECKING SYSTEM FOR DIAGNOSTIC TROUBLE CODES under DIAGNOSTIC TESTS.

4) Quickly depress and release RESUME/ACCEL switch. If vehicle speed does not increase by 2 MPH, repair is not complete. Check for related TSBs and return to DTC TEST: CHECKING SYSTEM FOR DIAGNOSTIC TROUBLE CODES under DIAGNOSTIC TESTS.

5) Press and hold COAST switch. Vehicle speed should decrease. If vehicle speed does not decrease, repair is not complete. Check for related TSBs and return to DTC TEST: CHECKING SYSTEM FOR DIAGNOSTIC TROUBLE CODES under DIAGNOSTIC TESTS.

6) Using caution, press and release brake pedal. If speed control does not disengage, repair is not complete. Check for related TSBs and return to DTC TEST: CHECKING SYSTEM FOR DIAGNOSTIC TROUBLE CODES under DIAGNOSTIC TESTS.

7) Bring vehicle speed to 25 MPH. Depress RESUME/ACCEL switch. If speed control does not resume to previously set speed, repair is not complete. Check for related TSBs and return to DTC TEST: CHECKING SYSTEM FOR DIAGNOSTIC TROUBLE CODES under DIAGNOSTIC TESTS.

8) Hold down SET switch. If vehicle did not decelerate, repair is not complete. Check for related TSBs and return to DTC TEST: CHECKING SYSTEM FOR DIAGNOSTIC TROUBLE CODES under DIAGNOSTIC TESTS.

9) Ensure vehicle speed is greater than 30 MPH and release SET switch. If vehicle did not adjust and set a new speed, repair is not complete. Check for related TSBs and return to DTC TEST: CHECKING SYSTEM FOR DIAGNOSTIC TROUBLE CODES under DIAGNOSTIC TESTS.

10) Depress and release CANCEL switch. If speed control did not disengage, repair is not complete. Check for related TSBs and return to DTC TEST: CHECKING SYSTEM FOR DIAGNOSTIC TROUBLE CODES under DIAGNOSTIC TESTS.

11) Bring vehicle speed to 35 MPH and engage speed control. Turn speed control ON/OFF switch to OFF position. If speed control disengages, repair is complete. If speed control did not disengage, repair is not complete. Check for related TSBs and return to DTC TEST: CHECKING SYSTEM FOR DIAGNOSTIC TROUBLE CODES under DIAGNOSTIC TESTS.

TEST VER-5A: OBD-II ROAD TEST

1) If PCM has been replaced, and correct VIN and mileage have not been programmed, a DTC will be set in ABS, Air bag and SKIM modules. If vehicle is equipped with Sentry Key Immobilizer Module (SKIM), secret key data must be updated to enable starting. See PROGRAMMING in appropriate ANTI-THEFT SYSTEMS article.

2) For ABS and air bag systems, enter correct VIN and mileage in PCM. Erase DTCs in ABS and Air bag modules. If all DTCs have not been repaired, return to DTC TEST: CHECKING SYSTEM FOR DIAGNOSTIC TROUBLE CODES under DIAGNOSTIC TESTS.

3) Connect scan tool to DLC. Ensure fuel tank is at least 1/4 full. Turn off all accessories. To verify an OBD-II DTC repair, PCM must run appropriate monitor(s) and increment a Good Trip. A component DTC will require 2 minutes of engine run time without any DTCs to increment a Good trip.

4) A monitor DTC will require using scan tool pretest screen to monitor enabling conditions for DTC to set. Turn engine off. Wait 10 seconds. Restart vehicle and run for 2 minutes. If Good Trips equal one or more, repair is complete. If any DTCs set, return to DTC TEST: CHECKING SYSTEM FOR DIAGNOSTIC TROUBLE CODES under DIAGNOSTIC TESTS.

CHRY
4-292

1999 ACCESSORIES & EQUIPMENT
Cruise Control Systems – Concorde, Intrepid, LHS & 300M (Cont.)

REMOVAL & INSTALLATION

WARNING: Vehicle is equipped with an air bag. Air bag must be deactivated before servicing speed control components on or around steering column. See AIR BAG RESTRAINT SYSTEMS – CARS article.

CAUTION: When battery is disconnected, vehicle computer and memory systems may lose memory data. Driveability problems may exist until computer systems have completed a relearn cycle. See COMPUTER RELEARN PROCEDURES in GENERAL INFORMATION before disconnecting battery.

BRAKE SWITCH

Removal – Fully depress brake pedal and rotate brake switch counterclockwise approximately 30 degrees. Remove brake switch from bracket. Depress lock tabs holding brake switch mounting bracket and separate harness connector from brake switch.

Installation – Connect harness connector to brake switch. Depress brake pedal and insert brake switch into keyed hole in mounting bracket. Rotate brake switch clockwise into locked position. Gently pull back on brake pedal until pedal will go no further. This causes the brake switch plunger to ratchet backward to the correct position. No further adjustment is required.

SPEED CONTROL SERVO

Removal – Remove speed control cable mounting bracket from servo. Remove servo mounting bracket. Disconnect wiring harness connector and vacuum hose from servo. Pull cable away from servo to expose retaining clip. Remove retaining clip and cable. Remove servo.

Installation – With throttle in full open position, align hole in speed control cable sleeve with hole in servo pin. Install retaining clip. To complete installation, reverse removal procedure.

SPEED CONTROL SWITCH

Removal & Installation – Speed control switches are mounted on the steering wheel and wired through clockspring device under air bag module. Turn ignition switch to OFF position. Deactivate air bag. See AIR BAG RESTRAINT SYSTEMS – CARS article. Remove 2 screws from side of each switch. Rock switch back and forth to remove switch from steering wheel. Disconnect speed control switch connector. To install switch, reverse removal procedure.

WIRING DIAGRAMS

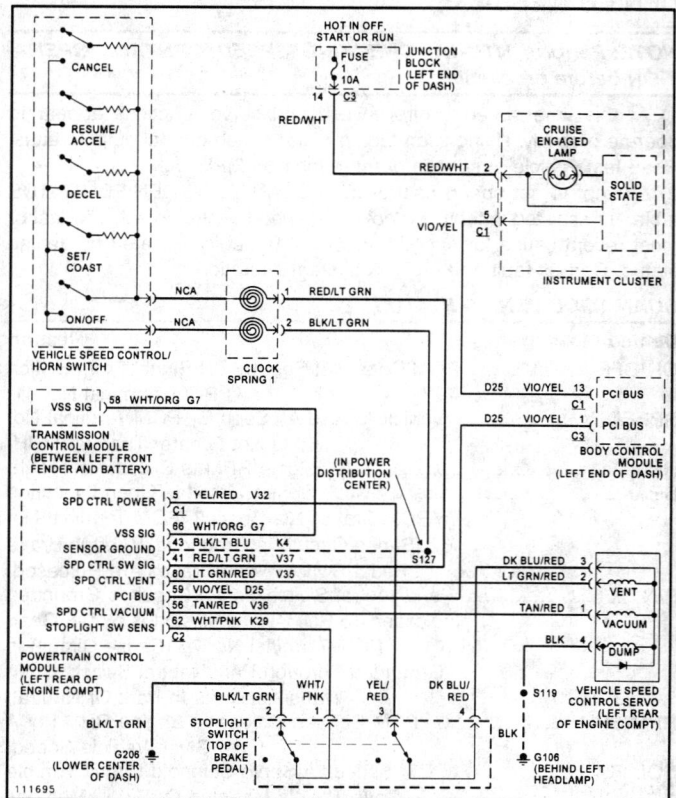

Fig. 6: Cruise Control System Wiring Diagram (Concorde, Intrepid, LHS & 300M)

Cruise Control Systems – Dakota, Durango, Ram Pickup, Ram Van & Ram Wagon

CAUTION: When battery is disconnected, vehicle computer and memory systems may lose memory data. Driveability problems may exist until computer systems have completed a relearn cycle. See COMPUTER RELEARN PROCEDURES article in GENERAL INFORMATION before disconnecting battery.

DESCRIPTION

The speed (cruise) control system is electronically controlled and vacuum operated. The electronic control is integrated into the Powertrain Control Module (PCM). System consists of the following components: Powertrain Control Module (PCM), servo, speed control switches, vacuum reservoir, vehicle speed sensor, speed control relay and brake switch.

System controls are located on each side of steering wheel air bag module and consist of ON/OFF, SET, RESUME/ACCEL, CANCEL AND COAST buttons. System is designed to operate at speeds above 30 MPH.

OPERATION

SYSTEM CONTROLS

To Set Speed Control – Press ON/OFF button to turn speed control system on. Accelerate to desired speed (minimum of 35 MPH) and press SET/COAST button. Vehicle speed will be maintained.

NOTE: Speed control system will automatically disengage when vehicle speed decreases to less than 35 MPH or increases to more than 85 MPH.

To Disengage Speed Control – Press brake pedal. Press clutch pedal (M/T). Press CANCEL button. Press ON/OFF button. If ON/OFF button is used, set speed will be erased from memory.

To Resume Previous Speed – If set speed has not been erased from memory and vehicle speed is more than 35 MPH, press RES/ACCEL button.

To Increase Speed – With speed control system on, increase set speed by rapidly pressing and releasing RES/ACCEL button. Each pressing of button will cause speed increase of 2 MPH. For example, pressing button 3 times will increase speed by 6 MPH. To increase speed gradually, hold RES/ACCEL button down until desired speed is reached. When button is released, new set speed will be maintained.

To Decrease Speed – With speed control system on, decrease set speed by pressing SET/COAST button. Vehicle speed will gradually decrease. Releasing button will set a new speed as long as vehicle speed is still more than 35 MPH.

COMPONENT LOCATIONS

COMPONENT LOCATIONS

Component	Location
ABS Control Module	
Ram Pickup	Left Side Of Engine Compartment
Ram Van/Wagon	Under Battery
Data Link Connector (DLC)	Lower Left Side Of Instrument Panel
Output Shaft Speed Sensor (OSS)	Left Side Of Transmission
Park/Neutral Position (PNP) Switch	Left Side Of Transmission
Powertrain Control Module (PCM)	
Dakota & Durango	Right Front Of Engine Compartment
Ram Pickup	Right Rear Corner Of Engine Compartment
Ram Van/Wagon	Under Hood Next To Wiper Motor

COMPONENT LOCATIONS (Cont.)

Component	Location
Vehicle Speed Sensor (VSS)	On Transmission Or Transfer Case Extension Housing

TROUBLE SHOOTING

ROAD TEST

Perform a road test to verify speed control malfunctions. Ensure speedometer operation is smooth without flutter at all speeds. Speedometer fluttering may cause surging in speed control system. For speedometer diagnosis, see appropriate INSTRUMENT PANELS article. If road test verifies a surge following speed control set and speedometer operates smoothly, see OVERSHOOT/UNDERSHOOT FOLLOWING SPEED CONTROL SET.

If road test verifies an inoperative system, and speedometer operates smoothly, check for:

- Diagnostic Trouble Codes (DTCs). See SELF-DIAGNOSTIC SYSTEM.
- Misadjusted brake switch. See BRAKE SWITCH under REMOVAL & INSTALLATION.
- Poor electrical connections at servo.
- Leaking vacuum reservoir, check valve, hoses or connections. See VACUUM SUPPLY under COMPONENT TESTS.
- Secure attachments of S/C servo cable.
- Smooth operation of throttle linkage.
- Defective PCM or wiring.
- Defective servo. See SPEED CONTROL SERVO under COMPONENT TESTS.

To verify a speed control electronic malfunction, use scan tool to check for DTCs. See SELF-DIAGNOSTIC SYSTEM. A speed control malfunction may occur without setting a DTC. If no DTCs are stored, go to CHECKING SPEED CONTROL OPERATION under SYSTEM TESTS.

OVERSHOOT/UNDERSHOOT FOLLOWING SPEED CONTROL SET

If operator repeatedly presses and releases set button with their foot off accelerator (lift foot set) to begin speed control operation, vehicle may accelerate and exceed desired set speed by 5 MPH and then decelerate to less than desired set speed before achieving desired set speed.

Speed Control (S/C) has as adaptive strategy that compensates for variations in S/C cable lengths. When S/C is set with vehicle operator's foot off accelerator pedal, S/C compensates for excessive S/C cable slack. If lift foot sets are continually used, speed control overshoot/undershoot condition will develop.

To "unlearn" overshoot/undershoot condition, operator must press and release set button while maintaining desired speed with accelerator pedal, then turn S/C switch to OFF position after waiting 10 seconds. This procedure must be repeated 10-15 times to completely unlearn overshoot/undershoot condition.

COMPONENT TESTS

WARNING: Vehicle is equipped with an air bag. Air bag must be deactivated before servicing speed control components on or around steering column. See appropriate AIR BAG RESTRAINT SYSTEMS article.

NOTE: For component locations, See COMPONENT LOCATIONS. For connector terminal identification, see CONNECTOR IDENTIFICATION. For wiring diagram, see WIRING DIAGRAMS.

BRAKE SWITCH

Disconnect brake switch 6-pin connector. Using an ohmmeter, check for continuity at brake switch. See Fig. 1. If continuity is not as specified in BRAKE SWITCH CONTINUITY table, check brake switch adjustment.

CHRY
4-294

1999 ACCESSORIES & EQUIPMENT
Cruise Control Systems – Dakota, Durango, Ram Pickup, Ram Van & Ram Wagon (Cont.)

See BRAKE SWITCH under REMOVAL & INSTALLATION. If brake switch adjustment is okay, replace defective brake switch.

BRAKE SWITCH CONTINUITY

Switch Plunger Position	Check Between Terminals	Continuity
Released	5 & 6	Yes
Depressed	1 & 2	Yes
	3 & 4	Yes

SPEED CONTROL SERVO

1) Start engine. Disconnect Speed Control (S/C) servo 4-pin connector. Turn S/C on. Using a voltmeter, check voltage at S/C servo connector terminal No. 3 (Dark Blue/Red wire). Battery voltage should exist when brake pedal is not depressed. If battery voltage exists, go to next step. If battery voltage does not exist, check circuit between brake switch and S/C servo. See WIRING DIAGRAMS.
2) Connect a jumper wire between S/C servo pin No. 3 and S/C servo connector terminal No. 3. Check voltage at S/C servo pins No. 1, 2 and 4. If battery voltage does not exist, replace S/C servo. If battery voltage exists, go to next step.
3) Turn ignition off. Check for continuity between S/C servo connector terminal No. 4 and ground. If continuity exists, test is complete. If continuity does not exist, repair open ground circuit as necessary.

VACUUM SUPPLY

Gasoline Engines – 1) Disconnect vacuum hose at speed control servo. Install vacuum gauge to disconnected vacuum hose. Start engine and observe gauge. Vacuum reading should be a minimum of 10 in. Hg. Turn engine off. Vacuum should continue to hold at a minimum of 10 in. Hg.
2) If vacuum is not as specified, check for kinked or leaking vacuum lines, defective check valve, defective vacuum reservoir or poor engine performance. If no problems are found, check speed control servo. See SPEED CONTROL SERVO.
Diesel Engines – 1) Disconnect vacuum hose at speed control servo. Install vacuum gauge to disconnected vacuum hose. Start engine and observe gauge. Vacuum reading should be a minimum of 25 in. Hg. A vacuum reservoir is not used on diesel vehicles.
2) If vacuum is not as specified, disconnect vacuum supply hose from vacuum pump. Install vacuum gauge to vacuum pump. Start engine and observe gauge. If vacuum reading is not 25 in. Hg or more, replace vacuum pump. If vacuum reading 25 in. Hg or more, go to next step.
3) Check all vacuum hoses to speed control servo, vacuum pump and heater-A/C system for leaks. Check vacuum check valve for leaks and proper operation. Vacuum check valve is located in vacuum hose between speed control servo and vacuum pump. If no problems are found, check speed control servo. See SPEED CONTROL SERVO.

CONNECTOR IDENTIFICATION

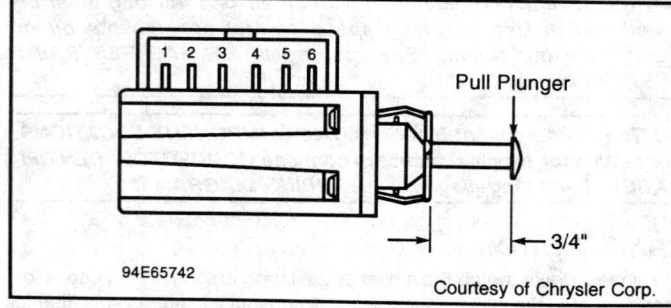

94E65742   Courtesy of Chrysler Corp.

Fig. 1: Identifying Brake Switch Terminals

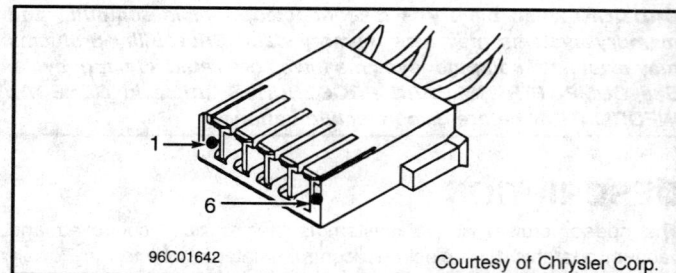

96C01642   Courtesy of Chrysler Corp.

Fig. 2: Identifying Brake Switch Harness Connector Terminals

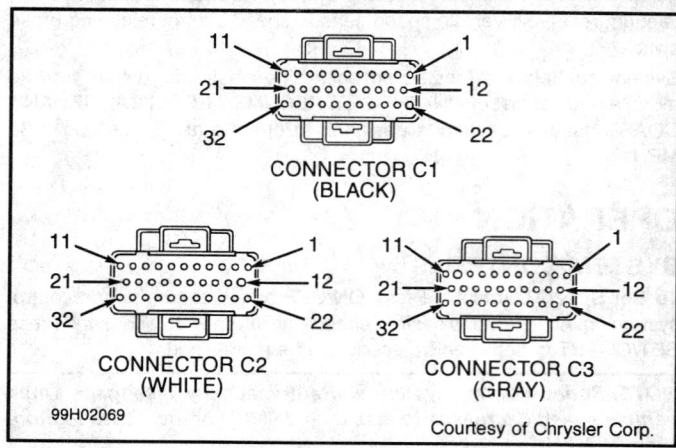

99H02069   Courtesy of Chrysler Corp.

Fig. 3: Identifying Powertrain Control Module (PCM) Connector Terminals

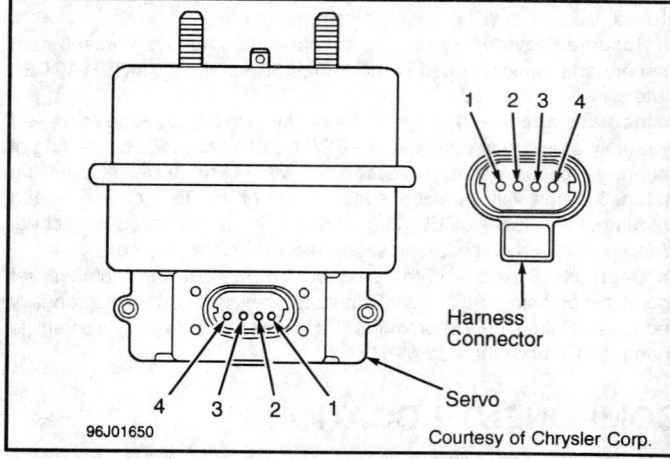

96J01650   Courtesy of Chrysler Corp.

Fig. 4: Identifying Speed Control (S/C) Servo Connector Terminals

SELF-DIAGNOSTIC SYSTEM

WARNING: Vehicle is equipped with an air bag. Air bag must be deactivated before servicing speed control components on or around steering column. See AIR BAG RESTRAINT SYSTEMS – TRUCKS article.

SERVICE PRECAUTIONS

Before proceeding with diagnosis, the following precautions must be followed:
- When using Diagnostic Trouble Code (DTC) tests for diagnosis, DO NOT skip any steps, or incorrect diagnosis may result. Always perform indicated verification procedure after repairs are made.

1999 ACCESSORIES & EQUIPMENT
Cruise Control Systems – Dakota, Durango, Ram Pickup, Ram Van & Ram Wagon (Cont.)

CHRY
4-295

- When using a jumper wire, ensure either jumper wire or circuit is fuse-protected.
- Before disconnecting connector from any control module, ensure ignition is off before removing connector.
- When checking voltage or continuity at any control module, probe connector for control module from pin side. DO NOT backprobe connector or probe wires through insulation.
- DO NOT cause short circuits when performing electrical tests. This will set additional Diagnostic Trouble Codes (DTCs), making diagnosis of original problem more difficult.
- Use specified test equipment when performing electrical tests.

RETRIEVING DIAGNOSTIC TROUBLE CODES

NOTE: Self-diagnostic tests are written specifically for Chrysler's Diagnostic Readout Box (DRB). If using a generic scan tool, ensure it is OBD-II certified. A generic scan tool may not be capable of performing all necessary test functions.

Ensure battery is fully charged. Turn ignition off. Connect scan tool to Data Link Connector (DLC). DLC is located under left side of instrument panel. Turn ignition on. Using scan tool manufacturer's instructions, record all DTCs displayed on scan tool. If ant DTCs are retrieved, perform appropriate test under DIAGNOSTIC TESTS. Once all repairs are made, clear DTCs. See CLEARING DIAGNOSTIC TROUBLE CODES. If no DTCs are retrieved and fault still exists, go to CHECKING SPEED CONTROL OPERATION under SYSTEM TESTS.

CLEARING DIAGNOSTIC TROUBLE CODES

Ensure ignition is off. Connect scan tool to DLC. Turn ignition on. Using screen prompts on scan tool, erase DTCs from PCM.

DIAGNOSTIC TESTS

DTC P0720: LOW OUTPUT SPEED SENSOR (OSS) RPM MORE THAN 15 MPH

DTC P0720 will set if output shaft speed is less than 60 RPM for 2.6 seconds when vehicle speed is more than 15 MPH.
Possible Causes:
- Defective Output Speed Sensor (OSS).
- OSS signal circuit open or shorted.
- OSS ground circuit open or shorted.
- Park/Neutral Position (PNP) switch DTC present.
- Defective PNP switch.
- Defective PCM.

1) Turn ignition on. Using scan tool, read DTCs. If DTC specific good trip is displayed and equal to zero, go to next step. If DTC specific good trip is equal to more than zero, go to step 13).
2) If there are any Park/Neutral Position (PNP) switch DTCs, repair PNP switch DTC first. Perform TEST VER-5A under VERIFICATION TESTS. If there are no PNP switch DTCs, go to next step.
3) Using scan tool, read PNP switch state. While observing scan tool, shift transmission through all positions. If scan tool did not display P/N and D/R in correct positions, repair PNP switch or circuit as necessary. Perform TEST VER-5A under VERIFICATION TESTS. If scan tool displayed P/N and D/R in correct positions, go to next step.
4) Raise drive wheels and support vehicle, allowing wheels to spin. Using scan tool, erase DTCs. Start engine. Using scan tool, read Output Speed Sensor (OSS). Shift transmission into first gear. While observing scan tool, allow wheels to spin at a speed less than 15 MPH. If scan tool displays OSS more than 60 RPM, go to next step. If scan tool displays OSS 60 RPM or less, go to step 7).
5) While wheels are spinning, wiggle wiring between OSS and PCM. If OSS reading dropped while wiggling, repair intermittent short or open circuit. Perform TEST VER-5A under VERIFICATION TESTS. If OSS reading did not drop, go to next step.

6) Using scan tool, erase DTCs. Road test vehicle. Read DTCs. If DTC P0720 returns, replace PCM. Perform TEST VER-5A under VERIFICATION TESTS. If DTC P0720 did not return, go to step 13).
7) Turn ignition off. Disconnect PCM. Inspect connectors. Clean or repair as necessary. Using an ohmmeter, measure resistance between ground and OSS signal circuit at PCM connector C2, terminal No. 28 (Light Green/Black wire on Ram Pickup; Light Green/White wire on all other models). If resistance is less than 5 ohms, repair short to ground. Perform TEST VER-5A under VERIFICATION TESTS.
8) Using an ohmmeter, measure resistance between ground and OSS ground circuit at PCM connector C2, terminal No. 25 (Dark Blue/Black wire). If resistance is less than 5 ohms, repair short to ground. Perform TEST VER-5A under VERIFICATION TESTS. If resistance is 5 ohms or more, go to next step.
9) Disconnect OSS. Using an ohmmeter, measure resistance across OSS terminals. If resistance is not 300-1200 ohms, replace OSS. Perform TEST VER-5A under VERIFICATION TESTS. If resistance is 300-1200 ohms, go to next step.
10) Using an ohmmeter, measure resistance of OSS signal circuit between PCM connector C2, terminal No. 28 and OSS connector (Light Green/Black wire on Ram Pickup; Light Green/White wire on all other models). If resistance is more than 5 ohms, repair open circuit. Perform TEST VER-5A under VERIFICATION TESTS. If resistance is 5 ohms or less, go to next step.
11) Using an ohmmeter, measure resistance of OSS ground circuit between PCM connector C2, terminal No. 25 and OSS connector (Dark Blue/Black wire). If resistance is more than 5 ohms, repair open circuit. Perform TEST VER-5A under VERIFICATION TESTS. If resistance is 5 ohms or less, go to next step.
12) Reconnect OSS. Using an ohmmeter, measure resistance between PCM connector C2, terminals No. 25 (Dark Blue/Black wire) and No. 28 (Light Green/Black wire on Ram Pickup; Light Green/White wire on all other models). If resistance is 300-1200 ohms, replace PCM. Perform TEST VER-5A under VERIFICATION TESTS. If resistance is not 300-1200 ohms, go to next step.
13) Inspect wiring and connectors. repair as necessary. Perform TEST VER-5A under VERIFICATION TESTS. If wiring and connectors are okay, go to next step.
14) Conditions required to set DTC are not present at this time. Check freeze frame data to determine conditions when DTC was set. Raise drive wheels and support vehicle, allowing wheels to spin. Using scan tool, read OSS. Shift transmission into first gear. While observing scan tool, allow wheels to spin at a speed less than 15 MPH. Wiggle wiring between OSS and PCM. If OSS reading dropped while wiggling, repair intermittent short or open circuit. Perform TEST VER-5A under VERIFICATION TESTS. If OSS reading did not drop, no problem is indicated at this time.

DTC P1595: SPEED CONTROL SOLENOID CIRCUITS

Speed Control (S/C) solenoid circuits are monitored when engine is running, S/C switch is on and battery voltage is more than 10.4 volts. DTC P1595 will set if vacuum and vent solenoids do not respond when actuated by PCM.
Possible Causes:
- Ground circuit open.
- S/C brake switch output circuit open.
- S/C power supply circuit open or shorted.
- S/C servo defective.
- S/C vacuum solenoid control circuit open or shorted.
- S/C vent solenoid control circuit open or shorted.
- Brake switch defective or out of adjustment.

CHRY
4-296

1999 ACCESSORIES & EQUIPMENT
Cruise Control Systems – Dakota, Durango, Ram Pickup,
Ram Van & Ram Wagon (Cont.)

- Defective PCM.

NOTE: For component locations, see COMPONENT LOCATIONS. For connector terminal identification, see CONNECTOR IDENTIFICATION. For wiring diagram, see WIRING DIAGRAMS.

1) Turn ignition on. Turn Speed Control (S/C) on. Using scan tool, actuate S/C vent solenoid. If speed control servo clicks, go to next step. If S/C servo does not click, go to step **7**).

2) Using scan tool, actuate S/C vacuum solenoid. If S/C servo clicks, go to next step. If S/C servo does not click, go to step **6**).

3) Turn ignition on. Using scan tool, actuate S/C vacuum solenoid. Wiggle wiring harness between S/C servo and brake switch to PCM while scan tool is still actuating speed control vacuum solenoid. If wiggling did not cause an interruption of S/C servo actuation, go to next step. If wiggling caused an interruption of S/C servo actuation, repair wiring harness as necessary. Perform TEST VER-4A under VERIFICATION TESTS.

4) Turn ignition off. Inspect S/C wiring and connectors. Clean or repair as necessary. Perform TEST VER-4A under VERIFICATION TESTS. If wiring and connectors are okay, go to next step.

5) Using scan tool, actuate S/C vent solenoid. Wiggle wiring harness between S/C servo and brake switch to PCM while scan tool is still actuating speed control vacuum solenoid. If wiggling did not cause interruption of S/C servo actuation, test is complete. If wiggling caused interruption of S/C servo actuation, repair wiring harness as necessary. Perform TEST VER-4A under VERIFICATION TESTS.

6) Using scan tool, actuate S/C vent solenoid. Wiggle wiring harness between S/C servo and brake switch to PCM while scan tool is still actuating speed control vacuum solenoid. If wiggling did not cause interruption of S/C servo actuation, go to next step. If wiggling caused interruption of S/C servo actuation, repair wiring harness as necessary. Perform TEST VER-4A under VERIFICATION TESTS.

NOTE: Ensure brake pedal is not depressed during the following steps.

7) Turn ignition off. Disconnect S/C servo 4-pin connector. Inspect all related wiring and connectors and repair as necessary. Turn ignition on. Turn S/C switch on. Using a 12-volt test light, probe brake switch output circuit at S/C servo connector terminal No. 3 (Dark Blue/Red wire). If test light is illuminated and bright, go to next step. If test light is dim or not illuminated, go to step **13**).

8) Turn ignition off. Using an ohmmeter, check resistance of ground circuit at S/C servo connector terminal No. 4 (Black wire). If resistance is 5 ohms or more, repair open ground circuit. Perform TEST VER-4A under VERIFICATION TESTS. If resistance is less than 5 ohms, go to next step.

9) Disconnect PCM. Inspect connectors. Clean or repair as necessary. Using an ohmmeter, measure resistance between ground and S/C vacuum solenoid control circuit at S/C servo connector terminal No. 1 (Tan/Red wire). If resistance is less than 5 ohms, repair short to ground. Perform TEST VER-4A under VERIFICATION TESTS. If resistance is 5 ohms or more, go to next step.

10) Using an ohmmeter, check resistance between ground and S/C vent solenoid control circuit at S/C servo connector terminal No. 2 (Light Green/Red wire). If resistance is less than 5 ohms, repair short to ground. Perform TEST VER-4A under VERIFICATION TESTS. If resistance is 5 ohms or more, go to next step.

11) Using an ohmmeter, measure resistance of S/C vacuum solenoid control circuit between S/C servo connector terminal No. 1 and PCM connector C3, terminal No. 4 (Tan/Red wire). If resistance is 5 ohms or more, repair open circuit. Perform TEST VER-4A under VERIFICATION TESTS. If resistance is less than 5 ohms, go to next step.

12) Using an ohmmeter, check resistance of S/C vent solenoid control circuit between S/C servo connector terminal No. 2 and PCM connector C3, terminal No. 5 (Light Green/Red wire). If resistance is 5 ohms or more, repair open circuit. Perform TEST VER-4A under VERIFICATION

TESTS. If resistance is less than 5 ohms, replace S/C servo. Perform TEST VER-4A under VERIFICATION TESTS.

13) Using an ohmmeter, check resistance between ground and brake switch output circuit at S/C servo connector terminal No. 3 (Dark Blue/Red wire). If resistance is less than 5 ohms, repair short to ground. Perform TEST VER-4A under VERIFICATION TESTS. If resistance is 5 ohms or more, go to next step.

14) Reconnect PCM. Disconnect brake switch connector. Turn ignition on. Turn S/C on. Using a 12-volt test light, probe S/C power supply circuit at brake switch connector terminal No. 3 (Yellow/Red wire). If test light is illuminated and bright, go to next step. If test light is not illuminated or dim, go to step **17**).

15) Turn ignition off. Using an ohmmeter, check resistance of S/C brake switch output circuit between S/C servo connector terminal No. 3 and brake switch connector terminal No. 4 (Dark Blue/Red wire). If resistance is 5 ohms or more, repair open circuit. Perform TEST VER-4A under VERIFICATION TESTS. If resistance is less than 5 ohms, go to next step.

16) Check brake switch adjustment. See BRAKE SWITCH under REMOVAL & INSTALLATION. Adjust as necessary. Perform TEST VER-4A under VERIFICATION TESTS. If brake switch adjustment is okay, replace brake switch. Perform TEST VER-4A under VERIFICATION TESTS.

17) Turn ignition off. Disconnect PCM. Inspect connectors. Clean or repair as necessary. Using an ohmmeter, measure resistance of S/C power supply circuit between PCM connector C3, terminal No. 11 and brake switch connector terminal No. 3 (Yellow/Red wire). If resistance is 5 ohms or more, repair open circuit. Perform TEST VER-4A under VERIFICATION TESTS. If resistance is less than 5 ohms, replace PCM. Perform TEST VER-4A under VERIFICATION TESTS.

DTC P1596: SPEED CONTROL SWITCH ALWAYS HIGH

DTC P1596 will set if an open circuit is detected in Speed Control (S/C) switch circuit when ignition is on.
Possible Causes:
- Defective clockspring.
- S/C switch ground circuit open.
- Defective ON/OFF switch.
- Defective PCM.
- S/C switch signal circuit open or shorted to voltage.

NOTE: For component locations, see COMPONENT LOCATIONS. For connector terminal identification, see CONNECTOR IDENTIFICATION. For wiring diagram, see WIRING DIAGRAMS.

1) Turn ignition on. Using scan tool, read S/C inputs. While observing display, press S/C ON/OFF switch several times and leave on. If scan tool displays S/C switch OFF and ON, go to next step. If scan tool does not display OFF and ON, go to step **3**).

2) Using scan tool, measure S/C switch voltage. While observing display, wiggle wiring between S/C switch and PCM. If voltage was more than 4.9 volts at any time during wiggling, repair wiring as necessary. Perform TEST VER-4A under VERIFICATION TESTS. If voltage was 4.9 volts or less during wiggling, test is complete.

3) Turn ignition off. Disconnect S/C ON/OFF switch. Inspect connector. Clean or repair as necessary. Using an ohmmeter, measure resistance of S/C switch ground circuit. If resistance is 5 ohms or more, repair open ground circuit. Perform TEST VER-4A under VERIFICATION TESTS. If resistance is less than 5 ohms, go to next step.

4) Turn ignition on. Using a voltmeter, measure voltage on S/C switch signal circuit. If voltage is more than 6 volts, repair short to voltage. Perform TEST VER-4A under VERIFICATION TESTS. If voltage is 6 volts or less, go to next step.

5) Turn ignition off. Disconnect PCM. Inspect connectors. Clean or repair as necessary. Using an ohmmeter, measure resistance of S/C switch signal circuit between ON/OFF switch connector and PCM connector C3, terminal No. 32 (White/Light Green wire on Ram Van &

1999 ACCESSORIES & EQUIPMENT
Cruise Control Systems – Dakota, Durango, Ram Pickup, Ram Van & Ram Wagon (Cont.)

CHRY
4-297

Ram Wagon; Red/Light Green wire on all other models). If resistance is less than 5 ohms, go to next step. If resistance is 5 ohms or more, go to step 7).

6) Using an ohmmeter, measure resistance across ON/OFF switch. Resistance should be 20,300-20,700 ohms. If resistance is not as specified, replace ON/OFF switch. Perform TEST VER-4A under VERIFICATION TESTS. If resistance is as specified, replace PCM. Perform TEST VER-4A under VERIFICATION TESTS.

7) Disconnect clockspring 5-pin connector. Clockspring 5-pin connector is located behind lower steering column shroud. Inspect connectors. Clean or repair as necessary. Using an ohmmeter, measure resistance of S/C switch signal circuit between PCM connector C3, terminal No. 32 and clockspring connector (White/Light Green wire on Ram Van and Ram Wagon; Red/Light Green wire on all other models). If resistance is 5 ohms or more, repair open circuit. Perform TEST VER-4A under VERIFICATION TESTS. If resistance is less than 5 ohms, replace clockspring. See appropriate AIR BAG RESTRAINT SYSTEMS article. Perform TEST VER-4A under VERIFICATION TESTS.

DTC P1597: SPEED CONTROL SWITCH ALWAYS LOW

DTC P1597 will set if Speed Control (S/C) switch voltage is less than 0.39 volts for 2 minutes when ignition is on and battery voltage is more than 10.4 volts.

Possible Causes:
- S/C ON/OFF switch defective.
- S/C RESUME/ACCEL switch defective.
- S/C switch signal circuit shorted to ground.
- Defective PCM.
- Defective clockspring.

NOTE: For component locations, see COMPONENT LOCATIONS. For connector terminal identification, see CONNECTOR IDENTIFICATION. For wiring diagram, see WIRING DIAGRAMS.

1) Turn ignition on. Using scan tool, read S/C switch voltage. If voltage is less than one volt, go to next step. If voltage is one volt or more, condition to set DTC is not present at this time. Test is complete.

2) While observing scan tool, disconnect S/C ON/OFF switch. If S/C switch voltage changes to 5 volts, replace S/C ON/OFF switch. Perform TEST VER-4A under VERIFICATION TESTS. If voltage does not change to 5 volts, go to next step.

3) While observing scan tool, disconnect S/C RESUME/ACCEL switch. If S/C switch voltage changes to 5 volts, replace S/C RESUME/ACCEL switch. Perform TEST VER-4A under VERIFICATION TESTS. If voltage does not change to 5 volts, go to next step.

4) Turn ignition off. Ensure both S/C switches are still disconnected. Using an ohmmeter, check resistance between S/C switch connector terminals (S/C switch signal circuit and S/C switch ground circuit). If resistance is less than 5 ohms, repair short circuit. Perform TEST VER-4A under VERIFICATION TESTS. If resistance is 5 ohms or more, go to next step.

5) Disconnect clockspring 4-pin connector. Clockspring 4-pin connector is located behind steering wheel. Inspect connector. Clean or repair as necessary. Using an ohmmeter, check resistance between ground and S/C switch signal circuit at clockspring connector (Dark Green/Red wire on all models except Ram Van and Ram Wagon; wire color is not available for Ram Van and Ram Wagon). If resistance is less than 5 ohms, repair short to ground. Perform TEST VER-4A under VERIFICATION TESTS. If resistance is 5 ohms or more, go to next step.

6) Disconnect PCM. Inspect connectors. Clean or repair as necessary. Using an ohmmeter, check resistance between ground and S/C switch signal circuit at either S/C switch connector (Dark Green/Red wire on all models except Ram Van and Ram Wagon; wire color is not available for Ram Van and Ram Wagon). If resistance is less than 5 ohms, repair short to ground. Perform TEST VER-4A under VERIFICATION TESTS. If resistance is 5 ohms or more, replace PCM. Perform TEST VER-4A under VERIFICATION TESTS.

DTC P1683: SPEED CONTROL POWER RELAY CIRCUIT

DTC P1683 will set if Speed Control (S/C) power supply circuit is open or shorted when S/C is turned on.

Possible Causes:
- Brake switch out of adjustment.
- S/C brake switch output circuit open or shorted.
- Defective S/C servo.
- Defective brake switch.
- S/C vacuum or vent solenoid control circuits open or shorted.
- Defective PCM.
- Ground circuit open.
- S/C power supply circuit open.

NOTE: For component locations, see COMPONENT LOCATIONS. For connector terminal identification, see CONNECTOR IDENTIFICATION. For wiring diagram, see WIRING DIAGRAMS.

NOTE: Ensure brake pedal is not depressed during the following steps.

1) Turn ignition off. Disconnect S/C servo connector. Inspect connector. Clean or repair as necessary. Turn ignition on. Using scan tool, actuate S/C relay. Using a 12-volt test light, probe S/C brake switch output circuit at S/C servo connector terminal No. 3 (Dark Blue/Red wire). If test light is illuminated and bright, go to next step. If test light is dim or not illuminated, go to step 7).

2) Turn ignition off. Using an ohmmeter, check resistance of ground circuit at S/C servo connector terminal No. 4 (Black wire). If resistance is 5 ohms or more, repair open ground circuit. Perform TEST VER-4A under VERIFICATION TESTS. If resistance is less than 5 ohms, go to next step.

3) Disconnect PCM. Inspect connectors. Clean or repair as necessary. Using an ohmmeter, measure resistance of S/C vacuum solenoid control circuit between PCM connector C3, terminal No. 4 and S/C servo connector terminal No. 1 (Tan/Red wire). If resistance is 5 ohms or more, repair open circuit. Perform TEST VER-4A under VERIFICATION TESTS. If resistance is less than 5 ohms, go to next step.

4) Using an ohmmeter, check resistance between ground and S/C vacuum solenoid control circuit at S/C servo connector terminal No. 1 (Tan/Red wire). If resistance is less than 5 ohms, repair short to ground. Perform TEST VER-4A under VERIFICATION TESTS. If resistance is 5 ohms or more, go to next step.

5) Using an ohmmeter, check resistance of S/C vent solenoid control circuit between PCM connector C3, terminal No. 5 and S/C servo connector terminal No. 2 (Light Green/Red wire). If resistance is 5 ohms or more, repair open circuit. Perform TEST VER-4A under VERIFICATION TESTS. If resistance is less than 5 ohms, go to next step.

6) Using an ohmmeter, check resistance between ground and S/C vent solenoid control circuit at S/C servo connector terminal No. 2 (Light Green/Red wire). If resistance is less than 5 ohms, repair short to ground. Perform TEST VER-4A under VERIFICATION TESTS. If resistance is 5 ohms or more, replace S/C servo. Perform TEST VER-4A under VERIFICATION TESTS.

7) Turn ignition off. Disconnect brake switch connector. Inspect connectors. Clean or repair as necessary. Turn ignition on. Using scan tool, actuate S/C solenoid. Using a 12-volt test light, probe S/C power supply circuit at brake switch connector terminal No. 4 (Yellow/Red wire). If test light is illuminated and bright, go to next step. If test light is not illuminated or dim, go to step 10).

8) Check brake switch adjustment. See BRAKE SWITCH under REMOVAL & INSTALLATION. Adjust as necessary. Perform TEST VER-4A under VERIFICATION TESTS. If brake switch adjustment is okay, go to next step.

9) Using an ohmmeter, check resistance of brake switch output circuit between brake switch connector terminal No. 3 and S/C servo connector terminal No. 3 (Dark Blue/Red wire). If resistance is more than 5 ohms,

CHRY
4-298

1999 ACCESSORIES & EQUIPMENT
Cruise Control Systems – Dakota, Durango, Ram Pickup, Ram Van & Ram Wagon (Cont.)

repair open circuit. Perform TEST VER-4A under VERIFICATION TESTS. If resistance is 5 ohms or less, replace brake switch. Perform TEST VER-4A under VERIFICATION TESTS.

10) Turn ignition off. Using an ohmmeter, check resistance between ground and S/C brake switch output circuit at S/C servo connector terminal No. 3 (Dark Blue/Red wire). If resistance is less than 5 ohms, repair short to ground. Perform TEST VER-4A under VERIFICATION TESTS. If resistance is 5 ohms or more, go to next step.

11) Disconnect PCM. Inspect connectors. Clean or repair as necessary. Using an ohmmeter, check resistance of S/C power supply circuit between PCM connector C3, terminal No. 11 and brake switch connector terminal No. 4 (Yellow/Red wire). If resistance is 5 ohms or more, repair open circuit. Perform TEST VER-4A under VERIFICATION TESTS. If resistance is less than 5 ohms, replace PCM. Perform TEST VER-4A under VERIFICATION TESTS.

DTC P1899: PARK/NEUTRAL POSITION (PNP) SWITCH STUCK IN PARK OR IN GEAR (A/T MODELS)

Possible Causes:
- PNP switch defective.
- PNP switch sense circuit open or shorted.
- PNP switch stuck.
- PCM defective.

NOTE: For component locations, see COMPONENT LOCATIONS. For connector terminal identification, see CONNECTOR IDENTIFICATION. For wiring diagram, see WIRING DIAGRAMS.

1) Turn ignition on. Using scan tool, read PNP switch state. While observing scan tool, move gear selector between Park and Reverse. If scan tool displays P/N and D/R, go to next step. If scan tool does not display P/N and D/R, go to step 3).

2) Turn ignition off. Inspect wiring and connectors related to PNP switch. Repair as necessary. Perform TEST VER-5A under VERIFICATION TESTS. If wiring and connectors are okay, condition to set DTC is not present at this time. Test is complete. Use freeze frame data to determine conditions when DTC was set.

3) Turn ignition off. Disconnect PCM. Inspect connectors. Clean or repair as necessary. Using an ohmmeter, check resistance between ground and PNP switch sense circuit at PCM connector C1, terminal No. 6 (Black/White wire). While observing ohmmeter, move gear selector from Park to Reverse and back to Park. If resistance switched from less than 10 ohms to more than 10 ohms, replace PCM. Perform TEST VER-5A under VERIFICATION TESTS. If resistance was less than 10 ohms at all times, go to next step. If resistance was more than 10 ohms at all times, go to step 5).

4) Disconnect PNP switch. Inspect connectors. Clean or repair as necessary. Using an ohmmeter, check resistance between ground and PNP switch sense circuit. If resistance is less than 5 ohms, repair short to ground. Perform TEST VER-5A under VERIFICATION TESTS. If resistance is 5 ohms or more, repair or replace stuck PNP switch. Perform TEST VER-5A under VERIFICATION TESTS.

5) Using an ohmmeter, check resistance of PNP switch circuit between PNP switch connector and PCM connector C1, terminal No. 6 (Black/White wire). If resistance is 5 ohms or more, repair open circuit. Perform TEST VER-5A under VERIFICATION TESTS. If resistance is less than 5 ohms, replace PNP switch. Perform TEST VER-5A under VERIFICATION TESTS.

SYSTEM TESTS

NOTE: For component locations, See COMPONENT LOCATIONS. For connector terminal identification, see CONNECTOR IDENTIFICATION. For wiring diagram, see WIRING DIAGRAMS.

CHECKING SPEED CONTROL OPERATION

NOTE: Perform this test only if there are no DTCs.

1) Turn ignition on. Using scan tool, monitor S/C switch inputs. Press S/C ON/OFF switch several times. If scan tool displays speed control switch on and off, go to next step. If scan tool does not display speed control switch on and off, go to NTC-3: SPEED CONTROL ON/OFF SWITCH.

2) While observing scan tool, press RESUME/ACCEL switch several times. If scan tool displays RESUME/ACCEL switch PRESSED and RELEASED, go to next step. If scan tool does not display PRESSED and RELEASED, go to NTC-4: SPEED CONTROL RESUME/ACCEL SWITCH.

3) While observing scan tool, press brake pedal several times. If scan tool displays brake pedal PRESSED and RELEASED, go to next step. If scan tool does not display brake pedal PRESSED and RELEASED, go to NTC-1: BRAKE SWITCH SENSE.

4) Turn S/C on. On A/T models, move gear selector to Drive. If scan tool displays park neutral switch D/R, go to next step. If scan tool does not display park neutral switch D/R, go to DTC P1899: PARK/NEUTRAL POSITION SWITCH STUCK IN PARK OR IN GEAR under DIAGNOSTIC TESTS.

5) On all models, using scan tool, actuate S/C vent solenoid. Using a 12-volt test light, backprobe S/C brake switch output circuit at S/C servo connector terminal No. 3 (Dark Blue/Red wire). If test light is illuminated and bright, go to next step. If test light is dim or is not illuminated, go to NTC-1: BRAKE SWITCH SENSE.

6) Start engine and let idle for one minute. Turn engine off. Turn ignition on (engine off). Using scan tool, actuate S/C servo solenoids. If throttle opens and closes, go to NTC-2: CHECKING FOR SPEED CONTROL DENIED MESSAGE. If throttle does not open and close, inspect throttle cable and linkage. Check vacuum supply. See VACUUM SUPPLY under COMPONENT TESTS. Repair as necessary. Perform TEST VER-4A under VERIFICATION TESTS.

7) While observing scan tool, press CANCEL switch several times. If scan tool displays PRESSED and RELEASED, go to next step. If scan tool does not display PRESSED and RELEASED, replace CANCEL switch. Perform TEST VER-4A under VERIFICATION TESTS.

8) Turn ignition off. Disconnect S/C servo connector. Using an ohmmeter, check resistance of ground circuit at S/C servo connector terminal No. 4 (Black wire). If resistance is 5 ohms or more, repair open ground circuit. Perform TEST VER-4A under VERIFICATION TESTS. If resistance is less than 5 ohms, go to next step.

9) Reconnect S/C servo connector. Turn ignition and S/C on. While observing scan tool, press SET switch several times. If scan tool displays PRESSED and RELEASED, go to next step. If scan tool does not display PRESSED and RELEASED, replace SET switch. Perform TEST VER-4A under VERIFICATION TESTS.

10) Turn ignition off. Disconnect S/C servo connector. Inspect terminals. If any terminal is damaged, pushed out or miswired, repair as necessary. Perform TEST VER-4A under VERIFICATION TESTS. If terminals are okay, go to next step.

11) Disconnect S/C servo connector. Disconnect PCM connectors. Inspect connectors. Clean or repair as necessary. Using an ohmmeter, check resistance of S/C vacuum solenoid control circuit between PCM connector C3, terminal No. 4 and S/C servo connector terminal No. 1 (Tan/Red wire). If resistance is 5 ohms or more, repair open circuit. Perform TEST VER-4A under VERIFICATION TESTS. If resistance is less than 5 ohms, go to next step.

1999 ACCESSORIES & EQUIPMENT

CHRY
4-299

Cruise Control Systems – Dakota, Durango, Ram Pickup, Ram Van & Ram Wagon (Cont.)

12) Turn S/C on. While observing scan tool, press COAST switch several times. If scan tool displays PRESSED and RELEASED, go to next step. If scan tool does not display PRESSED and RELEASED, replace COAST switch. Perform TEST VER-4A under VERIFICATION TESTS.

13) Using an ohmmeter, check resistance of S/C vent solenoid control circuit between PCM connector C3, terminal No. 5 and S/C servo connector terminal No. 2 (Light Green/Red wire). If resistance is 5 ohms or more, repair open circuit. Perform TEST VER-4A under VERIFICATION TESTS. If resistance is less than 5 ohms, replace S/C servo. Perform TEST VER-4A under VERIFICATION TESTS.

NTC-1: BRAKE SWITCH SENSE

Possible Causes:
- Ground circuit open.
- Defective brake switch.
- Brake switch sense circuit open or shorted.
- Defective PCM.

1) Turn ignition off. Disconnect brake switch connector. Inspect connector. Clean or repair as necessary. Turn ignition on. Using a voltmeter, measure voltage of brake switch sense circuit at brake switch White/Pink wire. If voltage is more than 10 volts, go to next step. If voltage is 10 volts or less, go to step 3).

2) Connect a jumper wire between ground and brake switch connector White/Pink wire. Using scan tool, read brake switch input status. If scan tool displays brake switch released, replace brake switch. Perform TEST VER-4A under VERIFICATION TESTS. If scan tool does not display brake switch released, repair open ground circuit. Perform TEST VER-4A under VERIFICATION TESTS.

3) Disconnect PCM connectors. Inspect connectors. Clean or repair as necessary. Using an ohmmeter, measure resistance between ground and brake switch sense circuit at PCM connector C3, terminal No. 24 (White/Pink wire). If resistance less than 5 ohms, repair short to ground. Perform TEST VER-4A under VERIFICATION TESTS. If resistance is 5 ohms or more, go to next step.

4) Using an ohmmeter, measure resistance of brake switch sense circuit between PCM connector C3, terminal No. 24 and brake switch White/Pink wire. If resistance is 5 ohms or more, repair open brake switch sense circuit. Perform TEST VER-4A under VERIFICATION TESTS. If resistance is less than 5 ohms, replace PCM. Perform TEST VER-4A under VERIFICATION TESTS.

NTC-2: CHECKING FOR SPEED CONTROL DENIED MESSAGE

At this time speed control switch and servo functions appear to operate properly. Using scan tool, monitor speed control output status. Road test vehicle at speeds more than 30 MPH. Attempt to set speed control. See SCAN TOOL DENIED STATUS table. Items listed in table will not allow speed control to set. The last or most recent cause for speed control not to set is indicated by denied status. Correct fault and recheck system operation.

SCAN TOOL DENIED STATUS

Denied Message	Reason
ON/OFF	PCM Does Not See An ON Signal From Switch At PCM Terminal No. 41
SPEED	Vehicle Speed As Seen By PCM Terminal No. 66 Is Not Greater Than 36 MPH
RPM	Engine RPM Is Excessively High
BRAKE	Brake Switch Sense Circuit Is Open Indicating That Brakes Are Applied
P/N	Park/Neutral Switch Sense Circuit Is Grounded Indicating That Transmission Is In Park Or Neutral
RPM/SPD	PCM Senses Excessive Engine RPM For A Given Vehicle Speed
SOL FLT	PCM Senses A Servo Solenoid Circuit Trouble Code That Is Maturing Or Set In Memory

NTC-3: SPEED CONTROL ON/OFF SWITCH

Possible Causes:
- Signal circuit open or shorted.
- S/C ON/OFF switch defective.
- S/C RESUME/ACCEL switch defective.
- Defective PCM.
- Defective clockspring.

1) Turn ignition on. Using scan tool, read S/C switch voltage. If voltage is more than 4 volts, go to next step. If voltage is 4 volts or less, go to step 4).

2) Turn ignition off. Disconnect S/C ON/OFF switch. Inspect connector. Clean or repair as necessary. Connect a jumper wire between ground and S/C switch signal circuit at S/C ON/OFF switch connector (Dark Green/Red wire on all models except Ram Van and Ram Wagon; wire color is not available for Ram Van and Ram Wagon). Turn ignition on. Using scan tool, read S/C switch voltage. If voltage is less than one volt, replace S/C ON/OFF switch. Perform TEST VER-4A under VERIFICATION TESTS. If voltage is one volt or more, go to next step.

3) Using a voltmeter, measure voltage on S/C switch signal circuit. If voltage is less than 4 volts, repair high resistance in S/C switch signal circuit. Perform TEST VER-4A under VERIFICATION TESTS. If voltage is more than 6 volts, repair short to voltage. Perform TEST VER-4A under VERIFICATION TESTS. If voltage is 4-6 volts, replace PCM. Perform TEST VER-4A under VERIFICATION TESTS.

4) Turn ignition off. Disconnect S/C ON/OFF switch. Disconnect PCM. Inspect connectors. Clean or repair as necessary. Using an ohmmeter, measure resistance between ground and S/C switch signal circuit at PCM connector C3, terminal No. 32 (White/Light Green wire on Ram Van & Ram Wagon; Red/Light Green wire on all other models). If resistance is less than 5 ohms, repair short to ground. Perform TEST VER-4A under VERIFICATION TESTS. If resistance is 5 ohms or more, go to next step.

5) Reconnect PCM. Ensure S/C ON/OFF switch is still disconnected. Turn ignition on. Using scan tool, read S/C switch voltage. If voltage is more than 4 volts, replace ON/OFF switch. Perform TEST VER-4A under VERIFICATION TESTS. If voltage is 4 volts or less, go to next step.

6) Disconnect RESUME/ACCEL switch. Using scan tool, read S/C switch voltage. If voltage is more than 4 volts, replace RESUME/ACCEL switch. Perform TEST VER-4A under VERIFICATION TESTS. If voltage is 4 volts or less, go to next step.

7) Disconnect clockspring connector located behind lower steering column shroud. Inspect connector. Clean or repair as necessary. Using scan tool, read S/C switch voltage. If voltage is more than 4 volts, replace clockspring. See AIR BAG RESTRAINT SYSTEMS – TRUCKS article. Perform TEST VER-4A under VERIFICATION TESTS. If voltage is 4 volts or less, test is complete.

NTC-4: SPEED CONTROL RESUME/ACCEL SWITCH

Possible Causes:
- Ground circuit open.
- RESUME/ACCEL switch defective.
- Signal circuit open.

1) Turn ignition off. Disconnect RESUME/ACCEL switch. Inspect connectors. Clean or repair as necessary. Connect a jumper wire between ground and S/C switch signal circuit at RESUME/ACCEL switch connector (Dark Green/Red wire on all models except Ram Van and Ram Wagon; wire color is not available for Ram Van and Ram Wagon). Turn ignition on. Using scan tool, read S/C switch voltage. If voltage is less than one volt, replace RESUME/ACCEL switch. Perform TEST VER-4A under VERIFICATION TESTS. If voltage is one volt or more, go to next step.

2) Turn ignition off. Using an ohmmeter, check resistance of RESUME/ACCEL switch ground circuit at RESUME/ACCEL switch connector. If resistance is 5 ohms or more, repair open ground circuit. Perform TEST

CHRY
4-300

1999 ACCESSORIES & EQUIPMENT
Cruise Control Systems – Dakota, Durango, Ram Pickup, Ram Van & Ram Wagon (Cont.)

VER-4A under VERIFICATION TESTS. If resistance is less than 5 ohms, repair open S/C switch signal circuit. Perform TEST VER-4A under VERIFICATION TESTS.

VERIFICATION TESTS

TEST VER-4A

NOTE: If PCM has been replaced and correct VIN and mileage have not been programmed, a DTC will be set in ABS and air bag modules. If vehicle is equipped with a Sentry Key Immobilizer Module (SKIM), sentry key data must be updated to enable starting. See COMPUTER RELEARN PROCEDURES article in GENERAL INFORMATION.

1) If vehicle is not equipped with a diesel engine, go to next step. If vehicle is equipped with a diesel engine, and PCM has been disconnected or replaced, battery has been disconnected, or Accelerator Pedal Position Sensor (APPS) has been disconnected or replaced, APPS calibration must be programmed into PCM (diesel only). Turn ignition on. Slowly press accelerator pedal to floor and slowly release. DO NOT attempt to adjust screws or disassemble APPS. Go to next step.
2) On all engines, if vehicle is equipped with ABS or air bag, enter correct VIN and mileage in PCM. Erase DTCs in ABS and air bag modules. Inspect vehicle to ensure all engine and speed control system components are connected. Reassemble and reconnect components as necessary. Using scan tool, erase DTCs from PCM.
3) Road test vehicle at a speed greater than 35 MPH. Turn S/C switch on. Press and release SET button. If S/C does not engage, repair is not complete. Check for related TSBs and return to TROUBLE SHOOTING, if necessary. If speed control engages, go to next step
4) Quickly depress and release RESUME/ACCEL switch. If vehicle speed increases by 2 MPH, go to next step. If vehicle speed does not increase by 2 MPH, repair is not complete. Check for related TSBs and return to TROUBLE SHOOTING, if necessary.
5) Press and hold COAST switch. Vehicle speed should decrease. If vehicle speed decreases, go to next step. If vehicle speed does not decrease, repair is not complete. Check for related TSBs and return to TROUBLE SHOOTING, if necessary.
6) Using caution, depress and release brake pedal. If S/C disengages, go to next step. If S/C does not disengage, repair is not complete. Check for related TSBs and return to TROUBLE SHOOTING, if necessary.
7) Bring vehicle speed to 35 MPH. Depress speed control RESUME/ACCEL switch. If vehicle resumes to previously set speed, go to next step. If vehicle does not resume to previously set speed, repair is not complete. Check for related TSBs and return to TROUBLE SHOOTING, if necessary.
8) Hold down SET switch. Vehicle speed should decrease. If vehicle speed decreases, go to next step. If vehicle speed did not decrease, repair is not complete. Check for related TSBs and return to TROUBLE SHOOTING, if necessary.
9) Ensure vehicle speed is more than 35 MPH and release SET switch. If vehicle sets a new speed, go to next step. If vehicle did not set a new speed, repair is not complete. Check for related TSBs and return to TROUBLE SHOOTING, if necessary.
10) Depress and release CANCEL switch. If S/C disengages, go to next step. If S/C did not disengage, repair is not complete. Check for related TSBs and return to TROUBLE SHOOTING, if necessary.
11) Ensure vehicle speed is greater than 35 MPH. Engage speed control. Turn S/C on/off switch to OFF position. If speed control disengages, system is operating correctly. Repair is complete. If speed control does not disengage, repair is not complete. Check for related TSBs and return to TROUBLE SHOOTING, if necessary.

TEST VER-5A

NOTE: If PCM has been replaced and correct VIN and mileage have not been programmed, a DTC will be set in ABS and air bag modules. If vehicle is equipped with a Sentry Key Immobilizer Module (SKIM), sentry key data must be updated to enable starting. See COMPUTER RELEARN PROCEDURES article in GENERAL INFORMATION.

1) If vehicle is not equipped with a diesel engine, go to next step. If vehicle is equipped with a diesel engine, and PCM has been disconnected or replaced, battery has been disconnected, or Accelerator Pedal Position Sensor (APPS) has been disconnected or replaced, APPS calibration must be programmed into PCM (diesel only). Turn ignition on. Slowly press accelerator pedal to floor and slowly release. DO NOT attempt to adjust screws or disassemble APPS. Go to next step.
2) On all engines, if vehicle is equipped with ABS or air bag, enter correct VIN and mileage in PCM. Erase DTCs in ABS and air bag modules. Inspect vehicle to ensure all engine and speed control system components are connected.
3) If there are any DTCs that have not been repaired, go to SELF-DIAGNOSTIC SYSTEM. After all DTCs have been repaired, run appropriate monitor for previously repaired DTC.
4) Connect scan tool to DLC. Ensure fuel tank is at least 1/4 full. Turn off all accessories. Allow PCM to run appropriate monitor and increment appropriate good trip. Enabling conditions must be met before monitor will run.
5) Using scan tool, monitor pretest enabling conditions until all conditions have been met. Once enabling conditions have been met, monitor appropriate monitor.
6) If repaired DTC has reset or was seen in monitor while on road test, repair is not complete. Check for TSBs or flash updates and return to TROUBLE SHOOTING.
7) If appropriate monitor ran, good trip counter incremented and no DTCs have been set, repair is complete.

REMOVAL & INSTALLATION

WARNING: Vehicle is equipped with an air bag. Air bag must be deactivated before servicing speed control components on or around steering column. See AIR BAG RESTRAINT SYSTEMS – TRUCKS article.

CAUTION: When battery is disconnected, vehicle computer and memory systems may lose memory data. Driveability problems may exist until computer systems have completed a relearn cycle. See COMPUTER RELEARN PROCEDURES article in GENERAL INFORMATION before disconnecting battery.

BRAKE SWITCH

Removal – Fully depress brake pedal and rotate brake switch counterclockwise approximately 30 degrees. Remove brake switch from bracket. Depress lock tabs holding brake switch mounting bracket and separate harness connector from brake switch.
Installation – 1) Before installing brake switch, reset adjustable plunger by pulling on plunger head until plunger reaches end of travel. Connect harness connector to brake switch. Depress brake pedal and insert brake switch into keyed hole in mounting bracket. Rotate brake switch clockwise into locked position.
2) Gently pull back on brake pedal until pedal will go no further. This causes the brake switch plunger to ratchet backward to the correct position. No further adjustment is required.

SPEED CONTROL SERVO

Removal (Except Ram Van & Ram Wagon) – 1) Disconnect negative battery cable. Disconnect electrical connector and vacuum hose from

Cruise Control Systems – Dakota, Durango, Ram Pickup, Ram Van & Ram Wagon (Cont.)

servo. Using finger pressure only, push servo cable connector from throttle body bellcrank pin. DO NOT pull cable connector perpendicular to bellcrank.

2) Remove 2 servo cable mounting nuts. Pull servo cable sleeve away from mounting bracket to expose cable retaining clip. Remove retaining clip. Remove servo.

Removal (Ram Van & Ram Wagon) – 1) Disconnect negative battery cable. Remove engine cover. Remove air cleaner assembly. Using finger pressure only, push servo cable connector from throttle body bellcrank pin. DO NOT pull cable connector perpendicular to bellcrank.

2) Remove right headlight assembly. Disconnect vacuum hose and electrical connector at servo. Remove 2 servo mounting bracket bolts. Remove 2 servo cable mounting nuts. Pull servo cable sleeve away from mounting bracket to expose cable retaining clip. Remove retaining clip. Remove servo.

Installation (All Models) – With throttle in full open position, align hole in speed control cable sleeve with hole in servo pin. Install retaining clip. To complete installation, reverse removal procedure. Tighten mounting bolts/nuts to 75 INCH lbs. (8.5 N.m).

SPEED CONTROL SWITCHES

Removal & Installation – Turn ignition off. Disconnect negative battery cable. Wait 2 minutes for air bag system to discharge reserve voltage. Remove 2 screws holding air bag assembly to steering column. Separate air bag assembly from steering column and disconnect air bag, horn and speed control switch connectors. Remove screws securing speed control switch to air bag assembly. Separate speed control switch from air bag assembly. To install, reverse removal procedure.

WIRING DIAGRAMS

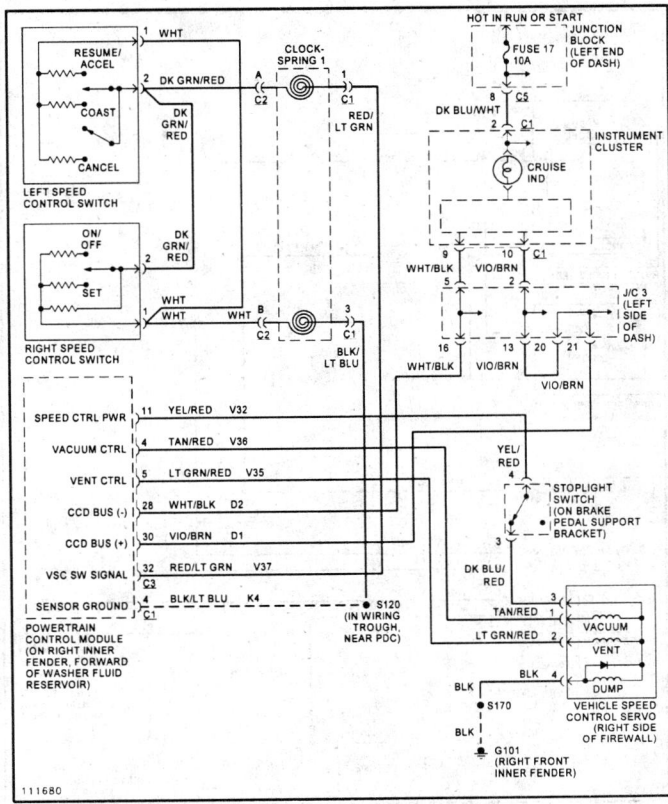

Fig. 6: Cruise Control System Wiring Diagram (Durango)

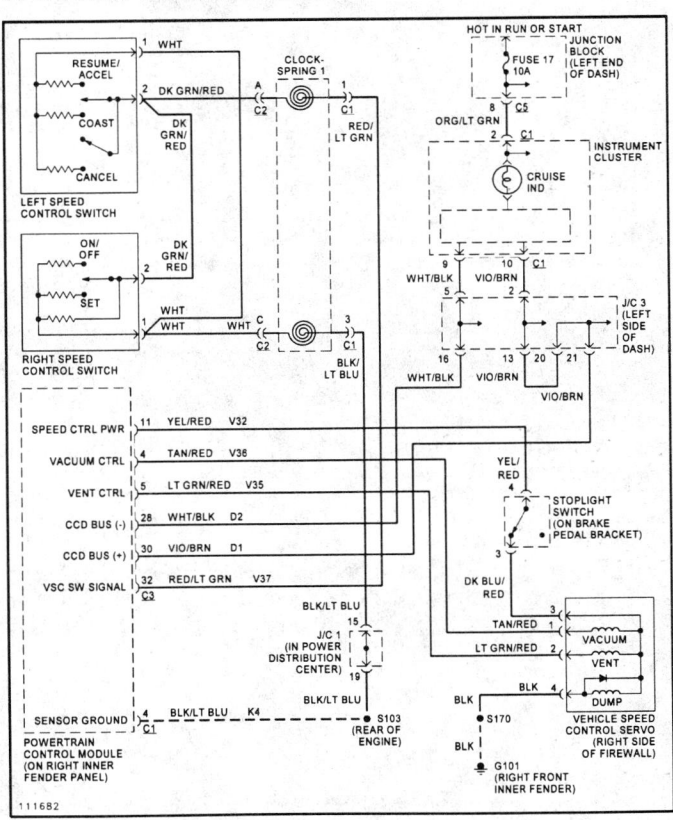

Fig. 5: Cruise Control System Wiring Diagram (Dakota)

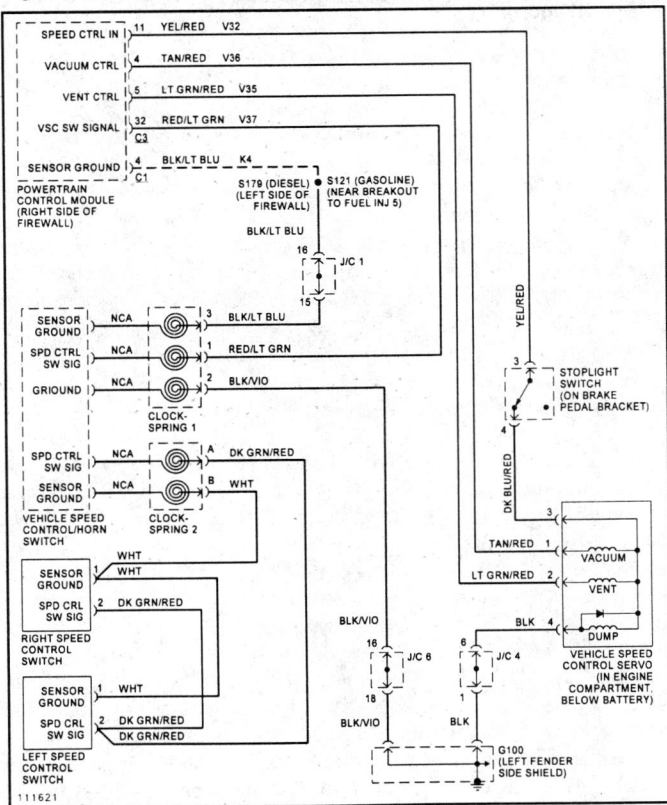

Fig. 7: Cruise Control System Wiring Diagram (Ram Pickup)

CHRY
4-302

1999 ACCESSORIES & EQUIPMENT
Cruise Control Systems – Dakota, Durango, Ram Pickup, Ram Van & Ram Wagon (Cont.)

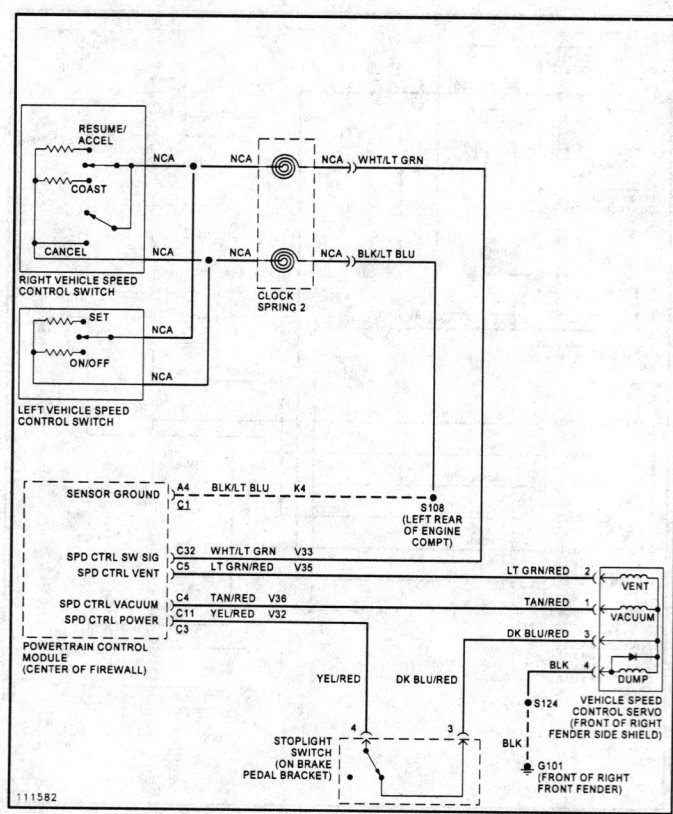

Fig. 8: Cruise Control System Wiring Diagram (Ram Van & Ram Wagon)

CAUTION: *When battery is disconnected, vehicle computer and memory systems may lose memory data. Driveability problems may exist until computer systems have completed a relearn cycle. See COMPUTER RELEARN PROCEDURES article in GENERAL INFORMATION before disconnecting battery.*

DESCRIPTION

The speed (cruise) control system is electronically controlled and vacuum operated. The electronic control is integrated into the Powertrain Control Module (PCM) located in left front corner of engine compartment. System consists of the following components: PCM, servo, speed control switches, vacuum reservoir, vehicle speed sensor, speed control relay and brake switch.

System controls are located on each side of steering wheel air bag module and consist of ON/OFF, CANCEL, RES/ACCEL and SET/COAST buttons. System is designed to operate at speeds above 30 MPH.

OPERATION

SYSTEM CONTROLS

To Set Speed Control – Press ON/OFF button to turn speed control system on. Accelerate to desired speed (minimum of 30 MPH) and press SET/COAST button. Vehicle speed will be maintained.

NOTE: *Speed control system will automatically disengage when vehicle speed decreases to less than 30 MPH or increases to more than 85 MPH.*

To Disengage Speed Control – Press brake pedal. Press clutch pedal (M/T). Press CANCEL button. Press ON/OFF button. If ON/OFF button is used, set speed will be erased from memory.

To Resume Previous Speed – If set speed has not been erased from memory and vehicle speed is more than 35 MPH, press RES/ACCEL button.

To Increase Speed – With speed control system on, increase set speed by rapidly pressing and releasing RES/ACCEL button. Each pressing of button will cause speed increase of 2 MPH. For example, pressing button 3 times will increase speed by 6 MPH. To increase speed gradually, hold RES/ACCEL button down until desired speed is reached. When button is released, new set speed will be maintained.

To Decrease Speed – With speed control system on, decrease set speed by pressing SET/COAST button. Vehicle speed will gradually decrease. Releasing button will set a new speed as long as vehicle speed is still more than 35 MPH.

COMPONENT LOCATIONS

COMPONENT LOCATIONS

Component	Location
Body Control Module (BCM)	Left End Of Instrument Panel On Junction Block
Data Link Connector (DLC)	Lower Left Side Of Instrument Panel
Park/Neutral Position (PNP) Switch	Left Front Side Of Transmission
Powertrain Control Module (PCM)	Left Front Corner Of Engine Compartment
Transmission Control Module (TCM)	Left Front Corner Of Engine Compartment

TROUBLE SHOOTING

ROAD TEST

Perform a road test to verify speed control malfunctions. Ensure speedometer operation is smooth without flutter at all speeds. Speedometer fluttering may cause surging in speed control system. For speedometer diagnosis, see INSTRUMENT PANELS article. If road test verifies a surge following speed control set and speedometer operates smoothly, see OVERSHOOT/UNDERSHOOT FOLLOWING SPEED CONTROL SET.

If road test verifies an inoperative system, and speedometer operates smoothly, check for:

- Diagnostic Trouble Codes (DTCs). See SELF-DIAGNOSTIC SYSTEM.
- Misadjusted brake switch. See BRAKE SWITCH under REMOVAL & INSTALLATION.
- Poor electrical connections at servo.
- Leaking vacuum reservoir, check valve, hoses or connections. See VACUUM SUPPLY under COMPONENT TESTS.
- Secure attachments of S/C servo cable.
- Smooth operation of throttle linkage.
- Defective PCM or wiring. See CHECKING POWERTRAIN CONTROL MODULE (PCM) & WIRING under SYSTEM TESTS.
- Defective servo. See SPEED CONTROL SERVO under COMPONENT TESTS.

To verify a speed control electronic malfunction, use a scan tool to check for DTCs. See SELF-DIAGNOSTIC SYSTEM. A speed control malfunction may occur without setting a DTC. If no DTCs are stored, go to CHECKING SPEED CONTROL OPERATION under SYSTEM TESTS.

SPEED CONTROL SLOWS DOWN BY ITSELF

Test Vehicle Speed Sensor (VSS). See DTC P0500: NO VEHICLE SPEED SENSOR SIGNAL under DIAGNOSTIC TESTS. Replace VSS, if necessary. If VSS is okay, perform the following:

- Check for defective speed control switch. See NTC-4: SPEED CONTROL ON/OFF SWITCH or NTC-5: SPEED CONTROL SET/RESUME SWITCH under SYSTEM TESTS.
- Perform vacuum supply test. See VACUUM SUPPLY under COMPONENT TESTS.
- Perform speed control servo test. See SPEED CONTROL SERVO under COMPONENT TESTS.
- Check for defective PCM. See CHECKING POWERTRAIN CONTROL MODULE (PCM) & WIRING under SYSTEM TESTS.
- On A/T models, check for transmission Diagnostic Trouble Codes (DTCs). See appropriate ELECTRONIC CONTROLS article in AUTOMATIC TRANSMISSIONS in appropriate MITCHELL® TRANSMISSION SERVICE & REPAIR manual.

OVERSHOOT/UNDERSHOOT FOLLOWING SPEED CONTROL SET

If operator repeatedly presses and releases set button with their foot off accelerator (lift foot set) to begin speed control operation, vehicle may accelerate and exceed desired set speed by 5 MPH and then decelerate to less than desired set speed before achieving desired set speed.

Speed Control (S/C) has as adaptive strategy that compensates for variations in S/C cable lengths. When S/C is set with vehicle operator's foot off accelerator pedal, S/C compensates for excessive S/C cable slack. If lift foot sets are continually used, speed control overshoot/undershoot condition will develop.

To "unlearn" overshoot/undershoot condition, operator must press and release set button while maintaining desired speed with accelerator pedal, then turn S/C switch to OFF position after waiting 10 seconds. This procedure must be repeated 10-15 times to completely unlearn overshoot/undershoot condition.

COMPONENT TESTS

WARNING: Vehicle is equipped with an air bag. Air bag must be deactivated before servicing speed control components on or around steering column. See appropriate AIR BAG RESTRAINT SYSTEMS article.

NOTE: For component locations, See COMPONENT LOCATIONS. For connector terminal identification, see CONNECTOR IDENTIFICATION. For wiring diagram, see WIRING DIAGRAMS.

BRAKE SWITCH

Disconnect brake switch 6-pin connector. Using an ohmmeter, check for continuity at brake switch. *See Fig. 1.* If continuity is not as specified in BRAKE SWITCH CONTINUITY table, check brake switch adjustment. See BRAKE SWITCH under REMOVAL & INSTALLATION. If brake switch adjustment is okay, replace defective brake switch.

BRAKE SWITCH CONTINUITY

Switch Plunger Position	Check Between Terminals	Continuity
Released	5 & 6	Yes
Depressed	1 & 2	Yes
	3 & 4	Yes

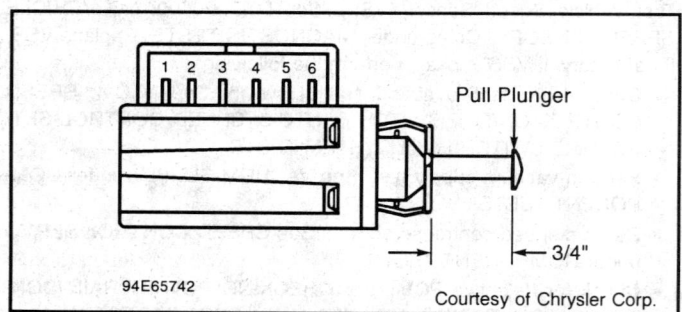

Fig. 1: Identifying Brake Switch Terminals

SPEED CONTROL SERVO

1) Turn ignition switch and speed control switch to ON position, but do not start engine. Disconnect Speed Control (S/C) servo 4-pin connector. Connect a jumper wire between S/C servo harness connector terminal No. 3 and S/C servo terminal No. 3. *See Fig. 5.* Using jumper wires, connect S/C servo terminals No. 2 and 4 to ground.
2) Using a hand-held vacuum pump, apply 10-15 in. Hg of vacuum to S/C servo vacuum nipple. Throttle cable should not retract. If throttle cable retracts, replace S/C servo. If throttle cable does not retract, connect S/C servo terminal No. 1 to ground. Throttle cable should now retract and hold position for at least one minute.
3) If throttle cable does not remain retracted, replace S/C servo. If throttle cable remains retracted, remove jumper wire from S/C servo terminal No. 3. Throttle cable should return to released position. If throttle cable does not return to released position, replace S/C servo. If servo functions as described, no problem is indicated at this time.

VACUUM SUPPLY

1) Disconnect vacuum hose at speed control servo. Install vacuum gauge to disconnected vacuum hose. Start engine and observe gauge. Vacuum reading should be a minimum of 10 in. Hg. Turn engine off. Vacuum should continue to hold at a minimum of 10 in. Hg.
2) If vacuum is not as specified, check for kinked or leaking vacuum lines, defective check valve, defective vacuum reservoir and/or poor engine performance. If no problems are found, check speed control servo. See SPEED CONTROL SERVO.

CONNECTOR IDENTIFICATION

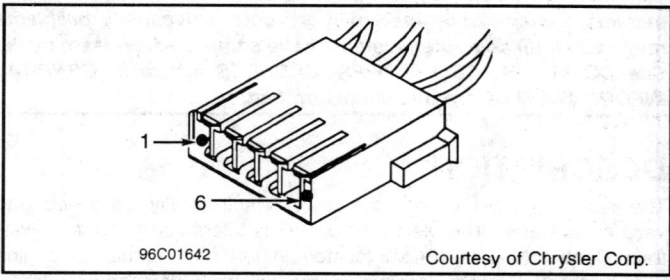

Fig. 2: Identifying Brake Switch Harness Connector Terminals

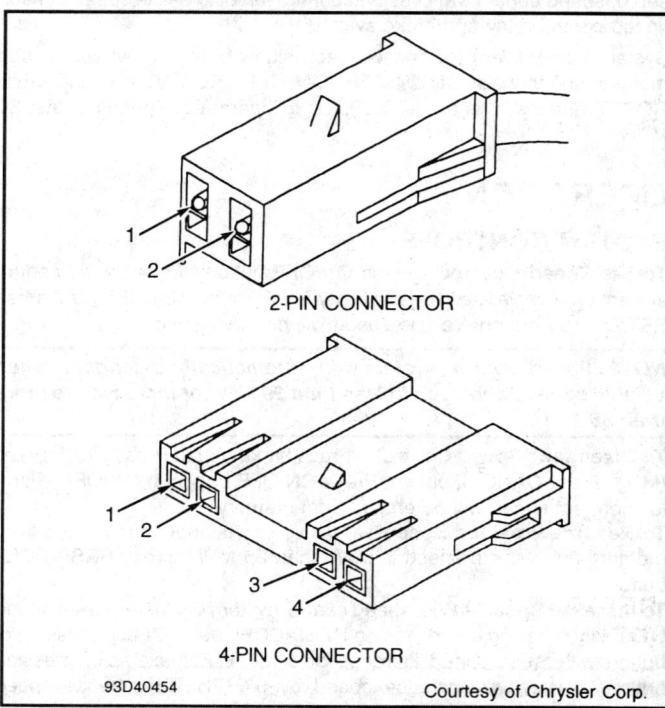

Fig. 3: Identifying Clockspring Connector Terminals

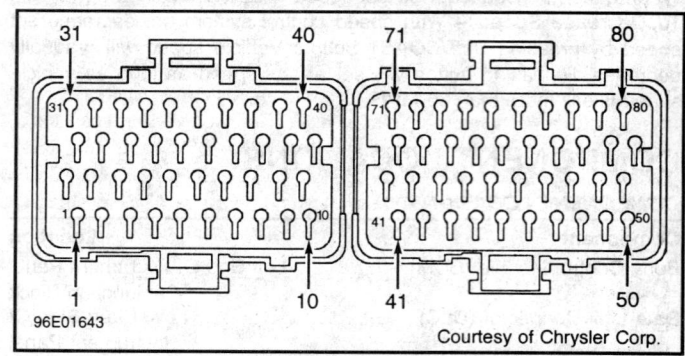

Fig. 4: Identifying Powertrain Control Module (PCM) Connector Terminals

SELF-DIAGNOSTIC SYSTEM

WARNING: Vehicle is equipped with an air bag. Air bag must be deactivated before servicing speed control components on or around steering column. See appropriate AIR BAG RESTRAINT SYSTEMS article.

SERVICE PRECAUTIONS

Before proceeding with diagnosis, the following precautions must be followed:

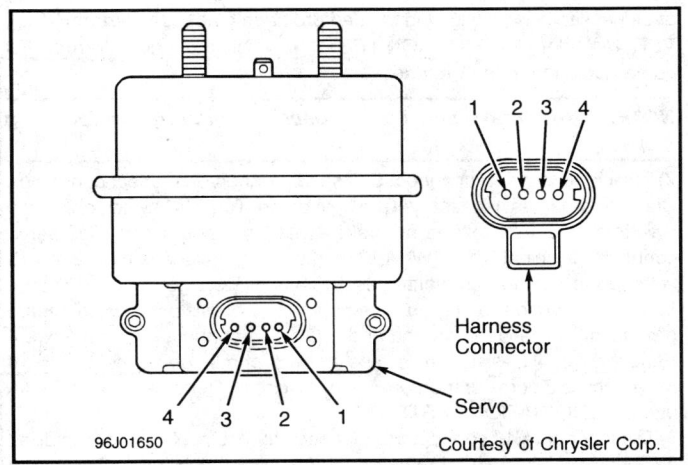

96J01650   Courtesy of Chrysler Corp.

Fig. 5: Identifying Speed Control (S/C) Servo Connector Terminals

- When using Diagnostic Trouble Code (DTC) tests for diagnosis, DO NOT skip any steps, or incorrect diagnosis may result. Always perform indicated verification procedure after repairs are made.
- When using a jumper wire, ensure either jumper wire or circuit is fuse-protected.
- Before disconnecting connector from any control module, ensure ignition is off before removing connector.
- When checking voltage or continuity at any control module, probe connector for control module from pin side. DO NOT backprobe connector or probe wires through insulation.
- DO NOT cause short circuits when performing electrical tests. This will set additional DTCs, making diagnosis of original problem more difficult.
- Use specified test equipment when performing electrical tests.

RETRIEVING DIAGNOSTIC TROUBLE CODES (DTCs)

NOTE: Self-diagnostic tests are written specifically for Chrysler's Diagnostic Readout Box (DRB). If using a generic scan tool, ensure it is OBD-II certified. A generic scan tool may not be capable of performing all necessary test functions.

Ensure battery is fully charged. Turn ignition off. Connect scan tool to Data Link Connector (DLC). *See Fig. 6.* Turn ignition on. Using scan tool manufacturer's instructions, record all DTCs displayed on scan tool. If any DTCs exist, perform appropriate test under DIAGNOSTIC TESTS. Clear DTCs after repairs are completed. See CLEARING DIAGNOSTIC TROUBLE CODES. If no DTCs are retrieved and fault still exists, go to CHECKING SPEED CONTROL OPERATION under SYSTEM TESTS.

CLEARING DIAGNOSTIC TROUBLE CODES

Ensure ignition is off. Turn ignition on. Using screen prompts on scan tool, erase DTC from PCM.

DIAGNOSTIC TESTS

DTC P0500: NO VEHICLE SPEED SENSOR SIGNAL

Possible Causes:
- VSS defective.
- 8-Volt supply circuit open or shorted.
- VSS circuit open or shorted.
- Speedometer pinion gear defective.

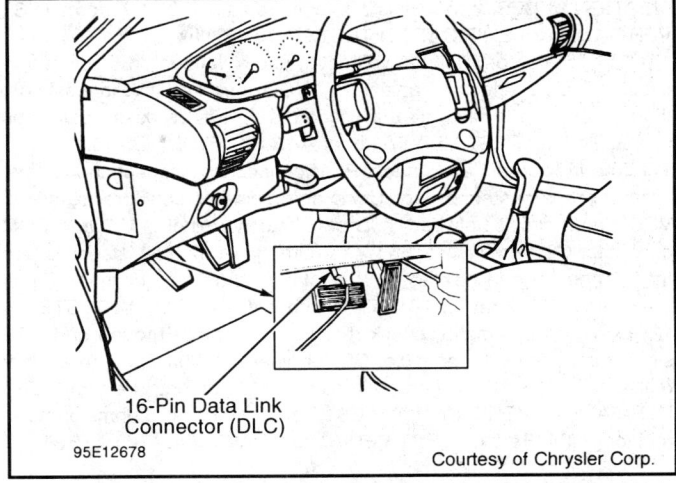

95E12678   Courtesy of Chrysler Corp.

Fig. 6: Locating Data Link Connector (DLC)

- PCM defective.

NOTE: For component locations, See COMPONENT LOCATIONS. For connector terminal identification, see CONNECTOR IDENTIFICATION. For wiring diagram, see WIRING DIAGRAMS.

WARNING: Keep hands and feet clear of rotating wheels.

1) Raise and support vehicle under lower control arms, allowing drive wheels to spin free. Start engine. Using scan tool, read Vehicle Speed Sensor (VSS). Put transmission in any forward gear. If scan tool displays more than zero MPH, go to next step. If scan tool does not display more than zero MPH, go to step **3)**.

2) Inspect wiring and connectors. Repair as necessary. Perform TEST VER-5A under VERIFICATION TESTS. If wiring and connectors are okay, go to next step.

3) Turn ignition off. Disconnect VSS connector. Inspect connector. Clean or repair as necessary. Turn ignition on. Using a voltmeter, check voltage on VSS signal circuit at VSS connector terminal No. 3 (White/Orange wire). If voltage is more than 4 volts, go to next step. If voltage is 4 volts or less, go to step **10)**.

4) Using a voltmeter, check voltage on 8-volt supply circuit at VSS connector terminal No. 1 (Orange wire). If voltage is more than 7 volts, go to next step. If voltage is 7 volts or less, repair open circuit. Perform TEST VER-5A under VERIFICATION TESTS.

5) Connect one end of jumper wire to VSS connector terminal No. 3 (White/Orange wire). Turn ignition on. Using scan tool, read VSS signal. While observing scan tool display, quickly and repeatedly tap other end of jumper wire to sensor ground circuit at VSS connector terminal No. 2 (Black/Light Blue wire). If scan tool displays more than zero MPH, go to next step. If scan tool does not display more than zero MPH, go to step **7)**.

6) Turn ignition off. Remove VSS. Inspect speedometer pinion gear. Repair as necessary. Perform TEST VER-5A under VERIFICATION TESTS. If pinion gear is okay, replace VSS. Perform TEST VER-5A under VERIFICATION TESTS.

7) Turn ignition off. Using an ohmmeter, check resistance of sensor ground circuit between ground and VSS connector terminal No. 2 (Black/Light Blue wire). If resistance is less than 5 ohms, go to next step. If resistance is 5 ohms or more, repair open circuit. Perform TEST VER-5A under VERIFICATION TESTS.

8) Disconnect PCM connectors. Using an ohmmeter, check resistance of VSS signal circuit between VSS connector terminal No. 3 and PCM connector C2, terminal No. 66 (White/Orange wire). If resistance is less than 5 ohms, go to next step. If resistance is 5 ohms or more, repair open circuit. Perform TEST VER-5A under VERIFICATION TESTS.

9) Inspect connector terminals. If any terminal is damaged, pushed out or miswired, repair as necessary. Perform TEST VER-5A under VERI-

FICATION TESTS. If terminals are okay, replace PCM. Perform TEST VER-5A under VERIFICATION TESTS.

10) Turn ignition on. Using a voltmeter, check voltage on 8-volt supply circuit at VSS connector terminal No. 1 (Orange wire). If voltage is more than 7 volts, go to next step. If voltage is 7 volts or less, repair open circuit. Perform TEST VER-5A under VERIFICATION TESTS.

11) Turn ignition off. Disconnect PCM connectors. Inspect connectors. Clean or repair as necessary. Using an ohmmeter, check resistance of VSS signal circuit between VSS connector terminal No. 3 and PCM connector C2, terminal No. 66 (White/Orange wire). If resistance is less than 5 ohms, go to next step. If resistance is 5 ohms or more, repair open circuit. Perform TEST VER-5A under VERIFICATION TESTS.

12) Using an ohmmeter, check resistance between ground and VSS signal circuit at PCM connector C2, terminal 66 (White/Orange wire). If resistance is less than 5 ohms, repair short to ground. Perform TEST VER-5A under VERIFICATION TESTS. If resistance is 5 ohms or more, replace PCM. Perform TEST VER-5A under VERIFICATION TESTS.

DTC P1595: SPEED CONTROL SOLENOID CIRCUITS OR DTC P1683: SPEED CONTROL POWER RELAY CIRCUIT

NOTE: Both DTCs are diagnosed using the same test.

DTC P1595 will set if vacuum and vent solenoids do not respond when actuated by PCM. DTC P1683 will set if Speed Control (S/C) power supply circuit is open or shorted.
Possible Causes:
- Ground circuit open.
- brake switch output circuit open.
- S/C power supply circuit open or shorted.
- S/C servo defective.
- S/C vacuum solenoid control circuit open or shorted.
- S/C vent solenoid control circuit open or shorted.
- Brake switch defective or out of adjustment.
- Defective PCM.

NOTE: For component locations, See COMPONENT LOCATIONS. For connector terminal identification, see CONNECTOR IDENTIFI-CATION. For wiring diagram, see WIRING DIAGRAMS.

1) Turn ignition on. Turn S/C on. Using scan tool, actuate S/C vent solenoid. If speed control servo clicks, go to next step. If S/C servo does not click, go to step **7**).

2) Using scan tool, actuate S/C vacuum solenoid. If S/C servo clicks, go to next step. If S/C servo does not click, go to step **6**).

3) Turn ignition on. Turn S/C on. Using scan tool, actuate S/C vent solenoid. Wiggle wiring harness between S/C servo, brake switch and PCM. If wiggling interrupted S/C servo actuation, repair wiring harness as necessary where wiggling caused problem to appear. Perform TEST VER-4Aunder VERIFICATION TESTS. If wiggling did not interrupt S/C servo actuation, go to next step.

4) Turn ignition off. Inspect wiring and connectors. Repair as necessary. Perform TEST VER-4A under VERIFICATION TESTS. If wiring and connectors are okay, go to next step.

5) Turn ignition on. Turn S/C on. Using scan tool, actuate S/C vacuum solenoid. Wiggle wiring harness between S/C servo, brake switch and PCM. If wiggling interrupted S/C servo actuation, repair wiring harness as necessary where wiggling caused problem to appear. Perform TEST VER-4A under VERIFICATION TESTS. If wiggling did not interrupt S/C servo actuation, symptom does not exist at this time.

6) Turn ignition on. Turn S/C on. Using scan tool, actuate S/C vent solenoid. Wiggle wiring harness between S/C servo, brake switch and PCM. If wiggling interrupted S/C servo actuation, repair wiring harness as necessary where wiggling caused problem to appear. Perform TEST VER-4A under VERIFICATION TESTS. If wiggling did not interrupt S/C servo actuation, go to next step.

NOTE: Ensure brake pedal is not depressed during the following steps.

7) Turn ignition off. Disconnect S/C servo connector. Inspect connector. Clean or repair as necessary. Turn ignition on. Turn S/C switch on. Using a voltmeter, check voltage on brake switch output circuit at S/C servo connector terminal No. 3 (White/Brown wire). If voltage is more than 10 volts, go to next step. If voltage is 10 volts or less, go to step **15**).

8) Turn ignition off. Using an ohmmeter, check resistance of S/C servo ground circuit between ground and S/C servo connector terminal No. 4 (Black wire). If resistance is less than 5 ohms, go to next step. If resistance is 5 ohms or more, repair open circuit. Perform TEST VER-4A under VERIFICATION TESTS.

9) Disconnect PCM connectors. Inspect connectors. Clean or repair as necessary. Using an ohmmeter, check resistance of S/C vacuum solenoid control circuit between S/C servo connector terminal No. 1 and PCM connector C2, terminal No. 78 (Tan/Red wire). If resistance is less than 5 ohms, go to next step. If resistance is 5 ohms or more, repair open circuit. Perform TEST VER-4A under VERIFICATION TESTS.

10) Using an ohmmeter, check resistance between ground and S/C vacuum solenoid control circuit at S/C servo connector terminal No. 1 (Tan/Red wire). If resistance is less than 5 ohms, repair short to ground. Perform TEST VER-4A under VERIFICATION TESTS. If resistance is 5 ohms or more, go to next step.

11) Using an ohmmeter, check resistance of S/C vent solenoid control circuit between S/C servo connector terminal No. 2 and PCM connector C2, terminal No. 80 (Light Green/Red wire). If resistance is less than 5 ohms, go to next step. If resistance is 5 ohms or more, repair open circuit. Perform TEST VER-4A under VERIFICATION TESTS.

12) Using an ohmmeter, check resistance between ground and S/C vent solenoid control circuit at S/C servo connector terminal No. 2 (Light Green/Red wire). If resistance is less than 5 ohms, repair short to ground. Perform TEST VER-4A under VERIFICATION TESTS. If resistance is 5 ohms or more, go to next step.

13) Disconnect brake switch connector. Inspect connector. Clean or repair as necessary. Using an ohmmeter, check resistance of S/C power supply circuit between PCM connector C1, terminal No. 5 and brake switch connector terminal No. 3 (Yellow/Red wire). If resistance is less than 5 ohms, go to next step. If resistance is 5 ohms or more, repair open circuit. Perform TEST VER-4A under VERIFICATION TESTS.

14) Using an ohmmeter, check resistance between ground and brake switch output circuit at brake switch terminal No. 3 (Yellow/Red wire). If resistance is less than 5 ohms, repair short to ground. Perform TEST VER-4A under VERIFICATION TESTS. If resistance is 5 ohms or more, replace S/C servo. Perform TEST VER-4A under VERIFICATION TESTS.

15) Turn S/C and ignition off. Disconnect brake switch connector. Inspect connectors. Clean or replace as necessary. Turn ignition on. Using a voltmeter, check voltage of S/C power supply circuit at brake switch connector terminal No. 3 (Yellow/Red wire). If voltage is more than 10 volts, go to next step. If voltage is 10 volts or less, go to step **19**).

16) Turn ignition off. Using an ohmmeter, check resistance between ground and brake switch output circuit at S/C servo connector terminal No. 3 (White/Brown wire). If resistance is less than 5 ohms, repair short to ground. Perform TEST VER-4A under VERIFICATION TESTS. If resistance is 5 ohms or more, go to next step.

17) Check brake switch adjustment. See BRAKE SWITCH under REMOVAL & INSTALLATION. Adjust as necessary. Perform TEST VER-4A under VERIFICATION TESTS. If brake switch adjustment is okay, go to next step.

18) Using an ohmmeter, check resistance of brake switch output circuit between brake switch connector terminal No. 4 and S/C servo connector terminal No. 3 (White/Brown wire). If resistance is more than 5 ohms, repair open circuit. Perform TEST VER-4A under VERIFICATION TESTS. If resistance is 5 ohms or less, replace brake switch. Perform TEST VER-4A under VERIFICATION TESTS.

19) Using an ohmmeter, check resistance between ground and brake switch output circuit at S/C servo connector terminal No. 3 (White/Brown wire). If resistance is less than 5 ohms, repair short to ground. Perform TEST VER-4A under VERIFICATION TESTS. If resistance is 5 ohms or more, go to next step.

20) Using an ohmmeter, check resistance of S/C power supply circuit between PCM connector C1 terminal No. 5 and brake switch connector terminal No. 3 (Yellow/Red wire). If resistance is less than 5 ohms, go to next step. If resistance is 5 ohms or more, repair open circuit. Perform TEST VER-4A under VERIFICATION TESTS.

21) Using an ohmmeter, check resistance of S/C servo ground circuit between ground and S/C servo connector terminal No. 4 (Black wire). If resistance is less than 5 ohms, replace PCM. Perform TEST VER-4A under VERIFICATION TESTS. If resistance is 5 ohms or more, repair open circuit. Perform TEST VER-4A under VERIFICATION TESTS.

DTC P1596: SPEED CONTROL SWITCH ALWAYS HIGH

DTC P1596 will set if open circuit is detected in Speed Control (S/C) switch circuit.

Possible Causes:

- Intermittent wiring harness defect.
- S/C switch ground circuit open.
- S/C switch signal circuit shorted to voltage.
- Defective PCM.
- Defective S/C switch.
- Defective clockspring.

NOTE: *For component locations, See COMPONENT LOCATIONS. For connector terminal identification, see CONNECTOR IDENTIFICATION. For wiring diagram, see WIRING DIAGRAMS.*

NOTE: *Speed control switch wire colors are not available from manufacturer.*

1) Using scan tool, read speed control inputs. While observing scan tool display, push S/C ON/OFF switch several times and leave on. If scan tool displays speed control switch off and on, go to next step. If scan tool does not display speed control switch off and on, go to step **3)**.

2) Using scan tool, monitor switch voltage while wiggling wiring between PCM and S/C switch. If voltage was more than 4.9 volts at any time while wiggling, repair wiring. Perform TEST VER-4A under VERIFICATION TESTS. If voltage was 4.9 volts or less while wiggling, symptom does not exist at this time.

3) Turn ignition off. Disconnect S/C ON/OFF switch connector (located behind S/C ON/OFF switch). Using an ohmmeter, check resistance between ground and S/C switch ground circuit terminal of S/C ON/OFF switch connector. See WIRING DIAGRAMS. If resistance is less than 5 ohms, go to next step. If resistance is 5 ohms or more, repair open ground circuit. Perform TEST VER-4A under VERIFICATION TESTS.

4) Turn ignition on. Using a voltmeter, check voltage of S/C signal circuit on S/C ON/OFF switch connector. See WIRING DIAGRAMS. If voltage is 4.8 volts or less, go to next step. If voltage is more than 4.8 volts, repair short to voltage on signal circuit. Perform TEST VER-4A under VERIFICATION TESTS.

5) Turn ignition off. Disconnect PCM. Inspect connectors. Clean or repair as necessary. Using an ohmmeter, check resistance of S/C switch signal circuit between S/C ON/OFF switch and PCM connector C2, terminal No. 41 (Red/Light Green wire). If resistance is less than 5 ohms, go to step **7)**.

6) Using an ohmmeter, check resistance across S/C ON/OFF switch terminals. If resistance is 25,000 ohms or more, replace S/C ON/OFF switch. Perform TEST VER-4A under VERIFICATION TESTS. If resistance is less than 25,000 ohms, replace PCM. Perform TEST VER- 4A under VERIFICATION TESTS.

7) Disconnect 4-pin clockspring connector located behind steering column shrouds. Using an ohmmeter, check resistance of S/C switch signal circuit between 4-pin clockspring connector and PCM connector terminal No. 41 (Red/Light Green wire). If resistance is less than 5 ohms, replace clockspring. See appropriate AIR BAG RESTRAINT SYSTEMS article. Perform TEST VER-4A under VERIFICATION TESTS. If resistance is 5 ohms or more, repair open signal circuit between 4-pin clockspring connector and PCM connector terminal No. 41. Perform TEST VER-4A under VERIFICATION TESTS.

DTC P1597: SPEED CONTROL SWITCH ALWAYS LOW

DTC P1597 will set if Speed Control (S/C) switch voltage is less than 4.5 volts for 2 minutes while battery voltage is more than 10.4 volts.

Possible Causes:

- S/C switch signal circuit shorted to ground or sensor ground.
- Defective S/C switch.
- Defective PCM.

NOTE: *For component locations, See COMPONENT LOCATIONS. For connector terminal identification, see CONNECTOR IDENTIFICATION. For wiring diagram, see WIRING DIAGRAMS.*

1) Using scan tool, record all DTCs and freeze frame data. Erase DTCs. Read speed control switch voltage. If voltage is less than one volt, go to next step. If voltage is one volt or more, symptom does not exist at this time.

2) Turn ignition off. Disconnect S/C ON/OFF switch. Inspect connectors. Clean or repair as necessary. Using an ohmmeter, check resistance between S/C switch signal circuit and sensor ground circuit across S/C ON/OFF switch connector terminals. If resistance is 5 ohms or more, go to next step. If resistance is less than 5 ohms, repair short to sensor ground on speed control switch signal circuit. Perform TEST VER-4A under VERIFICATION TESTS.

3) Turn ignition on. Using scan tool, read S/C switch voltage. If voltage is 5 volts, replace S/C switch. Perform TEST VER-4A under VERIFICATION TESTS. If voltage is less than 5 volts, go to next step.

4) Disconnect PCM connector C2. Inspect connector. Clean or repair as necessary. Using an ohmmeter, check resistance between ground and S/C switch signal circuit at PCM connector C2, terminal No. 41 (Red/Light Green wire). If resistance is less than 5 ohms, repair short to ground. Perform TEST VER-4A under VERIFICATION TESTS. If resistance is 5 ohms or more, replace PCM. Perform TEST VER-4A under VERIFICATION TESTS.

SYSTEM TESTS

NOTE: *For component locations, See COMPONENT LOCATIONS. For connector terminal identification, see CONNECTOR IDENTIFICATION. For wiring diagram, see WIRING DIAGRAMS.*

CHECKING POWERTRAIN CONTROL MODULE (PCM) & WIRING

1) Disconnect PCM connector C2. Remove both Speed Control (S/C) switches and disconnect wire connectors. Using an ohmmeter, check for continuity between PCM connector C2, terminal No. 41 (Red/Light Green wire) and terminal No. 1 of each S/C switch connector. *See Fig. 4.* If continuity exists, go to next step. If continuity does not exist, repair open circuit.

2) Using an ohmmeter, check for continuity between ground and PCM connector C2, terminal No. 41 (Red/Light Green wire). *See Fig. 4.* If continuity exists, repair short circuit. If continuity does not exist, test switches. See appropriate NTC TEST.

3) Reconnect S/C switches and PCM connector C2. Disconnect S/C servo connector. Turn ignition on. Turn S/C switch on. Using a voltmeter, check voltage at S/C servo connector terminal 3 (White/Brown wire). Battery voltage should exist. If battery voltage exists, go to next step. If battery voltage does not exist, go to step **16)**.

4) Turn S/C and ignition off. Using an ohmmeter, place positive lead on S/C servo terminal No. 3 and negative lead on terminal No. 4. If continuity does not exist, replace S/C servo. If resistance is 50 ohms or more, clean terminals and retest. If resistance is less than 50 ohms, go to next step.

5) Using an ohmmeter, place positive lead on S/C servo terminal No. 3 and negative lead on terminal No. 2. If continuity does not exist, replace S/C servo. If resistance is 50 ohms or more, clean terminals and retest. If resistance is less than 50 ohms, go to next step.

6) Using an ohmmeter, place positive lead on S/C servo terminal No. 3 and negative lead on terminal No. 1. If continuity does not exist, replace S/C servo. If resistance is 50 ohms or more, clean terminals and retest. If resistance is less than 50 ohms, go to next step.

7) Using an ohmmeter, check for continuity between ground and S/C servo connector terminal No. 4 (Black wire). If continuity does not exist, repair open ground circuit. If continuity exists, go to next step.

8) Disconnect PCM connectors. Using an ohmmeter, check for continuity between S/C servo connector terminal No. 1 and PCM connector C2, terminal No. 78 (Tan/Red wire). If continuity does not exist, repair open circuit. If continuity exists, go to next step.

9) Using an ohmmeter, check for continuity between ground and S/C servo connector terminal No. 1 (Tan/Red wire). If continuity exists, repair short circuit. If continuity does not exist, go to next step.

10) Using an ohmmeter, check for continuity between S/C servo connector terminal No. 2 and PCM connector C2, terminal No. 80 (Light Green/Red wire). If continuity does not exist, repair open circuit. If continuity exists, go to next step.

11) Using an ohmmeter, check for continuity between ground and S/C servo connector terminal No. 2 (Light Green/Red wire). If continuity exists, repair short circuit. If continuity does not exist, go to next step.

12) Using an ohmmeter, check for continuity between S/C servo connector terminals No. 1 and 2. If continuity exists, repair short circuit. If continuity does not exist, go to next step.

13) Reconnect S/C servo connector. Ensure brake pedal is not pressed. Using an ohmmeter, check for continuity between ground and PCM connector C2, terminal No. 62 (White/Pink wire). If continuity exists, go to step **15**). If continuity does not exist, test brake switch. See BRAKE SWITCH under COMPONENT TESTS. If brake switch is okay, go to next step.

14) Using an ohmmeter, check for continuity between PCM connector C2, terminal No. 62 and brake switch connector terminal No. 1 (White/Pink wire). If continuity does not exist, repair open circuit. If continuity exists, repair open circuit between brake switch connector terminal No. 2 and ground (Black/Tan wire).

15) Ensure transmission is in Park or Neutral. Using an ohmmeter, check for continuity between ground and PCM connector C2, terminal No. 76 (Brown/Yellow wire). If continuity does not exist, test Park/Neutral Position (PNP) switch and wiring. See NTC-2: PARK/NEUTRAL POSITION (PNP) SWITCH. If continuity exists, go to next step.

16) Turn S/C and ignition off. Using an ohmmeter, check for continuity between S/C servo connector terminal No. 3 and PCM connector C1, terminal No. 5 (Yellow/Red wire). If continuity exists, go to next step. If continuity does not exist, test brake switch. See BRAKE SWITCH under COMPONENT TESTS. If brake switch is okay, go to step **18**).

17) Using an ohmmeter, check for continuity between ground and S/C servo connector terminal No. 3 (White/Brown wire). If continuity exists, repair short circuit. If continuity does not exist, replace PCM.

18) Using an ohmmeter, check for continuity between S/C servo connector terminal No. 3 and brake switch connector terminal No. 4 (White/Brown wire). If continuity does not exist, repair open circuit. If continuity exists, go to next step.

19) Using an ohmmeter, check for continuity between brake switch terminal No. 3 and PCM connector C1, terminal No. 5 (Yellow/Red wire). If continuity does not exist, repair open circuit. If continuity exists, no problem is indicated at this time.

CHECKING SPEED CONTROL OPERATION

NOTE: *Perform this test only if there are no Diagnostic Trouble Codes (DTCs).*

1) Turn ignition on. Using scan tool, monitor Speed Control (S/C) switch inputs. Turn S/C switch on. If scan tool displays S/C switch ON, go to next step. If scan tool does not display S/C switch ON, go to NTC-4: SPEED CONTROL ON/OFF SWITCH.

2) While observing scan tool, press SET switch several times. If scan tool displays PRESSED and RELEASED, go to next step. If scan tool does not display PRESSED and RELEASED, go to NTC-5: SPEED CONTROL SET/RESUME SWITCH.

3) While observing scan tool, press brake pedal several times. If scan tool displays brake pedal PRESSED and RELEASED, go to next step (A/T) or go to step **5**) (M/T). If scan tool does not display brake pedal PRESSED and RELEASED, go to NTC-1: BRAKE SWITCH SENSE.

4) On A/T models, move gear selector to Drive. If scan tool displays park neutral switch D/R, go to next step. If scan tool does not display park neutral switch D/R, go to NTC-2: PARK/NEUTRAL POSITION (PNP) SWITCH.

5) On all models, press cancel switch several times. If scan tool displays cancel switch PRESSED or RELEASED, go to next step. If scan tool does not display cancel switch PRESSED or RELEASED, replace cancel switch. Perform TEST VER-4A under VERIFICATION TESTS.

6) While observing scan tool, press resume switch several times. If scan tool displays resume switch PRESSED or RELEASED, go to next step. If scan tool does not display resume switch PRESSED or RELEASED, replace SET/RESUME switch. Perform TEST VER-4A under VERIFICATION TESTS.

7) Turn ignition off. Disconnect S/C servo connector. Inspect connector. Clean or repair as necessary. Turn ignition on. Using scan tool, actuate S/C vent solenoid. Using voltmeter, check voltage on brake switch circuit at S/C servo connector terminal No. 3 (White/Brown wire). If voltage is more than 10 volts, go to next step. If voltage is 10 volts or less, go to step **16**).

8) Start engine and let idle for one minute. Turn engine off. Turn ignition on (engine off). Using scan tool, actuate S/C servo solenoids. If throttle opens and closes, go to NTC-3: CHECKING FOR SPEED CONTROL DENIED MESSAGE. If throttle does not open and close, go to next step.

9) Turn ignition off. Inspect throttle cable. If throttle cable is disconnected or damaged, repair as necessary. Perform TEST VER-4A under VERIFICATION TESTS. If throttle cable is okay, go to next step.

10) Turn ignition off. Disconnect S/C servo connector. Using an ohmmeter, check resistance between ground and S/C servo connector terminal No. 4 (Black wire). If resistance is less than 5 ohms, go to next step. If resistance is 5 ohms or more, repair open ground circuit. Perform TEST VER-4A under VERIFICATION TESTS.

11) Disconnect vacuum supply hose from S/C servo. Connect vacuum gauge to supply hose. Start engine. If vacuum gauge does not read manifold vacuum, repair vacuum supply leak or restriction. Perform TEST VER-4A under VERIFICATION TESTS. If vacuum gauge reads manifold vacuum, go to next step.

12) Turn ignition off. Disconnect S/C servo and PCM connectors. Inspect terminals. Clean or repair as necessary. Using an ohmmeter, check resistance of S/C vacuum solenoid control circuit between PCM connector C2, terminal No. 78 and S/C servo connector terminal No. 1 (Tan/Red wire). If resistance is less than 5 ohms, go to next step. If resistance is 5 ohms or more, repair open circuit. Perform TEST VER-4A under VERIFICATION TESTS.

13) Using an ohmmeter, check resistance of S/C vent solenoid control circuit between PCM connector C2, terminal No. 80 and S/C servo connector terminal No. 2 (Light Green/Red wire). If resistance is less than 5 ohms, go to next step. If resistance is 5 ohms or more, repair open circuit. Perform TEST VER-4A under VERIFICATION TESTS.

14) Inspect S/C servo connector terminals. If any terminal is damaged, pushed out or miswired, repair as necessary. Perform TEST VER-4A under VERIFICATION TESTS. If terminals are okay, go to next step.

15) Reconnect S/C servo and PCM connectors. Disconnect vacuum supply hose from S/C servo. Attach vacuum gauge to supply hose. Start engine. Turn engine off. Observe vacuum gauge. If vacuum does not hold for 10 seconds, repair vacuum leak or restriction. Perform TEST VER-4A under VERIFICATION TESTS. If vacuum holds for at least 10 seconds, replace S/C servo. Perform TEST VER-4A under VERIFICATION TESTS.

16) Turn ignition off. Using an ohmmeter, check resistance between ground and brake switch output circuit at S/C servo connector terminal No. 3 (White/Brown wire). If resistance is less than 5 ohms, repair short to ground. Perform TEST VER-4A under VERIFICATION TESTS. If resistance is 5 ohms or more, go to next step.

17) Turn ignition off. Disconnect brake switch connector. Inspect connector. Clean or repair as necessary. Turn ignition on. Using scan tool, ensure S/C vent solenoid is still actuated. using a voltmeter, check voltage on S/C power supply circuit at brake switch connector terminal No. 3 (Yellow/Red wire). If voltage is more than 10 volts, go to next step. If voltage is 10 volts or less, go to step **22)**.

18) Turn ignition off. Check brake switch adjustment. See BRAKE SWITCH under REMOVAL & INSTALLATION. Adjust as necessary. Perform TEST VER-4A under VERIFICATION TESTS. If brake switch adjustment is okay, replace brake switch. Perform TEST VER-4A under VERIFICATION TESTS. Go to next step.

19) Disconnect S/C servo connector. Using an ohmmeter, check resistance of S/C servo ground circuit between ground and S/C servo connector terminal No. 4 (Black wire). If resistance is 5 ohms or more, repair open ground circuit. Perform TEST VER-4A under VERIFICATION TESTS. If resistance is less than 5 ohms, go to next step.

20) Disconnect brake switch connector. Inspect connector terminals. If any terminal is damaged, pushed out or miswired, repair as necessary. Perform TEST VER-4A under VERIFICATION TESTS. If terminals are okay, go to next step.

21) Disconnect S/C servo connector. Inspect connector terminals. If any terminal is damaged, pushed out or miswired, repair as necessary. Perform TEST VER-4A under VERIFICATION TESTS. If terminals are okay, no problem is indicated at this time.

22) Turn ignition off. Disconnect S/C servo connector. Using an ohmmeter, check resistance of S/C servo ground circuit between ground and S/C servo connector terminal No. 4 (Black wire). If resistance is 5 ohms or more, repair open circuit. Perform TEST VER-4A under VERIFICATION TESTS. If resistance is less than 5 ohms, go to next step.

23) Disconnect brake switch connector. Inspect connector terminals. If any terminal is damaged, pushed out or miswired, repair as necessary. Perform TEST VER-4A under VERIFICATION TESTS. If terminals are okay, go to next step.

24) Disconnect S/C servo connector. Inspect connector terminals. If any terminal is damaged, pushed out or miswired, repair as necessary. Perform TEST VER-4A under VERIFICATION TESTS. If terminals are okay, go to next step.

25) Disconnect PCM connectors. Using an ohmmeter, check resistance of S/C power supply circuit between PCM connector C1, terminal No. 5 and brake switch connector terminal No. 3 (Yellow/Red wire). If resistance is 5 ohms or more, repair open circuit. Perform TEST VER-4A under VERIFICATION TESTS. If resistance is less than 5 ohms, replace PCM. Perform TEST VER-4A under VERIFICATION TESTS.

NTC-1: BRAKE SWITCH SENSE

Possible Causes:
- Ground circuit open.
- Defective brake switch.
- Brake switch sense circuit open or shorted.
- Defective PCM.

1) Turn ignition off. Disconnect brake switch connector. Inspect connector. Clean or repair as necessary. Turn ignition on. Using a voltmeter, check voltage of brake switch sense circuit at brake switch connector terminal No. 1 (White/Pink wire). If voltage is more than 10 volts, go to next step. If voltage is 10 volts or less, go to step **3)**.

2) Connect a jumper wire between ground and brake switch connector terminal No. 1 (White/Pink wire). Using scan tool, read brake switch input status. If scan tool displays brake switch RELEASED, replace brake switch. Perform TEST VER-4A under VERIFICATION TESTS. If scan tool does not display brake switch RELEASED, repair open ground circuit. Perform TEST VER-4A under VERIFICATION TESTS.

3) Turn ignition off. Disconnect PCM connectors. Inspect connector terminals. If any terminal is damaged, pushed out or miswired, repair as necessary. Perform TEST VER-4A under VERIFICATION TESTS. If terminals are okay, go to next step.

4) Using an ohmmeter, check resistance between ground and brake switch sense circuit at PCM connector C2, terminal No. 62 (White/Pink

wire). If resistance less than 5 ohms, repair short to ground. Perform TEST VER-4A under VERIFICATION TESTS. If resistance is 5 ohms or more, go to next step.

5) Using an ohmmeter, check resistance of brake switch sense circuit between PCM connector C2, terminal No. 62 and brake switch terminal No. 1 (White/Pink wire). If resistance is 5 ohms or more, repair open brake switch sense circuit. Perform TEST VER-4A under VERIFICATION TESTS. If resistance is less than 5 ohms, replace PCM. Perform TEST VER-4A under VERIFICATION TESTS.

NTC-2: PARK/NEUTRAL POSITION (PNP) SWITCH

Possible Causes:
- PNP switch sense circuit shorted to ground.
- Defective PNP switch.
- Defective PCM.

1) Disconnect PCM connectors. Disconnect Park/Neutral Position (PNP) switch connector. Inspect connectors. Clean or repair as necessary. Using an ohmmeter, check resistance between ground and PNP sense circuit at PCM connector C2, terminal No. 76 (Brown/Yellow wire). If resistance is less than 5 ohms, repair short to ground. Perform TEST VER-4A under VERIFICATION TESTS. If resistance is 5 ohms or more, go to next step.

2) Connect PNP switch connector. Place transmission in Drive. Using an ohmmeter, check resistance between ground and PNP sense circuit at PCM connector C2, terminal No. 76 (Brown/Yellow wire). If resistance is less than 5 ohms, replace PNP switch. Perform TEST VER-4A under VERIFICATION TESTS. If resistance is 5 ohms or more, replace PCM. Perform TEST VER-4A under VERIFICATION TESTS.

NTC-3: CHECKING FOR SPEED CONTROL DENIED MESSAGE

At this time speed control switch and servo functions appear to operate properly. Using scan tool, monitor speed control output status. Road test vehicle at speeds more than 35 MPH. Attempt to set speed control. See SCAN TOOL DENIED STATUS table. Items listed in table will not allow speed control to set. The last or most recent cause for speed control not to set is indicated by denied status. Correct fault and recheck system operation.

SCAN TOOL DENIED STATUS

Denied Message	Reason
ON/OFF	PCM Does Not See An ON Signal From Switch At PCM Terminal No. 41
SPEED	Vehicle Speed As Seen By PCM Terminal No. 66 Is Not Greater Than 30 MPH
RPM	Engine RPM Is Excessively High
BRAKE	Brake Switch Sense Circuit Is Open Indicating That Brakes Are Applied
P/N	Park/Neutral Switch Sense Circuit Is Grounded Indicating That Transmission Is In Park Or Neutral
RPM/SPD	PCM Senses Excessive Engine RPM For A Given Vehicle Speed
SOL FLT	PCM Senses A Servo Solenoid Circuit Trouble Code That Is Maturing Or Set In Memory

NTC-4: SPEED CONTROL ON/OFF SWITCH

Possible Causes:
- Ground circuit open.
- Speed Control (S/C) SET/RESUME switch voltage more than 4 volts.
- S/C switch signal circuit shorted to voltage or ground.
- S/C ON/OFF switch voltage less than one volt or more than 4 volts.
- Defective PCM.

NOTE: Speed control switch wire colors are not available from manufacturer.

1) Using scan tool, read S/C switch voltage. If voltage is more than 4 volts, go to next step. If voltage is 4 volts or less, go to step **5)**.

2) Turn ignition off. Disconnect S/C ON/OFF switch. Inspect connector. Clean or repair as necessary. Turn ignition on. Using a voltmeter, check voltage on S/C ON/OFF switch signal circuit. See WIRING DIAGRAMS. If voltage is more than 6 volts, repair short to voltage. Perform TEST VER-4A under VERIFICATION TESTS. If voltage is 6 volts or less, go to next step.

3) Turn ignition off. Connect a jumper wire between S/C ON/OFF switch signal circuit (at S/C ON/OFF switch) and ground. See WIRING DIA-GRAMS. Turn ignition on. Using scan tool, read S/C switch voltage. If voltage is less than one volt, replace S/C ON/OFF switch. Perform TEST VER-4A under VERIFICATION TESTS. If voltage is one volt or more, go to next step.

4) Using a voltmeter, check voltage S/C switch signal circuit at S/C ON/OFF switch connector. See WIRING DIAGRAMS. If voltage is more than 4 volts, repair open ground circuit. Perform TEST VER-4A under VERIFICATION TESTS. If voltage is 4 volts or less, replace PCM. Perform TEST VER-4A under VERIFICATION TESTS.

5) Turn ignition off. Disconnect S/C SET/RESUME switch. Inspect connector. Clean or repair as necessary. Turn ignition on. Using scan tool, read S/C switch voltage. If voltage is more than 4 volts, replace S/C SET/RESUME switch. Perform TEST VER-4A under VERIFICATION TESTS. If voltage is 4 volts or less, go to next step.

6) Turn ignition off. Disconnect S/C ON/OFF switch. Turn ignition on. Using scan tool, read S/C switch voltage. If voltage is more than 4 volts, replace S/C ON/OFF switch. Perform TEST VER-4A under VERIFICA-TION TESTS. If voltage is 4 volts or less, go to next step.

7) Turn ignition off. Disconnect PCM. Inspect connectors. Clean or repair as necessary. Using an ohmmeter, measure resistance between ground and S/C switch signal circuit at S/C switch connector. See WIRING DIAGRAMS. If resistance is less than 5100 ohms, repair short to ground. Perform TEST VER-4A under VERIFICATION TESTS. If resistance is 5100 ohms or more, replace PCM. Perform TEST VER- 4A under VERIFICATION TESTS.

NTC-5: SPEED CONTROL SET/RESUME SWITCH

Possible Causes:
- Open circuit.
- Defective SET/RESUME switch.

NOTE: Speed control switch wire colors are not available from manufacturer.

1) Turn ignition off. Disconnect Speed Control (S/C) SET/RESUME switch. Inspect connector. Clean or repair as necessary. Using an ohmmeter, check resistance of ground circuit between S/C SET/RESUME switch connector and ground. If resistance is 5 ohms or more, repair open ground circuit. Perform TEST VER-4A under VERIFICA-TION TESTS. If resistance is less than 5 ohms, go to next step.

2) Connect a jumper wire between ground and S/C switch signal circuit at S/C switch connector. See WIRING DIAGRAMS. Turn ignition on. Using scan tool, read S/C switch voltage. If voltage is less than one volt, replace S/C SET/RESUME switch. Perform TEST VER-4A under VERI-FICATION TESTS. If voltage is one volt or more, replace clockspring. See appropriate AIR BAG RESTRAINT SYSTEMS article. Perform TEST VER-4A under VERIFICATION TESTS.

VERIFICATION TESTS

TEST VER-4A

NOTE: If PCM has been replaced and correct VIN and mileage have not been programmed, a DTC will be set in ABS and air bag modules.

1) If vehicle is equipped with ABS or air bag, enter correct VIN and mileage in PCM. Erase DTCs in ABS and air bag modules. Inspect vehicle to ensure all engine and speed control system components are connected. Reassemble and reconnect components as necessary. Using scan tool, erase DTCs from PCM.

2) Road test vehicle at a speed greater than 30 MPH. Turn Speed Control (S/C) switch on. Depress and release S/C SET switch. If speed control engages, go to next step. If speed control does not engage, repair is not complete. Check for related Technical Service Bulletins (TSBs) and return to test that directed you here or perform appropriate test under SYSTEM TESTS.

3) Quickly depress and release RESUME/ACCEL switch. Vehicle speed should increase by 2 MPH. If vehicle speed increases by 2 MPH, go to next step. If vehicle speed does not increase by 2 MPH, repair is not complete. Return to test that directed you here or perform appropriate test under SYSTEM TESTS.

4) Press and hold COAST switch. Vehicle speed should decrease. If vehicle speed decreases, go to next step. If vehicle speed does not decrease, repair is not complete. Return to test that directed you here or perform appropriate test under SYSTEM TESTS.

5) Using caution, depress and release brake pedal. If speed control disengages, go to next step. If speed control does not disengage, repair is not complete. Return to test that directed you here or perform appropriate test under SYSTEM TESTS.

6) Bring vehicle speed to 25 MPH. Depress speed control RESUME/ACCEL switch. Vehicle should resume to previously set speed. If vehicle speed resumes to previously set speed, go to next step. If vehicle does not resume to previously set speed, repair is not complete. Return to test that directed you here or perform appropriate test under SYSTEM TESTS.

7) Hold down SET switch. Vehicle speed should decrease. If vehicle speed decreases, go to next step. If vehicle speed does not decrease, repair is not complete. Return to test that directed you here or perform appropriate test under SYSTEM TESTS.

8) Ensure vehicle speed is more than 30 MPH and release SET switch. Vehicle should set a new speed. If vehicle sets a new speed, go to next step. If vehicle does not adjust and set a new vehicle speed, repair is not complete. Return to test that directed you here or perform appropriate test under SYSTEM TESTS.

9) Depress and release CANCEL switch. Speed control should disengage. If speed control disengages, go to next step. If S/C does not disengage, repair is not complete. Return to test that directed you here or perform appropriate test under SYSTEM TESTS.

10) Ensure vehicle speed is greater than 35 MPH. Engage speed control. Turn S/C switch off. If speed control disengages, system is operating correctly. Repair is complete. If speed control does not disengage, repair is not complete. Return to test that directed you here or perform appropriate test under SYSTEM TESTS.

TEST VER-5A

NOTE: If PCM has been replaced and correct VIN and mileage have not been programmed, a DTC will be set in ABS and air bag modules.

1) If vehicle is equipped with ABS or air bag, enter correct VIN and mileage in PCM. Erase DTCs in ABS and air bag modules. Inspect vehicle to ensure all engine and speed control system components are connected. Reassemble and reconnect components as necessary.

2) After all DTCs have been repaired, appropriate monitor for previously repaired DTC must be run. Connect scan tool to DLC. Ensure fuel tank is at least 1/4 full. Turn off all accessories. Allow PCM to run appropriate monitor(s).

3) Enabling conditions must be met before PCM will run monitor. Using scan tool, monitor pretest enabling conditions until all conditions have been met. Once enabling conditions have been met, monitor appropriate monitor.

4) If repaired DTC has reset or was seen in monitor while on road test, repair is not complete. Check for Technical Service Bulletins (TSBs) or flash updates and return to test that directed you here or perform appropriate test under SYSTEM TESTS.

5) If appropriate monitor ran, good trip counter incremented and no DTCs have been set, repair is complete.

REMOVAL & INSTALLATION

WARNING: Vehicle is equipped with an air bag. Air bag must be deactivated before servicing speed control components on or around steering column. See appropriate AIR BAG RESTRAINT SYSTEMS article.

CAUTION: When battery is disconnected, vehicle computer and memory systems may lose memory data. Driveability problems may exist until computer systems have completed a relearn cycle. See COMPUTER RELEARN PROCEDURES in GENERAL INFORMATION before disconnecting battery.

BRAKE SWITCH

Removal – Fully depress brake pedal and rotate brake switch counterclockwise about 30 degrees. Pull brake switch rearward and remove from bracket. Depress lock tabs holding brake switch mounting bracket and separate harness connector from brake switch.

Installation – 1) Before installing brake switch, reset adjustable plunger by pulling on plunger head until plunger reaches end of travel. Connect harness connector to brake switch. Depress brake pedal and insert brake switch into keyed hole in mounting bracket. Rotate brake switch clockwise into locked position.

2) Gently pull back on brake pedal until pedal will go no further. This causes the brake switch plunger to ratchet backward to the correct position. No further adjustment is required.

SPEED CONTROL SERVO

Removal & Installation – Disconnect wiring harness connector and vacuum hose from servo. Remove nuts holding cable to servo. Remove pin holding cable to servo. Remove servo. To install, install pin holding cable to servo. Install nuts holding cable to servo. Tighten retaining nuts to 60 INCH lbs. (7 N.m). To complete installation, reverse removal procedure.

SPEED CONTROL SWITCH

Removal & Installation – 1) Speed control switches are mounted on the steering wheel and wired through clockspring device under air bag module.

2) Turn ignition off. Deactivate air bag. See appropriate AIR BAG RESTRAINT SYSTEMS article. Remove 2 screws from side of each switch. Rock switch back and forth to remove switch from steering wheel. Disconnect speed control switch connector. To install switch, reverse removal procedure.

WIRING DIAGRAMS

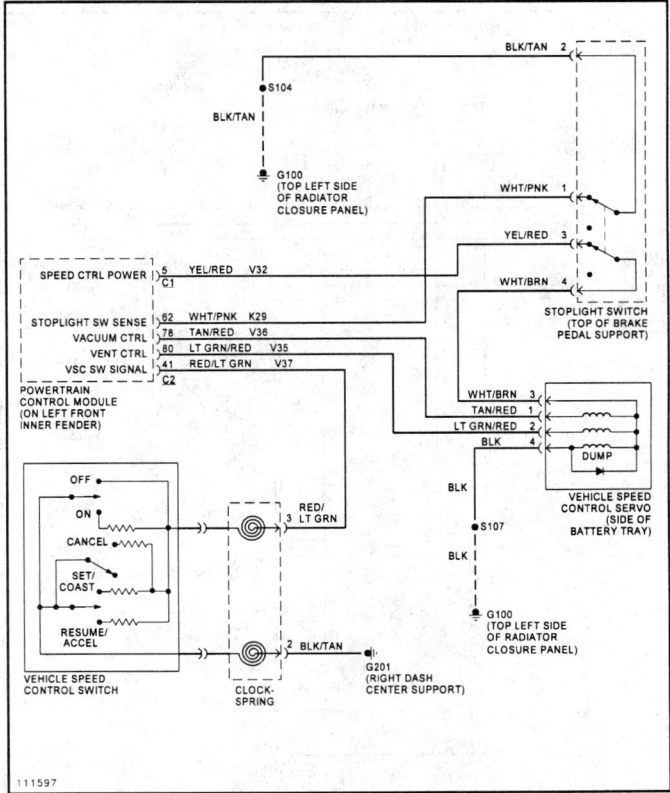

Fig. 7: Cruise Control Wiring Diagram (Neon)

WIRING DIAGRAMS

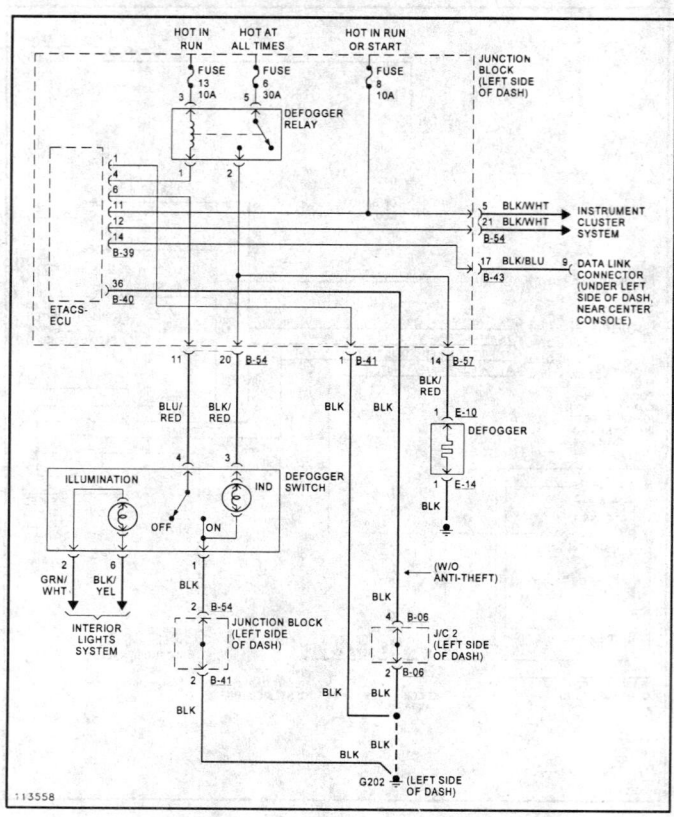

Fig. 1: Rear Window & Mirror Defogger Wiring Diagram (Avenger & Sebring Coupe)

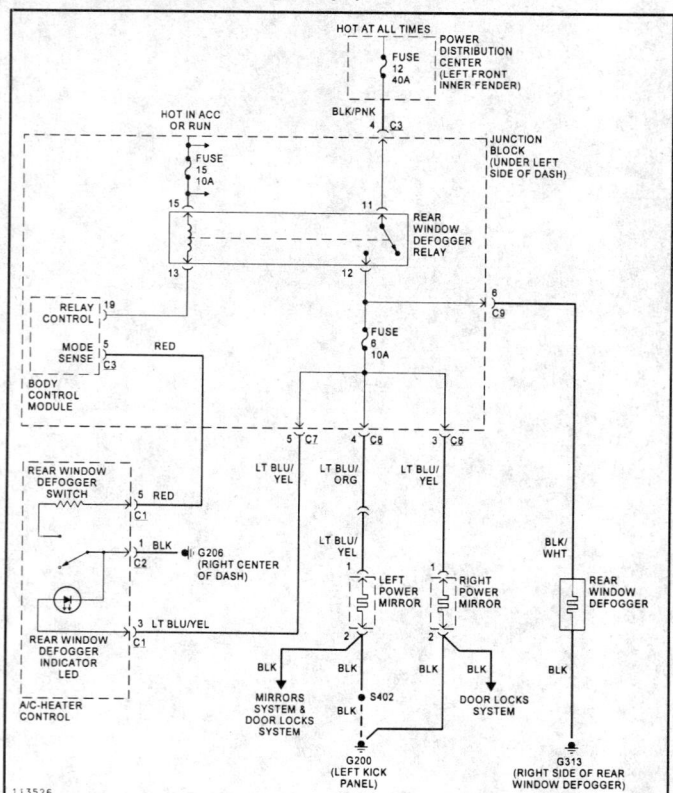

Fig. 2: Rear Window & Mirror Defogger Wiring Diagram (Breeze, Cirrus & Stratus)

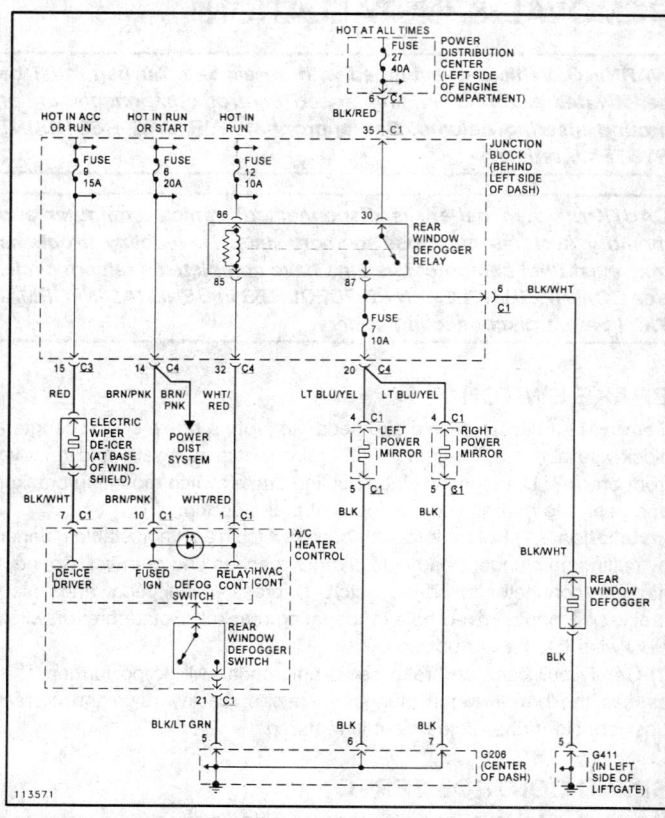

Fig. 3: Rear Window & Mirror Defogger Wiring Diagram (Caravan, Town & Country, & Voyager)

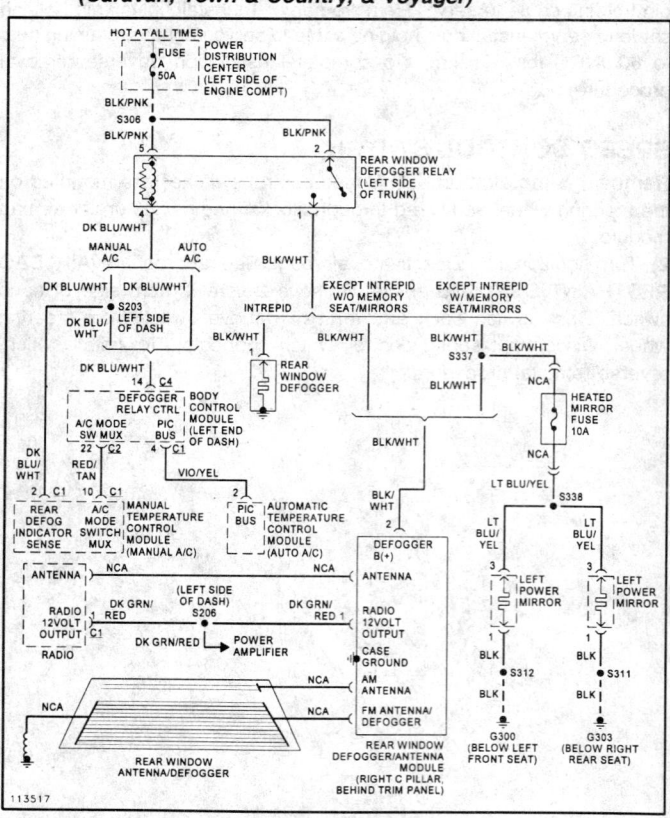

Fig. 4: Rear Window & Mirror Defogger Wiring Diagram (Concorde, Intrepid, LHS & 300M)

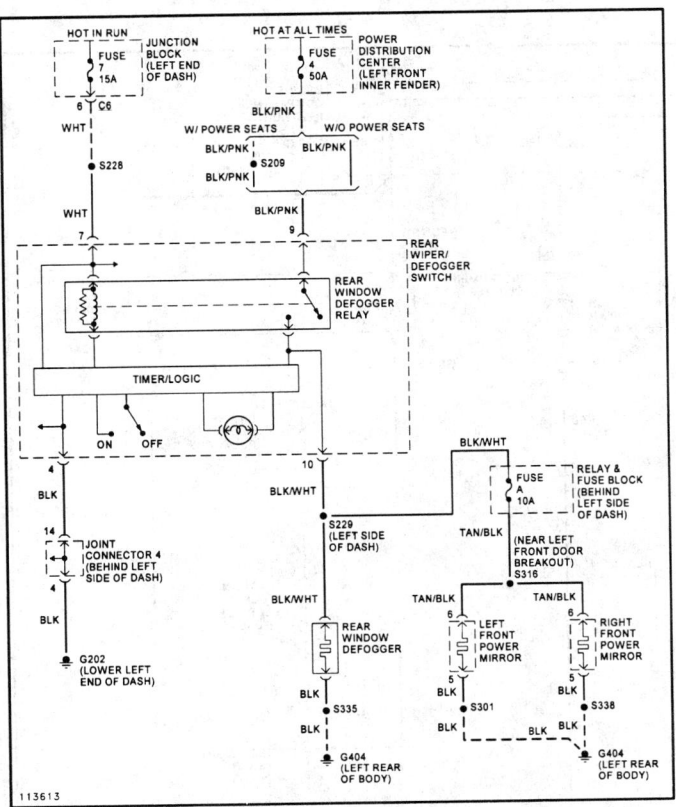

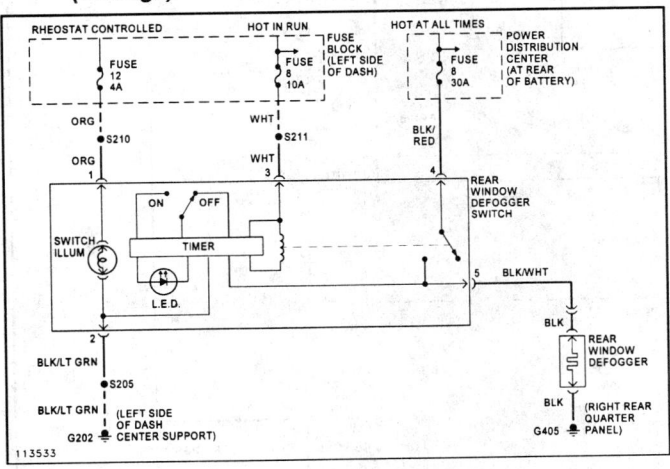

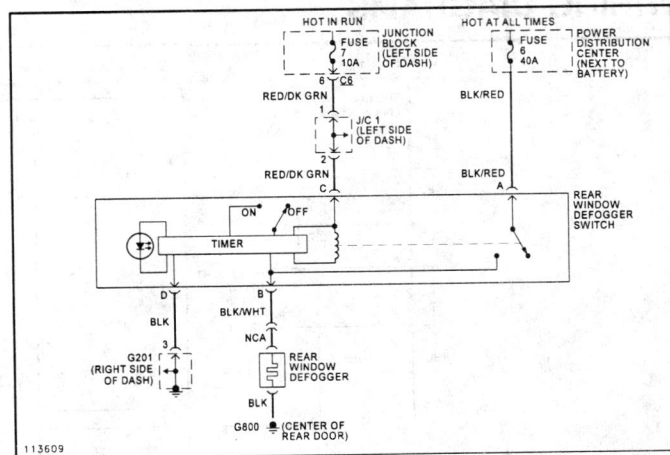

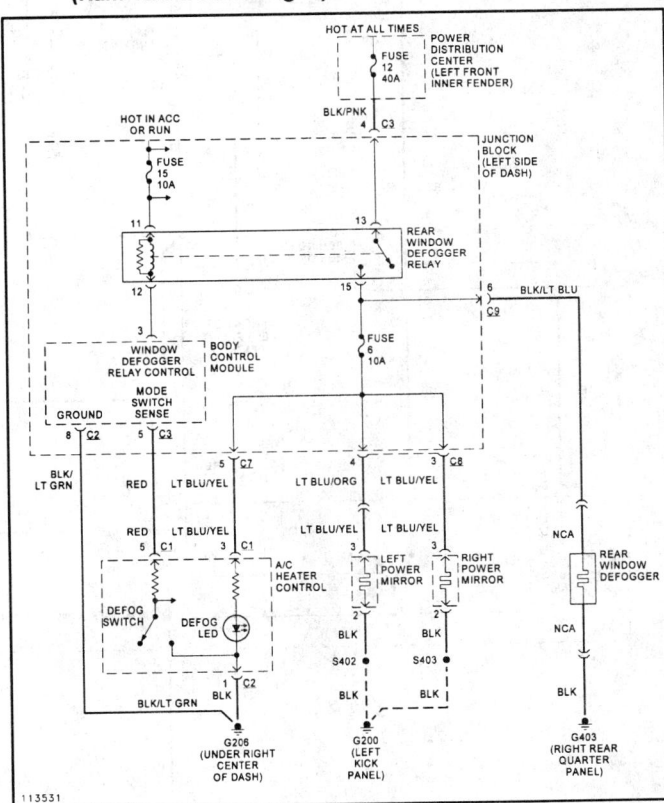

Fig. 5: Rear Window & Mirror Defogger Wiring Diagram (Durango)

Fig. 6: Rear Window & Mirror Defogger Wiring Diagram (Neon)

Fig. 7: Rear Window & Mirror Defogger Wiring Diagram (Ram Van & Ram Wagon)

Fig. 8: Rear Window & Mirror Defogger Wiring Diagram (Sebring Convertible)

WIRING DIAGRAMS

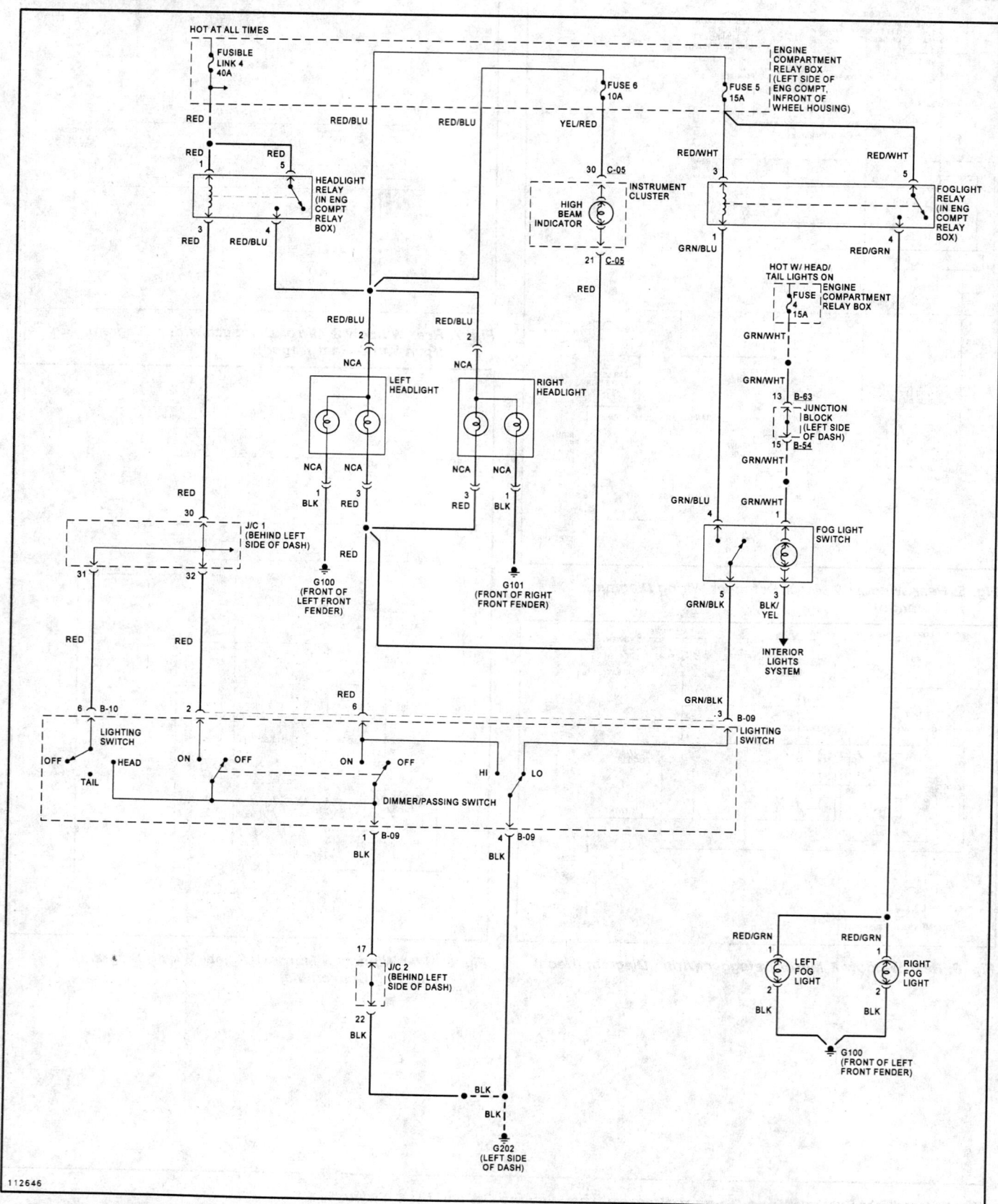

Fig. 1: Headlight System Wiring Diagram (Avenger & Sebring Coupe)

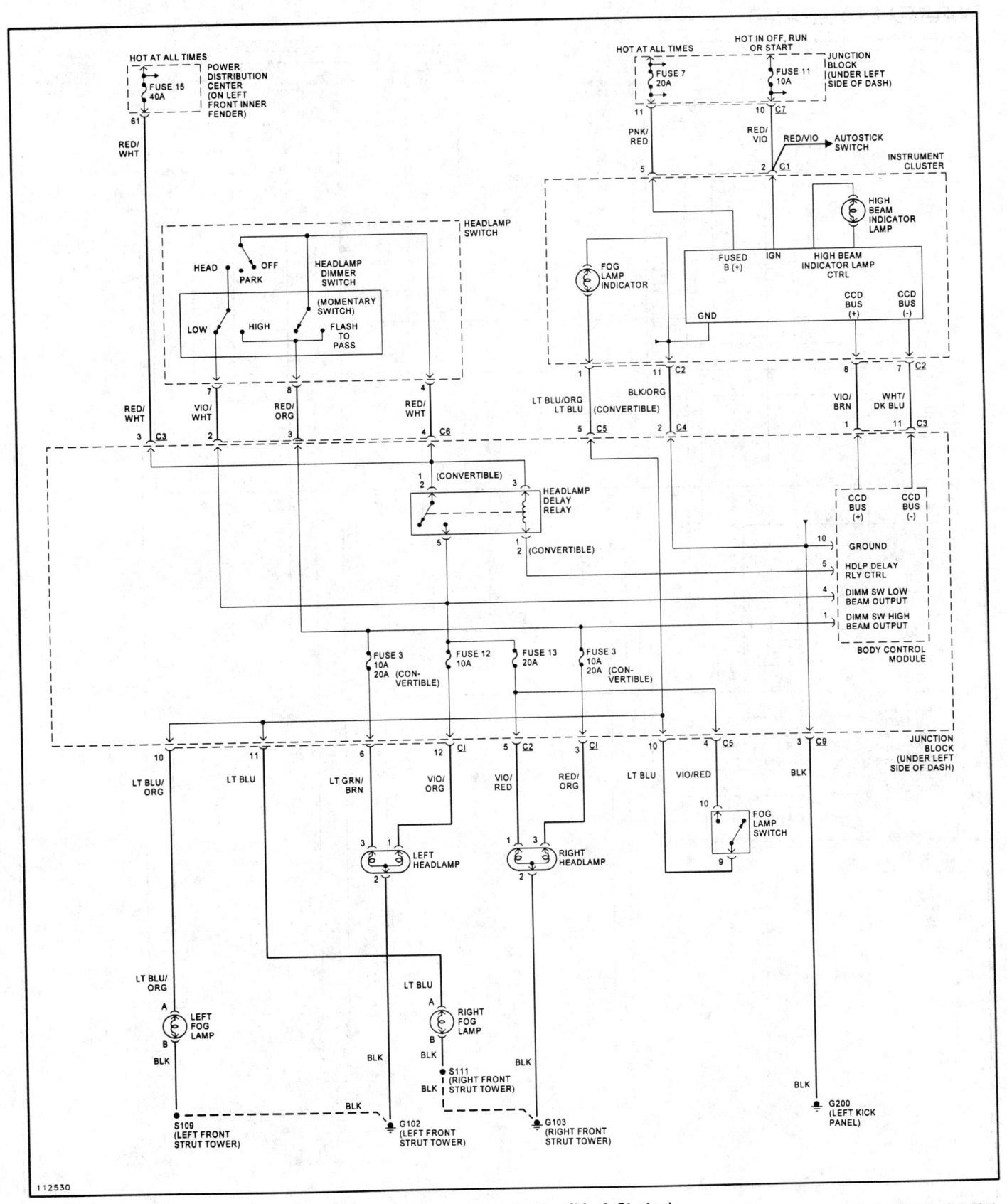

Fig. 2: Headlight System Wiring Diagram (Breeze, Cirrus, Sebring Convertible & Stratus)

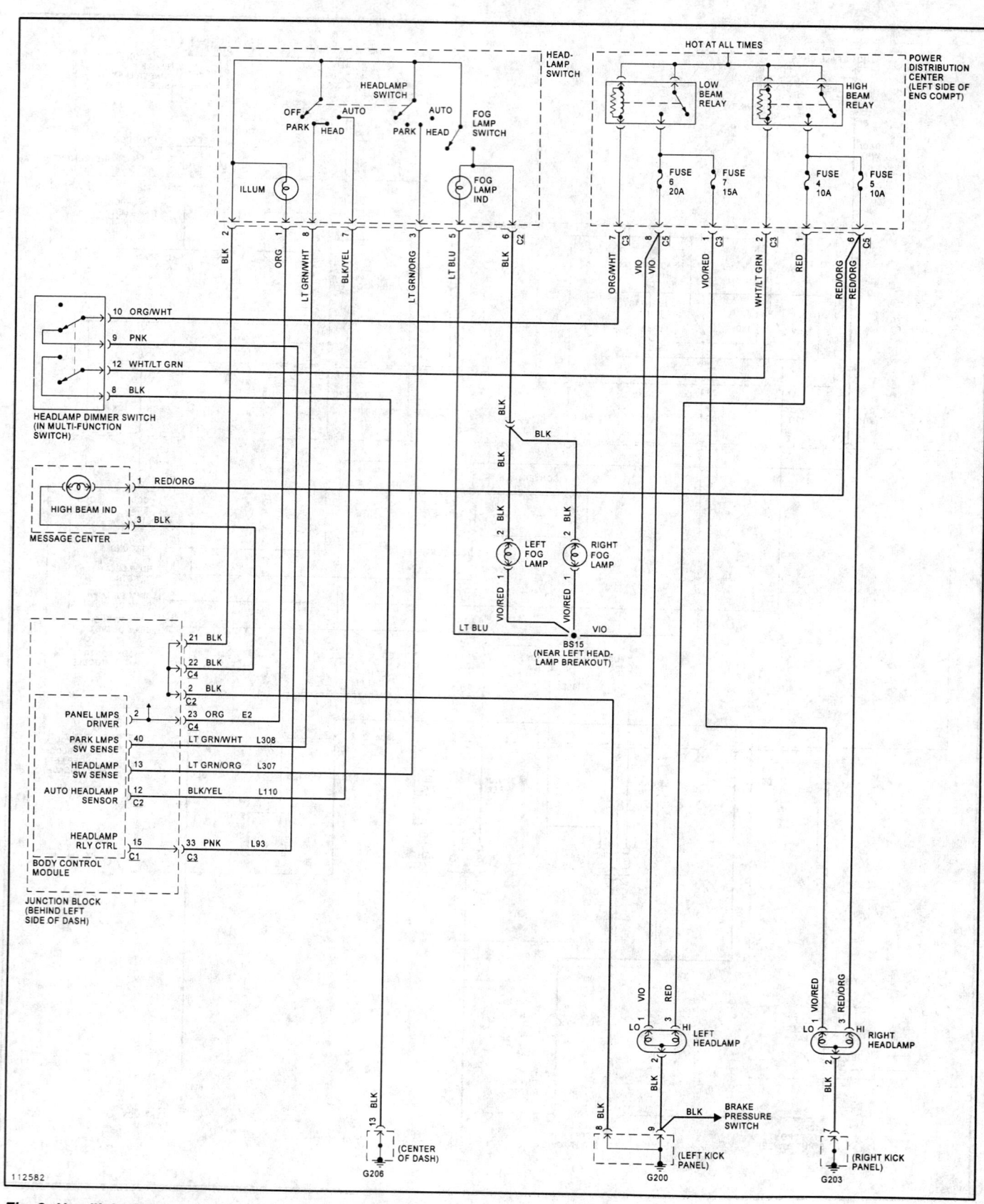

Fig. 3: Headlight System Wiring Diagram (Caravan & Voyager)

112582

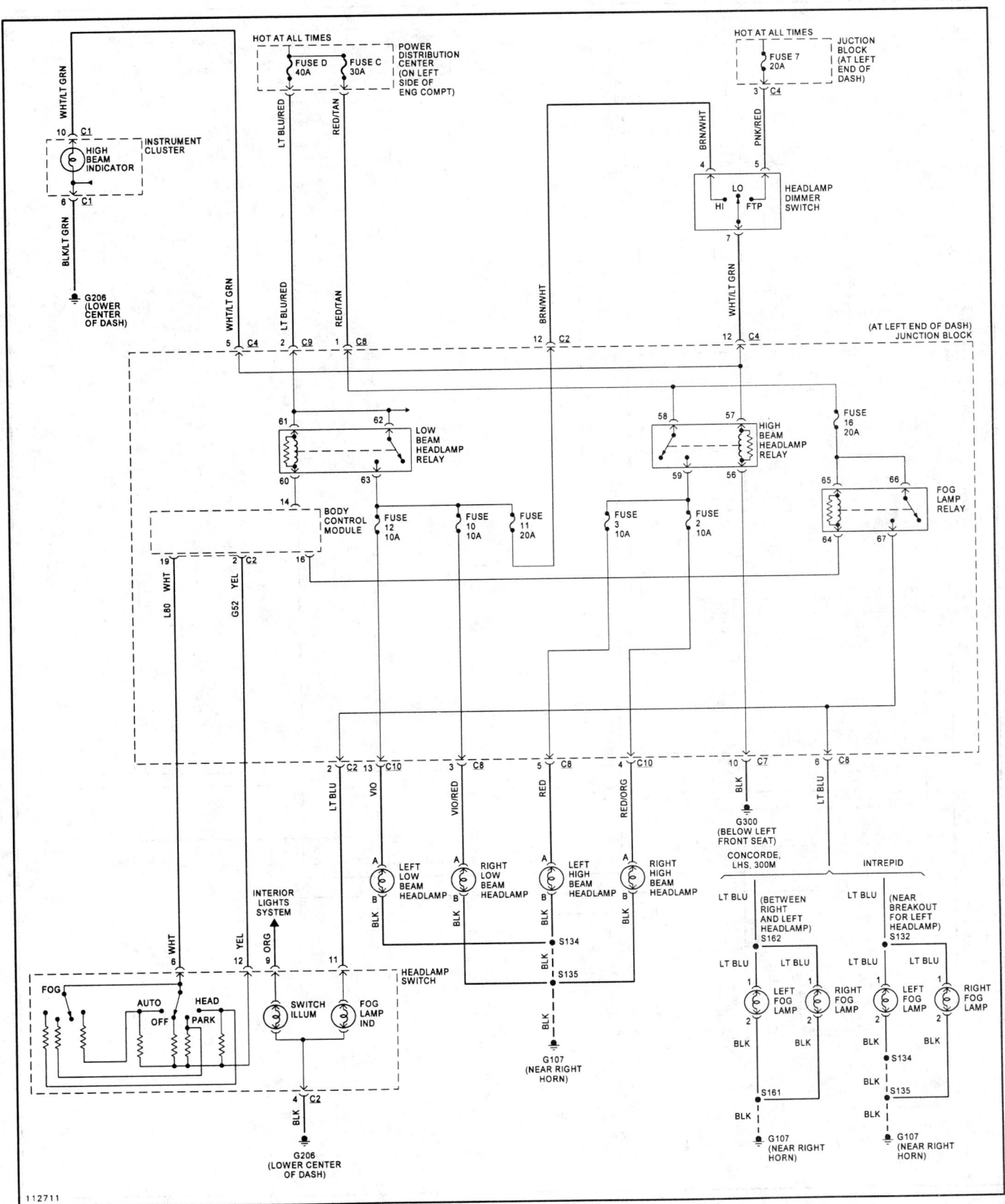

Fig. 4: Headlight System Wiring Diagram (Concorde, Intrepid, LHS & 300M)

112711

1999 ACCESSORIES & EQUIPMENT
Headlight Systems (Cont.)

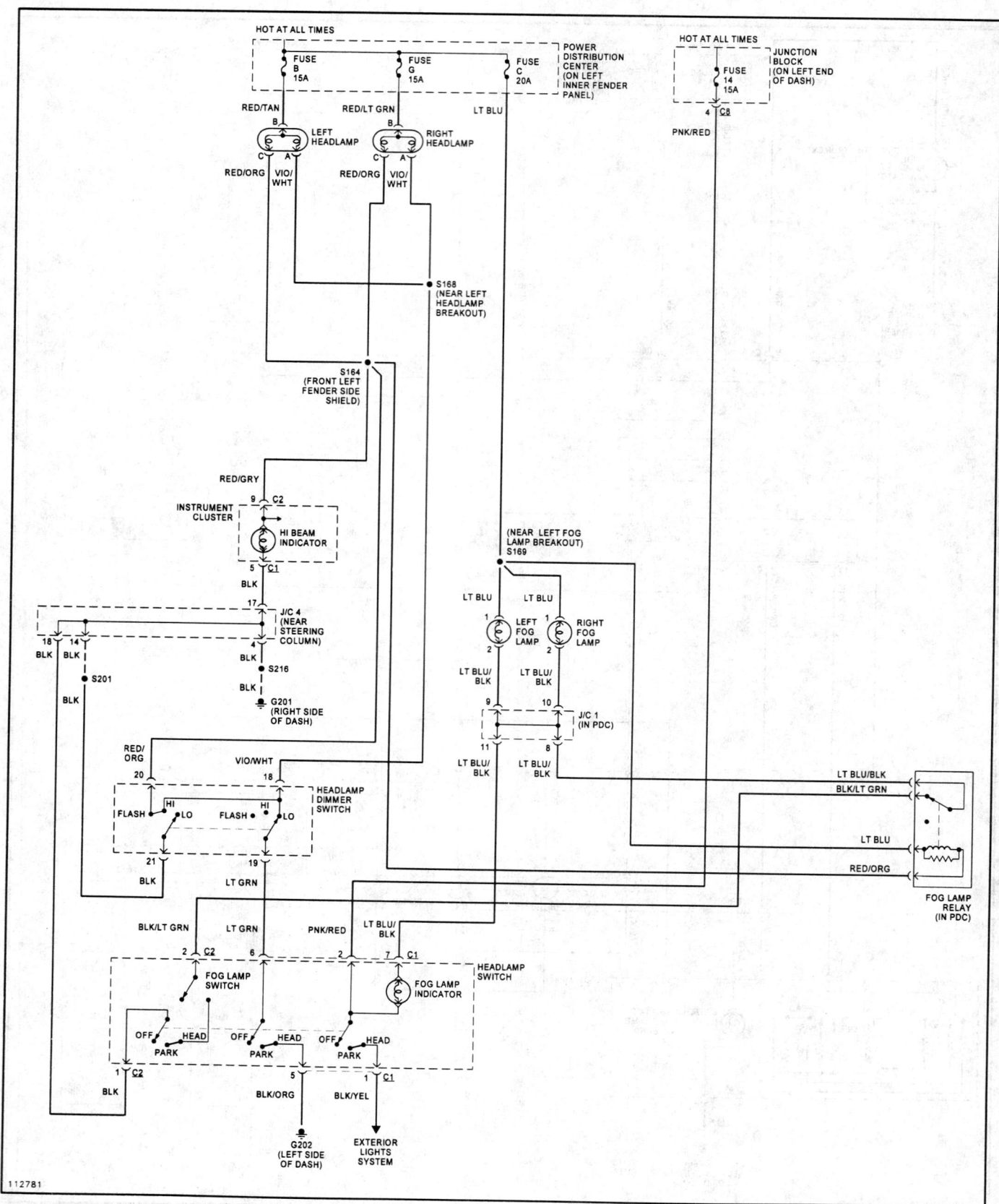

Fig. 5: Headlight System Wiring Diagram (Dakota – With Track)

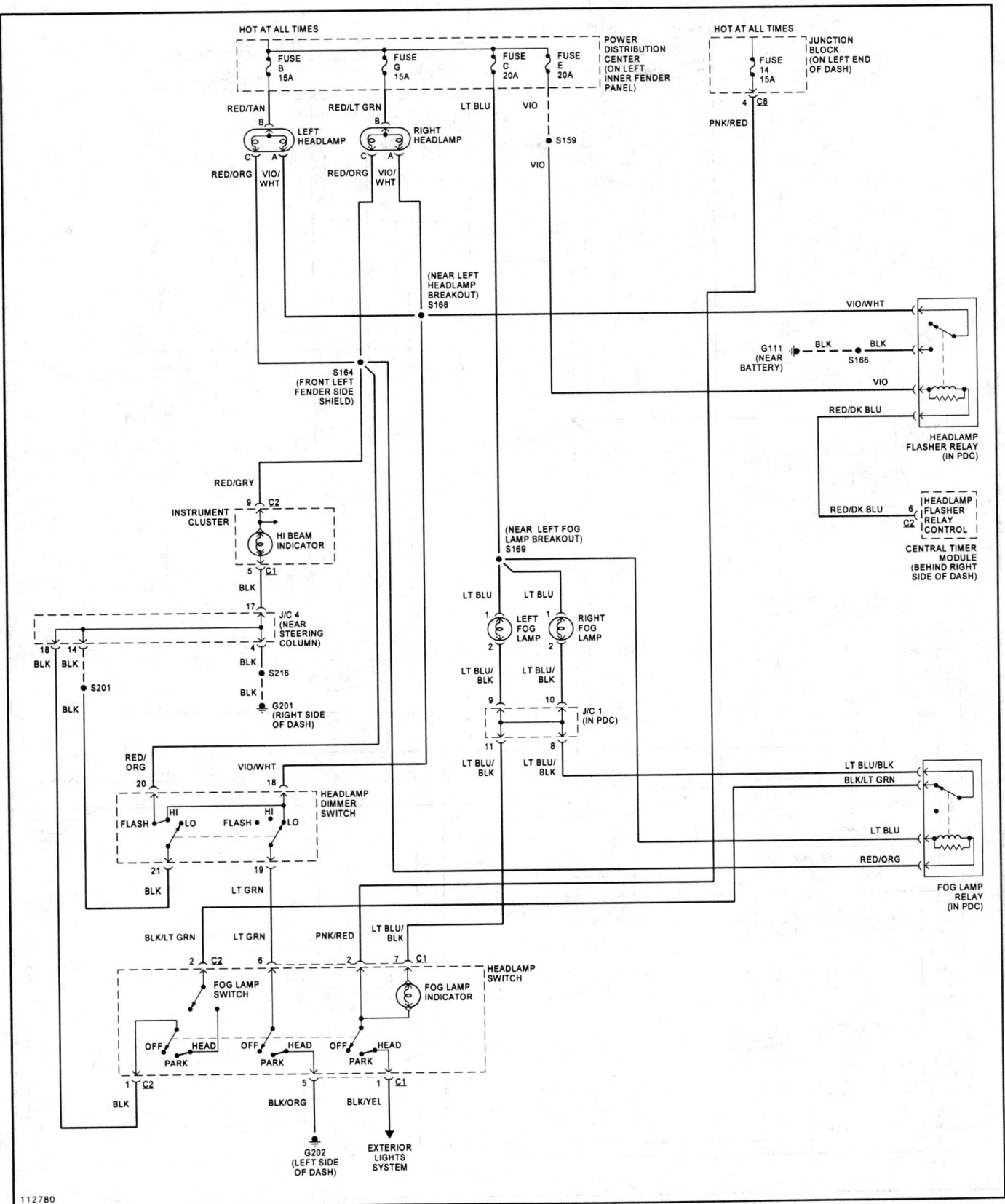

Fig. 6: Headlight System Wiring Diagram (Dakota – Without Track)

112780

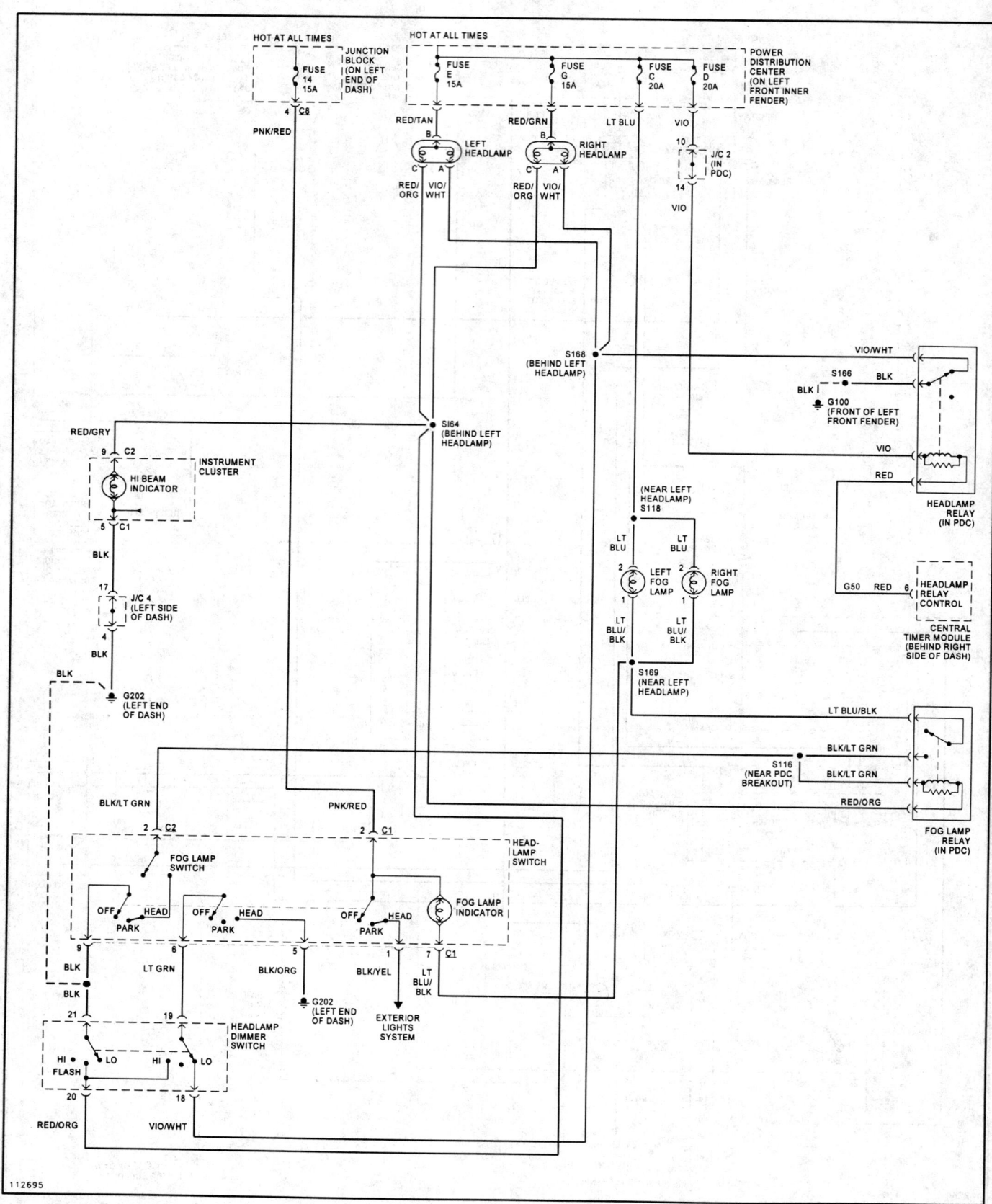

Fig. 7: Headlight System Wiring Diagram (Durango)

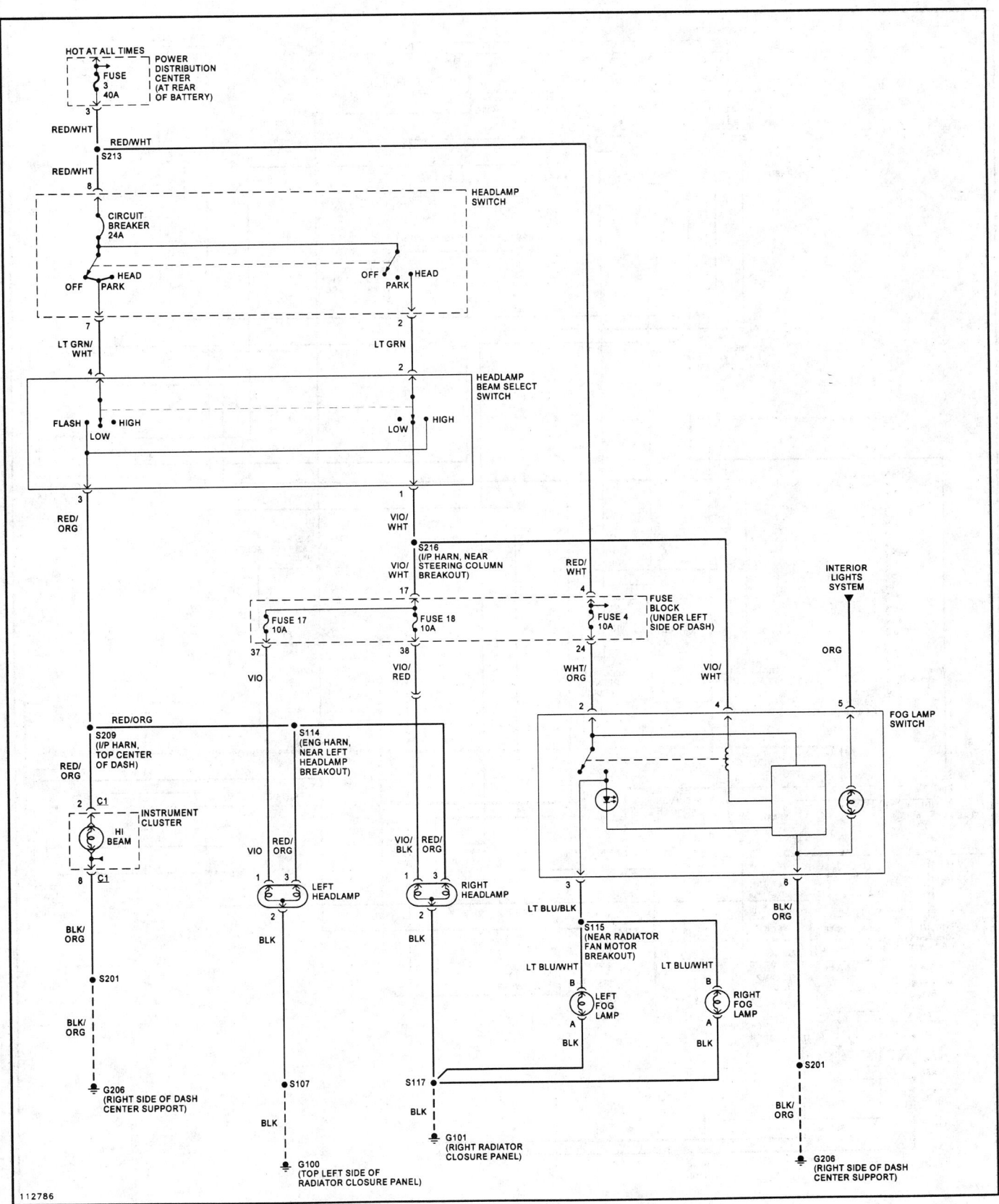

Fig. 8: Headlight System Wiring Diagram (Neon)

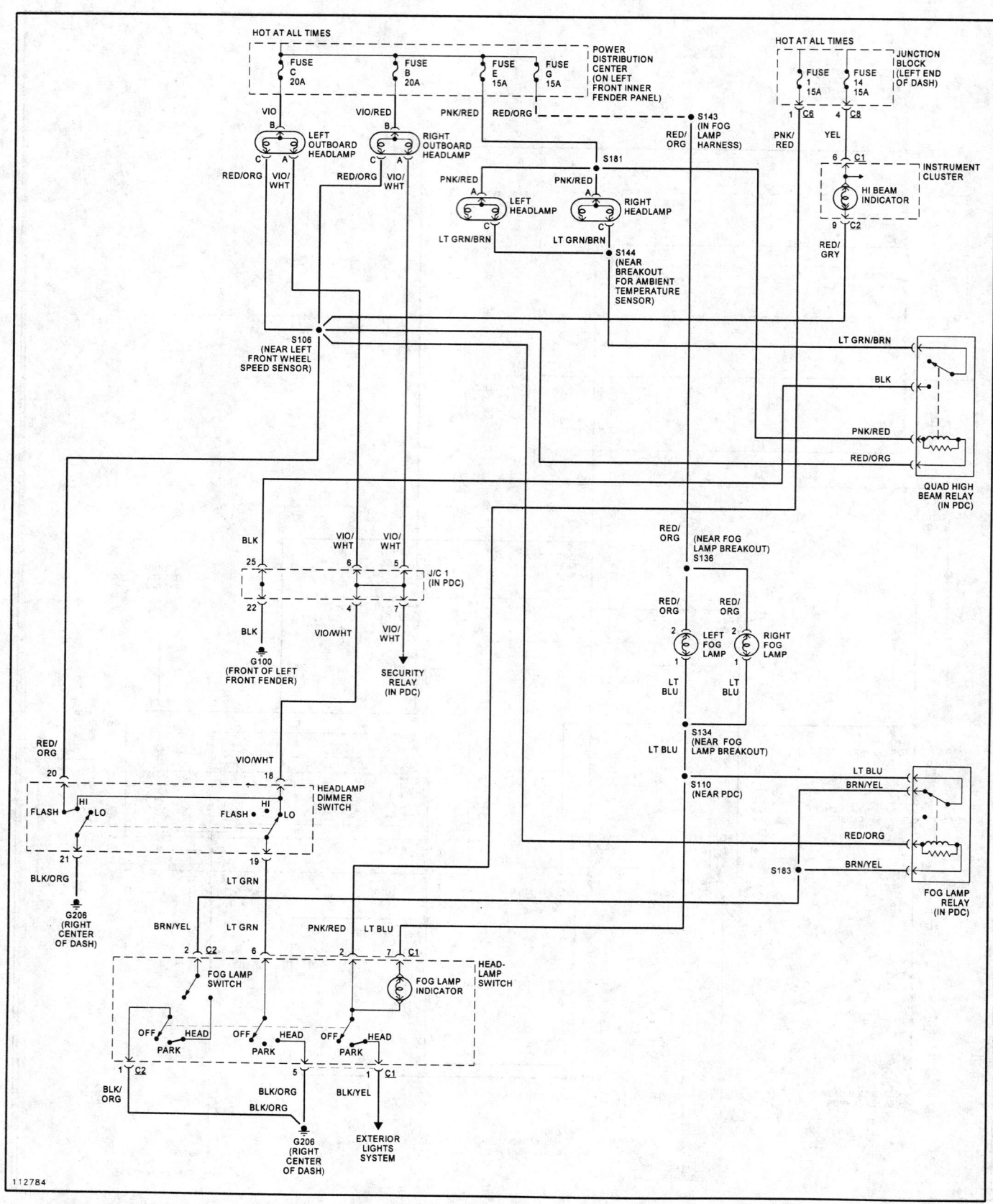

Fig. 9: Headlight System Wiring Diagram (Ram Pickup – With Quad Headlights)

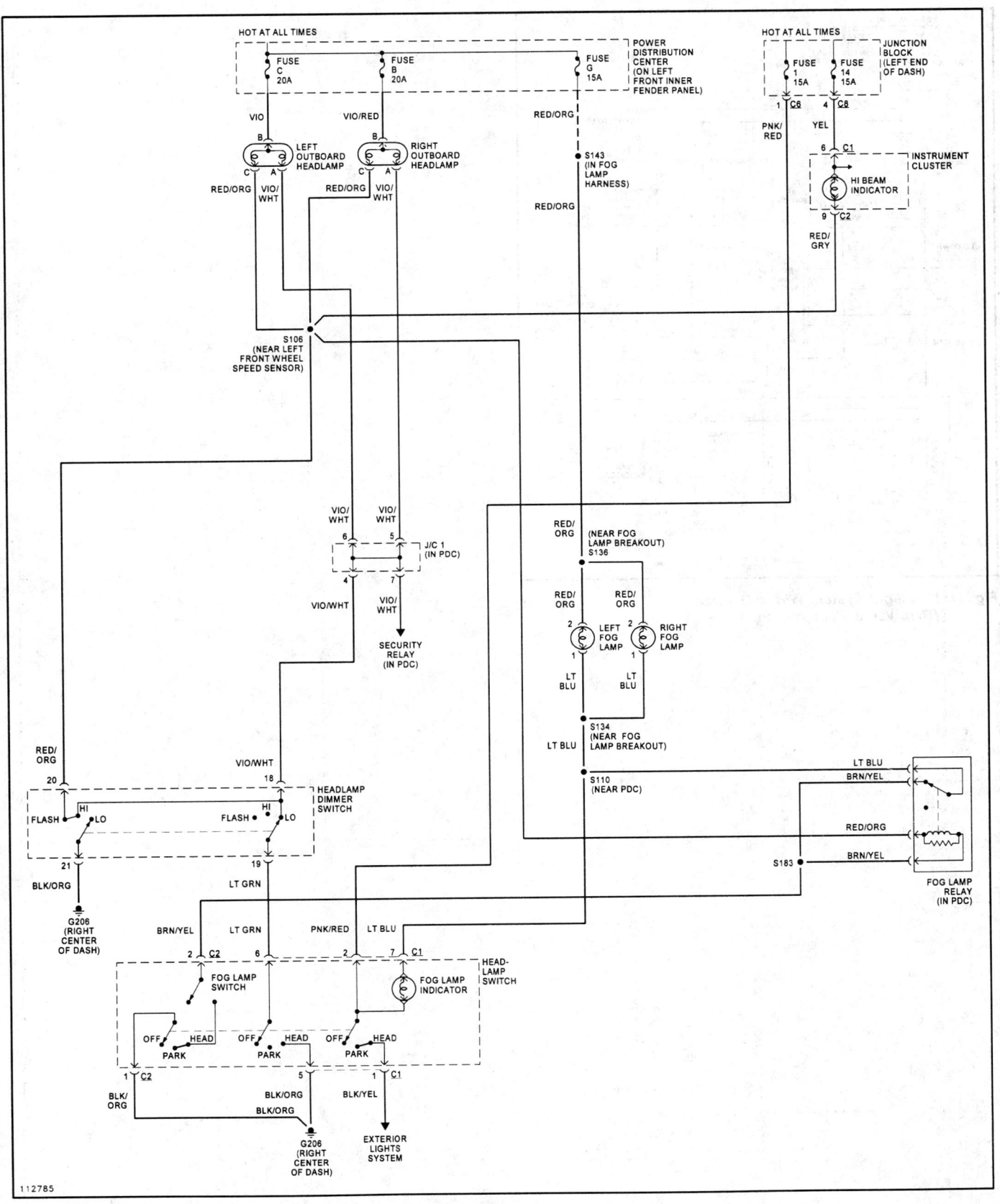

Fig. 10: Headlight System Wiring Diagram (Ram Pickup – Without Quad Headlights)

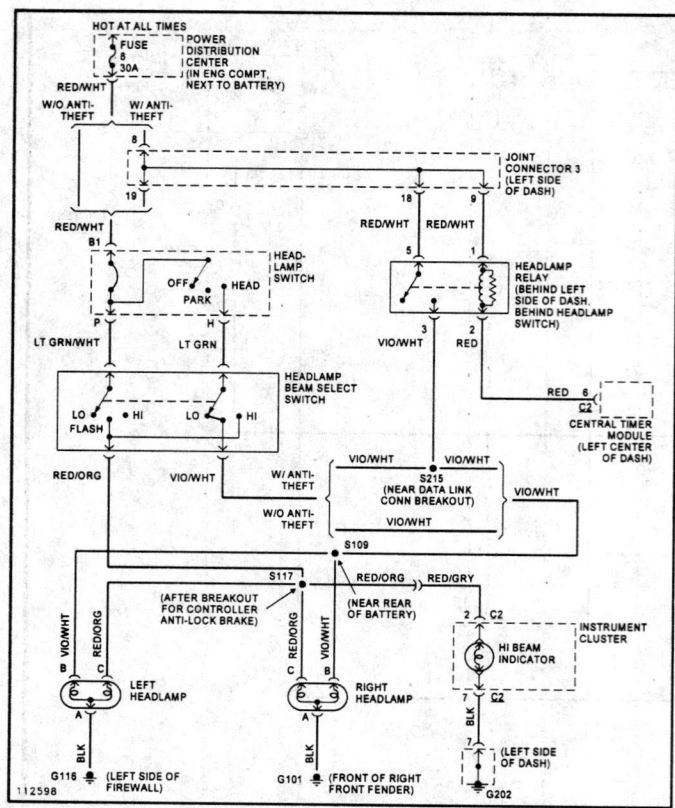

Fig. 11: Headlight System Wiring Diagram (Ram Van & Ram Wagon)

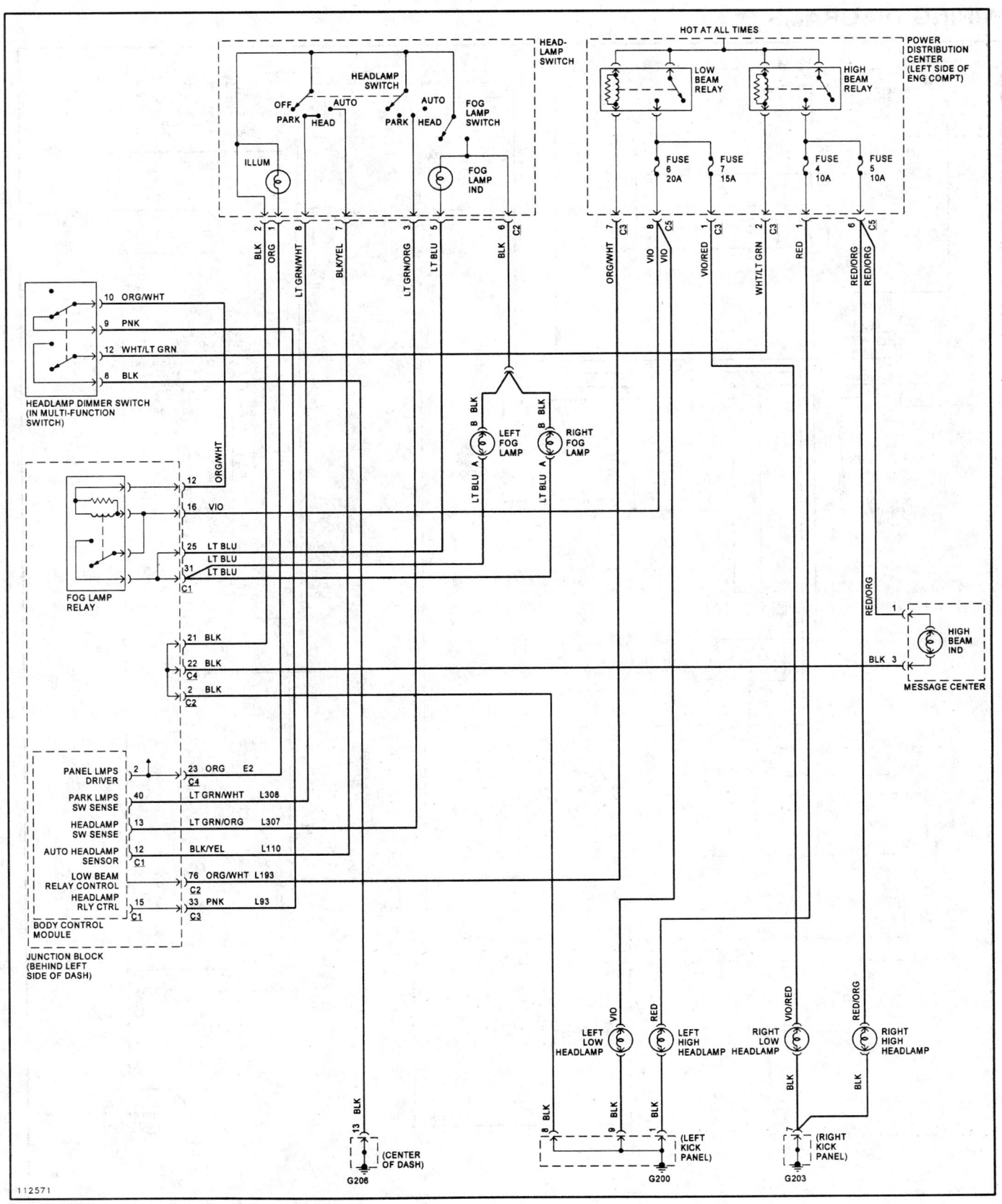

Fig. 12: Headlight System Wiring Diagram (Town & Country)

112571

1999 ACCESSORIES & EQUIPMENT
Daytime Running Lights

WIRING DIAGRAMS

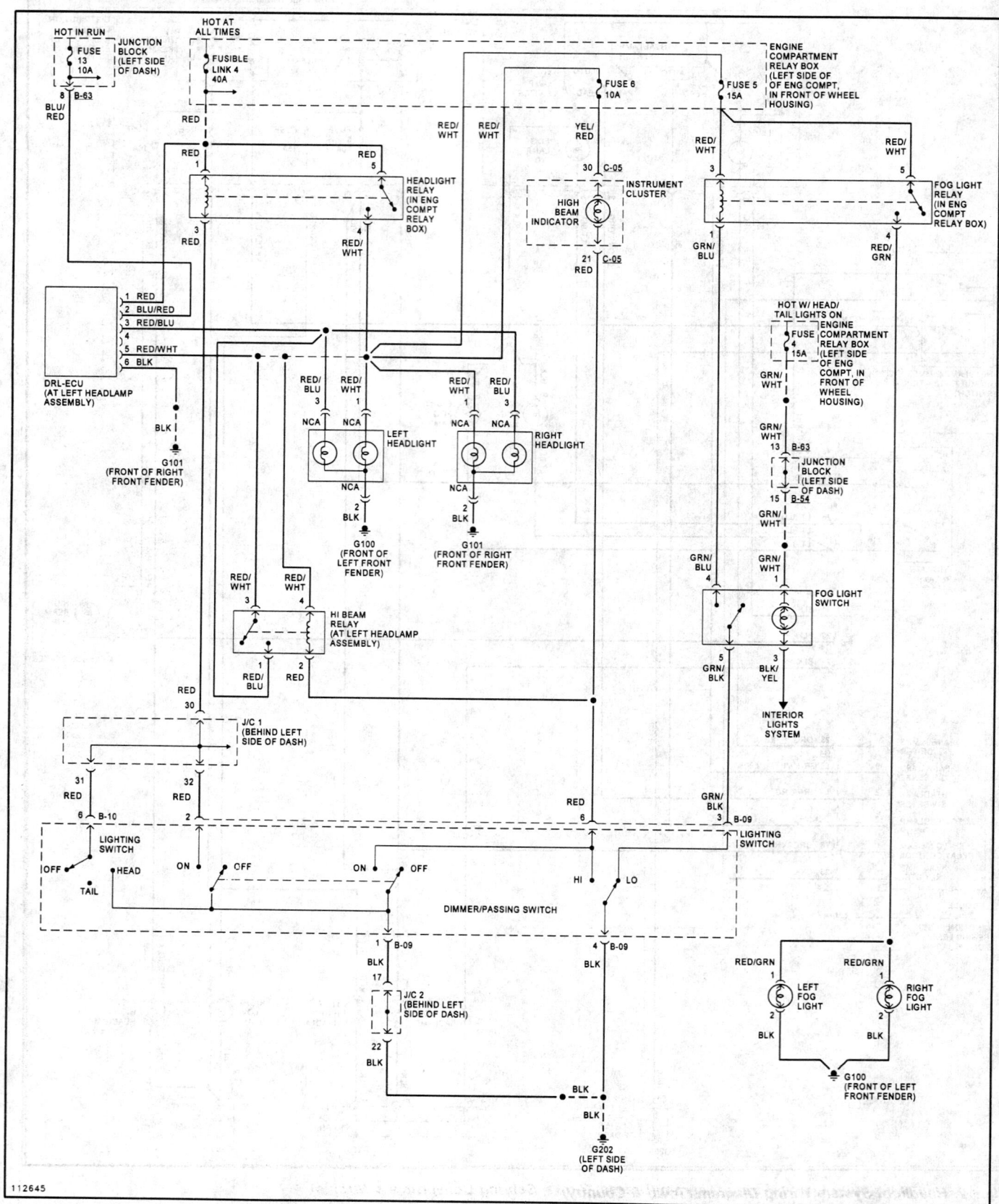

Fig. 1: Daytime Running Lights Wiring Diagram (Avenger & Sebring Coupe)

112645

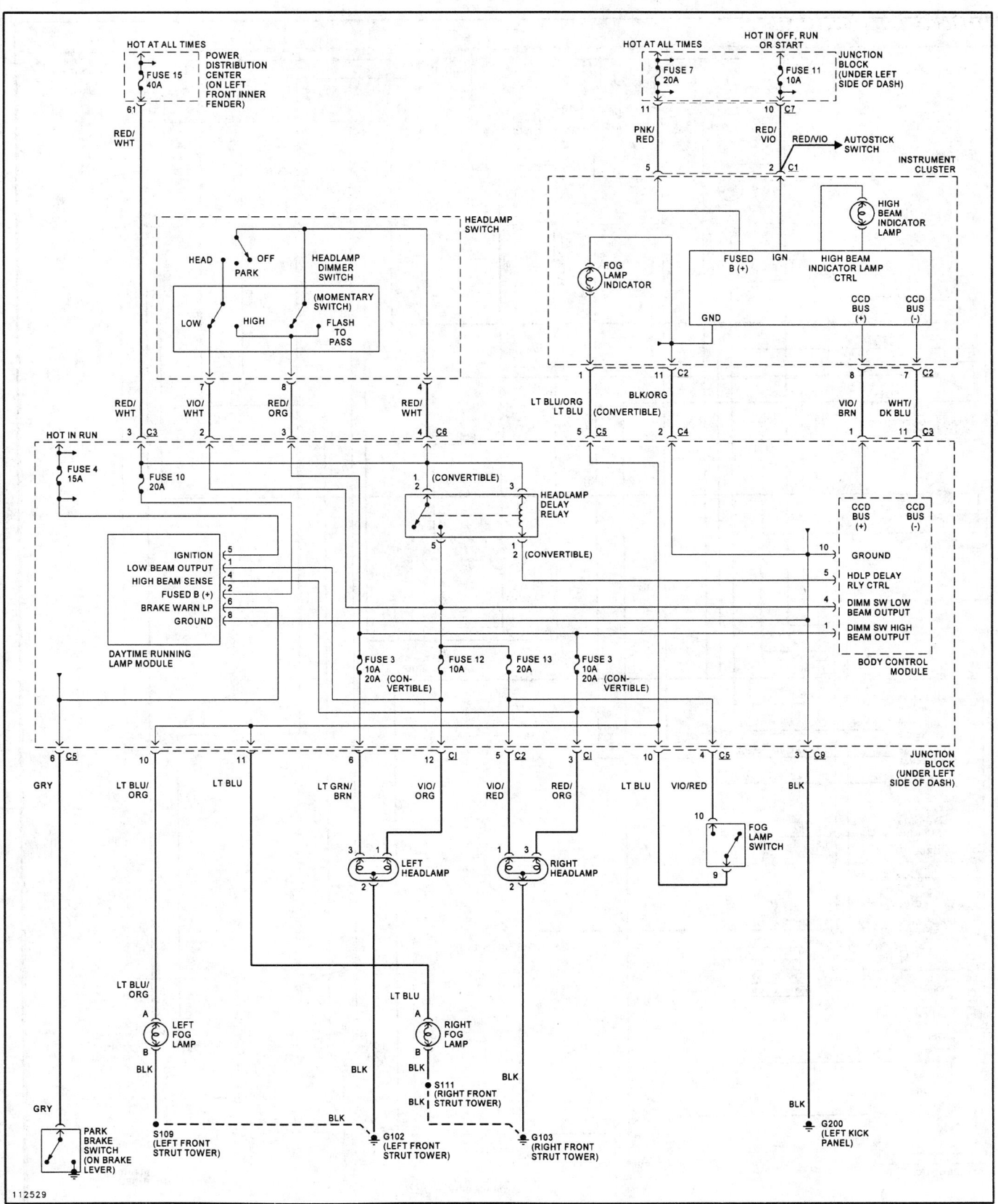

Fig. 2: Daytime Running Lights Wiring Diagram (Breeze, Cirrus, Sebring Convertible & Stratus)

112529

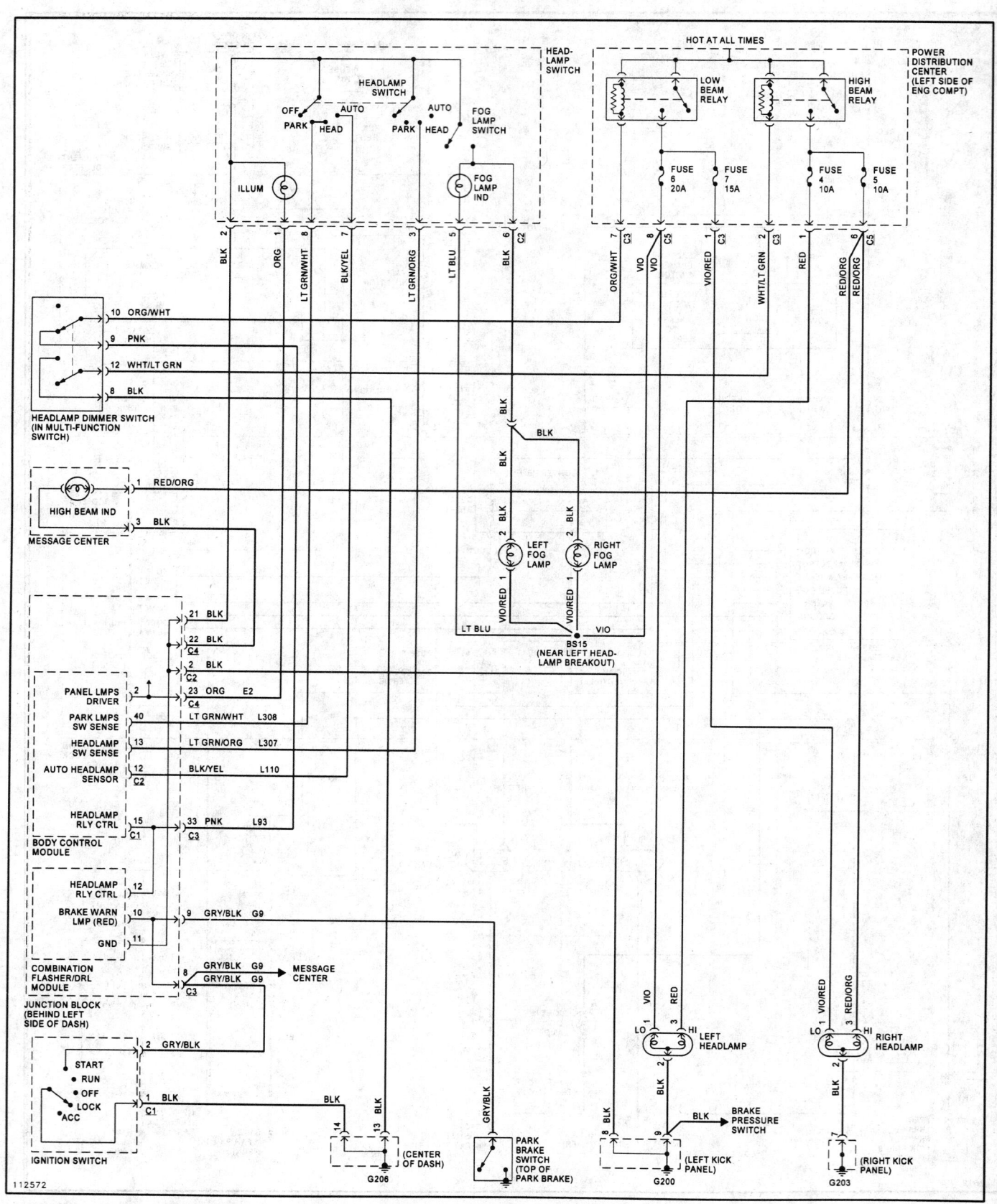

Fig. 3: Daytime Running Lights Wiring Diagram (Caravan & Voyager)

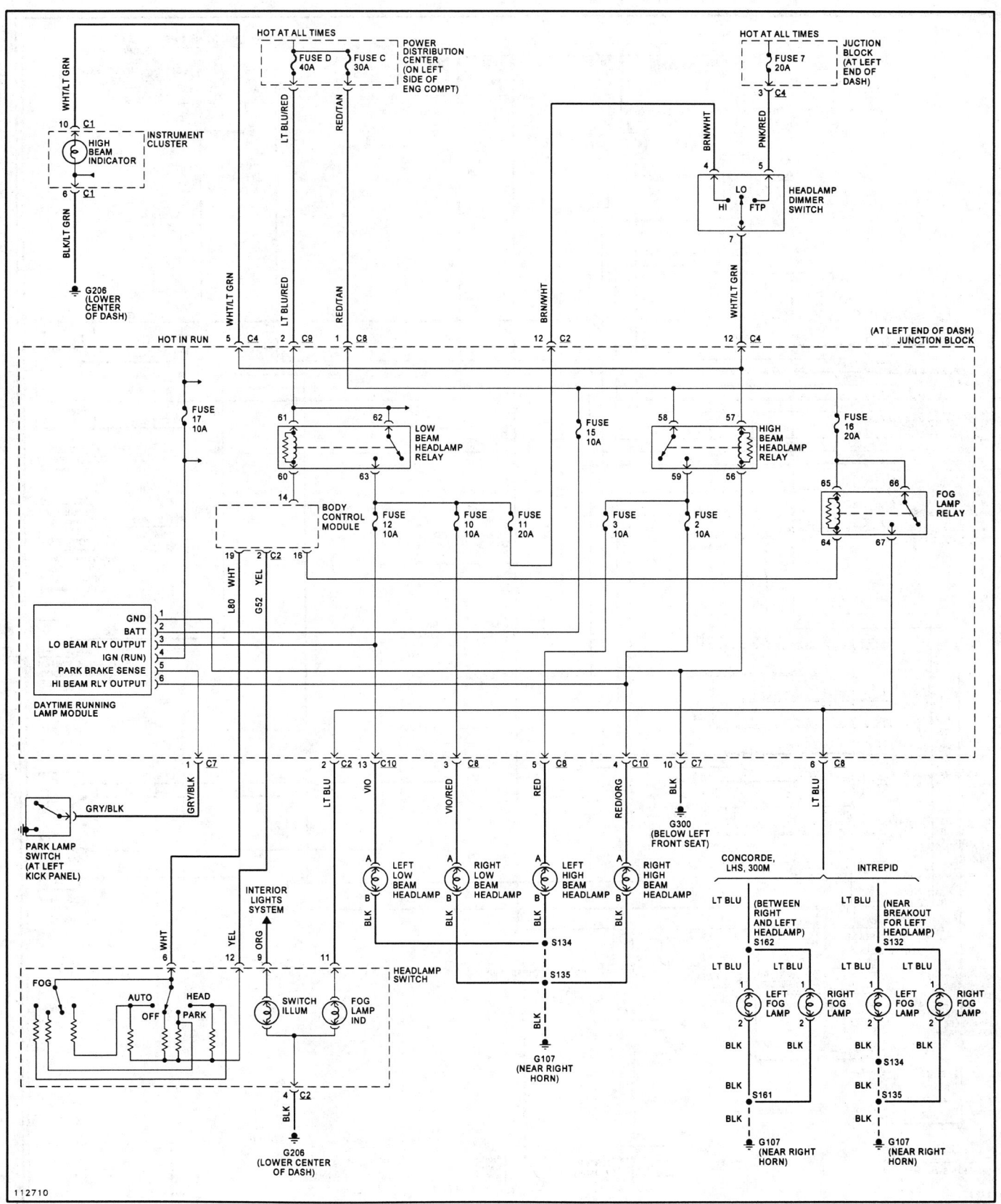

Fig. 4: Daytime Running Lights Wiring Diagram (Concorde, Intrepid, LHS & 300M)

112710

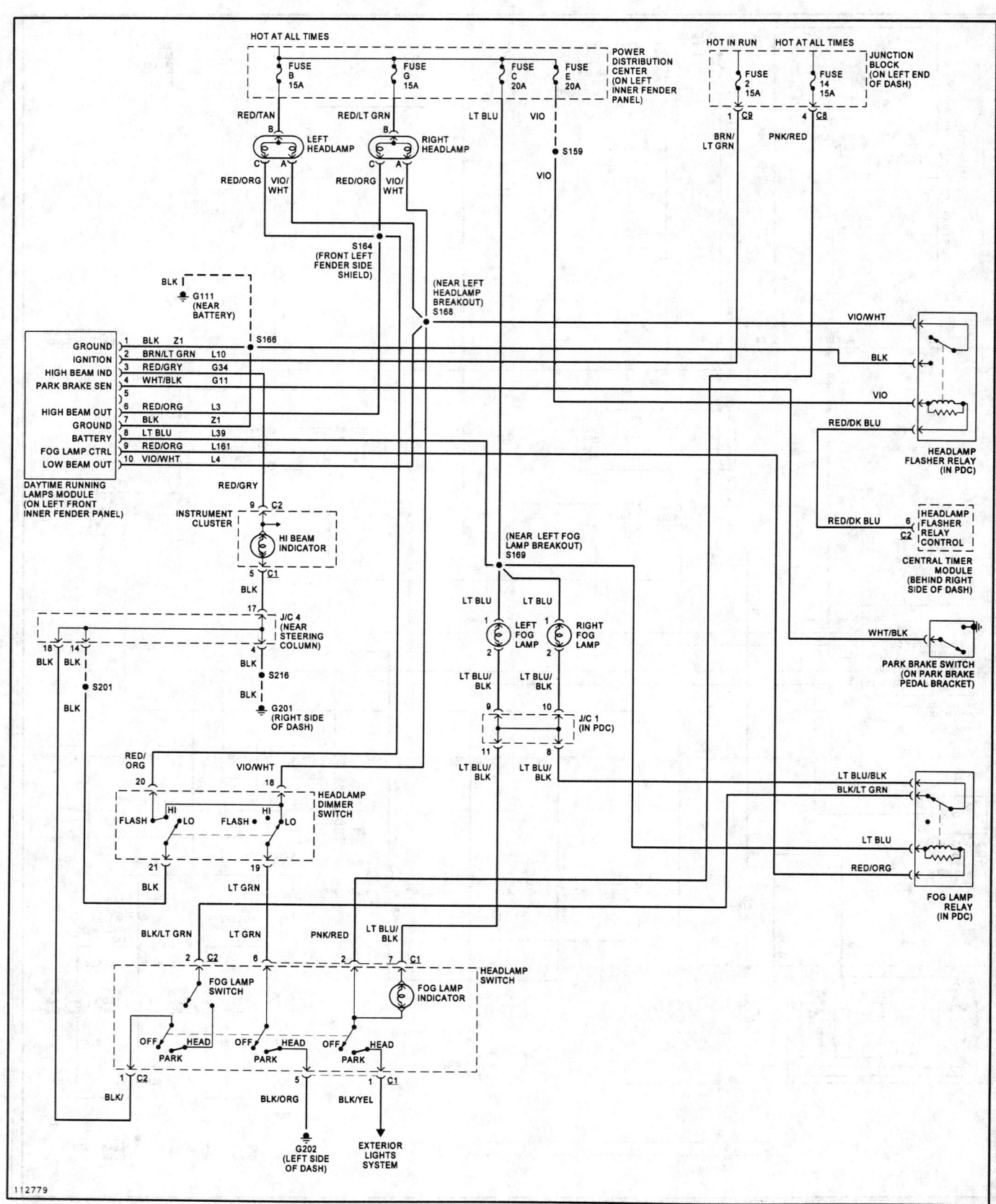

Fig. 5: Daytime Running Lights Wiring Diagram (Dakota)

112779

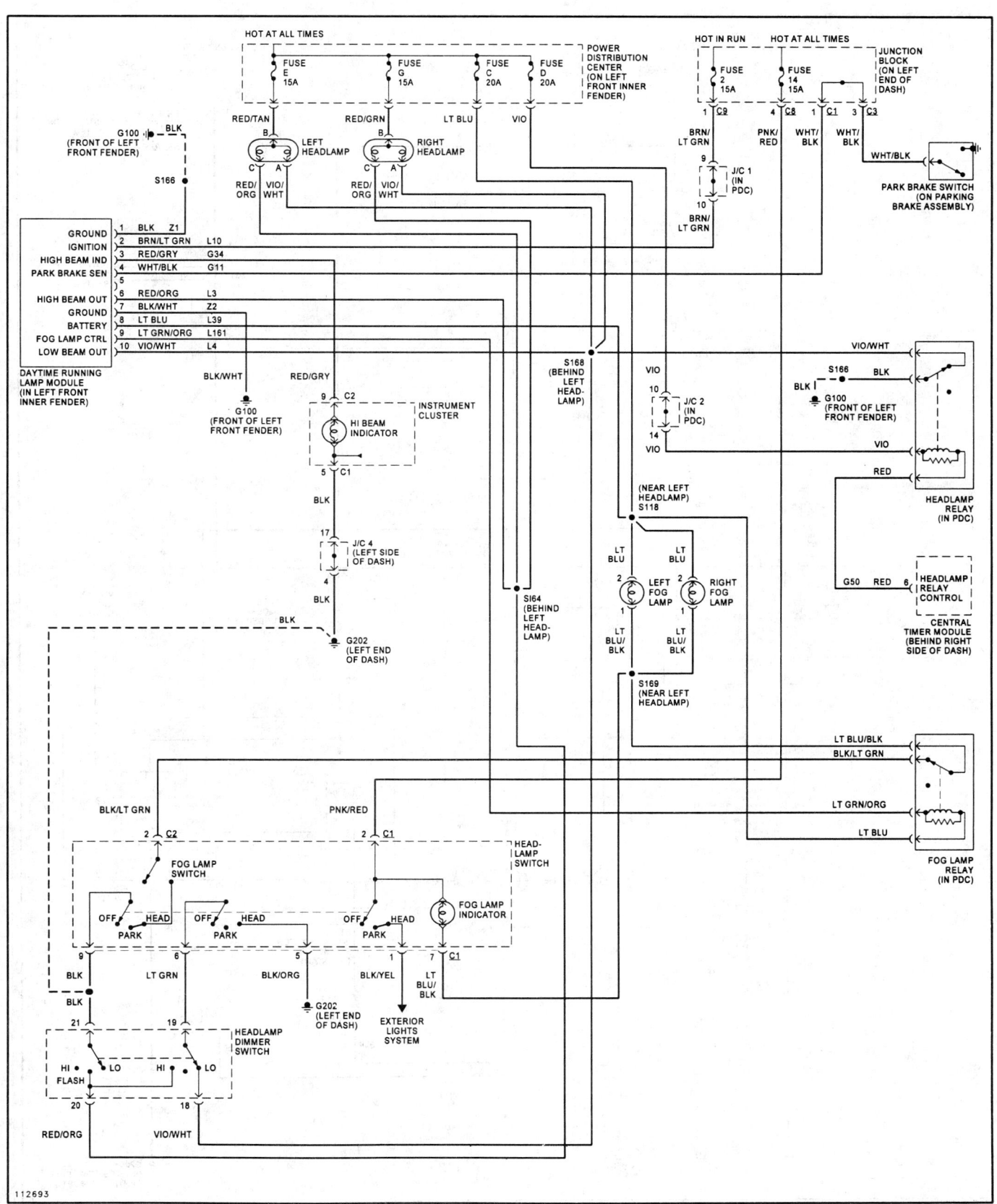

Fig. 6: Daytime Running Lights Wiring Diagram (Durango)

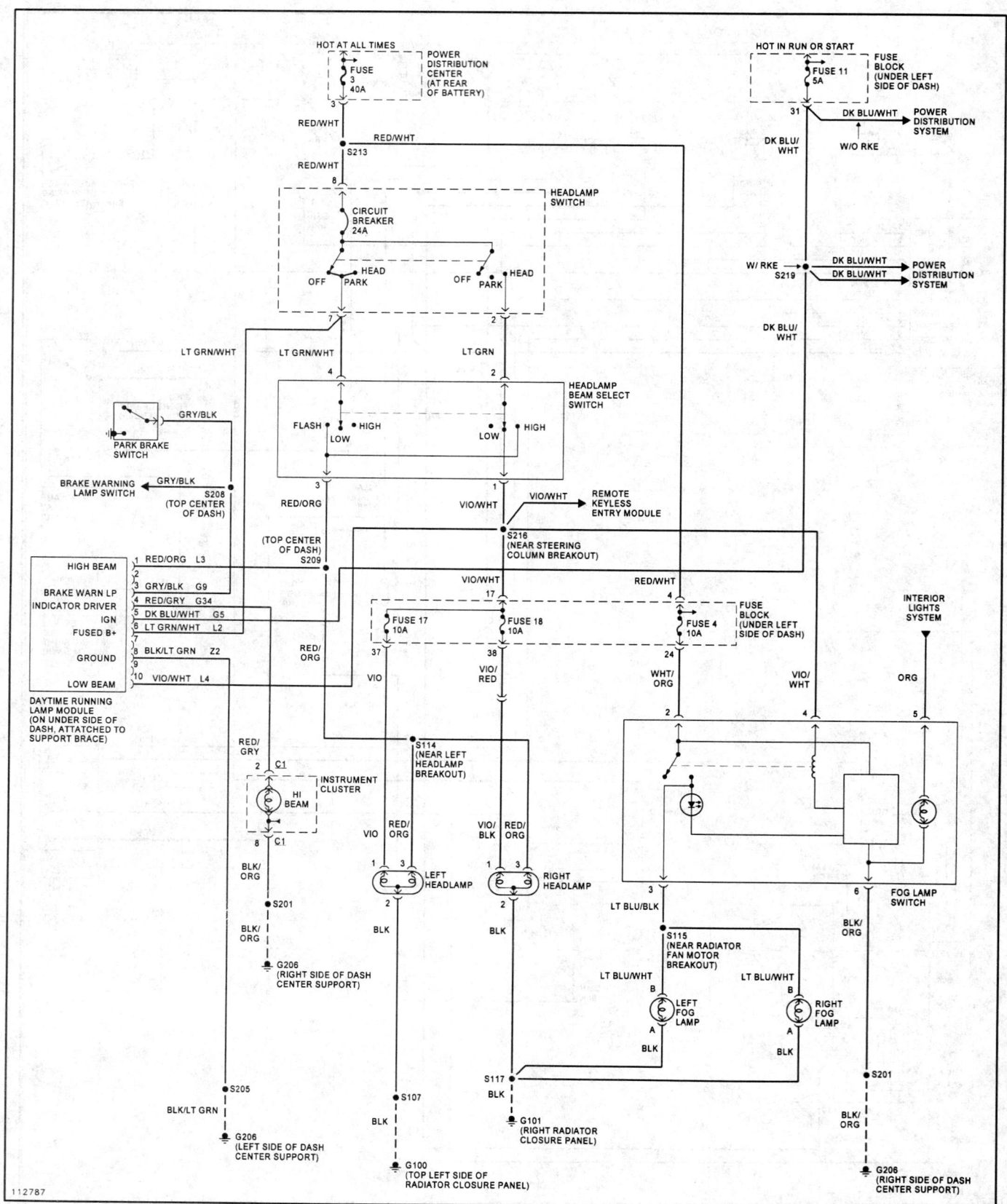

Fig. 7: Daytime Running Lights Wiring Diagram (Neon)

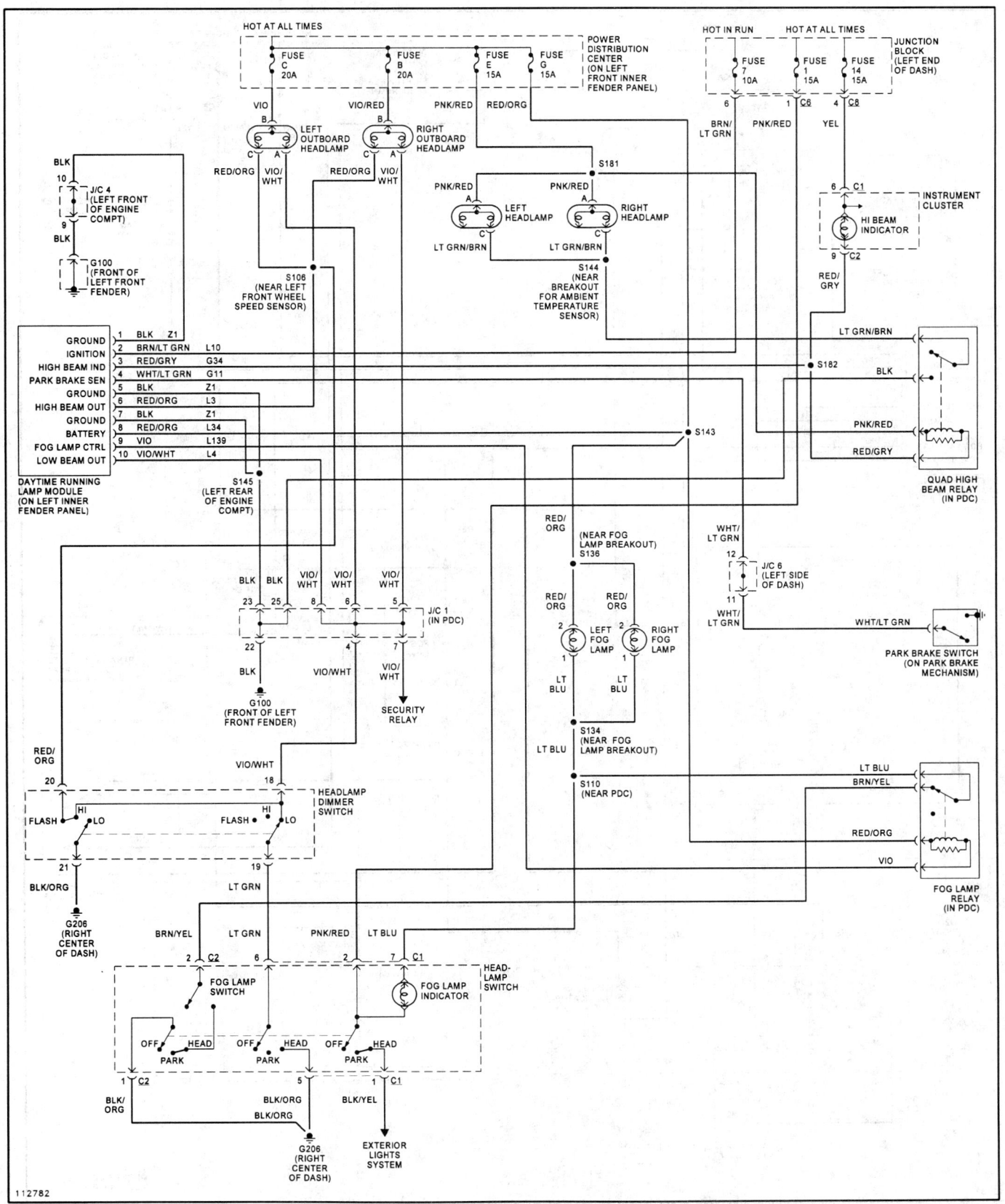

Fig. 8: Daytime Running Lights Wiring Diagram (Ram Pickup – With Quad Headlights)

112782

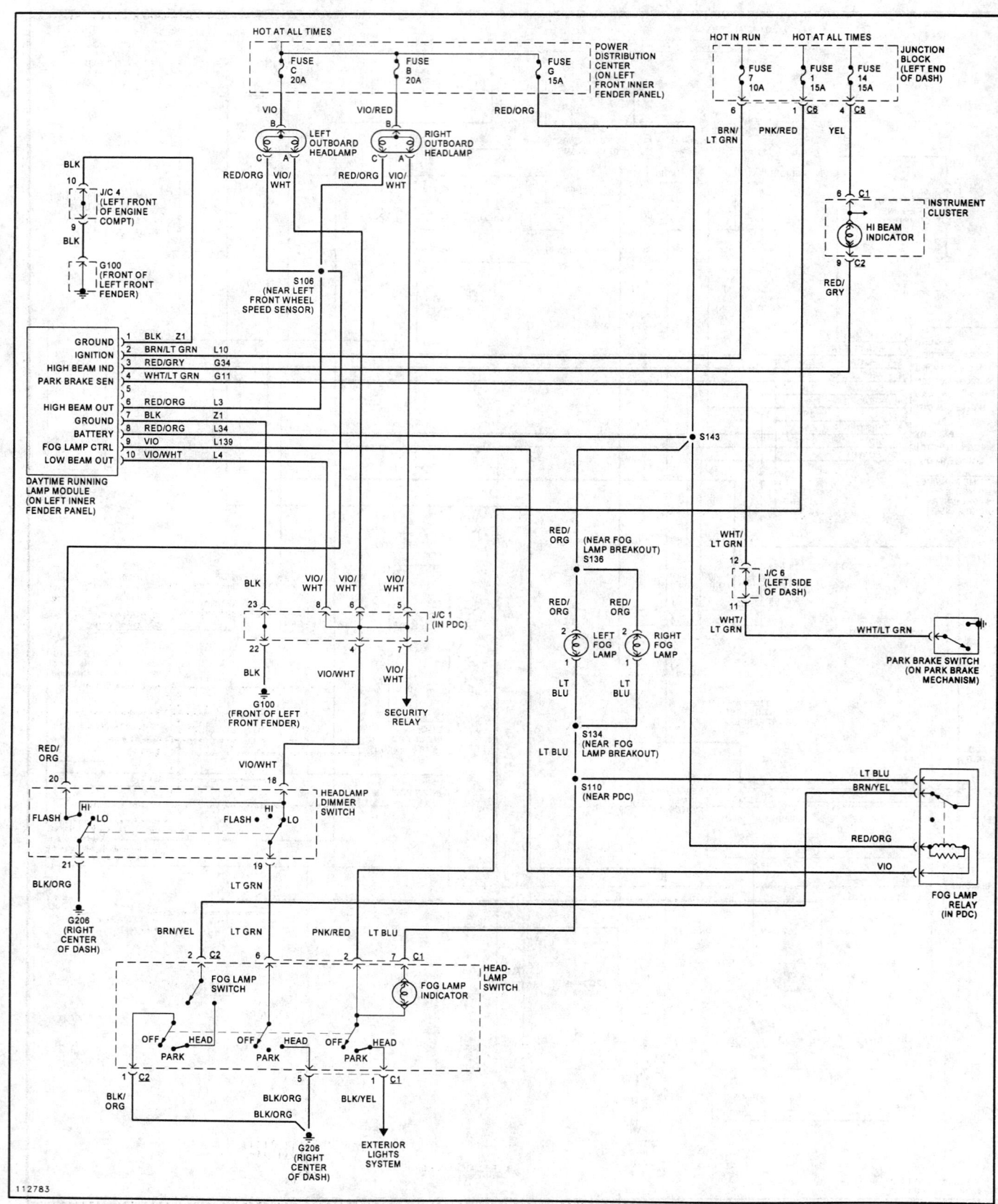

Fig. 9: Daytime Running Lights Wiring Diagram (Ram Pickup – Without Quad Headlights)

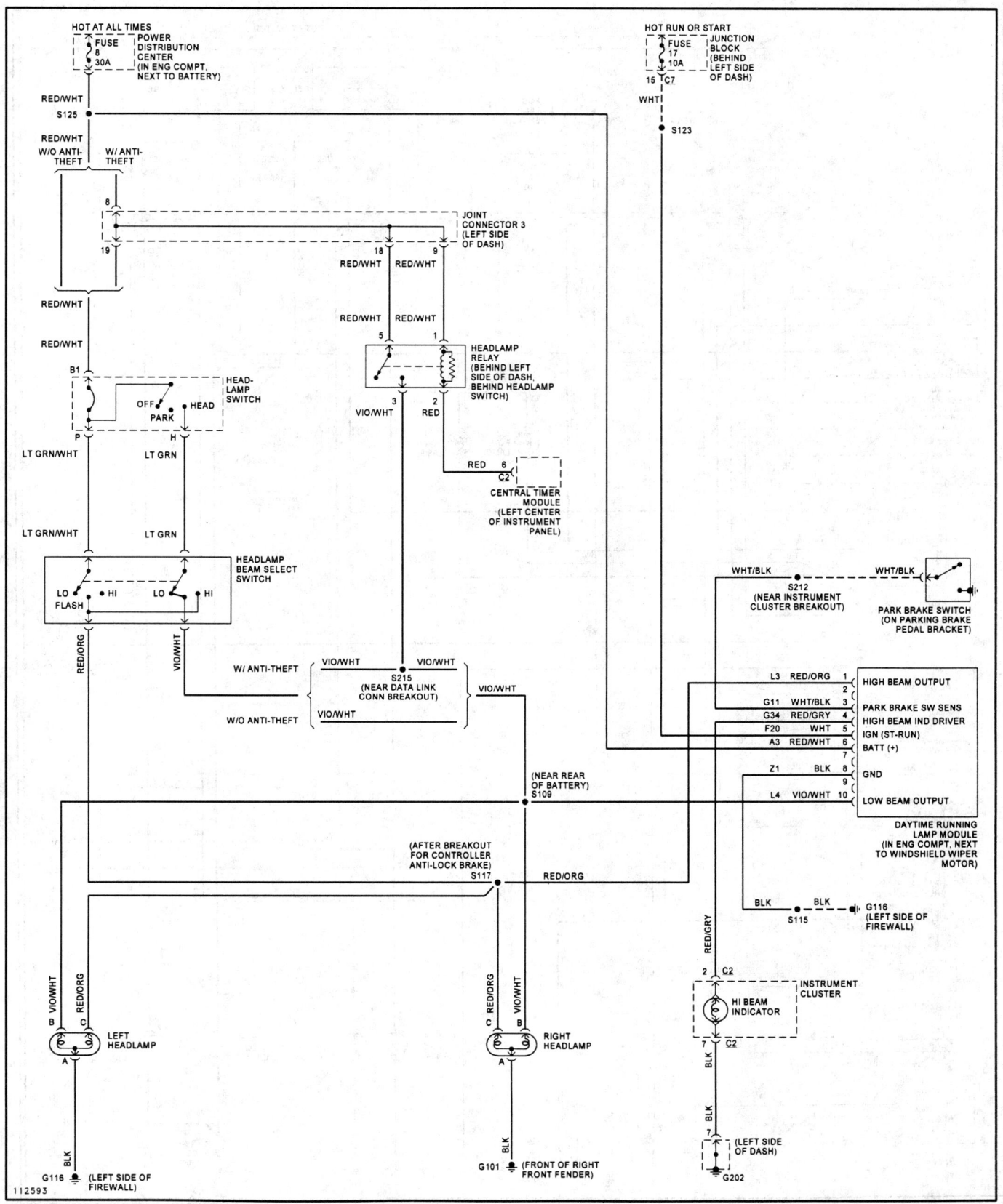

Fig. 10: Daytime Running Lights Wiring Diagram (Ram Van & Ram Wagon)

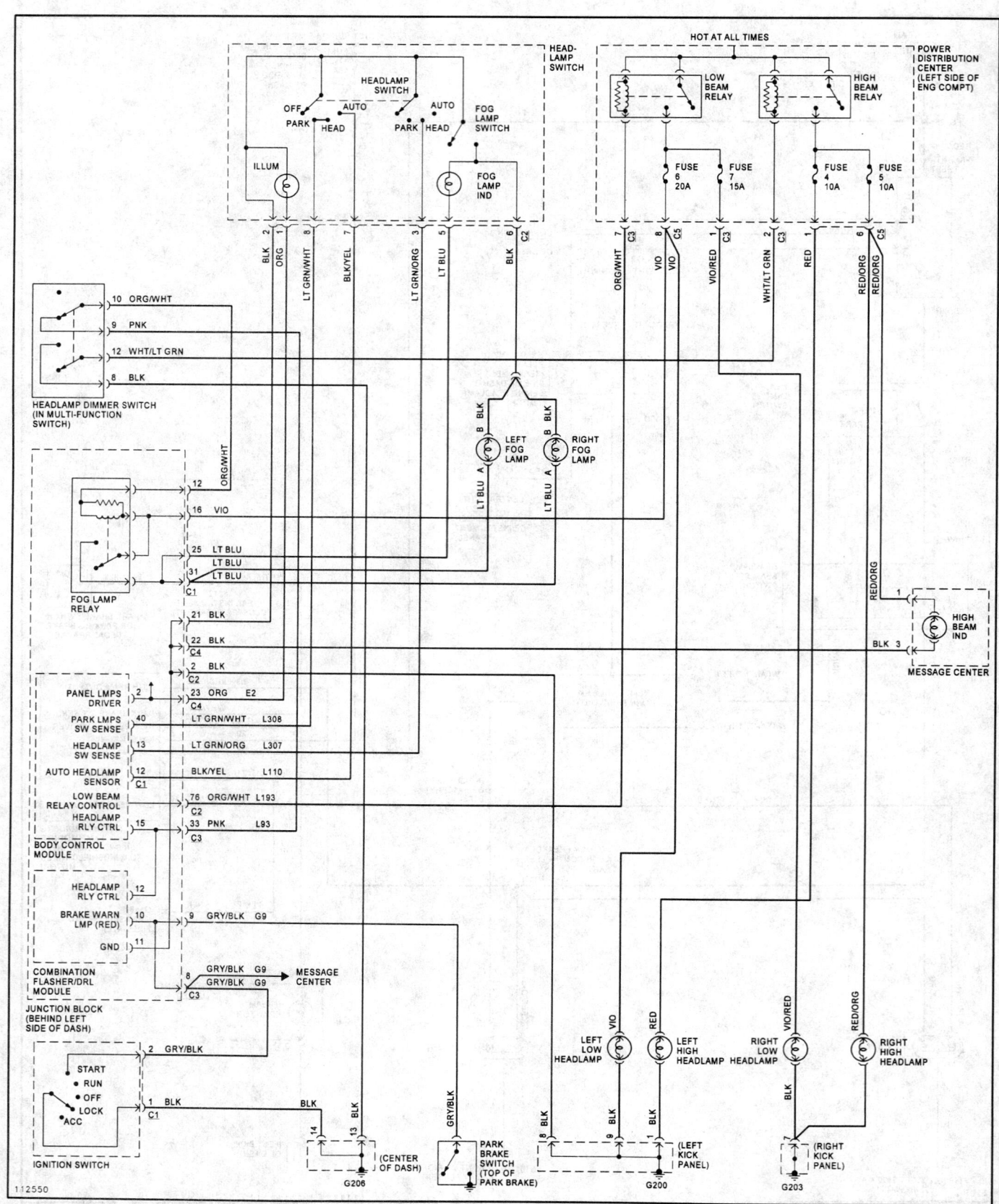

Fig. 11: Daytime Running Lights Wiring Diagram (Town & Country)

WIRING DIAGRAMS

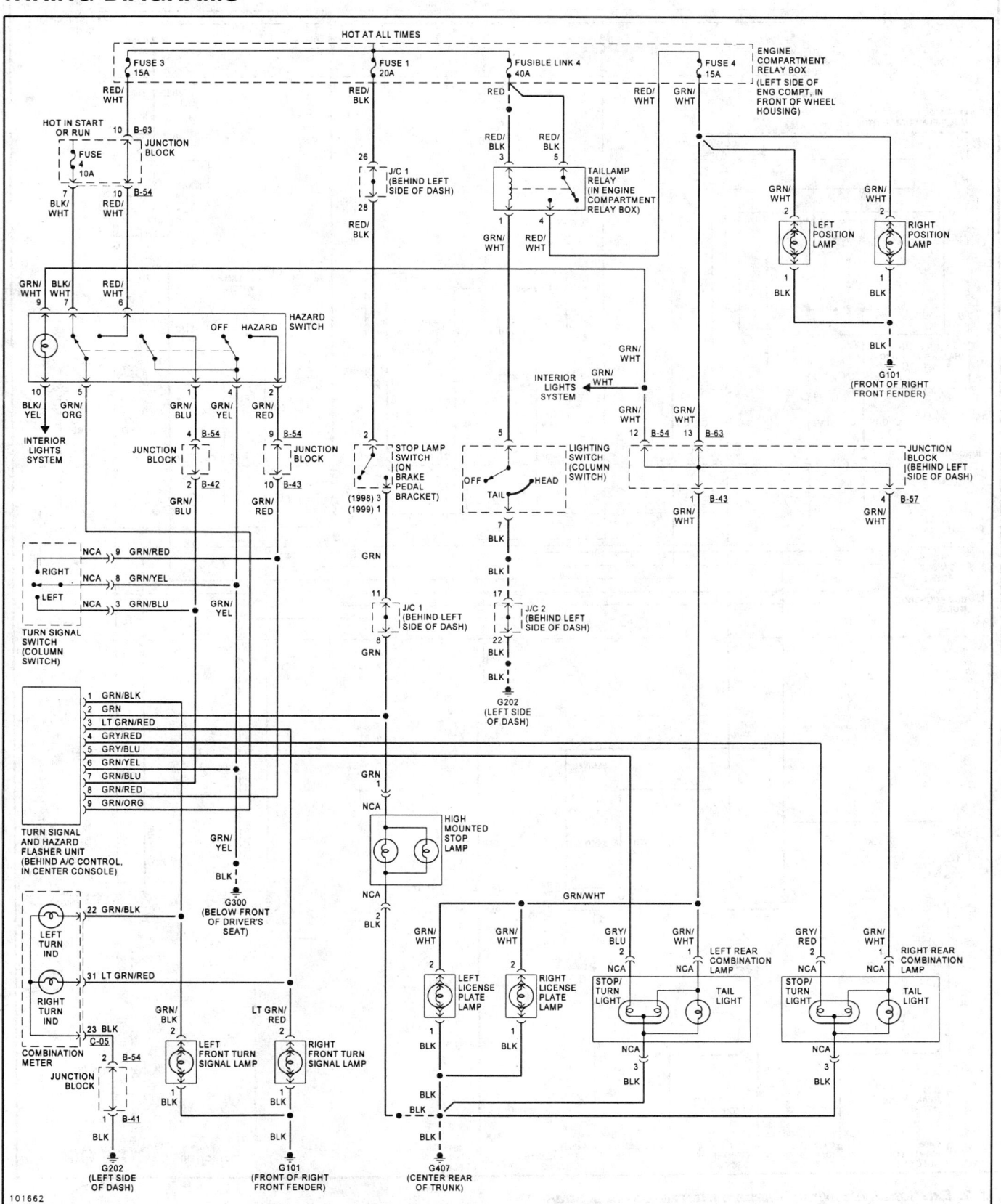

Fig. 1: Exterior Lights Wiring Diagram (Avenger)

101662

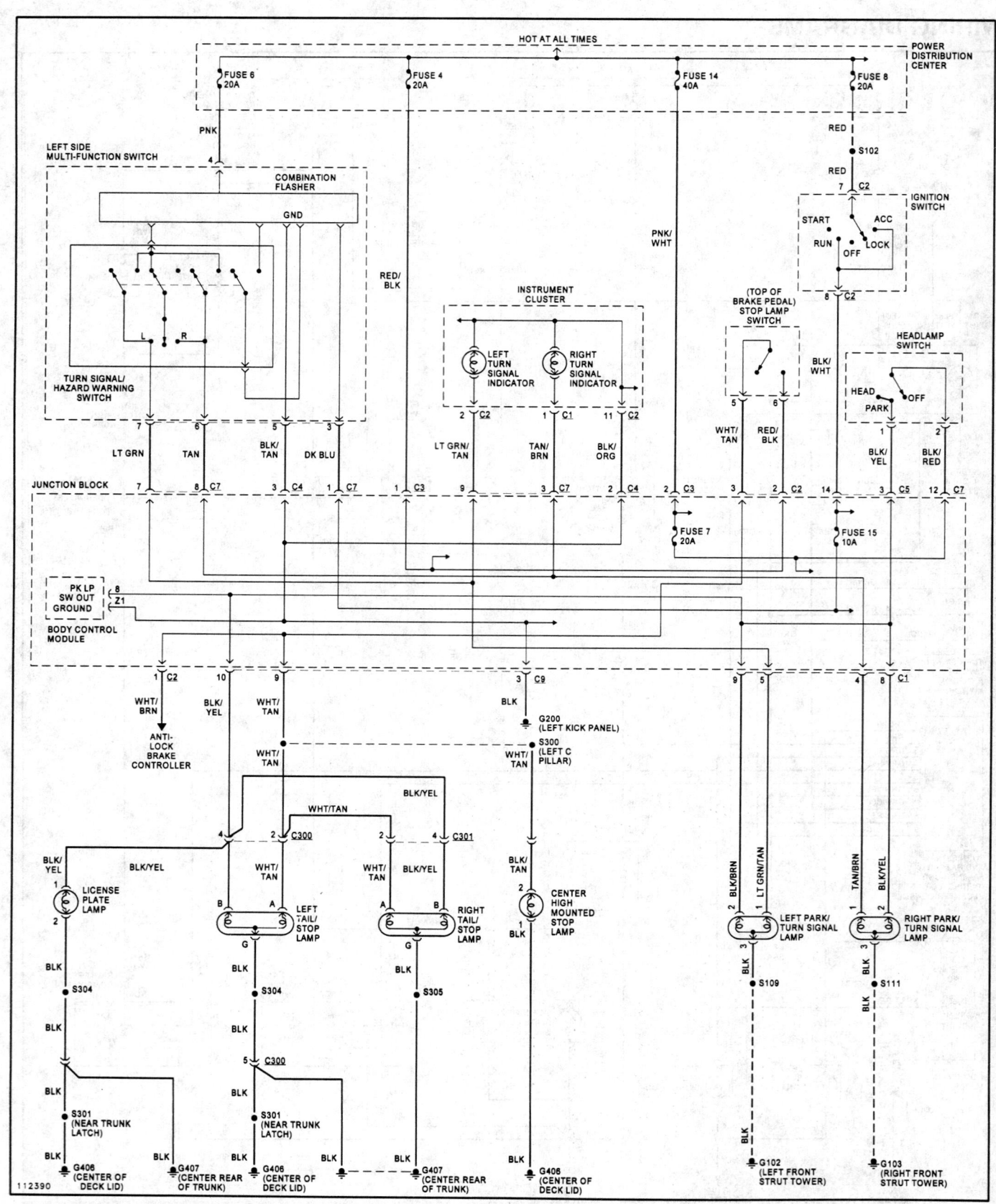

Fig. 2: Exterior Lights Wiring Diagram (Breeze, Cirrus & Stratus)

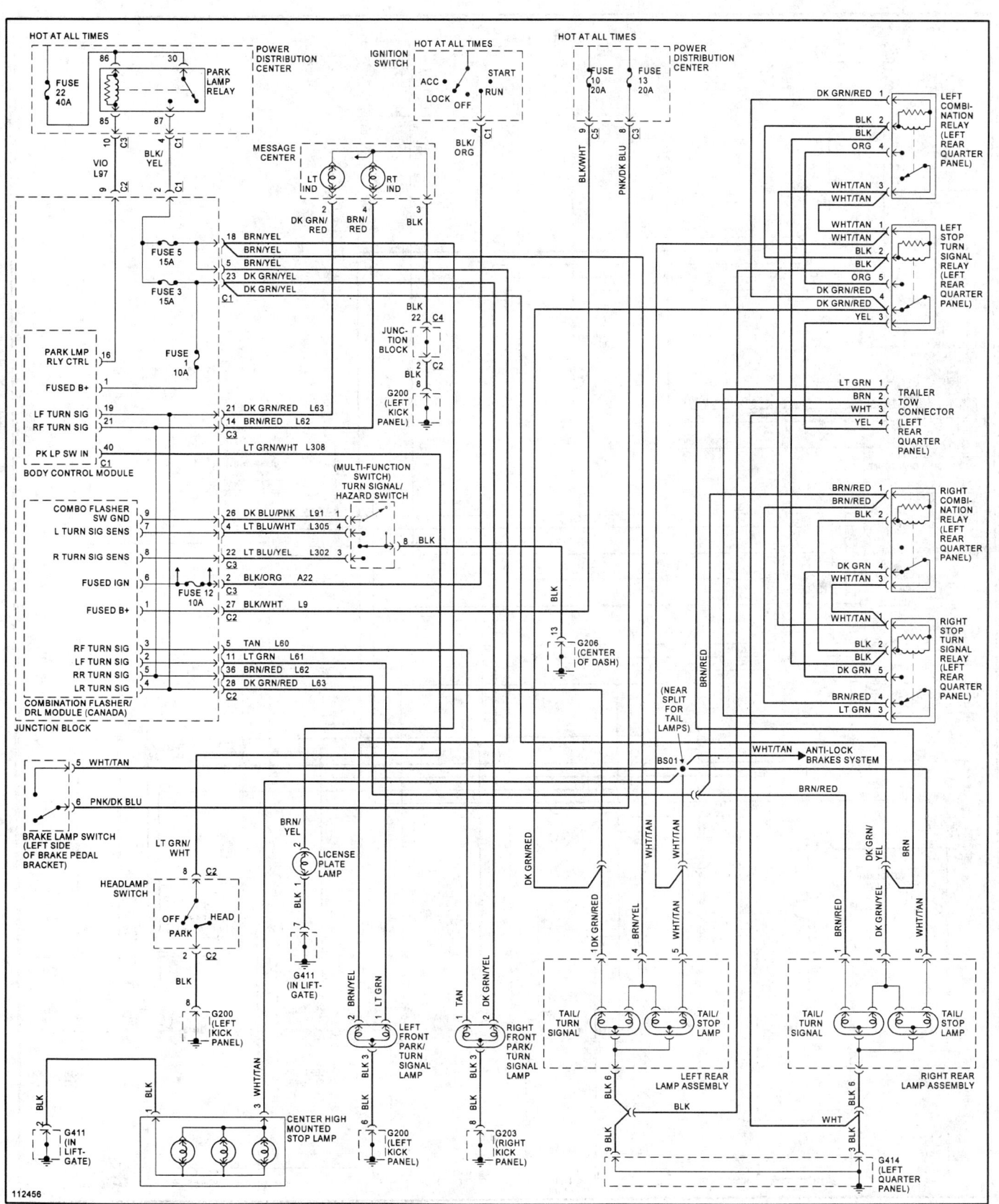

Fig. 3: Exterior Lights With Trailer Towing Wiring Diagram (Caravan, Town & Country, & Voyager)

112456

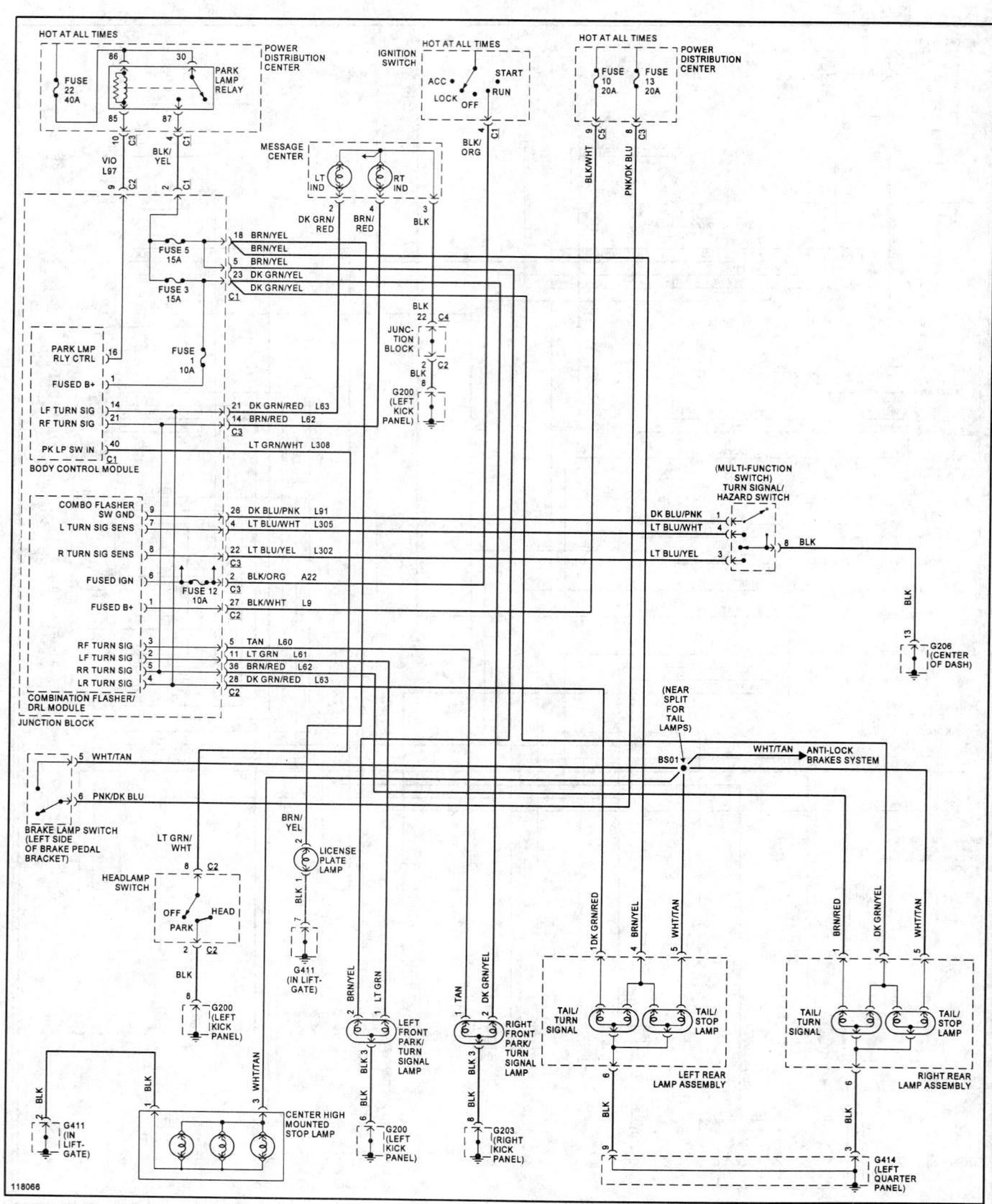

Fig. 4: Exterior Lights Without Trailer Towing Wiring Diagram (Caravan, Town & Country, & Voyager)

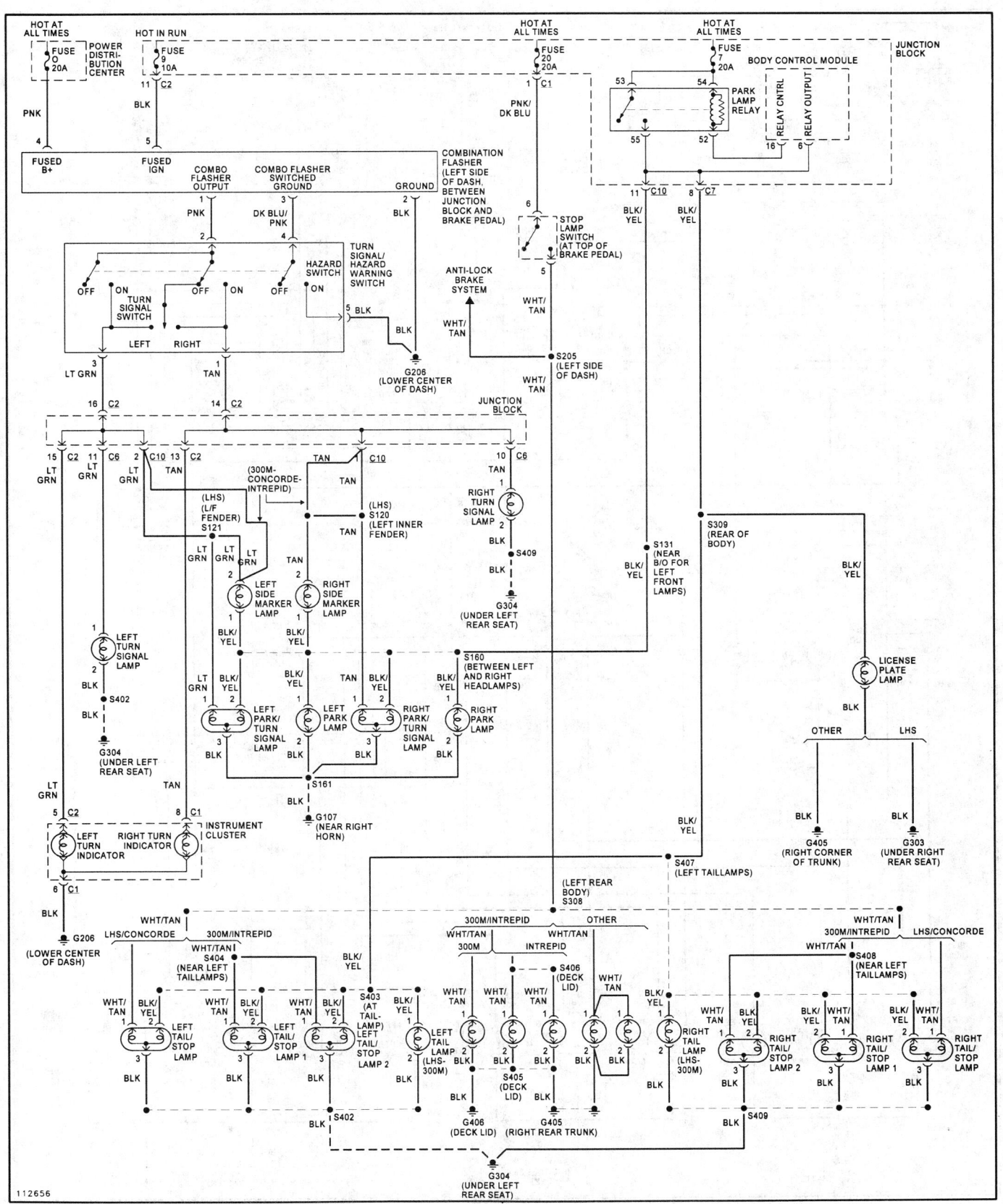

Fig. 5: Exterior Lights Wiring Diagram (Concorde, Intrepid, LHS & 300M)

112656

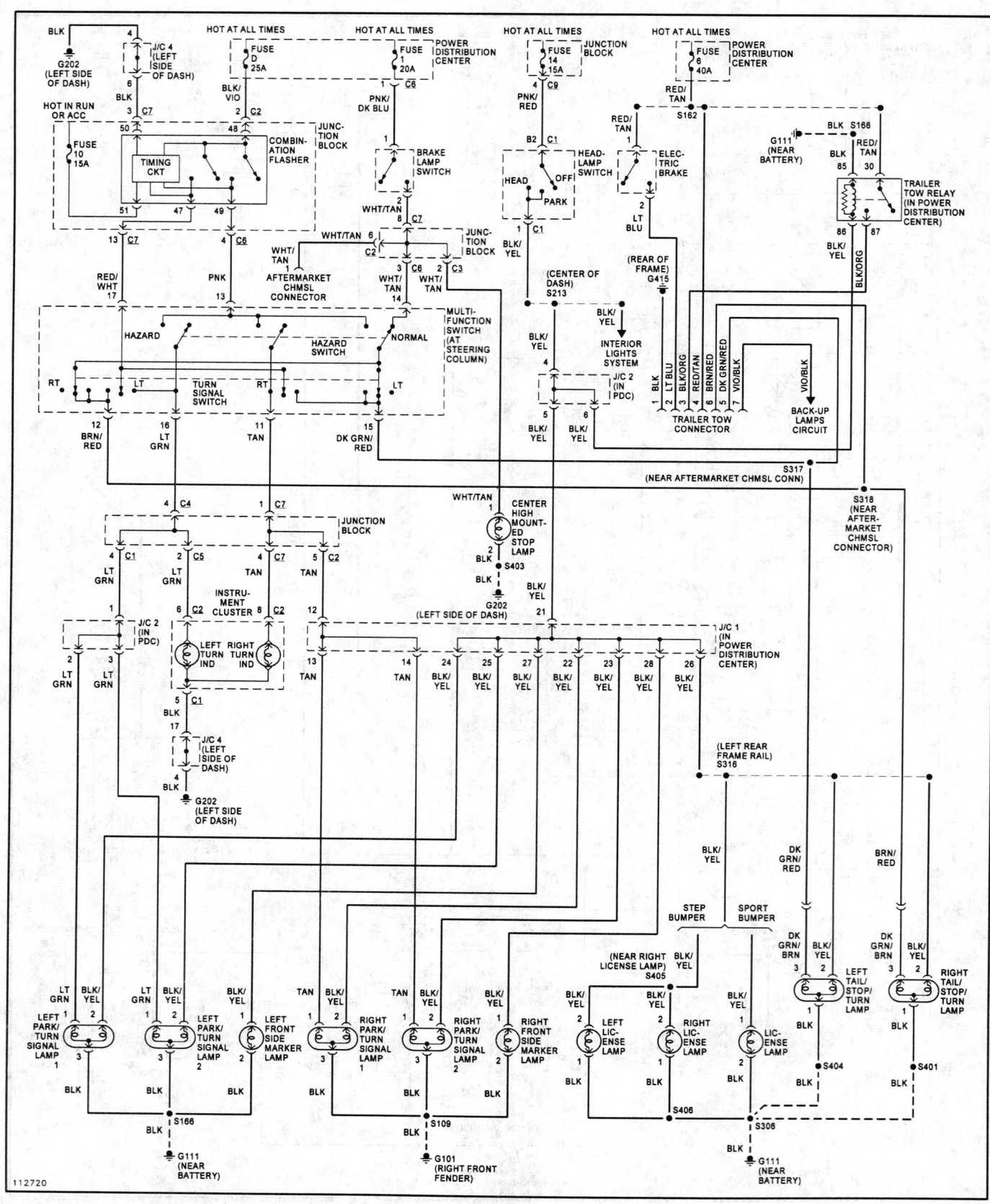

Fig. 6: Exterior Lights & Trailer Connector Wiring Diagram (Dakota)

112720

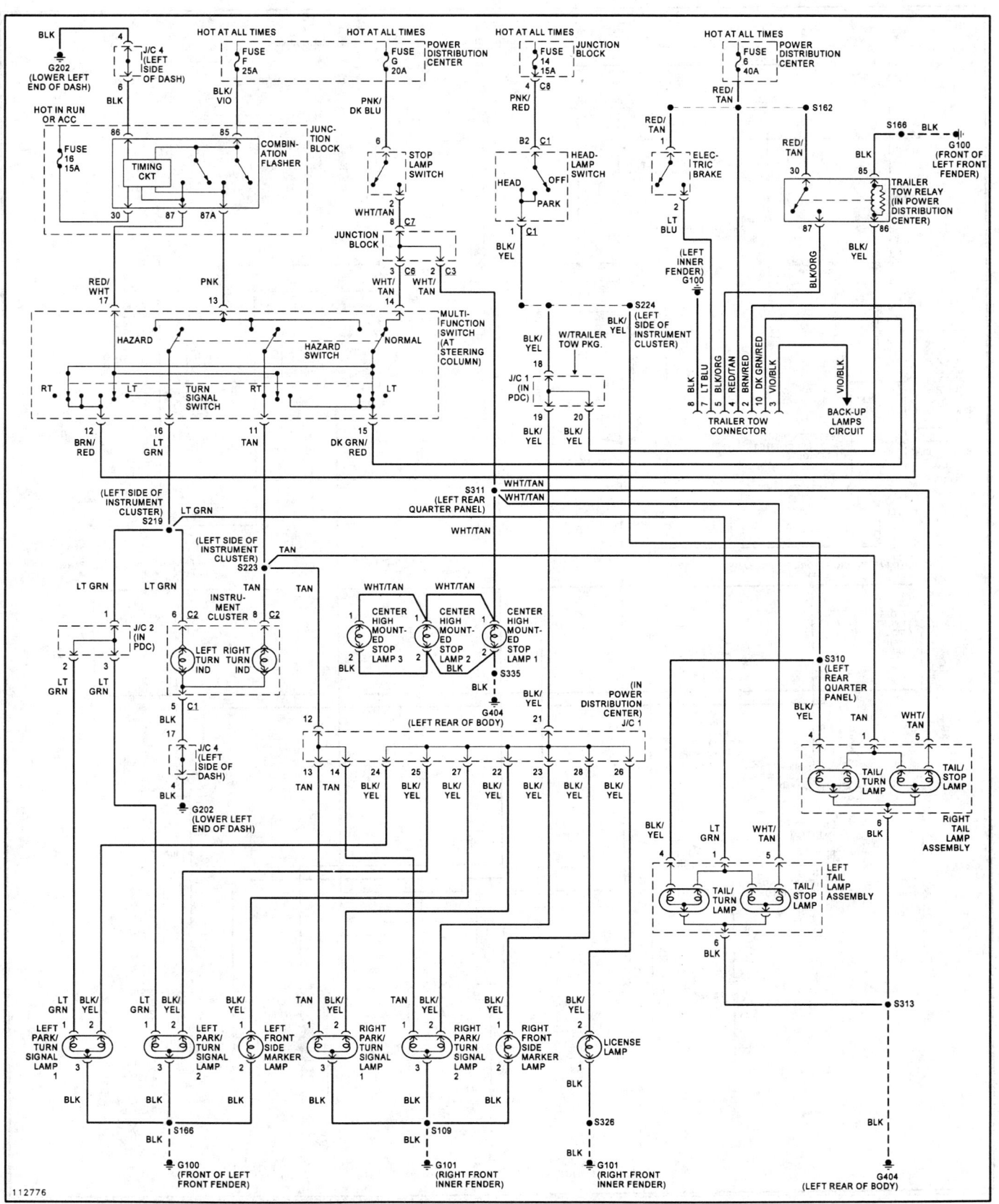

Fig. 7: Exterior Lights Wiring Diagram (Durango)

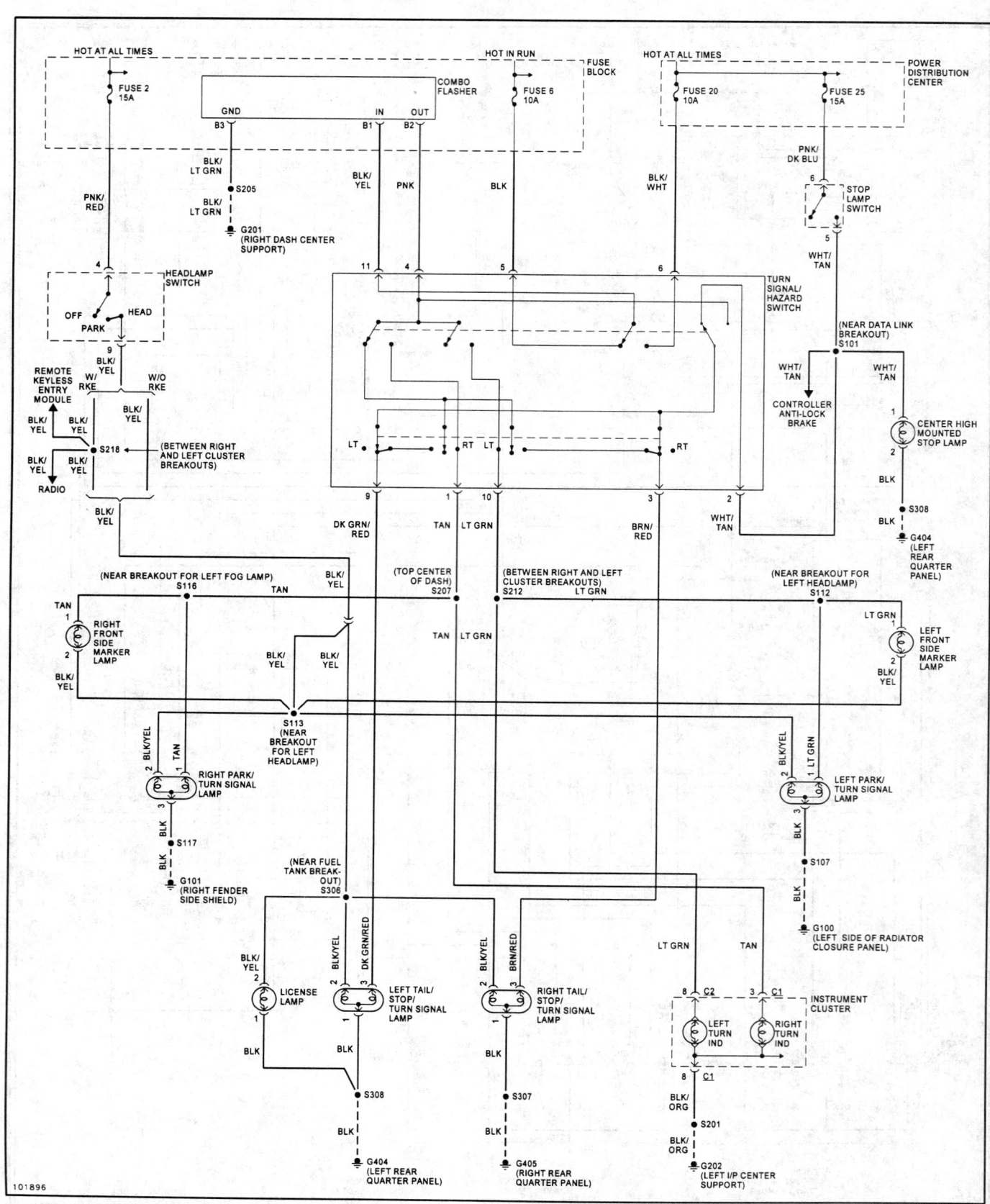

Fig. 8: Exterior Lights Wiring Diagram (Neon)

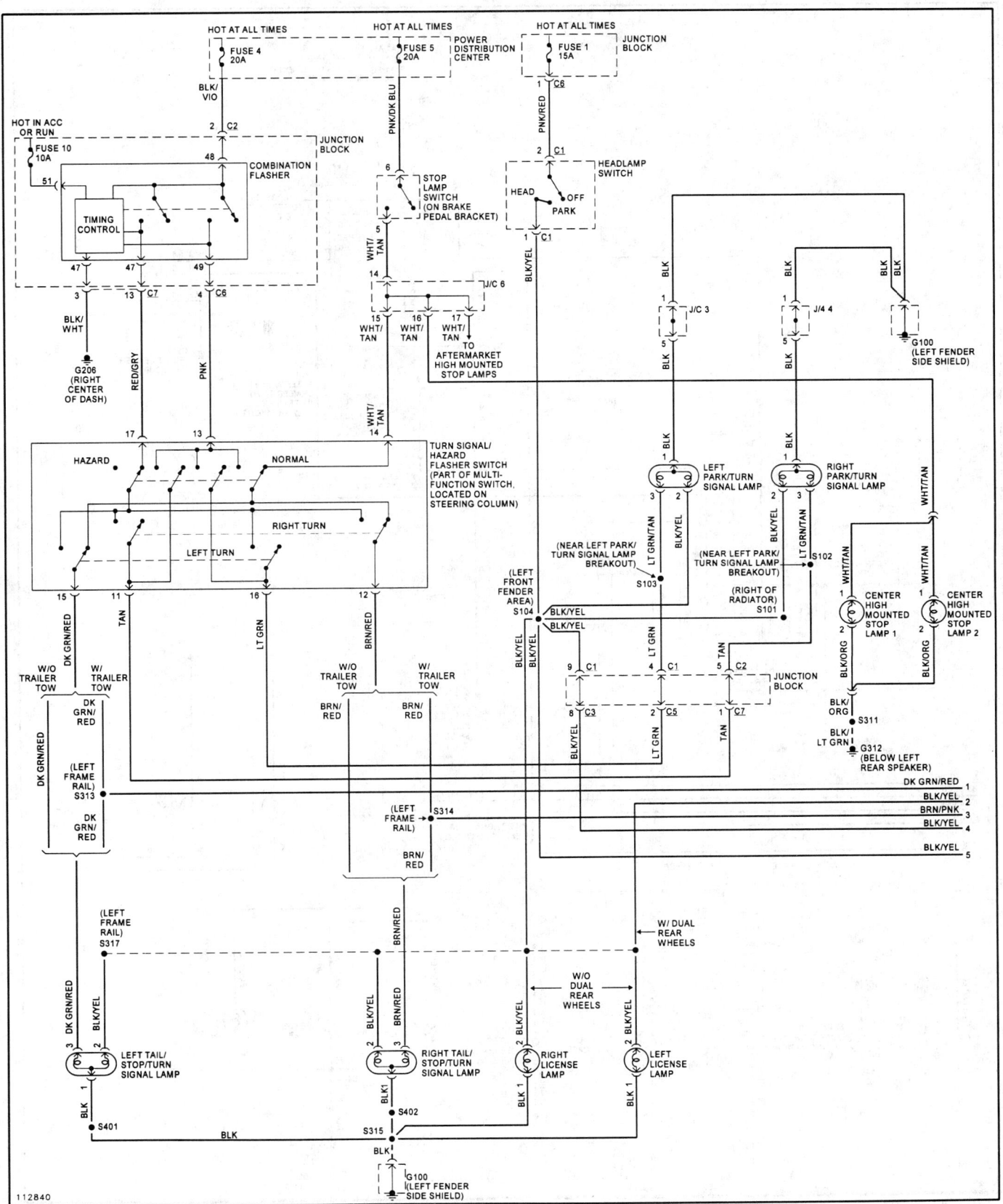

Fig. 9: Exterior Lights & Trailer Connector Wiring Diagram (Ram Pickup – 1 Of 2)

112840

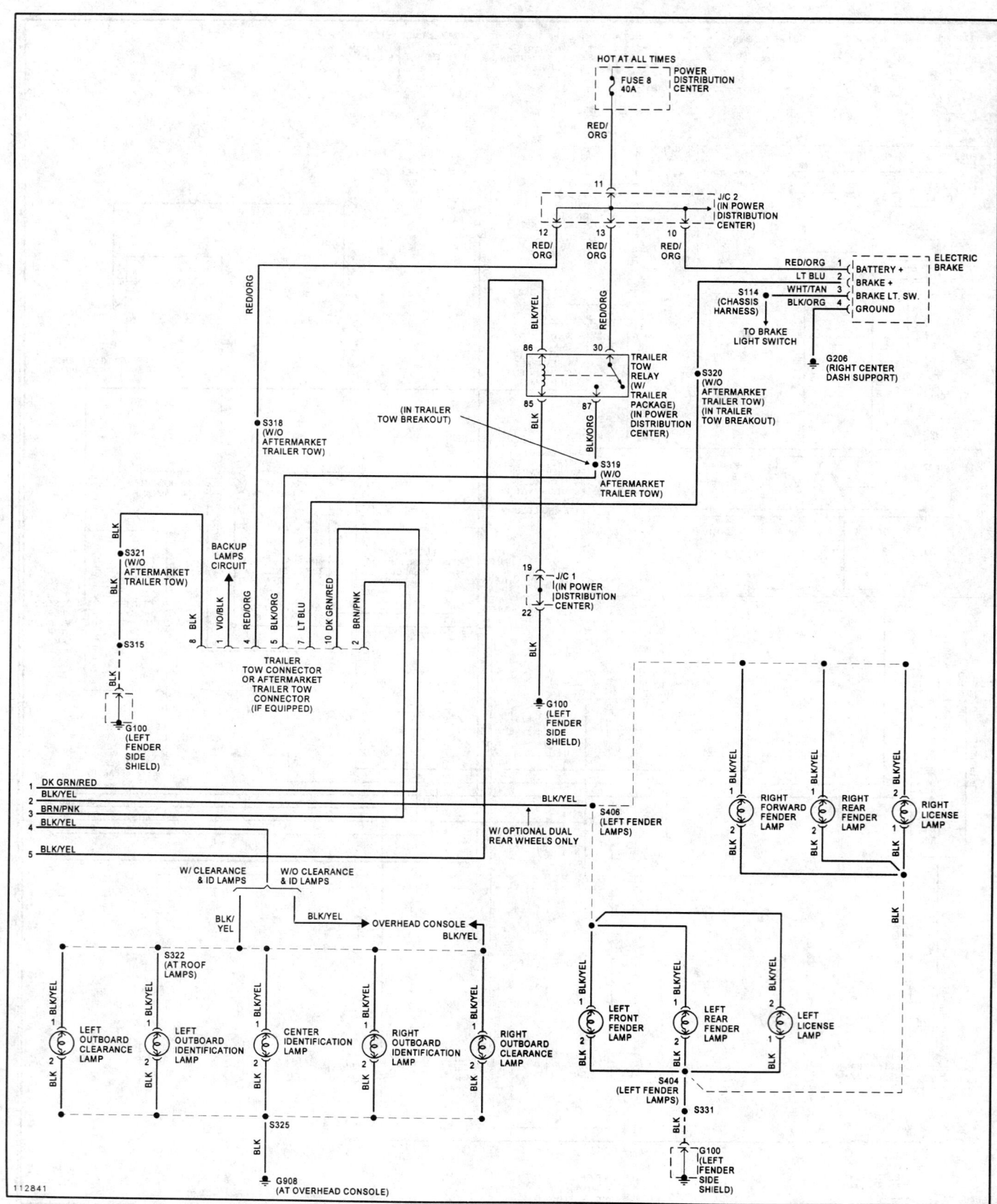

Fig. 10: Exterior Lights & Trailer Connector Wiring Diagram (Ram Pickup – 2 Of 2)

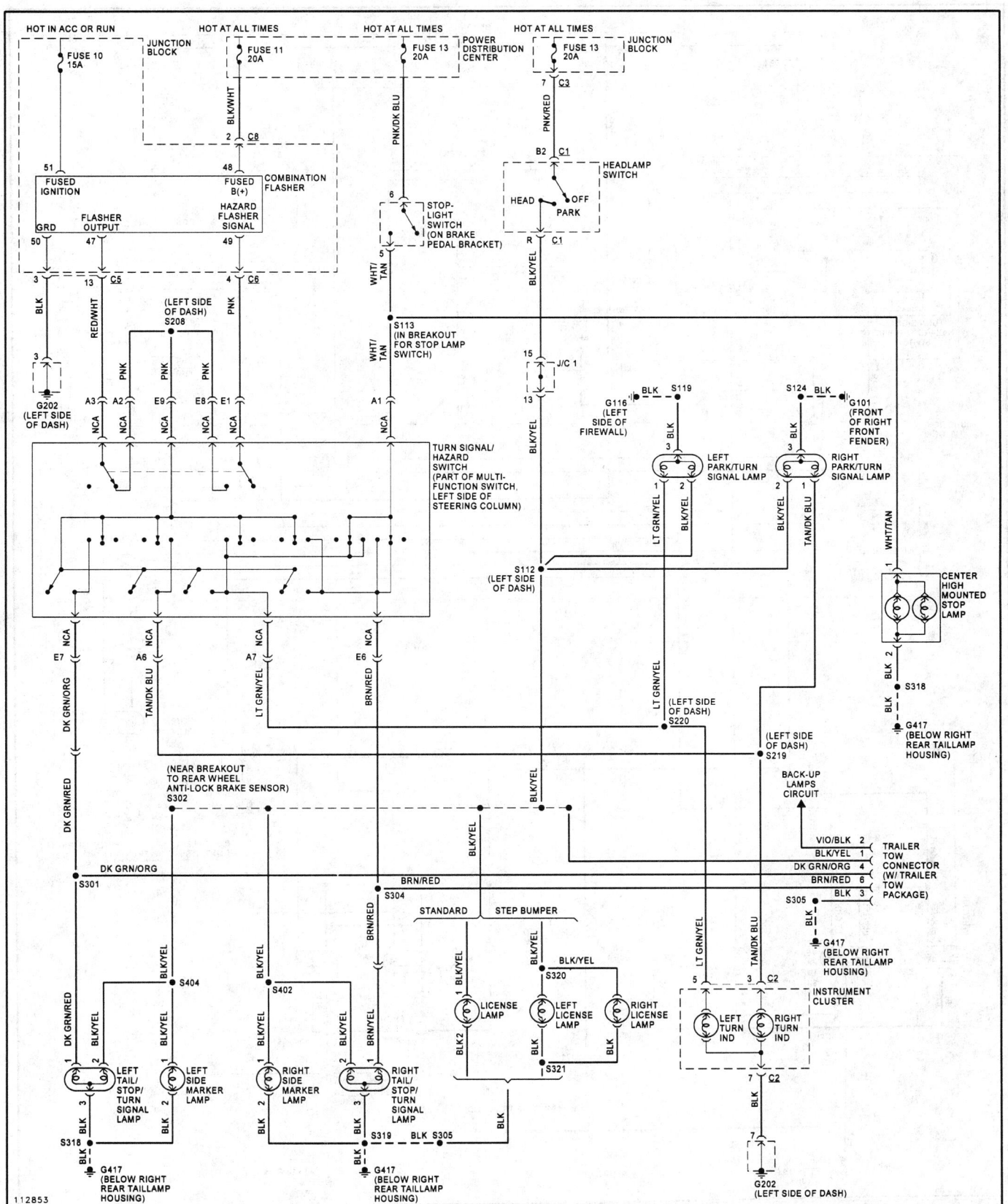

Fig. 11: Exterior Lights & Trailer Connector Wiring Diagram (Ram Van & Ram Wagon)

112853

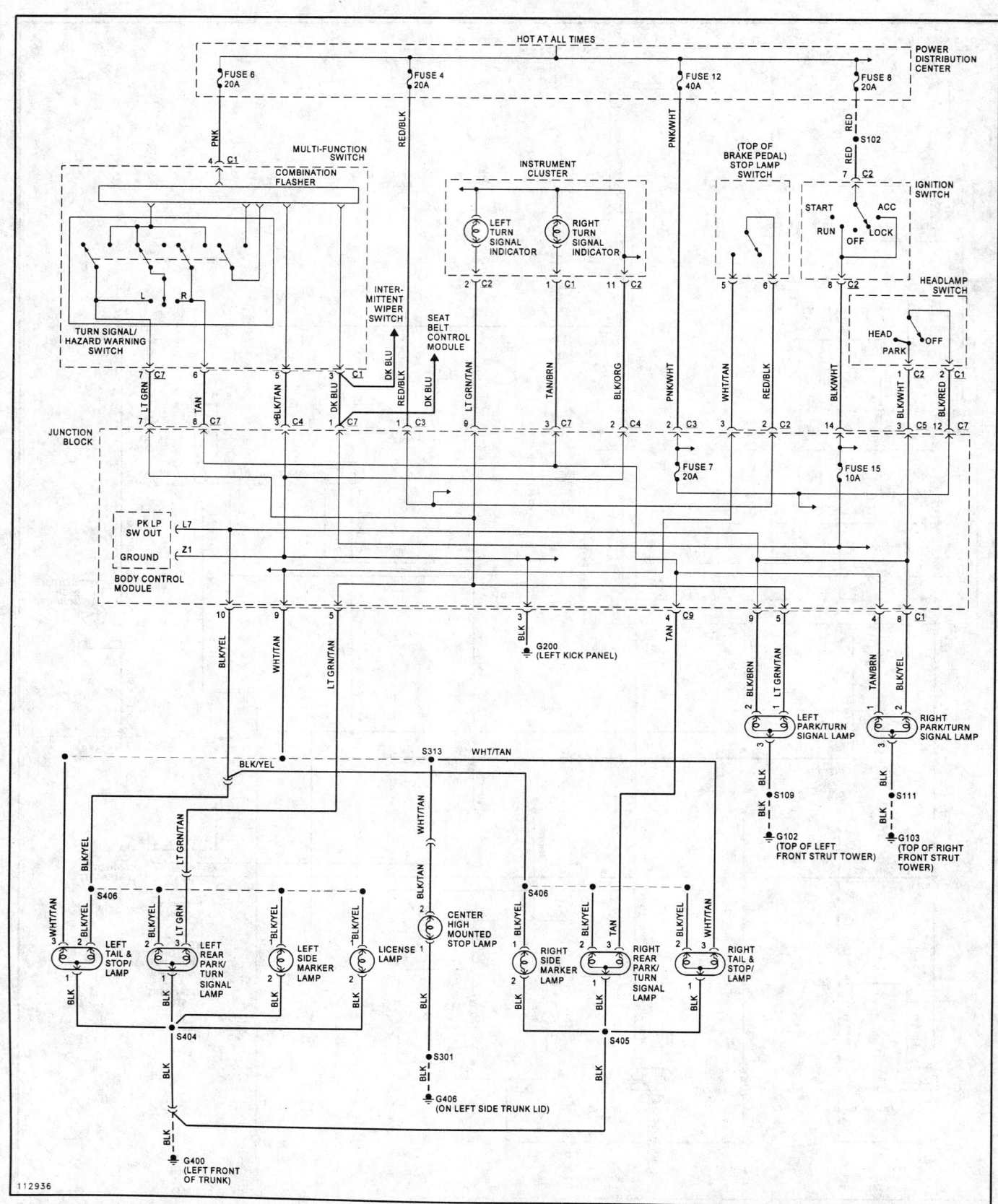

Fig. 12: Exterior Lights Wiring Diagram (Sebring Convertible)

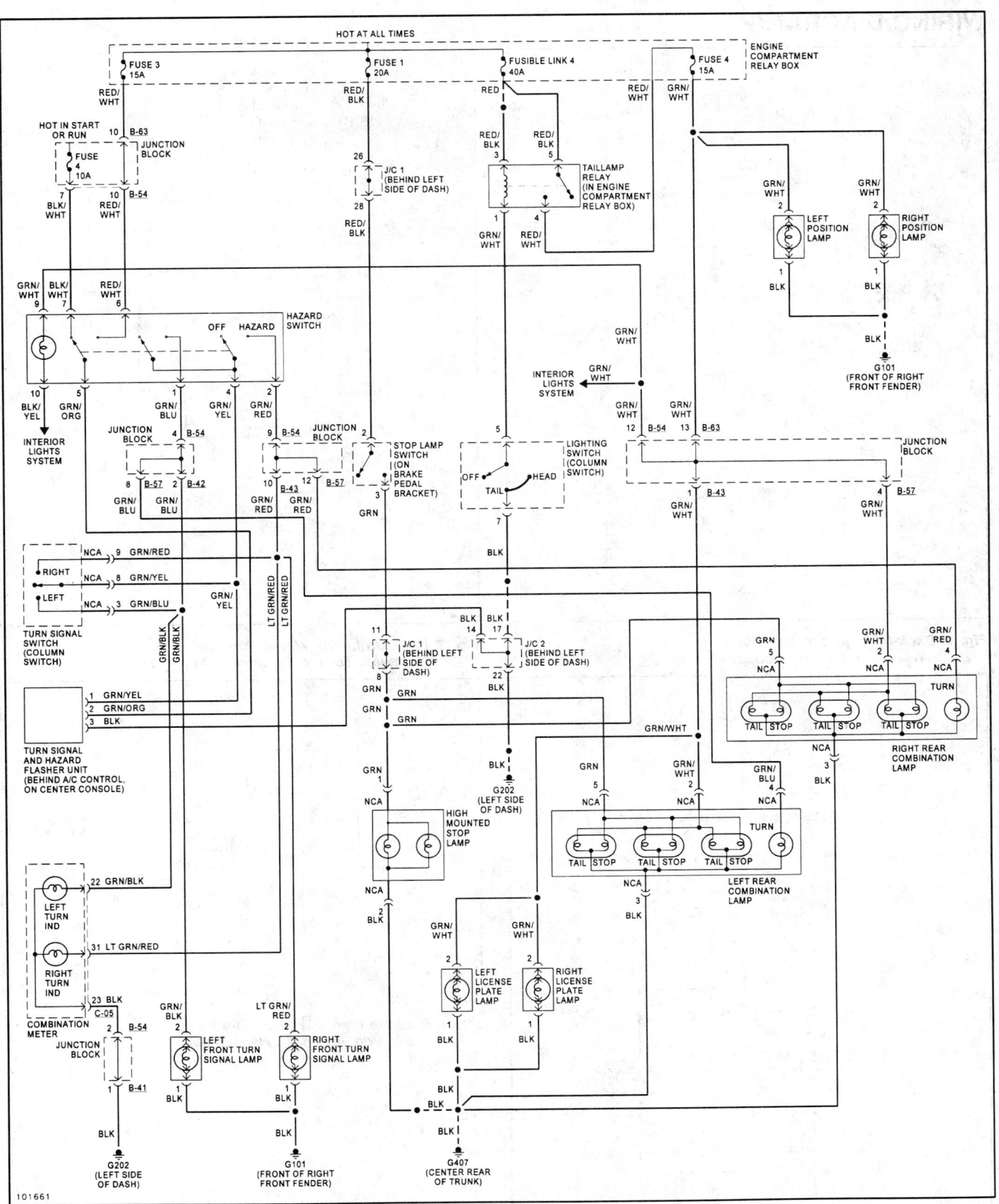

Fig. 13: Exterior Lights Wiring Diagram (Sebring Coupe)

101661

WIRING DIAGRAMS

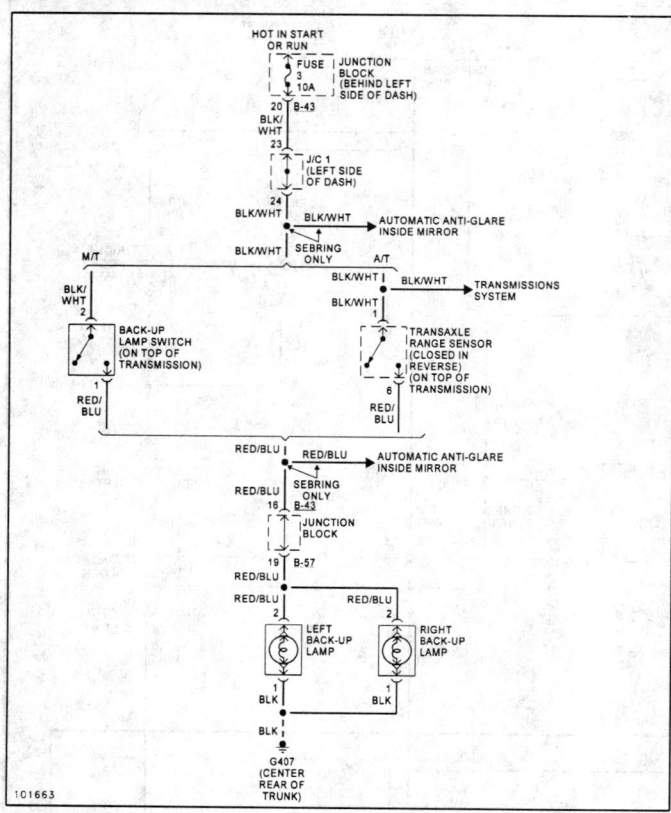

Fig. 1: Back-Up Lights Wiring Diagram
(Avenger & Sebring Coupe)

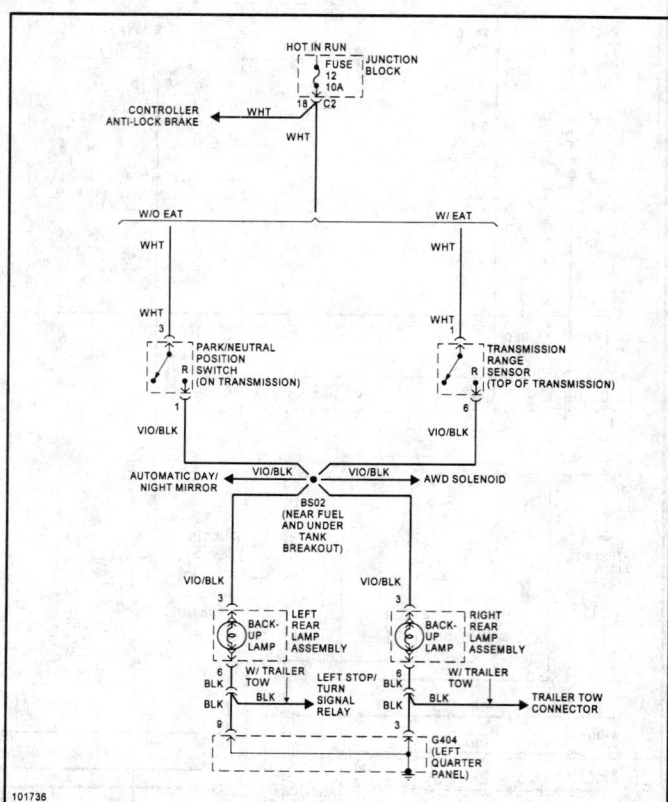

Fig. 3: Back-Up Lights Wiring Diagram
(Caravan, Town & Country, & Voyager)

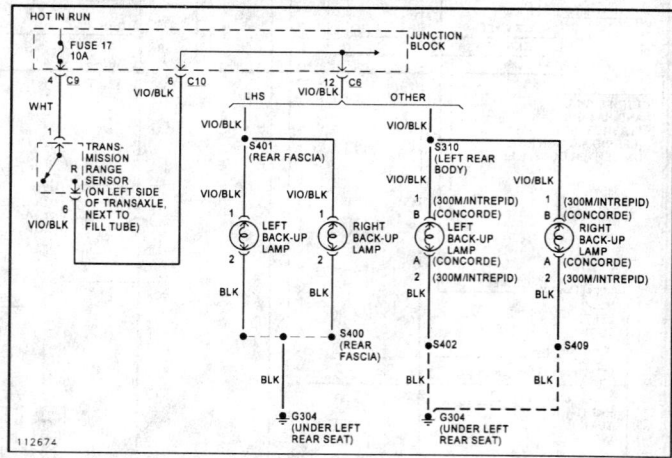

Fig. 4: Back-Up Lights Wiring Diagram
(Concorde, Intrepid, LHS & 300M)

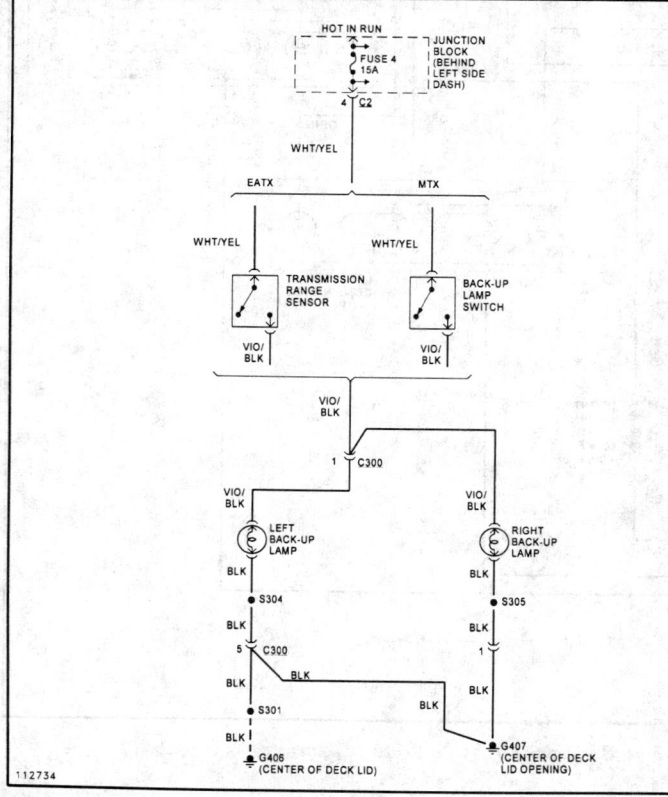

Fig. 2: Back-Up Lights Wiring Diagram
(Breeze, Cirrus & Stratus)

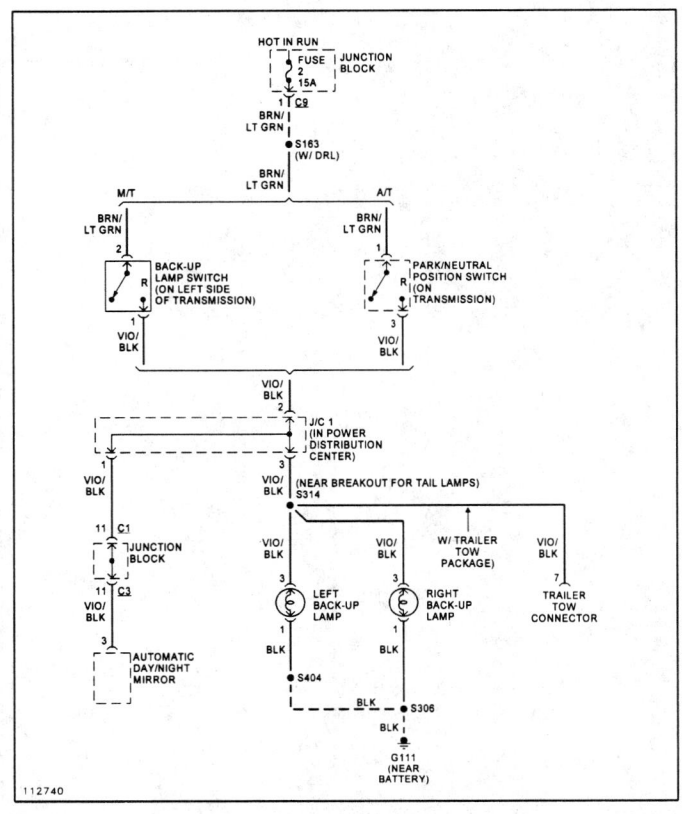

Fig. 5: Back-Up Lights Wiring Diagram (Dakota)

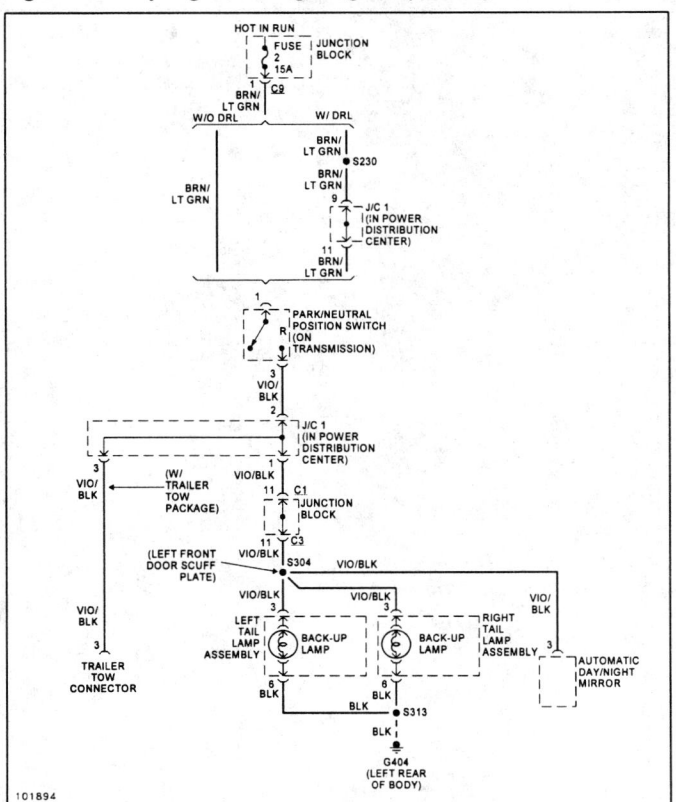

Fig. 6: Back-Up Lights Wiring Diagram (Durango)

Fig. 7: Back-Up Lights Wiring Diagram (Neon)

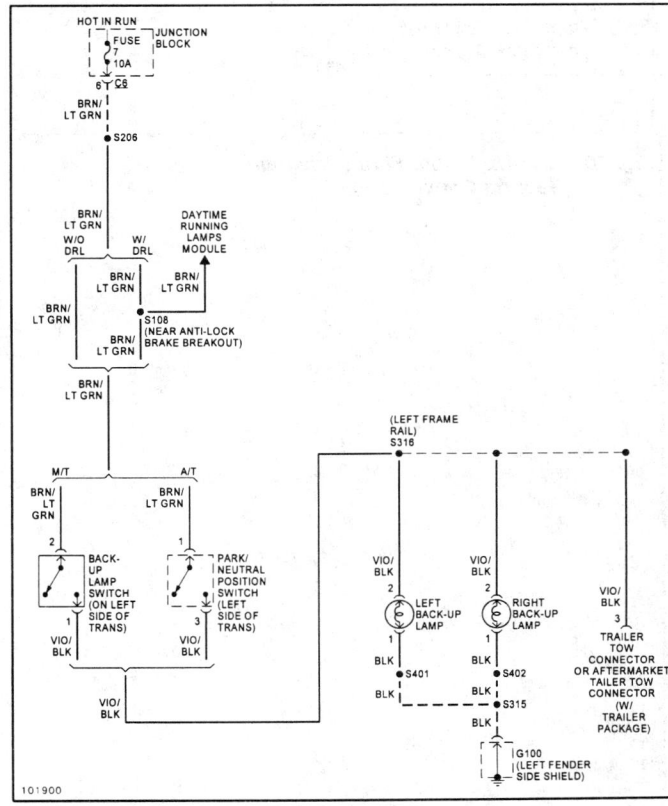

Fig. 8: Back-Up Lights Wiring Diagram (Ram Pickup)

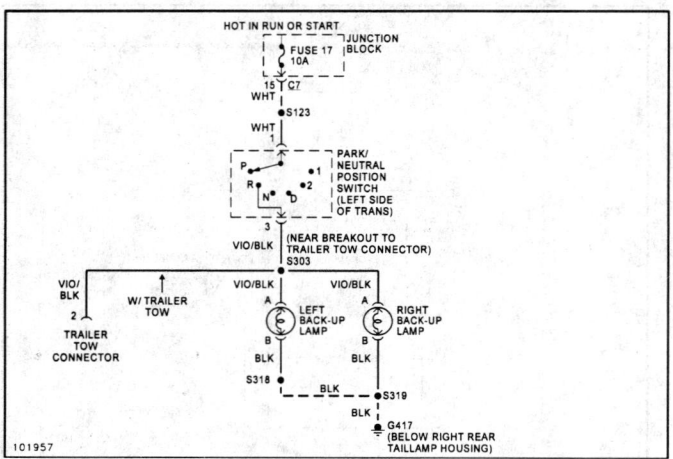

Fig. 9: Back-Up Lights Wiring Diagram
(Ram Van & Ram Wagon)

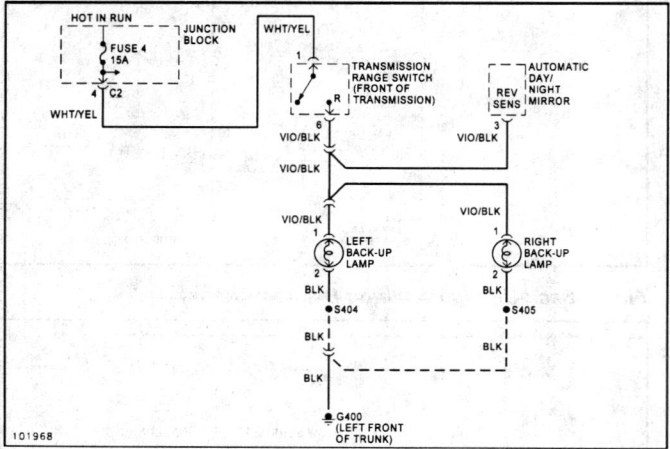

Fig. 10: Back-Up Lights Wiring Diagram
(Sebring Convertible)

WIRING DIAGRAMS

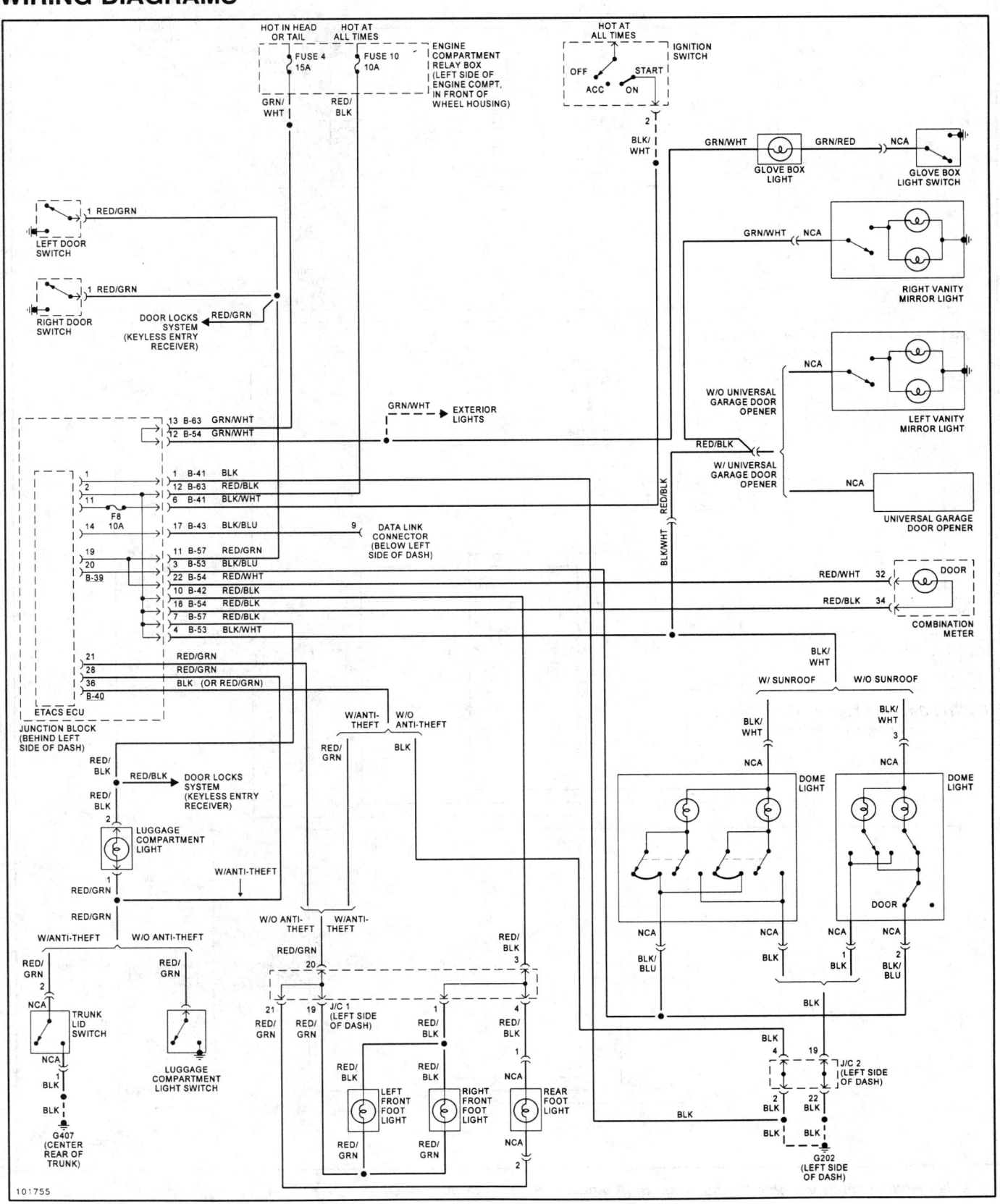

Fig. 1: Illumination/Interior Lights Wiring Diagram (Avenger & Sebring Coupe – 1 Of 2)

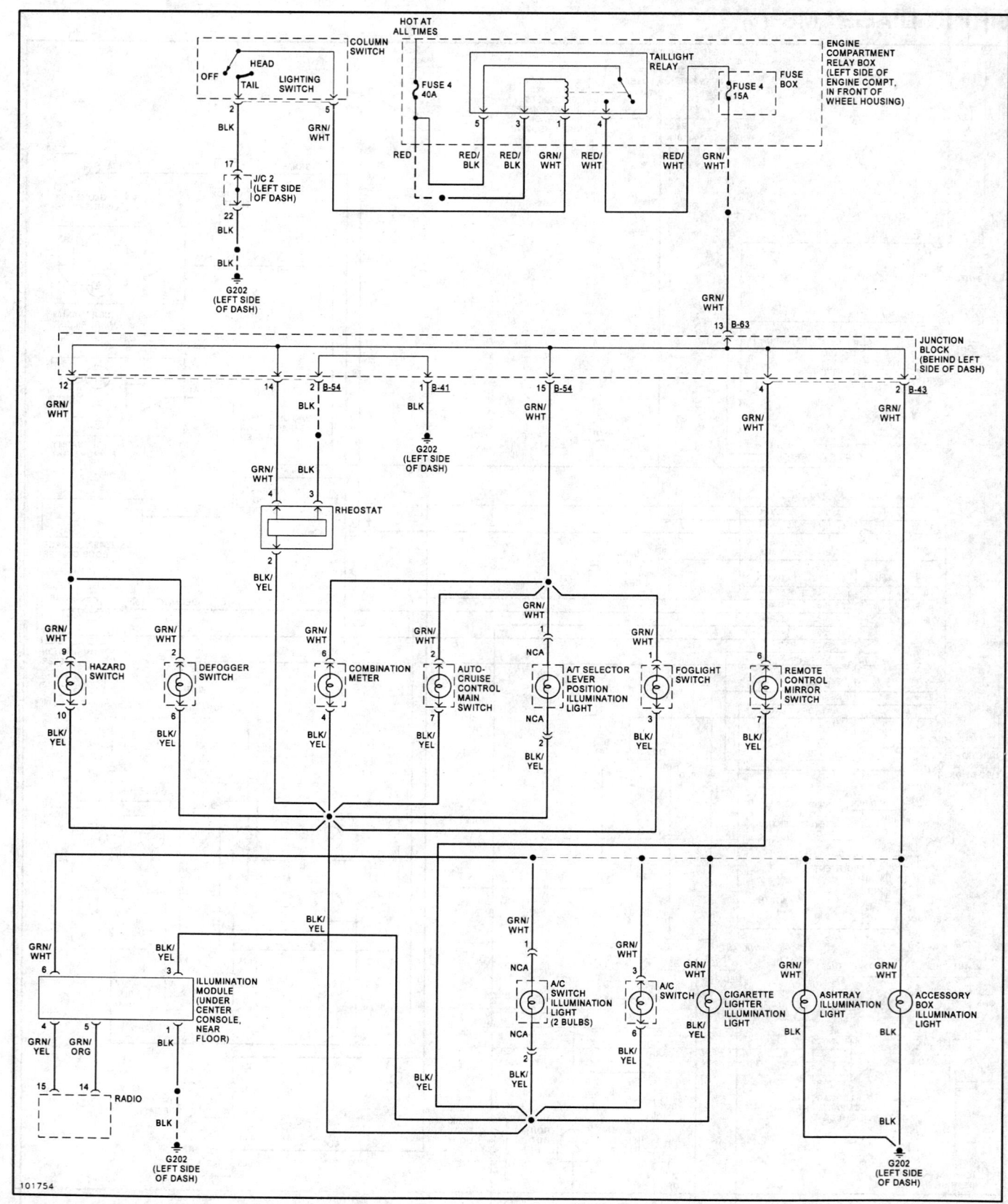

Fig. 2: Illumination/Interior Lights Wiring Diagram (Avenger & Sebring Coupe – 2 Of 2)

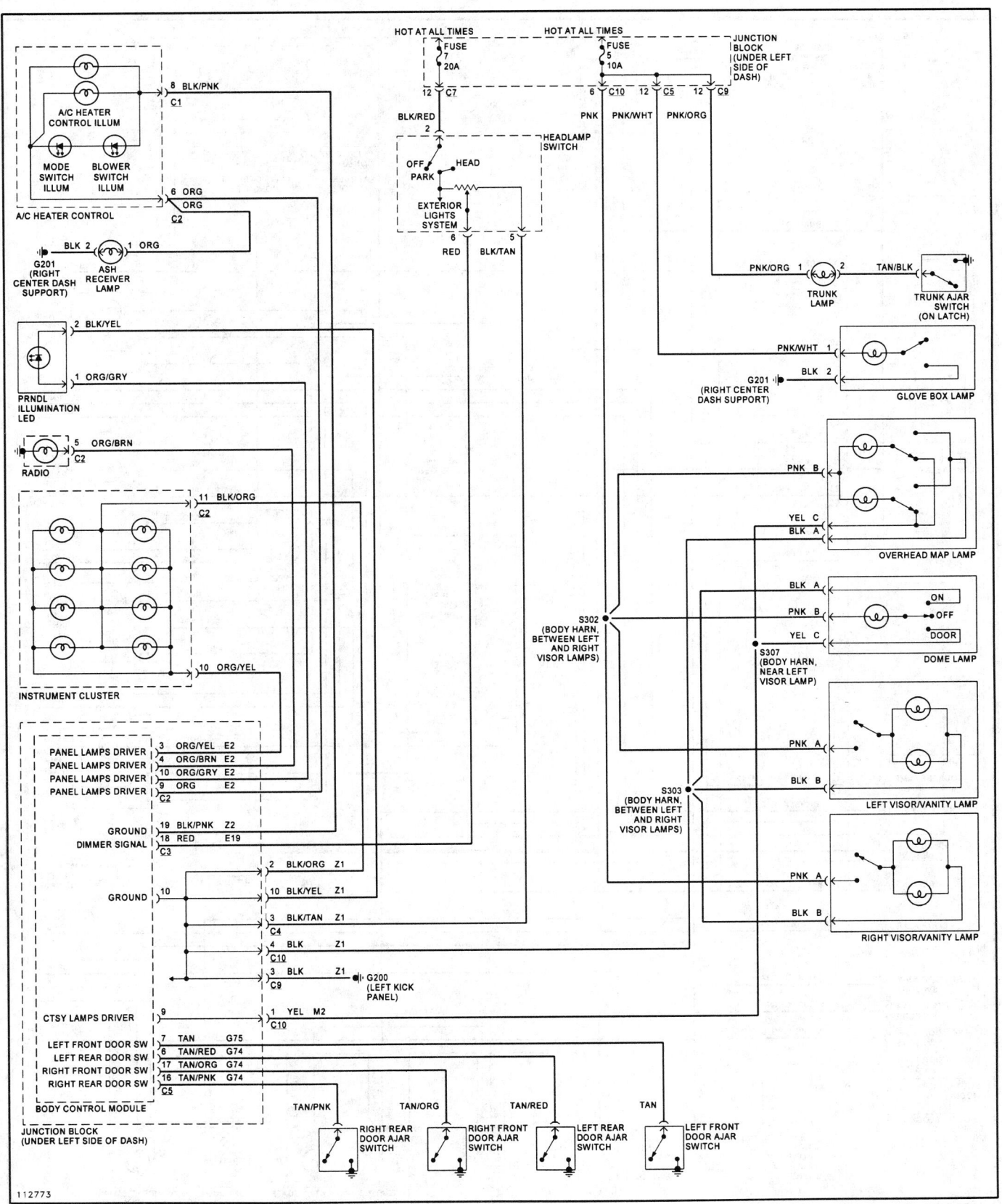

Fig. 3: Illumination/Interior Lights Wiring Diagram (Breeze, Cirrus & Stratus)

112773

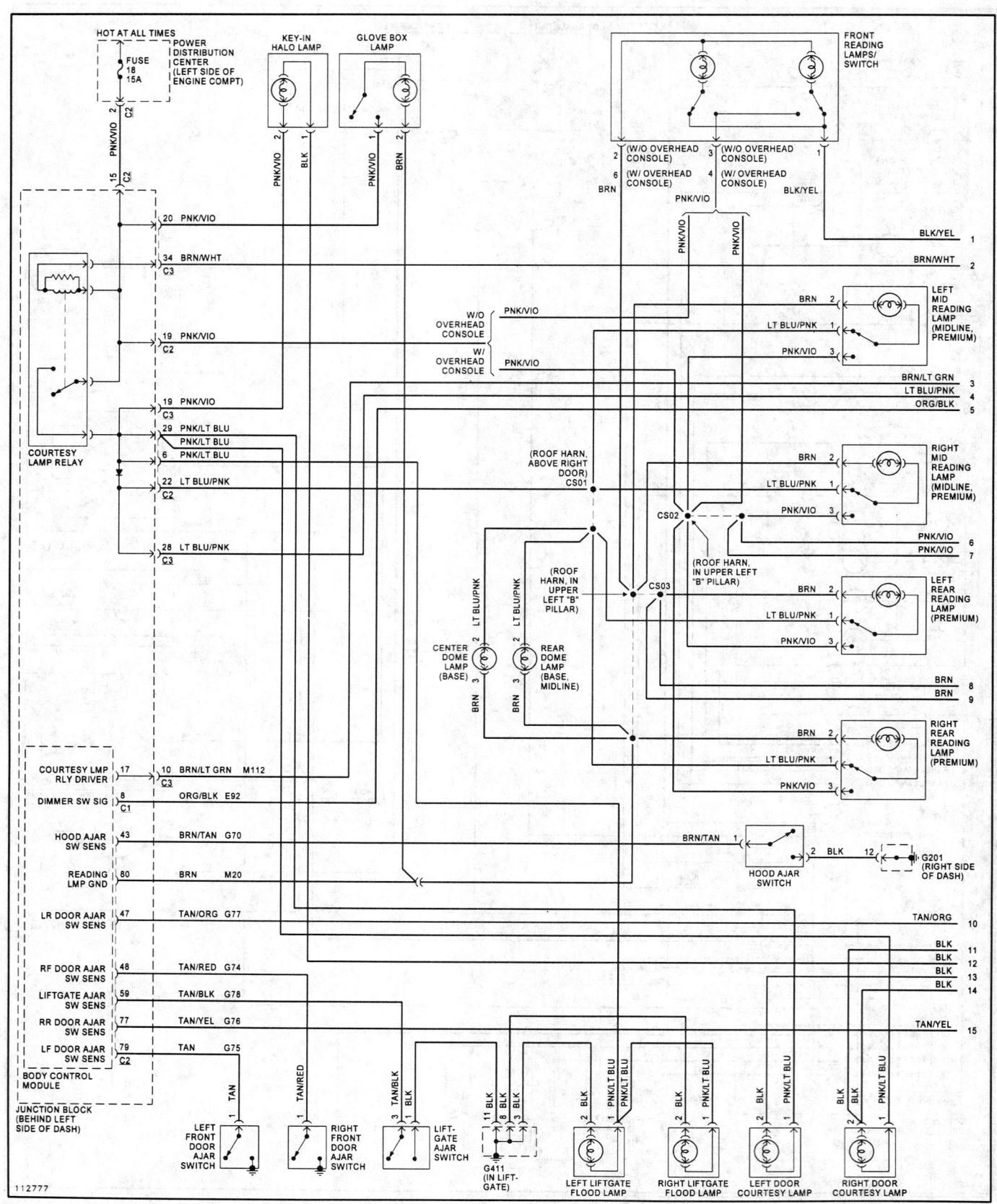

Fig. 4: Illumination/Interior Lights Wiring Diagram (Caravan, Town & Country, & Voyager – 1 Of 2)

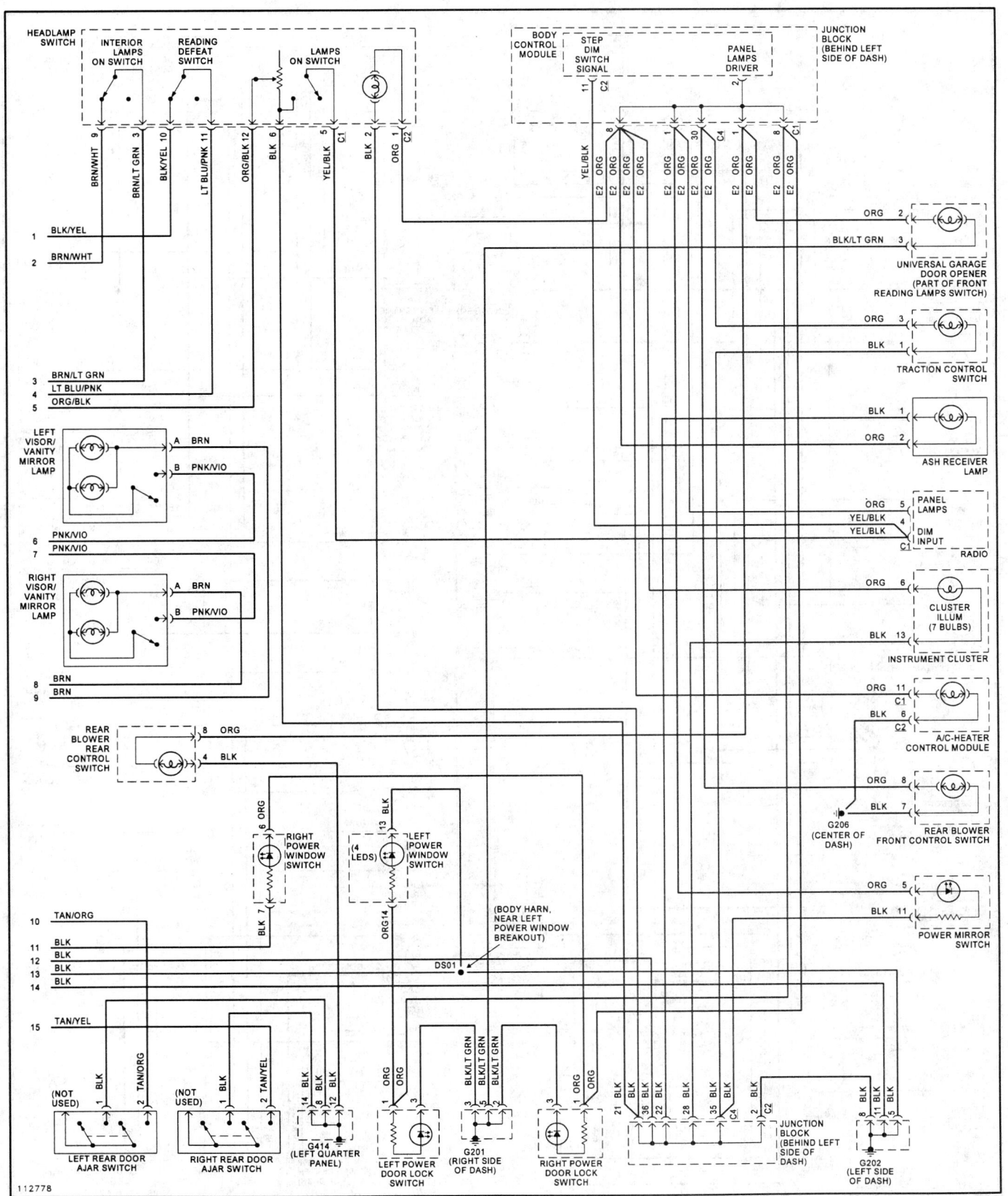

Fig. 5: Illumination/Interior Lights Wiring Diagram (Caravan, Town & Country, & Voyager – 2 Of 2)

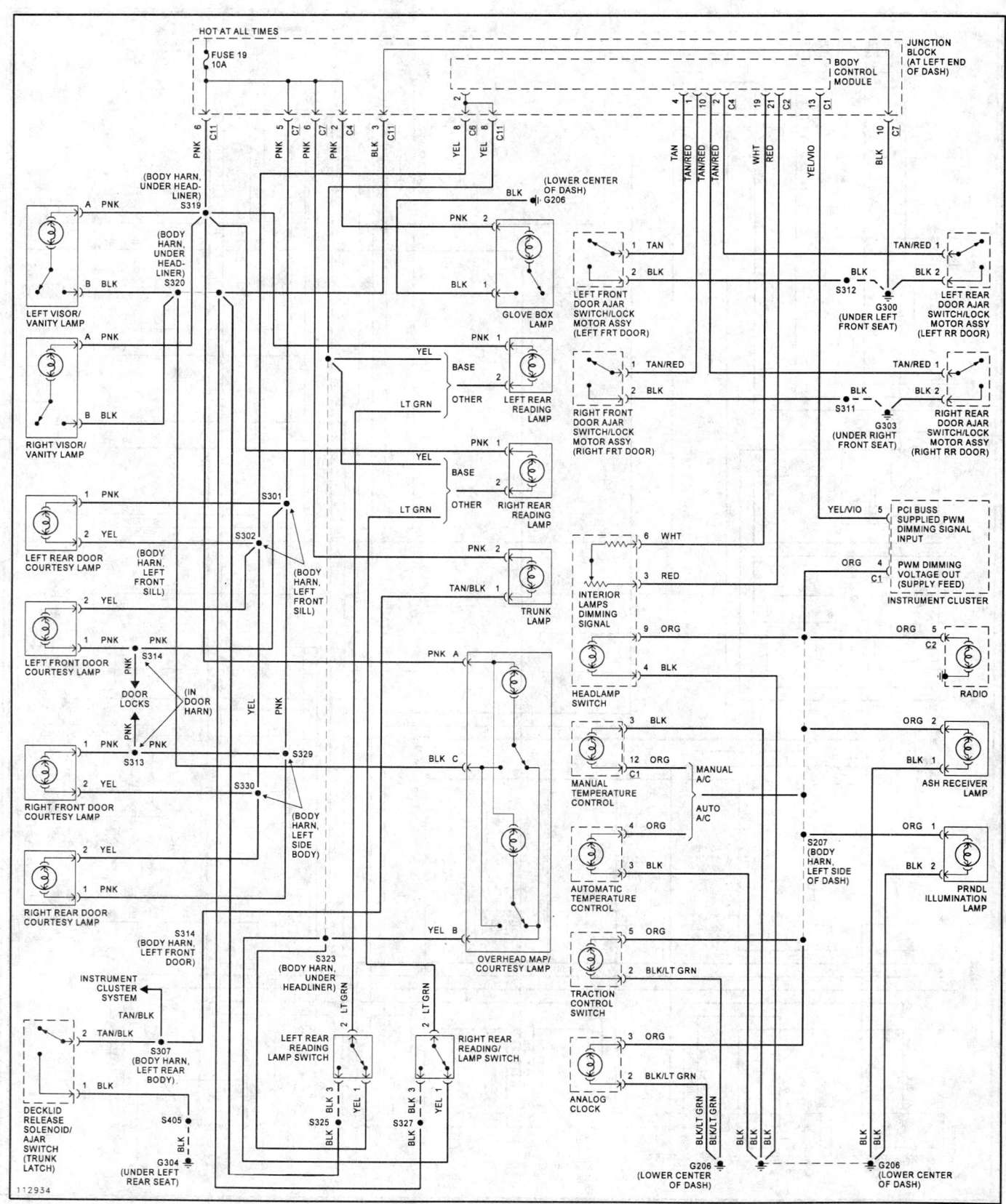

Fig. 6: Illumination/Interior Lights Wiring Diagram (Concorde, Intrepid, LHS & 300M)

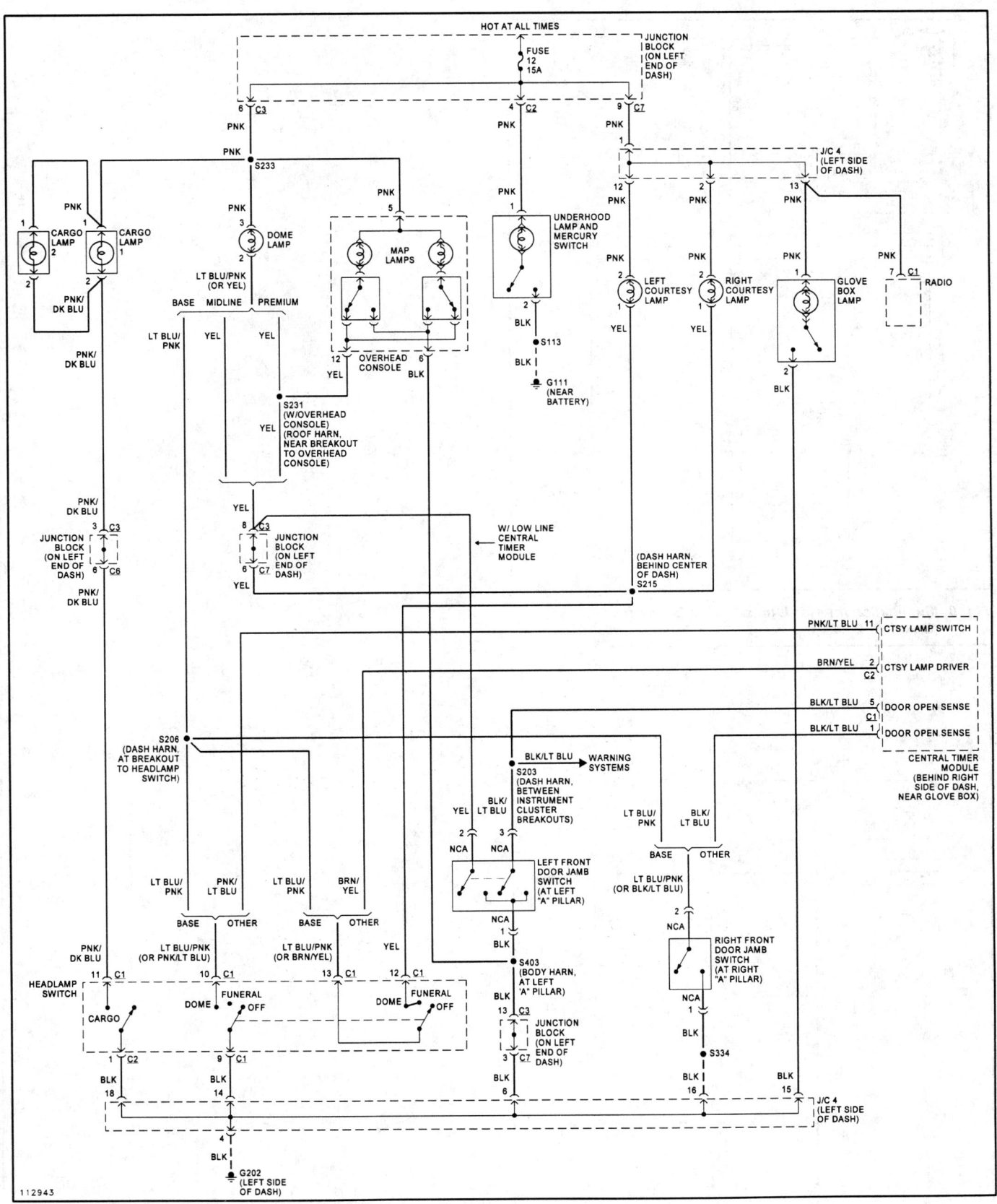

Fig. 7: Illumination/Interior Lights Wiring Diagram (Dakota – 1 Of 2)

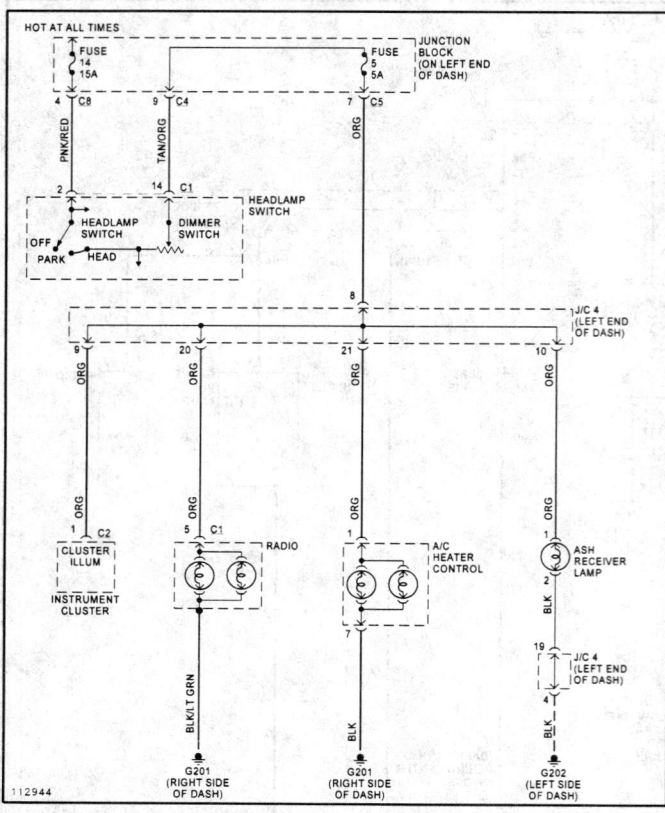

**Fig. 8: Illumination/Interior Lights Wiring Diagram
(Dakota – 2 Of 2)**

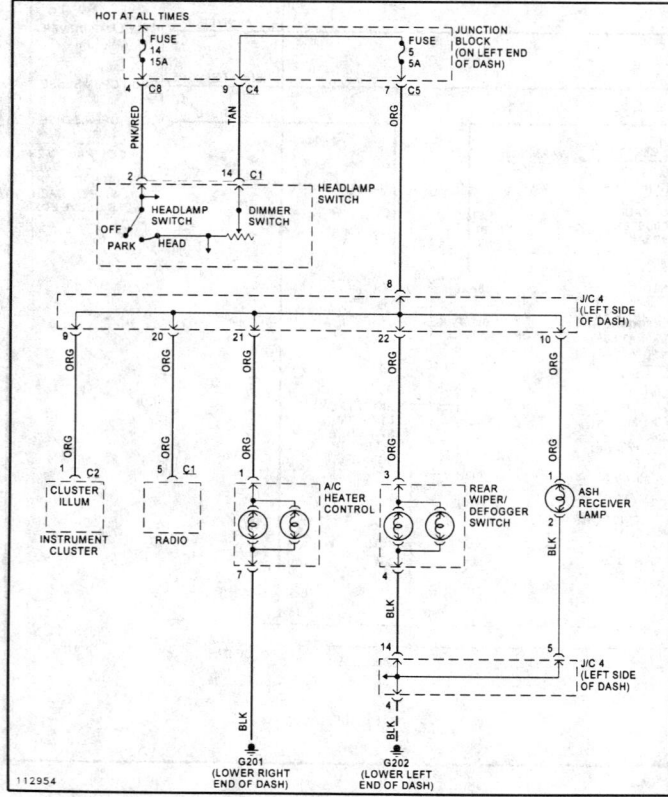

**Fig. 9: Illumination/Interior Lights Wiring Diagram
(Durango – 1 Of 2)**

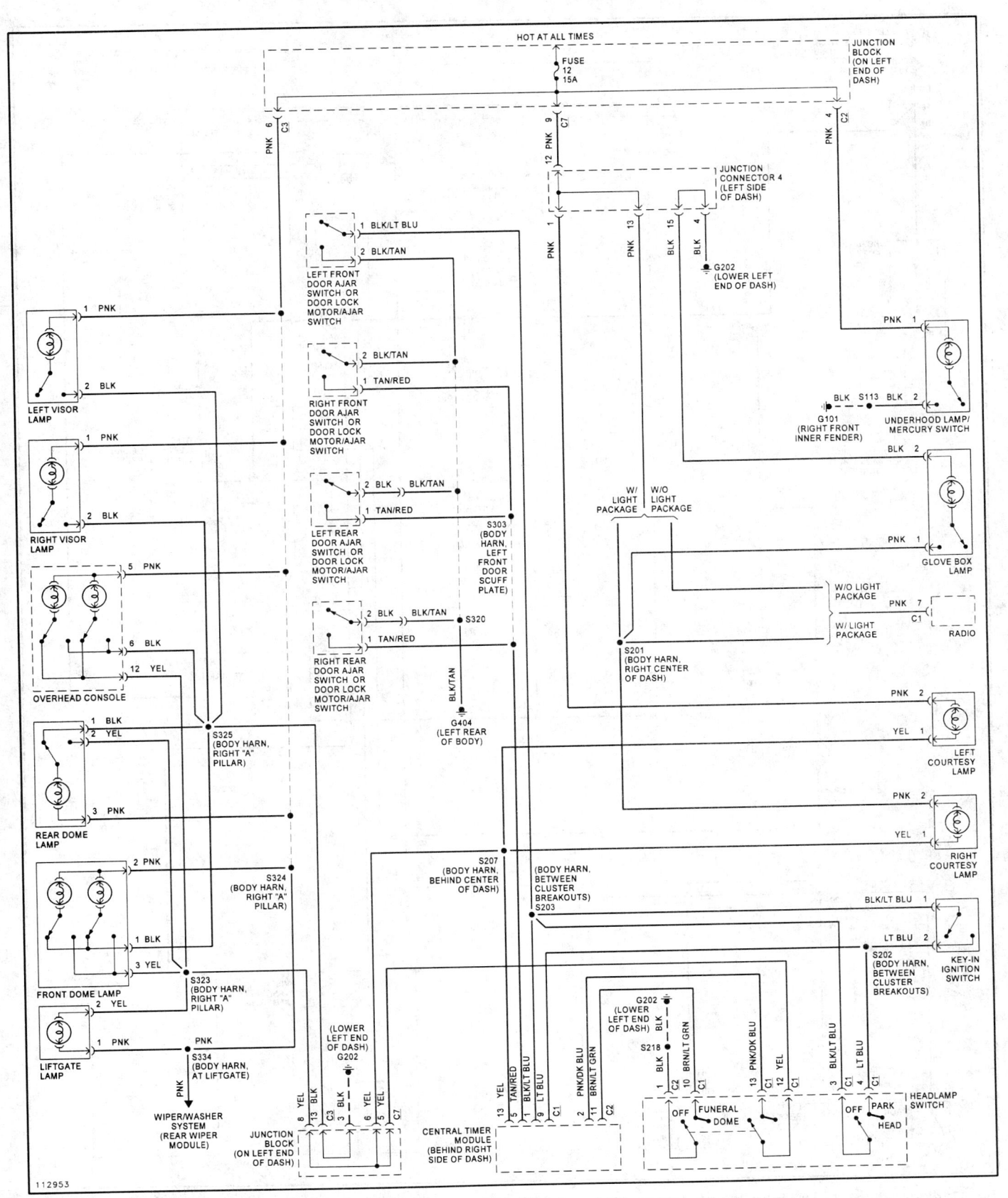

Fig. 10: Illumination/Interior Lights Wiring Diagram (Durango – 2 Of 2)

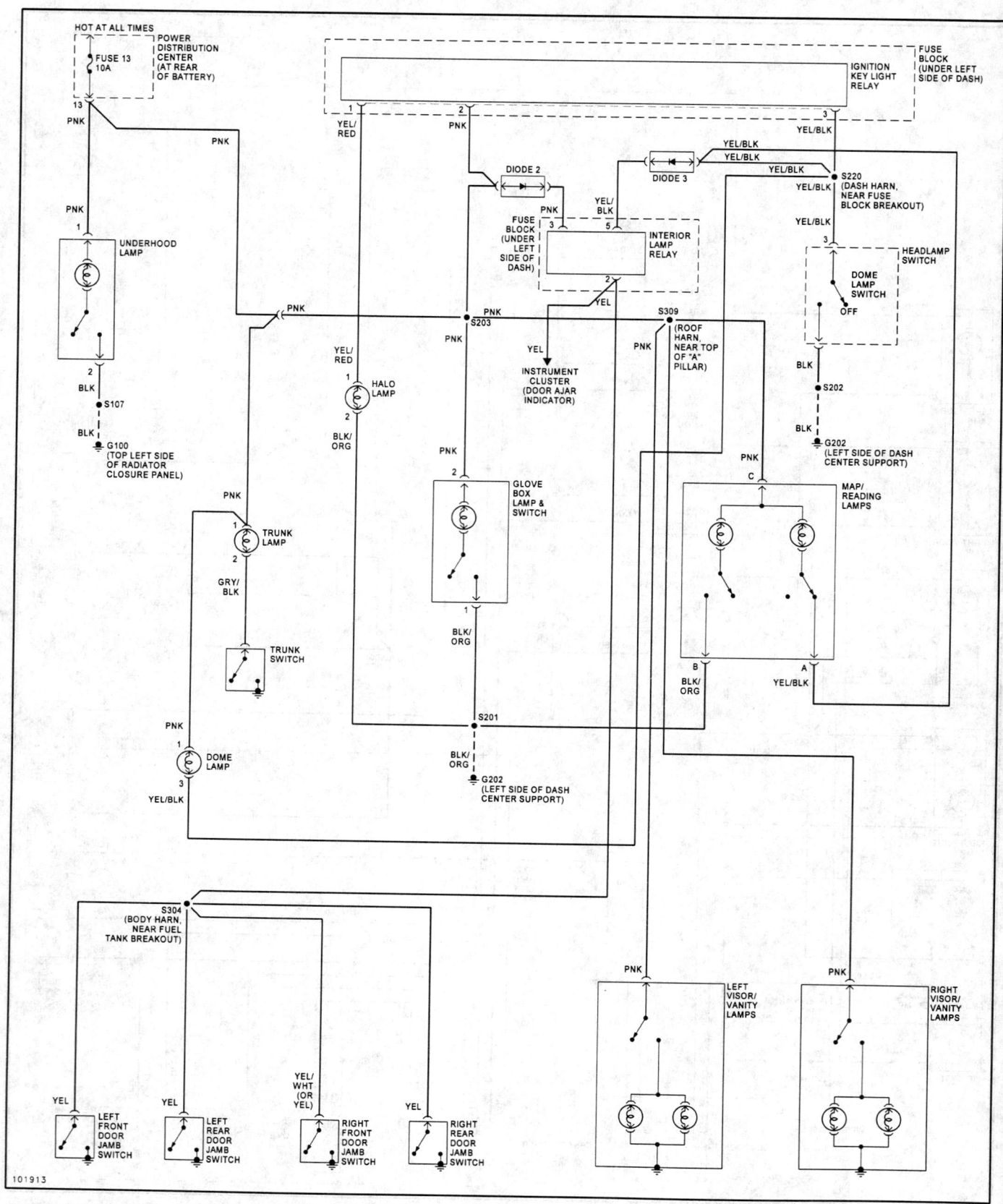

Fig. 11: Illumination/Interior Lights Wiring Diagram (Neon – 1 Of 2)

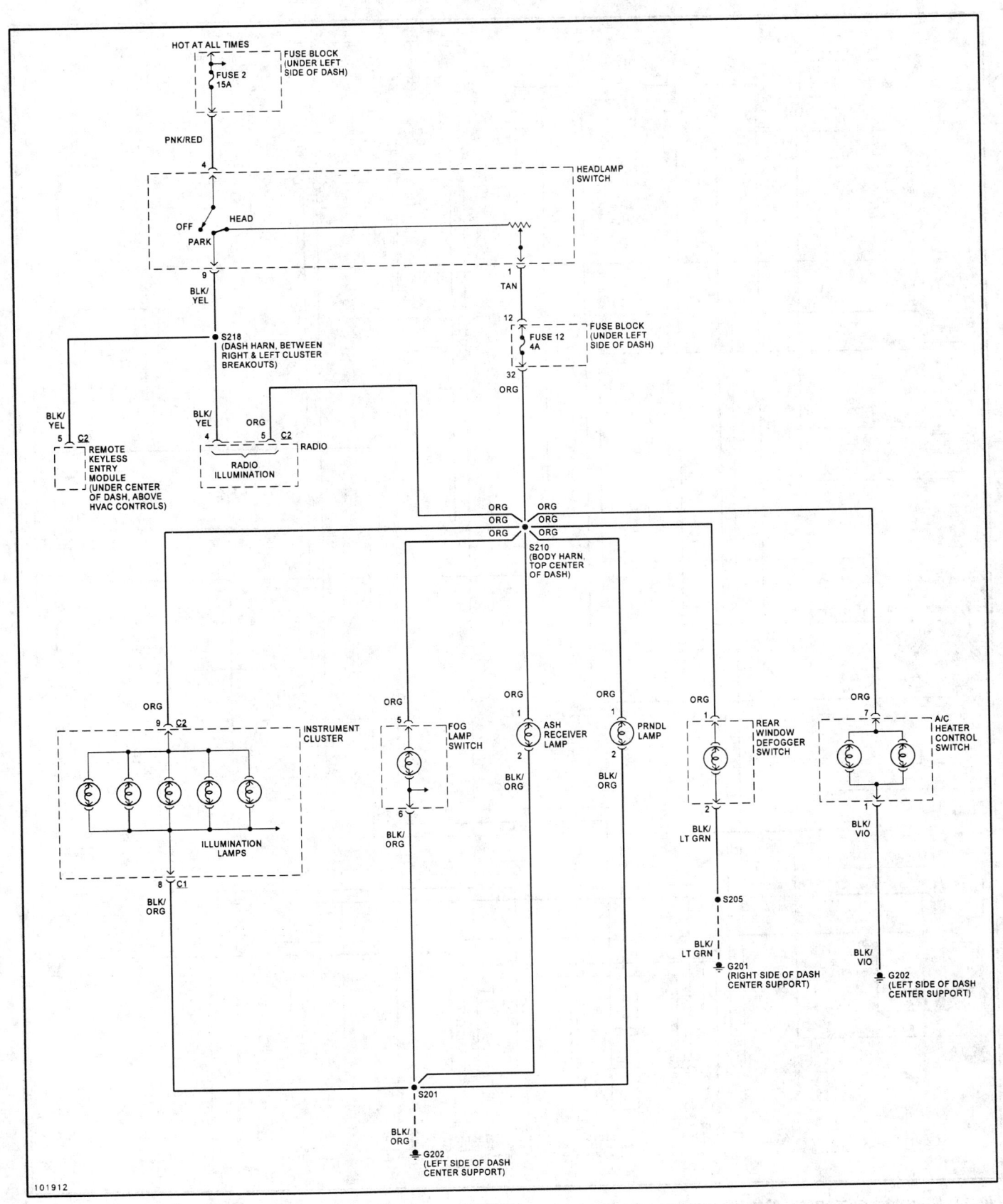

Fig. 12: Illumination/Interior Lights Wiring Diagram (Neon – 2 Of 2)

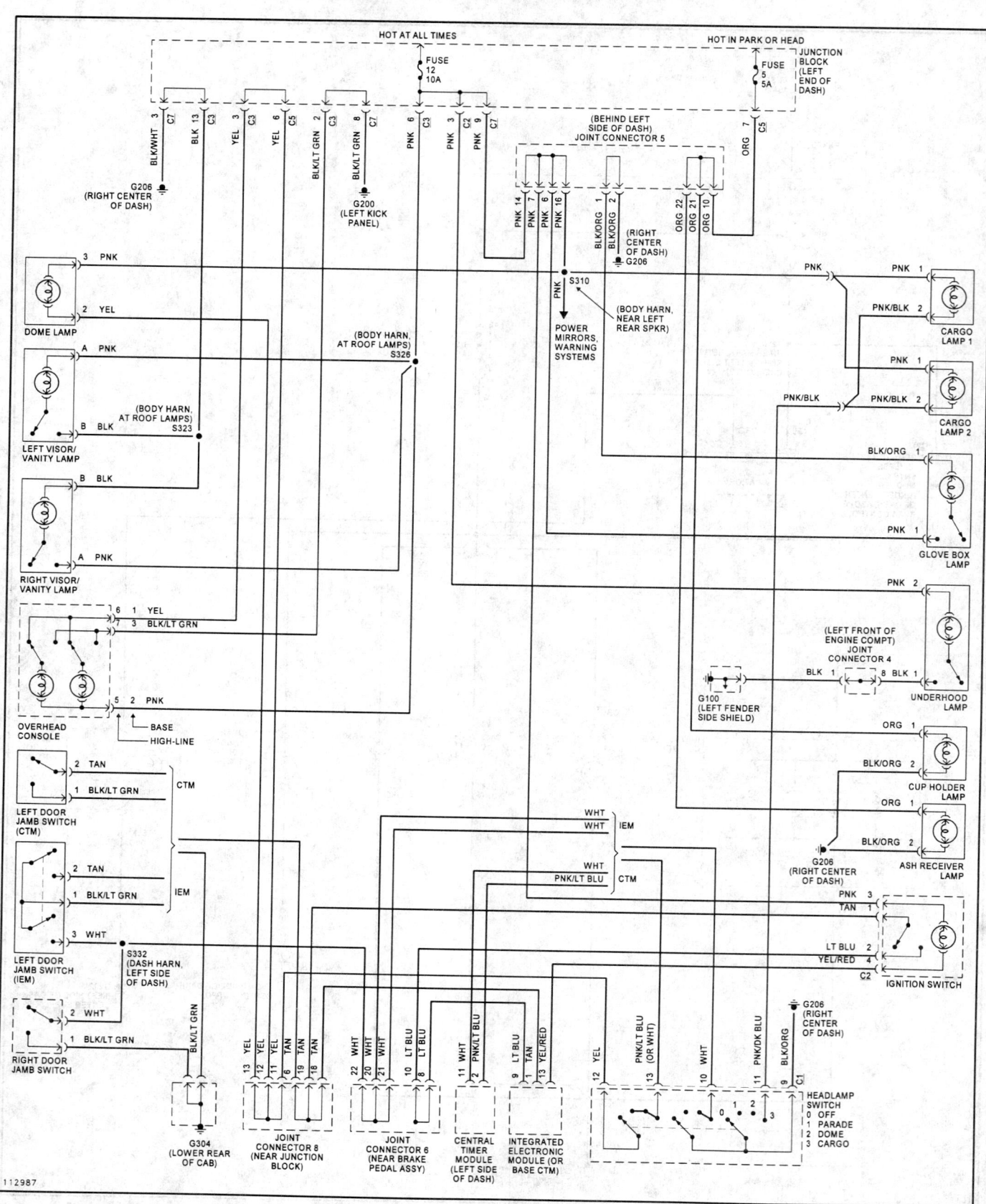

Fig. 13: Illumination/Interior Lights Wiring Diagram (Ram Pickup – 1 Of 2)

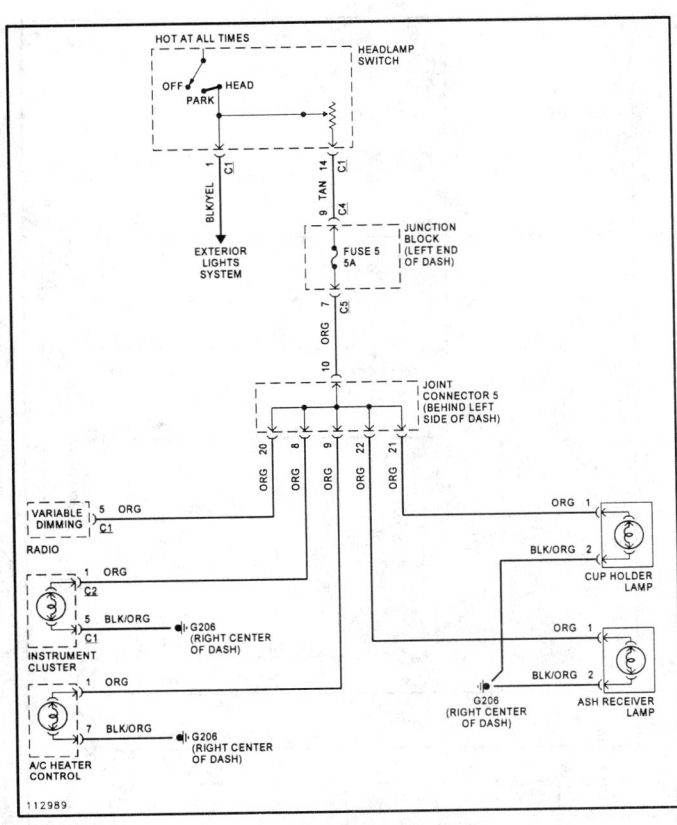

Fig. 14: Illumination/Interior Lights Wiring Diagram
(Ram Pickup – 2 Of 2)

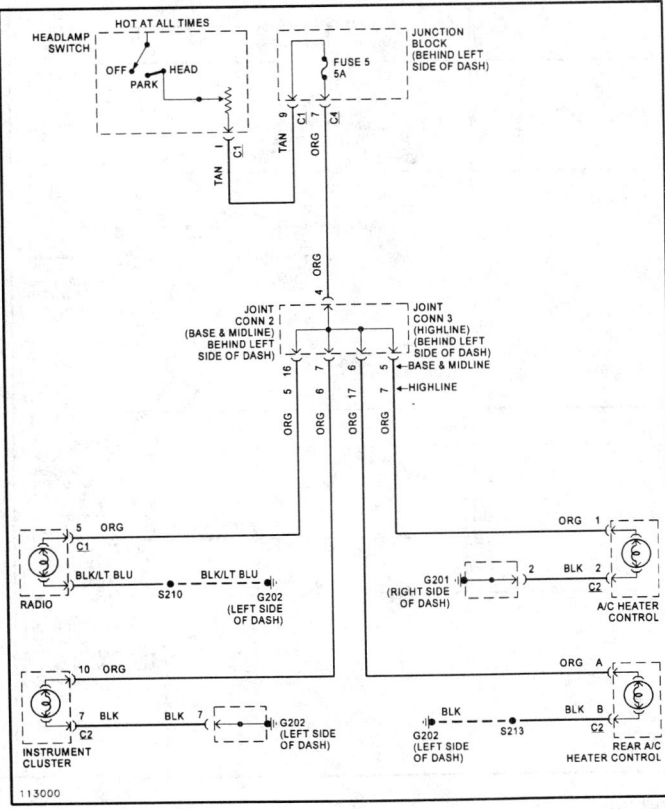

Fig. 15: Illumination/Interior Lights Wiring Diagram
(Ram Van & Ram Wagon – 1 Of 2)

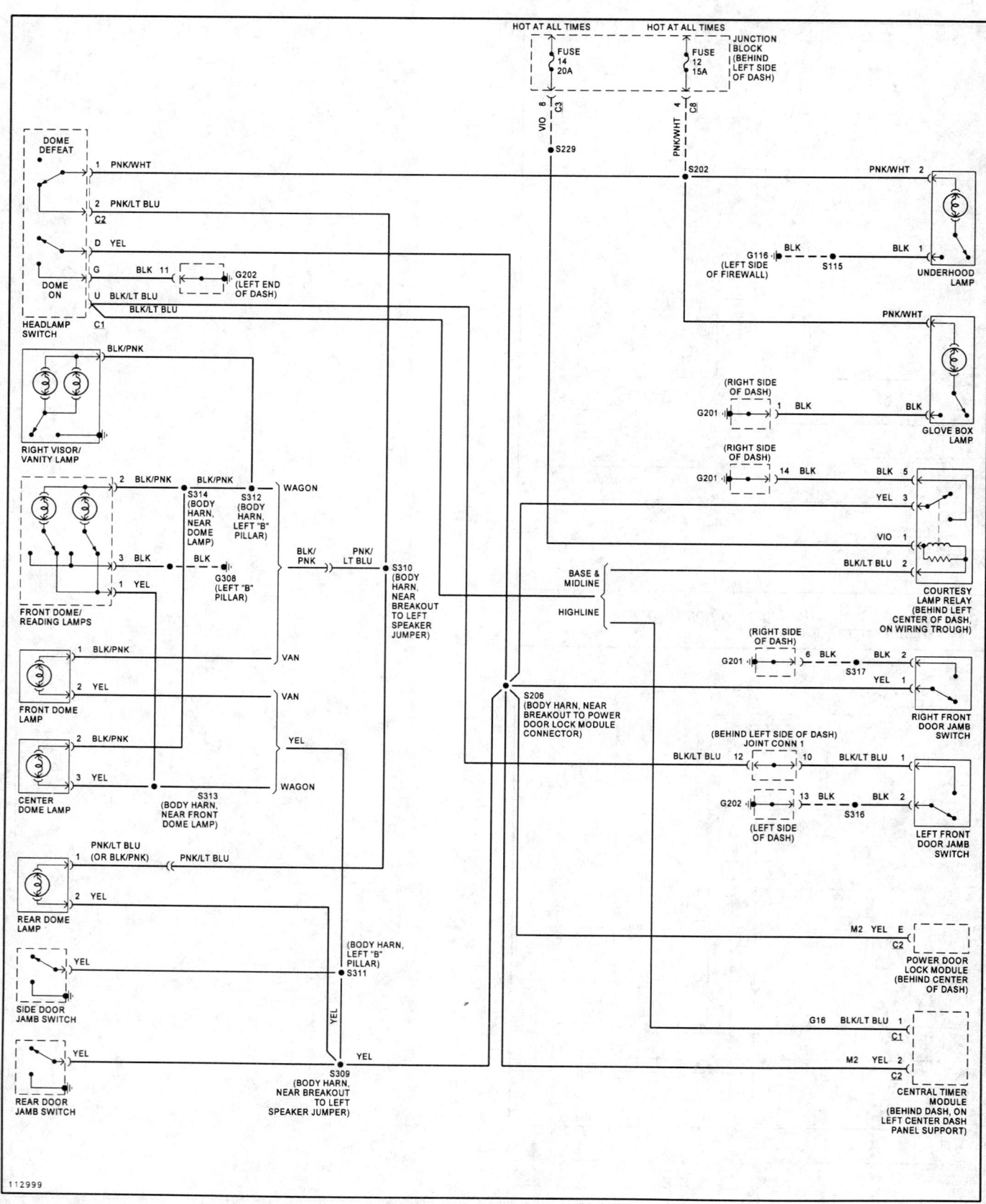

Fig. 16: Illumination/Interior Lights Wiring Diagram (Ram Van & Ram Wagon – 2 Of 2)

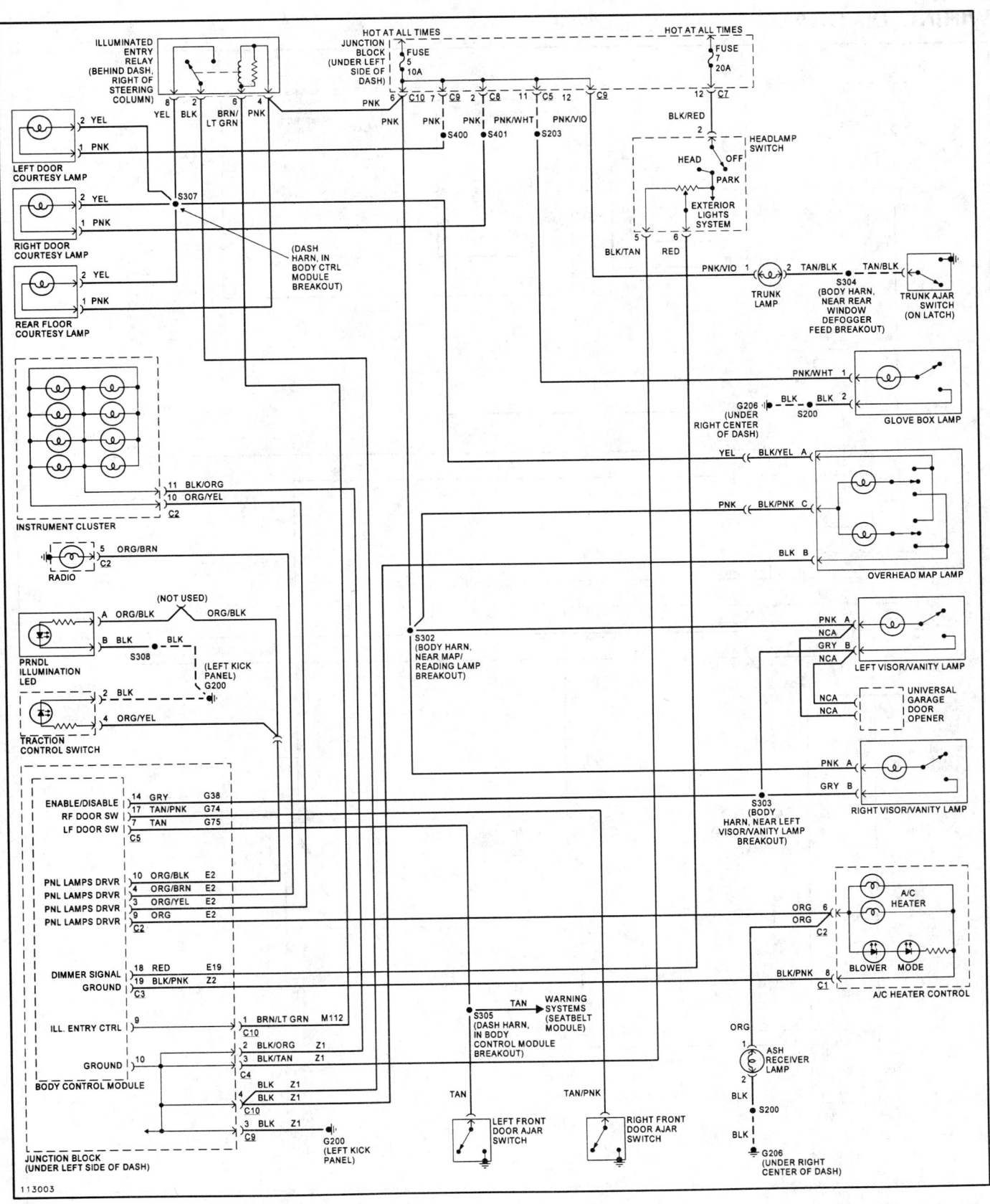

Fig. 17: Illumination/Interior Lights Wiring Diagram (Sebring Convertible)

113003

WIRING DIAGRAMS

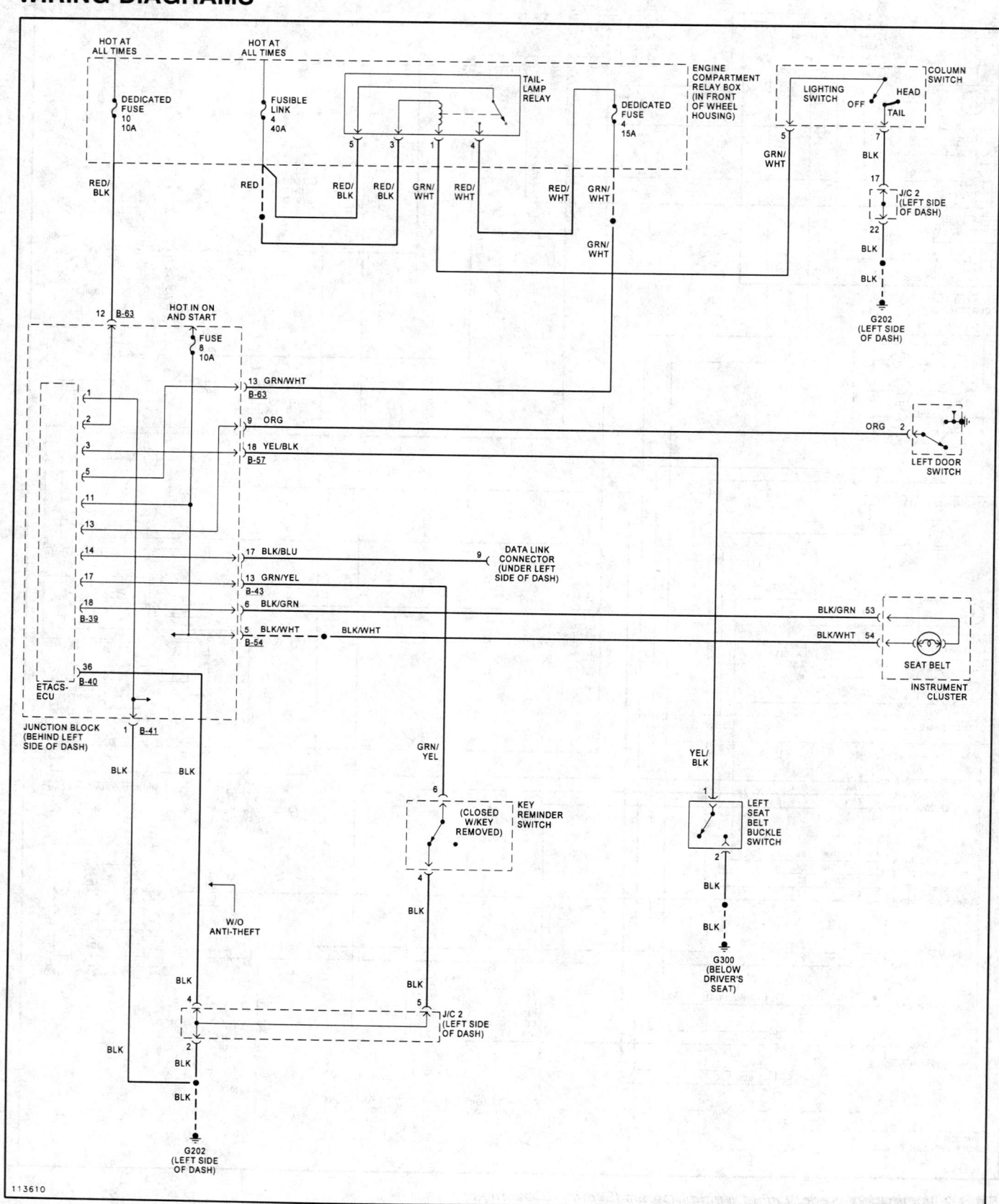

Fig. 1: Warning Systems Wiring Diagram (Avenger & Sebring Coupe)

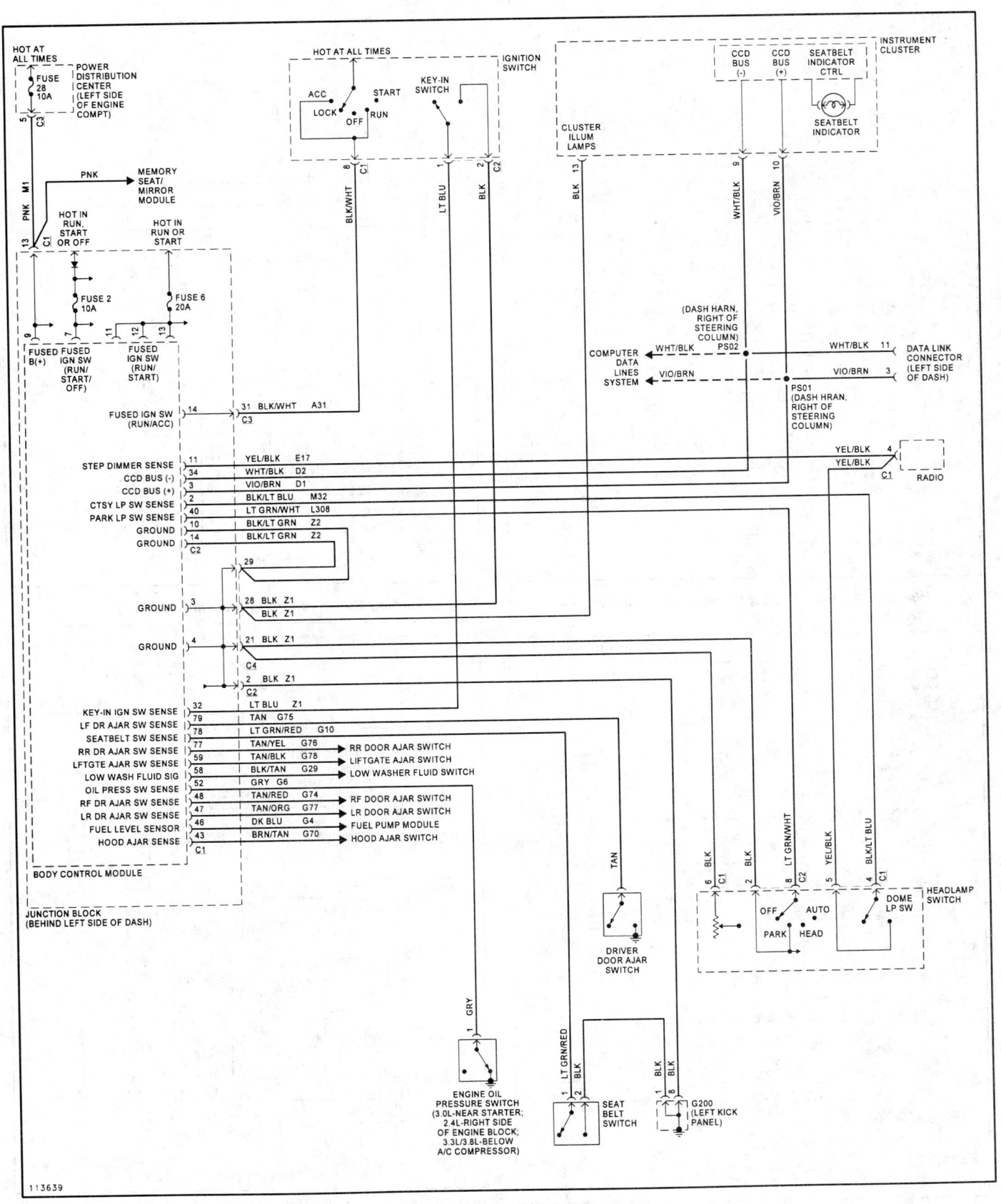

Fig. 2: Warning Systems Wiring Diagram (Caravan, Town & Country, & Voyager)

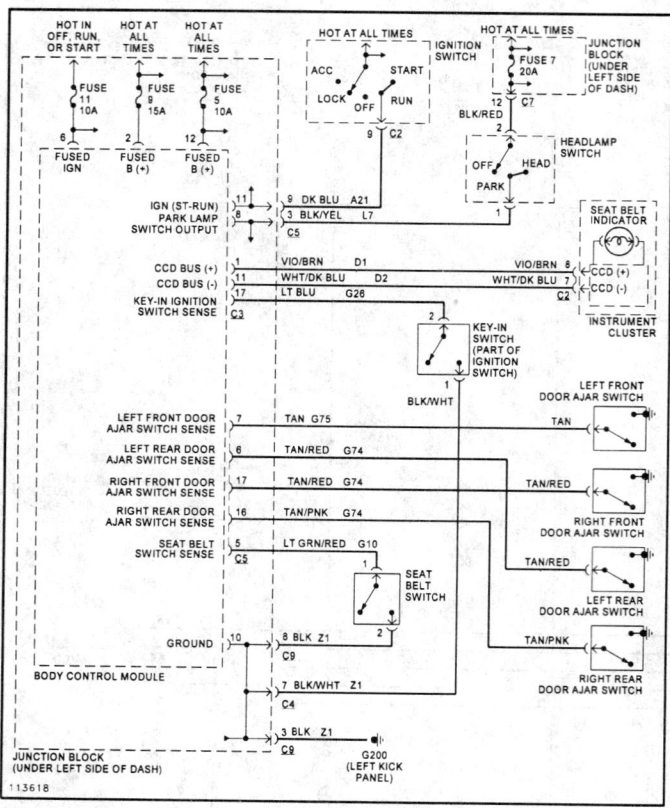

Fig. 3: Warning Systems Wiring Diagram (Breeze, Cirrus & Stratus)

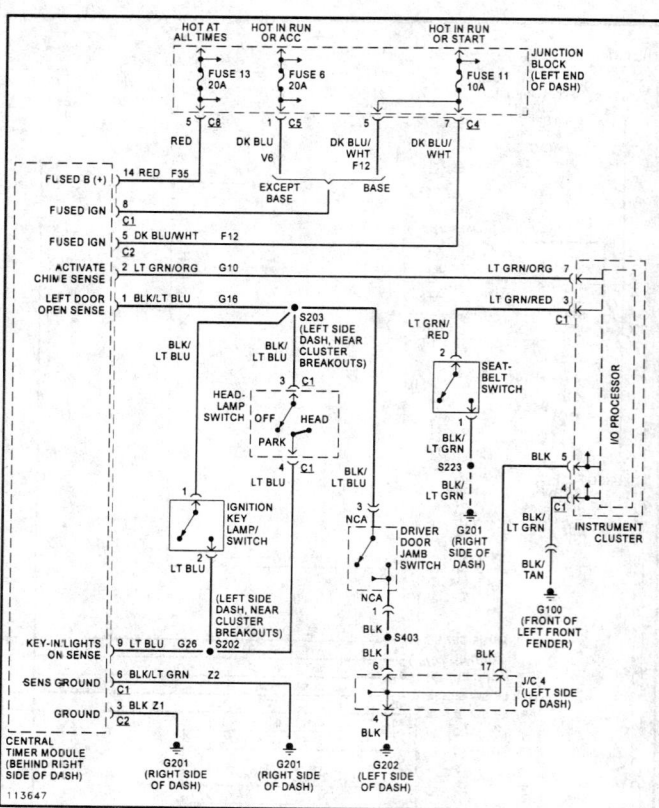

Fig. 5: Warning Systems Wiring Diagram (Dakota)

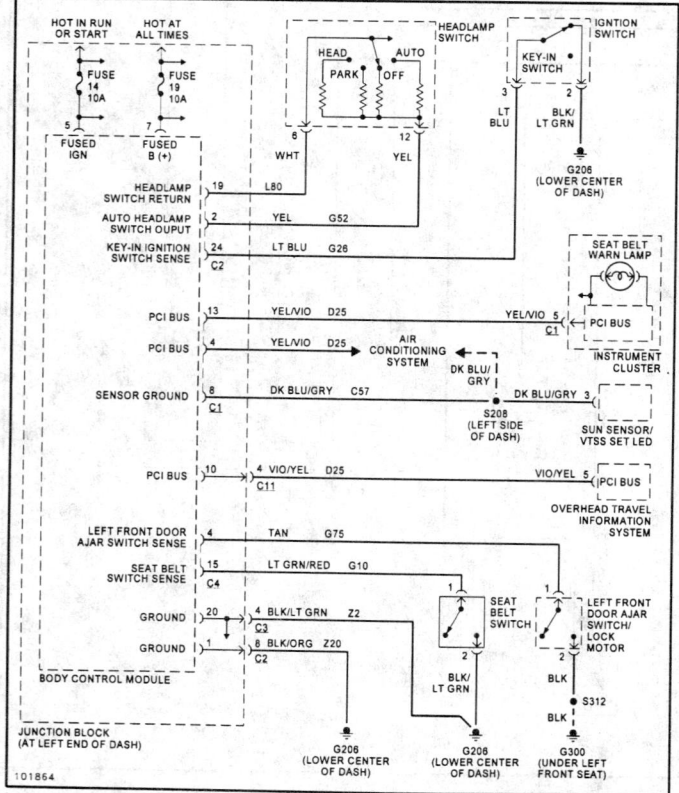

Fig. 4: Warning Systems Wiring Diagram (Concorde, Intrepid, LHS & 300M)

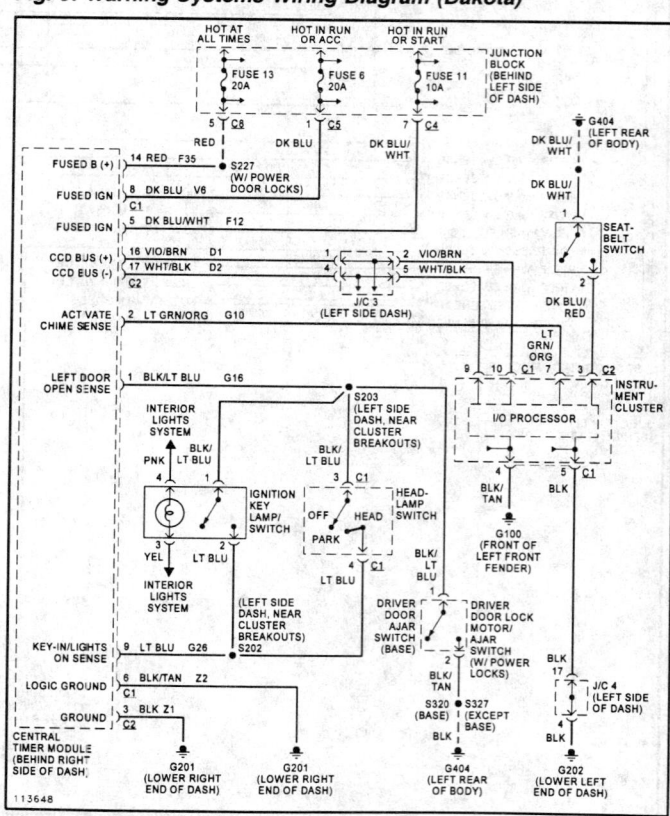

Fig. 6: Warning Systems Wiring Diagram (Durango)

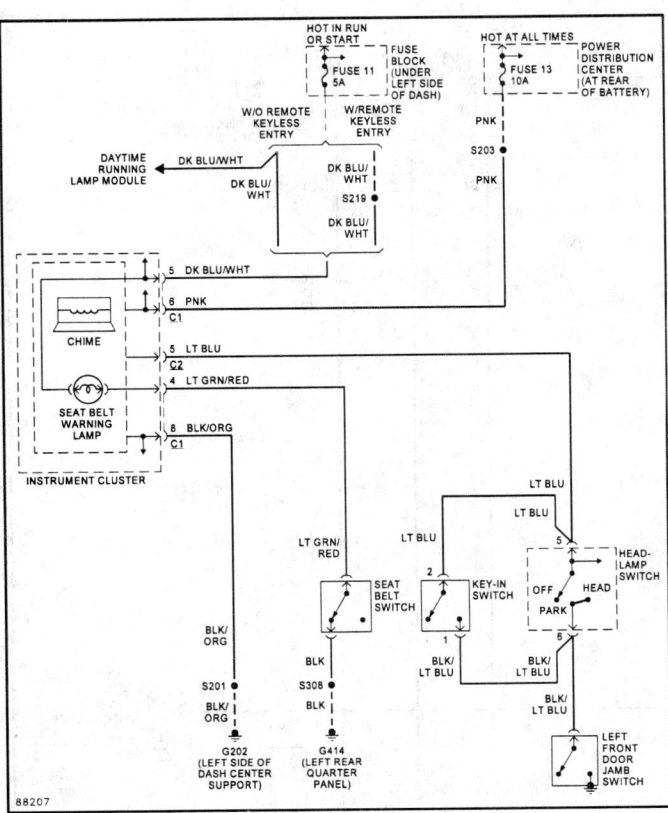

Fig. 7: Warning Systems Wiring Diagram (Neon)

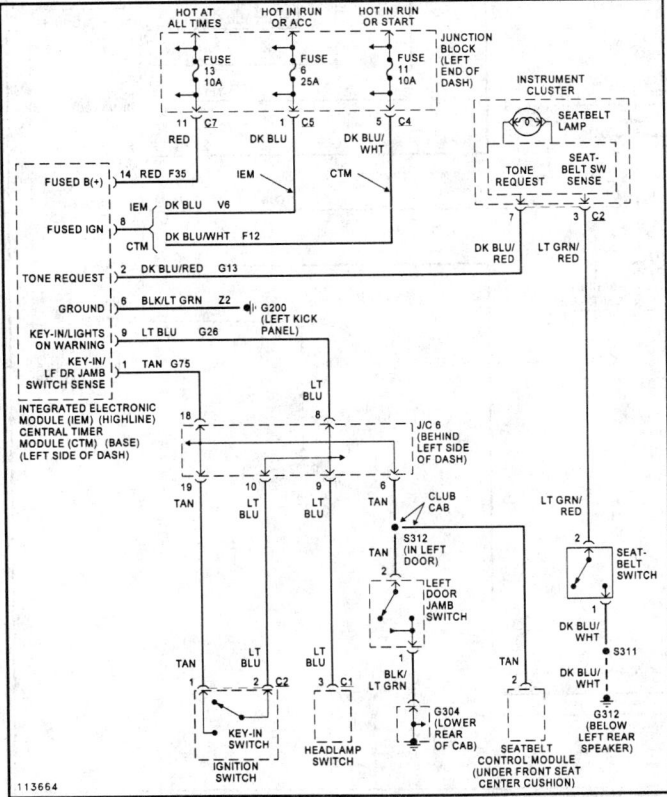

Fig. 8: Warning Systems Wiring Diagram (Ram Pickup)

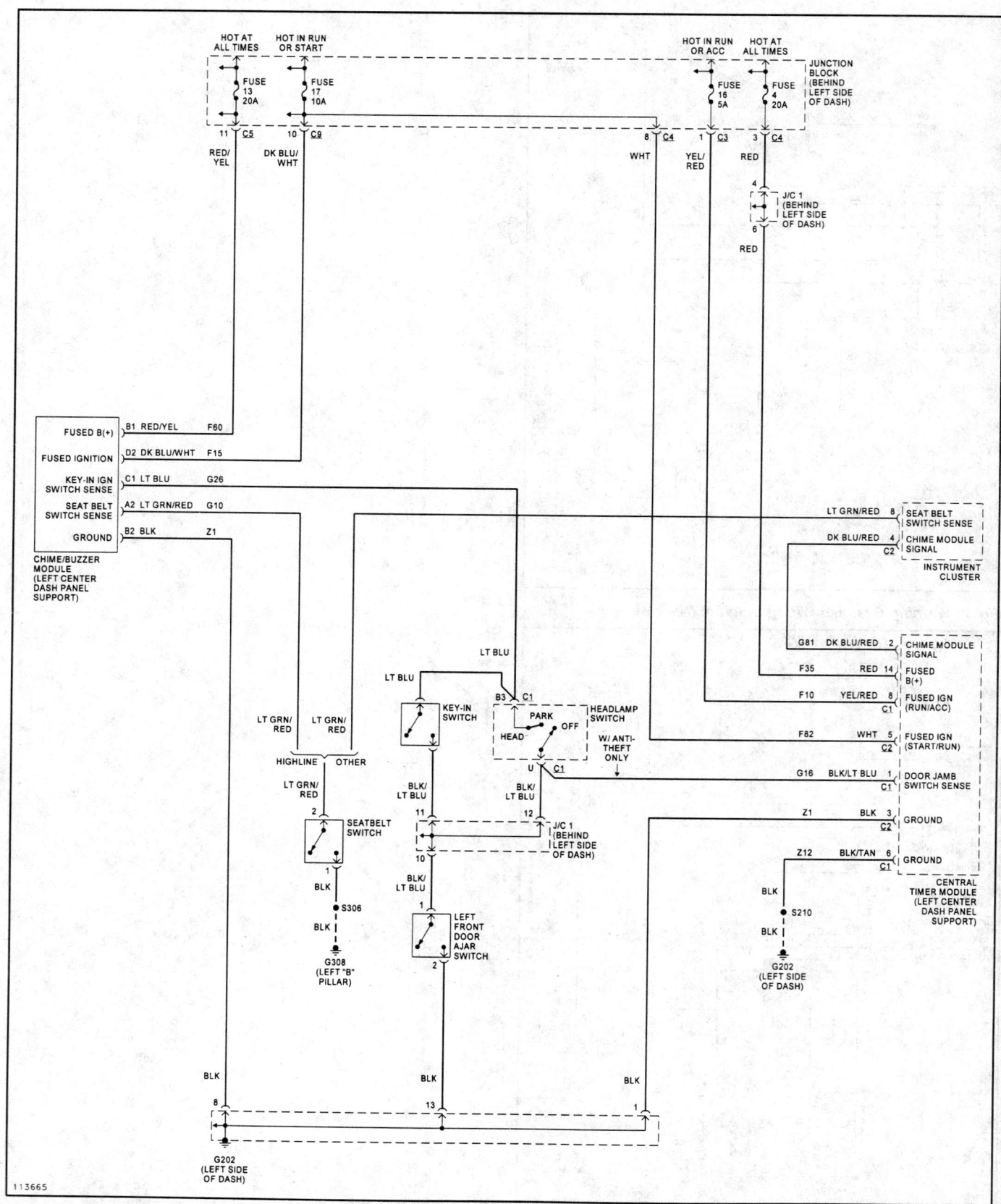

Fig. 9: Warning Systems Wiring Diagram (Ram Van & Ram Wagon)

113665

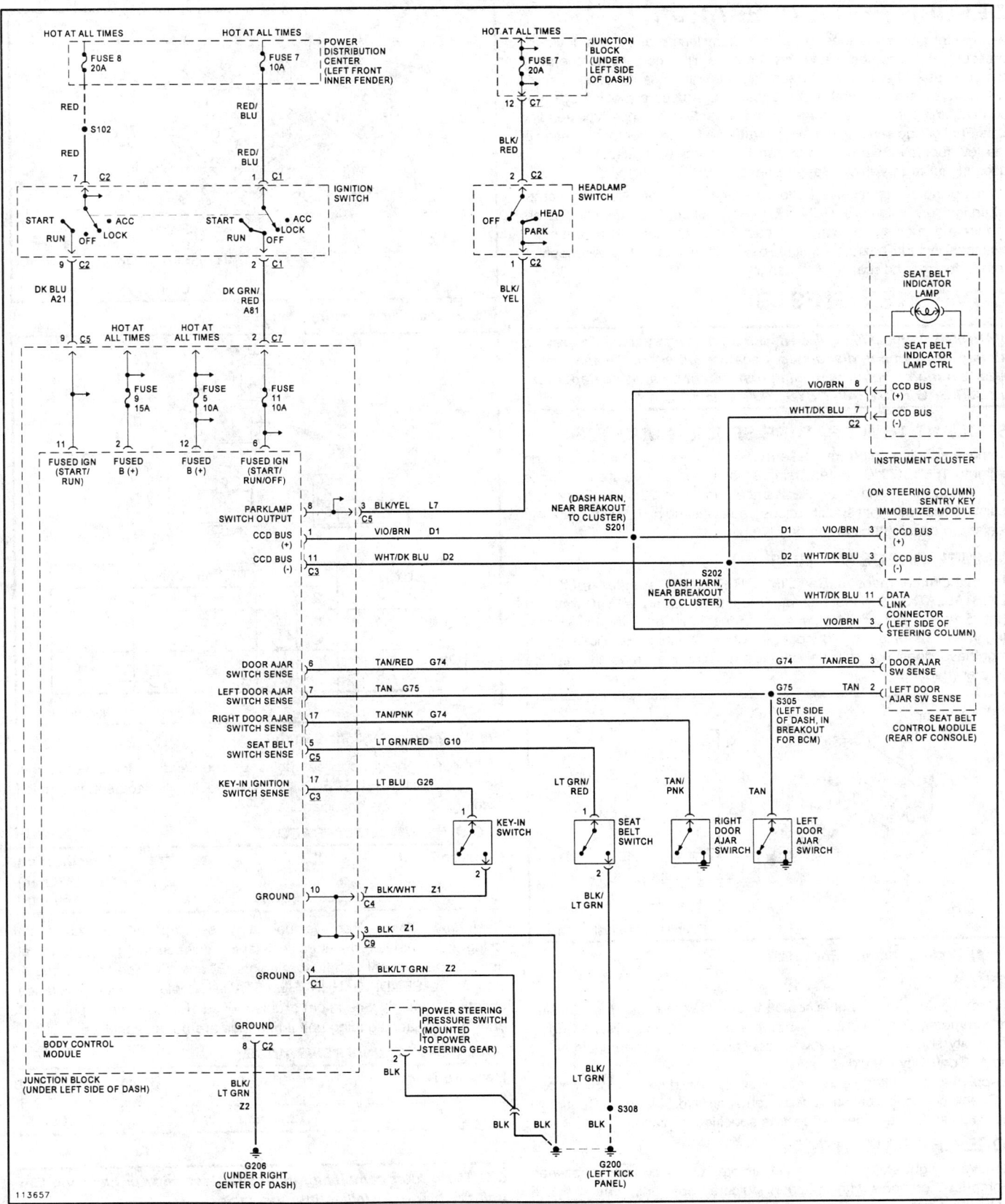

Fig. 10: Warning Systems Wiring Diagram (Sebring Convertible)

113657

1999 ACCESSORIES & EQUIPMENT
Analog Instrument Panels – Avenger & Sebring Coupe

DESCRIPTION & OPERATION

Instrument cluster gauges include: coolant temperature, fuel level, oil pressure, speedometer and tachometer. The coolant temperature gauge uses a thermistor-type sending unit, oil pressure gauge uses a bimetal-type sending unit, turbo boost gauge uses a moving coil type sending unit and the fuel gauge uses a variable resistance-type sending unit. Fuel gauge sending unit has an attached thermistor for operation of the low fuel level warning indicator. Speedometer is electric type and uses signal from Vehicle Speed Sensor (VSS).

Warning indicators receive battery voltage from fuse No. 8 (10-amp) when ignition switch is in RUN or START position. All warning indicators require a ground signal to activate each indicator light. Instrument panel switches include hazard, foglight, panel illumination dimmer rheostat, rear defogger and rear wiper/washer.

COMPONENT TESTS

WARNING: Vehicle is equipped with an air bag system. To prevent air bag deployment, disconnect negative battery cable and wait at least 2 minutes before servicing instrument cluster. See appropriate AIR BAG RESTRAINT SYSTEMS article.

COOLANT TEMPERATURE SENDING UNIT TEST

Remove sending unit from intake manifold. Dip sensor end of sending unit into 158°F (70°C) water. Using an ohmmeter, measure resistance between terminal and case. Resistance should be 90.5-117.5 ohms. If resistance is not within specifications, replace sending unit. Apply thread sealant to sending unit before installing.

DIMMER RHEOSTAT TEST

Remove dimmer rheostat. See DIMMER RHEOSTAT under REMOVAL & INSTALLATION. Connect dimmer rheostat to battery with 40-watt test light. *See Fig. 1.* Turn rheostat knob to full right and full left positions. Brightness of bulb should change without flashing or flickering. If brightness does not change or does not change smoothly, replace dimmer rheostat.

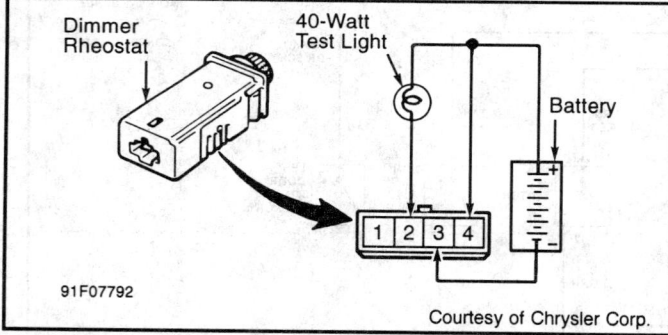

Fig. 1: Testing Dimmer Rheostat

RELAY TEST

1) Remove relay from engine compartment relay box. *See Fig. 2.* Using an ohmmeter, check continuity between relay terminals No. 1 and 3. Continuity should exist. Check for continuity between terminals No. 4 and 5. Continuity should not exist.
2) Apply battery voltage to relay terminal No. 1 and ground terminal No. 3. Check continuity between relay terminals No. 4 and 5. Continuity should exist. If relay does not test as specified, replace relay.

FOGLIGHT SWITCH TEST

Remove foglight switch. Using an ohmmeter, check continuity between appropriate terminals with switch in indicated positions. *See Fig. 3.* If continuity is not as specified, replace foglight switch.

FUEL GAUGE SENDING UNIT TEST

Float Height Measurement – Remove fuel gauge sending unit from fuel tank. Move float to highest point and measure height between point "F" and sending unit cover flange. *See Fig. 4.* Move float to lowest point

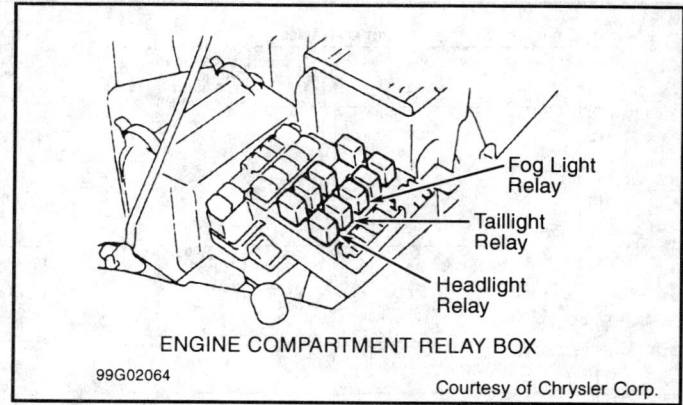

ENGINE COMPARTMENT RELAY BOX

99G02064

Courtesy of Chrysler Corp.

Fig. 2: Locating & Testing Relays

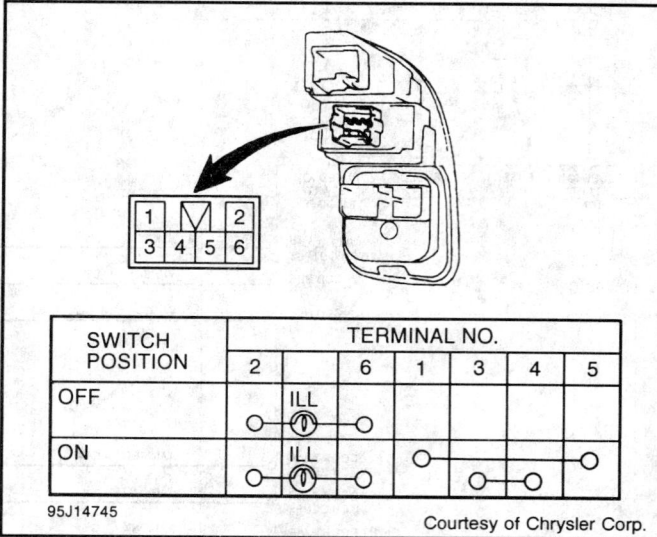

SWITCH POSITION	TERMINAL NO.					
	2	ILL	6	1	3	4	5
OFF	○	⊗	○				
ON	○	⊗	○	○	○ — ○		○

95J14745

Courtesy of Chrysler Corp.

Fig. 3: Testing Foglight Switch

and measure height between point "E" and sending unit cover flange. See FLOAT HEIGHT SPECIFICATIONS table. Replace sending unit if readings are not as specified.

FLOAT HEIGHT SPECIFICATIONS

Measure Point	Specification
F	1.13" (28.6 mm)
E	6.3" (160 mm)

Resistance Test – Remove fuel gauge sending unit from fuel tank. Using an ohmmeter, measure resistance between fuel gauge terminal and ground terminal with float at points "E" and "F". *See Figs. 4 and 5.* See FUEL SENDING UNIT RESISTANCE table. Ensure resistance changes smoothly when float arm is moved slowly between points "E" and "F". Replace sending unit if readings are not as specified.

FUEL SENDING UNIT RESISTANCE

Measure Point	Resistance (Ohms)
F	2-6
E	105-119

CAUTION: After completing thermistor test, wipe or blow sending unit dry before installing into fuel tank.

Thermistor Test – 1) Remove fuel gauge sending unit from fuel tank. Using 12-volt test light with a 3.4-watt bulb, connect positive battery terminal to fuel gauge sending unit connector. *See Fig. 6.* Use jumper wire to ground fuel gauge sending unit connector to battery.

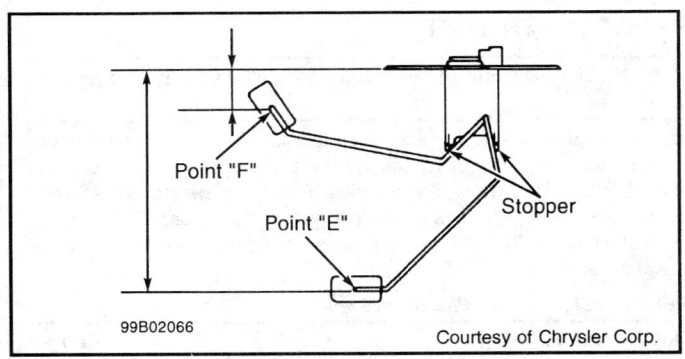

Fig. 4: Measuring Float Height

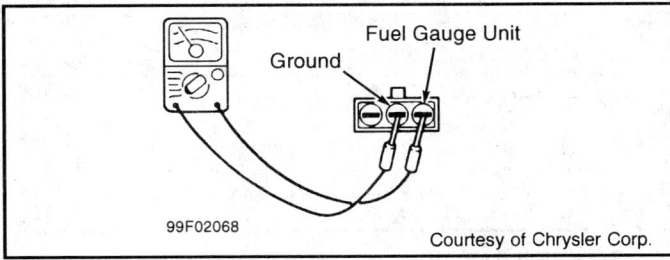

Fig. 5: Measuring Fuel Gauge Sending Unit Resistance

2) Submerge thermistor in container of water. If test light does not come on, thermistor is okay. If test light comes on, replace thermistor.

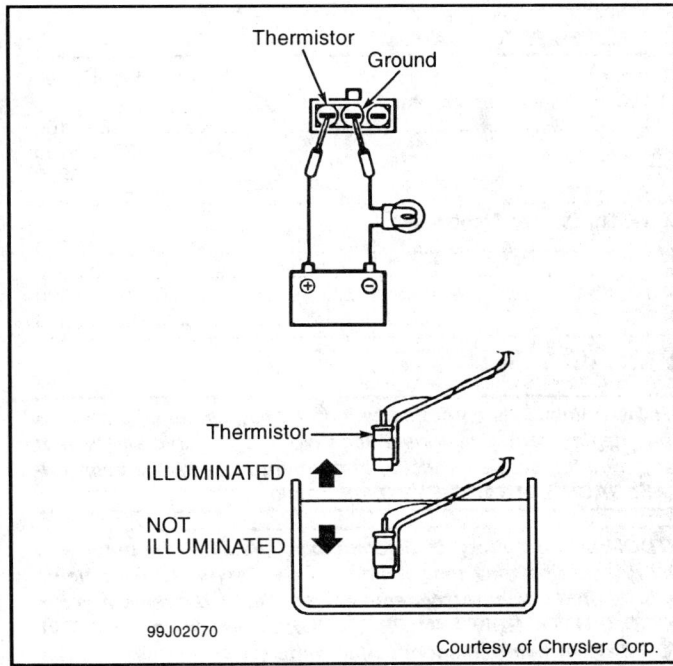

Fig. 6: Testing Thermistor

HAZARD WARNING SWITCH TEST

Remove hazard switch. See HAZARD WARNING LIGHT SWITCH, REAR DEFOGGER SWITCH & REAR WIPER/WASHER SWITCH under REMOVAL & INSTALLATION. Using an ohmmeter, check continuity between specified switch terminals with switch in appropriate position. See HAZARD WARNING SWITCH RESISTANCE table. See Fig. 7. If continuity is not as specified, replace hazard switch.

HAZARD WARNING SWITCH RESISTANCE

Switch Position	Between Terminals
OFF	5 & 7; [1]9 & 10
ON	1, 2 & 4; 5 & 6; [1]9 & 10

[1] – Terminals No. 9 and 10 are switch illumination circuit.

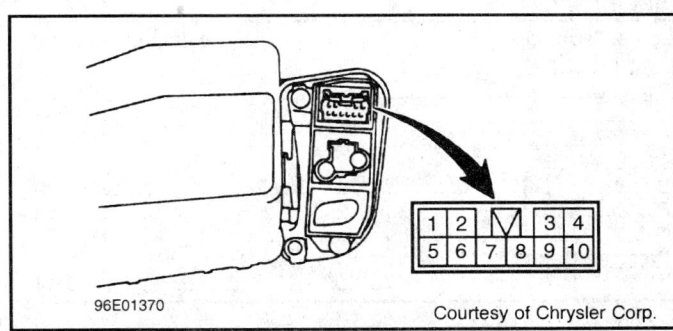

Fig. 7: Identifying Hazard Warning Switch Connector Terminals

VEHICLE SPEED SENSOR (VSS)

1) Remove VSS from transaxle. Apply battery voltage to VSS terminal No. 1 and ground terminal No. 2. Connect a 3-10 k/ohms resistor between VSS terminals No. 1 and 3. See Fig. 8.

2) Using voltmeter, check voltage between terminals No. 2 and 3 while turning VSS shaft. Voltage should pulse 8 times each time shaft is turned one revolution. Replace VSS if voltage does not pulse as specified.

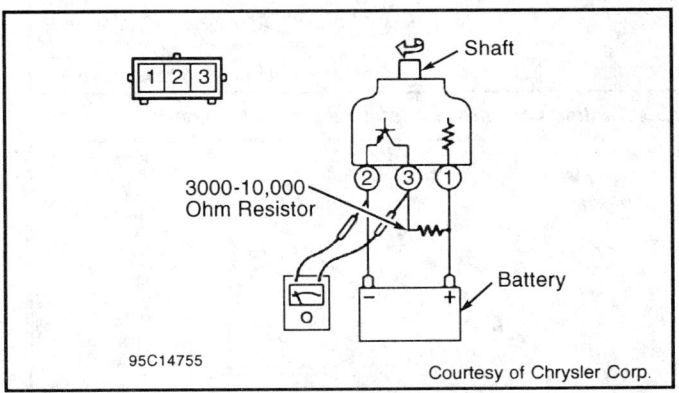

Fig. 8: Testing Vehicle Speed Sensor (VSS)

SYSTEM TESTS

INSTRUMENT CLUSTER GAUGE TESTS

CAUTION: DO NOT touch printed circuit board when inserting test probe into "A" terminal of gauge during resistance test.

NOTE: Perform step 1) of following test before removing instrument cluster to check a suspected faulty gauge.

1) Locate and disconnect harness connector from suspected faulty gauge sending unit. Ground sending unit harness connector using 12-volt test light with a 3.4-watt bulb. Turn ignition switch to RUN position. Test light should illuminate slightly and suspect gauge needle should move. If test light comes on and gauge needle moves, go to next step. If test light comes on but gauge needle does not move, replace gauge. If test light does not come on and gauge needle does not move, repair wiring harness as necessary.

2) To check for excessive resistance in gauge, remove instrument cluster to gain access to gauge. See INSTRUMENT CLUSTER

CHRY
4-376

1999 ACCESSORIES & EQUIPMENT
Analog Instrument Panels – Avenger & Sebring Coupe (Cont.)

GAUGES under REMOVAL & INSTALLATION. To prevent false reading, remove ignition terminal screw/nut from area "A" on coolant temperature and fuel gauges. *See Fig. 9 or 10.*

3) On all gauges, measure resistance between specified gauge terminals. See GAUGE RESISTANCE table. *See Figs. 9, 10 or 11.* Replace gauge if readings are not as specified.

GAUGE RESISTANCE

Gauge & Terminals	Resistance (Ohms)
Coolant Temperature Gauge	
A-B	161-197
A-C	51.3-56.7
B-C	210-256
Fuel Gauge	
A-B	219-279
A-C	102-152
B-C	112-132
Oil Pressure Gauge	
A-B	40-44

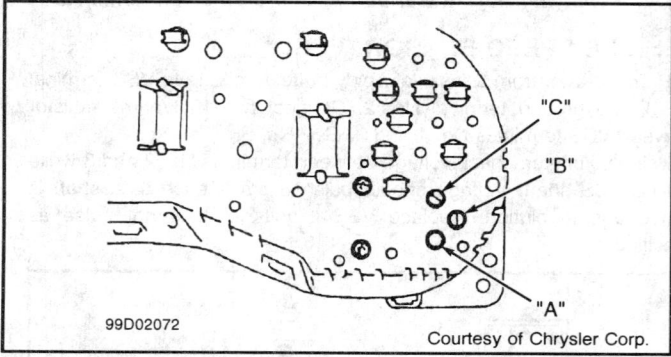

Fig. 9: Testing Coolant Temperature Gauge Resistance

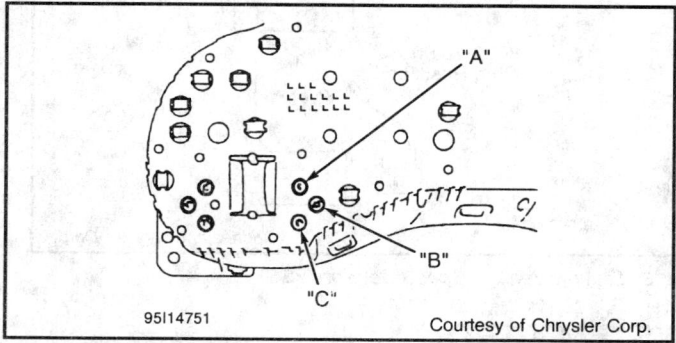

Fig. 10: Testing Fuel Gauge Resistance

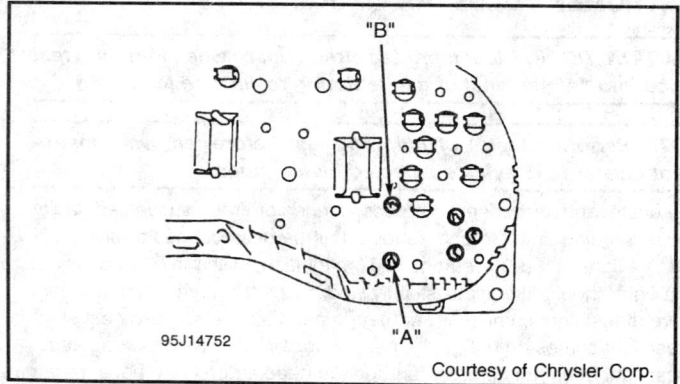

Fig. 11: Testing Oil Pressure Gauge Resistance

SPEEDOMETER TEST

CAUTION: DO NOT operate clutch suddenly or vary speed rapidly during testing.

Ensure tire pressure is correct. Position front wheels of vehicle on speedometer tester drum. Chock rear wheels. Apply parking brake. Attach a chain to rear tie-down holes located in rear of wheelwell. Ensure speedometer ranges are within specification. See SPEEDOMETER SPECIFICATIONS table. If ranges are not as specified, replace speedometer.

SPEEDOMETER SPECIFICATIONS

Standard Values	Allowable Range
MPH	
20	19-22
40	38-44
60	57-66
80	76-88
100	94-110
KM/H	
40	37-44
80	75-88
120	113-132
160	150-176

TACHOMETER TEST

Connect inductive-type engine tachometer to high tension cable. Start engine and compare tachometers at specified engine speed. See TACHOMETER SPECIFICATIONS table. Replace tachometer if difference is excessive.

TACHOMETER SPECIFICATIONS

Engine RPM	Allowable Range
8000 R/Min. Display Tachometer	
1000	900-1100
3000	2850-3150
5000	4750-5250
6000	5700-6300
9000 R/Min. Display Tachometer	
700	630-770
3000	2890-3220
5000	4900-5300
7000	6950-7350

REMOVAL & INSTALLATION

WARNING: Vehicle is equipped with an air bag system. To prevent air bag deployment, disconnect negative battery cable and wait at least 2 minutes before servicing instrument cluster. See appropriate AIR BAG RESTRAINT SYSTEMS article.

CAUTION: When battery is disconnected, vehicle computer and memory systems may lose memory data. Driveability problems may exist until computer systems have completed a relearn cycle. See COMPUTER RELEARN PROCEDURES article in GENERAL INFORMATION before disconnecting battery.

INSTRUMENT CLUSTER & GAUGES

Removal & Installation – 1) Remove screws, and pull out bezel and instrument cluster assembly. Remove sockets and bulbs. Remove cluster lens and faceplate by depressing retaining tabs on housing and separating both from cluster housing. *See Fig. 12.*

2) Remove gauge retaining nuts from printed circuit board. Remove gauge(s) from cluster housing. To install, reverse removal procedure.

HAZARD WARNING LIGHT SWITCH, REAR DEFOGGER SWITCH & REAR WIPER/WASHER SWITCH

Removal & Installation – 1) Remove stoppers from glove box. *See Fig. 13.* Remove center air outlet assembly. Remove rear wiper/washer

1999 ACCESSORIES & EQUIPMENT
Analog Instrument Panels – Avenger & Sebring Coupe (Cont.)

CHRY
4-377

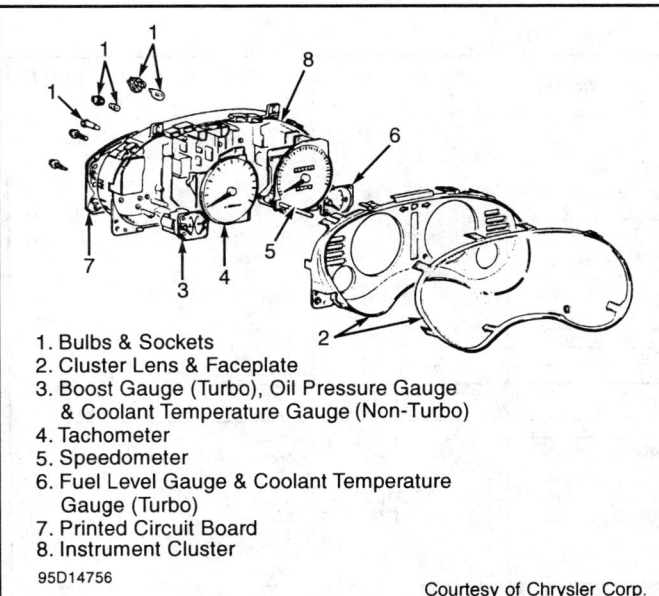

1. Bulbs & Sockets
2. Cluster Lens & Faceplate
3. Boost Gauge (Turbo), Oil Pressure Gauge
   & Coolant Temperature Gauge (Non-Turbo)
4. Tachometer
5. Speedometer
6. Fuel Level Gauge & Coolant Temperature
   Gauge (Turbo)
7. Printed Circuit Board
8. Instrument Cluster

95D14756

Courtesy of Chrysler Corp.

Fig. 12: Exploded View Of Instrument Cluster

switch. Remove holder from center air outlet assembly. Remove hazard warning light switch and rear defogger switch.

2) To install, reverse removal procedure. When installing center air outlet assembly, turn cool air by-pass lever fully downward. Pull cool air by-pass damper lever on heater unit fully forward, then attach cable to pin on lever. Push outer cable upward into dash until all slack is gone, then secure cable with clip.

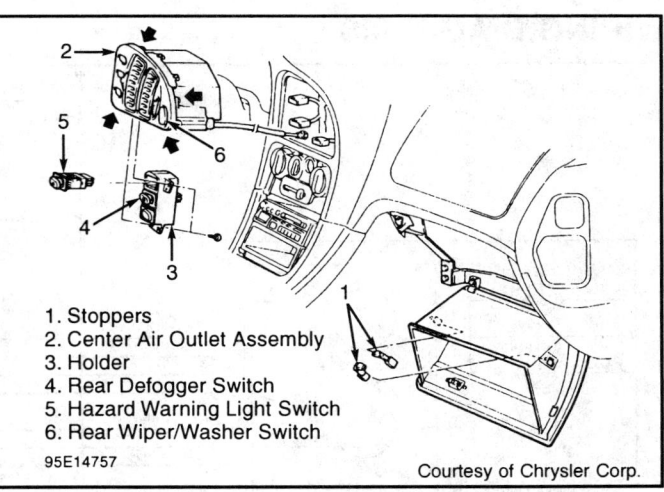

1. Stoppers
2. Center Air Outlet Assembly
3. Holder
4. Rear Defogger Switch
5. Hazard Warning Light Switch
6. Rear Wiper/Washer Switch

95E14757

Courtesy of Chrysler Corp.

Fig. 13: Removing Instrument Panel Switches

DIMMER RHEOSTAT

Removal & Installation – Remove lower instrument panel on driver's side. Remove dimmer rheostat. To install, reverse removal procedure.

CHRY
4-378

1999 ACCESSORIES & EQUIPMENT
Analog Instrument Panels – Avenger & Sebring Coupe (Cont.)

WIRING DIAGRAMS

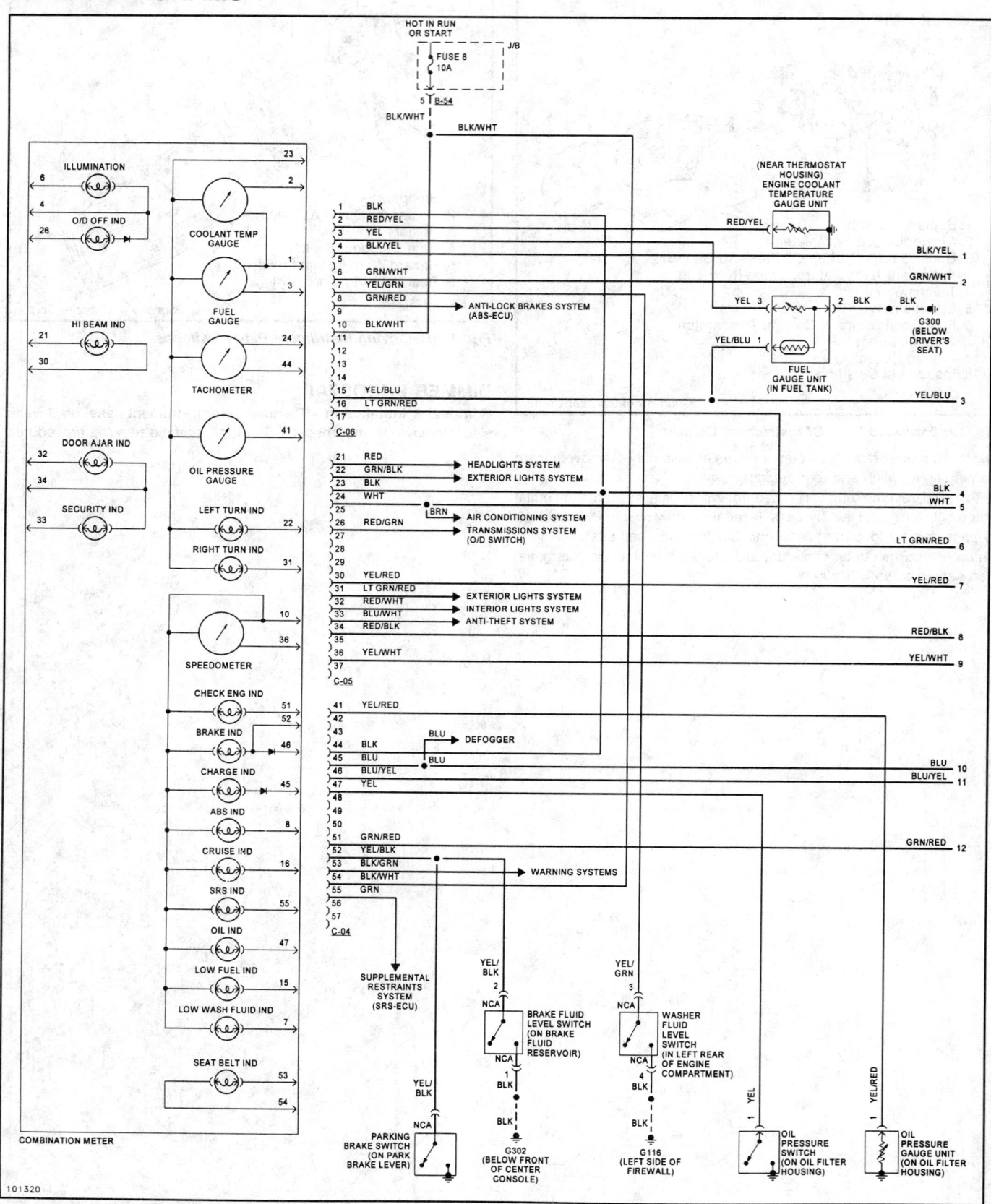

Fig. 14: Analog Instrument Panel Wiring Diagram (Avenger & Sebring Coupe – 1 Of 2)

1999 ACCESSORIES & EQUIPMENT
Analog Instrument Panels – Avenger & Sebring Coupe (Cont.)

CHRY
4-379

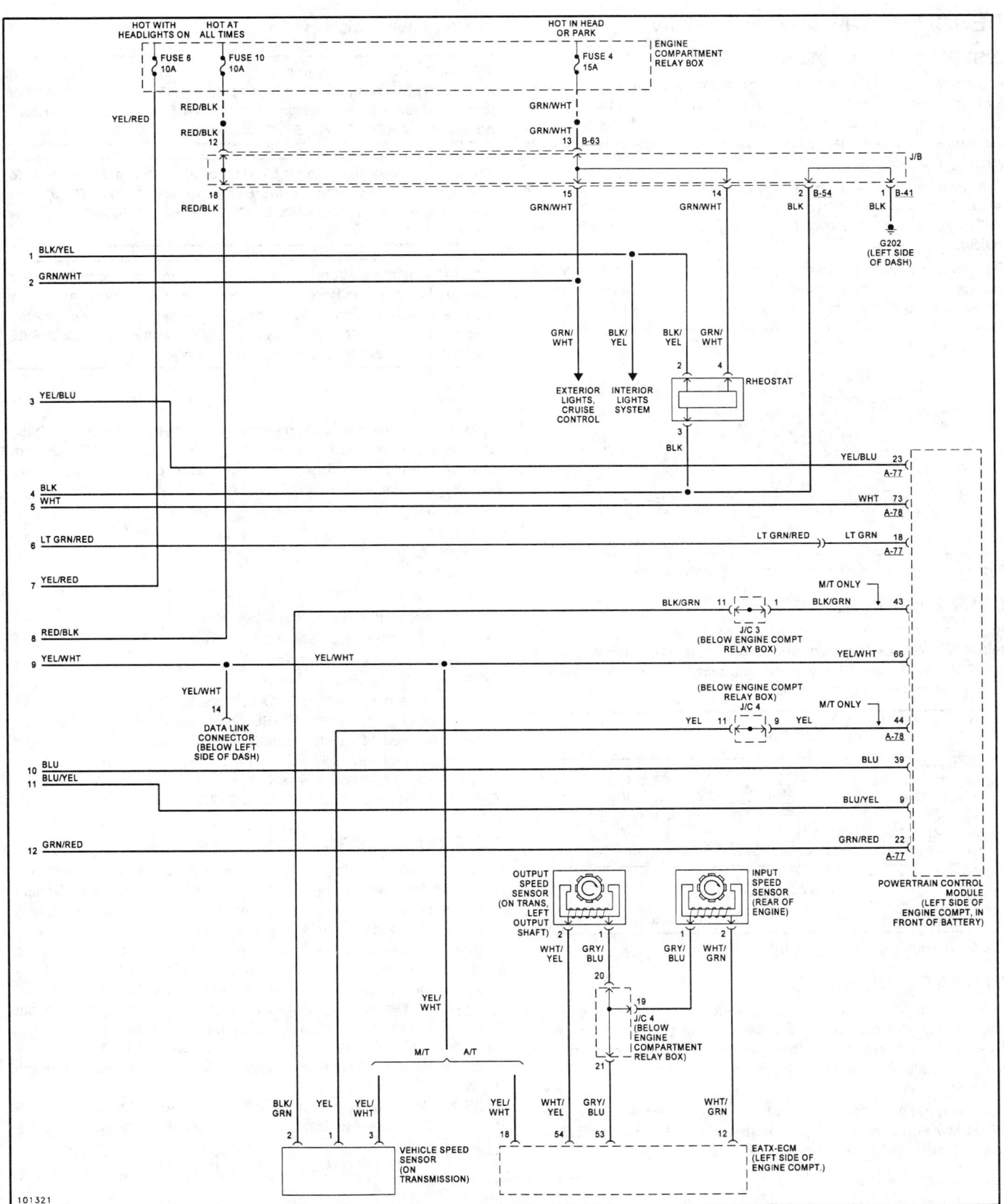

Fig. 15: Analog Instrument Panel Wiring Diagram (Avenger & Sebring Coupe – 2 Of 2)

1999 ACCESSORIES & EQUIPMENT
Analog Instrument Panels
Breeze, Cirrus, Sebring Convertible & Stratus

DESCRIPTION & OPERATION

INSTRUMENT CLUSTER

Analog instrument cluster is an electro-mechanical module which receives most of its information from Body Control Module (BCM) through Chrysler Collision Detection (CCD) bus. Instrument cluster contains speedometer, tachometer, fuel gauge, temperature gauge and warning indicators. *See Fig. 1.*

Speedometer contains a removable odometer/transmission range indicator (A/T). Various warning indicators are used to warn of system malfunctions. A printed circuit board provides power to gauges and indicator lights.

Gauges are magnetic air-core type. When ignition switch is in OFF position, gauge pointers should rest at or below low graduation. Gauge readings are accurate only when ignition switch is in RUN position.

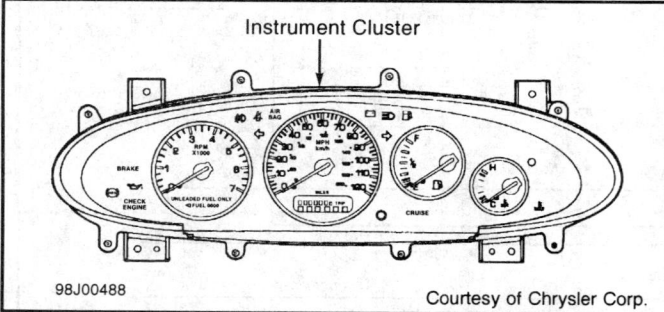

Instrument Cluster

98J00488   Courtesy of Chrysler Corp.

Fig. 1: Identifying Instrument Cluster Components

GEAR SHIFT INDICATOR

Two types of gear shift indicator are used. The standard type and autostick. Autostick equipped vehicles have a special shift indicator. *See Fig. 2.* When in autostick mode, a box around appropriate gear will be illuminated to display gear position.

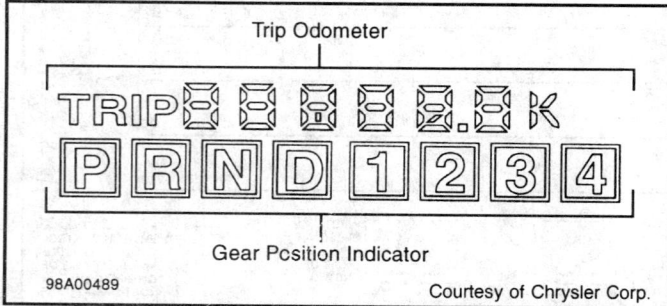

Trip Odometer

Gear Position Indicator

98A00489   Courtesy of Chrysler Corp.

Fig. 2: Identifying Autostick Shift Indicator

WARNING INDICATORS

Warning indicators include CHECK ENGINE, AIR BAG, charging system, oil pressure, temperature, low fuel, seat belt, CRUISE (if equipped), BRAKE, ABS (if equipped), high beam, fog (if equipped), security system (if equipped), turn signal and traction control ON/OFF (Sebring Convertible only).

Brake warning indicator will light when parking brake is applied, brake fluid is low in reservoir, hydraulic system fails, ABS warning indicator malfunctions or ABS system fails.

SYSTEM TESTS

WARNING: Vehicle is equipped with an air bag system. To prevent air bag deployment, disconnect negative battery cable and wait at least 2 minutes before servicing instrument cluster. See appropriate AIR BAG RESTRAINT SYSTEMS article.

NOTE: Testing of instrument cluster requires using a scan tool to check circuits connected to the Body Control Module (BCM). See appropriate BODY CONTROL COMPUTER – INTRODUCTION article.

CAUTION: When battery is disconnected, vehicle computer and memory systems may lose memory data. Driveability problems may exist until computer systems have completed a relearn cycle. See COMPUTER RELEARN PROCEDURES article in GENERAL INFORMATION before disconnecting battery.

QUICK TEST

1) As a quick diagnosis, instrument cluster will perform a function check immediately after ignition is switched to RUN or START position. Electronic display, odometer/transmission range indicator and all warning lights will illuminate for a brief period EXCEPT:

- CRUISE
- Fog Lamps
- High Beam
- Low Fuel
- Turn Signals
- Oil Pressure (Sebring Convertible)
- Security System LED (Sebring Convertible)
- BRAKE (Sebring Convertible)
- TRAC OFF (Sebring Convertible)

2) If cluster is not receiving CCD bus messages, cluster will appear non-functional except for the NO BUS message displayed and continuously illuminated AIR BAG warning indicator. On Breeze, Cirrus and Stratus, ABS and MIL lights will also be illuminated. If instrument cluster is not receiving CCD bus messages, repair communications concern. See appropriate VEHICLE COMMUNICATIONS article.

SELF-DIAGNOSTICS

Press and hold odometer/trip reset button while turning ignition switch to OFF, then RUN position. This will cycle an electronic display segment check and illumination in sequence of all CCD bus activated warning indicators. There are 4 check functions:

CHECK 1 (Gauge Display Check) –If all gauges fail to move, replace printed circuit. If any gauge fail to move, replace gauge assembly. If any gauge is not in proper position, replace printed circuit.

CHECK 2 (Warning Light Display Check) –If any light does not illuminate, check bulb. If bulb is okay, replace printed circuit.

CHECK 3 (Vacuum Fluorescent (VF) Display Check) –If any VF segment does not illuminate, replace odometer/transmission range indicator.

CHECK 4 (Transmission Range VF Display, A/T Check) –If any VF segment does not illuminate, replace odometer/transmission range indicator.

Analog Instrument Panels
Breeze, Cirrus, Sebring Convertible & Stratus (Cont.)

REMOVAL & INSTALLATION

WARNING: Vehicle is equipped with an air bag system. To prevent air bag deployment, disconnect negative battery cable and wait at least 2 minutes before servicing instrument cluster. See appropriate AIR BAG RESTRAINT SYSTEMS article.

INSTRUMENT CLUSTER

Removal – 1) Disconnect negative battery cable and wait at least 2 minutes. Remove left end cover by pulling outward. Tilt steering column down to its lowest position. Remove instrument cluster center bezel by disengaging 4 clips. *See Fig. 3.*

2) Remove 4 instrument cluster hood mounting screws. Three screws are located behind center bezel and one screw is located at left end of hood. Pull hood rearward to disengage 8 clips.

3) On models equipped with Compass/Temperature Mini Trip Computer (CMTC), pull hood rearward only about 3 inches. Reach through radio opening and disconnect CMTC wire connector. Remove cluster hood.

4) Remove 4 instrument cluster mounting screws. *See Fig. 3.* Disconnect wire connectors from instrument cluster by pulling instrument cluster rearward. Remove instrument cluster.

Disassembly – 1) To remove gauges or speedometer/tachometer, remove mask/lens retaining screws and remove mask/lens. Disconnect odometer/transmission range indicator connector from printed circuit board. Remove screws attaching speedometer/tachometer to housing. Remove speedometer/tachometer. Remove fuel/temperature gauge by removing attaching screws

2) To remove printed circuit board, remove 6 cluster back cover retaining screws and back cover. Disconnect odometer/transmission range indicator connector from printed circuit board. Remove 9 printed circuit board mounting screws and printed circuit board. There are 2 screws located at base of each wire connector.

Reassembly & Installation – To reassemble and install instrument cluster, reverse removal and disassembly procedures.

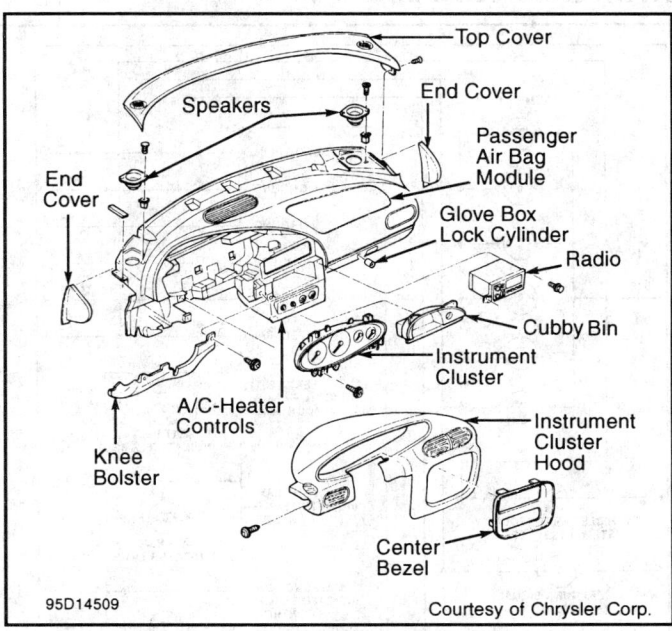

95D14509   Courtesy of Chrysler Corp.

Fig. 3: Exploded View Of Instrument Cluster

**CHRY
4-382**

1999 ACCESSORIES & EQUIPMENT
Analog Instrument Panels
Breeze, Cirrus, Sebring Convertible & Stratus (Cont.)

WIRING DIAGRAMS

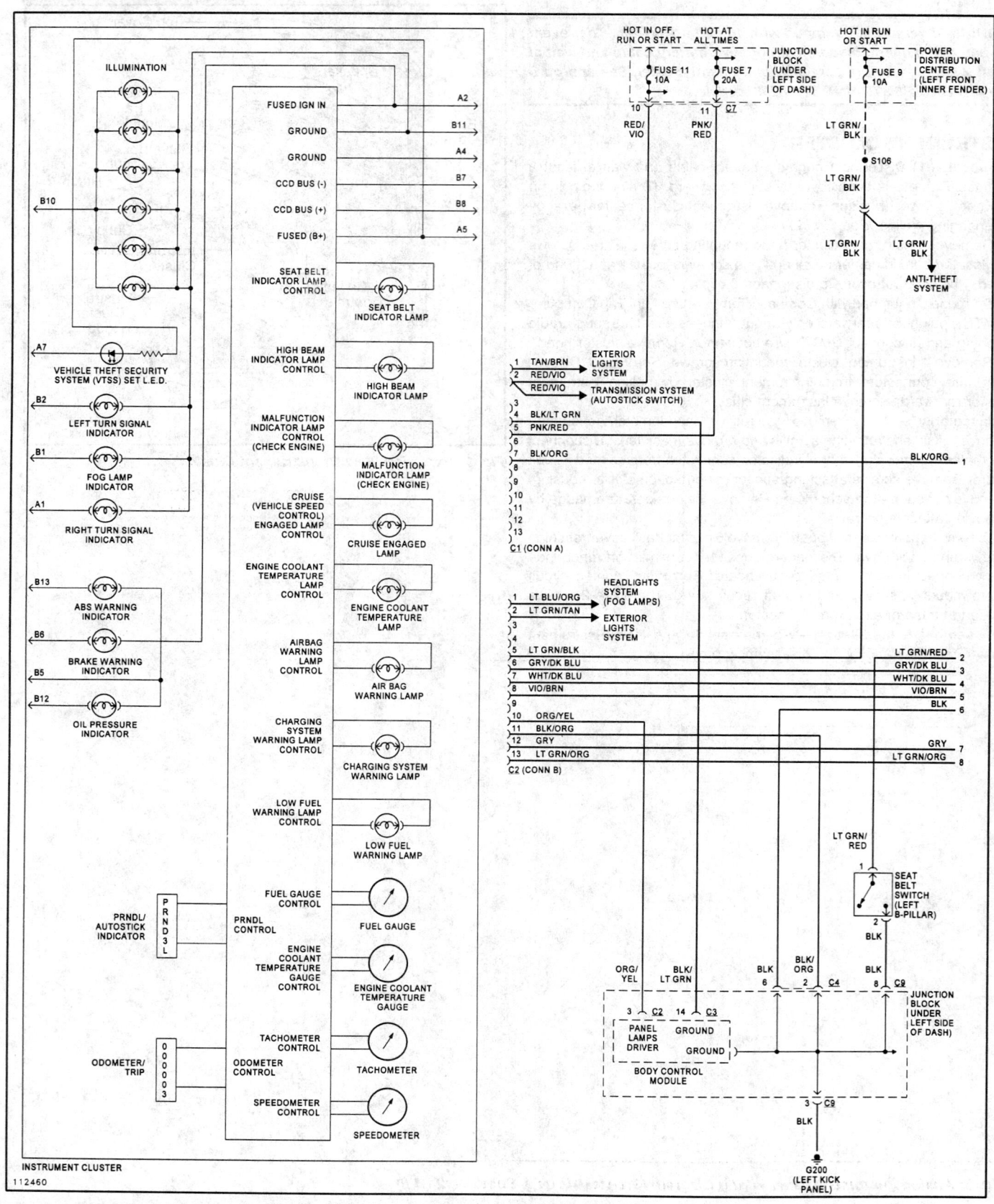

Fig. 4: Analog Instrument Panel Wiring Diagram (Breeze, Cirrus & Stratus – 1 Of 2)

1999 ACCESSORIES & EQUIPMENT
Analog Instrument Panels
Breeze, Cirrus, Sebring Convertible & Stratus (Cont.)

CHRY
4-383

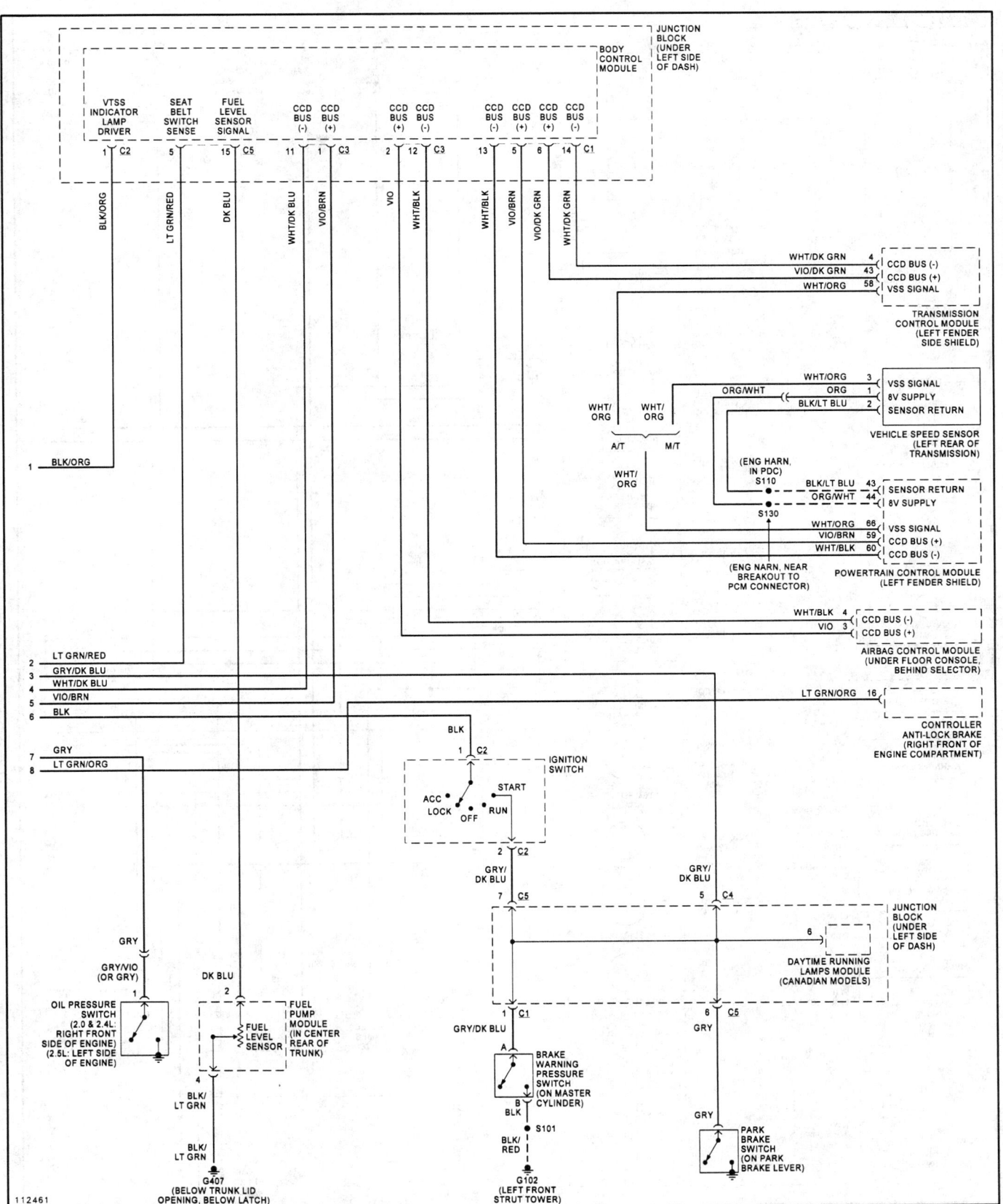

Fig. 5: Analog Instrument Panel Wiring Diagram (Breeze, Cirrus & Stratus – 2 Of 2)

CHRY
4-384

1999 ACCESSORIES & EQUIPMENT
Analog Instrument Panels
Breeze, Cirrus, Sebring Convertible & Stratus (Cont.)

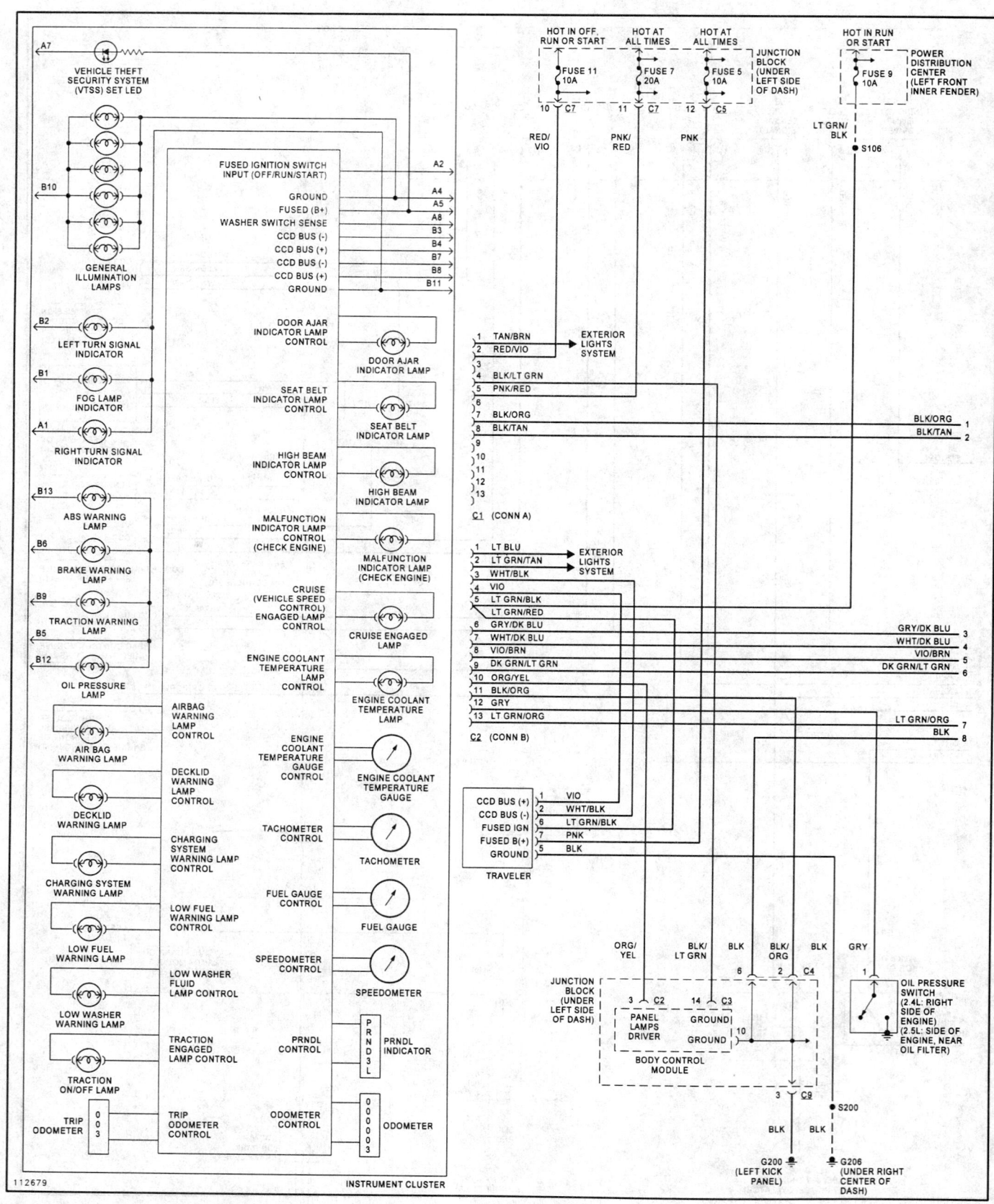

Fig. 6: Analog Instrument Panel Wiring Diagram (Sebring Convertible – 1 Of 2)

1999 ACCESSORIES & EQUIPMENT
Analog Instrument Panels
Breeze, Cirrus, Sebring Convertible & Stratus (Cont.)

CHRY
4-385

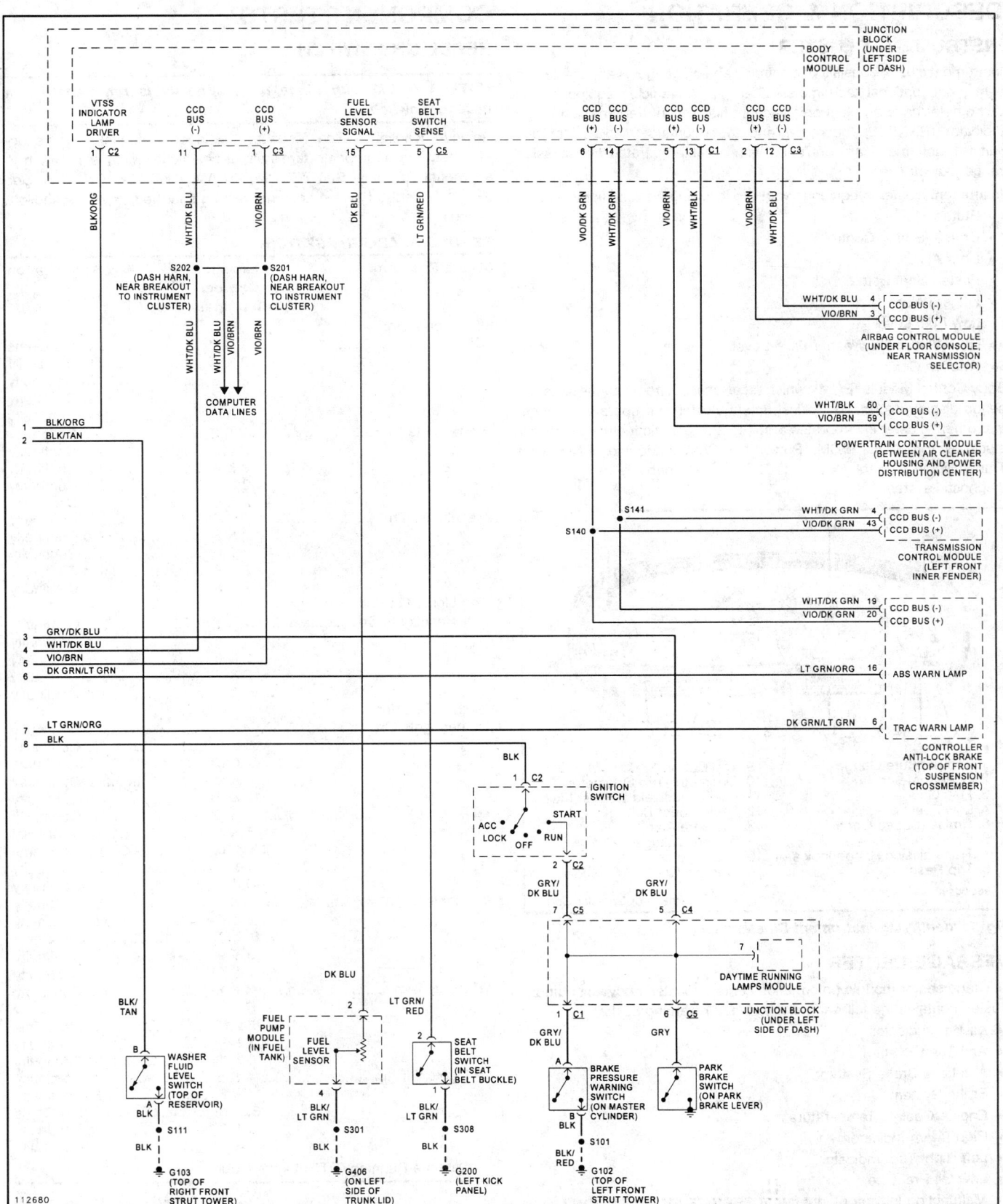

Fig. 7: Analog Instrument Panel Wiring Diagram (Sebring Convertible – 2 Of 2)

1999 ACCESSORIES & EQUIPMENT
Analog Instrument Panels
Caravan, Town & Country, & Voyager

DESCRIPTION & OPERATION

INSTRUMENT CLUSTER

Instrument cluster consists of electronic analog gauges, various warning lights, and optional tachometer. *See Fig. 1.* Vehicles equipped with tachometer have an electronic vacuum fluorescent transmission range indicator (PRND3L), odometer and trip odometer display. Vehicles without tachometer are equipped with a cable-operated transmission range indicator.

Instrument cluster is equipped with the following warning lights:

- Battery
- Cruise (Speed Control)
- Door Ajar
- Fasten Seat Belt
- Liftgate Ajar
- Low Fuel Level
- Low Windshield Washer Fluid Level
- Traction Control

Body Control Module (BCM), which receives input from various sensors, sends display information to instrument cluster and operates gauges. Instrument cluster incorporates a self-test diagnostic feature to identify electronic problems. BCM, Powertrain Control Module (PCM) and Transmission Control Module (TCM) are continuously monitored by diagnostic system.

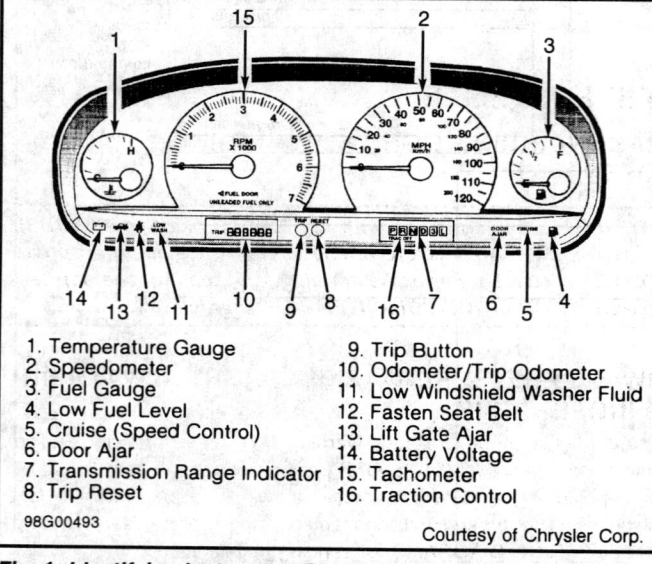

1. Temperature Gauge
2. Speedometer
3. Fuel Gauge
4. Low Fuel Level
5. Cruise (Speed Control)
6. Door Ajar
7. Transmission Range Indicator
8. Trip Reset
9. Trip Button
10. Odometer/Trip Odometer
11. Low Windshield Washer Fluid
12. Fasten Seat Belt
13. Lift Gate Ajar
14. Battery Voltage
15. Tachometer
16. Traction Control

98G00493   Courtesy of Chrysler Corp.

Fig. 1: Identifying Instrument Cluster Components

MESSAGE CENTER

Message center module (information center), located above instrument cluster, contains the following display and/or warning lights:

- Air Bag Indicator
- Anti-Theft System
- Anti-Lock Brake System
- Brake System
- Engine Coolant Temperature
- High Beam Indicator
- Left/Right Turn Indicator
- Low Oil Pressure
- Malfunction Indicator Light (MIL)/ SERVICE ENGINE SOON Light.

COMPONENT TESTS

HEADLIGHT SWITCH

NOTE: A DVOM with diode test capability is required to test headlight switch.

Remove headlight switch. Measure resistance or continuity as necessary between appropriate terminals at headlight switch with switch in appropriate position. See TESTING HEADLIGHT SWITCH table. *See Fig. 2.* If headlight switch does not test as specified, replace headlight switch.

TESTING HEADLIGHT SWITCH

Switch Position	Measure Between Terminals	Specification
8-Pin Connector		
Off	1 & 2	5.2 Ohms
	2 & 5	No Continuity
	2 & 6	No Continuity
	2 & 7	No Continuity
	2 & 8	No Continuity
Park Lights On	2 & 3	No Continuity
	2 & 5	No Continuity
	2 & 6	No Continuity
	2 & 7	No Continuity
	2 & 8	Continuity
Headlights On	2 & 3	Continuity
	2 & 5	No Continuity
	2 & 6	No Continuity
	2 & 7	No Continuity
	2 & 8	Continuity
Fog Lights On With Parking		
Or Headlights On	2 & 3	Continuity
	2 & 6	Continuity
	2 & 8	Continuity
	2 & 5	Diode Continuity
	2 & 7	No Continuity
12-Pin Connector		
Dome Lights On	4 & 6	Continuity
	5 & 6	No Continuity
	6 & 12	8000-12,000 Ohms
	3 & 9	Continuity
	10 & 11	No Continuity
DTR Mode [1]	4 & 6	No Continuity
	5 & 6	Continuity
	6 & 12	8000-12,000 Ohms
	3 & 9	Continuity
	10 & 11	Continuity
I/P Lights Bright	4 & 6	No Continuity
	5 & 6	No Continuity
	6 & 12	8000-12,000 Ohms
	3 & 9	Continuity
	10 & 11	Continuity
I/P Lights Dim	4 & 6	No Continuity
	5 & 6	No Continuity
	6 & 12	0-500 Ohms
	3 & 9	Continuity
	10 & 11	Continuity
I/P Lights Off	4 & 6	No Continuity
	5 & 6	No Continuity
	6 & 12	0-500 Ohms
	3 & 9	No Continuity
	10 & 11	Continuity

[1] – Daytime Running (DTR) Lights Mode.

Analog Instrument Panels
Caravan, Town & Country, & Voyager (Cont.)

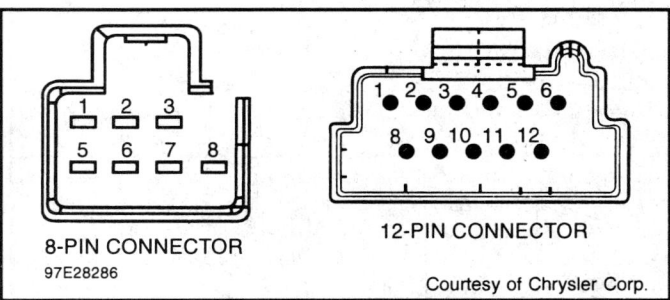

8-PIN CONNECTOR
97E28286

12-PIN CONNECTOR

Courtesy of Chrysler Corp.

Fig. 2: Identifying Headlight Switch Connectors

SELF-DIAGNOSTIC SYSTEM

WARNING: Vehicle is equipped with an air bag system. To prevent air bag deployment, disconnect negative battery cable and wait at least 2 minutes before servicing instrument cluster. See appropriate AIR BAG RESTRAINT SYSTEMS article.

NOTE: Testing of instrument panel and gauges requires using a scan tool to check circuits connected to Body Control Module (BCM). See appropriate BODY CONTROL COMPUTER TESTS article.

1) With ignition switch in OFF position, press and hold TRIP and RESET buttons while turning ignition switch to ON position. Continue to hold TRIP and RESET buttons until odometer window displays CODE (about 5 seconds). If problem exists, system will display diagnostic trouble codes. See DIAGNOSTIC CODE CHART table. If no problem exists, Code 999 (end test) will be displayed.

DIAGNOSTIC CODE CHART

Code	Description
110	Cluster Memory Fault
111	Cluster Calibration Fault
905	No CCD Bus Message From TCM
921	Odometer Fault From BCM
940	No CCD Bus Message From PCM
999	End Of Codes

2) After diagnostic code display ends, instrument cluster will go into each of the following tests in order: dim test, calibration test, odometer segment test then electronic transmission range indicator segment test.

DIM TEST

CHEC-0 will be displayed in odometer window. Instrument cluster will dim Vacuum Florescent (VF) display. If VF displays do not dim, a problem in instrument cluster exists. See appropriate BODY CONTROL COMPUTER TESTS article.

CALIBRATION TEST

CHEC-1 will be displayed in odometer window. Each of instrument cluster gauges will move sequentially through each calibration point. See GAUGE CALIBRATIONS table. If gauge needle is not calibrated properly, a problem in instrument cluster exists. See appropriate BODY CONTROL COMPUTER TESTS article for gauge recalibration procedures.

GAUGE CALIBRATIONS

Gauge Sequence	Calibration Point
Speedometer	
1	0 MPH
2	20 MPH
3	55 MPH
4	75 MPH
Tachometer	

GAUGE CALIBRATIONS (Cont.)

Gauge Sequence	Calibration Point
1	0 RPM
2	1000 RPM
3	3000 RPM
4	6000 RPM
Fuel Gauge	
1	Empty
2	1/8
3	1/4
4	Full
Temperature Gauge	
1	Cold
2	Low Normal
3	High Normal
4	Hot

ODOMETER SEGMENT TEST

CHEC-2 will be displayed in odometer window. Each segment of odometer will light sequentially. If any segment does not light, replace instrument cluster.

ELECTRONIC TRANSMISSION RANGE INDICATOR SEGMENT TEST

CHEC-3 will be displayed in odometer window. Each segment of electronic transmission range indicator will light sequentially. If any segment does not light, replace instrument cluster.

SYSTEM TESTS

BRAKE WARNING LIGHT ALWAYS ON OR INOPERATIVE

NOTE: If vehicle is equipped with Anti-Lock Brake System (ABS), see appropriate ANTI-LOCK article in BRAKES in appropriate MITCHELL® manual. For brake warning light testing, see appropriate BODY CONTROL COMPUTER TESTS article.

LOW OIL PRESSURE WARNING LIGHT ALWAYS ON OR INOPERATIVE

1) Start engine. If oil pressure warning light stays on with engine running, turn ignition switch to OFF position and go to step **3)** . If oil pressure warning light fails to come on with ignition switch in ON position, check for broken or disconnected wiring at oil pressure sending unit. See WIRING DIAGRAMS for sending unit location.

2) If wiring is okay, disconnect sending unit. Using jumper wire, ground sending unit wiring harness connector. If oil pressure warning light fails to come on, check for problems in circuit wiring, burned out bulb, disconnected bulb socket in message center, or faulty BCM. See appropriate BODY CONTROL COMPUTER TESTS article. Repair or replace as necessary.

3) Remove sending unit. Connect a test oil pressure gauge in its place. Start engine and note reading. If reading is 4.0 psi or more at idle, replace oil pressure sending unit.

TEMPERATURE WARNING LIGHT INOPERATIVE

Turn ignition switch to ON position. Disconnect temperature switch. Using a jumper wire, ground wiring harness connector to known-good ground. If temperature warning light fails to come on, check for problems in circuit wiring, burned out bulb, disconnected bulb socket in instrument cluster or faulty BCM. See appropriate BODY CONTROL COMPUTER TESTS article. Repair or replace as necessary.

1999 ACCESSORIES & EQUIPMENT
Analog Instrument Panels
Caravan, Town & Country, & Voyager (Cont.)

REMOVAL & INSTALLATION

WARNING: Vehicle is equipped with an air bag system. To prevent air bag deployment, disconnect negative battery cable and wait at least 2 minutes before servicing instrument cluster. See appropriate AIR BAG RESTRAINT SYSTEMS article.

CAUTION: When battery is disconnected, vehicle computer and memory systems may lose memory data. Driveability problems may exist until computer systems have completed a relearn cycle. See COMPUTER RELEARN PROCEDURES article in GENERAL INFORMATION before disconnecting battery.

NOTE: Gauges are contained in a subdial assembly within instrument cluster. DO NOT attempt to service gauges separately. If a gauge becomes faulty, replace subdial assembly.

BODY CONTROL MODULE

Removal & Installation – 1) Disconnect negative battery cable. Remove left underdash cover and knee bolster reinforcement. Disconnect wire connectors from bottom of Body Control Module (BCM). *See Fig. 3.*

2) Remove bolts holding junction block to dash panel mounting bracket. Remove junction block from mounting bracket. Remove screws holding BCM to junction block. Slide BCM downward to disengage guide studs. Remove BCM from junction block. To install, reverse removal procedure.

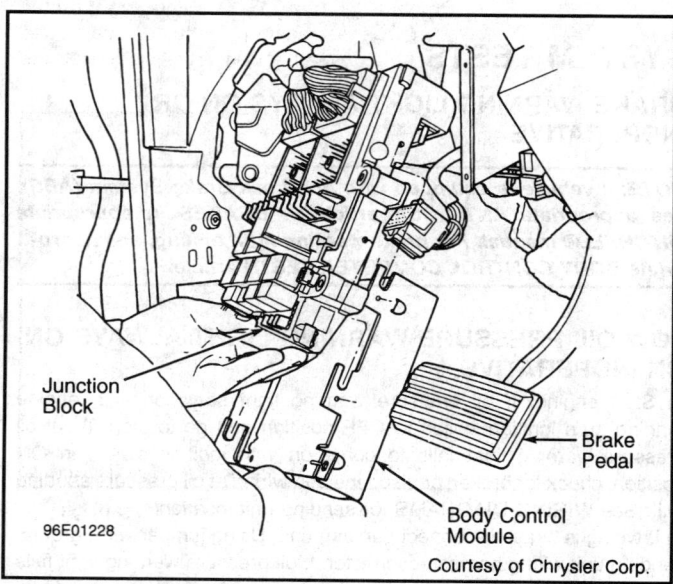

Fig. 3: Identifying Body Control Module

HEADLIGHT SWITCH

Removal & Installation – Remove instrument cluster bezel. See INSTRUMENT CLUSTER BEZEL. Remove headlight switch bezel-to-instrument cluster bezel screws. Unplug wire connectors from headlight switch and power mirror switch. Remove headlight switch bezel from cluster bezel. *See Fig. 4.* To install, reverse removal procedure.

INSTRUMENT CLUSTER BEZEL

Removal & Installation – 1) Disconnect negative battery cable. Remove lower steering column cover. Remove over steering column bezel screws from cluster bezel. Disengage clips holding over column bezel to cluster bezel. Disconnect traction control switch (if equipped). Remove over column bezel. Remove left end cover. Remove screw at left end of cluster bezel and headlight switch.

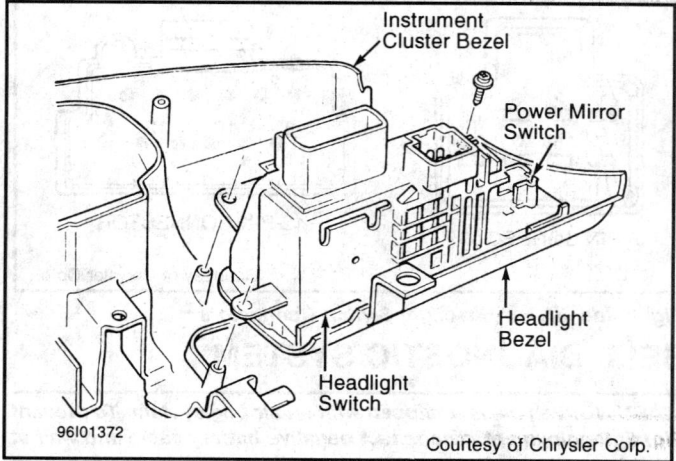

Fig. 4: Removing Headlight Switch

2) Remove cluster bezel-to-instrument panel screws from each side of steering column. Disengage clip holding cluster bezel to instrument panel above right vent louver. Carefully separate cluster bezel from instrument panel. *See Fig. 5.* Unplug wire connectors from back of bezel. To install, reverse removal procedure.

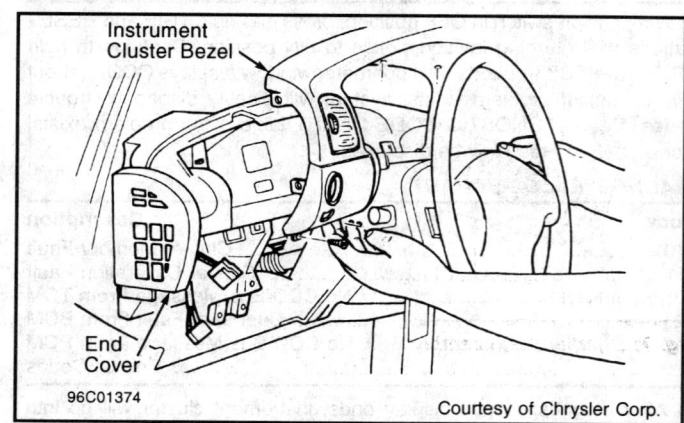

Fig. 5: Removing Instrument Cluster Bezel

INSTRUMENT CLUSTER

Removal & Installation (Mechanical Transmission Range Indicator) – 1) Remove lower steering column cover and metal knee-blocker panel. Disconnect transmission range indicator cable from shift lever by flexing end of transmission shift cable rearward. Disconnect clip holding indicator cable to shift cable bracket. Remove instrument cluster bezel. See INSTRUMENT CLUSTER BEZEL. Remove instrument cluster-to-instrument panel screws.

2) Rotate top of instrument cluster rearward. *See Fig. 6.* Unplug wire connectors from cluster. Remove instrument cluster carefully while guiding range indicator and guide tube through opening. Remove instrument cluster. To install, reverse removal procedure.

Removal & Installation (Electronic Transmission Range Selector) – 1) Remove instrument cluster bezel. See INSTRUMENT CLUSTER BEZEL. Remove instrument cluster-to-instrument panel screws.

2) Rotate top of cluster rearward. *See Fig. 6.* Unplug wire connectors from back of cluster. Remove instrument cluster. To install, reverse removal procedure.

INSTRUMENT CLUSTER SUBDIAL

Removal & Installation – Remove instrument cluster. See INSTRUMENT CLUSTER. Remove cluster lens-to-cluster screws and remove lens. If equipped with mechanical transmission range indicator, guide shift indicator cable through cluster shell. Disconnect temperature/fuel

1999 ACCESSORIES & EQUIPMENT
Analog Instrument Panels
Caravan, Town & Country, & Voyager (Cont.)

CHRY
4-389

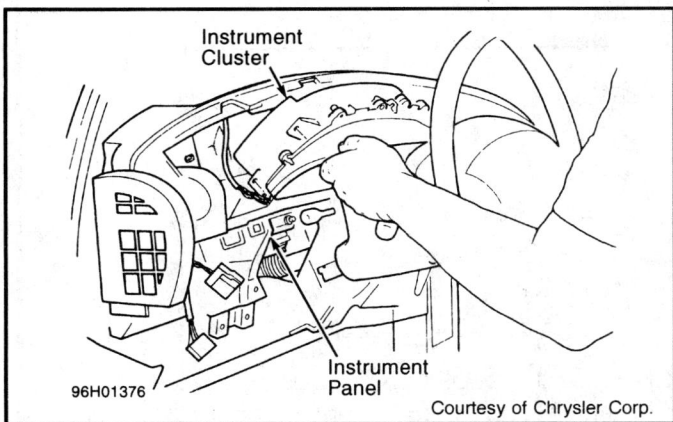

Fig. 6: Removing Instrument Cluster

gauge and tachometer terminals from connectors in cluster by pulling subdial assembly straight out, away from cluster. *See Fig. 7*. To install, reverse removal procedure.

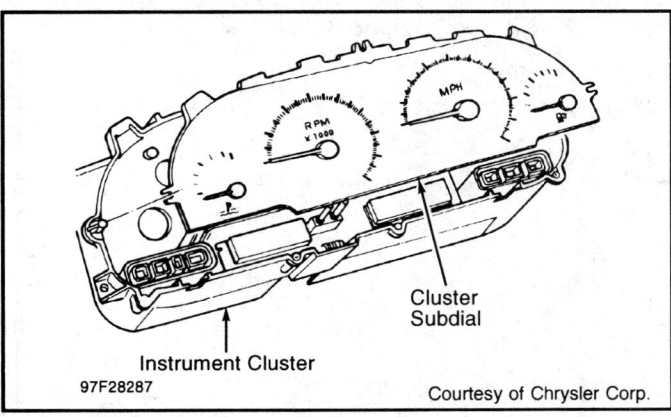

Fig. 7: Subdial Disassembly

PRINTED CIRCUIT BOARD

Removal & Installation – Remove instrument cluster. See INSTRUMENT CLUSTER. Remove 3 screws and instrument cluster back cover. Disconnect electronic cluster wire connector. *See Fig. 8*. Remove screws holding wire connector insulator to instrument cluster shell and printed circuit board. Remove printed circuit board-to-cluster shell screws. Remove circuit board. To install, reverse removal procedure.

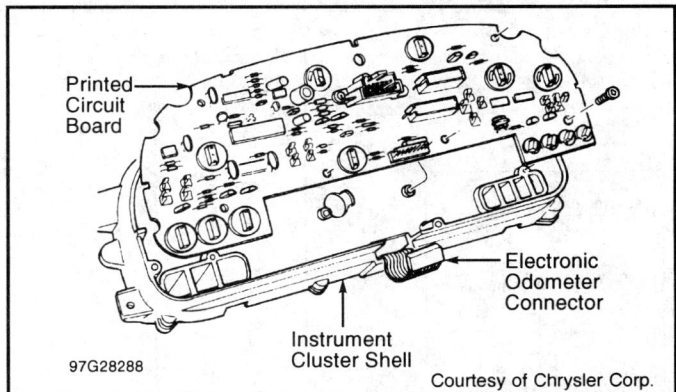

Fig. 8: Printed Circuit Board Disassembly

MESSAGE CENTER

Removal & Installation – Remove "A" pillar trim. Using a trim stick, remove instrument panel top cover by disengaging clips at rear edge. *See Fig. 9*. Unplug wire connector from back of message center. Remove screws attaching message center to instrument panel top cover. Remove message center. To install, reverse removal procedure.

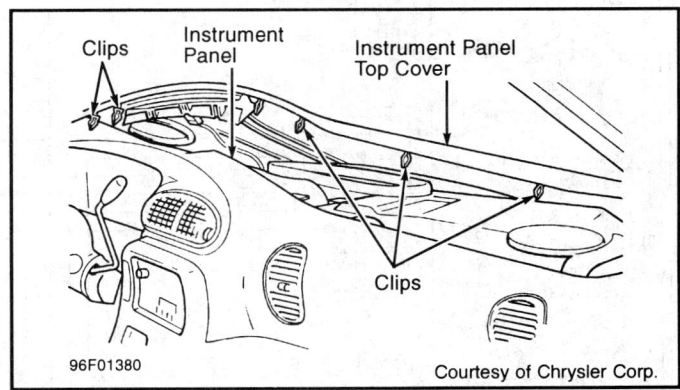

Fig. 9: Identifying Instrument Panel Top Cover Clip Locations

CHRY
4-390

1999 ACCESSORIES & EQUIPMENT
Analog Instrument Panels
Caravan, Town & Country, & Voyager (Cont.)

WIRING DIAGRAMS

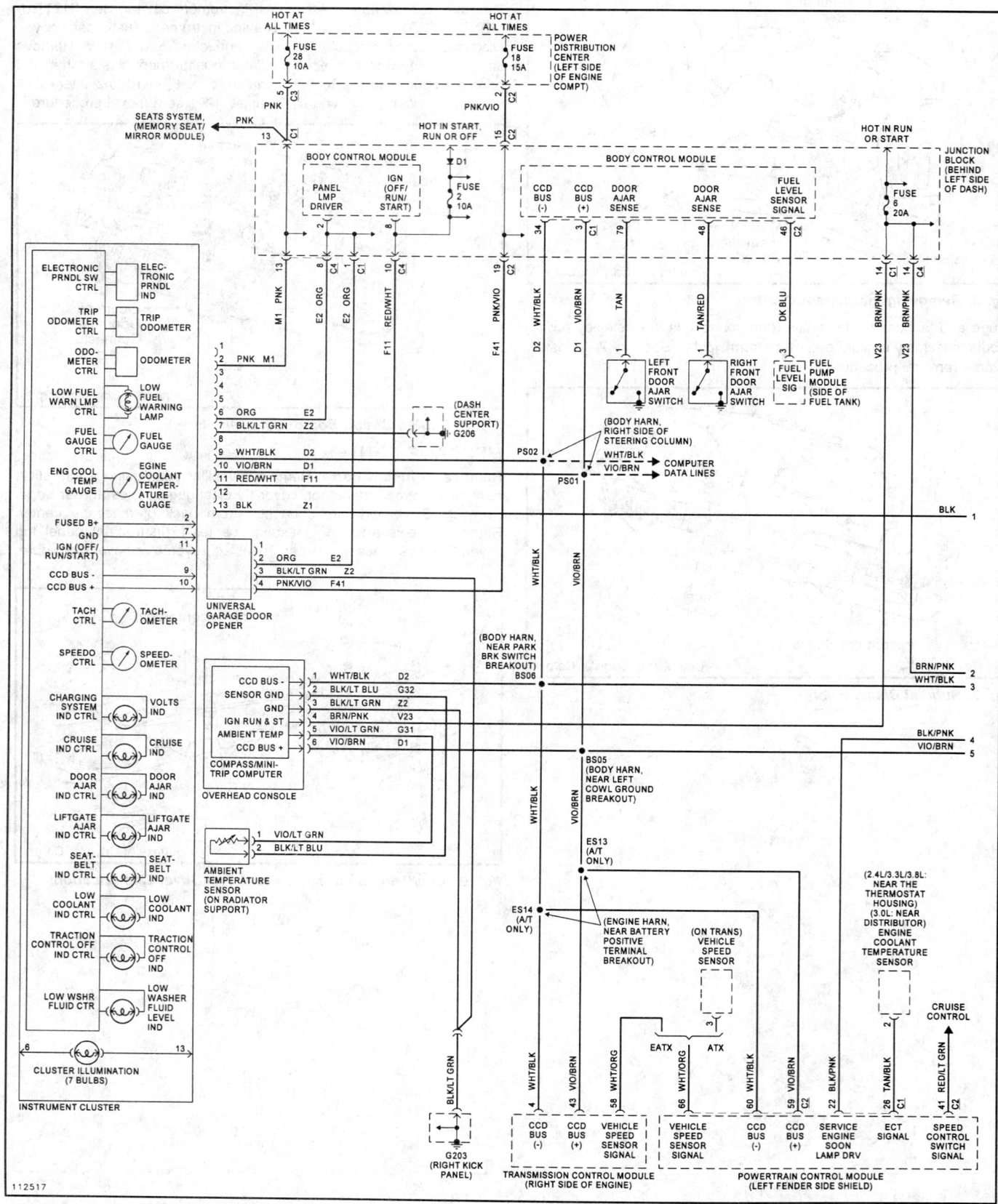

Fig. 10: Analog Instrument Panel Wiring Diagram (Caravan, Town & Country, & Voyager – 1 Of 2)

112517

1999 ACCESSORIES & EQUIPMENT
Analog Instrument Panels
Caravan, Town & Country, & Voyager (Cont.)

CHRY
4-391

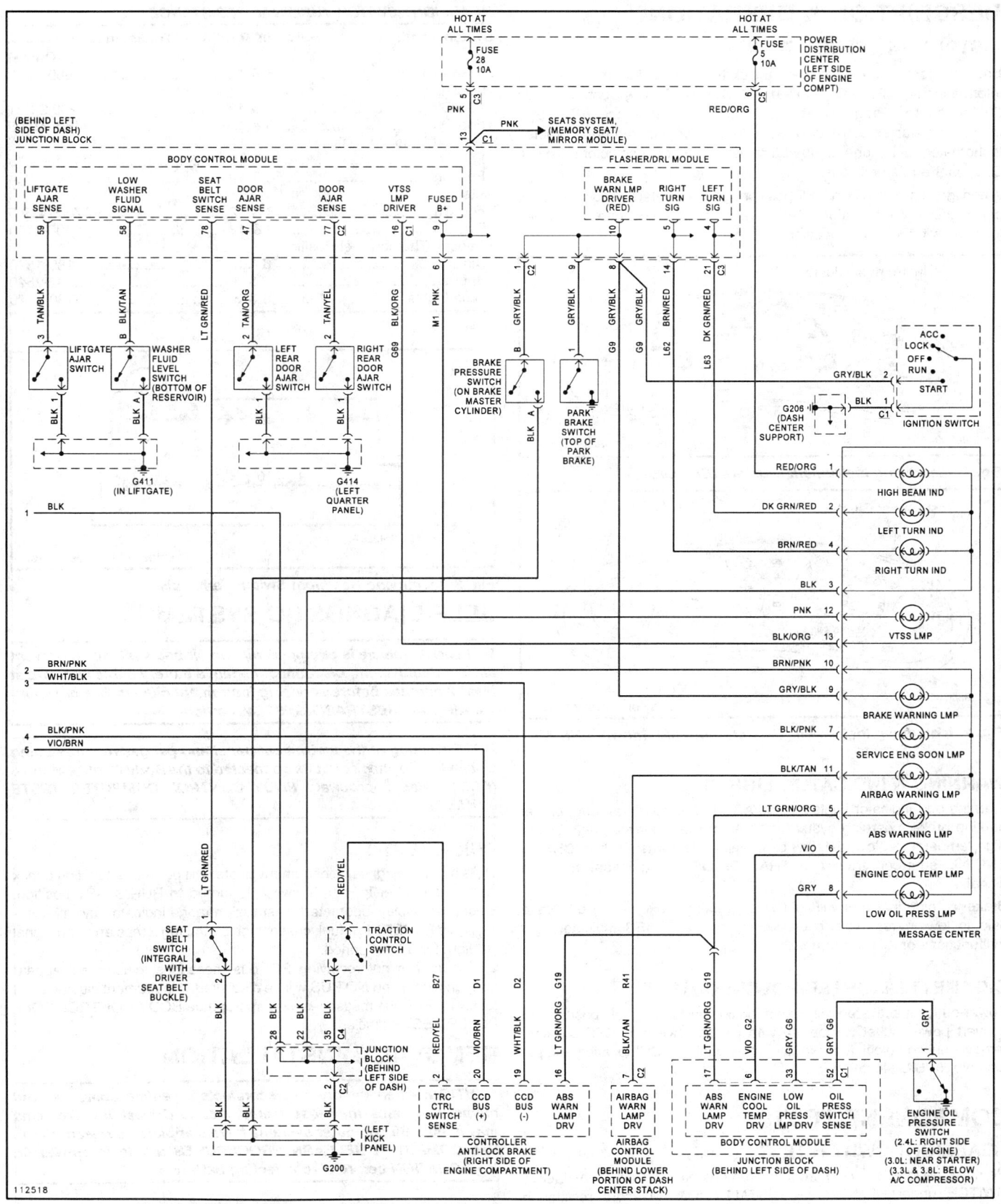

Fig. 11: Analog Instrument Panel Wiring Diagram (Caravan, Town & Country, & Voyager – 2 Of 2)

112518

1999 ACCESSORIES & EQUIPMENT
Analog Instrument Panels
Concorde, Intrepid, LHS & 300M

DESCRIPTION & OPERATION

INSTRUMENT CLUSTER

Both clusters are electro-mechanical type, receiving most of their information from Body Control Module (BCM) or Timing Control Module (TCM) through Programmable Communication Interface (PCI) bus. Instrument cluster consists of speedometer, odometer/trip odometer, tachometer, fuel gauge, temperature gauge and gear selector indicator. Gauges are magnetic air-core type. *See Fig. 1 or 2.*

When ignition switch is in OFF position, gauge pointers should rest at or below the low graduation. Gauge readings are accurate only when ignition switch is in ON position.

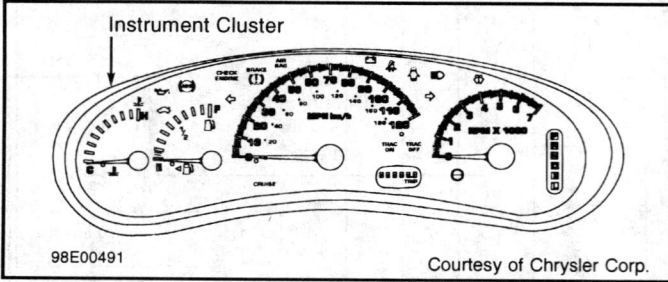

Fig. 1: Identifying Instrument Clusters (Concorde)

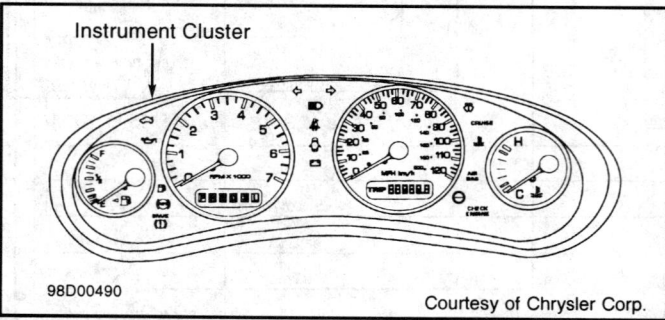

Fig. 2: Identifying Instrument Clusters (Intrepid Shown; LHS & 300M Similar)

WARNING & INDICATOR LIGHTS

Warning and indicator lights include ABS (if equipped), air bag, brake/parking brake, charging system voltage, cruise, door ajar, high beam, high temperature, low fuel, low oil pressure, low washer fluid, CHECK ENGINE, seat belt, trunk ajar, TRAC ON/OFF (if equipped), and turn signals.

Brake warning indicator will light when parking brake is applied, brake fluid is low in reservoir, hydraulic system fails, ABS indicator light malfunctions or ABS system fails.

CIGARETTE LIGHTER/POWER OUTLET

Power outlet is activated only when ignition switch is in ON position. To convert power outlet to operate with ignition switch in OFF position, remove junction block fuse No. 6 from its original "IGN" location and put fuse No. 6 "BAT" location.

COMPONENT TESTS

HEADLIGHT SWITCH TEST

Remove headlight switch from instrument panel. See HEADLIGHT SWITCH under REMOVAL & INSTALLATION. Measure resistance between specified switch terminals with switch in appropriate position. See HEADLIGHT SWITCH TERMINAL RESISTANCE table. *See Fig. 3.* If resistance is not as specified, replace headlight switch.

HEADLIGHT SWITCH TERMINAL RESISTANCE

Switch Position	Between Terminals	Resistance (Ohms)
All Switches Off	6 & 12	3600-5400
Headlights On		
Fog Off	6 & 12	209.2-231
Fog On	6 & 12	446.5-493.5
Parking Lights On		
Fog Off	6 & 12	44.65-49.35
Fog On	6 & 12	64.6-71.4
Auto		
Fog Off	6 & 12	370.5-409.5
Fog On	6 & 12	400-1100
Rheostat Thumbwheel Position		
Dim	6 & 3	180-1870
Bright	6 & 3	2280-2520
Dome Lights	6 & 3	3230-3570

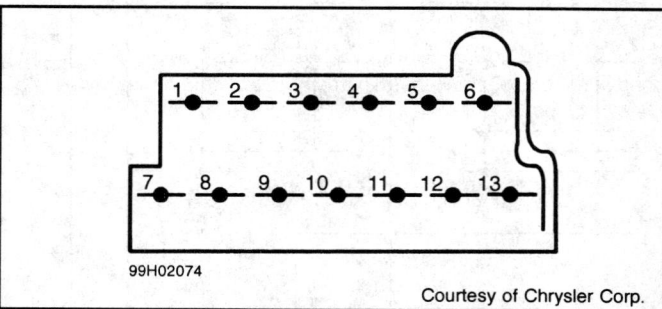

Fig. 3: Identifying Headlight Switch Terminals

SELF-DIAGNOSTIC SYSTEM

WARNING: Vehicle is equipped with an air bag system. To prevent air bag deployment, disconnect negative battery cable and wait at least 2 minutes before servicing instrument cluster. See appropriate AIR BAG RESTRAINT SYSTEMS article.

NOTE: Testing of the instrument panel and gauges requires using a scan tool to check circuits connected to the Body Control Module (BCM). See appropriate BODY CONTROL COMPUTER TESTS article.

QUICK TEST

1) As a quick diagnosis, instrument cluster will perform a function check immediately after ignition is switch is turned to RUN/START position. Electronic display, odometer/transmission range indicator and all warning lights EXCEPT low fuel, cruise, high beam, fog lamps and turn signal will light for a brief period.
2) If cluster is not receiving PCI bus messages, cluster will appear non-functional and NO BUS will be displayed. If instrument cluster is not receiving PCI bus messages, see appropriate BODY CONTROL COMPUTER TESTS article.

REMOVAL & INSTALLATION

CAUTION: When battery is disconnected, vehicle computer and memory systems may lose memory data. Driveability problems may exist until computer systems have completed a relearn cycle. See COMPUTER RELEARN PROCEDURES article in GENERAL INFORMATION before disconnecting battery.

HEADLIGHT SWITCH

Removal & Installation – Disconnect negative battery cable. Remove instrument panel left side cover cap. Remove steering column shroud

1999 ACCESSORIES & EQUIPMENT
Analog Instrument Panels
Concorde, Intrepid, LHS & 300M (Cont.)

CHRY
4-393

cover. Tilt steering column to lowest position. Remove all necessary components to access cluster bezel mounting screws. Remove screws. Using Trim Stick (#C-4755), pry out instrument cluster bezel. Disconnect headlight switch wiring and remove bezel. Remove 3 switch retaining screws and remove switch. To install, reverse removal procedure.

INSTRUMENT CLUSTER & BEZEL

NOTE: To service any instrument cluster component, instrument cluster must be removed from instrument panel.

Removal & Installation – 1) Disconnect negative battery cable. Remove instrument panel left side cover cap. Remove steering column shroud cover. Tilt steering column to lowest position. Remove all necessary components to access cluster bezel mounting screws. Remove screws. Using Trim Stick (#C-4755), pry out instrument cluster bezel. Disconnect headlight switch wiring and remove bezel.

2) Remove instrument cluster screws. Pull cluster away from panel. Instrument cluster wire harness connectors are self-aligning. About 30 lbs. (9 kg.) force will be required to disengage cluster from wire connectors and upper clips. Tabs are provided in lower corners for hook type tool to aid in removal. To install, reverse removal procedure.

SPEEDOMETER/TACHOMETER, GAUGES, GEAR SELECT INDICATOR & ODOMETER

NOTE: Use illustration for cluster identification. See Fig. 1 or 2.

Removal & Installation – 1) Remove instrument cluster. See INSTRUMENT CLUSTER & BEZEL. Remove back cover retaining screws. *See Fig. 4.* Disconnect gear select indicator and odometer connectors from printed circuit board. Remove mask/lens retaining screws and remove mask/lens.

2) Remove speedometer/tachometer assembly from cluster. Speedometer/tachometer are serviced as one component. Remove odometer retaining screws and remove odometer. Remove gear shift indicator retaining screws and remove indicator. To install, place odometer assembly in NEW speedometer/tachometer assembly. To complete installation, reverse removal procedure.

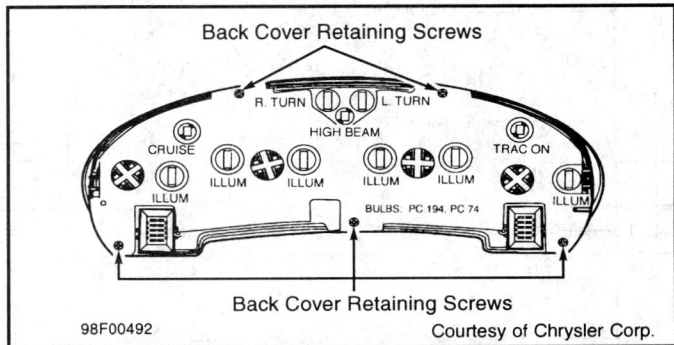

Fig. 4: Rear View Of Instrument Cluster (Intrepid, LHS & 300M Shown; Concorde Is Similar)

CHRY
4-394

1999 ACCESSORIES & EQUIPMENT
Analog Instrument Panels
Concorde, Intrepid, LHS & 300M (Cont.)

WIRING DIAGRAMS

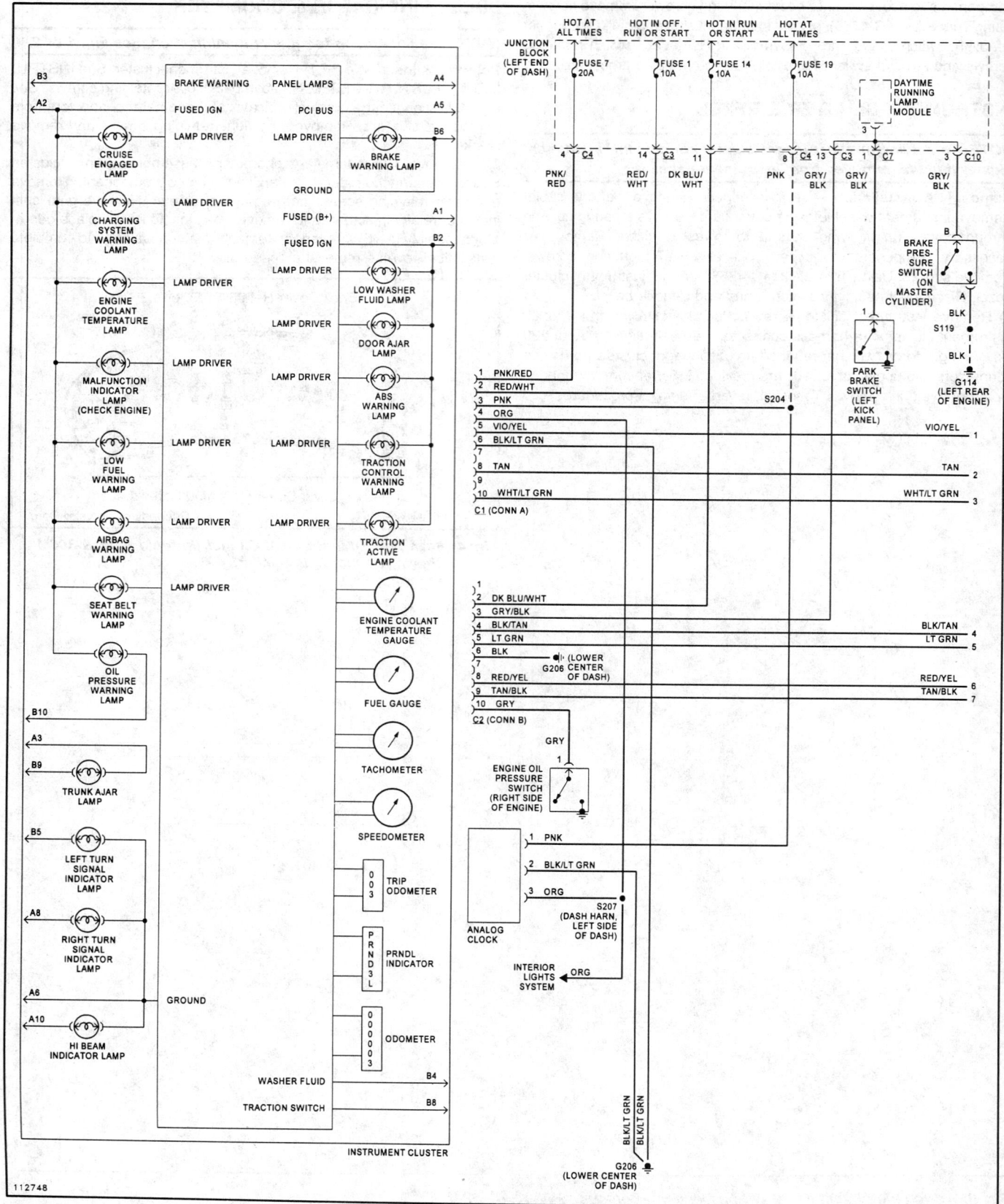

Fig. 5: Analog Instrument Panel Wiring Diagram (Concorde & Intrepid – 1 Of 2)

1999 ACCESSORIES & EQUIPMENT
Analog Instrument Panels
Concorde, Intrepid, LHS & 300M (Cont.)

CHRY
4-395

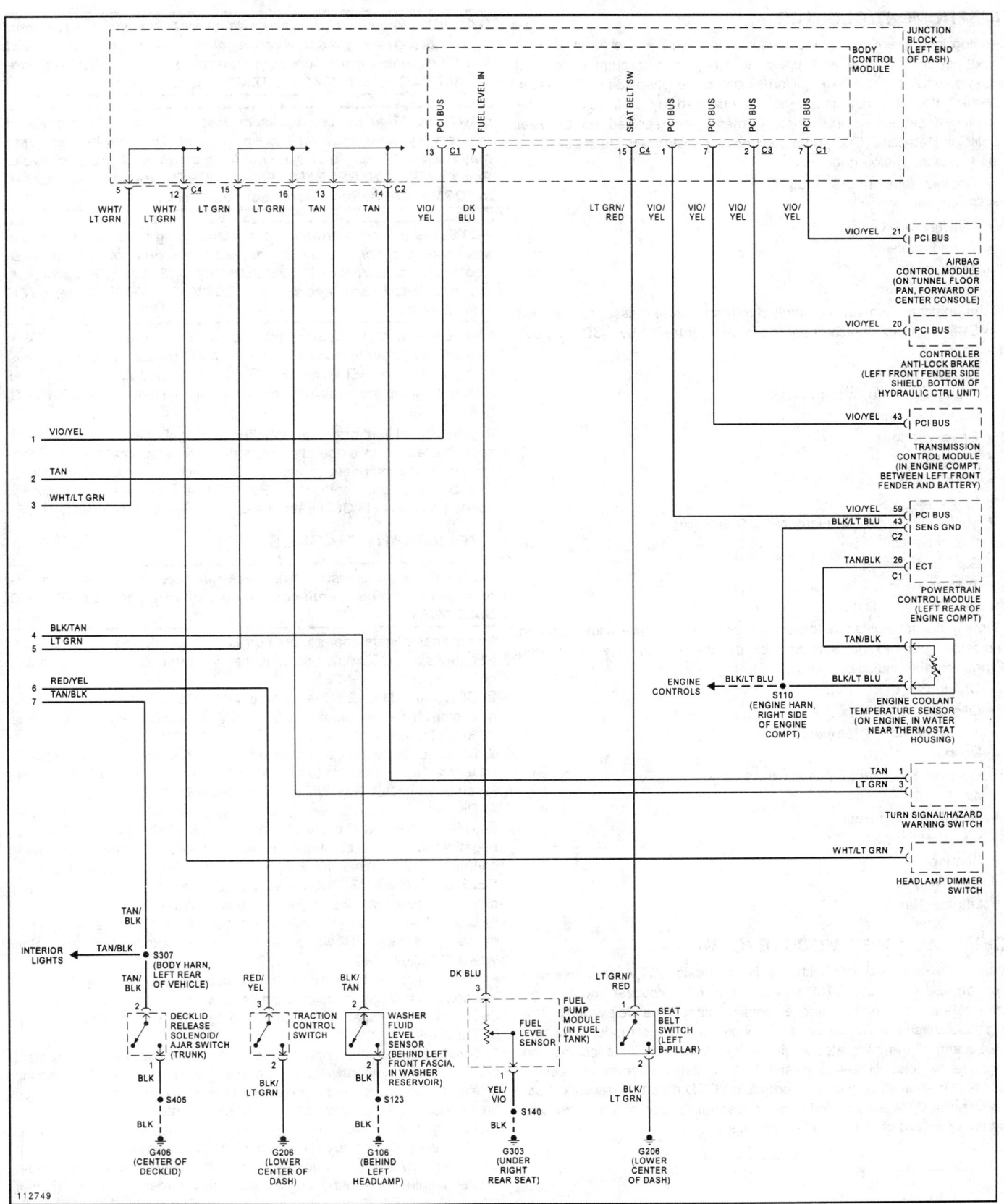

Fig. 6: Analog Instrument Panel Wiring Diagram (Concorde & Intrepid – 2 Of 2)

112749

1999 ACCESSORIES & EQUIPMENT
Analog Instrument Panels – Dakota & Durango

DESCRIPTION & OPERATION

INSTRUMENT CLUSTER

Analog instrument cluster includes warning lights and electromagnetic type gauges. Voltage is supplied to all gauges through instrument cluster circuit board when ignition switch is the ON or START position. Current flow through gauge coil is changed by instrument cluster electronic circuitry in response to messages received on Chrysler Collision Detection (CCD) data bus network. Instrument cluster includes the following analog gauges:

- Coolant Temperature Gauge
- Fuel Gauge
- Oil Pressure Gauge
- Speedometer
- Tachometer
- Voltmeter

Some indicator lights are controlled in response to messages received on CCD data bus. Indicator lights that are controlled by CCD data bus include:

- Air Bag
- Anti-Lock Brake System (ABS)
- Brake Warning
- Check Gauges
- Cruise On
- Door Ajar (Durango)
- Low Fuel
- Malfunction Indicator Light (MIL), Check Engine
- Overdrive Off
- Seat Belt Reminder
- Transmission Oil Temperature (A/T)
- Upshift (M/T – Dakota)

Some indicator lights are programmable. This feature allows certain indicator lights to be activated or deactivated using a scan tool. Programmable indicator lights include:

- Cruise-On
- Overdrive-Off
- Transmission Oil Temperature
- Upshift

The following indicator lights are hard-wired:

- 4WD
- Headlight High Beam
- Low Washer Fluid
- Security
- Turn Signals
- Liftgate Ajar

CENTRAL TIMER MODULE (CTM)

Vehicle is equipped with either a base version CTM or a high-line version. Base model CTM serves as a chime/buzzer module, an intermittent wipe module and an ignition lamp time delay relay. The high-line version CTM provides all functions of base model CTM, but also controls and integrates additional electronic functions included on high-line vehicles. High-line version CTM contains a central processing unit and interfaces with other modules on CCD data bus network. Both versions of CTM are located under passenger's side of the instrument panel, outboard of the glove box opening.

SELF-DIAGNOSTIC SYSTEM

WARNING: Vehicle is equipped with an air bag system. To prevent air bag deployment, disconnect negative battery cable and wait at least 2 minutes before servicing instrument cluster. See appropriate AIR BAG RESTRAINT SYSTEMS article.

CAUTION: When battery is disconnected, vehicle computer and memory systems may lose memory data. Driveability problems may exist until computer systems have completed a relearn cycle. See COMPUTER RELEARN PROCEDURES article in GENERAL INFORMATION before disconnecting battery.

NOTE: Testing of instrument panel and gauges requires using a scan tool to check circuits connected to various control modules. See appropriate VEHICLE COMMUNICATIONS article. For any testing not listed, see appropriate BODY CONTROL COMPUTER TESTS article.

If all gauges and/or indicator lights are inoperative, see PRELIMINARY DIAGNOSIS. If an individual gauge or CCD bus controlled indicator is inoperative, see SELF-DIAGNOSTICS. If an individual hard wired indicator light is inoperative, see appropriate system test and WIRING DIAGRAMS.

If an individual light or gauge is malfunctioning that is not listed, ensure appropriate system is operating properly before instrument panel repair. Diagnosis of appropriate system and Chrysler Collision Detection (CCD) data bus should be performed. For CCD data bus testing, check for opens and shorts in CCD data bus circuits. See WIRING DIAGRAMS.

PRELIMINARY DIAGNOSIS

NOTE: There are 2 instrument cluster connectors. These connectors look the same. Identify connectors by wire color. See WIRING DIAGRAMS.

1) If indicator lights operate, but no gauges operate, go to next step. If all gauges and CCD data bus controlled indicator lights are inoperative, go to step **5)**.

2) Check fuse No. 12 (15-amp) in junction block. If fuse is okay, go to next step. If fuse is blown, repair short circuit and replace fuse. See WIRING DIAGRAMS.

3) Check for battery voltage at fuse No. 12 (15-amp) in junction block. If battery voltage exists, go to next step. If battery voltage does not exist, repair open circuit. See WIRING DIAGRAMS.

4) Disconnect negative battery cable. Remove instrument cluster. See INSTRUMENT CLUSTER under REMOVAL & INSTALLATION. Connect negative battery cable. Check for battery voltage at instrument cluster connector C1, terminal No. 6 (Pink wire). If battery voltage exists, go to SELF-DIAGNOSTICS. If battery voltage does not exist, repair open circuit to instrument cluster. See WIRING DIAGRAMS.

5) Check fuse No. 17 (10-amp) in junction block. If fuse is okay, go to next step. If fuse is blown, repair short circuit and replace fuse. See WIRING DIAGRAMS.

6) Turn ignition on. Check for battery voltage at fuse No. 17 (10-amp) in junction block. If battery voltage exists, go to next step. If battery voltage does not exist, repair open circuit to ignition switch. See WIRING DIAGRAMS.

7) Turn ignition off. Disconnect negative battery cable. Install instrument cluster. Connect negative battery cable. Turn ignition on. Set parking brake. If Red brake warning light illuminates, go to next step. If Red brake warning lamp does not illuminate, go to step **9)**.

8) Turn ignition off. Turn parking lights on and adjust instrument panel lights dimmer rheostat to full bright position. If instrument panel lights are on, go to step **10)**. If instrument panel lights are off, repair instrument cluster illumination ground circuit between instrument cluster connector C1 terminal No. 5 (Black wire) and ground. See WIRING DIAGRAMS.

9) Remove instrument cluster. See INSTRUMENT CLUSTER under REMOVAL & INSTALLATION. Connect negative battery cable. Turn ignition on. Measure voltage between ground and terminal No. 2

(Orange/Light Green wire on Dakota; Dark Blue/White wire on Durango) at instrument cluster Black connector C1. If battery voltage is present, go to SELF-DIAGNOSTICS. If battery voltage is not present, locate and repair open circuit.

10) Remove instrument cluster. See INSTRUMENT CLUSTER REMOVAL & INSTALLATION. Check continuity between ground and terminal No. 4 (Black/Tan or Black/Light Green wire) at instrument cluster Black connector C1. If continuity exists, go to SELF- DIAGNOS-TICS. If continuity does not exist, locate and repair open in ground circuit between instrument cluster connector C1 terminal No. 4 (Black/Tan or Black/Light Green wire) and ground.

SELF-DIAGNOSTICS

1) With ignition off, press and hold trip odometer RESET button while turning ignition switch to ON position. Continue to hold RESET button until odometer window displays CHEC (about 10 seconds). If problem exists, system will display Diagnostic Trouble Codes (DTCs). See DIAGNOSTIC CODE CHART table. For repairs of DTCs, see appropri-

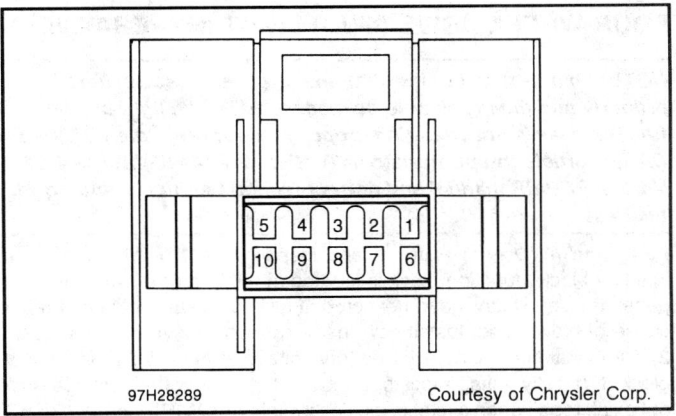

97H28289 — Courtesy of Chrysler Corp.

Fig. 1: Identifying Instrument Cluster Connector Terminals

ate BODY CONTROL COMPUTER TESTS article.

DIAGNOSTIC TROUBLE CODE (DTC) CHART

DTC	Description	Correction
110	Cluster CPU, RAM or EEPROM Fault	Replace Instrument Cluster
900	CCD Bus Inoperative	Check CCD Bus Connections At Cluster; Check Cluster Fuses; Check CCD Bus Bias; Check CCD Bus Voltage; Check CCD Bus Terminations
920	Not Receiving VSS Message From PCM	Check PCM Software Level; Using Scan Tool, Verify VSS Message Is Sent By PCM
921	Not Receiving Distance Pulse Message From PCM	Check PCM Software Level; Using Scan Tool, Verify Distance Pulse Message Is Sent By PCM
940	Not Receiving Air Bag Light On Message From Air Bag Module	Check CCD Bus Connections At PCM; Check ACM Fuse
950	Not Receiving ABS Light On Message From Anti-lock Brake Control Module	Check CCD BUs Connections At Anti-Lock Control Module
999	Undefined Error	Record DTC; Press RESET Button To Continue Self-Diagnostic Test

2) If no DTCs appear, cluster will begin odometer walking segment test. First all segments will be illuminated, then each segment in sequence. If any segment does not illuminate, repeat test to confirm and replace instrument cluster. When walking segment test is complete, bulb check will start.

3) If any bulb does not light, remove instrument cluster and check bulb and bulb holder. See INSTRUMENT CLUSTER under REMOVAL & INSTALLATION. Ensure bulb holder is properly installed. If bulb and bulb holder are okay, replace instrument cluster. If any LED does not light, replace instrument cluster. When bulb check is complete, gauge actuator test will start.

4) Each gauge needle should stop at 3 calibration points, then return to relaxed position. If any gauge does not perform as specified, remove instrument cluster. See INSTRUMENT CLUSTER under REMOVAL & INSTALLATION. Inspect all connections between printed circuit board and gauge terminals, repair as necessary. If connections are okay, replace instrument cluster. Instrument will automatically exit self-diagnostics when test is complete.

SYSTEM TESTS

NOTE: *There are 2 instrument cluster connectors. These connectors look the same. Identify connectors by wire color. See WIRING DIAGRAMS.*

BRAKE WARNING LIGHT INDICATOR TEST

1) Ensure parking brake is released. Turn ignition on. If brake warning light stays on, check and repair hydraulic brake system as necessary. See appropriate DISC & DRUM article in BRAKES in appropriate MITCHELL® manual.

2) If brake warning light does not illuminate when ignition is on, check fuse No. 17 (10-amp) in junction block. Junction block is located at left end cover of instrument panel. If fuse is okay, go to next step. If fuse is blown, locate and repair cause of blown fuse. Install new fuse and recheck system operation.

3) Turn ignition on. Check for battery voltage at fuse No. 17 in junction block. If battery voltage exists, go to next step. If battery voltage does not exist, repair open circuit to ignition switch. See WIRING DIAGRAMS.

4) Turn ignition off. Disconnect negative battery cable. Disconnect parking brake switch connector. Switch is located at base of parking brake lever. Ensure parking brake lever is released. Check continuity between ground and parking brake switch terminal. If continuity does not exist, go to next step. If continuity exists, adjust or replace parking brake switch.

5) Ensure parking brake switch is still disconnected. Turn ignition off. Remove instrument cluster. See INSTRUMENT CLUSTER under REMOVAL & INSTALLATION. Check continuity between ground and park brake switch connector. If continuity does not exist, go to next step. If continuity exists, repair short to ground between instrument cluster and park brake switch. See WIRING DIAGRAMS.

6) Check continuity of White/Black wire between park brake switch connector and terminal No. 3 at instrument cluster connector C1. *See Fig. 1.* If continuity does not exist, repair open White/Black wire. If continuity exists, see SELF- DIAGNOSTICS under SELF-DIAGNOSTIC SYSTEM.

FOUR WHEEL DRIVE (4WD) LIGHT INOPERATIVE

NOTE: This test assumes that the transfer case is functioning properly and the problem to be diagnosed is with light or switch. If transfer case is not operating properly, see appropriate TRANSFER CASES article in appropriate MITCHELL® TRANSMISSION SERVICE & REPAIR manual and correct fault(s) before continuing with this test.

Full Time 4WD – 1) Remove and inspect fuse No. 17 (10-amp) in junction block. Junction block is located at left end cover of instrument panel. If fuse is okay, go to next step. If fuse is blown, locate and repair cause of blown fuse. Install new fuse and recheck system operation.
2) Turn ignition on. Check for battery voltage at fuse No. 17 in junction block. If battery voltage exists, go to next step. If battery voltage does not exist, repair open circuit to ignition switch. See WIRING DIAGRAMS.
3) Turn ignition off. Disconnect negative battery cable. Disconnect 4WD switch connector. 4WD switch connector is located on front frame. Check continuity between 4WD switch connector terminal "A" (Black wire) and ground. *See Fig. 2.* If continuity does not exist, repair open Black wire between 4WD switch and ground. If continuity exists, go to next step.
4) Connect battery cable. Turn ignition on. Install jumper wire between 4WD switch connector terminal "B" (Black/White wire) and ground. 4WD light should illuminate. If light illuminates, replace 4WD switch. If light does not illuminate, go to next step.
5) Turn ignition off. Disconnect negative battery cable. Ensure 4WD switch is still disconnected. Remove instrument cluster. See INSTRUMENT CLUSTER under REMOVAL & INSTALLATION. Check continuity between ground and instrument cluster connector C1 terminal No. 8 (Black/White wire). *See Fig. 1.* If continuity does not exist, go to next step. If continuity exists, repair short to ground in Black/White wire.
6) Check continuity of Black/White wire between 4WD switch connector and terminal No. 8 at instrument cluster connector C1. If continuity does not exist, repair open Black/White wire. If continuity exists, replace bulb.

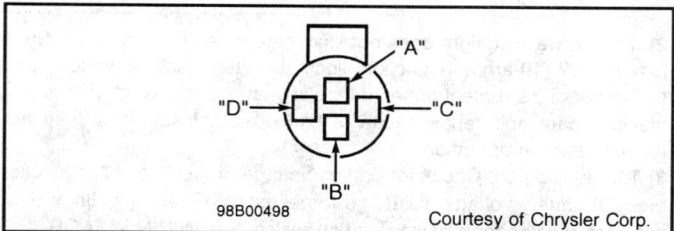

98B00498   Courtesy of Chrysler Corp.

Fig. 2: Identifying 4WD Switch Connector Terminals

Part Time 4WD – 1) Remove and inspect fuse No. 17 (10-amp) in junction block. Junction block is located at left end cover of instrument panel. If fuse is okay, go to next step. If fuse is blown, locate and repair cause of blown fuse. Install new fuse and recheck system operation.
2) Turn ignition on. Check for battery voltage at fuse No. 17 in junction block. If battery voltage exists, go to next step. If battery voltage does not exist, repair open circuit to junction block. See WIRING DIAGRAMS.
3) Turn ignition off. Disconnect negative battery cable. Disconnect 4WD switch connector. 4WD switch connector is located on front frame. Check continuity between 4WD switch connector terminal "A" (Black wire) and ground. *See Fig. 2.* If continuity does not exist, repair open Black wire between 4WD switch and ground. If continuity exists, go to next step.
4) Connect battery cable. Turn ignition on. Install jumper wire between 4WD switch connector terminal "D" (Black/Gray wire) and ground. 4WD light should illuminate. If light illuminates, replace 4WD switch. If light does not illuminate, go to next step.
5) Turn ignition off. Disconnect negative battery cable. Ensure 4WD switch is still disconnected. Disconnect anti-lock brake control module connector. Anti-lock brake control module is located at left side of engine compartment on left side inner fenderwell. Remove instrument cluster. See INSTRUMENT CLUSTER under REMOVAL & INSTALLATION.

Check continuity between ground and instrument cluster connector C2 terminal No. 10 (Black/Gray wire). *See Fig. 1.* If continuity does not exist, go to next step. If continuity exists, repair short to ground in Black/Gray wire.
6) Check continuity of Black/Gray wire between 4WD switch connector and terminal No. 10 at instrument cluster connector C2. If continuity does not exist, repair open Black/Gray wire. If continuity exists, replace bulb.

INSTRUMENT CLUSTER ILLUMINATION TEST

1) This test assumes that all exterior lighting controlled by headlight switch are functioning properly. If exterior lighting is not functioning properly, correct fault(s) before continuing with this test.
2) Check and replace illumination bulbs as necessary and retest. If bulbs are okay, check fuse No. 5 (5-amp) in junction block. Junction block is located at left end cover of instrument panel. If fuse is okay, go to next step. If fuse is blown, repair short circuit and replace fuse.
3) Using headlight switch, turn parking lights on. Connect voltmeter between ground and fuse No. 5 in junction block. Observing voltmeter, rotate headlight switch knob counterclockwise to just before interior lights detent, then rotate knob clockwise. Voltage reading should change from battery voltage to zero volts. If voltage is as specified, go to next step. If voltage is not as specified, locate and repair open circuit between headlight switch and junction block.
4) Disconnect negative battery cable. Remove instrument cluster. See INSTRUMENT CLUSTER under REMOVAL & INSTALLATION. Turn headlight switch off. Remove fuse No. 5 from junction block. Check continuity between ground and terminal No. 1 (Orange wire) at instrument cluster connector C2. *See Fig. 1.* If continuity does not exist, go to next step. If continuity exists, locate and repair short to ground in Orange wire.
5) Install fuse No. 5 in junction block. Connect negative battery cable. Using headlight switch, turn parking lights on. Rotate headlight switch knob counterclockwise to just before interior lights detent. Check for battery voltage at terminal No. 1 (Orange wire) at instrument cluster connector C2. If battery voltage is not present, locate and repair open circuit. If battery voltage is present, no problem is indicated. Recheck instrument cluster illumination bulb(s) and bulb holders. Repair as necessary.

LIFTGATE AJAR INDICATOR INOPERATIVE TEST (DURANGO)

1) Check fuse No. 17 (10-amp) in junction block. Junction block is located at left end cover of instrument panel. If fuse is okay, go to next step. If fuse is blown, locate and repair cause of blown fuse and retest.
2) Turn ignition on. Check for battery voltage at fuse No. 17 in junction block. If battery voltage exists, go to next step. If battery voltage does not exist, repair open circuit to ignition switch. See WIRING DIAGRAMS.
3) Unplug liftgate ajar switch connector. Check continuity between liftgate ajar switch connector Black wire and ground. If continuity does not exist, repair open Black wire between liftgate ajar switch and ground. If continuity exists, go to next step.
4) Install jumper wire between outside terminals of liftgate ajar switch harness connector. Turn ignition on. Warning light should come on. Remove jumper wire. Light should go off. If light operates okay, replace liftgate ajar switch. If light does not operate okay, go to next step.
5) Ensure liftgate ajar switch connector is still disconnected. Disconnect negative battery cable. Remove instrument cluster bezel and cluster assembly. See INSTRUMENT CLUSTER under REMOVAL & INSTALLATION. Disconnect instrument cluster connectors. Check continuity between instrument cluster connector C2 terminal No. 4 (Tan/Black wire) and ground. *See Fig. 1.* If continuity exists, repair liftgate ajar sense circuit (Tan/Black wire) for short to ground. See WIRING DIAGRAMS. If no continuity exists, go to next step.
6) Check continuity of Tan/Black wire between instrument cluster connector C2 terminal No. 4 and liftgate ajar switch connector. If continuity exists, replace faulty bulb. If continuity does not exist, repair open liftgate ajar sense circuit. See WIRING DIAGRAMS.

LOW WASHER INDICATOR INOPERATIVE TEST

1) Check fuse No. 17 (10-amp) in junction block. Junction block is located at left end cover of instrument panel. If fuse is okay, go to next step. If fuse is blown, locate and repair cause of blown fuse and retest.
2) Turn ignition on. Check for battery voltage at fuse No. 17 in junction block. If battery voltage exists, go to next step. If battery voltage does not exist, repair open circuit to junction block. See WIRING DIAGRAMS.
3) Unplug washer fluid level switch connector. Install jumper wire between both terminals of harness connector. Turn ignition on. Warning light should come on. Remove jumper wire. Light should go off. If light operates okay, replace washer fluid level switch. If light does not operate okay, go to next step.
4) Turn ignition off. Check continuity in Black wire between washer fluid level switch connector and ground. If continuity exists, go to next step. If no continuity exists, repair open Black wire.
5) Ensure washer fluid level switch connector is still disconnected. Disconnect negative battery cable. Remove instrument cluster. See INSTRUMENT CLUSTER under REMOVAL & INSTALLATION. Disconnect instrument cluster connectors. Check continuity between instrument cluster connector C2 terminal No. 2 (Dark Blue wire on Dakota; Tan/White wire on Durango) and ground. *See Fig. 1.* If continuity exists, repair washer fluid level sense circuit (Dark Blue wire on Dakota; Tan/White wire on Durango) for short to ground. See WIRING DIAGRAMS. If no continuity exists, go to next step.
6) Check continuity between instrument cluster connector C2 terminal No. 2 (Dark Blue wire on Dakota; Tan/White wire on Durango) and washer fluid level switch connector (Black/Tan wire on Dakota; Tan/White wire on Durango). If continuity exists, replace faulty bulb. If no continuity exists, repair open washer fluid level sense circuit. See WIRING DIAGRAMS.

SECURITY LIGHT TEST

1) Check fuse No. 17 (10-amp) in junction block. Junction block is located at left end cover of instrument panel. If fuse is okay, go to next step. If fuse is blown, locate and repair cause of blown fuse and retest.
2) Turn ignition on. Check for battery voltage at fuse No. 17 in junction block. If battery voltage exists, go to next step. If battery voltage does not exist, locate and repair open circuit to ignition switch. See WIRING DIAGRAMS.
3) Ensure ignition is off. Disconnect negative battery cable. Unplug Central Timing Module (CTM). CTM is located behind right kick panel. Connect negative battery cable. Install jumper wire between CTM 18-pin Black connector C2 terminal No. 8 (Yellow wire on Dakota; Black/Orange wire on Durango) and ground. *See Fig. 3.* If security light comes on, see appropriate ANTI-THEFT SYSTEMS article. If security light does not come on, go to next step.
4) Disconnect negative battery cable. Remove instrument cluster. See INSTRUMENT CLUSTER under REMOVAL & INSTALLATION. Disconnect instrument cluster connectors. Check continuity between junction block and instrument cluster connector C1 terminal No. 6 (Pink wire). *See Fig. 1.* If continuity exists, go to next step. If no continuity exists, repair open Pink wire.
5) Check continuity of Yellow wire on Dakota or Black/Orange wire on Durango between CTM 18-pin Black connector C2 terminal No. 8 and instrument cluster connector C1 terminal No. 1. If continuity exists, replace faulty bulb. If no continuity exists, repair open Yellow or Black/Orange wire. See WIRING DIAGRAMS.

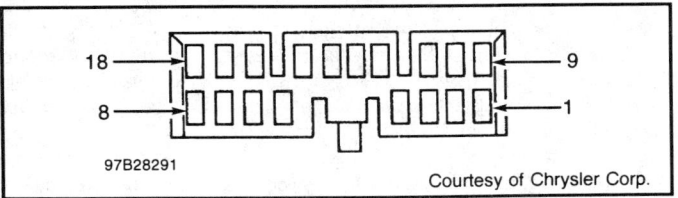

97B28291
Courtesy of Chrysler Corp.

Fig. 3: Connector View Of CTM Connector

LEFT & RIGHT TURN SIGNAL INDICATORS INOPERATIVE TEST

1) This test will diagnosis an inoperative turn signal indicator light and circuit. Disconnect negative battery cable. Remove instrument cluster leaving wire harnesses connected. See INSTRUMENT CLUSTER under REMOVAL & INSTALLATION.
2) Connect negative battery cable. Turn hazard flashers on. Backprobe instrument cluster connector C2 terminals No. 6 (Light Green wire) and No. 8 (Tan wire) for pulsing voltage. If pulsing voltage is not present on either terminal, repair appropriate wire between instrument cluster connector C2 and multi-function switch. If pulsing voltage is present, replace appropriate turn signal indicator bulb.

REMOVAL & INSTALLATION

WARNING: Vehicle is equipped with an air bag system. To prevent air bag deployment, disconnect negative battery cable and wait at least 2 minutes before servicing instrument cluster. See appropriate AIR BAG RESTRAINT SYSTEMS article.

CAUTION: When battery is disconnected, vehicle computer and memory systems may lose memory data. Driveability problems may exist until computer systems have completed a relearn cycle. See COMPUTER RELEARN PROCEDURES article in GENERAL INFORMATION before disconnecting battery.

CENTRAL TIMER MODULE (CTM)

Removal & Installation – 1) Disconnect negative battery cable. Remove glove box. Remove right-side glove box bracket screws from instrument panel. Remove screws holding CTM bracket to right glove box bracket. *See Fig. 4.*
2) Remove right glove box bracket. Pull CTM with bracket into glove box opening and disconnect connectors. Remove CTM from instrument panel. To install CTM, reverse removal procedure. Ensure mounting tab is engaged in slot in instrument panel end bracket.

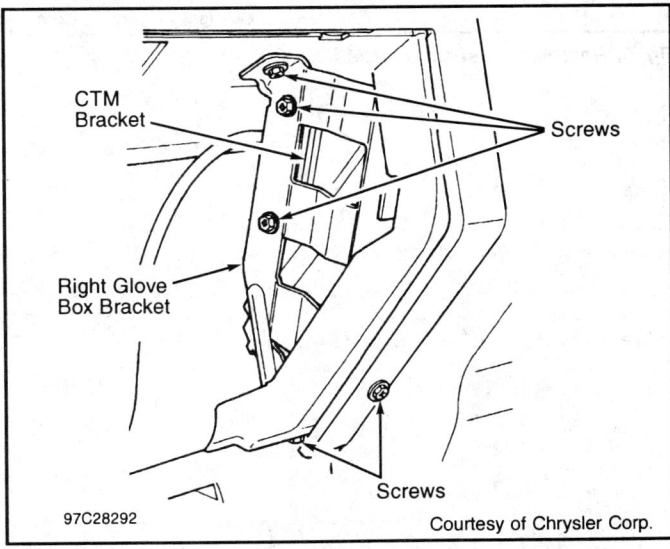

CTM Bracket

Screws

Right Glove Box Bracket

Screws

97C28292
Courtesy of Chrysler Corp.

Fig. 4: Removing CTM From Instrument Panel

INSTRUMENT CLUSTER

Removal & Installation – 1) Disconnect negative battery cable. Turn ignition switch to UNLOCK position. Set parking brake. On A/T equipped models, place shift lever into "L" position.
2) On all models, place tilt wheel in lowest position, if equipped. Using a wide, flat-blade tool, pry around edge of instrument cluster bezel to release 9 snap clip retainers. *See Fig. 5.* Pull instrument cluster bezel back far enough to unplug fog lamp switch, if equipped. Remove instrument cluster bezel.

3) Remove instrument cluster screws. Move cluster rearward. On A/T equipped models, remove shift indicator. See GEAR SELECTOR INDICATOR. On all models, disconnect cluster wiring connectors. Remove instrument cluster from instrument panel. *See Fig. 6*. To install instrument cluster, reverse removal procedure.

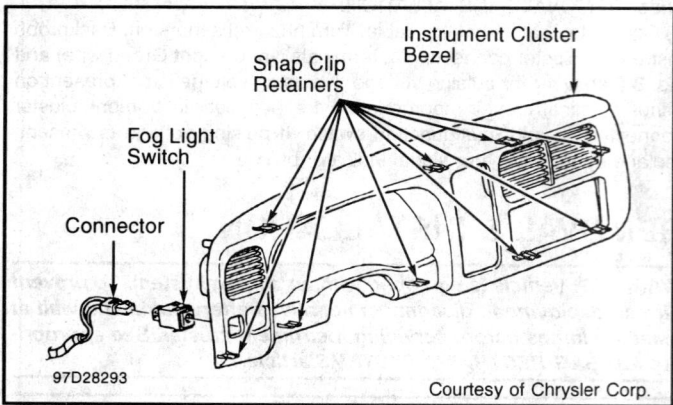

Fig. 5: Removing Instrument Cluster Bezel

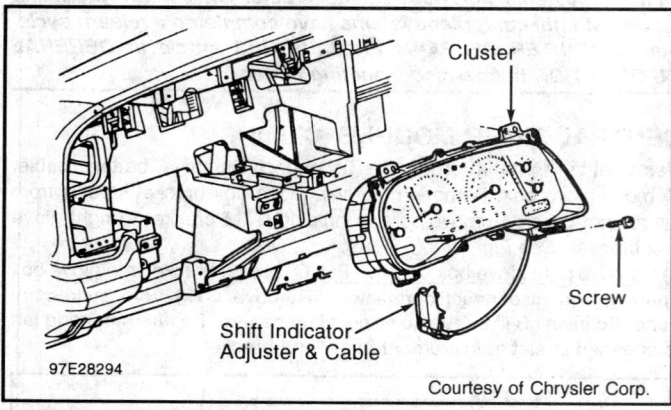

Fig. 6: Removing Instrument Cluster

GEAR SELECTOR INDICATOR

Removal & Installation – Remove instrument cluster. See INSTRUMENT CLUSTER. Remove screws and gear selector indicator mechanism from rear of instrument cluster. Remove lower steering column and knee bolster cover. Remove loop end of gear selector indicator mechanism cable lever on left side of steering column. To install, reverse removal procedure.

HEADLIGHT SWITCH

Removal & Installation – 1) Disconnect negative battery cable. Turn ignition switch to UNLOCK position. Set parking brake. On A/T equipped models, place shift lever into "L" position. Remove screws holding headlight switch to instrument cluster. Pull headlight switch out far enough to remove connectors.

2) Pull headlight switch knob out to on position. Press headlight switch knob and shaft release button located on top of switch and remove knob and shaft from headlight switch. Remove push nut from switch mounting bracket. Remove headlight switch. To install switch, reverse removal procedure.

WIRING DIAGRAMS

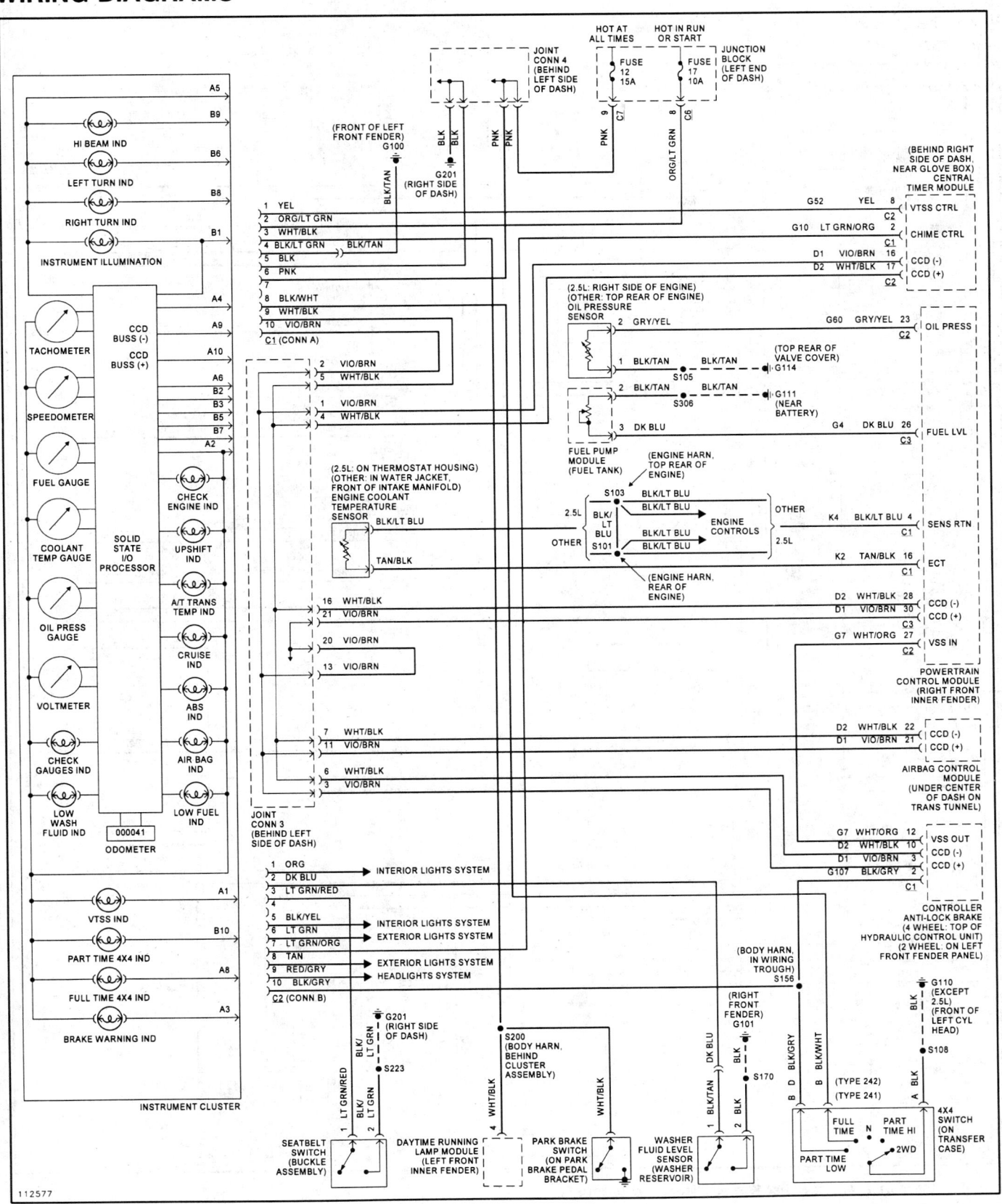

Fig. 7: Analog Instrument Panel Wiring Diagram (Dakota)

112577

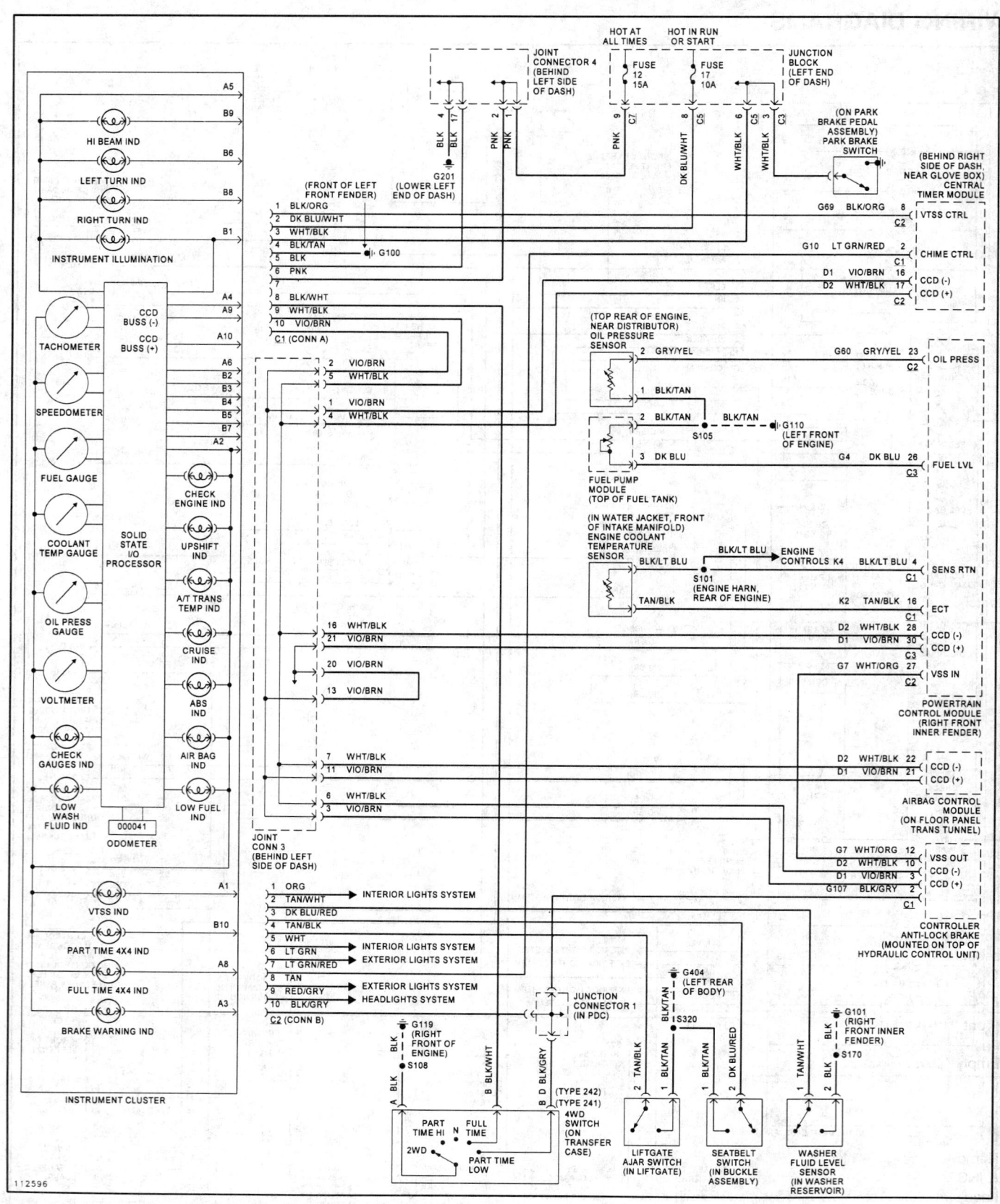

Fig. 8: Analog Instrument Panel Wiring Diagram (Durango)

DESCRIPTION

Instrument cluster gauges include coolant temperature, fuel level, speedometer and tachometer (if equipped). All gauges are magnetic type. Speedometer and odometer are electronically driven.

When ignition switch in OFF position, gauge pointers should rest at or below low graduation. Gauge readings are accurate ONLY when ignition switch is in ON position.

Low fuel level and oil pressure are indicated by warning lights. Other indicator and warning lights include ABS, AIR BAG, battery (charging system), BRAKE, door ajar, high beam, low fuel, oil pressure, CHECK ENGINE, seat belt reminder and turn signals. Instrument panel switches include foglight, headlight and rear defogger.

COMPONENT TESTS

WARNING: Vehicle is equipped with an air bag system. To prevent air bag deployment, disconnect negative battery cable and wait at least 2 minutes before servicing instrument cluster. See appropriate AIR BAG RESTRAINT SYSTEMS article.

FOGLIGHT SWITCH TEST

Remove foglight switch. See FOGLIGHT & REAR DEFOGGER SWITCHES under REMOVAL & INSTALLATION. Using jumper wires, apply battery voltage to switch terminals No. 2 and 4. *See Fig. 1.* Connect a test light to ground. Probe switch terminal No. 3 with test light and press foglight switch button. Foglight switch LED and test light should illuminate. If LED or test light does not illuminate, replace foglight switch.

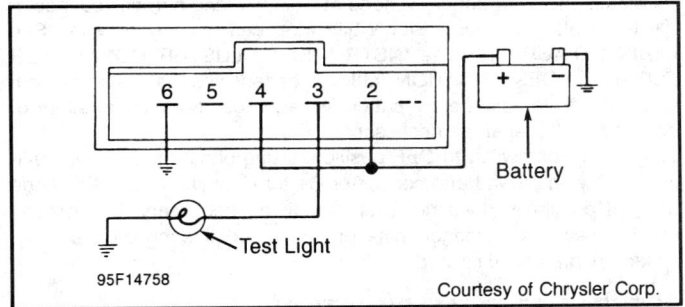

Fig. 1: Testing Foglight Switch

FUEL LEVEL SENSOR

Using ohmmeter, measure resistance between sensor signal and sensor ground terminals of fuel pump module connector with fuel lever sensor in indicated positions. See FUEL LEVEL SENSOR RESISTANCE table. *See Fig. 2.*

FUEL LEVEL SENSOR RESISTANCE

Float Position	Resistance (Ohms)
Full	50-90
Empty	1020-1080

HEADLIGHT SWITCH

Remove headlight switch. See HEADLIGHT SWITCH under REMOVAL & INSTALLATION. Check resistance or continuity between appropriate headlight switch terminals with headlight switch in appropriate position. See HEADLIGHT SWITCH RESISTANCE SPECIFICATIONS table. *See Fig. 3.* If switch does not test as specified, replace headlight switch.

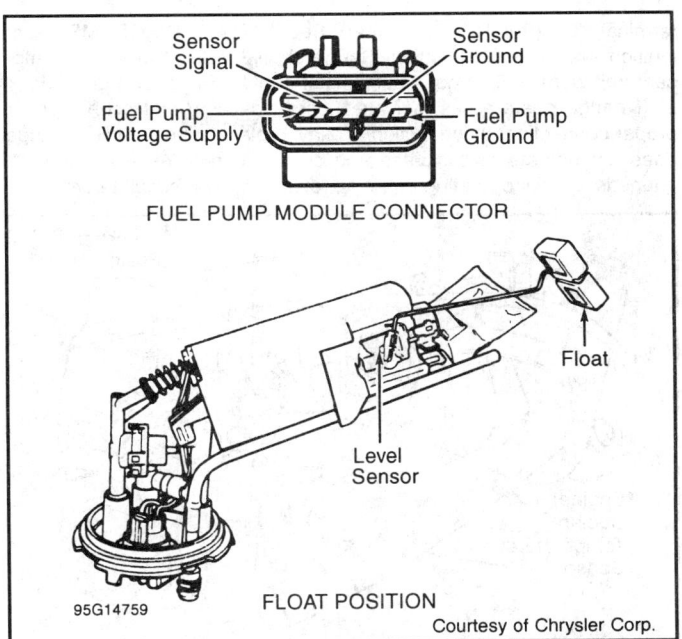

Fig. 2: Testing Fuel Level Sensor

HEADLIGHT SWITCH RESISTANCE SPECIFICATIONS

Switch Position	Between Terminals	Specification
Off	B1 & P	Continuity
Park	B1 & P; B2 & R; B3 & U	Continuity
On	B1 & P; B1 & H; B2 & R; B3 & U	Continuity
Instrument Panel Dimmer [1]		
Full Counterclockwise	D & Ground	Continuity
Between Stops	B2 & R	0.2-5.5 Ohms
Full Clockwise	B2 & R	No Continuity

[1] – With headlight switch in ON or PARK position.

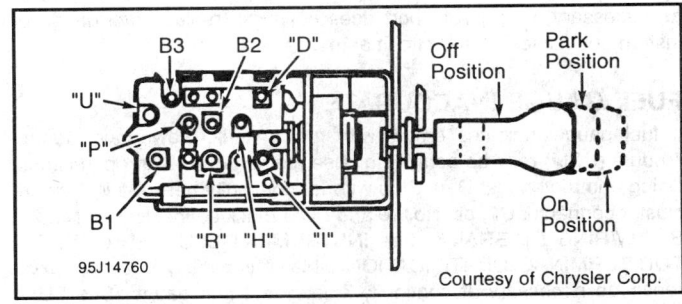

Fig. 3: Testing Headlight Switch

VEHICLE SPEED SENSOR (VSS)

NOTE: This test only applies to vehicle equipped with M/T. Vehicles with A/T use input and output shaft sensors to determine vehicle speed.

If a problem is suspected with Vehicle Speed Sensor (VSS) or circuit. Retrieve Diagnostic Trouble Codes (DTCs) from PCM. See appropriate SELF-DIAGNOSTICS article in ENGINE PERFORMANCE in appropriate MITCHELL® manual.

SYSTEM TESTS

COOLANT TEMPERATURE GAUGE INOPERATIVE

1) Disconnect coolant temperature sensor connector. *See Fig. 4.* Turn ignition switch to ON position. Gauge should read at lowest position. Turn ignition switch to OFF position. Ground sending unit connector

terminal "C" (Purple/Yellow wire). See WIRING DIAGRAMS. Turn ignition switch to ON position. Gauge should read at maximum. After seat belt warning light goes out, cluster should chime for 8 seconds.
2) If gauge operates as indicated, check sending unit connector for proper connection. If connection is okay, replace sending unit. If gauge does not operate as indicated and chime sounds, replace gauge. If gauge is still not operating properly, replace printed circuit board.

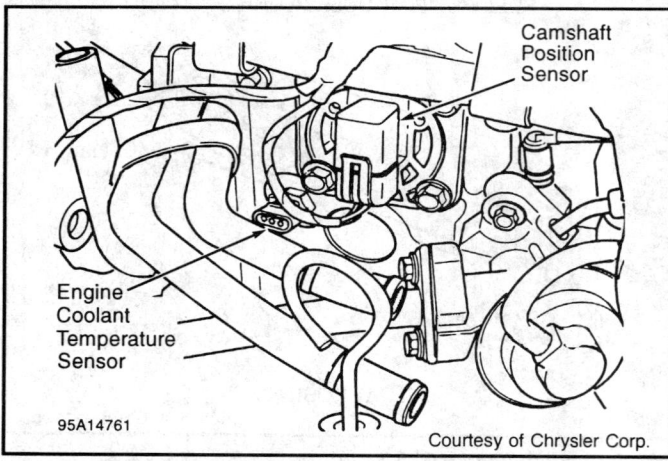

95A14761

Courtesy of Chrysler Corp.

Fig. 4: Locating Coolant Temperature Sensor

FUEL GAUGE INOPERATIVE

1) Disconnect fuel gauge sending unit connector. Turn ignition switch to ON position. Gauge should read at lowest position. Turn ignition switch to OFF position. Ground sending unit connector terminal No. 3 (Dark Blue wire). Turn ignition switch to ON position. Gauge should read at maximum. If gauge does not operate as indicated, go to next step. If gauge operates as indicated, check sending unit connector for proper connection. If connection is okay, check fuel level sensor. See FUEL LEVEL SENSOR.
2) Disconnect instrument cluster connector. Check wiring between instrument cluster connector and fuel gauge sending unit connector for open or short. See WIRING DIAGRAMS. If open or short exists, repair as necessary. If open or short does not exist, replace fuel gauge or instrument cluster printed circuit as necessary.

FUEL GAUGE INACCURATE

If fuel gauge indicates empty with fuel in tank, Powertrain Control Module (PCM) may be sending a false reading due to an open circuit. Using ohmmeter, test Dark Blue wire for continuity between instrument cluster connector C2, pin No. 10 and PCM Black connector, pin No. 23. See WIRING DIAGRAMS. See INSTRUMENT CLUSTER CONNECTOR TERMINAL IDENTIFICATION table. If continuity does not exist, repair as necessary. If continuity exists, test fuel gauge. See FUEL GAUGE INOPERATIVE.

INSTRUMENT CLUSTER CONNECTOR TERMINAL IDENTIFICATION

Connector & Terminal	Circuit
Connector C1	
1	Door Ajar
2	High Beam
3	Right Turn
4	Seat Belt
5	Ignition Feed
6	Battery
7	Tachometer Signal
8	Ground
9	Air Bag
10	Speed Signal
Connector C2	
1	Oil Pressure
2	Anti-Lock Brake System (ABS)

INSTRUMENT CLUSTER CONNECTOR TERMINAL IDENTIFICATION (Cont.)

Connector & Terminal	Circuit
3	CHECK ENGINE Light
4	Engine Temperature
5	Key In, Headlights On
6	Brake
7	Charging System
8	Left Turn
9	Illumination
10	Fuel Level

LOW FUEL WARNING LIGHT INOPERATIVE

Verify fuel gauge is operating correctly. If fuel gauge is okay, check for burned-out bulb or bad connection. If low fuel warning light still does not operate under a low fuel condition, replace printed circuit board.

LOW OIL PRESSURE WARNING LIGHT MALFUNCTION

1) Turn ignition switch to ON position. If warning light does not illuminate, check for a loose or open wire at oil pressure switch located at front of engine. If wire is okay, go to next step.
2) Turn ignition switch to OFF position. Disconnect oil pressure switch connector. Using jumper wire, ground connector. Turn ignition switch to ON position. If warning light does not illuminate, check for burned-out bulb or disconnected socket. If warning light illuminates, check oil pressure. If oil pressure is okay, replace oil pressure switch.

MULTIPLE INSTRUMENT CLUSTER GAUGES INOPERATIVE

1) Remove instrument cluster. See INSTRUMENT CLUSTER under REMOVAL & INSTALLATION. Turn ignition switch to ON position. Using voltmeter, check for battery voltage at cluster wiring harness connector C1, terminals No. 5 (Dark Blue/White wire) and No. 6 (Pink wire). See WIRING DIAGRAMS. See INSTRUMENT CLUSTER CONNECTOR TERMINAL IDENTIFICATION table. If battery voltage exists at both terminals, go to next step. If battery voltage does not exist at either or both terminals, repair as necessary.
2) Turn ignition switch to OFF position. Using ohmmeter, check continuity between ground and connector C1 terminal No. 8 (Black/Orange wire). If continuity does not exist, repair as necessary. If continuity exists, check for damaged pins or connector. If connector is okay, replace printed circuit board.

SPEEDOMETER MALFUNCTION

NOTE: Vehicles with M/T use a vehicle speed sensor to determine vehicle speed. Vehicles with A/T use input and output shaft sensors to determine vehicle speed.

If a problem is suspected with Vehicle Speed Sensor (VSS), output shaft sensor, input shaft sensor or circuit. Retrieve Diagnostic Trouble Codes (DTCs) from PCM. See appropriate SELF-DIAGNOSTICS article in ENGINE PERFORMANCE in appropriate MITCHELL® manual.

TACHOMETER MALFUNCTION

1) Remove instrument cluster. See INSTRUMENT CLUSTER under REMOVAL & INSTALLATION. Using voltmeter, check for battery voltage at instrument cluster connector C1 terminal No. 6 (Pink wire). See WIRING DIAGRAMS. See INSTRUMENT CLUSTER CONNECTOR TERMINAL IDENTIFICATION table. If battery voltage exists, go to next step. If battery voltage does not exist, repair as necessary.
2) Turn ignition switch to ON position. Check for battery voltage at instrument cluster connector C1 terminal No. 5 (Dark Blue/White wire). If battery voltage exists, go to next step. If battery voltage does not exist, repair as necessary.
3) Turn ignition switch to OFF position. Using ohmmeter, check continuity between ground and connector C1 terminal No. 8 (Black/Orange wire). If continuity exists, go to next step. If continuity does not exist, repair as necessary.

4) Using voltmeter in AC mode, check voltage between ground and connector C1 terminal No. 7 (Gray/Light Blue wire) with engine running. If reading is less than one volt, go to next step. If reading is at least one volt, replace tachometer. If tachometer still does not work properly, replace printed circuit board.

5) Turn ignition switch to OFF position. Using ohmmeter, check continuity in Gray/Light Blue wire between connector C1 terminal No. 7 and Powertrain Control Module (PCM) connector terminal No. 73. If continuity does not exist, repair as necessary. If continuity exists, check PCM connector for damaged or pushed-out pins. Repair connector as necessary. If PCM connector is okay, replace PCM.

REMOVAL & INSTALLATION

WARNING: Vehicle is equipped with an air bag system. To prevent air bag deployment, disconnect negative battery cable and wait at least 2 minutes before servicing instrument cluster. See appropriate AIR BAG RESTRAINT SYSTEMS article.

CAUTION: When battery is disconnected, vehicle computer and memory systems may lose memory data. Driveability problems may exist until computer systems have completed a relearn cycle. See COMPUTER RELEARN PROCEDURES article in GENERAL INFORMATION before disconnecting battery.

FOGLIGHT & REAR DEFOGGER SWITCHES

Removal & Installation – Remove instrument panel top cover and cluster bezel by lifting up lower outer areas of cluster bezel and rear edge of top cover to disengage clips. Pull top cover and bezel rearward to disengage forward pins from instrument panel. Disengage switch bezel latches and pull assembly rearward. Disconnect wire connectors and remove switch from bezel. To install, reverse removal procedure.

HEADLIGHT SWITCH

Removal & Installation – **1)** Remove steering column cover and liner. Remove 3 screws attaching headlight switch mounting plate to instrument panel. Pull switch and mounting plate rearward. Disconnect 9-pin connector and ground wiring from switch.

2) Pull switch to ON position. Depress release button on bottom of switch and remove switch knob and shaft. Snap switch bezel out of mounting plate to access retaining nut. Using Phillips screwdriver, remove retaining nut. Remove switch. To install, reverse removal procedure.

INSTRUMENT CLUSTER

Removal & Installation – **1)** Disconnect negative battery cable to ensure no DTCs are generated. Remove instrument panel top cover and cluster bezel by lifting up lower outer areas of cluster bezel and rear edge of top cover to disengage clips. Pull top cover and bezel rearward to disengage forward pins from instrument panel.

2) Remove 4 screws attaching cluster housing to base panel. Pulling cluster rearward, disconnect cluster from base panel. Remove instrument cluster. To install, reverse removal procedure.

INSTRUMENT CLUSTER GAUGES

CAUTION: DO NOT damage cluster overlays while handling or storing. Set cluster in face up position, or gauge operation will be damaged.

Removal & Installation – Remove instrument cluster. See INSTRUMENT CLUSTER. Remove 7 screws attaching printed circuit board cover. It is not necessary to remove foam pad to access bottom screws. Disconnect odometer connector. Remove lens attaching screws and lens. Gently pry out gauge assembly. To install, reverse removal procedure. *See Fig. 5.*

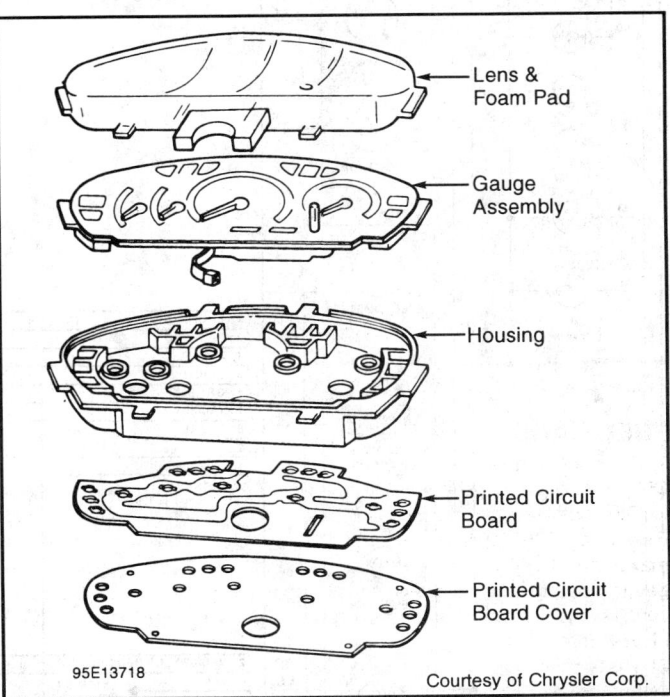

95E13718　　　　Courtesy of Chrysler Corp.

Lens & Foam Pad

Gauge Assembly

Housing

Printed Circuit Board

Printed Circuit Board Cover

Fig. 5: Exploded View Of Instrument Cluster

VEHICLE SPEED SENSOR (VSS)

Removal & Installation – Remove VSS connector. Ensure weather seal is on connector. Remove VSS retaining bolt. Pull VSS and pinion gear assembly from transaxle. If necessary, use flat-blade screwdriver to pry assembly loose. To install, reverse removal procedure. Seat VSS until proper gear engagement is obtained. Tighten bolt to 60 INCH lbs. (7 N.m).

WIRING DIAGRAMS

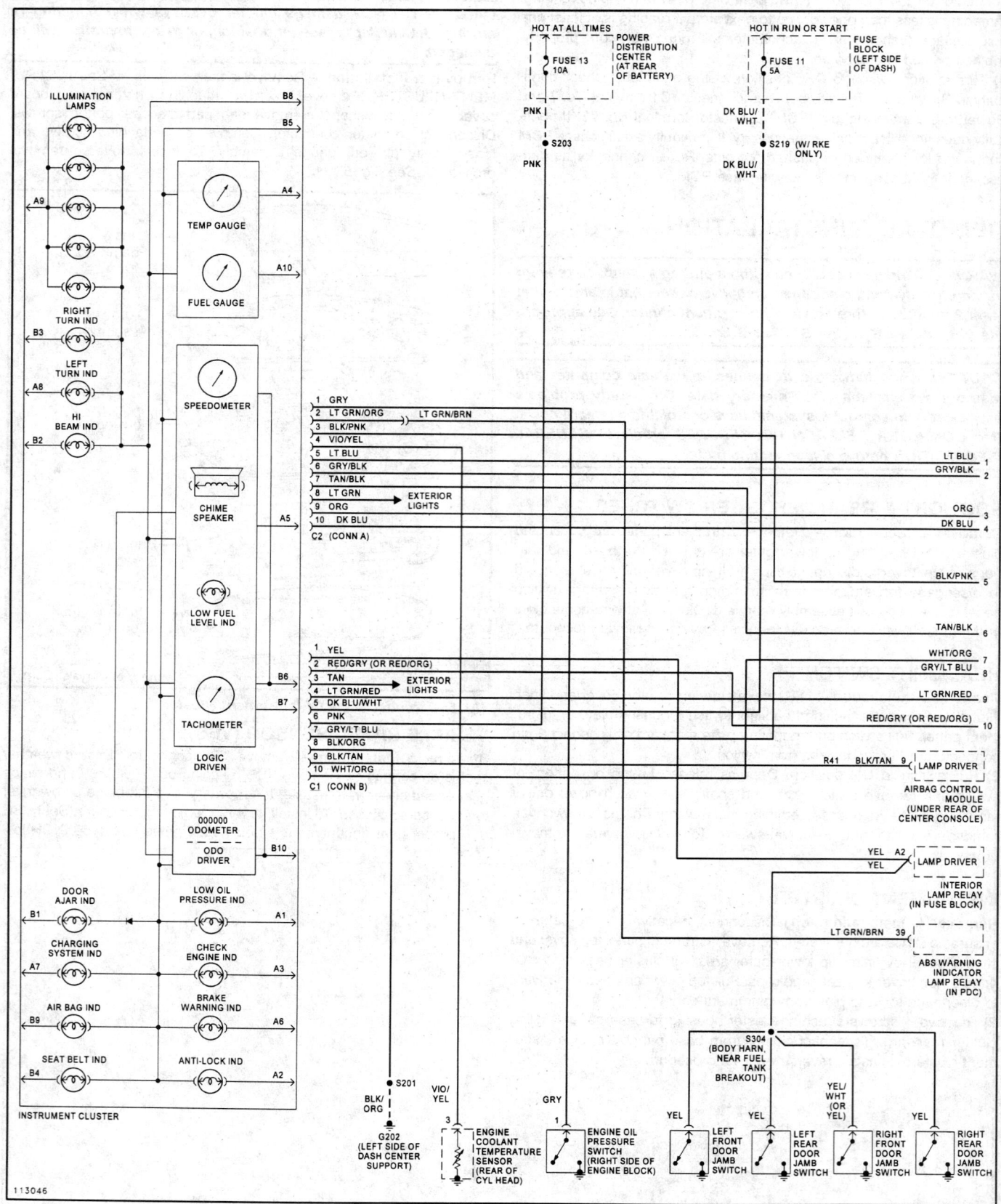

Fig. 6: Analog Instrument Panel Wiring Diagram (Neon – 1 Of 2)

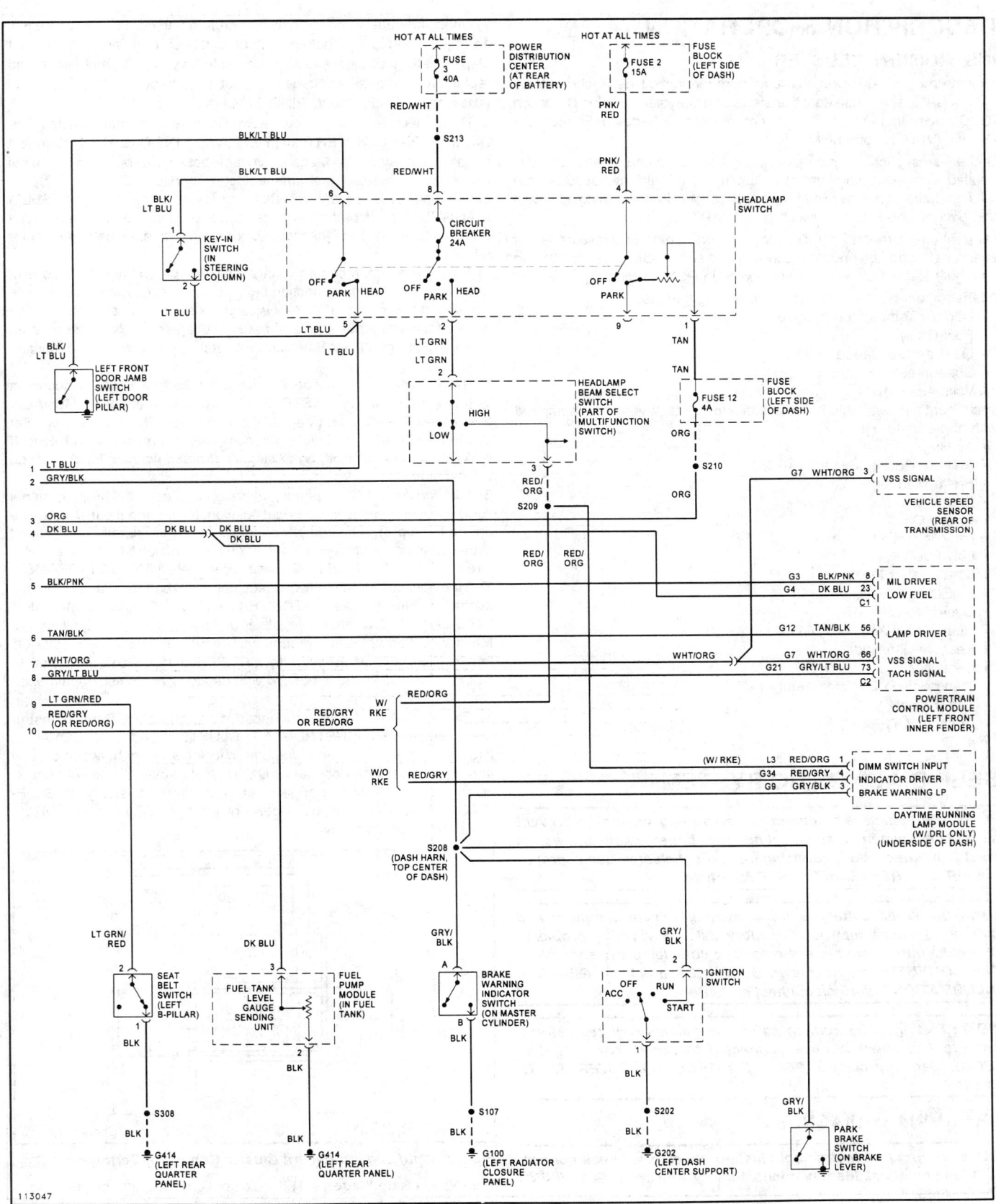

Fig. 7: Analog Instrument Panel Wiring Diagram (Neon – 2 Of 2)

1999 ACCESSORIES & EQUIPMENT
Analog Instrument Panels
Ram Pickup, Ram Van & Ram Wagon

DESCRIPTION & OPERATION

INSTRUMENT CLUSTER

All instrument cluster gauges are air core magnetic type. Tachometer is optional. All gauges use data transferred on Chrysler Collision Detection (CCD) bus. Instrument cluster incorporates a Vacuum Fluorescent Display (VFD) for odometer display.

Brake warning light illuminates when ignition is on and parking brake is applied. Brake warning light also illuminates if brake hydraulic system failure occurs during service brake application. Brake warning light bulb test occurs when ignition switch is in START position.

Oil pressure warning light illuminates when engine oil pressure is not sufficient to open oil pressure sending unit switch. Oil pressure warning light bulb test occurs with ignition switch in RUN position.

All instrument clusters include these analog gauges:
- Coolant Temperature Gauge
- Fuel Gauge
- Oil Pressure Gauge
- Speedometer
- Voltmeter

Instrument clusters include these indicator lights, if vehicle is equipped with appropriate option:
- Air Bag
- Anti-Lock Brake System (ABS)
- Brake Warning
- Check Gauges
- Cruise On
- Headlight High Beam
- Low Fuel
- Low Washer Fluid
- CHECK ENGINE
- Overdrive Off
- Rear Wheel Anti-Lock (RWAL)
- Seat Belt Reminder
- Security
- Transmission Oil Temperature (A/T)
- Turn Signal
- Upshift (M/T)
- 4WD

SELF-DIAGNOSTIC SYSTEM

WARNING: Vehicle is equipped with an air bag system. To prevent air bag deployment, disconnect negative battery cable and wait at least 2 minutes before servicing instrument cluster. See appropriate AIR BAG RESTRAINT SYSTEMS article.

CAUTION: When battery is disconnected, vehicle computer and memory systems may lose memory data. Driveability problems may exist until computer systems have completed a relearn cycle. See COMPUTER RELEARN PROCEDURES article in GENERAL INFORMATION before disconnecting battery.

NOTE: Testing of instrument panel and gauges requires using a scan tool to check circuits connected to Body Control Module (BCM). See appropriate BODY CONTROL COMPUTER TESTS article.

PRELIMINARY DIAGNOSIS

NOTE: There are 2 instrument cluster connectors. These connectors look identical. Identify connectors by wire color. See WIRING DIAGRAMS.

Ram Pickup – 1) If CCD bus controlled indicator lights and gauges do not operate, go to step **4)**. If indicator lights operate and all gauges do not operate, go to next step.

2) Check for battery voltage between ground and both sides of fuse No. 14 in junction block. If battery voltage exists on both sides, go to next step. If battery voltage exists on one side only, repair short circuit and replace fuse. If battery voltage does not exist on both sides, locate and repair open circuit. See WIRING DIAGRAMS.

3) Disconnect negative battery cable. Remove instrument cluster. See INSTRUMENT CLUSTER under REMOVAL & INSTALLATION. Connect negative battery cable. Measure voltage between ground and terminal No. 6 (Yellow wire) of instrument cluster connector C1. *See Fig. 1.* If battery voltage is present, reinstall instrument cluster and go to SELF-DIAGNOSTICS. If battery voltage is not present, repair open circuit between fuse No. 14 in junction block and instrument cluster connector C1.

4) Turn ignition on. Measure voltage between ground and both sides of fuse No. 17 (10-amp) in junction block. If battery voltage exists on both sides, go to next step. If battery voltage exists on one side only, repair short circuit and replace fuse. If battery voltage does not exist on both sides, repair open Dark Blue wire between ignition switch and junction block.

5) Turn ignition off. Disconnect negative battery cable. Reconnect instrument cluster. See INSTRUMENT CLUSTER under REMOVAL & INSTALLATION. Connect negative battery cable. Turn ignition on. Set parking brake and observe instrument cluster brake warning light. If brake warning light is off, go to step **7)**. If brake warning light is on, go to next step.

6) Turn ignition off. Turn parking lights on and adjust instrument panel lights dimmer rheostat to full bright position. If instrument panel lights are on, go to step **8)**. If instrument panel lights are off, repair open ground circuit to instrument cluster connector C1 terminal No. 4 (Black/Light Green wire) or No. 5 (Black/Orange wire). See WIRING DIAGRAMS.

7) Turn ignition off and disconnect negative battery cable. Remove instrument cluster. See INSTRUMENT CLUSTER under REMOVAL & INSTALLATION. Connect negative battery cable. Turn ignition on. Measure voltage between ground and instrument cluster connector C1 terminal No. 2 (Dark Blue/White wire). If battery voltage exists, go to SELF-DIAGNOSTICS. If battery voltage does not exist, repair open Dark Blue/White wire.

8) Turn ignition off. Disconnect negative battery cable. Remove instrument cluster. See INSTRUMENT CLUSTER under REMOVAL & INSTALLATION. Using an ohmmeter, check continuity between ground and instrument cluster connector C1 terminals No. 4 (Black/Light Green wire) and No. 5 (Black/Orange wire). If continuity exists, go to SELF-DIAGNOSTICS. If continuity does not exist, repair open Black/Light Green or Black/Orange wire.

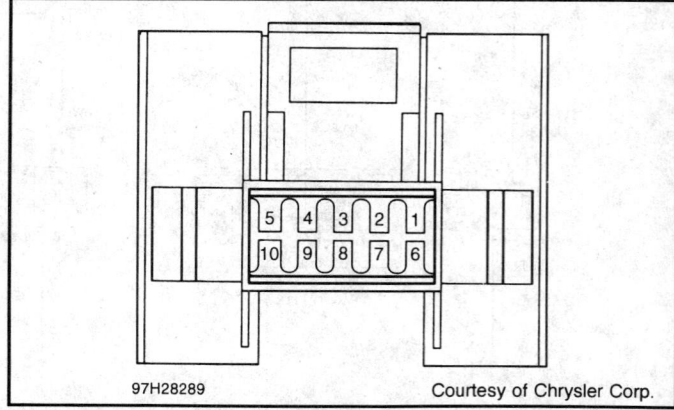

97H28289   Courtesy of Chrysler Corp.

Fig. 1: Identifying Instrument Cluster Connector Terminals

Ram Van & Ram Wagon – 1) If indicator lights operate, but all gauges are inoperative, go to next step. If all gauges and CCD bus-controlled indicator lights are inoperative, go to step **5)**.

2) Check fuse No. 12 (15-amp) in junction block. If fuse is okay, go to next step. If any fuse is blown, repair short circuit and replace fuse.

1999 ACCESSORIES & EQUIPMENT
Analog Instrument Panels
Ram Pickup, Ram Van & Ram Wagon (Cont.)

CHRY
4-409

3) Measure voltage between ground and fuse No. 12 in junction block. If battery voltage is present, go to next step. If battery voltage is not present, repair open circuit.

4) Disconnect negative battery cable. Remove instrument cluster. See INSTRUMENT CLUSTER under REMOVAL & INSTALLATION. Reconnect negative battery cable. Measure voltage between ground and terminal No. 6 (Pink/White wire) of instrument cluster connector C1. *See Fig. 1.* If battery voltage is present, reinstall instrument cluster and go to SELF- DIAGNOSTICS. If battery voltage is not present, repair open circuit between fuse No. 12 (15-amp) in junction block and instrument cluster connector C1 and go to next step.

5) Remove and inspect fuse No. 11 (10-amp) in junction block. If fuse is okay, go to next step. If fuse is blown, locate and repair cause of blown fuse. Install new fuse and recheck system operation.

6) Turn ignition on. Measure voltage between ground and power side (Dark Blue/White wire) of fuse No. 11 (10-amp) in junction block. If battery voltage is present, go to step **8)**. If battery voltage is not present, locate and repair open circuit to fuse No. 11. See WIRING DIAGRAMS.

7) Turn ignition off and disconnect negative battery cable. Install instrument cluster. Connect negative battery cable. Turn ignition on. Set parking brake and observe instrument cluster brake warning light. If brake warning light is on, go to next step. If brake warning light is off, go to step **9)**.

8) Turn ignition off. Turn parking lights on and adjust instrument panel lights dimmer rheostat to full bright position. If instrument panel lights are on, go to step **10)**. If instrument panel lights are off, repair instrument cluster illumination ground circuit between instrument cluster connector C2 terminal No. 7 (Black wire) and ground. See WIRING DIAGRAMS.

9) Turn ignition off and disconnect negative battery cable. Remove instrument cluster. See INSTRUMENT CLUSTER under REMOVAL & INSTALLATION. Connect negative battery cable. Turn ignition on. Measure voltage between ground and terminal No. 2 (Dark Blue/White wire) at instrument cluster connector C1. If battery voltage is present, go to SELF-DIAGNOSTICS. If battery voltage is not present, repair open circuit between junction block fuse No. 11 and instrument cluster.

10) Turn ignition off and disconnect negative battery cable. Remove instrument cluster. See INSTRUMENT CLUSTER under REMOVAL & INSTALLATION. Check continuity between ground and terminal No. 4 (Black/Dark Green wire) at instrument cluster connector C1. If continuity exists, go to SELF-DIAGNOSTICS. If continuity does not exist, locate and repair open in ground circuit.

SELF-DIAGNOSTICS

1) With ignition off, press and hold trip odometer RESET button while turning ignition switch to ON position. Continue to hold RESET button until odometer window displays CHEC (about 10 seconds). Release RESET button. If problem exists, system will display Diagnostic Trouble Codes (DTC). See DIAGNOSTIC CODE CHART table. For repairs of DTCs, see appropriate BODY CONTROL COMPUTER TESTS article.

DIAGNOSTIC TROUBLE (DTC) CODE CHART

DTC	Description	Correction
110	Cluster CPU, RAM Or EEPROM Fault	Replace Cluster
900	CCD Bus Inoperative	Check CCD Bus Connections At Cluster; Check Cluster Fuses; Check CCD Bus Bias; Check CCD Bus Voltage; Check CCD Bus Terminations
920	Not Receiving VSS Message From PCM	Check PCM Software Level; Use Scan Tool To Verify VSS Signal Is Sent By PCM
921	Not Receiving Distance Pulse Message From PCM	Check PCM Software Level; Use Scan Tool To Verify Distance Pulse Message Is Sent By PCM
940	Not Receiving Air Bag Light On Message From Air Bag Module	Check CCD Bus Connections At ACM; Check ACM Fuse
950	Not Receiving ABS Light On Message From Anti-lock Brake Control Module	Check CCD Bus Connections At Anti-Lock Control Module; Check Anti-Lock Control Module Fuse
999	Undefined Error	Record Failure Message; Press RESET Button To Continue Self-Diagnostic Test

2) If no DTCs appear, cluster will start a walking segment test. First, all segments will be illuminated, then each segment in sequence. If any segment does not illuminate, repeat test to confirm and replace instrument cluster. When walking segment test is complete, bulb check will start.

3) If any bulb does not light, remove instrument cluster and check bulb and bulb holder. See INSTRUMENT CLUSTER under REMOVAL & INSTALLATION. Ensure bulb holder is properly installed in cluster. If bulb and bulb holder are okay, replace instrument cluster. If LED does not light, replace instrument cluster. When bulb check is complete, gauge actuator test will start.

4) Each gauge needle should stop at 3 calibration points, then return to relaxed position. If any gauge does not perform as specified, remove instrument cluster. See INSTRUMENT CLUSTER under REMOVAL & INSTALLATION. Inspect all connections between printed circuit board and gauge terminals, repair as necessary. If connections are okay, replace instrument cluster. Instrument cluster will automatically exit self-diagnostics when test is complete.

SYSTEM TESTS

NOTE: There are 2 instrument cluster connectors. These connectors look identical. Identify connector by wire color. See WIRING DIAGRAMS.

BRAKE WARNING LIGHT INOPERATIVE

1) Ensure parking brake is released. Turn ignition on. If brake warning light stays on, check and repair hydraulic brake system as necessary. See appropriate DISC & DRUM article in BRAKES in appropriate MITCHELL® manual.

2) If brake warning light does not illuminate when ignition is on, check fuse No. 17 (10-amp) on Ram Pickup or fuse No. 11 (10-amp) on Ram Van and Ram Wagon in junction block. Junction block is located at left end cover of instrument panel. If fuse is okay, go to next step. If fuse is blown, locate and repair cause of blown fuse. Install new fuse and recheck system operation.

3) Turn ignition on. Measure voltage between ground and power side of fuse No. 17 on Ram Pickup or fuse No. 11 on Ram Van and Ram Wagon. If battery voltage is present, go to next step. If battery voltage is not present, locate and repair open circuit between to junction block. See WIRING DIAGRAMS.

CHRY
4-410

1999 ACCESSORIES & EQUIPMENT
Analog Instrument Panels
Ram Pickup, Ram Van & Ram Wagon (Cont.)

4) Turn ignition off. Disconnect negative battery cable. Disconnect parking brake switch connector. Switch is located at base of parking brake lever. Ensure parking brake lever is released. Check continuity between ground and parking brake switch terminal. If continuity does not exist, go to next step. If continuity exists, adjust or replace parking brake switch.

5) Ensure parking brake switch is still disconnected. Turn ignition off. Remove instrument cluster. See INSTRUMENT CLUSTER under REMOVAL & INSTALLATION. Check continuity between ground and park brake switch connector. If continuity does not exist, go to next step. If continuity exists, repair short to ground between instrument cluster and park brake switch.

6) Check continuity between park brake switch connector and instrument cluster connector C1, terminal No. 3 (White/Pink wire on Ram Van and Ram Wagon; White/Light Green wire on Ram Pickup). *See Fig. 1.* If continuity does not exist, repair open circuit. See WIRING DIAGRAMS. If continuity exists, see PRELIMINARY DIAGNOSIS under SELF-DIAGNOSTIC SYSTEM.

FOUR WHEEL DRIVE (4WD) LIGHT INOPERATIVE (RAM PICKUP)

1) Remove and inspect fuse No. 17 (10-amp) in junction block. Junction block is located at left end cover of instrument panel. If fuse is okay, go to next step. If fuse is blown, locate and repair cause of blown fuse. Install new fuse and recheck system operation.

2) Turn ignition on. Measure voltage between ground and power side of fuse No. 17. If battery voltage is present, go to next step. If battery voltage is not present, locate and repair open circuit between ignition switch and junction block.

3) Turn ignition off. Disconnect negative battery cable. Disconnect 4WD switch connector. 4WD switch connector is located at right side of front axle. Check continuity between 4WD switch connector Black wire and ground. If continuity does not exist, repair open Black wire between 4WD switch and ground. If continuity exists, go to next step.

4) Reconnect battery cable. Turn ignition on. Install jumper wire between 4WD switch connector terminals. 4WD light should illuminate. If light illuminates, replace 4WD switch. If light does not illuminate, go to next step.

5) Turn ignition off. Disconnect negative battery cable. Ensure 4WD switch is still disconnected. Remove instrument cluster. See INSTRUMENT CLUSTER under REMOVAL & INSTALLATION. Check continuity between ground and instrument cluster connector C2 terminal No. 10 (Gray wire). *See Fig. 1.* If continuity does not exist, go to next step. If continuity exists, repair short to ground in wire between instrument cluster and 4WD switch.

6) Check continuity of wire between 4WD switch connector and terminal No. 10 at instrument cluster connector C2. If continuity does not exist, repair open wire. If continuity exists, replace bulb.

LOW WASHER FLUID LIGHT INOPERATIVE

1) Remove and inspect fuse No. 17 (10-amp) on Ram Pickup or fuse No. 11 (10-amp) on Ram Van and Ram Wagon in junction block. Junction block is located at left end cover of instrument panel. If fuse is okay, go to next step. If fuse is blown, locate and repair cause of blown fuse. Install new fuse and recheck system operation.

2) Turn ignition on. Measure voltage between ground and power side of fuse No. 14 (10-amp) on Ram Pickup or fuse No. 11 (10-amp) on Ram Van and Ram Wagon. If battery voltage is present, go to next step. If battery voltage is not present, locate and repair open circuit between ignition switch and junction block.

3) Turn ignition off. Disconnect washer fluid level sensor connector. Install jumper wire between washer fluid level sensor connector terminals. Turn ignition on. Low washer fluid level light should illuminate. Disconnect jumper wire and light should go off. If light performs as specified, replace washer fluid level sensor. If light does not perform as specified, go to next step.

4) Turn ignition off. Check continuity between ground and washer fluid level sensor connector Black wire. If continuity does not exist, repair open Black wire between washer fluid level sensor and ground. If continuity exists, go to next step.

5) Ensure washer fluid level sensor is still disconnected. Turn ignition off. Remove instrument cluster. See INSTRUMENT CLUSTER under REMOVAL & INSTALLATION. Check continuity between ground and instrument cluster connector C2 terminal No. 2 (Black/White wire) on Ram Pickup and terminal No. 9 (Black/Gray wire) on Ram Van and Ram Wagon. If continuity does not exist, go to next step. If continuity exists, repair short to ground in White/Black or Black/Gray wire between instrument cluster and washer fluid level sensor.

6) Check continuity of Black/White wire on Ram Pickup or Black/Gray wire on Ram Van and Ram Wagon between washer fluid level sensor connector and instrument cluster connector C2 terminal No. 2 on Ram Pickup or terminal No. 9 on Ram Van and Ram Wagon. *See Fig. 1.* If continuity does not exist, repair open Black/White wire on Ram Pickup or Black/Gray wire on Ram Van and Ram Wagon. If continuity exists, replace bulb.

WAIT-TO-START LIGHT INOPERATIVE (RAM PICKUP – DIESEL)

1) Remove and inspect fuse No. 17 (10-amp) in junction block. Junction block is located at left end cover of instrument panel. If fuse is okay, go to next step. If fuse is blown, locate and repair cause of blown fuse. Install new fuse and recheck system operation.

2) Turn ignition on. Measure voltage between ground and power side of fuse No. 17. If battery voltage is present, go to next step. If battery voltage is not present, locate and repair open circuit between Power Distribution Center (PDC) and junction block.

3) Disconnect negative battery cable. Remove instrument cluster. See INSTRUMENT CLUSTER under REMOVAL & INSTALLATION. Check for battery voltage between ground and instrument cluster connector C1 terminal No. 2 (Dark Blue/White wire). *See Fig. 1.* Turn ignition on. If battery voltage exists, go to next step. If battery voltage does not exist, repair open Dark Blue/White wire between junction block and instrument cluster.

4) Turn ignition off. Disconnect Powertrain Control Module (PCM) White connector C2. PCM is located at firewall in right side of engine compartment. Connector C2 is center connector. Check continuity between ground and instrument cluster connector C1 terminal No. 8 (Orange/Black wire). If continuity does not exist, go to next step. If continuity exists, repair short to ground in Orange/Black wire between instrument cluster and ground.

5) Install instrument cluster. Connect battery cable. Install jumper wire between PCM White connector C2 terminal No. 20 (Orange/Black wire) and ground. *See Fig. 2.* Turn ignition on. Wait-to-start light should illuminate. If wait-to-start light illuminates, see appropriate SELF-DIAGNOSTICS article in ENGINE PERFORMANCE in appropriate MITCHELL® manual. If wait-to-start light does not illuminate, see SELF-DIAGNOSTICS.

1999 ACCESSORIES & EQUIPMENT
Analog Instrument Panels
Ram Pickup, Ram Van & Ram Wagon (Cont.)

CHRY
4-411

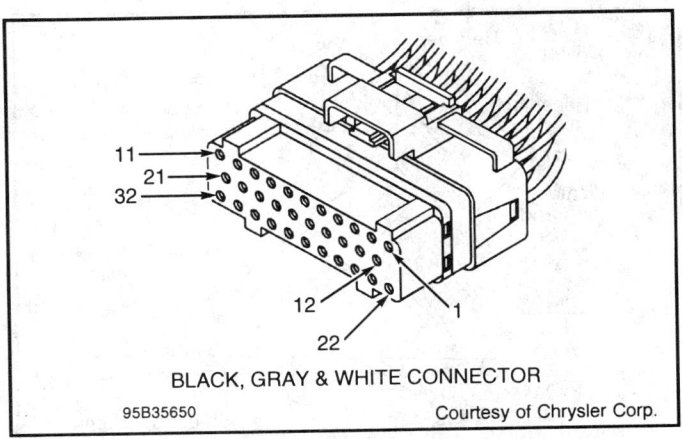

BLACK, GRAY & WHITE CONNECTOR

95B35650   Courtesy of Chrysler Corp.

Fig. 2: Identifying PCM Connector Terminals

REMOVAL & INSTALLATION

WARNING: Vehicle is equipped with an air bag system. To prevent air bag deployment, disconnect negative battery cable and wait at least 2 minutes before servicing instrument cluster. See appropriate AIR BAG RESTRAINT SYSTEMS article.

CAUTION: When battery is disconnected, vehicle computer and memory systems may lose memory data. Driveability problems may exist until computer systems have completed a relearn cycle. See COMPUTER RELEARN PROCEDURES article in GENERAL INFORMATION before disconnecting battery.

INSTRUMENT CLUSTER

Removal & Installation (Ram Pickup) – 1) Disconnect negative battery cable. On A/T models, turn ignition switch to UNLOCK position and shift gear selector to "1" position. On models equipped with tilt steering wheel, tilt wheel to lowest position. On all models, open power outlet door and remove instrument cluster bezel retaining screw. Pry cluster bezel away from clips securing it to instrument panel. *See Fig. 3.* Disconnect electrical connectors from power outlet to cluster bezel.

2) Remove 4 instrument cluster screws. On A/T models, shift gear selector to PARK position. On all models, pull cluster rearward, and disconnect 2 electrical connectors. On A/T models, pull cluster rearward enough to gain access to shift indicator retaining screws in back of instrument cluster. Remove shift indicator. Remove instrument cluster. To install, reverse removal procedure.

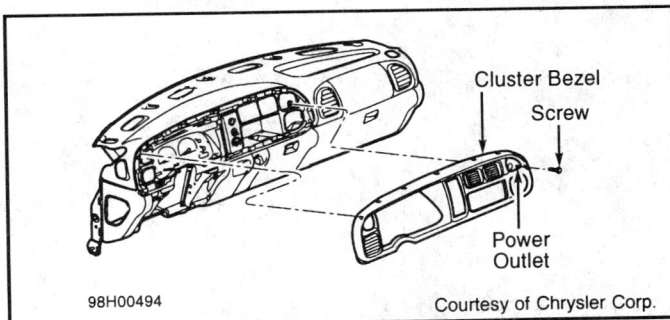

98H00494   Courtesy of Chrysler Corp.

Fig. 3: Removing Instrument Cluster Bezel (Ram Pickup)

Removal & Installation (Ram Van & Ram Wagon) – 1) Disconnect negative battery cable. Turn ignition switch to UNLOCK position, set parking brake and shift gear selector to "1" position. On models equipped with tilt steering wheel, tilt wheel to lowest position. On all models, pry cluster bezel away from clips securing it to instrument panel. *See Fig. 4.* Pull left side of bezel far enough to clear trip odometer reset button and remove bezel.

2) Remove 4 instrument cluster screws. Shift gear selector into PARK position. Pull cluster rearward, and disconnect 2 electrical connectors. Pull cluster rearward enough to gain access to shift indicator retaining screws in back of instrument cluster. Remove shift indicator. Remove instrument cluster. To install, reverse removal procedure.

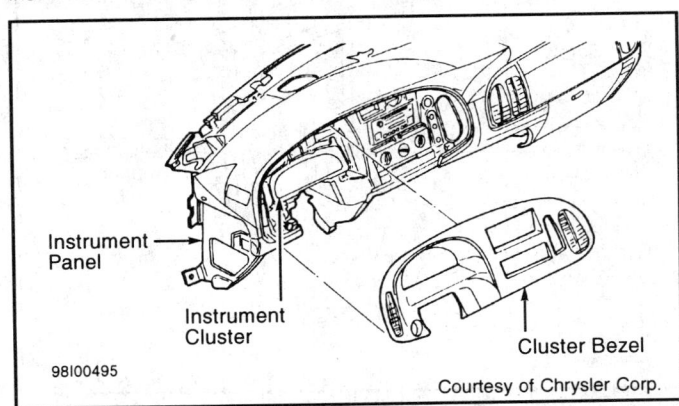

98I00495   Courtesy of Chrysler Corp.

*Fig. 4: Exploded View Of Instrument Panel
(Ram Van & Ram Wagon)*

CENTRAL TIMER MODULE (CTM)

NOTE: Before removing Central Timer Module (CTM) use scan tool to view settings for programmable features. Use these settings to program replacement CTM.

Removal & Installation (Ram Pickup) – 1) Disconnect negative battery cable. Remove left underdash cover and knee bolster reinforcement. Remove 2 CTM retaining screws at right side of underdash opening. *See Fig. 5.*

2) Slide CTM down into opening far enough to gain access to connectors. Disconnect harness connectors and remove CTM from underdash. To install, reverse removal procedure. Reprogram new CTM. See appropriate BODY CONTROL COMPUTER TESTS article.

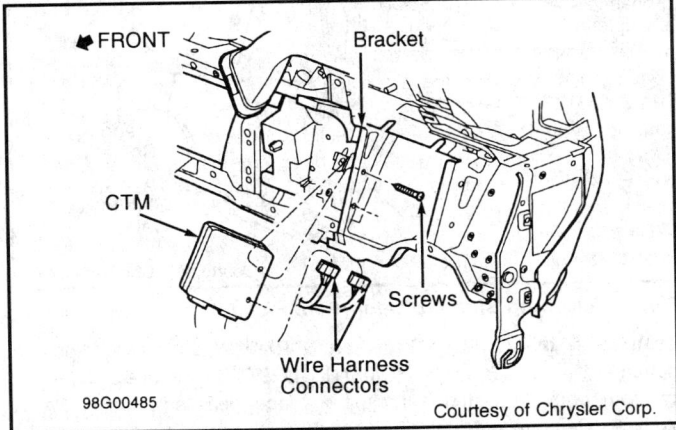

98G00485   Courtesy of Chrysler Corp.

Fig. 5: Identifying CTM Location (Ram Pickup)

Removal & Installation (Ram Van & Ram Wagon) – 1) Disconnect negative battery cable. Remove engine cover. Remove 3 CTM retaining screws from left center instrument panel support. *See Fig. 6.*

2) Slide CTM away from mounting enough to gain access to connectors. Disconnect harness connectors and remove CTM from underdash. To install, reverse removal procedure. Reprogram new CTM. See appropriate BODY CONTROL COMPUTER TESTS article.

SHIFT INDICATOR

Removal & Installation (Ram Pickup) – 1) Remove instrument cluster. See INSTRUMENT CLUSTER. Remove shift indicator from back of instrument cluster. Place gear selector in PARK position. Remove

CHRY
4-412

1999 ACCESSORIES & EQUIPMENT
Analog Instrument Panels
Ram Pickup, Ram Van & Ram Wagon (Cont.)

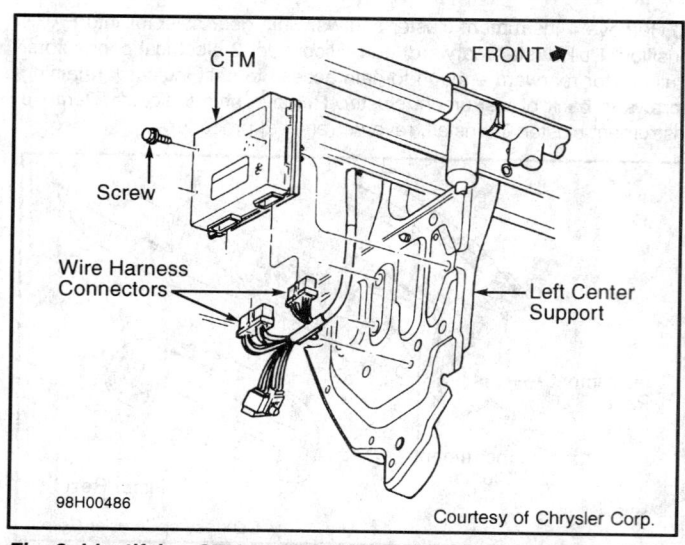

Fig. 6: Identifying CTM Location (Ram Van & Ram Wagon)

steering column opening cover and knee blocker. Steering column cover has retaining clips on upper half and will require prying or lifting with flat bladed tool to remove.

2) Remove loop end of shift indicator cable from lever on left side of steering column. *See Fig. 7.* Squeeze side of plastic adjuster bracket and remove shift indicator assembly. To install, reverse removal procedure.

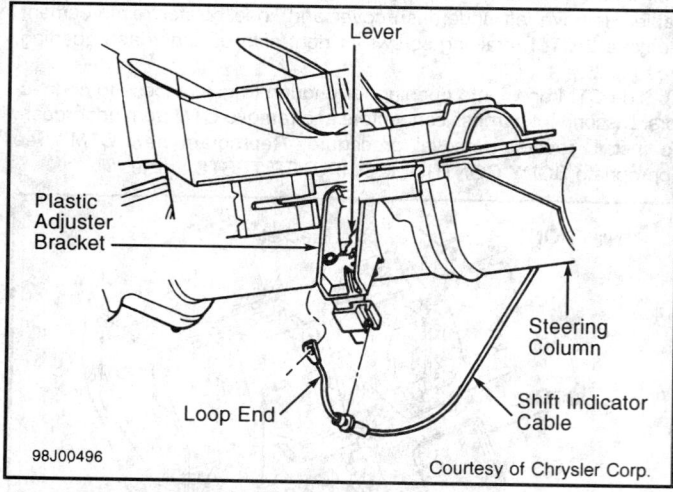

Fig. 7: Removing Shift Indicator (Ram Pickup)

Removal & Installation (Ram Van & Ram Wagon) – 1) Remove instrument cluster. See INSTRUMENT CLUSTER. Remove shift indicator from back of instrument cluster. Place gear selector in PARK position. Remove left instrument panel end cap. Remove 5 screws retaining steering column opening cover. Steering column cover has 4 retaining clips on upper half and will require prying or lifting with flat bladed tool to remove. Remove steering column opening cover.

2) Remove park brake release handle and data Link Connector (DLC). Remove knee blocker. Squeeze side of shift selector indicator cable housing retainer and remove retainer from plastic adjuster bracket on right side of steering column. *See Fig. 8.* Guide shift indicator cable out through slot. Disconnect loop end of shift indicator cable from hook on actuator. Remove shift indicator. To install, reverse removal procedure.

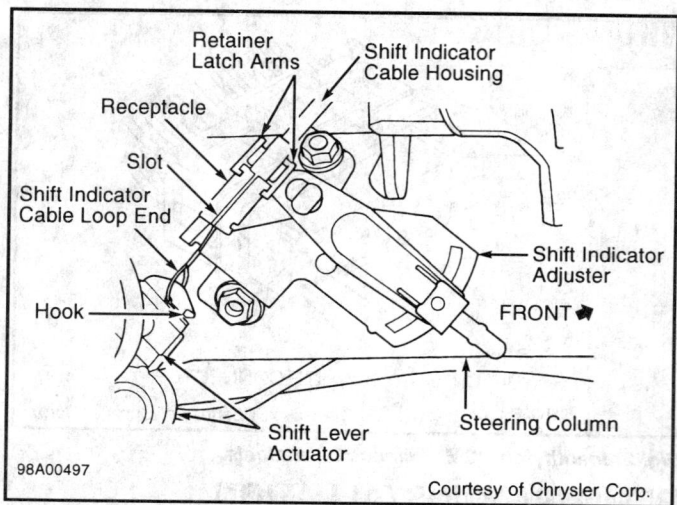

Fig. 8: Removing Shift Indicator (Ram Van & Ram Wagon)

HEADLIGHT SWITCH

Removal & Installation (Ram Pickup) – 1) Disconnect negative battery cable. Open power outlet door and remove instrument cluster bezel retaining screw. Pry cluster bezel from clips securing it to instrument panel. *See Fig. 3.* Disconnect electrical connectors from power outlet to cluster bezel. Remove cluster bezel.

2) Remove 3 screws and headlight switch. Disconnect electrical connectors. Pull knob and stem to stop. Hold down button on top of switch and remove switch. Remove 2 screws and bezel. To install switch, reverse removal procedure.

Removal & Installation (Ram Van & Ram Wagon) – 1) Disconnect negative battery cable. Turn ignition switch to UNLOCK position and shift gear selector to "1" position. On models equipped with tilt steering wheel, tilt wheel to lowest position. On all models, pry cluster bezel away from clips securing it to instrument panel. *See Fig. 4.* Pull left side of bezel far enough to clear trip odometer reset button and remove bezel.

2) Remove switch bezel attaching screws. Remove switch, and disconnect wiring harness. Pull headlight switch knob to on position. Hold down button on top of switch and remove knob and shaft assembly. Remove switch spanner nut and remove bezel from switch. To install switch, reverse removal procedure.

1999 ACCESSORIES & EQUIPMENT
Analog Instrument Panels
Ram Pickup, Ram Van & Ram Wagon (Cont.)

CHRY
4-413

WIRING DIAGRAMS

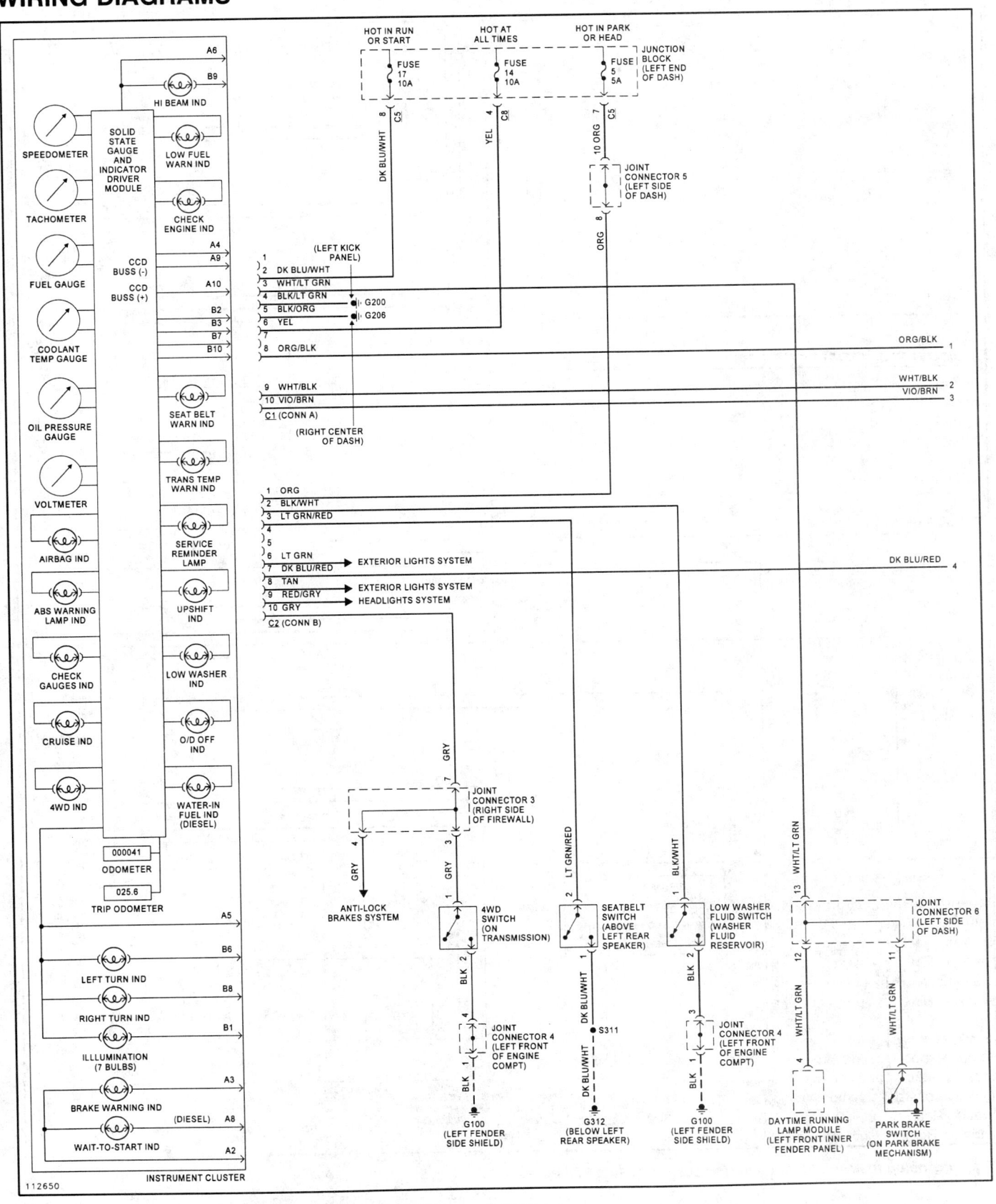

Fig. 9: Analog Instrument Panel Wiring Diagram (Ram Pickup – 1 Of 2)

CHRY
4-414

1999 ACCESSORIES & EQUIPMENT
Analog Instrument Panels
Ram Pickup, Ram Van & Ram Wagon (Cont.)

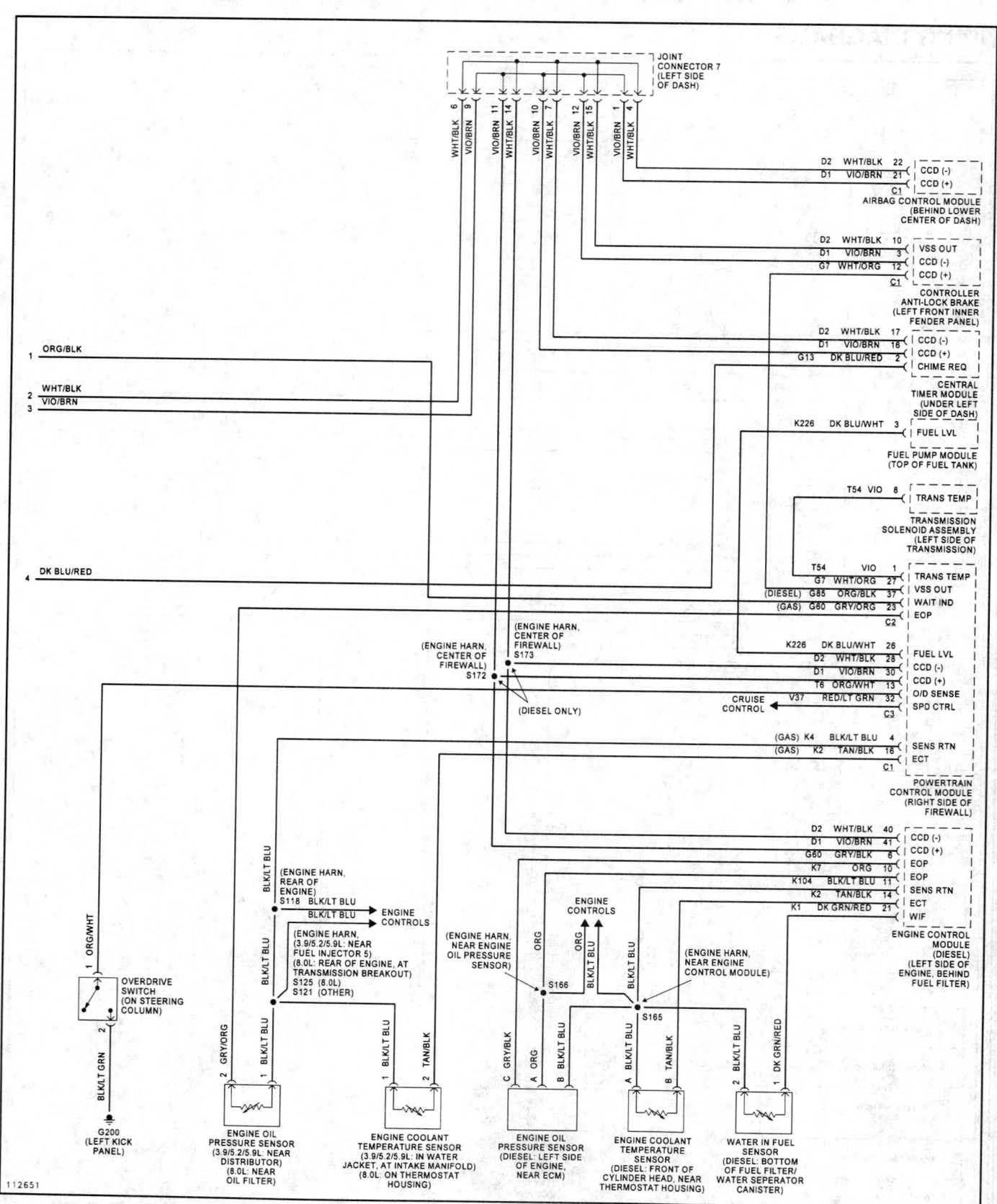

Fig. 10: Analog Instrument Panel Wiring Diagram (Ram Pickup – 2 Of 2)

1999 ACCESSORIES & EQUIPMENT
Analog Instrument Panels
Ram Pickup, Ram Van & Ram Wagon (Cont.)

CHRY
4-415

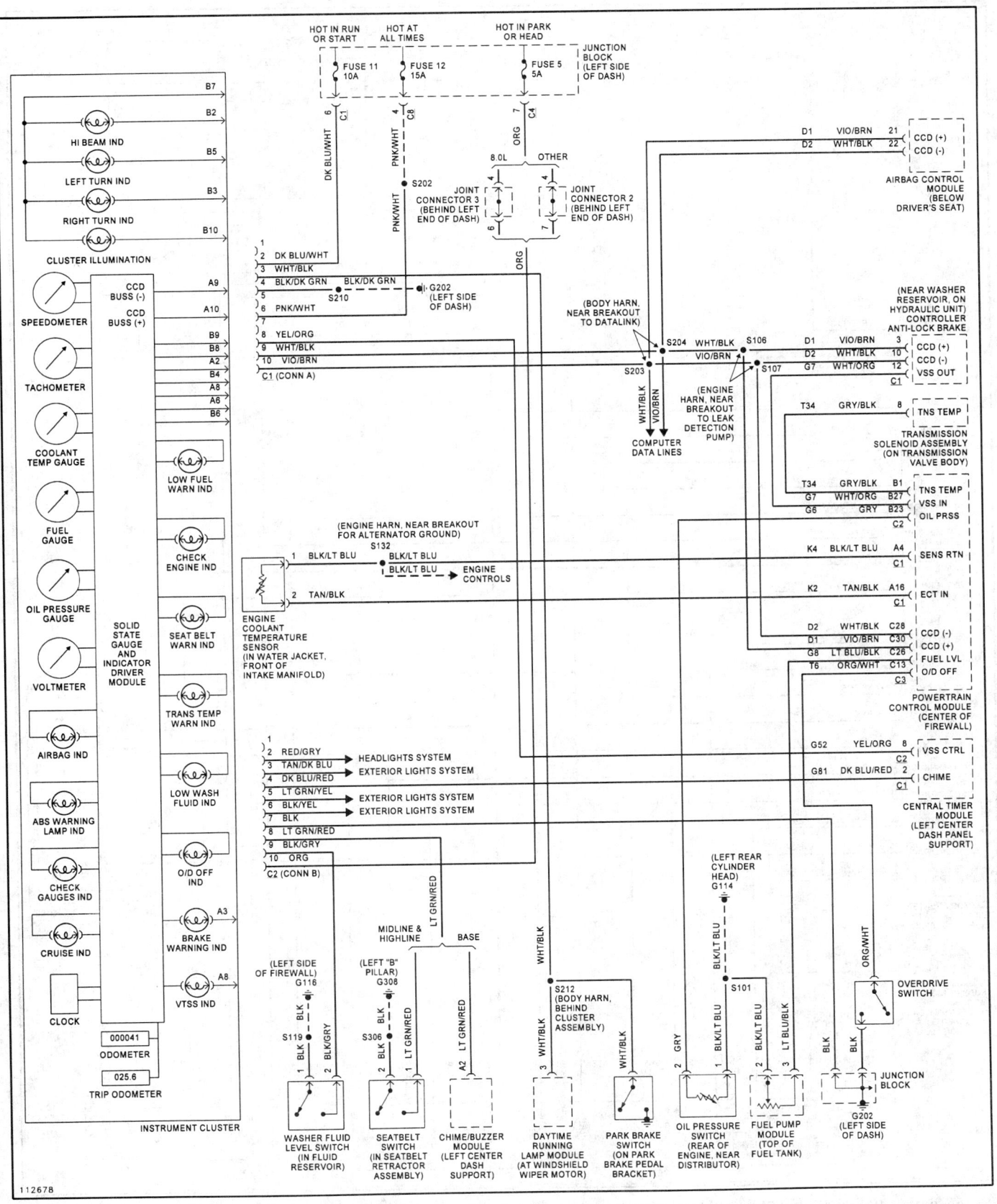

Fig. 11: Analog Instrument Panel Wiring Diagram (Ram Van & Ram Wagon)

112678

1999 ACCESSORIES & EQUIPMENT
Memory Systems

WIRING DIAGRAMS

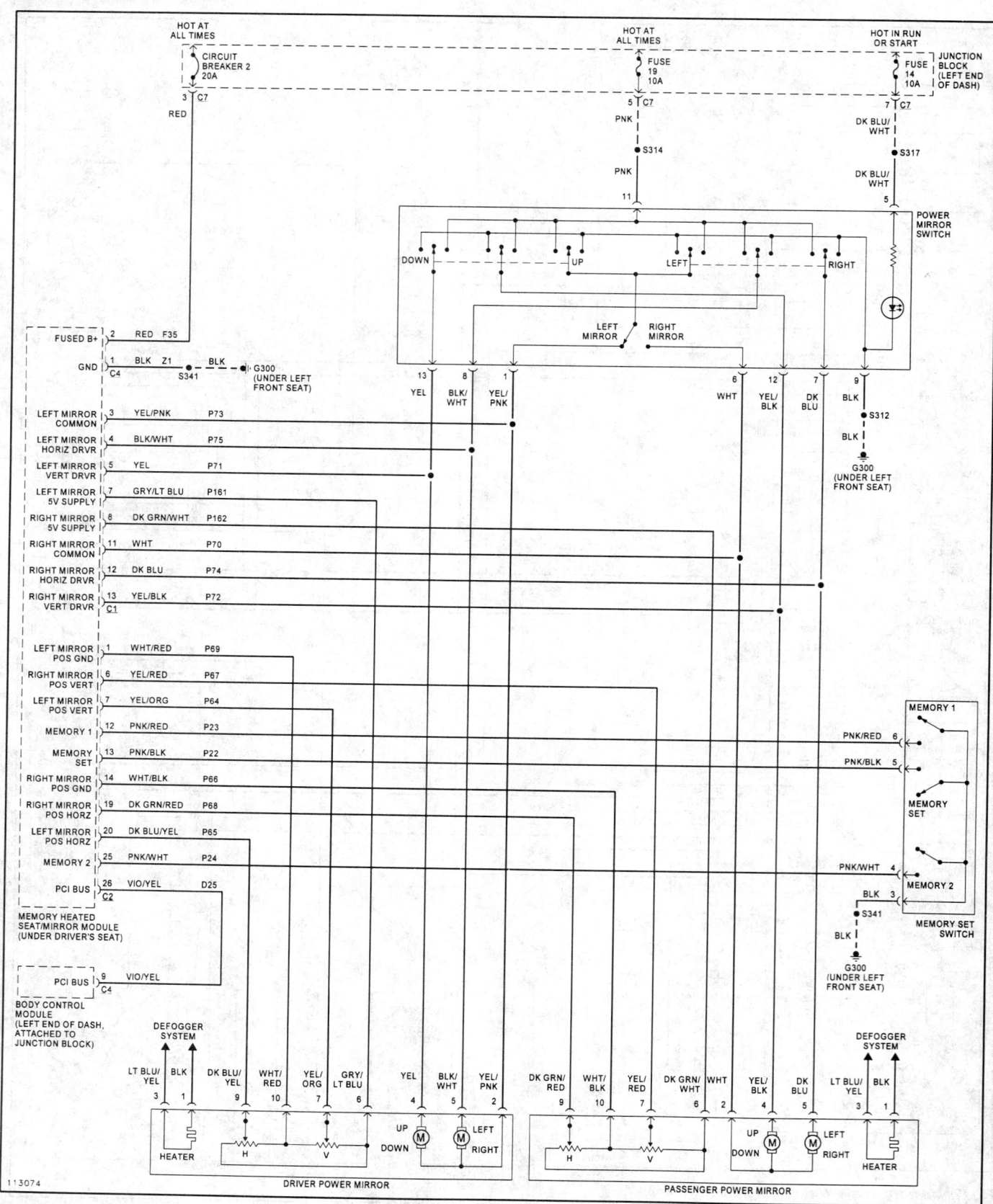

Fig. 1: Memory Mirrors Wiring Diagram (LHS & 300M)

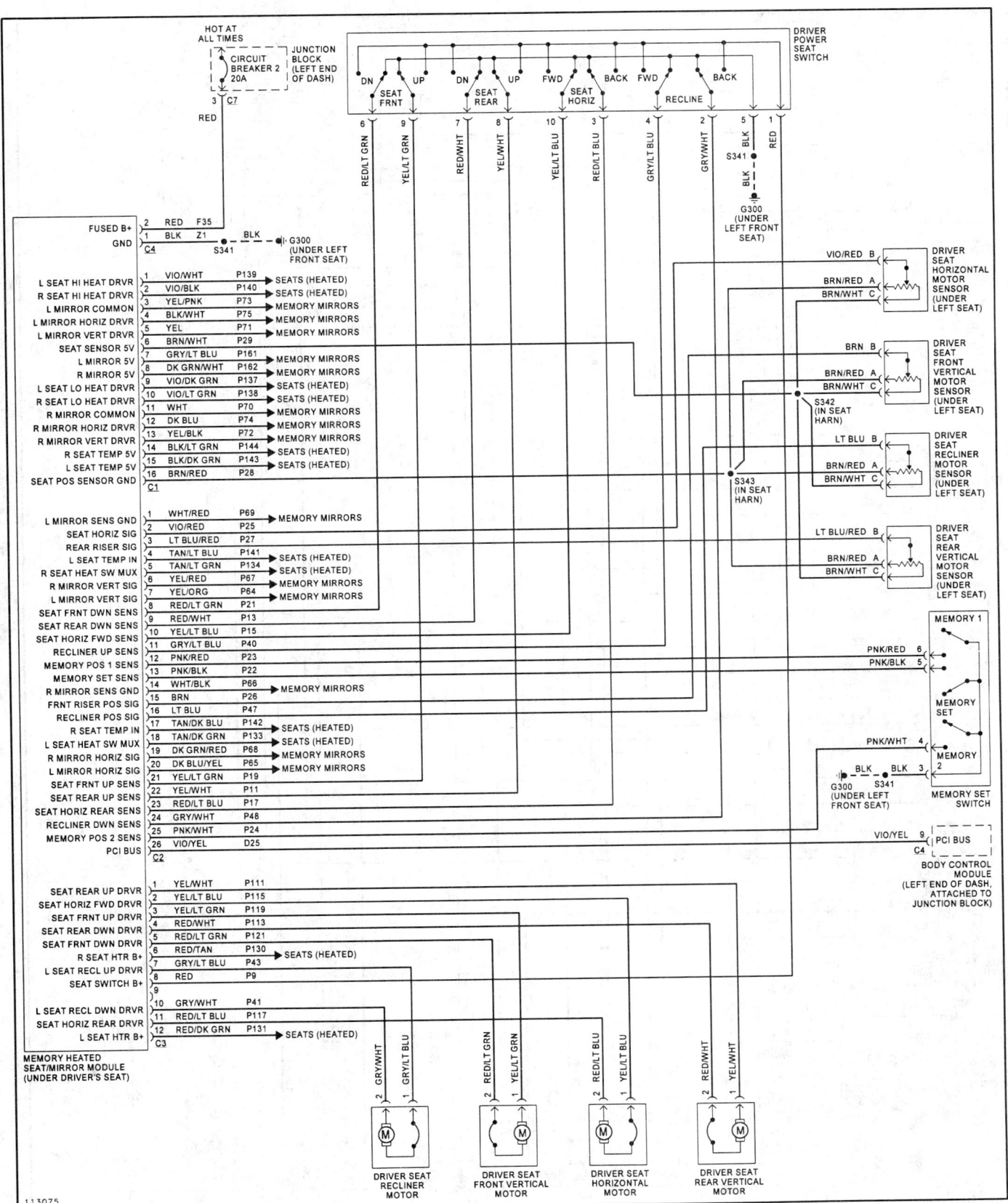

Fig. 2: Memory Seats Wiring Diagram (LHS & 300M)

113075

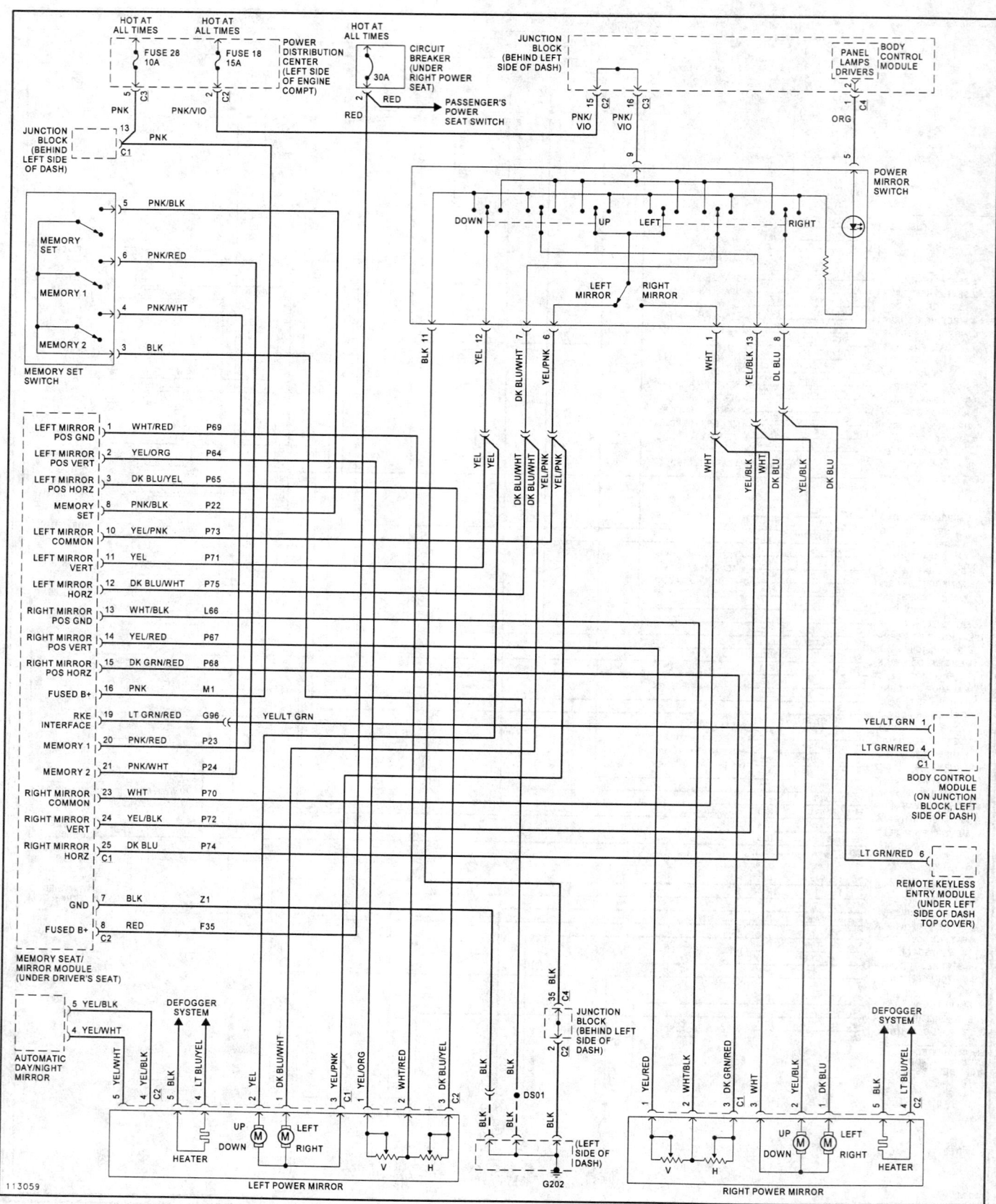

Fig. 3: Memory Mirrors Wiring Diagram (Town & Country)

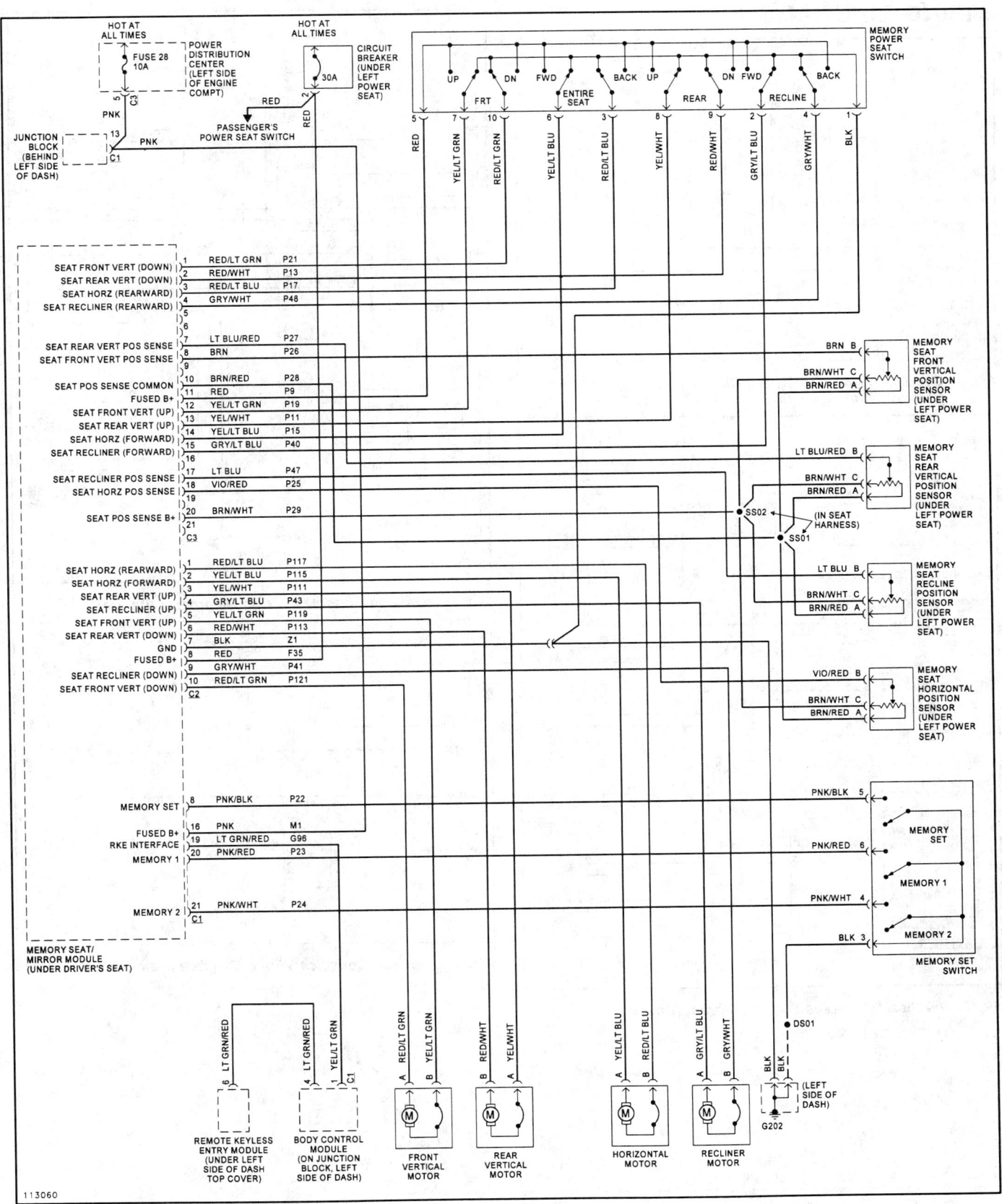

Fig. 4: Memory Seats Wiring Diagram (Town & Country)

WIRING DIAGRAMS

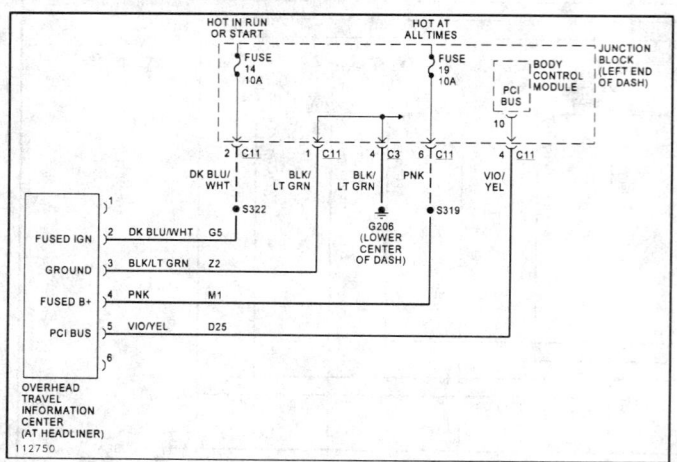

Fig. 1: Overhead Consoles Wiring Diagram
(Concorde, Intrepid, LHS & 300M)

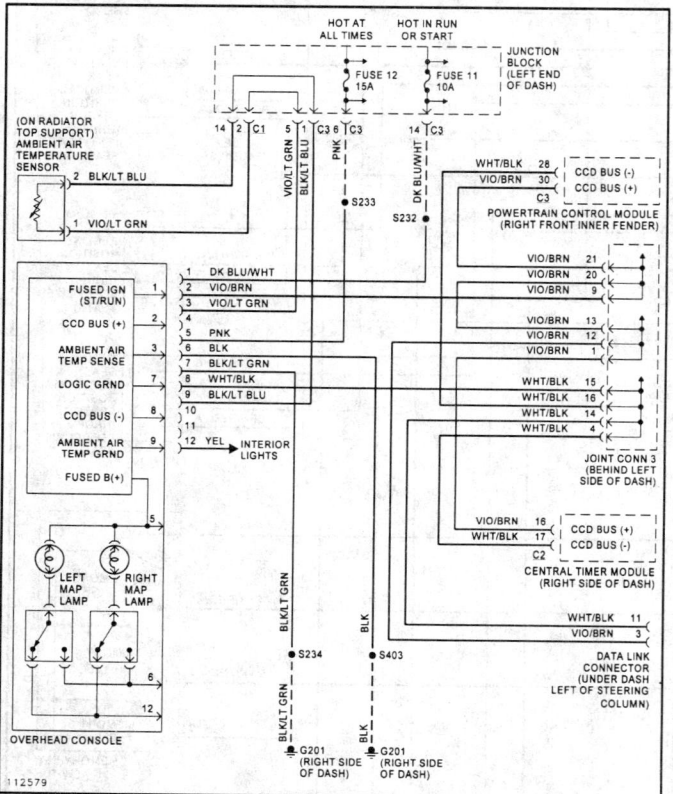

Fig. 2: Overhead Consoles Wiring Diagram (Dakota)

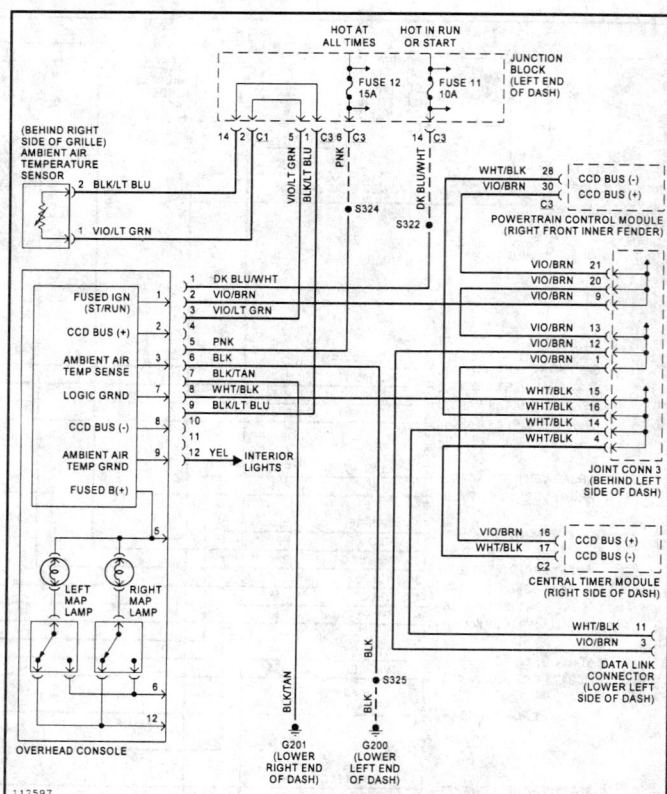

Fig. 3: Overhead Consoles Wiring Diagram (Durango)

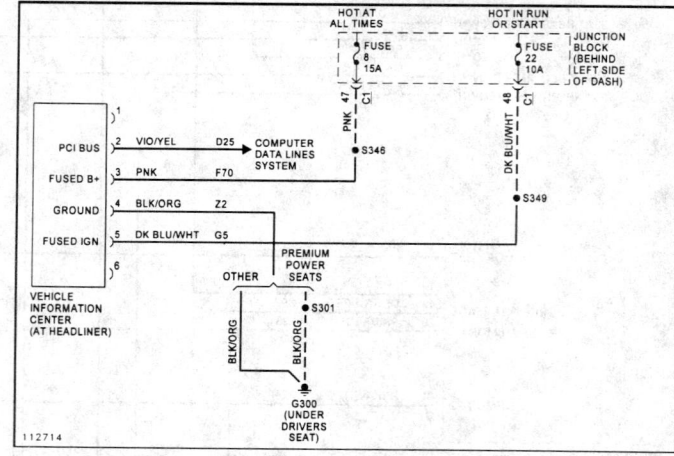

Fig. 4: Overhead Consoles Wiring Diagram (Ram Pickup)

Power Antennas

WIRING DIAGRAMS

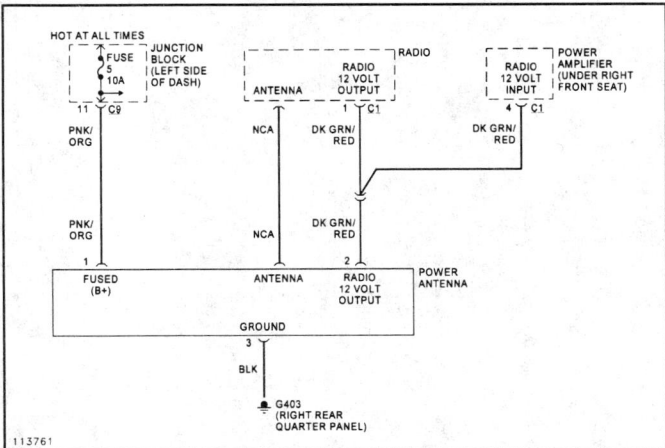

Fig. 1: Power Antennas Wiring Diagram (Sebring Convertible)

1999 ACCESSORIES & EQUIPMENT
Power Convertible Tops

WIRING DIAGRAMS

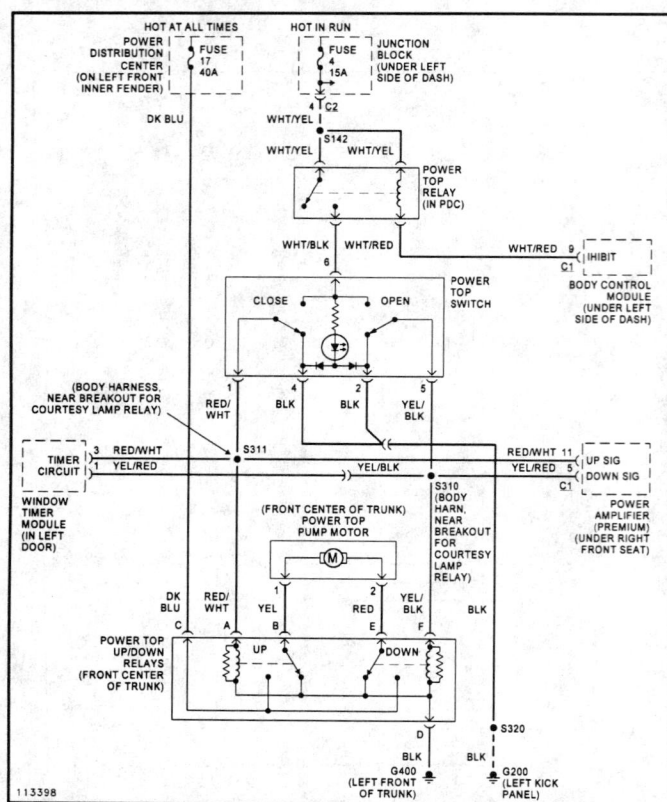

Fig. 1: Power Convertible Tops Wiring Diagram (Sebring Convertible)

NOTE: For models with remote keyless entry system, see appropriate wiring diagram in REMOTE KEYLESS ENTRY SYSTEMS article.

WIRING DIAGRAMS

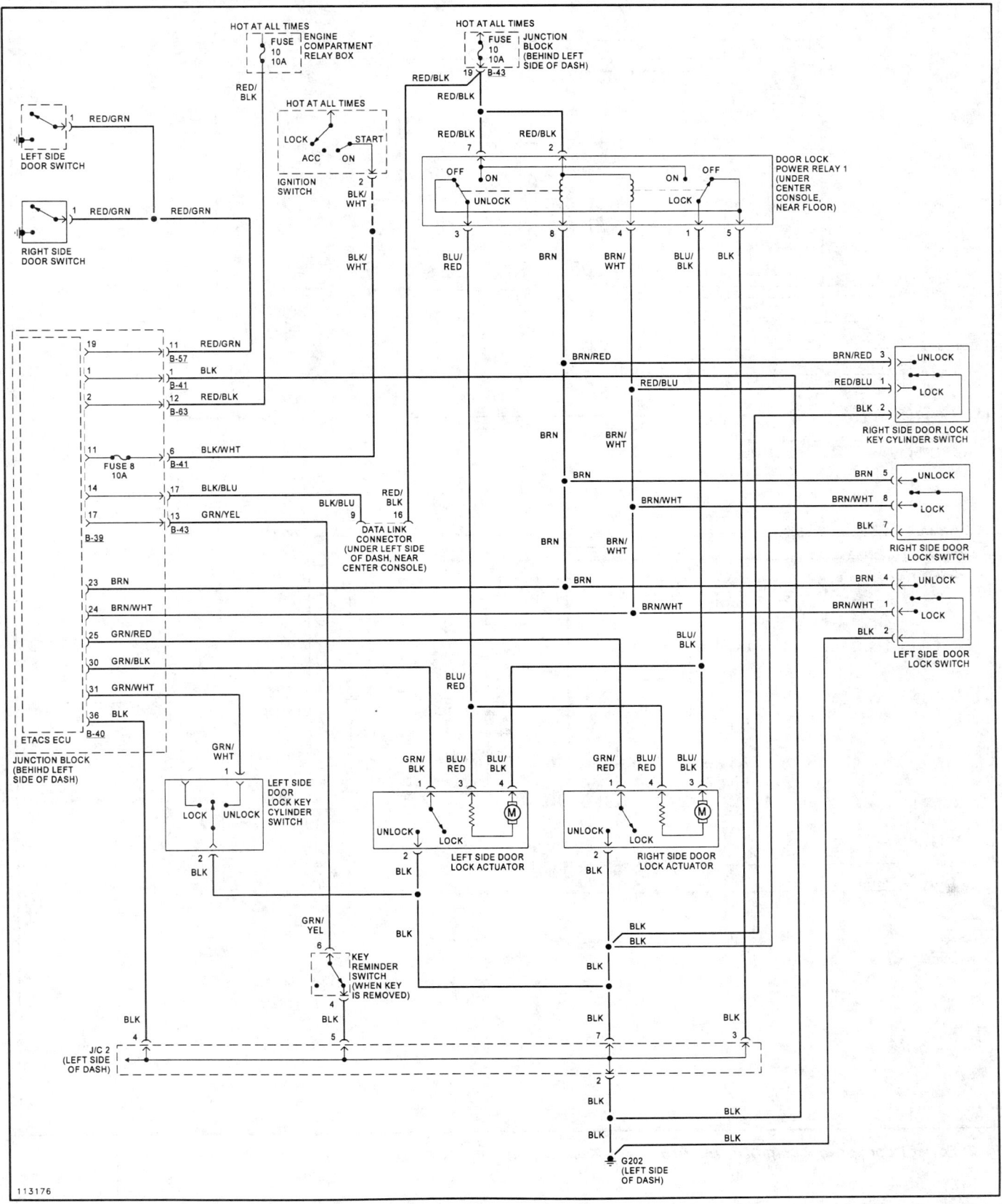

Fig. 1: Power Door Locks Wiring Diagram (Avenger & Sebring Coupe)

113176

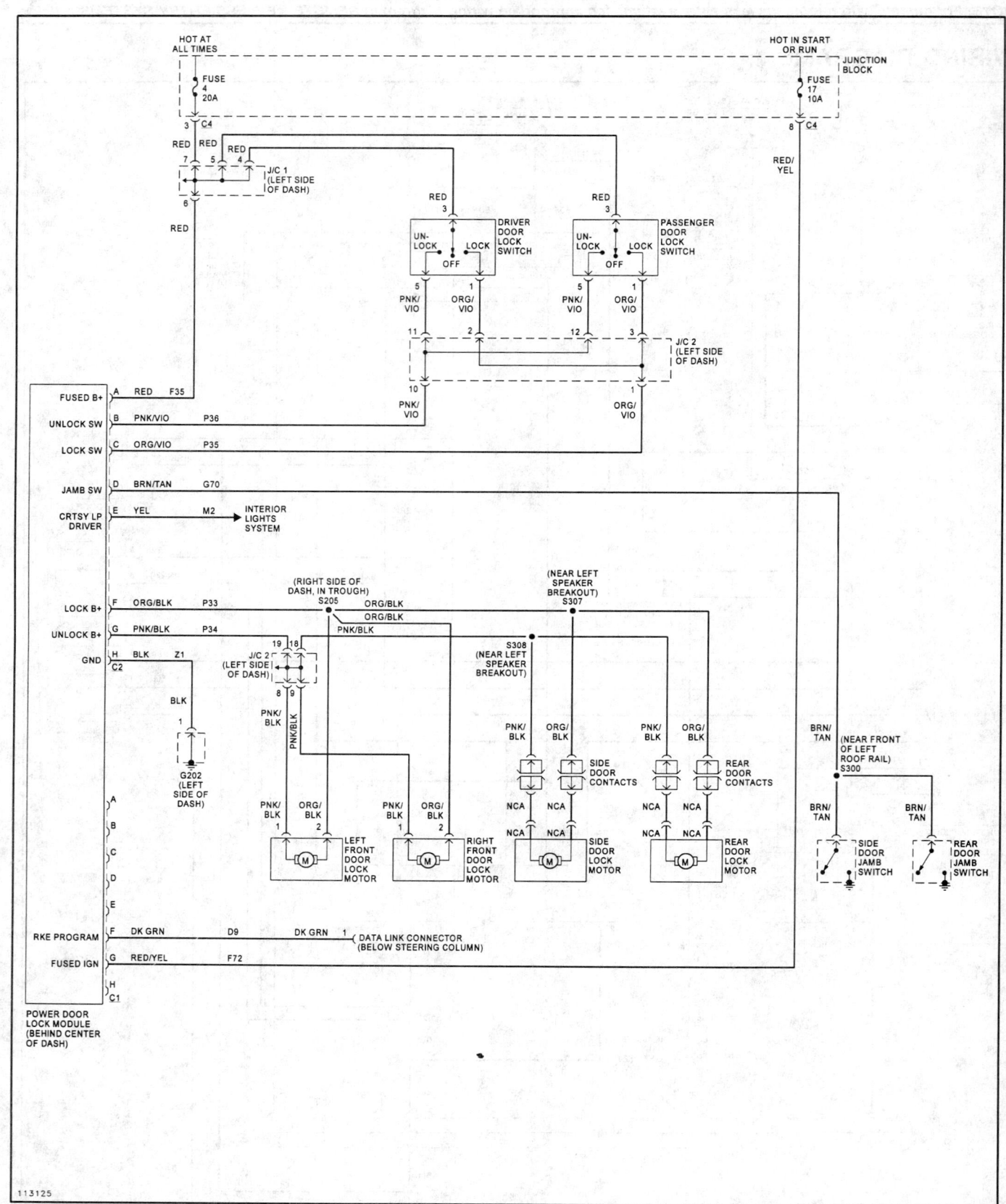

Fig. 2: Power Door Locks Wiring Diagram (Ram Van & Ram Wagon)

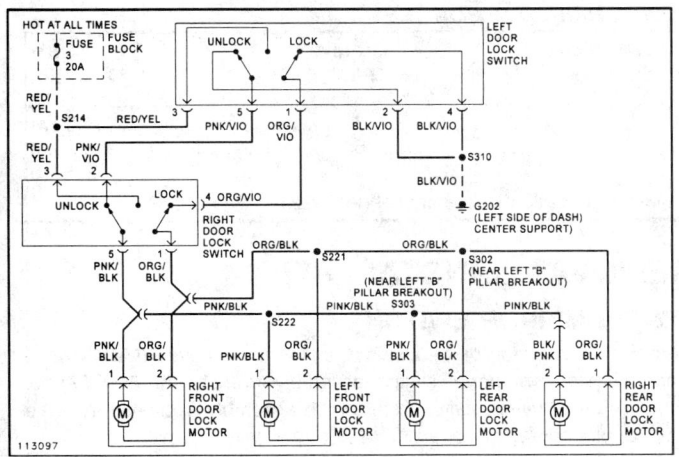

Fig. 3: Power Door Locks Wiring Diagram (Neon)

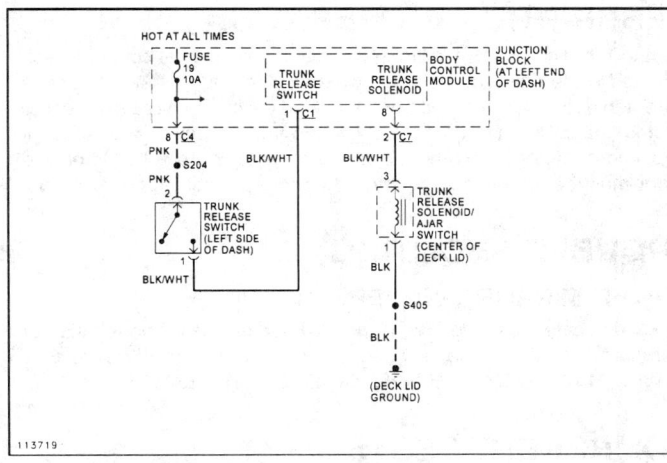

Fig. 5: Power Trunk Release Wiring Diagram (Concorde, Intrepid, LHS & 300M)

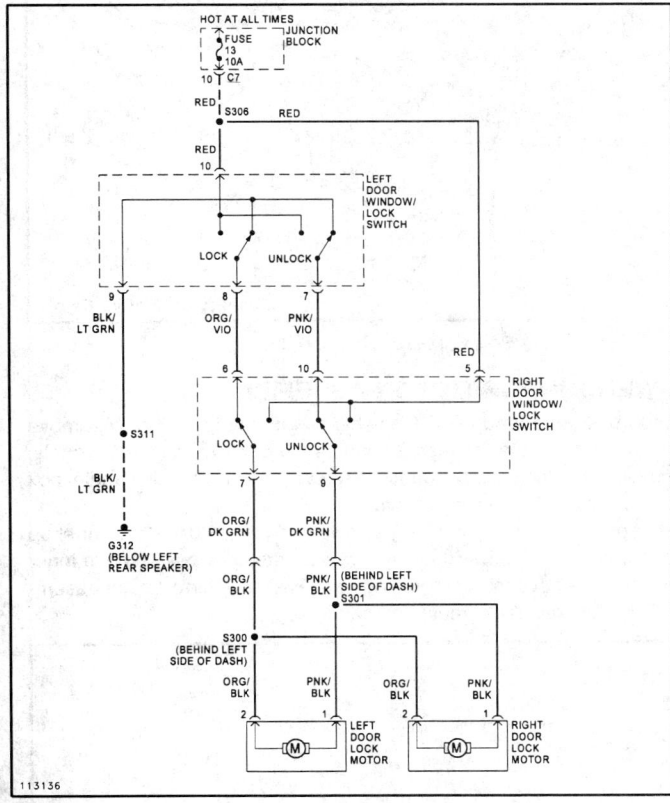

Fig. 4: Power Door Locks Wiring Diagram (Ram Pickup)

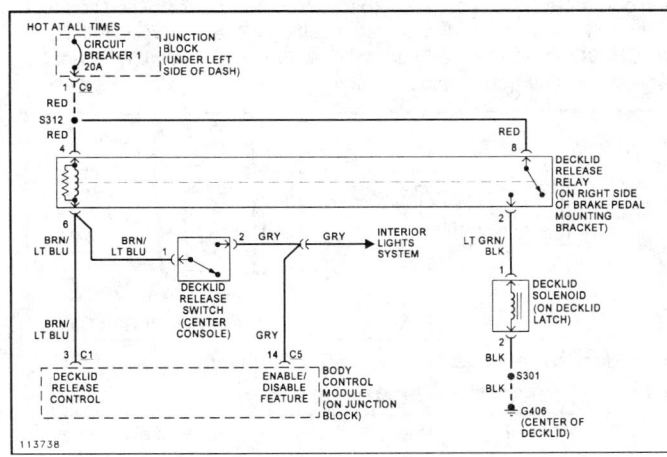

Fig. 6: Power Decklid Release Wiring Diagram (Sebring Convertible)

DESCRIPTION & OPERATION

Electric remote control mirrors are controlled by a dual-control switch mounted on left side of instrument panel. The left/right switch directs current to desired mirror. The horizontal/vertical switch directs current to electric motor in mirror assembly to control up/down and left/right adjustment. Motor is located inside mirror/motor assembly. Motor and mirror must be removed and serviced as an assembly.

TROUBLE SHOOTING

POWER MIRRORS INOPERATIVE

Check dedicated fuse No. 12 (10-amp). Fuse is located on left side of instrument panel. If fuse is good, check power mirror switch. See POWER MIRROR SWITCH under COMPONENT TESTS.

COMPONENT TESTS

POWER MIRROR SWITCH

Using ohmmeter, check continuity between power mirror switch connector pins with switch in designated position. See POWER MIRROR SWITCH CONTINUITY TEST table. See Fig. 1. If continuity is not as specified, replace power mirror switch.

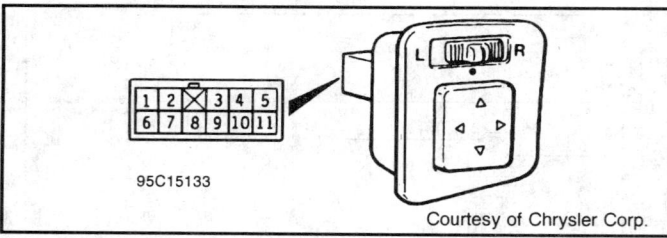

Fig. 1: Identifying Power Mirror Switch Connector Pins

POWER MIRROR SWITCH CONTINUITY TEST

Switch Position (Mirror Angle)	[1] Continuity Between Pins
Mirror Selector In Left Position	
Up	3 & 4; 5 & 10
Down	3 & 5; 4 & 10
Left	3 & 11; 4 & 10
Right	3 & 4; 10 & 11
Mirror Selector In Right Position	
Up	3 & 4; 9 & 10
Down	3 & 9; 4 & 10
Left	3 & 8; 4 & 10
Right	3 & 4; 8 & 10

[1] – Use illustration to identify connector pins. See Fig. 1.

POWER MIRROR MOTOR

Connect one jumper lead to battery voltage. Connect another jumper lead to chassis ground. Connect other ends of jumper leads to appropriate pins in mirror motor connector. See POWER MIRROR MOTOR TEST table. See Fig. 2. Motors should move in appropriate direction and stop at end of mirror travel. If mirror does not operate as specified, replace mirror/motor assembly.

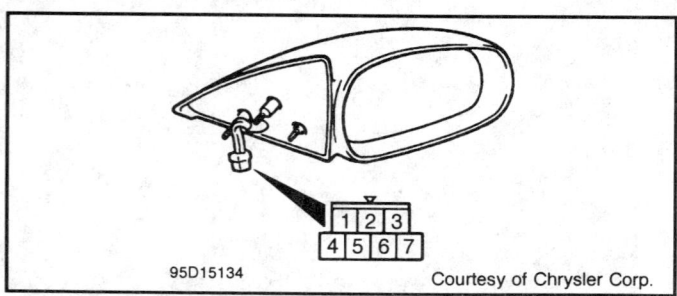

Fig. 2: Identifying Power Mirror Motor Connector Pins

POWER MIRROR MOTOR TEST

Apply 12 Volts To Pin No. [1]	[1] Ground Pin	Mirror Operation
7	5	Up
5	7	Down
5	6	Left
6	5	Right

[1] – Use illustration to identify connector pins. See Fig. 2.

REMOVAL & INSTALLATION

POWER MIRROR SWITCH

Removal & Installation – Using Ornament Remover (MB990784), remove instrument panel switch assembly from dash. See Fig. 3. Remove power mirror switch from switch assembly. To install, reverse removal procedure.

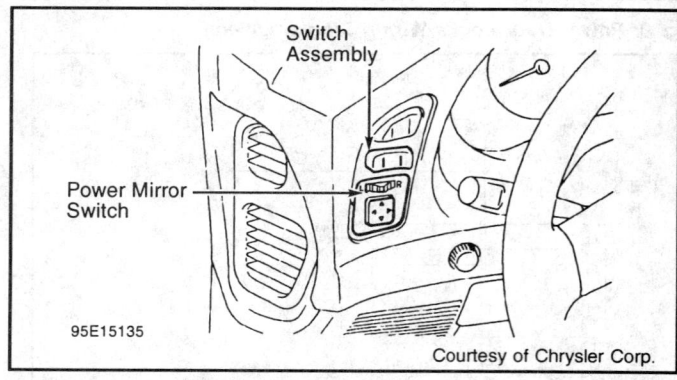

Fig. 3: Removing Power Mirror Switch

POWER MIRROR/MOTOR ASSEMBLY

Removal & Installation – 1) On vehicles with manual window, remove window crank handle clip, handle and bezel. See Fig. 4. On all models, remove pull handle box mounting screw, and slide pull handle box towards front of vehicle to remove.

2) Remove door panel mounting screws and clips. Push door panel up to separate panel from window inner weatherstrip clips. Remove inner trim cover. Remove mirror mounting nuts. Remove mirror/motor assembly. To install, reverse removal procedure.

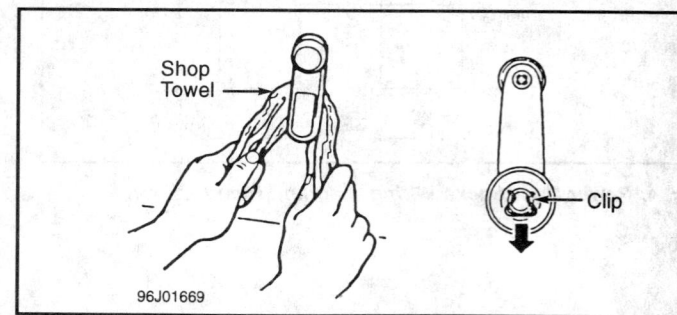

Fig. 4: Removing Window Crank Handle (Manual Window)

WIRING DIAGRAMS

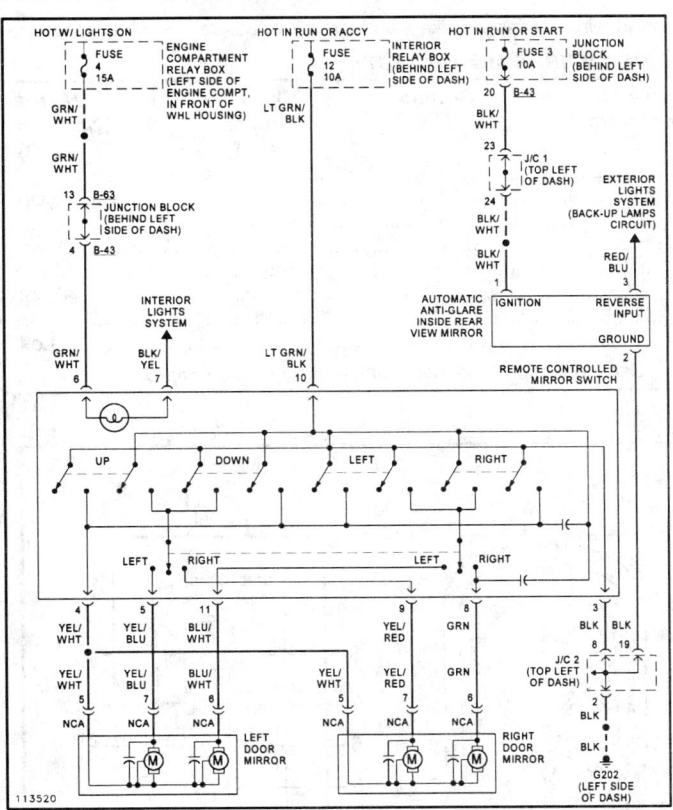

Fig. 5: Power Mirror System Wiring Diagram
(Avenger & Sebring Coupe)

1999 ACCESSORIES & EQUIPMENT
Power Mirrors
Breeze, Cirrus, Neon, Sebring Convertible & Stratus

DESCRIPTION & OPERATION

The power side mirrors are controlled by a single switch assembly located on driver's door panel. The switch has a rocker button marked left and right for mirror selection, and 4 buttons for mirror movement. *See Fig. 2.*

All vehicles are equipped with an ignition-off draw fuse, which helps prevent battery discharge during storage. This fuse is included in power mirror circuitry. Check fuse if mirrors are inoperative. The power mirror motor is an integral part of mirror assembly, and cannot be replaced separately.

Heated mirrors are available on Breeze, Cirrus, Sebring Convertible and Stratus with power mirrors and rear window defogger. Heated mirror is controlled by rear window defogger switch. Mirror should get warm when rear window defogger is activated.

COMPONENT TESTS

HEATED MIRROR

1) Access power mirror harness connector. See POWER MIRROR ASSEMBLY under REMOVAL & INSTALLATION. Using ohmmeter, check continuity between mirror harness connector terminal No. 2 (Black wire) and ground. *See Fig. 3* . Continuity should exist. Repair as necessary. Go to next step.

2) Turn rear window defogger switch on. Check for voltage at mirror harness connector terminal No. 1 (Light Blue/Yellow wire) and ground. If battery voltage exists, go to step **5)**. If battery voltage does not exist, check fuses No. 5 and 6 in junction block, located under driver's side of instrument panel. Check fuse No. 12 in Power Distribution Center (PDC). Replace fuse, if necessary. Go to next step.

3) Remove Heater/Ventilation Air Conditioning (HVAC) control unit. See HVAC CONTROL UNIT under REMOVAL & INSTALLATION. Using an ohmmeter, measure resistance between HVAC control unit 8-pin connector terminals No. 5 and 8. *See Fig. 1.* Press defogger switch. If resistance is 500-520 ohms, go to next step. If resistance is not 500-520 ohms, replace HVAC control unit.

4) If battery voltage still does not exist at mirror harness connector terminal No. 1 (Light Blue/Yellow wire), repair wiring. See WIRING DIAGRAMS.

5) Remove mirror glass. Check wiring between mirror and connector. If wiring is okay, replace mirror.

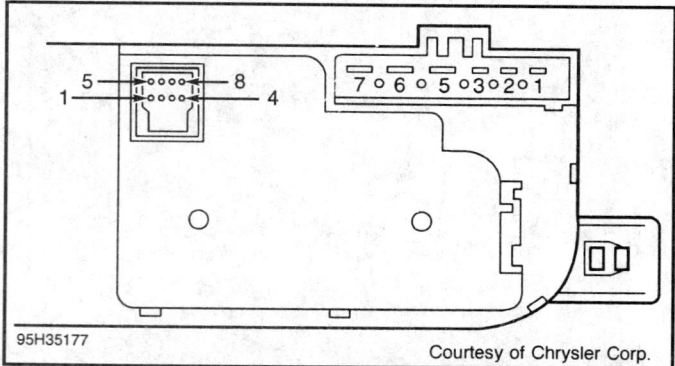

Fig. 1: Identifying HVAC Control Unit Connector Terminals

POWER MIRROR MOTOR

1) Remove mirror switch. See POWER MIRROR SWITCH under REMOVAL & INSTALLATION. Disconnect wiring harness connector at switch.

2) Connect one end of jumper wire to 12-volt source. Connect one end of second jumper wire to a good body ground. Connect remaining end of each jumper wire to specified mirror switch pins on harness side (not switch side). *See Fig. 3.* See POWER MIRROR MOTOR TEST table. If mirror operation is not as specified in table, check circuit for broken or

shorted wire. If wiring is okay, replace mirror assembly as necessary.

POWER MIRROR MOTOR TEST

Apply 12 Volts To Pin No. [1]	Ground Pin	Mirror Operation (Right)	Mirror Operation (Left)
4	5	Up	
8	5		Up
5	4	Down	
5	8		Down
6	3	Right	
6	7		Right
3	6	Left	
7	6		Left

[1] – Use illustration to identify connector pins. *See Fig. 33.*

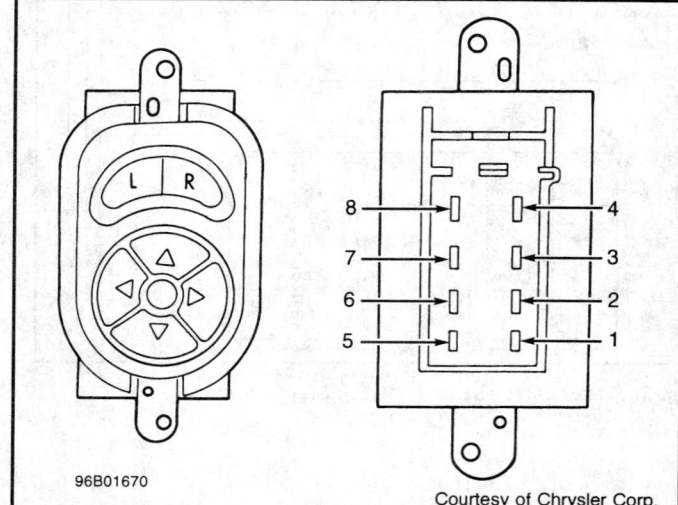

Fig. 2: Identifying Power Mirror Switch Pins

POWER MIRROR SWITCH

1) Remove power mirror switch. See POWER MIRROR SWITCH under REMOVAL & INSTALLATION. Remove power mirror switch from its mounting position. Disconnect switch from wiring harness.

2) Place mirror selector in appropriate position. See POWER MIRROR SWITCH CONTINUITY TEST table. Check for continuity between specified switch pins with mirror switch in position indicated. *See Fig. 2.* If continuity is not as specified, replace switch.

POWER MIRROR SWITCH CONTINUITY TEST

Application	Continuity Between Pins
Mirror Angle [1]	1 & 5; 2 & 8
Up	1 & 5; 2 & 8
Down	1 & 8; 2 & 5
Left	1 & 6; 2 & 7
Right	1 & 7; 2 & 6
Mirror Angle [2]	
Up	1 & 5; 2 & 4
Down	1 & 4; 2 & 5
Left	1 & 6; 2 & 3
Right	1 & 3; 2 & 6

[1] – With power mirror switch in LEFT (L) position.
[2] – With power mirror switch in RIGHT (R) position.

Power Mirrors
Breeze, Cirrus, Neon, Sebring Convertible & Stratus (Cont.)

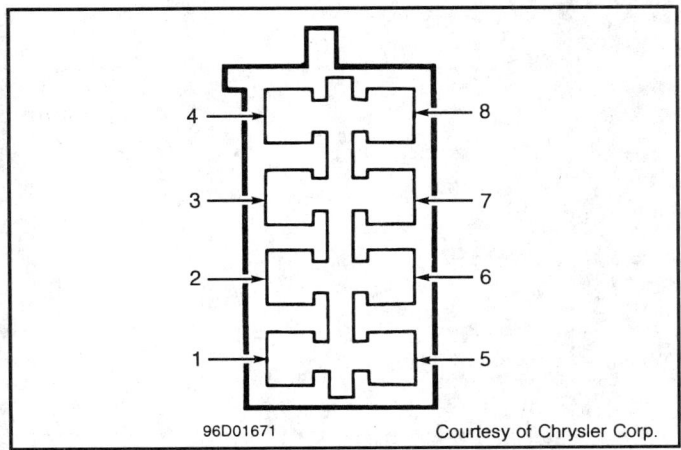

96D01671   Courtesy of Chrysler Corp.

Fig. 3: Identifying Mirror Connector Pins

REMOVAL & INSTALLATION

POWER MIRROR SWITCH

Removal & Installation (Except Sebring Convertible) – 1) Lower window to full down position. If equipped with manual windows, remove window crank. Remove speaker grille from door panel. Remove screws attaching door panel-to-door from around speaker. Remove screw cap and screw attaching arm rest pull cup-to-support bracket. Remove screw cap and screw attaching door latch handle-to-door panel. Disengage clips attaching door panel-to-outer edges of door.

2) Lift door panel upward to disengage upper retainer channel. Pull top of door panel away from door. Remove clip attaching latch linkage-to-door handle. Disconnect power mirror switch connector. Remove door panel. Remove screws attaching mirror switch-to-door panel. To install, reverse removal procedure.

Removal & Installation (Sebring Convertible) – Place small flat-blade tool into slot above L-R selector of power mirror switch. Push against power mirror switch and lift up to release switch assembly from door trim. Disconnect power mirror switch connector. To install, reverse removal procedure.

POWER MIRROR ASSEMBLY

Removal & Installation – Remove door panel. See POWER MIRROR SWITCH. For Sebring Convertible, use EXCEPT SEBRING CONVERTIBLE procedure. On all models, remove screws attaching mirror bezel-to-door. Disconnect mirror wiring connector. Disengage mirror wiring harness connector from door. Remove mirror mounting nuts. Remove mirror. To install, reverse removal procedure.

HVAC CONTROL UNIT

Removal & Installation – Disconnect negative battery cable. Pull center bezel rearward to disengage 4 retaining clips. Remove screws from cubby bin. Remove HVAC control unit attaching screws. Pull HVAC control unit outward to disconnect 2 electrical connectors and 2 control cables. Remove HVAC control unit. To install, reverse removal procedure.

WIRING DIAGRAMS

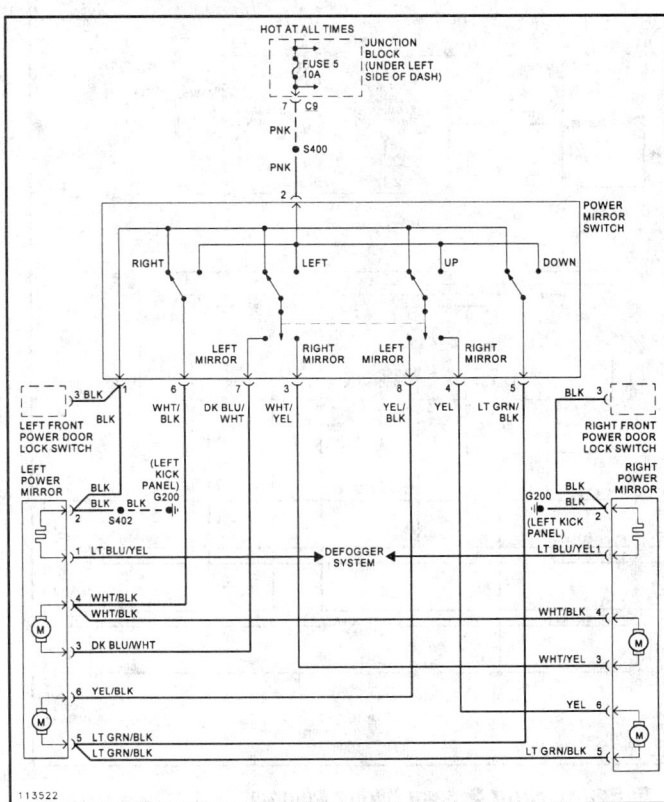

*Fig. 4: Power Mirror System Wiring Diagram
(Breeze, Cirrus & Stratus)*

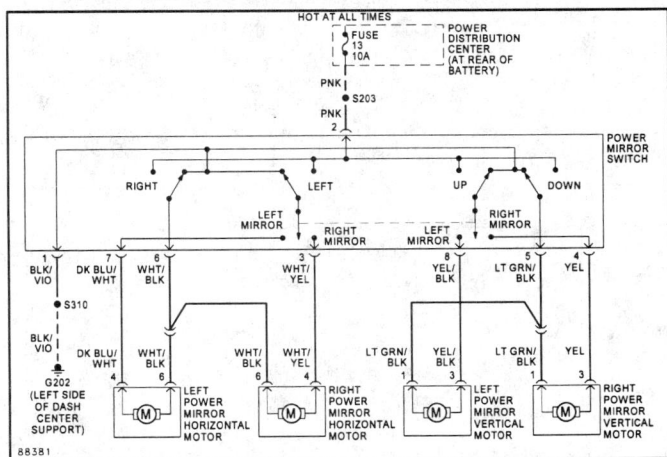

Fig. 5: Power Mirror System Wiring Diagram (Neon)

CHRY
4-430

1999 ACCESSORIES & EQUIPMENT
Power Mirrors
Breeze, Cirrus, Neon, Sebring Convertible & Stratus (Cont.)

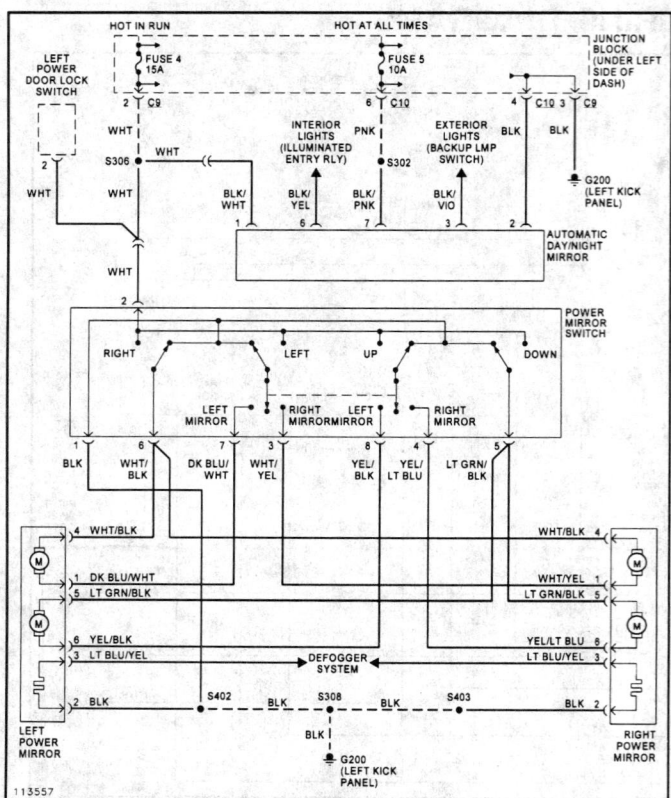

Fig. 6: Power Mirror System Wiring Diagram
(Sebring Convertible)

Power Mirrors – Caravan, Dakota, Durango, Ram Pickup, Ram Van, Ram Wagon, Town & Country, & Voyager

DESCRIPTION

Outside power rear view mirrors consist of door-mounted mirrors with internal motor drive and backing plate. On Caravan, Town & Country, and Voyager, mirrors are controlled by a rocker switch for left or right mirror selection and a platform button for up, down, right and left movement. On Dakota, Durango, Ram Pickup, Ram Van and Ram Wagon, mirrors are controlled by a single, multifunction, joystick-type switch assembly. On all models, mirror motors are integral with mirror assemblies and cannot be serviced separately. On Dakota and Durango, fold-away rear view mirrors are optional.

Dakota, Durango and Ram Pickup are equipped with an automatic dimming day/night inside mirror. The mirror uses 2 photocell sensors to monitor ambient and rear facing light levels. The mirror automatically adjusts its reflectance to reduce headlight glare from vehicles approaching from the rear. The mirror is controlled by an off/on switch located on the mirror bottom.

Caravan, Ram Pickup, Town & Country and Voyager have optional heated outside mirrors. On Caravan, Town & Country and Voyager, heated mirror is activated whenever the rear defogger is on. On Ram Pickup, heated mirror is activated by switch in dash. A timer turns off mirror heater after about 10 minutes.

COMPONENT TESTS

AUTOMATIC DAY/NIGHT INSIDE MIRROR

1) Turn ignition switch to ON position with transmission in Neutral or Park. Place mirror switch in ON position (switch LED illuminated). Cover forward facing sensor with a dark cloth or tape to exclude any ambient light. *See Fig. 1.*

2) Shine a light into rear-facing sensor. Observe whether or not mirror darkens. With mirror darkened, place transmission in Reverse. Mirror should return to normal. If conditions of steps **1)** and **2)** are met, mirror is operating correctly. If conditions are not met, go to next step.

3) Turn ignition on. Check for battery voltage at fuse No. 11 in junction block. If battery voltage exists on both sides of fuse, go to next step. If battery voltage does not exist, repair circuit to junction block. See WIRING DIAGRAMS. If fuse is blown, repair short circuit and replace fuse.

4) Check for battery voltage at day/night mirror wire connector terminal No. 1 (Dark Blue/White wire). If battery voltage exists, go to next step. If battery voltage does not exist, repair open circuit between mirror and junction block.

5) Check for continuity between ground and day/night mirror wire connector terminal No. 2 (Black wire). If continuity exists, go to next step. If continuity does not exist, repair open ground circuit.

6) Check for battery voltage at day/night mirror wire connector terminal No. 3 (Violet/Black wire) with transmission in Reverse. If battery voltage exists, replace mirror. If battery voltage does not exist, check back-up light circuit. See WIRING DIAGRAMS.

POWER MIRROR MOTOR

Caravan, Town & Country, & Voyager – Disconnect harness connector from mirror and headlight switch. Using 2 jumper wires, connect one jumper to a 12-volt source and the other jumper wire to a good ground. Connect other end of jumper wires to specified switch terminals as specified. See POWER MIRROR MOTOR TEST (CARAVAN, TOWN & COUNTRY, & VOYAGER) table. If mirror operation is not as specified, check for open or short circuit between switch and power mirror. Repair as necessary. If wiring harness is okay, replace mirror assembly as necessary. *See Fig. 2.*

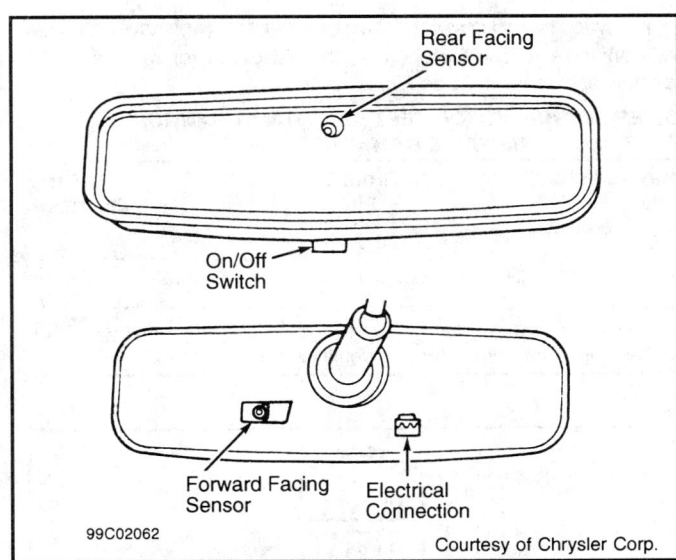

Fig. 1: Identifying Automatic Day/Night Mirror

POWER MIRROR MOTOR TEST
(CARAVAN, TOWN & COUNTRY, & VOYAGER)

Apply 12 Volts To Pin	Ground Pin	Mirror Operation (Right)	Mirror Operation (Left)
Switch Connector [1]			
12	6		Up
7	6		Left
6	12		Down
6	7		Right
13	1	Up	
8	1	Left	
1	13	Down	
1	8	Right	
5	11	[2]	[2]

[1] – Use illustration for connector pin identification. *See Fig. 2.*
[2] – Used for switch illumination. No mirror movement will be observed.

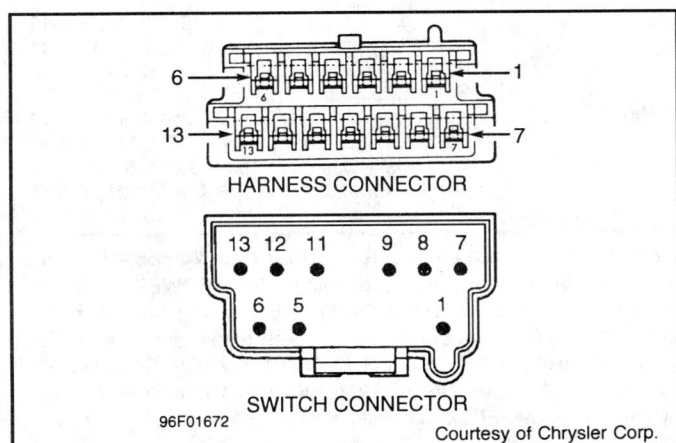

Fig. 2: Identifying Power Mirror Switch Connector Pins (Caravan, Town & Country, & Voyager)

Dakota, Durango, Ram Pickup, Ram Van & Ram Wagon – Disconnect harness connector from mirror and headlight switch. Using 2 jumper wires, connect one jumper to a 12-volt source and the other to a good ground. If tests do not agree with POWER MIRROR MOTOR

CHRY
4-432

1999 ACCESSORIES & EQUIPMENT
Power Mirrors – Caravan, Dakota, Durango, Ram Pickup, Ram Van, Ram Wagon, Town & Country, & Voyager (Cont.)

TEST (DAKOTA, DURANGO, RAM PICKUP, RAM VAN & RAM WAGON) table, check for open or shorted circuit, or replace mirror assembly as necessary. *See Fig. 3.*

POWER MIRROR MOTOR TEST (DAKOTA, DURANGO, RAM PICKUP, RAM VAN & RAM WAGON)

Apply 12 Volts To Pin	Ground Pin	Mirror Operation
Switch Connector [1]		
3	1	Up
2	1	Left
1	3	Down
1	2	Right

[1] – See Fig. 3 for connector pin identification.

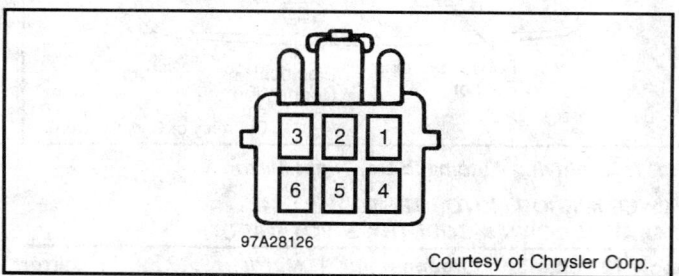

Fig. 3: Identifying Power Mirror Connector Pins (Dakota, Durango, Ram Pickup, Ram Van & Ram Wagon)

POWER MIRROR SWITCH

Caravan, Town & Country, & Voyager – Remove switch and disconnect wiring connector. See POWER MIRROR SWITCH under REMOVAL & INSTALLATION. Using an ohmmeter, check continuity between power mirror switch terminals with switch in appropriate position. See POWER MIRROR SWITCH CONTINUITY TEST (CARAVAN, TOWN & COUNTRY, & VOYAGER) table. *See Fig. 2.* If results differ from table, replace switch.

POWER MIRROR SWITCH CONTINUITY TEST (CARAVAN, TOWN & COUNTRY, & VOYAGER)

Mirror Selector Position	Mirror Angle	Continuity Between Pins
"L" (Left)	Up	9 & 12; 6 & 11; 9 & 13
	Down	9 & 6; 12 & 11; 13 & 11
	Left	9 & 7; 6 & 11; 9 & 8
	Right	9 & 6; 7 & 11; 8 & 11
"R" (Right)	Up	9 & 13; 1 & 11; 9 & 12
	Down	9 & 1; 13 & 11; 12 & 11
	Left	9 & 8; 1 & 11; 9 & 7
	Right	9 & 1; 8 & 11; 7 & 11
Illumination		5 & 11

Dakota, Durango, Ram Pickup, Ram Van & Ram Wagon – Remove switch and disconnect wiring connector. See POWER MIRROR SWITCH under REMOVAL & INSTALLATION. Using an ohmmeter, check continuity between power mirror switch terminals with switch in appropriate position. See POWER MIRROR SWITCH CONTINUITY TEST (DAKOTA, DURANGO, RAM PICKUP, RAM VAN & RAM WAGON) table. *See Fig. 4.* If results differ from table, replace switch.

POWER MIRROR SWITCH CONTINUITY TEST (DAKOTA, DURANGO, RAM PICKUP, RAM VAN & RAM WAGON)

Mirror Selector Position	Mirror Angle	Continuity Between Pins
"L" (Left)	Up	1 & 7; 3 & 8; 4 & 7
	Down	1 & 8; 3 & 7; 4 & 8
	Left	2 & 7; 3 & 8; 5 & 7
	Right	2 & 8; 3 & 7; 5 & 8
"R" (Right)	Up	1 & 7; 4 & 7; 6 & 8
	Down	1 & 8; 4 & 8; 6 & 7
	Left	2 & 7; 5 & 7; 6 & 8
	Right	2 & 8; 5 & 8; 6 & 7

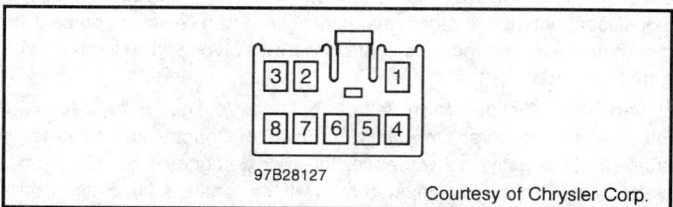

Fig. 4: Identifying Power Mirror Motor Switch Connector Pins (Dakota, Durango, Ram Pickup, Ram Van & Ram Wagon)

POWER MIRROR DEFOGGER

NOTE: On Caravan, Town & Country and Voyager, heated mirror is controlled by rear window defogger switch. Heated mirror is on whenever rear window defogger is on.

Caravan, Town & Country, & Voyager – 1) Mirror should be warm to touch with rear window defogger activated. If mirror is not warm to touch, check fuse No. 12 (10-amp) in junction block. Repair short circuit and replace fuse as necessary. Check for battery voltage at mirror harness connector Light Blue/Yellow wire with rear window defogger switch on. If battery voltage does not exist, repair wiring as necessary. See WIRING DIAGRAMS. If battery voltage exists, go to next step.
2) Apply voltage to Light Blue/Yellow wire at heated mirror and ground Black wire at heated mirror. Mirror should become warm to touch. If mirror is not warm to touch, remove mirror and test wires for continuity. If no continuity exists, repair wires. If wires are okay, replace mirror. To test defogger switch, see appropriate wiring diagram in REAR WINDOW DEFOGGERS article.

NOTE: On Ram Pickup, heated mirror is controlled by mirror defogger switch.

Ram Pickup – 1) Turn ignition on. While watching instrument panel voltmeter, turn heated mirror switch on. Voltmeter needle should deflect. With heated mirror on, mirror should be warm to touch after 3-4 minutes. If system operates as described, system is okay at this time.
2) If system does not operate as described, go to next step. Illuminated indicator light means only that voltage exists at heated mirror relay.
3) Ensure ignition is on. Check fuses in Power Distribution Center (PDC) and junction block. Ensure fuses are fully seated and connections are secure. If mirrors are still inoperative, problem is in heated mirror control, mirror heating grid and/or heated mirror harness or connectors. If turning switch on causes a large deflection in instrument panel voltmeter, check for a short circuit in system. Repair as necessary.

REMOVAL & INSTALLATION

CAUTION: When battery is disconnected, vehicle computer and memory systems may lose memory data. Driveability problems may exist until computer systems have completed a relearn cycle. See COMPUTER RELEARN PROCEDURES article in GENERAL INFORMATION before disconnecting battery.

HEATED MIRROR SWITCH

Removal & Installation (Ram Pickup) – Heated mirror switch is part of HVAC control unit. See appropriate AUTOMATIC A/C-HEATER SYSTEMS article in appropriate MITCHELL® AIR CONDITIONING & HEATING SERVICE & REPAIR manual.

POWER MIRROR SWITCH

Removal & Installation (Caravan, Town & Country, & Voyager) – 1) Remove cover from over steering column. Remove screws holding instrument cluster bezel to dash (above cluster lens). Remove screws holding instrument cluster bezel to dash from each side of steering column. Disconnect clip holding instrument cluster bezel to dash from above right vent louver.

2) Separate instrument cluster bezel from dash. Disconnect wires from back of bezel. Disengage lock tabs above and below mirror switch. Pull mirror switch from headlight switch bezel. To install, reverse removal procedure.

Removal & Installation (Dakota & Durango) – 1) Pull power mirror switch control knob rearward to remove it from switch body. Remove nut securing switch to door trim panel. Pull door latch handle to open position and remove screw securing trim panel to door. Remove manual window crank handle, if equipped. Release locking tab on power window/lock switch, if equipped. Remove power window/lock switch and unplug connector.

2) Remove remaining screws from door trim panel. Using a trim stick, pry perimeter of trim panel away from door sufficiently to unplug power mirror switch connector. Remove power mirror switch. To install, reverse removal procedure.

Removal & Installation (Ram Pickup) – 1) Remove door pull cup from door trim panel. Reach through door pull cup opening to release locking tab on power window/lock switch. Remove power window/lock switch and unplug connector.

2) Using a trim stick, pry perimeter of trim panel away from door. Remove door trim panel. Unplug power mirror switch connector. Remove power mirror switch. To install, reverse removal procedure.

Removal & Installation (Ram Van & Ram Wagon) – Disconnect battery. Remove knee blocker and lower instrument panel cover. Remove mirror control knob by pulling straight out. Remove inside hood release handle screws and lower handle. Reach under instrument panel and disconnect switch connector. Remove 2 switch mounting plate screws and pull switch from panel. Remove switch-to-mounting plate nut and remove switch. To install, reverse removal procedure.

POWER MIRROR ASSEMBLY

Removal & Installation (Caravan, Town & Country, & Voyager) – Remove screw and power mirror front cover. Remove 3 mirror attaching screws and pull mirror away from door. Disconnect mirror electrical connectors. To install, reverse removal procedure.

Removal & Installation (Dakota & Durango) – 1) Unscrew door lock knob. Remove power window/lock switch assembly by inserting a screwdriver in notch at forward end of switch housing to release locking tabs. Pull switch assembly forward and out from door panel. Remove trim plug from top of trim panel. Remove screw under trim plug.

2) Remove 2 screws from bottom of door trim panel. Remove arm rest screw. Using a trim stick, pry trim panel away from door. Roll door watershield away from lower rear corner of door to expose panel access. Reach inside door and disconnect mirror wiring connector.

3) Remove 3 mirror nuts and pull mirror loose from door. Feed wiring harness out through hole in outer door panel. To install, reverse removal procedure.

Removal & Installation (Ram Pickup, Ram Van & Ram Wagon) – 1) Raise window to full up position. Remove remote door latch control handle. Remove power window/lock switch by inserting thin-blade screwdriver into switch housing forward notch and depressing locking tab. Pull switch bezel out and forward to remove from door panel.

2) Remove 2 screws from bottom (front and rear) of trim panel. Using trim stick, pry trim panel away from door. Roll door watershield away from lower rear corner of door to expose panel access. Reach inside door and disconnect mirror wiring connector.

NOTE: Spray silicone on mounting bracket cover grommet to prevent grommet from coming off when cover is moved up on mirror stem.

3) Remove mirror mounting bracket cover and slide up on mirror stem. Remove mirror mounting bracket nuts. Pull mirror loose from door and feed wiring harness out through hole in outer door panel. To install, reverse removal procedure.

WIRING DIAGRAMS

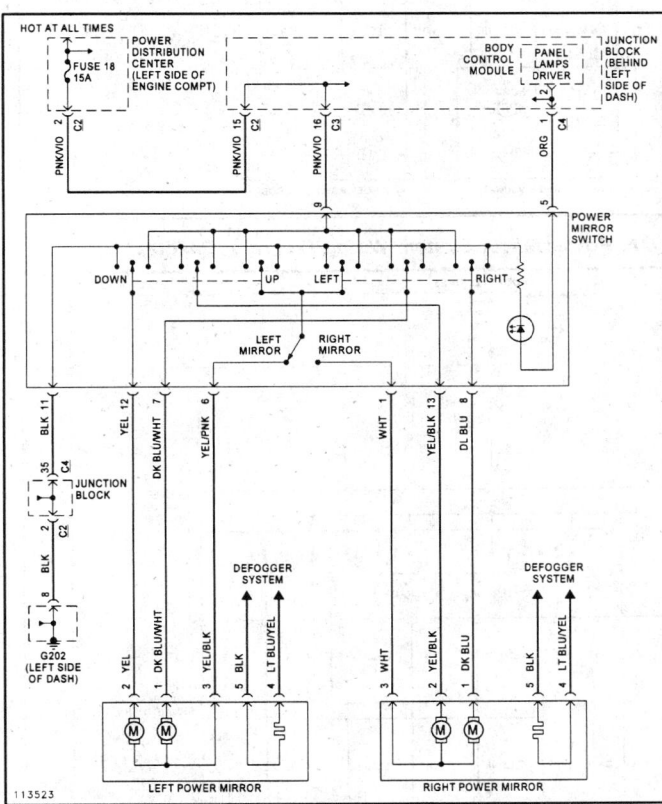

Fig. 5: Power Mirror System Wiring Diagram (Caravan, Town & Country, & Voyager)

CHRY
4-434

1999 ACCESSORIES & EQUIPMENT
Power Mirrors – Caravan, Dakota, Durango, Ram Pickup, Ram Van, Ram Wagon, Town & Country, & Voyager (Cont.)

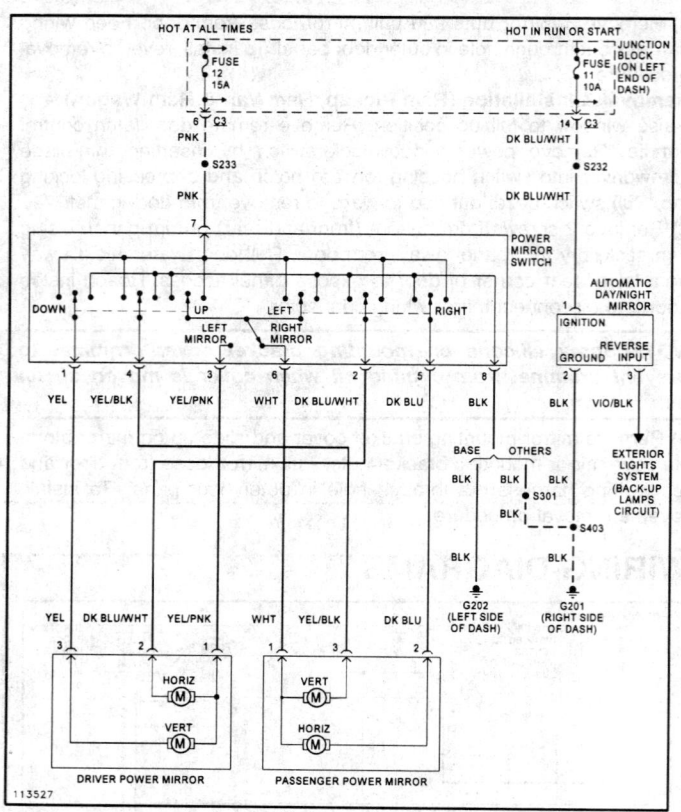

Fig. 6: *Power Mirror System Wiring Diagram (Dakota)*

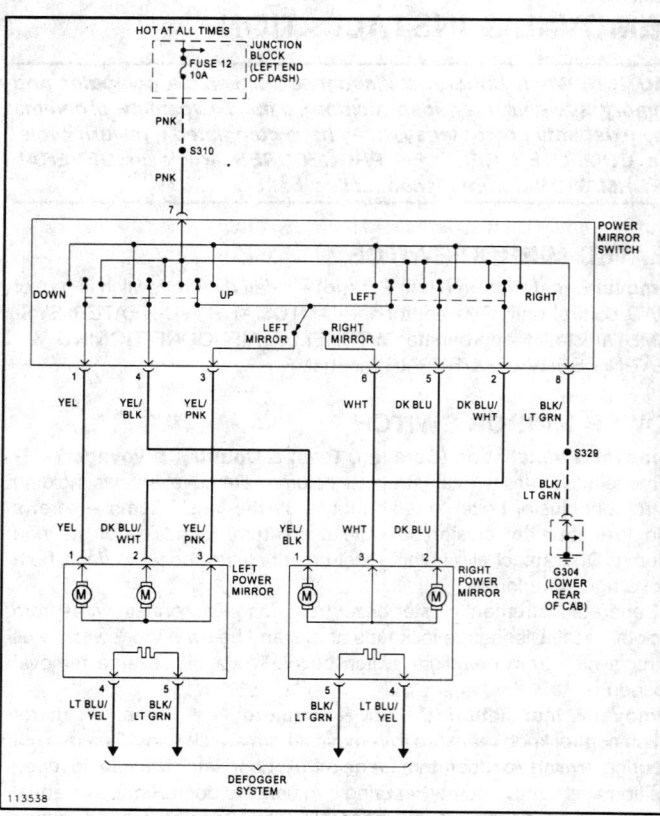

Fig. 8: *Power Mirror System Wiring Diagram (Ram Pickup)*

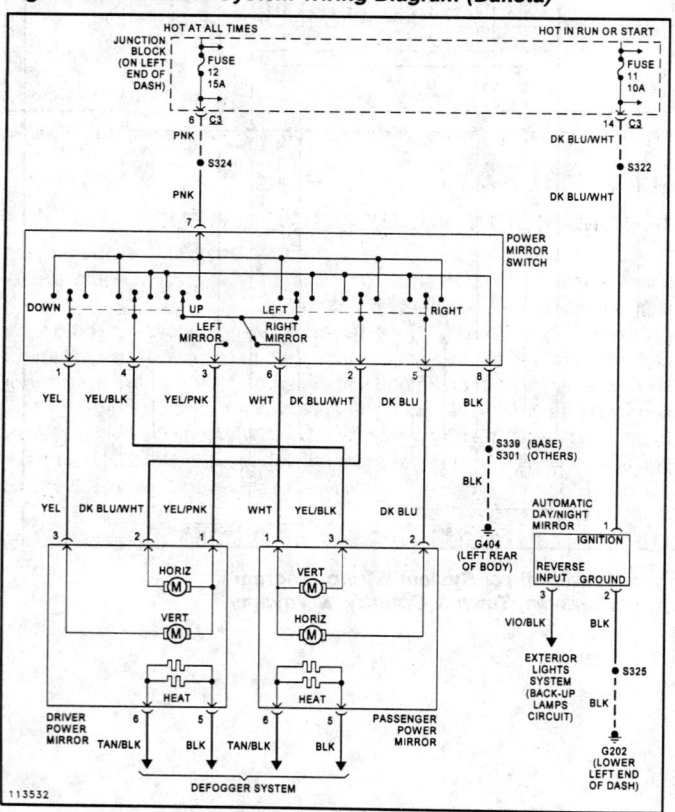

Fig. 7: *Power Mirror System Wiring Diagram (Durango)*

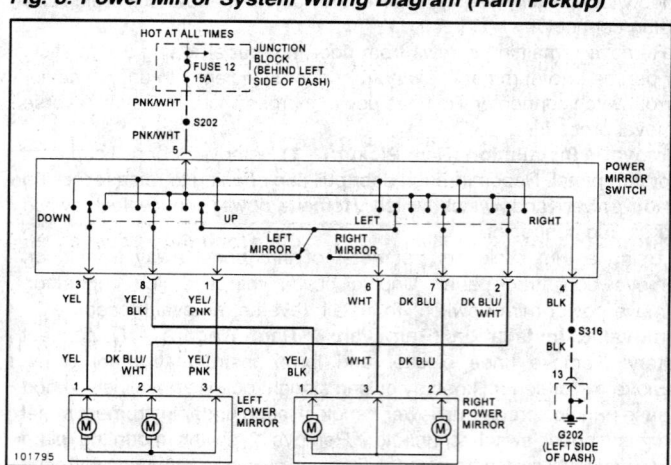

Fig. 9: *Power Mirror System Wiring Diagram (Ram Van & Ram Wagon)*

DESCRIPTION & OPERATION

Electric remote control mirrors are controlled by a single switch assembly located on driver's door trim panel. The rocker button switch uses "L" (left) and "R" (right) for mirror selection and a round platform which is tilted in direction of desired mirror movement. See Fig. 1.

The motors which operate the mirrors are part of mirror assembly and cannot be replaced separately. All vehicles are equipped with an ignition-off draw fuse which is used when vehicle is originally shipped from factory. This fuse is located behind instrument panel access cover, by driver's door, and helps to prevent battery discharge during storage. This fuse is included in power mirror circuitry and should be checked if mirrors are inoperative. Only models equipped with rear window defogger and memory mirrors are available with heated mirrors.

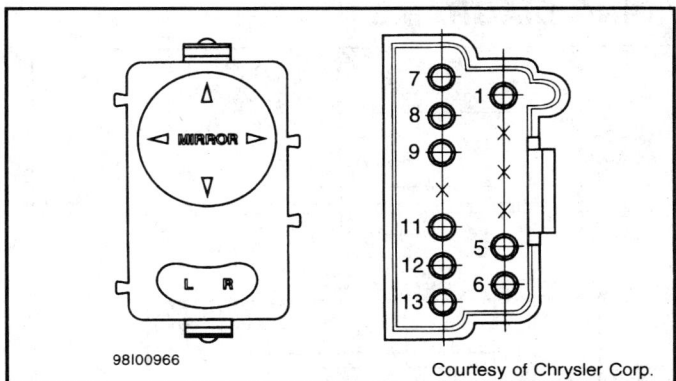

Fig. 1: Identifying Power Mirror Switch

COMPONENT TESTS

POWER MIRROR SWITCH

Remove power mirror switch. See POWER MIRROR SWITCH under REMOVAL & INSTALLATION. Using an ohmmeter, check continuity between power mirror switch terminals with switch in appropriate position. See POWER MIRROR SWITCH CONTINUITY TEST table. See Fig. 1. If continuity is not as specified, replace switch.

POWER MIRROR SWITCH CONTINUITY TEST

Mirror Selector Position	Mirror Angle	Continuity Between Pins
"L" (Left)	Up	1 & 9; 11 & 12; 12 & 13
	Down	1 & 11; 9 & 12; 9 & 13
	Left	1 & 9; 7 & 11; 8 & 11
	Right	1 & 11; 7 & 9; 8 & 9
"R" (Right)	Up	2 & 9; 11 & 12; 11 & 13
	Down	6 & 11; 9 & 12; 9 & 13
	Left	6 & 9; 7 & 11; 8 & 11
	Right	6 & 11; 7 & 9; 8 & 9

POWER MIRROR MOTOR

Disconnect power mirror switch connector. See POWER MIRROR SWITCH under REMOVAL & INSTALLATION. Connect one end of a jumper wire to a 12-volt source and other end to specified power mirror switch connector terminals. Connect one end of another jumper wire to a good ground and other end to specified power mirror switch connector terminals. See POWER MIRROR MOTOR TEST table. If mirror does not operate as specified, check for open or shorted circuit or replace power mirror assembly. See Fig. 2.

POWER MIRROR MOTOR TEST

Apply 12 Volts To Pin	Ground Pin	Mirror Operation (Right)	Mirror Operation (Left)
Switch Connector [1]			
12	6	Up	
13	1		Up
6	12	Down	
1	13		Down
6	7	Right	
1	8		Right
7	6	Left	
8	1		Left
Door Connector [1]			
6	2	Up	Up
2	6	Down	Down
2	5	Right	Right
5	2	Left	Left
1	3	[2]	[2]

[1] – See Fig. 2 for connector pin identification.
[2] – Used for mirror heater. No mirror movement will be observed.

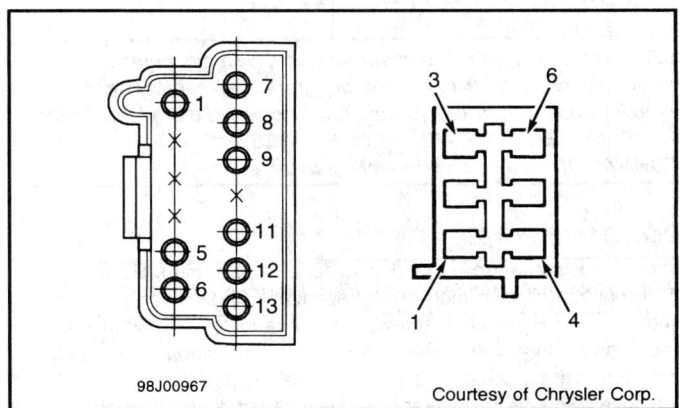

Fig. 2: Identifying Power Mirror Switch & Door Connector Pins

SYSTEM TESTS

AUTOMATIC DAY/NIGHT INSIDE MIRROR

1) Turn ignition switch to ON position with transmission in Park. Place mirror switch in HI position. Cover forward facing sensor with a dark cloth to exclude any ambient light. See Fig. 3.

2) Shine a light into rear facing sensor. Observe whether or not mirror darkens. With mirror darkened, place transmission in Reverse. Mirror should return to normal. If conditions in steps 1) and 2) are met, mirror is operating correctly. If conditions are not met, go to next step.

3) Test voltage at 3-pin harness connector. With ignition switch in RUN position, pin No. 1 should have battery voltage, pin No. 2 should have continuity to ground and, with transmission in Reverse, pin No. 3 should have battery voltage. See Fig. 3.

4) If circuits are okay, replace mirror. If circuits are not okay, check wiring harness. See WIRING DIAGRAMS.

1999 ACCESSORIES & EQUIPMENT
Power Mirrors – Concorde, Intrepid, LHS & 300M (Cont.)

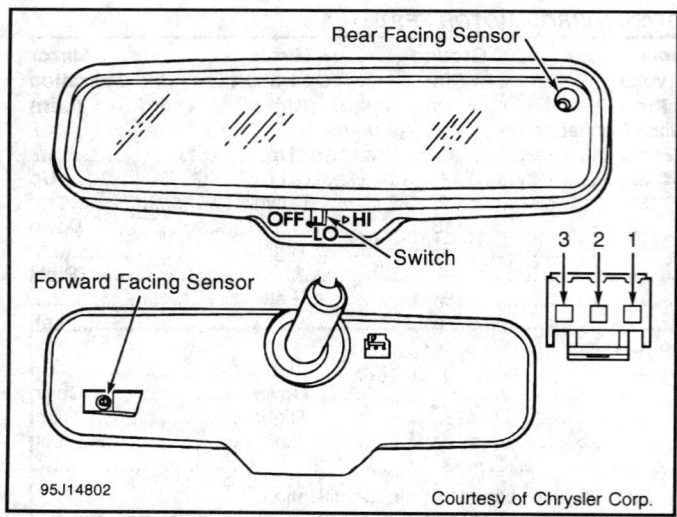

Fig. 3: Identifying Automatic Day/Night Mirror

REMOVAL & INSTALLATION

CAUTION: *When battery is disconnected, vehicle computer and memory systems may lose memory data. Driveability problems may exist until computer systems have completed a relearn cycle. See COMPUTER RELEARN PROCEDURES article in GENERAL INFORMATION before disconnecting battery.*

DOOR TRIM PANEL

Removal & Installation – 1) Remove speaker flag (trim). Using a trim tool, disengage clips holding rear of speaker grille to door trim panel. Remove grille. Remove 3 screws from bottom of door trim panel. Remove screw in pull cup. Remove screw behind plug in door handle bezel. Remove 2 screws in instrument panel interface area.

2) Remove 3 screws in speaker area. Using a trim tool, disengage clips holding door trim panel to door. Lift door trim panel upward and disconnect linkage from door handle. Disconnect wiring from door trim panel. Remove door trim panel. To install, reverse removal procedure.

POWER MIRROR SWITCH

Removal & Installation – Remove door trim panel. See DOOR TRIM PANEL. Using a trim tool, remove power mirror switch. Disconnect wiring from switch. To install, reverse removal procedure.

POWER MIRROR ASSEMBLY

Removal & Installation – 1) Remove front door trim panel. See DOOR TRIM PANEL. Remove window frame trim. Disconnect power mirror motor wire connector. Remove nuts holding mirror to door.

2) Separate mirror from door. Disengage wire harness plug from door. Feed wire harness through door to outside of vehicle. To install, reverse removal procedure. Verify mirror operation before installing trim panel.

WIRING DIAGRAMS

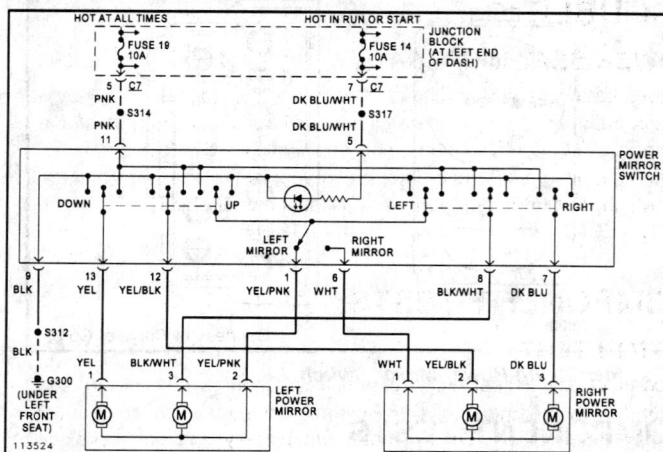

Fig. 4: Power Mirror System Wiring Diagram (Concorde, Intrepid, LHS & 300M)

DESCRIPTION

The power seat system consists of 3 reversible motors coupled through cables to worm gear box assemblies, a control switch assembly and a wiring harness. Power seats can be adjusted up-and-down, forward-and-backward and tilted forward-and-backward.

OPERATION

Power seat control switches are located on the outboard side of the seat, near the floor. Front switch controls up and down adjustment of front portion of seat. Rear switch controls up and down adjustment of rear portion of seat. Used in conjunction, seat may be tilted to desired position. Center switch controls forward and backward seat adjustment.

TROUBLE SHOOTING

POWER SEAT INOPERATIVE

Ensure battery is fully charged. Check fusible link No. 8 in engine compartment relay box. Ensure all connections are clean, tight and not damaged. With dome light on, apply seat switch in direction of failure. If dome light dims, seat motor is operating, indicating mechanical jam. If dome light does not dim, perform individual compoents. See COMPONENT TESTS.

COMPONENT TESTS

MOTOR TEST

Disconnect power seat motor connectors. Connect terminals of each motor directly to battery voltage. Reverse test leads to check operation in opposite direction. Ensure motor turns freely and each adjusting mechanism operates in correct direction. If there is any malfunction, replace entire power seat adjuster assembly.

POWER SEAT SWITCH TEST

Remove power seat switch. Check switch continuity with switch in specified positions. See Fig. 1. See POWER SEAT SWITCH CONTINUITY TEST table.

POWER SEAT SWITCH CONTINUITY TEST

Switch Position	Continuity Between Pins
Off	None
Front Riser Up	9 & 10; 11 & 14
Front Riser Down	8 & 11; 10 & 14
Center Switch Forward	2 & 3; 4 & 14
Center Switch Rearward	1 & 4; 3 & 14
Rear Riser Up	6 & 12; 7 & 14
Rear Riser Down	5 & 7; 12 & 14

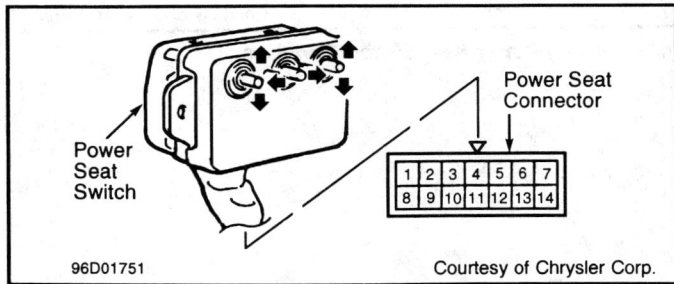

96D01751   Courtesy of Chrysler Corp.

Fig. 1: Identifying Power Seat Switch Terminals

REMOVAL & INSTALLATION

CAUTION: When battery is disconnected, vehicle computer and memory systems may lose memory data. Driveability problems may exist until computer systems have completed a relearn cycle. See COMPUTER RELEARN PROCEDURES article in GENERAL INFORMATION before disconnecting battery.

POWER SEAT ASSEMBLY

Removal & Installation – Use illustration for power seat assembly removal, disassembly and installation. See Fig. 2.

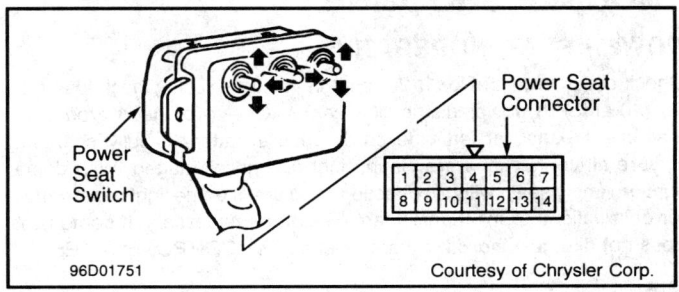

96D01751   Courtesy of Chrysler Corp.

Fig. 2: Removing Power Seat Assembly

WIRING DIAGRAMS

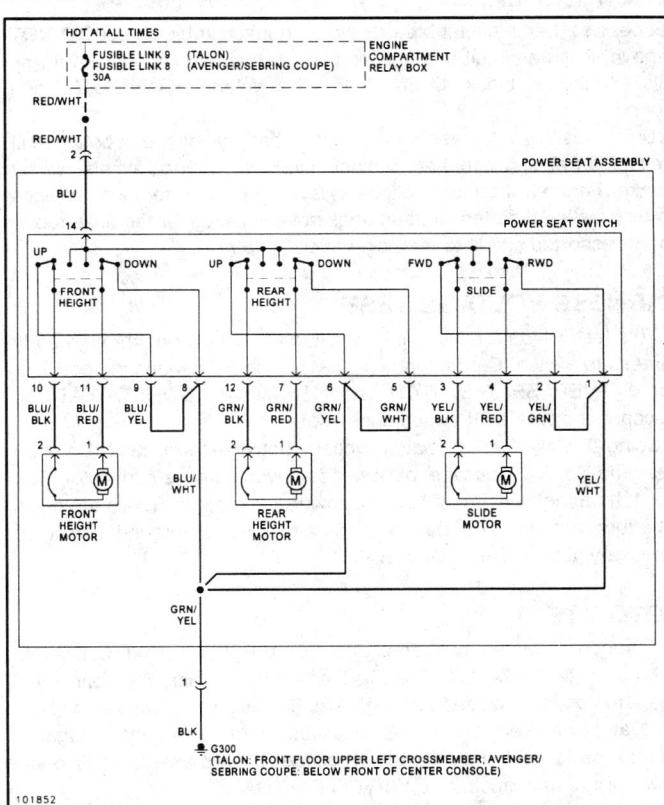

Fig. 3: Power Seat System Wiring Diagram (Avenger & Sebring Coupe)

DESCRIPTION & OPERATION

Power seat can be adjusted in 8 different directions: up, down, forward, back, tilt forward, tilt rearward, seat back recliner up and seat back recliner down. The power seat system receives battery power through a 20-amp circuit breaker in the junction block. Battery voltage is available to power seat system at all times. An 8-way switch directs power to 4 permanent-magnet, reversible motors. The motors are coupled through cables to worm gear box assemblies located in the seat tracks, providing the various seat movements.

TROUBLE SHOOTING

POWER SEAT INOPERATIVE

Check circuit breaker No. 1 (20-amp) in junction block. Check fuse No. 15 (40-amp) in power distribution center. Check for good ground at instrument panel, at left side cowl. Ensure battery is fully charged. Ensure all connections are clean, tight and not damaged. With dome light on, apply seat switch in direction of failure. If dome light dims, check for obstructions or mechanical jam. Repair as necessary. If dome light does not dim, test individual components. See COMPONENT TESTS.

COMPONENT TESTS

CIRCUIT BREAKER TEST

1) Loosen 20-amp circuit breaker No. 1 in junction block, but DO NOT remove. Ensure circuit breaker terminals remain in contact with terminals in junction block. Connect negative voltmeter lead to a good ground.

2) Using positive voltmeter lead, check for battery voltage at both circuit breaker terminals. If battery voltage exists at both terminals, circuit breaker is good. If battery voltage exists at only one terminal, replace circuit breaker. If battery voltage does not exist at either terminal, repair open or shorted circuit to circuit breaker.

HARNESS VOLTAGE TEST

1) This test will determine whether voltage is continuous through body harness to switch. Remove power seat switch from mounting position. See POWER SEAT SWITCH under REMOVAL & INSTALLATION. Disconnect power seat switch connector.

2) Using DVOM, check for battery voltage between terminals No. 1 (Red wire) and No. 5 (Black wire) at power seat with harness connector. See Fig. 1. If battery voltage and exists, power and ground circuits are okay. If battery voltage does not exist, repair power or ground circuit as necessary. See WIRING DIAGRAMS.

MOTOR TEST

1) Remove power seat switch. See POWER SEAT SWITCH under REMOVAL & INSTALLATION. Disconnect wiring harness connector. Measure voltage between terminals No. 5 (Black wire) and No. 1 (Red wire) at power seat switch harness connector. If battery voltage is present, go to next step. If battery voltage is not present, repair open power or ground circuit. See WIRING DIAGRAMS.

2) Using 2 jumper wires, connect one wire to battery supply. Connect second jumper wire to chassis ground. Connect other end of wires to pins as described in MOTOR TESTS AT SEAT CONNECTOR table to check seat action. See Fig. 1. If motor still does not work, check wiring between switch connector and motor. Repair wiring as necessary. If wiring is okay, replace motor.

POWER SEAT MOTOR & HARNESS TEST

Apply Voltage To Terminal	Apply Ground To Terminal	Seat Action
7	10	Front Up
10	7	Front Down
6	3	Forward
3	6	Backward
8	9	Rear Up
9	8	Rear Down
2	4	Seatback Up
4	2	Seatback Down

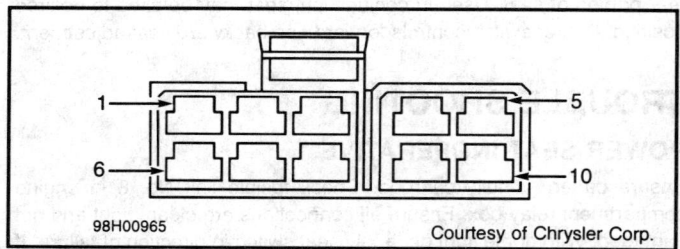

98H00965   Courtesy of Chrysler Corp.

Fig. 1: Identifying Power Seat Motor Connector Terminals

POWER SEAT SWITCH TEST

Remove power seat switch. See POWER SEAT SWITCH under REMOVAL & INSTALLATION. Check switch continuity between indicated terminals with switch in specified positions. See Fig. 2. See POWER SEAT SWITCH CONTINUITY TEST table. Replace switch if continuity is not as specified.

POWER SEAT SWITCH CONTINUITY TEST

Switch Position	Continuity Between Terminals
Off	1 & 2; 1 & 3; 1 & 4; 1 & 6; 1 & 7; 1 & 8; 1 & 9; 1 & 10
Forward	5 & 6; 1 & 3
Backward	5 & 3; 1 & 6
Front Tilt Up	5 & 4; 1 & 10
Front Tilt Down	5 & 10; 1 & 7
Rear Tilt Up	5 & 8; 1 & 9
Rear Tilt Down	5 & 9; 1 & 8
Recliner Up	5 & 2; 1 & 4
Recliner Down	5 & 4; 1 & 2

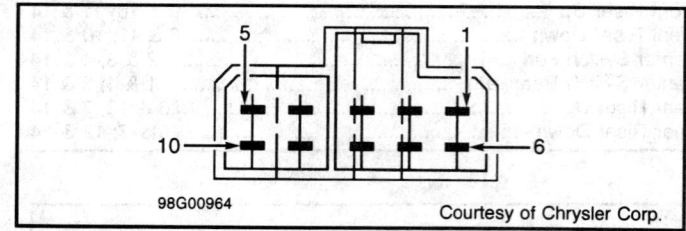

98G00964   Courtesy of Chrysler Corp.

Fig. 2: Testing Power Seat Switch Terminals

REMOVAL & INSTALLATION

CAUTION: When battery is disconnected, vehicle computer and memory systems may lose memory data. Driveability problems may exist until computer systems have completed a relearn cycle. See COMPUTER RELEARN PROCEDURES article in GENERAL INFORMATION before disconnecting battery.

POWER SEAT SWITCH

Removal & Installation – Remove left cushion side shield. Disconnect wiring from switch. Remove switch knobs. Remove switch mounting screws and switch. To install, reverse removal procedure.

SEAT ASSEMBLY

Removal & Installation – Remove front mounting bolts from floor pan. Adjust seat forward to access rear mounting bolts. Remove rear mounting bolts from floor pan. Disconnect negative battery cable. Disconnect wiring harness at carpet. Remove seat assembly from vehicle. To install, reverse removal procedure.

SEAT TRACK

Removal & Installation – Remove seat assembly from vehicle. See SEAT ASSEMBLY. Place seat on a clean area. Remove 2 seatback mounting bolts and 2 seatback recliner bolts. Remove 4 seat track mounting bolts from cushion pan. Remove seat track. To install, reverse removal procedure.

WIRING DIAGRAMS

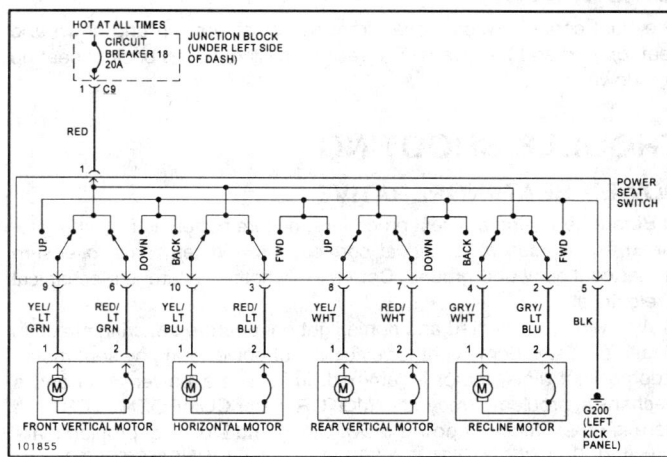

Fig. 3: Power Seat System Wiring Diagram (Breeze, Cirrus & Stratus)

DESCRIPTION

The power seats can be adjusted in 8 directions: up and down, forward and backward, tilt forward and backward, and recline up and down. Power seat system consists of 4 reversible motors and transmission located on seat tracks. Circuit is protected by fuse No. 26 (40- amp) in Power Distribution Center (PDC) and a 30-amp circuit breaker located in wire harness under driver's seat.

OPERATION

The front control switch moves front and/or of seat up and down and seat forward-and-backward. The recliner switch moves back of seat up and down.

TROUBLE SHOOTING

POWER SEAT INOPERATIVE

1) Before beginning any test procedure, ensure battery is fully charged. Clean and tighten all electrical connections and terminals to ensure proper continuity and ground. Determine whether failure is mechanical or electrical.

2) With wiring connected and dome light on, operate switch in direction of failure. Watch dome light for evidence of power drain by seat motor. If dome light dims, motor is jammed, indicating a power drain and a mechanical problem. Proceed to MOTOR under COMPOENT TESTS. If there is no evidence of power draw, wiring and electrical problems are indicated. See CIRCUIT BREAKER under COMPONENT TESTS.

COMPONENT TESTS

CIRCUIT BREAKER

1) Locate 30-amp circuit breaker under driver's seat. Circuit breaker also protects passenger's power seat track circuit. Check both sides of circuit breaker connector for battery voltage.

2) If battery voltage exists on both sides, circuit breaker is good. If battery voltage exists on only one side, circuit breaker is defective. Replace circuit breaker. If battery voltage does not exist on either side, check for open or shorted circuit to fuse box. Repair as necessary. If battery voltage exists on both sides, check motor. See MOTOR. If motor is okay, check switch. See POWER SEAT SWITCH.

HARNESS VOLTAGE TEST

1) This test will determine whether voltage is continuous through body harness to switch. Remove power seat switch from mounting position. See POWER SEAT SWITCH under REMOVAL & INSTALLATION. Disconnect power seat switch 10-pin Green connector.

2) Using DVOM, check for battery voltage between terminals No. 5 (Red wire) and No. 1 (Black wire) at power seat with harness connector. See Fig. 1. If battery voltage and exists, power and ground circuits are okay. If battery voltage does not exist, repair power or ground circuit as necessary. See WIRING DIAGRAMS.

MOTOR

1) This test will by-pass switch to determine if switch or specified motor is at fault. Remove power seat position switch and disconnect it from wiring harness. See POWER SEAT SWITCH under REMOVAL & INSTALLATION.

2) Check for voltage between terminals No. 5 (Red wire) and No. 1 (Black wire) at power seat switch harness connector. If battery voltage exists, go to next step. If battery voltage does not exist, repair open or ground circuits as necessary.

3) Using 2 jumper wires, connect one wire to battery supply. Connect second jumper wire to chassis ground. Connect other end of wires to pins as described in MOTOR TESTS AT SEAT CONNECTOR table to check seat action. See Fig. 1. If motor still does not work, check wiring between switch connector and motor. Repair wiring as necessary. If wiring is okay, replace motor.

MOTOR TESTS AT SEAT CONNECTOR

Terminal No. To: Battery (Ground)	Left Seat Action	Right Seat Action
7 (10)	Front Riser Up	Front Riser Down
10 (7)	Front Riser Down	Front Riser Up
6 (3)	Forward	Forward
3 (6)	Backward	Backward
8 (9)	Rear Riser Up	Rear Riser Down
9 (8)	Rear Riser Down	Rear Riser Up
2 (4)	Recliner Up	Recliner Up
4 (2)	Recliner Down	Recliner Down

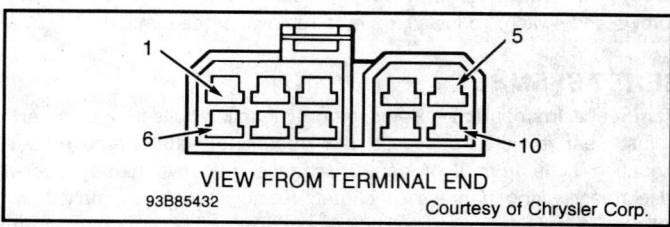

VIEW FROM TERMINAL END
93B85432
Courtesy of Chrysler Corp.

Fig. 1: Identifying Power Seat Motor Switch Connector Terminals

POWER SEAT SWITCH

Remove switch from mounting position. See POWER SEAT SWITCH under REMOVAL & INSTALLATION. Using ohmmeter, check continuity between specified pins at power seat switch. See POWER SEAT SWITCH CONTINUITY TEST table. See Fig. 2. If continuity does not exist between specified pins, replace switch.

POWER SEAT SWITCH CONTINUITY TEST

Switch Position	Left Seat Switch Pin	Right Seat Switch Pin
Off	1 & 2	1 & 2
	1 & 3	1 & 3
	1 & 4	1 & 4
	1 & 6	1 & 6
	1 & 7	1 & 7
	1 & 8	1 & 8
	1 & 9	1 & 9
	1 & 10	1 & 10
Front Riser Up	1 & 10	1 & 7
	5 & 7	5 & 10
Front Riser Down	1 & 7	1 & 10
	5 & 10	5 & 7
Center Switch Forward	1 & 3	1 & 3
	5 & 6	5 & 6
Center Switch Rearward	1 & 6	1 & 6
	3 & 5	3 & 5
Rear Riser Up	1 & 9	1 & 8
	5 & 8	5 & 9
Rear Riser Down	1 & 8	1 & 9
	5 & 9	5 & 8
Recliner Up	1 & 4	1 & 4
	2 & 5	2 & 5
Recliner Down	1 & 2	1 & 2
	4 & 5	4 & 5

REMOVAL & INSTALLATION

CAUTION: When battery is disconnected, vehicle computer and memory systems may lose memory data. Driveability problems may exist until computer systems have completed a relearn cycle. See COMPUTER RELEARN PROCEDURES article in GENERAL INFORMATION before disconnecting battery.

SEAT ASSEMBLY

Removal & Installation – Disconnect negative battery cable. Remove seat riser mounting nuts from below floor pan. Disconnect wiring

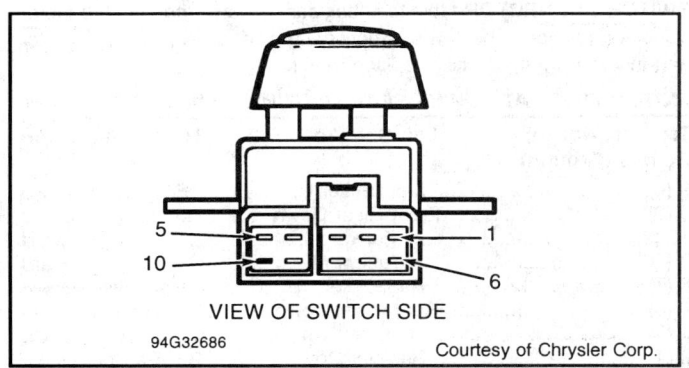

VIEW OF SWITCH SIDE

94G32686

Courtesy of Chrysler Corp.

Fig. 2: Identifying Power Seat Switch Terminals

harness at carpet. Remove seat assembly. To install, reverse removal procedure. Tighten nuts to 44 ft. lbs. (60 N.m).

SEAT MOTORS

Removal & Installation – Seat motors are not removable or serviceable. If seat motor(s) fails, replace seat position adjuster assembly.

SEAT POSITION ADJUSTER TRACK

Removal & Installation – 1) Remove seat assembly. See SEAT ASSEMBLY. Remove seat cushion side covers. Remove seat track front and rear covers. Remove bolts attaching cushion pan to seat track. Disconnect wire connectors and remove seat cushion from seat.
2) Disengage J-strip retainers holding seat cover to cushion. Remove cushion pan from cover and pad. Remove nut attaching recliner to seat back frame. Remove bolts attaching seat back frame to seat back. Remove stud on seat back frame from recliner. Remove seat back.
3) To install, transfer recliner, wire harness and trim covers to replacement seat track. To complete installation, reverse removal procedure.

POWER SEAT SWITCH

Removal & Installation – Disconnect negative battery cable. Remove left cushion side shield. Disconnect wiring from switch. Remove switch from side cover. For installation, reverse removal procedure.

TRANSMISSIONS

Removal & Installation – Transmissions are not removable or serviceable. If transmissions fail, replace seat position adjuster.

WIRING DIAGRAMS

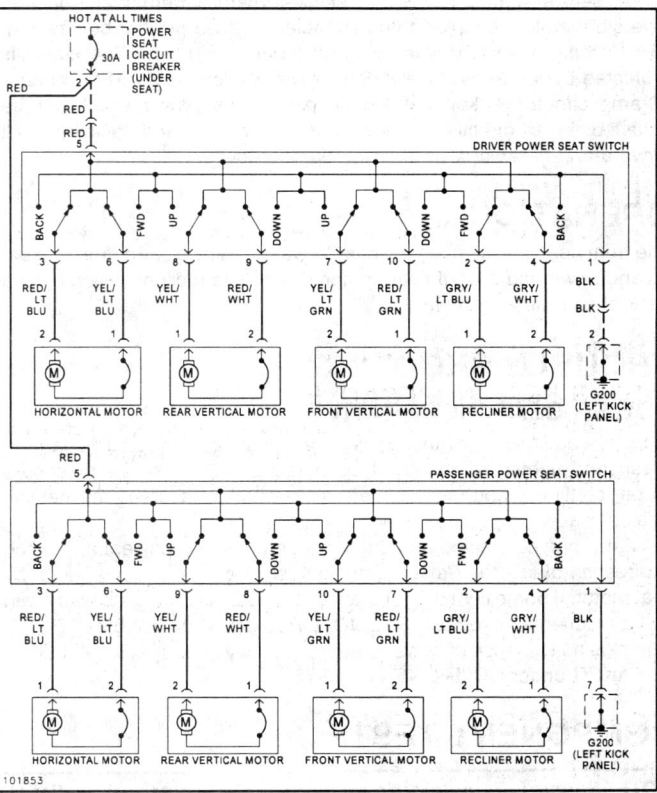

Fig. 3: Power Seat System Wiring Diagram (Caravan, Town & Country & Voyager)

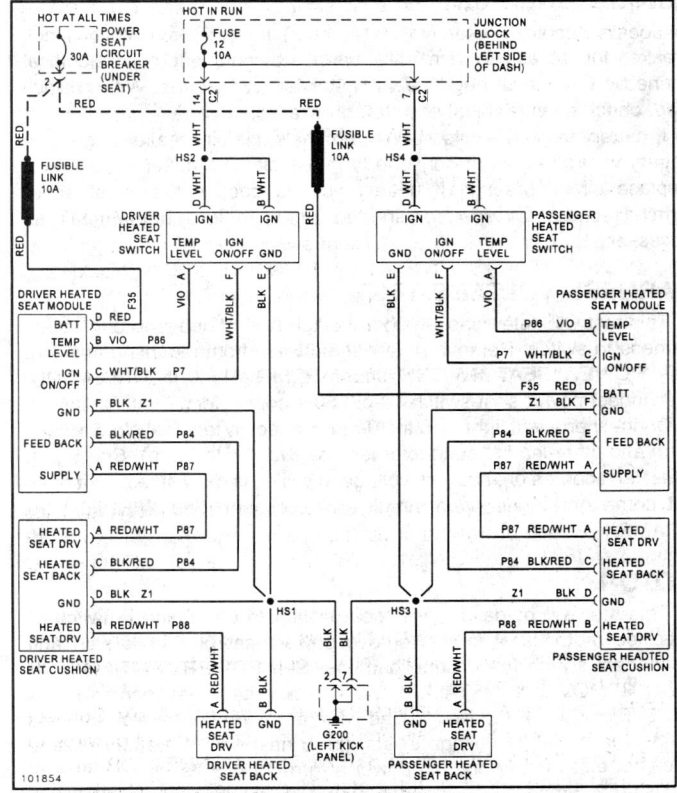

Fig. 4: Power Heated Seat System Wiring Diagram (Caravan, Town & Country & Voyager)

1999 ACCESSORIES & EQUIPMENT
Power Seats – Concorde, Intrepid, LHS & 300M

DESCRIPTION

Power seat system consists of 4 single-armature, permanent-magnet, reversible motors coupled through cables to 2 worm gear box assemblies, a control switch assembly and a wiring harness. The circuit is protected by a 40-amp fuse in Power Distribution Center (PDC) and a 20-amp circuit breaker in the fuse panel. The power seats can be adjusted in 8 directions: up-and-down, forward-and-backward, tilt forward-and-backward, and recline up-and-down.

OPERATION

The front control switch moves seat forward and backward, front of seat up and down and rear of seat up and down. The recliner switch moves back of seat up and down.

TROUBLE SHOOTING

POWER SEAT INOPERATIVE

1) Before beginning any test procedure, ensure battery is fully charged. Clean and tighten all electrical connections and terminals to ensure proper continuity and ground. Determine whether failure is mechanical or electrical.
2) With wiring connected and dome light on, operate power seat switch in direction of failure. Watch dome light for evidence of power drain by seat motor. If dome light dims, motor is jammed, indicating a power drain and a mechanical problem. See MOTOR under COMPONENT TESTS. If there is no evidence of power draw, wiring may be faulty. See CIRCUIT BREAKER under COMPONENT TESTS.

COMPONENT TESTS

NOTE: *Repair information on memory/heated seats not available. See WIRING DIAGRAMS.*

CIRCUIT BREAKER

1) Locate circuit breaker No. 2 (20-amp) in fuse box. Move circuit breaker for access to terminals, while maintaining proper electrical connection. Connect negative voltmeter lead to ground. With positive lead, check each terminal of circuit breaker for voltage.
2) If battery voltage exists at both terminals, circuit breaker is good. If battery voltage exists at only one terminal, circuit breaker is defective. Replace circuit breaker. If battery voltage does not exist at either terminal, check for open or shorted circuit to fuse box. Repair as necessary.

HARNESS VOLTAGE TEST

1) This test will determine whether voltage is continuous through body harness to switch. Remove power seat switch from mounting position. See POWER SEAT SWITCH under REMOVAL & INSTALLATION. Disconnect power seat switch 10-pin Blue connector.
2) Connect one test light lead to 10-pin connector, terminal No. 5 (Black wire) and other lead to connector terminal No. 1 (Red wire). *See Fig. 1.* If test light comes on, harness voltage to switch is okay. If test light does not come on, repair open circuit as necessary. See WIRING DIA-GRAMS.

MOTOR

1) This test will by-pass power seat switch to determine if switch or specified motor is at fault. Remove power seat position switch and disconnect switch from wiring harness. See POWER SEAT SWITCH under REMOVAL & INSTALLATION. Check voltage between terminals No. 5 (Black wire) and No. 1 (Red wire) at power seat switch harness connector. If battery voltage exists, go to next step. If battery voltage does not exist, repair open in power or ground circuits.
2) Using 2 jumper wires, connect one jumper wire to battery supply. Connect second jumper wire to chassis ground. Connect other end of wires to pins as described in MOTOR TESTS AT POWER SEAT

SWITCH CONNECTOR table to check seat action. *See Fig. 1.* If motor still does not work, check wiring between power seat switch connector and motor. If wiring is okay, replace motor.

MOTOR TESTS AT POWER SEAT SWITCH CONNECTOR

Terminal No. To: Battery (Ground)	Left Seat Action	Right Seat Action
9 (6)	Front Riser Up	Front Riser Down
6 (9)	Front Riser Down	Front Riser Up
10 (3)	Forward	Forward
3 (10)	Backward	Backward
8 (7)	Rear Riser Up	Rear Riser Down
7 (8)	Rear Riser Down	Rear Riser Up
4 (2)	Recliner Up	Recliner Up
2 (4)	Recliner Down	Recliner Down

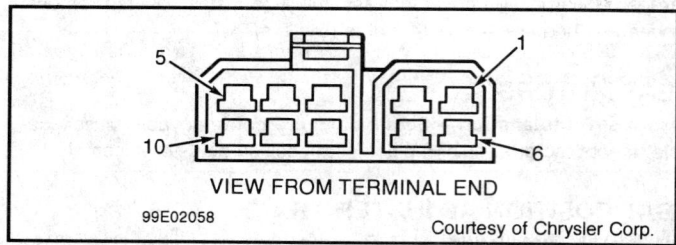

VIEW FROM TERMINAL END

99E02058

Courtesy of Chrysler Corp.

Fig. 1: Identifying Power Seat Switch Connector Terminals

POWER SEAT SWITCH

Remove power seat switch from mounting position. See POWER SEAT SWITCH under REMOVAL & INSTALLATION. Using ohmmeter, check continuity between specified power seat switch pins. See POWER SEAT SWITCH CONTINUITY TEST table. *See Fig. 2.* If continuity does not exist between specified pins as specified, replace power seat switch.

POWER SEAT SWITCH CONTINUITY TEST

Switch Position	Left Seat Switch Pins	Right Seat Switch Pins
Off	5 & 2	5 & 2
	5 & 3	5 & 3
	5 & 4	5 & 4
	5 & 6	5 & 6
	5 & 7	5 & 7
	5 & 8	5 & 8
	5 & 9	5 & 9
	5 & 10	5 & 10
Front Riser Up	5 & 6	5 & 9
	1 & 9	1 & 6
Front Riser Down	1 & 6	1 & 9
	5 & 9	5 & 6
Center Switch Forward	1 & 10	1 & 10
	3 & 5	3 & 5
Center Switch Rearward	1 & 3	1 & 3
	5 & 10	5 & 10
Rear Riser Up	1 & 8	1 & 7
	5 & 7	5 & 8
Rear Riser Down	1 & 7	1 & 8
	5 & 8	5 & 7
Recliner Up	1 & 4	1 & 4
	2 & 5	2 & 5
Recliner Down	1 & 2	1 & 2
	4 & 5	4 & 5

1999 ACCESSORIES & EQUIPMENT
Power Seats – Concorde, Intrepid, LHS & 300M (Cont.)

CHRY
4-443

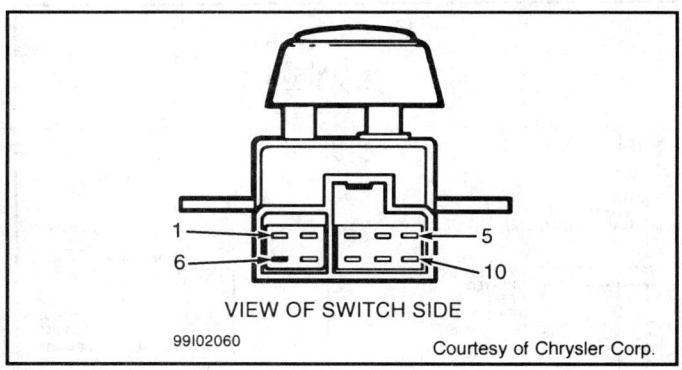

VIEW OF SWITCH SIDE

99102060 — Courtesy of Chrysler Corp.

Fig. 2: Identifying Power Seat Switch Terminals

REMOVAL & INSTALLATION

CAUTION: When battery is disconnected, vehicle computer and memory systems may lose memory data. Driveability problems may exist until computer systems have completed a relearn cycle. See COMPUTER RELEARN PROCEDURES article in GENERAL INFORMATION before disconnecting battery.

SEAT ASSEMBLY

Removal & Installation – Remove adjuster mounting bolts and nuts from floor pan. Move seat position adjuster for access. Disconnect negative battery cable. Disconnect wiring harness at carpet. Remove seat assembly. To install, reverse removal procedure. Tighten adjuster-to-floor pan mounting bolts and nuts to 44-59 INCH lbs. (60-80 N.m).

SEAT MOTORS

Removal & Installation – Seat motors are not removable or serviceable. If seat motor(s) fails, replace seat position adjuster assembly.

SEAT POSITION ADJUSTER TRACK

Removal & Installation – Remove seat assembly. See SEAT ASSEMBLY. Remove 2 seat back mounting screws and 2 seat back recliner screws. Remove 4 seat track mounting screws. *See Fig. 3.* Remove track from seat. To install, reverse removal procedure.

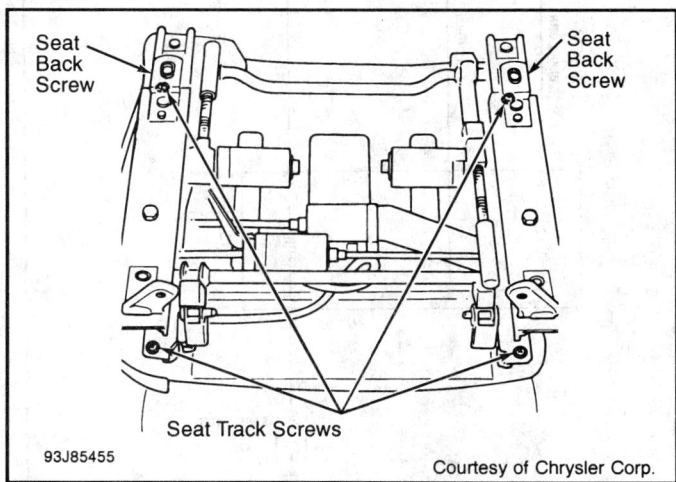

Seat Back Screw

Seat Back Screw

Seat Track Screws

93J85455 — Courtesy of Chrysler Corp.

Fig. 3: Removing Seat Adjuster Track

POWER SEAT SWITCH

Removal & Installation – Disconnect negative battery cable. Remove left cushion side shield. *See Fig. 4.* Disconnect wiring from switch. Remove switch knobs. Remove 4 screws. Remove switch. For installation, reverse removal procedure.

TRANSMISSIONS

Removal & Installation – Transmissions are not removable or serviceable. If transmissions fail, replace seat position adjuster.

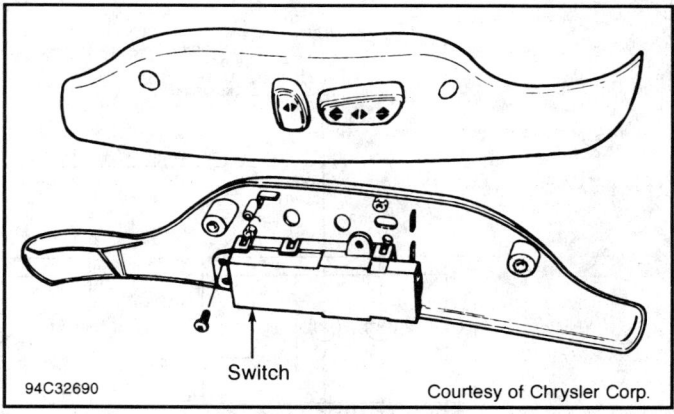

Switch

94C32690 — Courtesy of Chrysler Corp.

Fig. 4: Removing Power Seat Switch

WIRING DIAGRAMS

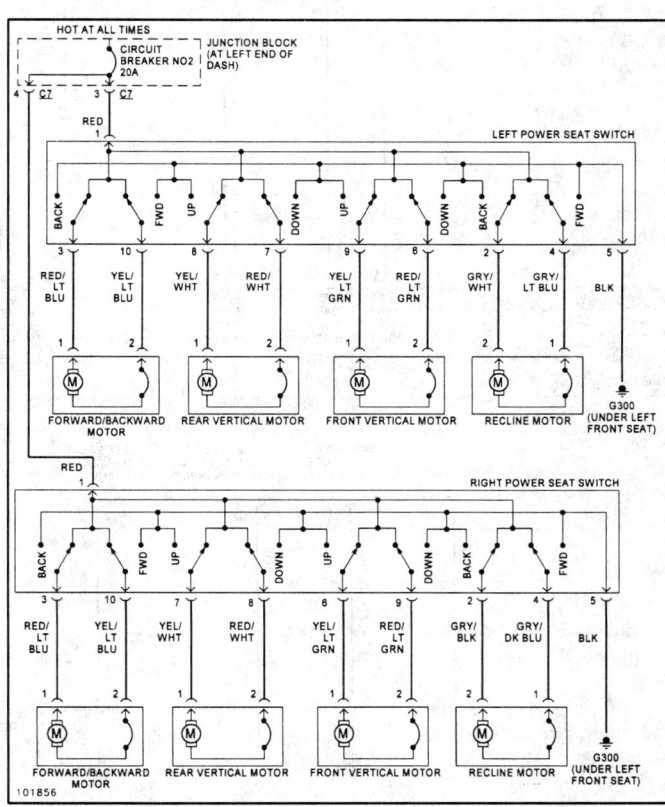

Fig. 5: Power Seat System Wiring Diagram (Concorde, Intrepid, LHS & 300M)

CHRY
4-444

1999 ACCESSORIES & EQUIPMENT
Power Seats – Concorde, Intrepid, LHS & 300M (Cont.)

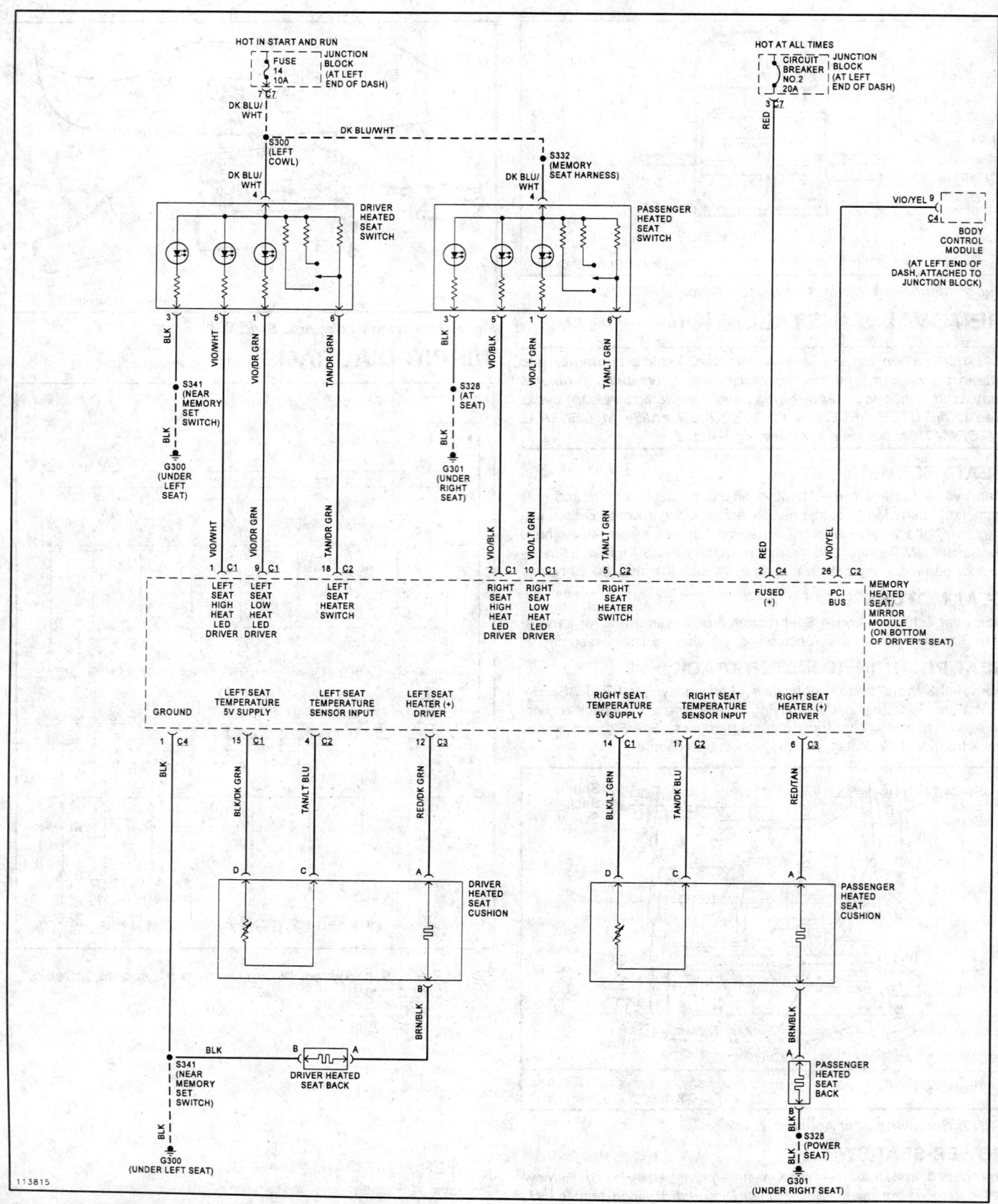

Fig. 6: Heated Seat System Wiring Diagram (LHS & 300M)

113815

DESCRIPTION & OPERATION

Driver's power seat can be adjusted in 6 different directions: up, down, forward, backward, tilt forward, or tilt rearward. The power seat system consists of a 6-way switch, motor assembly, seat adjuster, motor cable, housing and wiring harness.

The power seat system receives battery power through circuit breaker in instrument panel fuse box. Battery voltage is available to power seat system at all times. Three permanent magnet reversible motors are coupled through cables to worm gear box assemblies located in the seat tracks, providing the various seat movements.

TROUBLE SHOOTING

NOTE: Before any testing is attempted, the battery should be fully charged and all connections and terminals cleaned and tightened to ensure proper continuity and chassis grounds.

POWER SEAT INOPERATIVE

With dome light on, apply power seat switch in direction of failure. If dome light dims, power seat may be jamming. Check for binding or obstructions. If dome light does not dim, check individual components. See COMPONENT TESTS.

COMPONENT TESTS

POWER SEAT SWITCH

Remove power seat switch. See POWER SEAT SWITCH under REMOVAL & INSTALLATION. Using an ohmmeter, check continuity between power seat switch terminals with switch in appropriate position. See POWER SEAT SWITCH TEST table. *See Fig. 1.* If continuity does not exist between appropriate terminals with switch in appropriate position, replace switch. If continuity exists between appropriate terminals with switch in appropriate position, power seat switch is okay.

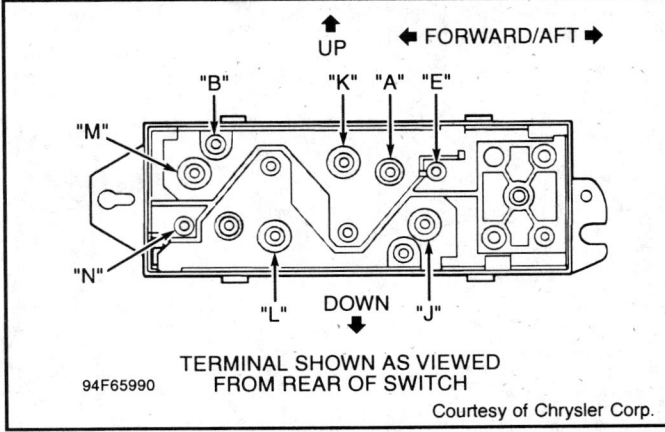

TERMINAL SHOWN AS VIEWED
FROM REAR OF SWITCH

94F65990

Courtesy of Chrysler Corp.

Fig. 1: Identifying Power Seat Switch Terminals

POWER SEAT SWITCH CONTINUITY TEST

Switch Position	Continuity Between Terminals
Off	B & E; B & J; B & K; B & L; B & M; B & N
Entire Seat	
Up	A & E; A & M; B & J; B & N
Down	A & J; A & N; B & E; B & M
Forward	A & L; B & K
Rearward	A & K; B & L
Front Of Seat	
Up	A & M; B & N
Down	A & N; B & M
Rear Of Seat	
Up	A & E; B & J
Down	A & J; B & E

SYSTEM TESTS

POWER SEAT INOPERATIVE

1) Operate power seat switch to move all 3 motors in each direction. If seat fails to move in more than one direction, go to next step. If seat fails to move in one direction only, move seat momentarily in opposite direction and test again. If seat still fails to move in one direction only, see POWER SEAT SWITCH under COMPONENT TESTS.

2) On Dakota, check circuit breaker No. 21 (20-amp) in junction block. Replace circuit breaker as necessary and recheck system operation. On Durango, check fuse No. 4 (50-amp) in Power Distribution Center. Replace fuse as necessary and recheck system operation. If fuse is okay, go to next step.

3) On all models, disconnect power seat switch harness connector. Check for battery voltage at power seat switch connector terminal "A" (Red/Black wire) on Dakota or terminal "B" (Black/Pink wire) on Durango. *See Fig. 1.* On all models, if battery voltage exists, go to next step. If battery voltage does not exist, repair open circuit to junction block

4) Check for continuity between ground and Black wire terminal "B" on Dakota or terminal "A" on Durango. *See Fig. 1.* On all models, if continuity exists, go to next step. If continuity does not exist, repair open ground circuit.

5) Test power seat switch. See POWER SEAT SWITCH under COMPONENT TESTS. If switch is okay, check for open or short circuit in wire harness between power seat switch and inoperative power seat motor. Repair circuits as necessary. If circuits are okay, replace power seat adjuster and motor assembly.

REMOVAL & INSTALLATION

CAUTION: When battery is disconnected, vehicle computer and memory systems may lose memory data. Driveability problems may exist until computer systems have completed a relearn cycle. See COMPUTER RELEARN PROCEDURES article in GENERAL INFORMATION before disconnecting battery.

SEAT ASSEMBLY

Removal & Installation – Remove 4 bolts/nuts attaching seat frame to floor pan. Remove 2 bolts holding power seat to center seat section. Disconnect power seat wiring harness connector located under seat. Remove seat from vehicle. To install, reverse removal procedure. Tighten seat mounting screws to 21 ft. lbs. (29 N.m).

POWER SEAT ADJUSTERS & MOTORS

NOTE: Seat motors are not serviced separately. If any segment of power seat adjustment mechanism is faulty, replace adjusters and motors as an assembly.

Removal & Installation – Disconnect negative battery cable. Remove seat assembly. See SEAT ASSEMBLY. Disconnect seat motor harness connectors. Release harness retainers from adjusters/motors assembly. Remove 4 screws attaching adjusters/motors assembly to seat. Remove adjusters/motors as an assembly. To install, reverse removal procedure.

POWER SEAT SWITCH

Removal & Installation – Disconnect negative battery cable. Remove recliner lever retaining screw and remove lever. Remove 3 screws holding switch and bezel to seat. Pull switch and bezel away from seat enough to disconnect power seat switch harness connector. Disconnect power seat switch harness connector. Remove 2 screws holding switch to bezel. Remove switch from bezel. To install, reverse removal procedure.

WIRING DIAGRAMS

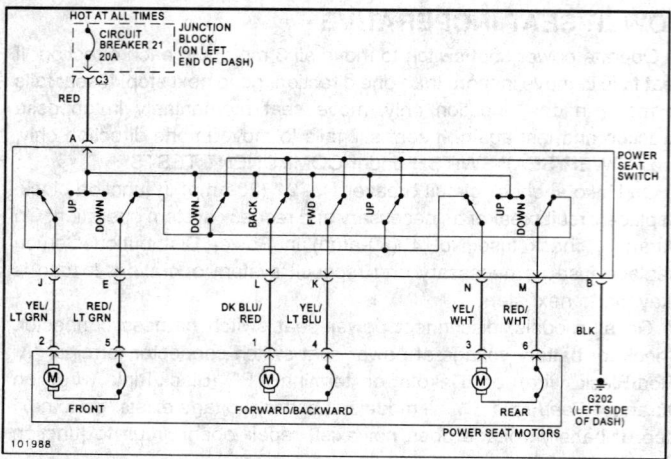

Fig. 2: Power Seat System Wiring Diagram (Dakota)

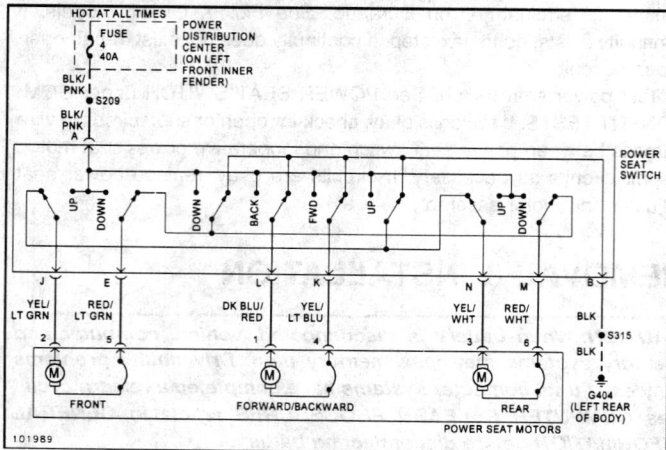

Fig. 3: Power Seat System Wiring Diagram (Durango)

DESCRIPTION & OPERATION

Driver's power seat can be adjusted in 6 different directions: up, down, forward, back, tilt forward, or tilt rearward. The power seat system consists of a 6-way switch, motor assembly, seat adjuster, motor cable, housing and wiring harness.

The power seat system receives battery power through circuit breaker and a fuse in the Power Distribution Center (PDC). Battery voltage is available to power seat system at all times. Three permanent magnet reversible motors are coupled through cables to worm gear box assemblies located in the seat tracks, providing the various seat movements.

On Ram Pickup with extended cab (club cab and quad cab), driver's seat also includes power operated lumbar support. Lumbar support can be inflated or deflated as needed, using additional switch. On seats with lumbar support, seat back remains at same height, while seat cushion raises and lowers. On seats without lumbar support, entire seat raises and lowers. On all seats, entire seat moves forward and backward.

TROUBLE SHOOTING

NOTE: *Before any testing is attempted, the battery should be fully charged and all connections and terminals cleaned and tightened to ensure proper continuity and chassis grounds.*

POWER SEAT INOPERATIVE

With dome light on, apply power seat switch in direction of failure. If dome light dims, power seat may be jamming. Check for binding or obstructions. If dome light does not dim, check individual components. See COMPONENT TESTS.

COMPONENT TESTS

HARNESS VOLTAGE TEST

NOTE: *This test will determine whether or not voltage is continuous through body harness to power seat switch.*

1) Remove power seat switch from mounting position and disconnect switch from wiring harness. See POWER SEAT SWITCH under REMOVAL & INSTALLATION.
2) Connect test light lead to ground terminal (Black wire on Ram Van and Ram Wagon; Black/Orange wire on Ram Pickup) at power seat switch harness connector. Using test light, probe power supply wire (Red/Light Blue wire) at power seat switch harness connector.
3) If test light comes on, power and ground circuits to power seat switch are good. If test light does not come on, check ground circuit. See WIRING DIAGRAMS. Repair as necessary. If ground circuit is okay, check power supply. See CIRCUIT BREAKER. Check ground circuit for continuity.

CIRCUIT BREAKER

1) Circuit breaker is located in fuse block. On Ram Van and Ram Wagon, fuse block is located under glove box door. On Ram Pickup, fuse block is located at extreme left end of instrument panel under protective cover. On all models, pull circuit breaker outward slightly, ensuring circuit breaker terminals still contact terminals in fuse block. Connect negative voltmeter lead to ground. With positive lead, check each terminal of circuit breaker for voltage.
2) If battery voltage exists at both terminals, circuit breaker is good. If battery voltage exists at only one terminal, circuit breaker is defective. Replace circuit breaker. If battery voltage does not exist at either terminal, check for open or shorted circuit to fuse box. Repair as necessary.

MOTOR

1) Operate power seat switch to move all 3 seat motors. Seat should move in all directions. If one or more motors operate, see POWER SEAT SWITCH. If no motors operate, go to next step.

2) Check circuit breaker in fuse block. See CIRCUIT BREAKER. If circuit breaker is good, go to next step. If circuit breaker is faulty, replace circuit breaker and retest system.
3) Remove power seat switch. See POWER SEAT SWITCH under REMOVAL & INSTALLATION. Check for battery voltage at power supply (Red wire on Ram Van and Ram Wagon; Red/Light Blue wire on Ram Pickup). If battery voltage exists, go to next step. If battery voltage does not exist, repair open in wire.
4) Check for continuity between switch connector ground circuit (Black wire on Ram Van and Ram Wagon; Black/Orange wire on Ram Pickup) and ground. If continuity exists, go to next step. If continuity does not exist, repair open in wire.
5) Test power seat switch. See POWER SEAT SWITCH. Replace switch as necessary and retest system. If switch tests good, check wiring harness between switch connector and motor. Repair as necessary. If wiring is okay, replace defective power seat adjuster/motors assembly.

POWER SEAT SWITCH

Remove switch from mounting position. See POWER SEAT SWITCH under REMOVAL & INSTALLATION. Using an ohmmeter, check continuity between power seat switch terminals as indicated. See POWER SEAT SWITCH CONTINUITY TEST (RAM PICKUP) or POWER SEAT SWITCH CONTINUITY TEST (RAM VAN & RAM WAGON) table. *See Fig. 1 or 2.* If continuity does not exist as specified, replace switch. If continuity exists as specified, switch is okay.

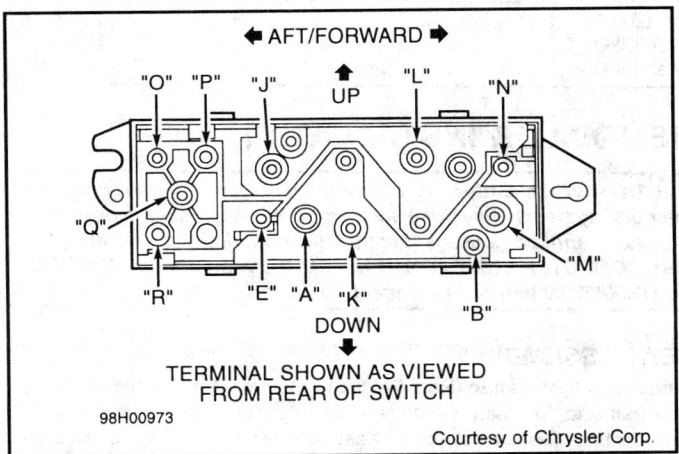

Fig. 1: *Testing Power Seat Switch Terminals (Ram Pickup)*

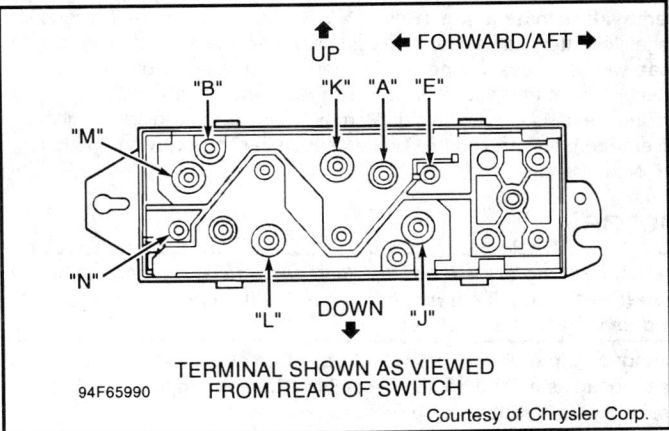

Fig. 2: *Testing Power Seat Switch Terminals (Ram Van & Ram Wagon)*

CHRY
4-448

1999 ACCESSORIES & EQUIPMENT
Power Seats – Ram Pickup, Ram Van & Ram Wagon (Cont.)

POWER SEAT SWITCH CONTINUITY TEST (RAM PICKUP)

Switch Position	Continuity Between Terminals
Off	B & N; B & J; B & M; B & E; B & K; B & L
Vertical Up	A & E; A & M; B & N; B & J
Vertical Down	A & J; A & N; B & M; B & E
Horizontal Forward	B & K; A & L
Horizontal Aft	B & L; A & K
Front Tilt Up	B & N; A & M
Front Tilt Down	A & N; B & M
Rear Tilt Up	A & E; B & J
Rear Tilt Down	A & J; B & E
Extended Cab	
Lumbar Off	O & P; P & R
Lumbar Up (Inflate)	O & P; Q & R
Lumbar Down (Deflate)	O & R; Q & P

POWER SEAT SWITCH CONTINUITY TEST (RAM VAN & RAM WAGON)

Switch Position	Continuity Between Terminals
Off	B & N; B & J; B & M; B & E; B & K; B & L
Vertical Up	B & M; B & E; A & N; A & J
Vertical Down	B & N; B & J; A & M; A & E
Horizontal	
Forward	B & K; A & L
Horizontal Aft	B & L; A & K
Front Tilt Up	B & M; A & N
Front Tilt Down	B & N; A & M
Rear Tilt Up	B & E; A & J
Rear Tilt Down	B & J; A & E

REMOVAL & INSTALLATION

CAUTION: When battery is disconnected, vehicle computer and memory systems may lose memory data. Driveability problems may exist until computer systems have completed a relearn cycle. See COMPUTER RELEARN PROCEDURES article in GENERAL INFORMATION before disconnecting battery.

SEAT ASSEMBLY

Removal & Installation (Ram Pickup) – Remove 4 bolts/nuts attaching seat frame to floor pan. Remove 2 bolts holding power seat to center seat section. Disconnect power seat wire harness connector located under seat. Remove seat from vehicle. To install, reverse removal procedure. Tighten seat mounting screws to 21 ft. lbs. (29 N.m).

Removal & Installation (Ram Van & Ram Wagon) – Disconnect negative battery cable. Remove seat riser rear shield. Disconnect power seat wire harness connector located under seat. Remove 4 nuts attaching seat frame to floor pan. The rear nuts are accessed by lifting up the seat riser rear shield. Remove seat from vehicle. To install, reverse removal procedure. Tighten seat mounting screws to 55 ft. lbs. (75 N.m).

MOTOR

NOTE: Seat motors are not serviced separately. If any segment of power seat adjustment mechanism is faulty, replace motor, cables and seat track assembly as a unit.

Removal & Installation (Ram Pickup) – Remove 4 bolts/nuts attaching seat to adjuster and motor assembly. Remove adjuster and motor assembly. To install, reverse removal procedure.

NOTE: If seat is in raised position, it is possible to remove seat and/or adjuster and motor assembly without removing seat riser. If seat can not be raised to full height, entire seat and riser assembly must be removed from vehicle.

Removal & Installation (Ram Van & Ram Wagon) – If seat cannot be raised to full height, remove seat. See SEAT ASSEMBLY. Remove 4

nuts attaching seat to riser. Disconnect wiring between seat switch and motor. Remove seat cushion frame from adjuster and motor assembly. Remove adjuster and motor assembly from riser. To install, reverse removal procedure. Tighten seat adjuster bolts to 17 ft. lbs. (23 N.m).

POWER SEAT SWITCH

Removal & Installation (Ram Pickup Without Lumbar Support) – Disconnect negative battery cable. Remove 2 screws holding switch and bezel to seat. Pull switch from seat far enough to access connector, and disconnect connector. Remove 2 screws holding switch to bezel. Remove switch from bezel. To install, reverse removal procedure.

Removal & Installation (Ram Pickup With Lumbar Support) – Disconnect negative battery cable. Remove recliner lever. Remove 3 screws holding side shield to seat. Pull shield from seat far enough to access connector, and disconnect connector. Remove 2 screws holding switch to shield. Remove switch from shield. To install, reverse removal procedure.

Removal & Installation (Ram Van & Ram Wagon) – Remove seat adjuster and motors assembly from seat. See MOTOR. Remove 2 switch bezel mounting screws from inside seat cushion frame. Disconnect switch wire connector. Remove 2 power seat switch-to-bezel screws. To install, reverse removal procedure. Tighten screws to 20 INCH lbs. (2.2 N.m).

POWER LUMBAR ADJUSTER & MOTOR

Removal & Installation – Disconnect negative battery cable. Remove driver's seat back. Disconnect wiring connector. Disconnect clips and remove power lumbar adjuster and motor assembly. To install, reverse removal procedures.

WIRING DIAGRAMS

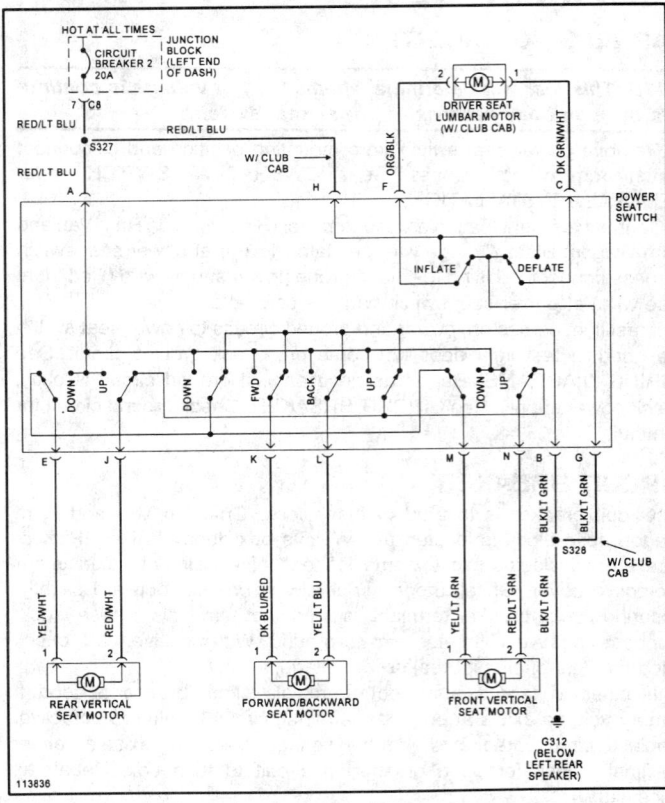

Fig. 3: Power Seat System Wiring Diagram (Ram Pickup)

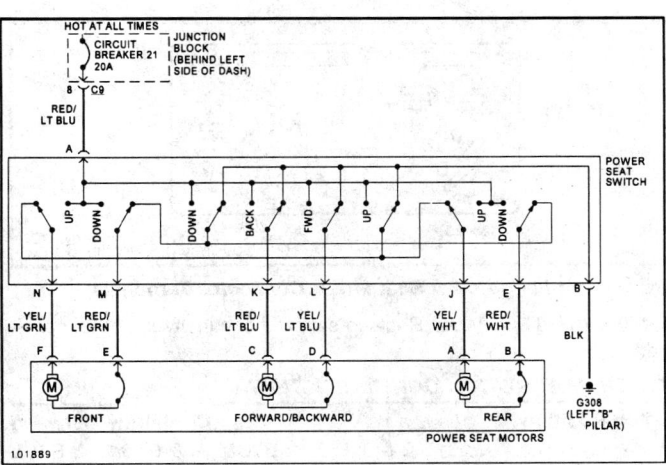

Fig. 4: Power Seat System Wiring Diagram
(Ram Van & Ram Wagon)

DESCRIPTION & OPERATION

Power seat can be adjusted in 6 different directions: up, down, forward, back, tilt forward or tilt rearward. The power seat system receives battery power through a 20-amp circuit breaker in the junction block. Battery voltage is available to power seat system at all times. A 6-way switch directs power to 3 permanent-magnet reversible motors. The motors are coupled through cables to worm gear box assemblies located in the seat tracks, providing the various seat movements.

TROUBLE SHOOTING

POWER SEAT INOPERATIVE

Check circuit breaker No. 18 (20-amp) in junction block. Check fuse No. 15 (40-amp) in power distribution center. Check for good ground at instrument panel, left side cowl. Ensure battery is fully charged. Ensure all connections are clean, tight and not damaged. With dome light on, apply seat switch in direction of failure. If dome light dims, check for obstructions or mechanical jam. Repair as necessary. If dome light does not dim, test individual components.

COMPONENT TESTS

CIRCUIT BREAKER

1) Pull out 20-amp circuit breaker No. 18 from junction block, but DO NOT remove. Ensure circuit breaker terminals remain in contact with terminals in junction block. Connect negative voltmeter lead to a good ground.

2) Using positive voltmeter lead, check for battery voltage at both circuit breaker terminals. If battery voltage exists at both terminals, circuit breaker is good. If battery voltage exists at only one terminal, replace circuit breaker. If battery voltage does not exist at both terminals, repair open or shorted circuit to circuit breaker.

HARNESS VOLTAGE TEST

Remove power seat switch. Disconnect wiring from switch. Connect test light leads to harness connector terminals "A" and "B". See WIRING DIAGRAMS. If test light comes on, wiring is okay. If test light does not come on, check 20-amp circuit breaker, power circuit, and ground circuit. Repair circuit(s) as necessary.

MOTOR

1) Remove power seat switch. See POWER SEAT SWITCH under REMOVAL & INSTALLATION. Disconnect wiring harness connector. Check voltage between terminals "A" and "B" at power seat switch harness connector. If battery voltage exists, go to next step. If battery voltage does not exist, repair open in ground or power circuit.

2) Connect a jumper wire between positive battery terminal and specified terminal of power seat motor connector. See POWER SEAT MOTOR TEST table. See Fig. 1. Connect another jumper wire between ground and specified terminal of power seat motor connector. Replace motor if it does not operate as specified.

POWER SEAT MOTOR TEST

Apply Battery To Terminal	Ground Terminal	Seat Action
J	E	Front Up
E	J	Front Down
K	L	Forward
L	K	Backward
N	M	Rear Up
M	N	Rear Down

POWER SEAT SWITCH

Remove switch. See POWER SEAT SWITCH under REMOVAL & INSTALLATION. Check continuity between indicated terminals with switch in specified positions. See Fig. 2. See POWER SEAT SWITCH

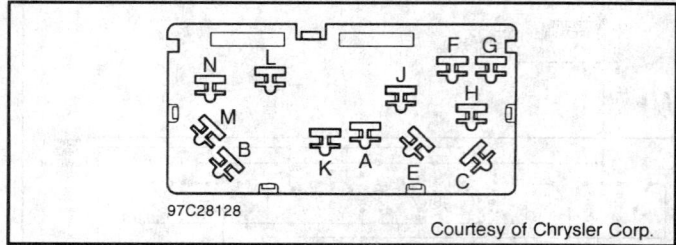
97C28128
Courtesy of Chrysler Corp.

Fig. 1: Identifying Power Seat Motor Connector Terminals

CONTINUITY TEST table. Replace switch if continuity is not as specified.

POWER SEAT SWITCH CONTINUITY TEST

Switch Position	Continuity Between
Off	B & J; B & N; B & M; B & E; B & K; B & L
Vertical Up	B & M; B & E; A & N; A & J
Vertical Down	B & N; B & J; A & M; A & E
Horizontal	
Forward	B & L; S & K
Horizontal Aft	B & K; A & L
Front Tilt Up	B & E; S & J
Front Tilt Down	A & E; B & J
Rear Tilt Up	A & N; B & N

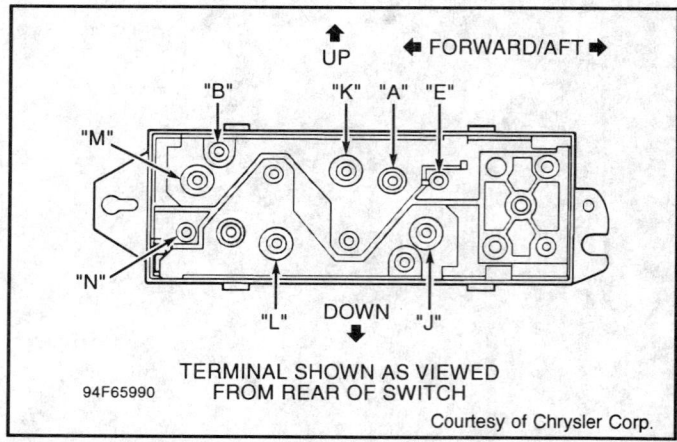
94F65990

TERMINAL SHOWN AS VIEWED FROM REAR OF SWITCH

Courtesy of Chrysler Corp.

Fig. 2: Testing Power Seat Switch Terminals

REMOVAL & INSTALLATION

CAUTION: When battery is disconnected, vehicle computer and memory systems may lose memory data. Driveability problems may exist until computer systems have completed a relearn cycle. See COMPUTER RELEARN PROCEDURES article in GENERAL INFORMATION before disconnecting battery.

POWER SEAT SWITCH

Removal & Installation – Remove left cushion side shield. Disconnect wiring from switch. Remove switch mounting screws and switch. To install, reverse removal procedure.

SEAT ASSEMBLY

Removal & Installation – Remove front mounting bolts from floor pan. Adjust seat forward to access rear mounting bolts. Remove rear mounting bolts from floor pan. Disconnect negative battery cable. Disconnect wiring harness at carpet. Remove seat assembly from vehicle. To install, reverse removal procedure.

SEAT TRACK

Removal & Installation – Remove seat assembly from vehicle. See SEAT ASSEMBLY. Place seat on a clean area. Remove 2 seat back mounting bolts and 2 seat back recliner bolts. Remove 4 seat track mounting bolts from cushion pan. Remove seat track. To install, reverse removal procedure.

WIRING DIAGRAMS

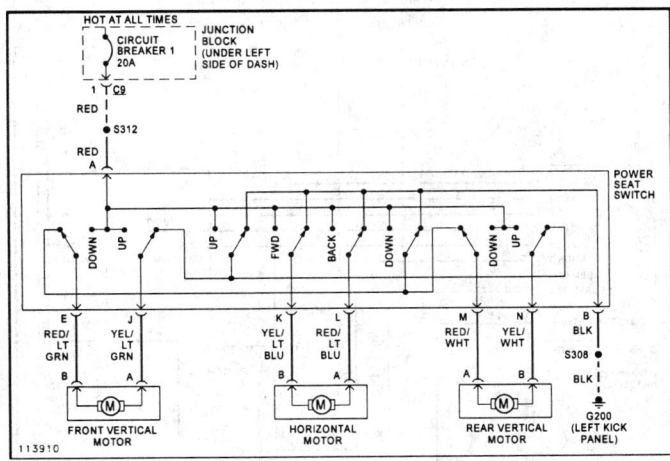

Fig. 3: Power Seat System Wiring Diagram (Sebring Convertible)

WIRING DIAGRAMS

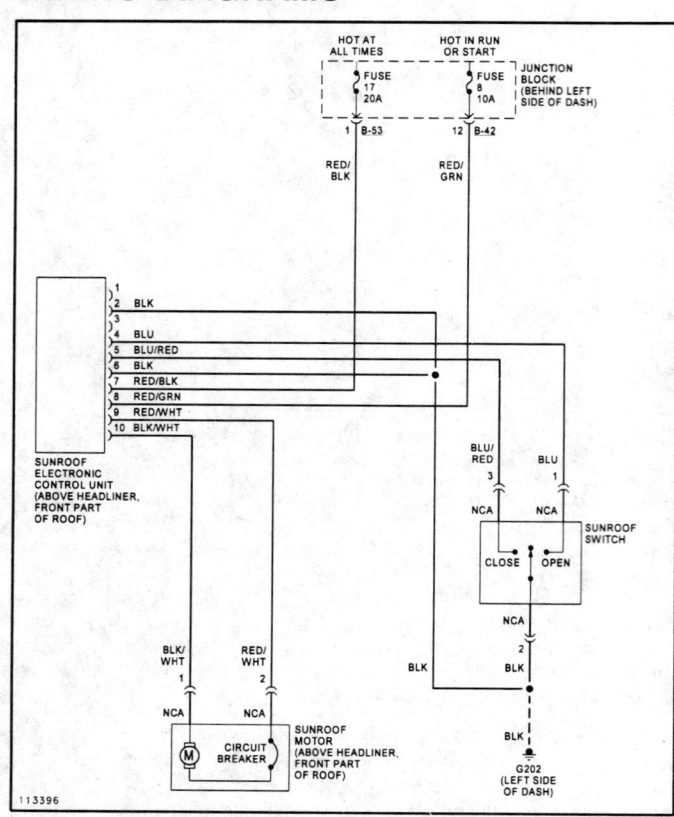

**Fig. 1: Power Sun Roof System Wiring Diagram
(Avenger & Sebring Coupe)**

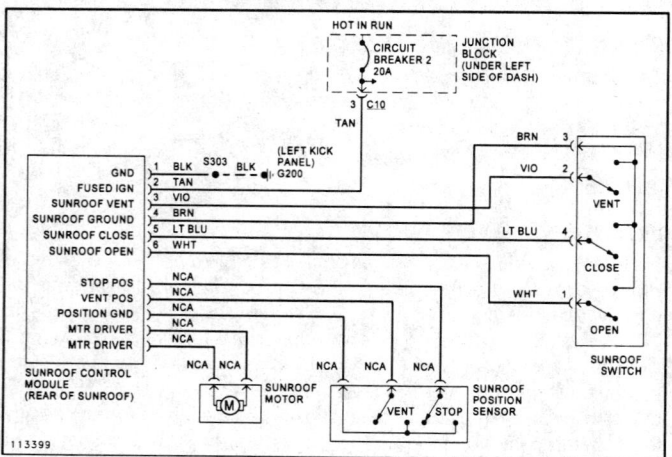

**Fig. 2: Power Sun Roof System Wiring Diagram
(Breeze, Cirrus & Stratus)**

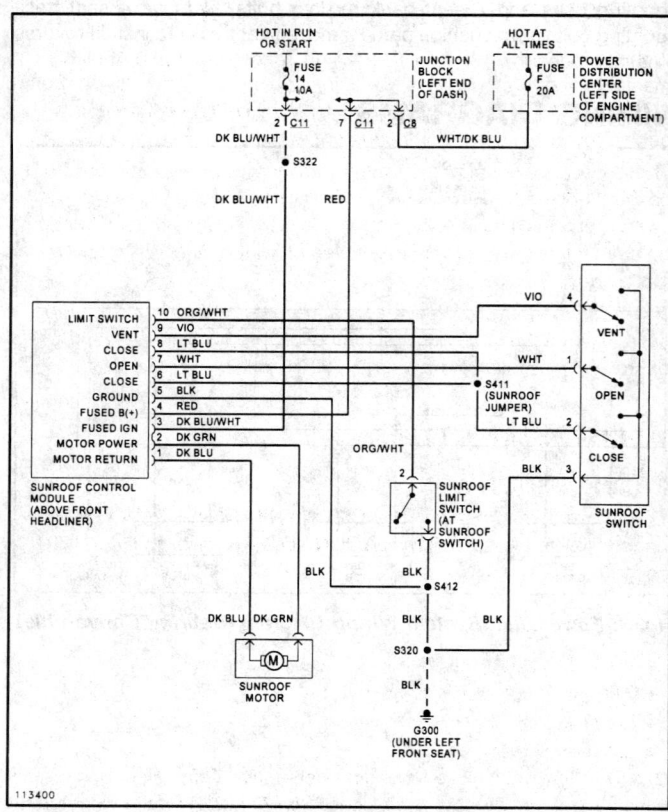

**Fig. 3: Power Sun Roof System Wiring Diagram
(Concorde, Intrepid, LHS & 300M)**

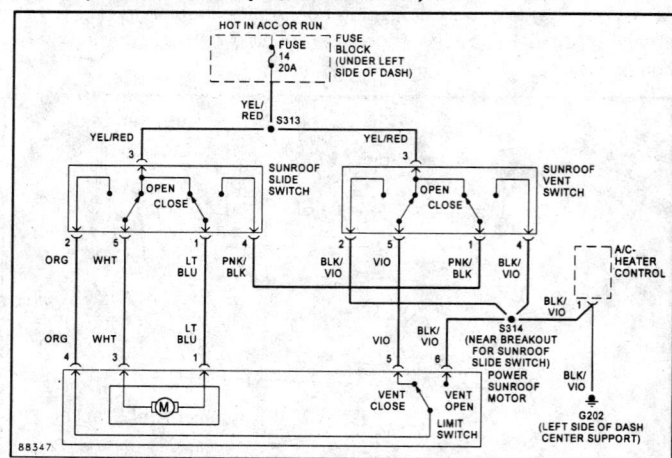

Fig. 4: Power Sun Roof System Wiring Diagram (Neon)

DESCRIPTION & OPERATION

With the ignition switch in RUN position, battery voltage is applied to the master power window switch via the Electronic Timer Alarm Control System (ETACS) Electronic Control Unit (ECU). ETACS-ECU is located behind lower left corner of instrument panel.

The driver's power window switch provides power and ground for the passenger's power window switch and motor. The master power window switch contains a solid state control unit that allow the driver's window to be completely lowered with one press of switch. A lock switch prevents passenger's window operation.

The ETACS ECU allows windows to be operated for approximately 30 seconds after the ignition key is turned to OFF position. Windows will not operate when doors are opened.

ADJUSTMENTS

FRONT WINDOW

1) Remove door trim panel. See DOOR TRIM PANEL & WATERSHIELD under REMOVAL & INSTALLATION. Loosen fasteners for following components:
- Delta sash.
- Equalizer arm bracket.
- Window guide front track.
- Window guide rear track.
- Up stop.
- Inner stabilizer.

2) Lower window before loosening delta sash bolts. See Fig. 1. Raise window and adjust to specifications. See Fig. 2. Remove weatherstriping from area to be measured (one area at a time). Push up stops against lift arm bracket of regulator. Tighten bolts. Ensure dimensions "a" and "d" are held while tightening front and rear guide tracks. Tighten equalizer arm bracket bolts. Align delta sash to front edge of window and tighten bolts.

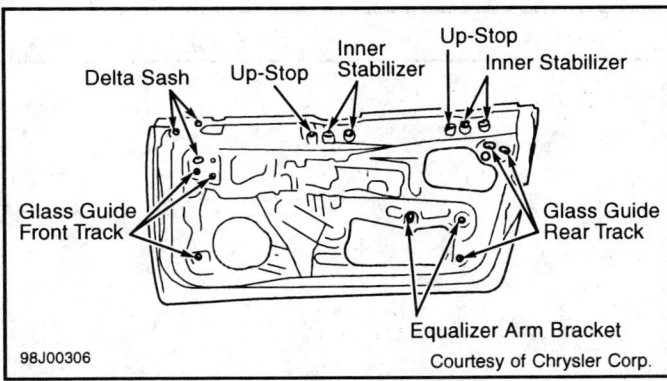

Delta Sash   Up-Stop   Inner Stabilizer   Up-Stop   Inner Stabilizer

Glass Guide Front Track   Glass Guide Rear Track

Equalizer Arm Bracket

98J00306   Courtesy of Chrysler Corp.

Fig. 1: Identifying Window Adjustment Bolts

3) Open and close door. Raise and lower window. Ensure window operates smoothly. Check window gaps. See GLASS CATCH GAP table. Adjust as necessary.

NOTE: If clearance is too small, window will ride over glass catch. If clearance is too large, wind noise may occur at high vehicle speeds.

GLASS CATCH GAP

Location	Dimension In. (mm)
Section A-A	
1	.10-.19 (2.4-4.6)
2	.03-.11 (.8-2.8)
Section B-B	
1	.11-.21 (2.8-5.3)
2	.05-.13 (1.2-3.2)
Section C-C	
1	.49-.57 (12.4-14.4)

NOTE: In following step, if clearance is too small, window will be damaged. If clearance is too large, rattling will occur.

4) Close door and raise window fully. Check window gaps. See Fig. 3. See GLASS CATCH GAP table. Adjust as necessary. Raise window fully and close door. Recheck gaps. Glass catch and weatherstrip should be parallel and both upstops should touch at same time when window is fully raised.

NOTE: In following step, if tilt is too small, window will ride over glass catch. If tilt is too large, door will be hard to close and window will not fully seat.

5) Raise window fully. Close door until top of window touches weatherstrip at top of center pillar. Measure gap between top of door edge and top of quarter panel. Gap should be .59-.98 in. (15-25 mm). Adjust as necessary. When all adjustments are completed, install door trim panel.

COMPONENT TESTS

CIRCUIT BREAKER TEST

Circuit breaker is incorporated with window motor. Press UP switch to fully close window. Continue to press switch for 40 seconds. Release UP switch and immediately press DOWN switch. If window begins to open within 60 seconds, circuit breaker is okay. Replace circuit breaker as necessary.

POWER WINDOW RELAY

1) Remove power window relay from fuse/relay block located under left side of instrument panel. See Fig. 4. Check continuity between power window relay terminals No. 1 and 3. See Fig. 5. Continuity should exist. Check continuity between power window relay terminals No. 4 and 5. Continuity should not exist. If continuity is as specified, go to next step. If continuity is not as specified, replace relay.

2) Using jumper wires and a 12-volt power source, apply battery positive to relay terminal No. 1 and battery negative to relay terminal No. 3. Continuity should exist between relay terminals No. 4 and 5. If continuity does not exist, replace relay.

POWER WINDOW MOTOR

1) Remove door trim panel. See DOOR TRIM PANEL & WATERSHIELD under REMOVAL & INSTALLATION. Disconnect window motor connector. Using jumper wires, apply battery voltage to one window motor terminal and battery negative to other terminal. Motor should operate, unless window is already at maximum travel. Reverse jumper wires. Window should move in opposite direction.

2) If window does not move in either direction, check window/regulator for freedom of movement. Remove screws holding glass lift plate to regulator. Slide window up and down by hand to ensure it moves freely in glass channels. If window slides freely, check regulator assembly. Repair window/regulator as necessary. If window slides freely and window/regulator is okay, replace window motor. If motor operates in

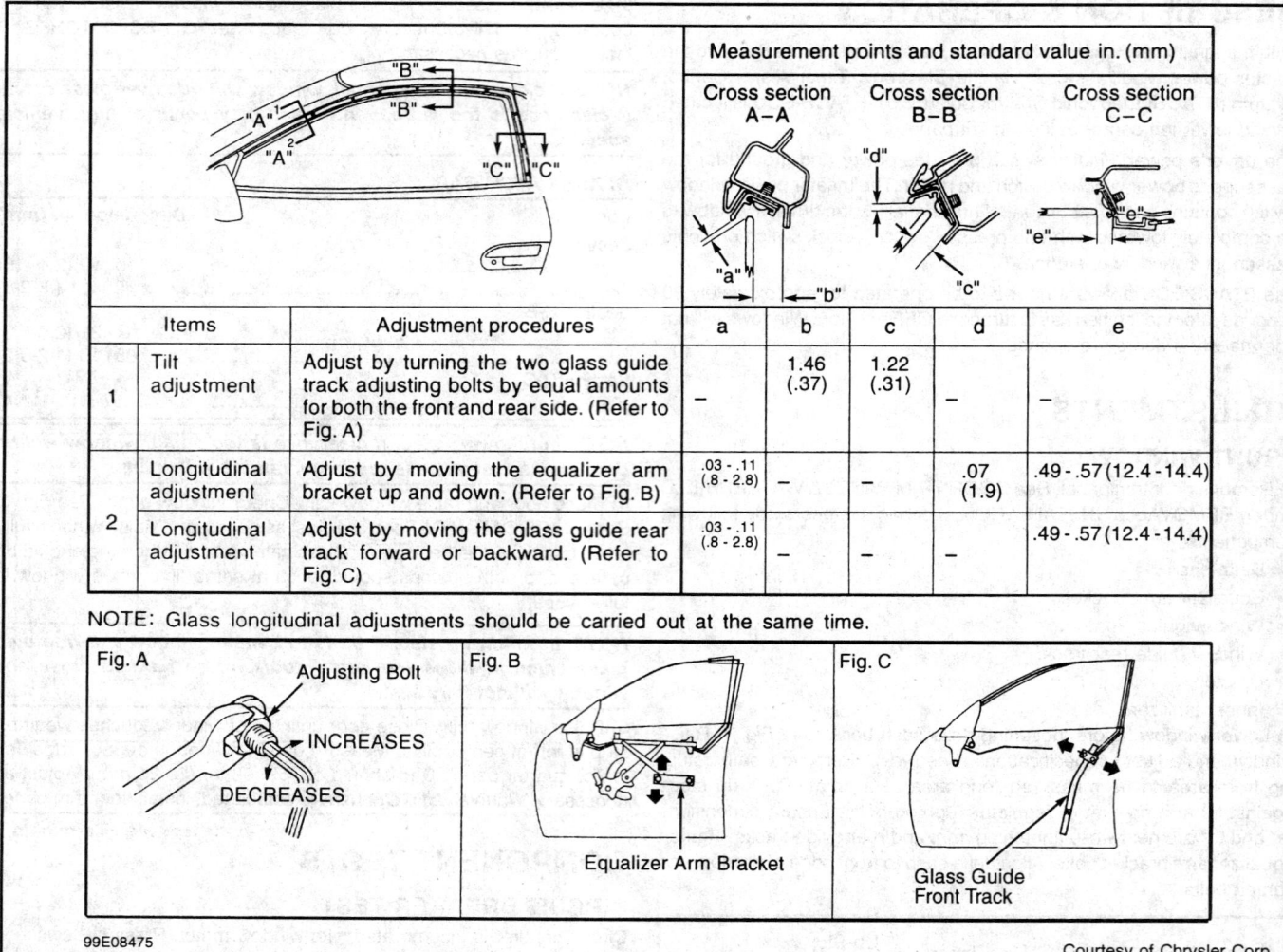

Items	Adjustment procedures	a	b	c	d	e
			Measurement points and standard value in. (mm)			
1 Tilt adjustment	Adjust by turning the two glass guide track adjusting bolts by equal amounts for both the front and rear side. (Refer to Fig. A)	–	1.46 (.37)	1.22 (.31)	–	–
2 Longitudinal adjustment	Adjust by moving the equalizer arm bracket up and down. (Refer to Fig. B)	.03 - .11 (.8 - 2.8)	–	–	.07 (1.9)	.49 - .57 (12.4 - 14.4)
Longitudinal adjustment	Adjust by moving the glass guide rear track forward or backward. (Refer to Fig. C)	.03 - .11 (.8 - 2.8)	–	–	–	.49 - .57 (12.4 - 14.4)

NOTE: Glass longitudinal adjustments should be carried out at the same time.

Fig. A Adjusting Bolt INCREASES DECREASES

Fig. B Equalizer Arm Bracket

Fig. C Glass Guide Front Track

99E08475

Courtesy of Chrysler Corp.

Fig. 2: Identifying Window Adjustments

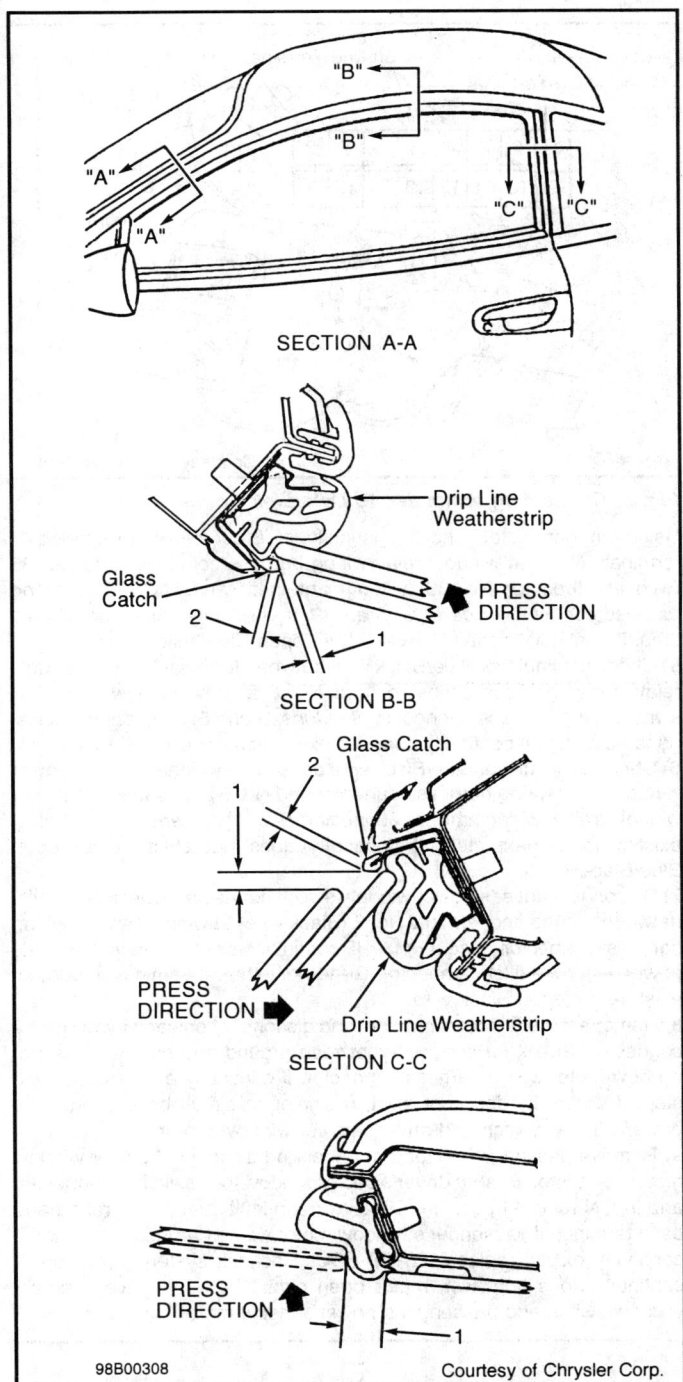

Fig. 3: Identifying Window Gap Adjustments

one direction only, replace motor. See POWER WINDOW MOTOR under REMOVAL & INSTALLATION.

POWER WINDOW SWITCH

Remove power window switch from trim panel. See POWER WINDOW SWITCH under REMOVAL & INSTALLATION. Using ohmmeter, check window switch continuity. See appropriate WINDOW SWITCH CONTINUITY table. *See Fig. 6 or 7.* Replace window switch as necessary.

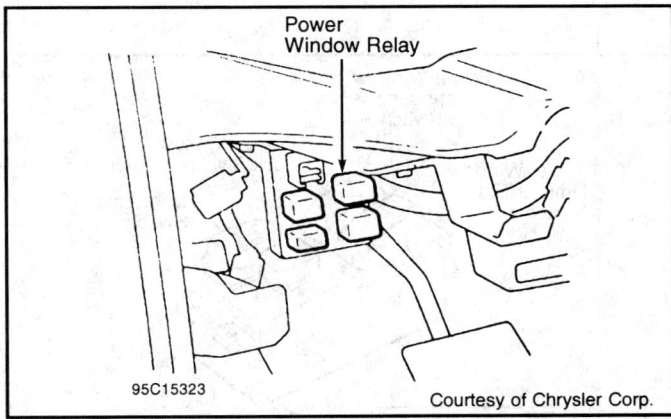

Fig. 4: Locating Power Window Relay

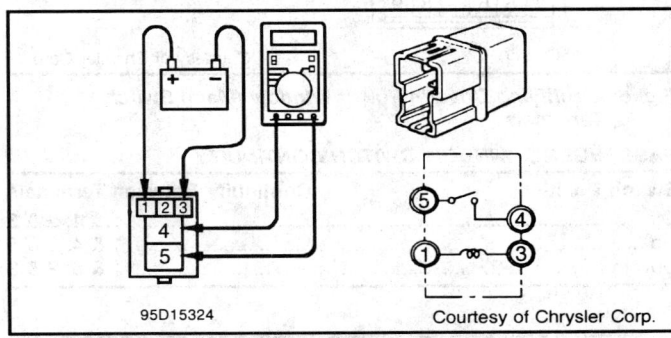

Fig. 5: Identifying Power Window Relay Terminals

DRIVER'S WINDOW SWITCH CONTINUITY

Switch Position	Continuity Between Terminals
Driver's Side Switch	
Off	2, 6 & 9
Up	2 & 6; 8 & 9
Down Or Auto Down	6 & 8; 2 & 9
Passenger's Side Switch	
Off	3 & 7
Up	3 & 8
Down	7 & 8
Window Lock Switch	
Normal	2 & 3; 2 & 7
Lock	1

[1] – Continuity should not exist between terminal No. 2 and terminals No. 3 and 7.

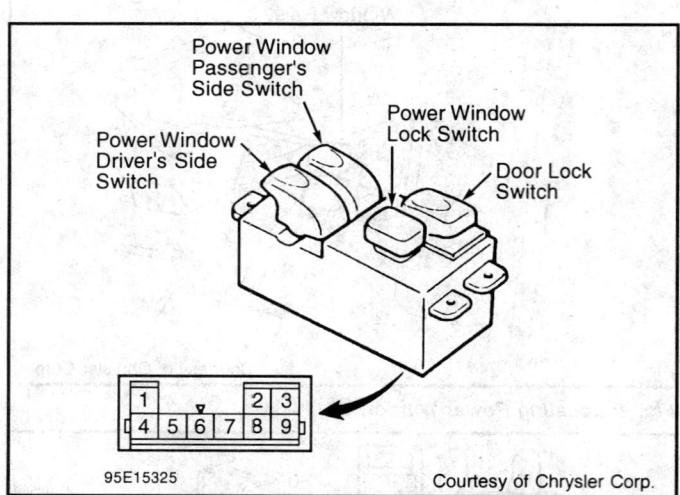

Fig. 6: Identifying Driver's Power Window (Main) Switch Terminals

PASSENGER'S WINDOW SWITCH CONTINUITY

Switch Position	Continuity Between Terminals
Off	1 & 4; 2 & 3
Up	1 & 4; 3 & 6
Down	1 & 6; 2 & 3

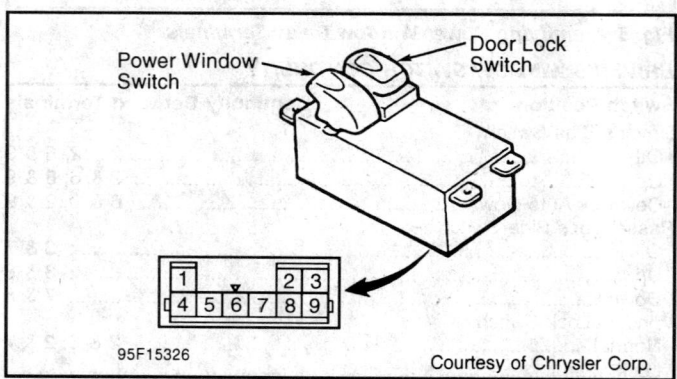

Fig. 7: Identifying Passenger's Power Window Switch Terminals

SYSTEM TESTS

POWER WINDOWS INOPERATIVE

1) Connect voltmeter, using Trouble Code Check Harness (MB991529), to Data Link Connector (DLC) ETACS terminal and ground terminal. *See Fig. 8.* Turn ignition on. Operate power window switch while monitoring voltmeter. If voltmeter deflects once each time switch is operated, go to next step. If voltmeter does not deflect, inspect and repair circuit between ignition switch and ETACS-ECU. See WIRING DIAGRAMS.

2) Check window relay. See POWER WINDOW RELAY under COMPONENT TESTS. Replace as necessary. Inspect driver's and passenger's window switch. See POWER WINDOW SWITCH under COMPONENT TESTS. Replace as necessary. Inspect both power window motors. See POWER WINDOW MOTOR under COMPONENT TESTS. Replace as necessary. If all components are okay, go to next step.

3) Remove power window relay. *See Fig. 4.* Turn ignition on. Using DVOM, check voltage at terminals No. 1 (Red/White wire) and No. 5 (Red/White wire) at window relay wiring harness connector. *See Fig. 5.* If battery voltage exists at both terminals, go to next step. If battery voltage does not exist at one or both terminals, inspect and repair power supply circuits to relay. See WIRING DIAGRAMS.

4) Turn ignition off. Disconnect ETACS-ECU connector B-40. ETACS-ECU is located behind lower left corner of instrument panel. See Fig. .

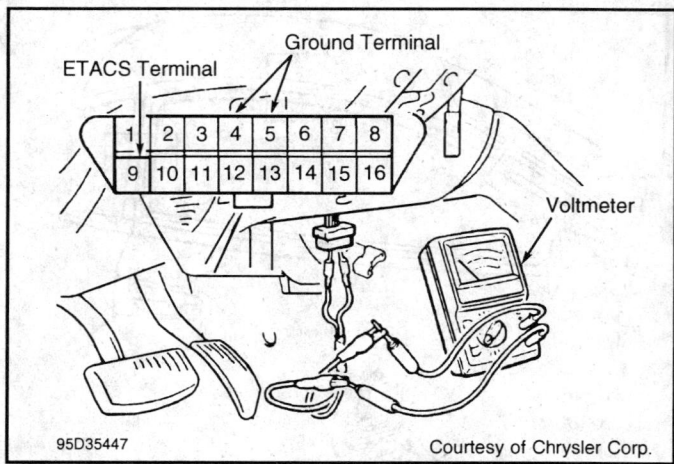

Fig. 8: Connecting Voltmeter To Data Link Connector

Using an ohmmeter, check continuity of Blue/Yellow wire between terminals No. 3 at window relay wiring harness connector and No. 35 (with anti-theft) or No. 33 (without anti-theft) at ETACS-ECU wiring harness connector. *See Figs. 5 and 9.* If continuity exists, go to next step. If continuity does not exist, repair open Blue/Yellow wire.

5) Check continuity of Blue/Black wire between terminal No. 4 at window relay wiring harness connector and No. 8 at driver's power window switch wiring harness connector. *See Figs. 5 and 6.* If continuity exists, go to next step. If continuity does not exist, repair open Blue/Black wire.

6) Check continuity of Blue/Black wire between terminals No. 4 at power window relay wiring harness connector and No. 6 at passenger's power window switch wiring harness connector. *See Figs. 5 and 7.* If continuity exists, go to next step. If continuity does not exist, repair open Blue/Black wire.

7) Disconnect driver's power window switch connector. Check continuity between ground and terminal No. 2 (Black wire) at window switch wiring harness connector. *See Fig. 6.* If continuity exists, connect driver's power window switch connector. Go to next step. If continuity does not exist, repair open Black wire.

8) Remove driver's door trim panel and disconnect power window motor connector. Check for continuity between ground and both terminals of window motor wiring harness connector. If continuity exists, go to next step. If continuity does not exist, repair open circuit between driver's power window switch and driver's power window motor.

9) Remove passenger's door trim panel and disconnect power window motor connector. Ensure driver's power window lock switch is connected and in ON (unlock) position. Check for continuity between ground and each terminal of passenger's window motor wiring harness connector. If continuity exists, replace ETACS-ECU. Recheck system operation. If continuity does not exist, repair open circuit between driver's power window switch and passenger's power window motor.

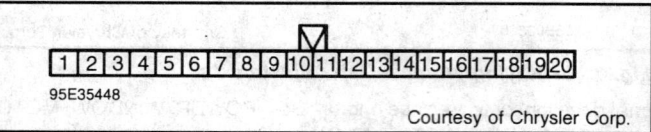

Fig. 9: Identifying ETACS-ECU Connector B39

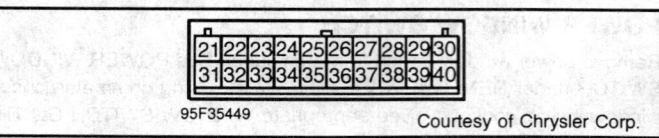

Fig. 10: Identifying ETACS-ECU Connector B40 (With Anti-Theft)

POWER WINDOWS OPERATIONAL WITH DOOR OPEN, IGNITION OFF

1) Connect voltmeter to Data Link Connector (DLC) ETACS terminal and ground terminal. *See Fig. 8.* Open and close driver's and passenger's

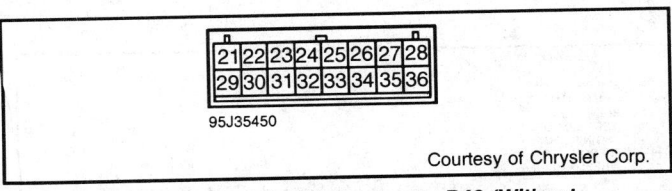

95J35450

Courtesy of Chrysler Corp.

Fig. 11: Identifying ETACS-ECU Connector B40 (Without Anti-Theft)

door while monitoring voltmeter. If voltmeter deflects once each time a door is opened, go to next step. If voltmeter does not deflect, check for open or short in door switch circuits. See appropriate wiring diagram in REMOTE KEYLESS ENTRY SYSTEMS article.

2) Turn ignition switch to ON position, then to OFF position while monitoring voltmeter. If voltmeter deflects once switch is operated, replace ETACS-ECU. ETACS-ECU is located behind lower left corner of instrument panel. If voltmeter does not deflect, inspect and repair ignition switch circuits. See appropriate wiring diagram in POWER DISTRIBUTION article in WIRING DIAGRAMS.

POWER WINDOWS NOT OPERATIONAL WITH IGNITION OFF

Only possible cause for this fault is a faulty ETACS-ECU. Replace ETACS-ECU. ETACS-ECU is located behind lower left corner of instrument panel.

POWER WINDOWS OPERATIONAL FOR MORE THAN 30 SECONDS WITH IGNITION OFF

Only possible cause for this fault is a faulty ETACS-ECU. Replace ETACS-ECU. ETACS-ECU is located behind lower left corner of instrument panel.

ONLY PASSENGER'S POWER WINDOW SWITCH OPERATIONAL

1) Check driver's window switch connector for loose, corroded or damaged terminals. Repair as necessary and recheck system operation. If connector is okay, go to next step.
2) Check driver's window switch. See POWER WINDOW SWITCH under COMPONENT TESTS. Replace switch as necessary. If switch is okay, disconnect power window relay. See Fig. 4.
3) Check continuity of Blue/Black wire between terminals No. 4 at window relay wiring harness connector and No. 8 at driver's window switch wiring harness connector. See Figs. 5 and 6. Repair wiring as necessary. See WIRING DIAGRAMS.

PASSENGER'S POWER WINDOW OPERABLE ONLY WITH DRIVER'S SWITCH

1) Check passenger's window switch connector for loose, corroded or damaged terminals. Repair as necessary and recheck system operation. If connector is okay, go to next step.
2) Check passenger's window switch. See POWER WINDOW SWITCH under COMPONENT TESTS. Replace switch as necessary. If switch is okay, disconnect power window relay. See Fig. 4.
3) Check continuity of Blue/Black wire between terminals No. 4 at window relay wiring harness connector and No. 6 at passenger's window switch wiring harness connector. See Figs. 5 and 7. Repair wiring as necessary. See WIRING DIAGRAMS.

REMOVAL & INSTALLATION

DOOR TRIM PANEL & WATERSHIELD

Removal & Installation – 1) Remove pull-handle box from door trim panel. Remove door handle cover. Disconnect window switch connector. Remove door trim panel.
2) Remove pull handle bracket. Remove door release handle assembly. Remove speaker assembly with cover. Remove watershield. To install, reverse removal procedure.

POWER WINDOW MOTOR

Removal & Installation – Remove window regulator. See WINDOW REGULATOR. Remove motor from regulator assembly. To install, reverse removal procedure.

POWER WINDOW SWITCH

Removal & Installation – Remove pull-handle box from door trim panel. Disconnect window switch connector. Remove switch from pull-handle box. To install, reverse removal procedure.

WINDOW REGULATOR

Removal & Installation – Remove door trim panel and watershield. See DOOR TRIM PANEL & WATERSHIELD. Remove up stop bolts. See Fig. 12. Remove inner stabilizers. Remove delta sash. Remove glass retaining screws and glass. Remove window regulator bolts. Remove window regulator and motor as an assembly. To install, reverse removal procedure.

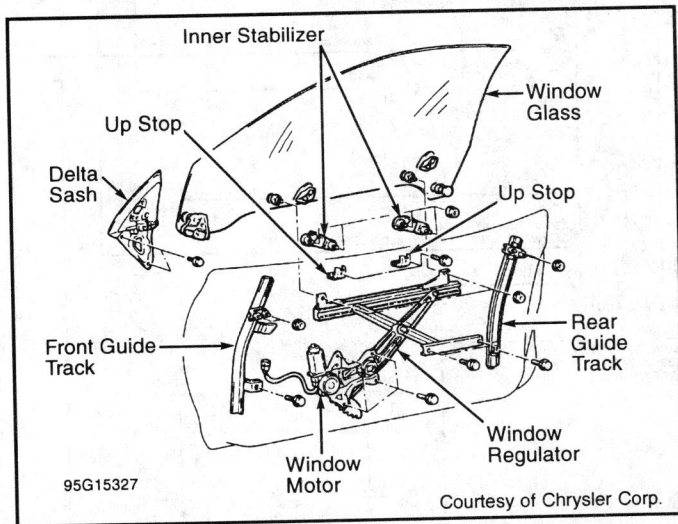

95G15327

Courtesy of Chrysler Corp.

Fig. 12: Removing Power Window Motor & Regulator Assembly

WIRING DIAGRAMS

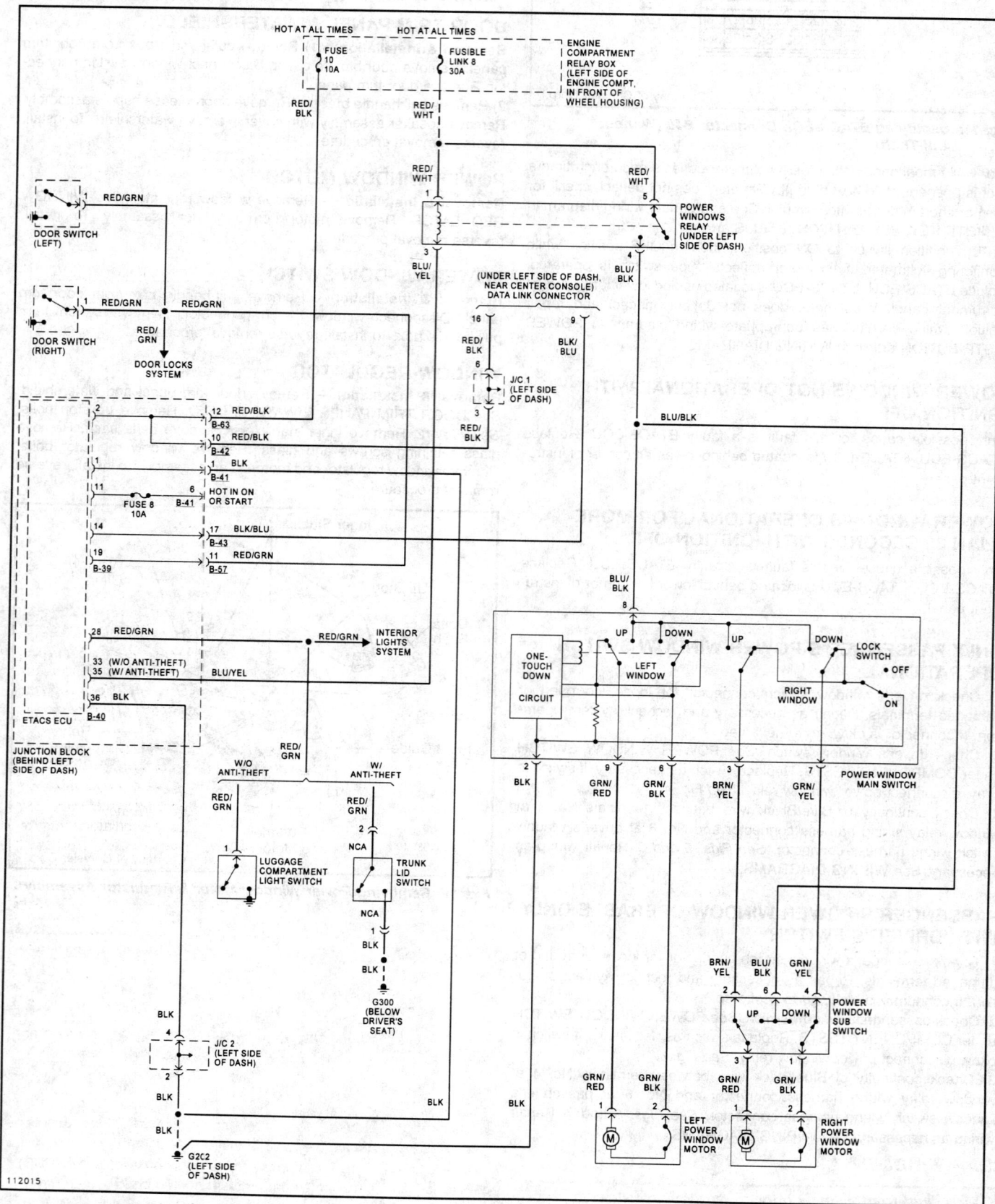

Fig. 13: Power Window System Wiring Diagram (Avenger & Sebring Coupe)

1999 ACCESSORIES & EQUIPMENT
Power Windows
Breeze, Cirrus, Sebring Convertible & Stratus

DESCRIPTION & OPERATION

Power windows are operated by a permanent magnet type electric motor mounted in each door. Master control switch provides ground to each motor. Circuit breaker No. 2 (20-amp), located in junction block, is used to protect power window circuit. Changing polarity at each motor will cause motor to rotate in reverse direction.

Driver's master control switch has a lock-out feature that restricts passenger window operation when it is engaged. All switches are illuminated with LEDs located inside switch. LEDs have power all the time, except when lock-out feature is engaged.

On Breeze, Cirrus and Stratus, master switch has an Auto-Down feature. Pressing switch to second detent will move driver's window to full down position. Moving switch during travel will cancel Auto-Down feature.

On Sebring Convertible, power window system utilizes a window drop relay assembly that allow windows to be automatically lowered when convertible top is raised or lowered. Assembly consists of 2 relays and a window timer module, all located inside driver's door. When power top switch is pressed up or down, windows are lowered about 1-3 inches so windows are clear of top while raising or lowering.

ADJUSTMENTS

FRONT WINDOW

NOTE: Ensure door is aligned to body before adjusting window. Lower rear window completely while adjusting front window.

FRONT WINDOW

Up-Stop Adjustment – Remove door panel, if not already removed. See DOOR TRIM PANEL under REMOVAL & INSTALLATION. Loosen up-stop nut and bolt. *See Figs. 1 and 2.* Remove weatherstrip only at area being adjusted and measured. Close door and raise window. Adjust up-stop until window is at proper height. *See Fig. 3.* Tighten up-stop nut. Check that forward up-stop fully contacts hook on window. Adjust contact bolt on forward up-stop as necessary. Install door trim panel.

Inboard/Outboard Adjustment – Remove door panel, if not already removed. See DOOR TRIM PANEL under REMOVAL & INSTALLATION. Loosen lower in/out jackscrew nuts. *See Fig. 4.* Remove weatherstrip only at area being adjusted and measured. Close door and raise window. Using an Allen wrench, rotate jackscrews until in/out position at top edge of window is at proper position. *See Fig. 3.* Tighten all fasteners. Install door trim panel.

Front/Rear Adjustment – Remove door panel, if not already removed. See DOOR TRIM PANEL under REMOVAL & INSTALLATION. Lower window to full down position. Loosen window retaining bolts. Raise window to full up position. Adjust window. *See Fig. 3.* Tighten 2 accessible window retaining bolts. Lower window and tighten remaining window retaining bolt. Raise window to full up position. Ensure front of window is positioned correctly. To check adjustment, slide a piece of paper between window and weatherstrip. Some tension should be felt.

NOTE: Adjustment verification must be done whenever front window is adjusted, after all adjustments are done.

Adjustment Verification – Raise rear window to full up position. Close door. Raise and lower window fully. Ensure that:
- Front window operates smoothly.
- Front window maintains proper alignment.
- Rear window weatherstrip seals against front window If any problems exist, adjust rear window and/or readjust front window.

REAR WINDOW

NOTE: Adjust front window prior to performing following procedures.

Up-Stop Adjustment – Remove quarter trim panel. See QUARTER TRIM PANEL under REMOVAL & INSTALLATION. Loosen up-stop nuts.

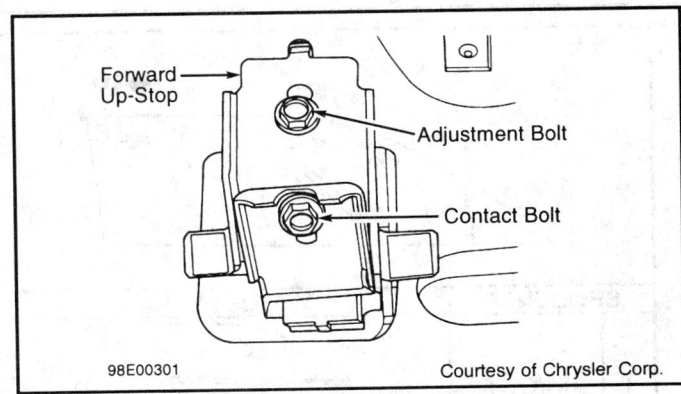

98E00301   Courtesy of Chrysler Corp.

Fig. 1: Adjusting Front Window Forward Up-Stop

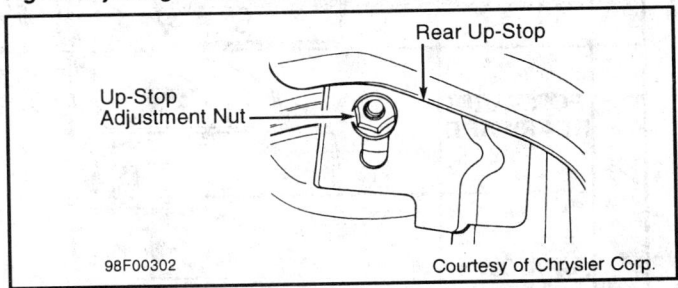

98F00302   Courtesy of Chrysler Corp.

Fig. 2: Adjusting Front Window Rear Up-Stop

See Fig. 5. Raise rear window. Using an Allen wrench, adjust up-stop until window is at proper height. *See Fig. 5.* Tighten up-stop nut. Cycle rear window and verify adjustment. Install door trim panel.

Inboard/Outboard Adjustment – Remove quarter trim panel, if not already removed. See QUARTER TRIM PANEL under REMOVAL & INSTALLATION. Loosen adjustment jackscrew nuts. *See Fig. 5.* Raise rear window. Using an Allen wrench, rotate jackscrew until in/out position at top edge of window is at proper position. *See Fig. 5.* Tighten up-stop nut. Cycle rear window and verify adjustment. Install door trim panel.

Front/Rear Adjustment – Remove quarter trim panel, if not already removed. See QUARTER TRIM PANEL under REMOVAL & INSTALLATION. Lower window to full down position. Loosen window retaining bolts. *See Fig. 5.* Raise window to full up position. Adjust window. *See Fig. 5.* Tighten bolts. Raise window to full up position. Ensure front of window is positioned correctly. To check adjustment, slide a piece of paper between window and weatherstrip. Some tension should be felt.

NOTE: Adjustment verification must be done whenever rear window is adjusted, after all adjustments are done.

Adjustment Verification – Raise front window to full up position. Raise and lower rear window fully. Ensure that;
- Rear window operates smoothly.
- Rear window maintains proper alignment.
- Rear window weatherstrip seals against front window If any problems exist, adjust front window and/or readjust rear window.

TROUBLE SHOOTING

- Check circuit breaker No. 2 (20-amp) in junction block. Junction block is located under left side of instrument panel.
- Check fuse No. 16 (40-amp) in Power Distribution Center (PDC). PDC is located in engine compartment next to battery.
- Check for good ground at instrument panel, left side cowl.

CHRY
4-460

1999 ACCESSORIES & EQUIPMENT
Power Windows
Breeze, Cirrus, Sebring Convertible & Stratus (Cont.)

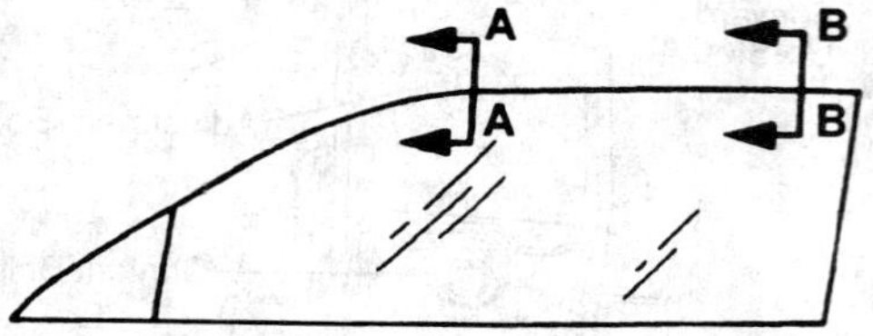

| | | MEASUREMENT LOCATIONS AND THEIR VALUES | | | |
| | | SECTION A-A | | SECTION B-B | |
SEQUENCE	ADJUSTMENT	W	X	Y	Z
1	IN/OUT	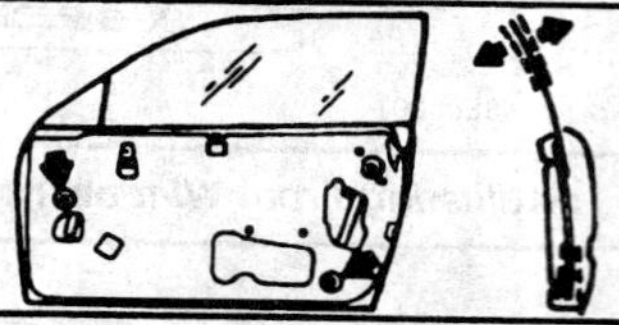	20.0mm ±2mm		20.0mm ±2mm
2	FORWARD/ REARWARD	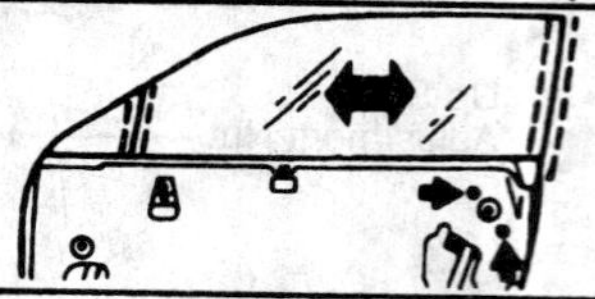 10.0mm ±2mm		10.0mm ±2mm	
	UP/DOWN	 10.0mm ±2mm		10.0mm ±2mm	

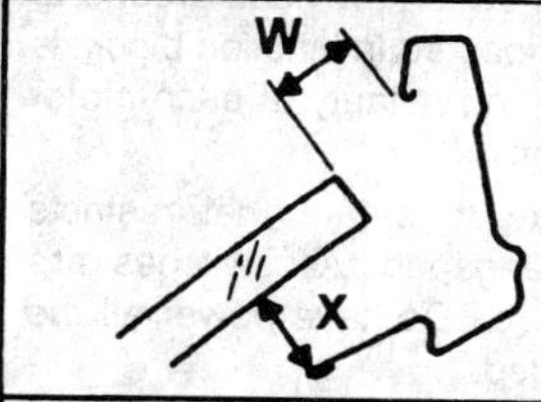

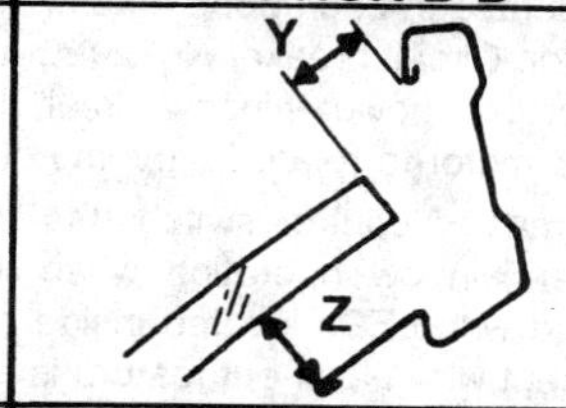

NOTE: Forward / Rearward and Up/Down adjustment are to be made at the same time.

98G00303

Courtesy of Chrysler Corp.

Fig. 3: Front Window Adjustment Measurements

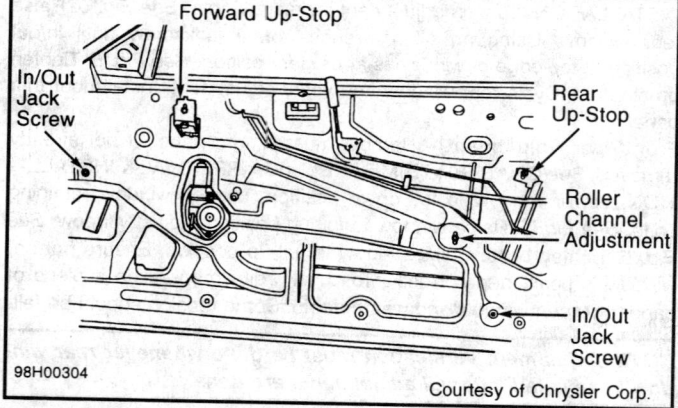

98H00304

Courtesy of Chrysler Corp.

Fig. 4: Adjusting Front Window Inboard/Outboard

1999 ACCESSORIES & EQUIPMENT
Power Windows
Breeze, Cirrus, Sebring Convertible & Stratus (Cont.)

CHRY
4-461

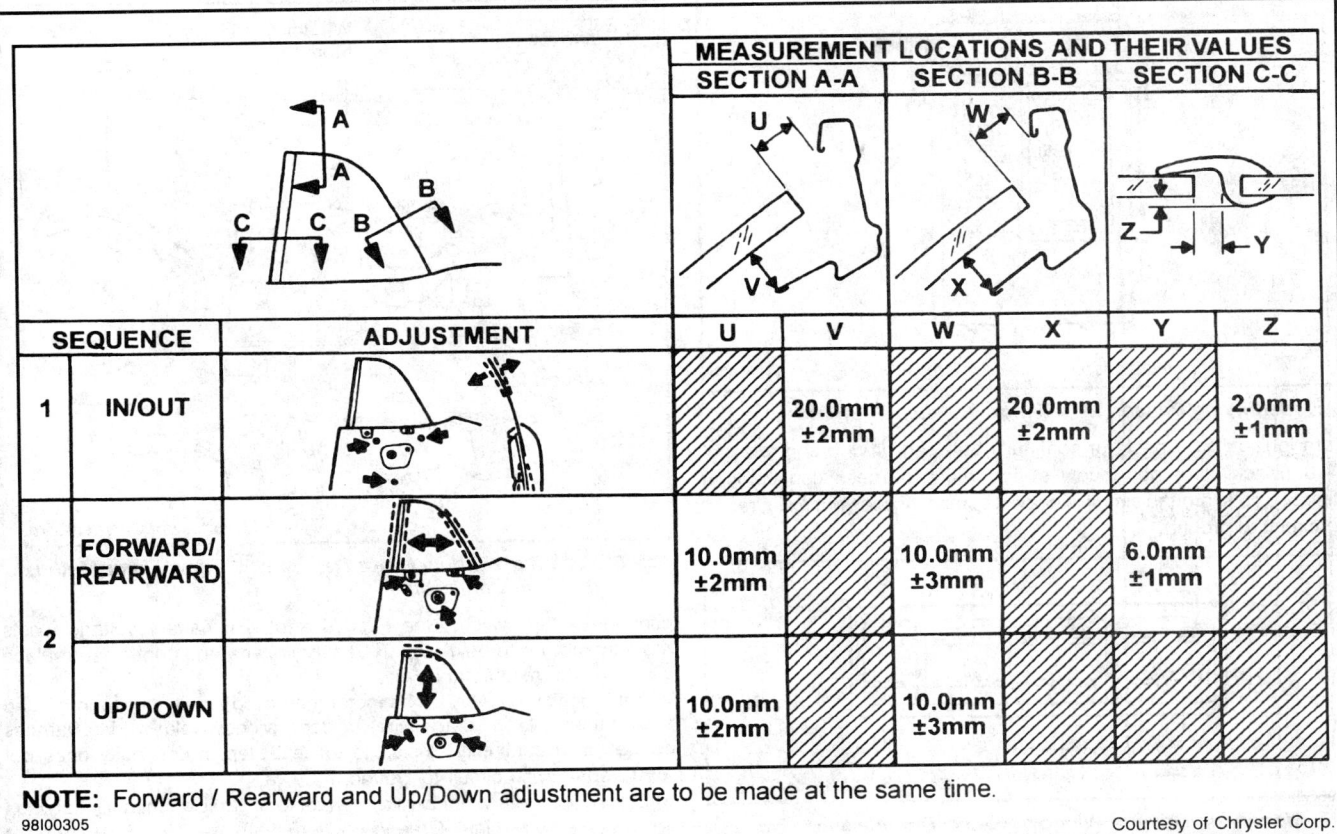

	SEQUENCE	ADJUSTMENT	U	V	W	X	Y	Z
1	IN/OUT			20.0mm ±2mm		20.0mm ±2mm		2.0mm ±1mm
2	FORWARD/ REARWARD		10.0mm ±2mm		10.0mm ±3mm		6.0mm ±1mm	
2	UP/DOWN		10.0mm ±2mm		10.0mm ±3mm			

MEASUREMENT LOCATIONS AND THEIR VALUES — SECTION A-A (U, V), SECTION B-B (W, X), SECTION C-C (Y, Z)

NOTE: Forward / Rearward and Up/Down adjustment are to be made at the same time.

98I00305

Courtesy of Chrysler Corp.

Fig. 5: Adjusting Rear Window

COMPONENT TESTS

WINDOW MOTOR

1) Remove appropriate door trim panel. See DOOR TRIM PANEL under REMOVAL & INSTALLATION. Disconnect window motor connector. Using jumper wires, apply battery voltage across window motor terminals. Motor should operate, unless it is already at maximum travel. Reverse jumper wires. Motor should operate in opposite direction.

2) If window does not move in either direction, remove screws holding glass lift plate to regulator. Slide window up and down by hand to ensure it moves freely in glass channels. If window slides freely, check regulator assembly. Repair window/regulator as necessary. If window/regulator is okay, replace window motor. If motor operates in one direction only, replace motor. See WINDOW MOTOR under REMOVAL & INSTALLATION.

WINDOW SWITCH

Remove power window switch. See appropriate WINDOW SWITCH under REMOVAL & INSTALLATION. Using an ohmmeter, check power window switch continuity. See appropriate WINDOW SWITCH CONTINUITY table. *See Fig. 6 or 7.* If continuity is not as specified, replace power window switch.

WINDOW SWITCH CONTINUITY (DRIVER'S)

Switch Position	Continuity Between Terminals
Off	2 & 10; 3 & 10; 4 & 10; 7 & 10; 8 & 10; 9 & 10; 10 & 11; 10 & 12
Up	
Left Front	1 & 7; 8 & 10
Right Front	1 & 12; 10 & 11
Left Rear	3 & 10; 1 & 2
Right Rear	1 & 4; 9 & 10

WINDOW SWITCH CONTINUITY (DRIVER'S) (Cont.)

Switch Position	Continuity Between Terminals
Down	
Left Front	1 & 8; 7 & 10
Right Front	1 & 11; 10 & 12
Left Rear	3 & 1; 2 & 10
Right Rear	4 & 10; 1 & 9
Window Lock	
Breeze, Cirrus & Stratus	1 & 5
Sebring Convertible	[1]

[1] – Not applicable.

WINDOW SWITCH CONTINUITY (PASSENGER'S)

Switch Position	Continuity Between Terminals
Off	2 & 5; 1 & 4
Up	1 & 4; 5 & 6
Down	2 & 5; 1 & 6

SYSTEM TESTS

POWER CIRCUIT

1) Remove driver's door trim panel. See DOOR TRIM PANEL under REMOVAL & INSTALLATION. Disconnect driver's power window switch connector. Turn ignition on.

2) Measure voltage between ground and terminal No. 1 (Tan wire) at power window wiring harness connector. *See Fig. 7.* If battery voltage is present, go to next step. If battery voltage is not present, check circuit breaker No. 2 (20 amp). Repair as necessary. If circuit breaker is okay, check for an open circuit between ignition switch and power window switch connector.

CHRY
4-462

1999 ACCESSORIES & EQUIPMENT
Power Windows
Breeze, Cirrus, Sebring Convertible & Stratus (Cont.)

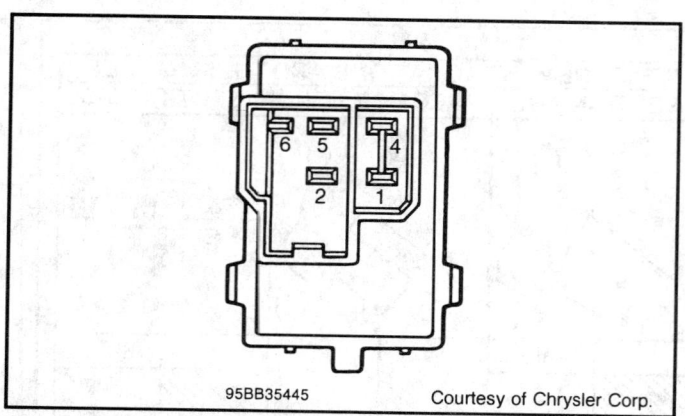

Fig. 6: *Identifying Passenger's Window Switch Terminals*

3) Turn ignition off. Check for continuity between ground and terminal No. 10 (Black wire) at window switch wiring harness connector. If continuity exists, ground circuit is okay. If continuity does not exist, repair open circuit to ground.

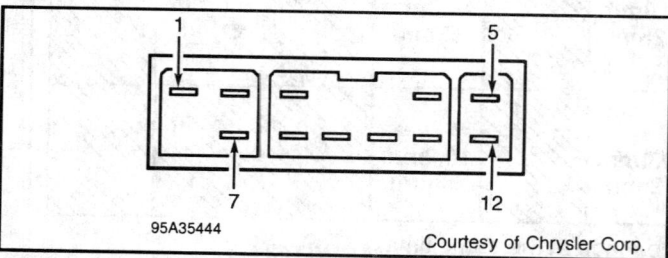

Fig. 7: *Identifying Driver's Window Switch Terminals*

WINDOW DROP RELAY ASSEMBLY (SEBRING CONVERTIBLE)

All Windows Do Not Lower When Convertible Top Switch Is Pressed – 1) Remove driver's door panel. See DOOR TRIM PANEL under REMOVAL & INSTALLATION. Disconnect window timer module connector. *See Fig. 8.* Turn ignition on.

2) Using DVOM, measure voltage between ground and terminal No. 1 (Yellow/Red wire) and No. 2 (Tan wire) at window timer module wiring harness connector. *See Fig. 9.* If battery voltage is present, go to next step. If battery voltage is not present, check circuit breaker No. 2 (20-amp) in junction block. Replace as necessary. If circuit breaker is okay, repair open in circuit.

3) Turn ignition off. Using ohmmeter, check for continuity between ground and terminal No. 9 (Black wire) at window timer module harness connector. If continuity exists, go to next step. If continuity does not exist, repair open circuit to ground.

NOTE: *In the following steps, a DVOM must be used when testing for voltage signal. Voltage signal is present for only 280-380 milliseconds.*

4) Connect window timer module connector. Connect DVOM negative lead to ground. Backprobing connector, measure voltage at terminal No. 7 (Light Green/Red wire) of window timer module wiring harness connector while pressing convertible top switch. *See Fig. 9.*

5) Voltage should be displayed for 280-380 seconds. If no voltage is present, replace window timer module. If voltage is displayed, inspect power window circuit connections for loose, corroded or damaged terminals. Repair as necessary.

Front Window(s) Do Not Lower When Convertible Top Switch Is Pressed – 1) Remove driver's door trim panel. See DOOR TRIM PANEL under REMOVAL & INSTALLATION. Turn ignition on. Using DVOM, measure voltage between ground and terminal No. 4 (Light Green/Red wire) at each window relay wiring harness connector while pressing

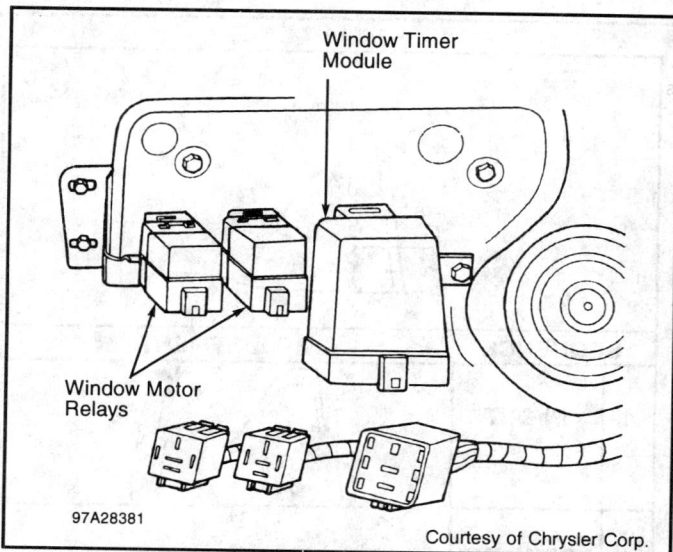

Fig. 8: *Locating Window Motor Relays & Window Timer Module (Sebring Convertible)*

convertible top switch. *See Figs. 8 and 9.* If battery voltage exists momentarily, go to next step. If battery voltage does not exist, replace window timer module and retest.

2) Turn ignition off. Using ohmmeter, check continuity between ground and terminal No. 6 (Black wire) at each window relay wiring harness connector. If continuity exists, go to next step. If continuity does not exist, repair open circuit to ground.

3) Disconnect both window relay connectors. Check continuity between terminals No. 4 (Light Green/Wire terminal) and No. 6 (Black wire terminal) at each relay. Terminals may also be marked on relay housing as No. 85 and 86. If continuity does not exist, replace relay and retest. If continuity exists, inspect power window circuit connections for loose, corroded or damaged terminals. Repair as necessary.

Rear Window(s) Do Not Lower When Convertible Top Switch Is Pressed – 1) Remove driver's door panel. See DOOR TRIM PANEL under REMOVAL & INSTALLATION. Turn ignition switch on. Using DVOM, measure voltage between ground and terminals No. 4 (Red/Black wire) and No. 6 (Dark Green/White wire) at window timer module wiring harness connector. *See Figs. 8 and 9.*

2) Press convertible top switch. If battery voltage exists, inspect power window circuit connections for loose, corroded or damaged terminals. Repair as necessary. If battery voltage does not exist, replace window timer module.

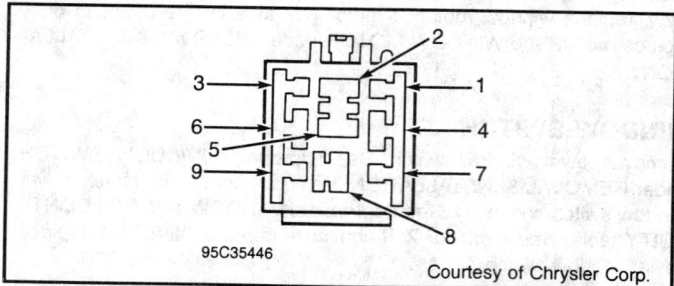

Fig. 9: *Identifying Window Timer Module & Window Motor Relay Wiring Harness Connector Terminal (Sebring Convertible)*

REMOVAL & INSTALLATION
DOOR TRIM PANEL

Removal & Installation (Front) – 1) Lower window to full-down position, if possible. Disengage clips holding speaker grille to trim panel.

1999 ACCESSORIES & EQUIPMENT
Power Windows
Breeze, Cirrus, Sebring Convertible & Stratus (Cont.)

CHRY
4-463

Remove screws securing door trim panel to door. Disengage clips holding perimeter of trim panel to door. Lift trim panel upward and disengage panel from upper retainer channel.

2) Tilt trim panel away from door. Disengage clip holding latch linkage to back of inside door handle. Disconnect connectors as necessary. Remove door trim panel. To install, reverse removal procedure.

Removal & Installation (Rear) – 1) Open rear door and lower window, if possible. Remove screw cap and screw from bottom of arm rest pull cup. Remove screw behind door handle. Disengage clips holding perimeter of trim panel to rear door.

2) Disengage trim panel from inner belt weatherstrip at top of door. Separate top of trim panel from door. Disengage clip securing linkage to latch handle. Separate linkage from latch handle. Lift trim up and off lock button. Remove rear door trim panel from door. To install, reverse removal procedure.

QUARTER TRIM PANEL (SEBRING CONVERTIBLE)

Removal & Installation – 1) Lower convertible top. Remove rear seat cushion and rear seat back. Remove door sill trim panel. Remove push-in fastener holding quarter trim panel to door sill panel. Remove speaker grille. Remove vertical screws holding quarter trim panel to inner quarter panel.

2) Remove screws securing quarter trim panel to inner quarter panel through speaker opening. Remove screws securing quarter trim panel to inner quarter panel at rear of trim panel.

3) Pull trim panel from inner quarter panel and disconnect speaker wiring connector. Remove push-in fasteners holding quarter trim panel to inner quarter panel at front of trim panel. Remove quarter trim panel. To install, reverse removal procedure.

WINDOW REGULATOR

Removal & Installation – 1) Remove door trim panel. See DOOR TRIM PANEL. Remove plastic watershield from door. Remove nuts securing window glass to regulator roller channel. Secure glass in full-up position. Mark position of rear roller channel bolt for installation reference and remove bolt. Disconnect power window motor connector.

2) Loosen rear roller channel bolt. Separate roller channel from inner door panel. Loosen window regulator-to-inner door panel bolts. Separate bolt heads from key-hole slots in inner door panel. Remove window regulator through large hole in inner door panel. To install, reverse removal procedure.

WINDOW MOTOR

WARNING: Keep fingers clear of sector gear teeth. Regulator movement may cause fingers to be pinched in sector gear teeth.

Removal – Move window to full up position, if possible. Remove door trim panel. See DOOR TRIM PANEL. Remove window regulator. See WINDOW REGULATOR. Disconnect wiring connector from power window motor. Using a "C" clamp, clamp sector gear to regulator mounting plate to prevent regulator movement. *See Fig. 10.* Remove 3 power window motor mounting bolts. Remove motor from regulator.

Installation – Install motor on regulator so motor engages sector gear teeth. Rotate motor as necessary to align 3 motor mounting bolts. Tighten motor mounting bolts to 50-70 INCH lbs. (5.6-8.0 N.m). Install regulator assembly. Using window switch, test window motor operation. To complete installation, reverse removal procedure.

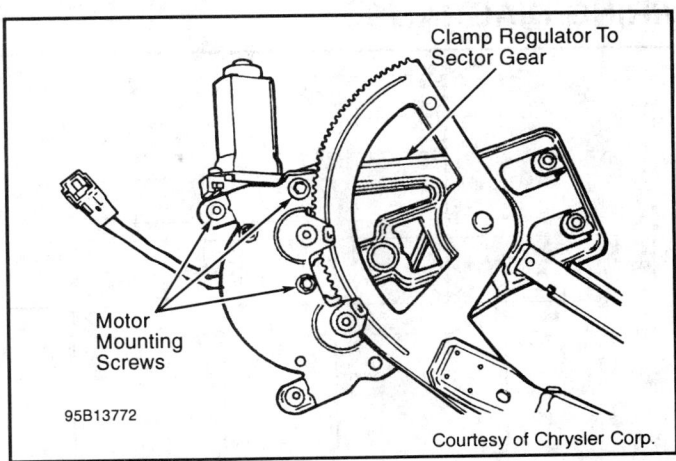

Courtesy of Chrysler Corp.

Fig. 10: Removing Window Motor

DRIVER'S WINDOW SWITCH

Removal & Installation (Breeze, Cirrus & Stratus) – Remove driver's door trim panel. See DOOR TRIM PANEL. Remove 3 switch mounting screws. Disconnect switch connector and remove switch. To install, reverse removal procedure.

Removal & Installation (Sebring Convertible) – Using a trim stick, gently pry up on center rear of switch bezel. With rear of switch bezel raised, pull front of switch bezel up. Disconnect wiring harness connectors as necessary. Remove screws and window switch from door trim panel. To install, reverse removal procedure.

PASSENGER'S WINDOW SWITCH

Removal & Installation (Breeze, Cirrus & Stratus) – Remove passenger's door trim panel. See DOOR TRIM PANEL. Disconnect switch connector and carefully pry switch from bezel. To install, reverse removal procedure.

Removal & Installation (Sebring Convertible) – Using a trim stick, gently pry up on center rear of switch bezel. With rear of switch bezel raised, pull front of switch bezel up. Disconnect wiring harness connectors as necessary. Remove screws and window switch from door trim panel. To install, reverse removal procedure.

1999 ACCESSORIES & EQUIPMENT
Power Windows
Breeze, Cirrus, Sebring Convertible & Stratus (Cont.)

WIRING DIAGRAMS

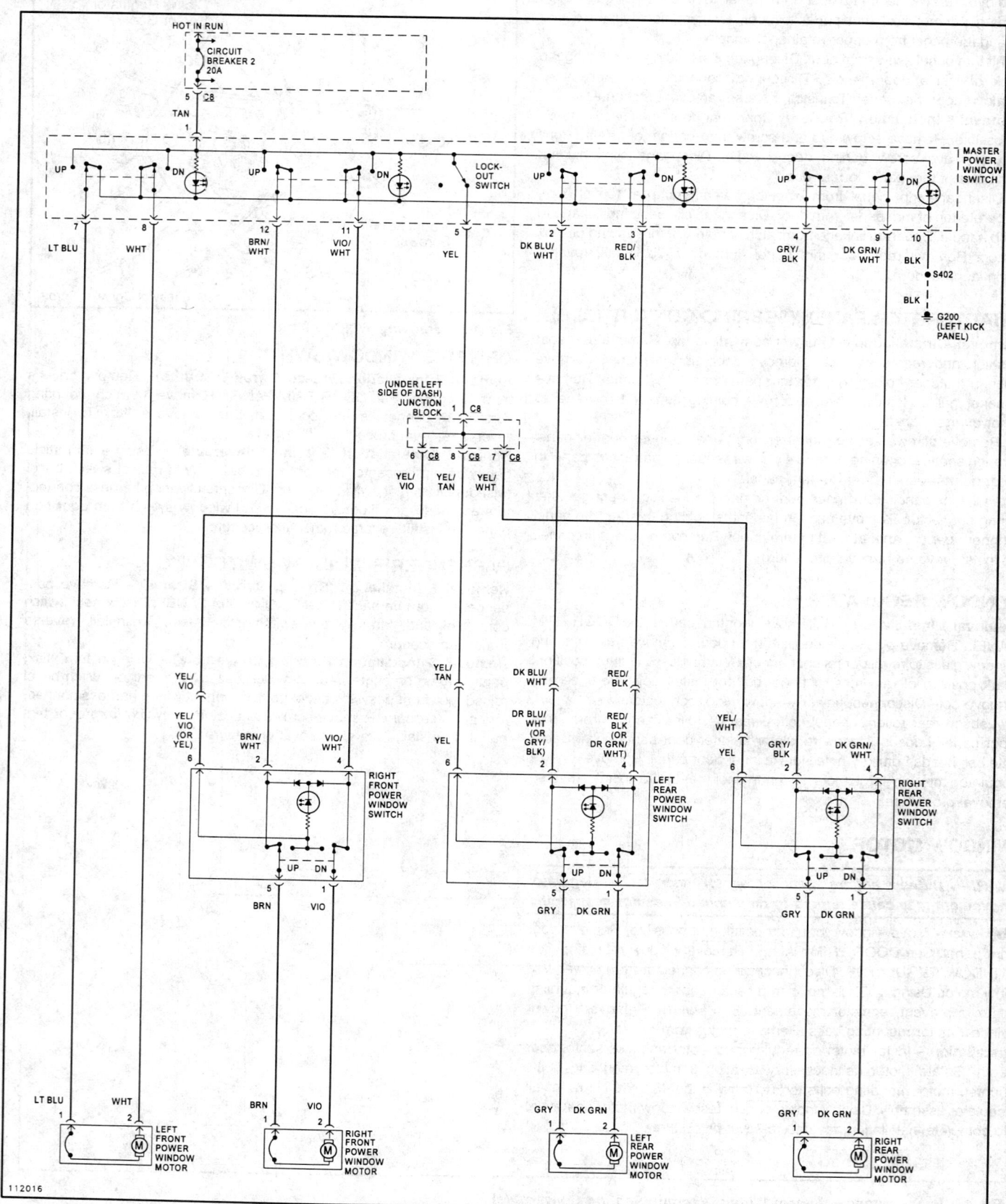

Fig. 11: Power Window System Wiring Diagram (Breeze, Cirrus & Stratus)

Power Windows
Breeze, Cirrus, Sebring Convertible & Stratus (Cont.)

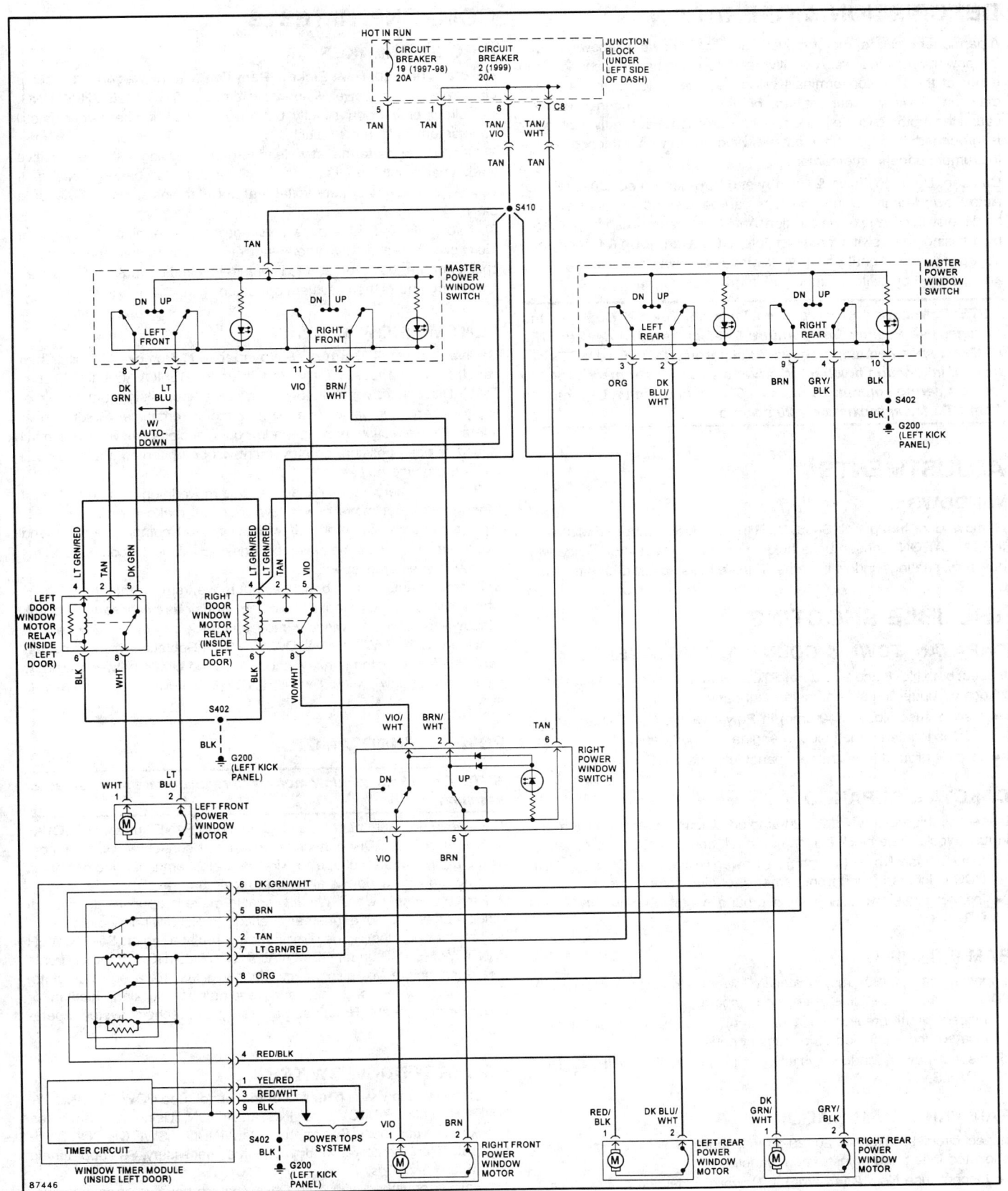

Fig. 12: Power Window System Wiring Diagram (Sebring Convertible)

1999 ACCESSORIES & EQUIPMENT
Power Windows – Caravan, Dakota, Durango, Ram Pickup, Ram Van, Ram Wagon, Town & Country, & Voyager

DESCRIPTION & OPERATION

A permanent magnet motor moves each of the power windows, including power vent windows. A positive and negative battery connection to either of the 2 motor terminals will cause the motor to rotate in one direction. Reversing current through these same 2 connections will cause the motor to rotate in the opposite direction. Each individual motor is grounded through the master switch by a wire attached to the instrument panel reinforcement.

Caravan, Durango, Town & Country and Voyager are equipped with an Auto Down feature. Drivers window can be lowered without having to hold the switch in the down position. Auto Down feature can be activated by pressing down switch past first detent. Caravan, Town & Country and Voyager have optional power vent windows. Power rear vent windows are operated by switches mounted in driver's door panel.

NOTE: Power window circuits on Caravan, Town & Country, and Voyager use Positive Temperature Coefficient (PTC) devices. The PTC is a specified amperage solid-state resettable fuse. PTCs are located in junction box behind driver's side of instrument panel, to left of steering column. To reset PTC, all current must be removed from PTC for approximately 20 seconds.

ADJUSTMENTS
WINDOWS

Remove door trim panel. See DOOR TRIM PANEL under REMOVAL & INSTALLATION. Loosen bolts holding window to regulator. Raise window fully, seating window in frame. Tighten bolts. Install door trim panel.

TROUBLE SHOOTING
CARAVAN, TOWN & COUNTRY, & VOYAGER

Inspect both No. 8 and 9 (9-amp) PTCs in junction block. Junction block is located under left side of instrument panel.
- Inspect fuse No. 23 (40-amp) in Power Distribution Center (PDC). PDC is located on left side of engine compartment.
- Inspect ground at instrument panel left side cowl.

DAKOTA & DURANGO

Inspect circuit breaker No. 20 (20-amp on Dakota, 25-amp on Durango) in fuse block. Fuse block is located on left end of instrument panel.
- Inspect fuse No. 9 (40-amp) in Power Distribution Center (PDC). PDC is located in left front corner of engine compartment.
- Inspect power window system ground circuit. See WIRING DIAGRAMS.

RAM PICKUP

Inspect fuse No. 2 (30-amp) located in Power Distribution Center (PDC). PDC is located in left side of engine compartment.
- Inspect circuit breaker No. 1 (20-amp) in fuse block. Fuse block is located under left side of instrument panel.
- Inspect power window system ground circuit. See WIRING DIAGRAMS.

RAM VAN & RAM WAGON

Inspect circuit breaker No. 20 (20-amp) in junction block. Junction block is located in left end of instrument panel.
- Inspect fuse No. 12 (40-amp) in Power Distribution Center (PDC). PDC is located in left side of engine compartment.
- Inspect power window system ground circuit. See WIRING DIAGRAMS.

COMPONENT TESTS
CIRCUIT BREAKER

Dakota, Durango, Ram Pickup, Ram Van & Ram Wagon – 1) Locate circuit breaker for power window system. See TROUBLE SHOOTING. Pull circuit breaker out slightly, but ensure circuit breaker terminals still contact terminals in fuse block.

2) Connect voltmeter negative lead to ground. Using voltmeter positive lead, check both terminals of circuit breaker for battery voltage. If voltmeter indicates battery voltage at both terminals, circuit breaker is okay.

3) If voltmeter indicates battery voltage at one terminal only, replace faulty circuit breaker. If voltmeter indicates no voltage at either terminal, check for an open or shorted circuit to circuit breaker. Repair as necessary and recheck system operation.

VENT WINDOW MOTOR

Caravan, Town & Country, & Voyager – 1) Remove "D" pillar trim panel. See "D" PILLAR TRIM PANEL under REMOVAL & INSTALLATION. Disconnect vent window motor connector. Using jumper wires, apply battery voltage to vent window motor terminals. Motor should rotate in one direction, moving window open or closed. If window is in full closed or open position, no movement will be observed and motor will make a grunting noise.

2) Reverse battery leads. Window should move in opposite direction. If window does not move or window does not make a grunting noise, replace vent window motor. If window moved completely open and closed, motor should be reversed one more time to complete a full window movement inspection.

3) If motor grunts and window does not move, remove motor assembly. Check window motor crank for binding. Repair as necessary. Recheck window operation. If window moves, check power window switch continuity. See POWER WINDOW SWITCH. Replace switch as necessary. If window switch is okay, check for open circuit between window motor and window switch. See WIRING DIAGRAMS. Repair as necessary.

POWER WINDOW MOTOR

NOTE: On Dakota, window motor and regulator are serviced as an assembly.

1) Remove door trim panel. See DOOR TRIM PANEL under REMOVAL & INSTALLATION. Disconnect window motor connector. Using jumper wires, apply battery voltage to window motor terminals. Motor should operate, unless window is already at maximum travel.

2) Reverse jumper wires. Window should move in opposite direction. If window does not move in either direction, replace window motor.

3) If motor operates in one direction only, replace motor. See POWER WINDOW MOTOR under REMOVAL & INSTALLATION. If motor grunts and does not move, disconnect window glass from regulator plate. Check window glass, tracks and regulator for sticking, binding or improper adjustment. Repair as necessary and recheck system operation.

POWER WINDOW SWITCH

1) Remove window switch from door trim panel. See POWER WINDOW SWITCH under REMOVAL & INSTALLATION. Using an ohmmeter, check switch continuity. See appropriate WINDOW SWITCH CONTINUITY table. Replace power window switch as necessary. See appropriate illustration. *See Figs. 1 - 6.*

2) Vehicles equipped with Auto Down feature have electronic components in switch to actuate Auto Down. To test, check switch continuity, reconnect switch, turn ignition on and test feature. If Auto Down does not work, replace switch.

Power Windows – Caravan, Dakota, Durango, Ram Pickup, Ram Van, Ram Wagon, Town & Country, & Voyager (Cont.)

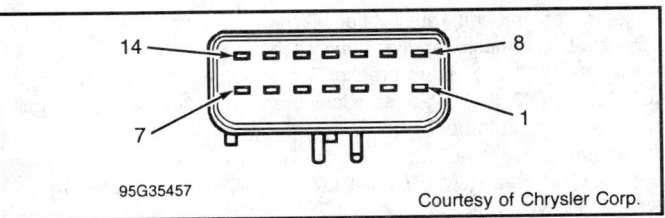

95G35457
Courtesy of Chrysler Corp.

Fig. 1: Identifying Driver's Window Switch Terminals (Caravan, Durango, Town & Country, & Voyager)

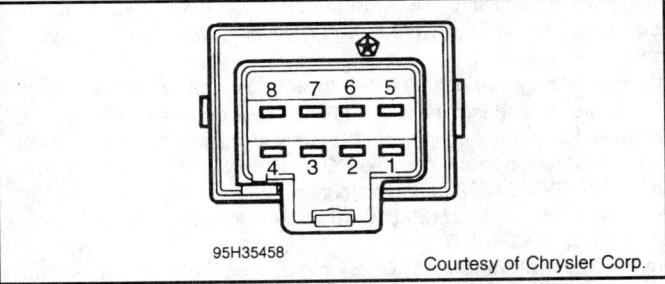

95H35458
Courtesy of Chrysler Corp.

Fig. 2: Identifying Passenger's Window Switch & Vent Switch Terminals (Caravan, Town & Country, & Voyager)

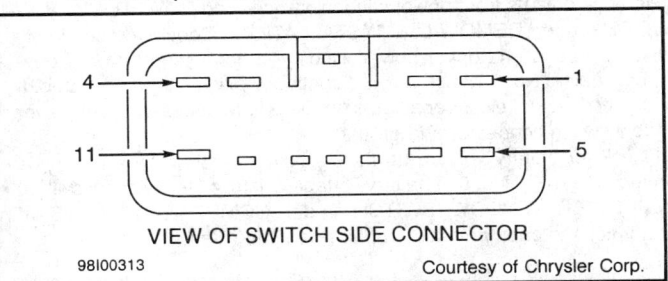

VIEW OF SWITCH SIDE CONNECTOR

98I00313
Courtesy of Chrysler Corp.

Fig. 3: Identifying Driver's & Passenger's Power Window Switch Terminals (Dakota & Ram Pickup)

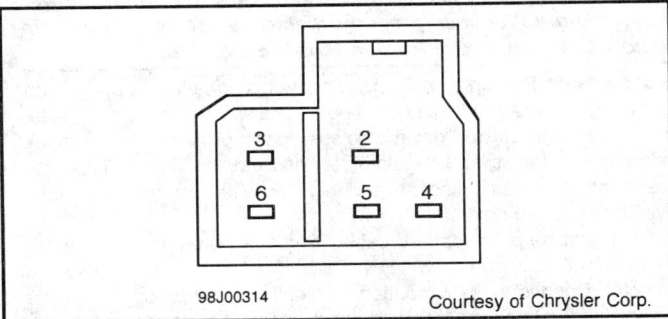

98J00314
Courtesy of Chrysler Corp.

Fig. 4: Identifying Passenger's Power Window Switch Terminals (Durango)

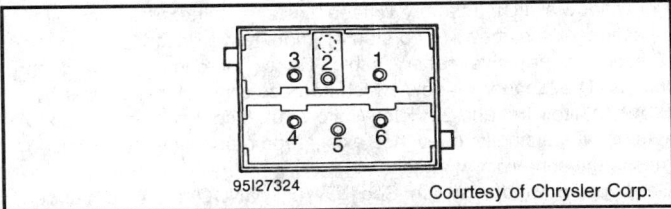

95I27324
Courtesy of Chrysler Corp.

Fig. 5: Identifying Driver's Power Window Switch Terminals (Ram Van & Ram Wagon)

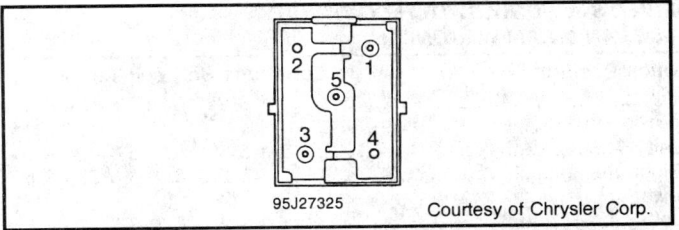

95J27325
Courtesy of Chrysler Corp.

Fig. 6: Identifying Passenger's Power Window Switch Terminals (Ram Van & Ram Wagon)

DRIVER'S WINDOW SWITCH CONTINUITY (CARAVAN, TOWN & COUNTRY & VOYAGER)

Switch Position	Continuity Between Terminals
Off	1 & 13; 2 & 13; 3 & 13; 4 & 13; 5 & 13; 6 & 13, 7 & 13; 8 & 13
Up	
Driver's Side	8 & 11
Passenger's Side	4 & 9
Down	
Driver's Side [1]	6 & 11
Passenger's Side	2 & 9
Auto-Down	
Driver Side's [1]	6 & 11
Vent Open	
Left	7 & 11
Right	1 & 9
Vent Close	
Left	3 & 9
Right	5 & 11

[1] – Connect battery voltage to terminal No. 9 and ground to terminal No. 13 before testing.

DRIVER'S WINDOW SWITCH CONTINUITY (DAKOTA & RAM PICKUP)

Switch Position	Continuity Between Terminals
Off	1 & 3; 2 & 3; 3 & 4; 3 & 6
Up	
Left	3 & 4; 5 & 6
Right	1 & 5; 2 & 3
Down	
Left	3 & 6; 4 & 5
Right	1 & 3; 2 & 5
Light	3 & 5

DRIVER'S WINDOW SWITCH CONTINUITY (DURANGO)

Switch Position	Continuity Between Terminals
Off	2 & 5; 3 & 5; 5 & 6; 5 & 11; 5 & 12; 5 & 13; 5 & 14
Up	
Left Front [1]	4 & 6
Right Front	2 & 5; 3 & 4
Left Rear	4 & 14; 5 & 13
Right Rear	4 & 12; 5 & 11
Down	
Left Front [1]	5 & 6
Right Front	2 & 4; 3 & 5
Left Rear	4 & 13; 5 & 14
Right Rear	4 & 11; 5 & 12
Auto-Down	
Left Front	[1]
Power Window Lock-Out	4 & 7

[1] – Vehicles equipped with Auto Down feature have electronic components in switch to actuate Auto Down. To test, check switch continuity, reconnect switch, turn ignition on and test feature. If Auto Down does not work, replace switch.

CHRY
4-468

1999 ACCESSORIES & EQUIPMENT
Power Windows – Caravan, Dakota, Durango, Ram Pickup, Ram Van, Ram Wagon, Town & Country, & Voyager (Cont.)

DRIVER'S WINDOW SWITCH CONTINUITY (RAM VAN & RAM WAGON)

Switch Position	Continuity Between Terminals
Off	1 & 2; 2 & 3; 3 & 4; 4 & 6
Up	
Left	1 & 5; 2 & 3; 3 & 4; 4 & 6
Right	1 & 2; 2 & 4; 3 & 5; 4 & 6
Down	
Left	1 & 2; 2 & 3; 3 & 4; 5 & 6
Right	1 & 2; 2 & 3; 3 & 6; 4 & 5

PASSENGER'S WINDOW SWITCH CONTINUITY (CARAVAN, TOWN & COUNTRY, & VOYAGER)

Switch Position	Continuity Between Terminals
Off	2 & 5; 3 & 8
Up	4 & 8
Down	4 & 5

PASSENGER'S WINDOW SWITCH CONTINUITY (DAKOTA & RAM PICKUP)

Switch Position	Continuity Between Terminals
Off	1 & 4; 2 & 3
Up	2 & 3; 4 & 11
Down	1 & 4; 3 & 11
Light	8 & 11

PASSENGER'S WINDOW SWITCH CONTINUITY (DURANGO)

Switch Position	Continuity Between Terminals
Off	2 & 5; 3 & 6
Up	2 & 5; 3 & 4
Down	3 & 6; 4 & 5

PASSENGER'S WINDOW SWITCH CONTINUITY (RAM VAN & RAM WAGON)

Switch Position	Continuity Between Terminals
Off	1 & 4; 2 & 3
Up	1 & 4; 3 & 5
Down	2 & 3; 1 & 5

SYSTEM TESTS

ALL WINDOWS INOPERATIVE

Caravan, Town & Country, & Voyager – 1) Check Positive Temperature Coefficient (PTC) for power window system. See TROUBLE SHOOTING. Replace PTC as necessary. If PTC is okay, go to next step.
2) Remove driver's power window switch. See POWER WINDOW SWITCH under REMOVAL & INSTALLATION. Turn ignition on. Using test light, connect ground lead to harness connector terminal No. 13 (Black Wire). Check for voltage by touching test light probe to harness connector terminals No. 9 (Tan/Dark Green Wire) and No. 11 (Tan Wire).
3) If test light illuminates, ground circuit and circuit between battery and switch are okay. If test light does not illuminate, check power and ground circuits. See WIRING DIAGRAMS.
Dakota & Ram Pickup – 1) Check circuit breaker for power window system. See TROUBLE SHOOTING. Replace circuit breaker as necessary. If circuit breaker is okay, go to next step.
2) Remove driver's front power window switch. See POWER WINDOW SWITCH under REMOVAL & INSTALLATION. Check for continuity between ground and terminal No. 3 at driver power window switch wiring harness connector. See WIRING DIAGRAMS. If continuity exists, go to next step. If continuity does not exist, repair open in Black/Light Green wire (Ram Pickup) or Black wire (Dakota) between driver power window switch connector and ground.
3) Turn ignition on. Measure voltage between ground and terminal No. 5 (Tan wire) at driver's power window switch wiring harness connector. If battery voltage is present, check driver power window switch. See POWER WINDOW SWITCH under COMPONENT TESTS. If battery

voltage is not present, repair open Tan wire between driver power window switch connector and ignition switch. See WIRING DIAGRAMS.
Durango – 1) Check circuit breaker for power window system. See TROUBLE SHOOTING. Replace circuit breaker as necessary. If circuit breaker is okay, go to next step.
2) Disconnect negative battery cable. Remove driver's front power window switch. See POWER WINDOW SWITCH under REMOVAL & INSTALLATION.
3) Check for continuity between ground and terminal No. 5 (Black wire) at driver's power window switch wiring harness connector. See WIRING DIAGRAMS. If continuity exists, go to next step. If continuity does not exist, repair open in Black wire between driver's power window switch connector and ground.
4) Reconnect negative battery cable. Turn ignition on. Measure voltage between ground and terminal No. 4 (Tan wire) at driver's power window switch wiring harness connector. If battery voltage is present, check driver's power window switch. See POWER WINDOW SWITCH under COMPONENT TESTS. If battery voltage is not present, repair open Tan wire between driver power window switch connector and ignition switch. See WIRING DIAGRAMS.
Ram Van & Ram Wagon – 1) Check circuit breaker for power window system. See TROUBLE SHOOTING. Replace circuit breaker as necessary. If circuit breaker is okay, go to next step.
2) Remove driver's front power window switch. See POWER WINDOW SWITCH under REMOVAL & INSTALLATION. Check for continuity between ground and driver power window switch wiring harness connector terminal No. 2 (Black wire). If continuity exists, go to next step. If continuity does not exist, repair open in Black wire between driver power window switch connector and ground.
3) Check for battery voltage at driver's power window switch harness connector terminal No. 5. If battery voltage exists, check window switch. See POWER WINDOW SWITCH under COMPONENT TESTS. If battery voltage does not exist, repair open Tan wire.

ONE WINDOW INOPERATIVE

NOTE: Window glass must be free to slide up and down for power window motor to function properly. If glass is not free to move up and down, motor will overload and trip the circuit breaker.

Dakota & Ram Pickup – 1) Place window glass halfway between up and down positions. Verify glass can be moved slightly from side to side, front to rear, and up and down. If glass does not move freely, check window glass, tracks and regulator for sticking, binding or improper adjustment. Repair as necessary and recheck system operation. If glass moves freely, go to next step.
2) Disconnect negative battery cable. Remove power window switch from door with inoperative window. Disconnect power window switch connector. Connect negative battery cable. Turn ignition on. Check for battery voltage at power window switch harness connector terminal No. 5 (driver's window) or terminal No. 11 (passenger's window). If battery voltage does not exist, repair open Tan wire between junction block and power window switch. If battery voltage exists, go to next step (inoperative passenger's window) or go step 4) (inoperative driver's window).
3) Disconnect negative battery cable. Check for continuity between ground and passenger window switch harness connector terminals No. 1 (Brown/White wire) and 2 (Violet/White wire). If continuity exists, go to next step. If continuity does not exist, repair open circuit in wiring harness between window switches.
4) Check power window switch. See POWER WINDOW SWITCH under COMPONENT TESTS. Replace faulty power window switch as necessary. If switch is okay, go to next step.
5) Check for continuity between window switch wiring connector terminals and corresponding window motor wire connector terminals of inoperative power window. If continuity exists in all circuits, power window switch and switch circuits are okay. Check power window motor. See POWER WINDOW MOTOR under COMPONENT TESTS. If con-

tinuity does not exist in one or more circuits, repair open circuit(s) as necessary. Recheck system operation.

Durango – 1) Place window glass halfway between up and down positions. Verify glass can be moved slightly from side to side, front to rear, and up and down. If glass does not move freely, check window glass, tracks and regulator for sticking, binding or improper adjustment. Repair as necessary and recheck system operation. If glass moves freely, and is not driver's window, go to next step. If driver's window is inoperative, check power window motor. See POWER WINDOW MOTOR under COMPONENT TESTS. If Auto Down feature is the only problem, replace driver's switch. If switch LED is the only problem, replace unlit switch.

2) Disconnect negative battery cable. Remove power window switch from door with inoperative window. See POWER WINDOW SWITCH under REMOVAL & INSTALLATION. Connect negative battery cable. Turn ignition on. Check for battery voltage at power window switch harness connector Yellow wire. If battery voltage does not exist, repair open circuit to master window switch. If battery voltage exists, go to next step.

3) Test power window switch continuity. See POWER WINDOW SWITCH under COMPONENT TESTS. Replace faulty switch as necessary. If switch is okay, go to next step.

4) Check for continuity in each circuit between master window switch and switch for inoperative window. See WIRING DIAGRAMS. If continuity does not exist in any circuit, repair open circuit as necessary. If continuity exists in all circuits, test power window motor. See POWER WINDOW MOTOR under COMPONENT TESTS.

Ram Van & Ram Wagon – 1) Place window glass halfway between up and down positions. Verify glass can be moved slightly from side to side, front to rear, and up and down. If glass does not move freely, check window glass, tracks and regulator for sticking or binding. Repair as necessary and recheck system operation. If glass moves freely, go to next step.

2) Disconnect negative battery cable. Disconnect and remove power window switch in door with inoperative window. See POWER WINDOW SWITCH under REMOVAL & INSTALLATION. Connect negative battery cable. Turn ignition on. Measure voltage between passenger power window switch wiring harness connector terminal (Tan wire) or driver power window switch wiring harness connector terminal (Tan wire) and ground. See WIRING DIAGRAMS. If battery voltage is not present, repair open Tan wire as necessary. If battery voltage exists, and inoperative window is on driver side, go to step **4)**. If battery voltage exists, and inoperative window is on passenger side, go to next step.

NOTE: Passenger's power window switch is grounded through driver's power window switch.

3) Disconnect negative battery cable. Check continuity between ground and passenger's power window switch harness connector terminals No. 2 (Brown/White wire) and No. 4 (Violet/White wire). See WIRING DIAGRAMS. If continuity exists on both circuits, go to step **5)**. If continuity does not exist on either or both circuits, repair open circuit.

4) Check power window switch. See POWER WINDOW SWITCH under COMPONENT TESTS. Replace faulty power window switch as necessary. If switch is okay, go to next step.

5) Using an ohmmeter, check continuity of each circuit between inoperative power window switch wiring harness connector and corresponding power window motor wiring harness connector terminal. See WIRING DIAGRAMS. If continuity does not exist in one or more circuits, repair open circuit(s) as necessary. Recheck system operation. If continuity exists in all circuits, power window switch and switch circuits are okay. Check power window motor. See POWER WINDOW MOTOR under COMPONENT TESTS.

REMOVAL & INSTALLATION

CAUTION: When battery is disconnected, vehicle computer and memory systems may lose memory data. Driveability problems may exist until computer systems have completed a relearn cycle. See COMPUTER RELEARN PROCEDURES article in GENERAL INFORMATION before disconnecting battery.

DOOR TRIM PANEL

Removal & Installation (Caravan, Town & Country, & Voyager) – 1) Using a trim stick, pry courtesy light from door trim. Disconnect courtesy light connector. Remove door assist handle (if equipped). Remove door pull cup (if equipped). Remove screws attaching trim panel to door below map pocket (if equipped). Using a trim stick, remove screw cover from switch panel.

2) Remove screws securing switch panel to door trim and remove panel. Using a trim stick, remove seat/mirror memory switch (if equipped). Remove screw securing door trim to door panel from behind inside latch release handle.

3) Disengage clips holding door trim to door frame around perimeter of panel. Tilt top of trim panel away from door to gain access to latch linkage. Disengage clip holding linkage rod to inside latch release handle. Separate linkage rod from latch handle. Remove door trim panel. To install, reverse removal procedure.

Removal & Installation (Dakota & Durango) – Lower window to full down position, if possible. Remove screws attaching trim panel to door. Lift panel up and outward to release retainers. Disconnect door handle linkage and all wiring. remove trim panel. To install, reverse removal procedure.

Removal & Installation (Ram Pickup) – Lower window to full down position, if possible. Remove screws attaching trim panel to door. Remove window switch. Using trim tool, disconnect clips around edge of door. Lift panel up and outward to release retainers. Disconnect door handle linkage and all wiring. remove trim panel. To install, reverse removal procedure.

Removal & Installation (Ram Van & Ram Wagon) – Remove screw attaching trim panel pull cup to door. Remove screw attaching door handle bezel to door. Remove screws attaching trim panel to door. Using trim tool, disconnect clips around edge of trim panel. Remove trim panel. To install, reverse removal procedure.

"D" PILLAR TRIM PANEL

Removal & Installation (Caravan, Town & Country, & Voyager – Left Side) – 1) Remove rear header trim cover. Remove liftgate sill plate. On long wheelbase models, remove second rear seat belt turning loop. On short wheelbase models, remove bolt securing second rear seat belt lower anchor to quarter panel.

2) On all models, remove jack storage cover. Remove "D" panel retaining screws. Using a trim stick, gently pry around perimeter of "D" pillar trim panel and separate trim panel from inner quarter panel. Disconnect rear speaker connector (if equipped).

3) On short wheelbase models, pass seat belt through slot in "D" pillar. On all models, remove "D" pillar trim panel. To install, reverse removal procedure.

Removal & Installation (Caravan, Town & Country, & Voyager – Right Side) – 1) Remove rear header trim cover. Remove liftgate sill plate. On long wheelbase models, remove second rear seat belt turning loop. On short wheelbase models, remove bolt securing second rear seat belt lower anchor to quarter panel. Remove quarter panel trim bolster.

2) On all models, remove "D" panel retaining screws. Disengage hidden "D" pillar trim panel clips. Separate "D" pillar trim panel from "D" pillar. Disconnect rear speaker connector (if equipped). Remove trim panel. To install, reverse removal procedure.

CHRY
4-470

1999 ACCESSORIES & EQUIPMENT
Power Windows – Caravan, Dakota, Durango, Ram Pickup, Ram Van, Ram Wagon, Town & Country, & Voyager (Cont.)

POWER WINDOW MOTOR

Removal & Installation (Caravan, Town & Country, & Voyager) – 1) Disconnect negative battery cable. Remove door trim panel. See DOOR TRIM PANEL. Remove watershield. Tape window in its existing position. Cut and discard window motor tie wrap. Disconnect window motor connector. Remove window motor mounting screws/nuts.

2) Remove window motor and cables from door and allow to hang from door. Do not remove drum and cables at this time. Install NEW window motor in door. Tighten screws/nuts to 30-40 INCH lbs. (3.4-4.5 N.m). Remove drum cover plate from faulty window motor. See Fig. 7. Lift cable guide, drum and cables from motor.

CAUTION: DO NOT allow drum to separate from cable guide, by dropping drum or letting cables unwind.

---

3) Install cable guide and drum into new window motor. To install drum onto window motor shaft, a slight rotation of drum may be necessary.

4) Using needle nose pliers, rotate drum. If drum still does not align with motor shaft, with aid of an assistant, lower window glass 1-2 inches. Drum will rotate when glass is lowered.

5) Install cover plate onto window motor. Connect window motor connector. Remove tape holding window in place. Test window operation. To complete installation, reverse removal procedure.

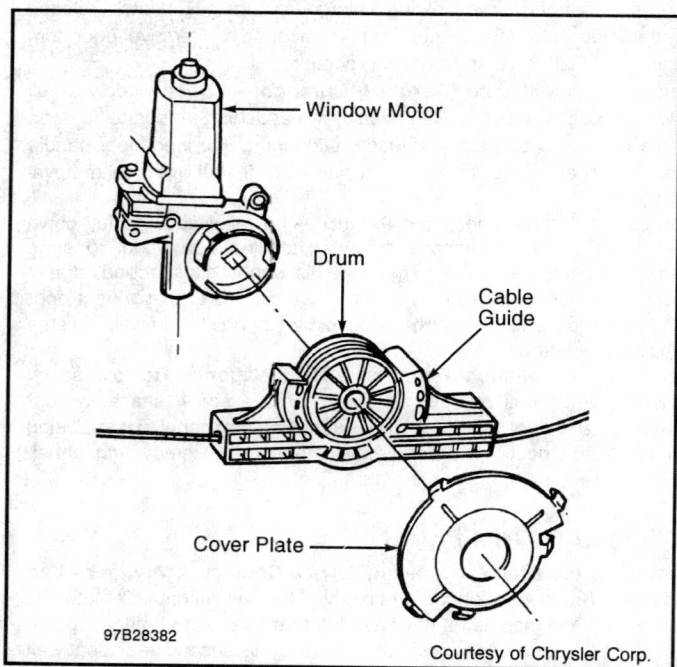

Fig. 7: Removing Power Window Motor (Caravan, Town & Country, & Voyager)

NOTE: On Dakota and Durango, power window motor is integral to window regulator unit. If power window motor is faulty, entire window regulator must be replaced.

Removal & Installation (Dakota & Durango) – 1) Remove door trim panel. See DOOR TRIM PANEL. Remove watershield. Remove inner and outer belt weatherstrip. Lower glass enough to align regulator arm-to-glass nuts with access holes in inner door panel.

2) Remove front glass run channel. Remove nuts attaching glass to regulator arm. Separate glass from regulator arm. Lift glass upward and remove from door. See Fig. 8.

3) Disconnect window motor wire connector. Loosen bolts in slotted holes attaching window regulator to inner door panel. Remove remain-

ing window regulator mounting bolts. Remove window regulator and motor assembly through access hole in inner door panel. To install, reverse removal procedure.

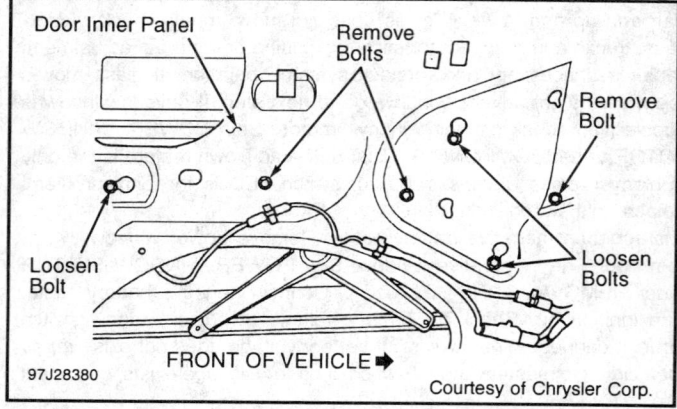

Fig. 8: Removing Power Window Motor (Dakota & Durango)

NOTE: On Ram Pickup, power window motor is integral to window regulator unit. If power window motor is faulty, entire window regulator must be replaced.

Removal & Installation (Ram Pickup) – Remove door trim panel. See DOOR TRIM PANEL. Remove watershield. Remove nuts attaching window to regulator. Remove window from door or tape window in raised position. Disconnect power window motor connector. Remove regulator screws. See Fig. 9. Remove window motor and regulator as an assembly. To install, reverse removal procedure.

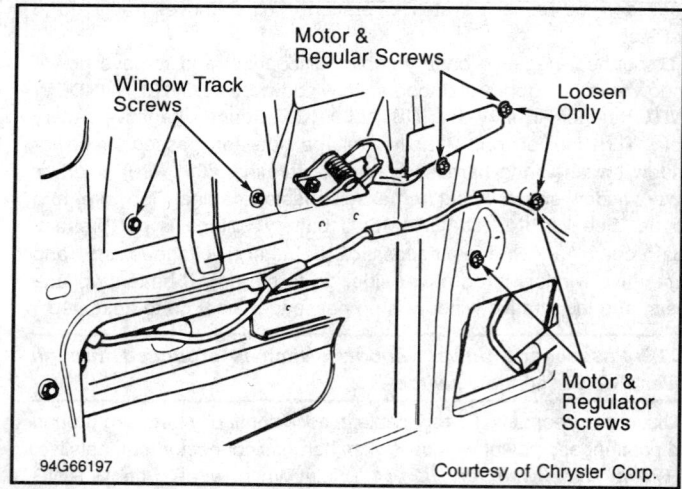

Fig. 9: Removing Window Motor & Regulator Mounting Screws (Ram Pickup)

NOTE: On Ram Van and Ram Wagon, power window motor is integral to window regulator unit. If power window motor is faulty, entire window regulator must be replaced.

Removal & Installation (Ram Van & Ram Wagon) – 1) Remove door trim panel. See DOOR TRIM PANEL. Remove inside door handle actuator. Disconnect window motor wire connector. Remove watershield. Remove inner and outer belt weatherstrip from door.

2) Lower glass enough to expose window glass-to-regulator bolts. Loosen window glass-to-regulator bolts. Loosen bolts at front and rear glass channels. Lift glass upward while rotating forward to remove.

1999 ACCESSORIES & EQUIPMENT
Power Windows – Caravan, Dakota, Durango, Ram Pickup, Ram Van, Ram Wagon, Town & Country, & Voyager (Cont.)

CHRY
4-471

3) Remove bolts attaching window regulator to inner door panel. Remove window regulator assembly. To install, reverse removal procedure. Tighten window glass-to-regulator bolts to 96 INCH lbs. (11 N.m).

POWER VENT WINDOW MOTOR

Removal & Installation (Caravan, Town & Country, & Voyager) – Remove "D" pillar trim panel. See "D" PILLAR TRIM PANEL. Disconnect power vent motor connector. Remove nut securing crank to vent glass. *See Fig. 10.* Remove bolts securing power vent motor to "D" pillar. Remove power vent motor. Remove crank from motor. To install, cycle motor to open position. Install crank in open position to new motor. To complete installation, reverse removal procedure.

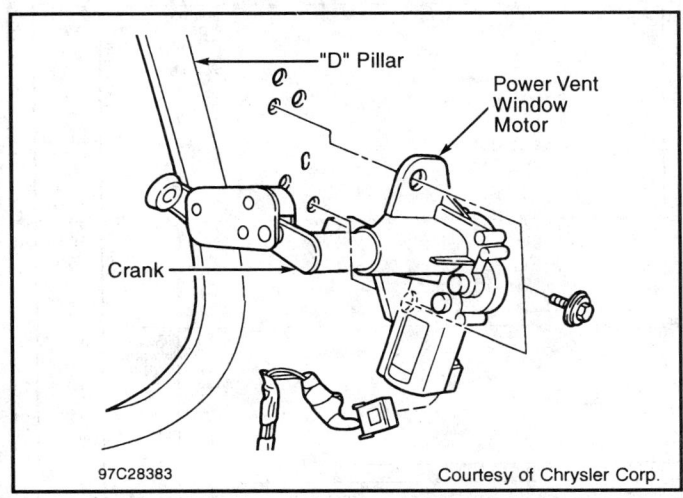

97C28383   Courtesy of Chrysler Corp.

Fig. 10: Removing Power Vent Motor (Caravan, Town & Country, & Voyager)

POWER WINDOW SWITCH

Removal & Installation (Caravan, Town & Country, & Voyager) – Disconnect negative battery cable. Using a trim stick, remove screw cover from switch panel. Remove screws securing switch panel to door trim. Disconnect wiring connector. Remove switch assembly from panel. Remove door lock switch retaining screws. To install, reverse removal procedure.

Removal & Installation (Ram Van & Ram Wagon) – Disconnect negative battery cable. Remove door trim panel. See DOOR TRIM PANEL. Remove mirror flag bezel. Remove screws attaching window switch mounting plate to mirror flag bezel. Using a thin screwdriver, gently pry snap clips at sides of window switch receptacle from rear of mounting plate. Pull switch out of receptacle. To install, reverse removal procedure. Tighten mounting screws to 20 INCH lbs. (2.2 N.m).

Removal & Installation (Dakota & Ram Pickup) – Disconnect negative battery cable. Using a trim stick, gently pry upper edge of switch bezel to release retainer securing bezel to door trim panel. Pull switch and bezel away from door trim panel and disconnect switch wire connector. To install, reverse removal procedure.

Removal & Installation (Durango) – Disconnect negative battery cable. Remove door trim panel. See DOOR TRIM PANEL. On driver's door, remove screws from back side of door trim panel and remove switch and bezel. On passenger's doors, gently pry snap clips at sides of window switch receptacle on back of door trim panel switch bezel. On all doors, remove power window switch from bezel. To install, reverse removal procedure.

1999 ACCESSORIES & EQUIPMENT
Power Windows – Caravan, Dakota, Durango, Ram Pickup, Ram Van, Ram Wagon, Town & Country, & Voyager (Cont.)

WIRING DIAGRAMS

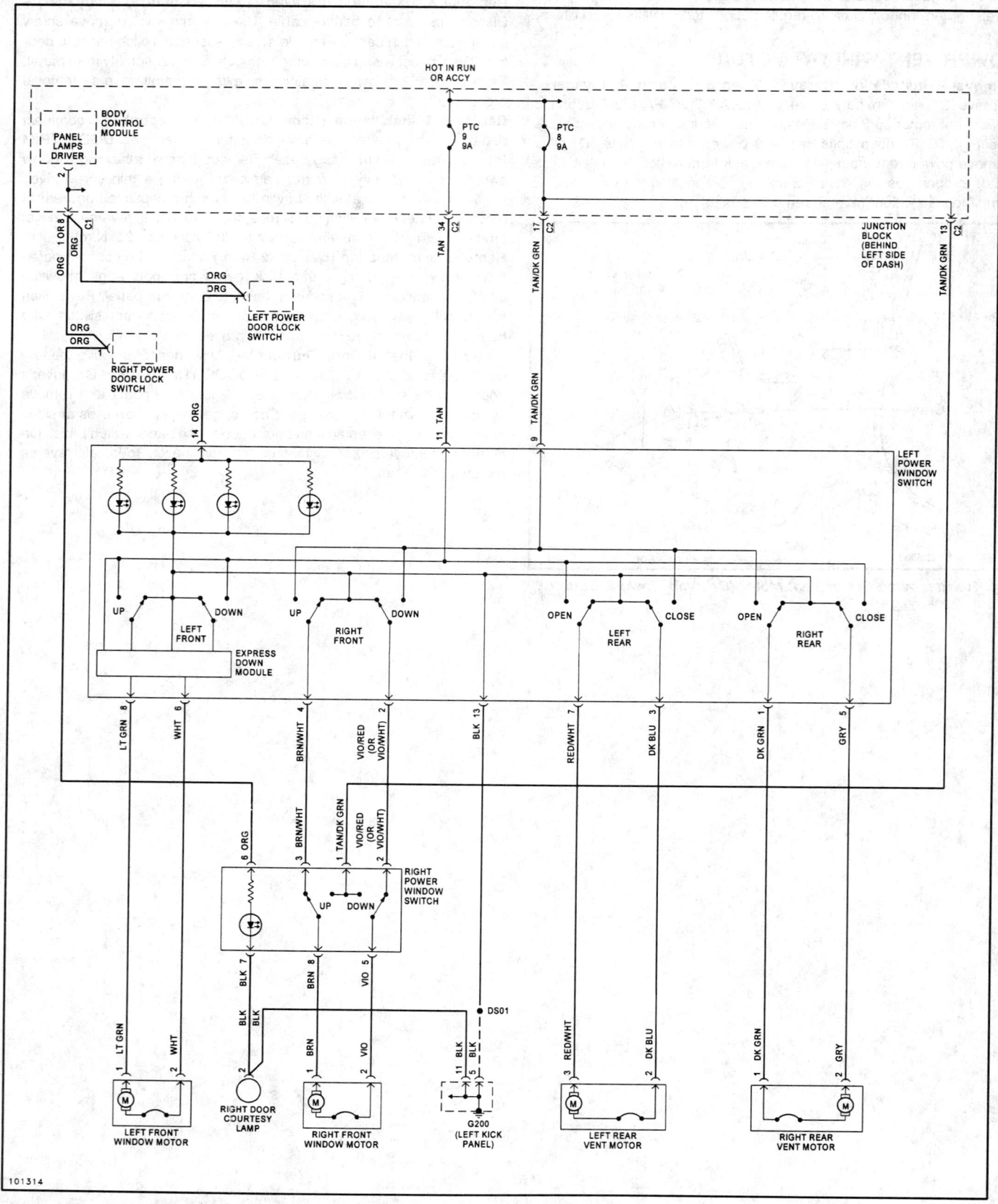

Fig. 11: Power Window System Wiring Diagram (Caravan, Town & Country, & Voyager)

101314

1999 ACCESSORIES & EQUIPMENT

CHRY
4-473

Power Windows – Caravan, Dakota, Durango, Ram Pickup, Ram Van, Ram Wagon, Town & Country, & Voyager (Cont.)

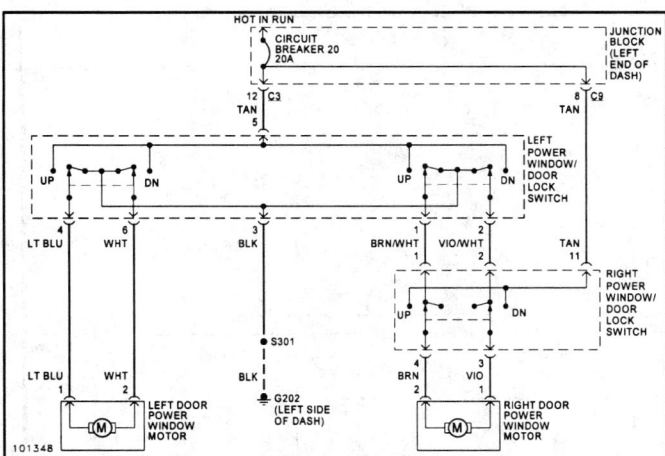

Fig. 12: Power Window System Wiring Diagram (Dakota)

CHRY
4-474

1999 ACCESSORIES & EQUIPMENT
Power Windows – Caravan, Dakota, Durango, Ram Pickup, Ram Van, Ram Wagon, Town & Country, & Voyager (Cont.)

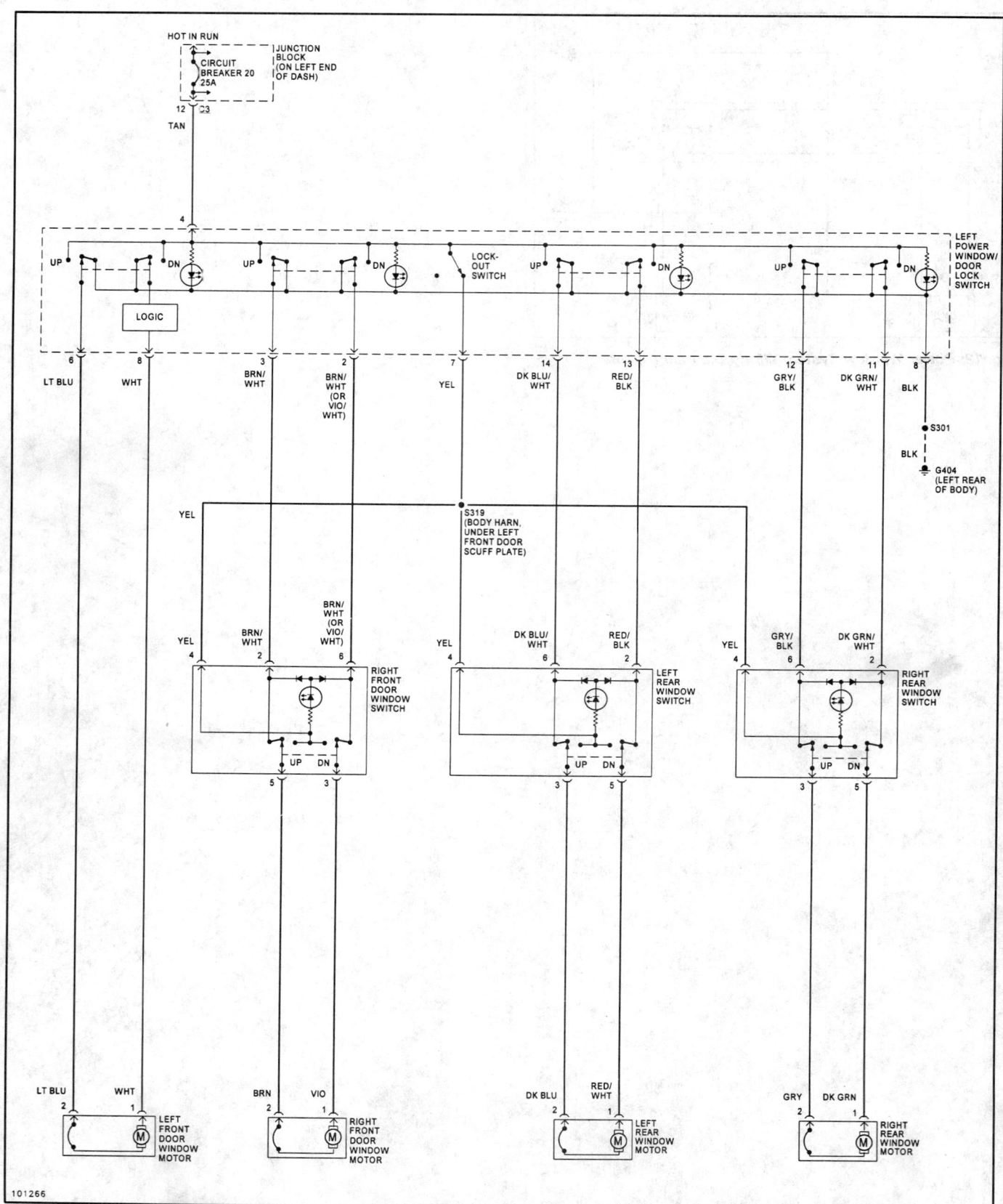

Fig. 13: Power Window System Wiring Diagram (Durango)

101266

Power Windows – Caravan, Dakota, Durango, Ram Pickup, Ram Van, Ram Wagon, Town & Country, & Voyager (Cont.)

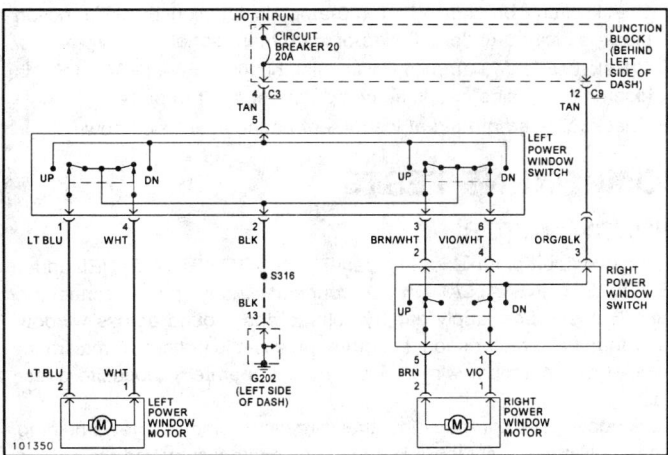

Fig. 14: Power Window System Wiring Diagram (Ram Pickup)

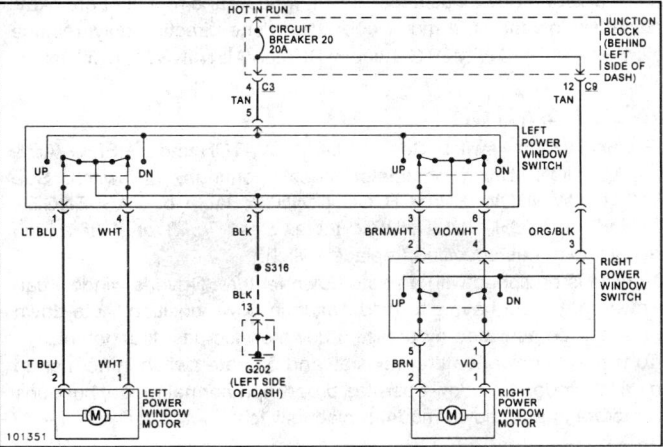

Fig. 15: Power Window System Wiring Diagram (Ram Van & Ram Wagon)

1999 ACCESSORIES & EQUIPMENT
Power Windows – Concorde, Intrepid, LHS & 300M

DESCRIPTION & OPERATION

Power windows are operated by a permanent-magnet electric motor mounted in each door. Driver's power window switch provides ground to each motor. A 20-amp circuit breaker is used to protect circuit. Electric motor operation is changed by reversing electric current flow.

ADJUSTMENTS

FRONT WINDOW

Remove door trim panel. See DOOR TRIM PANEL under REMOVAL & INSTALLATION. Loosen adjustment bolt. *See Fig. 1*. Position glass in weatherstrip to achieve smooth operation. Push glass rearward and apply slight downward pressure on scissor channel. Tighten adjustment bolt. Install door trim panel.

REAR WINDOW

Remove door trim panel. See DOOR TRIM PANEL under REMOVAL & INSTALLATION. Loosen adjustment bolt. *See Fig. 2*. Position glass in weatherstrip to achieve smooth operation. Push window toward rear. Apply slight downward pressure on scissor channel. Tighten adjustment bolt. Install door trim panel.

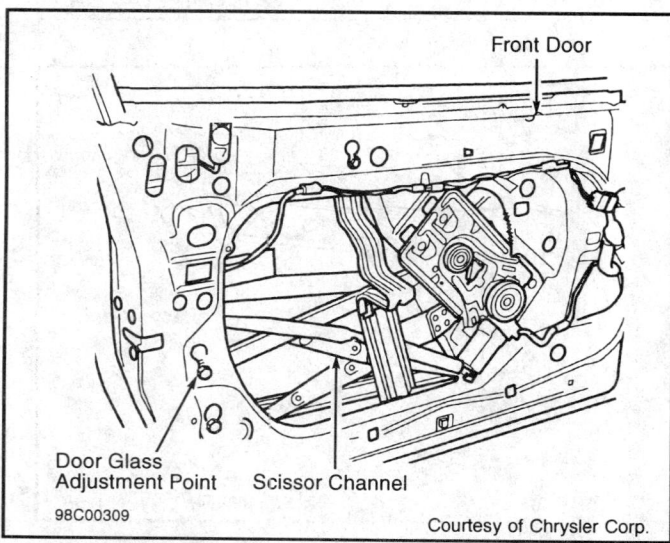

Fig. 1: Adjusting Front Window

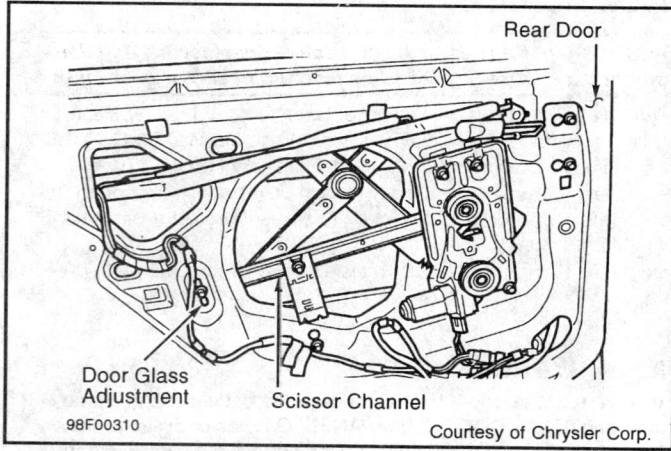

Fig. 2: Adjusting Rear Window

TROUBLESHOOTING

- Check circuit breaker No. 1 (20-amp) in junction block. Junction block is located under left side of instrument panel.
- Check fuse "J" (40-amp) in Power Distribution Center (PDC). PDC is located in left side of engine compartment, next to battery.
- Check for good ground at instrument panel, at left side cowl.

COMPONENT TESTS

WINDOW MOTOR

1) Remove appropriate door trim panel. See DOOR TRIM PANEL under REMOVAL & INSTALLATION. Disconnect window motor connector. Using jumper wires, apply battery voltage and ground across window motor terminals. Motor should operate, unless it is already at maximum travel. Reverse jumper wires. Motor should operate in opposite direction.

2) If window does not move in either direction, remove screws holding glass lift plate to regulator. Slide window up and down by hand to ensure it moves freely in glass channels. Check regulator assembly. Repair window and/or regulator as necessary. If window and regulator are okay, replace window motor. If motor operates in one direction only, replace motor. See WINDOW MOTOR under REMOVAL & INSTALLATION.

WINDOW SWITCH

1) Remove window switch. See WINDOW SWITCH under REMOVAL & INSTALLATION. Using ohmmeter, check continuity of switch. See DRIVER'S WINDOW SWITCH CONTINUITY table or PASSENGER WINDOW SWITCH CONTINUITY table. *See Fig. 3 or 4*. If switch continuity is not as specified, replace switch.

2) Vehicle is equipped with an auto down feature. Driver's window can be lowered without having to hold switch in down position. Auto down feature can be activated by pressing down switch past first detent.

3) To test auto down feature, reinstall and operate switch in normal up and down mode. If window operates properly in normal mode, but does not operate in auto down mode, replace switch.

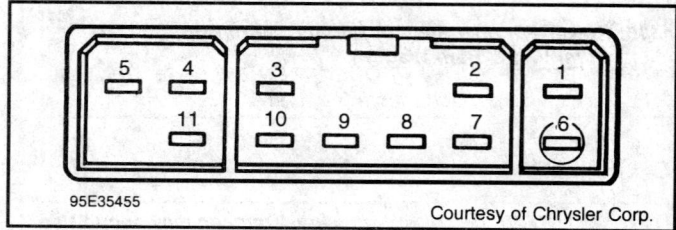

Fig. 3: Identifying Driver's Window Switch Terminals

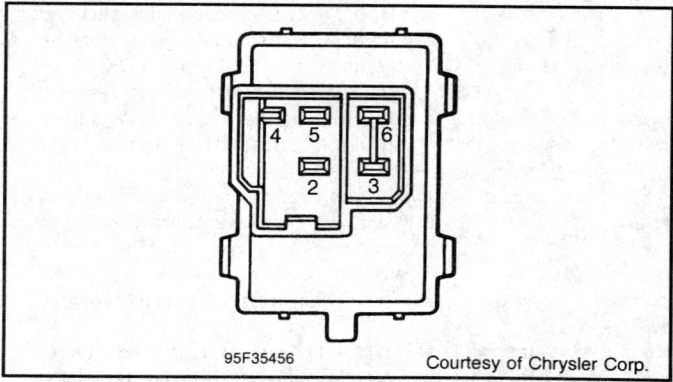

Fig. 4: Identifying Passenger's Window Switch Terminals

1999 ACCESSORIES & EQUIPMENT
Power Windows – Concorde, Intrepid, LHS & 300M (Cont.)

CHRY
4-477

DRIVER'S WINDOW SWITCH CONTINUITY

Switch Position	Continuity Between Terminals
OFF	2 & 8; 3 & 8; 4 & 8; 6 & 8; 7 & 8; 8 & 9; 8 & 10; 8 & 11
Up	
Driver's	5 & 11; 8 & 10
Passenger's	5 & 6; 7 & 8
Left Rear	3 & 8; 4 & 5
Right Rear	2 & 5; 8 & 9
Down	
Driver's	5 & 10; 8 & 11
Passenger's	5 & 7; 6 & 8
Left Rear	3 & 5; 4 & 8
Right Rear	2 & 8; 5 & 9
Window Lock	1 & 5

PASSENGER'S WINDOW SWITCH CONTINUITY

Switch Position	Continuity Between Terminals
Off	2 & 5; 3 & 6
Up	3 & 6; 4 & 5
Down	2 & 5; 3 & 4

SYSTEM TESTS

POWER SUPPLY

Remove driver's door trim panel. See DOOR TRIM PANEL under REMOVAL & INSTALLATION. Disconnect window switch harness connector. Connect positive lead of voltmeter to window switch connector terminal No. 1 (Tan wire). Connect negative lead of voltmeter to terminal No. 10 (Black wire). If battery voltage exists, check window switch. See WINDOW SWITCH under COMPONENT TESTS. If battery voltage does not exist, check circuit breaker No. 1 in junction block. If circuit breaker is okay, repair open circuit.

REMOVAL & INSTALLATION

CAUTION: When battery is disconnected, vehicle computer and memory systems may lose memory data. Driveability problems may exist until computer systems have completed a relearn cycle. See COMPUTER RELEARN PROCEDURES article in GENERAL INFORMATION before disconnecting battery.

DOOR TRIM PANEL

CAUTION: DO NOT pry on door trim panel. Damage may occur. Use trim tool.

Removal & Installation (Front Door) – 1) Disengage clips securing front of door speaker grille to trim panel, and separate grille. Remove screws securing trim panel to door from inside speaker opening.
2) Remove screws from bottom of door. Remove door pull cup. Remove screw securing trim panel to door from behind inside latch handle. Remove remaining screws. Using trim tool, disengage clips securing door trim panel to door.
3) Lift trim panel upward to disengage channel retainer at top of trim and tilt panel outward. Disconnect all wiring harness connectors. Disengage clip holding linkage rod to inside latch handle.
4) Lift trim panel upward to disengage hook retainers at bottom of panel. Disconnect remaining harness connector clips. To install, reverse removal procedure.
Removal & Installation (Rear Door) – 1) Remove door handle bezel. Remove screw behind bezel. Remove pull cup. Remove remaining screws. Using trim tool, disengage clips securing door trim panel to door.
2) Lift trim panel upward to disengage channel retainer at top of trim and tilt panel outward. Disengage clip holding linkage rod to inside latch handle and separate rod from handle. Remove trim panel from door. To install, reverse removal procedure.

WINDOW REGULATOR

Removal & Installation – 1) Remove door trim panel. See DOOR TRIM PANEL. Remove door cup support bracket. Disconnect window from regulator. See Fig. 5 or 6. Disconnect window motor harness connector. Loosen all bolts connecting regulator to door. Slide regulator free from door and rotate regulator out of access hole in door.
2) To install regulator, reverse removal procedure. Align window. See ADJUSTMENTS.

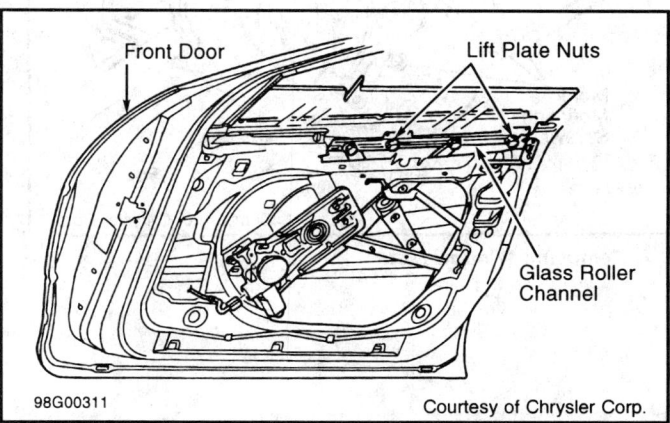

Fig. 5: Disconnecting Front Window

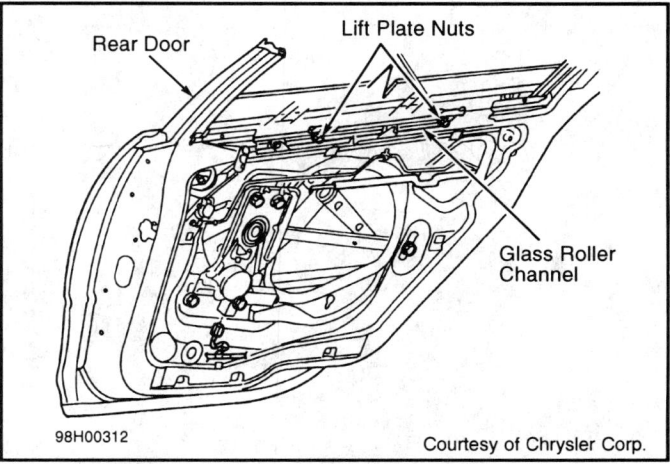

Fig. 6: Disconnecting Rear Window

WINDOW MOTOR

WARNING: Keep fingers clear of sector gear teeth. Regulator movement may cause fingers to be pinched in sector gear teeth.

Removal & Installation – 1) Raise window to full-up position, if possible. Disconnect battery. Remove door trim panel. See DOOR TRIM PANEL. Remove window regulator. See WINDOW REGULATOR.
2) Disconnect wire connector from motor. Using a "C" clamp, clamp sector gear to regulator mounting plate to prevent regulator movement. See Fig. 7.
3) Remove motor from regulator. To install, reverse removal procedure. Tighten motor mounting screws to 50-70 INCH lbs. (5.6-8.0 N.m). Adjust window alignment, if necessary. See ADJUSTMENTS.

WINDOW SWITCH

Removal & Installation – Disconnect negative battery cable. Remove door trim panel. See DOOR TRIM PANEL. On master switch, remove switch screws and switch. On passenger's switch, remove switch from bezel. On all switches, disconnect connector. To install, reverse removal procedure.

CHRY
4-478

1999 ACCESSORIES & EQUIPMENT
Power Windows – Concorde, Intrepid, LHS & 300M (Cont.)

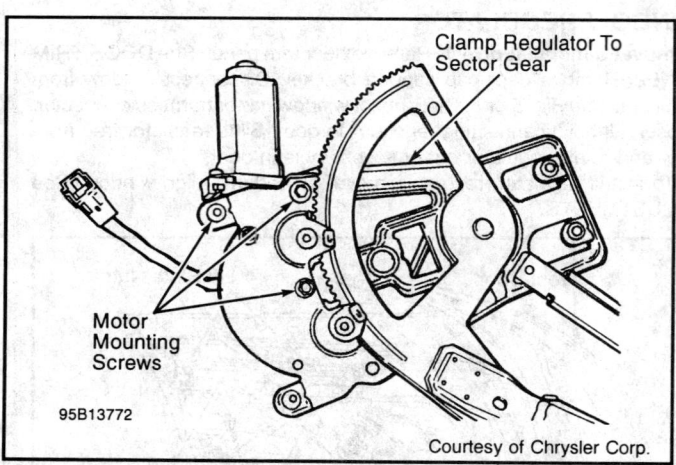

Clamp Regulator To
Sector Gear

Motor
Mounting
Screws

95B13772

Courtesy of Chrysler Corp.

Fig. 7: Removing Window Motor

1999 ACCESSORIES & EQUIPMENT
Power Windows – Concorde, Intrepid, LHS & 300M (Cont.)

CHRY
4-479

WIRING DIAGRAMS

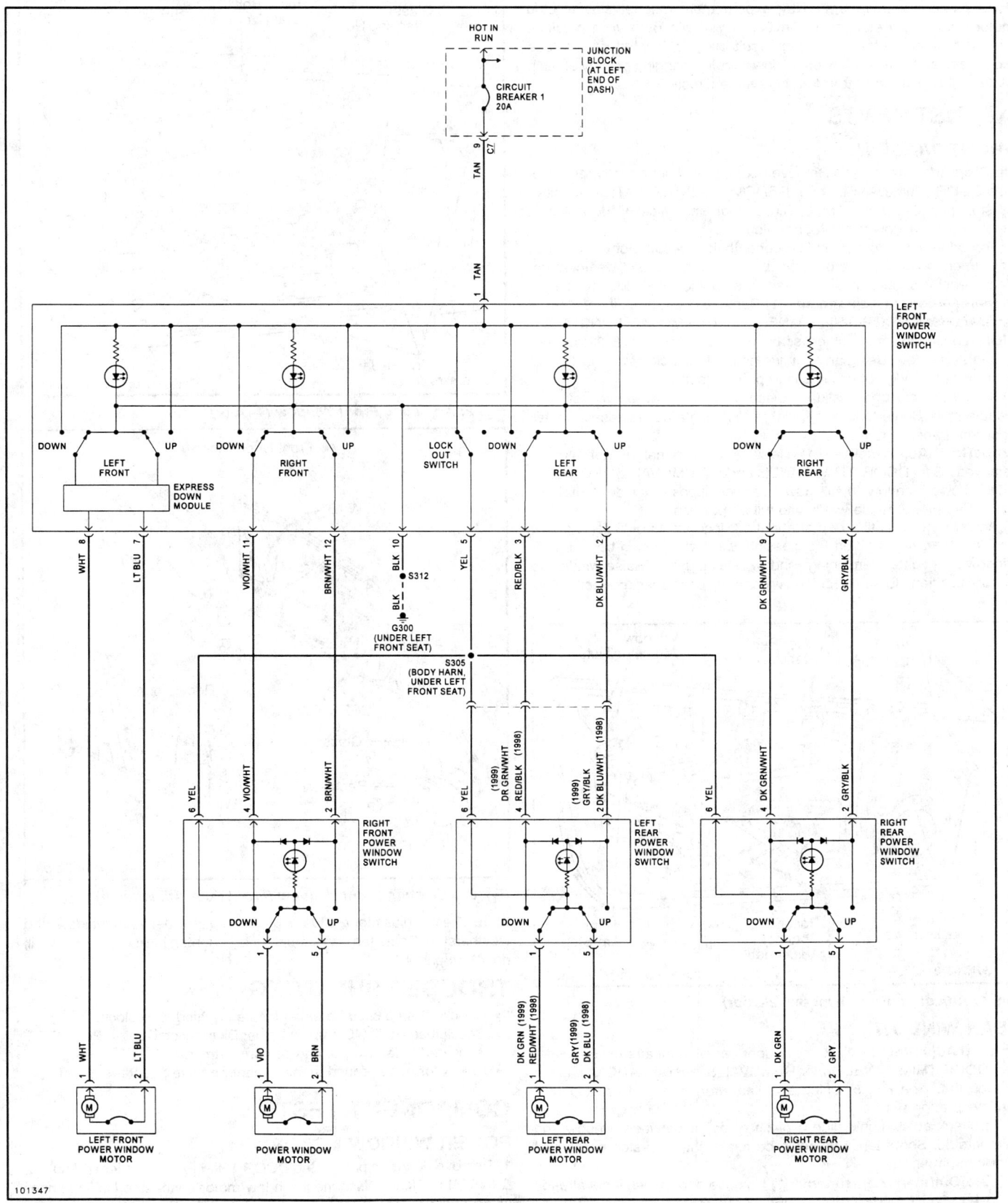

Fig. 8: Power Window System Wiring Diagram (Concorde, Intrepid, LHS & 300M)

DESCRIPTION & OPERATION

Power windows are operated by a permanent magnet type electric motor mounted in each door. Driver's power window switch provides ground to each motor. A 30-amp circuit breaker, located behind fuse block, is used to protect power window circuit. Changing polarity at each motor will cause motor to rotate in reverse direction.

ADJUSTMENTS

FRONT WINDOW

Up-Stop Adjustment – 1) Remove door panel, if not already removed. See DOOR TRIM PANEL under REMOVAL & INSTALLATION. Loosen up-stop nut. *See Fig. 1 or 2*. Close door and raise window. Adjust up-stop until window is at proper height.

2) Top edge of window should be beneath lip of weatherstrip. To check adjustment, slide a piece of paper between window and weatherstrip. Some tension should be felt. Tighten up-stop nut. Install door trim panel.

Inboard/Outboard Adjustment – 1) Remove door panel, if not already removed. See DOOR TRIM PANEL under REMOVAL & INSTALLATION. Loosen lower in/out jackscrew nuts. *See Fig. 1 or 2*. Close door and raise window. Using an Allen wrench, rotate jackscrews until in/out position at top edge of window is at proper position.

2) To check adjustment, slide a piece of paper between window and weatherstrip. Some tension should be felt. Tighten all fasteners. Install door trim panel.

Front/Rear Adjustment – 1) Remove door panel, if not already removed. See DOOR TRIM PANEL under REMOVAL & INSTALLATION. Lower window to full down position. Loosen window retaining bolts. *See Fig. 3*. Raise window to full up position.

2) Adjust window until a gap of about 1/2 inch exists between window and "B" pillar trim. Tighten 2 accessible window retaining bolts. Lower window and tighten remaining window retaining bolt. Raise window to full up position. Ensure front of window is positioned correctly. *See Fig. 4*.

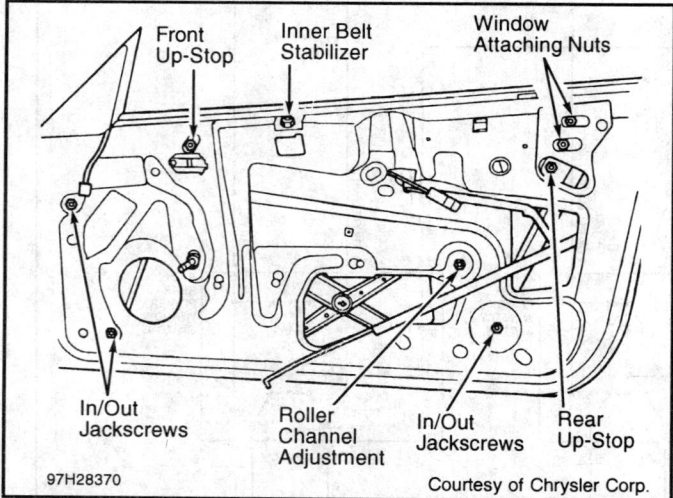

Fig. 1: Adjusting Front Window (2-Door)

REAR WINDOW

Up-Stop Adjustment – 1) Remove door panel, if not already removed. See DOOR TRIM PANEL under REMOVAL & INSTALLATION. Loosen up-stop nut. *See Fig. 5*. Using an Allen wrench, adjust up-stop until window is at proper height.

2) To check adjustment, slide a piece of paper between window and weatherstrip. Some tension should be felt. Tighten up-stop nut. Install door trim panel.

Inboard/Outboard Adjustment – 1) Remove door panel, if not already removed. See DOOR TRIM PANEL under REMOVAL & INSTALLATION. Loosen lower jackscrew nut. *See Fig. 5*. Using an Allen wrench, rotate jackscrew until in/out position at top edge of window is at proper position.

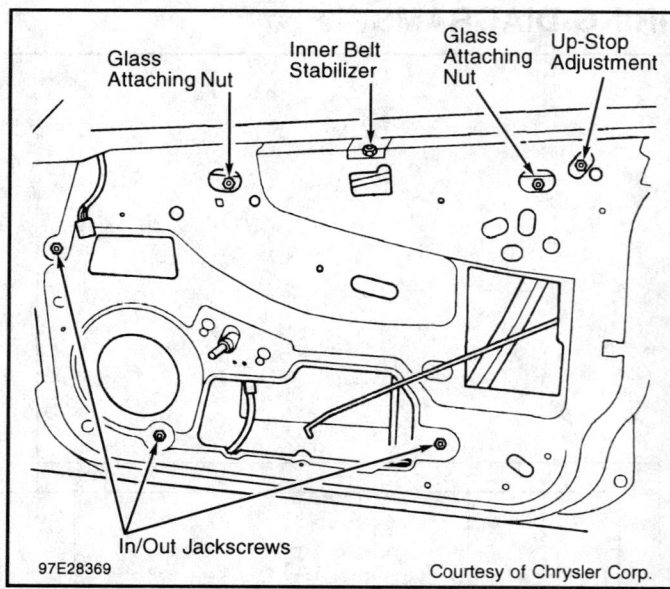

Fig. 2: Adjusting Front Window (4-Door)

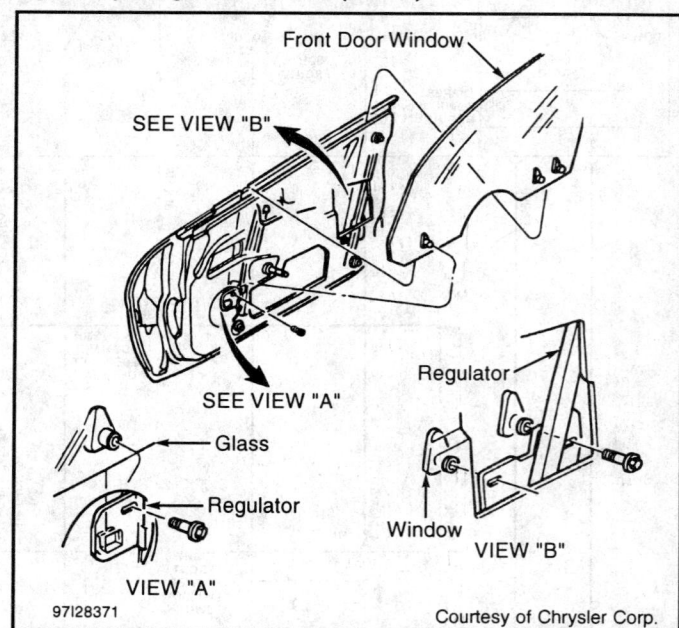

Fig. 3: Adjusting Front Window (Front/Rear Adjustment)

2) To check adjustment, slide a piece of paper between window and weatherstrip. Some tension should be felt. Tighten jackscrew nut. Install door trim panel.

TROUBLE SHOOTING

- Check 30-amp circuit breaker located behind fuse block.
- Check fuse No. 2 (40-amp) in Power Distribution Center (PDC). PDC is located in left side of engine compartment.
- Check for good ground at instrument panel left center support.

COMPONENT TESTS

POWER WINDOW MOTOR

1) Remove door trim panel. See DOOR TRIM PANEL under REMOVAL & INSTALLATION. Disconnect window motor connector. Using jumper wires, apply battery voltage to one window motor terminal and ground to other terminal. Motor should operate, unless window is already at maximum travel. Reverse jumper wires. Window should move in opposite direction.

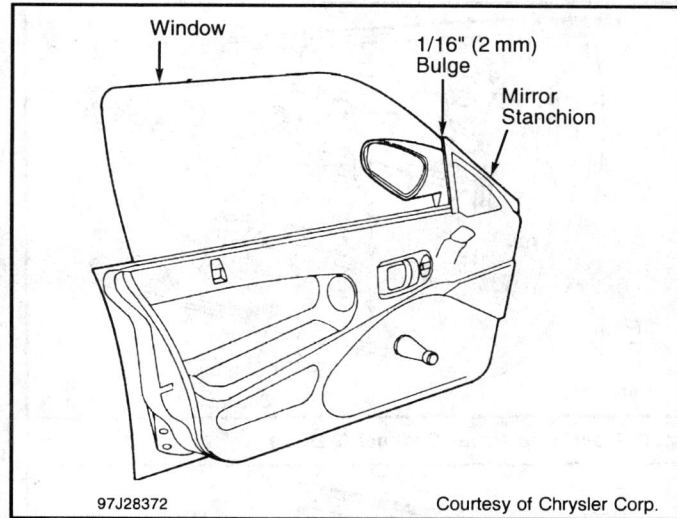

Fig. 4: Identifying Proper Front Window Position

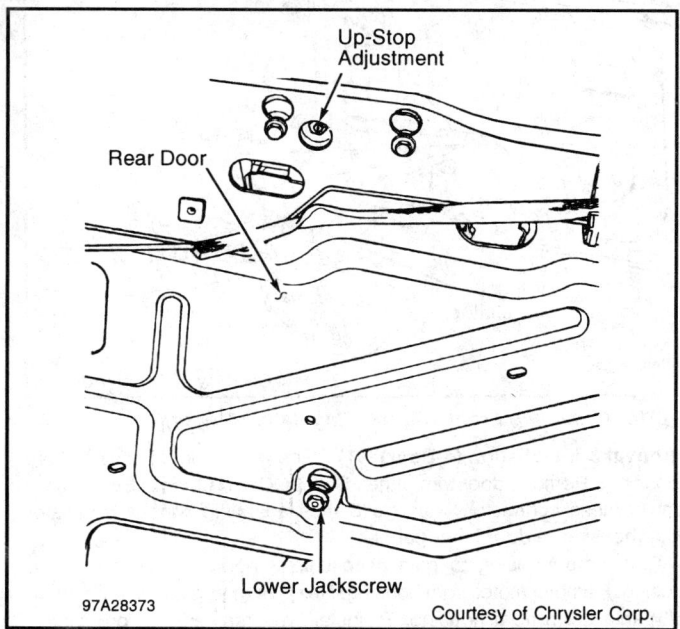

Fig. 5: Adjusting Rear Window

2) If window does not move in either direction, check window/regulator for freedom of movement. Remove screws holding glass lift plate to regulator. Slide window up and down by hand to ensure it moves freely in glass channels. If window slides freely, check regulator assembly. Repair window/regulator as necessary. If window slides freely and window/regulator is okay, replace window motor.

POWER WINDOW SWITCH

Remove power window switch. Using an ohmmeter, check continuity between appropriate switch terminals. See DRIVER'S WINDOW SWITCH CONTINUITY table or PASSENGER'S SWITCH CONTINUITY table. *See Fig. 6 or 7.* If continuity is not as specified, replace power window switch.

DRIVER'S WINDOW SWITCH CONTINUITY

Switch Position	Continuity Between Terminals
Off	1 & 2; 1 & 4; 1 & 5; 1 & 6; 2 & 4; 2 & 5; 2 & 6; 4 & 5; 4 & 6; 5 & 6
Up	
Driver's	1 & 3; 2 & 4
Passenger's	3 & 5; 4 & 6
Down	
Driver's	1 & 4; 2 & 3
Passenger's	3 & 6; 4 & 5

PASSENGER'S WINDOW SWITCH CONTINUITY

Switch Position	Continuity Between Terminals
Off	2 & 5; 1 & 4
Up	1 & 4; 3 & 5
Down	1 & 3; 2 & 5

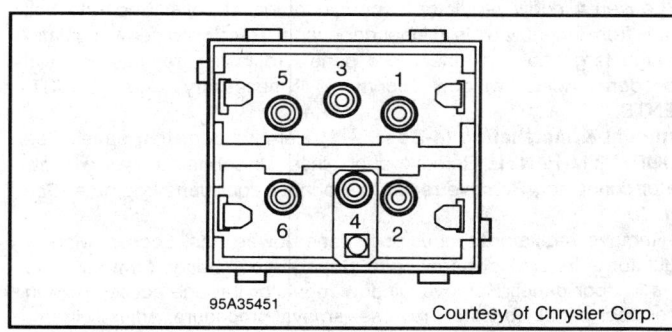

Fig. 6: Identifying Driver's Window Switch Terminals

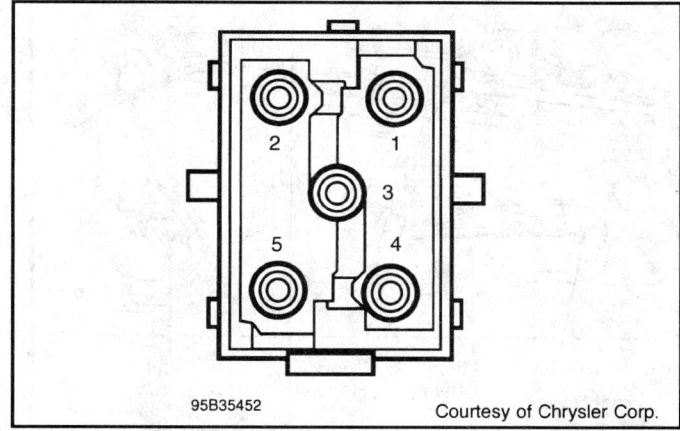

Fig. 7: Identifying Passenger's Window Switch Terminals

SYSTEM TESTS

CIRCUIT WIRING

Remove inoperative window switch. Turn ignition on. Using voltmeter, check voltage across harness connector terminal No. 4 (positive lead) and No. 3 (negative lead). If battery voltage exists, check switch. See POWER WINDOW SWITCH under COMPONENT TESTS. If battery voltage does not exist, check 30 amp circuit breaker behind fuse block. Check wiring and ground. See WIRING DIAGRAMS.

REMOVAL & INSTALLATION

DOOR TRIM PANEL

Removal & Installation – 1) Open door. Lower door glass. Remove door pull cup. While pulling door release handle, remove screw securing trim panel to door from behind inside door release handle.

2) Disengage hidden clips securing trim panel to door from around perimeter of panel. Tilt trim panel outward to clear locator pins on backside of panel. Disengage trim panel from retainer channel at top of door.

3) Move trim panel away from door and disengage clip holding door latch linkage to back of inside door handle. Separate latch rod from handle. Disconnect harness connectors for power door lock switch, mirror switch and power window switch. Remove trim panel from vehicle. To install, reverse removal procedure.

WINDOW REGULATOR

Removal & Installation (2-Door) – 1) Remove door trim panel. See DOOR TRIM PANEL. Disconnect power window motor connector. Remove regulator lift channel-to-window nuts. *See Fig. 8.* Secure window in up position.

2) Mark position of rear bolt of roller channel-to-inner door panel for installation reference, and remove bolt. *See Fig. 9.* Loosen front roller channel bolt. Separate roller channel from door panel.

3) Loosen window regulator-to-inner door panel bolts. Separate bolt heads from key-hole slots in inner door panel. Remove window regulator through large hole in inner door panel. To install, reverse removal procedure. Adjust window alignment, if necessary. See ADJUST-MENTS.

Removal & Installation (4-Door) – 1) Remove door trim panel. See DOOR TRIM PANEL. Remove door glass. Disconnect power window motor connector. Remove regulator- to-inner door panel top nuts. *See Fig. 10.*

2) Remove regulator-to-inner door panel lower nuts. Loosen window regulator-to-inner door panel bolts. Separate bolt heads from key-hole slots in door panel. Remove window regulator through access hole in inner door panel. To install, reverse removal procedure. Adjust window alignment, if necessary. See ADJUSTMENTS.

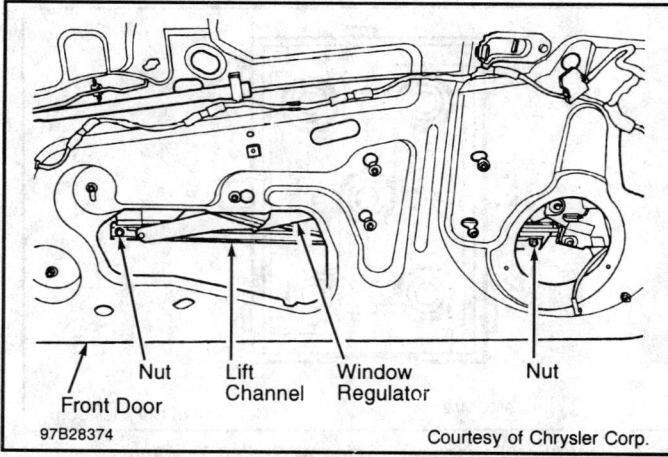

Fig. 8: Identifying Regulator Lift Channel (2-Door)

WINDOW MOTOR

WARNING: Keep fingers clear of sector gear teeth. Regulator movement may cause fingers to be pinched in sector gear teeth.

Removal (2-Door) – 1) Raise window to full-up position, if possible. Remove door trim panel. See DOOR TRIM PANEL. Remove window regulator. See WINDOW REGULATOR. Disconnect power window motor connector.

2) Using a "C" clamp, clamp sector gear to regulator mounting plate to prevent regulator movement. *See Fig. 11.* Remove 3 power window motor mounting bolts. Remove motor from regulator.

Installation – 1) Install motor on regulator so motor engages sector gear teeth. Rotate motor as necessary to align 3 motor mounting bolts. Tighten motor mounting bolts to 50-70 INCH lbs. (5.6-8.0 N.m).

2) Using window switch, test window motor operation. To complete installation, reverse removal procedure. Adjust window alignment, if necessary. See ADJUSTMENTS.

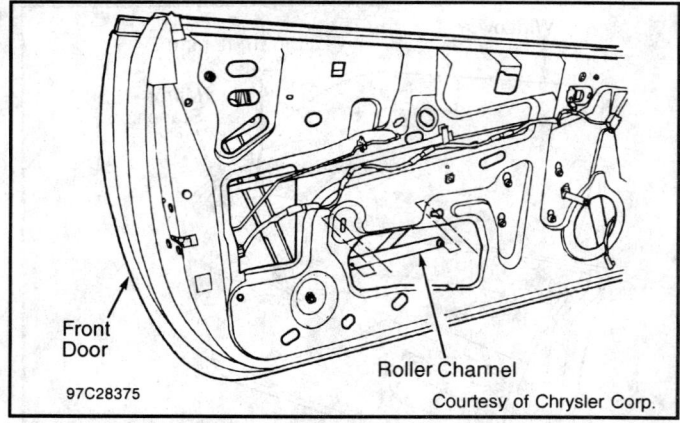

Fig. 9: Identifying Roller Channel (2-Door)

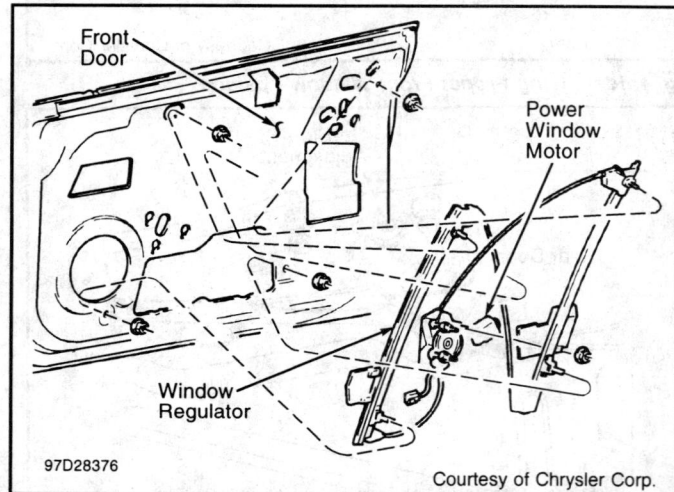

Fig. 10: Removing Front Window Regulator (4-Door)

Removal & Installation (4-Door) – 1) Place window in middle position, if possible. Remove door trim panel. See DOOR TRIM PANEL. Disconnect harness connector. Remove 3 nuts attaching window regulator motor/housing to door inner panel.

2) Turn motor/housing to gain access to 3 nuts attaching motor to housing. Remove motor from housing. Remove motor, taking care not to pull cable drum from housing. To install, reverse removal procedure. Adjust window alignment, if necessary. See ADJUSTMENTS.

WINDOW SWITCH

Removal & Installation – Insert flat bladed screwdriver into slot on bottom of switch bezel. Pry bezel from door trim panel. Disconnect switch connector. Remove switch by releasing tabs from bezel. To install, reverse removal procedure.

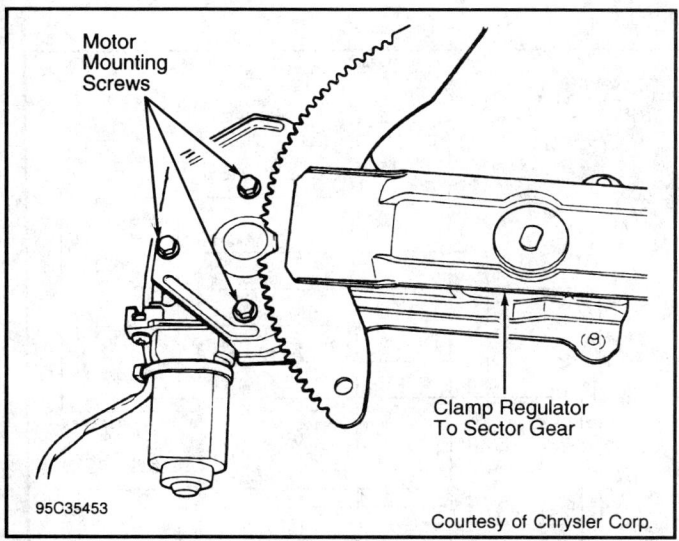

Fig. 11: Removing Window Motor

WIRING DIAGRAMS

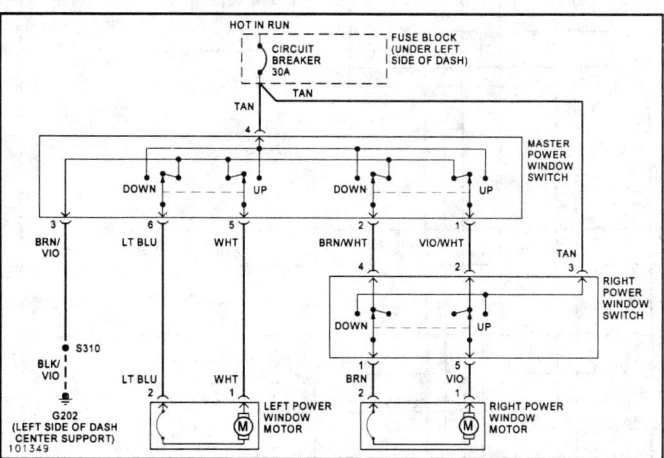

Fig. 12: Power Window System Wiring Diagram (Neon)

1999 ACCESSORIES & EQUIPMENT
Remote Keyless Entry Systems

WIRING DIAGRAMS

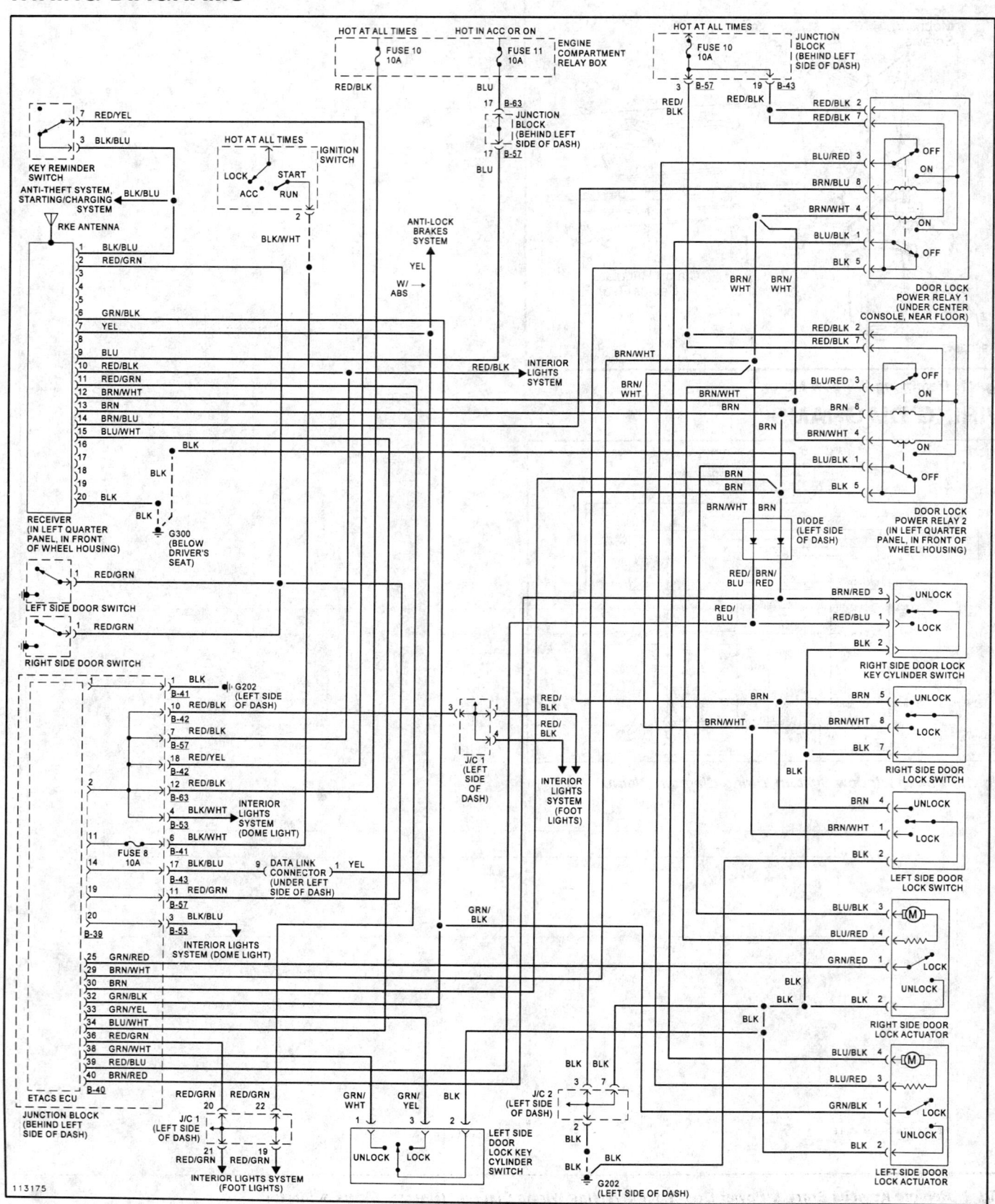

Fig. 1: Remote Keyless Entry & Power Door Lock Systems Wiring Diagram (Avenger & Sebring Coupe)

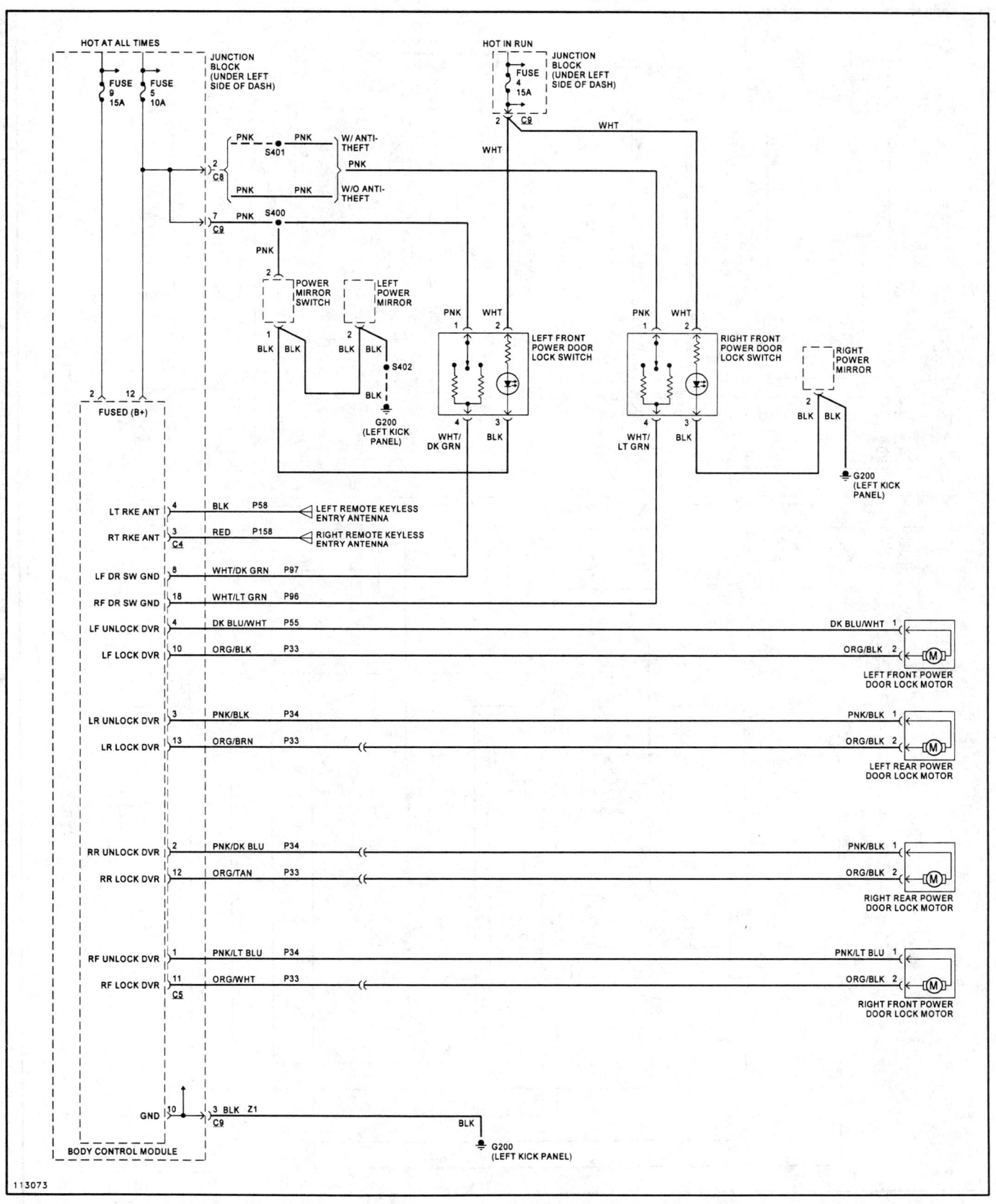

Fig. 2: Remote Keyless Entry & Power Door Lock Systems Wiring Diagram (Breeze, Cirrus & Stratus)

113073

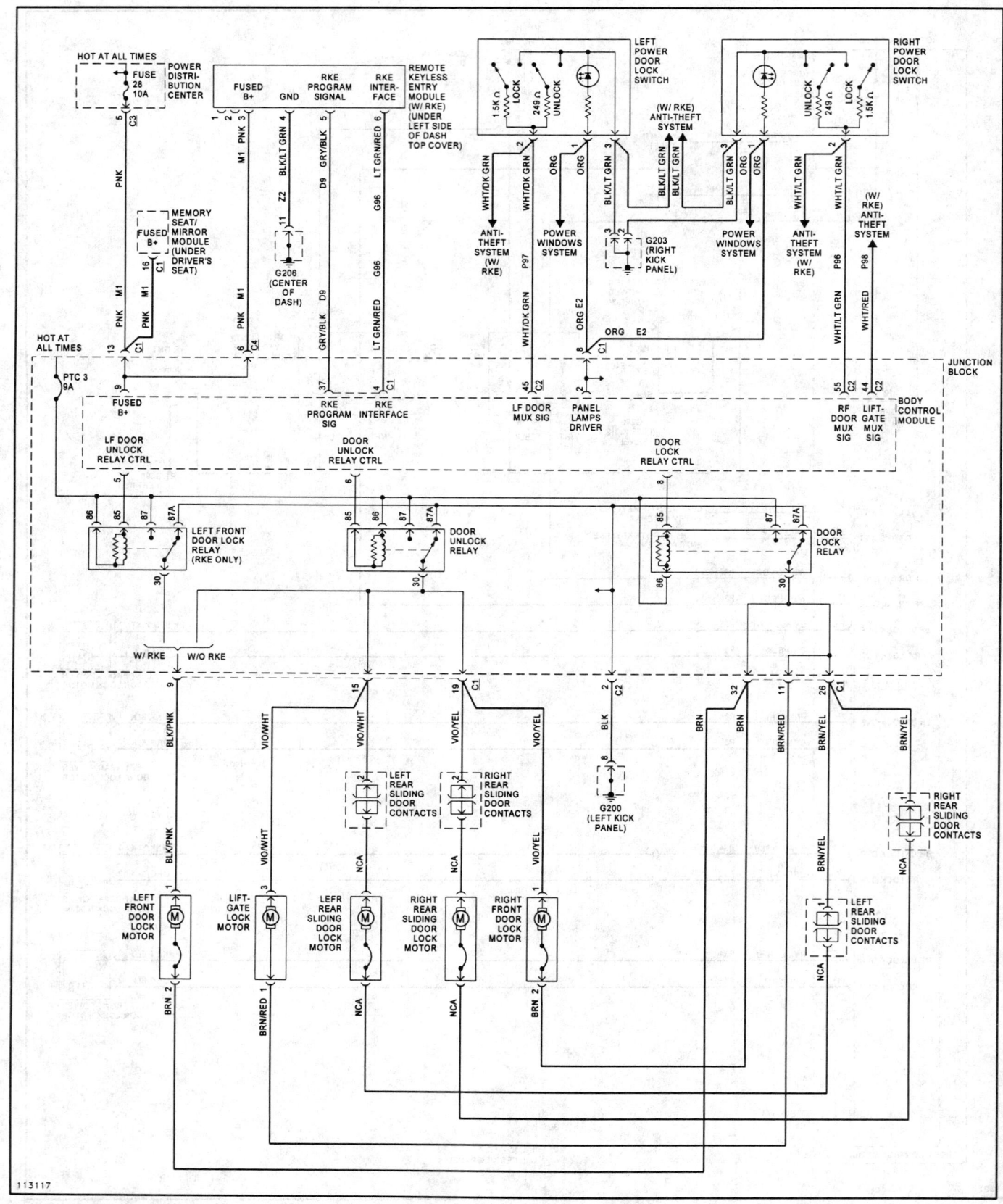

Fig. 3: Remote Keyless Entry & Power Door Lock Systems Wiring Diagram (Caravan, Town & Country, & Voyager)

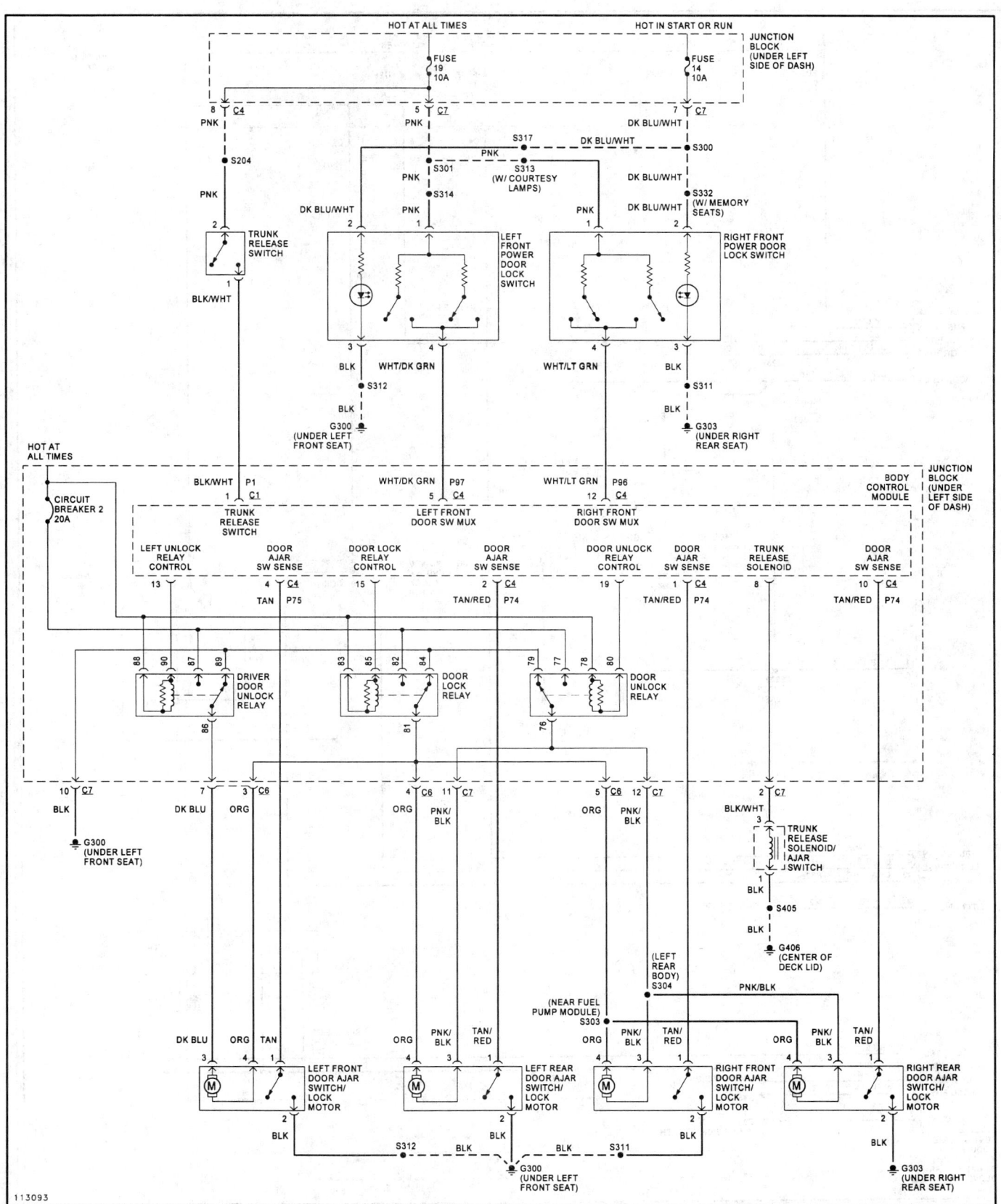

Fig. 4: Remote Keyless Entry & Power Door Lock Systems Wiring Diagram (Concorde, Intrepid, LHS & 300M)

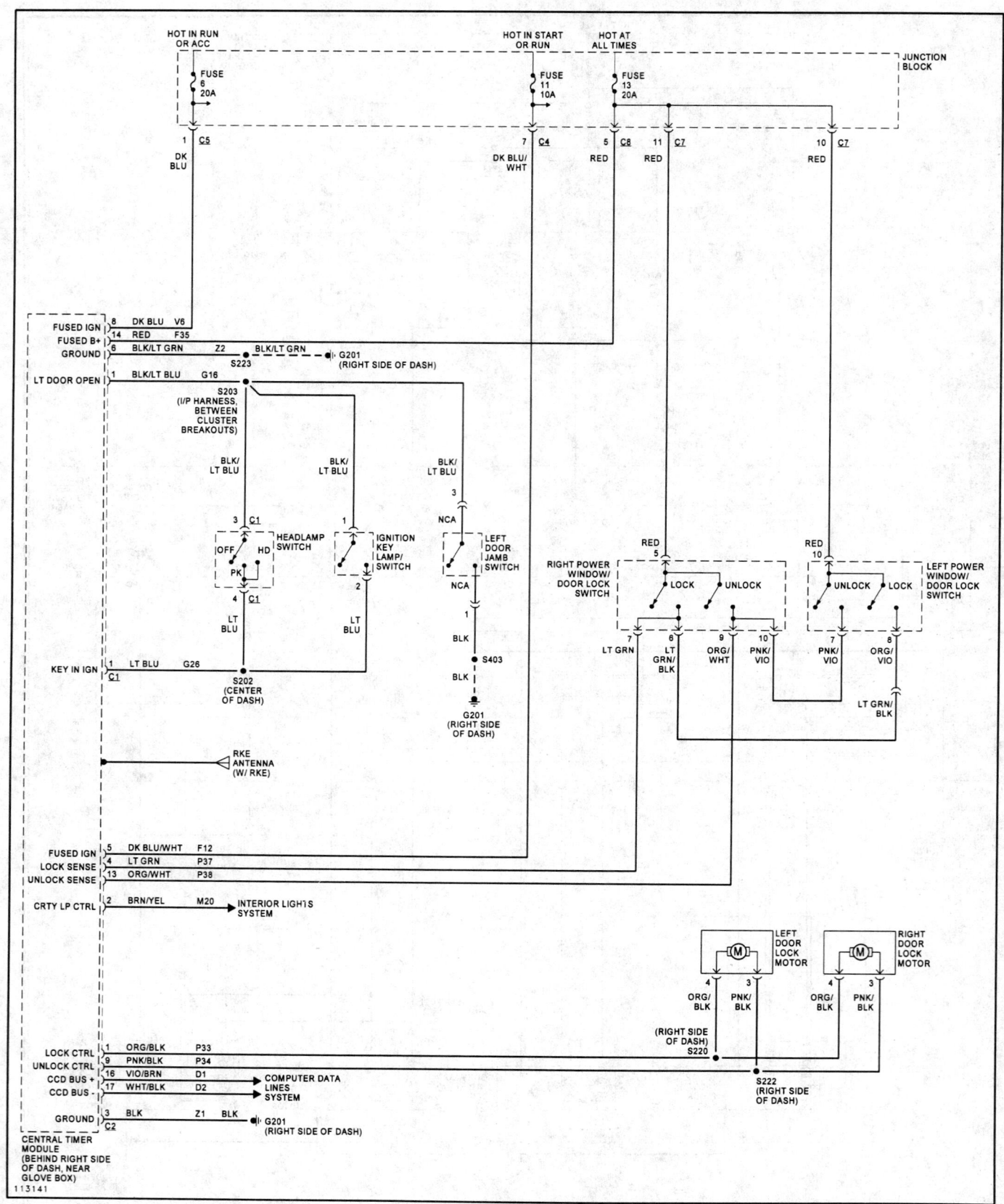

Fig. 5: Remote Keyless Entry & Power Door Lock Systems Wiring Diagram (Dakota)

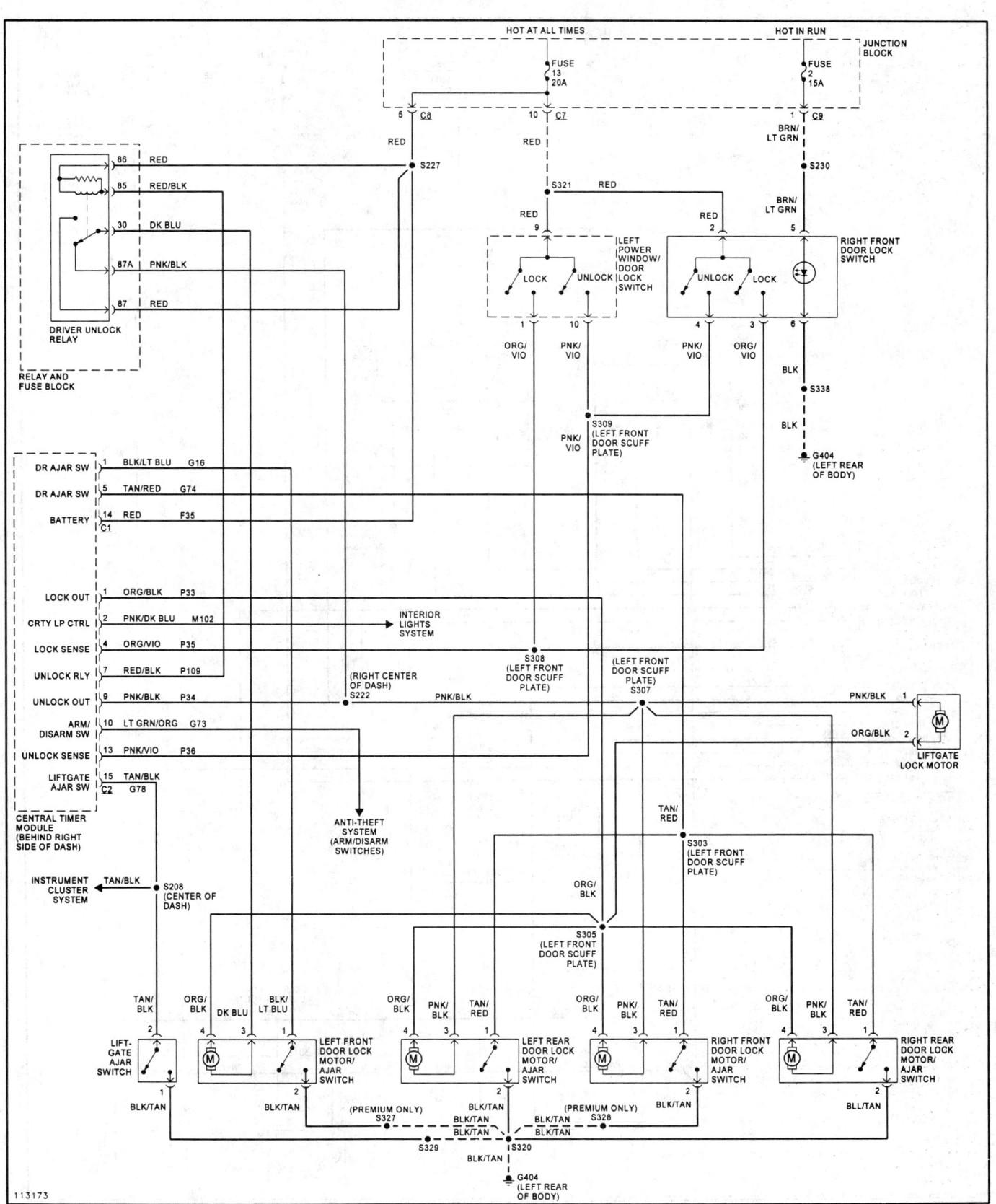

Fig. 6: Remote Keyless Entry & Power Door Lock Systems Wiring Diagram (Durango)

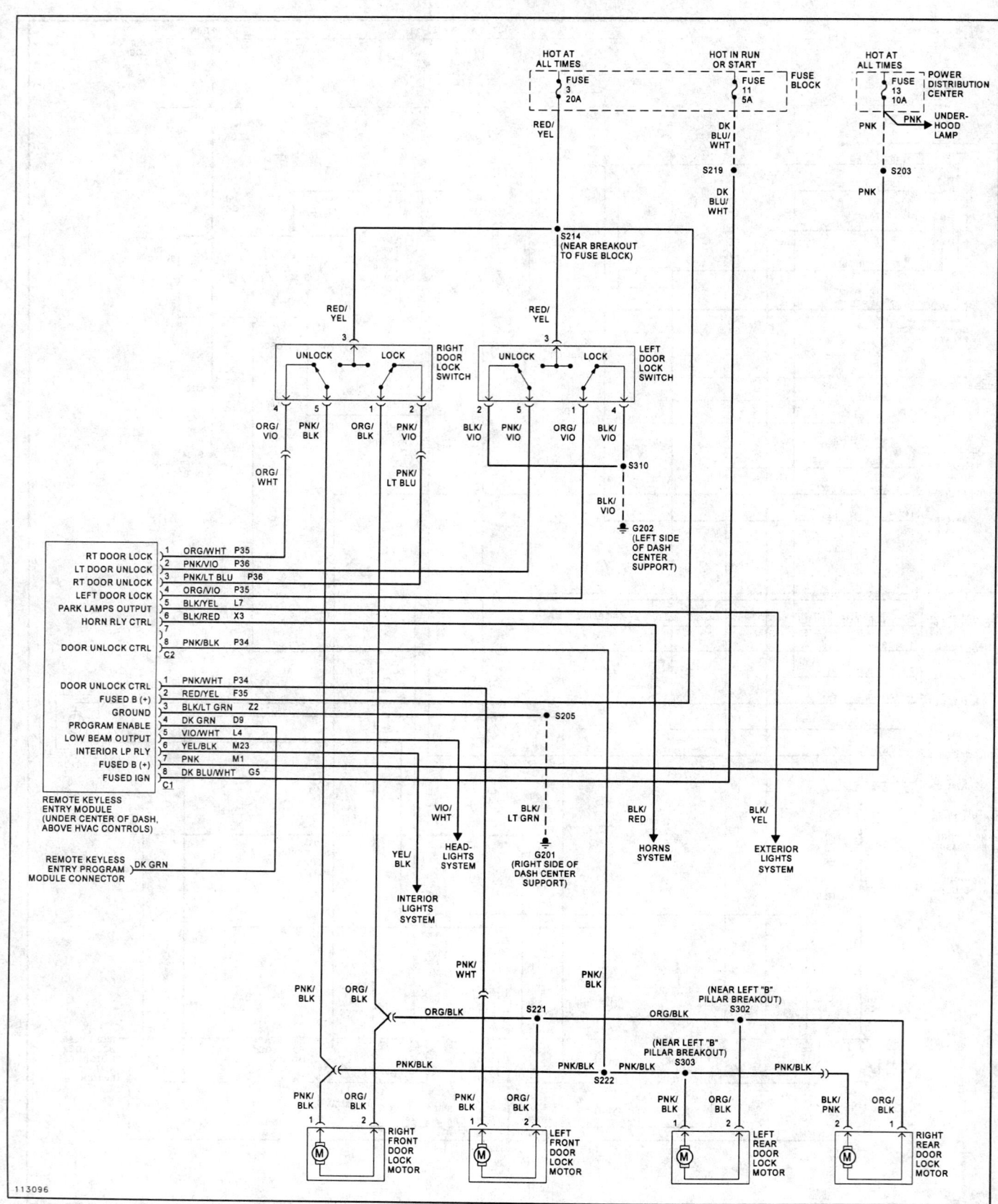

Fig. 7: Remote Keyless Entry & Power Door Lock Systems Wiring Diagram (Neon)

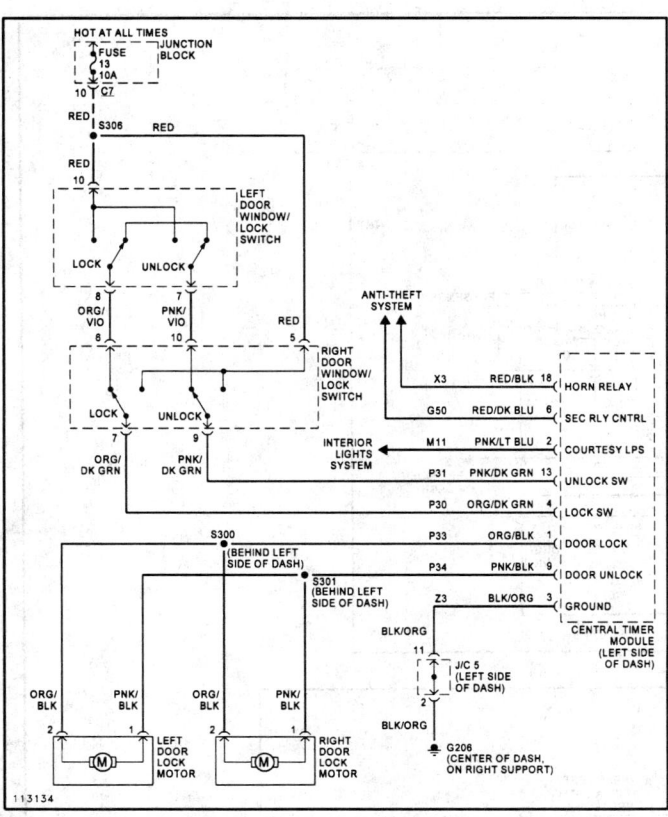

Fig. 8: Remote Keyless Entry & Power Door Lock Systems Wiring Diagram (Ram Pickup)

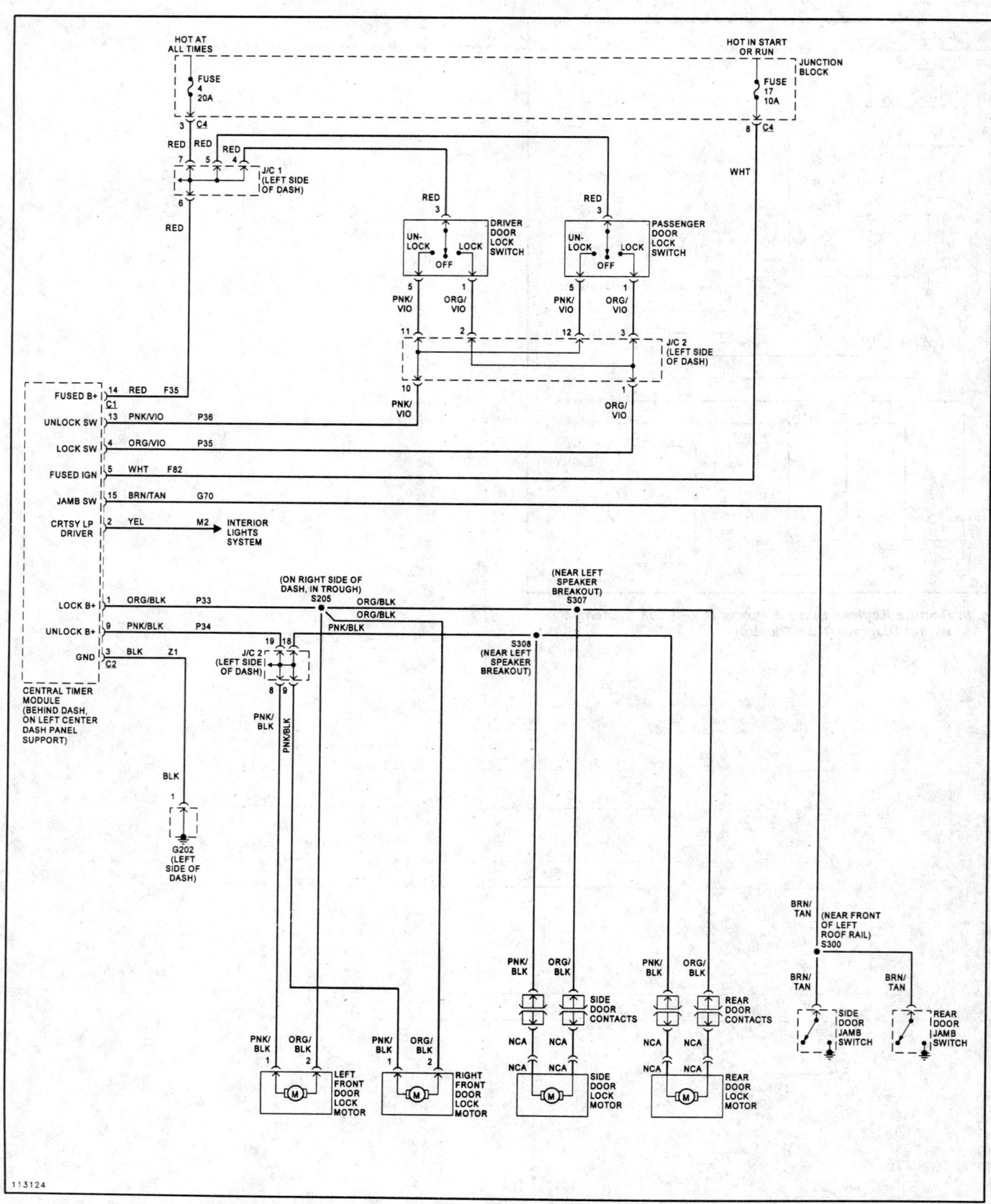

Fig. 9: Remote Keyless Entry & Power Door Lock Systems Wiring Diagram (Ram Van & Ram Wagon)

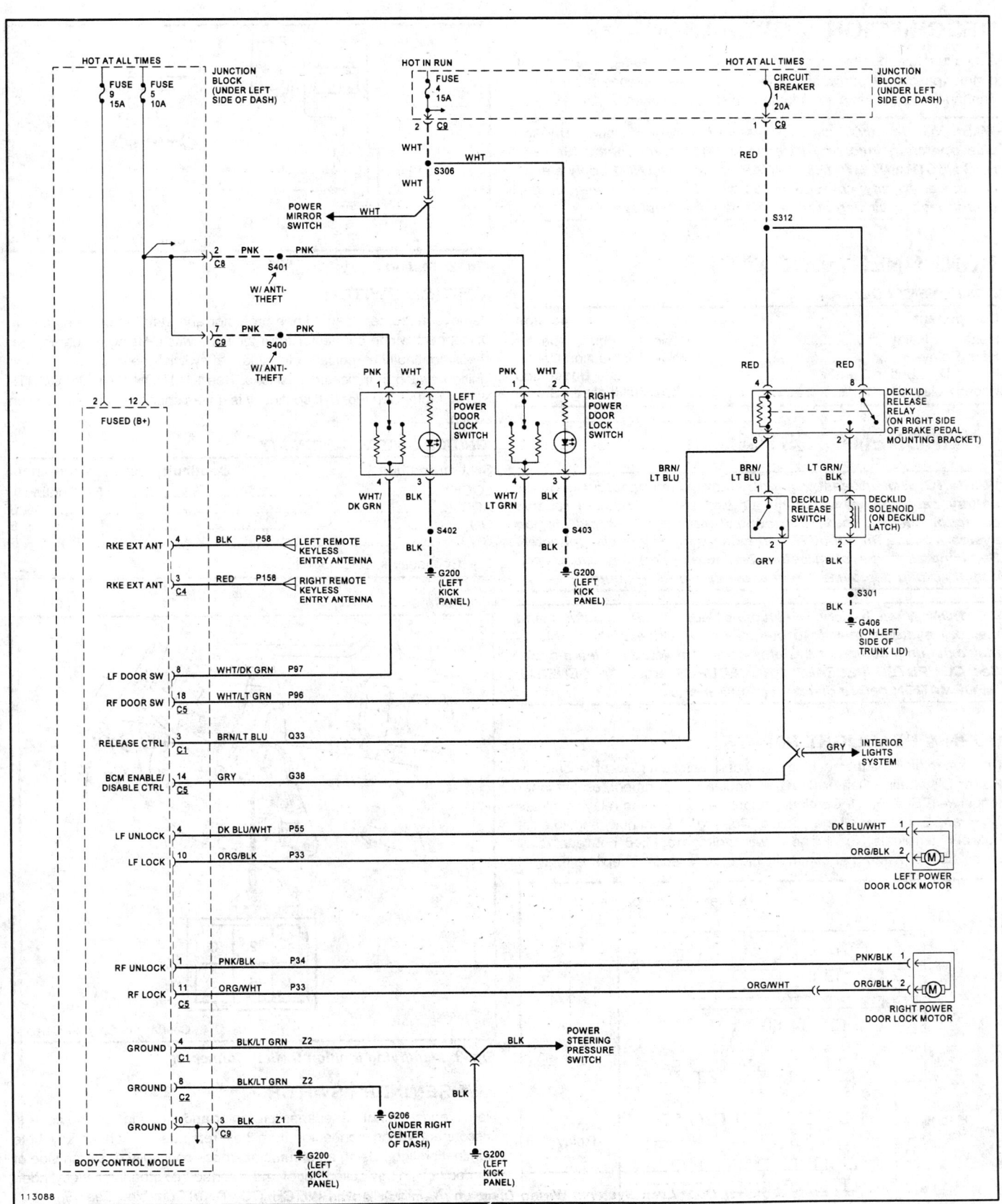

Fig. 10: Remote Keyless Entry & Power Door Lock Systems Wiring Diagram (Sebring Convertible)

113088

1999 ACCESSORIES & EQUIPMENT
Steering Column Switches
Avenger & Sebring Coupe

DESCRIPTION & OPERATION

A multifunction (combination) switch incorporates headlight, turn signal, dimmer/passing, wiper/washer and cruise control switches into one unit. The ignition switch is also mounted on steering column.

WARNING: Deactivate air bag system before performing any service operation involving steering column components. See AIR BAG RESTRAINT SYSTEMS – CARS article. DO NOT apply electrical power to any component on steering column without first disconnecting air bag module. Air bag may deploy.

COMPONENT LOCATIONS

COMPONENT LOCATIONS

Component	Location
Headlight Relay	Power Distribution Center
Horn Relay	Power Distribution Center
Power Distribution Center	Underhood
Wiper Relay	On Multifunction Switch

COMPONENT TESTS

WARNING: Wait at least 2 minutes after disconnecting negative battery cable before servicing air bag system. System reserve capacitor, integral to air bag control module, maintains air bag system voltage for about 2 minutes after battery is disconnected. Servicing air bag system before 2-minute period may cause accidental air bag deployment and possible personal injury.

CAUTION: When battery is disconnected, vehicle computer and memory systems may lose memory data. Driveability problems may exist until computer systems have completed a relearn cycle. See COMPUTER RELEARN PROCEDURES article in GENERAL INFORMATION before disconnecting battery.

HORN & HEADLIGHT RELAYS

Remove relay to be tested. Horn relay and headlight relay are located in Power Distribution Center (PDC) in engine compartment, on left inner fenderwell. *See Fig. 1.* Continuity should exist between relay terminals No. 1 and 3 without voltage applied. *See Fig. 2.* Continuity should exist between terminals No. 4 and 5 wtih voltage applied between relay terminals No. 1 and 3. If continuity is not as specified, replace relay.

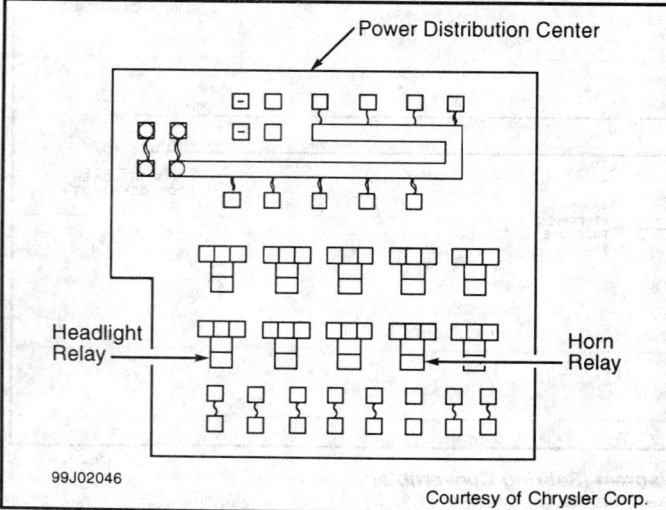

Fig. 1: Identifying Relay Locations

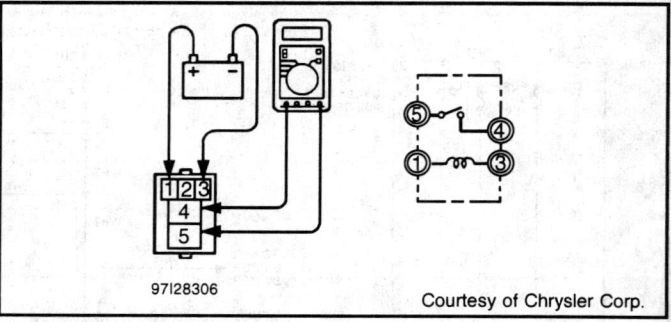

Fig. 2: Testing Relay

IGNITION SWITCH

Remove instrument panel knee protector and steering column covers. Disconnect wiring connector from ignition switch. Using an ohmmeter, check continuity at indicated terminals at switch side of connector with ignition switch in indicated positions. See IGNITION SWITCH CONTINUITY table. *See Fig. 3.* If continuity is not as specified, replace ignition switch.

IGNITION SWITCH CONTINUITY

Switch Position	Continuity Between Terminals
LOCK	[1] No Continuity
ACC	1 & 6
ON	1, 2, 4 & 6
START	1, 2, 3 & 5

[1] – Continuity should not exist.

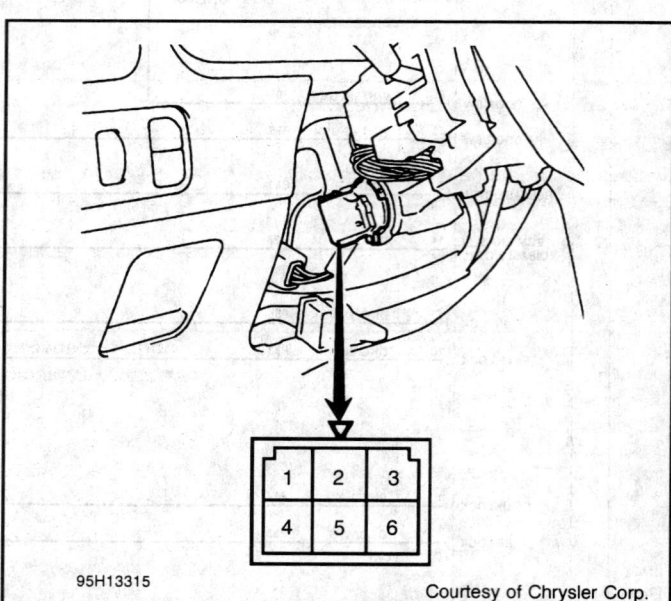

Fig. 3: Identifying Ignition Switch Connector

KEY REMINDER SWITCH

Remove instrument panel knee protector and steering column covers. Disconnect wiring connector from key reminder switch or key hole illumination light. Using an ohmmeter, check continuity at switch side of connector with key pulled out of and inserted into steering lock cylinder. See KEY REMINDER SWITCH CONTINUITY table. *See Fig. 4.* If continuity is not as specified, replace key reminder switch.

1999 ACCESSORIES & EQUIPMENT
Steering Column Switches
Avenger & Sebring Coupe (Cont.)

CHRY
4-495

KEY REMINDER SWITCH CONTINUITY

Key Position	Continuity Between Terminals
Removed	
Key Reminder Switch	[1] 4 & 6
Key Hole Illumination	1 & 2
Inserted	
Key Reminder Switch	[2]
Key Hole Illumination	1 & 2

[1] – On vehicles with anti-theft system, continuity should also exist between terminals No. 3 and 7.
[2] – Continuity shold not exist.

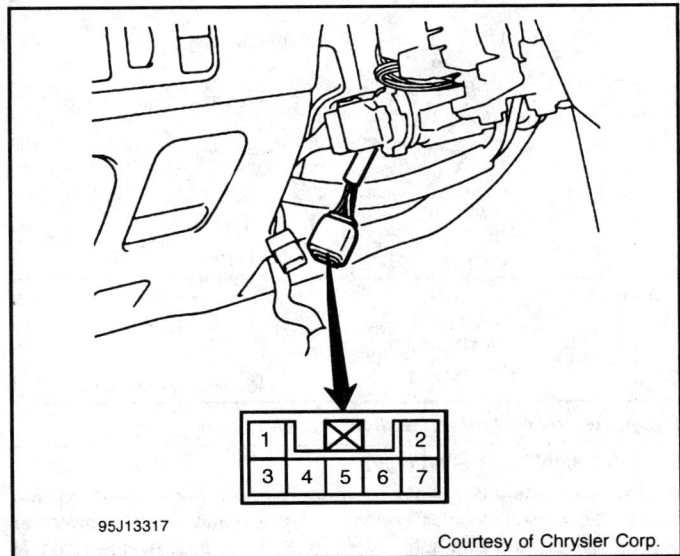

95J13317   Courtesy of Chrysler Corp.

Fig. 4: Identifying Key Reminder Switch Connector

HEADLIGHT SWITCH

Remove instrument panel knee protector and steering column covers. Disconnect switch connector at steering column. Check continuity between indicated switch terminals. See HEADLIGHT SWITCH CONTINUITY table. *See Fig. 5.* If continuity is not as specified, replace headlight switch.

HEADLIGHT SWITCH CONTINUITY

Switch Position	Continuity Between Connector/Terminals
Headlight Switch	
Off	[1]
Tail	A/6 & B/5, B/5 & B/7
Head	A/6 & B/5, A/1 & B/3, A/1 & B/6, B/5 & A/7
Dimmer/Passing Switch	
Low Beam	A/3 & A/4
High Beam	A/4 & A/6
Passing	[2] A/1, A/2 & A/6

[1] – Continuity should not exist.
[2] – When dimmer switch is in low-beam position, continuity also exists between terminals No. 3 and 4 of connector "A". When dimmer switch is in high-beam position, continuity also exists between terminals No. 4 and 6 of connector "A".

TURN SIGNAL SWITCH

Remove instrument panel knee protector and steering column covers. Disconnect switch connector at steering column. Check continuity between switch terminals. *See Fig. 5.* See TURN SIGNAL SWITCH CONTINUITY table. Replace switch as necessary.

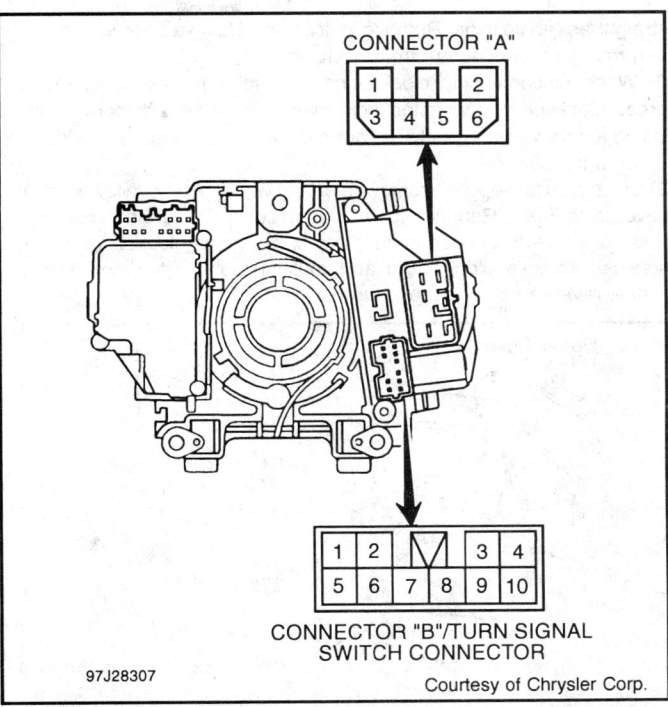

97J28307   Courtesy of Chrysler Corp.

Fig. 5: Identifying Headlight, Dimmer/Passing & Turn Signal Switch Connector Terminals

TURN SIGNAL SWITCH CONTINUITY

Switch Position	[1] Continuiuy Between Terminals
Off	[2]
Right Turn	8 & 9
Left Turn	3 & 8

[1] – Check at connector "B"
[2] – Continuity should not exist.

WIPER/WASHER SWITCH

For wiper/washer switch testing, see appropriate WIPER/WASHER SYSTEMS article.

REMOVAL & INSTALLATION

WARNING: Deactivate air bag system before performing any service operation involving steering column components. See AIR BAG RESTRAINT SYSTEMS – CARS article. DO NOT apply electrical power to any component on steering column without first disconnecting air bag module. Air bag may deploy.

CAUTION: When battery is disconnected, vehicle computer and memory systems may lose memory data. Driveability problems may exist until computer systems have completed a relearn cycle. See COMPUTER RELEARN PROCEDURES article in GENERAL INFORMATION before disconnecting battery.

CAUTION: Before removing steering wheel, position front wheels in a straight-ahead position and lock steering column by removing ignition key. Failure to do so could damage clockspring or require clockspring readjustment.

MULTIFUNCTION SWITCH

NOTE: Multifunction switch may also be referred to as combination or column switch.

Removal & Installation – 1) Disconnect and isolate negative battery cable. Wait at least 2 minutes. Set steering wheel and front wheels to

CHRY
4-496

1999 ACCESSORIES & EQUIPMENT
Steering Column Switches
Avenger & Sebring Coupe (Cont.)

straight-ahead position. Remove ignition key. Using a socket, remove air bag module mounting nut from back side.

2) When disconnecting clockspring connector from air bag module, press clockspring connector lock toward outer side to spread open. Using a screwdriver, gently pry out connector. Store air bag aside face up on a flat surface.

3) Using a suitable puller, remove steering wheel. Remove lower column cover. *See Fig. 6.* Remove upper column cover. Disconnect clockspring and body wiring harness connectors and remove clockspring retainer screws. Remove clockspring and multifunction switch assembly. To install, reverse removal procedure.

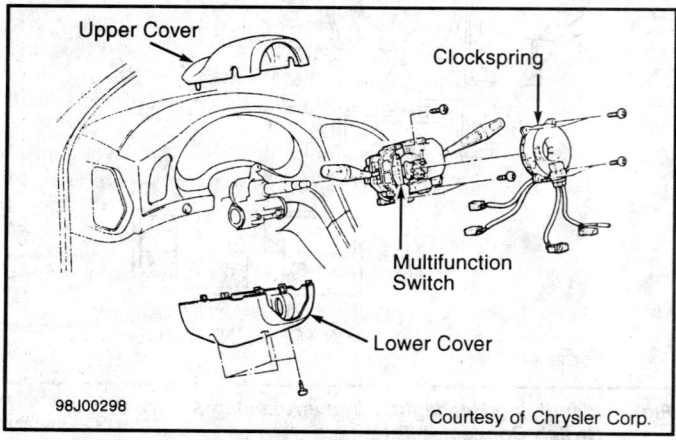

Fig. 6: Exploded View Of Steering Column Components

CLOCKSPRING

NOTE: See AIR BAG RESTRAINT SYSTEMS – CARS article.

IGNITION LOCK CYLINDER

Removal – 1) Disconnect and isolate negative battery cable. Wait at least 2 minutes. Set steering wheel and front wheels to straight-ahead position. Remove ignition key. Using a socket, remove air bag module mounting nut from back side. Using suitable puller, remove steering wheel.

2) Remove hood release handle. Remove knee protector. Remove upper and lower steering column covers. Remove clockspring and multifunction switch. Insert ignition key. Rotate switch to ACC position. Using a small punch or similar tool, push in lock pin. *See Fig. 7.* Pull lock cylinder from housing.

Installation – Insert ignition key into lock cylinder. Insert lock cylinder into housing, and rotate it to ACC position. Push lock cylinder into housing until lock pin clicks into position. To complete installation, reverse removal procedure.

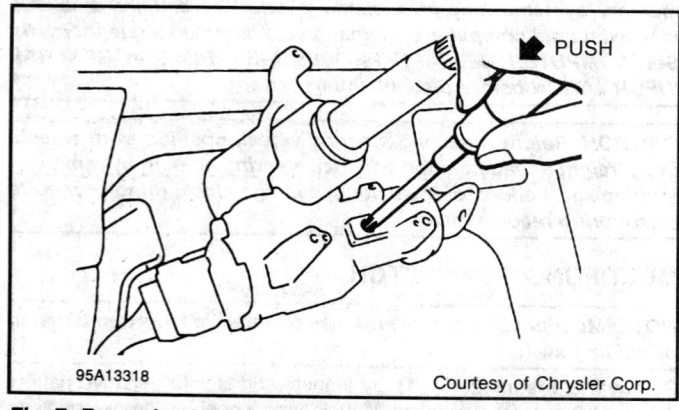

Fig. 7: Removing Ignition Lock Cylinder & Interlock Cable

IGNITION SWITCH

Removal & Installation – Remove upper and lower steering column covers. Disconnect electrical connector. Remove ignition switch. *See Fig. 8.* To install, reverse removal procedure.

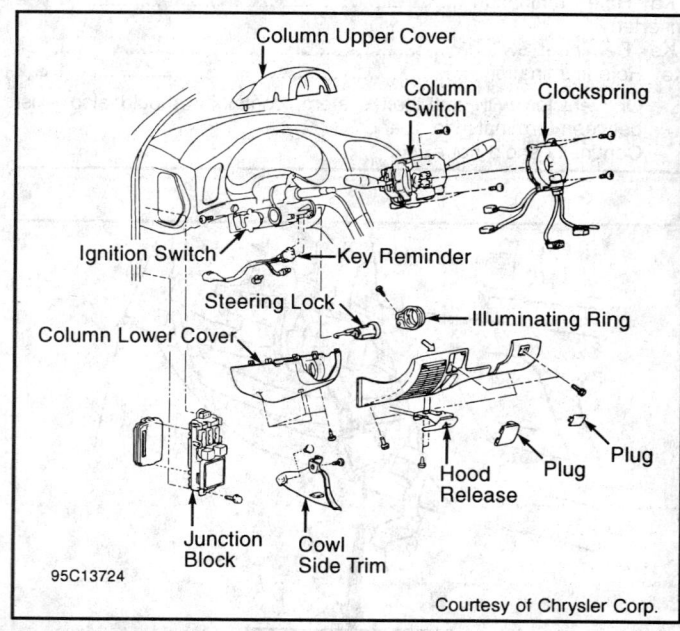

Fig. 8: Removing Ignition Switch

KEY REMINDER SWITCH

Removal & Installation – Remove upper and lower steering column covers. Disconnect electrical connector. Remove key reminder switch or keyhole illuminating ring light. *See Fig. 8.* To install, reverse removal procedure.

TORQUE SPECIFICATIONS

TORQUE SPECIFICATIONS

Application	Ft. Lbs. (N.m)
Steering Wheel Nut	30 (41)
	INCH Lbs. (N.m)
Air Bag Module Screws	53 (6)

WIRING DIAGRAMS

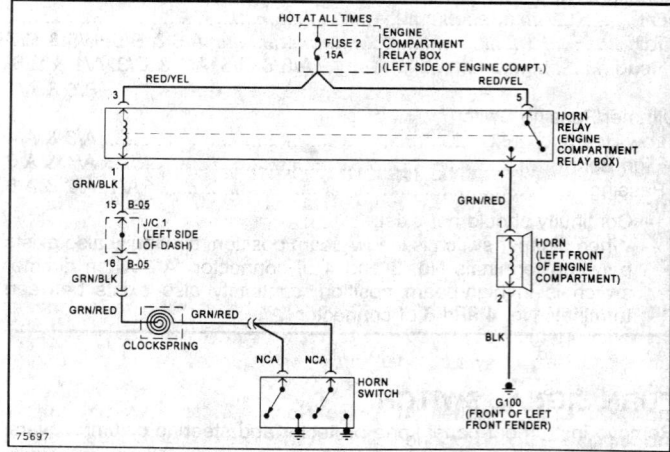

Fig. 9: Horn System Wiring Diagram (Avenger & Sebring Coupe)

Steering Column Switches
Breeze, Cirrus, Sebring Convertible & Stratus

DESCRIPTION & OPERATION

A multifunction (combination) switch incorporates headlight, passing, fog lamp, turn signal, hazard, panel dimmer and wiper/washer switches in one unit. *See Fig. 1*. The ignition switch and multifunction switch are mounted on steering column.

WARNING: Deactivate air bag system before performing any service operation involving steering column components. See AIR BAG RESTRAINT SYSTEMS – CARS article. Do not apply electrical power to any component on steering column without first disconnecting air bag module. Air bag may deploy.

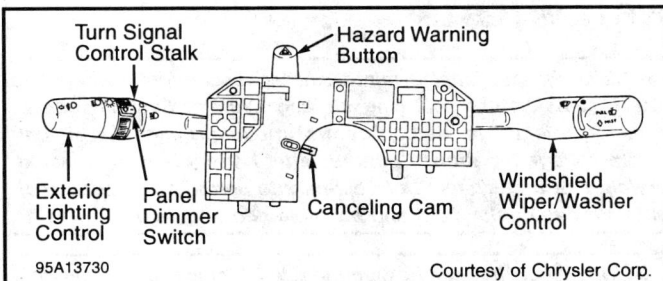

Fig. 1: Locating Multifunction Switch Controls

COMPONENT LOCATIONS

Component	Location
Flasher Relay	Multifunction Switch
Horn	Inner Right Front Frame Rail
Horn Fuse No. 8	Junction Block
Horn Fuse No. 14	Power Distribution Center
Horn Relay	Junction Block
Junction Block	Under Driver Side Instrument Panel
Power Distribution Center (PDC)	Left Front of Engine Compartment

TROUBLE SHOOTING

HORN SYSTEM

NOTE: If horn sounds continuously, disconnect relay and horn to prevent damage to system.

Horn Sounds Continuously – Check for faulty horn relay, shorted circuit or faulty horn switch.
Horn Sounds Intermittently When Wheel Is Turned – Check for faulty horn switch or shorted circuit.
Horn Does Not Work – Check for blown fuse, faulty power distribution center, open circuit, faulty horn or faulty horn switch.
Fuse Blows When Horn Sounds Or Without Sounding Horn – Check for short circuit.

TURN SIGNAL AND HAZARD FLASHER SYSTEM

Turn Signals Flashes At Twice Normal Rate – Check for blown exterior light, faulty switch or open circuit.
Interior Light Okay, Exterior Light Dim & Flashes Quickly – Check for poor exterior light connection or ground.
Hazard Flashers Inoperative – Check for blown fuse, faulty hazard flasher or open circuit in feed wire to hazard switch. Also check for faulty turn signal/hazard switch, open circuit or grounded circuit in wiring to external lights.
Indicator Light Flashes At Twice Normal Rate, External Lights Inoperative – Check for open circuit in wire to external light(s) or blown exterior light.
Turn Signals Inoperative – Check for faulty fuse, faulty flasher or loose bulkhead connection. Also check for open circuit in wiring to external

light(s), open circuit to flasher unit, open circuit in feed wire to turn signal switch, faulty turn signal/hazard switch, open or grounded circuit to exterior lights or bad bulbs.
Turn Signals Do Not Cancel After Turn – Check for broken canceling pawl on turn signal switch, or broken or loose canceling cam.
Indicator Light Inoperative, External Lights Okay – Burned-out indicator bulb in instrument cluster. Faulty contact. Open circuit.

COMPONENT TESTS

IGNITION SWITCH

1) Remove instrument panel knee protector and steering column covers. Disconnect wiring connectors from ignition switch. Using an ohmmeter, check continuity at switch side of connector. *See Figs. 2 and 3.* See IGNITION SWITCH CONTINUITY and IGNITION SWITCH CIRCUIT FUNCTIONS table.
2) Operate ignition switch while checking continuity between terminals. *See Figs. 2 and 3.* Replace ignition switch assembly if continuity is not as specified.

IGNITION SWITCH CONTINUITY

Switch Position	Continuity Between Terminals
ACC	
Connector C1	No Continuity
Connector C2	7 & 8
LOCK	
Connector C1	No Continuity
Connector C2	No Continuity
OFF	
Connector C1	1 & 2
RUN	
Connector C1	1 & 2
Connector C2	3 & 4; 7 & 8; 7 & 9
START	
Connector C1	1 & 2
Connector C2	1 & 2; 7 & 9; 7 & 10

IGNITION SWITCH CIRCUIT FUNCTIONS

Pin No. (Wire Color)	Function
Connector C1	
1 (RED/LT BLU)	Battery Feed To Ignition
2 (DK GRN/RED)	Ignition Switch Output (OFF/RUN/START)
Connector C2	
1 (BLK)	Ground
2 (GRY/DK BLU)	Red Brake Warning Light Driver
3 (PNK/BLK)	Battery Feed To Ignition
4 (BLK/ORG)	Ignition Switch Output (RUN)
5	Not Used
6	Not Used
7 (RED)	Battery Feed To Ignition
8 (BLK/WHT)	Ignition Switch Output (ACC/RUN)
9 (DK BLU)	Ignition Switch Output (START/RUN)
10 (YEL)	Ignition Switch Output (START)

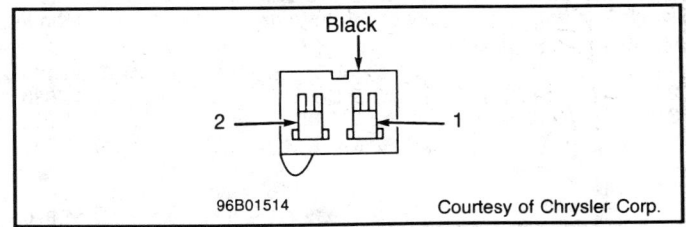

Fig. 2: Identifying Ignition Switch Connector C1 Terminals

CHRY
4-498

1999 ACCESSORIES & EQUIPMENT
Steering Column Switches
Breeze, Cirrus, Sebring Convertible & Stratus (Cont.)

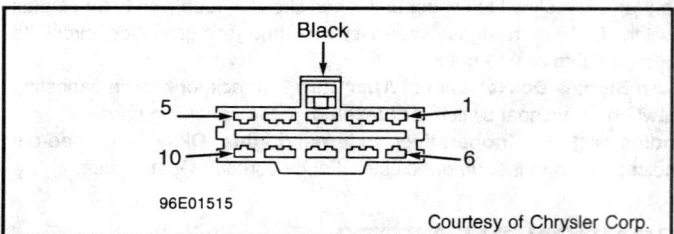

Fig. 3: Identifying Ignition Switch Connector C2 Terminals

KEY-IN REMINDER SWITCH

Key-in reminder switch is built into ignition switch assembly. If key-in switch requires service, ignition switch assembly must be replaced.

MULTIFUNCTION SWITCH

Remove instrument panel knee protector and steering column covers. Disconnect switch connector at steering column. Check continuity and resistance between indicated switch terminals with switch in specified positions. See MULTIFUNCTION SWITCH CONTINUITY table and MULTIFUNCTION SWITCH RESISTANCE table. *See Fig. 4.* If continuity is not as specified, replace multifunction switch.

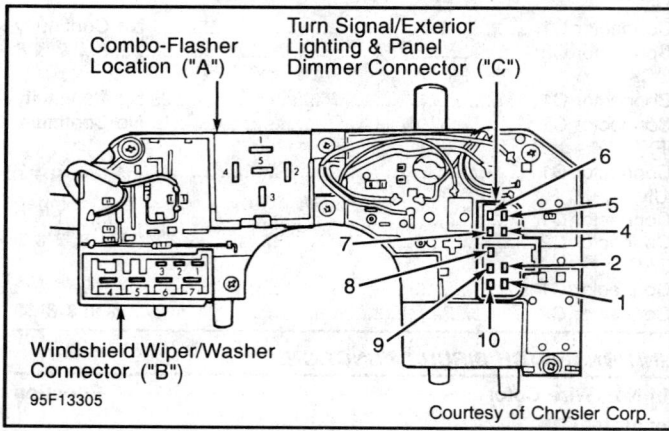

Fig. 4: Identifying Multifunction Switch Connectors

MULTIFUNCTION SWITCH CONTINUITY

Switch Position	Continuity Between Terminals
Turn Signal/Hazard	
With Hazard Warning Off	
Left	A1 & B7
Right	A1 & B6
With Hazard Warning On	
Left, Right Or Off	A1 & B6; A2 & A5; A1 & B7; B6 & B7
Foglights On	C9 & C10
Headlights	
Park	C1 & C2
Low Beam	C1 & C2; C4 & C7
High Beam	C1 & C2; C4 & C8
Flash	C4 & C8

MULTIFUNCTION SWITCH RESISTANCE

Switch Position	Between Terminals	Ohms
Instrument Panel Dimmer		
1	A2 & C6	Less Than 100
2	A2 & C6	300-2630
3 To 8	A2 & C6	Varies
9	A2 & C6	4990-10,500
Wiper		
Intermittent		
1	B2 & B3	11,870
2	B2 & B3	9870

MULTIFUNCTION SWITCH RESISTANCE (Cont.)

Switch Position	Between Terminals	Ohms
3	B2 & B3	7870
4	B2 & B3	5870
5	B2 & B3	3870
6	B2 & B3	1870
Low	B2 & B3	1250
High	B2 & B3	1820
Mist	B2 & B3	1250
Washer	B1 & B3	[1]

[1] – Continuity should exist.

SYSTEM TESTS

WARNING: Wait at least 2 minutes after disconnecting negative battery cable before servicing air bag system. System reserve capacitor, integral to air bag control module, maintains air bag system voltage for about 2 minutes after battery is disconnected. Servicing air bag system before 2-minute period may cause accidental air bag deployment and possible personal injury.

CAUTION: When battery is disconnected, vehicle computer and memory systems may lose memory data. Driveability problems may exist until computer systems have completed a relearn cycle. See COMPUTER RELEARN PROCEDURES article in GENERAL INFORMATION before disconnecting battery.

NOTE: For additional test information, see appropriate BODY CONTROL COMPUTER TESTS, CRUISE CONTROL SYSTEMS and WIPER/WASHER SYSTEMS articles.

HORN INOPERATIVE

1) Check fuse No. 14 (40-amp) in Power Distribution Center (PDC) and fuse No. 8 (20-amp) in junction block. Junction block is located under left front of instrument panel. If fuses are okay, go to next step. If either fuse is blown, go to step **7)**.

2) Remove horn relay from junction block. Using ohmmeter, check for continuity to ground at horn relay terminal No. 7 in junction block while pressing horn switch. *See Fig. 5.* If continuity exists, go to next step. If continuity does not exist, go to step **4)**.

3) Connect jumper wire between horn relay terminal No. 8 and horn relay terminal No. 10 in junction block. If horns do not sound, go to step **5)**. If horns sound, replace horn relay.

4) Remove air bag/horn pad from steering wheel. See HORN SWITCH under REMOVAL & INSTALLATION. Using ohmmeter, check for continuity between horn switch connector terminals while pressing horn switch. If continuity does not exist, replace air bag/horn pad. If continuity exists, repair open in wiring between horn switch and horn relay. See WIRING DIAGRAMS.

5) Install horn relay. Disconnect horn electrical connectors. Using voltmeter, check for voltage between horn harness terminals while pressing horn switch. If no voltage exists, go to next step. If voltage exists, replace horn(s).

6) Check for voltage between Dark Green/Pink wire terminal at horn and ground while pressing horn switch. If voltage exists, repair horn ground circuit. If voltage does not exist, repair open in Dark Green/Pink wire(s) between horn and horn relay.

7) Ensure battery is fully charged and terminal connections are okay. Go to next step. Check voltage at both sides of fuse No. 8. If voltage exists at both sides, go to step **2)**. If voltage does not exist on one side of fuse, fuse is blown. Go to next step.

8) Remove fuse. Connect ammeter across fuse terminals. Check amperage draw of horn circuit. If amperage draw is greater than 20 amps without horn switch depressed, circuit is grounded between fuse

1999 ACCESSORIES & EQUIPMENT
Steering Column Switches
Breeze, Cirrus, Sebring Convertible & Stratus (Cont.)

CHRY
4-499

and horn relay. Go to next step. If amperage draw is greater than 20 amps with horn switch depressed, circuit is grounded between horn relay and horn. Go to step **11**).

9) Remove horn relay from junction block. If amperage draw drops to zero amps, horn switch or circuit is shorted. See **WIRING DIAGRAMS**. If amperage draw does not drop, go to next step.

10) Disconnect both horns. If amperage draw does not drop with both horns disconnected and horn switch depressed, go to step **12**). If amperage draw drops, go to next step.

11) Ensure one horn connector is disconnected and other horn connector is connected. If amperage draw drops with one horn disconnected and other horn sounds, reverse procedure, and replace faulty horn.

12) Ensure both horn connectors are disconnected. Check continuity between horn relay terminal No. 10 and ground. If continuity does not exist, no problem is indicated at this time. Test is complete. If continuity exists, repair shorted circuit. If amperage draw does not drop to zero amps, repair short in junction block.

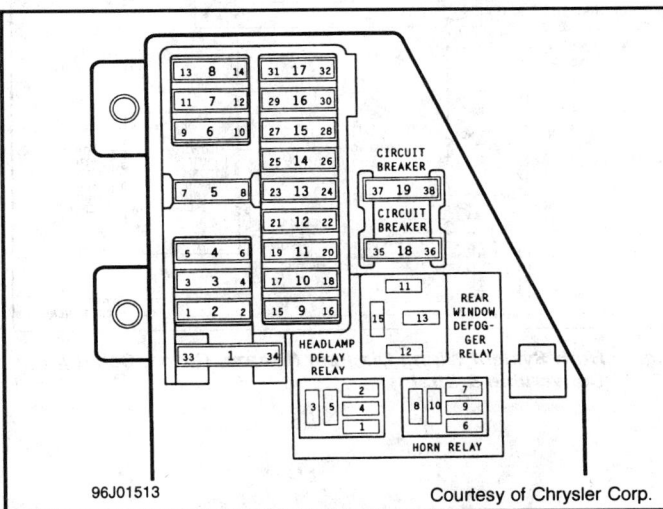

96J01513　　　　　　　Courtesy of Chrysler Corp.

Fig. 5: Identifying Horn Relay Terminals In Junction Block

REMOVAL & INSTALLATION

WARNING: Deactivate air bag system before performing any service operation involving steering column components. See AIR BAG RESTRAINT SYSTEMS – CARS article. Do not apply electrical power to any component on steering column without first deactivating air bag system. Air bag may deploy.

CAUTION: If battery is disconnected, vehicle computer and memory systems may lose memory data. Driveability problems may exist until computer systems have completed a relearn cycle. See COMPUTER RELEARN PROCEDURES article in GENERAL INFORMATION before disconnecting battery.

HORN SWITCH

Removal & Installation – Disconnect and isolate negative battery cable. Remove screws holding air bag module/horn switch to steering wheel. Lifting module to gain access, remove electrical connector. Place air bag module face up on a clean surface. If contact area is bad, replace air bag/horn switch. If mounting bracket or bushings are bad, replace steering wheel. To install, reverse removal procedure.

MULTIFUNCTION SWITCH

Removal & Installation – 1) Disconnect negative battery cable. Remove upper steering column cover. Remove multifunction switch mounting screws. See Fig. 6. Disconnect electrical connectors. Lift switch straight up to remove.

2) To install, reverse removal procedure. Tighten multifunction switch retaining screws to 20 INCH lbs. (2.3 N.m). Tighten steering column cover retaining screws to 17 INCH lbs. (2 N.m).

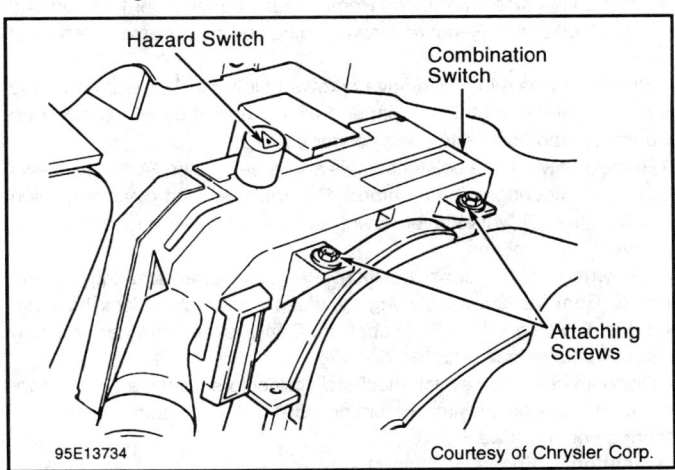

95E13734　　　　　　Courtesy of Chrysler Corp.

Fig. 6: Removing Multifunction Switch

IGNITION LOCK CYLINDER

Removal – Disconnect negative battery cable from auxiliary jumper terminal on left side strut tower. Remove upper steering column shroud. Pull lower shroud down far enough to access lock cylinder retaining tab. Place lock cylinder in RUN position. Depress retaining tab and remove lock cylinder. *See Fig. 7.*

Installation – 1) Insert ignition key into lock cylinder. Turn key to RUN position (retaining tab can be depressed). Shaft at end of lock cylinder aligns with socket in end of housing. To align socket with lock cylinder, ensure socket is in RUN position.

2) Align lock cylinder with grooves in housing. Slide lock cylinder into housing until tab sticks through opening in housing. Turn ignition switch to OFF position. Remove key. Install steering column shrouds. Connect negative battery cable.

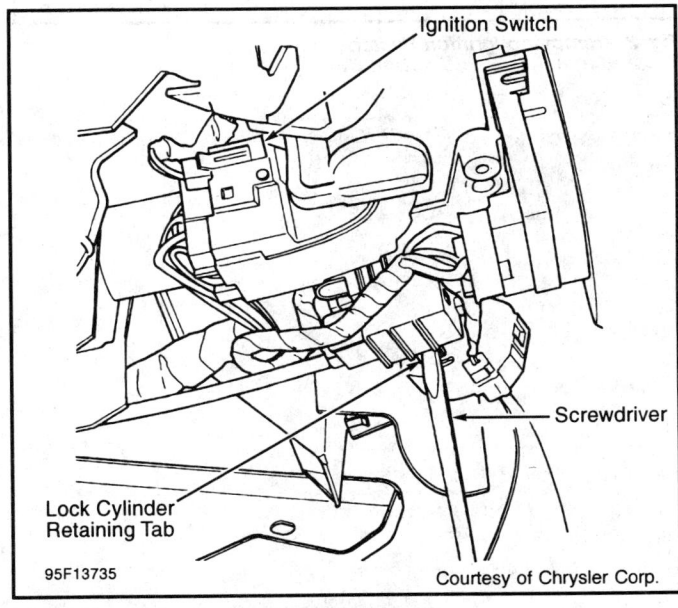

95F13735　　　　　　Courtesy of Chrysler Corp.

Fig. 7: Removing Ignition Lock Cylinder

CHRY
4-500

1999 ACCESSORIES & EQUIPMENT
Steering Column Switches
Breeze, Cirrus, Sebring Convertible & Stratus (Cont.)

IGNITION SWITCH

Removal – 1) Disconnect battery negative cable from auxiliary jumper terminal on left side strut tower. Remove fuse panel cover from left end of instrument panel. Remove screw holding end of instrument panel top cover.

2) Pull center bezel off. Remove screws holding instrument panel top cover to center of instrument panel. Pull instrument panel top cover up enough to gain access to knee bolster screws.

3) Remove lower knee bolster screws and knee bolster. Remove screws from lower steering column shroud. Pull lower shroud clear of ignition cylinder. Hold tilt wheel lever down, and slide lower shroud forward to remove it from column.

4) Tilt wheel to full down position. Remove upper steering column shroud. Remove screws holding multifunction switch to lock housing. *See Fig. 6.* Place key in RUN position. Depress lock cylinder retaining tab and remove lock cylinder. *See Fig. 7.*

5) Disconnect ignition switch electrical connectors. Using a No. 10 Torx bit, remove ignition switch mounting screw. Pull ignition switch from steering column. *See Fig. 8.*

Installation – Ensure ignition switch and actuator shaft are in RUN position. Carefully install ignition switch. Switch will snap over the retaining tabs. To complete installation, reverse removal procedure.

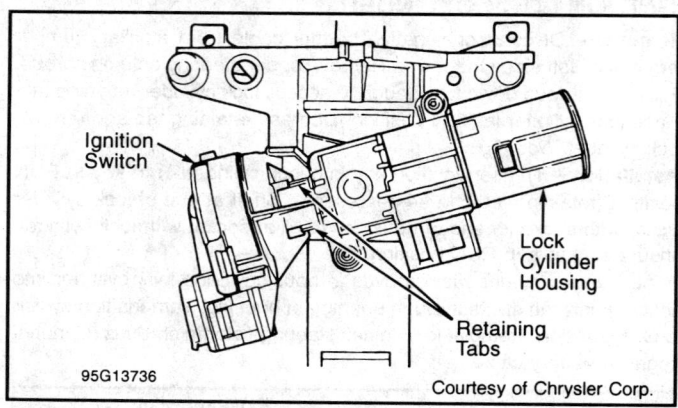

Fig. 8: Removing Ignition Switch

TORQUE SPECIFICATIONS

TORQUE SPECIFICATIONS

Application	Ft. Lbs. (N.m)
Steering Wheel Nut	45 (61)

	INCH Lbs. (N.m)
Air Bag Module Bolts	80-90 (9-10)
Multifunction Switch Screws	20 (2.3)
Steering Column Shroud Screws	17 (2)

WIRING DIAGRAMS

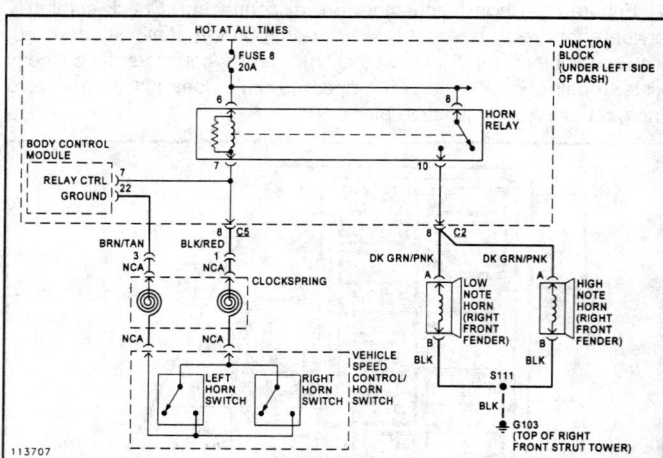

Fig. 9: Horn System Wiring Diagram (Breeze, Cirrus, Sebring Convertible & Stratus)

NOTE: Canadian vehicles are equipped with Daytime Running Lights (DRL).

WARNING: Deactivate air bag system before performing any service operation involving steering column components. See appropriate AIR BAG RESTRAINT SYSTEMS article. DO NOT apply electrical power to any component on steering column without first deactivating air bag system. Air bag may deploy.

DESCRIPTION

Turn signal, hazard flasher, headlight beam selector, windshield wipers, pulse wipe and windshield wash systems use a common switch assembly (multifunction switch), mounted within upper steering column housing. Chime will sound after turn signal is on more than .5 mile.

Ignition switch and lock cylinder are incorporated into an assembly attached to side of steering column. Lock cylinder can be serviced as a separate unit, but requires removal of ignition switch assembly.

COMPONENT LOCATIONS

COMPONENT LOCATIONS

Component	Location
Body Control Module	Behind Junction Block
DRL/Combination Relay	Junction Block Cavities 3 & 4
Junction Block	Under Dash, Behind Knee Bolster
Horns	Left Front Wheelwell
Horn Relay	Power Distribution Center
Turn Signal/Flasher Relay	Junction Block Cavity 4

TROUBLE SHOOTING

HORN

NOTE: If horn sounds continuously, unplug horn relay in Power Distribution Center (PDC) to prevent system damage.

Horn Sounds Continuously – Check horn relay. Check horn switch. See HORN under SYSTEM TESTS. Check horn relay control circuit for short between horn switch and horn relay. See WIRING DIAGRAMS. Check for pinched horn switch wire under driver's air bag module.

Horn Sounds Intermittently As Wheel Is Turned – Check horn relay control circuit for short between horn switch and horn relay. See WIRING DIAGRAMS. Check for pinched horn switch wire under driver's air bag module. Check horn switch. See HORN under SYSTEM TESTS.

Horn Inoperative – Check fuse No. 6 in PDC and fuse No. 7 in junction block. Check for open circuit to horn relay. See WIRING DIAGRAMS. Check for faulty horn relay, faulty horn or faulty horn switch. See HORN under SYSTEM TESTS.

Horn Fuse Blows – Check for shorted circuit in horn or horn wiring. See WIRING DIAGRAMS.

TURN SIGNALS WITH DAYTIME RUNNING LIGHTS (CANADIAN VEHICLES)

Hazard Flashers Inoperative – Check fuse No. 10 in Power Distribution Center (PDC). Check wiring and connections between PDC and junction block. Check multifunction switch ground. See WIRING DIAGRAMS. Check for faulty combination flasher/DRL module or connections. Check for faulty multifunction switch. See appropriate test under COMPONENT TESTS.

Turn Signals Inoperative (Hazard Flashers Okay) – Check fuse No. 12 in junction block. Check for loose connections in junction block. See WIRING DIAGRAMS. Check for faulty combination flasher/DRL module. See COMBINATION FLASHER/DRL MODULE (CANADIAN VEHICLES) under COMPONENT TESTS. Check for faulty multifunction switch. See MULTIFUNCTION SWITCH under COMPONENT TESTS.

Left Turn Signal Flashes Fast (Right Turn Signal Okay) – Use hazard flashers to check system. Check for faulty left front or left rear bulb or circuit. Check for poor connections in junction block. See WIRING DIAGRAMS. Check for faulty multifunction switch. See MULTIFUNCTION SWITCH under COMPONENT TESTS.

Right Turn Signal Flashes Fast (Left Turn Signal Okay) – Use hazard flashers to check system. Check for faulty right front or right rear bulb or circuit. Check for poor connections in junction block. See WIRING DIAGRAMS. Check for faulty multifunction switch. See MULTIFUNCTION SWITCH under COMPONENT TESTS.

Both Turn Signal Indicator Lights Inoperative (External Lights Okay) – Check for faulty ground connection to cowl ground splice. See WIRING DIAGRAMS.

One Turn Signal Indicator Light Inoperative (External Lights Okay) – Check for faulty indicator bulb in instrument cluster. Check wiring and connections between junction block and instrument cluster. See WIRING DIAGRAMS.

Daytime Running Lights Do Not Come On While Driving (Turn Signals & Hazard Flashers Okay) – Check for faulty ground circuit at instrument panel stud. Check for faulty ground through junction block. Check for grounded park brake input circuit (brake light in instrument panel will be lit unless bulb is bad). Check for grounded headlight switch sense circuit between headlight switch and BCM. Check for grounded headlight relay control circuit between headlight dimmer switch and BCM. See WIRING DIAGRAMS. Check for shorted headlight switch (high or low beam lit with switch off) or ignition switch. See appropriate test under COMPONENT TESTS.

TURN SIGNALS WITHOUT DAYTIME RUNNING LIGHTS (U.S. VEHICLES)

Hazard Flashers Inoperative – Check fuse No. 10 in Power Distribution Center (PDC). Check wiring and connections between PDC and junction block. Check multifunction switch ground. See WIRING DIAGRAMS. check for faulty combination flasher or connections. Check for faulty multifunction switch. See appropriate test under COMPONENT TESTS.

Turn Signals Inoperative (Hazard Flashers Okay) – Check fuse No. 12 in junction block. Check for loose connections in junction block. See WIRING DIAGRAMS. Check for faulty combination flasher. See COMBINATION FLASHER/DRL MODULE (CANADIAN VEHICLES) under COMPONENT TESTS. Check for faulty multifunction switch. See MULTIFUNCTION SWITCH under COMPONENT TESTS.

Left Turn Signals Inoperative (Hazard Flashers & Right Turn Signals Okay) – Check for poor connections between combination flasher and multifunction switch. Check for faulty combination flasher or multifunction switch. See appropriate test under COMPONENT TESTS.

Left Turn Signal Flashes Fast (Right Turn Signal Okay) – Use hazard flashers to check system. Check for faulty left front or left rear bulb or circuit. Check for poor connections in junction block. See WIRING DIAGRAMS. Check for faulty multifunction switch. See MULTIFUNCTION SWITCH under COMPONENT TESTS.

Right Turn Signal Flashes Fast (Left Turn Signal Okay) – Use hazard flashers to check system. Check for faulty right front or right rear bulb or circuit. Check for poor connections in junction block. See WIRING DIAGRAMS. Check for faulty multifunction switch. See MULTIFUNCTION SWITCH under COMPONENT TESTS.

Both Turn Signal Indicator Lights Inoperative (External Lights Okay) – Check for faulty ground connection to cowl ground splice. See WIRING DIAGRAMS.

One Turn Signal Indicator Light Inoperative (External Lights Okay) – Check for faulty indicator bulb in instrument cluster. Check wiring and connections between junction block and instrument cluster. See WIRING DIAGRAMS.

CHRY
4-502

1999 ACCESSORIES & EQUIPMENT
Steering Column Switches
Caravan, Town & Country, & Voyager (Cont.)

COMPONENT TESTS

CAUTION: When battery is disconnected, vehicle computer and memory systems may lose memory data. Driveability problems may exist until computer systems have completed a relearn cycle. See COMPUTER RELEARN PROCEDURES article in GENERAL INFORMATION before disconnecting battery.

COMBINATION FLASHER/DRL MODULE (CANADIAN VEHICLES)

Component testing is not available from manufacturer. Check circuits. See COMBINATION FLASHER/DRL MODULE CIRCUIT FUNCTIONS table.

COMBINATION FLASHER/DRL MODULE CIRCUIT FUNCTIONS

Terminal No. (Wire Color)	Circuit Function
1 (BLK/WHT)	Battery Input
2 (LT GRN)	Left Front Turn Signal Output
3 (TAN)	Right Front Turn Signal Output
4 (DK GRN/RED)	Left Rear Turn Signal Output
5 (BRN/RED)	Right Rear Turn Signal Output
6 (BLK/ORG)	Ignition Input
7 (LT BLU/WHT)	Left Turn Signal Input
8 (LT BLU/YEL)	Right Turn Signal Input
9 (DK BLU/PNK)	Hazard Flasher Input
10 (GRY/BLK)	Park Brake Switch Input
11 (BLK)	Ground
12 (RED/YEL)	Headlight Relay Switch Input

COMBINATION FLASHER

Component testing is not available from manufacturer. Check circuits. See COMBINATION FLASHER CIRCUIT FUNCTIONS table.

COMBINATION FLASHER CIRCUIT FUNCTIONS

Terminal No. (Wire Color)	Circuit Function
1 (BLK/WHT)	Battery Input
2 (LT GRN)	Left Front Turn Signal Output
3 (TAN)	Right Front Turn Signal Output
4 (DK GRN/RD)	Left Rear Turn Signal Output
5 (BRN/RED)	Right Rear Turn Signal Output
6 (BLK/ORG)	Ignition Input
7 (LT BLU/WHT)	Left Turn Signal Input
8 (LT BLU/YEL)	Right Turn Signal Input
9 (DK BLU/PNK)	Hazard Flasher Input

IGNITION SWITCH

NOTE: For ignition switch circuit function, see IGNITION SWITCH CIRCUIT FUNCTIONS table. See Figs. 1 and 2.

Remove ignition switch. See IGNITION SWITCH & LOCK CYLINDER under REMOVAL & INSTALLATION. Check continuity between appropriate ignition switch terminals with switch in appropriate position. See IGNITION SWITCH CONTINUITY table. See Figs. 1 and 2. If continuity is not as specified, replace ignition switch.

IGNITION SWITCH CONTINUITY

Switch Position	Connector	[1] Continuity Between Terminals
ACC	C1	7 & 8
ACC	C3	[2]
OFF/LOCK	C1	[2]
OFF/LOCK	C3	[2]
UNLOCK	C1	1 & 2
UNLOCK	C3	1 & 2
RUN	C1	3 & 4; 7 & 8; 7 & 9
RUN	C3	1 & 2
START	C1	1 & 2; 7 & 9; 7 & 10
START	C3	1 & 2

IGNITION SWITCH CONTINUITY (Cont.)

Switch Position	Connector	[1] Continuity Between Terminals

[1] – When key is in ignition switch continuity should exists between terminals No. 1 and 2 of connector C2. When key is not in ignition switch continuity should not exist between terminals No. 1 and 2 of connector C2.

[2] – Continuity should not exists between any terminals.

IGNITION SWITCH CIRCUIT FUNCTIONS

Terminal No. (Wire Color)	Circuit Function
Connector C1	
1 (BLK)	Ground
2 (GRY/BLK)	Red Brake Warning Light Driver
3 (PNK/BLK)	Battery Feed To Ignition
4 (BLK/ORG)	Ignition Switch Output (RUN)
5	Not Used
6	Not Used
7 (RED)	Battery Feed To Ignition
8 (BLK/WHT)	Ignition Switch Output (ACC/RUN)
9 (DK BLU)	Ignition Switch Output (START/RUN)
10 (YEL)	Ignition Switch Output (START)
Connector C3	
1 (PNK)	Battery Feed To Ignition
2 (DK GRN/RED)	Ignition Switch Output (OFF/START/RUN)

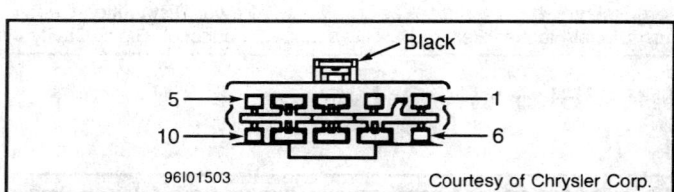

Fig. 1: Identifying Ignition Switch Connector C1 Terminals (Harness Side Shown)

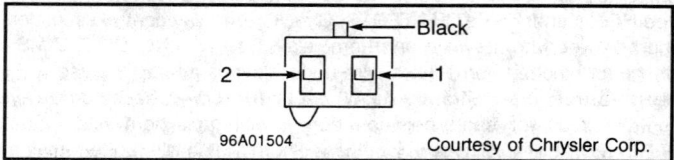

Fig. 2: Identifying Ignition Switch Connector C3 Terminals (Harness Side Shown)

MULTIFUNCTION SWITCH

NOTE: For additional testing, see appropriate CRUISE CONTROL SYSTEMS and WIPER/WASHER SYSTEMS articles.

Headlight Beam Select & Turn Signal/Hazard Warning Switch Circuits – Disconnect negative battery cable. Remove multifunction switch. See MULTIFUNCTION SWITCH under REMOVAL & INSTALLATION. Check continuity between appropriate multifunction switch terminals with switch in appropriate position. See MULTIFUNCTION SWITCH CONTINUITY table. See Fig. 3. If continuity is not as specified, replace multifunction switch.

MULTIFUNCTION SWITCH CONTINUITY

Switch Position	Continuity Between Terminals
Left Turn	4 & 8
Right Turn	3 & 8
Hazard	1 & 8
Low Beam	9 & 10
High Beam	8 & 12

1999 ACCESSORIES & EQUIPMENT
Steering Column Switches
Caravan, Town & Country, & Voyager (Cont.)

CHRY
4-503

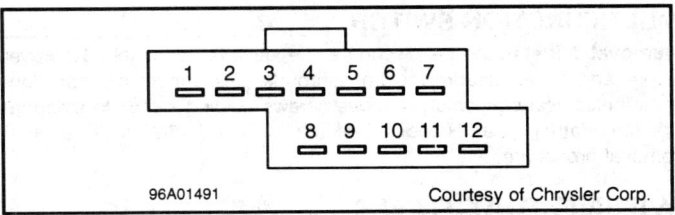

96A01491   Courtesy of Chrysler Corp.

Fig. 3: Identifying Multifunction Switch Terminals

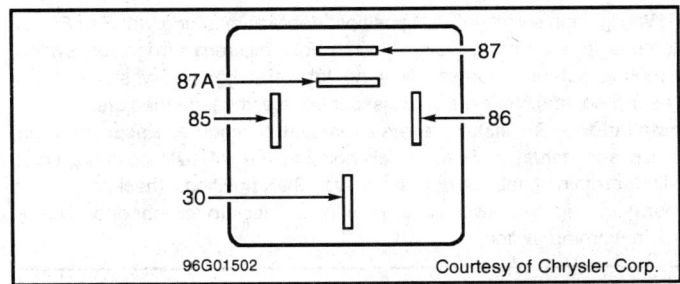

96G01502   Courtesy of Chrysler Corp.

Fig. 4: Identifying Horn Relay Terminals In Power Distribution Center

SYSTEM TESTS

HORN

Horns Will Not Sound – **1)** Check fuse No. 6 (40-amp) in Power Distribution Center (PDC) and fuse No. 7 (20-amp) in junction block. If fuses are okay, go to next step. If either fuse is blown, replace fuse and ensure horns are functioning. If horns sound and fuse does not blow, repair is complete. If fuse blows again, go to step **7**).

2) Remove horn relay from junction block. Check continuity between ground and horn relay terminal No. 85 in while pressing horn switch. *See Fig. 4.* If continuity exists, go to next step. If continuity does not exist, go to step **4**).

3) Connect jumper wire between horn relay terminals No. 30 and 87 in PDC. If horns do not sound, go to step **5**). If horns sound, replace horn relay.

4) Remove air bag/horn pad from steering wheel. See HORN SWITCH under REMOVAL & INSTALLATION. While pressing horn switch, check continuity between horn switch terminals (component side). If continuity does not exist, replace horn switch. If continuity exists, repair open in wiring between horn switch and horn relay.

5) Install air bag/horn pad, if removed. Install horn relay. Disconnect horn connectors. Check for voltage between horn harness terminals while pressing horn switch. If voltage does not exist, go to next step. If voltage exists, replace horn(s).

6) Check for voltage between horn harness connector Dark Green/Red wire terminal and ground while pressing horn. If voltage exists, repair horn ground circuit. If voltage does not exist, repair open in Dark Green/Red wire(s) between horn and horn relay.

7) Check battery and battery terminals. Clean, repair or replace as necessary. Check amperage draw of system by connecting ammeter across fuse terminals. If amperage is more than 20 amps without switch depressed, a short exists between fuse and relay. Go to next step. If amperage is more than 20 amps with switch depressed, a short exists between relay and horn. Go to step **9**).

8) Remove horn relay from junction block. If amperage drops to zero amps, horn switch or circuit is shorted. Repair as necessary. If amperage does not change, junction block is shorted. Repair as necessary.

9) Disconnect horns, one at a time. If amperage drops and other horn sounds, replace faulty horn. Disconnect both horns. If amperage does not change, go to next step.

10) With both horns disconnected, check continuity between horn harness connector Dark Green/Red wire terminal and ground. If continuity exists, repair shorted circuit between junction block and horns. If continuity does not exist, no problem is indicated at this time. Test is complete.

Horns Sound Continuously – **1)** Remove horn relay from junction block. Check continuity between horn relay terminal No. 85 in power distribution center and ground. *See Fig. 4.* If continuity exists, go to next step. If continuity does not exist, replace horn relay.

2) Remove air bag/horn pad from steering wheel. See HORN SWITCH under REMOVAL & INSTALLATION. Disconnect horn switch connector. Install horn relay. If horns do not sound, replace air bag/horn pad. If horns sound, repair short to ground between clockspring and junction block.

REMOVAL & INSTALLATION

WARNING: Deactivate air bag system before performing any service operation involving steering column components. See appropriate AIR BAG RESTRAINT SYSTEMS article. Do not apply electrical power to any component on steering column without first deactivating air bag system. Air bag may deploy.

CAUTION: When battery is disconnected, vehicle computer and memory systems may lose memory data. Driveability problems may exist until computer systems have completed a relearn cycle. See COMPUTER RELEARN PROCEDURES article in GENERAL INFORMATION before disconnecting battery.

HORN SWITCH

Removal & Installation – **1)** Disconnect negative battery cable. Wait at least 2 minutes. Remove air bag/horn switch screws. Separate air bag module from steering wheel. Disconnect air bag, horn switch and cruise control (if equipped) electrical connectors. Remove screws and cruise control switches (if equipped).

2) Remove nuts holding air bag cover retainers to back of air bag module. Remove retainers from air bag module. Disengage air bag module from channels in air bag cover/horn switch. *See Fig. 5.* Remove air bag cover/horn switch from air bag module. To install, reverse removal procedure.

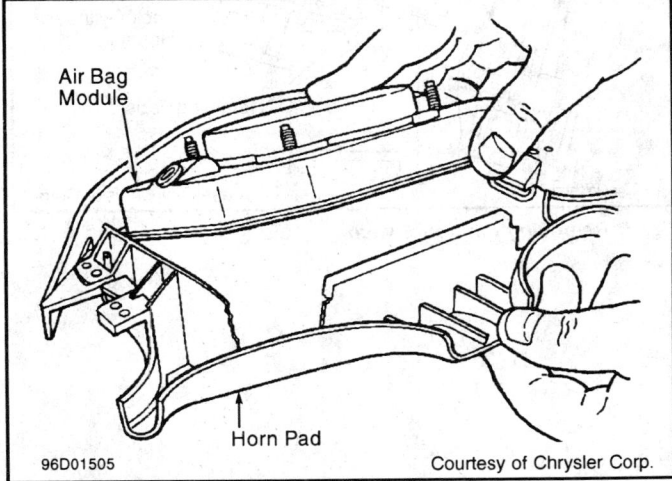

96D01505   Courtesy of Chrysler Corp.

Fig. 5: Removing Air Bag Cover/Horn Switch

IGNITION SWITCH & LOCK CYLINDER

Removal – **1)** Disconnect negative battery cable. Remove steering column cover retaining screws. Remove cable from parking brake release handle. Remove screws holding steering column shrouds. Remove lower steering column shroud.

CHRY
4-504

1999 ACCESSORIES & EQUIPMENT
Steering Column Switches
Caravan, Town & Country, & Voyager (Cont.)

2) With ignition switch in RUN position, depress retaining tab. *See Fig. 6.* Remove lock cylinder. Using No. 10 Torx bit, remove ignition switch mounting screw. Depress retaining tab, and gently pry switch from steering column. *See Fig. 7.* Disconnect electrical connectors.

Installation – To install, reverse removal procedure. Ensure ignition switch and actuator shaft in lock housing are in RUN position. Lock cylinder retaining tab will depress only in RUN position. Check for proper operation of ignition switch in all positions. Check for proper operation of key-in warning switch.

MULTIFUNCTION SWITCH

Removal & Installation – Disconnect negative battery cable. Remove upper and lower steering column shrouds. Disconnect multifunction switch electrical connector. Remove screws holding switch to steering column adapter collar. Remove multifunction switch. To install, reverse removal procedure.

WIRING DIAGRAMS

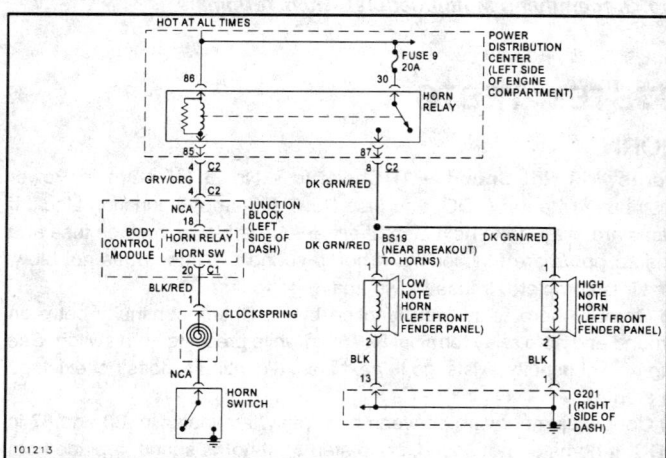

**Fig. 8: Horn System Wiring Diagram
(Caravan, Town & Country, & Voyager)**

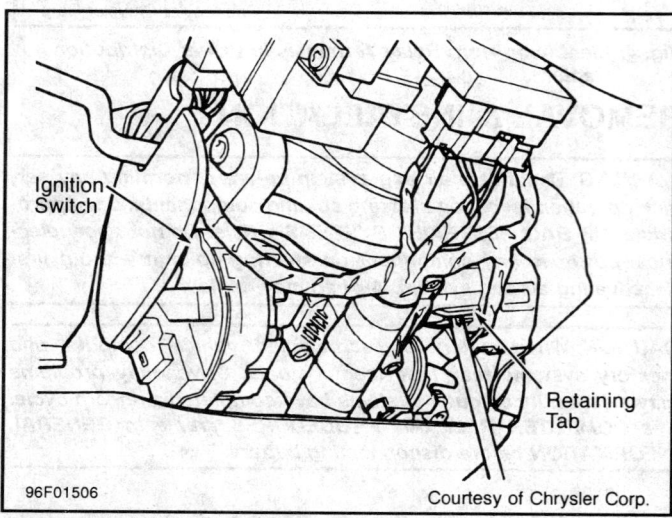

Fig. 6: Removing Lock Cylinder

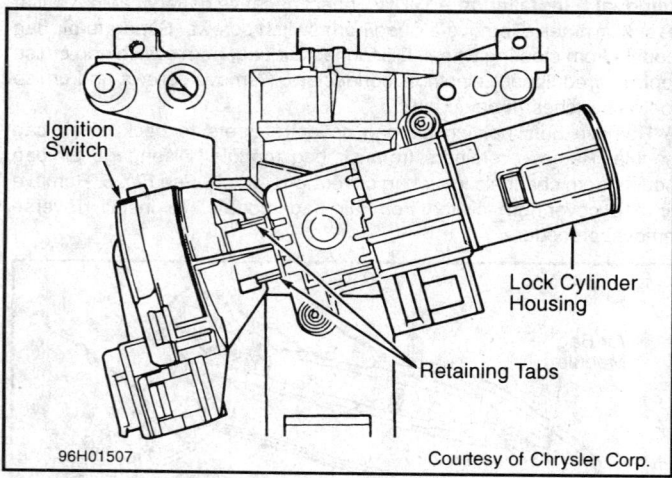

Fig. 7: Removing Ignition Switch

1999 ACCESSORIES & EQUIPMENT
Steering Column Switches
Concorde, Intrepid, LHS & 300M

WARNING: Deactivate air bag system before performing any service operation involving steering column components. See appropriate AIR BAG RESTRAINT SYSTEMS article. DO NOT apply electrical power to any component on steering column without first deactivating air bag system. Air bag may deploy.

DESCRIPTION & OPERATION

A multifunction (combination) switch incorporates headlight, turn signal, dimmer/passing, wiper/washer and hazard warning switches into one unit. Ignition switch is also mounted on steering column. Cruise control switches are mounted on each side of horn pad on steering wheel.

COMPONENT LOCATIONS

COMPONENT LOCATIONS

Component	Location
Combination Flasher Relay	Next To Junction Block
Left Horn	Left Front Wheelwell
Right Horn	Right Front Frame Rail
Horn Fuse No. 18	Junction Block
Horn Relay	Junction Block
Junction Block	Under Driver's Side Instrument Panel

ADJUSTMENTS

COLUMN SHIFT INTERLOCK

NOTE: Interlock cassette for column shift models can only be adjusted one time. When installing a new ignition lock cylinder, interlock cassette must be replaced.

Interlock cassette slides into housing behind lock cylinder. Cable at rear of cassette attaches to a locking arm on shifter mechanism. Ensure latch rotates freely on shifter gate. Ensure shifter is in Park and key is removed. Install cable over hook on locking arm. Slide cassette into housing until it locks in place. Push in adjustment tab until fully seated.

FLOOR SHIFT INTERLOCK

1) Remove shifter handle and console bezel. Loosen locking clip on interlock cable. Turn ignition switch to RUN position. Remove interlock cable from shifter housing. Slide cable out of groove in interlock lever.
2) Check cable inner wire with ignition switch in LOCK position. Cable inner wire should not move. Check cable inner wire with ignition switch in RUN position. Cable inner wire should move freely when pulled and return to bottomed out position when released. If cable inner wire does not work as specified, cable is improperly installed or kinked.
3) Put shifter in Park. Put steering column in full up position. Slide interlock cable inner wire into groove in adjustment lever with end of cable seated in groove. Slip cable into housing until it snaps in place. Ensure shifter is in Park. Remove key from ignition. Loosen locking clip and allow cable to self-adjust to correct position. Push locking clip down to lock cable in place.
4) Put steering column in full down position. Check interlock adjustment. With ignition switch in LOCK position, shifter should be locked in Park. With ignition switch in RUN position (engine off), move shifter to Reverse. Key should not be able to be removed. Put shifter in Park, turn ignition switch to LOCK position. Key should be able to be removed. If interlock does not operate as specified, readjust cable. Install shifter handle and console bezel.

TROUBLE SHOOTING

HORN SYSTEM

NOTE: If horn sounds continuously, disconnect relay and horn to prevent damage to system.

Horn Sounds Continuously – Check horn relay. See HORN RELAY under COMPONENT TESTS. Check horn switch. See HORN SWITCH under COMPONENT TESTS. Check horn relay control circuit for short to ground. See WIRING DIAGRAMS. Check for pinched horn switch wire under driver's air bag module.
Horn Sounds Intermittently When Wheel Is Turned – Check for pinched horn switch wire under driver's air bag module. Check horn relay control circuit for short to ground in steering column. See WIRING DIAGRAMS. Check horn switch. See HORN SWITCH under COMPONENT TESTS.
Horn Inoperative – Check fuse No. 18 in junction block. Check for open horn relay control circuit or horn relay power circuit. See WIRING DIAGRAMS. Check horn, horn switch and horn relay. See appropriate test under COMPONENT TESTS.
Fuse Blows When Horn Sounds Or Without Sounding Horn – Check for short circuit in horn or horn wiring. See WIRING DIAGRAMS.

TURN SIGNAL AND HAZARD FLASHER SYSTEM

System Does Not Flash On One Side & Indicator Light Flashes At Twice Normal Rate – Check for faulty exterior light bulb. Check for open exterior light circuit or poor exterior light ground circuit. Check multifunction switch. See MULTIFUNCTION SWITCH under COMPONENT TESTS.
Indicator Light Flashes At Twice Normal Rate (External Light Flashes Rapidly Or No Flash) – Check for loose or corroded connection at exterior light. Check for poor ground at exterior light.
Hazard Flashers Inoperative – Check fuse "O" in Power Distribution Center (PDC). Check for faulty combination flasher. Check for open circuit in feed wire to hazard switch. Check for open or grounded circuit in wiring to external lights. Check multifunction switch. See MULTIFUNCTION SWITCH under COMPONENT TESTS.
Indicator Light Flashes At Twice Normal Rate (External Light Inoperative) – Check for open exterior light circuit. Check for faulty bulb.
System Does Not Flash On Either Side – Check for blown fuse. Check for faulty combination flasher or faulty bulbs. Check for loose bulkhead connector. Check for open circuit to combination flasher, multifunction switch or wiring to exterior lights. Check multifunction switch. See MULTIFUNCTION SWITCH under COMPONENT TESTS.
Turn Signals Do Not Cancel After Turn – Check for broken canceling pawl on turn signal switch. Check for broken or loose canceling cam on clockspring. Check for sticking canceling pawl.
Indicator Light Inoperative (External Lights Okay) – Check for burned-out indicator bulb in instrument cluster.

COMPONENT TESTS

CAUTION: When battery is disconnected, vehicle computer and memory systems may lose memory data. Driveability problems may exist until computer systems have completed a relearn cycle. See COMPUTER RELEARN PROCEDURES article in GENERAL INFORMATION before disconnecting battery.

NOTE: For additional testing, see appropriate CRUISE CONTROL SYSTEMS and WIPER/WASHER SYSTEMS articles.

HORN RELAY

1) Remove horn relay from junction block. Check continuity between relay terminals No. 74 and 75. *See Fig. 1.* If continuity exists, replace relay. If continuity does not exist, check continuity between relay terminals No. 72 and 73. If continuity does not exist, replace relay. If continuity exists, go to next step.

CHRY
4-506

1999 ACCESSORIES & EQUIPMENT
Steering Column Switches
Concorde, Intrepid, LHS & 300M (Cont.)

2) Using jumper wires, connect positive battery voltage to relay terminal No. 73 and ground to relay terminal No. 72. Continuity should exist between terminals No. 74 and 75. If continuity does not exist, replace relay. If continuity exists, relay is okay. Go to HORN RELAY CIRCUIT under SYSTEM TESTS.

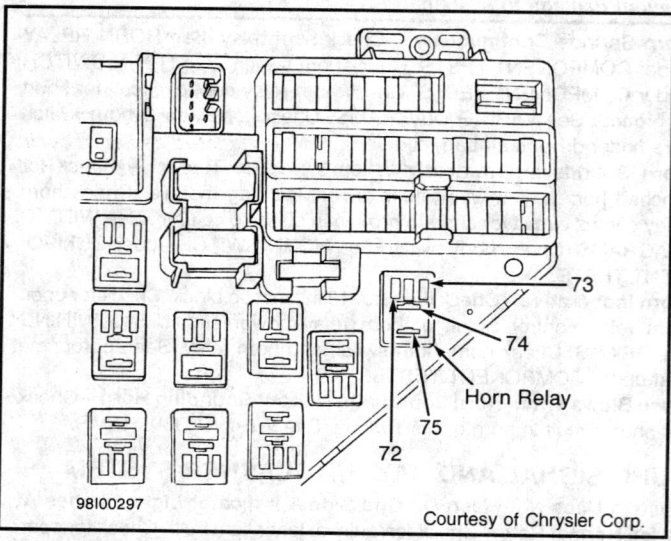

Fig. 1: Identifying Horn Relay Terminals In Junction Block

HORN SWITCH

Check continuity between horn switch connector Black/Red wire terminal and ground. When horn switch is depressed continuity should exist. Repeat for other horn switch. If continuity is not as specified, replace horn switch.

IGNITION SWITCH

NOTE: For ignition switch circuit function, see IGNITION SWITCH CIRCUIT FUNCTIONS table.

Remove ignition switch. See IGNITION SWITCH under REMOVAL & INSTALLATION. Check continuity between appropriate switch terminals with switch in specified position. See IGNITION SWITCH CONTINUITY table. See Fig. 2. If continuity is not as specified, replace ignition switch.

IGNITION SWITCH CONTINUITY

Switch Position	[1] Continuity Between Terminals
ACC	5 & 6
LOCK	[2]
OFF	4 & 6
RUN	1, 4, 5 & 6; 7 & 10
START	1, 4, 6 & 8

[1] – With key in ignition, continuity exists between terminals No. 2 and 3 for key-in switch.
[2] – Continuity should not exist between any terminals.

IGNITION SWITCH CIRCUIT FUNCTIONS

Terminal No. (Wire Color)	Circuit Description
1 (DK BLU/WHT)	Ignition Switch Output (START/RUN)
2 (BLK/LT GRN)	Ground
3 (LT BLU)	Key-In Ignition Switch Sense
4 (DK GRN/RED)	Ignition Switch Output (OFF/START/RUN)
5 (BLK/WHT)	Ignition Switch Output (ACC/RUN)
6 (RED)	Battery Feed To Ignition
7 (BLK/ORG)	Ignition Switch Output (RUN)
8 (YEL)	Ignition Switch Output (START)
9	Not Used
10 (PNK/BLK)	Battery Feed To Ignition

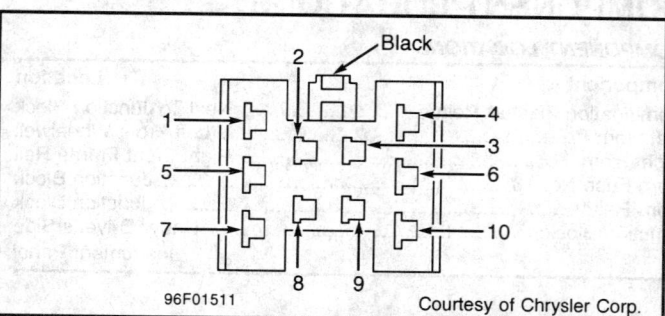

Fig. 2: Identifying Ignition Switch Connector Terminals

MULTIFUNCTION SWITCH

NOTE: For washer/wiper portion of multifunction switch testing, see appropriate WASHER/WIPER SYSTEMS article.

Disconnect negative battery cable. Disconnect multifunction switch connector. Check continuity between appropriate switch terminals with switch in specified position. See MULTIFUNCTION SWITCH TESTING tables. See Figs. 3 and 4. If continuity is not as specified, replace switch.

MULTIFUNCTION SWITCH TESTING

Switch Position	Continuity Between Terminals
Turn Signals	
Neutral	1 & 2
Left	6 & 7
Right	7 & 8
Hazards On	2 & 3; 4 & 5; 6 & 7; 7 & 8
Head Lights	
Low Beam	5 & 7
High Beam	4 & 7
Flash-To-Pass	4 & 6

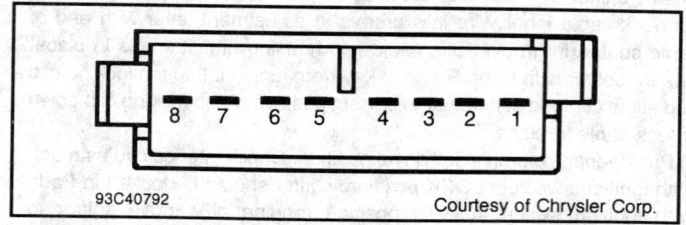

Fig. 3: Identifying Turn Signal & Hazard Flasher Switch Terminals

1999 ACCESSORIES & EQUIPMENT
Steering Column Switches
Concorde, Intrepid, LHS & 300M (Cont.)

CHRY
4-507

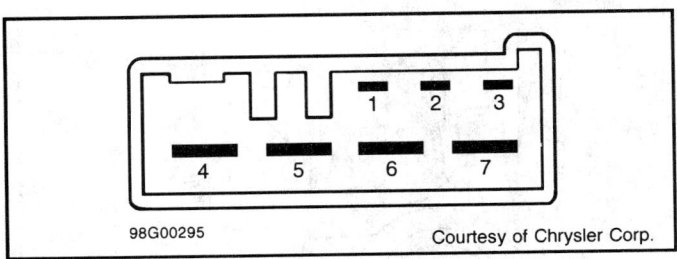

98G00295   Courtesy of Chrysler Corp.

Fig. 4: Identifying Dimmer Switch Terminals

SYSTEM TESTS

HORN

1) Disconnect horn connector. Connect voltmeter between ground and horn connector Dark Green/Red wire terminal. Depress horn switch. Repeat for other horn. If battery voltage does not exist, check horn relay circuit. See HORN RELAY CIRCUIT. If battery voltage exists, go to next step.

2) Check continuity between ground and Black wire terminal at horn connector. Repeat for other horn. If continuity exists, replace appropriate horn. If continuity does not exist, repair open in appropriate Black wire.

HORN RELAY CIRCUIT

1) Remove horn relay from junction block located under left side of instrument panel. Connect ohmmeter between horn relay terminal No. 72 in junction block and ground. *See Fig. 1.* When horn switch is pressed, continuity should exist. When horn switch is not pressed, continuity should not exist. If continuity is as specified, go to next step. If continuity is not as specified, go to next step.

2) Test horn switch. See under HORN SWITCHCOMPONENT TESTS. If horn switch is okay, repair open in Black/Red wire or clockspring as necessary. If horn switch is not okay, replace horn switch.

3) Check for voltage at horn relay terminals No. 73 and 74 in junction block. If battery voltage does not exist at both terminals, go to step 7). If battery voltage exists at both terminals, go to next step.

4) Connect a jumper wire between horn relay terminals No. 74 and 75 in junction block. If horns sound, replace horn relay. If horns do not sound, go to next step.

5) Test horn relay. See under HORN RELAY COMPONENT TEST. If relay is okay, go to next step. If relay is not okay, replace relay.

6) Disconnect horn connector. Check continuity in Dark Green/Red wire between relay terminal No. 75 in junction block and horn connector. If continuity exists, check horns. See HORN. If continuity does not exist, repair open in Dark Green/Red wire.

7) Inspect fuse No. 18 (20-amp) in junction block. If fuse is okay, go to next step. If fuse is blown, repair short circuit.

8) Check for voltage at fuse No. 18. If battery voltage exists, repair open in junction block. If battery voltage does not exist. repair power distribution circuit. See appropriate wiring diagram in POWER DISTRIBUTION article in WIRING DIAGRAMS.

REMOVAL & INSTALLATION

WARNING: Deactivate air bag system before performing any service operation involving steering column components. See appropriate AIR BAG RESTRAINT SYSTEMS article. Do not apply electrical power to any component on steering column without first deactivating air bag system. Air bag may deploy.

CAUTION: When battery is disconnected, vehicle computer and memory systems may lose memory data. Driveability problems may exist until computer systems have completed a relearn cycle. See COMPUTER RELEARN PROCEDURES article in GENERAL INFORMATION before disconnecting battery.

STEERING WHEEL & HORN SWITCH

Removal – 1) Lock steering column by rotating steering wheel 1/2 turn clockwise from straight-ahead position. Remove key. Disconnect and isolate negative battery cable and wait at least 2 minutes. Remove cruise control switches or cover plates.

2) Remove air bag module retaining screws. Lift air bag module enough to disconnect air bag and horn connectors. Place module on bench with pad facing upward. Push horn switch locking tab inward, and remove horn switch. Remove steering wheel retaining nut and steering wheel.

Installation – Align master splines on steering wheel and shaft. Guide Yellow horn lead through small round hole. Guide air bag and cruise control leads through larger slotted hole. Install steering wheel using care not to pinch wires under steering wheel. Tighten steering wheel retaining nut to 45 ft. lbs. (61 N.m). To complete installation, reverse removal procedure. Tighten air bag module retaining screws to 89 INCH lbs. (10 N.m).

MULTIFUNCTION SWITCH

NOTE: Multifunction switch may be referred to as combination switch.

Removal & Installation – Disconnect and isolate negative battery cable. Remove tilt lever. Remove steering column covers. Remove retaining screws and multifunction switch. Disconnect connectors. To install, reverse removal procedure.

IGNITION SWITCH

Removal & Installation – 1) Disconnect and isolate negative battery cable. Remove tilt lever. Remove steering column covers. Remove Sentry Key Immobilizer Module (SKIM) if equipped. Remove multifunction switch. Disconnect electrical connector. Remove retaining screws and ignition switch.

2) To install, reverse removal procedure. A tab on ignition switch indexes to a notch in lock cylinder housing. *See Fig. 5.* Slot in end of switch fits over shaft in end of lock cylinder housing. Using key, rotate lock cylinder to align ignition switch with lock cylinder housing.

LOCK CYLINDER

NOTE: Interlock cassette for column shift models can only be adjusted one time. When installing a new ignition lock cylinder, interlock cassette must be replaced.

Removal – Disconnect and isolate negative battery cable. Remove tilt lever. Remove steering column covers. Turn ignition switch to RUN position. Press tab and pull lock cylinder from housing. *See Fig. 6.*

Installation – 1) Insert key into lock cylinder. Rotate ignition switch to RUN position (retaining tab can be pressed inward). Socket in housing must be in RUN position. Align shaft at end of lock cylinder with socket in housing. *See Fig. 7.*

2) Align lock cylinder with grooves in housing. Insert lock cylinder until tab engages hole in housing. Turn ignition switch to OFF position and remove key. If vehicle is equipped with column shift and new lock

CHRY
4-508

1999 ACCESSORIES & EQUIPMENT
Steering Column Switches
Concorde, Intrepid, LHS & 300M (Cont.)

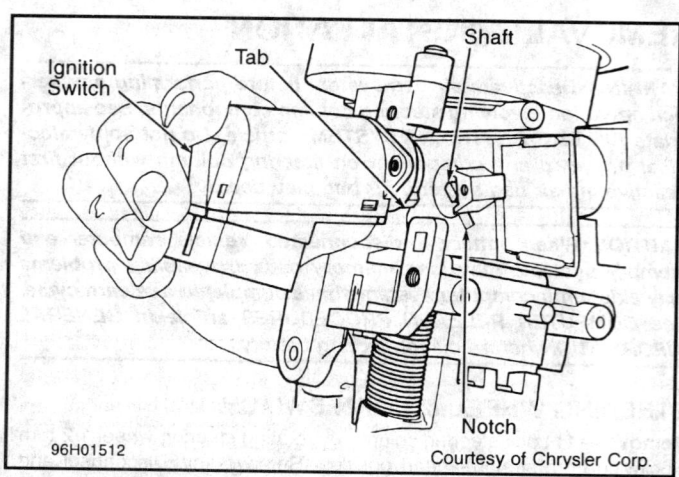

Fig. 5: Installing Ignition Switch

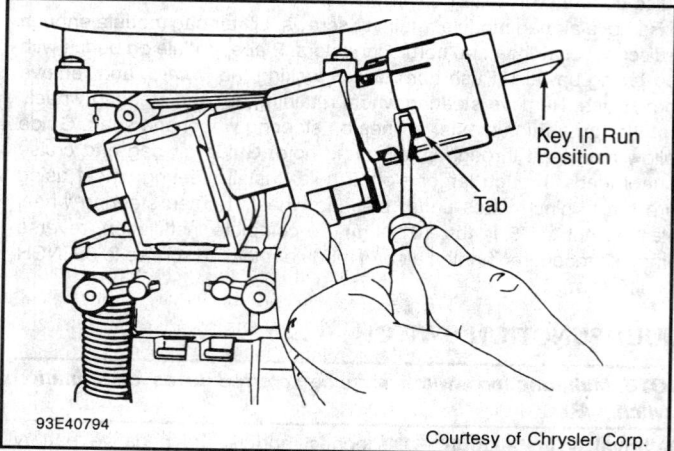

Fig. 6: Removing Lock Cylinder

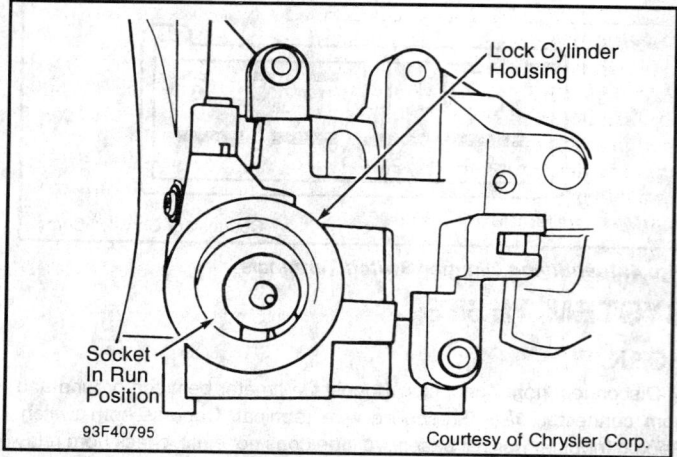

Fig. 7: Aligning Socket In Housing

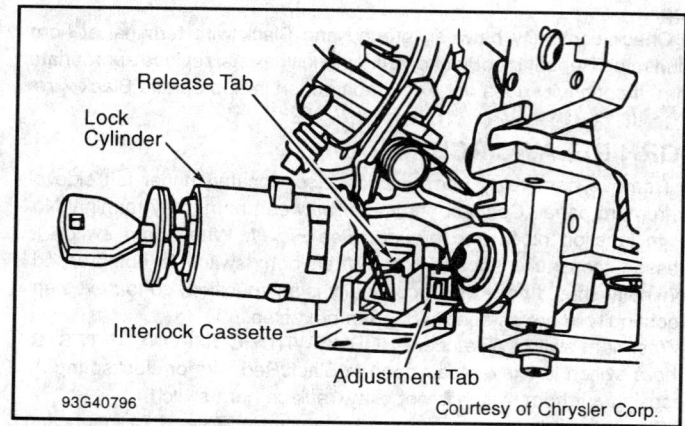

Fig. 8: Identifying Interlock Cassette

WIRING DIAGRAMS

cylinder was installed, go to next step. If vehicle is equipped with floor shift, adjust interlock cable. See FLOOR SHIFT INTERLOCK under ADJUSTMENTS. Reverse removal procedure to complete installation.

3) Press release tab on interlock cassette. *See Fig. 8.* Slide interlock cassette from housing. Disengage cable from locking arm on shifter mechanism.

4) Ensure latch rotates freely on shifter shaft. Set shifter lever in Park. Install cable over hook on shifter mechanism locking arm. Insert NEW cassette until it locks into position. Press adjustment tab until it stops. To complete installation, reverse removal procedure.

TORQUE SPECIFICATIONS

TORQUE SPECIFICATIONS

Application	Ft. Lbs. (N.m)
Steering Wheel Retaining Nut	45 (61)
	INCH Lbs. (N.m)
Air Bag Module Retaining Screws	89 (10)

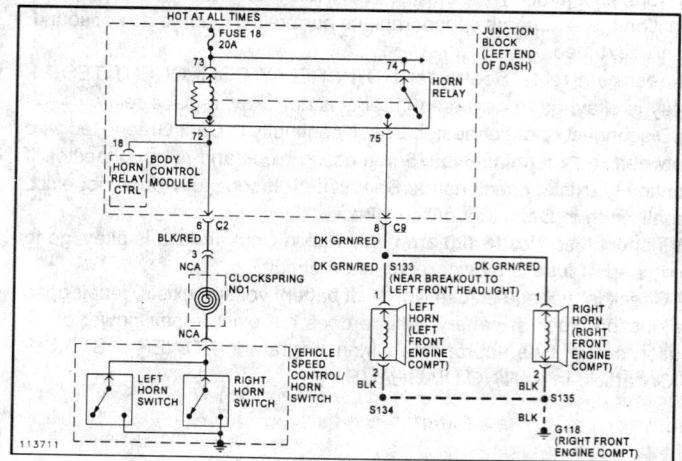

Fig. 9: Horn System Wiring Diagram (Concorde, Intrepid, LHS & 300M)

1999 ACCESSORIES & EQUIPMENT
Steering Column Switches
Dakota, Durango & Ram Pickup

WARNING: Deactivate air bag system before performing any service operation involving steering column components. See appropriate AIR BAG RESTRAINT SYSTEMS article. DO NOT apply electrical power to any component on steering column without first disconnecting air bag module. Air bag may deploy. Wait at least 2 minutes after disconnecting negative battery cable before servicing air bag system. System reserve capacitor, integral to ACM, maintains air bag system voltage for about 2 minutes after battery is disconnected. Servicing air bag system before 2-minute period may cause accidental air bag deployment and possible personal injury.

DESCRIPTION

Turn signal, hazard flasher, headlight beam selector, headlight flash-to-pass, windshield wipe, pulse wipe and windshield wash systems use a common switch assembly (multifunction switch) mounted within upper steering column housing.

Ignition switch and lock cylinder are incorporated into an assembly attached to side of steering column. Ignition switch assembly can be serviced as a separate unit, but requires removal of lock cylinder.

COMPONENT LOCATIONS

COMPONENT LOCATIONS

Component	Location
Combination Flasher Relay	Junction Block
Horn	In Right Front Corner Of Engine Compartment
Horn Relay	In Power Distribution Center
Junction Block	Under Left Side Of Instrument Panel
Power Distribution Center	In Left Side Of Engine Compartment, On Left Inner Panel
Relay/Flasher Module	Under Right Side Of Instrument Panel, Behind Glove Box

TROUBLE SHOOTING

TURN SIGNAL AND HAZARD FLASHER SYSTEM

Bulbs Burn Out Rapidly – Check charging system. See appropriate GENERATORS & REGULATORS article in STARTING & CHARGING SYSTEMS.

Hazard Flashers Inoperative – Blown fuse. Faulty hazard flasher. Open circuit in feed wire to hazard switch. Faulty turn signal/hazard switch. Open or grounded circuit in wiring to external lights.

Hazard Warning Lights Okay To Front Lights Only – Faulty external bulbs. Faulty contact in turn signal/hazard switch. Open circuit between hazard switch and turn signal switch. Open or grounded circuit in wiring to rear lights.

Hazard Warning Lights Okay To Rear Lights Only – Faulty external bulbs. Faulty contact in turn signal/hazard switch. Open or grounded circuit in wiring to front lights.

Indicator Light Inoperative, External Lights Okay – Burned-out indicator bulb in instrument cluster. Faulty contact. Open circuit.

Indicator Light Okay, External Lights Inoperative – Open circuit in wiring to external light(s).

Indicator Light Okay, External Lights Glow Dimly Or Do Not Flash – Loose or corroded external light connections. Poor ground circuit at external light(s).

Turn Signals Do Not Cancel After Turn – Broken canceling pawl on turn signal switch. Improperly aligned canceling cam. Broken or loose canceling cam.

Turn Signals Inoperative (Both Sides) – Blown fuse. Faulty turn signal flasher. Loose bulkhead connector. Loose or faulty rear wiring harness or terminals. Open circuit to turn signal flasher. Open circuit in feed wire to turn signal switch. Faulty switch connections. Open or grounded circuit in wiring to external lights.

Turn Signal Inoperative (One Side) – Faulty external bulb. Poor ground at external light. Open circuit in wiring to external light(s). Faulty turn signal/hazard switch.

COMPONENT TESTS

CAUTION: When battery is disconnected, vehicle computer and memory systems may lose memory data. Driveability problems may exist until computer systems have completed a relearn cycle. See COMPUTER RELEARN PROCEDURES article in GENERAL INFORMATION before disconnecting battery.

NOTE: For additional testing procedures, see appropriate CRUISE CONTROL SYSTEMS and WIPER/WASHER SYSTEMS articles.

NOTE: For component locations, see COMPONENT LOCATIONS.

HORN RELAY

1) Remove horn relay from Power Distribution Center (PDC). Use label on PDC cover to identify and locate relay. Check continuity between relay terminals No. 87A and 30. *See Fig. 1.* If continuity does not exist, replace relay. If continuity exists, go to next step.

2) Check continuity between relay terminals No. 30 and 87. If continuity exists, replace relay. If continuity does not exist, check resistance between relay terminals No. 85 and 86. If resistance is not 70-80 ohms, replace relay. If resistance is 70-80 ohms, go to next step.

3) Using jumper wires, connect positive battery voltage to relay terminal No. 86 and ground to relay terminal No. 85. Continuity should exist between terminals No. 30 and 87. Continuity should not exist between relay terminals No. 87A and 30. If continuity is not as specified, replace relay. If continuity is as specified, relay is okay. Go to HORN RELAY CIRCUIT test under SYSTEM TESTS.

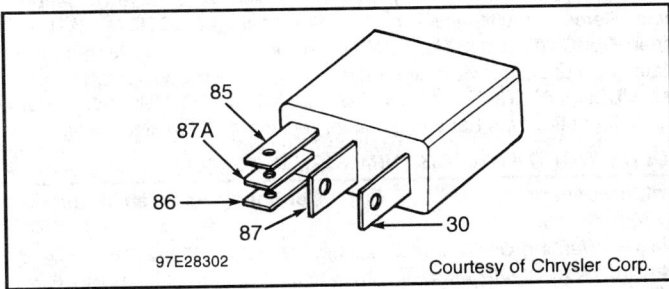

97E28302   Courtesy of Chrysler Corp.

Fig. 1: Identifying Horn Relay Terminals

IGNITION SWITCH

NOTE: For ignition switch circuit identification, see IGNITION SWITCH CIRCUIT FUNCTIONS table.

Remove ignition switch. See IGNITION SWITCH under REMOVAL & INSTALLATION. Check continuity between appropriate ignition switch terminals with switch in specified position. See IGNITION SWITCH CONTINUITY table. *See Fig. 2.*

CHRY
4-510

1999 ACCESSORIES & EQUIPMENT
Steering Column Switches
Dakota, Durango & Ram Pickup (Cont.)

IGNITION SWITCH CONTINUITY

Switch Position	Continuity Between Terminals
ACC	6 & 7
OFF	[1]
RUN	2 & 7; 4 & 5; 6 & 7
START	[2] 1 & 7; 2 & 7

[1] – Continuity should not exist between any terminals with key removed.

[2] – Continuity should also exist between terminal No. 3 and case ground.

IGNITION SWITCH CIRCUIT FUNCTIONS

Terminal No. (Wire Color)	Circuit
1 (DK BLU/YEL)	Ignition Switch Output (START)
2 (DK BLU)	Ignition Switch Output (START/RUN)
3 (GRY/BLK) [1]	Red Brake Warning Light Driver
4 (PNK/BLK)	Battery Feed To Ignition
5 (BLK/ORG)	Ignition Switch Output (RUN)
6 (BLK/WHT)	Ignition Switch Output (ACC/RUN)
7 (RED)	Battery Feed To Ignition

[1] – White wire on Dakota and Durango.

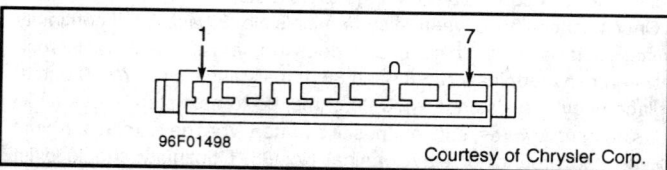

Fig. 2: Identifying Ignition Switch Connector Terminals (Harness Side)

MULTIFUNCTION SWITCH

Turn Signal/Hazard Warning Switch – Disconnect negative battery cable. Remove multifunction switch. See MULTIFUNCTION SWITCH under REMOVAL & INSTALLATION. Check continuity between appropriate multifunction switch terminals with switch in specified position. See MULTIFUNCTION SWITCH TURN SIGNAL TESTING table. See Fig. 3. If continuity is not as specified, replace multifunction switch.

MULTIFUNCTION SWITCH TURN SIGNAL TESTING

Switch Position	Continuity Between Terminals
Neutral	
Hazard Warning On	11, 12, 13, 15 & 16
Hazard Warning Off	12, 14 & 15
Left	12 & 14; 15, 16 & 17
Right	14 & 15; 11, 12 & 17
Optional Corner Lights	
Left	22 & 23
Right	23 & 24

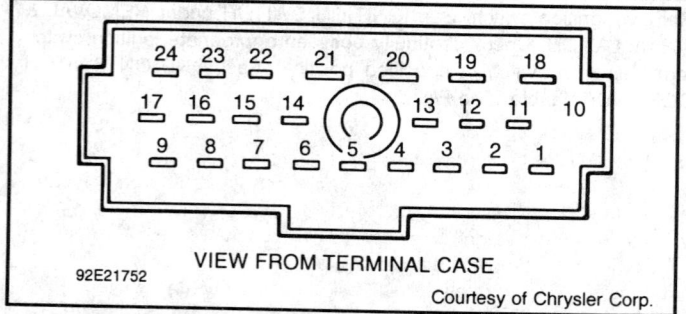

VIEW FROM TERMINAL CASE

Courtesy of Chrysler Corp.

Fig. 3: Identifying Multifunction Switch Terminals

SYSTEM TESTS

HORN

1) Check resistance between horn mounting bracket and ground. If resistance is zero ohms, go to next step. If resistance is not zero ohms, repair horn ground connection.

2) Check for battery voltage at horn harness connector when horn switch is pressed. If battery voltage exists, replace horn. If battery voltage does not exist, go to next step.

3) Test horn relay. See HORN RELAY under COMPONENT TESTS. If relay is okay, check horn circuit. See HORN RELAY CIRCUIT. If relay is not okay, replace horn relay.

HORN RELAY CIRCUIT

1) Remove horn relay from Power Distribution Center (PDC). Measure voltage between ground and horn relay terminals No. 30 and 86 in PDC. See Fig. 4. If battery voltage exists at both terminals, go to next step. If battery voltage does not exist at one or both terminals, repair open circuit to PDC.

2) Disconnect both horn connectors. Check continuity between horn relay terminal No. 87 in PDC and Dark Green/Red wire at each horn harness connector. If continuity exists, go to next step. If continuity does not exist, repair open in Dark Green/Red wire.

3) Check continuity between ground and relay terminal No. 85 in PDC. With horn switch depressed, continuity should exist. With horn switch released, continuity should not exist. If continuity is not as specified, go to HORN SWITCH. If continuity is as specified, no fault is indicated in relay circuits.

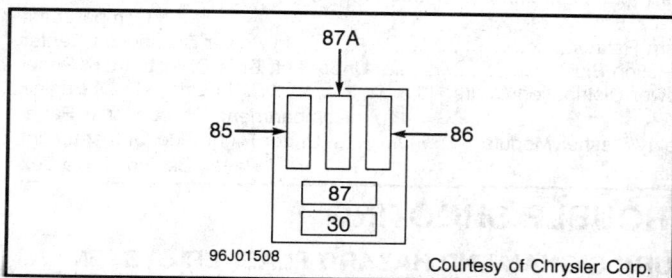

Fig. 4: Identifying Horn Relay Terminals In PDC

HORN SWITCH

1) Disconnect negative battery cable. Remove steering column opening cover from instrument panel. Check continuity between ground and metal steering column jacket. If continuity exists, go to next step. If continuity does not exist, check for proper installation of steering column mounting nuts.

2) Disable air bag system and remove driver's air bag module. See appropriate AIR BAG RESTRAINT SYSTEMS article. Remove horn relay from Power Distribution Center (PDC). Use label on PDC cover to identify and locate relay. Check continuity between horn relay terminal No. 85 in PDC and Black/Red wire at steering column horn switch connector. See Fig. 4. If continuity does not exist, repair open Black/Red wire. If continuity exists, go to next step.

3) Check continuity between ground and Black/Red wire at steering column horn switch connector. If continuity does not exist, go to next step. If continuity exists, repair short to ground in Black/Red wire.

4) Continuity between horn switch terminal and ground. Continuity should exist with horn switch depressed. Continuity should not exist without horn switch depressed. If continuity is not as specified, replace horn switch. If continuity is as specified, install horn relay and go to HORN under COMPONENT TESTS.

TURN SIGNAL & HAZARD WARNING SYSTEMS

1) If bulbs burn out rapidly, check charging system for overcharging condition. See appropriate GENERATORS & REGULATORS article in

1999 ACCESSORIES & EQUIPMENT
Steering Column Switches
Dakota, Durango & Ram Pickup (Cont.)

CHRY
4-511

STARTING & CHARGING SYSTEMS. If charging system is okay, go to next step. If charging system is not okay, repair as necessary.

2) If problem is turn signals failing to cancel after a turn, inspect multifunction switch or cancelling cam lobes on clockspring for damage or improper installation. If problem exists, repair as necessary. If problem does not exist, go to next step.

3) Turn ignition on. Actuate turn signal switch or hazard warning switch. Observe turn signal indicator light(s) in instrument cluster. If flash rate is very high, check for a bulb that is not lit or is dimly lit. Repair circuit or replace bulb as necessary. If turn signals fail to light, go to next step.

4) Turn ignition off. Check turn signal fuse in junction block and/or hazard warning fuse in PDC. If fuses are okay, go to next step. If either fuse is blown, repair short circuit and replace fuse.

5) Check for battery voltage at hazard warning fuse in PDC. Turn ignition on. Check for battery voltage at turn signal fuse in junction block. If battery voltage exists, go to next step. If battery voltage does not exist, repair open circuit to battery or ignition switch as necessary.

6) Turn ignition off. Disconnect negative battery cable. Remove combination flasher from junction block and replace with a known good unit. Connect battery cable and test operation of turn signal and hazard warning systems. If operation is okay, discard faulty flasher. If operation is not okay, go to next step.

7) Turn ignition on. Check for battery voltage at combination flasher terminals No. 51 and 48 in junction block. If battery voltage exists, go to next step. If battery voltage does not exist, repair open circuit to fuse in junction block or PDC as necessary.

8) Disconnect negative battery cable. Check continuity between combination flasher terminal No. 50 and ground. If continuity exists, go to next step. If continuity does not exist, repair open ground circuit.

9) Disconnect multifunction switch harness connector. Check continuity between junction block terminal No. 4 and multifunction switch terminal No. 13 (Pink wire). If continuity exists, go to next step. If continuity does not exist, repair open in Pink wire between multifunction switch and junction block.

10) Check continuity between junction block terminal No. 13 and multifunction switch terminal No. 17 (Red/White wire). If continuity exists, test multifunction switch. See MULTIFUNCTION SWITCH under COMPONENT TESTS. If continuity does not exist, repair open in Red/White wire between junction block and multifunction switch.

REMOVAL & INSTALLATION

WARNING: Deactivate air bag system before performing any service operation involving steering column components. See appropriate AIR BAG RESTRAINT SYSTEMS article. DO NOT apply electrical power to any component on steering column without first deactivating air bag system. Air bag may deploy.

CAUTION: When battery is disconnected, vehicle computer and memory systems may lose memory data. Driveability problems may exist until computer systems have completed a relearn cycle. See COMPUTER RELEARN PROCEDURES article in GENERAL INFORMATION before disconnecting battery.

HORN SWITCH

NOTE: Horn switch removal and installation information for Dakota and Durango is not provided by manufacturer.

Removal & Installation – Disconnect negative battery cable. Remove 4 air bag nuts from back of steering wheel. Pull air bag module back far enough to disconnect wiring connectors. Remove air bag module. To install, reverse removal procedure. Tighten air bag nuts to 90-97 INCH lbs. (9-11 N.m).

IGNITION SWITCH

CAUTION: DO NOT bump, jolt or hammer on steering shaft and gearshift tube.

Removal – Remove lock cylinder. See LOCK CYLINDER. Remove 3 tamper-proof Torx screws. *See Fig. 5.* Gently pull switch away from column. Release connector locks on wiring connectors and remove switch from connectors.

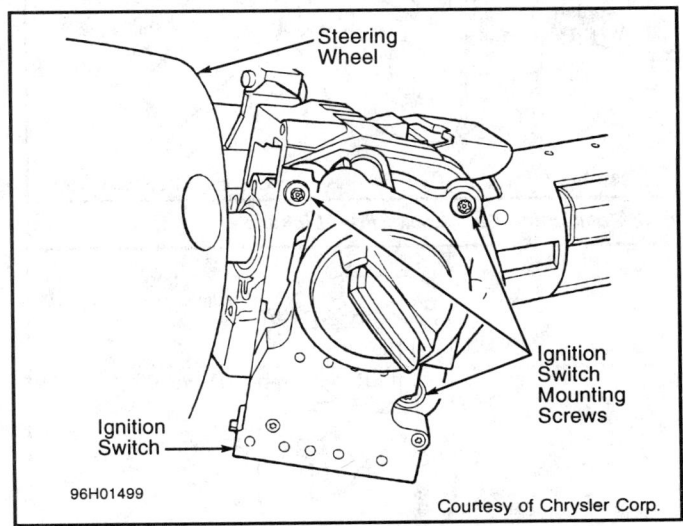

96H01499

Courtesy of Chrysler Corp.

Fig. 5: Removing Ignition Switch Mounting Screws

Installation – 1) Rotate flag on ignition switch to RUN position. This allows lock cylinder to mesh with switch. With key in lock cylinder, turn lock cylinder to RUN position so retaining pin can be depressed. Install lock cylinder in ignition switch (aligning slot) until retaining pin engages. Turn key to OFF or LOCK position.

2) Pull on lock cylinder to ensure retaining pin is retained in ignition switch and cylinder will not come out. On vehicles with automatic transmission, ensure shifter is in Park and dowel pin on ignition switch is in Park position. Ensure ignition switch is in LOCK position. On all models, ensure flag on ignition switch is properly indexed in Park position. The flag operates steering lock.

3) On vehicles with automatic transmission, apply a light coating of grease to park lock dowel and park lock slider linkage. *See Fig. 6.* Slide park lock slider linkage forward completely, then back .25" (6 mm). Apply a light coating of grease to column lock flag.

4) Carefully install ignition switch on steering column, ensuring flag is positioned above steering wheel lock lever, dowel pins on switch align in holes on steering column and park lock dowel pin slides into park lock slider linkage (automatic transmission only). *See Fig. 7.* Tighten mounting screws to 22-30 INCH lbs. (2.5-3.5 N.m).

5) Connect wiring connectors to ignition switch. Install upper and lower steering column covers. Tighten screws to 17 INCH lbs. (2 N.m). Install tilt lever (if equipped). Reconnect negative battery cable. Check for proper operation of ignition switch in all positions. Check for proper steering wheel lock operation. Check for proper automatic shift lock operation.

LOCK CYLINDER

Removal – Disconnect and isolate negative battery cable. On tilt columns, remove tilt lever. Remove upper and lower steering column covers. Place shifter in Park (if vehicle has automatic transmission). With key inserted and ignition switch in RUN position, press on retaining pin. *See Fig. 8.* Remove lock cylinder.

Installation – 1) With key in lock cylinder, turn lock cylinder to RUN position so retaining pin can be depressed. Install lock cylinder in ignition switch (aligning slot) until retaining pin engages. Turn key to

CHRY
4-512

1999 ACCESSORIES & EQUIPMENT
Steering Column Switches
Dakota, Durango & Ram Pickup (Cont.)

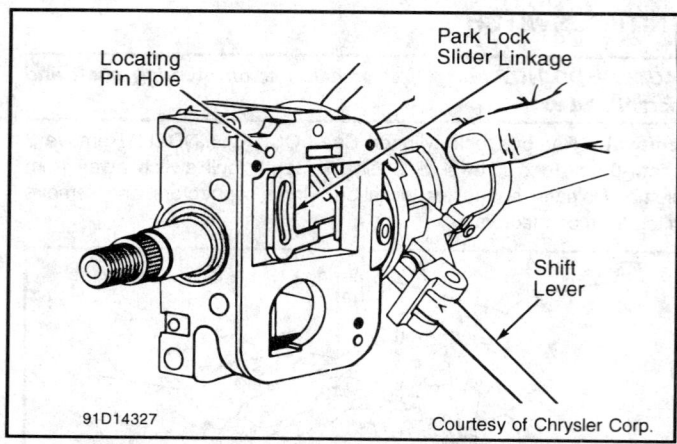

Fig. 6: Positioning Park Lock Slider Linkage

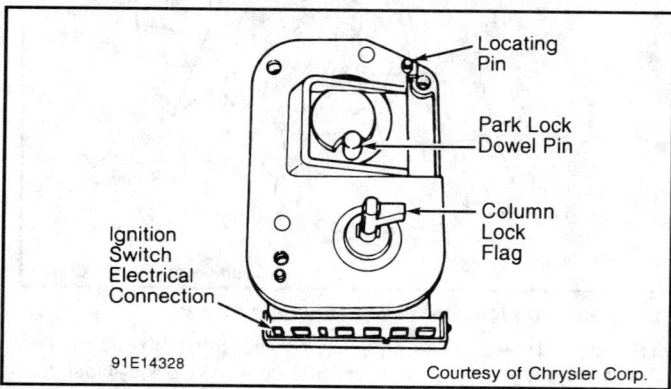

Fig. 7: Positioning Column Lock Flag

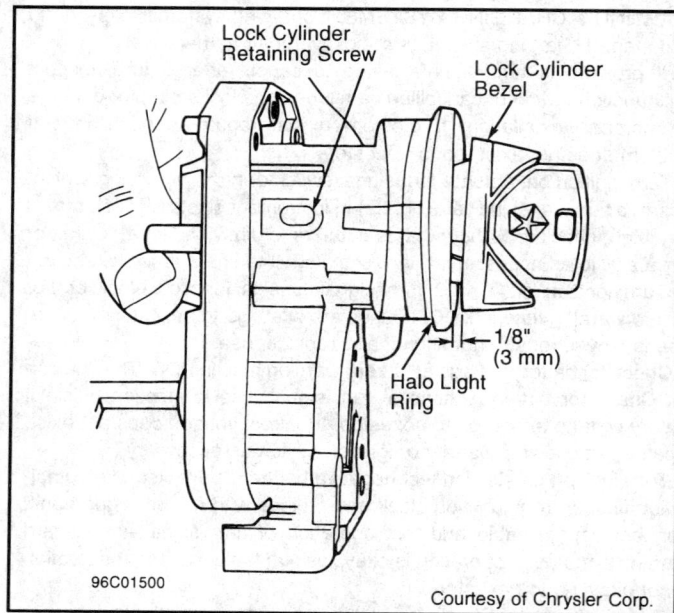

Fig. 8: Removing Lock Cylinder

OFF or LOCK position. Pull on lock cylinder to ensure retaining pin is retained in ignition switch and cylinder will not come out.

2) Install upper and lower steering column covers. Tighten screws to 17 INCH lbs. (2 N.m). Install tilt lever (if equipped). Connect negative battery cable. Check for proper operation of ignition switch in all positions. Check for proper steering wheel lock operation. Check for proper automatic shift lock operation.

MULTIFUNCTION SWITCH

Removal & Installation – Disconnect negative battery cable. On tilt columns, remove tilt lever. On all models, remove upper and lower steering column covers. Remove tamper-proof Torx screws. Pull switch away from column, and loosen connector screw (screw remains in connector). Remove switch. To install, reverse removal procedure. Tighten screws to specification. See TORQUE SPECIFICATIONS.

TORQUE SPECIFICATIONS

TORQUE SPECIFICATIONS

Application	INCH Lbs. (N.m)
Air Bag Retaining Nuts	90-97 (9-11)
Ignition Switch Mounting Screw	22-30 (2.5-3.5)
Multifunction Switch Connector Screw	17 (2)
Multifunction Switch Mounting Screw	17 (2)
Steering Column Cover Screw	17 (2)

WIRING DIAGRAMS

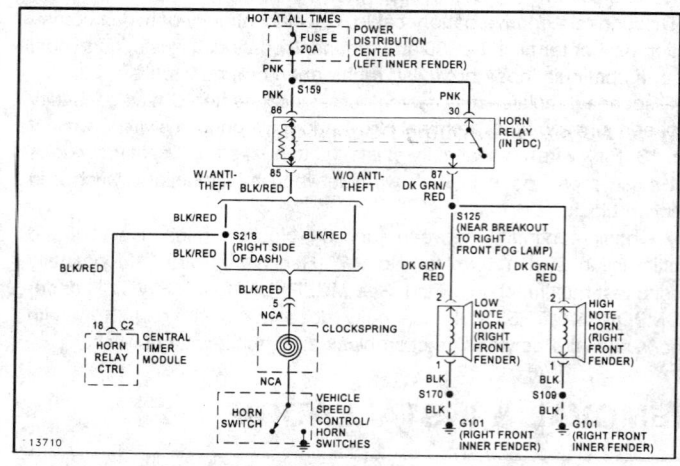

Fig. 9: Horn System Wiring Diagram (Dakota)

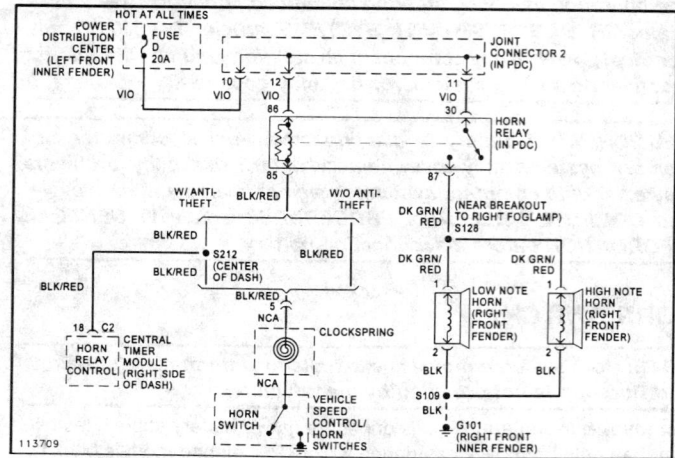

Fig. 10: Horn System Wiring Diagram (Durango)

1999 ACCESSORIES & EQUIPMENT
Steering Column Switches
Dakota, Durango & Ram Pickup (Cont.)

CHRY
4-513

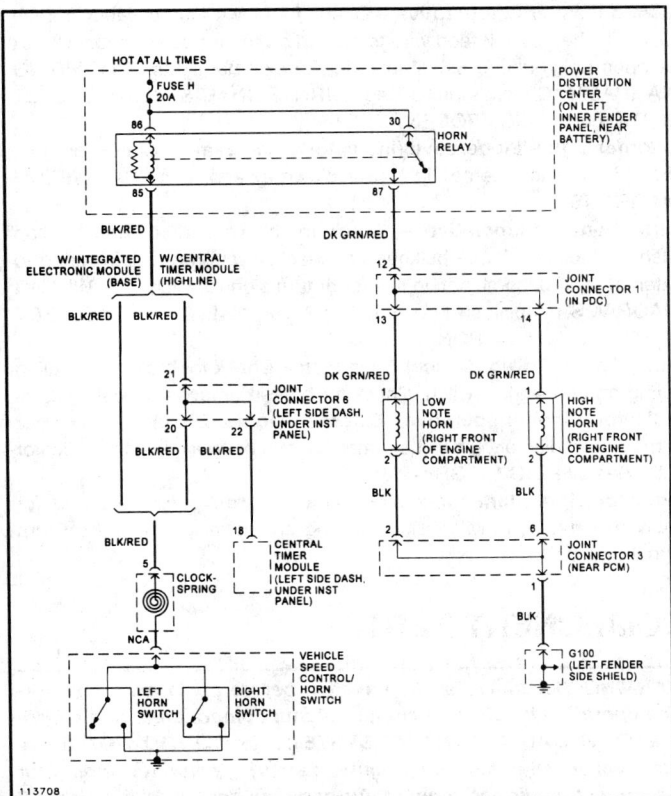

Fig. 11: Horn System Wiring Diagram (Ram Pickup)

WARNING: Deactivate air bag system before performing any service operation involving steering column components. See appropriate AIR BAG RESTRAINT SYSTEMS article. DO NOT apply electrical power to any component on steering column without first deactivating air bag system. Air bag may deploy.

DESCRIPTION & OPERATION

A multifunction (combination) switch incorporates turn signal, dimmer/passing and wiper/washer switches in one unit. Ignition switch and multifunction switch are mounted on steering column. *See Figs. 1 and 6.*

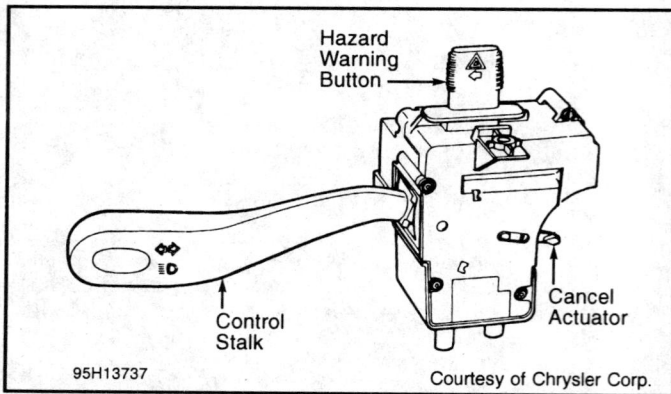

Fig. 1: Locating Multifunction Switch Controls

COMPONENT LOCATIONS

COMPONENT LOCATIONS

Component	Location
Combination Flasher Relay	Fuse Block
Horn	Left Front Wheelwell
Horn Fuse	Power Distribution Center
Horn Relay	Power Distribution Center
Fuse Block	Under Driver Side Instrument Panel
Power Distribution Center (PDC)	On Battery Tray

TROUBLE SHOOTING

HORN SYSTEM

NOTE: If horn sounds continuously, disconnect relay and horn to prevent damage to system.

Horn Sounds Continuously – Check horn relay. See HORN RELAY under COMPONENT TESTS. Check horn relay control circuit for short to ground. Check for pinched horn switch wire under driver's air bag module. Check horn switch. See HORN SWITCH under COMPONENT TESTS.

Horn Sounds Intermittently When Wheel Is Turned – Check horn relay control circuit for short to ground in steering column. See WIRING DIAGRAMS. Check for pinched horn switch wire under driver's air bag module. Check horn switch. See HORN SWITCH under COMPONENT TESTS.

Horn Inoperative – Check fuse No. 23 in Power Distribution Center (PDC). Check for open horn relay circuits. See WIRING DIAGRAMS. Check for faulty horn or horn switch. See appropriate test under COMPONENT TESTS.

Horn Fuse Blows – Check for short circuit in horn or horn wiring. See WIRING DIAGRAMS.

TURN SIGNAL & HAZARD FLASHER SYSTEM

Turn Signals Flash At Twice Normal Rate – Check for faulty exterior bulb or open circuit to exterior bulb. See WIRING DIAGRAMS. Check switch. See TURN SIGNAL & BEAM SELECT SWITCH under COMPONENT TESTS.

Turn Signals Dim & Flash Quickly (Indicator Light Okay) – Check for poor exterior light connection or ground. See WIRING DIAGRAMS.

Hazard Flashers Inoperative – Check for blown fuse or faulty combination flasher. Check feed wire to hazard switch for open circuit. Check for open or grounded circuit in wiring to external lights. See WIRING DIAGRAMS. Check switch. See TURN SIGNAL & BEAM SELECT SWITCH under COMPONENT TESTS.

External Lights Inoperative (Indicator Light Okay) – Check for open circuit in wire to external light(s) or blown exterior bulb. See WIRING DIAGRAMS.

Turn Signals Inoperative – Check for blown fuse or combination flasher. Check for loose bulkhead connection, open circuit in wiring to external light(s), combination flasher or turn signal switch. See WIRING DIAGRAMS. Check switch. See TURN SIGNAL & BEAM SELECT SWITCH under COMPONENT TESTS.

Turn Signals Do Not Cancel After Turn – Check for broken canceling spring on turn signal switch. Check for broken or loose canceling cam.

Indicator Light Inoperative (External Lights Okay) – Check for burned-out indicator bulb in instrument cluster or open circuit to indicator bulb. See WIRING DIAGRAMS.

Indicator Light Illuminates When Brakes Are Applied – Check for faulty multifunction switch or cancelling spring mispositioned on turn signal switch.

COMPONENT TESTS

WARNING: Deactivate air bag system before performing any service operation involving steering column components. See appropriate AIR BAG RESTRAINT SYSTEMS article. DO NOT apply electrical power to any component on steering column without first disconnecting air bag module. Air bag may deploy. Wait at least 2 minutes after disconnecting negative battery cable before servicing air bag system. System reserve capacitor, integral to ACM, maintains air bag system voltage for about 2 minutes after battery is disconnected. Servicing air bag system before 2-minute period may cause accidental air bag deployment and possible personal injury.

CAUTION: When battery is disconnected, vehicle computer and memory systems may lose memory data. Driveability problems may exist until computer systems have completed a relearn cycle. See COMPUTER RELEARN PROCEDURES article in GENERAL INFORMATION before disconnecting battery.

NOTE: For additional testing information, see appropriate BODY CONTROL COMPUTER TESTS article, CRUISE CONTROL SYSTEMS article or WIPER/WASHER SYSTEMS article.

HORN RELAY

1) Remove horn relay from Power Distribution Center (PDC). Use label on PDC cover to identify and locate relay. Check continuity between relay terminals No. 87A and 30. If continuity does not exist, replace relay. If continuity exists, go to next step.

2) Measure resistance between relay terminals No. 30 and 87. If continuity exists, replace relay. If continuity does not exist, check resistance between relay terminals No. 85 and 86. If resistance is not 70-80 ohms, replace relay. If resistance is 70-80 ohms, go to next step.

3) Using jumper wires, connect positive battery voltage to relay terminal No. 86 and ground to relay terminal No. 85. Continuity should exist between terminals No. 30 and 87. Continuity should not exist between relay terminals No. 87A and 30. If continuity is not as specified, replace relay. If continuity is as specified, relay is okay.

IGNITION SWITCH

NOTE: For ignition switch circuit identification, See IGNITION SWITCH CIRCUIT FUNCTIONS table.

NOTE: Key-in reminder switch is built into ignition switch assembly. If key-in switch requires service, ignition switch assembly must be replaced.

Remove ignition switch. See IGNITION SWITCH under REMOVAL & INSTALLATION. Check continuity between specified terminals with switch in appropriate position. See IGNITION SWITCH CONTINUITY table. *See Fig. 2.* Replace switch if continuity is not as specified.

IGNITION SWITCH CONTINUITY

Switch Position	Continuity Between Terminals
ACC	7 & 8
LOCK	[1]
RUN	3 & 4; 7 & 8; 7 & 9
START	1 & 2; 7 & 9; 7 & 10

[1] – Continuity should not exist between any terminals.

IGNITION SWITCH CIRCUIT FUNCTIONS

Terminal No. (Wire Color)	Circuit Function
1 (BLK)	Ground
2 (GRY/BLK)	Red Brake Warning Light Driver
3 (PNK/BLK)	Battery Feed To Ignition
4 (BLK/ORG)	Ignition Switch Output (RUN)
5	Not Used
6	Not Used
7 (RED)	Battery Feed To Ignition
8 (BLK/WHT)	Ignition Switch Output (ACC/RUN)
9 (DK BLU)	Ignition Switch Output (RUN/START)
10 (YEL)	Ignition Switch Output (START)

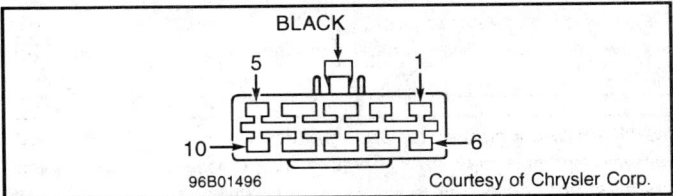

Fig. 2: Identifying Ignition Switch Terminals

MULTIFUNCTION SWITCH

NOTE: For wiper switch testing procedures, see appropriate WIPER/WASHER SYSTEMS article.

Turn Signal & Headlight Select Switch – Remove steering column covers. Remove multifunction switch mounting screws. Disconnect switch connector at steering column. Check continuity between specified terminals with switch in appropriate position. See TURN SIGNAL & HEADLIGHT SELECT SWITCH CONTINUITY table. *See Fig. 3.* Replace switch if continuity is not as specified.

TURN SIGNAL & HEADLIGHT SELECT SWITCH CONTINUITY

Switch Position	Continuity Between Terminals
Hazards On	B & E; C & H; C & I; C & J; C & K
Headlights	
Low	B2 & L
High	B2 & H
Flash-To-Pass	B1 & H
Turn Signals [1]	
Neutral	A & E; F & H; F & K
Left	A & E; C & I; C & K; F & H
Right	A & E; C & J; C & H; F & K

[1] – Ensure hazard switch is off.

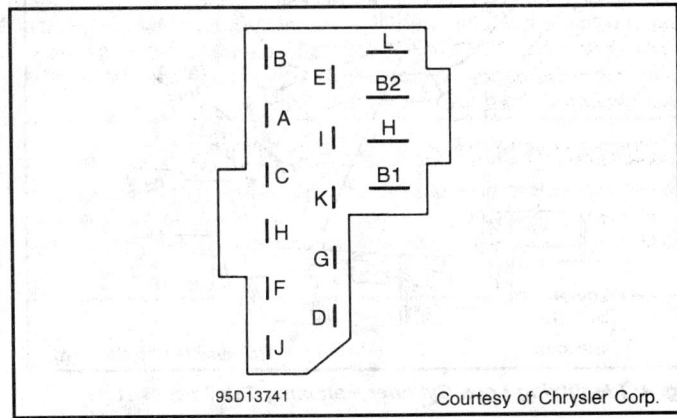

Fig. 3: Identifying Multifunction Switch Connector Terminals

REMOVAL & INSTALLATION

CAUTION: If battery is disconnected, vehicle computer and memory systems may lose memory data. Driveability problems may exist until computer systems have completed a relearn cycle. See COMPUTER RELEARN PROCEDURES article in GENERAL INFORMATION before disconnecting battery.

WARNING: Deactivate air bag system before performing any service operation involving steering column components. See appropriate AIR BAG RESTRAINT SYSTEMS article. DO NOT apply electrical power to any component on steering column without first deactivating air bag system. Air bag may deploy.

HORN SWITCH

NOTE: Horn switch is integral with driver's air bag module.

Removal & Installation – Disconnect negative battery cable. Wait 2 minutes for air bag system capacitor to discharge. Remove speed control switches from steering wheel and disconnect switch wires. Remove 2 bolts holding air bag module to sides of steering wheel. Lift air bag module and disconnect air bag squib and horn wire. To install, reverse removal procedure. Tighten air bag module bolts to 90-100 INCH lbs. (10-11 N.m) .

MULTIFUNCTION SWITCH

NOTE: Multifunction switch may also be referred to as combination switch.

Removal & Installation – Disconnect negative battery cable. Remove upper and lower steering column covers. Remove multifunction switch mounting screws. Disconnect wire connectors. Lift switch straight up to remove. To install, reverse removal procedure. Tighten multifunction switch and steering column cover retaining screws to 17 INCH lbs. (2 N.m).

IGNITION LOCK CYLINDER

Removal – Disconnect negative battery cable. Place ignition switch in RUN position. Through hole in lower shroud, depress retaining tab and remove lock cylinder. *See Fig. 4.*

Installation – 1) Insert ignition key into lock cylinder. Turn ignition switch to RUN position (retaining tab can be depressed).

2) Shaft at end of lock cylinder aligns with socket in end of housing. To align socket with lock cylinder, ensure socket is in RUN position.

3) Align lock cylinder with the grooves in housing. Slide lock cylinder into housing until tab sticks through opening in housing. Turn ignition switch to OFF position. Remove key. Connect negative battery cable.

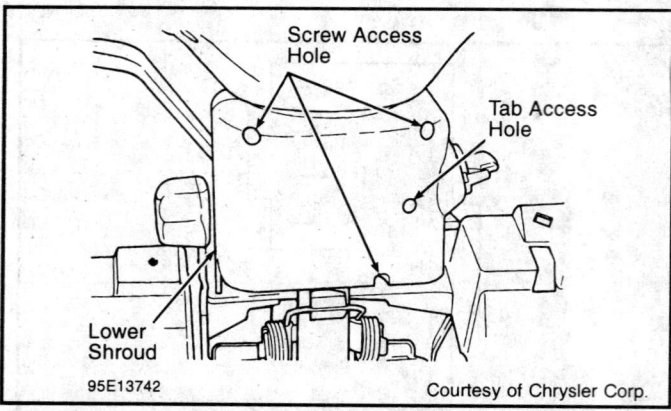

Fig. 4: Identifying Lock Cylinder Retaining Tab Access Hole

IGNITION SWITCH

Removal – 1) Disconnect negative battery cable. Place ignition switch in RUN position. Through hole in lower shroud, depress retaining tab and remove lock cylinder. *See Fig. 4.*

2) Remove upper and lower column shrouds from column. Disconnect electrical connectors from ignition switch. Using a No. 10 Torx bit, remove ignition switch mounting screw. Depress retaining tabs and pull ignition switch from steering column. *See Figs. 5 and 6.*

Installation – Ensure ignition switch and actuator shaft are in RUN position. Carefully install ignition switch. Switch will snap over the retaining tabs. To complete installation, reverse removal procedure.

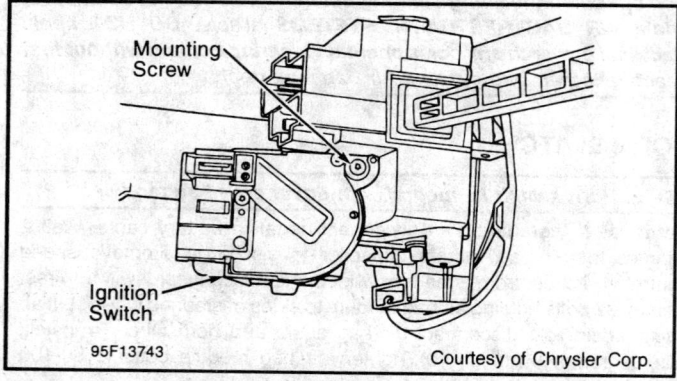

Fig. 5: Locating Ignition Switch Mounting Screw

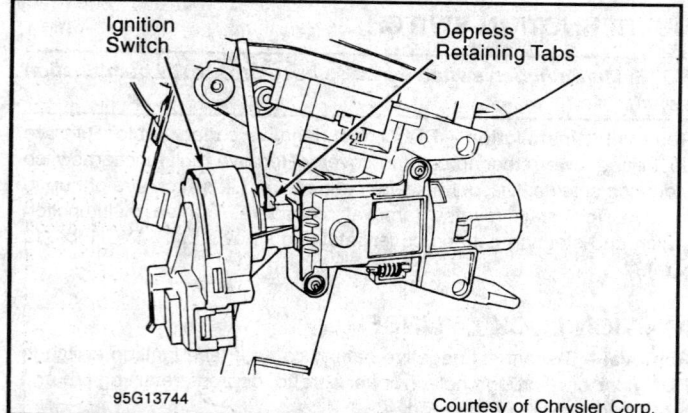

Fig. 6: Removing Ignition Switch

TORQUE SPECIFICATIONS

TORQUE SPECIFICATIONS	
Application	Ft. Lbs. (N.m)
Steering Wheel Nut	45 (61)
	INCH Lbs. (N.m)
Air Bag Securing Screws	53 (6)
Multifunction Switch Screws	17 (2)
Steering Column Cover Screws	17 (2)

WIRING DIAGRAMS

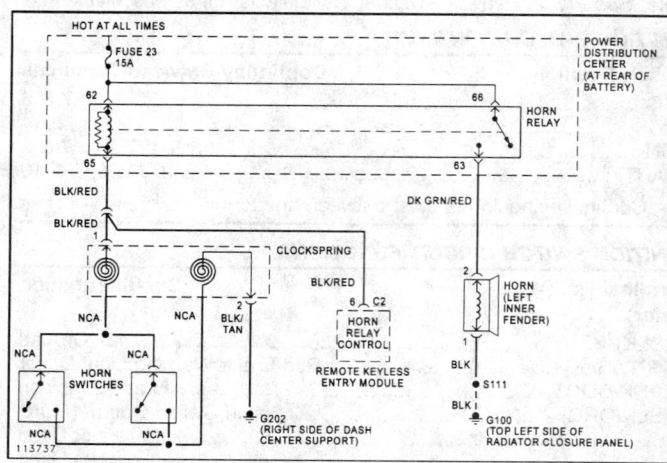

Fig. 7: Horn System Wiring Diagram (Neon)

DESCRIPTION & OPERATION

A multifunction switch incorporates turn signals, hazard warning flasher, autolamp dimmer/passing, horn and wiper/washer switches in one unit. Ignition switch and multifunction switch are mounted on steering column. All steering column switches are connected through 48- pin steering column connector located at base of steering column.

WARNING: Deactivate air bag system before performing any service operation involving steering column components. See AIR BAG RESTRAINT SYSTEMS – TRUCKS article. DO NOT apply electrical power to any component on steering column without first disconnecting air bag module. Air bag may deploy. Wait at least 2 minutes after disconnecting negative battery cable before servicing air bag system. System reserve capacitor, integral to ACM, maintains air bag system voltage for about 2 minutes after battery is disconnected. Servicing air bag system before 2-minute period may cause accidental air bag deployment and possible personal injury.

COMPONENT LOCATIONS

COMPONENT LOCATIONS

Component	Location
Combination Flasher Relay	Junction Block
Hazard Fuse	Power Distribution Center
Horn	Under Left Headlamp
Horn Relay	Junction Block
Junction Block	Left End Of Instrument Panel
Power Distribution Center	Left Front Corner Of Engine Compartment
Turn Signal Fuse	Junction Block

COMPONENT TESTS

CAUTION: When battery is disconnected, vehicle computer and memory systems may lose memory data. Driveability problems may exist until computer systems have completed a relearn cycle. See COMPUTER RELEARN PROCEDURES article in GENERAL INFORMATION before disconnecting battery.

HORN

1) Disconnect suspect horn connector. Check continuity between Black wire terminal and ground. If continuity exists, go to next step. If continuity does not exist, repair open ground circuit.
2) Check for battery voltage at Dark Green/Red wire terminal of horn connector with horn switch depressed. If battery voltage exists, replace faulty horn. If battery voltage does not exist, repair horn circuit as necessary.

HORN RELAY

1) Remove end cap from left side of instrument panel. Remove horn relay from junction block. Check for continuity between relay terminals No. 87A and 30. *See Fig. 1.* If continuity does not exist, replace relay. If continuity exists, go to next step.
2) Check for continuity between terminals No. 30 and 87. If continuity exists, replace relay. If continuity does not exist, check resistance between terminals No. 85 and 86. If resistance is not 70-80 ohms, replace relay. If resistance is 70-80 ohms, go to next step.
3) Using jumper wires, connect battery voltage across relay terminals No. 85 and 86. Continuity should exist between terminals No. 30 and 87. Continuity should not exist between terminals No. 87A and 30. If continuity is not as specified, replace relay.

HORN RELAY CIRCUIT

1) Check for battery voltage at horn relay terminals No. 30 and 86 in junction block. *See Fig. 1.* If battery voltage exists, go to next step. If battery voltage does not exist, repair open circuit between horn relay and fuse in PDC.

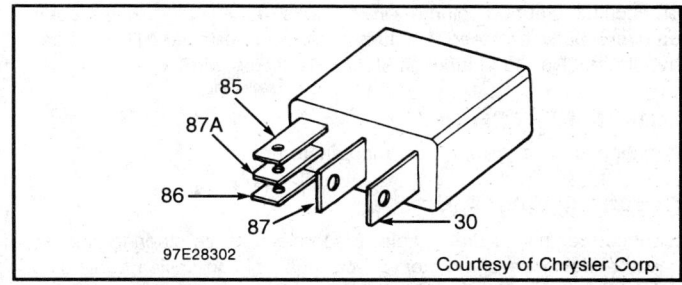

Fig. 1: Identifying Horn Relay Terminals

97E28302   Courtesy of Chrysler Corp.

2) Check for continuity between horn relay terminal No. 87 in junction block and each horn wire harness connector. If continuity exists, go to next step. If continuity does not exist, repair open circuit between junction block and horns.
3) Check for continuity between horn relay terminal No. 85 in junction block and ground. Continuity should exist when horn switch is depressed, and continuity should not exist with switch released. If continuity is not as specified, replace switch. See HORN SWITCH.

HORN SWITCH

1) Disconnect negative battery cable. Remove knee blocker from instrument panel. Check for continuity between metal steering column jacket and ground. If continuity exists, go to next step. If continuity does not exist, ensure steering column is installed correctly.
2) Remove air bag module from steering wheel. See AIR BAG RESTRAINT SYSTEMS – TRUCKS article. Disconnect horn switch wire connector from air bag module. Remove horn relay from junction block. Check for continuity between steering column half of horn switch wire connector and ground. If continuity does not exist, go to next step. If continuity exists, check horn contact. See HORN CONTACT.
3) Check for continuity between steering column half of horn switch wire connector and horn relay terminal No. 85 in junction block. If continuity exists, go to next step. If continuity does not exist, check horn tower. See HORN TOWER.
4) Check for continuity between horn switch wires on air bag module. If continuity exists, replace horn switch. If continuity does not exist, go to next step.
5) Depress horn switch and check for continuity between horn switch wires on air bag module. If continuity does not exist, replace horn switch.

HORN TOWER

Disconnect negative battery cable. Remove air bag module from steering wheel. See AIR BAG RESTRAINT SYSTEMS – TRUCKS article. Disconnect horn switch wire connector from air bag module. Remove lower steering column shroud. Check for continuity between steering column half of horn switch wire connector and electrically conductive disc on lower surface of turn signal cancel cam. Continuity should exist. If continuity does not exist, see HORN CONTACT.

HORN CONTACT

1) Disconnect negative battery cable. Remove air bag module from steering wheel. See AIR BAG RESTRAINT SYSTEMS – TRUCKS article. Disconnect horn switch wire connector from air bag module. Remove lower steering column shroud. Ensure horn contact on upper surface of multifunction switch housing is contacting electrically conductive disc on lower surface of turn signal cancel cam. Ensure horn contact moves freely in and out of multifunction switch housing. If horn contact operates as specified, go to next step. If horn contact does not operate as specified, replace multifunction switch.
2) Disconnect steering column wire connector. Check for continuity between horn contact and metal jacket of steering column. If continuity exists, repair short circuit in steering column wire harness or multifunction switch. If continuity does not exist, go to next step.
3) Check for continuity between horn contact and steering column connector terminal A11. *See Fig. 2.* If continuity does not exist, repair

CHRY
4-518

1999 ACCESSORIES & EQUIPMENT
Steering Column Switches – Ram Van & Ram Wagon (Cont.)

open circuit in steering column wire harness. If continuity exists, repair open circuit between steering column connector terminal A11 and horn relay terminal No. 85 in junction block (Black/Red wire).

IGNITION SWITCH

Information is not available from manufacturer.

MULTIFUNCTION SWITCH

Disconnect negative battery cable. Disconnect 48-pin steering column connector. Using an ohmmeter, check multifunction switch continuity. See MULTIFUNCTION SWITCH CONTINUITY table. *See Fig. 2.*

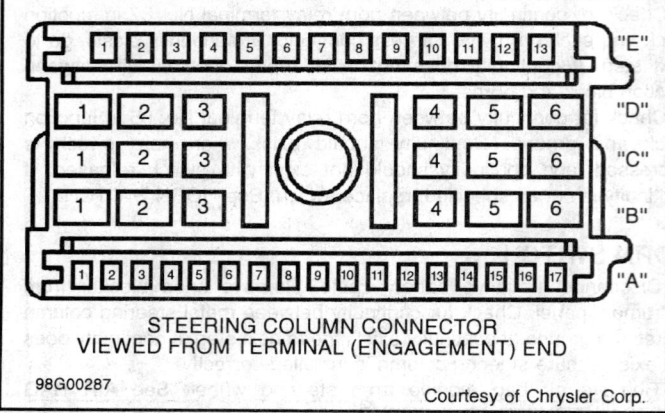

STEERING COLUMN CONNECTOR
VIEWED FROM TERMINAL (ENGAGEMENT) END

98G00287   Courtesy of Chrysler Corp.

Fig. 2: Identifying Steering Column Connector Terminals

MULTIFUNCTION SWITCH CONTINUITY

Turn Signal Switch Position	Hazard Warning Switch Position	Continuity Between Terminals
NEUTRAL	OFF	A1 & E2, A1 & E6, A1 & E7, A2 & A3, E2 & E6, E2 & E7
LEFT	OFF	A1 & E2, A1 & E6, A2 & A3, A7 & E9, E2 & E6, E7 & E9
RIGHT	OFF	A1 & E2, A1 & E7, A2 & A3, A6 & E9, E2 & E7, E6 & E9
NEUTRAL	ON	A6 & E9, A7 & E9, E1 & E8, E2 & E6, E2 & E7, E2 & E9, E6 & E9, E7 & E9

SYSTEM TESTS

WARNING: Deactivate air bag system before performing any service operation involving steering column components. See AIR BAG RESTRAINT SYSTEMS – TRUCKS article. DO NOT apply electrical power to any component on steering column without first disconnecting air bag module. Air bag may deploy. Wait at least 2 minutes after disconnecting negative battery cable before servicing air bag system. System reserve capacitor, integral to air bag control module, maintains air bag system voltage for about 2 minutes after battery is disconnected. Servicing air bag system before 2-minute period may cause accidental air bag deployment and possible personal injury.

CAUTION: When battery is disconnected, vehicle computer and memory systems may lose memory data. Driveability problems may exist until computer systems have completed a relearn cycle. See COMPUTER RELEARN PROCEDURES article in GENERAL INFORMATION before disconnecting battery.

TURN SIGNAL & HAZARD WARNING SYSTEM

1) If turn signals flash at a high rate, check for a bulb that is burned out or dimly lit. Repair circuit or replace bulb as necessary. If turn signals fail to light, go to next step.

2) Check turn signal fuse in junction block and hazard warning fuse in Power Distribution Center (PDC). If either fuse is blown, repair shorted circuit and replace fuse. If fuses are okay, go to next step.

3) Check for battery voltage at hazard warning fuse in PDC. Turn ignition on. Check for battery voltage at turn signal fuse in junction block. If battery voltage exists, go to next step. If battery voltage does not exist, repair open circuit between PDC and battery or between junction block and ignition switch.

4) Turn ignition off. Disconnect negative battery cable. Replace combination flasher with a known good unit. Connect negative battery cable. Test operation of turn signal and hazard warning systems. If operation is okay, repair is complete. If operation is not okay, go to next step.

5) Turn ignition on. Check for battery voltage at combination flasher terminals No. 48 and 51 in junction block. *See Fig. 3.* If battery voltage does not exist at both terminals, repair open circuit as necessary. If battery voltage exists at both terminals, go to next step.

6) Turn ignition off. Disconnect negative battery cable. Check for continuity between combination flasher terminal No. 50 in junction block and ground. *See Fig. 3.* If continuity exists, go to next step. If continuity does not exist, repair open ground circuit.

7) Disconnect steering column wire harness connector. Check continuity of Red/White wire between junction block connector C5, terminal No. 13 and steering column connector terminal No. A3. Continuity should exist. Also check continuity of Pink wire between junction block connector C6, terminal No. 4 and steering column connector terminal No. E1. *See Fig. 2.* If continuity does not exist, repair open circuit as necessary. If continuity exists, see MULTIFUNCTION SWITCH under COMPONENT TESTS.

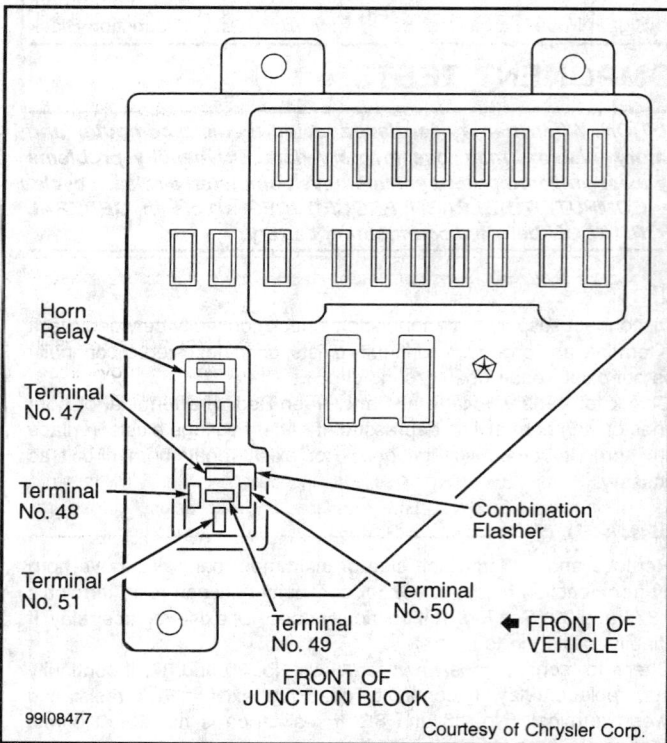

Horn Relay

Terminal No. 47

Terminal No. 48

Terminal No. 51

Combination Flasher

Terminal No. 50

Terminal No. 49

◄ FRONT OF VEHICLE

FRONT OF JUNCTION BLOCK

99I08477   Courtesy of Chrysler Corp.

Fig. 3: Identifying Combination Flasher Terminals In Junction Block

1999 ACCESSORIES & EQUIPMENT
Steering Column Switches – Ram Van & Ram Wagon (Cont.)

CHRY
4-519

REMOVAL & INSTALLATION

WARNING: Deactivate air bag system before performing any service operation involving steering column components. See AIR BAG RESTRAINT SYSTEMS – Trucks article. DO NOT apply electrical power to any component on steering column without first disconnecting air bag module. Air bag may deploy. Wait at least 2 minutes after disconnecting negative battery cable before servicing air bag system. System reserve capacitor, integral to air bag control module, maintains air bag system voltage for about 2 minutes after battery is disconnected. Servicing air bag system before 2-minute period may cause accidental air bag deployment and possible personal injury.

CAUTION: When battery is disconnected, vehicle computer and memory systems may lose memory data. Driveability problems may exist until computer systems have completed a relearn cycle. See COMPUTER RELEARN PROCEDURES article in GENERAL INFORMATION before disconnecting battery.

HORN SWITCH

Removal & Installation – Disconnect and isolate negative battery cable. Wait 2 minutes for air bag system capacitor to discharge. Remove air bag module screws from back of steering wheel. Pull air bag module back far enough to disconnect 2 wire harness connectors on air bag module. Remove air bag module. Remove 2 horn switch screws. Disconnect electrical connector. To install, reverse removal procedure. Tighten fasteners to specification. See TORQUE SPECIFICATIONS.

HORN RELAY

Removal & Installation – Disconnect negative battery cable. Remove end cap from left side of instrument panel. Remove horn relay from junction block. To install, reverse removal procedure.

IGNITION SWITCH & LOCK CYLINDER

NOTE: Lock cylinder removal is not necessary for ignition switch removal.

Removal – 1) Disconnect negative battery cable. Ensure shifter is in PARK position. Remove tilt lever by pulling it straight out. Remove upper and lower steering column shrouds. If removing ignition switch only, go to step **3)**. If removing lock cylinder, go to next step.

2) Insert ignition key and hold in START position. Insert a 1/16" pin punch into lock cylinder retainer pin access hole. *See Fig. 4.* Push in pin punch while releasing key to RUN position. Pull out lock cylinder.

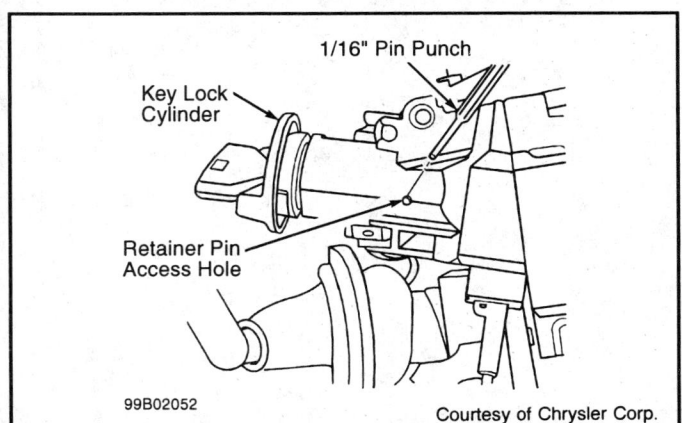

99B02052   Courtesy of Chrysler Corp.

Fig. 4: Removing Lock Cylinder

3) Lock cylinder removal is not necessary for ignition switch removal. Remove alarm switch. *See Fig. 5.* Press in on retaining clip with a small screwdriver while rotating switch 1/4 turn for removal. *See Fig. 6.*

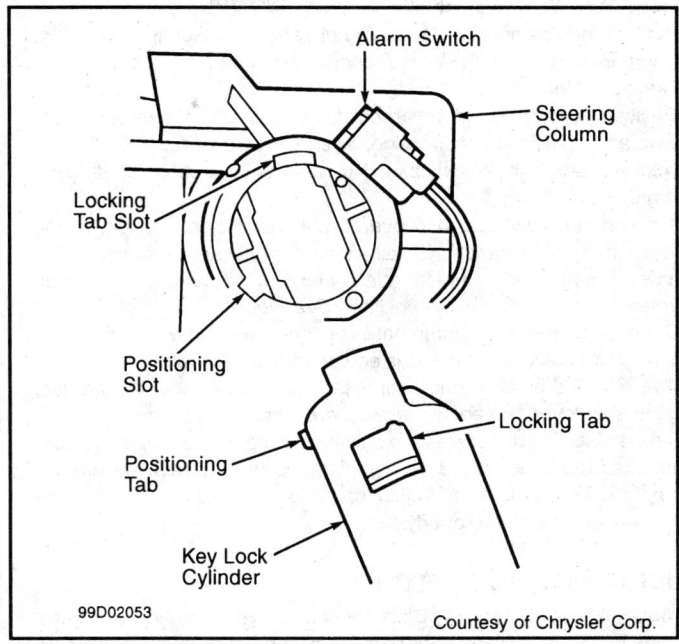

99D02053   Courtesy of Chrysler Corp.

Fig. 5: Installing Lock Cylinder

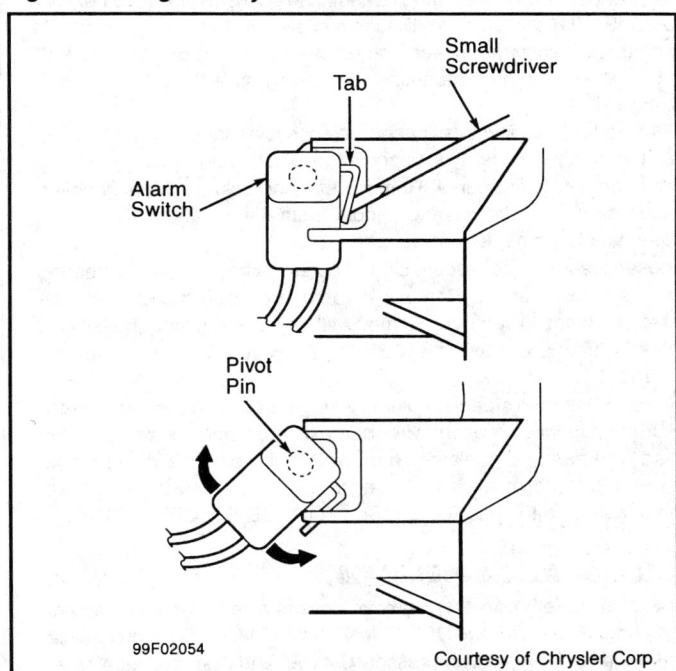

99F02054   Courtesy of Chrysler Corp.

Fig. 6: Removing & Installing Alarm Switch

NOTE: All steering column wiring harnesses and tie wraps must be installed in original locations to prevent damage to harness. Note positions of wiring harnesses and tie wraps before removal.

4) Remove knee blocker from instrument panel. On vehicles equipped with overdrive transmission, unclip OD wire harness at ignition switch. On all models, cut necessary tie wraps.

5) Remove 2 ignition switch mounting screws. Disconnect steering column wiring harness 48-pin connector. Separate 17-pin and 13-pin connectors from 18-pin connector. Separate multifunction switch wiring harnesses from ignition switch wiring harness. Remove ignition switch.

CHRY
4-520

1999 ACCESSORIES & EQUIPMENT
Steering Column Switches – Ram Van & Ram Wagon (Cont.)

Installation – 1) If lock cylinder was not removed, go to step **3)**. To install lock cylinder, insert key into lock cylinder. Align positioning tab on lock cylinder with positioning slot on steering column. *See Fig. 5.* Locking tab should align with locking tab slot.

2) Push in lock cylinder until retaining pin engages. Rotate key to OFF position. Ensure lock cylinder is properly retained by attempting to pull out lock cylinder.

3) Position switch and wiring harness to steering column. Install switch screws and tighten to specification. See TORQUE SPECIFICATIONS. Carefully route ignition switch wiring harness to bottom of steering column.

4) On vehicles equipped with overdrive transmission, clip OD wiring harness to ignition switch. On all models, route alarm switch wiring harness around ignition switch. Attach alarm switch to steering column by rotating and snapping into position. *See Fig. 6.*

5) Connect all steering column harness connectors. Install tie wraps in their original locations. If vehicle is equipped with tilt steering, operate tilt mechanism and ensure wiring harnesses do not bind. On all vehicles, operate shift lever and ensure wiring harnesses do not bind.

6) Before installing upper steering column shroud, ensure plastic spacer is attached to upper shroud. To complete installation, reverse removal procedure. Ensure ignition switch operates properly. Ensure column shift interlock operates properly.

MULTIFUNCTION SWITCH

Removal & Installation – 1) Disconnect negative battery cable. Wait 2 minutes for air bag system capacitor to discharge. Remove driver's side air bag module from steering wheel. See AIR BAG RESTRAINT SYSTEMS – TRUCKS article. Disconnect electrical connectors from air bag module. Disconnect speed control switch connectors, if equipped. Remove steering wheel mounting nut. Using suitable puller, remove steering wheel.

2) Remove fuse block access panel. Remove 5 steering column opening cover mounting screws. Pry upper edge of steering column opening cover from instrument panel. Remove steering column opening cover. Remove parking brake release handle, data link connector and hood release handle from knee blocker.

3) Loosen 2 screws that secure slotted holes of knee blocker to steering column support bracket. Remove 4 remaining screws and pull knee blocker rearward to remove. Remove tilt lever (if equipped). Remove steering column upper and lower covers. Remove 2 lower wire harness tie straps.

4) Remove bolt from steering column wiring harness connector. Disconnect 2 multifunction switch wire harness connectors from steering column wire harness insulator. Remove 2 multifunction switch screws. Remove multifunction switch. To install, reverse removal procedure. Tighten fasteners to specification. See TORQUE SPECIFICATIONS.

TURN SIGNAL CANCEL CAM

Removal & Installation – 1) Remove driver's side air bag module and clockspring. See AIR BAG RESTRAINT SYSTEMS – TRUCKS article. Using Shaft Lock Shield Compressor (C-4156) and Compressor Adapter (7100), remove retaining ring from upper steering column shaft. Remove shaft lock shield from upper steering column shaft. Remove turn signal cancel cam.

2) Lubricate conductive disc on lower surface of turn signal cancel cam with synthetic grease. Position turn signal cancel cam on steering column shaft. Position shaft lock shield onto shaft. Ensure shaft lock shield splines are aligned with splines on shaft. Install NEW retaining ring on shaft lock shield compressor.

3) Install compressor adapter and lock shield compressor on upper steering column shaft. Compress shaft lock shield far enough to install retaining ring into groove on upper shaft. To complete installation, reverse removal procedure. Tighten fasteners to specification. See TORQUE SPECIFICATIONS.

TORQUE SPECIFICATIONS

TORQUE SPECIFICATIONS	
Application	**Ft. Lbs. (N.m)**
Steering Wheel Retaining Nut	45 (61)
	INCH Lbs. (N.m)
Driver's Air Bag Module	90 (10.2)
Ignition Switch Screws	12 (1.4)
Lower Steering Column Shroud	30 (3.4)
Multifunction Switch Screws	53 (6)
Steering Column Harness	
Connector	40 (4.5)
Upper Steering Column Shroud	12 (1.4)

WIRING DIAGRAMS

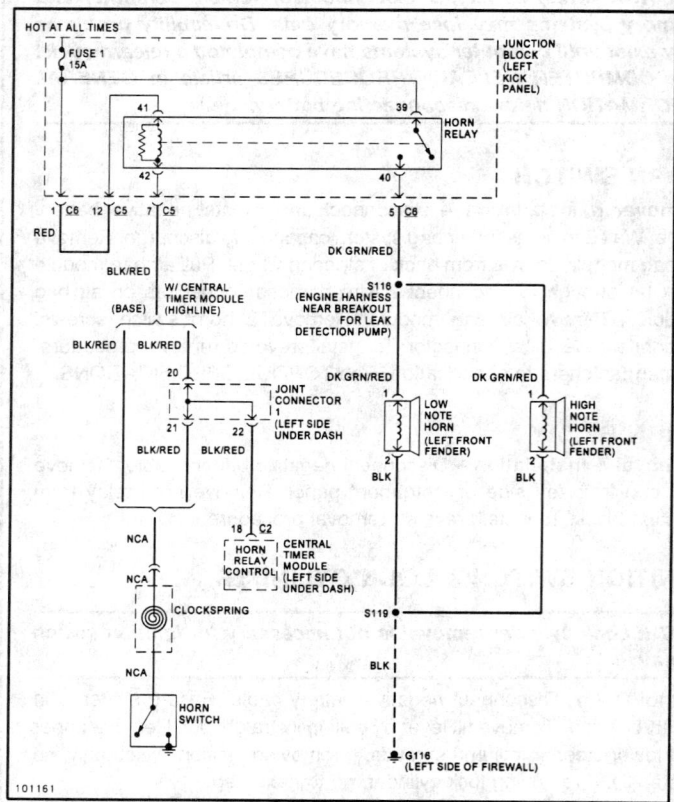

***Fig. 7: Horn System Wiring Diagram
(Ram Van & Ram Wagon)***

DESCRIPTION & OPERATION

Windshield wiper/washer system is a 2-speed intermittent system. Wiper motor is ferrite-magnet type. Wiper motor uses a 3-brush arrangement to control motor speed. Intermittent wiper relay for windshield wiper/washer system is located in wiper/washer switch. Windshield wiper/washer is activated by switch lever located on left side of steering column.

ADJUSTMENTS

WIPER ARM ADJUSTMENT

Adjust wiper and blade assembly so clearances between blade edges and ceramic line are within specification. *See Fig. 1.*

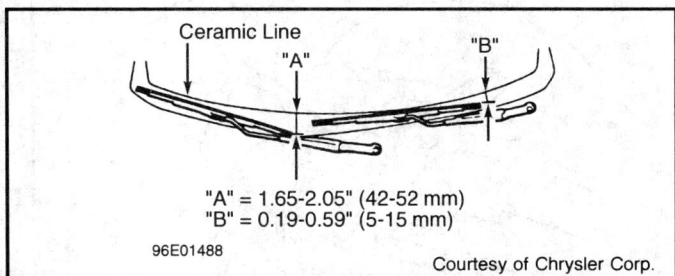

"A" = 1.65-2.05" (42-52 mm)
"B" = 0.19-0.59" (5-15 mm)

96E01488   Courtesy of Chrysler Corp.

Fig. 1: Adjusting Windshield Wiper Blades

TROUBLE SHOOTING

WIPERS & WASHER DO NOT OPERATE

Check fuse No. 9 (20-amp) in junction block. Check ground circuit. See WIRING DIAGRAMS.

ONLY LOW-SPEED OR HIGH-SPEED IS INOPERATIVE

Check wiper switch. See WINDSHIELD WIPER/WASHER SWITCH under COMPONENT TESTS.

WIPERS DO NOT STOP

Check wiper motor, intermittent wiper relay and wiper switch. See appropriate test under COMPONENT TESTS.

INTERMITTENT FUNCTION IS INOPERATIVE

Check voltage at steering column switch with intermittent wiper relay energized. See INTERMITTENT WIPER under SYSTEM TESTS.

INTERMITTENT OPERATION CANNOT BE VARIED

Check variable intermittent wiper control switch and intermittent wiper relay. See appropriate test under COMPONENT TESTS.

WASHER IS INOPERATIVE BUT WIPERS OPERATE

Check washer motor. See WINDSHIELD WASHER MOTOR under COMPONENT TESTS.

WASHER & WASHER ACTIVATED WIPER ARE INOPERATIVE

Check washer switch. See WINDSHIELD WIPER/WASHER SWITCH under COMPONENT TESTS.

WASHER ACTIVATED WIPER IS INOPERATIVE

Check intermittent wiper relay. See INTERMITTENT WIPER RELAY under COMPONENT TESTS. Check washer switch. See WINDSHIELD WIPER/WASHER SWITCH under COMPONENT TESTS.

COMPONENT TESTS

INTERMITTENT WIPER RELAY

Windshield intermittent wiper relay is an integral part of windshield wiper/washer switch assembly. Turn ignition switch to ACC position. Turn wiper/washer switch to INT position. *See Fig. 2.* Intermittent

operation cycling time should be about 3 seconds in fast mode and about 12 seconds in slow mode. If intermittent operation cycling time is not as specified, replace windshield wiper/washer switch assembly.

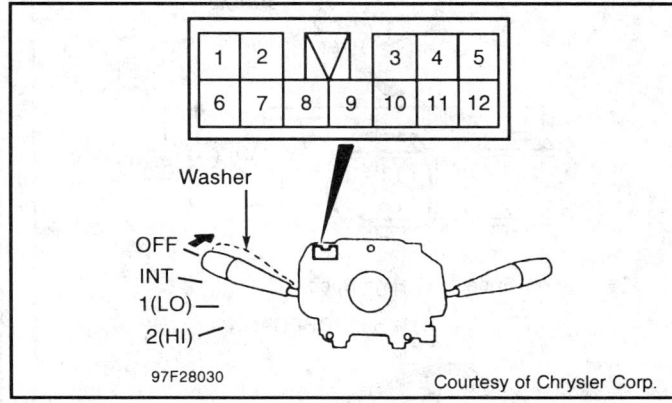

97F28030   Courtesy of Chrysler Corp.

Fig. 2: Testing Windshield Wiper/Washer Switch

WINDSHIELD WIPER/WASHER SWITCH

Disconnect wiper switch connector at steering column. Check continuity between appropriate switch terminals with switch in appropriate position. *See Fig. 2.* See WIPER/WASHER SWITCH CONTINUITY table. Replace switch as necessary.

WIPER/WASHER SWITCH CONTINUITY

Switch Position	Terminals
Wiper Switch	
Off	7 & 8
INT	7 & 8
1 (LO)	8 & 10
2 (HI)	9 & 10
Washer Switch (ON)	6 & 10

WINDSHIELD WIPER MOTOR

NOTE: DO NOT remove motor and link assembly when checking.

Disconnect wiper motor connector. Using jumper wires, connect battery voltage to motor. *See Fig. 3.* Ensure motor operates properly in low and high speeds. To ensure motor stops in park position, run wiper at low speed. Disconnect battery to stop motor. Reconnect battery as shown. Ensure motor starts turning at low speed and then stops at park position. Replace motor as necessary.

WINDSHIELD WASHER MOTOR

With washer motor installed, fill washer tank with water. With battery connected as illustrated, ensure water squirts out strongly. *See Fig. 4.*

SYSTEM TESTS

INTERMITTENT WIPER

Access multifunction switch. Turn ignition on. Using a voltmeter, back-probe wiper/washer switch terminal No. 7. *See Fig. 2.* Voltage should switch from zero volts to battery voltage continuously. If voltage does not exist, check intermittent wiper relay and wiper switch. See appropriate test under COMPONENT TESTS. If battery voltage exists, check intermittent wiper relay. See INTERMITTENT WIPER RELAY under COMPONENT TESTS.

CHRY
4-522

1999 ACCESSORIES & EQUIPMENT
Wiper/Washer Systems – Avenger & Sebring Coupe (Cont.)

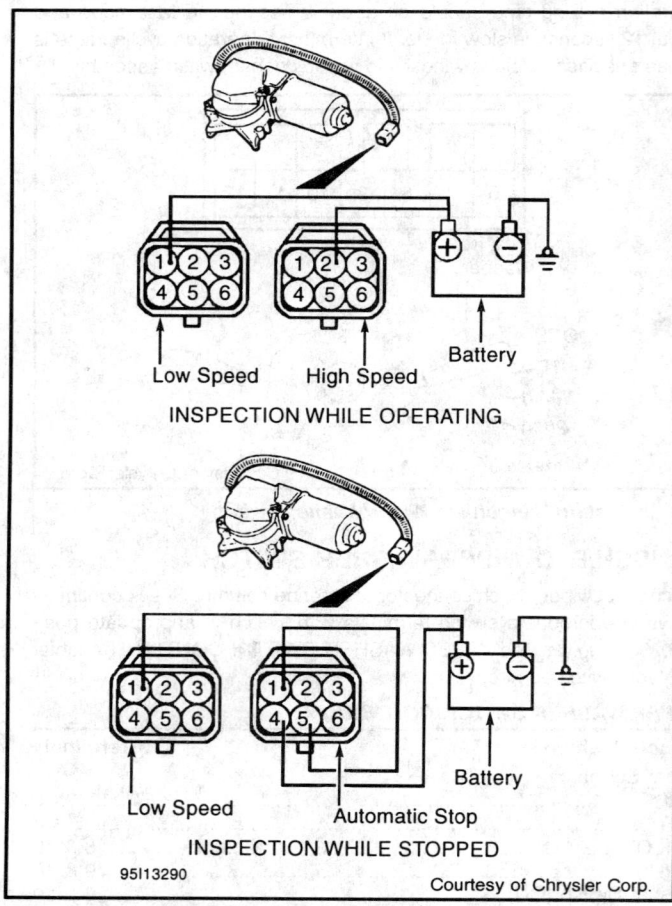

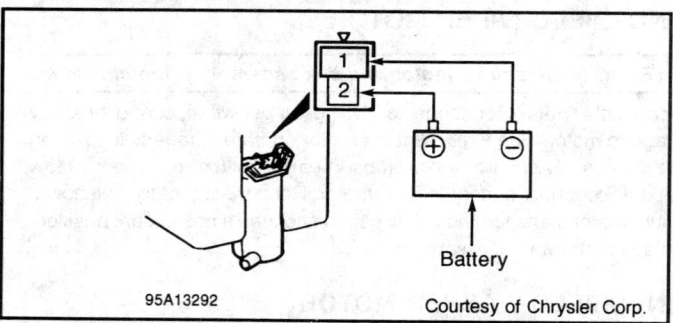

Fig. 3: Testing Windshield Wiper Motor

Fig. 4: Testing Windshield Washer Motor

REMOVAL & INSTALLATION

WARNING: On vehicles equipped with air bag restraint system, see appropriate AIR BAG RESTRAINT SYSTEMS article before servicing steering wheel or column. Use extreme caution to avoid personal injury and vehicle damage.

CAUTION: When battery is disconnected, vehicle computer and memory systems may lose memory data. Driveability problems may exist until computer systems have completed a relearn cycle. See COMPUTER RELEARN PROCEDURES article in GENERAL INFORMATION before disconnecting battery.

WINDSHIELD WIPER MOTOR & LINK ASSEMBLY

Removal & Installation – Remove wiper arms and blades. Remove front deck garnish. Disconnect motor wire connector. Remove wiper motor and link assembly. To install, reverse removal procedure.

WINDSHIELD INTERMITTENT WIPER RELAY

Removal & Installation – This relay is an integral part of windshield wiper/washer switch assembly. *See Fig. 5.* See WINDSHIELD WIPER/WASHER SWITCH.

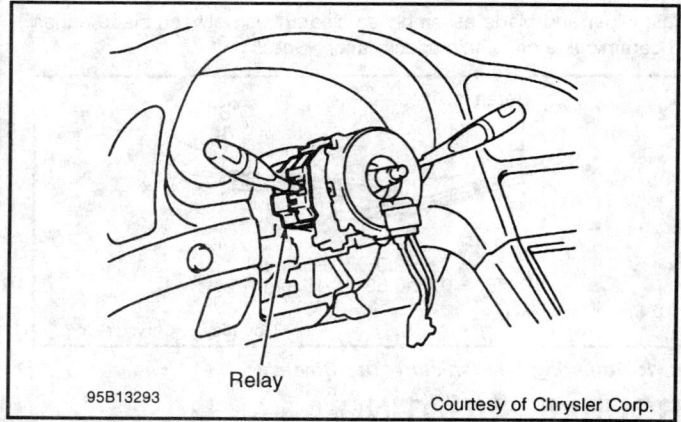

Fig. 5: Locating Intermittent Wiper Relay

WINDSHIELD WIPER/WASHER SWITCH

WARNING: Failure to follow air bag service precautions may result in air bag deployment and personal injury. After component replacement, perform an air bag system operational check to ensure proper system operation.

Removal & Installation – 1) Disconnect negative battery cable and insulate terminal. Wait at least 60 seconds after disconnecting battery to perform any further operation.

2) Set steering wheel and front wheels to straight-ahead position, and remove ignition key. Using a socket, remove air bag module mounting nut from back side. When disconnecting clockspring connector from air bag module, press clockspring connector lock toward outer side to spread open. Using a screwdriver, gently pry out connector. Store air bag aside, face up, on a flat surface.

3) Using a suitable puller, remove steering wheel. Remove upper and lower column covers. Remove multifunction switch assembly. If necessary, disconnect clockspring and body wiring harness connectors, and remove clockspring. To install, reverse removal procedure.

1999 ACCESSORIES & EQUIPMENT
Wiper/Washer Systems – Avenger & Sebring Coupe (Cont.)

CHRY
4-523

WIRING DIAGRAMS

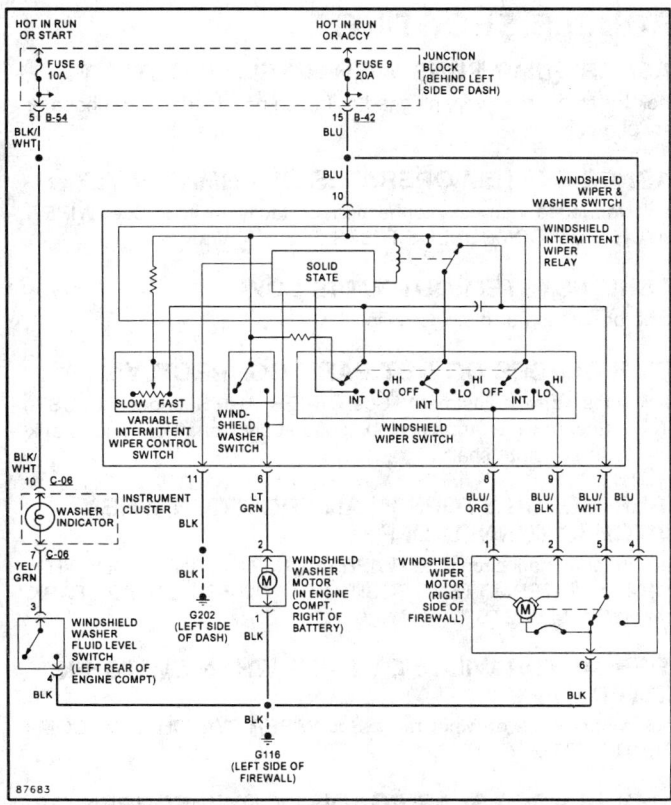

Fig. 6: Front Wiper/Washer System Wiring Diagram (Avenger & Sebring Coupe)

1999 ACCESSORIES & EQUIPMENT
Wiper/Washer Systems
Breeze, Cirrus, Sebring Convertible & Stratus

DESCRIPTION & OPERATION

Windshield wiper/washer system has normal wipe (low and high speeds), intermittent wipe, wiper after wash and mist wipe functions. Wiper functions are selected using multifunction switch located on a stalk mounted on steering column.

Intermittent functions of wiper/washer system are controlled by Body Control Module (BCM). BCM is located on junction block. Junction block is located under left side of instrument panel. *See Fig. 1.* Wiper/washer system uses intermittent and high/low wiper relays located in Power Distribution Center (PDC). PDC is located next to air cleaner cover and Powertrain Control Module (PCM).

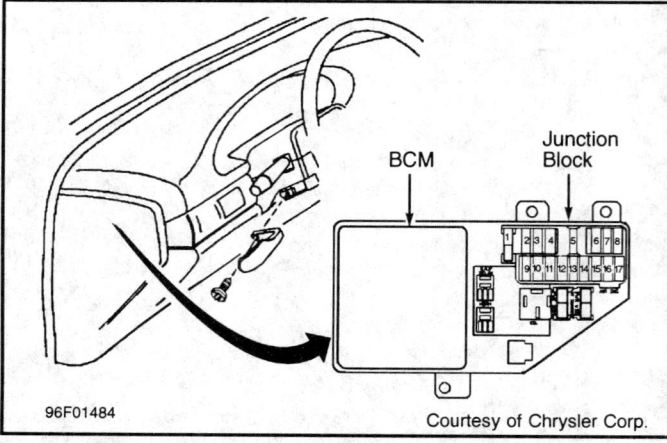

Fig. 1: Locating BCM & Junction Block

ADJUSTMENTS

WIPER ARMS

NOTE: During high speed wet windshield operation, right blade tip may ride over cowl screen. This is normal.

1) Lift wiper arms away from glass. With ignition in ON or ACC position, operate wipers in low speed. Turn wipers off and let wipers park. Turn ignition off.
2) Carefully lower arms and blades to windshield. Measure distance of blade tips to cowl screen edge. *See Fig. 2.* Measurement should be .710-1.65″ (18-42 mm). If measurement is not within specification, check for worn parts.
3) If blade tip strikes cowl screen or molding, remove arm. Remove molded keyway from pivot shaft by cutting or breaking it off. File surface smooth. Position arm on windshield and tighten nut to 27-32 ft. lbs. (37-43 N.m).

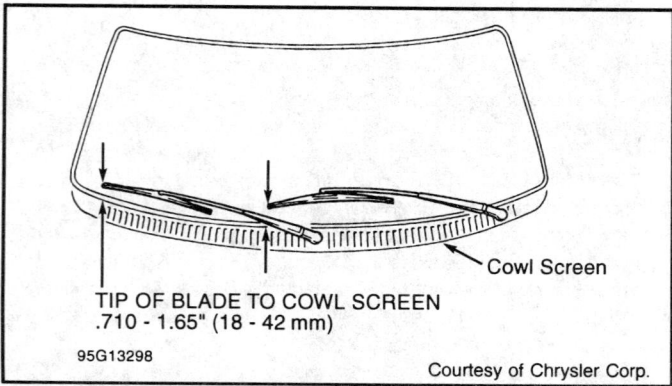

TIP OF BLADE TO COWL SCREEN
.710 - 1.65" (18 - 42 mm)

Fig. 2: Adjusting Windshield Wiper Arms

TROUBLE SHOOTING

WASHER PUMP RUNS WITH NO FLUID OUTPUT

Check for empty reservoir, plugged or frozen nozzle, damaged hose or faulty pump.

WASHER SYSTEM OPERATES INTERMITTENTLY

Check for loose harness connection or faulty switch. See WIPER SWITCH under COMPONENT TESTS.

WASHER SYSTEM OUTPUT IS LOW

Check for pinched or blocked hose.

WIPER BLADES DO NOT PARK CORRECTLY

Check wiper arm adjustment. See WIPER ARMS under ADJUSTMENTS. Ensure wiper arms are not loose at pivot shaft or motor crank is not loose at output shaft.

WIPER MOTOR STOPS IN ANY POSITION WHEN SWITCH IS TURNED OFF

Check for open park circuit. See WIPER RUNS CONTINUOUSLY WITH SWITCH IN INTERMITTENT POSITION & WIPERS DO NOT PARK under SYSTEM TESTS.

WIPER MOTOR WILL NOT STOP WHEN SWITCH IS TURNED OFF

Check wiper switch or wiper relay. See WIPER SWITCH under COMPONENT TESTS.

WIPER BLADES SLAP AGAINST COWL SCREEN OR WINDOW MOLDINGS

Check wiper arm adjustment. See WIPER ARMS under ADJUSTMENTS.

WIPER BLADE CHATTER

Check for worn or dirty blades, twisted wiper arm, bent blade or weather checked blade.

KNOCKING NOISE DURING OPERATION

Check for worn linkage bushings or excessive motor end play.

WIPERS INOPERATIVE

Check wiper fuse, short in harness or switch, faulty motor, open power supply or ground circuits or poor ground. See WIPERS INOPERATIVE under SYSTEM TESTS.

COMPONENT TESTS

WARNING: For all vehicles equipped with air bag restraint systems, see appropriate AIR BAG RESTRAINT SYSTEMS article before servicing steering wheel or column. Use extreme caution to avoid personal injury and vehicle damage.

NOTE: If problem occurs in electronic components, wiring, wiper switch or wiper motor, a Diagnostic Trouble Code (DTC) will be stored in BCM. For testing procedures, see appropriate BODY CONTROL COMPUTER TESTS article.

WIPER SWITCH

For complete multifunction switch testing, see appropriate STEERING COLUMN SWITCHES article. Disconnect wiper switch harness connector. Check continuity between appropriate terminals with switch in specified position. See WIPER SWITCH CONTINUITY table. *See Fig. 3.* If continuity is not as specified, replace multifunction switch.

1999 ACCESSORIES & EQUIPMENT
Wiper/Washer Systems
Breeze, Cirrus, Sebring Convertible & Stratus (Cont.)

CHRY
4-525

WIPER SWITCH CONTINUITY

Position	Terminals	Resistance (k/ohms)
Intermittent	2 & 3	[1]
Delay Level		
1	2 & 3	11.87
2	2 & 3	9.87
3	2 & 3	7.87
4	2 & 3	5.87
5	2 & 3	3.87
6	2 & 3	1.87
LOW	2 & 3	1.25
HIGH	2 & 3	1.82
MIST (On)	2 & 3	1.25
WASH (On)	1 & 3	[1]

[1] – Continuity should exist.

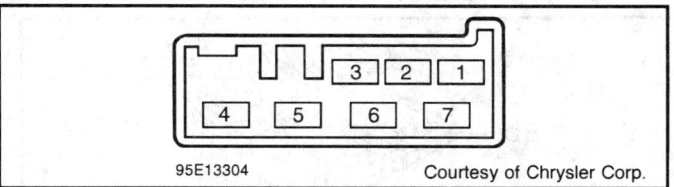

95E13304   Courtesy of Chrysler Corp.

Fig. 3: Identifying Wiper Switch Terminals

SYSTEM TESTS

WARNING: All vehicles are equipped with air bag restraint systems. See appropriate AIR BAG RESTRAINT SYSTEMS article before servicing steering wheel or column. Use extreme caution to avoid personal injury and vehicle damage.

NOTE: If problem occurs in electronic components, wiring, wiper switch or wiper motor, a Diagnostic Trouble Code (DTC) will be stored in BCM. For testing procedures, see appropriate BODY CONTROL COMPUTER TESTS article.

WIPERS INOPERATIVE

1) Check fuse No. 15 (10-amp) in junction block and fuses No. 8 (20-amp) and 18 (40-amp) in Power Distribution Center (PDC). See Figs. 4 and 5. If fuses are okay, go to next step. If fuses are blown, replace fuses and check motor operation in all switch positions. If motor is still inoperative and fuse does not blow, go to next step. If replacement fuse blows, go to step **11)**.

2) Disconnect wiper motor connector. Using jumper wire, connect battery voltage to wiper motor terminal "B". Connect another jumper wire to ground and wiper motor terminal "C". See Fig. 6. If wipers do not operate at low speed, go to step **4)**. If wipers operate at low speed, go to next step.

3) Connect positive jumper wire to wiper motor terminal "A". Ensure negative jumper wire is still connected to wiper motor terminal "C". If wipers do not operate at high speed, go to next step. If wipers operate at high speed, go to step **5)**.

4) Check continuity between ground and wiper motor connector terminal "C". If continuity exists, replace wiper motor. If continuity does not exist, repair open ground circuit.

5) Remove intermittent wiper relay from PDC. Check for battery voltage at intermittent wiper relay terminal No. 29 in PDC. See Fig. 5. If battery voltage exists, go to next step. If battery voltage dose not exist, check fuse No. 18 (40-amp) in PDC. Check Red/Gray wire between PDC and intermittent wiper relay. Repair as necessary.

6) Remove high/low relay from PDC. Check continuity between high/low wiper relay terminal No. 28 and wiper motor connector terminal "A" (Red/Yellow wire). See Fig. 5. Check continuity between high/low wiper relay terminal No. 11 and wiper motor connector terminal "B" (Brown/

Orange wire). If continuity exists in both wires, go to next step. If continuity does not exist in one or both wires, repair open in appropriate wire.

7) Check for continuity between high/low wiper relay terminal No. 36 and intermittent wiper relay terminal No. 37. See Fig. 5. If continuity exists, check for faulty relays. If relays are okay, go to next step. If continuity does not exist, repair open in appropriate wire.

8) Disconnect Body Control Module (BCM) Black 14-pin connector. Check continuity between BCM Black 14-pin connector terminal No. 7 and intermittent wiper relay terminal No. 15. See Figs. 5 and 7. If continuity exists, go to next step. If continuity does not exist, repair as necessary.

9) Using voltmeter, connect positive lead to BCM White 22-pin connector terminal No. 10 (Dark Green/Yellow wire) and negative lead to ground. See Fig. 8. Turn ignition on. Slowly move wiper switch from OFF position through each position to HIGH. If voltage increases from zero to about 10 volts in HIGH position, replace BCM. If no voltage exists, go to next step.

10) Check continuity between multifunction switch connector terminal No. 2 (Dark Green/Yellow wire) and BCM White 22-pin connector terminal No. 10 (Dark Green/Yellow wire). See Fig. 8. If continuity exists, go to next step. If continuity does not exist, repair open Dark Green/Yellow wire between multifunction switch and BCM. See WIRING DIAGRAMS.

11) Disconnect wiper motor connector and replace fuse No. 15 in junction block. If fuse does not blow, go to step **2)**. If fuse blows, wiper control circuitry is at fault. Repair as necessary. See WIRING DIAGRAMS.

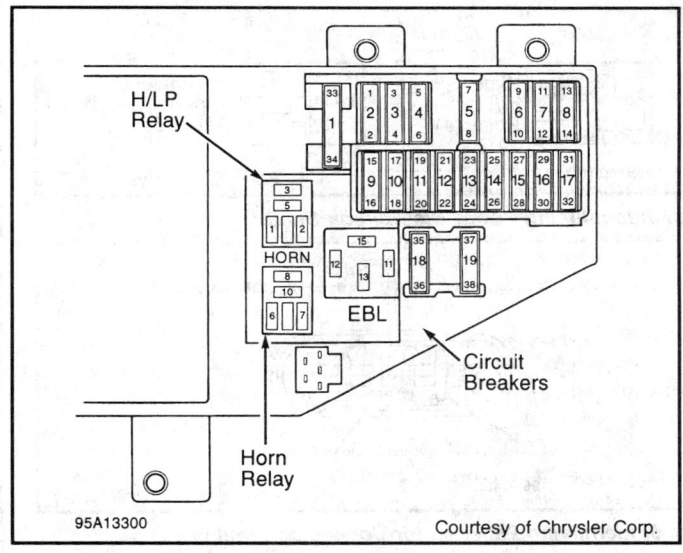

95A13300   Courtesy of Chrysler Corp.

Fig. 4: Identifying Junction Block

WIPERS RUN SLOWLY AT ALL SPEEDS

Disconnect wiper motor connector. Remove wiper arm and blade assemblies. Disconnect motor drive link from motor. Connect ammeter between negative battery terminal and wiper motor harness connector terminal "C" (Black wire). Connect battery positive wire to wiper motor harness connector terminal "B" (Brown/Orange wire). If average ammeter reading is more than 6 amps, replace wiper motor. If motor runs and average ammeter reading is less than 6 amps, ensure wiper linkage or pivots are not binding or stuck. When replacing drive link nut, tighten nut to 98-106 INCH lbs. (11-12 N.m).

CHRY
4-526

1999 ACCESSORIES & EQUIPMENT
Wiper/Washer Systems
Breeze, Cirrus, Sebring Convertible & Stratus (Cont.)

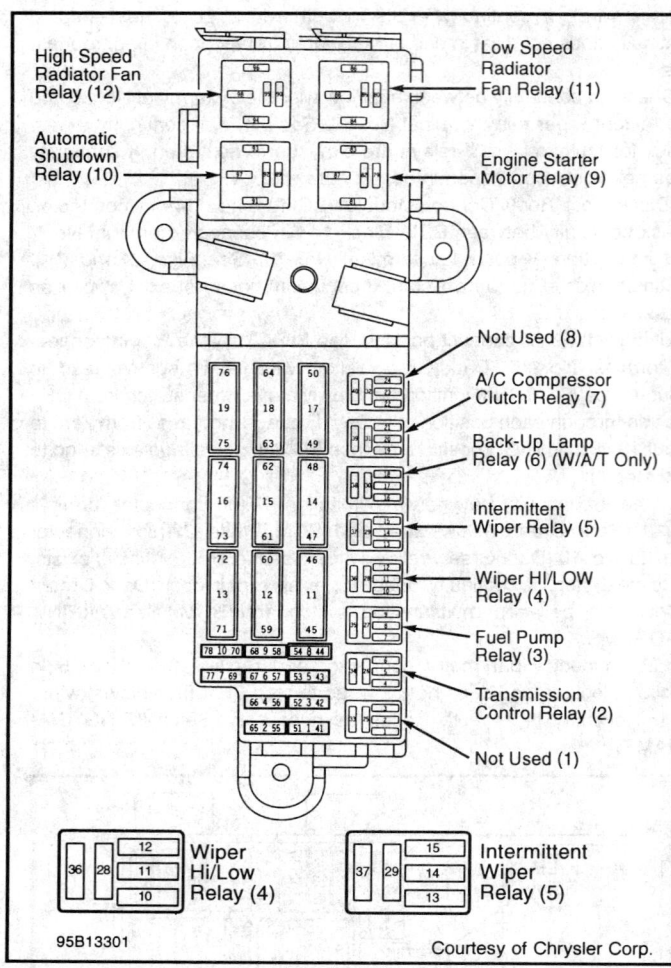

Fig. 5: Identifying Power Distribution Center

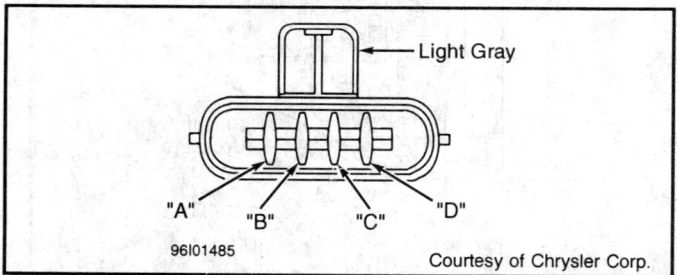

Fig. 6: Identifying Wiper Motor Connector Terminals

WIPERS OPERATE AT ONE SPEED ONLY

1) Disconnect wiper motor connector. Connect a jumper wire between positive battery terminal and wiper motor terminal "B". Connect another jumper wire between ground and wiper motor terminal "C". *See Fig. 6.* If motor runs at low speed, go to next step. If motor does not run at low speed, replace wiper motor.

2) Connect jumper wire between positive battery terminal and wiper motor terminal "A". Connect second jumper wire between ground and wiper motor terminal "C". *See Fig. 6.* If motor runs at high speed, go to next step. If motor does not run at high speed, replace wiper motor.

3) Remove high/low relay from Power Distribution Center (PDC). Check continuity between high/low wiper relay terminal No. 11 and wiper motor connector terminal "B" (Brown/Orange wire). *See Fig. 5.* If continuity exists, go to next step. If continuity does not exist, repair open Brown/Orange wire.

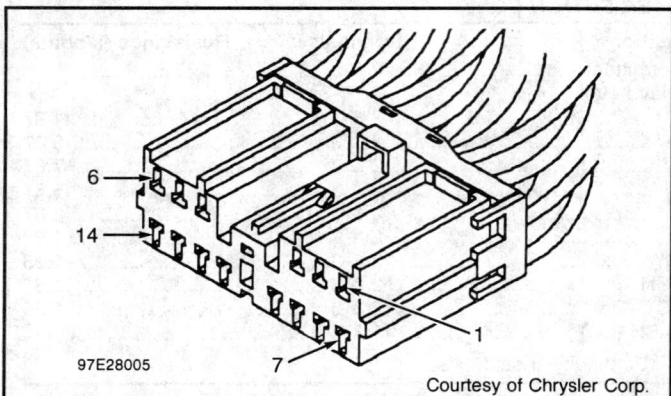

Fig. 7: Identifying BCM Black 14-Pin Connector

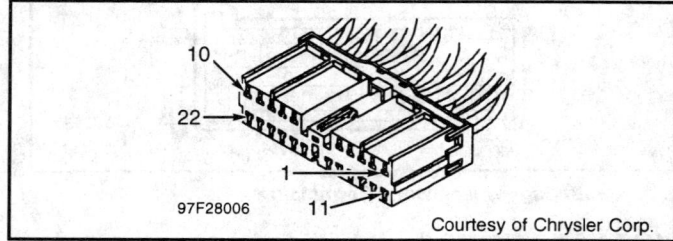

Fig. 8: Identifying BCM White 22-Pin Connector

4) Check continuity between high/low wiper relay terminal No. 28 and wiper motor harness connector terminal "A" (Red/Yellow wire). *See Fig. 5.* If continuity exists, check for faulty high/low wiper relay. If continuity does not exist, repair as necessary.

WIPERS RUN AT HIGH SPEED WITH SWITCH IN ANY POSITION

1) Disconnect wiper motor connector. Connect jumper wire between positive battery terminal and wiper motor terminal "B". Connect another jumper wire between ground and wiper motor terminal "C". *See Fig. 6.* If motor runs at low speed, go to next step. If motor does not run at low speed, replace wiper motor.

2) Check for faulty high/low wiper relay. Check for crossed wires in harness from high/low wiper relay and wiper motor. Disconnect BCM Black 14-pin connector. Remove intermittent wiper relay from Power Distribution Center (PDC). Check continuity between ground and BCM Black 14-pin connector terminal No. 8. *See Fig. 7.* If continuity exists, repair short to ground. If continuity does not exist, replace BCM.

WIPERS RUN AT LOW SPEED WITH SWITCH IN HIGH SPEED POSITION

Check for faulty high/low wiper relay. Replace if necessary. If relay is okay, check continuity between high/low wiper relay terminal No. 12 and BCM Black 14-pin connector terminal No. 8 (Violet/Pink wire). *See Figs. 5 and 7.* If continuity does not exist, repair open Violet/Pink wire. If continuity exists, check for faulty wiper switch. See WIPER SWITCH under COMPONENT TESTS. Replace switch if necessary. Check for binding linkage. Repair as necessary. If switch and linkage are okay, go to MOTOR RUNS SLOWLY AT ALL SPEEDS.

WIPERS RUN WITH SWITCH OFF

Disconnect BCM Black 14-pin connector Check continuity between ground and BCM 14-pin connector terminal No. 2 (Tan/Red wire) when wipers are in park position. *See Fig. 7.* If continuity does not exist, check park switch. See WIPER RUNS CONTINUOUSLY WITH SWITCH IN INTERMITTENT POSITION & WIPERS DO NOT PARK under SYSTEM TESTS. Replace wiper motor as necessary. If park switch is okay, check continuity of Tan/Red wire. Repair open circuit as necessary. If continuity

1999 ACCESSORIES & EQUIPMENT
Wiper/Washer Systems
Breeze, Cirrus, Sebring Convertible & Stratus (Cont.)

CHRY
4-527

exists, check wiper switch. See WIPER SWITCH under COMPONENT TESTS. Replace switch if necessary. If wiper switch is okay, replace BCM.

WIPER RUNS CONTINUOUSLY WITH SWITCH IN INTERMITTENT POSITION & WIPERS DO NOT PARK

1) Check continuity between ground and wiper motor terminal "D". *See Fig. 6.* If continuity does not exist, go to next step. If continuity exists, replace wiper motor.

2) With motor in PARK position, check continuity between wiper motor terminals "C" and "D". If continuity exists, go to next step. If continuity does not exist, replace wiper motor.

3) Disconnect wiper motor connector. Disconnect BCM Black 14-pin connector. Check continuity between wiper motor harness connector terminal "D" (White/Gray wire) and BCM Black 14-pin connector terminal No. 2 (White/Gray wire). *See Fig. 7.* If continuity does not exist, repair open in White/Gray wire. If continuity exists, test wiper motor.

WIPERS DO NOT RUN WHEN WASHER MOTOR IS TURNED ON

Using voltmeter, backprobe positive lead to BCM Black 14-pin connector terminal No. 10 and negative lead to ground. *See Fig. 7.* Engage washer switch so washer motor runs continuously. If reading is zero volts, check wiring between washer motor and BCM. Repair as necessary. If battery voltage exists, disconnect BCM Black 14-pin connector and recheck voltage at BCM Black 14-pin connector terminal No. 10. If voltage does not exist, check multifunction switch. Replace as needed. If switch is okay, replace BCM. If voltage exists, repair short in wiring.

UNABLE TO ADJUST INTERMITTENT SPEED

Test wiper switch. See WIPER SWITCH under COMPONENT TESTS. Replace if necessary.

WINDSHIELD WASHER INOPERATIVE

1) If washer pump does not run, go to next step. If washer pump runs, but fluid does not flow, check for blocked, loose or broken washer hoses or nozzles. Repair as necessary.

2) Check wiper switch. See WIPER SWITCH TEST under COMPONENT TESTS. If wiper switch is not okay, replace wiper switch. If wiper switch is okay, go to next step.

3) Using jumper wires, apply battery voltage to washer pump. If pump does not operate, replace washer pump. If pump operates, see appropriate BODY CONTROL COMPUTER TESTS article

REMOVAL & INSTALLATION

WARNING: On vehicles equipped with air bag restraint system, see appropriate AIR BAG RESTRAINT SYSTEMS article before servicing steering wheel or column. Use extreme caution to avoid personal injury and vehicle damage.

CAUTION: When battery is disconnected, vehicle computer and memory systems may lose memory data. Driveability problems may exist until computer systems have completed a relearn cycle. See COMPUTER RELEARN PROCEDURES article in GENERAL INFORMATION before disconnecting battery.

MULTIFUNCTION SWITCH

Removal & Installation – 1) Disconnect negative battery cable. Remove upper steering column cover. Remove 2 multifunction switch mounting screws. Disconnect electrical connectors. Lift straight up and remove multifunction switch.
2) To install, reverse removal procedure. Tighten multifunction switch mounting screws to 20 INCH lbs. (2.3 N.m). Tighten steering column cover screw to 17 INCH lbs. (2 N.m).

WASHER RESERVOIR

Removal & Installation – Disconnect fluid hose from in-line connector at top of right shock tower. Partially remove bumper fascia as needed to gain access to washer reservoir. Disconnect electrical connector. Slide reservoir rearward, and drop down and away from vehicle. Drain reservoir. Disconnect washer hose. To install, reverse removal procedure. Tighten reservoir nuts/screw to 80-124 INCH lbs. (9-14 N.m).

WASHER RESERVOIR PUMP

Removal & Installation – Remove reservoir. See WASHER RESERVOIR. While firmly grasping pump, twist and pull pump away from reservoir and out of grommet. DO NOT puncture reservoir. Remove and discard rubber grommet. To install, reverse removal procedure. Use NEW rubber grommet.

WIPER MOTOR & LINKAGE

Removal & Installation – 1) Remove wiper arms and blades. Remove cowl screen. Remove 3 wiper motor mounting screws and partially remove wiper motor assembly. Disconnect drive linkage from motor output crank. Using a ball joint/tie rod separator, separate ball cap from ball. Remove nuts and wiper motor. Disconnect wiper motor connector.
2) To install, reverse removal procedure. Tighten mounting screws to 89-106 INCH lbs. (10-12 N.m). Ensure motor connector seal is properly positioned. If removed, tighten motor crank nut to 19-23 ft. lbs. (25-30 N.m).

WIRING DIAGRAMS

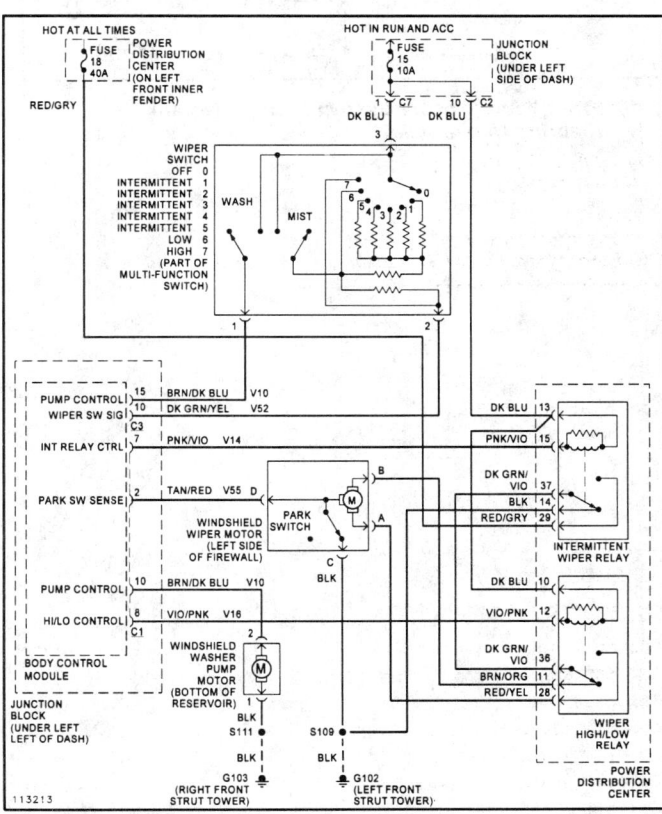

Fig. 9: Front Wiper/Washer System Wiring Diagram (Breeze, Cirrus & Stratus)

CHRY
4-528

1999 ACCESSORIES & EQUIPMENT
Wiper/Washer Systems
Breeze, Cirrus, Sebring Convertible & Stratus (Cont.)

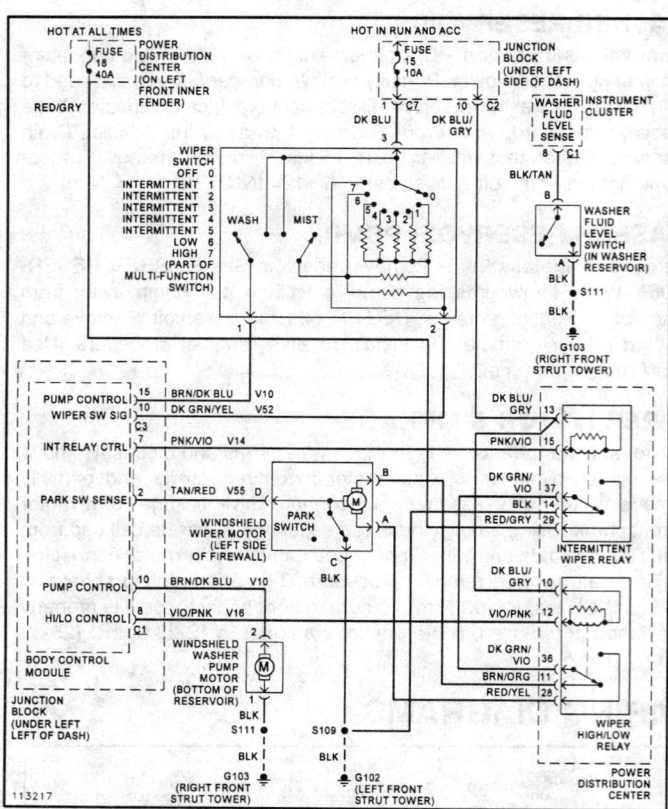

Fig. 10: Front Wiper/Washer System Wiring Diagram (Sebring Convertible)

Wiper/Washer Systems
Caravan, Town & Country, & Voyager

DESCRIPTION & OPERATION

A permanent magnet wiper motor is used in both conventional and intermittent wiper systems. Front intermittent (delay) wiper system includes a 1/2-18 second delay mode at 10 MPH or more, and 1-36 second delay mode at less than 10 MPH. Rear intermittent (delay) wiper system includes a 7 second delay mode at less than 50 MPH, and 5 second delay mode at more than 50 MPH. Washer system consists of an electric pump, sealed motor, reservoir, rubber hoses and nozzles.

Front delay, washer systems and rear wiper systems are controlled by the Body Control Computer (BCM). Some models are also equipped with an intermittent rear wiper/washer system, which is controlled by the BCM.

ADJUSTMENTS

WIPER ARMS

1) Ensure wiper blades and wiper arm spring tension are okay. While applying water to windshield, observe wiper low speed operation. If wiper element is not rolling over when wiper direction reverses, extension bar portion of wiper arm needs to be twisted in proper direction.
2) To twist extension bar portion of wiper arm, use 2 small adjustable wrenches positioned 2" (50 mm) apart on wiper arm extension rod. Twist extension rod slightly in opposite direction while holding wrench closest to pivot stationary.
3) Cycle wipers to park position. Ensure distances between wiper blades and above cowling are as specified in illustration. *See Fig. 1.*

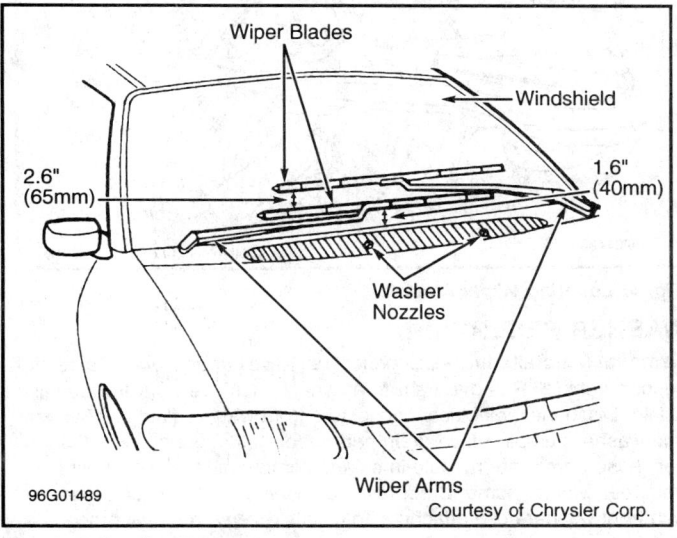

96G01489
Courtesy of Chrysler Corp.

Fig. 1: Adjusting Wiper Arms

TROUBLE SHOOTING

WIPERS DO NOT PARK PROPERLY

Check wiper arm adjustment. Ensure wiper arms are not loose on pivot shaft. See WIPER ARMS under ADJUSTMENTS. Ensure wiper linkage is not loose.

WIPERS DO NOT PARK

Check for open wiper motor park circuit. See appropriate BODY CONTROL COMPUTER TESTS article. Check for faulty wiper switch, wiper motor, or BCM. See FRONT WIPER/WASHER SWITCH under COMPONENT TESTS.

WIPERS DO NOT STOP WHEN SWITCH IS TURNED OFF

Check for faulty wiper switch, wiper motor, or BCM. See appropriate BODY CONTROL COMPUTER TESTS article.

BLADES CHATTER

Check for foreign substance on blades or glass. Ensure wiper arms are not twisted. Check for worn bent or damaged blades.

BLADES SLAP AGAINST WINDSHIELD MOLDING ON DRY GLASS

Check for loose or improperly positioned arms on pivot shaft. Check for loose wiper motor crank or drive components.

WIPERS KNOCK AT REVERSAL

Check for worn linkage bushings. Check for armature end play in wiper motor.

WIPER FUSE BLOWS

Disconnect wiper motor. If fuse does not blow, replace wiper motor. If fuse blows, repair short in wiper switch or wiring. See WIRING DIAGRAMS.

WIPERS INOPERATIVE

Check voltage at motor. Check motor ground. Check wiper switch, ground circuit and wiring. See appropriate BODY CONTROL COMPUTER TESTS article.

COMPONENT TESTS

WARNING: For all vehicles equipped with air bag restraint systems, see appropriate AIR BAG RESTRAINT SYSTEMS article before servicing steering wheel or column. Use extreme caution to avoid personal injury and vehicle damage.

NOTE: If problem occurs in electronic components, wiring, wiper switch or wiper motor, a Diagnostic Trouble Code (DTC) will be stored in BCM. For testing, see appropriate BODY CONTROL COMPUTER TESTS article.

FRONT WIPER/WASHER SWITCH

NOTE: Wiper/washer switch is part of multifunction steering column switch. If wiper/washer switch fails, entire multifunction switch must be replaced.

Disconnect wiper/washer switch connector. Measure resistance between appropriate switch terminals with switch in specified position. See WIPER/WASHER SWITCH CONTINUITY TEST table. *See Fig. 2.* If continuity is not as specified, replace multifunction switch.

WIPER/WASHER SWITCH CONTINUITY TEST

Switch Position	Between Terminals	Resistance (Ohms)
Off	6 & 7	[1]
Delay		
1	6 & 7	7920-8080
2	6 & 7	5940-6060
3	6 & 7	4455-4545
4	6 & 7	3465-3535
5	6 & 7	2475-2525
6	6 & 7	1485-1515
Low	6 & 7	990-1010
High	6 & 7	990-1010
Wash	6 & 11	[2]

[1] – Continuity should not exist.
[2] – Continuity should exist.

CHRY
4-530

1999 ACCESSORIES & EQUIPMENT
Wiper/Washer Systems
Caravan, Town & Country, & Voyager (Cont.)

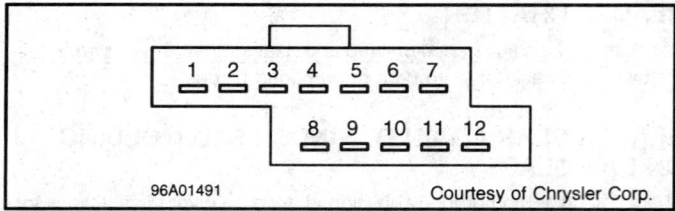

Fig. 2: Identifying Front Wiper/Washer Switch Terminals

REMOVAL & INSTALLATION

> WARNING: For all vehicles equipped with air bag restraint systems, see appropriate AIR BAG RESTRAINT SYSTEMS article before servicing steering wheel or column. Use extreme caution to avoid personal injury and vehicle damage.

> CAUTION: When battery is disconnected, vehicle computer and memory systems may lose memory data. Driveability problems may exist until computer systems have completed a relearn cycle. See COMPUTER RELEARN PROCEDURES article in GENERAL INFORMATION before disconnecting battery.

FRONT WIPER MOTOR

Removal & Installation – 1) Remove wiper module. See WIPER MODULE. Remove wiper linkage and motor mount plate from wiper module. Disconnect electrical connectors from back of wiper motor.
2) Remove wiper linkage from motor crank. DO NOT remove crank from motor. Remove bolts and wiper motor. To install, reverse removal procedure. Operate wiper motor to ensure wiper motor parks when wiper switch is turned off.

WIPER MODULE

> CAUTION: DO NOT allow wiper module to rest on master cylinder reservoir, or damage to brake system may result.

Removal & Installation – 1) Remove wiper arms. Remove cowl cover. Open hood. Disconnect positive lock on wiper module electrical connector. See Fig. 3. Disconnect wiper module electrical connector from engine compartment wiring harness. Disconnect washer hose from coupling inside unit.
2) Disconnect drain tubes from nipples on bottom of wiper module. Remove wiper module-to-lower windshield fence nuts. Remove wiper module-to-dash panel bolts. See Fig. 4.
3) Remove wiper module. DO NOT allow wiper module to rest on brake master cylinder reservoir. To install, reverse removal procedure.

FRONT WIPER/WASHER SWITCH

> NOTE: Wiper/washer switch is part of multifunction steering column switch. If wiper/washer switch fails, entire multifunction switch must be replaced.

Removal & Installation – Disconnect negative battery cable. Remove tilt lever (if equipped). Remove steering column upper and lower covers to access switch connector. Remove switch electrical connector. Remove screws and multifunction switch. To install, reverse removal procedure.

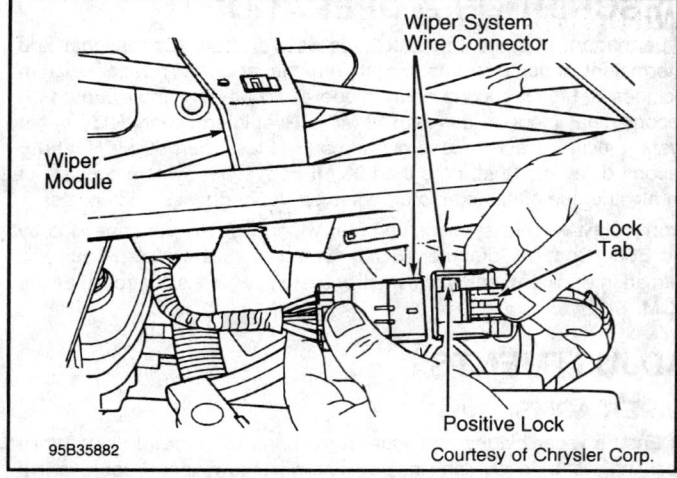

Fig. 3: Locating Wiper Module Connector

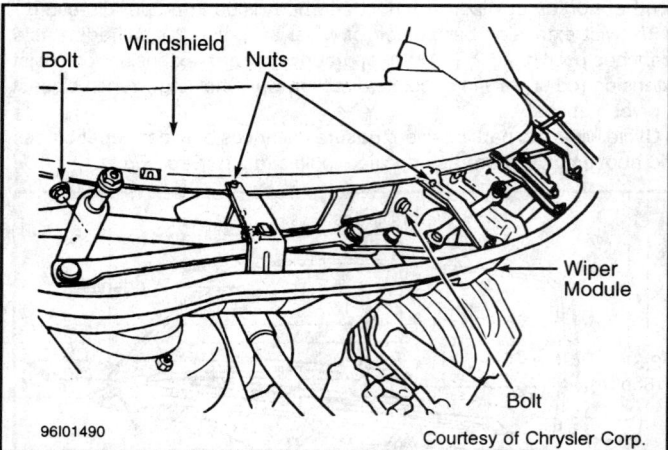

Fig. 4: Locating Wiper Module

WASHER RESERVOIR

Removal & Installation – Disconnect negative battery cable. Raise and support vehicle. Remove right front wheel. Remove right front splash shield. Disconnect electrical connectors from washer fluid level sensor and washer pumps. Place drain pan under hose connections. Disconnect hose from wiper module in engine compartment. Disconnect hose from rear washer pump. Drain reservoir. Remove screws and reservoir with front washer hose attached. To install, reverse removal procedure.

REAR WIPER MOTOR

Removal & Installation – Disconnect negative battery cable. Remove rear wiper arm. Open liftgate and remove liftgate trim panel. Disconnect rear wiper motor electrical connector. Remove screws and wiper motor from liftgate. To install, reverse removal procedure.

1999 ACCESSORIES & EQUIPMENT
Wiper/Washer Systems
Caravan, Town & Country, & Voyager (Cont.)

CHRY
4-531

WIRING DIAGRAMS

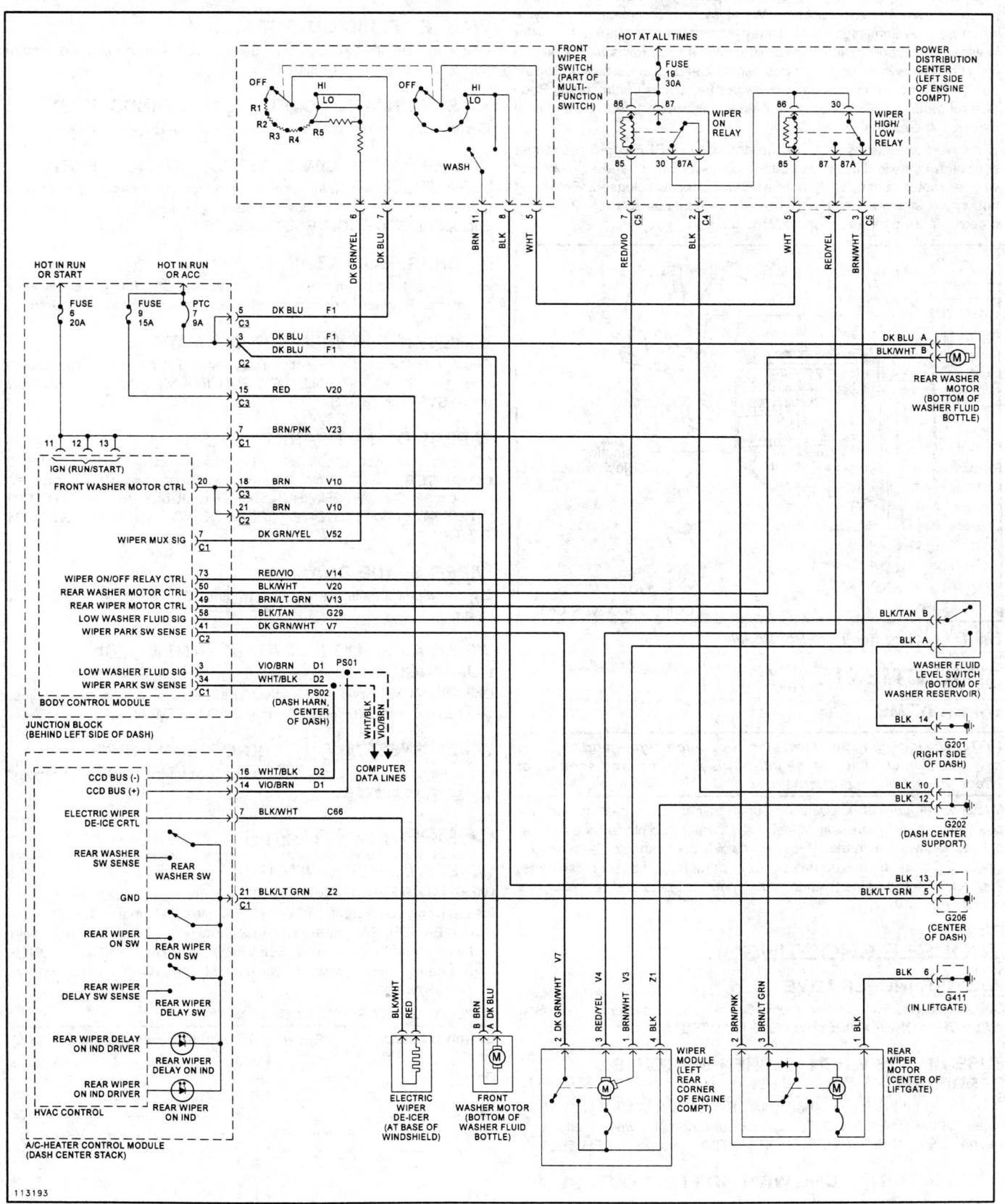

Fig. 5: Front & Rear Wiper/Washer System Wiring Diagram (Caravan, Town & Country, & Voyager)

113193

DESCRIPTION & OPERATION

Intermittent wiper system is standard. At speeds greater than 10 MPH, delay mode range is 1/2-18 seconds. At speeds less than 10 MPH, delay mode doubles to 1-36 seconds. Wiper system completes wipe cycle when wiper switch is turned off. Delay is controlled by a variable resistor in wiper switch and 2 relays. Intermittent wiper relay turns wipers on and off. High/low wiper relay changes wiper speed. Blades park in lowest portion of wipe pattern. Intermittent wiper function is controlled by Body Control Module (BCM) located in passenger compartment, behind right kick panel. *See Fig. 1.*

Windshield washer system can be activated in OFF position of wiper control switch. Holding wash button depressed will operate wipers and washer motor continuously until washer button is released. Releasing button will stop washer pump, but wipers continue to cycle 2-3 times before wipers park and module turns off.

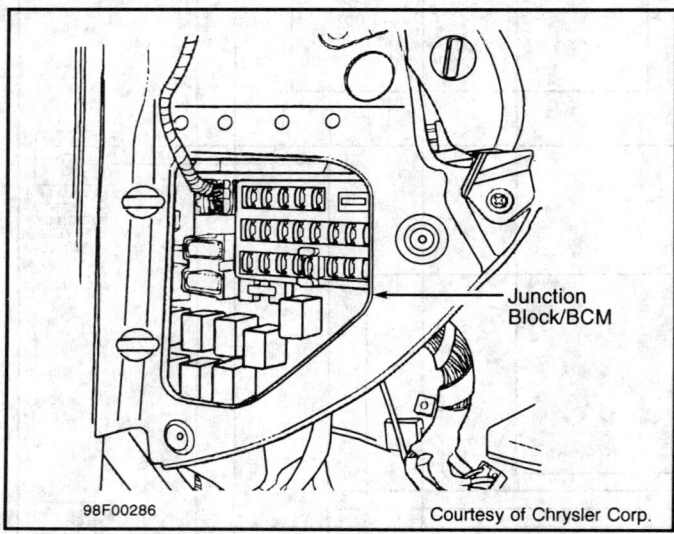

98F00286   Courtesy of Chrysler Corp.

Junction Block/BCM

Fig. 1: Locating Body Control Module

ADJUSTMENTS
WIPER ARMS

NOTE: During high-speed wet glass operation, right-hand blade tip may override cowl screen slightly. This is normal and should not affect wiper system performance.

Cycle wiper into park position. Turn ignition off. Wiper blades are positioned to "tic" marks on windshield. Driver's side blade should be on or between two "tic" marks. Passenger's side blade should be on or near single "tic" mark. If arms do not align, check for bent, worn or loose parts. Align blades and tighten wiper nuts. Operate wipers and recheck park position.

TROUBLE SHOOTING
WASHER INOPERATIVE

Check fuse No. 5 in junction block. Check washer system circuit. See WASHER INOPERATIVE under SYSTEM TESTS.

FUSE BLOWS WHEN WASHER SWITCH IS DEPRESSED

Check for short in wiper/washer switch. See WIPER/WASHER SWITCH under COMPONENT TESTS. Check for short in washer circuit or washer pump. See WASHER INOPERATIVE under SYSTEM TESTS.

WASHER PUMP RUNS WITH NO FLUID OUTPUT

Check fluid level in reservoir. Check for blocked hose or nozzle, misrouted hose or defective nozzle check valve.

WASHER SYSTEM OPERATES INTERMITTENTLY

Check for intermittent open circuit or faulty pump. See WASHER INOPERATIVE under SYSTEM TESTS.

WASHER FLUID OUTPUT IS LOW

Check for partially blocked hose, misrouted hoses or miswired washer pump. See WIRING DIAGRAMS.

WASHER NOZZLE OVERSHOOTS WINDSHIELD

Ensure nozzle is fully seated in place. Adjust nozzle jets using safety pin.

WASHER FLUID LEVEL INDICATOR INOPERATIVE

Check for loose fluid level sensor connector, open circuit to fluid level sensor or defective fluid level sensor. For testing procedures, see appropriate BODY CONTROL COMPUTER TESTS article.

WASHER FLUID LEAKING

Ensure filler tube is not loose or disconnected. Check pump and sensor grommets. Replace, if necessary. Check reservoir for cracks or defects.

WIPER MOTOR WILL NOT OPERATE

Check for blown fuse, defective relay, defective motor or open circuit. See WIPER MOTOR WILL NOT RUN IN ANY SWITCH POSITION under SYSTEM TESTS.

WIPERS DO NOT PARK

Check for open park circuit or BCM. See appropriate BODY CONTROL COMPUTER TESTS article. Perform appropriate test. Check for open park circuit. See WIPERS RUN CONTINUOUSLY WITH SWITCH IN INTERMITTENT POSITION & WIPERS DO NOT PARK under SYSTEM TESTS.

WIPER BLADE CHATTER

Ensure wiper arm is not bent or twisted. Check for damaged wiper blade.

WIPER ARMS DO NOT MOVE WITH MOTOR RUNNING

Check for loose wiper arm on pivot shaft. If wiper arm is loose, adjust wiper arms. See WIPER ARMS under ADJUSTMENTS.

WIPER SYSTEM MAKES KNOCKING NOISE

Check for loose wiper arms, linkage pivots or motor crank. Check motor for excessive backlash.

COMPONENT TESTS
WIPER/WASHER SWITCH

Wiper/washer switch is part of multifunction switch. Disconnect multifunction switch connector. See WIPER SWITCH under REMOVAL & INSTALLATION. Measure resistance between switch terminals with switch in appropriate position. See WIPER/WASHER SWITCH CONTINUITY table. *See Fig. 2.* If resistance is not as specified, replace wiper/washer switch.

WIPER/WASHER SWITCH CONTINUITY

Switch Position	Between Terminals	Resistance (k/ohms)
OFF	1 & 3	300 Or More
Delay Level		
1	1 & 3	9.72
2	1 & 3	8.22
3	1 & 3	6.61
4	1 & 3	5.12
5	1 & 3	3.67
6	1 & 3	2.22
LOW	1 & 3	1.02
HIGH	1 & 3	0.51

WIPER/WASHER SWITCH CONTINUITY (Cont.)

Switch Position	Between Terminals	Resistance (k/ohms)
WASH	1 & 2	 1

1 – Continuity should exist.

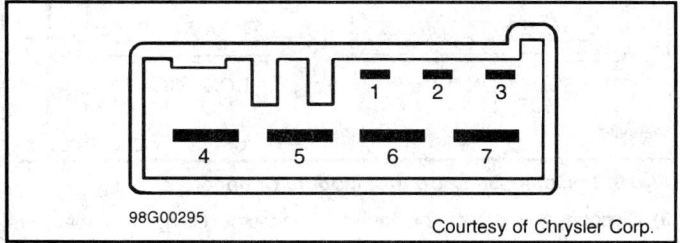

98G00295 Courtesy of Chrysler Corp.

Fig. 2: Identifying Wiper/Washer Switch Terminals

SYSTEM TESTS

WARNING: All vehicles are equipped with air bag restraint systems. See appropriate AIR BAG RESTRAINT SYSTEMS article before servicing steering wheel or column. Use extreme caution to avoid personal injury and vehicle damage.

NOTE: If problem occurs in electronic components, wiring, wiper switch or wiper motor, a Diagnostic Trouble Code (DTC) will be stored in BCM. For testing procedures, see appropriate BODY CONTROL COMPUTER TESTS article.

WIPERS INOPERATIVE

1) Check fuse No. 5 in junction block and fuse "M" in power distribution center. *See Figs. 3 and 4.* If fuses are okay, go to next step. If either fuse is blown, replace fuse and check system operation. If wipers are still inoperative and fuses are okay, go to next step. If replacement fuse blows, locate and repair short circuit. See WIRING DIAGRAMS.

2) Disconnect wiper motor harness connector. Connect a jumper wire between positive battery terminal and wiper motor terminal No. 2 (component side). Connect another jumper wire between negative battery terminal and wiper motor terminal No. 5 (component side). *See Fig. 5.* If wipers operate at low speed, go to next step. If wipers do not operate at low speed, replace wiper motor.

3) Connect positive jumper wire to wiper motor terminal No. 1 (component side). Connect negative jumper wire to wiper motor terminal No. 5 (component side). If wipers operate at high speed, go to next step. If wipers do not operate at high speed, replace wiper motor.

4) Check continuity between ground and wiper motor harness connector terminal No. 5 (Black wire). If continuity exists, go to next step. If continuity does not exist, repair open Black wire.

5) Remove intermittent wiper relay. Turn wiper switch on. Check for battery voltage at intermittent wiper relay terminals "A" (Red/Orange wire) and "D" (Red/Orange wire). *See Fig. 4.* If battery voltage exists, go to next step. If battery voltage does not exist, repair open circuit between fuse "M" and intermittent wiper relay in power distribution center.

6) Remove high/low wiper relay. Check continuity in Red/Yellow wire between high/low wiper relay terminal "D" and wiper motor harness connector terminal No. 1. *See Figs. 4 and 5.* Check continuity in Brown/White wire between high/low wiper relay terminal "E" and wiper motor connector terminal No. 2. If continuity exists, go to next step. If continuity does not exist, repair open Red/Yellow wire and/or Brown/White wire.

7) Check continuity in Dark Green wire between high/low wiper relay terminal "B" and intermittent wiper relay terminal "B". If continuity does not exist, repair open Dark Green wire. If continuity exists, check for faulty relays. If relays are okay, go to next step.

8) Turn ignition off. Disconnect Body Control Module (BCM) White 12-pin harness connector C3. *See Fig. 6.* Check continuity in Red/Violet wire between BCM harness connector C3 terminal No. 4 and intermit-

tent wiper relay terminal "C". If continuity exists, go to next step. If continuity does not exist, repair open Red/Violet wire.

9) Disconnect BCM Black 24-pin harness connector C2. Check voltage at BCM harness connector C2 terminal No. 8 (Dark Green/Red wire) . Turn ignition on. Slowly move wiper switch from OFF position through each position to HIGH position. If zero volts exists, go to next step. If voltage increases from zero volts to about 10 volts in HIGH position, replace BCM.

10) Turn ignition off. Check continuity in Dark Green/Red wire between wiper switch connector terminal No. 3 and BCM harness connector C2 terminal No. 8. If continuity exists, go to next step. If continuity does not exist, repair open Dark Green/Red wire.

11) Turn ignition on. Measure voltage at wiper switch connector terminal No. 1 (Dark Blue wire). If battery voltage exists, replace wiper switch. If battery voltage does not exist, repair open circuit to fuse No. 5 in junction block.

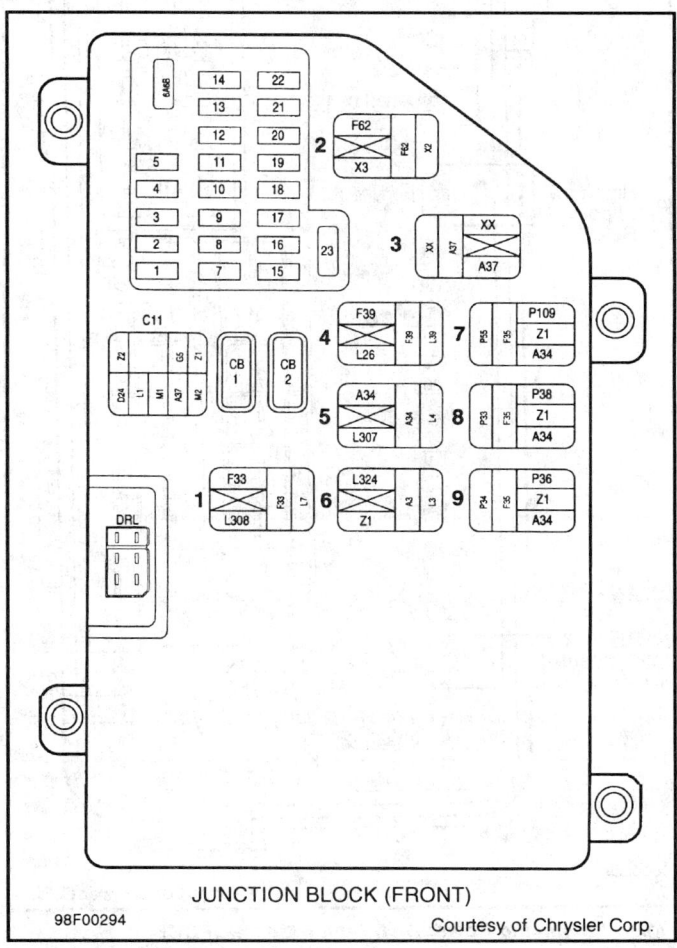

JUNCTION BLOCK (FRONT)

98F00294 Courtesy of Chrysler Corp.

Fig. 3: Identifying Junction Block

WIPERS RUN SLOWLY AT ALL SPEEDS

Disconnect wiper motor harness connector. Remove wiper arms and blades. Disconnect motor drive link from motor. Connect an ammeter between negative battery terminal and wiper motor terminal No. 5 (component side). Connect jumper wire from positive battery terminal to wiper motor terminal No. 2 (component side). *See Fig. 5.* If average ammeter reading is more than 10 amps, replace wiper motor. If motor runs and average ammeter reading is less than 10 amps, check wiper linkage pivots for binding. Repair as necessary. When replacing drive link nut, tighten nut to 98-106 INCH lbs. (11-12 N.m).

WIPERS RUN AT ONE SPEED ONLY

1) If wiper motor will not run on low speed, go to next step. If wiper motor will not run on high speed, go to step 3).

CHRY
4-534

1999 ACCESSORIES & EQUIPMENT
Wiper/Washer Systems – Concorde, Intrepid, LHS & 300M (Cont.)

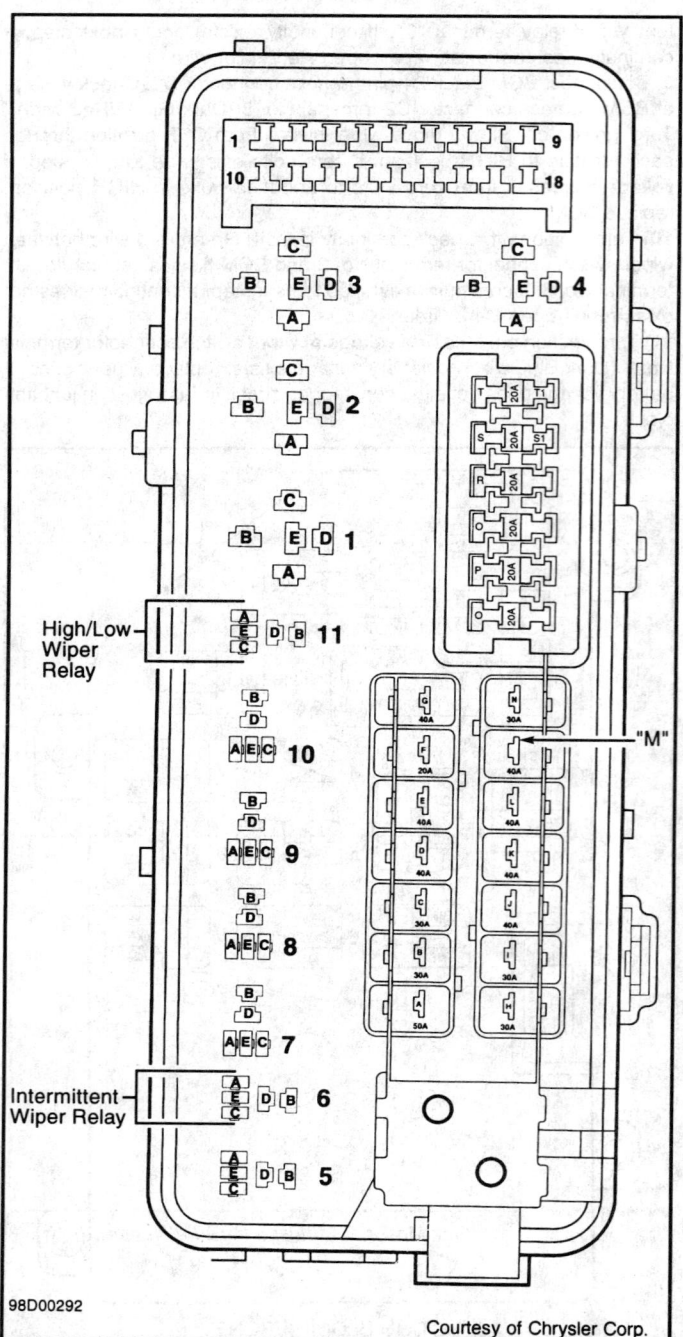

Fig. 4: Identifying Power Distribution Center (PDC)

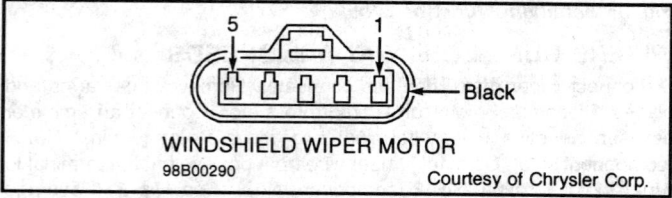

Fig. 5: Identifying Wiper Motor Connector

2) Disconnect wiper motor harness connector. Using a jumper wire, connect battery voltage to wiper motor terminal No. 2 (component side). Connect a second jumper wire between ground and wiper motor terminal No. 5 (component side). *See Fig. 5.* If motor runs, go to step **4)**. If motor does not run, replace wiper motor.

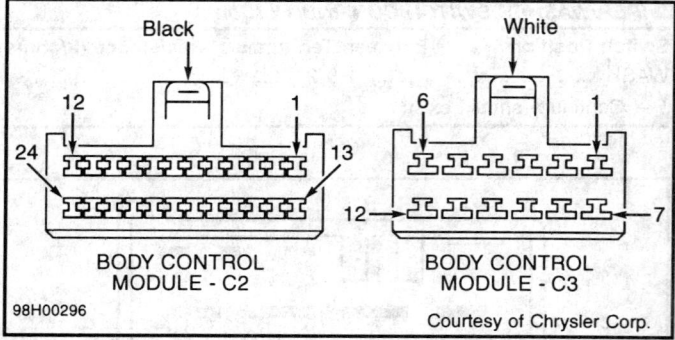

Fig. 6: Locating Body Control Module Connectors

3) Disconnect wiper motor harness connector. Using a jumper wire, connect battery voltage to wiper motor terminal No. 1 (component side). Connect a second jumper wire between ground and wiper motor terminal No. 5 (component side). If motor runs, go to step **5)**. If motor does not run, replace wiper motor.

4) Remove high/low wiper relay from power distribution center. Check continuity in Brown/White wire between high/low wiper relay terminal "E" and wiper motor connector terminal No. 2. *See Figs. 4 and 5.* If continuity exists, go to next step. If continuity does not exist, repair open Brown/White wire.

5) Check continuity in Red/Yellow wire between of high/low wiper relay terminal "D" and wiper motor connector terminal No. 1. If continuity exists, check for faulty high/low wiper relay. If continuity does not exist, repair open Red/Yellow wire.

WIPERS OPERATE AT HIGH SPEED WITH SWITCH IN ANY POSITION

1) Disconnect wiper motor harness connector. Using a jumper wire, connect battery voltage to wiper motor connector terminal No. 2 (component side). Connect a second jumper wire between ground and wiper motor connector terminal No. 5 (component side). *See Fig. 5.* If motor runs at low speed, go to next step. If motor runs at high speed, replace motor.

2) Check for faulty high/low wiper relay. Check for crossed wires between wiper motor and high/low wiper relay. See WIRING DIAGRAMS. If problem exists, repair as necessary. If problem does not exist, go to next step.

3) Turn ignition off. Disconnect Body Control Module (BCM) White 12-pin C3 connector and remove high/low wiper relay. *See Figs. 4 and 6.* Check continuity between ground and BCM connector C3 terminal No. 12 (Violet wire). If continuity exists, repair short to ground. If continuity does not exist, replace BCM.

WIPERS RUN AT LOW SPEED WITH SWITCH IN HIGH SPEED POSITION

1) Remove high/low relay from power distribution center. *See Fig. 4.* Check for faulty high/low wiper relay. If relay is faulty, replace relay. If relay is okay, go to next step.

2) Disconnect Body Control Module (BCM) White 12-pin harness connector C3. Check continuity in Violet wire between high/low wiper relay terminal "C" and BCM harness connector C3 terminal No. 12. *See Figs. 4 and 6.* If continuity does not exist, repair open Violet wire. If continuity exists, go to next step.

3) Check wiper switch. See WIPER/WASHER SWITCH under COMPONENT TESTS. If wiper/washer switch is defective, replace wiper switch. If wiper/washer switch is okay, check for binding linkage. See MOTOR RUNS SLOWLY AT ALL SPEEDS.

WIPERS RUN WITH SWITCH OFF

1) Check wiper motor wiring harness for short between low speed motor feed terminal No. 2 (Brown/White wire), or high speed motor feed terminal No. 1 (Red/Yellow wire) and voltage. See WIRING DIAGRAMS. If circuit is shorted to voltage, repair as necessary. If circuit is not shorted to voltage, go to next step.

2) Check for faulty wiper intermittent wiper relay or high/low relay. If either relay is faulty, replace appropriate relay. If relays are okay, go to next step.

3) Check Dark Green wire between intermittent wiper relay cavity "B" and high/low relay cavity "B" for short to voltage. If circuit is shorted to voltage, repair as necessary. If circuit is not shorted to voltage, go to next step.

4) Turn ignition off. Disconnect Body Control Module (BCM) White 12-pin harness connector C3. *See Fig. 6.* Check continuity between ground and BCM harness connector C3 terminal No. 4 (Red/Violet wire). If continuity exists, repair short to ground. If continuity does not exist, go to next step.

5) Check continuity in Red/Violet wire between BCM harness connector C3 terminal No. 4 and intermittent wiper relay terminal "C". If continuity does not exist, repair open Red/Violet wire. If continuity exists, go to next step.

6) Disconnect BCM Black 24-pin harness connector C2. Turn ignition on. Measure voltage at BCM harness connector C2 terminal No. 8 (Dark Green/Red wire). If voltage is zero volts, replace BCM. If voltage is more than zero volts, but less than 10 volts, check wiper switch and wiring. See WIPER/WASHER SWITCH under COMPONENT TESTS. See WIRING DIAGRAMS. If voltage is 10-15 volts, check Dark Green/Red wire for short to voltage.

WIPERS RUN CONTINUOUSLY WITH SWITCH IN INTERMITTENT POSITION & WIPERS DO NOT PARK

1) Disconnect wiper motor harness connector. Check continuity between ground and wiper motor terminal No. 4 (component side). *See Fig. 5.* If continuity exists, replace wiper motor. If continuity does not exist, go to next step.

2) Check continuity between wiper motor terminals No. 4 and 5 (component side) with wiper motor in park position. If continuity exists, go to next step. If continuity does not exist, replace wiper motor.

3) Disconnect Body Control Module (BCM) White 12-pin harness connector C3. Check continuity in Tan/Red wire between wiper motor harness connector terminal No. 4 and BCM harness connector C3 terminal No. 3. If continuity does not exist, repair open Tan/Red wire. If continuity exists, test wiper motor. See MOTOR WILL NOT RUN IN ANY SWITCH POSITION.

WIPERS DO NOT RUN WHEN WASHER IS ENGAGED

Turn ignition off. Disconnect Body Control Module (BCM) Black 24-pin harness connector C2. With washer switch engaged so that washer runs continuously, measure voltage at BCM harness connector C2 terminal No. 7 (Brown wire). If battery voltage exists, replace BCM. If voltage is zero volts, check circuit between wiper/washer switch terminal No. 2 and BCM connector C2 terminal No. 7 (Brown wire). Repair as necessary.

WASHER INOPERATIVE

1) If washer pump operates, and fluid does not flow, check for blocked, loose, broken or misrouted washer hoses. Repair as necessary. If washer pump does not operate, check fuse No. 5 in junction block. If fuse is blown, repair short circuit and replace fuse. If fuse is okay, go to next step.

2) Check for damaged or corroded terminals in wiper motor harness connector. Repair as necessary. If wiper motor connector is okay, check wiper/washer switch. See WIPER/WASHER SWITCH under COMPONENT TESTS. Replace switch if necessary. If switch is okay, go to next step.

3) Disconnect wiper switch harness connector. Turn ignition on. Measure voltage at wiper switch harness connector terminal No. 1 (Dark Blue wire). If battery voltage exists, go to next step. If battery voltage does not exist, repair open Dark Blue wire.

4) Connect wiper switch harness connector. Disconnect washer pump harness connector. With washer switch depressed, measure voltage at washer pump harness connector Brown wire terminal. If battery voltage exists, go to next step. If battery voltage does not exist, repair open Brown wire.

5) Check continuity between ground and washer pump harness connector Black wire terminal. If continuity exists, go to next step. If continuity does not exist, repair open Black wire.

6) Using jumper wires, apply battery voltage to washer pump. If washer pump does not operate, replace washer pump. If washer pump operates, test is complete.

REMOVAL & INSTALLATION

WARNING: On vehicles equipped with air bag restraint system, see appropriate AIR BAG RESTRAINT SYSTEMS article before servicing steering wheel or column. Use extreme caution to avoid personal injury and vehicle damage.

CAUTION: When battery is disconnected, vehicle computer and memory systems may lose memory data. Driveability problems may exist until computer systems have completed relearn cycle. See COMPUTER RELEARN PROCEDURES article in GENERAL INFORMATION before disconnecting battery.

WIPER MOTOR

Removal & Installation – 1) Disconnect negative battery cable. remove wiper module assembly. See WIPER MODULE ASSEMBLY. *See Fig. 7.* Disconnect motor from wiper module linkage using a ball and socket wedge. Remove 3 motor mounting screws.

2) Lift motor out of assembly. Disconnect motor harness grommet from assembly. To install, reverse removal procedure. Tighten motor crank nut to 98-124 INCH lbs. (11-14 N.m). Tighten motor mounting screws to 98-106 INCH lbs. (11-12 N.m).

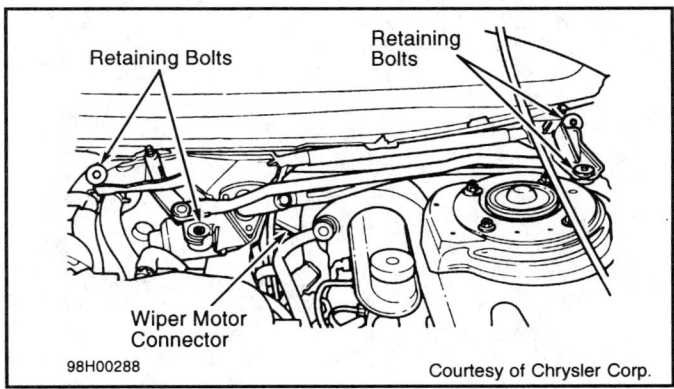

Fig. 7: Identifying Wiper Motor & Linkage Module Assembly

Retaining Bolts

Retaining Bolts

Wiper Motor Connector

98H00288

Courtesy of Chrysler Corp.

WIPER MODULE ASSEMBLY

Removal & Installation – 1) Disconnect negative battery cable. Remove wiper arms and blades and disconnect hoses from in-line connectors. Ensure in-line connectors are retained for reassembly. Remove rear hood seal with cowl top plastic screen, and disconnect washer hose at in-line connector. Retain in-line connector.

2) Remove strut crossbrace. Remove wiper module assembly bolts, lift assembly and disconnect wiring. Remove assembly. To install, reverse removal procedure. Ensure wiper module assembly and motor are in park position before installing wiper arms and blades.

WIPER SWITCH

Removal & Installation – 1) Disable air bag system. See appropriate AIR BAG RESTRAINT SYSTEMS article. Tilt column up and unsnap lower steering column shroud from upper steering column shroud. Tilt column down and remove upper shroud. Tilt column up and remove steering column tilt lever screw at base of lever. Remove tilt lever and lower shroud.

2) Using a screwdriver in place of lever, tilt column down. Remove 2 mounting screws on switch and partially remove switch. Remove wiring

CHRY
4-536

1999 ACCESSORIES & EQUIPMENT
Wiper/Washer Systems – Concorde, Intrepid, LHS & 300M (Cont.)

from hooks, and disconnect 2 electrical connections on multifunction switch. Remove switch. To install, reverse removal procedure.

WINDSHIELD WASHER RESERVOIR

Removal & Installation – Disconnect battery terminals. Raise and support vehicle. Remove left side of front bumper fascia to access reservoir as necessary. Disconnect electrical connectors from reservoir pump and float sensor. Disconnect washer hose, and block outlet to prevent leakage. Pull filler tube from rear of washer reservoir. Remove 4 mounting bolts and remove reservoir. To install, reverse removal procedure. Tighten reservoir retaining nuts and screw to 80-124 INCH lbs. (9-14 N.m).

WINDSHIELD WASHER PUMP

Removal & Installation – Remove liquid from reservoir. Remove reservoir. See WINDSHIELD WASHER RESERVOIR. Gently pry pump away from reservoir and out of grommet. DO NOT puncture reservoir. Discard rubber grommet. To install, reverse removal procedure using NEW grommet.

WIRING DIAGRAMS

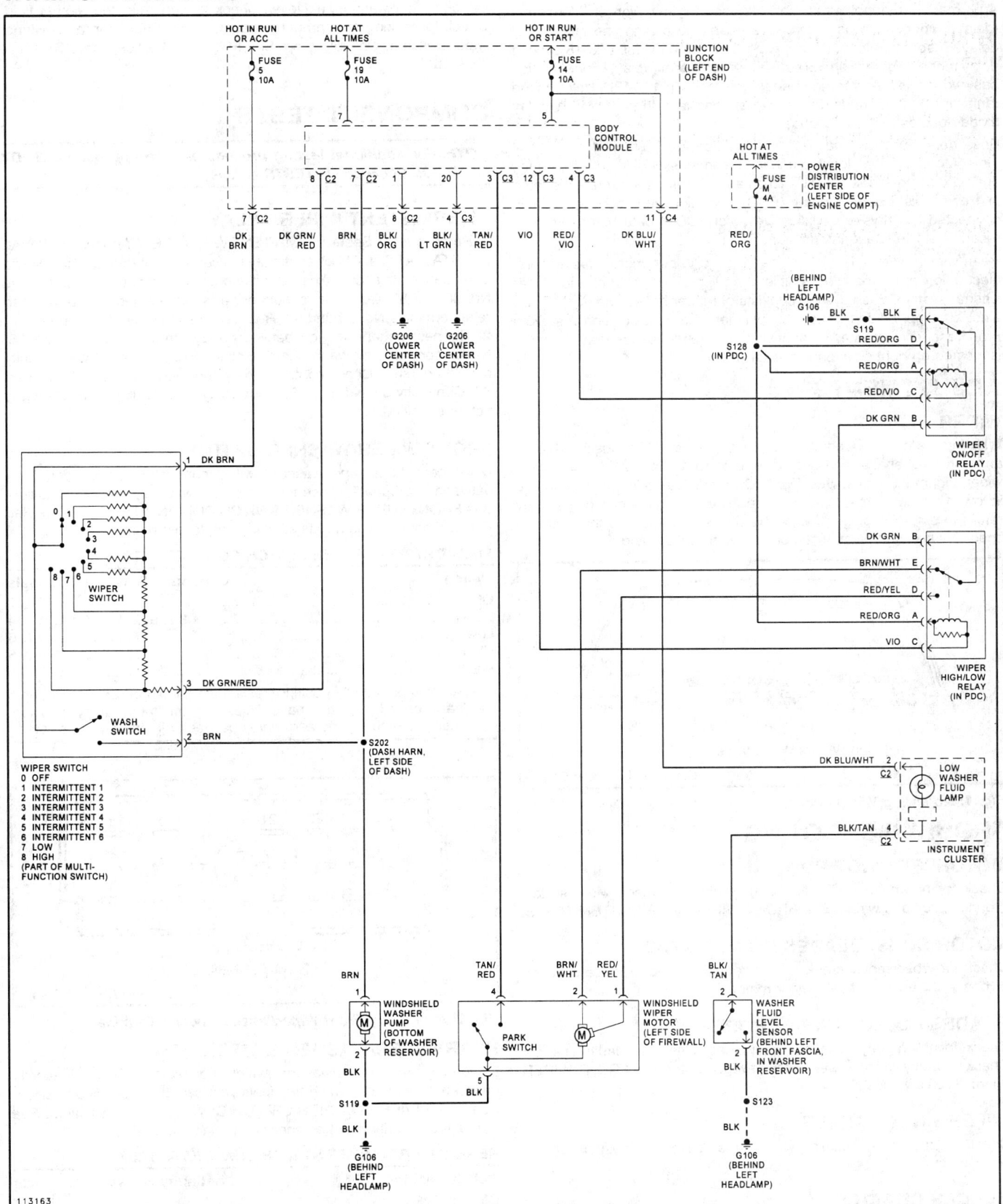

Fig. 8: Front Wiper/Washer System Wiring Diagram

113163

DESCRIPTION & OPERATION

A permanent magnet wiper motor is used for low, high or intermittent (delay) wiper functions. There is a base and a high line intermittent delay. Base intermittent (delay) wiper function provides a .5-18 second delay mode. High line speed sensitive intermittent (delay) wiper function has two ranges. At vehicle speeds greater than 10 MPH, delay mode range is .5-18 seconds. At vehicle speeds less than 10 MPH, delay mode doubles to 1-36 seconds.

Base delay function and high line function are controlled by Central Timer Module (CTM), located under passenger side of instrument panel, outboard of glove box. CTM switches an intermittent wiper relay, located in Power Distribution Center (PDC). On high line models, CTM is connected to Chrysler Collision Detection (CCD) data bus network to receive vehicle speed information.

Rear wiper system is single speed only. Wiper motor has integral electronic control module. Vehicle is equipped with a front and a rear washer system. Each system consists of rubber hoses and nozzles, an electric pump, sealed motor, low washer fluid indicator and reservoir. Front reservoir is located on right side inner fender panel. Rear reservoir is located on right side inner quarter panel.

ADJUSTMENTS

WIPER BLADES

With wiper arms removed, cycle wiper motor into PARK position. Mount arms on pivot shafts, and ensure wipers are within 0.59" (15.0 mm) of wiper alignment marks. See Fig. 1. On rear wiper, align blade with line in lower blackout area. Operate wiper blades, and check whether they return to proper position. If wiper blades do not return to this position, check linkage and pivot assembly for wear and binding.

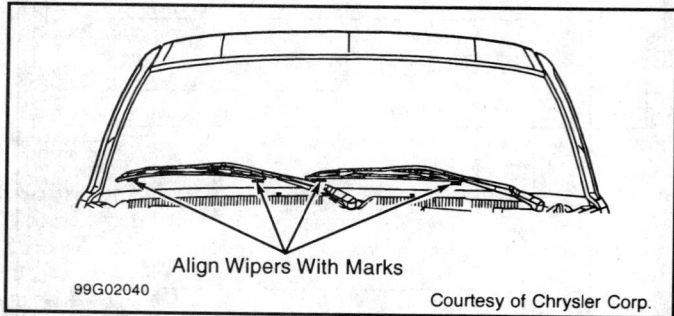

Align Wipers With Marks

99G02040   Courtesy of Chrysler Corp.

Fig. 1: Adjusting Wiper Blades

TROUBLE SHOOTING

MOTOR WILL NOT RUN

Check for blown fuse. Check voltage at motor. Check wiper switch, ground circuit and wiring. See FRONT WIPER under SYSTEM TESTS.

MOTOR RUNS, BLADES DO NOT MOVE

Check for loose motor crank, disconnected linkage or loose arms on pivot shaft. Check for faulty wiper motor.

BLADES DO NOT PARK PROPERLY

Check for improperly installed wiper arms. Check for faulty linkage. Check for faulty wiring, wiper switch or wiper motor. See FRONT WIPER under SYSTEM TESTS.

WIPER KNOCK NOISE

Check for improperly installed wiper arms. Check for faulty linkage or wiper motor.

BLADES CHATTER

Check for foreign substance on blades or glass. Check for twisted arm holding blade at wrong angle to glass. Check for bent or damaged blades.

WASHERS DO NOT OPERATE

Check for low washer fluid level. Check for contaminated washer fluid. Check for leaking or improperly routed hoses. Check for faulty wiring, wiper switch or washer pump. See FRONT WASHER under SYSTEM TESTS.

COMPONENT TESTS

NOTE: For additional testing procedures, see appropriate BODY CONTROL COMPUTER TESTS article.

INTERMITTENT WIPER RELAY

1) Remove relay. See INTERMITTENT WIPER RELAY under REMOVAL & INSTALLATION. Check continuity between relay terminals No. 30 and 87A. Continuity should exist. Check continuity between relay terminals No. 30 and 87. Continuity should not exist. Check resistance between relay terminals No. 85 and 86. Resistance should be 70-80 ohms.
2) Connect battery voltage between relay terminals No. 85 and 86. Check continuity between relay terminals No. 30 and 87A. Continuity should not exist. Check continuity between relay terminals No. 30 and 87. Continuity should exist. Replace relay if continuity or resistance is not as specified.

FRONT WIPER/WASHER SWITCH

Disconnect front wiper/washer switch connector. Check continuity between appropriate switch terminals with switch in specified position. See FRONT WIPER/WASHER SWITCH CONTINUITY TEST table. See Fig. 2. If continuity is not as specified, replace switch.

FRONT WIPER/WASHER SWITCH CONTINUITY TEST

Switch Position	Continuity Between Terminals
Off	6 & 7
Delay [1]	8 & 9; 2 & 4; 1 & 2; 1 & 4
Low	4 & 6
High	4 & 5
Wash	3 & 4

[1] – At maximum delay position, resistance should be 270-330 k/ohms between all terminal pairs listed. At minimum delay position, resistance should be zero ohms between all terminal pairs listed.

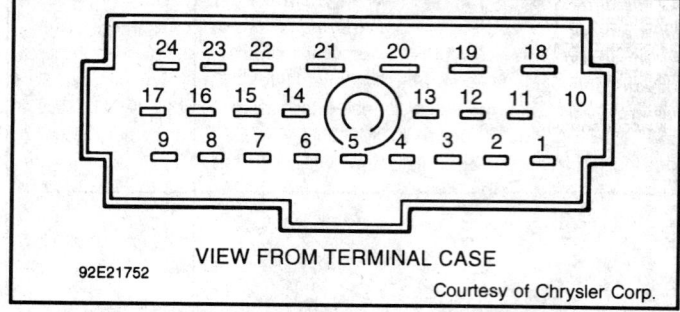

24 23 22   21   20   19   18
17 16 15 14   5   13 12 11 10
9 8 7 6   5   4 3 2 1

VIEW FROM TERMINAL CASE

92E21752   Courtesy of Chrysler Corp.

Fig. 2: Identifying Front Wiper/Washer Switch Terminals

REAR WIPER/WASHER SWITCH

Disconnect rear wiper/washer switch connector. Check continuity between appropriate switch terminals with switch in specified position. See REAR WIPER/WASHER SWITCH CONTINUITY TEST table. See Fig. 3. If continuity is not as specified replace switch.

REAR WIPER/WASHER SWITCH CONTINUITY TEST

Switch Position	Continuity Between Terminals
Off	3 & 4
Wiper	2 & 7
Washer	7 & 8

VIEW OF SWITCH SIDE
OF CONNECTOR

98I00289

Courtesy of Chrysler Corp.

Fig. 3: Identifying Rear Wiper/Washer Switch Terminals

SYSTEM TESTS

FRONT WASHER

NOTE: Following testing applies when pump does not operate. If pump operates, see TROUBLE SHOOTING. For additional testing procedures, see appropriate BODY CONTROL COMPUTER TESTS article.

---

1) Turn ignition on. Turn wiper switch on. If wipers operate, go to next step. If wipers do not operate, diagnose wiper problem first. See FRONT WIPER.

2) Turn wiper switch off. Depress washer switch. Washer pump and wipers should operate while switch is depressed. Wipers should operate about 3 sweeps after switch is released. If wipers are okay but washer is not, go to next step. If washer is okay but wipers are not, go to step **5)**.

3) Turn ignition off. Disconnect negative battery cable. Disconnect washer pump harness connector. Measure resistance between washer pump harness connector Black wire terminal and ground. If resistance is more than zero ohms, repair open in Black wire. If resistance is zero ohms, go to next step.

4) Connect negative battery cable. Turn ignition on. While depressing washer switch, check voltage at washer pump harness connector Brown wire terminal. If battery voltage exists, replace pump. If battery voltage does not exist, repair open in Brown wire.

5) Turn ignition off. Disconnect negative battery cable. Access CTM and disconnect CTM harness 14-pin connector. Connect negative battery cable. Turn ignition on. With washer switch depressed, check voltage at CTM harness 14-pin connector terminal No. 10 (Brown wire) . *See Fig. 4.* If battery voltage exists, check intermittent relay. See INTERMITTENT WIPER RELAY under COMPONENT TESTS. If battery voltage does not exist, repair open in Brown wire.

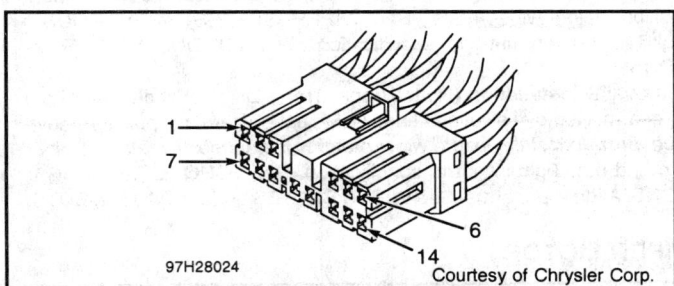

97H28024

Courtesy of Chrysler Corp.

Fig. 4: Identifying Central Timer Module 14-Pin Harness Connector Terminals

FRONT WIPER

NOTE: Wiper system utilizes a Central Timer Module (CTM) to control intermittent functions of wiper system. If problem is only pulse wipe or wipe-after-wash, see FRONT WASHER.

---

1) Check fuse in junction block. If fuse is blown, replace fuse and repair short as necessary. If fuse is okay, go to next step.

2) Turn ignition on. Check for battery voltage at fuse. If battery voltage does not exist, repair open circuit between fuse and ignition switch. If battery voltage exists, go to next step.

3) Turn ignition off. Disconnect negative battery cable. Disconnect multifunction switch harness connector. Connect negative battery cable. Turn ignition on. Check for battery voltage at multifunction switch harness connector terminal No. 4 (Dark Blue wire). *See Fig. 2.* If battery voltage exists, go to next step. If battery voltage does not exist, repair open in Dark Blue wire between fuse and multifunction switch.

4) If problem is intermittent wipe feature only, go to next step. If problem is with all wiper modes or only HI and/or LO speed modes, go to step **7)**.

5) Turn ignition off. Disconnect negative battery cable. Disconnect CTM 14-pin harness connector. Check continuity between multifunction switch harness connector terminal No. 3 (Brown wire) and CTM 14-pin harness connector terminal No. 10 (Brown wire). If continuity does not exist, repair open in Brown wire. If continuity exists, go to next step.

6) Check continuity between multifunction switch harness connector terminal No. 2 (Dark Green/Red wire) and CTM 14-pin harness connector terminal No. 3 (Dark Green/Red wire). If continuity does not exist, repair open in Dark Green/Red wire. If continuity exists, check intermittent relay. See INTERMITTENT WIPER RELAY under COMPONENT TESTS.

7) Check continuity between multifunction switch harness connector terminal No. 6 and 9 (both Violet wires). If continuity does not exist, repair open in Violet wire. If continuity exists, go to next step.

8) Check multifunction (wiper/washer) switch. See FRONT WIPER/WASHER SWITCH under COMPONENT TESTS. If switch tests okay, connect switch and go to next step. If switch does not test okay, replace switch.

9) Turn ignition off. Disconnect negative battery cable. Access wiper linkage and wiper motor harness connector. Check resistance between wiper motor harness connector terminal No. 4 (Black wire) and ground. *See Fig. 5.* If resistance is more than zero ohms, repair in Black wire. If resistance is zero ohms, go to next step.

10) Connect negative battery cable. Turn ignition on. Check voltage by backprobing at wiper motor terminals listed with wiper switch in specified position. See SWITCH POSITION VOLTAGE TEST table. If battery voltage does not exist at any terminal, repair open in appropriate wire. If battery voltage exists at all terminals and wiper motor does not operate properly, replace wiper motor. To check park switch, go to next step.

SWITCH POSITION VOLTAGE TEST

Switch Position	Terminal
All	1
Low	5
High	6

11) Check voltage at wiper motor park switch by backprobing wiper motor connector terminal No. 2 (Dark Green/Yellow wire) with multifunction switch in low or high position, then move switch to off. Voltage should vary between battery voltage and zero volts while wiper motor is cycling. Battery voltage should be present when switch is turned off, and zero volts when wipers return to park position. If voltage is not as specified, replace wiper motor.

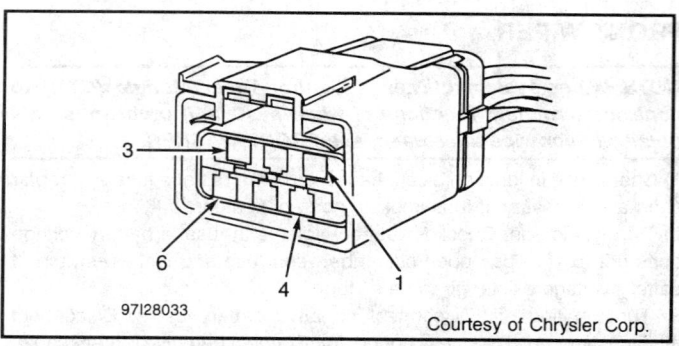

97128033   Courtesy of Chrysler Corp.

Fig. 5: Identifying Wiper Motor Harness Connector Terminals

REAR WASHER

NOTE: Following testing applies when pump does not operate. If pump operates, see TROUBLE SHOOTING.

1) Turn ignition on. Turn rear wiper switch on. If rear wipers operate, go to next step. If rear wipers do not operate, diagnose rear wiper problem first. See REAR WIPER.

2) Turn ignition off. Disconnect negative battery cable. Disconnect rear washer pump harness connector. Check resistance between rear washer pump harness connector terminal "B" (Black wire) and ground. If resistance is more than zero ohms, repair open in Black wire. If resistance is zero ohms, go to next step.

3) Connect negative battery cable. Turn ignition on. While depressing washer switch, check voltage at rear washer pump harness connector terminal "A" (Black/White wire). If battery voltage exists, replace pump. If battery voltage does not exist, go to next step.

4) Turn ignition off. Disconnect negative battery cable. Disconnect rear wiper/washer switch harness connector. Disconnect rear wiper motor harness connector. Check continuity between rear washer pump harness connector terminal "A" (Black/White wire) and ground. If continuity exists, repair short to ground in Black/White wire. If continuity does not exist, go to next step.

5) Check continuity between rear washer pump harness connector terminal "A" (Black/White wire) and rear wiper/washer switch harness connector terminal No. 8 (Black/White wire). If continuity does not exist, repair open in Black/White wire. If continuity exists, replace switch.

REAR WIPER

NOTE: If problem involves only rear wipe-after-wash mode, check circuit between washer motor and rear wiper motor. See WIRING DIAGRAMS.

1) Check fuses. If fuses are okay, go to next step. If fuses are blown, replace fuse(s) and repair circuit(s) as necessary.

2) Disconnect negative battery cable. Disconnect rear wiper/washer switch connector. Connect negative battery cable. Turn ignition on. Check voltage at rear wiper/washer switch connector terminal No. 7 (White wire). *See Fig. 3.* If battery voltage exists, go to next step. If voltage does not exist, repair open in White wire between junction block and rear wiper/washer switch connector.

3) Turn ignition off. Disconnect negative battery cable. Check continuity between rear wiper/washer switch connector terminal No. 4 (Black wire) and ground. If continuity exists, go to next step. If continuity does not exist, repair open in Black wire.

4) Test rear wiper/washer switch. See REAR WIPER/WASHER SWITCH under COMPONENT TESTS. If switch is not okay, replace rear wiper/washer switch. If switch is okay, go to next step.

5) Disconnect rear wiper motor connector. Connect negative battery cable. Check voltage at rear wiper motor connector terminal No. 4 (Pink wire). If battery voltage exists, go to next step. If voltage does not exist, repair open in Pink wire between junction block and rear wiper motor connector.

6) Turn ignition off. Disconnect negative battery cable. Check continuity between rear wiper motor connector terminal No. 1 (Black wire) and ground. If continuity exists, go to next step. If continuity does not exist, repair open in Black wire.

7) Check continuity between rear wiper motor connector terminal No. 3 (Brown/Orange wire) and ground. If continuity does not exist, go to next step. If continuity exists, repair short to ground in Brown/Orange wire.

8) Check continuity between rear wiper motor connector terminal No. 3 (Brown/Orange wire) and rear wiper/washer switch connector terminal No. 2 (Brown/Orange wire). If continuity exists, replace wiper motor. If continuity does not exist, repair open in Brown/Orange wire.

REMOVAL & INSTALLATION

WARNING: For all vehicles equipped with air bag restraint systems, see appropriate AIR BAG RESTRAINT SYSTEMS article before servicing steering wheel or column. Use extreme caution to avoid personal injury and vehicle damage.

CAUTION: When battery is disconnected, vehicle computer and memory systems may lose memory data. Driveability problems may exist until computer systems have completed a relearn cycle. See COMPUTER RELEARN PROCEDURES article in GENERAL INFORMATION before disconnecting battery.

CENTRAL TIMER MODULE (CTM)

NOTE: When installing new high line CTM, use scan tool to determine customer preferred settings before replacement. Settings must be enabled/disabled using scan tool.

Removal & Installation – Disconnect battery. Remove glove box. Remove CTM bracket fasteners. Pull out CTM and bracket. Disconnect CTM harness connector(s). Remove CTM and bracket. To install, reverse removal procedure.

INTERMITTENT WIPER RELAY

Removal & Installation – Intermittent wiper relay is located in Power Distribution Center (PDC) in engine compartment. Remove cover and remove relay. To install, reverse removal procedure.

WIPER ARMS

NOTE: DO NOT pry wiper arms off pivot shaft. Damage may result, allowing wiper to come loose. Use battery terminal puller to remove wiper arms.

Removal & Installation (Front Wiper Arm) – Open hood. Lift and remove pivot shaft cover from wiper arm. Remove pivot shaft nut and using puller, remove wiper arm. To install, ensure wiper motor is in park position. Align wiper arms. See WIPER BLADES under ADJUSTMENTS. Tighten nuts to specification. See TORQUE SPECIFICATIONS.

Removal & Installation (Rear Wiper Arm) – Lift pivot shaft cover from wiper arm. Remove pivot shaft nut. Using battery terminal puller, remove wiper arm. To install, ensure wiper motor is in park position. Install wiper arm and nut. Tighten nut to specification. See TORQUE SPECIFICATIONS. Align wiper arms. See WIPER BLADES under ADJUSTMENTS.

WIPER MOTOR

NOTE: Front wiper linkage and motor module is replaced as a unit.

Removal & Installation (Front) – 1) Disconnect negative battery cable. Remove wiper arms. See WIPER ARMS. Open hood. Remove weatherstrip from front edge of cowl grille. Disconnect cowl grille fasteners.

2) Lift cowl grille. Disconnect washer supply hose. Disconnect vacuum supply hose from vacuum reservoir. Remove cowl grille. Disconnect wiper motor harness connector. Remove wiper linkage and wiper motor.

3) To install, reverse removal procedure. Tighten fasteners to specification. See TORQUE SPECIFICATIONS. Install wiper arms. See WIPER BLADES under ADJUSTMENTS.

Removal & Installation (Rear) – 1) Disconnect negative battery cable. Remove wiper arm. See WIPER ARMS. Carefully pry off pivot shaft bezel nut cover. Disconnect washer hose (if equipped) and remove pivot shaft bezel nut and grommet.

2) Pull upper trim panel outward to disengage spring clips and remove. Remove screws and pull lower trim panel outward to disengage spring clips, disconnect wiring and remove. Disconnect wiper motor wiring. Remove motor and bracket.

3) To install, install motor and bracket loosely, then center shaft from outside and install pivot shaft bezel nut and grommet. To complete installation, reverse removal procedure. Tighten nuts and screws to specification. See TORQUE SPECIFICATIONS. Install wiper arm. See WIPER BLADES under ADJUSTMENTS.

FRONT WIPER/WASHER SWITCH

NOTE: Front wiper/washer switch is part of multifunction steering column switch. If wiper/washer switch fails, entire multifunction switch must be replaced.

Removal & Installation – 1) Disconnect negative battery cable. Remove tilt lever (if equipped). Remove steering column upper and lower covers to access switch connector. Remove switch connector. Remove multifunction switch tamperproof screws.

2) Gently pull switch away from column and loosen connector screw (screw remains in connector). Remove switch. To install, reverse removal procedure. Tighten screws and nuts to specification. See TORQUE SPECIFICATIONS. Ensure switch is functioning properly.

REAR WIPER/WASHER SWITCH

Removal & Installation – Disconnect negative battery cable. Remove lower panel from instrument panel. Remove switch from lower panel. To install, reverse removal procedure. Tighten screws and nuts to specification. See TORQUE SPECIFICATIONS. Ensure switch is functioning properly.

WASHER MOTOR

Removal & Installation (Front) – Disconnect negative battery cable. Remove air cleaner. Drain fluid from reservoir. Remove reservoir screws, reservoir and pump assembly. Disconnect electrical connector and rubber hose from bottom of pump. Pry pump away from reservoir. DO NOT puncture reservoir. Remove and discard grommet. To install, reverse removal procedure. Use a NEW rubber grommet.

Removal & Installation (Rear) – 1) Disconnect negative battery cable. Remove right rear quarter panel trim from vehicle interior. Disconnect washer supply hose from check valve located on right liftgate opening pillar. Siphon washer fluid from supply hose.

2) Disconnect supply hose from washer pump. Disconnect wiring. Disconnect vent hose. Remove reservoir screws. Lift reservoir and pump assembly clear of body and disconnect fill hose. Remove reservoir and pump.

3) Pry pump away from reservoir. DO NOT puncture reservoir. Remove and discard grommet. To install, reverse removal procedure. Use a NEW rubber grommet.

TORQUE SPECIFICATIONS

TORQUE SPECIFICATIONS

Application	INCH Lbs. (N.m)
Central Timer Module	20 (2.2)
Front Wiper	
Switch Screws	17 (2)
Pivot Shaft Nut	212 (24)
Module Mounting Bolts	72 (8)
Rear Wiper	
Pivot Shaft Nut	160 (18)
Wiper/Washer Switch	17 (2)

WIRING DIAGRAMS

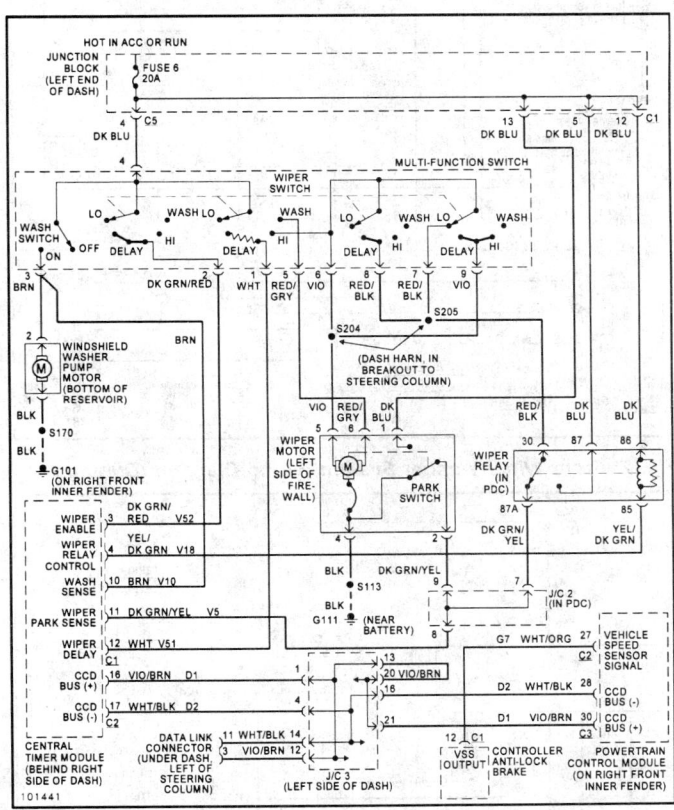

Fig. 6: Front Wiper/Washer System Wiring Diagram (Dakota)

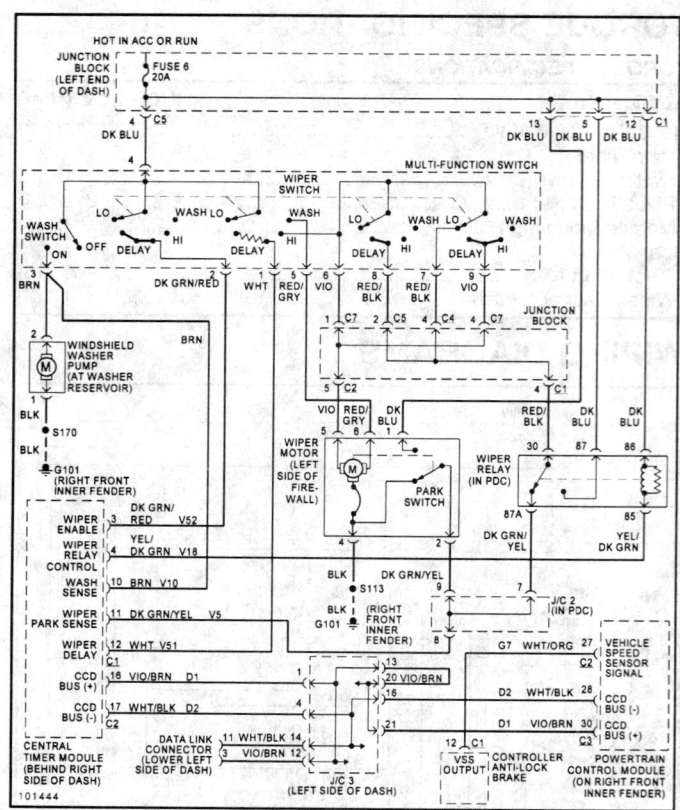

Fig. 7: Front Wiper/Washer System Wiring Diagram (Durango)

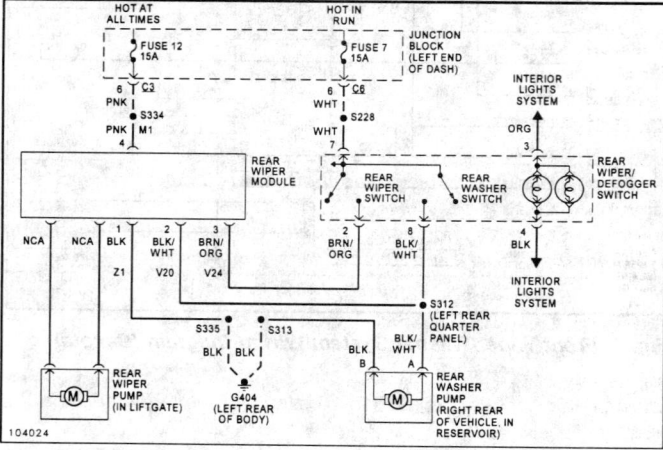

Fig. 8: Rear Wiper/Washer System Wiring Diagram (Durango)

DESCRIPTION & OPERATION

Windshield wiper/washer system is a 2-speed intermittent system. Wiper motor is ferrite-magnet type. Wiper motor uses a 3-brush arrangement to control motor speed. Windshield wiper/washer is activated by switch lever located on right side of steering column.

Intermittent wiper system has, in addition to low and high speed, a delay and a pulse wipe mode. Delay mode has a range of 1-15 seconds. Pulse wipe is triggered by momentarily moving the stalk lever into WASH position while wiper switch is in either OFF or DELAY position.

Intermittent wiper function is integral to the wiper switch. All electronics and relay are contained within switch assembly. Washer system will spray windshield and operate wipers until switch is released, followed by about 2 cycles of wipers. Wiper blades are of an unequal length. Left wiper is 20.7" (525 mm) and right wiper is 17.7" (450 mm). DO NOT exchange blades.

ADJUSTMENTS

WIPER ARMS

1) With ignition switch in ON or ACC position, cycle wiper motor to park position. Turn ignition switch to OFF position.
2) Lift wiper blade off windshield and release it. Heel of blade should be within 3/16" (5 mm) of park line mark on windshield. *See Fig. 1.*
3) If blade tip strikes cowl screen or molding due to long term normal wear, reposition wiper blade heel slightly above park line. Ensure wipers are in park position before adjustment.

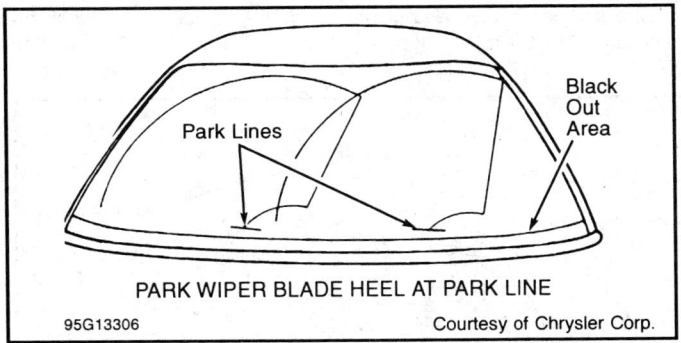

Fig. 1: Adjusting Wiper Arms

TROUBLE SHOOTING

WARNING: For all vehicles equipped with air bag restraint systems, see appropriate AIR BAG RESTRAINT SYSTEMS article before servicing steering wheel or column. Use extreme caution to avoid personal injury and vehicle damage.

WIPERS PARK IN WRONG POSITION

Check wiper arm adjustment. See WIPER ARMS under ADJUSTMENTS.

WIPERS RUN WHEN SWITCH IS TURNED OFF

Check for faulty wiper switch and park switch ground. See WIPER SWITCH under COMPONENT TESTS.

WIPER BLADES SLAP AGAINST COWL SCREEN OR WINDOW MOLDINGS

Wiper arms not adjusted properly. See WIPER ARMS under ADJUSTMENTS.

BLADES CHATTER

Check for foreign substance on glass or blades. Check wiper arms for damage. Ensure blades are not bent or at wrong angle on glass.

WIPER KNOCK AT REVERSAL

Worn linkage bushings. Excessive wiper motor armature end play.

WIPER MOTOR WILL NOT RUN

Check for blown fuse or open circuit. Check for faulty wiper motor or poor ground. See WIPERS INOPERATIVE under SYSTEM TESTS.

COMPONENT TESTS

WIPER SWITCH

Disconnect wiper switch connector. See WIPER SWITCH under REMOVAL & INSTALLATION. Check continuity between appropriate switch terminals with switch in specified position. See WIPER/WASHER SWITCH CONTINUITY table. *See Fig. 2.* Replace switch if continuity is not as specified.

WIPER/WASHER SWITCH CONTINUITY

Switch Position	Continuity Between Terminals
Off	P2 & "L"
Low	P1 & "L"
High	P1 & "H"
Wash	P1 & "W"
Intermittent	[1]

[1] – Can not be checked.

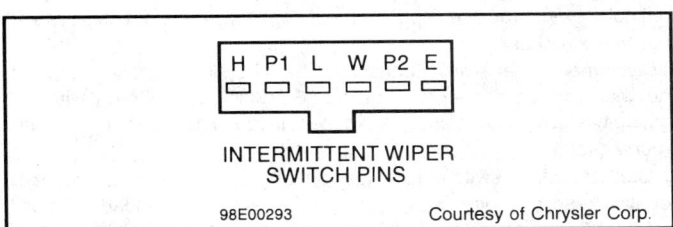

INTERMITTENT WIPER SWITCH PINS

98E00293   Courtesy of Chrysler Corp.

Fig. 2: Identifying Wiper Switch Terminals

SYSTEM TESTS

WARNING: For all vehicles equipped with air bag restraint systems, see appropriate AIR BAG RESTRAINT SYSTEMS article before servicing steering wheel or column. Use extreme caution to avoid personal injury and vehicle damage.

WIPERS DO NOT PARK PROPERLY

1) Ensure wiper arms are not loose on pivot shaft. Check wiper arm adjustment. See WIPER ARMS under ADJUSTMENTS. If wiper arm adjustment is not okay, adjust as necessary. If wiper arm adjustment is okay, go to next step.
2) If motor crank is loose at output shaft, remove wiper module. See WIPER MOTOR & LINKAGE MODULE under REMOVAL & INSTALLATION. Remove motor crank, without rotating motor shaft. Ensure crank mounting are is clean. Install motor crank. Tighten nut to 98-106 INCH lbs. (11-12 N.m) without rotating motor shaft.

WIPERS DO NOT PARK

Ensure wiper motor is not in PARK position. Disconnect wiper motor connector. Using jumper wire, apply battery voltage to wiper motor terminal No. 4 (component side). Connect another jumper wire between wiper motor terminals No. 3 and 2 (component side). *See Fig. 3.* Replace motor if it does not return to park position.

WIPERS INOPERATIVE

1) Check fuse No. 15 (20-amp) in junction block. *See Fig. 4.* If fuse is okay, go to next step. If fuse is blown, replace and check motor operation in all switch positions. If motor is still inoperative and fuse does not blow, go to next step. If replacement fuse blows, go to step 9).

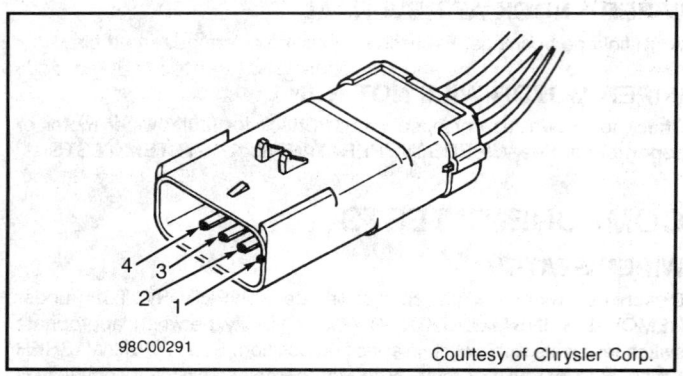

98C00291   Courtesy of Chrysler Corp.

Fig. 3: Identifying Wiper Motor Connector (Component Side)

2) Disconnect wiper motor connector. Connect a jumper wire between positive battery terminal and wiper motor terminal No. 2 (Brown/White wire). *See Fig. 3*. Connect another jumper wire to negative battery terminal and motor ground strap. If wiper motor operates at low speed, go to next step. If wiper motor does not operate at low speed, go to step **4)**.

3) Move positive jumper wire to wiper motor terminal No. 1 (Red/Yellow wire). If motor operates at high speed, go to step **5)**. If wiper motor does not operate at high speed, go to next step.

4) Check continuity between ground and wiper motor ground strap. If continuity exists, replace wiper motor. If continuity does not exist, repair open ground circuit.

5) Disconnect wiper switch connector. Check continuity between ground and wiper switch connector terminal "E" (Black/Light Green wire). If continuity exists, go to next step. If continuity does not exist, repair open ground circuit.

6) Connect wiper switch. Turn ignition on. Using voltmeter, connect negative lead to motor ground strap. Connect positive lead to wiper switch connector terminal P1 (Dark Blue wire). *See Figs. 2 and 5*. If battery voltage exists, go to next step. If battery voltage does not exist, repair wiring as necessary. See WIRING DIAGRAMS.

7) Connect voltmeter positive lead to wiper switch connector terminal "L" (Brown/White wire). Move wiper stalk to LOW position. If battery voltage exists, go to next step. If battery voltage does not exist, replace wiper switch.

8) Connect voltmeter positive lead to wiper switch connector terminal "H" (Red/Yellow wire). Move wiper stalk to HIGH position. If battery voltage exists, go to next step. If battery voltage does not exist, replace wiper switch.

9) Disconnect wiper motor connector, and replace fuse No. 15 in fuse block. If fuse does not blow, replace motor. If fuse blows, disconnect wiper switch and replace fuse. If fuse does not blow, replace switch. If fuse blows, repair short circuit in wiring as necessary. See WIRING DIAGRAMS.

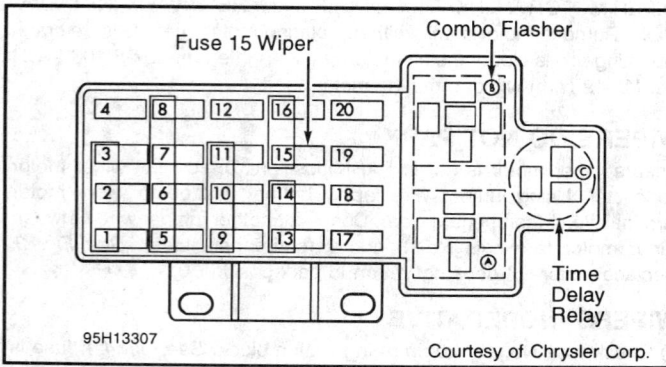

Fuse 15 Wiper   Combo Flasher

95H13307   Courtesy of Chrysler Corp.

Fig. 4: Identifying Junction Block

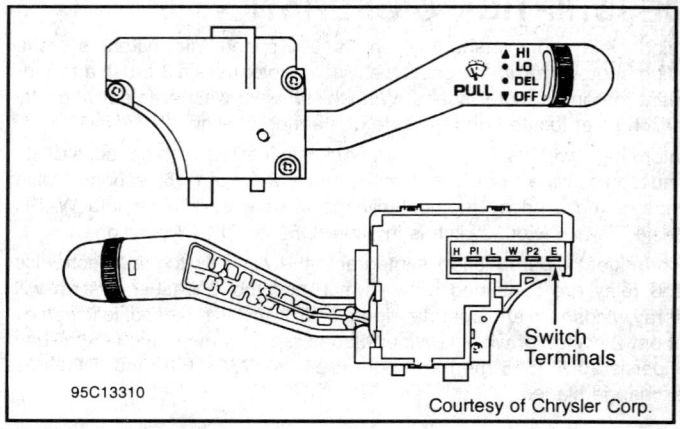

95C13310   Courtesy of Chrysler Corp.

Fig. 5: Identifying Wiper Switch & Terminals

WIPERS RUN SLOWLY AT ALL SPEEDS

1) Disconnect wiper motor connector. Remove wiper arms and cowl screen. Disconnect motor drive linkage from motor. Connect an ammeter between positive battery terminal and wiper motor connector terminal No. 4 (Dark Blue wire). If motor runs and average ammeter reading is more than 6 amps, go to next step. If motor runs and average ammeter reading is less than 6 amps, go to step **3)**.

2) Using an ohmmeter, check high and low speed circuits for a short to ground. See WIRING DIAGRAMS. Repair as necessary.

3) Check wiper linkage and pivots for binding or damage. Repair as necessary. Tighten drive link nut to 98-106 INCH lbs. (11-12 N.m). *See Fig. 6*.

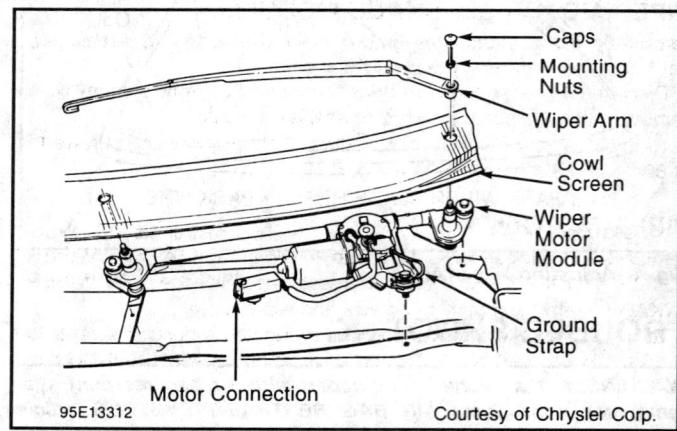

95E13312   Courtesy of Chrysler Corp.

Fig. 6: Identifying Wiper Motor & Linkage Module

WIPERS RUN AT HIGH SPEED WITH SWITCH IN LOW SPEED POSITION OR WIPERS RUN AT LOW SPEED WITH SWITCH IN HIGH SPEED POSITION

Check for crossed wires in wiper motor wire connector. Check for crossed wires in harness connector from wiper switch to motor. See WIRING DIAGRAMS. If wires are not crossed, replace wiper switch.

WIPERS RUN CONTINUOUSLY WITH SWITCH IN INTERMITTENT POSITION & WIPERS DO NOT PARK

Turn ignition off. Check for good ground at wiper motor ground strap. Repair ass necessary. With wiper motor in park position, use ohmmeter to check for continuity between wiper motor connector terminal No. 3 (Dark Green/Yellow wire) and ground strap. If continuity exists, replace wiper switch. If continuity does not exist, replace wiper motor.

WIPERS DO NOT RUN WHEN WASHER IS ENGAGED OR WIPERS INOPERATIVE IN INTERMITTENT POSITION

Check for good ground at wiper motor ground strap and at wiper switch terminal "E" (Black/Light Green wire). If ground circuits are okay, replace wiper switch. If ground circuits are not okay, repair wiring as necessary. See WIRING DIAGRAMS.

WASHER INOPERATIVE

1) If pump does not operate, go to next step. If pump operates, but fluid does not flow, or if washer output is low, check for blocked, loose or broken hoses. Check for plugged or frozen nozzle. Repair as necessary.
2) Test wiper switch. See WIPER SWITCH under COMPONENT TESTS. Replace switch, if necessary. If system operates intermittently, check connections at washer pump. Repair as necessary.

REMOVAL & INSTALLATION

WARNING: On vehicles equipped with air bag restraint system, see appropriate AIR BAG RESTRAINT SYSTEMS article before servicing steering wheel or column. Use extreme caution to avoid personal injury and vehicle damage.

WIPER ARMS

Removal & Installation – Remove caps and wiper mounting nuts. Remove wiper arms. *See Fig. 6.* To install, ensure wiper module is in PARK position. Reverse removal procedure. Adjust wiper arms. See WIPER ARMS under ADJUSTMENTS.

WIPER MOTOR & LINKAGE MODULE

Removal & Installation – 1) Remove wiper arms and blades. Remove rear hood seal with cowl top plastic screen.
2) Disconnect wiper motor electrical connector at front plenum wall. Remove mounting screws and remove wiper module.
3) To install, reverse removal procedure. Tighten mounting screws to 60-80 INCH lbs. (7-9 N.m). *See Fig. 6.*

WIPER MOTOR

Removal & Installation – 1) Remove wiper module. See WIPER MOTOR & LINKAGE MODULE. Remove wiper linkage. See WIPER LINKAGE. Remove mounting screws and wiper motor.
2) To install, reverse removal procedure. Tighten mounting screws to 45-55 INCH lbs. (5-6 N.m). Tighten drive link nut to 98-106 INCH lbs. (11-12 N.m).

WIPER LINKAGE

Removal & Installation – Remove wiper module. See WIPER MOTOR & LINKAGE MODULE. Disconnect wiper linkage by inserting screwdriver between ball cap and linkage, and lifting straight up while screwdriver is twisted. To install, reverse removal procedure. Use pliers or hand to press ball cap straight onto ball stud.

WIPER SWITCH

Removal & Installation – Remove 3 screws holding steering column shroud. Remove upper half of shroud. Remove mounting screw on switch, and remove switch. Disconnect electrical connector. To install, reverse removal procedure.

WASHER RESERVOIR

Removal & Installation – 1) Remove filler neck. Raise vehicle on hoist. Disconnect wire connector from reservoir pump. Disconnect washer hose at pump, and drain reservoir.
2) Remove reservoir screw. Remove reservoir through fender opening. To install, reverse removal procedure. Tighten reservoir screw to 20-29 INCH lbs. (2.2-3.3 N.m).

WASHER PUMP

Removal & Installation – 1) Raise vehicle on hoist. Disconnect wire connector from reservoir pump. Disconnect washer hose at pump, and drain reservoir.
2) Gently pry pump away from reservoir and out of grommet. DO NOT puncture reservoir during removal. Remove rubber grommet and discard. To install, reverse removal procedure. Use NEW grommet for installation.

WASHER NOZZLE

Removal & Installation – 1) Vehicle has 2 identical hood-mounted nozzles, each with 2 apertures. *See Fig. 7.* Nozzles should be adjusted to illustrated pattern. *See Fig. 8.*
2) To replace nozzle, disconnect washer fluid hose. Using needle-nose pliers, squeeze locking tabs on nozzle. When installing, ensure both tabs are securely snapped into place. Connect washer fluid hose and adjust nozzles to conform to correct pattern. *See Fig. 8.*

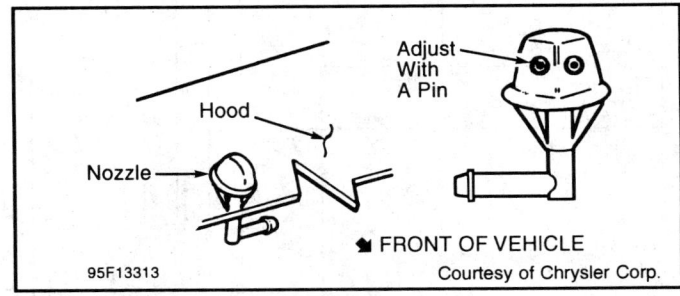

Fig. 7: Identifying Washer Nozzles

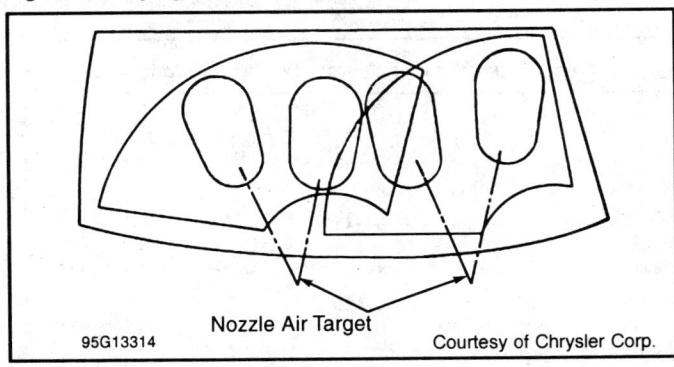

Fig. 8: Windshield Washer Pattern

WIRING DIAGRAMS

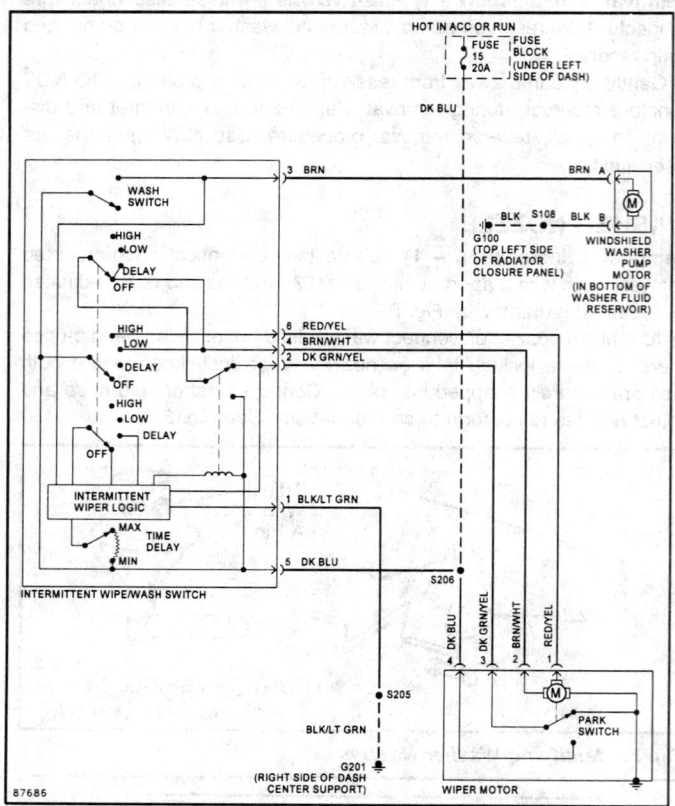

Fig. 9: Interval Wiper/Washer System Wiring Diagram (Neon)

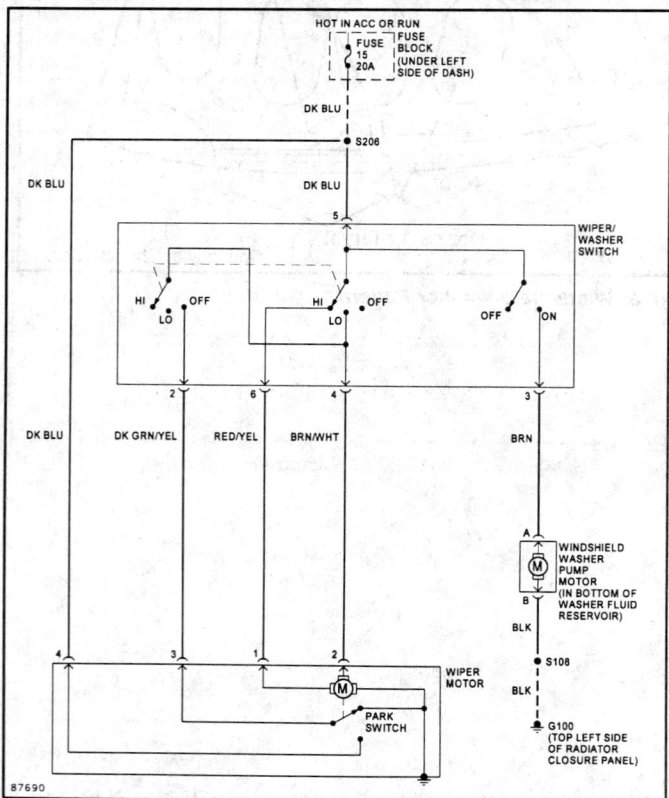

Fig. 10: 2-Speed Wiper/Washer System Wiring Diagram (Neon)

DESCRIPTION & OPERATION

A permanent magnet wiper motor is used for low, high or intermittent (delay) wiper functions. Base intermittent (delay) wiper function provides a .5-18 second delay mode. On high-line models, delay function is speed sensitive. At vehicle speeds greater than 10 MPH, delay mode range is 1/2-18 seconds. At vehicle speeds less than 10 MPH, delay mode doubles to 1-36 seconds.

Delay function is controlled by Central Timer Module (CTM), located under passenger side of instrument panel, outboard of glove box. CTM switches an intermittent wiper relay, located in Power Distribution Center (PDC). On high line models, CTM is connected to Chrysler Collision Detection (CCD) data bus network to receive vehicle speed information for delay function.

Washer system consists of rubber hoses and nozzles, an electric pump, sealed motor, low washer fluid indicator (if equipped) and reservoir.

ADJUSTMENTS

WIPER BLADES

With wiper arms removed, cycle wiper motor into PARK position. Mount arms on pivot shafts, and ensure distances are as specified. *See Fig. 1.* Operate wiper blades, and check whether they return to proper position. If wiper blades do not return to this position, check linkage and pivot assembly for wear and binding.

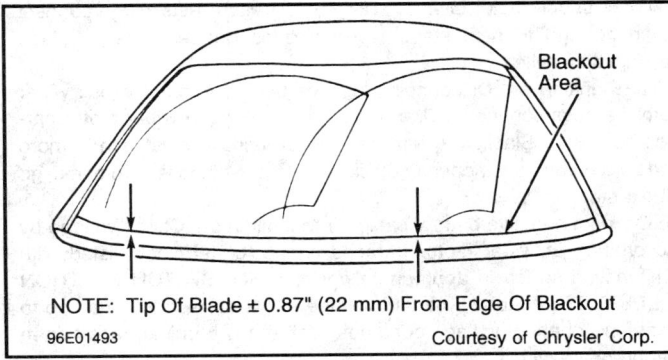

NOTE: Tip Of Blade ± 0.87" (22 mm) From Edge Of Blackout

96E01493   Courtesy of Chrysler Corp.

Fig. 1: Adjusting Wiper Blades

TROUBLE SHOOTING

MOTOR WILL NOT RUN

Check for blown fuse. Check voltage at motor. Check wiper switch, ground circuit and wiring.

MOTOR RUNS, BLADES DO NOT MOVE

Check for loose motor crank, disconnected linkage or loose arms on pivot shaft. Check for faulty wiper motor.

BLADES DO NOT PARK PROPERLY

Check for improperly installed wiper arms. Check for faulty linkage. Check for faulty wiring, wiper switch or wiper motor.

WIPER KNOCK NOISE

Check for improperly installed wiper arms. Check for faulty linkage or wiper motor.

BLADES CHATTER

Check for foreign substance on blades or glass. Check for twisted arm holding blade at wrong angle to glass. Check for bent or damaged blades.

WASHERS DO NOT OPERATE

Check for low washer fluid level. Check for contaminated washer fluid. Check for leaking or improperly routed hoses. Check for faulty wiring, wiper switch or washer pump.

COMPONENT TESTS

INTERMITTENT WIPER RELAY

1) Remove relay. See INTERMITTENT WIPER RELAY under REMOVAL & INSTALLATION. Check continuity between relay terminals No. 30 and 87A. Continuity should exist. Check continuity between relay terminals No. 30 and 87. Continuity should not exist. Check resistance between relay terminals No. 85 and 86. Resistance should be 70-80 ohms.

2) Connect battery voltage between relay terminals No. 85 and 86. Check continuity between relay terminals No. 30 and 87A. Continuity should not exist. Check continuity between relay terminals No. 30 and 87. Continuity should exist. Replace relay if continuity or resistance is not as specified.

WIPER/WASHER SWITCH

NOTE: Wiper/washer switch is part of multifunction steering column switch. If wiper/washer switch fails, entire multifunction switch must be replaced.

Disconnect wiper/washer switch connector. Check continuity between appropriate switch terminals with switch in specified position. See WIPER/WASHER CONTINUITY TEST table. *See Fig. 2.* Replace multifunction switch if continuity is not as specified.

WIPER/WASHER CONTINUITY TEST

Switch Position	Between Terminals
Off	6 & 7
Delay [1]	8 & 9; 2 & 4; 1 & 2; 1 & 4
Low	4 & 6
High	4 & 5
Wash	3 & 4

[1] – At maximum delay position, resistance should be 270-330 k/ohms between all terminal pairs listed. At minimum delay position, resistance should be zero when ohmmeter is set on high ohm scale between all terminal pairs listed.

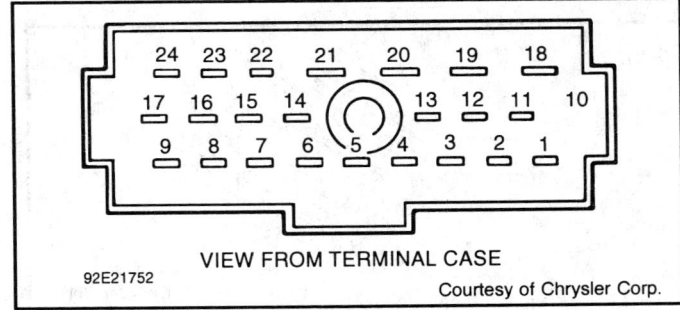

VIEW FROM TERMINAL CASE

92E21752   Courtesy of Chrysler Corp.

Fig. 2: Identifying Wiper/Washer Switch Terminals

SYSTEM TESTS

WARNING: All vehicles are equipped with air bag restraint systems. See appropriate AIR BAG RESTRAINT SYSTEMS article before servicing steering wheel or column. Use extreme caution to avoid personal injury and vehicle damage.

NOTE: If problem occurs in electronic components, wiring, wiper switch or wiper motor, a Diagnostic Trouble Code (DTC) will be stored in BCM. For testing procedures, see appropriate BODY CONTROL COMPUTER TESTS article.

WASHER

NOTE: Following testing applies when pump does not operate. If pump operates, see TROUBLE SHOOTING.

1) Turn ignition on. Turn wiper switch on. If wipers operate, go to next step. If wipers do not operate, diagnose wiper problem first. See WIPER.

2) Turn wiper switch off. Depress washer switch. Washer pump and wipers should operate while switch is depressed. Wipers should operate about 3 sweeps after switch is released. If wipers are okay but washer is not, go to next step. If washer is okay but wipers are not, go to step 5).

3) Turn ignition off. Disconnect negative battery cable. Disconnect washer pump harness connector. Check resistance between washer pump harness connector Black wire terminal and ground. If resistance is more than zero ohms, repair open in Black wire. If resistance is zero ohms, go to next step.

4) Connect negative battery cable. Turn ignition on. While depressing washer switch, check voltage at washer pump harness connector Brown wire terminal. If battery voltage exists, replace pump. If battery voltage does not exist, repair open in Brown wire.

5) Turn ignition off. Disconnect negative battery cable. Access CTM and disconnect CTM harness connector. Connect negative battery cable. Turn ignition on. With washer switch depressed, check voltage at CTM 14-pin harness connector terminal No. 10 (Brown wire). *See Fig. 3*. If battery voltage exists, check intermittent relay. See INTERMITTENT WIPER RELAY under COMPONENT TESTS. If battery voltage does not exist, repair open in Brown wire.

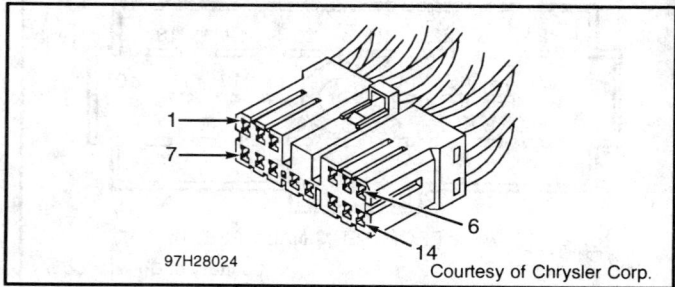

97H28024   Courtesy of Chrysler Corp.

Fig. 3: Identifying Central Timer Module 14-Pin Harness Connector Terminals

WIPER

NOTE: This testing applies to base model Ram Pickup. For high line Ram Pickup testing, see appropriate BODY CONTROL COMPUTER TESTS article.

NOTE: Wiper system utilizes a Central Timer Module (CTM) to control intermittent functions of wiper system. If problem is only pulse wipe or wipe-after-wash, see WASHER.

1) Check fuse No. 6 (25-amp) in junction block. If fuse is blown, replace fuse and repair short as necessary. If fuse is okay, go to next step.

2) Turn ignition on. Check for battery voltage at fuse. If battery voltage does not exist, repair open circuit between fuse and ignition switch as necessary. If battery voltage exists, go to next step.

3) Turn ignition off. Disconnect negative battery cable. Disconnect multifunction switch harness connector. Connect negative battery cable. Turn ignition on. Check for battery voltage at multifunction switch harness connector terminal No. 4 (Dark Blue wire). *See Fig. 2*. If battery voltage exists, go to next step. If battery voltage does not exist, repair open in Dark Blue wire between fuse and multifunction switch.

4) If problem is intermittent wipe feature only, go to next step. If problem is with all wiper modes or only HI and/or LO speed modes, go to step 7).

5) Turn ignition off. Disconnect negative battery cable. Disconnect CTM 14-pin harness connector. Check continuity between multifunction switch harness connector terminal No. 1 (White/Dark Blue wire) and CTM 14-pin harness connector terminal No. 12 (White/Dark Blue wire). *See Fig. 3*. If continuity does not exist, repair open in White/Dark Blue wire. If continuity exists, go to next step.

6) Check continuity between multifunction switch harness connector terminal No. 2 (Violet wire) and CTM 14-pin harness connector terminal No. 3 (Violet wire). If continuity does not exist, repair open in Violet wire. If continuity exists, check intermittent relay. See INTERMITTENT WIPER RELAY under COMPONENT TESTS.

7) Check continuity between multifunction switch harness connector terminals No. 6 (Brown/White wire) and No. 9 (Brown/White wire). If continuity does not exist, repair open in Brown/White wire. If continuity exists, go to next step.

8) Check multifunction (wiper/washer) switch. See WIPER/WASHER SWITCH under COMPONENT TESTS. If switch tests okay, connect switch and go to next step. If switch does not test okay, replace multifunction switch.

9) Turn ignition off. Disconnect negative battery cable. Access wiper motor harness connector. Check resistance between wiper motor harness connector Black wire terminal and ground. If resistance is more than zero ohms, repair open in Black wire. If resistance is zero ohms, go to next step.

10) Connect negative battery cable. Turn ignition on. Check voltage by backprobing at wiper motor harness connector terminals listed with multifunction switch in appropriate position. See SWITCH POSITION VOLTAGE TEST table. If battery voltage exists at each terminal, go to next step. If battery voltage does not exist at any terminal, repair open in appropriate wire.

SWITCH POSITION VOLTAGE TEST

Switch Position	Wiper Motor Terminal
Any	3
Low	4
High	1

11) Check voltage by backprobing wiper motor connector terminal No. 2 (Dark Green wire) with multifunction switch in LO or HI position, then move switch to OFF. Voltage should vary between battery voltage and zero volts while wiper motor is cycling. Battery voltage should be present when switch is turned off, and zero volts when wipers return to park position. If voltage is not as specified, replace wiper motor.

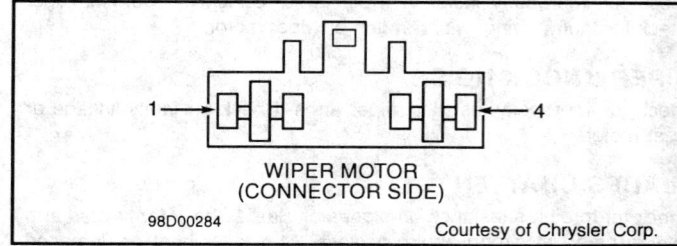

WIPER MOTOR
(CONNECTOR SIDE)

98D00284   Courtesy of Chrysler Corp.

Fig. 4: Identifying Wiper Motor Harness Connector Terminals

REMOVAL & INSTALLATION

WARNING: For all vehicles equipped with air bag restraint systems, see appropriate AIR BAG RESTRAINT SYSTEMS article before servicing steering wheel or column. Use extreme caution to avoid personal injury and vehicle damage.

CAUTION: When battery is disconnected, vehicle computer and memory systems may lose memory data. Driveability problems may exist until computer systems have completed a relearn cycle. See COMPUTER RELEARN PROCEDURES article in GENERAL INFORMATION before disconnecting battery.

CENTRAL TIMER MODULE (CTM)

NOTE: When installing new high line CTM, use scan tool to determine customer preferred settings before replacement. Settings must be enabled/disabled using scan tool.

Removal & Installation – Disconnect negative battery cable. Remove driver's side knee bolster. Remove CTM from bracket on inboard side of instrument panel steering column opening. Disconnect harness connectors. To install, reverse removal procedure.

INTERMITTENT WIPER RELAY

Removal & Installation – Intermittent wiper relay is located in Power Distribution Center (PDC) in engine compartment. Remove cover and remove relay. To install, reverse removal procedures

WIPER ARMS

Removal & Installation – Open hood. Lift wiper and slide latch to hold wiper off of windshield. With a rocking motion, remove wiper arm. To install, ensure wiper motor is in park position. Slide wiper arm on shaft. Align wiper arms. See WIPER BLADES under ADJUSTMENTS.

WIPER MOTOR

NOTE: Wiper linkage and motor module is replaced as a unit.

Removal & Installation – **1)** Disconnect negative battery cable. Remove wiper arms. See WIPER ARMS. Remove weatherstrip along front edge of cowl. Release plastic anchor screws. Lift cowl grille from vehicle. Remove washer hose from "Y" fitting. Set grille aside.
2) Remove wiper linkage mounting bolts. Turn linkage over and disconnect harness connector from wiper motor. Remove wiper linkage and motor module. To install, reverse removal procedure. Align wiper arms. See WIPER BLADES under ADJUSTMENTS.

WIPER/WASHER SWITCH

NOTE: Wiper/washer switch is part of multifunction steering column switch. If wiper/washer switch fails, entire multifunction switch must be replaced.

Removal & Installation – **1)** Disconnect negative battery cable. Remove tilt lever (if equipped). Remove steering column upper and lower covers to access switch connector. Remove switch connector. Remove multifunction switch tamperproof screws.
2) Gently pull switch away from column and loosen connector screw (screw remains in connector). Remove switch. To install, reverse removal procedure. Tighten screws and nuts to specification. See TORQUE SPECIFICATIONS. Ensure switch is functioning properly.

WASHER RESERVOIR

Removal & Installation – Disconnect negative battery cable. Drain cooling system. Disconnect upper radiator hose from radiator. Disconnect harness connectors from washer pump and washer fluid level sensor. Remove washer supply hose from washer pump and drain washer fluid. While pulling reservoir away from fan shroud, lift reservoir upward to disengage mounting tabs from fan shroud. Remove washer reservoir. To install, reverse removal procedure.

WASHER MOTOR

Removal & Installation – Disconnect negative battery cable. Remove hose from washer pump. Drain fluid from reservoir. Disconnect harness connectors from washer pump. Pry pump away from reservoir, being careful not to puncture reservoir. Remove and discard grommet. To install, reverse removal procedure. Use a NEW rubber grommet.

TORQUE SPECIFICATIONS

TORQUE SPECIFICATIONS

Application	INCH Lbs. (N.m)
Central Timer Module Screws	15 (1.6)
Multifunction Switch Mounting Screws	17 (2)
Wiper Motor Mounting Screws	72 (8)
Wiper/Washer Switch Screws	17 (2)

WIRING DIAGRAMS

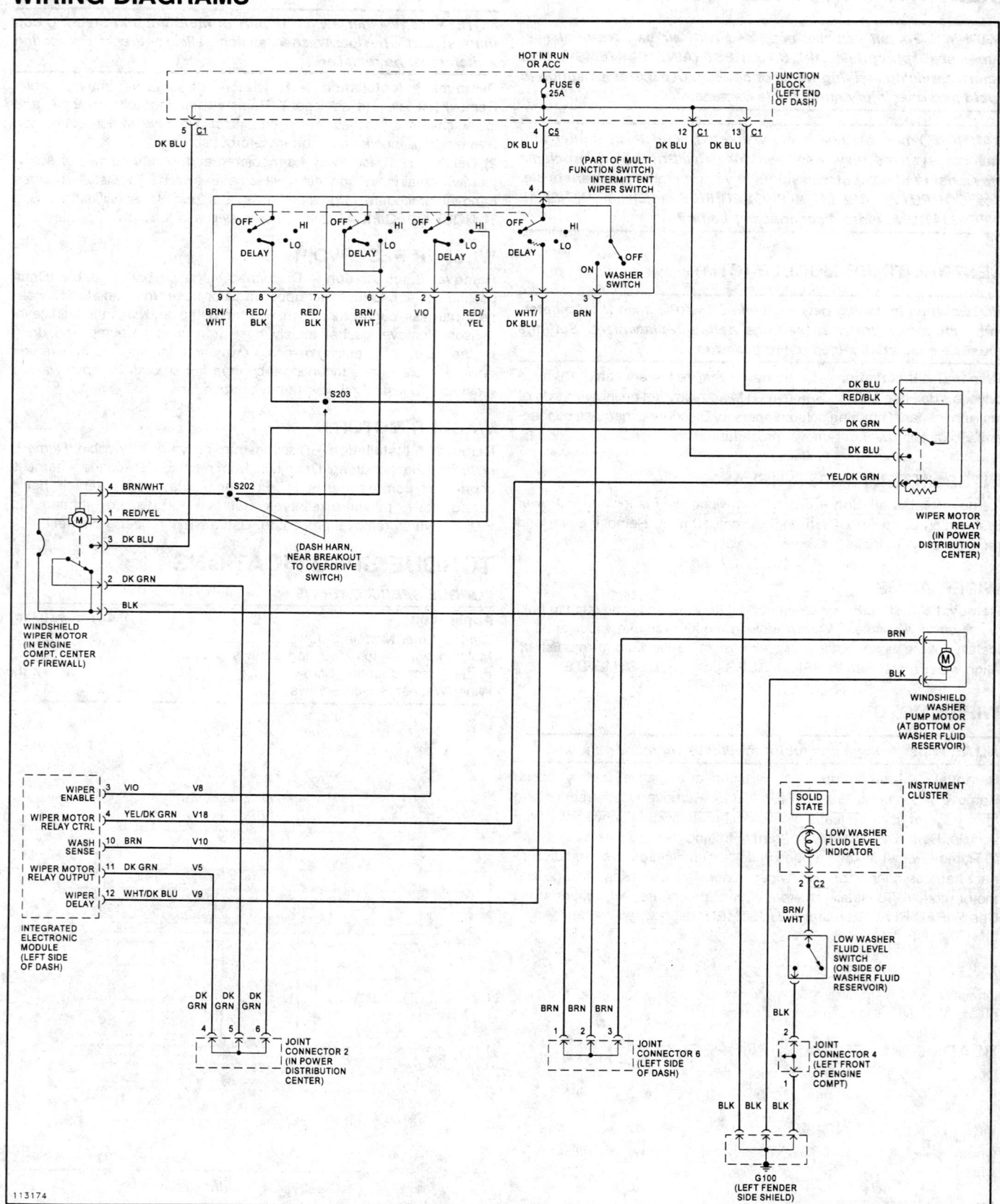

Fig. 5: Wiper/Washer System Wiring Diagram (Ram Pickup)

113174

DESCRIPTION & OPERATION

A permanent magnet wiper motor is used for low, high or intermittent (delay) wiper functions. On vehicles without Vehicle Theft Security System (VTSS), base delay function is controlled by an intermittent wiper module located behind glove box. Intermittent (delay) wiper function provides a .5-14 second delay mode.

On vehicles with Vehicle Theft Security System (VTSS), delay function is speed sensitive. At vehicle speeds greater than 10 MPH, delay mode range is .5-14 seconds. At vehicle speeds less than 10 MPH, delay mode doubles to 1-28 seconds. Delay function is controlled by Central Timer Module (CTM), located under passenger's side of instrument panel, right of glove box. CTM switches an intermittent wiper relay, located behind glove box. CTM is connected to Chrysler Collision Detection (CCD) data bus network to receive vehicle speed information.

Washer system consists of rubber hoses and nozzles, an electric pump, sealed motor, low washer fluid indicator and reservoir, located on right side inner fender panel.

ADJUSTMENTS

WIPER BLADES

With wiper arms removed, cycle wiper motor into park position. Mount arms on pivot shafts, adjust passenger's side to 1-3″ (25-75 mm) and driver's side to 1.6-3.5″ (40-90 mm). See Fig. 1. Operate wiper blades, and check whether they return to proper position. If wiper blades do not return to this position, check linkage and pivot assembly for wear and binding.

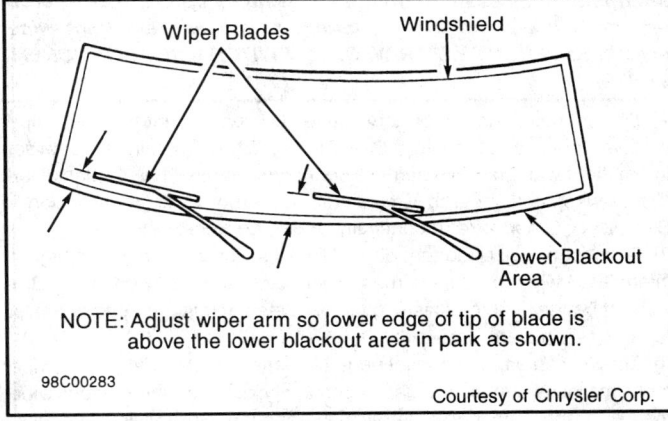

NOTE: Adjust wiper arm so lower edge of tip of blade is above the lower blackout area in park as shown.

98C00283

Courtesy of Chrysler Corp.

Fig. 1: Adjusting Wiper Blades

TROUBLE SHOOTING

MOTOR WILL NOT RUN

Check for blown fuse. Check voltage at motor. Check wiper switch, ground circuit and wiring. See WIPER under SYSTEM TESTS.

MOTOR RUNS, BLADES DO NOT MOVE

Check for loose motor crank, disconnected linkage or loose arms on pivot shaft. Check for faulty wiper motor.

BLADES DO NOT PARK PROPERLY

Check for improperly installed wiper arms. Check for faulty linkage. Check for faulty wiring, wiper switch or wiper motor.

WIPER KNOCK NOISE

Check for improperly installed wiper arms. Check for faulty linkage or wiper motor.

BLADES CHATTER

Check for foreign substance on blades or glass. Check for twisted arm holding blade at wrong angle to glass. Check for bent or damaged blades.

WASHERS DO NOT OPERATE

Check for low washer fluid level. Check for contaminated washer fluid. Check for leaking or improperly routed hoses. Check for faulty wiring, wiper switch or washer pump. See WASHER under SYSTEM TESTS.

COMPONENT TESTS

INTERMITTENT WIPER RELAY

1) Remove relay. See INTERMITTENT WIPER RELAY under REMOVAL & INSTALLATION. Check continuity between relay terminals No. 30 and 87A. Continuity should exist. Check continuity between relay terminals No. 30 and 87. Continuity should not exist. Check resistance between relay terminals No. 85 and 86. Resistance should be 70-80 ohms.

2) Connect battery voltage between relay terminals No. 85 and 86. Check continuity between relay terminals No. 30 and 87A. Continuity should not exist. Check continuity between relay terminals No. 30 and 87. Continuity should exist. Replace relay if continuity or resistance is not as specified.

WIPER/WASHER SWITCH

NOTE: Wiper/washer switch is part of multifunction switch. If wiper/washer switch fails, entire multifunction switch must be replaced.

Disconnect multifunction switch connector. Check continuity between appropriate multifunction switch terminals with switch in appropriate position. See WIPER/WASHER CONTINUITY TEST table. See Fig. 2. Replace multifunction switch if continuity is not as specified.

WIPER/WASHER SWITCH CONTINUITY TEST

Switch Position	Between Terminals
Off	A13 & E5
Delay	A14 & E4; A17 & E5
Delay [1]	A15 & E4
Low	E5 & E4
High	E3 & E4
Wash	A16 & E4

[1] – At maximum (first) delay position, resistance should be 18 k/ohms, at second delay position, resistance should be 12 k/ohms, at third delay position, resistance should be 6.2 k/ohms, at fourth delay position, resistance should be 3.3 k/ohms, at minimum delay (fifth) position, resistance should be zero ohms.

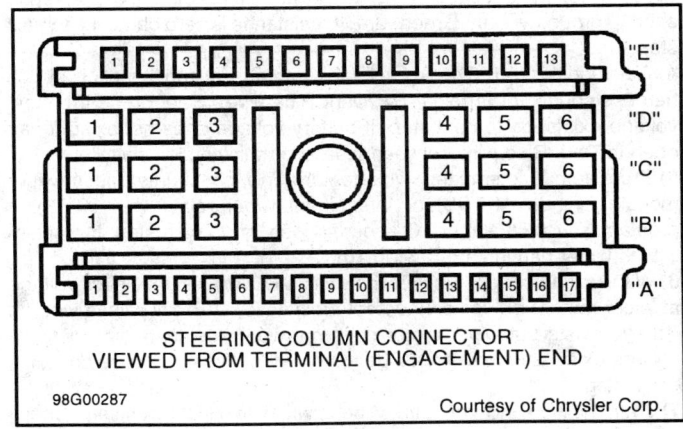

STEERING COLUMN CONNECTOR
VIEWED FROM TERMINAL (ENGAGEMENT) END

98G00287

Courtesy of Chrysler Corp.

Fig. 2: Identifying Wiper/Washer Switch Terminals

CHRY
4-552

1999 ACCESSORIES & EQUIPMENT
Wiper/Washer Systems – Ram Van & Ram Wagon (Cont.)

SYSTEM TESTS

WASHER

NOTE: Following testing applies when pump does not operate. If pump operates, see TROUBLE SHOOTING.

1) Turn ignition on. Turn wiper switch on. If wipers operate, go to next step. If wipers do not operate, diagnose wiper problem first. See WIPER.

2) Turn wiper switch off. Depress washer switch. Washer pump and wipers should operate while switch is depressed. Wipers should operate about 3 sweeps after switch is released. If wipers are okay, but washer is not, go to next step. If washer is okay, but wipers are not, go to step **5)**.

3) Turn ignition off. Disconnect negative battery cable. Disconnect washer pump harness connector. Measure resistance between washer pump harness connector Black wire terminal and ground. If resistance is more than zero ohms, repair open in Black wire. If resistance is zero ohms, go to next step.

4) Connect negative battery cable. Turn ignition on. While depressing washer switch, check voltage at washer pump harness connector Brown wire terminal. If battery voltage exists, replace pump. If battery voltage does not exist, repair open in Brown wire.

5) On vehicles with Vehicle Theft Security System (VTSS), go to next step. On vehicles without VTSS, turn ignition off. Disconnect negative battery cable. Access intermittent wiper module and disconnect connector. Connect negative battery cable. Turn ignition on. With washer switch depressed, check voltage at intermittent wiper module connector terminal No. 7 (Brown wire). If battery voltage exists, check intermittent wiper module. See INTERMITTENT WIPER MODULE. If battery voltage does not exist, repair open in Brown wire.

6) Turn ignition off. Disconnect negative battery cable. Access CTM and disconnect CTM connector. Connect negative battery cable. Turn ignition on. With washer switch depressed, check voltage at CTM connector terminal No. 10 (Brown wire). If battery voltage exists, check intermittent relay. See INTERMITTENT WIPER RELAY under COMPONENT TESTS. If battery voltage does not exist, repair open Brown wire.

WIPER

NOTE: If problem is only pulse wipe or wipe-after-wash, see WASHER.

1) Check fuse No. 6 (20-amp) in junction block. If fuse is blown, repair short circuit and replace fuse. If fuse is okay, go to next step.

2) Turn ignition on. Check for battery voltage at fuse. If battery voltage does not exist, repair open circuit between fuse and ignition switch. If battery voltage exists, go to next step.

3) Turn ignition off. Check resistance between wiper motor connector terminal No. 3 (Dark Green wire) and ground. If resistance exists, repair short to ground in Dark Green wire. If resistance is zero ohms, go to next step.

4) Turn ignition on. Check for battery voltage at multifunction switch harness connector terminal E4 (Dark Blue wire). *See Fig. 2.* If battery voltage exists, go to next step. If battery voltage does not exist, repair open in Dark Blue wire between fuse and multifunction switch.

5) If problem is intermittent wipe feature only, check intermittent wiper module (without V TSS) or intermittent wiper relay (with VTSS). If problem is with HI and/or LO speed modes, go to next step. If problem is with wiper parking, go to step **10)**.

6) With ignition still on, turn wiper switch to LOW position. Check voltage at wiper motor harness connector terminal No. 1 (Brown/White wire). If voltage exists but wiper motor does not work, replace wiper motor. If voltage exists and motor runs, go to step **8)**. If voltage does not exist, go to step **8)**.

7) With ignition still on, turn wiper switch to HIGH position. Check voltage at wiper motor harness connector terminal No. 4 (Red/Light Blue wire). If voltage exists but wiper motor does not work, replace wiper motor. If voltage does not exist, go to step **9)**.

8) With ignition still on, turn wiper switch to LOW position. Check voltage at wiper switch harness connector terminal E5 (Brown/White wire). If voltage exists, repair open in Brown/White wire between multifunction switch and motor. If voltage does not exist, check multifunction switch. See FRONT WIPER/WASHER SWITCH under COMPONENT TESTS.

9) With ignition still on, turn wiper switch to HIGH position. Check voltage at wiper switch harness connector terminal E3 (Red/Light Blue wire). If voltage exists, repair open in Red/Light Blue wire between multifunction switch and motor. If voltage does not exist, check multifunction switch. See FRONT WIPER/WASHER SWITCH under COMPONENT TESTS.

10) Turn ignition on. Check voltage at wiper motor connector terminal No. 2 (Dark Blue wire). If battery voltage exists, go to next step. If battery voltage does not exist, repair open in Dark Blue wire.

11) Turn ignition on. Turn wiper switch to LOW. With wiper motor running, backprobe wiper motor connector terminal No. 3 (Dark Green wire) with voltmeter. Battery voltage should exist when wipers are cycling across windshield, and no voltage when wipers are cycling through park position. If voltage is not as specified, replace wiper motor. If voltage is as specified, go to next step.

12) If vehicle is not equipped with VTSS, check intermittent wiper module. See INTERMITTENT WIPER MODULE. If vehicle is equipped with VTSS, check intermittent wiper relay. See INTERMITTENT WIPER RELAY under COMPONENT TESTS.

INTERMITTENT WIPER MODULE

NOTE: Intermittent wiper module is only used on vehicles without Vehicle Theft Security System (VTSS). If problem occurs in all intermittent modes, perform the following symptom tests. If problem does not occur in all intermittent modes, test front wiper switch. See FRONT WIPER/WASHER SWITCH under COMPONENT TESTS.

1) Disconnect negative battery cable. Disconnect intermittent wiper module harness connector. *See Fig. 3.* Check continuity between intermittent wiper module harness connector terminal No. 4 (Black/Dark Green wire) and ground. If continuity does not exist, repair open in Black/Dark Green wire. If continuity exists, go to next step.

2) Connect negative battery cable. Turn ignition on. Check voltage at intermittent wiper module harness connector terminal No. 1 (Dark Blue wire). If battery voltage exists, go to next step. If voltage does not exist, repair open in Dark Blue wire.

3) Turn ignition off. Disconnect negative battery cable. Disconnect wiper motor harness connector. Check continuity between intermittent wiper module harness connector terminal No. 3 (Dark Green wire) and wiper motor harness connector terminal No. 3 (Dark Green wire). If continuity exists, go to next step. If continuity does not exist, repair open in Dark Green wire.

4) Disconnect multifunction switch harness connector. Check continuity between multifunction switch harness connector terminal A13 (Dark Green/White wire) and intermittent wiper module harness connector terminal No. 2 (Dark Green/White wire). *See Fig. 2.* If continuity exists, go to next step. If continuity does not exist, repair open in Dark Green/White wire.

5) Check continuity between multifunction switch harness connector terminal A15 (White/Brown wire) and intermittent wiper module harness connector terminal No. 6 (White/Brown wire). If continuity exists, go to next step. If continuity does not exist, repair open in White/Brown wire.

6) Check continuity between multifunction switch harness connector terminal A17 (Dark Green/Yellow wire) and intermittent wiper module harness connector terminal No. 8 (Dark Green/Yellow wire). If continuity exists, go to next step. If continuity does not exist, repair open in Dark Green/Yellow wire.

7) Check wiper/washer switch portion of multifunction switch. See FRONT WIPER/WASHER SWITCH test. If switch is okay, replace intermittent wiper module. If switch is not okay, replace switch.

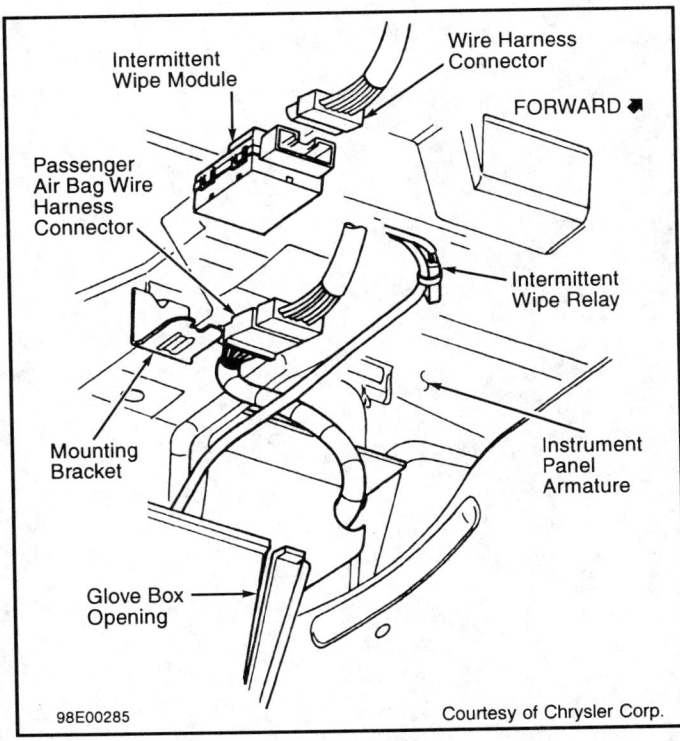

Intermittent Wipe Module

Wire Harness Connector

FORWARD ◄

Passenger Air Bag Wire Harness Connector

Intermittent Wipe Relay

Mounting Bracket

Instrument Panel Armature

Glove Box Opening

98E00285

Courtesy of Chrysler Corp.

Fig. 3: Locating Intermittent Wiper Module

REMOVAL & INSTALLATION

WARNING: For all vehicles equipped with air bag restraint systems, see appropriate AIR BAG RESTRAINT SYSTEMS article before servicing steering wheel or column. Use extreme caution to avoid personal injury and vehicle damage.

CAUTION: When battery is disconnected, vehicle computer and memory systems may lose memory data. Driveability problems may exist until computer systems have completed a relearn cycle. See COMPUTER RELEARN PROCEDURES article in GENERAL INFORMATION before disconnecting battery.

CENTRAL TIMER MODULE (CTM)

NOTE: When installing new CTM, use scan tool to determine customer preferred settings before replacement. Settings must be enabled/disabled using scan tool.

Removal & Installation – Disconnect battery. Remove engine cover. Remove CTM from inboard side of left instrument panel support. Disconnect CTM harness connectors. To install, reverse removal procedure.

INTERMITTENT WIPER MODULE

Removal & Installation – Intermittent wiper module is located above glove box. Disconnect negative battery cable. Fully open glove box door. Push intermittent wiper module forward to disengage mounting slot from blade of bracket. Disconnect intermittent wiper module harness connector. *See Fig. 3.* Remove intermittent wiper module. To install, reverse removal procedure.

INTERMITTENT WIPER RELAY

Removal & Installation – Intermittent wiper relay is located above glove box. Disconnect negative battery cable. Fully open glove box door. Remove tape securing relay to wiring harness. *See Fig. 3.* Remove relay. To install, reverse removal procedure.

WIPER ARMS

Removal & Installation – Lift wiper and slide latch to hold wiper off of windshield. Disconnect washer hose from wiper arm. With a rocking motion, remove wiper arm. To install, ensure wiper motor is in park position. Slide wiper arm on shaft. Align wiper arms. See WIPER BLADES under ADJUSTMENTS.

WIPER MOTOR

Removal & Installation – 1) Disconnect negative battery cable. Remove wiper arms. Open hood. Remove cowl cover fasteners and gently pry ends to release snap clips. Remove cowl cover. Disconnect wiper motor wiring harness connector. Remove crank arm by prying drive link from crank arm ball stud with 2 suitable screwdrivers. DO NOT apply pressure or pry on plastic drive link bushing, or bushing and linkage may be damaged.

2) Remove 3 bolts and wiper motor. Remove crank arm-to-motor drive shaft nut. Remove crank arm from motor. To install, reverse removal procedure. Tighten nuts and screws to specification. See TORQUE SPECIFICATIONS. Install wiper arms. See WIPER BLADES under ADJUSTMENTS.

FRONT WIPER/WASHER SWITCH

NOTE: Front wiper/washer switch is part of multifunction switch. If wiper/washer switch fails, entire multifunction switch must be replaced.

Removal & Installation – 1) Disconnect negative battery cable. Remove driver's side air bag module. See appropriate AIR BAG RESTRAINT SYSTEMS article. Disconnect speed control switch connectors, if equipped. Remove steering wheel mounting nut. Using suitable puller, remove steering wheel.

2) Remove fuse block access panel. Remove 5 steering column opening cover mounting screws. Pry upper edge of steering column opening cover from instrument panel. Remove steering column opening cover. Remove parking brake release handle, data link connector and hood release handle from knee bolster.

3) Loosen 2 screws that secure slotted holes of knee bolster to steering column support bracket. Remove 4 remaining screws and pull knee bolster rearward to remove. Remove tilt lever (if equipped). Remove steering column upper and lower covers. Remove 2 lower wire harness tie straps.

4) Remove bolt from steering column wire harness connector. Disconnect 2 multifunction switch harness connectors from steering column wire harness insulator. Remove 2 multifunction switch screws. Remove multifunction switch. To install, reverse removal procedure. Tighten screws and nuts to specification. See TORQUE SPECIFICATIONS.

WASHER RESERVOIR

Removal & Installation – Disconnect negative battery cable. Disconnect harness connectors from washer pump and washer fluid level sensor. Disconnect washer supply hose from washer pump and drain reservoir. Remove screws at top of reservoir. Lift washer reservoir upward to disengage mounting tab from slot in radiator panel. Remove washer reservoir. To install, reverse removal procedure.

WASHER MOTOR

Removal & Installation – Remove washer reservoir. See WASHER RESERVOIR. Disconnect washer pump harness connector. Carefully pry washer pump from rubber grommet in washer reservoir. DO NOT puncture reservoir. To install, reverse removal procedure. Use NEW rubber grommet

CHRY
4-554

1999 ACCESSORIES & EQUIPMENT
Wiper/Washer Systems – Ram Van & Ram Wagon (Cont.)

TORQUE SPECIFICATIONS

TORQUE SPECIFICATIONS

Application	INCH Lbs. (N.m)
Central Timer Module Screw	20 (2.2)
Cowl Cover Screw	17 (2)
Wiper Motor Mounting Screw	105 (12)
Wiper Pivot Mounting Screw	95 (11)
Steering Wheel Nut	[1]

[1] – Tighten nut to 45 ft. lbs. (61 N.m)

Wiper/Washer Systems – Ram Van & Ram Wagon (Cont.)

WIRING DIAGRAMS

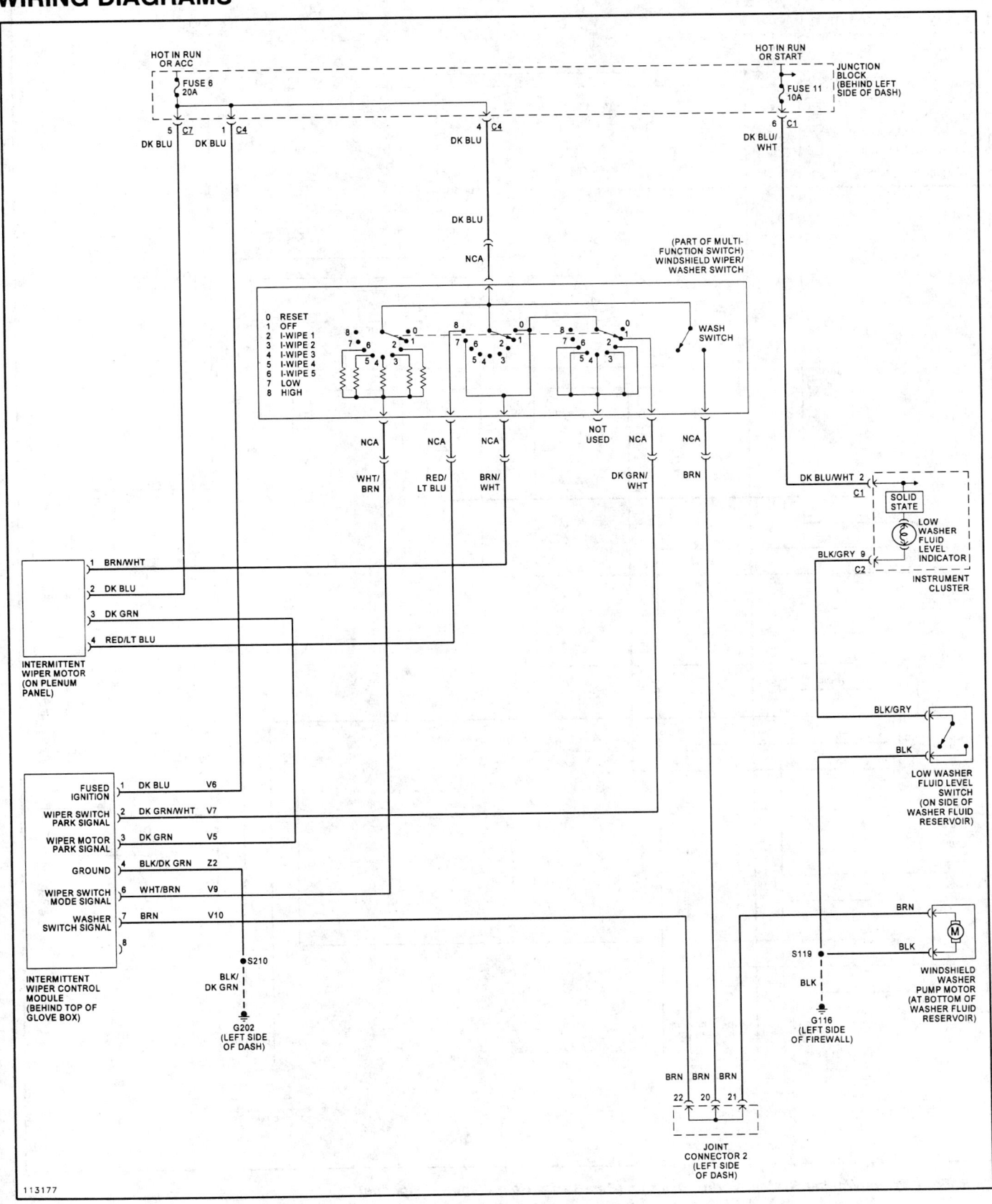

Fig. 4: Front Wiper/Washer System Wiring Diagram (Ram Van & Ram Wagon – Standard)

CHRY
4-556

1999 ACCESSORIES & EQUIPMENT
Wiper/Washer Systems – Ram Van & Ram Wagon (Cont.)

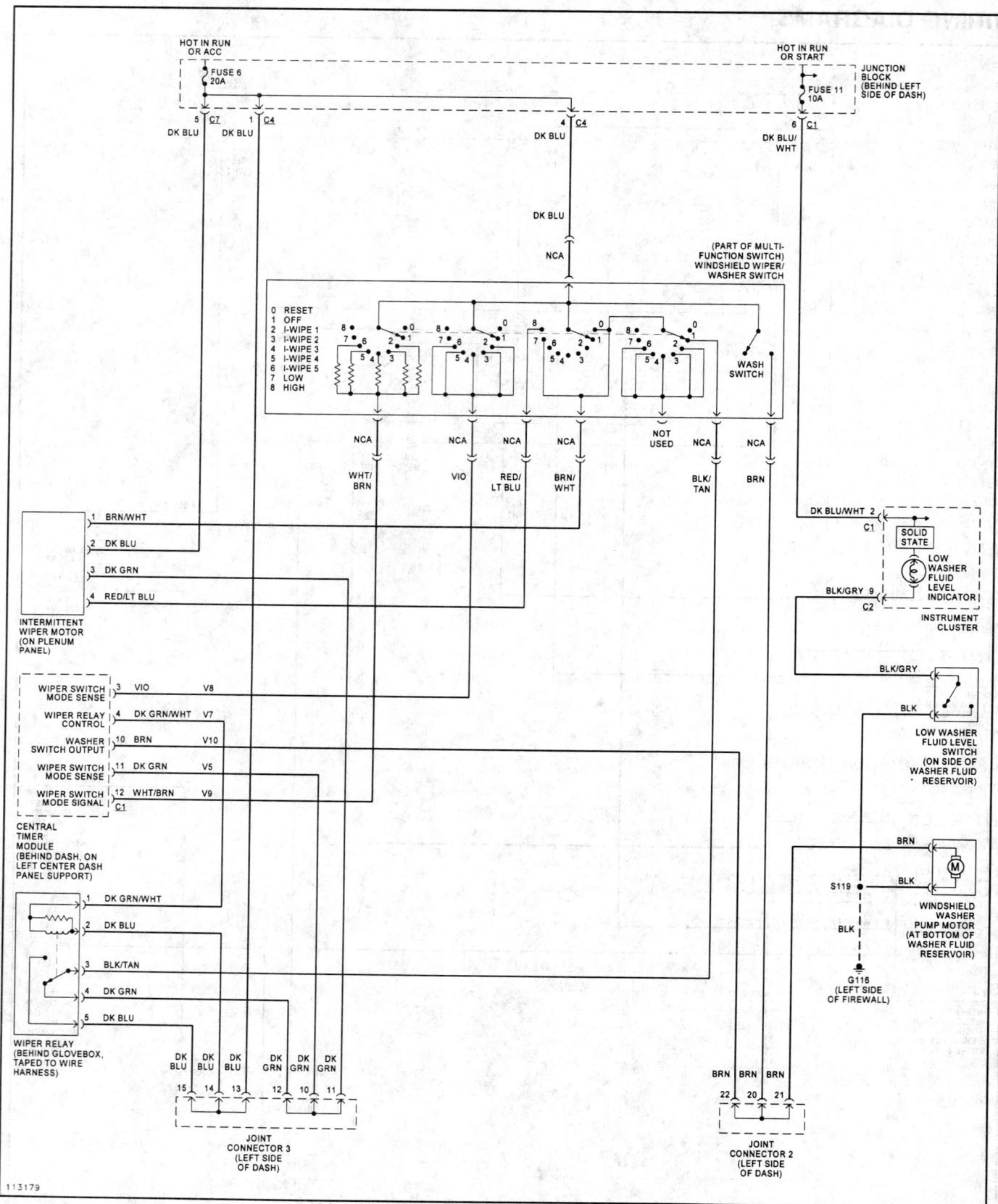

Fig. 5: Front Wiper/Washer System Wiring Diagram (Ram Van & Ram Wagon – Highline)

1999 JEEP
Contents

ACCESSORIES & EQUIPMENT (Cont.)

ACCESSORIES & EQUIPMENT (Cont.)

ACCESSORIES & EQUIPMENT (Cont.)

ACCESSORIES & EQUIPMENT (Cont.)

Cherokee, Grand Cherokee, Wrangler

DESCRIPTION

Mitsubishi permanent-magnet gear reduction starter is used on all models. A planetary gear set transmits power between starter motor and pinion shaft. Four permanent magnets are used, eliminating potential field wire-to-frame shorts. All models use a starter relay in starter circuit between the battery and starter solenoid terminal.

TROUBLE SHOOTING

CHEROKEE 2.5L & WRANGLER 2.5L

NOTE: *For additional trouble shooting, see TROUBLE SHOOTING article in GENERAL INFORMATION.*

Starter motor shims can be added or removed to correct starter noise. Shim thickness is .015" (.381 mm). Shims may be stacked if additional thickness is necessary. Identify symptom and repair as necessary.

High Frequency Whine Before Engine Starts; Engine Starts Okay – Probable cause is excessive distance between pinion gear and flywheel/drive plate gear. To repair, move starter motor toward flywheel/drive plate by removing starter shim(s), if possible.

High Frequency Whine After Engine Starts With Ignition Key Released; Engine Starts Okay – Probable cause is insufficient distance between pinion gear and flywheel/drive plate gear. Noise may be intermittent. To repair, move starter motor away from flywheel/drive plate by adding starter shim(s). Inspect for damage, excessive wear and excessive runout. Replace flywheel/drive plate as necessary.

ON-VEHICLE TESTING

CAUTION: *When battery is disconnected, vehicle computer and memory systems may lose memory data. Driveability problems may exist until computer systems have completed a relearn cycle. See COMPUTER RELEARN PROCEDURES article in GENERAL INFORMATION before disconnecting battery.*

CRANKING TEST

NOTE: *Ensure engine is at normal operating temperature. High viscosity oil, extreme cold temperatures, or tight engine will increase amperage draw.*

1) Using a battery load tester, connect positive and negative leads to battery. Connect inductive ammeter pick-up to positive battery cable. Ensure all lights and accessories are off. Place A/T in Park, or M/T in Neutral. Apply parking brake. Unplug Automatic Shut Down (ASD) relay from Power Distribution Center (PDC). Refer to PDC cover for relay location. PDC is located in engine compartment. On M/T models, depress clutch pedal.

CAUTION: *During cranking, DO NOT draw battery voltage down to less than 9.6 volts. Use care not to overheat starter.*

2) Crank engine and observe voltmeter reading. If voltage drops below 9.6 volts, recharge and test battery. Retest voltage. If voltage remains less than 9.6 volts, bench test starter. See BENCH TESTING. If voltage remains above 9.6 volts, observe amperage reading. If amperage draw is less than specified, perform circuit resistance tests. See STARTER SPECIFICATIONS table. Also see CIRCUIT RESISTANCE TESTS.

3) If voltage reads more than 12.5 volts, and starter does not turn, problem is in battery, relay, solenoid, ignition switch, park/neutral switch, clutch switch or wiring. Check each component until problem is found. If voltage is more than 12.5 volts and starter cranks very slowly, perform circuit resistance tests. See CIRCUIT RESISTANCE TESTS.

CIRCUIT RESISTANCE TESTS

NOTE: *If excessive resistance is not found in circuits being tested, remove starter and proceed to BENCH TESTING.*

NOTE: *A voltmeter accurate to one tenth of a volt will be needed for the following tests.*

Ensure battery is fully charged. Ensure A/T is in Park or M/T is in Neutral and parking brake is applied. Disconnect Automatic Shut Down (ASD) relay so engine will not start. ASD relay is located in Power Distribution Center (PDC). Refer to PDC cover for proper relay location. Clutch pedal must be depressed on M/T models. Perform all listed tests in the order given.

Battery Connection Resistance Test – Connect voltmeter positive lead to negative battery cable clamp. Connect voltmeter negative lead to negative battery post. Crank engine and observe voltmeter reading. If voltage is greater than 0.2 volt, repair poor contact between cable clamp and post. Perform same procedure to positive battery post and cable clamp.

Ground Connection Resistance Test – Connect voltmeter negative lead to negative battery post. Connect voltmeter positive lead to engine block, near negative battery cable grounding point. Crank engine and observe voltmeter reading. If voltage is greater than 0.2 volt, repair poor ground connection or replace ground cable.

Starter Ground Connection Resistance Test – Connect voltmeter negative lead to negative battery post. Connect voltmeter positive lead to starter housing. Crank engine and observe voltmeter reading. If voltmeter reading indicates more than 0.2 volt, repair poor starter-to-ground connection.

Positive Battery Cable Resistance Test – 1) Remove starter heat shield (if equipped) to gain access to starter solenoid connections. Connect voltmeter negative lead to starter solenoid battery terminal and voltmeter positive lead to positive battery post.

2) Crank engine and observe voltmeter reading. If voltage reads more than 0.2 volt, correct poor connection between battery cable and starter solenoid or replace positive battery cable.

SOLENOID CIRCUIT TEST

NOTE: *Perform this procedure before testing starter relay circuit and starter relay. Ensure transmission is in Park (A/T) or Neutral (M/T) and parking brake is applied.*

1) Ensure battery is fully charged. Ensure solenoid connections are not loose or corroded. Remove starter relay from Power Distribution Center (PDC). Refer to PDC cover for proper relay location. PDC is located in engine compartment.

2) Connect a remote starter switch or jumper wire between starter relay connector terminal No. 87 and positive battery post. See Fig. 1 or 2. If engine cranks, solenoid and starter are good. Go to STARTER RELAY CIRCUIT TEST.

3) If engine fails to crank, or if solenoid chatters, check wiring and connectors from starter relay connector to starter solenoid terminal for loose or corroded connections. Clean and retest. If engine still fails to crank, remove starter and proceed to SOLENOID TEST under BENCH TESTING.

STARTER RELAY TEST

NOTE: *Perform SOLENOID CIRCUIT TEST under ON-VEHICLE TESTING before testing starter relay.*

1) Remove starter relay from Power Distribution Center (PDC). PDC is located in engine compartment. Refer to PDC label for starter relay identification.

2) Using an ohmmeter, check for continuity between starter relay terminals No. 30 and 87A. See Fig. 1 or 2. If no continuity exists, replace starter relay. Check for continuity between starter relay terminals No. 30 and 87. If continuity exists, replace starter relay. If relay tests as specified, go to next step.

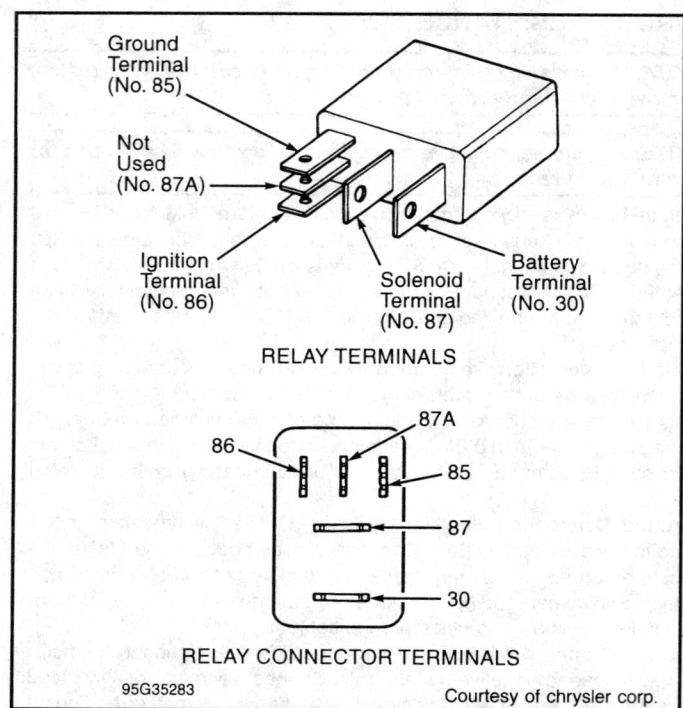

Fig. 1: Identifying Starter Relay Terminals (Grand Cherokee)

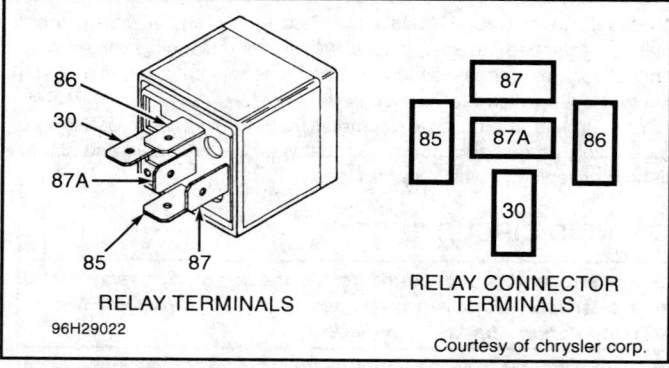

Fig. 2: Identifying Starter Relay Terminals (Cherokee & Wrangler)

3) Check resistance between starter relay terminals No. 85 and 86. If resistance is not 70-80 ohms, replace starter relay. If resistance is okay, go to next step.

4) Connect a 12-volt power source to starter relay terminals No. 85 and 86. Continuity should exist between starter relay terminals No. 30 and 87. No continuity should exist between starter relay terminals No. 30 and 87A. Replace starter relay if it does not test as specified. If starter relay tests as specified, go toSTARTER RELAY CIRCUIT TEST.

STARTER RELAY CIRCUIT TEST

NOTE: Perform SOLENOID CIRCUIT TEST under ON-VEHICLE TESTING before testing starter relay circuit.

1) Ensure battery is fully charged. Remove starter relay from Power Distribution Center (PDC). Refer to PDC cover for proper relay location. PDC is located in engine compartment. Depress clutch pedal on M/T models.

2) Connect a jumper wire between starter relay connector terminals No. 30 and 87. *See Fig. 1 or 2.* If engine does not crank, go to SOLENOID TEST under BENCH TESTING. If engine cranks, go to next step.

3) Turn ignition on. Check for battery voltage at starter relay connector terminal No. 30. If voltage is not present, repair open in wiring from starter relay connector to battery.

4) If voltage is present at starter relay connector terminal No. 30, ensure battery voltage is also present at starter relay connector terminal No. 86. Check for voltage with ignition switch in START position. If voltage is not present, go to next step. If voltage is present, circuit is okay. Go to step **6**).

5) If voltage is not present at starter relay connector terminal No. 86, repair open or short in wiring from ignition switch to starter relay connector. If circuit to ignition switch is okay, check ignition switch. See IGNITION SWITCH TEST under ON-VEHICLE TESTING.

6) Check for continuity to ground at starter relay connector terminal No. 85. If continuity exists, circuit is okay. If continuity does not exist, go to next step.

7) If vehicle is equipped with an A/T, check for an open or short to park/neutral position switch. See PARK/NEUTRAL POSITION SWITCH under ON-VEHICLE TESTING. If vehicle is equipped with a M/T, repair circuit to ground as required.

IGNITION SWITCH TEST

WARNING: Deactivate air bag system before performing any service operation involving steering column components. See appropriate AIR BAG RESTRAINT SYSTEMS article in ACCESSORIES & EQUIPMENT.

1) Disconnect negative battery cable. Remove ignition switch. See appropriate STEERING COLUMN SWITCHES article in ACCESSORIES & EQUIPMENT. With ignition switch in ON position, check for continuity between ignition switch terminals No. 1 and 7 (terminals No. 3 and 10 on Wrangler). See WIRING DIAGRAMS. If continuity exists, replace ignition switch. If continuity does not exist, go to next step.

2) With ignition switch in START position, check for continuity between ignition switch terminals No. 1 and 7 (terminals No. 3 and 10 on Wrangler). See WIRING DIAGRAMS. If continuity exists, ignition switch is okay. If continuity does not exist, replace ignition switch.

NOTE: For additional information, refer to TEST NS-1A in appropriate SELF-DIAGNOSTICS article in ENGINE PERFORMANCE.

PARK/NEUTRAL POSITION SWITCH

1) Place gear selector lever in Park. Disconnect negative battery cable. Raise and support vehicle. Disconnect Park/Neutral switch connector. Using an ohmmeter, check for continuity between switch center terminal and good ground. If continuity exists, go to next step. If continuity does not exist, replace faulty switch.

2) Place gear selector lever in Reverse. Check for continuity between switch center terminal and good ground. If continuity does not exist, switch is okay. If continuity exists, replace faulty switch.

NOTE: Also refer to TEST NTC-10A in appropriate SELF-DIAGNOSTICS article in ENGINE PERFORMANCE.

CLUTCH PEDAL POSITION SWITCH

WARNING: Deactivate air bag system before performing any service operation involving steering column components. See appropriate AIR BAG RESTRAINT SYSTEMS article in ACCESSORIES & EQUIPMENT.

1) Disconnect negative battery cable. Disconnect clutch pedal position switch connector. Switch is located on clutch pedal push rod. Using an ohmmeter, check for continuity between the two cavities in switch half of connector with clutch pedal released. If continuity does not exist, switch is okay. If continuity exists, replace faulty switch.

2) Depress clutch pedal. Check for continuity between the two cavities in switch half of connector. If continuity does not exist, replace faulty switch. If continuity exists, switch is okay, check ignition switch. See IGNITION SWITCH TEST.

BENCH TESTING

SOLENOID TEST

1) Remove starter. Using an ohmmeter, test for continuity between field terminal (large terminal connected to starter body) and solenoid terminal (small terminal). Continuity should exist.

2) Test for continuity between solenoid terminal and solenoid housing. Continuity should exist. If continuity does not exist in either test, solenoid has open circuit. Replace solenoid.

REMOVAL & INSTALLATION

STARTER

Removal & Installation (2.5L) – Disconnect negative battery cable. Raise and support vehicle. Disconnect battery cable and solenoid feed wire from starter solenoid. Remove starter mounting bolts, starter and starter motor shims (if equipped). To install, reverse removal procedure.

Removal & Installation (4.0L & 4.7L) – Disconnect negative battery cable. Raise and support vehicle. Disconnect starter battery cable and solenoid feed wire. Remove starter from flywheel housing. To install, reverse removal procedure.

OVERHAUL

NOTE: Manufacturer does not recommend disassembling and servicing starters. If starter is found defective, a new unit must be installed.

STARTER SPECIFICATIONS

STARTER SPECIFICATIONS

Application	Specification
Cranking Test	
Test Voltage	12.5 Volts
Minimum Voltage	9.6 Volts
Amperage Draw	
2.5L	130 Amps
4.0L & 4.7L	160 Amps
No-Load Test @ 11.2 Volts	
Maximum Amps	
2.5L, 4.0L & 4.7L	90 Amps
Minimum RPM	
2.5L	2600 RPM
4.0L	2500 RPM
4.7L	2400 RPM

TORQUE SPECIFICATIONS

TORQUE SPECIFICATIONS

Application	Ft. Lbs. (N.m)
Starter-To-Block Bolts	
2.5L	33 (45)
4.0L	
Upper Bolt	40 (54)
Lower Bolt	30 (41)
4.7L	50 (68)

WIRING DIAGRAMS

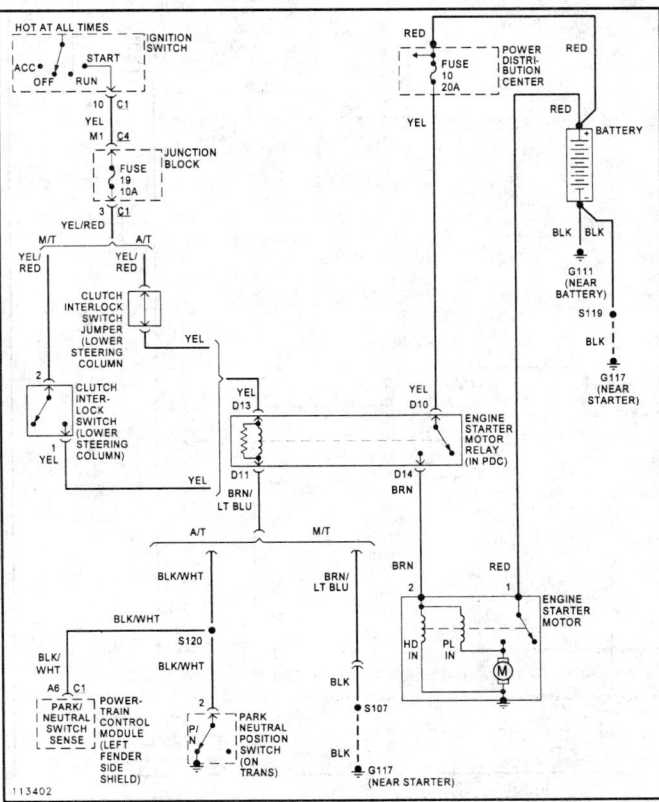

Fig. 3: Starting System Wiring Diagram (Cherokee – 2.5L)

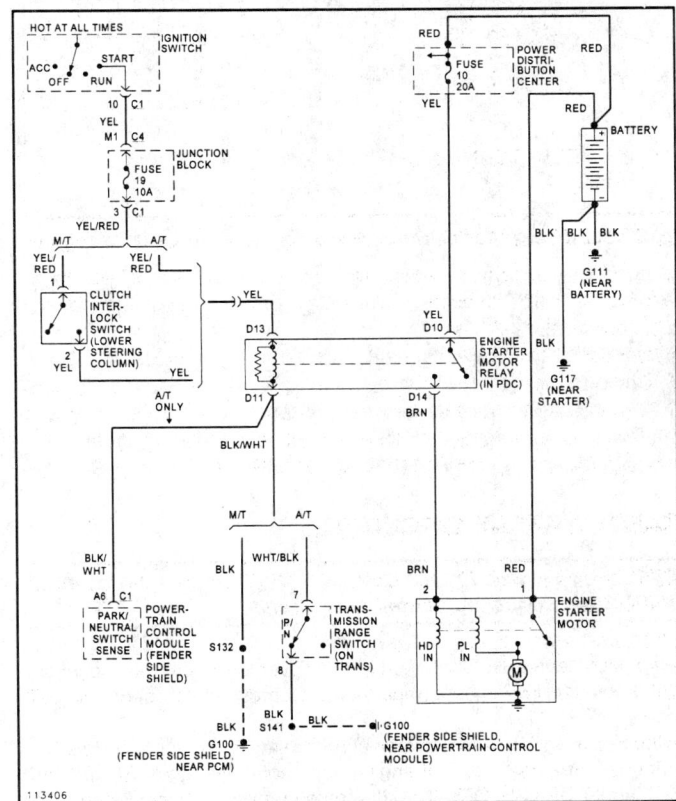

Fig. 4: Starting System Wiring Diagram (Cherokee – 4.0L)

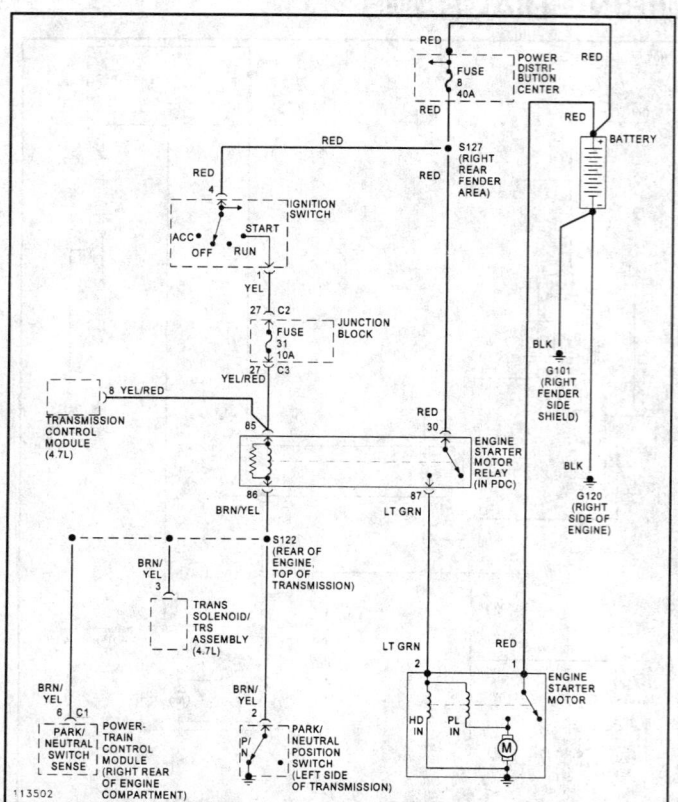

Fig. 5: Starting System Wiring Diagram (Grand Cherokee)

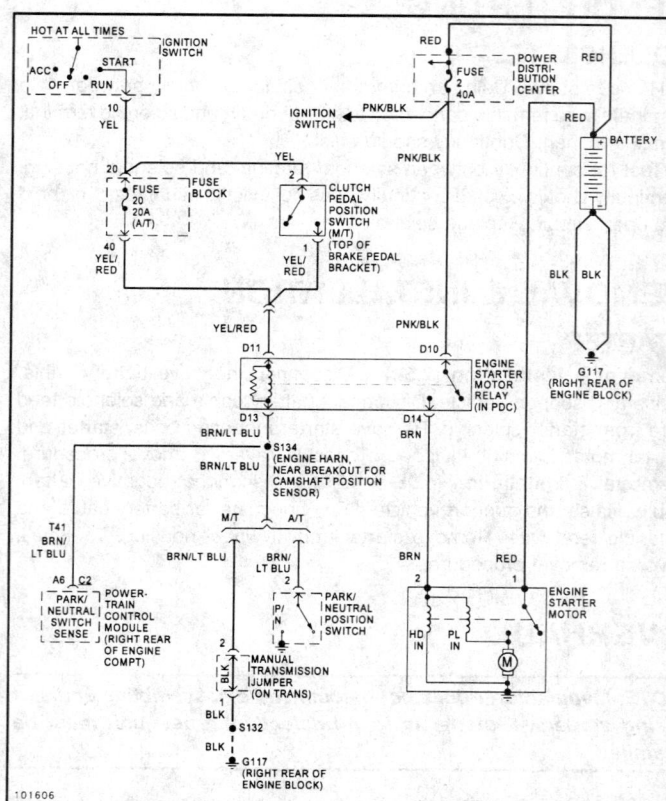

Fig. 6: Starting System Wiring Diagram (Wrangler)

Cherokee, Grand Cherokee, Wrangler

MODEL IDENTIFICATION

Vehicle body codes are used throughout self-diagnostic tests. See BODY CODE DESIGNATION table for model identification.

BODY CODE DESIGNATION

Model Name	Body Type
Cherokee	XJ
Grand Cherokee	WJ
Wrangler	TJ

DESCRIPTION

Charging system consists of a Powertrain Control Module (PCM), generator, Malfunction Indicator Light (MIL) and battery. Generator consists of a rotor, stator, rectifiers, front and rear covers and drive pulley. Generator is serviced as a complete unit only. Voltage regulation is controlled by the Powertrain Control Module (PCM). Electronic Voltage Regulator (EVR) is not a separate component, but a circuit located within the PCM. If EVR circuit is defective, PCM must be replaced.

OPERATION

The amount of amperage produced by the generator is controlled by Electronic Voltage Regulator (EVR) circuitry within the PCM. EVR circuity is connected in series with the generator field driver terminal and ground. A Battery Temperature Sensor (BTS), located in battery tray, is used to sense battery temperature. Sensed battery temperature and data from monitored line voltage is used by PCM to adjust battery charging rate. This is accomplished by cycling the ground path to control the strength of generator rotor magnetic field. PCM then compensates and regulates generator amperage output accordingly.

The PCM monitors critical input to control fuel injection, ignition, emission and other engine management functions. The PCM is also programmed to monitor charging system related circuits:
- Battery feed to PCM.
- Generator field control.
- Battery charging voltage (high and low).

If a problem is sensed in a monitored circuit, a Diagnostic Trouble Code (DTC) will be stored in PCM memory and Malfunction Indicator Light (MIL) will illuminate, provided specific criteria have been met. DTCs can be read using MIL, Chrysler's Diagnostic Readout Box (DRB-III), or a generic scan tool.

NOTE: *DTC is erased from memory if failure does not reoccur after 50 engine starts.*

Certain DTCs cause MIL to illuminate and PCM to enter limp-in mode. In limp-in mode, PCM attempts to compensate for particular component failure by substituting information from other sources. This allows vehicle operation until proper repairs are made.

ADJUSTMENTS

BELT TENSION

BELT ADJUSTMENT

Application	Tension In Lbs. (kg)
Serpentine Belt	
Cherokee & Wrangler	
New Belt [1]	180-200 (81.72-90.80)
Used Belt	140-160 (63.56-72.64)
Grand Cherokee	[2]

[1] – Belt is considered new if used less than 15 minutes.
[2] – Equipped with automatic belt tensioner.

TROUBLE SHOOTING

NOTE: *For additional trouble shooting, see TROUBLE SHOOTING article in GENERAL INFORMATION.*

INITIAL CHECKS

Before proceeding with charging system diagnosis, ensure following conditions are met:
- Battery is fully charged and in good condition.
- Battery cables are in good condition with connections clean and secure.
- Generator belt is in good condition and properly tightened. See BELT ADJUSTMENT.
- Generator and PCM wiring harness connections are clean and tight.
- Engine ground strap is in place.

UNSTEADY OR LOW CHARGING

Check for loose generator belt, charging resistance too high, loose generator ground wire, corroded battery terminals or faulty generator. See BELT ADJUSTMENT.

OVERCHARGING

Check for grounded generator field wiring or faulty generator. See WIRING DIAGRAMS.

NOISY GENERATOR

Check for worn or frayed drive belt, loose generator mounting, or faulty generator. See TORQUE SPECIFICATIONS table for generator mounting bolt tension.

SELF-DIAGNOSTIC SYSTEM

If a problem is sensed in a monitored circuit, a Diagnostic Trouble Code (DTC) will be stored in PCM and MIL will come on, provided specific criteria are met. PCM will then enter limp-in mode, substituting information from other sources to compensate for component failure. Vehicle is operational in limp-in mode, but driveability may not be optimal.

A specific DTC results from a particular system failure. DTC only indicates problem circuit. It does not identify specific component failure in the circuit.

If problem is repaired or ceases to exist, PCM automatically clears DTC after 50 ignition on-off cycles. DTCs can also be cleared using scan tool. See CLEARING DTCS.

PRECAUTIONS

Before proceeding with diagnosis, observe following precautions:
- Ensure battery is fully charged.
- Probe PCM connector from pin side. DO NOT backprobe PCM connector or probe wires through insulation.
- DO NOT cause short circuits when performing electrical tests. This will set additional DTCs, making diagnosis of original problem more difficult.
- DO NOT use a test light in place of a voltmeter.
- Always begin repair with lowest DTC number (MIL) or first DTC displayed (scan tool).
- Always perform appropriate verification (VER) test after repairs are made.
- Always disconnect scan tool after use.
- Always disconnect scan tool before charging battery.

ON-BOARD DIAGNOSTICS

CAUTION: Before entering on-board diagnostics, check charging system for other problems. See INITIAL CHECKS under TROUBLE SHOOTING. DO NOT connect scan tool to vehicle if battery charger is connected, as scan tool damage will result.

NOTE: PCM cannot diagnose every charging system problem. If fault still exists after performing self-diagnostic procedures, proceed to ON-VEHICLE TESTING.

RETRIEVING DTCS

NOTE: Self-diagnostic tests are written specifically for Chrysler's Diagnostic Readout Box (DRB-III) scan tool. A generic scan tool may also be used for system diagnostics, but may have limited diagnostic capability.

Using Scan Tool – 1) Ensure battery is fully charged. Connect scan tool to Data Link Connector (DLC). DLC is located below instrument panel, near steering column.
2) Using scan tool manufacturer's instructions, retrieve and record DTCs displayed on scan tool and proceed to SELF-DIAGNOSTIC TESTS. Once repairs are made, clear DTCs from PCM memory. See CLEARING DTCS.

CLEARING DTCS

PCM automatically clears DTCs from PCM memory after 50 ignition on-off cycles. DTCs can also be cleared using scan tool by following scan tool manufacturer's instructions.

SCAN TOOL PROBLEMS & ERROR MESSAGES

Blank Message Screen – Check for loose cable connections or bad cable. If cable connections and cable are okay, check voltage at DLC terminal No. 16 (Pink/White wire on Wrangler; Pink/Red wire on Grand Cherokee; Tan/Black wire on Cherokee). Voltage should be at least 11 volts. If voltage is not as specified, check wiring circuit and necessary fuses. See WIRING DIAGRAMS.
NO RESPONSE Message – See TEST NS-6A in appropriate SELF-DIAGNOSTICS article in ENGINE PERFORMANCE in appropriate MITCHELL® manual.

NOTE: For more information on scan tool and PCM diagnostics, see appropriate SELF-DIAGNOSTICS article in ENGINE PERFORMANCE in appropriate MITCHELL® manual.

SELF-DIAGNOSTIC TESTS

NOTE: When using diagnostic tests, DO NOT skip any steps in chart, or incorrect diagnosis may result. Ensure battery is fully charged.

DTC TEST: CHECKING SYSTEM FOR DIAGNOSTIC TROUBLE CODES

1) Attempt to start engine. If necessary, crank engine for up to 10 seconds. Read and record DTCs. See RETRIEVING DTCS under SELF-DIAGNOSTIC SYSTEM. If scan tool screen is blank or displays NO RESPONSE, see SCAN TOOL PROBLEMS & ERROR MESSAGES under SELF-DIAGNOSTIC SYSTEM.
2) If DTCs are displayed, see SCAN TOOL DTC MESSAGES table. Only DTCs relating to charging system are listed. For all other DTCs, see appropriate SELF-DIAGNOSTICS article in ENGINE PERFORMANCE in appropriate MITCHELL® manual. If no DTCs are displayed, go to TEST CH-1A: CHARGING SYSTEM NO CODE TEST.

SCAN TOOL DTC MESSAGES

Scan Tool Display	DTC
GENERATOR FIELD NOT SWITCHING PROPERLY	P0622
BATTERY TEMPERATURE SENSOR VOLTAGE TOO HIGH	P1492
BATTERY TEMPERATURE SENSOR VOLTAGE TOO LOW	P1493
CHARGING SYSTEM VOLTAGE TOO HIGH	P1594
CHARGING SYSTEM VOLTAGE TOO LOW	P1682

DTC P0622: GENERATOR FIELD NOT SWITCHING PROPERLY

NOTE: DTC is set when PCM attempts to regulate generator field with no result during monitoring. Possible causes are generator field resistance greater than 5 ohms, open generator field driver circuit, generator field driver circuit shorted to ground, defective generator or PCM.

1) Record all DTC's and clear codes. Check all charging system related connectors for loose, corroded or damaged terminals. Repair as necessary. Using scan tool, actuate generator field driver circuit. Using a voltmeter, backprobe generator field driver circuit on generator field connector. See WIRING DIAGRAMS. If voltage shifts from low to high, go to next step. If voltage does not shift from low to high, go to step 4).

NOTE: To identify field terminals, measure voltage between ground and each field terminal with engine running. Positive field terminal voltage should be 12.5-14.5 volts. Negative field terminal voltage should be 3-8 volts less than battery voltage.

2) Turn ignition on. Using scan tool, actuate generator field driver circuit. Using external voltmeter, measure voltage between ground and generator field source terminal on 2-wire connector on rear of generator. See WIRING DIAGRAMS. If voltage is more than 10 volts, go to next step. If voltage is 10 volts or less, repair open in generator field source circuit between generator and PCM. Perform TEST VER-3A.
3) Wiggle wiring harness from generator to PCM. Using scan tool, read DTCs with actuator test still running. If generator field driver circuit DTC sets, repair wiring harness as necessary where wiggling caused problem to appear. If DTC does not set, fault is currently not present. Test is complete. Perform TEST VER-3A.

NOTE: To identify field terminals, measure voltage between ground and each field terminal with engine running. Positive field terminal voltage should be 12.5-14.5 volts. Negative field terminal voltage should be 3-8 volts less than battery voltage.

4) Turn ignition on. Using scan tool, actuate generator field driver circuit. Using external voltmeter, measure voltage between ground and generator field source terminal (positive terminal) on 2-wire connector on rear of generator. See WIRING DIAGRAMS. If voltage is more than 10 volts, go to next step. If voltage is 10 volts or less, repair open in generator field source circuit between generator and PCM. Perform TEST VER-3A.
5) Turn ignition off. Disconnect PCM harness connector. Disconnect field harness connector on rear of generator. Disconnect battery connections. Using an ohmmeter, measure resistance between generator field terminals on generator. If resistance is 5 ohms or more, repair or replace generator. Perform TEST VER-3A. If resistance is less than 5 ohms, go to next step.
6) Using an ohmmeter, check resistance of generator field driver circuit between generator field harness connector and PCM harness connector. See WIRING DIAGRAMS. If resistance is 5 ohms or more, repair open generator field driver circuit. Perform TEST VER-3A. If resistance is less than 5 ohms, go to next step.
7) With generator field connector disconnected, measure resistance from either generator field terminal (on back of generator) to ground. If resistance is less than 5 ohms, repair or replace shorted generator. If resistance is 5 ohms or more, replace PCM. Perform TEST VER-3A.

DTC P1492: BATTERY TEMP SENSOR VOLTAGE TOO HIGH

1) Ensure ignition is on. Read Battery Temperature Sensor (BTS) voltage using scan tool. If BTS voltage is greater than 4.9 volts, go to next step. If BTS voltage is 4.9 volts or less, go to step 6).

2) Disconnect BTS connector. BTS is located in bottom of battery tray. Connect jumper wire between ground and terminal No. 2 (Pink/Yellow or Violet/Light Green wire) on BTS harness connector. Turn ignition on. Using scan tool, read BTS voltage. If BTS voltage is less than one volt, go to next step. repair open BTS ground circuit. Perform TEST VER-5A. If BTS voltage is one volt or more, go to next step.

3) Turn ignition off. Move jumper wire between BTS harness connector terminals. Turn ignition on. Using scan tool, read BTS voltage. If BTS voltage is less than one volt, replace BTS. Perform TEST VER-5A. If BTS voltage is one volt or more, remove jumper wire and go to next step.

4) Measure voltage between ground and terminal No. 2 (Pink/Yellow wire) on BTS harness connector. If voltage is greater than 6 volts, repaie BTS sensor signal circuit for short to voltage. Perform TEST VER-5A. If voltage is 6 volts or less, go to next step.

5) Turn ignition off. Disconnect Powertrain Control Module (PCM) connector. Using an ohmmeter, check resistance of BTS signal circuit between ground and terminal No. 2 on BTS harness connector. See WIRING DIAGRAMS. If resistance is less than 5 ohms, replace PCM. Perform TEST VER-5A. If resistance is 5 ohms or greater, repair open BTS signal circuit. Perform TEST VER-5A.

6) While observing scan tool BTS voltage, wiggle wiring harness for BTS sensor. If voltage changes, repair wiring harness as necessary where wiggling caused problem to appear. Perform TEST VER-5A. If voltage does not change, inspect all related wiring and connectors and repair as necessary. If no problems were found with wiring and connectors, DTC may have been set by intermittent condition.

DTC P1493: BATTERY TEMP SENSOR VOLTAGE TOO LOW

1) Ensure ignition is on. Using scan tool, read Battery Temperature Sensor (BTS) voltage. If BTS voltage is less than .5 volts, go to next step. If BTS voltage is .5 volts or greater, go to step 5).

2) Turn ignition off. Disconnect BTS connector. BTS is located in bottom of battery tray. Turn ignition on. Read Battery Temperature Sensor (BTS) voltage. If BTS voltage is greater than 4 volts, replace BTS. Perform TEST VER-5A. If BTS voltage is 4 volts or less, go to next step.

3) Ensure ignition is off and BTS is disconnected. Disconnect Powertrain Control Module (PCM) connector. Using an ohmmeter, measure resistance of BTS signal circuit between ground and terminal No. 2 on BTS harness connector. See WIRING DIAGRAMS. If resistance is less than 5 ohms, repair BTS signal circuit for short to ground. Perform TEST VER-5A. If resistance is 5 ohms or greater, go to next step.

4) Measure resistance between BTS harness connector terminals. See WIRING DIAGRAMS. If resistance is less than 5 ohms, repair BTS signal circuit shorted to sensor gound circuit. Perform TEST VER-5A. If resistance is 5 ohms or greater, replace PCM. Perform TEST VER-5A.

5) While observing scan tool BTS voltage, wiggle wiring harness for BTS sensor. If voltage changes, repair wiring harness as necessary where wiggling caused problem to appear. Perform TEST VER-5A. If voltage does not change, inspect all related wiring and connectors and repair as necessary. If no problems were found with wiring and connectors, inspect all related wiring and connectors and repair as necessary. If no problems were found with wiring and connectors, DTC may have been set by intermittent condition.

DTC P1594: CHARGING SYSTEM VOLTAGE TOO HIGH

NOTE: DTC is set when monitored battery voltage is one volt below charging system upper limit threshold for 25 seconds. PCM turns off field driver and monitors battery voltage. If voltage remains high, DTC P1594 is set. Possible causes are generator field driver circuit shorted to ground, shorted generator or Powertrain Control Module (battery temperature and/or charging voltage).

1) Ensure battery is fully charged, and generator belt tension and condition are okay. Using scan tool, actuate generator field driver. Using a voltmeter, backprobe generator field connector. Measure voltage between ground and terminal No. 1 (Dark Green wire) on generator field connector. See WIRING DIAGRAMS . If voltage shifts from low to high, go to next step. If voltage does not shift from low to high, go to step 6).

2) Using scan tool, stop generator field driver actuation. Start engine. Using scan tool, read target charging voltage. If target charging voltage is more than 13 volts, go to step 4). If target charging voltage is 13 volts or less, go to next step.

3) Measure underhood temperature near battery using scan tool temperature probe. Using scan tool, read battery temperature sensor temperature. If scan tool display is within 10 degrees of actual underhood temperature, go to next step. If scan tool display is not within 10 degrees of actual underhood temperature, replace BTS. Perform TEST VER-3A.

4) Start engine. Manually set engine speed to 1600 RPM. Using scan tool, read and compare voltage and target charging voltage. Observe voltage for up to 5 minutes (if necessary) for a one volt difference between voltage and target charging voltage. If difference between voltage and target charging voltage is one volt or less, go toTEST CH-1A . If difference between voltage and target charging voltage is more than one volt, replace Powertrain Control Module (PCM). Perform TEST VER-3A.

5) Turn ignition off. Disconnect PCM harness connector. Disconnect field harness connector on rear of generator. Using an ohmmeter, measure resistance of generator field driver circuit between PCM connector and ground. If resistance is 5 ohms or more, go to next step. If resistance is less than 5 ohms, repair short to ground on generator field driver circuit. Perform TEST VER-3A.

6) With generator field connector disconnected, measure resistance from either generator field terminal (on back of generator) to ground. If resistance is less than 5 ohms, repair or replace shorted generator. If resistance is 5 ohms or more, replace PCM. Perform TEST VER-3A.

DTC P1682: CHARGING SYSTEM VOLTAGE TOO LOW

NOTE: DTC is set when monitored battery voltage is one volt below charging system lower limit threshold for 25 seconds. PCM turns off field driver and monitors battery voltage. If voltage remains low, DTC P1682 is set. Possible causes are open high resistance in battery supply circuit between generator and battery, open field driver circuit, high resistance in ground circuit, defective generator or defective battery temperature sensor.

1) Ensure battery is fully charged. Start engine. Using scan tool, read voltage goal. If voltage goal is more than 15.1 volts, go to next step. If voltage goal is 15.1 volts or less, go to step 4).

2) Ensure engine is at normal operating temperature. Using scan tool, read Battery Temperature Sensor (BTS) temperature. Measure underhood temperature. If BTS temperature is within 10 degrees of actual underhood temperature, go to step 4). If BTS temperature is not within 10 degrees of actual underhood temperature, go to next step.

3) Turn ignition off. Disconnect BTS harness connector. BTS is mounted in bottom of battery tray. Connect jumper wire across BTS harness connector terminals. Turn ignition on. Using scan tool, read BTS voltage. If voltage is zero, replace BTS. Perform TEST VER-3A. If voltage is present, replace PCM. Perform TEST VER-3A.

4) Start engine and manually set engine speed to 1600 RPM. Using scan tool, read and compare target voltage and charging voltage. If difference between target voltage and charging voltage is more than one volt, go to next step. If difference between target voltage and charging voltage is one volt or less, go to step 12).

NOTE: Before starting engine, ensure all test equipment wires are clear of moving engine parts.

5) Connect an external voltmeter between generator B+ terminal and battery positive terminal. Start engine. If voltage is .4 volt or less, go to next step. If voltage is more than .4 volt, repair B+ circuit for high resistance between generator and battery. Perform TEST VER-3A.

6) Turn ignition off. Connect an external voltmeter between generator case and battery negative terminal. Start engine. If voltage is .1 volt or less, go to next step. If voltage is more than .1 volt, repair generator ground for high resistance between generator case and battery negative terminal. Perform TEST VER-3A.

7) With ignition on and engine not running, acutate generator field. Using voltmeter, measure voltage between ground and each generator field terminal. If voltage on both terminals is less than 3 volts, go to next step. If voltage for either terminal is 3 volts or greater, charging system is currently functioning correctly. Perform TEST VER-3A.

8) Turn ignition off. Disconnect Powertrain Control Module (PCM) harness connector. Using ohmmeter, measure resistance between ground and generator field driver terminal on PCM harness connector. See WIRING DIAGRAMS. If resistance is less than 5 ohms, repair field driver circuit for short to ground. Perform TEST VER-3A. If resistance is 5 ohms or greater, go to next step.

9) Disconnect generator field connector. Measure resistance of generator field driver circuit between PCM and generator field harness connector. See WIRING DIAGRAMS. If resistance is less than 5 ohms, go to next step. If resistance is 5 ohms or greater, repair open field driver circuit. Perform TEST VER-3A.

10) Using ohmmeter, measure resistance between ground and generator field source terminal on PCM harness connector. See WIRING DIAGRAMS. If resistance is less than 5 ohms, repair field source circuit for short to ground. Perform TEST VER-3A. If resistance is 5 ohms or greater, go to next step.

11) Disconnect generator field connector. Measure resistance of generator field source circuit between PCM and generator field harness connector. See WIRING DIAGRAMS. If resistance is less than 5 ohms, replace PCM. Perform TEST VER-3A. If resistance is 5 ohms or greater, repair open field source circuit.

NOTE: Before starting engine, ensure all test equipment wires are clear of moving engine parts.

12) Connect an external voltmeter between generator B+ terminal and battery positive terminal. Start engine. If voltage is .4 volt or less, go to next step. If voltage is more than .4 volt, repair B+ circuit for high resistance between generator and battery. Perform TEST VER-3A.

13) Turn ignition off. Connect an external voltmeter between generator case and battery negative terminal. Start engine. If voltage is .1 volt or less, test is complete. If voltage is more than .1 volt, repair generator ground for high resistance between generator case and battery negative terminal. Perform TEST VER-3A.

TEST CH-1A: CHARGING SYSTEM NO CODE TEST

1) Verify battery condition. Charge or replace battery as necessary. Inspect generator belt tension and condition. Replace generator belt as necessary. Start engine. Turn on all accessories. Set engine speed to 2000 RPM for 30 seconds, then return to idle. Read Diagnostic Trouble Codes (DTCs). See SCAN TOOL DTC MESSAGES table. If any charging system DTCs are set, perform appropriate test. If no charging system DTCs are set, go to next step.

2) With ignition on and engine off, read and record battery voltage using scan tool. Using voltmeter, measure and record voltage between battery posts. If voltage difference is less than one volt, test is complete. If voltage difference is one volt or greater, go to next step.

3) Turn ignition on with engine off. Using scan tool, actuate generator field. Using voltmeter, backprobe generator field terminals on back of generator. Measure voltage between ground and each field terminal. *See Fig. 1.* Voltage should cycle from zero volts to battery voltage every 1.4 seconds at both terminals. While observing scan tool, wiggle field terminal wiring harness back to Powertrain Control Module (PCM). If any interruption of voltage cycling occurred, repair wiring harness where wiggling caused failure. Perform TEST VER-3A. If wiggling did not interrupt voltage cycling, go to next step.

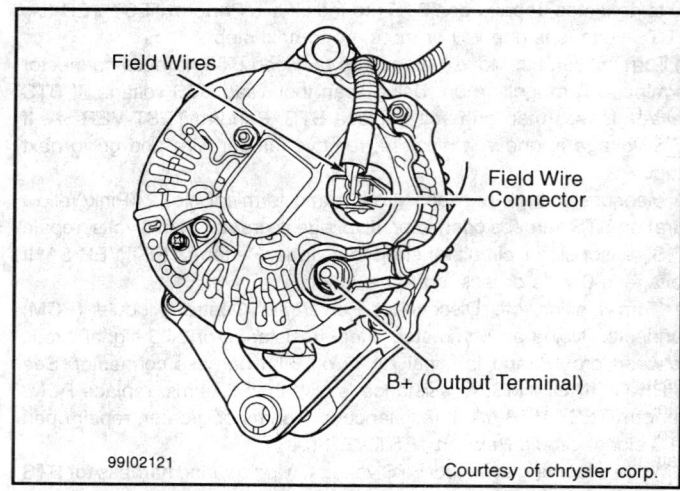

Fig. 1: Identifying Generator Terminals (Denso Generator)

4) Using an external voltmeter, check voltage between generator B+ terminal located on rear of generator and battery positive terminal. *See Fig. 1.* Ensure voltmeter wires are clear of moving engine parts. Start engine and observe voltmeter. If voltage is .4 volt or less, go to next step. If voltage is more than .4 volt, repair high resistance between generator B+ terminal and battery positive terminal. Perform TEST VER-3A.

5) Using scan tool, read DTCs. If any charging system DTCs are set, see SCAN TOOL DTC MESSAGES table and perform appropriate test. If no charging system trouble codes are set, go to next step.

6) Turn ignition off. Using an external voltmeter, check voltage between generator case and battery negative terminal. Start engine. If voltage is greater than .1 volt, repair high resistance between generator battery negative terminal and battery negative terminal. Perform TEST VER-3A. If voltage is .1 volt or less, go to next step.

7) With ignition on and engine off, read and record battery voltage using scan tool. Turn ignition off. Disconnect PCM connector. Turn ignition on. Using voltmeter, measure voltage between ground and terminal No. 22 on PCM connector C1. If voltage is within one volt of scan tool voltage, repair high resistance between PCM connector terminal No. 22 and battery positive terminal. Perform TEST VER-3A. If voltage is not within one volt of scan tool voltage, replace PCM. Perform TEST VER-3A.

TEST VER-2A: ROAD TEST VERIFICATION

CAUTION: If PCM is changed, correct VIN and mileage have to be programmed or ABS and SRS DTCs will be set.

1) If PCM has been replaced, go to next step. If ECM has been replaced or battery has been disconnected on diesel powered vehicles, go to step **3)**. If neither module has been replaced, go to step **4)**.

2) Connect scan tool to Data Link Connector (DLC). DLC is located below driver's side of instrument panel. Using scan tool, enter correct VIN and mileage into PCM. Using scan tool manufacturer's instructions, clear DTCs from ABS and SRS modules.

3) Programming of Accelerator Pedal Position Sensor (APPS) is necessary if ECM has been replaced or battery has been disconnected on diesel powered vehicles. Ensure all components are connected. Turn ignition on. Slowly depress accelerator pedal to floor, then slowly release. APPS is now programmed. Go to next step.

4) Inspect vehicle to ensure all engine components are connected. Reassemble and reconnect components as necessary.

5) Check if initial symptom still exists. If initial or another symptom exists, repair is not complete. Check for Technical Service Bulletins (TSBs) that apply to symptom.

6) If any DTCs have not been diagnosed, go to appropriate test and finish diagnosing remaining DTCs as necessary. If all DTCs have been diagnosed, go to next step.

7) Using scan tool, erase DTCs from PCM. Using scan tool, reset all values in adaptive memory. Disconnect scan tool. If no other DTCs remain, repair is now complete.

TEST VER-3A: CHARGING VERIFICATION

CAUTION: If PCM is changed, correct VIN and mileage have to be programmed or ABS and SRS DTCs will be set.

1) If PCM has been replaced, go to next step. If ECM has been replaced or battery has been disconnected on diesel powered vehicles, go to step 3). If neither module has been replaced, go to step 4).

2) Connect scan tool to Data Link Connector (DLC). DLC is located below driver's side of instrument panel. Using scan tool, enter correct VIN and mileage into PCM. Using scan tool manufacturer's instructions, clear DTCs from ABS and SRS modules.

3) Programming of Accelerator Pedal Position Sensor (APPS) is necessary if ECM has been replaced or battery has been disconnected on diesel powered vehicles. Ensure all components are connected. Turn ignition on. Slowly depress accelerator pedal to floor, then slowly release. APPS is now programmed. Go to next step.

4) Inspect vehicle to ensure all engine components are connected. Reassemble and reconnect components as necessary.

5) To ensure no charging system problem exists, start engine. Perform OUTPUT VOLTAGE TEST under ON-VEHICLE TESTING. Increase engine speed to 2000 RPM for at least 30 seconds. Allow engine to idle. Turn engine off.

6) Using scan tool, check for stored DTCs. If repaired DTC has reset, repair is not complete. Check for related Technical Service Bulletins (TSBs) and return to DTC TEST, if necessary. If another DTC exists, go to appropriate DTC test and follow specified procedure. If no other DTCs exist, repair is now complete.

TEST VER-5A: ROAD TEST VERIFICATION

CAUTION: If PCM is changed, correct VIN and mileage have to be programmed or ABS and SRS DTCs will be set.

1) If PCM has been replaced, go to next step. If ECM has been replaced or battery has been disconnected on diesel powered vehicles, go to step 3). If neither module has been replaced, go to step 4).

2) Connect scan tool to Data Link Connector (DLC). DLC is located below driver's side of instrument panel. Using scan tool, enter correct VIN and mileage into PCM. Using scan tool manufacturer's instructions, clear DTCs from ABS and SRS modules.

3) Programming of Accelerator Pedal Position Sensor (APPS) is necessary if ECM has been replaced or battery has been disconnected on diesel powered vehicles. Ensure all components are connected. Turn ignition on. Slowly depress accelerator pedal to floor, then slowly release. APPS is now programmed. Go to next step.

4) Connect scan tool to Data Link Connector (DLC). DLC is located below driver's side of instrument panel. Using scan tool, enter correct VIN and mileage into PCM. Using scan tool manufacturer's instructions, clear DTCs from ABS and SRS modules.

5) Inspect vehicle to ensure all engine components are connected. Reassemble and reconnect components as necessary.

6) If any DTCs have not been diagnosed, go to appropriate test and finish diagnosing remaining DTCs as necessary. If all DTCs have been diagnosed, go to next step.

7) Connect scan tool to DLC connector. Ensure fuel tank is at least 25 percent full. Turn off all accessories.

8) Using scan tool OBDII monitor, verify DTC repair. See scan tool instructions. Allow PCM to run appropriate monitor(s) and increment a global good trip (drive cycle). Enabling conditions must be met before PCM will run OBDII monitor. Scan tool monitor pretest screen will display enabling conditions.

9) If repaired DTC has reset or was seen in OBDII monitor while on road test, repair is not complete. Check for any TSBs and return to appropriate test. Repair as needed.

10) If any other DTCs are set, repair as needed. If OBDII monitor is run and good trip counter is incremented and no new DTCs are set, repair is successful and complete. Erase DTCs. See CLEARING CODES.

ON-VEHICLE TESTING

CAUTION: When battery is disconnected, vehicle computer and memory systems may lose memory data. Driveability problems may exist until computer systems have completed a relearn cycle. See COMPUTER RELEARN PROCEDURES article in GENERAL INFORMATION before disconnecting battery.

VOLTAGE DROP TEST

NOTE: VOLTAGE DROP TEST determines amount of resistance in circuits between generator and battery.

1) Ensure battery is in condition and is fully charged. Clean battery terminals (if necessary). Using external voltmeter, connect positive lead to generator B+ terminal stud (not the nut). Connect voltmeter negative lead to positive battery post. Connect tachometer to engine. Fully engage parking brake, and place gear selector in Neutral position. Start engine and run for 2 minutes to allow for warm-up.

2) Turn A/C system on, A/C-heater blower motor to high speed and headlights on high beam. Increase engine speed to 2400 RPM. Voltmeter reading should not be more than 0.6 volts.

3) If voltage drop is more than 0.6 volts, inspect, clean and tighten all connections between generator B+ terminal and positive battery post. Voltage drop test may be performed at each connection to locate connection with excessive resistance. If resistance tests are satisfactory, reduce engine speed, turn off all electrical loads and ignition switch.

4) Using external voltmeter, connect positive lead to generator ground terminal stud (not the nut). Connect voltmeter negative lead to negative battery post. Connect tachometer to engine. Fully engage parking brake, and place gear selector in Neutral position. Start engine and run for 2 minutes to allow for warm-up.

5) Turn A/C system on, A/C-heater blower motor to high speed and headlights on high beam. Increase engine speed to 2400 RPM. Voltmeter reading should not be more than 0.3 volts.

6) If voltage drop is more than 0.3 volt, inspect, clean and tighten all connections between generator ground terminal and negative battery post. Voltage drop test may be performed at each connection to locate connection with excessive resistance. If resistance tests are satisfactory, reduce engine speed and turn off all electrical loads and ignition switch.

1999 STARTING & CHARGING SYSTEMS
Generators & Regulators (Cont.)

CURRENT OUTPUT TEST

CAUTION: Generator has 2 field terminals: generator field driver (Dark Green wire) and generator field source (other than Dark Green wire). DO NOT connect generator field source terminal to ground.

NOTE: Perform VOLTAGE DROP TEST before continuing with this test. Perform test soon after starting engine, as charging amperage will drop quickly. A volt/amp tester equipped with both a battery load control (carbon pile rheostat) and an inductive type pick-up clamp is required to perform the following test.

1) Ensure battery is in good condition and is fully charged. Clean battery terminals (if necessary). Connect volt/amp tester leads to battery. Ensure carbon pile is in OFF position before connecting leads. Connect inductive pick-up clamp.

NOTE: Depending on volt/amp tester manufacturer, load may be applied automatically. Refer to volt/amp tester manufacturer's instructions.

2) Connect tachometer to engine. Start engine and raise engine speed to 2500 RPM. Slowly adjust rheostat control (load) on volt/amp tester until highest amperage reading is obtained. DO NOT allow voltage to drop less than 12 volts.
3) Note reading on ammeter. Generator amperage reading should be more than the minimum amperage rating specification. See GENERATOR SPECIFICATIONS table. If amperage reading is less than minimum specification, go to step 5). If amperage reading is more than minimum specification, go to next step.
4) Rotate load control knob to OFF position. Continue to hold engine speed at 2500 RPM. Output amperage should change to less than 20-amps, indicating EVR circuity is okay and charging system is functioning properly. It may take several minutes for amperage to change. If output amperage does not change to less than 20-amps, perform SELF-DIAGNOSTIC SYSTEM.
5) Connect a jumper wire between ground and generator field driver terminal (Dark Green wire) on back of generator. Start engine, and immediately reduce engine speed to idle. Adjust carbon pile and engine speed in increments until engine speed is 1250 RPM and voltmeter reads 15 volts. DO NOT allow voltage to exceed 16 volts.
6) Note reading on volt/amp tester. Generator amperage reading should be more than the minimum amperage rating specification. See GENERATOR SPECIFICATIONS. If amperage reading is less than minimum specification, replace generator. If amperage reading is more than minimum specification, a fault exists in EVR circuitry. Perform SELF-DIAGNOSTIC SYSTEM.

GENERATOR APPLICATION

Application	Case Number [1]	Minimum Output (Amps)
Cherokee		
2.5L		
81-Amp	56005684AB	57
4.0L		
117-Amp	56005684AB	88
Grand Cherokee		
4.0L		
136-Amp	56041322	100
4.7L		
136-Amp	56041324	100
Wrangler		
2.5L & 4.0L		
124-Amp	56041822AA	90

[1] – Part number is located on back of generator.

OUTPUT VOLTAGE TEST

1) Before performing this test, ensure battery is fully charged. Connect voltmeter leads across battery terminals. Record voltage with ignition switch and all electrical loads off. Fully engage parking brake, and place gear selector in Park position.
2) Start engine and operate at normal operating temperature. Record voltage with engine speed at 1500 RPM and no electrical loads. Voltage should not be greater than voltage recorded in step 1) by more than 2.5 volts. If voltage is not as specified, go to SELF-DIAGNOSTIC SYSTEM.
3) Record voltage with engine speed at 2000 RPM, blower motor on high and headlights on high beam. Voltage should be more than 0.5 volt above battery voltage previously recorded in step 1). If voltage is less than 0.5 volt above previously recorded battery voltage, go to SELF-DIAGNOSTIC SYSTEM. If voltage tests are satisfactory, reduce engine speed, and turn off blower motor, headlights and ignition switch.

BATTERY TEMPERATURE SENSOR

Disconnect sensor wiring connector. Sensor is located under the battery. Using an ohmmeter, connect leads to sensor terminals. With ambient temperature of 75-80°F (25°C), reading should be 9000-11,000 ohms. If reading is above or below specification, replace sensor.

BENCH TESTING

NOTE: Generator is not serviceable. Replace generator if defective.

TORQUE SPECIFICATIONS

TORQUE SPECIFICATIONS

Application	Ft. Lbs. (N.m)
Generator Mounting Bolts	41 (56)

WIRING DIAGRAMS

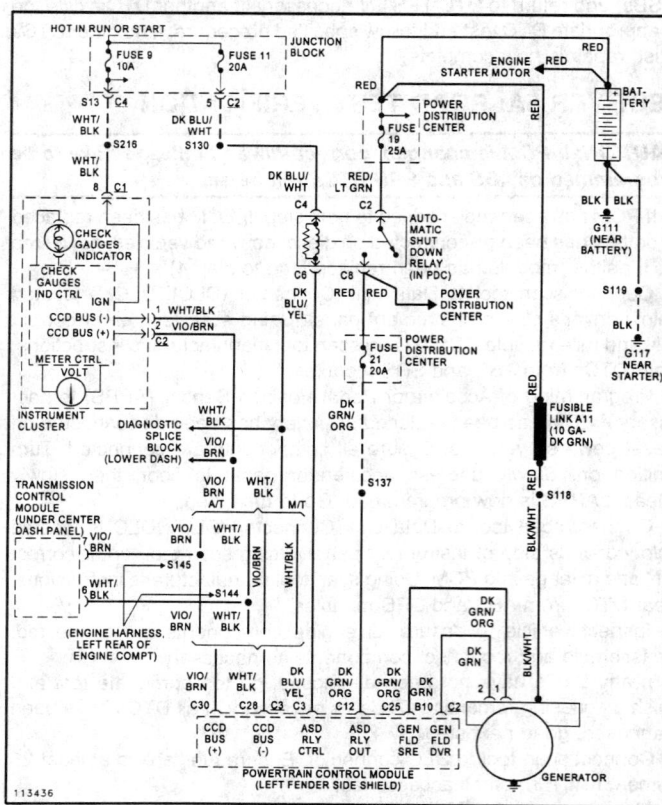

Fig. 2: Charging System Wiring Diagram (Cherokee)

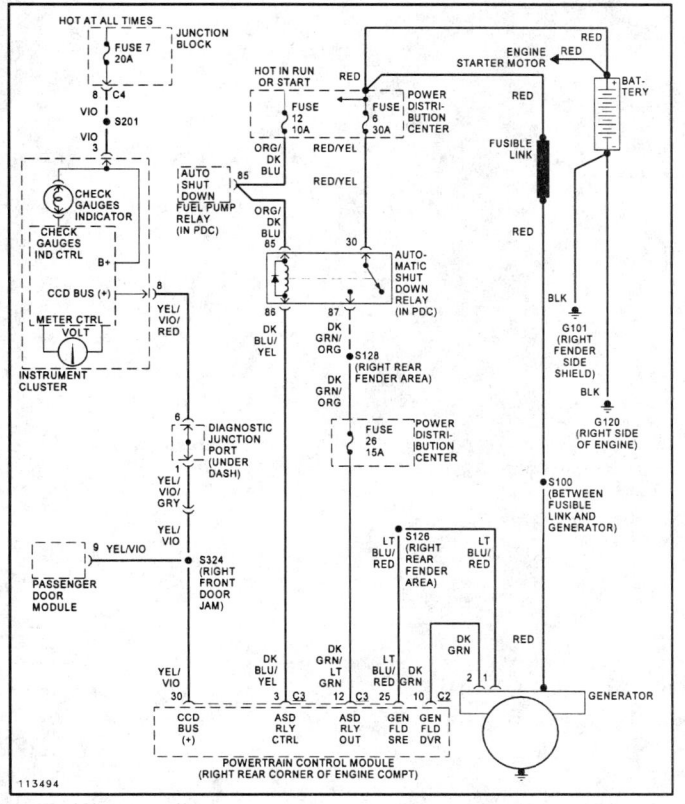

Fig. 3: Charging System Wiring Diagram (Grand Cherokee)

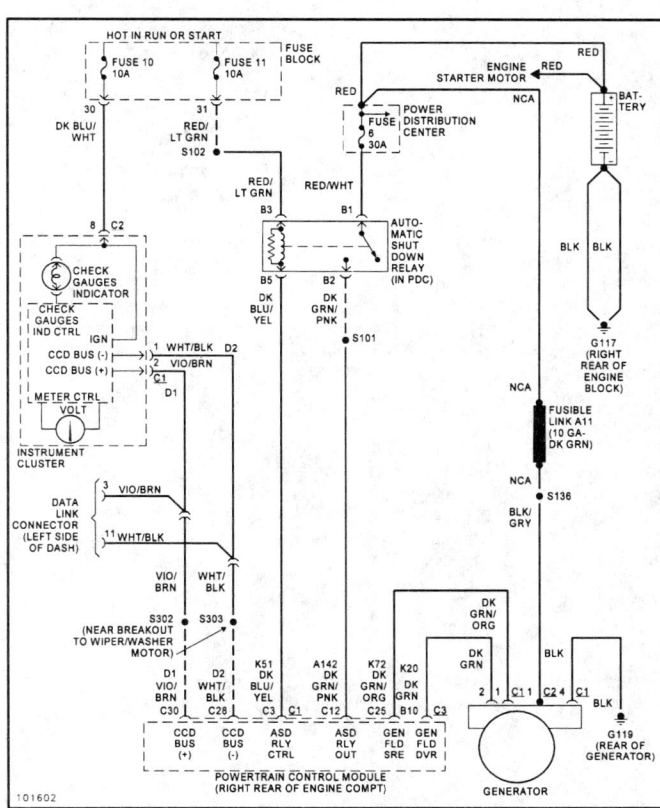

Fig. 4: Charging System Wiring Diagram (Wrangler)

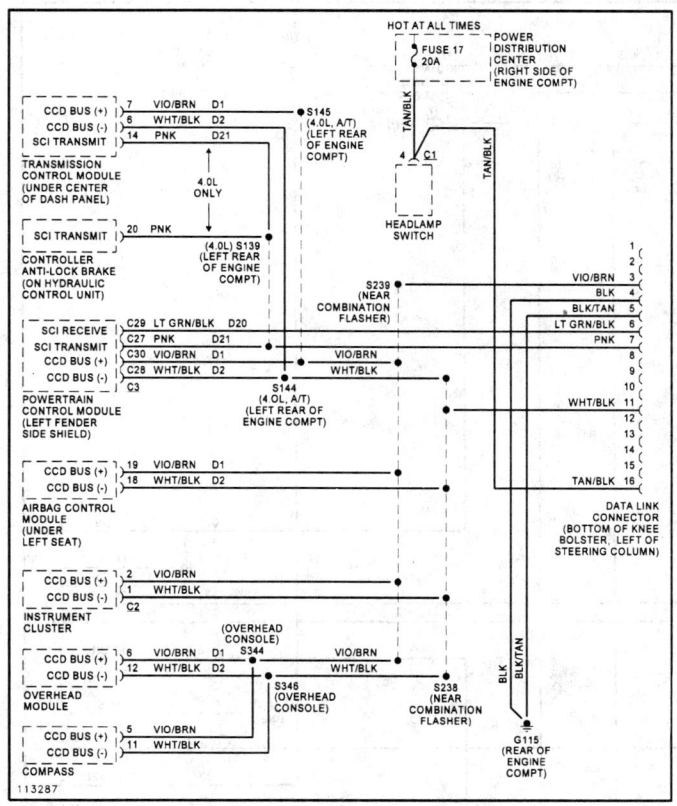

Fig. 1: Data Link Connectors Wiring Diagram (Cherokee)

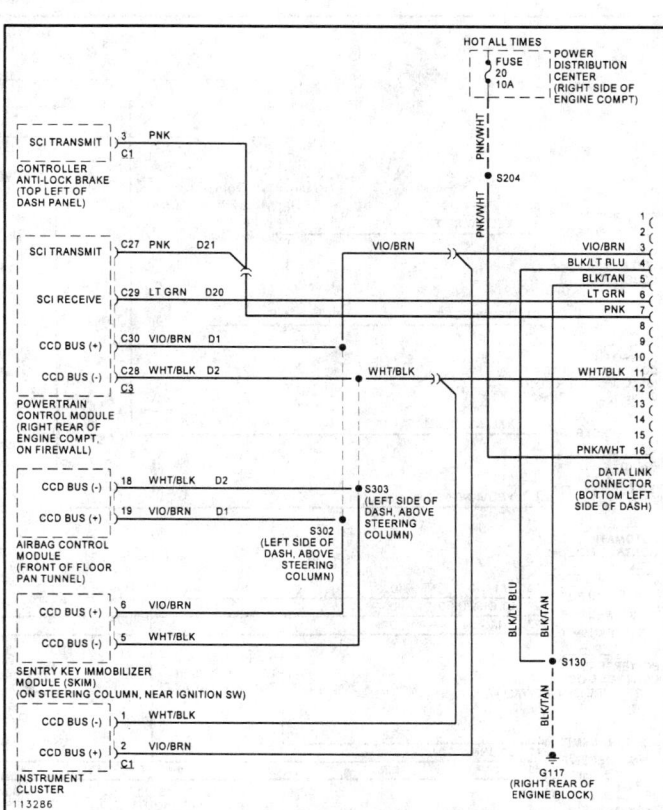

Fig. 2: Data Link Connectors Wiring Diagram (Wrangler)

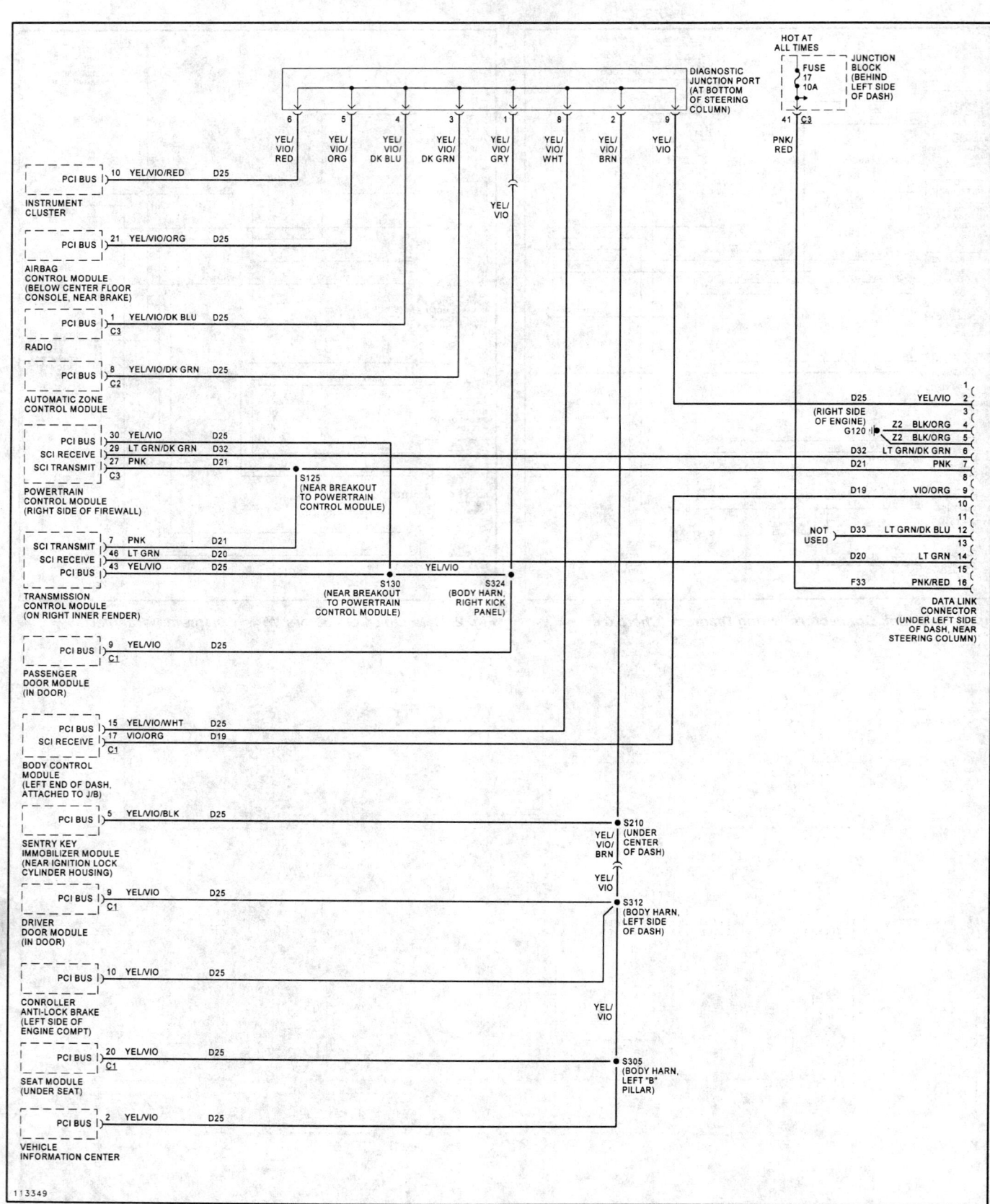

Fig. 3: Data Link Connectors Wiring Diagram (Grand Cherokee)

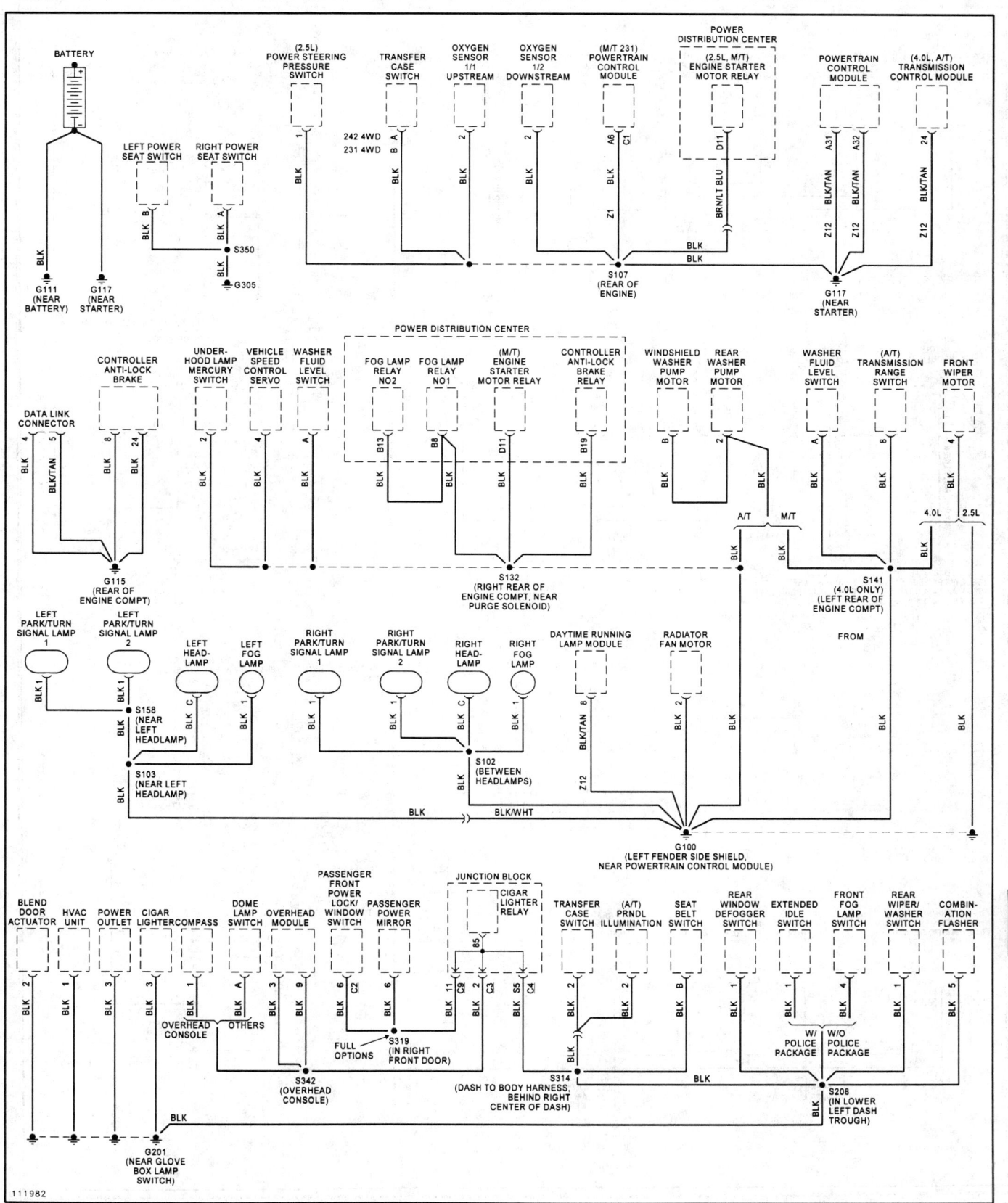

Fig. 1: Ground Distribution Wiring Diagram (Cherokee – 1 Of 2)

111982

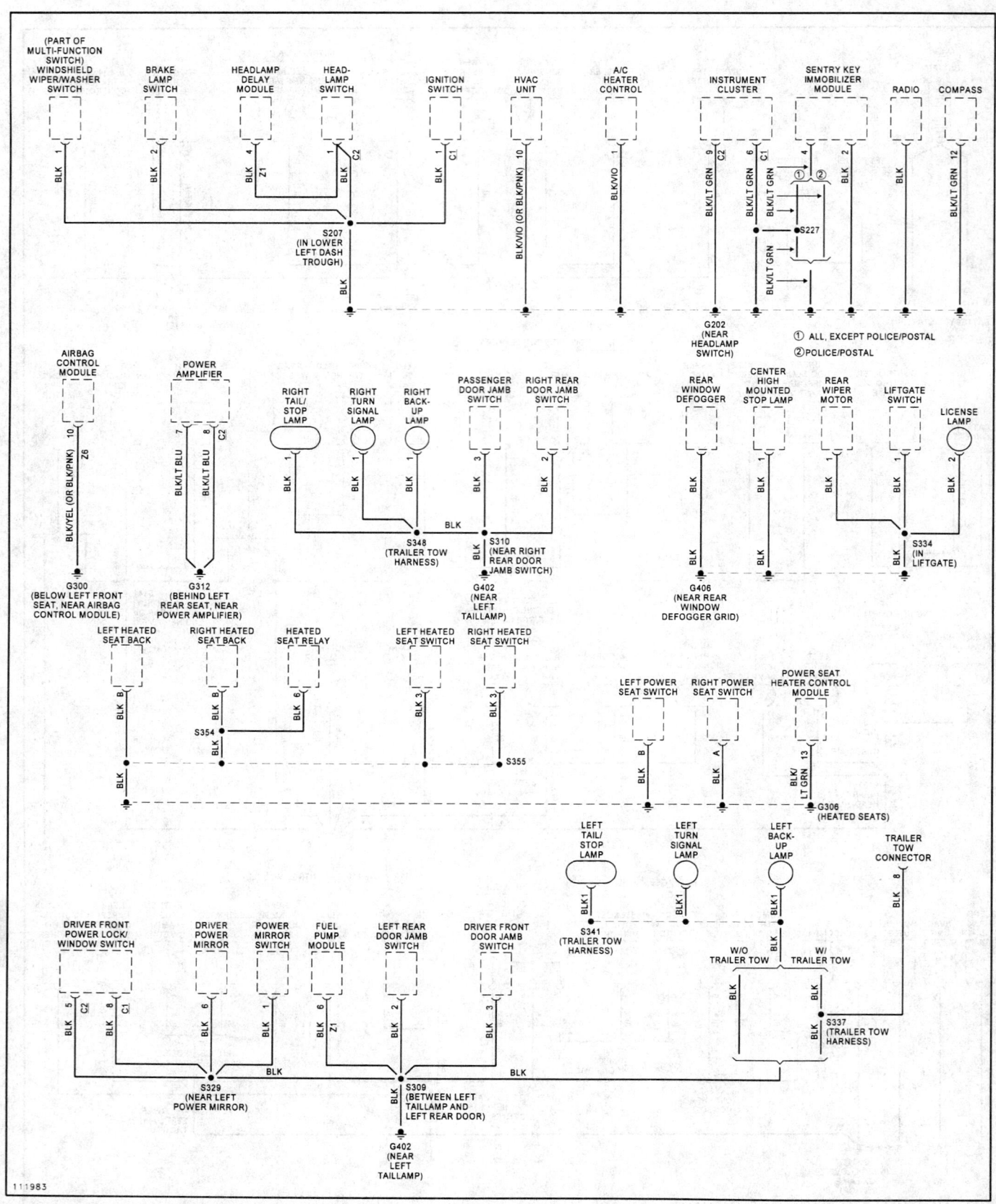

Fig. 2: Ground Distribution Wiring Diagram (Cherokee – 2 Of 2)

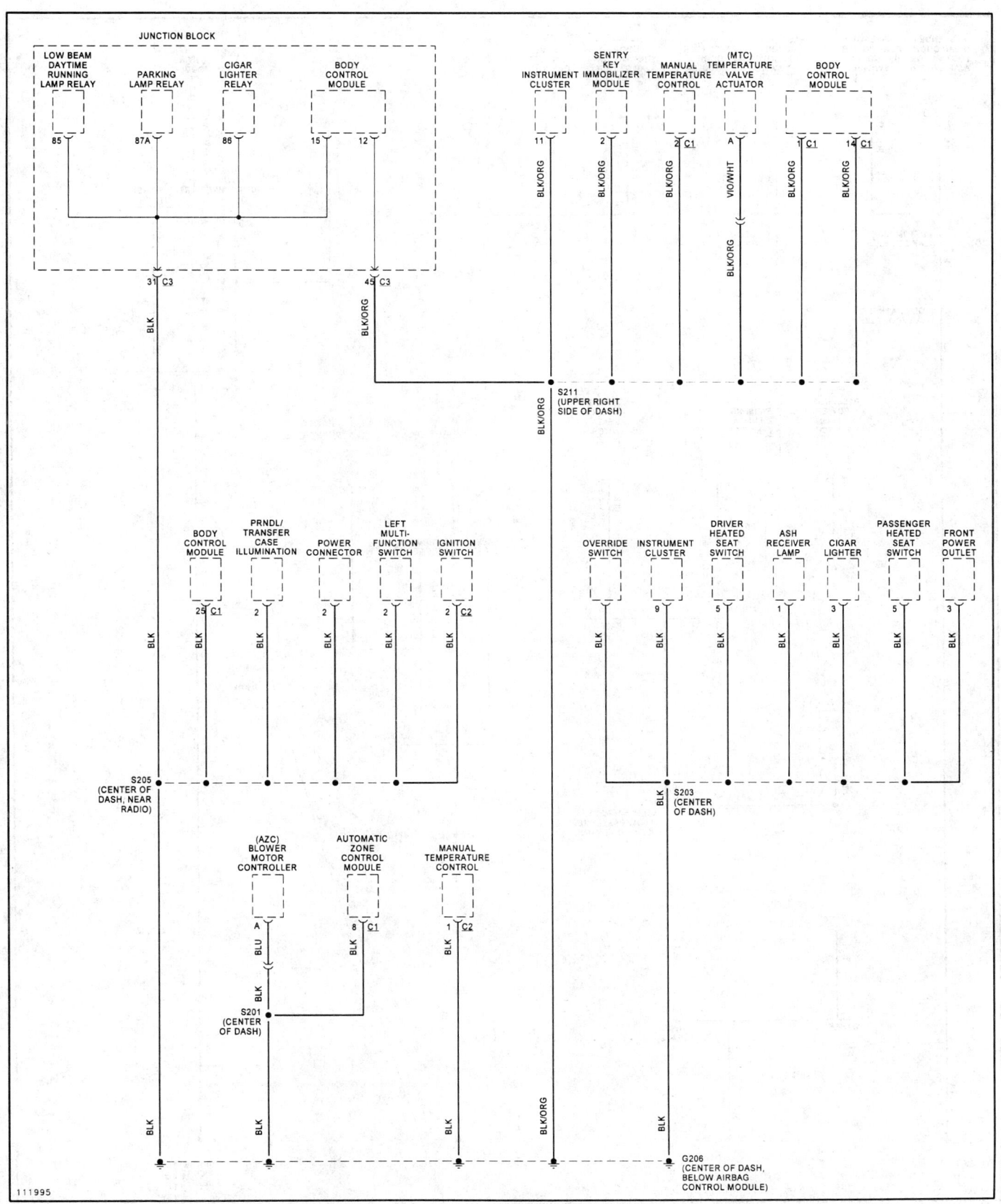

Fig. 3: Ground Distribution Wiring Diagram (Grand Cherokee – 1 Of 4)

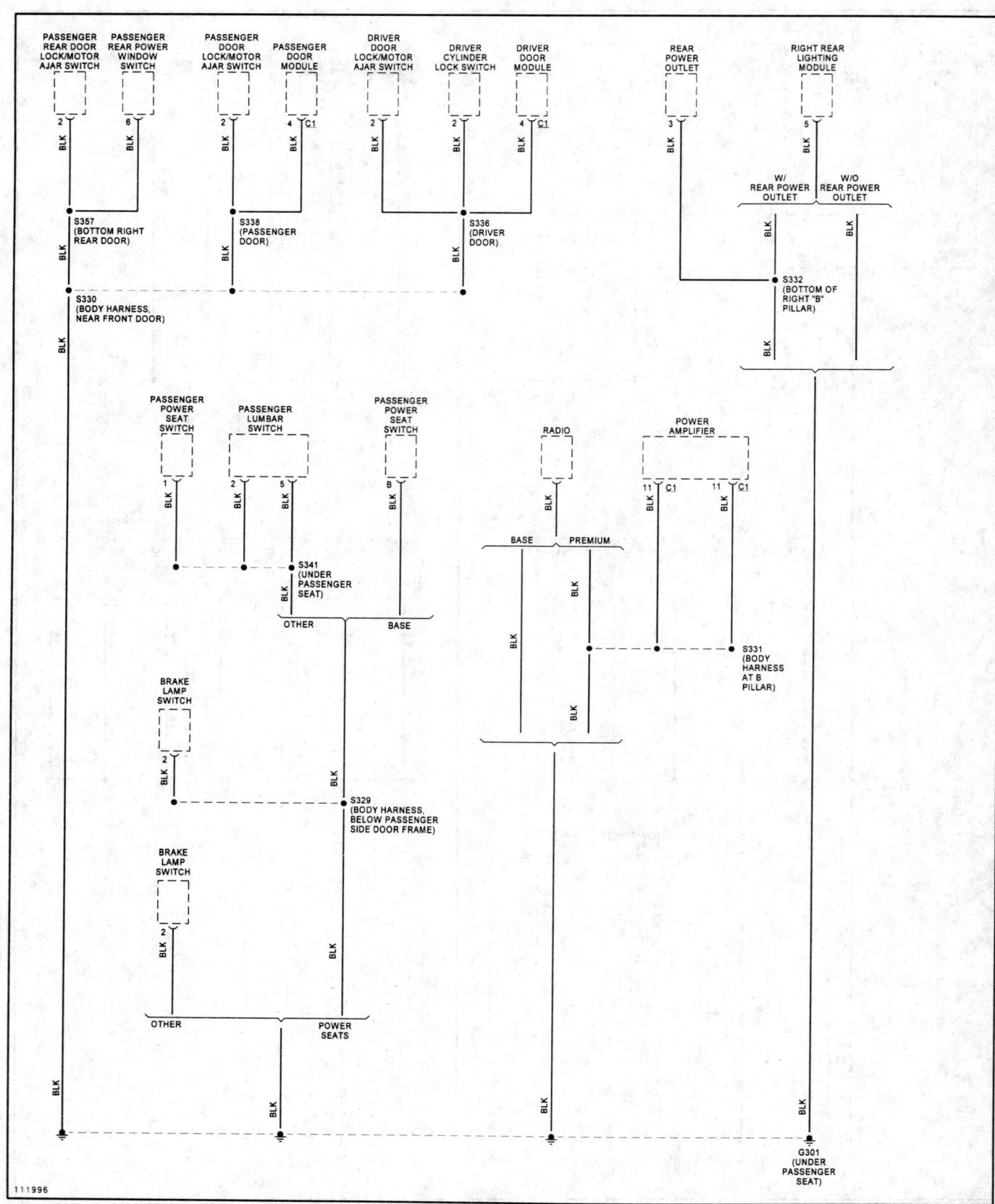

Fig. 4: Ground Distribution Wiring Diagram (Grand Cherokee – 2 Of 4)

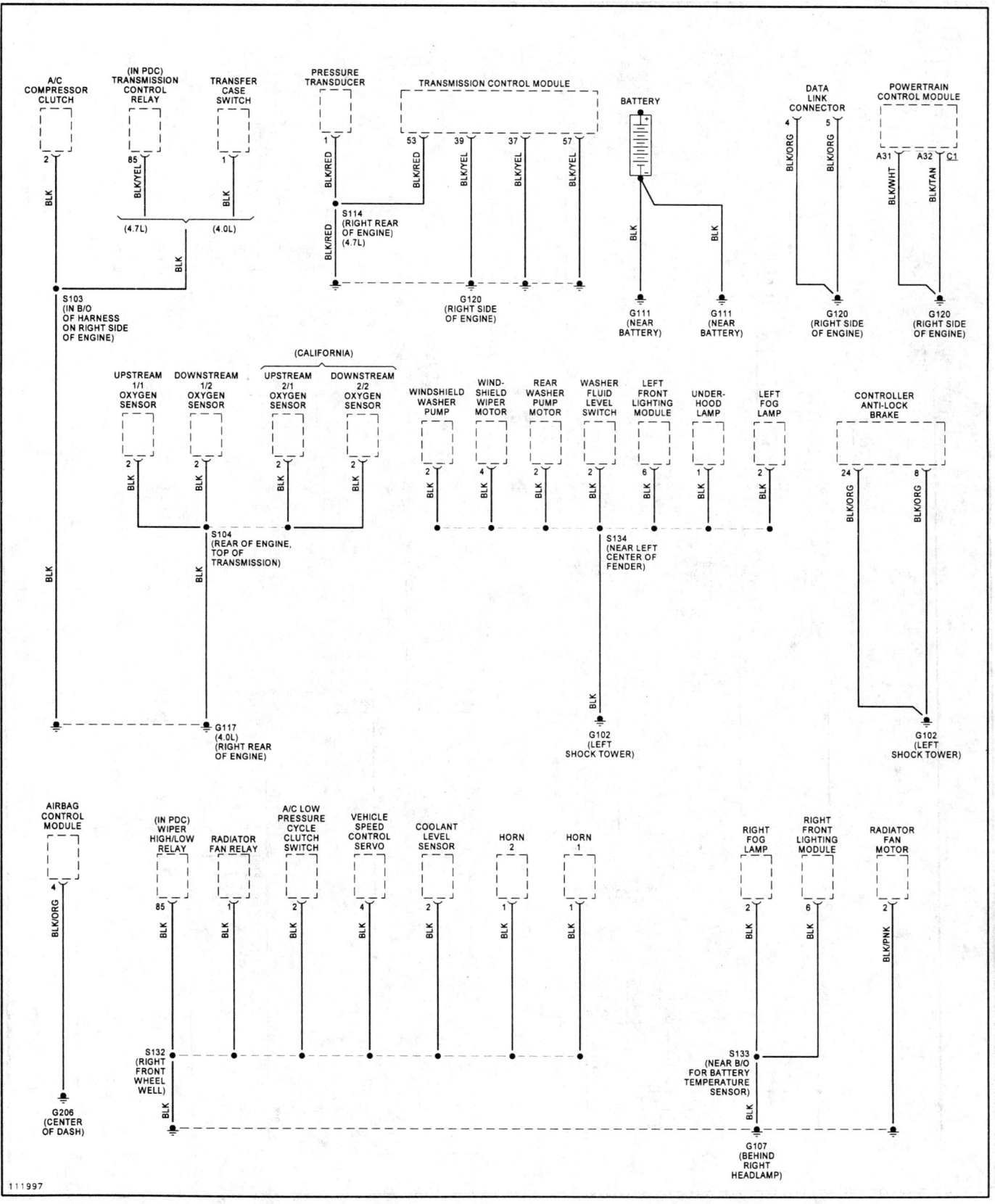

Fig. 5: Ground Distribution Wiring Diagram (Grand Cherokee – 3 Of 4)

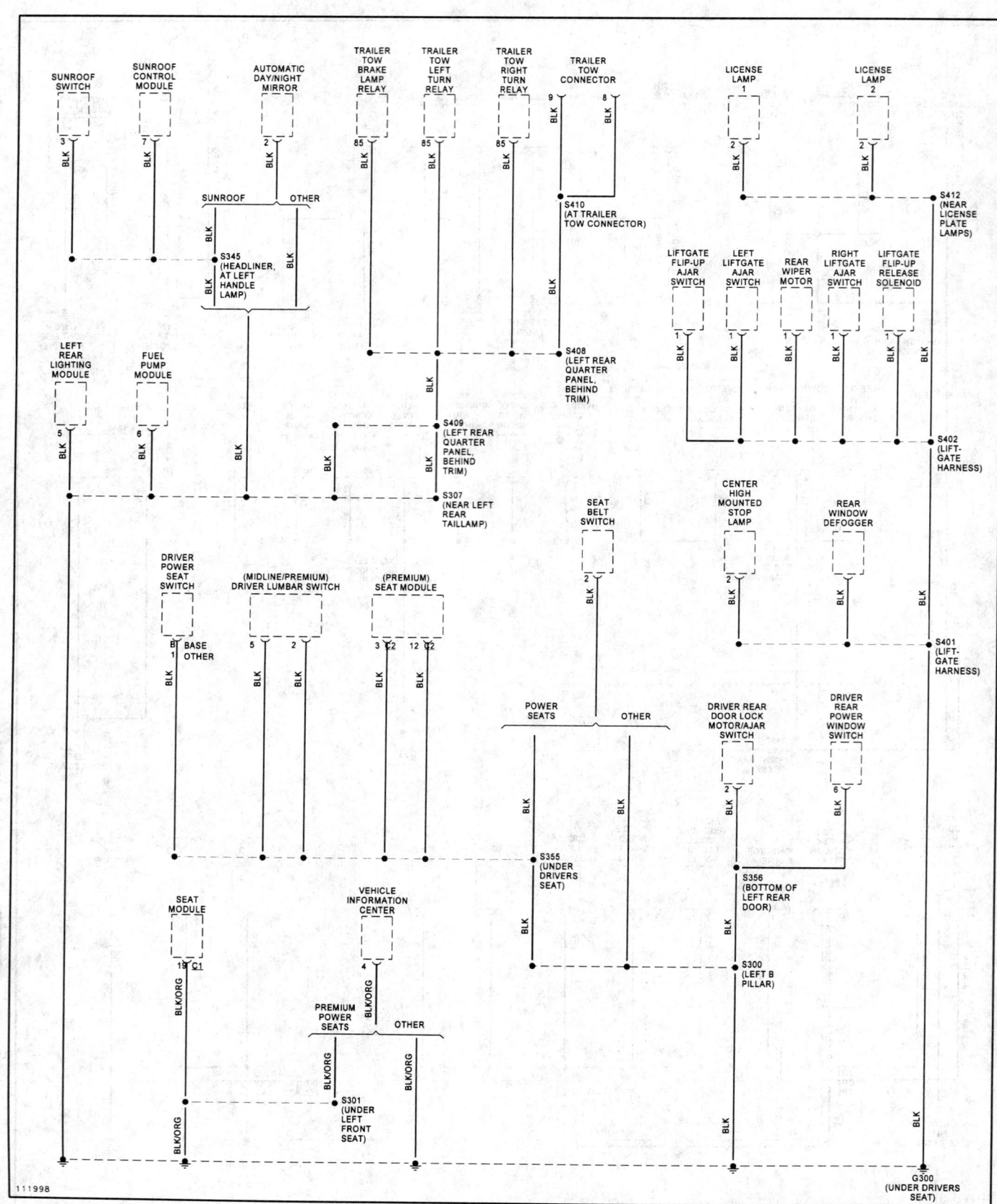

Fig. 6: Ground Distribution Wiring Diagram (Grand Cherokee – 4 Of 4)

1999 WIRING DIAGRAMS
Ground Distribution (Cont.)

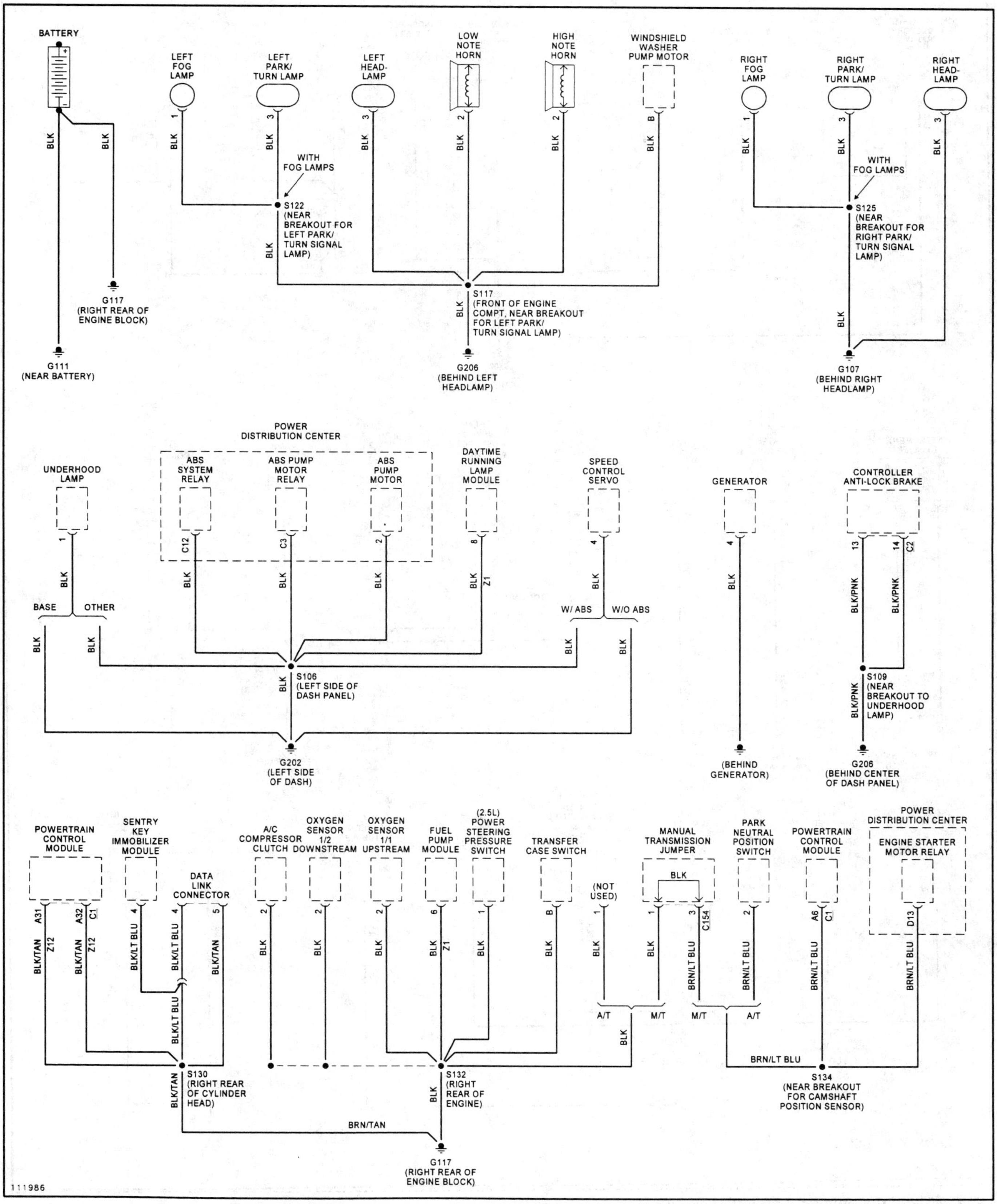
BATTERY
BLK
BLK
G117 (RIGHT REAR OF ENGINE BLOCK)
G111 (NEAR BATTERY)
LEFT FOG LAMP
LEFT PARK/ TURN LAMP
LEFT HEAD-LAMP
LOW NOTE HORN
HIGH NOTE HORN
WINDSHIELD WASHER PUMP MOTOR
WITH FOG LAMPS
S122 (NEAR BREAKOUT FOR LEFT PARK/ TURN SIGNAL LAMP)
S117 (FRONT OF ENGINE COMPT, NEAR BREAKOUT FOR LEFT PARK/ TURN SIGNAL LAMP)
G206 (BEHIND LEFT HEADLAMP)
RIGHT FOG LAMP
RIGHT PARK/ TURN LAMP
RIGHT HEAD-LAMP
WITH FOG LAMPS
S125 (NEAR BREAKOUT FOR RIGHT PARK/ TURN SIGNAL LAMP)
G107 (BEHIND RIGHT HEADLAMP)
POWER DISTRIBUTION CENTER
UNDERHOOD LAMP
ABS SYSTEM RELAY
ABS PUMP MOTOR RELAY
ABS PUMP MOTOR
DAYTIME RUNNING LAMP MODULE
SPEED CONTROL SERVO
GENERATOR
CONTROLLER ANTI-LOCK BRAKE
BASE
OTHER
W/ ABS
W/O ABS
BLK/PNK
S106 (LEFT SIDE OF DASH PANEL)
G202 (LEFT SIDE OF DASH)
(BEHIND GENERATOR)
S109 (NEAR BREAKOUT TO UNDERHOOD LAMP)
G206 (BEHIND CENTER OF DASH PANEL)
POWERTRAIN CONTROL MODULE
SENTRY KEY IMMOBILIZER MODULE
DATA LINK CONNECTOR
A/C COMPRESSOR CLUTCH
OXYGEN SENSOR 1/2 DOWNSTREAM
OXYGEN SENSOR 1/1 UPSTREAM
FUEL PUMP MODULE
(2.5L) POWER STEERING PRESSURE SWITCH
TRANSFER CASE SWITCH
(NOT USED)
MANUAL TRANSMISSION JUMPER
PARK NEUTRAL POSITION SWITCH
POWERTRAIN CONTROL MODULE
POWER DISTRIBUTION CENTER
ENGINE STARTER MOTOR RELAY
BLK/TAN
BLK/LT BLU
BRN/LT BLU
A/T
M/T
S130 (RIGHT REAR OF CYLINDER HEAD)
S132 (RIGHT REAR OF ENGINE)
S134 (NEAR BREAKOUT FOR CAMSHAFT POSITION SENSOR)
BRN/TAN
G117 (RIGHT REAR OF ENGINE BLOCK)
111986

Fig. 7: Ground Distribution Wiring Diagram (Wrangler – 1 Of 2)

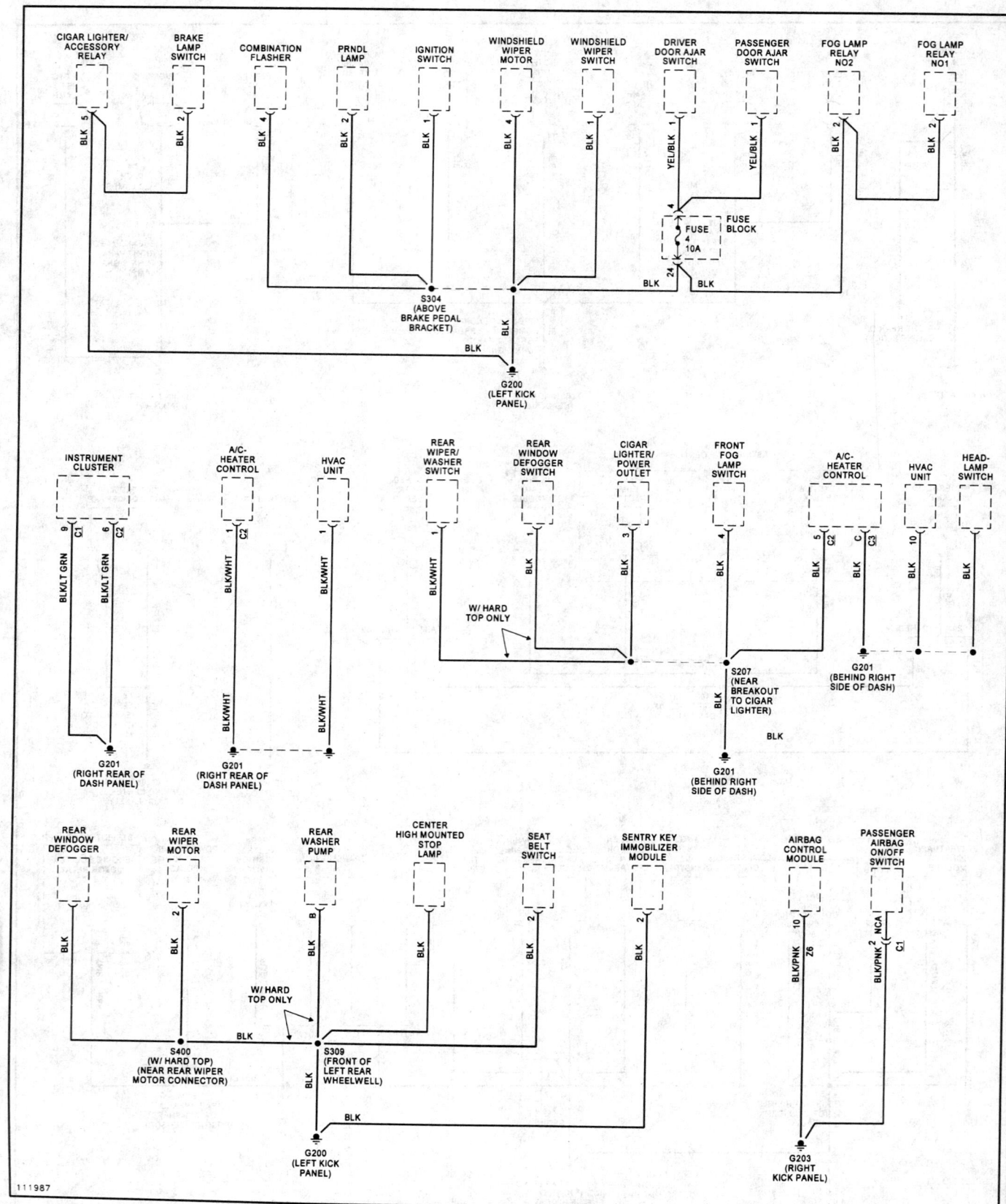

Fig. 8: Ground Distribution Wiring Diagram (Wrangler – 2 Of 2)

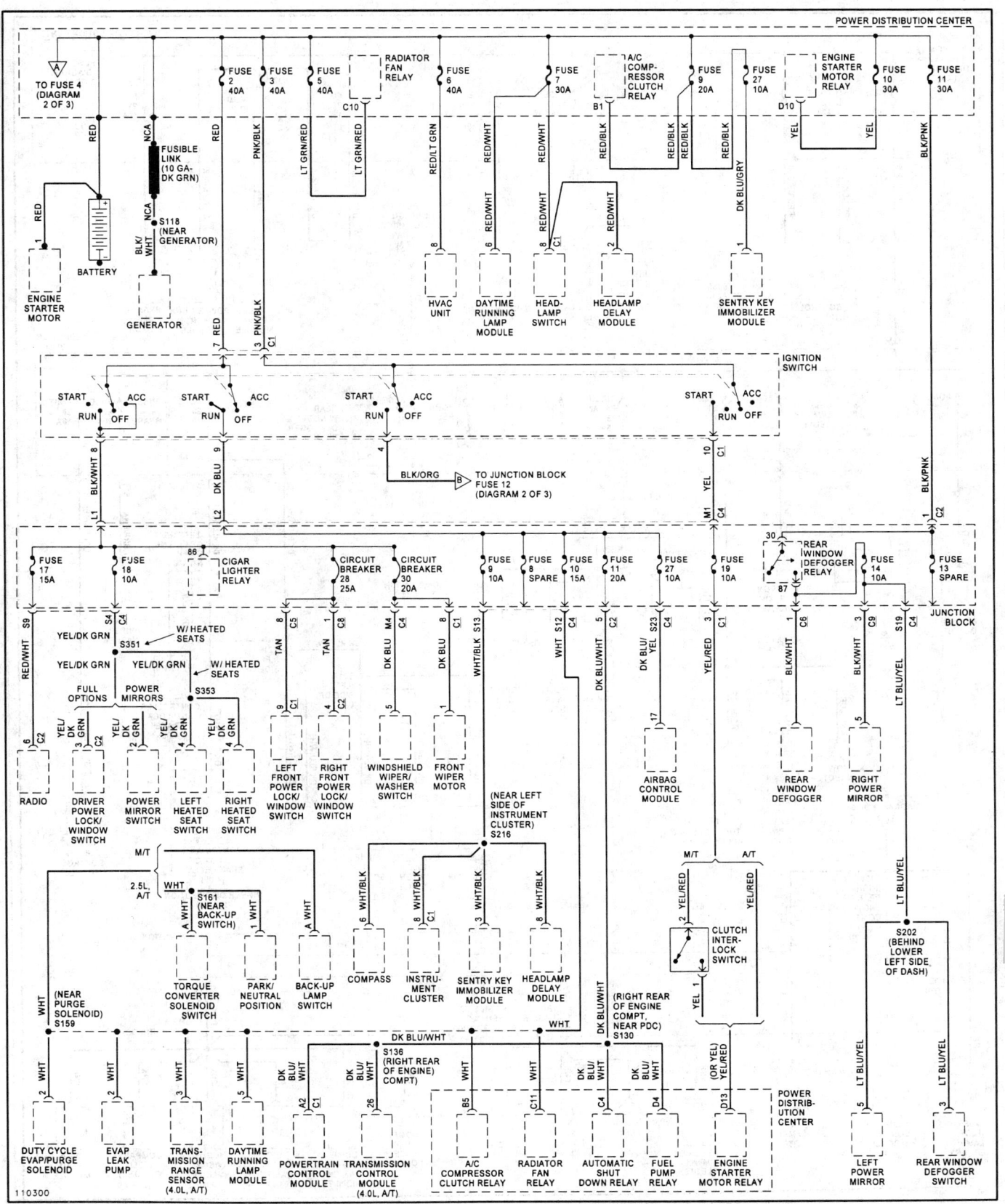

Fig. 1: Power Distribution Wiring Diagram (Cherokee – 1 Of 3)

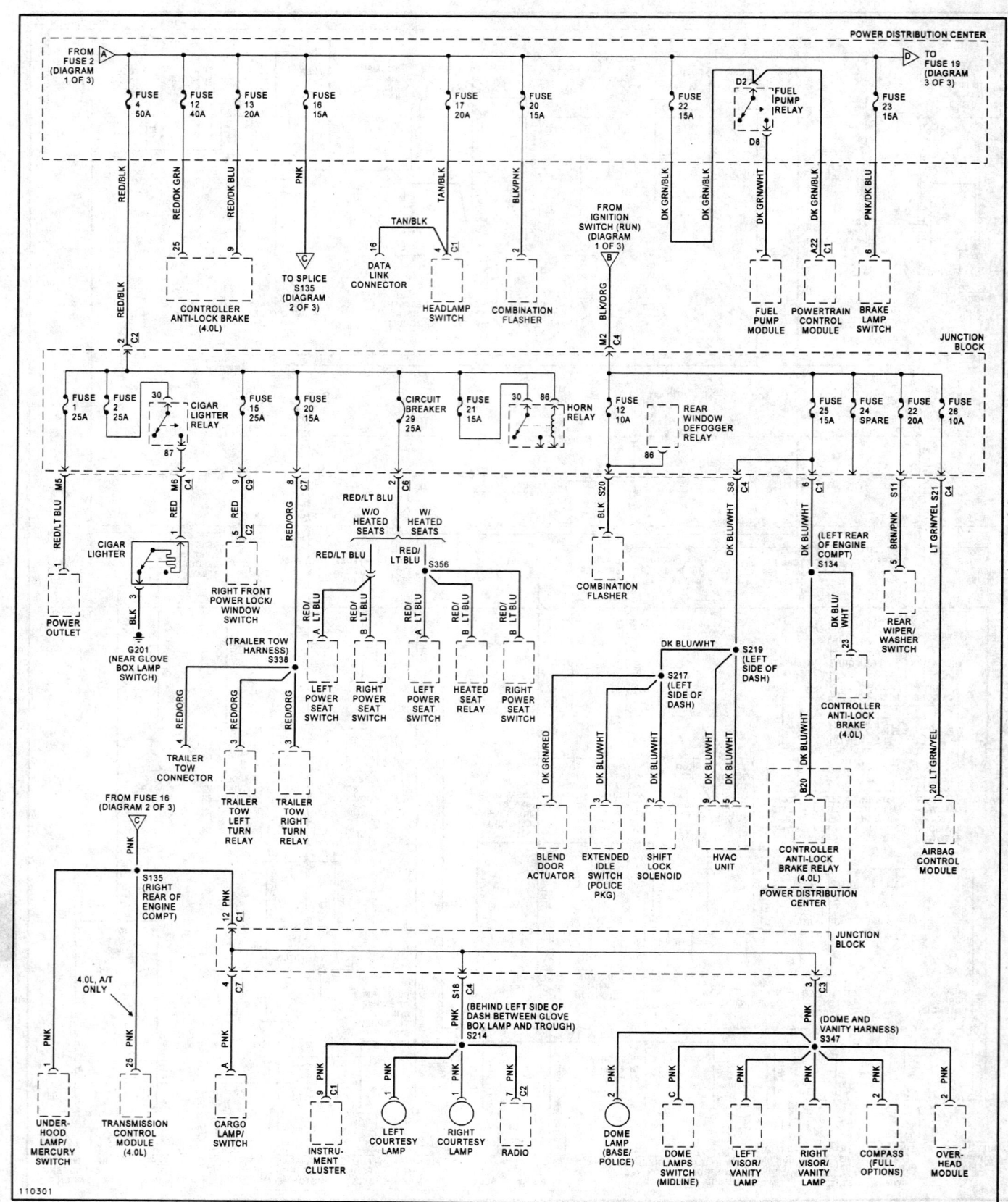

Fig. 2: Power Distribution Wiring Diagram (Cherokee – 2 Of 3)

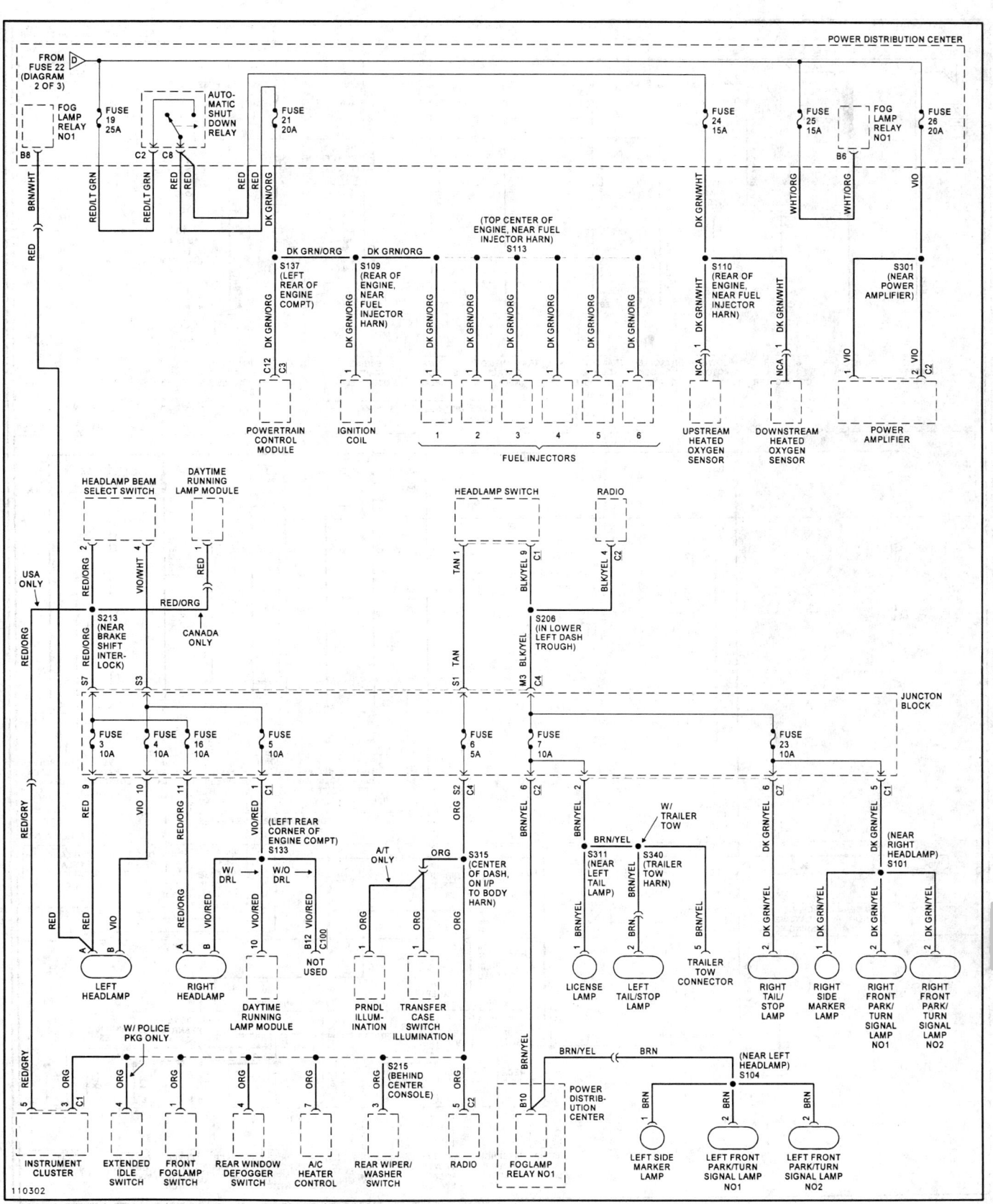

Fig. 3: Power Distribution Wiring Diagram (Cherokee – 3 Of 3)

110302

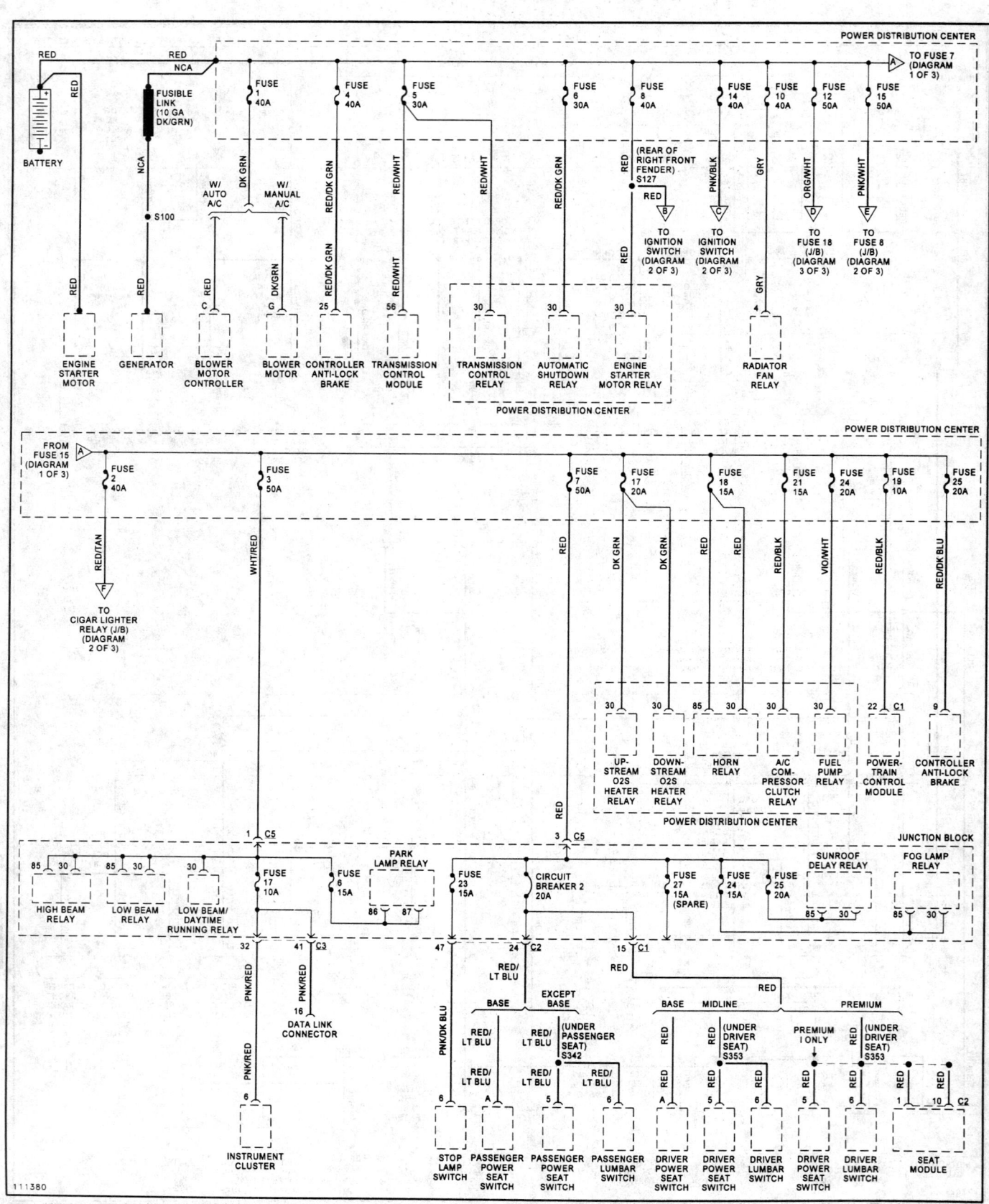

Fig. 4: Power Distribution Wiring Diagram (Grand Cherokee – 1 Of 3)

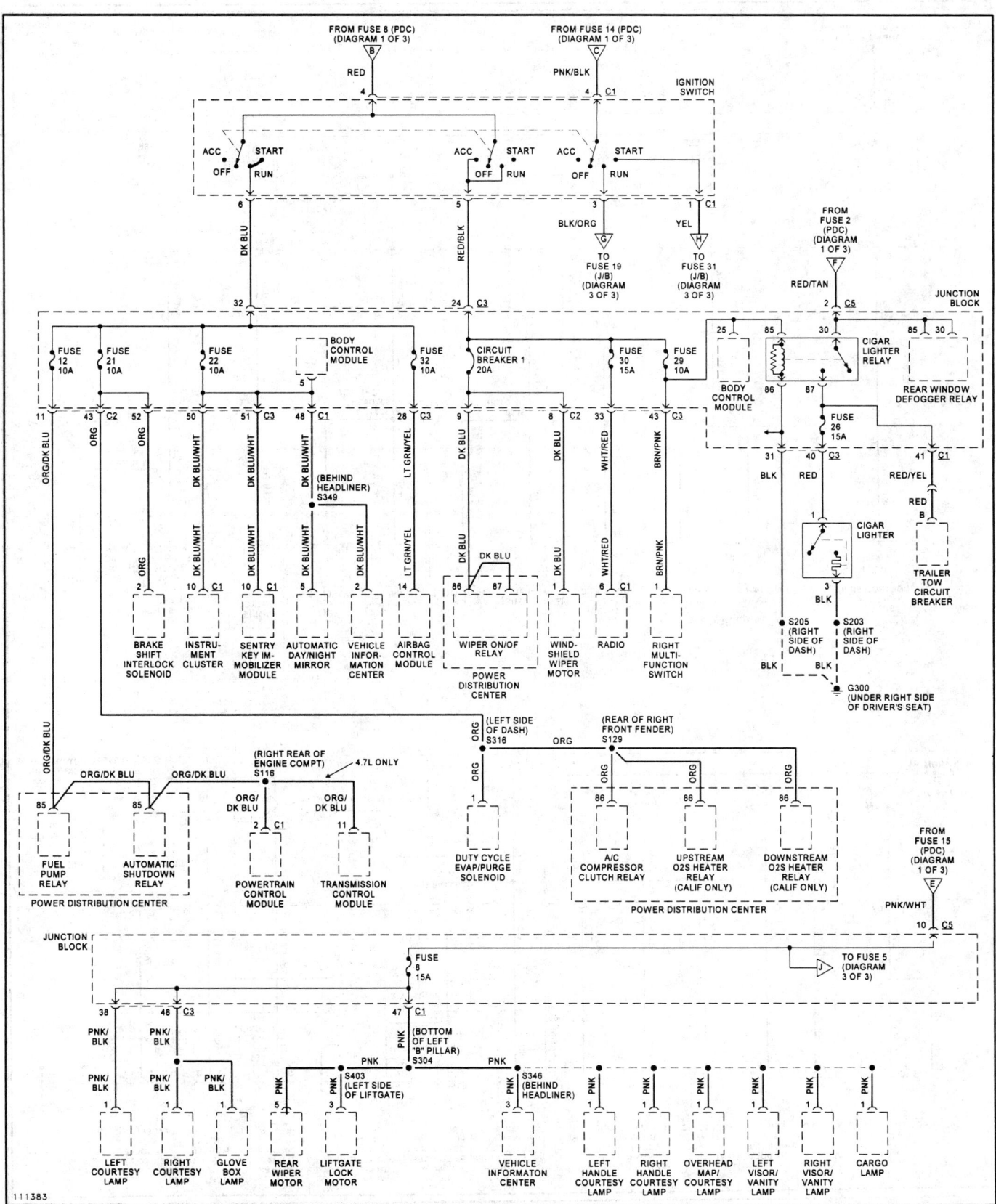

Fig. 5: Power Distribution Wiring Diagram (Grand Cherokee – 2 Of 3)

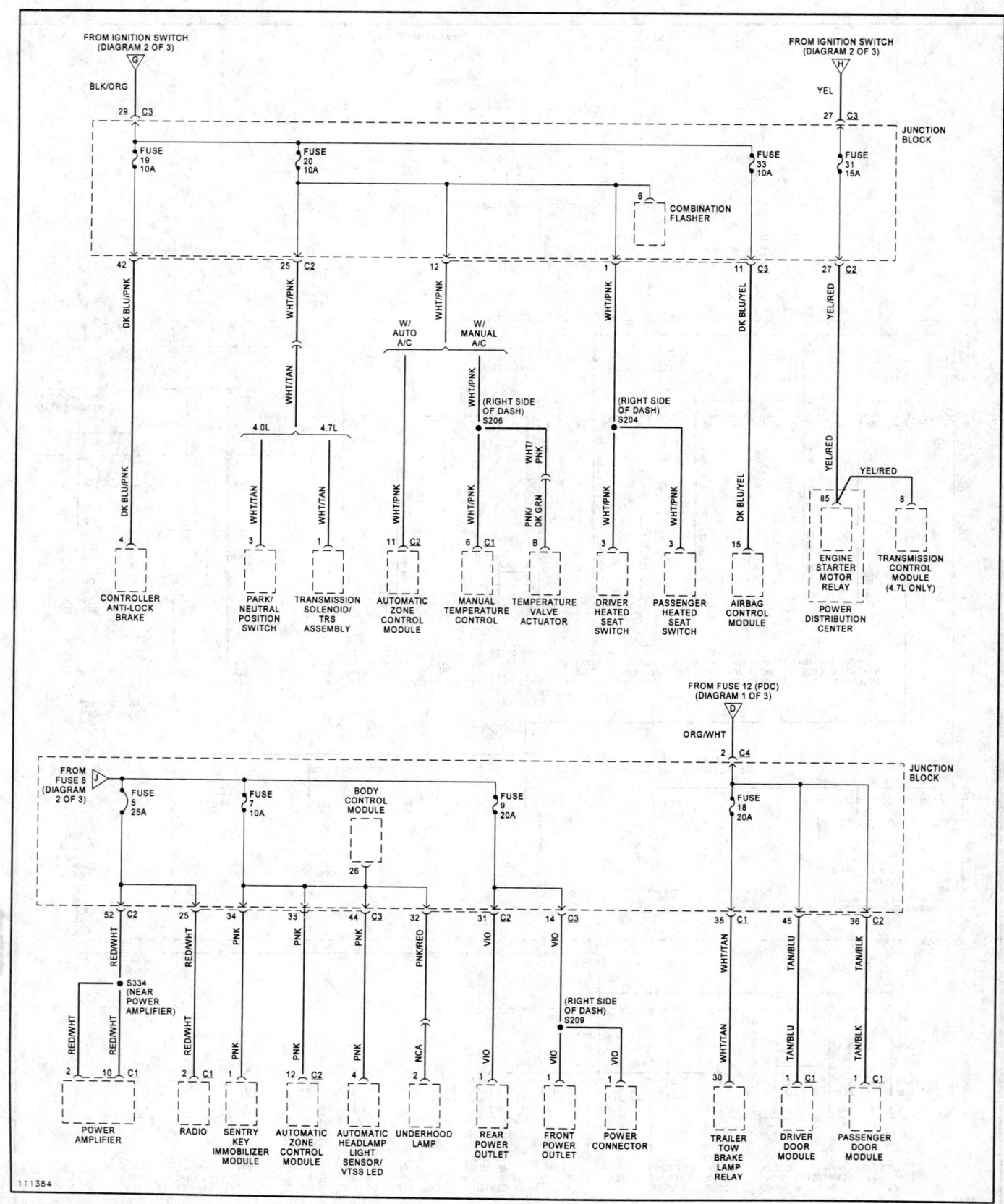

Fig. 6: Power Distribution Wiring Diagram (Grand Cherokee – 3 Of 3)

111384

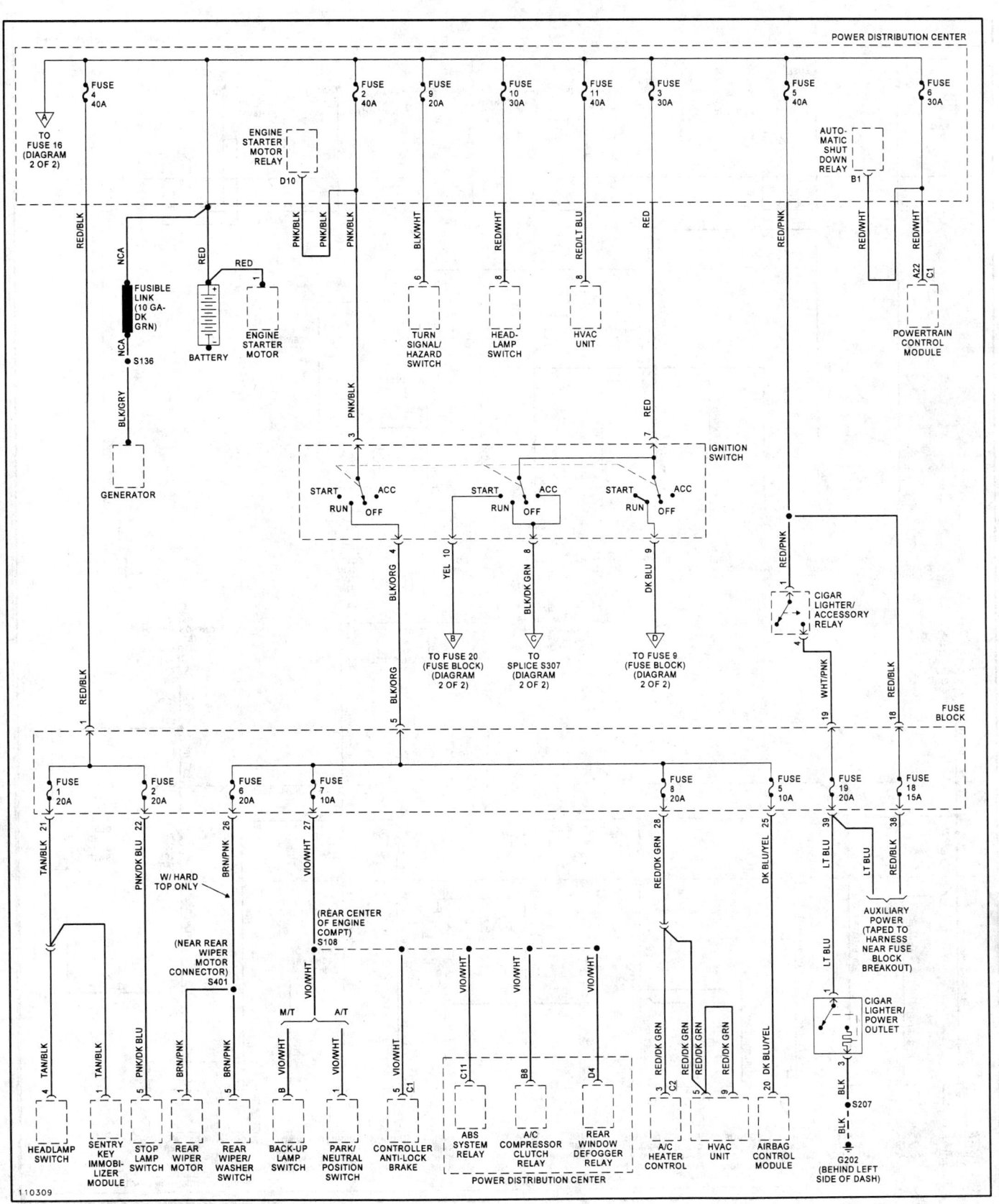

Fig. 7: Power Distribution Wiring Diagram (Wrangler – 1 Of 2)

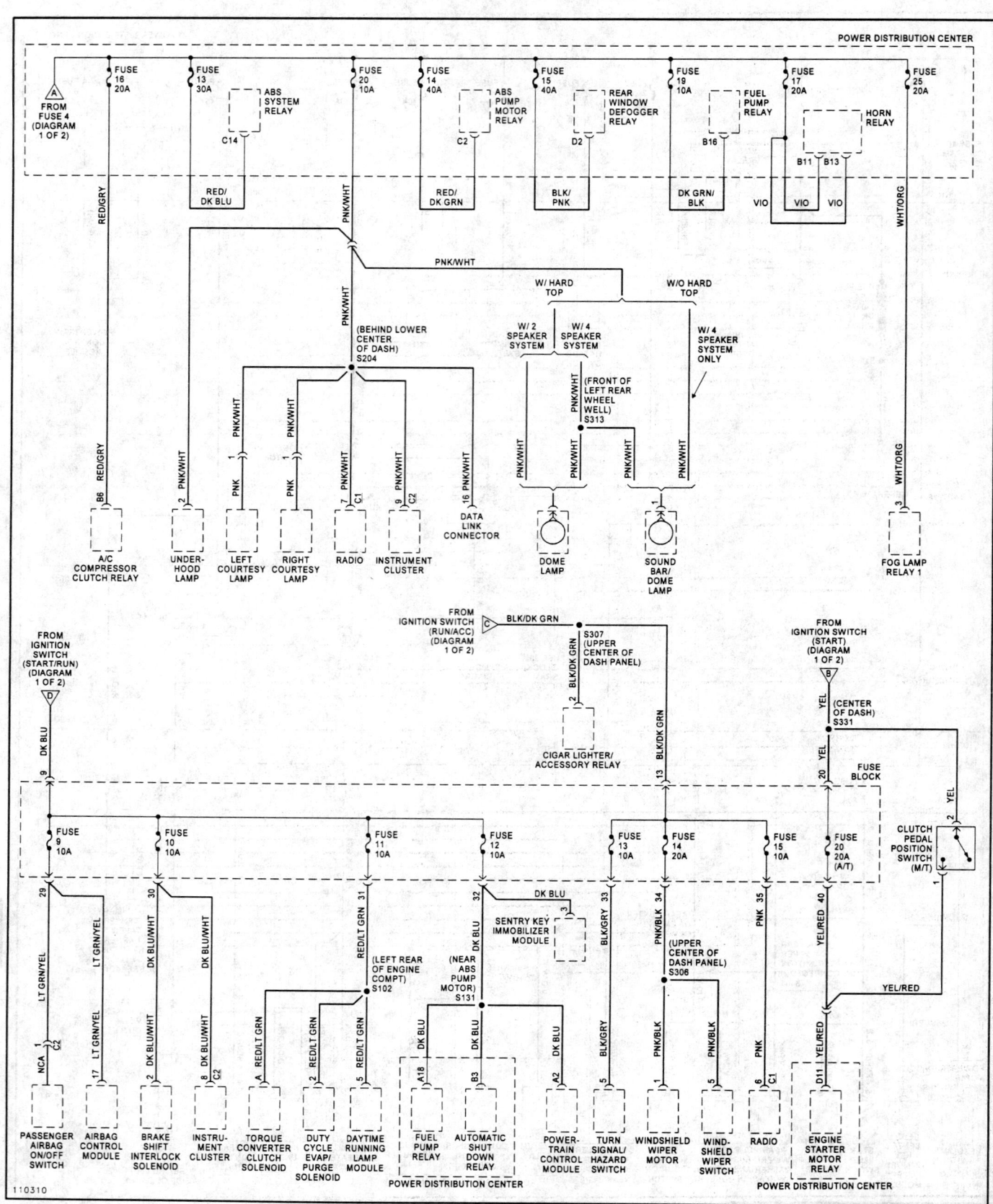

Fig. 8: Power Distribution Wiring Diagram (Wrangler – 2 Of 2)

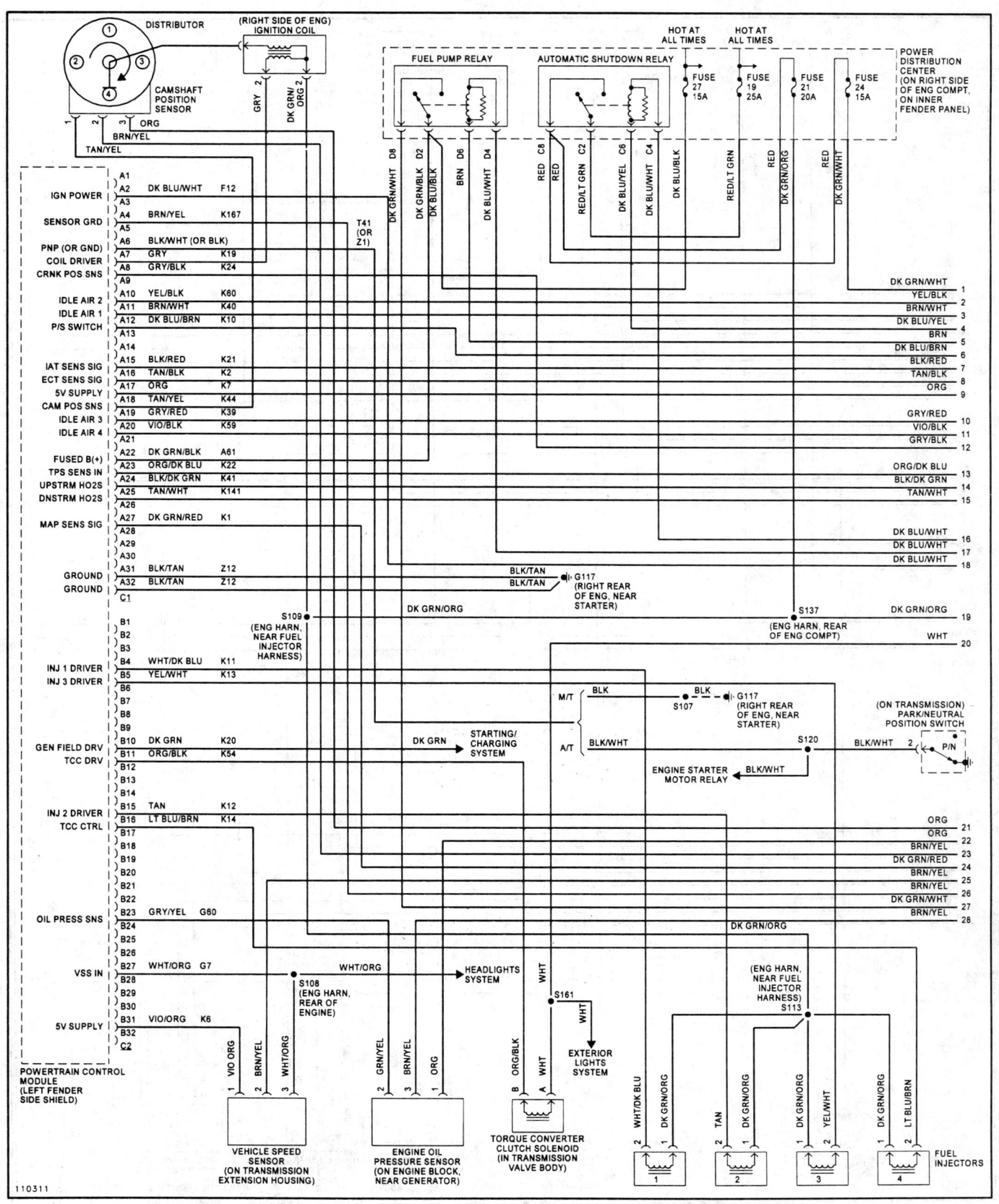

Fig. 1: PCM Wiring Diagram (Cherokee – 2.5L – 1 Of 3)

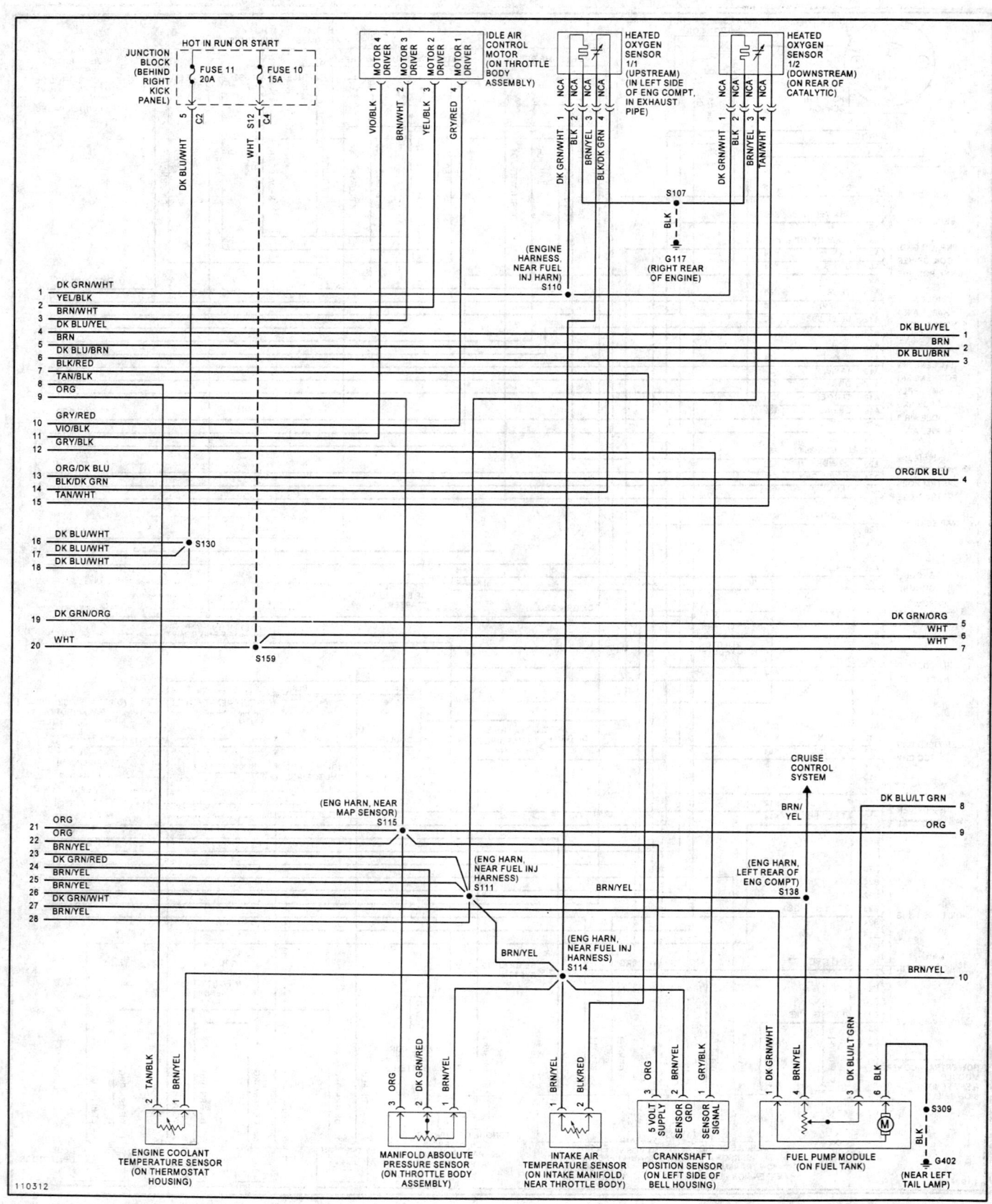

Fig. 2: PCM Wiring Diagram (Cherokee – 2.5L – 2 Of 3)

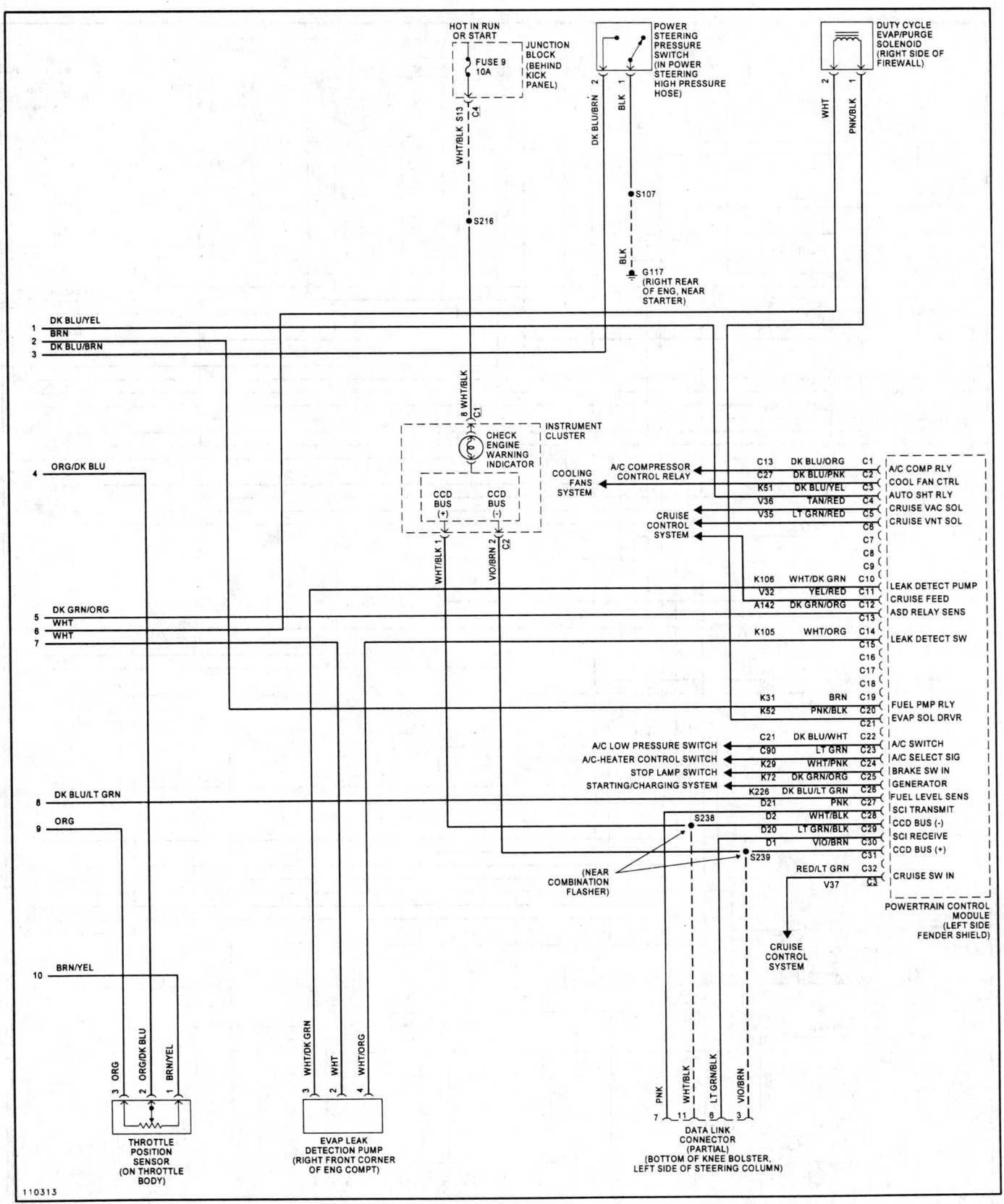

Fig. 3: PCM Wiring Diagram (Cherokee – 2.5L – 3 Of 3)

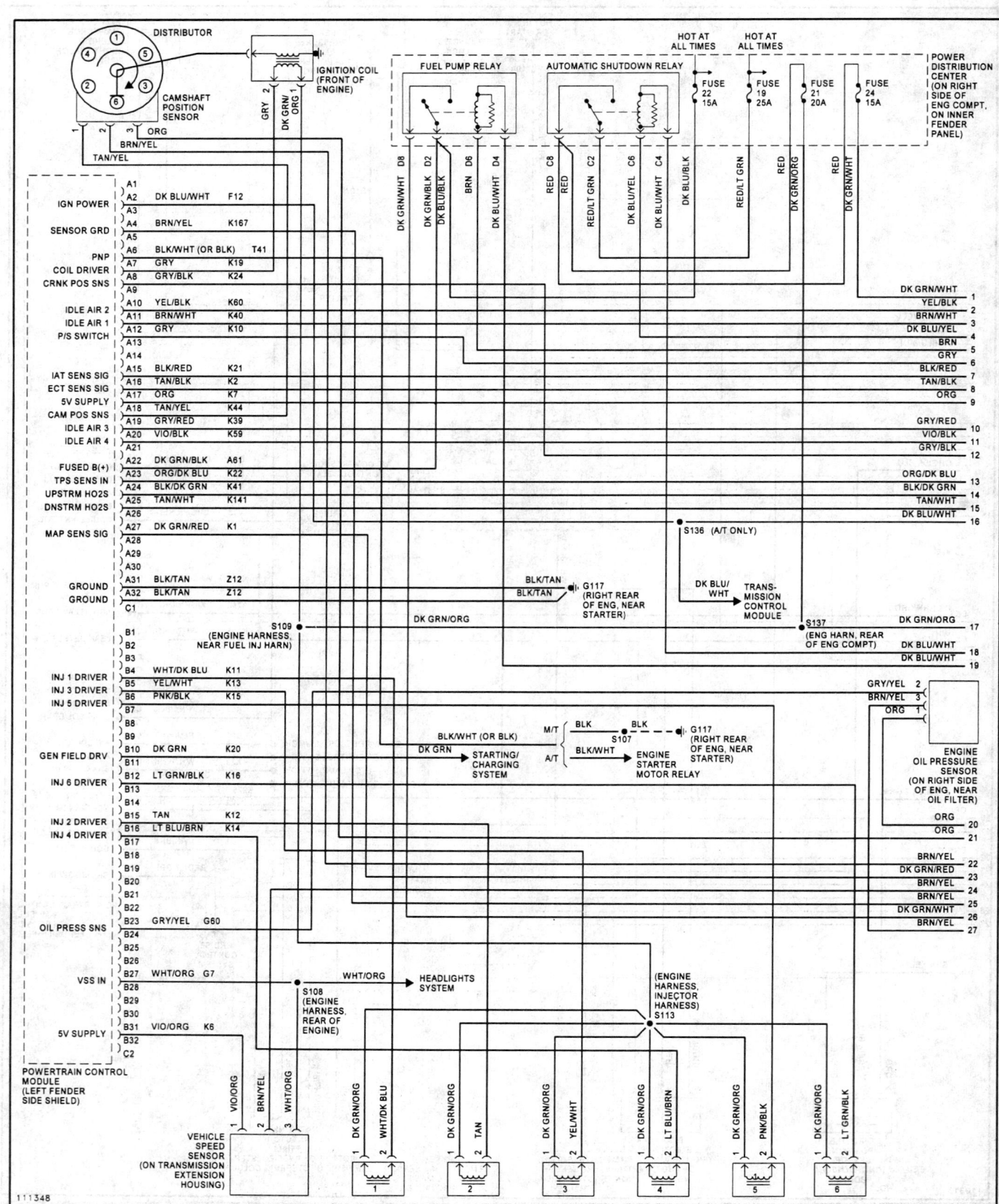

Fig. 4: PCM Wiring Diagram (Cherokee – 4.0L – 1 Of 3)

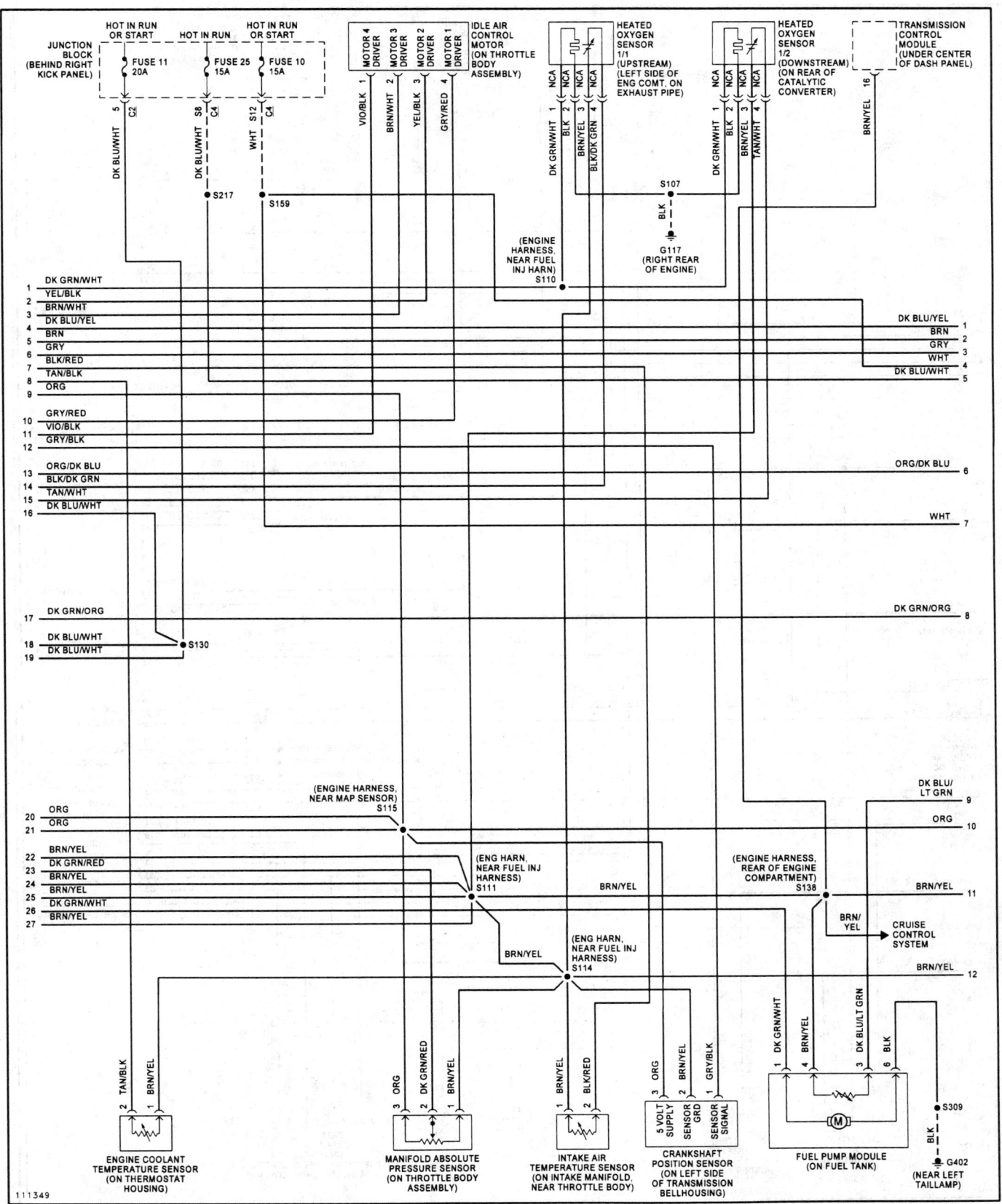

Fig. 5: PCM Wiring Diagram (Cherokee – 4.0L – 2 Of 3)

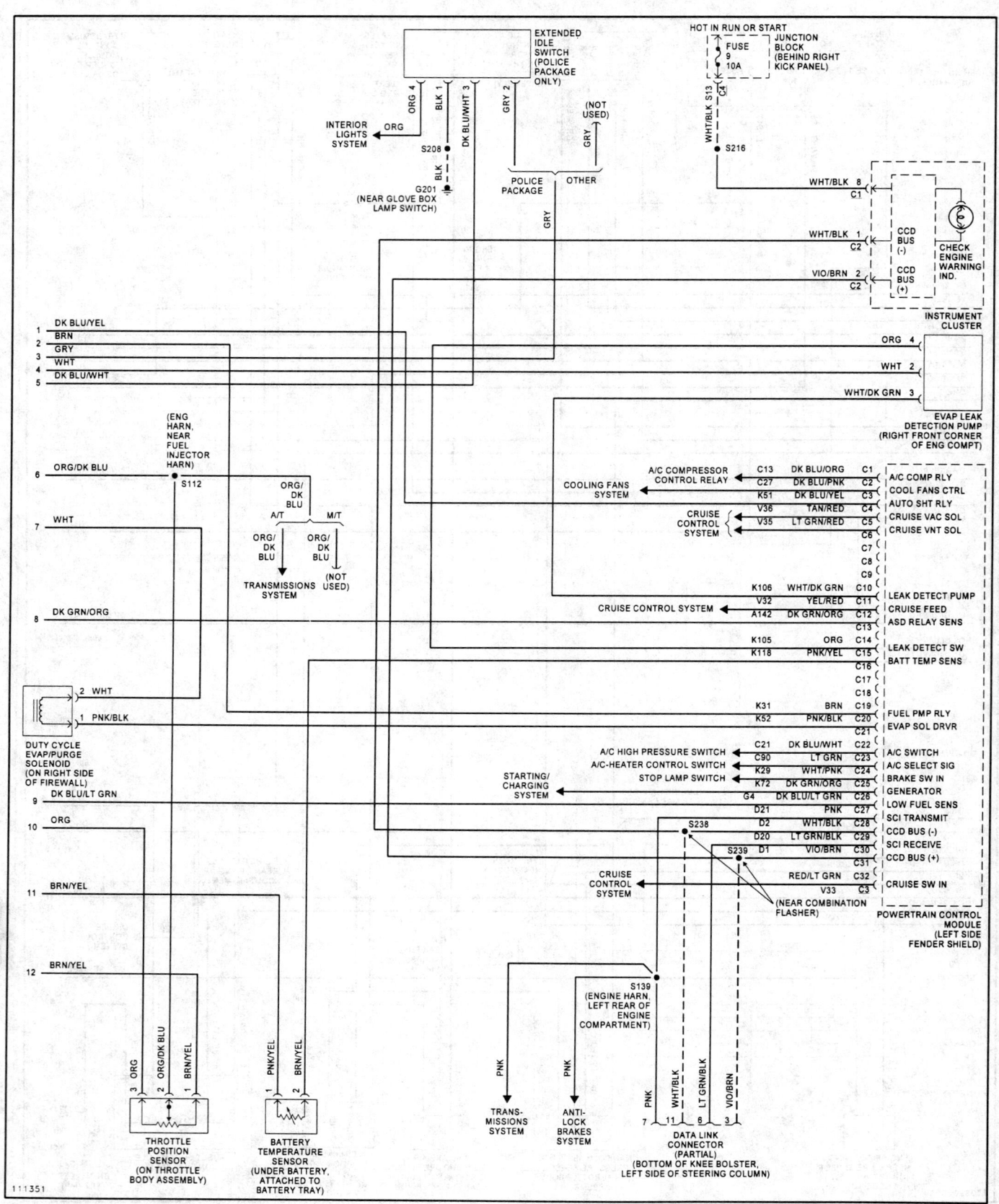

Fig. 6: PCM Wiring Diagram (Cherokee – 4.0L – 3 Of 3)

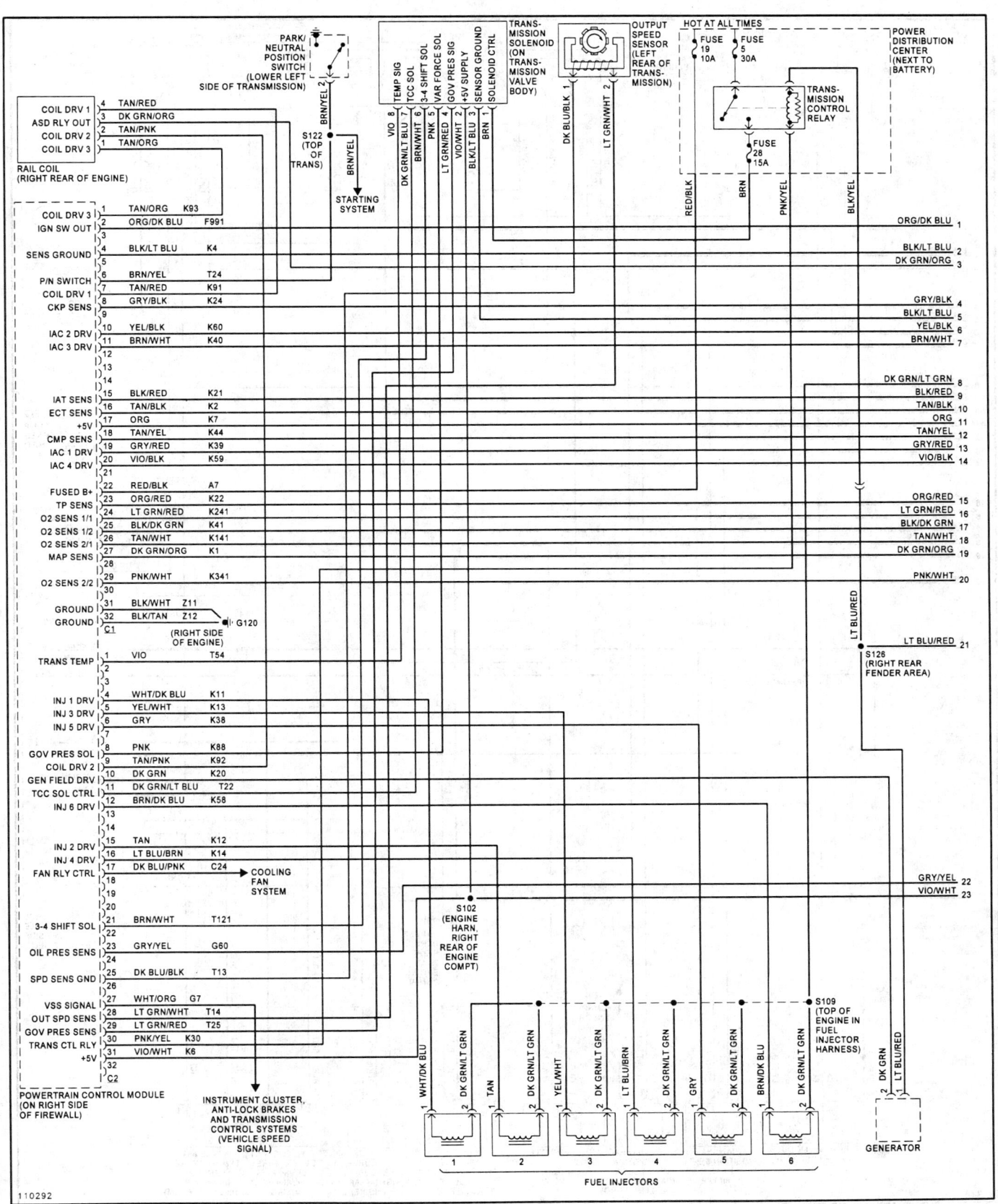

Fig. 7: PCM Wiring Diagram (Grand Cherokee – 4.0L – 1 Of 3)

110292

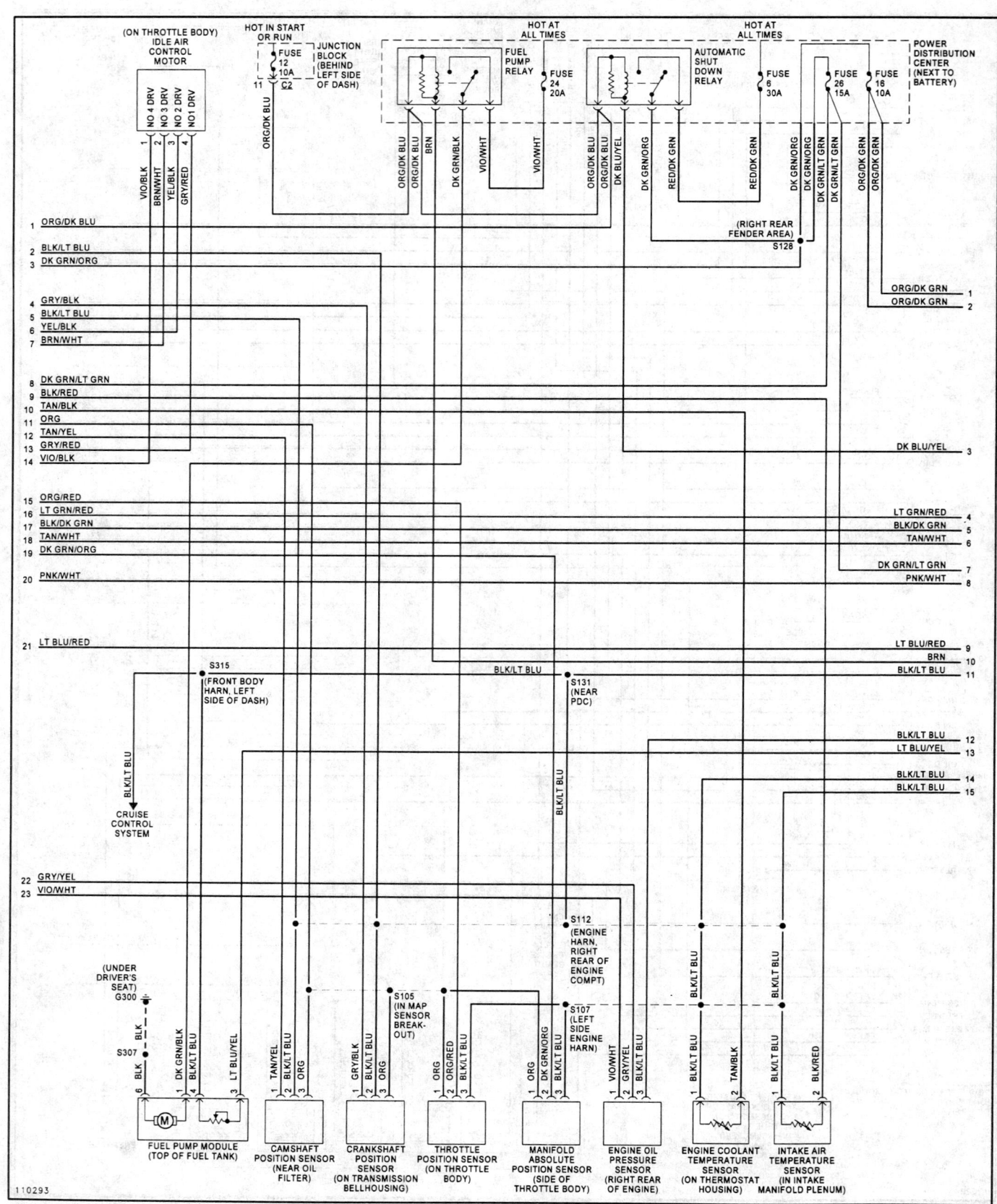

Fig. 8: PCM Wiring Diagram (Grand Cherokee – 4.0L – 2 Of 3)

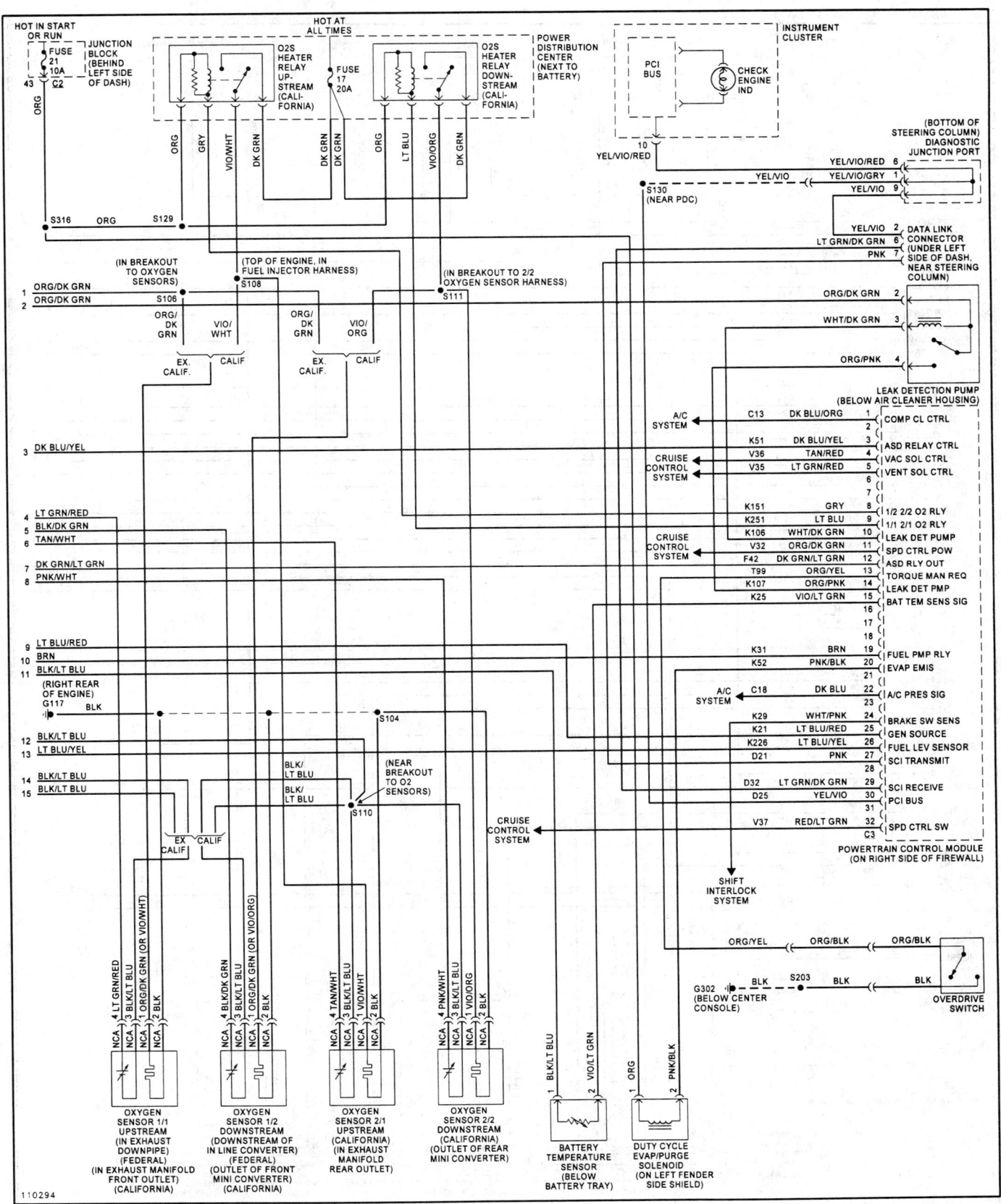

Fig. 9: PCM Wiring Diagram (Grand Cherokee – 4.0L – 3 Of 3)

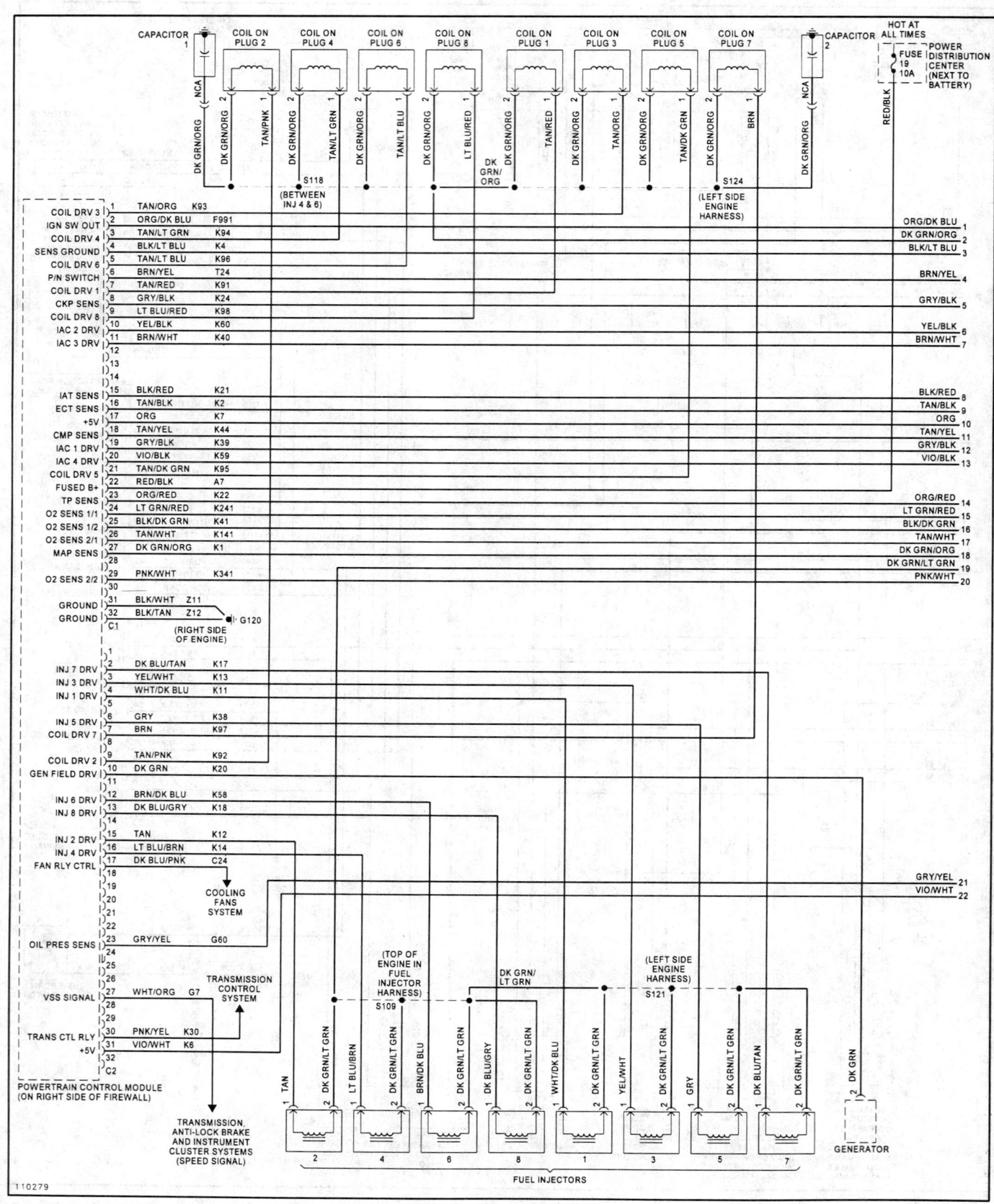

Fig. 10: PCM Wiring Diagram (Grand Cherokee – 4.7L – 1 Of 3)

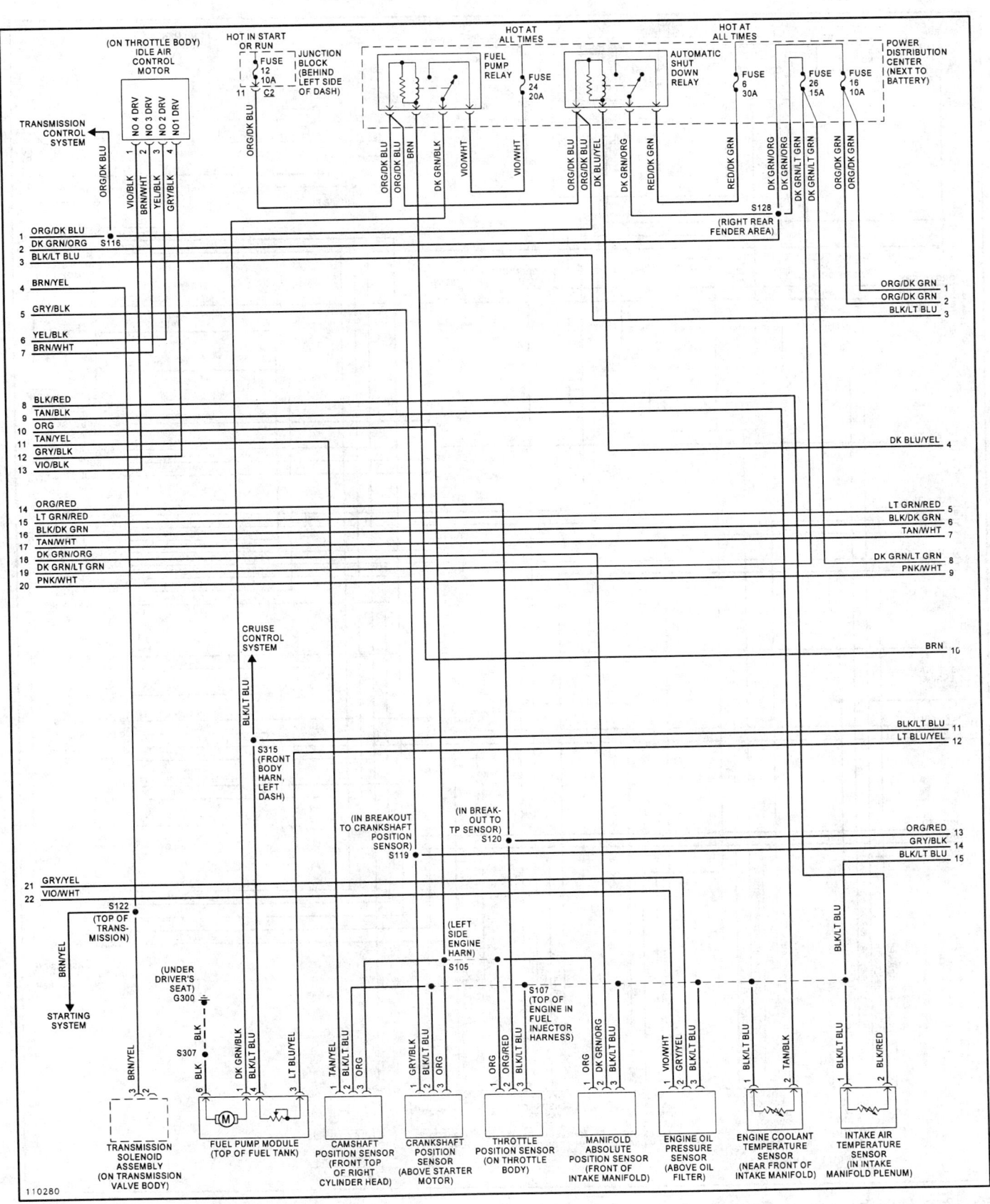

Fig. 11: PCM Wiring Diagram (Grand Cherokee – 4.7L – 2 Of 3)

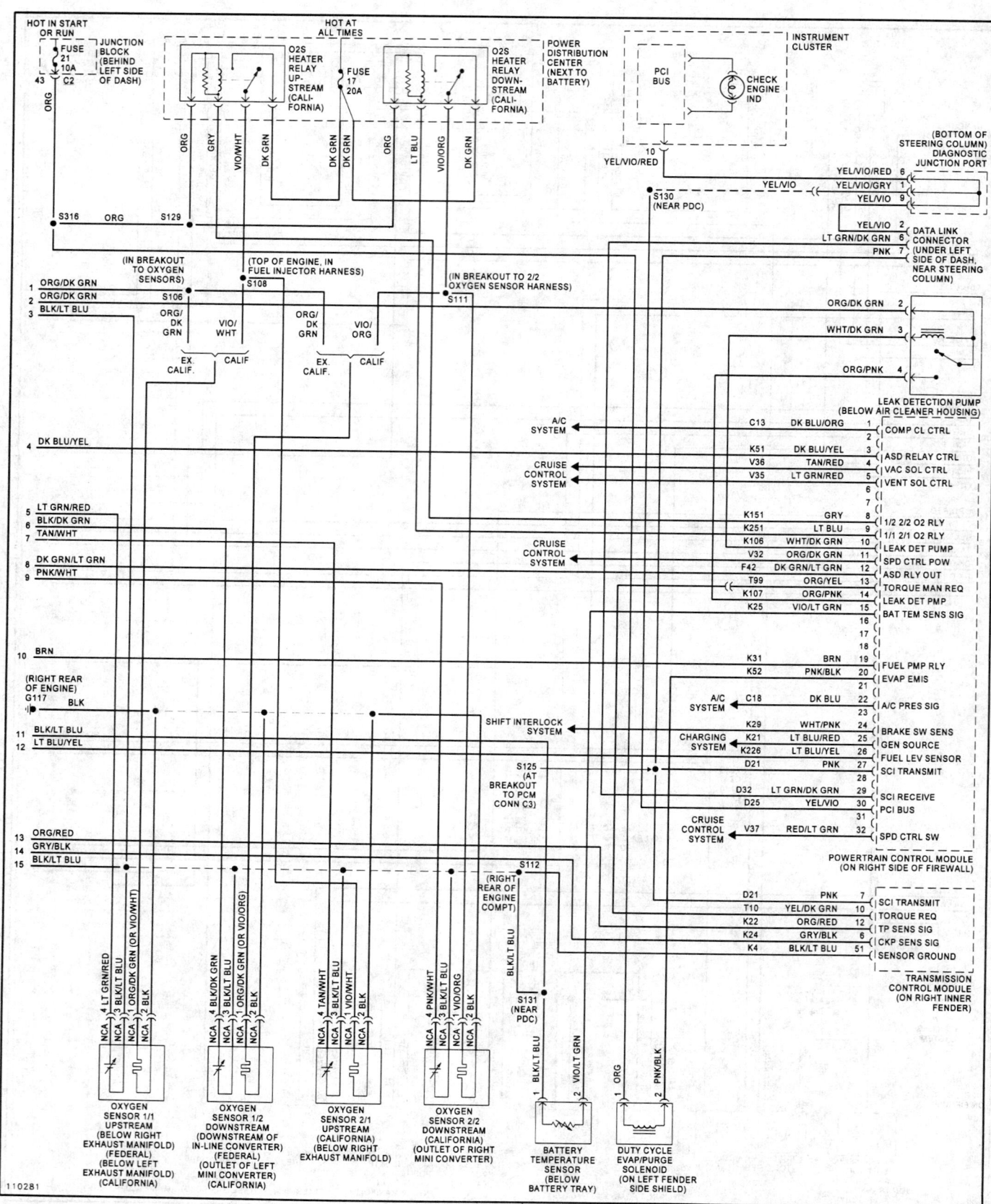

Fig. 12: PCM Wiring Diagram (Grand Cherokee – 4.7L – 3 Of 3)

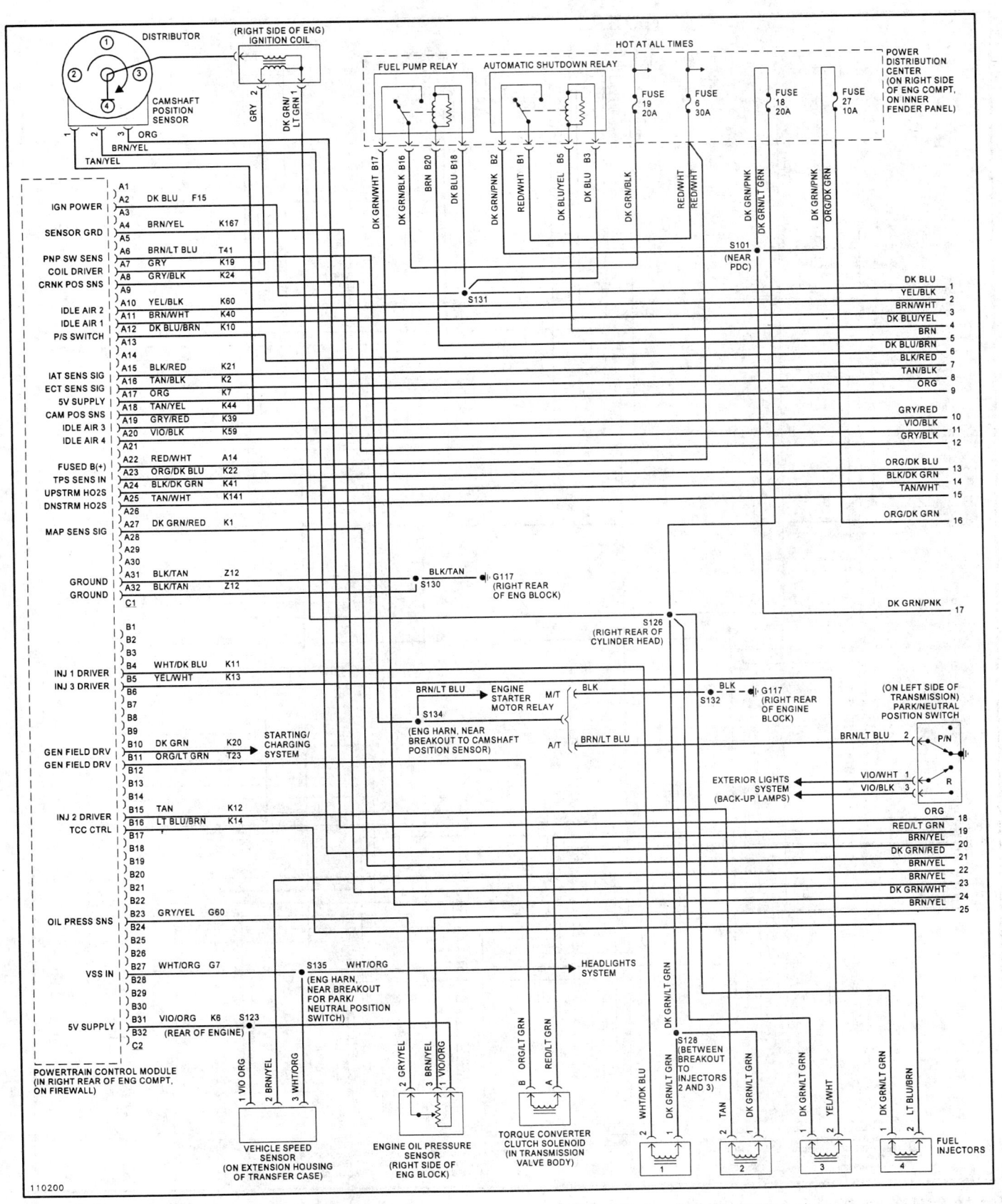

Fig. 13: PCM Wiring Diagram (Wrangler – 2.5L – 1 Of 3)

110200

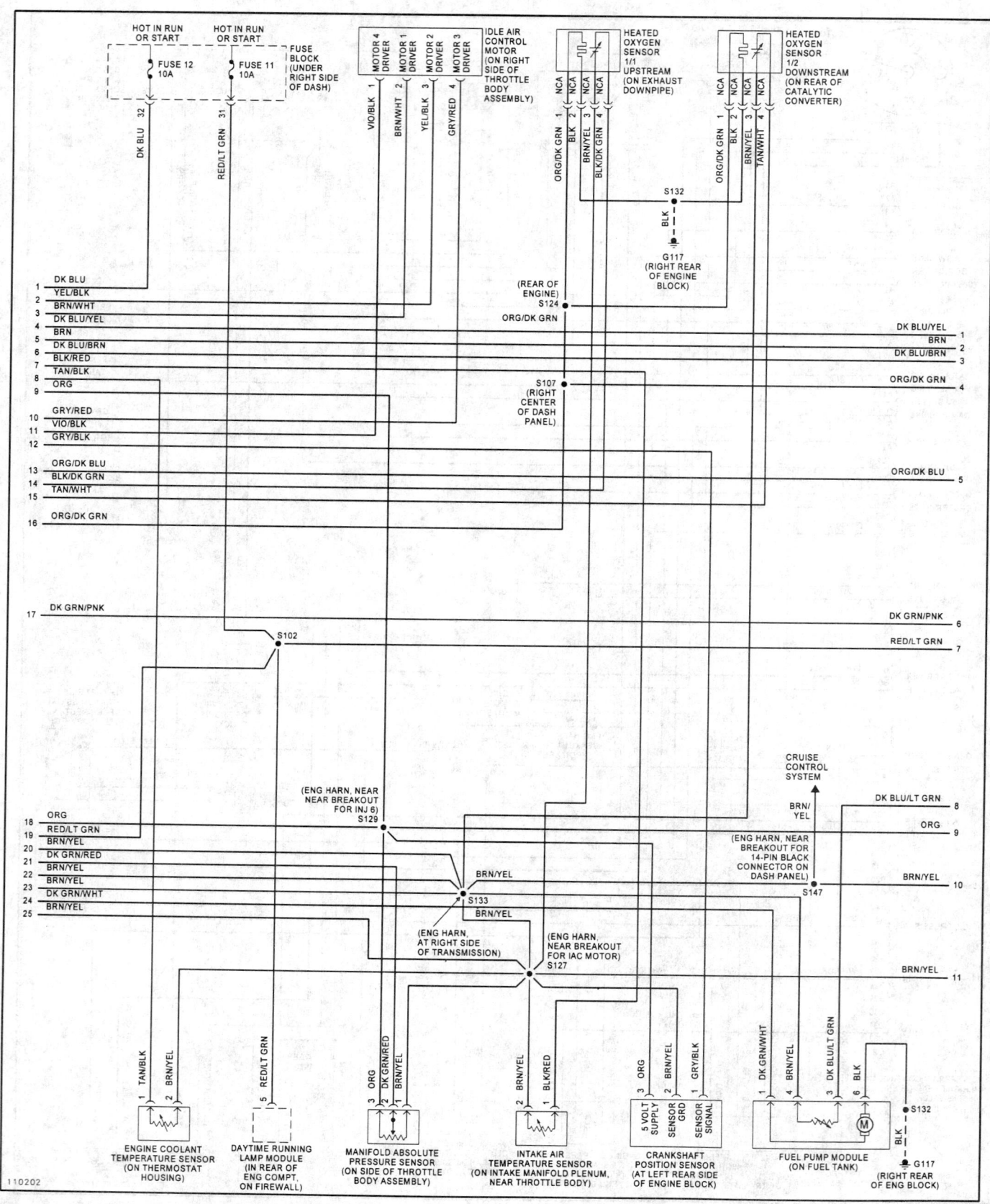

Fig. 14: PCM Wiring Diagram (Wrangler – 2.5L – 2 Of 3)

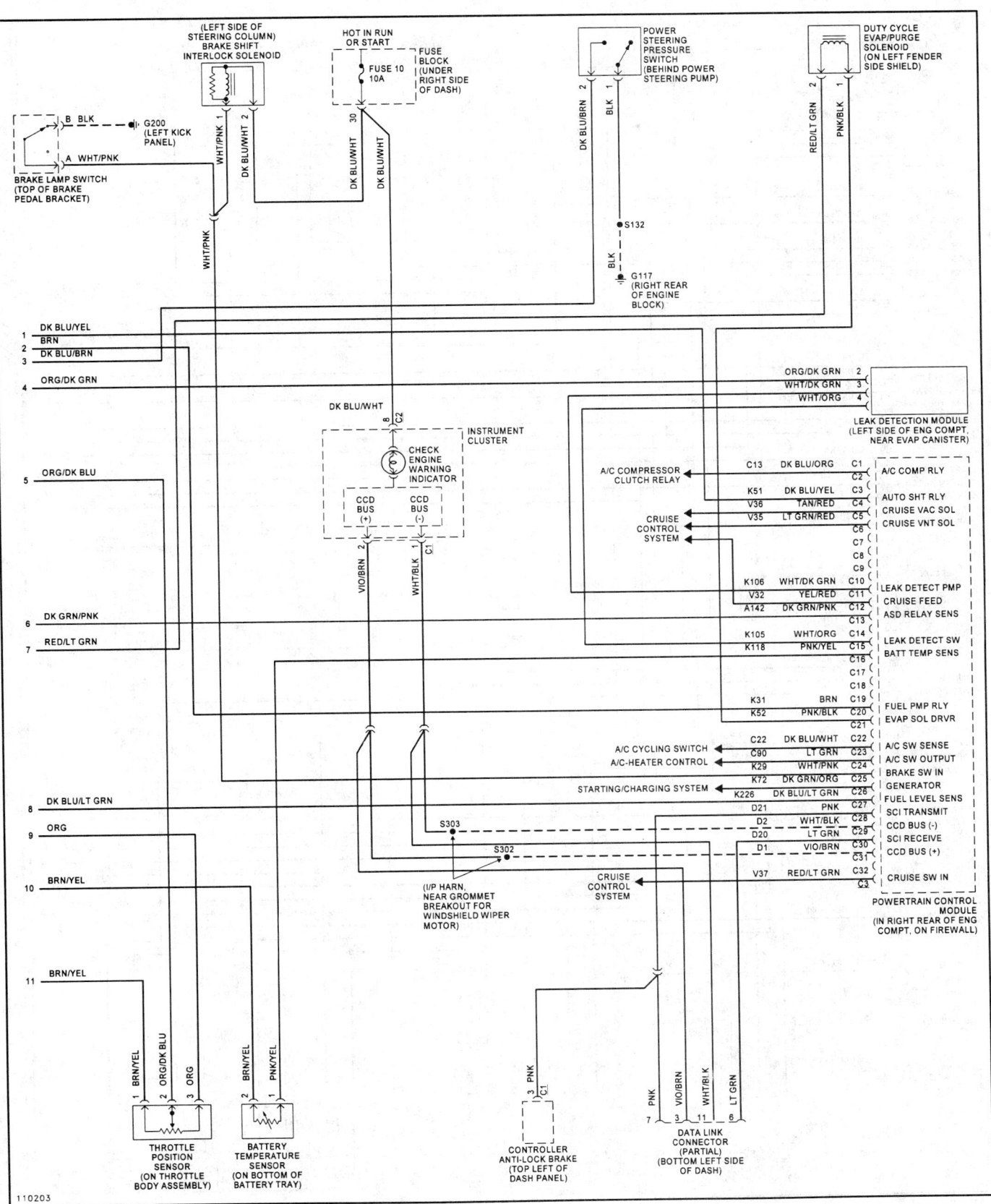

Fig. 15: PCM Wiring Diagram (Wrangler – 2.5L – 3 Of 3)

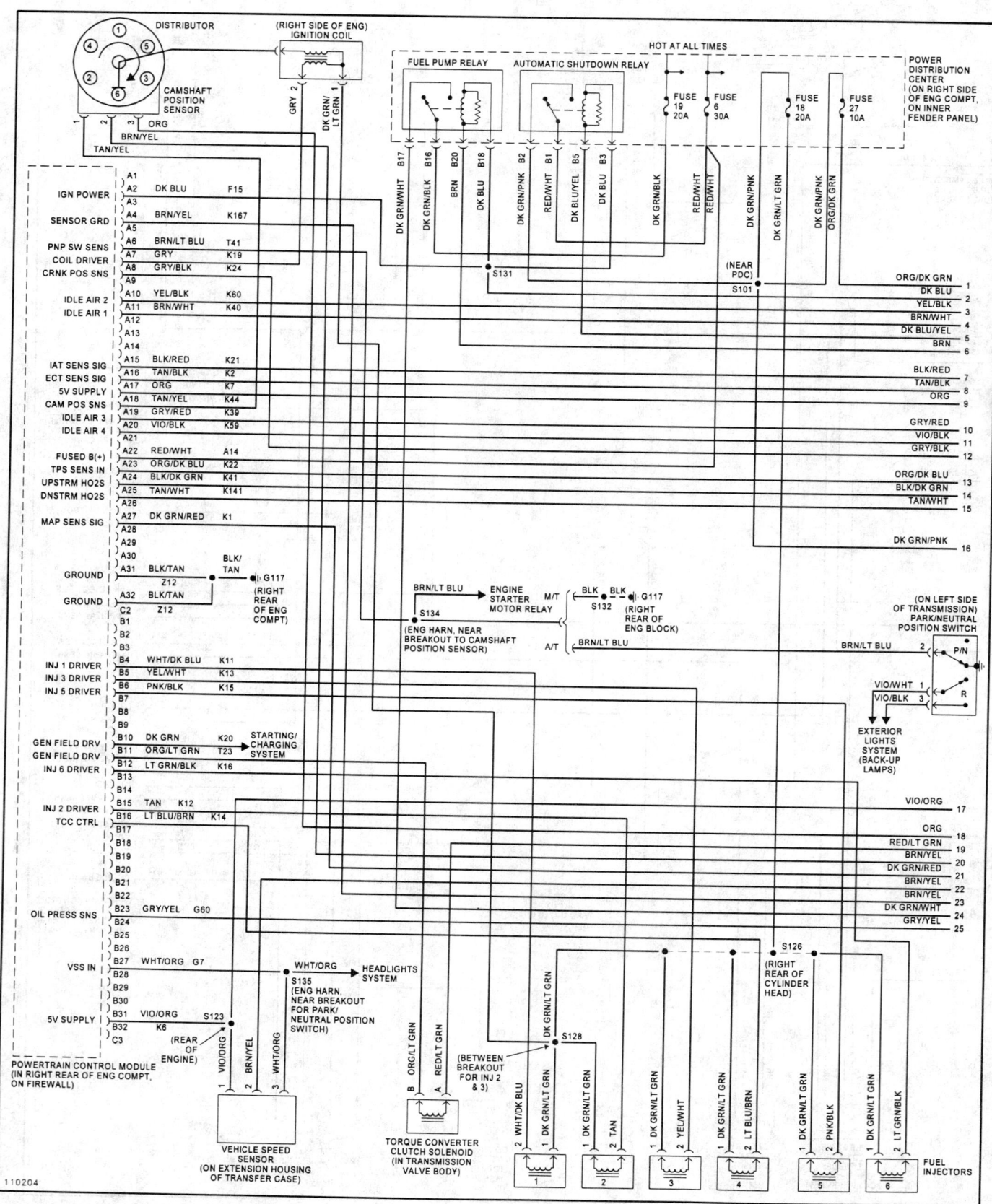

Fig. 16: PCM Wiring Diagram (Wrangler – 4.0L – 1 Of 3)

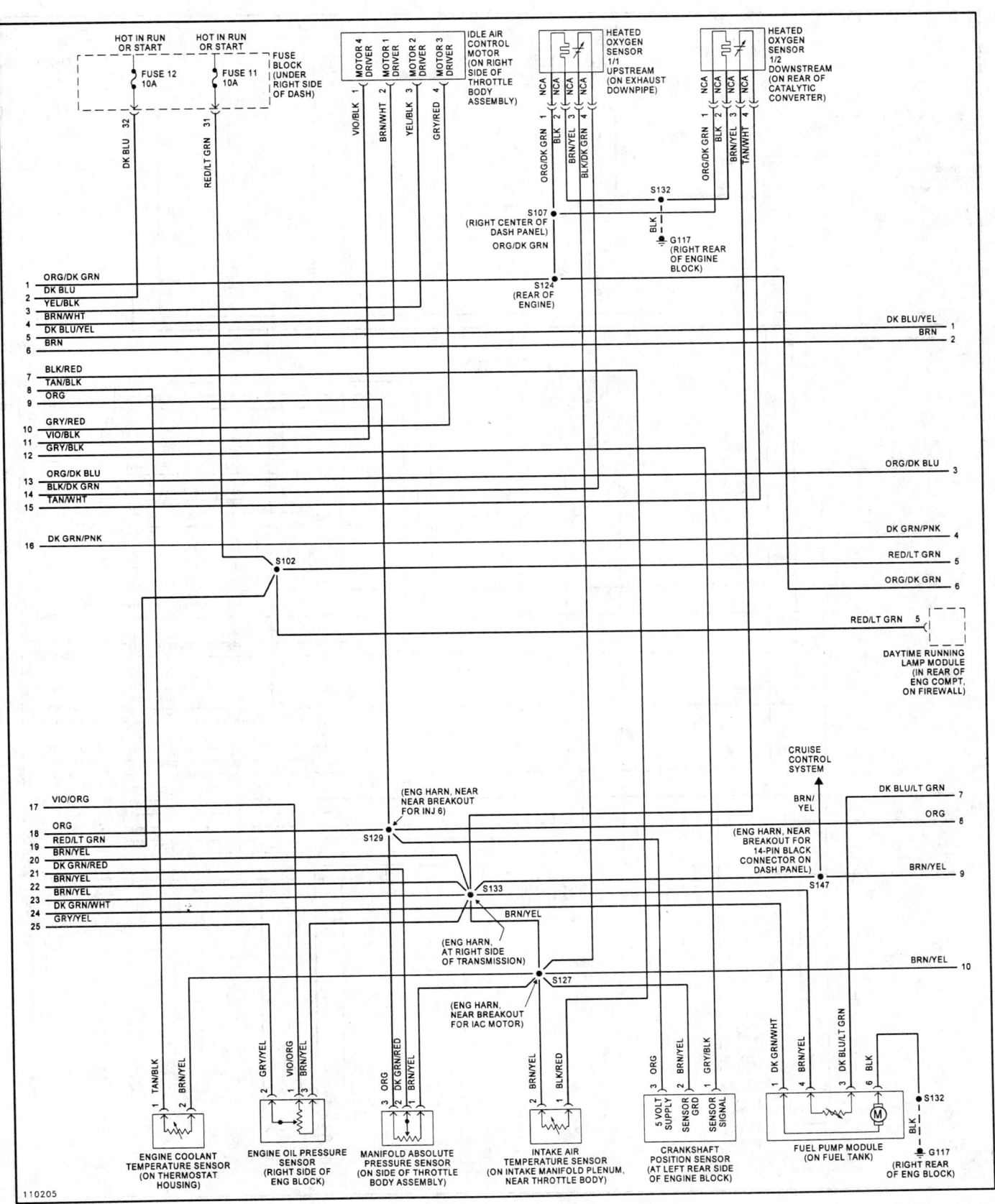

Fig. 17: PCM Wiring Diagram (Wrangler – 4.0L – 2 Of 3)

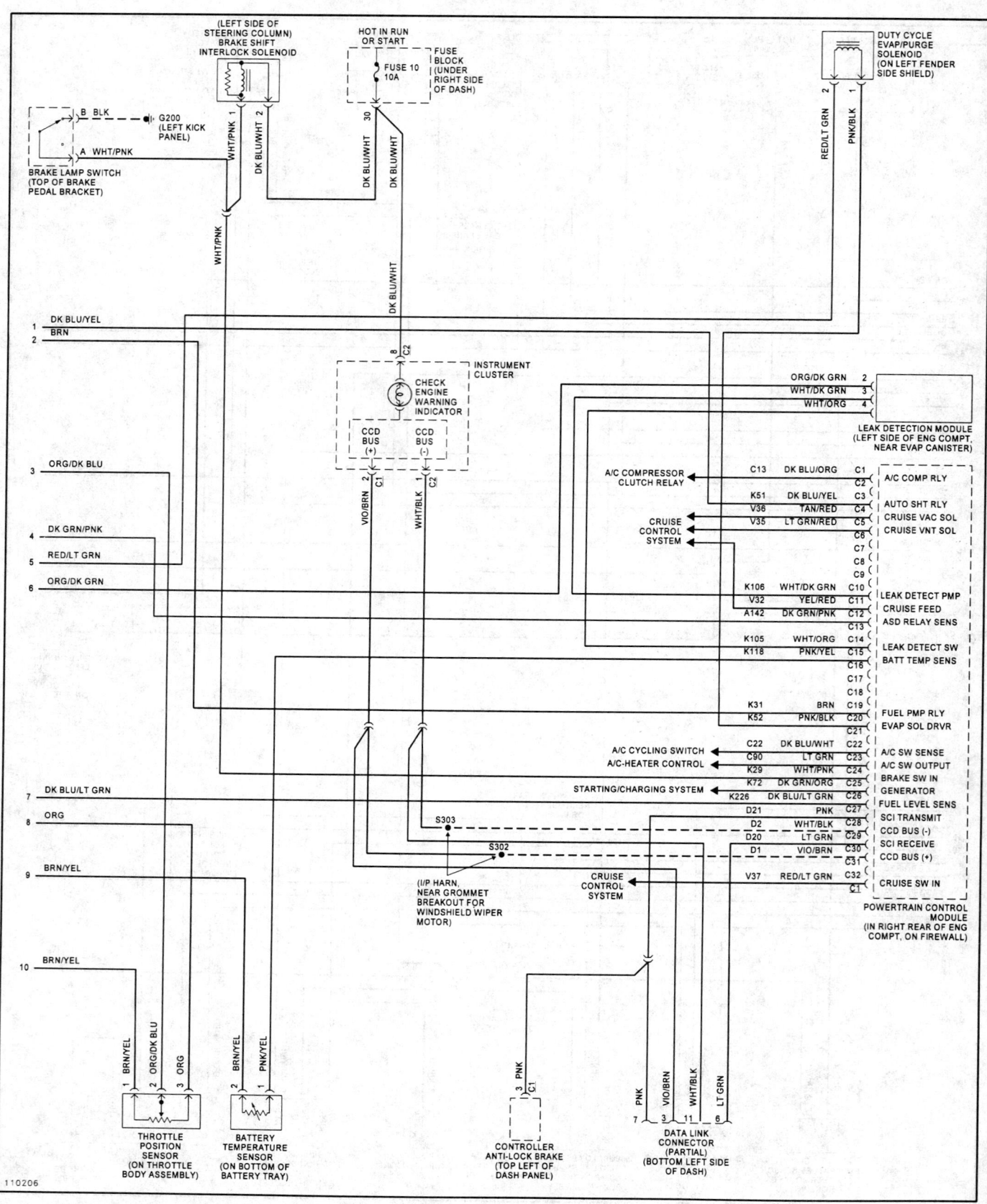

Fig. 18: PCM Wiring Diagram (Wrangler – 4.0L – 3 Of 3)

1999 WIRING DIAGRAMS
Electric Cooling Fans

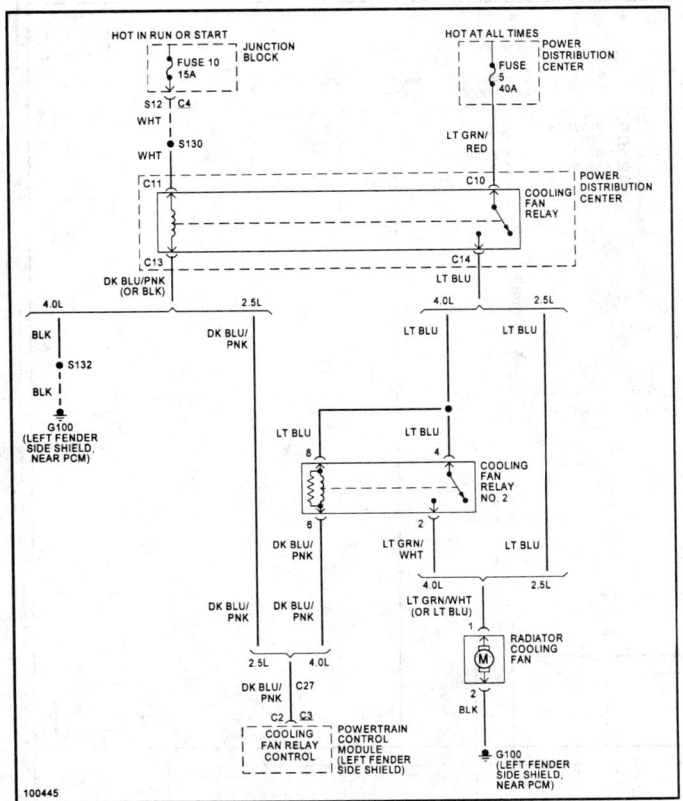

Fig. 1: Electric Cooling Fans Wiring Diagram (Cherokee)

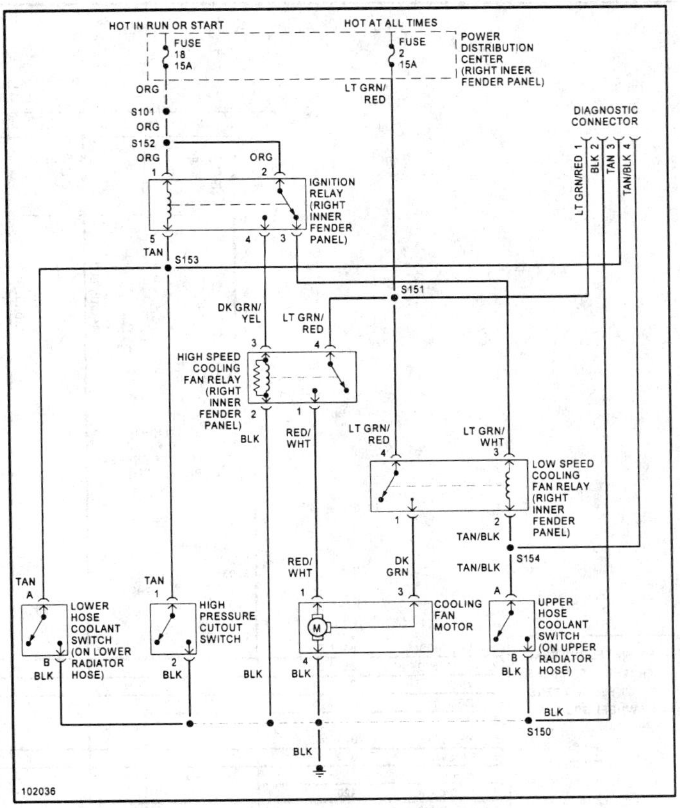

Fig. 2: Electric Cooling Fans Wiring Diagram (Grand Cherokee)

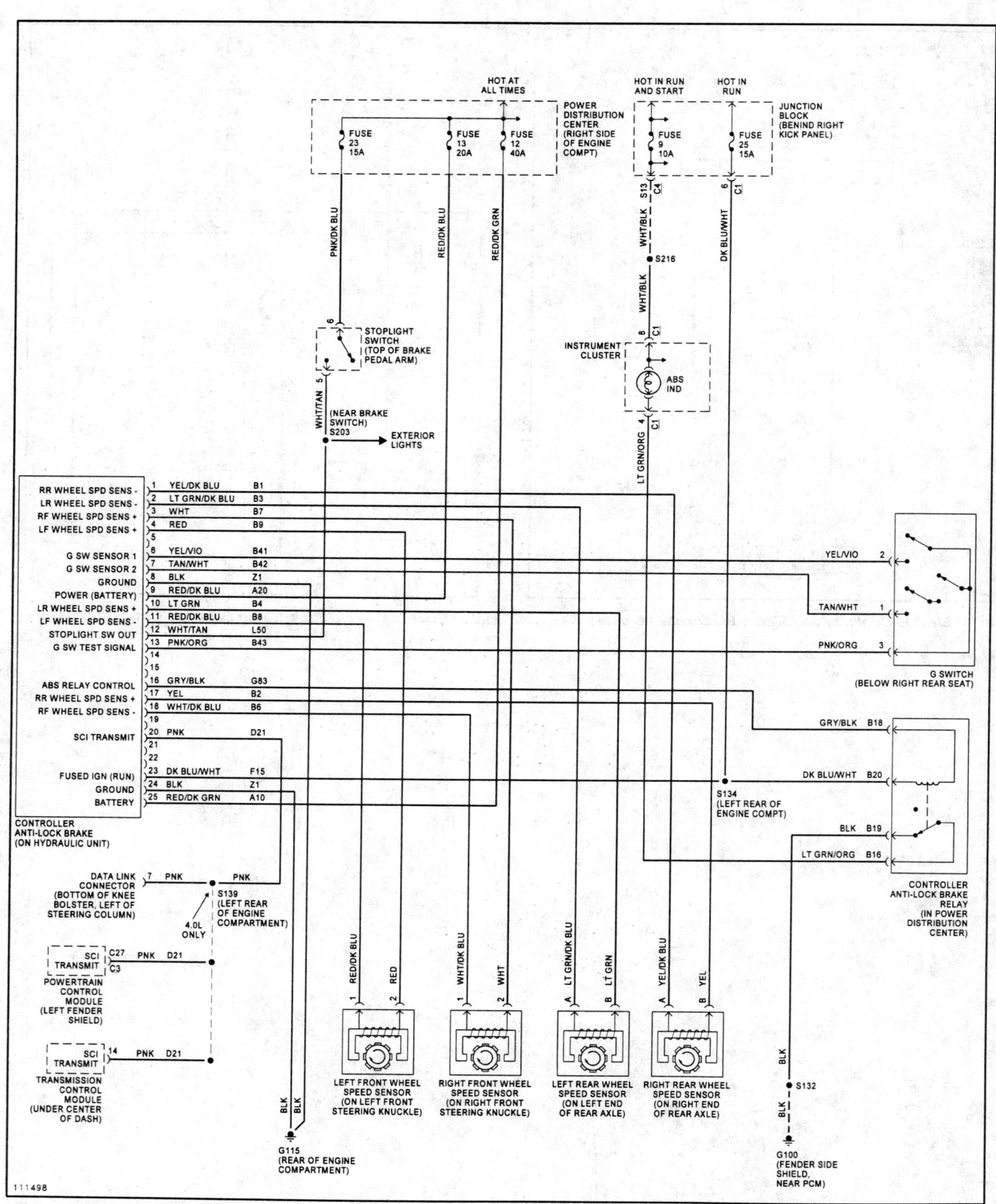

Fig. 1: Anti-Lock Brake System Wiring Diagram (Cherokee)

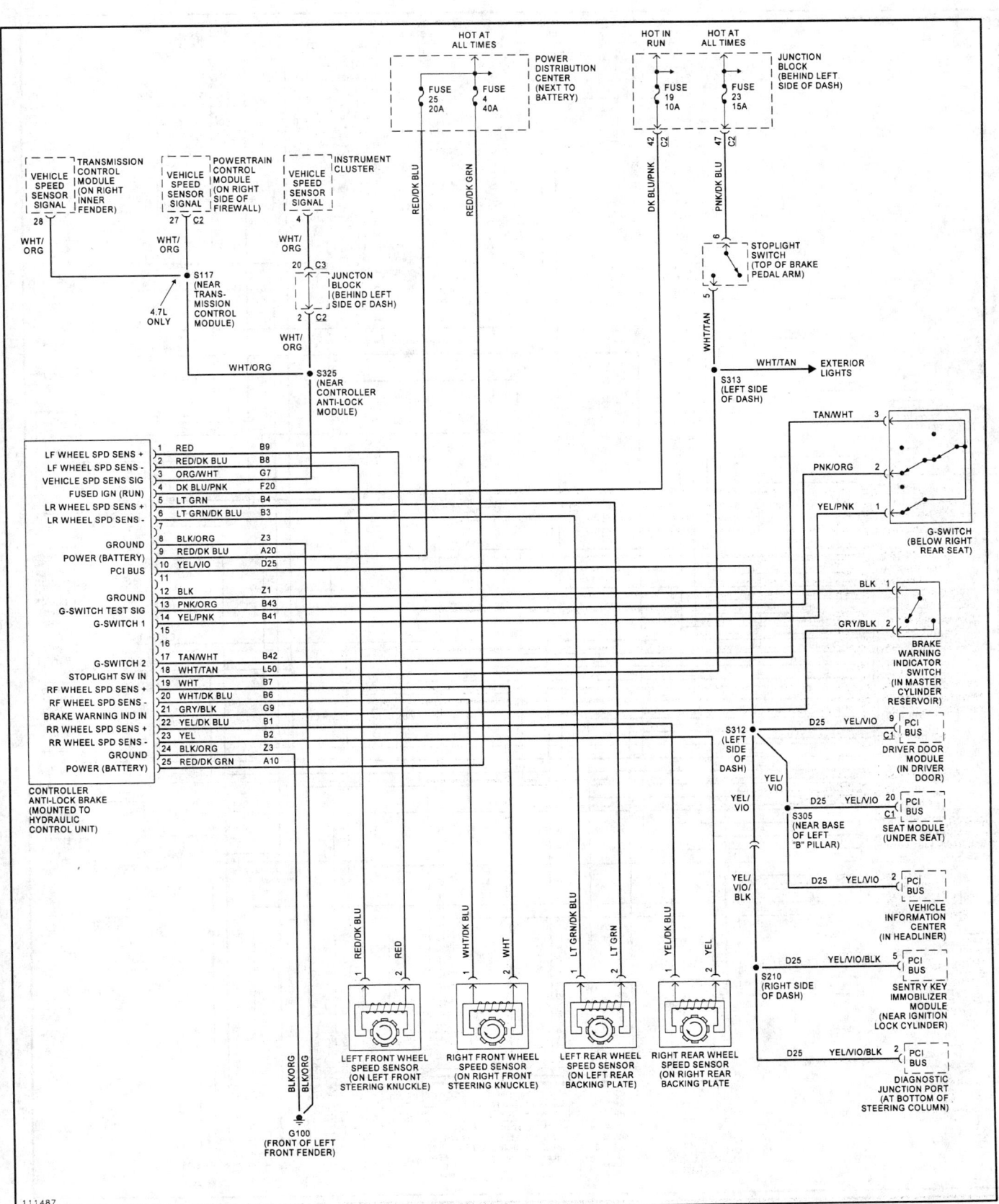

Fig. 2: Anti-Lock Brake System Wiring Diagram (Grand Cherokee)

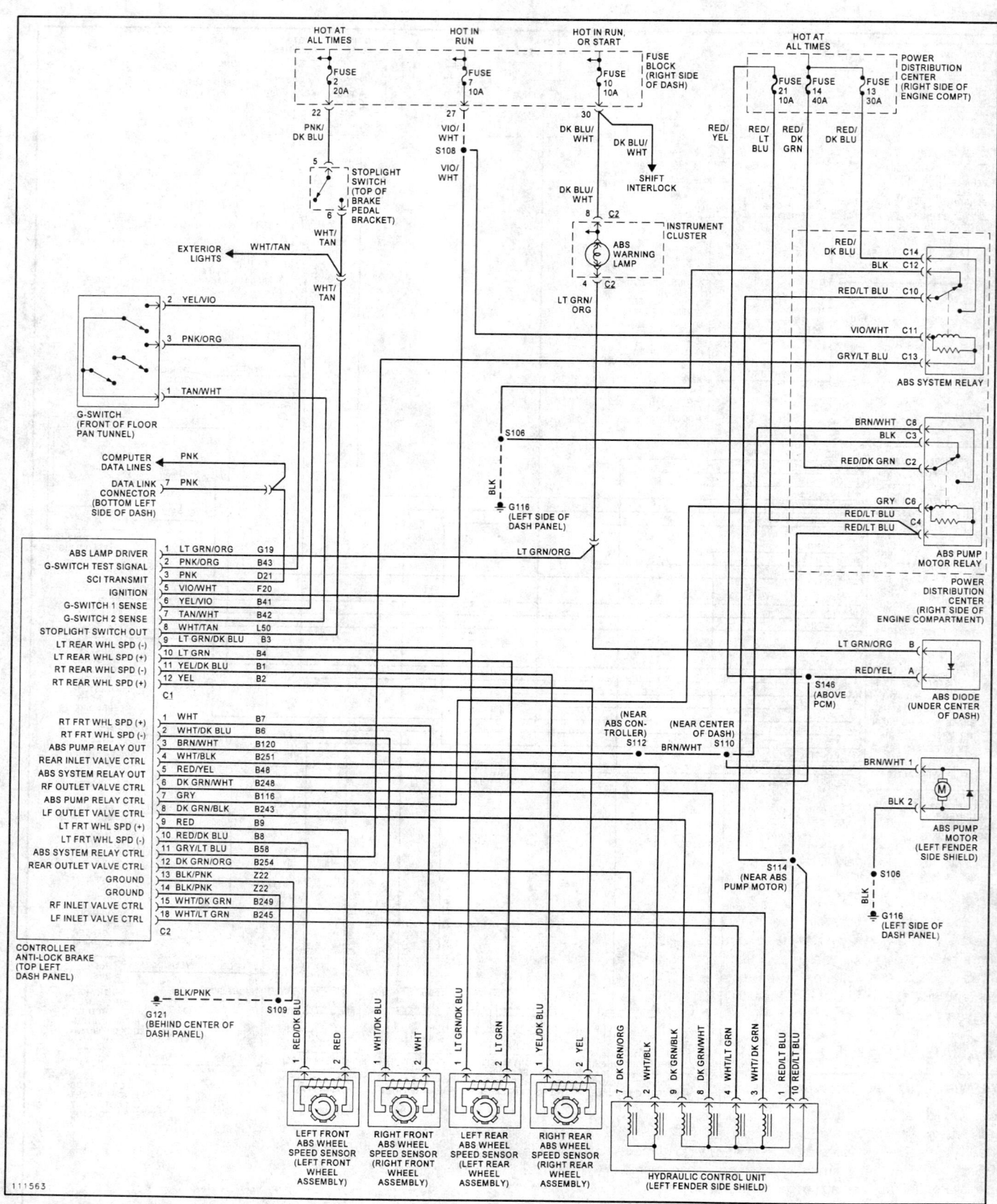

Fig. 3: Anti-Lock Brake System Wiring Diagram (Wrangler)

Air Bag Restraint Systems

Cherokee, Grand Cherokee, Wrangler

NOTE: For information on air bag DIAGNOSIS & TESTING or DISPOSAL PROCEDURES, see MITCHELL® AIR BAG SERVICE & REPAIR MANUAL, DOMESTIC & IMPORTED MODELS.

WARNING: To avoid injury from accidental air bag deployment, read and carefully follow all WARNINGS and SERVICE PRECAUTIONS.

DESCRIPTION & OPERATION

Supplemental Restraint System (SRS) is designed to work in conjunction with seat belts. SRS increases driver and passenger protection from serious injury during a front-end collision. Driver-side air bag is stored in a module in steering wheel hub. Passenger-side air bag is stored in the instrument panel, above glove box. All air bags are covered by a pad bearing the air bag SRS logo.

Air bags inflate and deflate within 1/10th of a second of impact sensor switches closing. This creates a cushion of air between driver and steering wheel, and passenger and instrument panel.

System consists of an AIR BAG warning light, clockspring, driver and passenger-side air bag modules, Air Bag Control Module (ACM), one impact sensor (located inside ACM) and an energy reserve capacitor. The ACM monitors system, stores fault codes (messages) and provides information to AIR BAG warning light and Data Link Connector (DLC). See DATA LINK CONNECTOR LOCATION table. When a malfunction occurs, a fault code is stored and AIR BAG warning light is activated for more than 12 seconds.

When impact sensors register sufficient deceleration force during a front-end collision, an electrical charge is sent from ACM to air bag module inflator via the clockspring. Inflator actuates and produces nitrogen gas, which inflates air bag.

Wrangler is equipped with a passenger-side airbag on/off switch located on front end of console. Switch position can be changed by using ignition key only. When passenger-side airbag is disabled, OFF indicator on switch is illuminated when ignition is turned on.

AIR BAG WARNING LIGHT

Whenever ignition switch is in RUN or START position, AIR BAG warning light on instrument panel will illuminate for 6-8 seconds and then turn off. This signifies ACM has checked the system and found it is functioning properly. If AIR BAG warning light illuminates for 12 seconds or more, stays on all the time or does not come on, a system malfunction exists and trouble code will be stored.

IMPACT SENSOR

All models are equipped with one impact sensor located inside ACM. Impact sensor is an accelerometer that measures deceleration. During a front-end collision, a signal is sent that completes an electrical circuit to inflators. Inflators actuate and produce nitrogen gas, which inflates each air bag. Impact sensor is calibrated for a specific vehicle and react to severity and direction of vehicle impact.

AIR BAG MODULE

WARNING: DO NOT attempt to disassemble air bag modules. Air bag modules are not serviceable.

Driver-Side – Air bag module is mounted on front face of steering wheel. A protective cover is fitted to front of air bag module bearing the SRS air bag logo. Air bag module contains air bag cushion, pyrotechnic-type inflator and supporting components. Air bag module is a sealed unit and is not serviceable. Inflator assembly is mounted to studs on back of airbag module housing. The inflator seals the opening in airbag cushion so it can discharge gas directly into cushion with proper electrical signal. Once air bag cushion is fully inflated, gas escapes from bag through vents, away from driver.

Passenger-Side – The passenger-side air bag module is mounted to instrument panel mounting bracket. Module is covered by a protective door bearing the SRS air bag logo. When supplied electrical signal, inflator will discharge argon gas directly into air bag. When air bag inflates, protective door will pivot aside allowing air bag to deploy. Following deployment, airbag quickly deflates by venting this gas through porous material on end panels of airbag cushion.

AIR BAG CONTROL MODULE (ACM)

Impact sensor, energy reserve capacitor and On-Board Diagnostics (OBD) are an integral part of ACM. ACM monitors critical input and output circuits within air bag system, ensuring they are operating correctly. Some circuits are tested continuously; others are checked only under certain conditions. ACM provides information about air bag system through AIR BAG warning light and Data Link Connector (DLC). See DATA LINK CONNECTOR LOCATION table. When a fault code (message) occurs, AIR BAG warning light will be activated for 12 seconds or more. For ACM location, see AIR BAG CONTROL MODULE LOCATIONS table.

AIR BAG CONTROL MODULE LOCATIONS

Application	Location
Cherokee	Under Driver's Seat
Grand Cherokee	Underneath Floor Console, near Parking Brake Lever Assembly
Wrangler	Under Instrument Panel, On Transmission Tunnel

DATA LINK CONNECTOR (DLC)

DATA LINK CONNECTOR LOCATION

Application	Location
All Models	Under Left Side Of Instrument Panel, Left Of Steering Column

CLOCKSPRING

Clockspring connects air bag module to steering column wiring, completing air bag system circuit. Inside clockspring is a flat, ribbon-like tape of conductive material, which winds and unwinds with steering wheel movement. Clockspring is the most fragile part of air bag system. Clockspring must be centered properly to allow 1 1/2 steering wheel turns in either direction. If clockspring is not centered properly, it can break from stretching or fatigue.

SHORTING BAR

Shorting bar is a device internal to the initiator's (squib) connectors that automatically shorts squib terminals when connector is disconnected.

SYSTEM OPERATION CHECK

WARNING: To avoid possible injury from accidental air bag deployment after repairs, disconnect and isolate negative battery cable. Turn ignition switch to ON position. Ensure no one is inside vehicle and connect negative battery cable. Turn ignition off.

Turn ignition on and observe AIR BAG warning light. AIR BAG warning light should come on for 6-8 seconds, then go out, indicating system is functioning properly. If AIR BAG warning light either fails to come on, blinks on and off, or comes on and stays on, a system malfunction exists. Repair as necessary. See MITCHELL® AIR BAG SERVICE & REPAIR MANUAL, DOMESTIC & IMPORTED MODELS.

SERVICE PRECAUTIONS

The following precautions should be observed when working with air bag system:
• Disable air bag system before servicing any air bag system or steering column component. Failure to do this could result in

accidental air bag deployment and possible personal injury. See DISABLING & ACTIVATING AIR BAG SYSTEM.

- To avoid possible injury from accidental air bag deployment after repairs, disconnect and isolate negative battery terminal. Turn ignition switch to ON position. Ensure no one is inside vehicle and connect negative battery cable. Turn ignition off. Turn ignition on and ensure AIR BAG warning light is working properly and no system faults are indicated. See SYSTEM OPERATION CHECK.
- Before disconnecting ACM, ensure ignition is off and negative battery cable is disconnected.
- Air Bag Control Module (ACM) contains impact sensor which enables SRS to deploy air bags. DO NOT connect ACM connector while battery is connected. Ensure ACM and mounting bracket are securely installed to vehicle whenever ACM is electrically connected to SRS and battery is connected.
- Always wear safety glasses when servicing or handling an air bag.
- Air bag module must be stored in its original special container until used for service. It must be stored in a clean, dry place, away from sources of extreme heat, sparks and high electrical energy.
- When placing a live air bag on a bench or other surface, always face air bag and trim cover up, away from surface. This will reduce motion of module if accidentally deployed.
- Because of critical system operating requirements, DO NOT attempt to service any air bag components. Corrections are only made by replacing defective part.
- Electrical sources should never be allowed near inflator on the back of air bag module.
- DO NOT probe connectors with an ohmmeter unless specifically instructed to do so. Ohmmeters are self-powered and could deploy air bags.
- When carrying a live air bag module, trim cover should be pointed away from your body to minimize injury in case of accidental deployment.
- DO NOT probe any wire through insulator, as this will damage it and eventually cause failure due to corrosion.
- If air bag system is not fully functional for any reason, vehicle should not be driven until system is repaired and again becomes operational. DO NOT remove bulbs, modules, sensors or other components or in any way disable system from operating normally. If air bag system is not functional, park vehicle until it is repaired and functions properly.
- When battery is disconnected, vehicle computer and memory systems may lose memory data. Driveability problems may exist until computer systems have completed a relearn cycle. See COMPUTER RELEARN PROCEDURES in GENERAL INFORMATION before disconnecting battery.

DISABLING & ACTIVATING AIR BAG SYSTEM

WARNING: Wait at least 2 minutes after disconnecting negative battery cable before servicing air bag system. System reserve capacitor, integral to air bag control module, maintains air bag system voltage for about 2 minutes after battery is disconnected. Servicing air bag system before 2-minute period may cause accidental deployment of air bags and possible personal injury. DO NOT use computer system memory saving devices. Enough voltage to deploy air bags may be provided from device.

CAUTION: When battery is disconnected, vehicle computer and memory systems may lose memory data. Driveability problems may exist until computer systems have completed a relearn cycle. See COMPUTER RELEARN PROCEDURES article in GENERAL INFORMATION before disconnecting battery.

DISABLING & ACTIVATING SYSTEM FOR REPAIRS

1) To disable air bag system for repairs, ensure ignition switch is in OFF position. Disconnect and isolate negative battery cable. WAIT at least 2 minutes after disconnecting negative battery cable before servicing air bag system.

2) To activate air bag system, disconnect and isolate negative battery cable. Turn ignition switch to ON position. Ensure no one is inside vehicle and connect negative battery cable.

3) Observe AIR BAG warning light. Warning light should come on for 6-8 seconds and then go out, indicating system is functioning properly. If warning light fails to illuminate, or illuminates and stays on, a system malfunction exists. Repair as necessary. See MITCHELL® AIR BAG SERVICE & REPAIR MANUAL, DOMESTIC & IMPORTED MODELS.

REMOVAL & INSTALLATION

WARNING: Failure to follow air bag service precautions may result in air bag deployment and personal injury. See SERVICE PRECAUTIONS. Air bag parts are not interchangeable between models. Always use NEW parts and correct part number for vehicle being worked on. After component replacement, always perform a system operation check to ensure proper system operation. See SYSTEM OPERATION CHECK.

CAUTION: When battery is disconnected, vehicle computer and memory systems may lose memory data. Driveability problems may exist until computer systems have completed a relearn cycle. DO NOT use computer system memory saving devices. Enough voltage to deploy air bags may be provided from device. See COMPUTER RELEARN PROCEDURES in GENERAL INFORMATION before disconnecting battery.

AIR BAG CONTROL MODULE (ACM)

WARNING: ACM contains impact sensor, which enables SRS to activate air bag. To avoid accidental air bag deployment, DO NOT connect ACM electrically to system unless it is bolted to vehicle. DO NOT strike or kick ACM. If ACM is accidentally dropped during installation, it must be replaced

Removal (Cherokee) – 1) Before proceeding, follow air bag service precautions. See SERVICE PRECAUTIONS. Disable air bag system. See DISABLING & ACTIVATING AIR BAG SYSTEM.

2) ACM is located under driver's seat. Remove driver's seat-to-floor pan bolts/nuts. Disconnect seat belt buckle warning light connector and power seat motor connector (if equipped). Remove driver's seat from vehicle.

3) Remove ACM cover screws. *See Fig. 1.* Pull ACM cover back far enough to access and release ACM wiring harness retainer from slotted hole near rear of cover. Remove ACM cover.

4) Squeeze 2 connector latch tabs, and remove connector from ACM. Remove ACM mounting bracket-to-floor pan seat mounting bracket screws. Remove ACM.

Installation – 1) Install ACM with arrow pointing toward front of vehicle. Tighten ACM mounting screws to specification. See TORQUE SPECIFICATIONS table. Connect ACM connector, ensuring connector latches are fully engaged.

2) Position ACM cover over ACM. Ensure wiring harness retainer is installed correctly in slotted hole of ACM cover. To complete installation, reverse removal procedure. DO NOT connect negative battery cable at this time. See DISABLING & ACTIVATING AIR BAG SYSTEM.

Removal (Grand Cherokee) – 1) Before proceeding, follow air bag service precautions. See SERVICE PRECAUTIONS. Disable air bag system. See DISABLING & ACTIVATING AIR BAG SYSTEM.

2) ACM is located underneath floor console, near parking brake lever assembly. Set parking brake. Place transmission shift lever and transfer case lever in full rearward position. Remove mat from front of bin and remove screws under mat.

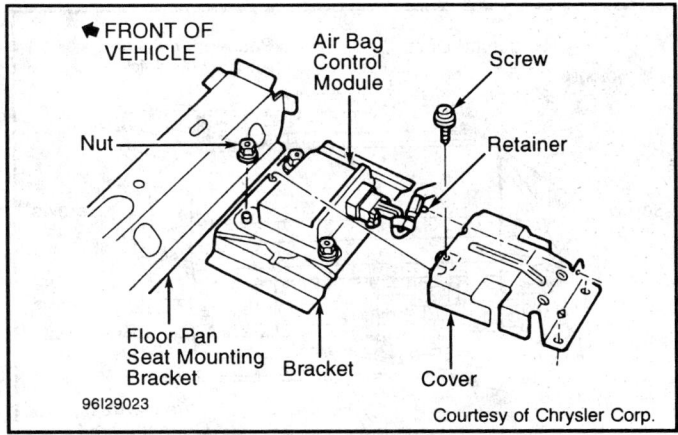

Fig. 1: Locating Air Bag Control Module (Cherokee)

3) Remove screws attaching rear bin to console. Remove rear bin. Pull rear cupholder outward to access screws. Remove screws attaching rear of console to floor. To remove console, lift upward and rearward.

4) Remove nut attaching center console bracket to stud on transmission tunnel in front of ACM. *See Fig. 2.* Remove center console bracket. Disconnect ACM wire connector. Remove 4 ACM mounting screws. Remove ACM.

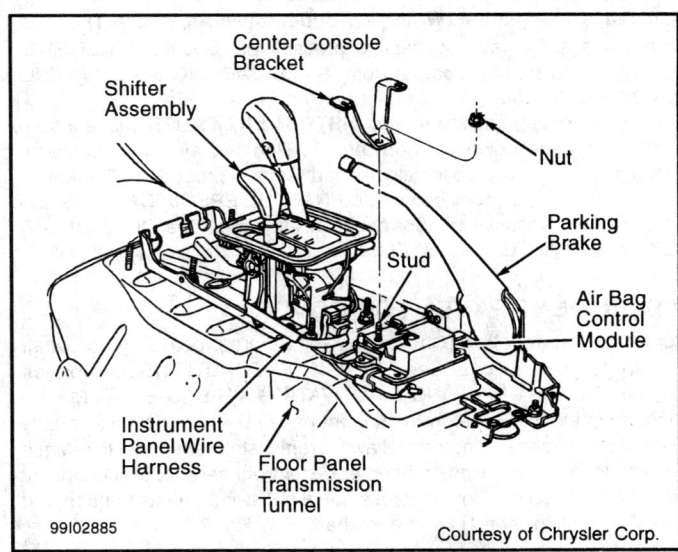

Fig. 2: Identifying Center Console Bracket (Grand Cherokee)

Installation – 1) Position ACM on floor bracket with arrow pointing toward front of vehicle. Ensure keyway on bottom of ACM housing is aligned and ACM is flush with floor bracket. Install ACM mounting screws and tighten to specification. See TORQUE SPECIFICATIONS.

2) Reconnect ACM wire connector. To complete installation, reverse removal procedure. DO NOT connect negative battery cable at this time. See DISABLING & ACTIVATING AIR BAG SYSTEM.

Removal (Wrangler) – 1) Before proceeding, follow air bag service precautions. See SERVICE PRECAUTIONS. Disable air bag system. See DISABLING & ACTIVATING AIR BAG SYSTEM.

CAUTION: *Always replace ACM and ACM mounting bracket as an assembly. Replacement modules include a NEW mounting bracket. DO NOT mount NEW ACM to old mounting bracket.*

2) ACM is located under instrument panel, on transmission tunnel. *See Fig. 3.* Pull carpet back from area under heater-A/C housing floor duct. If vehicle is equipped with ABS, remove acceleration switch and mounting bracket from transmission tunnel.

3) Remove 4 ACM mounting bracket screws. Slide ACM and mounting bracket out from under heater floor duct enough to access ACM wire

connector. Disconnect ACM connector. Pull 2 white locks out about .12″ (3.0 mm). Squeeze 2 connector latch tabs and pull connector from ACM. *See Fig. 4.* Remove ACM.

Installation – 1) Reconnect ACM wire connector. Ensure connector latches are fully engaged and connector locks are pushed in. Install ACM with arrow pointing toward front of vehicle. Install and tighten mounting screws to specification. See TORQUE SPECIFICATIONS table.

2) To complete installation, reverse removal procedure. DO NOT connect negative battery cable at this time. See DISABLING & ACTIVATING AIR BAG SYSTEM.

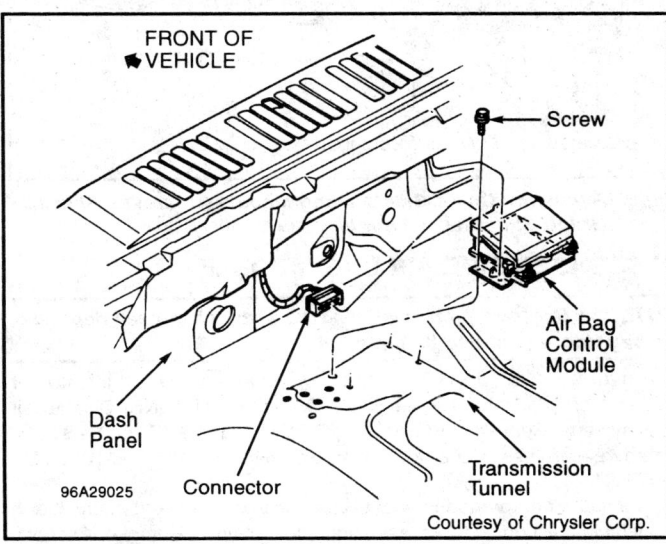

Fig. 3: Locating Air Bag Control Module (Wrangler)

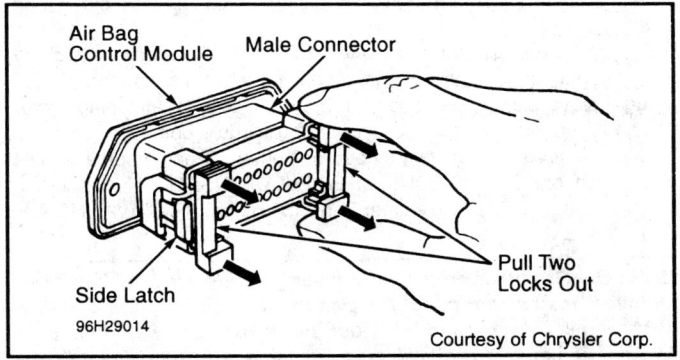

Fig. 4: Disconnect ACM Connector (Wrangler)

DRIVER-SIDE AIR BAG MODULE

NOTE: *When removing a deployed air bag, wear eye protection, rubber gloves and a long-sleeve shirt. Powder residue from air bag deployment may irritate skin and eyes.*

Removal – 1) Before proceeding, follow air bag service precautions. See SERVICE PRECAUTIONS. Disable air bag system. See DISABLING & ACTIVATING AIR BAG SYSTEM. Air bag module is mounted on face of steering wheel. *See Fig. 5.*

CAUTION: *Clockspring must be replaced whenever replacing a deployed air bag. See CLOCKSPRING under REMOVAL & INSTALLATION.*

2) Ensure wheels are pointed straight-ahead and steering wheel is locked. Remove air bag module-to-steering wheel screws from back side of steering wheel. Lift air bag module and disconnect wiring harness connectors from rear of module.

Installation – Connect wiring harness connectors to rear of air bag module, and secure module to steering wheel. Tighten air bag module-to-steering wheel screws to specification. See TORQUE SPECIFICATIONS table. DO NOT connect negative battery cable at this time. See DISABLING & ACTIVATING AIR BAG SYSTEM.

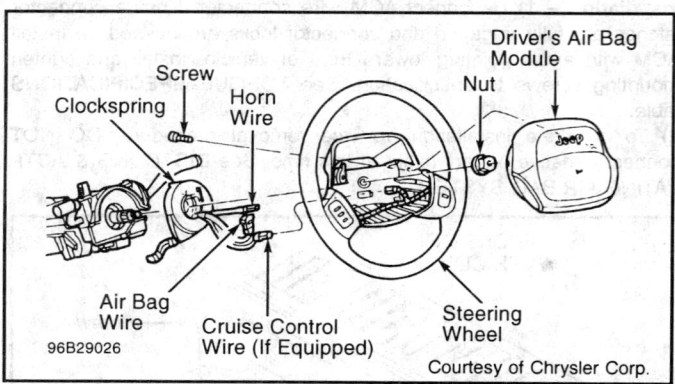

Fig. 5: Removing Driver-Side Air Bag Module (Cherokee Shown; Grand Cherokee & Wrangler Are Similar)

PASSENGER-SIDE AIR BAG MODULE

NOTE: On Cherokee, if passenger-side air bag has been deployed, air bag door must also be replaced.

Removal & Installation (Cherokee) – 1) Before proceeding, follow air bag service precautions. See SERVICE PRECAUTIONS. Disable air bag system. See DISABLING & ACTIVATING AIR BAG SYSTEM. Remove instrument panel top cover. See INSTRUMENT PANEL TOP COVER.

2) Unplug air bag module connector located between module and windshield. Disconnect harness connector retainer. Remove 4 screws attaching upper air bag door flange to instrument panel. Remove 2 screws attaching upper module mounting brackets. Roll glove box down.

3) Reach through glove box opening and remove 4 screws attaching lower air bag door flange to instrument panel reinforcement. Reach through glove box opening and remove 2 screws attaching lower module mounting bracket. Remove air bag module unit.

4) To install, reverse removal procedure. Tighten air bag module screws to specification. See TORQUE SPECIFICATIONS. DO NOT connect negative battery cable at this time. See DISABLING & ACTIVATING AIR BAG SYSTEM.

NOTE: On Grand Cherokee, if passenger-side air bag has been deployed, instrument panel top pad must be replaced and instrument panel structural duct must be inspected. See Fig. 6. If instrument panel structural duct is damaged, instrument panel must be replaced.

Removal & Installation (Grand Cherokee) – 1) Before proceeding, follow air bag service precautions. See SERVICE PRECAUTIONS. Disable air bag system. See DISABLING & ACTIVATING AIR BAG SYSTEM. Remove instrument panel top pad. See INSTRUMENT PANEL TOP PAD. Disconnect passenger-side air bag module wire connector. Remove 4 passenger-side air bag module screws. Remove air bag module.

2) To install, reverse removal procedure. Tighten air bag module screws to specification. See TORQUE SPECIFICATIONS. DO NOT connect negative battery cable at this time. See DISABLING & ACTIVATING AIR BAG SYSTEM.

NOTE: On Wrangler, if passenger-side air bag has been deployed, instrument panel assembly must be replaced. Replacement instrument panel is equipped with a NEW passenger air bag module and air bag door.

Removal (Wrangler; Deployed Air Bag) – Before proceeding, follow air bag service precautions. See SERVICE PRECAUTIONS. Disable air bag system. See DISABLING & ACTIVATING AIR BAG SYSTEM. Remove instrument panel. See INSTRUMENT PANEL.

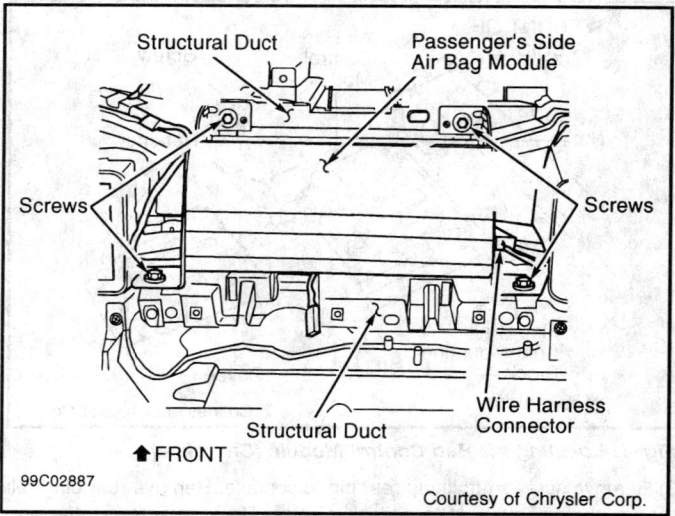

Fig. 6: Identifying Instrument Panel Structural Duct

Installation – Remove all reusable components from old instrument panel to NEW instrument panel. To complete installation, reverse removal procedure. DO NOT connect negative battery cable at this time. See DISABLING & ACTIVATING AIR BAG SYSTEM.

Removal & Installation (Wrangler; Undeployed Air Bag) – 1) Before proceeding, follow air bag service precautions. See SERVICE PRECAUTIONS. Disable air bag system. See DISABLING & ACTIVATING AIR BAG SYSTEM.

2) Remove instrument panel. See INSTRUMENT PANEL. Place instrument panel face down on work bench. Remove air bag module-to-instrument panel nuts. To install, reverse removal procedure. Tighten air bag module nuts to specification. See TORQUE SPECIFICATIONS. DO NOT connect negative battery cable at this time. See DISABLING & ACTIVATING AIR BAG SYSTEM.

INSTRUMENT PANEL TOP COVER

Removal & Installation (Cherokee) – 1) Before proceeding, follow air bag service precautions. See SERVICE PRECAUTIONS. Disable air bag system. See DISABLING & ACTIVATING AIR BAG SYSTEM.

2) Remove trim panel below instrument panel. Using a trim stick, gently pry instrument panel center bezel away from instrument panel to release 6 snap clip retainers. Remove center bezel from vehicle. Pull headlight switch knob to on position. Depress headlight switch release button and remove headlight switch knob and shaft. See Fig. 7.

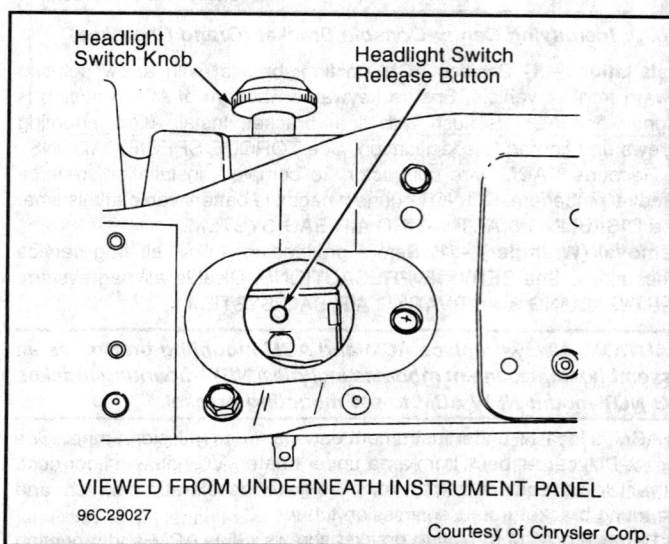

Fig. 7: Removing Headlight Switch Shaft (Cherokee)

3) Disengage 2 ends of steering column sight shield from each other at connector located below lower steering column cover. *See Fig. 8.* Remove 4 screws behind instrument cluster bezel that retain bezel to instrument panel. Using a trim stick, gently pry around perimeter of instrument cluster bezel and remove bezel.

4) Using a trim stick, gently pry rear edge (nearest passenger compartment) of instrument panel top cover up and away from top of instrument panel. *See Fig. 9.* Lift rear edge of top cover up and away from instrument panel until all rear snap clip retainers (7) on top cover are disengaged. Pull top cover sharply rearwards to disengage 4 front snap clip retainers.

5) Remove top cover from vehicle. To install, reverse removal procedure. DO NOT connect negative battery cable at this time. See DISABLING & ACTIVATING AIR BAG SYSTEM.

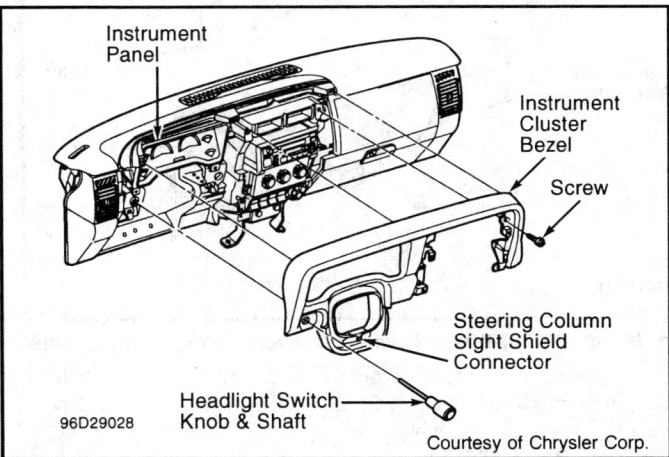

Fig. 8: Removing Instrument Cluster Bezel (Cherokee)

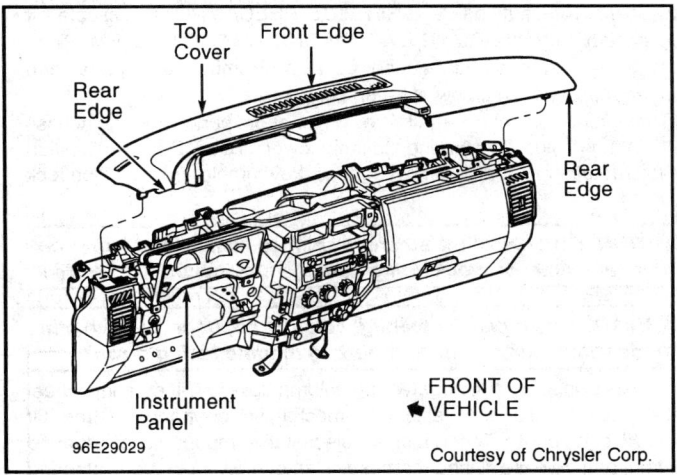

Fig. 9: Removing Instrument Panel Top Cover (Cherokee)

Removal & Installation (Grand Cherokee) – Before proceeding, follow air bag service precautions. See SERVICE PRECAUTIONS. Disable air bag system. See DISABLING & ACTIVATING AIR BAG SYSTEM. Using a trim stick, gently pry rear edge of top cover upward enough to disengage 4 snap clip retainers. Remove top cover. To install, reverse removal procedure.

INSTRUMENT PANEL TOP PAD (GRAND CHEROKEE)

Removal – **1)** Before proceeding, follow air bag service precautions. See SERVICE PRECAUTIONS. Disable air bag system. See DISABLING & ACTIVATING AIR BAG SYSTEM.

2) Remove A-pillar trim panels. Remove instrument panel top cover. See INSTRUMENT PANEL TOP COVER. Remove 4 nuts holding instrument panel top pad to studs on instrument panel. If vehicle is equipped with instrument panel speakers, remove speakers from instrument panel top pad. Disconnect wire connectors from speakers and secure wires aside.

3) Remove security indicator/light sensor screws assembly from instrument panel top pad and set aside. Remove cluster bezel. See CLUSTER BEZEL. Remove 4 instrument cluster-to-instrument panel screws. Pull top of cluster downward and rearward enough to disconnect instrument cluster wire connector. Remove instrument cluster.

4) Remove 3 screws holding steering column opening cover to instrument panel. Pull steering column opening cover rearward to disengage 3 snap clips. Remove steering column opening cover. Roll glove box down. Remove 4 screws holding instrument panel end cap to instrument panel. Pull instrument panel end cap rearward enough to disengage snap clip. Remove end cap.

5) Remove 3 screws holding lower right center bezel to glove box opening. Pull lower right center bezel rearward enough to disengage 2 snap clips. Remove lower right center bezel. Remove glove box lamp and switch. Remove 2 large screws holding instrument panel top pad to instrument panel structural duct.

6) Remove 2 small screws holding panel outlet vents to instrument panel structural duct. Using a trim stick, gently pry 4 corners of center upper bezel and center lower bezel away from instrument panel. Disconnect instrument panel wire connectors from center lower bezel. Remove both center bezels.

7) Remove 4 radio mounting screws. Remove 4 heater-A/C control screws. Pull radio and heater-A/C control out enough to access screws holding top pad to instrument panel structural duct. Remove all screws holding perimeter of top pad to instrument panel structural duct.

8) Remove front bin from floor console. Working through front bin opening, loosen 2 nuts holding center floor tunnel bracket to studs on transmission tunnel. Slide center floor tunnel bracket rearward enough to disengage locating hole in lower flange of top pad from locating pin on instrument panel structural duct. Remove instrument panel top pad.

Installation – Transfer components being reused to new instrument panel top pad. Position top pad over instrument panel structural duct and studs on dash panel. Route wire harness in its original location. To complete installation, reverse removal procedure. Tighten fasteners to specification. See TORQUE SPECIFICATIONS. DO NOT connect negative battery cable at this time. See DISABLING & ACTIVATING AIR BAG SYSTEM.

CLUSTER BEZEL

Removal & Installation (Grand Cherokee) – **1)** Disconnect negative battery cable. Tilt steering wheel to lowest position. Using a trim stick, gently pry corners of cluster bezel away from instrument panel to disengage retaining clips. Carefully roll top of cluster bezel rearward over top of steering column and remove. DO NOT scratch cluster lens with cluster bezel retaining clips.

2) To install, carefully align lower cluster bezel retaining clips with receptacles in instrument panel. Push firmly on cluster bezel to engage lower retaining clips. Align upper retaining clips and engage into instrument panel receptacles. Reconnect negative battery cable.

INSTRUMENT PANEL

Removal (Grand Cherokee) – **1)** Before proceeding, follow air bag service precautions. See SERVICE PRECAUTIONS. Disable air bag system. See DISABLING & ACTIVATING AIR BAG SYSTEM. Place front wheels in a straight-ahead position. Remove trim panel and support bracket from below steering column.

2) Ensure steering wheel in straight ahead position. Remove A-pillar trim panels. Remove instrument panel top cover. See INSTRUMENT PANEL TOP COVER. Remove 4 nuts holding instrument panel to dash panel. Using a trim stick, pry scuff plates from door sills and remove. Remove trim panels from cowl sides.

3) Set parking brake. Place transmission shift lever and transfer case lever in full rearward position. Remove mat from front of bin and remove screws under mat. Remove screws attaching rear bin to console. Remove rear bin. Pull rear cupholder outward to access screws. Remove screws attaching rear of console to floor. Lift console upward and remove.

4) Remove instrument panel fuse cover. Remove cluster bezel. See CLUSTER BEZEL. Remove 3 screws holding steering column opening cover to instrument panel. Pull steering column opening cover rearward to disengage 3 snap clips. Remove steering column opening cover.

5) Remove 4 screws holding instrument panel steering column bracket to instrument panel steering column support bracket. Remove instrument panel steering column bracket. Remove steering column shrouds. Disconnect wire connectors from clockspring, multifunction switches, ignition switch, shifter interlock solenoid and Sentry Key Immobilizer Module (if equipped).

6) Turn ignition switch to ON position. Remove shifter interlock cable connector from ignition lock housing receptacle. Turn ignition switch to LOCK position. Remove bolt holding coupler to lower steering column shaft. Remove 4 nuts holding steering column to instrument panel steering column support bracket.

7) Ensure steering column is locked. Remove steering column. Disconnect body wire harness bulkhead connectors, Ignition Off Draw (IOD) wire connector and power supply connector from junction block. *See Fig. 10.* Disconnect wire connectors from ACM, parking brake switch and shifter.

8) Remove 2 nuts holding instrument panel ground eyelets to studs on transmission tunnel. Disengage wire harness retainers from transmission tunnel. Remove instrument panel-to-center floor tunnel bracket. Remove screw holding driver-side floor duct to heater-A/C housing.

9) If vehicle is equipped with manual heater-A/C system, disconnect vacuum harness connector located behind driver-side floor duct. Remove screw holding instrument panel steering column support bracket to heater-A/C housing. Remove screw holding instrument panel steering column support bracket to intermediate bracket on driver-side dash panel.

10) Remove nut holding instrument panel steering column support bracket to stud on driver-side cowl plenum panel. Remove 2 screws holding instrument panel to driver-side cowl side inner panel. Remove 4 screws holding instrument panel end cap to instrument panel. Pull instrument panel end cap rearward enough to disengage snap clip. Remove end cap.

11) Remove 3 screws holding lower right center bezel to glove box opening. Pull lower right center bezel rearward enough to disengage 2 snap clips. Remove lower right center bezel. Disconnect instrument panel bulkhead connector from lower cavity of inline connector on passenger-side cowl side inner panel.

12) Disconnect radio antenna coaxial cable at connector near right cowl side inner panel. Disconnect 2 instrument panel wire connectors from heater-A/C housing connectors located near blower motor. Remove 2 screws holding passenger-side instrument panel structural duct to heater-A/C housing.

13) Remove 2 screws holding instrument panel to passenger-side cowl side inner panel. With aid of an assistant, lift instrument panel upward off studs near windshield and to disengage plastic hook formations on instrument panel structural duct from holes at cowl side inner panels. Pull instrument panel rearward and remove through driver's door.

Installation – 1) Loosen 3 nuts holding instrument panel intermediate bracket and accelerator pedal assembly to studs on dash panel. With aid of an assistant, hang instrument panel on studs on dash panel. Ensure plastic hook formations are engaged in holes at cowl side inner panels. Install, but do not tighten, 2 screws holding ends of instrument panel to cowl side inner panels.

2) Install and tighten screws holding instrument panel structural duct to heater-A/C housing. Install and tighten screw holding instrument panel steering column support bracket to driver-side end of heater-A/C housing. Tighten 2 screws holding ends of instrument panel to cowl side inner panels to specification.

3) Install and tighten screw holding instrument panel steering column support bracket to intermediate bracket on dash panel. Tighten 3 nuts holding instrument panel intermediate bracket and accelerator pedal assembly to studs on dash panel.

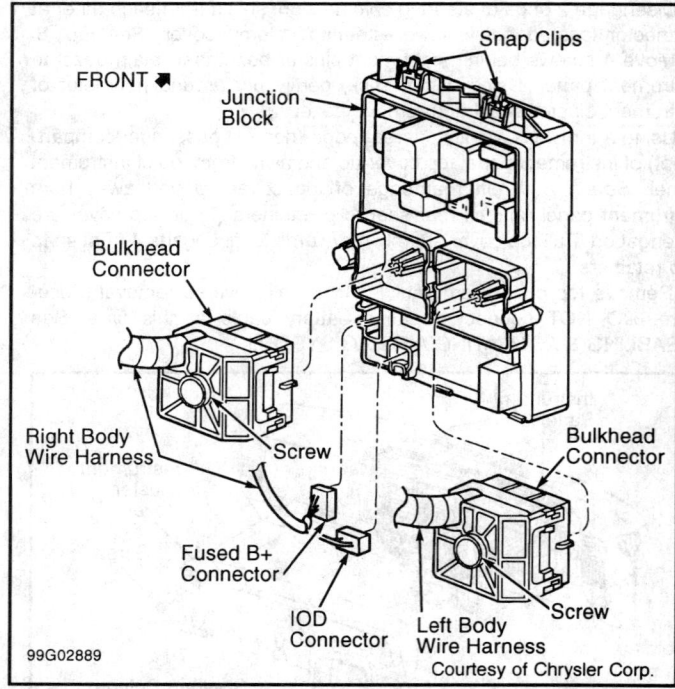

Fig. 10: Identifying Wiring Harness Connectors In Junction Block

4) To complete installation, reverse removal procedure. Tighten all fasteners to specification. See TORQUE SPECIFICATIONS. DO NOT connect negative battery cable at this time. See DISABLING & ACTIVATING AIR BAG SYSTEM.

Removal & Installation (Wrangler) – 1) Before proceeding, follow air bag service precautions. See SERVICE PRECAUTIONS. Disable air bag system. See DISABLING & ACTIVATING AIR BAG SYSTEM. Place front wheels in a straight-ahead position. Remove trim panel and support bracket from below steering column.

2) Turn ignition on. Insert small screwdriver or pin punch through access hole in right side of steering column lower cover. Depress ignition tumbler retaining pin and remove ignition key tumbler from ignition lock housing.

CAUTION: DO NOT allow steering shaft to rotate in steering column at any time, or clockspring damage may occur.

WARNING: Never place steering column on floor or any other surface with steering wheel or air bag module facing down.

3) Remove upper and lower steering column covers. Tilt steering wheel to its lowest position and release tilt mechanism control cable from tilt lever (if equipped). Disconnect all electrical components of steering column and release wiring harness. Remove lock-pin from steering column coupler. Remove steering column mounting nuts and remove steering column from vehicle.

4) Reach through lower steering column opening and disconnect 100-pin connector, located near cowl side panel. Disconnect side window demister/defroster ducting from A/C-heater housing for driver-side window. Remove glove box assembly. Reach through glove box opening and disconnect temperature control cable from A/C-heater housing.

5) Disconnect side window demister/defroster ducting for passenger-side window. Disconnect electrical and vacuum harness connectors. Disconnect passenger-side air bag module connector. Disconnect antenna, radio connector and radio ground strap (if equipped).

6) Remove 2 nuts securing lower air bag module bracket to studs of dash panel. Remove 2 bolts from instrument panel located near door hinge pillars. Using a trim stick, remove instrument panel top cover. Remove 4 nuts securing top of instrument panel to dash panel. With the aid of an assistant, remove instrument panel from vehicle.

7) To install, reverse removal procedure. DO NOT connect negative battery cable at this time. See DISABLING & ACTIVATING AIR BAG SYSTEM.

CLOCKSPRING

CAUTION: Failure to position wheels in the straight-ahead position with steering wheel locked when removing steering wheel could damage clockspring and/or require clockspring to be readjusted.

NOTE: Clockspring is self-centering and will automatically lock in the centered position when steering wheel is removed. Adjustment is only required if centering position is disturbed.

Removal (Cherokee & Wrangler) – 1) If replacing a deployed air bag, clockspring must be replaced. Before proceeding, follow air bag service precautions. See SERVICE PRECAUTIONS. Disable air bag system. See DISABLING & ACTIVATING AIR BAG SYSTEM.

2) Clockspring is located behind steering wheel. Ensure front wheels are pointed straight ahead, and lock steering wheel. Remove driver-side air bag module. See DRIVER-SIDE AIR BAG MODULE. Disconnect cruise control connector (if equipped).

3) Remove steering wheel nut. Using Steering Wheel Puller (C-3428B), remove steering wheel. When steering wheel is removed, self-centering clockspring will automatically lock in place. Set tilt steering column to its fully raised position (if equipped). Remove cover from bottom of steering column. Turn ignition on.

4) Insert a small punch into access hole in right side of lower steering column cover and depress ignition lock cylinder retainer tumbler. While holding retaining tumbler depressed, pull ignition lock cylinder and key out of ignition lock housing.

5) On models with tilt steering, set tilt steering to its lowest position. On models without tilt steering, loosen 2 upper steering column mounting bolts. On all models, remove upper and lower steering column covers. Disconnect clockspring connectors. Remove clockspring. *See Fig. 11.*

6) If reusing clockspring, lock clockspring rotor to clockspring case to maintain centering. Insert a stiff wire through index hole at 11 o'clock position in centered clockspring and case. *See Fig. 11.* Bend wire over to prevent it from falling out.

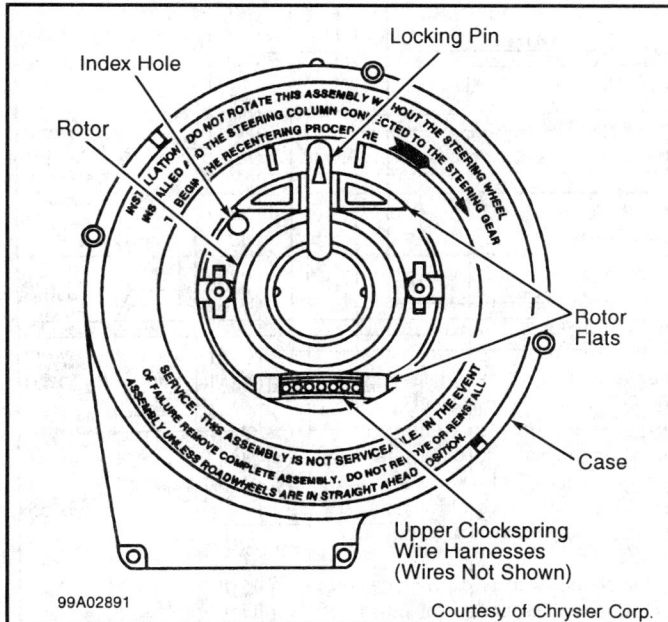

99A02891   Courtesy of Chrysler Corp.

Fig. 11: Identifying Clockspring (Cherokee & Wrangler)

Installation – Snap clockspring onto steering column. If clockspring centering adjustment is disturbed, adjust clockspring before installing steering wheel. See CLOCKSPRING CENTERING under ADJUSTMENTS. Connect clockspring wiring connectors. Install steering column covers. To complete installation, reverse removal procedure.

Removal (Grand Cherokee) – 1) If replacing a deployed air bag, clockspring must be replaced. Before proceeding, follow air bag service precautions. See SERVICE PRECAUTIONS. Disable air bag system. See DISABLING & ACTIVATING AIR BAG SYSTEM.

2) Clockspring is located behind steering wheel. Ensure front wheels are pointed straight ahead, and lock steering wheel. Remove driver-side air bag module. See DRIVER-SIDE AIR BAG MODULE. Disconnect upper clockspring connector. Remove steering wheel nut.

3) Using Steering Wheel Puller (C-3894A), remove steering wheel. Ensure jaws of puller are seated into pockets on sides of steering wheel hub. If reusing clockspring, DO NOT damage clockspring with puller. Remove upper and lower steering column covers. Disconnect lower clockspring connectors.

4) Remove 2 screws holding clockspring to steering column housing. Slide clockspring off steering column shaft. Clockspring cannot be repaired and must be replaced if faulty or damaged.

Installation – 1) Replacement clockspring is centered with a locking pin installed. DO NOT remove locking pin until clockspring is installed on steering column. If clockspring centering adjustment is disturbed, adjust clockspring before installing steering wheel. See CLOCKSPRING CENTERING under ADJUSTMENTS.

2) While holding centered clockspring hub and case together, slide clockspring over steering column shaft. Align 3 pins in clockspring hub with 3 holes in hub of turn signal cancelling cam. Uppermost pin in clockspring is oblong and will only fit in oblong hole. *See Fig. 12.* Install and tighten 2 clockspring mounting screws. To complete installation, reverse removal procedure.

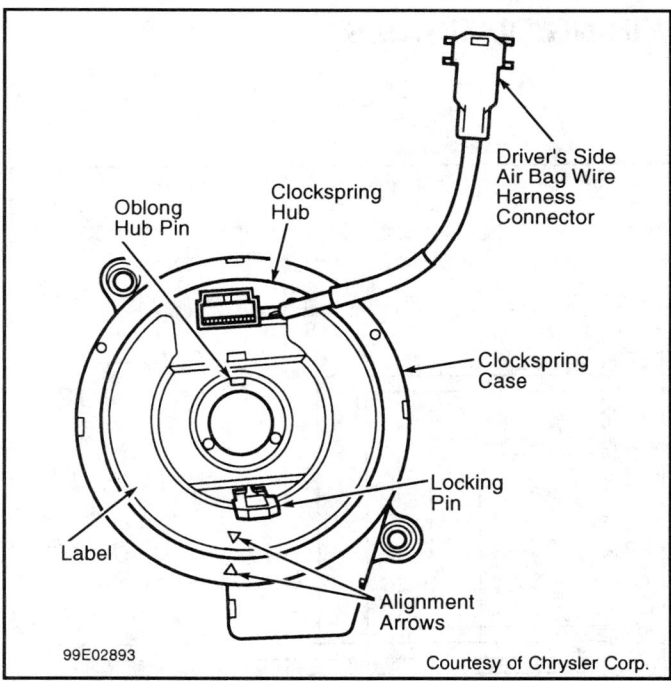

99E02893   Courtesy of Chrysler Corp.

Fig. 12: Identifying Clockspring (Grand Cherokee)

ADJUSTMENTS

CLOCKSPRING CENTERING

CAUTION: If rotating part of clockspring is not positioned properly with steering column and front wheels, clockspring failure may result. The following procedure must be used to center clockspring.

1) Before proceeding, follow air bag service precautions. See SERVICE PRECAUTIONS. Disable air bag system. See DISABLING & ACTIVATING AIR BAG SYSTEM.

2) Place front wheels in straight-ahead position. If clockspring is not already removed, remove driver-side air bag module and clockspring.

See DRIVER-SIDE AIR BAG MODULE and CLOCKSPRING. Rotate clockspring rotor in clockwise direction to the end of its travel. Do not apply excessive torque.

3) From the end of its travel, rotate rotor 2 1/2 full turns in counterclockwise direction. On Cherokee and Wrangler, if clockspring wiring is not at the bottom, rotate clockspring another 1/2 turn. *See Fig. 11.* On Grand Cherokee, align arrows and ensure oblong pin is at uppermost position. *See Fig. 12.*

4) On all models, install clockspring and driver-side air bag module. See CLOCKSPRING and DRIVER-SIDE AIR BAG MODULE. DO NOT connect negative battery cable at this time. See DISABLING & ACTIVATING AIR BAG SYSTEM.

TORQUE SPECIFICATIONS

TORQUE SPECIFICATIONS

Application	Ft. Lbs. (N.m)
Steering Wheel Nut	45 (61)
Steering Column Lower Shaft Coupler Bolt (Grand Cherokee)	36 (49)
	INCH Lbs. (N.m)
Air Bag Control Module	
Nuts (Cherokee)	65 (7.3)
Nuts (Grand Cherokee)	70 (7.9)
Screws (Wrangler)	95 (10.7)
Driver-Side Air Bag Module Screws	90 (10.2)
Passenger-Side Air Bag Module Bolts/Nuts	105 (11.9)

WIRING DIAGRAMS

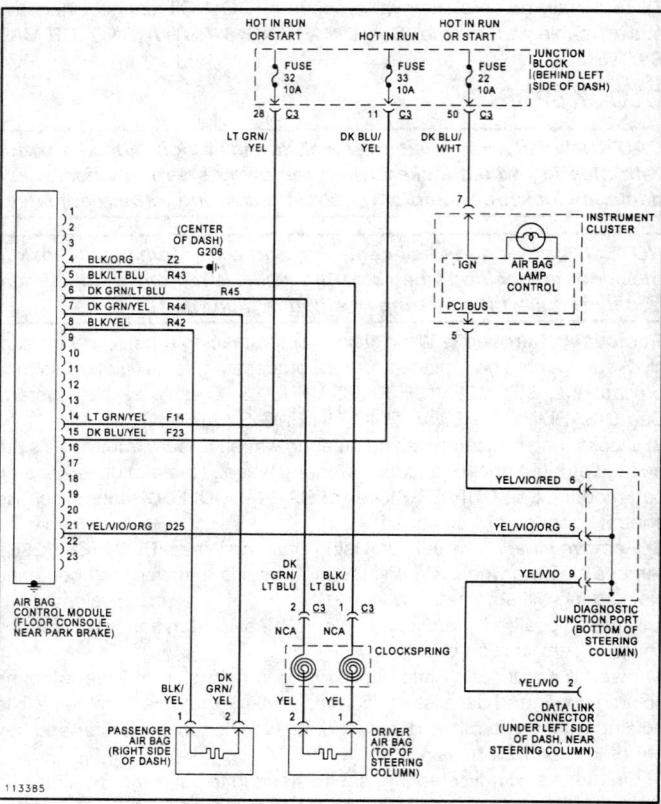

Fig. 14: Air Bag System Wiring Diagram (Grand Cherokee)

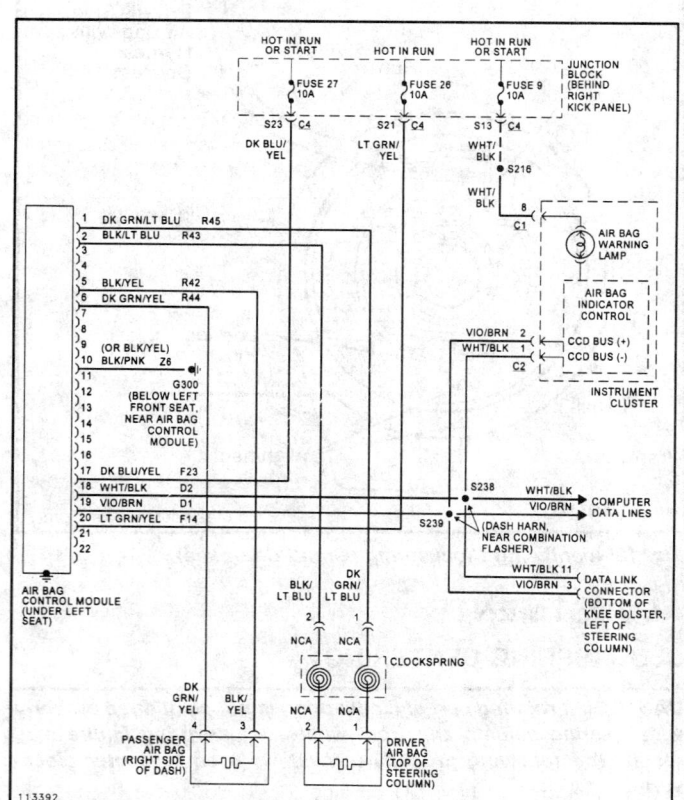

Fig. 13: Air Bag System Wiring Diagram (Cherokee)

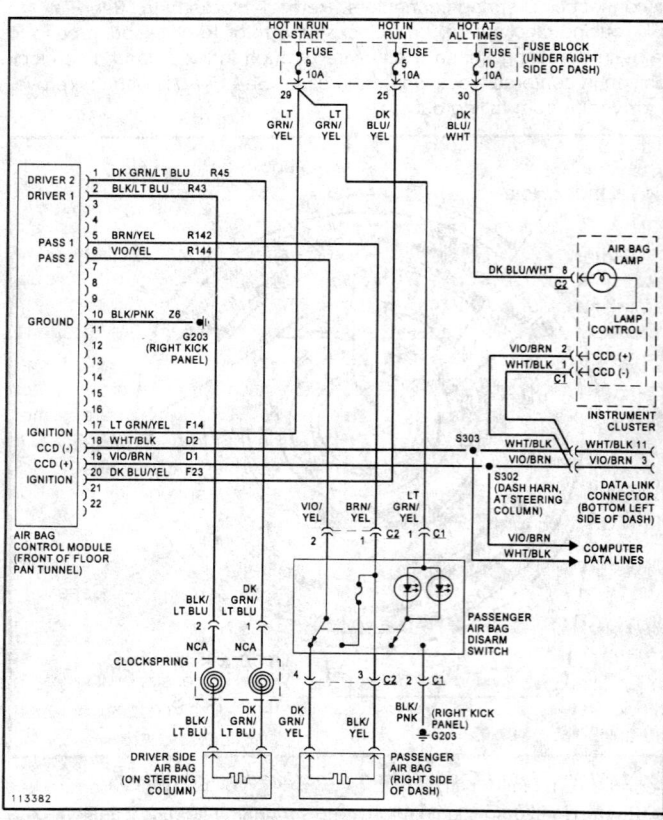

Fig. 15: Air Bag System Wiring Diagram (Wrangler)

WARNING: Vehicle is equipped with Supplemental Restraint System (SRS). See SERVICE PRECAUTIONS in appropriate AIR BAG RESTRAINT SYSTEMS article before working around instrument panel area.

DESCRIPTION

Anti-theft system is an optional feature. System is called Sentry Key Immobilizer System (SKIS). System features a Sentry Key Immobilizer Module (SKIM), which is designed to provide passive protection from unauthorized entry by preventing engine from starting when system is armed. Other components include a warning indicator, transponder and Powertrain Control Module (PCM).

SKIM is installed on steering column, near ignition switch. A transponder is located under molded rubber cap of ignition key head. SKIM warning indicator is located in instrument cluster. SKIS performs a self-test each time ignition switch is turned to ON position. If a system malfunction is detected, a Diagnostic Trouble Code (DTC) will be stored. SKIS can be diagnosed and DTC's retrieved using a DRB scan tool.

SKIM module contains a Radio Frequency (RF) transceiver and a central processing unit, which contains SKIS programming logic. SKIS logic allows for communication over Chrysler Collision Detection (CCD) data bus network with PCM, instrument cluster and DRB scan tool. SKIM transmits and receives RF signals through a tuned antenna enclosed within a molded plastic ring that is part of the SKIM housing.

SKIM is also programmed with a unique "secret key" code and a security code. SKIM keeps secret code in memory and sends code over CCD data bus to PCM, which also stores code in memory. SKIM also sends code to each of "smart key" transponders. SKIM also stores Vehicle Identification Number (VIN).

OPERATION

When ignition switch is turned to ON or START position, SKIM sends a signal to key transponder. SKIM then receives a signal back from key when it is inserted into the ignition switch. This signal is sent to PCM. If signal is correct, vehicle is allowed to be started. If signal is incorrect, SKIM will send an invalid key signal to PCM. PCM will enable or disable the engine starting process depending on signal received.

SKIM also controls indicator lamp. When ignition is turned ON position, SKIM will turn on warning indicator for about 3 seconds as a bulb circuit check. It then turns out warning indicator for about one second. A self-test is then performed by SKIS, and if a problem is detected, warning indicator is turned on again, indicating a system problem, or that system is inoperative. If an invalid key is detected, warning indicator will flash, and engine cannot be started.

Sentry key transponder has a unique identification code programmed into it at factory. Transponder is within range of SKIM antenna ring when it is inserted into ignition switch. SKIM compares transponder signal to code stored in memory and determines whether key is valid or not. Additional keys can be programmed for use. Key transponder cannot be repaired and must be replaced if faulty.

PROGRAMMING

TRANSPONDER PROGRAMMING

1) Additional keys can be programmed, up to a total of 8 per vehicle. Obtain manufacturer transponder blanks matching ignition key lock cylinder key codes. Insert one of the valid smart keys into ignition switch, and turn ignition on.

2) Leave ignition on for at least 3 seconds, but not longer than 15 seconds. Turn ignition off. Remove smart key No. 1 and install smart key No. 2. Turn ignition on. After 10 seconds, indicator lamp will flash and an audible chime will be heard. The system has entered the customer learn programming mode.

3) Within 50 seconds, turn ignition off. Remove valid smart key and insert a blank key. Turn ignition on. After 10 seconds, indicator lamp will

stop flashing and another audible chime will be heard. This indicates that the new key has been successfully programmed. Repeat procedure for each new key needing programming.

SYSTEM TESTS

WARNING: Vehicle is equipped with Supplemental Restraint System (SRS). See SERVICE PRECAUTIONS in appropriate AIR BAG RESTRAINT SYSTEMS article before working around instrument panel area.

SENTRY KEY IMMOBILIZER SYSTEM (SKIS)

NOTE: Manufacturer recommends using DRB scan tool and body diagnostic procedures to check SKIS system. See BODY CONTROL COMPUTER INTRODUCTION article. If DRB scan tool is not available, the following test can be used but results may not prove conclusive in diagnosis of SKIS system.

Cherokee – 1) Check fuse No. 9 (10-amp) in junction block and fuse No. 27 (10-amp) in Power Distribution Center (PDC). Junction block is located behind right kick panel. PDC is located on right side of engine compartment. If fuses are okay, go to next step. If fuse(s) are blown, locate and repair cause of blown fuse. Install new fuse and check operation.

2) Disconnect negative battery cable. Disconnect SKIM connector. See SKIM MODULE under REMOVAL & INSTALLATION. Using an ohmmeter, check continuity between ground and terminal No. 2 (Black/Light Green wire) at SKIM connector. *See Fig. 1.* If continuity exists, go to next step. If continuity does not exist, locate and repair open in Black/Light Green wire.

3) Connect negative battery cable. Using voltmeter, check for battery voltage at terminal No. 1 (Dark Blue/Gray wire) of SKIM connector. If battery voltage exists, go to next step. If battery voltage does not exist, locate and repair open in Dark Blue/Gray wire between junction block and SKIM connector.

4) Turn ignition on. Using voltmeter, check for battery voltage at terminal No. 3 (White/Black wire) of SKIM connector. If battery voltage exists, test is complete. Use DRB scan tool and diagnostic procedures to provide further diagnostics. If battery voltage does not exist, locate and repair open in White/Black wire between junction block and SKIM connector.

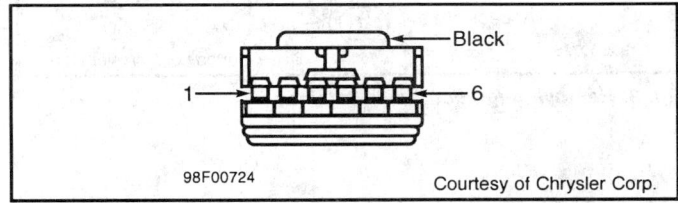

98F00724   Courtesy of Chrysler Corp.

Fig. 1: Identifying SKIM 6-Pin Harness Connector Terminals

Wrangler – 1) Check fuses No. 1 (20-amp) and No. 12 (10-amp) in junction block. Junction block is located behind glove box. If fuses are okay, go to next step. If fuse(s) are blown, locate and repair cause of blown fuse. Install new fuse and check operation.

2) Disconnect negative battery cable. Disconnect SKIM connector. See SKIM MODULE under REMOVAL & INSTALLATION. Check continuity between ground and terminal No. 2 (Black wire) at SKIM connector. *See Fig. 1.* If continuity exists, go to next step. If continuity does not exist, locate and repair open in Black wire.

3) Connect negative battery cable. Check for battery voltage at terminal No. 1 (Tan/Black wire) of SKIM connector. If battery voltage exists, go to next step. If battery voltage does not exist, locate and repair open in Tan/Black wire between fuse block and SKIM connector.

4) Turn ignition switch to ON position. Check for battery voltage at terminal No. 3 (Dark Blue wire) of SKIM connector. If battery voltage exists, test is complete. Use DRB scan tool and diagnostic procedures to provide further diagnostics. If battery voltage does not exist, locate and repair open in Dark Blue wire between junction block and SKIM connector.

REMOVAL & INSTALLATION

SKIM MODULE

Removal & Installation – 1) Before proceeding, follow air bag service precautions. See SERVICE PRECAUTIONS in AIR BAG RESTRAINT SYSTEMS article. Place front wheels in straight-ahead position. Remove knee bolster from under instrument panel.

2) Turn ignition on. Insert small screwdriver or pin punch into access hole in right side of steering column lower cover. Depress ignition tumbler retaining pin and remove ignition key tumbler from ignition lock housing. *See Fig. 2.*

3) Move tilt steering lever to full downward position (if equipped). Remove upper and lower steering column covers. Disconnect steering column wire harness retainer from tab on top of SKIM module mounting bracket. Disconnect electrical connector from SKIM. *See Fig. 3.*

4) Mounting bracket has a clip securing SKIM to steering column jacket. Pull down on connector end of mounting bracket to release clip. Rotate module and mounting bracket down, and then to the side, away from steering column. Slide SKIM antenna ring from around lock cylinder housing. Remove module from vehicle.

5) To install, reverse removal procedure. If a new module is installed, a DRB scan tool must be used to initialize module and program key transponders.

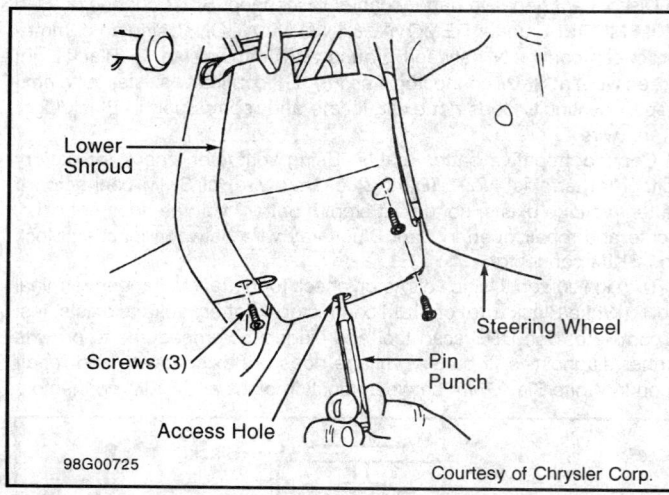

Fig. 2: Removing Ignition Lock Retainer

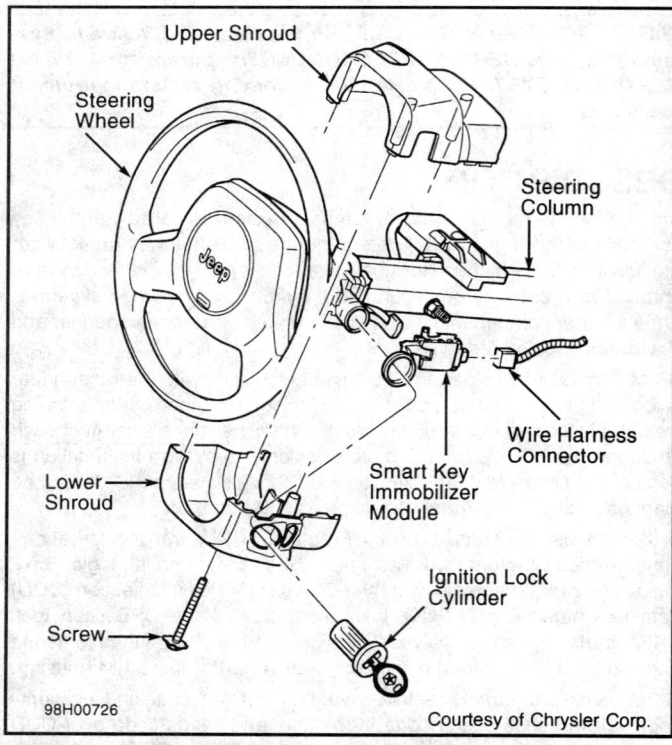

Fig. 3: Removing SKIM Module From Steering Column

WIRING DIAGRAMS

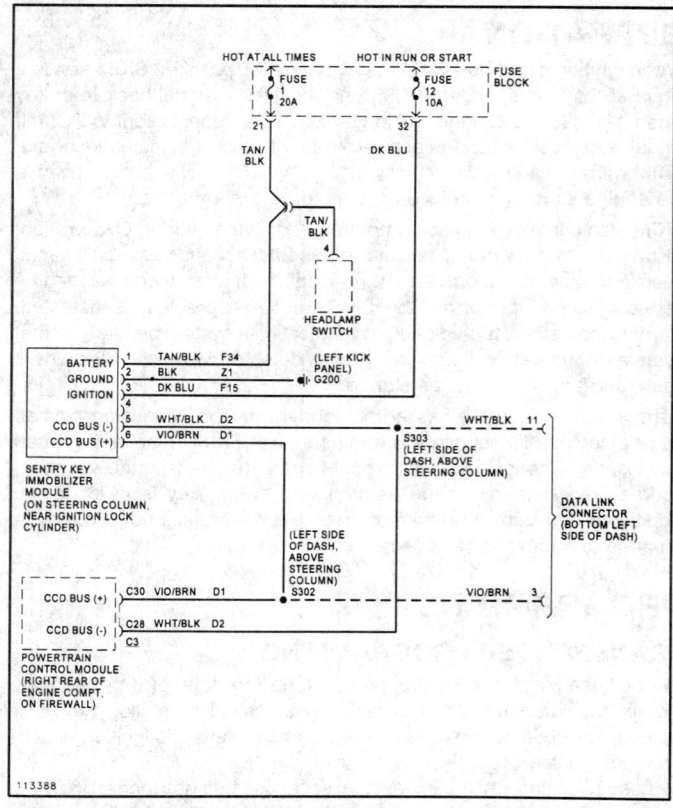

Fig. 4: Anti-Theft System Wiring Diagram (Wrangler)

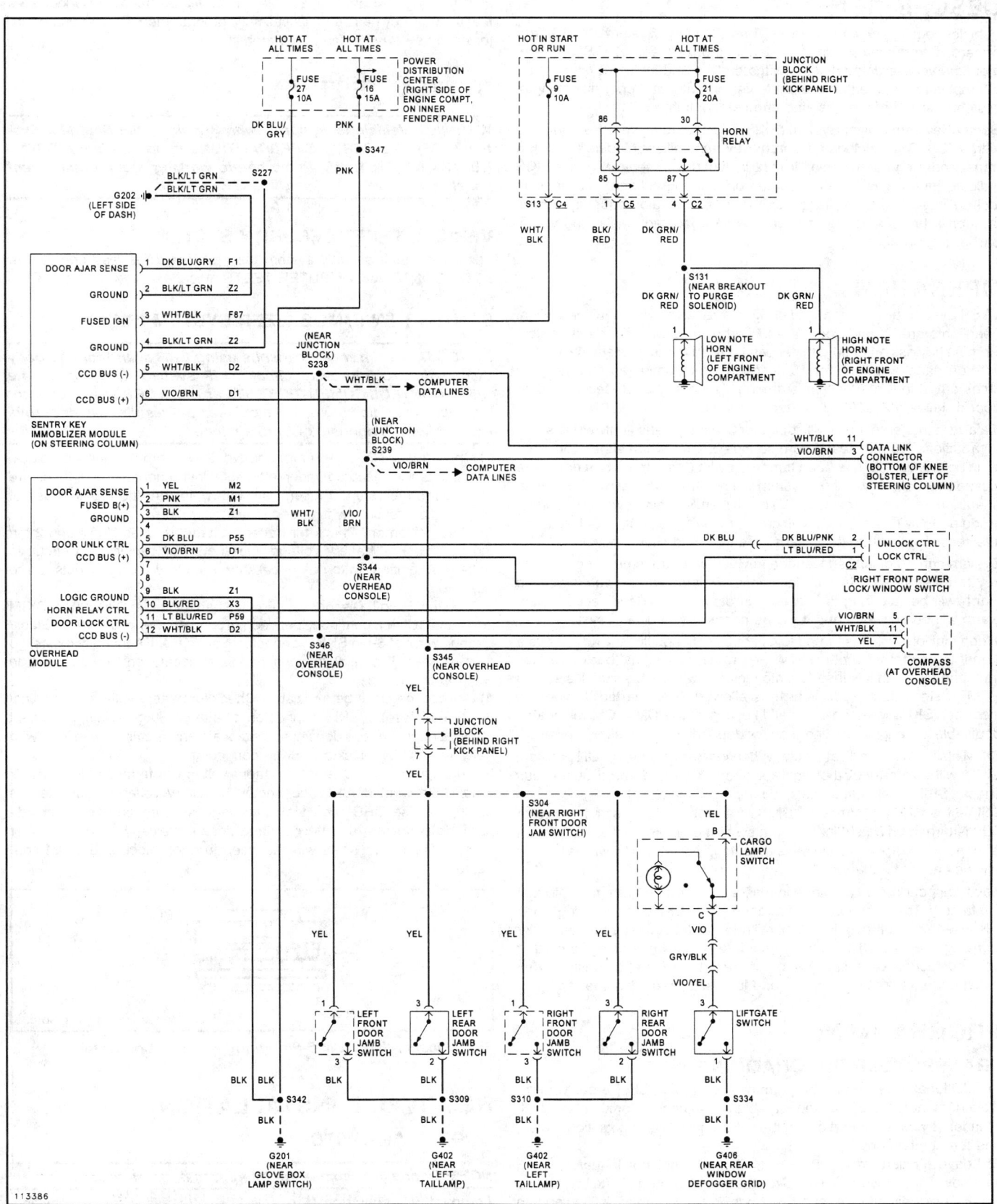

Fig. 5: Anti-Theft System Wiring Diagram (Cherokee)

113386

DESCRIPTION

Vehicles equipped with Vehicle Theft Security System (VTSS) are protected from vehicle theft and unauthorized entry. VTSS system monitors vehicle doors, liftgate, liftgate glass and ignition system. If an attempt is made to enter or operate vehicle without proper disarming of system, vehicle horn will sound and exterior lights will flash.

Sentry Key Immobilizer System (SKIS) is standard on vehicles equipped with VTSS. SKIS includes a Sentry Key Immobilizer Module (SKIM), a transponder on each ignition key (2 included with vehicle) and a SKIS indicator lamp. The SKIM is located on steering column, near ignition lock cylinder. The SKIM transmits and receives radio frequency signals through a tuned antenna enclosed within a molded plastic ring that is part of the SKIM housing.

OPERATION

VTSS system arms when ignition key is removed from ignition switch, headlights are off and doors are locked using power door lock switch. Remote keyless entry transmitter can be used to arm system. A indicator light on panel will flash for 15 seconds after illuminated entry system times out to indicate system is arming. At the end of 15 seconds, if no door or tailgate is opened, system is armed.

If alarm is triggered, horn will sound for 3 minutes, and lights will flash for an additional 15 minutes. If horn sounds 3 times when either front door is unlocked, vehicle has been tampered with (tamper alert). If doors are locked manually or with key, system will not arm (manual override). If an unauthorized entry does occur, VTSS system signals Powertrain Control Module (PCM) to prevent vehicle from being driven. PCM reduces injector pulse width to zero, causing a start and stall condition.

System can be disarmed with the keyless entry transmitter or by using key to enter vehicle. In both instances, if alarm was activated, vehicle alarm will be terminated. If battery is disconnected and reconnected, alarm will be activated and it will be necessary to disarm system.

When ignition switch is turned to ON or START positions, SKIM sends a signal to key transponder. SKIM then receives a signal back from key transponder when it is inserted into ignition switch. This signal is sent to PCM. If signal is correct, vehicle is allowed to be started. If signal is incorrect, SKIM will send an invalid key signal to PCM. PCM will enable or disable the engine starting process depending on the signal received.

SKIM also controls indicator light. When ignition is turned to ON position, SKIM will turn on indicator light for about 3 seconds as a bulb circuit check. SKIM then turns out indicator light for about one second. A self-test is then performed by SKIS. If a problem is detected, indicator light is turned on again, indicating a system problem, or that the system is inoperative. If an invalid key is detected, indicator light will flash, and engine cannot be started.

Key transponder has a unique identification code programmed into it at the factory. Transponder is within range of the SKIM antenna ring when it is inserted into the ignition lock cylinder. SKIM compares transponder signal to code stored in memory and determines whether key is valid or not. Additional keys can be programmed for use in ignition. Key transponder cannot be repaired and it must be replaced if faulty.

PROGRAMMING

TRANSPONDER PROGRAMMING

1) Additional keys can be programmed, up to a total of 8 per vehicle. Obtain manufacturer transponder blanks matching ignition key lock cylinder key codes. Insert one of the valid smart keys into ignition switch, and turn ignition on.

2) Leave ignition on for at least 3 seconds, but not longer than 15 seconds. Turn ignition off. Remove smart key No. 1 and install smart key No. 2. Turn ignition on. After 10 seconds, indicator lamp will flash and an audible chime will be heard. The system has entered the customer learn programming mode.

3) Within 50 seconds, turn ignition off. Remove valid smart key and insert a blank key. Turn ignition on. After 10 seconds, indicator lamp will

stop flashing and another audible chime will be heard. This indicates that the new key has been successfully programmed. Repeat procedure for each new key needing programming.

SYSTEM TESTS

WARNING: Vehicle is equipped with Supplemental Restraint System (SRS). See SERVICE PRECAUTIONS in appropriate AIR BAG RESTRAINT SYSTEMS article before working around instrument panel area.

VEHICLE THEFT SECURITY SYSTEM

For vehicle theft security system testing procedures, see appropriate BODY CONTROL COMPUTER TESTS article.

SENTRY KEY IMMOBILIZER SYSTEM (SKIS)

NOTE: Manufacturer recommends using DRB scan tool and body diagnostic procedures to check SKIS system. See appropriate BODY CONTROL COMPUTER TESTS article. If DRB scan tool is not available, the following test can be used but results may not prove conclusive in diagnosis of SKIS system.

1) Check fuses No. 7 (10-amp) and No. 22 (10-amp) in junction block. Junction block is located under left side of instrument panel. If fuses are okay, go to next step. If fuse(s) are blown, locate and repair cause of blown fuse. Install new fuse and check operation.

2) Turn ignition on. Check for battery voltage at fuses No. 7 and 22 in junction block. If battery voltage does not exist, repair open circuit to battery or ignition switch as necessary. If battery voltage exists, go to next step.

3) Turn ignition off. Disconnect negative battery cable. Disconnect SKIM connector. Check continuity between ground and terminal No. 2 (Black/Orange wire) at 6-pin SKIM connector. See Fig. 1. If continuity exists, go to next step. If continuity does not exist, locate and repair open in Black/Orange wire.

4) Connect negative battery cable. Check for battery voltage at terminal No. 1 (Pink wire) of SKIM connector. If battery voltage exists, go to next step. If battery voltage does not exist, locate and repair open in Pink wire between junction block and SKIM connector.

5) Turn ignition on. Check for battery voltage at terminal No. 3 (Dark Blue/White wire) of SKIM connector. If battery voltage exists, test is complete. Use DRB scan tool and diagnostic procedures to provide further diagnostics. If battery voltage does not exist, locate and repair open in Dark Blue/White wire between junction block and SKIM connector.

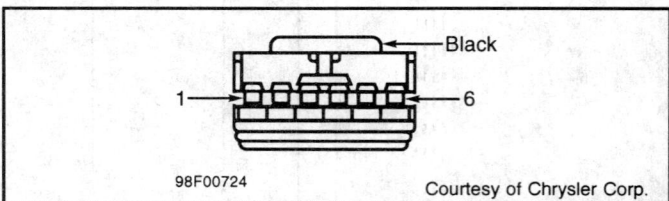

98F00724   Courtesy of Chrysler Corp.

Fig. 1: Identifying SKIM 6-Pin Wiring Harness Connector Terminals

REMOVAL & INSTALLATION
DOOR AJAR SWITCH

NOTE: Door ajar switches are integral to door latches.

Removal & Installation (Front) – Position glass to full up position. Remove door trim panel. Remove glass run channel. Remove 3 door latch mounting screws. Disconnect all rods and wire connector from door latch. Remove door latch. To install, reverse removal procedure. Tighten door latch mounting screws to 84 INCH lbs. (7 N.m).

Removal & Installation (Rear) – Remove door trim panel. Remove door latch mounting screws. Disconnect rods and wire connector from door latch. Remove door latch. To install, reverse removal procedure. Tighten door latch mounting screws to 95 INCH lbs. (10 N.m).

DOOR LOCK CYLINDER SWITCH

NOTE: Door lock cylinder switches are integral to door lock cylinders.

Removal & Installation – Remove door trim panel. Remove outside door handle. Remove lock cylinder retainer screw. Separate lock cylinder from door handle. Disconnect wire connector. To install, reverse removal procedure.

LIFTGATE AJAR SWITCHES

NOTE: Liftgate ajar switches are integral to liftgate latches.

Removal & Installation – Remove liftgate trim panel. Disconnect wire connector from latch. Disconnect outside handle link from latch. Remove latch mounting screws. Remove latch. To install, reverse removal procedure. Tighten latch mounting screws to 60 INCH lbs. (7 N.m).

LIFTGLASS AJAR SWITCH

NOTE: Liftglass ajar switch is integral to liftglass latch.

Removal & Installation – Remove liftgate trim panel. Remove liftglass latch nuts. Disconnect wire connectors from latch. Remove liftglass latch. To install, reverse removal procedure. Tighten latch nuts to 100 INCH lbs. (11 N.m).

BODY CONTROL MODULE (BCM)

Removal & Installation – Disconnect negative battery cable. Remove instrument panel fuse cover. Disconnect wire connectors from BCM. Remove 4 BCM-to-junction block screws. Pull BCM from junction block and remove. To install, reverse removal procedure. Tighten BCM mounting screws to 20 INCH lbs. (2.2 N.m).

HORN RELAY

Removal & Installation – Disconnect negative battery cable. Remove cover from Power Distribution Center (PDC). PDC is located in engine compartment, near battery. Remove horn relay from PDC. Refer to label on PDC for relay identification and location. To install, reverse removal procedure.

VTSS LED

NOTE: VTSS LED is integral to auto head light sensor.

Removal & Installation – Disconnect negative battery cable. Using a trim stick, remove instrument panel top cover by prying rear edge of top cover enough to disengage 4 snap clip retainers. Remove auto head light sensor screw. Disconnect wire connector from auto head light sensor. Remove auto head light sensor. To install, reverse removal procedure.

WIRING DIAGRAMS

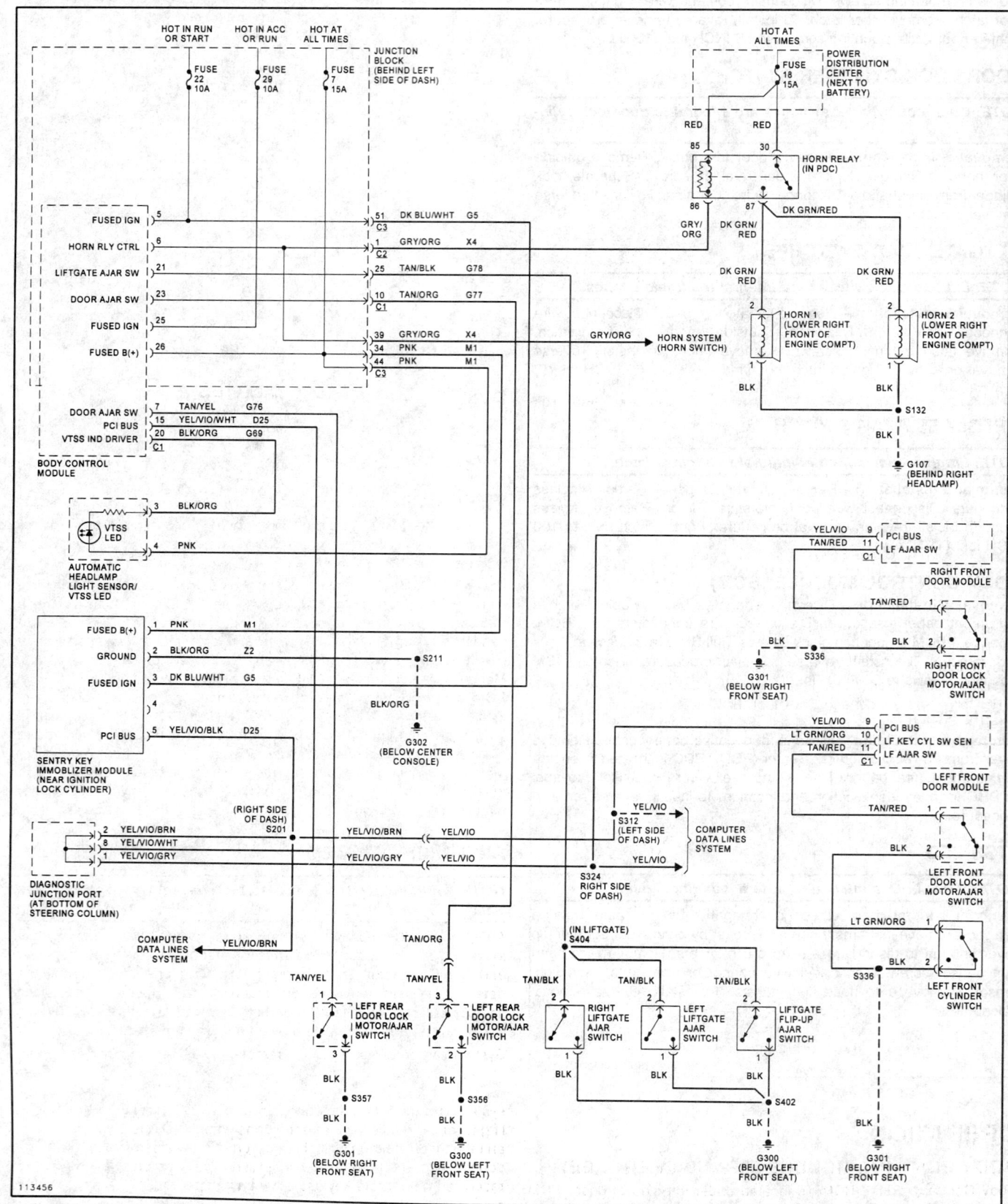

Fig. 2: Anti-Theft System Wiring Diagram (Grand Cherokee)

Cherokee, Grand Cherokee, Wrangler

IDENTIFICATION

Body Identification

Application	Body
Cherokee	XJ
Grand Cherokee	WJ
Wrangler	TJ

DESCRIPTION

NOTE: Self-diagnostic tests are written specifically for Chrysler's Diagnostic Readout Box (DRB) scan tool. A generic scan tool may not be capable of performing all necessary test functions.

The body control computer system consists of a combination of modules that either communicate over the Chrysler Collision Detection (CCD) bus system or Programmable Communication Interface (PCI) bus system. Through the CCD (Cherokee and Wrangler) or PCI (Grand Cherokee) bus, information related to the operation of vehicle components and circuits are relayed to the appropriate system module(s). This reduces the complexity of vehicle wiring and size of wiring harness.

Body control computer systems covered in BODY CONTROL COMPUTER TESTS articles are as follows:

- Chime System (WJ Body)
- Compass/Mini-Trip Computer (CMTC) (XJ and WJ Bodies)
- Exterior Lighting (WJ Body)
- Instrument Cluster (All)
- Interior Lighting (WJ Body)
- Power Door Locks (XJ and WJ Body)
- Power Windows (WJ Body)
- Sentry Key Immobilizer System (SKIS) (All)
- Vehicle Theft Security System (VTSS) (All)
- Wipers (WJ Body)

Body control computer fault messages are accessed through 16-pin Data Link Connector (DLC) using Chrysler's Diagnostic Readout Box (DRB) scan tool or generic scan tool. DLC is located on left side of steering column, above brake pedal. *See Fig. 1.*

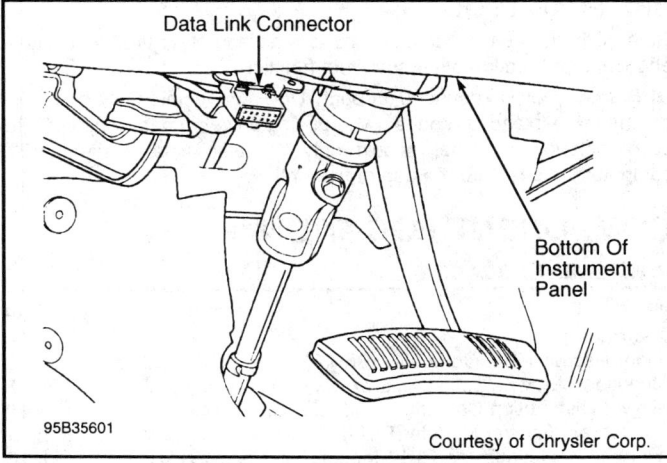

Courtesy of Chrysler Corp.

Fig. 1: Locating 16-Pin Data Link Connector

OPERATION

BODY CONTROL MODULE (GRAND CHEROKEE)

Body Control Module (BCM) is located under left side of dash. BCM controls many of the vehicle's electrical functions and features by providing power or ground to a variety of systems. BCM contains a central processing unit and interfaces with other modules in the vehicle on the PCI data bus network.

BCM is the only module that has the capability of providing both "bias" and "termination" on the PCI bus system. See PCI BUS SYSTEM (GRAND CHEROKEE). Systems are monitored by BCM through voltage drops.

CCD BUS SYSTEM (CHEROKEE & WRANGLER)

The Chrysler Collision Detection (CCD) bus is a pair of twisted wires traveling from module-to-module receiving and delivering coded information. The code identifies the message and its importance. When multiple messages attempt to access CCD bus at once, code assigns priority ranking.

The 2 twisted wires used by the CCD bus system are called bus "+" (positive) and bus "–" (negative). Both wires carry approximately 2.5 volts. The network consists of some modules with "bias" and some with "termination".

Bias is the part of the voltage divider network that places both bus "+" and bus "–" at 2.5 volts. Termination is the part of the circuitry required to complete the voltage divider network and also provide some electromagnetic protection for the CCD bus. Terminations in all CCD applications have approximately 120 ohms resistance.

COMPASS/MINI-TRIP COMPUTER (CMTC)

Compass/mini-trip computer consists of a mini/trip computer module, electronic compass and thermometer. Compass/mini-trip computer module is self-calibrated and requires no adjustment.

INSTRUMENT CLUSTER

Instrument cluster includes a speedometer, tachometer, fuel gauge, oil pressure gauge, water temperature gauge, voltmeter and a series of warning lights.

Powertrain Control Module (PCM) sends signals necessary for instrument cluster to position gauges. Instrument cluster receives these messages from bus and translates them into gauge positions. BCM sends status of all indicator lights and dimming level to instrument cluster over bus when ignition switch is in RUN or START positions. Malfunction indicator light (CHECK ENGINE) status is sent to BCM from PCM over bus. Vacuum florescent odometer/trip display works when ignition switch is in RUN or START positions. BCM stores mileage information that odometer displays. If bus is not functioning, odometer will display dashes instead of the mileage. BCM sends mileage message and dimming level message to vacuum fluorescent display when ignition switch is in the RUN position. All other instrument cluster features only work when the ignition switch is in the RUN position.

ANTI-THEFT SYSTEM

NOTE: Anti-theft system may also be referred to as Vehicle Theft Security System (VTSS).

Anti-theft system monitors vehicle doors, ignition switch, power door locks and door key cylinder switches to determine if alarm should trigger and prevent engine from starting. When an unauthorized entry is detected, system responds by sounding horn, flashing headlights, flashing taillights and flashing parking lights for 3 minutes. BCM also sends a message to PCM to prevent engine from starting.

System can be armed by using remote keyless entry transmitter or by pressing power door lock switch when exiting vehicle. Anti-theft system uses a security light located above instrument cluster to indicate when system is armed. System can be disarmed by unlocking a front door, liftgate or by remote keyless entry transmitter. If vehicle is tampered with anti-theft indicator light will change from a slow steady flash to a quick double flash and horn chirp will not function when unlock command is received from remote keyless entry transmitter.

Panic alert mode flashes headlight and taillights, pulses horn and disarms alarm. Driver can exit panic alert mode by either pushing panic button on remote keyless entry transmitter or by driving vehicle above 15 MPH.

Whenever BCM is replaced, anti-theft system must be enabled by unlocking doors with key one time or by using scan tool. This allows BCM to see that the vehicle is equipped with an anti-theft system.

DOOR MODULES

Door modules are used to reduce wiring complexity, and to facilitate faster and easier diagnosis. One door module is located in each front door. Door modules control power door locks, driver window express down, memory recall functions for memory seats and mirrors, keyless entry system and power mirrors.

PCI BUS SYSTEM (GRAND CHEROKEE)

The Programmable Communication Interface (PCI) bus system consists of a single wire. The BCM acts as a splice to connect each module and Data Link Connector (DLC). Each module uses its local ground as bus reference. If more than one module is trying to access the PCI bus at one time, code being sent determines which message has higher priority, and is then allowed to access bus first. Communication over the bus is essential to proper operation of vehicles on-board diagnostic systems and DRB. Problems with operation of bus or DRB must be corrected before proceeding with diagnostic testing. See appropriate VEHICLE COMMUNICATIONS article.

POWER WINDOWS

Power windows can be raised or lowered from driver's door module or individual door switch. Driver's door module has a lockout switch that prevents windows from being operated from any switch except driver's door. When this switch is pressed, it also shuts off individual door switch LEDs.

POWER DOOR LOCKS

When lock button on remote keyless entry transmitter is pressed, all doors will lock, illuminated entry will turn off and anti-theft system will arm. When transmitter unlock button is pressed one time, left front door will unlock, illuminated entry will turn on and anti-theft system will disarm. When transmitter button is pressed a second time, all other doors will unlock.

Passenger's door module contains remote keyless entry receiver. When passenger's door module receives a valid signal from remote keyless entry transmitter, it will send a signal on the bus to lock or unlock doors. Remote keyless entry transmitter uses radio frequency signals to communicate with remote keyless entry receiver.

WIPER SYSTEM

Wiper system provides driver with normal wipe (low and high speeds), intermittent wipe, wipe after wash and pulse wipe functions. Low and high speeds are directly controlled by multifunction switch. Intermittent wiper function is controlled through intermittent wiper relay and BCM. BCM uses vehicle speed input to double normal delay times when vehicle speed is less than 10 MPH.

SELF-DIAGNOSTIC SYSTEM

CAUTION: When battery is disconnected, vehicle computer and memory systems may lose memory data. Driveability problems may exist until computer systems have completed a relearn cycle. See COMPUTER RELEARN PROCEDURES article in GENERAL INFORMATION before disconnecting battery.

PRETEST INSPECTION

Before proceeding with diagnosis, the following precautions MUST be followed:

- Vehicle must have a fully charged battery and functional charging system.
- When testing voltage or continuity at any control module, use terminal side and not wire end. DO NOT probe a wire through insulation.

- Always start at IDENTIFYING VEHICLE EQUIPMENT & SYSTEM PROBLEMS under SYSTEM ID TEST in appropriate BODY CONTROL COMPUTER TESTS article. Starting with any other test may result in incorrect results.
- Only perform test steps indicated. It is not necessary to perform all steps in a test.
- BODY CONTROL COMPUTER - VEHICLE COMMUNICATIONS article should only be used when instructed by another test.
- Turn ignition switch to OFF position before disconnecting or connecting components.
- Use extreme care when connecting or disconnecting wiring during testing to prevent accidental grounding or shorting.
- Unless instructed to do so in test steps, DO NOT use a test light in place of a voltmeter.
- Always disconnect scan tool after use.
- Always disconnect scan tool before charging battery.
- Always perform appropriate VERIFICATION TESTS after repairs are made.

DIAGNOSTIC PROCEDURE

NOTE: Before proceeding with diagnosis, certain precautions must be followed. See PRETEST INSPECTION under SELF-DIAGNOSTIC SYSTEM.

Diagnostic procedures are designed to detect system faults as quickly as possible. Body control computer system diagnostic fault messages are accessed through Data Link Connector (DLC). *See Fig. 1.* Chrysler's Diagnostic Readout Box (DRB) scan tool or generic scan tool, is used to access information from DLC.

A 1999 diagnostic program cartridge, scan tool, body diagnostics cable, jumper wires and digital volt/ohmmeter will be needed for testing. Proceed to IDENTIFYING VEHICLE EQUIPMENT & SYSTEM PROBLEMS under SYSTEM ID TEST in appropriate BODY CONTROL COMPUTER TESTS article.

GENERIC SCAN TOOL

Self-diagnostic tests are written specifically for Chrysler's Diagnostic Readout Box (DRB) scan tool. A generic scan tool can be used, but may not be capable of performing all necessary test functions.

DRB SCAN TOOL

Refer to DRB scan tool instructions to read and clear fault messages, and when performing other scan tool function.

DRB scan tool is grounded through DLC connector. Only one volt/ohmmeter test lead is required when using volt/ohmmeter option. DRB scan tool volt/ohmmeter should only be used when body control computer tests require the use of this option.

COMPONENT LOCATION

COMPONENT LOCATION

Description	Location
Cherokee	
Compass/Mini-Trip Computer (CMTC)	Fig. 3
Junction Block	Fig. 5
Power Distribution Center	In Engine Compartment
Powertrain Control Module (PCM)	Left Inner Fender
Remote Keyless Entry (RKE) Module	Fig. 3
Transmission Control Module (TCM)	Fig. 7
Grand Cherokee	
Airbag Control Module (ACM)	Under Center Console, Beside Parking Brake Handle
Body Control Module (BCM)	Fig. 2
Controller Anti-Lock Brake (CAB) Module	Mounted To Hydraulic Control Unit
Compass/Mini-Trip Computer (CMTC)	Fig. 3

COMPONENT LOCATION (Cont.)

Description	Location
Diagnostic Junction Port	Fig. 4
Junction Block	Fig. 4
Memory Seat Module (MSM)	Under Driver's Seat
Powertrain Control Module (PCM)	Right Rear Corner Of Engine Compartment
Remote Keyless Entry (RKE) Module	Fig. 3
Sentry Key Immobilizer Module (SKIM)	Fig. 6
Transmission Control Module (TCM)	In Front Of PCM
Wrangler	
Airbag Control Module (ACM)	In Front Of Center Console
Powertrain Control Module (PCM)	Next To Battery

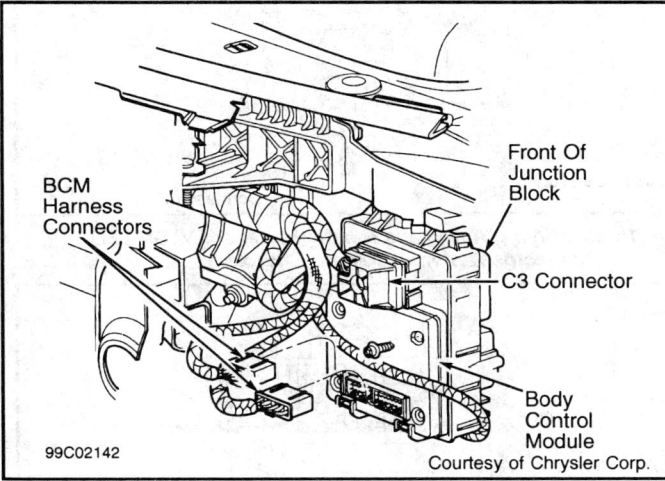

Fig. 2: Identifying Body Control Module (Grand Cherokee)

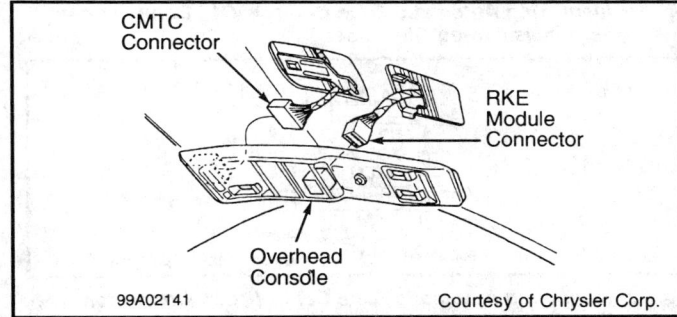

Fig. 3: Locating CMTC & RKE Module Connectors (Cherokee Shown; Grand Cherokee Is Similar)

CONNECTOR IDENTIFICATION

NOTE: For terminal identification of body control system connectors, see Figs. 8-47. Connector terminal numbers are molded into connectors. If connector terminal identification differs from that shown in figure, use wire colors to ensure correct circuit is being tested.

CONNECTOR IDENTIFICATION DIRECTORY

Connector	Fig.
Air Bag Control Module (Cherokee & Wrangler)	8
Air Bag Control Module (Grand Cherokee)	9
Automatic Headlight Sensor/VTSS LED (Grand Cherokee)	10
Automatic Zone Control "C1" (Grand Cherokee)	11
Automatic Zone Control "C2" (Grand Cherokee)	12
Body Control Module "C1" (Grand Cherokee)	13
Compass Mini-Trip Computer (Cherokee & Wrangler)	14

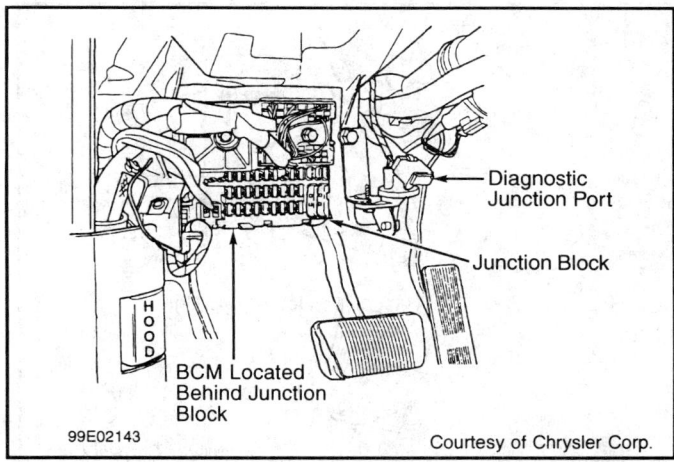

Fig. 4: Locating Diagnostic Junction Port (Grand Cherokee)

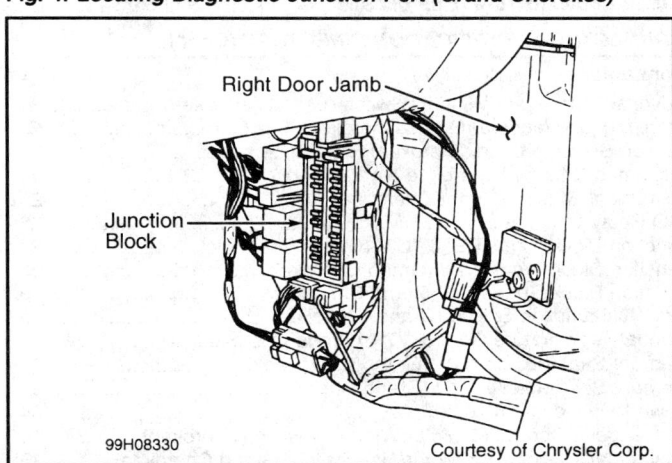

Fig. 5: Locating Junction Block (Cherokee)

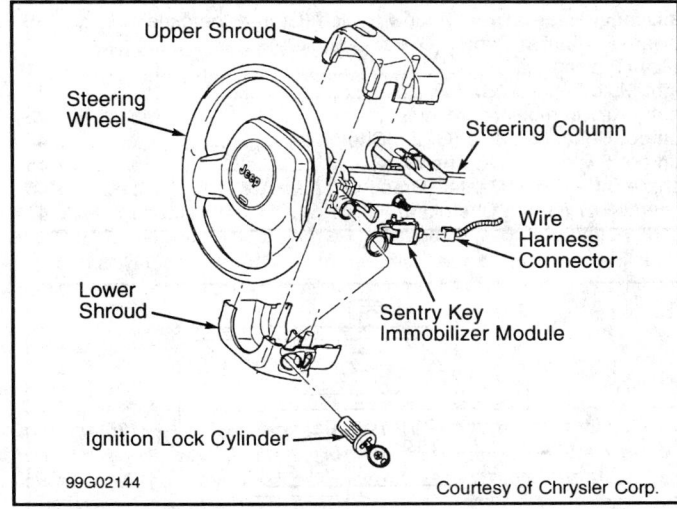

Fig. 6: Locating SKIM (Typical)

CONNECTOR IDENTIFICATION DIRECTORY (Cont.)

Connector	Fig.
Data Link Connector	15
Diagnostic Junction Port (Grand Cherokee)	16
Driver's Door Lock Motor/Ajar Switch (Grand Cherokee)	17
Driver's Door Module "C1" (Grand Cherokee)	18
Driver's Door Module "C2" (Grand Cherokee)	19
Driver's Rear Door Lock Motor/Ajar Switch (Grand Cherokee)	20

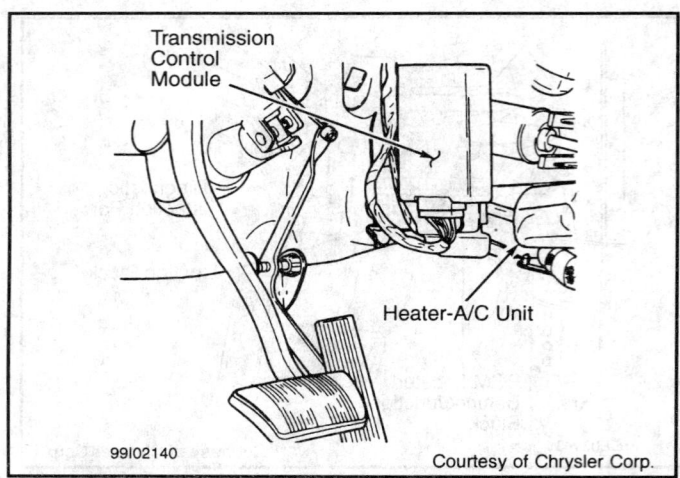

Transmission Control Module

Heater-A/C Unit

99I02140

Courtesy of Chrysler Corp.

Fig. 7: Locating TCM (Cherokee)

CONNECTOR IDENTIFICATION DIRECTORY (Cont.)

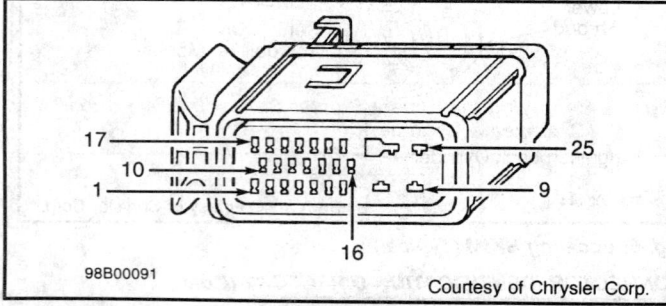

98B00091

Courtesy of Chrysler Corp.

Fig. 8: Identifying Air Bag Control Module Connector Terminals (Cherokee & Wrangler)

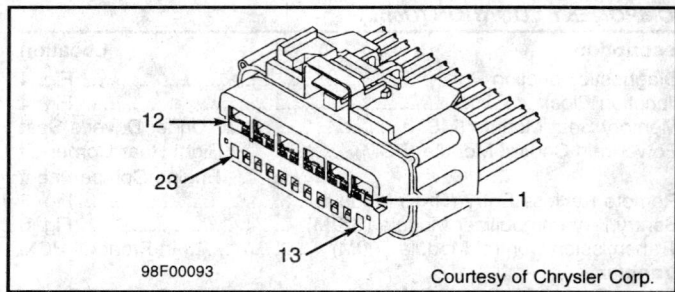

98F00093

Courtesy of Chrysler Corp.

Fig. 9: Identifying Airbag Control Module Connector Terminals (Grand Cherokee)

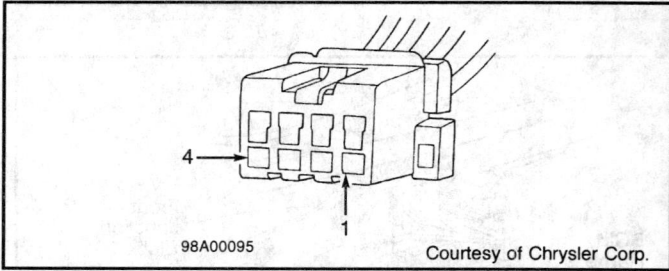

98A00095

Courtesy of Chrysler Corp.

Fig. 10: Identifying Automatic Headlight Sensor/VTSS LED Connector Terminals (Grand Cherokee)

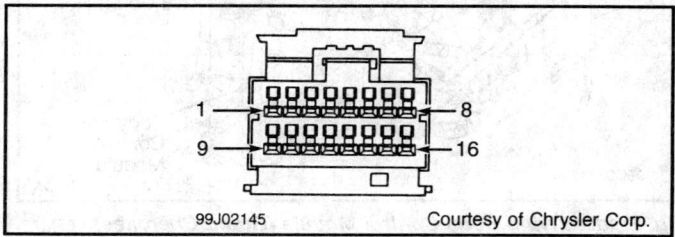

99J02145

Courtesy of Chrysler Corp.

Fig. 11: Identifying Automatic Zone Control "C1" Connector Terminals (Grand Cherokee)

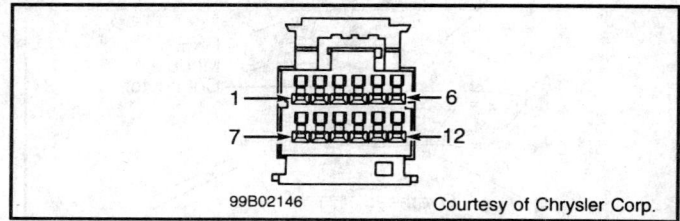

99B02146

Courtesy of Chrysler Corp.

Fig. 12: Identifying Automatic Zone Control "C2" Connector Terminals (Grand Cherokee)

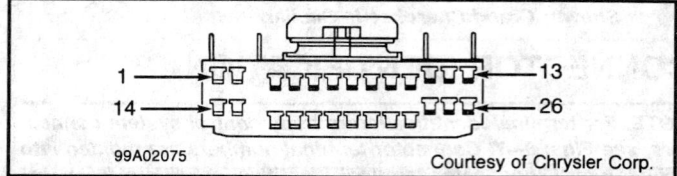

99A02075

Courtesy of Chrysler Corp.

Fig. 13: Identifying Body Control Module "C1" Connector Terminals (Grand Cherokee)

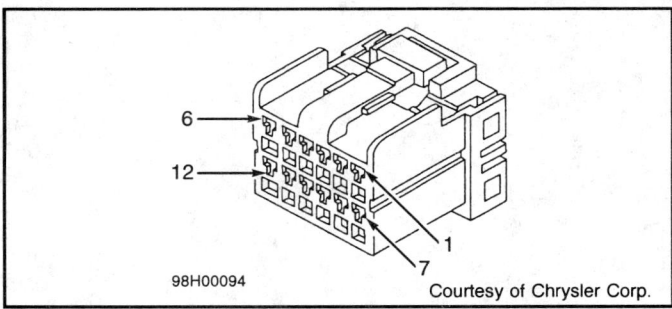

Fig. 14: Identifying Compass Mini-Trip Computer Connector Terminals (Cherokee & Warngler)

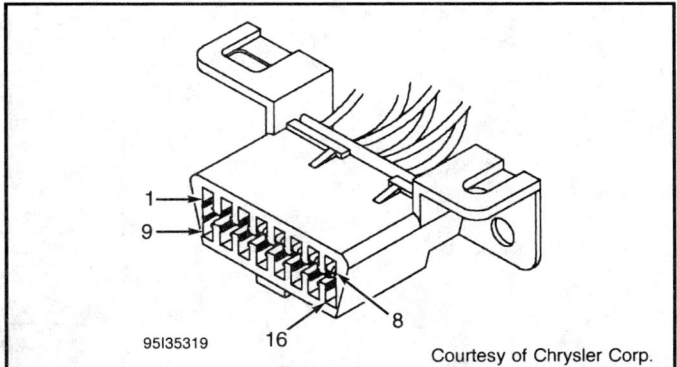

Fig. 15: Identifying Data Link Connector Terminals

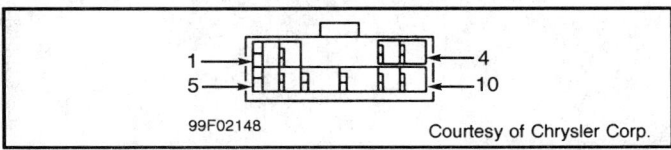

Fig. 16: Identifying Diagnostic Junction Port Connector Terminals (Grand Cherokee)

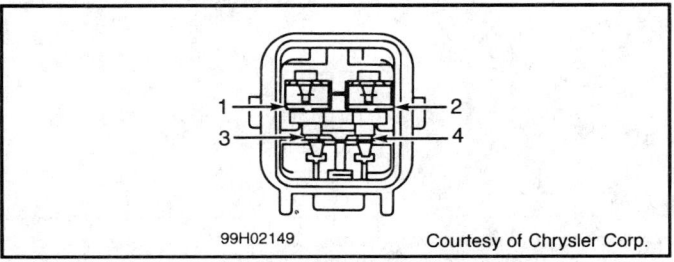

Fig. 17: Identifying Driver's Door Lock Motor/Ajar Switch Connector Terminals (Grand Cherokee)

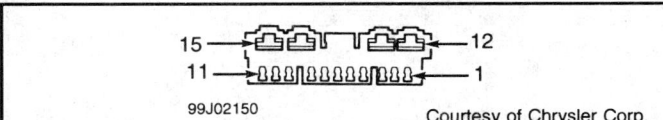

Fig. 18: Identifying Driver's Door Module "C1" Connector Terminals (Grand Cherokee)

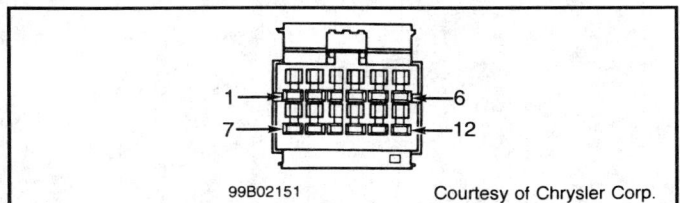

Fig. 19: Identifying Driver's Door Module "C2" Connector Terminals (Grand Cherokee)

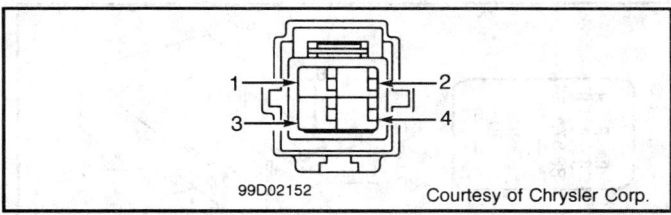

Fig. 20: Identifying Driver's Rear Door Lock Motor/Ajar Switch Connector Terminals (Grand Cherokee)

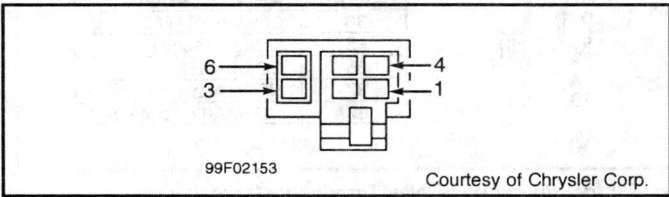

Fig. 21: Identifying Driver's Rear Power Window Switch Connector Terminals (Grand Cherokee)

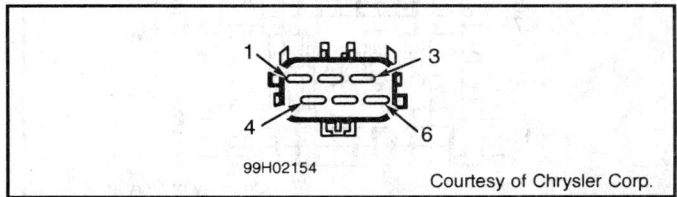

Fig. 22: Identifying Front Lighting Module Connector Terminals (Grand Cherokee)

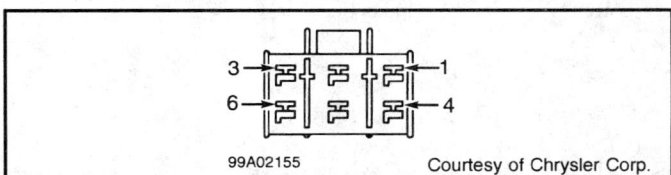

Fig. 23: Identifying Ignition Switch Connector Terminals (Grand Cherokee)

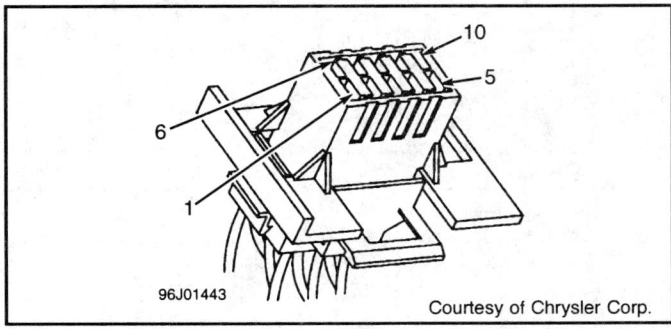

Fig. 24: Identifying Instrument Cluster Connector Terminals (Cherokee & Wrangler)

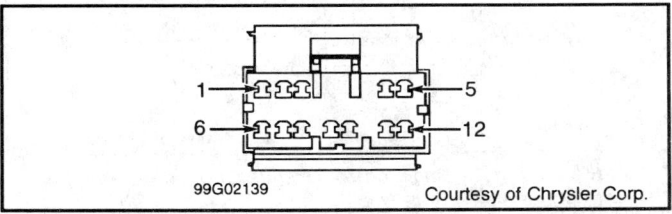

Fig. 25: Identifying Instrument Cluster Connector Terminals (Grand Cherokee)

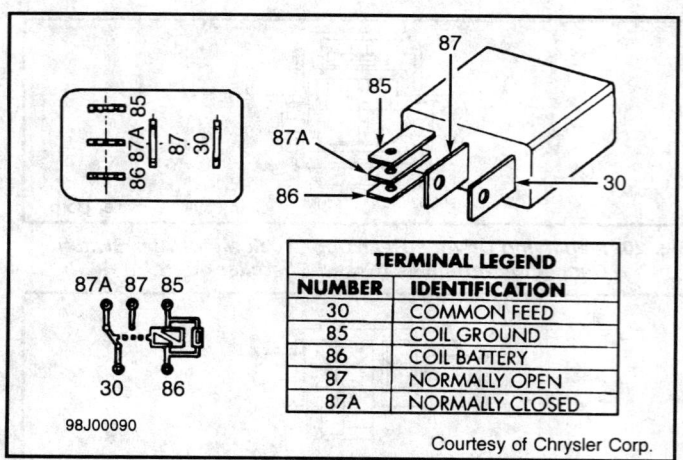

TERMINAL LEGEND	
NUMBER	**IDENTIFICATION**
30	COMMON FEED
85	COIL GROUND
86	COIL BATTERY
87	NORMALLY OPEN
87A	NORMALLY CLOSED

98J00090

Courtesy of Chrysler Corp.

Fig. 26: Identifying ISO Relay Terminals (Typical)

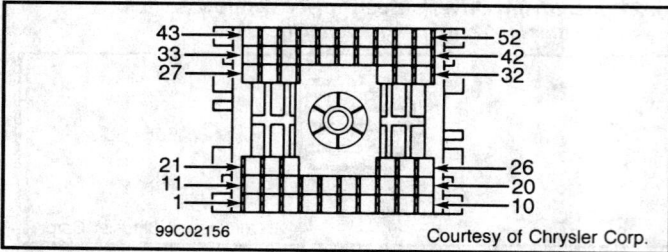

99C02156

Courtesy of Chrysler Corp.

Fig. 27: Identifying Junction Block "C1", "C2" & "C3" Connector Terminals (Grand Cherokee)

1999 ACCESSORIES & EQUIPMENT
Body Control Computer Introduction (Cont.)

Low Beam/ Daytime Running Light Relay
Cigar Lighter Relay
Sunroof Delay Relay
Combination Flasher
Rear Window Defogger Relay
Circuit Breaker No. 1
Spare Relay
High Beam Relay
Spare Relay
Low Beam Relay
Circuit Breaker No. 2
FogLight Relay
Park Light Relay
Spare Relay
C1
C2
SEE REAR VIEW
JUNCTION BLOCK FRONT VIEW
99E02157
Courtesy of Chrysler Corp.

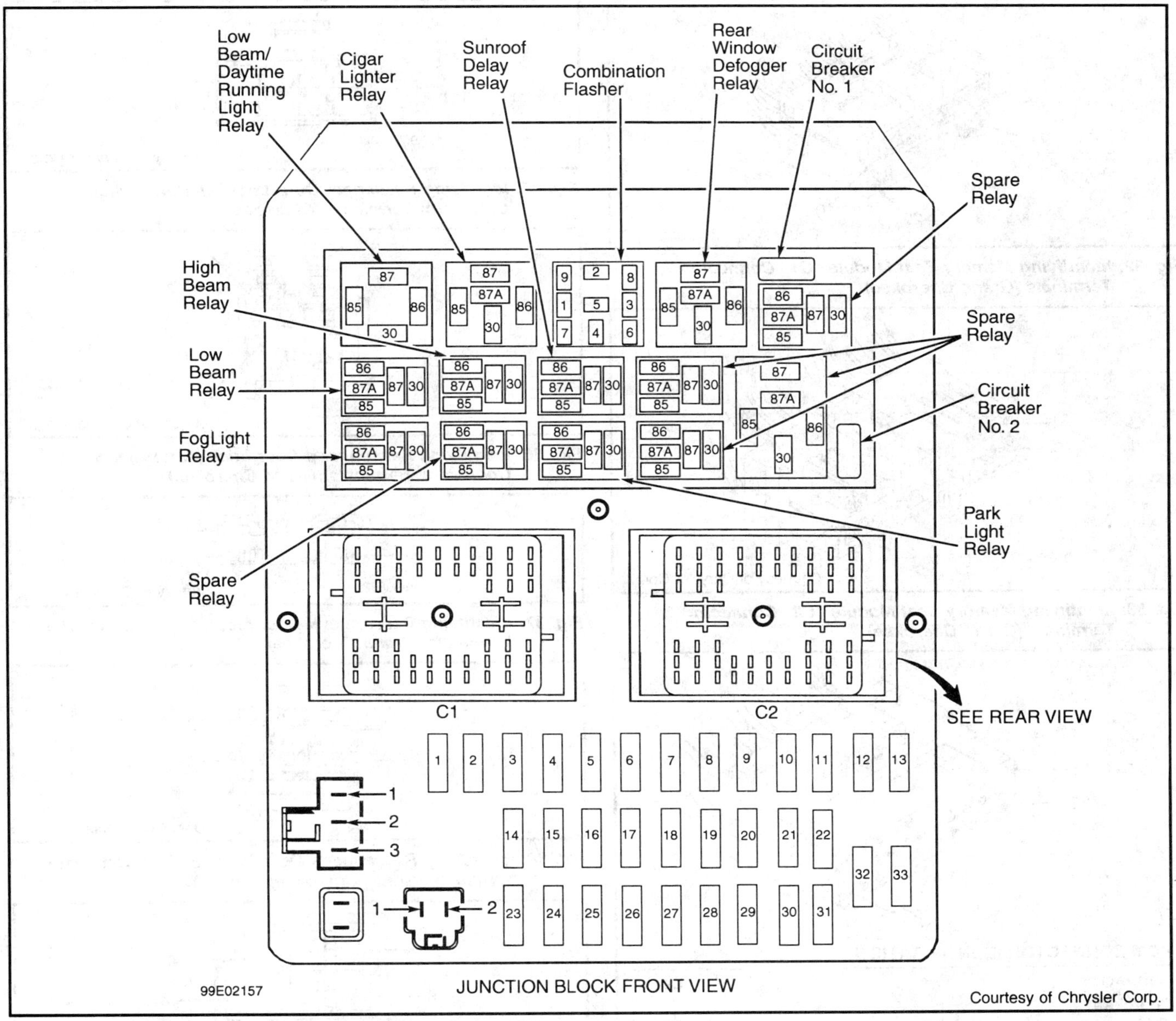

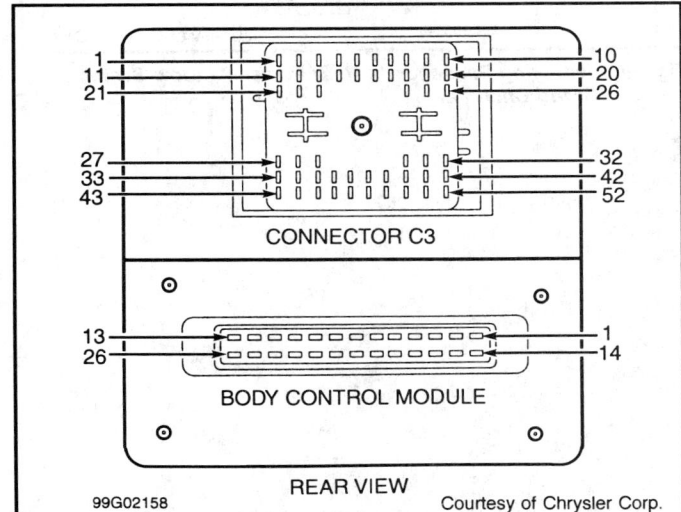

Fig. 28: Identifying Junction Block – Front View (Grand Cherokee)

CONNECTOR C3
BODY CONTROL MODULE
REAR VIEW
99G02158
Courtesy of Chrysler Corp.

Fig. 29: Identifying Junction Block – Rear View (Grand Cherokee)

99I02159
Courtesy of Chrysler Corp.

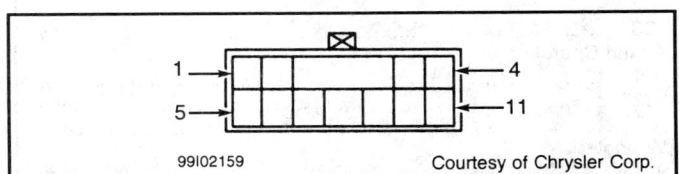

Fig. 30: Identifying Left Multi-Function Switch Connector Terminals (Grand Cherokee)

99G08320
Courtesy of Chrysler Corp.

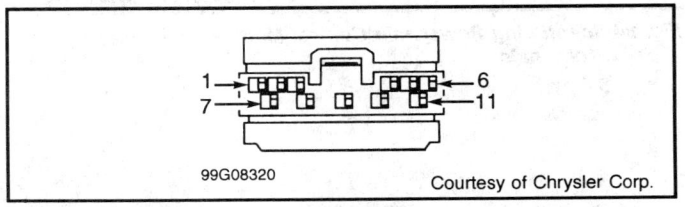

Fig. 31: Identifying Manual Temperature Control "C1" Connector (Grand Cherokee)

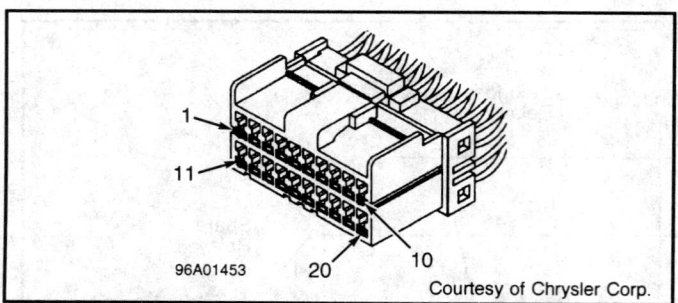

96A01453

Courtesy of Chrysler Corp.

Fig. 32: Identifying Memory Seat Module "C1" Connector Terminals (Grand Cherokee)

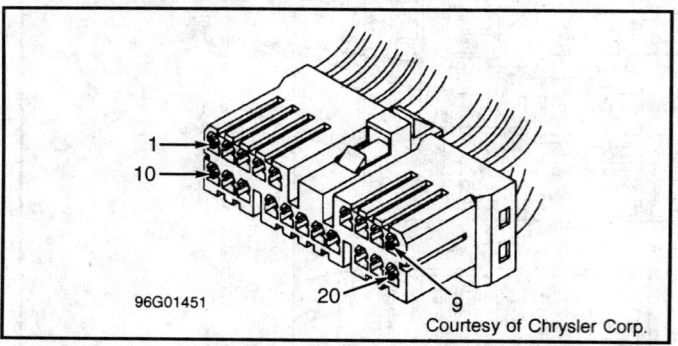

96G01451

Courtesy of Chrysler Corp.

Fig. 33: Identifying Memory Seat Module "C2" Connector Terminals (Grand Cherokee)

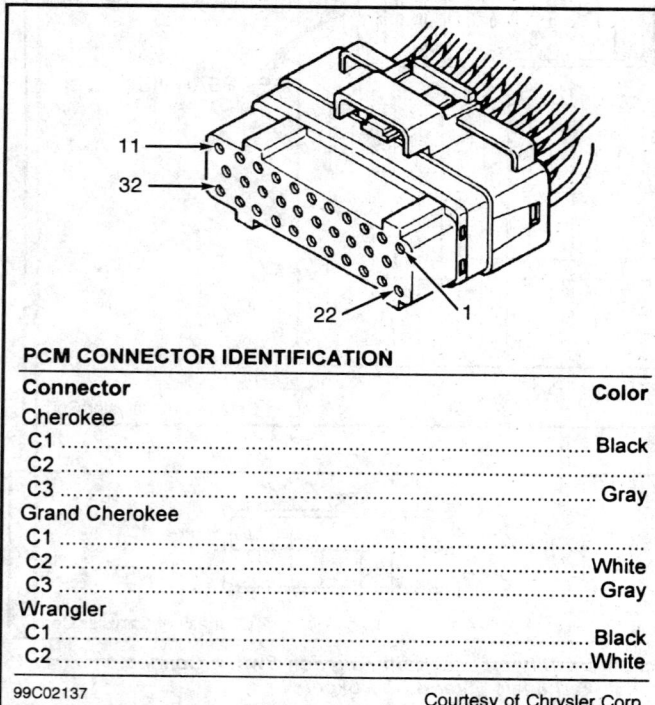

PCM CONNECTOR IDENTIFICATION

Connector	Color
Cherokee	
C1	Black
C2	
C3	Gray
Grand Cherokee	
C1	
C2	White
C3	Gray
Wrangler	
C1	Black
C2	White

99C02137

Courtesy of Chrysler Corp.

Fig. 34: Identifying Powertrain Control Module Connector Terminals

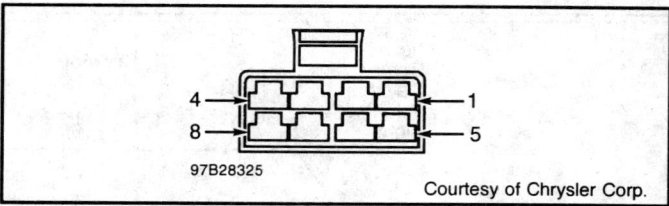

97B28325

Courtesy of Chrysler Corp.

Fig. 35: Idenifying Passenger Door Lock/Window Switch Connector Terminals (Cherokee)

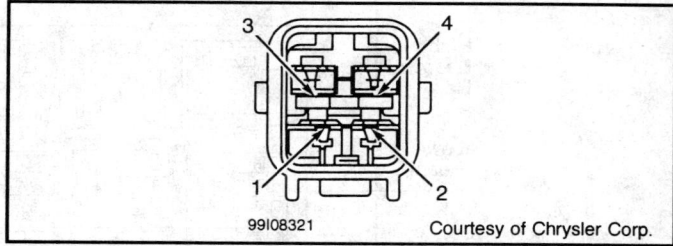

99I08321

Courtesy of Chrysler Corp.

Fig. 36: Identifying Passenger's Door Lock Motor/Ajar Switch Connector Terminals (Grand Cherokee)

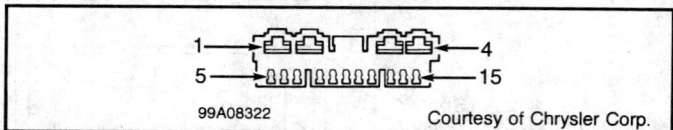

99A08322

Courtesy of Chrysler Corp.

Fig. 37: Identifying Passenger's Door Module "C1" Connector Terminals (Grand Cherokee)

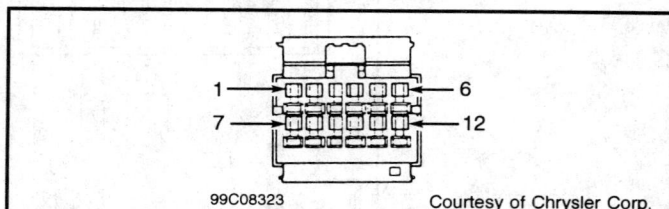

99C08323

Courtesy of Chrysler Corp.

Fig. 38: Identifying Passenger's Door Module "C2" Connector Terminals (Grand Cherokee)

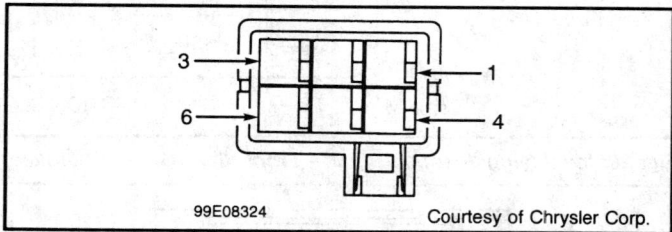

99E08324

Courtesy of Chrysler Corp.

Fig. 39: Identifying Passenger's Rear Power Window Switch (Grand Cherokee)

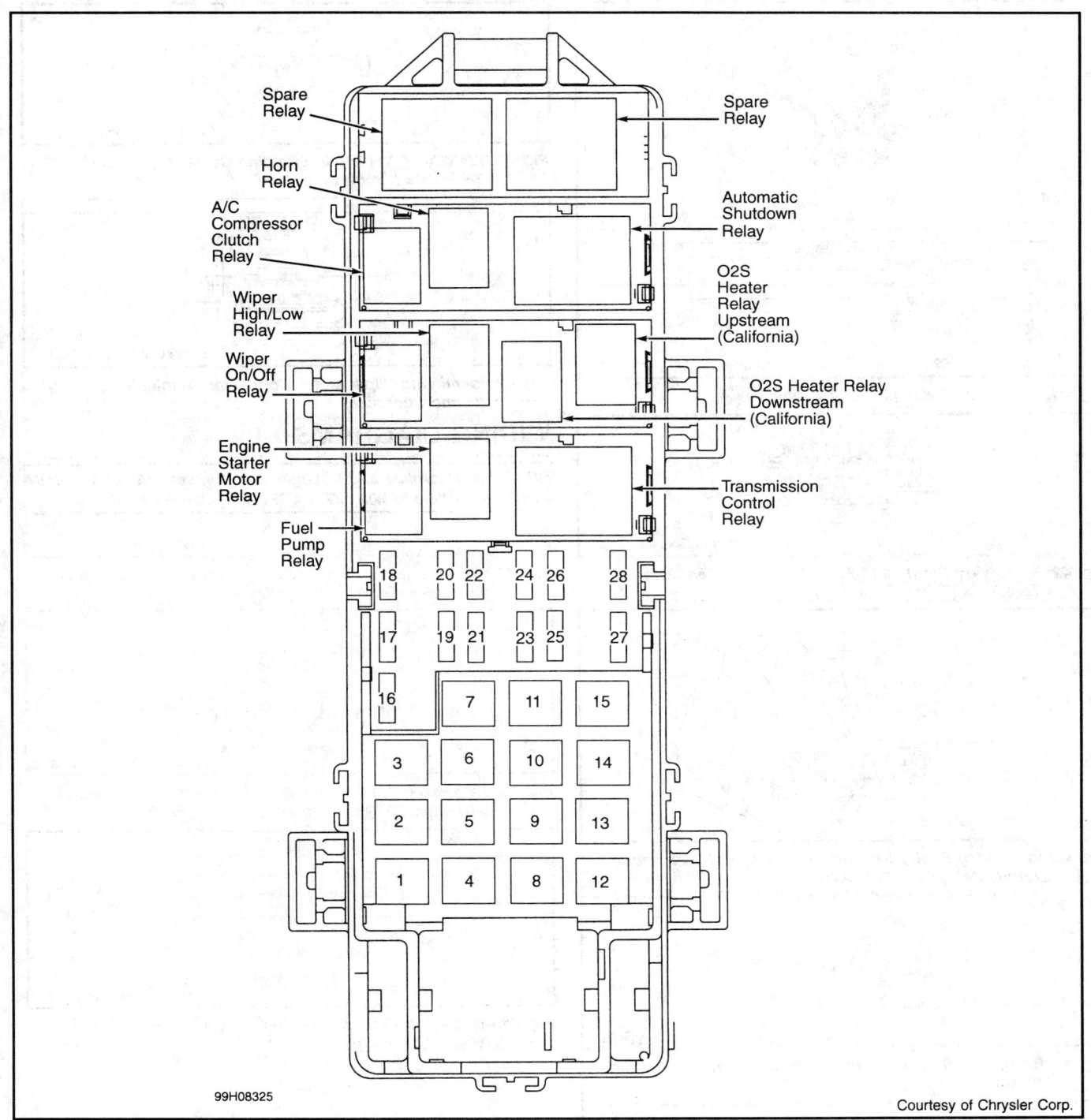

Fig. 40: Top View Of Power Distribution Center (Grand Cherokee)

99H08325

Courtesy of Chrysler Corp.

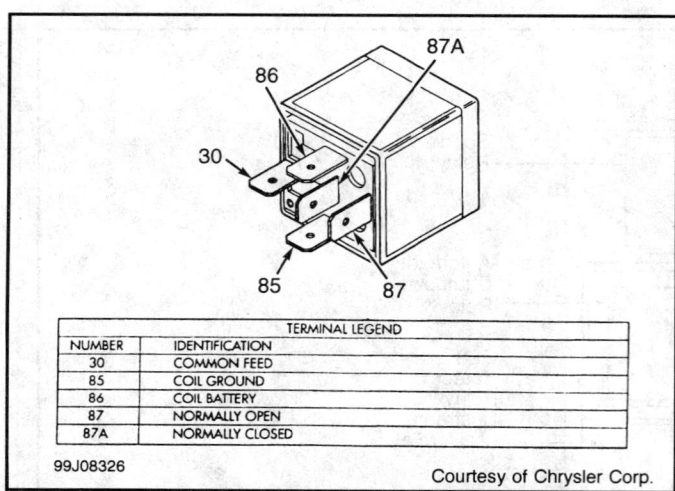

Fig. 41: Identifying Relay (Typical) Terminals

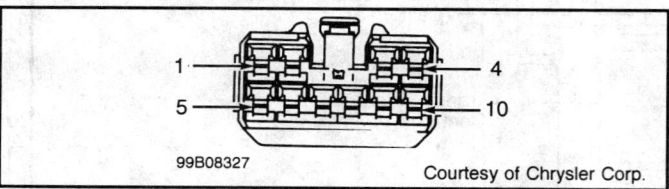

Fig. 42: Identifying Right Multi-Function Switch Connector Terminals (Grand Cherokee)

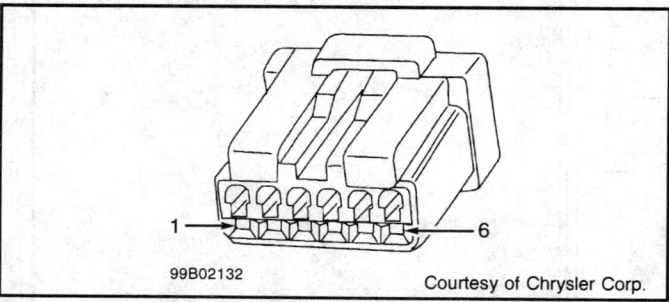

Fig. 43: Identifying Sentry Key Immobilizer Module Connector Terminals

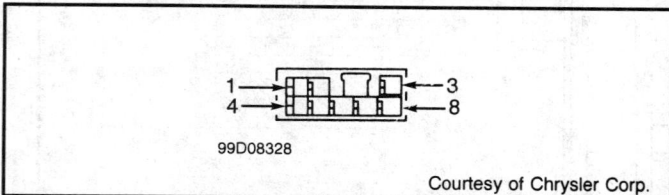

Fig. 44: Identifying Sunroof Control Module Connector Terminals (Grand Cherokee)

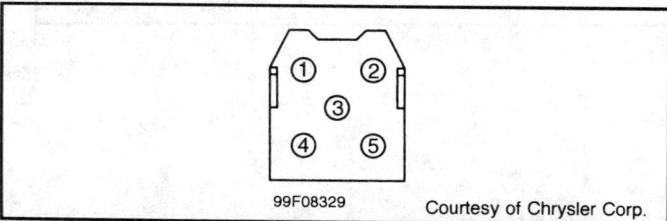

Fig. 45: Identifying Sunroof Switch Connector Terminals (Grand Cherokee)

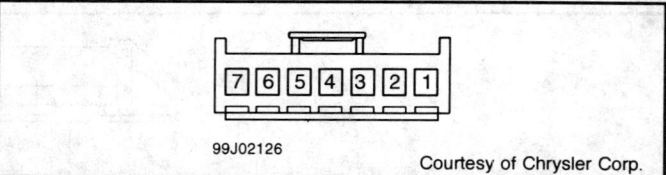

Fig. 46: Identifying Vehicle Information Center Connector Terminals (Grand Cherokee)

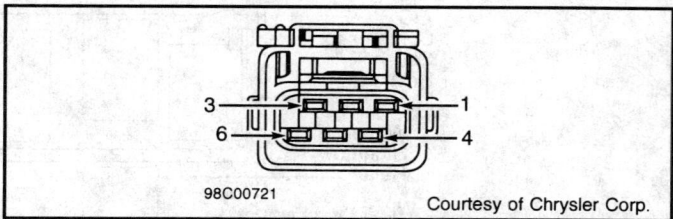

Fig. 47: Identifying Wiper Motor Connector Terminals (Grand Cherokee)

WIRING DIAGRAMS

NOTE: For Cherokee and Wrangler models, see DATA LINK CONNECTORS article in WIRING DIAGRAMS.

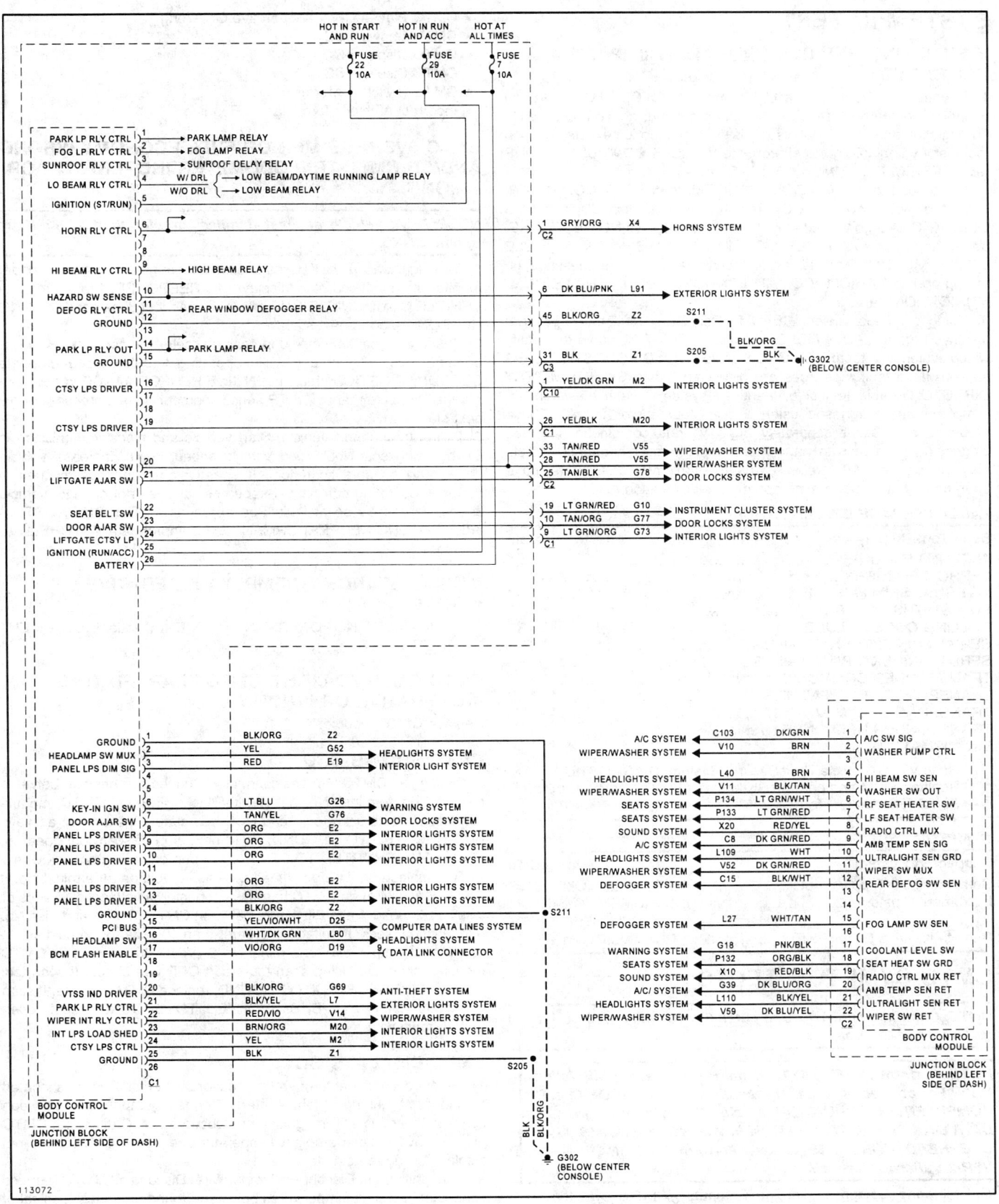

Fig. 48: BCM Wiring Diagram (Grand Cherokee)

SYSTEM ID TEST

IDENTIFYING VEHICLE EQUIPMENT & SYSTEM PROBLEMS

1) Connect scan tool to Data Link Connector (DLC). DLC is a 16-pin connector located on left side of steering column, above brake pedal. Turn ignition on. If scan tool display is not blank, go to next step. If scan tool display is blank, go to appropriate VEHICLE COMMUNICATIONS test in VEHICLE COMMUNICATIONS article.

2) Using scan tool, select BODY SYSTEM, then BODY COMPUTER. Scan tool will perform a CCD bus test. If scan tool displays BUS OPERATIONAL, go to next step. If scan tool displays NO RESPONSE, go to appropriate VEHICLE COMMUNICATIONS test in VEHICLE COMMUNICATIONS article. If scan tool displays any other message, go to appropriate VEHICLE COMMUNICATIONS test in VEHICLE COMMUNICATIONS article.

3) Using scan tool, select READ DTCs. If any fault messages are displayed, go to FAULT MESSAGE IDENTIFICATION table to identify which system is affected. Go to applicable test in DIAGNOSTIC TESTS section. If no fault messages are displayed, go to SYMPTOM TEST DIRECTORY table for list of identified systems. Fault messages or symptoms are diagnosed using a scan tool and/or DVOM. These problems may occur separately or in various combinations. When diagnosing a system with many apparent problems, a sequence of tests may be required. After repairs, ensure problem(s) or failure(s) have been corrected by performing appropriate verification test.

FAULT MESSAGE IDENTIFICATION

Scan Tool Display	Affected System
ANTENNA FAILURE	[1], [2]
EEPROM FAILURE	[1] VTSS
INTERNAL SKIM FAILURE	[2]
PCM STATUS FAILURE	[1] VTSS
ROLLING CODE FAILURE	[1] VTSS
SERIAL LINK EXTERNAL FAILURE	[1] VTSS
SERIAL LINK EXTERNAL FAILURE [3]	[1] VTSS
TRANSPONDER COMMUNICATION FAILURE	[1] VTSS
TRANSPONDER CRC FAILURE	[1] VTSS
TRANSPONDER ID MISMATCH	[1] VTSS
TRANSPONDER RESPONSE MISMATCH	[1] VTSS
VIN MISMATCH	[1] VTSS

[1] – Go to VTSS (Vehicle Theft Security System) DIAGNOSTIC TESTS.
[2] – Replace SKIM and perform SKIM INITIALIZATION PROCEDURE.
[3] – Sending secret key to PCM.

SYMPTOM TEST DIRECTORY

Suspected System	Proceed To
Computer Mini-Trip Computer	CMTC SYMPTOM TESTS
Instrument Cluster	INSTRUMENT SYMPTOM CLUSTER TESTS
Remote Keyless Entry (RKE)	RKE SYMPTOM TESTS

CMTC SYMPTOM TESTS

NOTE: Compass Mini-Trip Computer (CMTC) may also be known as Overhead Console.

NOTE: Perform SYSTEM ID TEST before proceeding with following tests. For connector terminal identification, see BODY CONTROL COMPUTER INTRODUCTION article. For wiring diagrams, see DATA LINK CONNECTORS article in WIRING DIAGRAMS. Also see OVERHEAD CONSOLES article. Perform VERIFICATION TEST: VER-2A after each repair.

The following Compass Mini-Trip Computer (CMTC) symptoms are covered:

- CMTC Average MPH Or Fuel Economy Wrong
- CMTC Trip Odometer Inoperative Or Wrong
- CMTC Distance To Empty Inoperative Or Wrong
- CMTC Fails To Light

- CMTC Elapsed Time Inoperative Or Wrong
- CMTC Shows CCD
- CMTC Displays OC
- CMTC Displays SC
- CMTC Switch Inoperative
- Incorrect Ambient Temperature Reading

CMTC AVERAGE MPH OR FUEL ECONOMY WRONG AND/OR CMTC TRIP ODOMETER INOPERATIVE OR WRONG

NOTE: Drive vehicle at least 3 miles (greater than 25 MPH) to update CMTC.

1) Turn ignition on. Using scan tool, read engine information under monitor display. If scan tool displays NO RESPONSE, see appropriate VEHICLE COMMUNICATIONS article. If scan tool does not display NO RESPONSE, go to next step.

2) Observe TP sensor while depressing accelerator pedal. If TP sensor percent does not increase while operating throttle, see appropriate SELF-DIAGNOSTICS article in ENGINE PERFORMANCE in appropriate MITCHELL® manual. If TP sensor percent does increase, go to next step.

3) Raise and support vehicle. Start vehicle and place transmission in Drive. Using scan tool, read vehicle speed signal. Increase vehicle speed and observe scan tool. If speed signal changes, system is currently operating correctly. If speed signal does not change, vehicle speed signal may be at fault. See appropriate SELF-DIAGNOSTICS article in ENGINE PERFORMANCE in appropriate MITCHELL® manual .

CMTC DISTANCE TO EMPTY INOPERATIVE OR WRONG

See ONE GAUGE NOT OPERATING PROPERLY under INSTRUMENT CLUSTER TESTS.

CMTC FAILS TO LIGHT, CMTC ELAPSED TIME INOPERATIVE OR WRONG

Replace CMTC module.

CMTC SHOWS CCD

1) Disconnect CMTC harness connector. Connect jumper wire between ground and terminal No. 11 (White/Black wire) on CMTC module connector. Using scan tool, read CCD bus status. If scan tool displays BUS SHORTED TO GROUND, go to next step. If scan tool does not display BUS SHORTED TO GROUND, repair open White/Black wire.

2) Turn ignition on. Using voltmeter, measure voltage at terminal No. 6 (White/Black wire) on CMTC harness connector. If voltage is 10 volts or less, repair open White/Black wire between CMTC module and fuse No. 9 in junction block. If voltage is greater than 10 volts, go to next step.

3) Connect jumper wire to terminal No. 5 (Violet/Brown wire) on CMTC module connector. Using scan tool, read CCD bus status. If scan tool displays BUS SHORTED TO GROUND, replace CMTC module. If scan tool does not display BUS SHORTED TO GROUND, repair open Violet/Brown wire.

CMTC DISPLAYS OC

1) Disconnect ambient temperature sensor connector. Sensor is located behind front bumper (right center). Connect jumper wire between connector terminals. Turn ignition on. Observe CMTC display. If CMTC displays SC, replace ambient temperature sensor. If CMTC does not display SC, go to next step.

2) Turn ignition off. Disconnect jumper wire. Disconnect CMTC harness connector. Connect jumper wires between ground and each terminal of ambient temperature sensor harness connector. Using ohmmeter, measure resistance between ground and terminal No. 4 (Violet/Light Green wire) on CMTC harness connector. If resistance is less than 5 ohms, go to next step. If resistance is 5 ohms or greater, repair open sensor signal circuit.

3) With jumper wires still connected, measure resistance at terminal No. 10 (Black/Light Blue wire) on CMTC connector. If resistance is less than 5 ohms, replace CMTC module. If resistance is 5 ohms or greater, repair open Black/Light Blue wire.

CMTC DISPLAYS SC

1) Disconnect ambient temperature sensor connector. Sensor is located behind front bumper (right center). Turn ignition on. Observe CMTC display. If CMTC displays OC, replace ambient temperature sensor. If CMTC does not display OC, go to next step.

2) Turn ignition off. Disconnect CMTC harness connector. Using ohmmeter, measure resistance between ground and terminal No. 4 (Violet/Light Green wire) on CMTC harness connector. If resistance is less than 25 ohms, repair sensor signal circuit for short to ground. If resistance is 25 ohms or greater, go to next step.

3) Measure resistance at terminal No. 10 (Black/Light Blue wire) on CMTC connector. If resistance is less than 5 ohms, repair Black/Light Blue wire for short to ground. If resistance is 5 ohms or greater, replace CMTC module.

CMTC SWITCH INOPERATIVE

1) Turn ignition off. Using scan tool, select COMPASS/MINI-TRIP, then INPUT/OUTPUT DISPLAY. If scan tool displays either button PRESSED, replace button assembly module. If scan tool displays either button PRESSED, go to next step.

2) Monitor scan tool display. Press STEP button. If scan tool displays button PRESSED, go to next step. If scan tool does not display button PRESSED, replace button assembly module.

3) Press US/M button. If scan tool displays button PRESSED, test is complete. If scan tool does not display button PRESSED, replace button assembly module.

INCORRECT AMBIENT TEMPERATURE READING

1) Disconnect and remove ambient temperature sensor. Sensor is located behind front bumper, right of center. Using external ohmmeter, measure resistance between sensor terminals and compare with AMBIENT TEMPERATURE SENSOR SPECIFICATIONS table. If resistance measurement does not correspond with AMBIENT TEMPERATURE SENSOR SPECIFICATIONS table, replace sensor. If sensor is within specification, go to next step.

AMBIENT TEMPERATURE SENSOR SPECIFICATIONS

Ambient Temperature	k/ohms
32°F (0°C)	29.3-36.0
50°F (10°C)	18.0-22.0
68°F (20°C)	11.4-13.6
77°F (25°C)	9.1-10.8
86°F (30°C)	7.4-8.7
104°F (40°C)	4.9-5.7
122°F (50°C)	3.3-3.8

2) Close all vehicle doors and ensure all lights are off. Wait one minute. Using external ohmmeter, measure resistance between ground and terminal No. 1 (Black/Light Blue wire) on ambient temperature sensor harness connector. If resistance is less than 5 ohms, go to next step. If resistance is 5 ohms or greater, go to **6)**.

3) Connect ambient temperature sensor. Disconnect CMTC connector. Using external ohmmeter, measure resistance between terminals No. 4 and No. 10 on CMTC harness connector. Compare with AMBIENT TEMPERATURE SENSOR SPECIFICATIONS table. If resistance measurement does not correspond with AMBIENT TEMPERATURE SENSOR SPECIFICATIONS table, go to next step. If sensor is within specification, replace CMTC module.

4) Disconnect ambient temperature sensor. Using external ohmmeter, measure resistance between ground and terminal No. 1 (Black/Light Blue wire) on sensor connector. If resistance is less than 500 k/ohms, repair Black/Light Blue wire for partial short to ground. If resistance is 500 k/ohms or greater, go to next step.

5) Move ohmmeter lead to terminal No. 2 (Violet/Light Green wire) on sensor connector. If resistance is less than 500 k/ohms, repair Violet/

Light Green wire for partial short to ground. If resistance is 500 k/ohms or greater, repair Violet/Light Green wire for short to Black/Light Blue wire.

6) Using external ohmmeter, measure resistance of Black/Light Blue wire between terminal No. 10 on CMTC harness connector and terminal No. 2 on ambient temperature sensor harness connector. If resistance is less than 5 ohms, replace CMTC. If resistance is 5 ohms or greater, repair open Black/Light Blue wire.

INSTRUMENT CLUSTER SYMPTOM TESTS

NOTE: Perform SYSTEM ID TEST before proceeding with following tests. For connector terminal identification, see BODY CONTROL COMPUTER INTRODUCTION article. For wiring diagrams, see DATA LINK CONNECTORS article in WIRING DIAGRAMS. Also see appropriate INSTRUMENT PANELS article. Perform VERIFICATION TEST: VER-2A after each repair.

The following instrument cluster symptoms are covered:
- All Gauges Not Operating
- Any CCD Cluster Warning Light Not Operating
- Any Hard Wired Warning Light Not Operating
- One Gauge Not Operating Properly

ALL GAUGES NOT OPERATING

1) Turn ignition on. Using scan tool, select ELECTRO/MECH CLUSTER. If scan tool displays BUS OPERATIONAL, go to next step. If scan tool displays any other message, see appropriate VEHICLE COMMUNICATIONS article. If scan tool displays NO RESPONSE, see appropriate VEHICLE COMMUNICATIONS article.

2) Using scan tool, select BODY, then BODY COMPUTER. Select SYSTEM TEST, then PCM MONITOR. If scan tool displays PCM ACTIVE ON THE BUS, go to next step. If scan tool does not display PCM ACTIVE ON THE BUS, see appropriate VEHICLE COMMUNICATIONS article.

3) Disconnect left instrument cluster 10-pin connector C1. Turn ignition on. Using external voltmeter, measure voltage between ground and terminal No. 9 (Pink wire) on instrument cluster harness connector. If voltage is 10 volts or less, repair open Pink wire. If voltage is more than 10 volts, replace instrument cluster.

ANY CCD CLUSTER WARNING LIGHT NOT OPERATING

1) Turn ignition on. Using scan tool, select ELECTRO/MECH CLUSTER. If scan tool displays BUS OPERATIONAL, go to next step. If scan tool displays any other message, see appropriate VEHICLE COMMUNICATIONS article. If scan tool displays NO RESPONSE, see appropriate VEHICLE COMMUNICATIONS article.

2) Using scan tool, select BODY, then BODY COMPUTER. Select SYSTEM TEST, then PCM MONITOR. If scan tool displays PCM ACTIVE ON THE BUS, go to next step. If scan tool does not display PCM ACTIVE ON THE BUS, see appropriate VEHICLE COMMUNICATIONS article.

3) Ensure ignition is off. Push and hold trip odometer reset button. Turn ignition on. Release button. Instrument cluster should enter self-test and actuate all CCD controlled indicator lights. If any indicator light did not illuminate, go to next step. If all indicator lights illuminate, system is functioning correctly.

4) Remove instrument cluster and inspect suspected indicator light bulb. Replace bulb(s) as needed. If bulb(s) is okay, replace instrument cluster.

ANY HARD WIRED WARNING LIGHT NOT OPERATING

1) Remove instrument cluster and inspect suspected indicator light bulb. Replace bulb(s) as needed. If bulb(s) is okay, go to next step.

2) If ABS, 4WD or brake warning lights are not functioning, go to next step. If high beam or turn signal indicator lights are not functioning, go to step **4)**.

3) Turn ignition on. Backprobe jumper wire between ground and appropriate terminal on instrument cluster harness connector. See INSTRUMENT CLUSTER INDICATOR LIGHT TERMINAL IDENTIFICATION table. If suspect indicator light does not illuminate, replace instrument cluster. If indicator light illuminates, inspect applicable circuit between ground and instrument cluster for open. Repair as needed.

4) Turn ignition off. Using ohmmeter, measure resistance between ground and terminal No. 6 (Black/Light Green wire) on instrument cluster left harness connector. If resistance is less than 5 ohms, go to next step. If resistance is 5 ohms or greater, repair open Black/Light Green wire.

5) Backprobe jumper wire between battery voltage source and appropriate terminal on instrument cluster harness connector. See INSTRUMENT CLUSTER INDICATOR LIGHT TERMINAL IDENTIFICATION table. If suspect indicator light does not illuminate, replace instrument cluster. If indicator light illuminates, inspect applicable circuit between ground and appropriate switch for open. Repair as needed.

INSTRUMENT CLUSTER INDICATOR LIGHT TERMINAL IDENTIFICATION

Indicator Light	Connector Location	Terminal No.
ABS	Left	4
Brake	Left	2
High Beam	Left	5
Left Turn Signal	Left	10
Right Turn Signal	Right	6
Part-Time 4WD	Right	5
Full-Time 4WD	Right	7

ONE GAUGE NOT OPERATING PROPERLY

1) Using scan tool, read DTCs. If any engine performance related codes are displayed, see appropriate SELF-DIAGNOSTICS article in ENGINE PERFORMANCE in appropriate MITCHELL® manual. If no engine performance related codes are displayed, go to next step.

2) Turn ignition off. Push and hold down trip odometer reset button. Turn ignition on. DO NOT start engine. Release trip odometer reset button. Compare operation of suspect gauge(s) with actuator test chart. See Fig. 1.

3) Instrument cluster will exit self-diagnostics mode at completion of test, or if ignition switch is turned off. If instrument cluster gauge(s) and/or indicator light(s) do not respond properly during actuator test, replace instrument cluster. If all gauges and indicator lights function correctly, system is currently functioning correctly.

RKE SYMPTOM TESTS

NOTE: Perform SYSTEM ID TEST before proceeding with following tests. For connector terminal identification, see BODY CONTROL COMPUTER INTRODUCTION article. For wiring diagrams, see DATA LINK CONNECTORS article in WIRING DIAGRAMS. Also see POWER DOOR LOCKS & REMOTE KEYLESS ENTRY SYSTEMS article. Perform VERIFICATION TEST: VER-2A after each repair.

The following RKE symptoms are covered:
• Illuminated Entry Inoperative
• Remote Keyless Entry Inoperative

ILLUMINATED ENTRY INOPERATIVE

1) Connect scan tool to DLC. Turn ignition on. If scan tool screen is blank, go to appropriate VEHICLE COMMUNICATIONS test in VEHICLE COMMUNICATIONS article.

2) Operate power door locks from door switches. If door locks operate correctly, go to next step. If door locks do not operate correctly, go to POWER DOOR LOCKS & REMOTE KEYLESS ENTRY SYSTEMS article.

3) Using scan tool, select SYSTEM MONITORS, then CCD BUS TEST. If scan tool displays BUS OPERATIONAL, go to next step. If scan tool does not display BUS OPERATIONAL, go to appropriate VEHICLE COMMUNICATIONS test in VEHICLE COMMUNICATIONS article.

4) Ensure ignition is in OFF position. Using RKE transmitter, operate door locks. If door locks operate correctly, go to next step. If door locks do not operate correctly, go to step 7).

5) Check courtesy light operation by opening and closing doors, and using dash switch. If courtesy lights operate correctly, go to next step. If courtesy lights do not operate, go to ILLUMINATION/INTERIOR LIGHTS article.

NOTE: Remote Keyless Entry (RKE) module may also be known as overhead module.

6) Ensure ignition is in OFF position. Disconnect RKE module connector. RKE module is mounted in roof or overhead console. Close all doors. Connect jumper wire between ground and terminal No. 1 (Yellow wire) on RKE module harness connector. If courtesy lights illuminate, replace RKE module. If courtesy lights do not illuminate, repair open Yellow wire.

7) Ensure RKE transmitter batteries are fully charged. Replace as needed. Using scan tool, program transmitter. Follow scan tool instructions. Using RKE transmitter, operate door locks. If door locks operate correctly, test is complete. If door locks do not operate correctly, go to next step.

8) Disconnect RKE module connector. RKE module is mounted in roof or overhead console. Using voltmeter, measure voltage between ground and terminal No. 2 (Pink wire) on RKE module harness connector. If voltage is 10 volts or greater, go to next step. If voltage is less than 10 volts, repair open Pink wire.

9) Connect jumper wire between ground and terminal No. 5 (Dark Blue wire) on RKE module harness connector. If door lock motor operates, go to next step. If door lock motor does not operate, go to step 12).

10) Connect jumper wire between ground and terminal No. 11 (Light Blue/Red wire) on RKE module harness connector. If door lock motor operates, replace RKE module. If door lock motor does not operate, go to next step.

11) Disconnect passenger door module 8-pin harness connector. Connect jumper wire between ground and terminals No. 5 and 11 on RKE module harness connector. Using ohmmeter, measure resistance between ground and terminal No. 2 (Dark Blue/Pink wire) on passenger door module 8-pin harness connector. If resistance is less than 5 ohms, go to step 14). If resistance is 5 ohms or greater, repair open Dark Blue/Pink wire.

12) Disconnect passenger door module 8-pin harness connector. Connect jumper wire between ground and terminals No. 5 and 11 on RKE module harness connector. Using ohmmeter, measure resistance between ground and terminal No. 2 (Dark Blue/Pink wire) on passenger door module 8-pin harness connector. If resistance is less than 5 ohms, go to next step. If resistance is 5 ohms or greater, repair open Dark Blue/Pink wire.

13) Ensure passenger door module 8-pin harness connector is connected. Connect jumper wire between ground and terminal No. 11 (Light Blue/Red wire) on RKE module harness connector. If door lock motor operates, replace RKE module. If door lock motor does not operate, go to next step.

14) Disconnect passenger door module 8-pin harness connector. Connect jumper wire between ground and terminals No. 5 and 11 on RKE module harness connector. Using ohmmeter, measure resistance between ground and terminal No. 1 (Light Blue/Red wire) on passenger door module 8-pin harness connector. If resistance is less than 5 ohms, replace passenger door module. If resistance is 5 ohms or greater, repair open Light Blue/Red wire.

REMOTE KEYLESS ENTRY INOPERATIVE

1) Connect scan tool to DLC. Turn ignition on. If scan tool screen is blank, go to appropriate VEHICLE COMMUNICATIONS test in VEHICLE COMMUNICATIONS article.

2) Operate power door locks from door switches. If door locks operate correctly, go to next step. If door locks do not operate correctly, go to POWER DOOR LOCKS & REMOTE KEYLESS ENTRY SYSTEMS article.

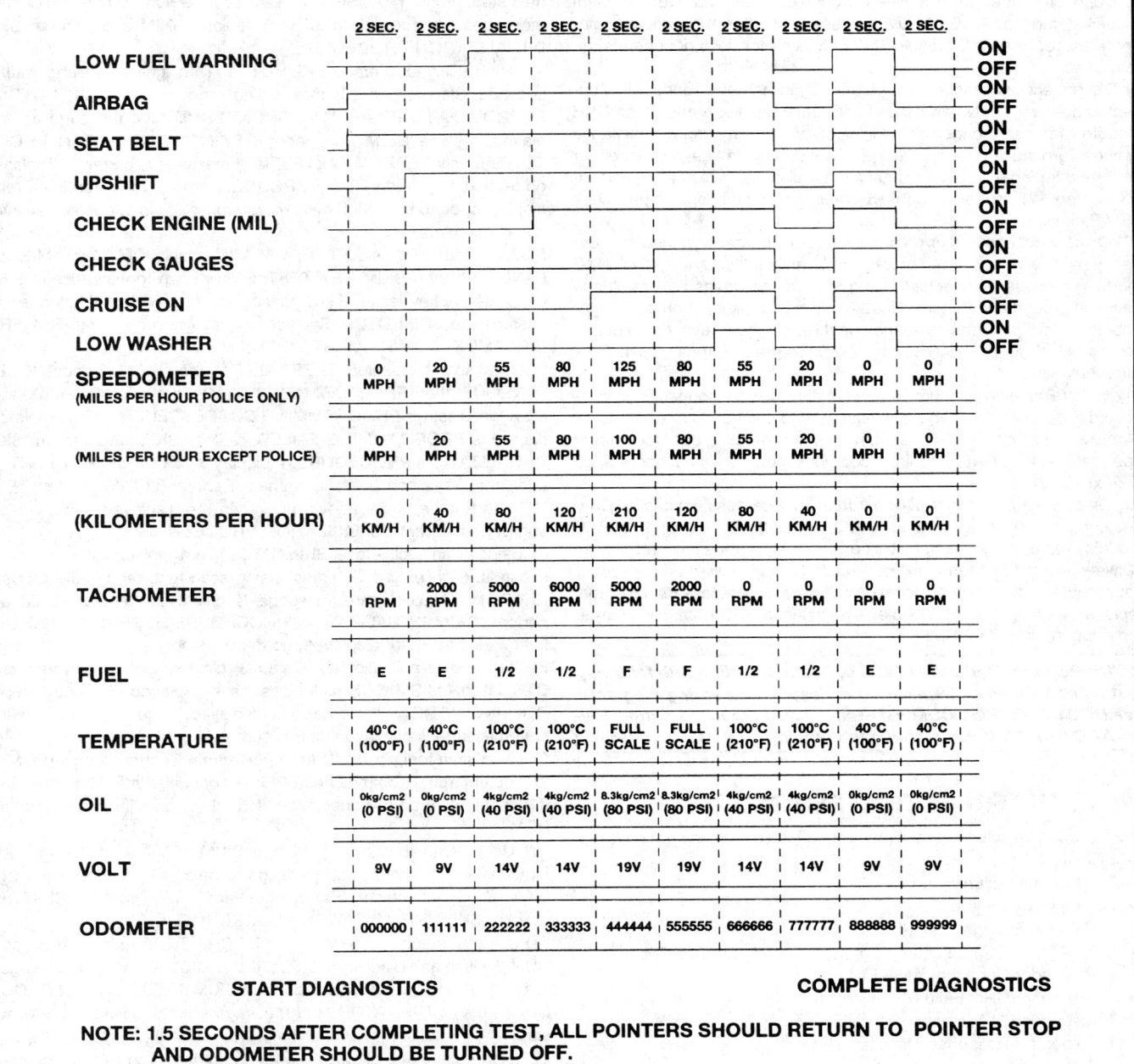

	2 SEC.	2 SEC.	2 SEC.	2 SEC.	2 SEC.	2 SEC.	2 SEC.	2 SEC.	2 SEC.	2 SEC.	
LOW FUEL WARNING											ON/OFF
AIRBAG											ON/OFF
SEAT BELT											ON/OFF
UPSHIFT											ON/OFF
CHECK ENGINE (MIL)											ON/OFF
CHECK GAUGES											ON/OFF
CRUISE ON											ON/OFF
LOW WASHER											ON/OFF
SPEEDOMETER (MILES PER HOUR POLICE ONLY)	0 MPH	20 MPH	55 MPH	80 MPH	125 MPH	80 MPH	55 MPH	20 MPH	0 MPH	0 MPH	
(MILES PER HOUR EXCEPT POLICE)	0 MPH	20 MPH	55 MPH	80 MPH	100 MPH	80 MPH	55 MPH	20 MPH	0 MPH	0 MPH	
(KILOMETERS PER HOUR)	0 KM/H	40 KM/H	80 KM/H	120 KM/H	210 KM/H	120 KM/H	80 KM/H	40 KM/H	0 KM/H	0 KM/H	
TACHOMETER	0 RPM	2000 RPM	5000 RPM	6000 RPM	5000 RPM	2000 RPM	0 RPM	0 RPM	0 RPM	0 RPM	
FUEL	E	E	1/2	1/2	F	F	1/2	1/2	E	E	
TEMPERATURE	40°C (100°F)	40°C (100°F)	100°C (210°F)	100°C (210°F)	FULL SCALE	FULL SCALE	100°C (210°F)	100°C (210°F)	40°C (100°F)	40°C (100°F)	
OIL	0kg/cm2 (0 PSI)	0kg/cm2 (0 PSI)	4kg/cm2 (40 PSI)	4kg/cm2 (40 PSI)	8.3kg/cm2 (80 PSI)	8.3kg/cm2 (80 PSI)	4kg/cm2 (40 PSI)	4kg/cm2 (40 PSI)	0kg/cm2 (0 PSI)	0kg/cm2 (0 PSI)	
VOLT	9V	9V	14V	14V	19V	19V	14V	14V	9V	9V	
ODOMETER	000000	111111	222222	333333	444444	555555	666666	777777	888888	999999	

START DIAGNOSTICS   COMPLETE DIAGNOSTICS

NOTE: 1.5 SECONDS AFTER COMPLETING TEST, ALL POINTERS SHOULD RETURN TO POINTER STOP AND ODOMETER SHOULD BE TURNED OFF.

96C29035

Courtesy of Chrysler Corp.

Fig. 1: Instrument Cluster Actuator Test

3) Using scan tool, select SYSTEM MONITORS, then CCD BUS TEST. If scan tool displays BUS OPERATIONAL, go to next step. If scan tool does not display BUS OPERATIONAL, go to appropriate VEHICLE COMMUNICATIONS test in VEHICLE COMMUNICATIONS article.

4) Using scan tool, select THEFT ALARM, then MISCELLANEOUS. Select PROGRAM RKE. Follow scan tool instructions and program all transmitters. Operate door locks using transmitter. If door locks operate properly, test is complete. If door locks do not operate properly, go to next step.

5) Ensure RKE transmitter batteries are fully charged. Replace as needed. Using scan tool, program transmitter. Follow scan tool instruc-

tions. Using RKE transmitter, operate door locks. If door locks operate correctly, test is complete. If door locks do not operate correctly, go to next step.

NOTE: Remote Keyless Entry (RKE) module may also be known as overhead module.

6) Disconnect RKE module connector. RKE module is mounted in roof or overhead console. Using voltmeter, measure voltage between ground and terminal No. 2 (Pink wire) on RKE module harness connector. If voltage is 10 volts or greater, go to next step. If voltage is less than 10 volts, repair open Pink wire.

7) Connect jumper wire between ground and terminal No. 5 (Dark Blue wire) on RKE module harness connector. If door lock motor operates, go to next step. If door lock motor does not operate, go to step 10).

8) Connect jumper wire between ground and terminal No. 11 (Light Blue/Red wire) on RKE module harness connector. If door lock motor operates, replace RKE module. If door lock motor does not operate, go to next step.

9) Disconnect passenger door module 8-pin harness connector. Connect jumper wire between ground and terminals No. 5 and 11 on RKE module harness connector. Using ohmmeter, measure resistance between ground and terminal No. 2 (Dark Blue/Pink wire) on passenger door module 8-pin harness connector. If resistance is less than 5 ohms, go to step **12)**. If resistance is 5 ohms or greater, repair open Dark Blue/Pink wire.

10) Disconnect passenger door module 8-pin harness connector. Connect jumper wire between ground and terminals No. 5 and 11 on RKE module harness connector. Using ohmmeter, measure resistance between ground and terminal No. 2 (Dark Blue/Pink wire) on passenger door module 8-pin harness connector. If resistance is less than 5 ohms, go to next step. If resistance is 5 ohms or greater, repair open Dark Blue/Pink wire.

11) Ensure passenger door module 8-pin harness connector is connected. Connect jumper wire between ground and terminal No. 11 (Light Blue/Red wire) on RKE module harness connector. If door lock motor operates, replace RKE module. If door lock motor does not operate, go to next step.

12) Disconnect passenger door module 8-pin harness connector. Connect jumper wire between ground and terminals No. 5 and 11 on RKE module harness connector. Using ohmmeter, measure resistance between ground and terminal No. 1 (Light Blue/Red wire) on passenger door module 8-pin harness connector. If resistance is less than 5 ohms, replace passenger door module. If resistance is 5 ohms or greater, repair open Light Blue/Red wire.

NOTE: Perform SYSTEM ID TEST before proceeding with following tests. For connector terminal identification and wiring diagrams, see BODY CONTROL COMPUTER INTRODUCTION. Perform VERIFICATION TEST: VER-2A after each repair.

VTSS DIAGNOSTIC TESTS

The following vehicle theft security system fault messages are covered:
- EEPROM Failure
- PCM Status Failure
- Rolling Code Failure
- Serial Link External Failure
- Serial Link External Failure – Sending Secret Key To PCM
- Transponder Communication Failure
- Transponder CRC Failure
- Transponder ID Mismatch
- Transponder Response Mismatch
- VIN Mismatch

EEPROM FAILURE

NOTE: Sentry Key Immobilizer System (SKIS) diagnosis may require use of all spare keys.

1) Ensure battery is fully charged. Using scan tool, read and record SKIM DTCs. Erase SKIM DTCs. Turn ignition off, then back to RUN position. After 3 minutes, read SKIM DTCs. If only EEPROM FAILURE fault message is currently displayed or was previously recorded, go to next step. If TRANSPONDER ID or RESPONSE MISMATCH fault message is displayed, go to step **3)**. If VIN MISMATCH & ROLLING CODE FAILURE fault message is displayed, test is complete. If VIN MISMATCH fault message is displayed, go to step **8)**.

2) If EEPROM FAILURE fault message was previously recorded but did not reset after DTCs were erased, go to next step. If EEPROM FAILURE fault message is currently displayed, replace SKIM and perform SKIM INITIALIZATION PROCEDURE.

3) If EEPROM FAILURE fault message is not currently displayed with TRANSPONDER ID or RESPONSE MISMATCH fault message, go to

next step. If only TRANSPONDER ID or RESPONSE MISMATCH fault messages are currently displayed, replace SKIM and perform SKIM INITIALIZATION PROCEDURE.

4) Using scan tool, erase SKIM DTCs. Turn ignition off and wait 10 seconds. Start engine 20 times. Using scan tool, read SKIM DTCs. If EEPROM FAILURE and TRANSPONDER ID fault message are displayed, replace SKIM and perform SKIM INITIALIZATION PROCEDURE. If only EEPROM FAILURE fault message is currently displayed, go to next step. If only TRANSPONDER ID fault message is currently displayed, go to step **6)**. If neither fault message is currently displayed, test is complete.

5) Using scan tool, select THEFT ALARM, then SKIM. Select MISCELLANEOUS, then SKIM KEY TEST. Follow scan tool instructions. Test key in sentry key tester. If key passes, go to next step. If key does not pass, erase SKIM DTCs. Replace and program new key. See PROGRAMMING BLANK SMART KEY USING SCAN TOOL.

6) Using scan tool, select THEFT ALARM, then SKIM. Select MISCELLANEOUS, then PROGRAM NEW KEY. Read status of current key. If scan tool displays PROGRAMMING SUCCESSFUL, test is complete. If display is PROGRAMMING FAILED, replace SKIM and perform SKIM INITIALIZATION PROCEDURE. If display is MAXIMUM KEY LIMIT, no additional keys can be programmed. Perform VERIFICATION TEST: VER-2A If none of the above messages are displayed, replace SKIM and perform SKIM INITIALIZATION PROCEDURE.

7) Using scan tool, erase SKIM DTCs. Turn ignition off and wait 10 seconds. Start engine 20 times. Using scan tool, read SKIM DTCs. If EEPROM FAILURE fault message is displayed, replace SKIM and perform SKIM INITIALIZATION PROCEDURE. If EEPROM FAILURE fault message is not displayed, go to next step.

8) Start engine and allow to idle for 3 minutes. Using scan tool, read DTCs. If VIN MISMATCH fault message is displayed, go to next step. If ROLLING CODE fault message is displayed, go to step **13)**. If neither fault message is displayed, test is complete.

9) Using scan tool, read VIN from Powertrain Control Module (PCM). If VIN output from PCM matches VIN on door jamb plate, go to next step. If VIN output from PCM does not match VIN on door jamb plate, replace PCM.

10) Using scan tool, read VIN from SKIM. If VIN output from SKIM matches VIN on door jamb plate, go to next step. If VIN output from SKIM does not match VIN on door jamb plate, replace SKIM and perform SKIM INITIALIZATION PROCEDURE.

11) Using scan tool, erase VIN MISMATCH DTC. Turn ignition switch to RUN position and read SKIM DTCs. If VIN MISMATCH fault message is still present, replace SKIM and perform SKIM INITIALIZATION PROCEDURE. If VIN MISMATCH fault message is not displayed, go to next step.

12) Start engine and allow to idle for 3 minutes. Using scan tool, erase SKIM DTCs. Read SKIM DTCs. If SKIM MISMATCH fault message is still present, replace SKIM and perform SKIM INITIALIZATION PROCEDURE. If SKIM MISMATCH fault message is not displayed, test is complete.

13) Using scan tool, erase SKIM DTCs. Select THEFT ALARM, then SKIM. If scan tool displays NO RESPONSE, go to appropriate VEHICLE COMMUNICATIONS test in VEHICLE COMMUNICATIONS article. If scan tool does not display NO RESPONSE,

14) Using scan tool, select BODY, then BODY COMPUTER. Select SYSTEM TEST, then PCM MONITOR. If scan tool displays PCM ACTIVE ON THE BUS, go to next step. If scan tool does not display PCM ACTIVE ON THE BUS, see appropriate VEHICLE COMMUNICATIONS article.

15) Using scan tool, select ENGINE, then read DTCs. If scan tool displays any PCM related DTCs, see appropriate SELF-DIAGNOSTICS article in ENGINE PERFORMANCE in appropriate MITCHELL® manual. If scan tool does not display any PCM related DTCs, replace smart key immobilizer module. Perform SKIM INITIALIZATION PROCEDURE.

PCM STATUS FAILURE

1) Using scan tool, select ENGINE, then read DTCs. If scan tool displays any PCM related DTCs, see appropriate SELF-DIAGNOSTICS article in ENGINE PERFORMANCE in appropriate MITCHELL® manual. If scan tool does not display any PCM related DTCs, go to next step.

2) Ensure battery is fully charged. Using scan tool, read and record SKIM DTCs. Erase SKIM DTCs. Turn ignition off, then back to RUN position. After 3 minutes, read SKIM DTCs. If PCM STATUS FAILURE fault message is currently displayed, go to next step. If PCM STATUS FAILURE fault message is not currently displayed, go to step 6).

3) Using scan tool, erase SKIM DTCs. Select THEFT ALARM, then SKIM. If scan tool displays NO RESPONSE, go to appropriate VEHICLE COMMUNICATIONS test in VEHICLE COMMUNICATIONS article. If scan tool does not display NO RESPONSE, go to next step.

4) Using scan tool, select BODY, then BODY COMPUTER. Select SYSTEM TEST, then PCM MONITOR. If scan tool displays PCM ACTIVE ON THE BUS, go to next step. If scan tool does not display PCM ACTIVE ON THE BUS, see appropriate VEHICLE COMMUNICATIONS article.

5) Using scan tool, select ENGINE, then read DTCs. If scan tool displays any PCM related DTCs, see appropriate SELF-DIAGNOSTICS article in ENGINE PERFORMANCE in appropriate MITCHELL® manual. If scan tool does not display any PCM related DTCs, replace SKIM. Perform SKIM INITIALIZATION PROCEDURE.

6) Using scan tool, erase SKIM DTCs. Turn ignition off and wait 10 seconds. Start engine 20 times. Using scan tool, read SKIM DTCs. If any SKIM DTCs are displayed, go to next step. If no fault message are currently displayed, test is complete.

7) Using scan tool, erase SKIM DTCs. Select THEFT ALARM, then SKIM. If scan tool displays NO RESPONSE, go to appropriate VEHICLE COMMUNICATIONS test in VEHICLE COMMUNICATIONS article. If scan tool does not display NO RESPONSE, go to next step.

8) Using scan tool, select BODY, then BODY COMPUTER. Select SYSTEM TEST, then PCM MONITOR. If scan tool displays PCM ACTIVE ON THE BUS, go to next step. If scan tool does not display PCM ACTIVE ON THE BUS, see appropriate VEHICLE COMMUNICATIONS article.

9) Using scan tool, select ENGINE, then read DTCs. If scan tool displays any PCM related DTCs, see appropriate SELF-DIAGNOSTICS article in ENGINE PERFORMANCE in appropriate MITCHELL® manual. If scan tool does not display any PCM related DTCs, replace smart key immobilizer module. Perform SKIM INITIALIZATION PROCEDURE.

ROLLING CODE FAILURE

1) Using scan tool, select ENGINE, then read DTCs. If scan tool displays any PCM related DTCs, see appropriate SELF-DIAGNOSTICS article in ENGINE PERFORMANCE in appropriate MITCHELL® manual. If scan tool does not display any PCM related DTCs, go to next step.

2) Ensure battery is fully charged. Using scan tool, read and record SKIM DTCs. Erase SKIM DTCs. Turn ignition off, then back to RUN position. After 3 minutes, read SKIM DTCs. If only ROLLING CODE FAILURE fault message is currently displayed or was previously recorded, go to next step. If VIN MISMATCH with or without EEPROM FAILURE fault message is displayed, test is complete.

3) Using scan tool, erase SKIM DTCs. Select THEFT ALARM, then SKIM. If scan tool displays NO RESPONSE, go to appropriate VEHICLE COMMUNICATIONS test in VEHICLE COMMUNICATIONS article. If scan tool does not display NO RESPONSE, go to next step.

4) Using scan tool, select BODY, then BODY COMPUTER. Select SYSTEM TEST, then PCM MONITOR. If scan tool displays PCM ACTIVE ON THE BUS, go to next step. If scan tool does not display PCM ACTIVE ON THE BUS, see appropriate VEHICLE COMMUNICATIONS article.

5) Using scan tool, select ENGINE, then read DTCs. If scan tool displays any PCM related DTCs, see appropriate SELF-DIAGNOSTICS article in ENGINE PERFORMANCE in appropriate MITCHELL® manual. If scan tool does not display any PCM related DTCs, replace SKIM. Perform SKIM INITIALIZATION PROCEDURE.

6) Using scan tool, erase SKIM DTCs. Turn ignition off and wait 10 seconds. Start engine 20 times. Using scan tool, read SKIM DTCs. If any SKIM DTCs are displayed, go to next step. If no fault message are currently displayed, test is complete.

7) Using scan tool, erase SKIM DTCs. Select THEFT ALARM, then SKIM. If scan tool displays NO RESPONSE, go to appropriate VEHICLE COMMUNICATIONS test in VEHICLE COMMUNICATIONS article. If scan tool does not display NO RESPONSE, go to next step.

8) Using scan tool, select BODY, then BODY COMPUTER. Select SYSTEM TEST, then PCM MONITOR. If scan tool displays PCM ACTIVE ON THE BUS, go to next step. If scan tool does not display PCM ACTIVE ON THE BUS, see appropriate VEHICLE COMMUNICATIONS article.

9) Using scan tool, select ENGINE, then read DTCs. If scan tool displays any PCM related DTCs, see appropriate SELF-DIAGNOSTICS article in ENGINE PERFORMANCE in appropriate MITCHELL® manual. If scan tool does not display any PCM related DTCs, replace SKIM. Perform SKIM INITIALIZATION PROCEDURE.

SERIAL LINK EXTERNAL FAILURE

1) Using scan tool, select ENGINE, then read DTCs. If scan tool displays any PCM related DTCs, see appropriate SELF-DIAGNOSTICS article in ENGINE PERFORMANCE in appropriate MITCHELL® manual. If scan tool does not display any PCM related DTCs, go to next step.

2) Ensure battery is fully charged. Using scan tool, read and record SKIM DTCs. Erase SKIM DTCs. Turn ignition off, then back to RUN position. After 3 minutes, read SKIM DTCs. If SERIAL LINK EXTERNAL FAILURE fault message is currently displayed or was previously recorded, go to next step. If SERIAL LINK EXTERNAL FAILURE fault message is not displayed, go to step 7).

3) Using scan tool, erase SKIM DTCs. Select THEFT ALARM, then SKIM. If scan tool displays NO RESPONSE, go to appropriate VEHICLE COMMUNICATIONS test in VEHICLE COMMUNICATIONS article. If scan tool does not display NO RESPONSE, go to next step.

4) Using scan tool, select BODY, then BODY COMPUTER. Select SYSTEM TEST, then PCM MONITOR. If scan tool displays PCM ACTIVE ON THE BUS, go to next step. If scan tool does not display PCM ACTIVE ON THE BUS, see appropriate VEHICLE COMMUNICATIONS article.

5) Using scan tool, select ENGINE, then read DTCs. If scan tool displays any PCM related DTCs, see appropriate SELF-DIAGNOSTICS article in ENGINE PERFORMANCE in appropriate MITCHELL® manual. If scan tool does not display any PCM related DTCs, replace SKIM. Perform SKIM INITIALIZATION PROCEDURE.

6) Using scan tool, erase SKIM DTCs. Turn ignition off and wait 10 seconds. Start engine 20 times. Using scan tool, read SKIM DTCs. If any SKIM DTCs are displayed, go to next step. If no fault message are currently displayed, test is complete.

7) Using scan tool, erase SKIM DTCs. Select THEFT ALARM, then SKIM. If scan tool displays NO RESPONSE, go to appropriate VEHICLE COMMUNICATIONS test in VEHICLE COMMUNICATIONS article. If scan tool does not display NO RESPONSE, go to next step.

8) Using scan tool, select BODY, then BODY COMPUTER. Select SYSTEM TEST, then PCM MONITOR. If scan tool displays PCM ACTIVE ON THE BUS, go to next step. If scan tool does not display PCM ACTIVE ON THE BUS, see appropriate VEHICLE COMMUNICATIONS article.

9) Using scan tool, select ENGINE, then read DTCs. If scan tool displays any PCM related DTCs, see appropriate SELF-DIAGNOSTICS article in ENGINE PERFORMANCE in appropriate MITCHELL® manual. If scan tool does not display any PCM related DTCs, replace smart key immobilizer module. Perform SKIM INITIALIZATION PROCEDURE.

SERIAL LINK EXTERNAL FAILURE – SENDING SECRET KEY TO PCM

1) Using scan tool, select ENGINE, then read DTCs. If scan tool displays any PCM related DTCs, see appropriate SELF-DIAGNOSTICS article in ENGINE PERFORMANCE in appropriate MITCHELL® manual. If scan tool does not display any PCM related DTCs, go to next step.

2) Ensure battery is fully charged. Using scan tool, read and record SKIM DTCs. Erase SKIM DTCs. Turn ignition off, then back to RUN position. After 3 minutes, read SKIM DTCs. If SERIAL LINK EXTERNAL FAILURE fault message is currently displayed, go to next step. If SERIAL LINK EXTERNAL FAILURE fault message is not displayed, DTC is not current.

3) Using scan tool, erase SKIM DTCs. Attempt another secret key transfer to PCM. Using scan tool, read DTCs. If SERIAL LINK EXTERNAL fault message is displayed, go to next step. If SERIAL LINK EXTERNAL fault message is not displayed, test is complete.

4) Using scan tool, erase SKIM DTCs. Select THEFT ALARM, then SKIM. If scan tool displays NO RESPONSE, go to appropriate VEHICLE COMMUNICATIONS test in VEHICLE COMMUNICATIONS article. If scan tool does not display NO RESPONSE, go to next step.

5) Using scan tool, select BODY, then BODY COMPUTER. Select SYSTEM TEST, then PCM MONITOR. If scan tool displays PCM ACTIVE ON THE BUS, go to next step. If scan tool does not display PCM ACTIVE ON THE BUS, see appropriate VEHICLE COMMUNICATIONS article.

6) Using scan tool, select ENGINE, then read DTCs. If scan tool displays any PCM related DTCs, see appropriate SELF-DIAGNOSTICS article in ENGINE PERFORMANCE in appropriate MITCHELL® manual. If scan tool does not display any PCM related DTCs, replace SKIM. Perform SKIM INITIALIZATION PROCEDURE.

TRANSPONDER COMMUNICATION FAILURE

1) Ensure battery is fully charged. Using scan tool, read and record SKIM DTCs. Erase SKIM DTCs. Turn ignition off, then back to RUN position. After 3 minutes, read SKIM DTCs. If TRANSPONDER COMMUNICATION FAILURE fault message is currently displayed or was previously recorded, go to next step. If TRANSPONDER COMMUNICATION FAILURE fault message is not displayed, go to step **3)**.

2) Using scan tool, select THEFT ALARM, then SKIM. Select MISCELLANEOUS, then SKIM KEY TEST. Follow scan tool instructions. Test key in sentry key tester. If key passes, replace SKIM. Perform SKIM INITIALIZATION PROCEDURE. If key does not pass, erase SKIM DTCs. Replace and program new key. See PROGRAMMING BLANK SMART KEY USING SCAN TOOL.

3) Start engine several times using each of vehicle's keys. Using scan tool, read SKIM DTCs. If TRANSPONDER fault message is displayed, replace SKIM. Perform SKIM INITIALIZATION PROCEDURE. If TRANSPONDER fault message is not displayed, test is complete.

TRANSPONDER CRC FAILURE

1) Ensure battery is fully charged. Using scan tool, read and record SKIM DTCs. Erase SKIM DTCs. Turn ignition off, then back to RUN position. After 3 minutes, read SKIM DTCs. If TRANSPONDER CRC FAILURE fault message is currently displayed or was previously recorded, go to next step. If TRANSPONDER CRC FAILURE fault message is not displayed, go to step **3)**.

2) Using scan tool, select THEFT ALARM, then SKIM. Select MISCELLANEOUS, then SKIM KEY TEST. Follow scan tool instructions. Test key in sentry key tester. If key passes, replace SKIM. Perform SKIM INITIALIZATION PROCEDURE. If key does not pass, erase SKIM DTCs. Replace and program new key. See PROGRAMMING BLANK SMART KEY USING SCAN TOOL.

3) Start engine several times using each of vehicle's keys. Using scan tool, read SKIM DTCs. If TRANSPONDER fault message is displayed, replace SKIM. Perform SKIM INITIALIZATION PROCEDURE. If TRANSPONDER fault message is not displayed, test is complete.

TRANSPONDER ID MISMATCH/TRANSPONDER RESPONSE MISMATCH

1) Ensure battery is fully charged. Using scan tool, read and record SKIM DTCs. Erase SKIM DTCs. Turn ignition off, then back to RUN position. After 3 minutes, read SKIM DTCs. If only TRANSPONDER ID MISMATCH or TRANSPONDER RESPONSE MISMATCH FAILURE fault message is currently displayed or was previously recorded, go to next step. If EEPROM failure fault message is also displayed, go to step **4)**.

2) If TRANSPONDER ID MISMATCH or TRANSPONDER RESPONSE MISMATCH FAILURE fault message are currently displayed, go to **7)**. If TRANSPONDER ID MISMATCH or TRANSPONDER RESPONSE MISMATCH FAILURE are previously recorded, but now not currently displayed, go to next step.

3) Start engine several times using each of vehicle's keys. Using scan tool, read SKIM DTCs. If a TRANSPONDER fault message is displayed, replace SKIM. Perform SKIM INITIALIZATION PROCEDURE. If no TRANSPONDER fault message is not displayed, test is complete.

4) If TRANSPONDER ID MISMATCH or TRANSPONDER RESPONSE MISMATCH FAILURE fault message are currently displayed, replace SKIM. Perform SKIM INITIALIZATION PROCEDURE. If TRANSPONDER ID MISMATCH or TRANSPONDER RESPONSE MISMATCH FAILURE was previously recorded, but now not currently displayed with EEPROM failure, go to next step.

5) Using scan tool, erase SKIM DTCs. Turn ignition off and wait 10 seconds. Start engine 20 times. Using scan tool, read SKIM DTCs. If EEPROM and TRANSPONDER fault messages are displayed, replace SKIM. Perform SKIM INITIALIZATION PROCEDURE. If only EEPROM failure is displayed, go to next step. If only TRANSPONDER fault message is displayed, go to step **7)**. If neither fault message is displayed, test is complete.

6) Using scan tool, erase SKIM DTCs. Turn ignition off and wait 10 seconds. Start engine 20 times. Using scan tool, read SKIM DTCs. If EEPROM fault message is displayed, replace SKIM. Perform SKIM INITIALIZATION PROCEDURE. If EEPROM failure is not displayed, test is complete.

7) Using scan tool, select THEFT ALARM, then SKIM. Select MISCELLANEOUS, then SKIM KEY TEST. Follow scan tool instructions. Test key in sentry key tester. If key passes, go to next step. If key does not pass, erase SKIM DTCs. Replace and program new key. See PROGRAMMING BLANK SMART KEY USING SCAN TOOL.

8) Using scan tool, select THEFT ALARM, then SKIM. Select MISCELLANEOUS, then PROGRAM NEW KEY. Read status of current key. If scan tool displays PROGRAMMING SUCCESSFUL, test is complete. If display is PROGRAMMING FAILED, replace SKIM and perform SKIM INITIALIZATION PROCEDURE. If display is MAXIMUM KEY LIMIT, no additional keys can be programmed. Perform VERIFICATION TEST: VER-2A If none of the above messages are displayed, replace SKIM and perform SKIM INITIALIZATION PROCEDURE.

VIN MISMATCH

1) Using scan tool, select ENGINE and read DTCs. If EEPROM fault message is present, go to PCM FAILURE EEPROM WRITE DENIED test in appropriate SELF-DIAGNOSTICS article in ENGINE PERFORMANCE in appropriate MITCHELL® manual. If EEPROM fault message is present, go to next step.

2) Ensure battery is fully charged. Using scan tool, read and record SKIM DTCs. Erase SKIM DTCs. Turn ignition off, then back to RUN position. After 3 minutes, read SKIM DTCs. If only VIN MISMATCH fault message is currently displayed or was previously recorded, go to next step. If EEPROM FAILURE fault message is also displayed, go to step **3)**. If ROLLING CODE FAILURE fault message is displayed with or without EEPROM FAILURE fault message is displayed, go to step **4)**.

3) Using scan tool, erase SKIM DTCs. Turn ignition off and wait 10 seconds. Start engine 20 times. Using scan tool, read SKIM DTCs. If EEPROM fault message is displayed, replace SKIM. Perform SKIM INITIALIZATION PROCEDURE. If EEPROM failure is not displayed, go to next step.

4) Start engine and allow to idle for 3 minutes. Using scan tool, read SKIM DTCs. If VIN MISMATCH fault message is displayed, go to next step. If ROLLING CODE fault message is displayed, go to step **9)**. If none of the above fault messages are present, test is complete.

5) Using scan tool, read VIN from Powertrain Control Module (PCM). If VIN output from PCM matches VIN on door jamb plate, go to next step. If VIN output from PCM does not match VIN on door jamb plate, replace PCM.

6) Using scan tool, read VIN from SKIM. If VIN output from SKIM matches VIN on door jamb plate, go to next step. If VIN output from SKIM does not match VIN on door jamb plate, replace SKIM and perform SKIM INITIALIZATION PROCEDURE.

7) Using scan tool, erase VIN MISMATCH DTC. Turn ignition switch to RUN position and read SKIM DTCs. If VIN MISMATCH fault message is still present, replace SKIM and perform SKIM INITIALIZATION PROCEDURE. If VIN MISMATCH fault message is not displayed, go to next step.

8) Start engine and allow to idle for 3 minutes. Using scan tool, erase SKIM DTCs. Read SKIM DTCs. If SKIM MISMATCH fault message is still present, replace SKIM and perform SKIM INITIALIZATION PROCEDURE. If SKIM MISMATCH fault message is not displayed, test is complete.

9) Using scan tool, erase SKIM DTCs. Select THEFT ALARM, then SKIM. If scan tool displays NO RESPONSE, go to appropriate VEHICLE COMMUNICATIONS test in VEHICLE COMMUNICATIONS article. If scan tool does not display NO RESPONSE, then

10) Using scan tool, select BODY, then BODY COMPUTER. Select SYSTEM TEST, then PCM MONITOR. If scan tool displays PCM ACTIVE ON THE BUS, go to next step. If scan tool does not display PCM ACTIVE ON THE BUS, see appropriate VEHICLE COMMUNICATIONS article.

11) Using scan tool, select ENGINE, then read DTCs. If scan tool displays any PCM related DTCs, see appropriate SELF-DIAGNOSTICS article in ENGINE PERFORMANCE in appropriate MITCHELL® manual. If scan tool does not display any PCM related DTCs, replace smart key immobilizer module. Perform SKIM INITIALIZATION PROCEDURE.

VERIFICATION TEST: VER-2A

BODY VERIFICATION TEST

1) Reconnect all previously disconnected components and connectors. If BCM was replaced, turn ignition on for at least 15 seconds.

2) Ensure ignition is on. Erase all DTCs using scan tool. Turn ignition off and wait 5 seconds. Turn ignition on and fully operate system that was malfunctioning.

3) If system is not operating properly, go to SYMPTOM ID TEST. Using scan tool, read Body DTCs. If any DTCs are present, go to SYMPTOM ID TEST. If no DTCs are present, system is operating correctly and customer's complaint cannot be duplicated, repair is complete.

SKIM INITIALIZATION PROCEDURE

GENERAL INFORMATION

SECURED ACCESS mode is not required to check programmed status of key.

If PCM is replaced, unique secret key data must be transferred from SKIM to PCM. This procedure requires SKIM to be placed in SECURED ACCESS mode using 4-digit PIN code.

If 3 attempts are made to enter secured access mode using an incorrect PIN, SECURED ACCESS mode will be locked out for one hour. To exit lock out mode, turn ignition switch to RUN/START position continuously for one hour. Ensure all accessories are turned off. Monitor battery state and connect battery charger is necessary.

To program smart keys using "customer programming method" requires 2 valid smart keys. See owner's manual.

INITIALIZATION PROCEDURE

1) Obtain vehicle's unique PIN number assigned to it's original SKIM module from vehicle owner or Chrysler's customer center.

2) Using scan tool, select THEFT ALARM, SKIM, then MISCELLANEOUS. Select SKIM MODULE REPLACED function.

3) Enter SECURED ACCESS mode using unique 4-digit PIN number.

4) Program vehicle's VIN number into SKIM's memory.

5) Program country code into SKIM's memory (U.S.).

6) Transfer vehicle's unique Secret Key data from PCM. This process will require SKIM module to be in SECURED ACCESS mode. The PIN number must be entered into scan tool before SKIM will enter SECURED ACCESS mode. Once SECURED ACCESS mode is active, SKIM will remain in that mode for 60 seconds.

7) Program all customer keys into SKIM's memory. This requires that SKIM be in SECURED ACCESS mode. The SKIM will immediately exit SECURED ACCESS mode after each key is programmed.

PROGRAMMING BLANK SMART KEY USING SCAN TOOL

1) Once key blank is cut, insert key into ignition switch. Turn ignition switch to RUN position. Using scan tool, select THEFT ALARM, then SKIM. Select MISCELLANEOUS, then PROGRAM NEW KEY. Enter 4-digit PIN code. When programming is completed, SKIM will exit SECURED ACCESS mode and display status of key. One of five different status messages maybe displayed as follows:

- PROGRAMMING SUCCESSFUL is displayed if SKIM smart key programming succeeds.
- LEARNED KEY IN IGNITION is displayed if key in the ignition has already been programmed into vehicle's SKIM.
- 8 KEYS ALREADY LEARNED, PROGRAMMING NOT DONE is displayed if eight keys have already been programmed into SKIM. If a new key needs to be added due to a lost or defective key, the ERASE ALL KEYS function has to be performed. Original 7 keys plus additional new key may then be reprogrammed into SKIM.
- PROGRAMMING NOT ATTEMPTED is displayed after an ERASE ALL KEYS function is executed.
- PROGRAMING KEY FAILED is displayed if further diagnosis is required.

2) To program additional keys, turn ignition off. Remove current programmed key and insert next new blank key. Turn ignition switch to RUN position. Re-enter SECURED ACCESS mode function and repeat PROGRAM NEW KEY procedure.

SYSTEM ID TEST

IDENTIFYING VEHICLE EQUIPMENT & SYSTEM PROBLEMS

1) Connect scan tool to Data Link Connector (DLC). DLC is a 16-pin connector located on left side of steering column, above brake pedal. Turn ignition on. If scan tool display is not blank, go to next step. If scan tool display is blank, go to appropriate test in VEHICLE COMMUNICATIONS article.

2) Using scan tool, select BODY SYSTEM, then BODY COMPUTER. Scan tool will perform a CCD bus test. If scan tool displays BUS OPERATIONAL, go to next step. If scan tool displays NO RESPONSE, go to appropriate test in VEHICLE COMMUNICATIONS article. If scan tool displays any other message, go to appropriate test in VEHICLE COMMUNICATIONS article.

3) Using scan tool, select READ DTCs. If any fault messages are displayed, go to FAULT MESSAGE IDENTIFICATION table to identify which system is affected. Go to applicable test in appropriate DIAGNOSTIC TESTS section. If no fault messages are displayed, go to SYMPTOM TEST DIRECTORY table for list of identified systems. Fault messages or symptoms are diagnosed using a scan tool and/or DVOM. These problems may occur separately or in various combinations. When diagnosing a system with many apparent problems, a sequence of tests may be required. After repairs, ensure problem(s) or failure(s) have been corrected by performing appropriate verification test.

FAULT MESSAGE IDENTIFICATION

Scan Tool Display	[1] Affected System
BATTERY IOD DISCONNECT AT BCM	2
BCM EEPROM CHECKSUM FAILURE	2
BCM FLASH CHECKSUM FAILURE	2
BCM J1850 BUS MESSAGE FAULTS - MESSAGES NOT RECEIVED	2
BCM MATURED FAULT PRESENT	2
DDM MESSAGE NOT RECEIVED	2
MIC MESSAGE NOT RECEIVED BY BCM	2
PCM MESSAGE NOT RECEIVED BY BCM	2
PDM MESSAGE NOT RECEIVED BY BCM	2
FOG LAMP RELAY CKT SHORTED HI	Exterior Lighting
FOG LAMP RELAY CKT SHORTED LO/OPEN	Exterior Lighting
HAZARD RELAY CKT SHORTED HI	Exterior Lighting
HEADLAMP SW OPEN CKT	Exterior Lighting
HEADLAMP SW SHORT TO GROUND	Exterior Lighting
HIGH BEAM RELAY CKT SHORTED HI	Exterior Lighting
LOW BEAM RELAY CKT SHORTED HI	Exterior Lighting
LOW BEAM RELAY CKT SHORTED LO/OPEN	Exterior Lighting
PARK LAMP RELAY CKT SHORTED HI	Exterior Lighting
PARK LAMP RELAY CKT SHORTED LO/OPEN	Exterior Lighting
ABS LAMP CKT SHORT	3
ABS LAMP OPEN	Instrument Cluster
ABS MESSAGE NOT RECEIVED BY MIC	Instrument Cluster
ACM MESSAGE NOT RECEIVED BY MIC	Instrument Cluster
AIRBAG LAMP DRIVER FAILURE	3
AIRBAG LAMP OPEN	Instrument Cluster
BCM MESSAGES NOT RECEIVED BY MIC	Instrument Cluster
BRAKE LAMP CKT SHORT	Instrument Cluster
BRAKE LAMP OPEN	3
JTEC MESSAGE NOT RECEIVED BY MIC	Instrument Cluster
SKIM MESSAGE NOT RECEIVED BY MIC	Instrument Cluster
DIM SW OPEN CKT	Interior Lighting
DIM SW SHORT TO GROUND	Interior Lighting
LAMP FADE FAILURE SHORT TO BATT	Interior Lighting
LOAD SHED FAILURE SHORT TO BATT	Interior Lighting
PANEL LAMP DRIVER FAILURE	Interior Lighting
AMBIENT TEMP	Overhead Console
AMBIENT TEMP SENSOR CKT SHORT TO GND	Overhead Console
COOLANT LEVEL SWITCH CIRCUIT OPEN	Overhead Console

FAULT MESSAGE IDENTIFICATION (Cont.)

Scan Tool Display	[1] Affected System
EVIC INTERNAL FAILURE	4
EVIC NOT RECEIVING BUS MESSAGES	Overhead Console
ACCESSORY DELAY RELAY SHORTED HI	Power Top
ANTENNA FAILURE	6 VTSS
EEPROM FAILURE	6 VTSS
INTERNAL SKIM FAILURE	5
PCM STATUS FAILURE	6 VTSS
ROLLING CODE FAILURE	6 VTSS
SERIAL LINK EXTERNAL FAILURE	6 VTSS
SERIAL LINK INTERNAL FAILURE	5
TRANSPONDER COMMUNICATION FAILURE	6 VTSS
TRANSPONDER CRC FAILURE	6 VTSS
TRANSPONDER ID MISMATCH	6 VTSS
TRANSPONDER RESPONSE MISMATCH	6 VTSS
VIN MISMATCH	6 VTSS
WASHER FLUID SENSOR FAILURE	Windshield Wiper
WIPER ON/OFF RELAY SHORTED HIGH	Windshield Wiper
WIPER ON/OFF RELAY SHORTED LOW/OPEN CIRCUIT	Windshield Wiper
WIPER PARK FAILURE	Windshield Wiper
WIPER SWITCH MUX CKT OPEN	Windshield Wiper
WIPER SWITCH MUX CKT SHORT TO GROUND	Windshield Wiper

1 – Go to applicable TESTS section.
2 – Go to VEHICLE COMMUNICATIONS article.
3 – Replace instrument cluster circuit board.
4 – Replace vehicle information center module in overhead console.
5 – Replace SKIM and perform SKIM INITIALIZATION PROCEDURE.
6 – Vehicle Theft Security System.

SYMPTOM TEST DIRECTORY

Suspected System	Proceed To
Exterior Lights	EXTERIOR LIGHTING SYMPTOM TESTS
Instrument Cluster	INSTRUMENT CLUSTER SYMPTOM TESTS
Interior Lights	INTERIOR LIGHTING SYMPTOM TESTS
Power Door Locks	POWER DOOR LOCK/REMOTE KEYLESS ENTRY (RKE) SYMPTOM TESTS
Remote Keyless Entry (RKE)	POWER DOOR LOCK/REMOTE KEYLESS ENTRY (RKE) SYMPTOM TESTS
Power Top	POWER TOP SYMPTOM TESTS
Power Windows	POWER WINDOW SYMPTOM TESTS
Vehicle Theft Security System	VEHICLE THEFT SECURITY SYSTEM SYMPTOM TESTS
Windshield Wiper/Washer	WINDSHIELD WIPER/WASHER SYSTEM SYMPTOM TESTS

EXTERIOR LIGHTING DIAGNOSTIC TESTS

NOTE: *Perform SYSTEM ID TEST before proceeding with following tests. For connector terminal identification and wiring diagrams, see BODY CONTROL COMPUTER INTRODUCTION article. Perform VERIFICATION TEST: VER-2A after each repair.*

The following exterior lighting scan tool fault messages are covered:

- FOG LAMP RELAY CKT SHORTED HI
- FOG LAMP RELAY CKT SHORTED LO/OPEN
- HAZARD RELAY CKT SHORTED HI
- HEADLAMP SW OPEN CKT
- HEADLAMP SW SHORT TO GROUND
- HIGH BEAM RELAY CKT SHORTED HI

1999 ACCESSORIES & EQUIPMENT
Body Control Computer Tests – Grand Cherokee (Cont.)

**JEEP
4-35**

- LOW BEAM RELAY CKT SHORTED HI
- LOW BEAM RELAY CKT SHORTED LO/OPEN
- PARK LAMP RELAY CKT SHORTED HI
- PARK LAMP RELAY CKT SHORTED LO/OPEN

FOG LAMP RELAY CKT SHORTED HI

1) Remove fog light relay from junction block. Replace relay with known good component. Operate fog lights. If fog lights operate correctly, replace relay. If fog lights do not operate correctly, go to next step.
2) Ensure ignition is off. Remove fog light relay from junction block. Remove Body Control Module (BCM) from junction block. Turn ignition on. Using voltmeter, measure voltage between ground and terminal No. 86 on fog light relay socket. If voltage is greater than one volt, replace junction block. If voltage is one volt or less, replace BCM.

FOG LAMP RELAY CKT SHORTED LO/OPEN

1) Ensure fog light relay is present in junction block. Install relay if necessary. Inspect junction block fuse No. 24. If fuse is blown, go to next step. If fuse is okay, go to step **5)**.
2) Turn ignition on. Using voltmeter, measure voltage between ground and B+ terminal on fuse No. 24 socket. If voltage is greater than 10 volts, go to next step. If voltage is 10 volts or less, replace junction block.
3) Install known good relay in junction block. Operate fog lights. If fog lights operate correctly, replace relay. If fog lights do not operate correctly, go to next step.
4) Using ohmmeter, measure resistance between ground and terminal No. 87 (relay output circuit) on fog light relay socket. If resistance is less than 5 ohms, repair relay output circuit for short to ground and replace fuse No. 24. If resistance is 5 ohms or greater, replace fuse No. 24.
5) Remove fog light relay from junction block. Using voltmeter, measure voltage between ground and terminals No. 30 and 85 on fog light relay socket. If voltage is greater than 10 volts on both circuits, go to next step. If voltage is 10 volts or less on either circuit, replace junction block.
6) Turn ignition on. Using voltmeter, measure voltage between ground and B+ terminal on fuse No. 24 socket. If voltage is greater than 10 volts, go to next step. If voltage is 10 volts or less, replace junction block.
7) Install known good relay in junction block. Operate fog lights. If fog lights operate correctly, replace relay. If fog lights do not operate correctly, go to next step.
8) Turn ignition off. Ensure fog light relay is removed. Disconnect Body Control Module (BCM) from back of junction block. Using ohmmeter, measure resistance between terminal No. 2 on internal BCM connector and terminal No. 86 on fog light relay socket. If resistance is less than 5 ohms, replace BCM. If resistance is 5 ohms or greater, replace junction block.
9) Turn ignition off. Remove fog light from junction block. Remove Body Control Module (BCM) from back of junction block. Using ohmmeter, measure resistance between ground and terminal No. 86 on fog light relay socket. If resistance is less than 5 ohms, go to next step. If resistance is 10 ohms or greater, replace junction block.
10) Disconnect a fog light bulb connector. Using ohmmeter, measure resistance of Light Blue wire between fog light bulb connector and terminal No. 86 on fog light relay socket. If resistance is less than 5 ohms, go to next step. If resistance is 5 ohms or greater, repair open Light Blue wire.
11) Using scan tool, select INPUT/OUTPUT under BODY. Read FOG LAMP SWITCH STATE. Turn fog light switch from OFF to ON position while monitoring scan tool. If fog light switch status changes, replace Body Control Module (BCM). If fog light switch status does not change, go to next step.
12) Using scan tool, select INPUT/OUTPUTS under BODY. Monitor FOG LAMP SWITCH STATE. Disconnect left multi-function switch connector. Connect jumper between terminal No. 1 and 4 on multi-function switch harness connector. If FOG LAMP SWITCH STATE changes when jumper wire is connected, replace left multi-function switch. If FOG LAMP SWITCH STATE does not change when jumper wire is connected, go to next step.
13) Ensure ignition is off. Disconnect left multi-function switch connector. Disconnect BCM C2 connector. Using ohmmeter, measure resistance

between ground and terminal No. 1 (White/Tan wire). If resistance is less than 5 ohms, repair White/Tan wire for short to ground. If resistance is 5 ohms or greater, replace Body Control Module (BCM).

HAZARD RELAY CKT SHORTED HI

1) Remove combination flasher from junction block. Using scan tool, erase DTCs. Operate either panic feature on Remote Keyless Entry (RKE) fob or trigger vehicle theft security system. Read BCM DTCs. If HAZARD RELAY CKT SHORTED HI DTC reset, go to next step. If HAZARD RELAY CKT SHORTED HI DTC did not reset, replace combination flasher.
2) Ensure ignition is off. Remove Body Control Module (BCM) from back of junction block. Turn ignition on. Using voltmeter, measure voltage between ground and terminal No. 9 (hazard switch sense circuit) on combination flasher socket. If voltage is greater than one volt, repair hazard switch sense circuit for short to voltage. If voltage is one volt or less, replace BCM.

HEADLAMP SW OPEN CKT

1) Disconnect left multi-function switch connector. Turn ignition on. Connect jumper wire between terminals No. 4 (White/Dark Green wire) and 11 (Yellow wire) on left multi-function switch harness connector. Using scan tool, select SENSORS under BODY. Read HEADLAMP SW VOLTS. If scan tool displays zero volts, replace left multi-function switch. If scan tool does not display zero volts, go to next step.
2) Turn ignition off. Disconnect Body Control Module (BCM) C1 connector. Using ohmmeter, measure resistance of Yellow wire between terminal No. 11 on left multi-function switch harness connector and terminal No. 2 on BCM C1 harness connector. If resistance is less than 5 ohms, go to next step. If resistance is 5 ohms or greater, repair open Yellow wire.
3) Measure resistance of White/Dark Green wire between terminal No. 4 on left multi-function switch harness connector and terminal No. 16 on BCM C1 harness connector. If resistance is less than 5 ohms, replace BCM. If resistance is 5 ohms or greater, repair open White/Dark Green wire.

HEADLAMP SW SHORT TO GROUND

1) Disconnect left multi-function switch connector. Turn ignition on. Using scan tool, select SENSORS under BODY. Read HEADLAMP SW VOLTS. If scan tool displays 5 volts, replace left multi-function switch. If scan tool does not display 5 volts, go to next step.
2) Turn ignition off. Disconnect Body Control Module (BCM) C1 connector. Using ohmmeter, measure resistance between ground and terminal No. 11 (Yellow wire) on left multi-function switch harness connector. If resistance is less than 5 ohms, repair Yellow wire for short to ground. If resistance is 5 ohms or greater, replace BCM.

HIGH BEAM RELAY CKT SHORTED HI

1) Install known good high beam relay in junction block. Operate high beam head lights. If high beam head lights operate correctly, replace relay. If high beam head lights do not operate correctly, go to next step.
2) Ensure ignition is off. Remove high beam relay from junction block. Remove Body Control Module (BCM) from junction block. Turn ignition on. Using voltmeter, measure voltage between ground and terminal No. 86 on high beam relay socket. If voltage is greater than one volt, replace junction block. If voltage is one volt or less, replace BCM.

LOW BEAM RELAY CKT SHORTED HI

1) Install known good low beam relay in junction block. Operate low beam head lights. If low beam head lights operate correctly, replace relay. If low beam head lights do not operate correctly, go to next step.
2) Ensure ignition is off. Remove low beam relay from junction block. Remove Body Control Module (BCM) from junction block. Turn ignition on. Using voltmeter, measure voltage between ground and terminal No. 86 on low beam relay socket. If voltage is greater than one volt, replace junction block. If voltage is one volt or less, replace BCM.

JEEP
4-36

1999 ACCESSORIES & EQUIPMENT
Body Control Computer Tests – Grand Cherokee (Cont.)

LOW BEAM RELAY CKT SHORTED LO/OPEN

1) Ensure low beam relay is installed in junction block. Install if necessary. Remove low beam relay from junction block. Using voltmeter, measure voltage between ground and terminals No. 30 and 85 on low beam relay socket. If voltage is greater than 10 volts on both circuits, go to next step. If voltage is 10 volts or less on either circuit, replace junction block.

2) Install known good relay in junction block. Operate low beam headlights. If low beam headlights operate correctly, replace relay. If low beam headlights do not operate correctly, go to next step.

3) Turn ignition off. Ensure low beam headlight relay is removed. Disconnect Body Control Module (BCM) from back of junction block. Using ohmmeter, measure resistance between terminal No. 4 on internal BCM connector and terminal No. 86 on fog light relay socket. If resistance is less than 5 ohms, replace BCM. If resistance is 5 ohms or greater, replace junction block.

4) Install low beam headlight relay. Ensure BCM is disconnected. Turn ignition is on. If headlights are illuminated, replace junction block. If headlights are not illuminated, replace BCM.

PARK LAMP RELAY CKT SHORTED HI

1) Install known good park lamp relay in junction block. Operate parking lights. If parking lights operate correctly, replace relay. If parking lights do not operate correctly, go to next step.

2) Ensure ignition is off. Remove park lamp relay from junction block. Remove Body Control Module (BCM) from junction block. Turn ignition on. Using voltmeter, measure voltage between ground and terminal No. 86 on park lamp socket. If voltage is greater than one volt, replace junction block. If voltage is one volt or less, replace BCM.

PARK LAMP RELAY CKT SHORTED LO/OPEN

1) Remove park lamp relay from junction block. Using ohmmeter, measure resistance between ground and terminals No. 30 and 85 (park lamp relay output circuit) on park lamp relay socket. If resistance is less than .6 ohms, repair park lamp relay output circuit for short to ground. If resistance is .6 ohms or greater on either circuit, replace junction block fuse No. 6.

2) Install known good relay in junction block. Operate parking lights. If parking lights operate correctly, replace relay. If parking lights do not operate correctly, go to next step.

3) Turn ignition on. Using voltmeter, measure voltage between ground and B+ terminal on fuse No. 6 socket. If voltage is greater than 10 volts, go to next step. If voltage is 10 volts or less, replace junction block.

4) Remove park lamp relay from junction block. Measure voltage between ground and terminals No. 85 and 87 in park lamp relay socket. If voltage is greater than 10 volts on both circuits, go to next step. If voltage is 10 volts or less on either circuit, replace junction block.

5) Turn ignition off. Ensure park lamp relay is removed. Disconnect Body Control Module (BCM) from back of junction block. Using ohmmeter, measure resistance between terminal No. 1 on internal BCM connector and terminal No. 86 on park lamp relay socket. If resistance is less than 5 ohms, replace BCM. If resistance is 5 ohms or greater, replace junction block.

EXTERIOR LIGHTING SYMPTOM TESTS

NOTE: Perform SYSTEM ID TEST before proceeding with following tests. For connector terminal identification and wiring diagrams, see BODY CONTROL COMPUTER INTRODUCTION article. Perform VERIFICATION TEST: VER-2A after each repair.

The following exterior lighting symptoms are covered:
- Auto Headlights Will Not Turn Off
- Auto Headlights Will Not Turn On
- Fog Lights Will Not Turn Off
- Fog Lights Will Not Turn On
- High Beam Headlights Will Not Turn Off
- High Beam Headlights Will Not Turn On
- Low Beam Headlights Will Not Turn Off
- Low Beam Headlights Will Not Turn On
- Parking Lights Will Not Turn Off
- Parking Lights Will Not Turn On

AUTO HEADLIGHTS WILL NOT TURN ON

1) Using scan tool, select SENSORS. Shine light on auto headlight sensor. Auto headlight sensor is located under dash top cover. *See Fig. 1.* Read and record AUTO HEADLAMP SENSE VOLTS. Cover sensor and read voltage. Voltage should range from zero to 5 volts. If voltage is within voltage range, go to next step. If voltage remains above 4.8 volts, go to step **3)**. If voltage remains below .5 volts, go to step **6)**.

2) Using scan tool, select BODY SENSORS. Read HEADLAMP SW VOLTS. Rotate headlight switch through all positions. Compare with HEADLIGHT SWITCH VOLTAGE SPECIFICATIONS table. If voltage is within specification, test is complete. If voltage is not within specification, replace left multifunction switch.

HEADLIGHT SWITCH VOLTAGE SPECIFICATIONS

Headlight Switch Position	Volts
OFF	4.4
Parking Lights ON	3.2
Headlights ON	2.0
Auto Headlights ON	.6

3) Using scan tool, select body sensors. Read HEADLAMP SW VOLTS. Rotate headlight switch through all positions. Compare with HEADLIGHT SWITCH VOLTAGE SPECIFICATIONS table. If voltage is within specification, go to next step. If voltage is not within specification, replace left multifunction switch.

4) Disconnect auto headlight sensor connector. Connect jumper wire between terminals No. 1 (White wire) and 2 (Black/Yellow wire) on auto headlight sensor harness connector. Using scan tool, read AUTO HEADLAMP VOLTS. If voltage is less than .5 volts, replace auto headlight sensor. If voltage is .5 volts or greater, go to next step.

5) Disconnect Body Control Module (BCM) C2 harness connector. Using ohmmeter, measure resistance of Black/Yellow wire between terminal No. 2 on auto headlight sensor harness connector and terminal No. 21 on BCM C2 harness connector. If resistance is less than 5 ohms, replace BCM. If resistance is 5 ohms or greater, repair open Black/Yellow wire.

6) Using scan tool, select body sensors. Read HEADLAMP SW VOLTS. Rotate headlight switch through all positions. Compare with HEADLIGHT SWITCH VOLTAGE SPECIFICATIONS table. If voltage is within specification, go to next step. If voltage is not within specification, replace left multifunction switch.

7) Disconnect auto headlight sensor connector. Using scan tool, read AUTO HEADLAMP VOLTS. If voltage is greater than 4.8 volts, replace auto headlight sensor. If voltage is 4.8 volts or less, go to next step.

8) Disconnect Body Control Module (BCM) C2 harness connector. Using ohmmeter, measure resistance between ground and terminal No. 2 (Black/Yellow wire) on auto headlight sensor harness connector. If resistance is less than 5 ohms, repair Black/Yellow wire for short to ground. If resistance is 5 ohms or greater, replace BCM.

FOG LAMPS WILL NOT TURN OFF

1) Using scan tool, select BODY INPUT/OUTPUTS. Monitor FOG LAMP SWITCH STATE. Turn fog light switch from ON to OFF position. If FOG LAMP SWITCH STATE changes when switch is operated, go to next step. If FOG LAMP SWITCH STATE does not change when switch is operated, go to step **14)**.

2) Inspect fuse No. 24 in junction block. If fuse is blown, go to next step. If fuse is okay, go to step **8)**.

3) Remove fog light relay from junction block. Install known good relay. Install known good relay. Operate fog lights. If fog lights operate correctly, replace defective fog light relay. If fog lights do not operate correctly, go to next step.

4) Turn ignition off. Remove fog light from junction block. Remove Body Control Module (BCM) from back of junction block. Using ohmmeter, measure resistance between ground and terminal No. 86 on fog light

Body Control Computer Tests – Grand Cherokee (Cont.)

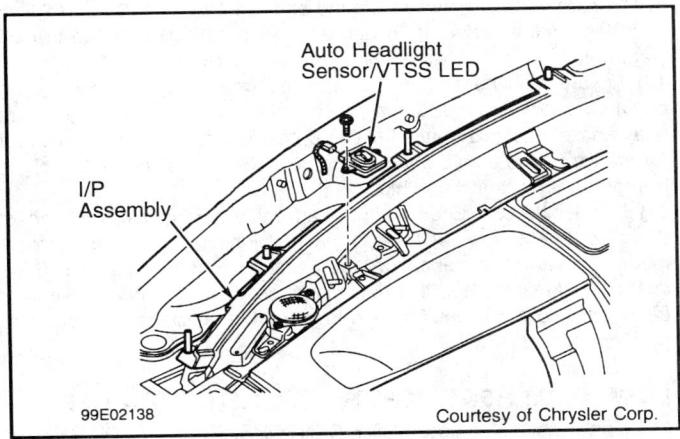

Auto Headlight Sensor/VTSS LED

I/P Assembly

99E02138

Courtesy of Chrysler Corp.

Fig. 1: Locating Auto Headlight Sensor

relay socket. If resistance is less than 10 ohms, replace junction block. If resistance is 10 ohms or greater, go to next step.

5) Disconnect a fog light bulb connector. Using ohmmeter, measure resistance of Light Blue wire between fog light bulb connector and terminal No. 86 on fog light relay socket. If resistance is less than 5 ohms, go to next step. If resistance is 5 ohms or greater, repair open Light Blue wire.

6) Ensure fog light relay is removed from junction block. If fog lights are illuminated, repair relay output circuit (Light Blue wire) from terminal No. 86 on fog light relay socket to fog lights. If fog lights are not illuminated, go to next step.

7) Measure resistance between ground and terminal No. 86 (relay output circuit) on fog light relay socket. If resistance is less than 5 ohms, repair relay output circuit for short to ground and replace fuse No. 24. If resistance is 5 ohms or greater, replace fuse No. 24.

8) Remove fog light relay from junction block. Install known good relay. Operate fog lights. If fog lights operate correctly, replace defective fog light relay. If fog lights do not operate correctly, go to next step.

9) Turn ignition off. Remove fog light from junction block. Remove Body Control Module (BCM) from back of junction block. Using ohmmeter, measure resistance between ground and terminal No. 87 on fog light relay socket. If resistance is less than 10 ohms, replace junction block. If resistance is 10 ohms or greater, go to next step.

10) Disconnect a fog light bulb connector. Using ohmmeter, measure resistance of Light Blue wire between fog light bulb connector and terminal No. 86 on fog light relay socket. If resistance is less than 5 ohms, go to next step. If resistance is 5 ohms or greater, repair open Light Blue wire.

11) Ensure fog light relay is removed from junction block. If fog lights are illuminated, repair relay output circuit (Light Blue wire) from terminal No. 86 on fog light relay socket to fog lights for short to battery. If fog lights are not illuminated, go to next step.

12) Turn ignition on. Using voltmeter, measure voltage between ground and B+ terminal on fuse No. 24 socket. If voltage is greater than 10 volts, go to next step. If voltage is 10 volts or less, replace junction block.

13) Turn ignition off. Ensure fog light relay is removed. Disconnect Body Control Module (BCM) from back of junction block. Using ohmmeter, measure resistance between terminal No. 2 on internal BCM connector and terminal No. 86 on fog light relay socket. If resistance is less than 5 ohms, replace BCM. If resistance is 5 ohms or greater, replace junction block.

14) Using scan tool, select BODY INPUT/OUTPUTS. Monitor FOG LAMP SWITCH STATE. Disconnect left multi-function switch connector. Connect jumper between terminal No. 1 and 4 on multi-function switch harness connector. If FOG LAMP SWITCH STATE changes when jumper wire is connected, replace left multi-function switch. If FOG LAMP SWITCH STATE does not change when jumper wire is connected, go to next step.

15) Remove fog light relay from junction block. Install known good relay. Install known good relay. Operate fog lights. If fog lights operate correctly, replace defective fog light relay. If fog lights do not operate correctly, go to next step.

16) Remove fog light relay from junction block. If fog lights are illuminated, repair relay output circuit (Light Blue wire) from terminal No. 86 on fog light relay socket to fog lights for short to battery. If fog lights are not illuminated, go to next step.

17) Ensure ignition is off. Disconnect left multi-function switch connector. Disconnect BCM C2 connector. Using ohmmeter, measure resistance between ground and terminal No. 1 (White/Tan wire). If resistance is less than 5 ohms, repair White/Tan wire for short to ground. If resistance is 5 ohms or greater, go to next step.

18) Ensure fog light relay is removed from junction block. Remove BCM from junction block. Using ohmmeter, measure resistance between ground and terminal No. 86 on fog light relay socket. If resistance is less than 10 ohms, replace junction block. If resistance is 10 ohms or greater, replace BCM.

FOG LAMPS WILL NOT TURN ON

1) Using scan tool, select BODY INPUT/OUTPUTS. Monitor FOG LAMP SWITCH STATE. Turn fog light switch from ON to OFF position. If FOG LAMP SWITCH STATE changes when switch is operated, go to next step. If FOG LAMP SWITCH STATE does not change when switch is operated, go to step **12**).

2) Inspect fuse No. 24 in junction block. If fuse is blown, go to next step. If fuse is okay, go to step **7**).

3) Disconnect a fog light bulb connector. Using ohmmeter, measure resistance of Light Blue wire between fog light bulb connector and terminal No. 86 on fog light relay socket. If resistance is less than 5 ohms, go to next step. If resistance is 5 ohms or greater, repair open Light Blue wire.

4) Turn ignition on. Using voltmeter, measure voltage between ground and B+ terminal on fuse No. 24 socket. If voltage is greater than 10 volts, go to next step. If voltage is 10 volts or less, replace junction block.

5) Remove fog light relay from junction block. Install known good relay. Operate fog lights. If fog lights operate correctly, replace defective fog light relay. If fog lights do not operate correctly, go to next step.

6) Using ohmmeter, measure resistance between ground and terminal No. 87 (relay output circuit) on fog light relay socket. If resistance is less than 5 ohms, repair relay output circuit for short to ground and replace fuse No. 24. If resistance is 5 ohms or greater, replace fuse No. 24.

7) Disconnect a fog light bulb connector. Using ohmmeter, measure resistance of Light Blue wire between fog light bulb connector and terminal No. 86 on fog light relay socket. If resistance is less than 5 ohms, go to next step. If resistance is 5 ohms or greater, repair open Light Blue wire.

8) Turn ignition on. Using voltmeter, measure voltage between ground and B+ terminal on fuse No. 24 socket. If voltage is greater than 10 volts, go to next step. If voltage is 10 volts or less, replace junction block.

9) Remove fog light relay from junction block. Install known good relay. Install known good relay. Operate fog lights. If fog lights operate correctly, replace defective fog light relay. If fog lights do not operate correctly, go to next step.

10) Turn ignition off. Ensure fog light relay is removed. Disconnect Body Control Module (BCM) from back of junction block. Using ohmmeter, measure resistance between terminal No. 2 on internal BCM connector and terminal No. 86 on fog light relay socket. If resistance is less than 5 ohms, replace BCM. If resistance is 5 ohms or greater, replace junction block.

11) Ensure fog light relay is removed from junction block. Remove BCM from junction block. Using ohmmeter, measure resistance between ground and terminal No. 86 on fog light relay socket. If resistance is less than 10 ohms, replace junction block. If resistance is 10 ohms or greater, replace BCM.

12) Ensure ignition is off. Disconnect left multi-function switch connector. Disconnect BCM C2 connector. Using ohmmeter, measure resistance

JEEP
4-38

1999 ACCESSORIES & EQUIPMENT
Body Control Computer Tests – Grand Cherokee (Cont.)

between ground and terminal No. 1 (White/Tan wire). If resistance is less than 5 ohms, repair White/Tan wire for short to ground. If resistance is 5 ohms or greater, go to next step.

13) Using scan tool, select INPUT/OUTPUTS under BODY. Monitor FOG LAMP SWITCH STATE. Disconnect left multi-function switch connector. Connect jumper between terminal No. 1 and 4 on multi-function switch harness connector. If FOG LAMP SWITCH STATE changes when jumper wire is connected, replace left multi-function switch. If FOG LAMP SWITCH STATE does not change when jumper wire is connected, replace Body Control Module (BCM).

HIGH BEAM HEAD LIGHTS WILL NOT TURN OFF

1) Using scan tool, select BODY INPUT/OUTPUTS. Monitor HIGH BEAM SWITCH STATE. Turn high beam switch from OFF to ON position. If HIGH BEAM SWITCH STATE changes when switch is operated, go to next step. If HIGH BEAM SWITCH STATE does not change when switch is operated, repair Brown wire (high beam switch sense) between left multi-function switch and Body Control Module (BCM) for short to ground.

2) Remove high beam relay from junction block. Install known good relay. Operate high beam headlights. If high beam headlights operate correctly, replace defective high beam relay. If high beam lights do not operate correctly, go to next step.

3) Ensure high beam relay is removed from junction block. If high beam head lights are illuminated, repair relay output circuit (Red or Red/Orange wire) from terminal No. 87 on high beam relay socket to head lights. If high beam head lights are not illuminated, go to next step.

4) Ensure ignition is off. Disconnect left multi-function switch connector. Disconnect BCM C2 connector. Using ohmmeter, measure resistance between ground and terminal No. 6 (Brown wire). If resistance is less than 5 ohms, repair Brown wire for short to ground. If resistance is 5 ohms or greater, replace BCM.

HIGH BEAM HEAD LIGHTS WILL NOT TURN ON

1) Using scan tool, select BODY SENSORS. Read HEADLAMP SW VOLTS. Rotate headlight switch through all positions. Compare with HEADLIGHT SWITCH VOLTAGE SPECIFICATIONS table. If voltage is within specification, go to next step. If voltage is not within specification, replace left multifunction switch.

2) Inspect fuse No. 16 in junction block. Replace as needed and go to next step.

3) Inspect fuse No. 3 in junction block. If fuse is blown, go to next step. If fuse is okay, go to step 7).

4) Remove high beam relay from junction block. Install known good relay. Operate high beam headlights. If high beam headlights operate correctly, replace defective high beam relay. If high beam lights do not operate correctly, go to next step.

5) Turn ignition off. Ensure high beam relay is removed. Disconnect Body Control Module (BCM) from back of junction block. Using ohmmeter, measure resistance between terminal No. 9 on internal BCM connector and terminal No. 86 on high beam relay socket. If resistance is less than 5 ohms, go to next step. If resistance is 5 ohms or greater, replace junction block.

6) Using ohmmeter, measure fused high beam output circuit between ground and fuses No. 3 and 16 on junction block. If resistance is less than .4 ohms, repair fused high beam relay output circuit for short to ground. Replace open fuse(s). If resistance is .4 ohms or greater, go to next step.

7) Remove high beam relay from junction block. Install known good relay. Operate high beam headlights. If high beam headlights operate correctly, replace defective high beam relay. If high beam lights do not operate correctly, go to next step.

8) Turn ignition off. Ensure high beam relay is removed. Disconnect Body Control Module (BCM) from back of junction block. Using ohmmeter, measure resistance between terminal No. 9 on internal BCM connector and terminal No. 86 on high beam relay socket. If resistance is less than 5 ohms, go to next step. If resistance is 5 ohms or greater, replace junction block.

9) Measure voltage between ground and terminals No. 30 and 85 on high beam relay socket. If voltage is greater than 10 volts, go to next step. If voltage is 10 volts or less, replace junction block.

10) Ensure high beam relay is removed from junction block. Using ohmmeter, measure resistance between terminal No. 87 on high beam relay socket and relay output circuit on fuses No. 3 and 16 sockets. If resistance is less than 5 ohms, go to next step. If resistance is 5 ohms or greater, replace junction block.

11) Turn ignition off. Ensure high beam relay is removed. Disconnect Body Control Module (BCM) from back of junction block. Using ohmmeter, measure resistance between ground and terminal No. 9 on internal BCM connector. If resistance is less than 5 ohms, repair high beam relay control circuit for short to ground. If resistance is 5 ohms or greater, replace BCM.

LOW BEAM HEADLIGHTS WILL NOT TURN OFF

1) Using scan tool, select BODY SENSORS. Read HEADLAMP SW VOLTS. Rotate headlight switch through all positions. Compare with HEADLIGHT SWITCH VOLTAGE SPECIFICATIONS table. If voltage is within specification, go to next step. If voltage is not within specification, replace left multifunction switch.

2) Remove low beam relay from junction block. Install known good relay. Operate low beam headlights. If low beam headlights operate correctly, replace defective low beam relay. If low beam headlights do not operate correctly, go to next step.

3) Remove low beam relay from junction block. If low beam headlights are illuminated, repair relay output circuit (Violet or Violet/Red wire) from terminal No. 87 on low beam headlight relay socket to low beam headlights for short to battery. If low beam headlights are not illuminated, go to next step.

4) Turn ignition off. Install low beam relay. Remove Body Control Module (BCM) from junction block. Turn ignition on. If low beam headlights are no longer illuminated, replace BCM. If low beam headlights are illuminated, replace junction block.

LOW BEAM HEADLIGHTS WILL NOT TURN ON

1) Inspect junction block fuses No. 14 and 15. If either fuse is open, go to next step. If both fuses are okay, go to step 3).

2) Remove low beam relay from junction block. Remove junction block fuses No. 14 and 15. Using ohmmeter, measure resistance between ground and terminal No. 87 on low beam relay socket. If resistance is less than 5 ohms, repair low beam relay output circuit for short to ground. If resistance is 5 ohms or greater, replace fuse(s).

3) Using scan tool, select BODY SENSORS. Read HEADLAMP SW VOLTS. Rotate headlight switch through all positions. Compare with HEADLIGHT SWITCH VOLTAGE SPECIFICATIONS table. If voltage is within specification, go to next step. If voltage is not within specification, replace left multifunction switch.

4) Install known good relay in low beam relay socket. Operate low beam headlights. If low beam headlights operate correctly, replace defective relay. If low beam headlights do not operate correctly, go to next step.

5) Remove low beam relay from junction block. Ensure junction block fuses No. 14 and 15 are installed. Using ohmmeter, measure resistance between terminal No. 87 on low beam relay socket and either right or left front light module harness connector. If resistance is less than 5 ohms, replace Body Control Module (BCM). If resistance is 5 ohms or greater, replace junction block.

PARKING LIGHTS WILL NOT TURN OFF

1) Remove parking light relay from junction block. Install known good relay in junction block. Operate parking lights. If parking lights operate correctly, replace defective parking light relay. If parking lights do not operate correctly, go to next step.

2) Using scan tool, select BODY SENSORS. Read HEADLAMP SW VOLTS. Rotate headlight switch through all positions. Compare with HEADLIGHT SWITCH VOLTAGE SPECIFICATIONS table. If voltage is within specification, go to next step. If voltage is not within specification, replace left multifunction switch.

1999 ACCESSORIES & EQUIPMENT
Body Control Computer Tests – Grand Cherokee (Cont.)

JEEP
4-39

3) Remove parking lights relay from junction block. If parking lights are not illuminated, go to next step. If parking lights are illuminated, repair parking light output circuit between relay and parking light bulbs.

4) Ensure parking light relay is installed. Turn ignition off. Remove Body Control Module (BCM) from back of junction block. Turn ignition on. If parking lights are not illuminated, replace BCM. If parking lights are illuminated, replace junction block.

PARKING LIGHT WILL NOT TURN ON

1) Remove parking light relay from junction block. Install known good relay in junction block. Operate parking lights. If parking lights operate correctly, replace defective parking light relay. If parking lights do not operate correctly, go to next step.

2) Using scan tool, select BODY SENSORS. Read HEADLAMP SW VOLTS. Rotate headlight switch through all positions. Compare with HEADLIGHT SWITCH VOLTAGE SPECIFICATIONS table. If voltage is within specification, go to next step. If voltage is not within specification, replace left multifunction switch.

3) Remove parking light relay from junction block. Disconnect appropriate lighting module connector. Using ohmmeter, measure resistance of parking light output circuit between terminal 30 on parking light relay socket and appropriate lighting module harness connector. If resistance is less than 5 ohms, replace BCM. If resistance is 5 ohms or greater, repair open parking light output circuit.

INSTRUMENT CLUSTER DIAGNOSTIC TESTS

NOTE: Perform SYSTEM ID TEST before proceeding with following tests. For connector terminal identification and wiring diagrams, see BODY CONTROL COMPUTER INTRODUCTION article. Perform VERIFICATION TEST: VER-2A after each repair.

The following instrument cluster scan tool fault messages are covered:
- ABS LAMP OPEN
- ABS MESSAGE NOT RECEIVED BY MIC
- ACM MESSAGE NOT RECEIVED BY MIC
- AIRBAG LAMP OPEN
- BCM MESSAGES NOT RECEIVED BY MIC
- JTEC MESSAGE NOT RECEIVED BY MIC
- SKIM MESSAGE NOT RECEIVED BY MIC

ABS LAMP OPEN

Turn ignition off. Replace ABS bulb. Turn ignition on. If ABS indicator light illuminates, test is complete. If ABS indicator light does not illuminate, replace instrument cluster circuit board.

ABS MESSAGE NOT RECEIVED BY MIC

Turn ignition on. Using scan tool, select ABS MODULE. If ABS module responds, test is complete. If ABS module does not respond, go to appropriate test in VEHICLE COMMUNICATIONS article.

ACM MESSAGE NOT RECEIVED BY MIC

Turn ignition on. Using scan tool, select ACM MODULE. If ACM module responds, test is complete. If ACM module does not respond, go to appropriate test in VEHICLE COMMUNICATIONS article.

AIRBAG LAMP OPEN

Turn ignition off. Replace airbag bulb. Turn ignition on. If airbag indicator light illuminates, test is complete. If airbag indicator light does not illuminate, replace instrument cluster circuit board.

BCM MESSAGES NOT RECEIVED BY MIC

Turn ignition on. Using scan tool, select BCM. If BCM responds, test is complete. If BCM does not respond, go to appropriate test in VEHICLE COMMUNICATIONS article.

JTEC MESSAGE NOT RECEIVED BY MIC

Turn ignition on. Using scan tool, select BODY CONTROLLER & SYSTEM TEST. If scan tool displays PCM ACTIVE ON THE BUS, test is complete. If scan tool does not display PCM ACTIVE ON THE BUS, go to appropriate test in VEHICLE COMMUNICATIONS article.

SKIM MESSAGE NOT RECEIVED BY MIC

Turn ignition on. Using scan tool, select THEFT ALARM, then SKIM. If SKIM responds, test is complete. If SKIM does not respond, go to appropriate test in VEHICLE COMMUNICATIONS article.

INSTRUMENT CLUSTER SYMPTOM TESTS

NOTE: Perform SYSTEM ID TEST before proceeding with following tests. For connector terminal identification and wiring diagrams, see BODY CONTROL COMPUTER INTRODUCTION article. Perform VERIFICATION TEST: VER-2A after each repair.

The following instrument cluster symptoms are covered:
- Air Bag Indicator Not Operating Properly
- All Gauges Not Operating
- All Indicators Not Operating
- Brake Indicator Not Operating Properly
- Check Engine Indicator Not Operating Properly
- Check Gauges Indicator Not Operating Properly
- Cruise Indicator Not Operating Properly
- Fuel Gauge Not Operating Properly
- High Beam Indicator Not Operating Properly
- Low Fuel Indicator Not Operating Properly
- O/D OFF Indicator Not Operating Properly
- Oil Pressure Gauge Not Operating Properly
- Seat Belt Indicator Not Operating Properly
- Sentry Key Immobilizer System Indicator (SKIS) Not Operating Properly
- Speedometer Not Operating Properly
- Tachometer Not Operating Properly
- Temperature Gauge Not Operating Properly
- Trans Over Temp Indicator Not Operating Properly

AIR BAG INDICATOR NOT OPERATING PROPERLY

1) Press and hold TRIP/RESET button on instrument panel. Turn ignition switch to RUN position. MIC self-test will start. If air bag indicator light illuminates, go to next step. If air bag indicator light does not illuminate, go to step **3)**.

2) Using scan tool, read instrument cluster and air bag DTCs. If any DTCs are present, go to appropriate INSTRUMENT PANELS and/or AIR BAG RESTRAINT SYSTEMS article. If no DTCs are present, go to next step.

3) Remove and inspect air bag indicator light bulb. Replace as needed. If bulb is okay, replace instrument cluster printed circuit board.

ALL GAUGES NOT OPERATING

1) Turn ignition off. Remove and inspect junction block fuse No. 22. If fuse is blown, go to step **12)**. If fuse is okay, go to next step.

2) Ensure ignition is off. Disconnect instrument cluster connector. Turn ignition on. Using voltmeter, measure voltage between ground and terminal No. 6 (Pink/Red wire) on instrument cluster harness connector. If voltage is less than 10.5 volts, go to next step. If voltage is 10.5 volts or greater, go to step **8)**.

3) Remove and junction block inspect fuse No. 17. If fuse is blown, go to next step. If fuse is okay, go to step **5)**.

4) Replace junction block fuse No. 17. Turn on ignition. Inspect fuse. If fuse is blown, go to next step. If fuse is okay, test is complete.

5) Turn ignition off. Ensure instrument cluster connector is disconnected. Using ohmmeter, measure resistance between ground and terminals No. 9 (Black/Orange wire) and 11 (Black wire). If resistance is less than

JEEP
4-40

1999 ACCESSORIES & EQUIPMENT
Body Control Computer Tests – Grand Cherokee (Cont.)

5 ohms for both circuits, go to next step. If resistance is 5 ohms or greater on either circuit, repair suspect open circuit.

6) Remove junction block fuse No. 17. Measure resistance between terminal No. 6 (Pink/Red wire) on instrument cluster harness connector and output terminal of junction block fuse No. 17. If resistance is less than 5 ohms, go to next step. If resistance is 5 ohms or greater, repair open Pink/Red wire.

7) Measure resistance between ground and terminal No. 6 (Pink/Red wire) on instrument cluster harness connector. If resistance is 100 ohms or less, repair Pink/Red wire for short to ground. Replace fuse No. 17. If resistance is greater than 100 ohms, go to step **9**).

8) Turn ignition off. Ensure instrument cluster connector is disconnected. Using ohmmeter, measure resistance between ground and terminals No. 9 (Black/Orange wire) and 11 (Black wire). If resistance is less than 5 ohms for both circuits, go to next step. If resistance is 5 ohms or greater on either circuit, repair suspect open circuit.

9) Connect Scope Input Cable (CH 7058) to channel No. 1 connector on scan tool. Connect Red and Black test probe cable with Probe Adapter (CH7062) to scope input cable. Select DRB STANDALONE. Select LAB SCOPE, then LIVE. Select 12 VOLT SQUARE WAVE. Press F2 for scope. Press F2 and use down arrow to set voltage range to 20 volts. Press F2. Ensure instrument cluster connector is disconnected. Connect Black lead to chassis ground. Connect Red lead to terminal No. 10 (Yellow/Violet/Red wire) on instrument cluster harness connector. Turn ignition on. If voltage displayed on scan tool lab scope pluses from zero to about 7.5 volts, go to next step. If voltage is zero volts, repair open Yellow/Violet/Red wire.

10) Ensure ignition is on. Measure voltage between ground and terminal No. 7 (Dark Blue/White wire) on instrument cluster harness connector. If voltage is greater than 10.5 volts, go to next step. If voltage is 10.5 volts or less, repair open Dark Blue/White wire.

11) Turn ignition off. Remove junction block fuse No. 22. Using ohmmeter, measure resistance between ground and terminal No. 7 (Dark Blue/White wire) on instrument cluster harness connector. If resistance is less 5 ohms, repair Dark Blue/White wire for short to ground. Replace junction block fuse No. 22. If resistance is 5 ohms or more, go to next step.

12) Replace junction block fuse No. 22. Turn ignition on. Inspect fuse. If fuse is blown, go to next step. If fuse is okay, test is complete.

13) Ensure instrument cluster connector is disconnected. Turn ignition on. Measure voltage between ground and terminal No. 6 (Pink/Red wire) on instrument cluster harness connector. If voltage is less than 10.5 volts, go to next step. If voltage is 10.5 volts or greater, go to step **18**).

14) Remove and inspect junction block fuse No. 17. If fuse is blown, go to next step. If fuse is okay, go to step **18**).

15) Turn ignition off. Remove and replace junction block fuse No. 17. Turn on ignition. Inspect junction block fuse No. 17. If fuse is blown, go to next step. If fuse is okay, test is complete.

16) Turn ignition off. Remove junction block fuse No. 17. Disconnect instrument cluster connector. Using ohmmeter, measure resistance between terminal No. 6 (Pink/Red wire) on instrument cluster harness connector and output terminal of junction block fuse No. 17. If resistance is less than 5 ohms, go to next step. If resistance is 5 ohms or greater, repair open Pink/Red wire.

17) Turn ignition off. Using ohmmeter, measure resistance between ground and terminals No. 9 (Black/Orange wire) and 11 (Black wire). If resistance is less than 5 ohms for both circuits, go to step **20**). If resistance is 5 ohms or greater on either circuit, repair suspect open circuit.

18) Turn ignition off. Disconnect instrument cluster connector. Using ohmmeter, measure resistance between ground and terminals No. 9 (Black/Orange wire) and 11 (Black wire). If resistance is less than 5 ohms for both circuits, go to step **20**). If resistance is 5 ohms or greater on either circuit, repair suspect open circuit.

19) Remove junction block fuse No. 17. Using ohmmeter, measure resistance between terminal No. 6 (Pink/Red wire) on instrument cluster harness connector and output terminal of junction block fuse No. 17. If resistance is less than 5 ohms, go to next step. If resistance is 5 ohms or greater, repair open Pink/Red wire.

20) Measure resistance between ground and terminal No. 6 (Pink/Red wire) on instrument cluster harness connector. If resistance 100 ohms or less, repair Pink/Red wire for short to ground. Replace fuse No. 17. If resistance is greater than 100 ohms, go to step **22**).

21) Using ohmmeter, measure resistance between ground and terminals No. 9 (Black/Orange wire) and 11 (Black wire). If resistance is less than 5 ohms for both circuits, go to next step. If resistance is 5 ohms or greater on either circuit, repair suspect open circuit.

22) Remove junction block fuse No. 22. Using ohmmeter, measure resistance between ground and terminal No. 7 (Dark Blue/White wire) on instrument cluster harness connector. If resistance is less 5 ohms, repair Dark Blue/White wire for short to ground. Replace junction block fuse No. 22. If resistance is 5 ohms or more, go to next step.

23) Connect Scope Input Cable (CH 7058) to channel No. 1 connector on scan tool. Connect Red and Black test probe cable with Probe Adapter (CH7062) to scope input cable. Select DRB STANDALONE. Select LAB SCOPE, then LIVE. Select 12 VOLT SQUARE WAVE. Press F2 for scope. Press F2 and use down arrow to set voltage range to 20 volts. Press F2. Ensure instrument cluster connector is disconnected. Connect Black lead to chassis ground. Connect Red lead to terminal No. 10 (Yellow/Violet/Red wire) on instrument cluster harness connector. Turn ignition on. If voltage displayed on scan tool lab scope pluses from zero to about 7.5 volts, go to next step. If voltage is zero volts, repair open Yellow/Violet/Red wire.

24) Turn ignition on. Using voltmeter, measure voltage between ground and terminal No. 7 (Dark Blue/White wire) on instrument cluster harness connector. If voltage is less than 10.5 volts, repair open Dark Blue/White wire. If voltage is 10.5 volts or greater, replace instrument cluster circuit board.

ALL INDICATORS NOT OPERATING

NOTE: All indicator lights except turn signals and Part Time 4WD indicator lights are PCI bus controlled.

1) Cycle ignition switch off, then on (RUN position). If PCI bus driven indicator lights illuminate, go to next step. If indicator lights do not illuminate, go to step **3**).

2) Connect Scope Input Cable (CH 7058) to channel No. 1 connector on scan tool. Connect Red and Black test probe cable with Probe Adapter (CH7062) to scope input cable. Select DRB STANDALONE. Select LAB SCOPE, then LIVE. Select 12 VOLT SQUARE WAVE. Press F2 for scope. Press F2 and use down arrow to set voltage range to 20 volts. Press F2. Ensure instrument cluster connector is disconnected. Connect Black lead to chassis ground. Connect Red lead to terminal No. 10 (Yellow/Violet/Red wire) on instrument cluster harness connector. Turn ignition on. If voltage displayed on scan tool lab scope pluses from zero to about 7.5 volts, go to next step. If voltage is zero volts, repair open Yellow/Violet/Red wire.

3) Turn ignition off. Remove and inspect junction block fuse No. 22. If fuse is blown, go to step **8**). If fuse is okay, go to next step.

4) Disconnect instrument cluster connector. Using ohmmeter, measure resistance between ground and terminals No. 9 (Black/Orange wire) and 11 (Black wire). If resistance is less than 5 ohms for both circuits, go to next step. If resistance is 5 ohms or greater on either circuit, repair suspect open circuit.

5) Turn ignition on. Using voltmeter, measure voltage between ground and terminal No. 6 (Pink/Red wire) on instrument cluster harness connector. If voltage is less than 10.5 volts, go to next step. If voltage is 10.5 volts or greater, go to step **17**).

6) Remove and junction block inspect fuse No. 17. If fuse is blown, go to next step. If fuse is okay, go to step **14**).

7) Replace junction block fuse No. 17. Turn ignition on. Inspect fuse. If fuse is blown, go to next step. If fuse is okay, test is complete.

8) Replace junction block fuse No. 22. Turn ignition on. Inspect fuse. If fuse is blown, go to next step. If fuse is okay, test is complete.

9) Disconnect instrument cluster connector. Using ohmmeter, measure resistance between ground and terminals No. 9 (Black/Orange wire) and

1999 ACCESSORIES & EQUIPMENT
Body Control Computer Tests – Grand Cherokee (Cont.)

JEEP
4-41

11 (Black wire). If resistance is less than 5 ohms for both circuits, go to next step. If resistance is 5 ohms or greater on either circuit, repair suspect open circuit.

10) Turn ignition on. Using voltmeter, measure voltage between ground and terminal No. 6 (Pink/Red wire) on instrument cluster harness connector. If voltage is less than 10.5 volts, go to next step. If voltage is 10.5 volts or greater, go to step 16).

11) Remove and junction block inspect fuse No. 17. If fuse is blown, go to next step. If fuse is okay, go to step 13).

12) Replace junction block fuse No. 17. Turn ignition on. Inspect fuse. If fuse is blown, go to next step. If fuse is okay, test is complete.

13) Turn ignition off. Remove junction block fuse No. 22. Using ohmmeter, measure resistance between ground and terminal No. 7 (Dark Blue/White wire) on instrument cluster harness connector. If resistance is less 5 ohms, repair Dark Blue/White wire for short to ground. Replace junction block fuse No. 22. If resistance is 5 ohms or more, go to next step.

14) Remove junction block fuse No. 17. Ensure instrument cluster connector is disconnected. Using ohmmeter, measure resistance between terminal No. 6 (Pink/Red wire) on instrument cluster harness connector and output terminal of junction block fuse No. 17. If resistance is less than 5 ohms, go to next step. If resistance is 5 ohms or greater, repair open Pink/Red wire.

15) Measure resistance between ground and terminal No. 6 (Pink/Red wire) on instrument cluster harness connector. If resistance is 100 ohms or less, repair Pink/Red wire for short to ground. Replace fuse No. 17. If resistance is greater than 100 ohms, go to step 17).

16) Remove junction block fuse No. 22. Using ohmmeter, measure resistance between ground and terminal No. 7 (Dark Blue/White wire) on instrument cluster harness connector. If resistance is less 5 ohms, repair Dark Blue/White wire for short to ground. Replace junction block fuse No. 22. If resistance is 5 ohms or more, go to next step.

17) Connect Scope Input Cable (CH 7058) to channel No. 1 connector on scan tool. Connect Red and Black test probe cable with Probe Adapter (CH7062) to scope input cable. Select DRB STANDALONE. Select LAB SCOPE, then LIVE. Select 12 VOLT SQUARE WAVE. Press F2 for scope. Press F2 and use down arrow to set voltage range to 20 volts. Press F2. Ensure instrument cluster connector is disconnected. Connect Black lead to chassis ground. Connect Red lead to terminal No. 10 (Yellow/Violet/Red wire) on instrument cluster harness connector. Turn ignition on. If voltage displayed on scan tool lab scope pluses from zero to about 7.5 volts, go to next step. If voltage is zero volts, repair open Yellow/Violet/Red wire.

18) Turn ignition on. Using voltmeter, measure voltage between ground and terminal No. 7 (Dark Blue/White wire) on instrument cluster harness connector. If voltage is less than 10.5 volts, repair open Dark Blue/White wire. If voltage is 10.5 volts or greater, replace instrument cluster circuit board.

BRAKE INDICATOR NOT OPERATING PROPERLY

1) Cycle ignition from OFF to ON position. If Red brake warning light illuminates for about 4 seconds and then goes out, go to next step. If Red brake warning light does not illuminate for about 4 seconds and then go out, go to step 6).

2) Turn ignition off. Disconnect parking brake switch. Measure resistance between ground and parking brake switch component terminal. Pull up on parking brake handle. If resistance is zero ohms, go to next step. If resistance is not zero ohms, replace parking brake switch.

3) Disconnect instrument cluster connector. Using ohmmeter, measure resistance between ground and terminal (Gray/Black wire) on parking brake switch harness connector. If resistance is less than 5 ohms, repair Gray/Black wire for short to ground. If resistance is 5 ohms or greater, go to next step.

4) Measure resistance of Gray/Black wire between terminal No. 5 on instrument cluster harness connector and terminal on parking brake switch harness connector. If resistance is less than 5 ohms, go to next step. If resistance is 5 ohms or greater, repair open Gray/Black wire.

5) Using voltmeter, measure voltage between ground and terminal (Gray/Black wire) on parking brake switch harness connector. If any voltage is present, repair Gray/Black wire for short to voltage. If no voltage is present, test is complete.

6) Turn ignition off. Disconnect parking brake switch. Measure resistance between ground and parking brake switch component terminal. Pull up on parking brake handle. If resistance is zero ohms, go to next step. If resistance is not zero ohms, replace parking brake switch.

7) Remove and inspect Red brake warning light bulb. Replace as needed. If bulb is okay, go to next step.

8) Disconnect instrument cluster connector. Using ohmmeter, measure resistance between ground and terminal (Gray/Black wire) on parking brake switch harness connector. If resistance is less than 5 ohms, repair Gray/Black wire for short to ground. If resistance is 5 ohms or greater, go to next step.

9) Measure resistance of Gray/Black wire between terminal No. 5 on instrument cluster harness connector and terminal on parking brake switch harness connector. If resistance is less than 5 ohms, go to next step. If resistance is 5 ohms or greater, repair open Gray/Black wire.

10) Using voltmeter, measure voltage between ground and terminal (Gray/Black wire) on parking brake switch harness connector. If any voltage is present, repair Gray/Black wire for short to voltage. If no voltage is present, replace instrument cluster circuit board.

CHECK ENGINE INDICATOR NOT OPERATING PROPERLY

1) Cycle ignition from OFF to ON position. If CHECK ENGINE indicator light illuminates for about 4 seconds and then goes out, go to next step. If CHECK ENGINE indicator light does not illuminate for about 4 seconds and then go out, go to step 3).

2) Using scan tool, read ENGINE DTCs. If any PCM DTCs are present, go to appropriate SELF-DIAGNOSTICS article in ENGINE PERFORMANCE in appropriate MITCHELL® manual. If no PCM DTCs are present, test is complete.

3) Remove and inspect CHECK ENGINE bulb. Replace as needed. If bulb is okay, go to next step.

4) Using scan tool, read ENGINE DTCs. If any PCM DTCs are present, go to appropriate SELF-DIAGNOSTICS article in ENGINE PERFORMANCE in appropriate MITCHELL® manual. If no PCM DTCs are present, replace instrument printed circuit board.

CHECK GAUGES INDICATOR NOT OPERATING PROPERLY

NOTE: Check gauges indicator is activated by engine temperature, battery voltage or low oil pressure.

1) If CHECK GAUGES indicator light is illuminated, inspect engine temperature, battery voltage or low oil pressure. Repair as needed. If CHECK GAUGES indicator light is not illuminated, go to next step.

2) Cycle ignition from OFF to ON position. If CHECK GAUGES indicator light illuminates for about 4 seconds and then goes out, test is complete. If CHECK GAUGES indicator light does not illuminate for about 4 seconds and then go out, go to next step.

3) Remove and inspect CHECK GAUGES bulb. Replace as needed. If bulb is okay, replace instrument cluster circuit board.

CRUISE INDICATOR NOT OPERATING PROPERLY

1) Cycle ignition from OFF to ON position. If CRUISE indicator light illuminates for about 4 seconds and then goes out, go to next step. If CRUISE indicator light does not illuminate for about 4 seconds and then go out, go to step 3).

2) Using scan tool, read ENGINE DTCs. If any PCM DTCs are present, go to appropriate SELF-DIAGNOSTICS article in ENGINE PERFORMANCE in appropriate MITCHELL® manual. If no PCM DTCs are present, test is complete.

3) Using scan tool, read ENGINE DTCs. If any PCM DTCs are present, go to appropriate SELF-DIAGNOSTICS article in ENGINE PERFORMANCE in appropriate MITCHELL® manual. If no PCM DTCs are present, go to next step.

4) Remove and inspect CRUISE bulb. Replace as needed. If bulb is okay, replace instrument printed circuit board.

JEEP
4-42

1999 ACCESSORIES & EQUIPMENT
Body Control Computer Tests – Grand Cherokee (Cont.)

FUEL GAUGE NOT OPERATING PROPERLY

NOTE: During MIC self-test, all gauges should move from minimum position to full scale and back to minimum position.

1) Ensure ignition is off. Press and hold TRIP/RESET button on instrument panel. Turn ignition switch to RUN position. MIC self-test will start. If all gauges pass self-test, go to next step. If fuel gauge fails self-test, replace defective fuel gauge pack. If all gauges fail self-test, replace instrument cluster printed circuit board.
2) Using scan tool, read ENGINE DTCs. If any PCM DTCs are present, go to appropriate SELF-DIAGNOSTICS article in ENGINE PERFORMANCE in appropriate MITCHELL® manual. If no PCM DTCs are present, test is complete.

HIGH BEAM INDICATOR NOT OPERATING PROPERLY

1) Ensure ignition is off. Press and hold TRIP/RESET button on instrument panel. Turn ignition switch to RUN position. MIC self-test will start. If HIGH BEAM indicator light illuminates for about 4 seconds and then goes out, go to next step. If HIGH BEAM indicator light does not illuminate for about 4 seconds and then go out, go to step 3).
2) Using scan tool, read BODY DTCs. If any DTCs related to exterior lighting are present, go to SYSTEM ID TEST. If no DTCs related to exterior lighting are present, test is complete.
3) Using scan tool, read BODY DTCs. If any DTCs related to exterior lighting are present, go to SYSTEM ID TEST. If no DTCs related to exterior lighting are present, go to next step.
4) Remove and inspect HIGH BEAM bulb. Replace as needed. If bulb is okay, replace instrument printed circuit board.

LOW FUEL INDICATOR NOT OPERATING PROPERLY

1) Inspect operation of fuel gauge. Repair as needed. See INSTRUMENT PANELS article. If fuel gauge operating correctly, go to next step.
2) Ensure ignition is off. Press and hold TRIP/RESET button on instrument panel. Turn ignition switch to RUN position. MIC self-test will start. If LOW FUEL indicator light illuminates for about 4 seconds and then goes out, test is complete. If LOW FUEL indicator light does not illuminate for about 4 seconds and then go out, go to next step.
3) Remove and inspect LOW BEAM indicator bulb. Replace as needed. If bulb is okay, replace instrument printed circuit board.

O/D OFF INDICATOR NOT OPERATING PROPERLY

1) Ensure ignition is off. Press and hold TRIP/RESET button on instrument panel. Turn ignition switch to RUN position. MIC self-test will start. If O/D OFF indicator light illuminates for about 4 seconds and then goes out, go to next step. If O/D OFF indicator light does not illuminate for about 4 seconds and then go out, go to step 3).
2) Using scan tool, read ENGINE DTCs. If any PCM DTCs are present, go to appropriate SELF-DIAGNOSTICS article in ENGINE PERFORMANCE in appropriate MITCHELL® manual. If no PCM DTCs are present, test is complete.
3) Using scan tool, read ENGINE DTCs. If any PCM DTCs are present, go to appropriate SELF-DIAGNOSTICS article in ENGINE PERFORMANCE in appropriate MITCHELL® manual. If no PCM DTCs are present, go to next step.
4) Remove and inspect HIGH BEAM bulb. Replace as needed. If bulb is okay, replace instrument printed circuit board.

OIL PRESSURE GAUGE NOT OPERATING PROPERLY

1) Start engine. Read and record oil pressure displayed on instrument cluster. Turn ignition off. Press and hold TRIP/RESET button on instrument panel. Turn ignition switch to RUN position. MIC self-test will start. Oil pressure gauge should sweep from zero to full scale (high position), and back to zero. If oil pressure gauge passes self-test, go to next step. If oil pressure gauge fails self-test, replace instrument cluster printed circuit board.

2) Turn ignition switch on with engine not running. Monitor oil pressure gauge. If oil pressure gauge is stuck in high position, see P0523: OIL PRESSURE SENSOR VOLTS HIGH in appropriate SELF-DIAGNOSTICS article in ENGINE PERFORMANCE in appropriate MITCHELL® manual. If oil pressure gauge is not stuck in high position, go to next step.
3) Start engine and monitor oil pressure on instrument cluster gauge. If oil pressure gauge is stuck in low/zero position, see P0522: OIL PRESSURE SENSOR VOLTS LOW in appropriate SELF-DIAGNOSTICS article in ENGINE PERFORMANCE in appropriate MITCHELL® manual. If oil pressure gauge is not stuck in low/zero position, go to next step.
4) Turn ignition off. Remove oil pressure sensor. Oil pressure sensor is located on right rear of engine block on 4.0L or beside oil filter on 4.7L engine. Install oil pressure gauge. Start and idle engine. Read oil pressure. If oil pressure is 4.0 lbs. psi or less at idle, possible mechanical problem may be contributing to low oil pressure. If oil pressure is greater than 4.0 lbs. psi at idle, go to next step.
5) Connect Scope Input Cable (CH 7058) to channel No. 1 connector on scan tool. Connect Red and Black test probe cable with Probe Adapter (CH7062) to scope input cable. Select DRB STANDALONE. Select LAB SCOPE, then LIVE. Select 12 VOLT SQUARE WAVE. Press F2 for scope. Press F2 and use down arrow to set voltage range to 20 volts. Press F2. Ensure instrument cluster connector is disconnected. Connect Black lead to chassis ground. Connect Red lead to terminal No. 10 (Yellow/Violet/Red wire) on instrument cluster harness connector. Turn ignition on. If voltage displayed on scan tool lab scope pluses from zero to about 7.5 volts, test is complete. If voltage is zero volts, repair open Yellow/Violet/Red wire.

SEAT BELT INDICATOR NOT OPERATING PROPERLY

1) Turn ignition switch to RUN position. MIC self-test will begin. If seat belt indicator light illuminates for about 4 seconds and then goes out, test is complete. If seat belt indicator light does not illuminate for about 4 seconds and then go out, go to next step.
2) Remove and inspect SEAT BELT bulb. Replace as needed. If bulb is okay, replace instrument printed circuit board.

SENTRY KEY IMMOBILIZER SYSTEM INDICATOR (SKIS) NOT OPERATING PROPERLY

1) Ensure ignition is off. Press and hold TRIP/RESET button on instrument panel. Turn ignition switch to RUN position. MIC self-test will start. If SKIS indicator light illuminates for about 4 seconds and then goes out, go to next step. If SKIS indicator light does not illuminate for about 4 seconds and then go out, go to step 3).
2) Using scan tool, select VEHICLE THEFT/SECURITY, then SKIM DTCs. If any SKIM DTCs are present, go to appropriate ANTI-THEFT SYSTEMS article. If no SKIM DTCs are present, test is complete.
3) Using scan tool, select VEHICLE THEFT/SECURITY, then SKIM DTCs. If any SKIM DTCs are present, go to appropriate ANTI-THEFT SYSTEMS article. If no SKIM DTCs are present, go to next step.
4) Remove and inspect SKIS indicator bulb. Replace as needed. If bulb is okay, replace instrument printed circuit board.

SPEEDOMETER NOT OPERATING PROPERLY

1) Turn ignition off. Press and hold TRIP/RESET button on instrument panel. Turn ignition switch to RUN position. MIC self-test will start. All gauges including speedometer should sweep from zero to full scale, and back to zero. If all gauges passes self-test, go to next step. If speedometer fails self-test, replace speedometer gauge pack. If all gauges fail self-test, replace instrument cluster printed circuit board.
2) Using scan tool, read ENGINE DTCs. If any engine DTCs are present, go to appropriate SELF-DIAGNOSTICS article in ENGINE PERFORMANCE in appropriate MITCHELL® manual. If no engine DTCs are present, test is complete.

TACHOMETER NOT OPERATING PROPERLY

1) Turn ignition off. Press and hold TRIP/RESET button on instrument panel. Turn ignition switch to RUN position. MIC self-test will start. All

1999 ACCESSORIES & EQUIPMENT
Body Control Computer Tests – Grand Cherokee (Cont.)

JEEP
4-43

gauges including tachometer should sweep from zero to full scale, and back to zero. If all gauges passes self-test, go to next step. If tachometer fails self-test, replace tachometer gauge pack. If all gauges fail self-test, replace instrument cluster printed circuit test.

2) Using scan tool, read ENGINE DTCs. If any engine DTCs are present, go to appropriate SELF-DIAGNOSTICS article in ENGINE PERFORMANCE in appropriate MITCHELL® manual. If no engine DTCs are present, test is complete.

TEMPERATURE GAUGE NOT OPERATING PROPERLY

1) Turn ignition off. Press and hold TRIP/RESET button on instrument panel. Turn ignition switch to RUN position. MIC self-test will start. All gauges including temperature gauge should sweep from zero to full scale, and back to zero. If all gauges passes self-test, go to next step. If temperature gauge fails self-test, replace temperature gauge pack. If all gauges fail self-test, replace instrument cluster printed circuit test.

2) Using scan tool, read ENGINE DTCs. If any engine DTCs are present, go to appropriate SELF-DIAGNOSTICS article in ENGINE PERFORMANCE in appropriate MITCHELL® manual. If no engine DTCs are present, test is complete.

TRANS OVER TEMP INDICATOR NOT OPERATING PROPERLY

1) Ensure ignition is off. Press and hold TRIP/RESET button on instrument panel. Turn ignition switch to RUN position. MIC self-test will start. If TRANS OVER TEMP indicator light illuminates for about 4 seconds and then goes out, go to next step. If TRANS OVER TEMP indicator light does not illuminate for about 4 seconds and then go out, go to step **3)**.

2) Using scan tool, read TRANSMISSION DTCs. If any TRANSMISSION DTCs are present, go to appropriate ELECTRONIC CONTROLS article in AUTOMATIC TRANSMISSIONS in appropriate MITCHELL® TRANSMISSION SERVICE & REPAIR manual. If no TRANSMISSION DTCs are present, test is complete.

3) Using scan tool, read TRANSMISSION DTCs. If any TRANSMISSION DTCs are present, go to appropriate ELECTRONIC CONTROLS article in AUTOMATIC TRANSMISSIONS in appropriate MITCHELL® TRANSMISSION SERVICE & REPAIR manual. If no TRANSMISSION DTCs are present, go to next step.

4) Remove and inspect TRANS OVER TEMP indicator bulb. Replace as needed. If bulb is okay, replace instrument printed circuit board.

INTERIOR LIGHTING DIAGNOSTIC TESTS

NOTE: Perform SYSTEM ID TEST before proceeding with following tests. For connector terminal identification and wiring diagrams, see BODY CONTROL COMPUTER INTRODUCTION article. Perform VERIFICATION TEST: VER-2A after each repair.

The following interior lighting scan tool fault messages are covered:
- DIM SW OPEN CKT
- DIM SW SHORT TO GROUND
- LAMP FADE FAILURE SHORT TO BATTERY
- LOAD SHED FAILURE SHORT TO BATT
- PANEL LAMP DRIVER FAILURE

DIM SW OPEN CKT

1) Turn ignition off. Disconnect Body Control Module (BCM) C1 connector. Using ohmmeter, measure resistance between terminals No. 3 (Red wire) and 16 (White/Dark Green wire) on BCM C1 harness connector. Monitor ohmmeter while rotating panel lights dimmer switch. If resistance varies from 60 to 7900 ohms, replace BCM. If resistance does not vary from 60 to 7900 ohms, go to next step.

2) Disconnect left multi-function switch connector. Measure resistance of Red wire between terminal No. 3 on BCM C1 harness connector and

terminal No. 10 on left multi-function switch harness connector. If resistance is less than 5 ohms, go to next step. If resistance is 5 ohms or greater, repair open Red wire.

3) Ensure ignition is off. Using voltmeter, measure voltage between ground and terminal No. 3 (Red wire) on BCM C1 harness connector. If voltage is present, repair Red wire for short to voltage. If no voltage is present, go to next step.

4) Measure resistance of White/Dark Green wire between terminal No. 16 on BCM C1 harness connector and terminal No. 4 on left multi-function switch harness connector. If resistance is less than 5 ohms, go to next step. If resistance is 5 ohms or greater, repair open White/Dark Green wire wire.

5) Using voltmeter, measure voltage between ground and terminal No. 16 (White/Dark Green wire) on BCM C1 harness connector. If voltage is present, repair White/Dark Green wire for short to voltage. If no voltage is present, go to next step.

6) Ensure ignition is off. Connect Body Control Module (BCM) C1 connector. Disconnect left multi-function switch connector. Using ohmmeter, measure resistance between terminals No. 10 (Red wire) and 4 (White/Dark Green wire) on left multi-function switch harness connector. Monitor ohmmeter while rotating panel lights dimmer switch. If resistance varies from 60 to 7900 ohms, replace left multi-function switch. If resistance does not vary from 60 to 7900 ohms, replace BCM.

DIM SW SHORT TO GROUND

1) Turn ignition off. Disconnect Body Control Module (BCM) C1 connector. Using ohmmeter, measure resistance between ground and terminals No. 3 (Red wire) and 16 (White/Dark Green wire) on BCM C1 harness connector. If resistance is 1000 ohms or greater, replace BCM. If resistance is less than 1000 ohms, go to next step.

2) Disconnect left multi-function switch connector. Measure resistance between ground and terminal No. 10 (Red wire) on left multi-function switch harness connector. If resistance is 1000 ohms or greater, go to next step. If resistance is less than 1000 ohms, repair Red wire for short to ground.

3) Measure resistance between ground and terminal No. 4 (White/Dark Green wire) on left multi-function switch harness connector. If resistance is 1000 ohms or greater, go to next step. If resistance is less than 1000 ohms, repair White/Dark Green wire for short to ground.

4) Using ohmmeter, measure resistance between ground and terminals No. 10 (Red wire) and 4 (White/Dark Green wire) on left multi-function switch component connector. If resistance is 1000 ohms or greater, replace BCM. If resistance is less than 1000 ohms, replace left multi-function switch.

LAMP FADE FAILURE SHORT TO BATTERY

1) Turn ignition on. Using scan tool, read Body Control Module (BCM) DTCs. If LAMP FADE FAILURE SHORT TO BATTERY is displayed, go to next step. If LAMP FADE FAILURE SHORT TO BATTERY is not displayed, go to step **4)**.

2) Turn ignition off. Remove each of the following listed bulbs. Proceed with step. When step is completed, leave bulb out and remove another bulb. Repeat step until all bulbs are removed. Applicable bulbs are; instrument panel footwell (2), rear reading (2), front overhead (2) and liftgate.

Remove bulb. Turn ignition on. Using scan tool, erase BCM DTCs. Read Body Control Module (BCM) DTCs. If LAMP FADE FAILURE SHORT TO BATTERY is displayed, go to next step. If LAMP FADE FAILURE SHORT TO BATTERY is not displayed, remove another bulb and repeat step until defective bulb is found.

3) Turn ignition off. Disconnect junction block C1 connector. Turn ignition on. Measure voltage between ground and terminal No. 16 (Yellow/Dark Green wire) on junction block C1 harness connector. If any voltage is present, repair Yellow/Dark Green wire for short to voltage. If no voltage is present, go to step **6)**.

4) Turn ignition off. Disconnect junction block C1 connector. Turn ignition on. Measure voltage between ground and terminal No. 16 (Yellow/Dark

JEEP
4-44

1999 ACCESSORIES & EQUIPMENT
Body Control Computer Tests – Grand Cherokee (Cont.)

Green wire) on junction block C1 harness connector. If any voltage is present, repair Yellow/Dark Green wire for short to voltage. If no voltage is present, go to next step.

5) Turn ignition off. Remove each of the following listed bulbs. Proceed with step. When step is completed, leave bulb out and remove another bulb. Repeat step until all bulbs are removed. Applicable bulbs are; instrument panel footwell (2), rear reading (2), front overhead (2) and liftgate.

6) Remove bulb. Turn ignition on. Using scan tool, erase BCM DTCs. Read Body Control Module (BCM) DTCs. If LAMP FADE FAILURE SHORT TO BATTERY is displayed, replace BCM. If LAMP FADE FAILURE SHORT TO BATTERY is not displayed, remove another bulb and repeat step until defective bulb is found.

LOAD SHED FAILURE SHORT TO BATT

1) Turn ignition on. Using scan tool, read Body Control Module (BCM) DTCs. If LOAD SHED FAILURE SHORT TO BATT DTC is present, go to step **3)**. If LOAD SHED FAILURE SHORT TO BATT DTC is not present, go to next step.

2) Ensure both visor vanity mirror covers are closed (if equipped). close all doors. Ensure that rear reading lights and front map light switches are off. Open a door and observe rear reading and front map lights. If any lights fail to illuminate, check on/off switch. Retry light(s). If all four courtesy lights illuminate, go to next step. If any light does not illuminate, repair as needed. See ILLUMINATION/INTERIOR LIGHTS article.

3) Turn ignition off. Disconnect junction block C1 connector. Turn ignition on. Measure voltage between ground and terminal No. 26 (Yellow/Black wire) on junction block C1 harness connector. If voltage is present, repair Yellow/Black wire for short to voltage. If no voltage is present, replace BCM.

PANEL LAMP DRIVER FAILURE

1) Turn ignition off. Disconnect driver's heated seat switch. Turn ignition on. Using scan tool, erase BCM DTCs. Wait 5 seconds, then read BCM DTCs. If PANEL LAMP DRIVER FAILURE DTC is present, go to next step. If PANEL LAMP DRIVER FAILURE DTC is not present, repair driver's heated seat switch for short to ground.

2) Turn ignition off. Disconnect passenger's heated seat switch. Turn ignition on. Using scan tool, erase BCM DTCs. Wait 5 seconds, then read BCM DTCs. If PANEL LAMP DRIVER FAILURE DTC is present, go to next step. If PANEL LAMP DRIVER FAILURE DTC is not present, repair passenger's heated seat switch for short to ground.

3) Turn ignition off. Disconnect HVAC control panel connectors. Turn ignition on. Using scan tool, erase BCM DTCs. Wait 5 seconds, then read BCM DTCs. If PANEL LAMP DRIVER FAILURE DTC is present, go to next step. If PANEL LAMP DRIVER FAILURE DTC is not present, replace HVAC control panel.

4) Turn ignition off. Disconnect PRNDL/transfer case illumination device. Turn ignition on. Using scan tool, erase BCM DTCs. Wait 5 seconds, then read BCM DTCs. If PANEL LAMP DRIVER FAILURE DTC is present, go to next step. If PANEL LAMP DRIVER FAILURE DTC is not present, repair PRNDL illumination circuit for short to ground.

5) Turn ignition off. Disconnect ash tray light. Turn ignition on. Using scan tool, erase BCM DTCs. Wait 5 seconds, then read BCM DTCs. If PANEL LAMP DRIVER FAILURE DTC is present, go to next step. If PANEL LAMP DRIVER FAILURE DTC is not present, repair ash tray bulb or socket for short to ground.

6) Turn ignition off. Disconnect radio connectors. Turn ignition on. Using scan tool, erase BCM DTCs. Wait 5 seconds, then read BCM DTCs. If PANEL LAMP DRIVER FAILURE DTC is present, go to next step. If PANEL LAMP DRIVER FAILURE DTC is not present, replace radio.

7) Turn ignition off. Disconnect HVAC control panel connectors. Disconnect BCM C1 connector. Using ohmmeter, measure resistance between ground and terminal No. 10 (Orange wire) on BCM C1 harness connector. If resistance is less than 5 ohms, repair Orange wire for short to ground. If resistance is 5 ohms or greater, go to next step.

8) Disconnect PRNDL illumination unit connector. Using ohmmeter, measure resistance between ground and terminal No. 9 (Orange wire)

on BCM C1 harness connector. If resistance is less than 5 ohms, repair Orange wire for short to ground. If resistance is 5 ohms or greater, go to next step.

9) Disconnect radio connectors. Using ohmmeter, measure resistance between ground and terminal No. 13 (Orange wire) on BCM C1 harness connector. If resistance is less than 5 ohms, repair Orange wire for short to ground. If resistance is 5 ohms or greater, go to next step.

10) Disconnect ash tray light. Using ohmmeter, measure resistance between ground and terminal No. 8 (Orange wire) on BCM C1 harness connector. If resistance is less than 5 ohms, repair Orange wire for short to ground. If resistance is 5 ohms or greater, go to next step.

11) Disconnect driver's and passenger's heated seat switch connectors. Using ohmmeter, measure resistance between ground and terminal No. 12 (Orange wire) on BCM C1 harness connector. If resistance is less than 5 ohms, repair Orange wire for short to ground. If resistance is 5 ohms or greater, replace BCM.

INTERIOR LIGHTING SYMPTOM TESTS

NOTE: Perform SYSTEM ID TEST before proceeding with following tests. For connector terminal identification and wiring diagrams, see BODY CONTROL COMPUTER INTRODUCTION article. Perform VERIFICATION TEST: VER-2A after each repair.

The following interior lighting symptoms are covered:

- All Courtesy Lights Inoperative
- Ash Tray Light Inoperative
- Courtesy Lights Inoperative From Dome Light Switch Only
- Courtesy Lights Inoperative From Drivers Front Door Only
- VTSS Does Not Trip From Drivers Front Door
- Courtesy Lights Inoperative From Left Rear Door Only
- VTSS Does Not Trip From Left Rear Door
- Courtesy Lights Inoperative From Liftgate
- Courtesy Light Inoperative From Liftgate Flip-Up Glass Only
- VTSS Does Not Trip From Liftgate Flip-Up Glass Only
- Courtesy Lights Inoperative From Passenger Front Door Only
- VTSS Does Not Trip From Passenger Front Door
- Courtesy Lights Inoperative From Right Rear Door Only
- VTSS Does Not Trip From Right Rear Door
- Driver Door Courtesy Light Inoperative
- Glove Box Light Inoperative
- Heated Seat Switch Illumination Light Inoperative
- HVAC Control Illumination Lights Inoperative
- Instrument Panel Courtesy Lights Inoperative
- Liftgate Courtesy Light Disable Feature Inoperative
- Overhead, Rear & Liftgate Lights Inoperative
- Passenger Door Courtesy Light Inoperative
- PRNDL/T-Case Illumination Lights Inoperative
- Radio Illumination Lights Inoperative
- Reading & Vanity Lights Inoperative

ALL COURTESY LIGHTS INOPERATIVE

1) Turn ignition off. Remove and inspect junction block fuse No. 8. If fuse is blown, go to next step. If fuse is okay, go to step **3)**.

2) Remove junction block fuse No. 8. Using ohmmeter, measure resistance between ground and fused B+ (upper terminal) terminal on fuse No. 8 socket. If resistance is less than 5 ohms, repair fused B+ circuit for short to ground. Replace fuse No. 8. If resistance is 5 ohms or greater, replace fuse No. 8.

3) Remove junction block fuse No. 8. Remove driver's side rear seat overhead reading light lens cover. Using ohmmeter, measure resistance of Pink wire between fused B+ (upper terminal) terminal on fuse No. 8 socket and reading light fused B+ terminal. If resistance is less than 5 ohms, replace BCM. If resistance is 5 ohms or greater, repair open fused B+ circuit (Pink wire).

ASH TRAY LIGHT INOPERATIVE

1) Using scan tool, read BODY DTCs. If PARK LAMP RELAY CKT SHORTED LO/OPEN DTC is present, go to EXTERIOR LIGHTING

TESTS under DIAGNOSTIC TESTS. If PARK LAMP RELAY CKT SHORTED LO/OPEN DTC is not present, go to next step.

2) Remove and inspect ash tray light bulb. Replace as needed. If bulb is okay, go to next step.

3) Ensure ignition is off. Disconnect ash tray light connector. Using ohmmeter, measure resistance of Black wire between ground and ash tray light harness connector. If resistance is less than 5 ohms, go to next step. If resistance is greater than 5 ohms, repair open Black wire.

4) Ensure ash tray light connector is disconnected. Disconnect Body Control Module (BCM) C1 connector. Measure resistance between terminal No. 8 (Orange wire) on BCM C1 harness connector and ash tray light harness connector. If resistance is less than 5 ohms, replace BCM. If resistance is greater than 5 ohms, repair open Orange wire.

COURTESY LIGHTS INOPERATIVE FROM DOME LIGHT SWITCH ONLY

1) Turn ignition on. Using scan tool, read BODY DTCs. If any BODY DTCs are present, go to appropriate test. If BODY DTCs are not present, go to next step.

2) Turn ignition off. Disconnect left multi-function switch connector. Measure resistance between terminal No. 4 (White/Dark Green wire) and terminal No. 10 (Red wire) on left multi-function switch harness connector. Rotate dimmer dial on left multi-function switch while monitoring ohmmeter. If resistance ranges from 60 to 7900 ohms, replace Body Control Module (BCM). If resistance does not range from 60 to 7900 ohms, replace defective left multi-function switch.

COURTESY LIGHTS INOPERATIVE FROM DRIVERS FRONT DOOR ONLY/VTSS DOES NOT TRIP FROM DRIVERS FRONT DOOR

1) Open driver's door. Using scan tool, select BODY, DOOR MODULES, then INPUT/OUTPUT. Read DRV DOOR AJAR SW status. If scan tool displays CLOSED, replace Body Control Module (BCM). If scan tool does not display CLOSED, go to next step.

2) Remove inner door trim panel. Disconnect driver's door lock motor/ajar switch connector. Measure resistance between ground and terminal No. 2 (Black wire) on driver's door lock motor/ajar switch harness connector. If resistance is less than 5 ohms, go to next step. If resistance is 5 ohms or greater, repair open Black wire.

3) Disconnect driver's door module 15-pin connector. Measure resistance of Tan/Red wire between terminal No. 1 on driver's door lock motor/ajar switch harness connector and terminal No. 11 on driver's door module 15-pin harness connector. If resistance is less than 5 ohms, go to next step. If resistance is 5 ohms or greater, repair open Tan/Red wire.

4) Ensure driver's door is open. Connect driver's door lock motor/ajar switch connector. Measure resistance between ground and terminal No. 11 (Tan/Red wire) on driver's door module 15-pin harness connector. If resistance is less than 5 ohms, replace driver's door module. If resistance is 5 ohms or greater, replace driver's door lock motor/ajar assembly.

COURTESY LIGHTS INOPERATIVE FROM LEFT REAR DOOR ONLY/VTSS DOES NOT TRIP FROM LEFT REAR DOOR

1) Open left rear door. Using scan tool, select BODY, DOOR MODULES, then INPUT/OUTPUT. Read LEFT REAR DOOR AJAR SW status. If scan tool displays CLOSED, replace Body Control Module (BCM). If scan tool does not display CLOSED, go to next step.

2) Disconnect left rear door lock motor/ajar switch connector. Disconnect junction block C1 connector. Measure resistance between terminal No. 10 (Tan/Orange wire) on junction block C1 harness connector and terminal No. 1 (Tan/Yellow wire) on left rear door lock motor/ajar switch harness connector. If resistance is less than 5 ohms, go to next step. If resistance is 5 ohms or greater, repair open LR door ajar switch sense circuit.

3) Measure resistance between ground and terminal No. 2 (Black wire) on left rear door lock motor/ajar switch harness connector. If resistance is less than 5 ohms, go to next step. If resistance is 5 ohms or greater, repair open Black wire.

4) Ensure left rear door is open. Connect left rear door lock motor/ajar switch connector. Measure resistance between ground and terminal No. 10 (Tan/Orange wire) on junction block C1 harness connector. If resistance is less than 5 ohms and vehicle is not equipped with sentry key system, test is complete. If resistance is less than 5 ohms and vehicle is equipped with sentry key system, replace Body Control Module (BCM). If resistance is 5 ohms or greater, replace left rear door lock motor/ajar switch assembly.

COURTESY LIGHTS INOPERATIVE FROM LIFTGATE

1) Open liftgate. Using scan tool, select BODY, DOOR MODULES, then INPUT/OUTPUT. Read LIFTGATE SW status. If scan tool displays CLOSED, test is complete. If scan tool does not display CLOSED, go to next step.

2) Disconnect left, right and flip-up glass liftgate ajar switch connectors. Using ohmmeter, measure resistance between ground and terminal No. 1 (Black wire) on each liftgate ajar switch harness connector. If resistance is less than 5 ohms, go to next step. If resistance is 5 ohms or greater, repair open Black wire.

3) Disconnect junction block C1 connector. Measure resistance of Tan/Black wire between terminal No. 1 on each liftgate ajar switch harness connector and terminal No. 25 on junction block C1 harness connector. If resistance is less than 5 ohms, go to next step. If resistance is 5 ohms or greater, repair open Tan/Black wire.

4) Ensure latch of each liftgate switch is in unlatched position. Measure resistance between terminals on each liftgate ajar switch component connector. If resistance is less than 2 ohms for each switch, replace Body Control Module (BCM). If resistance is 2 ohms or greater on any switch, replace defective switch.

COURTESY LIGHTS INOPERATIVE FROM LIFTGATE FLIP-UP GLASS ONLY/VTSS DOES NOT TRIP FROM LIFTGATE FLIP-UP GLASS ONLY

1) Disconnect left and right liftgate ajar switch connectors. Using ohmmeter, measure resistance between ground and terminal No. 1 (Black wire) on each liftgate ajar switch harness connector. If resistance is less 5 ohms, go to next step. If resistance is 5 ohms or greater, repair open Black wire.

2) Disconnect junction block C1 connector. Measure resistance of Tan/Black wire between terminal No. 1 on each liftgate ajar switch harness connector and terminal No. 25 on junction block C1 harness connector. If resistance is less than 5 ohms, go to next step. If resistance is 5 ohms or greater, repair open Tan/Black wire.

3) Disconnect liftgate flip-up glass ajar switch connector. Ensure latch of switch is in unlatched position. Measure resistance between terminals on switch component connector. If resistance is less than 2 ohms, test is complete. If resistance is 2 ohms or greater, replace defective switch.

COURTESY LIGHTS INOPERATIVE FROM PASSENGER FRONT DOOR ONLY/VTSS DOES NOT TRIP FROM PASSENGER FRONT DOOR ONLY

1) Open passenger front door. Using scan tool, select BODY, DOOR MODULES, then INPUT/OUTPUT. Read PASS DOOR AJAR SW status. If scan tool displays CLOSED, replace Body Control Module (BCM). If scan tool does not display CLOSED, go to next step.

2) Disconnect passenger door lock motor/ajar switch connector. Using ohmmeter, measure resistance between ground and terminal No. 2 (Black wire) on passenger front door ajar switch harness connector. If resistance is less 5 ohms, go to next step. If resistance is 5 ohms or greater, repair open Black wire.

3) Disconnect passenger's front door module 15-pin connector. Measure resistance of Tan/Red wire between terminal No. 1 on passenger's front door lock motor/ajar switch harness connector and terminal No. 11

JEEP
4-46

1999 ACCESSORIES & EQUIPMENT
Body Control Computer Tests – Grand Cherokee (Cont.)

on passenger's front door module 15-pin harness connector. If resistance is less than 5 ohms, go to next step. If resistance is 5 ohms or greater, repair open Tan/Red wire.

4) Ensure passenger's front door is open. Connect passenger's front door lock motor/ajar switch connector. Measure resistance between ground and terminal No. 11 (Tan/Red wire) on passenger's front door module 15-pin harness connector. If resistance is less than 5 ohms, replace passenger's front door module. If resistance is 5 ohms or greater, replace passenger's front door lock motor/ajar assembly.

COURTESY LIGHTS INOPERATIVE FROM PASSENGER REAR DOOR ONLY/VTSS DOES NOT TRIP FROM PASSENGER REAR DOOR ONLY

1) Open right rear door. Using scan tool, select BODY, DOOR MODULES, then INPUT/OUTPUT. Read RIGHT REAR DOOR AJAR SW status. If scan tool displays CLOSED, replace Body Control Module (BCM). If scan tool does not display CLOSED, go to next step.

2) Disconnect right rear door lock motor/ajar switch connector. Using ohmmeter, measure resistance between ground and terminal No. 2 (Black wire) on right rear door ajar switch harness connector. If resistance is less 5 ohms, go to next step. If resistance is 5 ohms or greater, repair open Black wire.

3) Disconnect Body Control Module (BCM) C1 connector. Measure resistance of Tan/Yellow wire between terminal No. 7 on BCM C1 harness connector and terminal No. 1 on right rear door lock motor/ajar switch harness connector. If resistance is less than 5 ohms, go to next step. If resistance is 5 ohms or greater, repair open Tan/Yellow wire.

4) Ensure right rear door is open. Connect right rear door lock motor/ajar switch connector. Measure resistance between ground and terminal No. 7 (Tan/Yellow wire) on BCM C1 harness connector. If resistance is less than 5 ohms, replace Body Control Module (BCM). If resistance is 5 ohms or greater, replace right rear door lock motor/ajar switch assembly.

DRIVER'S DOOR COURTESY LIGHT INOPERATIVE

1) Remove and inspect driver's door courtesy light bulb. Replace as needed. If bulb is okay, go to next step.

2) Remove driver's door courtesy light bulb. Remove driver's door inner trim panel. Disconnect driver's door module 12-pin C2 connector. Using ohmmeter, measure resistance of Pink/Dark Green wire between terminal No. 9 on driver's door module 12-pin C2 harness connector and driver's door courtesy light bulb socket. If resistance is less than 5 ohms, go to next step. If resistance is 5 ohms or greater, repair open Pink/Dark Green wire.

3) Measure resistance of Black/Red wire between terminal No. 12 on driver's door module 12-pin C2 harness connector and driver's door courtesy light bulb socket. If resistance is less than 5 ohms, replace Body Control Module (BCM). If resistance is 5 ohms or greater, repair open Pink/Dark Green wire.

GLOVE BOX LIGHT INOPERATIVE

1) Remove and inspect glove box light bulb. Replace as needed. If bulb is okay, go to next step.

2) Disconnect glove box light connector. Using voltmeter, measure voltage between ground and terminal No. 1 (Pink/Black wire) on glove box light harness connector. If voltage is greater than 10.5 volts, go to next step. If voltage is 10.5 volts or less, repair open Pink/Black wire.

3) Connect test light between terminals on glove box light harness connector. If test light illuminates, replace defective glove box light switch. If test light does not illuminate, go to next step.

4) Disconnect Body Control Module (BCM) C1 connector. Using ohmmeter, measure resistance of Brown/Orange wire between terminal No. 2 on glove box light harness connector and terminal No. 23 on BCM C1 harness connector. If resistance is less than 5 ohms, replace BCM. If resistance is 5 ohms or greater, repair open Brown/Orange wire.

HEATED SEAT SWITCH ILLUMINATION LIGHT INOPERATIVE

1) Using scan tool, read BODY DTCs. If PARK LAMP RELAY CKT SHORTED LO/OPEN DTC is present, go to EXTERIOR LIGHTING

DIAGNOSTIC TESTS. If PARK LAMP RELAY CKT SHORTED LO/OPEN DTC is not present, go to next step.

2) Remove and inspect driver's heated seat switch light bulb. Replace as needed. If bulb is okay, go to next step.

3) Remove and inspect passenger's heated seat switch light bulb. Replace as needed. If bulb is okay, go to next step.

4) Turn ignition off. Disconnect driver's heated seat switch connector. Using ohmmeter, measure resistance between ground and terminal No. 5 (Black wire) on driver's heated seat switch harness connector. If resistance is less than 5 ohms, go to next step. If resistance is 5 ohms or greater, repair open Black wire.

5) Turn ignition off. Disconnect passenger's heated seat switch connector. Using ohmmeter, measure resistance between ground and terminal No. 5 (Black wire) on passenger's heated seat switch harness connector. If resistance is less than 5 ohms, go to next step. If resistance is 5 ohms or greater, repair open Black wire.

6) Disconnect Body Control Module (BCM) C1 connector. Measure resistance of Orange wire between terminal No. 2 on passenger's heated seat switch harness connector and terminal No. 12 on BCM C1 harness connector. If resistance is less than 5 ohms, go to next step. If resistance is 5 ohms or greater, repair open Orange wire.

7) Disconnect Body Control Module (BCM) C1 connector. Measure resistance of Orange wire between terminal No. 2 on driver's heated seat switch harness connector and terminal No. 12 on BCM C1 harness connector. If resistance is less than 5 ohms, replace BCM. If resistance is 5 ohms or greater, repair open Orange wire.

HVAC CONTROL ILLUMINATION LIGHTS INOPERATIVE

1) Using scan tool, read BODY DTCs. If PARK LAMP RELAY CKT SHORTED LO/OPEN DTC is present, go to EXTERIOR LIGHTING DIAGNOSTIC TESTS. If PARK LAMP RELAY CKT SHORTED LO/OPEN DTC is not present, go to next step.

2) Disconnect HVAC control panel harness connectors. On manual HVAC system, connect test light between terminals No. 2 (Black/Orange wire) and No. 7 (Orange wire) on manual HVAC 11-pin C1 harness connector. On automatic HVAC system, connect test light between terminal No. 8 (Black wire) on automatic HVAC 16-pin C1 harness connector and No. 6 (Orange wire) on automatic HVAC 12-pin C2 harness connector. Turn on panel lamps. If test light is illuminated, replace defective HVAC control panel assembly. If test light does not illuminate, go to next step.

3) Turn ignition off. Using ohmmeter, measure resistance between ground and appropriate HVAC system ground circuit. On manual HVAC system, connect ohmmeter to terminal No. 2 (Black/Orange wire) on manual HVAC 11-pin C1 harness connector. On automatic HVAC system, connect ohmmeter to terminal No. 8 (Black wire) on automatic HVAC 16-pin C1 harness connector. If resistance is less than 5 ohms, go to next step. If resistance is 5 ohms or greater, repair open ground circuit.

4) Disconnect Body Control Module (BCM) C1 connector. Measure resistance of Orange wire between terminal No. 10 on BCM C1 harness connector and appropriate HVAC system panel lights driver. On manual HVAC system, connect ohmmeter to terminal No. 7 on manual HVAC 11-pin C1 harness connector. On automatic HVAC system, connect ohmmeter to terminal No. 6 on automatic HVAC 12-pin C2 harness connector. If resistance is less than 5 ohms, replace defective BCM. If resistance is 5 ohms or greater, repair open panel lights driver circuit.

INSTRUMENT PANEL COURTESY LIGHTS INOPERATIVE

1) Remove and inspect inoperative instrument panel courtesy light. Replace as needed. If both bulbs are okay, go to next step.

2) Using voltmeter, measure voltage between ground and fused B+ terminal (Pink/Black wire) on either instrument panel courtesy light socket. If voltage is greater than 10 volts, go to next step. If voltage is less than 10 volts, repair open Pink/Black wire.

3) Turn ignition off. Disconnect Body Control Module C1 connector. Using ohmmeter, measure resistance of Yellow wire between terminal

1999 ACCESSORIES & EQUIPMENT
Body Control Computer Tests – Grand Cherokee (Cont.)

JEEP
4-47

No. 24 on BCM C1 harness connector and appropriate terminal on suspect instrument panel courtesy light socket. If resistance is less than 5 ohms, go to next step. If resistance is 5 ohms or greater, repair open Yellow wire.

4) Remove junction block fuse No. 8. Connect BCM C1 connector. Turn dome light switch to ON position. Backprobing BCM C1 harness connector, measure resistance between ground and terminal No. 24 (Yellow wire). If resistance is less than 5 ohms, test is complete. If resistance is 5 ohms or greater, replace BCM.

LIFTGATE COURTESY LIGHT DISABLE FEATURE INOPERATIVE

1) Disconnect cargo light connector. Using voltmeter, measure voltage between ground and terminal No. 1 (Pink wire) on cargo light harness connector. If voltage is greater than 10 volts, go to next step. If voltage is 10 volts or less, repair open Pink wire.

2) Disconnect junction block C1 connector. Using ohmmeter, measure resistance of Light Green/Orange wire between terminal No. 2 on cargo light harness connector and terminal No. 9 on junction block C1 harness connector. If resistance is less than 5 ohms, go to next step. If resistance is 5 ohms or greater, repair open Light Green/Orange wire.

3) Connect cargo light harness connector. Using voltmeter, backprobe cargo light harness connector. Measure voltage between ground and terminal No. 2 (Light Green/Orange wire) on cargo light harness connector. Operate disable switch while monitoring voltmeter. If voltage toggle between zero to about 10 volts, replace Body Control Module (BCM). If voltage does not toggle between zero to about 10 volts, replace cargo light assembly.

OVERHEAD, REAR & LIFTGATE COURTESY LIGHTS INOPERATIVE

1) Remove and inspect inoperative light bulb(s). Replace as needed. If all bulbs are okay, go to next step.

2) Using voltmeter, measure voltage between ground and terminal No. 1 (Pink wire) on suspect courtesy light assembly connector. If voltage is greater than 10 volts, go to next step. If voltage is 10 volts or less, repair open Pink wire.

3) Disconnect junction block C1 connector. Using ohmmeter, measure resistance of Yellow/Dark Green wire between terminal No. 3 on applicable courtesy light harness connector and terminal No. 16 on junction block C1 harness connector. If resistance is less than 5 ohms, go to next step. If resistance is 5 ohms or greater, repair open Yellow/Dark Green wire.

4) Remove junction block fuse No. 8. Connect junction block C1 connector. Turn dome light switch to ON position. Backprobing junction block C1 harness connector, measure resistance between ground and terminal No. 16 (Yellow/Light Green wire). If resistance is less than 5 ohms, test is complete. If resistance is 5 ohms or greater, replace BCM.

PASSENGER DOOR COURTESY LIGHT INOPERATIVE

1) Remove and inspect passenger's door courtesy light bulb. Replace as needed. If bulb is okay, go to next step.

2) Remove passenger's door courtesy light bulb. Remove passenger's door inner trim panel. Disconnect passenger's door module 12-pin C2 connector. Using ohmmeter, measure resistance of Pink/Dark Green wire between terminal No. 9 on passenger's door module 12-pin C2 harness connector and passenger's door courtesy light bulb socket. If resistance is less than 5 ohms, go to next step. If resistance is 5 ohms or greater, repair open Pink/Dark Green wire.

3) Measure resistance of Black/Red wire between terminal No. 12 on passenger's door module 12-pin C2 harness connector and passenger's door courtesy light bulb socket. If resistance is less than 5 ohms, replace Body Control Module (BCM). If resistance is 5 ohms or greater, repair open Pink/Dark Green wire.

PRNDL/T-CASE ILLUMINATION LIGHTS INOPERATIVE

1) Using scan tool, read BODY DTCs. If PARK LAMP RELAY CKT SHORTED LO/OPEN DTC is present, go to EXTERIOR LIGHTING DIAGNOSTIC TESTS. If PARK LAMP RELAY CKT SHORTED LO/OPEN DTC is not present, go to next step.

2) Disconnect PRNDL connector. Connect test light between PRNDL connector terminals. Turn on panel lamps. If test light illuminates, replace defective PRNDL illumination unit. If test light does not illuminate, go to next step.

3) Turn ignition off. Using ohmmeter, measure resistance between ground and terminal No. 2 (Black wire) on PRNDL connector. If resistance is less than 5 ohms, go to next step. If resistance is 5 ohms or greater, repair open Black wire.

4) Disconnect Body Control Module (BCM) C1 connector. Measure resistance of Light Blue wire between terminal No. 1 on PRNDL illumination unit connector and terminal No. 9 on BCM C1 connector. If resistance is less than 5 ohms, replace BCM. If resistance is 5 ohms or greater, repair open Light Blue wire.

RADIO ILLUMINATION LIGHTS INOPERATIVE

1) Using scan tool, read BODY DTCs. If PARK LAMP RELAY CKT SHORTED LO/OPEN DTC is present, go to EXTERIOR LIGHTING DIAGNOSTIC TESTS. If PARK LAMP RELAY CKT SHORTED LO/OPEN DTC is not present, go to next step.

2) Turn ignition off. Disconnect radio ground strap. Using ohmmeter, measure resistance between ground and ground strap terminal. If resistance is less than 5 ohms, go to next step. If resistance is 5 ohms or greater,

3) Disconnect radio 7-pin C1 connector. Connect test light between ground strap and terminal No. 5 (Orange wire) on radio 7-pin C1 harness connector. Turn on panel lights. If test light illuminates, replace defective radio. If test light does not illuminate, go to next step.

4) Turn ignition off. Disconnect Body Control Module (BCM) C1 connector. Measure resistance of Orange wire between terminal No. 5 on radio 7-pin C1 harness connector and terminal No. 13 on BCM C1 harness connector. If resistance is less than 5 ohms, replace BCM. If resistance is 5 ohms or greater, repair open Orange wire.

READING & VANITY LIGHTS INOPERATIVE

1) Ensure ignition is off. Disconnect junction block C1 connector. Using ohmmeter, measure resistance of Yellow/Black wire between terminal No. 2 on applicable vanity light harness connector and terminal No. 26 on junction block C1 harness connector. If resistance is less than 5 ohms, go to next step. If resistance is 5 ohms or greater, repair open Yellow/Black wire.

2) Remove junction block fuse No. 8. Connect junction block C1 connector. Backprobing junction block C1 harness connector, measure resistance between ground and terminal No. 26 (Yellow/Black wire). If resistance is less than 5 ohms, test is complete. If resistance is 5 ohms or greater, replace BCM.

OVERHEAD CONSOLE DIAGNOSTIC TESTS

NOTE: Perform SYSTEM ID TEST before proceeding with following tests. For connector terminal identification and wiring diagrams, see BODY CONTROL COMPUTER INTRODUCTION article. Perform VERIFICATION TEST: VER-2A after each repair.

The following overhead console diagnostic tests are covered:
- AMBIENT TEMP SENSOR CKT OPEN
- AMBIENT TEMP SENSOR CKT SHORT TO GND
- COOLANT LEVEL SWITCH CIRCUIT OPEN
- EVIC NOT RECEIVING BUS MESSAGES

AMBIENT TEMP SENSOR CKT OPEN

1) Disconnect ambient temperature sensor. Sensor is located on right side of front grille, next to headlight. Connect jumper wire between sensor harness connector terminals. Turn ignition on. Close all doors. If

JEEP
4-48

1999 ACCESSORIES & EQUIPMENT
Body Control Computer Tests – Grand Cherokee (Cont.)

overhead console displays SHORT CIRCUIT, replace ambient temperature sensor. If overhead console does not display SHORT CIRCUIT, go to next step.

2) Turn igniton off. Disconnect Body Control Module (BCM) connector. Measure resistance of Dark Green/Red wire between terminal No. 9 on BCM C2 harness connector and terminal No. 2 on ambient temperature sensor harness connector. If resistance is less than 2 ohms, go to next step. If resistance is 2 ohms or greater, repair open Dark Green/Red wire.

3) Connect BCM connector. Connect jumper wire between ground and terminal No. 2 (Dark Green/Red wire) on ambient temperature sensor harness connector. Turn ignition on. Close all doors. If overhead console displays SHORT CIRCUIT, repair open Dark Green/Red wire. If overhead console does not display SHORT CIRCUIT, go to next step.

4) Remove jumper wire. Turn ignition on. Close all doors. If overhead console displays OPEN CIRCUIT, replace ambient temperature sensor. If overhead console does not display OPEN CIRCUIT, go to next step.

5) Turn igniton off. Measure resistance between ground and terminal No. 2 (Dark Green/Red wire) on ambient temperature sensor harness connector. If resistance is less than 5 ohms, repair Dark Green/Red wire for short to ground. If resistance is 2 ohms or greater, go to next step.

6) Ensure ambient temperature sensor connector is disconnected. Turn ignition on. Using voltmeter, measure voltage between ground and terminal No. 2 (Dark Green/Red wire) on sensor harness connector. If voltage is greater than 4 volts, test is complete. If voltage is 4 volts or less, replace BCM.

AMBIENT TEMP SENSOR CKT SHORT TO GND

1) Disconnect ambient temperature sensor. Sensor is located on right side of front grille, next to headlight. Turn ignition on. Close all doors. If overhead console displays OPEN CIRCUIT, replace ambient temperature sensor. If overhead console does not display OPEN CIRCUIT, go to next step.

2) Connect jumper wire between ground and terminal No. 2 (Dark Green/Red wire) on ambient temperature sensor harness connector. Turn ignition on. Close all doors. If overhead console displays SHORT CIRCUIT, replace ambient temperature sensor. If overhead console does not display SHORT CIRCUIT, go to next step.

3) Turn igniton off. Disconnect Body Control Module (BCM) connector. Measure resistance between ground and terminal No. 2 (Dark Green/Red wire) on ambient temperature sensor harness connector. If resistance is less than 5 ohms, repair Dark Green/Red wire for short to ground. If resistance is 2 ohms or greater, go to next step.

4) Turn igniton off. Measure resistance of Dark Green/Red wire between terminal No. 9 on BCM C2 harness connector and terminal No. 2 on ambient temperature sensor harness connector. If resistance is less than 2 ohms, go to next step. If resistance is 2 ohms or greater, repair open Dark Green/Red wire.

5) Connect BCM connector. Connect jumper wire between ambient sensor harness connector terminals. Turn ignition on. Close all doors. If overhead console displays SHORT CIRCUIT, repair open ambient sensor signal circuit (Dark Green/Red wire). If overhead console does not display SHORT CIRCUIT, go to next step.

6) Ensure ambient temperature sensor connector is disconnected. Turn ignition on. Using voltmeter, measure voltage between ground and terminal No. 2 (Dark Green/Red wire) on sensor harness connector. If voltage is greater than 4 volts, test is complete. If voltage is 4 volts or less, replace BCM.

COOLANT LEVEL SWITCH CIRCUIT OPEN

1) Using scan tool, select BCM SENSORS. Turn ignition on. Read coolant level sensor voltage. If voltage is greater than 4.7 volts, go to next step. If voltage is 4.7 volts or less, test is complete.

2) Turn ignition off. Disconnect coolant level sensor. Sensor is mounted in coolant recovery tank. Using ohmmeter, measure resistance between ground and terminal No. 2 (Black wire) on sensor harness connector. If resistance is less than 5 ohms, go to next step. If resistance is 5 ohms or greater, repair open Black wire.

3) Measure resistance between coolant level sensor component connector. If resistance is less than 3500 ohms, connect sensor connector and go to next step. If resistance is 3500 ohms or greater, replace coolant level sensor.

4) Turn ignition on. Using scan tool, select BCM SENSORS. Using jumper wire, backprobe coolant level sensor connector terminals. If coolant level sensor voltage is less than one volt, go to next step. If voltage is one volt or greater, replace Body Control Module (BCM)

5) Disconnect coolant level sensor connector. Using scan tool, select BCM SENSORS. Turn ignition on. Connect jumper wire between ground and terminal No. 1 (Pink/Black wire) on coolant level sensor harness connector. Read coolant level sensor voltage. If voltage is greater than 4.7 volts, repair open Pink/Black wire. If voltage is 4.7 volts or less, test is complete.

EVIC NOT RECEIVING BUS MESSAGES

1) Turn ignition on. Using scan tool, access BODY CONTROL MODULE. If BCM responds, go to next step. If there is no response from BCM, go to appropriate test in VEHICLE COMMUNICATIONS article.

2) Using scan tool, select BODY CONTROLLER. Perform SYSTEM TEST. If scan tool displays PCM ACTIVE ON THE BUS, go to next step. If scan tool does not display PCM ACTIVE ON THE BUS, go to appropriate test in VEHICLE COMMUNICATIONS article.

3) Using scan tool, access BODY CONTROL MODULE. Select ELECTROMECHANICAL INSTRUMENT CLUSTER. If instrument cluster responds, test is complete. If instrument cluster does not respond, go to appropriate test in VEHICLE COMMUNICATIONS article.

POWER DOOR LOCK/REMOTE KEYLESS ENTRY (RKE) SYMPTOM TESTS

NOTE: Perform SYSTEM ID TEST before proceeding with following tests. For connector terminal identification and wiring diagrams, see BODY CONTROL COMPUTER INTRODUCTION article. Perform VERIFICATION TEST: VER-2A after each repair.

The following power door lock/remote keyless entry symptoms are covered:
- All Doors Excluding Driver's Door Fail To Lock/Unlock
- All Doors Excluding Driver's Door Fail To Lock
- All Doors Excluding Driver's Door Fail To Unlock
- All Locks Inoperative From Driver's Door Module
- All Locks Inoperative From Passenger's Door Module
- Automatic Door Locks Inoperative
- Doors Lock With Key In Ignition & Front Door Open
- Driver's Door Fails To Lock
- Driver's Door Fails To Lock & Unlock
- Driver's Door Fails To Unlock
- Driver's Rear Door Fails To Lock & Unlock
- Liftgate Lock Fails To Lock/Unlock
- Passenger Door Fails To Lock & Unlock
- Passenger Rear Door Fails To Lock & Unlock
- RKE Transmitter Inoperative

ALL DOORS EXCLUDING DRIVER'S DOOR FAIL TO LOCK/UNLOCK

1) Remove passenger front door inner trim panel. Disconnect door lock motor/ajar switch connector. Disconnect passenger door module 15-pin C1 connector. Using ohmmeter, measure resistance of Orange/Violet wire between terminal No. 5 on passenger door module 15-pin C1 harness connector and terminal No. 4 on door lock motor/ajar switch harness connector. If resistance is less than 5 ohms, go to next step. If resistance is 5 ohms or greater, repair open Orange/Violet wire.

2) Measure resistance of Pink/Violet wire between terminal No. 7 on passenger door module 15-pin C1 harness connector and terminal No. 3 on door lock motor/ajar switch harness connector. If resistance is less

1999 ACCESSORIES & EQUIPMENT
Body Control Computer Tests – Grand Cherokee (Cont.)

JEEP
4-49

than 5 ohms, replace passenger door module. If resistance is 5 ohms or greater, repair open Pink/Violet wire.

ALL DOORS EXCLUDING DRIVER'S DOOR FAILS TO LOCK

Remove passenger front door inner trim panel. Disconnect passenger door module 15-pin C1 connector. Using ohmmeter, measure resistance between ground and terminal No. 5 (Orange/Violet wire) on passenger door module 15-pin C1 harness connector. If resistance is less than 5 ohms, repair Orange/Violet wire for short to ground. If resistance is 5 ohms or greater, replace passenger door module.

ALL DOORS EXCLUDING DRIVER'S DOOR FAILS TO UNLOCK

Remove passenger front door inner trim panel. Disconnect passenger door module 15-pin C1 connector. Using ohmmeter, measure resistance between ground and terminal No. 7 (Pink/Violet wire) on passenger door module 15-pin C1 harness connector. If resistance is less than 5 ohms, repair Pink/Violet wire for short to ground. If resistance is 5 ohms or greater, replace passenger door module.

ALL LOCKS INOPERATIVE FROM DRIVER'S DOOR MODULE

Using scan tool, select BODY, then DOOR MODULES. If scan tool displays driver's door module PART NO. and VERSION NO., replace driver's door module. If scan tool does not display driver door module PART NO. and VERSION NO., go to appropriate test in VEHICLE COMMUNICATIONS article.

ALL LOCKS INOPERATIVE FROM PASSENGER'S DOOR MODULE

Using scan tool, select BODY, then DOOR MODULES. If scan tool displays passenger's door module PART NO. and VERSION NO., replace passenger's door module. If scan tool does not display passenger's door module PART NO. and VERSION NO., go to appropriate test in VEHICLE COMMUNICATIONS article.

AUTOMATIC DOOR LOCKS INOPERATIVE

1) Using scan tool, select CUSTOMER PREFERENCES. Read ROLLING DOOR LOCK status. If scan tool displays ROLLING DOOR LOCKS ENABLED, go to next step. If scan tool does not display ROLLING DOOR LOCKS ENABLED, enable auto door locks using scan tool. Retest system.

2) Using scan tool, read ENGINE DTCs. Repair any engine related DTCs before continuing. If no engine DTCs are present, replace passenger door module.

DOORS LOCK WITH KEY IN IGNITION & FRONT DOOR OPEN

1) Using scan tool, read KEY-IN IGNITON status. If scan tool displays CLOSED, go to next step. If scan tool does not display CLOSED, go to step 8).

2) Open driver's door. Using scan tool, select BODY, DOOR MODULES, then INPUT/OUTPUT. Read DRV DOOR AJAR SW. If scan tool displays CLOSED, go to next step. If scan tool does not display CLOSED, go to step 6).

3) Remove driver's inner door trim panel. Disconnect driver's door lock motor/ajar switch connector. Disconnect driver's door module 15-pin connector. Using ohmmeter, measure resistance of Tan/Red wire between terminal No. 1 on driver's door lock motor/ajar switch harness connector and terminal No. 11 on driver's door module 15-pin harness connector. If resistance is less than 5 ohms, go to next step. If resistance is 5 ohms or greater, repair open Tan/Red wire.

4) Measure resistance between ground and terminal No. 2 (Black wire) on driver's door lock motor/ajar switch harness connector. If resistance is less than 5 ohms, go to next step. If resistance is 5 ohms or greater, repair open Black wire.

5) Open driver's door. Connect driver's door lock motor/ajar switch connector. Measure resistance between ground and terminal No. 11 (Tan/Red wire) on driver's door module 15-pin harness connector. If resistance is less than 5 ohms, replace Body Control Module (BCM). If resistance is 5 ohms or greater, replace driver's door lock motor/ajar switch assembly.

6) Remove driver's inner door trim panel. Disconnect driver's door lock motor/ajar switch connector. Disconnect driver's door module 15-pin connector. Using ohmmeter, measure resistance of Tan/Red wire between terminal No. 1 on driver's door lock motor/ajar switch harness connector and terminal No. 11 on driver's door module 15-pin harness connector. If resistance is less than 5 ohms, go to next step. If resistance is 5 ohms or greater, repair open Tan/Red wire.

7) Measure resistance between ground and terminal No. 2 (Black wire) on driver's door lock motor/ajar switch harness connector. If resistance is less than 5 ohms, go to step 20). If resistance is 5 ohms or greater, repair open Black wire.

8) Open driver's door. Using scan tool, select BODY, DOOR MODULES, then INPUT/OUTPUT. Read DRV DOOR AJAR SW. If scan tool displays CLOSED, go to next step. If scan tool does not display CLOSED, go to step 15).

9) Remove driver's inner door trim panel. Disconnect driver's door lock motor/ajar switch connector. Disconnect driver's door module 15-pin connector. Using ohmmeter, measure resistance of Tan/Red wire between terminal No. 1 on driver's door lock motor/ajar switch harness connector and terminal No. 11 on driver's door module 15-pin harness connector. If resistance is less than 5 ohms, go to next step. If resistance is 5 ohms or greater, repair open Tan/Red wire.

10) Disconnect ignition switch 2-pin connector. Measure resistance between ground and terminal No. 2 (Black wire) on ignition switch 2-pin harness connector. If resistance is less than 5 ohms, go to next step. If resistance is 5 ohms or greater, repair open Black wire.

11) Connect jumper wire between ignition switch 2-pin harness connector terminals. Using scan tool, read KEY-IN IGNITON status. If scan tool displays CLOSED, replace ignition switch. If scan tool does not display CLOSED, go to next step.

12) Ensure ignition is off. Disconnect Body Control Module (BCM) C1 connector. Using ohmmeter, measure resistance of Light Blue wire between terminal No. 1 on ignition switch 2-pin harness connector and terminal No. 6 on BCM C1 harness connector. If resistance is less than 5 ohms, go to next step. If resistance is 5 ohms or greater, repair open Light Blue wire.

13) Measure resistance between ground and terminal No. 2 (Black wire) on driver's door lock motor/ajar switch harness connector. If resistance is less than 5 ohms, go to next step. If resistance is 5 ohms or greater, repair open Black wire.

14) Open driver's door. Connect driver's door lock motor/ajar switch connector. Measure resistance between ground and terminal No. 11 (Tan/Red wire) on driver's door module 15-pin harness connector. If resistance is less than 5 ohms, replace Body Control Module (BCM). If resistance is 5 ohms or greater, replace driver's door lock motor/ajar switch assembly.

15) Remove driver's inner door trim panel. Disconnect driver's door lock motor/ajar switch connector. Using ohmmeter, measure resistance between ground and terminal No. 2 (Black wire) on driver's door lock motor/ajar switch harness connector. If resistance is less than 5 ohms, go to next step. If resistance is 5 ohms or greater, repair open Black wire.

16) Disconnect driver's door module 15-pin connector. Using ohmmeter, measure resistance of Tan/Red wire between terminal No. 1 on driver's door lock motor/ajar switch harness connector and terminal No. 11 on driver's door module 15-pin harness connector. If resistance is less than 5 ohms, go to next step. If resistance is 5 ohms or greater, repair open Tan/Red wire.

17) Disconnect ignition switch 2-pin connector. Measure resistance between ground and terminal No. 2 (Black wire) on ignition switch 2-pin harness connector. If resistance is less than 5 ohms, go to next step. If resistance is 5 ohms or greater, repair open Black wire.

JEEP
4-50

1999 ACCESSORIES & EQUIPMENT
Body Control Computer Tests – Grand Cherokee (Cont.)

18) Connect jumper wire between ignition switch 2-pin harness connector terminals. Using scan tool, read KEY-IN IGNITON status. If scan tool displays CLOSED, replace ignition switch. If scan tool does not display CLOSED, go to next step.

19) Ensure ignition is off. Disconnect Body Control Module (BCM) C1 connector. Using ohmmeter, measure resistance of Light Blue wire between terminal No. 1 on ignition switch 2-pin harness connector and terminal No. 6 on BCM C1 harness connector. If resistance is less than 5 ohms, go to next step. If resistance is 5 ohms or greater, repair open Light Blue wire.

20) Open driver's door. Connect driver's door lock motor/ajar switch connector. Measure resistance between ground and terminal No. 11 (Tan/Red wire) on driver's door module 15-pin harness connector. If resistance is less than 5 ohms, replace driver door module. If resistance is 5 ohms or greater, replace driver's door lock motor/ajar switch assembly.

DRIVER DOOR FAILS TO LOCK

Remove driver's front door inner trim panel. Disconnect driver's door module 15-pin C1 connector. Using ohmmeter, measure resistance between ground and terminal No. 5 (Orange/Black wire) on driver's door module 15-pin C1 harness connector. If resistance is less than 20 ohms, repair Orange/Black wire for short to ground. If resistance is 20 ohms or greater, replace driver door module.

DRIVER'S DOOR FAILS TO LOCK & UNLOCK

1) Remove driver's front door inner trim panel. Disconnect driver's door module 15-pin C1 connector. Ensure driver's window is down and door is unlocked. Connect a jumper wire between terminals No. 4 (Black wire) and 5 (Orange/Black wire) on driver's door module 15-pin C1 harness connector. Connect jumper wire to terminal No. 7 (Pink/Black wire) and momentarily touch terminal No. 1 (Tan/Light Blue wire). If driver's door unlocks, replace driver's door module. If driver's door does not unlock, go to next step.

2) Disconnect door lock motor/ajar switch connector. Using ohmmeter, measure resistance of Orange/Black wire between terminal No. 5 on passenger door module 15-pin C1 harness connector and terminal No. 4 on door lock motor/ajar switch harness connector. If resistance is less than 5 ohms, go to next step. If resistance is 5 ohms or greater, repair open Orange/Black wire.

3) Disconnect door lock motor/ajar switch connector. Using ohmmeter, measure resistance of Pink/Black wire between terminal No. 7 on passenger door module 15-pin C1 harness connector and terminal No. 3 on door lock motor/ajar switch harness connector. If resistance is less than 5 ohms, replace defective door lock motor. If resistance is 5 ohms or greater, repair open Pink/Black wire.

DRIVER DOOR FAILS TO UNLOCK

Remove driver's front door inner trim panel. Disconnect driver's door module 15-pin C1 connector. Using ohmmeter, measure resistance between ground and terminal No. 7 (Pink/Black wire) on driver's door module 15-pin C1 harness connector. If resistance is less than 20 ohms, repair Pink/Black wire for short to ground. If resistance is 20 ohms or greater, replace driver door module.

DRIVER'S REAR DOOR FAILS TO LOCK & UNLOCK

1) Remove driver's rear door inner trim panel. Disconnect door lock motor/ajar switch connector. Ensure passenger door module connector is connected. Connect test light between terminals No. 3 (Pink/Violet wire) and 4 (Orange/Violet wire) on driver's rear door lock motor/ajar switch harness connector. Using scan tool, actuate PAS LOCK RELAY, then PAS UNLOCK RELAY while monitoring test light. If test light illuminates during actuation, replace door lock motor. If test light does not illuminate, go to next step.

2) Ensure ignition is off. Remove passenger's door inner trim panel. Disconnect passenger door module 15-pin C1 connector. Using ohmmeter, measure resistance of Orange/Violet wire between terminal No. 4 on driver's rear door lock motor/ajar switch harness connector and

terminal No. 5 on passenger door module 15-pin C1 connector. If resistance is less than 5 ohms, go to next step. If resistance is 5 ohms or greater, repair open Orange/Violet wire.

3) Measure resistance of Pink/Violet wire between terminal No. 3 on driver's rear door lock motor/ajar switch harness connector and terminal No. 7 on passenger door module 15-pin C1 connector. If resistance is less than 5 ohms, test is complete. If resistance is 5 ohms or greater, repair open Orange/Violet wire.

LIFTGATE LOCK FAILS TO LOCK/UNLOCK

1) Remove liftgate inner trim panel. Disconnect liftgate lock motor connector. Ensure passenger door module connector is connected. Connect test light between terminals No. 1 (Orange/Violet wire) and 2 (Pink/Violet wire) on liftgate door lock motor harness connector. Using scan tool, actuate PAS LOCK RELAY, then PAS UNLOCK RELAY while monitoring test light. If test light illuminates during actuation, replace liftgate lock motor. If test light does not illuminate, go to next step.

2) Ensure ignition is off. Remove passenger's door inner trim panel. Disconnect passenger door module 15-pin C1 connector. Using ohmmeter, measure resistance of Orange/Violet wire between terminal No. 1 on liftgate door lock motor harness connector and terminal No. 5 on passenger door module 15-pin C1 connector. If resistance is less than 5 ohms, go to next step. If resistance is 5 ohms or greater, repair open Orange/Violet wire.

3) Measure resistance of Pink/Violet wire between terminal No. 2 on liftgate door lock motor harness connector and terminal No. 7 on passenger door module 15-pin C1 connector. If resistance is less than 5 ohms, test is complete. If resistance is 5 ohms or greater, repair open Orange/Violet wire.

PASSENGER DOOR FAILS TO LOCK & UNLOCK

1) Remove passenger's door inner trim panel. Disconnect door lock motor/ajar switch connector. Ensure passenger door module connector is connected. Connect test light between terminals No. 3 (Pink/Violet wire) and 4 (Orange/Violet wire) on passenger's door lock motor/ajar switch harness connector. Using scan tool, actuate PAS LOCK RELAY, then PAS UNLOCK RELAY while monitoring test light. If test light illuminates during actuation, replace door lock motor. If test light does not illuminate, go to next step.

2) Ensure ignition is off. Disconnect passenger door module 15-pin C1 connector. Using ohmmeter, measure resistance of Orange/Violet wire between terminal No. 4 on passenger's door lock motor/ajar switch harness connector and terminal No. 5 on passenger door module 15-pin C1 connector. If resistance is less than 5 ohms, go to next step. If resistance is 5 ohms or greater, repair open Orange/Violet wire.

3) Measure resistance of Pink/Violet wire between terminal No. 3 on passenger's door lock motor/ajar switch harness connector and terminal No. 7 on passenger door module 15-pin C1 connector. If resistance is less than 5 ohms, test is complete. If resistance is 5 ohms or greater, repair open Orange/Violet wire.

PASSENGER REAR DOOR FAILS TO LOCK & UNLOCK

1) Remove passenger's rear door inner trim panel. Disconnect door lock motor/ajar switch connector. Ensure passenger door module connector is connected. Connect test light between terminals No. 3 (Pink/Violet wire) and 4 (Orange/Violet wire) on passenger's rear door lock motor/ajar switch harness connector. Using scan tool, actuate PAS LOCK RELAY, then PAS UNLOCK RELAY while monitoring test light. If test light illuminates during actuation, replace door lock motor. If test light does not illuminate, go to next step.

2) Ensure ignition is off. Remove passenger's door inner trim panel. Disconnect passenger door module 15-pin C1 connector. Using ohmmeter, measure resistance of Orange/Violet wire between terminal No. 4 on passenger's rear door lock motor/ajar switch harness connector and terminal No. 5 on passenger door module 15-pin C1 connector. If resistance is less than 5 ohms, go to next step. If resistance is 5 ohms or greater, repair open Orange/Violet wire.

1999 ACCESSORIES & EQUIPMENT
Body Control Computer Tests – Grand Cherokee (Cont.)

JEEP
4-51

3) Measure resistance of Pink/Violet wire between terminal No. 3 on passenger's rear door lock motor/ajar switch harness connector and terminal No. 7 on passenger door module 15-pin C1 connector. If resistance is less than 5 ohms, test is complete. If resistance is 5 ohms or greater, repair open Orange/Violet wire.

RKE TRANSMITTER INOPERATIVE

1) Ensure RKE transmitter batteries are fully charged. Replace as needed. Using scan tool, select BODY, DOOR MODULES, MISCELLANEOUS, then PROGRAM RKE. Program transmitter. Follow scan tool instructions. Exit PROGRAM RKE. Using RKE transmitter, operate door locks. If door locks operate correctly, test is complete. Program other transmitters as necessary. If door locks do not operate correctly, go to next step.

2) Acquire known good transmitter. Using scan tool, select BODY, DOOR MODULES, MISCELLANEOUS, then PROGRAM RKE. Program transmitter. Follow scan tool instructions. Exit PROGRAM RKE. Using RKE transmitter, operate door locks. If door locks operate correctly, replace transmitter. If door locks do not operate correctly, replace passenger door module.

POWER TOP DIAGNOSTIC TESTS

NOTE: Perform SYSTEM ID TEST before proceeding with following test. For connector terminal identification and wiring diagrams, see BODY CONTROL COMPUTER INTRODUCTION article. Perform VERIFICATION TEST: VER-2A after each repair.

ACCESSORY (SUNROOF) DELAY RELAY SHORTED HI

1) Remove sunroof delay relay from junction block. Measure resistance between terminals No. 85 and 86 on sunroof delay relay. If resistance is less than 65 ohms or greater than 85 ohms, replace relay. If resistance is 65-85 ohms, go to next step.

2) Disconnect Body Control Module (BCM) from junction block. Turn ignition on. Measure voltage between ground and terminal No. 3 on BCM internal junction block connector. If voltage is present, replace junction block. If no voltage is present, replace BCM.

POWER TOP (SUNROOF) SYMPTOM TESTS

NOTE: Perform SYSTEM ID TEST before proceeding with following tests. For connector terminal identification and wiring diagrams, see BODY CONTROL COMPUTER INTRODUCTION article. Perform VERIFICATION TEST: VER-2A after each repair.

The following power top symptoms are covered:
- Sunroof Fails To Close With Ignition Off
- Sunroof Fails To Open With Ignition Off
- Sunroof Fails To Close With Ignition On
- Sunroof Fails To Open With Ignition On

SUNROOF FAILS TO CLOSE WITH IGNITION OFF/SUNROOF FAILS TO OPEN WITH IGNITION OFF

NOTE: Sunroof is operational for about 45 seconds after ignition has been turned off. If either front door is opened, power to sunroof will be cut.

Ensure both front doors are closed. Attempt to open and close sunroof. If sunroof opens and closes normally, replace Body Control Module (BCM). If sunroof fails to open, go to SUNROOF FAILS TO OPEN WITH IGNITION ON. If sunroof fails to close, go to SUNROOF FAILS TO CLOSE WITH IGNITION ON.

SUNROOF FAILS TO CLOSE WITH IGNITION ON

1) Ensure ignition is off. Access sunroof module and motor assembly. Disconnect harness connector. Using voltmeter, measure voltage between ground and terminal No. 1 (Tan wire) on sunroof module and motor assembly harness connector. Turn ignition on. If voltage rises above 10.5 volts, go to next step. If voltage does not rise above 10.5 volts, go to step 6).

2) Disconnect sunroof switch connector. Using ohmmeter, measure resistance of Violet wire between terminal No. 3 on sunroof module and motor assembly harness connector and terminal No. 1 on sunroof switch harness connector. If resistance is less than 5 ohms, go to next step. If resistance is 5 ohms or greater, repair open Violet wire.

3) Measure resistance between ground and terminal No. 7 (Black wire) on sunroof module and motor assembly harness connector. If resistance is less than 5 ohms, go to next step. If resistance is 5 ohms or greater, repair open Black wire.

4) Measure resistance between ground and terminal No. 3 (Black wire) on sunroof switch harness connector. If resistance is less than 5 ohms, go to next step. If resistance is 5 ohms or greater, repair open Black wire.

5) Measure resistance between terminals No. 1 and 3 on sunroof switch component connector. Press vent/close button. If resistance is less than 5 ohms, replace power sunroof assembly. If resistance is 5 ohms or greater, replace sunroof switch.

6) Remove sunroof delay relay from junction block. Measure resistance between terminals No. 85 and 86 on sunroof delay relay. If resistance is less than 65 ohms or greater than 85 ohms, replace relay. If resistance is 65-85 ohms, go to next step.

7) Using voltmeter, measure voltage between terminals No. 30 and 85 on sunroof delay relay socket. If voltage is 10.5 volts or less , go to step 17). If voltage is greater than 10.5 volts, go to next step.

8) Disconnect Body Control Module (BCM) from junction block. Turn ignition on. Measure voltage between ground and terminal No. 3 on BCM internal junction block connector. If voltage is present, replace junction block. If no voltage is present, go to next step.

9) Turn ignition off. Using ohmmeter, measure resistance between terminal No. 86 on sunroof delay relay socket and terminal No. 3 on BCM internal junction block connector. If resistance is less than 5 ohms, go to next step. If resistance is 5 ohms or greater, replace junction block.

10) Ensure sunroof module and motor assembly connector is disconnected. Measure resistance of Tan wire between terminal No. 1 on sunroof module and motor assembly harness connector and terminal No. 87 on sunroof delay relay socket. If resistance is less than 5 ohms, go to next step. If resistance is 5 ohms or greater, repair open Tan wire.

11) Disconnect sunroof switch connector. Measure resistance of Violet wire between terminal No. 1 on sunroof switch harness connector and terminal No. 3 on sunroof module and motor assembly connector. If resistance is less than 5 ohms, go to next step. If resistance is 5 ohms or greater, repair open Violet wire.

12) Measure resistance of between ground and terminal No. 1 (Tan wire) on sunroof module and motor assembly harness connector. If resistance is less than 1000 ohms, repair Tan wire for short to ground. If resistance is 1000 ohms or greater, go to next step.

13) Measure resistance between ground and terminal No. 7 (Black wire) on sunroof module and motor assembly harness connector. If resistance is less than 5 ohms, go to next step. If resistance is 5 ohms or greater, repair open Black wire.

14) Measure resistance between ground and terminal No. 3 (Black wire) on sunroof switch harness connector. If resistance is less than 5 ohms, go to next step. If resistance is 5 ohms or greater, repair open Black wire.

15) Ensure ignition is off. Ensure sunroof delay relay is removed from junction block. Connect test light between terminals No. 85 and 86 on sunroof delay relay socket. Turn ignition on. If test light is illuminated, go to next step. If test light is not illuminated, replace Body Control Module (BCM).

16) Measure resistance between terminals No. 1 and 3 on sunroof switch component connector. Press vent/close button. If resistance is less than 5 ohms, go to next step. If resistance is 5 ohms or greater, replace sunroof switch.

17) Turn ignition off. Remove and inspect junction block fuse No. 25. If fuse is okay, replace junction block. If fuse is blown, go to next step.

18) Replace junction block fuse No. 25 with known good fuse. Turn ignition on, then off. Remove and inspect junction block fuse No. 25. If fuse is okay, test is complete. If fuse is blown, go to next step.

19) Ensure ignition is off. Remove sunroof delay relay from junction block. Disconnect Body Control Module (BCM) from junction block. Turn ignition on. Using voltmeter, measure voltage between ground and terminal No. 3 on BCM internal junction block connector. If voltage is present, replace junction block. If no voltage is present, go to next step.

20) Turn ignition off. Using ohmmeter, measure resistance between terminal No. 86 on sunroof delay relay socket and terminal No. 3 on BCM internal junction block connector. If resistance is less than 5 ohms, go to next step. If resistance is 5 ohms or greater, replace junction block.

21) Remove junction block fuse No. 25. Using ohmmeter, measure resistance between ground and terminal No. 30 on sunroof delay relay socket. If resistance is less than 5 ohms, replace junction block. If resistance is 5 ohms or greater, go to next step.

22) Ensure sunroof module and motor assembly connector is disconnected. Measure resistance of Tan wire between terminal No. 1 on sunroof module and motor assembly harness connector and terminal No. 87 on sunroof delay relay socket. If resistance is less than 5 ohms, go to next step. If resistance is 5 ohms or greater, repair open Tan wire.

23) Disconnect sunroof switch connector. Measure resistance of Violet wire between terminal No. 1 on sunroof switch harness connector and terminal No. 3 on sunroof module and motor assembly harness connector. If resistance is less than 5 ohms, go to next step. If resistance is 5 ohms or greater, repair open Violet wire.

24) Measure resistance of between ground and terminal No. 1 (Tan wire) on sunroof module and motor assembly harness connector. If resistance is less than 1000 ohms, repair Tan wire for short to ground. If resistance is 1000 ohms or greater, go to next step.

25) Measure resistance between ground and terminal No. 7 (Black wire) on sunroof module and motor assembly harness connector. If resistance is less than 5 ohms, go to next step. If resistance is 5 ohms or greater, repair open Black wire.

26) Measure resistance between ground and terminal No. 3 (Black wire) on sunroof switch harness connector. If resistance is less than 5 ohms, go to next step. If resistance is 5 ohms or greater, repair open Black wire.

27) Measure resistance between terminals No. 1 and 3 on sunroof switch component connector. Press vent/close button. If resistance is less than 5 ohms, go to next step. If resistance is 5 ohms or greater, replace sunroof switch.

28) Ensure ignition is off. Ensure sunroof delay relay is removed from junction block. Connect test light between terminals No. 85 and 86 on sunroof delay relay socket. Turn ignition on. If test light is illuminated, go to next step. If test light is not illuminated, replace Body Control Module (BCM).

29) Ensure ignition is off. Install sunroof delay relay. Access sunroof module and motor assembly. Disconnect harness connector. Using voltmeter, measure voltage between ground and terminal No. 1 (Tan wire) on sunroof module and motor assembly harness connector. Turn ignition on. If test light is illuminated, replace sunroof module and motor assembly. If test light does not illuminate, replace sunroof delay relay.

SUNROOF FAILS TO OPEN WITH IGNITION ON

1) Ensure ignition is off. Access sunroof module and motor assembly. Disconnect harness connector. Using voltmeter, measure voltage between ground and terminal No. 1 (Tan wire) on sunroof module and motor assembly harness connector. Turn ignition on. If voltage rises above 10.5 volts, go to next step. If voltage does not rise above 10.5 volts, go to step 6).

2) Disconnect sunroof switch connector. Using ohmmeter, measure resistance of White wire between terminal No. 4 on sunroof module and motor assembly harness connector and terminal No. 5 on sunroof switch harness connector. If resistance is less than 5 ohms, go to next step. If resistance is 5 ohms or greater, repair open Tan wire.

3) Measure resistance between ground and terminal No. 7 (Black wire) on sunroof module and motor assembly harness connector. If resistance is less than 5 ohms, go to next step. If resistance is 5 ohms or greater, repair open Black wire.

4) Measure resistance between ground and terminal No. 3 (Black wire) on sunroof switch harness connector. If resistance is less than 5 ohms, go to next step. If resistance is 5 ohms or greater, repair open Black wire.

5) Measure resistance between terminals No. 3 and 5 on sunroof switch component connector. Press open button. If resistance is less than 5 ohms, replace power sunroof assembly. If resistance is 5 ohms or greater, replace sunroof switch.

6) Remove sunroof delay relay from junction block. Measure resistance between terminals No. 85 and 86 on sunroof delay relay. If resistance is less than 65 ohms or greater than 85 ohms, replace relay. If resistance is 65-85 ohms, go to next step.

7) Using voltmeter, measure voltage between terminals No. 30 and 85 on sunroof delay relay socket. If voltage is 10.5 volts or less , go to step 17). If voltage is greater than 10.5 volts, go to next step.

8) Disconnect Body Control Module (BCM) from junction block. Turn ignition on. Measure voltage between ground and terminal No. 3 on BCM internal junction block connector. If voltage is present, replace junction block. If no voltage is present, go to next step.

9) Turn ignition off. Using ohmmeter, measure resistance between terminal No. 86 on sunroof delay relay socket and terminal No. 3 on BCM internal junction block connector. If resistance is less than 5 ohms, go to next step. If resistance is 5 ohms or greater, replace junction block.

10) Ensure sunroof module and motor assembly connector is disconnected. Measure resistance of Tan wire between terminal No. 1 on sunroof module and motor assembly harness connector and terminal No. 87 on sunroof delay relay socket. If resistance is less than 5 ohms, go to next step. If resistance is 5 ohms or greater, repair open Tan wire.

11) Disconnect sunroof switch connector. Measure resistance of White wire between terminal No. 5 on sunroof switch harness connector and terminal No. 4 on sunroof module and motor assembly harness connector. If resistance is less than 5 ohms, go to next step. If resistance is 5 ohms or greater, repair open White wire.

12) Measure resistance of between ground and terminal No. 1 (Tan wire) on sunroof module and motor assembly harness connector. If resistance is less than 1000 ohms, repair Tan wire for short to ground. If resistance is 1000 ohms or greater, go to next step.

13) Measure resistance between ground and terminal No. 7 (Black wire) on sunroof module and motor assembly harness connector. If resistance is less than 5 ohms, go to next step. If resistance is 5 ohms or greater, repair open Black wire.

14) Measure resistance between ground and terminal No. 3 (Black wire) on sunroof switch harness connector. If resistance is less than 5 ohms, go to next step. If resistance is 5 ohms or greater, repair open Black wire.

15) Ensure ignition is off. Ensure sunroof delay relay is removed from junction block. Connect test light between terminals No. 85 and 86 on sunroof delay relay socket. Turn ignition on. If test light is illuminated, go to next step. If test light is not illuminated, replace Body Control Module (BCM).

16) Measure resistance between terminals No. 3 and 5 on sunroof switch component connector. Press open button. If resistance is less than 5 ohms, go to next step. If resistance is 5 ohms or greater, replace sunroof switch.

17) Turn ignition off. Remove and inspect junction block fuse No. 25. If fuse is okay, replace junction block. If fuse is blown, go to next step.

18) Replace junction block fuse No. 25 with known good fuse. Turn ignition on, then off. Remove and inspect junction block fuse No. 25. If fuse is okay, test is complete. If fuse is blown, go to next step.

19) Ensure ignition is off. Remove sunroof delay relay from junction block. Disconnect Body Control Module (BCM) from junction block. Turn ignition on. Using voltmeter, measure voltage between ground and

1999 ACCESSORIES & EQUIPMENT
Body Control Computer Tests – Grand Cherokee (Cont.)

JEEP
4-53

terminal No. 3 on BCM internal junction block connector. If voltage is present, replace junction block. If no voltage is present, go to next step.

20) Turn ignition off. Using ohmmeter, measure resistance between terminal No. 86 on sunroof delay relay socket and terminal No. 3 on BCM internal junction block connector. If resistance is less than 5 ohms, go to next step. If resistance is 5 ohms or greater, replace junction block.

21) Remove junction block fuse No. 25. Using ohmmeter, measure resistance between ground and terminal No. 30 on sunroof delay relay socket. If resistance is less than 5 ohms, replace junction block. If resistance is 5 ohms or greater, go to next step.

22) Ensure sunroof module and motor assembly connector is disconnected. Measure resistance of Tan wire between terminal No. 1 on sunroof module and motor assembly harness connector and terminal No. 87 on sunroof delay relay socket. If resistance is less than 5 ohms, go to next step. If resistance is 5 ohms or greater, repair open Tan wire.

23) Disconnect sunroof switch connector. Measure resistance of White wire between terminal No. 5 on sunroof switch harness connector and terminal No. 4 on sunroof module and motor assembly harness connector. If resistance is less than 5 ohms, go to next step. If resistance is 5 ohms or greater, repair open White wire.

24) Measure resistance of between ground and terminal No. 1 (Tan wire) on sunroof module and motor assembly harness connector. If resistance is less than 1000 ohms, repair Tan wire for short to ground. If resistance is 1000 ohms or greater, go to next step.

25) Measure resistance between ground and terminal No. 7 (Black wire) on sunroof module and motor assembly harness connector. If resistance is less than 5 ohms, go to next step. If resistance is 5 ohms or greater, repair open Black wire.

26) Measure resistance between ground and terminal No. 3 (Black wire) on sunroof switch harness connector. If resistance is less than 5 ohms, go to next step. If resistance is 5 ohms or greater, repair open Black wire.

27) Measure resistance between terminals No. 3 and 5 on sunroof switch component connector. Press open button. If resistance is less than 5 ohms, go to next step. If resistance is 5 ohms or greater, replace sunroof switch.

28) Ensure ignition is off. Ensure sunroof delay relay is removed from junction block. Connect test light between terminals No. 85 and 86 on sunroof delay relay socket. Turn ignition on. If test light is illuminated, go to next step. If test light is not illuminated, replace Body Control Module (BCM).

29) Ensure ignition is off. Install sunroof delay relay. Access sunroof module and motor assembly. Disconnect harness connector. Using voltmeter, measure voltage between ground and terminal No. 1 (Tan wire) on sunroof module and motor assembly harness connector. Turn ignition on. If test light is illuminated, replace sunroof module and motor assembly. If test light does not illuminate, replace sunroof delay relay.

POWER WINDOW SYMPTOM TESTS

NOTE: Perform SYSTEM ID TEST before proceeding with following tests. For connector terminal identification and wiring diagrams, see BODY CONTROL COMPUTER INTRODUCTION article. Perform VERIFICATION TEST: VER-2A after each repair.

The following power window symptoms are covered:
* DRIVER REAR WINDOW INOPERATIVE FROM BOTH SWITCHES
* DRIVER'S REAR WINDOW INOPERATIVE FROM DDM
* DRIVER'S REAR WINDOW INOPERATIVE FROM REAR SWITCH
* DRIVER WINDOW INOPERATIVE
* PASSENGER'S REAR WINDOW INOPERATIVE FROM BOTH SWITCHES
* PASSENGER'S REAR WINDOW INOPERATIVE FROM DDM
* PASSENGER'S REAR WINDOW INOPERATIVE FROM REAR SWITCH
* PASSENGER'S WINDOW INOPERATIVE FROM BOTH SWITCHES
* PASSENGER WINDOW INOPERATIVE FROM DDM
* PASSENGER WINDOW INOPERATIVE FROM PDM

DRIVER REAR WINDOW INOPERATIVE FROM BOTH SWITCHES

1) Remove driver's rear door trim panel. Disconnect window motor connector. Connect jumper wire between ground and either terminal on window motor component connector. Connect second jumper wire to remaining window motor connector terminal and momentarily touch other end of jumper wire to available battery voltage source. Window motor should operate. Reverse jumper wire ends at window motor. Motor should operate in opposite direction. If motor operates as specified go to next step. If motor does not operate, replace motor.

2) Remove driver's door trim panel. Disconnect Driver's Door Module (DDM) 15-pin C1 connector. Disconnect driver's rear door window switch connector. Measure resistance between terminal No. 2 (Red/White wire) on DDM C1 harness connector and terminal No. 4 (Dark Green wire) on driver's rear door window switch harness connector. If resistance is less than 5 ohms, go to next step. If resistance is 5 ohms or greater, repair open down driver circuit.

3) Measure resistance between ground and terminal No. 4 (Dark Green wire) on driver's rear door window switch harness connector. If resistance is less than 100 ohms, repair Dark Green wire for short to ground. If resistance is 100 ohms or greater, go to next step.

4) Disconnect driver's rear door window motor connector. Measure resistance of Dark Green/White wire between terminal No. 5 on driver's rear door window switch harness connector and terminal No. 1 on window switch harness connector. If resistance is less than 5 ohms, go to next step. If resistance is 5 ohms or greater, repair open Dark Green/White wire.

5) Ensure Driver's Door Module (DDM) 15-pin C1 connector and driver's rear door window switch connector are disconnected. Measure resistance between terminal No. 3 (Dark Blue wire) on DDM C1 harness connector and terminal No.1 (Gray wire) on driver's rear door window switch harness connector. If resistance is less than 5 ohms, go to next step. If resistance is 5 ohms or greater, repair open down driver circuit.

6) Ensure window motor connector is connected. Connect jumper wire between terminals No. 2 (Red/White wire) and 4 (Black wire) on Driver's Door Module (DDM) 15-pin C1 harness connector. Connect second jumper wire to terminal No. 3 (Dark Blue wire) and momentarily touch other end of jumper wire to terminal No. 1 (Tan/Light Blue wire) on DDM C1 harness connector. Window motor should operate. Reverse jumper wire ends on terminals No. 2 and 3. Motor should operate in opposite direction. If motor operates as specified, replace DDM. If motor does not operate, go to next step.

7) Ensure driver's rear window switch and motor connectors are disconnected. Measure resistance between ground and terminal No. 1 (Dark Green wire) on driver's rear door window switch harness connector. If resistance is less than 100 ohms, repair Dark Green wire for short to ground. If resistance is 100 ohms or greater, go to next step.

8) Measure resistance between ground and terminal No. 1 (Gray wire) on driver's rear door window switch harness connector. If resistance is less than 100 ohms, repair Gray wire for short to ground. If resistance is 100 ohms or greater, go to next step.

9) Measure resistance of Gray/White wire between terminal No. 2 on driver's rear door window switch harness connector and terminal No. 2 on window switch harness connector. If resistance is less than 5 ohms, go to next step. If resistance is 5 ohms or greater, repair open Gray/White wire.

10) Inspect driver's rear window switch. Perform continuity check. See appropriate POWER WINDOWS article. Replace as needed. If switch is okay, go to next step.

11) Measure resistance between ground and terminal No. 1 (Gray wire) on driver's rear door window switch harness connector. If resistance is less than 100 ohms, repair Gray wire for short to ground. If resistance is 100 ohms or greater, test is complete.

DRIVER'S REAR WINDOW INOPERATIVE FROM DDM

Ensure driver's rear window is operable from it's own window switch. If no other causes for malfunction are present, replace driver's door module.

JEEP
4-54

1999 ACCESSORIES & EQUIPMENT
Body Control Computer Tests – Grand Cherokee (Cont.)

DRIVER'S REAR WINDOW INOPERATIVE FROM REAR SWITCH

1) Remove driver's rear door trim panel. Disconnect window switch connector. Using ohmmeter, measure resistance between ground and terminal No. 6 (Black wire) on driver's rear window switch harness connector. If resistance is less than 5 ohms, go to next step. If resistance is 5 ohms or greater, repair open Black wire.

2) Remove driver's rear window switch. Inspect window switch. Perform continuity check. See appropriate POWER WINDOWS article. Replace as needed. If switch is okay, test is complete.

DRIVER'S WINDOW INOPERATIVE

1) Turn ignition off. Remove driver's door trim panel. Disconnect Driver's Door Module (DDM) 15-pin C1 connector. Using ohmmeter, measure resistance between terminals No. 13 (Light Blue wire) and 15 (White wire) on DDM C1 harness connector. If resistance is less than 5 ohms, go to next step. If resistance is 5 ohms or greater, go to step **21**).

2) Measure resistance between ground and terminal No. 15 (White wire) on DDM C1 harness connector. If resistance is less than 1000 ohms, go to step **10**). If resistance is 1000 ohms or greater, go to next step.

3) Turn ignition on. Using voltmeter, measure voltage between ground and terminal No. 15 (White wire) on DDM C1 harness connector. If voltage is .02 volts or less, go to step **8**). If voltage is greater than .02 volts, go to next step.

4) Connect DDM connector. Using scan tool, select BODY, DOOR MODULES, then ACTUATORS. Actuate DRV F WIN UP RLY, then DRV F WIN DN RLY. If driver's window operates in both directions, replace DDM. If driver's window does not operate in both directions, go to next step.

5) Disconnect Driver's Door Module (DDM) 15-pin C1 connector. Disconnect driver's door window motor connector. Using voltmeter, measure voltage between ground and terminal No. 13 (Light Blue wire) on DDM C1 harness connector. If any voltage is present, repair Light Blue wire for short to voltage. If no voltage is present, go to next step.

6) Ensure window motor connector is connected. Connect jumper wire between terminals No. 4 (Black wire) and 15 (White wire) on DDM C1 harness connector. Connect second jumper wire to terminal No. 13 (Light Blue wire) and momentarily touch other end of jumper wire to terminal No. 1 (Tan/Light Blue wire) on DDM C1 harness connector. Window motor should operate. Reverse jumper wire ends on terminals No. 13 and 15. Motor should operate in opposite direction. If motor operates as specified, replace DDM. If motor does not operate, go to next step.

7) Ensure DDM C1 connector is disconnected. Disconnect driver's window motor connector. Using voltmeter, measure voltage between ground and terminal No. 15 (White wire) on DDM C1 harness connector. If any voltage is present, repair White wire for short to voltage. If no voltage is present, go to step **10**).

8) Connect DDM connector and window motor connector. Using scan tool, select BODY, DOOR MODULES, then ACTUATORS. Actuate DRV F WIN UP RLY, then DRV F WIN DN RLY. If driver's window operates in both directions, replace DDM. If driver's window does not operate in both directions, go to next step.

9) Ensure window motor connector is connected. Connect jumper wire between terminals No. 4 (Black wire) and 15 (White wire) on DDM C1 harness connector. Connect second jumper wire to terminal No. 13 (Light Blue wire) and momentarily touch other end of jumper wire to terminal No. 1 (Tan/Light Blue wire) on DDM C1 harness connector. Window motor should operate. Reverse jumper wire ends on terminals No. 13 and 15. Motor should operate in opposite direction. If motor operates as specified, replace DDM. If motor does not operate, inspect window mechanism. Repair as needed. If mechanism is okay, replace window motor.

10) Turn ignition on. Using voltmeter, measure voltage between ground and terminal No. 15 (White wire) on DDM C1 harness connector. If voltage is .02 volts or less, go to step **17**). If voltage is greater than .02 volts, go to next step.

11) Connect DDM connector. Using scan tool, select BODY, DOOR MODULES, then ACTUATORS. Actuate DRV F WIN UP RLY, then DRV

F WIN DN RLY. If driver's window operates in both directions, replace DDM. If driver's window does not operate in both directions, go to next step.

12) Disconnect Driver's Door Module (DDM) 15-pin C1 connector. Disconnect driver's door window motor connector. Using ohmmeter, measure resistance between ground and terminal No. 13 (Light Blue wire) on DDM C1 harness connector. If resistance is less than 100 ohms, repair Light Blue wire for short to ground. If resistance is 100 ohms or greater, go to next step.

13) Using voltmeter, measure voltage between ground and terminal No. 13 (Light Blue wire) on DDM C1 harness connector. If any voltage is present, repair Light Blue wire for short to voltage. If no voltage is present, go to next step.

14) Ensure window motor connector is connected. Connect jumper wire between terminals No. 4 (Black wire) and 15 (White wire) on DDM C1 harness connector. Connect second jumper wire to terminal No. 13 (Light Blue wire) and momentarily touch other end of jumper wire to terminal No. 1 (Tan/Light Blue wire) on DDM C1 harness connector. Window motor should operate. Reverse jumper wire ends on terminals No. 13 and 15. Motor should operate in opposite direction. If motor operates as specified, replace DDM. If motor does not operate, inspect window mechanism. Repair as needed. If mechanism is okay, replace window motor.

15) Disconnect driver's door window motor connector. Using ohmmeter, measure resistance between ground and terminal No. 15 (White wire) on DDM C1 harness connector. If resistance is less than 100 ohms, repair White wire for short to ground. If resistance is 100 ohms or greater, go to next step.

16) Using voltmeter, measure voltage between ground and terminal No. 15 (White wire) on DDM C1 harness connector. If any voltage is present, repair White wire for short to voltage. If no voltage is present, replace window motor.

17) Ensure DDM connector and window motor connector are connected. Using scan tool, select BODY, DOOR MODULES, then ACTUATORS. Actuate DRV F WIN UP RLY, then DRV F WIN DN RLY. If driver's window operates in both directions, replace DDM. If driver's window does not operate in both directions, go to next step.

18) Disconnect Driver's Door Module (DDM) 15-pin C1 connector. Disconnect driver's door window motor connector. Using ohmmeter, measure resistance between ground and terminal No. 13 (Light Blue wire) on DDM C1 harness connector. If resistance is less than 100 ohms, repair Light Blue wire for short to ground. If resistance is 100 ohms or greater, go to next step.

19) Ensure window motor connector is connected. Connect jumper wire between terminals No. 4 (Black wire) and 15 (White wire) on DDM C1 harness connector. Connect second jumper wire to terminal No. 13 (Light Blue wire) and momentarily touch other end of jumper wire to terminal No. 1 (Tan/Light Blue wire) on DDM C1 harness connector. Window motor should operate. Reverse jumper wire ends on terminals No. 13 and 15. Motor should operate in opposite direction. If motor operates as specified, replace DDM. If motor does not operate, inspect window mechanism. Repair as needed. If mechanism is okay, replace window motor.

20) Disconnect driver's door window motor connector. Using ohmmeter, measure resistance between ground and terminal No. 15 (White wire) on DDM C1 harness connector. If resistance is less than 100 ohms, repair White wire for short to ground. If resistance is 100 ohms or greater, replace window motor.

21) Measure resistance between ground and terminal No. 15 (White wire) on DDM C1 harness connector. If resistance is less than 1000 ohms, go to step **30**). If resistance is 1000 ohms or greater, go to next step.

22) Turn ignition on. Using voltmeter, measure voltage between ground and terminal No. 15 (White wire) on DDM C1 harness connector. If voltage is .02 volts or less, go to step **27**). If voltage is greater than .02 volts, go to next step.

23) Disconnect driver's window motor connector. Measure resistance of Light Blue wire between window motor harness connector and terminal

1999 ACCESSORIES & EQUIPMENT
Body Control Computer Tests – Grand Cherokee (Cont.)

JEEP
4-55

No. 13 on DDM C1 harness connector. If resistance is less than 5 ohms, go to next step. If resistance is 5 ohms or greater, repair open Light Blue wire.

24) Ensure DDM connector and window motor connector are connected. Using scan tool, select BODY, DOOR MODULES, then ACTUATORS. Actuate DRV F WIN UP RLY, then DRV F WIN DN RLY. If driver's window operates in both directions, replace DDM. If driver's window does not operate in both directions, go to next step.

25) Disconnect Driver's Door Module (DDM) 15-pin C1 connector. Disconnect driver's door window motor connector. Using voltmeter, measure voltage between ground and terminal No. 13 (Light Blue wire) on DDM C1 harness connector. If any voltage is present, repair Light Blue wire for short to voltage. If no voltage is present, go to next step.

26) Ensure window motor connector is connected. Connect jumper wire between terminals No. 4 (Black wire) and 15 (White wire) on DDM C1 harness connector. Connect second jumper wire to terminal No. 13 (Light Blue wire) and momentarily touch other end of jumper wire to terminal No. 1 (Tan/Light Blue wire) on DDM C1 harness connector. Window motor should operate. Reverse jumper wire ends on terminals No. 13 and 15. Motor should operate in opposite direction. If motor operates as specified, replace DDM. If motor does not operate, go to step 37).

27) Disconnect driver's window motor connector. Measure resistance of Light Blue wire between window motor harness connector and terminal No. 13 on DDM C1 harness connector. If resistance is less than 5 ohms, go to next step. If resistance is 5 ohms or greater, repair open Light Blue wire.

28) Ensure DDM connector and window motor connector are connected. Using scan tool, select BODY, DOOR MODULES, then ACTUATORS. Actuate DRV F WIN UP RLY, then DRV F WIN DN RLY. If driver's window operates in both directions, replace DDM. If driver's window does not operate in both directions, go to next step.

29) Ensure window motor connector is connected. Connect jumper wire between terminals No. 4 (Black wire) and 15 (White wire) on DDM C1 harness connector. Connect second jumper wire to terminal No. 13 (Light Blue wire) and momentarily touch other end of jumper wire to terminal No. 1 (Tan/Light Blue wire) on DDM C1 harness connector. Window motor should operate. Reverse jumper wire ends on terminals No. 13 and 15. Motor should operate in opposite direction. If motor operates as specified, replace DDM. If motor does not operate, go to step 43).

30) Turn ignition on. Using voltmeter, measure voltage between ground and terminal No. 15 (White wire) on DDM C1 harness connector. If voltage is .02 volts or less, go to step 38). If voltage is greater than .02 volts, go to next step.

31) Disconnect driver's window motor connector. Measure resistance of Light Blue wire between window motor harness connector and terminal No. 13 on DDM C1 harness connector. If resistance is less than 5 ohms, go to next step. If resistance is 5 ohms or greater, repair open Light Blue wire.

32) Ensure DDM connector and window motor connector are connected. Using scan tool, select BODY, DOOR MODULES, then ACTUATORS. Actuate DRV F WIN UP RLY, then DRV F WIN DN RLY. If driver's window operates in both directions, replace DDM. If driver's window does not operate in both directions, go to next step.

33) Disconnect Driver's Door Module (DDM) 15-pin C1 connector. Disconnect driver's door window motor connector. Using ohmmeter, measure resistance between ground and terminal No. 13 (Light Blue wire) on DDM C1 harness connector. If resistance is less than 100 ohms, repair Light Blue wire for short to ground. If resistance is 100 ohms or greater, go to next step.

34) Using voltmeter, measure voltage between ground and terminal No. 13 (Light Blue wire) on DDM C1 harness connector. If any voltage is present, repair Light Blue wire for short to voltage. If no voltage is present, go to next step.

35) Ensure window motor connector is connected. Connect jumper wire between terminals No. 4 (Black wire) and 15 (White wire) on DDM C1 harness connector. Connect second jumper wire to terminal No. 13 (Light Blue wire) and momentarily touch other end of jumper wire to

terminal No. 1 (Tan/Light Blue wire) on DDM C1 harness connector. Window motor should operate. Reverse jumper wire ends on terminals No. 13 and 15. Motor should operate in opposite direction. If motor operates as specified, replace DDM. If motor does not operate, go to next step.

36) Disconnect driver's door window motor connector. Using ohmmeter, measure resistance between ground and terminal No. 15 (White wire) on DDM C1 harness connector. If resistance is less than 100 ohms, repair White wire for short to ground. If resistance is 100 ohms or greater, go to next step.

37) Using voltmeter, measure voltage between ground and terminal No. 15 (White wire) on DDM C1 harness connector. If any voltage is present, repair White wire for short to voltage. If no voltage is present, go to step 43).

38) Disconnect driver's window motor connector. Measure resistance of Light Blue wire between window motor harness connector and terminal No. 13 on DDM C1 harness connector. If resistance is less than 5 ohms, go to next step. If resistance is 5 ohms or greater, repair open Light Blue wire.

39) Ensure DDM connector and window motor connector are connected. Using scan tool, select BODY, DOOR MODULES, then ACTUATORS. Actuate DRV F WIN UP RLY, then DRV F WIN DN RLY. If driver's window operates in both directions, replace DDM. If driver's window does not operate in both directions, go to next step.

40) Disconnect Driver's Door Module (DDM) 15-pin C1 connector. Disconnect driver's door window motor connector. Using ohmmeter, measure resistance between ground and terminal No. 13 (Light Blue wire) on DDM C1 harness connector. If resistance is less than 100 ohms, repair Light Blue wire for short to ground. If resistance is 100 ohms or greater, go to next step.

41) Ensure window motor connector is connected. Connect jumper wire between terminals No. 4 (Black wire) and 15 (White wire) on DDM C1 harness connector. Connect second jumper wire to terminal No. 13 (Light Blue wire) and momentarily touch other end of jumper wire to terminal No. 1 (Tan/Light Blue wire) on DDM C1 harness connector. Window motor should operate. Reverse jumper wire ends on terminals No. 13 and 15. Motor should operate in opposite direction. If motor operates as specified, replace DDM. If motor does not operate, go to next step.

42) Disconnect driver's door window motor connector. Using ohmmeter, measure resistance between ground and terminal No. 15 (White wire) on DDM C1 harness connector. If resistance is less than 100 ohms, repair White wire for short to ground. If resistance is 100 ohms or greater, go to next step.

43) Measure resistance of White wire between window motor harness connector and terminal No. 15 on DDM C1 harness connector. If resistance is less than 5 ohms, replace window motor. If resistance is 5 ohms or greater, repair open White wire.

PASSENGER'S REAR WINDOW INOPERATIVE FROM BOTH SWITCHES

1) Remove passenger's rear door trim panel. Disconnect window motor connector. Connect jumper wire between ground and either terminal on window motor component connector. Connect second jumper wire to remaining window motor connector terminal and momentarily touch other end of jumper wire to available battery voltage source. Window motor should operate. Reverse jumper wire ends at window motor. Motor should operate in opposite direction. If motor operates as specified go to next step. If motor does not operate, replace motor.

2) Disconnect passenger's rear door window motor connector. Measure resistance of Dark Green/White wire between terminal No. 5 on passenger's rear door window switch harness connector and terminal No. 1 on window switch harness connector. If resistance is less than 5 ohms, go to next step. If resistance is 5 ohms or greater, repair open Dark Green/White wire.

3) Measure resistance between ground and terminal No. 4 (Dark Green wire) on passenger's rear door window switch harness connector. If resistance is less than 100 ohms, repair Dark Green wire for short to ground. If resistance is 100 ohms or greater, go to next step.

4) Measure resistance of Gray/White wire between terminal No. 2 on passenger's rear door window switch harness connector and terminal No. 2 on window switch harness connector. If resistance is less than 5 ohms, go to next step. If resistance is 5 ohms or greater, repair open Gray/White wire.

5) Ensure passenger's rear window switch and motor connectors are disconnected. Measure resistance between ground and terminal No. 1 (Dark Green wire) on passenger's rear door window switch harness connector. If resistance is less than 100 ohms, repair Dark Green wire for short to ground. If resistance is 100 ohms or greater, go to next step.

6) Inspect passenger's rear window switch. Perform continuity check. See appropriate POWER WINDOWS article. Replace as needed. If switch is okay, go to next step.

7) Remove passenger's door trim panel. Disconnect Passenger's Door Module (PDM) 15-pin C1 connector. Disconnect passenger's rear door window switch connector. Measure resistance of Dark Green wire between terminal No. 2 (Red/White wire) on PDM C1 harness connector and terminal No. 4 on passenger's rear door window switch harness connector. If resistance is less than 5 ohms, go to next step. If resistance is 5 ohms or greater, repair open down driver circuit.

8) Ensure PDM 15-pin C1 connector is disconnected. Measure resistance between ground and terminal No. 1 (Gray wire) on passenger's rear door window switch harness connector. If resistance is less than 100 ohms, repair Gray wire for short to ground. If resistance is 100 ohms or greater, go to next step

9) Measure resistance between ground and terminal No. 4 (Dark Green wire) on passenger's rear door window switch harness connector. If resistance is less than 100 ohms, repair Dark Green wire for short to ground. If resistance is 100 ohms or greater, go to next step.

10) Ensure Passenger's Door Module (PDM) 15-pin C1 connector and passenger's rear door window switch connector are disconnected. Measure resistance of Gray wire between terminal No. 3 on PDM C1 harness connector and terminal No.1 on passenger's rear door window switch harness connector. If resistance is less than 5 ohms, go to next step. If resistance is 5 ohms or greater, repair open down driver circuit.

11) Ensure window motor connector is connected. Connect jumper wire between terminals No. 2 (Red/White wire) and 4 (Black wire) on Passenger's Door Module (PDM) 15-pin C1 harness connector. Connect second jumper wire to terminal No. 3 (Dark Blue wire) and momentarily touch other end of jumper wire to terminal No. 1 (Tan/Black wire) on PDM C1 harness connector. Window motor should operate. Reverse jumper wire ends on terminals No. 2 and 3. Motor should operate in opposite direction. If motor operates as specified, replace PDM. If motor does not operate, test is complete.

PASSENGER'S REAR WINDOW INOPERATIVE FROM DDM

Ensure passenger's rear window is operable from it's own window switch. If no other causes for malfunction are present, replace passenger's door module.

PASSENGER'S REAR WINDOW INOPERATIVE FROM REAR SWITCH

1) Remove passenger's rear door trim panel. Disconnect window switch connector. Using ohmmeter, measure resistance between ground and terminal No. 6 (Black wire) on passenger's rear window switch harness connector. If resistance is less than 5 ohms, go to next step. If resistance is 5 ohms or greater, repair open Black wire.

2) Remove passenger's rear window switch. Inspect window switch. Perform continuity check. See appropriate POWER WINDOWS article. Replace as needed. If switch is okay, test is complete.

PASSENGER'S WINDOW INOPERATIVE FROM BOTH SWITCHES

1) Remove passenger's door trim panel. Disconnect Passenger Door Module (PDM) 15-pin C1 connector. Connect jumper wire between terminals No. 4 (Black wire) and 15 (Violet wire) on PDM C1 harness connector. Connect second jumper wire to terminal No. 13 (Brown wire) and momentarily touch other end of jumper wire to terminal No. 1 (Tan/Black wire) on PDM C1 harness connector. Window motor should operate. Reverse jumper wire ends on terminals No. 13 and 15. Motor should operate in opposite direction. If motor operates as specified, replace PDM. If motor does not operate, go to next step.

2) Turn ignition off. Using ohmmeter, measure resistance between terminals No. 13 (Brown wire) and 15 (Violet wire) on PDM C1 harness connector. If resistance is less than 5 ohms, go to next step. If resistance is 5 ohms or greater, go to step 14).

3) Measure resistance between ground and terminal No. 15 (Violet wire) on PDM C1 harness connector. If resistance is less than 1000 ohms, go to step 7). If resistance is 1000 ohms or greater, go to next step.

4) Turn ignition on. Using voltmeter, measure voltage between ground and terminal No. 15 (Violet wire) on PDM C1 harness connector. If voltage is .02 volts or less, inspect window mechanism for binding. Repair as needed. If window mechanism is okay, replace window motor. If voltage is greater than .02 volts, go to next step.

5) Disconnect passenger's door window motor connector. Using voltmeter, measure voltage between ground and terminal No. 13 (Brown wire) on PDM C1 harness connector. If any voltage is present, repair Brown wire for short to voltage. If no voltage is present, go to next step.

6) Ensure PDM C1 connector is disconnected. Disconnect passenger's window motor connector. Using voltmeter, measure voltage between ground and terminal No. 15 (Violet wire) on PDM C1 harness connector. If any voltage is present, repair Violet wire for short to voltage. If no voltage is present, inspect window mechanism for binding. Repair as needed. If window mechanism is okay, replace window motor. If voltage is greater than .02 volts, go to next step.

7) Turn ignition on. Using voltmeter, measure voltage between ground and terminal No. 15 (Violet wire) on PDM C1 harness connector. If voltage is .02 volts or less, go to step 12). If voltage is greater than .02 volts, go to next step.

8) Ensure Passenger's Door Module (PDM) 15-pin C1 connector and door window motor connector are disconnected. Using ohmmeter, measure resistance between ground and terminal No. 13 (Brown wire) on PDM C1 harness connector. If resistance is less than 100 ohms, repair Brown wire for short to ground. If resistance is 100 ohms or greater, go to next step.

9) Using voltmeter, measure voltage between ground and terminal No. 13 (Brown wire) on PDM C1 harness connector. If any voltage is present, repair Brown wire for short to voltage. If no voltage is present, go to next step.

10) Disconnect driver's door window motor connector. Using ohmmeter, measure resistance between ground and terminal No. 15 (Violet wire) on DDM C1 harness connector. If resistance is less than 100 ohms, repair Violet wire for short to ground. If resistance is 100 ohms or greater, go to next step.

11) Using voltmeter, measure voltage between ground and terminal No. 15 (Violet wire) on DDM C1 harness connector. If any voltage is present, repair Violet wire for short to voltage. If no voltage is present, replace window motor.

12) Ensure Passenger's Door Module (PDM) 15-pin C1 connector and door window motor connector are disconnected. Using ohmmeter, measure resistance between ground and terminal No. 13 (Brown wire) on PDM C1 harness connector. If resistance is less than 100 ohms, repair Brown wire for short to ground. If resistance is 100 ohms or greater, go to next step.

13) Measure resistance between ground and terminal No. 15 (Violet wire) on PDM C1 harness connector. If resistance is less than 100 ohms, repair Violet wire for short to ground. If resistance is 100 ohms or greater, replace window motor.

14) Measure resistance between ground and terminal No. 15 (Violet wire) on PDM C1 harness connector. If resistance is less than 1000 ohms, go to step 21). If resistance is 1000 ohms or greater, go to next step.

15) Turn ignition on. Using voltmeter, measure voltage between ground and terminal No. 15 (Violet wire) on PDM C1 harness connector. If voltage is .02 volts or less, go to step 19). If voltage is greater than .02 volts, go to next step.

1999 ACCESSORIES & EQUIPMENT
Body Control Computer Tests – Grand Cherokee (Cont.)

JEEP
4-57

16) Ensure Passenger's Door Module (PDM) 15-pin C1 connector and door window motor connector. Using voltmeter, measure voltage between ground and terminal No. 13 (Brown wire) on PDM C1 harness connector. If any voltage is present, repair Brown wire for short to voltage. If no voltage is present, go to next step.

17) Measure resistance of Brown wire between window motor harness connector and terminal No. 13 on PDM C1 harness connector. If resistance is less than 5 ohms, go to next step. If resistance is 5 ohms or greater, repair open Brown wire.

18) Measure resistance of Violet wire between window motor harness connector and terminal No. 15 on PDM C1 harness connector. If resistance is less than 5 ohms, go to step **27)**. If resistance is 5 ohms or greater, repair open Violet wire.

19) Disconnect window motor connector. Measure resistance of Brown wire between window motor harness connector and terminal No. 13 on PDM C1 harness connector. If resistance is less than 5 ohms, go to next step. If resistance is 5 ohms or greater, repair open Brown wire.

20) Measure resistance of Violet wire between window motor harness connector and terminal No. 15 on PDM C1 harness connector. If resistance is less than 5 ohms, replace window motor. If resistance is 5 ohms or greater, repair open Violet wire.

21) Turn ignition on. Using voltmeter, measure voltage between ground and terminal No. 15 (Violet wire) on DDM C1 harness connector. If voltage is .02 volts or less, go to step **28)**. If voltage is greater than .02 volts, go to next step.

22) Ensure Passenger's Door Module (PDM) 15-pin C1 connector and door window motor connector. Using ohmmeter, measure resistance between ground and terminal No. 13 (Brown wire) on PDM C1 harness connector. If resistance is less than 100 ohms, repair Brown wire for short to ground. If resistance is 100 ohms or greater, go to next step.

23) Using voltmeter, measure voltage between ground and terminal No. 13 (Brown wire) on PDM C1 harness connector. If any voltage is present, repair Brown wire for short to voltage. If no voltage is present, go to next step.

24) Measure resistance of Brown wire between window motor harness connector and terminal No. 13 on PDM C1 harness connector. If resistance is less than 5 ohms, go to next step. If resistance is 5 ohms or greater, repair open Brown wire.

25) Measure resistance of Violet wire between window motor harness connector and terminal No. 15 on PDM C1 harness connector. If resistance is less than 5 ohms, replace window motor. If resistance is 5 ohms or greater, repair open Violet wire.

26) Ensure passenger's door window motor connector is disconnected. Using ohmmeter, measure resistance between ground and terminal No. 15 (Violet wire) on PDM C1 harness connector. If resistance is less than 100 ohms, repair Violet wire for short to ground. If resistance is 100 ohms or greater, go to next step.

27) Using voltmeter, measure voltage between ground and terminal No. 15 (Violet wire) on PDM C1 harness connector. If any voltage is present, repair Violet wire for short to voltage. If no voltage is present, replace window motor.

28) Using ohmmeter, measure resistance between ground and terminal No. 13 (Brown wire) on PDM C1 harness connector. If resistance is less than 100 ohms, repair Brown wire for short to ground. If resistance is 100 ohms or greater, go to next step.

29) Measure resistance of Brown wire between window motor harness connector and terminal No. 13 on PDM C1 harness connector. If resistance is less than 5 ohms, go to next step. If resistance is 5 ohms or greater, repair open Brown wire.

30) Measure resistance of Violet wire between window motor harness connector and terminal No. 15 on PDM C1 harness connector. If resistance is less than 5 ohms, go to next step. If resistance is 5 ohms or greater, repair open Violet wire.

31) Ensure passenger's door window motor connector is disconnected. Using ohmmeter, measure resistance between ground and terminal No. 15 (Violet wire) on PDM C1 harness connector. If resistance is less than 100 ohms, repair Violet wire for short to ground. If resistance is 100 ohms or greater, replace window motor.

PASSENGER'S WINDOW INOPERATIVE FROM DDM

Ensure passenger's window is operable from it's own window switch. If no other causes for malfunction are present, replace driver's door module.

PASSENGER'S WINDOW INOPERATIVE FROM PDM

Ensure passenger's window is operable from driver's door module. If no other causes for malfunction are present, replace passenger's door module.

VEHICLE THEFT SECURITY SYSTEM (VTSS) DIAGNOSTIC TESTS

NOTE: Perform SYSTEM ID TEST before proceeding with following tests. For connector terminal identification and wiring diagrams, see BODY CONTROL COMPUTER INTRODUCTION article. Perform VERIFICATION TEST: VER-2A after each repair.

The following VTSS scan tool fault messages are covered:
- ANTENNA FAILURE
- EEPROM FAILURE
- INTERNAL SKIM FAILURE
- HORN RELAY CKT SHORTED HI
- PCM STATUS FAILURE
- ROLLING CODE FAILURE
- SERIAL LINK EXTERNAL FAILURE
- TRANSPONDER CRC FAILURE
- TRANSPONDER COMMUNICATION FAILURE
- TRANSPONDER RESPONSE MISMATCH
- TRANSPONDER ID MISMATCHED
- VIN MISMATCH

ANTENNA FAILURE, EEPROM FAILURE OR INTERNAL SKIM FAILURE

Using scan tool, read and record SKIM DTCs. Erase DTCs. Turn ignition on. Wait 3 minutes. Read SKIM DTCs. If ANTENNA FAILURE, EEPROM FAILURE or INTERNAL SKIM FAILURE are present, replace Sentry Key Immobilizer Module (SKIM) and perform SKIM INITIALIZATION PROCEDURE. If ANTENNA FAILURE, EEPROM FAILURE or INTERNAL SKIM FAILURE are not present, test is complete

HORN RELAY CKT SHORTED HI

1) Remove horn relay from Power Distribution Center (PDC) and replace with known good relay. Using scan tool, erase DTCs. Operate either panic feature on RKE fob or trigger vehicle theft alarm. Read BCM DTCs. If HORN RELAY CKT SHORTED HI DTC is set, go to next step. If HORN RELAY CKT SHORTED HI DTC is not set, replace horn relay.

2) Turn ignition off. Remove horn relay. Remove Body Control Module (BCM) from rear junction block. Turn ignition on. Measure voltage between ground and terminal No. 86 on horn relay socket. If voltage is greater than one volt, repair horn relay control circuit for short to voltage. If voltage is one volt or less, replace BCM.

PCM STATUS FAILURE, ROLLING CODE FAILURE OR SERIAL LINK EXTERNAL FAILURE

Turn igniton on. Using scan tool, access BODY CONTROL MODULE. Select BODY CONTROLLER and SYSTEM TEST. If scan tool displays PCM ACTIVE ON BUS, test is complete. If scan tool displays PCM ACTIVE ON BUS, go to appropriate test in VEHICLE COMMUNICATIONS article.

TRANSPONDER CRC FAILURE, TRANSPONDER COMMUNICATION FAILURE, TRANSPONDER RESPONSE MISMATCH OR TRANSPONDER ID MISMATCHED

Using scan tool, select SKIM DIAGNOSTICS. Select SKIM KEY TEST. Follow scan tool instructions. Test key in sentry key tester. If key passes, replace SKIM. Perform SKIM INITIALIZATION PROCEDURE. If key does not pass, erase SKIM DTCs. Replace and program new key. See PROGRAMMING BLANK SMART KEY USING SCAN TOOL.

JEEP
4-58

1999 ACCESSORIES & EQUIPMENT
Body Control Computer Tests – Grand Cherokee (Cont.)

VIN MISMATCH

1) Record VIN from vehicle I.D. plate. Using scan tool, read VIN stored in PCM. Read VIN stored in Sentry Key Immobilizer Module (SKIM). Compare VIN number stored in modules memory to actual VIN. If only PCM has correct VIN, replace SKIM and perform SKIM INITIALIZATION PROCEDURESKIM INITIALIZATION PROCEDURE. If only SKIM has correct VIN, replace PCM. If both modules have correct VIN, go to next step. If neither module has correct VIN, replace SKIM, PCM and all vehicle keys. Perform SKIM INITIALIZATION PROCEDURE.

2) Using scan tool, erase SKIM DTCs. Turn ignition off. Turn ignition on. Wait 3 minutes. Read SKIM DTCs. If VIN MISMATCH DTC is present, replace SKIM and perform SKIM INITIALIZATION PROCEDURE. If VIN MISMATCH DTC is not present, test is complete.

VEHICLE THEFT SECURITY SYSTEM (VTSS) SYMPTOM TESTS

NOTE: Perform SYSTEM ID TEST before proceeding with following tests. For connector terminal identification and wiring diagrams, see BODY CONTROL COMPUTER INTRODUCTION article. Perform VERIFICATION TEST: VER-2A after each repair.

The following VTSS symptoms are covered:
- ALARM TRIPS WITHOUT CAUSE
- DRIVER'S DOOR KEY FAILS TO DISARM VTSS
- HAZARD LIGHTS FAIL TO FLASH WITH ALARM TRIPPED
- HEADLIGHTS FAIL TO FLASH WITH ALARM TRIPPED
- HORN FAILS TO SOUND WITH ALARM TRIPPED
- THEFT ALARM WILL NOT ARM
- ALARM DOES NOT TRIP FROM LIFTGATE
- VTSS INDICATOR INOPERATIVE

ALARM TRIPS WITHOUT CAUSE

Using scan tool, select VTSS, then MONITORS. Select ALARM TRIPPED BY. If no causes are displayed, test is complete. If a cause is listed, attempt to isolate intermittent alarm trigger cause using scan tool. Repair as needed.

DRIVER'S DOOR KEY FAILS TO DISARM VTSS

1) Using scan tool, select THEFT ALARM, VTSS, then SENSORS. Read DRV KEY CYL SW volts. Rotate key in door key cylinder from normal position to unlock position. If voltage changes from 5.0 to 1.6 volts, go to next step. If voltage does not change from 5.0 to 1.6 volts, go to step 3).

2) Remove and install Power Distribution Center (PDC) fuse No. 12. Retry VTSS. If system functions correctly, test is complete. If system does not operate correctly, replace Driver's Door Module (DDM).

3) Remove driver door trim panel. Disconnect driver's door cylinder lock switch connector. Using ohmmeter, measure resistance between ground and terminal No. 2 (Black wire) on door cylinder lock switch harness connector. If resistance is less than 5 ohms, go to next step. If resistance is greater than 5 ohms, repair open Black wire.

4) Disconnect Driver's Door Module (DDM) 15-pin C1 connector. Measure resistance between ground and terminal No. 10 (Light Green/Orange wire) on DDM C1 harness connector. If resistance is less than 5 ohms, repair Light Green/Orange wire for short to ground. If resistance is 5 ohms or greater, go to next step.

5) Measure resistance of Light Green/Orange wire between terminal No. 10 on DDM C1 harness connector and terminal No. 1 on door cylinder lock switch harness connector. If resistance is less than 5 ohms, go to next step. If resistance is 5 ohms or greater, repair open Light Green/Orange wire.

6) Measure resistance between driver's door lock cylinder terminals while holding key in unlock position. If resistance is 2000 ohms, replace DDM. If resistance is not 2000 ohms, replace driver's door lock cylinder switch assembly.

HAZARD LIGHTS FAIL TO FLASH WITH ALARM TRIPPED

Turn on hazard lights. If hazard lights function correctly, replace Body Control Module (BCM). If hazard lights do not function correctly, check

for related BCM DTCs. Repair as needed. If no related DTCs are present, see EXTERIOR LIGHTS article.

HEADLIGHTS FAIL TO FLASH WITH ALARM TRIPPED

Turn on low beam headlights. If low beam headlights operate correctly, replace Body Control Module (BCM). If low beam headlights do not function correctly, check for related BCM DTCs. Repair as needed. If no related DTCs are present, see HEADLIGHT SYSTEMS article.

HORN FAILS TO SOUND WITH ALARM TRIPPED

1) Press horn button on steering wheel. If horn operates properly, go to next step. If horn does not operate properly, check for related Body Control Module (BCM) DTCs. Repair as needed. If no related DTCs are present, see appropriate STEERING COLUMN SWITCHES article.

2) Remove horn relay from Power Distribution Center (PDC). Disconnect junction block C2 connector. Using ohmmeter, measure resistance of Gray/Orange wire between terminal No. 86 on horn relay socket and terminal No. 1 on junction block C2 harness connector. If resistance is less than 5 ohms, replace BCM. If resistance is 5 ohms or greater, repair open Gray/Orange wire.

THEFT ALARM WILL NOT ARM

1) Using scan tool, select VTSS, then MISCELLANEOUS. Check status of alarm. Enable alarm if necessary. Go to next step.

2) Inspect junction block fuse No. 7. If fuse is okay, go to next step. If fuse is blown, go to step 4).

3) Turn ignition off. Disconnect negative battery cable. Disconnect Body Control Module (BCM) from junction block. Reconnect negative battery cable. Turn ignition on. Using voltmeter, measure voltage between ground and terminal No. 26 on internal junction block BCM connector. If voltage is greater than 10 volts, replace BCM. If voltage is 10 volts or less, go to next step.

4) Turn ignition off. Remove junction block fuse No. 7. Measure resistance between ground and fused B+ terminal on fuse No. 7 socket. If resistance is less than 5 ohms, repair circuit for short to ground. Replace fuse. If resistance is 5 ohms or greater, replace defective fuse.

ALARM DOES NOT TRIP FROM LIFTGATE

1) Using scan tool, select BODY, DOOR MODULES, then INPUT/OUTPUT. Read LIFTGATE SW status. Open liftgate. If scan tool displays CLOSED, replace Body Control Module (BCM). If scan tool does not display CLOSED, go to next step.

2) Remove liftgate trim panel. Disconnect either liftgate ajar switch connector. Using ohmmeter, measure resistance between ground and terminal No. 1 (Black wire) on liftgate ajar switch harness connector. If resistance is less than 5 ohms, go to next step. If resistance is 5 ohms or greater, repair open Black wire.

3) Ensure ignition is off. Disconnect junction block C1 connector. Measure resistance of Tan/Black wire between terminal No. 25 on junction block C1 connector and terminal No. 2 on liftgate ajar switch harness connector. If resistance is less than 5 ohms, go to next step. If resistance is 5 ohms or greater, repair open Tan/Black wire.

4) Measure resistance across suspect liftgate ajar switch terminals. If resistance is less than 2 ohms, replace BCM. If resistance is 2 ohms or greater, replace defective ajar switch.

VTSS INDICATOR INOPERATIVE

1) Disconnect auto headlight sensor/VTSS LED connector. Auto headlight sensor/VTSS LED is located under dash top cover. *See Fig. 1.* Connect positive lead of voltmeter to battery voltage source. Connect negative lead to terminal No. 3 (Black/Orange wire) on auto headlight sensor/VTSS LED harness connector. Using scan tool, actuate VTSS indicator light. If voltage is greater than 10 volts, replace defective auto headlight sensor/VTSS LED assembly. If voltage is 10 volts or less, go to next step.

2) Turn ignition off. Disconnect Body Control Module (BCM) C1 connector. Using ohmmeter, measure resistance of Black/Orange wire between

1999 ACCESSORIES & EQUIPMENT
Body Control Computer Tests – Grand Cherokee (Cont.)

**JEEP
4-59**

terminal No. 20 on BCM C1 harness connector and terminal No. 3 on auto headlight sensor/VTSS LED harness connector. If resistance is less than 5 ohms, go to next step. If resistance is 5 ohms or greater, repair open Black/Orange wire.

3) Using voltmeter, measure voltage between ground and terminal No. 4 (Pink wire) on auto headlight sensor/VTSS LED harness connector. If voltage is less than 10 volts, repair open Pink wire. If voltage is greater than 10 volts, go to next step.

4) Connect BCM C1 connector. Using voltmeter, backprobe BCM C1 connector. Connect positive lead of voltmeter to battery voltage source. Connect negative lead to terminal No. 20 (Black/Orange wire) on BCM C1 harness connector. Using scan tool, actuate VTSS indicator light. If voltage is greater than 10 volts, test is complete. If voltage is 10 volts or less, replace BCM.

WINDSHIELD WIPER/WASHER SYSTEM DIAGNOSTIC TESTS

NOTE: Perform SYSTEM ID TEST before proceeding with following tests. For connector terminal identification and wiring diagrams, see BODY CONTROL COMPUTER INTRODUCTION article. Perform VERIFICATION TEST: VER-2A after each repair.

The following windshield wiper/washer system scan tool fault messages are covered:

- WASHER FLUID SENSOR FAILURE
- WIPER ON/OFF RELAY SHORTED HIGH
- WIPER ON/OFF RELAY SHORTED LOW/OPEN CIRCUIT
- WIPER PARK FAILURE
- WIPER SWITCH MUX CKT OPEN
- WIPER SWITCH MUX CKT SHORT TO GROUND

WASHER FLUID SENSOR FAILURE

1) Using scan tool, access BCM SENSORS. Turn ignition on. Read WASHER FLUID LEVEL SWITCH VOLTAGE. If scan tool displays voltage greater than 4.8 volts, go to next step. If voltage is 4.8 volts or less, go to step **5)**.

2) Inspect washer fluid level switch connector. Correct as needed. Go to next step.

3) Turn ignition off. Disconnect washer fluid level switch connector. Using ohmmeter, measure resistance is between ground and terminal No. 2 (Black wire) on switch harness connector. If resistance is less 5 ohms, go to next step. If resistance is 5 ohms or greater, repair open Black wire.

4) Measure resistance between washer fluid level switch component connector. If resistance is less than 3500 ohms, go to next step. If resistance is 3500 ohms or greater, replace washer fluid level switch.

5) Using scan tool, access BCM sensors. Turn ignition on. Backprobe a jumper wire between ground and terminal No. 1 (Black/Tan wire) on washer fluid level switch connector. Read WASHER FLUID LEVEL SWITCH VOLTAGE. If voltage is less than one volt, test is complete. If voltage is one volt or greater, replace Body Control Module (BCM).

WIPER ON/OFF RELAY SHORTED HIGH

1) Turn ignition on. Using scan tool, erase BCM DTCs. Turn ignition off, then on. Turn wiper switch to each intermittent position, then low and high speed positions. Read BCM DTCs. If scan tool displays WIPER ON/OFF RELAY SHORTED HIGH, go to next step. If scan tool does not display WIPER ON/OFF RELAY SHORTED HIGH, test is complete.

2) Turn ignition off. Remove wiper on/off relay from Power Distribution Center (PDC). Using ohmmeter, measure resistance between terminals No. 85 and 86 on relay. If resistance is less than 50 ohms, replace relay. If resistance is 50 ohms or greater, go to next step.

3) Disconnect Body Control Module (BCM) C1 connector. Turn ignition on. Using voltmeter, measure voltage between ground and terminal No. 22 (Red/Violet wire) on BCM C1 harness connector. If voltage is greater than one volt, repair Red/Violet wire for short to voltage. If voltage is one volt or less, go to next step.

4) With wiper on/off relay removed, measure voltage between terminal No. 85 on wiper on/off relay socket. If voltage is greater than one volt, replace BCM. If voltage is one volt or less, test is complete.

WIPER ON/OFF RELAY SHORTED LOW/OPEN CIRCUIT

1) Turn ignition on. Using scan tool, erase BCM DTCs. Turn ignition off, then on. Turn wiper switch to each intermittent position, then low and high speed positions. Read BCM DTCs. If scan tool displays WIPER ON/OFF RELAY SHORTED LOW/OPEN CIRCUIT, go to next step. If scan tool does not display WIPER ON/OFF RELAY SHORTED LOW/OPEN CIRCUIT, test is complete.

2) Remove circuit breaker No. 1 from junction block. Install known good circuit breaker. Operate wipers. If wipers function correctly, replace circuit breaker. If wipers does not function correctly, go to next step.

3) Remove wiper on/off relay. Remove junction block circuit breaker No. 1. Connect jumper wire between ground and fused ignition switch output on circuit breaker No. 1 socket. Using ohmmeter, measure resistance between ground and terminal No. 86 (Dark Blue wire) on wiper on/off relay socket. If resistance is less than 5 ohms, remove jumper wire and go to next step. If resistance is 5 ohms or greater, repair open Dark Blue wire.

4) Ensure wiper on/off relay and junction block circuit breaker No. 1 are disconnected. Measure resistance between ground and terminal No. 86 (fused ignition switch output circuit) on wiper on/off relay socket. If resistance is less than 10 ohms, repair fused ignition switch output circuit for short to ground. If resistance is greater than 10 ohms, go to next step.

5) Turn ignition off. Ensure junction block circuit breaker No. 1 is removed. Disconnect wiper motor connector. Using ohmmeter, measure resistance between ground and terminal No. 1 (Dark Blue wire) on wiper motor harness connector. If resistance is less than 5 ohms, repair Dark Blue wire for short to ground. If resistance is 5 ohms or greater, go to next step.

6) Turn ignition off. Remove both wiper relays from Power Distribution Center (PDC). Using ohmmeter, measure resistance between ground and terminal No. 30 (Yellow/Dark Green wire) on wiper on/off relay socket. If resistance is less than 10 ohms, repair Yellow/Dark Green wire for short to ground. If resistance is 10 ohms or greater, go to next step.

7) Measure resistance between ground and terminal No. 87 (Red/Yellow wire) on wiper high/low relay socket. If resistance is less than 10 ohms, repair Red/Yellow wire for short to ground. If resistance is 10 ohms or greater, go to next step.

8) Measure resistance between ground and terminal No. 87A (Brown/White wire) on wiper high/low relay socket. If resistance is less than 10 ohms, repair Brown/White wire for short to ground. If resistance is 10 ohms or greater, go to next step.

9) Ensure BCM C1 connector is disconnected. Connect jumper wire between ground and terminal No. 22 (Red/Violet wire) on BCM C1 harness connector. Using ohmmeter, measure resistance between ground and terminal No. 85 on wiper on/off relay socket. If resistance is less than 5 ohms, go to next step. If resistance is 5 ohms or greater, repair open Red/Violet wire.

10) Measure resistance between ground and terminal No. 85 (Red/Violet wire) on wiper on/off relay socket. If resistance is less than 5 ohms, repair Red/Violet wire for short to ground. If resistance is 5 ohms or greater, go to next step.

11) Ensure all components are connected except wiper on/off relay. Connect test light between terminals No. 85 and 86 on wiper on/off socket. Turn ignition on. Using scan tool, actuate wiper relay. If test light pulses on and off, test is complete. If test light does not pulse, stop wiper actuation and replace BCM.

WIPER PARK FAILURE

1) Turn ignition on. Using scan tool, erase BCM DTCs. Turn ignition off, then on. Turn wiper switch to each intermittent position, then low and high speed positions. Read BCM DTCs. If scan tool displays WIPER PARK FAILURE, go to next step. If scan tool does not display WIPER PARK FAILURE, test is complete.

JEEP
4-60

1999 ACCESSORIES & EQUIPMENT
Body Control Computer Tests – Grand Cherokee (Cont.)

2) Remove circuit breaker No. 1 from junction block. Install known good circuit breaker. Operate wipers. If wipers function correctly, replace circuit breaker. If wipers do not function correctly, go to next step.

3) Turn ignition off. Disconnect junction block C2 connector. Disconnect Body Control Module (BCM) from back of junction block. Measure resistance between terminal No. 20 on junction block BCM internal connector and terminal No. 33 on junction block C2 component connector. If resistance is less than 5 ohms, go to next step. If resistance is 5 ohms or greater, replace junction block.

4) Disconnect BCM C1 connector. Connect jumper wire between ground and terminal No. 22 (Red/Violet wire) on BCM C1 harness connector. Connect test light between ground and terminal No. 33 (Tan/Red wire) on junction block C2 harness connector. Turn ignition on. Operate wipers and observe test light. If test light pulses, replace BCM. If test light does not pulse, go to next step.

5) Disconnect wiper motor connector. Turn ignition on. Using voltmeter, measure voltage between ground and terminal No. 1 (Dark Blue wire). If voltage is greater than 10 volts, go to next step. If voltage is 10 volts or less, repair open Dark Blue wire.

6) Ensure all components are connected. Using test light, backprobe wiper motor connector. Connect test light between ground and terminal No. 2 (Tan/Red wire) on wiper motor connector. Turn wiper switch to position where wipers are operating correctly. If test light pulses, test is complete. If test light does not pulse, replace wiper motor.

WIPER SWITCH MUX CKT OPEN

1) Turn ignition on. Using scan tool, erase BCM DTCs. Turn ignition off, then on. Turn wiper switch to each intermittent position, then low and high speed positions. Read BCM DTCs. If scan tool displays WIPER SWITCH MUX CKT OPEN, go to next step. If scan tool does not display WIPER SWITCH MUX CKT OPEN, test is complete.

2) Turn ignition off. Disconnect right multi-function switch connector. Disconnect Body Control Module (BCM) C2 connector. Using ohmmeter, measure resistance of Dark Blue/Yellow wire between terminal No. 22 on BCM C2 harness connector and terminal No. 7 on right multi-function switch harness connector. If resistance is less than 5 ohms, go to next step. If resistance is 5 ohms or greater, repair open Dark Blue/Yellow wire.

3) Using ohmmeter, measure resistance of Dark Green/Red wire between terminal No. 11 on BCM C2 harness connector and terminal No. 8 on right multi-function switch harness connector. If resistance is less than 5 ohms, go to next step. If resistance is 5 ohms or greater, repair open Dark Green/Red wire.

4) Ensure wiper switch is in OFF position. Using ohmmeter, measure resistance between terminals No. 7 and 8 on right multi-function switch component connector. Rotate wiper switch to HIGH position while monitoring ohmmeter. If resistance is less than 40 ohms in any position, replace right multi-function switch. If resistance is not less than 40 ohms in any position, go to next step.

5) Ensure all components are connected. Using jumper wire, backprobe BCM C2 connector. Connect jumper wire between terminals No. 11 and 22 on BCM C2 connector. Turn ignition on. Using scan tool, read WIPER MODE SW VOLTS sensor. If sensor volts are greater than 4.8 volts, replace BCM. If sensor volts are 4.8 volts or less, test is complete.

WIPER SWITCH MUX CKT SHORT TO GROUND

1) Turn ignition on. Using scan tool, erase BCM DTCs. Turn ignition off, then on. Turn wiper switch to each intermittent position, then low and high speed positions. Read BCM DTCs. If scan tool displays WIPER SWITCH MUX CKT SHORT TO GROUND, go to next step. If scan tool does not display WIPER SWITCH MUX CKT SHORT TO GROUND, test is complete.

2) Turn ignition off. Turn ignition off. Disconnect right multi-function switch connector. Disconnect Body Control Module (BCM) C2 connector. Using ohmmeter, measure resistance between ground and terminal No. 11 (Dark Green/Red wire) on BCM C2 harness connector. If resistance is less than 5 ohms, repair Dark Green/Red wire for short to ground. If resistance is 5 ohms or greater, go to next step.

3) Ensure wiper switch is in OFF position. Using ohmmeter, measure resistance between terminals No. 7 and 8 on right multi-function switch component connector. Rotate wiper switch to HIGH position while monitoring ohmmeter. If resistance is less than 40 ohms in any position, replace right multi-function switch. If resistance is not less than 40 ohms in any position, go to next step.

4) Ensure BCM C2 connector is disconnected. Turn ignition on. Using scan tool, read WIPER MODE SW VOLTS sensor. If sensor volts are less than .3 volts, replace BCM. If sensor volts are .3 volts or greater, test is complete.

WINDSHIELD WIPER/WASHER SYSTEM SYMPTOM TESTS

NOTE: Perform SYSTEM ID TEST before proceeding with following tests. For connector terminal identification and wiring diagrams, see BODY CONTROL COMPUTER INTRODUCTION article. Perform VERIFICATION TEST: VER-2A after each repair.

The following windshield wiper/washer system symptoms are covered:

- REAR WASHER OPERATES CONSTANTLY WITH IGNITION ON
- REAR WASHER INOPERATIVE
- REAR WIPER INOPERATIVE
- REAR WIPER OPERATES CONSTANTLY WITH IGNITION ON
- REAR WIPER INOPERATIVE IN DELAY POSITION
- REAR WIPER INOPERATIVE IN ON POSITION
- REAR WIPERS MOVE TO PARK POSITION IN ON OR DELAY POSITION
- WASHER INOPERATIVE
- WASHER OPERATES CONSTANTLY WITH IGNITION ON
- WIPER INOPERATIVE IN LOW SPEED
- WIPER ERRATIC OPERATION IN INTERMITTENT SPEEDS
- WIPER INOPERATIVE WITH WASH FUNCTION
- WIPERS INOPERATIVE
- WIPER INOPERATIVE IN HIGH SPEED
- WIPER INTERMITTENT SPEEDS INOPERATIVE (ONE OR MORE)
- WIPER OPERATES CONSTANTLY WITH IGNITION ON

REAR WASHER OPERATES CONSTANTLY WITH IGNITION ON

1) Disconnect right multi-function switch connector. Disconnect rear washer motor connector. Turn ignition on. Measure voltage between ground and terminal No. 2 (Black/White wire) on rear washer pump harness connector. If voltage is greater than one volt, repair Black/White wire for short to voltage. If voltage is one volt or less, go to next step.

2) Connect right multi-function switch connector. Ensure rear washer pump switch is in OFF position. Using voltmeter, backprobe right multi-function switch connector. Measure voltage between ground and terminal No. 2 (Black/White wire). If voltage greater than .2 volts, replace right multi-function switch. If voltage is .2 volts or less, test is complete

REAR WASHER INOPERATIVE

1) Remove junction block fuse No. 29. Turn ignition on. Using voltmeter, measure voltage between ground and ignition switch output terminal on fuse No. 29 socket. If voltage is greater than 6 volts, go to next step. If voltage is 6 volts or less, repair open ignition switch output circuit.

2) Inspect junction block fuse No. 29. If fuse is blown, see if is fuse is okay, go to step **8)**.

3) Ensure ignition is off. Disconnect Body Control Module (BCM) from rear of junction block. Remove junction block fuse No. 29. Remove cigar lighter relay from junction block. Disconnect junction block C3 connector. Measure resistance between ground and ignition switch output terminal on fuse No. 29 socket. If resistance is less than 5 ohms, replace junction block. If resistance is 5 ohms or greater, go to next step.

4) Disconnect right multi-function switch connector. Ensure rear washer pump switch is in OFF position. Measure resistance between terminals No. 1 and 2 on right multi-function switch component connector. If

1999 ACCESSORIES & EQUIPMENT
Body Control Computer Tests – Grand Cherokee (Cont.)

JEEP
4-61

resistance is less than 5 ohms, replace right multi-function switch . If resistance is 5 ohms or greater, go to next step.

5) Ensure rear washer motor connector is connected. Ensure ignition is off. Using ohmmeter, measure resistance between ground and terminal No. 2 (Black/White wire) on rear washer motor harness connector. If resistance is less than 5 ohms, repair Black/White wire for short to ground. If resistance is 5 ohms or greater, go to next step.

6) Disconnect junction block C3 connector. Ensure right multi-function switch connector is disconnected. Measure resistance between ground and terminal No. 43 (Brown/Pink wire) on junction block C1 connector. If resistance is less than 5 ohms, repair Brown/Pink wire for short to ground. If resistance is 5 ohms or greater, go to next step.

7) Ensure rear washer motor connector is connected. Using ohmmeter, measure resistance between ground and terminal No. 2 (Black/White wire) on right multi-function switch harness connector. If resistance is less than 2.5 ohms, replace rear washer motor. If resistance is 2.5 ohms or greater, test is complete.

8) Disconnect rear washer motor connector. Ensure ignition is off. Using ohmmeter, measure resistance between ground and terminal No. 1 (Black wire) on rear washer motor harness connector. If resistance is less than 5 ohms, go to next step. If resistance is 5 ohms or greater, repair open Black wire.

9) Ensure ignition is off. Disconnect right multi-function switch connector. Disconnect junction block C3 connector. Measure resistance of Brown/Pink wire between terminal No. 43 on junction block C3 harness connector and terminal No. 1 on right multi-function switch harness connector. If resistance is less than 5 ohms, go to next step. If resistance is 5 ohms or greater, repair open Brown/Pink wire.

10) Remove junction block fuse No. 29. Measure resistance of fused ignition switch output circuit between fuse No. 29 and terminal No. 43 on junction block C3 connector. If resistance is less than 5 ohms, go to next step. If resistance is 5 ohms or greater, replace junction block.

11) Ensure ignition is off. Disconnect Body Control Module (BCM) C2 connector. Turn ignition on. Using voltmeter, measure voltage between ground and terminal No. 2 (Brown wire) on BCM C2 harness connector. Operate washer switch. If voltage is greater than 10 volts, go to next step. If voltage is 10 volts or less, repair open Brown wire.

12) Turn ignition off. Disconnect rear washer pump connector. Using ohmmeter, measure resistance between ground and terminal No. 1 (Black wire) on rear washer pump harness connector. If resistance is less than 5 ohms, go to next step. If resistance is 5 ohms or greater, repair open Black wire.

13) Connect test light between rear washer pump harness connector terminals. Depress rear washer switch. If test light illuminates, replace rear washer pump. If test light does not illuminate, test is complete.

REAR WIPER INOPERATIVE

1) Remove junction block fuse No. 8. Turn ignition on. Using voltmeter, measure voltage between ground and B+ terminal on fuse No. 8 socket. If voltage is greater than 10 volts, go to next step. If voltage is 10 volts or less, repair open B+ circuit.

2) Turn ignition off. Inspect junction block fuse No. 8. If fuse is blown, go to next step. If fuse is okay, go to step **5)**.

3) Disconnect rear wiper motor connector. Disconnect junction block C1 connector. Using ohmmeter, measure resistance between ground and terminal No. 47 (Pink wire) on junction block C1 harness connector. If resistance is less than 5 ohms, repair Pink wire for short to ground. Replace fuse No. 8. If resistance is 5 ohms or greater, go to next step.

4) Connect rear wiper motor connector. Using ohmmeter, backprobe rear wiper motor connector. Measure resistance ground and terminal No. 5 (Pink wire) on rear wiper motor harness connector. If resistance is less than 5 ohms, replace rear wiper motor. Replace fuse No. 8. If resistance is 5 ohms or greater, test is complete.

5) Disconnect rear wiper motor connector. Measure resistance between ground and terminal No. 1 (Black wire) on rear wiper motor harness connector. If resistance is less than 5 ohms, go to next step. If resistance is 5 ohms or greater, repair open Black wire.

6) Disconnect junction block C1 connector. Connect jumper between ground and terminal No. 47 (Pink wire) on junction block C1 harness

connector. Measure resistance between ground and terminal No. 5 (Pink wire) on rear wiper motor harness connector. If resistance is less than 5 ohms, go to next step. If resistance is 5 ohms or greater, repair open Pink wire.

7) Ensure all components are connected. Ensure rear liftgate and flip-up glass are properly closed and aligned. Using scan tool, select INPUT/OUTPUT under BODY CONTROL MODULE. Read LIFTGATE SW. If scan tool displays LIFTGATE SW: CLOSED, go to next step. If scan tool does not display LIFTGATE SW: CLOSED, go to step **15)**.

8) Disconnect junction block C1 connector. Remove liftgate trim panel. Disconnect liftgate flip-up ajar switch connector, right and left ajar switch connectors and rear wiper motor connector. Using ohmmeter, measure resistance between ground and terminal No. 25 (Tan/Black wire) on junction block C1 harness connector. If resistance is less than 5 ohms, repair Tan/Black wire for short to ground. If resistance is 5 ohms or greater, go to next step.

9) Measure resistance across each liftgate ajar switch terminals. Ensure switch is in closed position. If resistance is less than 2 ohms for either switch, replace defective switch. If resistance is 2 ohms or greater for both switches, go to next step.

10) Measure resistance across flip-up ajar switch terminals. Ensure switch is in closed position. If resistance is less than 2 ohms, replace defective switch. If resistance is 2 ohms or greater, go to next step.

11) Disconnect right multi-function switch connector. Ensure rear wiper motor connector is disconnected. Connect jumper wire between ground and terminal No. 2 (Brown/Light Green wire) on rear wiper motor harness connector. Using ohmmeter, measure resistance between ground and terminal No. 5 (Brown/Light Green wire) on right multi-function switch harness connector. If resistance is less than 5 ohms, go to next step. If resistance is 5 ohms or greater, repair open Brown/Light Green wire.

12) Connect jumper wire between ground and terminal No. 4 (Brown/Yellow wire) on rear wiper motor harness connector. Using ohmmeter, measure resistance between ground and terminal No. 6 (Brown/Yellow wire) on right multi-function switch harness connector. If resistance is less than 5 ohms, go to next step. If resistance is 5 ohms or greater, repair open Brown/Yellow wire.

13) Turn rear wiper switch to ON position. Measure resistance between terminals No. 1 and 5 on right multi-function switch component connector. If resistance is less than 5 ohms, go to next step. If resistance is 5 ohms or greater, replace right multi-function switch.

14) Ensure all components are connected. Ensure rear liftgate and flip-up glass are properly closed and aligned. Using scan tool, select INPUT/OUTPUT under BODY CONTROL MODULE. Read LIFTGATE SW. If scan tool displays LIFTGATE SW: CLOSED, replace rear wiper motor. If scan tool does not display LIFTGATE SW: CLOSED, go to next step.

15) Disconnect right multi-function switch connector. Ensure rear wiper motor connector is disconnected. Connect jumper wire between ground and terminal No. 2 (Brown/Light Green wire) on rear wiper motor harness connector. Using ohmmeter, measure resistance between ground and terminal No. 5 (Brown/Light Green wire) on right multi-function switch harness connector. If resistance is less than 5 ohms, go to next step. If resistance is 5 ohms or greater, repair open Brown/Light Green wire.

16) Connect jumper wire between ground and terminal No. 4 (Brown/Yellow wire) on rear wiper motor harness connector. Using ohmmeter, measure resistance between ground and terminal No. 6 (Brown/Yellow wire) on right multi-function switch harness connector. If resistance is less than 5 ohms, go to next step. If resistance is 5 ohms or greater, repair open Brown/Yellow wire.

17) Turn rear wiper switch to ON position. Measure resistance between terminals No. 1 and 5 on right multi-function switch component connector. If resistance is less than 5 ohms, go to next step. If resistance is 5 ohms or greater, replace right multi-function switch.

18) Turn rear wiper switch to DEL position. Measure resistance between terminals No. 1 and 6 on right multi-function switch component connector. If resistance is less than 5 ohms, go to next step. If resistance is 5 ohms or greater, replace right multi-function switch.

JEEP
4-62

1999 ACCESSORIES & EQUIPMENT
Body Control Computer Tests – Grand Cherokee (Cont.)

19) Connect rear wiper motor connector. Using ohmmeter, backprobe rear wiper motor connector. Measure resistance is less than 5 ohms, replace rear wiper motor. Replace fuse No. 8. If resistance is 5 ohms or greater, test is complete.

20) Ensure ignition is off. Connect rear wiper motor connector. Using ohmmeter, backprobe rear wiper motor connector. Measure resistance ground and terminal No. 5 (Pink wire) on rear wiper motor harness connector. If resistance is less than 5 ohms, test is complete. If resistance is 5 ohms or greater, replace rear wiper motor.

REAR WIPER OPERATES CONSTANTLY WITH IGNITION ON

1) Ensure ignition is off. Disconnect right multi-function switch connector. Disconnect rear wiper motor connector. Using voltmeter, measure voltage between ground and terminal No. 2 (Brown/Light Green wire) on rear wiper motor harness connector. If no voltage is present, go to next step. If any voltage is present, repair Brown/Light Green wire for short to voltage.

2) Using voltmeter, measure voltage between ground and terminal No. 4 (Brown/Yellow wire) on rear wiper motor harness connector. If no voltage is present, go to next step. If any voltage is present, repair Brown/Yellow wire for short to voltage.

3) Connect right multi-function switch connector. Turn ignition on. Ensure rear wiper switch is in OFF position. Using voltmeter, backprobe right multi-function switch connector. Measure voltage between ground and terminal No. 6 (Brown/Yellow wire). If voltage is greater than .2 volts, replace right multi-function switch. If voltage is .2 volts or less, go to next step.

4) Using voltmeter, backprobe right multi-function switch connector. Measure voltage between ground and terminal No. 5 (Brown/Light Green wire). If voltage is greater than .2 volts, replace right multi-function switch. If voltage is .2 volts or less, replace rear wiper motor.

REAR WIPER INOPERATIVE IN DELAY POSITION

1) Disconnect right multi-function switch connector and rear wiper motor connector. Connect jumper wire between ground and terminal No. 4 (Brown/Yellow wire) on rear wiper motor harness connector. Using ohmmeter, measure resistance between ground and terminal No. 6 (Brown/Yellow wire) on right multi-function switch harness connector. If resistance is less than 5 ohms, go to next step. If resistance is 5 ohms or greater, repair open Brown/Yellow wire.

2) Turn rear wiper switch to DEL position. Measure resistance between terminals No. 1 and 6 on right multi-function switch component connector. If resistance is less than 5 ohms, go to next step. If resistance is 5 ohms or greater, replace right multi-function switch.

3) Turn rear wiper switch to ON position. Measure resistance between terminals No. 1 and 5 on right multi-function switch component connector. If resistance is less than 5 ohms, go to next step. If resistance is 5 ohms or greater, replace right multi-function switch.

4) Connect jumper wire between ground and terminal No. 2 (Brown/Light Green wire) on rear wiper motor harness connector. Using ohmmeter, measure resistance between ground and terminal No. 5 (Brown/Light Green wire) on right multi-function switch harness connector. If resistance is less than 5 ohms, replace rear wiper motor. If resistance is 5 ohms or greater, repair open Brown/Light Green wire.

REAR WIPER INOPERATIVE IN ON POSITION

1) Disconnect right multi-function switch connector and rear wiper motor connector. Connect jumper wire between ground and terminal No. 2 (Brown/Light Green wire) on rear wiper motor harness connector. Using ohmmeter, measure resistance between ground and terminal No. 5 (Brown/Light Green wire) on right multi-function switch harness connector. If resistance is less than 5 ohms, go to next step. If resistance is 5 ohms or greater, repair open Brown/Light Green wire.

2) Turn rear wiper switch to ON position. Measure resistance between terminals No. 1 and 5 on right multi-function switch component connector. If resistance is less than 5 ohms, go to next step. If resistance is 5 ohms or greater, replace right multi-function switch.

3) Turn ignition on. Ensure rear wiper switch is in OFF position. Using voltmeter, backprobe right multi-function switch connector. Measure voltage between ground and terminal No. 6 (Brown/Yellow wire). If voltage is greater than .2 volts, replace multi-function switch. If voltage .2 volts or less, go to next step.

4) Turn ignition off. Disconnect right multi-function switch connector. Disconnect rear wiper motor connector. Turn ignition on. Measure voltage between ground and terminal No. 4 (Brown/Yellow wire) on rear wiper motor harness connector. If voltage is greater than .2 volts, repair Brown/Yellow wire for short to voltage. If voltage is .2 volts or less, go to next step.

5) Connect right multi-function switch connector. Turn ignition on. Ensure rear wiper switch is in OFF position. Using voltmeter, backprobe right multi-function switch connector. Measure voltage between ground and terminal No. 5 (Brown/Light Green wire). If voltage is greater than .2 volts, replace multi-function switch. If voltage .2 volts or less, go to next step.

6) Turn ignition off. Disconnect right multi-function switch connector. Ensure rear wiper motor connector is disconnected. Turn ignition on. Measure voltage between ground and terminal No. 2 (Brown/Light Green wire) on rear wiper motor harness connector. If voltage is greater than .2 volts, repair Brown/Light Green wire for short to voltage. If voltage is .2 volts or less, replace rear wiper motor.

REAR WIPERS MOVE TO PARK POSITION IN ON OR DELAY POSITION

1) Ensure rear liftgate and flip-up glass are properly closed and aligned. Using scan tool, select INPUT/OUTPUT under BODY CONTROL MODULE. Read LIFTGATE SW. If scan tool displays LIFTGATE SW: CLOSED, go to next step. If scan tool does not display LIFTGATE SW: CLOSED, test is complete.

2) Disconnect junction block C1 connector. Remove liftgate trim panel. Disconnect liftgate flip-up ajar switch connector, right and left ajar switch connectors and rear wiper motor connector. Using ohmmeter, measure resistance between ground and terminal No. 25 (Tan/Black wire) on junction block C1 harness connector. If resistance is less than 5 ohms, repair Tan/Black wire for short to ground. If resistance is 5 ohms or greater, go to next step.

3) Measure resistance across each liftgate ajar switch terminals. Ensure switch is in closed position. If resistance is less than 2 ohms for either switch, replace defective switch. If resistance is 2 ohms or greater for both switches, go to next step.

4) Measure resistance across flip-up ajar switch terminals. Ensure switch is in closed position. If resistance is less than 2 ohms, replace defective switch. If resistance is 2 ohms or greater, go to next step.

5) Ensure all components are connected. Ensure rear liftgate and flip-up glass are properly closed and aligned. Using scan tool, select INPUT/OUTPUT under BODY CONTROL MODULE. Read LIFTGATE SW. If scan tool displays LIFTGATE SW: CLOSED, replace rear wiper motor. If scan tool does not display LIFTGATE SW: CLOSED, test is complete.

WASHER INOPERATIVE

1) Remove junction block fuse No. 29. Turn ignition on. Using voltmeter, measure voltage between ground and ignition switch output terminal on fuse No. 29 socket. If voltage is greater than 10 volts, go to next step. If voltage is 10 volts or less, repair open ignition switch output circuit.

2) Inspect junction block fuse No. 29. If fuse is blown, go to next step. If is fuse is okay, go to step **8)**.

3) Ensure ignition is off. Disconnect right multi-function switch connector. Disconnect junction block C3 connector. Measure resistance between ground and terminal No. 23 (Brown/Pink wire) on junction block C3 harness connector. If resistance is less than 5 ohms, repair Brown/Pink wire for short to ground. If resistance is 5 ohms or greater, go to next step.

4) Ensure washer pump switch is in OFF position. Measure resistance between terminals No. 1 and 3 on right multi-function switch component connector. If resistance is less than 5 ohms, replace right multi-function switch . If resistance is 5 ohms or greater, go to next step.

5) Ensure ignition is off. Disconnect Body Control Module (BCM) from rear of junction block. Remove junction block fuse No. 29. Remove cigar lighter relay from junction block. Disconnect junction block C3 connector. Measure resistance between ground and ignition switch output terminal on fuse No. 29 socket. If resistance is less than 5 ohms, replace junction block. If resistance is 5 ohms or greater, go to next step.

6) Disconnect washer pump connector. Disconnect junction block C2 connector. Ensure right multi-function switch connector is disconnected. Measure resistance between ground and terminal No. 2 (Brown wire) on junction block C2 harness connector. If resistance is less than 5 ohms, repair Brown wire for short to ground. If resistance is 5 ohms or greater, go to next step.

7) Ensure ignition is off. Ensure washer motor connector is connected. Using ohmmeter, measure resistance between ground and terminal No. 3 (Brown wire) on right multi-function switch harness connector. If resistance is less than 2.5 ohms, replace washer motor. If resistance is 2.5 ohms or greater, test is complete.

8) Disconnect washer motor connector. Ensure ignition is off. Using ohmmeter, measure resistance between ground and terminal No. 2 (Black wire) on rear washer motor harness connector. If resistance is less than 5 ohms, go to next step. If resistance is 5 ohms or greater, repair open Black wire.

9) Ensure ignition is off. Disconnect right multi-function switch connector. Disconnect junction block C3 connector. Measure resistance of Brown/Pink wire between terminal No. 43 on junction block C3 harness connector and terminal No. 1 on right multi-function switch harness connector. If resistance is less than 5 ohms, go to next step. If resistance is 5 ohms or greater, repair Brown/Pink wire.

10) Measure resistance between terminals No. 1 and 3 on right multi-function switch harness component connector. Operate washer switch. If resistance is less than 5 ohms, go to next step. If resistance is 5 ohms or greater, replace multi-function switch.

11) Ensure ignition is off. Disconnect Body Control Module (BCM) C2 connector. Turn ignition on. Using voltmeter, measure voltage between ground and terminal No. 2 (Brown wire) on BCM C2 harness connector. Operate washer switch. If voltage is greater than 10 volts, go to next step. If voltage is 10 volts or less, repair open Brown wire.

12) Remove junction block fuse No. 29. Ensure junction block C3 connector is disconnected. Measure resistance of fused ignition switch output circuit between fuse No. 29 and terminal No. 43 on junction block C3 connector. If resistance is less than 5 ohms, go to next step. If resistance is 5 ohms or greater, replace junction block.

13) Ensure all components except washer pump are connected. Connect test light between washer pump harness connector terminals. Depress washer switch. If test light illuminates, replace rear washer pump. If test light does not illuminate, test is complete.

WASHER OPERATES CONSTANTLY WITH IGNITION ON

Ensure washer switch is in OFF position. Turn ignition on. Disconnect right multi-function switch connector. If washer stops operating, replace multi-function switch. If washer is operating, repair Brown wire (washer control switch output circuit) between Body Control Module (BCM) and washer pump for short to voltage.

WIPER INOPERATIVE IN LOW SPEED

1) Remove wiper high/low relay from Power Distribution Center (PDC). Install known good relay. Operate wipers. If wipers operate correctly, replace wiper high/low relay. If wipers do not operate correctly, go to next step.

2) Turn ignition on. Disconnect wiper motor connector. Turn wiper switch to low speed position. Using voltmeter, measure voltage between ground and terminal No. 5 (Brown/White wire) on wiper motor harness connector. If voltage is greater than 10 volts, replace wiper motor. If voltage is 10 volts or less, go to next step.

3) Turn ignition off. Remove wiper high/low relay from PDC. Using ohmmeter, measure resistance of Brown/White wire between terminal No. 87A on wiper high/low relay socket and terminal No. 5 on wiper

motor harness connector. If resistance is less than 10 ohms, test is complete. If resistance is 10 ohms or greater, repair open Brown/White wire.

WIPER ERRATIC OPERATION IN INTERMITTENT SPEEDS

1) Turn ignition off. Disconnect junction block C2 connector. Disconnect Body Control Module (BCM). Using ohmmeter, measure resistance between terminal No. 20 on BCM internal junction block connector and terminals No. 28 and 30 on junction block C2 harness connector. If resistance is less than 5 ohms on both circuits, go to next step. If resistance is 5 ohms or greater on either circuit, replace junction block.

2) Remove wiper on/off relay from Power Distribution Center (PDC). Energize relay by applying voltage to terminals No. 85 and 86. Check continuity between relay terminals No. 30 and 87. If continuity is present, go to next step. If continuity is not present, replace relay.

3) Measure resistance of Tan/Red wire between terminal No. 33 on junction block C2 harness connector and terminal No. 87A on wiper on/off relay socket. If resistance is less than 5 ohms, go to next step. If resistance is 5 ohms or greater, repair open Tan/Red wire.

4) Disconnect wiper motor connector. Measure resistance of Tan/Red wire between terminal No. 28 on junction block C2 harness connector and terminal No. 2 on wiper motor harness connector. If resistance is less than 5 ohms, go to next step. If resistance is 5 ohms or greater, repair open Tan/Red wire.

5) Turn on ignition. Using voltmeter, measure voltage between ground and terminal No. 1 (Dark Blue wire) on wiper motor connector. If voltage is greater than 10 volts, go to next step. If voltage is 10 volts or less, repair open Dark Blue wire.

6) Ensure all connectors are connected. Using test light, backprobe wiper motor connector. Connect test light between ground and terminal No. 2 (Tan/Red wire) on wiper motor connector. Turn wiper switch to a position where wiper are working properly and observe test light. If test light pulses, go to next step. If test light does not pulse, replace wiper motor.

7) Turn ignition off. Disconnect Body Control Module (BCM) from junction block. Disconnect BCM C1 connector. Connect jumper wire between ground and terminal No. 22 (Red/Violet wire) on BCM C1 harness connector. Connect test light between ground and terminal No. 20 on internal junction block connector. Turn ignition on. Turn wiper switch to a position where wiper are working properly and observe test light. If test light pulses, replace BCM. If test light does not pulse, test is complete.

WIPER INOPERATIVE WITH WASH FUNCTION

1) Turn ignition off. Disconnect Body Control Module (BCM) C2 connector. Turn ignition on. Using voltmeter, measure voltage between ground and terminal No. 2 (Brown wire) on BCM C2 harness connector. Operate washer switch. If voltage is greater than 10 volts, go to next step. If voltage is 10 volts or less, repair open Brown wire.

2) Using scan tool, select INPUT/OUTPUT under BODY CONTROL MODULE. Turn ignition on. Operate washer switch while monitoring scan tool display. If scan tool display changes from CLOSED to OPEN, replace BCM. If scan tool display does not change from CLOSED to OPEN, test is complete.

WIPERS INOPERATIVE

1) Replace wiper high/low relay in Power Distribution Center (PDC) with known good relay. If wipers operate correctly, replace wiper high/low relay. If wipers do not operate, go to next step.

2) Replace wiper on/off relay in Power Distribution Center (PDC) with known good relay. If wipers operate correctly, replace wiper on/off relay. If wipers do not operate, go to next step.

3) Turn ignition off. Disconnect wiper motor connector. Measure resistance between ground and terminal No. 4 (Black wire) on wiper motor harness connector. If resistance is less than 5 ohms, go to next step. If resistance is 5 ohms or greater, repair open Black wire.

4) Remove wiper on/off relay. Remove junction block circuit breaker No. 1. Connect jumper wire between ground and fused ignition switch output

JEEP
4-64

1999 ACCESSORIES & EQUIPMENT
Body Control Computer Tests – Grand Cherokee (Cont.)

on circuit breaker No. 1 socket. Using ohmmeter, measure resistance between ground and terminal No. 86 (Dark Blue wire) on wiper on/off relay socket. If resistance is less than 5 ohms, go to next step. If resistance is 5 ohms or greater, repair open Dark Blue wire.

5) Turn ignition off. Ensure both wiper relays are removed. Using ohmmeter, measure resistance of Yellow/Dark Green wire between terminal No. 30 on wiper on/off relay socket and terminal No. 30 on wiper high/low relay socket . If resistance is less than 10 ohms, go to next step. If resistance is 10 ohms or greater, repair open Yellow/Dark Green wire.

6) Ensure wiper on/off relay and junction block No. 1 circuit breaker are disconnected. Measure resistance between ground and terminal No. 86 (fused ignition switch output circuit) on wiper on/off relay socket. If resistance is less than 10 ohms, repair fused ignition switch output circuit for short to ground. If resistance is greater than 10 ohms, go to next step.

7) Disconnect Body Control Module (BCM) C1 connector. Turn ignition on. Using voltmeter, measure voltage between ground and terminal No. 22 (Red/Violet wire) on BCM C1 harness connector. If voltage is greater than one volt, repair Red/Violet wire for short to voltage. If voltage is one volt or less, go to next step.

8) Turn ignition off. Ensure both wiper relays are disconnected. Using ohmmeter, measure resistance between ground and terminal No. 30 (Yellow/Dark Green wire) on wiper on/off relay socket. If resistance is less than 10 ohms, repair Yellow/Dark Green wire for short to ground. If resistance is 10 ohms or greater, go to next step.

9) Measure resistance between ground and terminal No. 87A (Brown/White wire) on wiper high/low relay socket. If resistance is less than 10 ohms, repair Brown/White wire for short to ground. If resistance is 10 ohms or greater, go to next step.

10) Ensure BCM C1 connector is disconnected. Connect jumper wire between ground and terminal No. 22 (Red/Violet wire) on BCM C1 harness connector. Using ohmmeter, measure resistance between ground and terminal No. 85 on wiper on/off relay socket. If resistance is less than 5 ohms, go to next step. If resistance is 5 ohms or greater, repair open Red/Violet wire.

11) Ensure ignition is off. Ensure junction block C2 connector is disconnected. Remove junction block circuit breaker No. 1. Using ohmmeter, measure resistance between terminals No. 8 and 9 on junction block C1 harness connector and fused B+ terminal on circuit breaker No. 1 socket. If resistance is less than 5 ohms for both circuits, go to next step. If resistance is 5 ohms or greater for either circuit, replace junction block.

12) Ensure all connectors and components are connected. Disconnect wiper motor connector. Turn wiper switch to LO position. Using voltmeter, measure and record voltage between ground and terminal No. 5 (Brown/White wire) on wiper motor connector. Turn wiper switch to HIGH position. Using voltmeter, measure and record voltage between ground and terminal No. 6 (Red/Yellow wire) on wiper motor connector. If voltage for both circuits is greater than 10 volts, replace wiper motor. If voltage is 10 volts or less or either circuit, go to next step.

13) Turn wiper switch to LO position. Using scan tool, read wiper mode switch voltage. If voltage is about .82 volts, replace BCM. If voltage is not about .82 volts, test is complete.

WIPER INOPERATIVE IN HIGH SPEED

1) Replace wiper high/low relay in Power Distribution Center (PDC) with known good relay. If wipers operate correctly, replace wiper high/low relay. If wipers do not operate, go to next step.

2) Using ohmmeter, measure resistance between ground and terminal No. 85 (Black wire) on wiper high/low relay socket. If resistance is less than 5 ohms, repair open Black wire. If resistance is 5 ohms or greater, go to next step.

3) Disconnect right multi-function switch connector. Measure resistance of Violet wire between terminal No. 86 on wiper high/low relay socket and terminal No. 9 on multi-function switch harness connector. If resistance is less than 5 ohms, go to next step. If resistance is 5 ohms or greater, repair open Violet wire.

4) Measure resistance between ground and terminal No. 86 (Violet wire) on wiper high/low relay socket. If resistance is less than 5 ohms, repair Violet wire for short to ground. If resistance is 5 ohms or greater, go to next step.

5) Disconnect wiper motor connector. Measure resistance of Red/Yellow wire between terminal No. 6 on wiper motor harness connector and terminal No. 87 on wiper high/low relay socket. If resistance is less than 10 ohms, go to next step. If resistance is 10 ohms or greater, repair open Red/Yellow wire.

6) Turn ignition on. Turn wiper switch to HIGH position. Using voltmeter, measure voltage between ground and terminal No. 6 (Red/Yellow wire) on wiper motor connector. If voltage is greater than 10 volts, replace wiper motor. If voltage is 10 volts or less, go to next step.

7) Turn ignition off. Measure resistance between ground and terminal No. 87 (Red/Yellow wire) on wiper high/low relay socket. If resistance is less than 10 ohms, repair Red/Yellow wire for short to ground. If resistance is 10 ohms or greater, go to next step.

8) Ensure all components and connectors are connected. Turn ignition on. Turn wiper switch to HIGH position. Using voltmeter, backprobe right multi-function connector. Measure voltage between ground and terminal No. 9 (Violet wire). If voltage is greater than 5 volts, test is complete. If voltage is 5 volts or less, replace multi-function switch.

WIPER INTERMITTENT SPEEDS INOPERATIVE (ONE OR MORE)

1) Ensure ignition is off. Disconnect right multi-function switch connector. Disconnect Body Control Module (BCM) C2 connector. Using ohmmeter, measure resistance of Dark Blue/Yellow wire between terminal No. 22 on BCM C2 harness connector and terminal No. 7 on multi-function switch harness connector. If resistance is less than 5 ohms, go to next step. If resistance is 5 ohms or greater, repair open Dark Blue/Yellow wire.

2) Measure resistance of Dark Green/Red wire between terminal No. 11 on BCM C2 harness connector and terminal No. 8 on multi-function switch harness connector. If resistance is less than 5 ohms, go to next step. If resistance is 5 ohms or greater, repair open Dark Green/Red wire.

3) Ensure wiper switch is in OFF position. Measure resistance between terminals No. 7 and 8 on right multi-function switch component connector. Rotate switch to HIGH position. If resistance is less than 40 ohms in any position, replace multi-function switch. If resistance is not less than 40 ohms in any position, go to next step.

4) Ensure all connectors are connected. Using jumper wire, backprobe BCM C2 connector. Connect jumper wire between BCM C2 connector terminals No. 7 and 11. Turn ignition on. Using scan tool, read WIPER MODE SW VOLTS. If voltage is greater than 4.8 volts, replace BCM. If voltage is 4.8 volts or less, test is complete.

WIPER OPERATES CONSTANTLY WITH IGNITION ON

1) Replace wiper on/off relay in Power Distribution Center (PDC) with known good relay. If wipers operate correctly, replace wiper on/off relay. If wipers do not operate, go to next step.

2) Turn ignition off. Remove wiper high/low relay and on/off relay in Power Distribution Center (PDC). Using voltmeter, measure voltage between ground and terminal No. 30 (Yellow/Dark Green wire) on wiper high/low relay socket. If voltage is greater than 10 volts, repair Yellow/Dark Green wire for short to voltage. If voltage is 10 volts or less, go to next step.

3) Disconnect wiper motor connector. Turn ignition on. Measure voltage between ground and terminal No. 87A (Brown/White wire) on wiper high/low relay socket. If voltage is greater than 10 volts, repair Brown/White wire for short to voltage. If voltage is 10 volts or less, go to next step.

4) Measure voltage between ground and terminal No. 87 (Red/Yellow wire) on wiper high/low relay socket. If voltage is greater than 10 volts, repair Red/Yellow wire for short to voltage. If voltage is 10 volts or less, go to next step.

1999 ACCESSORIES & EQUIPMENT
Body Control Computer Tests – Grand Cherokee (Cont.)

JEEP
4-65

5) Using ohmmeter, measure resistance between ground and terminal No. 85 (Black wire) on wiper on/off relay socket. If resistance is less than 5 ohms, repair Black wire for short to ground. If resistance is 5 ohms or greater, go to next step.

6) Ensure ignition is off. Connect test light to terminals No. 85 and 86 on wiper on/off relay from Power Distribution Center (PDC). Turn ignition on. Using scan tool, actuate wiper relay. If test light pulses, test is complete. If test light does not pulse, replace Body Control Module (BCM).

VERIFICATION TEST: VER-2A

BODY VERIFICATION TEST

1) Reconnect all previously disconnected components and connectors. If BCM was replaced, turn ignition on for at least 15 seconds.

2) Ensure ignition is on. Erase all DTCs using scan tool. Turn ignition off and wait 5 seconds. Turn ignition on and fully operate system that was malfunctioning.

3) If system is not operating properly, go to SYMPTOM ID TEST. Using scan tool, read Body DTCs. If any DTCs are present, go to SYMPTOM ID TEST. If no DTCs are present, system is operating correctly and customer's complaint cannot be duplicated, repair is complete.

SKIM INITIALIZATION PROCEDURE

GENERAL INFORMATION

SECURED ACCESS mode is not required to check programmed status of key.

If PCM is replaced, unique secret key data must be transferred from SKIM to PCM. This procedure requires SKIM to be placed in SECURED ACCESS mode using 4-digit PIN code.

If 3 attempts are made to enter secured access mode using an incorrect PIN, SECURED ACCESS mode will be locked out for one hour. To exit lock out mode, turn ignition switch to RUN/START position continuously for one hour. Ensure all accessories are turned off. Monitor battery state and connect battery charger is necessary.

To program smart keys using "customer programming method" requires 2 valid smart keys. See owner's manual.

INITIALIZATION PROCEDURE

1) Obtain vehicle's unique PIN number assigned to it's original SKIM module from vehicle owner or Chrysler's customer center.

2) Using scan tool, select THEFT ALARM, SKIM, then MISCELLANEOUS. Select SKIM MODULE REPLACED function.

3) Enter SECURED ACCESS mode using unique 4-digit PIN number.

4) Program vehicle's VIN number into SKIM's memory.

5) Program country code into SKIM's memory (U.S.).

6) Transfer vehicle's unique Secret Key data from PCM. This process will require SKIM module to be in SECURED ACCESS mode. The PIN number must be entered into scan tool before SKIM will enter SECURED ACCESS mode. Once SECURED ACCESS mode is active, SKIM will remain in that mode for 60 seconds.

7) Program all customer keys into SKIM's memory. This requires that SKIM be in SECURED ACCESS mode. The SKIM will immediately exit SECURED ACCESS mode after each key is programmed.

PROGRAMMING BLANK SMART KEY USING SCAN TOOL

1) Once key blank is cut, insert key into ignition switch. Turn ignition switch to RUN position. Using scan tool, select THEFT ALARM, then SKIM. Select MISCELLANEOUS, then PROGRAM NEW KEY. Enter 4-digit PIN code. When programming is completed, SKIM will exit SECURED ACCESS mode and display status of key. One of five different status messages maybe displayed as follows:

- PROGRAMMING SUCCESSFUL is displayed if SKIM smart key programming succeeds.
- LEARNED KEY IN IGNITION is displayed if key in the ignition has already been programmed into vehicle's SKIM.
- 8 KEYS ALREADY LEARNED, PROGRAMMING NOT DONE is displayed if eight keys have already been programmed into SKIM. If a new key needs to be added due to a lost or defective key, the ERASE ALL KEYS function has to be performed. Original 7 keys plus additional new key may then be reprogrammed into SKIM.
- PROGRAMMING NOT ATTEMPTED is displayed after an ERASE ALL KEYS function is executed.
- PROGRAMMING KEY FAILED is displayed if further diagnosis is required.

2) To program additional keys, turn ignition off. Remove current programmed key and insert next new blank key. Turn ignition switch to RUN position. Re-enter SECURED ACCESS mode function and repeat PROGRAM NEW KEY procedure.

SYSTEM ID TEST

IDENTIFYING VEHICLE EQUIPMENT & SYSTEM PROBLEMS

1) Connect scan tool to Data Link Connector (DLC). DLC is a 16-pin connector located on left side of steering column, above brake pedal. Turn ignition on. If scan tool display is not blank, go to next step. If scan tool display is blank, go to appropriate VEHICLE COMMUNICATIONS test in VEHICLE COMMUNICATIONS article.

2) Using scan tool, select BODY SYSTEM, then BODY COMPUTER. Scan tool will perform a CCD bus test. If scan tool displays BUS OPERATIONAL, go to next step. If scan tool displays NO RESPONSE, go to appropriate VEHICLE COMMUNICATIONS test in VEHICLE COMMUNICATIONS article. If scan tool displays any other message, go to appropriate VEHICLE COMMUNICATIONS test in VEHICLE COMMUNICATIONS article.

3) Using scan tool, select READ DTCs. If any fault messages are displayed, go to FAULT MESSAGE IDENTIFICATION table to identify which system is affected. Go to applicable test in VTSS DIAGNOSTIC TESTS section. If no fault messages are displayed, go to SYMPTOM TEST DIRECTORY table for list of identified systems. Fault messages or symptoms are diagnosed using a scan tool and/or DVOM. These problems may occur separately or in various combinations. When diagnosing a system with many apparent problems, a sequence of tests may be required. After repairs, ensure problem(s) or failure(s) have been corrected by performing appropriate verification test.

FAULT MESSAGE IDENTIFICATION

Scan Tool Display	Affected System
ANTENNA FAILURE	[1],[2]
EEPROM FAILURE	[1]
INTERNAL SKIM FAILURE	[2]
PCM STATUS FAILURE	[1]
ROLLING CODE FAILURE	[1]
SERIAL LINK EXTERNAL FAILURE	[1]
SERIAL LINK EXTERNAL FAILURE	[1]
TRANSPONDER COMMUNICATION FAILURE	[1]
TRANSPONDER CRC FAILURE	[1]
TRANSPONDER ID MISMATCH	[1]
TRANSPONDER RESPONSE MISMATCH	[1]
VIN MISMATCH	[1]

[1] – Go to VTSS (Vehicle Theft Security System) DIAGNOSTIC TESTS.
[2] – Replace SKIM and perform SKIM INTIALIZATION PROCEDURE.
[3] – Sending secret key to PCM.

SYMPTOM TEST DIRECTORY

Suspected System	Proceed To
Instrument Cluster	INSTRUMENT CLUSTER SYMPTOM TESTS

INSTRUMENT CLUSTER SYMPTOM TESTS

NOTE: Perform SYSTEM ID TEST before proceeding with following tests. For connector terminal identification and wiring diagrams, see BODY CONTROL COMPUTER INTRODUCTION article. Perform VERIFICATION TEST: VER-2A after each repair.

The following instrument cluster symptoms are covered:

- All Gauges & Warning Lights Not Operating
- Any Or All CCD Cluster Warning Lights Not Operating
- Any Or All Hard Wired Warning Lights Not Operating
- Gauges Not Operating Properly

ALL GAUGES & WARNING LIGHTS NOT OPERATING

1) Turn ignition on. Using scan tool, select MIC CLUSTER. If scan tool displays BUS OPERATIONAL, go to next step. If scan tool displays any other message, see appropriate VEHICLE COMMUNICATIONS article. If scan tool displays NO RESPONSE, see appropriate VEHICLE COMMUNICATIONS article.

2) Turn ignition off. Remove and inspect fuse No. 10 from fuse block. Fuse block is located behind glove box. If fuse is open, go to next step. If fuse is not open, go to step **4)**.

3) Using external ohmmeter, measure resistance between ground and left terminal (terminal closest to fuse No. 14) on fuse No. 10 socket. If resistance is less than 5 ohms, repair fused ignition switch output circuit for short to ground. If resistance is 5 ohms or greater, replace fuse No. 10.

4) Disconnect instrument cluster Blue 10-pin connector C2. Turn ignition on. Using external voltmeter, measure voltage between ground and terminal No. 8 (Dark Blue/White wire) on instrument cluster Blue harness connector. If voltage is 10 volts or less, repair open Dark Blue/White wire. If voltage is more than 10 volts, go to next step.

5) Turn ignition off. Measure resistance between ground and terminal No. 6 (Black/Light Green wire) on instrument cluster Blue harness connector. If resistance is less than 5 ohms, replace instrument cluster. If resistance is 5 ohms or greater, repair open Black/Light Green wire.

ANY OR ALL CCD CLUSTER WARNING LIGHTS NOT OPERATING

1) Turn ignition on. Using scan tool, select MIC CLUSTER. If scan tool displays BUS OPERATIONAL, go to next step. If scan tool displays any other message, see appropriate VEHICLE COMMUNICATIONS article. If scan tool displays NO RESPONSE, see appropriate VEHICLE COMMUNICATIONS article.

2) Ensure ignition is off. Push and hold trip odometer reset button. Turn ignition on. Release button. Instrument cluster should enter self-test and actuate all CCD controlled indicator lights. If any indicator light did not illuminate, go to next step. If all indicator lights illuminate, system is functioning correctly.

3) Remove instrument cluster and inspect suspected indicator light bulb. Replace bulb(s) as needed. If bulb(s) is okay, replace instrument cluster.

ANY OR ALL HARD WIRED WARNING LIGHTS NOT OPERATING

1) Remove instrument cluster and inspect suspected indicator light bulb. Replace bulb(s) as needed. If bulb(s) is okay, go to next step.

2) If ABS, 4WD or brake warning lights are not functioning, go to next step. If high beam or turn signal indicator lights are not functioning, go to step **4)**.

3) Turn ignition on. Using jumper wire, backprobe between ground and appropriate terminal on instrument cluster harness connector. See INSTRUMENT CLUSTER INDICATOR LIGHT TERMINAL IDENTIFICATION table. If suspect indicator light does not illuminate, replace instrument cluster. If indicator light illuminates, inspect applicable circuit between ground and instrument cluster for open. Repair as needed.

4) Turn ignition off. Using ohmmeter, measure resistance between ground and terminal No. 6 (Black/Light Green wire) on instrument cluster Blue harness connector. If resistance is less than 5 ohms, go to next step. If resistance is 5 ohms or greater, repair open Black/Light Green wire.

5) Backprobe jumper wire between battery voltage source and appropriate terminal on instrument cluster harness connector. See INSTRUMENT CLUSTER INDICATOR LIGHT TERMINAL IDENTIFICATION table. If suspect indicator light does not illuminate, replace instrument cluster. If indicator light illuminates, inspect applicable circuit between ground and appropriate switch for open. For connector terminal identification and wiring diagrams, see BODY CONTROL COMPUTER INTRODUCTION. Repair as needed.

INSTRUMENT CLUSTER INDICATOR LIGHT TERMINAL IDENTIFICATION

Indicator Light	Connector Color	Terminal No.
ABS	Blue	4
Brake	Blue	2
High Beam	Blue	5
Left Turn Signal	Blue	10
Right Turn Signal	Green	6
4WD	Green	5

GAUGES NOT OPERATING PROPERLY

1) Using scan tool, read DTCs. If any engine performance related codes are displayed, see appropriate SELF-DIAGNOSTICS article in ENGINE PERFORMANCE in appropriate MITCHELL® manual. If no engine performance related codes are displayed, go to next step.

2) Turn ignition off. Push and hold down trip odometer reset button. Turn ignition on. DO NOT start engine. Release trip odometer reset button. Compare operation of suspect gauge(s) with actuator test chart. *See Fig. 1.*

3) Instrument cluster will exit self-diagnostics mode at completion of test, or if ignition switch is turned off. If instrument cluster gauge(s) and/or indicator light(s) do not respond properly during actuator test, replace instrument cluster. If all gauges and indicator lights function correctly, system is currently functioning correctly.

VTSS DIAGNOSTIC TESTS

NOTE: Perform SYSTEM ID TEST before proceeding with following tests. For connector terminal identification and wiring diagrams, see BODY CONTROL COMPUTER INTRODUCTION. Perform VERIFICATION TEST: VER-2A after each repair.

The following vehicle theft security system fault messages are covered:
- EEPROM Failure
- PCM Status Failure
- Rolling Code Failure
- Serial Link External Failure
- Serial Link External Failure – Sending Secret Key To PCM
- Transponder Communication Failure
- Transponder CRC Failure
- Transponder ID Mismatch
- Transponder Response Mismatch
- VIN Mismatch

EEPROM FAILURE

NOTE: Sentry Key Immobilizer System (SKIS) diagnosis may require use of all spare keys.

1) Ensure battery is fully charged. Using scan tool, read and record SKIM DTCs. Erase SKIM DTCs. Turn ignition off, then back to RUN position. After 3 minutes, read SKIM DTCs. If only EEPROM FAILURE fault message is currently displayed or was previously recorded, go to next step. If TRANSPONDER ID or RESPONSE MISMATCH fault message is displayed, go to step 3). If VIN MISMATCH & ROLLING CODE FAILURE fault message is displayed, test is complete. If VIN MISMATCH fault message is displayed, go to step 8).

2) If EEPROM FAILURE fault message was previously recorded but did not reset after DTCs were erased, go to next step. If EEPROM FAILURE fault message is currently displayed, replace SKIM and perform SKIM INITIALIZATION PROCEDURE.

3) If EEPROM FAILURE fault message is not currently displayed with TRANSPONDER ID or RESPONSE MISMATCH fault message, go to next step. If only TRANSPONDER ID or RESPONSE MISMATCH fault messages are currently displayed, replace SKIM and perform SKIM INITIALIZATION PROCEDURE.

4) Using scan tool, erase SKIM DTCs. Turn ignition off and wait 10 seconds. Start engine 20 times. Using scan tool, read SKIM DTCs. If EEPROM FAILURE and TRANSPONDER ID fault message are displayed, replace SKIM and perform SKIM INITIALIZATION PROCE-

DURE. If only EEPROM FAILURE fault message is currently displayed, go to next step. If only TRANSPONDER ID fault message is currently displayed, go to step 6). If neither fault message is currently displayed, test is complete.

5) Using scan tool, select THEFT ALARM, then SKIM. Select MISCEL-LANEOUS, then SKIM KEY TEST. Follow scan tool instructions. Test key in sentry key tester. If key passes, go to next step. If key does not pass, erase SKIM DTCs. Replace and program new key. See PROGRAMMING BLANK SMART KEY USING SCAN TOOL.

6) Using scan tool, select THEFT ALARM, then SKIM. Select MISCEL-LANEOUS, then PROGRAM NEW KEY. Read status of current key. If scan tool displays PROGRAMMING SUCCESSFUL, test is complete. If display is PROGRAMMING FAILED, replace SKIM and perform SKIM INITIALIZATION PROCEDURE. If display is MAXIMUM KEY LIMIT, no additional keys can be programmed. Perform VERIFICATION TEST: VER-2A If none of the above messages are displayed, replace SKIM and perform SKIM INITIALIZATION PROCEDURE.

7) Using scan tool, erase SKIM DTCs. Turn ignition off and wait 10 seconds. Start engine 20 times. Using scan tool, read SKIM DTCs. If EEPROM FAILURE fault message is displayed, replace SKIM and perform SKIM INITIALIZATION PROCEDURE. If EEPROM FAILURE fault message is not displayed, go to next step.

8) Start engine and allow to idle for 3 minutes. Using scan tool, read DTCs. If VIN MISMATCH fault message is displayed, go to next step. If ROLLING CODE fault message is displayed, go to step 13). If neither fault message is displayed, test is complete.

9) Using scan tool, read VIN from Powertrain Control Module (PCM). If VIN output from PCM matches VIN on door jamb plate, go to next step. If VIN output from PCM does not match VIN on door jamb plate, replace PCM.

10) Using scan tool, read VIN from SKIM. If VIN output from SKIM matches VIN on door jamb plate, go to next step. If VIN output from SKIM does not match VIN on door jamb plate, replace SKIM and perform SKIM INITIALIZATION PROCEDURE.

11) Using scan tool, erase VIN MISMATCH DTC. Turn ignition switch to RUN position and read SKIM DTCs. If VIN MISMATCH fault message is still present, replace SKIM and perform SKIM INITIALIZATION PROCEDURE. If VIN MISMATCH fault message is not displayed, go to next step.

12) Start engine and allow to idle for 3 minutes. Using scan tool, erase SKIM DTCs. Read SKIM DTCs. If SKIM MISMATCH fault message is still present, replace SKIM and perform SKIM INITIALIZATION PROCEDURE. If SKIM MISMATCH fault message is not displayed, test is complete.

13) Using scan tool, erase SKIM DTCs. Select THEFT ALARM, then SKIM. If scan tool displays NO RESPONSE, go to appropriate VEHICLE COMMUNICATIONS test in VEHICLE COMMUNICATIONS article. If scan tool does not display NO RESPONSE,

14) Using scan tool, select BODY, then BODY COMPUTER. Select SYSTEM TEST, then PCM MONITOR. If scan tool displays PCM ACTIVE ON THE BUS, go to next step. If scan tool does not display PCM ACTIVE ON THE BUS, see appropriate VEHICLE COMMUNICATIONS article.

15) Using scan tool, select ENGINE, then read DTCs. If scan tool displays any PCM related DTCs, see appropriate SELF-DIAGNOSTICS article in ENGINE PERFORMANCE in appropriate MITCHELL® manual. If scan tool does not display any PCM related DTCs, replace smart key immobilizer module. Perform SKIM INITIALIZATION PROCEDURE.

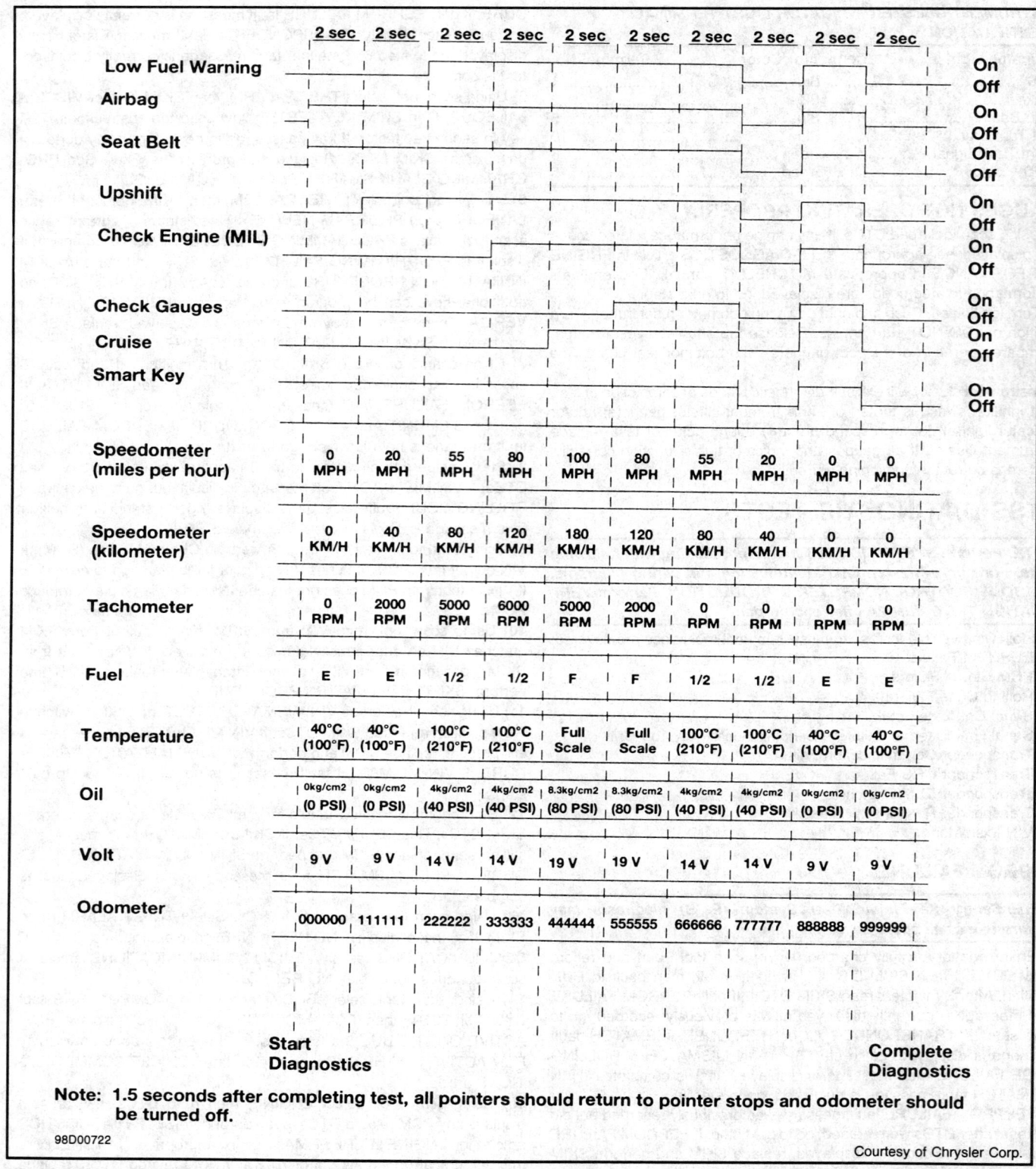

Fig. 1: Instrument Cluster Actuator Test

Note: 1.5 seconds after completing test, all pointers should return to pointer stops and odometer should be turned off.

98D00722

Courtesy of Chrysler Corp.

PCM STATUS FAILURE

1) Using scan tool, select ENGINE, then read DTCs. If scan tool displays any PCM related DTCs, see appropriate SELF-DIAGNOSTICS article in ENGINE PERFORMANCE in appropriate MITCHELL® manual. If scan tool does not display any PCM related DTCs, go to next step.
2) Ensure battery is fully charged. Using scan tool, read and record SKIM DTCs. Erase SKIM DTCs. Turn ignition off, then back to RUN position. After 3 minutes, read SKIM DTCs. If PCM STATUS FAILURE fault message is currently displayed, go to next step. If PCM STATUS FAILURE fault message is not currently displayed, go to step 6).
3) Using scan tool, erase SKIM DTCs. Select THEFT ALARM, then SKIM. If scan tool displays NO RESPONSE, go to appropriate VEHICLE COMMUNICATIONS test in VEHICLE COMMUNICATIONS article. If scan tool does not display NO RESPONSE, go to next step.

4) Using scan tool, select BODY, then BODY COMPUTER. Select SYSTEM TEST, then PCM MONITOR. If scan tool displays PCM ACTIVE ON THE BUS, go to next step. If scan tool does not display PCM ACTIVE ON THE BUS, see appropriate VEHICLE COMMUNICATIONS article.

5) Using scan tool, select ENGINE, then read DTCs. If scan tool displays any PCM related DTCs, see appropriate SELF-DIAGNOSTICS article in ENGINE PERFORMANCE in appropriate MITCHELL® manual. If scan tool does not display any PCM related DTCs, replace SKIM. Perform SKIM INITIALIZATION PROCEDURE.

6) Using scan tool, erase SKIM DTCs. Turn ignition off and wait 10 seconds. Start engine 20 times. Using scan tool, read SKIM DTCs. If any SKIM DTCs are displayed, go to next step. If no fault message are currently displayed, test is complete.

7) Using scan tool, erase SKIM DTCs. Select THEFT ALARM, then SKIM. If scan tool displays NO RESPONSE, go to appropriate VEHICLE COMMUNICATIONS test in VEHICLE COMMUNICATIONS article. If scan tool does not display NO RESPONSE, go to next step.

8) Using scan tool, select BODY, then BODY COMPUTER. Select SYSTEM TEST, then PCM MONITOR. If scan tool displays PCM ACTIVE ON THE BUS, go to next step. If scan tool does not display PCM ACTIVE ON THE BUS, see appropriate VEHICLE COMMUNICATIONS article.

9) Using scan tool, select ENGINE, then read DTCs. If scan tool displays any PCM related DTCs, see appropriate SELF-DIAGNOSTICS article in ENGINE PERFORMANCE in appropriate MITCHELL® manual. If scan tool does not display any PCM related DTCs, replace smart key immobilizer module. Perform SKIM INITIALIZATION PROCEDURE.

ROLLING CODE FAILURE

1) Using scan tool, select ENGINE, then read DTCs. If scan tool displays any PCM related DTCs, see appropriate SELF-DIAGNOSTICS article in ENGINE PERFORMANCE in appropriate MITCHELL® manual. If scan tool does not display any PCM related DTCs, go to next step.

2) Ensure battery is fully charged. Using scan tool, read and record SKIM DTCs. Erase SKIM DTCs. Turn ignition off, then back to RUN position. After 3 minutes, read SKIM DTCs. If only ROLLING CODE FAILURE fault message is currently displayed or was previously recorded, go to next step. If VIN MISMATCH with or without EEPROM FAILURE fault message is displayed, test is complete.

3) Using scan tool, erase SKIM DTCs. Select THEFT ALARM, then SKIM. If scan tool displays NO RESPONSE, go to appropriate VEHICLE COMMUNICATIONS test in VEHICLE COMMUNICATIONS article. If scan tool does not display NO RESPONSE, go to next step.

4) Using scan tool, select BODY, then BODY COMPUTER. Select SYSTEM TEST, then PCM MONITOR. If scan tool displays PCM ACTIVE ON THE BUS, go to next step. If scan tool does not display PCM ACTIVE ON THE BUS, see appropriate VEHICLE COMMUNICA-TIONS article.

5) Using scan tool, select ENGINE, then read DTCs. If scan tool displays any PCM related DTCs, see appropriate SELF-DIAGNOSTICS article in ENGINE PERFORMANCE in appropriate MITCHELL® manual. If scan tool does not display any PCM related DTCs, replace SKIM. Perform SKIM INITIALIZATION PROCEDURE.

6) Using scan tool, erase SKIM DTCs. Turn ignition off and wait 10 seconds. Start engine 20 times. Using scan tool, read SKIM DTCs. If any SKIM DTCs are displayed, go to next step. If no fault message are currently displayed, test is complete.

7) Using scan tool, erase SKIM DTCs. Select THEFT ALARM, then SKIM. If scan tool displays NO RESPONSE, go to appropriate VEHICLE COMMUNICATIONS test in VEHICLE COMMUNICATIONS article. If scan tool does not display NO RESPONSE, go to next step.

8) Using scan tool, select BODY, then BODY COMPUTER. Select SYSTEM TEST, then PCM MONITOR. If scan tool displays PCM ACTIVE ON THE BUS, go to next step. If scan tool does not display PCM ACTIVE ON THE BUS, see appropriate VEHICLE COMMUNICA-TIONS article.

9) Using scan tool, select ENGINE, then read DTCs. If scan tool displays any PCM related DTCs, see appropriate SELF-DIAGNOSTICS article in

ENGINE PERFORMANCE in appropriate MITCHELL® manual. If scan tool does not display any PCM related DTCs, replace SKIM. Perform SKIM INITIALIZATION PROCEDURE.

SERIAL LINK EXTERNAL FAILURE

1) Using scan tool, select ENGINE, then read DTCs. If scan tool displays any PCM related DTCs, see appropriate SELF-DIAGNOSTICS article in ENGINE PERFORMANCE in appropriate MITCHELL® manual. If scan tool does not display any PCM related DTCs, go to next step.

2) Ensure battery is fully charged. Using scan tool, read and record SKIM DTCs. Erase SKIM DTCs. Turn ignition off, then back to RUN position. After 3 minutes, read SKIM DTCs. If SERIAL LINK EXTERNAL FAILURE fault message is currently displayed or was previously recorded, go to next step. If SERIAL LINK EXTERNAL FAILURE fault message is not displayed, go to step 7).

3) Using scan tool, erase SKIM DTCs. Select THEFT ALARM, then SKIM. If scan tool displays NO RESPONSE, go to appropriate VEHICLE COMMUNICATIONS test in VEHICLE COMMUNICATIONS article. If scan tool does not display NO RESPONSE, go to next step.

4) Using scan tool, select BODY, then BODY COMPUTER. Select SYSTEM TEST, then PCM MONITOR. If scan tool displays PCM ACTIVE ON THE BUS, go to next step. If scan tool does not display PCM ACTIVE ON THE BUS, see appropriate VEHICLE COMMUNICA-TIONS article.

5) Using scan tool, select ENGINE, then read DTCs. If scan tool displays any PCM related DTCs, see appropriate SELF-DIAGNOSTICS article in ENGINE PERFORMANCE in appropriate MITCHELL® manual. If scan tool does not display any PCM related DTCs, replace SKIM. Perform SKIM INITIALIZATION PROCEDURE.

6) Using scan tool, erase SKIM DTCs. Turn ignition off and wait 10 seconds. Start engine 20 times. Using scan tool, read SKIM DTCs. If any SKIM DTCs are displayed, go to next step. If no fault message are currently displayed, test is complete.

7) Using scan tool, erase SKIM DTCs. Select THEFT ALARM, then SKIM. If scan tool displays NO RESPONSE, go to appropriate VEHICLE COMMUNICATIONS test in VEHICLE COMMUNICATIONS article. If scan tool does not display NO RESPONSE, go to next step.

8) Using scan tool, select BODY, then BODY COMPUTER. Select SYSTEM TEST, then PCM MONITOR. If scan tool displays PCM ACTIVE ON THE BUS, go to next step. If scan tool does not display PCM ACTIVE ON THE BUS, see appropriate VEHICLE COMMUNICA-TIONS article.

9) Using scan tool, select ENGINE, then read DTCs. If scan tool displays any PCM related DTCs, see appropriate SELF-DIAGNOSTICS article in ENGINE PERFORMANCE in appropriate MITCHELL® manual. If scan tool does not display any PCM related DTCs, replace smart key immobilizer module. Perform SKIM INITIALIZATION PROCEDURE.

SERIAL LINK EXTERNAL FAILURE – SENDING SECRET KEY TO PCM

1) Using scan tool, select ENGINE, then read DTCs. If scan tool displays any PCM related DTCs, see appropriate SELF-DIAGNOSTICS article in ENGINE PERFORMANCE in appropriate MITCHELL® manual. If scan tool does not display any PCM related DTCs, go to next step.

2) Ensure battery is fully charged. Using scan tool, read and record SKIM DTCs. Erase SKIM DTCs. Turn ignition off, then back to RUN position. After 3 minutes, read SKIM DTCs. If SERIAL LINK EXTERNAL FAILURE fault message is currently displayed, go to next step. If SERIAL LINK EXTERNAL FAILURE fault message is not displayed, DTC is not current.

3) Using scan tool, erase SKIM DTCs. Attempt another secret key transfer to PCM. Using scan tool, read DTCs. If SERIAL LINK EXTER-NAL fault message is displayed, go to next step. If SERIAL LINK EXTERNAL fault message is not displayed, test is complete.

4) Using scan tool, erase SKIM DTCs. Select THEFT ALARM, then SKIM. If scan tool displays NO RESPONSE, go to appropriate VEHICLE COMMUNICATIONS test in VEHICLE COMMUNICATIONS article. If scan tool does not display NO RESPONSE, go to next step.

5) Using scan tool, select BODY, then BODY COMPUTER. Select SYSTEM TEST, then PCM MONITOR. If scan tool displays PCM ACTIVE ON THE BUS, go to next step. If scan tool does not display PCM ACTIVE ON THE BUS, see appropriate VEHICLE COMMUNICATIONS article.

6) Using scan tool, select ENGINE, then read DTCs. If scan tool displays any PCM related DTCs, see appropriate SELF-DIAGNOSTICS article in ENGINE PERFORMANCE in appropriate MITCHELL® manual. If scan tool does not display any PCM related DTCs, replace SKIM. Perform SKIM INITIALIZATION PROCEDURE.

TRANSPONDER COMMUNICATION FAILURE

1) Ensure battery is fully charged. Using scan tool, read and record SKIM DTCs. Erase SKIM DTCs. Turn ignition off, then back to RUN position. After 3 minutes, read SKIM DTCs. If TRANSPONDER COMMUNICATION FAILURE fault message is currently displayed or was previously recorded, go to next step. If TRANSPONDER COMMUNICATION FAILURE fault message is not displayed, go to step 3).

2) Using scan tool, select THEFT ALARM, then SKIM. Select MISCELLANEOUS, then SKIM KEY TEST. Follow scan tool instructions. Test key in sentry key tester. If key passes, replace SKIM. Perform SKIM INITIALIZATION PROCEDURE. If key does not pass, erase SKIM DTCs. Replace and program new key. See PROGRAMMING BLANK SMART KEY USING SCAN TOOL.

3) Start engine several times using each of vehicle's keys. Using scan tool, read SKIM DTCs. If TRANSPONDER fault message is displayed, replace SKIM. Perform SKIM INITIALIZATION PROCEDURE. If TRANSPONDER fault message is not displayed, test is complete.

TRANSPONDER CRC FAILURE

1) Ensure battery is fully charged. Using scan tool, read and record SKIM DTCs. Erase SKIM DTCs. Turn ignition off, then back to RUN position. After 3 minutes, read SKIM DTCs. If TRANSPONDER CRC FAILURE fault message is currently displayed or was previously recorded, go to next step. If TRANSPONDER CRC FAILURE fault message is not displayed, go to step 3).

2) Using scan tool, select THEFT ALARM, then SKIM. Select MISCELLANEOUS, then SKIM KEY TEST. Follow scan tool instructions. Test key in sentry key tester. If key passes, replace SKIM. Perform SKIM INITIALIZATION PROCEDURE. If key does not pass, erase SKIM DTCs. Replace and program new key. See PROGRAMMING BLANK SMART KEY USING SCAN TOOL.

3) Start engine several times using each of vehicle's keys. Using scan tool, read SKIM DTCs. If TRANSPONDER fault message is displayed, replace SKIM. Perform SKIM INITIALIZATION PROCEDURE. If TRANSPONDER fault message is not displayed, test is complete.

TRANSPONDER ID MISMATCH/TRANSPONDER RESPONSE MISMATCH

1) Ensure battery is fully charged. Using scan tool, read and record SKIM DTCs. Erase SKIM DTCs. Turn ignition off, then back to RUN position. After 3 minutes, read SKIM DTCs. If only TRANSPONDER ID MISMATCH or TRANSPONDER RESPONSE MISMATCH FAILURE fault message is currently displayed or was previously recorded, go to next step. If EEPROM failure fault message is also displayed, go to step 4).

2) If TRANSPONDER ID MISMATCH or TRANSPONDER RESPONSE MISMATCH FAILURE fault message are currently displayed, go to step 7). If TRANSPONDER ID MISMATCH or TRANSPONDER RESPONSE MISMATCH FAILURE are previously recorded, but now not currently displayed, go to next step.

3) Start engine several times using each of vehicle's keys. Using scan tool, read SKIM DTCs. If a TRANSPONDER fault message is displayed, replace SKIM. Perform SKIM INITIALIZATION PROCEDURE. If no TRANSPONDER fault message is not displayed, test is complete.

4) If TRANSPONDER ID MISMATCH or TRANSPONDER RESPONSE MISMATCH FAILURE fault message are currently displayed, replace SKIM. Perform SKIM INITIALIZATION PROCEDURE. If TRANSPON-DER ID MISMATCH or TRANSPONDER RESPONSE MISMATCH FAILURE was previously recorded, but not currently displayed with EEPROM failure, go to next step.

5) Using scan tool, erase SKIM DTCs. Turn ignition off and wait 10 seconds. Start engine 20 times. Using scan tool, read SKIM DTCs. If EEPROM and TRANSPONDER fault messages are displayed, replace SKIM. Perform SKIM INITIALIZATION PROCEDURE. If only EEPROM failure is displayed, go to next step. If only TRANSPONDER fault message is displayed, go to step 7). If neither fault message is displayed, test is complete.

6) Using scan tool, erase SKIM DTCs. Turn ignition off and wait 10 seconds. Start engine 20 times. Using scan tool, read SKIM DTCs. If EEPROM fault message is displayed, replace SKIM. Perform SKIM INITIALIZATION PROCEDURE. If EEPROM failure is not displayed, test is complete.

7) Using scan tool, select THEFT ALARM, then SKIM. Select MISCELLANEOUS, then SKIM KEY TEST. Follow scan tool instructions. Test key in sentry key tester. If key passes, go to next step. If key does not pass, erase SKIM DTCs. Replace and program new key. See PROGRAMMING BLANK SMART KEY USING SCAN TOOL.

8) Using scan tool, select THEFT ALARM, then SKIM. Select MISCELLANEOUS, then PROGRAM NEW KEY. Read status of current key. If scan tool displays PROGRAMMING SUCCESSFUL, test is complete. If display is PROGRAMMING FAILED, replace SKIM and perform SKIM INITIALIZATION PROCEDURE. If display is MAXIMUM KEY LIMIT, no additional keys can be programmed. Perform VERIFICATION TEST: VER-2A If none of the above messages are displayed, replace SKIM and perform SKIM INITIALIZATION PROCEDURE.

VIN MISMATCH

1) Using scan tool, select ENGINE and read DTCs. If EEPROM fault message is present, go to PCM FAILURE EEPROM WRITE DENIED test in appropriate SELF-DIAGNOSTICS article in ENGINE PERFORMANCE in appropriate MITCHELL® manual. If EEPROM fault message is present, go to next step.

2) Ensure battery is fully charged. Using scan tool, read and record SKIM DTCs. Erase SKIM DTCs. Turn ignition off, then back to RUN position. After 3 minutes, read SKIM DTCs. If only VIN MISMATCH fault message is currently displayed or was previously recorded, go to next step. If EEPROM FAILURE fault message is also displayed, go to step 3). If ROLLING CODE FAILURE fault message is displayed with or without EEPROM FAILURE fault message is displayed, go to step 4).

3) Using scan tool, erase SKIM DTCs. Turn ignition off and wait 10 seconds. Start engine 20 times. Using scan tool, read SKIM DTCs. If EEPROM fault message is displayed, replace SKIM. Perform SKIM INITIALIZATION PROCEDURE. If EEPROM failure is not displayed, go to next step.

4) Start engine and allow to idle for 3 minutes. Using scan tool, read SKIM DTCs. If VIN MISMATCH fault message is displayed, go to next step. If ROLLING CODE fault message is displayed, go to step 9). If none of the above fault messages are present, test is complete.

5) Using scan tool, read VIN from Powertrain Control Module (PCM). If VIN output from PCM matches VIN on door jamb plate, go to next step. If VIN output from PCM does not match VIN on door jamb plate, replace PCM.

6) Using scan tool, read VIN from SKIM. If VIN output from SKIM matches VIN on door jamb plate, go to next step. If VIN output from SKIM does not match VIN on door jamb plate, replace SKIM and perform SKIM INITIALIZATION PROCEDURE.

7) Using scan tool, erase VIN MISMATCH DTC. Turn ignition switch to RUN position and read SKIM DTCs. If VIN MISMATCH fault message is still present, replace SKIM and perform SKIM INITIALIZATION PROCEDURE. If VIN MISMATCH fault message is not displayed, go to next step.

8) Start engine and allow to idle for 3 minutes. Using scan tool, erase SKIM DTCs. Read SKIM DTCs. If SKIM MISMATCH fault message is still present, replace SKIM and perform SKIM INITIALIZATION PROCEDURE. If SKIM MISMATCH fault message is not displayed, test is complete.

9) Using scan tool, erase SKIM DTCs. Select THEFT ALARM, then SKIM. If scan tool displays NO RESPONSE, go to appropriate VEHICLE COMMUNICATIONS test in VEHICLE COMMUNICATIONS article. If scan tool does not display NO RESPONSE,

10) Using scan tool, select BODY, then BODY COMPUTER. Select SYSTEM TEST, then PCM MONITOR. If scan tool displays PCM ACTIVE ON THE BUS, go to next step. If scan tool does not display PCM ACTIVE ON THE BUS, see appropriate VEHICLE COMMUNICATIONS article.

11) Using scan tool, select ENGINE, then read DTCs. If scan tool displays any PCM related DTCs, see appropriate SELF-DIAGNOSTICS article in ENGINE PERFORMANCE in appropriate MITCHELL® manual. If scan tool does not display any PCM related DTCs, replace smart key immobilizer module. Perform SKIM INITIALIZATION PROCEDURE.

VERIFICATION TEST: VER-2A

BODY VERIFICATION TEST

1) Reconnect all previously disconnected components and connectors. If BCM was replaced, turn ignition on for at least 15 seconds.

2) Ensure ignition is on. Erase all DTCs using scan tool. Turn ignition off and wait 5 seconds. Turn ignition on and fully operate system that was malfunctioning.

3) If system is not operating properly, go to SYMPTOM ID TEST. Using scan tool, read Body DTCs. If any DTCs are present, go to SYMPTOM ID TEST. If no DTCs are present, system is operating correctly and customer's complaint cannot be duplicated, repair is complete.

SKIM INITIALIZATION PROCEDURE

GENERAL INFORMATION

SECURED ACCESS mode is not required to check programmed status of key.

If PCM is replaced, unique secret key data must be transferred from SKIM to PCM. This procedure requires SKIM to be placed in SECURED ACCESS mode using 4-digit PIN code.

If 3 attempts are made to enter secured access mode using an incorrect PIN, SECURED ACCESS mode will be locked out for one hour. To exit lock out mode, turn ignition switch to RUN/START position continuously for one hour. Ensure all accessories are turned off. Monitor battery state and connect battery charger is necessary.

To program smart keys using "customer programming method" requires 2 valid smart keys. See owner's manual.

INITIALIZATION PROCEDURE

1) Obtain vehicle's unique PIN number assigned to it's original SKIM module from vehicle owner or Chrysler's customer center.

2) Using scan tool, select THEFT ALARM, SKIM, then MISCELLANEOUS. Select SKIM MODULE REPLACED function.

3) Enter SECURED ACCESS mode using unique 4-digit PIN number.

4) Program vehicle's VIN number into SKIM's memory.

5) Program country code into SKIM's memory (U.S.).

6) Transfer vehicle's unique Secret Key data from PCM. This process will require SKIM module to be in SECURED ACCESS mode. The PIN number must be entered into scan tool before SKIM will enter SECURED ACCESS mode. Once SECURED ACCESS mode is active, SKIM will remain in that mode for 60 seconds.

7) Program all customer keys into SKIM's memory. This requires that SKIM be in SECURED ACCESS mode. The SKIM will immediately exit SECURED ACCESS mode after each key is programmed.

PROGRAMMING BLANK SMART KEY USING SCAN TOOL

1) Once key blank is cut, insert key into ignition switch. Turn ignition switch to RUN position. Using scan tool, select THEFT ALARM, then SKIM. Select MISCELLANEOUS, then PROGRAM NEW KEY. Enter 4-digit PIN code. When programming is completed, SKIM will exit SECURED ACCESS mode and display status of key. One of five different status messages maybe displayed as follows:

- PROGRAMMING SUCCESSFUL is displayed if SKIM smart key programming succeeds.
- LEARNED KEY IN IGNITION is displayed if key in the ignition has already been programmed into vehicle's SKIM.
- 8 KEYS ALREADY LEARNED, PROGRAMMING NOT DONE is displayed if eight keys have already been programmed into SKIM. If a new key needs to be added due to a lost or defective key, the ERASE ALL KEYS function has to be performed. Original 7 keys plus additional new key may then be reprogrammed into SKIM.
- PROGRAMMING NOT ATTEMPTED is displayed after an ERASE ALL KEYS function is executed.
- PROGRAMMING KEY FAILED is displayed if further diagnosis is required.

2) To program additional keys, turn ignition off. Remove current programmed key and insert next new blank key. Turn ignition switch to RUN position. Re-enter SECURED ACCESS mode function and repeat PROGRAM NEW KEY procedure.

SYSTEM TESTS

NOTE: *For connector terminal identification, component location and wiring diagrams, see BODY CONTROL COMPUTER INTRODUCTION article. Perform VERIFICATION TEST: VER-2A after each repair.*

IDENTIFYING VEHICLE COMMUNICATION PROBLEMS

Battery must be fully charged before proceeding. Connect scan tool to Data Link Connector (DLC) to retrieve messages. Ensure ground circuit has continuity at terminal No. 4 on DLC. Ensure 12 volts exists at terminal No. 16 on DLC. See following list of vehicle communication symptoms and scan tool fault messages. Proceed to appropriate test. Always turn ignition off prior to disconnecting any module connector.

- BUS (+) & BUS (-) SHORTED TOGETHER
- BUS BIAS LEVEL TOO HIGH (CHEROKEE)
- BUS BIAS LEVEL TOO HIGH (WRANGLER)
- BUS BIAS LEVEL TOO LOW (CHEROKEE)
- BUS BIAS LEVEL TOO LOW (WRANGLER)
- BUS (+) & BUS (-) OPEN
- BUS (+) OPEN OR BUS (-) OPEN
- SCAN TOOL BLANK SCREEN
- NO BUS BIAS (CHEROKEE)
- NO BUS BIAS (WRANGLER)
- NO RESPONSE FROM AIRBAG CONTROL MODULE (CHEROKEE)
- NO RESPONSE FROM AIRBAG CONTROL MODULE (WRANGLER)
- NO RESPONSE FROM COMPASS MINI-TRIP COMPUTER (CMTC)
- NO RESPONSE FROM INSTRUMENT CLUSTER
- NO RESPONSE FROM POWERTRAIN CONTROL MODULE (PCM)
- NO RESPONSE FROM REMOTE KEYLESS ENTRY (RKE)
- NO RESPONSE FROM SENTRY KEY IMMOBILIZER MODULE (SKIM)
- NO RESPONSE FROM TRANSMISSION CONTROL MODULE (TCM)
- NO TERMINATION
- NOT RECEIVING BUS MESSAGES CORRECTLY
- SHORT TO 5 VOLTS
- SHORT TO BATTERY
- SHORT TO GROUND

BUS (+) & BUS (-) SHORTED TOGETHER

1) Turn ignition off. Disconnect Powertrain Control Module (PCM). Turn ignition on. If scan tool does not display BUS (+) & BUS (-) SHORTED TOGETHER, replace PCM. If scan tool displays BUS (+) & BUS (-) SHORTED TOGETHER, go to next step.

2) Turn ignition off. Disconnect Smart Key Immobilizer Module (SKIM). Turn ignition on. If scan tool does not display BUS (+) & BUS (-) SHORTED TOGETHER, replace SKIM. If scan tool displays BUS (+) & BUS (-) SHORTED TOGETHER, go to next step.

3) Turn ignition off. Disconnect instrument cluster. Turn ignition on. If scan tool does not display BUS (+) & BUS (-) SHORTED TOGETHER, replace instrument cluster circuit board. If scan tool displays BUS (+) & BUS (-) SHORTED TOGETHER, go to next step.

4) Turn ignition off and wait 2 minutes. Disconnect Airbag Control Module (ACM). Turn ignition on. If scan tool does not display BUS (+) & BUS (-) SHORTED TOGETHER, see MITCHELL® AIR BAG SERVICE & REPAIR, DOMESTIC CARS, LIGHT TRUCKS & VANS. If scan tool displays BUS (+) & BUS (-) SHORTED TOGETHER, go to next step.

5) Turn ignition off and wait 2 minutes. Disconnect Transmission Control Module (TCM) (if equipped). Turn ignition on. If scan tool does not display BUS (+) & BUS (-) SHORTED TOGETHER, replace TCM. If scan tool displays BUS (+) & BUS (-) SHORTED TOGETHER, go to next step.

6) Turn ignition off and wait 2 minutes. Disconnect Compass Mini-Trip Computer (CMTC) (if equipped). Turn ignition on. If scan tool does not display BUS (+) & BUS (-) SHORTED TOGETHER, replace CMTC. If scan tool displays BUS (+) & BUS (-) SHORTED TOGETHER, go to next step.

7) Turn ignition off and wait 2 minutes. Disconnect Remote Keyless Entry (RKE) module (if equipped). Turn ignition on. If scan tool does not display BUS (+) & BUS (-) SHORTED TOGETHER, replace RKE module. If scan tool displays BUS (+) & BUS (-) SHORTED TOGETHER, go to next step.

8) Turn ignition off. Disconnect scan tool from DLC. Using ohmmeter, measure resistance between terminals No. 3 (Violet/Brown wire) and No. 11 (White/Black wire) on DLC connector. If resistance is less than 100 ohms, repair short between Violet/Brown wire and White/Black wire. If resistance is 100 ohms or greater, replace scan tool cable or scan tool as necessary.

BUS BIAS LEVEL TOO LOW OR TOO HIGH (CHEROKEE)

1) Disconnect scan tool. Using an external voltmeter, measure voltage between ground and terminal No. 3 (Violet/Brown wire) on DLC connector. If voltage is not 1.8-2.6 volts, go to step **3)**. If voltage is 1.8-2.6 volts, go to next step.

2) Measure voltage between ground and terminal No. 11 (White/Black wire) on DLC connector. If voltage is not 1.8-2.6 volts, go to next step. If voltage is 1.8-2.6 volts, replace scan tool cable or scan tool.

3) Connect scan tool to DLC. Turn ignition off. Disconnect Powertrain Control Module (PCM). Turn ignition on. Perform CCD BUS test under SYSTEM MONITORS. If scan tool displays BUS OPERATIONAL, replace PCM. If scan tool does not display BUS OPERATIONAL, go to next step.

4) Turn ignition off. Disconnect Smart Key Immobilizer Module (SKIM). Turn ignition on. If scan tool displays BUS OPERATIONAL, replace SKIM. If scan tool does not display BUS OPERATIONAL, go to next step.

5) Turn ignition off and wait 2 minutes. Disconnect Airbag Control Module (ACM). Turn ignition on. If scan tool does displays BUS OPERATIONAL, see MITCHELL® AIR BAG SERVICE & REPAIR, DOMESTIC CARS, LIGHT TRUCKS & VANS. If scan tool does not display BUS OPERATIONAL, go to next step.

6) Turn ignition off. Disconnect Compass Mini-Trip Computer (CMTC). Turn ignition on. If scan tool displays BUS OPERATIONAL, replace CMTC. If scan tool does not display BUS OPERATIONAL, go to next step.

7) Turn ignition off. Disconnect Transmission Control Module (TCM). Turn ignition on. If scan tool displays BUS OPERATIONAL, replace TCM. If scan tool does not display BUS OPERATIONAL, go to next step.

8) Turn ignition off. Disconnect Remote Keyless Entry (RKE) module. Turn ignition on. If scan tool displays BUS OPERATIONAL, replace RKE module. If scan tool does not display BUS OPERATIONAL, go to next step.

9) Turn ignition off. Remove instrument cluster. Ensure interior lights are off. Using external ohmmeter, measure resistance between ground and terminal No. 6 (Black/Light Green wire) on left instrument cluster connector. If resistance is less than 5 ohms, go to next step. If resistance is 5 ohms or greater, repair open Black/Light Green wire.

10) Ensure PCM, SKIM AND ACM connectors are disconnected. Connect jumper wire between ground and terminal No. 11 (White/Black wire) on DLC connector. Using external ohmmeter, measure resistance between ground and terminal No. 1 (White/Black wire) on right instrument cluster connector. If resistance is less than 5 ohms, go to next step. If resistance is 5 ohms or greater, repair open White/Black wire.

11) Disconnect jumper wire. Measure resistance between ground and terminal No. 1 (White/Black wire) on right instrument cluster connector. If resistance is less than 1000 ohms, repair White/Black wire for short to ground. If resistance is 1000 ohms or greater, go to next step.

12) Connect jumper wire between ground and terminal No. 3 (Violet/Brown wire) on DLC connector. Using external ohmmeter, measure resistance between ground and terminal No. 2 (Violet/Brown wire) on right instrument cluster connector. If resistance is less than 5 ohms, go to next step. If resistance is 5 ohms or greater, repair open Violet/Brown wire.

13) Disconnect jumper wire. Measure resistance between ground and terminal No. 2 (Violet/Brown wire) on right instrument cluster Green connector. If resistance is less than 1000 ohms, repair Violet/Brown wire for short to ground. If resistance is 1000 ohms or greater, replace instrument cluster.

BUS BIAS LEVEL TOO LOW OR TOO HIGH (WRANGLER)

1) Disconnect scan tool. Using an external voltmeter, measure voltage between ground and terminal No. 3 (Violet/Brown wire) on DLC connector. If voltage is not 2.3-2.6 volts, go to step **3)**. If voltage is 2.3-2.6 volts, go to next step.

2) Measure voltage between ground and terminal No. 11 (White/Black wire) on DLC connector. If voltage is not 2.3-2.6 volts, go to next step. If voltage is 2.3-2.6 volts, replace scan tool cable or scan tool.

3) Connect scan tool to DLC. Turn ignition off. Disconnect Powertrain Control Module (PCM). Turn ignition on. Perform CCD BUS test under SYSTEM MONITORS. If scan tool displays BUS OPERATIONAL, replace PCM. If scan tool does not display BUS OPERATIONAL, go to next step.

4) Turn ignition off. Disconnect Smart Key Immobilizer Module (SKIM). Turn ignition on. If scan tool displays BUS OPERATIONAL, replace SKIM. If scan tool does not display BUS OPERATIONAL, go to next step.

5) Turn ignition off and wait 2 minutes. Disconnect Airbag Control Module (ACM). Turn ignition on. If scan tool does displays BUS OPERATIONAL, see ® AIR BAG SERVICE & REPAIR, DOMESTIC CARS, LIGHT TRUCKS & VANS. If scan tool does not display BUS OPERATIONAL, go to next step.

6) Turn ignition off. Remove instrument cluster. Ensure interior lights are off. Using external ohmmeter, measure resistance between ground and terminal No. 6 (Black/Light Green wire) on left instrument cluster Blue connector. If resistance is less than 5 ohms, go to next step. If resistance is 5 ohms or greater, repair open Black/Light Green wire.

7) Ensure PCM, SKIM AND ACM connectors are disconnected. Connect jumper wire between ground and terminal No. 11 (White/Black wire) on DLC connector. Using external ohmmeter, measure resistance between ground and terminal No. 1 (White/Black wire) on right instrument cluster Green connector. If resistance is less than 5 ohms, go to next step. If resistance is 5 ohms or greater, repair open White/Black wire.

8) Disconnect jumper wire. Measure resistance between ground and terminal No. 1 (White/Black wire) on right instrument cluster Green connector. If resistance is less than 1000 ohms, repair White/Black wire for short to ground. If resistance is 1000 ohms or greater, go to next step.

9) Connect jumper wire between ground and terminal No. 3 (Violet/Brown wire) on DLC connector. Using external ohmmeter, measure resistance between ground and terminal No. 2 (Violet/Brown wire) on right instrument cluster Green connector. If resistance is less than 5 ohms, go to next step. If resistance is 5 ohms or greater, repair open Violet/Brown wire.

10) Disconnect jumper wire. Measure resistance between ground and terminal No. 2 (Violet/Brown wire) on right instrument cluster Green connector. If resistance is less than 1000 ohms, repair Violet/Brown wire for short to ground. If resistance is 1000 ohms or greater, replace instrument cluster.

BUS (+) &/OR BUS (-) OPEN

1) Ensure ignition off. Disconnect scan tool. Using an external voltmeter, measure voltage between ground and DLC terminal No. 3 (Violet/Brown wire). If voltage is 2.3-2.6 volts, go to step **3)**. If voltage is not 2.3-2.6 volts, go to next step.

2) Measure voltage between ground and DLC terminal No. 11 (White/Black wire). If voltage is not 2.3-2.6 volts, go to next step. If voltage is 2.3-2.6 volts, replace scan tool cable or scan tool.

3) Connect jumper wire between ground and terminal No. 11 on DLC connector. Remove instrument cluster. Using external ohmmeter, measure resistance between ground and terminal No. 1 (White/Black wire) on right instrument cluster connector. If resistance is less than 5 ohms, go to next step. If resistance is 5 ohms or greater, repair open White/Black wire.

4) Disconnect jumper wire. Connect jumper wire between ground and terminal No. 3 on DLC connector. Measure resistance between ground and terminal No. 2 (Violet/Brown wire) on right instrument cluster connector. If resistance is less than 5 ohms, replace instrument cluster. If resistance is 5 ohms or greater, repair open Violet/Brown wire.

SCAN TOOL BLANK SCREEN

Using ohmmeter, check continuity between ground and terminals No. 4 and 5 on DLC. Continuity should exist. Repair as needed. Using voltmeter, measure voltage between ground and terminal No. 16 on DLC. Battery voltage should exist. If battery voltage is not present, inspect fuse No. 17 in Power Distribution Center (PDC). Replace as needed. If battery voltage is present, replace scan tool cable or scan tool as necessary.

NO BUS BIAS (CHEROKEE)

1) Disconnect scan tool. Using an external voltmeter, measure voltage between ground and DLC terminal No. 3 (Violet/Brown wire). If voltage is not 2.3-2.6 volts, go to step **3)**. If voltage is 2.3-2.6 volts, go to next step.

2) Measure voltage between ground and DLC terminal No. 11 (White/Black wire). If voltage is not 2.3-2.6 volts, go to next step. If voltage is 2.3-2.6 volts, replace scan tool cable or scan tool.

3) Ensure ignition is on. Using voltmeter, measure voltage between ground and fused ignition switch output terminal (White/Black wire) on junction block fuse No. 9. If voltage is greater than 10 volts, go to next step. If voltage is 10 volts or less, go to step **5)**.

4) Remove instrument cluster. Turn ignition on. Measure voltage between ground and terminal No. 8 (White/Black wire) on left instrument cluster harness connector. If voltage is 10 volts or less, repair open White/Black wire. If voltage is greater than 10 volts, replace instrument cluster.

5) Turn ignition off. Remove junction block fuse No. 9. Using ohmmeter, measure resistance between ground and fused ignition switch output terminal (White/Black wire) on junction block fuse No. 9. If resistance is 5 ohms or greater, go to next step. If resistance is less than 5 ohms, repair White/Black wire for short to ground. Replace fuse No. 9.

6) Turn ignition on. Using voltmeter, measure voltage between ground and ignition switch output terminal (Dark Blue wire) on junction block fuse No. 9. If voltage is greater than 10 volts, replace fuse. If voltage is 10 volts or less, repair open Dark Blue wire.

NO BUS BIAS (WRANGLER)

1) Disconnect scan tool. Using an external voltmeter, measure voltage between ground and DLC terminal No. 3 (Violet/Brown wire). If voltage is not 2.3-2.6 volts, go to step **3)**. If voltage is 2.3-2.6 volts, go to next step.

2) Measure voltage between ground and DLC terminal No. 11 (White/Black wire). If voltage is not 2.3-2.6 volts, go to next step. If voltage is 2.3-2.6 volts, replace scan tool cable or scan tool.

3) Disconnect instrument cluster connectors. Connect jumper wire between ground and terminal No. 3 (White/Black wire) on DLC connector. Using external ohmmeter, measure resistance between ground and terminal No. 2 (Violet/Brown wire) on right instrument cluster connector. If resistance is less than 5 ohms, go to next step. If resistance is 5 ohms or greater, repair open Violet/Brown wire.

4) Remove and inspect fuse No. 10. If fuse is open, go to next step. If fuse is okay, go to step **6)**.

5) Turn ignition off. Remove fuse block fuse No. 10. Using ohmmeter, measure resistance between ground and fused ignition switch output terminal (Dark Blue/White wire) on fuse block fuse No. 10. If resistance is 5 ohms or greater, replace fuse. If resistance is less than 5 ohms, repair Dark Blue/White wire for short to ground. Replace fuse No. 9.

6) Remove instrument cluster. Turn ignition on. Using external voltmeter, measure voltage between ground and terminal No. 8 (Dark Blue/White wire) on left instrument cluster harness connector. If voltage is 10 volts or less, repair open Dark Blue/White wire. If voltage is greater than 10 volts, go to next step.

7) Using external ohmmeter, measure resistance between ground and terminal No. 6 (Black/Light Green wire) on left instrument cluster connector. If resistance is less than 5 ohms, go to next step. If resistance is 5 ohms or greater, repair open Black/Light Green wire.

8) Connect jumper wire between ground and terminal No. 11 (White/Black wire) on DLC connector. Using external ohmmeter, measure resistance between ground and terminal No. 1 (White/Black wire) on right instrument cluster connector. If resistance is less than 5 ohms, go to next step. If resistance is 5 ohms or greater, repair open White/Black wire.

9) Disconnect jumper wire. Measure resistance between ground and terminal No. 1 (White/Black wire) on right instrument cluster connector. If resistance is less than 1000 ohms, repair White/Black wire for short to ground. If resistance is 1000 ohms or greater, go to next step.

10) Disconnect jumper wire. Measure resistance between ground and terminal No. 2 (Violet/Brown wire) on right instrument cluster connector. If resistance is less than 1000 ohms, repair Violet/Brown wire for short to ground. If resistance is 1000 ohms or greater, replace instrument cluster.

NO RESPONSE FROM AIR BAG CONTROL MODULE (CHEROKEE)

WARNING: Disconnect battery and wait 2 minutes before disconnecting airbag control module. If airbag control module is dropped, it must be replaced.

1) Remove fuse No. 27 from junction block. If fuse is blown, go to next step. If fuse is okay, go to step 7).

2) Turn ignition on. Using voltmeter, measure voltage between ground and ignition switch output run/start terminal on fuse No. 27 socket. If voltage is greater than 10 volts, go to next step. If voltage is 10 volts or less, repair open ignition switch output run/start circuit.

3) Turn ignition off. Using ohmmeter, measure resistance between ground and fused ignition switch output terminal on junction block fuse No. 27. If resistance is less than 5 ohms, go to next step. If resistance is 5 ohms or greater, go to step 5).

4) Ensure ignition is off. Disconnect battery and wait 2 minutes. Disconnect Airbag Control Module (ACM) connector. Using ohmmeter, measure resistance between ground and fused ignition switch output terminal on fuse No. 27. If resistance is less than 5 ohms, repair fused ignition switch output circuit for short to ground. Replace junction block fuse No. 27. If resistance is 5 ohms or greater, replace ACM. Replace junction block fuse No. 27.

5) Ensure ignition is off. Disconnect battery and wait 2 minutes. Disconnect Airbag Control Module (ACM) connector. Using ohmmeter, measure resistance between ground and terminal No. 17 (Dark Blue/Yellow wire) on ACM harness connector. If resistance is less than 5 ohms, repair Dark Blue/Yellow wire for short to ground. If resistance is 5 ohms or greater, go to next step.

6) Measure resistance of Dark Blue/Yellow wire between fused ignition switch output terminal on junction block fuse No. 27 and terminal No. 17 on ACM harness connector. If resistance is less than 5 ohms, replace junction block fuse No. 27. If resistance is 5 ohms or greater, repair open Dark Blue/Yellow wire. Replace junction block fuse No. 27.

7) Turn ignition on. Using voltmeter, measure voltage between ground and ignition switch output run/start terminal on fuse No. 27 socket. If voltage is greater than 10 volts, go to next step. If voltage is 10 volts or less, repair open ignition switch output run/start circuit.

8) Install fuse No. 27. Ensure ignition is off. Disconnect battery and wait 2 minutes. Disconnect Airbag Control Module (ACM) connector. Reconnect battery and turn ignition on. Using ohmmeter, measure voltage

between ground and terminal No. 17 (Dark Blue/Yellow wire) on ACM harness connector. If voltage is greater than 10 volts, go to next step. If voltage is 10 volts or less, repair open Dark Blue/Yellow wire.

9) Turn ignition off. Using ohmmeter, measure resistance between ground and terminal No. 10 (Black/Pink wire) on ACM harness connector. If resistance is less than 5 ohms, go to next step. If resistance is 5 ohms or greater, repair open Black/Pink wire.

10) Ensure ACM harness connector is disconnected and battery is connected. Turn ignition on. Using voltmeter, measure voltage between ground and terminal No. 19 (Violet/Brown wire) on ACM harness connector. If voltage is 1.8–2.6 volts, go to next step. If voltage is not 1.8–2.6 volts, repair open Violet/Brown wire.

11) Measure voltage between ground and terminal No. 18 (White/Black wire) on ACM harness connector. If voltage is 1.8–2.6 volts, go to next step. If voltage is not 1.8–2.6 volts, repair open White/Black wire.

NO RESPONSE FROM AIR BAG CONTROL MODULE (WRANGLER)

1) Remove and inspect fuse No. 9 from fuse block. Fuse block is behind glove compartment. If fuse is blown, go to next step. If fuse is okay, go to step 4).

2) Using ohmmeter, measure resistance between ground and fused ignition switch output terminal on fuse No. 9 socket. If resistance is less than 5 ohms, go to next step. If resistance is 5 ohms or greater, replace fuse No. 9.

3) Ensure ignition is off. Disconnect battery and wait 2 minutes. Disconnect Airbag Control Module (ACM) connector. Using ohmmeter, measure resistance between ground and fused ignition switch output terminal on fuse No. 9. If resistance is less than 5 ohms, repair fused ignition switch output circuit for short to ground. Replace fuse No. 9. If resistance is 5 ohms or greater, replace ACM. Replace fuse No. 9.

4) Using voltmeter, measure voltage between ground and ignition output terminal on fuse No. 9 socket. If voltage is 10 volts or less, repair open ignition switch output circuit. If voltage is more than 10 volts, go to next step.

5) Ensure ignition is off. Disconnect battery and wait 2 minutes. Disconnect Airbag Control Module (ACM) connector. Using voltmeter, measure voltage between ground and terminal No. 17 (Light Green/Yellow wire) on ACM harness connector. If voltage is 10 volts or less, repair open Light Green/Yellow wire. If voltage is greater than 10 volts, go to next step.

6) Turn ignition off. Using ohmmeter mode, measure resistance between ground and terminal No. 10 (Black/Pink wire) on ABSCM harness connector. If resistance is 5 ohms or greater, repair open Black/Pink wire. If resistance is less than 5 ohms, go to next step.

7) Turn ignition on. Using voltmeter, measure voltage between ground and terminal No. 19 (Violet/Brown wire) on ACM harness connector. If voltage is not 1.8-2.6 volts, repair open Violet/Brown wire. If voltage is 1.8-2.6 volts, go to next step.

8) Measure voltage between ground and terminal No. 18 (White/Black wire) on ACM connector. If voltage is not 1.8-2.6 volts, repair open White/Black wire. If voltage is 1.8-2.6 volts, replace ACM.

NO RESPONSE FROM COMPASS MINI-TRIP COMPUTER (CMTC)

1) Ensure ignition is off. Disconnect CMTC connector. Turn ignition on. Using voltmeter, measure voltage between ground and terminal No. 6 (White/Black wire) on CMTC harness connector. If voltage is greater than 10 volts, go to next step. If voltage is 10 volts or less, repair open White/Black wire.

2) Connect jumper wire between ground and terminal No. 12 (White/Black wire). Using scan tool, select BODY, BODY COMPUTER, then SYSTEM TEST. Perform CCD BUS test. If scan tool displays BUS SHORTED TO GROUND, go to next step. If scan tool displays BUS SHORTED TO GROUND, repair open White/Black wire.

3) Connect jumper wire between ground and terminal No. 6 (Violet/Brown wire). Using scan tool, perform BUS TEST. If scan tool displays BUS SHORTED TO GROUND, replace CMTC. If scan tool displays BUS SHORTED TO GROUND, repair open Violet/Brown wire.

NO RESPONSE FROM INSTRUMENT CLUSTER

1) Disconnect instrument cluster. Connect jumper between ground and terminal No. 2 (Violet/Brown wire) on instrument cluster right connector. Turn ignition on. Using scan tool, select BODY, BODY COMPUTER, then SYSTEM TEST. Perform CCD BUS test. If scan tool does not display BUS SHORT TO GROUND, repair open Violet/Brown wire. If scan tool displays BUS SHORT TO GROUND, go to next step.

2) Connect jumper between ground and terminal No. 1 (White/Black wire) on instrument cluster right connector. Perform CCD BUS test. If scan tool does not display BUS SHORT TO GROUND, repair open White/Black wire. If scan tool displays BUS SHORT TO GROUND, replace instrument cluster circuit board.

NO RESPONSE FROM POWERTRAIN CONTROL MODULE

1) If engine does not run, see appropriate article in ENGINE PERFORMANCE in appropriate MITCHELL® manual. If engine runs, turn ignition off. Disconnect Powertrain Control Module (PCM). Turn ignition on. Connect jumper wire between ground and terminal No. C30 (Violet/Brown wire) on PCM connector. Using scan tool, perform CCD BUS test. If scan tool does not display BUS SHORT TO GROUND, repair open Violet/Brown wire. If scan tool displays BUS SHORT TO GROUND, go to next step.

2) Move jumper wire to terminal No. C28 (White/Black wire) on PCM connector. Perform CCD BUS test. If scan tool does not display BUS SHORT TO GROUND, repair open White/Black wire. If scan tool displays BUS SHORT TO GROUND, replace PCM.

NO RESPONSE FROM REMOTE KEYLESS ENTRY (RKE)

1) Disconnect transmission control module. Disconnect RKE module connector. Connect jumper wire between ground and terminal No. 12 (White/Black wire). Turn ignition on. Using scan tool, select BODY, BODY COMPUTER, then SYSTEM TEST. Perform CCD BUS test. If scan tool displays BUS SHORTED TO GROUND, go to next step. If scan tool displays BUS SHORTED TO GROUND, repair open White/Black wire.

2) Ensure ignition is on. Using voltmeter, measure voltage between ground and terminal No. 2 (Pink wire) on RKE module harness connector. If voltage is greater than 10 volts, go to next step. If voltage is 10 volts or less, repair open Pink wire.

3) Using voltmeter, measure voltage between ground and terminal No. 8 (Pink wire) on RKE module harness connector. If voltage is greater than 10 volts, go to next step. If voltage is 10 volts or less, repair open Pink wire.

4) Connect jumper wire between ground and terminal No. 6 (Violet/Brown wire). Using scan tool, perform BUS TEST. If scan tool displays BUS SHORTED TO GROUND, replace RKE module. If scan tool displays BUS SHORTED TO GROUND, repair open Violet/Brown wire.

NO RESPONSE FROM SMART KEY IMMOBILIZER MODULE (SKIM)

1) Using scan tool, select BODY, BODY COMPUTER, then SYSTEM TEST. If scan tool displays PCM ACTIVE ON THE BUS, go to next step. If scan tool does not display PCM ACTIVE ON THE BUS, go to NO RESPONSE FROM POWERTRAIN CONTROL MODULE.

2) Turn ignition off. Disconnect Smart Key Immobilizer Module (SKIM) harness connector. Using ohmmeter, measure resistance between ground and terminals No. 2 and 4 (Black/Light Green wires) on SKIM connector. If resistance is less than 5 ohms, go to next step. If resistance is 5 ohms or greater, repair open Black/Light Green wire(s).

3) Using voltmeter, measure voltage between ground and terminal No. 1 (Dark Blue/Gray wire on Cherokee, Tan/Black wire on Wrangler) on SKIM connector. If voltage is 10 volts or less, repair open Dark Blue/Gray or Tan/Black wire. If voltage is greater than 10 volts, go to next step.

4) Turn ignition on. Using voltmeter, measure voltage between ground and terminal No. 3 (White/Black wire on Cherokee, Dark Blue wire on Wrangler) on SKIM connector. If voltage is 10 volts or less, repair open White/Black wire or Dark Blue wire. If voltage is greater than 10 volts, go to next step.

5) Connect jumper wire between ground and terminal No. 5 (White/Black wire) on SKIM connector. Using scan tool, perform CCD BUS test. If scan tool does not display BUS SHORT TO GROUND, repair open White/Black wire. If scan tool displays BUS SHORT TO GROUND, go to next step.

6) Move jumper wire between ground and terminal No. 6 (Violet/Brown wire) on SKIM connector. Using scan tool, perform CCD BUS test. If scan tool does not display BUS SHORT TO GROUND, repair open Violet/Brown wire. If scan tool displays BUS SHORT TO GROUND, replace SKIM. Using scan tool, reprogram keys.

NO RESPONSE FROM TRANSMISSION CONTROL MODULE (TCM)

1) Ensure ignition is off. Disconnect TCM connector. Turn ignition on. Using voltmeter, measure voltage between ground and terminal No. 26 (Dark Blue/White wire) on TCM harness connector. If voltage is greater than 10 volts, go to next step. If voltage is 10 volts or less, repair open Dark Blue/White wire.

2) Connect jumper wire between ground and terminal No. 6 (White/Black wire) on TCM harness connector. Using scan tool, select BODY, BODY COMPUTER, then SYSTEM TEST. Perform CCD BUS test. If scan tool displays BUS SHORTED TO GROUND, go to next step. If scan tool displays BUS SHORTED TO GROUND, repair open White/Black wire.

3) Connect jumper wire between ground and terminal No. 7 (Violet/Brown wire). Using scan tool, perform BUS TEST. If scan tool displays BUS SHORTED TO GROUND, replace TCM. If scan tool displays BUS SHORTED TO GROUND, repair open Violet/Brown wire.

NO TERMINATION

1) Ensure ignition off. Disconnect Powertrain Control Module (PCM) Gray connector. Connect jumper wire between ground and terminal C30 (Violet/Brown wire) on PCM Gray connector. Turn ignition on. Using scan tool, select SYSTEM MONITORS. Perform CCD BUS test. If scan tool does not display BUS SHORT TO GROUND, repair open Violet/Brown wire. If scan tool displays BUS SHORT TO GROUND, go to next step.

2) Move jumper wire to terminal C28 (White/Black wire) on PCM Gray connector. Perform CCD BUS test. If scan tool does not display BUS SHORT TO GROUND, repair open White/Black wire. If scan tool displays BUS SHORT TO GROUND, replace PCM and instrument cluster.

NOT RECEIVING BUS MESSAGES CORRECTLY

1) Turn ignition off. Disconnect Powertrain Control Module (PCM). Turn ignition on. If scan tool displays BUS OPERATIONAL, replace PCM. If scan tool does not display BUS OPERATIONAL, go to next step.

2) Turn ignition off. Disconnect Smart Key Immobilizer Module (SKIM). Turn ignition on. If scan tool displays BUS OPERATIONAL, replace SKIM. If scan tool does not display BUS OPERATIONAL, go to next step.

3) Turn ignition off. Disconnect instrument cluster. Turn ignition on. If scan tool displays BUS OPERATIONAL, replace instrument cluster circuit board. If scan tool does not display BUS OPERATIONAL, go to next step.

4) Turn ignition off and wait 2 minutes. Disconnect Airbag Control Module (ACM). Turn ignition on. If scan tool displays BUS OPERATIONAL, see MITCHELL® AIR BAG SERVICE & REPAIR, DOMESTIC CARS, LIGHT TRUCKS & VANS. If scan tool does not display BUS OPERATIONAL, go to next step.

5) Turn ignition off and wait 2 minutes. Disconnect Transmission Control Module (TCM) (if equipped). Turn ignition on. If scan tool displays BUS OPERATIONAL, replace TCM. If scan tool does not display BUS OPERATIONAL, go to next step.

6) Turn ignition off and wait 2 minutes. Disconnect Compass Mini-Trip Computer (CMTC) (if equipped). Turn ignition on. If scan tool displays BUS OPERATIONAL, replace CMTC. If scan tool does not display BUS OPERATIONAL, go to next step.

7) Turn ignition off and wait 2 minutes. Disconnect Remote Keyless Entry (RKE) module (if equipped). Turn ignition on. If scan tool displays BUS OPERATIONAL, replace RKE module. If scan tool does not display BUS OPERATIONAL, replace scan tool cable or scan tool as necessary.

BUS SHORT TO 5 VOLTS

1) Turn ignition off. Disconnect Powertrain Control Module (PCM). Turn ignition on. If scan tool does not display BUS SHORT TO 5 VOLTS, go to step **12)**. If scan tool displays BUS SHORT TO 5 VOLTS, go to next step.

2) Turn ignition off. Disconnect Transmission Control Module (TCM). Turn ignition on. If scan tool does not display BUS SHORT TO 5 VOLTS, go to step **10)**. If scan tool displays BUS SHORT TO 5 VOLTS, go to next step.

3) Turn ignition off. Disconnect instrument cluster. Turn ignition on. If scan tool does not display BUS SHORT TO 5 VOLTS, replace instrument cluster circuit board. If scan tool displays BUS SHORT TO 5 VOLTS, go to next step.

4) Turn ignition off. Disconnect Compass Mini-Trip Computer (CMTC). Turn ignition on. If scan tool does not display BUS SHORT TO 5 VOLTS, replace CMTC. If scan tool displays BUS SHORT TO 5 VOLTS, go to next step.

5) Turn ignition off. Disconnect Remote Keyless Entry (RKE) module. Turn ignition on. If scan tool does not display BUS SHORT TO 5 VOLTS, replace RKE module. If scan tool displays BUS SHORT TO 5 VOLTS, go to next step.

6) Turn ignition off and wait 2 minutes. Disconnect Sentry Key Immobilizer Module (SKIM). Turn ignition on. If scan tool does not display BUS SHORT TO 5 VOLTS, replace SKIM. If scan tool displays BUS SHORT TO 5 VOLTS, go to next step.

7) Turn ignition off and wait 2 minutes. Disconnect Airbag Control Module (ACM). Turn ignition on. If scan tool does not display BUS SHORT TO 5 VOLTS, replace ACM. If scan tool displays BUS SHORT TO 5 VOLTS, go to next step.

8) Ensure all previously disconnected modules are still disconnected. Disconnect scan tool from DLC. Using voltmeter, measure voltage between ground and terminal No. 3 (Violet/Brown wire) on DLC connector. If voltage is more than 4 volts, repair Violet/Brown wire for short to voltage. If voltage is 4 volts or less, go to next step.

9) Measure voltage between ground and terminal No. 11 (White/Black wire) on DLC connector. If voltage is more than 4 volts, repair White/Black wire for short to voltage. If voltage is less than 4 volts, replace scan tool cable or scan tool as necessary.

10) Turn ignition off. Measure resistance between terminals No. 4 (Light Green/White wire) and 7 (Violet/Brown wire) on TCM harness connector. If resistance is less than 100 ohms, repair shorted to Violet/Brown wire. If resistance is 100 ohms or greater, go to next step.

11) Measure resistance between terminals No. 4 (Light Green/White wire) and 6 (White/Black wire) on TCM harness connector. If resistance is less than 100 ohms, repair shorted to White/Black wire. If resistance is 100 ohms or greater, go to next step.

12) Turn ignition off. Using ohmmeter, measure resistance between terminal C30 (Violet/Brown wire) on Powertrain Control Module (PCM) Gray connector and terminal A17 (Orange wire) on PCM Black connector. If resistance is less than 800 ohms, repair short between Violet/Brown wire and Orange wire. If resistance is 800 ohms or greater, go to next step.

13) Measure resistance between terminal C28 (White/Black wire) on PCM Gray connector and terminal A17 (Orange wire) on PCM Black connector. If resistance is less than 800 ohms, repair short between White/Black and Orange wire. If resistance is 800 ohms or greater, go to next step.

14) Turn ignition off. Using ohmmeter, measure resistance between terminal C30 (Violet/Brown wire) on Powertrain Control Module (PCM) Gray connector and terminal B31 (Violet/Orange wire) on PCM Black connector. If resistance is less than 800 ohms, repair short between Violet/Brown wire and Violet/Orange wire. If resistance is 800 ohms or greater, go to next step.

15) Measure resistance between terminal C28 (White/Black wire) on PCM Gray connector and terminal B31 (Violet/Orange wire) on PCM Black connector. If resistance is less than 800 ohms, repair short between White/Black and Violet/Orange wire. If resistance is 800 ohms or greater, replace PCM.

BUS SHORT TO BATTERY

1) Turn ignition off. Disconnect Powertrain Control Module (PCM). Turn ignition on. If scan tool does not display BUS SHORT TO BATTERY, go to step **13)**. If scan tool displays BUS SHORT TO BATTERY, go to next step.

2) Turn ignition off. Disconnect Transmission Control Module (TCM). Turn ignition on. If scan tool does not display BUS SHORT TO BATTERY, replace TCM. If scan tool displays BUS SHORT TO BATTERY, go to next step.

3) Turn ignition off. Disconnect Compass Mini-Trip Computer (CMTC). Turn ignition on. If scan tool does not display BUS SHORT TO BATTERY, replace CMTC. If scan tool displays BUS SHORT TO BATTERY, go to next step.

4) Turn ignition off. Disconnect Remote Keyless Entry (RKE) module. Turn ignition on. If scan tool does not display BUS SHORT TO BATTERY, replace RKE module. If scan tool displays BUS SHORT TO BATTERY, go to next step.

5) Turn ignition off. Disconnect instrument cluster. Turn ignition on. If scan tool does not display BUS SHORT TO BATTERY, replace instrument cluster. If scan tool displays BUS SHORT TO BATTERY, go to next step.

6) Turn ignition off and wait 2 minutes. Disconnect Airbag Control Module (ACM). Turn ignition on. If scan tool does not display BUS SHORT TO BATTERY, replace ACM. If scan tool displays BUS SHORT TO BATTERY, go to next step.

7) Turn ignition off. Disconnect Smart Key Immobilizer Module (SKIM). Turn ignition on. If scan tool does not display BUS SHORT TO BATTERY, replace instrument cluster. If scan tool displays BUS SHORT TO BATTERY, go to next step.

8) Ensure all previously disconnected modules are still disconnected. Disconnect scan tool from DLC. Using external voltmeter, measure voltage between ground and terminal No. 3 (Violet/Brown wire) on DLC connector. If voltage is more than .2 volt, repair Violet/Brown wire for short to voltage. If voltage is .2 volt or less, go to next step.

9) Measure voltage between ground and terminal No. 11 (White/Black wire) on DLC connector. If voltage is more than .2 volt, repair White/Black wire for short to voltage. If voltage is less than .2 volt, replace scan tool cable or scan tool as necessary.

10) Ensure ignition is off. Using ohmmeter, measure resistance between ground and terminal No. 6 (Black/Light Green wire) on instrument cluster left harness connector. If resistance is less than 5 ohms, go to next step. If resistance 5 ohms or greater, repair open Black/Light Green wire.

11) Measure resistance between ground and terminals No. 3 and 9 (Black wires) on RKE module harness connector. If resistance is less than 5 ohms, go to next step. If resistance 5 ohms or greater, repair open Black wire.

12) Measure resistance between ground and terminal No. 12 (Black wire) on CMTC harness connector. If resistance is less than 5 ohms, go to next step. If resistance 5 ohms or greater, repair open Black wire.

13) Measure resistance between ground and terminal A31 (Black/Tan wire) on PCM Black connector. If resistance is less than 10 ohms, go to next step. If resistance is 10 ohms or greater, repair open Black/Tan wire.

14) Measure resistance between ground and A32 (Black/Tan wire) on PCM Black connector. If resistance is less than 5 ohms, replace PCM. If resistance is 5 ohms or greater, repair open Black/Tan wire.

BUS SHORT TO GROUND

1) Ensure ignition is in RUN position. Backprobe a jumper wire between terminals No. 4 (Black/Light Blue wire) and 5 (Black/Tan wire) on DLC connector. If scan tool does not display BUS SHORT TO GROUND, repair open Black/Tan wire. If scan tool displays BUS SHORT TO GROUND, remove jumper wire and go to next step.

2) Turn ignition off. Disconnect Powertrain Control Module (PCM). Turn ignition on. If scan tool does not display BUS SHORT TO GROUND, replace PCM. If scan tool displays BUS SHORT TO GROUND, go to next step.

3) Turn ignition off. Disconnect Transmission Control Module (TCM). Turn ignition on. If scan tool does not display BUS SHORT TO GROUND, replace TCM. If scan tool displays BUS SHORT TO GROUND, go to next step.

4) Turn ignition off. Disconnect Compass Mini-Trip Module (CMTC). Turn ignition on. If scan tool does not display BUS SHORT TO GROUND, replace CMTC. If scan tool displays BUS SHORT TO GROUND, go to next step.

5) Turn ignition off. Disconnect Remote Keyless Entry (RKE) module. Turn ignition on. If scan tool does not display BUS SHORT TO GROUND, replace RKE module. If scan tool displays BUS SHORT TO GROUND, go to next step.

6) Turn ignition off. Disconnect Smart Key Immobilizer Module (SKIM). Turn ignition on. If scan tool does not display BUS SHORT TO GROUND, replace SKIM. If scan tool displays BUS SHORT TO GROUND, go to next step.

7) Turn ignition off and wait 2 minutes. Disconnect Air Bag System Control Module (ABSCM). ABSCM is located under center console. Turn ignition on. If scan tool does not display BUS SHORT TO GROUND, replace ABSCM. If scan tool displays BUS SHORT TO GROUND, go to next step.

8) Ensure all previously disconnected modules are still disconnected. Turn ignition off. Disconnect instrument cluster. Turn ignition on. Disconnect scan tool from DLC. Using external ohmmeter, measure resistance between ground and terminal No. 3 (Violet/Brown wire) on DLC connector. If resistance is less than 700 ohms, repair Violet/Brown wire for short to ground. If resistance is 700 ohms or greater, go to next step.

9) Measure resistance between ground and terminal No. 11 (White/Black wire) on DLC connector. If resistance is less than 700 ohms, repair White/Black wire for short to ground. If resistance is 700 ohms or greater, replace instrument cluster.

VERIFICATION TEST: VER-2A

Body Verification Test – 1) Reconnect all previously disconnected components and connectors. If BCM was replaced, turn ignition on for at least 15 seconds.

2) Ensure ignition is on. Erase all DTCs using scan tool. Turn ignition off and wait 5 seconds. Turn ignition on and fully operate system that was malfunctioning.

3) If system is not operating properly, go to SYSTEM TESTS. Using scan tool, read Body DTCs. If any DTCs are present, go to SYSTEM TESTS. If no DTCs are present, system is operating correctly and customer's complaint cannot be duplicated, repair is complete.

SYSTEM TESTS

NOTE: For connector terminal identification, component location and wiring diagrams, see BODY CONTROL COMPUTER INTRODUCTION article. Perform appropriate VERIFICATION TEST after each repair. See VERIFICATION TESTS.

IDENTIFYING VEHICLE COMMUNICATION PROBLEMS

Battery must be fully charged before proceeding. Connect scan tool to Data Link Connector (DLC) to retrieve messages. Ensure ground circuit has continuity at terminal No. 4 on DLC. Ensure 12 volts exists at terminal No. 16 on DLC. See following list of vehicle communication symptoms and scan tool fault messages. Proceed to appropriate test. Always turn ignition off prior to disconnecting any module connector.

- BATTERY IOD DISCONNECT AT BCM
- BCM EEPROM CHECKSUM FAILURE
- BCM FLASH CHECKSUM FAILURE
- BCM J1850 BUS MESSAGE FAULTS – MESSAGES NOT RECEIVED
- BUS +/- SIGNAL OPEN FROM BCM
- BCM MATURED FAULT PRESENT
- DDM MESSAGE NOT RECEIVED
- BUS +/- SIGNALS OPEN FROM DDM
- MIC MESSAGE NOT RECEIVED BY BCM
- PCM MESSAGE NOT RECEIVED BY BCM
- PDM MESSAGE NOT RECEIVED BY BCM
- BUS +/- SIGNALS OPEN FROM PDM
- BUS +/- SIGNALS OPEN FROM ELECTRONIC VEHICLE INFORMATION CENTER
- BUS +/- SIGNALS OPEN FROM INSTRUMENT CLUSTER
- BUS +/- SIGNALS OPEN FROM SENTRY KEY IMMOBILIZER MODULE (SKIM)
- COMPLETE PCI BUS FAILURE
- NO RESPONSE FROM ACM
- NO RESPONSE FROM CAB CONTROLLER
- NO RESPONSE FROM PCM (PCI BUS)
- NO RESPONSE FROM PCM (SCI BUS)
- NO RESPONSE FROM TCM
- PCI BUS SHORT TO BATTERY
- PCI BUS SHORT TO GROUND

BATTERY IOD DISCONNECT AT BCM

1) Ensure scan tool is connected to DLC. Turn ignition on. Using scan tool, erase BCM DTCs. Turn ignition off, then on. Read DTCs. If scan tool displays BATTERY IOD DISCONNECT AT BCM, go to next step. If scan tool does not display BATTERY IOD DISCONNECT AT BCM, test is complete.
2) Remove and inspect Power Distribution Center (PDC) fuse No. 15. If fuse is okay, go to next step. If fuse is blown, replace fuse No. 15.
3) Using voltmeter, measure voltage between ground and fused B+ on junction block fuse No. 7. If voltage is greater than 10 volts, go to next step. If voltage is 10 volts or less, repair open Pink/White wire between junction block and PDC.
4) Remove and inspect junction block fuse No. 7. If fuse is okay, go to next step. If fuse is blown, go to step **7)**.
5) Ensure voltage is present at junction block fuse No. 7. Turn ignition off. Disconnect negative battery cable. Remove Body Control Module (BCM) from back of junction block. Reconnect battery negative cable. Turn ignition on. Measure voltage between ground and terminal No. 26 on junction block internal BCM connector. If voltage is greater than 10 volts, go to next step. If voltage is 10 volts or less, replace junction block.
6) Using scan tool, select VTSS, then MISCELLANEOUS. Check status of alarm. Enable alarm as necessary. If alarm is already armed, replace BCM.
7) Turn ignition off. Remove junction block fuse No. 7. Using voltmeter, measure voltage between ground and fused B+ terminal on fuse No. 7.

If resistance is less than 5 ohms, repair fused B+ circuit for short to ground. If resistance is 5 ohms or greater, replace defective fuse.

BCM EEPROM CHECKSUM FAILURE

Ensure scan tool is connected to DLC. Turn ignition on. Using scan tool, erase BCM DTCs. Turn ignition off, then on. Read DTCs. If scan tool displays BCM EEPROM CHECKSUM FAILURE, reflash or replace BCM. If scan tool does not display BCM EEPROM CHECKSUM FAILURE, test is complete.

BCM FLASH CHECKSUM FAILURE

Ensure scan tool is connected to DLC. Turn ignition on. Using scan tool, erase BCM DTCs. Turn ignition off, then on. Read DTCs. If scan tool displays BCM FLASH CHECKSUM FAILURE, reflash or replace BCM. If scan tool does not display BCM FLASH CHECKSUM FAILURE, test is complete.

BCM J1850 BUS MESSAGE FAULTS - MESSAGES NOT RECEIVED &/OR BUS +/- SIGNAL OPEN FROM BCM

1) Turn ignition on. Using scan tool, select PASSIVE RESTRAINTS, then select AIRBAG. Monitor scan tool display. Select ANTI-LOCK BRAKES. If scan tool displays version and/or part number for either module, go to next step. If scan tool does not display version and/or part number for either module, go to COMPLETE PCI BUS FAILURE.
2) Remove and inspect junction block fuse No. 22. If fuse is okay, go to next step. If fuse is blown, go to step **11)**.
3) Remove and inspect junction block fuse No. 29. If fuse is okay, go to next step. If fuse is blown, go to step **8)**.
4) Turn ignition on. Using voltmeter, backprobe BCM C1 connector. Measure voltage between ground and terminals No. 1 (Black/Orange wire), 14 (Black/Orange wire) and 25 (Black wire). If voltage is present on any circuit, repair suspect open circuit. If no voltage is present on all circuits, go to next step.
5) Turn ignition off. Disconnect negative battery cable. Remove BCM from rear of junction block. Reconnect battery negative cable. Turn ignition on. Measure voltage between ground and terminal No. 25 on junction block internal BCM connector. If voltage is greater than 10 volts, reconnect all components and go to next step. If voltage is 10 volts or less, replace junction block.
6) Connect Scope Input Cable (CH 7058) to channel No. 1 connector on scan tool. Connect Red and Black test probe cable with Probe Adapter (CH7062) to scope input cable. Select DRB STANDALONE. Select LAB SCOPE, then LIVE. Select 12 VOLT SQUARE WAVE. Press F2 for scope. Press F2 and use down arrow to set voltage range to 20 volts. Press F2. Connect Black lead to chassis ground. Backprobe Red lead to terminal No. 15 (Yellow/Violet/White wire) on BCM C1 harness connector. Turn ignition on. If voltage displayed on scan tool lab scope pluses from zero to about 7.5 volts, replace BCM. If voltage is zero volts, repair open Yellow/Violet/White wire.
7) Turn ignition off. Disconnect negative battery cable. Remove BCM from rear of junction block. Reconnect battery negative cable. Turn ignition on. Measure voltage between ground and terminal No. 5 on junction block internal BCM connector. If voltage is greater than 10 volts, replace BCM. If voltage is 10 volts or less, replace junction block.
8) Turn ignition on. Using voltmeter, backprobe BCM C1 connector. Measure voltage between ground and terminals No. 1 (Black/Orange wire), 14 (Black/Orange wire) and 25 (Black wire). If voltage is present on any circuit, repair suspect open circuit. If no voltage is present on all circuits, go to next step.
9) Turn ignition off. Disconnect negative battery cable. Remove BCM from rear of junction block. Reconnect battery negative cable. Measure resistance between ground and fused ignition switch output terminal on junction block fuse No. 29 socket. If resistance is less than 5 ohms, repair fused ignition switch output circuit for short to ground. If resistance is 5 ohms or greater, go to next step.
10) Disconnect negative battery cable. Connect BCM to rear of junction block. Reconnect battery negative cable. Measure resistance between

ground and fused ignition switch output terminal on junction block fuse No. 29 socket. If resistance is less than 5 ohms, replace BCM. If resistance is 5 ohms or greater, replace defective fuse.

11) Remove and inspect junction block fuse No. 29. If fuse is okay, go to next step. If fuse is blown, go to step **13**).

12) Turn ignition on. Using voltmeter, backprobe BCM C1 connector. Measure voltage between ground and terminals No. 1 (Black/Orange wire), 14 (Black/Orange wire) and 25 (Black wire). If voltage is present on any circuit, repair suspect open circuit. If no voltage is present on all circuits, go to next step.

13) Turn ignition off. Disconnect negative battery cable. Remove BCM from rear of junction block. Reconnect battery negative cable. Measure resistance between ground and terminal No. 5 on junction block internal BCM connector. If resistance is less than 5 ohms, replace junction block. If resistance is 5 ohms or greater, go to next step.

14) Disconnect negative battery cable. Connect BCM to rear of junction block. Reconnect battery negative cable. Measure resistance between ground and fused ignition switch output terminal on junction block fuse No. 22 socket. If resistance is less than 5 ohms, replace BCM. If resistance is 5 ohms or greater, replace defective fuse.

BCM MATURED FAULT PRESENT

1) Ensure scan tool is connected to DLC. Turn ignition on. Using scan tool, erase BCM DTCs. Turn ignition off, then on. Read DTCs. If scan tool displays BCM EEPROM CHECKSUM FAILURE, reflash or replace BCM. If scan tool does not display BCM EEPROM CHECKSUM FAILURE, go to next step.

2) Ensure scan tool is connected to DLC. Turn ignition on. Using scan tool, erase BCM DTCs. Turn ignition off, then on. Read DTCs. If scan tool displays BCM FLASH CHECKSUM FAILURE, reflash or replace BCM. If scan tool does not display BCM FLASH CHECKSUM FAILURE, go to next step.

3) Using scan tool, select ELECTROMECHANICAL INSTRUMENT CLUSTER. If scan tool displays MIC module version, go to next step. If scan tool does not display MIC module version, go to BUS +/- SIGNALS OPEN FROM INSTRUMENT CLUSTER.

4) Using scan tool, select BODY CONTROLLER, then PCM SYSTEM TEST. If scan tool displays PCM ACTIVE ON THE BUS, test is complete. If scan tool does not display PCM ACTIVE ON THE BUS, go to NO RESPONSE FROM PCM (PCI BUS).

DDM MESSAGE NOT RECEIVED &/OR BUS +/- SIGNALS OPEN FROM DDM

1) Remove Power Distribution Center (PDC) fuse No. 12. Measure voltage at B+ terminal on fuse No. 12 socket. If voltage is greater than 10 volts, go to next step. If voltage is 10 volts or less, repair open B+ circuit.

2) Remove and inspect PDC No. 12. If fuse is okay, go to step **7**). If fuse is blown, go to next step.

3) Using ohmmeter, measure resistance between ground and fused B+ terminal on PDC fuse No. 12 socket. If resistance is less than 5 ohms, go to next step. If resistance is 5 ohms or greater, replace defective fuse.

4) Remove PDC fuse No. 12. Disconnect DDM C1 connector. Measure resistance between ground and fused B+ terminal on PDC fuse No. 12 socket. If resistance is less than 5 ohms, repair fused B+ circuit for short to ground. If resistance is 5 ohms or greater, go to next step.

5) Connect Scope Input Cable (CH 7058) to channel No. 1 connector on scan tool. Connect Red and Black test probe cable with Probe Adapter (CH7062) to scope input cable. Select DRB STANDALONE. Select LAB SCOPE, then LIVE. Select 12 VOLT SQUARE WAVE. Press F2 for scope. Press F2 and use down arrow to set voltage range to 20 volts. Press F2. Connect Black lead to chassis ground. Backprobe Red lead to terminal No. 9 (Yellow/Violet wire) on DDM C1 harness connector. Turn ignition on. If voltage displayed on scan tool lab scope pluses from zero to about 7.5 volts, go to next step. If voltage is zero volts, repair open Yellow/Violet wire.

6) Disconnect DDM C1 connector. Using ohmmeter, measure resistance between ground and terminal No. 4 (Black wire) on C1 harness connector. If resistance is less than 5 ohms, replace DDM. If resistance is 5 ohms or greater, repair open Black wire.

7) Connect Scope Input Cable (CH 7058) to channel No. 1 connector on scan tool. Connect Red and Black test probe cable with Probe Adapter (CH7062) to scope input cable. Select DRB STANDALONE. Select LAB SCOPE, then LIVE. Select 12 VOLT SQUARE WAVE. Press F2 for scope. Press F2 and use down arrow to set voltage range to 20 volts. Press F2. Connect Black lead to chassis ground. Backprobe Red lead to terminal No. 9 (Yellow/Violet wire) on DDM C1 harness connector. Turn ignition on. If voltage displayed on scan tool lab scope pluses from zero to about 7.5 volts, go to next step. If voltage is zero volts, repair open Yellow/Violet wire.

8) Disconnect DDM C1 connector. Using ohmmeter, measure resistance between ground and terminal No. 4 (Black wire) on C1 harness connector. If resistance is less than 5 ohms, go to next step. If resistance is 5 ohms or greater, repair open Black wire.

9) Using voltmeter, measure voltage between ground and terminal No. 1 (Tan/Light Blue wire) on DDM C1 harness connector. If voltage is greater than 10 volts, replace DDM. If voltage is 10 volts or less, repair open Tan/Light Blue wire.

MIC MESSAGE NOT RECEIVED BY BCM

1) Remove and inspect junction block fuse No. 22. If fuse is okay, go to next step. If fuse is blown, go to step **6**).

2) Using scan tool, select ELECTROMECHANICAL INSTRUMENT CLUSTER. If scan tool displays MIC module version, go to next step. If scan tool does not display MIC module version, go to BUS +/- SIGNALS OPEN FROM INSTRUMENT CLUSTER.

3) Turn ignition off. Disconnect instrument cluster connector. Using ohmmeter, measure resistance between ground and terminals No. 9 (Black wire) and No. 11 (Black/Orange wire) on instrument cluster harness connector. If resistance is less than 5 ohms for both circuits, go to next step. If resistance is 5 ohms or greater on either circuit, repair open suspect circuit.

4) Connect Scope Input Cable (CH 7058) to channel No. 1 connector on scan tool. Connect Red and Black test probe cable with Probe Adapter (CH7062) to scope input cable. Select DRB STANDALONE. Select LAB SCOPE, then LIVE. Select 12 VOLT SQUARE WAVE. Press F2 for scope. Press F2 and use down arrow to set voltage range to 20 volts. Press F2. Connect Black lead to chassis ground. Backprobe Red lead to terminal No. 10 (Yellow/Violet/Red wire) on instrument cluster harness connector. Turn ignition on. If voltage displayed on scan tool lab scope pluses from zero to about 7.5 volts, go to next step. If voltage is zero volts, repair open Yellow/Violet/Red wire.

5) Turn ignition off. Remove junction block fuse No. 22. Measure resistance between ground and terminal No. 7 (Dark Blue/White wire) on instrument cluster harness connector. If resistance is less than 5 ohms, repair Dark Blue/White wire for short to ground. If resistance is 5 ohms or greater, go to step **11**).

6) Replace junction block fuse No. 22 with known good fuse. Turn ignition on, then off. Remove and inspect junction block fuse No. 22. If fuse is okay, test is complete. If fuse is blown, go to next step.

7) Using scan tool, select ELECTROMECHANICAL INSTRUMENT CLUSTER. If scan tool displays MIC module version, go to next step. If scan tool does not display MIC module version, go to BUS +/- SIGNALS OPEN FROM INSTRUMENT CLUSTER.

8) Turn ignition off. Disconnect instrument cluster connector. Using ohmmeter, measure resistance between ground and terminals No. 9 (Black wire) and No. 11 (Black/Orange wire) on instrument cluster harness connector. If resistance is less than 5 ohms for both circuits, go to next step. If resistance is 5 ohms or greater on either circuit, repair open suspect circuit.

9) Remove junction block fuse No. 22. Ensure instrument cluster connector is disconnected. Measure resistance between ground and terminal No. 7 (Dark Blue/White wire) on instrument cluster harness connector. If resistance is less than 5 ohms, repair Dark Blue/White wire for short to ground. If resistance is 5 ohms or greater, go to next step.

10) Connect Scope Input Cable (CH 7058) to channel No. 1 connector on scan tool. Connect Red and Black test probe cable with Probe

Adapter (CH7062) to scope input cable. Select DRB STANDALONE. Select LAB SCOPE, then LIVE. Select 12 VOLT SQUARE WAVE. Press F2 for scope. Press F2 and use down arrow to set voltage range to 20 volts. Press F2. Connect Black lead to chassis ground. Backprobe Red lead to terminal No. 10 (Yellow/Violet/Red wire) on instrument cluster harness connector. Turn ignition on. If voltage displayed on scan tool lab scope pluses from zero to about 7.5 volts, go to next step. If voltage is zero volts, repair open Yellow/Violet/Red wire.

11) Ensure instrument cluster connector is disconnected. Turn ignition on. Measure voltage between ground and terminal No. 7 (Dark Blue/White wire) on instrument cluster harness connector. If voltage is greater than 10.5 volts, replace instrument cluster circuit board. If voltage is 10.5 volts or less, repair open Dark Blue/White wire.

PCM MESSAGE NOT RECEIVED BY BCM

Using scan tool, select BODY CONTROLLER, then PCM SYSTEM TEST. If scan tool displays PCM ACTIVE ON THE BUS, test is complete. If scan tool does not display PCM ACTIVE ON THE BUS, go to NO RESPONSE FROM PCM (PCI BUS).

PDM MESSAGE NOT RECEIVED TO BCM &/OR BUS +/- SIGNALS OPEN FROM PDM

1) Remove and inspect Power Distribution Center (PDC) fuse No. 12. If fuse is okay, go to step **7)**. If fuse is open, go to next step.

2) Turn ignition off. Using ohmmeter, measure resistance between ground and fused B+ terminal on PDC fuse No. 12 socket. If resistance is less than 5 ohms, go to next step. If fuse is 5 ohms or greater, replace defective fuse.

3) Remove PDC fuse No. 12. Disconnect PDM C1 connector. Measure resistance between ground and fused B+ terminal on PDC fuse No. 12 socket. If resistance is less than 5 ohms, repair fused B+ circuit for short to ground. If fuse is 5 ohms or greater, go to next step.

4) Using voltmeter, measure voltage between ground and B+ terminal on PDC fuse No. 12. If voltage is less than 10 volts, repair open B+ circuit. If voltage is greater than 10 volts, go to next step.

5) Ensure PDM connector is disconnected. Using ohmmeter, measure resistance between ground and terminal No. 4 (Black wire) on PDM harness connector. If resistance is less than 5 ohms, replace PDM. If resistance is 5 ohms or greater, repair open Black wire.

6) Remove PDC fuse No. 12. Using voltmeter, measure voltage between ground and B+ terminal on PDC fuse No. 12. If voltage is less than 10 volts, repair open B+ circuit. If voltage is greater than 10 volts, go to next step.

7) Disconnect PDM C1 connector. Using ohmmeter, measure resistance between ground and terminal No. 4 (Black wire) on PDM harness connector. If resistance is less than 5 ohms, replace PDM. If resistance is 5 ohms or greater, repair open Black wire.

8) Connect Scope Input Cable (CH 7058) to channel No. 1 connector on scan tool. Connect Red and Black test probe cable with Probe Adapter (CH7062) to scope input cable. Select DRB STANDALONE. Select LAB SCOPE, then LIVE. Select 12 VOLT SQUARE WAVE. Press F2 for scope. Press F2 and use down arrow to set voltage range to 20 volts. Press F2. Connect Black lead to chassis ground. Backprobe Red lead to terminal No. 9 (Yellow/Violet wire) on PDM C1 harness connector. Turn ignition on. If voltage displayed on scan tool lab scope pluses from zero to about 7.5 volts, go to next step. If voltage is zero volts, repair open Yellow/Violet wire.

9) Ensure PDC fuse No. 12 is installed. Using voltmeter, measure voltage between ground and terminal No. 1 (Tan/Black wire) on PDM harness connector. If voltage is less than 10 volts, repair open Tan/Black wire. If voltage is greater than 10 volts, replace PDM.

BUS +/- SIGNALS OPEN FROM ELECTRONIC VEHICLE INFORMATION CENTER

1) Disconnect Vehicle Information Center (VIC) connector. Turn ignition on. Using voltmeter, measure voltage between ground and terminal No. 5 (Dark Blue/White wire) on VIC harness connector. If voltage is less than 10 volts, repair open Dark Blue/White wire. If voltage is greater than 10 volts, go to next step.

2) Measure voltage between ground and terminal No. 3 (Pink wire) on VIC harness connector. If voltage is less than 10 volts, repair open Pink wire. If voltage is greater than 10 volts, go to next step.

3) Turn ignition off. Disconnect negative battery cable. Using ohmmeter, measure resistance between ground and terminal No. 4 (Black/Orange wire) on VIC harness connector. If resistance is less than 2 ohms, go to next step. If resistance is 2 ohms or greater, repair open Black/Orange wire.

4) Connect Scope Input Cable (CH 7058) to channel No. 1 connector on scan tool. Connect Red and Black test probe cable with Probe Adapter (CH7062) to scope input cable. Select DRB STANDALONE. Select LAB SCOPE, then LIVE. Select 12 VOLT SQUARE WAVE. Press F2 for scope. Press F2 and use down arrow to set voltage range to 20 volts. Press F2. Connect Black lead to chassis ground. Backprobe Red lead to terminal No. 2 (Violet/Yellow wire) on VIC harness connector. Turn ignition on. If voltage displayed on scan tool lab scope pluses from zero to about 7.5 volts, replace VIC. If voltage is zero volts, repair open Violet/Yellow wire.

BUS +/- SIGNALS OPEN FROM INSTRUMENT CLUSTER

1) Remove and inspect junction block fuse No. 22. If fuse is okay, go to next step. If fuse is blown, go to step **5)**.

2) Turn ignition off. Disconnect instrument cluster connector. Using ohmmeter, measure resistance between ground and terminals No. 9 (Black wire) and No. 11 (Black/Orange wire) on instrument cluster harness connector. If resistance is less than 5 ohms for both circuits, go to next step. If resistance is 5 ohms or greater on either circuit, repair open suspect circuit.

3) Connect Scope Input Cable (CH 7058) to channel No. 1 connector on scan tool. Connect Red and Black test probe cable with Probe Adapter (CH7062) to scope input cable. Select DRB STANDALONE. Select LAB SCOPE, then LIVE. Select 12 VOLT SQUARE WAVE. Press F2 for scope. Press F2 and use down arrow to set voltage range to 20 volts. Press F2. Connect Black lead to chassis ground. Backprobe Red lead to terminal No. 10 (Yellow/Violet/Red wire) on instrument cluster harness connector. Turn ignition on. If voltage displayed on scan tool lab scope pluses from zero to about 7.5 volts, go to next step. If voltage is zero volts, repair open Yellow/Violet/Red wire.

4) Turn ignition off. Remove junction block fuse No. 22. Measure resistance between ground and terminal No. 7 (Dark Blue/White wire) on instrument cluster harness connector. If resistance is less than 5 ohms, repair Dark Blue/White wire for short to ground. If resistance is 5 ohms or greater, go to step **9)**.

5) Replace junction block fuse No. 22 with known good fuse. Turn ignition on, then off. Remove and inspect junction block fuse No. 22. If fuse is okay, test is complete. If fuse is blown, go to next step.

6) Turn ignition off. Using ohmmeter, measure resistance between ground and terminals No. 9 (Black wire) and No. 11 (Black/Orange wire) on instrument cluster harness connector. If resistance is less than 5 ohms for both circuits, go to next step. If resistance is 5 ohms or greater on either circuit, repair open suspect circuit.

7) Turn ignition off. Remove junction block fuse No. 22. Measure resistance between ground and terminal No. 7 (Dark Blue/White wire) on instrument cluster harness connector. If resistance is less than 5 ohms, repair Dark Blue/White wire for short to ground. Replace fuse No. 22. If resistance is 5 ohms or greater, install fuse No. 22 and go to next step.

8) Connect Scope Input Cable (CH 7058) to channel No. 1 connector on scan tool. Connect Red and Black test probe cable with Probe Adapter (CH7062) to scope input cable. Select DRB STANDALONE. Select LAB SCOPE, then LIVE. Select 12 VOLT SQUARE WAVE. Press F2 for scope. Press F2 and use down arrow to set voltage range to 20 volts. Press F2. Connect Black lead to chassis ground. Backprobe Red lead to terminal No. 10 (Yellow/Violet/Red wire) on instrument cluster harness connector. Turn ignition on. If voltage displayed on scan tool lab scope pluses from zero to about 7.5 volts, go to next step. If voltage is zero volts, repair open Yellow/Violet/Red wire.

9) Ensure instrument cluster connector is disconnected. Turn ignition on. Measure voltage between ground and terminal No. 7 (Dark Blue/White wire) on instrument cluster harness connector. If voltage is greater than 10.5 volts, replace instrument cluster circuit board. If voltage is 10.5 volts or less, repair open Dark Blue/White wire.

BUS +/- SIGNALS OPEN FROM SENTRY KEY IMMOBILIZER MODULE (SKIM)

1) Turn ignition on. Using scan tool, select BODY, select BODY COMPUTER. If scan tool displays NO RESPONSE FROM BCM, go to next step. If scan tool does not display NO RESPONSE FROM BCM, go to step **16**).

2) Using scan tool, select PASSIVE RESTRAINTS, then select AIRBAG. Monitor scan tool display. Select ANTI-LOCK BRAKES. If scan tool displays version and/or part number for either module, go to next step. If scan tool does not display version and/or part number for either module, go to COMPLETE PCI BUS FAILURE.

3) Remove and inspect junction block fuse No. 22. If fuse is blown, go to step **12**). If fuse is okay, go to next step.

4) Remove and inspect junction block fuse No. 29. If fuse is blown, go to step **9**). If fuse is okay, go to next step.

5) Turn ignition on. Using voltmeter, backprobe BCM C1 connector. Measure voltage between ground and terminals No. 1 (Black/Orange wire), No. 14 (Black/Orange wire) and No. 25 (Black wire). If voltage is present on any circuit, repair suspect open circuit. If no voltage is present on all circuits, go to next step.

6) Turn ignition off. Disconnect negative battery cable. Remove BCM from rear of junction block. Reconnect battery negative cable. Turn ignition on. Measure voltage between ground and terminal No. 25 on junction block internal BCM connector. If voltage is greater than 10 volts, reconnect all components and go to next step. If voltage is 10 volts or less, replace junction block.

7) Connect Scope Input Cable (CH 7058) to channel No. 1 connector on scan tool. Connect Red and Black test probe cable with Probe Adapter (CH7062) to scope input cable. Select DRB STANDALONE. Select LAB SCOPE, then LIVE. Select 12 VOLT SQUARE WAVE. Press F2 for scope. Press F2 and use down arrow to set voltage range to 20 volts. Press F2. Connect Black lead to chassis ground. Backprobe Red lead to terminal No. 15 (Yellow/Violet/White wire) on BCM C1 harness connector. Turn ignition on. If voltage displayed on scan tool lab scope pluses from zero to about 7.5 volts, replace BCM. If voltage is zero volts, repair open Yellow/Violet/White wire.

8) Turn ignition off. Disconnect negative battery cable. Remove BCM from rear of junction block. Reconnect battery negative cable. Turn ignition on. Measure voltage between ground and terminal No. 5 on junction block internal BCM connector. If voltage is greater than 10 volts, replace BCM. If voltage is 10 volts or less, replace junction block.

9) Turn ignition on. Using voltmeter, backprobe BCM C1 connector. Measure voltage between ground and terminals No. 1 (Black/Orange wire), No. 14 (Black/Orange wire) and No. 25 (Black wire). If voltage is present on any circuit, repair suspect open circuit. If no voltage is present on all circuits, go to next step.

10) Turn ignition off. Disconnect negative battery cable. Remove BCM from rear of junction block. Reconnect battery negative cable. Measure resistance between ground and fused ignition switch output terminal on junction block fuse No. 29 socket. If resistance is less than 5 ohms, repair fused ignition switch output circuit for short to ground. If resistance is 5 ohms or greater, go to next step.

11) Disconnect negative battery cable. Connect BCM to rear of junction block. Reconnect battery negative cable. Measure resistance between ground and fused ignition switch output terminal on junction block fuse No. 29 socket. If resistance is less than 5 ohms, replace BCM. If resistance is 5 ohms or greater, replace defective fuse.

12) Remove and inspect junction block fuse No. 29. If fuse is blown, go to step **14**). If fuse is okay, go to next step.

13) Turn ignition on. Using voltmeter, backprobe BCM C1 connector. Measure voltage between ground and terminals No. 1 (Black/Orange wire), No. 14 (Black/Orange wire) and No. 25 (Black wire). If voltage is

present on any circuit, repair suspect open circuit. If no voltage is present on all circuits, go to next step.

14) Turn ignition off. Disconnect negative battery cable. Remove BCM from rear of junction block. Reconnect battery negative cable. Measure resistance between ground and terminal No. 5 on junction block internal BCM connector. If resistance is less than 5 ohms, replace junction block. If resistance is 5 ohms or greater, go to next step.

15) Disconnect negative battery cable. Connect BCM to rear of junction block. Reconnect battery negative cable. Measure resistance between ground and fused ignition switch output terminal on junction block fuse No. 22 socket. If resistance is less than 5 ohms, replace BCM. If resistance is 5 ohms or greater, replace defective fuse.

16) Inspect junction block fuses No. 7 and 22. If fuse No. 7 is blown, go to next step. If fuse No. 22 is blown, go to step **23**). If both fuses are okay, go to step **18**).

17) Turn ignition off. Disconnect negative battery cable. Disconnect SKIM connector. Using ohmmeter, measure resistance between ground and terminal No. 1 (Pink wire) on SKIM harness connector. If resistance is less than 5 ohms, repair Pink wire for short to ground. Replace defective fuse. If resistance is 5 ohms or greater, replace defective fuse.

18) Measure resistance between ground and terminal No. 2 (Black/Orange wire) on SKIM harness connector. If resistance is less than 5 ohms, go to next step. If resistance is 5 ohms or greater, repair open Black/Orange wire.

19) Ensure battery is connected. Using voltmeter, measure voltage between ground and terminal No. 1 (Pink wire) on SKIM harness connector. If voltage is 10 volts or less, repair open Pink wire. If voltage is greater than 10 volts, go to next step.

20) Remove and inspect junction block fuse No. 22. If fuse is blown, go to step **23**). If fuse is okay, go to next step.

21) Turn ignition on. Using voltmeter, measure voltage between ground and terminal No. 3 (Dark Blue/White wire) on SKIM harness connector. If voltage is 10 volts or less, repair open Dark Blue/White wire. If voltage is greater than 10 volts, go to next step.

22) Ensure SKIM connector is disconnected. Connect Scope Input Cable (CH 7058) to channel No. 1 connector on scan tool. Connect Red and Black test probe cable with Probe Adapter (CH7062) to scope input cable. Select DRB STANDALONE. Select LAB SCOPE, then LIVE. Select 12 VOLT SQUARE WAVE. Press F2 for scope. Press F2 and use down arrow to set voltage range to 20 volts. Press F2. Connect Black lead to chassis ground. Backprobe Red lead to terminal No. 5 (Yellow/Violet/Brown wire) on SKIM harness connector. Turn ignition on. If voltage displayed on scan tool lab scope pluses from zero to about 7.5 volts, replace BCM. If voltage is zero volts, repair open Yellow/Violet/Brown wire.

23) Turn ignition off. Using ohmmeter, measure resistance between ground and terminal No. 3 (Dark Blue/White wire) on SKIM harness connector. If resistance is less than 5 ohms, repair Dark Blue/White wire for short to ground. Replace fuse No. 22. If resistance is 5 ohms or greater, replace fuse No. 22.

COMPLETE PCI BUS FAILURE

1) Connect Breakout Box (J-1962) to DLC. Connect scan tool to breakout box. Connect Scope Input Cable (CH 7058) to channel No. 1 connector on scan tool. Connect Red and Black test probe cable with Probe Adapter (CH7062) to scope input cable. Select DRB STANDALONE. Select LAB SCOPE, then LIVE. Select 12 VOLT SQUARE WAVE. Press F2 for scope. Press F2 and use down arrow to set voltage range to 20 volts. Press F2. Connect Black lead to breakout box port No. 4. Connect Red lead to terminal No. 2. Turn ignition on. If voltage displayed on scan tool lab scope pluses from zero to about 7.5 volts, go to next step. If voltage is zero volts, go to PCI BUS SHORT TO GROUND. If a constant voltage is displayed, go to PCI BUS SHORT TO BATTERY.

2) Remove driver's side knee blocker below steering column. Inspect junction port connector. Splice connector should be fully seated. Correct as needed. If splice is correctly seated, go to next step.

3) Turn ignition off. Ensure breakout box is connected to DLC. Disconnect splice from junction port connector. Using ohmmeter, measure resistance of Yellow/Violet wire between terminal No. 2 on breakout box and terminal No. 9 on junction port. If resistance is less than 5 ohms, test is complete. If resistance is 5 ohms or greater, repair open Yellow/Violet wire.

NO RESPONSE FROM ACM

1) Turn igniton off. Disconnect battery and wait 2 minutes. Disconnect Airbag Control Module (ACM) connector. Using ohmmeter, measure resistance between ground and terminal No. 4 (Black/Orange wire) on ACM harness connector. If resistance is less than 5 ohms, go to next step. If resistance is 5 ohms or greater, repair open Black/Orange wire.
2) Measure resistance between ground and terminal No. 4 on ACM component connector. If resistance is less than 5 ohms, go to next step. If resistance is 5 ohms or greater, replace ACM.
3) Ensure ignition is off. Remove driver's side knee blocker below steering column. Disconnect junction port splice connector. Using ohmmeter, measure resistance of Yellow/Violet/Orange wire between terminal No. 21 on ACM harness connector and terminal No. 5 on junction port. If resistance is less than 5 ohms, go to next step. If resistance is 5 ohms or greater, repair open Yellow/Violet/Orange wire.
4) Ensure ACM connector is disconnected. Connect battery. Turn ignition on. Using voltmeter, measure voltage between ground and terminals No. 14 (Light Green/Yellow wire) and No. 15 (Dark Blue/Yellow wire) on ACM harness connector. Voltage should be greater than 10 volts on both circuits. If voltage is within specification, replace ACM. If voltage is not within specification on either circuit, repair suspect open circuit.

NO RESPONSE FROM CAB CONTROLLER

1) Using scan tool, select PASSIVE RESTRAINTS, then select AIRBAG. Monitor scan tool display. Select ANTI-LOCK BRAKES. If scan tool displays version and/or part number for either module, go to next step. If scan tool does not display version and/or part number for either module, go to COMPLETE PCI BUS FAILURE.
2) Remove and inspect junction block fuse No. 19. If fuse is blown, go to next step. If fuse is okay, go to step **6)**.
3) Visually inspect Dark Blue/Pink wire from Controller Anti-Lock Brake (CAB) to junction block. Ensure harness is not damaged or chafing against ground source. Repair as needed. If harness is okay, go to next step.
4) Turn ignition off. Remove junction block fuse No. 19. Disconnect CAB connector. Connect test light between 12 volts and terminal No. 4 (Dark Blue/Pink wire) on CAB harness connector. If test light is illuminated, repair Dark Blue/Pink wire for short to ground. If light is not illuminated, test is complete.
5) Ensure ignition is off. Remove driver's side knee blocker below steering column. Disconnect junction port splice connector. Using ohmmeter, measure resistance of Yellow/Violet wire between terminal No. 10 on CAB harness connector and terminal No. 2 on junction port. If resistance is less than 5 ohms, go to next step. If resistance is 5 ohms or greater, repair open Yellow/Violet/Orange wire.
6) Ensure junction block fuse No. 19 is removed. Measure resistance of Dark Blue/Pink wire between terminal No. 4 on CAB harness connector and fused ignition switch output terminal on fuse No. 19 socket. If resistance is less than 5 ohms, go to next step. If resistance is 5 ohms or greater, repair open Dark Blue/Pink wire.
7) Measure resistance between ground and terminals No. 8 and 24 (Black/Orange wires) on CAB harness connector. If resistance is less than 5 ohms for both circuits, replace CAB. If resistance is 5 ohms or greater on either circuit, repair suspect open circuit.

NO RESPONSE FROM PCM (PCI BUS)

1) Turn ignition on. Using scan tool, select BODY, then BCM. Determine if communication was able to be established. Select BODY, then DOOR MODULES. Determine if communication was able to be established. Select ANTI-LOCK BRAKES. Determine if communication was able to be established. Select BODY, then ELECTRO-MECHANICAL CLUS-TER. Determine if communication was able to be established. Select PASSIVE RESTRAINTS, then AIRBAG. Determine if communication

was able to be established. If communication is possible with all modules, go to next step. If communication cannot be established with one or more modules, go to COMPLETE PCI BUS FAILURE.
2) Using scan tool, read PCM DTCs. If scan tool cannot read PCM DTCs, go to NO RESPONSE FROM PCM (SCI BUS). Turn ignition off. Disconnect PCM connectors. Connect Scope Input Cable (CH 7058) to channel No. 1 connector on scan tool. Connect Red and Black test probe cable with Probe Adapter (CH7062) to scope input cable. Select DRB STANDALONE. Select LAB SCOPE, then LIVE. Select 12 VOLT SQUARE WAVE. Press F2 for scope. Press F2 and use down arrow to set voltage range to 20 volts. Press F2. Connect Black lead to terminal No. 31 (Black/White wire). Connect Red lead to terminal No. 30 (Yellow/Violet wire). Turn ignition on. If voltage displayed on scan tool lab scope pluses from zero to about 7.5 volts, replace PCM. If voltage is zero volts, repair open Yellow/Violet wire.

NO RESPONSE FROM PCM (SCI BUS)

1) Using scan tool, attempt to read DTCs. If ignition was on when NO RESPONSE message was displayed, go to next step. If ignition is not on, turn ignition on and attempt to read DTCs.
2) Substitute scan tool cable. Attempt to read DTCs. If NO RESPONSE is displayed, go to next step. If NO RESPONSE is not displayed, replace scan tool cable.
3) Turn ignition off. Using ohmmeter, measure resistance between ground and terminals No. 4 and 5 (Black/Orange wires) on DLC. If resistance is less than 5 ohms for both circuits, go to next step. If resistance is 5 ohms or greater on either circuit, repair open suspect circuit.
4) Disconnect PCM connectors. Disconnect scan tool from DLC. Using ohmmeter, measure resistance of Light Green/Dark Green wire between terminal No. 29 on PCM C3 harness connector and terminal No. 6 on DLC. If resistance is less than 5 ohms, go to next step. If resistance is 5 ohms or greater, repair open Light Green/Dark Green wire.
5) Using ohmmeter, measure resistance between ground and terminal No. 6 (Light Green/Dark Green wire) on DLC. If resistance is less than 5 ohms, repair open Light Green/Dark Green wire. If resistance is 5 ohms or greater, go to next step.
6) Measure resistance of Pink wire between terminal No. 27 on PCM C3 harness connector and terminal No. 7 on DLC. If resistance is less than 5 ohms, go to next step. If resistance is 5 ohms or greater, repair open Pink wire.
7) Measure resistance between ground and terminal No. 7 (Pink wire) on DLC. If resistance is less than 5 ohms, repair open Pink wire. If resistance is 5 ohms or greater, go to next step.
8) Connect scan tool to another vehicle. Turn ignition on. Using scan tool, read DTCs. If scan tool displays NO RESPONSE, replace scan tool. If scan tool does not display NO RESPONSE, replace PCM in original vehicle.

NO RESPONSE FROM TCM

Using scan tool, erase BCM DTCs. Turn ignition off, then on. Using scan tool, read TCM DTCs. If scan tool displays NO RESPONSE, replace TCM. If scan tool does not display NO RESPONSE, test is complete. Ensure applicable connectors are not damaged when taking voltage or resistance measurements.

PCI BUS SHORT TO BATTERY

NOTE: Additional DTCs will be set during following test. Any module connected to PCI bus may set a DTC when junction port splice is removed. Always reconnect junction port splice when testing is completed.

1) Remove driver's side knee blocker below steering column. Locate junction port connector. Remove splice connector from junction port connector. Turn ignition and all accessories on. Measure voltage between ground and terminal No. 8 (Yellow/Violet/White wire) on junction port connector. If voltage is greater than one volt, go to next step. If voltage is one volt or less, go to step **35)**.

2) Measure voltage between ground and terminal No. 4 (Yellow/Violet/Dark Blue wire) on junction port connector. If voltage is greater than one volt, go to next step. If voltage is one volt or less, go to step 9).

3) Ensure ignition and all accessories are on. Measure voltage between ground and terminal No. 2 (Yellow/Violet wire) on DLC. If voltage is present, repair Yellow/Violet wire for short to voltage. If no voltage is present, go to next step.

4) Turn ignition off. Measure voltage between ground and terminal No. 2 (Yellow/Violet/Brown wire) on junction port connector. If voltage is greater than one volt, go to next step if vehicle is equipped with Vehicle Information Center (VIC). If vehicle is not equipped with VIC, go to step 6). If voltage is one volt or less, go to step 8).

5) Ensure ignition is off. Disconnect VIC connector. Turn ignition and all accessories on. Measure voltage between ground and terminal No. 2 (Yellow/Violet/Brown wire) on junction port connector. If voltage is greater than one volt, replace VIC. If voltage is one volt or less, go to next step.

6) Turn ignition off. Disconnect Controller Anti-Lock Brake (CAB). Disconnect Driver's Door Module (DDM). Ensure VIC connector is disconnected. Disconnect Memory Seat Module (MSM). Ensure junction port splice connector is removed. Turn ignition and all accessories on. Measure voltage between ground and terminal No. 2 (Yellow/Violet/Brown wire) on junction port connector. If voltage is greater than one volt, repair Yellow/Violet/Brown wire for short to voltage. If voltage is one volt or less, go to next step.

7) Turn ignition off. Connect all modules except CAB. Turn ignition and all accessories on. Measure voltage between ground and terminal No. 2 (Yellow/Violet/Brown wire) on junction port connector. If voltage is greater than one volt, replace CAB. If voltage is one volt or less, connect CAB and go to next step.

8) Ensure ignition and all accessories are on. Measure voltage between ground and terminal No. 5 (Yellow/Violet/Orange wire) on junction port connector. If voltage is greater than one volt, go to step 99). If voltage is one volt or less, go to step 63).

9) Ensure ignition and all accessories are on. Measure voltage between ground and terminal No. 2 (Yellow/Violet wire) on DLC. If voltage is present, repair Yellow/Violet wire for short to voltage. If no voltage is present, go to next step.

10) Turn ignition off. Measure voltage between ground and terminal No. 2 (Yellow/Violet/Brown wire) on junction port connector. If voltage is greater than one volt, go to next step if vehicle is equipped with Vehicle Information Center (VIC). If vehicle is not equipped with VIC, go to step 12). If voltage is one volt or less, go to step 17).

11) Ensure ignition is off. Disconnect VIC connector. Turn ignition and all accessories on. Measure voltage between ground and terminal No. 2 (Yellow/Violet/Brown wire) on junction port connector. If voltage is greater than one volt, replace VIC. If voltage is one volt or less, go to next step.

12) Turn ignition off. Disconnect Controller Anti-Lock Brake (CAB). Disconnect Driver's Door Module (DDM). Ensure VIC connector is disconnected. Disconnect Memory Seat Module (MSM). Ensure junction port splice connector is removed. Turn ignition and all accessories on. Measure voltage between ground and terminal No. 2 (Yellow/Violet/Brown wire) on junction port connector. If voltage is greater than one volt, repair Yellow/Violet/Brown wire for short to voltage. If voltage is one volt or less, go to next step.

13) Turn ignition off. Connect all modules except CAB. Turn ignition and all accessories on. Measure voltage between ground and terminal No. 2 (Yellow/Violet/Brown wire) on junction port connector. If voltage is greater than one volt, replace CAB. If voltage is one volt or less, connect CAB and go to next step.

14) Ensure ignition and all accessories are on. Measure voltage between ground and terminal No. 5 (Yellow/Violet/Orange wire) on junction port connector. If voltage is greater than one volt, go to step 99). If voltage is one volt or less, go to next step.

15) Ensure ignition and all accessories are on. Measure voltage between ground and terminal No. 1 (Yellow/Violet/Gray wire) on junction port connector. If voltage is greater than one volt, go to step 25). If voltage is one volt or less, go to next step.

16) Ensure ignition and all accessories are on. Measure voltage between ground and terminal No. 6 (Yellow/Violet/Red wire) on junction port connector. If voltage is greater than one volt, go to step 111). If voltage is one volt or less, go to step 32).

17) Ensure ignition and all accessories are on. Measure voltage between ground and terminal No. 5 (Yellow/Violet/Orange wire) on junction port connector. If voltage is greater than one volt, go to next step. If voltage is one volt or less, go to step 24).

18) Ensure ignition and all accessories are on. Measure voltage between ground and terminal No. 1 (Yellow/Violet/Gray wire) on junction port connector. If voltage is greater than one volt, go to next step. If voltage is one volt or less, go to step 30).

19) Turn ignition off. Disconnect Powertrain Control Module (PCM). Turn ignition and all accessories on. Measure voltage between ground and terminal No. 1 (Yellow/Violet/Gray wire) on junction port connector. If voltage is greater than one volt, replace PCM. If voltage is one volt or less, go to next step if vehicle is equipped with Sentry Key Immobilizer System (SKIS). If vehicle is not equipped with SKIS, go to step 21).

20) Turn ignition off. Connect PCM connectors. Disconnect Sentry Key Immobilizer Module (SKIM). Turn ignition and all accessories on. Measure voltage between ground and terminal No. 1 (Yellow/Violet/Gray wire) on junction port connector. If voltage is greater than one volt, replace SKIM. If voltage is one volt or less, go to next step.

21) Turn ignition off. Disconnect PCM connectors. Disconnect Transmission Control Module (TCM) connector, Passenger Door Module (PDM) connector, SKIM connector and remote CD changer (if equipped) connector. Turn ignition and all accessories on. Measure voltage between ground and terminal No. 1 (Yellow/Violet/Gray wire) on junction port connector. If voltage is greater than one volt, repair Yellow/Violet/Gray wire for short to voltage. If voltage is one volt or less, go to next step if vehicle is equipped with 45RFE 4-speed A/T. If vehicle is equipped with remote CD changer, go to step 23). If voltage is one volt or less and vehicle is not equipped with 45RFE 4-speed A/T and remote CD changer, go to step 34).

22) Turn ignition off. Connect all module connectors except TCM connector. Turn ignition and all accessories on. Measure voltage between ground and terminal No. 1 (Yellow/Violet/Gray wire) on junction port connector. If voltage is greater than one volt, replace TCM. If voltage is one volt or less and vehicle is equipped with remote CD changer, go to next step. If vehicle is not equipped with remote CD changer, go to step 34).

23) Turn ignition off. Connect TCM connector. Disconnect remote CD changer connector. Turn ignition and all accessories on. Measure voltage between ground and terminal No. 2 (Yellow/Violet/Brown wire) on junction port connector. If voltage is greater than one volt, replace remote CD changer. If voltage is one volt or less, go to step 34).

24) Ensure ignition and all accessories are on. Measure voltage between ground and terminal No. 1 (Yellow/Violet/Gray wire) on junction port connector. If voltage is greater than one volt, go to next step. If voltage is one volt or less, go to step 31).

25) Turn ignition off. Disconnect Powertrain Control Module (PCM). Turn ignition and all accessories on. Measure voltage between ground and terminal No. 1 (Yellow/Violet/Gray wire) on junction port connector. If voltage is greater than one volt, replace PCM. If voltage is one volt or less and vehicle is equipped with Sentry Key Immobilizer System (SKIS), go to next step. If vehicle is not equipped with SKIS, go to step 27).

26) Turn ignition off. Connect PCM connectors. Disconnect Sentry Key Immobilizer Module (SKIM) module. Turn ignition and all accessories on. Measure voltage between ground and terminal No. 1 (Yellow/Violet/Gray wire) on junction port connector. If voltage is greater than one volt, replace SKIM. If voltage is one volt or less, go to next step.

27) Turn ignition off. Disconnect PCM connectors. Disconnect Transmission Control Module (TCM) connector, Passenger Door Module (PDM) connector, SKIM connector and remote CD changer (if equipped) connector. Turn ignition and all accessories on. Measure voltage between ground and terminal No. 1 (Yellow/Violet/Gray wire) on junction port connector. If voltage is greater than one volt, repair Yellow/Violet/Gray wire for short to voltage. If voltage is one volt or less, go to next

step if vehicle is equipped with 45RFE 4-speed A/T. If vehicle is equipped with remote CD changer, go to step 29). If voltage is one volt or less and vehicle is not equipped with 45RFE 4-speed A/T and remote CD changer, go to step 30).

28) Turn ignition off. Connect all module connectors except TCM connector. Turn ignition and all accessories on. Measure voltage between ground and terminal No. 1 (Yellow/Violet/Gray wire) on junction port connector. If voltage is greater than one volt, replace TCM. If voltage is one volt or less and vehicle is equipped with remote CD changer, go to next step. If vehicle is not equipped with remote CD changer, go to step 30).

29) Turn ignition off. Connect TCM connector. Disconnect remote CD changer connector. Turn ignition and all accessories on. Measure voltage between ground and terminal No. 2 (Yellow/Violet/Brown wire) on junction port connector. If voltage is greater than one volt, replace remote CD changer. If voltage is one volt or less, connect remote CD changer and go to next step.

30) Ensure ignition and all accessories are on. Measure voltage between ground and terminal No. 6 (Yellow/Violet/Red wire) on junction port connector. If voltage is greater than one volt, go to step 111). If voltage is one volt or less, go to step 34).

31) Ensure ignition and all accessories are on. Measure voltage between ground and terminal No. 6 (Yellow/Violet/Red wire) on junction port connector. If voltage is greater than one volt, go to next step. If voltage is one volt or less, go to step 33).

32) Ensure ignition and all accessories are on. Measure voltage between ground and terminal No. 3 (Yellow/Violet/Dark Green wire) on junction port connector. If voltage is greater than one volt, go to step 111). If voltage is one volt or less, go to step 34).

33) Ensure ignition and all accessories are on. Measure voltage between ground and terminal No. 3 (Yellow/Violet/Dark Green wire) on junction port connector. If voltage is greater than one volt, go to next step. If voltage is one volt or less, go to next step.

34) Turn ignition off. Disconnect BCM connectors. Turn ignition and all accessories on. Measure voltage between ground and terminal No. 8 (Yellow/Violet/White wire) on junction port connector. If voltage is greater than one volt, repair Yellow/Violet/White wire for short to voltage. If voltage is one volt or less, replace BCM

35) Ensure ignition and all accessories are on. Measure voltage between ground and terminal No. 4 (Yellow/Violet/Dark Blue wire) on junction port connector. If voltage is greater than one volt, go to next step. If voltage is one volt or less, go to step 64).

36) Ensure ignition and all accessories are on. Measure voltage between ground and terminal No. 2 (Yellow/Violet wire) on DLC connector. If voltage is present, repair Yellow/Violet wire for short to voltage. If no voltage is present, go to next step.

37) Measure voltage between ground and terminal No. 2 (Yellow/Violet/Brown wire) on junction port connector. If voltage is greater than one volt, go to next step. If voltage is one volt or less, go to step 51).

38) Turn ignition off. Disconnect Controller Anti-Lock Brake (CAB) module. Disconnect Driver's Door Module (DDM). Disconnect VIC connector. Disconnect Memory Seat Module (MSM). Ensure junction port splice connector is removed. Turn ignition and all accessories on. Measure voltage between ground and terminal No. 2 (Yellow/Violet/Brown wire) on junction port connector. If voltage is greater than one volt, repair Yellow/Violet/Brown wire for short to voltage. If voltage is one volt or less, go to next step.

39) Turn ignition off. Connect all modules except CAB module. Turn ignition and all accessories on. Measure voltage between ground and terminal No. 2 (Yellow/Violet/Brown wire) on junction port connector. If voltage is greater than one volt, replace CAB module. If voltage is one volt or less, connect CAB module connector and go to next step.

40) Ensure ignition and all accessories are on. Measure voltage between ground and terminal No. 5 (Yellow/Violet/Orange wire) on junction port connector. If voltage is greater than one volt, go to step 99). If voltage is one volt or less, go to next step.

41) Measure voltage between ground and terminal No. 1 (Yellow/Violet/Gray wire) on junction port connector. If voltage is greater than one volt,

go to next step. If voltage is one volt or less and vehicle is equipped with Vehicle Information Center (VIC), go to step 48). If vehicle is not equipped with VIC, go to step 49).

42) Turn ignition off. Disconnect Powertrain Control Module (PCM). Turn ignition and all accessories on. Measure voltage between ground and terminal No. 1 (Yellow/Violet/Gray wire) on junction port connector. If voltage is greater than one volt, replace PCM. If voltage is one volt or less, go to next step if vehicle is equipped with Sentry Key Immobilizer System (SKIS). If vehicle is not equipped with SKIS, go to step 44).

43) Turn ignition off. Connect PCM connectors. Disconnect Sentry Key Immobilizer Module (SKIM). Turn ignition and all accessories on. Measure voltage between ground and terminal No. 1 (Yellow/Violet/Gray wire) on junction port connector. If voltage is greater than one volt, replace SKIM. If voltage is one volt or less, go to next step.

44) Turn ignition off. Disconnect PCM connectors. Disconnect Transmission Control Module (TCM) connector, Passenger Door Module (PDM) connector, SKIM connector and remote CD changer (if equipped) connector. Turn ignition and all accessories on. Measure voltage between ground and terminal No. 1 (Yellow/Violet/Gray wire) on junction port connector. If voltage is greater than one volt, repair Yellow/Violet/Gray wire for short to voltage. If voltage is one volt or less, go to next step if vehicle is equipped with 45RFE 4-speed A/T. If vehicle is equipped with remote CD changer, go to step 46). If vehicle is equipped with Vehicle Information Center (VIC), go to step 47). If voltage is one volt or less and vehicle is not equipped with 45RFE 4-speed A/T, remote CD changer or VIC, go to step 55).

45) Turn ignition off. Connect all module connectors except TCM connector. Turn ignition and all accessories on. Measure voltage between ground and terminal No. 1 (Yellow/Violet/Gray wire) on junction port connector. If voltage is greater than one volt, replace TCM. If voltage is one volt or less and vehicle is equipped with remote CD changer, go to next step. If voltage is one volt or less and vehicle is equipped Vehicle Information Center (VIC), go to step 47). If vehicle is not equipped with remote CD changer or VIC, go to next step 55).

46) Turn ignition off. Connect TCM connector. Disconnect remote CD changer connector. Turn ignition and all accessories on. Measure voltage between ground and terminal No. 2 (Yellow/Violet/Brown wire) on junction port connector. If voltage is greater than one volt, replace remote CD changer. If voltage is one volt or less and vehicle is equipped Vehicle Information Center (VIC), and go to next step. If voltage is one volt or less and vehicle is not equipped with VIC, go to step 55).

47) Turn ignition off. Connect CD changer connector. Disconnect remote VIC connector. Turn ignition and all accessories on. Measure voltage between ground and terminal No. 2 (Yellow/Violet/Brown wire) on junction port connector. If voltage is greater than one volt, replace VIC. If voltage is one volt or less, go to step 55).

48) Turn ignition off. Disconnect Vehicle Information Center (VIC) connector. Turn ignition and all accessories on. Measure voltage between ground and terminal No. 2 (Yellow/Violet/Brown wire) on junction port connector. If voltage is greater than one volt, replace VIC. If voltage is one volt or less, connect VIC connector and go to next step.

49) Ensure ignition and all accessories are on. Measure voltage between ground and terminal No. 6 (Yellow/Violet/Red wire) on junction port connector. If voltage is greater than one volt, go to step 111). If voltage is one volt or less, go to next step.

50) Measure voltage between ground and terminal No. 3 (Yellow/Violet/Dark Green wire) on junction port connector. If voltage is greater than one volt, go to step 113). If voltage is one volt or less, go to step 63).

51) Ensure ignition and all accessories are on. Measure voltage between ground and terminal No. 5 (Yellow/Violet/Orange wire) on junction port connector. If voltage is greater than one volt, go to next step. If voltage is one volt or less, go to step 56).

52) Measure voltage between ground and terminal No. 1 (Yellow/Violet/Gray wire) on junction port connector. If voltage is greater than one volt, go to step 113). If voltage is one volt or less, go to step 63).

53) Turn ignition off. Disconnect Powertrain Control Module (PCM). Turn ignition and all accessories on. Measure voltage between ground and terminal No. 1 (Yellow/Violet/Gray wire) on junction port connector. If voltage is greater than one volt, replace PCM. If voltage is one volt or

less, go to next step if vehicle is equipped with Sentry Key Immobilizer System (SKIS). If vehicle is not equipped with SKIS, go to step **58**).

54) Turn ignition off. Connect PCM connectors. Disconnect Sentry Key Immobilizer Module (SKIM). Turn ignition and all accessories on. Measure voltage between ground and terminal No. 1 (Yellow/Violet/Gray wire) on junction port connector. If voltage is greater than one volt, replace SKIM. If voltage is one volt or less, go to step **58**).

55) Ensure all modules are connected. Turn ignition and all accessories on. Measure voltage between ground and terminal No. 6 (Yellow/Violet/Red wire) on junction port connector. If voltage is greater than one volt, go to step **111**). If voltage is one volt or less, go to step **58**).

56) Measure voltage between ground and terminal No. 1 (Yellow/Violet/Gray wire) on junction port connector. If voltage is greater than one volt, go to next step. If voltage is one volt or less, go to step **61**).

57) Turn ignition off. Disconnect Powertrain Control Module (PCM). Turn ignition and all accessories on. Measure voltage between ground and terminal No. 1 (Yellow/Violet/Gray wire) on junction port connector. If voltage is greater than one volt, replace PCM. If voltage is one volt or less, go to next step.

58) Turn ignition off. Disconnect PCM connectors. Disconnect Transmission Control Module (TCM) connector, Passenger Door Module (PDM) connector, SKIM connector and remote CD changer (if equipped) connector. Turn ignition and all accessories on. Measure voltage between ground and terminal No. 1 (Yellow/Violet/Gray wire) on junction port connector. If voltage is greater than one volt, repair Yellow/Violet/Gray wire for short to voltage. If voltage is one volt or less, go to next step if vehicle is equipped with 45RFE 4-speed A/T. If vehicle is equipped with remote CD changer, go to step **60**). If voltage is one volt or less and vehicle is not equipped with 45RFE 4-speed A/T or remote CD changer, go to step **63**).

59) Turn ignition off. Connect all module connectors except TCM connector. Turn ignition and all accessories on. Measure voltage between ground and terminal No. 1 (Yellow/Violet/Gray wire) on junction port connector. If voltage is greater than one volt, replace TCM. If voltage is one volt or less and vehicle is equipped with remote CD changer, go to next step. If vehicle is not equipped with remote CD changer, go to step **63**).

60) Turn ignition off. Connect TCM connector. Disconnect remote CD changer connector. Turn ignition and all accessories on. Measure voltage between ground and terminal No. 2 (Yellow/Violet/Brown wire) on junction port connector. If voltage is greater than one volt, replace remote CD changer. If voltage is one volt or less, go to step **63**).

61) Ensure all modules are connected. Turn ignition and all accessories on. Measure voltage between ground and terminal No. 6 (Yellow/Violet/Red wire) on junction port connector. If voltage is greater than one volt, go to next step. If voltage is one volt or less, go to next step.

62) Ensure ignition and all accessories are on. Measure voltage between ground and terminal No. 3 (Yellow/Violet/Dark Green wire) on junction port connector. If voltage is greater than one volt, go to next step. If voltage is one volt or less, go to next step.

63) Turn ignition off. Disconnect radio PCI bus connector (if equipped). Turn ignition and all accessories on. Measure voltage between ground and terminal No. 4 (Yellow/Violet/Dark Blue wire). If voltage is greater than one volt or if vehicle is not equipped with PCI bus radio connector, repair Yellow/Violet/Dark Blue wire for short to voltage. If voltage is one volt or less, replace radio.

64) Ensure ignition and all accessories are on. Measure voltage between ground and terminal No. 2 (Yellow/Violet wire) on DLC. If voltage is present, repair Yellow/Violet wire for short to voltage. If no voltage is present, go to next step.

65) Ensure all modules are connected. Measure voltage between ground and terminal No. 2 (Yellow/Violet/Brown wire) on junction port connector. If voltage is greater than one volt, go to next step. If voltage is one volt or less, go to step **89**).

66) Turn ignition and all accessories on. Measure voltage between ground and terminal No. 5 (Yellow/Violet/Orange wire) on junction port connector. If voltage is greater than one volt, go to next step. If voltage is one volt or less, go to step **74**).

67) Turn ignition off. Disconnect Controller Anti-Lock Brake (CAB). Disconnect Driver's Door Module (DDM). Ensure VIC connector is disconnected. Disconnect Memory Seat Module (MSM). Ensure junction port splice connector is removed. Turn ignition and all accessories on. Measure voltage between ground and terminal No. 2 (Yellow/Violet/Brown wire) on junction port connector. If voltage is greater than one volt, repair Yellow/Violet/Brown wire for short to voltage. If voltage is one volt or less, go to next step.

68) Turn ignition off. Reconnect all modules. Turn ignition and all accessories on. Measure voltage between ground and terminal No. 1 (Yellow/Violet/Gray wire) on junction port connector. If voltage is greater than one volt, go to next step. If voltage is one volt or less, go to step **99**).

69) Turn ignition off. Disconnect Powertrain Control Module (PCM). Turn ignition and all accessories on. Measure voltage between ground and terminal No. 1 (Yellow/Violet/Gray wire) on junction port connector. If voltage is greater than one volt, replace PCM. If voltage is one volt or less, go to next step if vehicle is equipped with Sentry Key Immobilizer System (SKIS). If vehicle is not equipped with SKIS, go to step **71**).

70) Turn ignition off. Connect PCM connectors. Disconnect Sentry Key Immobilizer Module (SKIM). Turn ignition and all accessories on. Measure voltage between ground and terminal No. 1 (Yellow/Violet/Gray wire) on junction port connector. If voltage is greater than one volt, replace SKIM. If voltage is one volt or less, go to next step.

71) Turn ignition off. Disconnect PCM connectors. Disconnect Transmission Control Module (TCM) connector, Passenger Door Module (PDM) connector, SKIM connector and remote CD changer (if equipped) connector. Turn ignition and all accessories on. Measure voltage between ground and terminal No. 1 (Yellow/Violet/Gray wire) on junction port connector. If voltage is greater than one volt, repair Yellow/Violet/Gray wire for short to voltage. If voltage is one volt or less, go to next step if vehicle is equipped with 45RFE 4-speed A/T. If vehicle is equipped with remote CD changer, go to step **72**). If voltage is one volt or less and vehicle is not equipped with 45RFE 4-speed A/T and remote CD changer, go to step **99**).

72) Turn ignition off. Connect all module connectors except TCM connector. Turn ignition and all accessories on. Measure voltage between ground and terminal No. 1 (Yellow/Violet/Gray wire) on junction port connector. If voltage is greater than one volt, replace TCM. If voltage is one volt or less and vehicle is equipped with remote CD changer, go to next step. If vehicle is not equipped with remote CD changer, go to step **99**).

73) Turn ignition off. Connect TCM connector. Disconnect remote CD changer connector. Turn ignition and all accessories on. Measure voltage between ground and terminal No. 2 (Yellow/Violet/Brown wire) on junction port connector. If voltage is greater than one volt, replace remote CD changer. If voltage is one volt or less, go to step **99**).

74) Turn ignition off. Disconnect Controller Anti-Lock Brake (CAB). Disconnect Driver's Door Module (DDM), Vehicle Information Center (VIC) and Memory Seat Module (MSM). Ensure junction port splice connector is removed. Turn ignition and all accessories on. Measure voltage between ground and terminal No. 2 (Yellow/Violet/Brown wire) on junction port connector. If voltage is greater than one volt, repair Yellow/Violet/Brown wire for short to voltage. If voltage is one volt or less, go to next step.

75) Turn ignition off. Reconnect all modules. Turn ignition and all accessories on. Measure voltage between ground and terminal No. 1 (Yellow/Violet/Gray wire) on junction port connector. If voltage is greater than one volt, go to next step. If voltage is one volt or less, go to step **85**).

76) Turn ignition off. Disconnect Powertrain Control Module (PCM). Turn ignition and all accessories on. Measure voltage between ground and terminal No. 1 (Yellow/Violet/Gray wire) on junction port connector. If voltage is greater than one volt, replace PCM. If voltage is one volt or less, go to next step if vehicle is equipped with Sentry Key Immobilizer System (SKIS). If vehicle is not equipped with SKIS, go to step **77**).

77) Turn ignition off. Connect PCM connectors. Disconnect Sentry Key Immobilizer Module (SKIM). Turn ignition and all accessories on. Measure voltage between ground and terminal No. 1 (Yellow/Violet/Gray wire) on junction port connector. If voltage is greater than one volt, replace SKIM. If voltage is one volt or less, go to next step.

78) Turn ignition off. Disconnect PCM connectors. Disconnect Transmission Control Module (TCM) connector, Passenger Door Module (PDM) connector, SKIM connector and remote CD changer (if equipped) connector. Turn ignition and all accessories on. Measure voltage between ground and terminal No. 1 (Yellow/Violet/Gray wire) on junction port connector. If voltage is greater than one volt, repair Yellow/Violet/Gray wire for short to voltage. If voltage is one volt or less, go to next step if vehicle is equipped with 45RFE 4-speed A/T. If vehicle is equipped with remote CD changer, go to step **80)**. If voltage is one volt or less and vehicle is not equipped with 45RFE 4-speed A/T and remote CD changer, go to step **81)**.

79) Turn ignition off. Connect all module connectors except TCM connector. Turn ignition and all accessories on. Measure voltage between ground and terminal No. 1 (Yellow/Violet/Gray wire) on junction port connector. If voltage is greater than one volt, replace TCM. If voltage is one volt or less and vehicle is equipped with remote CD changer, go to next step. If vehicle is not equipped with remote CD changer, go to step **81)**.

80) Turn ignition off. Connect TCM connector. Disconnect remote CD changer connector. Turn ignition and all accessories on. Measure voltage between ground and terminal No. 2 (Yellow/Violet/Brown wire) on junction port connector. If voltage is greater than one volt, replace remote CD changer. If voltage is one volt or less, connect remote CD changer and go to next step.

81) Turn ignition off. Disconnect Controller Anti-Lock Brake (CAB) module. Turn ignition and all accessories on. Measure voltage between ground and terminal No. 2 (Yellow/Violet/Brown wire) on junction port connector. If voltage is greater than one volt, replace CAB module. If voltage is one volt or less, connect CAB module and go to next step.

82) Ensure all modules are connected. Turn ignition and all accessories on. Measure voltage between ground and terminal No. 6 (Yellow/Violet/Red wire) on junction port connector. If voltage is greater than one volt, go to step **111)**. If voltage is one volt or less, go to next step.

83) Ensure ignition and all accessories are on. Measure voltage between ground and terminal No. 3 (Yellow/Violet/Dark Green wire) on junction port connector. If voltage is greater than one volt, go to step **113)**. If voltage is one volt or less and vehicle is equipped with Vehicle Information Center (VIC), go to next step. If vehicle is not equipped with VIC, go to step **108)**.

84) Turn ignition off. Disconnect VIC connector. Turn ignition and all accessories on. Measure voltage between ground and terminal No. 2 (Yellow/Violet/Brown wire) on junction port connector. If voltage is greater than one volt, replace VIC module. If voltage is one volt or less, connect VIC module connector and go to next step.

85) Ensure ignition and all accessories are on. Measure voltage between ground and terminal No. 6 (Yellow/Violet/Red wire) on junction port connector. If voltage is greater than one volt, go to step **111)**. If voltage is one volt or less, go to next step.

86) Turn ignition off. Disconnect Controller Anti-Lock Brake (CAB) module. Turn ignition and all accessories on. Measure voltage between ground and terminal No. 2 (Yellow/Violet/Brown wire) on junction port connector. If voltage is greater than one volt, replace CAB. If voltage is one volt or less, connect CAB and go to next step.

87) Ensure ignition and all accessories are on. Measure voltage between ground and terminal No. 3 (Yellow/Violet/Dark Green wire) on junction port connector. If voltage is greater than one volt, go to next step. If voltage is one volt or less and vehicle is equipped with Vehicle Information Center (VIC), go to next step. If vehicle is not equipped with VIC, test is complete.

88) Turn ignition off. Disconnect VIC connector. Turn ignition and all accessories on. Measure voltage between ground and terminal No. 2 (Yellow/Violet/Brown wire) on junction port connector. If voltage is greater than one volt, replace VIC module. If voltage is one volt or less, connect VIC module connector. Test is complete.

89) Ensure ignition and all accessories are on. Measure voltage between ground and terminal No. 5 (Yellow/Violet/Orange wire) on junction port connector. If voltage is greater than one volt, go to next step. If voltage is one volt or less, go to step **100)**.

90) Measure voltage between ground and terminal No. 1 (Yellow/Violet/Gray wire) on junction port connector. If voltage is greater than one volt, go to next step. If voltage is one volt or less, go to step **97)**.

91) Turn ignition off. Disconnect Powertrain Control Module (PCM). Turn ignition and all accessories on. Measure voltage between ground and terminal No. 1 (Yellow/Violet/Gray wire) on junction port connector. If voltage is greater than one volt, replace PCM. If voltage is one volt or less, go to next step.

92) Turn ignition off. Disconnect PCM connectors. Disconnect Transmission Control Module (TCM) connector, Passenger Door Module (PDM) connector, SKIM connector and remote CD changer (if equipped) connector. Turn ignition and all accessories on. Measure voltage between ground and terminal No. 1 (Yellow/Violet/Gray wire) on junction port connector. If voltage is greater than one volt, repair Yellow/Violet/Gray wire for short to voltage. If voltage is one volt or less, go to next step if vehicle is equipped with 45RFE 4-speed A/T. If vehicle is equipped with remote CD changer, go to step **94)**. If voltage is one volt or less and vehicle is not equipped with 45RFE 4-speed A/T or remote CD changer, go to step **95)**.

93) Turn ignition off. Connect all module connectors except TCM connector. Turn ignition and all accessories on. Measure voltage between ground and terminal No. 1 (Yellow/Violet/Gray wire) on junction port connector. If voltage is greater than one volt, replace TCM. If voltage is one volt or less and vehicle is equipped with remote CD changer, go to next step. If vehicle is not equipped with remote CD changer, go to step **95)**.

94) Turn ignition off. Connect TCM connector. Disconnect remote CD changer connector. Turn ignition and all accessories on. Measure voltage between ground and terminal No. 2 (Yellow/Violet/Brown wire) on junction port connector. If voltage is greater than one volt, replace remote CD changer. If voltage is one volt or less, connect CD changer and go to next step.

95) Ensure all modules are connected. Turn ignition and all accessories on. Measure voltage between ground and terminal No. 6 (Yellow/Violet/Red wire) on junction port connector. If voltage is greater than one volt, go to next step. If voltage is one volt or less and vehicle is equipped with Sentry Key Immobilizer System (SKIS), go to next step. If vehicle is equipped with Automatic Temperature Control (ATC), go to step **98)**. If voltage is one volt or less and vehicle is not equipped with SKIS or ATC, test is complete.

96) Turn ignition off. Disconnect Sentry Key Immobilizer Module (SKIM). Turn ignition and all accessories on. Measure voltage between ground and terminal No. 1 (Yellow/Violet/Gray wire) on junction port connector. If voltage is greater than one volt, replace SKIM. If voltage is one volt or less, connect SKIM and go to step **98)**.

97) Ensure ignition and all accessories are on. Measure voltage between ground and terminal No. 6 (Yellow/Violet/Red wire) on junction port connector. If voltage is greater than one volt, go to step **110)**. If voltage is one volt or less, go to next step.

98) Ensure ignition and all accessories are on. Measure voltage between ground and terminal No. 3 (Yellow/Violet/Dark Green wire) on junction port connector. If voltage is greater than one volt, go to step **113)**. If voltage is one volt or less, go to next step.

99) Turn ignition off and wait 2 minutes. Disconnect Airbag Control Module (ACM). Turn ignition and all accessories on. Measure voltage between ground and terminal No. 5 (Yellow/Violet/Orange wire) on junction port connector. If voltage is greater than one volt, repair Yellow/Violet/Orange wire for short to voltage. If voltage is one volt or less, turn ignition off. Disconnect battery and replace ACM.

100) Turn ignition off. Ensure all modules are connected. Turn ignition and all accessories on. Measure voltage between ground and terminal No. 1 (Yellow/Violet/Gray wire) on junction port connector. If voltage is greater than one volt, go to next step. If voltage is one volt or less, go to step **109)**.

101) Ensure ignition and all accessories are on. Measure voltage between ground and terminal No. 6 (Yellow/Violet/Red wire) on junction port connector. If voltage is greater than one volt, go to step **111)**. If voltage is one volt or less, go to next step.

102) Turn ignition off. Disconnect PCM connectors. Disconnect Transmission Control Module (TCM) connector, Passenger Door Module (PDM) connector, SKIM connector and remote CD changer (if equipped) connector. Turn ignition and all accessories on. Measure voltage between ground and terminal No. 1 (Yellow/Violet/Gray wire) on junction port connector. If voltage is greater than one volt, repair Yellow/Violet/Gray wire for short to voltage. If voltage is one volt or less, go to next step if vehicle is equipped with 45RFE 4-speed A/T. If vehicle is equipped with remote CD changer, go to step **104)**. If voltage is one volt or less and vehicle is equipped with Automatic Temperature Control (ATC), go to step **105)**. If vehicle is not equipped with 45RFE 4-speed A/T, remote CD changer or Automatic Temperature Control (ATC), test is complete.

103) Turn ignition off. Connect all module connectors except TCM connector. Turn ignition and all accessories on. Measure voltage between ground and terminal No. 1 (Yellow/Violet/Gray wire) on junction port connector. If voltage is greater than one volt, replace TCM. If voltage is one volt or less and vehicle is equipped with remote CD changer, go to next step. If voltage is one volt or less and vehicle is equipped with Automatic Temperature Control (ATC), go to step **105)**. If vehicle is not equipped with remote CD changer or ATC, test is complete.

104) Turn ignition off. Connect TCM connector. Disconnect remote CD changer connector. Turn ignition and all accessories on. Measure voltage between ground and terminal No. 2 (Yellow/Violet/Brown wire) on junction port connector. If voltage is greater than one volt, replace remote CD changer. If voltage is one volt or less, connect CD changer and go to next step.

105) Ensure ignition and all accessories are on. Measure voltage between ground and terminal No. 3 (Yellow/Violet/Dark Green wire) on junction port connector. If voltage is greater than one volt, go to step **113)**. If voltage is one volt or less, go to next step.

106) Turn ignition off. Disconnect Powertrain Control Module (PCM). Turn ignition and all accessories on. Measure voltage between ground and terminal No. 1 (Yellow/Violet/Gray wire) on junction port connector. If voltage is greater than one volt, replace PCM. If voltage is one volt or less and vehicle is equipped with Sentry Key Immobilizer System (SKIS), go to next step. If vehicle is not equipped with SKIS, go to step **108)**.

107) Turn ignition off. Disconnect Sentry Key Immobilizer Module (SKIM). Turn ignition and all accessories on. Measure voltage between ground and terminal No. 1 (Yellow/Violet/Gray wire) on junction port connector. If voltage is greater than one volt, replace SKIM. If voltage is one volt or less, connect SKIM and go to next step.

108) Turn ignition off. Disconnect Passenger's Door Module (PDM). Turn ignition and all accessories on. Measure voltage between ground and terminal No. 1 (Yellow/Violet/Gray wire) on junction port connector. If voltage is greater than one volt, test is complete. If voltage is one volt or less, test is complete.

109) Ensure ignition and all accessories are on. Measure voltage between ground and terminal No. 6 (Yellow/Violet/Red wire) on junction port connector. If voltage is greater than one volt, go to next step. If voltage is one volt or less, go to step **112)**.

110) Ensure ignition and all accessories are on. Measure voltage between ground and terminal No. 3 (Yellow/Violet/Dark Green wire) on junction port connector. If voltage is greater than one volt, go to step **113)**. If voltage is one volt or less, go to next step.

111) Turn ignition off. Disconnect instrument cluster. Turn ignition and all accessories on. Measure voltage between ground and terminal No. 6 (Yellow/Violet/Red wire) on junction port connector. If voltage is greater than one volt, repair Yellow/Violet/Red wire for short to voltage. If voltage is one volt or less, replace instrument cluster.

112) Ensure ignition and all accessories are on. Measure voltage between ground and terminal No. 3 (Yellow/Violet/Dark Green wire) on junction port connector. If voltage is greater than one volt, go to next step. If voltage is one volt or less, test is complete.

113) Turn ignition off. Disconnect Automatic Zone Control (AZC) module. Turn ignition and all accessories on. Measure voltage between ground and terminal No. 3 (Yellow/Violet/Dark Green wire) on junction

port connector. If voltage is greater than one volt, repair Yellow/Violet/Dark Green wire for short to voltage. If voltage is one volt or less, test is complete.

PCI BUS SHORT TO GROUND

NOTE: Additional DTCs will be set during following test. Any module connected to PCI bus may set a DTC when junction port splice is removed. Always reconnect junction port splice when testing is completed. Ensure ignition is off and disconnect negative battery cable before proceeding with testing.

NOTE: Junction port connector may also be known as diagnostic junction port connector.

1) Ensure ignition is off. Disconnect negative battery cable. Remove driver's side knee blocker below steering column. Locate junction port connector. Remove splice connector from junction port connector. Turn ignition and all accessories on. Using ohmmeter, measure resistance between ground and terminal No. 8 (Yellow/Violet/White wire) on junction port connector. If resistance is less than 9000 ohms, go to next step. If resistance is 9000 ohms or greater, go to step **40)**.

2) Measure resistance between ground and terminal No. 4 (Yellow/Violet/Dark Blue wire) on junction port connector. If resistance is less than 9000 ohms, go to next step. If resistance is 9000 ohms or greater, go to step **10)**.

3) Access DLC. Check continuity between terminals No. 2 (Yellow/Violet wire) and No. 4 (Black/Orange wire) on DLC. If continuity exists, repair Yellow/Violet wire for short to ground. If continuity does not exist, go to next step.

4) Check continuity between ground and terminal No. 2 (Yellow/Violet/Brown wire) on junction port connector. If continuity exists and vehicle is equipped with Vehicle Information Center (VIC), go to next step. If vehicle is not equipped with VIC, go to step **6)**. If continuity does not exist, go to step **9)**.

5) Disconnect VIC module. Measure resistance between ground and terminal No. 2 (Yellow/Violet/Brown wire) on junction port connector. If resistance is less than 500 ohms, replace VIC. If resistance is 500 ohms or greater, connect VIC connector and go to next step.

6) Disconnect Controller Anti-Lock Brake (CAB). Disconnect Driver's Door Module (DDM), VIC connector and Memory Seat Module (MSM). Ensure junction port splice connector is removed. Measure resistance between ground and terminal No. 2 (Yellow/Violet/Brown wire) on junction port connector. If resistance is less than 5 ohms, repair Yellow/Violet/Brown wire for short to ground. If resistance is 5 ohms or greater, go to next step.

7) Connect all module connectors except DDM connector. Measure resistance between ground and terminal No. 2 (Yellow/Violet/Brown wire) on junction port connector. If resistance is less than 500 ohms or if resistance is 500 ohms or greater, go to next step if vehicle is equipped with Memory Seat Module (MSM). If vehicle is not equipped with MSM, go to step **9)**.

8) Disconnect MSM. Measure resistance between ground and terminal No. 2 (Yellow/Violet/Brown wire) on junction port connector. If resistance is less than 500 ohms, connect MSM and go to next step. If resistance is 500 ohms or greater, replace MSM.

9) Measure resistance between ground and terminal No. 5 (Yellow/Violet/Orange wire) on junction port connector. If resistance is less than 9000 ohms, go to step 84. If resistance is 9000 ohms or greater, go to step **56)**.

10) Access DLC. Check continuity between terminals No. 2 (Yellow/Violet wire) and No. 4 (Black/Orange wire) on DLC. If continuity exists, repair Yellow/Violet wire for short to ground. If continuity does not exist, go to next step.

11) Check continuity between ground and terminal No. 2 (Yellow/Violet/Brown wire) on junction port connector. If continuity exists and vehicle is equipped with Vehicle Information Center (VIC), go to next step. If vehicle is not equipped with VIC, go to step **13)**. If continuity does not exist, go to step **25)**.

12) Disconnect VIC module. Measure resistance between ground and terminal No. 2 (Yellow/Violet/Brown wire) on junction port connector. If resistance is less than 500 ohms, replace VIC. If resistance is 500 ohms or greater, connect VIC connector and go to next step.

13) Disconnect Controller Anti-Lock Brake (CAB). Disconnect Driver's Door Module (DDM), VIC connector and Memory Seat Module (MSM). Ensure junction port splice connector is removed. Measure resistance between ground and terminal No. 2 (Yellow/Violet/Brown wire) on junction port connector. If resistance is less than 5 ohms, repair Yellow/Violet/Brown wire for short to ground. If resistance is 5 ohms or greater, go to next step.

14) Connect all module connectors except DDM connector. Measure resistance between ground and terminal No. 2 (Yellow/Violet/Brown wire) on junction port connector. If resistance is less than 500 ohms or if resistance is 500 ohms or greater, go to next step.

15) Connect DDM connector. Measure resistance between ground and terminal No. 5 (Yellow/Violet/Orange wire) on junction port connector. If resistance is less than 9000 ohms, go to step **84)**. If resistance is 9000 ohms or greater, go to next step.

16) Check continuity between ground and terminal No. 1 (Yellow/Violet/Gray wire) on junction port connector. If continuity exists, go to next step. If continuity does not exist, go to step **23)**.

17) Disconnect Powertrain Control Module (PCM), Transmission Control Module (TCM), Passenger Door Module (PDM), Sentry Key Immobilizer Module (SKIM) and remote CD changer connectors. Check continuity between ground and terminal No. 1 (Yellow/Violet/Gray wire) on junction port connector. If continuity exists, go to next step. If continuity does not exist and vehicle is equipped with remote CD changer, go to next step. If vehicle is equipped with 45RFE 4-speed A/T, go to step **19)**. If continuity does not exist and vehicle is equipped with Memory Seat Module (MSM), go to step **20)**. If vehicle is not equipped with remote CD changer, 45RFE 4-speed A/T or MSM, go to step **21)**.

18) Connect all disconnected modules except remote CD changer. Measure resistance between ground and terminal No. 1 (Yellow/Violet/Gray wire) on junction port connector. If resistance is less than 500 ohms, replace remote CD changer. If resistance is 500 ohms or greater and vehicle is equipped with 45RFE 4-speed A/T, go to next step. If vehicle is equipped with MSM, go to step **20)**. If resistance is 500 ohms or greater and vehicle is not equipped with 45RFE 4-speed A/T or MSM, go to step **21)**.

19) Connect remote CD changer connector. Disconnect TCM connector. Measure resistance between ground and terminal No. 1 (Yellow/Violet/Gray wire) on junction port connector. If resistance is less than 500 ohms, replace TCM. If resistance is 500 ohms or greater and vehicle is equipped with MSM, go to next step. If vehicle is not equipped with MSM, go to step **21)**.

20) Connect TCM connector. Disconnect MSM connector. Measure resistance between ground and terminal No. 1 (Yellow/Violet/Gray wire) on junction port connector. If resistance is less than 500 ohms, replace MSM. If resistance is 500 ohms or greater, go to next step.

21) Connect MSM connector. Disconnect Passenger Door Module (PDM) connector. Measure resistance between ground and terminal No. 1 (Yellow/Violet/Gray wire) on junction port connector. If resistance is less than 500 ohms or if resistance is 500 ohms or greater, go to next step.

22) Connect PDM connector. Measure resistance between ground and terminal No. 6 (Yellow/Violet/Red wire) on junction port connector. If resistance is less than 1500 ohms, go to step **96)**. If resistance is 1500 ohms or greater, go to step **39)**.

23) Connect PDM connector. Measure resistance between ground and terminal No. 6 (Yellow/Violet/Red wire) on junction port connector. If resistance is less than 500 ohms and vehicle is equipped with Memory Seat Module (MSM), go to next step. If vehicle is equipped with Automatic Temperature Control (ATC), go to step **37)**. If vehicle is not equipped with MSM or ATC, test is complete.

24) Disconnect MSM connector. Measure resistance between ground and terminal No. 1 (Yellow/Violet/Gray wire) on junction port connector. If resistance is less than 500 ohms, replace MSM. If resistance is 500 ohms or greater, go to step **37)**.

25) Measure resistance between ground and terminal No. 5 (Yellow/Violet/Orange wire) on junction port connector. If resistance is less than 9000 ohms, go to next step. If resistance is 9000 ohms or greater, go to step **32)**.

26) Measure resistance between ground and terminal No. 1 (Yellow/Violet/Gray wire) on junction port connector. If resistance is less than 5 ohms, go to next step. If resistance is 5 ohms or greater, go to step **31)**.

27) Disconnect Powertrain Control Module (PCM), Transmission Control Module (TCM), Passenger Door Module (PDM), Sentry Key Immobilizer Module (SKIM) and remote CD changer connectors. Check continuity between ground and terminal No. 1 (Yellow/Violet/Gray wire) on junction port connector. If continuity exists, repair Yellow/Violet/Gray wire for short to ground. If continuity does not exist and vehicle is equipped with remote CD changer, go to next step. If vehicle is equipped with 45RFE 4-speed A/T, go to step **29)**. If vehicle is not equipped with remote CD changer or 45RFE 4-speed A/T, go to step **30)**.

28) Connect all disconnected modules except remote CD changer. Measure resistance between ground and terminal No. 1 (Yellow/Violet/Gray wire) on junction port connector. If resistance is less than 500 ohms, replace remote CD changer. If resistance is 500 ohms or greater and vehicle is equipped with 45RFE 4-speed A/T, go to next step. If vehicle is not equipped with 45RFE 4-speed A/T, go to step **30)**.

29) Connect remote CD changer connector. Disconnect TCM connector. Measure resistance between ground and terminal No. 1 (Yellow/Violet/Gray wire) on junction port connector. If resistance is less than 500 ohms, replace TCM. If resistance is 500 ohms or greater, go to next step.

30) Connect TCM connector. Disconnect Passenger Door Module (PDM) connector. Measure resistance between ground and terminal No. 1 (Yellow/Violet/Gray wire) on junction port connector. If resistance is less than 500 ohms or if resistance is 500 ohms or greater, go to step **39)**.

31) Connect PDM connector. Measure resistance between ground and terminal No. 6 (Yellow/Violet/Red wire) on junction port connector. If resistance is less than 1500 ohms, go to step **96)**. If resistance is 1500 ohms or greater, go to step 84.

32) Measure resistance between ground and terminal No. 1 (Yellow/Violet/Gray wire) on junction port connector. If resistance is less than 5 ohms, go to next step. If resistance is 5 ohms or greater, go to step **36)**.

33) Disconnect Powertrain Control Module (PCM), Transmission Control Module (TCM), Passenger Door Module (PDM), Sentry Key Immobilizer Module (SKIM) and remote CD changer connectors. Check continuity between ground and terminal No. 1 (Yellow/Violet/Gray wire) on junction port connector. If continuity exists, repair Yellow/Violet/Gray wire for short to ground. If continuity does not exist and vehicle is equipped with remote CD changer, go to next step. If vehicle is equipped with 45RFE 4-speed A/T, go to step **29)**. If vehicle is not equipped with remote CD changer or 45RFE 4-speed A/T, go to step **35)**.

34) Connect all disconnected modules except remote CD changer. Measure resistance between ground and terminal No. 1 (Yellow/Violet/Gray wire) on junction port connector. If resistance is less than 500 ohms, replace remote CD changer. If resistance is 500 ohms or greater and vehicle is equipped with 45RFE 4-speed A/T, go to next step. If resistance is 500 ohms or greater and vehicle is not equipped with 45RFE 4-speed A/T, go to step **39)**.

35) Connect remote CD changer connector. Disconnect TCM connector. Measure resistance between ground and terminal No. 1 (Yellow/Violet/Gray wire) on junction port connector. If resistance is less than 500 ohms, replace TCM. If resistance is 500 ohms or greater, go to step **39)**.

36) Measure resistance between ground and terminal No. 6 (Yellow/Violet/Red wire) on junction port connector. If resistance is less than 1500 ohms, go to next step. If resistance is 1500 ohms or greater, go to step **38)**.

37) Measure resistance between ground and terminal No. 3 (Yellow/Violet/Dark Green wire) on junction port connector. If resistance is less than 9000 ohms, go to step **98)**. If resistance is 9000 ohms or greater, go to step **39)**.

38) Measure resistance between ground and terminal No. 3 (Yellow/Violet/Dark Green wire) on junction port connector. If resistance is less than 9000 ohms or if resistance is 9000 ohms or greater, go to next step.

39) Disconnect Body Control Module (BCM) connectors. Measure resistance between ground and terminal No. 8 (Yellow/Violet/White wire) on junction port connector. If resistance is less than 9000 ohms, repair Yellow/Violet/White wire for short to voltage. If resistance is 9000 ohms or greater, replace BCM.

40) Measure resistance between ground and terminal No. 4 (Yellow/Violet/Dark Blue wire) on junction port connector. If resistance is less than 9000 ohms, go to next step. If resistance is 9000 ohms or greater, go to step **57)**.

41) Access DLC. Check continuity between terminals No. 2 (Yellow/Violet wire) and 4 (Black/Orange wire) on DLC. If continuity exists, repair Yellow/Violet wire for short to ground. If continuity does not exist, go to next step.

42) Check continuity between ground and terminal No. 2 (Yellow/Violet/Brown wire) on junction port connector. If continuity exists and vehicle is equipped with Vehicle Information Center (VIC), go to next step. If vehicle is not equipped with VIC, go to step **44)**. If continuity does not exist, go to step **47)**.

43) Disconnect VIC module. Measure resistance between ground and terminal No. 2 (Yellow/Violet/Brown wire) on junction port connector. If resistance is less than 500 ohms, replace VIC. If resistance is 500 ohms or greater, go to next step.

44) Disconnect Controller Anti-Lock Brake (CAB). Disconnect Driver's Door Module (DDM), VIC connector and Memory Seat Module (MSM). Ensure junction port splice connector is removed. Measure resistance between ground and terminal No. 2 (Yellow/Violet/Brown wire) on junction port connector. If resistance is less than 5 ohms, repair Yellow/Violet/Brown wire for short to ground. If resistance is 5 ohms or greater, go to next step.

45) Connect all module connectors except DDM connector. Measure resistance between ground and terminal No. 2 (Yellow/Violet/Brown wire) on junction port connector. If resistance is less than 500 ohms or if resistance is 500 ohms or greater, go to next step.

46) Connect DDM connector. Measure resistance between ground and terminal No. 5 (Yellow/Violet/Orange wire) on junction port connector. If resistance is less than 9000 ohms, go to step **84)**. If resistance is 9000 ohms or greater, go to step **48)**.

47) Measure resistance between ground and terminal No. 5 (Yellow/Violet/Orange wire) on junction port connector. If resistance is less than 9000 ohms, go to next step. If resistance is 9000 ohms or greater, go to step **50)**.

48) Measure resistance between ground and terminal No. 1 (Yellow/Violet/Gray wire) on junction port connector. If resistance is less than 5 ohms, go to step **51)**. If resistance is 5 ohms or greater, go to next step.

49) Measure resistance between ground and terminal No. 6 (Yellow/Violet/Red wire) on junction port connector. If resistance is less than 1500 ohms, go to step **96)**. If resistance is 1500 ohms or greater, go to step **56)**.

50) Measure resistance between ground and terminal No. 1 (Yellow/Violet/Gray wire) on junction port connector. If resistance is less than 5 ohms, go to next step. If resistance is 5 ohms or greater, go to step **54)**.

51) Disconnect Powertrain Control Module (PCM), Transmission Control Module (TCM), Passenger Door Module (PDM), Sentry Key Immobilizer Module (SKIM) and remote CD changer connectors. Check continuity between ground and terminal No. 1 (Yellow/Violet/Gray wire) on junction port connector. If continuity exists, repair Yellow/Violet/Gray wire for short to ground. If continuity does not exist and vehicle is equipped with remote CD changer, go to next step. If vehicle is equipped with 45RFE 4-speed A/T, go to step **53)**. If vehicle is not equipped with remote CD changer or 45RFE 4-speed A/T, go to step **56)**.

52) Connect all disconnected modules except remote CD changer. Measure resistance between ground and terminal No. 1 (Yellow/Violet/

Gray wire) on junction port connector. If resistance is less than 500 ohms, replace remote CD changer. If resistance is 500 ohms or greater and vehicle is equipped with 45RFE 4-speed A/T, go to next step. If resistance is 500 ohms or greater and vehicle is not equipped with 45RFE 4-speed A/T, go to step **56)**.

53) Connect remote CD changer connector. Disconnect TCM connector. Measure resistance between ground and terminal No. 1 (Yellow/Violet/Gray wire) on junction port connector. If resistance is less than 500 ohms, replace TCM. If resistance is 500 ohms or greater, go to step **56)**.

54) Measure resistance between ground and terminal No. 6 (Yellow/Violet/Red wire) on junction port connector. If resistance is less than 1500 ohms or if resistance is 1500 ohms or greater, go to next step.

55) Measure resistance between ground and terminal No. 3 (Yellow/Violet/Dark Green wire) on junction port connector. If resistance is less than 9000 ohms or if resistance is 9000 ohms or greater, go to next step.

56) Disconnect radio PCI bus connector. Measure resistance between ground and terminal No. 4 (Yellow/Violet/Dark Blue wire) on junction port connector. If resistance is less than 9000 ohms, repair Yellow/Violet/Dark Blue wire for short to ground. If resistance is 9000 ohms or greater, replace radio.

57) Access DLC. Check continuity between terminals No. 2 (Yellow/Violet wire) and 4 (Black/Orange wire) on DLC. If continuity exists, repair Yellow/Violet wire for short to ground. If continuity does not exist, go to next step.

58) Check continuity between ground and terminal No. 2 (Yellow/Violet/Brown wire) on junction port connector. If continuity exists, go to next step. If continuity does not exist, go to step **75)**.

59) Measure resistance between ground and terminal No. 5 (Yellow/Violet/Orange wire) on junction port connector. If resistance is less than 9000 ohms, go to step **84)**. If resistance is 9000 ohms or greater, go to step **60)**.

60) Disconnect Controller Anti-Lock Brake (CAB). Disconnect Driver's Door Module (DDM), Vehicle Information Center (VIC) and Memory Seat Module (MSM). Ensure junction port splice connector is removed. Measure resistance between ground and terminal No. 2 (Yellow/Violet/Brown wire) on junction port connector. If resistance is less than 5 ohms, repair Yellow/Violet/Brown wire for short to ground. If resistance is 5 ohms or greater, go to next step.

61) Connect all module connectors except DDM connector. Measure resistance between ground and terminal No. 2 (Yellow/Violet/Brown wire) on junction port connector. If resistance is less than 500 ohms or if resistance is 500 ohms or greater, go to next step.

62) Measure resistance between ground and terminal No. 1 (Yellow/Violet/Gray wire) on junction port connector. If resistance is less than 5 ohms, go to next step. If resistance is 5 ohms or greater, go to step **69)**.

63) Disconnect Powertrain Control Module (PCM), Transmission Control Module (TCM), Passenger Door Module (PDM), Sentry Key Immobilizer Module (SKIM) and remote CD changer connectors. Check continuity between ground and terminal No. 1 (Yellow/Violet/Gray wire) on junction port connector. If continuity exists, repair Yellow/Violet/Gray wire for short to ground. If continuity does not exist and vehicle is equipped with remote CD changer, go to next step. If vehicle is equipped with 45RFE 4-speed A/T, go to step **65)**. If continuity does not exist and vehicle is equipped with Vehicle Information Center (VIC), go to step **66)**. If vehicle is equipped with Memory Seat Module (MSM), go to step **67)**. If vehicle is not equipped with remote CD changer, 45RFE 4-speed A/T, VIC or MSM, go to step **68)**.

64) Connect all disconnected modules except remote CD changer. Measure resistance between ground and terminal No. 1 (Yellow/Violet/Gray wire) on junction port connector. If resistance is less than 500 ohms, replace remote CD changer. If resistance is 500 ohms or greater and vehicle is equipped with 45RFE 4-speed A/T, go to next step. If vehicle is equipped with Vehicle Information Center (VIC), go to step **66)**. If resistance is 500 ohms or greater and vehicle is equipped with Memory Seat Module (MSM), go to step **67)**. If vehicle is not equipped with 45RFE 4-speed A/T, VIC or MSM, go to step **68)**.

65) Connect remote CD changer connector. Disconnect TCM connector. Measure resistance between ground and terminal No. 1 (Yellow/Violet/Gray wire) on junction port connector. If resistance is less than 500 ohms, replace TCM. If resistance is 500 ohms or greater and vehicle is equipped with Vehicle Information Center (VIC), go to next step. If vehicle is equipped with Memory Seat Module (MSM), go to step **67)**. If vehicle is not equipped with VIC or MSM, go to step **68)**.

66) Disconnect Controller Anti-Lock Brake (CAB). Measure resistance between ground and terminal No. 2 (Yellow/Violet/Brown wire) on junction port connector. If resistance is less than 500 ohms, replace Vehicle Information Center (VIC). If resistance is 500 ohms or greater and vehicle is equipped with Memory Seat Module (MSM), go to next step. If vehicle is not equipped with MSM, go to step **67)**.

67) Connect Controller Anti-Lock Brake (CAB). Disconnect Memory Seat Module (MSM). Measure resistance between ground and terminal No. 2 (Yellow/Violet/Brown wire) on junction port connector. If resistance is less than 500 ohms, go to next step. If resistance is 500 ohms or greater, replace MSM.

68) Measure resistance between ground and terminal No. 6 (Yellow/Violet/Red wire) on junction port connector. If resistance is less than 1500 ohms, go to step **96)**. If resistance is 1500 ohms or greater, go to step **90)**.

69) Measure resistance between ground and terminal No. 6 (Yellow/Violet/Red wire) on junction port connector. If resistance is less than 1500 ohms and vehicle is equipped with Vehicle Information Center (VIC), go to next step. If vehicle is not equipped with VIC, go to step 96. If resistance is 1500 ohms or greater and vehicle is equipped with VIC, go to step **71)**. If vehicle is equipped with Automatic Temperature Control (ATC), go to step **72)**. If resistance is 1500 ohms or greater and vehicle is equipped with Memory Seat Module (MSM), go to step **73)**. If vehicle is not equipped with VIC, ATC or MSM, test is complete.

70) Disconnect Controller Anti-Lock Brake (CAB). Measure resistance between ground and terminal No. 2 (Yellow/Violet/Brown wire) on junction port connector. If resistance is less than 500 ohms, replace Vehicle Information Center (VIC). If resistance is 500 ohms or greater, go to step **96)**.

71) Disconnect Controller Anti-Lock Brake (CAB). Measure resistance between ground and terminal No. 2 (Yellow/Violet/Brown wire) on junction port connector. If resistance is less than 500 ohms, replace Vehicle Information Center (VIC). If resistance is 500 ohms or greater, go to next step.

72) Connect Controller Anti-Lock Brake (CAB). Measure resistance between ground and terminal No. 3 (Yellow/Violet/Dark Green wire) on junction port connector. If resistance is less than 9000 ohms and vehicle is equipped with Memory Seat Module (MSM), go to next step. If vehicle is equipped with Automatic Temperature Control (ATC), go to step **98)**. If resistance is 9000 ohms or greater and vehicle is equipped with Memory Seat Module (MSM), go to step **74)**. If vehicle is not equipped with MSM, test is complete.

73) Disconnect Memory Seat Module (MSM). Measure resistance between ground and terminal No. 2 (Yellow/Violet/Brown wire) on junction port connector. If resistance is less than 500 ohms, go to step **98)**. If resistance is 500 ohms or greater, replace MSM.

74) Disconnect Memory Seat Module (MSM). Measure resistance between ground and terminal No. 2 (Yellow/Violet/Brown wire) on junction port connector. If resistance is less than 500 ohms, test is complete. If resistance is 500 ohms or greater, replace MSM.

75) Measure resistance between ground and terminal No. 5 (Yellow/Violet/Orange wire) on junction port connector. If resistance is less than 9000 ohms, go to next step. If resistance is 9000 ohms or greater, go to step **85)**.

76) Measure resistance between ground and terminal No. 1 (Yellow/Violet/Gray wire) on junction port connector. If resistance is less than 5 ohms, go to next step. If resistance is 5 ohms or greater, go to step **82)**.

77) Disconnect Powertrain Control Module (PCM), Transmission Control Module (TCM), Passenger Door Module (PDM), Sentry Key Immobilizer Module (SKIM) and remote CD changer connectors. Check continuity between ground and terminal No. 1 (Yellow/Violet/Gray wire) on junction port connector. If continuity exists, repair Yellow/Violet/Gray wire for short to ground. If continuity does not exist and vehicle is equipped with remote CD changer, go to next step. If vehicle is equipped with 45RFE

4-speed A/T, go to step **79)**. If vehicle is not equipped with remote CD changer or 45RFE 4-speed A/T, go to step **80)**.

78) Connect all disconnected modules except remote CD changer. Measure resistance between ground and terminal No. 1 (Yellow/Violet/Gray wire) on junction port connector. If resistance is less than 500 ohms, replace remote CD changer. If resistance is 500 ohms or greater and vehicle is equipped with 45RFE 4-speed A/T, go to next step. If vehicle is not equipped with 45RFE 4-speed A/T, go to step **80)**.

79) Connect remote CD changer connector. Disconnect TCM connector. Measure resistance between ground and terminal No. 1 (Yellow/Violet/Gray wire) on junction port connector. If resistance is less than 500 ohms, replace TCM. If resistance is 500 ohms or greater, go to next step.

80) Measure resistance between ground and terminal No. 6 (Yellow/Violet/Red wire) on junction port connector. If resistance is less than 1500 ohms, go to step **96)**. If resistance is 1500 ohms or greater, go to next step.

81) Disconnect Passenger Door Module (PDM). Measure resistance between ground and terminal No. 1 (Yellow/Violet/Gray wire) on junction port connector. If resistance is less than 500 ohms or if resistance is 500 ohms or greater, go to step **83)**.

82) Connect PDM connector. Measure resistance between ground and terminal No. 6 (Yellow/Violet/Red wire) on junction port connector. If resistance is less than 1500 ohms, go to step **95)**. If resistance is 1500 ohms or greater, go to next step.

83) Measure resistance between ground and terminal No. 3 (Yellow/Violet/Dark Green wire) on junction port connector. If resistance is less than 9000 ohms, go to step **98)**. If resistance is 9000 ohms or greater, go to next step.

84) Measure resistance between ground and terminal No. 5 (Yellow/Violet/Orange wire) on junction port connector. If resistance is less than 9000 ohms, repair Yellow/Violet/Orange wire for short to ground. If resistance is 9000 ohms or greater, replace Airbag Control Module (ACM).

85) Measure resistance between ground and terminal No. 1 (Yellow/Violet/Gray wire) on junction port connector. If resistance is less than 5 ohms, go to next step. If resistance is 5 ohms or greater, go to step **94)**.

86) Measure resistance between ground and terminal No. 6 (Yellow/Violet/Red wire) on junction port connector. If resistance is less than 1500 ohms, go to step **96)**. If resistance is 1500 ohms or greater, go to next step.

87) Disconnect Powertrain Control Module (PCM), Transmission Control Module (TCM), Passenger Door Module (PDM), Sentry Key Immobilizer Module (SKIM) and remote CD changer connectors. Check continuity between ground and terminal No. 1 (Yellow/Violet/Gray wire) on junction port connector. If continuity exists, repair Yellow/Violet/Gray wire for short to ground. If continuity does not exist and vehicle is equipped with remote CD changer, go to next step. If vehicle is equipped with 45RFE 4-speed A/T, go to step **89)**. If continuity does not exist and vehicle is equipped with Automatic Temperature Control (ATC), go to step **90)**. If vehicle is not equipped with remote CD changer, 45RFE 4-speed A/T or ATC, test is complete.

88) Connect all disconnected modules except remote CD changer. Measure resistance between ground and terminal No. 1 (Yellow/Violet/Gray wire) on junction port connector. If resistance is less than 500 ohms, replace remote CD changer. If resistance is 500 ohms or greater and vehicle is equipped with 45RFE 4-speed A/T, go to next step. If vehicle is equipped with Automatic Temperature Control (ATC), go to step **90)**. If vehicle is not equipped with 45RFE 4-speed A/T or ATC, test is complete.

89) Connect remote CD changer connector. Disconnect TCM connector. Measure resistance between ground and terminal No. 1 (Yellow/Violet/Gray wire) on junction port connector. If resistance is less than 500 ohms, replace TCM. If resistance is 500 ohms or greater, go to next step.

90) Connect TCM connector. Measure resistance between ground and terminal No. 3 (Yellow/Violet/Dark Green wire) on junction port connector. If resistance is less than 9000 ohms, go to step **98)**. If resistance is 9000 ohms or greater, go to next step.

91) Disconnect Passenger Door Module (PDM). Measure resistance between ground and terminal No. 1 (Yellow/Violet/Gray wire) on junction port connector. If resistance is less than 500 ohms or if resistance is 500 ohms or greater, go to next step.

92) Connect Passenger Door Module (PDM). Disconnect Powertrain Control Module (PCM). Measure resistance between ground and terminal No. 1 (Yellow/Violet/Gray wire) on junction port connector. If resistance is less than 500 ohms, replace PCM. If resistance is 500 ohms or greater and vehicle is equipped with Sentry Key Immobilizer System (SKIS), go to next step. If vehicle is not equipped with SKIS, test is complete.

93) Connect PCM. Disconnect Sentry Key Immobilizer Module (SKIM). Measure resistance between ground and terminal No. 1 (Yellow/Violet/Gray wire) on junction port connector. If resistance is less than 500 ohms or if resistance is 500 ohms or greater, test is complete.

94) Measure resistance between ground and terminal No. 6 (Yellow/Violet/Red wire) on junction port connector. If resistance is less than 1500 ohms, go to next step. If resistance is 1500 ohms or greater, go to step **97)**.

95) Measure resistance between ground and terminal No. 3 (Yellow/Violet/Dark Green wire) on junction port connector. If resistance is less than 9000 ohms, go to step **98)**. If resistance is 9000 ohms or greater, go to next step.

96) Disconnect instrument cluster connector. Measure resistance between ground and terminal No. 6 (Yellow/Violet/Red wire) on junction port connector. If resistance is less than 1500 ohms, repair Yellow/Violet/Red wire for short to ground. If resistance is 1500 ohms or greater, replace instrument cluster.

97) Measure resistance between ground and terminal No. 3 (Yellow/Violet/Dark Green wire) on junction port connector. If resistance is less than 9000 ohms, go to next step. If resistance is 9000 ohms or greater, test is complete.

98) Disconnect Automatic Temperature Control (ATC) (if equipped). Check continuity between ground and terminal No. 3 (Yellow/Violet/Dark Green wire) on junction port connector. If continuity exists, repair Yellow/Violet/Dark Green wire for short to ground. If continuity does not exist, replace ATC. If vehicle is not equipped with ATC, repair Yellow/Violet/Dark Green wire for short to ground.

VERIFICATION TESTS

ABS VERIFICATION TEST

1) Turn ignition off. Connect all previously disconnected components and connectors.

2) Turn ignition on. Using scan tool, erase DTCs. Read DTCs. If any DTCs are present, go to IDENTIFYING VEHICLE COMMUNICATION PROBLEMS.

3) If not DTCs are present, road test vehicle for at least 5 minutes. Perform several ABS braking stops.

4) Using scan tool, read DTCs. If any DTCs are present, go to IDENTIFYING VEHICLE COMMUNICATION PROBLEMS. If no DTCs are present, test is complete.

BODY VERIFICATION TEST

1) Reconnect all previously disconnected components and connectors. If BCM was replaced, turn ignition on for at least 15 seconds.

2) Ensure ignition is on. Erase all DTCs using scan tool. Turn ignition off and wait 5 seconds. Turn ignition on and fully operate system that was malfunctioning.

3) If system is not operating properly, go to IDENTIFYING VEHICLE COMMUNICATION PROBLEMS. Using scan tool, read Body DTCs. If any DTCs are present, go to IDENTIFYING VEHICLE COMMUNICATION PROBLEMS. If no DTCs are present, system is operating correctly and customer's complaint cannot be duplicated, repair is complete.

PCI BUS TEST

1) Connect Breakout Box (J-1962) to DLC. Connect scan tool to breakout box. Connect Scope Input Cable (CH 7058) to channel No. 1 connector on scan tool.

2) Connect Red and Black test probe cable with Probe Adapter (CH7062) to scope input cable. Select DRB STANDALONE. Select LAB SCOPE, then LIVE. Select 12 VOLT SQUARE WAVE.

3) Press F2 for scope. Press F2 and use down arrow to set voltage range to 20 volts. Press F2. Connect Black lead to breakout box port No. 4. Connect Red lead to terminal No. 2.

4) Turn ignition on. If voltage displayed on scan tool lab scope pluses from zero to about 7.5 volts, repair is not complete. Go to appropriate symptom. If voltage is zero volts, go to PCI BUS SHORT TO GROUND. If a constant voltage is displayed, go to PCI BUS SHORT TO BATTERY.

45RFE 4-SPEED A/T VERIFICATION TEST

1) Turn ignition off. Connect all previously disconnected components and connectors. Turn ignition on. Using scan tool, erase DTCs.

2) Using scan tool, display transmission temperature. Start and run engine until transmission temperature is above 110°F. Ensure transmission fluid level is correct.

3) Road test vehicle. Using scan tool, monitor engine RPM. Perform 15–20 upshifts from standing start to 45 MPH with a constant throttle opening of 20–25 degrees.

4) Below 25 MPH, perform 5–8 WOT kickdown type downshifts to 1st gear. Allow at least 5 seconds in 2nd and/or 3rd gear between downshifts. Using scan tool, read DTCs during road test.

5) If any DTCs are present, go to IDENTIFYING VEHICLE COMMUNICATION PROBLEMS. If no DTCs are present, system is operating correctly and customer's complaint cannot be duplicated, repair is complete.

SKIM INITIALIZATION PROCEDURE

General Information – SECURED ACCESS mode is not required to check programmed status of key.

If PCM is replaced, unique secret key data must be transferred from SKIM to PCM. This procedure requires SKIM to be placed in SECURED ACCESS mode using 4-digit PIN code.

If 3 attempts are made to enter secured access mode using an incorrect PIN, SECURED ACCESS mode will be locked out for one hour. To exit lock out mode, turn ignition switch to RUN/START position continuously for one hour. Ensure all accessories are turned off. Monitor battery state and connect battery charger is necessary.

To program smart keys using "customer programming method" requires 2 valid smart keys. See owner's manual.

Initialization Procedure – **1)** Obtain vehicle's unique PIN number assigned to it's original SKIM module from vehicle owner or Chrysler's customer center.

2) Using scan tool, select THEFT ALARM, SKIM, then MISCELLANEOUS. Select SKIM MODULE REPLACED function.

3) Enter SECURED ACCESS mode using unique 4-digit PIN number.

4) Program vehicle's VIN number into SKIM's memory.

5) Program country code into SKIM's memory (U.S.).

6) Transfer vehicle's unique Secret Key data from PCM. This process will require SKIM module to be in SECURED ACCESS mode. The PIN number must be entered into scan tool before SKIM will enter SECURED ACCESS mode. Once SECURED ACCESS mode is active, SKIM will remain in that mode for 60 seconds.

7) Program all customer keys into SKIM's memory. This requires that SKIM be in SECURED ACCESS mode. The SKIM will immediately exit SECURED ACCESS mode after each key is programmed.

PROGRAMMING BLANK SMART KEY USING SCAN TOOL

1) Once key blank is cut, insert key into ignition switch. Turn ignition switch to RUN position. Using scan tool, select THEFT ALARM, then SKIM. Select MISCELLANEOUS, then PROGRAM NEW KEY. Enter 4-digit PIN code. When programming is completed, SKIM will exit SECURED ACCESS mode and display status of key. One of five different status messages maybe displayed as follows:

- PROGRAMMING SUCCESSFUL is displayed if SKIM smart key programming succeeds.

- LEARNED KEY IN IGNITION is displayed if key in the ignition has already been programmed into vehicle's SKIM.
- 8 KEYS ALREADY LEARNED, PROGRAMMING NOT DONE is displayed if eight keys have already been programmed into SKIM. If a new key needs to be added due to a lost or defective key, the ERASE ALL KEYS function has to be performed. Original 7 keys plus additional new key may then be reprogrammed into SKIM.
- PROGRAMMING NOT ATTEMPTED is displayed after an ERASE ALL KEYS function is executed.
- PROGRAMING KEY FAILED is displayed if further diagnosis is required.

2) To program additional keys, turn ignition off. Remove current programmed key and insert next new blank key. Turn ignition switch to RUN position. Re-enter SECURED ACCESS mode function and repeat PROGRAM NEW KEY procedure.

CAUTION: When battery is disconnected, vehicle computer and memory systems may lose memory data. Driveability problems may exist until computer systems have completed a relearn cycle. See COMPUTER RELEARN PROCEDURES article in GENERAL INFORMATION before disconnecting battery.

DESCRIPTION

The speed (cruise) control system is electronically controlled and vacuum operated. The electronic control is integrated into the Powertrain Control Module (PCM). System consists of the following components: PCM, servo, speed control switches, vacuum reservoir, vehicle speed sensor, speed control relay and brake switch.

System controls are located on each side of steering wheel air bag module and consist of ON/OFF, SET, RESUME/ACCEL, CANCEL AND COAST buttons. System is designed to operate at speeds above 35 MPH.

OPERATION

SYSTEM CONTROLS

To Set Speed Control – Press ON/OFF button to turn speed control system on. Accelerate to desired speed (minimum of 35 MPH) and press SET/COAST button. Vehicle speed will be maintained.

NOTE: Speed control system will automatically disengage when vehicle speed decreases to less than 35 MPH or increases to more than 85 MPH.

To Disengage Speed Control – Press brake pedal. Press clutch pedal. Press CANCEL button. Press ON/OFF button. If ON/OFF button is used, set speed will be erased from memory.
To Resume Previous Speed – If set speed has not been erased from memory and vehicle speed is more than 35 MPH, press RES/ACCEL button.
To Increase Speed – With speed control system on, increase set speed by rapidly pressing and releasing RES/ACCEL button. Each pressing of button will cause speed increase of 2 MPH. For example, pressing button 3 times will increase speed by 6 MPH. To increase speed gradually, hold RES/ACCEL button down until desired speed is reached. When button is released, new set speed will be maintained.
To Decrease Speed – With speed control system on, decrease set speed by pressing SET/COAST button. Vehicle speed will gradually decrease. Releasing button will set a new speed as long as vehicle speed is still more than 35 MPH.

COMPONENT LOCATIONS

COMPONENT LOCATIONS

Component	Location
Powertrain Control Module (PCM)	
Wrangler	Right Side Of Firewall In Engine Compartment
Cherokee	Left Front Corner Of Engine Compartment
Data Link Connector (DLC)	Lower Left Side Of Instrument Panel
Park/Neutral Position (PNP)	
Switch	Left Side Of Transmission
Vehicle Speed Sensor (VSS)	On Transmission Or Transfer Case Extension Housing

TROUBLE SHOOTING

ROAD TEST

Perform a road test to verify speed control malfunctions. Ensure speedometer operation is smooth without flutter at all speeds. Speedometer fluttering may cause surging in speed control system. For speedometer diagnosis, see appropriate INSTRUMENT PANELS

article. If road test verifies a surge following speed control set and speedometer operates smoothly, see OVERSHOOT/UNDERSHOOT FOLLOWING SPEED CONTROL SET.

If road test verifies an inoperative system, and speedometer operates smoothly, check for:
- Diagnostic Trouble Codes (DTCs). See SELF-DIAGNOSTIC SYSTEM.
- Misadjusted brake switch. See BRAKE SWITCH under REMOVAL & INSTALLATION.
- Poor electrical connections at servo.
- Leaking vacuum reservoir, check valve, hoses or connections. See VACUUM SUPPLY under COMPONENT TESTS.
- Secure attachments of S/C servo cable.
- Smooth operation of throttle linkage.
- Defective PCM or wiring.
- Defective servo. See SPEED CONTROL SERVO under COMPONENT TESTS.

To verify a speed control electronic malfunction, use a scan tool to check for DTCs. See SELF-DIAGNOSTIC SYSTEM. A speed control malfunction may occur without setting a DTC. If no DTCs are stored, go to CHECKING SPEED CONTROL OPERATION under SYSTEM TESTS.

OVERSHOOT/UNDERSHOOT FOLLOWING SPEED CONTROL SET

If operator repeatedly presses and releases set button with their foot off accelerator (lift foot set) to begin speed control operation, vehicle may accelerate and exceed desired set speed by 5 MPH and then decelerate to less than desired set speed before achieving desired set speed.

Speed Control (S/C) has as adaptive strategy that compensates for variations in S/C cable lengths. When S/C is set with vehicle operator's foot off accelerator pedal, S/C compensates for excessive S/C cable slack. If lift foot sets are continually used, speed control overshoot/undershoot condition will develop.

To "unlearn" overshoot/undershoot condition, operator must press and release set button while maintaining desired speed with accelerator pedal, then turn S/C switch to OFF position after waiting 10 seconds. This procedure must be repeated 10-15 times to completely unlearn overshoot/undershoot condition.

COMPONENT TESTS

WARNING: Vehicle is equipped with an air bag. Air bag must be deactivated before servicing speed control components on or around steering column. See AIR BAG RESTRAINT SYSTEMS article.

NOTE: For component location, See COMPONENT LOCATIONS. For connector terminal identification, see CONNECTOR IDENTIFICATION. For wiring diagram, see WIRING DIAGRAMS.

BRAKE SWITCH

Disconnect brake switch 6-pin connector. Using an ohmmeter, check for continuity at brake switch. *See Fig. 1.* If continuity is not as specified in BRAKE SWITCH CONTINUITY table, check brake switch adjustment. See BRAKE SWITCH under REMOVAL & INSTALLATION. If brake switch adjustment is okay, replace defective brake switch.

BRAKE SWITCH CONTINUITY

Switch Plunger Position	Check Between Terminals No.	Continuity
Released	5 & 6	Yes
Depressed	1 & 2	Yes
	3 & 4	Yes

SPEED CONTROL SERVO

1) Start engine. Disconnect Speed Control (S/C) servo 4-pin connector. Turn speed control switch to ON position. Using a voltmeter, check voltage at S/C servo connector terminal No. 3 (Dark Blue/Red wire). Battery voltage should exist when brake pedal is NOT depressed.

2) Connect a jumper wire between S/C servo pin No. 3 and S/C servo connector terminal No. 3. Check voltage at S/C servo pins No. 1, 2 and 4. If battery voltage does not exist, replace S/C servo.

3) Turn ignition off. Check for continuity between S/C servo connector terminal No. 4 and ground. Continuity should exist. Repair open ground circuit as necessary.

VACUUM SUPPLY

1) Disconnect vacuum hose at speed control servo. Install vacuum gauge to disconnected vacuum hose. Start engine and observe gauge. Vacuum reading should be a minimum of 10 in. Hg. Turn engine off. Vacuum should continue to hold at a minimum of 10 in. Hg.

2) If vacuum is not as specified, check for kinked or leaking vacuum lines, defective check valve, defective vacuum reservoir or poor engine performance. If no problems are found, check speed control servo. See SPEED CONTROL SERVO.

CONNECTOR IDENTIFICATION

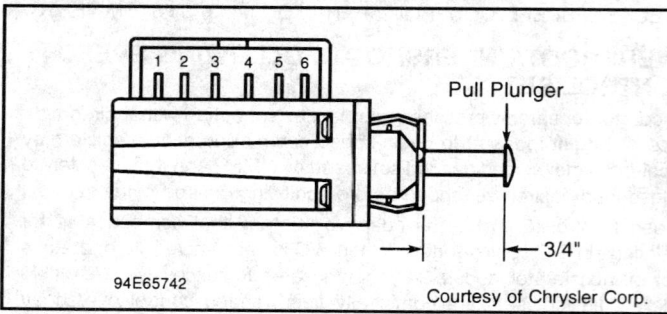

Fig. 1: Identifying Brake Switch Terminals

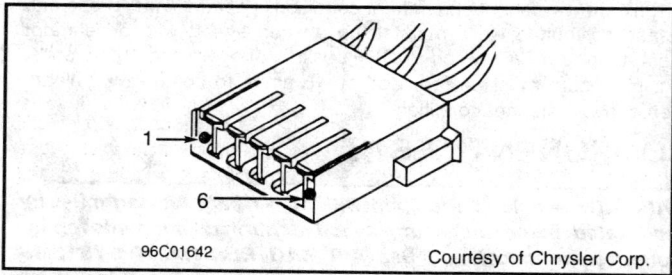

Fig. 2: Identifying Brake Switch Harness Connector Terminals

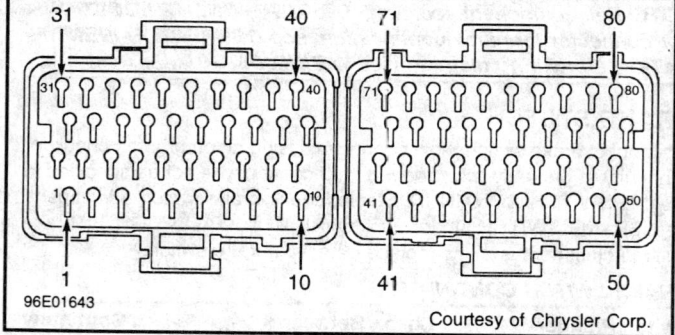

Fig. 3: Identifying Powertrain Control Module (PCM) Connector Terminals

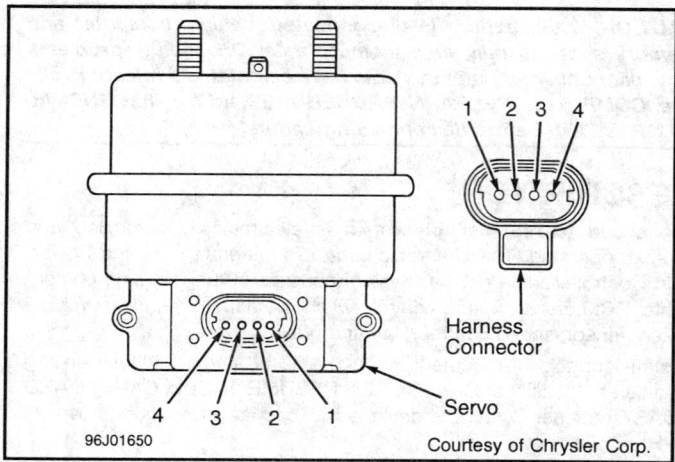

Fig. 4: Identifying Speed Control (S/C) Servo Connector Terminals

SELF-DIAGNOSTIC SYSTEM

WARNING: Vehicle is equipped with an air bag. Air bag must be deactivated before servicing speed control components on or around steering column. See AIR BAG RESTRAINT SYSTEMS article.

SERVICE PRECAUTIONS

Before proceeding with diagnosis, the following precautions must be followed:

- When using Diagnostic Trouble Code (DTC) tests for diagnosis, DO NOT skip any steps, or incorrect diagnosis may result. Always perform indicated verification procedure after repairs are made.
- When using a jumper wire, ensure either jumper wire or circuit is fuse-protected.
- Before disconnecting connector from any control module, ensure ignition is off before removing connector.
- When checking voltage or continuity at any control module, probe connector for control module from pin side. DO NOT backprobe connector or probe wires through insulation.
- DO NOT cause short circuits when performing electrical tests. This will set additional DTCs, making diagnosis of original problem more difficult.
- Use specified test equipment when performing electrical tests.

RETRIEVING DIAGNOSTIC TROUBLE CODES

NOTE: Self-diagnostic tests are written specifically for Chrysler's Diagnostic Readout Box (DRB). If using a generic scan tool, ensure it is OBD-II certified. A generic scan tool may not be capable of performing all necessary test functions.

Ensure battery is fully charged. Turn ignition off. Connect scan tool to Data Link Connector (DLC). DLC is located under left side of instrument panel. Turn ignition on. Using scan tool manufacturer's instructions, record all DTCs displayed on scan tool. If any DTCs are retrieved, perform appropriate test under DIAGNOSTIC TESTS. Once all repairs are made, clear DTCs. See CLEARING DIAGNOSTIC TROUBLE CODES. If no DTCs are retrieved and fault still exists, go to CHECKING SPEED CONTROL OPERATION under SYSTEM TESTS.

CLEARING DIAGNOSTIC TROUBLE CODES

Ensure ignition is off. Connect scan tool to DLC. Turn ignition on. Using screen prompts on scan tool, erase DTCs from PCM.

DIAGNOSTIC TESTS

DTC P0500: NO VEHICLE SPEED SENSOR SIGNAL

Vehicle Speed Sensor (VSS) is monitored when engine temperature is more than 104°F (40°C), MAP vacuum is 15-16 in. Hg and engine speed is 1400-3000 RPM. DTC P0500 will set if there is no signal from VSS for more than 15 seconds on 2 consecutive trips.

Possible Causes:

- VSS defective.
- 5-volt supply circuit open.
- VSS circuit open or shorted.
- Speedometer pinion gear defective.
- PCM defective.

NOTE: For connector terminal identification, see CONNECTOR IDENTIFICATION. For wiring diagram, see WIRING DIAGRAMS.

WARNING: Keep hands and feet clear of rotating wheels.

1) Raise drive wheels to spin free. Start engine. Using scan tool, read Vehicle Speed Sensor (VSS). Put transmission in any forward gear. If scan tool displays more than zero MPH, go to next step. If scan tool does not display more than zero MPH, go to step 3).

2) Condition to set DTC is not present at this time. Inspect wiring and connectors for possible intermittent problems. Check for Technical Service Bulletins (TSBs). Repair as necessary. Perform TEST VER-5A under VERIFICATION TESTS.

3) Raise vehicle. Inspect VSS adapter. If VSS adapter is not seated or positioned properly, repair as necessary. Perform TEST VER-5A under VERIFICATION TESTS. If VSS adapter is okay, go to next step.

4) Turn ignition off. Disconnect VSS connector. Inspect connectors. Clean or repair as necessary. Turn ignition on. Using a voltmeter, check voltage on VSS 5-volt supply circuit at VSS connector terminal No. 1 (Violet/Orange wire). If voltage is 4 volts or less, repair open circuit. Perform TEST VER-5A under VERIFICATION TESTS. If voltage is more than 4 volts, go to next step.

5) Turn ignition off. Connect jumper wire to VSS signal circuit at VSS connector terminal No. 3 (White/Orange wire). Turn ignition on. Using scan tool, read VSS signal. While observing scan tool, tap other end of jumper wire to sensor ground circuit at VSS connector terminal No. 2 (Brown/Yellow wire). If scan tool displays more than zero MPH, go to next step. If scan tool does not display more than zero MPH, go to step 7).

6) Turn ignition off. Remove VSS. Inspect speedometer pinion gear. Repair as necessary. Perform TEST VER-5A under VERIFICATION TESTS. If pinion gear is okay, replace VSS. Perform TEST VER-5A under VERIFICATION TESTS.

7) Turn ignition off. Disconnect PCM connectors. Inspect connectors. Clean or repair as necessary. Using an ohmmeter, check resistance of sensor ground circuit at VSS connector terminal No. 2 (Brown/Yellow wire). If resistance is 5 ohms or more, repair open circuit. Perform TEST VER-5A under VERIFICATION TESTS. If resistance is less than 5 ohms, go to next step.

8) Using an ohmmeter, check resistance of VSS signal circuit at VSS connector terminal No. 3 (White/Orange wire). If resistance is 5 ohms or more, repair open circuit. Perform TEST VER-5A under VERIFICATION TESTS. If resistance is less than 5 ohms, go to next step.

9) Using an ohmmeter, check resistance between ground and VSS signal circuit at VSS connector terminal No. 3 (White/Orange wire). If resistance is less than 5 ohms, repair short circuit. Perform TEST VER-5A under VERIFICATION TESTS. If resistance is 5 ohms or more, go to next step.

10) Using an ohmmeter, check resistance between ground and sensor ground circuit at VSS connector terminal No. 2 (Brown/Yellow wire). If resistance is less than 5 ohms, repair short circuit. Perform TEST VER-5A under VERIFICATION TESTS. If resistance is 5 ohms or more, replace PCM. Perform TEST VER-5A under VERIFICATION TESTS.

DTC P1595: SPEED CONTROL SOLENOID CIRCUITS

NOTE: This test applies to Wrangler only. Information for Cherokee is not available from manufacturer.

Speed Control (S/C) solenoid circuits are monitored when engine is running, S/C switch is on and battery voltage is more than 10.4 volts. DTC P1595 will set if vacuum and vent solenoids do not respond when actuated by PCM.

Possible Causes:

- Ground circuit open.
- S/C brake switch output circuit open.
- S/C power supply circuit open or shorted.
- S/C servo defective.
- S/C vacuum solenoid control circuit open or shorted.
- S/C vent solenoid control circuit open or shorted.
- Brake switch defective or out of adjustment.
- Defective PCM.

NOTE: For component location, see COMPONENT LOCATIONS. For connector terminal identification, see CONNECTOR IDENTIFICATION. For wiring diagram, see WIRING DIAGRAMS.

1) Turn ignition on. Turn Speed Control (S/C) on. Using scan tool, actuate S/C vent solenoid. If speed control servo clicks, go to next step. If S/C servo does not click, go to step 7).

2) Using scan tool, actuate S/C vacuum solenoid. If S/C servo clicks, go to next step. If S/C servo does not click, go to step 6).

3) Turn ignition off. Inspect S/C wiring and connectors. Clean or repair as necessary. Perform TEST VER-4A under VERIFICATION TESTS. If wiring and connectors are okay, go to next step.

4) Turn ignition on. Using scan tool, actuate S/C vacuum solenoid. Wiggle wiring harness between S/C servo and brake switch to PCM while scan tool is still actuating speed control vacuum solenoid. If wiggling did not cause an interruption of S/C servo actuation, go to next step. If wiggling caused an interruption of S/C servo actuation, repair wiring harness as necessary. Perform TEST VER-4A under VERIFICATION TESTS.

5) Using scan tool, actuate S/C vent solenoid. Wiggle wiring harness between S/C servo and brake switch to PCM while scan tool is still actuating speed control vacuum solenoid. If wiggling did not cause interruption of S/C servo actuation, test is complete. If wiggling caused interruption of S/C servo actuation, repair wiring harness as necessary. Perform TEST VER-4A under VERIFICATION TESTS.

6) Using scan tool, actuate S/C vent solenoid. Wiggle wiring harness between S/C servo and brake switch to PCM while scan tool is still actuating speed control vacuum solenoid. If wiggling did not cause interruption of S/C servo actuation, go to next step. If wiggling caused interruption of S/C servo actuation, repair wiring harness as necessary. Perform TEST VER-4A under VERIFICATION TESTS.

NOTE: Ensure brake pedal is NOT depressed during the following steps.

7) Turn ignition off. Disconnect S/C servo 4-pin connector. Inspect all related wiring and connectors and repair as necessary. Turn ignition on. Turn S/C switch on. Using a 12-volt test light, probe brake switch output circuit at S/C servo connector terminal No. 3 (Dark Blue/Red wire). If test light is illuminated and bright, go to next step. If test light is dim or not illuminated, go to step 13).

8) Turn ignition off. Using an ohmmeter, check resistance of ground circuit at S/C servo connector terminal No. 4 (Black wire). If resistance is 5 ohms or more, repair open ground circuit. Perform TEST VER-4A under VERIFICATION TESTS. If resistance is less than 5 ohms, go to next step.

9) Disconnect PCM connectors. Inspect connectors. Clean or repair as necessary. Using an ohmmeter, check resistance between ground and S/C vacuum solenoid control circuit at S/C servo connector terminal No. 1 (Tan/Red wire). If resistance is less than 5 ohms, repair short to ground. Perform TEST VER-4A under VERIFICATION TESTS. If resistance is 5 ohms or more, go to next step.

10) Using an ohmmeter, check resistance between ground and S/C vent solenoid control circuit at S/C servo connector terminal No. 2 (Light Green/Red wire). If resistance is less than 5 ohms, repair short to ground. Perform TEST VER-4A under VERIFICATION TESTS. If resistance is 5 ohms or more, go to next step.

11) Using an ohmmeter, check resistance of S/C vacuum solenoid control circuit between S/C servo connector terminal No. 1 and PCM connector C3, terminal No. C4 (Tan/Red wire). If resistance is 5 ohms or more, repair open circuit. Perform TEST VER-4A under VERIFICATION TESTS. If resistance is less than 5 ohms, go to next step.

12) Using an ohmmeter, check resistance of S/C vent solenoid control circuit between S/C servo connector terminal No. 2 and PCM connector C3, terminal No. 5 (Light Green/Red wire). If resistance is 5 ohms or more, repair open circuit. Perform TEST VER-4A under VERIFICATION TESTS. If resistance is less than 5 ohms, replace S/C servo. Perform TEST VER-4A under VERIFICATION TESTS.

13) Using an ohmmeter, check resistance between ground and brake switch output circuit at S/C servo connector terminal No. 3 (Dark Blue/Red wire). If resistance is less than 5 ohms, repair short to ground. Perform TEST VER-4A under VERIFICATION TESTS. If resistance is 5 ohms or more, go to next step.

14) Disconnect brake switch connector. Turn ignition on. Using a 12-volt test light, probe S/C power supply circuit at brake switch connector terminal No. 3 (Yellow/Red wire). If test light is illuminated and bright, go to next step. If test light is not illuminated or dim, go to step **17)**.

15) Turn ignition off. Using an ohmmeter, check resistance of S/C brake switch output circuit between S/C servo connector terminal No. 3 and brake switch connector terminal No. 4 (Dark Blue/Red wire). If resistance is 5 ohms or more, repair open circuit. Perform TEST VER-4A under VERIFICATION TESTS. If resistance is less than 5 ohms, go to next step.

16) Check brake switch adjustment. Adjust as necessary. Perform TEST VER-4A under VERIFICATION TESTS. If brake switch adjustment is okay, replace brake switch. Perform TEST VER-4A under VERIFICATION TESTS.

17) Turn ignition off. Disconnect PCM connectors. Inspect connectors. Clean or repair as necessary. Using an ohmmeter, check resistance of S/C power supply circuit between PCM connector C3, terminal No. 11 and brake switch connector terminal No. 3 (Yellow/Red wire). If resistance is 5 ohms or more, repair open circuit. Perform TEST VER-4A under VERIFICATION TESTS. If resistance is less than 5 ohms, replace PCM. Perform TEST VER-4A under VERIFICATION TESTS.

DTC P1597: SPEED CONTROL SWITCH ALWAYS LOW

NOTE: This test applies to Wrangler only. Information for Cherokee is not available from manufacturer.

DTC P1597 will set if Speed Control (S/C) switch voltage is less than 0.39 volts for 2 minutes when ignition is on and battery voltage is more than 10.4 volts.
Possible Causes:
- S/C ON/OFF switch defective.
- S/C RESUME/ACCEL switch defective.
- S/C switch signal circuit shorted to ground.
- Defective PCM.
- Defective clockspring.

NOTE: For component location, see COMPONENT LOCATIONS. For connector terminal identification, see CONNECTOR IDENTIFICATION. For wiring diagram, see WIRING DIAGRAMS.

1) Turn ignition on. Using scan tool, read S/C switch volts. If voltage is less than one volt, go to next step. If voltage is one volt or more, no problem is indicated at this time.

2) While observing scan tool, disconnect S/C ON/OFF switch. If S/C switch voltage changes to 5 volts, replace S/C ON/OFF switch. Perform TEST VER-4A under VERIFICATION TESTS. If voltage does not change to 5 volts, go to next step.

3) While observing scan tool, disconnect S/C RESUME/ACCEL switch. If S/C switch voltage changes to 5 volts, replace S/C RESUME/ACCEL switch. Perform TEST VER-4A under VERIFICATION TESTS. If voltage does not change to 5 volts, go to next step.

4) Turn ignition off. Ensure both S/C switches are still disconnected. Using an ohmmeter, check resistance between S/C switch connector terminals (S/C switch signal circuit and S/C switch ground circuit). If resistance is less than 5 ohms, repair short circuit. Perform TEST VER-4A under VERIFICATION TESTS. If resistance is 5 ohms or more, go to next step.

5) Reconnect RESUME/ACCEL switch. Disconnect clockspring 4-pin connector. Inspect connectors. Clean or repair as necessary. Using an ohmmeter, check resistance between ground and S/C switch signal circuit at clockspring 4-pin connector terminal No. 2 (Red/Light Green wire). If resistance is less than 5 ohms, go to next step. If resistance is 5 ohms or more, replace clockspring. Perform TEST VER-4A under VERIFICATION TESTS.

6) Disconnect RESUME/ACCEL switch. Disconnect PCM connectors. Inspect connectors. Clean or repair as necessary. Using an ohmmeter, check resistance between ground and S/C switch signal circuit at clockspring 4-pin connector terminal No. 2 (Red/Light Green wire). If resistance is less than 5 ohms, repair short to ground. Perform TEST VER-4A under VERIFICATION TESTS. If resistance is 5 ohms or more, replace PCM. Perform TEST VER-4A under VERIFICATION TESTS.

DTC P1683: SPEED CONTROL POWER RELAY CIRCUIT OR 12-VOLT DRIVER CIRCUIT

NOTE: This test applies to Wrangler only. Information for Cherokee is not available from manufacturer.

DTC P1683 will set if Speed Control (S/C) power supply circuit is open or shorted when S/C is turned on.
Possible Causes:
- Brake switch out of adjustment.
- S/C brake switch output circuit open or shorted.
- Defective S/C servo.
- Defective brake switch.
- S/C vacuum or vent solenoid control circuits open or shorted.
- Defective PCM.
- Ground circuit open.
- S/C power supply circuit open.

NOTE: For component location, see COMPONENT LOCATIONS. For connector terminal identification, see CONNECTOR IDENTIFICATION. For wiring diagram, see WIRING DIAGRAMS.

NOTE: Ensure brake pedal is not depressed during the following steps.

1) Turn ignition off. Disconnect S/C servo connector. Inspect connectors. Clean or repair as necessary. Turn ignition on. Using scan tool, actuate S/C relay. Using a 12-volt test light, probe S/C brake switch output circuit at S/C servo connector terminal No. 3 (Dark Blue/Red wire). If test light is illuminated and bright, go to next step. If test light is not illuminated or dim, go to step **7)**.

2) Turn ignition off. Using an ohmmeter, check resistance of ground circuit at S/C servo connector terminal No. 4 (Black wire). If resistance is 5 ohms or more, repair open ground circuit. Perform TEST VER-4A under VERIFICATION TESTS. If resistance is less than 5 ohms, go to next step.

3) Disconnect PCM connectors. Inspect connectors. Clean or repair as necessary. Using an ohmmeter, check resistance of S/C vacuum solenoid control circuit between PCM connector C3, terminal No. 4 and S/C servo connector terminal No. 1 (Tan/Red wire). If resistance is 5 ohms or more, repair open circuit. Perform TEST VER-4A under VERIFICATION TESTS. If resistance is less than 5 ohms, go to next step.

4) Using an ohmmeter, check resistance between ground and S/C vacuum solenoid control circuit at S/C servo connector terminal No. 1

(Tan/Red wire). If resistance is less than 5 ohms, repair short to ground. Perform TEST VER-4A under VERIFICATION TESTS. If resistance is 5 ohms or more, go to next step.

5) Using an ohmmeter, check resistance of S/C vent solenoid control circuit between PCM connector C3, terminal No. 5 and S/C servo connector terminal No. 2 (Light Green/Red wire). If resistance is 5 ohms or more, repair open circuit. Perform TEST VER-4A under VERIFICATION TESTS. If resistance is less than 5 ohms, go to next step.

6) Using an ohmmeter, check resistance between ground and S/C vent solenoid control circuit at S/C servo connector terminal No. 1 (Light Green/Red wire). If resistance is less than 5 ohms, repair short to ground. Perform TEST VER-4A under VERIFICATION TESTS. If resistance is 5 ohms or more, replace S/C servo. Perform TEST VER-4A under VERIFICATION TESTS.

7) Turn ignition off. Disconnect brake switch connector. Inspect connectors. Clean or repair as necessary. Turn ignition on. Using scan tool, actuate S/C solenoid. Using a 12-volt test light, probe S/C power supply circuit at brake switch connector terminal No. 3 (Yellow/Red wire). If test light is illuminated and bright, go to next step. If test light is not illuminated or dim, go to step **11)**.

8) Turn ignition off. Disconnect S/C servo connector. Inspect connectors. Clean or repair as necessary. Using an ohmmeter, check resistance between ground and S/C brake switch output circuit at S/C servo connector terminal No. 3 (Dark Blue/Red wire). If resistance is less than 5 ohms, repair short to ground. Perform TEST VER-4A under VERIFICATION TESTS. If resistance is 5 ohms or more, go to next step.

9) Using an ohmmeter, check resistance of brake switch output circuit between brake switch connector terminal No. 4 and S/C servo connector terminal No. 3 (Dark Blue/Red wire). If resistance is more than 5 ohms, repair open circuit. Perform TEST VER-4A under VERIFICATION TESTS. If resistance is 5 ohms or less, go to next step.

10) Check brake switch adjustment. Adjust as necessary. Perform TEST VER-4A under VERIFICATION TESTS. If brake switch adjustment is okay, replace brake switch. Perform TEST VER-4A under VERIFICATION TESTS.

11) Turn ignition off. Using an ohmmeter, check resistance between ground and S/C brake switch output circuit at S/C servo connector terminal No. 3 (Dark Blue/Red wire). If resistance is less than 5 ohms, repair short to ground. Perform TEST VER-4A under VERIFICATION TESTS. If resistance is 5 ohms or more, go to next step.

12) Disconnect PCM connectors. Inspect connectors. Clean or repair as necessary. Using an ohmmeter, check resistance of S/C power supply circuit between PCM connector C3, terminal No. 11 and brake switch connector terminal No. 3 (Yellow/Red wire). If resistance is 5 ohms or more, repair open circuit. Perform TEST VER-4A under VERIFICATION TESTS. If resistance is less than 5 ohms, replace PCM. Perform TEST VER-4A under VERIFICATION TESTS. .

DTC P1899: PARK/NEUTRAL POSITION (PNP) SWITCH STUCK IN PARK OR IN GEAR

NOTE: This test applies to Wrangler only. Information for Cherokee is not available from manufacturer.

Possible Causes:
- PNP switch defective.
- PNP switch sense circuit open or shorted.
- PNP switch stuck.
- PCM defective.

NOTE: For component location, see COMPONENT LOCATIONS. For connector terminal identification, see CONNECTOR IDENTIFICATION. For wiring diagram, see WIRING DIAGRAMS.

1) Turn ignition on. Using scan tool, read PNP switch state. While observing scan tool, move gear selector between Park and Reverse. If scan tool displays P/N and D/R, go to next step. If scan tool does not display P/N and D/R, go to step **3)**.

2) Turn ignition off. Inspect wiring and connectors related to PNP switch. Repair as necessary. Perform TEST VER-2A under VERIFICATION TESTS. If wiring and connectors are okay, test is complete.

3) Turn ignition off. Disconnect PCM. Inspect connectors. Clean or repair as necessary. Using an ohmmeter, check resistance between ground and PNP switch sense circuit at PCM connector C1, terminal No. 6 (Brown/Light Blue wire). While observing ohmmeter, move gear selector from Park to Reverse and back to Park. If resistance switched from less than 10 ohms to more than 10 ohms, replace PCM. Perform TEST VER-2A under VERIFICATION TESTS. If resistance was less than 10 ohms at all times, go to next step. If resistance was more than 10 ohms at all times, go to step **5)**.

4) Disconnect PNP switch. Inspect connectors. Clean or repair as necessary. Using an ohmmeter, check resistance between ground and PNP switch sense circuit. If resistance is less than 5 ohms, repair short to ground. Perform TEST VER-2A under VERIFICATION TESTS. If resistance is 5 ohms or more, repair or replace stuck PNP switch. Perform TEST VER-2A under VERIFICATION TESTS.

5) Using an ohmmeter, check resistance of PNP switch circuit between PNP switch connector and PCM connector C1, terminal No. 6 (Brown/Light Blue wire). If resistance is 5 ohms or more, repair open circuit. Perform TEST VER-2A under VERIFICATION TESTS. If resistance is less than 5 ohms, replace PNP switch. Perform TEST VER-2A under VERIFICATION TESTS.

SYSTEM TESTS

NOTE: For component location, See COMPONENT LOCATIONS. For connector terminal identification, see CONNECTOR IDENTIFICATION. For wiring diagram, see WIRING DIAGRAMS.

CHECKING SPEED CONTROL OPERATION

NOTE: Perform this test only if there are no DTCs.

1) Turn ignition on. Using scan tool, monitor S/C switch inputs. Press S/C ON/OFF switch several times. If scan tool displays speed control switch on and off, go to next step. If scan tool does not display speed control switch on and off, go to NTC-3: SPEED CONTROL ON/OFF SWITCH.

2) While observing scan tool, press RESUME/ACCEL switch several times. If scan tool displays RESUME/ACCEL switch PRESSED and RELEASED, go to next step. If scan tool does not display PRESSED and RELEASED, go to NTC-4: SPEED CONTROL RESUME/ACCEL SWITCH.

3) While observing scan tool, press brake pedal several times. If scan tool displays brake pedal PRESSED and RELEASED, go to next step. If scan tool does not display brake pedal PRESSED and RELEASED, go to NTC-1: BRAKE SWITCH SENSE.

4) While observing scan tool, press CANCEL switch several times. If scan tool displays PRESSED and RELEASED, go to next step. If scan tool does not display PRESSED and RELEASED, replace CANCEL switch. Perform TEST VER-4A under VERIFICATION TESTS.

5) Turn S/C on. While observing scan tool, move gear selector to Drive. If scan tool displays park neutral switch D/R, go to next step. If scan tool does not display park neutral switch D/R, go to DTC P1899: PARK/ NEUTRAL POSITION SWITCH STUCK IN PARK OR IN GEAR under DIAGNOSTIC TESTS.

6) Using scan tool, actuate S/C vent solenoid. Using a 12-volt test light, backprobe S/C brake switch output circuit at S/C servo connector terminal No. 3 (Dark Blue/Red wire). If test light is illuminated and bright, go to next step. If test light is dim or is not illuminated, go to NTC-1: BRAKE SWITCH SENSE.

7) Start engine and let idle for one minute. Turn engine off. Turn ignition on (engine off). Using scan tool, actuate S/C servo solenoids. If throttle opens and closes, go to NTC-2: CHECKING FOR SPEED CONTROL DENIED MESSAGE. If throttle does not open and close, go to next step.

8) Turn ignition off. Inspect throttle cable. Repair as necessary. Perform TEST VER-4A under VERIFICATION TESTS. If throttle cable is okay, go to next step.

9) Using an ohmmeter, check resistance of ground circuit at S/C servo connector terminal No. 4 (Black wire). If resistance is 5 ohms or more, repair open ground circuit. Perform TEST VER-4A under VERIFICATION TESTS. If resistance is less than 5 ohms, go to next step.

10) Turn S/C on. While observing scan tool, press COAST switch several times. If scan tool displays PRESSED and RELEASED, go to next step. If scan tool does not display PRESSED and RELEASED, replace COAST switch. Perform TEST VER-4A under VERIFICATION TESTS.

11) Turn ignition off. Disconnect vacuum supply hose from S/C servo. Attach vacuum gauge to disconnected hose. Start engine. If vacuum gauge does not read manifold vacuum, repair vacuum leak or restriction. Perform TEST VER-4A under VERIFICATION TESTS. If vacuum gauge reads manifold vacuum, go to next step.

12) While observing scan tool, press SET switch several times. If scan tool displays PRESSED and RELEASED, go to next step. If scan tool does not display PRESSED and RELEASED, replace SET switch. Perform TEST VER-4A under VERIFICATION TESTS.

13) Turn ignition off. Disconnect S/C servo connector. Inspect terminals. If any terminal is damaged, pushed out or miswired, repair as necessary. Perform TEST VER-4A under VERIFICATION TESTS. If terminals are okay, go to next step.

14) Reconnect S/C servo connector. Start engine and let idle for one minute with vacuum gauge still attached to S/C servo vacuum supply hose. Turn engine off. If vacuum does not hold for 10 seconds, replace vacuum check valve. Perform TEST VER-4A under VERIFICATION TESTS. If vacuum holds for at least 10 seconds, go to next step.

15) Disconnect S/C servo connector. Disconnect PCM connectors. Inspect connectors. Clean or repair as necessary. Using an ohmmeter, check resistance of S/C vacuum solenoid control circuit between PCM connector C3, terminal No. 4 and S/C servo connector terminal No. 1 (Tan/Red wire). If resistance is 5 ohms or more, repair open circuit. Perform TEST VER-4A under VERIFICATION TESTS. If resistance is less than 5 ohms, go to next step.

16) Using an ohmmeter, check resistance of S/C vent solenoid control circuit between PCM connector C3, terminal No. 5 and S/C servo connector terminal No. 2 (Light Green/Red wire). If resistance is 5 ohms or more, repair open circuit. Perform TEST VER-4A under VERIFICATION TESTS. If resistance is less than 5 ohms, replace S/C servo. Perform TEST VER-4A under VERIFICATION TESTS.

NTC-1: BRAKE SWITCH SENSE

Possible Causes:
- Ground circuit open.
- Defective brake switch.
- Brake switch sense circuit open or shorted.
- Defective PCM.

1) Turn ignition off. Disconnect brake switch connector. Inspect connector. Clean or repair as necessary. Turn ignition on. Using a voltmeter, check voltage of brake switch sense circuit at brake switch connector terminal No. 1 (White/Pink wire). If voltage is more than 10 volts, go to next step. If voltage is 10 volts or less, go to step 3).

2) Connect a jumper wire between ground and brake switch connector terminal No. 1 (White/Pink wire). Using scan tool, read brake switch input status. If scan tool displays brake switch released, replace brake switch. Perform TEST VER-4A under VERIFICATION TESTS. If scan tool does not display brake switch released, repair open ground circuit. Perform TEST VER-4A under VERIFICATION TESTS.

3) Turn ignition off. Disconnect PCM connectors. Inspect connector terminals. If any terminal is damaged, pushed out or miswired, repair as necessary. Perform TEST VER-4A under VERIFICATION TESTS. If terminals are okay, go to next step.

4) Disconnect PCM connectors. Inspect connectors. Clean or repair as necessary. Using an ohmmeter, check resistance between ground and brake switch sense circuit at PCM connector C3, terminal No. 24 (White/Pink wire). If resistance less than 5 ohms, repair short to ground. Perform TEST VER-4A under VERIFICATION TESTS. If resistance is 5 ohms or more, go to next step.

5) Using an ohmmeter, check resistance of brake switch sense circuit between PCM connector C3, terminal No. 24 and brake switch terminal No. 1 (White/Pink wire). If resistance is 5 ohms or more, repair open

brake switch sense circuit. Perform TEST VER-4A under VERIFICATION TESTS. If resistance is less than 5 ohms, replace PCM. Perform TEST VER-4A under VERIFICATION TESTS.

NTC-2: CHECKING FOR SPEED CONTROL DENIED MESSAGE

At this time speed control switch and servo functions appear to operate properly. Using scan tool, monitor speed control output status. Road test vehicle at speeds more than 30 MPH. Attempt to set speed control. See SCAN TOOL DENIED STATUS table. Items listed in table will not allow speed control to set. The last or most recent cause for speed control not to set is indicated by denied status.

SCAN TOOL DENIED STATUS

Denied Message	Reason
ON/OFF	PCM Does Not See An ON Signal From Switch At PCM Terminal No. 41
SPEED	Vehicle Speed As Seen By PCM Terminal No. 66 Is Not Greater Than 36 MPH
RPM	Engine RPM Is Excessively High
BRAKE	Brake Switch Sense Circuit Is Open Indicating Brakes Are Applied
P/N	Park/Neutral Switch Sense Circuit Is Grounded Indicating That Transmission Is In Park Or Neutral
RPM/SPD	PCM Senses Excessive Engine RPM For A Given Vehicle Speed
SOL FLT	PCM Senses A Servo Solenoid Circuit Trouble Code That Is Maturing Or Set In Memory

NTC-3: SPEED CONTROL ON/OFF SWITCH

Possible Causes:
- Signal circuit open or shorted.
- S/C ON/OFF switch defective.
- S/C RESUME/ACCEL switch defective.
- Defective PCM.
- Defective clockspring.

1) Turn ignition on. Using scan tool, read S/C switch voltage. If voltage is more than 4 volts, go to next step. If voltage is 4 volts or less, go to step 4).

2) Disconnect S/C ON/OFF switch. Inspect connectors. Clean or repair as necessary. Using a voltmeter, check voltage on S/C switch signal circuit. If voltage is more than 6 volts, repair short to voltage. Perform TEST VER-4A under VERIFICATION TESTS. If voltage is less than 4 volts, repair high resistance or open circuit. Perform TEST VER-4A under VERIFICATION TESTS. If voltage is 4-6 volts, go to next step.

3) Turn ignition off. Connect a jumper wire between S/C switch signal circuit and ground. Turn ignition on. Using scan tool, read S/C switch voltage. If voltage is less than one volt, replace S/C ON/OFF switch. Perform TEST VER-4A under VERIFICATION TESTS. If voltage is one volt or more, replace PCM. Perform TEST VER-4A under VERIFICATION TESTS.

4) Disconnect S/C ON/OFF switch. Inspect connectors. Clean or repair as necessary. Turn ignition on. Using scan tool, read S/C switch voltage. If voltage is more than 4 volts, replace S/C ON/OFF switch. Perform TEST VER-4A under VERIFICATION TESTS. If voltage is 4 volts or less, go to next step.

5) Disconnect S/C RESUME/ACCEL switch. Using scan tool, read S/C switch voltage. If voltage is more than 4 volts, replace RESUME/ACCEL switch. Perform TEST VER-4A under VERIFICATION TESTS. If voltage is 4 volts or less, go to next step.

6) Disconnect clockspring connector. Inspect connectors. Clean or repair as necessary. Using scan tool, read S/C switch voltage. If voltage is more than 4 volts, replace clockspring. Perform TEST VER-4A under VERIFICATION TESTS. If voltage is 4 volts or less, go to next step.

7) Turn ignition off. Disconnect PCM. Inspect connectors. Clean or repair as necessary. Using an ohmmeter, check resistance between ground and S/C switch signal circuit. If resistance is less than 5 ohms, repair short to ground. Perform TEST VER-4A under VERIFICATION TESTS. If resistance is 5 ohms or more, replace PCM. Perform TEST VER-4A under VERIFICATION TESTS.

NTC-4: SPEED CONTROL RESUME/ACCEL SWITCH

Possible Causes:
- Ground circuit open.
- RESUME/ACCEL switch defective.
- Signal circuit open.

1) Turn ignition off. Disconnect RESUME/ACCEL switch. Inspect connectors. Clean or repair as necessary. Connect a jumper wire between S/C switch signal circuit and ground. Turn ignition on. Using scan tool, read S/C switch voltage. If voltage is less than one volt, replace RESUME/ACCEL switch. Perform TEST VER-4A under VERIFICATION TESTS. If voltage is one volt or more, go to next step.

2) Turn ignition off. Using an ohmmeter, check resistance of RESUME/ACCEL switch ground circuit at RESUME/ACCEL switch connector. If resistance is 5 ohms or more, repair open ground circuit. Perform TEST VER-4A under VERIFICATION TESTS. If resistance is less than 5 ohms, repair open S/C switch signal circuit. Perform TEST VER-4A under VERIFICATION TESTS.

VERIFICATION TESTS

TEST VER-2A

NOTE: If PCM has been replaced and correct VIN and mileage have not been programmed, a DTC will be set in ABS and air bag modules. If vehicle is equipped with a Sentry Key Immobilizer Module (SKIM), sentry key data must be updated to enable starting. See COMPUTER RELEARN PROCEDURES article in GENERAL INFORMATION.

1) Inspect vehicle to ensure all engine components are connected. Reassemble and reconnect components as necessary. If any DTCs have not been repaired, go to SELF-DIAGNOSTIC SYSTEM. If all DTCs have been repaired, perform appropriate verification test.

2) If this verification procedure is being performed following a No Trouble Code (NTC) test, check if initial symptom still exists. If initial or another symptom exists, repair is not complete. Check for Technical Service Bulletins (TSBs) or flash updates and return to TROUBLE SHOOTING.

3) Using scan tool, erase DTCs and reset all values in PCM. Disconnect scan tool. Road test vehicle. Use all accessories related to repair. Ensure initial symptom does not exist.

4) Using scan tool, read Global Good Trips. If Global Good Trips is zero, repair is not complete. Check for related TSBs or flash updates and return to TROUBLE SHOOTING.

5) Using scan tool, check for stored DTCs. If repaired DTC or another DTC has set, repair is not complete. Check for related TSBs and return to TROUBLE SHOOTING. If no other DTCs exist, and Global Good Trips is more than zero, repair is complete.

TEST VER-4A

NOTE: If PCM has been replaced and correct VIN and mileage have not been programmed, a DTC will be set in ABS and air bag modules. If vehicle is equipped with a Sentry Key Immobilizer Module (SKIM), sentry key data must be updated to enable starting. See COMPUTER RELEARN PROCEDURES article in GENERAL INFORMATION.

1) If vehicle is equipped with ABS or air bag, enter correct VIN and mileage in PCM. Erase DTCs in ABS and air bag modules. Inspect vehicle to ensure all engine and speed control system components are connected. Reassemble and reconnect components as necessary. Using scan tool, erase DTCs from PCM.

2) Road test vehicle at a speed greater than 35 MPH. Turn S/C switch on. Press and release SET button. If S/C does not engage, repair is not complete. Check for related TSBs and return to TROUBLE SHOOTING, if necessary. If speed control engages, go to next step

3) Quickly depress and release RESUME/ACCEL switch. If vehicle speed increases by 2 MPH, go to next step. If vehicle speed does not increase by 2 MPH, repair is not complete. Check for related TSBs and return to TROUBLE SHOOTING, if necessary.

4) Press and hold COAST switch. If vehicle speed decreases, go to next step. Vehicle speed should decrease. If vehicle speed does not decrease, repair is not complete. Check for related TSBs and return to TROUBLE SHOOTING, if necessary.

5) Using caution, depress and release brake pedal. If S/C disengages, go to next step. If S/C does not disengage, repair is not complete. Check for related TSBs and return to TROUBLE SHOOTING, if necessary.

6) Bring vehicle speed to 35 MPH. Depress speed control RESUME/ACCEL switch. If vehicle resumes to previously set speed, go to next step. If vehicle does not resume to previously set speed, repair is not complete. Check for related TSBs and return to TROUBLE SHOOTING, if necessary.

7) Hold down SET switch. If vehicle speed decreases, go to next step. If vehicle speed did not decrease, repair is not complete. Check for related TSBs and return to TROUBLE SHOOTING, if necessary.

8) Ensure vehicle speed is more than 35 MPH and release SET switch. If vehicle set a new speed, go to next step. If vehicle does not set a new speed, repair is not complete. Check for related TSBs and return to TROUBLE SHOOTING, if necessary.

9) Depress and release CANCEL switch. If S/C disengages, go to next step. If S/C did not disengage, repair is not complete. Check for related TSBs and return to TROUBLE SHOOTING, if necessary.

10) Ensure vehicle speed is greater than 35 MPH. Engage speed control. Turn S/C on/off switch to OFF position. If speed control disengages, system is operating correctly. Repair is complete. If speed control does not disengage, repair is not complete. Check for related TSBs and return to TROUBLE SHOOTING, if necessary.

TEST VER-5A

NOTE: If PCM has been replaced and correct VIN and mileage have not been programmed, a DTC will be set in ABS and air bag modules. If vehicle is equipped with a Sentry Key Immobilizer Module (SKIM), sentry key data must be updated to enable starting. See COMPUTER RELEARN PROCEDURES article in GENERAL INFORMATION.

1) If vehicle is equipped with ABS or air bag, enter correct VIN and mileage in PCM. Erase DTCs in ABS and air bag modules. Inspect vehicle to ensure all engine and speed control system components are connected.

2) If there are any DTCs that have not been repaired, go to SELF-DIAGNOSTIC SYSTEM. After all DTCs have been repaired, run appropriate monitor for previously repaired DTC.

3) Connect scan tool to DLC. Ensure fuel tank is at least 1/4 full. Turn off all accessories. Allow PCM to run appropriate monitor and increment appropriate good trip. Enabling conditions must be met before monitor will run.

4) Using scan tool, monitor pretest enabling conditions until all conditions have been met. Once enabling conditions have been met, monitor appropriate monitor.

5) If repaired DTC has reset or was seen in monitor while on road test, repair is not complete. Check for TSBs or flash updates and return to TROUBLE SHOOTING.

6) If appropriate monitor ran, good trip counter incremented and no DTCs have been set, repair is complete.

REMOVAL & INSTALLATION

WARNING: Vehicle is equipped with an air bag. Air bag must be deactivated before servicing speed control components on or around steering column. See AIR BAG RESTRAINT SYSTEMS article.

CAUTION: When battery is disconnected, vehicle computer and memory systems may lose memory data. Driveability problems may exist until computer systems have completed a relearn cycle. See COMPUTER RELEARN PROCEDURES article in GENERAL INFORMATION before disconnecting battery.

BRAKE SWITCH

Removal – Fully depress brake pedal and rotate brake switch counterclockwise approximately 30 degrees. Remove brake switch from bracket. Depress lock tabs holding brake switch mounting bracket and separate harness connector from brake switch.

Installation – 1) Before installing brake switch, reset adjustable plunger by pulling on plunger head until plunger reaches end of travel. Connect harness connector to brake switch. Depress brake pedal and insert brake switch into keyed hole in mounting bracket. Rotate brake switch clockwise into locked position.

2) Gently pull back on brake pedal until pedal will go no further. This causes the brake switch plunger to ratchet backward to the correct position. No further adjustment is required.

SPEED CONTROL SERVO

Removal – 1) Disconnect negative battery cable. Disconnect electrical connector and vacuum hose from servo. Using finger pressure only, push servo cable connector from throttle body bellcrank pin. DO NOT pull cable connector perpendicular to bellcrank.

2) Remove 2 servo mounting nuts. Pull servo cable sleeve away from mounting bracket to expose cable retaining clip. Remove retaining clip. Remove servo.

Installation – With throttle in full open position, align hole in speed control cable sleeve with hole in servo pin. Install retaining clip. To complete installation, reverse removal procedure. Tighten mounting nuts to 75 INCH lbs. (8.5 N.m).

SPEED CONTROL SWITCHES

Removal & Installation – Turn ignition switch to OFF position. Disconnect negative battery cable. Wait 2 minutes for air bag system to discharge reserve voltage. Remove 2 screws holding air bag assembly to steering column. Separate air bag assembly from steering column and disconnect air bag, horn and speed control switch connectors. Remove screws securing speed control switch to air bag assembly. Separate speed control switch from air bag assembly. To install, reverse removal procedure.

WIRING DIAGRAMS

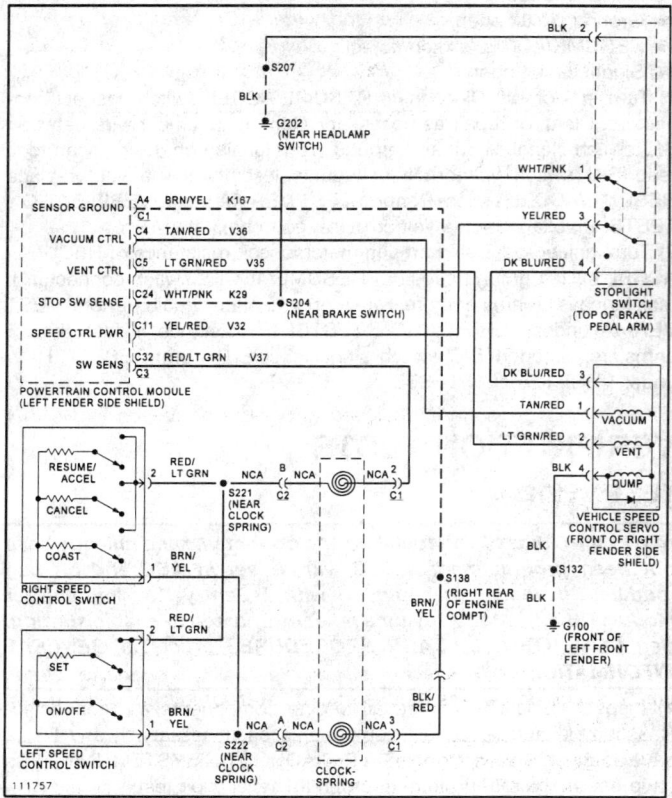

Fig. 5: Cruise Control System Wiring Diagram (Cherokee)

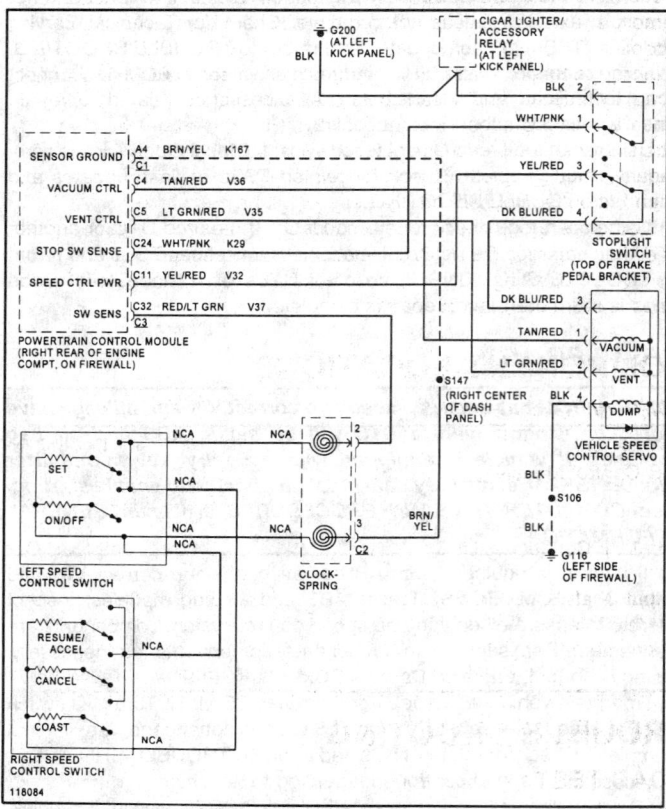

Fig. 6: Cruise Control System Wiring Diagram (Wrangler)

CAUTION: When battery is disconnected, vehicle computer and memory systems may lose memory data. Driveability problems may exist until computer systems have completed a relearn cycle. See COMPUTER RELEARN PROCEDURES article in GENERAL INFORMATION before disconnecting battery.

DESCRIPTION

The speed (cruise) control system is electronically controlled and vacuum operated. The electronic control is integrated into the Powertrain Control Module (PCM) located on right side of firewall. System consists of the following components: PCM, servo, speed control switches, vacuum reservoir, vehicle speed sensor, speed control relay and brake switch.

System controls are located on each side of steering wheel air bag module and consist of ON/OFF, SET, RESUME/ACCEL, CANCEL AND COAST buttons. System is designed to operate at speeds above 35 MPH.

OPERATION

SYSTEM CONTROLS

To Set Speed Control – Press ON/OFF button to turn speed control system on. Accelerate to desired speed (minimum of 35 MPH) and press SET/COAST button. Vehicle speed will be maintained.

NOTE: Speed control system will automatically disengage when vehicle speed decreases to less than 35 MPH or increases to more than 85 MPH.

To Disengage Speed Control – Press brake pedal. Press CANCEL button. Press ON/OFF button. If ON/OFF button is used, set speed will be erased from memory.

To Resume Previous Speed – If set speed has not been erased from memory and vehicle speed is more than 35 MPH, press RES/ACCEL button.

To Increase Speed – With speed control system on, increase set speed by rapidly pressing and releasing RES/ACCEL button. Each pressing of button will cause speed increase of 2 MPH. For example, pressing button 3 times will increase speed by 6 MPH. To increase speed gradually, hold RES/ACCEL button down until desired speed is reached. When button is released, new set speed will be maintained.

To Decrease Speed – With speed control system on, decrease set speed by pressing SET/COAST button. Vehicle speed will gradually decrease. Releasing button will set a new speed as long as vehicle speed is still more than 35 MPH.

COMPONENT LOCATIONS

COMPONENT LOCATIONS

Component	Location
ABS Control Module	Left Side Of Engine Compartment Near Master Cylinder
Data Link Connector (DLC)	Lower Left Side Of Instrument Panel
Output Shaft Speed (OSS) Sensor	Left Side Of Transmission
Park/Neutral Position (PNP) Switch	Left Side Of Transmission
Powertrain Control Module (PCM)	Right Side Of Firewall In Engine Compartment

TROUBLE SHOOTING

ROAD TEST

Perform a road test to verify speed control malfunctions. Ensure speedometer operation is smooth without flutter at all speeds. Speedometer fluttering may cause surging in speed control system. For speedometer diagnosis, see appropriate INSTRUMENT PANELS article. If road test verifies a surge following speed control set and speedometer operates smoothly, see OVERSHOOT/UNDERSHOOT FOLLOWING SPEED CONTROL SET.

If road test verifies an inoperative system, and speedometer operates smoothly, check for:
- DTCs. See SELF-DIAGNOSTIC SYSTEM.
- Misadjusted brake switch. See BRAKE SWITCH under REMOVAL & INSTALLATION.
- Poor electrical connections at servo.
- Leaking vacuum reservoir, check valve, hoses or connections. See VACUUM SUPPLY under COMPONENT TESTS.
- Secure attachments of S/C servo cable.
- Smooth operation of throttle linkage.
- Defective PCM or wiring.
- Defective servo. See DTC P1595: SPEED CONTROL SOLENOID CIRCUITS OR DTC P1683: SPEED CONTROL POWER RELAY OR 12-VOLT DRIVER CIRCUIT under DIAGNOSTIC TESTS.

To verify a speed control electronic malfunction, use a scan tool to check for DTCs. See SELF-DIAGNOSTIC SYSTEM. A speed control malfunction may occur without setting a DTC. If no DTCs are stored, go to CHECKING SPEED CONTROL OPERATION under SYSTEM TESTS.

OVERSHOOT/UNDERSHOOT FOLLOWING SPEED CONTROL SET

If operator repeatedly presses and releases set button with their foot off accelerator (lift foot set) to begin speed control operation, vehicle may accelerate and exceed desired set speed by 5 MPH and then decelerate to less than desired set speed before achieving desired set speed.

Speed Control (S/C) has as adaptive strategy that compensates for variations in S/C cable lengths. When S/C is set with vehicle operator's foot off accelerator pedal, S/C compensates for excessive S/C cable slack. If lift foot sets are continually used, speed control overshoot/undershoot condition will develop.

To "unlearn" overshoot/undershoot condition, operator must press and release set button while maintaining desired speed with accelerator pedal, then turn S/C switch off after waiting 10 seconds. This procedure must be repeated 10-15 times to completely unlearn overshoot/undershoot condition.

COMPONENT TESTS

WARNING: Vehicle is equipped with an air bag. Air bag must be deactivated before servicing speed control components on or around steering column. See AIR BAG RESTRAINT SYSTEMS article.

NOTE: For component locations, See COMPONENT LOCATIONS. For connector terminal identification, see CONNECTOR IDENTIFICATION. For wiring diagram, see WIRING DIAGRAMS.

BRAKE SWITCH

Disconnect brake switch 6-pin connector. Using an ohmmeter, check for continuity at brake switch. *See Fig. 1.* If continuity is not as specified in BRAKE SWITCH CONTINUITY table, check brake switch adjustment. See BRAKE SWITCH under REMOVAL & INSTALLATION. If brake switch adjustment is okay, replace defective brake switch.

BRAKE SWITCH CONTINUITY

Switch Plunger Position	Check Between Terminals No.	Continuity
Released	5 & 6	Yes
Depressed	1 & 2	Yes
	3 & 4	Yes

VACUUM SUPPLY

1) Disconnect vacuum hose at speed control servo. Install vacuum gauge to disconnected vacuum hose. Start engine and observe gauge. Vacuum reading should be a minimum of 10 in. Hg. Turn engine off. Vacuum should continue to hold at a minimum of 10 in. Hg.

2) If vacuum is not as specified, check for kinked or leaking vacuum lines, defective check valve, defective vacuum reservoir or poor engine performance.

CONNECTOR IDENTIFICATION

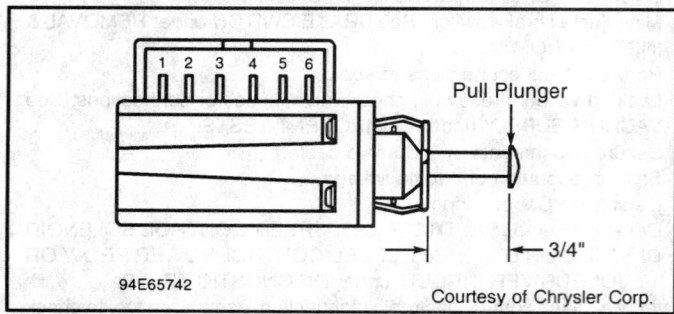

94E65742   Courtesy of Chrysler Corp.

Fig. 1: Identifying Brake Switch Terminals

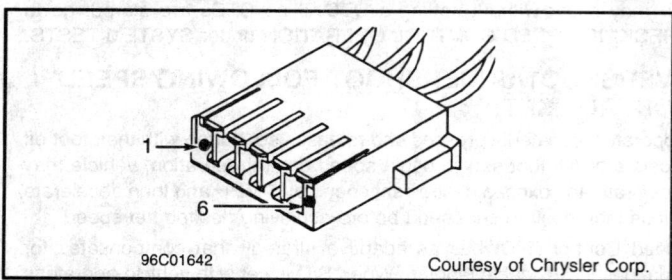

96C01642   Courtesy of Chrysler Corp.

Fig. 2: Identifying Brake Switch Harness Connector Terminals

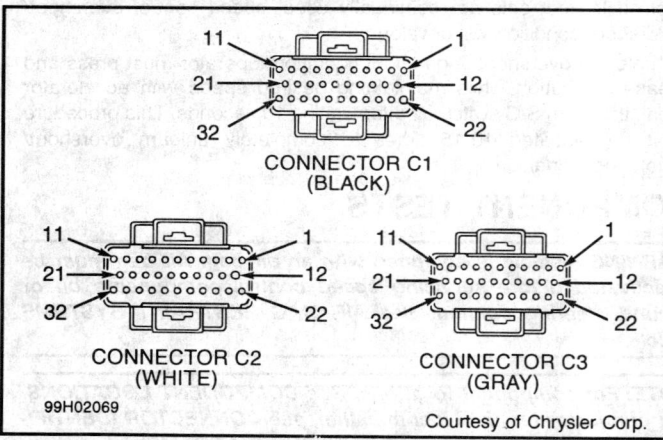

CONNECTOR C1
(BLACK)

CONNECTOR C2
(WHITE)

CONNECTOR C3
(GRAY)

99H02069   Courtesy of Chrysler Corp.

Fig. 3: Identifying Powertrain Control Module (PCM) Connector Terminals

SELF-DIAGNOSTIC SYSTEM

WARNING: Vehicle is equipped with an air bag. Air bag must be deactivated before servicing speed control components on or around steering column. See AIR BAG RESTRAINT SYSTEMS article.

SERVICE PRECAUTIONS

Before proceeding with diagnosis, the following precautions must be followed:

- When using Diagnostic Trouble Code (DTC) tests for diagnosis, DO NOT skip any steps, or incorrect diagnosis may result. Always perform indicated verification procedure after repairs are made.
- When using a jumper wire, ensure either jumper wire or circuit is fuse-protected.
- Before disconnecting connector from any control module, ensure ignition is off before removing connector.

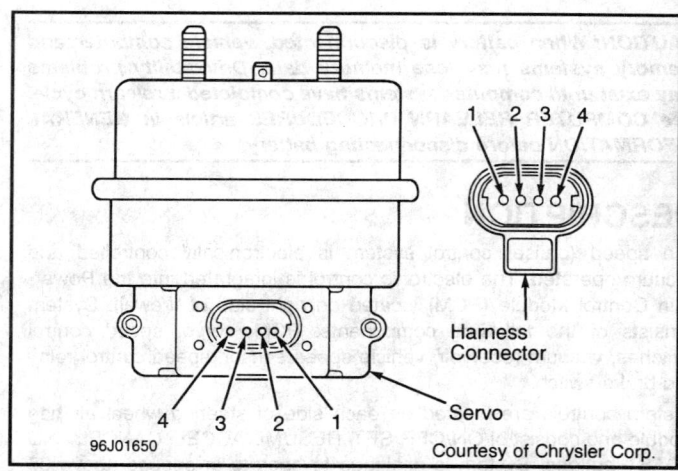

Harness
Connector

Servo

96J01650   Courtesy of Chrysler Corp.

Fig. 4: Identifying Speed Control (S/C) Servo Connector Terminals

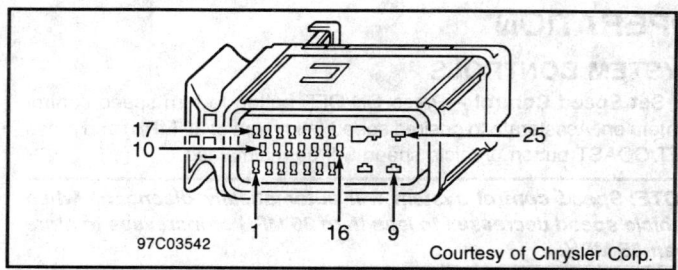

97C03542   Courtesy of Chrysler Corp.

Fig. 5: Identifying ABS Control Module Connector Terminals

- When checking voltage or continuity at any control module, probe connector for control module from pin side. DO NOT backprobe connector or probe wires through the insulation.
- DO NOT cause short circuits when performing electrical tests. This will set additional DTCs, making diagnosis of original problem more difficult.
- Use specified test equipment when performing electrical tests.

RETRIEVING DIAGNOSTIC TROUBLE CODES

NOTE: Self-diagnostic tests are written specifically for Chrysler's Diagnostic Readout Box (DRB). If using a generic scan tool, ensure it is OBD-II certified. A generic scan tool may not be capable of performing all necessary test functions.

Ensure battery is fully charged. Turn ignition off. Connect scan tool to Data Link Connector (DLC). DLC is located under left side of instrument panel. Turn ignition on. Using scan tool manufacturer's instructions, record all DTCs displayed on scan tool. If any DTCs are retrieved, perform appropriate test under DIAGNOSTIC TESTS. Once all repairs are made, clear DTCs. See CLEARING DIAGNOSTIC TROUBLE CODES. If no DTCs are retrieved and fault still exists, go to CHECKING SPEED CONTROL OPERATION under SYSTEM TESTS.

CLEARING DIAGNOSTIC TROUBLE CODES

Ensure ignition is off. Connect scan tool to DLC. Turn ignition on. Using screen prompts on scan tool, erase DTCs from PCM.

DIAGNOSTIC TESTS

DTC P0500: NO VEHICLE SPEED SENSOR SIGNAL

Vehicle Speed Sensor (VSS) is monitored when engine temperature is more than 104°F (40°C), MAP vacuum is 15-16 in. Hg and output shaft speed is more than 64 RPM. DTC P0500 will set if there is no VSS signal from ABS control module for more than 15 seconds on 2 consecutive trips.

Possible Causes:

- VSS defective.
- 5-volt supply circuit open.
- VSS circuit open or shorted.
- Speedometer pinion gear defective.
- ABS DTCs present.
- ABS control module defective.
- PCM defective.

NOTE: For connector terminal identification, see CONNECTOR IDENTIFICATION. For wiring diagram, see WIRING DIAGRAMS.

1) Using scan tool, read DTCs. If good trip counter for DTC P0500 is not displayed and equal to zero, go to step 6). If any ABS DTCs are present, repair ABS system. See ANTI-LOCK – TEVES MARK 20 article in BRAKES in appropriate MITCHELL® manual. Perform TEST VER-5A under VERIFICATION TESTS.

2) Turn ignition off. Disconnect PCM and ABS control module. Using an ohmmeter, measure resistance between ground and VSS signal circuit at PCM connector C2, terminal No. 27 (White/Orange wire). If resistance is less than 5 ohms, repair short to ground. Perform TEST VER-5A under VERIFICATION TESTS. If resistance is 5 ohms or more, go to next step.

3) Using an ohmmeter, measure resistance of VSS signal circuit between PCM connector C2, terminal No. 27 and ABS control module terminal No. 3 (White/Orange wire). If resistance is more than 5 ohms, repair open circuit. Perform TEST VER-5A under VERIFICATION TESTS. If resistance is 5 ohms or less, go to next step.

4) Reconnect PCM. Turn ignition on. Using a voltmeter, measure voltage on VSS signal circuit at ABS control module connector terminal No. 3 (White/Orange wire). If voltage is more than 6 volts, repair short to voltage. Perform TEST VER-5A under VERIFICATION TESTS. If voltage is 6 volts or less, go to next step.

5) Turn ignition off. Connect one end of jumper wire to VSS signal circuit at ABS control module terminal No. 3 (White/Orange wire). Turn ignition on. Quickly and repeatedly tap other end of jumper wire to ground. Using scan tool, read VSS display. If scan tool displays VSS more than zero MPH, replace ABS control module. Perform TEST VER-5A under VERIFICATION TESTS. If scan tool displays zero MPH, replace PCM. Perform TEST VER-5A under VERIFICATION TESTS.

6) Conditions required to set DTC are not present at this time. Use freeze frame data to help duplicate conditions that set DTC. Inspect wiring and connectors for potential intermittent problems. Check for Technical Service Bulletins (TSBs) that apply. Repair as necessary. Perform TEST VER-5A under VERIFICATION TESTS.

DTC P1595: SPEED CONTROL SOLENOID CIRCUITS OR DTC P1683: SPEED CONTROL POWER RELAY OR 12-VOLT DRIVER CIRCUIT

DTC P1595 will set if PCM actuates Speed Control (S/C) vacuum and vent solenoids, but they do not respond. Vehicle speed must be greater than 35 MPH, transmission must be in Drive and S/C must be on with SET switch depressed.

DTC P1683 will set if S/C power supply circuit is open or shorted. Ignition and S/C must be on.

Possible Causes:
- S/C servo ground circuit open.
- S/C brake switch output circuit open.
- S/C power supply circuit open or shorted.
- S/C servo defective.
- S/C vacuum solenoid control circuit open or shorted.
- S/C vent solenoid control circuit open or shorted.
- Brake switch defective or out of adjustment.
- Defective PCM.

NOTE: For component locations, see COMPONENT LOCATIONS. For connector terminal identification, see CONNECTOR IDENTIFICATION. For wiring diagram, see WIRING DIAGRAMS.

1) Turn ignition on. Turn Speed Control (S/C) on. Using scan tool, actuate S/C vent solenoid. If S/C servo does not click, go to step 9).

Actuate S/C vacuum solenoid. If S/C servo does not click, go to step 4). If both solenoids click, go to next step.

2) Using scan tool, actuate S/C vent solenoid. Wiggle wiring harness between S/C servo and brake switch to PCM. If wiggling caused an interruption of S/C servo actuation, repair wiring harness as necessary. Perform TEST VER-4A under VERIFICATION TESTS. If wiggling did not cause an interruption, inspect wiring and connectors. Repair as necessary. Perform TEST VER-4A under VERIFICATION TESTS. If wiring and connectors are okay, go to next step.

3) Using scan tool, actuate S/C vacuum solenoid. Wiggle wiring harness between S/C servo and brake switch to PCM. If wiggling caused an interruption of S/C servo actuation, repair wiring harness as necessary. Perform TEST VER-4A under VERIFICATION TESTS. If wiggling did not cause an interruption, test is complete.

4) Using scan tool, actuate S/C vent solenoid. Wiggle wiring harness between S/C servo and brake switch to PCM. If wiggling caused an interruption of S/C servo actuation, repair wiring harness as necessary. Perform TEST VER-4A under VERIFICATION TESTS. If wiggling did not cause an interruption, go to next step.

NOTE: Ensure brake pedal is NOT depressed during the following steps.

5) Turn ignition off. Disconnect S/C servo 4-pin connector. Turn ignition on. Turn S/C switch on. Using scan tool, actuate S/C vacuum solenoid. Using a 12-volt test light, probe brake switch output circuit at S/C servo connector terminal No. 3 (Dark Blue/Red wire). If test light is dim or is not illuminated, go to step 13). If test light illuminates, go to next step.

6) Turn ignition off. Using an ohmmeter, measure resistance of ground circuit at S/C servo connector terminal No. 4 (Black wire). If resistance is 5 ohms or more, repair open ground circuit. Perform TEST VER-4A under VERIFICATION TESTS. If resistance is less than 5 ohms, go to next step.

7) Disconnect PCM. Inspect connectors. Clean or repair as necessary. Using an ohmmeter, measure resistance of S/C vacuum solenoid control circuit between S/C servo connector terminal No. 2 and PCM connector C3, terminal No. 5 (Light Green/Red wire). If resistance is 5 ohms or more, repair open circuit. Perform TEST VER-4A under VERIFICATION TESTS. If resistance is less than 5 ohms, go to next step.

8) Using an ohmmeter, measure resistance between ground and S/C vacuum solenoid control circuit at S/C servo connector terminal No. 2 (Light Green/Red wire). If resistance is less than 5 ohms, repair short to ground. Perform TEST VER-4A under VERIFICATION TESTS. If circuit is not shorted to ground, replace S/C servo. Perform TEST VER-4A under VERIFICATION TESTS.

NOTE: Ensure brake pedal is NOT depressed during the following steps.

9) Turn ignition off. Disconnect S/C servo connector. Inspect connectors. Clean or repair as necessary. Turn ignition and S/C on. Using scan tool, actuate S/C vacuum solenoid. Using a 12-volt test light, probe S/C brake switch output circuit at S/C servo connector terminal No. 3 (Dark Blue/Red wire). If test light is dim or is not illuminated, go to step 13). If test light illuminates, go to next step.

10) Turn ignition off. Using an ohmmeter, measure resistance of ground circuit at S/C servo connector terminal No. 4 (Black wire). If resistance is 5 ohms or more, repair open ground circuit. Perform TEST VER-4A under VERIFICATION TESTS. If resistance is less than 5 ohms, go to next step.

11) Disconnect PCM. Inspect connectors. Clean or repair as necessary. Using an ohmmeter, measure resistance of S/C vent solenoid control circuit between S/C servo connector terminal No. 1 and PCM connector C3, terminal No. 4 (Tan/Red wire). If resistance is 5 ohms or more, repair open circuit. Perform TEST VER-4A under VERIFICATION TESTS. If resistance is less than 5 ohms, go to next step.

12) Using an ohmmeter, measure resistance between ground and S/C vent solenoid control circuit at S/C servo connector terminal No. 1 (Tan/Red wire). Is resistance is less than 5 ohms, repair short to ground.

Perform TEST VER-4A under VERIFICATION TESTS. If resistance is 5 ohms or more, replace S/C servo. Perform TEST VER-4A under VERIFICATION TESTS.

NOTE: *Ensure brake pedal is NOT depressed during the following step.*

13) Turn ignition off. Check brake switch adjustment. See BRAKE SWITCH under REMOVAL & INSTALLATION. Adjust as necessary. Perform TEST VER-4A under VERIFICATION TESTS. If brake switch adjustment is okay, disconnect brake switch. Using an ohmmeter, measure resistance between brake switch terminals No. 3 and 4. *See Fig. 1.* If resistance is 5 ohms or more, replace brake switch. Perform TEST VER-4A under VERIFICATION TESTS. If resistance is less than 5 ohms, go to next step.

14) Disconnect PCM. Inspect connectors. Clean or repair as necessary. Using an ohmmeter, measure resistance between ground and S/C power supply circuit at brake switch connector terminal No. 3 (Orange/Dark Green wire). If resistance is less than 5 ohms, repair short to ground. Perform TEST VER-4A under VERIFICATION TESTS. If resistance is 5 ohms or more, go to next step.

15) Using an ohmmeter, measure resistance of S/C power supply circuit between PCM connector C3, terminal No. 11 and brake switch connector terminal No. 3 (Orange/Dark Green wire). If resistance is 5 ohms or more, repair open circuit. Perform TEST VER-4A under VERIFICATION TESTS. If resistance is less than 5 ohms, go to next step.

16) Disconnect S/C servo. Inspect connectors. Clean or repair as necessary. Using an ohmmeter, measure resistance between ground and S/C brake switch output circuit at S/C servo connector terminal No. 3 (Dark Blue/Red wire). If resistance is less than 5 ohms, repair short to ground. Perform TEST VER-4A under VERIFICATION TESTS. If resistance is 5 ohms or more, go to next step.

17) Using an ohmmeter, measure resistance of S/C brake switch output circuit between brake switch connector terminal No. 4 and S/C servo connector terminal No. 3 (Dark Blue/Red wire). If resistance is more than 5 ohms, repair open circuit. Perform TEST VER-4A under VERIFICATION TESTS. If resistance is 5 ohms or less, replace PCM. Perform TEST VER-4A under VERIFICATION TESTS.

DTC P1596: SPEED CONTROL SWITCH ALWAYS HIGH

DTC P1596 will set if voltage on Speed Control (S/C) switch signal circuit is more than 4.8 volts for more than 2 minutes.
Possible Causes:
- S/C switch ground circuit open.
- S/C ON/OFF switch defective.
- S/C switch signal circuit open or shorted to voltage.
- Defective PCM.

NOTE: *For component locations, see COMPONENT LOCATIONS. For connector terminal identification, see CONNECTOR IDENTIFICATION. For wiring diagram, see WIRING DIAGRAMS.*

1) Turn ignition on. Using scan tool, monitor S/C inputs. While observing scan tool, press S/C ON/OFF switch several times. If scan tool did not display S/C switch off and on, go to next step. If scan tool displayed S/C ON/OFF switch off and on, inspect wiring and connectors. Repair as necessary. Perform TEST VER-4A under VERIFICATION TESTS. If wiring and connectors are okay, no problem is indicated at this time.
2) Turn ignition off. Disconnect S/C ON/OFF switch. Disconnect clockspring connector C1, located behind steering wheel (S/C switch side). Inspect connectors. Clean or repair as necessary. Using an ohmmeter, measure resistance of S/C switch ground circuit between S/C ON/OFF switch connector and clockspring connector (Black/Light Blue wire). If resistance is 5 ohms or more, repair open ground circuit. Perform TEST VER-4A under VERIFICATION TESTS. If resistance is less than 5 ohms, go to next step.
3) Disconnect clockspring connector C2, located behind lower steering column shroud. Disconnect PCM. Inspect connectors. Clean or repair as necessary. Using an ohmmeter, measure resistance of S/C switch

ground circuit between clockspring connector and PCM connector C1, terminal No. 4 (Black/Light Blue wire). If resistance is 5 ohms or more, repair open circuit. Perform TEST VER-4A under VERIFICATION TESTS. If resistance is less than 5 ohms, go to next step.
4) Using an ohmmeter, measure resistance across S/C ON/OFF switch terminals. If resistance is 20,300-20,77 ohms, go to next step. If resistance is not 20,300-20,700 ohms, replace S/C ON/OFF switch. Perform TEST VER-4A under VERIFICATION TESTS.
5) Using an ohmmeter, measure resistance between clockspring connector C1, terminal No. 5 and clockspring connector C2, terminal No. 5 (Black/Light Blue wire). Measure resistance between clockspring connector C1, terminal No. 6 and clockspring connector C2, terminal No. 6 (Red/Light Green wire). If resistance is more than 5 ohms on either circuit, replace clockspring. Perform TEST VER-4A under VERIFICATION TESTS. If resistance is less than 5 ohms, go to next step.
6) Reconnect all previously disconnected electrical connectors except S/C ON/OFF switch 2-pin connector. Turn ignition on. Using a voltmeter, measure voltage on S/C switch signal circuit at ON/OFF switch connector (Red/Light Green wire). If voltage is more than 6 volts, repair short to voltage. Perform TEST VER-4A under VERIFICATION TESTS. If voltage is 6 volts or less, go to next step.
7) Turn ignition off. Disconnect clockspring connector C2, located behind lower steering column shroud. Disconnect PCM. Using an ohmmeter, measure resistance of S/C switch signal circuit between PCM connector C3, terminal No. 32 and clockspring connector C2, terminal No. 6 (Red/Light Green wire). If resistance is 5 ohms or more, repair open circuit. Perform TEST VER-4A under VERIFICATION TESTS. If resistance is less than 5 ohms, go to next step.
8) Disconnect clockspring connector C1 located behind steering wheel. Using an ohmmeter, measure resistance of S/C switch signal circuit between clockspring connector and ON/OFF switch connector (Red/Light Green wire). If resistance is 5 ohms or more, repair open circuit. Perform TEST VER-4A under VERIFICATION TESTS. If resistance is less than 5 ohms, replace PCM. Perform TEST VER-4A under VERIFICATION TESTS.

DTC P1597: SPEED CONTROL SWITCH ALWAYS LOW

DTC P1597 will set if Speed Control (S/C) switch voltage is less than 0.39 volts for 2 minutes when ignition is on and battery voltage is more than 10.4 volts.
Possible Causes:
- S/C ON/OFF switch defective.
- S/C RESUME/ACCEL switch defective.
- S/C switch signal circuit shorted to ground.
- Defective PCM.
- Defective clockspring.

NOTE: *For component locations, see COMPONENT LOCATIONS. For connector terminal identification, see CONNECTOR IDENTIFICATION. For wiring diagram, see WIRING DIAGRAMS.*

1) Turn ignition on. Using scan tool, read S/C switch voltage. If voltage is less than one volt, disconnect ON/OFF switch. If voltage changes to 5 volts, replace ON/OFF switch. Perform TEST VER-4A under VERIFICATION TESTS. If voltage does not change to 5 volts, go to next step. If voltage is one volt or more, inspect wiring and connectors. Repair as necessary. Perform TEST VER-4A under VERIFICATION TESTS. If wiring and connectors are okay, no problem is indicated at this time.
2) Turn ignition off. Disconnect RESUME/ACCEL switch. Inspect connectors. Clean or repair as necessary. Turn ignition on. Using scan tool, read S/C switch volts. If voltage changed to more than 4 volts, replace RESUME/ACCEL switch. Perform TEST VER-4A under VERIFICATION TESTS. If voltage did not change to more than 4 volts, go to next step.
3) Turn ignition off. Disconnect clockspring 6-pin connector (instrument panel side). Using scan tool, read S/C switch voltage. If voltage changed to 5 volts, replace clockspring. Perform TEST VER-4A under VERIFICATION TESTS. If voltage did not change to 5 volts, go to next step.
4) Reconnect clockspring. Disconnect S/C ON/OFF switch and PCM. Inspect connectors. Clean or repair as necessary. Using an ohmmeter,

measure resistance across ON/OFF switch terminals. If resistance is less than 5 ohms, repair short to sensor ground. Perform TEST VER-4A under VERIFICATION TESTS. If resistance is 5 ohms or more, go to next step.

5) Using an ohmmeter, measure resistance between ground and S/C switch signal circuit at PCM connector C3, terminal No. 32 (Red/Light Green wire). If resistance is less than 5 ohms, repair short to ground. Perform TEST VER-4A under VERIFICATION TESTS. If resistance is 5 ohms or more, replace PCM. Perform TEST VER-4A under VERIFICA-TION TESTS.

SYSTEM TESTS

NOTE: For component locations, See COMPONENT LOCATIONS. For connector terminal identification, see CONNECTOR IDENTIFI-CATION. For wiring diagram, see WIRING DIAGRAMS.

CHECKING SPEED CONTROL OPERATION

NOTE: Perform this test only if there are no DTCs.

1) Turn ignition on. Using scan tool, monitor S/C switch inputs. While observing display, press brake pedal several times. If scan tool displays PRESSED and RELEASED, go to next step. If scan tool does not display brake switch PRESSED and RELEASED, go to NTC-1: BRAKE SWITCH SENSE.

2) Turn ignition off. Disconnect S/C servo. Inspect connectors. Clean or repair as necessary. Using an ohmmeter, measure resistance between ground and S/C servo connector terminal No. 4 (Black wire). If resistance is 5 ohms or more, repair open ground circuit. Perform TEST VER-4A under VERIFICATION TESTS. If resistance is less than 5 ohms, go to next step.

3) Reconnect S/C servo. Turn ignition on. While observing scan tool, press ON/OFF switch several times. If scan tool does not display ON/OFF switch PRESSED and RELEASED, go to step **14)**. If scan tool displays PRESSED and RELEASED, inspect wiring and connectors. Repair as necessary. Perform TEST VER-4A under VERIFICATION TESTS. If wiring and connectors are okay, go to next step.

4) Using scan tool, monitor P/N switch inputs. While observing display, shift transmission into Drive. If scan tool does not display P/N switch D/R, go to NTC-2: CHECKING PARK/NEUTRAL POSITION (PNP) SWITCH OPERATION. If scan tool displays P/N switch D/R, inspect throttle cable and linkage. Repair as necessary. Perform TEST VER-4A under VERIFICATION TESTS. If throttle cable and linkage are okay, go to next step.

5) While observing scan tool, press SET switch several times. If scan tool does not display SET switch PRESSED and RELEASED, replace left S/C switch. Perform TEST VER-4A under VERIFICATION TESTS. If scan tool displays PRESSED and RELEASED, read DTCs. If DTC P0500 is set, go to DTC P0500: NO VEHICLE SPEED SENSOR SIGNAL under DIAGNOSTIC TESTS.

6) While observing scan tool, press RESUME switch several times. If scan tool displays RESUME switch PRESSED and RELEASED, go to next step. If scan tool does not display PRESSED and RELEASED, go to step **9)**.

7) While observing scan tool, press CANCEL switch several times. If scan tool does not display CANCEL switch PRESSED and RELEASED, replace right S/C switch. Perform TEST VER-4A under VERIFICATION TESTS. If scan tool displays CANCEL switch PRESSED and RELEASED, go to next step.

8) While observing scan tool, press COAST switch. If scan tool does not display COAST switch PRESSED and RELEASED, replace right S/C switch. Perform TEST VER-4A under VERIFICATION TESTS. If scan tool displays COAST switch PRESSED and RELEASED, go to next step.

9) Turn ignition off. Disconnect RESUME/ACCEL switch. Inspect connectors. Clean or repair as necessary. Using an ohmmeter, measure resistance of sensor ground circuit at RESUME/ACCEL switch connector (Black/Light Blue wire). If resistance is 5 ohms or more, repair open

ground circuit. Perform TEST VER-4A under VERIFICATION TESTS. If resistance is less than 5 ohms, go to next step.

10) Reconnect RESUME/ACCEL switch. Start engine and let idle for one minute. Turn engine off. Turn ignition on (engine off). Using scan tool, actuate S/C servo solenoids. If throttle does not open and close, go to VACUUM SUPPLY test under COMPONENT TESTS. Repair as necessary. Perform TEST VER-4A under VERIFICATION TESTS. If throttle opens and closes, go to next step.

11) Using scan tool, monitor S/C output status. Road test vehicle at speed greater than 35 MPH and attempt to set speed control. If speed control does not set, speed control denied status will indicate reason for speed control not to set. See SCAN TOOL DENIED STATUS table. Press continue on scan tool. Repair as necessary. Go to next step.

12) Turn ignition off. Disconnect both S/C switches. Using an ohmmeter, measure resistance between S/C ON/OFF switch connector Red/Light Green wire and RESUME/ACCEL switch connector Red/Light Green wire. If resistance is 5 ohms or more, repair open circuit. Perform TEST VER-4A under VERIFICATION TESTS. If resistance is less than 5 ohms, go to next step.

13) Reconnect ON/OFF switch. Connect a jumper wire between RESUME/ACCEL switch connector terminals. Turn ignition on. Using scan tool, read S/C switch voltage. If voltage is less than one volt, replace right S/C switch. Perform TEST VER-4A under VERIFICATION TESTS. If voltage is one volt or more, go to next step.

14) Turn ignition off. Inspect wiring and connectors. Repair as necessary. Perform TEST VER-4A under VERIFICATION TESTS. If wiring and connectors are okay, turn ignition on. Using scan tool, read S/C switch voltage. If voltage is 4.2 volts or less, go to step **17)**. If voltage is more than 4.2 volts, go to next step.

15) Using scan tool, monitor P/N switch inputs. While observing display, shift transmission into Drive. If scan tool does not display P/N switch D/R, go to NTC-2: CHECKING PARK/NEUTRAL POSITION (PNP) SWITCH OPERATION. If scan tool displays P/N switch D/R, inspect throttle cable and linkage. Repair as necessary. Perform TEST VER-4A under VERIFICATION TESTS. If throttle cable and linkage are okay, go to next step.

16) Using scan tool, read DTCs. If DTC P0500 is displayed, go to DTC P0500: NO VEHICLE SPEED SENSOR SIGNAL under DIAGNOSTIC TESTS. Repair as necessary.

17) Using scan tool, monitor P/N switch inputs. While observing display, shift transmission into Drive. If scan tool does not display P/N switch D/R, go to NTC-2: CHECKING PARK/NEUTRAL SWITCH OPERA-TION. If scan tool displays P/N switch D/R, disconnect ON/OFF switch. Using scan tool, read S/C switch voltage. If voltage is more than 4.2 volts, replace ON/OFF switch. Perform TEST VER-4A under VERIFI-CATION TESTS. If voltage is 4.2 volts or less, go to next step.

18) Inspect throttle cable and linkage. Repair as necessary. Perform TEST VER-4A under VERIFICATION TESTS. If throttle cable and linkage are okay, read DTCs. If DTC P0500 is displayed, go to DTC P0500: NO VEHICLE SPEED SENSOR SIGNAL under DIAGNOSTIC TESTS. Repair as necessary. If DTC P0500 is not displayed, go to next step.

19) Disconnect RESUME/ACCEL switch. Using scan tool, read S/C switch voltage. If voltage is now more than 4.2 volts, replace RESUME/ACCEL switch. Perform TEST VER-4A under VERIFICATION TESTS. If voltage is 4.2 volts or less, go to next step.

20) Start engine and let idle for one minute. Turn engine off. Turn ignition on (engine off). Using scan tool, actuate S/C servo solenoids. If throttle does not open and close, go to VACUUM SUPPLY test under COMPO-NENT TESTING. If throttle opens and closes, go to next step.

21) Using scan tool, monitor S/C output status. Road test vehicle at speed greater than 35 MPH and attempt to set speed control. If speed control does not set, speed control denied status will indicate reason for speed control not to set. See SCAN TOOL DENIED STATUS table. Press continue on scan tool. Repair as necessary. Test is complete.

SCAN TOOL DENIED STATUS

Denied Message	Reason
ON/OFF	PCM Does Not See An ON Signal From Switch At PCM Terminal No. 41
SPEED	Vehicle Speed As Seen By PCM Terminal No. 66 Is Not Greater Than 36 MPH
RPM	Engine RPM Is Excessively High
BRAKE	Brake Switch Sense Circuit Is Open Indicating That Brakes Are Applied
P/N	Park/Neutral Switch Sense Circuit Is Grounded Indicating That Transmission Is In Park Or Neutral
RPM/SPD	PCM Senses Excessive Engine RPM For A Given Vehicle Speed
SOL FLT	PCM Senses A Servo Solenoid Circuit Trouble Code That Is Maturing Or Set In Memory

NTC-1: BRAKE SWITCH SENSE

Possible Causes:
- Ground circuit open.
- Defective brake switch.
- Brake switch sense circuit open or shorted.
- Defective PCM.

1) Turn ignition off. Disconnect brake switch. Inspect connector. Clean or repair as necessary. Using an ohmmeter, measure resistance between ground and brake switch connector terminal No. 2 (Black wire). If resistance is 5 ohms or more, repair open ground circuit. Perform TEST VER-4A under VERIFICATION TESTS. If resistance is less than 5 ohms, go to next step.

2) Disconnect PCM. Inspect connectors. Clean or repair as necessary. Using an ohmmeter, measure resistance of brake switch sense circuit between PCM connector C3, terminal No. 24 and brake switch connector terminal No. 1 (White/Pink wire). If resistance is 5 ohms or more, repair open circuit. Perform TEST VER-4A under VERIFICATION TESTS. If resistance is less than 5 ohms, go to next step.

3) Disconnect ABS control module. Inspect connectors. Clean or repair as necessary. Using an ohmmeter, measure resistance between ground and brake switch sense circuit at brake switch connector terminal No. 1 (White/Pink wire). If resistance is less than 5 ohms, repair short to ground. Perform TEST VER-4A under VERIFICATION TESTS. If resistance is 5 ohms or more, go to next step.

NOTE: Ensure brake pedal is NOT depressed during the following step.

4) Reconnect PCM and ABS control module. Using an ohmmeter, measure resistance between brake switch terminals No. 1 and 5. *See Fig. 1.* If resistance is 5 ohms or more, replace brake switch. Perform TEST VER-4A under VERIFICATION TESTS. If resistance is less than 5 ohms, replace PCM. Perform TEST VER-4A under VERIFICATION TESTS.

NTC-2: CHECKING PARK/NEUTRAL POSITION (PNP) SWITCH OPERATION

1) Turn ignition on. Using scan tool, read PNP switch state. While observing display, shift transmission through all positions. If scan tool does not display P/N and D/R in correct gear positions, go to next step. If scan tool displays P/N and D/R in correct gear positions, test is complete.

2) Turn ignition off. Disconnect PCM and PNP switch. Inspect connectors. Clean or repair as necessary. Using an ohmmeter, measure resistance between ground and PNP sense circuit at PNP switch connector (Brown/Yellow wire). If resistance is less than 5 ohms, repair short to ground. Perform TRANSMISSION DTC VERIFICATION TEST under VERIFICATION TESTS. If resistance is 5 ohms or more, go to next step.

3) Using an ohmmeter, measure resistance of PNP sense circuit between PNP switch connector and PCM connector C1, terminal No. 6 (Brown/Yellow wire). If resistance is 5 ohms or more, repair open circuit. Perform TRANSMISSION DTC VERIFICATION TEST under VERIFICATION TESTS. If resistance is less than 5 ohms, go to next step.

4) Reconnect PNP switch. Using an ohmmeter, measure resistance between ground and PNP sense circuit at PCM connector C1, terminal No. 6 (Brown/Yellow wire). While observing ohmmeter, shift transmission through all positions. If resistance does not change from more than 10 ohms to less than 10 ohms, replace PNP switch. Perform TRANSMISSION DTC VERIFICATION TEST under VERIFICATION TESTS. If resistance changes from more than 10 ohms to less than 10 ohms, replace PCM. Perform TRANSMISSION DTC VERIFICATION TEST under VERIFICATION TESTS.

VERIFICATION TESTS

TEST VER-4A

NOTE: If PCM has been replaced and correct VIN and mileage have not been programmed, a DTC will be set in ABS and air bag modules. If vehicle is equipped with a Sentry Key Immobilizer Module (SKIM), sentry key data must be updated to enable starting. See COMPUTER RELEARN PROCEDURES article in GENERAL INFORMATION.

1) If vehicle is equipped with ABS or air bag, enter correct VIN and mileage in PCM. Erase DTCs in ABS and air bag modules. Inspect vehicle to ensure all engine and speed control system components are connected. Reassemble and reconnect components as necessary. Using scan tool, erase DTCs from PCM.

2) Road test vehicle at a speed greater than 35 MPH. Turn S/C switch on. Press and release SET button. If S/C does not engage, repair is not complete. Check for related TSBs and return to TROUBLE SHOOTING, if necessary. If speed control engages, go to next step.

3) Quickly depress and release RESUME/ACCEL switch. If vehicle speed increases by 2 MPH, go to next step. If vehicle speed does not increase by 2 MPH, repair is not complete. Check for related TSBs and return to TROUBLE SHOOTING, if necessary.

4) Press and hold COAST switch. Vehicle speed should decrease. If vehicle speed decreases, go to next step. If vehicle speed does not decrease, repair is not complete. Check for related TSBs and return to TROUBLE SHOOTING, if necessary.

5) Using caution, depress and release brake pedal. If S/C disengages, go to next step. If S/C does not disengage, repair is not complete. Check for related TSBs and return to TROUBLE SHOOTING, if necessary.

6) Bring vehicle speed to 35 MPH. Depress speed control RESUME/ACCEL switch. If vehicle resumes to previously set speed, go to next step. If vehicle does not resume to previously set speed, repair is not complete. Check for related TSBs and return to TROUBLE SHOOTING, if necessary.

7) Hold down SET switch. If vehicle speed decreases, go to next step. If vehicle speed does not decrease, repair is not complete. Check for related TSBs and return to TROUBLE SHOOTING, if necessary.

8) Ensure vehicle speed is more than 35 MPH and release SET switch. If vehicle sets a new speed, go to next step. If vehicle does not set a new speed, repair is not complete. Check for related TSBs and return to TROUBLE SHOOTING, if necessary.

9) Depress and release CANCEL switch. If S/C disengages, go to next step. If S/C does not disengage, repair is not complete. Check for related TSBs and return to TROUBLE SHOOTING, if necessary.

10) Ensure vehicle speed is greater than 35 MPH. Engage speed control. Turn S/C ON/OFF switch to OFF position. If speed control disengages, system is operating correctly. Repair is complete. If speed control does not disengage, repair is not complete. Check for related TSBs and return to TROUBLE SHOOTING, if necessary.

TEST VER-5A

NOTE: If PCM has been replaced and correct VIN and mileage have not been programmed, a DTC will be set in ABS and air bag modules. If vehicle is equipped with a Sentry Key Immobilizer Module (SKIM), sentry key data must be updated to enable starting. See COMPUTER RELEARN PROCEDURES article in GENERAL INFORMATION.

1) If vehicle is equipped with ABS or air bag, enter correct VIN and mileage in PCM. Erase DTCs in ABS and air bag modules. Inspect vehicle to ensure all engine and speed control system components are connected. If there are any DTCs that have not been repaired, go to SELF-DIAGNOSTIC SYSTEM. After all DTCs have been repaired, go to next step.

2) Ensure fuel tank is at least 1/4 full. Allow PCM to run appropriate monitor and increment appropriate good trip. Enabling conditions must be met before monitor will run. Using scan tool, monitor pretest enabling conditions until all conditions have been met. Once enabling conditions have been met, monitor appropriate monitor.

3) If repaired DTC has reset or was seen in monitor while on road test, repair is not complete. Check for TSBs or flash updates and return to TROUBLE SHOOTING.

4) If appropriate monitor ran, good trip counter incremented and no DTCs have been set, repair is complete.

TRANSMISSION DTC VERIFICATION TEST

NOTE: If PCM has been replaced and correct VIN and mileage have not been programmed, a DTC will be set in ABS and air bag modules. If vehicle is equipped with a Sentry Key Immobilizer Module (SKIM), sentry key data must be updated to enable starting. See COMPUTER RELEARN PROCEDURES article in GENERAL INFORMATION.

1) Inspect vehicle to ensure that all engine components are properly installed and connected. If any DTCs have not been repaired, go to SELF-DIAGNOSTIC SYSTEM and repair as necessary. Connect scan tool to DLC. Ensure fuel tank is at least 1/4 full.

2) Start engine and run until transmission temperature is more than 110°F (43°C). Check transmission fluid level. Adjust fluid level as necessary. Road test vehicle. Make 15-20 upshifts (1-2, 2-3 & 3-4). Perform shifts from a standing start to 45 MPH with a constant throttle opening of 20-25 degrees. Make 5-8 wide open throttle kick-downs with vehicle speed less than 25 MPH. Allow at least 5 seconds between kick-downs.

3) For a specific DTC, road test vehicle under similar conditions when DTC was set. If DTC sets during road test, go to SELF-DIAGNOSTIC SYSTEM and repair as necessary. If no DTCs set, repair is complete.

REMOVAL & INSTALLATION

WARNING: Vehicle is equipped with an air bag. Air bag must be deactivated before servicing speed control components on or around steering column. See AIR BAG RESTRAINT SYSTEMS article.

CAUTION: When battery is disconnected, vehicle computer and memory systems may lose memory data. Driveability problems may exist until computer systems have completed a relearn cycle. See COMPUTER RELEARN PROCEDURES article in GENERAL INFORMATION before disconnecting battery.

BRAKE SWITCH

Removal – Remove steering column cover and lower trim panel for switch access, if necessary. Fully depress brake pedal and rotate brake switch counterclockwise approximately 30 degrees. Remove brake switch from bracket. Depress lock tabs holding brake switch mounting bracket and separate harness connector from brake switch.

Installation – 1) Before installing brake switch, reset adjustable plunger by pulling on plunger head until plunger reaches end of travel. Connect harness connector to brake switch. Depress brake pedal and insert brake switch into keyed hole in mounting bracket. Rotate brake switch clockwise into locked position.

2) Gently pull back on brake pedal until pedal will go no further. This causes the brake switch plunger to ratchet backward to the correct position. No further adjustment is required. To complete installation, reverse removal procedure.

SPEED CONTROL SERVO

Removal – 1) Disconnect both battery cables and remove battery. Remove air cleaner housing from top of throttle body. Using finger pressure only, push servo cable connector from throttle body bellcrank pin. DO NOT pull cable connector perpendicular to bellcrank. Disconnect wiring at battery tray.

2) Disconnect positive battery cable from Power Distribution Center (PDC). Loosen PDC from battery tray. Remove 3 battery tray bolts. Disconnect battery temperature sensor and remove battery tray. Disconnect electrical connector and vacuum hose from servo. Remove 2 servo mounting nuts. Pull servo cable sleeve away from mounting bracket to expose cable retaining clip. Remove retaining clip. Remove servo.

Installation – With throttle in full open position, align hole in speed control cable sleeve with hole in servo pin. Install retaining clip. To complete installation, reverse removal procedure. Tighten mounting nuts to 75 INCH lbs. (8.5 N.m).

SPEED CONTROL SWITCHES

Removal & Installation – Turn ignition off. Disconnect negative battery cable. Wait 2 minutes for air bag system to discharge reserve voltage. Remove 2 screws holding air bag assembly to steering column. Separate air bag assembly from steering column and disconnect air bag, horn and speed control switch connectors. Remove screws securing speed control switch to air bag assembly. Separate speed control switch from air bag assembly. To install, reverse removal procedure.

WIRING DIAGRAMS

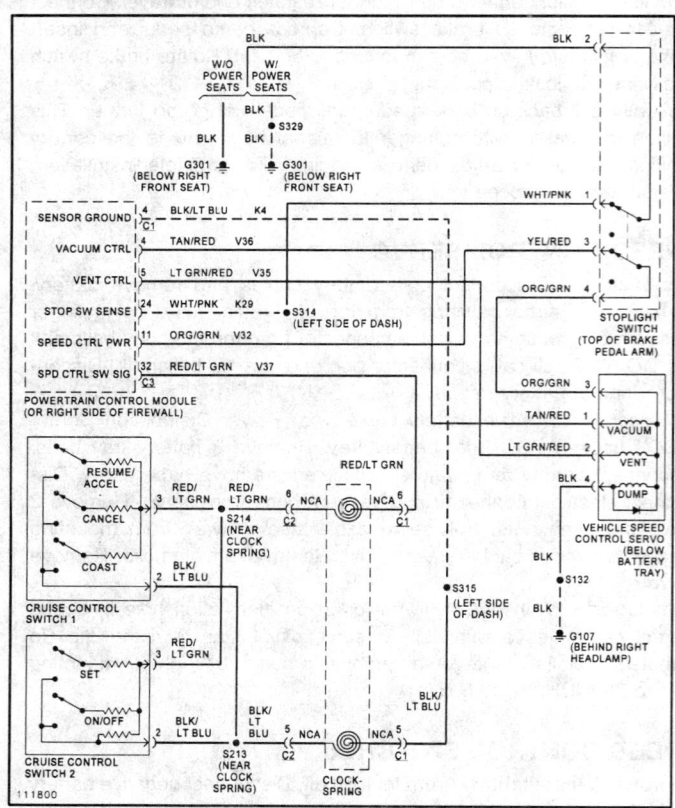

Fig. 6: Cruise Control System Wiring Diagram (Grand Cherokee)

WIRING DIAGRAMS

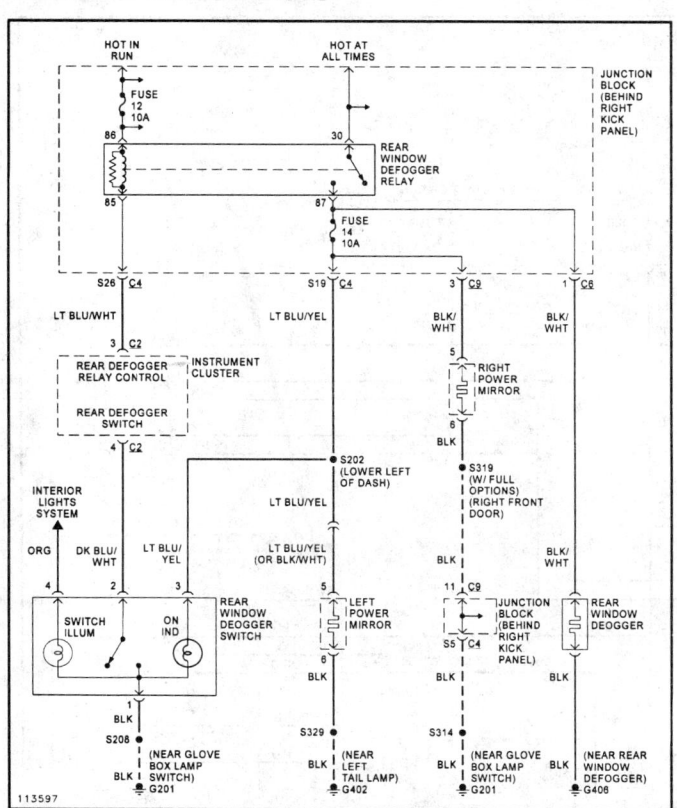

Fig. 1: Rear Window & Mirror Defogger Wiring Diagram (Cherokee)

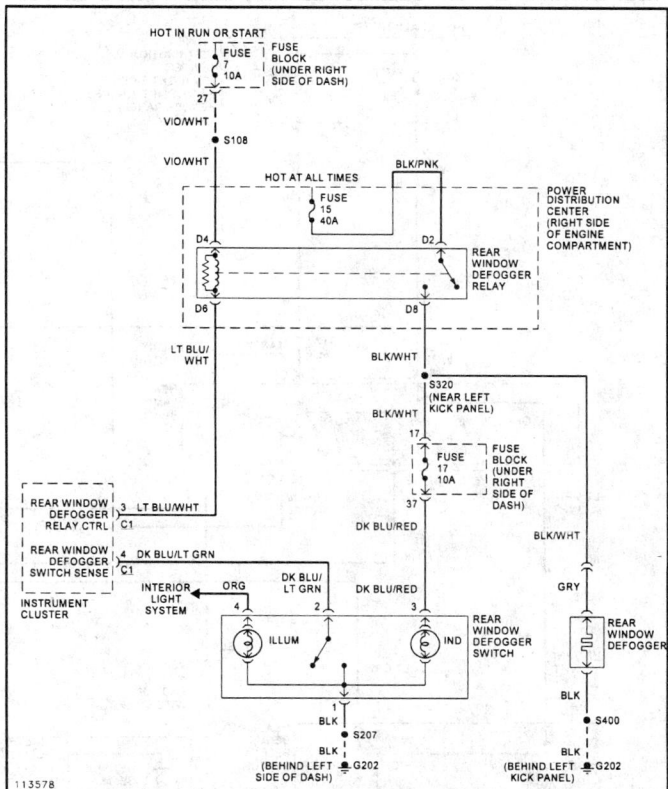

Fig. 3: Rear Window & Mirror Defogger Wiring Diagram (Wrangler)

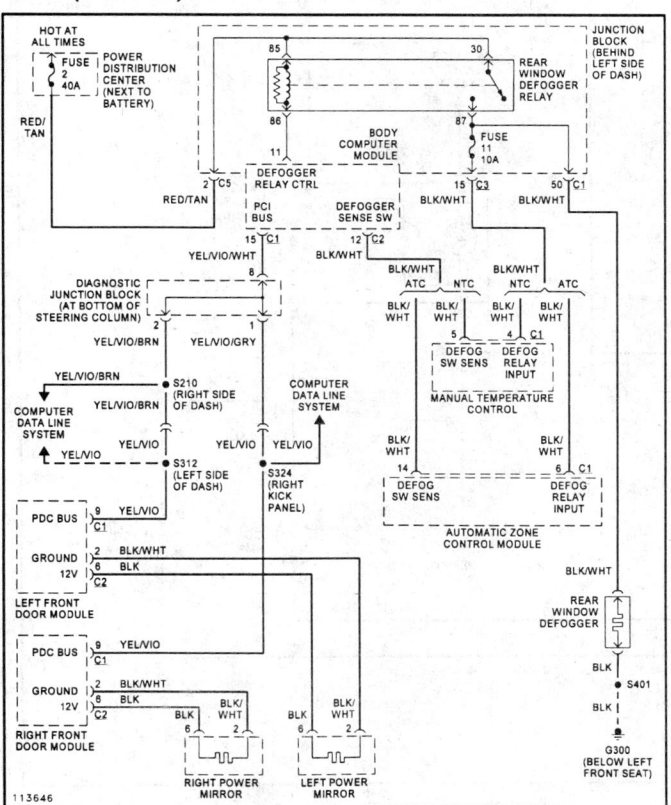

Fig. 2: Rear Window & Mirror Defogger Wiring Diagram (Grand Cherokee)

WIRING DIAGRAMS

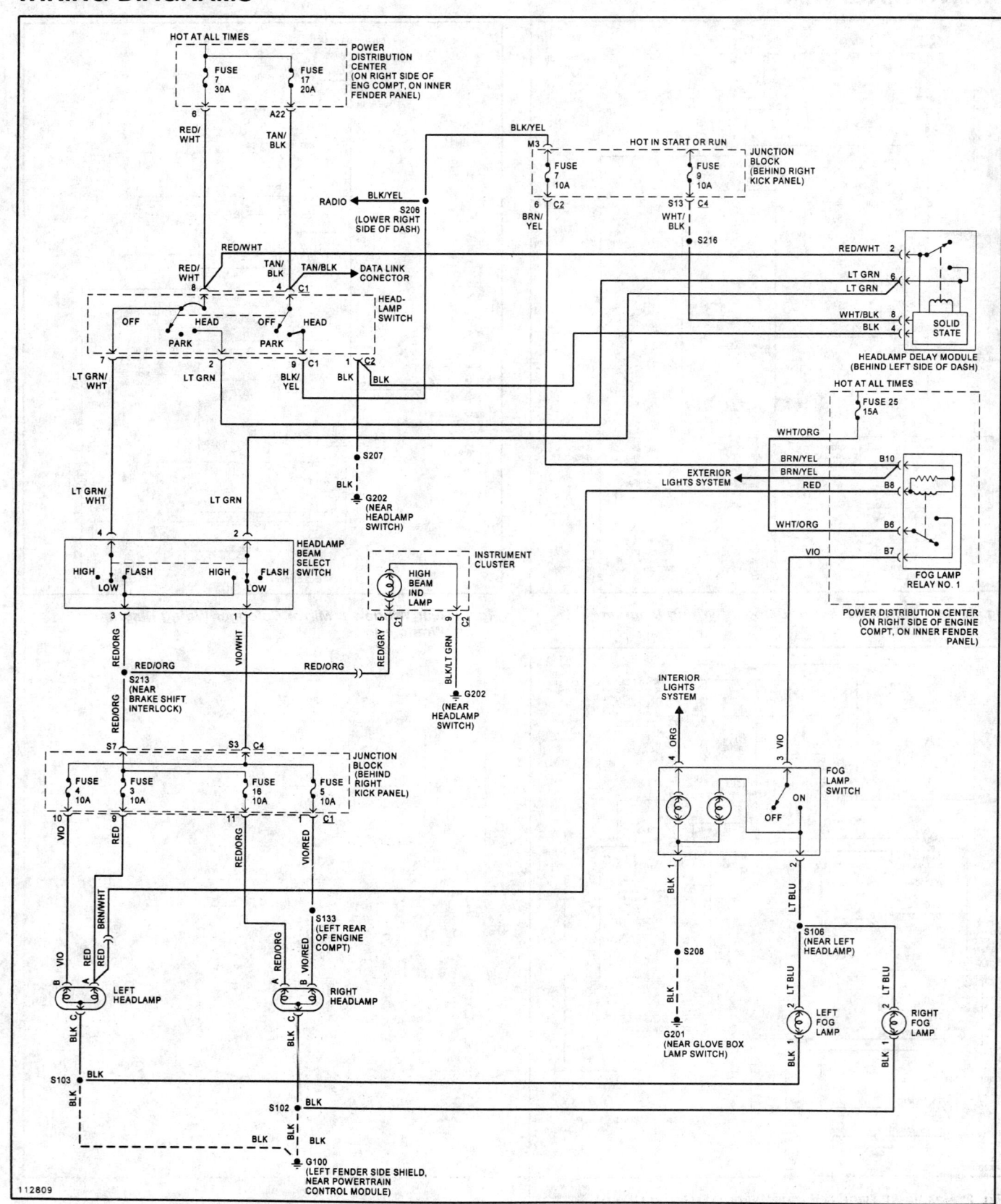

Fig. 1: Headlight System Wiring Diagram (Cherokee)

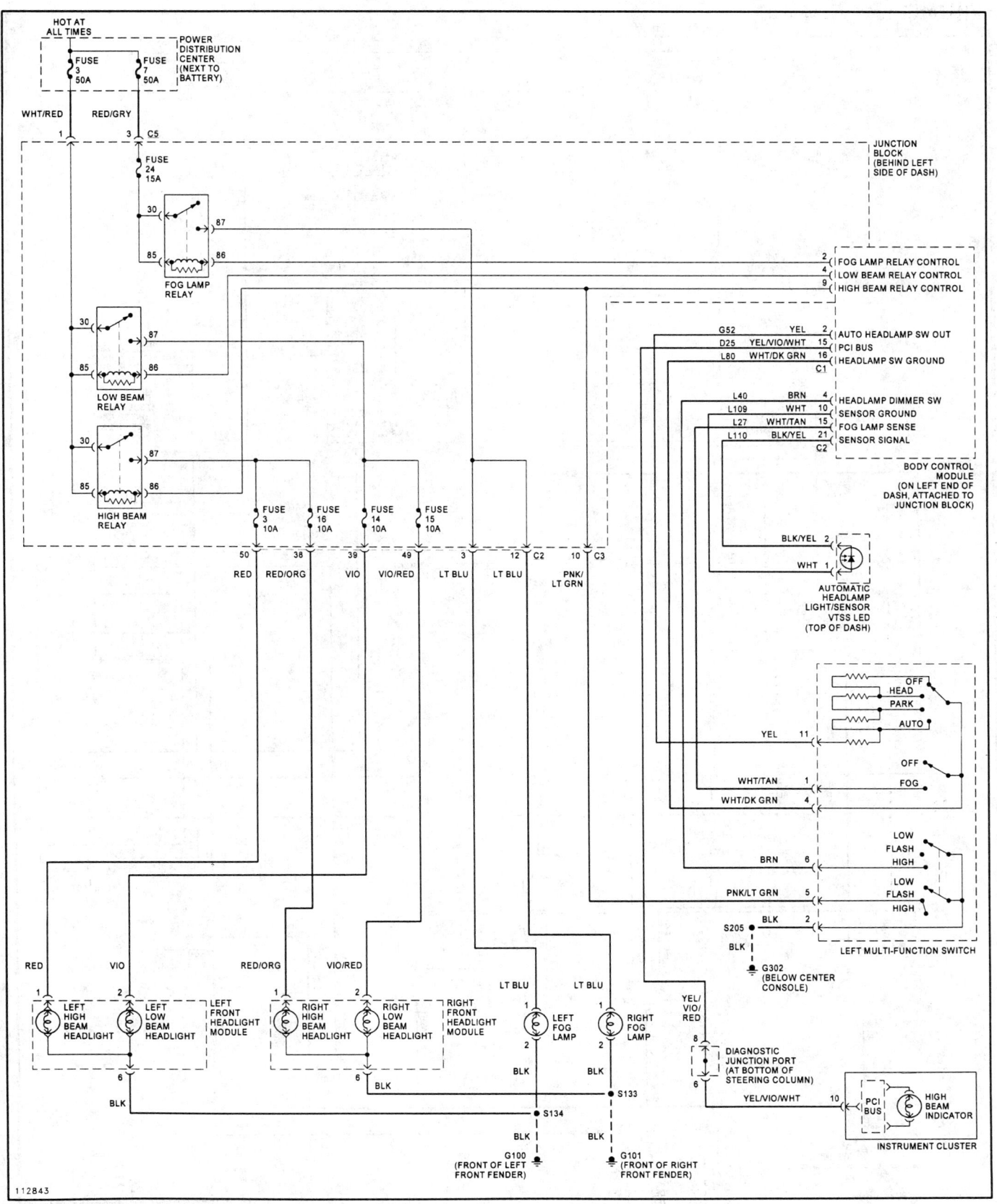

Fig. 2: Headlight System Wiring Diagram (Grand Cherokee)

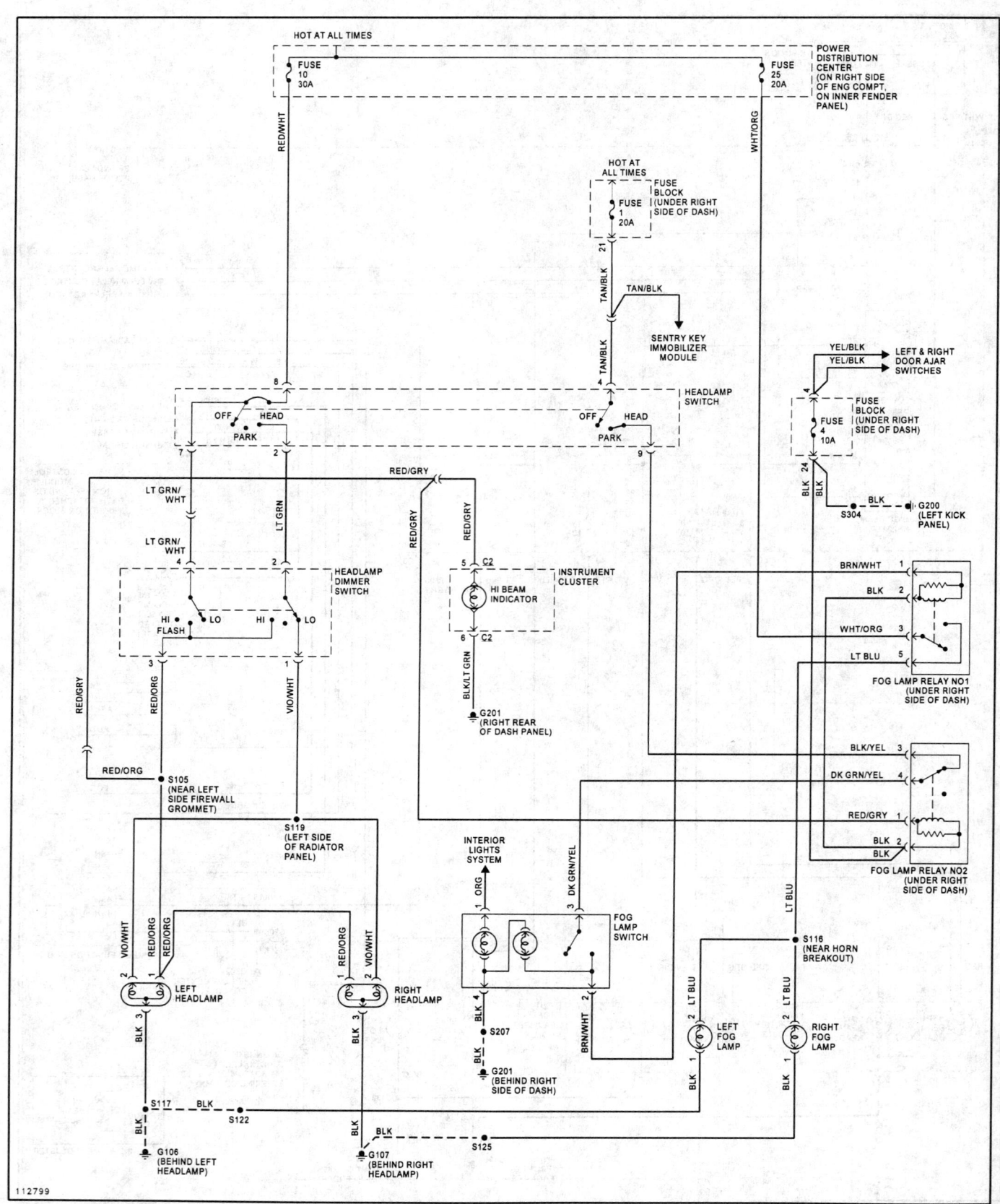

Fig. 3: Headlight System Wiring Diagram (Wrangler)

WIRING DIAGRAMS

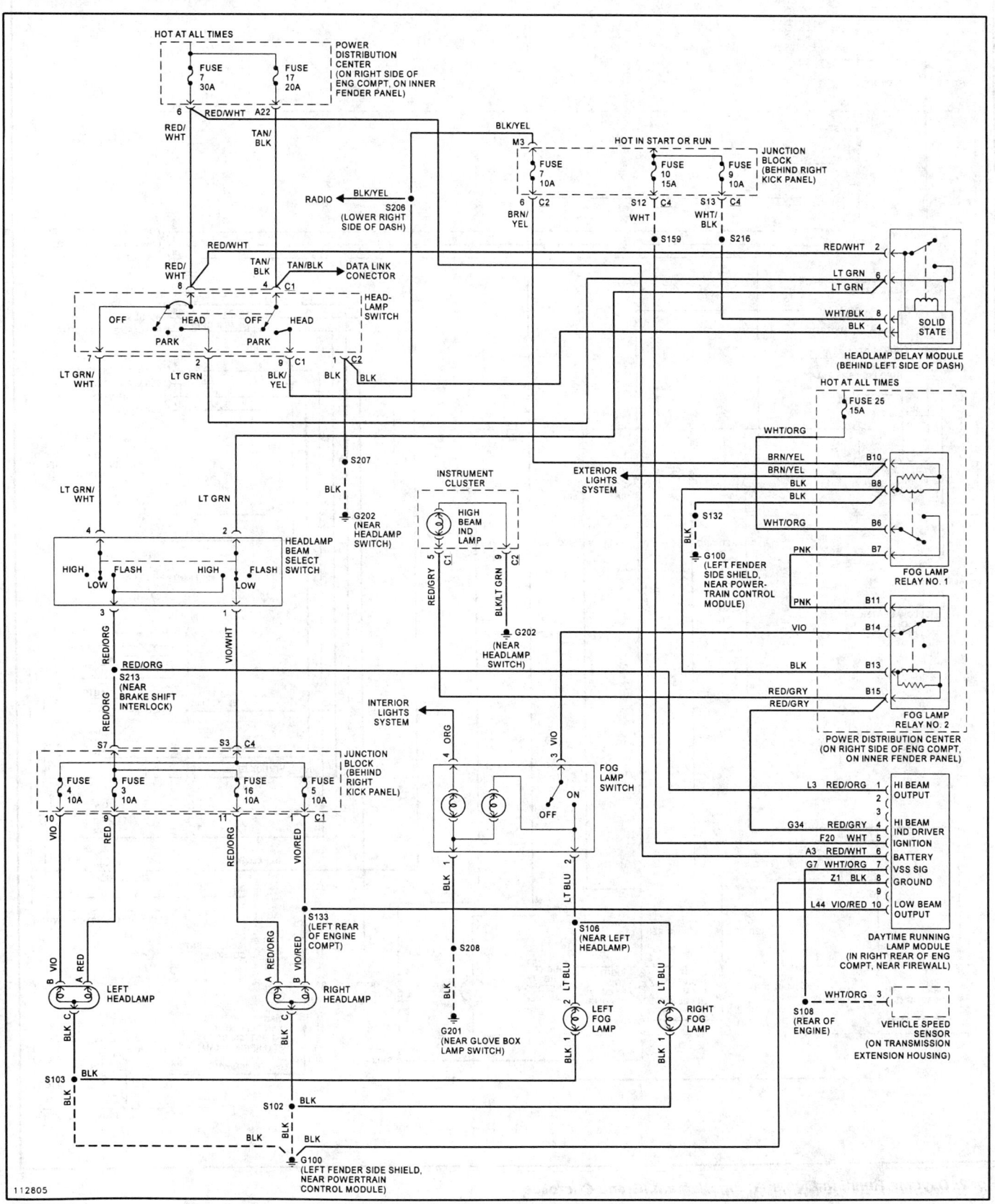

Fig. 1: Daytime Running Lights Wiring Diagram (Cherokee)

112805

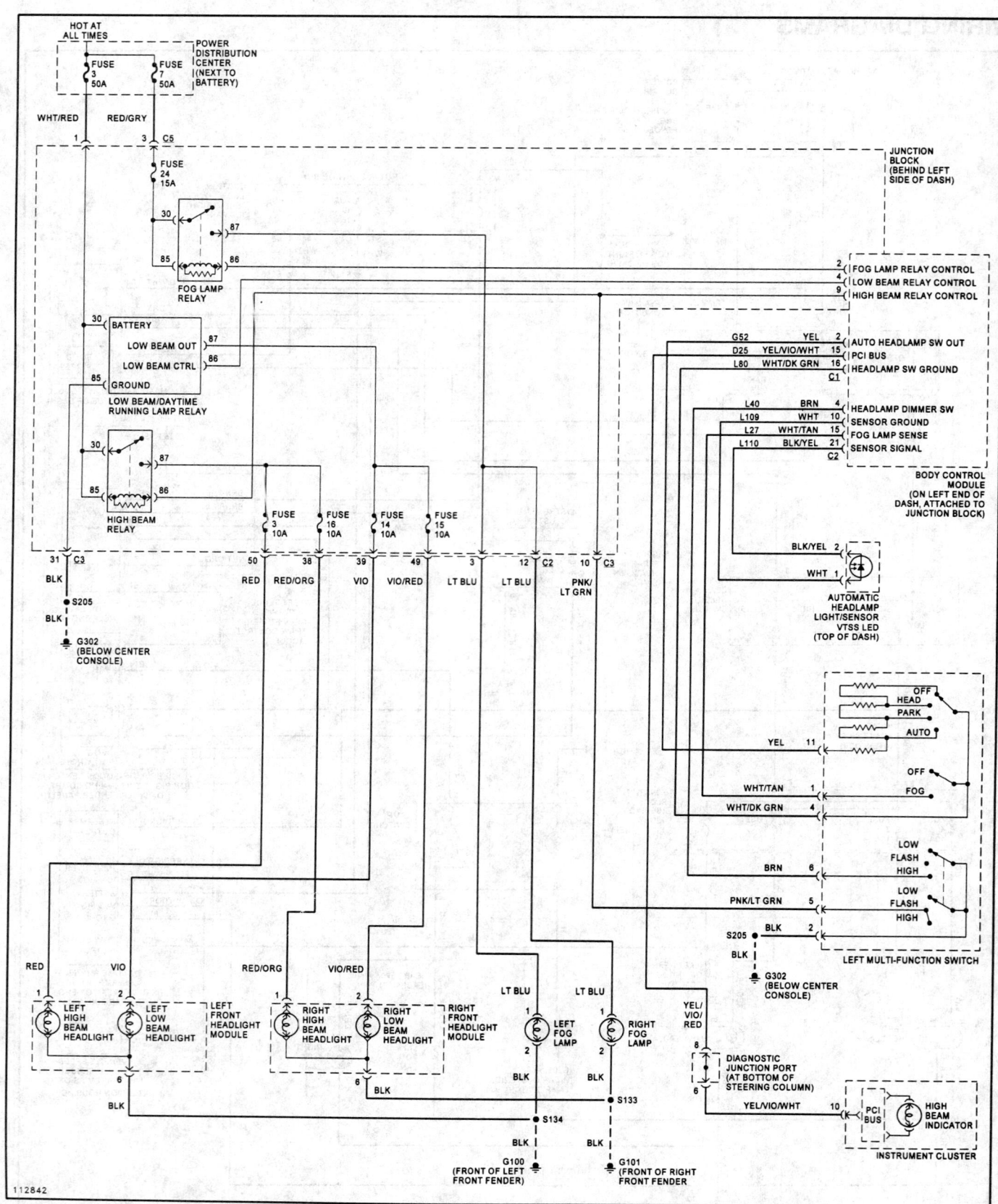

Fig. 2:. Daytime Running Lights Wiring Diagram (Grand Cherokee)

1999 ACCESSORIES & EQUIPMENT

Daytime Running Lights (Cont.)

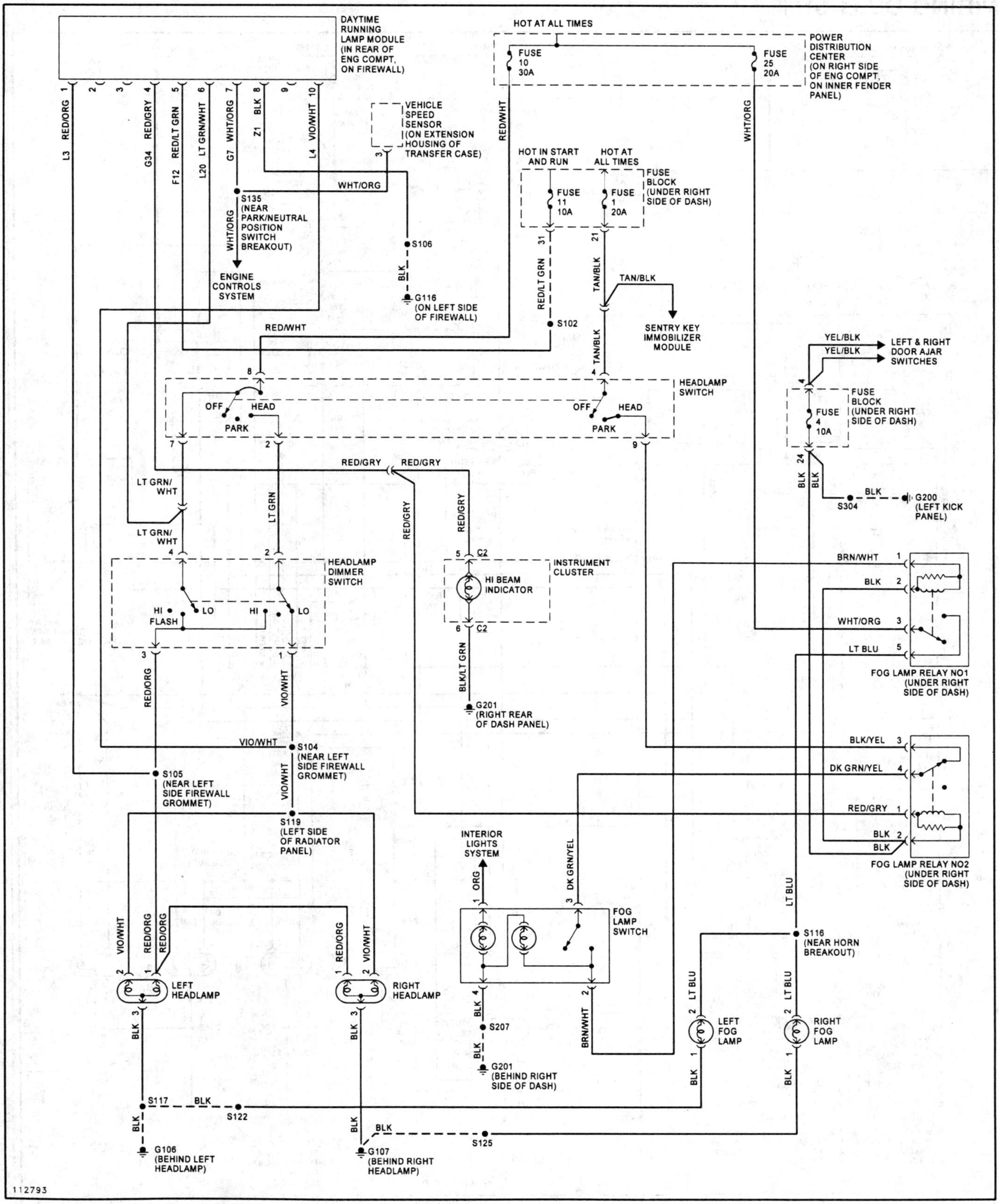

Fig. 3: Daytime Running Lights Wiring Diagram (Wrangler)

WIRING DIAGRAMS

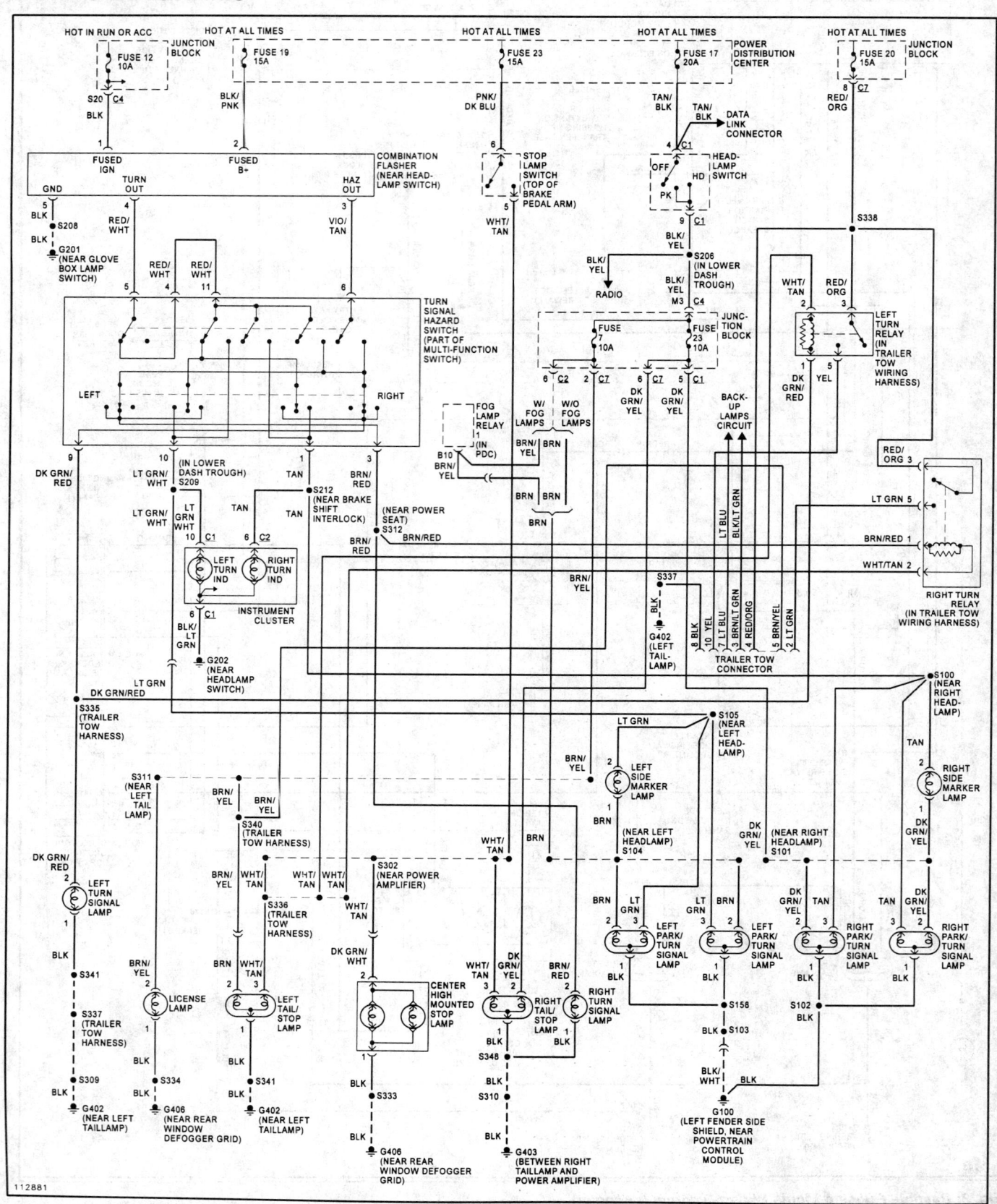

Fig. 1: Exterior Lights & Trailer Connector Wiring Diagram (Cherokee)

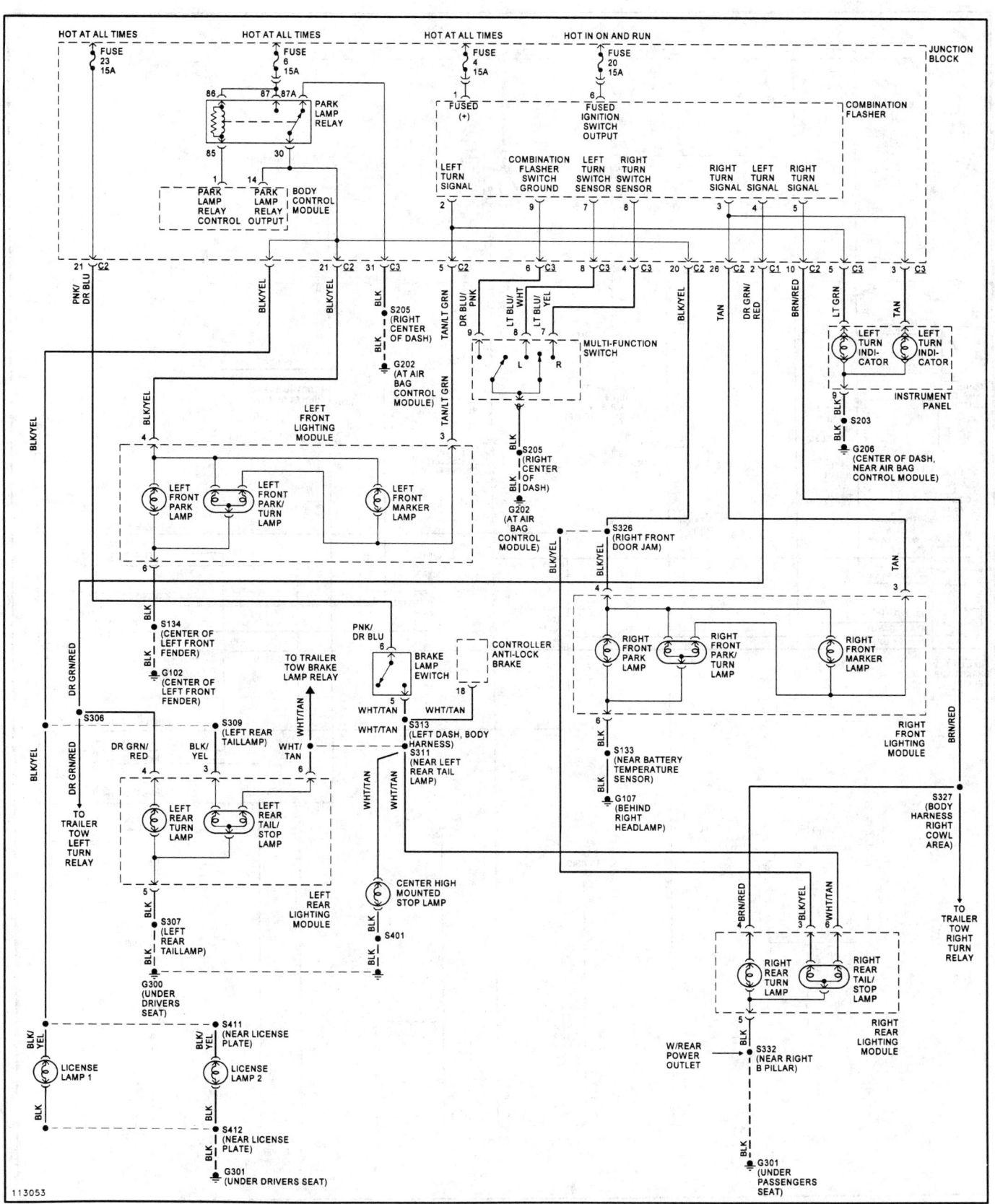

Fig. 2: Exterior Lights & Trailer Connector Wiring Diagram (Grand Cherokee)

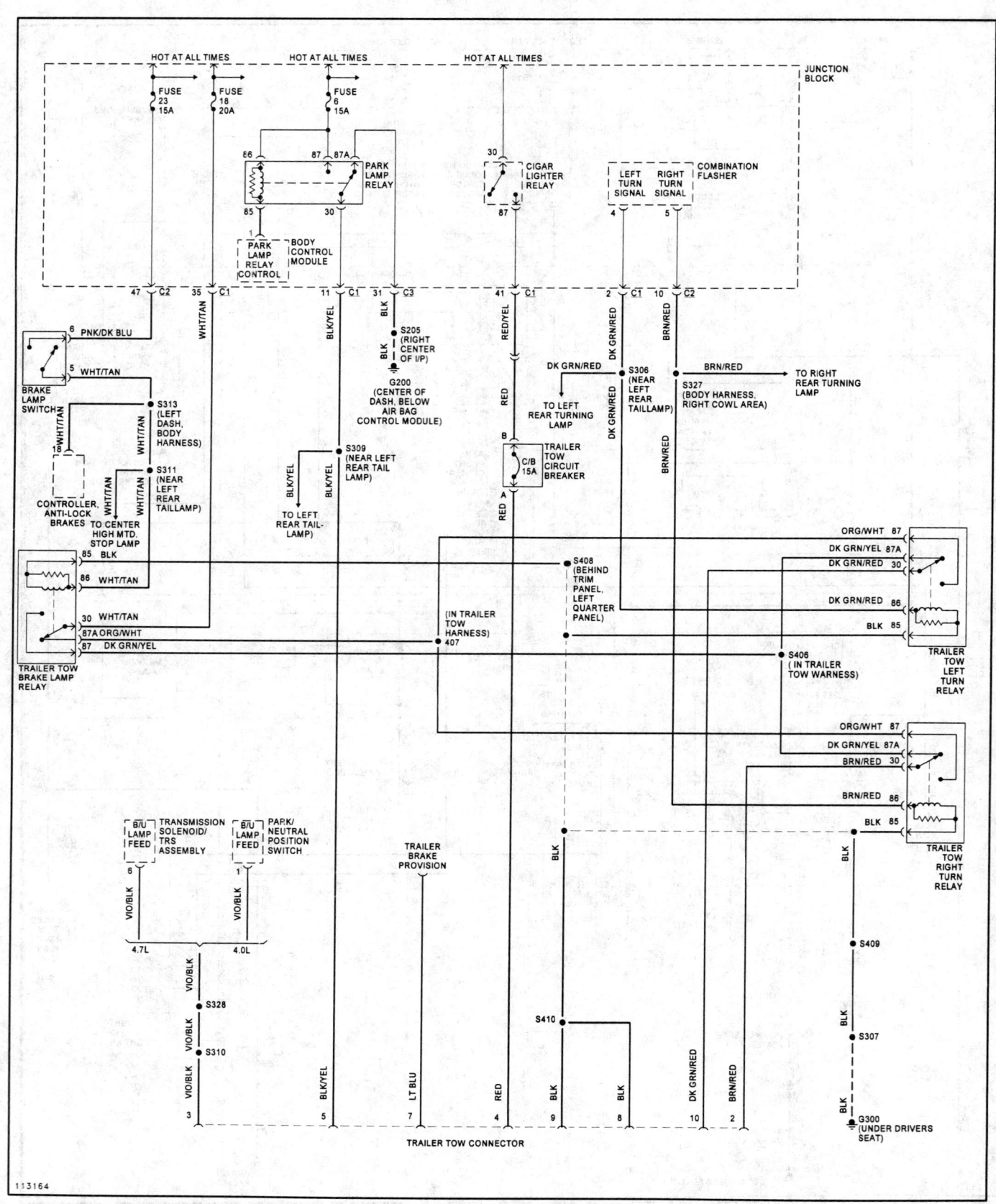

Fig. 3: Trailer Tow Circuit Wiring Diagram (Grand Cherokee)

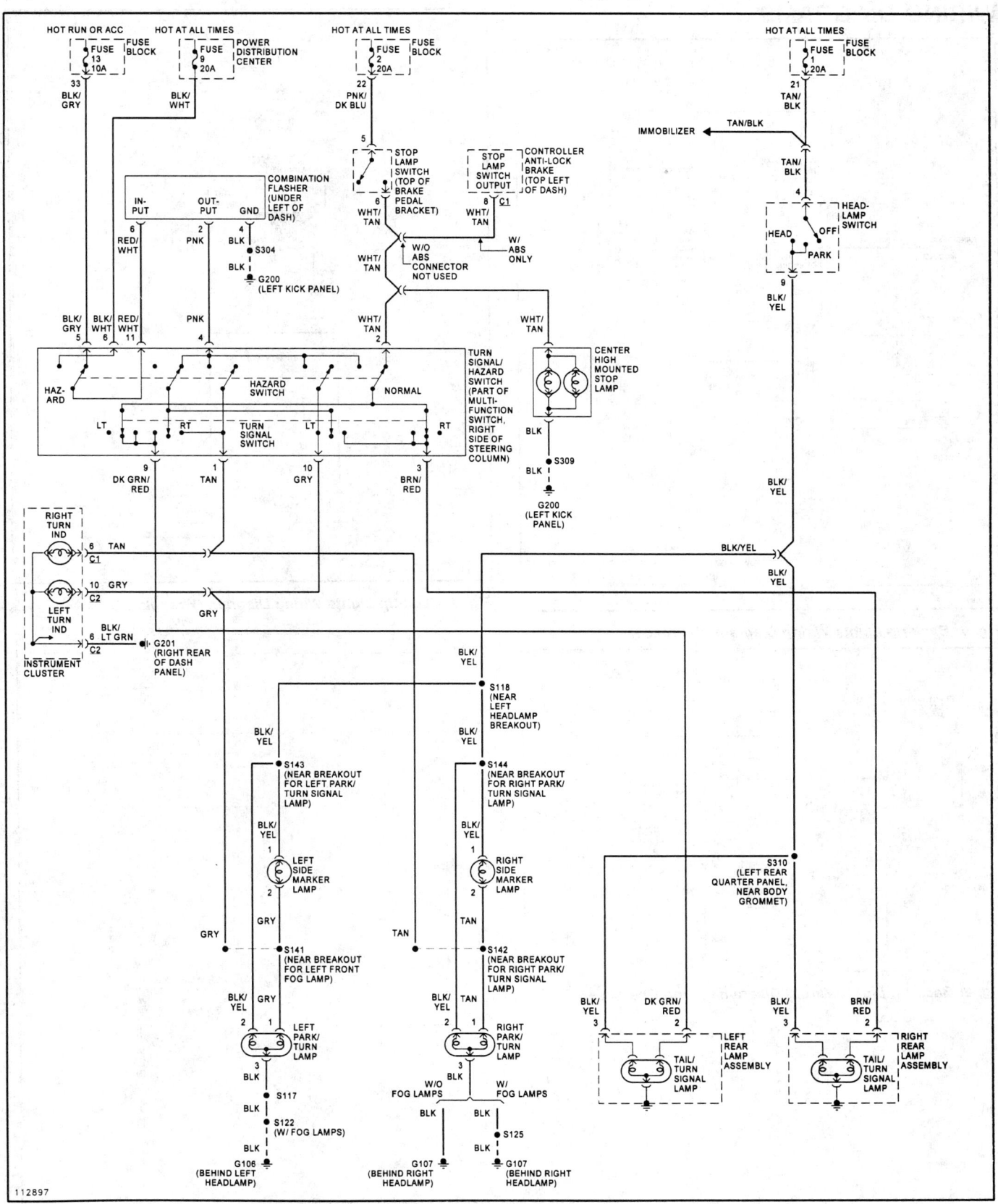

Fig. 4: Exterior Lights Wiring Diagram (Wrangler)

1999 ACCESSORIES & EQUIPMENT

Back-Up Lights

WIRING DIAGRAMS

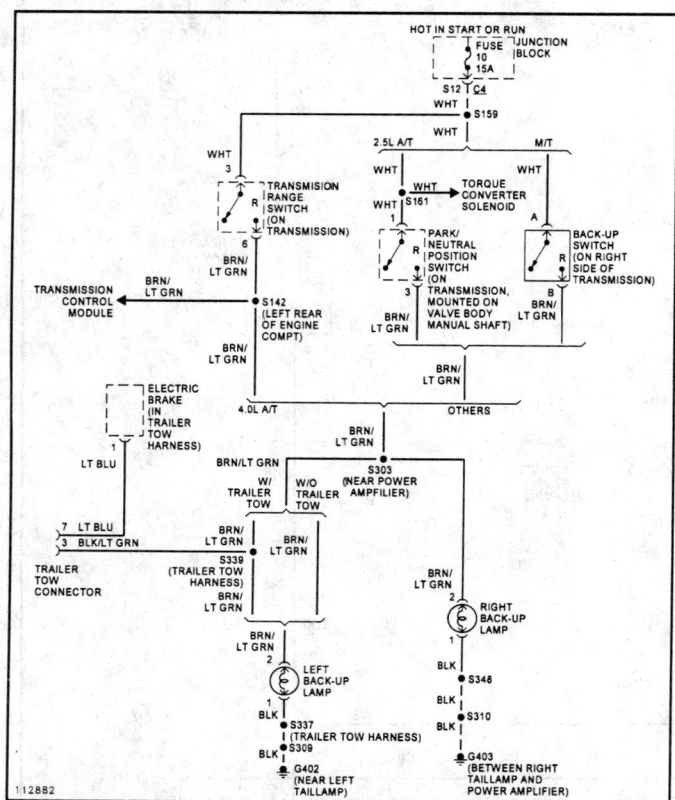

Fig. 1: Back-Up Lights Wiring Diagram (Cherokee)

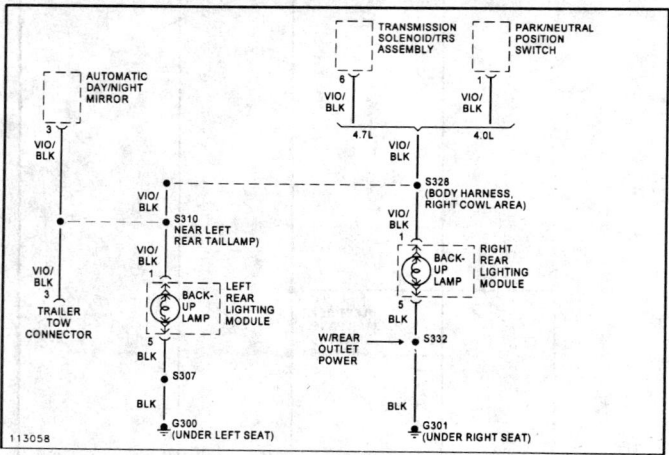

Fig. 2: Back-Up Lights Wiring Diagram (Grand Cherokee)

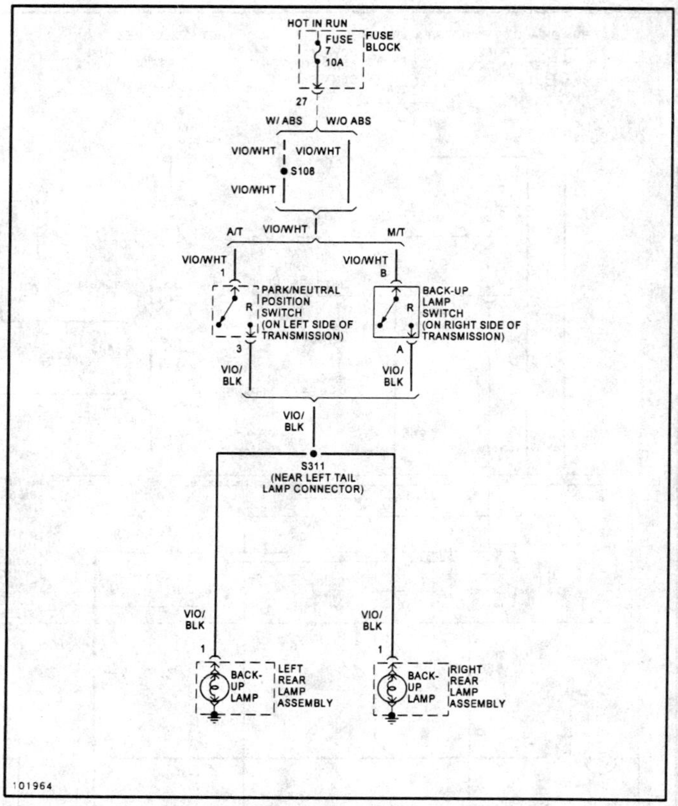

Fig. 3: Back-Up Lights Wiring Diagram (Wrangler)

WIRING DIAGRAMS

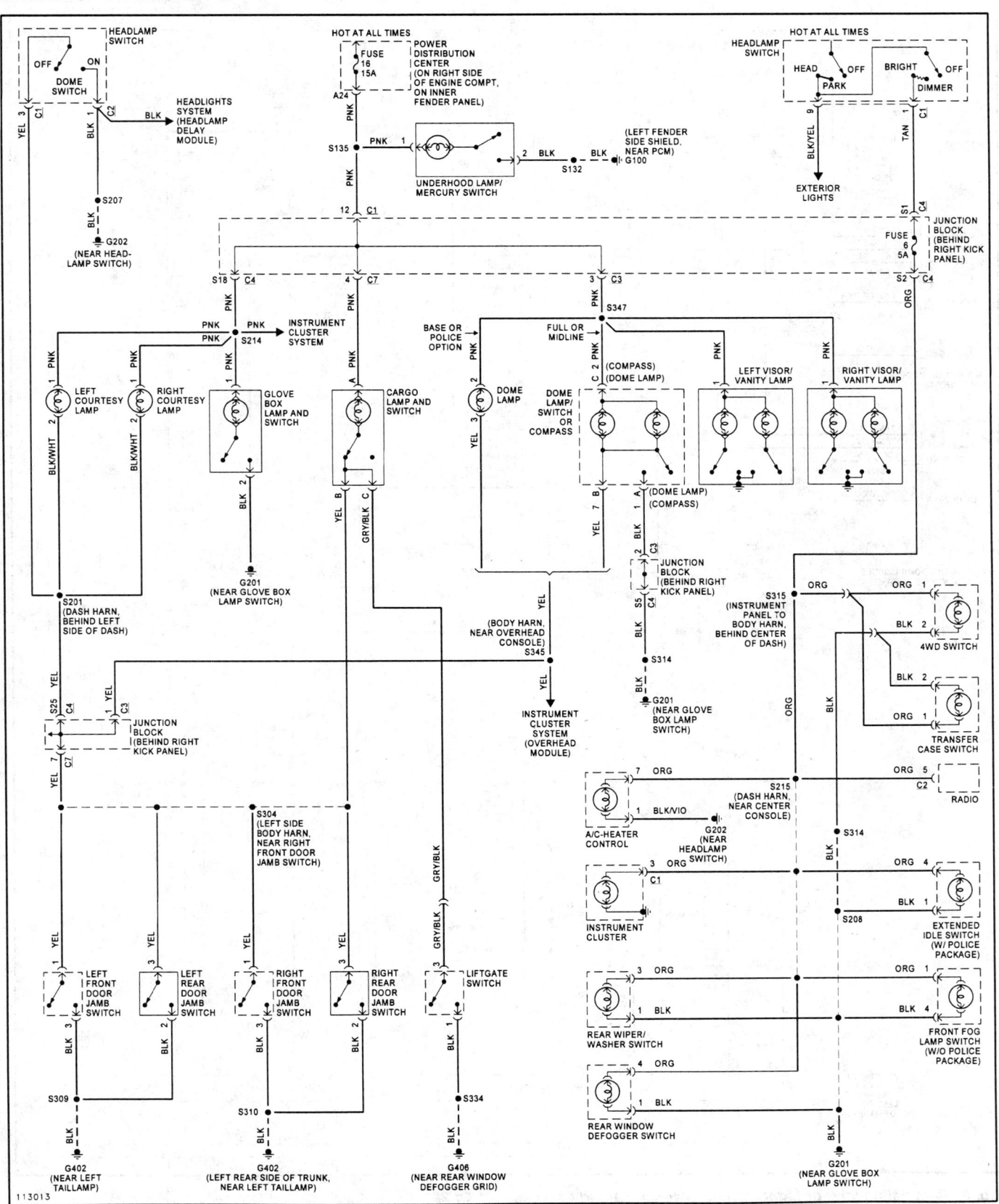

Fig. 1: Illumination/Interior Lights Wiring Diagram (Cherokee)

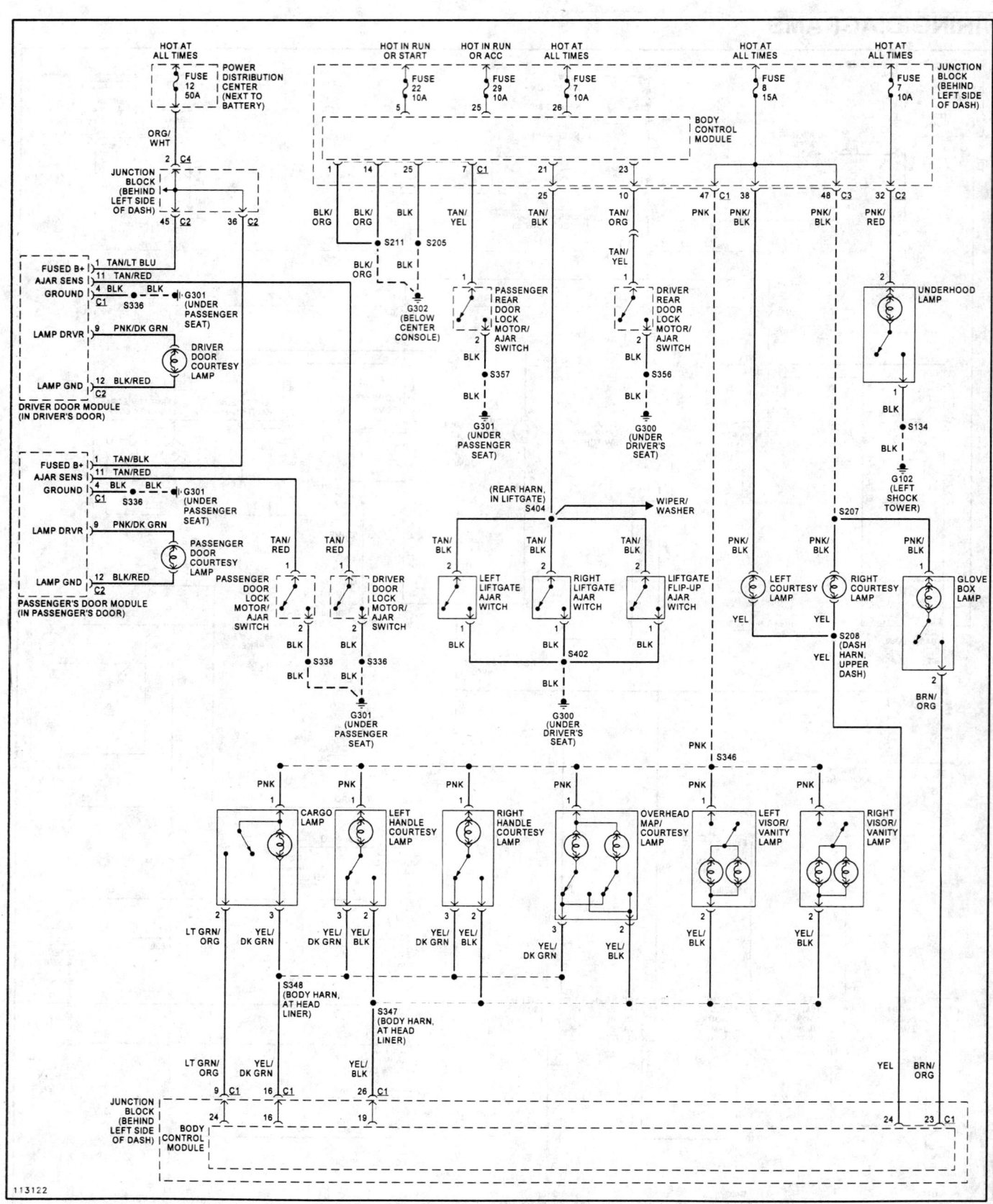

Fig. 2: Illumination/Interior Lights Wiring Diagram (Grand Cherokee – 1 Of 2)

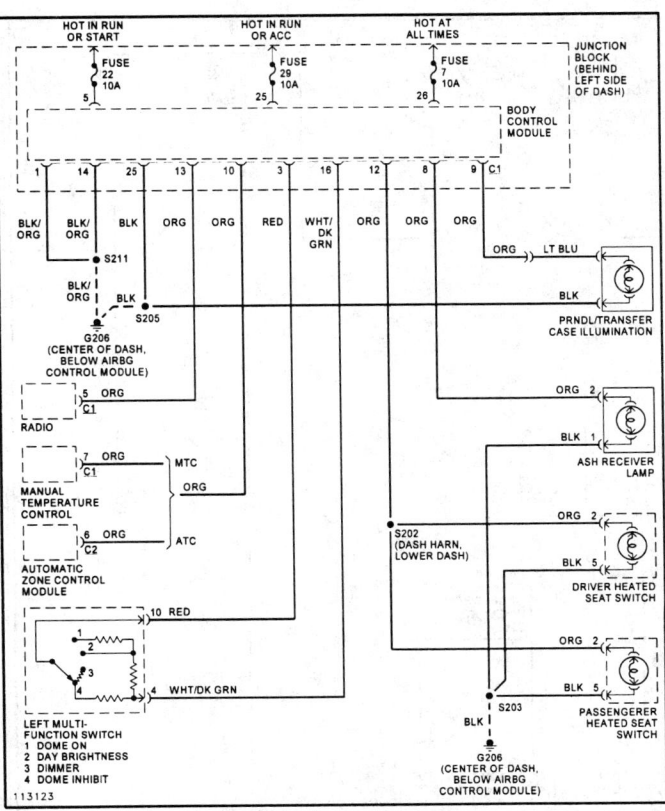

*Fig. 3: Illumination/Interior Lights Wiring Diagram
(Grand Cherokee – 2 Of 2)*

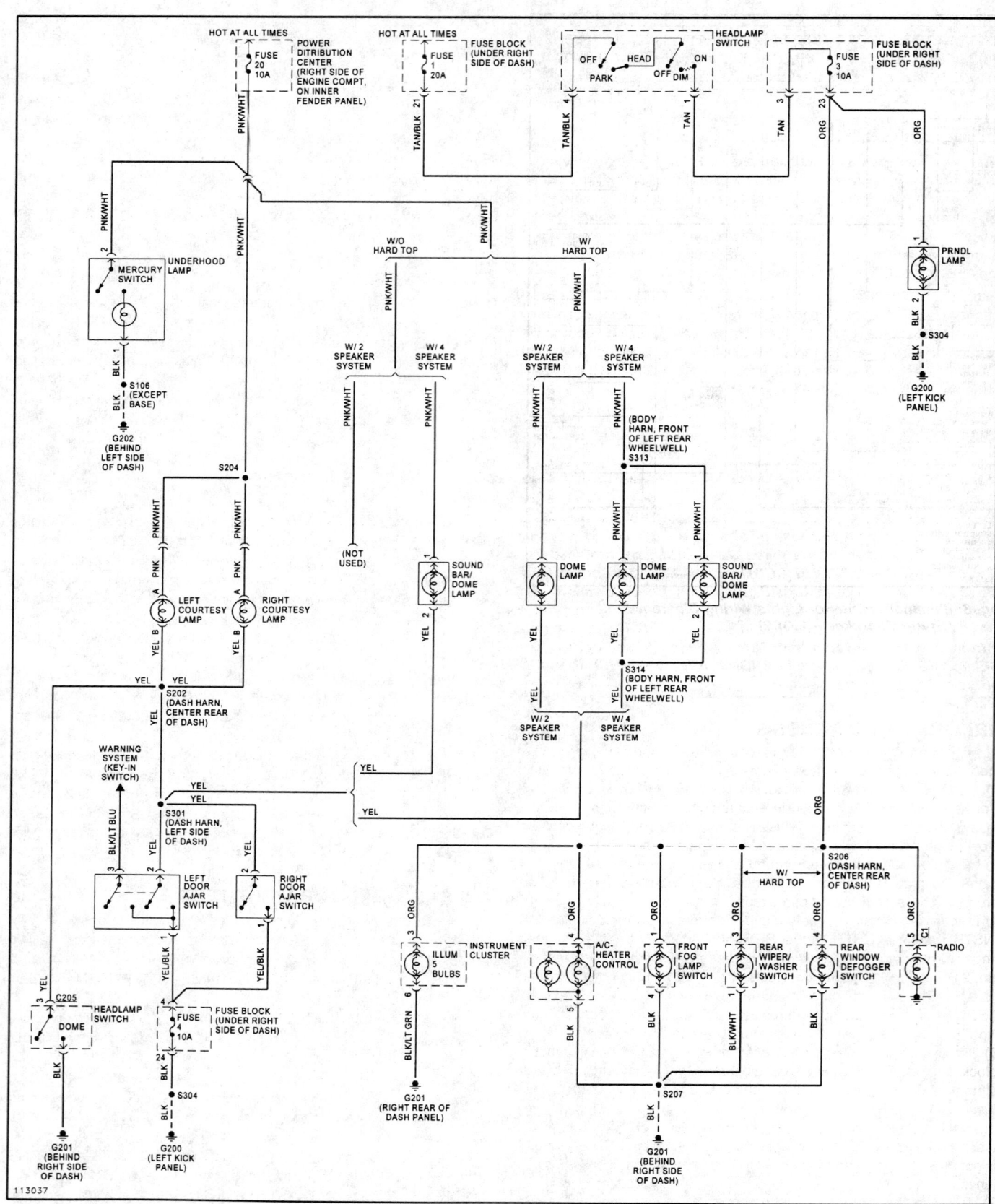

Fig. 4: Illumination/Interior Lights Wiring Diagram (Wrangler)

WARNING: Vehicle is equipped with Supplemental Restraint System (SRS). See SERVICE PRECAUTIONS in AIR BAG RESTRAINT SYSTEMS article before working around instrument panel area.

DESCRIPTION

Vehicle may be equipped with a low-line or high-line instrument cluster. Both instrument clusters are electro-mechanical units that utilize integrated circuitry and information carried on the Chrysler Collision Detection (CCD) data bus network for control of all gauges and many of the indicator lights. High-line cluster replaces some of the indicator lights found in the low-line cluster with analog gauges. High-line cluster also adds a CHECK GAUGES light and a LOW FUEL warning light.

Both instrument clusters are equipped with circuitry that has self-diagnostic actuator test capability. Instrument cluster is serviced as a complete unit. If instrument cluster gauge or circuit board is faulty, entire instrument cluster must be replaced. Cluster lens, hood and mask, rear housing cover and odometer reset knob boot are replaceable. Individual bulbs and bulb holders can also be serviced.

SYSTEM TESTS

NOTE: For instrument cluster circuit and terminal identification, see WIRING DIAGRAMS.

NOTE: For diagnosis and testing of systems not covered in this article, manufacturer recommends using DRB scan tool to check Chrysler Collision Detection (CCD) and/or Powertrain Control Module (PCM) circuits. For CCD data bus testing, check for opens and shorts in CCD data bus circuits. See appropriate wiring diagram in DATA LINK CONNECTORS article in WIRING DIAGRAMS. For more information on scan tool and PCM diagnostics, see appropriate SELF-DIAGNOSTICS article in ENGINE PERFORMANCE in appropriate MITCHELL® manual.

PRELIMINARY DIAGNOSIS

1) If indicator lights operate but all gauges are inoperative, go to next step. If all gauges and indicator lights are inoperative, go to step **5)**.
2) Remove and inspect fuse No. 16 (15-amp) in Power Distribution Center (PDC). PDC is located in engine compartment, near battery. If fuse is okay, go to next step. If fuse is blown, locate and repair cause of blown fuse. Install new fuse and recheck system operation.
3) Measure voltage between ground and power side of fuse No. 16. If battery voltage is present, go to next step. If battery voltage is not present, locate and repair open circuit.
4) Disconnect negative battery cable. Remove instrument cluster. See INSTRUMENT CLUSTER under REMOVAL & INSTALLATION. Connect negative battery cable. Measure voltage between ground and terminal No. 9 (Pink wire) at instrument cluster 10-pin Black connector. If battery voltage is present, reinstall instrument cluster and go to ACTUATOR TEST. If battery voltage is not present, repair open circuit between fuse No. 16 in PDC and instrument cluster 10-pin Black connector.
5) Remove and inspect fuse No. 9 (10-amp) in junction block. Junction block is located behind right side kick panel. If fuse is okay, go to next step. If fuse is blown, locate and repair cause of blown fuse. Install new fuse and recheck system operation.
6) Turn ignition on. Measure voltage between ground and power side of fuse No. 9. If battery voltage is present, go to next step. If battery voltage is not present, locate and repair open circuit between ignition switch and junction block.
7) Turn ignition off. Install instrument cluster. Turn ignition on. Set parking brake and observe instrument cluster BRAKE warning light. If warning light is on, go to next step. If warning light is off, go to step **9)**.
8) Turn parking lights on and adjust instrument panel lights dimmer rheostat to full bright position. If instrument panel lights are on, go to ACTUATOR TEST. If instrument panel lights are off, go to step **10)**.

9) Turn ignition off. Disconnect negative battery cable. Remove instrument cluster. See INSTRUMENT CLUSTER under REMOVAL & INSTALLATION. Connect negative battery cable. Turn ignition on. Measure voltage between ground and terminal No. 8 (White/Black wire) at instrument cluster 10-pin Black connector. If battery voltage is present, go to ACTUATOR TEST. If battery voltage is not present, locate and repair open circuit.
10) Remove instrument cluster. See INSTRUMENT CLUSTER under REMOVAL & INSTALLATION. Check continuity between ground and terminal No. 6 (Black/Light Green wire) at instrument cluster 10-pin Black connector. If continuity exists, go to ACTUATOR TEST. If continuity does not exist, locate and repair open in ground circuit.

ACTUATOR TEST

Diagnostic Aids – Instrument actuator test will put instrument cluster into self-diagnostic mode. In this mode, instrument cluster will position each of the gauge needles at various specified calibration points, and turn all Chrysler Collision Detection (CCD) data bus message-controlled indicator lights on and off at specified time intervals. *See Fig. 1 or 2.* Successful completion of actuator test will confirm instrument cluster circuitry, gauges and indicator lights are capable of operating properly. If test is successful, a problem may still exist with CCD data bus, Powertrain Control Module (PCM), Air Bag Control Module (ACM), Sentry Key Immobilizer Module (SKIM) or inputs to one of these modules.

If an individual gauge does not respond properly or at all during actuator test, remove instrument cluster. Check tightness of suspect gauge mounting screws on printed circuit board. If screws are loose, reinstall instrument cluster and retest. If screws are tight, replace instrument cluster. If an individual indicator light does not illuminate during actuator test, remove instrument cluster. Check indicator light bulb and bulb holder. Repair as necessary and retest. If indicator bulb is okay and bulb holder is installed properly, replace instrument cluster.
Actuator Test – **1)** Turn ignition off. Depress and hold down trip odometer RESET button. Turn ignition on. DO NOT start engine. Release trip odometer reset button. Compare operation of suspect gauge(s) and/or indicator light(s) with chart. *See Fig. 1 or 2.*
2) Instrument cluster will exit self-diagnostics mode at completion of test, if ignition switch is turned off or if VSS signal is detected by PCM, indicating that vehicle is moving. If instrument cluster gauge(s) and/or indictor light(s) do not respond properly during actuator test, see DIAGNOSTIC AIDS before replacing instrument cluster. Repeat actuator test if necessary.

AIR BAG INDICATOR LIGHT TEST

1) If AIR BAG warning light illuminates for 12 seconds or more, or stays on all the time, a system malfunction exists and trouble code will be stored. For air bag system testing procedures, see DIAGNOSIS & TESTING MITCHELL® AIR BAG SERVICE & REPAIR MANUAL, DOMESTIC & IMPORTED MODELS.
2) If AIR BAG indicator light does not illuminate when ignition is on, replace air bag indicator bulb and retest. If AIR BAG indicator light still does not illuminate, perform PRELIMINARY DIAGNOSIS.
3) If after performing preliminary diagnosis and actuator test, air bag indicator light and instrument cluster circuitry is okay, diagnosis of air bag system and Chrysler Collision Detection (CCD) data bus should be performed.
4) For air bag system testing procedures, see DIAGNOSIS & TESTING MITCHELL® AIR BAG SERVICE & REPAIR MANUAL, DOMESTIC & IMPORTED MODELS. For CCD data bus testing, check for opens and shorts in CCD data bus circuits. See appropriate wiring diagram in DATA LINK CONNECTORS article in WIRING DIAGRAMS.

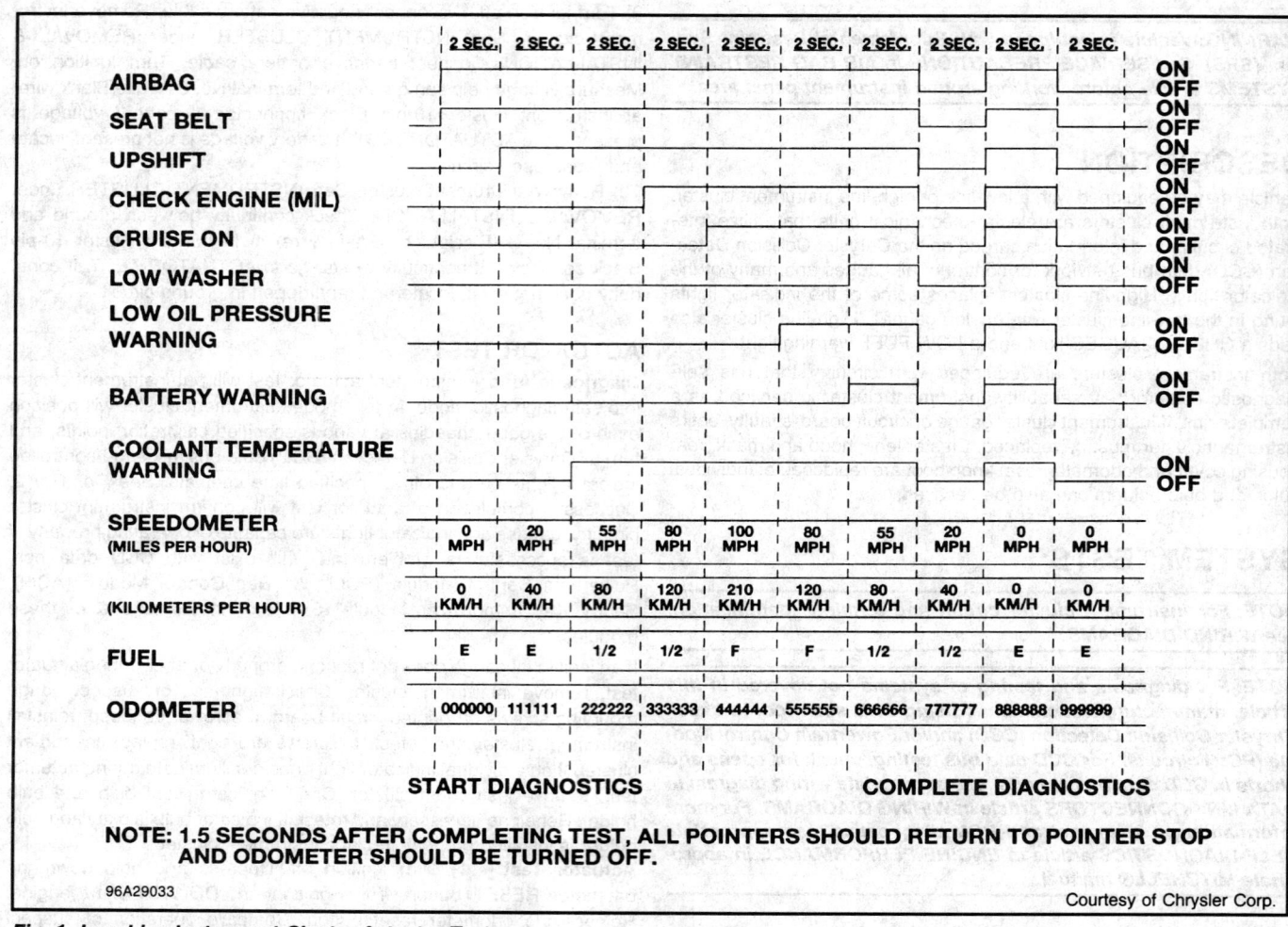

NOTE: 1.5 SECONDS AFTER COMPLETING TEST, ALL POINTERS SHOULD RETURN TO POINTER STOP
AND ODOMETER SHOULD BE TURNED OFF.

96A29033

Courtesy of Chrysler Corp.

Fig. 1: Low-Line Instrument Cluster Actuator Test

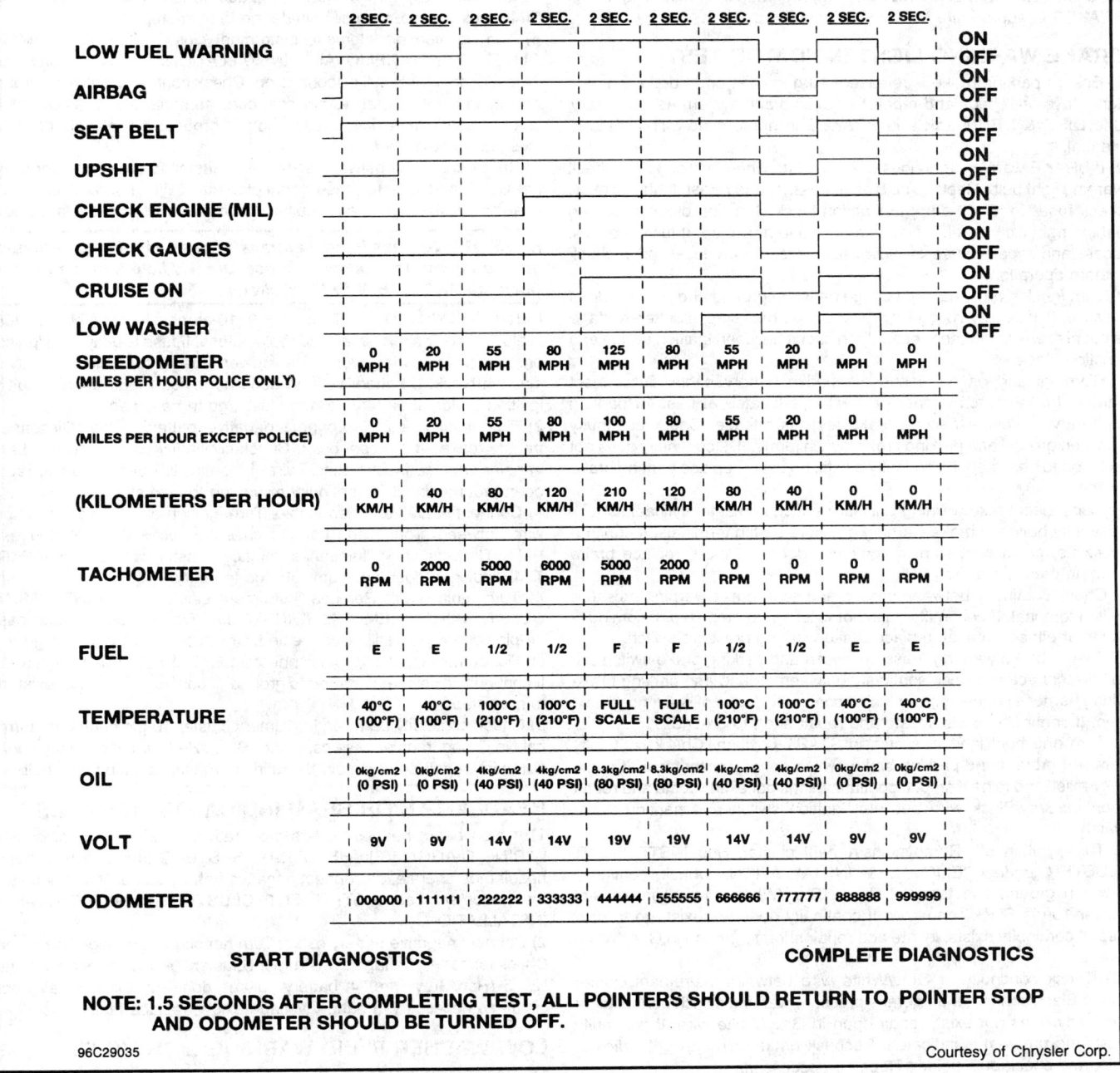

Fig. 2: High-Line Instrument Cluster Actuator Test

ANTI-LOCK BRAKE INDICATOR LIGHT TEST

1) If Anti-Lock Brake System (ABS) warning light stays on all the time, a system malfunction exists and trouble code will be stored. For ABS testing, see appropriate ANTI-LOCK article in BRAKES in appropriate MITCHELL® manual.

2) If ABS light does not illuminate when ignition is on, check fuse No. 9 (10-amp) in junction block. Junction block is located behind right kick panel. If fuse is okay, go to next step. If fuse is blown, locate and repair cause of blown fuse. Install new fuse and recheck system operation.

3) Turn ignition on. Measure voltage between ground and power side of fuse No. 9. If battery voltage is present, go to next step. If battery voltage is not present, locate and repair open circuit between ignition switch and junction block.

4) Disconnect negative battery cable. Remove instrument cluster. See INSTRUMENT CLUSTER under REMOVAL & INSTALLATION. Connect negative battery cable. Turn ignition on, and within 5 seconds check continuity between ground and terminal No. 4 (Light Green/Orange wire) at instrument cluster 10-pin Black connector. Continuity should exist for 5 seconds, and should not exist after 5 seconds. If continuity is as specified, replace ABS indicator bulb and retest. If continuity is not as specified, go to next step.

5) Turn ignition off. Disconnect negative battery cable. Disconnect Controller Anti-Lock Brake (CAB) relay in Power Distribution Center (PDC). PDC is located in engine compartment, near battery. Refer to label on PDC cover for relay identification and location.

6) Check continuity between ground and terminal No. 4 (Light Green/Orange wire) at instrument cluster 10-pin Black connector. If continuity does not exist, go to next step. If continuity exist, locate and repair short to ground in Light Green/Orange wire.

7) Check continuity of Light Green/Orange wire between instrument cluster 10-pin Black connector and CAB relay connector in PDC. If continuity does not exist, repair open in Light Green/Orange wire. If continuity exists, check ABS. See appropriate ANTI-LOCK article in BRAKES in appropriate MITCHELL® manual.

BRAKE WARNING LIGHT INDICATOR TEST

1) Ensure parking brake is released. Turn ignition on. If brake warning light stays on, check and repair hydraulic brake system as necessary. See DISC & DRUM article in BRAKES in appropriate MITCHELL® manual.

2) If BRAKE warning light does not illuminate when ignition is on, check warning light bulb. Replace bulb as necessary and retest. If bulb is okay, check fuse No. 9 (10-amp) in junction block. Junction block is located behind right kick panel. If fuse is okay, go to next step. If fuse is blown, locate and repair cause of blown fuse. Install new fuse and recheck system operation.

3) Turn ignition on. Measure voltage between ground and power side of fuse No. 9. If battery voltage is present, go to next step. If battery voltage is not present, locate and repair open circuit between ignition switch and junction block.

4) Turn ignition off. Disconnect negative battery cable. Disconnect parking brake switch connector. Switch is located at base of parking brake lever. Ensure parking brake lever is release. Check continuity between ground and parking brake switch terminal. If continuity does not exist, go to next step. If continuity exists, adjust or replace parking brake switch.

5) Disconnect brake warning pressure switch at master cylinder. Check continuity between brake warning pressure switch terminals. If continuity exists, go to next step. If continuity does not exist, replace brake warning pressure switch.

6) Check continuity between ground and each brake warning pressure switch terminal. If continuity does not exist, go to next step. If continuity exists at either terminal, replace brake warning pressure switch.

7) Ensure brake warning pressure switch and parking brake switch are still disconnected. Check continuity between ground and parking brake wiring harness connector terminal. If continuity does not exist, go to next step. If continuity exists, locate and repair short to ground.

8) Turn and hold ignition switch in START position. Check continuity between ground and parking brake switch connector terminal. If continuity exists, go to next step. If continuity does not exist, locate and repair open in Gray/Black wire between ignition switch and parking brake switch.

9) Turn ignition off. Remove instrument cluster. See INSTRUMENT CLUSTER under REMOVAL & INSTALLATION. Check continuity between ground and terminal No. 2 (Gray/White wire) at instrument cluster 10-pin Black connector. If continuity does not exist, go to next step. If continuity exists, locate and repair short to ground in Gray/White wire.

10) Check continuity of Gray/White wire between instrument cluster 10-pin Black connector and brake pressure warning switch connector. If continuity does not exist, repair open in Gray/White wire. If continuity exists, no problem is indicated. Recheck brake warning light indicator bulb, and check bulb holder. Repair as necessary.

FOUR WHEEL DRIVE (4WD) INDICATOR LIGHT TEST

NOTE: This test assumes that transfer case and linkage are operating properly. The following procedure will help locate a short or open in Full Time 4WD light circuit.

Full-Time 4WD – 1) Check fuse No. 9 (10-amp) in junction block. If fuse is blown, repair short circuit and replace fuse. If fuse is okay, turn ignition on. Check for battery voltage at power side of fuse No. 9. If battery voltage does not exist, repair open circuit to ignition switch. If battery voltage exists, go to next step.

2) Turn ignition off. Disconnect negative battery cable. Disconnect transfer case 14-pin connector. Check continuity between ground and transfer case connector Black wire. If continuity does not exist, repair open ground circuit. If continuity exists, go to next step.

3) Connect negative battery cable. Turn ignition on. Connect a jumper wire between ground and transfer case connector Black/White wire. If

FULL TIME indicator illuminates, replace transfer case switch. If FULL TIME indicator does not illuminate, go to next step.

4) Turn ignition off. Remove instrument cluster. See INSTRUMENT CLUSTER under REMOVAL & INSTALLATION. Ensure transfer case 14-pin connector is still disconnected. Check continuity between ground and instrument cluster 10-pin connector terminal No. 7 (Black/White wire). If continuity exists, repair short to ground. If continuity does not exist, go to next step.

5) Check continuity between instrument cluster 10-pin connector terminal No. 7 and transfer case connector Black/White wire. If continuity does not exist, repair open circuit. If continuity exists, replace faulty bulb.

NOTE: This test assumes that transfer case and linkage are operating properly. The following procedure will help locate a short or open in PART TIME 4WD lamp circuit.

Part-Time 4WD – 1) Check fuse No. 9 (10-amp) in junction block. If fuse is blown, repair short circuit and replace fuse. If fuse is okay, turn ignition on. Check for battery voltage at power side of fuse No. 9 cavity in junction block. If battery voltage does not exist, repair open circuit to ignition switch. If battery voltage exists, go to next step.

2) Turn ignition off. Disconnect negative battery cable. Disconnect transfer case 14-pin connector. Check continuity between ground and transfer case connector Black wire. If continuity does not exist, repair open ground circuit. If continuity exists, go to next step.

3) Connect negative battery cable. Turn ignition on. Connect a jumper wire between ground and transfer case connector Black/Red wire. If PART TIME indicator illuminates, replace transfer case switch. If PART TIME indicator does not illuminate, go to next step.

4) Turn ignition off. Remove instrument cluster. See INSTRUMENT CLUSTER under REMOVAL & INSTALLATION. Ensure transfer case 14-pin connector is still disconnected. Check continuity between ground and instrument cluster 10-pin connector terminal No. 5 (Black/Red wire). If continuity exists, repair short to ground. If continuity does not exist, go to next step.

5) Check continuity between instrument cluster 10-pin connector terminal No. 7 and transfer case connector Black/Red wire. If continuity does not exist, repair open circuit. If continuity exists, replace faulty bulb.

HEADLAMP HIGH BEAM INDICATOR LIGHT TEST

1) If high beam headlamps are inoperative, repair high beams. See WIRING DIAGRAMS in HEADLIGHT SYSTEMS article. If high beam headlamps operate, disconnect negative battery cable. Remove instrument cluster. See INSTRUMENT CLUSTER under REMOVAL & INSTALLATION.

2) Connect negative battery cable. Turn headlights and high beams on. Check for battery voltage at instrument cluster 10-pin connector terminal No. 5 (Red/Gray wire). If battery voltage does not exist, repair open circuit as necessary. If battery voltage exists, replace faulty bulb.

LOW WASHER FLUID WARNING LIGHT TEST

1) Check fuse No. 9 (10-amp) in junction block. If fuse is blown, repair short circuit and replace fuse. If fuse is okay, turn ignition on. Check for battery voltage at fuse No. 9. If battery voltage does not exist, repair open circuit to ignition switch. If battery voltage exists, go to next step.

2) Turn ignition off. Disconnect washer fluid level sensor. Connect a jumper wire between washer fluid level sensor connector terminals. Turn ignition on. LOW WASHER light should illuminate. Disconnect jumper wire. LOW WASHER light should turn off. If indicator operates as specified, replace washer fluid level sensor. If indicator does not operate as specified, go to next step.

3) Turn ignition off. Check continuity between ground and washer fluid level sensor connector Black wire. If continuity does not exist, repair open ground circuit. If continuity exists, go to next step.

4) Disconnect negative battery cable. Remove instrument cluster. See INSTRUMENT CLUSTER under REMOVAL & INSTALLATION. With washer fluid level sensor still disconnected, check continuity between ground and instrument cluster 10-pin connector terminal No. 7 (Black/Light Blue wire). If continuity exists, repair short to ground. If continuity does not exist, go to next step.

5) Check continuity of Black/Light Blue wire between washer fluid level sensor and instrument cluster. If continuity does not exist, repair open circuit. If continuity exists, replace faulty bulb.

TURN SIGNAL INDICATOR LAMP TEST

1) Disconnect negative battery cable. Remove instrument cluster. See INSTRUMENT CLUSTER under REMOVAL & INSTALLATION. Connect negative battery cable. Actuate hazard warning switch.

2) Check for battery voltage at instrument cluster 10-pin connector terminals No. 6 (Tan wire) and No. 10 (Light Green/White wire). There should be a switching battery voltage signal. If battery voltage does not exist, repair open circuit to turn signal switch. If battery voltage exists, replace faulty bulb(s).

REMOVAL & INSTALLATION

WARNING: Vehicle is equipped with Supplemental Restraint System (SRS). See SERVICE PRECAUTIONS in AIR BAG RESTRAINT SYSTEMS article before working around instrument panel area.

INSTRUMENT CLUSTER

Removal & Installation – Disconnect negative battery cable. Remove instrument cluster bezel. See INSTRUMENT CLUSTER BEZEL. Remove 4 instrument cluster retaining screws. Pull instrument cluster rearward and disengage 2 self-locking wire harness connectors. Remove instrument cluster. To install, reverse removal procedure.

INSTRUMENT CLUSTER BEZEL

Removal & Installation – **1)** Disconnect negative battery cable. Remove trim panel below instrument panel. Remove knee bolster. Using a trim stick, gently pry instrument panel center bezel away from instrument panel to release 6 snap clip retainers. Remove center bezel from vehicle. Pull headlight switch knob to on position. Depress headlight switch release button and remove headlight switch knob and shaft. *See Fig. 3.*

2) Disengage 2 ends of steering column sight shield from each other at connector located below lower steering column cover. *See Fig. 4.* Set tilt steering column (if equipped) to its lowest position. Remove 4 screws behind instrument cluster bezel that retain bezel to instrument panel. Using a trim stick, gently pry around perimeter of instrument cluster bezel, and remove bezel.

3) To install, reverse removal procedure, ensuring 2 ends of steering column sight shield connector are completely engaged.

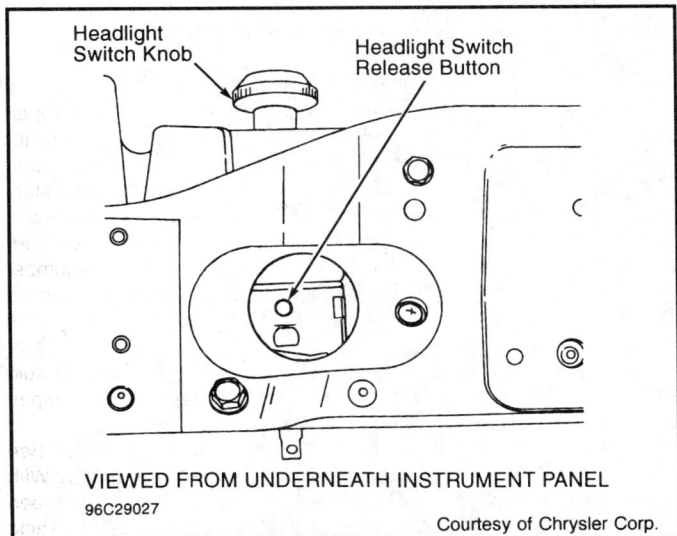

VIEWED FROM UNDERNEATH INSTRUMENT PANEL

96C29027

Courtesy of Chrysler Corp.

Fig. 3: Removing Headlight Switch Shaft

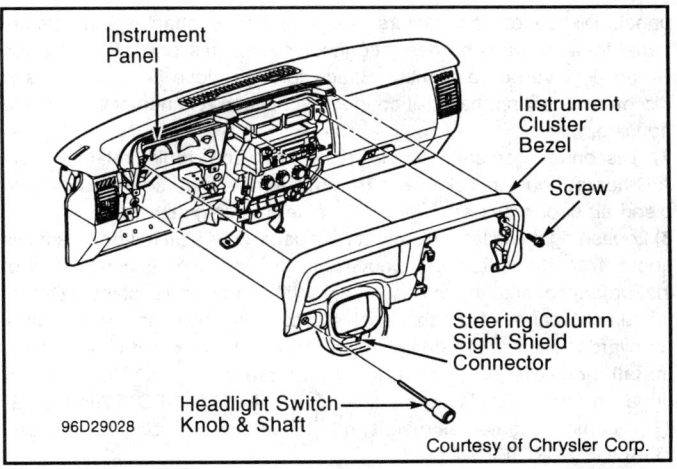

96D29028

Courtesy of Chrysler Corp.

Fig. 4: Removing Instrument Cluster Bezel

HEADLIGHT SWITCH

WARNING: If headlight switch was on, allow dimmer resistor to cool for 5 minutes to avoid burning fingers.

Removal & Installation – Disconnect negative battery cable. Remove trim panel below instrument panel. Remove knee bolster. Place headlight switch control knob in ON position. Reach under instrument panel and depress headlight switch release button. *See Fig. 3.* Pull switch control knob and shaft outward. Remove headlight switch retaining nut from front of instrument panel. Disconnect headlight switch connector. Remove headlight switch from instrument panel. To install, reverse removal procedure.

INSTRUMENT PANEL

Removal – **1)** Before proceeding, follow air bag service precautions. See SERVICE PRECAUTIONS in AIR BAG RESTRAINT SYSTEMS article. Disconnect negative battery cable. Place front wheels in straight-ahead position. Remove left and right cowl side inner trim panels. If equipped with tilt steering column, place column in fully raised position. Remove 3 screws attaching steering column opening cover. Using a trim stick, gently pry around opening cover to release snap retainers. Remove opening cover.

2) Remove 2 screws attaching knee blocker to instrument panel. Disengage lower mounting tabs, and remove knee blocker. Using a trim stick, gently pry instrument panel center bezel away from instrument panel to release 6 snap clip retainers. Remove center bezel from vehicle. Using a trim stick, gently pry rear edge of instrument panel cover up and away from instrument panel to release 7 snap clip retainers. Pull top cover sharply rearward to release 4 snap clip retainers at front of top panel near windshield base. Remove top cover.

3) Remove floor console from transmission tunnel. Peel back carpeting enough to access instrument panel center support bracket mounting nuts. Remove 2 nuts attaching center support bracket to bottom of instrument panel. Remove 2 nuts attaching center support bracket to transmission tunnel. Remove center support bracket.

4) Disable air bag system and remove driver air bag module. See AIR BAG RESTRAINT SYSTEMS article. Remove steering wheel using appropriate puller. Turn ignition on. Insert small screwdriver or pin punch into access hole in right side of steering column lower cover. Depress ignition tumbler retaining pin and remove ignition key tumbler from ignition lock housing. Remove screws attaching steering column upper and lower covers, and separate covers.

5) On A/T models, disconnect shifter interlock cable. Remove steering column mounting nuts and remove steering column from vehicle.

CAUTION: DO NOT allow steering shaft to rotate in steering column at any time. Clockspring damage may occur.

6) Remove screws attaching instrument panel-to-body and instrument panel-to-headlamp and dash wiring connectors near left cowl side inner panel. Disconnect connectors. Remove screw attaching instrument panel-to-floor wire harness connector and disconnect connector. Remove glove box assembly. Reach through glove box opening and disconnect vacuum harness connector between A/C-heater control and housing.

7) Disconnect antenna, radio connector and radio retainer from A/C-heater housing kick cover. Remove temperature control cable and blend air door crank arm from A/C-heater housing as a unit.

8) Loosen right and left side instrument panel cowl side roll-down screws about 1/4". *See Fig. 5.* Remove screws and nuts attaching top of instrument panel to top of dash panel. With aid of an assistant, lift top of instrument panel off dash panel studs. Pull lower instrument panel rearward to clear cowl side roll-down screws. Remove instrument panel.

Installation – To install, reverse removal procedure. DO NOT connect negative battery cable at this time. See AIR BAG RESTRAINT SYSTEMS article. Tighten all mounting nuts and bolts to specification. See TORQUE SPECIFICATIONS.

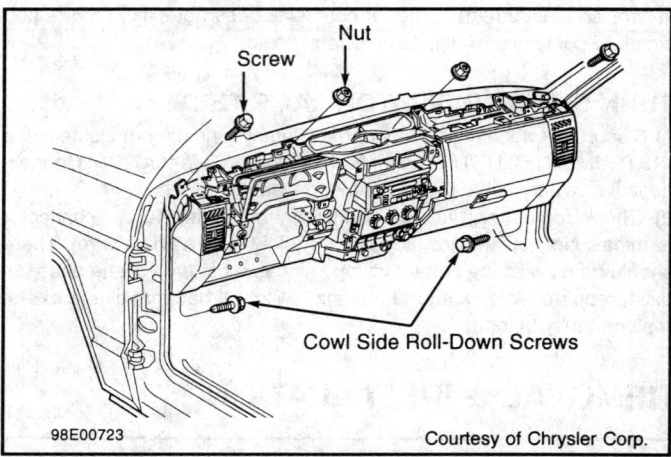

Courtesy of Chrysler Corp.

Fig. 5: Removing Instrument Panel Assembly

TORQUE SPECIFICATIONS

TORQUE SPECIFICATIONS

Application	Ft. Lbs. (N.m)
Instrument Panel Cowl Side Roll Down Screws	21 (28)
Steering Column Coupler Bolt	36 (49)
Steering Column Mounting Nuts	17 (23)
Steering Wheel Nut	40 (54)
	INCH Lbs. (N.m)
Instrument Panel Top-to-Dash Panel Nuts	60 (7)
Instrument Panel Top-to-Dash Panel Screws	60 (7)
Wire Harness Connector Screws	35 (4)

WIRING DIAGRAMS

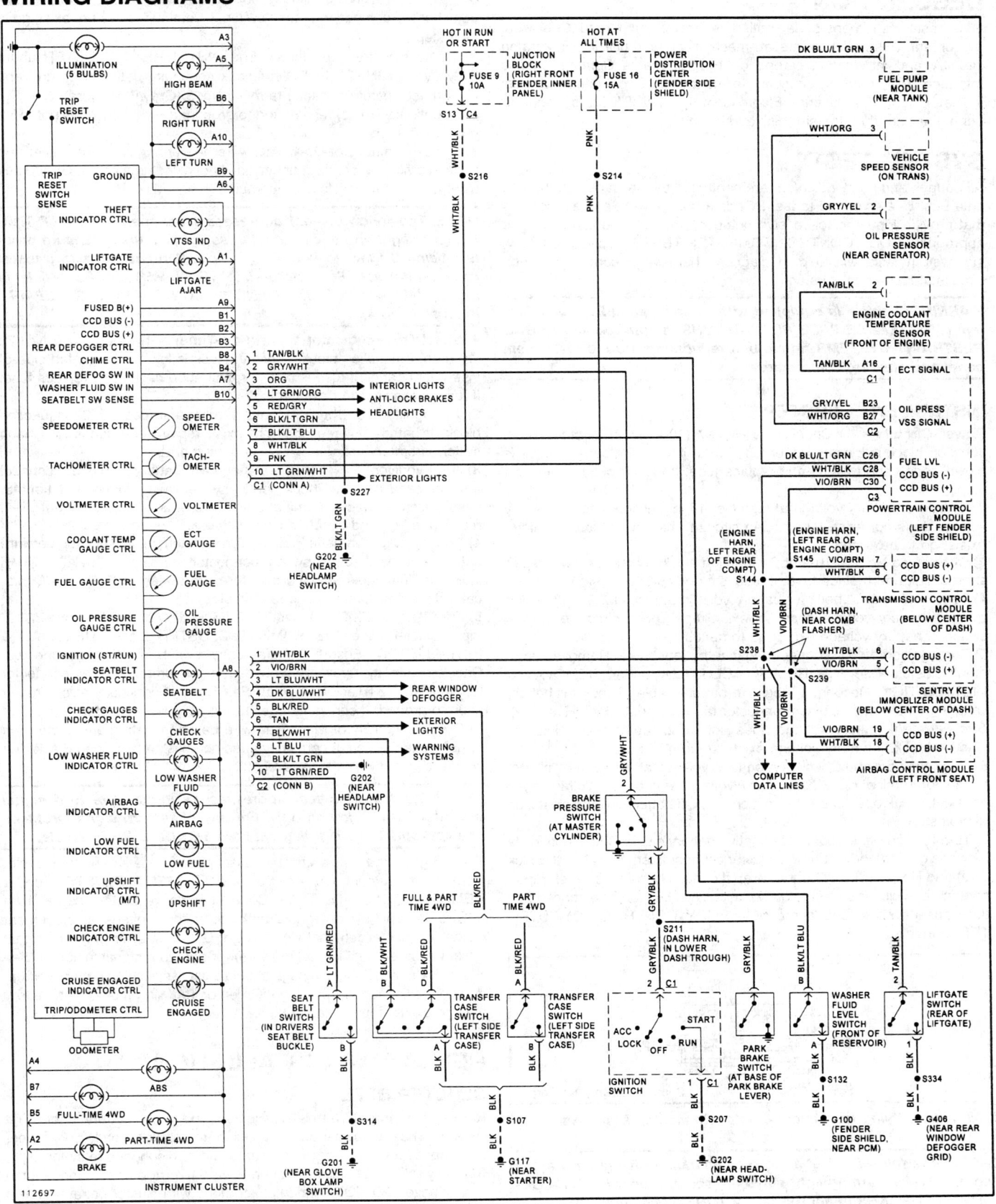

Fig. 6: Instrument Cluster Wiring Diagram (Cherokee)

DESCRIPTION

One basic instrument panel option is offered on Grand Cherokee. Instrument cluster is an electro-mechanical unit utilizing integrated circuitry and information carried on Programmable Communications Interface (PCI) data bus network for control of all gauges, and most indicator lights. A Vacuum Fluorescent Display (VFD) is used for odometer and trip odometer display functions.

SYSTEM TESTS

All gauges and most indicators are controlled by messages on the PCI data bus. Use scan tool to test PCI data bus network and all modules that provide inputs to, or receive outputs from instrument cluster. See appropriate BODY CONTROL COMPUTER TESTS article. The following system tests will help to diagnose hard-wired components and circuits of instrument cluster.

WARNING: *Vehicle is equipped with Supplemental Restraint System (SRS). See SERVICE PRECAUTIONS in appropriate AIR BAG RESTRAINT SYSTEMS article before working around instrument panel and steering column area.*

INSTRUMENT CLUSTER

Power Circuits – 1) Check fuse No. 17 (10-amp) in junction block. Junction block is located under left side of instrument panel. If fuse is blown, repair short circuit and replace fuse. If fuse is okay, go to next step.
2) Check for battery voltage at fuse No. 17 in junction block. If battery voltage does not exist, repair open circuit to battery. If battery voltage exists, go to next step.
3) Check fuse No. 22 (10-amp) in junction block. If fuse is blown, repair short circuit and replace fuse. If fuse is okay, go to next step.
4) Turn ignition on. Check for battery voltage at fuse No. 22 in junction block. If battery voltage does not exist, repair open circuit to ignition switch. If battery voltage exists, go to next step.
5) Turn ignition off. Disconnect negative battery cable. Remove instrument cluster. See INSTRUMENT CLUSTER under REMOVAL & INSTALLATION. Reconnect negative battery cable. Check for battery voltage at instrument cluster connector terminal No. 6 (Pink/Red wire). *See Fig. 1.* If battery voltage does not exist, repair open circuit to junction block. If battery voltage exists, go to next step.
6) Turn ignition on. Check for battery voltage at instrument cluster connector terminal No. 7 (Dark Blue/White wire). If battery voltage does not exist, repair open circuit to junction block. If battery voltage exists, go to next step.
7) Turn ignition off. Disconnect negative battery cable. Check continuity between ground and instrument cluster connector terminals No. 9 (Black wire) and No. 11 (Black/Orange wire). If continuity does not exist, repair open ground circuit(s). If continuity exists, use scan tool to diagnose PCI data bus network. See appropriate BODY CONTROL COMPUTER TESTS article.

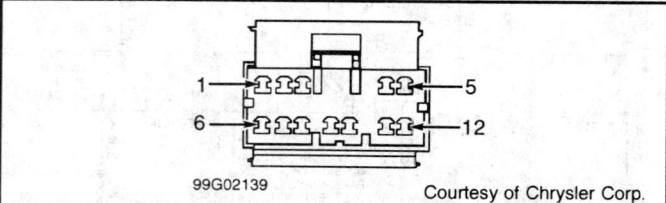

99G02139   Courtesy of Chrysler Corp.

Fig. 1: Identifying Instrument Cluster Connector Terminals

NOTE: *The following test addresses an inoperative brake warning light. If brake warning light stays on, see appropriate ANTI-LOCK article in BRAKES in appropriate MITCHELL® manual.*

Brake Warning Light – 1) Turn ignition off. Disconnect negative battery cable. Disconnect parking brake switch. Ensure parking brake is released. Check continuity between ground and parking brake switch connector terminal. Continuity should not exist. If continuity exists, adjust or replace parking brake switch. If continuity does not exist, go to next step.
2) Remove instrument cluster. See INSTRUMENT CLUSTER under REMOVAL & INSTALLATION. Check continuity between ground and instrument cluster connector terminal No. 5 (Gray/Black wire). *See Fig. 1.* If continuity exists, repair short to ground. If continuity does not exist, go to next step.
3) Check continuity of Gray/Black wire between instrument cluster and parking brake switch. If continuity does not exist, repair open Gray/Black wire. If continuity exists, replace bulb.

NOTE: *The following test addresses an inoperative PART TIME indicator light and does not address light accuracy. Ensure problem being diagnosed is with light or switch and not with transfer case or linkage. See appropriate TRANSFER CASES article in appropriate MITCHELL® TRANSMISSION SERVICE & REPAIR manual.*

4-Wheel Drive Indicator Light (Part-Time) – 1) Check fuse No. 22 (10-amp) in junction block. Junction block is located under left side of instrument panel. If fuse is blown, repair short circuit and replace fuse. If fuse is okay, go to next step.
2) Turn ignition on. Check for battery voltage at fuse No. 22 in junction block. If battery voltage does not exist, repair open circuit to ignition switch. If battery voltage exists, go to next step.
3) Turn ignition off. Disconnect negative battery cable. Disconnect transfer case switch. Check continuity between ground and transfer case switch connector terminal Black wire. If continuity does not exist, repair open ground circuit. If continuity exists, go to next step.
4) Connect negative battery cable. Turn ignition on. Install a jumper wire between transfer case switch connector terminals. If PART TIME indicator illuminates, replace transfer case switch. If PART TIME indicator does not illuminate, go to next step.
5) Turn ignition off. Disconnect negative battery cable. Remove instrument cluster. See INSTRUMENT CLUSTER under REMOVAL & INSTALLATION. Ensure transfer case switch is still disconnected. Check continuity between ground and instrument cluster connector terminal No. 12 (Black/Red wire). *See Fig. 1.* If continuity exists, repair short to ground. If continuity does not exist, go to next step.
6) Check continuity of Black/Red wire between instrument cluster and transfer case switch. If continuity does not exist, repair open Black/Red wire. If continuity exists, replace bulb.

NOTE: *The following test addresses an inoperative turn signal indicator light condition only. For any other turn signal problem, see appropriate wiring diagram in EXTERIOR LIGHTS article.*

Turn Signal Indicator Light – Disconnect negative battery cable. Remove instrument cluster. See INSTRUMENT CLUSTER under REMOVAL & INSTALLATION. Connect negative battery cable. Turn hazard warning system on. Check for battery voltage at instrument cluster connector terminal No. 1 (Light Green wire) for left turn signal indicator, or terminal No. 2 (Tan wire) for right turn signal indicator. *See Fig. 1.* Switching battery voltage should exist. If switching battery voltage does not exist, repair open Light Green or Tan wire. If switching battery voltage exists, replace faulty bulb.

REMOVAL & INSTALLATION

CLUSTER BEZEL

Removal & Installation – Disconnect negative battery cable. Tilt steering wheel to lowest position. Using a trim stick, gently pry corners of cluster bezel away from instrument panel to disengage retaining clips. Carefully roll top of cluster bezel rearward over top of steering column and remove. DO NOT scratch cluster lens with cluster bezel retaining clips. To install, carefully align lower cluster bezel retaining clips with receptacles in instrument panel. Push firmly on cluster bezel to engage lower retaining clips. Align upper retaining clips and engage into instrument panel receptacles. Connect negative battery cable.

INSTRUMENT CLUSTER

Removal & Installation – Remove cluster bezel. See CLUSTER BEZEL. Remove 4 instrument cluster-to-instrument panel screws. Pull top of cluster downward and rearward enough to disconnect instrument cluster wire connectors. Remove instrument cluster. To install, reverse removal procedure.

CLUSTER BULBS

NOTE: Illumination bulbs and indicator bulbs are different. DO NOT interchange illumination bulbs with indicator bulbs. Incorrect bulbs may overheat and cause damage to instrument cluster, circuit board or gauges.

Removal & Installation – Disconnect negative battery cable. Remove instrument cluster. See INSTRUMENT CLUSTER. Turn bulb holder counterclockwise about 60 degrees and pull out of circuit board. To install, reverse removal procedure.

CLUSTER LENS, HOOD & MASK

Removal & Installation – 1) Disconnect negative battery cable. Remove trip odometer reset knob. *See Fig. 2.* Remove instrument cluster. See INSTRUMENT CLUSTER.

2) Disengage 8 snap clips securing cluster lens to cluster hood and gently pull lens away from hood. Gently pull lens, hood and mask away from housing.

3) Gently lift gauge mask away from locating pins on front of cluster circuit and gauge housing. To install, reverse removal procedure.

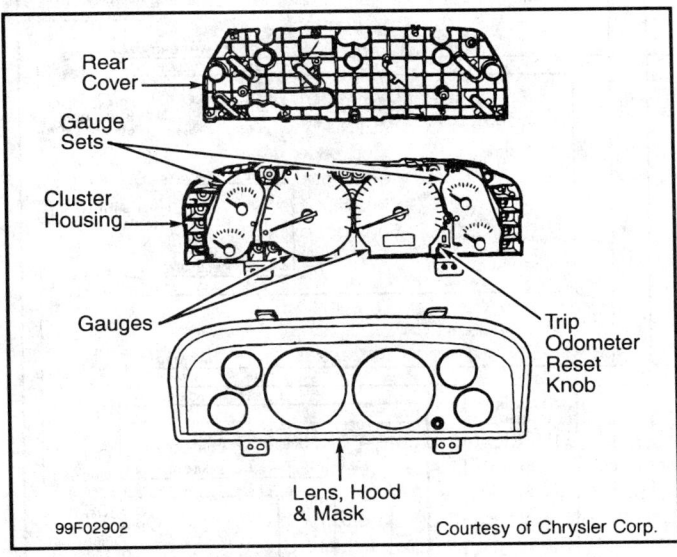

Fig. 2: Identifying Instrument Cluster Components

CLUSTER HOUSING REAR COVER

Removal & Installation – Disconnect negative battery cable. Remove instrument cluster. See INSTRUMENT CLUSTER. Remove 7 rear cover screws. *See Fig. 3.* Disengage 6 latches that secure upper and lower edges of rear cover to cluster housing. To install, reverse removal procedure.

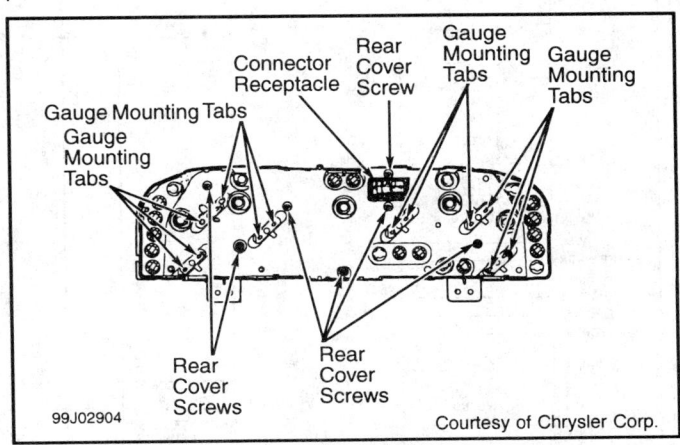

Fig. 3: Identifying Rear Cover Screws

GAUGES

Removal & Installation – 1) Disconnect negative battery cable. Remove trip odometer reset knob. Remove instrument cluster. See INSTRUMENT CLUSTER. Remove cluster lens, hood and mask. See CLUSTER LENS, HOOD & MASK. Remove cluster housing rear cover. See CLUSTER HOUSING REAR COVER.

2) From rear of cluster housing, carefully straighten small metal mounting tabs that secure gauge or gauge set to circuit board. *See Fig. 3.* From front of cluster housing, carefully pull gauge or gauge set straight out of gauge mounting cavity in cluster housing. To install, reverse removal procedure.

WIRING DIAGRAMS

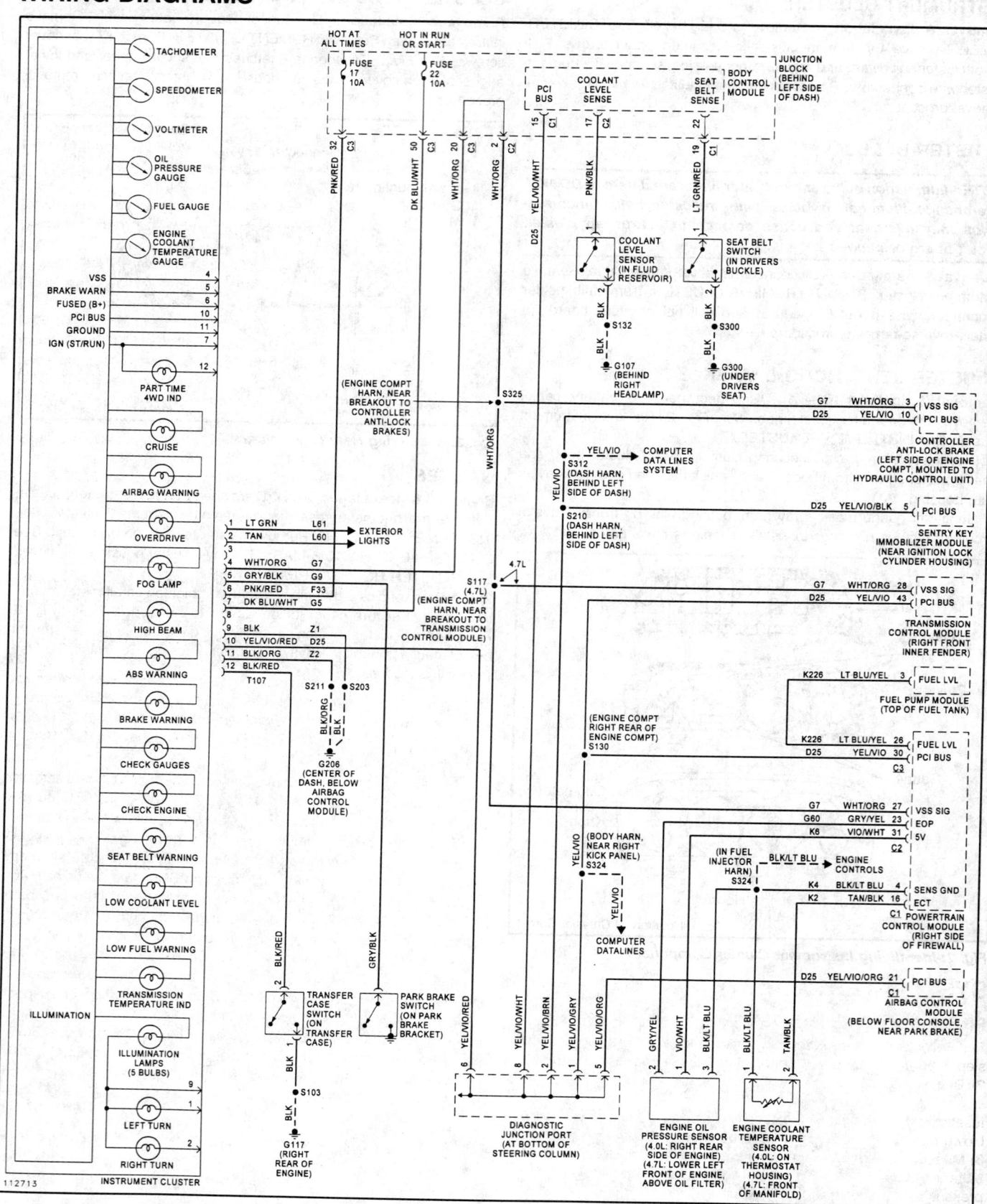

Fig. 4: Instrument Cluster Wiring Diagram (Grand Cherokee)

DESCRIPTION

One basic instrument panel option is offered. Instrument cluster is an electro-mechanical unit utilizing integrated circuitry and information carried on Chrysler Collision Detection (CCD) data bus network for control of all gauges and most indicator lights. Instrument cluster is equipped with circuitry that has self-diagnostic actuator test capability. Instrument cluster is serviced as a complete unit. If an instrument cluster gauge or circuit board is faulty, entire instrument cluster must be replaced. Cluster lens and individual bulbs can be serviced.

COMPONENT TESTS

ACCESSORY RELAY

1) Remove accessory relay. Relay is located under left side of instrument panel. Using an ohmmeter, check relay continuity. Continuity should exist between relay terminals No. 87A and 30. See Fig. 1. No continuity should exist between relay terminals No. 87 and 30. Replace relay as necessary. If continuity is as specified, go to next step.

2) Check resistance between relay terminals No. 85 and 86. If resistance is not 70-80 ohms, replace relay. If resistance is 70-80 ohms, connect 12-volt power source to relay terminal No. 86, and ground terminal No. 85. Continuity should exist between terminals No. 30 and 87.

3) No continuity should exist between terminals No. 87A and 30. If continuity is not as specified, replace relay. If continuity is as specified, relay is okay.

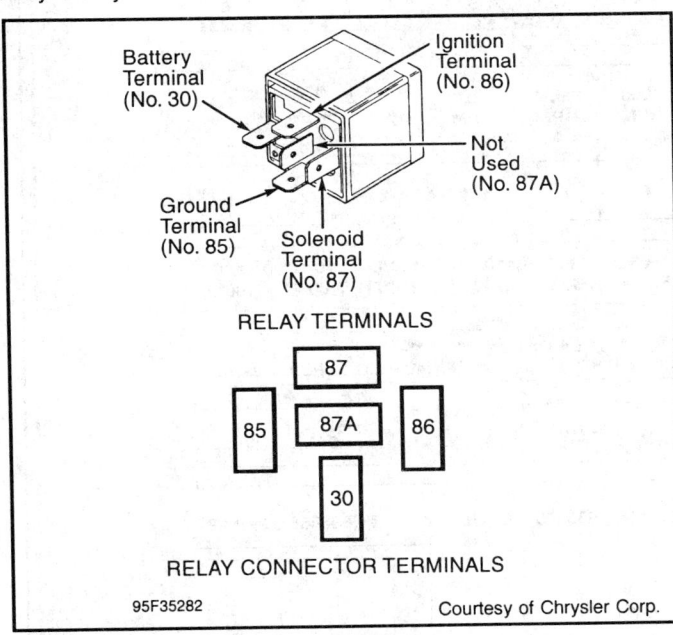

95F35282   Courtesy of Chrysler Corp.

Fig. 1: Identifying Defogger Relay Terminals

SYSTEM TESTS

PRELIMINARY DIAGNOSIS

1) If indicator lights operate, but all gauges are inoperative, go to next step. If all gauges and indicator lights are inoperative, go to step **5)**.

2) Remove and inspect fuse No. 17 (10-amp) in Power Distribution Center (PDC). PDC is located in engine compartment, near battery. If fuse is okay, go to next step. If fuse is blown, locate and repair cause of blown fuse. Install new fuse and recheck system operation.

3) Measure voltage between ground and power side of fuse No. 17. If battery voltage is present, go to next step. If battery voltage is not present, locate and repair open circuit.

4) Disconnect negative battery cable. Remove instrument cluster. See INSTRUMENT CLUSTER under REMOVAL & INSTALLATION. Connect negative battery cable. Measure voltage between ground and instrument cluster Blue connector, terminal No. 9 (Pink/White wire). If battery voltage is present, reinstall instrument cluster and go to ACTUATOR TEST. If battery voltage is not present, repair open circuit between fuse No. 17 in PDC and instrument cluster 10-pin Blue connector.

5) Remove and inspect fuse No. 10 (10-amp) in fuse box. Fuse box is located behind glove box. If fuse is okay, go to next step. If fuse is blown, locate and repair cause of blown fuse. Install new fuse and recheck system operation.

6) Turn ignition on. Measure voltage between ground and power side of fuse No. 10. If battery voltage is present, go to next step. If battery voltage is not present, locate and repair open circuit between ignition switch and fuse box. Install instrument cluster.

7) Turn ignition on. Set parking brake and observe instrument cluster BRAKE warning light. If warning light is on, go to next step. If warning light is off, go to step **9)**.

8) Turn parking lights on and adjust instrument panel lights dimmer rheostat to full bright position. If instrument panel lights are on, go to ACTUATOR TEST. If instrument panel lights are off, go to step **10)**.

9) Disconnect negative battery cable. Remove instrument cluster. See INSTRUMENT CLUSTER under REMOVAL & INSTALLATION. Connect negative battery cable. Turn ignition on. Measure voltage between ground and instrument cluster Blue connector, terminal No. 8 (Dark Blue/White Green wire). If battery voltage is present, go to ACTUATOR TEST. If battery voltage is not present, locate and repair open circuit.

10) Remove instrument cluster. See INSTRUMENT CLUSTER under REMOVAL & INSTALLATION. Check continuity between ground and instrument cluster Blue connector, terminal No. 6 (Black/Light Green wire). If continuity exists, go to ACTUATOR TEST. If continuity does not exist, locate and repair open in ground circuit.

ACTUATOR TEST

Diagnostic Aids – Instrument actuator test will put instrument cluster into self-diagnostic mode. In this mode, instrument cluster will position each of the gauge needles at various specified calibration points, and turn all Chrysler Collision Detection (CCD) data bus message-controlled indicator lights on and off at specified time intervals. See Fig. 2. Successful completion of actuator test will confirm that instrument cluster circuitry, gauges and indicator lights are capable of operating properly. If test is successful, a problem may still exist with CCD data bus, Powertrain Control Module (PCM) or Air Bag Control Module (ACM).

If an individual gauge does not respond properly or at all during actuator test, remove instrument cluster. See INSTRUMENT CLUSTER under REMOVAL & INSTALLATION. Check tightness of suspect gauge mounting screws on printed circuit board. If screws are loose, reinstall instrument cluster and retest. If screws are tight, replace instrument cluster. If an individual indicator light does not illuminate during actuator test, remove instrument cluster. Check indicator light bulb and bulb holder. Repair as necessary and retest. If indicator bulb is okay and bulb holder is installed properly, replace instrument cluster.

Actuator Test – **1)** Turn ignition off. Depress and hold down trip odometer RESET button. Turn ignition on. DO NOT start engine. Release trip odometer reset button. Compare operation of suspect gauge(s) and/or indicator light(s) with chart. See Fig. 2.

2) Instrument cluster will exit self-diagnostics mode at completion of test, or if ignition switch is turned off. If instrument cluster gauge(s) and/or indicator light(s) do not respond properly during actuator test, see DIAGNOSTIC AIDS before replacing instrument cluster. Repeat actuator test if necessary.

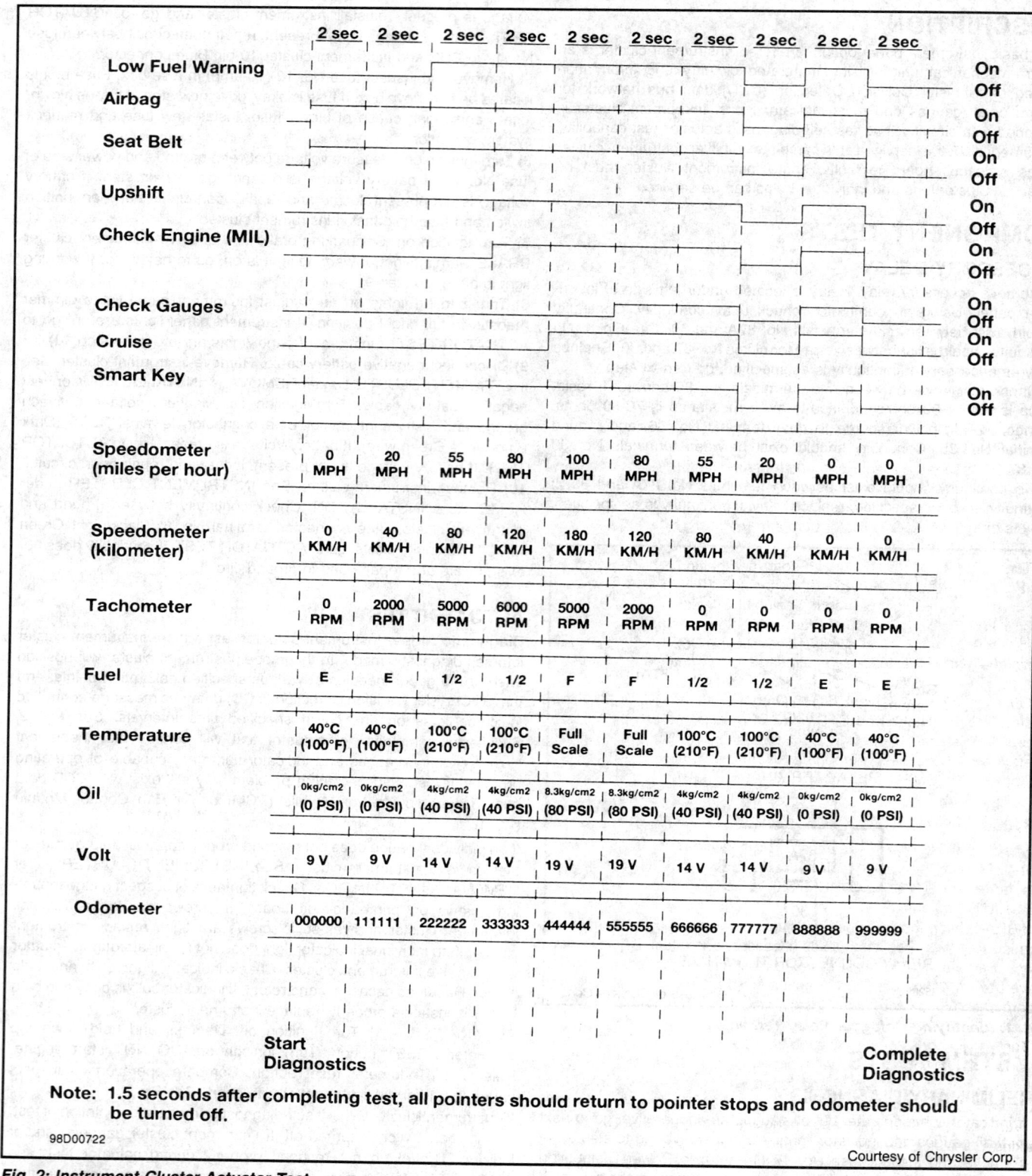

Fig. 2: Instrument Cluster Actuator Test

Courtesy of Chrysler Corp.

Note: 1.5 seconds after completing test, all pointers should return to pointer stops and odometer should be turned off.

98D00722

AIR BAG INDICATOR LIGHT TEST

1) If AIR BAG warning light illuminates for 12 seconds or more, or stays on all the time, a system malfunction exists and trouble code will be stored. For air bag system testing procedures, see MITCHELL® AIR BAG SERVICE & REPAIR MANUAL, DOMESTIC & IMPORTED MODELS.

2) If air bag indicator light does not illuminate when ignition is on, replace air bag indicator bulb and retest. If air bag indicator light still does not illuminate, perform PRELIMINARY DIAGNOSIS.

3) If after performing preliminary diagnosis and actuator test, air bag indicator light and instrument cluster circuitry is okay, diagnosis of air bag system and Chrysler Collision Detection (CCD) data bus should be performed.

4) For air bag system testing procedures, see DIAGNOSIS & TESTING MITCHELL® AIR BAG SERVICE & REPAIR MANUAL, DOMESTIC & IMPORTED MODELS. For CCD data bus testing, check for opens and shorts in CCD data bus circuits. See appropriate VEHICLE COMMUNICATIONS article.

ANTI-LOCK BRAKE INDICATOR LIGHT TEST

1) If Anti-Lock Brake System (ABS) warning light stays on all the time, a system malfunction exists and trouble code will be stored. For ABS testing, see appropriate ANTI-LOCK article in BRAKES in appropriate MITCHELL® manual.

2) If ABS light does not illuminate when ignition is on, check fuse No. 10 (10-amp) in fuse box. Fuse box is located behind glove box. If fuse is okay, go to next step. If fuse is blown, locate and repair cause of blown fuse. Install new fuse and recheck system operation.

3) Turn ignition on. Measure voltage between ground and power side of fuse No. 10. If battery voltage is present, go to next step. If battery voltage is not present, locate and repair open circuit between ignition switch and fuse box.

4) Disconnect negative battery cable. Remove instrument cluster. See INSTRUMENT CLUSTER under REMOVAL & INSTALLATION. Connect negative battery cable. Turn ignition on and, within 5 seconds, check continuity between ground and instrument cluster Blue connector, terminal No. 4 (Light Green/Orange wire). Continuity should exist for 5 seconds, and should not exist after 5 seconds. If continuity is as specified, replace ABS indicator bulb and retest. If continuity is not as specified, go to next step.

5) Turn ignition off. Disconnect negative battery cable. Disconnect Controller Anti-Lock Brake (CAB) connector. CAB is located under instrument panel to right of steering column. Check continuity between ground and instrument cluster Blue connector, terminal No. 4 (Light Green/Orange wire). If continuity does not exist, go to next step. If continuity exists, locate and repair short to ground in Light Green/Orange wire.

6) Check continuity of Light Green/Orange wire between instrument cluster Blue connector and CAB relay connector in PDC. If continuity does not exist, repair open in Light Green/Orange wire. If continuity exists, check ABS. See appropriate ANTI-LOCK article in BRAKES in appropriate MITCHELL® manual.

BRAKE WARNING LIGHT INDICATOR TEST

1) Ensure parking brake is released. Turn ignition on. If brake warning light stays on, check and repair hydraulic brake system as necessary. See appropriate DISC & DRUM article in BRAKES in appropriate MITCHELL® manual.

2) If BRAKE warning light does not illuminate when ignition is on, check warning light bulb. Replace bulb as necessary and retest. If bulb is okay, check fuse No. 10 (10-amp) in fuse box. Fuse box is located behind glove box. If fuse is okay, go to next step. If fuse is blown, locate and repair cause of blown fuse. Install new fuse and recheck system operation.

3) Turn ignition on. Measure voltage between ground and power side of fuse No. 10. If battery voltage is present, go to next step. If battery voltage is not present, locate and repair open circuit between ignition switch and fuse box.

4) Turn ignition off. Disconnect negative battery cable. Disconnect parking brake switch connector. Switch is located at base of parking brake lever. Ensure parking brake lever is released. Check continuity between ground and parking brake switch terminal. If continuity does not exist, go to next step. If continuity exists, adjust or replace parking brake switch.

5) Disconnect brake warning pressure switch at master cylinder. Check continuity between brake warning pressure switch terminals. If continuity exists, go to next step. If continuity does not exist, replace brake warning pressure switch.

6) Check continuity between ground and each brake warning pressure switch terminal. If continuity does not exist, go to next step. If continuity exists at either terminal, replace brake warning pressure switch.

7) Ensure brake warning pressure switch and parking brake switch are still disconnected. Check continuity between ground and parking brake wiring harness connector terminal. If continuity does not exist, go to next step. If continuity exists, locate and repair short to ground.

8) Turn and hold ignition switch in START position. Check continuity between ground and parking brake switch wiring harness connector terminal. If continuity exists, go to next step. If continuity does not exist, locate and repair open in Gray/Black wire between ignition switch and parking brake switch.

9) Turn ignition off. Remove instrument cluster. See INSTRUMENT CLUSTER under REMOVAL & INSTALLATION. Check continuity between ground and instrument cluster Blue connector, terminal No. 2 (Gray/White wire). If continuity does not exist, go to next step. If continuity exists, locate and repair short to ground in Gray/White wire.

10) Check continuity of Gray/White wire between instrument cluster Blue connector and brake pressure warning switch connector. If continuity does not exist, repair open in Gray/White wire. If continuity exists, no problem is indicated. Recheck brake warning light indicator bulb, and check bulb holder. Repair as necessary.

CHECK GAUGES INDICATOR LIGHT TEST

1) If CHECK GAUGES indicator light stays on with ignition on, or comes on while driving and there is no unusual gauge readings, diagnosis of Powertrain Control Module (PCM) and Chrysler Collision Detection (CCD) data bus should be performed.

2) For PCM testing, see appropriate SELF-DIAGNOSTICS article in ENGINE PERFORMANCE in appropriate MITCHELL® manual. For CCD data bus testing, see appropriate VEHICLE COMMUNICATIONS article.

3) If CHECK GAUGES indicator light does not illuminate when ignition is on, replace bulb with a known-good bulb. If CHECK GAUGES indicator light is still off, and coolant temperature gauge, oil pressure gauge, or voltmeter are giving an indication that should trigger check gauges indicator light, perform ACTUATOR TEST.

INSTRUMENT CLUSTER ILLUMINATION TEST

1) This test assumes that all exterior lighting controlled by headlight switch are functioning properly. If exterior lighting is not functioning properly, correct fault(s) before continuing with this test.

2) Check and replace illumination bulbs as necessary and retest. If bulbs are okay, remove and inspect fuse No. 12 (10-amp) in fuse box. Fuse box is located behind glove box. If fuse is okay, go to next step. If fuse is blown, locate and repair cause of blown fuse and retest.

3) Using headlight switch, turn parking lights on. Connect voltmeter between ground and power side of fuse No. 12. Observing voltmeter, rotate headlight switch knob counterclockwise to just before interior lights detent, then rotate knob clockwise. Voltage reading should change from battery voltage to zero volts. If voltage is as specified, go to next step. If voltage is not as specified, locate and repair open circuit between headlight switch and fuse box.

4) Disconnect negative battery cable. Remove instrument cluster. See INSTRUMENT CLUSTER under REMOVAL & INSTALLATION. Turn headlight switch off. Remove fuse No. 12 from fuse box. Check continuity between ground and instrument cluster Blue connector, terminal No. 3 (Orange wire). If continuity does not exist, go to next step. If continuity exists, locate and repair short to ground in Orange wire.

5) Install fuse No. 12 in fuse box. Connect negative battery cable. Using headlight switch, turn parking lights on. Rotate headlight switch knob counterclockwise to just before interior lights detent. Measure voltage between ground and instrument cluster Blue connector, terminal No. 3 (Orange wire). If battery voltage is not present, locate and repair open circuit. If battery voltage is present, no problem is indicated. Recheck instrument cluster illumination bulb(s) and bulb holders. Repair as necessary.

REMOVAL & INSTALLATION

WARNING: Vehicle is equipped with Supplemental Restraint System (SRS). See SERVICE PRECAUTIONS in AIR BAG RESTRAINT SYSTEMS article before working around instrument panel area.

CAUTION: When battery is disconnected, vehicle computer and memory systems may lose memory data. Driveability problems may exist until computer systems have completed a relearn cycle. See COMPUTER RELEARN PROCEDURES in GENERAL INFORMATION before disconnecting battery.

INSTRUMENT PANEL

Removal & Installation – 1) Before proceeding, follow air bag service precautions. See SERVICE PRECAUTIONS in AIR BAG RESTRAINT SYSTEMS article. Place front wheels in straight-ahead position. Remove trim panel and support bracket from below steering column.
2) Turn ignition on. Insert small screwdriver or pin punch into access hole in right side of steering column lower cover. Depress ignition tumbler retaining pin and remove ignition key tumbler from ignition lock housing.
3) Remove upper and lower steering column covers. Tilt steering wheel to its lowest position and release tilt mechanism control cable from tilt lever (if equipped). Disconnect all electrical components of steering column and release wiring harness. Remove lock-pin from steering column coupler. Remove steering column mounting nuts and remove steering column from vehicle.

CAUTION: DO NOT allow steering shaft to rotate in steering column at any time, or clockspring damage may occur.

WARNING: Never place steering column on floor or any other surface with steering wheel or air bag module facing down.

4) Reach through lower steering column opening and disconnect 100-pin connector located near cowl side panel. Disconnect side window demister/defroster ducting from A/C-heater housing for driver's side window. Remove glove box assembly. Reach through glove box opening and disconnect temperature control cable from A/C-heater housing.
5) Disconnect side window demister/defroster ducting for passenger's side window. Disconnect electrical and vacuum harness connectors. Disconnect passenger side air bag module connector. Disconnect antenna, radio connector and radio ground strap (if equipped).
6) Remove 2 nuts securing lower air bag module bracket to studs of dash panel. Remove 2 bolts from instrument panel located near door hinge pillars. Using a trim stick, remove instrument panel top cover. Remove 4 nuts securing top of instrument panel to dash panel. With the aid of an assistant, remove instrument panel from vehicle.
7) To install, reverse removal procedure. DO NOT connect negative battery cable at this time. See AIR BAG RESTRAINT SYSTEMS article.

INSTRUMENT CLUSTER BEZEL

Removal & Installation – 1) Disconnect negative battery cable. Set tilt steering column (if equipped) to fully raised position. Remove steering column cover from bottom of instrument panel. Using a trim stick, carefully pry instrument top cover away from instrument panel.
2) Lift and remove instrument top panel from instrument panel. Remove 2 lower screws securing instrument cluster bezel to instrument panel. Remove 3 upper screws securing instrument cluster bezel to top of instrument panel and remove bezel. To install, reverse removal procedure.

INSTRUMENT CLUSTER

Removal & Installation – Remove cluster bezel. See INSTRUMENT CLUSTER BEZEL. Remove 4 screws securing instrument cluster to instrument panel. Pull cluster rearward and disconnect 2 instrument cluster wire connectors. Remove instrument cluster. To install, reverse removal procedure.

CLUSTER LENS

Removal & Installation – Remove cluster bezel. See INSTRUMENT CLUSTER BEZEL. Remove instrument cluster. See INSTRUMENT CLUSTER. Remove trip odometer reset knob by pulling it off switch stem. Depress snap clips securing cluster lens to cluster housing and gently pull lens away from housing. To install, reverse removal procedure.

INSTRUMENT CLUSTER BULBS

Removal & Installation – Remove cluster bezel. See INSTRUMENT CLUSTER BEZEL. Remove instrument cluster. See INSTRUMENT CLUSTER. Turn bulb holder clockwise and remove holder and bulb. To install, reverse removal procedure.

HEADLIGHT SWITCH

Removal & Installation – Disconnect negative battery cable. Pull switch out to full on position. Reach under instrument panel and depress switch knob and shaft release button on top of switch. With button depressed, pull knob and shaft from switch. Remove knee bolster. Remove switch mounting nut. Disconnect wiring connector. Remove switch. To install, reverse removal procedure.

WIRING DIAGRAMS

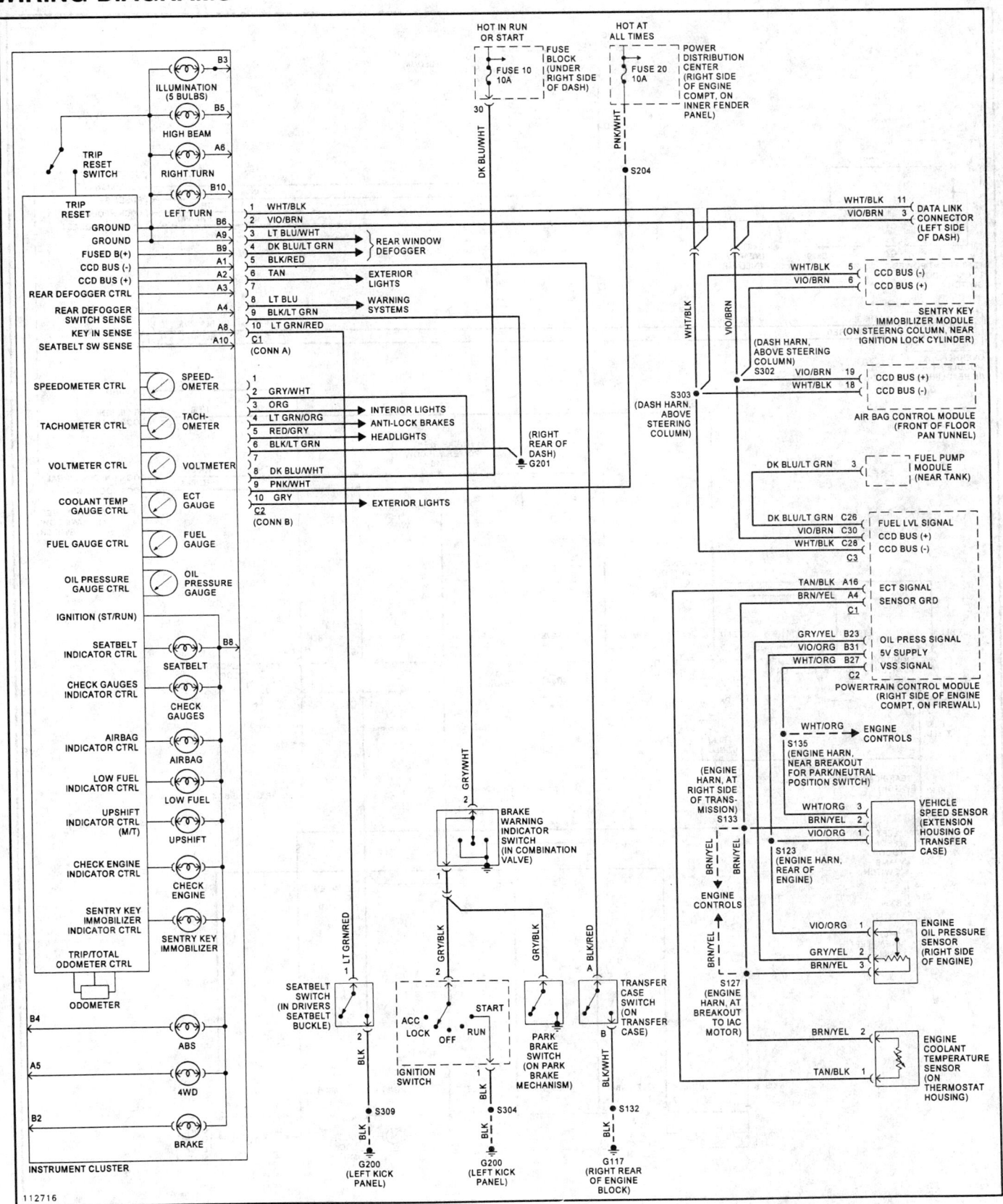

Fig. 3: Instrument Cluster Wiring Diagram (Wrangler)

112716

WIRING DIAGRAMS

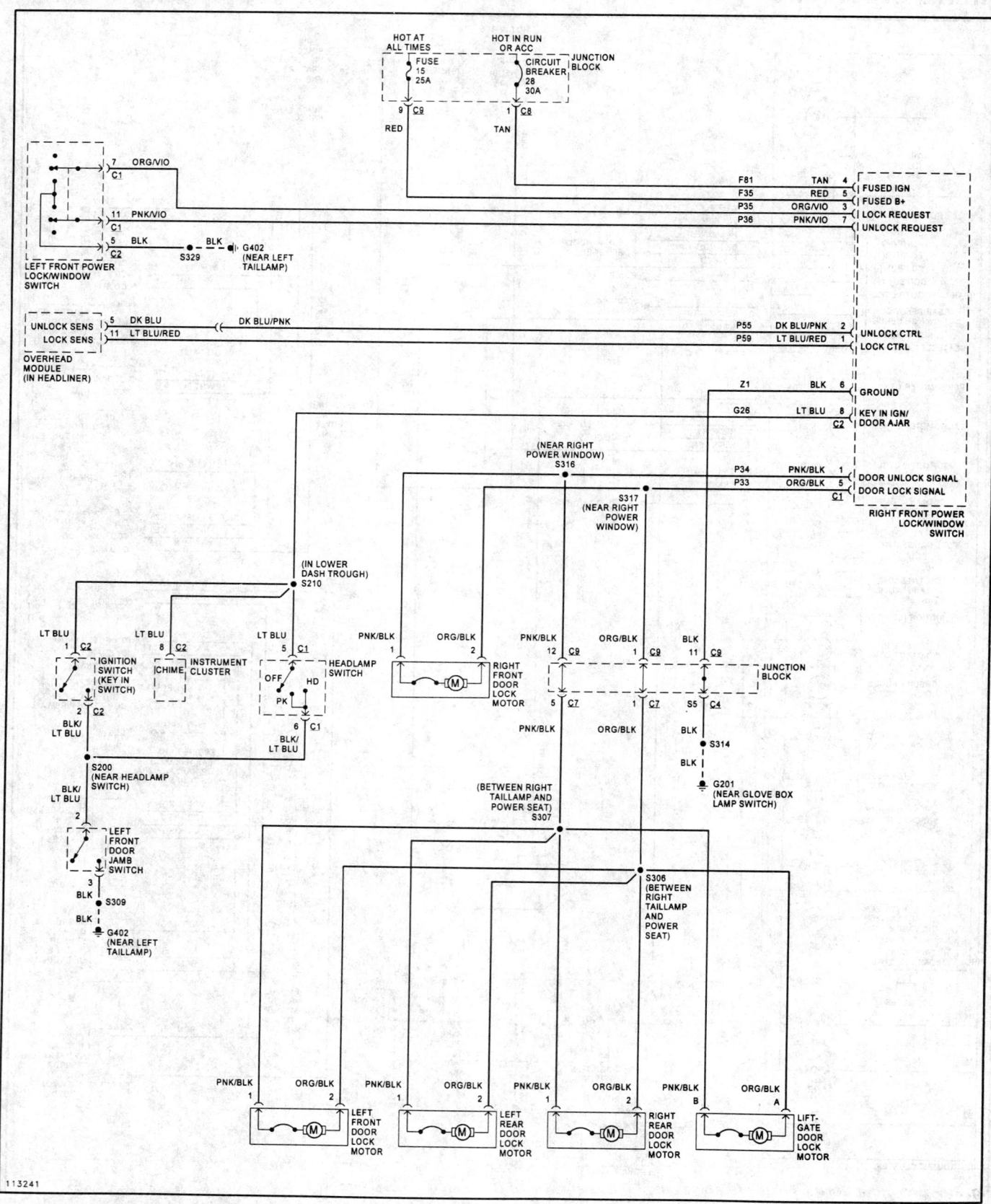

Fig. 1: Power Door Locks & Remote Keyless Entry System Wiring Diagram (Cherokee)

1999 ACCESSORIES & EQUIPMENT
Power Door Locks & Remote Keyless Entry Systems (Cont.)

JEEP
4-141

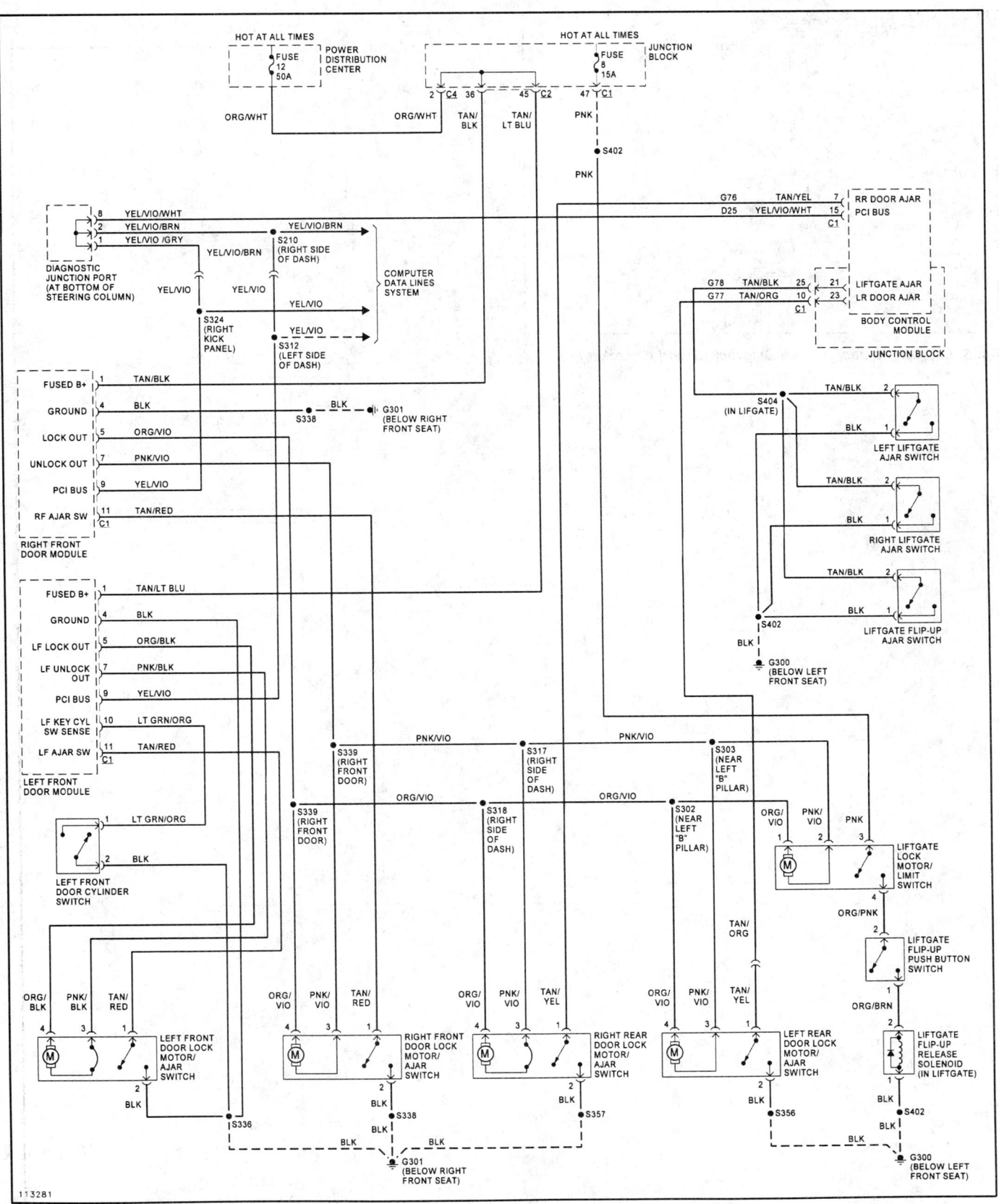

Fig. 2: Power Door Locks & Remote Keyless Entry System Wiring Diagram (Grand Cherokee)

JEEP
4-142

1999 ACCESSORIES & EQUIPMENT
Power Door Locks & Remote Keyless Entry Systems (Cont.)

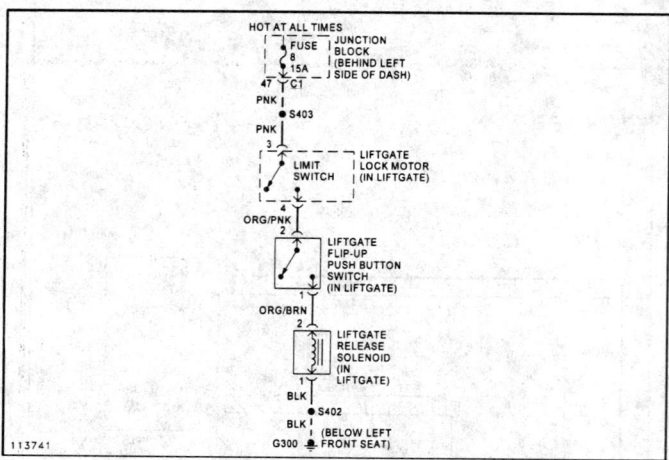

Fig. 3: Liftgate Release Wiring Diagram (Grand Cherokee)

WIRING DIAGRAMS

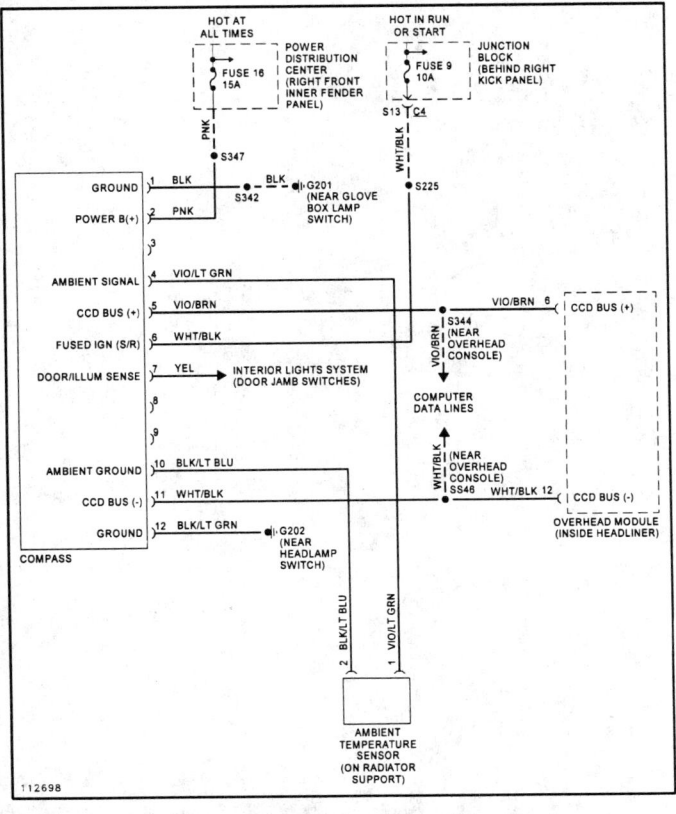

Fig. 1: Overhead Console Wiring Diagram (Cherokee)

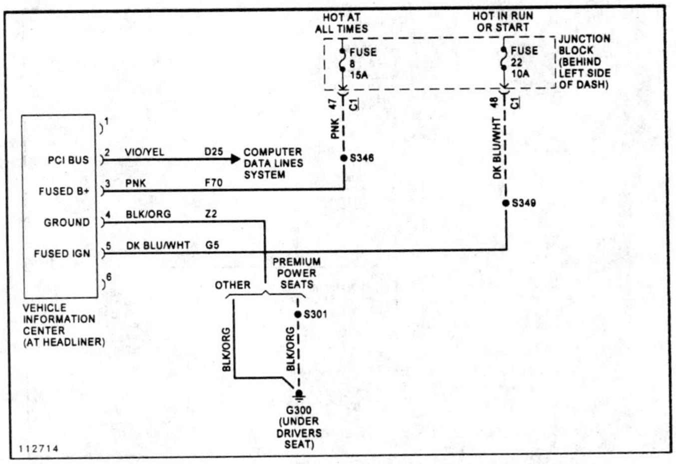

Fig. 2: Overhead Console Wiring Diagram (Grand Cherokee)

WIRING DIAGRAMS

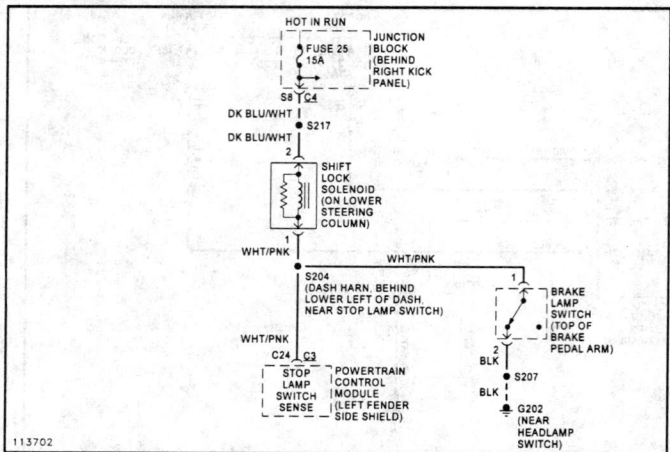

Fig. 1: Shift Interlock System Wiring Diagram (Cherokee)

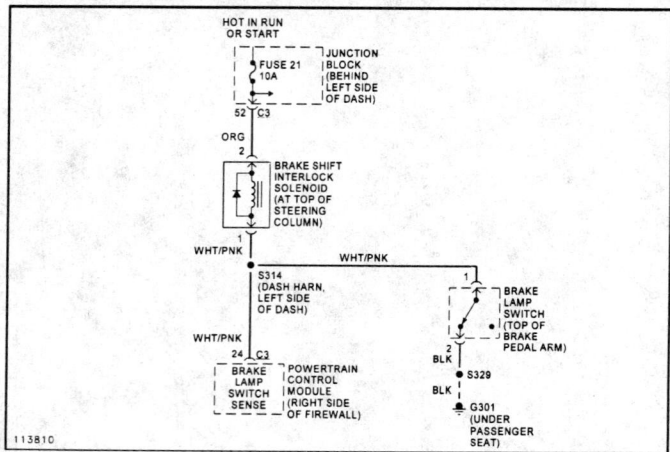

Fig. 2: Shift Interlock System Wiring Diagram (Grand Cherokee)

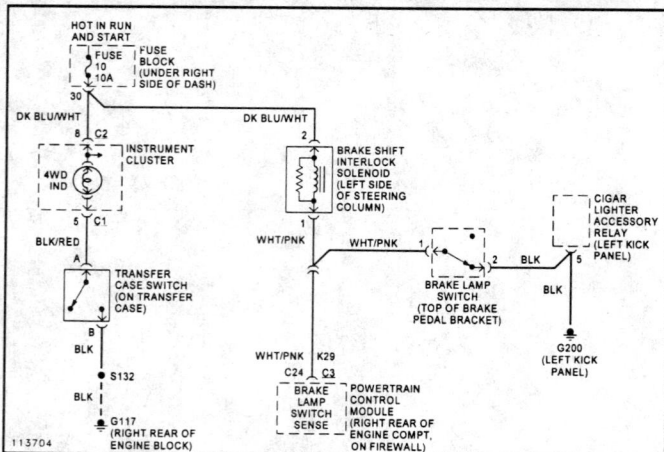

Fig. 3: Shift Interlock System Wiring Diagram (Wrangler)

WIRING DIAGRAMS

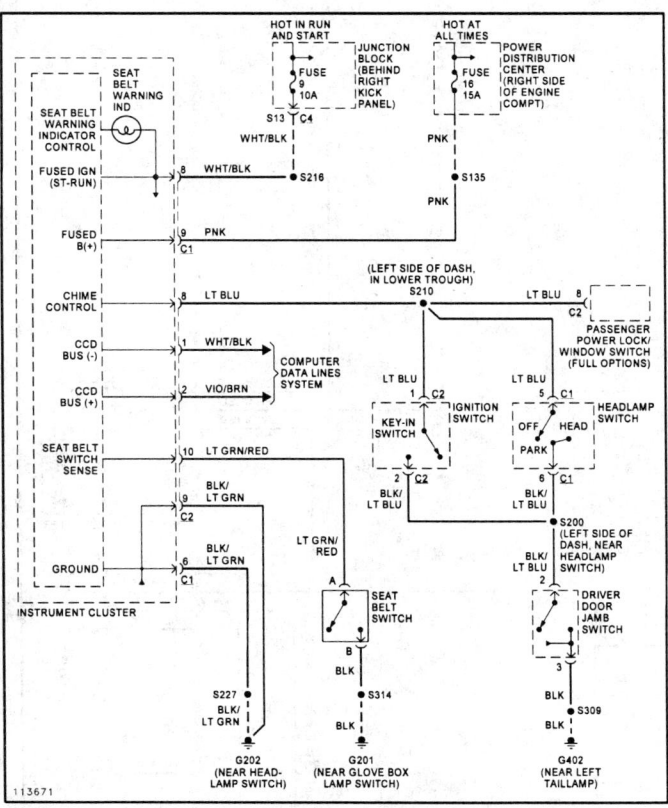

Fig. 1: Warning System Wiring Diagram (Cherokee)

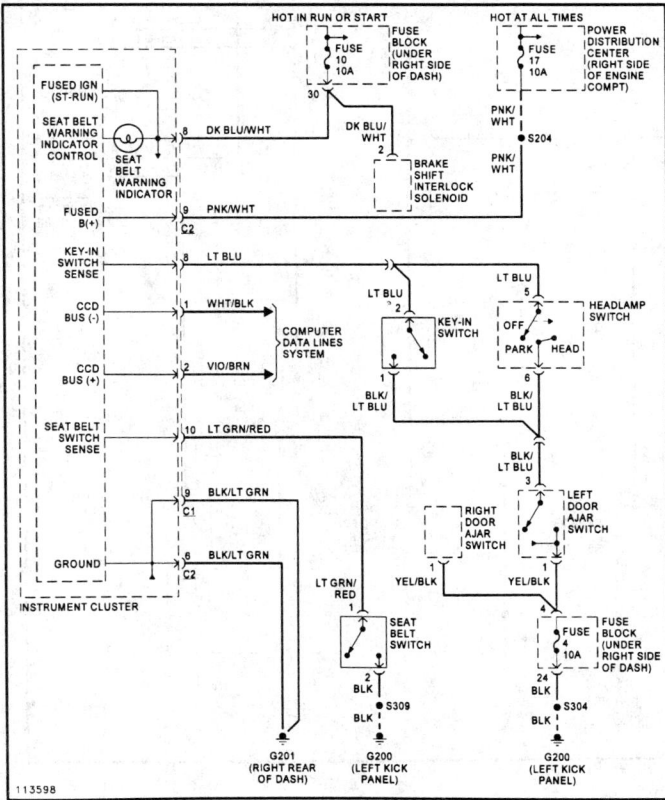

Fig. 2: Warning System Wiring Diagram (Wrangler)

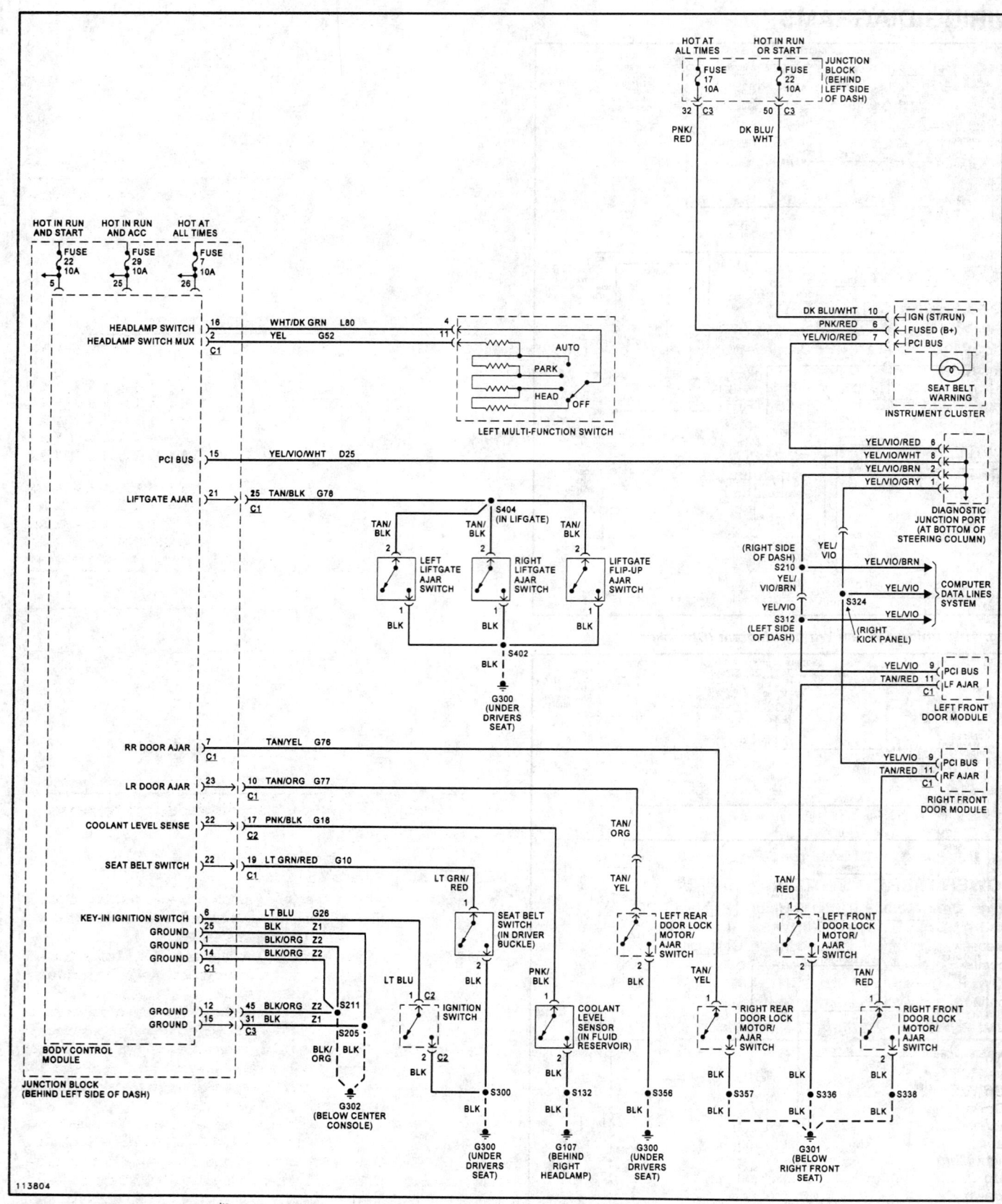

Fig. 3: Warning System Wiring Diagram (Grand Cherokee)

113804

DESCRIPTION & OPERATION

Right and left mirrors are controlled by a single multifunction switch on driver's door trim panel. On vehicles with power windows and door locks, multifunction switch is integral to Driver Door Module (DDM). On vehicles without power windows and door locks, a stand-alone switch is used. A 3 position rocker-type switch is moved to select left (left mirror control), right (right mirror control) or center to turn power mirrors off. Then one of 4 directional control buttons is depressed to control movement of selected mirror up, down, left or right. These buttons control polarity of voltage to 2 motors within each mirror. The side mirrors may be equipped with a heating element for defogging. The heating function is activated by rear window defogger switch.

COMPONENT TESTS

POWER MIRROR MOTOR

1) Remove door trim panel. See FRONT DOOR TRIM PANEL under REMOVAL & INSTALLATION. Disconnect power mirror 6-pin connector. Connect jumper wire to ground.
2) Connect second jumper wire to 12-volt power source. Connect each jumper wire as indicated in POWER MIRROR MOTOR TEST table. *See Fig. 1.* If mirror does not function as specified, replace power mirror.

POWER MIRROR MOTOR TEST

Connect 12 Volts To Terminal No.	Connect Ground To Terminal No.	Mirror Reaction
1	4	Up
4	1	Down
2	3	Left
3	2	Right
5	6	Heater

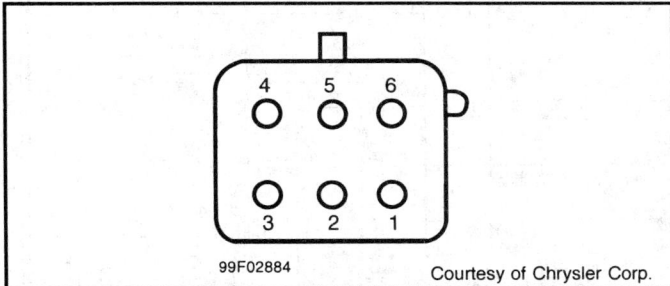

Fig. 1: Identifying Power Mirror 6-Pin Connector Terminals

POWER MIRROR SWITCH

Driver Door Module (DDM) Switch – Remove DDM. See DRIVER DOOR MODULE under REMOVAL & INSTALLATION. Place mirror select switch in left or right mirror mode. Continuity should exist between specified terminals when each control button is depressed. See DDM POWER MIRROR SWITCH CONTINUITY TEST table. *See Fig. 2.* If continuity is not as specified, replace DDM.

DDM POWER MIRROR SWITCH CONTINUITY TEST

Switch Position	Terminals No.
Left Mirror	
Up	1 & 3; 2 & 5
Down	2 & 3; 1 & 5
Right	3 & 6; 2 & 5
Left	2 & 3; 5 & 6
Right Mirror	
Up	3 & 7; 2 & 5
Down	2 & 3; 5 & 7
Right	3 & 4; 2 & 5
Left	2 & 3; 4 & 5

Stand-Alone Switch – Disconnect negative battery cable. Remove power window switch. See STAND-ALONE POWER MIRROR SWITCH

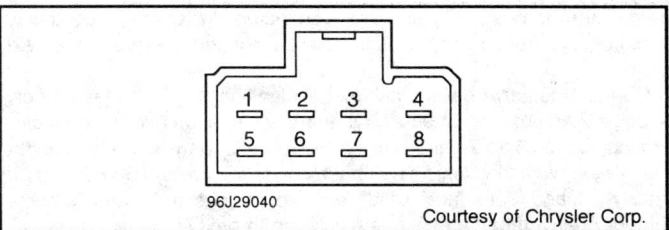

Fig. 2: Identifying DDM Power Mirror Switch Connector Terminals

under REMOVAL & INSTALLATION. Place mirror select switch in left or right mirror mode. Continuity should exist between specified terminals when each control button is depressed. See STAND-ALONE POWER MIRROR SWITCH CONTINUITY. *See Fig. 3.* If continuity is not as specified, replace switch.

STAND-ALONE POWER MIRROR SWITCH CONTINUITY

Switch Position	Terminals No.
Left Mirror	
Off	1 & 5; 1 & 6; 1 & 7; 1 & 8
Up	2 & 8; 1 & 5; 1 & 6; 1 & 7
Down	2 & 5; 1 & 6; 1 & 7; 1 & 8
Left	2 & 7; 1 & 5; 1 & 6; 1 & 8
Right	2 & 6; 1 & 5; 1 & 7; 1 & 8
Right Mirror	
Off	1 & 3; 1 & 4; 1 & 5; 1 & 6
Up	2 & 4; 1 & 3; 1 & 5; 1 & 6
Down	2 & 5; 1 & 3; 1 & 4; 1 & 6
Left	2 & 3; 1 & 4; 1 & 5; 1 & 6
Right	2 & 6; 1 & 3; 1 & 4; 1 & 5

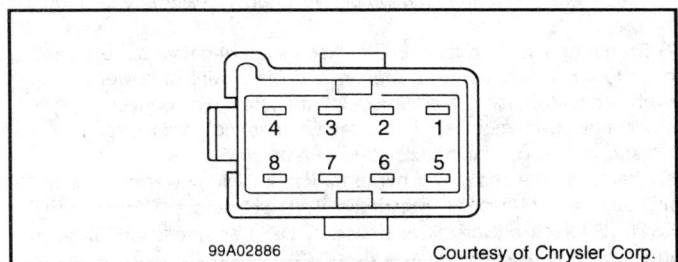

Fig. 3: Identifying Stand-Alone Power Mirror Switch Terminals

SYSTEM TESTS

POWER MIRROR SYSTEM

1) Check fuse No. 18 (10-amp) in junction block. Junction block is located behind right kick panel. If fuse is blown, repair short circuit and replace fuse. If fuse is okay, go to next step.
2) Turn ignition on. Check for battery voltage at fuse in junction block. If battery voltage does not exist, repair open circuit between ignition switch and junction block. If battery voltage exists, go to next step.
3) If problem being diagnosed is inoperative illumination of power mirror switch buttons on Driver Door Module (DDM), go to next step. If problem being diagnosed is inoperative power mirror heating grid, go to step **6)**. If problem being diagnosed is inoperative power mirror, go to step **10)**.
4) Check circuit breaker No. 28 (25-amp) in junction block. Replace as necessary. If circuit breaker is okay, go to next step.
5) Turn ignition off. Disconnect negative battery cable. Remove driver's door trim panel. See FRONT DOOR TRIM PANEL under REMOVAL & INSTALLATION. Disconnect DDM. Connect negative battery cable. Turn ignition on. Check for battery voltage at DDM 12-pin connector terminal No. 9 (Tan wire). *See Fig. 2.* If battery voltage does not exist, repair open circuit to circuit breaker No. 28 in junction block. If battery voltage exists, replace DDM.
6) Disconnect negative battery cable. Remove door trim panel. See FRONT DOOR TRIM PANEL under REMOVAL & INSTALLATION. Disconnect wire connector from mirror. Check for continuity **between**

ground and harness side of mirror connector Black wire. If continuity does not exist, repair open ground circuit. If continuity exists, go to next step.

7) Connect negative battery cable. Turn ignition on. Turn rear window defogger system on. Check for battery voltage at mirror connector terminal No. 5 (Black/White wire on models with power windows; Light Blue/Yellow wire on vehicles without power windows). *See Fig. 1.* If battery voltage does not exist, repair open circuit to rear window defogger relay. If battery voltage exists, go to next step.

8) Check for continuity between ground and mirror side of mirror connector (Black/White wire on models with power windows; Light Blue/Yellow wire on models without power windows). If continuity does not exist, replace mirror. If continuity exists, go to next step.

9) Measure resistance between mirror side of mirror connector Black wire terminal and Light Blue/Yellow wire terminal (on vehicles without power windows) or Black/White wire (on vehicles with power windows). Resistance should be 10-16 ohms with an ambient temperature of 70°F (21°C). If resistance is not as specified, replace mirror.

10) Disconnect negative battery cable. On models with power windows, go to next step. On models without power windows, remove power mirror switch. See STAND-ALONE POWER MIRROR SWITCH under REMOVAL & INSTALLATION. Disconnect power mirror switch. Connect negative battery cable. Turn ignition on. Check for battery voltage at power mirror switch connector terminal No. 2 (Yellow/Dark Green wire). If battery voltage does not exist, repair open circuit between power mirror switch and junction block. If battery voltage exists, go to step **12**).

11) On models with power windows, remove door trim panel See FRONT DOOR TRIM PANEL under REMOVAL & INSTALLATION. Disconnect DDM 8-pin connector. Connect negative battery cable. Turn ignition on. Check for battery voltage at DDM connector terminal No. 3 (Yellow Dark Green wire). If battery voltage does not exist, repair open circuit between DDM and junction block. If battery voltage exists, go to next step.

12) On all models, turn ignition off. Disconnect negative battery cable. Check for continuity between ground and Black wire of power window switch connector (stand-alone models) or DDM 8-pin connector (power window-equipped models). If continuity does not exist, repair open ground circuit. If continuity exists, go to next step.

13) Check stand-alone power mirror switch or DDM power mirror switch continuity. See POWER MIRROR SWITCH under COMPONENT TESTS. Replace power mirror switch or DDM as necessary. If power mirror switch is okay, go to next step.

14) Test power mirror motor. See POWER MIRROR MOTOR test under COMPONENT TESTS. Replace mirror as necessary. If power mirror is okay, repair wiring between mirror and switch.

REMOVAL & INSTALLATION

FRONT DOOR TRIM PANEL

NOTE: When removing door trim panel, start at bottom of panel. Pry panel free with wide, flat prying tool.

Removal & Installation – 1) Lower window to full down position. Remove window crank, if equipped. Remove door trim panel attaching screws. Using a trim stick, separate trim panel fasteners from door inner panel.

2) Lift door trim upwards and away from door to disengage top of panel from inner weather-stripping. Pull door trim panel out far enough to access inside door latch release and lock linkage rods near back of inside door remote controls.

3) Disconnect ends of latch release and lock linkage rods and remove rod ends from inside door remote controls. Disconnect door lock, window or mirror connectors, if equipped. Remove door trim panel from door. To install, reverse removal procedure.

STAND-ALONE POWER MIRROR SWITCH

Removal & Installation – Disconnect negative battery cable. Using a trim stick, gently pry around edge of switch to release snap clips. Pull

switch out enough to access wire connector. Disconnect wire connector. To install, reverse removal procedure.

DRIVER DOOR MODULE

Removal & Installation – Door module is mounted to door trim panel. Remove front door trim panel. See FRONT DOOR TRIM PANEL. Remove door module retaining screws. Remove door module from trim panel. To install, reverse removal procedure.

POWER MIRROR ASSEMBLY

Removal & Installation – Disconnect negative battery cable. Remove front door trim panel. See FRONT DOOR TRIM PANEL. Remove power mirror mounting trim cover screw. Using a trim stick, gently pry power mirror mounting trim cover away from door and remove cover. Disconnect power mirror connector. Remove 3 mirror mounting screws. Remove mirror from door. To install, reverse removal procedure.

WIRING DIAGRAMS

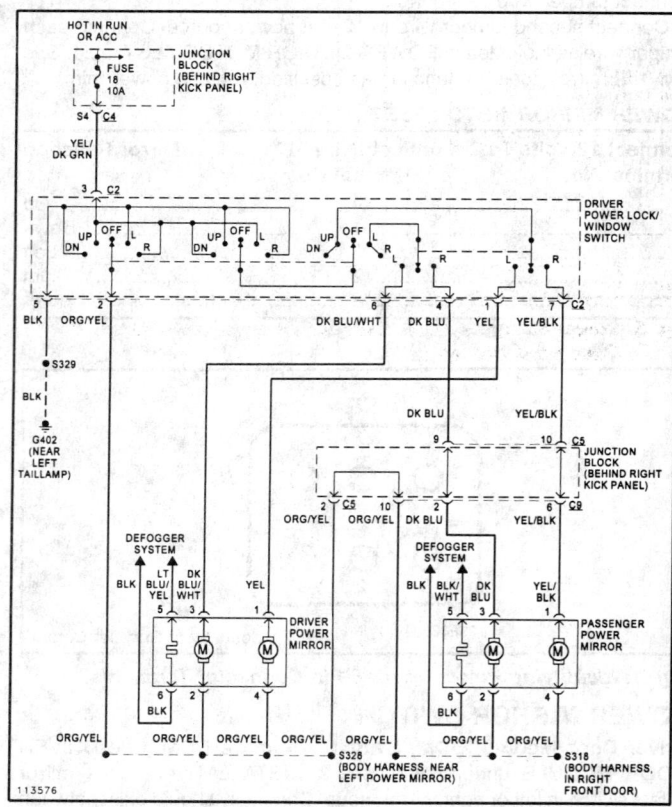

Fig. 4: Power Mirror System (With Full Options) Wiring Diagram (Cherokee)

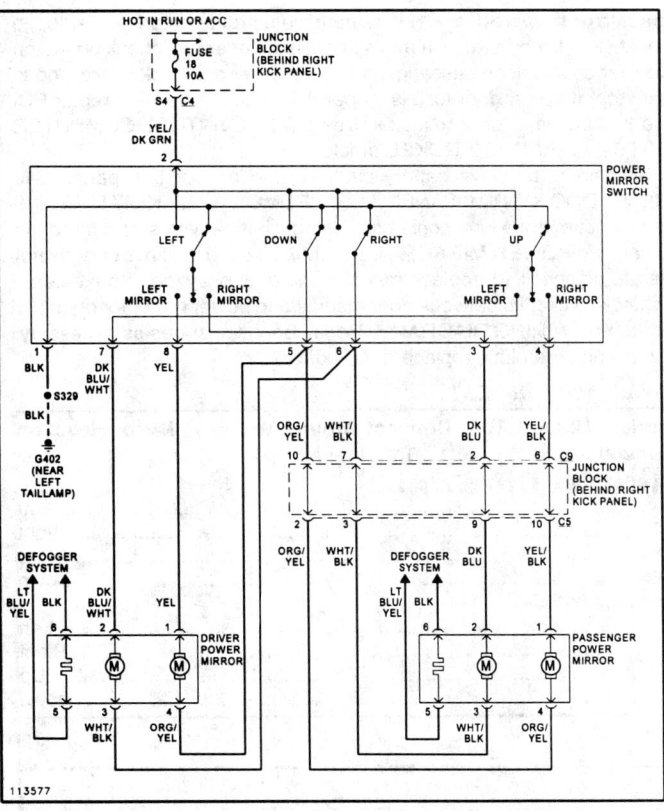

Fig. 5: Power Mirror System (Except Full Options) Wiring Diagram (Cherokee)

DESCRIPTION & OPERATION

Right and left mirrors are controlled by a multifunction switch on driver's door trim panel. Switch is integral to Driver Door Module (DDM). A 3 position rocker-type switch is moved to select left (left mirror control), right (right mirror control) or center to turn power mirrors off. Then one of 4 directional control buttons is depressed to control movement of selected mirror up, down, left or right. These buttons control polarity of voltage to 2 motors within each mirror.

The side mirrors are equipped with a heating element for defogging. The heating function is activated by rear window defogger switch. Vehicle may also have an electronic memory option, which can control both outside mirror positions when either driver 1 or 2 switches are depressed, or when doors are unlocked using remote keyless entry transmitters for driver 1 or 2.

Vehicle may be equipped with an optional automatic day/night inside rear view mirror, which automatically adjusts to reduce glare during night driving. Mirror switch at bottom of mirror can be used to manually turn mirror on or off. Additionally, the driver's side mirror may include this option, which is controlled by the same circuit as the rear view mirror.

The automatic day/night inside rear view mirror is controlled by 2 light-sensitive photocells. Outside light level is measured by a sensor on backside of mirror housing. A second sensor, located inside the mirror, detects approaching rear lights. The mirror locks in normal position whenever transmission gear selector is placed in Reverse position.

SYSTEM TESTS

POWER MIRROR SYSTEM

NOTE: Manufacturer recommends using DRB scan tool to check power mirror system. If DRB scan tool is not available, the following tests can be used to diagnose hard-wired components of power system, but results may be inconclusive. In order to obtain conclusive testing of power mirror system, Programmable Communications Interface (PCI) data bus network and all modules that provide inputs to, or receive outputs from power mirror system, must be checked. See BODY CONTROL COMPUTER TESTS – GRAND CHEROKEE article.

Both Mirrors Inoperative – 1) Check operation of driver's power lock switch. If all doors lock and unlock, replace Driver Door Module (DDM). If door locks are inoperative, check operation of passenger's power lock switch. If all doors lock and unlock, replace DDM. If door locks are inoperative, go to next step.

2) Check fuse No. 12 (50-amp) in Power Distribution Center (PDC). If fuse is blown, repair short circuit and replace fuse. If fuse is okay, check for battery voltage at fuse No. 12 in PDC. If battery voltage does not exist, repair open circuit to battery. If battery exists, go to next step.

3) Disconnect negative battery cable. Remove driver's door trim panel. See FRONT DOOR TRIM PANEL under REMOVAL & INSTALLATION. Disconnect DDM 15-pin connector. Check for continuity between ground and DDM 15-pin connector terminal No. 4 (Black wire). *See Fig. 1.* If continuity does not exist, repair open circuit. If continuity exists, go to next step.

4) Reconnect negative battery cable. Check for battery voltage at DDM 15-pin connector terminal No. 1 (Tan/Light Blue wire). If battery voltage does not exist, repair open circuit between DDM and PDC. If battery voltage exists, replace DDM.

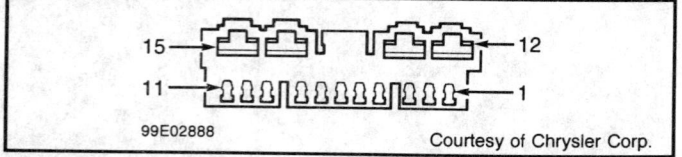

99E02888   Courtesy of Chrysler Corp.

Fig. 1: Identifying Driver's Door Module (DDM) 15-Pin Connector Terminals

One Mirror Inoperative – 1) If inoperative mirror is on driver's side, go to next step. If inoperative mirror is on passenger's side, check operation of power door lock on passenger's side. If power door lock is okay, go to next step. If power door lock is inoperative, use scan tool to repair PCI data bus between door modules. See BODY CONTROL COMPUTER TESTS – GRAND CHEROKEE article.

2) Disconnect negative battery cable. Remove door trim panel. See FRONT DOOR TRIM PANEL under REMOVAL & INSTALLATION. Disconnect mirror wiring connector. Using 2 jumper wires, test mirror as indicated in POWER MIRROR TEST table. *See Fig. 2.* If mirror does not operate as specified, replace mirror. If mirror is okay, go to next step.

3) Check all circuits between door module and power mirror for opens or shorts. See WIRING DIAGRAMS. Repair opens or shorts as necessary. If all circuits are okay, replace door module.

POWER MIRROR TEST

Connect 12 Volts To Terminal No.	Connect Ground To Terminal No.	Mirror Reaction
Driver's Side		
6	12	Left
12	6	Right
11	12	Up
12	11	Down
Passenger's Side		
1	7	Left
7	1	Right
8	7	Up
7	8	Down

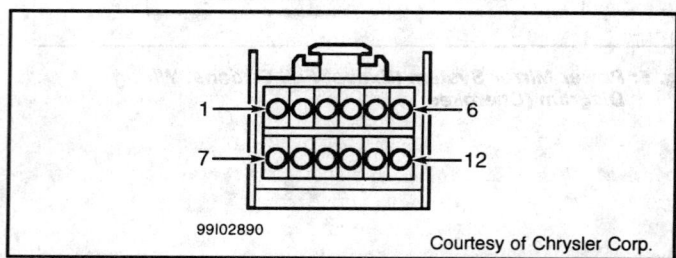

99I02890   Courtesy of Chrysler Corp.

Fig. 2: Identifying Power Mirror 12-Pin Connector Terminals

HEATED MIRROR INOPERATIVE

1) If both mirror heaters are inoperative, see appropriate wiring diagram in REAR WINDOW DEFOGGERS & HEATED MIRRORS article. If only one mirror heater is inoperative, disconnect negative battery terminal. Remove front door trim panel on side of inoperative mirror. See FRONT DOOR TRIM PANEL under REMOVAL & INSTALLATION.

2) Disconnect power mirror 12-pin connector from door module. Check for continuity between terminals "B" (Black wire) and "F" at mirror 12-pin connector. *See Fig. 2.* If continuity does not exist, replace power mirror. If continuity exists, use scan tool to test door module and PCI data bus. See BODY CONTROL COMPUTER TESTS – GRAND CHEROKEE article.

DRIVER'S OUTSIDE POWER MIRROR DOES NOT DARKEN

1) Ensure automatic day/night rear view mirror is functioning properly before continuing with this test. See AUTOMATIC DAY/NIGHT INSIDE REAR VIEW MIRROR test. If rear view mirror functions properly, go to next step. If rear view mirror does not function properly, repair as necessary. After repair is completed, recheck outside power mirror operation. If outside power mirror still does not darken, go to next step.

2) Disconnect negative battery cable. Remove driver's door trim panel. See FRONT DOOR TRIM PANEL under REMOVAL & INSTALLATION. Disconnect power mirror connector. Connect a voltmeter between power mirror wiring harness connector terminals No. 7 (Yellow/Red wire) and No. 10 (Yellow/White wire). While observing voltmeter, perform steps **6)** and **7)** in AUTOMATIC DAY/NIGHT INSIDE REAR VIEW MIRROR test.

3) A voltmeter reading of 1.4-1.5 volts indicates power mirror is receiving a proper dimming signal. If voltage is as specified, replace outside power mirror. If voltage is not as specified, repair wiring harness between outside power mirror connector and automatic day/night inside rear view mirror.

AUTOMATIC DAY/NIGHT INSIDE REAR VIEW MIRROR

1) Check fuse No. 22 (10-amp) in junction block. Junction block is located under left side of instrument panel. If fuse is okay, go to next step. If fuse is blown, check for cause of fuse to blow. Repair as necessary. Replace fuse and recheck system operation.

2) Turn ignition on. Check for battery voltage at fuse No. 22 in junction block. If battery voltage is present, go to next step. If battery voltage is not present, repair open in Dark Blue wire between ignition switch and junction block.

3) Disconnect 7-pin harness connector from rear view mirror. Ensure ignition is on. Measure voltage between ground and terminal No. 1 (Dark Blue/White wire) at rear view mirror wiring harness connector. *See Fig. 3*. If battery voltage is present, go to next step. If battery voltage is not present, repair open in Dark Blue/White wire between fuse box and rear view mirror connector.

4) Turn ignition off. Check for continuity between ground and terminal No. 2 (Black wire) at rear view mirror harness connector. If continuity exists, go to next step. If continuity does not exist, repair open in Black wire ground circuit.

5) Turn ignition on. Set parking brake. Place transmission gear selector lever in Reverse. Measure voltage between ground and terminal No. 3 (Violet/Black wire) at rear view mirror harness connector. If battery voltage is present, reconnect rear view mirror connector and go to next step. If battery voltage is not present, locate and repair open circuit.

6) Place transmission gear selector lever in Neutral. Place rear view mirror switch in ON position (switch LED is lighted). Completely cover forward facing sensor. *See Fig. 4*. Shine light into rear facing sensor. If mirror darkens, go to next step. If mirror does not darken, replace mirror.

7) With mirror still darkened, place transmission gear selector lever in Reverse. Mirror should return to normal. If mirror operates as specified, system is functioning properly. Test is complete. If mirror does not return to normal, replace mirror.

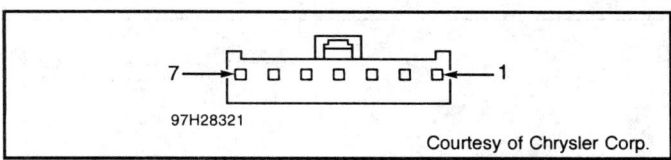

Fig. 3: Identifying Electronic Inside Rear View Mirror Wiring Harness Connector Terminals

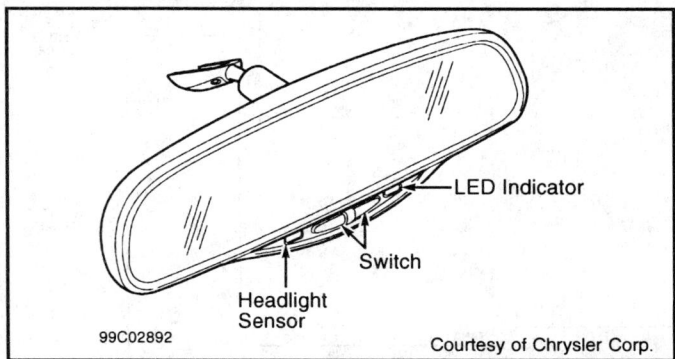

Fig. 4: Identifying Inside Rear View Mirror

NO MIRROR MEMORY

For diagnosis of power mirror memory system, check power memory system for open and short circuits. See WIRING DIAGRAMS.

REMOVAL & INSTALLATION

FRONT DOOR TRIM PANEL

Removal & Installation – Remove plug from mirror flag bezel. Remove trim panel attaching screws. Using trim stick, detach trim panel push-in fasteners. Lift trim panel upward and separate from door. Disconnect all necessary wire connectors. Disconnect latch rods from inside handle actuator. Remove trim panel. To install, reverse removal procedure.

DRIVER DOOR MODULE

Removal & Installation – Door module is mounted to door trim panel. Remove front door trim panel. See FRONT DOOR TRIM PANEL. Disconnect door module connectors and door courtesy light connector (if equipped). Remove door module-to-trim panel screws. Remove door module from trim panel. To install, reverse removal procedure.

POWER MIRROR ASSEMBLY

Removal & Installation – Disconnect negative battery cable. Remove front door trim panel. See FRONT DOOR TRIM PANEL. Disconnect power mirror connector. Remove mirror flag seal from inner panel. Remove 3 mirror mounting nuts. Remove mirror from door. To install, reverse removal procedure. Tighten mirror mounting nuts to 65 INCH lbs. (7.4 N.m).

WIRING DIAGRAMS

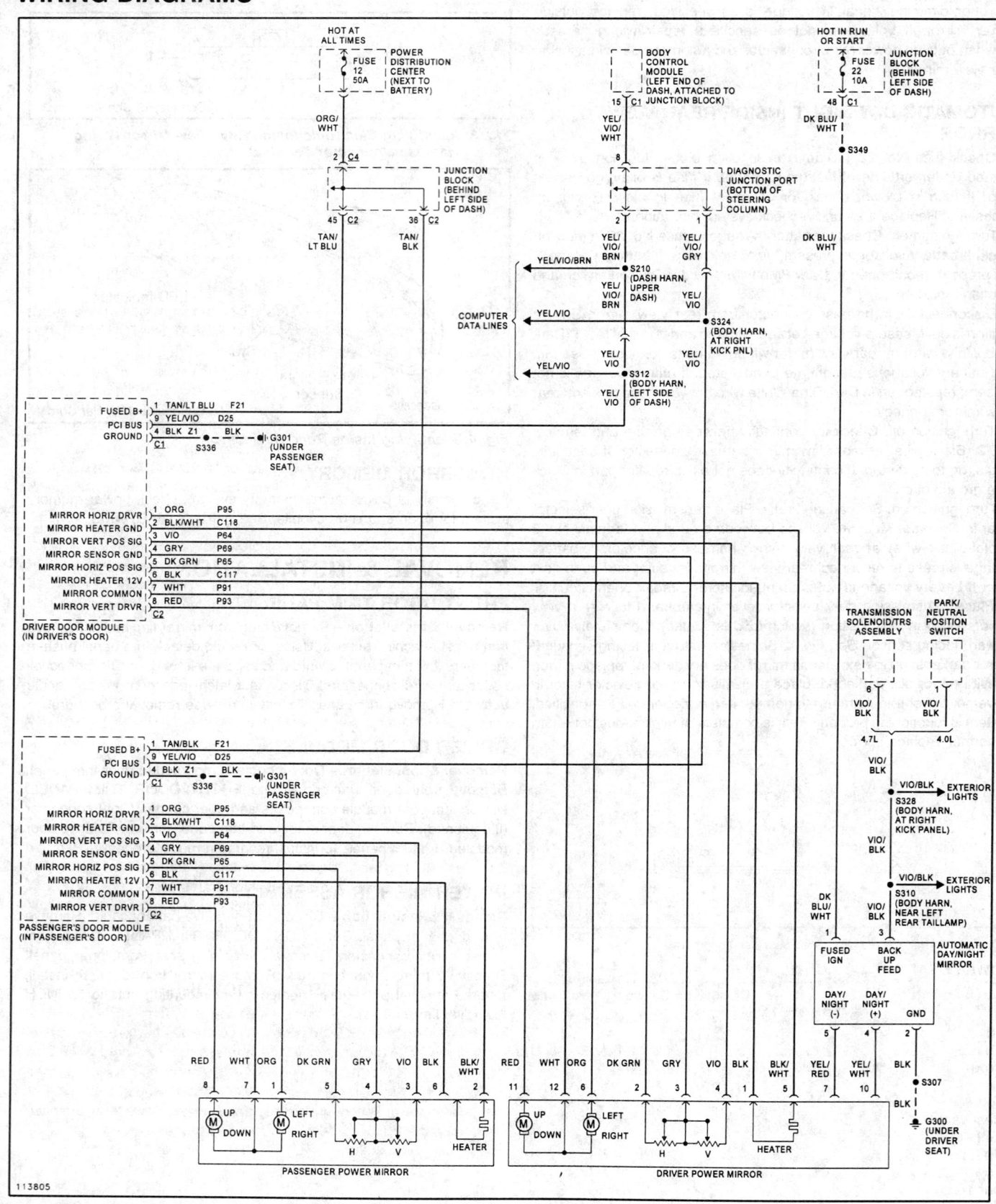

Fig. 5: Power Mirror System Wiring Diagram (Grand Cherokee)

Power Seats – Cherokee

DESCRIPTION & OPERATION

The power seat can be adjusted in 6 different ways using the power seat switch. The switch is located on the lower outboard side of seat cushion frame. There are 3 reversible motors that operate the power seat adjuster. The motors are connected to worm drive gearboxes that move the seat adjuster through a combination of screw-type drive units.

TROUBLE SHOOTING

POWER SEAT INOPERATIVE

Ensure battery is fully charged. Ensure all connections are clean, tight and not damaged. With dome light on, apply seat switch in direction of failure. If dome light dims, check for obstructions or mechanical jam. Repair as necessary. If dome light does not dim, test individual components. See COMPONENT TESTS.

COMPONENT TESTS

CIRCUIT BREAKER TEST

1) Locate circuit breaker No. 29 (25-amp), located in fuse box behind right kick panel. Pull circuit breaker out slightly. Ensure circuit breaker terminals still make contact with mating terminals in fuse box.
2) Measure voltage between ground and each terminal of circuit breaker No. 29. If battery voltage is not present at either circuit breaker terminal, repair open between battery and fuse box. If battery voltage is present at only one circuit breaker terminal, replace faulty circuit breaker.

POWER SEAT SWITCH TEST

Remove power seat switch. See POWER SEAT SWITCH under REMOVAL & INSTALLATION. Using an ohmmeter, check for continuity between switch terminals. See appropriate POWER SEAT SWITCH CONTINUITY table. See Fig. 1. Continuity should exist between terminals as specified. Replace switch as necessary. If switch is okay, see POWER SEAT ADJUSTER/MOTOR TEST.

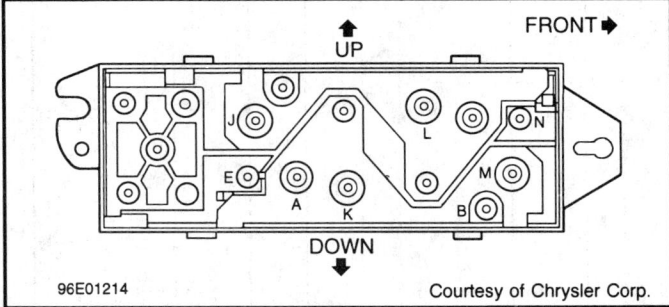

Fig. 1: Identifying Power Seat Switch Terminals

POWER SEAT SWITCH CONTINUITY (DRIVER'S)

Switch Position	Continuity Between Terminals
Off	B & E; B & J; B & K; B & L; B & M; B & N
Vertical	
Up	A & J; A & M; B & E; B & N
Down	A & E; A & N; B & J; B & M
Horizontal	
Forward	A & L; B & K
Rearward	A & K; B & L
Front Tilt	
Up	A & M; B & N
Down	A & N; B & M
Rear Tilt	
Up	A & J; B & E
Down	A & E; B & J

POWER SEAT SWITCH CONTINUITY (PASSENGER'S)

Switch Position	Continuity Between Terminals
Off	A & E; A & J; A & K; A & L; A & M; A & N
Vertical	
Up	A & J; A & N; B & E; B & M
Down	A & E; A & M; B & J; B & N
Horizontal	
Forward	A & L; B & K
Rearward	A & K; B & L
Front Tilt	
Up	A & M; B & N
Down	A & N; B & M
Rear Tilt	
Up	A & J; B & E
Down	A & E; B & J

POWER SEAT ADJUSTER/MOTOR TEST

1) Operate power seat switch so that all 3 motors have been energized. If one or more motors operate, see POWER SEAT SWITCH TEST. If no motors operate, go to next step.
2) Check circuit breaker. See CIRCUIT BREAKER TEST. Replace circuit breaker as necessary and recheck system operation. If circuit breaker is okay, remove power seat switch. See POWER SEAT SWITCH under REMOVAL & INSTALLATION.
3) Using a voltmeter, measure voltage between ground and Red/Light Blue wire (terminal "A" on driver's seat or terminal "B" on passenger's seat) at power seat switch harness connector. If battery voltage is present, go to next step. If battery voltage is not present, repair open in Red/Light Blue wire between circuit breaker and power seat switch.
4) Using an ohmmeter, check for continuity between ground and Black wire (terminal "A" on driver's seat or terminal "B" on passenger's seat) at power seat harness connector. If continuity exists, go to next step. If continuity does not exist, repair open in Black wire between power seat switch connector and ground.
5) Test power seat switch. See POWER SEAT SWITCH TEST. Replace switch as necessary and recheck system operation. If switch is okay, check wiring harness between power seat adjuster motor assembly and power seat switch harness connector. Repair as necessary. If wiring is okay, replace faulty power seat adjuster/motor assembly. Recheck system operation.

REMOVAL & INSTALLATION

POWER SEAT SWITCH

Removal & Installation – Disconnect negative battery cable. Remove 3 screws retaining seat side shield to outboard seat cushion frame. Pull seat side shield away from seat cushion frame far enough to access power seat switch connector. Disconnect power seat switch connector. Remove seat side shield. Remove power seat switch from seat side shield. To install, reverse removal procedure.

POWER SEAT ADJUSTERS/MOTORS

Removal & Installation – Move power seat adjuster to full-up position and full-forward position (if possible). Disconnect negative battery cable. Disconnect seat belt switch wiring harness from inboard seat belt. Remove bolts/nuts that secure seat adjuster frame to floor pan. Disconnect power seat wiring harness connector. Remove seat from vehicle. Disconnect power seat motor connectors. Remove power seat adjuster/motor assembly. To install, reverse removal procedure.

WIRING DIAGRAMS

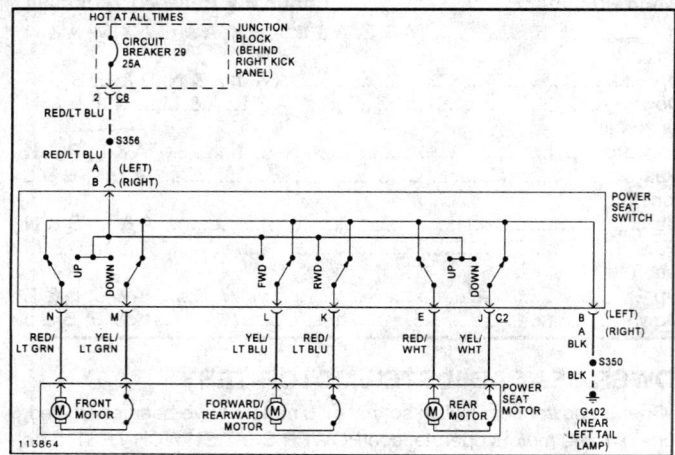

Fig. 2: Power Seat System Wiring Diagram (Cherokee)

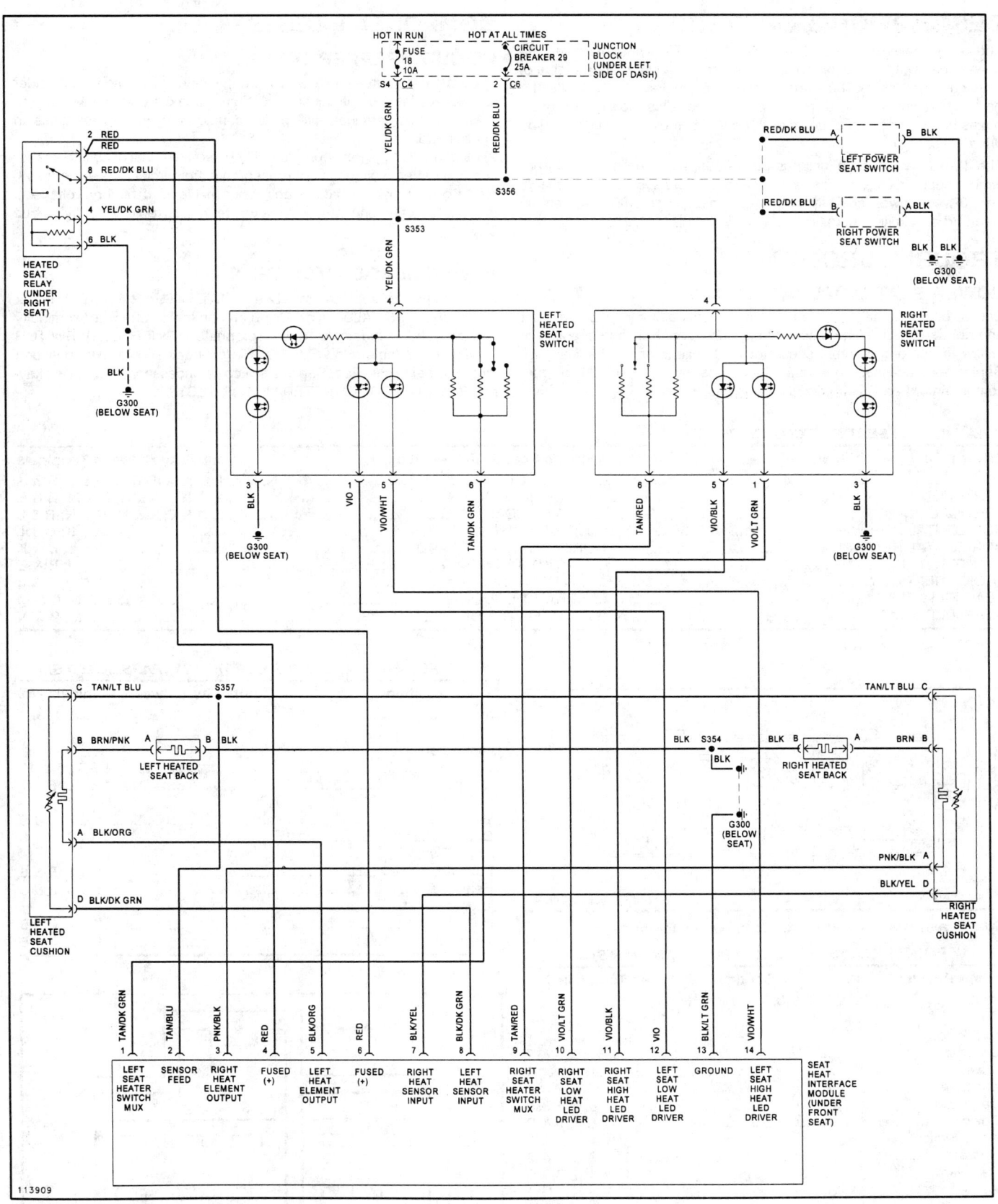

Fig. 3: Heated Seat System Wiring Diagram (Cherokee)

113909

DESCRIPTION & OPERATION

The 6-way power seat can be adjusted in 6 different ways using the power seat switch. The switch is located on the lower outboard side of seat cushion frame. There are 3 reversible motors that operate the power seat adjuster. The motors are connected to worm drive gearboxes that move the seat adjuster through a combination of screw-type drive units.

The 10-way power seat includes power seat back recliner and power lumbar support. Heated seat system and memory system are available on 10-way power seat system. Additionally, a memory system is standard on Limited models.

TROUBLE SHOOTING

POWER SEAT INOPERATIVE

Ensure battery is fully charged. Ensure all connections are clean, tight and not damaged. With dome light on, apply seat switch in direction of failure. If dome light dims, check for obstructions or mechanical jam. Repair as necessary. If dome light does not dim, test individual components. See COMPONENT TESTING.

COMPONENT TESTS

CIRCUIT BREAKER TEST

1) Locate circuit breaker No. 2 (20-amp), located in junction block under left side of instrument panel. Pull circuit breaker out slightly. Ensure circuit breaker terminals still make contact with mating terminals in junction block.
2) Measure voltage between ground and each terminal of circuit breaker No. 2. If battery voltage is not present at either circuit breaker terminal, repair open between battery and junction block. If battery voltage is present at only one circuit breaker terminal, replace faulty circuit breaker.

POWER SEAT SWITCH TEST

Remove power seat switch. See POWER SEAT SWITCH under REMOVAL & INSTALLATION. Using an ohmmeter, check for continuity between switch terminals. See appropriate POWER SEAT SWITCH CONTINUITY table. *See Fig. 1 or 2.* Continuity should exist between terminals being checked. Replace switch as necessary. If switch is okay, see POWER SEAT ADJUSTER/MOTOR TEST.

6-WAY POWER SEAT SWITCH CONTINUITY

Driver's Seat Switch Position	Passenger's Seat Switch Position	Continuity Between Terminals
OFF	OFF	B & N; B & J; B & M; B & E; B & L; B & K
VERTICAL UP	VERTICAL DOWN	A & J; A & N; B & M; B & E
VERTICAL DOWN	VERTICAL UP	A & E; A & M; B & N; B & J
HORIZONTAL FORWARD	HORIZONTAL FORWARD	A & K; B & L
HORIZONTAL REARWARD	HORIZONTAL REARWARD	A & L; B & K
FRONT TILT UP	FRONT TILT DOWN	A & J; B & E
FRONT TILT DOWN	FRONT TILT UP	A & E; B & J
REAR TILT UP	REAR TILT DOWN	A & N; B & M
REAR TILT DOWN	REAR TILT UP	A & M; B & N

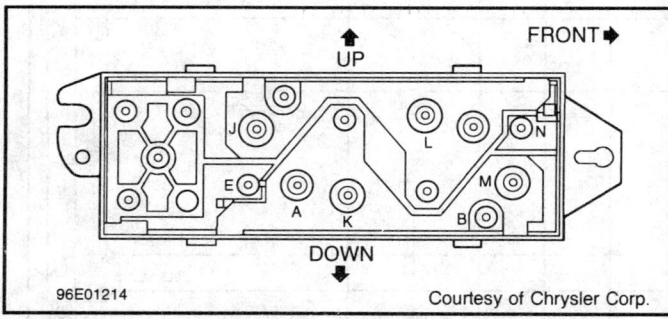

Fig. 1: Identifying 6-Way Power Seat Switch Terminals

10-WAY POWER SEAT SWITCH CONTINUITY (DRIVER'S)

Switch Position	Continuity Between Terminals No.
Off	1 & 2; 1 & 3; 1 & 4; 1 & 6; 1 & 7; 1 & 8; 1 & 9; 1 & 10
Front Riser	
Up	1 & 10; 5 & 7
Down	1 & 7; 5 & 10
Rear Riser	
Up	1 & 9; 5 & 8
Down	1 & 8; 5 & 9
Center Switch	
Forward	1 & 3; 5 & 6
Rearward	1 & 6; 3 & 5
Recliner	
Up	1 & 4; 2 & 5
Down	1 & 2; 4 & 5

10-WAY POWER SEAT SWITCH CONTINUITY (PASSENGER'S)

Switch Position	Continuity Between Terminals No.
Off	1 & 2; 1 & 3; 1 & 4; 1 & 6; 1 & 7; 1 & 8; 1 & 9; 1 & 10
Front Riser	
Up	1 & 7; 5 & 10
Down	1 & 10; 5 & 7
Rear Riser	
Up	1 & 8; 5 & 9
Down	1 & 9; 5 & 8
Center Switch	
Forward	1 & 3; 5 & 6
Rearward	1 & 6; 3 & 5
Recliner	
Up	1 & 4; 2 & 5
Down	1 & 2; 4 & 5

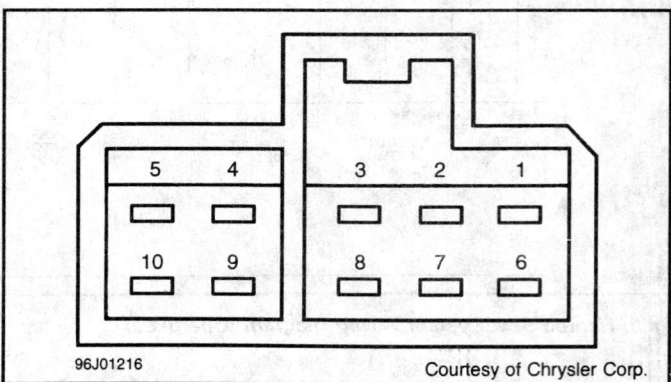

Fig. 2: Identifying 10-Way Power Seat Switch Terminals

POWER LUMBAR SWITCH TEST

Remove power lumbar switch. See POWER LUMBAR SWITCH under REMOVAL & INSTALLATION. Using an ohmmeter, check power lumbar switch continuity. See POWER LUMBAR SWITCH CONTINUITY table. *See Fig. 3.* Replace switch as necessary and recheck system operation. If switch is okay, go to POWER LUMBAR ADJUSTER/MOTOR TEST.

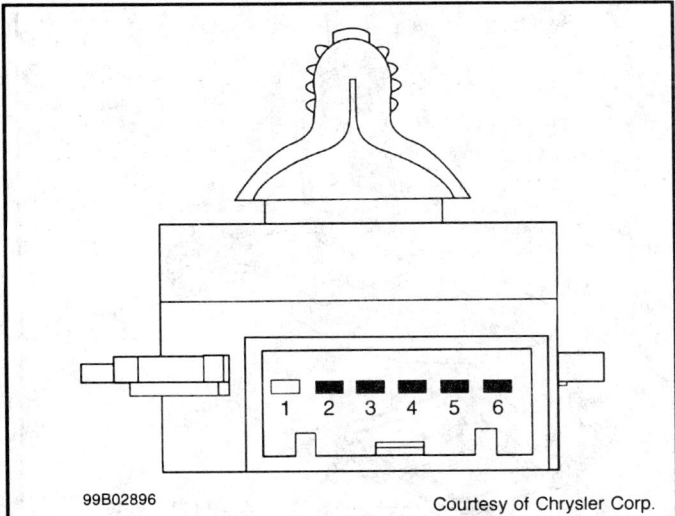

99B02896   Courtesy of Chrysler Corp.

Fig. 3: Identifying Power Lumbar Switch Terminals

POWER LUMBAR SWITCH CONTINUITY

Application	Continuity Between Terminals No.
Driver's Seat Switch Position	
Off	2 & 4; 3 & 5
Forward	3 & 5; 4 & 6
Rearward	2 & 4; 3 & 6
Passenger's Seat Switch Position	
Off	2 & 4; 3 & 5
Rearward	3 & 5; 4 & 6
Forward	2 & 4; 3 & 6

POWER LUMBAR ADJUSTER/MOTOR TEST

1) Operate power lumbar switch in both directions. If power lumbar is inoperative in both directions, go to next step. If power lumbar operates in one direction only, move adjuster a short distance in opposite direction and test again to ensure adjuster is not at its travel limit. If power lumbar still operates in one direction only, see POWER LUMBAR SWITCH TEST.

2) Check circuit breaker. See CIRCUIT BREAKER TEST. Replace circuit breaker as necessary. Recheck system operation. If circuit breaker is okay, remove outboard seat cushion side shield. Disconnect power lumbar switch wire harness connector. Check for battery voltage at power lumbar switch connector terminal No. 6 (Red wire on driver's side; Red/Light Blue wire on passenger's side). If battery voltage is present, go to next step. If battery voltage is not present, repair open circuit to junction block.

3) Using an ohmmeter, check for continuity between ground and terminals No. 2 (Black wire) and No. 5 (Black wire) at power lumbar switch wiring harness connector. If continuity exists in both wires, go to next step. If continuity does not exist in one or both wires, repair open in appropriate Black wire between power lumbar switch and ground.

4) Test power lumbar switch. See POWER LUMBAR SWITCH TEST. Replace switch as necessary and recheck system operation. If switch is okay, check circuits between power lumbar adjuster motor and power lumbar switch for shorts or opens. Repair as necessary. If circuits are okay, replace faulty seat back frame.

POWER RECLINER ADJUSTER/MOTOR TEST

1) Operate power recliner switch in both directions. If power recliner operates in one direction only, move seat in opposite direction and test again to ensure adjuster is not at its travel limit. If power recliner still operates in one direction only, see POWER SEAT SWITCH TEST. If power recliner is inoperative in both directions, go to next step.

2) Check circuit breaker. See CIRCUIT BREAKER TEST. Replace circuit breaker as necessary and recheck system operation. If circuit breaker is okay, remove outboard seat cushion side shield. Disconnect power seat switch connector. Check for battery voltage at power seat switch connector terminal No. 5 (Red wire on driver's side; Red/Light Blue wire on passenger's side). If battery voltage is present, go to next step. If battery voltage is not present, repair open circuit to junction block.

3) Using an ohmmeter, check for continuity between ground and terminal No. 1 (Black wire) at power seat wiring harness connector. If continuity exists, go to next step. If continuity does not exist, repair open in Black wire between power seat switch and ground.

4) Test power seat switch. See POWER SEAT SWITCH TEST. Replace switch as necessary and recheck system operation. If switch is okay, check circuits between power seat recliner and power seat switch for opens or shorts. Repair as necessary. If circuits are okay, replace faulty power recliner assembly and recheck system operation.

POWER SEAT ADJUSTER/MOTOR TEST

1) Operate power seat switch to move all 3 motors. If seat adjuster fails to operate in only one direction, move adjuster a short distance in opposite direction and test again to ensure that adjuster is not at its travel limit. If seat adjuster still fails to operate in only one direction, see POWER SEAT SWITCH TEST. If seat adjuster fails to operate in more than one direction, go to next step.

2) Check circuit breaker. See CIRCUIT BREAKER TEST. Replace circuit breaker as necessary and recheck system operation. If circuit breaker is okay, remove outboard seat cushion side shield. Disconnect power seat switch wire connector.

3) Check for battery voltage at power seat switch connector terminal "A" (Red wire on driver's side; Red/Light Blue wire on passenger's side) for 6-way power seat or terminal No. 5 (Red wire on driver's side; Red/Light Blue wire on passenger's side) for 10-way power seat. If battery voltage exists, go to next step. If battery voltage does not exist, repair open circuit to junction block.

4) Using an ohmmeter, check for continuity between ground and terminal "B" (Black wire) for 6-way power seat or terminal No. 1 (Black wire) for 10-way power seat at power seat switch connector. If continuity exists, go to next step. If continuity does not exist, repair open in Black wire between power seat switch and ground.

5) Test power seat switch. See POWER SEAT SWITCH TEST. Replace switch as necessary and recheck system operation. If switch is okay, check circuits between power seat switch and power seat adjuster for opens or shorts. Repair as necessary. If circuits are okay, replace faulty power seat adjuster/motor assembly and recheck system operation.

REMOVAL & INSTALLATION

MEMORY SEAT MODULE

NOTE: After installation, initialize memory seat module. Move each power seat adjuster motor, including power recliner and power lumbar motors, through full range of motion using power seat switches. This is required so that memory seat module will function properly.

Removal & Installation – 1) Move seat to full-up position and full-forward position (if possible). Disconnect seat belt switch wiring harness from inboard seat belt. Remove screw securing each rear seat track cover to rear of seat tracks, and remove covers. Remove screw securing each seat track to floor pan.

2) Move seat to full-rearward position (if possible). Remove single screw securing front of each seat track to floor pan. Disconnect negative battery cable. Carefully tilt seat back toward outboard side of vehicle. Remove wiring harness retainers from seat adjuster top rail.

3) Slide memory seat module off mounting bracket slide tabs far enough to disconnect wiring harness connectors. Remove module from under seat cushion. To install, reverse removal procedure.

POWER SEAT SWITCH

Removal & Installation – 1) Disconnect negative battery cable. On models with 10-way power seat, use a trim stick to pry power seat and power recliner switch knobs off switch stems. On all models, remove 3 screws securing seat cushion side shield to seat cushion frame.
2) Pull side shield away from seat cushion far enough to disconnect power seat switch connector. Remove screws securing switch to inside of side shield. Remove switch from side shield. To install, reverse removal procedure.

POWER LUMBAR SWITCH

Removal & Installation – Disconnect negative battery cable. Remove screws securing seat cushion side shield to seat cushion frame. Pull side shield away from seat cushion far enough to disconnect power lumbar switch connector. Remove screws securing switch to inside of side shield. Remove switch from side shield. To install, reverse removal procedure.

POWER LUMBAR ADJUSTER/MOTOR

Removal & Installation – Remove power recliner adjuster and motor from seatback frame. See POWER RECLINER ADJUSTER/MOTOR. Remove all seatback trim from seatback. Remove seatback frame assembly with lumbar adjuster and motor. *See Fig. 4*. To install, reverse removal procedure.

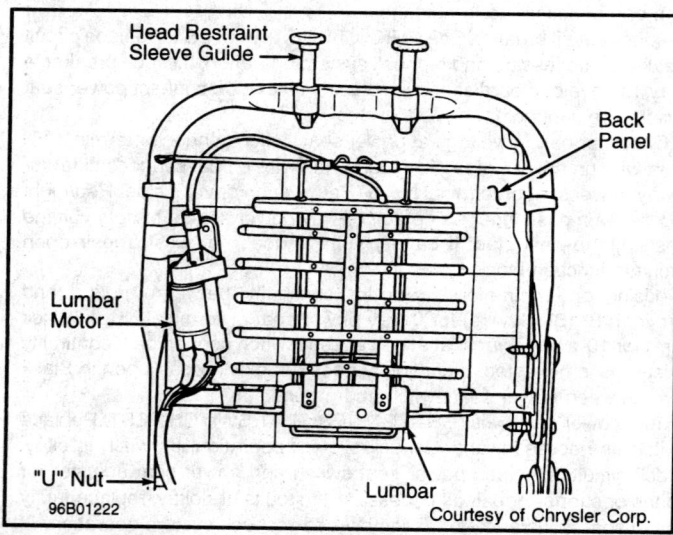

Fig. 4: Identifying Power Lumbar Components

POWER RECLINER ADJUSTER/MOTOR

Removal & Installation – 1) Move power seat adjuster to full-up position and full-forward position (if possible). Remove 3 screws securing outboard seat cushion side shield to seat cushion frame. Pull shield away from seat to access power recliner adjuster lower bracket.
2) Adjust seatback with power recliner switch so both bolts in power recliner adjuster lower bracket can be accessed. Disconnect negative battery cable. Remove 2 bolts securing power recliner adjuster lower bracket to seat cushion frame. Remove inboard seatback pivot bolt.
3) Disconnect wiring harness connectors. Pull back seatback cover far enough to access bolts securing power recliner adjuster upper bracket to seatback frame. Remove power recliner adjuster and motor assembly from seatback frame. See Fig. 5. To install, reverse removal procedure.

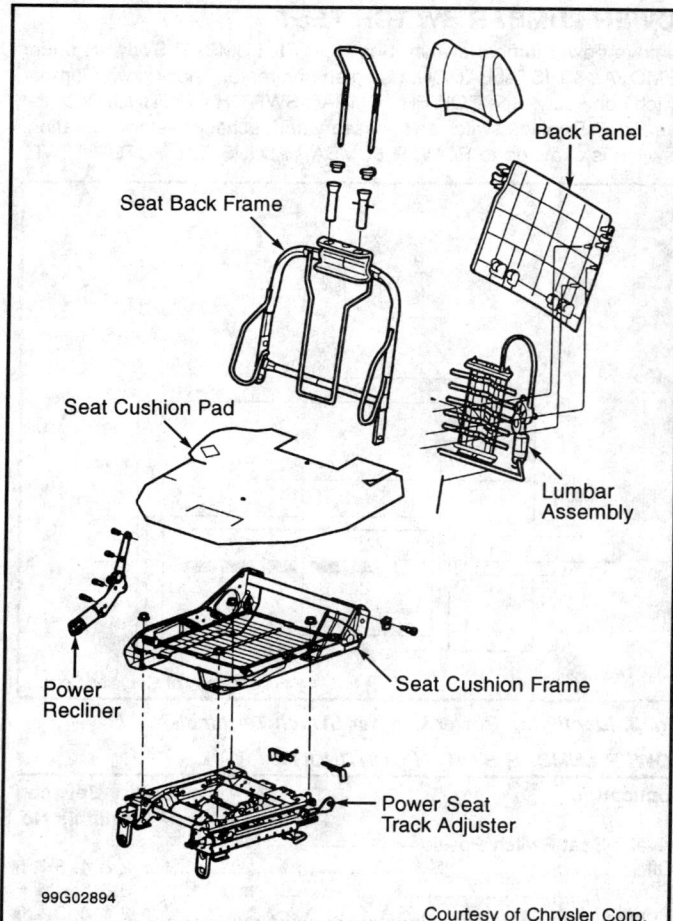

Fig. 5: Identifying Power Seat Components

POWER SEAT ADJUSTERS/MOTORS

Removal & Installation – Move power seat adjuster to full-up position and full-forward position (if possible). Disconnect negative battery cable. Disconnect seat belt switch wiring harness from inboard seat belt. Remove bolts/nuts that secure seat adjuster frame to floor pan. Disconnect power seat wiring harness connector. Remove seat from vehicle. Disconnect power seat motor connectors. Remove power seat adjuster/motor assembly. To install, reverse removal procedure.

WIRING DIAGRAMS

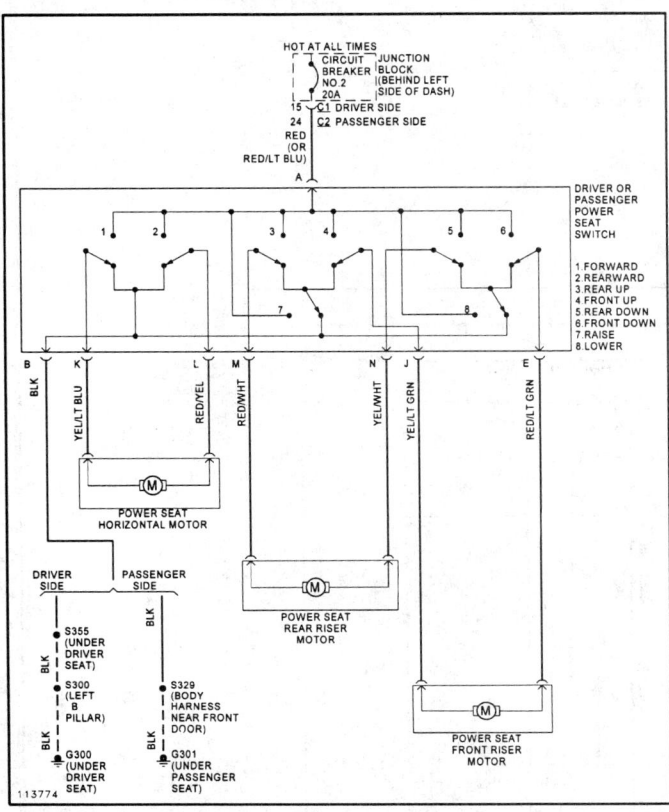

Fig. 6: Base Power Seat System Wiring Diagram (Grand Cherokee)

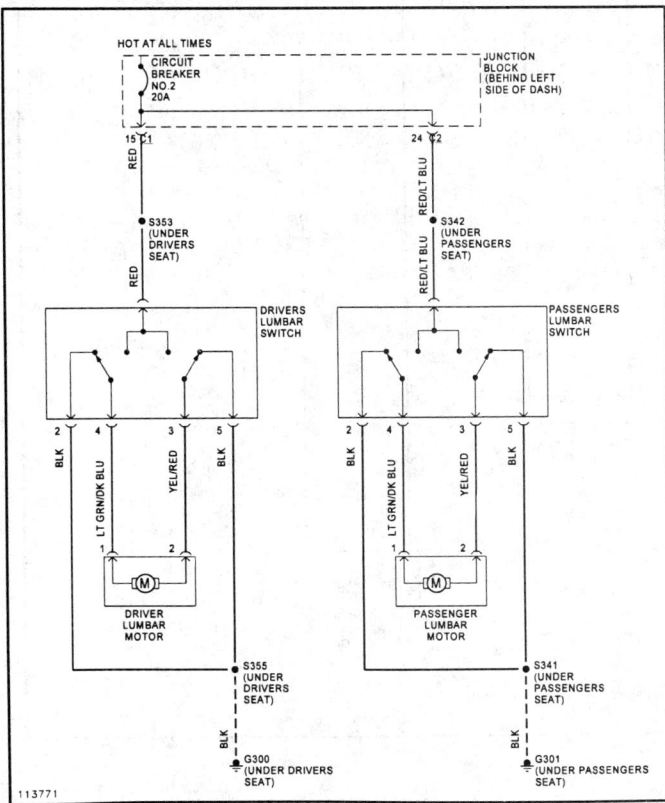

Fig. 7: Lumbar Power Seat System Wiring Diagram (Grand Cherokee)

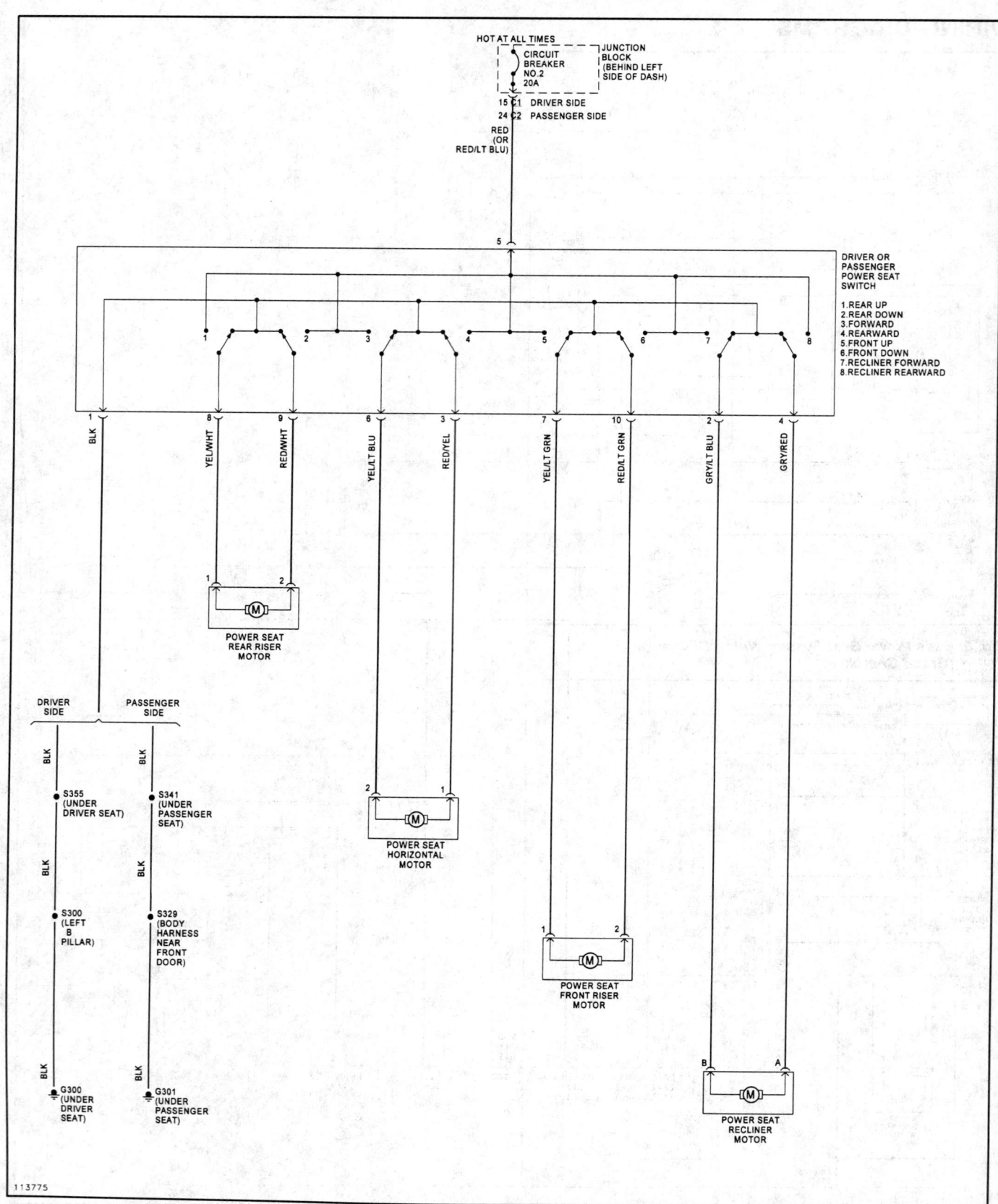

Fig. 8: Midline Power Seat System Wiring Diagram (Grand Cherokee)

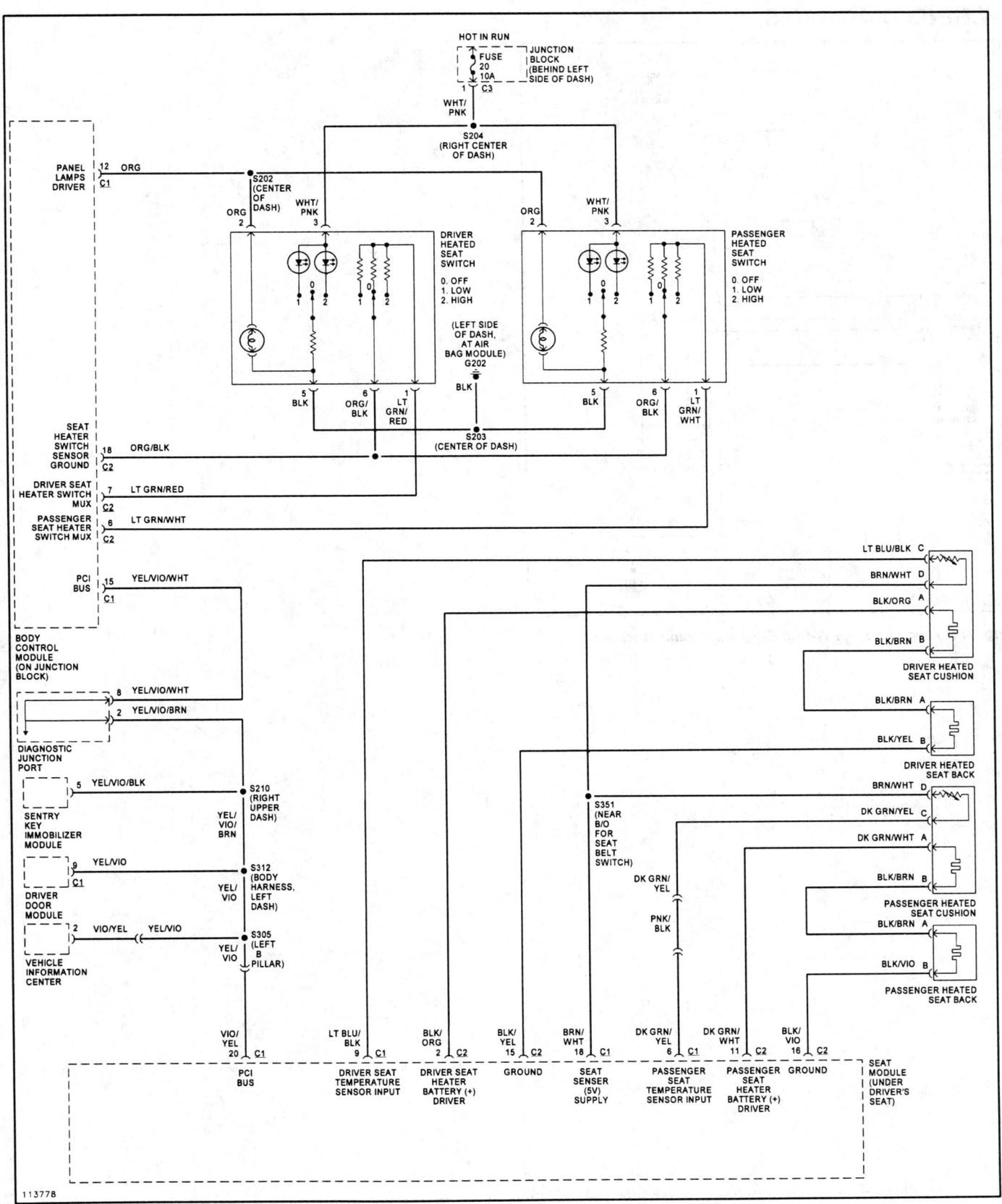

Fig. 9: Heated Seat System Wiring Diagram (Grand Cherokee)

WIRING DIAGRAMS

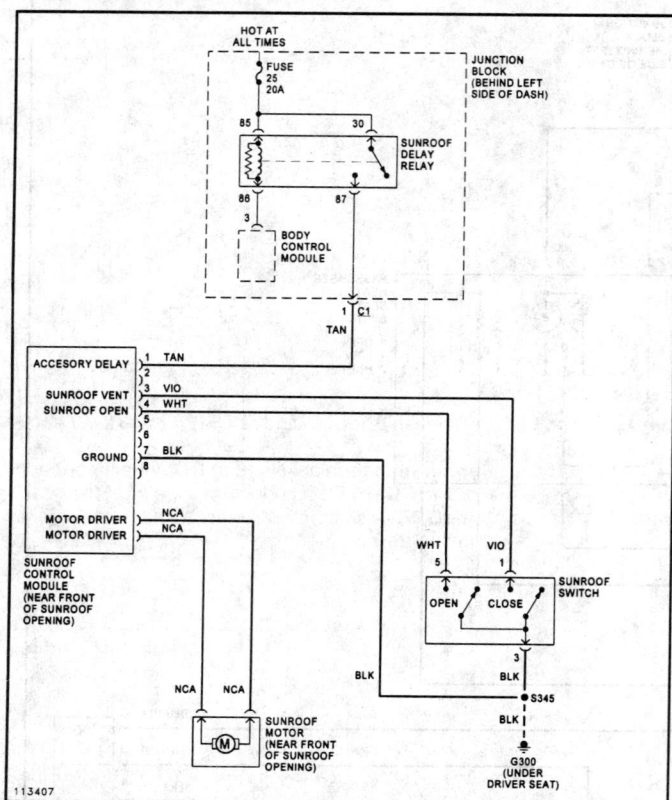

Fig. 1: Power Sun Roof Wiring Diagram (Grand Cherokee)

DESCRIPTION & OPERATION

Power windows are an optional feature on Cherokee. The power window system allows all door windows to be opened or closed by operating a switch on trim panel for each door. The master switch on driver's door trim panel can be operated to open or close any window. A lock-out switch on driver's door trim panel allows driver to disable all passenger door window switches.

Front door power window switches and power window lockout switch are integral to Driver Door Module (DDM) or Passenger Door Module (PDM), respectively. Rear door power window switches are stand alone units. An automatic resetting circuit breaker, located in fuse box is used to protect power window system circuit.

CIRCUIT BREAKER

1) Locate circuit breaker No. 28 in fuse box. Fuse box is located behind right kick panel. Pull out circuit breaker No. 28 slightly. Ensure circuit breaker terminals still contact terminals in fuse box. Turn ignition on. Measure voltage between ground and each terminal of circuit breaker No. 28.

2) If battery voltage is not present at either circuit breaker terminal, repair open between ignition switch and fuse box. If battery voltage is present at only one circuit breaker terminal, replace faulty circuit breaker.

DOOR MODULE

DIAGNOSTIC AIDS

Driver Door Module (DDM) contains master switches and lockout switch for power window system. The passenger front power window switch and rear power window switches (4-door models only) are supplied battery current through DDM power window lockout switch. In addition, ground for each individual power window switch is supplied through the DDM master switch. The one-touch down feature circuitry within the DDM will not operate power window motor if door glass, window regulator, or gearbox mechanism is stuck, obstructed or is binding. If driver front power window operates properly, but one-touch down feature is inoperative, replace faulty DDM. If problem being diagnosed is an inoperative power window switch illumination light but power window switch operates properly, replace faulty door module.

DOOR MODULE TESTING

Remove door module. See DOOR MODULE under REMOVAL & INSTALLATION. Check door module power window switch and/or power window lockout switch continuity. See POWER WINDOW SWITCH. Replace faulty door module as necessary. If switch(es) is okay, see POWER WINDOW MOTOR.

POWER WINDOW SWITCH

FRONT POWER WINDOW SWITCH

1) Front power window switch is integral to front door module. Remove suspect door module. See DOOR MODULE under REMOVAL & INSTALLATION.
2) With switch in specified position, check switch continuity. Continuity should exist between terminals being tested. See DRIVER DOOR MODULE POWER WINDOW SWITCH CONTINUITY or PASSENGER DOOR MODULE POWER WINDOW SWITCH CONTINUITY table. See Figs. 1 and 2.
3) If continuity is as specified, go to POWER WINDOW MOTOR. If continuity check is not as specified, replace faulty door module.

REAR POWER WINDOW SWITCH

1) Remove rear power window switch from door trim panel. See POWER WINDOW SWITCH under REMOVAL & INSTALLATION. With switch in specified position, check switch continuity.
2) Continuity should exist between terminals being tested. See REAR POWER WINDOW SWITCH CONTINUITY table. See Fig. 3. If continu-ity is as specified, go to POWER WINDOW MOTOR. If continuity is not as specified, replace faulty switch.

DRIVER DOOR MODULE POWER WINDOW SWITCH CONTINUITY

Switch Position	Check Continuity Between Terminals No.
Power Windows [1]	
Off	1 & 8; 2 & 8; 3 & 8; 4 & 8; 5 & 8; 6 & 8; 8 & 10; 8 & 12
Right Rear Down	1 & 9; 2 & 8
Right Rear Up	2 & 9; 1 & 8
Right Front Up	3 & 9; 6 & 8
Left Rear Up	4 & 9; 8 & 10
Left Front Up	5 & 9; 8 & 12
Right Front Down	6 & 9; 3 & 8
Left Rear Down	9 & 10; 4 & 8
Left Front Down	9 & 1; 5 & 8
Lock-Out Switch [2]	

[1] – Check continuity at Driver Door Module (DDM) 12-pin Blue connector. See Fig. 1.
[2] – Check for continuity between terminal No. 8 at DDM 8-pin connector and terminal No. 9 at DDM 12-pin connector. See Figs. 1 and 2. With lockout switch off (up position), continuity should exist. With lockout switch on (down position), continuity should not exist.

PASSENGER DOOR MODULE POWER WINDOW SWITCH CONTINUITY

Switch Position	[1] Check Continuity Between Terminals No.
Off	2 & 3; 4 & 9
Up	2 & 3; 9 & 10
Down	2 & 10; 4 & 9

[1] – Check continuity at Passenger Door Module (PDM) 12-pin Blue connector. See Fig. 1.

REAR POWER WINDOW SWITCH CONTINUITY

Switch Position	Check Continuity Between Terminals No.
Off	1 & 4; 2 & 5
Up	1 & 6; 2 & 5
Down	1 & 4; 5 & 6

POWER WINDOW MOTOR

NOTE: Before performing power window motor test, ensure power window switch is functioning properly. See POWER WINDOW SWITCH. Window glass must be free to slide up and down for power window motor to function properly. If glass does not move freely, motor will overload and trip the circuit breaker.

1) Remove door trim panel of window motor to be tested. See DOOR TRIM PANEL under REMOVAL & INSTALLATION. Disconnect power window motor connector. Using a 12-volt power source, connect 12-volts to one terminal of motor connector and ground to other terminal. Motor should operate.

NOTE: If window is in full up or full down position, motor will not operate in that direction by design.

2) Reverse 12-volt power source connections at motor connector. Motor should operate in opposite direction. If motor operates as specified, check wiring harness between power window switch and window motor. Also check window travel through complete opening and closing cycle. Check window for sticking, binding or improper adjustment. If window travel is not as specified, repair as necessary.

SYSTEM TESTS

ALL WINDOWS INOPERATIVE

1) Check circuit breaker for power window system. See CIRCUIT BREAKER. Replace circuit breaker as necessary. If circuit breaker is okay, go to next step.

2) Disconnect negative battery cable. Remove Driver Door Module (DDM). See DOOR MODULE under REMOVAL & INSTALLATION. Check for continuity between ground and terminal No. 5 (Black wire) at DDM 8-pin wiring harness connector. *See Fig. 2.* If continuity exists, go to next step. If continuity does not exist, repair open in Black wire ground circuit.

3) Reconnect negative battery cable. Turn ignition on. Measure voltage between ground and terminal No. 9 (Tan wire) at DDM 12-pin connector. *See Fig. 1.* If battery voltage is not present, repair open in Tan wire. If battery voltage is present, DDM power and ground circuits are okay. See DOOR MODULE.

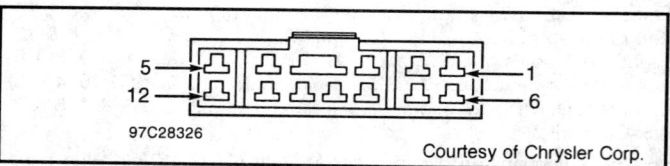

97C28326
Courtesy of Chrysler Corp.

Fig. 1: Identifying Door Module 12-Pin Wiring Harness Connector Terminals

ONE WINDOW INOPERATIVE

NOTE: Window glass must be free to slide up and down for power window motor to function properly. If glass is not free to move up and down, motor will overload and trip the circuit breaker.

1) Place window glass halfway between up and down positions. Verify glass can be moved slightly from side to side, front to rear, and up and down. If glass does not move freely, adjust glass or repair as necessary. If glass moves freely, go to next step.

2) Check power window switch continuity. See POWER WINDOW SWITCH. Replace faulty door module or power window switch as necessary. If switch is okay and driver's door window is inoperative, see POWER WINDOW MOTOR. If switch is okay and any door window is inoperative besides driver's window, go to next step.

3) Using an ohmmeter, check continuity of each circuit between inoperative Passenger Door Module (PDM) or power window switch wiring harness connector and corresponding Driver Door Module (DDM) wiring harness connector terminal. *See Figs. 1- 3.* See WIRING DIAGRAM.

4) If continuity exists in all circuits, power window switch and switch circuits are okay. See POWER WINDOW MOTOR. If continuity does not exist in one or more circuits, repair open circuit(s) as necessary.

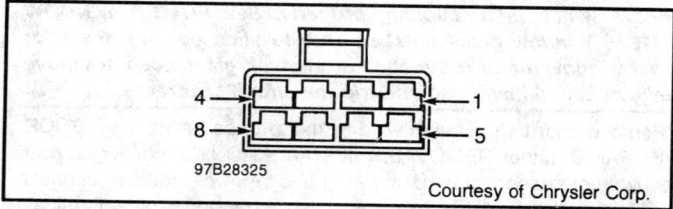

97B28325
Courtesy of Chrysler Corp.

Fig. 2: Identifying Door Module 8-Pin Wiring Harness Connector Terminals

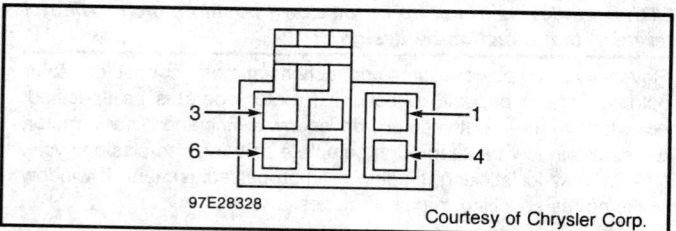

97E28328
Courtesy of Chrysler Corp.

Fig. 3: Identifying Rear Power Window Switch Wiring Harness Connector Terminals

REMOVAL & INSTALLATION
DOOR TRIM PANEL

Removal & Installation (Front Door Panel) – 1) Disconnect negative battery cable. Remove door panel screws. Using a trim stick, and starting at bottom of trim panel, gently pry around perimeter of trim panel.

2) Lift door trim upwards and away from door to disengage top of panel from inner weather-stripping. Pull door trim panel out far enough to access inside door latch release and lock linkage rods near back of inside door remote controls.

3) Disconnect ends of latch release and lock linkage rods and remove rod ends from inside door remote controls. Disconnect door module connectors. Remove door trim panel from door. To install, reverse removal procedure.

Removal & Installation (Rear Door Panel) – 1) Disconnect negative battery cable. Put window in down position. Remove door trim panel mounting screws. Using trim stick, beginning at bottom of door panel, gently pry around perimeter of trim panel.

2) Pull trim panel outward and disconnect handle-to-latch rods. Disconnect power window wiring harness connector. Remove trim panel from door. To install, reverse removal procedure.

DOOR MODULE

Removal & Installation – Door module is mounted to inside of front door trim panel. Remove front door trim panel. See DOOR TRIM PANEL. Remove screws securing door module to door trim panel. Remove door module from trim panel. To install, reverse removal procedure.

POWER WINDOW MOTOR

NOTE: Power window motor and mechanism is integral to power window regulator. If power window motor or mechanism is faulty, window regulator assembly must be replaced.

Removal & Installation (Front Window Motor) – 1) Disconnect negative battery cable. Remove front door trim panel. See DOOR TRIM PANEL. Pry up on weatherstrip corner and remove inner and outer weather-stripping. *See Fig. 4.* Put window in up position.

2) Remove bolts securing glass to regulator assembly. Carefully lift glass upward and out of door. Loosen regulator assembly mounting bolts/nuts. *See Fig. 5.*

3) Lift regulator assembly upward to release assembly from key hole slots. Remove regulator assembly through access hole in inner door panel. To install, reverse removal procedure.

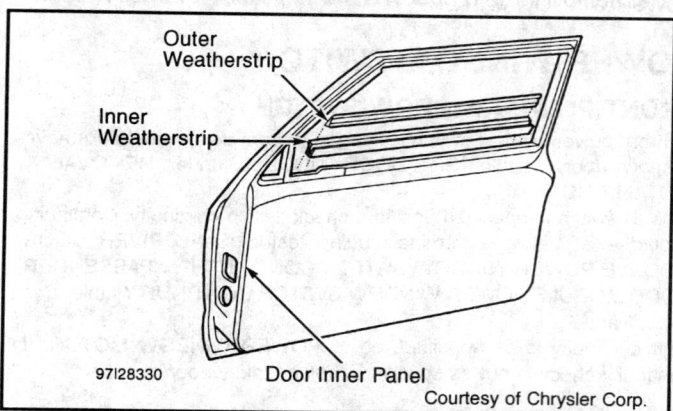

Outer Weatherstrip
Inner Weatherstrip
Door Inner Panel
97I28330
Courtesy of Chrysler Corp.

Fig. 4: Removing Front Window Weather-Stripping

Removal & Installation (Rear Window Motor) – 1) Disconnect negative battery cable. Remove rear door trim panel. See DOOR TRIM PANEL. Remove bolt securing glass to regulator assembly, and support glass. Remove lower regulator mounting bolts. *See Fig. 6.*

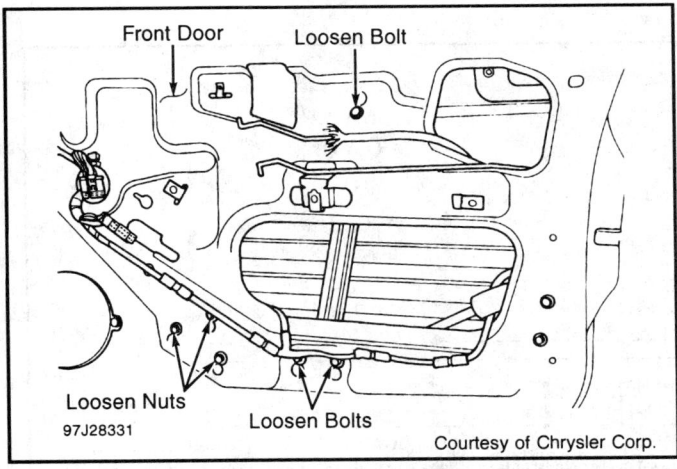

Fig. 5: Identifying Front Window Regulator Assembly Mounting Bolts

2) Remove window motor nuts. Loosen upper regulator mounting bolt. Disconnect window motor connector. Remove regulator and window motor assembly. To install, reverse removal procedure.

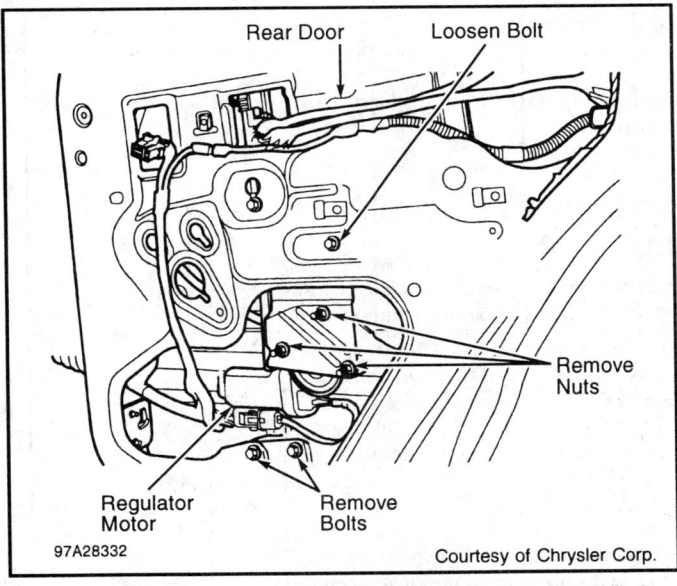

Fig. 6: Removing Rear Door Window Regulator & Power Window Assembly

POWER WINDOW SWITCH

NOTE: Front door power window switches and power window lockout switch are integral to Driver Door Module (DDM) or Passenger Door Module (PDM). If switch is faulty, door module must be replaced. See DOOR MODULE.

Removal & Installation (Rear Window Switch) – Disconnect negative battery cable. Remove rear door trim panel. See DOOR TRIM PANEL. Unsnap switch from receptacle in trim panel. To install, reverse removal procedure.

WIRING DIAGRAMS

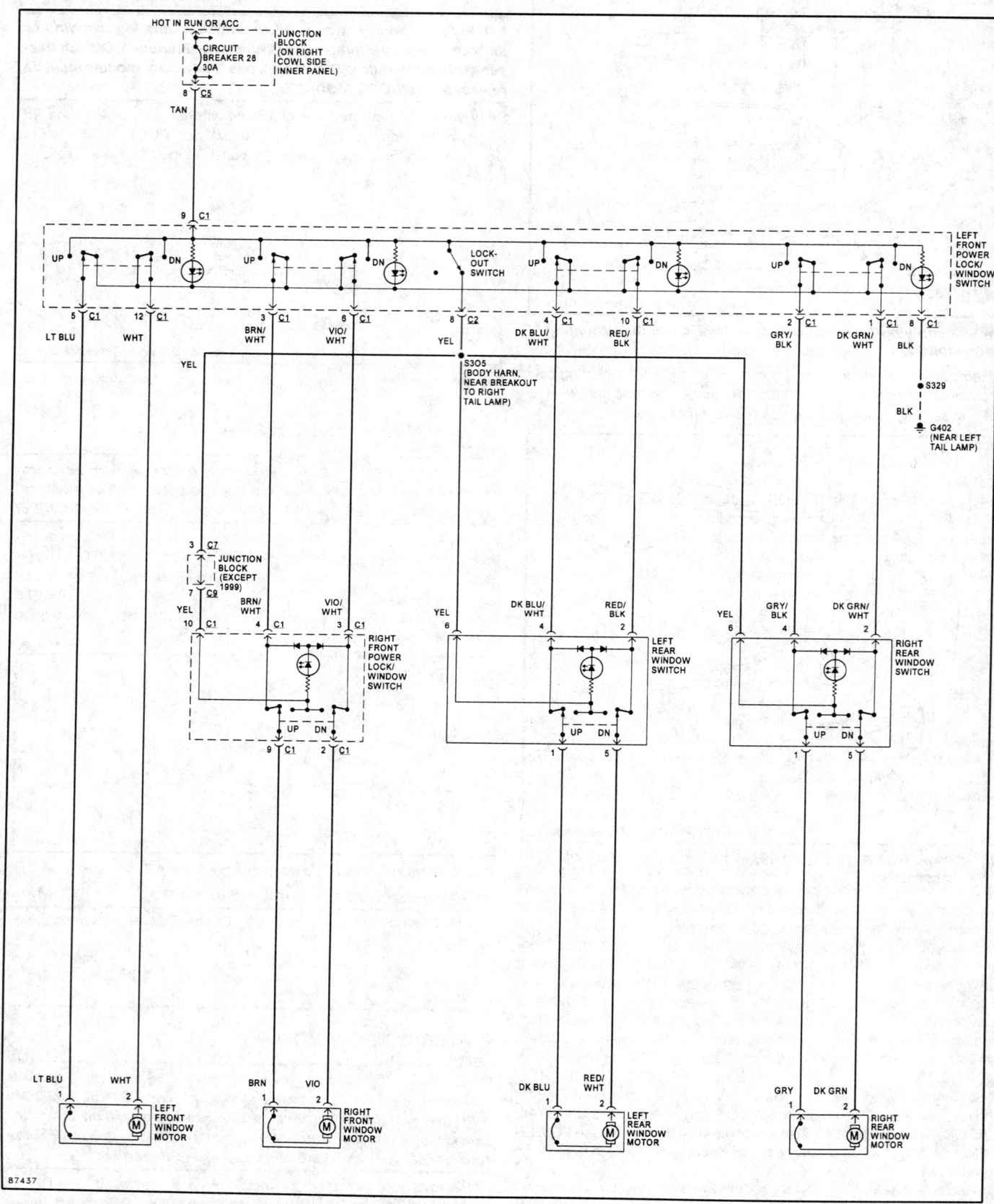

Fig. 7: Power Window System Wiring Diagram (Cherokee)

DESCRIPTION & OPERATION

Power windows are a standard feature on Grand Cherokee. The power window system allows all door windows to be opened or closed by operating a switch on trim panel for each door. The master switch on driver's door trim panel can be operated to open or close any window. A lock-out switch on drivers door trim panel allow driver to disable all passenger door window switches.

Power windows can be operated for up to 45 seconds after ignition is turned off, or until a front door is opened, whichever comes first. Front door power window switches and power window lock-out switch are integral to Driver Door Module (DDM) or Passenger Door Module (PDM), respectively. Rear door power window switches are stand alone units.

COMPONENT TESTS

DOOR MODULE

Diagnostic Aids – If problem being diagnosed is a rear door window that won't operate from rear door switch, but does operate from driver's master switch, see POWER WINDOW SWITCH. If problem is a passenger front or rear window that operates from that door switch, but does not operate from driver master switch, use scan tool to diagnose door modules and PCI data bus circuits. See BODY CONTROL COMPUTER – GRAND CHEROKEE article.

Door Module Testing – 1) Disconnect negative battery cable. Remove front door trim panel. See DOOR TRIM PANEL under REMOVAL & INSTALLATION. Verify door module connectors are properly connected. Repair as necessary and recheck system operation. If connectors are properly connected, go to next step.

2) Disconnect door module 15-pin connector. Using an ohmmeter, check for continuity between ground and terminal No. 4 (Black wire) at door module 15-pin wiring harness connector. *See Fig. 1 or 3.* If continuity exists, go to next step. If continuity does not exist, repair open ground circuit.

3) Connect negative battery cable. Using a voltmeter, measure voltage between ground and terminal No. 1 (Tan/Light Blue wire) at door module 15-pin wiring harness connector. If battery voltage is present, go to next step (inoperative front window), or go to step **7)** (inoperative rear window). If battery voltage is not present, repair open circuit to PDC.

4) Disconnect negative battery cable. Disconnect inoperative power window motor connector. Using an ohmmeter, check for continuity between ground and terminals No. 13 (Light Brown wire on driver's side; Brown wire on passenger's side) and 15 (White wire on driver's side; Violet wire on passenger's side) at door module 15-pin wiring harness connector. Continuity should not exist at either terminal. If continuity does not exist, go to next step. If continuity exists, repair short to ground.

5) Check for continuity on circuits between door module connector and window motor connector. If continuity does not exist, repair open circuit as necessary. If continuity exists, go to next step.

6) Reconnect door module connector. Disconnect window motor connector. Connect negative battery cable. Turn ignition on. Connect a voltmeter between window motor wiring harness connector terminals. Battery voltage should be present with power window switch in up or down position. No voltage should be present with switch in neutral (off) position. If voltage is not as specified, replace door module. If voltage is as specified, door module test is complete. Go to POWER WINDOW MOTOR.

7) Disconnect negative battery cable. Remove rear door power window switch. See POWER WINDOW SWITCH under REMOVAL & INSTALLATION. Check rear door power window switch continuity. See POWER WINDOW SWITCH. Replace switch as necessary. If switch is okay, go to next step.

8) Reconnect rear door power window switch connector. Disconnect inoperative power window motor connector. Check for continuity between ground and terminal No. 3 (Dark Blue wire on driver's side or Gray wire on passenger's side) and terminal No. 2 (Red/White wire on driver's side or Dark Green wire on passenger's side) at door module

15-pin wiring harness connector. If continuity does not exist, go to next step. If continuity exists, repair short to ground in appropriate circuit.

9) Check for continuity of circuits between door module connector and power window motor connector of inoperative window. If continuity does not exist, repair open circuit. If continuity exists, go to next step.

10) Reconnect door module connector. Connect negative battery cable. Turn ignition on. Measure voltage between ground and each terminal of power window motor wiring harness connector. With power window switch in neutral position (off), battery voltage should be present at each terminal. Also, each terminal should have battery voltage in one other switch position, either up or down. If voltage is not as specified, replace door module. If voltage is as specified, go to POWER WINDOW MOTOR for testing.

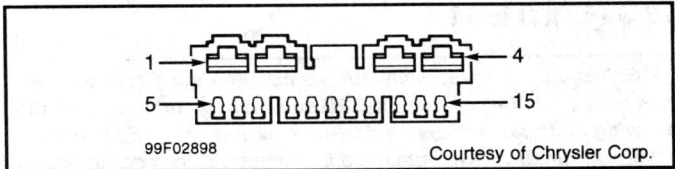

99F02898   Courtesy of Chrysler Corp.

Fig. 1: Identifying Passenger Door Module 15-Pin Connector Terminals

POWER WINDOW SWITCH

NOTE: The following test is for rear door power window switches. Front door power window switches are integral to door modules. For front door power window switch testing, see DOOR MODULE.

Disconnect negative battery cable. Remove rear power window switch from door trim panel. See POWER WINDOW SWITCH under REMOVAL & INSTALLATION. With switch in specified position, check switch continuity. See REAR POWER WINDOW SWITCH CONTINUITY table. *See Fig. 2.* Replace switch as necessary. If switch is okay, go to POWER WINDOW MOTOR.

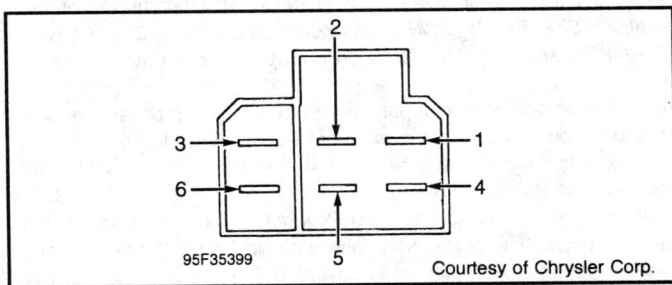

95F35399   Courtesy of Chrysler Corp.

Fig. 2: Identifying Rear Power Window Switch Terminals

REAR POWER WINDOW SWITCH CONTINUITY

Switch Position	Check Between Terminals No.
All Positions (LED)	3 & 6
Off	1 & 2; 4 & 5
Up	1 & 2; 5 & 6
Down	2 & 6; 4 & 5

POWER WINDOW MOTOR

NOTE: Before performing power window motor test, ensure power window switch is functioning properly. See POWER WINDOW SWITCH. Window glass must be free to slide up and down for power window motor to function properly. If glass does not move freely, motor will overload and trip the circuit breaker.

1) Remove door trim panel of window motor to be tested. See DOOR TRIM PANEL under REMOVAL & INSTALLATION. Disconnect power window motor connector. Using a 12-volt power source, connect 12-volts to one terminal of motor connector and ground to other terminal. Motor should operate.

NOTE: If window is at full extent of its travel in full up or full down position, motor is designed to no longer operate in that direction.

2) Reverse 12-volt power source connections at motor connector. Motor should operate in opposite direction. If motor operates as specified, check wiring harness between power window switch and window motor. Also, check window travel through complete opening and closing cycle. Check window for sticking, binding or improper adjustment. If window travel is not as specified, repair as necessary.

SYSTEM TESTS

NOTE: Manufacturer recommends using DRB scan tool to diagnose power window system. If DRB scan tool is not available, the following tests can be used to diagnose hard-wired components of power system, but results may be inconclusive. In order to obtain conclusive testing of power window system, Programmable Communications Interface (PCI) data bus network and all modules that provide inputs to, or receive outputs from power window system, must be checked. See BODY CONTROL COMPUTER TESTS – GRAND CHEROKEE article.

ALL WINDOWS INOPERATIVE

NOTE: Driver Door Module (DDM) circuitry controls output to left front and left rear power window motors. Passenger Door Module (PDM) circuitry controls output to right front and right rear power window motors. See WIRING DIAGRAMS.

1) Check operation of driver's power lock switch. If all door locks operate, use scan tool to check BCM, DDM and PCI data bus for proper operation. See BODY CONTROL COMPUTER TESTS – GRAND CHEROKEE article. If door locks do not operate properly, go to next step.

2) Check operation of passenger's power lock switch. If passenger side doors lock and unlock, but driver's door does not, go to step **5)**. If all power door locks and power windows are inoperative from both front door switches, go to next step.

3) Check fuse No. 12 (50-amp) in Power Distribution Center (PDC) located in engine compartment. If fuse is blown, repair short circuit and replace fuse. If fuse is okay, go to next step.

4) Check for battery voltage at fuse No. 12 in PDC. If battery voltage does not exist, repair open circuit between battery and PDC. If battery voltage exists, go to next step.

5) Disconnect negative battery cable. Remove driver's door trim panel. Disconnect DDM 15-pin connector. Check for continuity between ground and DDM 15-pin connector terminal No. 4 (Black wire). *See Fig. 3.* If continuity does not exist, repair open ground circuit. If continuity exists, go to next step.

6) Reconnect negative battery cable. Check for battery voltage at DDM 15-pin connector terminal No. 9 (Yellow/Violet wire). If battery voltage does not exist, repair open circuit between battery and PDC. If battery voltage exists, replace DDM.

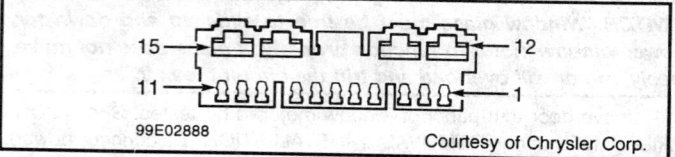

99E02888   Courtesy of Chrysler Corp.

Fig. 3: Identifying Driver Door Module (DDM) 15-Pin Wiring Harness Connector Terminals

PASSENGER'S SIDE FRONT AND REAR WINDOWS INOPERATIVE

If driver's side front and rear windows operate, but passenger's side front and rear windows do not, use scan tool to check PCI data bus for proper operation. See BODY CONTROL COMPUTER TESTS – GRAND CHEROKEE article.

ONE WINDOW INOPERATIVE

NOTE: Window glass must be free to slide up and down for power window motor to function properly. If glass is not free to move up and down, motor will overload and trip the circuit breaker.

Place window glass halfway between up and down positions. Verify glass can be moved slightly from side to side, front to rear, and up and down. If glass is not free to move, adjust or replace glass as necessary. If glass moves freely, go to DOOR MODULE under COMPONENT TESTS.

REMOVAL & INSTALLATION
DOOR TRIM PANEL

Removal & Installation (Front Door Panel) – Remove plug from mirror flag bezel. Remove trim panel attaching screws. Using trim stick, detach trim panel push-in fasteners. Lift trim panel upward and separate from door. Disconnect all necessary wire connectors. Disconnect latch rods from inside handle actuator. Remove trim panel. To install, reverse removal procedure.

Removal & Installation (Rear Door Panel) – **1)** Disconnect negative battery cable. Remove bezel near inside door latch release handle by inserting a flat-blade screwdriver in notched end and prying gently upward.

2) Remove door trim panel mounting screw located in bezel opening, near inside door latch release handle. Remove trim cap and screw near rear of door armrest. Using trim stick, beginning at bottom of door panel, gently pry around perimeter of trim panel. Pull door panel out and disconnect power window switch connector. Remove trim panel. To install, reverse removal procedure.

DOOR MODULE

Removal & Installation – Door module is mounted to inside of front door trim panel. Remove front door trim panel. See DOOR TRIM PANEL. Remove screws securing door module to door trim panel. Remove door module from trim panel. To install, reverse removal procedure.

POWER WINDOW MOTOR

Removal & Installation – Disconnect negative battery cable. Remove window regulator. See WINDOW REGULATOR. Remove screws holding window motor to regulator. Remove window motor. To install, reverse removal procedure. Tighten window motor mounting screws to 80 INCH lbs. (9 N.m).

WINDOW REGULATOR

Front Door – **1)** Lower glass to full down position. Remove door trim panel. See DOOR TRIM PANEL. Remove inner and outer belt weatherstrips. Raise glass to 3/4 up position. Remove door insulator. Remove clips attaching glass to lift plate. Push bottom of glass outward to disengage studs. Lift glass out of door.

2) Loosen window regulator-to-door bolts. Remove uppermost window regulator-to-door bolt. *See Fig. 4.* Lift regulator upward to disengage bolts from door. Disconnect power window motor wire connector. Remove regulator through access hole. To install, reverse removal procedure.

Rear Door – **1)** Remove door trim panel. See DOOR TRIM PANEL. Lower window glass. Pull run weatherstrip from fixed glass. Remove fixed glass module fasteners. Remove fixed glass module. Raise and support window glass.

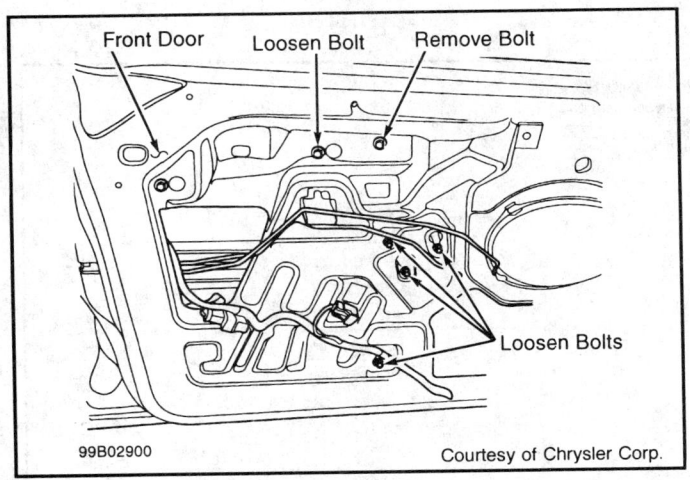

Front Door   Loosen Bolt   Remove Bolt

Loosen Bolts

99B02900   Courtesy of Chrysler Corp.

Fig. 4: Removing Front Window Regulator

2) Remove clips attaching window glass to lift plate. Remove window glass. Remove window regulator mounting bolts. Remove window regulator. To install, reverse removal procedure. Operate window and check operation.

POWER WINDOW SWITCH

NOTE: Front door power window switches are integral to Driver Door Module (DDM) and Passenger Door Module (PDM). If switch is faulty, door module must be replaced. See DOOR MODULE.

Removal & Installation (Rear Window Switch) – Remove rear door trim panel. See DOOR TRIM PANEL. Disconnect power window switch connector. Unsnap switch from receptacle in trim panel. To install, reverse removal procedure.

WIRING DIAGRAMS

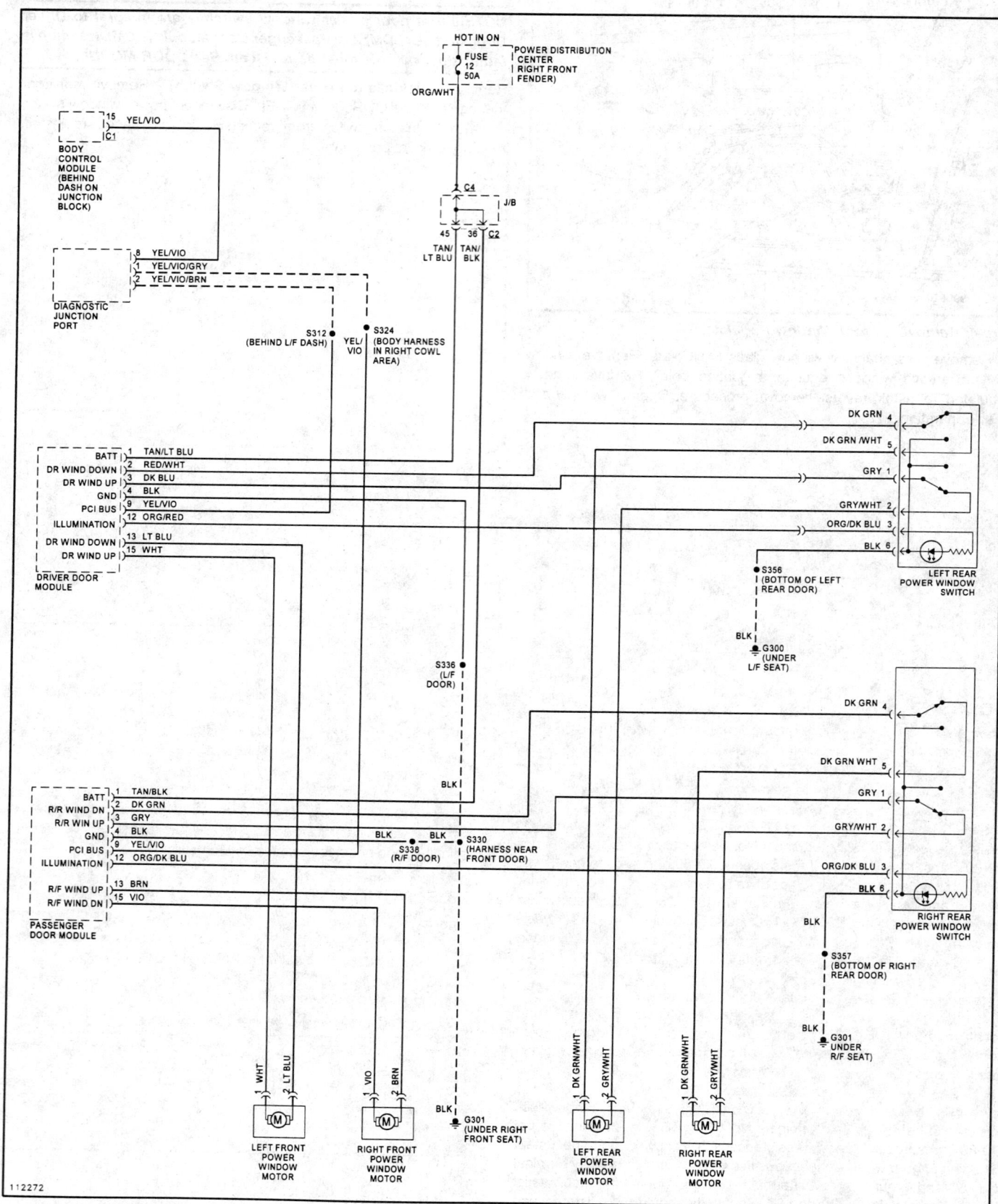

Fig. 5: Power Window System Wiring Diagram (Grand Cherokee)

DESCRIPTION & OPERATION

Multifunction switch incorporates headlight dimmer/passing, turn signal, and hazard warning switches into one unit. *See Fig. 1.* The ignition switch is mounted on steering column.

WARNING: All models are equipped with air bag system. To avoid injury from accidental air bag deployment, read and carefully follow all WARNINGS and SERVICE PRECAUTIONS. See AIR BAG RESTRAINT SYSTEMS article. DO NOT apply electrical power to any component on steering column without first deactivating air bag system. Air bag may deploy.

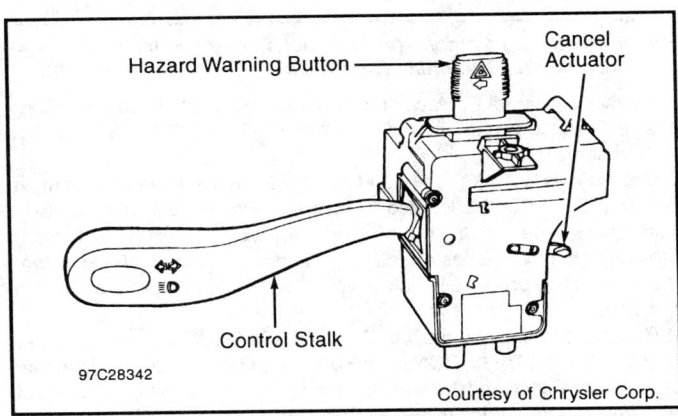

Fig. 1: Identifying Multifunction Switch

COMPONENT TESTS

HAZARD SWITCH

See TURN SIGNAL/HAZARD WARNING SWITCH under SYSTEM TESTS.

HORN RELAY

Cherokee – 1) Remove horn relay from fuse box located behind right kick panel. Using an ohmmeter, check for continuity between relay terminals No. 87A and 30. *See Fig. 2.* If continuity does not exist, replace relay. If continuity exists, go to next step.

2) Check for continuity between relay terminals No. 30 and 87. If continuity exists, replace relay. If continuity does not exist, check resistance between relay terminals No. 85 and 86. If resistance is not 70-80 ohms, replace relay. If resistance is 70-80 ohms, go to next step.

3) Using jumper wires, connect positive battery voltage to relay terminal No. 86 and ground to relay terminal No. 85. Continuity should exist between terminals No. 30 and 87. Continuity should not exist between relay terminals No. 87A and 30. If continuity is not as specified, replace relay. If continuity is as specified, relay is okay. Go to HORN RELAY CIRCUIT TEST.

Wrangler – 1) Remove horn relay from Power Distribution Center (PDC) located in engine compartment. Use label on PDC cover to identify and locate relay. Using an ohmmeter, check for continuity between relay terminals No. 87A and 30. *See Fig. 3.* If continuity does not exist, replace relay. If continuity exists, go to next step.

2) Check for continuity between relay terminals No. 30 and 87. If continuity exists, replace relay. If continuity does not exist, check resistance between relay terminals No. 85 and 86. If resistance is not 70-80 ohms, replace relay. If resistance is 70-80 ohms, go to next step.

3) Using jumper wires, connect positive battery voltage to relay terminal No. 86 and ground to relay terminal No. 85. Continuity should exist between terminals No. 30 and 87. Continuity should not exist between relay terminals No. 87A and 30. If continuity is not as specified, replace relay. If continuity is as specified, relay is okay. Go to HORN RELAY CIRCUIT TEST.

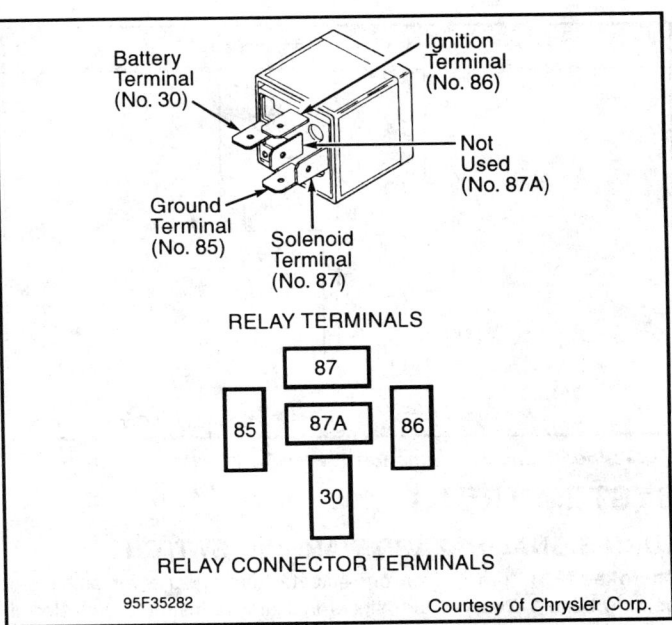

Fig. 2: Identifying Horn Relay Terminals (Cherokee)

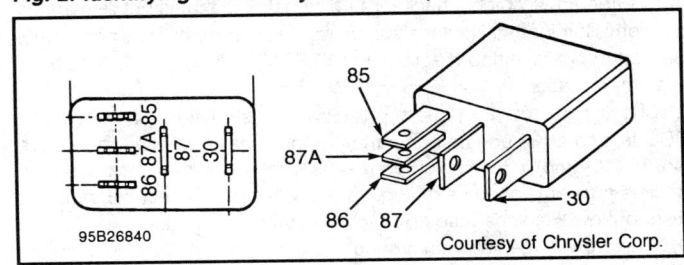

Fig. 3: Identifying Horn Relay Terminals (Wrangler)

IGNITION SWITCH

1) Disconnect negative battery cable. Remove upper and lower steering column covers. Disconnect ignition switch connector.

2) With ignition switch in ON position, check for continuity between ignition switch terminals No. 3 (Pink/Black wire terminal) and No. 10 (Yellow wire terminal). If continuity does not exist, go to next step. If continuity exists, replace ignition switch.

3) With ignition switch in START position, check for continuity between ignition switch terminals No. 3 and 10. If continuity exists, switch is okay. If continuity does not exist, replace ignition switch.

MULTIFUNCTION SWITCH

Disconnect multifunction switch connector. See MULTIFUNCTION SWITCH under REMOVAL & INSTALLATION for access to multifunction switch connector. Check multifunction switch continuity. See MULTIFUNCTION SIGNAL SWITCH CONTINUITY table. *See Fig. 4.* Replace multifunction switch as necessary.

MULTIFUNCTION SIGNAL SWITCH CONTINUITY

Switch Position	Continuity Between Terminals
Hazard Switch	B & E; C & H; C & K; C & I; C & J
Turn Signal Switch	
Neutral	F & H; F & K; A & E
Left	F & H; C & K; C & I; A & E
Right	F & K; C & H; C & J; A & E

WIPER SWITCH

For wiper switch testing information, see appropriate WIPER/WASHER SYSTEMS article.

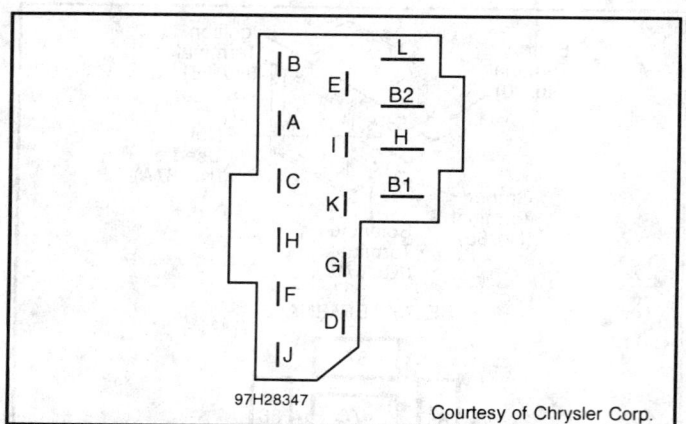

97H28347

Courtesy of Chrysler Corp.

Fig. 4: Identifying Multifunction Switch Terminals

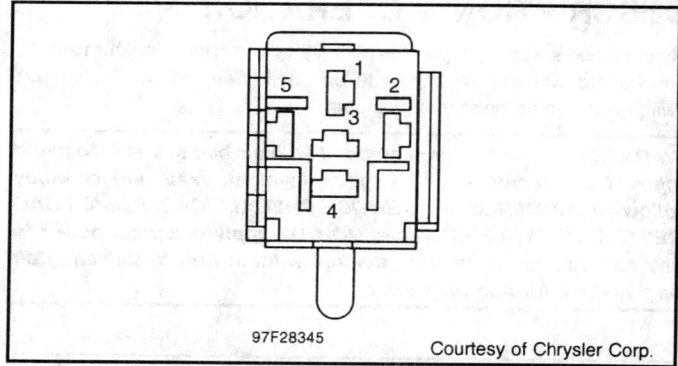

97F28345

Courtesy of Chrysler Corp.

Fig. 5: Identifying Combination Flasher Wiring Harness Connector Terminals (Cherokee)

SYSTEM TESTS

TURN SIGNAL/HAZARD WARNING SWITCH

Cherokee – 1) Turn ignition on. Actuate turn signal lever or hazard warning button. Observe turn signal indicator in instrument cluster. If turn signal indicator is off, go to next step. If turn signal indicator flash rate is abnormally high, check for turn signal bulb that is not illuminated or poorly illuminated. Replace bulb or repair circuit to bulb as necessary. See appropriate wiring diagram in EXTERIOR LIGHTS article. Check system operation.

2) Check fuse No. 20 (15-amp) in Power Distribution Center (PDC). PDC is located in engine compartment, near battery. Also, check fuse No. 12 (10-amp) in fuse box. Fuse box is located behind right kick panel. If fuses are okay, go to next step. If fuse(s) is blown, check for cause of fuse to blow. Replace fuse and recheck system operation.

3) Measure voltage between ground and power side of fuse No. 20 (Red wire) in fuse holder at PDC. If battery voltage is not present, repair open circuit. If battery voltage is present, turn ignition switch on. Measure voltage between ground and power side of fuse No. 12 (Black/Orange wire) in fuse holder at fuse box. If battery voltage is present, go to next step. If battery voltage is not present, repair open circuit.

4) Turn ignition off. Remove combination flasher from fuse box. Install a known-good combination flasher. Turn ignition on. Check turn signal and hazard flasher operation. If system does not function properly, remove test flasher and go to next step. If system operates properly, replace faulty combination flasher.

5) Turn ignition on. Turn hazard warning flasher on. Measure voltage between ground and terminal No. 1 (Black wire) at combination flasher wiring harness connector. See Fig. 5. If battery voltage is present, go to next step. If battery voltage is not present, go to step **8)**.

6) Turn ignition off. Measure voltage between ground and terminal No. 2 (Black/Pink wire) at combination flasher wiring harness connector. If battery voltage is present, go to next step. If battery voltage is not present, go to step **8)**.

7) Check for continuity between ground and terminal No. 5 (Black wire) at combination flasher wiring harness connector. If continuity exists, go to next step. If continuity does not exist, repair open Black wire between combination flasher wiring harness connector and ground.

8) Disconnect multifunction switch connector. See MULTIFUNCTION SWITCH under REMOVAL & INSTALLATION for access to multifunction switch connector. Check continuity of Red/White and Violet/Tan wires between multifunction switch connector and combination flasher wiring harness connector. See WIRING DIAGRAMS. If continuity does not exist in one or both wires, repair open circuit as necessary. If continuity exists in both wires, check multifunction switch. See MULTIFUNCTION SWITCH under COMPONENT TESTS.

Wrangler – 1) Turn ignition on. Actuate turn signal lever or hazard warning button. Observe turn signal indicator in instrument cluster. If turn signal indicator is off, go to next step. If turn signal indicator flash rate is abnormally high, check for turn signal bulb that is not illuminated

or poorly illuminated. Replace bulb or repair circuit to bulb as necessary. See appropriate wiring diagram in EXTERIOR LIGHTS article. Check system operation.

2) Check fuses No. 3 (30-amp) and No. 9 (20-amp) in Power Distribution Center (PDC). PDC is located in engine compartment, near battery. Also, check fuse No. 13 (10-amp) in fuse box. Fuse box is located behind glove box. If fuses are okay, go to next step. If fuse(s) is blown, check for cause of fuse to blow. Replace fuse and recheck system operation.

3) Remove combination flasher. See COMBINATION FLASHER under REMOVAL & INSTALLATION. Install a known-good combination flasher. Check turn signal and hazard flasher operation. If system does not function properly, remove test flasher and go to next step. If system operates properly, replace faulty combination flasher.

4) Turn ignition on. Measure voltage between ground and terminal No. 6 (Red/White wire) at combination flasher wiring harness connector. See Fig. 6. If battery voltage is present, go to next step. If battery voltage is not present, go to step **7)**.

5) Turn ignition off. Turn hazard warning switch on. Measure voltage between ground and terminal No. 6 (Red/White wire) at combination flasher wiring harness connector. If battery voltage is present, turn hazard warning switch off and go to next step. If battery voltage is not present, go to step **7)**.

6) Check for continuity between ground and terminal No. 4 (Black wire) at combination flasher wiring harness connector. If continuity exists, go to next step. If continuity does not exist, repair open Black wire between combination flasher wiring harness connector and ground.

7) Disconnect multifunction switch connector. See MULTIFUNCTION SWITCH under REMOVAL & INSTALLATION for access to multifunction switch connector. Check continuity of Red/White wire between terminal No. 11 at multifunction switch connector and terminal No. 6 at combination flasher wiring harness connector. See Figs. 6 and 7. If continuity exists, go to next step. If continuity does not exist, repair open Red/White wire between multifunction switch wiring harness connector and combination flasher wiring harness connector.

8) Check continuity of Pink wire between terminal No. 4 at multifunction switch wiring harness connector and terminal No. 2 at combination wiring harness connector. If continuity does not exist, repair open Pink wire between multifunction switch and combination flasher connector. If continuity exists, check multifunction switch. See MULTIFUNCTION SWITCH under COMPONENT TESTS.

HORN SWITCH CIRCUIT TEST

Cherokee – 1) Disconnect negative battery cable. Remove lower steering column cover. Using an ohmmeter, check for continuity between ground and metal steering column jacket. If continuity exists, go to next step. If continuity does not exist, check for proper installation of steering column mounting nuts.

2) Disable air bag system and remove driver air bag module. See AIR BAG RESTRAINT SYSTEMS article. Remove horn relay from fuse box. Fuse box is located behind right kick panel. Check for continuity between ground and Black/Red wire at steering column horn switch

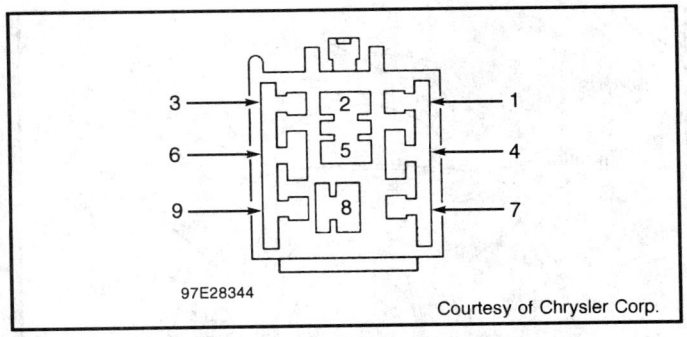

Fig. 6: Identifying Combination Flasher Wiring Harness Connector Terminals (Wrangler)

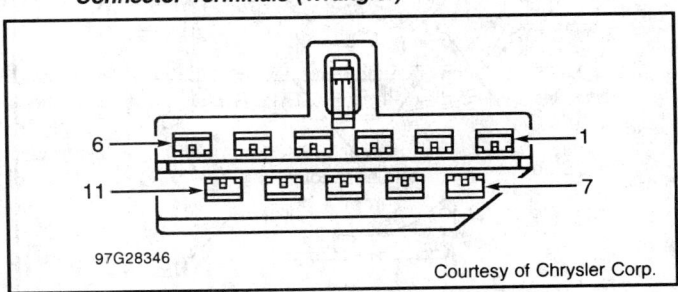

Fig. 7: Identifying Multifunction Switch Wiring Harness Connector Terminals (Wrangler)

connector. If continuity does not exist, go to next step. If continuity exists, repair short to ground in Black/Red wire.

3) Check continuity of Black/Red wire between steering column horn switch connector and terminal No. 85 at horn relay wiring harness connector. *See Fig. 2.* If continuity does not exist, repair open Black/Red wire. If continuity exists, check for continuity between horn switch wires (power and ground circuits) at air bag module.

4) Continuity should exist with horn switch depressed. Continuity should not exist with horn switch released. If continuity is not as specified, replace horn switch. If continuity is as specified, install horn relay and go to HORN CIRCUIT TEST.

Wrangler – 1) Disconnect negative battery cable. Remove lower steering column cover. Using an ohmmeter, check for continuity between ground and metal steering column jacket. If continuity exists, go to next step. If continuity does not exist, check for proper installation of steering column mounting nuts.

2) Disable air bag system and remove driver air bag module. See AIR BAG RESTRAINT SYSTEMS article. Remove horn relay from Power Distribution Center (PDC). PDC is located in engine compartment, near battery. Use label on PDC cover to identify and locate relay. Check for continuity between ground and Red/Yellow wire at steering column horn switch connector. If continuity does not exist, go to next step. If continuity exists, repair short to ground in Red/Yellow wire.

3) Check continuity of Red/Yellow wire between steering column horn switch connector and terminal No. 15 at horn relay wiring harness connector. *See Fig. 8.* If continuity does not exist, repair open Red/Yellow wire. If continuity exists, check for continuity between horn switch wires (power and ground circuits) at air bag module.

4) Continuity should exist with horn switch depressed. Continuity should not exist with horn switch released. If continuity is not as specified, replace horn switch. If continuity is as specified, install horn relay and go to HORN CIRCUIT TEST.

HORN RELAY CIRCUIT TEST

Cherokee – 1) Check fuse No. 21 (15-amp) in fuse box, located behind right kick panel. If fuse is blown, check for cause of fuse to blow. Replace fuse and check horn operation. If fuse is okay, go to next step.

2) Remove horn relay from fuse box, located behind right kick panel. Measure voltage between ground and horn relay wiring harness connector terminals for relay terminals No. 30 and 86. See WIRING DIAGRAMS. If battery voltage is present at both terminals, go to next

step. If battery voltage is not present at one or both terminals, repair open circuit between horn wiring harness connector and battery.

3) Disconnect both horn connectors. Using an ohmmeter, check continuity of Dark Green/Red wire between horn relay wiring harness connector and each horn wiring harness connector. If continuity exists, go to next step. If continuity does not exist, repair open Dark Green/Red wire.

4) Using an ohmmeter, check for continuity between ground and Black/Red wire at relay wiring harness connector. With horn switch depressed, continuity should exist. With horn switch released, continuity should not exist. If continuity is not as specified, go to HORN SWITCH CIRCUIT TEST. If continuity is as specified, no fault is indicated in relay circuits.

Wrangler – 1) Check fuse No. 17 (20-amp) in Power Distribution Center (PDC). PDC is located in engine compartment, near battery. If fuse is blown, check for cause of fuse to blow. Replace fuse and check horn operation. If fuse is okay, go to next step.

2) Remove horn relay from PDC. Use label on PDC cover to identify and locate relay. Measure voltage between ground and terminals No. 11 (Violet wire) and No. 13 (Violet wire) at relay wiring harness connector. *See Fig. 8.* If battery voltage is present at both terminals, go to next step. If battery voltage is not present at one or both terminals, repair open Violet wire.

3) Disconnect both horn connectors. Using an ohmmeter, check continuity of White/Red wire between terminal No. 12 at relay wiring harness connector and each horn wiring harness connector. If continuity exists, go to next step. If continuity does not exist, repair open White/Red wire.

4) Using an ohmmeter, check for continuity between ground and terminal No. 15 (Red/Yellow wire) at relay wiring harness connector. With horn switch depressed, continuity should exist. With horn switch released, continuity should not exist. If continuity is not as specified, go to HORN SWITCH CIRCUIT TEST. If continuity is as specified, no fault is indicated in relay circuits.

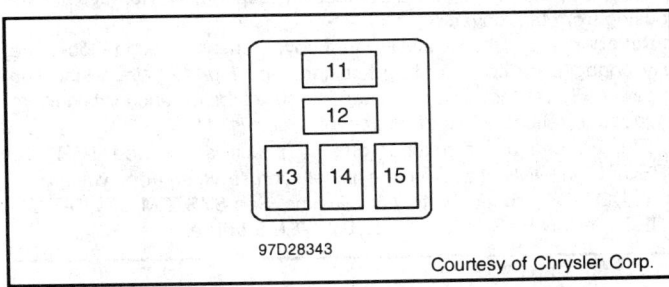

Fig. 8: Identifying Horn Relay Wiring Harness Connector Terminals (Wrangler)

HORN CIRCUIT TEST

Cherokee – 1) Check for continuity between ground and horn mounting bracket(s). Continuity should exist. If continuity does not exist, clean and tighten horn mounting hardware. If continuity exists, go to next step.

2) Disconnect horn connector(s). Using a voltmeter, measure voltage between ground and Dark Green/Red wire(s). Voltage should be zero volts. If any voltage exists, repair short circuit or replace faulty horn relay. If voltage is zero volts, go to next step.

3) Depress horn switch. Battery voltage should now exist at Dark Green/Red wire(s). If battery voltage does not exist, repair horn circuit. If battery voltage exists, replace horn(s).

Wrangler – 1) Disconnect horn connector. Using an ohmmeter, check for continuity between ground and Black wire at horn wiring harness connector. If no continuity exists, go to next step. If continuity does exist, repair open Black wire between ground and horn wiring harness connector.

2) Depress horn switch. Using a voltmeter, measure voltage between ground and White/Red wire at horn wiring harness connector. If battery voltage is not present, repair open White/Red wire. If battery voltage is present, replace horn.

REMOVAL & INSTALLATION

WARNING: Deactivate air bag system before performing any service operation involving steering column components. See AIR BAG RESTRAINT SYSTEMS article.

HORN

Removal & Installation (Cherokee) – 1) Horns are located behind front bumper and are mounted to left and right radiator closure panel braces. Disconnect negative battery cable. Raise and support vehicle. Remove front underbody splash shield.

2) Remove horn mounting bracket bolt. Lower horn bracket and disconnect horn connector. Remove horn and horn bracket as an assembly. To install, reverse removal procedure. Tighten horn bracket bolt to specification. See TORQUE SPECIFICATIONS.

Removal & Installation (Wrangler) – Horns are mounted on left inner fender, ahead of wheelwell in engine compartment. Disconnect negative battery cable. Disconnect horn connectors. Remove horn bracket mounting bolt(s). Remove horn. To install, reverse removal procedure.

HORN SWITCH

NOTE: Horn switch is an integral part of air bag module trim cover. If horn switch is defective, replace trim cover.

Removal – 1) Disconnect negative battery cable. Disable air bag system and remove driver air bag module. See AIR BAG RESTRAINT SYSTEMS article. Remove plastic horn switch feed wire retainer(s) from studs on air bag module housing. *See Fig. 9.*

2) Remove upper and lower trim cover retainers from air bag housing studs *See Fig. 10*. Remove horn switch ground wire eyelet from upper air bag module housing stud. Release 4 trim cover locking blocks from lip around outside edge of air bag housing. *See Fig. 11*. Remove air bag housing from trim cover.

Installation – 1) When installing trim cover, ensure locking blocks are fully engaged on lip of air bag housing. *See Fig. 12*. When installing upper and lower trim cover retainers, ensure tabs on each retainer are engaged in retainer slots of trim cover. *See Fig. 11*.

2) Tighten trim cover retainer nuts to specification. See TORQUE SPECIFICATIONS. To complete installation, reverse removal procedure. DO NOT connect battery at this time. See SYSTEM OPERATION CHECK in AIR BAG RESTRAINT SYSTEMS article.

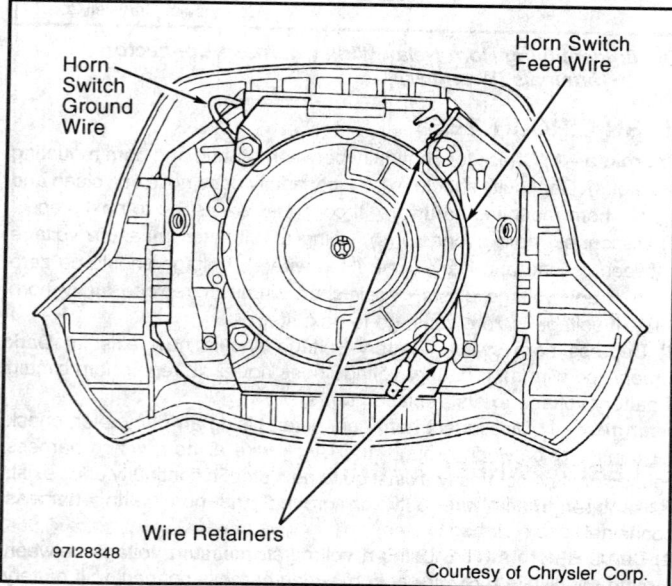

Fig. 9: Identifying Horn Switch Wires (Wrangler Shown; Cherokee Is Similar)

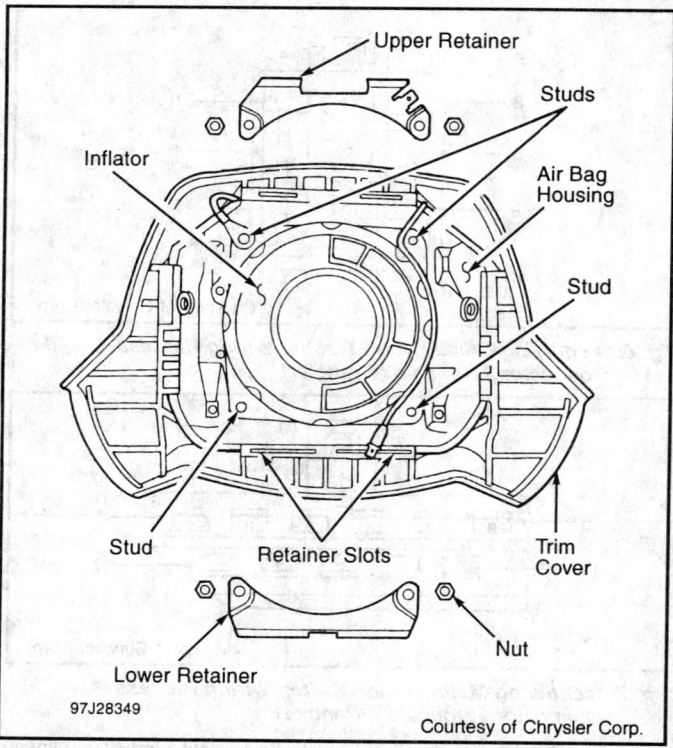

Courtesy of Chrysler Corp.

Fig. 10: Identifying Trim Cover Retainers (Wrangler Shown; Cherokee Is Similar)

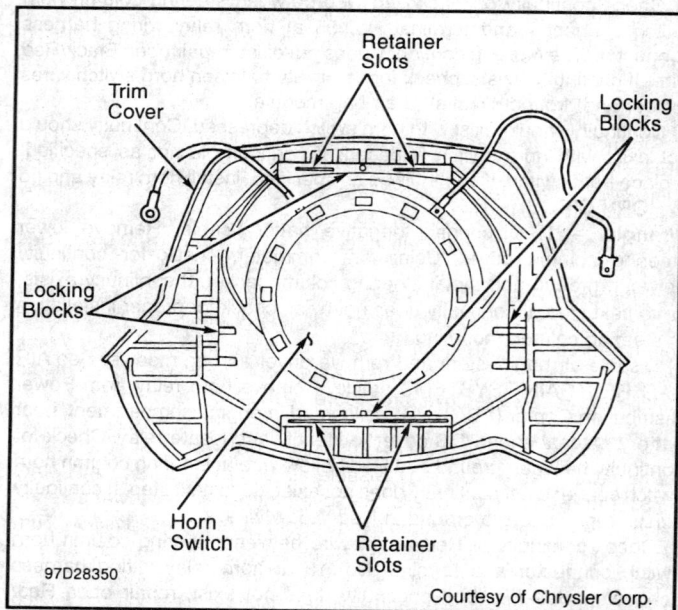

Courtesy of Chrysler Corp.

Fig. 11: Identifying Trim Cover Locking Blocks (Wrangler Shown; Cherokee Is Similar)

IGNITION KEY CYLINDER

Removal – Disconnect negative battery cable. On A/T models, place shifter in Park position. On all models, turn ignition on. Insert small screwdriver into access hole in right side of steering column lower cover. Push screwdriver up and pull key cylinder from ignition switch housing.

Installation – 1) On A/T models, ensure shifter is in Park position. On all models, position key cylinder into steering column as it normally would be in ON position. Press key cylinder into steering column until it snaps into position. Check mechanical operation of switch. On A/T models, go to next step. On M/T models, go to step **3).**

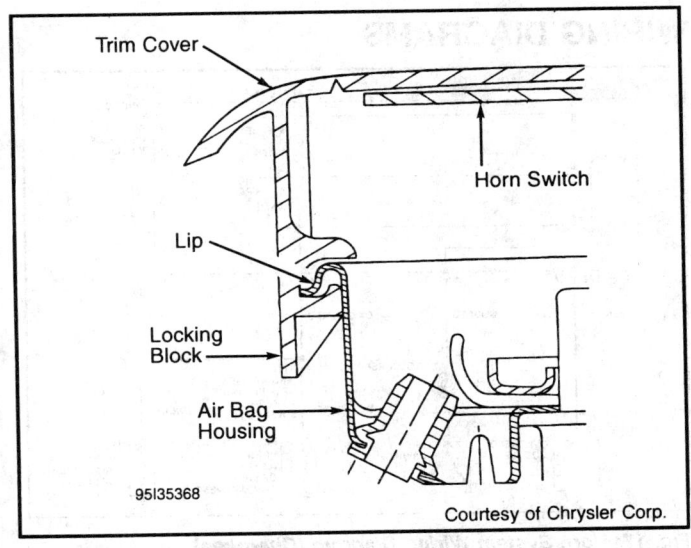

Fig. 12: Installing Trim Cover

2) On A/T models, remove ignition key and ensure transmission lever is locked in Park position. If key is difficult to remove, shift lever-to-steering column cable may be out of adjustment. Adjust as necessary. To complete installation, reverse removal procedure. Check electrical operation of ignition switch.

3) On M/T models, ensure ignition switch key cannot be removed until release lever is operated. If ignition key can be removed without operating release lever, release lever mechanism may be defective. Release lever mechanism is not serviced separately. If release lever mechanism is defective, replace steering column. To complete installation, reverse removal procedure. Check electrical operation of ignition switch.

IGNITION SWITCH

Removal – Remove ignition key cylinder. See IGNITION KEY CYLINDER. Remove lower steering column cover. Disconnect ignition switch connectors. Using tamper proof Torx bit, remove tamper proof screw from ignition switch. See Fig. 13. Using a small screwdriver, push locking tab and remove ignition switch from steering column. See Fig. 14.

Installation – Rotate ignition switch slot to ON position. See Fig. 15. Connect ignition switch connectors. Place ignition switch on steering column and install tamper proof screw. Ensure connector locking tabs are fully seated. Install lower steering column cover. To complete installation, reverse removal procedure.

MULTIFUNCTION SWITCH

Removal & Installation – 1) Disable air bag system. See AIR BAG RESTRAINT SYSTEMS article. Remove trim panel from lower steering column. Set tilt steering column (if equipped) to its highest position. Turn ignition on. Insert small screwdriver into access hole in right side of steering column lower cover.

2) Push up on screwdriver and pull key cylinder from ignition switch housing. Remove lower steering column cover retaining screws. Set tilt steering column (if equipped) to its lowest position. Remove upper and lower steering column covers. Remove 2 screws securing multifunction switch water shield to top of steering column. See Fig. 16.

3) Remove screw from bottom of water shield. Lift multifunction switch with water shield away from steering column. Disconnect multifunction switch connectors. Remove multifunction switch and water shield as an assembly. Gently pull water shield over hazard warning switch knob and remove shield from switch. To install, reverse removal procedure.

COMBINATION FLASHER

Removal & Installation – Combination flasher is located underneath instrument panel, right side of steering column. Disconnect negative battery cable. Remove lower steering column cover and knee bolster.

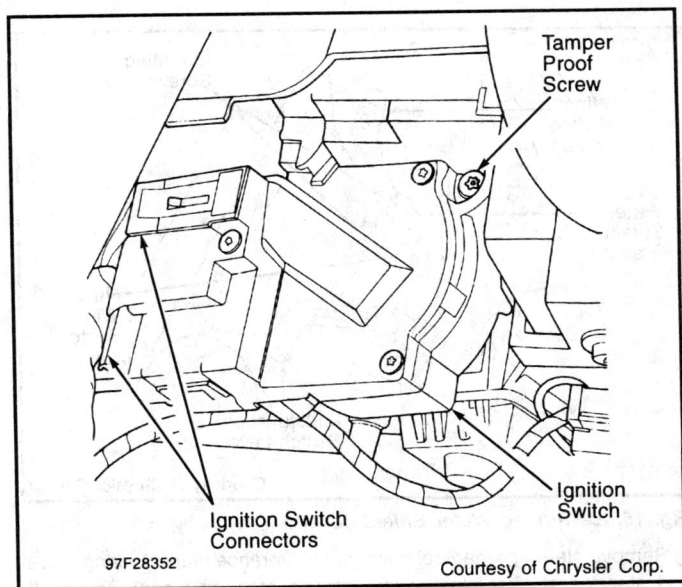

Fig. 13: Identifying Ignition Switch Tamper Proof Screw

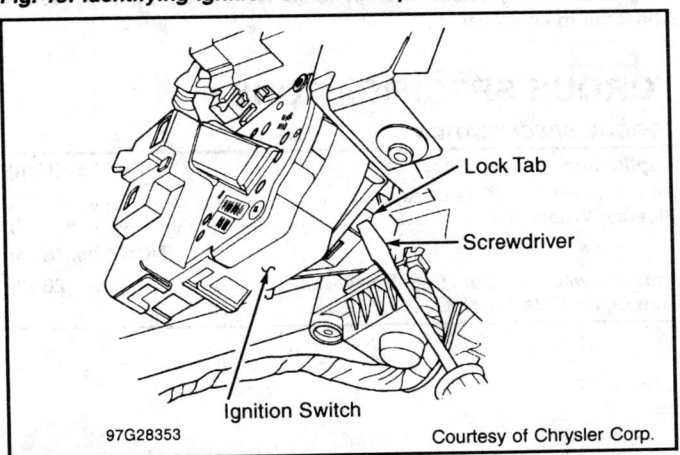

Fig. 14: Removing Ignition Switch

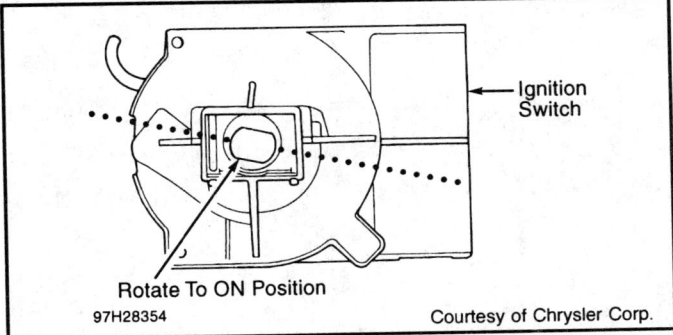

Fig. 15: Setting Ignition Switch To ON Position

Remove combination flasher retaining screw. Disconnect flasher connector. Remove combination flasher. To install, reverse removal procedure.

STEERING WHEEL & HORN PAD

Removal & Installation – 1) Ensure steering wheel is in straight-ahead position. Disable air bag system and remove driver air bag module. See AIR BAG RESTRAINT SYSTEMS article. Disconnect cruise control and remote radio switch connectors (if equipped).

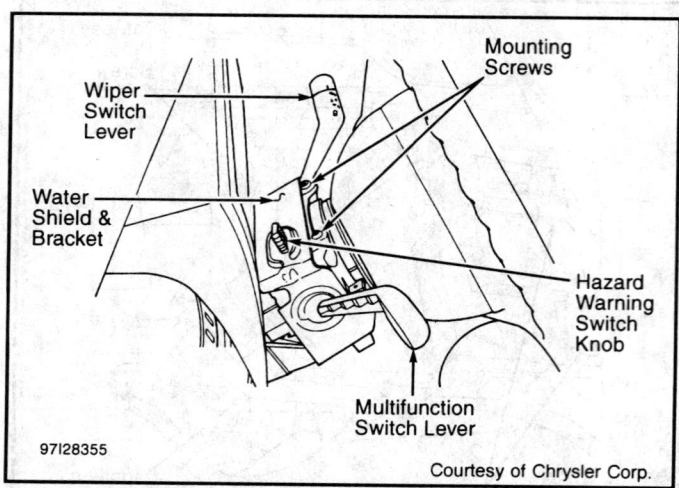

Fig. 16: Identifying Water Shield Screws

2) Remove steering wheel retaining nut. Reference mark steering wheel and steering shaft. Using puller, remove steering wheel. To install, reverse removal procedure. Align reference marks. Tighten steering wheel nut to specification.

TORQUE SPECIFICATIONS

TORQUE SPECIFICATIONS

Application	Ft. Lbs. (N.m)
Horn Bracket Bolt (Cherokee)	21 (28)
Steering Wheel Nut	40 (54)

	INCH Lbs. (N.m)
Ignition Switch Tamper Proof Screw	26 (3)
Trim Cover Retainer Nuts	90 (10)

WIRING DIAGRAMS

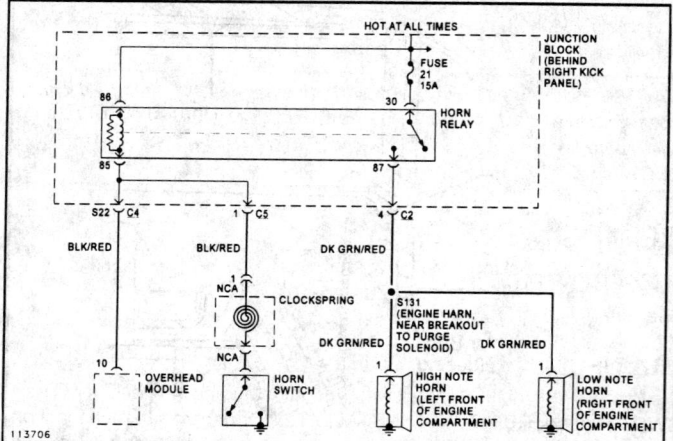

Fig. 17: Horn System Wiring Diagram (Cherokee)

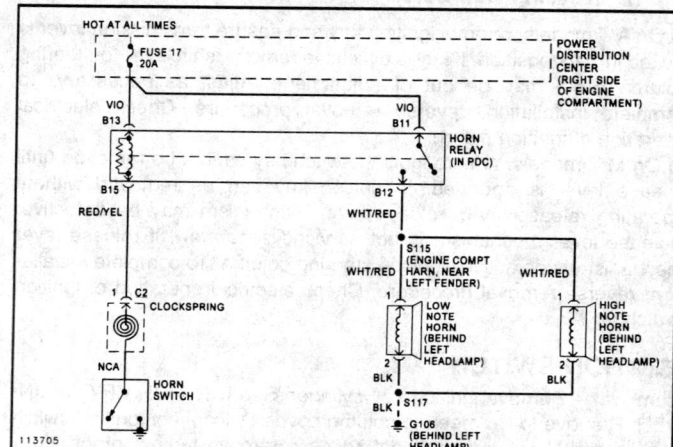

Fig. 18: Horn System Wiring Diagram (Wrangler)

DESCRIPTION & OPERATION

Multifunction switch incorporates headlight dimmer/passing, turn signal, windshield wiper/washer and hazard warning switches into one unit. The ignition switch is mounted on steering column.

WARNING: Vehicle is equipped with air bag system. To avoid injury from accidental air bag deployment, read and carefully follow all WARNINGS and SERVICE PRECAUTIONS. See AIR BAG RESTRAINT SYSTEMS article.

COMPONENT TESTS

HAZARD SWITCH

See MULTIFUNCTION SWITCH.

MULTIFUNCTION SWITCH

Disconnect left multifunction switch connector. See MULTIFUNCTION SWITCH under REMOVAL & INSTALLATION for access to multifunction switch connector. Using an ohmmeter, check for continuity in multifunc-tion switch terminals with switch turned to indicated positions. *See Fig. 1.* See MULTIFUNCTION SWITCH CONTINUITY table. If continuity is not as specified, replace multifunction switch assembly.

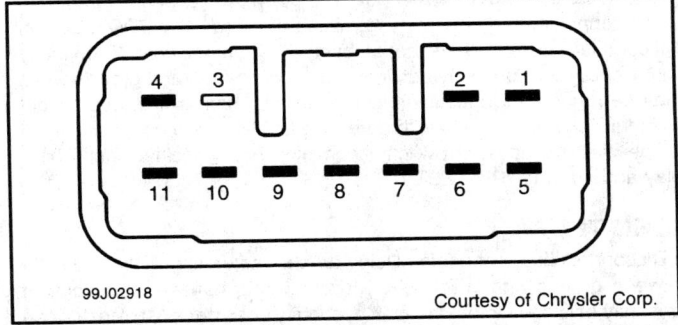

99J02918

Courtesy of Chrysler Corp.

Fig. 1: Identifying Multifunction Switch Terminals

MULTIFUNCTION SWITCH CONTINUITY

Switch Position	Continuity Between Terminals No.	Resistance Between Terminals No.	Ohms
Turn Signal Switch			
Neutral	None		
Left	2 & 8		
Right	2 & 7		
Hazard Switch On	2 & 9		
Exterior Light Switch			
Off		4 & 11	3743-3824
Park Lamps On		4 & 11	901-926
Headlights On		4 & 11	345-358
Auto Headlights On		4 & 11	74-81
Fog Lamps On	1 & 2		
Flash To Pass	2 & 5		
High Beam On	2 & 6		
Interior Light Switch			
Dome Lamp Disable On		4 & 9	63-70
Instrument Panel Dimmer			
Position 1		4 & 9	198-208
Position 2		4 & 9	551-569
Position 3		4 & 9	905-929
Position 4		4 & 9	1258-1290
Position 5		4 & 9	1611-1651
Position 6		4 & 9	1965-2011
Parade Mode On		4 & 9	3534-3611
Dome Lamp Enable On		4 & 9	7811-7974

HORN RELAY

1) Remove horn relay from Power Distribution Center (PDC). Use label on PDC cover to identify and locate relay. Using an ohmmeter, check for continuity between relay terminals No. 87A and 30. *See Fig. 2.* If continuity does not exist, replace relay. If continuity exists, go to next step.

2) Check for continuity between relay terminals No. 30 and 87. If continuity exists, replace relay. If continuity does not exist, check resistance between relay terminals No. 85 and 86. If resistance is not 70-80 ohms, replace relay. If resistance is 70-80 ohms, go to next step.

3) Using jumper wires, connect positive battery voltage to relay terminal No. 86 and ground to relay terminal No. 85. Continuity should exist between terminals No. 30 and 87. Continuity should not exist between relay terminals No. 87A and 30. If continuity is not as specified, replace relay. If continuity is as specified, relay is okay. Go to HORN RELAY CIRCUIT TEST.

HORN SWITCH TEST

1) Disconnect negative battery cable. Remove steering column opening cover. Using an ohmmeter, check for continuity between ground and

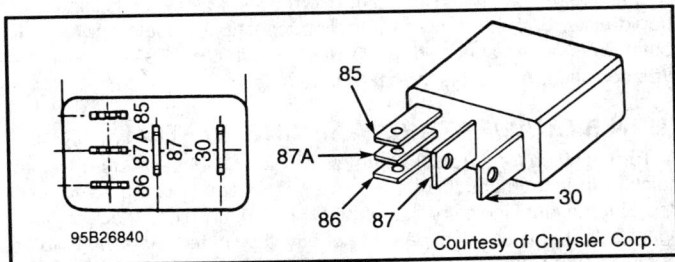

95B26840

Courtesy of Chrysler Corp.

Fig. 2: Identifying Horn Relay Terminals

metal steering column jacket. If continuity exists, go to next step. If continuity does not exist, check for proper installation of steering column.

2) Disable air bag system and remove driver air bag module. See AIR BAG RESTRAINT SYSTEMS article. Unplug horn switch connector from air bag module. Remove horn relay from Power Distribution Center (PDC). PDC is located in engine compartment, near battery. Use label on PDC cover to identify and locate relay. Check for continuity between ground and Gray/Orange wire at steering column horn switch connector. If continuity does not exist, go to next step. If continuity exists, repair short to ground in Gray/Orange wire.

3) Check continuity of Gray/Orange wire between steering column horn switch connector and horn relay terminal No. 86 cavity in PDC. *See Fig. 2.* If continuity does not exist, repair open Gray/Orange wire. If continuity exists, check for continuity between horn switch feed and ground wires at air bag module. Continuity should exist with horn switch depressed. Continuity should not exist with horn switch released. If continuity is not as specified, replace horn switch. If continuity is as specified, install horn relay and go to HORN TEST.

HORN TEST

1) Disconnect horn connector. Using an ohmmeter, check for continuity between ground and Black wire at horn wiring harness connector. If continuity exists, go to next step. If continuity does not exist, repair open Black wire between ground and horn wiring harness connector.

2) Depress horn switch. Using a voltmeter, measure voltage between ground and Dark Green/Red wire at horn wiring harness connector. If battery voltage is not present, repair open Dark Green/Red wire. If battery voltage is present, replace horn.

IGNITION SWITCH

Information is not available from manufacturer. See appropriate wiring diagram in POWER DISTRIBUTION article in WIRING DIAGRAMS.

WIPER SWITCH

For wiper switch testing information, see appropriate WIPER/WASHER SYSTEMS article.

SYSTEM TESTS

HORN RELAY CIRCUIT TEST

1) Check fuse No. 18 (15-amp) in Power Distribution Center (PDC). PDC is located in engine compartment, near battery. If fuse is okay, go to next step. If fuse is blown, repair cause of blown fuse. Replace fuse and check horn operation.

2) Remove horn relay from PDC. Use label on PDC cover to identify and locate relay. Check for battery voltage at relay terminals No. 30 and 85 cavities in PDC. *See Fig. 2.* If battery voltage does not exist, at one or both terminals, repair open circuit. If battery voltage exists, go to next step.

3) Disconnect both horn connectors. Using an ohmmeter, check for continuity between horn connectors (Dark Green/Red wires) and horn relay terminal No. 87 cavity in PDC. If continuity does not exist, repair open circuit(s). If continuity exists, go to next step.

4) Using an ohmmeter, check for continuity between ground and relay terminal No. 86 cavity in PDC. With horn switch depressed, continuity should exist. With horn switch released, continuity should not exist. If continuity is not as specified, go to HORN SWITCH TEST. If continuity is as specified, no fault is indicated in relay circuits.

TURN SIGNAL/HAZARD WARNING SYSTEM

1) Turn ignition on. Actuate turn signal lever. Observe turn signal indicator in instrument cluster. If turn signal indicator is off, go to next step. If turn signal indicator flash rate is abnormally high, check for turn signal bulb that is not illuminated or poorly illuminated. Replace bulb or repair circuit to bulb as necessary. See appropriate wiring diagram in EXTERIOR LIGHTS article. Check system operation.

2) Check fuses No. 4 (15-amp) and 20 (10-amp) in junction block. Junction block is located under left side of instrument panel. If fuses are okay, go to next step. If fuse(s) is blown, check for cause of blown fuse. Replace fuse and recheck system operation.

3) Check for battery voltage at fuse No. 4 in junction block. If battery voltage does not exist, repair open circuit between junction block and ignition switch. If battery voltage exists, turn ignition on. Check for battery voltage at fuse No. 20 in junction block. If battery voltage does not exist, repair open circuit between junction block and battery. See

appropriate wiring diagram in POWER DISTRIBUTION article in WIRING DIAGRAMS. If battery voltage exists, go to next step.

4) Turn ignition off. Disconnect negative battery cable. Remove combination flasher from fuse box. Install a known-good combination flasher. Check turn signal and hazard flasher operation. If system does not function properly, remove test flasher and go to next step. If system operates properly, replace faulty combination flasher.

5) Turn ignition on. Check for battery voltage at combination flasher terminal No. 6 cavity in junction block. *See Fig. 3.* If battery voltage does not exist, repair open circuit to ignition switch. If battery voltage exists, go to next step.

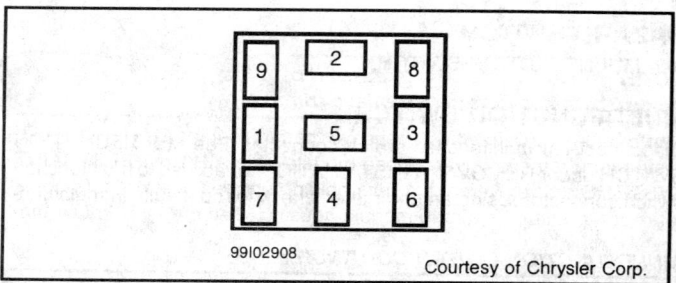

99102908   Courtesy of Chrysler Corp.

Fig. 3: Identifying Combination Flasher Cavities In Junction Block

6) Turn ignition off. Check for battery voltage at combination flasher terminal No. 1 cavity in junction block. *See Fig. 3.* If battery voltage does not exist, repair open circuit in junction block. If battery voltage exists, go to next step.

7) Check for continuity between ground and terminal No. 5 (Black wire) at combination flasher wiring harness connector in fuse box. If continuity exists, go to next step. If continuity does not exist, repair open Black wire between ground and combination flasher connector.

8) Disconnect multifunction switch connector. See MULTIFUNCTION SWITCH under REMOVAL & INSTALLATION for access to multifunction switch connector. Check for continuity between ground and multifunction switch connector terminal No. 2 (Black wire) If continuity does not exist, repair open ground circuit. If continuity exists, go to next step.

9) Check for continuity between ground and multifunction switch connector terminal No. 9 (Dark Blue/Pink wire). If continuity exists, repair short to ground. If continuity does not exist, go to next step.

10) Check for continuity of hazard switch sense circuit between multifunction switch connector terminal No. 9 (Dark Blue/Pink wire) and combination flasher terminal No. 9 cavity in junction block. *See Fig. 3.* If continuity does not exist, repair open circuit. If continuity exists, go to next step.

11) Check for continuity between ground and multifunction switch connector terminal No. 8 (Light Blue/White wire). If continuity exists, repair short to ground. If continuity does not exist, go to next step.

12) Check for continuity of left turn switch sense circuit between multifunction switch connector terminal No. 8 (Light Blue/White wire) and combination flasher terminal No. 7 cavity in junction block. If continuity does not exist, repair open circuit. If continuity exists, go to next step.

13) Check for continuity between ground and multifunction switch connector terminal No. 7 (Light Blue/Yellow wire). If continuity exists, repair short to ground. If continuity does not exist, go to next step.

14) Check for continuity of right turn switch sense circuit between multifunction switch connector terminal No. 7 (Light Blue/Yellow wire) and combination flasher terminal No. 8 in junction block. If continuity does not exist, repair open circuit. If continuity exists, test multifunction switch continuity. See MULTIFUNCTION SWITCH under COMPONENT TESTS.

REMOVAL & INSTALLATION

WARNING: Deactivate air bag system before performing any service operation involving steering column components. See AIR BAG RESTRAINT SYSTEMS article.

HORN

Removal & Installation – Disconnect negative battery cable. Raise and support vehicle. Remove radiator lower air deflector. Disconnect horn connectors. Remove horn mounting bolt. Remove horn. To install, reverse removal procedure.

HORN SWITCH

NOTE: Horn switch is an integral part of air bag module trim cover. If horn switch is defective, replace trim cover.

Removal – **1)** Disconnect negative battery cable. Disable air bag system and remove driver air bag module. See AIR BAG RESTRAINT SYSTEMS article. Remove 4 nuts holding upper and lower trim cover retainers to studs on airbag module housing. *See Fig. 4.* Remove trim cover retainers. *See Fig. 5.*

2) Disengage horn switch feed wire connector retainer from upper trim cover retainer. Disconnect horn switch ground wire from air bag module housing. Disengage 4 trim cover locking blocks from lip around outside edge of airbag housing. *See Fig. 6.*

3) Remove housing from cover. Remove horn switch and tray as a unit from pouch on retaining strap of airbag module. *See Fig. 7.*

Installation – **1)** Install horn switch and tray as a unit into pouch on retaining strap of airbag module. Ensure tray is facing airbag module and horn switch wires are positioned correctly. *See Fig. 7.*

2) When installing trim cover, ensure locking blocks are fully engaged on lip of air bag housing. *See Fig. 8.* Ensure horn switch wires are not pinched between airbag housing and trim cover locking blocks. When installing upper and lower trim cover retainers, ensure tabs on each retainer are engaged in retainer slots of trim cover. *See Fig. 6.*

3) Tighten trim cover retainer nuts to specification. See TORQUE SPECIFICATIONS. To complete installation, reverse removal procedure. DO NOT connect battery at this time. See SYSTEM OPERATION CHECK in AIR BAG RESTRAINT SYSTEMS article.

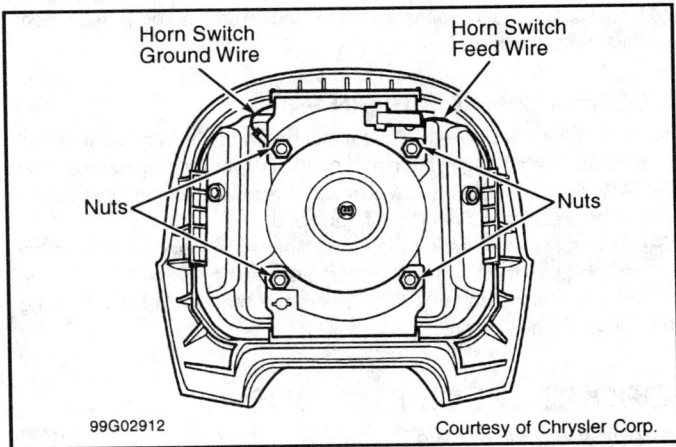

Fig. 4: Removing Air Bag Trim Cover

IGNITION SWITCH

Removal – **1)** Disconnect negative battery cable. Place transmission into Park. If removing lock cylinder only, go to next step. If removing ignition switch only, go to step **3)**.

2) Tilt steering wheel to full up position. Turn ignition switch to RUN position. While pressing retaining pin, pull lock cylinder from housing. *See Fig. 9.* Note position of alignment tang at end of cylinder for installation reference.

3) Remove steering column opening cover from instrument panel. Remove upper and lower steering column shrouds. Remove 2 upper

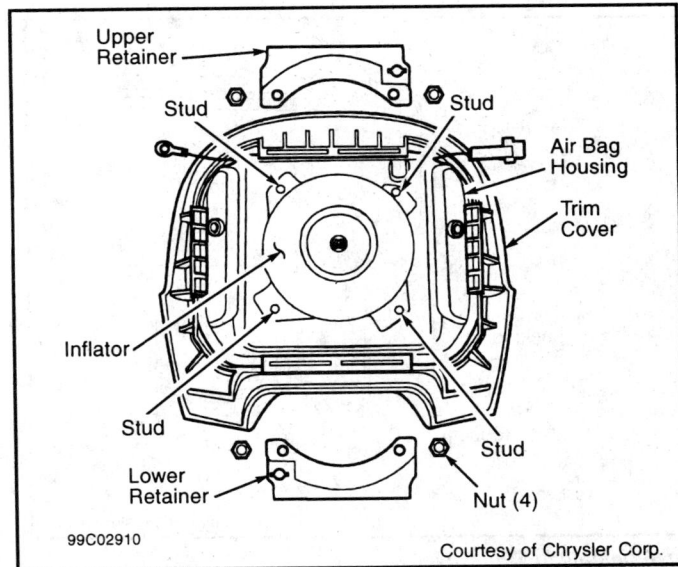

Fig. 5: Identifying Trim Cover Retainers

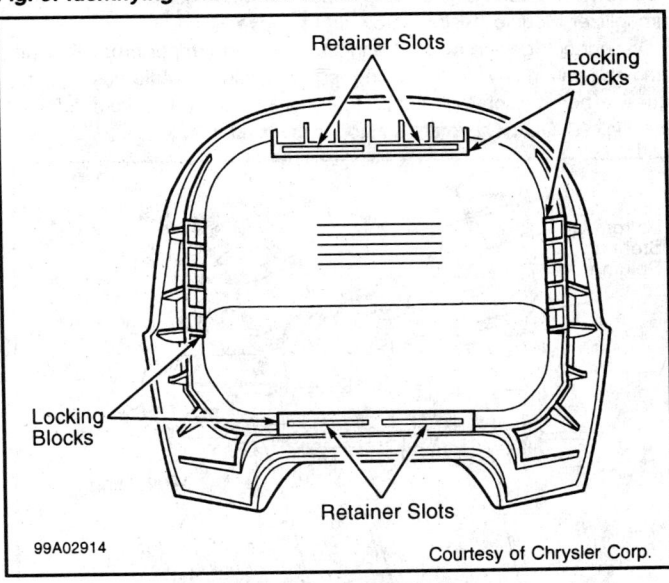

Fig. 6: Identifying Trim Cover Locking Blocks

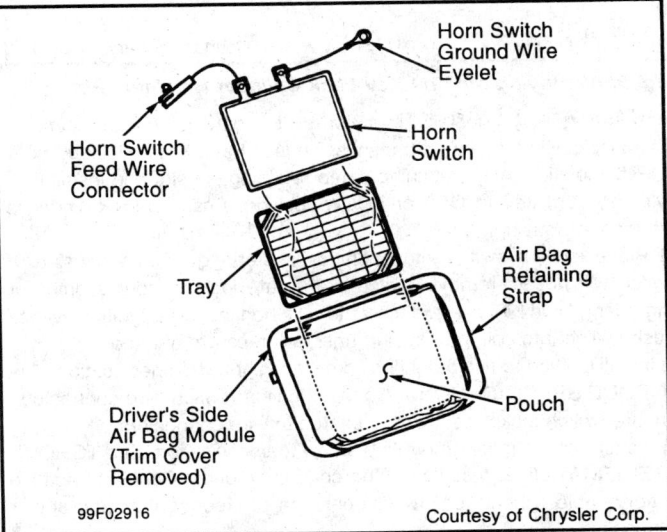

Fig. 7: Removing Horn Switch

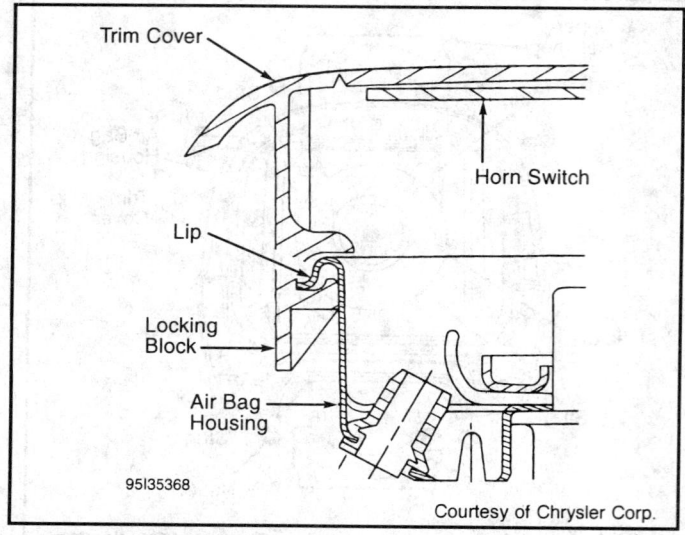

Fig. 8: Installing Trim Cover

fixed column shroud screws and remove shroud. Remove Sentry Key Immobilizer Module (SKIM) screw and remove SKIM.

4) Disconnect ignition switch connectors. Using tamper-proof Torx bit, remove ignition switch mounting screw. Using needle-nose pliers, squeeze both switch lock tabs. Gently pull switch away from column. *See Fig. 10.* DO NOT rotate ignition lock cylinder.

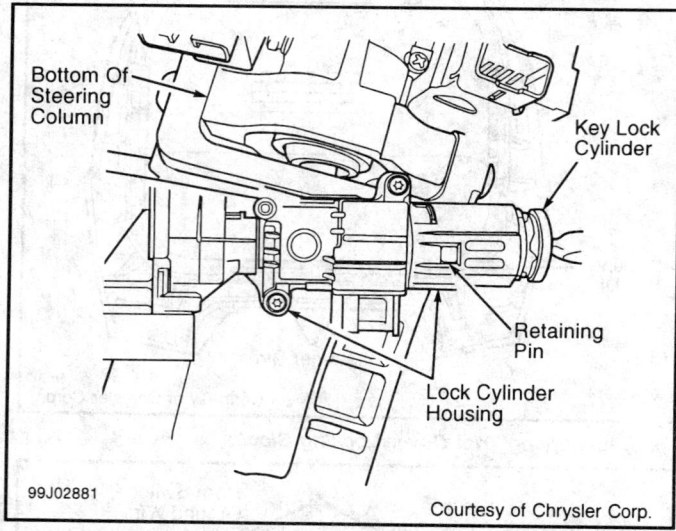

Fig. 9: Identifying Ignition Key Lock Cylinder Retaining Pin

Installation – 1) If installing ignition switch only, go to next step. To install lock cylinder, ensure transmission is in Park. Rotate lock cylinder to RUN position. Align retaining pin to retaining pin slot and install lock cylinder. Turn key to OFF or LOCK position. Ensure lock cylinder is retained in housing.

2) Place ignition switch into opening on steering column housing. If switch will not fit, remove switch and rotate lock cylinder slightly for alignment. DO NOT use excessive force when installing ignition switch. Push switch into column housing until lock tabs are engaged.

3) Install ignition switch mounting screw and tighten to specification. See TORQUE SPECIFICATIONS. Connect ignition switch wire connectors. Ensure switch lock tabs are fully seated in wire connectors.

4) Install SKIM. Tighten mounting screw to specification. See TORQUE SPECIFICATIONS. Install steering column shrouds. Connect negative battery cable. Check for proper operation of steering lock and shifter interlock.

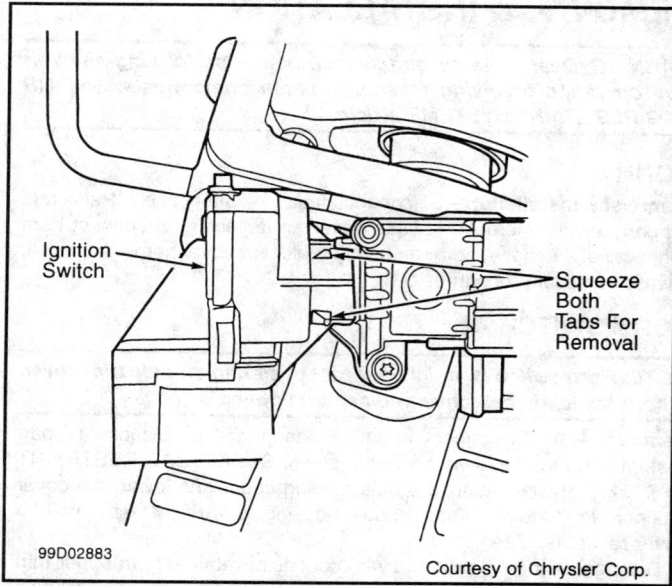

Fig. 10: Removing Ignition Switch

IGNITION KEY LOCK CYLINDER

Removal & Installation – See IGNITION SWITCH.

MULTIFUNCTION SWITCH

Removal & Installation – 1) Disconnect negative battery cable. Remove screw holding lower tilting steering column shroud to multifunction switch mounting housing. Unsnap 2 halves of tilting steering column shroud and remove from column.

2) Disconnect multifunction switch wire connector. Remove 2 multifunction switch mounting screws. Remove multifunction switch.

3) To install, position multifunction switch onto multifunction switch housing. Tighten screws to specification. See TORQUE SPECIFICATIONS. Connect multifunction switch wire connector.

4) Position lower tilting steering column shroud onto steering column and install screw. Install upper tilting steering column shroud. Reconnect negative battery cable.

STEERING WHEEL & HORN PAD

Removal & Installation – 1) Ensure steering wheel is in straight-ahead position. Disable air bag system and remove driver air bag module. See AIR BAG RESTRAINT SYSTEMS article. Disconnect cruise control and remote radio switch connectors (if equipped).

2) Remove steering wheel retaining nut. Reference mark steering wheel and steering shaft. Using puller, remove steering wheel. To install, reverse removal procedure. Align reference marks. Tighten steering wheel nut to specification.

TORQUE SPECIFICATIONS

TORQUE SPECIFICATIONS

Application	Ft. Lbs. (N.m)
Steering Wheel Nut	35 (47)

	INCH Lbs. (N.m)
Ignition Switch Mounting Screws	30 (3)
Lower Tilting Steering Column Shroud Screw	17 (1.9)
Multifunction Switch Retaining Screws	22 (2.5)
Sentry Key Immobilizer Module (SKIM) Screw	30 (3)
Trim Cover Retainer Nuts	60 (6.8)

WIRING DIAGRAMS

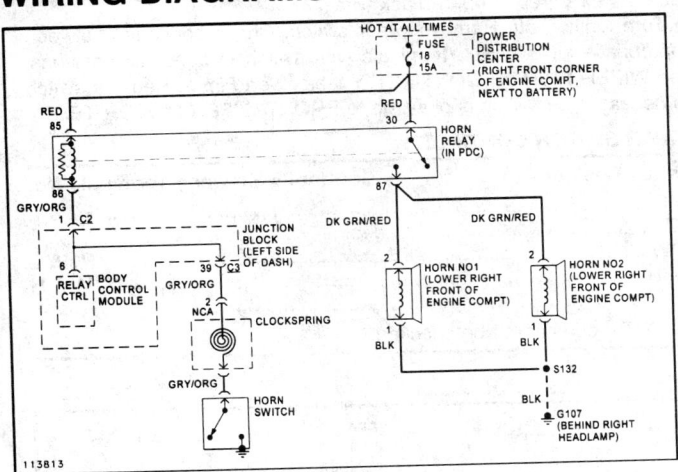

Fig. 11: Horn System Wiring Diagram (Grand Cherokee)

DESCRIPTION & OPERATION

All models use a 2-speed windshield wiper system with electrically operated front washer system. On Cherokee, intermittent wiper system is standard equipment and rear wiper/washer system is available as an option. On Wrangler, intermittent wiper system is optional and rear wiper/washer system is standard equipment on hardtop models. On all models, front wiper/washer system is controlled by a switch mounted on right side of steering column. Rear wiper/washer system is controlled by a switch located on accessory switch panel on instrument panel.

ADJUSTMENTS

WIPER ARMS

Cherokee – With wiper arm(s) removed, cycle wiper motor into park position. Mount wiper arm(s) on pivot shaft(s). On front wiper arm, ensure distance between tip of wiper blade and upper edge of lower windshield molding is as specified. On rear wiper arm, ensure distance between tip of wiper blade and upper edge of lower liftgate glass seal is as specified. See WIPER ARM HEIGHT SPECIFICATIONS table.

Wrangler – With wiper arm(s) removed, cycle wiper motor into park position. Mount wiper arm(s) on pivot shaft(s). On front wiper arms, ensure distance between tip of wiper blade and upper edge of lower windshield blackout area is as specified. On rear wiper arms, ensure distance between tip of wiper arm and upper edge of liftglass is as specified. See WIPER ARM HEIGHT SPECIFICATIONS table.

WIPER ARM HEIGHT SPECIFICATIONS

Application	In. (mm)
Cherokee	
Front Wiper	
Driver's Side	.90-2.04 (23-52)
Passenger's Side	1.29-2.44 (33-62)
Rear Wiper	1.06-1.38 (27-35)
Wrangler	
Front Wiper	0-.59 (0-15)
Rear Wiper	0-3.14 (0-80)

SYSTEM TESTS

CAUTION: When battery is disconnected, vehicle computer and memory systems may lose memory data. Driveability problems may exist until computer systems have completed a relearn cycle. See COMPUTER RELEARN PROCEDURES article in GENERAL INFORMATION before disconnecting battery.

WARNING: Vehicle is equipped with an air bag restraint system. Failure to follow air bag service precautions may result in air bag deployment and personal injury. See SERVICE PRECAUTIONS in appropriate AIR BAG RESTRAINT SYSTEMS article. DO NOT apply electrical power to any component on steering column without first deactivating air bag system. Air bag may deploy.

FRONT WIPER SWITCH TEST

Cherokee – 1) Check circuit breaker No. 30 (20-amp) from junction block. Junction block is located behind right kick panel. Replace circuit breaker as necessary and recheck wiper operation. If circuit breaker is okay, go to next step.
2) Disconnect wiper switch connector. Turn ignition on. Measure voltage between ground and terminal No. 5 (Dark Blue wire) at wiper switch harness connector. *See Fig. 1.* If battery voltage exists, go to next step. If battery voltage is not present, repair open Dark Blue wire between junction block and wiper switch.
3) If problem being diagnosed involves only pulse wipe, wipe after wash, or intermittent wipe modes, go to next step. If problem being diagnosed is other than pulse wipe, wipe after wash, or intermittent wipe modes, go to step 5).
4) Turn ignition off. Disconnect negative battery cable. Check continuity between ground and terminal No. 1 (Black wire) at wiper switch harness

connector. If continuity exists, replace faulty wiper switch. If continuity does not exist, repair open Black wire.
5) Turn ignition off. Remove wiper switch. Check continuity between appropriate wiper switch terminals with switch in specified positions. See WIPER SWITCH CONTINUITY table. *See Fig. 2.* Replace switch as necessary. If switch is okay, go to FRONT WIPER MOTOR TEST.

WIPER SWITCH CONTINUITY

Switch Position	Continuity Between Terminals No.
OFF	P2 & L
INT	1
LOW	P1 & L
HIGH	P1 & H
WASH	P1 & W

1 – INT mode cannot be checked.

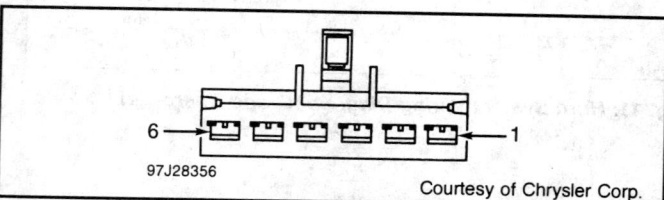

Fig. 1: Identifying Front Wiper Switch Harness Connector Terminals

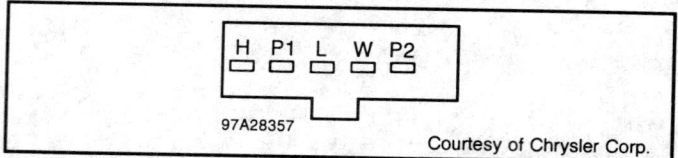

Fig. 2: Identifying Front Wiper Switch Terminals

Wrangler – 1) Remove and inspect fuse No. 14 (20-amp) from junction block. Junction block is located behind glove box. Replace fuse as necessary and recheck wiper operation. If fuse is okay, go to next step.
2) Disconnect wiper switch connector. Turn ignition on. Measure voltage between ground and terminal No. 5 (Pink/Black wire) at wiper switch harness connector. *See Fig. 1.* If battery voltage exists, go to next step. If battery voltage does not exist, repair open in Pink/Black wire between junction block and wiper switch connector.
3) If problem being diagnosed involves only pulse wipe, wipe after wash, or intermittent wipe modes, go to next step. If problem being diagnosed is other than pulse wipe, wipe after wash, or intermittent wipe modes, go to step 5).
4) Turn ignition off. Disconnect negative battery cable. Check continuity between ground and terminal No. 1 (Black wire) at wiper switch harness connector. If continuity exists, replace faulty wiper switch. If continuity does not exist, repair open Black wire.
5) Turn ignition off. Remove wiper switch. Check continuity between appropriate wiper switch terminals with switch in specified positions. See WIPER SWITCH CONTINUITY table. *See Fig. 2.* Replace switch as necessary. If switch is okay, go to FRONT WIPER MOTOR TEST.

FRONT WIPER MOTOR TEST

1) Disconnect front wiper motor connector. Check continuity between ground and terminal No. 4 (Black wire) at wiper motor harness connector. *See Fig. 3.* If continuity exists, go to next step. If continuity does not exist, repair open Black wire.
2) Turn ignition on. Measure voltage between ground and terminal No. 1 (Dark Blue wire on Cherokee; Pink/Black wire on Wrangler) at wiper motor harness connector. If battery voltage is present, go to next step. If battery voltage is not present, repair open circuit between wiper motor connector and junction block.
3) Turn ignition off. Disconnect negative battery cable. Disconnect front wiper switch connector. Check continuity between ground and terminals No. 2 (Dark Green/Yellow wire), No. 5 (Brown/White wire) and No. 6

(Brown/Violet wire on Cherokee; Red/Yellow wire on Wrangler) at front wiper motor harness connector. If continuity does not exist in any wires, go to next step. If continuity exists in any wire, repair short to ground as necessary.

4) Check continuity of the following wires.

- Dark Green/Yellow wire between terminals No. 2 at front wiper motor wiring harness connector and No. 2 at wiper switch wiring harness connector. See Figs. 1 and 3.
- Brown/Violet wire on Cherokee or Red/Yellow wire on Wrangler between terminals No. 6 at from wiper motor wiring harness connector and No. 6 at wiper switch wiring harness connector.
- Brown/White wire between terminals No. 5 at front wiper motor wiring harness connector and No. 4 at wiper switch wiring harness connector.

If continuity exists in each wire checked, replace faulty wiper motor. If continuity does not exist in one or more wires, repair open circuit as necessary.

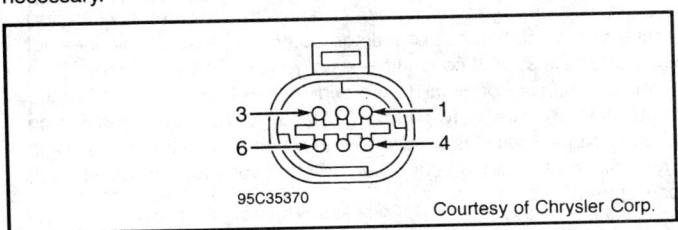

95C35370   Courtesy of Chrysler Corp.

Fig. 3: Identifying Front Wiper Motor Wiring Harness Connector Terminals (Cherokee Shown; Wrangler Is Similar)

FRONT WASHER PUMP TEST

1) Turn ignition on. Place wiper switch in HIGH or LOW position. If wipers do not operate, go to FRONT WIPER MOTOR TEST. If wipers operate, place wiper switch in OFF position and go to next step.

2) Turn ignition off. Disconnect front washer pump connector. See Fig. 4 or 5. Check continuity between ground and Black wire terminal at front washer pump connector. If continuity exists, go to next step. If continuity does not exist, repair open in Black wire.

3) Turn ignition on. Measure voltage between ground and Brown wire terminal at front washer pump connector while depressing washer switch. If battery voltage does not exist, go to next step. If battery voltage exists, replace faulty pump.

4) Turn ignition off. Disconnect negative battery cable. Disconnect front wiper switch connector. Check continuity between ground and terminal No. 3 (Brown wire) at wiper switch harness connector. If continuity does not exist, go to next step. If continuity exists, repair short to ground in Brown wire.

5) Check continuity of Brown wire between terminal No. 3 at wiper switch harness connector and front washer pump connector. If continuity does not exist, repair open Brown wire. If continuity exists, replace faulty front wiper switch.

REAR WIPER SWITCH TEST

1) Check fuse No. 22 (Cherokee) or No. 6 (Wrangler) in junction block. Junction block is located behind right kick panel (Cherokee) or behind glove box (Wrangler). If fuse is okay, go to next step. If fuse is blown, check for cause of fuse to blow and repair as necessary. Recheck rear wiper operation.

2) Disconnect negative battery cable. Remove rear wiper switch. Connect negative battery cable. Turn ignition on. Measure voltage between ground and terminal No. 5 (Brown/Pink wire) at rear wiper switch harness connector. See Fig. 6. If battery voltage exists, go to next step. If battery voltage does not exist, repair open circuit between ignition switch and rear wiper switch connector.

3) Turn ignition off. Disconnect negative battery cable. Check continuity between ground and terminal No. 1 (Black wire on Cherokee; Black/White wire on Wrangler) at rear wiper switch harness connector. If continuity exists, go to next step. If continuity does not exist, repair open in Black or Black/White wire.

4) Check continuity between appropriate rear wiper switch terminal with switch in specified position. See REAR WIPER SWITCH CONTINUITY

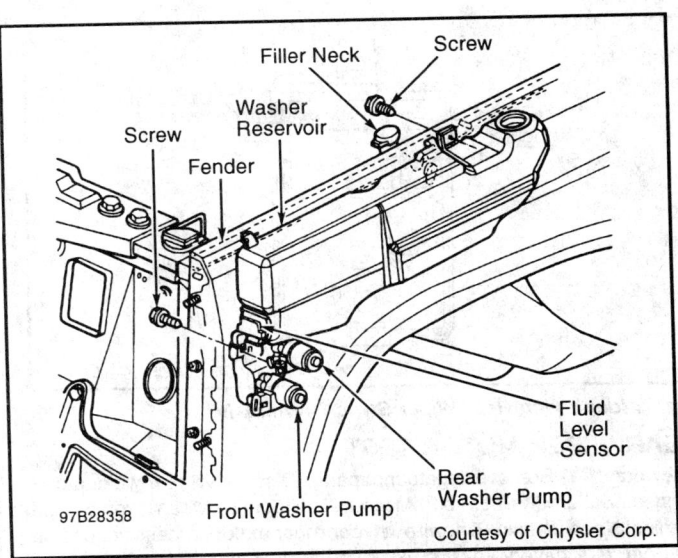

97B28358   Courtesy of Chrysler Corp.

Fig. 4: Locating Front/Rear Washer Pump Motors (Cherokee)

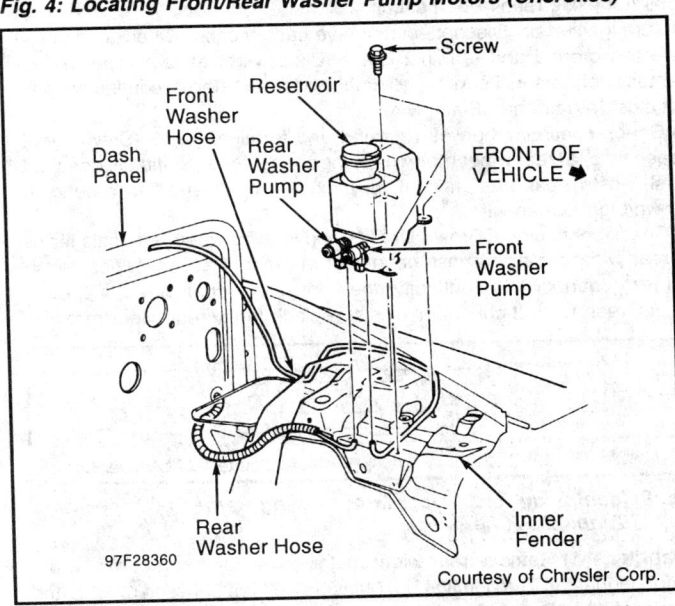

97F28360   Courtesy of Chrysler Corp.

Fig. 5: Locating Front/Rear Washer Pump Motors (Wrangler)

table. See Fig. 7. Replace switch if continuity is not as specified. If rear wiper switch is okay, install wiper switch and go to REAR WIPER MOTOR TEST.

REAR WIPER SWITCH CONTINUITY

Switch Position	Continuity Between Terminals No.
OFF	2 & 5; 4 & 5
WASH	4 & 5
Wipe	1 & 4
Illumination Light	1 & 3

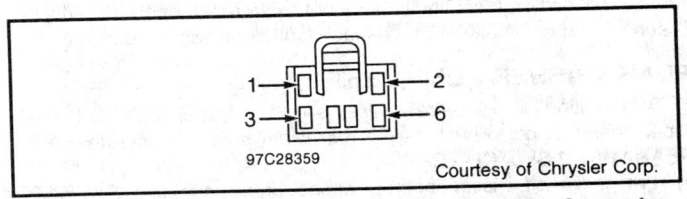

97C28359   Courtesy of Chrysler Corp.

Fig. 6: Identifying Rear Wiper Switch Wiring Harness Connector Terminals (Cherokee Shown; Wrangler Is Similar)

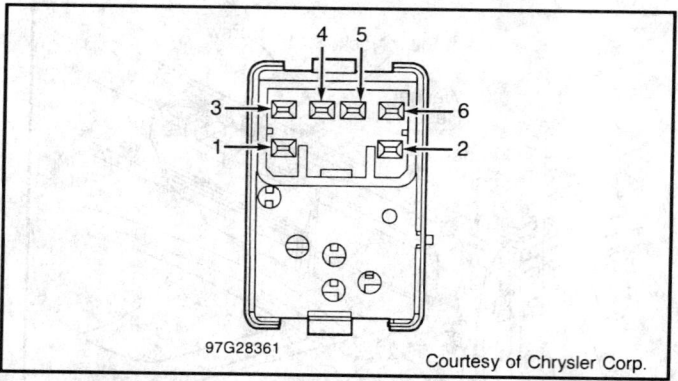

Fig. 7: Identifying Rear Wiper Switch Terminals

REAR WIPER MOTOR TEST

Cherokee – 1) Remove liftgate trim panel. Disconnect rear wiper motor connector. Turn ignition on. Measure voltage between ground and terminal No. 4 (Brown/Pink wire) at rear wiper motor harness connector. *See Fig. 8*. If battery voltage exists, go to next step. If battery voltage does not exist, repair open circuit.

2) Turn ignition off. Disconnect negative battery cable. Check continuity between ground and terminal No. 1 (Black wire) at rear wiper motor harness connector. If continuity exists, go to next step. If continuity does not exist, repair open Black wire.

3) Check continuity between ground and terminal No. 3 (Brown/Light Green wire) at rear wiper motor harness connector. If continuity does not exist, go to next step. If continuity exists, repair short to ground in Brown/Light Green wire.

4) Check continuity of Brown/Light Green wire between terminals No. 3 at rear wiper motor harness connector and No. 4 at rear wiper switch harness connector. If continuity does not exist, repair open in Brown/Light Green wire. If continuity exists, replace faulty rear wiper motor.

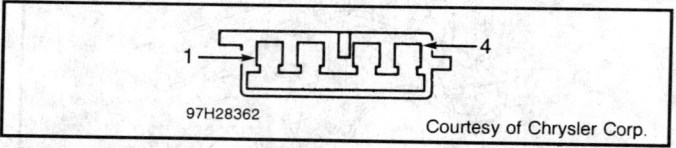

Fig. 8: Identifying Rear Wiper Motor Wiring Harness Connector Terminals (Cherokee)

Wrangler – 1) Remove rear wiper motor cover. Disconnect rear wiper motor connector. Turn ignition on. Measure voltage between ground and terminal No. 1 (Brown/Pink wire) at rear wiper motor harness connector. *See Fig. 9*. If battery voltage exists, go to next step. If battery voltage does not exist, repair open circuit.

2) Turn ignition off. Disconnect negative battery cable. Check continuity between ground and terminal No. 2 (Black wire) at rear wiper motor harness connector. If continuity exists, go to next step. If continuity does not exist, repair open Black wire.

3) Check continuity between ground and terminal No. 3 (Black/Light Green wire) at rear wiper motor harness connector. If continuity does not exist, go to next step. If continuity exists, repair short to ground in Black/Light Green wire.

4) Check continuity of Black/Light Green wire between terminals No. 3 at rear wiper motor harness connector and No. 4 at rear wiper switch harness connector. If continuity does not exist, repair open Black/Light Green wire. If continuity exists, replace faulty rear wiper motor.

REAR WASHER PUMP TEST

1) Turn ignition on. Place rear wiper switch in WIPE position. If rear wiper operates, go to next step. If rear wiper does not operate, go to REAR WIPER SWITCH TEST.

2) Turn ignition off. Disconnect rear washer pump connector. *See Fig. 4 or 5*. Check continuity between ground and Black wire terminal at rear washer pump harness connector. If continuity exists, go to next step. If continuity does not exist, repair open Black wire.

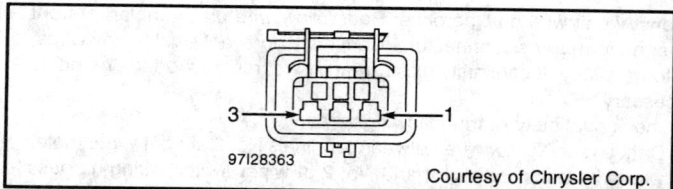

Fig. 9: Identifying Rear Wiper Motor Wiring Harness Connector Terminals (Wrangler)

3) Turn ignition on. Measure voltage between ground and Black/White wire (Cherokee) or Violet/Orange wire (Wrangler) at rear washer pump harness connector while depressing rear washer switch. If battery voltage does not exist, go to next step. If battery voltage exists, replace rear washer pump.

4) Turn ignition off. Disconnect negative battery cable. Disconnect rear wiper switch connector. Check continuity between ground and terminal No. 2 (Black/White wire on Cherokee; Violet/Orange wire on Wrangler) at rear wiper switch harness connector. *See Fig. 6*. If continuity does not exist, go to next step. If continuity exists, repair short to ground.

5) Check continuity of Black/White wire (Cherokee) or Violet/Orange wire (Wrangler) wire between terminal No. 2 at rear wiper switch harness connector and rear washer pump harness connector. If continuity exists, replace faulty rear wiper switch. If continuity does not exist, repair open circuit.

REMOVAL & INSTALLATION
FRONT WIPER SWITCH

WARNING: Deactivate air bag system before performing any service operation involving steering column components. See AIR BAG RESTRAINT SYSTEMS article.

Removal & Installation – 1) Disable air bag system. See appropriate AIR BAG RESTRAINT SYSTEMS article. Remove trim cover from bottom of instrument panel. Set tilt steering column to its fully raised position (if equipped). Turn ignition on.

2) Insert a small punch into access hole in right side of lower steering column cover and depress ignition lock cylinder retainer tumbler. While holding retaining tumbler depressed, pull ignition lock cylinder and key out of ignition lock housing.

3) On models with tilt steering, set tilt steering to its lowest position. On models without tilt steering, loosen 2 upper steering column mounting bolts. On all models, remove upper and lower steering column covers. Remove 2 screws securing multifunction switch water shield to top of steering column. *See Fig. 10*.

4) Remove screw from bottom of water shield. Lift multifunction switch with water shield away from steering column. Disconnect multifunction switch connectors. Remove multifunction switch and water shield as an assembly.

5) Gently pull front wiper switch up and away from right side of steering column to access wiring harness connector. Disconnect connector and remove wiper switch. To install, reverse removal procedure.

FRONT WIPER ARMS

CAUTION: DO NOT use a screwdriver or prying tool to remove wiper arm. Wiper arm may distort, causing wiper arm to come off pivot shaft.

Removal & Installation – 1) Lift wiper arm. Pull wiper arm locking latch out to its holding position and release wiper arm. Arm will remain off windshield with latch in this position. Using a rocking motion, remove wiper arm from pivot.

2) Install wiper arm and blade with wiper motor in park position. On Cherokee, mount wiper arms on pivot shafts so distance between tip of wiper blade and upper edge of lower windshield molding is .90-2.04" (23-52 mm) on driver's side or 1.29-2.44" (3-62 mm) on passenger's side.

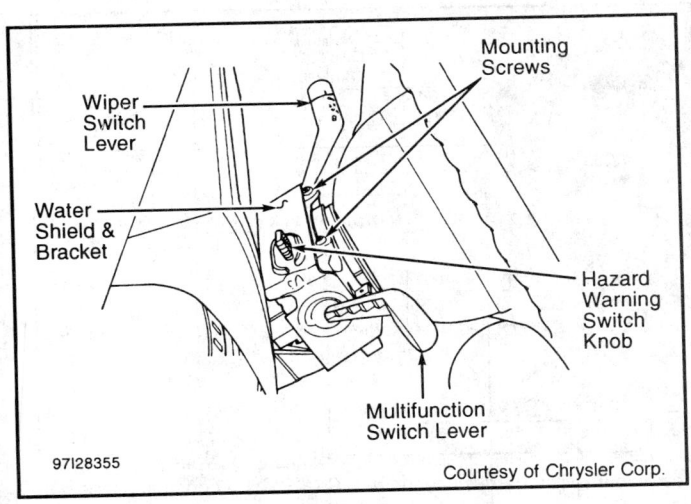

Wiper Switch Lever

Water Shield & Bracket

Mounting Screws

Hazard Warning Switch Knob

Multifunction Switch Lever

97I28355

Courtesy of Chrysler Corp.

Fig. 10: Identifying Water Shield Screws

3) On Wrangler, mount wiper arms on pivot shafts so distance between tip of wiper blade and upper edge of lower windshield blackout area is 0-.59" (0-15 mm). On all models, lift wiper arm away from windshield slightly, relieving spring tension on locking latch.

4) Push latch into locked position and slowly release arm until wiper blade rests on windshield. Operate wipers with windshield wet. Turn wiper switch off and check for correct wiper arm positioning. Readjust as necessary.

FRONT WIPER MOTOR

Removal & Installation (Cherokee) – 1) Disconnect negative battery cable. Remove wiper arms. See FRONT WIPER ARMS. Remove 8 cowl grille retaining screws. Lift cowl grille panel and disconnect washer hose. Remove cowl grille panel.

2) Disconnect wiper motor connector. Open hood. Remove cowl mounting bracket nuts. Remove 4 screws retaining wiper motor to cowl. Remove wiper motor and linkage as an assembly. Remove screws retaining wiper motor to wiper linkage. Remove motor. To install, reverse removal procedure.

Removal & Installation (Wrangler) – 1) Disconnect negative battery cable. Remove front wiper arms. See FRONT WIPER ARMS. Open hood. Pull back each end of hood seal from dash panel to access screw on each end of cowl grille panel. Remove screws. Close hood.

2) Remove screw from center of cowl grille panel. Remove 4 screws securing cowl grille panel near base of windshield. Carefully remove cowl grille panel from vehicle. Disconnect wiper motor connector. Remove 3 wiper linkage cowl mounting bracket screws.

3) Remove wiper motor and linkage as an assembly. Release retainer securing wiper motor connector to wiper linkage assembly bracket. Remove wiper motor crank arm nut. Remove screws retaining wiper motor to wiper linkage assembly bracket. Remove wiper motor. To install, reverse removal procedure.

FRONT WASHER MOTOR

Removal & Installation (Cherokee) – 1) Washer motor is press fit into reservoir. Raise and support vehicle. Remove left front inner wheelwell splash shield. Disconnect washer supply hose from pump. Drain washer fluid from reservoir.

2) Disconnect washer pump connector. Gently pry washer pump out of rubber grommet seal in reservoir. Remove and discard rubber grommet. To install, reverse removal procedure. Use NEW grommet when installing pump.

Removal & Installation (Wrangler) – Remove reservoir mounting screws and reservoir. Disconnect washer pump connectors. Disconnect hoses from pumps. Drain reservoir. Gently pry washer pump out of rubber grommet seal in reservoir. Remove and discard rubber grommet. To install, reverse removal procedure. Use NEW grommet when installing pump.

REAR WIPER SWITCH

Removal & Installation (Cherokee) – 1) Rear wiper switch is located in accessory switch bezel, located below A/C-heater control panel. Disconnect negative battery cable. Using a trim stick, gently pry around perimeter of instrument panel center bezel and remove bezel. Remove accessory switch bezel retaining screws.

2) Pull accessory switch bezel out far enough to access wiring harness connectors. Disconnect connectors. Remove accessory switch bezel. Using a thin bladed screwdriver, remove rear wiper switch from accessory switch bezel.

3) To install, reverse removal procedure. When installing rear wiper switch, ensure both switch snap retainers are fully engaged in accessory switch bezel.

Removal & Installation (Wrangler) – 1) Rear wiper switch is located in accessory switch bezel, located below A/C-heater control panel. Disconnect negative battery cable. Using a trim stick, gently pry instrument panel top cover away from instrument panel.

2) Remove top cover. Remove 2 screws securing top of center bezel. Remove ashtray and ashtray housing. Using a trim stick, pry lower edge of center bezel away from instrument panel. Lift lower edge of center bezel to release 4 snap clip retainers and remove bezel.

3) Remove 4 accessory switch bezel retaining screws. Pull accessory switch bezel out and disconnect wiring harness connectors. Remove accessory switch bezel. Using a thin bladed screwdriver, remove rear wiper switch from accessory switch bezel.

4) To install, reverse removal procedure. When installing rear wiper switch, ensure both switch snap retainers are fully engaged in accessory switch bezel.

REAR WIPER ARM

Removal & Installation (Cherokee) – 1) Lift pivot cover and remove retaining nut. Remove wiper arm from wiper motor output shaft. Install rear wiper arm with wiper motor in park position. Place rear wiper blade on glass so blade is parallel to liftgate glass opening.

2) Install wiper arm retaining nut. Operate rear wiper on wet liftgate glass. Turn wiper off. Wiper blade should now be in park position. Distance between tip of wiper blade and upper edge of window seal should be 1.06-1.38" (27-35 mm). Readjust wiper arm position if necessary.

Removal & Installation (Wrangler) – 1) Lift wiper arm. Pull wiper arm locking latch out to its holding position and release wiper arm. Arm will remain off windshield with latch in this position. Using a rocking motion, remove wiper arm from pivot.

2) Install wiper arm and blade with wiper motor in park position. Mount wiper arm on pivot shaft so distance between tip of wiper blade and upper edge of liftglass is 0-3.14" (0-80 mm). Lift wiper arm away from liftglass slightly, relieving spring tension on locking latch.

3) Push latch into locked position and slowly release arm until wiper blade rests on liftglass. Operate wipers with liftglass wet. Turn wiper switch off and check for correct wiper arm positioning. Readjust as necessary.

REAR WIPER MOTOR

Removal & Installation (Cherokee) – 1) Disconnect negative battery cable. Remove wiper arm. See REAR WIPER ARM. Remove wiper motor output shaft retaining nut. Pull bezel and seal out far enough to access washer supply hose. Disconnect washer supply hose. Remove bezel and seal.

2) Open liftgate. Using a trim stick, gently pry screw covers from liftgate assist handle. Remove liftgate assist handle screws and handle. Remove liftgate trim panel screws. Using a trim stick, gently pry lower edges of trim panel away from liftgate.

3) Remove liftgate trim panel. Disconnect rear wiper motor connector. Remove rear wiper motor mounting bracket-to-liftgate inner panel screws. Remove rear wiper motor and mounting bracket as an assembly. To install, reverse removal procedure.

Removal & Installation (Wrangler) – 1) Disconnect negative battery cable. Remove rear wiper arm. See REAR WIPER ARM. Remove wiper motor cover. Disconnect wiper motor connector. Loosen, but DO NOT remove, right liftglass hinge nut.

2) Carefully pull on motor until output shaft clears hole in liftglass. Move wiper motor towards right side of vehicle until slotted hole in motor mounting bracket clears grommet under right liftglass hinge nut. Remove wiper motor. To install, reverse removal procedure.

REAR WASHER MOTOR

Removal & Installation – Rear washer pump is located next to front washer pump. See FRONT WASHER MOTOR.

TORQUE SPECIFICATIONS

TORQUE SPECIFICATIONS

Application	Ft. Lbs. (N.m)
Cherokee	
Rear Wiper Arm Retaining Nut	13 (18)
	INCH Lbs. (N.m)
Front Wiper Motor	
Mounting Screws & Nuts	53 (6)
Rear Wiper Motor	
Mounting Screws	44 (5)
Mounting Nut	27 (3)
Wrangler	
Crank Arm Nut	101 (11.5)
Front Wiper Motor Mounting Screws	53 (6)
Module Bracket Screws	70 (9)
Rear Wiper Motor Output Shaft Nut	30 (3.3)

WIRING DIAGRAMS

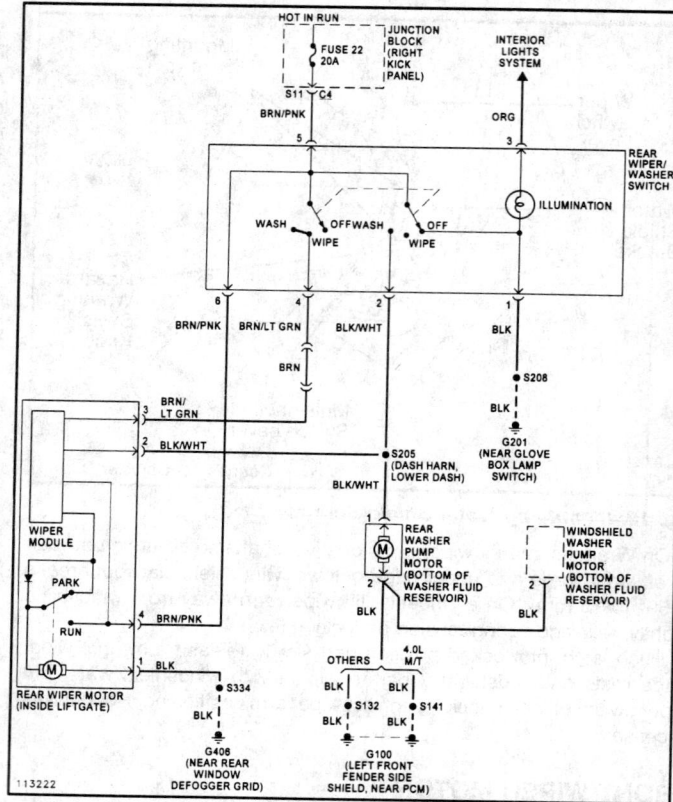

Fig. 12: Rear Wiper/Washer System Wiring Diagram (Cherokee)

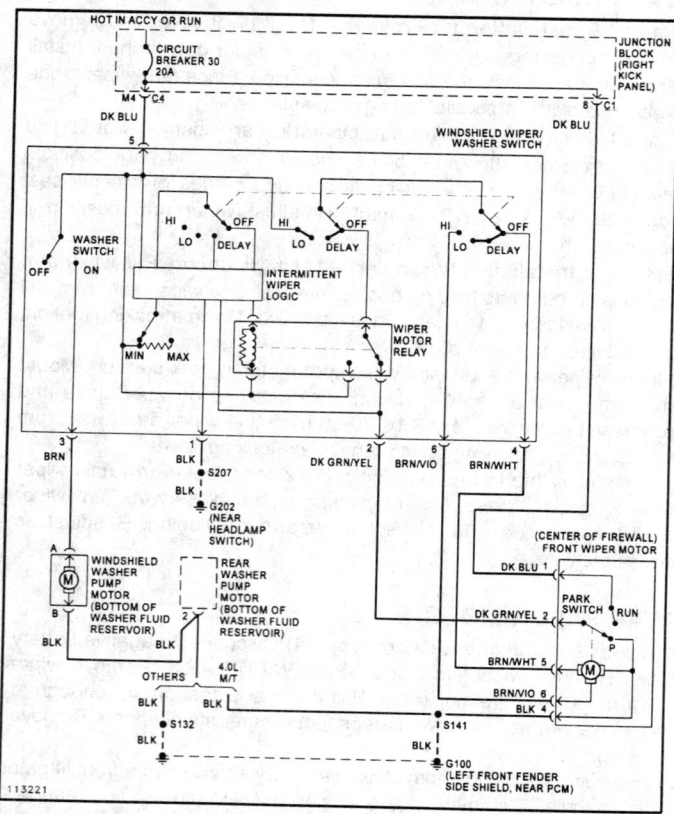

Fig. 11: Front Wiper/Washer System Wiring Diagram (Cherokee)

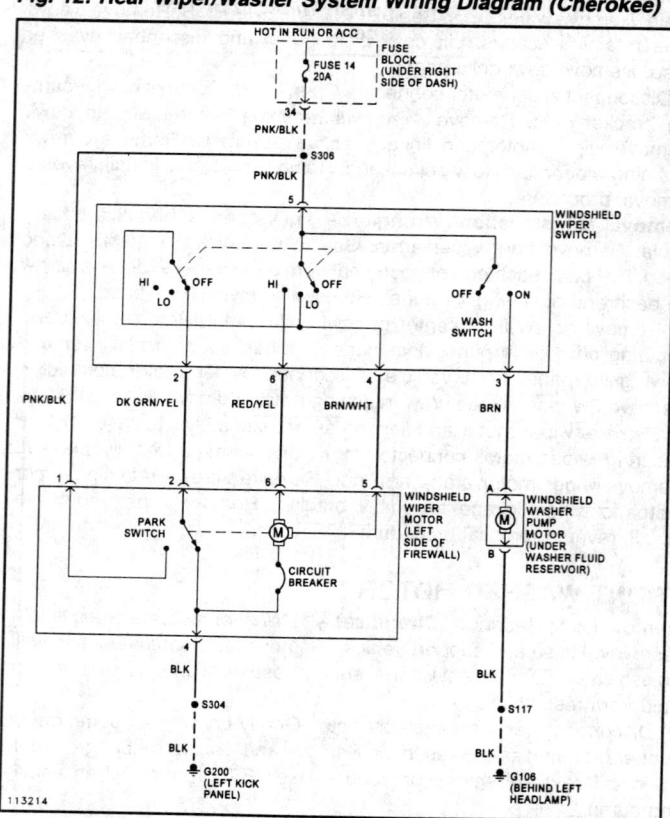

Fig. 13: Front Wiper/Washer System Wiring Diagram (Wrangler – 2-Speed Wipers)

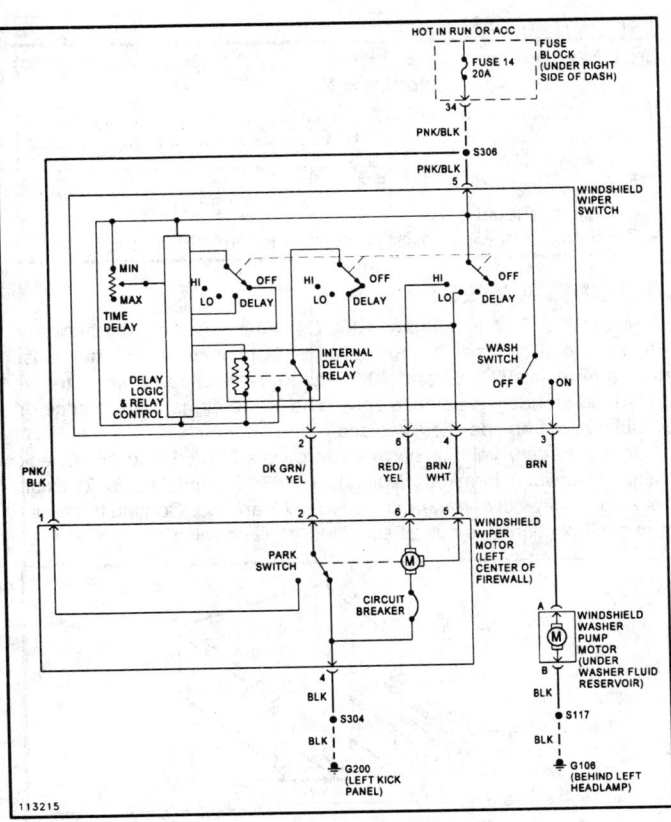

Fig. 14: Front Wiper/Washer System Wiring Diagram (Wrangler – Interval Wipers)

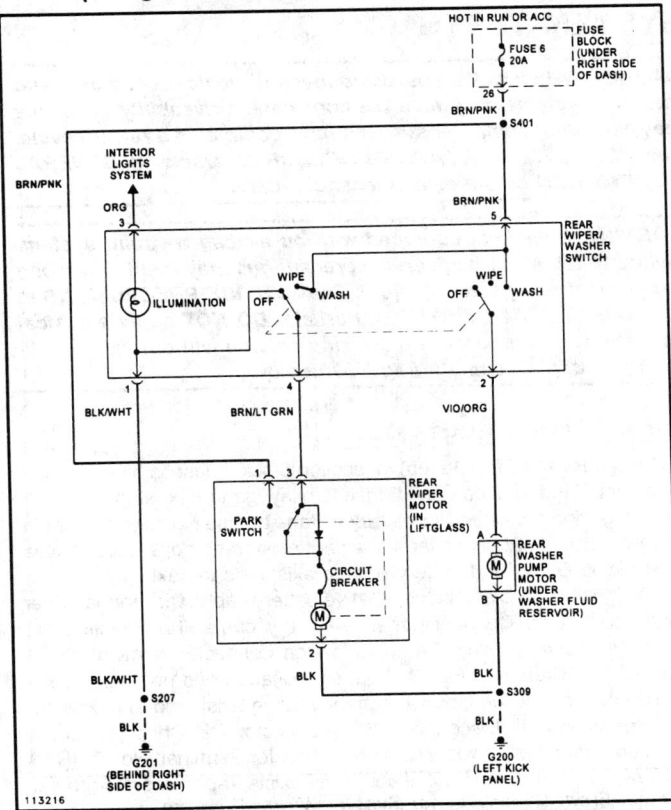

Fig. 15: Rear Wiper/Washer System Wiring Diagram (Wrangler)

DESCRIPTION & OPERATION

Grand Cherokee uses an intermittent wiper system and electric washer. Intermittent wiper function is controlled by the Body Control Module (BCM). Vehicle is equipped with a rear wiper/washer system.

ADJUSTMENTS

WIPER ARMS

With wiper arms removed, cycle wiper motor into park position. Mount wiper arms on pivot shafts. Align lower edge of wiper blades with alignment lines near lower edge of windshield glass. *See Fig. 1.* Install wiper arm nut and tighten to specification. See TORQUE SPECIFICATIONS.

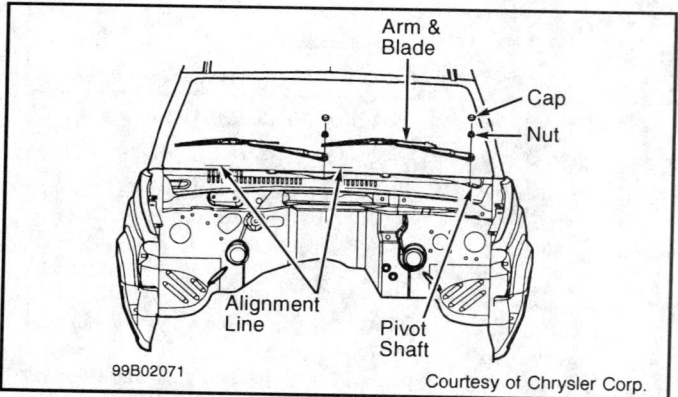

Fig. 1: Aligning Wiper Arms

COMPONENT TESTS

CAUTION: When battery is disconnected, vehicle computer and memory systems may lose memory data. Driveability problems may exist until computer systems have completed a relearn cycle. See COMPUTER RELEARN PROCEDURES article in GENERAL INFORMATION before disconnecting battery.

WARNING: Vehicle is equipped with an air bag restraint system. Failure to follow air bag service precautions may result in air bag deployment and personal injury. See SERVICE PRECAUTIONS in AIR BAG RESTRAINT SYSTEMS article. DO NOT apply electrical power to any component on steering column without first deactivating air bag system. Air bag may deploy.

WIPER SWITCH TEST

Disconnect negative battery cable. Disconnect wiper switch connector. Measure resistance and/or continuity between appropriate wiper switch terminals with switch in specified position. See WIPER SWITCH TEST table. If resistance or continuity is not as specified, replace wiper switch.

WIPER SWITCH TEST

Switch Position	Between Terminals No.	Resistance (Ohms)
Front Wiper		
OFF	7 & 8	4286-4379
DELAY 1	7 & 8	1445-1480
DELAY 2	7 & 8	847-870
DELAY 3	7 & 8	556-573
DELAY 4	7 & 8	367-380
DELAY 5	7 & 8	218-229
LOW	7 & 8	99-106
HIGH	7 & 8	99-106
HIGH	1 & 9	...¹
MIST	7 & 8	49-56
WASH	1 & 3	...¹
Rear Wiper		

WIPER SWITCH TEST (Cont.)

Switch Position	Between Terminals No.	Resistance (Ohms)
OFF	2	...²
DELAY	1 & 6	...¹
ON	1 & 5	...¹
WASH	1, 5 & 6	...¹

¹ – Continuity should exist.
² – Continuity should not exist between any terminals.

WIPER RELAY TEST

1) Remove high/low relay from PDC. Continuity should exist between terminals No. 87A and 30. *See Fig. 2.* Continuity should not exist between terminals No. 87 and 30. Measure resistance between terminals No. 85 and 86. Resistance should be 70-80 ohms. If resistance or continuity is not as specified, replace relay.

2) Connect battery voltage between terminals No. 85 and 86. Check continuity between terminals No. 30 and 87. Continuity should exist. Check continuity between terminals No. 87A and 30. Continuity should not exist. If continuity is not as specified, replace relay.

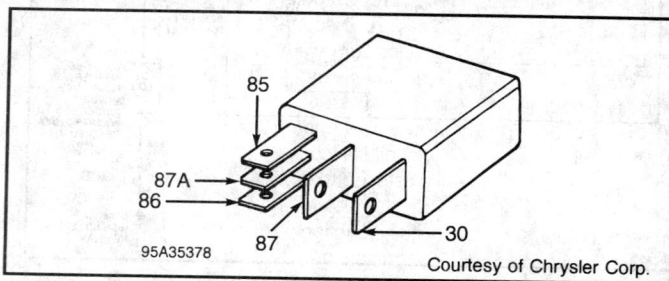

Fig. 2: Identifying Wiper Relay Terminals

SYSTEM TESTS

CAUTION: When battery is disconnected, vehicle computer and memory systems may lose memory data. Driveability problems may exist until computer systems have completed a relearn cycle. See COMPUTER RELEARN PROCEDURES article in GENERAL INFORMATION before disconnecting battery.

WARNING: Vehicle is equipped with an air bag restraint system. Failure to follow air bag service precautions may result in air bag deployment and personal injury. See SERVICE PRECAUTIONS in AIR BAG RESTRAINT SYSTEMS article. DO NOT apply electrical power to any component on steering column without first deactivating air bag system. Air bag may deploy.

FRONT WIPER SYSTEM

1) Check fuse No. 29 (10-amp) in junction block. If fuse is blown, repair short circuit and replace fuse. If fuse is okay, go to next step.

2) Turn ignition on. Check for battery voltage at fuse No. 29 (10-amp) in junction block. If battery voltage does not exist, repair open circuit. See WIRING DIAGRAMS. If battery voltage exists, go to next step.

3) Turn ignition off. Disconnect negative battery cable. Disconnect wiper switch connector. Connect negative battery cable. Turn ignition on. Check for battery voltage at wiper switch connector terminal No. 1 (Brown/Pink wire). *See Fig. 3.* If battery voltage does not exist, repair open circuit to junction block. If battery voltage exists, go to next step.

4) Turn ignition off. Disconnect BCM connector C2. Check continuity between ground and wiper switch connector terminal No. 7 (Dark Blue/Yellow wire). *See Fig. 4.* If continuity exists, repair short to ground. If continuity does not exist, go to next step.

5) Check continuity between wiper switch connector terminal No. 7 (Dark Blue/Yellow wire) and BCM connector C2 terminal No. 22 (Dark Blue/Yellow wire). If continuity does not exist, repair open circuit. If continuity exists, go to next step.

6) Check continuity between ground and wiper switch connector terminal No. 8 (Dark Green/Red wire). If continuity exists, repair short to ground. If continuity does not exist, go to next step.

7) Check continuity between wiper switch connector terminal No. 8 (Dark Green/Red wire) and BCM connector C2 terminal No. 11 (Dark Green/Red wire). If continuity does not exist, repair open circuit. If continuity exists, reconnect BCM and go to next step.

8) Test wiper switch. See WIPER SWITCH TEST under COMPONENT TESTS. If wiper switch in not okay, replace wiper switch. If wiper switch is okay, connect wiper switch connector and go to next step.

9) If wipers do not park, and all other functions are okay, go to next step. If wipers operate at low speed when intermittent delay is selected and wipers do not park, go to step **11)**. If wipers do not operate in any mode, go to step **14)**. If wipers do not operate at high speed, go to step **18)**.

10) Turn ignition off. Disconnect negative battery cable. Using a voltmeter, backprobe wiper motor connector terminal No. 1 (Dark Blue wire). *See Fig. 5.* Connect negative battery cable. Turn ignition on. If battery voltage does not exist, repair open circuit to junction block. If battery voltage exists, go to next step.

11) Turn ignition off. Disconnect negative battery cable. Disconnect wiper motor connector. Disconnect 52-pin instrument panel connector from junction block (connector C2). Disconnect wiper motor connector. Check continuity between ground and wiper motor connector terminal No. 2 (Tan/Red wire). If continuity exists, repair short to ground. If continuity does not exist, go to next step.

12) Check continuity between wiper motor connector terminal No. 2 (Tan/Red wire) and junction block connector C2 terminal No. 28 (Tan/Red wire). If continuity exists, go to next step. If continuity does not exist, repair open circuit.

13) Connect wiper motor and junction block connectors. Connect negative battery cable. Turn ignition on. Backprobe wiper motor connector terminal No. 2 (Tan/Red wire). Turn wipers on. Check for battery voltage. Voltage should switch between battery voltage and zero volts. Turn wipers off. Battery voltage should exist until wipers park. If voltage is not as specified, replace wiper motor. If voltage is as specified, use scan tool to diagnose BCM. See appropriate BODY CONTROL COMPUTER TESTS article.

14) Check continuity between ground and wiper motor connector terminal No. 4 (Black wire). If continuity does not exist, repair open ground circuit. If continuity exists, go to next step.

15) Remove circuit breaker No. 1 (20-amp) from junction block. Connect negative battery cable. Turn ignition on. Check for battery voltage at circuit breaker terminal in junction block (ignition switch side). If battery voltage does not exist, repair open circuit to ignition switch. If battery voltage exists, go to next step.

16) Turn ignition off. Disconnect negative battery cable. Install circuit breaker No. 1 in junction block. Connect negative battery cable. Turn ignition on. Check for battery voltage at circuit breaker No. 1 in junction block (output side). If battery voltage does not exist, replace circuit breaker. If battery voltage exists, go to next step.

17) Test wiper on/off relay. See WIPER RELAY TEST. If wiper on/off relay is not okay, replace wiper on/off relay. If wiper on/off relay is okay, go to next step.

18) Test wiper high/low relay. See WIPER RELAY TEST. If wiper high/low relay is not okay, replace wiper high/low relay. If wiper high/low relay is okay, replace wiper motor.

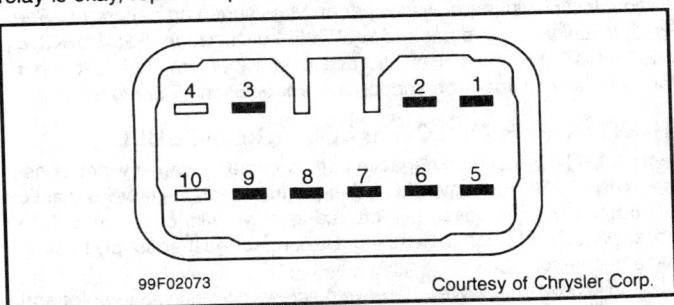

99F02073   Courtesy of Chrysler Corp.

Fig. 3: Identifying Wiper Switch Connector Terminals

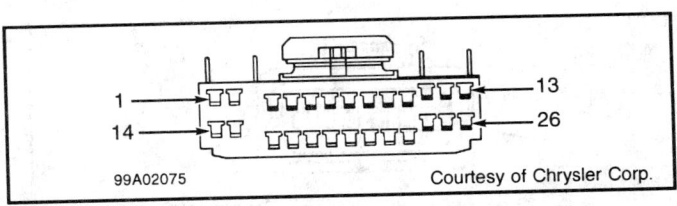

99A02075   Courtesy of Chrysler Corp.

Fig. 4: Identifying Body Control Module (BCM) Connector Terminals

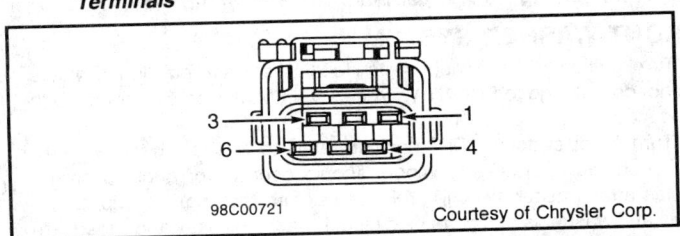

98C00721   Courtesy of Chrysler Corp.

Fig. 5: Identifying Front Wiper Motor Connector Terminals

REAR WIPER SYSTEM

1) Ensure instrument panel dimmer switch is not turned to the extreme up position. Open liftgate. Interior lights should illuminate. Close all doors, liftgate and liftgate glass. Interior lights should turn off after about 30 seconds. If interior lights do not operate as specified, go to step **9)**. If interior lights are okay, go to next step.

2) Check fuse No. 8 (15-amp) in junction block. If fuse is blown, repair short circuit and replace fuse. If fuse is okay, go to next step.

3) Check for battery voltage at fuse No. 8. If battery voltage does not exist, repair open circuit to Power Distribution Center (PDC). If battery voltage exists, go to next step.

4) Check fuse No. 29 (10-amp) in junction block. If fuse is blown, repair short circuit and replace fuse. If fuse is okay, go to next step.

5) Turn ignition on. Check for battery voltage at fuse No. 29. If battery voltage does not exist, repair open circuit to ignition switch. If battery voltage exists, go to next step.

6) Disconnect negative battery cable. Disconnect wiper switch connector. Connect negative battery cable. Turn ignition on. Check for battery voltage at wiper switch connector terminal No. 1 (Brown/Pink wire). *See Fig. 3.* If battery voltage does not exist, repair open circuit to junction block. If battery voltage exists, go to next step.

7) Turn ignition off. Test wiper switch. See WIPER SWITCH TEST under COMPONENT TESTS. If wiper switch is not okay, replace wiper switch. If wiper switch is okay, go to next step.

8) Remove liftgate inner trim panel. Disconnect rear wiper motor connector. Check continuity between ground and rear wiper motor connector terminal No. 1 (Black wire). *See Fig. 6.* If continuity does not exist, repair open ground circuit. If continuity exists, go to next step.

9) Check continuity between ground and rear wiper motor connector terminal No. 3 (Tan/Black wire). Continuity should exist when liftgate or glass is open. Continuity should not exist when liftgate and glass are closed. If continuity is not as specified, repair liftgate ajar sense circuit as necessary. If continuity is as specified, go to next step.

10) Connect negative battery cable. Check for battery voltage at rear wiper motor connector terminal No. 5 (Pink wire). If battery voltage does not exist, repair open circuit to junction block. If battery voltage exists, go to next step.

11) Turn ignition on. Turn rear wiper switch to DELAY position. Check for battery voltage at rear wiper motor connector terminal No. 4 (Brown/Yellow wire). If battery voltage does not exist, repair open circuit to wiper switch. If battery voltage exists, go to next step.

12) Turn rear wiper switch on. Check for battery voltage at rear wiper motor connector terminal No. 2 (Brown/Light Green wire). If battery voltage does not exist, repair open circuit to wiper switch. If battery voltage exists, replace rear wiper motor.

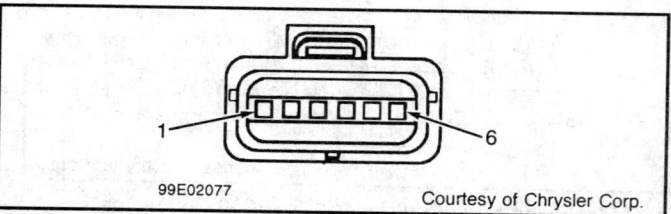

99E02077   Courtesy of Chrysler Corp.

Fig. 6: Identifying Rear Wiper Motor Connector Terminals

FRONT WASHER SYSTEM

1) Turn ignition on. Turn wiper switch to LOW or HIGH position. If wipers do not operate, go to FRONT WIPER SYSTEM. If wipers operate, go to next step.

2) Turn wiper switch to OFF position. Actuate washer switch. Washer pump should operate and wipers should operate for about 3 sweep cycles after washer switch is released before they park. If wipers are okay and washer is not, go to next step. If washer is okay and wipers are not, go to step 5).

3) Turn ignition off. Disconnect negative battery cable. Disconnect washer pump connector. Check continuity between ground and washer pump connector Black wire terminal. If continuity does not exist, repair open ground circuit. If continuity exists, go to next step.

4) Connect negative battery cable. Turn ignition on. While washer switch is actuated, check for battery voltage at washer pump connector Brown wire terminal. If battery voltage does not exist, repair open circuit to wiper switch. If battery voltage exists, replace washer pump.

5) Turn ignition off. Disconnect negative battery cable. Disconnect BCM connector C2. Connect negative battery cable. Turn ignition on. While washer switch is actuated, check for battery voltage at BCM connector C2 terminal No. 2 (Brown wire). If battery voltage does not exist, repair open washer pump control switch output circuit to wiper switch. If battery voltage does exist, use scan tool to diagnose BCM. See BODY CONTROL COMPUTER TESTS – GRAND CHEROKEE article.

REAR WASHER SYSTEM

1) Turn ignition on. Turn rear wiper switch to ON position. If rear wiper does not operate, go to REAR WIPER SYSTEM. If rear wiper is okay, go to next step.

2) Turn ignition off. Disconnect negative battery cable. Disconnect rear washer pump connector. Check continuity between ground and washer pump connector Black wire terminal. If continuity does not exist, repair open ground circuit. If continuity exists, go to next step.

3) Connect negative battery cable. Turn ignition on. While rear washer switch is actuated, check for battery voltage at rear washer pump connector Black/White wire terminal. If battery voltage does not exist, repair open circuit to wiper switch. If battery voltage exists, replace washer pump.

WIPER HIGH/LOW RELAY CIRCUIT TEST

1) Remove wiper high/low relay and wiper on/off relay from Power Distribution Center (PDC). Check continuity between high/low connector terminal No. 30 and on/off relay connector terminal No. 30. See Fig. 2. If continuity does not exist, repair open circuit in PDC. If continuity exists, go to next step.

2) Disconnect wiper motor connector. Check continuity between high/low relay connector terminal No. 87A and wiper motor connector terminal No. 5 (Brown/White wire). See Fig. 5. If continuity does not exist, repair open high/low relay low-speed output circuit. If continuity exists, go to next step.

3) Check continuity between high/low relay connector terminal No. 87 and wiper motor connector terminal No. 6 (Red/Yellow wire). If continuity does not exist, repair open high/low relay high-speed output circuit. If continuity exists, go to next step.

4) Turn ignition on. Turn wiper switch to HIGH position. Check for battery voltage at high/low relay connector terminal No. 86. If battery voltage does not exist, repair open circuit to wiper switch. If battery voltage exists, go to next step.

5) Turn ignition off. Check continuity between ground and high/low relay connector terminal No. 85. If continuity does not exist, repair open ground circuit. If continuity exists, test wiper high/low relay. See WIPER RELAY TEST.

WIPER ON/OFF RELAY CIRCUIT TEST

1) Remove wiper high/low relay and wiper on/off relay from PDC. Check continuity between high/low relay connector terminal No. 30 and on/off relay connector terminal No. 30. See Fig. 2. If continuity does not exist, repair open circuit in PDC. If continuity exists, go to next step.

2) Disconnect wiper motor connector. Check continuity between high/low relay connector terminal No. 87A and wiper motor connector terminal No. 2 (Tan/Red wire). See Fig. 5. If continuity does not exist, repair open park switch sense circuit. If continuity exists, go to next step.

3) Turn ignition on. Check for battery voltage at on/off relay connector terminal No. 87. If battery voltage does not exist, repair open circuit to junction block. If battery voltage exists, go to next step.

4) Check for battery voltage at on/off relay connector terminal No. 86. If battery voltage does not exist, repair open circuit to junction block. If battery voltage exists, go to next step.

5) Turn ignition off. Check continuity between on/off relay connector terminal No. 85 and BCM connector C1 terminal No. 22 (Red/Violet wire). If continuity does not exist, repair open on/off relay control circuit to BCM. If continuity exists, use scan tool to diagnose BCM. See BODY CONTROL COMPUTER TESTS – GRAND CHEROKEE article.

REMOVAL & INSTALLATION

WIPER SWITCH

WARNING: Deactivate air bag system before performing any service operation involving steering column components. See AIR BAG RESTRAINT SYSTEMS article.

Removal & Installation – Disable air bag system. See AIR BAG RESTRAINT SYSTEMS article. Remove screw from lower steering column shroud. Remove upper and lower steering column shrouds. Disconnect wiper switch connector. Remove 2 wiper switch screws. Remove wiper switch. To install, reverse removal procedure. Tighten wiper switch screws to 22 INCH lbs. (2.5 N.m). Tighten lower steering column shroud screw to 17 INCH lbs. (1.9 N.m).

WIPER ARMS

CAUTION: DO NOT use a screwdriver or prying tool to remove wiper arm. Wiper arm may distort, causing wiper arm to come off pivot shaft.

Removal (Front Or Rear) – Carefully remove plastic cap from wiper arm nut. Remove wiper arm nut. Using a battery terminal puller, remove wiper arm.

Installation (Front) – Install wiper arm with wiper motor in Park position. Install wiper arm onto pivot shaft. Ensure wiper arms are aligned. See WIPER ARM ADJUSTMENT under ADJUSTMENTS. Install wiper arm nut and tighten to specification. See TORQUE SPECIFICATIONS. Install plastic cap over wiper arm nut.

Installation (Rear) – Install wiper arm with wiper motor in PARK position. Install wiper arm with wiper arm positioned on park ramp. See Fig. 7. Install wiper arm nut and tighten to specification. See TORQUE SPECIFICATIONS. Install plastic cap over wiper arm nut. Lift wiper blade and place wiper arm support in Park position. See Fig. 8.

FRONT WIPER MOTOR & LINKAGE MODULE

Removal – 1) Disconnect negative battery cable. Remove wiper arms. See WIPER ARMS. Remove hood-to-plenum seal. Remove 6 plastic nuts from cowl grille cover. Lift left end of cowl grille cover enough to access windshield washer plumbing. Disconnect washer supply hose at in-line connector.

2) Remove cowl grille cover. Remove 4 screws holding wiper motor and linkage module to cowl plenum panel. Lift left end of wiper motor and

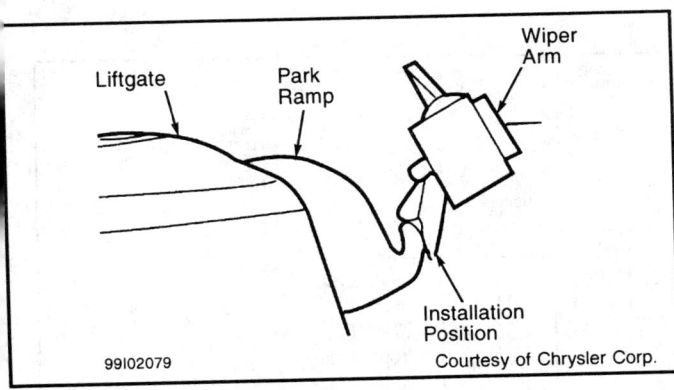

99I02079   Courtesy of Chrysler Corp.

Fig. 7: Installing Rear Wiper Arm

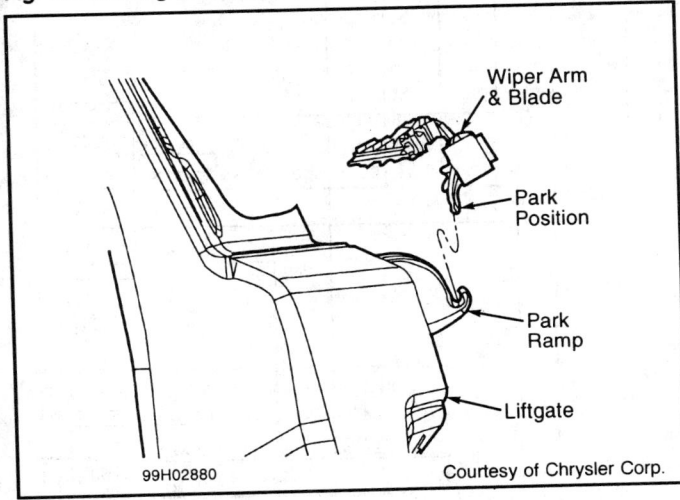

99H02880   Courtesy of Chrysler Corp.

Fig. 8: Parking Wiper Arm

linkage module enough to access wiper motor wire connector. Disconnect wiper motor wire connector. Remove wiper motor and linkage module.

Installation – 1) Position wiper motor and linkage module into cowl plenum. Lift left end of wiper motor and linkage module and connect wiper motor wire connector. Install one wiper motor and linkage module screw on right end of module. Install remaining screws from left to right. Tighten to specification. See TORQUE SPECIFICATIONS.

2) Position cowl grille cover onto cowl plenum. Lift left end of cowl grille cover enough to access windshield washer plumbing. Connect washer supply hose. Install 6 plastic cowl grille cover nuts in the following sequence:

- Install one short nut on third stud from right side.
- Install remaining short nut on second stud from left side.
- Install long nuts on right and left end studs.
- Install remaining long nuts on third stud from left side and second stud from right side.

3) Starting from ends and working towards center, install hood-to-plenum seal. Install wiper arms. See WIPER ARMS. Connect negative battery cable.

REAR WIPER MOTOR MODULE

Removal – 1) Disconnect negative battery cable. Remove wiper arm. See WIPER ARMS. Using a door trim panel removal tool, carefully pry nut cover from wiper motor output shaft. Remove nut holding wiper motor output shaft to outer liftgate panel. Remove bezel and gasket from wiper motor output shaft.

2) Remove liftgate inside trim panel. Disconnect wiper motor wire connector. Loosen wiper motor bracket mounting nuts. Slide wiper motor module forward enough to disengage mounting nuts from keyed holes. Remove wiper motor module.

Installation – 1) Position wiper motor module to liftgate inner panel. Insert wiper motor output shaft through hole in liftgate outer panel. Engage mounting nuts into keyed holes of liftgate inner panel. Center wiper motor output shaft in liftgate outer panel mounting hole. Install gasket, bezel and mounting nut. Tighten nut to specification. See TORQUE SPECIFICATIONS.

2) Install wiper motor module mounting nuts. Tighten nuts to specification. See TORQUE SPECIFICATIONS. Connect wiper motor wire connector. To complete installation, reverse removal procedure.

WASHER RESERVOIR

Removal – 1) Disconnect negative battery cable. Remove left front fender liner. Remove air cleaner housing. Disconnect 2 washer fluid hoses from in-line connectors located near washer fluid filler neck. Remove washer fluid reservoir filler cap. Remove filler neck screw.

2) Raise and support vehicle. Disconnect washer pump wire connectors. Remove 2 washer reservoir mounting screws. Pull bottom of washer reservoir rearward enough to access washer fluid level sensor wire connector. Disconnect washer fluid level sensor wire connector. Remove washer reservoir.

Installation – To install, reverse removal procedure. Tighten fasteners to specification. See TORQUE SPECIFICATIONS.

WASHER PUMP

NOTE: Washer pumps can be removed without removing washer reservoir.

Removal – Disconnect negative battery cable. Raise and support vehicle. Remove left front fender liner. Disconnect washer pump wire connector. Disconnect washer hose from pump and allow washer fluid to drain. Using a suitable flat-bladed tool, gently pry washer pump out of rubber grommet in reservoir.

Installation – Install a NEW rubber grommet into washer reservoir. Install washer pump into reservoir. To complete installation, reverse removal procedure.

WASHER FLUID LEVEL SENSOR

NOTE: Washer fluid level sensor can be removed without removing washer reservoir.

Removal – 1) Disconnect negative battery cable. Remove washer fluid filler neck screw. Raise and support vehicle. Remove left front fender liner. Disconnect washer fluid hose from rearmost washer pump and allow fluid to drain. Remove 2 washer reservoir mounting screws.

2) Pull bottom of washer reservoir rearward enough to access washer fluid level sensor wire connector. Disconnect washer fluid level sensor wire connector. Using a suitable flat-bladed tool, gently pry washer fluid level sensor out of reservoir. Remove washer fluid level sensor and float from reservoir.

Installation – Install NEW rubber grommet into washer reservoir. Install float and washer fluid level sensor into washer reservoir with wire connector pointing downward. To complete installation, reverse removal procedure. Tighten washer reservoir filler neck screw to specification. See TORQUE SPECIFICATIONS.

TORQUE SPECIFICATIONS

TORQUE SPECIFICATIONS

Application	INCH Lbs. (N.m)
Wiper Arm Retaining Nut	210 (23.7)
Front	160 (18)
Rear	
Wiper Module	72 (8)
Front	47 (5.3)
Rear	
Rear Wiper Motor Output	43 (4.8)
Shaft-To-Outer Liftgate Panel Nut	
Washer Reservoir Screws	66 (7.4)

WIRING DIAGRAMS

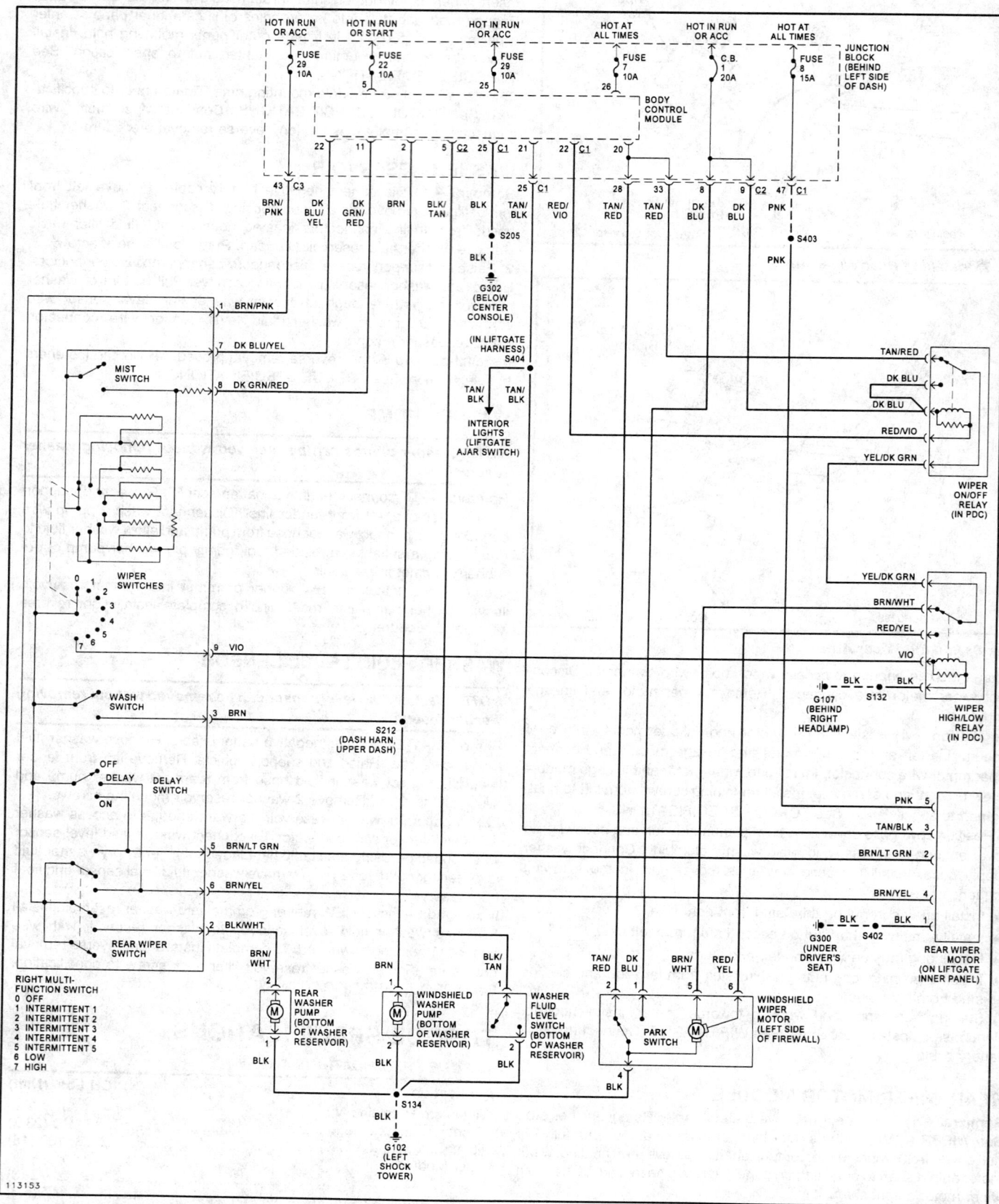

Fig. 9: Wiper/Washer System Wiring Diagram (Grand Cherokee)

NOTES

NOTES

NOTES

NOTES

NOTES

NOTES

NOTES

NOTES

NOTES

NOTES

NOTES

NOTES